Sporting News
BOOKS

HOCKEY GUIDE

2005-2006 EDITION

CONTENTS

Editors: Paul Grant, Zach Bodendieck, Ray Slover. **Cover design and page layout by:** Chad Painter.

ON THE COVER: Martin St. Louis by Kent Smith for TSN; Joe Sakic by Scott Rovak for TSN; Martin Brodeur by John Cordes for TSN; Jarome Iginla by Dilip Vishwanat / TSN Archives. ON THE BACK COVER: Sidney Crosby and Mario Lemieux by Tobin Grimshaw / AP.

NHL statistics compiled by STATS, Inc., a News Corporation company; 8130 Lehigh Avenue, Morton Grove, IL 60053. STATS is a trademark of Sports Team Analysis and Tracking Systems, Inc.

ISBN: 0-89204-776-3

10 9 8 7 6 5 4 3 2 1

EXPLANATION OF FOOTNOTES AND ABBREVIATIONS

* League leader.
. . . Statistic unavailable, unofficial or mathematically impossible to calculate.
— Statistic inapplicable.

POSITIONS: C: center. **D:** defenseman. **G:** goaltender. **LW:** left winger. **RW:** right winger.

STATISTICS: A: assists. **GAA:** goals-against average. **G:** goals. **GA:** goals against. **GP:** games played. **L:** losses. **Min.:** minutes. **PIM.:** penalties in minutes. **+/-:** plus/minus. **PP:** power-play goals. **Pts:** points. **SH:** shorthanded goals. **SO:** shutouts. **SV%:** save percentage. **T:** ties. **W:** wins.

TEAMS: Bloom. Jefferson: Bloomington Jefferson. **Chem. Litvinov:** Chemopetrol Litvinov. **Chem. Litvinov Jrs.:** Chemopetrol Litvinov Juniors. **Culver Mil. Acad.:** Culver Military Academy. **Czech. Olympic team:** Czechoslovakian Olympic team. **Czech Rep. Oly. team:** Czech Republic Olympic team. **Czechosla. Jr. national:** Czechoslavakian Junior national team. **Det. Little Caesars:** Detroit Little Caesars. **Djur. Stockholm:** Djurgarden Stockholm. **Dynamo-Energ. Yek.:** Dynamo-Energiya Yekaterinburg. **Dyn.-Energiya 2 Yek.:** Dynamo-Energiya 2 Yekaterinburg. **Dynamo Ust-Kameno.:** Dynamo Ust-Kamenogorsk. **Fin. Olympic team:** Finnish Olympic team. **German Oly. team:** German Olympic team. **HC Ceske Bude.:** HC Ceske Budejovice. **HK 32 Lip. Mikulas:** HK 32 Liptovsky Mikulas. **IS Banska Byst.:** IS Banska Bystrica. **Kiek.-Karhut Jodusuu:** Kiekko-Karhut Jodusuu. **Krylja Sov. Moscow:** Krylja Sovetov Moscow. **Mass.-Lowell:** Massachusetts-Lowell. **Metal. Cherepovets:** Metallurg Cherepovets. **Metal. Magnitogorsk:** Metallurg Magnitogorsk. **Metallurg-2 Novok.:** Metallurg-2 Novokuznetsk. **MoDo Ornsk. Jrs.:** Modo Ornskoldsvik Jrs. **Motor Ceske Bude.:** Motor Ceske Budejovice. **N. Yarmouth Acad.:** North Yarmouth Academy. **N. Arizona Univ.:** Northern Arizona University. **N. Michigan Univ.:** Northern Michigan University. **NW Americans Jr. B:** Northwest Americans Junior B. **Poji. Pardubice Jrs.:** Pojistovna Pardubice Juniors. **Prin. Edward Island:** Prince Edward Island. **Rus. Olympic team:** Russian Olympic team. **Sault Ste. Marie:** Sault Sainte Marie. **Sever. Cherepovets:** Severstal Cherepovets. **Slovakian Oly. team:** Slovakian Olympic team. **Sov. Olympic team:** Soviet Olympic team. **Spisska N.V.:** Spisska Nova Ves. **Stad. Hradec Kralove:** Stadion Hradec Kralove. **Swed. Olympic team:** Swedish Olympic team. **Tor. Nizhny Nov.:** Torpedo Nizhny Novgorod. **Torpedo Ust-Kam.:** Torpedo Ust-Kamenogorsk. **Ukrainian Oly. team:** Ukrainian Olympic team. **Unif. Olympic team:** Unified Olympic team. **Univ. of New Hamp.:** University of New Hampshire. **Univ. of West. Ontario:** University of Western Ontario. **V. Frolunda Goteborg:** Vastra Frolunda Goteborg.

LEAGUES: AAHL: All American Hockey League. **ACHL:** Atlantic Coast Hockey League. **AHL:** American Hockey League. **AJHL:** Alberta Junior Hockey League. **AMHL:** Alberta Minor Hockey League. **AUAA:** Atlantic Universities Athletic Association. **BCJHL:** British Columbia Junior Hockey League. **CAHL:** Central Alberta Hockey League. **CAJHL:** Central Alberta Junior Hockey League. **Can. College:** Canadian College. **Can.HL:** Canadian Hockey League. **CCHA:** Central Collegiate Hockey Association. **CHL:** Central Hockey League. **CIS:** Commonwealth of Independent States. **CJHL:** Central Junior A Hockey League. **COJHL:** Central Ontario Junior Hockey League. **CPHL:** Central Professional Hockey League. **CWUAA:** Canada West University Athletic Association. **Conn. H.S.:** Connecticut High School. **Czech.:** Czechoslovakia. **Czech. Jrs.:** Czech Republic Junior. **Czech Rep.:** Czech Republic. **ECAC:** Eastern College Athletic Conference. **ECAC-II:** Eastern College Athletic Conference, Division II. **ECHL:** East Coast Hockey League. **EEHL:** Eastern European Hockey League. **EHL:** Eastern Hockey League. **EURO:** Euroliga. **Fin.:** Finland. **Ger.:** Germany. **GWHC:** Great Western Hockey Conference. **Hoc. East:** Hockey East. **IHL:** International Hockey League. **Ill. H.S.:** Illinois High School. **Indiana H.S.:** Indiana High School. **Int'l:** International. **KIJHL:** Kootenay International Junior Hockey League. **Mass. H.S.:** Massachusetts High School. **Md. H.S.:** Maryland High School. **Met. Bos.:** Metro Boston. **Mich. H.S.:** Michigan High School. **Minn. H.S.:** Minnesota High School. **MJHL:** Manitoba Junior Hockey League. **MTHL:** Metro Toronto Hockey League. **NAHL:** North American Hockey League. **NAJHL:** North American Junior Hockey League. **N.B. H.S.:** New Brunswick High School. **NCAA-II:** National Collegiate Athletic Association, Division II. **N.D. H.S.:** North Dakota High School. **NEJHL:** New England Junior Hockey League. **NHL:** National Hockey League. **N.H. H.S.:** New Hampshire High School. **N.J. H.S.:** New Jersey High School. **Nia. D. Jr. C:** Niagara District Junior C. **NSJHL:** Nova Scotia Junior Hockey League. **N.S. Jr. A:** Nova Scotia Junior A. **N.Y. H.S.:** New York High School. **NYMJHL:** New York Major Junior Hockey League. **NYOHL:** North York Ontario Hockey League. **ODHA:** Ottawa & District Hockey Association. **OHA:** Ontario Hockey Association. **OHA Jr. A:** Ontario Hockey Association Junior A. **OHA Mjr. Jr. A:** Ontario Hockey Association Major Junior A. **OHA Senior:** Ontario Hockey Association Senior. **OHL:** Ontario Hockey League. **O.H.S.:** Ohio High School. **OJHA:** Ontario Junior Hockey Association. **OJHL:** Ontario Junior Hockey League. **OMJHL:** Ontario Major Junior Hockey League. **OPJHL:** Ontario Provincial Junior Hockey League. **OUAA:** Ontario Universities Athletic Association. **PCJHL:** Peace Caribou Junior Hockey League. **PEIHA:** Prince Edward Island Hockey Association. **PEIJHL:** Prince Edward Island Junior Hockey League. **Penn. H.S.:** Pennsylvania High School. **QMJHL:** Quebec Major Junior Hockey League. **R.I. H.S.:** Rhode Island High School. **Rus. Div II, III:** Russian Division II, III. **SAJHL:** Southern Alberta Junior Hockey League. **SJHL:** Saskatchewan Junior Hockey League. **Sask. H.S.:** Saskatchewan High School. **SOJHL:** Southern Ontario Junior Hockey League. **Swed. Jr.:** Sweden Junior. **Switz.:** Switzerland. **TBAHA:** Thunder Bay Amateur Hockey Association. **TBJHL:** Thunder Bay Junior Hockey League. **UHL:** United Hockey League. **USHL:** United States Hockey League. **USHS:** United States High School. **USSR:** Union of Soviet Socialist Republics. **Vt. H.S.:** Vermont High School. **W. Germany, W. Ger.:** West Germany. **WCHA:** Western Collegiate Hockey Association. **WCHL:** Western Canada Hockey League. **WHA:** World Hockey Association. **WHL:** Western Hockey League. **Wisc. H.S.:** Wisconsin High School. **Yukon Sr.:** Yukon Senior.

THE NEW NHL

Changes to the NHL's on-ice product as included in the new collective bargaining agreement:

SHOOTOUTS

If a game is tied at the end of regulation time, teams play a 4-on-4, sudden-death overtime period. If the game remains tied at the end of the 5-minute overtime, a shootout (3 shooters per team; if teams still tied after 3 shots, then sudden death) is used. If a game is tied 3-3 after regulation and goes to a shootout, the final score of the game will be 4-3, regardless the number of goals scored in the shootout. Individual statistics will not be kept from shootouts. Also, a goalie will not be charged with a loss should he lose in overtime or in a shootout. Instead, such a decision will be added to a goalie's OT column (the same as team standings—W-L-OT).

SMALLER GOALIE EQUIPMENT

Goalie equipment has been reduced by about 11 percent. In addition to a 1-inch reduction (to 11 inches) in the width of legpads, the blocking glove, upper-body protector, pants and jersey also have been reduced in size.

REPOSITIONED LINES

The neutral-zone edges of the blue lines are 64 feet from the attacking goal line and 75 feet from the end boards in the attacking zone. The goal lines are 11 feet from the end boards, 2 feet closer to the end boards than previously. The size of the neutral zone has been reduced to 50 feet (from 54 feet).

OFFSIDES

Passes from behind the defensive blue line to the attacking blue line are considered legal. The center red line is used only to determine icing. The tag-up rule permits play to continue if offensive players who preceded the puck into the zone return to the blue line and "tag" it.

ICING

Icing offenses are still penalized by a faceoff in the defensive zone of the team that ices the puck. A team that iced the puck cannot make a line change before the ensuing faceoff. Touch icing remains the practice, although linesmen have discretion to wave off apparent icing infractions if they are deemed the result of an attempted pass.

INSTIGATOR RULE

A player who instigates a fight in the final 5 minutes of a game receives a game misconduct and an automatic 1-game suspension. The length of the suspension doubles for each additional incident. As well, the player's coach will be fined $10,000—a fine that would double for each such incident.

PUCK-HANDLING GOALTENDERS

Goaltenders may play the puck behind the goal line only in a trapezoid-shaped area defined by lines that begin 6 feet from either goal post and extend diagonally to points 28 feet apart at the end boards. Goaltenders who play the puck behind the goal line but outside the designated puck-handling area will be penalized for delay of game.

DELAY OF GAME

Officials have been instructed to enforce zero tolerance on interference, hooking and holding/obstruction. Further to this goal, goaltenders will be penalized for delaying the game if they freeze the puck unnecessarily, as will a player who shoots the puck directly over the glass in his defending zone.

UNSPORTSMANLIKE CONDUCT

In addition to the minor penalty for unsportsmanlike conduct-diving that may be assessed by the referee during a game, hockey operations will review game videos and assess fines to players who dive or embellish a fall or a reaction, or who feign injury in an attempt to draw penalties. Postgame consequences range according to frequency of offense from a warning letter to a 1-game suspension.

RIVALRY-HEAVY SCHEDULE

Each club will play 8 games against each of its 4 division rivals (32 total). Each club will play 4 games against each of the 10 nondivision clubs in its conference (40 total). Each club will play 10 interconference games, hosting one game each against all 5 clubs from a designated division and traveling for 1 game each against all 5 clubs from a different division. For 2005-06, Northeast Division teams will host the Pacific Division and visit the Northwest Division; Atlantic teams will host the Northwest and visit the Central; and Southeast teams will host the Central and visit the Pacific. Division vs. division assignments will rotate annually.

ANAHEIM MIGHTY DUCKS
WESTERN CONFERENCE, PACIFIC DIVISION

Mighty Ducks Schedule
Home games shaded.

October

SUN	MON	TUE	WED	THU	FRI	SAT
2	3	4	5 CHI	6	7	8 NAS
9	10 EDM	11	12	13	14 COB	15
16 MIN	17	18	19 STL	20	21 DET	22
23 PHO	24	25 LA	26 CAL	27	28 STL	29
30 PHO	31					

November

SUN	MON	TUE	WED	THU	FRI	SAT
		1 NAS	2	3 COL	4 SJ	5
6 MIN	7	8	9	10	11	12 PHO
13 DAL	14	15	16 DAL	17	18 COL	19
20 VAN	21	22 PHO	23 DAL	24	25 DET	26
27 CHI	28	29	30 PHO			

December

SUN	MON	TUE	WED	THU	FRI	SAT
				1	2	3 ATL
4	5	6 CAR	7	8 BUF	9	10 MON
11	12 TOR	13	14 TB	15	16 LA	17
18 SJ	19	20 SJ	21 STL	22	23	24
25	26	27	28 COB	29	30	31 STL

January

SUN	MON	TUE	WED	THU	FRI	SAT
1 NAS	2	3	4	5	6 DAL	7 MIN
8	9 LA	10	11	12	13 WAS	14
15	16 BOS	17	18	19 OTT	20	21 FLA
22	23 LA	24	25 EDM	26 SJ	27	28 LA
29	30 LA	31				

February

SUN	MON	TUE	WED	THU	FRI	SAT
			1 SJ	2	3	4 SJ
5	6 EDM	7	8 CAL	9	10 VAN	11
12 CHI	13	14	15	16	17	18
19	20	21	22	23	24	25
26	27	28				

March

SUN	MON	TUE	WED	THU	FRI	SAT
			1 DET	2	3 MIN	4
5 COB	6	7 SJ	8	9	10	11 PHO
12 PHO	13	14	15 DET	16	17 CHI	18
19 COB	20 DAL	21	22 COL	23	24 NAS	25 PHO
26	27	28 COL	29 DAL	30	31 DAL	

April

SUN	MON	TUE	WED	THU	FRI	SAT
						1
2 VAN	3	4 LA	5	6 DAL	7	8 LA
9	10 VAN	11 CAL	12	13 EDM	14	15 SJ
16	17 CAL	18	19	20	21	22

2005-06 SEASON
CLUB DIRECTORY

Executive vice president, general manager
Brian Burke
Vice president of hockey operation
Bob Murray
Assistant general manager
Chuck Fletcher
Assistant general manager
David McNab
Director of professional scouting
Rick Paterson
Head coach
Randy Carlyle
Director of communications/team services
Alex Gilchrist
Manager of communications/team services
Merit Tully
Communications and team services coordinator
Ryan Lichtenfels
Strength and conditioning coordinator
Sean Skahan
Equipment manager
Mark O'Neill
Assistant equipment manager
John Allaway

TOP FOUR DRAFT CHOICES

2005

Rd.-Overall	Ht., Wt.	Amateur league, team	Position
1-2 BOBBY RYAN	6-1, 213	OHL Owen Sound	RW
2-31 BRENDAN MIKKELSON	6-2, 180	WHL Portland	D
3-63 JASON BAILEY	6-0, 205	U.S. National	RW
5-127 BOBBY BOLT	6-3, 219	OHL Kingston	LW

2004

Rd.-Overall	Ht., Wt.	Amateur league, team	Position
1-9 LADISLAV SMID	6-3, 202	Czech Liberec	D
2-39 JORDAN SMITH	6-1, 207	OHL Sault Ste. Marie	D
3-74 KYLE KLUBERTANZ	6-0, 178	USHL Green Bay	D
3-75 TIM BRENT	5-11, 177	OHL St. Michael's	C

MISCELLANEOUS DATA

Home ice (capacity)
The Arrowhead Pond of Anaheim (17,174)
Address
2695 E. Katella Avenue
P.O. Box 61077
Anaheim, CA 92803-6177
Business phone
714-940-2900
Ticket information
877-945-3946
Website
www.mightyducks.com
Training site
Anaheim
Club colors
Purple, jade, silver and white
Radio affiliation
Mighty 1090 AM
TV affiliation
KCAL (Channel 9), FOX Sports West 2 (Cable)

ATLANTA THRASHERS

EASTERN CONFERENCE, SOUTHEAST DIVISION

ATLANTA THRASHERS

Thrashers Schedule

Home games shaded.

October

SUN	MON	TUE	WED	THU	FRI	SAT
2	3	4	5 FLA	6	7 WAS	8 WAS
9	10	11	12 MON	13	14 TOR	15 NYR
16	17	18	19	20 TB	21	22 NJ
23	24	25 NYI	26	27 PIT	28	29 TB
30	31					

November

SUN	MON	TUE	WED	THU	FRI	SAT
	1 TB	2	3	4 WAS	5 PHI	6
7	8	9 PIT	10	11 TB	12 CAR	13
14	15	16 NYI	17	18 PHI	19 TOR	20
21	22 MON	23	24 NYR	25	26 FLA	27 CAR
28	29 CAR	30				

December

SUN	MON	TUE	WED	THU	FRI	SAT
			1 TOR	2	3 ANA	4
5 PHO	6 SJ	7	8	9 COL	10	11 CHI
12	13 DET	14	15 NJ	16	17 FLA	18
19	20	21	22 WAS	23 NJ	24	25
26 MON	27	28 PHI	29	30 BUF	31	

January

SUN	MON	TUE	WED	THU	FRI	SAT
						1 WAS
2 OTT	3	4 CAR	5	6 PIT	7 PIT	8
9	10	11 WAS	12	13 STL	14	15
16	17	18 DAL	19 LA	20	21 TB	22
23	24 BOS	25	26 CAR	27	28 CAR	29
30	31 BUF					

February

SUN	MON	TUE	WED	THU	FRI	SAT
		1	2	3 FLA	4 FLA	5
6	7 TOR	8	9 OTT	10	11 MON	12
13	14	15	16	17	18	19
20	21	22	23	24	25	26
27	28					

March

SUN	MON	TUE	WED	THU	FRI	SAT
		1 BUF	2 BOS	3	4 WAS	5
6 FLA	7	8 NYR	9	10 OTT	11	12 NYR
13	14	15	16 NYI	17	18 PHI	19
20 BUF	21 BOS	22	23 NJ	24	25 NYI	26
27	28	29	30 TB	31		

April

SUN	MON	TUE	WED	THU	FRI	SAT
					1 CAR	2
3 OTT	4	5 FLA	6 TB	7	8 CAR	9
10	11 TB	12	13 WAS	14	15 BOS	16
17 WAS	18 FLA	19	20	21	22	23

2005-06 SEASON

CLUB DIRECTORY

Owners/Atlanta Spirit, LLC
Bruce Levenson (governor), Rutherford Seydel (alt. gov.), Steve Belkin, Michael Gearon, Ed Peskowitz

Investors/Atlanta Spirit, LLC
Todd Foreman, Michael Gearon Sr., Bud Seretean, Beau Turner, Dominique Wilkins

President and c.e.o./alt. gov.
Bernard J. Mullin

Exec. v.p. and G.M./alt. gov.
Don Waddell

Exec. v.p. and chief marketing officer
Lou DePaoli

Exec. v.p. and chief financial officer
Bill Duffy

Senior v.p., broadcast and corporate partnerships
Tracy White

Senior v.p., communications
Tom Hughes

Senior v.p., ticket sales and services
Jeff Morander

V.p., marketing/advertising/branding
Jim Pfeifer

V.p. and assistant g.m.
Larry Simmons

Head coach
Bob Hartley

Assistant coaches
Brad McCrimmon, Steve Weeks

Director of player personnel
Jack Ferriera

Dir. of amateur scouting and player dev.
Dan Marr

Head scout
Marcel Comeau

Senior director of team services
Michele Zarzaca

Senior director of public relations
Rob Koch

Manager of media relations
John Heid

Assistant director of communications
Brian Potter

Head trainer
Craig Brewer

Assistant athletic trainer
Stephen Roberts

Equipment manager
Bobby Stewart

Assistant equipment manager
Joe Guilmet, Jim Guilmet

Strength and conditioning coach
Ray Bear

Massage therapist
Inar Treiguts

Video/hockey operations coordinator
Tony Borgford

TOP FOUR DRAFT CHOICES

2005

Rd.-Overall	Ht., Wt.	Amateur league, team	Position
1-16 ALEX BOURRET	5-9, 209	QMJHL Lewiston	RW
2-41 ONDREJ PAVELEC	6-2, 177	Czech Jr. Kladno	G
2-49 CHAD DENNY	6-2, 210	QMJHL Lewiston	D
2-53 ANDREW KOZEK	5-10, 175	BCHL South Surrey	W

2004

Rd.-Overall	Ht., Wt.	Amateur league, team	Position
1-10 BORIS VALABIK	6-7, 212	OHL Kitchener	D
2-40 GRANT LEWIS	6-3, 190	ECAC Dartmouth	D
3-76 SCOTT LEHMAN	6-1, 194	OHL St. Michael's	D
4-106 CHAD PAINCHAUD	5-11, 172	OHL Mississauga	LW

MISCELLANEOUS DATA

Home ice (capacity)
Philips Arena (18,545)

Address
One Philips Drive
Atlanta, GA 30303

Business phone
404-827-5300

Ticket information
404-584-7825

Website
www.atlantathrashers.com

Training site
Ice Forum, Duluth, GA

Club colors
Navy, blue, copper, bronze and gold

Radio affiliation
WQXI (790 AM), WLKQ (102.3 FM)

TV affiliation
Turner South, WUPA/UPN (Channel 69)

BOSTON BRUINS
EASTERN CONFERENCE/NORTHEAST DIVISION

Bruins Schedule
Home games shaded.

October

SUN	MON	TUE	WED	THU	FRI	SAT
2	3	4	5 MON	6	7 BUF	8 PIT
9	10 TB	11	12	13 FLA	14	15 OTT
16	17	18 MON	19	20 BUF	21	22 PIT
23	24 TOR	25	26 CAR	27 TOR	28	29 NJ
30	31					

November

SUN	MON	TUE	WED	THU	FRI	SAT
		1 NYI	2	3 FLA	4	5 PIT
6	7	8 PHI	9	10 OTT	11	12 NYI
13	14	15	16	17 TOR	18	19 BUF
20 NYR	21	22	23 TOR	24	25 PHI	26 OTT
27	28	29 NJ	30			

December

SUN	MON	TUE	WED	THU	FRI	SAT
				1 OTT	2	3 EDM
4 VAN	5	6	7 COL	8	9	10
11 PHO	12	13	14	15 MIN	16	17 CAL
18	19	20	21	22 TOR	23 TOR	24
25	26	27 WAS	28 FLA	29	30 TB	31

January

SUN	MON	TUE	WED	THU	FRI	SAT
1	2 PHI	3	4	5 OTT	6	7 TB
8	9	10 SJ	11	12 LA	13	14 DAL
15	16 ANA	17	18	19 PHI	20	21 NYR
22	23 WAS	24 ATL	25	26 WAS	27	28 NYI
29	30 OTT	31				

February

SUN	MON	TUE	WED	THU	FRI	SAT
			1	2 MON	3	4 MON
5 CAR	6	7	8 PIT	9 NJ	10	11 TB
12	13	14	15	16	17	18
19	20	21	22	23	24	25
26	27	28				

March

SUN	MON	TUE	WED	THU	FRI	SAT
			1 CAR	2 ATL	3	4 BUF
5	6	7 BUF	8	9 MON	10	11 NYI
12 BUF	13	14 TOR	15	16 OTT	17	18 CAR
19	20 NYR	21 ATL	22	23	24 NJ	25 BUF
26	27 FLA	28	29 BUF	30	31	

April

SUN	MON	TUE	WED	THU	FRI	SAT
						1 MON
2	3	4 MON	5	6 TOR	7	8 NYR
9	10 WAS	11 OTT	12	13 MON	14	15 ATL

2005-06 SEASON
CLUB DIRECTORY

Owner and governor
Jeremy M. Jacobs
Alternative governors
Charles Jacobs, Jeremy Jacobs Jr., Louis Jacobs
President and alternate governor
Harry Sinden
Senior assistant to the president
Nate Greenberg
V.p., g.m. and alternate governor
Mike O'Connell
Assistant general manager
Jeff Gorton
Executive vice presidents
Richard Krezwick, Charles Jacobs
Chief legal officer
Michael Wall
Chief financial officer
Jessica Rahuba
Director of administration
Dale Hamilton-Powers
Assistant to the president
Joe Curnane
Team travel coordinator/admin. asst.
Carol Gould
Coach
Mike Sullivan
Assistant coaches
Wayne Cashman, Norm Maciver
Goaltending consultant
Bob Essensa
Director of pro scouting & player dev.
Sean Coady
Director of amateur scouting
Scott Bradley
Scouting staff
Nikolai Bobrov, Gerry Cheevers, Adam Creighton, Daniel Dore, Oto Huscak, Mike McGraw, Tom McVie, Tom Songin, Svenake Svensson
Director of media relations
Heidi Holland
Media relations manager
Ryan Nadeau
Director of marketing and community relations
Sue Byrne
Strength & conditioning coach
John Whitesides
Athletic trainer
Don Del Negro
Physical therapist
Scott Waugh
Equipment manager
Peter Henderson
Assistant equipment managers
Chris "Muggsy" Aldrich
Keith Robinson

TOP FOUR DRAFT CHOICES

2005

Rd.-Overall	Ht., Wt.	Amateur league, team	Position
1-22 MATT LASHOFF	6-1, 201	OHL Kitchener	D
2-39 PETR KALUS	6-1, 186	Czech Jr. Vitkovice	C
3-83 MIKKO LEHTONEN	6-3, 196	Finland Jr. Espoo	RW
4-100 JONATHAN SIGALET	6-1, 185	CCHA Bowling Green	D

2004

Rd.-Overall	Ht., Wt.	Amateur league, team	Position
2-63 DAVID KREJCI	5-11, 176	Czech Jr. Kladno	C
2-64 MARTINS KARSUMS	5-10, 177	QMJHL Moncton	RW
4-108 ASHTON ROME	6-0, 191	WHL Moose Jaw	RW
5-134 KRIS VERSTEEG	5-9, 159	WHL Lethbridge	RW

MISCELLANEOUS DATA

Home ice (capacity)
TD Banknorth Garden (17,565)
Address
TD Banknorth Garden, 100 Legends Way Boston, MA 02114-1303
Business phone
617-624-1900
Ticket information
(617) 624-BEAR
Website
www.bostonbruins.com
Training site
Ristuccia Memorial Arena (Wilmington, MA)
Club colors
Gold, black and white
Radio affiliation
WBZ (1030 AM) & Bruins Radio Net.
TV affiliation
UPN38 & NESN

BUFFALO SABRES
EASTERN CONFERENCE, NORTHEAST DIVISION

Sabres Schedule
Home games shaded.

October

SUN	MON	TUE	WED	THU	FRI	SAT
2	3	4	5 NYI	6	7 BOS	8 OTT
9	10 PIT	11	12	13 TB	14	15 FLA
16	17	18	19	20 BOS	21	22 NYR
23	24	25	26 WAS	27	28 NJ	29 NYI
30	31					

November

SUN	MON	TUE	WED	THU	FRI	SAT
		1	2 OTT	3	4 MON	5 MON
6	7	8	9 CAR	10	11 TOR	12 OTT
13	14	15 NJ	16	17 WAS	18	19 BOS
20	21	22 NYR	23 NYI	24	25 MON	26
27 WAS	28	29 PIT	30			

December

SUN	MON	TUE	WED	THU	FRI	SAT
				1 MON	2 SJ	3
4 COL	5	6	7	8 ANA	9	10
11 MIN	12	13	14 DAL	15	16 PIT	17 PIT
18	19 PHI	20	21	22 FLA	23 TB	24
25	26 NYI	27	28	29 TOR	30 ATL	31

January

SUN	MON	TUE	WED	THU	FRI	SAT
1 FLA	2	3	4	5 TB	6	7 NJ
8	9	10	11	12 PHO	13	14 LA
15	16 EDM	17	18	19 VAN	20	21 CAL
22	23	24 NYR	25	26 TOR	27	28
29	30	31 ATL				

February

SUN	MON	TUE	WED	THU	FRI	SAT
			1	2 PHI	3	4 OTT
5	6	7 MON	8	9 MON	10	11 FLA
12 CAR	13	14	15	16	17	18
19	20	21	22	23	24	25
26	27	28				

March

SUN	MON	TUE	WED	THU	FRI	SAT
			1 ATL	2	3 TOR	4 BOS
5	6	7 BOS	8	9 TB	10	11 PHI
12 BOS	13	14 WAS	15	16 TOR	17	18 OTT
19	20 ATL	21	22 CAR	23	24 OTT	25 BOS
26	27 NYR	28	29 BOS	30 NJ	31	

April

SUN	MON	TUE	WED	THU	FRI	SAT
						1 TOR
2	3 TOR	4	5 OTT	6	7 PHI	8 OTT
9	10	11	12 MON	13	14	15 MON
16 TOR	17	18 CAR	19	20	21	22

2005-06 SEASON
CLUB DIRECTORY

Owner
B. Thomas Golisano
Managing partner
Lawrence Quinn
Chief operating officer
Daniel DiPofi
Director of public relations
Michael Gilbert
Director of marketing
Rob Kopacz
General manager
Darcy Regier
Head coach
Lindy Ruff
Assistant coaches
Scott Arneil, Brian McCutcheon
Manager of publications & hockey information
Kevin Snow
Media relations coordinator
Chris Bandura
Director of player personnel
Jim Benning
Professional scout
Kevin Devine
Scouting staff
Bo Berglund, Jon Christiano, Iouri Khmylev, Paul Merritt, Rudy Migay, Darryl Plandowski, Mike Racicot, David Volek
Strength & conditioning coach
Doug McKenney
Goaltender coach
Jim Corsi
Administrative assistant coach
Jeff Holbrook
Head equipment manager
Rip Simonick
Assistant equipment manager
George Babcock
Team doctor
John Marzo

TOP FOUR DRAFT CHOICES

2005

Rd.-Overall	Ht., Wt.	Amateur league, team	Position
1-13 MAREK ZAGRAPAN	6-0, 195	QMJHL Chicoutimi	C
2-48 PHILIPPE GOGULLA	6-2, 176	Germany Koln	W
3-87 MARC-ANDRE GRAGNANI	6-1, 180	QMJHL P.E.I.	D
4-96 CHRIS BUTLER	6-1, 178	USHL Sioux City	D

2004

Rd.-Overall	Ht., Wt.	Amateur league, team	Position
1-13 DREW STAFFORD	6-1, 202	WCHA U. of North Dakota	RW
2-43 MICHAEL FUNK	6-4, 199	WHL Portland	D
3-71 ANDREJ SEKERA	6-0, 187	Slovakia Jr. Trencin	D
5-145 MICHAL VALENT	6-2, 176	Slovakia Jr. Martin	G

MISCELLANEOUS DATA

Home ice (capacity)
HSBC Arena (18,690)
Address
HSBC Arena
One Seymour H. Knox III Plaza
Buffalo, NY 14203
Business phone
716-855-4100
Ticket information
888-223-6000
Website
www.sabres.com
Training site
Buffalo, NY
Club colors
Black, white, red, gray and silver
Radio affiliation
WGR (550 AM)
TV affiliation
MSG Network

CALGARY FLAMES
WESTERN CONFERENCE, NORTHWEST DIVISION

Flames Schedule

Home games shaded.

October

SUN	MON	TUE	WED	THU	FRI	SAT
2	3	4	5 MIN	6	7 COB	8
9 DET	10 COL	11	12	13 DAL	14	15 EDM
16	17 PHO	18	19	20 EDM	21	22 DAL
23 LA	24	25	26 ANA	27 PHO	28	29 SJ
30	31					

November

SUN	MON	TUE	WED	THU	FRI	SAT
		1 MIN	2	3 COB	4	5 VAN
6	7 VAN	8	9	10 PHO	11	12 COL
13	14 MIN	15	16 DET	17	18 CHI	19
20	21 COL	22	23 SJ	24	25 EDM	26
27	28	29 NAS	30			

December

SUN	MON	TUE	WED	THU	FRI	SAT
				1 DET	2	3 PIT
4	5	6 PHI	7 NJ	8	9	10 OTT
11	12	13	14	15	16	17 BOS
18	19 EDM	20	21 LA	22	23 VAN	24
25	26 VAN	27 NAS	28	29 MIN	30	31 EDM

January

SUN	MON	TUE	WED	THU	FRI	SAT
1	2 CHI	3	4	5	6 TOR	7 VAN
8	9	10 NYR	11	12 NYI	13	14 MIN
15	16	17	18	19 MON	20	21 BUF
22	23 EDM	24 COL	25	26 CHI	27	28
29 CHI	30 STL	31				

February

SUN	MON	TUE	WED	THU	FRI	SAT
			1 COB	2	3 VAN	4
5	6 SJ	7	8 ANA	9	10 STL	11
12	13	14	15	16	17	18
19	20	21	22	23	24	25
26	27	28 VAN				

March

SUN	MON	TUE	WED	THU	FRI	SAT
			1	2 STL	3	4 SJ
5	6	7 NAS	8	9 DAL	10	11
12 COL	13 COL	14	15	16 EDM	17	18 NAS
19 MIN	20	21 MIN	22	23 STL	24 COB	25
26 DAL	27	28	29 LA	30	31 COL	

April

SUN	MON	TUE	WED	THU	FRI	SAT
						1 EDM
2	3 DET	4	5 PHO	6	7 MIN	8 VAN
9	10	11 ANA	12	13 COL	14	15 LA
16	17 ANA	18	19	20	21	22

2005-06 SEASON
CLUB DIRECTORY

Co-owners
N. Murray Edwards, Harley N. Hotchkiss, Alvin G. Libin, Allan P. Markin, J.R. (Bud) McCaig, Byron J. Seaman, Daryl K. Seaman, Clayton H. Riddell

President & chief executive officer
Ken King

General manager/head coach
Darryl Sutter

Vice president, hockey administration
Michael Holditch

Vice president, building operations
Libby Raines

Vice president, business development
Jim Peplinski

Vice president, advertising/marketing
Jim Bagshaw

Vice president, sales
Rollie Cyr

Director, hockey administration
Mike Burke

Special assistant to the G.M.
Al MacNeil

Assistant coaches
Jim Playfair, Rich Preston, Rob Cookson

Development coach
Jamie Hislop

Goaltending coach
David Marcoux

Team services manager
Kelly Chesla

Director of scouting
Tod Button

Director of amateur scouting
Mike Sands

Pro scouts
Ron Sutter, Tom Webster

Scouts
Tomas Jelinek, Randy Hansch, Sergei Samoilov, Al Tuer, Craig Demetrick, Fred Devereaux, Ralph Schmidt, Anders Steen, Rich Thibeau

Athletic therapist
Morris Boyer

Assistant athletic therapist
Gerry Kurylowich

Strength & conditioning coach
Rich Hesketh

Equipment manager
Gus Thorson

Assistant equipment manager
Les Jarvis

Team physicians
Dr. Kelly Brett, Dr. Jim Thorne

Team dentist
Dr. Bill Blair

V.p., communications
Peter Hanlon

Manager, media relations
Sean O'Brien

Admin. assistant, communications
Bernie Hargrave

TOP FOUR DRAFT CHOICES

2005

Rd.-Overall	Ht., Wt.	Amateur league, team	Position
1-26 MATT PELECH	6-3, 220	OHL Sarnia	D
3-69 GORD BALDWIN	6-5, 199	WHL Medicine Hat	D
3-74 DAN RYDER	5-10, 193	OHL Peterborough	C
4-111 J.D. WATT	6-1, 198	WHL Vancouver	RW

2004

Rd.-Overall	Ht., Wt.	Amateur league, team	Position
1-24 KRIS CHUCKO	6-2, 190	BCHL Salmon Arm	LW
3-70 BRANDON PRUST	5-11, 191	OHL London	C/LW
3-98 DUSTIN BOYD	6-0, 186	WHL Moose Jaw	C
4-118 AKI SEITSONEN	6-3, 206	WHL Prince Albert	C

MISCELLANEOUS DATA

Home ice (capacity)
Pengrowth Saddledome (17,439)

Address
P.O. Box 1540, Station M, Calgary, Alta. T2P 3B9

Business phone
403-777-2177

Ticket information
403-777-0000

Website
www.calgaryflames.com

Training site
Pengrowth Saddledome

Club colors
Red, white, gold and black

Radio affiliation
The Fan 960 (960 AM)

TV affiliations
Rogers Sportsnet, CBC, TSN, PPV

CAROLINA HURRICANES

EASTERN CONFERENCE, SOUTHEAST DIVISION

Hurricanes Schedule

Home games shaded.

October

SUN	MON	TUE	WED	THU	FRI	SAT
2	3	4	5 TB	6	7 PIT	8 NYI
9	10	11	12 WAS	13	14	15 NJ
16	17	18	19	20 TOR	21	22 WAS
23	24 OTT	25	26 BOS	27	28 PHI	29 PIT
30	31					

November

SUN	MON	TUE	WED	THU	FRI	SAT
		1	2	3 TOR	4	5 FLA
6	7	8	9 BUF	10	11 FLA	12 ATL
13	14	15 OTT	16	17 NYR	18	19 NYR
20 TB	21	22 OTT	23	24	25 TOR	26
27 ATL	28	29 ATL	30			

December

SUN	MON	TUE	WED	THU	FRI	SAT
				1	2 DAL	3 PHO
4	5	6 ANA	7	8 LA	9	10 SJ
11	12	13 CHI	14	15 COB	16	17 NJ
18	19	20 TB	21	22	23 FLA	24
25	26 TB	27	28 OTT	29 PHI	30	31 MON

January

SUN	MON	TUE	WED	THU	FRI	SAT
1	2	3	4 ATL	5	6 NYI	7 NYI
8	9	10 DET	11	12	13 NAS	14
15 STL	16	17 PHI	18	19 NYI	20	21 WAS
22	23 MON	24	25 FLA	26 ATL	27	28 ATL
29	30	31 MON				

February

SUN	MON	TUE	WED	THU	FRI	SAT
			1	2	3 NJ	4
5 BOS	6	7	8	9 TB	10 PIT	11
12 BUF	13	14	15	16	17	18
19	20	21	22	23	24	25
26	27	28				

March

SUN	MON	TUE	WED	THU	FRI	SAT
			1 BOS	2	3 FLA	4 PIT
5	6 NYR	7	8 PHI	9	10	11 FLA
12 FLA	13	14 NYR	15	16 MON	17	18 BOS
19	20	21 TOR	22 BUF	23	24	25 WAS
26	27 TB	28	29 WAS	30	31 FLA	

April

SUN	MON	TUE	WED	THU	FRI	SAT
						1 ATL
2	3 WAS	4	5 WAS	6	7 WAS	8 ATL
9	10	11 NJ	12	13	14 TB	15 TB
16	17	18 BUF	19	20	21	22

2005-06 SEASON

CLUB DIRECTORY

Owner/governor
Peter Karmanos Jr.
General partner
Thomas Thewes
President/general manager
Jim Rutherford
Vice president/asst. general manager
Jason Karmanos
Chief financial officer
Mike Amendola
V.p., business operations
Matt West
V.p.,general manager
Davin Olsen
Head coach
Peter Laviolette
Assistant coaches
Jeff Daniels
Kevin McCarthy
Goaltending coach/pro scout
Sheldon Ferguson
Director of amateur scouting
Sheldon Ferguson
Director of professional scouting
Marshall Johnston
Amateur scouts
Martin Madden
Tony MacDonald
Bert Marshall
Pro scout
Claude Larose, Ron Smith
Video coordinator
Chris Huffine
Head athletic therapist/strength and conditioning coach
Peter Friesen
Equipment managers
Skip Cunningham
Bob Gorman
Wally Tatomir
Director of media relations
Mike Sundheim
Manager of media relations
Kyle Hanlin

TOP FOUR DRAFT CHOICES

2005

Rd.-Overall	Ht., Wt.	Amateur league, team	Position
1-3 JACK JOHNSON	6-1, 201	U.S. National	D
2-58 NATHAN HAGEMO	5-11, 192	WCHA U. of Minnesota	D
3-64 JOE BARNES	6-3, 212	WHL Saskatoon	C
4-94 JAKUB VOJTA	6-0, 194	Czech Jr. Sparta	D

2004

Rd.-Overall	Ht., Wt.	Amateur league, team	Position
1-4 ANDREW LADD	6-2, 200	WHL Calgary	LW
2-38 JUSTIN PETERS	6-0, 209	OHL St. Michael's	G
3-69 CASEY BORER	6-2, 197	WCHA St. Cloud State	D
4-109 BRETT CARSON	6-4, 220	WHL Calgary	D

MISCELLANEOUS DATA

Home ice (capacity)
RBC Center (18,730)
Address
1400 Edwards Mill Road
Raleigh, NC 27607
Business phone
919-467-7825
Ticket information
866-NHL-CANES (645-2263)
Website
www.carolinahurricanes.com
Training site
RecZone
Club colors
Red, white, black and silver
Radio affiliation
102.9 FM)
TV affiliation
FOX Sports Net

CHICAGO BLACKHAWKS
WESTERN CONFERENCE, CENTRAL DIVISION

Blackhawks Schedule
Home games shaded.

October

SUN	MON	TUE	WED	THU	FRI	SAT
2	3	4	5 ANA	6	7 SJ	8
9 COB	10	11 STL	12	13	14 COL	15 SJ
16	17	18 VAN	19	20	21	22
23 MIN	24	25 NAS	26	27 DET	28	29 DET
30	31					

November

SUN	MON	TUE	WED	THU	FRI	SAT
		1 DET	2 STL	3	4 DAL	5
6 PHO	7	8	9	10 STL	11 LA	12
13 EDM	14	15	16	17	18 CAL	19 EDM
20	21	22 VAN	23	24	25	26 LA
27 ANA	28	29	30 LA			

December

SUN	MON	TUE	WED	THU	FRI	SAT
				1	2 TB	3 FLA
4	5	6	7 NYR	8	9	10
11 ATL	12	13 CAR	14	15 NAS	16 STL	17
18 DAL	19	20	21 NAS	22	23 DET	24
25	26 COB	27	28 STL	29	30 COB	31

January

SUN	MON	TUE	WED	THU	FRI	SAT
1	2 CAL	3 EDM	4	5 VAN	6	7
8 NAS	9	10 WAS	11 PHI	12	13 PIT	14
15 NJ	16	17 NYI	18	19 COL	20 MIN	21
22 MIN	23	24	25	26 CAL	27	28
29 CAL	30	31				

February

SUN	MON	TUE	WED	THU	FRI	SAT
			1	2 STL	3	4 NAS
5	6	7 PHO	8 SJ	9	10	11 LA
12 ANA	13	14	15	16	17	18
19	20	21	22	23	24	25
26	27	28				

March

SUN	MON	TUE	WED	THU	FRI	SAT
			1 NAS	2	3 VAN	4
5 DAL	6	7 COB	8	9 COL	10	11 DET
12 DET	13	14	15 COB	16	17 ANA	18
19 PHO	20	21	22	23 PHO	24 DAL	25
26 SJ	27	28	29 STL	30	31 DET	

April

SUN	MON	TUE	WED	THU	FRI	SAT
						1 COB
2	3 COL	4	5 NAS	6	7 EDM	8 NAS
9	10	11 MIN	12	13 DET	14	15 COB
16 COB	17	18 STL	19	20	21	22

2005-06 SEASON
CLUB DIRECTORY

President
William W. Wirtz
Senior vice president
Robert J. Pulford
Vice president
Peter R. Wirtz
General manager
Dale Tallon
Hockey operations consultant
Rick Dudley
Head coach
Trent Yawney
Assistant coaches
Denis Savard
Bruce Cassidy
Strength and conditioning coach
Phil Walker
Goaltending consultant
Vladislav Tretiak
Goaltending coach
Stephane Waite
Scouts
Ron Anderson, Bruce Franklin, Tim Higgins, Rob Pulford
Chief amateur scout
Michel Dumas
European scouting coordinator
Sakari Pietela
Assistant to the G.M.
Stan Bowman
Head trainer
Michael Gapski
Equipment manager
Troy Parchman
Massage therapist
Pawel Prylinski
Executive director of communications
Jim De Maria
Director of community outreach
Jim Blaney
Manager of p.r. and team services
Tony Ommen
Exec. dir. of marketing and sales
Jim Sofranko
Manager, game operations
Ben Broder
Manager, community outreach
Angela Armbruster
Director of In-Kind Giving
Barbara Davidson
Director of ticket operations
James K. Bare
Sales manager
Doug Ryan
Website producer
Adam Kempenaar
Executive assistant
Alison Finley

TOP FOUR DRAFT CHOICES

2005

Rd.-Overall	Ht., Wt.	Amateur league, team	Position
1-7 JACK SKILLE	6-1, 198	U.S. National	RW
2-43 MICHAEL BLUNDEN	6-3 213	OHL Erie	RW
2-54 DAN BERTRAM	5-11, 175	HE Boston College	RW
3-68 EVAN BROPHEY	6-1, 194	OHL Belleville	C/LW

2004

Rd.-Overall	Ht., Wt.	Amateur league, team	Position
1-3 CAMERON BARKER	6-3, 214	WHL Medicine Hat	D
2-32 DAVE BOLLAND	5-11, 171	OHL London	C/RW
2-41 BRYAN BICKELL	6-3, 210	OHL Ottawa	LW
2-45 RYAN GARLOCK	6-0, 202	OHL Windsor	C

MISCELLANEOUS DATA

Home ice (capacity)
United Center (20,500)
Address
1901 W. Madison Street
Chicago, IL 60612
Business phone
312-455-7000
Ticket information
312-943-7000
Website
www.chicagoblackhawks.com
Training site
Chicago
Club colors
Red, black and white
Radio affiliation
WSCR (670 AM)
TV affiliation
FOX Sports Chicago

COLORADO AVALANCHE
WESTERN CONFERENCE, NORTHWEST DIVISION

Avalanche Schedule
Home games shaded.

October

SUN	MON	TUE	WED	THU	FRI	SAT
2	3	4	5 EDM	6	7	8 DAL
9	10 CAL	11	12 NAS	13	14 CHI	15
16	17	18	19 LA	20	21 EDM	22 VAN
23	24	25 EDM	26	27 VAN	28	29 VAN
30	31					

November

SUN	MON	TUE	WED	THU	FRI	SAT
		1	2	3 ANA	4	5 DAL
6	7	8 SJ	9	10 VAN	11	12 CAL
13	14 EDM	15	16 PHO	17	18 ANA	19 LA
20	21 CAL	22	23 DET	24	25 COB	26
27 VAN	28	29 EDM	30 VAN			

December

SUN	MON	TUE	WED	THU	FRI	SAT
				1	2	3
4 BUF	5	6	7 BOS	8	9 NJ	10 PIT
11	12 OTT	13	14	15	16	17 NYI
18 NYR	19	20 NAS	21	22 MIN	23 MIN	24
25	26 PHO	27	28 LA	29	30 SJ	31 PHO

January

SUN	MON	TUE	WED	THU	FRI	SAT
1	2	3 NAS	4	5 MIN	6	7 COB
8	9 STL	10	11 MON	12	13	14 PHI
15	16	17 TOR	18	19 CHI	20	21 DET
22	23	24 CAL	25	26 DAL	27	28 VAN
29	30	31 MIN				

February

SUN	MON	TUE	WED	THU	FRI	SAT
			1	2 NAS	3	4 DET
5	6	7 EDM	8	9 MIN	10 COB	11
12 DET	13	14	15	16	17	18
19	20	21	22	23	24	25
26	27	28 MIN				

March

SUN	MON	TUE	WED	THU	FRI	SAT
			1	2 COB	3	4 DAL
5 MIN	6	7 STL	8	9 CHI	10	11
12 CAL	13 CAL	14	15	16	17	18
19 SJ	20 LA	21	22 ANA	23	24	25 STL
26 EDM	27	28 ANA	29	30	31 CAL	

April

SUN	MON	TUE	WED	THU	FRI	SAT
						1
2	3 CHI	4	5 SJ	6	7	8 STL
9 MIN	10	11 PHO	12	13 CAL	14	15 VAN
16	17 EDM	18	19	20	21	22

2005-06 SEASON

CLUB DIRECTORY

Owner & governor
E. Stanley Kroenke
Alternate governor, president & general manager
Pierre Lacroix
Head coach
Joel Quenneville
Assistant coaches
Jacques Cloutier, Tony Granato
Director of player personnel
Brad Smith
Assistant to the general manager
Greg Sherman
Special assistant to the president
Michel Goulet
Director of player dev./goaltending coach
Craig Billington
Senior director of hockey administration
Charlotte Grahame
Video coordinator
Bryan Vines
Team services assistant
Ronnie Jameson
Hockey administration assistant
Andrea Furness
Chief scout
Jim Hammett
Pro scout
Garth Joy
Scouts
Glen Cochrane, Paul Fixter, Luc Gauthier, Alan Hepple, Kiril Ladygin, Chris O'Sullivan, Don Paarup, Richard Pracey, Joni Lehto
Strength and conditioning coach
Paul Goldberg
Head athletic trainer
Matt Sokolowski
Assistant athletic trainer
Scott Woodward
Massage therapist
Gregorio Pradera
Inventory manager
Wayne Flemming
Head equipment manager
Mark Miller
Assistant equipment managers
Terry Geer, Cliff Halstead
Senior v.p., communications & team services
Jean Martineau
Director of communications
Damen Zier
Director of media services/Internet
Brendan McNicholas

TOP FOUR DRAFT CHOICES

2005

Rd.-Overall	Ht., Wt.	Amateur league, team	Position
2-34 RYAN STOA	6-3, 200	U.S. National team	C
2-44 PAUL STASTNY	6-0, 201	WCHA U. OF Denver	C
2-47 TOM FRITSCHE	5-11, 183	CCHA Ohio State	LW
2-52 CHRIS DURAND	6-1, 186	WHL Seattle	C

2004

Rd.-Overall	Ht., Wt.	Amateur league, team	Position
1-21 WOJTEK WOLSKI	6-3, 200	OHL Brampton	LW
2-55 VICTOR ORESKOVICH	6-2, 216	USHL Green Bay	RW
3-72 DENIS PARSHIN	5-10, 165	Russia II Central Army	LW
5-154 R. DEMEN-WILLAUME	6-3, 196	Sweden Jr. Frolunda	D

MISCELLANEOUS DATA

Home ice (capacity)
Pepsi Center (18,007)
Address
1000 Chopper Cr.
Denver, CO 80204
Business phone
303-405-1100
Ticket information
303-405-1100
Website
www.coloradoavalanche.com
Training site
South Suburban Family Sports Center - Englewood, CO
Club colors
Burgundy, silver, blue and black
Radio affiliation
950am KKFN - "The Fan" via the Altitude Radio Network
TV affiliation
Altitude Sports & Entertainment

COLUMBUS BLUE JACKETS

WESTERN CONFERENCE, CENTRAL DIVISION

Blue Jackets Schedule

Home games shaded.

October

SUN	MON	TUE	WED	THU	FRI	SAT
2	3	4	5 WAS	6	7 CAL	8
9 CHI	10	11	12 SJ	13	14 ANA	15
16 LA	17	18	19	20	21 SJ	22 DET
23	24 DET	25	26 NAS	27	28 MIN	29 MIN
30	31					

November

SUN	MON	TUE	WED	THU	FRI	SAT
		1 EDM	2	3 CAL	4 VAN	5
6	7	8	9 STL	10	11 EDM	12
13 LA	14	15	16 STL	17	18 DAL	19
20 PHO	21	22	23 NAS	24	25 COL	26 STL
27	28	29	30 MIN			

December

SUN	MON	TUE	WED	THU	FRI	SAT
				1 STL	2	3
4	5	6	7	8 NYI	9 ATL	10
11 NJ	12	13 PHI	14	15 CAR	16	17 NAS
18	19	20 DET	21 DAL	22	23 NAS	24
25	26 CHI	27	28 ANA	29	30 CHI	31 DET

January

SUN	MON	TUE	WED	THU	FRI	SAT
1	2	3	4	5 SJ	6	7 COL
8 PHO	9	10	11 PIT	12	13 TB	14 FLA
15	16 NYR	17	18 DET	19	20 STL	21 NAS
22	23	24 VAN	25	26	27 MIN	28 NAS
29	30	31				

February

SUN	MON	TUE	WED	THU	FRI	SAT
			1 CAL	2 EDM	3	4
5	6 VAN	7	8 LA	9	10 COL	11 NAS
12	13	14	15	16	17	18
19	20	21	22	23	24	25
26	27	28				

March

SUN	MON	TUE	WED	THU	FRI	SAT
			1	2 COL	3	4 LA
5 ANA	6	7 CHI	8	9 PHO	10	11 EDM
12	13 STL	14	15 CHI	16	17 VAN	18
19 ANA	20	21 PHO	22	23	24 CAL	25 DET
26	27	28 SJ	29	30	31 STL	

April

SUN	MON	TUE	WED	THU	FRI	SAT
						1 CHI
2	3 NAS	4	5	6	7 DET	8 DET
9	10	11 DAL	12	13 STL	14	15 CHI
16 CHI	17	18 DAL	19	20	21	22

2005-06 SEASON

CLUB DIRECTORY

Owner/governor
John H. McConnell

Alternate governor
John P. McConnell

President/g.m./alternate governor
Doug MacLean

Exec. v.p./assistant general manager
Jim Clark

Head coach
Gerard Gallant

Associate coach
Dean Blais

Assistant coach
Gord Murphy

Goaltending coach/pro scout
Rick Wamsley

Director of amateur scouting
Don Boyd

Amateur scouts
Sam McMaster, Wayne Smith, John Williams

Director of player development
Paul Castron

Pro scout
Peter Dineen

Director of pro scouting
Bob Strumm

Hockey operations manager
Chris MacFarland

Video coordinator
Dan Singleton

Athletic trainer
Chris Mizer

Equipment manager
Tim LeRoy

Assistant equipment manager
Jamie Healy

Director of communications
Todd Sharrock

TOP FOUR DRAFT CHOICES

2005

Rd.-Overall	Ht., Wt.	Amateur league, team	Position
1-6 GILBERT BRULE	5-10, 175	WHL Vancouver	C
2-55 ADAM MCQUAID	6-3, 197	OHL Sudbury	D
3-67 KRIS RUSSELL	5-10, 160	WHL Medicine Hat	D
4-101 JARED BOLL	6-1, 190	USHL Lincoln	RW

2004

Rd.-Overall	Ht., Wt.	Amateur league, team	Position
1-8 ALEXANDRE PICARD	6-2, 190	QMJHL Lewiston	LW
2-46 ADAM PINEAULT	6-1, 193	HE Boston College	RW
2-59 KYLE WHARTON	6-2, 185	OHL Ottawa	D
3-93 DANIEL LACOSTA	6-1, 186	OHL Owen Sound	G

MISCELLANEOUS DATA

Home ice (capacity)
Nationwide Arena (18,136)

Office address
Nationwide Arena
200 W. Nationwide Blvd.
Columbus, OH 43215

Business phone
614-246-4625

Ticket information
1-800-645-2657

Website
www.bluejackets.com

Training site
Ice Haus at Nationwide Arena

Club colors
Capital Blue, Red, Silver, Electric Green

Radio affiliation
WBNS (1460 AM), WWCD (101.1 FM)

TV affiliation
Fox Sports Net Ohio

DALLAS STARS
WESTERN CONFERENCE, PACIFIC DIVISION

Stars Schedule

Home games shaded.

October

SUN	MON	TUE	WED	THU	FRI	SAT
2	3	4	5 LA	6	7	8 COL
9	10	11 PHO	12	13 CAL	14 EDM	15
16 VAN	17	18	19	20 LA	21	22 CAL
23	24	25	26 SJ	27	28 EDM	29 PHO
30	31					

November

SUN	MON	TUE	WED	THU	FRI	SAT
		1	2 LA	3	4 CHI	5 COL
6	7 EDM	8	9	10 NAS	11	12 SJ
13 ANA	14	15	16 ANA	17	18 COB	19
20	21	22	23 ANA	24	25 PHO	26 NAS
27	28	29	30 SJ			

December

SUN	MON	TUE	WED	THU	FRI	SAT
				1	2 CAR	3
4	5	6	7 FLA	8	9	10 TOR
11	12	13	14 BUF	15 OTT	16	17
18 CHI	19 MIN	20	21 COB	22	23 PHO	24
25	26 STL	27 DET	28	29 STL	30	31 LA

January

SUN	MON	TUE	WED	THU	FRI	SAT
1	2 LA	3	4 VAN	5	6 ANA	7
8 DET	9 MIN	10	11	12 WAS	13	14 BOS
15	16 MON	17	18 ATL	19	20 TB	21
22	23 PHO	24	25 STL	26 COL	27	28 DET
29	30 SJ	31				

February

SUN	MON	TUE	WED	THU	FRI	SAT
			1 NAS	2	3	4 STL
5	6 NAS	7	8	9 PHO	10 SJ	11
12 LA	13	14	15	16	17	18
19	20	21	22	23	24	25
26	27	28				

March

SUN	MON	TUE	WED	THU	FRI	SAT
			1	2 PHO	3	4 COL
5 CHI	6	7 EDM	8	9 CAL	10	11 VAN
12	13 VAN	14	15	16 LA	17	18 SJ
19	20 ANA	21	22 MIN	23	24 CHI	25
26 CAL	27	28	29 ANA	30	31 ANA	

April

SUN	MON	TUE	WED	THU	FRI	SAT
						1 LA
2	3 SJ	4	5	6 ANA	7	8 PHO
9 SJ	10	11 COB	12	13	14	15 MIN
16	17 DET	18 COB	19	20	21	22

2005-06 SEASON
CLUB DIRECTORY

Chairman of the board and owner
Thomas O. Hicks
President
James R. Lites
V.p., business operations
Randy Locey
V.p., marketing and communications
Geoff Moore
V.p., finance and c.f.o.
Robert Hutson
General manager
Doug Armstrong
Assistant general manager
Francois Giguere, Les Jackson, Guy Carbonneau
Head coach
Dave Tippett
Associate coach
Rick Wilson
Assistant coaches
Mark Lamb, Andy Moog
Director of amateur scouting
Tim Bernhardt
Director of pro scouting
Doug Overton
Senior dir., communications
Rob Scichili
Director of media relations
Mark Janko
Manager of media and team services
Jason Rademan
Head athletic trainer
Dave Surprenant
Head equipment manager
Steve Sumner
Strength and conditioning coach
J.J. McQueen
Assistant athletic trainer
Craig Lowry

TOP FOUR DRAFT CHOICES

2005

Rd.-Overall	Ht., Wt.	Amateur league, team	Position
1-28 MATT NISKANEN	6-0, 194	USHSW Virginia	D
2-33 JAMES NEAL	6-2, 185	OHL Plymouth	LW
3-71 RICHARD CLUNE	5-11, 195	OHL Sarnia	LW
3-75 PERTTU LINDGREN	6-0, 185	Finland Jr. Ilves	C

2004

Rd.-Overall	Ht., Wt.	Amateur league, team	Position
1-28 MARK FISTRIC	6-2, 232	WHL Vancouver	D
2-34 JOHAN FRANSSON	6-1, 183	Sweden Lulea	D
2-52 RAYMOND SAWADA	6-2, 195	BCHL Nanaimo	RW
2-56 NIKLAS GROSSMAN	6-4, 187	Sweden Jr. Sodertalje	D

MISCELLANEOUS DATA

Home ice (capacity)
American Airlines Center (18,532)
Address
2500 Victory Avenue, Dallas, Texas 75219
Business phone
214-387-5500
Ticket information
214-467-8277
Website
www.dallasstars.com
Training site
Frisco, TX
Club colors
Green, black, gold
Radio affiliation
WBAP (820 AM)
TV affiliation
FOX Sports Southwest (Cable), KDFI (Channel 27)

DETROIT RED WINGS
WESTERN CONFERENCE, CENTRAL DIVISION

Red Wings Schedule
Home games shaded.

October

SUN	MON	TUE	WED	THU	FRI	SAT
2	3	4	5 STL	6 STL	7	8
9 CAL	10	11 VAN	12	13 LA	14	15 PHO
16	17 SJ	18	19	20	21 ANA	22 COB
23	24 COB	25	26	27 CHI	28	29 CHI
30	31					

November

SUN	MON	TUE	WED	THU	FRI	SAT
		1 CHI	2	3 EDM	4	5 PHO
6 STL	7	8	9 LA	10	11 MIN	12
13 VAN	14	15	16 CAL	17 EDM	18	19 STL
20	21 NAS	22	23 COL	24	25 ANA	26 SJ
27	28 LA	29	30			

December

SUN	MON	TUE	WED	THU	FRI	SAT
				1 CAL	2	3
4 NYI	5	6 NJ	7	8	9 WAS	10
11	12 PIT	13 ATL	14	15 FLA	16	17 TB
18	19	20 COB	21	22	23 CHI	24
25	26	27 DAL	28	29	30	31 COB

January

SUN	MON	TUE	WED	THU	FRI	SAT
1	2	3 MIN	4	5 STL	6 NAS	7
8 DAL	9	10 CAR	11	12 PHI	13	14 NYR
15	16	17	18 COB	19	20	21 COL
22	23 NAS	24 NAS	25	26 VAN	27	28 DAL
29	30 MIN	31				

February

SUN	MON	TUE	WED	THU	FRI	SAT
			1 STL	2	3	4 COL
5	6	7	8 NAS	9 NAS	10	11
12 COL	13	14	15	16	17	18
19	20	21	22	23	24	25
26	27	28 SJ				

March

SUN	MON	TUE	WED	THU	FRI	SAT
			1 ANA	2	3	4 PHO
5	6	7 PHO	8	9 LA	10	11 CHI
12 CHI	13	14	15 ANA	16	17	18 EDM
19 VAN	20	21 NAS	22	23 SJ	24	25 COB
26	27 STL	28	29	30	31 CHI	

April

SUN	MON	TUE	WED	THU	FRI	SAT
						1
2 MIN	3 CAL	4	5	6	7 COB	8 COB
9	10	11 EDM	12	13 CHI	14	15 STL
16	17 DAL	18 NAS	19	20	21	22

2005-06 SEASON
CLUB DIRECTORY

Owner/governor
Mike Ilitch
Owner/secretary-treasurer
Marian Ilitch
President, Ilitch Holdings/alt. governor
Christopher Ilitch
President, Ilitch Holdings/alt. governor
Denise Ilitch
Sr. vice president/alternate governor
Jim Devellano
General manager
Ken Holland
Assistant general manager
Jim Nill
Head coach
Mike Babcock
Assistant coach
Paul MacLean
Assistant coach
Todd McLellan
Goaltending consultant
Jim Bedard
NHL scouts
Mark Howe, Bob McCammon
Scouts
Hakan Andersson, Evgeni Erfilov, Bruce Haralson, Vladimir Havluj, David Kolb, Mark Leach, Joe McDonnell, Glenn Merkosky, Marty Stein
Athletic trainer
Piet VanZant
Equipment manager
Paul Boyer
Assistant athletic trainer
Russ Baumann
Masseur
Sergei Tchekmarev
Team physicians
David Collon, M.D.
Anthony Colucci, M.D.
Team dentist
C.J. Regula, D.M.D.
Senior director of communications
John Hahn
Community relations manager
AnneMarie Krappmann

TOP FOUR DRAFT CHOICES

2005

Rd.-Overall	Ht., Wt.	Amateur league, team	Position
1-19 JAKUB KINDL	6-2, 199	OHL Kitchener	D
2-42 JUSTIN ABDELKADER	6-1, 195	USHL Cedar Rapids	LW
3-80 CHRISTOFER LOFBERG	6-3, 189	Sweden Jr. Djurgarden	C
4-103 MATTIAS RITOLA	6-0, 192	Sweden Jr. Leksand	C/W

2004

Rd.-Overall	Ht., Wt.	Amateur league, team	Position
3-97 JOHAN FRANZEN	6-2, 207	Sweden Linkoping	C
4-128 EVAN MCGRATH	5-11, 181	OHL Kitchener	C
5-151 SIARHEI KOLASAU	6-4, 187	Belarus Minsk	D
5-162 TYLER HASKINS	6-1, 177	OHL St. Michael's	C

MISCELLANEOUS DATA

Home ice (capacity)
Joe Louis Arena (20,066)
Address
600 Civic Center Drive
Detroit, MI 48226
Business phone
313-396-7544
Ticket information
313-396-7575
Website
www.detroitredwings.com
Training site
Center I.C.E., Traverse City, Mich.
Club colors
Red and white
Radio affiliation
Team 1270 WXYT (AM)
TV affiliation
FOX Sports Net Detroit (Cable)

EDMONTON OILERS
WESTERN CONFERENCE, NORTHWEST DIVISION

Oilers Schedule
Home games shaded.

October

SUN	MON	TUE	WED	THU	FRI	SAT
2	3	4	5 COL	6	7	8 VAN
9	10 ANA	11 LA	12	13	14 DAL	15 CAL
16	17	18 PHO	19	20 CAL	21 COL	22
23	24	25 COL	26	27	28 DAL	29 NAS
30	31					

November

SUN	MON	TUE	WED	THU	FRI	SAT
		1 COB	2	3 DET	4 STL	5
6	7 DAL	8 NAS	9	10	11 COB	12
13 CHI	14 COL	15	16	17 DET	18	19 CHI
20	21 SJ	22	23 MIN	24	25 CAL	26
27	28	29 COL	30			

December

SUN	MON	TUE	WED	THU	FRI	SAT
				1 VAN	2	3 BOS
4	5	6	7	8 PHI	9	10 NYI
11	12	13 NJ	14	15 MON	16	17 VAN
18	19 CAL	20	21 VAN	22	23 LA	24
25	26 MIN	27	28 MIN	29	30 NAS	31 CAL

January

SUN	MON	TUE	WED	THU	FRI	SAT
1	2	3 CHI	4	5	6	7 TOR
8	9	10 PIT	11	12 NYR	13	14 OTT
15	16 BUF	17	18	19 SJ	20	21 PHO
22	23 CAL	24	25 ANA	26 LA	27	28
29 PHO	30	31				

February

SUN	MON	TUE	WED	THU	FRI	SAT
			1	2 COB	3	4 VAN
5	6 ANA	7 COL	8	9	10 MIN	11
12 STL	13	14	15	16	17	18
19	20	21	22	23	24	25
26	27	28				

March

SUN	MON	TUE	WED	THU	FRI	SAT
			1 STL	2	3 SJ	4
5 NAS	6	7 DAL	8	9 SJ	10	11 COB
12 MIN	13	14 MIN	15	16 CAL	17	18 DET
19	20	21 VAN	22	23 VAN	24	25 VAN
26 COL	27	28 MIN	29	30 LA	31	

April

SUN	MON	TUE	WED	THU	FRI	SAT
						1 CAL
2	3 PHO	4	5	6 MIN	7 CHI	8
9 STL	10	11 DET	12	13 ANA	14	15
16	17 COL	18	19	20	21	22

2005-06 SEASON
CLUB DIRECTORY

Owner
Edmonton Investors Group, Ltd.
Governor
Cal Nichols
Alternate governors
Bill Butler, Kevin Lowe
President & chief executive officer
Patrick LaForge
General manager
Kevin Lowe
Assistant general manager
Scott Howson
V.p. of hockey operations
Kevin Prendergast
Head coach
Craig MacTavish
Assistant coaches
Charlie Huddy, Bill Moores, Craig Simpson
Video coach
Brian Ross
Goaltending coach
Pete Peeters
Scouting staff
Bob Brown, Bill Dandy, Brad Davis, Lorne Davis, Morey Gare, Kent Hawley, Stu MacGregor, Chris McCarthy, Frank Musil, Kent Nilsson, Dave Semenko
Head medical trainer
Ken Lowe
Head equipment manager
Barrie Stafford
Equipment managers
Lyle Kulchisky, Jeff Lang
Massage therapist
Stewart Poirier
Team physician
Dr. David C. Reid
V.p. of communications/broadcasting
Allan Watt
Information coordinator
Steve Knowles
Coordinator of communications/media
J.J. Hebert
Vice president, finance
Darryl Boessenkool
V.p. of marketing
Stew MacDonald
V.p. of ticketing
Eric Upton
Director of ticketing
Sean Price
Director of broadcast
Don Metz

TOP FOUR DRAFT CHOICES

2005

Rd.-Overall	Ht., Wt.	Amateur league, team	Position
1-2 ANDREW COGLIANO	5-9, 178	OPJRA St. Michael's	C
2-36 TAYLOR CHORNEY	5-11, 182	USHSW Shattuck-St. Mary's	D
3-81 DANNY SYVRET	5-11, 203	OHL London	D
3-86 ROBBY DEE	6-1, 185	USHSW Breck	C/W

2004

Rd.-Overall	Ht., Wt.	Amateur league, team	Position
1-14 DEVAN DUBNYK	6-5, 194	WHL Kamloops	G
1-25 ROB SCHREMP	5-11, 197	OHL London	C
2-44 ROMAN TESLYUK	6-1, 195	WHL Kamloops	D
2-57 GEOFF PAUKOVICH	6-4, 208	U.S. National team	LW

MISCELLANEOUS DATA

Home ice (capacity)
Rexall Place (16,839)
Address
11230 110 Street
Edmonton, AB T5G 3H7
Business phone
780-414-4000
Ticket information
780-414-4625
Website
www.edmontonoilers.com
Training site
To be announced
Club colors
White, midnight blue, metallic copper and red
Radio affiliation
CHED (630 AM)
TV affiliation
SportsNet & CBXT-TV

FLORIDA PANTHERS

EASTERN CONFERENCE, SOUTHEAST DIVISION

Panthers Schedule

Home games shaded.

October

SUN	MON	TUE	WED	THU	FRI	SAT
2	3	4	5 ATL	6	7 TB	8 TB
9	10 NYI	11	12	13 BOS	14	15 BUF
16	17 NYR	18 NJ	19	20 WAS	21	22 OTT
23	24	25 PIT	26	27 PHI	28	29 WAS
30	31 TOR					

November

SUN	MON	TUE	WED	THU	FRI	SAT
		1 MON	2	3 BOS	4	5 CAR
6	7	8	9 NYR	10	11 CAR	12 PHI
13	14	15 MON	16	17 OTT	18	19 NYI
20	21	22	23 NJ	24	25 PIT	26 ATL
27	28 TOR	29	30			

December

SUN	MON	TUE	WED	THU	FRI	SAT
				1	2	3 CHI
4	5	6	7 DAL	8 SJ	9	10 LA
11	12	13 NAS	14	15 DET	16	17 ATL
18 WAS	19	20	21	22 BUF	23 CAR	24
25	26 PHI	27	28 BOS	29	30 MON	31

January

SUN	MON	TUE	WED	THU	FRI	SAT
1 BUF	2	3 NJ	4 NYI	5	6	7 NYR
8 WAS	9	10	11	12 STL	13	14 COB
15	16	17	18	19 PHO	20	21 ANA
22	23	24 TB	25 CAR	26	27 NJ	28
29	30 TOR	31				

February

SUN	MON	TUE	WED	THU	FRI	SAT
			1	2	3 ATL	4 ATL
5	6	7 WAS	8	9	10	11 BUF
12	13	14	15	16	17	18
19	20	21	22	23	24	25
26	27	28 TB				

March

SUN	MON	TUE	WED	THU	FRI	SAT
			1	2 MON	3 CAR	4
5	6 ATL	7	8	9 OTT	10	11 CAR
12 CAR	13	14	15 PHI	16	17 NYI	18 WAS
19	20 TB	21	22 WAS	23	24 NYR	25
26	27 BOS	28	29 PIT	30	31 CAR	

April

SUN	MON	TUE	WED	THU	FRI	SAT
						1 TB
2	3 TB	4	5 ATL	6	7 PIT	8
9 TB	10	11 TOR	12	13 OTT	14	15 WAS
16	17	18 ATL	19	20	21	22

2005-06 SEASON

CLUB DIRECTORY

General partner and chairman of the board/CEO/governor
Alan Cohen

Partner/president, Panthers Hockey LLLP & alternate governor
Jordan Zimmerman

Partners
Steve Cohen, David Epstein, Dr. Elliott Hahn, H. Wayne Huizenga, Bernie Kosar, Richard C. Lehman, M.D., Al Maroone, Michael Maroone, Cliff Viner

Alternate governor
William A. Torrey

Chief operating officer
Michael Yormark

Senior v.p., business relations/strategic partnerships
Pedro Goncalves

V.p. of finance/chief financial officer
Evelyn Lopez

V.p., arena operations
Brett Stefansson

General manager
Mike Keenan

Head coach
Jacques Martin

Assistant coach
Guy Charon

Director of hockey operations
Matt Loughran

Director of hockey operations
Jack Birch

Director of player development
Duane Sutter

Skating & skills instructor and scout
Paul Vincent

Director of scouting
Scott Luce

Head amateur scout
Darwin Bennett

Amateur scouts
Erin Ginnell, Ron Harris

European scouts
Niklas Blomgren, Jari Kekalainen

Part-time scouts
Vadim Podrezov, Dale Degray

Medical trainer/massage therapist
Jim Pizzutelli

V.p. of communications
Randy Sieminski

Manager of communications
Justin Copertino

Dir., game presentation and events
Greg Hanover

TOP FOUR DRAFT CHOICES

2005

Rd.-Overall	Ht., Wt.	Amateur league, team	Position
1-20 KENNDAL MCARDLE	5-11, 190	WHL Moose Jaw	LW
2-32 TYLER PLANTE	6-2, 191	WHL Brandon	G
3-90 DAN COLLINS	6-1, 185	OHL Plymouth	RW
4-93 OLIVIER LEGAULT	6-5, 238	QMJHL Lewiston	LW

2004

Rd.-Overall	Ht., Wt.	Amateur league, team	Position
1-7 ROSTISLAV OLESZ	6-1, 202	Czech Vitkovice	C
2-37 DAVID SHANTZ	6-1, 202	OHL Mississauga	G
2-53 DAVID BOOTH	6-0, 212	CCHA Michigan State	LW
4-105 EVAN SCHAFER	6-2, 221	WHL Prince Albert	D

MISCELLANEOUS DATA

Home ice (capacity)
Office Depot Center (19,250)

Address
One Panther Parkway
Sunrise, FL 33323

Business phone
954-835-7000

Ticket information
954-835-7825

Website
www.floridapanthers.com

Training site
incredible ICE in Coral Springs, FL

Club colors
Red, navy blue, yellow and gold

Radio affiliation
WQAM (560 AM)

TV affiliation
FOX SportsNet

LOS ANGELES KINGS

WESTERN CONFERENCE, PACIFIC DIVISION

Kings Schedule

Home games shaded.

October

SUN	MON	TUE	WED	THU	FRI	SAT
2	3	4	5 DAL	6 PHO	7	8
9 MIN	10	11 EDM	12	13 DET	14	15
16 COB	17	18	19 COL	20 DAL	21	22
23 CAL	24	25 ANA	26	27	28 SJ	29 STL
30	31					

November

SUN	MON	TUE	WED	THU	FRI	SAT
		1	2 DAL	3 PHO	4	5 NAS
6	7	8	9 DET	10	11 CHI	12
13 COB	14	15 NAS	16	17 VAN	18	19 COL
20	21	22 STL	23	24 NAS	25	26 CHI
27	28 DET	29	30 CHI			

December

SUN	MON	TUE	WED	THU	FRI	SAT
				1	2 OTT	3 MON
4	5	6 TOR	7	8 CAR	9	10 FLA
11	12	13	14 WAS	15	16 ANA	17 PHO
18	19 VAN	20	21 CAL	22	23 EDM	24
25	26 SJ	27	28 COL	29 PHO	30	31 DAL

January

SUN	MON	TUE	WED	THU	FRI	SAT
1	2 DAL	3	4	5 PHO	6	7 SJ
8	9 ANA	10	11	12 BOS	13	14 BUF
15	16	17 TB	18	19 ATL	20	21 SJ
22	23 ANA	24 SJ	25	26 EDM	27	28 ANA
29	30 ANA	31				

February

SUN	MON	TUE	WED	THU	FRI	SAT
			1	2 PHO	3	4
5	6	7 MIN	8 COB	9	10	11 CHI
12 DAL	13	14	15	16	17	18
19	20	21	22	23	24	25
26	27	28				

March

SUN	MON	TUE	WED	THU	FRI	SAT
			1	2 MIN	3	4 COB
5	6	7 MIN	8	9 DET	10	11 STL
12	13 SJ	14 PHO	15	16 DAL	17	18 STL
19	20 COL	21	22	23	24	25 NAS
26	27 VAN	28	29 CAL	30 EDM	31	

April

SUN	MON	TUE	WED	THU	FRI	SAT
						1 DAL
2	3 VAN	4 ANA	5	6 SJ	7	8 ANA
9	10	11	12	13 PHO	14	15 CAL
16	17 SJ	18	19	20	21	22

2005-06 SEASON

CLUB DIRECTORY

Owners
Philip F. Anschutz
Edward P. Roski, Jr.

President/CEO
Tim Leiweke

Sr. vice president, general manager
Dave Taylor

Coach
Andy Murray

Assistant coaches
Mark Hardy
Ray Bennett
John Van Boxmeer

Goaltending consultant
Andy Nowicki

V.p. of hockey operations, asst. g.m.
Kevin Gilmore

Director of player personnel
Bill O'Flaherty

Assistant to general manager
John Wolf

Director of amateur scouting
Al Murray

Pro scout—dir. of European evaluation
Rob Laird

Scouting staff
Vaclav Nedomansky, Brian Putnam, Parry Shockey, John Stanton, Jan Vopat, Ari Vuori, Glen Williamson, Michel Boucher, Jim Cassidy, Mike Donnelly, Viacheslav Golovin, Gary Harker, Jerry Sodomlak, Victor Tjumenev, Barry Martinelli

Vice president of sales and marketing
Chris McGowan

V.p., communications and broadcasting
Mike Altieri

Director, communications
Jeff Moeller

Manager, communications
Lee Callans

Trainers
Peter Demers, Peter Millar, Rick Burrill, Rick Garcia, Robert Zolg, Mike Kadar, Marco Yrjovuori

TOP FOUR DRAFT CHOICES

2005

Rd.-Overall	Ht., Wt.	Amateur league, team	Position
1-11 ANZE KOPITAR	6-4, 220	Sweden Jr. Sodertalje	C
2-50 DANY ROUSSIN	6-2, 200	QMJHL Rimouski	LW
2-60 T.J. FAST	6-1, 190	AJHL Camrose	D
3-72 JONATHAN QUICK	6-0, 180	USHSE Avon Old Farms	G

2004

Rd.-Overall	Ht., Wt.	Amateur league, team	Position
1-11 LAURI TUKONEN	6-2, 198	Finland Espoo	RW
3-95 PAUL BAIER	6-3, 212	USHSE Deerfield Academy	D
3-110 NED LUKACEVIC	6-0, 185	WHL Spokane	LW
5-143 ERIC NEILSON	6-1, 201	QMJHL Rimouski	RW

MISCELLANEOUS DATA

Home ice (capacity)
Staples Center (18,118)

Address
Staples Center
1111 South Figueroa St.
Los Angeles, CA 90015

Business phone
213-742-7100

Ticket information
888-546-4752

Website
www.lakings.com

Training site
El Segundo, CA

Club colors
Purple, silver, black and white

Radio affiliation
KSPN (710 AM)

TV affiliation
FOX Sports West

MINNESOTA WILD
WESTERN CONFERENCE, NORTHWEST DIVISION

Wild Schedule
Home games shaded.

October

SUN	MON	TUE	WED	THU	FRI	SAT
2	3	4	5 CAL	6	7	8 PHO
9 LA	10	11	12 VAN	13	14 VAN	15
16 ANA	17	18	19 SJ	20	21	22 STL
23 CHI	24	25 VAN	26	27	28 COB	29 COB
30	31					

November

SUN	MON	TUE	WED	THU	FRI	SAT
		1 CAL	2 VAN	3	4	5 SJ
6 ANA	7	8 PHO	9	10	11 DET	12
13	14 CAL	15	16	17	18	19 NAS
20	21	22	23 EDM	24	25 STL	26
27	28	29	30 COB			

December

SUN	MON	TUE	WED	THU	FRI	SAT
				1 NAS	2	3 NJ
4	5 NYR	6	7	8 PIT	9	10 PHI
11 BUF	12	13 NYI	14	15 BOS	16	17 MON
18	19 DAL	20	21	22 COL	23 COL	24
25	26 EDM	27	28 EDM	29 CAL	30	31 VAN

January

SUN	MON	TUE	WED	THU	FRI	SAT
1	2	3 DET	4	5 COL	6	7 ANA
8	9 DAL	10	11	12	13	14 CAL
15	16 OTT	17	18 TOR	19	20 CHI	21
22 CHI	23	24 PHO	25	26 NAS	27 COB	28
29	30 DET	31 COL				

February

SUN	MON	TUE	WED	THU	FRI	SAT
			1	2 SJ	3	4 PHO
5	6	7 LA	8	9 COL	10 EDM	11
12 VAN	13	14	15	16	17	18
19	20	21	22	23	24	25
26	27	28 COL				

March

SUN	MON	TUE	WED	THU	FRI	SAT
			1	2 LA	3 ANA	4
5 COL	6	7 LA	8	9	10 STL	11
12 EDM	13	14 EDM	15	16	17	18
19 CAL	20	21 CAL	22 DAL	23	24	25 SJ
26	27	28 EDM	29 VAN	30	31 VAN	

April

SUN	MON	TUE	WED	THU	FRI	SAT
						1
2 DET	3	4 STL	5	6 EDM	7 CAL	8
9 COL	10	11 CHI	12	13 NAS	14	15 DAL
16						

2005-06 SEASON
CLUB DIRECTORY

Chairman
Bob Naegele Jr.
Chief executive officer
Jac Sperling
President and general manager
Doug Risebrough
Assistant general manager/player personnel
Tom Thompson
Head coach
Jacques Lemaire
Assistant coaches
Mike Ramsey, Mario Tremblay
Assistant general manager/hockey operations
Tom Lynn
V.p. of communications and broadcasting
Bill Robertson
Manager of media relations/team services
Aaron Sickman
Head athletic therapist
Don Fuller

TOP FOUR DRAFT CHOICES

2005

Rd.-Overall	Ht., Wt.	Amateur league, team	Position
1-4 BENOIT POULIOT	6-3, 179	OHL Sudbury	LW
2-57 MATT KASSIAN	6-3, 232	WHL Kamloops	LW
3-65 KRISTOFER WESTBLOM	6-1, 155	WHL Kelowna	G
4-110 KYLE BAILEY	6-2, 182	WHL Portland	C

2004

Rd.-Overall	Ht., Wt.	Amateur league, team	Position
1-12 A.J. THELEN	6-3, 205	CCHA Michigan State	D
2-42 ROMAN VOLOSHENKO	6-1, 189	Russia Krylja	LW
3-78 PETER OLVECKY	6-2, 185	Slovakia Jr. Trencin	W
3-79 CLAYTON STONER	6-3, 225	WHL Tric-City	D

MISCELLANEOUS DATA

Home ice (capacity)
Xcel Energy Center (18,064)
Office address
317 Washington Street
St. Paul, MN 55102
Business phone
651-602-6000
Ticket information
651-222-9453
Website
www.wild.com
Training site
Parade Ice Garden, Minneapolis
Club colors
Red, green, gold and wheat
Radio affiliation
WCCO (830 AM)
TV affiliation
FOX Sports Net (Cable), KSTC TV (Channel 45)

MONTREAL CANADIENS
EASTERN CONFERENCE, NORTHEAST DIVISION

Canadiens Schedule
Home games shaded.

October

SUN	MON	TUE	WED	THU	FRI	SAT
2	3	4	5 BOS	6 NYR	7	8 TOR
9	10	11 OTT	12 ATL	13	14	15 TOR
16	17	18 BOS	19	20	21	22 NYI
23	24	25 PHI	26	27 OTT	28	29 NYR
30	31 NYR					

November

SUN	MON	TUE	WED	THU	FRI	SAT
	1 FLA	2	3	4 BUF	5 BUF	6
7	8 TB	9	10 PIT	11	12 TOR	13
14	15 FLA	16	17	18 NJ	19 WAS	20
21	22 ATL	23	24	25 BUF	26 TOR	27
28	29 OTT	30				

December

SUN	MON	TUE	WED	THU	FRI	SAT
			1 BUF	2	3 LA	4
5	6	7	8	9	10 ANA	11
12	13 PHO	14	15 EDM	16	17 MIN	18
19	20 OTT	21	22	23 WAS	24	25
26 ATL	27	28 TB	29	30 FLA	31 CAR	

January

SUN	MON	TUE	WED	THU	FRI	SAT
						1
2	3 PIT	4	5 NJ	6	7 OTT	8
9	10	11 COL	12	13	14 SJ	15
16 DAL	17	18	19 CAL	20	21 VAN	22
23 CAR	24	25 PHI	26 OTT	27	28 TOR	29
30	31 CAR					

February

SUN	MON	TUE	WED	THU	FRI	SAT
		1	2 BOS	3	4 BOS	5 PHI
6	7 BUF	8	9 BUF	10	11 ATL	12
13	14	15	16	17	18	19
20	21	22	23	24	25	26
27	28 NYI					

March

SUN	MON	TUE	WED	THU	FRI	SAT
		1	2 FLA	3	4 TB	5
6 PHI	7 TOR	8	9 BOS	10	11 NYR	12
13 TB	14	15	16 CAR	17	18 PIT	19
20 WAS	21 NYI	22	23 TOR	24	25 TOR	26 PIT
27	28 NYI	29	30 WAS	31		

April

SUN	MON	TUE	WED	THU	FRI	SAT
					1 BOS	2
3	4 BOS	5	6 OTT	7	8 NJ	9
10 OTT	11	12 BUF	13 BOS	14	15 BUF	16
17	18 NJ	19	20	21	22	23

2005-06 SEASON
CLUB DIRECTORY

Chairman and governor
George N. Gillett Jr.
Vice-chairman
Jeff Joyce
President of club de hockey Canadien and the Bell Centre
Pierre Boivin
Assistant to the president
Foster Gillett
Executive v.p., hockey and g.m.
Bob Gainey
Chief financial officer
Fred Steer
Vice-president, marketing and sales
Ray Lalonde
V.p., comm. and community relations
Donald Beauchamp
V.p., operations, Bell Centre
Alain Gauthier
Assistant general manager
André Savard
Director of hockey operations and Legal affairs
Julien BriseBois
Director of player personnel
Trevor Timmins
Director of pro scouting
Pierre Gauthier
Head coach
Claude Julien
Assistant coaches
Roland Melanson, Rick Green, Doug Jarvis
Pro scouts
Gordie Roberts, Richard Green
Amateur scouting coordinator
Pierre Dorion
Scouting staff
Elmer Benning, William A. Berglund, Hannu Laine, Dave Mayville, Craig Sarner, Antonin Routa, Nikolai Vakourov, Patrik Allvin
Equipment manager
Pierre Gervais
Assistants to the equipment manager
Robert Boulanger, Pierre Ouellette
Video supervisor
Mario Leblanc
Club physician and chief surgeon
Dr. David Mulder
Head athletic therapist
Graham Rynbend
Assistant to the athletic therapist
Jodi Van Rees
Strength & conditioning coordinator
Scott Livingston
Director of media relations
Dominick Saillant

TOP FOUR DRAFT CHOICES

2005

Rd.-Overall	Ht., Wt.	Amateur league, team	Position
1-5 CAREY PRICE	6-2, 222	WHL Tri-City	G
2-45 G. LATENDRESSE	6-1, 216	QMJHL Drummondville	RW
4-121 JURAJ MIKUS	6-1, 186	Slovakia Jr. Skalica	C/W
5-130 MATHIEU AUBIN	6-2, 190	QMJHL Lewiston	C

2004

Rd.-Overall	Ht., Wt.	Amateur league, team	Position
1-18 KYLE CHIPCHURA	6-2, 197	WHL Prince Albert	C
3-84 ALEXEI YEMELIN	6-0, 187	Russia Samara	D
4-100 JAMES WYMAN	6-1, 192	USHSW Blake	RW
5-150 MIKHAIL GRABOVSKI	5-11, 181	Russia Nizhnekamsk	F

MISCELLANEOUS DATA

Home ice (capacity)
Bell Centre (21,273)
Address
1260 rue de la Gauchetiere Ouest
Montreal, Que. H3B 5E8
Business phone
514-932-2582
Ticket information
1-800-361-4595
Website
www.canadiens.com
Training site
Centre Bell, Montreal
Club colors
Red, white and blue
Radio affiliation
CJAD (800 AM), CKAC (730 AM)
TV affiliation
RDS (33)

NASHVILLE PREDATORS

WESTERN CONFERENCE, CENTRAL DIVISION

NASHVILLE PREDATORS

Predators Schedule

Home games shaded.

October

SUN	MON	TUE	WED	THU	FRI	SAT
2	3	4	5 SJ	6	7	8 ANA
9	10	11	12 COL	13 PHO	14	15 STL
16	17	18	19	20 STL	21	22 SJ
23	24	25 CHI	26 COB	27	28	29 EDM
30	31					

November

SUN	MON	TUE	WED	THU	FRI	SAT
		1 ANA	2 SJ	3	4	5 LA
6	7	8 EDM	9	10 DAL	11	12 STL
13	14	15 LA	16	17	18	19 MIN
20	21 DET	22	23 COB	24 LA	25	26 DAL
27	28	29 CAL	30			

December

SUN	MON	TUE	WED	THU	FRI	SAT
				1 MIN	2	3 PHI
4	5	6	7 WAS	8 NYR	9	10 TB
11	12	13 FLA	14	15 CHI	16	17 COB
18	19	20 COL	21 CHI	22	23 COB	24
25	26	27 CAL	28 VAN	29	30 EDM	31

January

SUN	MON	TUE	WED	THU	FRI	SAT
1 ANA	2	3 COL	4 STL	5	6 DET	7
8 CHI	9	10 NYI	11 ATL	12	13 CAR	14
15 PIT	16	17	18	19 NJ	20	21 COB
22	23 DET	24 DET	25	26 MIN	27	28 COB
29	30	31				

February

SUN	MON	TUE	WED	THU	FRI	SAT
			1 DAL	2 COL	3	4 CHI
5	6 DAL	7	8 DET	9 DET	10	11 COB
12	13	14	15	16	17	18
19	20	21	22	23	24	25
26	27	28				

March

SUN	MON	TUE	WED	THU	FRI	SAT
			1 CHI	2 VAN	3	4
5 EDM	6	7 CAL	8	9 VAN	10	11 SJ
12	13	14 VAN	15	16 PHO	17	18 CAL
19	20 STL	21 DET	22	23	24 ANA	25 LA
26	27	28 PHO	29	30	31	

April

SUN	MON	TUE	WED	THU	FRI	SAT
						1 STL
2	3 COB	4	5 CHI	6 STL	7	8 CHI
9	10	11 STL	12	13 MIN	14	15 PHO
16	17	18 DET	19	20	21	22

2005-06 SEASON

CLUB DIRECTORY

Owner, chairman and governor
Craig Leipold
Exec. v.p./g.m., alternate governor
David Poile
V.p. finance and admin./ alt. gov.
Ed Lang
Exec. v. p. business affairs
Steve Violetta
Assistant general manager
Ray Shero
Senior v.p., comm./develpment
Gerry Helper
Director of communications
Ken Anderson
Communications coordinator
Tim Darling
Director of team services
Gregory Harvey
Head coach
Barry Trotz
Associate coach
Brent Peterson
Assistant
Peter Horachek
Director of player personnel
Paul Fenton
Strength and conditioning coach
David Good
Goaltending coach
Mitch Korn
Head athletic trainer
Dan Redmond
Assistant athletic trainer
Eric Claas
Equipment manager
Pete Rogers
Video coach
Robert Bouchard

TOP FOUR DRAFT CHOICES

2005

Rd.-Overall	Ht., Wt.	Amateur league, team	Position
1-18 RYAN PARENT	6-2, 183	OHL Guelph	D
3-78 TEEMU LAAKSO	6-0, 195	Finland Jr. IFK	D
3-79 CODY FRANSON	6-4, 205	WHL Vancouver	D
5-150 CAL O'REILLY	5-11, 180	OHL Windsor	C

2004

Rd.-Overall	Ht., Wt.	Amateur league, team	Position
1-15 ALEXANDER RADULOV	6-1, 178	Russia Tver	RW
3-81 VACLAV MEIDL	6-4, 198	OHL Plymouth	C
4-107 NICK FUGERE	6-2, 230	QMJHL Gatineau	LW
5-139 KYLE MOIR	6-2, 190	WHL Swift Current	G

MISCELLANEOUS DATA

Home ice (capacity)
Gaylord Entertainment Center (17,113)
Address
501 Broadway
Nashville, TN 37203
Business phone
615-770-2300
Ticket information
615-770-7825
Website
www.nashvillepredators.com
Training site
Centennial Sportsplex, Nashville
Club colors
Blue, gold, silver, steel and orange
Radio affiliation
WGFX 104.5 (The Zone) and WNSR Sports56
TV affiliation
FOX Sports Net

NEW JERSEY DEVILS
EASTERN CONFERENCE, ATLANTIC DIVISION

Devils Schedule
Home games shaded.

October

SUN	MON	TUE	WED	THU	FRI	SAT
2	3	4	5 PIT	6	7 PHI	8 NYR
9	10	11	12	13 NYR	14	15 CAR
16	17	18 FLA	19	20 PIT	21	22 ATL
23	24	25	26 TB	27	28 BUF	29 BOS
30	31					

November

SUN	MON	TUE	WED	THU	FRI	SAT
		1 PIT	2	3 NYR	4	5 NYR
6	7	8 NYI	9	10	11 WAS	12 WAS
13	14	15 BUF	16	17	18 MON	19 OTT
20	21	22	23 FLA	24	25 TB	26
27	28	29 BOS	30 PHI			

December

SUN	MON	TUE	WED	THU	FRI	SAT
				1	2	3 MIN
4	5	6 DET	7 CAL	8	9 COL	10
11 COB	12	13 EDM	14	15 ATL	16	17 CAR
18	19	20 NYR	21 NYI	22	23 ATL	24
25	26 TOR	27	28 WAS	29 PIT	30	31 TOR

January

SUN	MON	TUE	WED	THU	FRI	SAT
1	2	3 FLA	4	5 MON	6	7 BUF
8	9 PHI	10	11	12	13 VAN	14
15 CHI	16	17 STL	18	19 NAS	20	21 NYI
22 NYR	23	24 NYI	25	26 TB	27 FLA	28
29	30	31				

February

SUN	MON	TUE	WED	THU	FRI	SAT
			1 OTT	2	3 CAR	4 TOR
5	6	7 TB	8	9 BOS	10	11 NYI
12	13	14	15	16	17	18
19	20	21	22	23	24	25
26	27	28				

March

SUN	MON	TUE	WED	THU	FRI	SAT
			1 PHI	2 NYI	3	4 NYR
5	6	7 NYI	8	9	10 WAS	11 PIT
12	13	14 NYI	15	16 PIT	17	18
19 OTT	20	21 PHI	22	23 ATL	24 BOS	25
26 TOR	27	28 OTT	29	30 BUF	31	

April

SUN	MON	TUE	WED	THU	FRI	SAT
						1 PHI
2 PIT	3	4	5 PIT	6	7	8 MON
9 NYR	10	11 CAR	12	13 PHI	14	15
16 PHI	17	18 MON	19	20	21	22

2005-06 SEASON
CLUB DIRECTORY

CEO/president and general manager
Louis A. Lamoriello
Head coach
Larry Robinson
Assistant coaches
Jacques Laperriere
Bob Carpenter
John MacLean
Goaltending coach
Jacques Caron
Medical trainer
Bill Murray
Strength & conditioning coordinator
Michael Vasalani
Equipment manager
Rich Matthews
Assistant equipment manager
Alex Abasto
Director, public relations
Jeff Altstadter
VP, information & publications
Mike Levine

TOP FOUR DRAFT CHOICES

2005

Rd.-Overall	Ht., Wt.	Amateur league, team	Position
1-23 NICKLAS BERGFORS	5-11, 195	Sweden Jr. Sodertalje	W
2-38 JEFF FRAZEE	6-0, 184	U.S. National team	G
3-84 MARK FRASER	6-3, 195	OHL Kitchener	D
4-99 PATRICK DAVIS	6-2, 188	OHL Kitchener	LW

2004

Rd.-Overall	Ht., Wt.	Amateur league, team	Position
1-20 TRAVIS ZAJAC	6-2, 205	BCHL Salmon Arm	C
5-155 ALEX MIKHAILISHIN	6-4, 207	Russia Spartak 2	D
6-185 JOSH DISHER	6-1, 164	OHL Erie	G
7-216 P-L Leblond-Letourneau	6-2, 208	QMJHL Baie Comeau	LW

MISCELLANEOUS DATA

Home ice (capacity)
Continental Airlines Arena (19,040)
Address
P.O. Box 504
50 Route 120 North
East Rutherford, N.J. 07073
Business phone
201-935-6050
Ticket information
201-935-6050
Website
www.newjerseydevils.com
Training site
South Mountain Arena, West Orange, NJ
Club colors
Red, black and white
Radio affiliation
WFAN (660 AM)
TV affiliation
FOX Sports Net New York

NEW YORK ISLANDERS
EASTERN CONFERENCE, ATLANTIC DIVISION

Islanders Schedule
Home games shaded.

October

SUN	MON	TUE	WED	THU	FRI	SAT
2	3	4	5 BUF	6	7	8 CAR
9	10 FLA	11	12	13 WAS	14	15 PHI
16	17	18	19 NYR	20 NYR	21	22 MON
23	24	25 ATL	26	27 NYR	28	29 BUF
30	31					

November

SUN	MON	TUE	WED	THU	FRI	SAT
		1 BOS	2	3 PIT	4	5 OTT
6	7	8 NJ	9	10 PHI	11	12 BOS
13	14 PIT	15	16 ATL	17 TB	18	19 FLA
20	21	22	23 BUF	24	25 OTT	26 PHI
27	28	29 PHI	30			

December

SUN	MON	TUE	WED	THU	FRI	SAT
				1	2	3
4 DET	5	6 STL	7	8 COB	9	10 EDM
11	12	13 MIN	14	15	16	17 COL
18	19 TOR	20	21 NJ	22	23 OTT	24
25	26 BUF	27	28 NYR	29	30 OTT	31

January

SUN	MON	TUE	WED	THU	FRI	SAT
1	2 TB	3	4 FLA	5	6 CAR	7 CAR
8	9	10 NAS	11	12 CAL	13	14 VAN
15	16	17 CHI	18	19 CAR	20	21 NJ
22	23	24 NJ	25	26 PIT	27	28 BOS
29	30	31 WAS				

February

SUN	MON	TUE	WED	THU	FRI	SAT
			1	2 NYR	3	4 PIT
5	6 TB	7	8 PHI	9	10	11 NJ
12	13	14	15	16	17	18
19	20	21	22	23	24	25
26	27	28 MON				

March

SUN	MON	TUE	WED	THU	FRI	SAT
			1	2 NJ	3	4 PHI
5	6 WAS	7 NJ	8	9	10 TOR	11 BOS
12	13	14 NJ	15	16 ATL	17 FLA	18
19 TB	20	21 MON	22	23	24 PIT	25 ATL
26	27	28 MON	29 NYR	30	31 PIT	

April

SUN	MON	TUE	WED	THU	FRI	SAT
						1
2 PHI	3	4	5 TOR	6 NYR	7	8 WAS
9	10	11 NYR	12	13 TOR	14	15 PIT
16	17 PIT	18 PHI	19	20	21	22

2005-06 SEASON
CLUB DIRECTORY

Owner and governor
Charles B. Wang
Owner and alternate governor
Sanjay Kumar
Sr. v.p., operations and alt. governor
Michael J. Picker
Alt. governor and general counsel
Roy E. Reichbach
General manager and alt. governor
Mike Milbury
Manager, hockey administration
Joanne Holewa
Asst. Manager, hockey administration
Kerry Gwydir
Head coach
Steve Stirling
Assistant coaches
Dan Bylsma, Jack Capuano, Brad Shaw
Goaltending consultant
Sudarshan "Sudsie" Maharaj
Director of pro scouting
Ken Morrow
Asst. director of pro scouting
Kevin Maxwell
Head amateur scout
Tony Feltrin
Western scout
Earl Ingarfield
Ontario scout
Doug Gibson
Sweden/Finland amateur scout
Anders Kallur
US amateur scout
Jay Heinbuck
Czech Republic amateur scout
Karel Pavlik
Scouting staff
Jim Madigan, Mario Saraceno, Brian Hunter, Harri Rindell, Greg Morrow, Harkie Singh, Ryan Jankowski
Video coordinator
Bob Smith
Director of medical services
Dr. Elliot Pellman
Internist
Dr. Damion Martins
Team orthopedists
Dr. Elliott Hershman, Dr. Kenneth Montgomery, Dr. David Gazzaniga
Team dentists
Dr. Bruce Michnick, Dr. Jan Sherman
Head athletic trainer
Rich Campbell
Assistant athletic trainer
Andy Wetstein
Strength & conditioning coach
Garrett Timms
Equipment managers
Scott Moon, Thomas Kitz
V.p. communications
Chris Botta
Media relations assistant
Corey Witt

TOP FOUR DRAFT CHOICES

2005

Rd.-Overall	Ht., Wt.	Amateur league, team	Position
1-15 RYAN O'MARRA	6-1, 193	OHL Erie	C
2-46 DUSTIN KOHN	6-1, 182	WHL Calgary	D
3-76 SHEA GUTHRIE	6-0, 187	USHSE St. George's	W
5-144 MASI MARJAMAKI	6-2, 202	WHL Moose Jaw	RW

2004

Rd.-Overall	Ht., Wt.	Amateur league, team	Position
1-16 PETTERI NOKELAINEN	6-1, 190	Finland Saipa	C/W
2-47 BLAKE COMEAU	6-1, 198	WHL Kelowna	RW
3-82 SERGEI OGORDNIKOV	6-1, 185	Russia Tver	C
4-115 WES O'NEILL	6-4, 200	CCHA U. of Notre Dame	D

MISCELLANEOUS DATA

Home ice (capacity)
Nassau Veterans Memorial Coliseum (16,234)
Address
1535 Old Country Road
Plainview, NY 11803
Business phone
516-501-6700
Ticket information
1-800-882-4753
Website
www.newyorkislanders.com
Training site
Iceworks, Syosset, NY
Club colors
Blue and orange
Radio affiliation
Bloomberg Radio (1130 AM)
TV affiliation
FOX Sports Net New York

NEW YORK RANGERS
EASTERN CONFERENCE, ATLANTIC DIVISION

Rangers Schedule
Home games shaded.

October

SUN	MON	TUE	WED	THU	FRI	SAT
2	3	4	5 PHI	6 MON	7	8 NJ
9	10 WAS	11	12	13 NJ	14	15 ATL
16	17 FLA	18	19 NYI	20 NYI	21	22 BUF
23	24	25	26	27 NYI	28	29 MON
30	31 MON					

November

SUN	MON	TUE	WED	THU	FRI	SAT
		1	2	3 NJ	4	5 NJ
6	7 PIT	8	9 FLA	10 TB	11	12 PIT
13	14	15 TOR	16	17 CAR	18	19 CAR
20 BOS	21	22 BUF	23	24 ATL	25	26 WAS
27	28	29	30			

December

SUN	MON	TUE	WED	THU	FRI	SAT
				1 PIT	2	3 WAS
4	5 MIN	6	7 CHI	8 NAS	9	10 STL
11	12	13 VAN	14	15	16	17
18 COL	19	20 NJ	21	22 TB	23	24
25	26 OTT	27	28 NYI	29	30	31 PIT

January

SUN	MON	TUE	WED	THU	FRI	SAT
1	2	3 TB	4	5 PHI	6	7 FLA
8	9	10 CAL	11	12 EDM	13	14 DET
15	16 COB	17	18	19 PIT	20	21 BOS
22 NJ	23	24 BUF	25	26	27	28 PIT
29	30 PHI	31				

February

SUN	MON	TUE	WED	THU	FRI	SAT
			1 PIT	2 NYI	3	4 PHI
5	6	7	8 OTT	9	10 TOR	11 TOR
12	13	14	15	16	17	18
19	20	21	22	23	24	25
26	27	28				

March

SUN	MON	TUE	WED	THU	FRI	SAT
			1	2 PHI	3	4 NJ
5	6 CAR	7	8 ATL	9	10	11 MON
12 ATL	13	14 CAR	15	16 WAS	17	18 TOR
19	20 BOS	21	22 PHI	23	24 FLA	25 TB
26	27 BUF	28	29 NYI	30 OTT	31	

April

SUN	MON	TUE	WED	THU	FRI	SAT
						1
2	3	4 PHI	5	6 NYI	7	8 BOS
9 NJ	10	11 NYI	12	13 PIT	14	15 PHI
16	17	18 OTT	19	20	21	22

2005-06 SEASON
CLUB DIRECTORY

President and CEO, Cablevision Systems Corp.; chairman, MSG; Governor
James L. Dolan
Vice chairman, Cablevision Systems Corp.; vice chairman, MSG; alternate governor
Robert S. Lemle
President and G.M., alternate governor
Glen Sather
President & CEO of sports team operations
Steve Mills
Senior vice president of marketing & business operations
Mike Golub
Vice president, player development and assistant G.M.
Don Maloney
Head coach
Tom Renney
Vice president of hockey administration
Cameron Hope
Assistant coaches
Perry Pearm, Mike Pelino, Benoit Allaire
Special assistant, prospect development & community relations
Adam Graves
Head amateur staff
Gordie Clark
Amateur scouting staff
Ray Clearwater, Rich Brown, Andre Beaulieu, Bob Crocker, Jan Gajdosik, Ernie Gare, Christer Rockstom, Vladimir Lutchecko, Tim Murray, Shanon Sather
Head professional scout
Dave Brown
Professional scouting staff
Harry Howell, Gilles Leger, Nick Fotiu, Peter Stephen
Manager of scouting
Victor Saljanin
Video analyst
Jerry Dineen
V.p., public relations
John Rosasco
Director, public relations
Jason Vogel
Public relations coordinators
Dave Martella
Vice president, marketing
Jeanie Baumgartner
Director, marketing
Janet Duch
V.p. of sponsorship for NY Rangers & NY Knicks
Rob Scolaro
Medical trainer
Jim Ramsay
Equipment manager
Acacio Marques
Assistant equipment manager
James Johnson
Massage therapist
Bruce Lifrieri
Strength & conditioning coordinator
Reg Grant
Coaching staff assistant
Pat Boller

TOP FOUR DRAFT CHOICES

2005

Rd.-Overall	Ht., Wt.	Amateur league, team	Position
1-12 MARC STAAL	6-3, 196	OHL Sudbury	D
2-40 MICHAEL SAUER	6-2, 198	WHL Portland	D
2-56 MARC-ANDRE CLICHE	6-0, 175	QMJHL Lewiston	RW
3-66 BRODIE DUPONT	6-1, 192	WHL Calgary	C

2004

Rd.-Overall	Ht., Wt.	Amateur league, team	Position
1-6 AL MONTOYA	6' 1, 190	CCHA U. of Michigan	G
1-19 LAURI KORPIKOSKI	6' 1, 183	Finland Jr. TPS	C/W
2-36 DARIN OLVER	6' 0, 165	CCHA N. Michigan	C
2-48 DANE BYERS	6' 2, 189	WHL Prince Albert	LW

MISCELLANEOUS DATA

Home ice (capacity)
Madison Square Garden (18,200)
Address
2 Pennsylvania Plaza
New York, NY 10121
Business phone
212-465-6486
Ticket information
212-307-7171
Website
www.newyorkrangers.com
Training site
MSG Training Center—Greenburgh, NY
Club colors
Blue, red and white
Radio affiliation
MSG Radio
TV affiliation
MSG Network

OTTAWA SENATORS
EASTERN CONFERENCE, NORTHEAST DIVISION

Senators Schedule

Home games shaded.

October

SUN	MON	TUE	WED	THU	FRI	SAT
2	3	4	5 TOR	6	7	8 BUF
9	10 TOR	11 MON	12	13	14	15 BOS
16	17	18	19	20	21 TB	22 FLA
23	24 CAR	25	26	27 MON	28	29 TOR
30 PHI	31					

November

SUN	MON	TUE	WED	THU	FRI	SAT
		1	2 BUF	3 TB	4	5 NYI
6	7	8	9	10 BOS	11	12 BUF
13	14	15 CAR	16	17 FLA	18	19 NJ
20	21	22 CAR	23	24	25 NYI	26 BOS
27	28	29 MON	30			

December

SUN	MON	TUE	WED	THU	FRI	SAT
				1 BOS	2 LA	3
4	5	6	7	8	9 VAN	10 CAL
11	12 COL	13	14	15 DAL	16	17 TOR
18	19	20 MON	21	22 PHI	23 NYI	24
25	26 NYR	27	28 CAR	29	30 NYI	31

January

SUN	MON	TUE	WED	THU	FRI	SAT
1	2 ATL	3	4 WAS	5 BOS	6	7 MON
8	9	10 PHO	11	12 SJ	13	14 EDM
15	16 MIN	17	18	19 ANA	20	21 TOR
22	23 TOR	24	25	26 MON	27	28
29	30 BOS	31				

February

SUN	MON	TUE	WED	THU	FRI	SAT
			1 NJ	2 PIT	3	4 BUF
5	6 PIT	7	8 NYR	9 ATL	10	11 PHI
12	13	14	15	16	17	18
19	20	21	22	23	24	25
26	27	28				

March

SUN	MON	TUE	WED	THU	FRI	SAT
			1 PIT	2 WAS	3	4 TOR
5	6 TB	7	8	9 FLA	10 ATL	11
12 WAS	13	14 TB	15	16 BOS	17	18 BUF
19 NJ	20	21 PIT	22	23	24 BUF	25 PHI
26	27	28 NJ	29	30 NYR	31	

April

SUN	MON	TUE	WED	THU	FRI	SAT
						1 WAS
2	3 ATL	4	5 BUF	6 MON	7	8 BUF
9	10 MON	11 BOS	12	13 FLA	14	15 TOR
16	17	18 NYR	19	20	21	22

2005-06 SEASON

CLUB DIRECTORY

Owner, governor
Eugene Melnyk
President and CEO & alt. governor
Roy Mlakar
General manager
John Muckler
Chief operating officer
Cyril Leeder
Assistant general manager
Peter Chiarelli
Head coach
Bryan Murray
Assistant coaches
Greg Carvel
Randy Lee
Ron Low
John Paddock
Director of player personnel
Anders Hedberg
Vice president, broadcast
Jim Steel
Vice president, communications
Phil Legault
Director, communications
Steve Keogh
Head equipment manager
Scott Allegrino
Assistant equipment manager
Chris Cook
Head athletic trainer
Gerry Townend
Assistant athletic trainer
Andy Playter
Team doctor
Don Chow
Scouts
Vaclav Burda, George Fargher, Bob Janecyk, Frank Jay, Lewis Mangelluzzo, Nick Polano, Patrick Savard, Boris Shagus, Bill McCarthy

TOP FOUR DRAFT CHOICES

2005

Rd.-Overall	Ht., Wt.	Amateur league, team	Position
1-9 BRIAN LEE	6-2, 202	USHSW Moorhead	D
3-70 VITALY ANIKEYENKO	6-3, 220	Russia 3 Yaroslavl	D
4-95 CODY BASS	6-0, 191	OHL Mississauga	C
4-98 ILJA ZUBOV	6-0, 176	Russia 2 Chelyabinsk	C

2004

Rd.-Overall	Ht., Wt.	Amateur league, team	Position
1-23 ANDREJ MESZAROS	6-0, 198	Slovakia Trencin	D
2-58 KIRILL LYAMIN	6-3, 198	Russia CSKA	D
3-77 SHAWN WELLER	6-1, 188	EJHL Capital District	LW
3-87 PETER REGIN	6-1, 185	Denmark Jr. Herning	C/W

MISCELLANEOUS DATA

Home ice (capacity)
Corel Centre (19,153)
Address
1000 Palladium Drive
Ottawa, Ont. K2VIA5
Business phone
613-599-0250
Ticket information
613-599-0103
Website
www.ottawasenators.com
Training site
Ottawa
Club colors
Black, red and white
Radio affiliation
Team 1200 (1200 AM), English
Radio 1150 CJRC (1150 AM), French
TV affiliation
New RO, Rogers Sportsnet

PHILADELPHIA FLYERS
EASTERN CONFERENCE, ATLANTIC DIVISION

Flyers Schedule
Home games shaded.

October

SUN	MON	TUE	WED	THU	FRI	SAT
2	3	4	5 NYR	6	7 NJ	8
9	10	11 TOR	12	13	14 PIT	15 NYI
16	17	18	19	20	21	22 TOR
23	24	25 MON	26	27 FLA	28 CAR	29
30 OTT	31					

November

SUN	MON	TUE	WED	THU	FRI	SAT
		1	2	3 WAS	4	5 ATL
6	7	8 BOS	9	10 NYI	11	12 FLA
13	14 TB	15	16 PIT	17	18 ATL	19 PIT
20	21	22 TB	23	24	25 BOS	26 NYI
27	28	29 NYI	30 NJ			

December

SUN	MON	TUE	WED	THU	FRI	SAT
				1	2	3 NAS
4	5	6 CAL	7	8 EDM	9	10 MIN
11	12	13 COB	14	15 VAN	16	17 STL
18	19 BUF	20	21	22 OTT	23 PIT	24
25	26 FLA	27	28 ATL	29 CAR	30	31 WAS

January

SUN	MON	TUE	WED	THU	FRI	SAT
1	2 BOS	3	4	5 NYR	6 WAS	7
8	9 NJ	10	11 CHI	12 DET	13	14 COL
15	16	17 CAR	18	19 BOS	20	21 PIT
22	23 PIT	24	25 MON	26	27	28 TB
29	30 NYR	31				

February

SUN	MON	TUE	WED	THU	FRI	SAT
			1	2 BUF	3	4 NYR
5 MON	6	7	8 NYI	9	10 WAS	11 OTT
12	13	14	15	16	17	18
19	20	21	22	23	24	25
26	27	28				

March

SUN	MON	TUE	WED	THU	FRI	SAT
			1 NJ	2 NYR	3	4 NYI
5	6 MON	7	8 CAR	9	10	11 BUF
12 PIT	13	14	15 FLA	16	17 TB	18 ATL
19	20	21 NJ	22 NYR	23	24	25 OTT
26	27	28 TOR	29	30	31	

April

SUN	MON	TUE	WED	THU	FRI	SAT
						1 NJ
2 NYI	3	4 NYR	5	6	7 BUF	8 TOR
9	10	11 PIT	12	13 NJ	14	15 NYR
16 NJ	17	18 NYI	19	20	21	22

2005-06 SEASON
CLUB DIRECTORY

Chairman
Edward M. Snider
President
Ron Ryan
General manager
Bob Clarke
Executive vice president
Keith Allen
Assistant general manager
Paul Holmgren
Head coach
Ken Hitchcock
Assistant coaches
Wayne Fleming
Terry Murray
Goaltending coach
Reggie Lemelin
Director of pro hockey personnel
Ron Hextall
Pro scouts
Al Hill
Dean Lombardi
Scouts
John Chapman, Inge Hammarstrom, Vaclav Slansky, Simon Nolet, Dennis Patterson, Chris Pryor, Evgeny Zimin
Vice president of ticket operations
Cecilia Baker
Vice president, marketing and communications
Shawn Tilger
Senior Director of public relations
Zack Hill
Director of media services and publications
Joe Klueg
Publicist
Jill Lipson
Communications assistant
Katie Hammer
Athletic trainer/strength & conditioning coach
Jim McCrossin
Athletic trainer
Steve Lipinsky
Head equipment manager
Jim Evers
Equipment managers
Harry Bricker
Anthony Oratorio

TOP FOUR DRAFT CHOICES

2005

Rd.-Overall	Ht., Wt.	Amateur league, team	Position
1-29 STEVE DOWNIE	5-10, 192	OHL Windsor	RW
3-91 OSKARS BARTULIS	6-1, 184	QMJHL Moncton	D
4-119 JEREMY DUCHESNE	6-0, 201	QMJHL Halifax	G
5-152 JOSH BEAULIEU	6-0, 180	OHL London	C

2004

Rd.-Overall	Ht., Wt.	Amateur league, team	Position
1-23 ANDREJ MESZAROS	6-0, 198	Slovakia Trencin	D
2-58 KIRILL LYAMIN	6-3, 198	Russia CSKA	D
3-77 SHAWN WELLER	6-1, 188	EJHL Capital District	LW
3-87 PETER REGIN	6-1, 185	Denmark Jr. Herning	C/W

MISCELLANEOUS DATA

Home ice (capacity)
First Union Center (19,523)
Address
First Union Center
3601 South Broad Street
Philadelphia, PA 19148
Business phone
215-465-4500
Ticket information
215-218-7825
Website
www.philadelphiaflyers.com
Training site
Sovereign Bank Flyers Skate Zone, Voorhees, NJ
Club colors
Orange, white and black
Radio affiliation
WIP (610 AM)
TV affiliation
Comcast SportsNet (cable); UPN 57 WPSG-TV

PHOENIX COYOTES
WESTERN CONFERENCE, PACIFIC DIVISION

Coyotes Schedule
Home games shaded.

October

SUN	MON	TUE	WED	THU	FRI	SAT
2	3	4	5 VAN	6 LA	7	8 MIN
9	10	11 DAL	12	13 NAS	14	15 DET
16	17 CAL	18 EDM	19	20 VAN	21	22
23 ANA	24	25 STL	26	27 CAL	28	29 DAL
30 ANA	31					

November

SUN	MON	TUE	WED	THU	FRI	SAT
		1	2	3 LA	4	5 DET
6 CHI	7	8 MIN	9	10 CAL	11	12 ANA
13	14	15	16 COL	17	18	19 SJ
20 COB	21	22 ANA	23	24	25 DAL	26 VAN
27	28	29	30 ANA			

December

SUN	MON	TUE	WED	THU	FRI	SAT
				1	2	3 CAR
4	5 ATL	6	7	8	9	10
11 BOS	12	13 MON	14	15 TB	16	17 LA
18	19	20 STL	21	22 SJ	23 DAL	24
25	26 COL	27	28 SJ	29 LA	30	31 COL

January

SUN	MON	TUE	WED	THU	FRI	SAT
1	2	3	4	5 LA	6	7
8 COB	9	10 OTT	11	12 BUF	13	14 TOR
15	16 WAS	17	18	19 FLA	20	21 EDM
22	23 DAL	24 MIN	25	26 STL	27	28 SJ
29 EDM	30	31 VAN				

February

SUN	MON	TUE	WED	THU	FRI	SAT
			1	2 LA	3	4 MIN
5	6	7 CHI	8	9 DAL	10	11
12 SJ	13	14	15	16	17	18
19	20	21	22	23	24	25
26	27	28				

March

SUN	MON	TUE	WED	THU	FRI	SAT
			1	2 DAL	3	4 DET
5	6	7 DET	8	9 COB	10	11 ANA
12 ANA	13	14 LA	15	16 NAS	17	18
19 CHI	20	21 COB	22	23 CHI	24	25 ANA
26	27	28 NAS	29	30 SJ	31	

April

SUN	MON	TUE	WED	THU	FRI	SAT
						1 SJ
2	3 EDM	4	5 CAL	6	7	8 DAL
9	10 SJ	11 COL	12	13 LA	14	15 NAS
16 STL	17	18	19	20	21	22

2005-06 SEASON
CLUB DIRECTORY

Chairman and governor
Steve Ellman
Co-owner
Jerry Moyes
Managing partner
Wayne Gretzky
President and chief operating officer
Douglas Moss
Sr. executive v.p. of hockey operations
Cliff Fletcher
Executive v.p. and general manager
Michael Barnett
V.p. and asst. general nanager
Laurence Gilman
Head coach
Wayne Gretzky
Assistant coaches
Rick Bowness
Rick Tocchet
Barry Smith
Goaltending coach
Grant Fuhr
Video coordinator
Steve Peters
Massage therapist
Jukka Nieminen
Equipment managers
Stan Wilson
Tony Silva
Asst. equipment manager
Jason Rudee
V.p. of communications
Rich Nairn
Director of media relations
Rick Braunstein

TOP FOUR DRAFT CHOICES

2005

Rd.-Overall	Ht., Wt.	Amateur league, team	Position
1-17 MARTIN HANZAL	6-4, 198	Czech Jr. Budejovice	C
2-59 P-O PELLETIER	6-1, 175	QMJHL Drummondville	G
4-105 KEITH YANDLE	6-2, 195	USHSE Cushing Academy	D
5-148 ANTON KRYSANOV	6-3, 198	Russia Togliatti	C

2004

Rd.-Overall	Ht., Wt.	Amateur league, team	Position
1-5 BLAKE WHEELER	6-3, 185	USHSW Breck	RW
2-35 LOGAN STEPHENSON	6-2, 185	WHL Tri-City	D
2-50 ENVER LISIN	6-2, 190	RUS Saratov	RW
4-103 ROMAN TOMANEK	6-1, 176	Slovakia Povazka Bystrica	RW

MISCELLANEOUS DATA

Home ice (capacity)
Glendale Arena (17,799)
Address
5800 W. Glenn Avenue
Glendale, AZ 85301
Business phone
623-463-8800
Ticket information
480-563-PUCK
Website
www.phoenixcoyotes.com
Training site
Glendale, AZ
Club colors
Brick red, desert sand and black
Radio affiliation
KDUS (1060 AM) and KDKB (93.3 FM)
TV affiliation
FOX Sports Arizona, WB 6/61, KTVK (Channel 3)

PITTSBURGH PENGUINS

EASTERN CONFERENCE, ATLANTIC DIVISION

Penguins Schedule

Home games shaded.

October

SUN	MON	TUE	WED	THU	FRI	SAT
2	3	4	5 NJ	6	7 CAR	8 BOS
9	10 BUF	11	12	13	14 PHI	15 TB
16	17	18	19	20 NJ	21	22 BOS
23	24	25 FLA	26	27 ATL	28	29 CAR
30	31					

November

SUN	MON	TUE	WED	THU	FRI	SAT
		1 NJ	2	3 NYI	4	5 BOS
6	7 NYR	8	9 ATL	10 MON	11	12 NYR
13	14 NYI	15	16 PHI	17	18	19 PHI
20	21	22 WAS	23	24	25 FLA	26
27 TB	28	29 BUF	30			

December

SUN	MON	TUE	WED	THU	FRI	SAT
				1 NYR	2	3 CAL
4	5	6	7	8 MIN	9	10 COL
11	12 DET	13 STL	14	15	16 BUF	17 BUF
18	19	20	21	22	23 PHI	24
25	26	27 TOR	28	29 NJ	30	31 NYR

January

SUN	MON	TUE	WED	THU	FRI	SAT
1	2 TOR	3 MON	4	5	6 ATL	7 ATL
8	9	10 EDM	11 COB	12	13 CHI	14
15 NAS	16 VAN	17	18	19 NYR	20	21 PHI
22	23 PHI	24	25 WAS	26 NYI	27	28 NYR
29	30	31				

February

SUN	MON	TUE	WED	THU	FRI	SAT
			1 NYR	2 OTT	3	4 NYI
5	6 OTT	7	8 BOS	9	10 CAR	11 WAS
12	13	14	15	16	17	18
19	20	21	22	23	24	25
26	27	28				

March

SUN	MON	TUE	WED	THU	FRI	SAT
			1 OTT	2	3	4 CAR
5	6	7 TB	8 WAS	9	10	11 NJ
12 PHI	13	14	15	16 NJ	17	18 MON
19 TOR	20	21 OTT	22	23	24 NYI	25
26 MON	27	28	29 FLA	30	31 NYI	

April

SUN	MON	TUE	WED	THU	FRI	SAT
						1
2 NJ	3	4	5 NJ	6	7 FLA	8 TB
9	10	11 PHI	12	13 NYR	14	15 NYI
16	17 NYI	18 TOR	19	20	21	22

2005-06 SEASON

CLUB DIRECTORY

Chairman/CEO
Mario Lemieux

President and governor
Ken Sawyer

Executive v.p./general manager
Craig Patrick

Vice president & general counsel
Ted Black

Vice president & controller
Kevin Hart

V.p., communications/marketing
Tom McMillan

Vice president, sales and marketing
David Soltesz

General manager
Craig Patrick

Assistant general manager
Ed Johnston

Head coach
Eddie Olczyk

Assistant coaches
Randy Hillier, Joe Mullen

Head scout
Greg Malone

Goaltending coach/scout
Gilles Meloche

Scouts
Wayne Daniels, Chuck Grillo, Charlie Hodge, Mark Kelley, Richard Rose, Neil Shea

Pro scout
Rick Kehoe

Strength & conditioning coach
John Welday

Equipment manager
Steve Latin

Team physician
Dr. Charles Burke

Head athletic trainer
Mark Mortland

Senior director of ticketing
James Santilli

TOP FOUR DRAFT CHOICES

2005

Rd.-Overall	Ht., Wt.	Amateur league, team	Position
1-1 SIDNEY CROSBY	5-11, 193	QMJHL Rimouski	C
2-61 MICHAEL GERGEN	5-10, 185	USHSW Shattuck-St. Mary's	W
3-62 KRISTOPHER LETANG	5-11, 190	QMJHL Val d'Or	D
4-125 TOMMI LEINONEN	6-2, 185	Finland Jr. Karpat	D

2004

Rd.-Overall	Ht., Wt.	Amateur league, team	Position
1-2 EVGENI MALKIN	6-3, 186	Russia Magnitogorsk	C/W
2-31 JOH. SALMONSSON	6-2, 183	Sweden Djurgarden	W
2-61 ALEX GOLIGOSKI	5-11, 180	USHL Sioux Falls	D
3-67 NICK JOHNSON	6-1, 183	AJHL St. Albert	RW

MISCELLANEOUS DATA

Home ice (capacity)
Mellon Arena (16,958)

Address
Mellon Arena
66 Mario Lemieux Place
Pittsburgh, PA 15219

Business phone
412-642-1300

Ticket information
412-642-7367 and 1-800-642-7367

Website
www.pittsburghpenguins.com

Training site
Canonsburg, PA

Club colors
Black, gold and white

Radio affiliation
3WS (94.5FM), Fox Sports Radio 970AM

TV affiliation
Fox Sports Net Pittsburgh

ST. LOUIS BLUES
WESTERN CONFERENCE, CENTRAL DIVISION

Blues Schedule

Home games shaded.

October

SUN	MON	TUE	WED	THU	FRI	SAT
2	3	4	5 DET	6 DET	7	8 SJ
9	10	11 CHI	12	13	14	15 NAS
16	17	18	19 ANA	20 NAS	21	22 MIN
23	24	25 PHO	26	27	28 ANA	29 LA
30	31					

November

SUN	MON	TUE	WED	THU	FRI	SAT
		1	2 CHI	3	4 EDM	5
6 DET	7	8	9 COB	10 CHI	11	12 NAS
13	14	15	16 COB	17	18	19 DET
20	21	22 LA	23	24	25 MIN	26 COB
27	28	29	30			

December

SUN	MON	TUE	WED	THU	FRI	SAT
				1 COB	2	3
4	5	6 NYI	7	8 TB	9	10 NYR
11	12	13 PIT	14	15	16 CHI	17 PHI
18	19	20 PHO	21 ANA	22	23 SJ	24
25	26 DAL	27	28 CHI	29 DAL	30	31 ANA

January

SUN	MON	TUE	WED	THU	FRI	SAT
1	2 VAN	3	4 NAS	5 DET	6	7
8	9 COL	10	11	12 FLA	13 ATL	14
15 CAR	16	17 NJ	18	19 WAS	20 COB	21
22	23 VAN	24	25 DAL	26 PHO	27	28
29	30 CAL	31				

February

SUN	MON	TUE	WED	THU	FRI	SAT
			1 DET	2 CHI	3	4 DAL
5	6	7	8 VAN	9	10 CAL	11
12 EDM	13	14	15	16	17	18
19	20	21	22	23	24	25
26	27	28				

March

SUN	MON	TUE	WED	THU	FRI	SAT
			1 EDM	2 CAL	3	4
5 VAN	6	7 COL	8	9	10 MIN	11 LA
12	13 COB	14	15	16 SJ	17	18 LA
19	20 NAS	21 SJ	22	23 CAL	24	25 COL
26	27 DET	28	29 CHI	30	31 COB	

April

SUN	MON	TUE	WED	THU	FRI	SAT
						1 NAS
2	3	4 MIN	5	6 NAS	7	8 COL
9 EDM	10	11 NAS	12	13 COB	14	15 DET
16 PHO	17	18 CHI	19	20	21	22

2005-06 SEASON

CLUB DIRECTORY

Chairman of the board and owner
Bill Laurie
President & chief executive officer
Mark Sauer
Sr. vice president and general manager
Larry Pleau
Sr. v.p.,finance/ hockey administration
Jerry Jasiek
Sr. v.p. and G.M., Savvis Center
Dennis Petrullo
V.p. of sales
Bruce Affleck
V.p. of marketing
Jo Ann Miles
Head coach
Mike Kitchen
Assistant coach
Curt Fraser
Goaltending coach
Keith Allain
Athletic trainer
Ray Barile
Video coach
Jamie Kompon
Equipment manager
Bert Godin
Assistant equipment manager
Steve Wissman
Equipment assistant
Ray Halle
Director of broadcasts and communications
Chuck Menke
Communications assistants
Scott Bonanni
Rich Jankowski

TOP FOUR DRAFT CHOICES

2005

Rd.-Overall	Ht., Wt.	Amateur league, team	Position
1-24 T.J. OSHIE	5-10, 170	USHSW Warroad	C
2-37 SCOTT JACKSON	6-3, 200	WHL Seattle	D
3-85 BEN BISHOP	6-5, 205	NAHL Texas	G
5-156 RYAN REAVES	6-1, 193	WHL Brandon	RW

2004

Rd.-Overall	Ht., Wt.	Amateur league, team	Position
1-17 MAREK SCHWARZ	6-0, 180	Czech Sparta	G
2-49 CARL SODERBERG	6-3, 198	Sweden Malmo	C/W
3-83 VICTOR ALEXANDROV	5-11, 183	Russia Novokuznetsk	RW
4-116 MICHAL BIRNER	6-0, 183	Czech Jr. Slavia	LW

MISCELLANEOUS DATA

Home ice (capacity)
Savvis Center (19,022)
Address
1401 Clark
St. Louis, MO 63103
Business phone
314-622-2500; fax, 314-622-2582
Ticket information
314-241-1888
Website
www.stlouisblues.com
Training site
Ice Zone at St. Louis Mills, Hazelwood, MO
Club colors
Blue, gold, navy and white
Radio affiliation
KTRS (550 AM)
TV affiliation
KPLR (Channel 11) & FOX Sports Midwest

SAN JOSE SHARKS
WESTERN CONFERENCE, PACIFIC DIVISION

Sharks Schedule
Home games shaded.

October

SUN	MON	TUE	WED	THU	FRI	SAT
2	3	4	5 NAS	6	7 CHI	8 STL
9	10	11	12 COB	13	14	15 CHI
16	17 DET	18	19 MIN	20	21 COB	22 NAS
23	24	25	26 DAL	27	28 LA	29 CAL
30	31					

November

SUN	MON	TUE	WED	THU	FRI	SAT
		1	2 NAS	3	4 ANA	5 MIN
6	7	8 COL	9	10	11	12 DAL
13	14	15	16 VAN	17	18	19 PHO
20	21 EDM	22	23 CAL	24 VAN	25	26 DET
27	28	29	30 DAL			

December

SUN	MON	TUE	WED	THU	FRI	SAT
				1	2 BUF	3 TOR
4	5	6 ATL	7	8 FLA	9	10 CAR
11	12	13	14	15	16 WAS	17
18 ANA	19	20 ANA	21	22 PHO	23 STL	24
25	26 LA	27	28 PHO	29	30 COL	31

January

SUN	MON	TUE	WED	THU	FRI	SAT
1	2	3	4	5 COB	6	7 LA
8	9	10 BOS	11	12 OTT	13	14 MON
15	16 TB	17	18	19 EDM	20	21 LA
22	23	24 LA	25	26 ANA	27	28 PHO
29	30 DAL	31				

February

SUN	MON	TUE	WED	THU	FRI	SAT
			1 ANA	2 MIN	3	4 ANA
5	6 CAL	7	8 CHI	9	10 DAL	11
12 PHO	13	14	15	16	17	18
19	20	21	22	23	24	25
26	27	28 DET				

March

SUN	MON	TUE	WED	THU	FRI	SAT
			1	2	3 EDM	4 CAL
5	6	7 ANA	8	9 EDM	10	11 NAS
12	13 LA	14	15	16 STL	17	18 DAL
19 COL	20	21 STL	22	23 DET	24	25 MIN
26 CHI	27	28 COB	29	30 PHO	31	

April

SUN	MON	TUE	WED	THU	FRI	SAT
						1 PHO
2	3 DAL	4	5 COL	6 LA	7	8
9 DAL	10 PHO	11	12 VAN	13 VAN	14	15 ANA
16	17 LA	18	19	20	21	22

2005-06 SEASON
CLUB DIRECTORY

President, CEO and manager of the SJSEE Ownership Group
Greg Jamison
Exec. v.p. and general manager
Doug Wilson
Vice president & assistant g.m.
Wayne Thomas
Head coach
Ron Wilson
Assistant coaches
Tim Hunter
Rob Zettler
Goaltender coach
Warren Strelow
Strength & conditioning coach
Mac Read
Assistant to the general manager
Joe Will
Director of hockey administration
Rosemary Maher
Senior director of communications
Ken Arnold
Director of media relations
Scott Emmert
Media relations coordinator
Tom Holy
Head trainer
Ray Tufts
Equipment manager
Mike Aldrich
Assistant equipment managers
Kurt Harvey
Roy Sneesby
Team physician
Dr. Arthur J. Ting
Director of advertising and publicity
Andrew Ebel

TOP FOUR DRAFT CHOICES

2005

Rd.-Overall	Ht., Wt.	Amateur league, team	Position
1-8 DEVIN SETOGUCHI	5-11, 186	WHL Saskatoon	RW
2-35 MARC-EDOUARD VLASIC	6-1, 190	QMJHL Quebec	D
4-112 ALEX STALOCK	5-11, 170	USHL Cedar Rapids	G
5-140 TAYLOR DAKERS	6-1, 165	WHL Kootenay	G

2004

Rd.-Overall	Ht., Wt.	Amateur league, team	Position
1-22 LUKAS KASPAR	6-2, 202	Czech Litvinov	RW
3-94 THOMAS GREISS	6-1, 192	Germany Koln	G
4-126 TORREY MITCHELL	5-11, 175	USHSE Hotchkiss	C
4-129 JASON CHURCHILL	6-3, 184	QMJHL Halifax	G

MISCELLANEOUS DATA

Home ice (capacity)
HP Pavilion at San Jose (17,496)
Address
525 West Santa Clara Street
San Jose, CA 95113
Business phone
408-287-7070
Ticket information
408-287-7070
Website
sjsharks.com
Training site
Logitech Ice at San Jose
Club colors
Deep pacific teal, gray, burnt orange and black
Radio affiliation
KFOX (98.5 FM)
TV affiliation
FOX Sports Net

TAMPA BAY LIGHTNING

EASTERN CONFERENCE, SOUTHEAST DIVISION

Lightning Schedule

Home games shaded.

October

SUN	MON	TUE	WED	THU	FRI	SAT
2	3	4	5 CAR	6	7 FLA	8 FLA
9	10 BOS	11	12	13 BUF	14	15 PIT
16 WAS	17	18	19	20 ATL	21 OTT	22
23	24	25	26 NJ	27	28 WAS	29 ATL
30	31					

November

SUN	MON	TUE	WED	THU	FRI	SAT
		1 ATL	2	3 OTT	4	5 TOR
6	7	8 MON	9	10 NYR	11 ATL	12
13	14 PHI	15 WAS	16	17 NYI	18	19
20 CAR	21	22 PHI	23 WAS	24	25 NJ	26
27 PIT	28	29	30 TOR			

December

SUN	MON	TUE	WED	THU	FRI	SAT
				1	2 CHI	3
4	5	6	7	8 STL	9	10 NAS
11	12	13	14 ANA	15 PHO	16	17 DET
18	19	20 CAR	21	22 NYR	23 BUF	24
25	26 CAR	27	28 MON	29	30 BOS	31

January

SUN	MON	TUE	WED	THU	FRI	SAT
1	2 NYI	3 NYR	4	5 BUF	6	7 BOS
8	9	10	11	12	13 COB	14
15	16 SJ	17 LA	18	19	20 DAL	21 ATL
22	23	24 FLA	25	26 NJ	27	28 PHI
29 WAS	30	31 TOR				

February

SUN	MON	TUE	WED	THU	FRI	SAT
			1	2	3	4 WAS
5	6 NYI	7 NJ	8	9 CAR	10	11 BOS
12	13	14	15	16	17	18
19	20	21	22	23	24	25
26	27	28 FLA				

March

SUN	MON	TUE	WED	THU	FRI	SAT
			1	2	3	4 MON
5	6 OTT	7 PIT	8	9 BUF	10	11 TOR
12	13 MON	14 OTT	15	16	17 PHI	18
19 NYI	20 FLA	21	22	23 WAS	24	25 NYR
26	27 CAR	28	29	30 ATL	31	

April

SUN	MON	TUE	WED	THU	FRI	SAT
						1 FLA
2	3 FLA	4	5	6 ATL	7	8 PIT
9 FLA	10	11 ATL	12	13	14 CAR	15 CAR
16	17	18 WAS	19	20	21	22

2005-06 SEASON

CLUB DIRECTORY

Chief executive officer & governor
Tom Wilson

President
Ron Campbell

General manager
Jay Feaster

Head coach
John Tortorella

Associate coach
Craig Ramsay

Assistant coach
Jeff Reese

Vice president of public relations
Bill Wickett

Director of public relations
Jay Preble

Media relations manager
Brian Breseman

TOP FOUR DRAFT CHOICES

2005

Rd.-Overall	Ht., Wt.	Amateur league, team	Position
1-30 VLADIMIR MIHALIK	6-7, 222	Slovakia 2 Presov	D
3-73 RADEK SMOLENAK	6-2, 180	OHL Kingston	LW
3-89 CHRIS LAWRENCE	6-4, 199	OHL Sault Ste. Marie	C
4-92 MAREK BARTANUS	6-3, 194	Slovakia Jr. Kosice	RW

2004

Rd.-Overall	Ht., Wt.	Amateur league, team	Position
1-30 ANDY ROGERS	6-5, 206	WHL Calgary	D
2-65 MARK TOBIN	6-3, 204	QMJHL Rimouski	LW
4-102 MIKE LUNDIN	6-2, 180	HE U. of Maine	D
5-158 BRANDON ELLIOTT	6-4, 225	OHL Mississauga	D

MISCELLANEOUS DATA

Home ice (capacity)
St. Pete Times Forum (19,758)

Address
401 Channelside Drive
Tampa, Fla. 33602

Business phone
813-301-6500

Ticket information
813-301-6600

Website
www.tampabaylightning.com

Training site
Ice Sports Forum, Brandon, FL

Club colors
Black, blue, silver and white

Radio affiliation
WDAE (620 AM)

TV affiliation
Sunsports (Cable)

TORONTO MAPLE LEAFS

EASTERN CONFERENCE, NORTHEAST DIVISION

Maple Leafs Schedule

Home games shaded.

October

SUN	MON	TUE	WED	THU	FRI	SAT
2	3	4	5 OTT	6	7	8 MON
9	10 OTT	11 PHI	12	13	14 ATL	15 MON
16	17	18	19	20 CAR	21	22 PHI
23	24 BOS	25	26	27 BOS	28	29 OTT
30	31 FLA					

November

SUN	MON	TUE	WED	THU	FRI	SAT
		1	2	3 CAR	4	5 TB
6 WAS	7	8 WAS	9	10	11 BUF	12 MON
13	14	15 NYR	16	17 BOS	18	19 ATL
20	21	22	23 BOS	24	25 CAR	26 MON
27	28 FLA	29	30 TB			

December

SUN	MON	TUE	WED	THU	FRI	SAT
				1 ATL	2	3 SJ
4	5	6 LA	7	8	9	10 DAL
11	12 ANA	13	14	15	16	17 OTT
18	19 NYI	20	21	22 BOS	23 BOS	24
25	26 NJ	27 PIT	28	29 BUF	30	31 NJ

January

SUN	MON	TUE	WED	THU	FRI	SAT
1	2 PIT	3	4	5	6 CAL	7 EDM
8	9	10 VAN	11	12	13	14 PHO
15	16	17 COL	18 MIN	19	20	21 OTT
22	23 OTT	24	25	26 BUF	27	28 MON
29	30 FLA	31 TB				

February

SUN	MON	TUE	WED	THU	FRI	SAT
			1	2	3 WAS	4 NJ
5	6	7 ATL	8	9	10 NYR	11 NYR
12	13	14	15	16	17	18
19	20	21	22	23	24	25
26	27	28 WAS				

March

SUN	MON	TUE	WED	THU	FRI	SAT
			1	2	3 BUF	4 OTT
5	6	7 MON	8	9	10 NYI	11 TB
12	13	14 BOS	15	16 BUF	17	18 NYR
19 PIT	20	21 CAR	22	23 MON	24	25 MON
26 NJ	27	28 PHI	29	30	31	

April

SUN	MON	TUE	WED	THU	FRI	SAT
						1 BUF
2	3 BUF	4	5 NYI	6 BOS	7	8 PHI
9	10	11 FLA	12	13 NYI	14	15 OTT
16 BUF	17	18 PIT	19	20	21	22

2005-06 SEASON

CLUB DIRECTORY

Chairman of the board and NHL governor
Larry Tanenbaum
Alternate governors
John Ferguson, Dale Lastman, Dean Metcalf, Richard Peddie
President, CEO and alt. governor
Richard Peddie
Exec. v.p., chief operating officer
Tom Anselmi
Exec. v.p. and g.m., Air Canada Centre
Bob Hunter
Exec. V.P., Chief Financial Officer & Business Development
Ian Clarke
Vice president, communications & community development
John Lashway
Vice president, people
Mardi Walker
Sr. v.p. and general counsel & corporate secretary
Robin Brudner
General manager & Vice president
John Ferguson
Head Coach
Pat Quinn
Assistant general manager
Mike Penny
Assistant coaches
Keith Acton, Rick Ley
Player development coach
Paul Dennis
Community representatives
Wendel Clark, Darryl Sittler
Chief European scout
Thommie Bergman
Director, amateur scouting
Barry Trapp
Scouts
George Armstrong, Fred Bandel, Garth Malarchuk, Dave Morrison, Mike Palmateer, Mark Yannetti
European scouts
Peter Ahola, Jan Kovac, Nikolai Ladygin
Director, media relations
Pat Park
Coordinator, media relations
Dave Griffiths
Manager, hockey administration
Reid Mitchell
Director, community development
Bev Deeth
Equipment manager
Brian Papineau

TOP FOUR DRAFT CHOICES

2005

Rd.-Overall	Ht., Wt.	Amateur league, team	Position
1-21 TUUKKA RASK	6-2, 165	Finland Jr. Ilves	G
3-82 PHIL ORESKOVIC	6-3, 217	OHL Brampton	D
5-153 ALEX BERRY	6-2, 195	EJHL Junior Bruins	RW
6-173 JOHAN DAHLBERG	6-2, 194	Sweden Jr. MoDo	W

2004

Rd.-Overall	Ht., Wt.	Amateur league, team	Position
3-90 JUSTIN POGGE	6-3, 183	WHL Prince George	G
4-113 ROMAN KUKUMBERG	6-1, 196	Slovakia Trencin	F
5-157 DIMITRI VOROBIEV	6-1, 211	Russia Togliatti	D
6-187 ROBERT EARL	5-10, 184	WCHA U. of Wisconsin	LW

MISCELLANEOUS DATA

Home ice (capacity)
Air Canada Centre (18,819)
Address
Air Canada Centre
40 Bay Street
Toronto, Ont. M5J 2X2
Business phone
416-815-5700
Ticket information
416-815-5700
Website
www.mapleleafs.com
Training site
Toronto
Club colors
Blue and white
Radio affiliation
Talk 640 (640 AM)
TV affiliation
Leafs TV, CBC, TSN, Rogers Sportsn

VANCOUVER CANUCKS
WESTERN CONFERENCE, NORTHWEST DIVISION

Canucks Schedule
Home games shaded.

October

SUN	MON	TUE	WED	THU	FRI	SAT
2	3	4	5 PHO	6	7	8 EDM
9	10	11 DET	12 MIN	13	14 MIN	15
16 DAL	17	18 CHI	19	20 PHO	21	22 COL
23	24	25 MIN	26	27 COL	28	29 COL
30	31					

November

SUN	MON	TUE	WED	THU	FRI	SAT
		1	2 MIN	3	4 COB	5 CAL
6	7 CAL	8	9	10 COL	11	12
13 DET	14	15	16 SJ	17 LA	18	19
20 ANA	21	22 CHI	23	24 SJ	25	26 PHO
27 COL	28	29	30 COL			

December

SUN	MON	TUE	WED	THU	FRI	SAT
				1 EDM	2	3
4 BOS	5	6	7	8	9 OTT	10
11	12	13 NYR	14	15 PHI	16	17 EDM
18	19 LA	20	21 EDM	22	23 CAL	24
25	26 CAL	27	28 NAS	29	30	31 MIN

January

SUN	MON	TUE	WED	THU	FRI	SAT
1	2 STL	3	4 DAL	5 CHI	6	7 CAL
8	9	10 TOR	11	12	13 NJ	14 NYI
15	16 PIT	17	18	19 BUF	20	21 MON
22	23 STL	24 COB	25	26 DET	27	28 COL
29	30	31 PHO				

February

SUN	MON	TUE	WED	THU	FRI	SAT
			1	2	3 CAL	4 EDM
5	6 COB	7	8 STL	9	10 ANA	11
12 MIN	13	14	15	16	17	18
19	20	21	22	23	24	25
26	27	28 CAL				

March

SUN	MON	TUE	WED	THU	FRI	SAT
			1	2 NAS	3 CHI	4
5 STL	6	7	8	9 NAS	10	11 DAL
12	13 DAL	14 NAS	15	16	17 COB	18
19 DET	20	21 EDM	22	23 EDM	24	25 EDM
26	27 LA	28	29 MIN	30	31 MIN	

April

SUN	MON	TUE	WED	THU	FRI	SAT
						1
2 ANA	3 LA	4	5	6	7	8 CAL
9	10 ANA	11	12 SJ	13 SJ	14	15 COL
16						

2005-06 SEASON
CLUB DIRECTORY

Chairman/Gov.
John E McCaw, Jr.
Deputy chairman/alt. gov.
Francesco Aquilini
Deputy chairman/c.e.o. & president
Stanley McCammon
Sr. v.p./g.m./alternate governor
David Nonis
V.p./assistant general manager
Steve Tambellini
V.p./customer sales & services
Caley Denton
V.p./g.m./arena operations
Harvey Jones
V.p./finance
Victor de Bonis
V.p./broadcast and new media
Chris Hebb
V.p./people dev./admin
Susanne Haine
Head coach
Marc Crawford
Associate coaches
Jack McIlhargey, Mike Johnston
Assistant coach
Barry Smith
Strength & conditioning coach
Roger Takhashi
Director, media relations
Chris Brumwell
Manager/game entertainment
Karen Christiansen
Professional scout
Lucien DeBlois
European scout
Thomas Gradin
Russian scout
Sergei Chibisov
Chief amateur scout
Ron Delorme
Amateur scouts
Barry Dean, Ken Slater, Tim Lenardon, Mario Marois, Jack McCartan, Gary Lupul, John McMorrow, Jimmy Eagle
Equipment manager
Pat O'Neill
Assistant equipment trainer
Brian Hamilton
Medical trainer
Mike Burnstein
Assistant medical trainers
Jon Sanderson, Marty Dudgeon
Team doctors
Rui Avelar, Bill Regan
Team dentist
Dr. David Lawson
Team chiropractor
Dr. Sid Sheard
Team optometrist
Dr. Alan R. Boyco

TOP FOUR DRAFT CHOICES

2005

Rd.-Overall	Ht., Wt.	Amateur league, team	Position
1-10 LUC BOURDON	6-2, 199	QMJHL Val d'Or	D
2-51 MASON RAYMOND	6-0, 165	AJHL Camrose	LW
4-114 ALEXANDRE VINCENT	6-4, 193	QMJHL Chicoutimi	G
5-138 MATT BUTCHER	6-1, 185	BCHL Chilliwack	C

2004

Rd.-Overall	Ht., Wt.	Amateur league, team	Position
1-26 CORY SCHNEIDER	6-2, 195	USHSE Phillips-Andover	G
3-91 ALEXANDER EDLER	6-3, 194	Sweden II Jamtland	D
4-125 ANDREW SARAUER	6-4, 190	BCHL Langley	LW
5-159 MIKE BROWN	6-0, 210	CCHA U. of Michigan	RW

MISCELLANEOUS DATA

Home ice (capacity)
General Motors Place (18,630)
Address
800 Griffiths Way
Vancouver, B.C. V6B 6G1
Business phone
604-899-7400
Ticket information
604-899-4625
Website
www.canucks.com
Training site
Burnaby, B.C.
Club colors
Deep blue, sky blue, deep red, white and silver
Radio affiliation
CKNW (980 AM)
TV affiliation
Sportsnet (Cable)

WASHINGTON CAPITALS
EASTERN CONFERENCE, SOUTHEAST DIVISION

Capitals Schedule
Home games shaded.

October

SUN	MON	TUE	WED	THU	FRI	SAT
2	3	4	5 COB	6	7 ATL	8 ATL
9	10 NYR	11	12 CAR	13 NYI	14	15
16 TB	17	18	19	20 FLA	21	22 CAR
23	24	25	26 BUF	27	28 TB	29 FLA
30	31					

November

SUN	MON	TUE	WED	THU	FRI	SAT
		1	2	3 PHI	4 ATL	5
6 TOR	7	8 TOR	9	10	11 NJ	12 NJ
13	14	15 TB	16	17 BUF	18	19 MON
20	21	22 PIT	23 TB	24	25	26 NYR
27 BUF	28	29	30			

December

SUN	MON	TUE	WED	THU	FRI	SAT
				1	2	3 NYR
4	5	6	7 NAS	8	9 DET	10
11	12	13	14 LA	15	16 SJ	17
18 FLA	19	20	21	22 ATL	23 MON	24
25	26	27 BOS	28 NJ	29	30	31 PHI

January

SUN	MON	TUE	WED	THU	FRI	SAT
1 ATL	2	3	4 OTT	5	6 PHI	7
8 FLA	9	10 CHI	11	12 DAL	13 ANA	14
15	16 PHO	17	18	19 STL	20	21 CAR
22	23 BOS	24	25 PIT	26 BOS	27	28
29 TB	30	31 NYI				

February

SUN	MON	TUE	WED	THU	FRI	SAT
			1	2	3 TOR	4 TB
5	6	7 FLA	8	9	10 PHI	11 PIT
12	13	14	15	16	17	18
19	20	21	22	23	24	25
26	27	28 TOR				

March

SUN	MON	TUE	WED	THU	FRI	SAT
			1	2 OTT	3	4 ATL
5	6 NYI	7	8 PIT	9	10 NJ	11
12 OTT	13	14 BUF	15	16 NYR	17	18 FLA
19	20 MON	21	22 FLA	23 TB	24	25 CAR
26	27	28	29 CAR	30 MON	31	

April

SUN	MON	TUE	WED	THU	FRI	SAT
						1 OTT
2	3 CAR	4	5 CAR	6	7 CAR	8 NYI
9	10 BOS	11	12	13 ATL	14	15 FLA
16	17 ATL	18 TB	19	20	21	22

2005-06 SEASON
CLUB DIRECTORY

Chairman and majority owner
Ted Leonsis
President and governor
Dick Patrick
Vice president/general manager
George McPhee
Director, hockey operations/legal affairs
Don Fishman
Director of player personnel
Brian MacLellan
Head coach
Glen Hanlon
Assistant coaches
Jay Leach, Dean Evason
Goaltending coach
Dave Prior
Director of amateur scouting
Ross Mahoney
Pro scout
Larry Carriere
Amateur scouts
Steve Bowman, Ed McColgan, Ray Payne, Martin Pouliot, Steve Richmond
European scouts
Gleb Chistyakov, Vojtech Kucera
Team physician
Dr. Ben Shaffer
Trainer
Greg Smith
Assistant trainer
Tim Clark
Equipment manager
Doug Shearer
Assistant equipment manager
Craig Leydig
Equipment assistant
Brian Metzger
Strength and conditioning coach
Dana White
Massage therapist
Curt Millar
Senior director, communications
Kurt Kehl
Director of media relations
Nate Ewell

TOP FOUR DRAFT CHOICES

2005

Rd.-Overall	Ht., Wt.	Amateur league, team	Position
1-14 SASHA POKULOK	6-5, 220	ECAC Cornell	D
1-27 JOE FINLEY	6-7, 229	USHL Sioux Falls	D
4-109 ANDREW THOMAS	6-2, 196	WCHA U. of Denver	D
4-118 PATRICK MCNEILL	6-0, 195	OHL Saginaw	D

2004

Rd.-Overall	Ht., Wt.	Amateur league, team	Position
1-1 ALEXANDER OVECHKIN	6-2, 212	Russia Dynamo	LW
1-27 JEFF SCHULTZ	6-6, 212	WHL Calgary	D
1-29 MIKE GREEN	6-1, 198	WHL Saskatoon	D
2-33 CHRIS. BOURQUE	5-7, 170	USHSE Cushing Academy	C

MISCELLANEOUS DATA

Home ice (capacity)
MCI Center (18,277)
Address
MCI Center
401 9th Street, NW, Suite 750
Washington, DC 20004
Business phone
202-266-2200
Ticket information
202-266-2277
Website
www.washingtoncaps.com
Training site
Piney Orchard, MD
Club colors
Bronze, blue and black
Radio affiliation
WTEM (980 AM)
TV affiliation
Comcast SportsNet

SCHEDULE

DAY BY DAY

All times Eastern

Wednesday, Oct. 5
Montreal at Boston, 7 p.m.
N.Y. Islanders at Buffalo, 7 p.m.
N.Y. Rangers at Philadelphia, 7 p.m.
Columbus at Washington, 7 p.m.
Atlanta at Florida, 7 p.m.
Ottawa at Toronto, 8 p.m.
Pittsburgh at New Jersey, 7:30 p.m.
Carolina at Tampa Bay, 7:30 p.m.
St. Louis at Detroit, 7:30 p.m.
San Jose at Nashville, 8 p.m.
Anaheim at Chicago, 8:30 p.m.
Calgary at Minnesota, 8:30 p.m.
Los Angeles at Dallas, 8:30 p.m.
Colorado at Edmonton, 9:30 p.m.
Phoenix at Vancouver, 10 p.m.

Thursday, Oct. 6
Montreal at N.Y. Rangers, 7 p.m.
Detroit at St. Louis, 8 p.m.
Phoenix at Los Angeles, 10:30 p.m.

Friday, Oct. 7
New Jersey at Philadelphia, 7 p.m.
Atlanta at Washington, 7 p.m.
Pittsburgh at Carolina, 7 p.m.
Calgary at Columbus, 7 p.m.
Tampa Bay at Florida, 7:30 p.m.
Boston at Buffalo, 8 p.m.
San Jose at Chicago, 8:30 p.m.

Saturday, Oct. 8
Montreal at Toronto, 7 p.m.
Buffalo at Ottawa, 7 p.m.
Carolina at N.Y. Islanders, 7 p.m.
Washington at Atlanta, 7 p.m.
N.Y. Rangers at New Jersey, 7:30 p.m.
Boston at Pittsburgh, 7:30 p.m.
Florida at Tampa Bay, 7:30 p.m.
San Jose at St. Louis, 8 p.m.
Anaheim at Nashville, 8 p.m.
Colorado at Dallas, 8 p.m.
Vancouver at Edmonton, 10 p.m.
Minnesota at Phoenix, 10 p.m.

Sunday, Oct. 9
Calgary at Detroit, 4 p.m.
Columbus at Chicago, 7 p.m.
Minnesota at Los Angeles, 8 p.m.

Monday, Oct. 10
Florida at N.Y. Islanders, 1 p.m.
N.Y. Rangers at Washington, 1 p.m.
Pittsburgh at Buffalo, 7 p.m.
Toronto at Ottawa, 7:30 p.m.
Boston at Tampa Bay, 7:30 p.m.
Calgary at Colorado, 9 p.m.
Edmonton at Anaheim, 10:30 p.m.

Tuesday, Oct. 11
Philadelphia at Toronto, 7:30 p.m.
Ottawa at Montreal, 7:30 p.m.
Chicago at St. Louis, 8 p.m.
Phoenix at Dallas, 8:30 p.m.
Edmonton at Los Angeles, 10:30 p.m.

Wednesday, Oct. 12
Washington at Carolina, 7 p.m.
Vancouver at Detroit, 7:30 p.m.
Montreal at Atlanta, 7 p.m.
Vancouver at Minnesota, 8 p.m.
Nashville at Colorado, 9 p.m.
Columbus at San Jose, 10:30 p.m.

Thursday, Oct. 13
New Jersey at N.Y. Rangers, 7 p.m.
N.Y. Islanders at Washington, 7 p.m.
Boston at Florida, 7 p.m.
Buffalo at Tampa Bay, 7:30 p.m.
Dallas at Calgary, 9 p.m.
Nashville at Phoenix, 10 p.m.
Detroit at Los Angeles, 10:30 p.m.

Friday, Oct. 14
Pittsburgh at Philadelphia, 7 p.m.
Toronto at Atlanta, 7 p.m.
Vancouver at Minnesota, 8 p.m.
Chicago at Colorado, 9 p.m.
Dallas at Edmonton, 9 p.m.
Columbus at Anaheim, 10:30 p.m.

Saturday, Oct. 15
Toronto at Montreal, 7 p.m.
Boston at Ottawa, 7 p.m.
Atlanta at N.Y. Rangers, 7 p.m.
N.Y. Islanders at Philadelphia, 7 p.m.
Carolina at New Jersey, 7:30 p.m.
Tampa Bay at Pittsburgh, 7:30 p.m.
Buffalo at Florida, 7:30 p.m.
Nashville at St. Louis, 8 p.m.
Edmonton at Calgary, 10 p.m.
Detroit at Phoenix, 10 p.m.
Chicago at San Jose, 10:30 p.m.

Sunday, Oct. 16
Tampa Bay at Washington, 6 p.m.
Anaheim at Minnesota, 6 p.m.
Columbus at Los Angeles, 8 p.m.
Dallas at Vancouver, 10 p.m.

Monday, Oct. 17
Florida at N.Y. Rangers, 7 p.m.
San Jose at Detroit, 7:30 p.m.
Phoenix at Calgary, 9 p.m.

Tuesday, Oct. 18
Boston at Montreal, 7:30 p.m.
Florida at New Jersey, 7:30 p.m.
Phoenix at Edmonton, 9 p.m.
Chicago at Vancouver, 10 p.m.

Wednesday, Oct. 19
N.Y. Islanders at N.Y. Rangers, 7 p.m.
Anaheim at St. Louis, 8 p.m.
San Jose at Minnesota, 8 p.m.
Los Angeles at Colorado, 9 p.m.

Thursday, Oct. 20
Buffalo at Boston, 7 p.m.
N.Y. Rangers at N.Y. Islanders, 7 p.m.
Tampa Bay at Atlanta, 7 p.m.
Washington at Florida, 7 p.m.
Carolina at Toronto, 7:30 p.m.
New Jersey at Pittsburgh, 7:30 p.m.
St. Louis at Nashville, 8 p.m.
Los Angeles at Dallas, 8:30 p.m.
Edmonton at Calgary, 9 p.m.
Phoenix at Vancouver, 10 p.m.

Friday, Oct. 21
San Jose at Columbus, 7 p.m.
Ottawa at Tampa Bay, 7:30 p.m.
Anaheim at Detroit, 7:30 p.m.
Colorado at Edmonton, 9 p.m.

Saturday, Oct. 22
Pittsburgh at Boston, 7 p.m.
Philadelphia at Toronto, 7 p.m.
N.Y. Islanders at Montreal, 7 p.m.
Carolina at Washington, 7 p.m.
New Jersey at Atlanta, 7 p.m.
Detroit at Columbus, 7 p.m.
N.Y. Rangers at Buffalo, 7:30 p.m.
Ottawa at Florida, 7:30 p.m.
Minnesota at St. Louis, 8 p.m.
San Jose at Nashville, 8 p.m.
Calgary at Dallas, 8 p.m.
Colorado at Vancouver, 10 p.m.

Sunday, Oct. 23
Phoenix at Anaheim, 4 p.m.
Minnesota at Chicago, 7 p.m.
Calgary at Los Angeles, 10:30 p.m.

Monday, Oct. 24
Ottawa at Carolina, 7 p.m.
Detroit at Columbus, 7 p.m.
Boston at Toronto, 7:30 p.m.

Tuesday, Oct. 25
Atlanta at N.Y. Islanders, 7 p.m.
Philadelphia at Montreal, 7:30 p.m.
Florida at Pittsburgh, 7:30 p.m.
Chicago at Nashville, 8 p.m.
Vancouver at Minnesota, 8 p.m.
Edmonton at Colorado, 9 p.m.
St. Louis at Phoenix, 10 p.m.
Anaheim at Los Angeles, 10:30 p.m.

Wednesday, Oct. 26
Washington at Buffalo, 7 p.m.
Boston at Carolina, 7 p.m.
Nashville at Columbus, 7 p.m.
Tampa Bay at New Jersey, 7:30 p.m.
San Jose at Dallas, 8:30 p.m.
Calgary at Anaheim, 10:30 p.m.

Thursday, Oct. 27
Toronto at Boston, 7 p.m.
N.Y. Islanders at N.Y. Rangers, 7 p.m.
Florida at Philadelphia, 7 p.m.
Montreal at Ottawa, 7:30 p.m.
Atlanta at Pittsburgh, 7:30 p.m.
Chicago at Detroit, 7:30 p.m.
Vancouver at Colorado, 9 p.m.
Calgary at Phoenix, 10 p.m.

Friday, Oct. 28
Philadelphia at Carolina, 7 p.m.
Minnesota at Columbus, 7 p.m.

Buffalo at New Jersey, 7:30 p.m.
Washington at Tampa Bay, 7:30 p.m.
Edmonton at Dallas, 8:30 p.m.
St. Louis at Anaheim, 10:30 p.m.
San Jose at Los Angeles, 10:30 p.m.

Saturday, Oct. 29
New Jersey at Boston, 7 p.m.
Ottawa at Toronto, 7 p.m.
N.Y. Rangers at Montreal, 7 p.m.
Buffalo at N.Y. Islanders, 7 p.m.
Tampa Bay at Atlanta, 7 p.m.
Carolina at Pittsburgh, 7:30 p.m.
Washington at Florida, 7:30 p.m.
Edmonton at Nashville, 8 p.m.
Columbus at Minnesota, 8 p.m.
Detroit at Chicago, 8:30 p.m.
Vancouver at Colorado, 10 p.m.
Dallas at Phoenix, 10 p.m.
St. Louis at Los Angeles, 10:30 p.m.
Calgary at San Jose, 10:30 p.m.

Sunday, Oct. 30
Philadelphia at Ottawa, 7 p.m.
Phoenix at Anaheim, 8 p.m.

Monday, Oct. 31
Montreal at N.Y. Rangers, 7 p.m.
Florida at Toronto, 7:30 p.m.

Tuesday, Nov. 1
Boston at N.Y. Islanders, 7 p.m.
Florida at Montreal, 7:30 p.m.
Pittsburgh at New Jersey, 7:30 p.m.
Atlanta at Tampa Bay, 7:30 p.m.
Chicago at Detroit, 7:30 p.m.
Minnesota at Calgary, 9 p.m.
Columbus at Edmonton, 9 p.m.
Nashville at Anaheim, 10:30 p.m.

Wednesday, Nov. 2
Ottawa at Buffalo, 7 p.m.
Chicago at St. Louis, 8 p.m.
Los Angeles at Dallas, 8:30 p.m.
Minnesota at Vancouver, 10 p.m.
Nashville at San Jose, 10:30 p.m.

Thursday, Nov. 3
Florida at Boston, 7 p.m.
Pittsburgh at N.Y. Islanders, 7 p.m.
Washington at Philadelphia, 7 p.m.
Toronto at Carolina, 7 p.m.
Tampa Bay at Ottawa, 7:30 p.m.
N.Y. Rangers at New Jersey, 7:30 p.m.
Edmonton at Detroit, 7:30 p.m.
Anaheim at Colorado, 9 p.m.
Columbus at Calgary, 9 p.m.
Los Angeles at Phoenix, 9 p.m.

Friday, Nov. 4
Atlanta at Washington, 7 p.m.
Montreal at Buffalo, 8 p.m.
Edmonton at St. Louis, 8 p.m.
Chicago at Dallas, 8:30 p.m.
Columbus at Vancouver, 10 p.m.
San Jose at Anaheim, 10:30 p.m.

Saturday, Nov. 5
New Jersey at N.Y. Rangers, 1 p.m.
Nashville at Los Angeles, 4 p.m.
Pittsburgh at Boston, 7 p.m.
Tampa Bay at Toronto, 7 p.m.
Buffalo at Montreal, 7 p.m.
N.Y. Islanders at Ottawa, 7 p.m.
Atlanta at Philadelphia, 7 p.m.
Florida at Carolina, 7 p.m.
Phoenix at Detroit, 7:30 p.m.
Dallas at Colorado, 9 p.m.
Vancouver at Calgary, 10 p.m.
Minnesota at San Jose, 10:30 p.m.

Sunday, Nov. 6
Toronto at Washington, 5 p.m.
Phoenix at Chicago, 7 p.m.
Detroit at St. Louis, 7 p.m.
Minnesota at Anaheim, 8 p.m.

Monday, Nov. 7
Pittsburgh at N.Y. Rangers, 7 p.m.
Edmonton at Dallas, 8:30 p.m.
Vancouver at Calgary, 9 p.m.

Tuesday, Nov. 8
Boston at Philadelphia, 7 p.m.
Washington at Toronto, 7:30 p.m.
Tampa Bay at Montreal, 7:30 p.m.
N.Y. Islanders at New Jersey, 7:30 p.m.
Edmonton at Nashville, 8 p.m.
Phoenix at Minnesota, 8 p.m.
San Jose at Colorado, 9 p.m.

Wednesday, Nov. 9
Carolina at Buffalo, 7 p.m.
Pittsburgh at Atlanta, 7 p.m.
N.Y. Rangers at Florida, 7 p.m.
St. Louis at Columbus, 7 p.m.
Los Angeles at Detroit, 7:30 p.m.

Thursday, Nov. 10
Ottawa at Boston, 7 p.m.
N.Y. Islanders at Philadelphia, 7 p.m.
Montreal at Pittsburgh, 7:30 p.m.
N.Y. Rangers at Tampa Bay, 7:30 p.m.
Chicago at St. Louis, 8 p.m.
Dallas at Nashville, 8 p.m.
Calgary at Phoenix, 9 p.m.
Colorado at Vancouver, 10 p.m.

Friday, Nov. 11
New Jersey at Washington, 1 p.m.
Tampa Bay at Atlanta, 7 p.m.
Edmonton at Columbus, 7 p.m.
Carolina at Florida, 7:30 p.m.
Minnesota at Detroit, 7:30 p.m.
Toronto at Buffalo, 8 p.m.
Los Angeles at Chicago, 8:30 p.m.

Saturday, Nov. 12
Washington at New Jersey, 1 p.m.
Toronto at Montreal, 7 p.m.
Buffalo at Ottawa, 7 p.m.
Boston at N.Y. Islanders, 7 p.m.
Florida at Philadelphia, 7 p.m.
Atlanta at Carolina, 7 p.m.
N.Y. Rangers at Pittsburgh, 7:30 p.m.
St. Louis at Nashville, 8 p.m.
Anaheim at Phoenix, 9 p.m.
Colorado at Calgary, 10 p.m.
Dallas at San Jose, 10:30 p.m.

Sunday, Nov. 13
Los Angeles at Columbus, 5 p.m.
Edmonton at Chicago, 7 p.m.
Dallas at Anaheim, 8 p.m.
Detroit at Vancouver, 10 p.m.

Monday, Nov. 14
N.Y. Islanders at Pittsburgh, 7:30 p.m.
Philadelphia at Tampa Bay, 7:30 p.m.
Edmonton at Colorado, 9 p.m.
Minnesota at Calgary, 9 p.m.

Tuesday, Nov. 15
New Jersey at Buffalo, 7 p.m.
Tampa Bay at Washington, 7 p.m.
N.Y. Rangers at Toronto, 7:30 p.m.
Florida at Montreal, 7:30 p.m.
Carolina at Ottawa, 7:30 p.m.
Los Angeles at Nashville, 8 p.m.

Wednesday, Nov. 16
Pittsburgh at Philadelphia, 7 p.m.
N.Y. Islanders at Atlanta, 7 p.m.
St. Louis at Columbus, 7 p.m.
Detroit at Calgary, 9 p.m.
Colorado at Phoenix, 9 p.m.
Dallas at Anaheim, 10:30 p.m.
Vancouver at San Jose, 10:30 p.m.

Thursday, Nov. 17
Toronto at Boston, 7 p.m.
Washington at Buffalo, 7 p.m.
N.Y. Rangers at Carolina, 7 p.m.
Florida at Ottawa, 7:30 p.m.
N.Y. Islanders at Tampa Bay, 7:30 p.m.
Detroit at Edmonton, 9 p.m.
Vancouver at Los Angeles, 10:30 p.m.

Friday, Nov. 18
Atlanta at Philadelphia, 7 p.m.
Montreal at New Jersey, 7:30 p.m.
Columbus at Dallas, 8:30 p.m.
Chicago at Calgary, 9 p.m.
Colorado at Anaheim, 10:30 p.m.

Saturday, Nov. 19
Carolina at N.Y. Rangers, 1 p.m.
Buffalo at Boston, 7 p.m.
Atlanta at Toronto, 7 p.m.
Washington at Montreal, 7 p.m.
New Jersey at Ottawa, 7 p.m.
Philadelphia at Pittsburgh, 7:30 p.m.
N.Y. Islanders at Florida, 7:30 p.m.
St. Louis at Detroit, 7:30 p.m.
Nashville at Minnesota, 8 p.m.
Chicago at Edmonton, 10 p.m.
Colorado at Los Angeles, 10:30 p.m.
Phoenix at San Jose, 10:30 p.m.

Sunday, Nov. 20
Vancouver at Anaheim, 4 p.m.
Boston at N.Y. Rangers, 7 p.m.
Tampa Bay at Carolina, 7 p.m.
Columbus at Phoenix, 8 p.m.

Monday, Nov. 21
Nashville at Detroit, 7:30 p.m.
Calgary at Colorado, 9 p.m.
San Jose at Edmonton, 9 p.m.

Tuesday, Nov. 22
N.Y. Rangers at Buffalo, 7 p.m.
Tampa Bay at Philadelphia, 7 p.m.
Ottawa at Carolina, 7 p.m.
Atlanta at Montreal, 7:30 p.m.
Washington at Pittsburgh, 7:30 p.m.
Los Angeles at St. Louis, 8 p.m.
Anaheim at Phoenix, 9 p.m.
Chicago at Vancouver, 10 p.m.

Wednesday, Nov. 23
Buffalo at N.Y. Islanders, 7 p.m.
Tampa Bay at Washington, 7 p.m.
New Jersey at Florida, 7 p.m.
Nashville at Columbus, 7 p.m.
Boston at Toronto, 7:30 p.m.
Colorado at Detroit, 7:30 p.m.
Edmonton at Minnesota, 8 p.m.
Anaheim at Dallas, 8:30 p.m.
San Jose at Calgary, 9 p.m.

Thursday, Nov. 24
N.Y. Rangers at Atlanta, 7 p.m.
Los Angeles at Nashville, 8 p.m.
San Jose at Vancouver, 10 p.m.

Friday, Nov. 25
Philadelphia at Boston, 12 p.m.
Ottawa at N.Y. Islanders, 2 p.m.
St. Louis at Minnesota, 2 p.m.
Detroit at Anaheim, 4 p.m.
Toronto at Carolina, 7 p.m.
Colorado at Columbus, 7 p.m.
New Jersey at Tampa Bay, 7:30 p.m.
Pittsburgh at Florida, 7:30 p.m.
Montreal at Buffalo, 8 p.m.
Phoenix at Dallas, 8:30 p.m.
Edmonton at Calgary, 9 p.m.

Saturday, Nov. 26
N.Y. Islanders at Philadelphia, 2 p.m.
Montreal at Toronto, 7 p.m.
Boston at Ottawa, 7 p.m.
Washington at N.Y. Rangers, 7 p.m.
Florida at Atlanta, 7 p.m.
Columbus at St. Louis, 8 p.m.
Dallas at Nashville, 8 p.m.
Vancouver at Phoenix, 10 p.m.
Chicago at Los Angeles, 10:30 p.m.
Detroit at San Jose, 10:30 p.m.

Sunday, Nov. 27
Atlanta at Carolina, 5 p.m.
Pittsburgh at Tampa Bay, 5 p.m.
Buffalo at Washington, 3 p.m.
Chicago at Anaheim, 8 p.m.
Vancouver at Colorado, 9 p.m.

Monday, Nov. 28
Toronto at Florida, 7 p.m.
Detroit at Los Angeles, 10:30 p.m.

Tuesday, Nov. 29
Philadelphia at N.Y. Islanders, 7 p.m.
Carolina at Atlanta, 7 p.m.
Montreal at Ottawa, 7:30 p.m.
Boston at New Jersey, 7:30 p.m.
Buffalo at Pittsburgh, 7:30 p.m.
Calgary at Nashville, 8 p.m.
Colorado at Edmonton, 9 p.m.

Wednesday, Nov. 30
New Jersey at Philadelphia, 7 p.m.
Toronto at Tampa Bay, 7:30 p.m.
Columbus at Minnesota, 8 p.m.
Los Angeles at Chicago, 8:30 p.m.
San Jose at Dallas, 8:30 p.m.
Colorado at Vancouver, 10 p.m.
Phoenix at Anaheim, 10:30 p.m.

Thursday, Dec. 1
Ottawa at Boston, 7 p.m.
Pittsburgh at N.Y. Rangers, 7 p.m.
Toronto at Atlanta, 7 p.m.
Buffalo at Montreal, 7:30 p.m.
Calgary at Detroit, 7:30 p.m.
Columbus at St. Louis, 8 p.m.
Minnesota at Nashville, 8 p.m.
Vancouver at Edmonton, 9 p.m.

Friday, Dec. 2
Los Angeles at Ottawa, 7:30 p.m.
Chicago at Tampa Bay, 7:30 p.m.
San Jose at Buffalo, 8 p.m.
Carolina at Dallas, 8:30 p.m.

Saturday, Dec. 3
Minnesota at New Jersey, 1 p.m.
N.Y. Rangers at Washington, 7 p.m.
San Jose at Toronto, 7 p.m.
Los Angeles at Montreal, 7 p.m.
Calgary at Pittsburgh, 7:30 p.m.
Chicago at Florida, 7:30 p.m.
Philadelphia at Nashville, 8 p.m.
Carolina at Phoenix, 9 p.m.
Boston at Edmonton, 10 p.m.
Atlanta at Anaheim, 10:30 p.m.

Sunday, Dec. 4
N.Y. Islanders at Detroit, 5 p.m.
Buffalo at Colorado, 9 p.m.
Boston at Vancouver, 10 p.m.

Monday, Dec. 5
Minnesota at N.Y. Rangers, 7 p.m.
Atlanta at Phoenix, 9 p.m.

Tuesday, Dec. 6
Calgary at Philadelphia, 7 p.m.
Los Angeles at Toronto, 7:30 p.m.
New Jersey at Detroit, 7:30 p.m.
N.Y. Islanders at St. Louis, 8 p.m.
Carolina at Anaheim, 10:30 p.m.
Atlanta at San Jose, 10:30 p.m.

Wednesday, Dec. 7
Nashville at Washington, 7 p.m.
Calgary at New Jersey, 7:30 p.m.
N.Y. Rangers at Chicago, 8:30 p.m.
Florida at Dallas, 8:30 p.m.
Boston at Colorado, 9 p.m.

Thursday, Dec. 8
Anaheim at Buffalo, 7 p.m.
Edmonton at Philadelphia, 7 p.m.
N.Y. Islanders at Columbus, 7 p.m.
Minnesota at Pittsburgh, 7:30 p.m.
St. Louis at Tampa Bay, 7:30 p.m.
N.Y. Rangers at Nashville, 8 p.m.
Carolina at Los Angeles, 10:30 p.m.
Florida at San Jose, 10:30 p.m.

Friday, Dec. 9
Detroit at Washington, 7 p.m.
Columbus at Atlanta, 7 p.m.
Colorado at New Jersey, 7:30 p.m.
Ottawa at Vancouver, 10 p.m.

Saturday, Dec. 10
Minnesota at Philadelphia, 2 p.m.
Florida at Los Angeles, 4 p.m.
Dallas at Toronto, 7 p.m.
Anaheim at Montreal, 7 p.m.
Edmonton at N.Y. Islanders, 7 p.m.
Colorado at Pittsburgh, 7:30 p.m.
Nashville at Tampa Bay, 8 p.m.
N.Y. Rangers at St. Louis, 8 p.m.
Ottawa at Calgary, 10 p.m.
Carolina at San Jose, 10:30 p.m.

Sunday, Dec. 11
Chicago at Atlanta, 2 p.m.
Phoenix at Boston, 5 p.m.
New Jersey at Columbus, 5 p.m.
Buffalo at Minnesota, 7 p.m.

Monday, Dec. 12
Anaheim at Toronto, 7:30 p.m.
Pittsburgh at Detroit, 7:30 p.m.
Ottawa at Colorado, 9 p.m.

Tuesday, Dec. 13
Minnesota at N.Y. Islanders, 7 p.m.
Vancouver at N.Y. Rangers, 7 p.m.
Chicago at Carolina, 7 p.m.
Detroit at Atlanta, 7 p.m.
Nashville at Florida, 7 p.m.
Philadelphia at Columbus, 7 p.m.
Phoenix at Montreal, 7:30 p.m.
Edmonton at New Jersey, 7:30 p.m.
Pittsburgh at St. Louis, 8 p.m.

Wednesday, Dec. 14
Dallas at Buffalo, 7 p.m.
Tampa Bay at Anaheim, 10:30 p.m.
Washington at Los Angeles, 10:30 p.m.

Thursday, Dec. 15
Vancouver at Philadelphia, 7 p.m.
Columbus at Carolina, 7 p.m.
Dallas at Ottawa, 7:30 p.m.
Atlanta at New Jersey, 7:30 p.m.
Detroit at Florida, 8 p.m.
Chicago at Nashville, 8 p.m.
Boston at Minnesota, 8 p.m.
Montreal at Edmonton, 9 p.m.
Tampa Bay at Phoenix, 9 p.m.

Friday, Dec. 16
Buffalo at Pittsburgh, 7:30 p.m.
St. Louis at Chicago, 8:30 p.m.
Los Angeles at Anaheim, 10:30 p.m.
Washington at San Jose, 10:30 p.m.

Saturday, Dec. 17
Toronto at Ottawa, 7 p.m.
Colorado at N.Y. Islanders, 7 p.m.
New Jersey at Carolina, 7 p.m.
Florida at Atlanta, 7 p.m.
Pittsburgh at Buffalo, 7:30 p.m.
Detroit at Tampa Bay, 7:30 p.m.
Philadelphia at St. Louis, 8 p.m.
Columbus at Nashville, 8 p.m.
Montreal at Minnesota, 8 p.m.
Boston at Calgary, 10 p.m.
Edmonton at Vancouver, 10 p.m.
Phoenix at Los Angeles, 10:30 p.m.

Sunday, Dec. 18
Colorado at N.Y. Rangers, 5 p.m.
Florida at Washington, 6 p.m.
Dallas at Chicago, 7 p.m.
San Jose at Anaheim, 8 p.m.

Monday, Dec. 19
Buffalo at Philadelphia, 7 p.m.
N.Y. Islanders at Toronto, 7:30 p.m.
Dallas at Minnesota, 8 p.m.
Calgary at Edmonton, 9 p.m.
Los Angeles at Vancouver, 10 p.m.

Tuesday, Dec. 20
New Jersey at N.Y. Rangers, 7 p.m.
Tampa Bay at Carolina, 7 p.m.
Ottawa at Montreal, 7:30 p.m.
Columbus at Detroit, 7:30 p.m.
Colorado at Nashville, 8 p.m.
St. Louis at Phoenix, 9 p.m.
Anaheim at San Jose, 10:30 p.m.

Wednesday, Dec. 21
New Jersey at N.Y. Islanders, 7 p.m.
Dallas at Columbus, 7 p.m.
Nashville at Chicago, 8:30 p.m.
Los Angeles at Calgary, 9 p.m.
Edmonton at Vancouver, 10 p.m.
St. Louis at Anaheim, 10:30 p.m.

Thursday, Dec. 22
Toronto at Boston, 7 p.m.
Tampa Bay at N.Y. Rangers, 7 p.m.
Ottawa at Philadelphia, 7 p.m.
Washington at Atlanta, 7 p.m.
Buffalo at Florida, 7 p.m.
Minnesota at Colorado, 9 p.m.
San Jose at Phoenix, 9 p.m.

Friday, Dec. 23
Boston at Toronto, 7 p.m.
Ottawa at N.Y. Islanders, 7 p.m.
Montreal at Washington, 7 p.m.
Florida at Carolina, 7 p.m.
Nashville at Columbus, 7 p.m.
Atlanta at New Jersey, 7:30 p.m.
Philadelphia at Pittsburgh, 7:30 p.m.
Buffalo at Tampa Bay, 7:30 p.m.
Colorado at Minnesota, 8 p.m.
Detroit at Chicago, 8:30 p.m.
Phoenix at Dallas, 8:30 p.m.
Los Angeles at Edmonton, 9 p.m.
Calgary at Vancouver, 10 p.m.
St. Louis at San Jose, 10:30 p.m.

Monday, Dec. 26
N.Y. Islanders at Buffalo, 7 p.m.
Montreal at Atlanta, 7 p.m.
Philadelphia at Florida, 7 p.m.
Chicago at Columbus, 7 p.m.
New Jersey at Toronto, 7:30 p.m.
N.Y. Rangers at Ottawa, 7:30 p.m.
Carolina at Tampa Bay, 7:30 p.m.
Dallas at St. Louis, 8 p.m.
Phoenix at Colorado, 9 p.m.
Minnesota at Edmonton, 9 p.m.
Calgary at Vancouver, 10 p.m.
San Jose at Los Angeles, 10:30 p.m.

Tuesday, Dec. 27
Boston at Washington, 7 p.m.
Toronto at Pittsburgh, 7:30 p.m.
Detroit at Dallas, 8:30 p.m.
Nashville at Calgary, 9 p.m.

Wednesday, Dec. 28
N.Y. Rangers at N.Y. Islanders, 7 p.m.
Philadelphia at Atlanta, 7 p.m.
Boston at Florida, 7 p.m.
Anaheim at Columbus, 7 p.m.
Carolina at Ottawa, 7:30 p.m.
Washington at New Jersey, 7:30 p.m.
Montreal at Tampa Bay, 7:30 p.m.
St. Louis at Chicago, 8:30 p.m.
Los Angeles at Colorado, 9 p.m.
Minnesota at Edmonton, 9 p.m.
Nashville at Vancouver, 10 p.m.
Phoenix at San Jose, 10:30 p.m.

Thursday, Dec. 29
Philadelphia at Carolina, 7 p.m.
Buffalo at Toronto, 7:30 p.m.
New Jersey at Pittsburgh, 7:30 p.m.
St. Louis at Dallas, 8:30 p.m.
Minnesota at Calgary, 9 p.m.
Los Angeles at Phoenix, 9 p.m.

Friday, Dec. 30
N.Y. Islanders at Ottawa, 7:30 p.m.
Boston at Tampa Bay, 7:30 p.m.
Montreal at Florida, 7:30 p.m.
Atlanta at Buffalo, 8 p.m.
Columbus at Chicago, 8:30 p.m.
Nashville at Edmonton, 9 p.m.
Colorado at San Jose, 10:30 p.m.

Saturday, Dec. 31
N.Y. Rangers at Pittsburgh, 1 p.m.
Philadelphia at Washington, 1 p.m.
Anaheim at St. Louis, 6 p.m.
Vancouver at Minnesota, 6 p.m.
Toronto at New Jersey, 7 p.m.
Columbus at Detroit, 7 p.m.
Montreal at Carolina, 8 p.m.
Los Angeles at Dallas, 8 p.m.
Colorado at Phoenix, 8 p.m.
Edmonton at Calgary, 10 p.m.

Sunday, Jan. 1
Atlanta at Washington, 3 p.m.
Florida at Buffalo, 5 p.m.
Anaheim at Nashville, 8 p.m.

Monday, Jan. 2
Philadelphia at Boston, 1 p.m.
Chicago at Calgary, 3 p.m.
Tampa Bay at N.Y. Islanders, 7 p.m.
Ottawa at Atlanta, 7 p.m.
Pittsburgh at Toronto, 7:30 p.m.
Vancouver at St. Louis, 8 p.m.
Dallas at Los Angeles, 10:30 p.m.

Tuesday, Jan. 3
Tampa Bay at N.Y. Rangers, 7 p.m.
Pittsburgh at Montreal, 7:30 p.m.
Florida at New Jersey, 7:30 p.m.
Minnesota at Detroit, 7:30 p.m.
Nashville at Colorado, 9 p.m.
Chicago at Edmonton, 9 p.m.

Wednesday, Jan. 4
Florida at N.Y. Islanders, 7 p.m.
Ottawa at Washington, 7 p.m.
Atlanta at Carolina, 7 p.m.
Nashville at St. Louis, 8 p.m.
Vancouver at Dallas, 8:30 p.m.

Thursday, Jan. 5
Ottawa at Boston, 7 p.m.
Tampa Bay at Buffalo, 7 p.m.
Philadelphia at N.Y. Rangers, 7 p.m.
Montreal at New Jersey, 7:30 p.m.
St. Louis at Detroit, 7:30 p.m.
Colorado at Minnesota, 8 p.m.
Vancouver at Chicago, 8:30 p.m.
Phoenix at Los Angeles, 10:30 p.m.
Columbus at San Jose, 10:30 p.m.

Friday, Jan. 6
Philadelphia at Washington, 7 p.m.
N.Y. Islanders at Carolina, 7 p.m.
Pittsburgh at Atlanta, 7 p.m.
Detroit at Nashville, 8 p.m.
Anaheim at Dallas, 8:30 p.m.
Toronto at Calgary, 9 p.m.

Saturday, Jan. 7
Florida at N.Y. Rangers, 1 p.m.
Ottawa at Montreal, 2 p.m.
Columbus at Colorado, 3 p.m.
Tampa Bay at Boston, 7 p.m.
Carolina at N.Y. Islanders, 7 p.m.
Toronto at Edmonton, 7 p.m.
New Jersey at Buffalo, 7:30 p.m.
Atlanta at Pittsburgh, 7:30 p.m.
Anaheim at Minnesota, 8 p.m.
Calgary at Vancouver, 10 p.m.
Los Angeles at San Jose, 10:30 p.m.

Sunday, Jan. 8
Florida at Washington, 3 p.m.
Dallas at Detroit, 5 p.m.
Nashville at Chicago, 7 p.m.
Columbus at Phoenix, 8 p.m.

Monday, Jan. 9
Philadelphia at New Jersey, 7:30 p.m.
Dallas at Minnesota, 8 p.m.
St. Louis at Colorado, 9 p.m.
Los Angeles at Anaheim, 10:30 p.m.

Tuesday, Jan. 10
San Jose at Boston, 7 p.m.
Calgary at N.Y. Rangers, 7 p.m.
Chicago at Washington, 7 p.m.
Detroit at Carolina, 7 p.m.
Phoenix at Ottawa, 7:30 p.m.
Edmonton at Pittsburgh, 7:30 p.m.
N.Y. Islanders at Nashville, 8 p.m.
Toronto at Vancouver, 10 p.m.

Wednesday, Jan. 11
Nashville at Atlanta, 7 p.m.
Pittsburgh at Columbus, 7 p.m.
Philadelphia at Chicago, 8:30 p.m.
Montreal at Colorado, 9 p.m.

Thursday, Jan. 12
Los Angeles at Boston, 7 p.m.
Phoenix at Buffalo, 7 p.m.
Calgary at N.Y. Islanders, 7 p.m.
Edmonton at N.Y. Rangers, 7 p.m.
St. Louis at Florida, 7 p.m.
San Jose at Ottawa, 7:30 p.m.
Philadelphia at Detroit, 7:30 p.m.
Washington at Dallas, 8:30 p.m.

Friday, Jan. 13
Nashville at Carolina, 7 p.m.
St. Louis at Atlanta, 7 p.m.
Vancouver at New Jersey, 7:30 p.m.
Columbus at Tampa Bay, 7:30 p.m.
Pittsburgh at Chicago, 8:30 p.m.
Washington at Anaheim, 10:30 p.m.

Saturday, Jan. 14
Dallas at Boston, 2 p.m.
Colorado at Philadelphia, 2 p.m.
N.Y. Rangers at Detroit, 2 p.m.
Phoenix at Toronto, 7 p.m.
San Jose at Montreal, 7 p.m.

Vancouver at N.Y. Islanders, 7 p.m.
Los Angeles at Buffalo, 7:30 p.m.
Columbus at Florida, 7:30 p.m.
Calgary at Minnesota, 8 p.m.
Ottawa at Edmonton, 10 p.m.

Sunday, Jan. 15
St. Louis at Carolina, 1:30 p.m.
New Jersey at Chicago, 7 p.m.
Pittsburgh at Nashville, 8 p.m.

Monday, Jan. 16
Anaheim at Boston, 1 p.m.
Washington at Phoenix, 4 p.m.
N.Y. Rangers at Columbus, 7 p.m.
Dallas at Montreal, 7:30 p.m.
Vancouver at Pittsburgh, 7:30 p.m.
Ottawa at Minnesota, 8 p.m.
Tampa Bay at San Jose, 8 p.m.
Buffalo at Edmonton, 9 p.m.

Tuesday, Jan. 17
Carolina at Philadelphia, 7 p.m.
New Jersey at St. Louis, 8 p.m.
N.Y. Islanders at Chicago, 8:30 p.m.
Toronto at Colorado, 9 p.m.
Tampa Bay at Los Angeles, 10:30 p.m.

Wednesday, Jan. 18
Detroit at Columbus, 7 p.m.
Toronto at Minnesota, 8 p.m.
Atlanta at Dallas, 8:30 p.m.

Thursday, Jan. 19
Boston at Philadelphia, 7 p.m.
St. Louis at Washington, 7 p.m.
N.Y. Islanders at Carolina, 7 p.m.
Anaheim at Ottawa, 7:30 p.m.
N.Y. Rangers at Pittsburgh, 7:30 p.m.
New Jersey at Nashville, 8 p.m.
Colorado at Chicago, 8:30 p.m.
Montreal at Calgary, 9 p.m.
Florida at Phoenix, 9 p.m.
Buffalo at Vancouver, 10 p.m.
Atlanta at Los Angeles, 10:30 p.m.
Edmonton at San Jose, 10:30 p.m.

Friday, Jan. 20
St. Louis at Columbus, 7 p.m.
Chicago at Minnesota, 8 p.m.
Tampa Bay at Dallas, 8:30 p.m.

Saturday, Jan. 21
N.Y. Islanders at New Jersey, 12 p.m.
Philadelphia at Pittsburgh, 2 p.m.
Detroit at Colorado, 2 p.m.
San Jose at Los Angeles, 6 p.m.
N.Y. Rangers at Boston, 7 p.m.
Toronto at Ottawa, 7 p.m.
Tampa Bay at Atlanta, 7 p.m.
Carolina at Washington, 7:30 p.m.
Columbus at Nashville, 8 p.m.
Buffalo at Calgary, 9 p.m.
Edmonton at Phoenix, 9 p.m.
Montreal at Vancouver, 10 p.m.
Florida at Anaheim, 10:30 p.m.

Sunday, Jan. 22
New Jersey at N.Y. Rangers, 7 p.m.
Minnesota at Chicago, 7 p.m.

Monday, Jan. 23
Pittsburgh at Philadelphia, 7 p.m.
Boston at Washington, 7 p.m.
Montreal at Carolina, 7 p.m.
Toronto at Ottawa, 7:30 p.m.
Vancouver at St. Louis, 8 p.m.
Detroit at Nashville, 8 p.m.
Phoenix at Dallas, 8:30 p.m.
Calgary at Edmonton, 9 p.m.
Anaheim at Los Angeles, 10:30 p.m.

Tuesday, Jan. 24
New Jersey at N.Y. Islanders, 7 p.m.
Buffalo at N.Y. Rangers, 7 p.m.
Boston at Atlanta, 7 p.m.
Vancouver at Columbus, 7 p.m.
Florida at Tampa Bay, 7:30 p.m.
Nashville at Detroit, 7:30 p.m.
Phoenix at Minnesota, 8 p.m.
Calgary at Colorado, 9 p.m.
Los Angeles at San Jose, 10:30 p.m.

Wednesday, Jan. 25
Montreal at Philadelphia, 7 p.m.
Carolina at Florida, 7 p.m.
Washington at Pittsburgh, 7:30 p.m.
St. Louis at Dallas, 8:30 p.m.
Edmonton at Anaheim, 10:30 p.m.

Thursday, Jan. 26
Washington at Boston, 7 p.m.
Pittsburgh at N.Y. Islanders, 7 p.m.
Carolina at Atlanta, 7 p.m.
Buffalo at Toronto, 7:30 p.m.
Montreal at Ottawa, 7:30 p.m.
New Jersey at Tampa Bay, 7:30 p.m.
Vancouver at Detroit, 7:30 p.m.
Phoenix at St. Louis, 8 p.m.
Nashville at Minnesota, 8 p.m.
Calgary at Chicago, 8:30 p.m.
Dallas at Colorado, 9 p.m.
Edmonton at Los Angeles, 10:30 p.m.
Anaheim at San Jose, 10:30 p.m.

Friday, Jan. 27
Minnesota at Columbus, 7 p.m.
New Jersey at Florida, 7:30 p.m.

Saturday, Jan. 28
Tampa Bay at Philadelphia, 2 p.m.
Detroit at Dallas, 2 p.m.
Anaheim at Los Angeles, 4 p.m.
N.Y. Islanders at Boston, 7 p.m.
Montreal at Toronto, 7 p.m.
Pittsburgh at N.Y. Rangers, 7 p.m.
Atlanta at Carolina, 7 p.m.
Nashville at Columbus, 7 p.m.
San Jose at Phoenix, 9 p.m.
Vancouver at Colorado, 10 p.m.

Sunday, Jan. 29
Tampa Bay at Washington, 3 p.m.
Calgary at Chicago, 3 p.m.
Edmonton at Phoenix, 8 p.m.

Monday, Jan. 30
Philadelphia at N.Y. Rangers, 7 p.m.
Toronto at Florida, 7 p.m.
Boston at Ottawa, 7:30 p.m.
Calgary at St. Louis, 8 p.m.
Detroit at Minnesota, 8 p.m.
San Jose at Dallas, 8:30 p.m.
Los Angeles at Anaheim, 10:30 p.m.

Tuesday, Jan. 31
Washington at N.Y. Islanders, 7 p.m.
Buffalo at Atlanta, 7 p.m.
Carolina at Montreal, 7:30 p.m.
Toronto at Tampa Bay, 7:30 p.m.
Minnesota at Colorado, 9 p.m.
Vancouver at Phoenix, 9 p.m.

Wednesday, Feb. 1
Pittsburgh at N.Y. Rangers, 7 p.m.
Ottawa at New Jersey, 7:30 p.m.
St. Louis at Detroit, 7:30 p.m.
Nashville at Dallas, 8:30 p.m.
Columbus at Calgary, 9 p.m.
San Jose at Anaheim, 10:30 p.m.

Thursday, Feb. 2
Montreal at Boston, 7 p.m.
Philadelphia at Buffalo, 7 p.m.
N.Y. Rangers at N.Y. Islanders, 7 p.m.
Ottawa at Pittsburgh, 7:30 p.m.
Chicago at St. Louis, 8 p.m.
Colorado at Nashville, 8 p.m.
Columbus at Edmonton, 9 p.m.
Los Angeles at Phoenix, 9 p.m.
Minnesota at San Jose, 10:30 p.m.

Friday, Feb. 3
Toronto at Washington, 7 p.m.
Carolina at New Jersey, 7:30 p.m.
Atlanta at Florida, 7:30 p.m.
Vancouver at Calgary, 9 p.m.

Saturday, Feb. 4
Boston at Montreal, 1 p.m.
N.Y. Rangers at Philadelphia, 2 p.m.
Dallas at St. Louis, 2 p.m.
Chicago at Nashville, 2 p.m.
Detroit at Colorado, 2 p.m.
New Jersey at Toronto, 7 p.m.
Florida at Atlanta, 7 p.m.
Ottawa at Buffalo, 7:30 p.m.
N.Y. Islanders at Pittsburgh, 7:30 p.m.
Washington at Tampa Bay, 7:30 p.m.
Minnesota at Phoenix, 9 p.m.
Vancouver at Edmonton, 10 p.m.
Anaheim at San Jose, 10:30 p.m.

Sunday, Feb. 5
Carolina at Boston, 1 p.m.
Philadelphia at Montreal, 1 p.m.

Monday, Feb. 6
Tampa Bay at N.Y. Islanders, 7 p.m.
Pittsburgh at Ottawa, 7:30 p.m.
Nashville at Dallas, 8:30 p.m.
Anaheim at Edmonton, 9 p.m.
Columbus at Vancouver, 10 p.m.
Calgary at San Jose, 10:30 p.m.

Tuesday, Feb. 7
Florida at Washington, 7 p.m.
Atlanta at Toronto, 7:30 p.m.
Buffalo at Montreal, 7:30 p.m.
Tampa Bay at New Jersey, 7:30 p.m.
Los Angeles at Minnesota, 8 p.m.
Edmonton at Colorado, 9 p.m.
Chicago at Phoenix, 9 p.m.

Wednesday, Feb. 8
Ottawa at N.Y. Rangers, 7 p.m.
N.Y. Islanders at Philadelphia, 7 p.m.
Los Angeles at Columbus, 7 p.m.
Boston at Pittsburgh, 7:30 p.m.
Nashville at Detroit, 7:30 p.m.
Anaheim at Calgary, 9 p.m.

St. Louis at Vancouver, 10 p.m.
Chicago at San Jose, 10:30 p.m.

Thursday, Feb. 9
New Jersey at Boston, 7 p.m.
Montreal at Buffalo, 7 p.m.
Atlanta at Ottawa, 7:30 p.m.
Carolina at Tampa Bay, 7:30 p.m.
Detroit at Nashville, 8 p.m.
Colorado at Minnesota, 8 p.m.
Dallas at Phoenix, 9 p.m.

Friday, Feb. 10
Toronto at N.Y. Rangers, 7 p.m.
Washington at Philadelphia, 7 p.m.
Pittsburgh at Carolina, 7 p.m.
Colorado at Columbus, 7 p.m.
St. Louis at Calgary, 9 p.m.
Minnesota at Edmonton, 9 p.m.
Anaheim at Vancouver, 10 p.m.
Dallas at San Jose, 10:30 p.m.

Saturday, Feb. 11
N.Y. Islanders at New Jersey, 1 p.m.
Chicago at Los Angeles, 4 p.m.
N.Y. Rangers at Toronto, 6 p.m.
Tampa Bay at Boston, 7 p.m.
Atlanta at Montreal, 7 p.m.
Philadelphia at Ottawa, 7 p.m.
Pittsburgh at Washington, 7 p.m.
Florida at Buffalo, 7:30 p.m.
Columbus at Nashville, 8 p.m.

Sunday, Feb. 12
St. Louis at Edmonton, 4 p.m.
Dallas at Los Angeles, 4 p.m.
Buffalo at Carolina, 5 p.m.
Colorado at Detroit, 5 p.m.
San Jose at Phoenix, 8 p.m.
Chicago at Anaheim, 8 p.m.
Minnesota at Vancouver, 10 p.m.

Tuesday, Feb. 28
Montreal at N.Y. Islanders, 7 p.m.
Washington at Toronto, 7:30 p.m.
Florida at Tampa Bay, 7:30 p.m.
Minnesota at Colorado, 9 p.m.
Vancouver at Calgary, 9 p.m.
Detroit at San Jose, 10:30 p.m.

Wednesday, March 1
Atlanta at Buffalo, 7 p.m.
Boston at Carolina, 7 p.m.
Philadelphia at New Jersey, 7:30 p.m.
Ottawa at Pittsburgh, 7:30 p.m.
Nashville at Chicago, 8:30 p.m.
St. Louis at Edmonton, 9 p.m.
Detroit at Anaheim, 10:30 p.m.

Thursday, March 2
Atlanta at Boston, 7 p.m.
New Jersey at N.Y. Islanders, 7 p.m.
N.Y. Rangers at Philadelphia, 7 p.m.
Montreal at Florida, 7 p.m.
Washington at Ottawa, 7:30 p.m.
Vancouver at Nashville, 8 p.m.
Columbus at Colorado, 9 p.m.
St. Louis at Calgary, 9 p.m.
Dallas at Phoenix, 9 p.m.
Minnesota at Los Angeles, 10:30 p.m.

Friday, March 3
Florida at Carolina, 7 p.m.
Toronto at Buffalo, 8 p.m.
Vancouver at Chicago, 8:30 p.m.
San Jose at Edmonton, 9 p.m.
Minnesota at Anaheim, 10:30 p.m.

Saturday, March 4
Columbus at Los Angeles, 4 p.m.
Buffalo at Boston, 7 p.m.
Ottawa at Toronto, 7 p.m.
Philadelphia at N.Y. Islanders, 7 p.m.
Washington at Atlanta, 7 p.m.
N.Y. Rangers at New Jersey, 7:30 p.m.
Carolina at Pittsburgh, 7:30 p.m.
Montreal at Tampa Bay, 7:30 p.m.
Colorado at Dallas, 8 p.m.
Detroit at Phoenix, 9 p.m.
San Jose at Calgary, 10 p.m.

Sunday, March 5
Nashville at Edmonton, 4 p.m.
Columbus at Anaheim, 4 p.m.
Dallas at Chicago, 7 p.m.
Colorado at Minnesota, 7 p.m.
St. Louis at Vancouver, 10 p.m.

Monday, March 6
Carolina at N.Y. Rangers, 7 p.m.
Montreal at Philadelphia, 7 p.m.
N.Y. Islanders at Washington, 7 p.m.
Florida at Atlanta, 7 p.m.
Ottawa at Tampa Bay, 7:30 p.m.

Tuesday, March 7
Boston at Buffalo, 7 p.m.
New Jersey at N.Y. Islanders, 7 p.m.
Chicago at Columbus, 7 p.m.
Montreal at Toronto, 7:30 p.m.
Tampa Bay at Pittsburgh, 7:30 p.m.
Phoenix at Detroit, 7:30 p.m.
Colorado at St. Louis, 8 p.m.
Los Angeles at Minnesota, 8 p.m.
Nashville at Calgary, 9 p.m.
Dallas at Edmonton, 9 p.m.
San Jose at Anaheim, 10:30 p.m.

Wednesday, March 8
Carolina at Philadelphia, 7 p.m.
Pittsburgh at Washington, 7 p.m.
N.Y. Rangers at Atlanta, 7 p.m.

Thursday, March 9
Montreal at Boston, 7 p.m.
Tampa Bay at Buffalo, 7 p.m.
Ottawa at Florida, 7 p.m.
Phoenix at Columbus, 7 p.m.
Los Angeles at Detroit, 7:30 p.m.
Colorado at Chicago, 8:30 p.m.
Dallas at Calgary, 9 p.m.
Nashville at Vancouver, 10 p.m.
Edmonton at San Jose, 10:30 p.m.

Friday, March 10
Toronto at N.Y. Islanders, 7 p.m.
New Jersey at Washington, 7 p.m.
Ottawa at Atlanta, 7 p.m.
Minnesota at St. Louis, 8 p.m.

Saturday, March 11
Buffalo at Philadelphia, 2 p.m.
Nashville at San Jose, 4 p.m.
N.Y. Islanders at Boston, 7 p.m.
Tampa Bay at Toronto, 7 p.m.
N.Y. Rangers at Montreal, 7 p.m.
Edmonton at Columbus, 7 p.m.
New Jersey at Pittsburgh, 7:30 p.m.
Carolina at Florida, 7:30 p.m.
Chicago at Detroit, 7:30 p.m.
Los Angeles at St. Louis, 8 p.m.
Anaheim at Phoenix, 9 p.m.
Dallas at Vancouver, 10 p.m.

Sunday, March 12
Ottawa at Washington, 3 p.m.
Calgary at Colorado, 3 p.m.
Boston at Buffalo, 5 p.m.
Atlanta at N.Y. Rangers, 5 p.m.
Carolina at Florida, 5 p.m.
Detroit at Chicago, 7 p.m.
Edmonton at Minnesota, 7 p.m.
Philadelphia at Pittsburgh, 7:30 p.m.
Phoenix at Anaheim, 8 p.m.

Monday, March 13
Tampa Bay at Montreal, 7:30 p.m.
Columbus at St. Louis, 8 p.m.
Vancouver at Dallas, 8:30 p.m.
Colorado at Calgary, 9 p.m.
Los Angeles at San Jose, 10:30 p.m.

Tuesday, March 14
Buffalo at Washington, 7 p.m.
N.Y. Rangers at Carolina, 7 p.m.
Boston at Toronto, 7:30 p.m.
Tampa Bay at Ottawa, 7:30 p.m.
N.Y. Islanders at New Jersey, 7:30 p.m.
Vancouver at Nashville, 8 p.m.
Edmonton at Minnesota, 8 p.m.
Phoenix at Los Angeles, 10:30 p.m.

Wednesday, March 15
Philadelphia at Florida, 7 p.m.
Anaheim at Detroit, 7:30 p.m.
Columbus at Chicago, 8:30 p.m.

Thursday, March 16
Ottawa at Boston, 7 p.m.
Toronto at Buffalo, 7 p.m.
Washington at N.Y. Rangers, 7 p.m.
N.Y. Islanders at Atlanta, 7 p.m.
Carolina at Montreal, 7:30 p.m.
Pittsburgh at New Jersey, 7:30 p.m.
Phoenix at Nashville, 8 p.m.
Calgary at Edmonton, 9 p.m.
Dallas at Los Angeles, 10:30 p.m.
St. Louis at San Jose, 10:30 p.m.

Friday, March 17
Vancouver at Columbus, 7 p.m.
Philadelphia at Tampa Bay, 7:30 p.m.
N.Y. Islanders at Florida, 7:30 p.m.
Anaheim at Chicago, 8:30 p.m.

Saturday, March 18
Carolina at Boston, 12 p.m.
Dallas at San Jose, 4 p.m.
Pittsburgh at Montreal, 7 p.m.
Buffalo at Ottawa, 7 p.m.
Toronto at N.Y. Rangers, 7 p.m.
Florida at Washington, 7 p.m.
Philadelphia at Atlanta, 7 p.m.
Calgary at Nashville, 8 p.m.
Detroit at Edmonton, 10 p.m.
St. Louis at Los Angeles, 10:30 p.m.

Sunday, March 19
Phoenix at Chicago, 3 p.m.

N.Y. Islanders at Tampa Bay, 5 p.m.
Anaheim at Columbus, 5 p.m.
Calgary at Minnesota, 7 p.m.
Ottawa at New Jersey, 7:30 p.m.
Toronto at Pittsburgh, 7:30 p.m.
Colorado at San Jose, 8 p.m.
Detroit at Vancouver, 10 p.m.

Monday, March 20
Boston at N.Y. Rangers, 7 p.m.
Montreal at Washington, 7 p.m.
Buffalo at Atlanta, 7 p.m.
Tampa Bay at Florida, 7 p.m.
St. Louis at Nashville, 8 p.m.
Anaheim at Dallas, 8:30 p.m.
Colorado at Los Angeles, 10:30 p.m.

Tuesday, March 21
Atlanta at Boston, 7 p.m.
Montreal at N.Y. Islanders, 7 p.m.
New Jersey at Philadelphia, 7 p.m.
Phoenix at Columbus, 7 p.m.
Carolina at Toronto, 7:30 p.m.
Pittsburgh at Ottawa, 7:30 p.m.
Nashville at Detroit, 7:30 p.m.
San Jose at St. Louis, 8 p.m.
Calgary at Minnesota, 8 p.m.
Vancouver at Edmonton, 9 p.m.

Wednesday, March 22
Carolina at Buffalo, 7 p.m.
Philadelphia at N.Y. Rangers, 7 p.m.
Washington at Florida, 7 p.m.
Minnesota at Dallas, 8:30 p.m.
Colorado at Anaheim, 10:30 p.m.

Thursday, March 23
New Jersey at Atlanta, 7 p.m.
Toronto at Montreal, 7:30 p.m.
Washington at Tampa Bay, 7:30 p.m.
San Jose at Detroit, 7:30 p.m.
Calgary at St. Louis, 8 p.m.
Chicago at Phoenix, 9 p.m.
Edmonton at Vancouver, 10 p.m.

Friday, March 24
Calgary at Columbus, 7 p.m.
Boston at New Jersey, 7:30 p.m.
N.Y. Islanders at Pittsburgh, 7:30 p.m.
N.Y. Rangers at Florida, 7:30 p.m.
Ottawa at Buffalo, 8 p.m.
Chicago at Dallas, 8:30 p.m.
Nashville at Anaheim, 10:30 p.m.

Saturday, March 25
Buffalo at Boston, 7 p.m.
Toronto at Montreal, 7 p.m.
Atlanta at N.Y. Islanders, 7 p.m.
Ottawa at Philadelphia, 7 p.m.
Washington at Carolina, 7 p.m.
N.Y. Rangers at Tampa Bay, 7:30 p.m.
Columbus at Detroit, 7:30 p.m.
Colorado at St. Louis, 8 p.m.
San Jose at Minnesota, 8 p.m.
Anaheim at Phoenix, 9 p.m.
Edmonton at Vancouver, 10 p.m.
Nashville at Los Angeles, 10:30 p.m.

Sunday, March 26
Calgary at Dallas, 3 p.m.
San Jose at Chicago, 7 p.m.
Toronto at New Jersey, 7:30 p.m.
Montreal at Pittsburgh, 7:30 p.m.
Edmonton at Colorado, 9 p.m.

Monday, March 27
Florida at Boston, 7 p.m.
Buffalo at N.Y. Rangers, 7 p.m.
Tampa Bay at Carolina, 7 p.m.
Detroit at St. Louis, 8 p.m.
Los Angeles at Vancouver, 10 p.m.

Tuesday, March 28
Toronto at Philadelphia, 7 p.m.
San Jose at Columbus, 7 p.m.
N.Y. Islanders at Montreal, 7:30 p.m.
New Jersey at Ottawa, 7:30 p.m.
Anaheim at Colorado, 9 p.m.
Minnesota at Edmonton, 9 p.m.
Nashville at Phoenix, 9 p.m.

Wednesday, March 29
Boston at Buffalo, 7 p.m.
N.Y. Rangers at N.Y. Islanders, 7 p.m.
Washington at Carolina, 7 p.m.
Florida at Pittsburgh, 7:30 p.m.
St. Louis at Chicago, 8:30 p.m.
Anaheim at Dallas, 8:30 p.m.
Los Angeles at Calgary, 9 p.m.
Minnesota at Vancouver, 10 p.m.

Thursday, March 30
Washington at Montreal, 7:30 p.m.
N.Y. Rangers at Ottawa, 7:30 p.m.
Buffalo at New Jersey, 7:30 p.m.
Atlanta at Tampa Bay, 7:30 p.m.
Los Angeles at Edmonton, 9 p.m.
Phoenix at San Jose, 10:30 p.m.

Friday, March 31
Pittsburgh at N.Y. Islanders, 7 p.m.
Florida at Carolina, 7 p.m.
Chicago at Detroit, 7:30 p.m.
Columbus at St. Louis, 8 p.m.
Colorado at Calgary, 9 p.m.
Minnesota at Vancouver, 10 p.m.
Dallas at Anaheim, 10:30 p.m.

Saturday, April 1
New Jersey at Philadelphia, 2 p.m.
Buffalo at Toronto, 7 p.m.
Boston at Montreal, 7 p.m.
Washington at Ottawa, 7 p.m.
Carolina at Atlanta, 7 p.m.
Chicago at Columbus, 7 p.m.
Tampa Bay at Florida, 7:30 p.m.
St. Louis at Nashville, 8 p.m.
Calgary at Edmonton, 10 p.m.
Dallas at Los Angeles, 10:30 p.m.
Phoenix at San Jose, 10:30 p.m.

Sunday, April 2
Philadelphia at N.Y. Islanders, 1 p.m.
Detroit at Minnesota, 2 p.m.
New Jersey at Pittsburgh, 3 p.m.
Vancouver at Anaheim, 4 p.m.

Monday, April 3
Washington at Carolina, 7 p.m.
Buffalo at Toronto, 7:30 p.m.
Atlanta at Ottawa, 7:30 p.m.
Florida at Tampa Bay, 7:30 p.m.
Columbus at Nashville, 8 p.m.
San Jose at Dallas, 8:30 p.m.
Chicago at Colorado, 9 p.m.
Detroit at Calgary, 9 p.m.
Phoenix at Edmonton, 9 p.m.
Vancouver at Los Angeles, 10:30 p.m.

Tuesday, April 4
Philadelphia at N.Y. Rangers, 7 p.m.
Boston at Montreal, 7:30 p.m.
St. Louis at Minnesota, 8 p.m.
Los Angeles at Anaheim, 10:30 p.m.

Wednesday, April 5
Ottawa at Buffalo, 7 p.m.
Carolina at Washington, 7 p.m.
Atlanta at Florida, 7 p.m.
N.Y. Islanders at Toronto, 7:30 p.m.
Pittsburgh at New Jersey, 7:30 p.m.
Nashville at Chicago, 8:30 p.m.
San Jose at Colorado, 9 p.m.
Phoenix at Calgary, 9 p.m.

Thursday, April 6
Toronto at Boston, 7 p.m.
N.Y. Islanders at N.Y. Rangers, 7 p.m.
Montreal at Ottawa, 7:30 p.m.
Atlanta at Tampa Bay, 7:30 p.m.
Nashville at St. Louis, 8 p.m.
Edmonton at Minnesota, 8 p.m.
Dallas at Anaheim, 10:30 p.m.
San Jose at Los Angeles, 10:30 p.m.

Friday, April 7
Carolina at Washington, 7 p.m.
Pittsburgh at Florida, 7:30 p.m.
Columbus at Detroit, 7:30 p.m.
Philadelphia at Buffalo, 8 p.m.
Edmonton at Chicago, 8:30 p.m.
Minnesota at Calgary, 9 p.m.

Saturday, April 8
N.Y. Rangers at Boston, 2 p.m.
St. Louis at Colorado, 2 p.m.
Anaheim at Los Angeles, 6 p.m.
New Jersey at Montreal, 7 p.m.
Buffalo at Ottawa, 7 p.m.
Washington at N.Y. Islanders, 7 p.m.
Toronto at Philadelphia, 7 p.m.
Carolina at Atlanta, 7 p.m.
Detroit at Columbus, 7 p.m.
Pittsburgh at Tampa Bay, 7:30 p.m.
Chicago at Nashville, 8 p.m.
Calgary at Vancouver, 10 p.m.
Dallas at Phoenix, 10 p.m.

Sunday, April 9
Tampa Bay at Florida, 5 p.m.
Edmonton at St. Louis, 7 p.m.
N.Y. Rangers at New Jersey, 7:30 p.m.
Dallas at San Jose, 8 p.m.
Minnesota at Colorado, 9 p.m.

Monday, April 10
Washington at Boston, 7 p.m.
Ottawa at Montreal, 7:30 p.m.
Anaheim at Vancouver, 10 p.m.
San Jose at Phoenix, 10 p.m.

Tuesday, April 11
N.Y. Islanders at N.Y. Rangers, 7 p.m.
Pittsburgh at Philadelphia, 7 p.m.
New Jersey at Carolina, 7 p.m.
Florida at Toronto, 7:30 p.m.
Boston at Ottawa, 7:30 p.m.
Atlanta at Tampa Bay, 7:30 p.m.

Edmonton at Detroit, 7:30 p.m.
Nashville at St. Louis, 8 p.m.
Chicago at Minnesota, 8 p.m.
Columbus at Dallas, 8:30 p.m.
Phoenix at Colorado, 9 p.m.
Anaheim at Calgary, 9 p.m.

Wednesday, April 12
Montreal at Buffalo, 7 p.m.
San Jose at Vancouver, 10 p.m.

Thursday, April 13
Montreal at Boston, 7 p.m.
Toronto at N.Y. Islanders, 7 p.m.
Washington at Atlanta, 7 p.m.
St. Louis at Columbus, 7 p.m.
Florida at Ottawa, 7:30 p.m.
Philadelphia at New Jersey, 7:30 p.m.
N.Y. Rangers at Pittsburgh, 7:30 p.m.
Minnesota at Nashville, 8 p.m.
Detroit at Chicago, 8:30 p.m.
Colorado at Calgary, 9 p.m.
Anaheim at Edmonton, 9 p.m.
Los Angeles at Phoenix, 10 p.m.
Vancouver at San Jose, 10:30 p.m.

Friday, April 14
Tampa Bay at Carolina, 7 p.m.

Saturday, April 15
N.Y. Rangers at Philadelphia, 2 p.m.
Detroit at St. Louis, 2 p.m.
Minnesota at Dallas, 2 p.m.
Anaheim at San Jose, 4 p.m.
Ottawa at Toronto, 7 p.m.
Buffalo at Montreal, 7 p.m.
Pittsburgh at N.Y. Islanders, 7 p.m.
Boston at Atlanta, 7 p.m.
Chicago at Columbus, 7 p.m.
Carolina at Tampa Bay, 7:30 p.m.
Washington at Florida, 7:30 p.m.
Phoenix at Nashville, 8 p.m.
Colorado at Vancouver, 10 p.m.
Calgary at Los Angeles, 10:30 p.m.

Sunday, April 16
Philadelphia at New Jersey, 1 p.m.
Toronto at Buffalo, 5 p.m.
Columbus at Chicago, 7 p.m.
Phoenix at St. Louis, 7 p.m.

Monday, April 17
Atlanta at Washington, 7 p.m.
N.Y. Islanders at Pittsburgh, 7:30 p.m.
Dallas at Detroit, 7:30 p.m.
Colorado at Edmonton, 9 p.m.
Calgary at Anaheim, 10:30 p.m.
Los Angeles at San Jose, 10:30 p.m.

Tuesday, April 18
Philadelphia at N.Y. Islanders, 7 p.m.
Ottawa at N.Y. Rangers, 7 p.m.
Buffalo at Carolina, 7 p.m.
Atlanta at Florida, 7 p.m.
Dallas at Columbus, 7 p.m.
Pittsburgh at Toronto, 7:30 p.m.
New Jersey at Montreal, 7:30 p.m.
Washington at Tampa Bay, 7:30 p.m.
Detroit at Nashville, 8 p.m.
St. Louis at Chicago, 8:30 p.m.

2003-04 REVIEW

Regular season

Stanley Cup playoffs

2005 entry draft

2004 entry draft

REGULAR SEASON

2003-04 FINAL STANDINGS

EASTERN CONFERENCE

ATLANTIC DIVISION

	W	L	T	OTL	Pts.	GF	GA	Home	Away	Div. Rec.
Philadelphia Flyers	40	21	15	6	101	229	186	24-11-3-3	16-10-12-3	13-6-5-0
New Jersey Devils	43	25	12	2	100	213	164	22-13-5-1	21-12-7-1	14-7-2-1
New York Islanders	38	29	11	4	91	237	210	25-11-4-1	13-18-7-3	8-11-3-2
New York Rangers	27	40	7	8	69	206	250	13-21-3-4	14-19-4-4	11-10-1-2
Pittsbugh Penguins	23	47	8	4	58	190	303	13-22-6-0	10-25-2-4	6-12-5-1

NORTHEAST DIVISION

	W	L	T	OTL	Pts.	GF	GA	Home	Away	Div. Rec.
Boston Bruins	41	19	15	7	104	209	188	18-12-9-2	23-7-6-5	13-6-2-3
Toronto Maple Leafs	45	24	10	3	103	242	204	22-14-3-2	23-10-7-1	13-9-2-0
Ottawa Senators	43	23	10	6	102	262	189	23-8-5-5	20-15-5-1	9-10-4-1
Montreal Canadiens	41	30	7	4	93	208	192	23-13-4-1	18-17-3-3	9-13-1-1
Buffalo Sabres	37	34	7	4	85	220	221	21-13-4-3	16-21-3-1	10-8-3-3

SOUTHEAST DIVISION

	W	L	T	OTL	Pts.	GF	GA	Home	Away	Div. Rec.
Tampa Bay Lightning	46	22	8	6	106	245	192	24-10-4-3	22-12-4-3	13-8-3-0
Atlanta Thrashers	33	37	8	4	78	214	243	18-17-4-2	15-20-4-2	13-8-1-2
Carolina Hurricanes	28	34	14	6	76	172	209	13-18-8-2	15-16-6-4	8-10-5-1
Florida Panthers	28	35	15	4	75	188	221	16-15-7-3	12-20-8-1	8-10-5-1
Washington Capitals	23	46	10	3	59	186	253	13-20-6-2	10-26-4-1	9-10-4-1

WESTERN CONFERENCE

CENTRAL DIVISION

	W	L	T	OTL	Pts.	GF	GA	Home	Away	Div. Rec.
Detroit Red Wings	48	21	11	2	109	255	189	30-7-4-0	18-14-7-2	15-7-1-1
St. Louis Blues	39	30	11	2	91	191	198	23-11-7-0	16-19-4-2	12-9-2-1
Nashville Predators	38	29	11	4	91	216	217	22-10-7-2	16-19-4-2	11-9-2-1
Columbus Blue Jackets	25	45	8	4	62	177	238	17-18-4-2	8-27-4-2	9-13-0-2
Chicago Blackhawks	20	43	11	8	59	188	259	13-17-6-5	7-26-5-3	10-11-1-2

NORTHWEST DIVISION

	W	L	T	OTL	Pts.	GF	GA	Home	Away	Div. Rec.
Vancouver Canucks	43	24	10	5	101	235	194	21-13-7-0	22-11-3-5	10-7-6-1
Colorado Avalanche	40	22	13	7	100	236	198	19-14-6-2	21-8-7-5	12-7-4-1
Calgary Flames	42	30	7	3	94	200	176	21-14-5-1	21-16-2-2	11-7-4-1
Edmonton Oilers	36	29	12	5	89	221	208	22-12-4-3	14-17-8-2	7-12-3-2
Minnesota Wild	30	29	20	3	83	188	183	19-13-7-2	11-16-13-1	8-9-7-0

PACIFIC DIVISION

	W	L	T	OTL	Pts.	GF	GA	Home	Away	Div. Rec.
San Jose Sharks	43	21	12	6	104	219	183	24-8-7-2	19-13-5-4	15-6-3-0
Dallas Stars	41	26	13	2	97	194	175	26-7-8-0	15-19-5-2	9-8-6-1
Los Angeles Kings	28	29	16	9	81	205	217	15-16-9-1	13-13-7-8	9-9-5-1
Anaheim Mighty Ducks	29	35	10	8	76	184	213	19-11-7-4	10-24-3-4	8-10-4-2
Phoenix Coyotes	22	36	18	6	68	188	245	11-19-7-4	11-17-11-2	8-10-4-2

Note: OTL denotes overtime loss; teams receive two points for each victory, one for each tie and one for each overtime loss.

INDIVIDUAL LEADERS

SCORING

TOP SCORERS

Player, Team	GP	G	A	Pts.	+/-	PIM	SHG	PPG	ESG	GWG	GTG	OTG	Shots	ATOI
1. Martin St. Louis, Tampa Bay	82	38	56	94	35	24	8	8	22	7	0	1	212	20:34
2. Ilya Kovalchuk, Atlanta	81	41	46	87	-10	63	1	16	24	6	0	1	341	23:41
3. Joe Sakic, Colorado	81	33	54	87	11	42	1	13	19	3	1	0	253	20:15
4. Markus Naslund, Vancouver	78	35	49	84	24	58	0	5	30	6	0	4	296	19:22
5. Marian Hossa, Ottawa	81	36	46	82	4	46	1	14	21	5	1	0	233	18:37
6. Patrik Elias, New Jersey	82	38	43	81	26	44	3	9	26	9	0	4	300	18:46
7. Daniel Alfredsson, Ottawa	77	32	48	80	12	24	0	9	23	5	1	0	230	19:24
8. Cory Stillman, Tampa Bay	81	25	55	80	18	36	1	11	13	6	0	0	178	19:31
9. Robert Lang, Was-Det	69	30	49	79	4	24	0	10	20	3	1	0	163	21:17
10. Brad Richards, Tampa Bay	82	26	53	79	14	12	1	5	20	6	0	0	244	20:25
11. Alex Tanguay, Colorado	69	25	54	79	30	42	0	7	18	5	0	1	117	18:21
12. Milan Hejduk, Colorado	82	35	40	75	19	20	0	16	19	6	0	2	237	18:45
13. Mats Sundin, Toronto	81	31	44	75	11	52	1	11	19	10	0	1	226	19:52
14. Mark Recchi, Philadelphia	82	26	49	75	18	47	1	14	11	5	2	0	167	17:11
15. Jaromir Jagr, Was-NYR	77	31	43	74	-5	38	0	10	21	3	1	0	257	20:57
16. Jarome Iginla, Calgary	81	41	32	73	21	84	4	8	29	10	1	0	265	21:18
17. Steve Sullivan, Nashville	80	24	49	73	1	48	2	11	11	4	0	0	218	20:55
18. Joe Thornton, Boston	77	23	50	73	18	98	0	4	19	6	0	1	187	21:38
19. Keith Tkachuk, St. Louis	75	33	38	71	8	83	0	18	15	8	2	2	233	19:39
20. Scott Gomez, New Jersey	80	14	56	70	18	70	0	3	11	1	0	0	189	16:00
21. Bill Guerin, Dallas	82	34	35	69	14	109	0	9	25	10	1	2	263	18:41
22. Martin Havlat, Ottawa	68	31	37	68	12	46	0	13	18	7	0	1	175	16:43
23. Pavel Datsyuk, Detroit	75	30	38	68	-2	35	1	8	21	4	0	0	136	18:16
24. Shane Doan, Phoenix	79	27	41	68	-11	47	2	9	16	1	3	0	254	21:45
25. Brett Hull, Detroit	81	25	43	68	-4	12	0	10	15	6	1	2	200	16:53
26. Scott Walker, Nashville	75	25	42	67	4	94	3	9	13	3	0	1	157	20:03
27. Vincent Lecavalier, Tampa Bay	81	32	34	66	23	52	2	5	25	6	0	0	242	18:03
28. Sergei Fedorov, Anaheim	80	31	34	65	-5	42	2	9	20	6	1	1	268	21:04
29. Daniel Briere, Buffalo	82	28	37	65	-7	70	0	11	17	3	0	1	194	18:19
30. Mike Ribeiro, Montreal	81	20	45	65	15	34	0	7	13	5	1	1	103	17:04

GOALTENDING

TOP GOALTENDERS

(Based on save percentage, minimum 25 games played)

Goalie, Team	GP	Mins.	W	L	T	SA	GA	GAA	SV	SV%	SO
1. Dwayne Roloson, Minnesota	48	2,847	19	18	11	1,323	89	1.88	1,234	.933	5
2. Miikka Kiprusoff, Calgary	38	2,301	24	10	4	966	65	1.69	901	.933	4
3. Roberto Luongo, Florida	72	4,252	25	33	14	2,475	172	2.43	2,303	.931	7
4. Vesa Toskala, San Jose	28	1,541	12	8	4	760	53	2.06	707	.930	1
5. Andrew Raycroft, Boston	57	3,420	29	18	9	1,586	117	2.05	1,469	.926	3
6. David Aebischer, Colorado	62	3,703	32	19	9	1,703	129	2.09	1,574	.924	4
7. Evgeni Nabokov, San Jose	59	3,456	31	19	8	1,610	127	2.20	1,483	.921	9
8. Manny Legace, Detroit	41	2,325	23	10	5	1,019	82	2.12	937	.920	3
9. Jose Theodore, Montreal	67	3,961	33	28	5	1,860	150	2.27	1,710	.919	6
10. Martin Gerber, Anaheim	32	1,698	11	12	4	785	64	2.26	721	.918	2
11. Jussi Markkanen, Edmonton	33	1,638	10	14	3	793	65	2.38	728	.918	2
12. Marc Denis, Columbus	66	3,796	21	36	7	1,970	162	2.56	1,808	.918	5
13. Ed Belfour, Toronto	59	3,444	34	19	6	1,483	122	2.13	1,361	.918	10
14. Martin Prusek, Ottawa	29	1,528	16	6	3	651	54	2.12	597	.917	3
15. Martin Brodeur, New Jersey	75	4,555	38	26	11	1,845	154	2.03	1,691	.917	11
16. Robert Esche, Philadelphia	40	2,322	21	11	7	932	79	2.04	853	.915	3
17. Emmanuel Fernandez, Minnesota	37	2,166	11	14	9	1,056	90	2.49	966	.915	2
18. Dan Cloutier, Vancouver	60	3,539	33	21	6	1,554	134	2.27	1,420	.914	5
19. Jean-Sebastien Giguere, Anaheim	55	3,210	17	31	6	1,623	140	2.62	1,483	.914	3
20. Martin Biron, Buffalo	52	2,972	26	18	5	1,442	125	2.52	1,317	.913	2

STANLEY CUP PLAYOFFS

2003-04 RESULTS

CONFERENCE QUARTERFINALS

EASTERN CONFERENCE

Score	Winning goalie, GWG, Period, Time	
Tampa Bay 3 N.Y. Isles 0	Khabibulin	Roy 2 5:07
N.Y. Isles 3 Tampa Bay 0	DiPietro	Niinimaa 1 11:42
Tampa Bay 3 N.Y. Isles 0	Khabibulin	Richards 1 3:40
Tampa Bay 3 N.Y. Isles 0	Khabibulin	St. Louis 1 10:30
Tampa Bay 3 N.Y. Isles 2	Khabibulin	St. Louis 4 4:07

(Tampa Bay wins Eastern Conference quarterfinal, 4-1)

Score	Winning goalie, GWG, Period, Time	
Boston 3 Montreal 0	Raycroft	Gonchar 1 5:12
Boston 2 Montreal 1	Raycroft	Bergeron 4 1:26
Montreal 3 Boston 2	Theodore	Markov 2 13:32
Boston 4 Montreal 3	Raycroft	Murray 5 9:27
Montreal 5 Boston 1	Theodore	Kovalev 2 7:39
Montreal 5 Boston 2	Theodore	Perreault 2 14:23
Montreal 2 Boston 0	Theodore	Zednik 3 10:52

(Montreal wins Eastern Conference quarterfinal, 4-3)

Score	Winning goalie, GWG, Period, Time	
Phila. 3 New Jersey 2	Esche	Primeau 3 3:31
Phila. 3 New Jersey 2	Esche	Timander 3 10:31
New Jersey 4 Phila. 2	Brodeur	Elias 2 17:28
Phila. 3 New Jersey 0	Esche	Johnsson 1 1:18
Phila. 3 New Jersey 1	Esche	Markov 3 14:37

(Philadelphia wins Eastern Conference quarterfinal, 4-1)

Score	Winning goalie, GWG, Period, Time	
Ottawa 4 Toronto 2	Lalime	Hossa 2 10:40
Toronto 2 Ottawa 0	Belfour	Roberts 1 10:40
Toronto 2 Ottawa 0	Belfour	Nieuwendyk 2 1:30
Ottawa 4 Toronto 1	Lalime	Hossa 2 13:15
Toronto 2 Ottawa 0	Belfour	Domi 3 1:43
Ottawa 2 Toronto 1	Lalime	Fisher 5 1:47
Toronto 4 Ottawa 1	Belfour	Nieuwendyk 1 7:41

(Toronto wins Eastern Conference quarterfinal, 4-3)

WESTERN CONFERENCE

Score	Winning goalie, GWG, Period, Time	
Detroit 3 Nashville 1	Legace	Holmstrom 3 4:55
Detroit 2 Nashville 1	Legace	Schneider 3 17:15
Nashville 3 Detroit 1	Vokoun	Hall 1 19:45
Nashville 3 Detroit 0	Vokoun	Sullivan 1 10:44
Detroit 4 Nashville 1	Joseph	Hull 1 6:22
Detroit 2 Nashville 0	Joseph	Whitney 1 1:26

(Detroit wins Western Conference quarterfinal, 4-2)

Score	Winning goalie, GWG, Period, Time	
San Jose 1 St. Louis 0	Nabokov	Dimitrakos 4 9:16
San Jose 3 St. Louis 1	Nabokov	Marleau 2 3:52
St. Louis 4 San Jose 1	Osgood	Drake 2 17:24
San Jose 4 St. Louis 3	Nabokov	Koroloyuk 3 11:19
San Jose 3 St. Louis 1	Nabokov	Smith 2 9:34

(San Jose wins Western Conference quarterfinal, 4-1)

Score	Winning goalie, GWG, Period, Time	
Calgary 3 Vancouver 5	Cloutier	Ohlund 2 17:51
Calgary 2 Vancouver 1	Kiprusoff	Lombardi 1 3:56
Vancouver 2 Calgary 1	Hedberg	Cooke 3 1:29
Vancouver 0 Calgary 4	Kiprusoff	Yelle 2 0:58
Calgary 2 Vancouver 1	Kiprusoff	Iginla 3 5:37
Vancouver 5 Calgary 4	Auld	Morrison 6 2:28
Calgary 3 Vancouver 2	Kiprusoff	Gelinas 4 1:25

(Calgary wins Western Conference quarterfinal, 4-3)

Score	Winning goalie, GWG, Period, Time	
Colorado 3 Dallas 1	Aebischer	Tanguay 1 08:37
Colorado 5 Dallas 2	Aebische	Forsbrg 2 06:48
Dallas 4 Colorado 3	Turco	Ott 4 02:11
Colorado 3 Dallas 2	Aebischer	Svatos 5 05:18
Colorado 5 Dallas 1	Aebischer	Konowalchuk 2 01:41

(Colorado wins Western Conference quarterfinal, 4-1)

CONFERENCE SEMIFINALS

EASTERN CONFERENCE

Score	Winning goalie, GWG, Period, Time	
Tampa Bay 4 Montreal 0	Khabibulin	Fedotenko 2 2:52
Tampa Bay 3 Montreal 1	Khabibulin	Modin 1 8:33
Tampa Bay 4 Montreal 3	Khabibulin	Richards 4 1:05
Tampa Bay 3 Montreal 1	Khabibulin	Richards 2 17:14

(Tampa Bay wins Eastern Conference semifinal, 4-0)

Score	Winning goalie, GWG, Period, Time	
Philadelphia 3 Toronto 1	Esche	Ragnarsson 2 5:11
Philadelphia 2 Toronto 1	Esche	Zhamnov 3 8:25
Toronto 4 Philadelphia 1	Belfour	Ponikarovsky 2 6:42
Toronto 3 Philadelphia 1	Belfour	Sundin 2 7:45
Philadelphia 7 Toronto 2	Esche	Primeau 1 18:54
Philadelphia 3 Toronto 2	Esche	Roenick 4 7:39

(Philadelphia wins Eastern Conference semifinal, 4-2)

WESTERN CONFERENCE

Score	Winning goalie, GWG, Period, Time	
Calgary 2 Detroit 1	Kiprusoff	Nilson 4 2:39
Detroit 5 Calgary 2	Joseph	Yzerman 2 12:19
Calgary 3 Detroit 2	Kiprusoff	Donovan 2 12:24
Detroit 4 Calgary 2	Joseph	Dandenault 3 10:02
Calgary 1 Detroit 0	Kiprusoff	Conroy 2 16:07
Calgary 1 Detroit 0	Kiprusoff	Gelinas 4 19:13

(Calgary wins Western Conference semifinal, 4-2)

Score	Winning goalie, GWG, Period, Time	
San Jose 5 Colorado 2	Nabokov	Hannan 1 19:07
San Jose 4 Colorado 1	Nabokov	Marleau 2 19:36
San Jose 1 Colorado 0	Nabokov	Damphousse 3 8:59
Colorado 1 San Jose 0	Aebischer	Sakic 4 5:15
Colorado 2 San Jose 1	Aebischer	Sakic 4 1:54
San Jose 3 Colorado 1	Nabokov	Goc 2 8:59

(San Jose wins Western Conference semifinal, 4-2)

CONFERENCE FINALS

EASTERN CONFERENCE

Score	Winning goalie, GWG, Period, Time	
Tampa Bay 3 Phila. 1	Khabibulin	Richards 2 13:34
Phila. 6 Tampa Bay 2	Esche	Kapanen 1 11:17
Tampa Bay 4 Phila. 1	Khabibulin	Fedotenko 1 15:20
Phila. 3 Tampa Bay 2	Esche	Primeau 2 11:50
Tampa Bay 4 Phila. 2	Khabibulin	Richards 2 07:12
Phila. 5 Tampa Bay 4	Esche	Gagne 4 18:18
Tampa Bay 2 Phila. 1	Khabibulin	Modin 2 4:57

(Tampa Bay wins Eastern Conference final, 4-3)

WESTERN CONFERENCE

Score	Winning goalie, GWG, Period, Time	
Calgary 4 San Jose 3	Kiprusoff	Montador 4 18:43
Calgary 4 San Jose 1	Kiprusoff	Donovan 1 10:35
San Jose 3 Calgary 0	Nabokov	Damphousse 2 7:31
San Jose 4 Calgary 2	Nabokov	Damphousse 2 10:03
Calgary 3 San Jose 0	Kiprusoff	Iginla 1 6:27
Calgary 3 San Jose 1	Kiprusoff	Gelinas 2 13:02

(Calgary wins Western Conference final, 4-2)

STANLEY CUP FINALS

Score	Winning goalie	Game-winning goal scorer	Period	Time
Calgary 4 Tampa Bay 1	Kiprusoff	Iginla	2	15:21
Tampa Bay 4 Calgary 1	Khabibulin	Richards	3	2:51
Calgary 3 Tampa Bay 0	Kiprusoff	Simon	2	13:53
Tampa Bay 1 Calgary 0	Khabibulin	Richards	1	2:48
Calgary 3 Tampa Bay 2	Kiprusoff	Saprykin	4	14:40
Tampa Bay 3 Calgary 2	Khabibulin	St. Louis	5	0:33
Tampa Bay 2 Calgary 1	Khabibulin	Fedotenko	2	14:38

(Tampa Bay wins Stanley Cup finals, 4-3)

INDIVIDUAL LEADERS

SCORING

TOP SCORERS

	GP	G	A	Pts.	PIM
Brad Richards, TB	23	12	14	26	4
Martin St. Louis, TB	23	9	15	24	14
Jarome Iginla, Cal	26	13	9	22	45
Fredrik Modin, TB	23	8	11	19	10
Craig Conroy, Cal	26	6	11	17	12
Keith Primeau, Phi	18	9	7	16	22
Vincent Lecavalier, TB	23	9	7	16	25
Martin Gelinas, Cal	26	8	7	15	35
Ruslan Fedotenko, TB	22	12	2	14	14
Vincent Damphousse, SJ	17	7	7	14	20
Alexei Zhamnov, Phi	18	4	10	14	8
Dave Andreychuk, TB	23	1	13	14	14
Jeremy Roenick, Phi	18	4	9	13	8
Patrick Marleau, SJ	17	8	4	12	6
Joe Sakic, Col	11	7	5	12	8
Peter Forsberg, Col	11	4	7	11	12
Marcus Nilson, Cal	26	4	7	11	12
Saku Koivu, Mtl	11	3	8	11	10
Alex Kovalev, Mtl	11	6	4	10	8
Shean Donovan, Cal	24	5	5	10	23

GOALTENDING

TOP GOALTENDERS

(Based on save percentage, minimum seven games)

	GP	S%	W	L	GAA	SO	GA
C. Joseph, Det	9	.939	4	4	1.39	1	12
E. Nabokov, SJ	17	.935	10	7	1.71	3	30
N. Khabibulin, TB	23	.933	16	7	1.71	5	40
E. Belfour, Tor	13	.929	6	7	2.09	3	27
M. Kiprusoff, Cal	26	.928	15	11	1.85	5	51
A. Raycroft, Bos	7	.924	3	4	2.15	1	16
D. Aebischer, Col	11	.922	6	5	2.08	1	23
J. Theodore, Mtl	11	.919	4	7	2.39	1	27
R. Esche, Phi	18	.918	11	7	2.32	1	41
P. Lalime, Ott	7	.906	3	4	1.96	0	13

TEAM-BY-TEAM STATISTICS

BOSTON BRUINS

(Lost Eastern Conference quarterfinals to Montreal, 4-3)

SCORING

Pos., No.	GP	ATOI	G	A	Pts	+/-	PIM	PPG	SHG	GWG	OTG	Shots	S%
L 14 SERGEI SAMSONOV	7	17:17	2	5	7	2	0	0	0	0	0	13	15.4
C 92 MICHAEL NYLANDER	6	18:56	3	3	6	2	0	0	0	0	0	10	30.0
D 55 SERGEI GONCHAR	7	27:51	1	4	5	-4	4	1	0	1	0	19	5.3
C 37 *PATRICE BERGERON	7	17:13	1	3	4	5	0	0	0	1	1	20	5.0
R 27 GLEN MURRAY	7	19:56	2	1	3	-2	8	0	0	1	1	19	10.5
L 26 MIKE KNUBLE	7	19:44	2	0	2	-5	0	1	0	0	0	16	12.5
D 71 JIRI SLEGR	7	18:08	1	1	2	-1	0	0	0	0	0	22	4.5
D 44 NICK BOYNTON	7	24:43	0	2	2	1	2	0	0	0	0	18	.0
C 16 ANDY HILBERT	5	5:32	1	0	1	0	0	0	0	0	0	4	25.0
C 12 BRIAN ROLSTON	7	16:33	1	0	1	-5	8	0	0	0	0	14	7.1
C 39 TRAVIS GREEN	7	15:36	0	1	1	0	8	0	0	0	0	8	.0
D 25 HAL GILL	7	19:03	0	1	1	-2	4	0	0	0	0	11	.0
C 33 CRAIG MACDONALD	1	2:11	0	0	0	1	0	0	0	0	0	0	.0
L 40 TED DONATO	2	5:31	0	0	0	0	0	0	0	0	0	1	.0
L 17 ROB ZAMUNER	7	5:34	0	0	0	-1	0	0	0	0	0	3	.0
R 20 MARTIN LAPOINTE	7	15:20	0	0	0	-2	14	0	0	0	0	7	.0
D 21 SEAN O'DONNELL	7	19:52	0	0	0	1	0	0	0	0	0	2	.0
D 6 DAN MCGILLIS	7	18:37	0	0	0	-3	2	0	0	0	0	14	.0
L 11 P.J. AXELSSON	7	14:43	0	0	0	-2	4	0	0	0	0	10	.0
C 19 JOE THORNTON	7	21:30	0	0	0	-6	14	0	0	0	0	14	.0
G 1 *ANDREW RAYCROFT	7	63:52	0	0	0	0	2	0	0	0	0	0	.0

GOALTENDING

	GP	Mins.	GAA	W	L	EN	SO	GA	SA	SV%	PIM
*ANDREW RAYCROFT	7	447	2.15	3	4	3	1	16	210	.924	2

CALGARY FLAMES

(Lost Stanley Cup finals to Tampa Bay, 4-3)

SCORING

Pos., No.	GP	ATOI	G	A	Pts	+/-	PIM	PPG	SHG	GWG	OTG	Shots	S%
R 12 JAROME IGINLA	26	23:18	13	9	22	13	45	4	2	3	0	93	14.0
C 22 CRAIG CONROY	26	20:22	6	11	17	12	12	2	0	1	0	49	12.2
L 23 MARTIN GELINAS	26	15:57	8	7	15	10	35	2	0	3	2	51	15.7
L 26 MARCUS NILSON	26	19:24	4	7	11	0	12	0	0	1	1	37	10.8
R 16 SHEAN DONOVAN	24	15:26	5	5	10	0	23	0	0	2	0	43	11.6
D 4 JORDAN LEOPOLD	26	25:41	0	10	10	5	6	0	0	0	0	34	.0
D 28 ROBYN REGEHR	26	26:26	2	7	9	7	20	0	0	0	0	29	6.9
L 24 VILLE NIEMINEN	24	16:17	4	4	8	0	55	1	0	0	0	41	9.8
L 15 CHRIS SIMON	16	15:06	5	2	7	0	74	4	0	1	0	34	14.7
C 11 STEPHANE YELLE	23	17:03	3	3	6	-1	16	0	1	1	0	27	11.1
R 17 CHRIS CLARK	26	14:34	3	3	6	0	30	1	0	0	0	29	10.3
L 19 OLEG SAPRYKIN	26	14:00	3	3	6	1	14	1	0	1	1	53	5.7
C 18 *MATTHEW LOMBARDI	13	14:46	1	5	6	1	4	0	0	1	0	15	6.7
D 5 STEVE MONTADOR	20	17:43	1	2	3	4	6	0	0	1	1	44	2.3
D 21 ANDREW FERENCE	26	24:13	0	3	3	5	25	0	0	0	0	37	.0
L 33 KRZYSZTOF OLIWA	20	3:44	2	0	2	-1	6	0	0	0	0	16	12.5
D 2 MIKE COMMODORE	20	11:34	0	2	2	1	19	0	0	0	0	13	.0
D 3 DENIS GAUTHIER	6	18:33	0	1	1	2	4	0	0	0	0	3	.0
D 32 TONI LYDMAN	6	14:29	0	1	1	1	2	0	0	0	0	4	.0
D 44 RHETT WARRENER	24	24:05	0	1	1	1	6	0	0	0	0	27	.0
G 34 MIIKKA KIPRUSOFF	26	63:39	0	1	1	0	0	0	0	0	0	0	.0
R 7 *CHUCK KOBASEW	26	9:01	0	1	1	0	24	0	0	0	0	15	.0
G 1 ROMAN TUREK	1	19:29	0	0	0	0	0	0	0	0	0	0	.0
D 43 *BRENNAN EVANS	2	2:51	0	0	0	0	0	0	0	0	0	0	.0
L 10 DAVE LOWRY	10	9:26	0	0	0	-1	6	0	0	0	0	4	.0

GOALTENDING

	GP	Mins.	GAA	W	L	EN	SO	GA	SA	SV%	PIM
ROMAN TUREK	1	19	0.00	0	0	0	0	0	3	1.000	0
MIIKKA KIPRUSOFF	26	1655	1.85	15	11	2	5	51	710	.928	0

*rookie

COLORADO AVALANCHE

(Lost Western Conference semifinals to San Jose, 4-2)

SCORING

Pos., No.	GP	ATOI	G	A	Pts	+/-	PIM	PPG	SHG	GWG	OTG	Shots	S%
C 19 JOE SAKIC	11	21:15	7	5	12	0	8	1	1	2	2	35	20.0
C 21 PETER FORSBERG	11	19:02	4	7	11	6	12	1	0	1	0	16	25.0
R 23 MILAN HEJDUK	11	18:40	5	2	7	6	0	2	0	0	0	30	16.7
R 40 *MAREK SVATOS	11	12:29	1	5	6	3	2	0	0	1	1	25	4.0
D 4 ROB BLAKE	9	20:17	0	5	5	0	6	0	0	0	0	17	.0
L 22 STEVE KONOWALCHUK	11	18:15	4	0	4	-4	12	4	0	1	0	25	16.0
L 18 ALEX TANGUAY	8	15:46	2	2	4	1	2	1	0	1	0	6	33.3
D 6 BOB BOUGHNER	11	15:39	0	4	4	5	6	0	0	0	0	13	.0
D 52 ADAM FOOTE	11	25:06	0	4	4	-2	10	0	0	0	0	6	.0
R 8 TEEMU SELANNE	10	12:52	0	3	3	-2	2	0	0	0	0	9	.0
C 11 ANDREI NIKOLISHIN	11	15:40	0	2	2	-3	4	0	0	0	0	7	.0
R 38 MATTHEW BARNABY	11	12:22	0	2	2	-3	27	0	0	0	0	10	.0
D 3 KARLIS SKRASTINS	11	23:06	0	2	2	-2	2	0	0	0	0	14	.0
C 7 DARBY HENDRICKSON	6	11:51	1	0	1	-1	2	0	0	0	0	5	20.0
C 32 RIKU HAHL	7	12:08	1	0	1	0	2	0	0	0	0	12	8.3
R 13 DAN HINOTE	11	13:03	1	0	1	2	0	0	1	0	0	15	6.7
L 9 PAUL KARIYA	1	16:00	0	1	1	-1	0	0	0	0	0	2	.0
D 27 OSSI VAANANEN	11	22:06	0	1	1	3	18	0	0	0	0	4	.0
D 26 *JOHN-MICHAEL LILES	11	16:41	0	1	1	1	4	0	0	0	0	21	.0
G 35 TOMMY SALO	1	26:37	0	0	0	0	2	0	0	0	0	0	.0
D 34 KURT SAUER	3	11:56	0	0	0	0	0	0	0	0	0	1	.0
C 24 CHRIS GRATTON	11	12:13	0	0	0	-1	27	0	0	0	0	12	.0
G 1 DAVID AEBISCHER	11	60:12	0	0	0	0	2	0	0	0	0	0	.0

GOALTENDING

	GP	Mins.	GAA	W	L	EN	SO	GA	SA	SV%	PIM
TOMMY SALO	1	27	0.00	0	0	0	0	0	7	1.000	2
DAVID AEBISCHER	11	662	2.08	6	5	1	1	23	295	.922	2

DALLAS STARS

(Lost Western Conference quarterfinals to Colorado, 4-1)

SCORING

Pos., No.	GP	ATOI	G	A	Pts	+/-	PIM	PPG	SHG	GWG	OTG	Shots	S%
C 77 PIERRE TURGEON	5	15:53	1	3	4	-2	2	0	0	0	0	9	11.1
C 9 MIKE MODANO	5	23:16	1	2	3	-4	8	1	0	0	0	12	8.3
R 17 VALERI BURE	5	17:12	0	3	3	-1	0	0	0	0	0	9	.0
D 6 CHRIS THERIEN	5	17:04	2	0	2	1	0	0	0	0	0	6	33.3
D 56 SERGEI ZUBOV	5	28:00	1	1	2	-5	0	1	0	0	0	14	7.1
C 44 JASON ARNOTT	5	17:23	1	1	2	-1	2	1	0	0	0	11	9.1
C 39 NIKO KAPANEN	1	6:51	1	0	1	0	0	0	0	0	0	2	50.0
R 48 SCOTT YOUNG	4	15:05	1	0	1	1	2	1	0	0	0	9	11.1
C 29 STEVE OTT	4	6:54	1	0	1	0	0	0	0	1	1	3	33.3
D 43 PHILIPPE BOUCHER	5	23:57	1	0	1	-1	6	0	0	0	0	15	6.7
D 27 TEPPO NUMMINEN	4	19:12	0	1	1	-1	0	0	0	0	0	3	.0
L 72 SHAYNE CORSON	5	13:55	0	1	1	-5	12	0	0	0	0	2	.0
R 18 ROB DIMAIO	5	10:28	0	1	1	-2	2	0	0	0	0	2	.0
R 13 BILL GUERIN	5	20:08	0	1	1	-1	4	0	0	0	0	23	.0
D 24 RICHARD MATVICHUK	5	22:15	0	1	1	-4	8	0	0	0	0	5	.0
L 10 BRENDEN MORROW	5	21:29	0	1	1	0	4	0	0	0	0	10	.0
R 28 DAVID OLIVER	1	7:31	0	0	0	0	0	0	0	0	0	0	.0
D 5 *TREVOR DALEY	1	10:21	0	0	0	0	0	0	0	0	0	0	.0
D 32 DON SWEENEY	5	16:58	0	0	0	-2	2	0	0	0	0	2	.0
C 14 STU BARNES	5	14:58	0	0	0	-6	0	0	0	0	0	8	.0
R 26 JERE LEHTINEN	5	19:18	0	0	0	-4	0	0	0	0	0	11	.0
G 35 MARTY TURCO	5	65:00	0	0	0	0	0	0	0	0	0	0	.0

GOALTENDING

	GP	Mins.	GAA	W	L	EN	SO	GA	SA	SV%	PIM
MARTY TURCO	5	325	3.32	1	4	1	0	18	119	.849	0

*rookie

DETROIT RED WINGS

(Lost Western Conference semifinals to Calgary, 4-2)

SCORING

Pos., No.	GP	ATOI	G	A	Pts	+/-	PIM	PPG	SHG	GWG	OTG	Shots	S%
C 20 ROBERT LANG	12	18:10	4	5	9	-1	6	0	0	0	0	20	20.0
D 5 NICKLAS LIDSTROM	12	27:00	2	5	7	4	4	2	0	0	0	27	7.4
L 14 BRENDAN SHANAHAN	12	16:49	1	5	6	4	20	0	1	0	0	41	2.4
C 13 PAVEL DATSYUK	12	17:23	0	6	6	1	2	0	0	0	0	19	.0
C 19 STEVE YZERMAN	11	17:02	3	2	5	-1	0	0	0	1	0	18	16.7
R 17 BRETT HULL	12	15:15	3	2	5	0	4	1	0	1	0	39	7.7
L 96 TOMAS HOLMSTROM	12	11:26	2	2	4	0	10	1	0	1	0	20	10.0
L 40 HENRIK ZETTERBERG	12	17:16	2	2	4	0	4	0	0	0	0	23	8.7
C 33 KRIS DRAPER	12	18:28	1	3	4	1	6	0	0	0	0	23	4.3
L 41 RAY WHITNEY	12	11:55	1	3	4	-4	4	0	0	1	0	21	4.8
L 18 KIRK MALTBY	12	17:34	1	3	4	2	11	0	0	0	0	18	5.6
D 23 MATHIEU SCHNEIDER	12	26:29	1	2	3	2	8	1	0	1	0	32	3.1
D 11 MATHIEU DANDENAULT	12	13:32	1	1	2	-1	6	0	0	1	0	17	5.9
C 21 BOYD DEVEREAUX	3	6:36	1	0	1	0	0	0	0	0	0	3	33.3
D 8 JIRI FISCHER	11	11:29	1	0	1	-2	16	0	0	0	0	8	12.5
G 34 MANNY LEGACE	4	55:02	0	1	1	0	0	0	0	0	0	0	.0
R 32 STEVE THOMAS	6	8:17	0	1	1	1	2	0	0	0	0	10	.0
D 24 CHRIS CHELIOS	8	21:13	0	1	1	1	4	0	0	0	0	14	.0
D 2 DERIAN HATCHER	12	22:54	0	1	1	0	15	0	0	0	0	12	.0
R 25 DARREN MCCARTY	12	11:29	0	1	1	0	7	0	0	0	0	15	.0
D 4 JAMIE RIVERS	2	5:40	0	0	0	0	2	0	0	0	0	0	.0
C 29 JASON WILLIAMS	3	6:11	0	0	0	0	2	0	0	0	0	2	.0
D 15 JASON WOOLLEY	4	16:59	0	0	0	-1	0	0	0	0	0	3	.0
G 31 CURTIS JOSEPH	9	57:30	0	0	0	0	2	0	0	0	0	0	.0

GOALTENDING

	GP	Mins.	GAA	W	L	EN	SO	GA	SA	SV%	PIM
CURTIS JOSEPH	9	518	1.39	4	4	0	1	12	197	.939	2
MANNY LEGACE	4	220	2.18	2	2	0	0	8	84	.905	0

MONTREAL CANADIENS

(Lost Eastern Conference semifinals to Tampa Bay, 4-0)

SCORING

Pos., No.	GP	ATOI	G	A	Pts	+/-	PIM	PPG	SHG	GWG	OTG	Shots	S%
C 11 SAKU KOIVU	11	20:33	3	8	11	1	10	2	0	0	0	27	11.1
R 27 ALEX KOVALEV	11	20:10	6	4	10	2	8	1	0	1	0	29	20.7
R 20 RICHARD ZEDNIK	11	18:52	3	3	6	7	2	0	0	1	0	32	9.4
D 52 CRAIG RIVET	11	24:07	1	4	5	2	2	1	0	0	0	16	6.3
D 79 ANDREI MARKOV	11	22:52	1	4	5	3	8	0	0	1	0	18	5.6
C 94 YANIC PERREAULT	9	12:28	2	2	4	-3	0	0	0	1	0	15	13.3
D 43 PATRICE BRISEBOIS	11	22:29	2	1	3	-5	4	1	0	0	0	10	20.0
C 71 MIKE RIBEIRO	11	16:30	2	1	3	0	18	0	0	0	0	14	14.3
R 73 *MICHAEL RYDER	11	16:52	1	2	3	-5	4	0	0	0	0	36	2.8
C 38 JAN BULIS	11	17:23	1	1	2	-6	4	0	0	0	0	15	6.7
R 17 JASON WARD	5	15:39	0	2	2	-2	2	0	0	0	0	4	.0
C 34 JIM DOWD	11	15:34	0	2	2	-3	2	0	0	0	0	10	.0
G 60 JOSE THEODORE	11	61:39	0	2	2	0	0	0	0	0	0	0	.0
D 44 SHELDON SOURAY	11	23:55	0	2	2	-2	39	0	0	0	0	31	.0
R 37 NIKLAS SUNDSTROM	4	13:10	1	0	1	-1	2	0	0	0	0	5	20.0
L 15 DARREN LANGDON	9	3:15	1	0	1	0	6	0	0	0	0	2	50.0
L 26 PIERRE DAGENAIS	8	12:05	0	1	1	-1	6	0	0	0	0	17	.0
C 22 STEVE BEGIN	9	12:26	0	1	1	0	10	0	0	0	0	9	.0
C 90 JOE JUNEAU	11	10:53	0	1	1	-2	4	0	0	0	0	10	.0
G 30 MATHIEU GARON	1	11:54	0	0	0	0	0	0	0	0	0	0	.0
D 5 STEPHANE QUINTAL	4	13:02	0	0	0	-1	2	0	0	0	0	1	.0
D 8 *MICHAEL KOMISAREK	7	14:08	0	0	0	1	8	0	0	0	0	6	.0
D 51 FRANCIS BOUILLON	11	17:59	0	0	0	-6	7	0	0	0	0	13	.0

GOALTENDING

	GP	Mins.	GAA	W	L	EN	SO	GA	SA	SV%	PIM
MATHIEU GARON	1	12	.00	0	0	0	0	0	6	1.000	0
JOSE THEODORE	11	678	2.39	4	7	1	1	27	333	.919	0

*rookie

NASHVILLE PREDATORS

(Lost Western Conference quarterfinals to Detroit, 4-2)

SCORING

Pos., No.	GP	ATOI	G	A	Pts	+/-	PIM	PPG	SHG	GWG	OTG	Shots	S%
R 18 ADAM HALL	6	18:29	2	1	3	3	2	0	0	1	0	13	15.4
C 22 GREG JOHNSON	6	17:47	1	2	3	4	0	0	0	0	0	7	14.3
L 17 SCOTT HARTNELL	6	15:37	1	2	3	3	2	0	0	0	0	11	9.1
D 27 JASON YORK	6	21:27	0	3	3	2	4	0	0	0	0	9	.0
R 33 VLADIMIR ORSZAGH	6	16:08	2	0	2	-2	4	0	0	0	0	5	40.0
R 26 STEVE SULLIVAN	6	18:57	1	1	2	-4	6	0	0	1	0	13	7.7
D 2 *DAN HAMHUIS	6	20:29	0	2	2	-2	6	0	0	0	0	4	.0
C 9 SERGEI ZHOLTOK	6	10:33	1	0	1	-3	0	1	0	0	0	6	16.7
C 11 DAVID LEGWAND	6	15:41	1	0	1	1	8	0	1	0	0	8	12.5
D 5 BRAD BOMBARDIR	6	19:38	0	1	1	1	2	0	0	0	0	3	.0
R 24 SCOTT WALKER	6	20:09	0	1	1	-3	6	0	0	0	0	14	.0
L 10 MARTIN ERAT	6	14:08	0	1	1	-2	6	0	0	0	0	6	.0
L 19 JIM MCKENZIE	1	3:32	0	0	0	0	0	0	0	0	0	0	.0
D 3 MAREK ZIDLICKY	1	2:16	0	0	0	0	0	0	0	0	0	0	.0
D 34 SHANE HNIDY	5	12:31	0	0	0	0	6	0	0	0	0	4	.0
R 55 *JORDIN TOOTOO	5	5:09	0	0	0	0	4	0	0	0	0	2	.0
L 21 ANDREAS JOHANSSON	6	15:17	0	0	0	-3	0	0	0	0	0	5	.0
L 28 JEREMY STEVENSON	6	6:43	0	0	0	-1	8	0	0	0	0	3	.0
D 44 KIMMO TIMONEN	6	24:15	0	0	0	-3	10	0	0	0	0	9	.0
G 29 TOMAS VOKOUN	6	59:17	0	0	0	0	0	0	0	0	0	0	.0
D 4 MARK EATON	6	19:50	0	0	0	-2	2	0	0	0	0	6	.0

GOALTENDING

	GP	Mins.	GAA	W	L	EN	SO	GA	SA	SV%	PIM
TOMAS VOKOUN	6	356	2.02	2	4	0	1	12	197	.939	0

NEW JERSEY DEVILS

(Lost Eastern Conference quarterfinals to Philadelphia, 4-1)

SCORING

Pos., No.	GP	ATOI	G	A	Pts	+/-	PIM	PPG	SHG	GWG	OTG	Shots	S%
C 23 SCOTT GOMEZ	5	17:14	0	6	6	-2	0	0	0	0	0	17	.0
C 26 PATRIK ELIAS	5	18:58	3	2	5	-3	2	1	0	1	0	18	16.7
R 14 BRIAN GIONTA	5	15:41	2	3	5	-2	0	1	0	0	0	9	22.2
C 16 JAN HRDINA	5	13:22	2	0	2	0	2	0	0	0	0	7	28.6
D 7 *PAUL MARTIN	5	23:39	1	1	2	-4	4	1	0	0	0	9	11.1
R 15 JAMIE LANGENBRUNNER	5	15:04	0	2	2	0	2	0	0	0	0	11	.0
C 10 ERIK RASMUSSEN	5	14:44	0	2	2	1	2	0	0	0	0	4	.0
D 27 SCOTT NIEDERMAYER	5	27:21	1	0	1	-5	6	0	0	0	0	12	8.3
D 6 TOMMY ALBELIN	4	13:12	0	1	1	1	0	0	0	0	0	2	.0
D 28 BRIAN RAFALSKI	5	22:21	0	1	1	0	0	0	0	0	0	9	.0
C 8 IGOR LARIONOV	1	11:38	0	0	0	-1	0	0	0	0	0	0	.0
D 2 SEAN BROWN	1	11:20	0	0	0	-1	2	0	0	0	0	0	.0
D 25 *DAVID HALE	1	8:59	0	0	0	1	0	0	0	0	0	0	.0
R 22 VIKTOR KOZLOV	2	8:54	0	0	0	-1	0	0	0	0	0	2	.0
R 9 JIRI BICEK	2	12:25	0	0	0	-1	0	0	0	0	0	4	.0
D 19 RAYMOND GIROUX	4	15:15	0	0	0	1	0	0	0	0	0	3	.0
G 30 MARTIN BRODEUR	5	59:35	0	0	0	0	0	0	0	0	0	0	.0
R 24 TURNER STEVENSON	5	13:29	0	0	0	-2	0	0	0	0	0	9	.0
C 18 SERGEI BRYLIN	5	15:02	0	0	0	0	0	0	0	0	0	9	.0
L 20 JAY PANDOLFO	5	13:41	0	0	0	0	0	0	0	0	0	4	.0
L 12 JEFF FRIESEN	5	12:55	0	0	0	-2	4	0	0	0	0	11	.0
D 5 COLIN WHITE	5	19:40	0	0	0	-1	4	0	0	0	0	2	.0
C 11 JOHN MADDEN	5	14:51	0	0	0	0	0	0	0	0	0	13	.0

GOALTENDING

	GP	Mins.	GAA	W	L	EN	SO	GA	SA	SV%	PIM
MARTIN BRODEUR	5	298	2.62	1	4	1	0	13	133	.902	0

*rookie

NEW YORK ISLANDERS

(Lost Eastern Conference quarterfinals to Ottawa, 4-1)

SCORING

Pos., No.	GP	ATOI	G	A	Pts	+/-	PIM	PPG	SHG	GWG	OTG	Shots	S%
D 44 JANNE NIINIMAA	5	24:31	1	2	3	-2	2	1	0	1	0	4	25.0
R 37 MARK PARRISH	5	20:34	1	2	3	-4	0	0	0	0	0	12	8.3
C 55 JASON BLAKE	4	18:09	2	0	2	-2	2	0	0	0	0	9	22.2
L 12 OLEG KVASHA	5	16:05	1	0	1	-1	0	1	0	0	0	8	12.5
R 21 MARIUSZ CZERKAWSKI	5	10:43	0	1	1	-1	0	0	0	0	0	7	.0
D 4 ROMAN HAMRLIK	5	25:30	0	1	1	0	2	0	0	0	0	10	.0
C 79 ALEXEI YASHIN	5	15:32	0	1	1	-2	0	0	0	0	0	15	.0
C 38 DAVE SCATCHARD	5	16:17	0	1	1	-3	6	0	0	0	0	12	.0
R 45 ARRON ASHAM	5	8:44	0	1	1	0	4	0	0	0	0	8	.0
D 24 RADEK MARTINEK	5	12:11	0	1	1	2	0	0	0	0	0	4	.0
D 33 ERIC CAIRNS	1	3:53	0	0	0	-2	0	0	0	0	0	0	.0
R 20 STEVE WEBB	2	4:00	0	0	0	-1	6	0	0	0	0	1	.0
C 77 CLIFF RONNING	4	5:43	0	0	0	-2	0	0	0	0	0	3	.0
D 52 SVEN BUTENSCHON	4	7:42	0	0	0	-1	0	0	0	0	0	1	.0
C 27 MICHAEL PECA	5	23:00	0	0	0	-1	6	0	0	0	0	12	.0
D 3 ADRIAN AUCOIN	5	28:20	0	0	0	-6	6	0	0	0	0	12	.0
D 29 KENNY JONSSON	5	21:58	0	0	0	-4	2	0	0	0	0	2	.0
C 17 SHAWN BATES	5	17:13	0	0	0	-2	4	0	0	0	0	6	.0
R 7 *TRENT HUNTER	5	11:38	0	0	0	-2	4	0	0	0	0	6	.0
R 11 MATTIAS WEINHANDL	5	13:07	0	0	0	-2	2	0	0	0	0	10	.0
G 39 RICK DIPIETRO	5	60:34	0	0	0	0	0	0	0	0	0	0	.0

GOALTENDING

	GP	Mins.	GAA	W	L	EN	SO	GA	SA	SV%	PIM
39 RICK DIPIETRO	5	303	2.18	1	4	1	1	11	120	.908	0

OTTAWA SENATORS

(Lost Eastern Conference quarterfinals to Toronto, 4-3)

SCORING

Pos., No.	GP	ATOI	G	A	Pts	+/-	PIM	PPG	SHG	GWG	OTG	Shots	S%
R 18 MARIAN HOSSA	7	21:24	3	1	4	2	0	1	0	2	0	32	9.4
R 11 DANIEL ALFREDSSON	7	20:02	1	2	3	0	2	0	0	0	0	29	3.4
R 9 MARTIN HAVLAT	7	16:09	0	3	3	-1	2	0	0	0	0	14	.0
C 21 BRYAN SMOLINSKI	7	16:03	1	1	2	-2	4	0	0	0	0	10	10.0
L 26 VACLAV VARADA	7	12:03	1	1	2	0	4	0	0	0	0	10	10.0
D 3 ZDENO CHARA	7	24:38	1	1	2	3	8	0	0	0	0	12	8.3
C 14 RADEK BONK	7	18:29	0	2	2	2	0	0	0	0	0	15	.0
L 15 PETER SCHAEFER	7	14:25	0	2	2	1	4	0	0	0	0	11	.0
D 6 WADE REDDEN	7	26:46	1	0	1	-5	2	1	0	0	0	18	5.6
D 4 CHRIS PHILLIPS	7	20:26	1	0	1	2	12	1	0	0	0	15	6.7
C 28 TODD WHITE	7	18:03	1	0	1	-1	4	0	0	0	0	13	7.7
C 12 MIKE FISHER	7	16:11	1	0	1	0	4	0	0	1	1	13	7.7
L 20 *ANTOINE VERMETTE	4	11:35	0	1	1	-1	4	0	0	0	0	5	.0
D 5 GREG DE VRIES	7	17:50	0	1	1	-2	8	0	0	0	0	10	.0
R 25 CHRIS NEIL	7	6:45	0	1	1	0	19	0	0	0	0	1	.0
G 31 MARTIN PRUSEK	1	40:00	0	0	0	0	0	0	0	0	0	0	.0
D 7 CURTIS LESCHYSHYN	2	15:36	0	0	0	-1	0	0	0	0	0	1	.0
C 39 JASON SPEZZA	3	9:44	0	0	0	-1	2	0	0	0	0	1	.0
D 24 ANTON VOLCHENKOV	5	11:52	0	0	0	0	6	0	0	0	0	4	.0
L 10 PETER BONDRA	7	16:36	0	0	0	-4	6	0	0	0	0	16	.0
G 40 PATRICK LALIME	7	56:54	0	0	0	0	2	0	0	0	0	0	.0
D 2 BRIAN POTHIER	7	17:14	0	0	0	-2	6	0	0	0	0	8	.0

GOALTENDING

	GP	Mins.	GAA	W	L	EN	SO	GA	SA	SV%	PIM
MARTIN PRUSEK	1	40	1.50	0	0	0	0	1	15	.933	0
PATRICK LALIME	7	398	1.96	3	4	0	0	13	139	.906	2

*rookie

PHILADELPHIA FLYERS

(Lost Eastern Conference finals to Tampa Bay, 4-3)

SCORING

Pos., No.	GP	ATOI	G	A	Pts	+/-	PIM	PPG	SHG	GWG	OTG	Shots	S%
C 25 KEITH PRIMEAU	18	18:58	9	7	16	11	22	0	2	3	0	44	20.5
C 23 ALEXEI ZHAMNOV	18	18:39	4	10	14	-1	8	1	0	1	0	31	12.9
C 97 JEREMY ROENICK	18	18:04	4	9	13	4	8	2	0	1	1	49	8.2
C 26 MICHAL HANDZUS	18	18:33	5	5	10	7	10	0	0	0	0	23	21.7
L 24 SAMI KAPANEN	18	17:41	3	7	10	5	6	0	1	1	0	24	12.5
L 12 SIMON GAGNE	18	16:48	5	4	9	10	12	0	0	1	1	44	11.4
R 11 TONY AMONTE	18	14:41	3	5	8	7	6	2	0	0	0	26	11.5
D 5 KIM JOHNSSON	15	26:11	2	6	8	-3	8	0	0	1	0	22	9.1
R 8 MARK RECCHI	18	16:45	4	2	6	-3	4	2	0	0	0	33	12.1
D 3 MATTIAS TIMANDER	18	17:27	2	4	6	2	6	0	0	1	0	17	11.8
D 2 VLADIMIR MALAKHOV	17	24:56	1	5	6	9	12	0	0	0	0	38	2.6
D 28 MARCUS RAGNARSSON	14	21:58	1	4	5	3	14	0	0	1	0	12	8.3
L 10 JOHN LECLAIR	18	15:57	2	2	4	2	8	0	0	0	0	27	7.4
L 87 DONALD BRASHEAR	18	8:55	1	3	4	0	61	1	0	0	0	18	5.6
D 55 DANNY MARKOV	18	23:02	1	2	3	17	25	0	0	1	0	19	5.3
D 44 *JONI PITKANEN	15	12:13	0	3	3	-6	6	0	0	0	0	15	.0
L 20 RADOVAN SOMIK	10	8:07	1	1	2	1	4	0	0	0	0	5	20.0
R 19 BRANKO RADIVOJEVIC	18	9:56	1	1	2	-1	32	0	0	0	0	19	5.3
C 9 *PATRICK SHARP	12	6:11	1	0	1	-2	2	0	0	0	0	11	9.1
G 41 SEAN BURKE	1	40:00	0	0	0	0	0	0	0	0	0	0	.0
C 13 CLAUDE LAPOINTE	1	9:38	0	0	0	0	0	0	0	0	0	2	.0
L 29 TODD FEDORUK	1	6:42	0	0	0	-2	2	0	0	0	0	1	.0
D 36 DENNIS SEIDENBERG	3	7:36	0	0	0	1	0	0	0	0	0	2	.0
G 42 ROBERT ESCHE	18	58:55	0	0	0	0	8	0	0	0	0	0	.0

GOALTENDING

	GP	Mins.	GAA	W	L	EN	SO	GA	SA	SV%	PIM
SEAN BURKE	1	40	1.50	0	0	0	0	1	9	.889	0
ROBERT ESCHE	18	1061	2.32	11	7	1	1	41	498	.918	8

ST. LOUIS BLUES

(Lost Western Conference quarterfinals to San Jose, 4-1)

SCORING

Pos., No.	GP	ATOI	G	A	Pts	+/-	PIM	PPG	SHG	GWG	OTG	Shots	S%
C 18 MIKE SILLINGER	5	22:17	3	1	4	5	6	0	1	0	0	12	25.0
C 39 DOUG WEIGHT	5	19:23	2	1	3	-4	6	1	1	0	0	14	14.3
R 10 DALLAS DRAKE	5	16:44	1	1	2	-1	2	0	0	1	0	7	14.3
L 49 BRIAN SAVAGE	5	15:09	1	1	2	-3	0	0	0	0	0	10	10.0
L 7 KEITH TKACHUK	5	19:18	0	2	2	-1	10	0	0	0	0	12	.0
D 55 *CHRISTIAN BACKMAN	5	23:06	0	2	2	2	4	0	0	0	0	6	.0
C 26 PETR CAJANEK	5	19:27	0	2	2	3	2	0	0	0	0	8	.0
C 38 PAVOL DEMITRA	5	18:07	1	0	1	1	4	0	0	0	0	13	7.7
C 22 *MIKE DANTON	5	7:24	1	0	1	1	2	0	0	0	0	1	100.0
R 19 SCOTT MELLANBY	4	14:16	0	1	1	-4	2	0	0	0	0	3	.0
D 6 ERIC WEINRICH	5	23:35	0	1	1	-1	0	0	0	0	0	6	.0
G 30 CHRIS OSGOOD	5	57:25	0	1	1	0	0	0	0	0	0	0	.0
D 44 CHRIS PRONGER	5	27:53	0	1	1	1	16	0	0	0	0	8	.0
D 37 JEFF FINLEY	1	12:14	0	0	0	0	2	0	0	0	0	0	.0
R 33 ERIC BOGUNIECKI	1	12:52	0	0	0	0	0	0	0	0	0	2	.0
C 12 STEVE MARTINS	1	5:29	0	0	0	-1	0	0	0	0	0	0	.0
G 50 REINHARD DIVIS	1	18:25	0	0	0	0	0	0	0	0	0	0	.0
C 25 PASCAL RHEAUME	3	6:55	0	0	0	-1	2	0	0	0	0	2	.0
C 17 RYAN JOHNSON	3	6:11	0	0	0	0	0	0	0	0	0	2	.0
R 42 *MARK RYCROFT	3	9:41	0	0	0	-1	2	0	0	0	0	1	.0
D 28 *MATT WALKER	4	9:43	0	0	0	-2	0	0	0	0	0	3	.0
D 23 MURRAY BARON	5	18:55	0	0	0	0	6	0	0	0	0	6	.0
R 21 JAMAL MAYERS	5	12:55	0	0	0	1	0	0	0	0	0	6	.0
D 27 BRYCE SALVADOR	5	14:30	0	0	0	-2	2	0	0	0	0	6	.0

GOALTENDING

	GP	Mins.	GAA	W	L	EN	SO	GA	SA	SV%	PIM
REINHARD DIVIS	1	18	.00	0	0	0	0	0	8	1.000	0
CHRIS OSGOOD	5	287	2.51	1	4	0	0	12	109	.890	0

*rookie

SAN JOSE SHARKS

(Lost Western Conference finals to Calgary, 4-2)

SCORING

Pos., No.	GP	ATOI	G	A	Pts	+/-	PIM	PPG	SHG	GWG	OTG	Shots	S%
C 25 VINCENT DAMPHOUSSE	17	18:53	7	7	14	0	20	3	0	3	0	37	18.9
C 12 PATRICK MARLEAU	17	19:16	8	4	12	0	6	4	1	2	0	45	17.8
R 14 JONATHAN CHEECHOO	17	17:37	4	6	10	4	10	1	0	0	0	34	11.8
R 23 *NICHOLAS DIMITRAKOS	15	14:30	1	8	9	2	8	0	0	1	1	22	4.5
L 94 ALEXANDER KOROLYUK	17	16:40	5	2	7	0	10	2	0	1	0	42	11.9
D 2 MIKE RATHJE	17	23:25	1	5	6	1	13	0	0	0	0	14	7.1
D 22 SCOTT HANNAN	17	26:38	1	5	6	7	22	1	0	1	0	25	4.0
D 7 BRAD STUART	17	23:23	1	5	6	-4	13	0	0	0	0	28	3.6
C 18 MIKE RICCI	17	15:30	2	3	5	5	4	0	0	0	0	13	15.4
L 17 SCOTT THORNTON	12	12:30	2	2	4	1	22	0	0	0	0	15	13.3
C 10 ALYN MCCAULEY	11	14:17	2	1	3	0	2	0	0	0	0	11	18.2
R 13 TODD HARVEY	16	10:29	1	2	3	-3	2	0	0	0	0	11	9.1
C 15 WAYNE PRIMEAU	17	15:41	1	2	3	-7	4	0	0	0	0	28	3.6
L 28 NILS EKMAN	16	13:02	0	3	3	-2	8	0	0	0	0	29	.0
D 4 KYLE MCLAREN	16	24:08	0	3	3	-1	10	0	0	0	0	12	.0
C 57 *MARCEL GOC	5	7:07	1	1	2	1	0	0	0	1	0	1	100.0
D 5 *ROB DAVISON	5	9:01	0	2	2	0	4	0	0	0	0	2	.0
C 37 CURTIS BROWN	17	14:36	0	2	2	-5	18	0	0	0	0	23	.0
C 16 MARK SMITH	10	7:43	1	0	1	2	11	0	0	1	0	3	33.3
D 42 *TOM PREISSING	11	12:49	0	1	1	0	0	0	0	0	0	7	.0
D 6 JASON MARSHALL	17	14:43	0	1	1	1	25	0	0	0	0	13	.0
D 21 JIM FAHEY	2	4:41	0	0	0	0	0	0	0	0	0	0	.0
G 20 EVGENI NABOKOV	17	61:53	0	0	0	0	4	0	0	0	0	0	.0

GOALTENDING

	GP	Mins.	GAA	W	L	EN	SO	GA	SA	SV%	PIM
EVGENI NABOKOV	17	1052	1.71	10	7	2	3	30	461	.935	4

TAMPA BAY LIGHTNING

(Won Stanley Cup finals over Calgary, 4-3)

SCORING

Pos., No.	GP	ATOI	G	A	Pts	+/-	PIM	PPG	SHG	GWG	OTG	Shots	S%
C 19 BRAD RICHARDS	23	23:28	12	14	26	5	4	7	0	7	1	88	13.6
R 26 MARTIN ST. LOUIS	23	22:52	9	15	24	6	14	3	1	3	2	58	15.5
L 33 FREDRIK MODIN	23	20:46	8	11	19	7	10	3	0	2	0	50	16.0
C 4 VINCENT LECAVALIER	23	19:38	9	7	16	-2	25	2	0	0	0	76	11.8
R 17 RUSLAN FEDOTENKO	22	16:39	12	2	14	0	14	5	0	3	0	43	27.9
L 25 DAVE ANDREYCHUK	23	18:51	1	13	14	-2	14	0	0	0	0	30	3.3
D 22 DAN BOYLE	23	21:27	2	8	10	7	16	1	0	0	0	25	8.0
L 61 CORY STILLMAN	21	17:22	2	5	7	2	15	0	1	0	0	35	5.7
D 55 DARRYL SYDOR	23	21:49	0	6	6	-4	9	0	0	0	0	25	.0
C 27 TIM TAYLOR	23	14:17	2	3	5	-2	31	0	0	0	0	21	9.5
D 13 PAVEL KUBINA	22	22:53	0	4	4	0	50	0	0	0	0	29	.0
L 36 ANDRE ROY	21	6:11	1	2	3	3	61	0	0	1	0	11	9.1
L 29 *DIMITRY AFANASENKOV	23	13:05	1	2	3	-3	6	0	0	0	0	27	3.7
L 11 CHRIS DINGMAN	23	5:58	1	1	2	1	63	0	0	0	0	13	7.7
D 5 JASSEN CULLIMORE	11	15:14	0	2	2	7	6	0	0	0	0	7	.0
D 37 BRAD LUKOWICH	18	15:51	0	2	2	4	6	0	0	0	0	7	.0
D 21 CORY SARICH	23	19:10	0	2	2	1	25	0	0	0	0	32	.0
C 8 MARTIN CIBAK	6	7:35	0	1	1	0	0	0	0	0	0	3	.0
C 9 ERIC PERRIN	12	5:20	0	1	1	0	6	0	0	0	0	9	.0
G 47 JOHN GRAHAME	1	33:58	0	0	0	0	0	0	0	0	0	0	.0
D 2 STAN NECKAR	2	13:48	0	0	0	1	0	0	0	0	0	1	.0
R 7 BEN CLYMER	5	7:46	0	0	0	0	0	0	0	0	0	2	.0
D 44 NOLAN PRATT	20	18:05	0	0	0	0	8	0	0	0	0	10	.0
G 35 NIKOLAI KHABIBULIN	23	60:53	0	0	0	0	0	0	0	0	0	0	.0

GOALTENDING

	GP	Mins.	GAA	W	L	EN	SO	GA	SA	SV%	PIM
NIKOLAI KHABIBULIN	23	1401	1.71	16	7	1	5	40	598	.933	0
JOHN GRAHAME	1	34	3.53	0	0	0	0	2	17	.882	0

*rookie

TORONTO MAPLE LEAFS

(Lost Eastern Conference semifinals to Philadelphia, 4-2)

SCORING

Pos., No.	GP	ATOI	G	A	Pts	+/-	PIM	PPG	SHG	GWG	OTG	Shots	S%
C 13 MATS SUNDIN	9	18:24	4	5	9	-2	8	0	0	1	0	19	21.1
L 7 GARY ROBERTS	13	17:44	4	4	8	-3	10	2	0	1	0	19	21.1
D 24 BRYAN MCCABE	13	28:47	3	5	8	0	14	2	0	0	0	26	11.5
D 2 BRIAN LEETCH	13	28:29	0	8	8	1	6	0	0	0	0	23	.0
C 25 JOE NIEUWENDYK	9	15:23	6	0	6	0	4	1	0	2	0	23	26.1
R 89 ALEXANDER MOGILNY	13	16:27	2	4	6	-1	8	0	0	0	0	16	12.5
R 28 TIE DOMI	13	11:49	2	2	4	4	41	0	0	1	0	27	7.4
L 23 ALEXEI PONIKAROVSKY	13	14:20	1	3	4	-1	8	0	0	1	0	23	4.3
C 10 RON FRANCIS	12	15:27	0	4	4	0	2	0	0	0	0	14	.0
L 18 CHAD KILGER	13	11:40	2	1	3	0	0	0	0	0	0	16	12.5
D 15 TOMAS KABERLE	13	20:15	0	3	3	1	6	0	0	0	0	14	.0
R 16 DARCY TUCKER	12	13:54	2	0	2	-3	14	1	0	0	0	16	12.5
C 21 ROBERT REICHEL	12	17:10	0	2	2	4	8	0	0	0	0	18	.0
C 80 NIK ANTROPOV	13	15:56	0	2	2	1	18	0	0	0	0	18	.0
D 29 KAREL PILAR	1	20:48	1	0	1	1	0	0	0	0	0	2	50.0
C 39 CLARKE WILM	5	12:44	0	1	1	-1	2	0	0	0	0	5	.0
G 37 TREVOR KIDD	1	32:57	0	0	0	0	0	0	0	0	0	0	.0
R 19 MIKAEL RENBERG	2	10:31	0	0	0	0	4	0	0	0	0	2	.0
C 14 *MATT STAJAN	3	11:13	0	0	0	0	2	0	0	0	0	3	.0
D 9 CALLE JOHANSSON	4	12:11	0	0	0	-1	2	0	0	0	0	3	.0
R 3 WADE BELAK	4	9:58	0	0	0	0	14	0	0	0	0	0	.0
R 12 TOM FITZGERALD	10	13:26	0	0	0	0	6	0	0	0	0	9	.0
D 8 AKI BERG	10	14:51	0	0	0	-3	2	0	0	0	0	7	.0
D 22 KEN KLEE	11	18:44	0	0	0	-1	6	0	0	0	0	6	.0
G 20 ED BELFOUR	13	59:31	0	0	0	0	8	0	0	0	0	0	.0
D 27 BRYAN MARCHMENT	13	14:31	0	0	0	0	8	0	0	0	0	2	.0

GOALTENDING

	GP	Mins.	GAA	W	L	EN	SO	GA	SA	SV%	PIM
TREVOR KIDD	1	33	1.82	0	0	0	0	1	11	.909	0
ED BELFOUR	13	774	2.09	6	7	0	3	27	379	.929	8

VANCOUVER CANUCKS

(Lost Western Conference quarterfinals to Calgary, 4-3)

SCORING

Pos., No.	GP	ATOI	G	A	Pts	+/-	PIM	PPG	SHG	GWG	OTG	Shots	S%
L 19 MARKUS NASLUND	7	19:21	2	7	9	1	2	2	0	0	0	32	6.3
C 7 BRENDAN MORRISON	7	22:00	2	3	5	2	8	1	0	1	1	13	15.4
D 2 MATTIAS OHLUND	7	27:25	1	4	5	-6	13	0	0	1	0	15	6.7
C 24 MATT COOKE	7	18:23	3	1	4	3	12	0	0	1	0	15	20.0
C 33 HENRIK SEDIN	7	16:02	2	2	4	0	2	2	0	0	0	11	18.2
D 55 ED JOVANOVSKI	7	26:36	0	4	4	2	6	0	0	0	0	17	.0
D 6 SAMI SALO	7	22:59	1	2	3	-3	2	1	0	0	0	19	5.3
L 22 DANIEL SEDIN	7	16:03	1	2	3	0	0	1	0	0	0	13	7.7
L 14 GEOFF SANDERSON	7	12:54	1	1	2	-1	4	0	0	0	0	10	10.0
L 26 MARTIN RUCINSKY	7	17:01	1	1	2	-3	6	1	0	0	0	15	6.7
L 10 BRAD MAY	6	7:07	1	0	1	-3	6	0	0	0	0	6	16.7
L 37 JARKKO RUUTU	6	9:12	1	0	1	-3	10	0	0	0	0	2	50.0
D 3 BRENT SOPEL	7	23:54	0	1	1	-4	0	0	0	0	0	16	.0
C 13 ARTEM CHUBAROV	7	19:07	0	1	1	-3	0	0	0	0	0	5	.0
R 32 TYLER BOUCK	1	5:15	0	0	0	-1	0	0	0	0	0	0	.0
C 17 *JASON KING	1	6:21	0	0	0	0	0	0	0	0	0	0	.0
G 1 JOHAN HEDBERG	2	49:01	0	0	0	0	0	0	0	0	0	0	.0
D 23 MARC BERGEVIN	3	8:40	0	0	0	0	2	0	0	0	0	2	.0
G 39 DAN CLOUTIER	3	45:52	0	0	0	0	2	0	0	0	0	0	.0
G 35 *ALEXANDER AULD	3	73:53	0	0	0	0	0	0	0	0	0	0	.0
D 5 BRYAN ALLEN	4	14:37	0	0	0	0	2	0	0	0	0	1	.0
L 9 MIKE KEANE	7	12:18	0	0	0	-3	4	0	0	0	0	4	.0
C 16 TREVOR LINDEN	7	18:29	0	0	0	-3	6	0	0	0	0	4	.0
D 8 MAREK MALIK	7	20:02	0	0	0	1	10	0	0	0	0	6	.0

GOALTENDING

	GP	Mins.	GAA	W	L	EN	SO	GA	SA	SV%	PIM
DAN CLOUTIER	3	138	2.17	1	1	0	0	5	64	.922	2
*ALEXANDER AULD	3	222	2.43	1	2	0	0	9	88	.898	0
JOHAN HEDBERG	2	98	2.45	1	1	1	0	4	51	.922	0

*rookie

ENTRY DRAFT

JULY 30, 2005, Ottawa

FIRST ROUND

No.—Selecting club	Player	Pos.	Previous team (league/country)
1—Pittsburgh	Sidney Crosby	C	Rimouski (QMJHL)
2—Anaheim	Bobby Ryan	RW	Owen Sound (OHL)
3—Carolina	Jack Johnson	D	U.S. National team
4—Minnesota	Benoit Pouliot	LW	Sudbury (OHL)
5—Montreal	Carey Price	G	Tri-City (WHL)
6—Columbus	Gilbert Brule	C	Vancouver (WHL)
7—Chicago	Jack Skille	RW	U.S. National team
8—San Jose (from Atlanta)	Devin Setoguchi	RW	Saskatoon (WHL)
9—Ottawa	Brian Lee	D	Lincoln (USHL)
10—Vancouver	Luc Bourdon	D	Val d'Or (QMJHL)
11—Los Angeles	Anze Kopitar	C	Sodertalje Jr. (Sweden)
12—Rangers (from San Jose via Atlanta)	Marc Staal	D	Sudbury (OHL)
13—Buffalo	Marek Zagrapan	C	Chicoutimi (QMJHL)
14—Washington	Sasha Pokulok	D	Cornell (ECAC)
15—New York Islanders	Ryan O'Marra	C	Erie (OHL)
16—Atlanta (from N.Y. Rangers)	Alex Bourret	C	Lewiston (QMJHL)
17—Phoenix	Martin Hanzal	C	Budejovice (Czec Rep.)
18—Nashville	Ryan Parent	D	Guelph (OHL)
19—Detroit	Jacob Kindl	D	Kitchener (OHL)
20—Florida (from Philadelphia)	Kenndal McArdle	LW	Moose Jaw (WHL)
21—Toronto	Tuukka Rask	G	Ilves Jr. (Finland)
22—Boston	Matt Lashoff	D	Kitchener (OHL)
23—New Jersey	Niklas Bergfors	W	Sodertalje Jr. (Sweden)
24—St. Louis	T.J. Oshie	C	Warroad (USHSE)
25—Edmonton	Andrew Cogliano	C	St. Michael's (OPJHL)
26—Calgary	Matt Pelech	D	Sarnia (OHL)
27—Washington (from Colorado)	Joe Finley	D	Sioux Falls (USHL)
28—Dallas	Matthew Niskanen	D	Virginia (USHSE)
29—Philadelphia (from Florida)	Steve Downie	RW	Windsor (OHL)
30—Tampa Bay	Vladimir Mihalik	D	Presov (Slovakia)

SECOND ROUND

No.—Selecting club	Player	Pos.	Previous team (league/country)
31—Anaheim (from Tampa Bay)	Brendan Mikkelson	D	Portland (WHL)
32—Florida	Tyler Plante	G	Brandon (WHL)
33—Dallas	James Neal	LW	Plymouth (OHL)
34—Colorado	Ryan Stoa	C	U.S. National team
35—San Jose (from Calgary)	Marc-Edouard Vlasic	D	Quebec (WMJHL)
36—Edmonton	Taylor Chorney	D	Shattuck-St. Mary's (USHSW)
37—St. Louis	Scott Jackson	D	Salmon Arm (BCJHL)
38—New Jersey	Jeff Frazee	G	U.S. National team
39—Boston	Peter Kalus	C	Vitkovice (Czech Rep.)
40—N.Y. Rangers (from Toronto)	Mike Sauer	D	Portland (WHL)
41—Atlanta (from Phila. via Rangers)	Ondrej Pavelec	G	Kladno Jr. (Czech Rep.)
42—Detroit	Justin Abdelkader	LW	Cedar Rapids (USHL)
43—Chicago (from Nashville)	Michael Blunden	RW	Erie (OHL)
44—Colorado (from Phoenix)	Paul Stastny	C	Denver (WCHA)
45—New York Rangers	Guillaume Latendresse	RW	Drummondville (QMJHL)
46—New York Islanders	Dustin Kohn	D	Calgary (WHL)
47—Colorado (from Washington)	Tom Fritsche	LW	Ohio State (CCHA)
48—Buffalo	Philippe Gogulla	W	Kohn (Germany)
49—Atlanta (from San Jose)	Chad Denny	D	Lewiston (QMJHL)
50—Los Angeles	Dany Roussin	LW	Rimouski (QMJHL)
51—Vancouver	Mason Raymond	LW	Camrose (AJHL)
52—Colorado (from Ottawa via Wash.)	Chris Durand	C	Seattle (WHL)
53—Atlanta	Andrew Kozek	W	South Surrey (BCJHL)
54—Chicago	Dan Bertram	RW	Boston College (HE)
55—Columbus	Adam McQuaid	D	Sudbury (OHL)
56—N.Y. Rangers (from Montreal)	Marc-Andre Cliche	RW	Lewiston (QMJHL)
57—Minnesota	Matt Kassian	LW	Kamloops (WHL)
58—Carolina	Nathan Hagemo	D	Minnesota (WCHA)
59—Phoenix (from Anaheim)	Pier-Olivier Pelletier	G	Drummondville (QMJHL)
60—Los Angeles	T.J. Fast	D	Camrose (AJHL)
61—Pittsburgh	Michael Gergen	W	Shattuck-St. Mary's (USHSW)

THIRD ROUND

No.—Selecting club	Player	Pos.	Previous team (league/country)
62—Pittsburgh	Kristopher Letang	D	Val d'Or (QMJHL)
63—Anaheim	Jason Bailey	RW	U.S. National Team
64—Carolina	Joe Barnes	C	Saskatoon (WHL)
65—Minnesota	Kristofer Westblom	G	Kelowna (WHL)
66—N.Y. Rangers (from Montreal)	Brodie DuPont	C	Calgary (WHL)
67—Columbus	Kris Russell	D	Medicine Hat (WHL)
68—Chicago	Evan Brophey	C/LW	Belleville (OHL)
69—Calgary (from Atlanta via Carolina)	Gord Baldwin	D	Medicine Hat (WHL)
70—Ottawa	Vitaly Anikeyenko	D	Yaroslavl (Russia)
71—Dallas (from Vancouver)	Richard Clune	LW	Sarnia (OHL)
72—Los Angeles	Jonathan Quick	G	Avon (USHSE)
73—Tampa Bay (from San Jose)	Radek Smolenak	LW	Kingston (OHL)
74—Calgary (from Buffalo)	Dan Ryder	C	Peterborough (OHL)
75—Dallas (from Washington)	Perttu Lindgren	C	Ilves Jr. (Finland)
76—New York Islanders	Shea Guthrie	W	St. George's (USHSE)
77—New York Rangers	Dalyn Flatt	D	Saskatoon (WHL)
78—Carolina (from Phoenix)	Teemu Laasko	D	IFK Jr. (Finland)
79—Nashville	Cody Franson	D	Vancouver (WHL)
80—Detroit	Christofer Loftberg	C	Djurgarden Jr. (Sweden)
81—Edmonton (from Philadelphia)	Danny Syvret	D	London (OHL)
82—Toronto	Phil Oreskovic	D	Brampton (OHL)
83—Boston	Mikko Lehtonen	RW	Espoo Jr. (Finland)
84—New Jersey	Mark Fraser	D	Kitchener (OHL)
85—St. Louis	Ben Bishop	G	Texas (NAHL)
86—Edmonton	Robby Dee	C/W	Breck (USHSW)
87—Buffalo (from Calgary)	Marc-Andre Gragnani	D	P.E.I. (QMJHL)
88—Colorado	T.J. Hensick	C	Michigan (CCHA)
89—Tampa Bay (from Dallas via Phila.)	Chris Lawrence	C	Sault Ste. Marie (OHL)
90—Florida	Dan Collins	RW	Plymouth (OHL)
91—Philadelphia (from Tampa Bay)	Oskars Bartulis	D	Moncton (QMJHL)

FOURTH ROUND

No.—Selecting club	Player	Pos.	Previous team (league/country)
92—Tampa Bay	Marek Bartanus	RW	Kosice Jr. (Slovakia)
93—Florida	Olivier Legault	LW	Lewiston (QMJHL)
94—Carolina (from Dallas)	Jakub Vojta	D	Sparta Jr. (Czech Rep.)
95—Minnesota (from Colorado)	Cody Bass	C	Mississauga (OHL)
96—Buffalo (from Calgary)	Chris Butler	D	Sioux City (USHL)
97—Edmonton	Chris Vande Velde	C	Moorhead (USHSW)
98—Ottawa (from St. Louis)	Ilja Zubov	C	Chelyabinsk (Russia)
99—New Jersey	Patrick Davis	LW	Kitchener (OHL)
100—Boston	Jonathan Sigalet	D	Bowling Green (CCHA)
101—Carolina (from Toronto)	Jared Boll	RW	Lincoln (USHL)
102—Tampa Bay (from Philadelphia)	Blair Jones	C	Moose Jaw (WHL)
103—Detroit	Mattias Ritola	C/W	Leksand Jr. (Sweden)
104—Florida (from Nashville)	Matt Duffy	D	NHJ Monarchs (EJHL)
105—Phoenix	Keith Yandle	D	Cushing Academy (USHSE)
106—Boston	Vladimir Sobotka	C/W	Slavia Jr. (Czech Rep.)
107—New York Rangers	Tom Pyatt	C	Saginaw (OHL)
108—Chicago (from N.Y. Islanders)	Niklas Hjalmarsson	D	HV 71 Jr. (Sweden)
109—Washington	Andrew Thomas	D	U. of Denver (WCHA)
110—Minnesota (from Buffalo)	Kyle Bailey	C	Portland (WHL)
111—Calgary	J.D. Wyatt	RW	Vancouver (WHL)
112—San Jose	Alex Stalock	G	Cedar Rapids (USHL)
113—Chicago (from Los Angeles)	Nathan Davis	C/LW	Ohio (Miami) (CCHA)
114—Vancouver	Alexandre Vincent	G	Chicoutimi (QMJHL)
115—Ottawa	Janne Kolehmainen	LW	Saipa (Finland)
116—Atlanta	Jordan Lavallee	LW	Quebec (QMJHL)
117—Chicago	Denis Istomin	RW	Chelyabinsk (Russia)
118—Washington (from Boston)	Patrick McNeill	D	Saginaw (OHL)
119—Phoenix (from Columbus)	Jeremy Duchesne	G	Halifax (QMJHL)
120—Edmonton	Viatcheslav Trukhno	C	P.E.I. (QMJHL)
121—Montreal	Juraj Mikus	C/W	Skalica Jr. (Slovakia)
122—Minnesota	Morten Madsen	C/W	Frolunda Jr. (Sweden)
123—Carolina	Ondrej Otecenas	C/W	Trencin Jr. (Slovakia)
124—Colorado (from Anaheim)	Raymond Macias	D	Kamloops (WHL)
125—Pittsburgh	Tommi Leinonen	D	Karpat Jr. (Finland)

FIFTH ROUND

No.—Selecting club	Player	Pos.	Previous team (league/country)
126—Pittsburgh	Tim Crowder	RW	South Surrey (BCJHL)
127—Anaheim	Bobby Bolt	LW	Kingston (OHL)
128—Calgary (from Carolina)	Kevin Lalande	G	Belleville (OHL)
129—Minnesota	Anthony Aiello	D	Thayer Academy (USHSE)
130—Montreal	Mathieu Aubin	C	Lewiston (QMJHL)
131—Columbus	Tomas Popperle	G	Sparta (Czech Rep.)
132—Detroit	Darren Helm	C/LW	Medicine Hat (WHL)
133—Tampa Bay	Stanislav Lascek	RW	Chicoutimi (QMJHL)
134—Chicago	Brennan Turner	D	Notre Dame (SJHL)
135—Atlanta	Tomas Pospisil	RW	Trinec (Czech Rep. Jr.)
136—Ottawa	Tomas Kudelka	D	Zlin (Czech Rep. Jr.)
137—Detroit	Johan Ryno	W	Kumla (Sweden Jr.)
138—Vancouver	Matt Butcher	C	Chilliwack (BCJHL)
139—Los Angeles	Patrick Hersley	D	Malmo (Sweden Jr.)
140—San Jose	Taylor Dakers	G	Kootenay (WHL)
141—Anaheim (from San Jose)	Brian Salcido	D	Colorado College (WCHA)
142—Buffalo	Nathan Gerbe	C	U.S. National team
143—Washington	Daren Machesney	G	Brampton (OHL)
144—New York Islanders	Masi Marjamaki	RW	Moose Jaw (WHL)
145—Carolina	Timothy Kunes	D	Junior Falcons (EJHL)
146—Dallas	Tom Wandell	C/W	Sodertalje (Sweden Jr.)
147—New York Rangers	Trevor Koverko	D	Owen Sound (OHL)
148—Phoenix	Anton Krysanov	C	Togliatti (Russia)
149—San Jose	Derek Joslin	D	Ottawa (OHL)
150—Nashville	Cal O'Reilly	D	Windsor (OHL)
151—Detroit	Jeff May	D	Prince Albert (WHL)
152—Philadelphia	Josh Beaulieu	C	London (OHL)
153—Toronto	Alex Berry	RW	Junior Bruins (EJHL)
154—Boston	Wacey Rabbit	C	Saskatoon (WHL)
155—New Jersey	Mark Fayne	D	Noble & Greenough (USHSE)
156—St. Louis	Ryan Reaves	RW	Brandon (WHL)
157—Edmonton	Fredrik Pettersson	LW	Frolunda (Sweden Jr.)
158—Calgary	Matt Keetley	G	Medicine Hat (WHL)
159—Carolina (from Colorado)	Risto Korhonen	D	Karpat (Finland Jr.)
160—Dallas	Matt Watkins	RW	Vernon (BCJHL)
161—Florida	Brian Foster	G	Junior Monarch (EJHL)
162—San Jose (from Tampa Bay)	Paul Fenton	F	U. Mass-Amherst (HE)

SIXTH ROUND

No.—Selecting club	Player	Pos.	Previous team (league/country)
163—Tampa Bay	Marek Kvapil	RW	Saginaw (OHL)
164—Florida	Roman Deryuk	D	Spartak (Russia)
165—Tampa Bay (from Dallas)	Kevin Beech	G	Sudbury (OHL)
166—Colorado	Jason Lynch	D	Spokane (WHL)
167—Chicago (from Calgary)	Joseph Fallon	G	U. of Vermont (ECAC)
168—Colorado (from Edmonton)	Justin Mercier	C/W	U.S. National team
169—St. Louis	Mike Gauthier	D	Prince Albert (WHL)
170—New Jersey	Sean Zimmerman	D	Spokane (WHL)
171—St. Louis	Nicholas Drazenovic	C	Prince George (WHL)
172—Boston	Lukas Vantuch	C/W	Liberec (Czech Rep. Jr.)
173—Toronto	Johan Dahlberg	W	MoDo (Sweden Jr.)
174—Philadelphia	John Flatters	D	Red Deer (WHL)
175—Detroit	Juho Mielonen	D	Ilves (Finland Jr.)
176—Nashville	Ryan Maki	RW	Harvard (ECAC)
177—Columbus (from Phoenix)	Derek Reinhart	D	Regina (WHL)
178—New York Rangers	Greg Beller	W	Lake of the Woods (USHSW)
179—Calgary	Brett Sutter	C/LW	Kootenay (WHL)
180—New York Islanders	Tyrell Mason	D	Salmon Arm (BCJHL)
181—Washington	Tim Kennedy	LW	Sioux City (USHL)
182—Buffalo	Adam Dennis	G	London (OHL)
183—San Jose	William Colbert	D	Ottawa (OHL)
184—Los Angeles	Ryan McGinnis	D	Plymouth (OHL)
185—Vancouver	Kris Fredheim	D	Notre Dame (SJHL)
186—Ottawa	Dimitri Megalinsky	D	Yaroslavl (Russia)
187—Atlanta	Andrei Zubarev	D	UFA (Russia 3)
188—Chicago	Joe Charlebois	D	Sioux City (USHL)
189—Columbus	Kirill Starkov	C	Frolunda (Sweden Jr.)
190—Montreal	Matt D'Agostini	RW	Guelph (OHL)

No.—Selecting club	Player	Pos.	Previous team (league/country)
191—Buffalo (from Minnesota)	Vjateslav Buravchinkov	D	Krylja (Russia 2)
192—Carolina	Nicholas Blanchard	C	Chicoutimi (QMJHL)
193—San Jose (from Anaheim)	Tony Lucia	LW	Wayzata (USHSW)
194—Pittsburgh	Jean-Philippe Paquet	D	Shawinigan (QMJHL)

SEVENTH ROUND

No.—Selecting club	Player	Pos.	Previous team (league/country)
195—Pittsburgh	Joe Vitale	C	Sioux Falls (USHL)
196—New York Islanders	Nicholas Tuzzolino	D	Sarnia (OHL)
197—Anaheim	Jean-Philippe Levasseur	G	Rouyn-Noranda (QMJHL)
198—Carolina	Kyle Lawson	D	U.S. National team
199—Minnesota	Riley Emmerson	D	Tri-City (WHL)
200—Montreal	Siarhei Kastsitsyn	W	Gomel (Belarus)
201—Columbus	Trevor Hendrikx	D	Peterborough (OHL)
202—Chicago	David Kuchejda	RW	Budejovice (Czech Rep. Jr.)
203—Chicago (from Atlanta)	Adam Hobson	C	Spokane (WHL)
204—Ottawa	Colin Greening	C/LW	Upper Canada College (CCL)
205—Vancouver	Mario Bliznak	C	Dubinca (Slovakia Jr.)
206—Los Angeles	Josh Meyers	D	Sioux City (USHL)
207—Atlanta (from San Jose)	Myles Stoesz	D	Spokane (WHL)
208—Buffalo	Matt Generous	D	Junior Falcons (EJHL)
209—Washington	Ineligible claim		
210—New York Islanders	Luciano Aquino	C/LW	Brampton (OHL)
211—New York Rangers	Ryan Russell	C	Kooetnay (WHL)
212—Phoenix	Pat Brosnihan	RW	Worcester Academy (USHSE)
213—Nashville	Scott Todd	D	Windsor (OHL)
214—Detroit	Bretton Stamler	D	Seattle (WHL)
215—Philadelphia	Matthew Clackson	LW	Chicago (USHL)
216—Toronto	Anton Stralman	D	Skovde (Sweden 2)
217—Boston	Brock Bradford	C	Omaha (USHL)
218—New Jersey	Alexander Sundstrom	C/W	Bjorkloven (Sweden 2)
219—St. Louis	Nikolai Lemtygov	W	CSKA (Russia)
220—Edmonton	Matthew Glasser	LW	Fort McMurray (AJHL)
221—Calgary	Myles Rumsey	D	Swift Current (WHL)
222—Colorado	Kyle Cumiskey	D	Kelowna (WHL)
223—Dallas	Pat McGann	G	Illionois (USMHL)
224—Florida	Zach Bearson	RW	Waterloo (USHL)
225—Tampa Bay	John Wessbecker	D	Blake (USHSW)
226—Los Angeles	John Seymour	LW	Brampton (OHL)
227—Buffalo	Andrew Orpik	D	Thayer Academy (USHSE)
228—Toronto	Chad Rau	C	Des Moines (USHL)
229—Montreal	Philippe Paquet	D	Sallsbury (USHSE)
230—Nashville	Patric Hornqvlst	W	Vasby (Sweden 3)

Compensatory pick notes:

Pick 60 - assigned to Los Angeles for club not signing 2001 first-round pick David Steckel.
Pick 106 - assigned to Boston for loss of Group III free agent Brian Rolston.
Pick 111 - assigned to Calgary for loss of Group III free agent Craig Conroy.
Pick 118 - assigned to Boston for loss of Group III free agent Michael Nylander.
Pick 120 - assigned to Edmonton for loss of Group III free agent Petr Nedved.
Pick 132 - assigned to Detroit for loss of Group III free agent Dominik Hasek.
Pick 133 - assigned to Tampa Bay for loss of Group III free agent Jassen Cullimore.
Pick 137 - assigned to Detroit for loss of Group III free agent Brett Hull.
Pick 140 - assigned to San Jose for loss of Group III free agent Vincent Damphousse.
Pick 145 - assigned to Carolina for loss of Group III free agent Sean Hill.
Pick 146 - assigned to Dallas for loss of Group III free agent Richard Matvichuk.
Pick 149 - assigned to San Jose for loss of Group III free agent Mike Ricci.
Pick 171 - assigned to St. Louis for loss of Group III free agent Scott Mellanby.
Pick 179 - assigned to Calgary for loss of Group III free agent Kryzstof Oliwa.
Pick 196 - assigned to NY Islanders for loss of Group III free agent Alexander Karpovtsev.
Pick 226 - assigned to Los Angeles for the loss of a draft pick (acquired via trade) as a result of the shortening of the Entry Draft from nine to seven rounds.
Pick 227 - assigned to Buffalo for the loss of a draft pick (acquired via trade) as a result of the shortening of the Entry Draft from nine to seven rounds.
Pick 228 - assigned to Toronto for loss of Group III free agent Tom Fitzgerald.
Pick 229 - assigned to Montreal for loss of Group III free agent Darren Langdon.
Pick 230 - assigned to Nashville for loss of Group III free agent Wade Flaherty.

ENTRY DRAFT

JUNE 26-27, 2004, Raleigh, N.C.

FIRST ROUND

No.—Selecting club	Player	Pos.	Previous team (league)
1—Washington	Alexander Ovechkin	LW	Moscow Dynamo (Russia)
2—Pittsburgh	Evgeni Malkin	C/W	Magnitogorsk (Russia)
3—Chicago	Cameron Barker	D	Medicine Hat (WHL)
4—Carolina (from Columbus)	Andrew Ladd	LW	Calgary (WHL)
5—Phoenix	Blake Wheeler	RW	Breck School (U.S. high school)
6—New York Rangers	Al Montoya	G	Michigan (CCHA)
7—Florida	Rostislav Olesz	C	Vitkovice (Czech Republic)
8—Columbus (from Carolina)	Alexandre Picard	LW	Lewiston (QMJHL)
9—Anaheim	Ladislav Smid	D	Liberec (Czech Republic)
10—Atlanta	Boris Valabik	D	Kitchener (OHL)
11—Los Angeles	Lauri Tukonen	W	Espoo (Finland)
12—Minnesota	A.J. Thelen	D	Michigan State (CCHA)
13—Buffalo	Drew Stafford	RW	North Dakota (WCHA)
14—Edmonton	Devan Dubnyk	G	Kamloops (WHL)
15—Nashville	Alexander Radulov	RW	Moscow Dynamo (Russia)
16—New York Islanders	Petteri Nokelainen	C/W	SaiPa (Finland)
17—St. Louis	Marek Schwarz	G	Sparta (Czech Republic)
18—Montreal	Kyle Chipchura	C	Prince Albert (WHL)
19—New York Rangers (from Calgary)	Lauri Korpikoski	C/W	TPS (Finland)
20—New Jersey (from Dallas)	Travis Zajac	C	Salmon Arm (BCHL)
21—Colorado	Wojtek Wolski	LW	Brampton (OHL)
22—San Jose (from New Jersey via Dallas)	Lukas Kaspa	RW	Litvinov (Czech Republic)
23—Ottawa	Andrej Meszaros	D	Trencin (Slovakia)
24—Calgary (from Toronto via Rangers)	Kris Chucko	LW	Salmon Arm (BCHL)
25—Edmonton (from Philadelphia)	Rob Schremp	C	London (OHL)
26—Vancouver	Cory Schneider	G	Phillips Academy (USHSE)
27—Washington (from Boston)	Jeff Schultz	D	Calgary (WHL)
28—Dallas (from San Jose)	Mark Fistric	D	Vancouver (WHL)
29—Washington (from Detroit)	Mike Green	D	Saskatoon (WHL)
30—Tampa Bay	Andy Rogers	D	Calgary (WHL)

SECOND ROUND

No.—Selecting club	Player	Pos.	Previous team (league)
31—Pittsburgh	Johannes Salmonsson	W	Djurgarden (Sweden)
32—Chicago	Dave Bolland	C/RW	London (OHL)
33—Washington	Christopher Bourque	C	Cushing Academy, Mass. (USHSE)
34—Dallas (from Columbus)	Johan Fransson	D	Lulea (Sweden)
35—Phoenix	Logan Stephenson	D	Tri-City (WHL)
36—New York Rangers	Darin Olver	D	Northern Michigan (CCHA)
37—Florida (from N.Y. Rangers)	David Shantz	G	Mississauga (OHL)
38—Carolina	Justin Peters	G	St. Michael's (OHL)
39—Anaheim	Jordan Smith	D	Sault Ste. Marie (OHL)
40—Atlanta	Grant Lewis	D	Dartmouth (ECAC)
41—Chicago (from Los Angeles)	Bryan Bickell	LW	Ottawa (OHL)
42—Minnesota	Roman Voloshenko	LW	Krylja (Russia)
43—Buffalo	Michael Funk	D	Portland (WHL)
44—Edmonton	Roman Teslyuk	D	Kamloops (WHL)
45—Chicago (from Nashville)	Ryan Garlock	C	Windsor (OHL)
46—Columbus (from New York Rangers)	Adam Pineault	RW	Boston College.
47—New York Islanders	Blake Comeau	RW	Kelowna (WHL)
48—New York Rangers (from Edmonton)	Dane Byers	LW	Prince Albert (WHL)
49—St. Louis	Carl Soderberg	C/W	Malmo (Sweden)
50—Phoenix (from Dallas)	Enver Lisin	RW	Saratov (Russia)
51—New York Rangers (from Montreal)	Bruce Graham	C	Moncton (QMJHL)
52—Dallas (from San Jose)	Raymond Sawada	RW	Nanaimo (BCHL)
53—Florida (from Calgary)	David Booth	LW	Michigan State (CCHA)
54—Chicago (from Dallas)	Jakub Sindel	C	Sparta (Czech Republic)
55—Colorado	Victor Oreskovich	RW	Green Bay (USHL)
56—Dallas	Niklas Grossman	D	Sodertalje Jr. (Sweden)
57—Edmonton (from New Jersey)	Geoff Paukovich	LW	U.S. under-18 national team.
58—Ottawa	Kirill Lyamin	D	HC CSKA (Russia)
59—Columbus (from Toronto)	Kyle Wharton	D	Ottawa (OHL)
60—New York Rangers (from Philadelphia)	Brandon Dubinsky	C	Portland (WHL)

No.—Selecting club	Player	Pos.	Previous team (league)
61—Pittsburgh (from Vancouver)	Alex Goligoski	D	Sioux Falls (USHL)
62—Washington (from Boston)	Michail Yunkov	C/W	Krylja (Russia)
63—Boston (from San Jose)	David Krejci	C	Kladno Jr. (Czech Republic)
64—Boston (from Detroit)	Martins Karsums	RW	Moncton (QMJHL)
65—Tampa Bay	Mark Tobin	LW	Rimouski (QMJHL)

THIRD ROUND

No.—Selecting club	Player	Pos.	Previous team (league)
66—Washington	Sami Lepisto	D	Jokerit (Finland)
67—Pittsburgh	Nick Johnson	RW	St. Albert (AJHL)
68—Chicago	Adam Berti	LW	Oshawa (OHL)
69—Carolina (from Washington)	Casey Borer	D	St. Cloud State (WCHA)
70—Calgary (from Columbus)	Brandon Prust	C/LW	London (OHL)
71—Buffalo (from Phoenix)	Andrej Sekera	D	Trencin Jr. (Slovakia)
72—Colorado (from New York Rangers)	Denis Parshin	LW	CSKA (Russia)
73—New York Rangers (from Florida)	Zdenek Bahensky	RW	Litvinov (Czech Republic)
74—Anaheim (from Carolina)	Kyle Klubertanz	D	Green Bay (USHL)
75—Anaheim	Tim Brent	C	Toronto-St. Michael's (OHL)
76—Atlanta	Scott Lehman	D	Toronto-St. Michael's (OHL)
77—Ottawa (from Los Angeles)	Shawn Weller	LW	Capital District (EJHL)
78—Minnesota	Peter Olvecky	W	Trencin Jr. (Slovakia)
79—Minnesota (from Buffalo)	Clayton Stoner	D	Tri-City (WHL)
80—New York Rangers (from Edmonton)	Billy Ryan	C	Cushing Academy (USHSE)
81—Nashville	Vaclav Meidl	C	Plymouth (OHL)
82—New York Islanders	Sergei Ogordnikov	C	Tver (Russia)
83—St. Louis	Victor Alexandrov	RW	Novokuznetsk (Russia)
84—Montreal	Alexei Yemelin	D	Samara (Russia)
85—Pittsburgh (from Calgary)	Brian Gifford	C	Moorhead (USHSW)
86—Dallas	John Lammers	LW	Lethbridge (WHL)
87—Ottawa (from Colorado)	Peter Regin	C/W	Herning Jr. (Denmark)
88—Washington (from New Jersey)	Clayton Barthel	D	Seattle (WHL)
89—Ottawa	Jeff Glass	G	Kootenay (WHL)
90—Toronto	Justin Pogge	G	Prince George (WHL)
91—Vancouver (from San Jose)	Alexander Edler	D	Jamtland (Sweden)
92—Philadephia	Rob Bellamy	RW	New England (EJHL)
93—Columbus (from Vancouver)	Daniel Lacosta	G	Owen Sound (OHL)
94—San Jose (from Boston)	Thomas Greiss	G	Koln (Germany)
95—Los Angeles (from San Jose)	Paul Baier	D	Deerfield Academy (USHSE)
96—Columbus	Andrei Plehanov	D	Nizhnekampsk (Russia)
97—Detroit	Johan Franzen	C	Linkoping (Sweden)
98—Calgary (from Tampa Bay)	Dustin Boyd	C	Moose Jaw (WHL)

FOURTH ROUND

No.—Selecting club	Player	Pos.	Previous team (league)
99—Pittsburgh	Tyler Kennedy	C	Sault Ste. Marie (OHL)
100—Montreal (from Chicago)	James Wyman	RW	Blake, Minn. (USHSW)
101—Philadelphia (from Washington)	R.J. Anderson	D	Centennial, Minn. (USHSW)
102—Tampa Bay (from Columbus)	Mike Lundin	D	Maine (HE)
103—Phoenix	Roman Tomanek	RW	Povazka Bystrica (Slovakia)
104—Dallas (from N.Y. Rangers)	Frederik Naslund	RW	Vasteras (Sweden)
105—Florida	Evan Schafer	D	Prince Albert (WHL)
106—Atlanta (from Carolina)	Chad Painchaud	LW	Mississauga (OHL)
107—Nashville (from Anaheim)	Nick Fugere	LW	Gatineau (QMJHL)
108—Boston	Ashton Rome	RW	Moose Jaw (WHL)
109—Carolina (from Atlanta)	Brett Carson	D	Calgary (WHL)
110—Los Angeles	Ned Lukacevic	LW	Spokane (WHL)
111—Minnesota	Ryan Jones	F	Chatham (WJRB)
112—Edmonton (from Buffalo)	Liam Reddox	LW	Peterborough (OHL)
113—Toronto (from Edmonton)	Roman Kukumberg	F	Trencin (Slovakia)
114—Minnesota (from Nashville)	Patrick Bordeleau	LW	Val d'Or (QMJHL)
115—N.Y. Islanders	Wes O'Neill	D	Notre Dame (CCHA)
116—St. Louis	Michal Birner	LW	Slavia Jr. (Czech Republic)
117—Minnesota (from Montreal)	Julien Sprunger	RW	Fribourg (Switzerland)
118—Calgary	Aki Seitsonen	C	Prince Albert (WHL)
119—Phoenix (from Dallas)	Kevin Porter	C/LW	U.S. National Team.
120—Chicago (from Colorado)	Mitch Maunu	D	Windsor (OHL)
121—Calgary (from New Jersey)	Kristopher Hogg	LW	Kamloops (WHL)
122—Ottawa	Alexander Nikulin	C	RPL CSKA (Russia)
123—Chicago (from Toronto)	Karel Hromas	LW	Sparta Jr. (Czech Republic)
124—Philadelphia	David Laliberte	RW	P.E.I. (QMJHL)

No.—Selecting club	Player	Pos.	Previous team (league)
125—Vancouver	Andrew Sarauer	LW	Langley (BCHL)
126—San Jose (from Boston)	Torrey Mitchell	C	Hotchkiss School (Conn.)
127—N.Y. Rangers (from San Jose)	Ryan Callahan	RW	Guelph (OHL)
128—Detroit	Evan McGrath	C	Kitchener (OHL)
129—San Jose (from Tampa Bay)	Jason Churchill	G	Halifax (QMJHL)

FIFTH ROUND

No.—Selecting club	Player	Pos.	Previous team (league)
130—Pittsburgh	Michal Sersen	D	Rimouski (QMJHL)
131—Chicago	Trevor Kell	RW	London (OHL)
132—Washington	Oscar Hedman	D	Modo (Sweden)
133—Columbus	Petr Pohl	RW	Gatineau (QMJHL)
134—Boston (from Phoenix)	Kris Versteeg	RW	Lethbridge (WHL)
135—N.Y. Rangers	Roman Psurny	LW	Zlin Jr. (Czech Republic)
136—St. Louis (from Florida)	Nikita Nikitin	D	Omsk (Russia)
137—Carolina	Magnus Akerlund	G	HV 71 Jr. (Sweden)
138—Washington	Pasi Salonen	F	IFK Jr. (Finland)
139—Nashville (from Anaheim)	Kyle Moir	G	Swift Current (WHL)
140—Chicago	Jacob Dowell	C	Wisconsin (WCHA)
141—Ottawa	Jim McKenzie	RW	Sioux Falls (USHL)
142—Atlanta	Juraj Gracik	RW	Topolcany (Slovakia)
143—Los Angeles	Eric Neilson	RW	Rimouski (QMJHL)
144—Philadelphia (from Minnesota)	Chris Zarb	D	Tri-City (USHL)
145—Buffalo	Michal Valent	G	Martin Jr. (Slovakia)
146—Edmonton	Bryan Young	D	Peterborough (OHL)
147—Nashville	Janne Niskala	D	Lukko (Finland)
148—N.Y. Islanders	Steve Regier	LW	Medicine Hat (WHL)
149—Philadelphia (from St. Louis)	Gino Pisellini	RW	Plymouth (OHL)
150—Montreal	Mikhail Grabovski	F	Nizhnekamsk (Russia)
151—Detroit	Siarhei Kolasau	D	Minsk (Belarus)
152—Florida (from Calgary)	Bret Nasby	D	Oshawa (OHL)
153—San Jose (from Dallas)	Steven Zalewski	C	Northwood Prep. (USHSE)
154—Colorado	Richard Demen-Willaume	D	Frolunda Jr. (Sweden)
155—New Jersey	Alexander Mikhailishin	D	Spartak (Russia)
156—Ottawa	Roman Wick	RW	Kloten (Switzerland)
157—Toronto	Dimitri Vorobiev	D	Togliatti (Russia)
158—Tampa Bay (from Philadelphia)	Brandon Elliott	D	Mississauga (OHL)
159—Vancouver	Mike Brown	RW	Michigan (CCHA)
160—Boston	Ben Walter	D	Massachusetts-Lowell
161—Minnesota (from San Jose)	Jean-Claude Sawyer	D	Cape Breton (QMJHL)
162—Detroit	Tyler Haskins	C	Toronto-St. Michael's (OHL)
163—Tampa Bay	Dustin Collins	C/LW	Northern Michigan (CCHA)

SIXTH ROUND

No.—Selecting club	Player	Pos.	Previous team (league)
164—Pittsburgh	Moises Gutierrez	RW	Kamloops (WHL)
165—Chicago	Scott McCulloch	LW	Grande Prairie (AJHL)
166—Washington	Peter Guggisberg	F	Davos (Switzerland)
167—Columbus	Rob Page	D	Blake (USHSW)
168—Phoenix	Kevin Cormier	F	Moncton (MJAHL)
169—N.Y. Rangers	Jordan Foote	LW	Nanaimo (BCHL)
170—Philadelphia (from Florida)	Ladislav Scurko	C	Spisska Nova Ves Jr. (Slovakia)
171—Philadelphia (from Carolina)	Frederik Cabana	C/LW	Halifax (QMJHL)
172—Anaheim	Matt Auffrey	RW	U.S. National Team
173—Calgary (from Atlanta)	Adam Pardy	D	Cape Breton (QMJHL)
174—Los Angeles	Scott Parse	F	Nebraska-Omaha (CCHA)
175—Minnesota	Aaron Boogaard	RW	Tri-City (WHL)
176—Buffalo	Patrick Kaleta	RW	Peterborough (OHL)
177—Edmonton	Max Gordichuk	D	Kamloops (WHL)
178—Nashville	Michael Santorelli	C	Vernon (BCHL)
179—N.Y. Islanders	Jaroslav Mrazek	D	Sparta Jr. (Czech Republic)
180—St. Louis	Roman Polak	D	Vitkovice Jr. (Czech Republic)
181—Montreal	Loic Lacasse	G	Baie-Comeau (QMJHL)
182—Calgary	Fred Wikner	F	Frolunda Jr. (Sweden)
183—Dallas	Trevor Ludwig	D	Texas (NAHL)
184—Colorado	Derek Peltier	D	Cedar Rapids (USHL)
185—New Jersey	Josh Disher	G	Erie (OHL)
186—Atlanta (from Ottawa)	Dan Turple	G	Oshawa (OHL)
187—Toronto	Robert Earl	LW	Wisconsin (WCHA)

No.—Selecting club	Player	Pos.	Previous team (league)
188—Tampa Bay (from Philadelphia)	Jan Zapletal	D	Vsetin Jr. (Czech Republic)
189—Vancouver	Julien Ellis-Plante	G	Shawinigan (QMJHL)
190—Columbus (from Boston)	Lennart Petrell	C/W	IFK Jr. (Finland)
191—Tampa Bay (from San Jose)	Karri Ramo	G	Pelicans Jr. (Finland)
192—Detroit	Anton Axelsson	LW	Frolunda Jr. (Sweden)
193—Nasville (from Tampa Bay)	Kevin Schaeffer	D	Boston U. (HE)

SEVENTH ROUND

No.—Selecting club	Player	Pos.	Previous team (league)
194—Pittsburgh	Chris Peluso	D	Brainerd (USHSW)
195—Minnesota	Jean-Michel Rizk	RW	Saginaw (OHL)
196—Chicago	Petri Kontiola	C/W	Tappara (Finland)
197—Washington	Andrew Gordon	RW	Notre Dame (SJHL)
198—Columbus	Justin Vienneau	D	Shawinigan (QMJHL)
199—Phoenix	Chad Kolarik	C	U.S. National Team
200—Calgary (from N.Y. Rangers)	Matt Schneider	C	Tri-City (WHL)
201—San Jose (from Florida)	Michael Vernace	D	Brampton (OHL)
202—Carolina	Ryan Pottruff	D	London (OHL)
203—Anaheim	Gabriel Bouthillette	G	Gatineau (QMJHL)
204—Atlanta	Miikka Tuomainen	LW	Tuto (Finland)
205—Los Angeles	John Curry	RW	Sioux City (USHL)
206—Minnesota	Anton Khudobin	G	Magnitogorsk (Russia)
207—Buffalo	Mark Mancari	RW	Ottawa (OHL)
208—Edmonton	Stephane Goulet	RW	Quebec (QMJHL)
209—Nashville	Stanislav Balan	C	Zlin Jr. (Czech Republic)
210—N.Y. Islanders	Emil Axelsson	D	Orebero (Sweden)
211—St. Louis	David Fredriksson	F	HV 71 Jr. (Sweden)
212—Montreal	Jon Gleed	D	Cornell (ECAC)
213—Calgary	James Spratt	G	Sioux City (USHL)
214—Chicago (from Dallas)	Troy Brouwer	RW	Moose Jaw (WHL)
215—Colorado	Ian Keserich	G	Cleveland (NAHL)
216—New Jersey	Pierre-Luc Leblond-Letourneau	LW	Baie-Comeau (QMJHL)
217—New Jersey	Tyler Eckford	D	South Surrey (BCHL)
218—Dallas	Sergei Kukushin	F	Junost Minsk (Belarus)
219—Ottawa	Joe Cooper	RW	Miami-Ohio (CCHA)
220—Toronto	Maxim Semenov	D	Togliatti (Russia)
221—Los Angeles (from Philadelphia)	Daniel Taylor	G	Guelph (OHL)
222—Pittsburgh (from Vancouver)	Jordan Morrison	C	Peterborough (OHL)
223—Chicago	Jared Walker	C	Red Deer (WHL)
224—Boston	Matt Hunwick	D	Michigan (CCHA)
225—San Jose	David MacDonald	D	New England (EJHL)
226—Detroit	Steven Covington	RW	Calgary (WHL)
227—N.Y. Islanders (from Tampa Bay)	Chris Campoli	D	Erie (OHL)

EIGHTH ROUND

No.—Selecting club	Player	Pos.	Previous team (league)
228—Pittsburgh	David Brown	G	Notre Dame (CCHA)
229—Chicago	Eric Hunter	C	Prince George (WHL)
230—Washington	Justin Mrazek	G	Estevan (SJHL)
231—Columbus	Brian McGuirk	LW	Governor Dummer (USHSE)
232—Philadelphia (from Phoenix)	Martin Houle	G	Cape Breton (QMJHL)
233—Columbus (from N.Y. Rangers)	Matt Greer	F	White Bear Lake (USHSW)
234—San Jose (from Florida)	Derek MacIntyre	G	Sault Ste. Marie (NAHL)
235—Carolina	Jonas Fiedler	RW	Plymouth (OHL)
236—Anaheim	Matt Christie	C	Miami-Ohio (CCHA)
237—Atlanta	Mitch Carefoot	C	Cornell (ECAC)
238—Los Angeles	Yutaka Fukufuji	G	Japanese national team
239—Colorado (from Minnesota)	Brandon Yip	RW	Coquitlam (BCHL)
240—Phoenix	Aaron Gagnon	C	Seattle (WHL)
241—Buffalo	Mike Card	D	Kelowna (WHL)
242—Edmonton	Tyler Spurgeon	C	Kelowna (WHL)
243—Nashville	Denis Kulyash	D	CSKA (Russia)
244—N.Y. Islanders	Jason Pitton	LW	Sault Ste. Marie (OHL)
245—Tampa Bay (from St. Louis)	Justin Keller	LW	Kelowna (WHL)
246—Montreal	Gregory Stewart	LW	Peterborough (OHL)
247—N.Y. Rangers (from Calgary)	Jonathon Paiement	D	Lewiston (QMJHL)
248—Dallas	Lukas Vomela	D	Budejovice (Czech Republic)
249—Colorado	J.D. Corbin	LW	Denver (WCHA)
250—New Jersey	Nathan Perkovich	RW	Cedar Rapids (USHL)

No.—Selecting club	Player	Pos.	Previous team (league)
251—Ottawa	Matthew McIlvane	C	Chicago (USHL)
252—Toronto	Jan Steber	C/LW	Halifax (QMJHL)
253—Philadelphia	Travis Gawryletz	D	Trail (BCHL)
254—Vancouver	David Schulz	D	Swift Current (WHL)
255—Boston	Anton Hedman	F	Stocksund (Sweden)
256—Chicago (from San Jose)	Matthew Ford	RW	Sioux Falls (USHL)
257—Detroit	Gennady Stolyarov	RW	Tver (Russia)
258—Nashville (from Tampa Bay)	Pekka Rinne	G	Karpat (Finland)

NINTH ROUND

No.—Selecting club	Player	Pos.	Previous team (league)
259—Pittsburgh	Brian Ihnacak	C	Brown (ECAC)
260—Chicago	Marko Anttila	RW	Lempaala (Finland)
261—Phoenix	William Engasser	LW	Blake (USHSW)
262—Montreal	Mark Streit	D	Zurich (Switzerland)
263—Washington	Travis Morin	C	Minnesota St. (WCHA)
264—Los Angeles (from Columbus)	Valtteri Tenkanen	C/W	Jyvaskyla (Finland)
265—Phoenix	Daniel Winnik	C/LW	New Hampshire (HE)
266—N.Y. Rangers	Jakub Petruzalek	RW	Litvinov (Czech Republic)
267—Florida	Spencer Dillon	D	Salmon Arm (BCHL)
268—Carolina	Martin Vagner	D	Gatineau (QMJHL)
269—Anaheim	Janne Pesonen	F	Karpat (Finland)
270—Atlanta	Matthew Siddall	RW	Powell River (BCHL)
271—Columbus (from Los Angeles)	Grant Clitsome	D	Nepean (CJHL)
272—Minnesota	Kyle Wilson	C	Colgate (ECAC)
273—Buffalo	Dylan Hunter	LW	London (OHL)
274—Edmonton	Bjorn Bjurling	G	Djurgarden (Sweden)
275—Nashville	Craig Switzer	D	Salmon Arm (BCHL)
276—N.Y. Islanders	Sylvain Michaud	G	Drummondville (QMJHL)
277—St. Louis	Jonathon Michel Boutin	RW	Shawinigan (QMJHL)
278—Montreal	Alex Dulac-Lemelin	D	Baie-Comeau (QMJHL)
279—Calgary	Adam Cracknell	RW	Kootenay (WHL)
280—Dallas	Matt McKnight	F	Camrose (AJHL)
281—Colorado	Stephen McClellan	D	Catholic Memorial (USHS)
282—New Jersey	Valeri Klimov	D	Spartak (Russia)
283—Florida (from Ottawa)	Luke Beaverson	D	Green Bay (USHL)
284—Ottawa	John Wikner	LW	Frolunda Jr. (Sweden)
285—Toronto	Pierce Norton	RW	Thayer Academy (USHSE)
286—Philadelphia	Triston Grant	LW	Vancouver (WHL)
287—Vancouver	Jannik Hansen	W	Malmo Jr. (Sweden)
288—San Jose (from Boston)	Brian Mahoney-Wilson	G	Catholic Memorial (USHS)
289—San Jose	Christian Jensen	D	New Jersey Jr. Titans (independent)
290—Detroit	Nils Backstrom	D	Stocksund (Sweden)
291—Philadelphia (from Tampa Bay)	John Carter	C	Brewster Jr. Bulldogs (independent)

NHL HISTORY

Stanley Cup champions

All-Star games

Year-by-year standings

Award winners

The Sporting News awards

Hall of Fame

Team by team

STANLEY CUP CHAMPIONS

LIST OF WINNERS

The Stanley Cup was donated in 1893 to be awarded to signify supremacy in Canadian amateur hockey. Eventually, other teams, including professional clubs and clubs outside of Canada, began vying for the trophy. Since 1926 only NHL clubs have competed for the Stanley Cup.

Season	Club	Coach
1892-93	Montreal Amateur Athletic Association*	
1893-94	Montreal Amateur Athletic Association*	
1894-95	Montreal Victorias*	Mike Grant†
1895-96	(Feb. '96) Winnipeg Victorias*	J. Armitage†
1895-96	(Dec. '96) Montreal Victorias*	Mike Grant†
1896-97	Montreal Victorias*	Mike Grant†
1897-98	Montreal Victorias*	F. Richardson†
1898-99	Montreal Shamrocks*	H.J. Trihey†
1899-1900	Montreal Shamrocks*	H.J. Trihey†
1900-01	Winnipeg Victorias*	D.H. Bain†
1901-02	Montreal Am. Ath. Assn.*	C. McKerrow
1902-03	Ottawa Silver Seven*	A.T. Smith
1903-04	Ottawa Silver Seven*	A.T. Smith
1904-05	Ottawa Silver Seven*	A.T. Smith
1905-06	Montreal Wanderers*	Cecil Blachford†
1906-07	(Jan. '07) Kenora Thistles*	Tommy Phillips†
1906-07	(Mar. '07) Montreal Wanderers*	Cecil Blachford†
1907-08	Montreal Wanderers*	Cecil Blachford†
1908-09	Ottawa Senators*	Bruce Stuart†
1909-10	Montreal Wanderers*	Pud Glass†
1910-11	Ottawa Senators*	Bruce Stuart†
1911-12	Quebec Bulldogs*	C. Nolan
1912-13	Quebec Bulldogs*	Joe Malone†
1913-14	Toronto Blueshirts*	Scotty Davidson†
1914-15	Vancouver Millionaires*	Frank Patrick
1915-16	Montreal Canadiens*	George Kennedy
1916-17	Seattle Metropolitans*	Pete Muldoon
1917-18	Toronto Arenas	Dick Carroll
1919-20	Ottawa Senators	Pete Green
1920-21	Ottawa Senators	Pete Green
1921-22	Toronto St. Pats	George O'Donoghue
1922-23	Ottawa Senators	Pete Green
1923-24	Montreal Canadiens	Leo Dandurand
1924-25	Victoria Cougars*	Lester Patrick
1925-26	Montreal Maroons	Eddie Gerard
1926-27	Ottawa Senators	Dave Gill
1927-28	New York Rangers	Lester Patrick
1928-29	Boston Bruins	Cy Denneny
1929-30	Montreal Canadiens	Cecil Hart
1930-31	Montreal Canadiens	Cecil Hart
1931-32	Toronto Maple Leafs	Dick Irvin
1932-33	New York Rangers	Lester Patrick
1933-34	Chicago Black Hawks	Tommy Gorman
1934-35	Montreal Maroons	Tommy Gorman
1935-36	Detroit Red Wings	Jack Adams
1936-37	Detroit Red Wings	Jack Adams
1937-38	Chicago Black Hawks	Bill Stewart
1938-39	Boston Bruins	Art Ross
1939-40	New York Rangers	Frank Boucher
1940-41	Boston Bruins	Cooney Weiland
1941-42	Toronto Maple Leafs	Hap Day
1942-43	Detroit Red Wings	Jack Adams
1943-44	Montreal Canadiens	Dick Irvin
1944-45	Toronto Maple Leafs	Hap Day
1945-46	Montreal Canadiens	Dick Irvin
1946-47	Toronto Maple Leafs	Hap Day
1947-48	Toronto Maple Leafs	Hap Day
1948-49	Toronto Maple Leafs	Hap Day
1949-50	Detroit Red Wings	Tommy Ivan
1950-51	Toronto Maple Leafs	Joe Primeau
1951-52	Detroit Red Wings	Tommy Ivan
1952-53	Montreal Canadiens	Dick Irvin
1953-54	Detroit Red Wings	Tommy Ivan
1954-55	Detroit Red Wings	Jimmy Skinner
1955-56	Montreal Canadiens	Toe Blake
1956-57	Montreal Canadiens	Toe Blake
1957-58	Montreal Canadiens	Toe Blake
1958-59	Montreal Canadiens	Toe Blake
1959-60	Montreal Canadiens	Toe Blake
1960-61	Chicago Black Hawks	Rudy Pilous
1961-62	Toronto Maple Leafs	Punch Imlach
1962-63	Toronto Maple Leafs	Punch Imlach
1963-64	Toronto Maple Leafs	Punch Imlach
1964-65	Montreal Canadiens	Toe Blake
1965-66	Montreal Canadiens	Toe Blake
1966-67	Toronto Maple Leafs	Punch Imlach
1967-68	Montreal Canadiens	Toe Blake
1968-69	Montreal Canadiens	Claude Ruel
1969-70	Boston Bruins	Harry Sinden
1970-71	Montreal Canadiens	Al MacNeil
1971-72	Boston Bruins	Tom Johnson
1972-73	Montreal Canadiens	Scotty Bowman
1973-74	Philadelphia Flyers	Fred Shero
1974-75	Philadelphia Flyers	Fred Shero
1975-76	Montreal Canadiens	Scotty Bowman
1976-77	Montreal Canadiens	Scotty Bowman
1977-78	Montreal Canadiens	Scotty Bowman
1978-79	Montreal Canadiens	Scotty Bowman
1979-80	New York Islanders	Al Arbour
1980-81	New York Islanders	Al Arbour
1981-82	New York Islanders	Al Arbour
1982-83	New York Islanders	Al Arbour
1983-84	Edmonton Oilers	Glen Sather
1984-85	Edmonton Oilers	Glen Sather
1985-86	Montreal Canadiens	Jean Perron
1986-87	Edmonton Oilers	Glen Sather
1987-88	Edmonton Oilers	Glen Sather
1988-89	Calgary Flames	Terry Crisp
1989-90	Edmonton Oilers	John Muckler
1990-91	Pittsburgh Penguins	Bob Johnson
1991-92	Pittsburgh Penguins	Scotty Bowman
1992-93	Montreal Canadiens	Jacques Demers
1993-94	New York Rangers	Mike Keenan
1994-95	New Jersey Devils	Jacques Lemaire
1995-96	Colorado Avalanche	Marc Crawford
1996-97	Detroit Red Wings	Scotty Bowman
1997-98	Detroit Red Wings	Scotty Bowman
1998-99	Dallas Stars	Ken Hitchcock
1999-00	New Jersey Devils	Larry Robinson
2000-01	Colorado Avalanche	Bob Hartley
2001-02	Detroit Red Wings	Scotty Bowman
2002-03	New Jersey Devils	Pat Burns
2003-04	Tampa Bay Lightning	John Tortella
2004-05	No Cup awarded	

NOTE: 1918-19 series between Montreal and Seattle cancelled after five games because of influenza epidemic. 2004-05 series not contested because of lockout.

*Stanley Cups won by non-NHL clubs.

†Team captain.

ALL-STAR GAMES

RESULTS

Date	Site	Winning team, score	Losing team, score	Att.
2-14-34†	Maple Leaf Gardens, Toronto	Toronto Maple Leafs, 7	NHL All-Stars, 3	*14,000
11-3-37‡	Montreal Forum	NHL All-Stars, 6	Montreal All-Stars§, 5	8,683
10-29-39∞	Montreal Forum	NHL All-Stars, 5	Montreal Canadiens, 2	*6,000
10-13-47	Maple Leaf Gardens, Toronto	NHL All-Stars, 4	Toronto Maple Leafs, 3	14,169
11-3-48	Chicago Stadium	NHL All-Stars, 3	Toronto Maple Leafs, 1	12,794
10-10-49	Maple Leaf Gardens, Toronto	NHL All-Stars, 3	Toronto Maple Leafs, 1	13,541
10-8-50	Olympia Stadium, Detroit	Detroit Red Wings, 7	NHL All-Stars, 1	9,166
10-9-51	Maple Leaf Gardens, Toronto	First Team, 2	Second Team, 2	11,469
10-5-52	Olympia Stadium, Detroit	First Team, 1	Second Team, 1	10,680
10-3-53	Montreal Forum	NHL All-Stars, 3	Montreal Canadiens, 1	14,153
10-2-54	Olympia Stadium, Detroit	NHL All-Stars, 2	Detroit Red Wings, 2	10,689
10-2-55	Olympia Stadium, Detroit	Detroit Red Wings, 3	NHL All-Stars, 1	10,111
10-9-56	Montreal Forum	NHL All-Stars, 1	Montreal Canadiens, 1	13,095
10-5-57	Montreal Forum	NHL All-Stars, 5	Montreal Canadiens, 3	13,095
10-4-58	Montreal Forum	Montreal Canadiens, 6	NHL All-Stars, 3	13,989
10-3-59	Montreal Forum	Montreal Canadiens, 6	NHL All-Stars, 1	13,818
10-1-60	Montreal Forum	NHL All-Stars, 2	Montreal Canadiens, 1	13,949
10-7-61	Chicago Stadium	NHL All-Stars, 3	Chicago Blackhawks, 1	14,534
10-6-62	Maple Leaf Gardens, Toronto	Toronto Maple Leafs, 4	NHL All-Stars, 1	14,236
10-5-63	Maple Leaf Gardens, Toronto	NHL All-Stars, 3	Toronto Maple Leafs, 3	14,034
10-10-64	Maple Leaf Gardens, Toronto	NHL All-Stars, 3	Toronto Maple Leafs, 2	14,232
10-20-65	Montreal Forum	NHL All-Stars, 5	Montreal Canadiens, 2	14,284
1-18-67	Montreal Forum	Montreal Canadiens, 3	NHL All-Stars, 0	14,284
1-16-68	Maple Leaf Gardens, Toronto	Toronto Maple Leafs, 4	NHL All-Stars, 3	15,753
1-21-69	Montreal Forum	West Division, 3	East Division, 3	16,260
1-20-70	St. Louis Arena	East Division, 4	West Division, 1	16,587
1-19-71	Boston Garden	West Division, 2	East Division, 1	14,790
1-25-72	Met Sports Center, Bloomington, Minn.	East Division, 3	West Division, 2	15,423
1-30-73	Madison Square Garden, New York	East Division, 5	West Division, 4	16,986
1-29-74	Chicago Stadium	West Division, 6	East Division, 4	16,426
1-21-75	Montreal Forum	Wales Conference, 7	Campbell Conference, 1	16,080
1-20-76	The Spectrum, Philadelphia	Wales Conference, 7	Campbell Conference, 5	16,436
1-25-77	Pacific Coliseum, Vancouver	Wales Conference, 4	Campbell Conference, 3	15,607
1-24-78	Buffalo Memorial Auditorium	Wales Conference, 3	Campbell Conference, 2 (OT)	16,433
	1979 All-Star Game replaced by Challenge Cup series between Team NHL and Soviet Union			
2-5-80	Joe Louis Arena, Detroit	Wales Conference, 6	Campbell Conference, 3	21,002
2-10-81	The Forum, Los Angeles	Campbell Conference, 4	Wales Conference, 1	15,761
2-9-82	Capital Centre, Landover, Md.	Wales Conference, 4	Campbell Conference, 2	18,130
2-8-83	Nassau Coliseum, Long Island, N.Y.	Campbell Conference, 9	Wales Conference, 3	15,230
1-31-84	Meadowlands Arena, East Rutherford, N.J.	Wales Conference, 7	Campbell Conference, 6	18,939
2-12-85	Olympic Saddledome, Calgary	Wales Conference, 6	Campbell Conference, 4	16,683
2-4-86	Hartford Civic Center	Wales Conference, 4	Campbell Conference, 3 (OT)	15,126
	1987 All-Star Game replaced by Rendez-Vous '87 between Team NHL and Soviet Union			
2-9-88	St. Louis Arena	Wales Conference, 6	Campbell Conference, 5 (OT)	17,878
2-7-89	Northlands Coliseum, Edmonton	Campbell Conference, 9	Wales Conference, 5	17,503
1-21-90	Pittsburgh Civic Arena	Wales Conference, 12	Campbell Conference, 7	17,503
1-19-91	Chicago Stadium	Campbell Conference, 11	Wales Conference, 5	18,472
1-18-92	The Spectrum, Philadelphia	Campbell Conference, 10	Wales Conference, 6	17,380
2-6-93	Montreal Forum	Wales Conference, 16	Campbell Conference, 6	17,137
1-22-94	Madison Square Garden, New York	Eastern Conference, 9	Western Conference, 8	18,200
	1995 All-Star Game canceled because of NHL lockout			
1-20-96	FleetCenter, Boston	Eastern Conference, 5	Western Conference, 4	17,565
1-18-97	San Jose Arena	Eastern Conference, 11	Western Conference, 7	17,442
1-18-98	General Motors Place, Vancouver	North America, 8	World, 7	18,422
1-24-99	Ice Palace, Tampa	North America, 8	World, 6	19,758
2-6-00	Air Canada Centre, Toronto	World, 9	North America, 4	19,300
2-4-01	Pepsi Center, Denver	North America, 14	World, 12	18,646
2-2-02	Staples Center, Los Angeles	World, 8	North America, 5	18,118
2-2-03	Office Depot Center, Sunrise, Florida	Western Conference, 6	Eastern Conference, 5 (2OT; SO)	19,250
2-8-04	Xcel Energy Center, St. Paul, Minnesota	Eastern Conference 6	Western Conference 4	19,434
	2005 All-Star Game canceled because of NHL lockout			

*Estimated figure.

†Benefit game for Toronto Maple Leafs left winger Ace Bailey, who suffered a career-ending skull injury earlier in the season.

‡Benefit game for the family of Montreal Canadiens center Howie Morenz, who died of a heart attack earlier in the year.

§Montreal All-Star roster made up of players from Montreal Canadiens and Maroons.

∞Benefit game for the family of Montreal Canadiens defenseman Babe Siebert, who drowned earlier in the year.

MOST VALUABLE PLAYERS

Date	Player, All-Star Game team (regular-season team)
10-6-62	Eddie Shack, Toronto Maple Leafs
10-5-63	Frank Mahovlich, Toronto Maple Leafs
10-10-64	Jean Beliveau, All-Stars (Montreal Canadiens)
10-20-65	Gordie Howe, All-Stars (Detroit Red Wings)
1-18-67	Henri Richard, Montreal Canadiens
1-16-68	Bruce Gamble, Toronto Maple Leafs
1-21-69	Frank Mahovlich, East Div. (Detroit Red Wings)
1-20-70	Bobby Hull, East Div. (Chicago Blackhawks)
1-19-71	Bobby Hull, West Div. (Chicago Blackhawks)
1-25-72	Bobby Orr, East Division (Boston Bruins)
1-30-73	Greg Polis, West Division (Pittsburgh Penguins)
1-29-74	Garry Unger, West Division (St. Louis Blues)
1-21-75	Syl Apps Jr., Wales Conf. (Pittsburgh Penguins)
1-20-76	Peter Mahovlich, Wales Conf. (Montreal Canadiens)
1-25-77	Rick Martin, Wales Conference (Buffalo Sabres)
1-24-78	Billy Smith, Campbell Conf. (New York Islanders)
2-5-80	Reggie Leach, Campbell Conf. (Philadelphia Flyers)
2-10-81	Mike Liut, Campbell Conf. (St. Louis Blues)
2-9-82	Mike Bossy, Wales Conf. (New York Islanders)
2-8-83	Wayne Gretzky, Campbell Conf. (Edmonton Oilers)

Date	Player, All-Star Game team (regular-season team)
1-31-84	Don Maloney, Wales Conf. (New York Rangers)
2-12-85	Mario Lemieux, Wales Conf. (Pittsburgh Penguins)
2-4-86	Grant Fuhr, Campbell Conf. (Edmonton Oilers)
2-9-88	Mario Lemieux, Wales Conf. (Pittsburgh Penguins)
2-7-89	Wayne Gretzky, Campbell Conf. (Los Angeles Kings)
1-21-90	Mario Lemieux, Wales Conf. (Pittsburgh Penguins)
1-19-91	Vincent Damphousse, Camp. Conf. (Tor. Maple Leafs)
1-18-92	Brett Hull, Campbell Conf. (St. Louis Blues)
2-6-93	Mike Gartner, Wales Conf. (New York Rangers)
1-22-94	Mike Richter, Eastern Conf. (New York Rangers)
1-20-96	Ray Bourque, Eastern Conf. (Boston Bruins)
1-18-97	Mark Recchi, Eastern Conf. (Montreal Canadiens)
1-18-98	Teemu Selanne, North America (Ana. Mighty Ducks)
1-24-99	Wayne Gretzky, North America (New York Rangers)
2-6-00	Pavel Bure, World (Florida Panthers)
2-4-01	Bill Guerin, North America (Boston Bruins)
2-2-02	Eric Daze, North America (Chicago Blackhawks)
2-2-03	Dany Heatley, Eastern Conference (Atlanta Thrashers)
2-8-04	Joe Sakic, Western Conference (Colorado Avalanche)

YEAR-BY-YEAR STANDINGS

Note: Prior to 1926-27 season, clubs outside the NHL also competed for the Stanley Cup. Non-NHL clubs are denoted in parentheses. Sometimes playoff rounds were decided by total goals scored, rather than by games won.

1917-18

Team	W	L	T	Pts.	GF	GA
Montreal Canadiens	13	9	0	26	115	84
Toronto Arenas	13	9	0	26	108	109
Ottawa Senators	9	13	0	18	102	114
Montreal Wanderers	1	5	0	2	17	35

PLAYOFFS

Semifinals: Toronto 10 goals, Montreal Canadiens 7 goals (2-game series); Vancouver (PCHL) 3 goals, Seattle (PCHL) 2 goals (2-game series).

Stanley Cup finals: Toronto 3, Vancouver (PCHL) 2.

1918-19

Team	W	L	T	Pts.	GF	GA
Ottawa Senators	12	6	0	24	71	53
Montreal Canadiens	10	8	0	20	88	78
Toronto Arenas	5	13	0	10	64	92

PLAYOFFS

Semifinals: Seattle (PCHL) 7 goals, Vancouver 5 goals (2-game series); Montreal Canadiens 3, Ottawa 1.

Stanley Cup finals: Series between Montreal Canadiens and Seattle (PCHL) abandoned (with each team winning two games and one game tied) due to influenza epidemic.

1919-20

Team	W	L	T	Pts.	GF	GA
Ottawa Senators	19	5	0	38	121	64
Montreal Canadiens	13	11	0	26	129	113
Toronto St. Patricks	12	12	0	24	119	106
Quebec Bulldogs	4	20	0	8	91	177

PLAYOFFS

Semifinals: Seattle (PCHL) 7 goals, Vancouver (PCHL) 3 goals (2-game series).

Stanley Cup finals: Ottawa 3, Seattle (PCHL) 2.

1920-21

Team	W	L	T	Pts.	GF	GA
Toronto St. Patricks	15	9	0	30	105	100
Ottawa Senators	14	10	0	28	97	75
Montreal Canadiens	13	11	0	26	112	99
Hamilton Tigers	6	18	0	12	92	132

PLAYOFFS

Semifinals: Vancouver (PCHL) 2, Seattle (PCHL) 0; Ottawa 2, Toronto 0.

Stanley Cup finals: Ottawa 3, Vancouver (PCHL) 2.

1921-22

Team	W	L	T	Pts.	GF	GA
Ottawa Senators	14	8	2	30	106	84
Toronto St. Patricks	13	10	1	27	98	97
Montreal Canadiens	12	11	1	25	88	94
Hamilton Tigers	7	17	0	14	88	105

PLAYOFFS

Preliminaries: Regina (WCHL) 2 goals, Calgary (WCHL) 1 goal (2-game series); Regina (WCHL) 3, Edmonton (WCHL) 2; Vancouver (PCHL) 2, Seattle (PCHL) 0; Vancouver (PCHL) 5 goals, Regina (WCHL) 2 goals (2-game series); Toronto 5 goals, Ottawa 4 goals (2-game series).

Stanley Cup finals: Toronto 3, Vancouver (PCHL) 2.

1922-23

Team	W	L	T	Pts.	GF	GA
Ottawa Senators	14	9	1	29	77	54
Montreal Canadiens	13	9	2	28	73	61
Toronto St. Patricks	13	10	1	27	82	88
Hamilton Tigers	6	18	0	12	81	110

PLAYOFFS

Quarterfinals: Ottawa 3 goals, Montreal Canadiens 2 goals (2-game series); Vancouver (PCHL) 5 goals, Victoria (PCHL) 3 goals (2-game series). **Semifinals:** Ottawa 3, Vancouver (PCHL) 1; Edmonton (WCHL) 4 goals, Regina (WCHL) 3 goals (2-game series).

Stanley Cup finals: Ottawa 2, Edmonton (WCHL) 0.

1923-24

Team	W	L	T	Pts.	GF	GA
Ottawa Senators	16	8	0	32	74	54
Montreal Canadiens	13	11	0	26	59	48
Toronto St. Patricks	10	14	0	20	59	85
Hamilton Tigers	9	15	0	18	63	68

PLAYOFFS

First round: Vancouver (PCHL) 4 goals, Seattle (PCHL) 3 goals (2-game series); Calgary (WCHL) 4 goals, Regina (WCHL) 2 goals (2-game series). **Second round:** Montreal Canadiens 2, Ottawa 0; Calgary (WCHL) 2, Vancouver (PCHL) 1. **Third round:** Montreal Canadiens 2, Vancouver (PCHL) 0.

Stanley Cup finals: Montreal Canadiens 2, Calgary (WCHL) 0.

1924-25

Team	W	L	T	Pts.	GF	GA
Hamilton Tigers	19	10	1	39	90	60
Toronto St. Patricks	19	11	0	38	90	84
Montreal Canadiens	17	11	2	36	93	56
Ottawa Senators	17	12	1	35	83	66
Montreal Maroons	9	19	2	20	45	65
Boston Bruins	6	24	0	12	49	119

PLAYOFFS

Quarterfinals: Victoria (WCHL) 6 goals, Saskatoon (WCHL) 4 goals (2-game series). **Semifinals:** Montreal Canadiens 2, Toronto 0; Victoria (WCHL) 3 goals, Calgary (WCHL) 1 goal (2-game series).

Stanley Cup finals: Victoria (WCHL) 3, Montreal Canadiens 1.

1925-26

Team	W	L	T	Pts.	GF	GA
Ottawa Senators	24	8	4	52	77	42
Montreal Maroons	20	11	5	45	91	73
Pittsburgh Pirates	19	16	1	39	82	70
Boston Bruins	17	15	4	38	92	85
New York Americans	12	20	4	28	68	89
Toronto St. Patricks	12	21	3	27	92	114
Montreal Canadiens	11	24	1	23	79	108

PLAYOFFS

Quarterfinals: Victoria (WHL) 4 goals, Saskatoon (WHL) 3 goals (2-game series); Montreal Maroons 6 goals, Pittsburgh 4 goals (2-game series). **Semifinals:** Victoria (WHL) 5 goals, Edmonton (WHL) 3 goals (2-game series); Montreal Maroons 2 goals, Ottawa 1 goal (2-game series).

Stanley Cup finals: Montreal Maroons 3, Victoria (WHL) 1.

1926-27

AMERICAN DIVISION

Team	W	L	T	Pts.	GF	GA
New York Rangers	25	13	6	56	95	72
Boston Bruins	21	20	3	45	97	89
Chicago Blackhawks	19	22	3	41	115	116
Pittsburgh Pirates	15	26	3	33	79	108
Detroit Cougars	12	28	4	28	76	105

CANADIAN DIVISION

Team	W	L	T	Pts.	GF	GA
Ottawa Senators	30	10	4	64	89	69
Montreal Canadiens	28	14	2	58	99	67
Montreal Maroons	20	20	4	44	71	68
New York Americans	17	25	2	36	82	91
Toronto St. Patricks	15	24	5	35	79	94

PLAYOFFS

League quarterfinals: Montreal Canadiens 2 goals, Montreal Maroons 1 goal (2-game series); Boston 10 goals, Chicago 5 goals (2-game series). **Semifinals:** Ottawa 5 goals, Montreal Canadiens 1 goal (2-game series); Boston 3 goals, N.Y. Rangers 1 goal (2-game series).

Stanley Cup finals: Ottawa 2, Boston 0 (two ties).

1927-28

AMERICAN DIVISION

Team	W	L	T	Pts.	GF	GA
Boston Bruins	20	13	11	51	77	70
New York Rangers	19	16	9	47	94	79
Pittsburgh Pirates	19	17	8	46	67	76
Detroit Cougars	19	19	6	44	88	79
Chicago Blackhawks	7	34	3	17	68	134

CANADIAN DIVISION

Team	W	L	T	Pts.	GF	GA
Montreal Canadiens	26	11	7	59	116	48
Montreal Maroons	24	14	6	54	96	77
Ottawa Senators	20	14	10	50	78	57
Toronto Maple Leafs	18	18	8	44	89	88
New York Americans	11	27	6	28	63	128

PLAYOFFS

League quarterfinals: Montreal Maroons 3 goals, Ottawa 1 goal (2-game series); N.Y. Rangers 6 goals, Pittsburgh 4 goals (2-game series). **Semifinals:** Montreal Maroons 3 goals, Montreal Canadiens 2 goals (2-game series); N.Y. Rangers 5 goals, Boston 2 goals (2-game series).

Stanley Cup finals: N.Y. Rangers 3, Montreal Maroons 2.

1928-29

AMERICAN DIVISION

Team	W	L	T	Pts.	GF	GA
Boston Bruins	26	13	5	57	89	52
New York Rangers	21	13	10	52	72	65
Detroit Cougars	19	16	9	47	72	63
Pittsburgh Pirates	9	27	8	26	46	80
Chicago Blackhawks	7	29	8	22	33	85

CANADIAN DIVISION

Team	W	L	T	Pts.	GF	GA
Montreal Canadiens	22	7	15	59	71	43
New York Americans	19	13	12	50	53	53
Toronto Maple Leafs	21	18	5	47	85	69
Ottawa Senators	14	17	13	41	54	67
Montreal Maroons	15	20	9	39	67	65

PLAYOFFS

League quarterfinals: N.Y. Rangers 1 goal, N.Y. Americans 0 goals (2-game series); Toronto 7 goals, Detroit 2 goals (2-game series). **Semifinals:** Boston 3, Montreal Canadiens 0; N.Y. Rangers 2, Toronto 0.

Stanley Cup finals: Boston 2, N.Y. Rangers 0.

1929-30

AMERICAN DIVISION

Team	W	L	T	Pts.	GF	GA
Boston Bruins	38	5	1	77	179	98
Chicago Blackhawks	21	18	5	47	117	111
New York Rangers	17	17	10	44	136	143
Detroit Cougars	14	24	6	34	117	133
Pittsburgh Pirates	5	36	3	13	102	185

CANADIAN DIVISION

Team	W	L	T	Pts.	GF	GA
Montreal Maroons	23	16	5	51	141	114
Montreal Canadiens	21	14	9	51	142	114
Ottawa Senators	21	15	8	50	138	118
Toronto Maple Leafs	17	21	6	40	116	124
New York Americans	14	25	5	33	113	161

PLAYOFFS

League quarterfinals: Montreal Canadiens 3 goals, Chicago 2 goals (2-game series); N.Y. Rangers 6 goals, Ottawa 3 goals (2-game series). **Semifinals:** Boston 3, Montreal Maroons 1; Montreal Canadiens 2, N.Y. Rangers 0.

Stanley Cup finals: Montreal Canadiens 2, Boston 0.

1930-31

AMERICAN DIVISION

Team	W	L	T	Pts.	GF	GA
Boston Bruins	28	10	6	62	143	90
Chicago Blackhawks	24	17	3	51	108	78
New York Rangers	19	16	9	47	106	87
Detroit Falcons	16	21	7	39	102	105
Philadelphia Quakers	4	36	4	12	76	184

CANADIAN DIVISION

Team	W	L	T	Pts.	GF	GA
Montreal Canadiens	26	10	8	60	129	89
Toronto Maple Leafs	22	13	9	53	118	99
Montreal Maroons	20	18	6	46	105	106
New York Americans	18	16	10	46	76	74
Ottawa Senators	10	30	4	24	91	142

PLAYOFFS

League quarterfinals: Chicago 4 goals, Toronto 3 goals (2-game series); N.Y. Rangers 8 goals, Montreal Maroons 1 goal (2-game series). **Semifinals:** Montreal Canadiens 3, Boston 2; Chicago 3 goals, N.Y. Rangers 0 goals (2-game series).

Stanley Cup finals: Montreal Canadiens 3, Chicago 2.

1931-32

AMERICAN DIVISION

Team	W	L	T	Pts.	GF	GA
New York Rangers	23	17	8	54	134	112
Chicago Blackhawks	18	19	11	47	86	101
Detroit Falcons	18	20	10	46	95	108
Boston Bruins	15	21	12	42	122	117

CANADIAN DIVISION

Team	W	L	T	Pts.	GF	GA
Montreal Canadiens	25	16	7	57	128	111
Toronto Maple Leafs	23	18	7	53	155	127
Montreal Maroons	19	22	7	45	142	139
New York Americans	16	24	8	40	95	142

PLAYOFFS

League quarterfinals: Toronto 6 goals, Chicago 2 goals (2-game series); Montreal Maroons 3 goals, Detroit 1 goal (2-game series). **Semifinals:** N.Y. Rangers 3, Montreal Canadiens 1; Toronto 4 goals, Montreal Maroons 3 (2-game series).

Stanley Cup finals: Toronto 3, N.Y. Rangers 0.

1932-33

AMERICAN DIVISION

Team	W	L	T	Pts.	GF	GA
Boston Bruins	25	15	8	58	124	88
Detroit Red Wings	25	15	8	58	111	93
New York Rangers	23	17	8	54	135	107
Chicago Blackhawks	16	20	12	44	88	101

CANADIAN DIVISION

Team	W	L	T	Pts.	GF	GA
Toronto Maple Leafs	24	18	6	54	119	111
Montreal Maroons	22	20	6	50	135	119
Montreal Canadiens	18	25	5	41	92	115
New York Americans	15	22	11	41	91	118
Ottawa Senators	11	27	10	32	88	131

PLAYOFFS

League quarterfinals: Detroit 5 goals, Montreal Maroons 2 goals (2-game series); N.Y. Rangers 8 goals, Montreal Canadiens 5 goals (2-game series). **Semifinals:** Toronto 3, Boston 2; N.Y. Rangers 6 goals, Detroit 3 goals (2-game series).

Stanley Cup finals: N.Y. Rangers 3, Toronto 1.

1933-34

AMERICAN DIVISION

Team	W	L	T	Pts.	GF	GA
Detroit Red Wings	24	14	10	58	113	98
Chicago Blackhawks	20	17	11	51	88	83
New York Rangers	21	19	8	50	120	113
Boston Bruins	18	25	5	41	111	130

CANADIAN DIVISION

Team	W	L	T	Pts.	GF	GA
Toronto Maple Leafs	26	13	9	61	174	119
Montreal Canadiens	22	20	6	50	99	101
Montreal Maroons	19	18	11	49	117	122
New York Americans	15	23	10	40	104	132
Ottawa Senators	13	29	6	32	115	143

PLAYOFFS

League quarterfinals: Chicago 4 goals, Montreal Canadiens 3 goals (2-game series); Montreal Maroons 2 goals, N.Y. Rangers 1 goal (2-game series). **Semifinals:** Detroit 3, Toronto 2; Chicago 6 goals, Montreal Maroons 2 goals (2-game series).

Stanley Cup finals: Chicago 3, Detroit 1.

1934-35

AMERICAN DIVISION

Team	W	L	T	Pts.	GF	GA
Boston Bruins	26	16	6	58	129	112
Chicago Blackhawks	26	17	5	57	118	88
New York Rangers	22	20	6	50	137	139
Detroit Red Wings	19	22	7	45	127	114

CANADIAN DIVISION

Team	W	L	T	Pts.	GF	GA
Toronto Maple Leafs	30	14	4	64	157	111
Montreal Maroons	24	19	5	53	123	92
Montreal Canadiens	19	23	6	44	110	145
New York Americans	12	27	9	33	100	142
St. Louis Eagles	11	31	6	28	86	144

PLAYOFFS

League quarterfinals: Montreal Maroons 1 goal, Chicago 0 goals (2-game series); N.Y. Rangers 6 goals, Montreal Canadiens 5 goals (2-game series). **Semifinals:** Toronto 3, Boston 1; Montreal Maroons 5 goals, N.Y. Rangers 4 (2-game series).

Stanley Cup finals: Montreal Maroons 3, Toronto 0.

1935-36

AMERICAN DIVISION

Team	W	L	T	Pts.	GF	GA
Detroit Red Wings	24	16	8	56	124	103
Boston Bruins	22	20	6	50	92	83
Chicago Blackhawks	21	19	8	50	93	92
New York Rangers	19	17	12	50	91	96

CANADIAN DIVISION

Team	W	L	T	Pts.	GF	GA
Montreal Maroons	22	16	10	54	114	106
Toronto Maple Leafs	23	19	6	52	126	106
New York Americans	16	25	7	39	109	122
Montreal Canadiens	11	26	11	33	82	123

PLAYOFFS

League quarterfinals: Toronto 8 goals, Boston 6 goals (2-game series); N.Y. Americans 7 goals, Chicago 5 goals (2-game series). **Semifinals:** Detroit 3, Montreal Maroons 0; Toronto 2, N.Y. Americans 1.

Stanley Cup finals: Detroit 3, Toronto 1.

1936-37

AMERICAN DIVISION

Team	W	L	T	Pts.	GF	GA
Detroit Red Wings	25	14	9	59	128	102
Boston Bruins	23	18	7	53	120	110
New York Rangers	19	20	9	47	117	106
Chicago Blackhawks	14	27	7	35	99	131

CANADIAN DIVISION

Team	W	L	T	Pts.	GF	GA
Montreal Canadiens	24	18	6	54	115	111
Montreal Maroons	22	17	9	53	126	110
Toronto Maple Leafs	22	21	5	49	119	115
New York Americans	15	29	4	34	122	161

PLAYOFFS

League quarterfinals: Montreal Maroons 2, Boston 1; N.Y. Rangers 2, Toronto 0. **Semifinals:** Detroit 3, Montreal Canadiens 2; N.Y. Rangers 2, Montreal Maroons 0.

Stanley Cup finals: Detroit 3, N.Y. Rangers 2.

1937-38

AMERICAN DIVISION

Team	W	L	T	Pts.	GF	GA
Boston Bruins	30	11	7	67	142	89
New York Rangers	27	15	6	60	149	96
Chicago Blackhawks	14	25	9	37	97	139
Detroit Red Wings	12	25	11	35	99	133

CANADIAN DIVISION

Team	W	L	T	Pts.	GF	GA
Toronto Maple Leafs	24	15	9	57	151	127
New York Americans	19	18	11	49	110	111
Montreal Canadiens	18	17	13	49	123	128
Montreal Maroons	12	30	6	30	101	149

PLAYOFFS

League quarterfinals: N.Y. Americans 2, N.Y. Rangers 1; Chicago 2, Montreal Canadiens 1. **Semifinals:** Toronto 3, Boston 0; Chicago 2, N.Y. Americans 1.

Stanley Cup finals: Chicago 3, Toronto 1.

1938-39

Team	W	L	T	Pts.	GF	GA
Boston Bruins	36	10	2	74	156	76
New York Rangers	26	16	6	58	149	105
Toronto Maple Leafs	19	20	9	47	114	107
New York Americans	17	21	10	44	119	157
Detroit Red Wings	18	24	6	42	107	128
Montreal Canadiens	15	24	9	39	115	146
Chicago Blackhawks	12	28	8	32	91	132

PLAYOFFS

League quarterfinals: Toronto 2, N.Y. Americans 0; Detroit 2, Montreal 1. **Semifinals:** Boston 4, N.Y. Rangers 3; Toronto 2, Detroit 1.

Stanley Cup finals: Boston 4, Toronto 1.

1939-40

Team	W	L	T	Pts.	GF	GA
Boston Bruins	31	12	5	67	170	98
New York Rangers	27	11	10	64	136	77
Toronto Maple Leafs	25	17	6	56	134	110
Chicago Blackhawks	23	19	6	52	112	120
Detroit Red Wings	16	26	6	38	90	126
New York Americans	15	29	4	34	106	140
Montreal Canadiens	10	33	5	25	90	168

PLAYOFFS

League quarterfinals: Toronto 2, Chicago 0; Detroit 2, N.Y. Americans 1. **Semifinals:** N.Y. Rangers 4, Boston 2; Toronto 2, Detroit 0.

Stanley Cup finals: N.Y. Rangers 4, Toronto 2.

1940-41

Team	W	L	T	Pts.	GF	GA
Boston Bruins	27	8	13	67	168	102
Toronto Maple Leafs	28	14	6	62	145	99
Detroit Red Wings	21	16	11	53	112	102
New York Rangers	21	19	8	50	143	125
Chicago Blackhawks	16	25	7	39	112	139
Montreal Canadiens	16	26	6	38	121	147
New York Americans	8	29	11	27	99	186

PLAYOFFS

League quarterfinals: Detroit 2, N.Y. Rangers 1; Chicago 2, Montreal 1. **Semifinals:** Boston 4, Toronto 3; Detroit 2, Chicago 0.

Stanley Cup finals: Boston 4, Detroit 0.

1941-42

Team	W	L	T	Pts.	GF	GA
New York Rangers	29	17	2	60	177	143
Toronto Maple Leafs	27	18	3	57	158	136
Boston Bruins	25	17	6	56	160	118
Chicago Blackhawks	22	23	3	47	145	155
Detroit Red Wings	19	25	4	42	140	147
Montreal Canadiens	18	27	3	39	134	173
Brooklyn Americans	16	29	3	35	133	175

PLAYOFFS

League quarterfinals: Boston 2, Chicago 1; Detroit 2, Montreal 1. **Semifinals:** Toronto 4, New York 2; Detroit 2, Boston 0.

Stanley Cup finals: Toronto 4, Detroit 3.

1942-43

Team	W	L	T	Pts.	GF	GA
Detroit Red Wings	25	14	11	61	169	124
Boston Bruins	24	17	9	57	195	176
Toronto Maple Leafs	22	19	9	53	198	159
Montreal Canadiens	19	19	12	50	181	191
Chicago Blackhawks	17	18	15	49	179	180
New York Rangers	11	31	8	30	161	253

PLAYOFFS

League semifinals: Detroit 4, Toronto 2; Boston 4, Montreal 1.

Stanley Cup finals: Detroit 4, Boston 0.

1943-44

Team	W	L	T	Pts.	GF	GA
Montreal Canadiens	38	5	7	83	234	109
Detroit Red Wings	26	18	6	58	214	177
Toronto Maple Leafs	23	23	4	50	214	174
Chicago Blackhawks	22	23	5	49	178	187
Boston Bruins	19	26	5	43	223	268
New York Rangers	6	39	5	17	162	310

PLAYOFFS

League semifinals: Montreal 4, Toronto 1; Chicago 4, Detroit 1.

Stanley Cup finals: Montreal 4, Chicago 0.

1944-45

Team	W	L	T	Pts.	GF	GA
Montreal Canadiens	38	8	4	80	228	121
Detroit Red Wings	31	14	5	67	218	161
Toronto Maple Leafs	24	22	4	52	183	161
Boston Bruins	16	30	4	36	179	219
Chicago Blackhawks	13	30	7	33	141	194
New York Rangers	11	29	10	32	154	247

PLAYOFFS

League semifinals: Toronto 4, Montreal 2; Detroit 4, Boston 3.

Stanley Cup finals: Toronto 4, Detroit 3.

1945-46

Team	W	L	T	Pts.	GF	GA
Montreal Canadiens	28	17	5	61	172	134
Boston Bruins	24	18	8	56	167	156
Chicago Blackhawks	23	20	7	53	200	178
Detroit Red Wings	20	20	10	50	146	159
Toronto Maple Leafs	19	24	7	45	174	185
New York Rangers	13	28	9	35	144	191

PLAYOFFS

League semifinals: Montreal 4, Chicago 0; Boston 4, Detroit 1.

Stanley Cup finals: Montreal 4, Boston 1.

1946-47

Team	W	L	T	Pts.	GF	GA
Montreal Canadiens	34	16	10	78	189	138
Toronto Maple Leafs	31	19	10	72	209	172
Boston Bruins	26	23	11	63	190	175
Detroit Red Wings	22	27	11	55	190	193
New York Rangers	22	32	6	50	167	186
Chicago Blackhawks	19	37	4	42	193	274

PLAYOFFS

League semifinals: Montreal 4, Boston 1; Toronto 4, Detroit 1.

Stanley Cup finals: Toronto 4, Montreal 2.

1947-48

Team	W	L	T	Pts.	GF	GA
Toronto Maple Leafs	32	15	13	77	182	143
Detroit Red Wings	30	18	12	72	187	148
Boston Bruins	23	24	13	59	167	168
New York Rangers	21	26	13	55	176	201
Montreal Canadiens	20	29	11	51	147	169
Chicago Blackhawks	20	34	6	46	195	225

PLAYOFFS

League semifinals: Toronto 4, Boston 1; Detroit 4, New York 2.

Stanley Cup finals: Toronto 4, Detroit 0.

1948-49

Team	W	L	T	Pts.	GF	GA
Detroit Red Wings	34	19	7	75	195	145
Boston Bruins	29	23	8	66	178	163
Montreal Canadiens	28	23	9	65	152	126
Toronto Maple Leafs	22	25	13	57	147	161
Chicago Blackhawks	21	31	8	50	173	211
New York Rangers	18	31	11	47	133	172

PLAYOFFS

League semifinals: Detroit 4, Montreal 3; Toronto 4, Boston 1.
Stanley Cup finals: Toronto 4, Detroit 0.

1949-50

Team	W	L	T	Pts.	GF	GA
Detroit Red Wings	37	19	14	88	229	164
Montreal Canadiens	29	22	19	77	172	150
Toronto Maple Leafs	31	27	12	74	176	173
New York Rangers	28	31	11	67	170	189
Boston Bruins	22	32	16	60	198	228
Chicago Blackhawks	22	38	10	54	203	244

PLAYOFFS

League semifinals: Detroit 4, Toronto 3; New York 4, Montreal 1.
Stanley Cup finals: Detroit 4, New York 3.

1950-51

Team	W	L	T	Pts.	GF	GA
Detroit Red Wings	44	13	13	101	236	139
Toronto Maple Leafs	41	16	13	95	212	138
Montreal Canadiens	25	30	15	65	173	184
Boston Bruins	22	30	18	62	178	197
New York Rangers	20	29	21	61	169	201
Chicago Blackhawks	13	47	10	36	171	280

PLAYOFFS

League semifinals: Montreal 4, Detroit 2; Toronto 4, Boston 1.
Stanley Cup finals: Toronto 4, Montreal 1.

1951-52

Team	W	L	T	Pts.	GF	GA
Detroit Red Wings	44	14	12	100	215	133
Montreal Canadiens	34	26	10	78	195	164
Toronto Maple Leafs	29	25	16	74	168	157
Boston Bruins	25	29	16	66	162	176
New York Rangers	23	34	13	59	192	219
Chicago Blackhawks	17	44	9	43	158	241

PLAYOFFS

League semifinals: Detroit 4, Toronto 0; Montreal 4, Boston 3.
Stanley Cup finals: Detroit 4, Montreal 0.

1952-53

Team	W	L	T	Pts.	GF	GA
Detroit Red Wings	36	16	18	90	222	133
Montreal Canadiens	28	23	19	75	155	148
Boston Bruins	28	29	13	69	152	172
Chicago Blackhawks	27	28	15	69	169	175
Toronto Maple Leafs	27	30	13	67	156	167
New York Rangers	17	37	16	50	152	211

PLAYOFFS

League semifinals: Boston 4, Detroit 2; Montreal 4, Chicago 3.
Stanley Cup finals: Montreal 4, Boston 1.

1953-54

Team	W	L	T	Pts.	GF	GA
Detroit Red Wings	37	19	14	88	191	132
Montreal Canadiens	35	24	11	81	195	141
Toronto Maple Leafs	32	24	14	78	152	131
Boston Bruins	32	28	10	74	177	181
New York Rangers	29	31	10	68	161	182
Chicago Blackhawks	12	51	7	31	133	242

PLAYOFFS

League semifinals: Detroit 4, Toronto 1; Montreal 4, Boston 0.
Stanley Cup finals: Detroit 4, Montreal 3.

1954-55

Team	W	L	T	Pts.	GF	GA
Detroit Red Wings	42	17	11	95	204	134
Montreal Canadiens	41	18	11	93	228	157
Toronto Maple Leafs	24	24	22	70	147	135
Boston Bruins	23	26	21	67	169	188
New York Rangers	17	35	18	52	150	210
Chicago Blackhawks	13	40	17	43	161	235

PLAYOFFS

League semifinals: Detroit 4, Toronto 0; Montreal 4, Boston 1.
Stanley Cup finals: Detroit 4, Montreal 3.

1955-56

Team	W	L	T	Pts.	GF	GA
Montreal Canadiens	45	15	10	100	222	131
Detroit Red Wings	30	24	16	76	183	148
New York Rangers	32	28	10	74	204	203
Toronto Maple Leafs	24	33	13	61	153	181
Boston Bruins	23	34	13	59	147	185
Chicago Blackhawks	19	39	12	50	155	216

PLAYOFFS

League semifinals: Montreal 4, New York 1; Detroit 4, Toronto 1.
Stanley Cup finals: Montreal 4, Detroit 1.

1956-57

Team	W	L	T	Pts.	GF	GA
Detroit Red Wings	38	20	12	88	198	157
Montreal Canadiens	35	23	12	82	210	155
Boston Bruins	34	24	12	80	195	174
New York Rangers	26	30	14	66	184	227
Toronto Maple Leafs	21	34	15	57	174	192
Chicago Blackhawks	16	39	15	47	169	225

PLAYOFFS

League semifinals: Boston 4, Detroit 1; Montreal 4, New York 1.
Stanley Cup finals: Montreal 4, Boston 1.

1957-58

Team	W	L	T	Pts.	GF	GA
Montreal Canadiens	43	17	10	96	250	158
New York Rangers	32	25	13	77	195	188
Detroit Red Wings	29	29	12	70	176	207
Boston Bruins	27	28	15	69	199	194
Chicago Blackhawks	24	39	7	55	163	202
Toronto Maple Leafs	21	38	11	53	192	226

PLAYOFFS

League semifinals: Montreal 4, Detroit 0; Boston 4, New York 2.
Stanley Cup finals: Montreal 4, Boston 2.

1958-59

Team	W	L	T	Pts.	GF	GA
Montreal Canadiens	39	18	13	91	258	158
Boston Bruins	32	29	9	73	205	215
Chicago Blackhawks	28	29	13	69	197	208
Toronto Maple Leafs	27	32	11	65	189	201
New York Rangers	26	32	12	64	201	217
Detroit Red Wings	25	37	8	58	167	218

PLAYOFFS

League semifinals: Montreal 4, Chicago 2; Toronto 4, Boston 3.
Stanley Cup finals: Montreal 4, Toronto 1.

1959-60

Team	W	L	T	Pts.	GF	GA
Montreal Canadiens	40	18	12	92	255	178
Toronto Maple Leafs	35	26	9	79	199	195
Chicago Blackhawks	28	29	13	69	191	180
Detroit Red Wings	26	29	15	67	186	197
Boston Bruins	28	34	8	64	220	241
New York Rangers	17	38	15	49	187	247

PLAYOFFS

League semifinals: Montreal 4, Chicago 0; Toronto 4, Detroit 2.
Stanley Cup finals: Montreal 4, Toronto 0.

1960-61

Team	W	L	T	Pts.	GF	GA
Montreal Canadiens	41	19	10	92	254	188
Toronto Maple Leafs	39	19	12	90	234	176
Chicago Blackhawks	29	24	17	75	198	180
Detroit Red Wings	25	29	16	66	195	215
New York Rangers	22	38	10	54	204	248
Boston Bruins	15	42	13	43	176	254

PLAYOFFS

League semifinals: Chicago 4, Montreal 2; Detroit 4, Toronto 1.
Stanley Cup finals: Chicago 4, Detroit 2.

1961-62

Team	W	L	T	Pts.	GF	GA
Montreal Canadiens	42	14	14	98	259	166
Toronto Maple Leafs	37	22	11	85	232	180
Chicago Blackhawks	31	26	13	75	217	186
New York Rangers	26	32	12	64	195	207
Detroit Red Wings	23	33	14	60	184	219
Boston Bruins	15	47	8	38	177	306

PLAYOFFS

League semifinals: Chicago 4, Montreal 2; Toronto 4, New York 2.
Stanley Cup finals: Toronto 4, Chicago 2.

1962-63

Team	W	L	T	Pts.	GF	GA
Toronto Maple Leafs	35	23	12	82	221	180
Chicago Blackhawks	32	21	17	81	194	178
Montreal Canadiens	28	19	23	79	225	183
Detroit Red Wings	32	25	13	77	200	194
New York Rangers	22	36	12	56	211	233
Boston Bruins	14	39	17	45	198	281

PLAYOFFS

League semifinals: Toronto 4, Montreal 1; Detroit 4, Chicago 2.
Stanley Cup finals: Toronto 4, Detroit 1.

1963-64

Team	W	L	T	Pts.	GF	GA
Montreal Canadiens	36	21	13	85	209	167
Chicago Blackhawks	36	22	12	84	218	169
Toronto Maple Leafs	33	25	12	78	192	172
Detroit Red Wings	30	29	11	71	191	204
New York Rangers	22	38	10	54	186	242
Boston Bruins	18	40	12	48	170	212

PLAYOFFS

League semifinals: Toronto 4, Montreal 3; Detroit 4, Chicago 3.
Stanley Cup finals: Toronto 4, Detroit 3.

1964-65

Team	W	L	T	Pts.	GF	GA
Detroit Red Wings	40	23	7	87	224	175
Montreal Canadiens	36	23	11	83	211	185
Chicago Blackhawks	34	28	8	76	224	176
Toronto Maple Leafs	30	26	14	74	204	173
New York Rangers	20	38	12	52	179	246
Boston Bruins	21	43	6	48	166	253

PLAYOFFS

League semifinals: Chicago 4, Detroit 3; Montreal 4, Toronto 2.
Stanley Cup finals: Montreal 4, Chicago 3.

1965-66

Team	W	L	T	Pts.	GF	GA
Montreal Canadiens	41	21	8	90	239	173
Chicago Blackhawks	37	25	8	82	240	187
Toronto Maple Leafs	34	25	11	79	208	187
Detroit Red Wings	31	27	12	74	221	194
Boston Bruins	21	43	6	48	174	275
New York Rangers	18	41	11	47	195	261

PLAYOFFS

League semifinals: Montreal 4, Toronto 0; Detroit 4, Chicago 2.
Stanley Cup finals: Montreal 4, Detroit 2.

1966-67

Team	W	L	T	Pts.	GF	GA
Chicago Blackhawks	41	17	12	94	264	170
Montreal Canadiens	32	25	13	77	202	188
Toronto Maple Leafs	32	27	11	75	204	211
New York Rangers	30	28	12	72	188	189
Detroit Red Wings	27	39	4	58	212	241
Boston Bruins	17	43	10	44	182	253

PLAYOFFS

League semifinals: Toronto 4, Chicago 2; Montreal 4, New York 0.
Stanley Cup finals: Toronto 4, Montreal 2.

1967-68

EAST DIVISION

Team	W	L	T	Pts.	GF	GA
Montreal Canadiens	42	22	10	94	236	167
New York Rangers	39	23	12	90	226	183
Boston Bruins	37	27	10	84	259	216
Chicago Blackhawks	32	26	16	80	212	222
Toronto Maple Leafs	33	31	10	76	209	176
Detroit Red Wings	27	35	12	66	245	257

WEST DIVISION

Team	W	L	T	Pts.	GF	GA
Philadelphia Flyers	31	32	11	73	173	179
Los Angeles Kings	31	33	10	72	200	224

Team	W	L	T	Pts.	GF	GA
St. Louis Blues	27	31	16	70	177	191
Minnesota North Stars	27	32	15	69	191	226
Pittsburgh Penguins	27	34	13	67	195	216
Oakland Seals	15	42	17	47	153	219

PLAYOFFS

Division semifinals: Montreal 4, Boston 0; Chicago 4, New York 2; St. Louis 4, Philadelphia 3; Minnesota 4, Los Angeles 3. **Division finals:** Montreal 4, Chicago 1; St. Louis 4, Minnesota 3.

Stanley Cup finals: Montreal 4, St. Louis 0.

1968-69

EAST DIVISION

Team	W	L	T	Pts.	GF	GA
Montreal Canadiens	46	19	11	103	271	202
Boston Bruins	42	18	16	100	303	221
New York Rangers	41	26	9	91	231	196
Toronto Maple Leafs	35	26	15	85	234	217
Detroit Red Wings	33	31	12	78	239	221
Chicago Blackhawks	34	33	9	77	280	246

WEST DIVISION

Team	W	L	T	Pts.	GF	GA
St. Louis Blues	37	25	14	88	204	157
Oakland Seals	29	36	11	69	219	251
Philadelphia Flyers	20	35	21	61	174	225
Los Angeles Kings	24	42	10	58	185	260
Pittsburgh Penguins	20	45	11	51	189	252
Minnesota North Stars	18	43	15	51	189	270

PLAYOFFS

Division semifinals: Montreal 4, New York 0; Boston 4, Toronto 0; St. Louis 4, Philadelphia 0; Los Angeles 4, Oakland 3. **Division finals:** Montreal 4, Boston 2; St. Louis 4, Los Angeles 0.

Stanley Cup finals: Montreal 4, St. Louis 0.

1969-70

EAST DIVISION

Team	W	L	T	Pts.	GF	GA
Chicago Blackhawks	45	22	9	99	250	170
Boston Bruins	40	17	19	99	277	216
Detroit Red Wings	40	21	15	95	246	199
New York Rangers	38	22	16	92	246	189
Montreal Canadiens	38	22	16	92	244	201
Toronto Maple Leafs	29	34	13	71	222	242

WEST DIVISION

Team	W	L	T	Pts.	GF	GA
St. Louis Blues	37	27	12	86	224	179
Pittsburgh Penguins	26	38	12	64	182	238
Minnesota North Stars	19	35	22	60	224	257
Oakland Seals	22	40	14	58	169	243
Philadelphia Flyers	17	35	24	58	197	225
Los Angeles Kings	14	52	10	38	168	290

PLAYOFFS

Division semifinals: Chicago 4, Detroit 0; Boston 4, N.Y. Rangers 2; St. Louis 4, Minnesota 2; Pittsburgh 4, Oakland 0. **Division finals:** Boston 4, Chicago 0; St. Louis 4, Pittsburgh 2.

Stanley Cup finals: Boston 4, St. Louis 0.

1970-71

EAST DIVISION

Team	W	L	T	Pts.	GF	GA
Boston Bruins	57	14	7	121	399	207
New York Rangers	49	18	11	109	259	177
Montreal Canadiens	42	23	13	97	291	216
Toronto Maple Leafs	37	33	8	82	248	211
Buffalo Sabres	24	39	15	63	217	291
Vancouver Canucks	24	46	8	56	229	296
Detroit Red Wings	22	45	11	55	209	308

WEST DIVISION

Team	W	L	T	Pts.	GF	GA
Chicago Blackhawks	49	20	9	107	277	184
St. Louis Blues	34	25	19	87	223	208
Philadelphia Flyers	28	33	17	73	207	225
Minnesota North Stars	28	34	16	72	191	223
Los Angeles Kings	25	40	13	63	239	303
Pittsburgh Penguins	21	37	20	62	221	240
California Golden Seals	20	53	5	45	199	320

PLAYOFFS

Division semifinals: Montreal 4, Boston 3; N.Y Rangers 4, Toronto 2; Chicago 4, Philadelphia 0; Minnesota 4, St. Louis 2. **Division finals:** Montreal 4, Minnesota 2; Chicago 4, N.Y. Rangers 3.

Stanley Cup finals: Montreal 4, Chicago 3.

1971-72

EAST DIVISION

Team	W	L	T	Pts.	GF	GA
Boston Bruins	54	13	11	119	330	204
New York Rangers	48	17	13	109	317	192
Montreal Canadiens	46	16	16	108	307	205
Toronto Maple Leafs	33	31	14	80	209	208
Detroit Red Wings	33	35	10	76	261	262
Buffalo Sabres	16	43	19	51	203	289
Vancouver Canucks	20	50	8	48	203	297

WEST DIVISION

Team	W	L	T	Pts.	GF	GA
Chicago Blackhawks	46	17	15	107	256	166
Minnesota North Stars	37	29	12	86	212	191
St. Louis Blues	28	39	11	67	208	247
Pittsburgh Penguins	26	38	14	66	220	258
Philadelphia Flyers	26	38	14	66	200	236
California Golden Seals	21	39	18	60	216	288
Los Angeles Kings	20	49	9	49	206	305

PLAYOFFS

Division semifinals: Boston 4, Toronto 1; N.Y. Rangers 4, Montreal 2; Chicago 4, Pittsburgh 0; St. Louis 4, Minnesota 3. **Division finals:** N.Y. Rangers 4, Chicago 0; Boston 4, St. Louis 0.

Stanley Cup finals: Boston 4, N.Y. Rangers 2.

1972-73

EAST DIVISION

Team	W	L	T	Pts.	GF	GA
Montreal Canadiens	52	10	16	120	329	184
Boston Bruins	51	22	5	107	330	235
New York Rangers	47	23	8	102	297	208
Buffalo Sabres	37	27	14	88	257	219
Detroit Red Wings	37	29	12	86	265	243
Toronto Maple Leafs	27	41	10	64	247	279
Vancouver Canucks	22	47	9	53	233	339
New York Islanders	12	60	6	30	170	347

WEST DIVISION

Team	W	L	T	Pts.	GF	GA
Chicago Blackhawks	42	27	9	93	284	225
Philadelphia Flyers	37	30	11	85	296	256
Minnesota North Stars	37	30	11	85	254	230
St. Louis Blues	32	34	12	76	233	251
Pittsburgh Penguins	32	37	9	73	257	265

Team	W	L	T	Pts.	GF	GA
Los Angeles Kings	31	36	11	73	232	245
Atlanta Flames	25	38	15	65	191	239
California Golden Seals	16	46	16	48	213	323

PLAYOFFS

Division semifinals: Montreal 4, Buffalo 2; N.Y. Rangers 4, Boston 1; Chicago 4, St. Louis 1; Philadelphia 4, Minnesota 2. **Division finals:** Montreal 4, Philadelphia 1; Chicago 4, N.Y. Rangers 1.

Stanley Cup finals: Montreal 4, Chicago 2.

1973-74

EAST DIVISION

Team	W	L	T	Pts.	GF	GA
Boston Bruins	52	17	9	113	349	221
Montreal Canadiens	45	24	9	99	293	240
New York Rangers	40	24	14	94	300	251
Toronto Maple Leafs	35	27	16	86	274	230
Buffalo Sabres	32	34	12	76	242	250
Detroit Red Wings	29	39	10	68	255	319
Vancouver Canucks	24	43	11	59	224	296
New York Islanders	19	41	18	56	182	247

WEST DIVISION

Team	W	L	T	Pts.	GF	GA
Philadelphia Flyers	50	16	12	112	273	164
Chicago Blackhawks	41	14	23	105	272	164
Los Angeles Kings	33	33	12	78	233	231
Atlanta Flames	30	34	14	74	214	238
Pittsburgh Penguins	28	41	9	65	242	273
St. Louis Blues	26	40	12	64	206	248
Minnesota North Stars	23	38	17	63	235	275
California Golden Seals	13	55	10	36	195	342

PLAYOFFS

Division semifinals: Boston 4, Toronto 0; N.Y. Rangers 4, Montreal 2; Philadelphia 4, Atlanta 0; Chicago 4, Los Angeles 1. **Division finals:** Boston 4, Chicago 2; Philadelphia 4, N.Y. Rangers 3.

Stanley Cup finals: Philadelphia 4, Boston 2.

1974-75

PRINCE OF WALES CONFERENCE

ADAMS DIVISION

Team	W	L	T	Pts.	GF	GA
Buffalo Sabres	49	16	15	113	354	240
Boston Bruins	40	26	14	94	345	245
Toronto Maple Leafs	31	33	16	78	280	309
California Golden Seals	19	48	13	51	212	316

NORRIS DIVISION

Team	W	L	T	Pts.	GF	GA
Montreal Canadiens	47	14	19	113	374	225
Los Angeles Kings	42	17	21	105	269	185
Pittsburgh Penguins	37	28	15	89	326	289
Detroit Red Wings	23	45	12	58	259	335
Washington Capitals	8	67	5	21	181	446

CLARENCE CAMPBELL CONFERENCE

PATRICK DIVISION

Team	W	L	T	Pts.	GF	GA
Philadelphia Flyers	51	18	11	113	293	181
New York Rangers	37	29	14	88	319	276
New York Islanders	33	25	22	88	264	221
Atlanta Flames	34	31	15	83	243	233

SMYTHE DIVISION

Team	W	L	T	Pts.	GF	GA
Vancouver Canucks	38	32	10	86	271	254
St. Louis Blues	35	31	14	84	269	267
Chicago Blackhawks	37	35	8	82	268	241
Minnesota North Stars	23	50	7	53	221	341
Kansas City Scouts	15	54	11	41	184	328

PLAYOFFS

Preliminaries: Toronto 2, Los Angeles 1; Chicago 2, Boston 1; Pittsburgh 2, St. Louis 0; N.Y. Islanders 2, N.Y. Rangers 1. **Quarterfinals:** Philadelphia 4, Toronto 0; Buffalo 4, Chicago 1; Montreal 4, Vancouver 1; N.Y. Islanders 4, Pittsburgh 3. **Semifinals:** Philadelphia 4, N.Y. Islanders 3; Buffalo 4, Montreal 2.

Stanley Cup finals: Philadelphia 4, Buffalo 2.

1975-76

PRINCE OF WALES CONFERENCE

ADAMS DIVISION

Team	W	L	T	Pts.	GF	GA
Boston Bruins	48	15	17	113	313	237
Buffalo Sabres	46	21	13	105	339	240
Toronto Maple Leafs	34	31	15	83	294	276
California Golden Seals	27	42	11	65	250	278

NORRIS DIVISION

Team	W	L	T	Pts.	GF	GA
Montreal Canadiens	58	11	11	127	337	174
Los Angeles Kings	38	33	9	85	263	265
Pittsburgh Penguins	35	33	12	82	339	303
Detroit Red Wings	26	44	10	62	226	300
Washington Capitals	11	59	10	32	224	394

CLARENCE CAMPBELL CONFERENCE

PATRICK DIVISION

Team	W	L	T	Pts.	GF	GA
Philadelphia Flyers	51	13	16	118	348	209
New York Islanders	42	21	17	101	297	190
Atlanta Flames	35	33	12	82	262	237
New York Rangers	29	42	9	67	262	333

SMYTHE DIVISION

Team	W	L	T	Pts.	GF	GA
Chicago Blackhawks	32	30	18	82	254	261
Vancouver Canucks	33	32	15	81	271	272
St. Louis Blues	29	37	14	72	249	290
Minnesota North Stars	20	53	7	47	195	303
Kansas City Scouts	12	56	12	36	190	351

PLAYOFFS

Preliminaries: Buffalo 2, St. Louis 1; N.Y. Islanders 2, Vancouver 0; Los Angeles 2, Atlanta 0; Toronto 2, Pittsburgh 1. **Quarterfinals:** Montreal 4, Chicago 0; Philadelphia 4, Toronto 3; Boston 4, Los Angeles 3; N.Y. Islanders 4, Buffalo 2. **Semifinals:** Montreal 4, N.Y. Islanders 1; Philadelphia 4, Boston 1.

Stanley Cup finals: Montreal 4, Philadelphia 0.

1976-77

PRINCE OF WALES CONFERENCE

ADAMS DIVISION

Team	W	L	T	Pts.	GF	GA
Boston Bruins	49	23	8	106	312	240
Buffalo Sabres	48	24	8	104	301	220
Toronto Maple Leafs	33	32	15	81	301	285
Cleveland Barons	25	42	13	63	240	292

NORRIS DIVISION

Team	W	L	T	Pts.	GF	GA
Montreal Canadiens	60	8	12	132	387	171
Los Angeles Kings	34	31	15	83	271	241
Pittsburgh Penguins	34	33	13	81	240	252
Washington Capitals	24	42	14	62	221	307
Detroit Red Wings	16	55	9	41	183	309

CLARENCE CAMPBELL CONFERENCE

PATRICK DIVISION

Team	W	L	T	Pts.	GF	GA
Philadelphia Flyers	48	16	16	112	323	213
New York Islanders	47	21	12	106	288	193
Atlanta Flames	34	34	12	80	264	265
New York Rangers	29	37	14	72	272	310

SMYTHE DIVISION

Team	W	L	T	Pts.	GF	GA
St. Louis Blues	32	39	9	73	239	276
Minnesota North Stars	23	39	18	64	240	310
Chicago Blackhawks	26	43	11	63	240	298
Vancouver Canucks	25	42	13	63	235	294
Colorado Rockies	20	46	14	54	226	307

PLAYOFFS

Preliminaries: N.Y. Islanders 2, Chicago 0; Buffalo 2, Minnesota 0; Los Angeles 2, Atlanta 1; Toronto 2, Pittsburgh 1. **Quarterfinals:** Montreal 4, St. Louis 0; Philadelphia 4, Toronto 2; Boston 4, Los Angeles 2; N.Y. Islanders 4, Buffalo 0. **Semifinals:** Montreal 4, N.Y. Islanders 2; Boston 4, Philadelphia 0.

Stanley Cup finals: Montreal 4, Boston 0.

1977-78

PRINCE OF WALES CONFERENCE

ADAMS DIVISION

Team	W	L	T	Pts.	GF	GA
Boston Bruins	51	18	11	113	333	218
Buffalo Sabres	44	19	17	105	288	215
Toronto Maple Leafs	41	29	10	92	271	237
Cleveland Barons	22	45	13	57	230	325

NORRIS DIVISION

Team	W	L	T	Pts.	GF	GA
Montreal Canadiens	59	10	11	129	359	183
Detroit Red Wings	32	34	14	78	252	266
Los Angeles Kings	31	34	15	77	243	245
Pittsburgh Penguins	25	37	18	68	254	321
Washington Capitals	17	49	14	48	195	321

CLARENCE CAMPBELL CONFERENCE

PATRICK DIVISION

Team	W	L	T	Pts.	GF	GA
New York Islanders	48	17	15	111	334	210
Philadelphia Flyers	45	20	15	105	296	200
Atlanta Flames	34	27	19	87	274	252
New York Rangers	30	37	13	73	279	280

SMYTHE DIVISION

Team	W	L	T	Pts.	GF	GA
Chicago Blackhawks	32	29	19	83	230	220
Colorado Rockies	19	40	21	59	257	305
Vancouver Canucks	20	43	17	57	239	320
St. Louis Blues	20	47	13	53	195	304
Minnesota North Stars	18	53	9	45	218	325

PLAYOFFS

Preliminaries: Philadelphia 2, Colorado 0; Buffalo 2, N.Y. Rangers 1; Toronto 2, Los Angeles 0; Detroit 2, Atlanta 0. **Quarterfinals:** Montreal 4, Detroit 1; Boston 4, Chicago 0; Toronto 4, N.Y. Islanders 3; Philadelphia 4, Buffalo 1. **Semifinals:** Montreal 4, Toronto 0; Boston 4, Philadelphia 1.

Stanley Cup finals: Montreal 4, Boston 2.

1978-79

PRINCE OF WALES CONFERENCE

ADAMS DIVISION

Team	W	L	T	Pts.	GF	GA
Boston Bruins	43	23	14	100	316	270
Buffalo Sabres	36	28	16	88	280	263
Toronto Maple Leafs	34	33	13	81	267	252
Minnesota North Stars	28	40	12	68	257	289

NORRIS DIVISION

Team	W	L	T	Pts.	GF	GA
Montreal Canadiens	52	17	11	115	337	204
Pittsburgh Penguins	36	31	13	85	281	279
Los Angeles Kings	34	34	12	80	292	286
Washington Capitals	24	41	15	63	273	338
Detroit Red Wings	23	41	16	62	252	295

CLARENCE CAMPBELL CONFERENCE

PATRICK DIVISION

Team	W	L	T	Pts.	GF	GA
New York Islanders	51	15	14	116	358	214
Philadelphia Flyers	40	25	15	95	281	248
New York Rangers	40	29	11	91	316	292
Atlanta Flames	41	31	8	90	327	280

SMYTHE DIVISION

Team	W	L	T	Pts.	GF	GA
Chicago Blackhawks	29	36	15	73	244	277
Vancouver Canucks	25	42	13	63	217	291
St. Louis Blues	18	50	12	48	249	348
Colorado Rockies	15	53	12	42	210	331

PLAYOFFS

Preliminaries: Philadelphia 2, Vancouver 1; N.Y. Rangers 2, Los Angeles 0; Toronto 2, Atlanta 0; Pittsburgh 2, Buffalo 1. **Quarterfinals:** N.Y. Islanders 4, Chicago 0; Montreal 4, Toronto 0; Boston 4, Pittsburgh 0; N.Y. Rangers 4, Philadelphia 1. **Semifinals:** N.Y. Rangers 4, N.Y. Islanders 2; Montreal 4, Boston 3.

Stanley Cup finals: Montreal 4, N.Y. Rangers 1.

1979-80

PRINCE OF WALES CONFERENCE

ADAMS DIVISION

Team	W	L	T	Pts.	GF	GA
Buffalo Sabres	47	17	16	110	318	201
Boston Bruins	46	21	13	105	310	234
Minnesota North Stars	36	28	16	88	311	253
Toronto Maple Leafs	35	40	5	75	304	327
Quebec Nordiques	25	44	11	61	248	313

NORRIS DIVISION

Team	W	L	T	Pts.	GF	GA
Montreal Canadiens	47	20	13	107	328	240
Los Angeles Kings	30	36	14	74	290	313
Pittsburgh Penguins	30	37	13	73	251	303
Hartford Whalers	27	34	19	73	303	312
Detroit Red Wings	26	43	11	63	268	306

CLARENCE CAMPBELL CONFERENCE

PATRICK DIVISION

Team	W	L	T	Pts.	GF	GA
Philadelphia Flyers	48	12	20	116	327	254
New York Islanders	39	28	13	91	281	247

Team	W	L	T	Pts.	GF	GA
New York Rangers	38	32	10	86	308	284
Atlanta Flames	35	32	13	83	282	269
Washington Capitals	27	40	13	67	261	293

SMYTHE DIVISION

Team	W	L	T	Pts.	GF	GA
Chicago Blackhawks	34	27	19	87	241	250
St. Louis Blues	34	34	12	80	266	278
Vancouver Canucks	27	37	16	70	256	281
Edmonton Oilers	28	39	13	69	301	322
Winnipeg Jets	20	49	11	51	214	314
Colorado Rockies	19	48	13	51	234	308

PLAYOFFS

Preliminaries: Philadelphia 3, Edmonton 0; Buffalo 3, Vancouver 1; Montreal 3, Hartford 0; Boston 3, Pittsburgh 2; N.Y. Islanders 3, Los Angeles 1; Minnesota 3, Toronto 0; Chicago 3, St. Louis 0; N.Y. Rangers 3, Atlanta 1. **Quarterfinals:** Philadelphia 4, N.Y. Rangers 1; Buffalo 4, Chicago 0; Minnesota 4, Montreal 3; N.Y. Islanders 4, Boston 1. **Semifinals:** Philadelphia 4, Minnesota 1; N.Y. Islanders 4, Buffalo 2.

Stanley Cup finals: N.Y. Islanders 4, Philadelphia 2.

1980-81

PRINCE OF WALES CONFERENCE

ADAMS DIVISION

Team	W	L	T	Pts.	GF	GA
Buffalo Sabres	39	20	21	99	327	250
Boston Bruins	37	30	13	87	316	272
Minnesota North Stars	35	28	17	87	291	263
Quebec Nordiques	30	32	18	78	314	318
Toronto Maple Leafs	28	37	15	71	322	367

NORRIS DIVISION

Team	W	L	T	Pts.	GF	GA
Montreal Canadiens	45	22	13	103	332	232
Los Angeles Kings	43	24	13	99	337	290
Pittsburgh Penguins	30	37	13	73	302	345
Hartford Whalers	21	41	18	60	292	372
Detroit Red Wings	19	43	18	56	252	339

CLARENCE CAMPBELL CONFERENCE

PATRICK DIVISION

Team	W	L	T	Pts.	GF	GA
New York Islanders	48	18	14	110	355	260
Philadelphia Flyers	41	24	15	97	313	249
Calgary Flames	39	27	14	92	329	298
New York Rangers	30	36	14	74	312	317
Washington Capitals	26	36	18	70	286	317

SMYTHE DIVISION

Team	W	L	T	Pts.	GF	GA
St. Louis Blues	45	18	17	107	352	281
Chicago Blackhawks	31	33	16	78	304	315
Vancouver Canucks	28	32	20	76	289	301
Edmonton Oilers	29	35	16	74	328	327
Colorado Rockies	22	45	13	57	258	344
Winnipeg Jets	9	57	14	32	246	400

PLAYOFFS

Preliminaries: N.Y. Islanders 3, Toronto 0; St. Louis 3, Pittsburgh 2; Edmonton 3, Montreal 0; N.Y. Rangers 3, Los Angeles 1; Buffalo 3, Vancouver 0; Philadelphia 3, Quebec 2; Calgary 3, Chicago 0; Minnesota 3, Boston 0. **Quarterfinals:** N.Y. Islanders 4, Edmonton 2; N.Y. Rangers 4, St. Louis 2; Minnesota 4, Buffalo 1; Calgary 4, Philadelphia 3. **Semifinals:** N.Y. Islanders 4, N.Y. Rangers 0; Minnesota 4, Calgary 2.

Stanley Cup finals: N.Y. Islanders 4, Minnesota 1.

1981-82

PRINCE OF WALES CONFERENCE

ADAMS DIVISION

Team	W	L	T	Pts.	GF	GA
Montreal Canadiens	46	17	17	109	360	223
Boston Bruins	43	27	10	96	323	285
Buffalo Sabres	39	26	15	93	307	273
Quebec Nordiques	33	31	16	82	356	345
Hartford Whalers	21	41	18	60	264	351

PATRICK DIVISION

Team	W	L	T	Pts.	GF	GA
New York Islanders	54	16	10	118	385	250
New York Rangers	39	27	14	92	316	306
Philadelphia Flyers	38	31	11	87	325	313
Pittsburgh Penguins	31	36	13	75	310	337
Washington Capitals	26	41	13	65	319	338

CLARENCE CAMPBELL CONFERENCE

NORRIS DIVISION

Team	W	L	T	Pts.	GF	GA
Minnesota North Stars	37	23	20	94	346	288
Winnipeg Jets	33	33	14	80	319	332
St. Louis Blues	32	40	8	72	315	349
Chicago Blackhawks	30	38	12	72	332	363
Toronto Maple Leafs	20	44	16	56	298	380
Detroit Red Wings	21	47	12	54	270	351

SMYTHE DIVISION

Team	W	L	T	Pts.	GF	GA
Edmonton Oilers	48	17	15	111	417	295
Vancouver Canucks	30	33	17	77	290	286
Calgary Flames	29	34	17	75	334	345
Los Angeles Kings	24	41	15	63	314	369
Colorado Rockies	18	49	13	49	241	362

PLAYOFFS

Wales Conference division semifinals: Quebec 3, Montreal 2; Boston 3, Buffalo 1; N.Y. Islanders 3, Pittsburgh 2; N.Y. Rangers 3, Philadelphia 1. **Division finals:** Quebec 4, Boston 3; N.Y. Islanders 4, N.Y. Rangers 2. **Conference finals:** N.Y. Islanders 4, Quebec 0.

Campbell Conference division semifinals: Chicago 3, Minnesota 1; St. Louis 3, Winnipeg 1; Los Angeles 3, Edmonton 2; Vancouver 3, Calgary 0. **Division finals:** Chicago 4, St. Louis 2; Vancouver 4, Los Angeles 1. **Conference finals:** Vancouver 4, Chicago 1.

Stanley Cup finals: N.Y. Islanders 4, Vancouver 0.

1982-83

PRINCE OF WALES CONFERENCE

ADAMS DIVISION

Team	W	L	T	Pts.	GF	GA
Boston Bruins	50	20	10	110	327	228
Montreal Canadiens	42	24	14	98	350	286
Buffalo Sabres	38	29	13	89	318	285
Quebec Nordiques	34	34	12	80	343	336
Hartford Whalers	19	54	7	45	261	403

PATRICK DIVISION

Team	W	L	T	Pts.	GF	GA
Philadelphia Flyers	49	23	8	106	326	240
New York Islanders	42	26	12	96	302	226
Washington Capitals	39	25	16	94	306	283
New York Rangers	35	35	10	80	306	287
New Jersey Devils	17	49	14	48	230	338
Pittsburgh Penguins	18	53	9	45	257	394

CLARENCE CAMPBELL CONFERENCE

NORRIS DIVISION

Team	W	L	T	Pts.	GF	GA
Chicago Blackhawks	47	23	10	104	338	268
Minnesota North Stars	40	24	16	96	321	290
Toronto Maple Leafs	28	40	12	68	293	330
St. Louis Blues	25	40	15	65	285	316
Detroit Red Wings	21	44	15	57	263	344

SMYTHE DIVISION

Team	W	L	T	Pts.	GF	GA
Edmonton Oilers	47	21	12	106	424	315
Calgary Flames	32	34	14	78	321	317
Vancouver Canucks	30	35	15	75	303	309
Winnipeg Jets	33	39	8	74	311	333
Los Angeles Kings	27	41	12	66	308	365

PLAYOFFS

Wales Conference division semifinals: Boston 3, Quebec 1; Buffalo 3, Montreal 0; N.Y. Rangers 3, Philadelphia 0; N.Y. Islanders 3, Washington 1. **Division finals:** Boston 4, Buffalo 3; N.Y. Islanders 4, N.Y. Rangers 2. **Conference finals:** N.Y. Islanders 4, Boston 2.

Campbell Conference division semifinals: Chicago 3, St. Louis 1; Minnesota 3, Toronto 1; Edmonton 3, Winnipeg 0; Calgary 3, Vancouver 1. **Division finals:** Chicago 4, Minnesota 1; Edmonton 4, Calgary 1. **Conference finals:** Edmonton 4, Chicago 0.

Stanley Cup finals: N.Y. Islanders 4, Edmonton 0.

1983-84

PRINCE OF WALES CONFERENCE

ADAMS DIVISION

Team	W	L	T	Pts.	GF	GA
Boston Bruins	49	25	6	104	336	261
Buffalo Sabres	48	25	7	103	315	257
Quebec Nordiques	42	28	10	94	360	278
Montreal Canadiens	35	40	5	75	286	295
Hartford Whalers	28	42	10	66	288	320

PATRICK DIVISION

Team	W	L	T	Pts.	GF	GA
New York Islanders	50	26	4	104	357	269
Washington Capitals	48	27	5	101	308	226
Philadelphia Flyers	44	26	10	98	350	290
New York Rangers	42	29	9	93	314	304
New Jersey Devils	17	56	7	41	231	350
Pittsburgh Penguins	16	58	6	38	254	390

CLARENCE CAMPBELL CONFERENCE

NORRIS DIVISION

Team	W	L	T	Pts.	GF	GA
Minnesota North Stars	39	31	10	88	345	344
St. Louis Blues	32	41	7	71	293	316
Detroit Red Wings	31	42	7	69	298	323
Chicago Blackhawks	30	42	8	68	277	311
Toronto Maple Leafs	26	45	9	61	303	387

SMYTHE DIVISION

Team	W	L	T	Pts.	GF	GA
Edmonton Oilers	57	18	5	119	446	314
Calgary Flames	34	32	14	82	311	314
Vancouver Canucks	32	39	9	73	306	328
Winnipeg Jets	31	38	11	73	340	374
Los Angeles Kings	23	44	13	59	309	376

PLAYOFFS

Wales Conference division semifinals: Montreal 3, Boston 0; Quebec 3, Buffalo 0; N.Y. Islanders 3, N.Y. Rangers 2; Washington 3, Philadelphia 0. **Division finals:** Montreal 4, Quebec 2; N.Y. Islanders 4, Washington 1. **Conference finals:** N.Y. Islanders 4, Montreal 2.

Campbell Conference division semifinals: Minnesota 3, Chicago 2; St. Louis 3, Detroit 1; Edmonton 3, Winnipeg 0; Calgary 3, Vancouver 1. **Division finals:** Minnesota 4, St. Louis 3; Edmonton 4, Calgary 3. **Conference finals:** Edmonton 4, Minnesota 0.

Stanley Cup finals: Edmonton 4, N.Y. Islanders 1.

1984-85

PRINCE OF WALES CONFERENCE

ADAMS DIVISION

Team	W	L	T	Pts.	GF	GA
Montreal Canadiens	41	27	12	94	309	262
Quebec Nordiques	41	30	9	91	323	275
Buffalo Sabres	38	28	14	90	290	237
Boston Bruins	36	34	10	82	303	287
Hartford Whalers	30	41	9	69	268	318

PATRICK DIVISION

Team	W	L	T	Pts.	GF	GA
Philadelphia Flyers	53	20	7	113	348	241
Washington Capitals	46	25	9	101	322	240
New York Islanders	40	34	6	86	345	312
New York Rangers	26	44	10	62	295	345
New Jersey Devils	22	48	10	54	264	346
Pittsburgh Penguins	24	51	5	53	276	385

CLARENCE CAMPBELL CONFERENCE

NORRIS DIVISION

Team	W	L	T	Pts.	GF	GA
St. Louis Blues	37	31	12	86	299	288
Chicago Blackhawks	38	35	7	83	309	299
Detroit Red Wings	27	41	12	66	313	357
Minnesota North Stars	25	43	12	62	268	321
Toronto Maple Leafs	20	52	8	48	253	358

SMYTHE DIVISION

Team	W	L	T	Pts.	GF	GA
Edmonton Oilers	49	20	11	109	401	298
Winnipeg Jets	43	27	10	96	358	332
Calgary Flames	41	27	12	94	303	302
Los Angeles Kings	34	32	14	82	339	326
Vancouver Canucks	25	46	9	59	284	401

PLAYOFFS

Wales Conference division semifinals: Montreal 3, Boston 2; Quebec 3, Buffalo 2; Philadelphia 3, N.Y. Rangers 0; N.Y. Islanders 3, Washington 2. **Division finals:** Quebec 4, Montreal 3; Philadelphia 4, N.Y. Islanders 1. **Conference finals:** Philadelphia 4, Quebec 2.

Campbell Conference division semifinals: Minnesota 3, St. Louis 0; Chicago 3, Detroit 0; Edmonton 3, Los Angelse 0; Winnipeg 3, Calgary 1. **Division finals:** Chicago 4, Minnesota 2; Edmonton 4, Winnipeg 0. **Conference finals:** Edmonton 4, Chicago 2.

Stanley Cup finals: Edmonton 4, Philadelphia 1.

1985-86

PRINCE OF WALES CONFERENCE

ADAMS DIVISION

Team	W	L	T	Pts.	GF	GA
Quebec Nordiques	43	31	6	92	330	289
Montreal Canadiens	40	33	7	87	330	280
Boston Bruins	37	31	12	86	311	288
Hartford Whalers	40	36	4	84	332	302
Buffalo Sabres	37	37	6	80	296	291

PATRICK DIVISION

Team	W	L	T	Pts.	GF	GA
Philadelphia Flyers	53	23	4	110	335	241
Washington Capitals	50	23	7	107	315	272
New York Islanders	39	29	12	90	327	284
New York Rangers	36	38	6	78	280	276
Pittsburgh Penguins	34	38	8	76	313	305
New Jersey Devils	28	49	3	59	300	374

CLARENCE CAMPBELL CONFERENCE

NORRIS DIVISION

Team	W	L	T	Pts.	GF	GA
Chicago Blackhawks	39	33	8	86	351	349
Minnesota North Stars	38	33	9	85	327	305
St. Louis Blues	37	34	9	83	302	291
Toronto Maple Leafs	25	48	7	57	311	386
Detroit Red Wings	17	57	6	40	266	415

SMYTHE DIVISION

Team	W	L	T	Pts.	GF	GA
Edmonton Oilers	56	17	7	119	426	310
Calgary Flames	40	31	9	89	354	315
Winnipeg Jets	26	47	7	59	295	372
Vancouver Canucks	23	44	13	59	282	333
Los Angeles Kings	23	49	8	54	284	389

PLAYOFFS

Wales Conference division semifinals: Hartford 3, Quebec 0; Montreal 3, Boston 0; N.Y. Rangers 3, Philadelphia 2; Washington 3, N.Y. Islanders 0. **Division finals:** Montreal 4, Hartford 3; N.Y. Rangers 4, Washington 2. **Conference finals:** Montreal 4, N.Y. Rangers 1.

Campbell Conference division semifinals: Toronto 3, Chicago 0; St. Louis 3, Minnesota 2; Edmonton 3, Vancouver 0; Calgary 3, Winnipeg 0. **Division finals:** St. Louis 4, Toronto 3; Calgary 4, Edmonton 3. **Conference finals:** Calgary 4, St. Louis 3.

Stanley Cup finals: Montreal 4, Calgary 1.

1986-87

PRINCE OF WALES CONFERENCE

ADAMS DIVISION

Team	W	L	T	Pts.	GF	GA
Hartford Whalers	43	30	7	93	287	270
Montreal Canadiens	41	29	10	92	277	241
Boston Bruins	39	34	7	85	301	276
Quebec Nordiques	31	39	10	72	267	276
Buffalo Sabres	28	44	8	64	280	308

PATRICK DIVISION

Team	W	L	T	Pts.	GF	GA
Philadelphia Flyers	46	26	8	100	310	245
Washington Capitals	38	32	10	86	285	278
New York Islanders	35	33	12	82	279	281
New York Rangers	34	38	8	76	307	323
Pittsburgh Penguins	30	38	12	72	297	290
New Jersey Devils	29	45	6	64	293	368

CLARENCE CAMPBELL CONFERENCE

NORRIS DIVISION

Team	W	L	T	Pts.	GF	GA
St. Louis Blues	32	33	15	79	281	293
Detroit Red Wings	34	36	10	78	260	274
Chicago Blackhawks	29	37	14	72	290	310
Toronto Maple Leafs	32	42	6	70	286	319
Minnesota North Stars	30	40	10	70	296	314

SMYTHE DIVISION

Team	W	L	T	Pts.	GF	GA
Edmonton Oilers	50	24	6	106	372	284
Calgary Flames	46	31	3	95	318	289
Winnipeg Jets	40	32	8	88	279	271
Los Angeles Kings	31	41	8	70	318	341
Vancouver Canucks	29	43	8	66	282	314

PLAYOFFS

Wales Conference division semifinals: Quebec 4, Hartford 2; Montreal 4, Boston 0; Philadelphia 4, N.Y. Rangers 2; N.Y. Islanders 4, Washington 3. **Division finals:** Montreal 4, Quebec 3; Philadelphia 4, N.Y. Islanders 3. **Conference finals:** Philadelphia 4, Montreal 2.

Campbell Conference division semifinals: Toronto 4, St. Louis 2; Detroit 4, Chicago 0; Edmonton 4, Los Angeles 1; Winnipeg 4, Calgary 2. **Division finals:** Detroit 4, Toronto 3; Edmonton 4, Winnipeg 0. **Conference finals:** Edmonton 4, Detroit 1.

Stanley Cup finals: Edmonton 4, Philadelphia 3.

1987-88

PRINCE OF WALES CONFERENCE

ADAMS DIVISION

Team	W	L	T	Pts.	GF	GA
Montreal Canadiens	45	22	13	103	298	238
Boston Bruins	44	30	6	94	300	251
Buffalo Sabres	37	32	11	85	283	305
Hartford Whalers	35	38	7	77	249	267
Quebec Nordiques	32	43	5	69	271	306

PATRICK DIVISION

Team	W	L	T	Pts.	GF	GA
New York Islanders	39	31	10	88	308	267
Philadelphia Flyers	38	33	9	85	292	292
Washington Capitals	38	33	9	85	281	249
New Jersey Devils	38	36	6	82	295	296
New York Rangers	36	34	10	82	300	283
Pittsburgh Penguins	36	35	9	81	319	316

CLARENCE CAMPBELL CONFERENCE

NORRIS DIVISION

Team	W	L	T	Pts.	GF	GA
Detroit Red Wings	41	28	11	93	322	269
St. Louis Blues	34	38	8	76	278	294
Chicago Blackhawks	30	41	9	69	284	328
Toronto Maple Leafs	21	49	10	52	273	345
Minnesota North Stars	19	48	13	51	242	349

SMYTHE DIVISION

Team	W	L	T	Pts.	GF	GA
Calgary Flames	48	23	9	105	397	305
Edmonton Oilers	44	25	11	99	363	288
Winnipeg Jets	33	36	11	77	292	310
Los Angeles Kings	30	42	8	68	318	359
Vancouver Canucks	25	46	9	59	272	320

PLAYOFFS

Wales Conference division semifinals: Montreal 4, Hartford 2; Boston 4, Buffalo 2; New Jersey 4, N.Y. Islanders 2; Washington 4, Philadelphia 3. **Division finals:** Boston 4, Montreal 1; New Jersey 4, Washington 3. **Conference finals:** Boston 4, New Jersey 3.

Campbell Conference division semifinals: Detroit 4, Toronto 2; St. Louis 4, Chicago 1; Calgary 4, Los Angeles 1; Edmonton 4, Winnipeg 1. **Division finals:** Detroit 4, St. Louis 1; Edmonton 4, Calgary 0. **Conference finals:** Edmonton 4, Detroit 1.

Stanley Cup finals: Edmonton 4, Boston 0.

1988-89

PRINCE OF WALES CONFERENCE

ADAMS DIVISION

Team	W	L	T	Pts.	GF	GA
Montreal Canadiens	53	18	9	115	315	218
Boston Bruins	37	29	14	88	289	256
Buffalo Sabres	38	35	7	83	291	299
Hartford Whalers	37	38	5	79	299	290
Quebec Nordiques	27	46	7	61	269	342

PATRICK DIVISION

Team	W	L	T	Pts.	GF	GA
Washington Capitals	41	29	10	92	305	259
Pittsburgh Penguins	40	33	7	87	347	349
New York Rangers	37	35	8	82	310	307
Philadelphia Flyers	36	36	8	80	307	285
New Jersey Devils	27	41	12	66	281	325
New York Islanders	28	47	5	61	265	325

CLARENCE CAMPBELL CONFERENCE

NORRIS DIVISION

Team	W	L	T	Pts.	GF	GA
Detroit Red Wings	34	34	12	80	313	316
St. Louis Blues	33	35	12	78	275	285
Minnesota North Stars	27	37	16	70	258	278
Chicago Blackhawks	27	41	12	66	297	335
Toronto Maple Leafs	28	46	6	62	259	342

SMYTHE DIVISION

Team	W	L	T	Pts.	GF	GA
Calgary Flames	54	17	9	117	354	226
Los Angeles Kings	42	31	7	91	376	335
Edmonton Oilers	38	34	8	84	325	306
Vancouver Canucks	33	39	8	74	251	253
Winnipeg Jets	26	42	12	64	300	355

PLAYOFFS

Wales Conference division semifinals: Montreal 4, Hartford 0; Boston 4, Buffalo 1; Philadelphia 4, Washington 2; Pittsburgh 4, N.Y. Rangers 0. **Division finals:** Montreal 4, Boston 1; Philadelphia 4, Pittsburgh 3. **Conference finals:** Montreal 4, Philadelphia 2.

Campbell Conference division semifinals: Chicago 4, Detroit 2; St. Louis 4, Minnesota 1; Calgary 4, Vancouver 3; Los Angeles 4, Edmonton 3. **Division finals:** Chicago 4, St. Louis 1; Calgary 4, Los Angeles 0. **Conference finals:** Calgary 4, Chicago 1.

Stanley Cup finals: Calgary 4, Montreal 2.

1989-90

PRINCE OF WALES CONFERENCE

ADAMS DIVISION

Team	W	L	T	Pts.	GF	GA
Boston Bruins	46	25	9	101	289	232
Buffalo Sabres	45	27	8	98	286	248
Montreal Canadiens	41	28	11	93	288	234
Hartford Whalers	38	33	9	85	275	268
Quebec Nordiques	12	61	7	31	240	407

PATRICK DIVISION

Team	W	L	T	Pts.	GF	GA
New York Rangers	36	31	13	85	279	267
New Jersey Devils	37	34	9	83	295	288
Washington Capitals	36	38	6	78	284	275
New York Islanders	31	38	11	73	281	288
Pittsburgh Penguins	32	40	8	72	318	359
Philadelphia Flyers	30	39	11	71	290	297

CLARENCE CAMPBELL CONFERENCE

NORRIS DIVISION

Team	W	L	T	Pts.	GF	GA
Chicago Blackhawks	41	33	6	88	316	294
St. Louis Blues	37	34	9	83	295	279
Toronto Maple Leafs	38	38	4	80	337	358
Minnesota North Stars	36	40	4	76	284	291
Detroit Red Wings	28	38	14	70	288	323

SMYTHE DIVISION

Team	W	L	T	Pts.	GF	GA
Calgary Flames	42	23	15	99	348	265
Edmonton Oilers	38	28	14	90	315	283
Winnipeg Jets	37	32	11	85	298	290
Los Angeles Kings	34	39	7	75	338	337
Vancouver Canucks	25	41	14	64	245	306

PLAYOFFS

Wales Conference division semifinals: Boston 4, Hartford 3; Montreal 4, Buffalo 2; N.Y. Rangers 4, N.Y. Islanders 1; Washington 4, New Jersey 2. **Division finals:** Boston 4, Montreal 1; Washington 4, N.Y. Rangers 1. **Conference finals:** Boston 4, Washington 0.

Campbell Conference division semifinals: Chicago 4, Minnesota 3; St. Louis 4, Toronto 1; Los Angeles 4, Calgary 2; Edmonton 4, Winnipeg 3. **Division finals:** Chicago 4, St. Louis 3; Edmonton 4, Los Angeles 0. **Conference finals:** Edmonton 4, Chicago 2.

Stanley Cup finals: Edmonton 4, Boston 1.

1990-91

PRINCE OF WALES CONFERENCE

ADAMS DIVISION

Team	W	L	T	Pts.	GF	GA
Boston Bruins	44	24	12	100	299	264
Montreal Canadiens	39	30	11	89	273	249
Buffalo Sabres	31	30	19	81	292	278
Hartford Whalers	31	38	11	73	238	276
Quebec Nordiques	16	50	14	46	236	354

PATRICK DIVISION

Team	W	L	T	Pts.	GF	GA
Pittsburgh Penguins	41	33	6	88	342	305
New York Rangers	36	31	13	85	297	265
Washington Capitals	37	36	7	81	258	258
New Jersey Devils	32	33	15	79	272	264
Philadelphia Flyers	33	37	10	76	252	267
New York Islanders	25	45	10	60	223	290

CLARENCE CAMPBELL CONFERENCE

NORRIS DIVISION

Team	W	L	T	Pts.	GF	GA
Chicago Blackhawks	49	23	8	106	284	211
St. Louis Blues	47	22	11	105	310	250
Detroit Red Wings	34	38	8	76	273	298
Minnesota North Stars	27	39	14	68	256	266
Toronto Maple Leafs	23	46	11	57	241	318

SMYTHE DIVISION

Team	W	L	T	Pts.	GF	GA
Los Angeles Kings	46	24	10	102	340	254
Calgary Flames	46	26	8	100	344	263
Edmonton Oilers	37	37	6	80	272	272
Vancouver Canucks	28	43	9	65	243	315
Winnipeg Jets	26	43	11	63	260	288

PLAYOFFS

Wales Conference division semifinals: Boston 4, Hartford 2; Montreal 4, Buffalo 2; Pittsburgh 4, New Jersey 3; Washington

4, N.Y. Rangers 2. **Division finals:** Boston 4, Montreal 3; Pittsburgh 4, Washington 1. **Conference finals:** Pittsburgh 4, Boston 2.

Campbell Conference division semifinals: Minnesota 4, Chicago 2; St. Louis 4, Detroit 3; Los Angeles 4, Vancouver 2; Edmonton 4, Calgary 3. **Division finals:** Minnesota 4, St. Louis 2; Edmonton 4, Los Angeles 2. **Conference finals:** Minnesota 4, Edmonton 1.

Stanley Cup finals: Pittsburgh 4, Minnesota 2.

1991-92

PRINCE OF WALES CONFERENCE

ADAMS DIVISION

Team	W	L	T	Pts.	GF	GA
Montreal Canadiens	41	28	11	93	267	207
Boston Bruins	36	32	12	84	270	275
Buffalo Sabres	31	37	12	74	289	299
Hartford Whalers	26	41	13	65	247	283
Quebec Nordiques	20	48	12	52	255	318

PATRICK DIVISION

Team	W	L	T	Pts.	GF	GA
New York Rangers	50	25	5	105	321	246
Washington Capitals	45	27	8	98	330	275
Pittsburgh Penguins	39	32	9	87	343	308
New Jersey Devils	38	31	11	87	289	259
New York Islanders	34	35	11	79	291	299
Philadelphia Flyers	32	37	11	75	252	273

CLARENCE CAMPBELL CONFERENCE

NORRIS DIVISION

Team	W	L	T	Pts.	GF	GA
Detroit Red Wings	43	25	12	98	320	256
Chicago Blackhawks	36	29	15	87	257	236
St. Louis Blues	36	33	11	83	279	266
Minnesota North Stars	32	42	6	70	246	278
Toronto Maple Leafs	30	43	7	67	234	294

SMYTHE DIVISION

Team	W	L	T	Pts.	GF	GA
Vancouver Canucks	42	26	12	96	285	250
Los Angeles Kings	35	31	14	84	287	296
Edmonton Oilers	36	34	10	82	295	297
Winnipeg Jets	33	32	15	81	251	244
Calgary Flames	31	37	12	74	296	305
San Jose Sharks	17	58	5	39	219	359

PLAYOFFS

Wales Conference division semifinals: Montreal 4, Hartford 3; Boston 4, Buffalo 3; N.Y. Rangers 4, New Jersey 3; Pittsburgh 4, Washington 3. **Division finals:** Boston 4, Montreal 0; Pittsburgh 4, N.Y. Rangers 2. **Conference finals:** Pittsburgh 4, Boston 0.

Campbell Conference division semifinals: Detroit 4, Minnesota 3; Chicago 4, St. Louis 2; Vancouver 4, Winnipeg 3; Edmonton 4, Los Angeles 2. **Division finals:** Chicago 4, Detroit 0; Edmonton 4, Vancouver 2. **Conference finals:** Chicago 4, Edmonton 0.

Stanley Cup finals: Pittsburgh 4, Chicago 0.

1992-93

PRINCE OF WALES CONFERENCE

ADAMS DIVISION

Team	W	L	T	Pts.	GF	GA
Boston Bruins	51	26	7	109	332	268
Quebec Nordiques	47	27	10	104	351	300
Montreal Canadiens	48	30	6	102	326	280
Buffalo Sabres	38	36	10	86	335	297
Hartford Whalers	26	52	6	58	284	369
Ottawa Senators	10	70	4	24	202	395

PATRICK DIVISION

Team	W	L	T	Pts.	GF	GA
Pittsburgh Penguins	56	21	7	119	367	268
Washington Capitals	43	34	7	93	325	286
New York Islanders	40	37	7	87	335	297
New Jersey Devils	40	37	7	87	308	299
Philadelphia Flyers	36	37	11	83	319	319
New York Rangers	34	39	11	79	304	308

CLARENCE CAMPBELL CONFERENCE

NORRIS DIVISION

Team	W	L	T	Pts.	GF	GA
Chicago Blackhawks	47	25	12	106	279	230
Detroit Red Wings	47	28	9	103	369	280
Toronto Maple Leafs	44	29	11	99	288	241
St. Louis Blues	37	36	11	85	282	278
Minnesota North Stars	36	38	10	82	272	293
Tampa Bay Lightning	23	54	7	53	245	332

SMYTHE DIVISION

Team	W	L	T	Pts.	GF	GA
Vancouver Canucks	46	29	9	101	346	278
Calgary Flames	43	30	11	97	322	282
Los Angeles Kings	39	35	10	88	338	340
Winnipeg Jets	40	37	7	87	322	320
Edmonton Oilers	26	50	8	60	242	337
San Jose Sharks	11	71	2	24	218	414

PLAYOFFS

Wales Conference division semifinals: Buffalo 4, Boston 0; Montreal 4, Quebec 2; Pittsburgh 4, New Jersey 1; N.Y. Islanders 4, Washington 2. **Division finals:** Montreal 4, Buffalo 0; N.Y. Islanders 4, Pittsburgh 3. **Conference finals:** Montreal 4, N.Y. Islanders 1.

Campbell Conference division semifinals: St. Louis 4, Chicago 0; Toronto 4, Detroit 3; Vancouver 4, Winnipeg 2; Los Angeles 4, Calgary 2. **Division finals:** Toronto 4, St. Louis 3; Los Angeles 4, Vancouver 2. **Conference finals:** Los Angeles 4, Toronto 3.

Stanley Cup finals: Montreal 4, Los Angeles 1.

1993-94

EASTERN CONFERENCE

ATLANTIC DIVISION

Team	W	L	T	Pts.	GF	GA
New York Rangers	52	24	8	112	299	231
New Jersey Devils	47	25	12	106	306	220
Washington Capitals	39	35	10	88	277	263
New York Islanders	36	36	12	84	282	264
Florida Panthers	33	34	17	83	233	233
Philadelphia Flyers	35	39	10	80	294	314
Tampa Bay Lightning	30	43	11	71	224	251

NORTHEAST DIVISION

Team	W	L	T	Pts.	GF	GA
Pittsburgh Penguins	44	27	13	101	299	285
Boston Bruins	42	29	13	97	289	252
Montreal Canadiens	41	29	14	96	283	248
Buffalo Sabres	43	32	9	95	282	218
Quebec Nordiques	34	42	8	76	277	292
Hartford Whalers	27	48	9	63	227	288
Ottawa Senators	14	61	9	37	201	397

WESTERN CONFERENCE

CENTRAL DIVISION

Team	W	L	T	Pts.	GF	GA
Detroit Red Wings	46	30	8	100	356	275
Toronto Maple Leafs	43	29	12	98	280	243
Dallas Stars	42	29	13	97	286	265
St. Louis Blues	40	33	11	91	270	283
Chicago Blackhawks	39	36	9	87	254	240
Winnipeg Jets	24	51	9	57	245	344

PACIFIC DIVISION

Team	W	L	T	Pts.	GF	GA
Calgary Flames	42	29	13	97	302	256
Vancouver Canucks	41	40	3	85	279	276
San Jose Sharks	33	35	16	82	252	265
Mighty Ducks of Anaheim	33	46	5	71	229	251
Los Angeles Kings	27	45	12	66	294	322
Edmonton Oilers	25	45	14	64	261	305

PLAYOFFS

Eastern Conference quarterfinals: N.Y. Rangers 4, N.Y. Islanders 0; Washington 4, Pittsburgh 2; New Jersey 4, Buffalo 3; Boston 4, Montreal 3. **Semifinals:** N.Y. Rangers 4, Washington 1; New Jersey 4, Boston 2. **Finals:** N.Y. Rangers 4, New Jersey 3.

Western Conference quarterfinals: San Jose 4, Detroit 3; Vancouver 4, Calgary 3; Toronto 4, Chicago 2; Dallas 4, St. Louis 0. **Semifinals:** Toronto 4, San Jose 3; Vancouver 4, Dallas 1. **Finals:** Vancouver 4, Toronto 1.

Stanley Cup finals: N.Y. Rangers 4, Vancouver 3.

1994-95

EASTERN CONFERENCE

ATLANTIC DIVISION

Team	W	L	T	Pts.	GF	GA
Philadelphia Flyers	28	16	4	60	150	132
New Jersey Devils	22	18	8	52	136	121
Washington Capitals	22	18	8	52	136	120
New York Rangers	22	23	3	47	139	134
Florida Panthers	20	22	6	46	115	127
Tampa Bay Lightning	17	28	3	37	120	144
New York Islanders	15	28	5	35	126	158

NORTHEAST DIVISION

Team	W	L	T	Pts.	GF	GA
Quebec Nordiques	30	13	5	65	185	134
Pittsburgh Penguins	29	16	3	61	181	158
Boston Bruins	27	18	3	57	150	127
Buffalo Sabres	22	19	7	51	130	119
Hartford Whalers	19	24	5	43	127	141
Montreal Canadiens	18	23	7	43	125	148
Ottawa Senators	9	34	5	23	117	174

WESTERN CONFERENCE

CENTRAL DIVISION

Team	W	L	T	Pts.	GF	GA
Detroit Red Wings	33	11	4	70	180	117
St. Louis Blues	28	15	5	61	178	135
Chicago Blackhawks	24	19	5	53	156	115
Toronto Maple Leafs	21	19	8	50	135	146
Dallas Stars	17	23	8	42	136	135
Winnipeg Jets	16	25	7	39	157	177

PACIFIC DIVISION

Team	W	L	T	Pts.	GF	GA
Calgary Flames	24	17	7	55	163	135
Vancouver Canucks	18	18	12	48	153	148
San Jose Sharks	19	25	4	42	129	161
Los Angeles Kings	16	23	9	41	142	174
Edmonton Oilers	17	27	4	38	136	183
Mighty Ducks of Anaheim	16	27	5	37	125	164

PLAYOFFS

Eastern Conference quarterfinals: N.Y. Rangers 4, Quebec 2; Pittsburgh 4, Washington 3; Philadelphia 4, Buffalo 1; New Jersey 4, Boston 1. **Semifinals:** New Jersey 4, Pittsburgh 1; Philadelphia 4, N.Y. Rangers 0. **Finals:** New Jersey 4, Philadelphia 2.

Western Conference quarterfinals: Detroit 4, Dallas 1; Vancouver 4, St. Louis 3; Chicago 4, Toronto 3; San Jose 4, Calgary 3. **Semifinals:** Detroit 4, San Jose 0; Chicago 4, Vancouver 0. **Finals:** Detroit 4, Chicago 1.

Stanley Cup finals: New Jersey 4, Detroit 0.

1995-96

EASTERN CONFERENCE

ATLANTIC DIVISION

Team	W	L	T	Pts.	GF	GA
Philadelphia Flyers	45	24	13	103	282	208
New York Rangers	41	27	14	96	272	237
Florida Panthers	41	31	10	92	254	234
Washington Capitals	39	32	11	89	234	204
Tampa Bay Lightning	38	32	12	88	238	248
New Jersey Devils	37	33	12	86	215	202
New York Islanders	22	50	10	54	229	315

NORTHEAST DIVISION

Team	W	L	T	Pts.	GF	GA
Pittsburgh Penguins	49	29	4	102	362	284
Boston Bruins	40	31	11	91	282	269
Montreal Canadiens	40	32	10	90	265	248
Hartford Whalers	34	39	9	77	237	259
Buffalo Sabres	33	42	7	73	247	262
Ottawa Senators	18	59	5	41	191	291

WESTERN CONFERENCE

CENTRAL DIVISION

Team	W	L	T	Pts.	GF	GA
Detroit Red Wings	62	13	7	131	325	181
Chicago Blackhawks	40	28	14	94	273	220
Toronto Maple Leafs	34	36	12	80	247	252
St. Louis Blues	32	34	16	80	219	248
Winnipeg Jets	36	40	6	78	275	291
Dallas Stars	26	42	14	66	227	280

PACIFIC DIVISION

Team	W	L	T	Pts.	GF	GA
Colorado Avalanche	47	25	10	104	326	240
Calgary Flames	34	37	11	79	241	240
Vancouver Canucks	32	35	15	79	278	278
Mighty Ducks of Anaheim	35	39	8	78	234	247
Edmonton Oilers	30	44	8	68	240	304
Los Angeles Kings	24	40	18	66	256	302
San Jose Sharks	20	55	7	47	252	357

PLAYOFFS

Eastern Conference quarterfinals: Philadelphia 4, Tampa Bay 2; Pittsburgh 4, Washington 2; N.Y. Rangers 4, Montreal 2; Florida 4, Boston 1. **Semifinals:** Florida 4, Philadelphia 2; Pittsburgh 4, N.Y. Rangers 1. **Finals:** Florida 4, Pittsburgh 3.

Western Conference quarterfinals: Detroit 4, Winnipeg 2; Colorado 4, Vancouver 2; Chicago 4, Calgary 0; St. Louis 4, Toronto 2. **Semifinals:** Detroit 4, St. Louis 3; Colorado 4, Chicago 2. **Finals:** Colorado 4, Detroit 2.

Stanley Cup finals: Colorado 4, Florida 0.

1996-97

EASTERN CONFERENCE

ATLANTIC DIVISION

Team	W	L	T	Pts.	GF	GA
New Jersey Devils	45	23	14	104	231	182
Philadelphia Flyers	45	24	13	103	274	217
Florida Panthers	35	28	19	89	221	201
New York Rangers	38	34	10	86	258	231
Washington Capitals	33	40	9	75	214	231
Tampa Bay Lightning	32	40	10	74	217	247
New York Islanders	29	41	12	70	240	250

NORTHEAST DIVISION

Team	W	L	T	Pts.	GF	GA
Buffalo Sabres	40	30	12	92	237	208
Pittsburgh Penguins	38	36	8	84	285	280
Ottawa Senators	31	36	15	77	226	234
Montreal Canadiens	31	36	15	77	249	276
Hartford Whalers	32	39	11	75	226	256
Boston Bruins	26	47	9	61	234	300

WESTERN CONFERENCE

CENTRAL DIVISION

Team	W	L	T	Pts.	GF	GA
Dallas Stars	48	26	8	104	252	198
Detroit Red Wings	38	26	18	94	253	197
Phoenix Coyotes	38	37	7	83	240	243
St. Louis Blues	36	35	11	83	236	239
Chicago Blackhawks	34	35	13	81	223	210
Toronto Maple Leafs	30	44	8	68	230	273

PACIFIC DIVISION

Team	W	L	T	Pts.	GF	GA
Colorado Avalanche	49	24	9	107	277	205
Mighty Ducks of Anaheim	36	33	13	85	245	233
Edmonton Oilers	36	37	9	81	252	247
Vancouver Canucks	35	40	7	77	257	273
Calgary Flames	32	41	9	73	214	239
Los Angeles Kings	28	43	11	67	214	268
San Jose Sharks	27	47	8	62	211	278

PLAYOFFS

Eastern Conference quarterfinals: New Jersey 4, Montreal 1; Buffalo 4, Ottawa 3; Philadelphia 4, Pittsburgh 1; N.Y. Rangers 4, Florida 1. **Semifinals:** N.Y. Rangers 4, New Jersey 1; Philadelphia 4, Buffalo 1. **Finals:** Philadelphia 4, N.Y. Rangers 1.

Western Conference quarterfinals: Colorado 4, Chicago 2; Edmonton 4, Dallas 3; Detroit 4, St. Louis 2; Anaheim 4, Phoenix 3. **Semifinals:** Colorado 4, Edmonton 1; Detroit 4, Anaheim 0. **Finals:** Detroit 4, Colorado 2.

Stanley Cup finals: Detroit 4, Philadelphia 0.

1997-98

EASTERN CONFERENCE

ATLANTIC DIVISION

Team	W	L	T	Pts.	GF	GA
New Jersey Devils	48	23	11	107	225	166
Philadelphia Flyers	42	29	11	95	242	193
Washington Capitals	40	30	12	92	219	202
New York Islanders	30	41	11	71	212	225
New York Rangers	25	39	18	68	197	231
Florida Panthers	24	43	15	63	203	256
Tampa Bay Lightning	17	55	10	44	151	269

NORTHEAST DIVISION

Team	W	L	T	Pts.	GF	GA
Pittsburgh Penguins	40	24	18	98	228	188
Boston Bruins	39	30	13	91	221	194
Buffalo Sabres	36	29	17	89	211	187
Montreal Canadiens	37	32	13	87	235	208
Ottawa Senators	34	33	15	83	193	200
Carolina Hurricanes	33	41	8	74	200	219

WESTERN CONFERENCE

CENTRAL DIVISION

Team	W	L	T	Pts.	GF	GA
Dallas Stars	49	22	11	109	242	167
Detroit Red Wings	44	23	15	103	250	196
St. Louis Blues	45	29	8	98	256	204
Phoenix Coyotes	35	35	12	82	224	227
Chicago Blackhawks	30	39	13	73	192	199
Toronto Maple Leafs	30	43	9	69	194	237

PACIFIC DIVISION

Team	W	L	T	Pts.	GF	GA
Colorado Avalanche	39	26	17	95	231	205
Los Angeles Kings	38	33	11	87	227	225
Edmonton Oilers	35	37	10	80	215	224
San Jose Sharks	34	38	10	78	210	216
Calgary Flames	26	41	15	67	217	252
Mighty Ducks of Anaheim	26	43	13	65	205	261
Vancouver Canucks	25	43	14	64	224	273

PLAYOFFS

Eastern Conference quarterfinals: Ottawa 4, New Jersey 2; Washington 4, Boston 2; Buffalo 4, Philadelphia 1; Montreal 4, Pittsburgh 2. **Semifinals:** Washington 4, Ottawa 1; Buffalo 4, Montreal 0. **Finals:** Washington 4, Buffalo 2.

Western Conference quarterfinals: Edmonton 4, Colorado 3; Dallas 4, San Jose 2; Detroit 4, Phoenix 2; St. Louis 4, Los Angeles 0. **Semifinals:** Dallas 4, Edmonton 1; Detroit 4, St. Louis 2. **Finals:** Detroit 4, Dallas 2.

Stanley Cup finals: Detroit 4, Washington 0.

1998-99

EASTERN CONFERENCE

ATLANTIC DIVISION

Team	W	L	T	Pts.	GF	GA
New Jersey Devils	47	24	11	105	248	196
Philadelphia Flyers	37	26	19	93	231	196
Pittsburgh Penguins	38	30	14	90	242	225
New York Rangers	33	38	11	77	217	227
New York Islanders	24	48	10	58	194	244

NORTHEAST DIVISION

Team	W	L	T	Pts.	GF	GA
Ottawa Senators	44	23	15	103	239	179
Toronto Maple Leafs	45	30	7	97	268	231
Boston Bruins	39	30	13	91	214	181
Buffalo Sabres	37	28	17	91	207	175
Montreal Canadiens	32	39	11	75	184	209

SOUTHEAST DIVISION

Team	W	L	T	Pts.	GF	GA
Carolina Hurricanes	34	30	18	86	210	202
Florida Panthers	30	34	18	78	210	228
Washington Capitals	31	45	6	68	200	218
Tampa Bay Lightning	19	54	9	47	179	292

WESTERN CONFERENCE

CENTRAL DIVISION

Team	W	L	T	Pts.	GF	GA
Detroit Red Wings	43	32	7	93	245	202
St. Louis Blues	37	32	13	87	237	209
Chicago Blackhawks	29	41	12	70	202	248
Nashville Predators	28	47	7	63	190	261

PACIFIC DIVISION

Team	W	L	T	Pts.	GF	GA
Dallas Stars	51	19	12	114	236	168
Phoenix Coyotes	39	31	12	90	205	197
Anaheim Mighty Ducks	35	34	13	83	215	206
San Jose Sharks	31	33	18	80	196	191
Los Angeles Kings	32	45	5	69	189	222

NORTHWEST DIVISION

Team	W	L	T	Pts.	GF	GA
Colorado Avalanche	44	28	10	98	239	205
Edmonton Oilers	33	37	12	78	230	226
Calgary Flames	30	40	12	72	211	234
Vancouver Canucks	23	47	12	58	192	258

PLAYOFFS

Eastern Conference quarterfinals: Pittsburgh 4, New Jersey 3; Buffalo 4, Ottawa 0; Boston 4, Carolina 2; Toronto 4, Philadelphia 2. **Semifinals:** Toronto 4, Pittsburgh 2; Buffalo 4, Boston 2. **Finals:** Buffalo 4, Toronto 1.

Western Conference quarterfinals: Dallas 4, Edmonton 0; Colorado 4, San Jose 2; Detroit 4, Anaheim 0; St. Louis 4, Phoenix 3. **Semifinals:** Dallas 4, St. Louis 2; Colorado 4, Detroit 2. **Finals:** Dallas 4, Colorado 3.

Stanley Cup finals: Dallas 4, Buffalo 2.

1999-2000

EASTERN CONFERENCE

ATLANTIC DIVISION

Team	W	L	T	OTL	Pts.	GF	GA
Philadelphia Flyers	45	22	12	3	105	237	179
New Jersey Devils	45	24	8	5	103	251	203
Pittsburgh Penguins	37	31	8	6	88	241	236
New York Rangers	29	38	12	3	73	218	246
New York Islanders	24	48	9	1	58	194	275

NORTHEAST DIVISION

Team	W	L	T	OTL	Pts.	GF	GA
Toronto Maple Leafs	45	27	7	3	100	246	222
Ottawa Senators	41	28	11	2	95	244	210
Buffalo Sabres	35	32	11	4	85	213	204
Montreal Canadiens	35	34	9	4	83	196	194
Boston Bruins	24	33	19	6	73	210	248

SOUTHEAST DIVISION

Team	W	L	T	OTL	Pts.	GF	GA
Washington Capitals	44	24	12	2	102	227	194
Florida Panthers	43	27	6	6	98	244	209
Carolina Hurricanes	37	35	10	0	84	217	216
Tampa Bay Lightning	19	47	9	7	54	204	310
Atlanta Thrashers	14	57	7	4	39	170	313

WESTERN CONFERENCE

CENTRAL DIVISION

Team	W	L	T	OTL	Pts.	GF	GA
St. Louis Blues	51	19	11	1	114	248	165
Detroit Red Wings	48	22	10	2	108	278	210
Chicago Blackhawks	33	37	10	2	78	242	245
Nashville Predators	28	40	7	7	70	199	240

PACIFIC DIVISION

Team	W	L	T	OTL	Pts.	GF	GA
Dallas Stars	43	23	10	6	102	211	184
Los Angeles Kings	39	27	12	4	94	245	228
Phoenix Coyotes	39	31	8	4	90	232	228
San Jose Sharks	35	30	10	7	87	225	214
Mighty Ducks of Anaheim	34	33	12	3	83	217	227

NORTHWEST DIVISION

Team	W	L	T	OTL	Pts.	GF	GA
Colorado Avalanche	42	28	11	1	96	233	201
Edmonton Oilers	32	26	16	8	88	226	212
Vancouver Canucks	30	29	15	8	83	227	237
Calgary Flames	31	36	10	5	77	211	256

PLAYOFFS

Eastern Conference quarterfinals: Philadelphia 4, Buffalo 1; Pittsburgh 4, Washington 1; Toronto 4, Ottawa 2; New Jersey 4, Florida 0. **Semifinals:** Philadelphia 4, Pittsburgh 2; New Jersey 4, Toronto 2. **Finals:** New Jersey 4, Philadelphia 3.

Western Conference quarterfinals: San Jose 4, St. Louis 3; Dallas 4, Edmonton 1; Colorado 4, Phoenix 1; Detroit 4, Los Angeles 0. **Semifinals:** Dallas 4, San Jose 1; Colorado 4, Detroit 1. **Finals:** Dallas 4, Colorado 3.

Stanley Cup finals: New Jersey 4, Dallas 2.

2000-01

EASTERN CONFERENCE

ATLANTIC DIVISION

Team	W	L	T	OTL	Pts.	GF	GA
New Jersey Devils	48	19	12	3	111	295	195
Philadelphia Flyers	43	25	11	3	100	240	207
Pittsburgh Penguins	42	28	9	3	96	281	256
New York Rangers	33	43	5	1	72	250	290
New York Islanders	21	51	7	3	52	185	268

NORTHEAST DIVISION

Team	W	L	T	OTL	Pts.	GF	GA
Ottawa Senators	48	21	9	4	109	274	205
Buffalo Sabres	46	30	5	1	98	218	184
Toronto Maple Leafs	37	29	11	5	90	232	207
Boston Bruins	36	30	8	8	88	227	249
Montreal Canadiens	28	40	8	6	70	206	232

SOUTHEAST DIVISION

Team	W	L	T	OTL	Pts.	GF	GA
Washington Capitals	41	27	10	4	96	233	211
Carolina Hurricanes	38	32	9	3	88	212	225
Florida Panthers	22	38	13	9	66	200	246
Atlanta Thrashers	23	45	12	2	60	211	289
Tampa Bay Lightning	24	47	6	5	59	201	280

WESTERN CONFERENCE

CENTRAL DIVISION

Team	W	L	T	OTL	Pts.	GF	GA
Detroit Red Wings	49	20	9	4	111	253	202
St. Louis Blues	43	22	12	5	103	249	195
Nashville Predators	34	36	9	3	80	186	200
Chicago Blackhawks	29	40	8	5	71	210	246
Columbus Blue Jackets	28	39	9	6	71	190	233

PACIFIC DIVISION

Team	W	L	T	OTL	Pts.	GF	GA
Dallas Stars	48	24	8	2	106	241	187
San Jose Sharks	40	27	12	3	95	217	192
Los Angeles Kings	38	28	13	3	92	252	228
Phoenix Coyotes	35	27	17	3	90	214	212
Mighty Ducks of Anaheim	25	41	11	5	66	188	245

NORTHWEST DIVISION

Team	W	L	T	OTL	Pts.	GF	GA
Colorado Rockies	52	16	10	4	118	270	192
Edmonton Oilers	39	28	12	3	93	243	222
Vancouver Canucks	36	28	11	7	90	239	238
Calgary Flames	27	36	15	4	73	197	236
Minnesota Wild	25	39	13	5	68	168	210

PLAYOFFS

Eastern Conference quarterfinals: New Jersey 4, Carolina 2; Toronto 4, Ottawa 0; Pittsburgh 4, Washington 2; Buffalo 4, Philadelphia 2. **Semifinals:** New Jersey 4, Toronto 3; Pittsburgh 4, Buffalo 3. **Finals:** New Jersey 4, Pittsburgh 1.

Western Conference quarterfinals: Colorado 4, Vancouver 0; Los Angeles 4, Detroit 2; Dallas 4, Edmonton 2; St. Louis 4, San Jose 2. **Semifinals:** Colorado 4, Los Angeles 3; St. Louis 4, Dallas 0. **Finals:** Colorado 4, St. Louis 1.

Stanley Cup finals: Colorado 4, New Jersey 3.

2001-02

EASTERN CONFERENCE

NORTHEAST DIVISION

Team	W	L	T	OTL	Pts.	GF	GA
Boston Bruins	43	24	6	9	101	236	201
Toronto Maple Leafs	43	25	10	4	100	249	207
Ottawa Senators	39	27	9	7	94	243	208
Montreal Canadiens	36	31	12	3	87	207	209
Buffalo Sabres	35	35	11	1	82	213	200

ATLANTIC DIVISION

Team	W	L	T	OTL	Pts.	GF	GA
Philadelphia Flyers	42	27	10	3	97	234	192
New York Islanders	42	28	8	4	96	239	220
New Jersey Devils	41	28	9	4	95	205	187
New York Rangers	36	38	4	4	80	227	258
Pittsburgh Penguins	28	41	8	5	69	198	249

SOUTHEAST DIVISION

Team	W	L	T	OTL	Pts.	GF	GA
Carolina Hurricanes	35	26	16	5	91	217	217
Washington Capitals	36	33	11	2	85	228	240
Tampa Bay Lightning	27	40	11	4	69	178	219
Florida Panthers	22	44	10	6	60	180	250
Atlanta Thrashers	19	47	11	5	54	187	288

WESTERN CONFERENCE

CENTRAL DIVISION

Team	W	L	T	OTL	Pts.	GF	GA
Detroit Red Wings	51	17	10	4	116	251	187
St. Louis Blues	43	27	8	4	98	227	188
Chicago Blackhawks	41	27	13	1	96	216	207
Nashville Predators	28	41	13	0	69	196	230
Columbus Blue Jackets	22	47	8	5	57	164	255

PACIFIC DIVISION

Team	W	L	T	OTL	Pts.	GF	GA
San Jose Sharks	44	27	8	3	99	248	199
Phoenix Coyotes	40	27	9	6	95	228	210
Los Angeles Kings	40	27	11	4	95	214	190
Dallas Stars	36	28	13	5	90	215	213
Mighty Ducks of Anaheim	29	42	8	3	69	175	198

NORTHWEST DIVISION

Team	W	L	T	OTL	Pts.	GF	GA
Colorado Avalanche	45	28	8	1	99	212	169
Vancouver Canucks	42	30	7	3	94	254	211
Edmonton Oilers	38	28	12	4	92	205	182
Calgary Flames	32	35	12	3	79	201	220
Minnesota Wild	26	35	12	9	73	195	238

PLAYOFFS

Eastern Conference quarterfinals: Ottawa 4, Philadelphia 1; Montreal 4, Boston 2; Carolina 4, New Jersey 2; Toronto 4, N.Y. Islanders 3. **Semifinals:** Toronto 4, Ottawa 3; Carolina 4, Montreal 2. **Finals:** Carolina 4, Toronto 2.

Western Conference quarterfinals: San Jose 4, Phoenix 1; St. Louis 4, Chicago 1; Colorado 4, Los Angeles 3; Detroit 4, Vancouver 2. **Semifinals:** Colorado 4, San Jose 3; Detroit 4, St. Louis 1. **Finals:** Detroit 4, Colorado 3.

Stanley Cup finals: Detroit 4, Carolina 1.

2002-03

EASTERN CONFERENCE

NORTHEAST DIVISION

Team	W	L	T	OTL	Pts.	GF	GA
Ottawa Senators	52	21	8	1	113	263	182
Toronto Maple Leafs	44	28	7	3	98	236	208
Boston Bruins	36	31	11	4	87	245	237
Montreal Canadiens	30	35	8	9	77	206	234
Buffalo Sabres	27	37	10	8	72	190	219

ATLANTIC DIVISION

Team	W	L	T	OTL	Pts.	GF	GA
New Jersey Devils	46	20	10	6	108	216	166
Philadelphia Flyers	45	20	13	4	107	211	166
New York Islanders	35	34	11	2	83	224	231
New York Rangers	32	36	10	4	78	210	231
Pittsburgh Penguins	27	44	6	5	65	189	255

SOUTHEAST DIVISION

Team	W	L	T	OTL	Pts.	GF	GA
Tampa Bay Lightning	36	25	16	5	93	219	210
Washington Capitals	39	29	8	6	92	224	220
Atlanta Thrashers	31	39	7	5	74	226	284
Florida Panthers	24	36	13	9	70	176	237
Carolina Hurricanes	22	43	11	6	61	171	240

WESTERN CONFERENCE

CENTRAL DIVISION

Team	W	L	T	OTL	Pts.	GF	GA
Detroit Red Wings	48	20	10	4	110	269	203
St. Louis Blues	41	24	11	6	99	253	222
Chicago Blackhawks	30	33	13	6	79	207	226
Nashville Predators	27	35	13	7	74	183	206
Columbus Blue Jackets	29	42	8	3	69	213	263

PACIFIC DIVISION

Team	W	L	T	OTL	Pts.	GF	GA
Dallas Stars	46	17	15	4	111	245	169
Mighty Ducks of Anaheim	40	27	9	6	95	203	193
Los Angeles Kings	33	37	6	7	78	203	221
Phoenix Coyotes	31	35	11	5	78	204	230
San Jose Sharks	28	37	9	8	73	214	239

NORTHWEST DIVISION

Team	W	L	T	OTL	Pts.	GF	GA
Colorado Avalanche	42	19	13	8	105	251	194
Vancouver Canucks	45	23	13	1	104	264	208
Minnesota Wild	42	29	10	1	95	198	178
Edmonton Oilers	36	26	11	9	92	231	230
Calgary Flames	29	36	13	4	75	186	228

PLAYOFFS

Eastern Conference quarterfinals: Ottawa 4, N.Y. Islanders 1; New Jersey 4, Boston 1; Tampa Bay 4, Washington 2; Philadelphia 4, Toronto 2. **Semifinals:** Ottawa 4, Philadelphia 2; New Jersey 4, Tampa Bay 2. **Finals:** New Jersey 4, Ottawa 3.

Western Conference quarterfinals: Dallas 4, Edmonton 2; Anaheim 4, Detroit 0; Minnesota 4, Colorado 3; Vancouver 4, St. Louis 3. **Semifinals:** Anaheim 4, Dallas 2; Minnesota 4, Vancouver 3. **Finals:** Anaheim 4, Minnesota 0.

Stanley Cup finals: New Jersey 4, Anaheim 3.

AWARD WINNERS

LEAGUE AWARDS

ART ROSS TROPHY

(Leading scorer)

Season	Player, Team	Pts.
1917-18	Joe Malone, Montreal	48
1918-19	Newsy Lalonde, Montreal	32
1919-20	Joe Malone, Quebec Bulldogs	49
1920-21	Newsy Lalonde, Montreal	43
1921-22	Punch Broadbent, Ottawa	46
1922-23	Babe Dye, Toronto	37
1923-24	Cy Denneny, Ottawa	24
1924-25	Babe Dye, Toronto	46
1925-26	Nels Stewart, Montreal Maroons	42
1926-27	Bill Cook, N.Y. Rangers	37
1927-28	Howie Morenz, Montreal	51
1928-29	Ace Bailey, Toronto	32
1929-30	Cooney Weiland, Boston	73
1930-31	Howie Morenz, Montreal	51
1931-32	Harvey Jackson, Toronto	53
1932-33	Bill Cook, N.Y. Rangers	50
1933-34	Charlie Conacher, Toronto	52
1934-35	Charlie Conacher, Toronto	57
1935-36	Dave Schriner, N.Y. Americans	45
1936-37	Dave Schriner, N.Y. Americans	46
1937-38	Gordie Drillion, Toronto	52
1938-39	Toe Blake, Montreal	47
1939-40	Milt Schmidt, Boston	52
1940-41	Bill Cowley, Boston	62
1941-42	Bryan Hextall, N.Y. Rangers	56
1942-43	Doug Bentley, Chicago	73
1943-44	Herbie Cain, Boston	82
1944-45	Elmer Lach, Montreal	80
1945-46	Max Bentley, Chicago	61
1946-47	Max Bentley, Chicago	72
1947-48	Elmer Lach, Montreal	61
1948-49	Roy Conacher, Chicago	68
1949-50	Ted Lindsay, Detroit	78
1950-51	Gordie Howe, Detroit	86
1951-52	Gordie Howe, Detroit	86
1952-53	Gordie Howe, Detroit	95
1953-54	Gordie Howe, Detroit	81
1954-55	Bernie Geoffrion, Montreal	75
1955-56	Jean Beliveau, Montreal	88
1956-57	Gordie Howe, Detroit	89
1957-58	Dickie Moore, Montreal	84
1958-59	Dickie Moore, Montreal	96
1959-60	Bobby Hull, Chicago	81
1960-61	Bernie Geoffrion, Montreal	95
1961-62	Bobby Hull, Chicago	84
1962-63	Gordie Howe, Detroit	86
1963-64	Stan Mikita, Chicago	89
1964-65	Stan Mikita, Chicago	87
1965-66	Bobby Hull, Chicago	97
1966-67	Stan Mikita, Chicago	97
1967-68	Stan Mikita, Chicago	87
1968-69	Phil Esposito, Boston	126
1969-70	Bobby Orr, Boston	120
1970-71	Phil Esposito, Boston	152
1971-72	Phil Esposito, Boston	133
1972-73	Phil Esposito, Boston	130
1973-74	Phil Esposito, Boston	145
1974-75	Bobby Orr, Boston	135
1975-76	Guy Lafleur, Montreal	125
1976-77	Guy Lafleur, Montreal	136
1977-78	Guy Lafleur, Montreal	132
1978-79	Bryan Trottier, N.Y. Islanders	134
1979-80	Marcel Dionne, Los Angeles	137
1980-81	Wayne Gretzky, Edmonton	164
1981-82	Wayne Gretzky, Edmonton	212
1982-83	Wayne Gretzky, Edmonton	196
1983-84	Wayne Gretzky, Edmonton	205
1984-85	Wayne Gretzky, Edmonton	208
1985-86	Wayne Gretzky, Edmonton	215
1986-87	Wayne Gretzky, Edmonton	183
1987-88	Mario Lemieux, Pittsburgh	168
1988-89	Mario Lemieux, Pittsburgh	199
1989-90	Wayne Gretzky, Los Angeles	142
1990-91	Wayne Gretzky, Los Angeles	163
1991-92	Mario Lemieux, Pittsburgh	131
1992-93	Mario Lemieux, Pittsburgh	160
1993-94	Wayne Gretzky, Los Angeles	130
1994-95	Jaromir Jagr, Pittsburgh	70
1995-96	Mario Lemieux, Pittsburgh	161
1996-97	Mario Lemieux, Pittsburgh	122
1997-98	Jaromir Jagr, Pittsburgh	102
1998-99	Jaromir Jagr, Pittsburgh	127
1999-00	Jaromir Jagr, Pittsburgh	96
2000-01	Jaromir Jagr, Pittsburgh	121
2001-02	Jarome Iginla, Calgary	96
2002-03	Peter Forsberg, Colorado	106
2003-04	Martin St. Louis, Tampa Bay	94

The award was originally known as the Leading Scorer Trophy. The present trophy, first given in 1947, was presented to the NHL by Art Ross, former manager-coach of the Boston Bruins. In event of a tie, the player with the most goals receives the award.

MAURICE RICHARD TROPHY

(Leading goal scorer)

Season	Player, Team	Goals
1998-99	Teemu Selanne, Anaheim	47
1999-00	Pavel Bure, Florida	58
2000-01	Pavel Bure, Florida	59
2001-02	Jarome Iginla, Calgary	52
2002-03	Milan Hejduk, Colorado	50
2003-04	I. Kovalchuk, Atl., J. Iginla, Cal., R. Nash, Clm.	41

HART MEMORIAL TROPHY

(Most Valuable Player)

Season	Player, Team
1923-24	Frank Nighbor, Ottawa
1924-25	Billy Burch, Hamilton
1925-26	Nels Stewart, Montreal Maroons
1926-27	Herb Gardiner, Montreal
1927-28	Howie Morenz, Montreal
1928-29	Roy Worters, N.Y. Americans
1929-30	Nels Stewart, Montreal Maroons
1930-31	Howie Morenz, Montreal
1931-32	Howie Morenz, Montreal
1932-33	Eddie Shore, Boston
1933-34	Aurel Joliat, Montreal
1934-35	Eddie Shore, Boston
1935-36	Eddie Shore, Boston
1936-37	Babe Siebert, Montreal
1937-38	Eddie Shore, Boston
1938-39	Toe Blake, Montreal
1939-40	Ebbie Goodfellow, Detroit
1940-41	Bill Cowley, Boston
1941-42	Tom Anderson, Brooklyn
1942-43	Bill Cowley, Boston
1943-44	Babe Pratt, Toronto

Season	Player, Team
1944-45	Elmer Lach, Montreal
1945-46	Max Bentley, Chicago
1946-47	Maurice Richard, Montreal
1947-48	Buddy O'Connor, N.Y. Rangers
1948-49	Sid Abel, Detroit
1949-50	Chuck Rayner, N.Y. Rangers
1950-51	Milt Schmidt, Boston
1951-52	Gordie Howe, Detroit
1952-53	Gordie Howe, Detroit
1953-54	Al Rollins, Chicago
1954-55	Ted Kennedy, Toronto
1955-56	Jean Beliveau, Montreal
1956-57	Gordie Howe, Detroit
1957-58	Gordie Howe, Detroit
1958-59	Andy Bathgate, N.Y. Rangers
1959-60	Gordie Howe, Detroit
1960-61	Bernie Geoffrion, Montreal
1961-62	Jacques Plante, Montreal
1962-63	Gordie Howe, Detroit
1963-64	Jean Beliveau, Montreal
1964-65	Bobby Hull, Chicago
1965-66	Bobby Hull, Chicago
1966-67	Stan Mikita, Chicago
1967-68	Stan Mikita, Chicago
1968-69	Phil Esposito, Boston
1969-70	Bobby Orr, Boston
1970-71	Bobby Orr, Boston
1971-72	Bobby Orr, Boston
1972-73	Bobby Clarke, Philadelphia
1973-74	Phil Esposito, Boston
1974-75	Bobby Clarke, Philadelphia
1975-76	Bobby Clarke, Philadelphia
1976-77	Guy Lafleur, Montreal
1977-78	Guy Lafleur, Montreal
1978-79	Bryan Trottier, N.Y. Islanders
1979-80	Wayne Gretzky, Edmonton
1980-81	Wayne Gretzky, Edmonton
1981-82	Wayne Gretzky, Edmonton
1982-83	Wayne Gretzky, Edmonton
1983-84	Wayne Gretzky, Edmonton
1984-85	Wayne Gretzky, Edmonton
1985-86	Wayne Gretzky, Edmonton
1986-87	Wayne Gretzky, Edmonton
1987-88	Mario Lemieux, Pittsburgh
1988-89	Wayne Gretzky, Los Angeles
1989-90	Mark Messier, Edmonton
1990-91	Brett Hull, St. Louis
1991-92	Mark Messier, N.Y. Rangers
1992-93	Mario Lemieux, Pittsburgh
1993-94	Sergei Fedorov, Detroit
1994-95	Eric Lindros, Philadelphia
1995-96	Mario Lemieux, Pittsburgh
1996-97	Dominik Hasek, Buffalo
1997-98	Dominik Hasek, Buffalo
1998-99	Jaromir Jagr, Pittsburgh
1999-00	Chris Pronger, St. Louis
2000-01	Joe Sakic, Colorado
2001-02	Jose Theodore, Montreal
2002-03	Peter Forsberg, Colorado
2003-04	Martin St. Louis, Tampa Bay

JAMES NORRIS MEMORIAL TROPHY

(Outstanding defenseman)

Season	Player, Team
1953-54	Red Kelly, Detroit
1954-55	Doug Harvey, Montreal
1955-56	Doug Harvey, Montreal
1956-57	Doug Harvey, Montreal
1957-58	Doug Harvey, Montreal
1958-59	Tom Johnson, Montreal
1959-60	Doug Harvey, Montreal
1960-61	Doug Harvey, Montreal
1961-62	Doug Harvey, N.Y. Rangers
1962-63	Pierre Pilote, Chicago
1963-64	Pierre Pilote, Chicago
1964-65	Pierre Pilote, Chicago
1965-66	Jacques Laperriere, Montreal
1966-67	Harry Howell, N.Y. Rangers
1967-68	Bobby Orr, Boston
1968-69	Bobby Orr, Boston
1969-70	Bobby Orr, Boston
1970-71	Bobby Orr, Boston
1971-72	Bobby Orr, Boston
1972-73	Bobby Orr, Boston
1973-74	Bobby Orr, Boston
1974-75	Bobby Orr, Boston
1975-76	Denis Potvin, N.Y. Islanders
1976-77	Larry Robinson, Montreal
1977-78	Denis Potvin, N.Y. Islanders
1978-79	Denis Potvin, N.Y. Islanders
1979-80	Larry Robinson, Montreal
1980-81	Randy Carlyle, Pittsburgh
1981-82	Doug Wilson, Chicago
1982-83	Rod Langway, Washington
1983-84	Rod Langway, Washington
1984-85	Paul Coffey, Edmonton
1985-86	Paul Coffey, Edmonton
1986-87	Ray Bourque, Boston
1987-88	Ray Bourque, Boston
1988-89	Chris Chelios, Montreal
1989-90	Ray Bourque, Boston
1990-91	Ray Bourque, Boston
1991-92	Brian Leetch, N.Y. Rangers
1992-93	Chris Chelios, Chicago
1993-94	Ray Bourque, Boston
1994-95	Paul Coffey, Detroit
1995-96	Chris Chelios, Chicago
1996-97	Brian Leetch, N.Y. Rangers
1997-98	Rob Blake, Los Angeles
1998-99	Al MacInnis, St. Louis
1999-00	Chris Pronger, St. Louis
2000-01	Nicklas Lidstrom, Detroit
2001-02	Nicklas Lidstrom, Detroit
2002-03	Nicklas Lidstrom, Detroit
2003-04	Scott Niedermayer, New Jersey

VEZINA TROPHY

(Outstanding goaltender)

Season	Player, Team	GAA
1926-27	George Hainsworth, Montreal	1.52
1927-28	George Hainsworth, Montreal	1.09
1928-29	George Hainsworth, Montreal	0.98
1929-30	Tiny Thompson, Boston	2.23
1930-31	Roy Worters, N.Y. Americans	1.68
1931-32	Charlie Gardiner, Chicago	2.10
1932-33	Tiny Thompson, Boston	1.83
1933-34	Charlie Gardiner, Chicago	1.73
1934-35	Lorne Chabot, Chicago	1.83
1935-36	Tiny Thompson, Boston	1.71
1936-37	Normie Smith, Detroit	2.13
1937-38	Tiny Thompson, Boston	1.85
1938-39	Frank Brimsek, Boston	1.60
1939-40	Dave Kerr, N.Y. Rangers	1.60
1940-41	Turk Broda, Toronto	2.60
1941-42	Frank Brimsek, Boston	2.38
1942-43	Johnny Mowers, Detroit	2.48
1943-44	Bill Durnan, Montreal	2.18
1944-45	Bill Durnan, Montreal	2.42
1945-46	Bill Durnan, Montreal	2.60
1946-47	Bill Durnan, Montreal	2.30
1947-48	Turk Broda, Toronto	2.38
1948-49	Bill Durnan, Montreal	2.10
1949-50	Bill Durnan, Montreal	2.20

Season	Player, Team	GAA
1950-51	Al Rollins, Toronto	1.75
1951-52	Terry Sawchuk, Detroit	1.98
1952-53	Terry Sawchuk, Detroit	1.94
1953-54	Harry Lumley, Toronto	1.85
1954-55	Terry Sawchuk, Detroit	1.94
1955-56	Jacques Plante, Montreal	1.86
1956-57	Jacques Plante, Montreal	2.02
1957-58	Jacques Plante, Montreal	2.09
1958-59	Jacques Plante, Montreal	2.15
1959-60	Jacques Plante, Montreal	2.54
1960-61	Johnny Bower, Toronto	2.50
1961-62	Jacques Plante, Montreal	2.37
1962-63	Glenn Hall, Chicago	2.51
1963-64	Charlie Hodge, Montreal	2.26
1964-65	Terry Sawchuk, Toronto	2.56
	Johnny Bower, Toronto	2.38
1965-66	Lorne Worsley, Montreal	2.36
	Charlie Hodge, Montreal	2.58
1966-67	Glenn Hall, Chicago	2.38
	Denis DeJordy, Chicago	2.46
1967-68	Lorne Worsley, Montreal	1.98
	Rogatien Vachon, Montreal	2.48
1968-69	Glenn Hall, St. Louis	2.17
	Jacques Plante, St. Louis	1.96
1969-70	Tony Esposito, Chicago	2.17
1970-71	Ed Giacomin, N.Y. Rangers	2.16
	Gilles Villemure, N.Y. Rangers	2.30
1971-72	Tony Esposito, Chicago	1.77
	Gary Smith, Chicago	2.42
1972-73	Ken Dryden, Montreal	2.26
1973-74	Bernie Parent, Philadelphia	1.89
	Tony Esposito, Chicago	2.04
1974-75	Bernie Parent, Philadelphia	2.03
1975-76	Ken Dryden, Montreal	2.03
1976-77	Ken Dryden, Montreal	2.14
	Michel Larocque, Montreal	2.09
1977-78	Ken Dryden, Montreal	2.05
	Michel Larocque, Montreal	2.67
1978-79	Ken Dryden, Montreal	2.30
	Michel Larocque, Montreal	2.84
1979-80	Bob Sauve, Buffalo	2.36
	Don Edwards, Buffalo	2.57
1980-81	Richard Sevigny, Montreal	2.40
	Michel Larocque, Montreal	3.03
	Denis Herron, Montreal	3.50
1981-82	Billy Smith, N.Y. Islanders	2.97
1982-83	Pete Peeters, Boston	2.36
1983-84	Tom Barrasso, Buffalo	2.84
1984-85	Pelle Lindbergh, Philadelphia	3.02
1985-86	John Vanbiesbrouck, N.Y. Rangers	3.32
1986-87	Ron Hextall, Philadelphia	3.00
1987-88	Grant Fuhr, Edmonton	3.43
1988-89	Patrick Roy, Montreal	2.47
1989-90	Patrick Roy, Montreal	2.53
1990-91	Ed Belfour, Chicago	2.47
1991-92	Patrick Roy, Montreal	2.36
1992-93	Ed Belfour, Chicago	2.59
1993-94	Dominik Hasek, Buffalo	1.95
1994-95	Dominik Hasek, Buffalo	2.11
1995-96	Jim Carey, Washington	2.26
1996-97	Dominik Hasek, Buffalo	2.27
1997-98	Dominik Hasek, Buffalo	2.09
1998-99	Dominik Hasek, Buffalo	1.87
1999-00	Olaf Kolzig, Washington	2.24
2000-01	Dominik Hasek, Buffalo	2.11
2001-02	Jose Theodore, Montreal	2.11
2002-03	Martin Brodeur, New Jersey	2.02
2003-04	Martin Brodeur, New Jersey	2.02

The award was formerly presented to the goaltender(s) having played a minimum of 25 games for the team with the fewest goals scored against. Beginning with the 1981-82 season, it was awarded to the outstanding goaltender.

LESTER B. PEARSON AWARD

(Most outstanding player as selected by NHL Players' Association members)

Season	Player, Team
1970-71	Phil Esposito, Boston
1971-72	Jean Ratelle, N.Y. Rangers
1972-73	Bobby Clarke, Philadelphia
1973-74	Phil Esposito, Boston
1974-75	Bobby Orr, Boston
1975-76	Guy Lafleur, Montreal
1976-77	Guy Lafleur, Montreal
1977-78	Guy Lafleur, Montreal
1978-79	Marcel Dionne, Los Angeles
1979-80	Marcel Dionne, Los Angeles
1980-81	Mike Liut, St. Louis
1981-82	Wayne Gretzky, Edmonton
1982-83	Wayne Gretzky, Edmonton
1983-84	Wayne Gretzky, Edmonton
1984-85	Wayne Gretzky, Edmonton
1985-86	Mario Lemieux, Pittsburgh
1986-87	Wayne Gretzky, Edmonton
1987-88	Mario Lemieux, Pittsburgh
1988-89	Steve Yzerman, Detroit
1989-90	Mark Messier, Edmonton
1990-91	Brett Hull, St. Louis
1991-92	Mark Messier, N.Y. Rangers
1992-93	Mario Lemieux, Pittsburgh
1993-94	Sergei Fedorov, Detroit
1994-95	Eric Lindros, Philadelphia
1995-96	Mario Lemieux, Pittsburgh
1996-97	Dominik Hasek, Buffalo
1997-98	Dominik Hasek, Buffalo
1998-99	Jaromir Jagr, Pittsburgh
1999-00	Jaromir Jagr, Pittsburgh
2000-01	Joe Sakic, Colorado
2001-02	Jarome Iginla, Calgary
2002-03	Markus Naslund, Vancouver
2003-04	Martin St. Louis, Tampa Bay

WILLIAM M. JENNINGS TROPHY

(Leading goaltender)

Season	Player, Team	GAA
1981-82	Denis Herron, Montreal	2.64
	Rick Wamsley, Montreal	2.75
1982-83	Roland Melanson, N.Y. Islanders	2.66
	Billy Smith, N.Y. Islanders	2.87
1983-84	Pat Riggin, Washington	2.66
	Al Jensen, Washington	2.91
1984-85	Tom Barrasso, Buffalo	2.66
	Bob Sauve, Buffalo	3.22
1985-86	Bob Froese, Philadelphia	2.55
	Darren Jensen, Philadelphia	3.68
1986-87	Brian Hayward, Montreal	2.81
	Patrick Roy, Montreal	2.93
1987-88	Brian Hayward, Montreal	2.86
	Patrick Roy, Montreal	2.90
1988-89	Patrick Roy, Montreal	2.47
	Brian Hayward, Montreal	2.90
1989-90	Rejean Lemelin, Boston	2.81
	Andy Moog, Boston	2.89
1990-91	Ed Belfour, Chicago	2.47
1991-92	Patrick Roy, Montreal	2.36
1992-93	Ed Belfour, Chicago	2.59
1993-94	Dominik Hasek, Buffalo	1.95
	Grant Fuhr, Buffalo	3.68
1994-95	Ed Belfour, Chicago	2.28

Season	Player, Team	GAA
1995-96—	Chris Osgood, Detroit	2.17
	Mike Vernon, Detroit	2.26
1996-97—	Martin Brodeur, New Jersey	1.88
	Mike Dunham, New Jersey	2.55
1997-98—	Martin Brodeur, New Jersey	1.89
1998-99—	Ed Belfour, Dallas	1.99
	Roman Turek, Dallas	2.08
1999-00—	Roman Turek, St. Louis	1.95
2000-01—	Dominik Hasek, Buffalo	2.11
2001-02—	Patrick Roy, Colorado	1.94
2002-03—	Roman Cechmanek, Philadelphia	1.83
	Robert Esche, Philadelphia	2.20
	Martin Brodeur, New Jersey	2.02
2003-04—	Martin Brodeur, New Jersey	2.03

The award is presented to the goaltender(s) having played a minimum of 25 games for the team with the fewest goals scored against.

CALDER MEMORIAL TROPHY

(Rookie of the year)

Season Player, Team
1932-33—Carl Voss, Detroit
1933-34—Russ Blinco, Montreal Maroons
1934-35—Dave Schriner, N.Y. Americans
1935-36—Mike Karakas, Chicago
1936-37—Syl Apps, Toronto
1937-38—Cully Dahlstrom, Chicago
1938-39—Frank Brimsek, Boston
1939-40—Kilby Macdonald, N.Y. Rangers
1940-41—John Quilty, Montreal
1941-42—Grant Warwick, N.Y. Rangers
1942-43—Gaye Stewart, Toronto
1943-44—Gus Bodnar, Toronto
1944-45—Frank McCool, Toronto
1945-46—Edgar Laprade, N.Y. Rangers
1946-47—Howie Meeker, Toronto
1947-48—Jim McFadden, Detroit
1948-49—Pentti Lund, N.Y. Rangers
1949-50—Jack Gelineau, Boston
1950-51—Terry Sawchuk, Detroit
1951-52—Bernie Geoffrion, Montreal
1952-53—Lorne Worsley, N.Y. Rangers
1953-54—Camille Henry, N.Y. Rangers
1954-55—Ed Litzenberger, Chicago
1955-56—Glenn Hall, Detroit
1956-57—Larry Regan, Boston
1957-58—Frank Mahovlich, Toronto
1958-59—Ralph Backstrom, Montreal
1959-60—Bill Hay, Chicago
1960-61—Dave Keon, Toronto
1961-62—Bobby Rousseau, Montreal
1962-63—Kent Douglas, Toronto
1963-64—Jacques Laperriere, Montreal
1964-65—Roger Crozier, Detroit
1965-66—Brit Selby, Toronto
1966-67—Bobby Orr, Boston
1967-68—Derek Sanderson, Boston
1968-69—Danny Grant, Minnesota
1969-70—Tony Esposito, Chicago
1970-71—Gilbert Perreault, Buffalo
1971-72—Ken Dryden, Montreal
1972-73—Steve Vickers, N.Y. Rangers
1973-74—Denis Potvin, N.Y. Islanders
1974-75—Eric Vail, Atlanta
1975-76—Bryan Trottier, N.Y. Islanders
1976-77—Willi Plett, Atlanta
1977-78—Mike Bossy, N.Y. Islanders
1978-79—Bobby Smith, Minnesota
1979-80—Ray Bourque, Boston
1980-81—Peter Stastny, Quebec

Season Player, Team
1981-82—Dale Hawerchuk, Winnipeg
1982-83—Steve Larmer, Chicago
1983-84—Tom Barrasso, Buffalo
1984-85—Mario Lemieux, Pittsburgh
1985-86—Gary Suter, Calgary
1986-87—Luc Robitaille, Los Angeles
1987-88—Joe Nieuwendyk, Calgary
1988-89—Brian Leetch, N.Y. Rangers
1989-90—Sergei Makarov, Calgary
1990-91—Ed Belfour, Chicago
1991-92—Pavel Bure, Vancouver
1992-93—Teemu Selanne, Winnipeg
1993-94—Martin Brodeur, New Jersey
1994-95—Peter Forsberg, Quebec
1995-96—Daniel Alfredsson, Ottawa
1996-97—Bryan Berard, N.Y. Islanders
1997-98—Sergei Samsonov, Boston
1998-99—Chris Drury, Colorado
1999-00—Scott Gomez, New Jersey
2000-01—Evgeni Nabokov, San Jose
2001-02—Dany Heatley, Atlanta
2002-03—Barret Jackman, St. Louis
2003-04—Andrew Raycroft, Boston

The award was originally known as the Leading Rookie Award. It was renamed the Calder Trophy in 1936-37 and became the Calder Memorial Trophy in 1942-43, following the death of NHL President Frank Calder.

LADY BYNG MEMORIAL TROPHY

(Most gentlemanly player)

Season Player, Team
1924-25—Frank Nighbor, Ottawa
1925-26—Frank Nighbor, Ottawa
1926-27—Billy Burch, N.Y. Americans
1927-28—Frank Boucher, N.Y. Rangers
1928-29—Frank Boucher, N.Y. Rangers
1929-30—Frank Boucher, N.Y. Rangers
1930-31—Frank Boucher, N.Y. Rangers
1931-32—Joe Primeau, Toronto
1932-33—Frank Boucher, N.Y. Rangers
1933-34—Frank Boucher, N.Y. Rangers
1934-35—Frank Boucher, N.Y. Rangers
1935-36—Doc Romnes, Chicago
1936-37—Marty Barry, Detroit
1937-38—Gordie Drillon, Toronto
1938-39—Clint Smith, N.Y. Rangers
1939-40—Bobby Bauer, Boston
1940-41—Bobby Bauer, Boston
1941-42—Syl Apps, Toronto
1942-43—Max Bentley, Chicago
1943-44—Clint Smith, Chicago
1944-45—Bill Mosienko, Chicago
1945-46—Toe Blake, Montreal
1946-47—Bobby Bauer, Boston
1947-48—Buddy O'Connor, N.Y. Rangers
1948-49—Bill Quackenbush, Detroit
1949-50—Edgar Laprade, N.Y. Rangers
1950-51—Red Kelly, Detroit
1951-52—Sid Smith, Toronto
1952-53—Red Kelly, Detroit
1953-54—Red Kelly, Detroit
1954-55—Sid Smith, Toronto
1955-56—Earl Reibel, Detroit
1956-57—Andy Hebenton, N.Y. Rangers
1957-58—Camille Henry, N.Y. Rangers
1958-59—Alex Delvecchio, Detroit
1959-60—Don McKenney, Boston
1960-61—Red Kelly, Toronto
1961-62—Dave Keon, Toronto
1962-63—Dave Keon, Toronto

Season Player, Team
1963-64—Ken Wharram, Chicago
1964-65—Bobby Hull, Chicago
1965-66—Alex Delvecchio, Detroit
1966-67—Stan Mikita, Chicago
1967-68—Stan Mikita, Chicago
1968-69—Alex Delvecchio, Detroit
1969-70—Phil Goyette, St. Louis
1970-71—John Bucyk, Boston
1971-72—Jean Ratelle, N.Y. Rangers
1972-73—Gilbert Perreault, Buffalo
1973-74—John Bucyk, Boston
1974-75—Marcel Dionne, Detroit
1975-76—Jean Ratelle, N.Y. R.-Boston
1976-77—Marcel Dionne, Los Angeles
1977-78—Butch Goring, Los Angeles
1978-79—Bob MacMillan, Atlanta
1979-80—Wayne Gretzky, Edmonton
1980-81—Rick Kehoe, Pittsburgh
1981-82—Rick Middleton, Boston
1982-83—Mike Bossy, N.Y. Islanders
1983-84—Mike Bossy, N.Y. Islanders
1984-85—Jari Kurri, Edmonton
1985-86—Mike Bossy, N.Y. Islanders
1986-87—Joe Mullen, Calgary
1987-88—Mats Naslund, Montreal
1988-89—Joe Mullen, Calgary
1989-90—Brett Hull, St. Louis
1990-91—Wayne Gretzky, Los Angeles
1991-92—Wayne Gretzky, Los Angeles
1992-93—Pierre Turgeon, N.Y. Islanders
1993-94—Wayne Gretzky, Los Angeles
1994-95—Ron Francis, Pittsburgh
1995-96—Paul Kariya, Anaheim
1996-97—Paul Kariya, Anaheim
1997-98—Ron Francis, Pittsburgh
1998-99—Wayne Gretzky, N.Y. Rangers
1999-00—Pavol Demitra, St. Louis
2000-01—Joe Sakic, Colorado
2001-02—Ron Francis, Carolina
2002-03—Alexander Mogilny, Toronto
2003-04—Brad Richards, Tampa Bay

The award was originally known as the Lady Byng Trophy. After winning the award seven times, Frank Boucher received permanent possession and a new trophy was donated to the NHL in 1936. After Lady Byng's death in 1949, the NHL changed the name to Lady Byng Memorial Trophy.

CONN SMYTHE TROPHY

(Playoff MVP)

Season Player, Team
1964-65—Jean Beliveau, Montreal
1965-66—Roger Crozier, Detroit
1966-67—Dave Keon, Toronto
1967-68—Glenn Hall, St. Louis
1968-69—Serge Savard, Montreal
1969-70—Bobby Orr, Boston
1970-71—Ken Dryden, Montreal
1971-72—Bobby Orr, Boston
1972-73—Yvan Cournoyer, Montreal
1973-74—Bernie Parent, Philadelphia
1974-75—Bernie Parent, Philadelphia
1975-76—Reggie Leach, Philadelphia
1976-77—Guy Lafleur, Montreal
1977-78—Larry Robinson, Montreal
1978-79—Bob Gainey, Montreal
1979-80—Bryan Trottier, N.Y. Islanders
1980-81—Butch Goring, N.Y. Islanders
1981-82—Mike Bossy, N.Y. Islanders
1982-83—Billy Smith, N.Y. Islanders
1983-84—Mark Messier, Edmonton

Season Player, Team
1984-85—Wayne Gretzky, Edmonton
1985-86—Patrick Roy, Montreal
1986-87—Ron Hextall, Philadelphia
1987-88—Wayne Gretzky, Edmonton
1988-89—Al MacInnis, Calgary
1989-90—Bill Ranford, Edmonton
1990-91—Mario Lemieux, Pittsburgh
1991-92—Mario Lemieux, Pittsburgh
1992-93—Patrick Roy, Montreal
1993-94—Brian Leetch, N.Y. Rangers
1994-95—Claude Lemieux, New Jersey
1995-96—Joe Sakic, Colorado
1996-97—Mike Vernon, Detroit
1997-98—Steve Yzerman, Detroit
1998-99—Joe Nieuwendyk, Dallas
1999-00—Scott Stevens, New Jersey
2000-01—Patrick Roy, Colorado
2001-02—Niklas Lidstrom, Detroit
2002-03—Jean-Sebastien Giguere, Anaheim
2003-04—Brad Richards, Tampa Bay

FRANK J. SELKE TROPHY

(Best defensive forward)

Season Player, Team
1977-78—Bob Gainey, Montreal
1978-79—Bob Gainey, Montreal
1979-80—Bob Gainey, Montreal
1980-81—Bob Gainey, Montreal
1981-82—Steve Kasper, Boston
1982-83—Bobby Clarke, Philadelphia
1983-84—Doug Jarvis, Washington
1984-85—Craig Ramsay, Buffalo
1985-86—Troy Murray, Chicago
1986-87—Dave Poulin, Philadelphia
1987-88—Guy Carbonneau, Montreal
1988-89—Guy Carbonneau, Montreal
1989-90—Rick Meagher, St. Louis
1990-91—Dirk Graham, Chicago
1991-92—Guy Carbonneau, Montreal
1992-93—Doug Gilmour, Toronto
1993-94—Sergei Fedorov, Detroit
1994-95—Ron Francis, Pittsburgh
1995-96—Sergei Fedorov, Detroit
1996-97—Michael Peca, Buffalo
1997-98—Jere Lehtinen, Dallas
1998-99—Jere Lehtinen, Dallas
1999-00—Steve Yzerman, Detroit
2000-01—John Madden, New Jersey
2001-02—Michael Peca, N.Y. Islanders
2002-03—Jere Lehtinen, Dallas
2003-04—Kris Draper, Detroit

BILL MASTERTON MEMORIAL TROPHY

(Sportsmanship, dedication to hockey)

Season Player, Team
1967-68—Claude Provost, Montreal
1968-69—Ted Hampson, Oakland
1969-70—Pit Martin, Chicago
1970-71—Jean Ratelle, N.Y. Rangers
1971-72—Bobby Clarke, Philadelphia
1972-73—Lowell MacDonald, Pittsburgh
1973-74—Henri Richard, Montreal
1974-75—Don Luce, Buffalo
1975-76—Rod Gilbert, N.Y. Rangers
1976-77—Ed Westfall, N.Y. Islanders
1977-78—Butch Goring, Los Angeles
1978-79—Serge Savard, Montreal
1979-80—Al MacAdam, Minnesota

Season Player, Team
1980-81—Blake Dunlop, St. Louis
1981-82—Glenn Resch, Colorado
1982-83—Lanny McDonald, Calgary
1983-84—Brad Park, Detroit
1984-85—Anders Hedberg, N.Y. Rangers
1985-86—Charlie Simmer, Boston
1986-87—Doug Jarvis, Hartford
1987-88—Bob Bourne, Los Angeles
1988-89—Tim Kerr, Philadelphia
1989-90—Gord Kluzak, Boston
1990-91—Dave Taylor, Los Angeles
1991-92—Mark Fitzpatrick, N.Y. Islanders
1992-93—Mario Lemieux, Pittsburgh
1993-94—Cam Neely, Boston
1994-95—Pat LaFontaine, Buffalo
1995-96—Gary Roberts, Calgary
1996-97—Tony Granato, San Jose
1997-98—Jamie McLennan, St. Louis
1998-99—John Cullen, Tampa Bay
1999-00—Ken Daneyko, New Jersey
2000-01—Adam Graves, N.Y. Rangers
2001-02—Saku Koivu, Montreal
2002-03—Steve Yzerman, Detroit
2003-04—Bryan Berard, Chicago

Presented by the Professional Hockey Writers' Association to the player who best exemplifies the qualities of perseverance, sportsmanship and dedication to hockey.

JACK ADAMS AWARD

(Coach of the year)

Season Coach, Team
1973-74—Fred Shero, Philadelphia
1974-75—Bob Pulford, Los Angeles
1975-76—Don Cherry, Boston
1976-77—Scotty Bowman, Montreal
1977-78—Bobby Kromm, Detroit
1978-79—Al Arbour, N.Y. Islanders
1979-80—Pat Quinn, Philadelphia
1980-81—Red Berenson, St. Louis
1981-82—Tom Watt, Winnipeg
1982-83—Orval Tessier, Chicago
1983-84—Bryan Murray, Washington
1984-85—Mike Keenan, Philadelphia
1985-86—Glen Sather, Edmonton
1986-87—Jacques Demers, Detroit
1987-88—Jacques Demers, Detroit
1988-89—Pat Burns, Montreal
1989-90—Bob Murdoch, Winnipeg
1990-91—Brian Sutter, St. Louis
1991-92—Pat Quinn, Vancouver
1992-93—Pat Burns, Toronto
1993-94—Jacques Lemaire, New Jersey
1994-95—Marc Crawford, Quebec
1995-96—Scotty Bowman, Detroit
1996-97—Ted Nolan, Buffalo
1997-98—Pat Burns, Boston
1998-99—Jacques Martin, Ottawa
1999-00—Joel Quenneville, St. Louis
2000-01—Bill Barber, Philadelphia
2001-02—Bob Francis, Phoenix
2002-03—Jacques Lemaire, Minnesota
2003-04—John Tortorella, Tampa Bay

KING CLANCY TROPHY

(Humanitarian contributions)

Season Player, Team
1987-88—Lanny McDonald, Calgary
1988-89—Bryan Trottier, N.Y. Islanders
1989-90—Kevin Lowe, Edmonton
1990-91—Dave Taylor, Los Angeles
1991-92—Ray Bourque, Boston
1992-93—Dave Poulin, Boston
1993-94—Adam Graves, N.Y. Rangers
1994-95—Joe Nieuwendyk, Calgary
1995-96—Kris King, Winnipeg
1996-97—Trevor Linden, Vancouver
1997-98—Kelly Chase, St. Louis
1998-99—Rob Ray, Buffalo
1999-00—Curtis Joseph, Toronto
2000-01—Shjon Podein, Colorado
2001-02—Ron Francis, Carolina
2002-03—Brendan Shanahan, Detroit
2003-04—Jarome Iginla, Calgary

THE SPORTING NEWS AWARDS

PLAYER OF THE YEAR

1967-68—E. Div.: Stan Mikita, Chicago
W. Div.: Red Berenson, St. Louis
1968-69—E. Div.: Phil Esposito, Boston
W. Div.: Red Berenson, St. Louis
1969-70—E. Div.: Bobby Orr, Boston
W. Div.: Red Berenson, St. Louis
1970-71—E. Div.: Phil Esposito, Boston
W. Div.: Bobby Hull, Chicago
1971-72—E. Div.: Jean Ratelle, N.Y. Rangers
W. Div.: Bobby Hull, Chicago
1972-73—E. Div.: Phil Esposito, Boston
W. Div.: Bobby Clarke, Philadelphia
1973-74—E. Div.: Phil Esposito, Boston
W. Div.: Bernie Parent, Philadelphia
1974-75—Camp. Conf.: Bobby Clarke, Philadelphia
Wales Conf.: Guy Lafleur, Montreal
1975-76—Bobby Clarke, Philadelphia
1976-77—Guy Lafleur, Montreal
1977-78—Guy Lafleur, Montreal
1978-79—Bryan Trottier, N.Y. Islanders
1979-80—Marcel Dionne, Los Angeles
1980-81—Wayne Gretzky, Edmonton
1981-82—Wayne Gretzky, Edmonton
1982-83—Wayne Gretzky, Edmonton
1983-84—Wayne Gretzky, Edmonton
1984-85—Wayne Gretzky, Edmonton
1985-86—Wayne Gretzky, Edmonton
1986-87—Wayne Gretzky, Edmonton
1987-88—Mario Lemieux, Pittsburgh
1988-89—Mario Lemieux, Pittsburgh
1989-90—Mark Messier, Edmonton
1990-91—Brett Hull, St. Louis
1991-92—Mark Messier, N.Y. Rangers
1992-93—Mario Lemieux, Pittsburgh
1993-94—Sergei Fedorov, Detroit
1994-95—Eric Lindros, Philadelphia
1995-96—Mario Lemieux, Pittsburgh
1996-97—Dominik Hasek, Buffalo
1997-98—Dominik Hasek, Buffalo
1998-99—Jaromir Jagr, Pittsburgh
1999-00—Jaromir Jagr, Pittsburgh
2000-01—Joe Sakic, Colorado
2001-02—Jarome Iginla, Calgary
2002-03—Peter Forsberg, Colorado
2003-04—Martin St. Louis, Tampa Bay

ROOKIE OF THE YEAR

1967-68—E. Div.: Derek Sanderson, Boston
W. Div.: Bill Flett, Los Angeles
1968-69—E. Div.: Brad Park, N.Y. Rangers

W. Div.: Norm Ferguson, Oakland
1969-70—E. Div.: Tony Esposito, Chicago
W. Div.: Bobby Clarke, Philadelphia
1970-71—E. Div.: Gil Perreault, Buffalo
W. Div.: Jude Drouin, Minnesota
1971-72—E. Div.: Richard Martin, Buffalo
W. Div.: Gilles Meloche, California
1972-73—E. Div.: Steve Vickers, N.Y. Rangers
W. Div.: Bill Barber, Philadelphia
1973-74—E. Div.: Denis Potvin, N.Y. Islanders
W. Div.: Tom Lysiak, Atlanta
1974-75—Camp. Conf.: Eric Vail, Atlanta
Wales Conf.: Pierre Larouche, Pittsburgh
1975-76—Bryan Trottier, N.Y. Islanders
1976-77—Willi Plett, Atlanta
1977-78—Mike Bossy, N.Y. Islanders
1978-79—Bobby Smith, Minnesota
1979-80—Ray Bourque, Boston
1980-81—Peter Stastny, Quebec
1981-82—Dale Hawerchuk, Winnipeg
1982-83—Steve Larmer, Chicago
1983-84—Steve Yzerman, Detroit
1984-85—Mario Lemieux, Pittsburgh
1985-86—Wendel Clark, Toronto
1986-87—Ron Hextall, Philadelphia
1987-88—Joe Nieuwendyk, Calgary
1988-89—Brian Leetch, N.Y. Rangers
1989-90—Jeremy Roenick, Chicago
1990-91—Ed Belfour, Chicago
1991-92—Tony Amonte, N.Y. Rangers
1992-93—Teemu Selanne, Winnipeg
1993-94—Jason Arnott, Edmonton
1994-95—Peter Forsberg, Quebec
1995-96—Eric Daze, Chicago
1996-97—Bryan Berard, N.Y. Islanders
1997-98—Sergei Samsonov, Boston
1998-99—Chris Drury, Colorado
1999-00—Scott Gomez, New Jersey
2000-01—Evgeni Nabokov, San Jose
2001-02—Dany Heatley, Atlanta
2002-03—Henrik Zetterberg, Detroit
2003-04—Michael Ryder, Montreal

NHL COACH OF THE YEAR

1944-45—Dick Irvin, Montreal
1945-46—Johnny Gottselig, Chicago
1979-80—Pat Quinn, Philadelphia
1980-81—Red Berenson, St. Louis
1981-82—Herb Brooks, N.Y. Rangers
1982-83—Gerry Cheevers, Boston
1983-84—Bryan Murray, Washington
1984-85—Mike Keenan, Philadelphia
1985-86—Jacques Demers, St. Louis
1986-87—Jacques Demers, Detroit
1987-88—Terry Crisp, Calgary
1988-89—Pat Burns, Montreal
1989-90—Mike Milbury, Boston
1990-91—Tom Webster, Los Angeles
1991-92—Pat Quinn, Vancouver
1992-93—Pat Burns, Toronto
1993-94—Jacques Lemaire, New Jersey
1994-95—Marc Crawford, Quebec
1995-96—Scotty Bowman, Detroit
1996-97—Ken Hitchcock, Dallas
1997-98—Pat Burns, Boston
1998-99—Jacques Martin, Ottawa
1999-00—Joel Quenneville, St. Louis
2000-01—Scotty Bowman, Detroit
2001-02—Brian Sutter, Chicago
2002-03—Jacques Lemaire, Minnesota
2003-04—John Tortorella, Tampa Bay

NOTE: The Coach of the Year Award was not given from 1946-47 through 1978-79 seasons.

NHL EXECUTIVE OF THE YEAR

1972-73—Sam Pollock, Montreal
1973-74—Keith Allen, Philadelphia
1974-75—Bill Torrey, N.Y. Islanders
1975-76—Sam Pollock, Montreal
1976-77—Harry Sinden, Boston
1977-78—Ted Lindsay, Detroit
1978-79—Bill Torrey, N.Y. Islanders
1979-80—Scotty Bowman, Buffalo
1980-81—Emile Francis, St. Louis
1981-82—John Ferguson, Winnipeg
1982-83—David Poile, Washington
1983-84—David Poile, Washington
1984-85—John Ferguson, Winnipeg
1985-86—Emile Francis, Hartford
1986-87—John Ferguson, Winnipeg
1987-88—Cliff Fletcher, Calgary
1988-89—Bruce McNall, Los Angeles
1989-90—Harry Sinden, Boston
1990-91—Craig Patrick, Pittsburgh
1991-92—Neil Smith, N.Y. Rangers
1992-93—Cliff Fletcher, Toronto
1993-94—Bobby Clarke, Florida
1994-95—Bobby Clarke, Philadelphia
1995-96—Bryan Murray, Florida
1996-97—John Muckler, Buffalo
1997-98—Craig Patrick, Pittsburgh
1998-99—Craig Patrick, Pittsburgh
1999-00—Larry Pleau, St. Louis
2000-01—Brian Burke, Vancouver
2001-02—Mike Smith, Chicago
2002-03—Doug Risebrough, Minnesota
2003-04—Jay Feaster, Tampa Bay

THE SPORTING NEWS ALL-STAR TEAMS

(As selected by six hockey writers in 1944-45 and 1945-46 and by a vote of league players since 1967-68; no teams selected from 1946-47 through 1966-67)

1944-45

First team		Second team
Maurice Richard, Mon.	W	Bill Mosienko, Chi.
Toe Blake, Mon.	W	Sweeney Schriner, Tor.
Elmer Lach, Mon.	C	Bill Cowley, Bos.
Emile Bouchard, Mon.	D	Earl Seibert, Det.
Bill Hollett, Det.	D	Babe Pratt, Tor.
Bill Durnan, Mon.	G	Frank McCool, Tor.

1945-46

First team		Second team
Gaye Stewart, Tor.	LW	Doug Bentley, Chi.
Max Bentley, Chi.	C	Elmer Lach, Mon.
Bill Mosienko, Chi.	RW	Maurice Richard, Mon.
Emile Bouchard, Mon.	D	Jack Crawford, Bos.
Jack Stewart, Det.	D	Babe Pratt, Tor.
Bill Durnan, Mon.	G	Harry Lumley, Det.

1967-68

EAST DIVISION		WEST DIVISION
First team		First team
Bobby Hull, Chi.	LW	Ab McDonald, Pit.
Stan Mikita, Chi.	C	Red Berenson, St.L.
Gordie Howe, Det.	RW	Wayne Connelly, Min.
Bobby Orr, Bos.	D	Bill White, L.A.
Tim Horton, Tor.	D	Mike McMahon, Min.
Ed Giacomin, N.Y.R.	G	Glenn Hall, St.L.

Second team		Second team
Johnny Bucyk, Bos.	LW	Bill Sutherland, Phi.
Phil Esposito, Bos.	C	Ray Cullen, Min.
Rod Gilbert, N.Y.R.	RW	Bill Flett, L.A.
J.C. Tremblay, Mon.	D	Al Arbour, St.L.
Gary Bergman, Det.	D	Ed Van Impe, Phi.
Gump Worsley, Mon.	G	Doug Favell, Phi.

1968-69

EAST DIVISION		WEST DIVISION
First team		**First team**
Bobby Hull, Chi.	LW	Danny Grant, Min.
Phil Esposito, Bos.	C	Red Berenson, St.L.
Gordie Howe, Det.	RW	Norm Ferguson, Oak.
Bobby Orr, Bos.	D	Bill White, L.A.
Tim Horton, Tor.	D	Al Arbour, St.L.
Ed Giacomin, N.Y.R.	G	Glenn Hall, St.L.
Second team		**Second team**
Frank Mahovlich, Det.	LW	Ab McDonald, St.L.
Stan Mikita, Chi.	C	Ted Hampson, Oak.
Yvan Cournoyer, Mon.	RW	Claude LaRose, Min.
J.C. Tremblay, Mon.	D	Carol Vadnais, Oak.
Jim Neilson, N.Y.R.	D	Ed Van Impe, Phi.
Bruce Gamble, Tor.	G	Bernie Parent, Phi.

1969-70

EAST DIVISION		WEST DIVISION
Bobby Hull, Chi.	LW	Dean Prentice, Pit.
Stan Mikita, Chi.	C	Red Berenson, St.L.
Ron Ellis, Tor.	RW	Bill Goldsworthy, Min.
Bobby Orr, Bos.	D	Al Arbour, St.L.
Brad Park, N.Y.R.	D	Bob Woytowich, Pit.
Tony Esposito, Chi.	G	Bernie Parent, Phi.

1970-71

EAST DIVISION		WEST DIVISION
Johnny Bucyk, Bos.	LW	Bobby Hull, Chi.
Phil Esposito, Bos.	C	Stan Mikita, Chi.
Ken Hodge, Bos.	RW	Bill Goldsworthy, Min.
Bobby Orr, Bos.	D	Pat Stapleton, Chi.
J.C. Tremblay, Mon.	D	Bill White, Chi.
Ed Giacomin, N.Y.R.	G	Tony Esposito, Chi.

1971-72

EAST DIVISION		WEST DIVISION
Vic Hadfield, N.Y.R.	LW	Bobby Hull, Chi.
Phil Esposito, Bos.	C	Bobby Clarke, Phi.
Rod Gilbert, N.Y.R.	RW	Bill Goldsworthy, Min.
Bobby Orr, Bos.	D	Pat Stapleton, Chi.
Brad Park, N.Y.R.	D	Bill White, Chi.
Ken Dryden, Mon.	G	Tony Esposito, Chi.

1972-73

EAST DIVISION		WEST DIVISION
Frank Mahovlich, Mon.	LW	Dennis Hull, Chi.
Phil Esposito, Bos.	C	Bobby Clarke, Phi.
Mickey Redmond, Det.	RW	Bill Flett, Phi.
Bobby Orr, Bos.	D	Bill White, Chi.
Guy Lapointe, Mon.	D	Barry Gibbs, Min.
Ken Dryden, Mon.	G	Tony Esposito, Chi.

1973-74

EAST DIVISION		WEST DIVISION
First team		**First team**
Richard Martin, Buf.	LW	Lowell MacDonald, Pit.
Phil Esposito, Bos.	C	Bobby Clarke, Phi.
Ken Hodge, Bos.	RW	Bill Goldsworthy, Min.
Bobby Orr, Bos.	D	Bill White, Chi.
Brad Park, N.Y.R.	D	Barry Ashbee, Phi.
Gilles Gilbert, Bos.	G	Bernie Parent, Phi.
Second team		**Second team**
Frank Mahovlich, Mon.	LW	Dennis Hull, Chi.
Darryl Sittler, Tor.	C	Stan Mikita, Chi.
Mickey Redmond, Det.	RW	Jean Pronovost, Pit.
Guy Lapointe, Mon.	D	Don Awrey, St.L.
Borje Salming, Tor.	D	Dave Burrows, Pit.
Ed Giacomin, N.Y.R.	D	Tony Esposito, Chi.

1974-75

CAMPBELL CONFERENCE		WALES CONFERENCE
First team		**First team**
Steve Vickers, N.Y.R.	LW	Richard Martin, Buf.
Bobby Clarke, Phi.	C	Phil Esposito, Bos.
Rod Gilbert, N.Y.R.	RW	Guy Lafleur, Mon.
Denis Potvin, N.Y.I.	D	Bobby Orr, Bos.
Brad Park, N.Y.R.	D	Guy Lapointe, Mon.
Bernie Parent, Phi.	G	Rogie Vachon, L.A.
Second team		**Second team**
Eric Vail, Atl.	LW	Danny Grant, Det.
Stan Mikita, Chi.	C	Gilbert Perreault, Buf.
Reggie Leach, Phi.	RW	Rene Robert, Buf.
Jim Watson, Phi.	D	Borje Salming, Tor.
Phil Russell, Chi.	D	Terry Harper, L.A.
Gary Smith, Van.	G	Ken Dryden, Mon.

1975-76

First team		Second team
Bill Barber, Phi.	LW	Richard Martin, Buf.
Bobby Clarke, Phi.	C	Pete Mahovlich, Mon.
Guy Lafleur, Mon.	RW	Reggie Leach, Phi.
Denis Potvin, N.Y.I.	D	Guy Lapointe, Mon.
Brad Park, Bos.	D	Borje Salming, Tor.
Ken Dryden, Mon.	G	Glenn Resch, N.Y.I.

1976-77

First team		Second team
Steve Shutt, Mon.	LW	Clark Gillies, N.Y.I.
Marcel Dionne, L.A.	C	Gilbert Perreault, Buf.
Guy Lafleur, Mon.	RW	Lanny McDonald, Tor.
Larry Robinson, Mon.	D	Guy Lapointe, Mon.
Borje Salming, Tor.	D	Serge Savard, Mon.
	(tied)	Denis Potvin, N.Y.I.
Rogie Vachon, L.A.	G	Ken Dryden, Mon.

1977-78

First team		Second team
Clark Gillies, N.Y.I.	LW	Steve Shutt, Mon.
Bryan Trottier, N.Y.I.	C	Darryl Sittler, Tor.
Guy Lafleur, Mon.	RW	Terry O'Reilly, Bos.
Borje Salming, Tor.	D	Denis Potvin, N.Y.I.
Larry Robinson, Mon.	D	Serge Savard, Mon.
Ken Dryden, Mon.	G	Don Edwards, Buf.

1978-79

First team		Second team
Clark Gillies, N.Y.I.	LW	Bob Gainey, Mon.
Bryan Trottier, N.Y.I.	C	Marcel Dionne, L.A.
Guy Lafleur, Mon.	RW	Mike Bossy, N.Y.I.
Denis Potvin, N.Y.I.	D	Borje Salming, Tor.
Larry Robinson, Mon.	D	Serge Savard, Mon.
Ken Dryden, Mon.	G	Glenn Resch, N.Y.I.

1979-80

First team		Second team
Charlie Simmer, L.A.	LW	Steve Shutt, Mon.
Marcel Dionne, L.A.	C	Wayne Gretzky, Edm.
Guy Lafleur, Mon.	RW	Danny Gare, Buf.
Larry Robinson, Mon.	D	Barry Beck, Col., N.Y.R.
Borje Salming, Tor.	D	Mark Howe, Har.
Tony Esposito, Chi.	G	Don Edwards, Buf.

1980-81

First team		Second team
Charlie Simmer, L.A.	LW	Bill Barber, Phi.
Wayne Gretzky, Edm.	C	Marcel Dionne, L.A.
Mike Bossy, N.Y.I.	RW	Dave Taylor, L.A.
Randy Carlyle, Pit.	D	Larry Robinson, Mon.
Denis Potvin, N.Y.I.	D	Ray Bourque, Bos.
Mike Liut, St.L.	G	Don Beaupre, Min.

1981-82

First team		Second team
Mark Messier, Edm.	LW	John Tonelli, N.Y.I.
Wayne Gretzky, Edm.	C	Bryan Trottier, N.Y.I.
Mike Bossy, N.Y.I.	RW	Rick Middleton, Bos.
Doug Wilson, Chi.	D	Paul Coffey, Edm.
Ray Bourque, Bos.	D	Larry Robinson, Mon.
Bill Smith, N.Y.I.	G	Grant Fuhr, Edm.

1982-83

First team		Second team
Mark Messier, Edm.	LW	Michel Goulet, Que.
Wayne Gretzky, Edm.	C	Denis Savard, Chi.
Lanny McDonald, Cal.	RW	Mike Bossy, N.Y.I.
Mark Howe, Phi.	D	Ray Bourque, Bos.
Rod Langway, Was.	D	Paul Coffey, Edm.
Pete Peeters, Bos.	G	Andy Moog, Edm.

1983-84

First team		Second team
Michel Goulet, Que.	LW	John Ogrodnick, Det.
Wayne Gretzky, Edm.	C	Bryan Trottier, N.Y.I.
Rick Middleton, Bos.	RW	Mike Bossy, N.Y.I.
Ray Bourque, Bos.	D	Paul Coffey, Edm.
Rod Langway, Was.	D	Denis Potvin, N.Y.I.
Pat Riggin, Was.	G	Tom Barrasso, Buf.

1984-85

First team		Second team
Michel Goulet, Que.	LW	John Ogrodnick, Det.
Wayne Gretzky, Edm.	C	Dale Hawerchuk, Win.
Jari Kurri, Edm.	RW	Mike Bossy, N.Y.I.
Ray Bourque, Bos.	D	Rod Langway, Was.
Paul Coffey, Edm.	D	Doug Wilson, Chi.
Pelle Lindbergh, Phi.	G	Tom Barrasso, Buf.

1985-86

First team		Second team
Michel Goulet, Que.	LW	Mats Naslund, Mon.
Wayne Gretzky, Edm.	C	Mario Lemieux, Pit.
Mike Bossy, N.Y.I.	RW	Jari Kurri, Edm.
Paul Coffey, Edm.	D	Ray Bourque, Bos.
Mark Howe, Phi.	D	Larry Robinson, Mon.
John Vanbiesbrouck, N.Y.R.	G	Grant Fuhr, Edm.

1986-87

First team		Second team
Michel Goulet, Que.	LW	Luc Robitaille, L.A.
Wayne Gretzky, Edm.	C	Mark Messier, Edm.
Tim Kerr, Phi.	RW	Kevin Dineen, Har.
Ray Bourque, Bos.	D	Larry Murphy, Was.
Mark Howe, Phi.	D	Paul Coffey, Edm.
Mike Liut, Har.	G	Ron Hextall, Phi.

1987-88

First team		Second team
Luc Robitaille, L.A.	LW	Michel Goulet, Que.
Mario Lemieux, Pit.	C	Wayne Gretzky, Edm.
Cam Neely, Bos.	RW	Hakan Loob, Cal.
Ray Bourque, Bos.	D	Scott Stevens, Was.
Gary Suter, Cal.	D	Brad McCrimmon, Cal.
Grant Fuhr, Edm.	G	Tom Barrasso, Buf.

1988-89

First team		Second team
Luc Robitaille, L.A.	LW	Mats Naslund, Mon.
Mario Lemieux, Pit.	C	Wayne Gretzky, L.A.
Joe Mullen, Cal.	RW	Jari Kurri, Edm.
Paul Coffey, Pit.	D	Ray Bourque, Bos.
Chris Chelios, Mon.	D	Gary Suter, Cal.
Patrick Roy, Mon.	G	Mike Vernon, Cal.

1989-90

First team		Second team
Luc Robitaille, L.A.	LW	Brian Bellows, Min.
Mark Messier, Edm.	C	Pat LaFontaine, N.Y.I.
Brett Hull, St.L.	RW	Cam Neely, Bos.
Ray Bourque, Bos.	D	Doug Wilson, Chi.
Al MacInnis, Cal.	D	Paul Coffey, Pit.
Patrick Roy, Mon.	G	Daren Puppa, Buf.

1990-91

First team		Second team
Luc Robitaille, L.A.	LW	Kevin Stevens, Pit.
Wayne Gretzky, L.A.	C	Adam Oates, St.L.
Brett Hull, St.L.	RW	Cam Neely, Bos.
Ray Bourque, Bos.	D	Brian Leetch, N.Y.R.
Al MacInnis, Cal.	D	Chris Chelios, Chi.
Ed Belfour, Chi.	G	Patrick Roy, Mon.

1991-92

First team		Second team
Kevin Stevens, Pit.	LW	Luc Robitaille, L.A.
Mark Messier, N.Y.R.	C	Wayne Gretzky, L.A.
Brett Hull, St.L.	RW	Joe Mullen, Pit.
Brian Leetch, N.Y.R.	D	Phil Housley, Win.
Ray Bourque, Bos.	D	Chris Chelios, Chi.
Patrick Roy, Mon.	G	Kirk McLean, Van.

1992-93

First team		Second team
Luc Robitaille, L.A.	LW	Kevin Stevens, Pit.
Mario Lemieux, Pit.	C	Doug Gilmour, Tor.
Teemu Selanne, Win.	RW	Alexander Mogilny, Buf.
Chris Chelios, Chi.	D	Larry Murphy, Pit.
Ray Bourque, Bos.	D	Al Iafrate, Was.
Tom Barrasso, Pit.	G	Ed Belfour, Chi.

1993-94

First team		Second team
Adam Graves, N.Y.R.	LW	Dave Andreychuk, Tor.
Sergei Fedorov, Det.	C	Wayne Gretzky, L.A.
Cam Neely, Bos.	RW	Pavel Bure, Van.
Ray Bourque, Bos.	D	Brian Leetch, N.Y.R.
Scott Stevens, N.J.	D	Al MacInnis, Cal.
John Vanbiesbrouck, Fla.	G	Dominik Hasek, Buf.

1994-95

LW	John LeClair, Mon.-Phi.
C	Eric Lindros, Philadelphia
RW	Jaromir Jagr, Pittsburgh
D	Paul Coffey, Detroit
D	Ray Bourque, Boston
G	Dominik Hasek, Buffalo

1995-96

LW	Keith Tkachuk, Winnipeg
C	Mario Lemieux, Pittsburgh
RW	Jaromir Jagr, Pittsburgh
D	Chris Chelios, Chicago
D	Ray Bourque, Boston
G	Chris Osgood, Detroit

1996-97

LW	John LeClair, Philadelphia
C	Mario Lemieux, Pittsburgh
RW	Teemu Selanne, Anaheim

D	Chris Chelios, Chicago
D	Brian Leetch, N.Y. Rangers
G	Dominik Hasek, Buffalo

1997-98

LW	John LeClair, Philadelphia
C	Peter Forsberg, Colorado
RW	Teemu Selanne, Anaheim
D	Rob Blake, Los Angeles
D	Nicklas Lidstrom, Detroit
G	Dominik Hasek, Buffalo

1998-99

LW	Paul Kariya, Anaheim
C	Alexei Yashin, Ottawa
RW	Jaromir Jagr, Pittsburgh
D	Al MacInnis, St. Louis
D	Nicklas Lidstrom, Detroit
G	Dominik Hasek, Buffalo

1999-2000

LW	Paul Kariya, Anaheim
C	Steve Yzerman, Detroit
RW	Jaromir Jagr, Pittsburgh
D	Nicklas Lidstrom, Detroit
D	Chris Pronger, St. Louis
G	Roman Turek, St. Louis

2000-01

First team		Second team
Alexei Kovalev, Pit.	LW	Patrik Elias, N.J.
Joe Sakic, Col.	C	Mario Lemieux, Pit.
Jaromir Jagr, Pit.	RW	Pavel Bure, Fla.
Rob Blake, L.A.-Col.	D	Brian Leetch, N.Y.R.
Nicklas Lidstrom, Det.	D	Chris Pronger, St.L.
Martin Brodeur, N.J.	G	Sean Burke, Pho.

2001-02

LW	Markus Naslund, Vancouver
C	Joe Sakic, Colorado
RW	Jarome Iginla, Calgary
D	Rob Blake, Colorado
D	Nicklas Lidstrom, Detroit
G	Patrick Roy, Colorado

2002-03

First team		Second team
Markus Naslund, Van.	LW	Marian Hossa, Ottawa
Peter Forsberg, Colo.	C	Joe Thornton, Boston
Todd Bertuzzi, Van.	RW	Milan Hejduk, Colo.
Nicklas Lidstrom, Detroit	D	Rob Blake, Colorado
Al MacInnis, St. Louis	D	Sergei Gonchar, Was.
Martin Brodeur, N.J.	G	Marty Turco, Dallas

2003-04

First team		Second team
Markus Naslund, Vancouver	LW	Alex Tanguay, Colorado
Joe Sakic, Colorado	C	Joe Thornton, Boston
Martin St. Louis, Tampa Bay	RW	Jarome Iginla, Calgary
Nicklas Lidstrom, Detroit	D	Scott Niedermayer, N.J.
Zdeno Chara, Ottawa	D	Rob Blake, Colorado
Roberto Luongo, Florida	G	Martin Brodeur, N.J.

HOCKEY HALL OF FAME

ROSTER OF MEMBERS

NOTE: Leagues other than the NHL with which Hall of Fame members are associated are denoted in parentheses. Abbreviations: **AAHA:** Alberta Amateur Hockey Association. **AHA:** Amateur Hockey Association of Canada. **CAHL:** Canadian Amateur Hockey League. **EAA:** Eaton Athletic Association. **ECAHA:** Eastern Canada Amateur Hockey Association. **ECHA:** Eastern Canada Hockey Association. **FAHL:** Federal Amateur Hockey League. **IHL:** International Professional Hockey League. **MHL:** Manitoba Hockey League. **MNSHL:** Manitoba and Northwestern Senior Hockey League. **MPHL:** Maritime Pro Hockey League. **MSHL:** Manitoba Senior Hockey League. **NHA:** National Hockey Association. **NOHA:** Northern Ontario Hockey Association. **OHA:** Ontario Hockey Association. **OPHL:** Ontario Professional Hockey League. **PCHA:** Pacific Coast Hockey Association. **WCHL:** Western Canada Hockey League. **WHA:** World Hockey Association. **WHL:** Western Hockey League. **WinHL:** Winnipeg Hockey League. **WOHA:** Western Ontario Hockey Association.

PLAYERS

Player	Elec. year/ how elected*	Pos.†	First season	Last season	Stanley Cup wins‡	Teams as player
Abel, Sid	1969/P	C	1938-39	1953-54	3	Detroit Red Wings, Chicago Blackhawks
Adams, Jack	1959/P	C	1917-18	1926-27	2	Toronto Arenas, Vancouver Millionaires (PCHA), Toronto St. Pats, Ottawa Senators
Apps, Syl	1961/P	C	1936-37	1947-48	3	Toronto Maple Leafs
Armstrong, George	1975/P	RW	1949-50	1970-71	4	Toronto Maple Leafs
Bailey, Ace	1975/P	RW	1926-27	1933-34	1	Toronto Maple Leafs
Bain, Dan	1945/P	C	1895-96	1901-02	3	Winnipeg Victorias (MHL)
Baker, Hobey	1945/P	Ro.	1910	1915	0	Princeton University, St. Nicholas
Barber, Bill	1990/P	LW	1972-73	1983-84	2	Philadelphia Flyers
Barry, Marty	1965/P	C	1927-28	1939-40	2	New York Americans, Boston Bruins, Detroit Red Wings, Montreal Canadiens
Bathgate, Andy	1978/P	RW	1952-53	1974-75	1	New York Rangers, Toronto Maple Leafs, Detroit Red Wings, Pittsburgh Penguins, Vancouver Blazers (WHA)
Bauer, Bobby	1996/V	LW	1936-37	1951-52	2	Boston Bruins
Beliveau, Jean	1972/P	C	1950-51	1970-71	10	Montreal Canadiens
Benedict, Clint	1965/P	G	1917-18	1929-30	4	Ottawa Senators, Montreal Maroons
Bentley, Doug	1964/P	LW	1939-40	1953-54	0	Chicago Blackhawks, New York Rangers
Bentley, Max	1966/P	C	1940-41	1953-54	3	Chicago Blackhawks, Toronto Maple Leafs, New York Rangers
Blake, Toe	1966/P	LW	1934-35	1947-48	3	Montreal Maroons, Montreal Canadiens
Boivin, Leo	1986/P	D	1951-52	1969-70	0	Toronto Maple Leafs, Boston Bruins, Detroit Red Wings, Pittsburgh Penguins, Minnesota North Stars
Boon, Dickie	1952/P	D	1897	1905	2	Montreal Monarchs, Montreal AAA (CAHL), Montreal Wanderers (FAHL)
Bossy, Mike	1991/P	RW	1977-78	1986-87	4	New York Islanders
Bouchard, Butch	1966/P	D	1941-42	1955-56	4	Montreal Canadiens
Boucher, Frank	1958/P	C	1921-22	1943-44	2	Ottawa Senators, Vancouver Maroons, New York Rangers
Boucher, Georges	1960/P	F/D	1917-18	1931-32	4	Ottawa Senators, Montreal Maroons, Chicago Blackhawks
Bourque, Raymond	2004/P	D	1979-80	2000-01	1	Boston Bruins, Colorado Avalanche
Bower, Johnny	1976/P	G	1953-54	1969-70	0	New York Rangers, Toronto Maple Leafs
Bowie, Russell	1945/P	C	1898-99	1907-08	1	Montreal Victorias
Brimsek, Frank	1966/P	G	1938-39	1949-50	2	Boston Bruins, Chicago Blackhawks
Broadbent, Punch	1962/P	RW	1912-13	1928-29	4	Ottawa Senators, Montreal Maroons, New York Americans
Broda, Turk	1967/P	G	1936-37	1951-52	0	Toronto Maple Leafs
Bucyk, John	1981/P	LW	1955-56	1977-78	2	Detroit Red Wings, Boston Bruins
Burch, Billy	1974/P	C	1922-23	1932-33	0	Hamilton Tigers, New York Americans, Boston Bruins, Chicago Blackhawks
Cameron, Harry	1962/P	D	1912-13	1925-26	3	Toronto Blueshirts, Toronto Arenas, Montreal Wanderers, Ottawa Senators, Toronto St. Pats, Montreal Canadiens, Saskatoon (WCHL)
Cheevers, Gerry	1985/P	G	1961-62	1979-80	2	Toronto Maple Leafs, Boston Bruins, Cleveland Crusaders (WHA)
Clancy, King	1958/P	D	1921-22	1936-37	3	Ottawa Senators, Toronto Maple Leafs
Clapper, Dit	1947/P	RW	1927-28	1946-47	3	Boston Bruins
Clarke, Bobby	1987/P	C	1969-70	1983-84	2	Philadelphia Flyers
Cleghorn, Sprague	1958/P	D	1909-10	1927-28	3	New York Crescents, Renfrew Creamery Kings (NHA), Montreal Wanderers, Ottawa Senators, Toronto St. Pats, Montreal Canadiens, Boston Bruins
Coffey, Paul	2004/P	D	1980-81	2000-01	4	Edmonton Oilers, Pittsburgh Penguins, Los Angeles Kings, Detroit Red Wings, Hartford Whalers, Philadelphia Flyers, Chicago Blackhawks, Carolina Hurricanes, Boston Bruins
Colville, Neil	1967/P	C/D	1935-36	1948-49	1	New York Rangers
Conacher, Charlie	1961/P	RW	1929-30	1940-41	1	Toronto Maple Leafs, Detroit Red Wings, New York Americans
Conacher, Lionel	1994/V	D	1925-26	1936-37	2	Pittsburgh Pirates, New York Americans, Montreal Maroons, Chicago Blackhawks
Conacher, Roy	1998/V	LW	1938-39	1951-52	2	Boston Bruins, Detroit Red Wings, Chicago Blackhawks
Connell, Alex	1958/P	G	1924-25	1936-37	2	Ottawa Senators, Detroit Falcons, New York Americans, Montreal Maroons

Player	Elec. year/ how elected*	Pos.†	First season	Last season	Stanley Cup wins‡	Teams as player
Cook, Bill	1952/P	RW	1921-22	1936-37	2	Saskatoon (WCHL/WHL), New York Rangers
Cook, Bun	1995/V	LW	1926-27	1936-37	2	New York Rangers, Boston Bruins
Coulter, Art	1974/P	D	1931-32	1941-42	2	Chicago Blackhawks, New York Rangers
Cournoyer, Yvan	1982/P	RW	1963-64	1978-79	10	Montreal Canadiens
Cowley, Bill	1968/P	C	1934-35	1946-47	2	St. Louis Eagles, Boston Bruins
Crawford, Rusty	1962/P	LW	1912-13	1925-26	1	Quebec Bulldogs, Ottawa Senators, Toronto Arenas, Saskatoon (WCHL), Calgary (WCHL), Vancouver (WHL)
Darragh, Jack	1962/P	RW	1910-11	1923-24	4	Ottawa Senators
Davidson, Scotty	1950/P	RW	1912-13	1913-14	0	Toronto (NHA)
Day, Hap	1961/P	D	1924-25	1937-38	1	Toronto St. Pats, Toronto Maple Leafs, New York Americans
Delvecchio, Alex	1977/P	C	1950-51	1973-74	3	Detroit Red Wings
Denneny, Cy	1959/P	LW	1914-15	1928-29	5	Toronto Shamrocks (NHA), Toronto Blueshirts (NHA), Ottawa Senators, Boston Bruins
Dionne, Marcel	1992/P	C	1971-72	1988-89	0	Detroit Red Wings, Los Angeles Kings, New York Rangers
Drillon, Gord	1975/P	RW	1936-37	1942-43	1	Toronto Maple Leafs, Montreal Canadiens
Drinkwater, Graham	1950/P	F/D	1892-93	1898-99	5	Montreal Victorias
Dryden, Ken	1983/P	G	1970-71	1978-79	6	Montreal Canadiens
Dumart, Woody	1992/V	LW	1935-36	1953-54	2	Boston Bruins
Dunderdale, Tommy	1974/P	C	1906-07	1923-24	0	Winnipeg Maple Leafs (MHL), Montreal Shamrocks (NHA), Quebec Bulldogs (NHA), Victoria (PCHA), Portland (PCHA), Saskatoon (WCHL), Edmonton (WCHL)
Durnan, Bill	1964/P	G	1943-44	1949-50	2	Montreal Canadiens
Dutton, Red	1958/P	D	1921-22	1935-36	0	Calgary Tigers (WCHL), Montreal Maroons, New York Americans
Dye, Babe	1970/P	RW	1919-20	1930-31	1	Toronto St. Pats, Hamilton Tigers, Chicago Blackhawks, New York Americans, Toronto Maple Leafs
Esposito, Phil	1984/P	C	1963-64	1980-81	2	Chicago Blackhawks, Boston Bruins, New York Rangers
Esposito, Tony	1988/P	G	1968-69	1983-84	1	Montreal Canadiens, Chicago Blackhawks
Farrell, Arthur	1965/P	F	1896-97	1900-01	2	Montreal Shamrocks (AHA/CAHL)
Federko, Bernie	2002/P	C	1976-77	1989-90	0	St. Louis Blues, Detroit Red Wings
Fetisov, Viacheslav	2001/P	D	1974-75	1997-98	2	CSKA Moscow, New Jersey Devils, Detroit Red Wings
Flaman, Fern	1990/V	D	1944-45	1960-61	1	Boston Bruins, Toronto Maple Leafs
Foyston, Frank	1958/P	C	1912-13	1927-28	3	Toronto Blueshirts (NHA), Seattle Metropolitans (PCHA), Victoria Cougars (WCHL/WHL), Detroit Cougars
Fredrickson, Frank	1958/P	C	1920-21	1930-31	1	Victoria Aristocrats (PCHA), Victoria Cougars (PCHA/WCHL/WHL), Detroit Cougars, Boston Bruins, Pittsburgh Pirates, Detroit Falcons
Fuhr, Grant	2003/P	G	1979-80	1999-00	5	Victoria Cougars (WHL), Edmonton Oilers, Toronto Maple Leafs, Buffalo Sabres, St. Louis Blues, Calgary Flames
Gadsby, Bill	1970/P	D	1946-47	1965-66	0	Chicago Blackhawks, New York Rangers, Detroit Red Wings
Gainey, Bob	1992/P	LW	1973-74	1988-89	5	Montreal Canadiens
Gardiner, Chuck	1945/P	G	1927-28	1933-34	1	Chicago Blackhawks
Gardiner, Herb	1958/P	D	1921-22	1928-29	0	Calgary Tigers (WCHL), Montreal Canadiens, Chicago Blackhawks
Gardner, Jimmy	1962/P	LW	1900-01	1914-15	3	Montreal Hockey Club (CAHL), Montreal Wanderers (FAHL/ECHA/NHA), Calumet (IHL), Pittsburgh (IHL), Montreal Shamrocks (ECAHA),New Westminster Royals (PCHA), Montreal Canadiens (NHA)
Gartner, Mike	2001/P	RW	1978-79	1997-98	0	Cincinnati Stingers (WHA), Washington Capitals, Minnesota North Stars, New York Rangers, Toronto Maple Leafs, Phoenix Coyotes
Geoffrion, Boom Boom	1972/P	RW	1950-51	1967-68	6	Montreal Canadiens, New York Rangers
Gerard, Eddie	1945/P	F/D	1913-14	1922-23	4	Ottawa Senators (NHA/NHL), Toronto St. Pats
Giacomin, Eddie	1987/P	G	1965-66	1977-78	0	New York Rangers, Detroit Red Wings
Gilbert, Rod	1982/P	RW	1960-61	1977-78	0	New York Rangers
Gillies, Clark	2002/P	LW	1974-75	1987-88	4	New York Islanders, Buffalo Sabres
Gilmour, Billy	1962/P	RW	1902-03	1915-16	5	Ottawa Silver Seven (CAHL/FAHL/ECAHA), Montreal Victorias (ECAHA), Ottawa Senators (ECHA/NHA)
Goheen, Moose	1952/P	D	1914	1918	0	St. Paul Athletic Club, 1920 U.S. Olympic Team
Goodfellow, Ebbie	1963/P	C	1929-30	1942-43	3	Detroit Cougars, Detroit Falcons, Detroit Red Wings
Goulet, Michel	1998/P	LW	1978-79	1993-94	0	Birmingham Bulls (WHA), Quebec Nordiques, Chicago Blackhawks
Grant, Mike	1950/P	D	1893-94	1901-02	5	Montreal Victorias (AHA/CAHL), Montreal Shamrocks (CAHL)
Green, Shorty	1962/P	RW	1923-24	1926-27	0	Hamilton Tigers, New York Americans
Gretzky, Wayne	1999/P	C	1978-79	1998-99	4	Indianapolis Racers (WHA), Edmonton (WHA/NHL), Los Angeles Kings, St. Louis Blues, New York Rangers
Griffis, Si	1950/P	Ro./D	1902-03	1918-19	2	Rat Portage Thistles (MNSHL), Kenora Thistles (MSHL), Vancouver Millionaires (PCHA)
Hainsworth, George	1961/P	G	1923-24	1936-37	2	Saskatoon Crescents (WCHL/WHL), Montreal Canadiens, Toronto Maple Leafs

Player	Elec. year/ how elected*	Pos.†	First season	Last season	Stanley Cup wins‡	Teams as player
Hall, Glenn	1975/P	G	1952-53	1970-71	1	Detroit Red Wings, Chicago Blackhawks, St. Louis Blues
Hall, Joe	1961/P	F/D	1903-04	1918-19	2	Winnipeg (MSHL), Quebec Bulldogs (ECAHA/NHA), Brandon (MHL), Montreal (ECAHA), Montreal Shamrocks (ECAHA/NHA), Montreal Wanderers (ECHA), Montreal Canadiens
Harvey, Doug	1973/P	D	1947-48	1968-69	6	Montreal Canadiens, New York Rangers, Detroit Red Wings, St. Louis Blues
Hawerchuk, Dale	2001/P	C	1981-82	1996-97	0	Winnipeg Jets, Buffalo Sabres, St. Louis Blues, Philadelphia Flyers
Hay, George	1958/P	LW	1921-22	1933-34	0	Regina Capitals (WCHL), Portland Rosebuds (WHL), Chicago Blackhawks, Detroit Cougars, Detroit Falcons, Detroit Red Wings
Hern, Riley	1962/P	G	1906-07	1910-11	3	Montreal Wanderers (ECAHA/ECHA/NHA)
Hextall, Bryan	1969/P	RW	1936-37	1947-48	1	New York Rangers
Holmes, Hap	1972/P	G	1912-13	1927-28	0	Toronto Blueshirts (NHA), Seattle Metropolitans (PCHA), Toronto Arenas, Victoria Cougars (WCHL/WHL), Detroit Cougars
Hooper, Tom	1962/P	F	1904-05	1907-08	2	Rat Portage Thistles (MNSHL), Kenora Thistles (SHL), Montreal Wanderers (ECAHA), Montreal (ECAHA)
Horner, Red	1965/P	D	1928-29	1939-40	1	Toronto Maple Leafs
Horton, Tim	1977/P	D	1949-50	1973-74	4	Toronto Maple Leafs, New York Rangers, Pittsburgh Penguins, Buffalo Sabres
Howe, Gordie	1972/P	RW	1946-47	1979-80	4	Detroit Red Wings, Houston Aeros (WHA), New England Whalers (WHA), Hartford Whalers
Howe, Syd	1965/P	F/D	1929-30	1945-46	3	Ottawa Senators, Philadelphia Quakers, Toronto Maple Leafs, St. Louis Eagles, Detroit Red Wings
Howell, Harry	1979/P	D	1952-53	1975-76	0	New York Rangers, Oakland Seals, California Golden Seals, Los Angeles Kings, New York Golden Blades/Jersey Knights (WHA), San Diego Mariners (WHA), Calgary Cowboys (WHA)
Hull, Bobby	1983/P	LW	1957-58	1979-80	1	Chicago Blackhawks, Winnipeg Jets (WHA/NHL), Hartford Whalers
Hutton, Bouse	1962/P	G	1898-99	1903-04	1	Ottawa Silver Seven (CAHL)
Hyland, Harry	1962/P	RW	1908-09	1917-18	1	Montreal Shamrocks (ECHA), Montreal Wanderers (NHA), New Westminster Royals (PCHA), Ottawa Senators
Irvin, Dick	1958/P	C	1916-17	1928-29	0	Portland Rosebuds (PCHA), Regina Capitals (WCHL), Chicago Blackhawks
Jackson, Busher	1971/P	LW	1929-30	1943-44	1	Toronto Maple Leafs, New York Americans, Boston Bruins
Johnson, Ching	1958/P	D	1926-27	1937-38	2	New York Rangers, New York Americans
Johnson, Moose	1952/P	LW/D	1903-04	1921-22	4	Montreal AAA (CAHL), Montreal Wanderers (ECAHA/ECHA/NHA), New Westminster Royals (PCHA), Portland Rosebuds (PCHA), Victoria Aristocrats (PCHA)
Johnson, Tom	1970/P	D	1947-48	1964-65	6	Montreal Canadiens, Boston Bruins
Joliat, Aurel	1947/P	LW	1922-23	1937-38	3	Montreal Canadiens
Keats, Duke	1958/P	C	1915-16	1928-29	0	Toronto Blueshirts (NHA), Edmonton Eskimos (WCHL/WHL), Boston Bruins, Detroit Cougars, Chicago Blackhawks
Kelly, Red	1969/P	C	1947-48	1966-67	8	Detroit Red Wings, Toronto Maple Leafs
Kennedy, Ted	1966/P	C	1942-43	1956-57	5	Toronto Maple Leafs
Keon, Dave	1986/P	C	1960-61	1981-82	4	Toronto Maple Leafs, Minnesota Fighting Saints (WHA) Indianapolis Racers (WHA), New England Whalers (WHA), Hartford Whalers
Kharlamov, Valeri	2005/P	W	1967-68	1980-81	0	CSKA Moscow
Kurri, Jari	2001/P	C/RW	1980-81	1997-98	5	Edmonton Oilers, Los Angeles Kings, New York Rangers, Mighty Ducks of Anaheim, Colorado Avalanche
Lach, Elmer	1966/P	C	1940-41	1953-54	3	Montreal Canadiens
Lafleur, Guy	1988/P	RW	1971-72	1990-91	5	Montreal Canadiens, New York Rangers, Quebec Nordiques
LaFontaine, Pat	2003/P	C	1983-84	1997-98	0	New York Islanders, Buffalo Sabres, New York Rangers
Lalonde, Newsy	1950/P	C/Ro.	1904-05	1926-27	1	Cornwall (FAHL), Portage La Prairie (MHL), Toronto (OPHL), Montreal Canadiens (NHA/NHL), Renfrew Creamery Kings (NHA), Vancouver Millionaires (PCHA), Saskatoon Sheiks (WCHL), Saskatoon Crescents (WCHL/WHL), New York Americans
Langway, Rod	2002/P	D	1978-79	1992-93	1	Montreal Canadiens, Washington Capitals
Laperriere, Jacques	1987/P	D	1962-63	1973-74	6	Montreal Canadiens
Lapointe, Guy	1993/P	D	1968-69	1983-84	6	Montreal Canadiens, St. Louis Blues, Boston Bruins
Laprade, Edgar	1993/V	C	1945-46	1954-55	0	New York Rangers
Laviolette, Jack	1962/P	D/LW	1903-04	1917-18	1	Montreal Nationals (FAHL), Montreal Shamrocks (ECAHA/ECHA), Montreal Canadiens (NHA/NHL)
Lehman, Hugh	1958/P	G	1908-09	1927-28	1	Berlin Dutchmen (OPHL), Galt (OPHL), New Westminster Royals (PCHA), Vancouver Millionaires (PCHA), Vancouver Maroons (PCHA), Chicago Blackhawks
Lemaire, Jacques	1984/P	C	1967-68	1978-79	8	Montreal Canadiens

Player	Elec. year/ how elected*	Pos.†	First season	Last season	Stanley Cup wins‡	Teams as player
Lemieux, Mario	1997/P	C	1984-85	2002-03	2	Pittsburgh Penguins
LeSueur, Percy	1961/P	G	1905-06	1915-16	3	Smith Falls (FAHL), Ottawa Senators (ECAHA/ECHA/NHA), Toronto Shamrocks (NHA), Toronto Blueshirts (NHA)
Lewis, Herbie	1989/V	LW	1928-29	1938-39	2	Detroit Cougars, Detroit Falcons, Detroit Red Wings
Lindsay, Ted	1966/P	LW	1944-45	1964-65	4	Detroit Red Wings, Chicago Blackhawks
Lumley, Harry	1980/P	G	1943-44	1959-60	1	Detroit Red Wings, New York Rangers, Chicago Blackhawks, Toronto Maple Leafs, Boston Bruins
MacKay, Mickey	1952/P	C/Ro.	1914-15	1929-30	1	Vancouver Millionaires (PCHA), Vancouver Maroons (PCHA/WCHL/WHL), Chicago Blackhawks, Pittsburgh Pirates, Boston Bruins
Mahovlich, Frank	1981/P	LW	1956-57	1977-78	6	Toronto Maple Leafs, Detroit Red Wings, Montreal Canadiens, Toronto Toros (WHA), Birmingham Bulls (WHA)
Malone, Joe	1950/P	C/LW	1908-09	1923-24	3	Quebec (ECHA), Waterloo (OPHL), Quebec Bulldogs (NHA/NHL), Montreal Canadiens, Hamilton Tigers
Mantha, Sylvio	1960/P	D	1923-24	1936-37	3	Montreal Canadiens, Boston Bruins
Marshall, Jack	1965/P	C/D	1900-01	1916-17	6	Winnipeg Victorias, Montreal AAA (CAHL), Montreal Wanderers (FAHL/ECAHA/NHA), Ottawa Montagnards (FAHL), Montreal Shamrocks (ECAHA/ECHA), Toronto Blueshirts (NHA)
Maxwell, Fred	1962/P	Ro.	1914	1925	0	Winnipeg Monarchs (MSHL), Winnipeg Falcons (MSHL)
McDonald, Lanny	1992/P	RW	1973-74	1988-89	1	Toronto Maple Leafs, Colorado Rockies, Calgary Flames
McGee, Frank	1945/P	C/Ro.	1902-03	1905-06	4	Ottawa Silver Seven
McGimsie, Billy	1962/P	F	1902-03	1906-07	1	Rat Portage Thistles (MNSHL/MSHL), Kenora Thistles (MSHL)
McNamara, George	1958/P	D	1907-08	1916-17	1	Montreal Shamrocks (ECAHA/ECHA), Waterloo (OPHL), Toronto Tecumsehs (NHA), Toronto Ontarios (NHA), Toronto Blueshirts (NHA), Toronto Shamrocks (NHA), 228th Battalion (NHA)
Mikita, Stan	1983/P	C	1958-59	1979-80	1	Chicago Blackhawks
Moore, Dickie	1974/P	LW	1951-52	1967-68	6	Montreal Canadiens, Toronto Maple Leafs, St. Louis Blues
Moran, Paddy	1958/P	G	1901-02	1916-17	2	Quebec Bulldogs (CAHL/ECAHA/ECHA/NHA), Haileybury (NHA)
Morenz, Howie	1945/P	C	1923-24	1936-37	3	Montreal Canadiens, Chicago Blackhawks, New York Rangers
Mosienko, Bill	1965/P	RW	1941-42	1954-55	0	Chicago Blackhawks
Mullen, Joe	2000/P	RW	1979-80	1996-97	3	St. Louis Blues, Calgary Flames, Pittsburgh Penguins, Boston Bruins
Murphy, Larry	2004/P	D	1980-81	2000-01	4	Los Angeles Kings, Washington Capitals, Minnesota North Stars, Pittsburgh Penguins, Toronto Maple Leafs, Detroit Red Wings
Neely, Cam	2005/P	RW	1983-84	1995-96	0	Vancouver Canucks, Boston Bruins
Nighbor, Frank	1947/P	LW/C	1912-13	1929-30	5	Toronto Blueshirts (NHA), Vancouver Millionaires, (PCHA), Ottawa Senators, Toronto Maple Leafs
Noble, Reg	1962/P	LW/C/D	1916-17	1932-33	3	Toronto Blueshirts (NHA), Montreal Canadiens (NHA), Toronto Arenas, Toronto St. Pats, Montreal Maroons, Detroit Cougars, Detroit Falcons, Detroit Red Wings
O'Connor, Buddy	1988/V	C	1941-42	1950-51	2	Montreal Canadiens, New York Rangers
Oliver, Harry	1967/P	RW	1921-22	1936-37	1	Calgary Tigers (WCHL/WHL), Boston Bruins, New York Americans
Olmstead, Bert	1985/P	LW	1948-49	1961-62	5	Chicago Blackhawks, Montreal Canadiens, Toronto Maple Leafs
Orr, Bobby	1979/P	D	1966-67	1978-79	2	Boston Bruins, Chicago Blackhawks
Parent, Bernie	1984/P	G	1965-66	1978-79	2	Boston Bruins, Philadelphia Flyers, Toronto Maple Leafs, Philadelphia Blazers (WHA)
Park, Brad	1988/P	D	1968-69	1984-85	0	New York Rangers, Boston Bruins, Detroit Red Wings
Patrick, Lester	1947/P	D	1903-04	1926-27	3	Brandon, Westmount (CAHL), Montreal Wanderers (ECAHA), Edmonton Eskimos (AAHA), Renfrew Creamery Kings (NHA), Victoria Aristocrats (PCHA), Spokane Canaries (PCHA), Seattle Metropolitans (PCHA), Seattle Metropolitans(PCHA), Victoria Cougars (WHL), New York Rangers
Patrick, Lynn	1980/P	LW	1934-35	1945-46	1	New York Rangers
Perreault, Gilbert	1990/P	C	1970-71	1986-87	0	Buffalo Sabres
Phillips, Tommy	1945/P	LW	1902-03	1911-12	1	Montreal AAA (CAHL), Toronto Marlboros (OHA), Rat Portage Thistles, Kenora Thistles (MHL), Ottawa Ottawa Senators (ECAHA), Edmonton Eskimos (AAHA), Vancouver Millionaires (PCHA)
Pilote, Pierre	1975/P	D	1955-56	1968-69	1	Chicago Blackhawks, Toronto Maple Leafs
Pitre, Didier	1962/P	D/RW	1903-04	1922-23	0	Montreal Nationals (FAHL/CAHL), Montreal Shamrocks (ECAHA), Edmonton Eskimos (AAHA), Montreal Canadiens (NHA/NHL), Vancouver Millionaires (PCHA)

Player	Elec. year/ how elected*	Pos.†	First season	Last season	Stanley Cup wins‡	Teams as player
Plante, Jacques	1978/P	G	1952-53	1974-75	6	Montreal Canadiens, New York Rangers, St. Louis Blues, Toronto Maple Leafs, Boston Bruins, Edmonton Oilers (WHA)
Potvin, Denis	1991/P	D	1973-74	1987-88	4	New York Islanders
Pratt, Babe	1966/P	D	1935-36	1946-47	2	New York Rangers, Toronto Maple Leafs, Boston Bruins
Primeau, Joe	1963/P	C	1927-28	1935-36	1	Toronto Maple Leafs
Pronovost, Marcel	1978/P	D	1949-50	1969-70	5	Detroit Red Wings, Toronto Maple Leafs
Pulford, Bob	1991/P	LW	1956-57	1971-72	4	Toronto Maple Leafs, Los Angeles Kings
Pulford, Harvey	1945/P	D	1893-94	1907-08	4	Ottawa Silver Seven/Senators (AHA/CAHL/FAHL/ECAHA)
Quackenbush, Bill	1976/P	D	1942-43	1955-56	0	Detroit Red Wings, Boston Bruins
Rankin, Frank	1961/P	Ro.	1906	1914	0	Stratford (OHA), Eatons (EAA), Toronto St. Michaels (OHA)
Ratelle, Jean	1985/P	C	1960-61	1980-81	0	New York Rangers, Boston Bruins
Rayner, Chuck	1973/P	G	1940-41	1952-53	0	New York Americans, New York Rangers
Reardon, Ken	1966/P	D	1940-41	1949-50	1	Montreal Canadiens
Richard, Henri	1979/P	C	1955-56	1974-75	11	Montreal Canadiens
Richard, Rocket	1961/P	RW	1942-43	1959-60	8	Montreal Canadiens
Richardson, George	1950/P		1906	1912	0	14th Regiment, Queen's University
Roberts, Gordon	1971/P	LW	1909-10	1919-20	0	Ottawa Senators (NHA), Montreal Wanderers (NHA), Vancouver Millionaires (PCHA), Seattle Metropolitans (PCHA)
Robinson, Larry	1995/P	D	1972-73	1991-92	6	Montreal Canadiens, Los Angeles Kings
Ross, Art	1945/P	D	1904-05	1917-18	2	Westmount (CAHL), Brandon (MHL), Kenora Thistles (MHL), Montreal Wanderers (ECAHA/ECHA/NHA/NHL), Haileybury (NHA), Ottawa Senators (NHA)
Russell, Blair	1965/P	RW/C	1899-00	1907-08	0	Montreal Victorias (CAHL/ECAHA)
Russell, Ernie	1965/P	Ro./C	1904-05	1913-14	4	Montreal Winged Wheelers (CAHL), Montreal Wanderers (ECAHA/NHA)
Ruttan, Jack	1962/P		1905	1913	0	Armstrong's Point, Rustler, St. John's College, Manitoba Varsity (WSHL), Winnipeg (WinHL)
Salming, Borje	1996/P	D	1973-74	1989-90	0	Toronto Maple Leafs, Detroit Red Wings
Savard, Dennis	2000/P	C	1980-81	1996-97	1	Chicago Blackhawks, Montreal Canadiens, Tampa Bay Lightning
Savard, Serge	1986/P	D	1966-67	1982-83	7	Montreal Canadiens, Winnipeg Jets
Sawchuk, Terry	1971/P	G	1949-50	1969-70	4	Detroit Red Wings, Boston Bruins, Toronto Maple Leafs, Los Angeles Kings, New York Rangers
Scanlan, Fred	1965/P	F	1897-98	1902-03	3	Montreal Shamrocks (AHA/CAHL), Winnipeg Victorias (MSHL)
Schmidt, Milt	1961/P	C	1936-37	1954-55	2	Boston Bruins
Schriner, Sweeney	1962/P	LW	1934-35	1945-46	2	New York Americans, Toronto Maple Leafs
Seibert, Earl	1963/P	D	1931-32	1945-46	2	New York Rangers, Chicago Blackhawks, Detroit Red Wings
Seibert, Oliver	1961/P	D	1900	1906	0	Berlin Rangers (WOHA), Houghton (IHL), Guelph (OPHL), London (OPHL)
Shore, Eddie	1947/P	D	1924-25	1939-40	2	Regina Capitals (WCHL), Edmonton Eskimos (WHL), Boston Bruins, New York Americans
Shutt, Steve	1993/P	LW	1972-73	1984-85	5	Montreal Canadiens, Los Angeles Kings
Siebert, Babe	1964/P	LW/D	1925-26	1938-39	2	Montreal Maroons, New York Rangers, Boston Bruins, Montreal Canadiens
Simpson, Joe	1962/P	D	1921-22	1930-31	0	Edmonton Eskimos (WCHL), New York Americans
Sittler, Darryl	1989/P	C	1970-71	1984-85	0	Toronto Maple Leafs, Philadelphia Flyers, Detroit Red Wings
Smith, Alf	1962/P	RW	1894-95	1907-08	4	Ottawa Silver Seven/Senators (AHA/CAHL/FAHL/ECAHA), Kenora Thistles (MHL)
Smith, Billy	1993/P	G	1971-72	1988-89	4	Los Angeles Kings, New York Islanders
Smith, Clint	1991/V	C	1936-37	1946-47	1	New York Rangers, Chicago Blackhawks
Smith, Hooley	1972/P	RW	1924-25	1940-41	2	1924 Canadian Olympic Team, Ottawa Senators, Montreal Maroons, Boston Bruins, New York Americans
Smith, Tommy	1973/P	LW/C	1905-06	1919-20	1	Ottawa Vics (FAHL), Ottawa Senators (ECAHA), Brantford (OPHL), Moncton (MPHL), Quebec Bulldogs (NHA/NHL), Toronto Shamrocks (NHA), Montreal Canadiens (NHA)
Stanley, Allan	1981/P	D	1948-49	1968-69	4	New York Rangers, Chicago Blackhawks, Boston Bruins, Toronto Maple Leafs, Philadelphia Flyers
Stanley, Barney	1962/P	RW/D	1914-15	1927-28	1	Vancouver Millionaires (PCHA), Calgary Tigers (WCHL), Regina Capitals (WCHL), Edmonton Eskimos (WCHL/WHL), Chicago Blackhawks
Stastny, Peter	1998/P	C	1980-81	1994-95	0	Quebec Nordiques, New Jersey Devils, St. Louis Blues
Stewart, Black Jack	1964/P	D	1938-39	1951-52	2	Detroit Red Wings, Chicago Blackhawks
Stewart, Nels	1962/P	C	1925-26	1939-40	1	Montreal Maroons, Boston Bruins, New York Americans
Stuart, Bruce	1961/P	F	1989-99	1910-11	3	Ottawa Senators (CAHL/ECHA/NHA), Quebec Bulldogs

Player	Elec. year/ how elected*	Pos.†	First season	Last season	Stanley Cup wins‡	Teams as player
						(CAHL), Pittsburgh (IHL), Houghton (IHL), Portage Lake (IHL), Montreal Wanderers (ECAHA)
Stuart, Hod	1945/P	D	1898-99	1906-07	1	Ottawa Senators, Quebec Bulldogs, Calumet (IHL), Pittsburgh (IHL), Montreal Wanderers
Taylor, Cyclone	1947/P	D/Ro./C	1907-08	1922-23	2	Ottawa Senators (ECAHA/ECHA), Renfrew Creamery Kings (NHA), Vancouver Maroons (PCHA)
Thompson, Tiny	1959/P	G	1928-29	1939-40	1	Boston Bruins, Detroit Red Wings
Tretiak, Vladislav	1989/P	G	1969	1984	0	CSKA Moscow
Trihey, Harry	1950/P	C	1896-97	1900-01	2	Montreal Shamrocks (AHA/CAHL)
Trottier, Bryan	1997/P	C	1975-76	1993-94	6	New York Islanders, Pittsburgh Penguins
Ullman, Norm	1982/P	C	1955-56	1976-77	0	Detroit Red Wings, Toronto Maple Leafs, Edmonton Oilers (WHA)
Vezina, Georges	1945/P	G	1910-11	1925-26	2	Montreal Canadiens (NHA/NHL)
Walker, Jack	1960/P	LW/Ro.	1912-13	1927-28	3	Port Arthur, Toronto Blueshirts (NHA), Seattle Metropolitans (PCHA), Victoria Cougars (WCHL/WHL), Detroit Cougars
Walsh, Marty	1962/P	C	1905-06	1911-12	2	Queens University (OHA), Ottawa Senators (ECAHA/ECHA/NHA)
Watson, Harry E.	1962/P	C	1915	1931	0	St. Andrews (OHA), Aura Lee Juniors (OHA), Toronto Dentals (OHA), Toronto Granites (OHA), 1924 Canadian Olympic Team, Toronto National Sea Fleas (OHA)
Watson, Harry P.	1994/V	LW	1941-42	1956-57	5	Brooklyn Americans, Detroit Red Wings, Toronto Maple Leafs, Chicago Blackhawks
Weiland, Cooney	1971/P	C	1928-29	1938-39	2	Boston Bruins, Ottawa Senators, Detroit Red Wings
Westwick, Harry	1962/P	Ro.	1894-95	1907-08	4	Ottawa Senators/Silver Seven (AHA/CAHL/FAHL/ECAHA), Kenora Thistles
Whitcroft, Frederick	1962/P	Ro.	1906-07	1909-10	0	Kenora Thistles (MSHL), Edmonton Eskimos (AAHA), Renfrew Creamery Kings (NHA)
Wilson, Gord	1962/P	D	1918	1933	0	Port Arthur War Veterans (OHA), Iroquois Falls (NOHA), Port Arthur Bearcats (OHA)
Worsley, Gump	1980/P	G	1952-53	1973-74	4	New York Rangers, Montreal Canadiens, Minnesota North Stars
Worters, Roy	1969/P	G	1925-26	1936-37	0	Pittsburgh Pirates, New York Americans, Montreal Canadiens

*Denotes whether enshrinee was elected by regular election (P) or veterans committee (V).
†Primary positions played during career: C—center; D—defense; G—goaltender; LW—left wing; Ro.—rover; RW—right wing.
‡Stanley Cup wins column refers to wins as a player in the players section and as a coach in the coaches section.

BUILDERS

Builder	Election year	Stanley Cup wins‡	Designation for induction
Adams, Charles F.	1960		Founder, Boston Bruins (1924)
Adams, Weston W.	1972		President and chairman, Boston Bruins(1936-69)
Aheam, Frank	1962		Owner, Ottawa Senators (1924-34)
Ahearne, Bunny	1977		President, International Hockey Federation (1957-75)
Allan, Sir Montagu	1945		Donator of Allan Cup, awarded anually to senior amateur champion of Canada (1908)
Allen, Keith	1992	0	Coach, Philadelphia Flyers (1967-68 and 1968-69); general manager and executive, Philadelphia Flyers (1966-present)
Arbour, Al	1996	4	Coach, St. Louis Blues, New York Islanders, 1970-71, 1971-72 to 1972-73, 1973-74 through 1985-86 and 1988-89 to 1993-94; vice president of hockey operations and consultant, New York Islanders (1994 to 1998)
Ballard, Harold	1977		Owner and chief executive, Toronto Maple Leafs (1961-90)
Bauer, Father David	1989		Developer and coach of first Canadian National Hockey Team
Bickell, J.P.	1978		First president and chairman of the board, Toronto Maple Leafs (1927-51)
Bowman, Scotty	1991	9	Coach, St. Louis Blues, Montreal Canadiens, Buffalo Sabres, Pittsburgh Penguins, Detroit Red Wings (1967-68 through 1979-80, 1981-82 through 1986-87 and 1991-92 through 2001-02); general manager, St. Louis Blues, Buffalo Sabres (1969-70, 1970-71 and 1979-80 through 1986-87)
Brown, George V.	1961		U.S. hockey pioneer; organizer, Boston Athletic Association hockey team (1910); general manager, Boston Arena and Boston Garden (1934-37)
Brown, Walter A.	1962		Co-owner and president, Boston Bruins (1951-64); general manager, Boston Gardens
Buckland, Frank	1975		Amateur hockey coach and manager; president and treasurer, Ontario Hockey Association
Bush, Walter L.	2000		President, Minnesota North Stars (1967-1978); president, USA Hockey; vice president, International Ice Hockey Federation
Butterfield, Jack	1980		President, American Hockey League
Calder, Frank	1947		First president, National Hockey League (1917-43)
Campbell, Angus	1964		First president, Northern Ontario Hockey Association (1919); executive, Ontario

Builder	Election year	Stanley Cup wins‡	Designation for induction
			Hockey Association
Campbell, Clarence	1966		Referee (1929-40); president, National Hockey League (1946-77)
Cattarinich, Joseph	1977		General manager, Montreal Canadiens (1909-10); co-owner, Montreal Canadiens (1921-35)
Costello, Murray	2005	0	President, Canadian Hockey Association (1979-1998); Hockey Hall of Fame selection committee and board member; member of IIHF
Dandurand, Leo	1963	1	Co-owner, Montreal Canadiens (1921-35); coach, Montreal Canadiens (1920-21 through 1925-26 and 1934-35); general manager, Montreal Canadiens (1920-21 through 1934-35)
Dilio, Frank	1964		Secretary and president, Junior Amateur Hockey Association; registrar and secretary, Quebec Amateur Hockey League (1943-62)
Dudley, George	1958		President, Canadian Amateur Hockey Association (1940-42); treasurer, Ontario Hockey Association; president, International Ice Hockey Federation
Dunn, Jimmy	1968		President, Manitoba Amateur Hockey Association (1945-51); president, Canadian Amateur Hockey Association
Fletcher, Cliff	2004		General manager, Altanta and Calgary Flames, Toronto Maple Leafs (1972-1997), Phoenix Coyotes (2001); first G.M. to sign a Soviet player with official consent
Francis, Emile	1982	0	General manager, New York Rangers,St. Louis Blues, Hartford Whalers (1964-65 through 1988-89); coach, New York Rangers, St. Louis Blues (1965-66 through 1974-75, 1976-77, 1981-82 and 1982-83); president, Hartford Whalers (1983-1993)
Gibson, Jack	1976		Organizer, International League (1903-07), world's first professional hockey league
Gorman, Tommy	1963	2	Co-founder, National Hockey League (1917); coach, Ottawa Senators, New York Americans, Chicago Blackhawks, Montreal Maroons (1917-1938); general manager, Montreal Canadiens (1941-42 through 1945-46)
Griffiths, Frank	1993		Chairman, Vancouver Canucks (1974 through 1994)
Hanley, Bill	1986		Secretary-manager, Ontario Hockey Association
Hay, Charles	1974		Coordinator, 1972 series between Canada and Soviet Union; president, Hockey Canada
Hendy, Jim	1968		President, United States Hockey League; general manager, Cleveland Barons (AHL); publisher, Hockey Guide (1933-51)
Hewitt, Foster	1965		Hockey broadcaster
Hewitt, William	1947		Sports editor, Toronto Star; secretary, Ontario Hockey Association (1903-61); registrar and treasurer, Canadian Amateur Hockey Association
Hume, Fred	1962		Co-developer, Western Hockey League, New Westminster Royals
Ilitch, Mike	2003	3	Owner, Detroit Red Wings (1982-83 through 2002-03)
Imlach, Punch	1984	4	Coach, Toronto Maple Leafs, Buffalo Sabres (1958-59 through 1968-69, 1970-71, 1971-72 and 1979-80); general manager, Toronto Maple Leafs, Buffalo Sabres (1958-59 through 1968-69, 1970-71 through 1977-78 and 1979-80 through 1981-82)
Ivan, Tommy	1974	3	Coach, Detroit Red Wings, Chicago Blackhawks (1947-48 through 1953-54, 1956-57 and 1957-58); general manager, Chicago Blackhawks (1954-55 through 1976-77)
Jennings, Bill	1975		President, New York Rangers
Johnson, Bob	1992	1	Coach, Calgary Flames, Pittsburgh Penguins (1982-83 through 1986-87, 1990-91 and 1991-92)
Juckes, Gordon	1979		President, Saskatchewan Amateur Hockey Association; director, Canadian Amateur Hockey Association (1960-78)
Kilpatrick,General J.R.	1960		President, New York Rangers, Madison Square Garden; director, NHL Players' Pension Society; NHL Governor
Kilrea, Brian	2003		Player, Detroit Red Wings (1957-58) and Los Angeles Kings (1967-68); general manager and head coach, Ottawa 67's of the Ontario Hockey League (1974-75 through 1983-84, 1986-87 through 1993-94 and 1995-96 through 2002-03); assistant coach, New York Islanders (1984-85 through 1985-86)
Knox III, Seymour	1993		Chairman and president, Buffalo Sabres (1970-71 through 1995-96)
Leader, Al	1969		President, Western Hockey League (1944-69)
LeBel, Bob	1970		Founder and president, Interprovincial Senior League (1944-47); president, Quebec Amateur Hockey League, Canadian Amateur Hockey Association, International Ice Hockey Federation (1955-63)
Lockhart, Tommy	1965		Organizer and president, Eastern Amateur Hockey League, Amateur Hockey Association of the United States; business manager, New York Rangers
Loicq, Paul	1961		President and referee, International Ice Hockey Federation (1922-47)
Mariucci, John	1985		Minnesota hockey pioneer; coach, 1956 U.S. Olympic Team
Mathers, Frank	1992		Coach, president and general manager, Hershey Bears (AHL)
McLaughlin, Major Frederic	1963		Owner and first president, Chicago Blackhawks; general manager, Chicago Blackhawks (1926-27 through 1941-42)
Milford, Jake	1984		Coach, New York Rangers organization; general manager, Los Angeles Kings, Vancouver Canucks (1973-74 through 1981-82)
Molson, Senator Hartland De Montarville	1973		President and chairman, Montreal Canadiens (1957-68)
Morrison, Scotty	1999		Referee-in-chief; chairman, Hall of Fame
Murray, Monsignor Athol	1998		Founded hockey programs in Saskatchewan; founded Notre Dame College in Wilcox
Neilson, Roger	2002		Coach, Toronto Maple Leafs, Buffalo Sabres, Vancouver Canucks, Los Angeles Kings, New York Rangers, Florida Panthers, Philadelphia Flyers, Ottawa Senators (1977-78 through 1983-84, 1989-90 through 1994-95, 1997-98 through 1999-2000 and 2001-02
Nelson, Francis	1947		Sports editor, Toronto Globe; vice president, Ontario Hockey Association

Builder	Election year	Stanley Cup wins‡	Designation for induction
			(1903-05); Governor, Amateur Athletic Union of Canada
Norris, Bruce	1969		Owner, Detroit Red Wings, Olympic Stadium (1955-82)
Norris, James Sr.	1958		Co-owner, Detroit Red Wings (1933-43)
Norris, James Dougan	1962		Co-owner, Detroit Red Wings (1933-43), Chicago Blackhawks (1946-66)
Northey, William	1947		President, Montreal Amateur Athletic Association; managing director, Montreal Forum; first trustee, Allan Cup (1908)
O'Brien, J. Ambrose	1962		Organizer, National Hockey Association (1909); co-founder, Montreal Canadiens
O'Neil, Brian	1994		Director of administration, NHL (1966); executive director, NHL (1971); executive vice-president, NHL (1977)
Page, Fred	1993		President, Canadian Amateur Hockey Association (1966-68); chairman of the board, British Columbia Junior Hockey League (1983 through 1997)
Patrick, Craig	2001		Builder of U.S. National & Olympic programs; general manager, New York Rangers (1981 through 1986), general manager, Pittsburgh Penguins (1989 to present), coach, Pittsburgh Penguins (1989-90 and1996-97)
Patrick, Frank	1958		Co-organizer and president, Pacific Coast Hockey Association (1911); owner, manager, player/coach, Vancouver Millionaires (PCHA), managing director, National Hockey League (1933-34); coach, Boston Bruins (1934-35 and 1935-36); business manager, Montreal Canadiens (1941-42)
Pickard, Allan	1958		President, Saskatchewan Amateur Hockey Association, Saskatchewan Senior League (1933-34), Western Canada Senior League;governor, Saskatchewan Junior League, Western Canada Junior League; president, Canadian Amateur Hockey Association (1947-50)
Pilous, Rudy	1985	1	Coach, Chicago Blackhawks, Winnipeg Jets (1957-58 through 1962-63 and 1974-75); manager, Winnipeg Jets (WHA); scout, Detroit Red Wings, Los Angeles Kings
Poile, Bud	1990		General manager, Philadelphia Flyers, Vancouver Canucks (1967-68 through 1972-73); vice president, World Hockey Association; commissioner, Central Hockey League, International Hockey League
Pollock, Sam	1978		Director of personnel, Montreal Canadiens (1950-64); general manager, Montreal Canadiens (1964-65 through 1977-78)
Raymond, Sen. Donat	1958		President, Canadian Arena Company (Montreal Maroons, Montreal Canadiens) (1924-25 through 1955); chairman, Canadian Arena Company (1955-63)
Robertson, John Ross	1947		President, Ontario Hockey Association (1901-05)
Robinson, Claude	1947		First secretary, Canadian Amateur Hockey Association (1914); manager, 1932 Canadian Olympic Team
Ross, Philip	1976		Trustee, Stanley Cup (1893-1949)
Sabetzki, Gunther	1995		President, International Ice Hockey Federation (1975-1994)
Sather, Glen	1997	4	Coach, Edmonton Oilers (1976-89 and 1993-94); general manager, Edmonton Oilers (1979 to 2000); general manager, New York Rangers (2000 to present)
Selke, Frank	1960		Assistant general manager, Toronto Maple Leafs; general manager, Montreal Canadiens (1946-47 through 1963-64)
Sinden, Harry	1983	1	Coach, Boston Bruins (1966-67 through 1969-70, 1979-80 and 1984-85); coach, 1972 Team Canada; general manager, Boston Bruins (1972-73 through 1988-89); President, Boston bruins (1989-90 through present)
Smith, Frank	1962		Co-founder and secretary, Beaches Hockey League (later Metropolitan Toronto Hockey League (1911-62)
Smythe, Conn	1958	0	President, Toronto Maple Leafs, Maple Leaf Gardens, general manager, Toronto Maple Leafs (1927-28 through 1956-57); coach, Toronto Maple Leafs (1927-28 through 1930-31)
Snider, Ed	1988		Owner, Philadelphia Flyers (1967-68 through present)
Stanley of Preston, Lord	1945		Donator, Stanley Cup (1893)
Sutherland, Capt. James	1947		President, Ontario Hockey Association (1915-17); president, Canadian Amateur Hockey Association (1919-21)
Tarasov, Anatoli	1974		Coach, Soviet National Team
Torrey, Bill	1995		Executive vice president, California Seals; general manager, New York Islanders; president, Florida Panthers (1967-present)
Turner, Lloyd	1958		Co-organizer, Western Canadian Hockey League (1918); organizer, Calgary Tigers
Tutt, Thayer	1978		President, International Ice Hockey Federation (1966-69), Amateur Hockey Association of the United States
Voss, Carl	1974		President, U.S. Hockey League; first NHL referee-in-chief
Waghorne, Fred	1961		Pioneer and hockey official, Toronto Hockey League
Wirtz, Arthur	1971		Co-owner, Detroit Red Wings, Olympia Stadium, Chicago Stadium, St. Louis Arena, Madison Square Garden, Chicago Blackhawks
Wirtz, Bill	1976		President, Chicago Blackhawks (1966 through present); chairman, NHL Board of Governors
Ziegler, John	1987		President, National Hockey League (1977-92)

‡Stanley Cup wins column refers to wins as a player in the players section and as a coach in the builders section.

REFEREES/LINESMEN

Referee/linesman	Election year	First season	Last season	Position
Armstrong, Neil	1991	1957	1977	Linesman and referee
Ashley, John	1981	1959	1972	Referee
Chadwick, Bill	1964	1940	1955	Linesman and referee
D'Amico, John	1993	1964-65	1987-88	Linesman
Elliott, Chaucer	1961	1903	1913	Referee (OHA)
Hayes, George	1988	1946-47	1964-65	Linesman
Hewitson, Bobby	1963	1924	1934	Referee
Ion, Mickey	1961	1913	1943	Referee (PCHL/NHL)
Pavelich, Matt	1987	1956-57	1978-79	Linesman
Rodden, Mike	1962			Referee
Smeaton, Cooper	1961			Referee (NHA/NHL); referee-in-chief (NHL) (1931-37); trustee, Stanley Cup (1946-78)
Storey, Red	1967	1951	1959	Referee
Udvari, Frank	1973	1951-52	1965-66	Referee; supervisor of NHL officials
Van Hellemond, Andy	1999	1972-73	1995-96	Referee

TEAM BY TEAM

ANAHEIM MIGHTY DUCKS

YEAR-BY-YEAR RECORDS

	REGULAR SEASON						PLAYOFFS			
Season	W	L	T	OTL	Pts.	Finish	W	L	Highest round	Coach
1993-94	33	46	5	—	71	4th/Pacific	—	—		Ron Wilson
1994-95	16	27	5	—	37	6th/Pacific	—	—		Ron Wilson
1995-96	35	39	8	—	78	4th/Pacific	—	—		Ron Wilson
1996-97	36	33	13	—	85	2nd/Pacific	4	7	Conference semifinals	Ron Wilson
1997-98	26	43	13	—	65	6th/Pacific	—	—		Pierre Page
1998-99	35	34	13	—	83	3rd/Pacific	0	4	Conference quarterfinals	Craig Hartsburg
1999-00	34	33	12	3	83	5th/Pacific	—	—		Craig Hartsburg
2000-01	25	41	11	5	66	5th/Pacific	—	—		Craig Hartsburg, Guy Charron
2001-02	29	42	8	3	69	5th/Pacific	—	—		Bryan Murray
2002-03	40	27	9	6	95	2nd/Pacific	15	6	Stanley Cup finals	Mike Babcock
2003-04	29	35	10	8	76	4th/Pacific	—	—		Mike Babcock

FIRST-ROUND ENTRY DRAFT CHOICES

Year Player, Overall, Last amateur team (league)
1993—Paul Kariya, 4, University of Maine
1994—Oleg Tverdovsky, 2, Krylja Sovetov, CIS
1995—Chad Kilger, 4, Kingston (OHL)
1996—Ruslan Salei, 9, Las Vegas (IHL)
1997—Mikael Holmqvist, 18, Djurgarden Stockholm, Sweden
1998—Vitali Vishnevsky, 5, Torpedo Yaroslavl, Russia
1999—No first-round selection

Year Player, Overall, Last amateur team (league)
2000—Alexei Smirnov, 12, Dynamo, Russia
2001—Stanislav Chistov, 5, OMDK, Russia
2002—Joffrey Lupul, 7, Medicine Hat (WHL)
2003—Ryan Getzlaf, 19, Calgary (WHL)
Corey Perry, 28, London (OHL)
2004—Ladislav Smid, 9, Liberec, Czech. Rep.
2005—Bobby Ryan, 2, Owen Sound (OHL)

SINGLE-SEASON INDIVIDUAL RECORDS

FORWARDS/DEFENSEMEN

Most goals
52—Teemu Selanne, 1997-98

Most assists
62—Paul Kariya, 1998-99

Most points
109—Teemu Selanne, 1996-97

Most penalty minutes
285—Todd Ewen, 1995-96

Most power play goals
25—Teemu Selanne, 1998-99

Most shorthanded goals
3—Bob Corkum, 1993-94
Paul Kariya, 1995-96
Paul Kariya, 1996-97
Paul Kariya, 1999-00
Paul Kariya, 2000-01

Most games with three or more goals
3—Teemu Selanne, 1997-98

Most shots
429—Paul Kariya, 1998-99

GOALTENDERS

Most games
69—Guy Hebert, 1998-99

Most minutes
4,083—Guy Hebert, 1998-99

Most shots against
2,133—Guy Hebert, 1996-97

Most goals allowed
172—Guy Hebert, 1996-97

Lowest goals-against average
2.13—Jean-Sebastien Giguere, 2001-02

Most shutouts
8—Jean-Sebastien Giguere, 2002-03

Most wins
34—Jean-Sebastien Giguere, 2002-03

Most losses
31—Guy Hebert, 1999-2000
Jean-Sebastien Giguere, 2003-04

Most ties
12—Guy Hebert, 1996-97

ATLANTA THRASHERS

YEAR-BY-YEAR RECORDS

	REGULAR SEASON						PLAYOFFS			
Season	W	L	T	OTL	Pts.	Finish	W	L	Highest round	Coach
1999-00	14	57	7	4	39	5th/Southeast	—	—		Curt Fraser
2000-01	23	45	12	2	60	4th/Southeast	—	—		Curt Fraser
2001-02	19	47	11	5	54	5th/Southeast	—	—		Curt Fraser
2002-03	31	39	7	5	74	3rd/Southeast	—	—		C. Fraser, Don Waddell, Bob Hartley
2003-04	33	37	8	4	78	2nd/Southeast	—	—		Bob Hartley

FIRST-ROUND ENTRY DRAFT CHOICES

Year Player, Overall, Last amateur team (league)
1999—Patrik Stefan, 1, Long Beach (IHL)
2000—Dany Heatley, 2, Wisconsin (WCHA)
2001—Ilja Kovalchuk, 1, Spartak Jr., Russia
2002—Kari Lehtonen, 2, Jokerit, Finland
Jim Slater, 30, Michigan State (CCHA)

Year Player, Overall, Last amateur team (league)
2003—Braydon Coburn, 8, Portland (WHL)
2004—Boris Valabik, 10, Kitchener (OHL)
2005—Alex Bourret, 16, Lewiston (QMJHL)

SINGLE-SEASON INDIVIDUAL RECORDS

FORWARDS/DEFENSEMEN

Most goals
41—Dany Heatley, 2002-03
Ilya Kovalchuk, 2003-04

Most assists
49—Vyacheslav Kozlov, 2002-03

Most points
89—Dany Heatley, 2002-03

Most penalty minutes
226—Jeff Odgers, 2000-01

Most power play goals
19—Dany Heatley, 2002-03

Most shorthanded goals
3—Shean Donovan, 2000-01

Most games with three or more goals
2—Donald Audette, 2000-01
Ray Ferraro, 2000-01
Ilya Kovalchuk, 2003-04

Most shots
341—Ilya Kovalchuk, 2003-04

GOALTENDERS

Most games
64—Pasi Nurminen, 2003-04

Most minutes
3,738—Pasi Nurminen, 2003-04

Most shots against
1,956—Milan Hnilicka, 2001-02

Most goals allowed
179—Milan Hnilicka, 2001-02

Lowest goals-against average
2.78—Pasi Nurminen, 2003-04

Most shutouts
3—Milan Hnilicka, 2001-02
Pasi Nurminen, 2003-04

Most wins
25—Pasi Nurminen, 2003-04

Most losses
33—Milan Hnilicka, 2001-02

Most ties
10—Milan Hnilicka, 2001-02

BOSTON BRUINS

YEAR-BY-YEAR RECORDS

	REGULAR SEASON						PLAYOFFS			
Season	W	L	T	OTL	Pts.	Finish	W	L	Highest round	Coach
1924-25	6	24	0	—	12	6th	—	—		Art Ross
1925-26	17	15	4	—	38	4th	—	—		Art Ross
1926-27	21	20	3	—	45	2nd/American	*2	2	Stanley Cup finals	Art Ross
1927-28	20	13	11	—	51	1st/American	*0	1	Semifinals	Art Ross
1928-29	26	13	5	—	57	1st/American	5	0	Stanley Cup champ	Cy Denneny
1929-30	38	5	1	—	77	1st/American	3	3	Stanley Cup finals	Art Ross
1930-31	28	10	6	—	62	1st/American	2	3	Semifinals	Art Ross
1931-32	15	21	12	—	42	4th/American	—	—		Art Ross
1932-33	25	15	8	—	58	1st/American	2	3	Semifinals	Art Ross
1933-34	18	25	5	—	41	4th/American	—	—		Art Ross
1934-35	26	16	6	—	58	1st/American	1	3	Semifinals	Frank Patrick
1935-36	22	20	6	—	50	2nd/American	1	1	Quarterfinals	Frank Patrick
1936-37	23	18	7	—	53	2nd/American	1	2	Quarterfinals	Art Ross
1937-38	30	11	7	—	67	1st/American	0	3	Semifinals	Art Ross
1938-39	36	10	2	—	74	1st	8	4	Stanley Cup champ	Art Ross
1939-40	31	12	5	—	67	1st	2	4	Semifinals	Ralph (Cooney) Weiland
1940-41	27	8	13	—	67	1st	8	3	Stanley Cup champ	Ralph (Cooney) Weiland
1941-42	25	17	6	—	56	3rd	2	3	Semifinals	Art Ross
1942-43	24	17	9	—	57	2nd	4	5	Stanley Cup finals	Art Ross
1943-44	19	26	5	—	43	5th	—	—		Art Ross
1944-45	16	30	4	—	36	4th	3	4	League semifinals	Art Ross
1945-46	24	18	8	—	56	2nd	5	5	Stanley Cup finals	Dit Clapper
1946-47	26	23	11	—	63	3rd	1	4	League semifinals	Dit Clapper
1947-48	23	24	13	—	59	3rd	1	4	League semifinals	Dit Clapper
1948-49	29	23	8	—	66	2nd	1	4	League semifinals	Dit Clapper
1949-50	22	32	16	—	60	5th	—	—		George Boucher
1950-51	22	30	18	—	62	4th	†1	4	League semifinals	Lynn Patrick
1951-52	25	29	16	—	66	4th	3	4	League semifinals	Lynn Patrick
1952-53	28	29	13	—	69	3rd	5	6	Stanley Cup finals	Lynn Patrick
1953-54	32	28	10	—	74	4th	0	4	League semifinals	Lynn Patrick
1954-55	23	26	21	—	67	4th	1	4	League semifinals	Lynn Patrick, Milt Schmidt
1955-56	23	34	13	—	59	5th	—	—		Milt Schmidt
1956-57	34	24	12	—	80	3rd	5	5	Stanley Cup finals	Milt Schmidt
1957-58	27	28	15	—	69	4th	6	6	Stanley Cup finals	Milt Schmidt
1958-59	32	29	9	—	73	2nd	3	4	League semifinals	Milt Schmidt
1959-60	28	34	8	—	64	5th	—	—		Milt Schmidt
1960-61	15	42	13	—	43	6th	—	—		Milt Schmidt
1961-62	15	47	8	—	38	6th	—	—		Phil Watson
1962-63	14	39	17	—	45	6th	—	—		Phil Watson, Milt Schmidt
1963-64	18	40	12	—	48	6th	—	—		Milt Schmidt
1964-65	21	43	6	—	48	6th	—	—		Milt Schmidt
1965-66	21	43	6	—	48	5th	—	—		Milt Schmidt
1966-67	17	43	10	—	44	6th	—	—		Harry Sinden
1967-68	37	27	10	—	84	3rd/East	0	4	Division semifinals	Harry Sinden
1968-69	42	18	16	—	100	2nd/East	6	4	Division finals	Harry Sinden
1969-70	40	17	19	—	99	2nd/East	12	2	Stanley Cup champ	Harry Sinden
1970-71	57	14	7	—	121	1st/East	3	4	Division semifinals	Tom Johnson
1971-72	54	13	11	—	119	1st/East	12	3	Stanley Cup champ	Tom Johnson
1972-73	51	22	5	—	107	2nd/East	1	4	Division semifinals	Tom Johnson, Bep Guidolin
1973-74	52	17	9	—	113	1st/East	10	6	Stanley Cup finals	Bep Guidolin
1974-75	40	26	14	—	94	2nd/Adams	1	2	Preliminaries	Don Cherry
1975-76	48	15	17	—	113	1st/Adams	5	7	Semifinals	Don Cherry

Season	W	L	T	OTL	Pts.	Finish	W	L	Highest round	Coach
			REGULAR SEASON						PLAYOFFS	
1976-77	49	23	8	—	106	1st/Adams	8	6	Stanley Cup finals	Don Cherry
1977-78	51	18	11	—	113	1st/Adams	10	5	Stanley Cup finals	Don Cherry
1978-79	43	23	14	—	100	1st/Adams	7	4	Semifinals	Don Cherry
1979-80	46	21	13	—	105	2nd/Adams	4	6	Quarterfinals	Fred Creighton, Harry Sinden
1980-81	37	30	13	—	87	2nd/Adams	0	3	Preliminaries	Gerry Cheevers
1981-82	43	27	10	—	96	2nd/Adams	6	5	Division finals	Gerry Cheevers
1982-83	50	20	10	—	110	1st/Adams	9	8	Conference finals	Gerry Cheevers
1983-84	49	25	6	—	104	1st/Adams	0	3	Division semifinals	Gerry Cheevers
1984-85	36	34	10	—	82	4th/Adams	2	3	Division semifinals	Gerry Cheevers, Harry Sinden
1985-86	37	31	12	—	86	3rd/Adams	0	3	Division semifinals	Butch Goring
1986-87	39	34	7	—	85	3rd/Adams	0	4	Division semifinals	Butch Goring, Terry O'Reilly
1987-88	44	30	6	—	94	2nd/Adams	12	10	Stanley Cup finals	Terry O'Reilly
1988-89	37	29	14	—	88	2nd/Adams	5	5	Division finals	Terry O'Reilly
1989-90	46	25	9	—	101	1st/Adams	13	8	Stanley Cup finals	Mike Milbury
1990-91	44	24	12	—	100	1st/Adams	10	9	Conference finals	Mike Milbury
1991-92	36	32	12	—	84	2nd/Adams	8	7	Conference finals	Rick Bowness
1992-93	51	26	7	—	109	1st/Adams	0	4	Division semifinals	Brian Sutter
1993-94	42	29	13	—	97	2nd/Northeast	6	7	Conference semifinals	Brian Sutter
1994-95	27	18	3	—	57	3rd/Northeast	1	4	Conference quarterfinals	Brian Sutter
1995-96	40	31	11	—	91	2nd/Northeast	1	4	Conference quarterfinals	Steve Kasper
1996-97	26	47	9	—	61	6th/Northeast	—	—		Steve Kasper
1997-98	39	30	13	—	91	2nd/Northeast	2	4	Conference quarterfinals	Pat Burns
1998-99	39	30	13	—	91	3th/Northeast	6	6	Conference semifinals	Pat Burns
1999-00	24	33	19	6	73	5th/Northeast	—	—		Pat Burns
2000-01	36	30	8	8	88	4th/Northeast	—	—		Pat Burns, Mike Keenan
2001-02	43	24	6	9	101	1st/Northeast	2	4	Conference quarterfinals	Robbie Ftorek
2002-03	36	31	11	4	87	3rd/Northeast	1	4	Conference quarterfinals	Robbie Ftorek, Mike O'Connell
2003-04	41	19	15	7	104	1st/Northeast	3	4	Conference quarterfinals	Mike Sullivan

*Won-lost record does not indicate tie(s) resulting from two-game, total-goals series that year (two-game, total-goals series were played from 1917-18 through 1935-36).

†Tied after one overtime (curfew law).

FIRST-ROUND ENTRY DRAFT CHOICES

Year Player, Overall, Last amateur team (league)

1969—Don Tannahill, 3, Niagara Falls (OHL)
Frank Spring, 4, Edmonton (WCHL)
Ivan Boldirev, 11, Oshawa (OHL)
1970—Reggie Leach, 3, Flin Flon (WCHL)
Rick MacLeish, 4, Peterborough (OHL)
Ron Plumb, 9, Peterborough (OHL)
Bob Stewart, 13, Oshawa (OHL)
1971—Ron Jones, 6, Edmonton (WCHL)
Terry O'Reilly, 14, Oshawa (OHL)
1972—Mike Bloom, 16, St. Catharines (OHL)
1973—Andre Savard, 6, Quebec (QMJHL)
1974—Don Laraway, 18, Swift Current (WCHL)
1975—Doug Halward, 14, Peterborough (OHL)
1976—Clayton Pachal, 16, New Westminster (WCHL)
1977—Dwight Foster, 16, Kitchener (OHL)
1978—Al Secord, 16, Hamilton (OHL)
1979—Ray Bourque, 8, Verdun (QMJHL)
Brad McCrimmon, 15, Brandon (WHL)
1980—Barry Pederson, 18, Victoria (WHL)
1981—Norm Leveille, 14, Chicoutimi (QMJHL)
1982—Gord Kluzak, 1, Billings (WHL)
1983—Nevin Markwart, 21, Regina (WHL)
1984—Dave Pasin, 19, Prince Albert (WHL)
1985—No first-round selection
1986—Craig Janney, 13, Boston College

Year Player, Overall, Last amateur team (league)

1987—Glen Wesley, 3, Portland (WHL)
Stephane Quintal, 14, Granby (QMJHL)
1988—Robert Cimetta, 18, Toronto (OHL)
1989—Shayne Stevenson, 17, Kitchener (OHL)
1990—Bryan Smolinski, 21, Michigan State University
1991—Glen Murray, 18, Sudbury (OHL)
1992—Dmitri Kvartalnov, 16, San Diego (IHL)
1993—Kevyn Adams, 25, Miami of Ohio
1994—Evgeni Riabchikov, 21, Molot-Perm (Russia)
1995—Kyle McLaren, 9, Tacoma (WHL)
Sean Brown, 21, Belleville (OHL)
1996—Johnathan Aitken, 8, Medicine Hat (WHL)
1997—Joe Thornton, 1, Sault Ste. Marie (OHL)
Sergei Samsonov, 8, Detroit (IHL)
1998—No first-round selection
1999—Nicholas Boynton, 21, Ottawa (OHL)
2000—Lars Jonsson, 7, Leksand, Sweden
Martin Samuelsson, 27, MoDo, Sweden
2001—Shaone Morrisonn, 19, Kamloops (WHL)
2002—Hannu Toivonen, 29, HPK, Finland
2003—Mark Stuart, 21, Colorado College (WCHA)
2004—No first-round selection
2005—Matt Lashoff, 22, Kitchener (OHL)

SINGLE-SEASON INDIVIDUAL RECORDS

FORWARDS/DEFENSEMEN

Most goals
76—Phil Esposito, 1970-71

Most assists
102—Bobby Orr, 1970-71

Most points
152—Phil Esposito, 1970-71

Most penalty minutes
302—Jay Miller, 1987-88

Most power play goals
28—Phil Esposito, 1971-72

Most shorthanded goals
9—Brian Rolston, 2001-02

Most games with three or more goals
7—Phil Esposito, 1970-71

Most shots
550—Phil Esposito, 1970-71

GOALTENDERS

Most games
70—Frank Brimsek, 1949-50
Jack Gelineau, 1950-51
Eddie Johnston, 1964-64

Most minutes
4,200—Frank Brimsek, 1949-50
Jack Gelineau, 1950-51
Eddie Johnston, 1964-64

Most goals allowed
244—Frank Brimsek, 1949-50

Lowest goals-against average
1.18—Tiny Thompson, 1928-29

Most shutouts
15—Hal Winkler, 1927-28

Most wins
40—Pete Peeters, 1982-83

BUFFALO SABRES

YEAR-BY-YEAR RECORDS

	REGULAR SEASON						PLAYOFFS			
Season	W	L	T	OTL	Pts.	Finish	W	L	Highest round	Coach
1970-71	24	39	15	—	63	5th/East	—	—		Punch Imlach
1971-72	16	43	19	—	51	6th/East	—	—		Punch Imlach, Joe Crozier
1972-73	37	27	14	—	88	4th/East	2	4	Division semifinals	Joe Crozier
1973-74	32	34	12	—	76	5th/East	—	—		Joe Crozier
1974-75	49	16	15	—	113	1st/Adams	10	7	Stanley Cup finals	Floyd Smith
1975-76	46	21	13	—	105	2nd/Adams	4	5	Quarterfinals	Floyd Smith
1976-77	48	24	8	—	104	2nd/Adams	2	4	Quarterfinals	Floyd Smith
1977-78	44	19	17	—	105	2nd/Adams	3	5	Quarterfinals	Marcel Pronovost
1978-79	36	28	16	—	88	2nd/Adams	1	2	Preliminaries	Marcel Pronovost, Bill Inglis
1979-80	47	17	16	—	110	1st/Adams	9	5	Semifinals	Scotty Bowman
1980-81	39	20	21	—	99	1st/Adams	4	4	Quarterfinals	Roger Neilson
1981-82	39	26	15	—	93	3rd/Adams	1	3	Division semifinals	Jim Roberts, Scotty Bowman
1982-83	38	29	13	—	89	3rd/Adams	6	4	Division finals	Scotty Bowman
1983-84	48	25	7	—	103	2nd/Adams	0	3	Division semifinals	Scotty Bowman
1984-85	38	28	14	—	90	3rd/Adams	2	3	Divison semifinals	Scotty Bowman
1985-86	37	37	6	—	80	5th/Adams	—	—		Jim Schoenfeld, Scotty Bowman
1986-87	28	44	8	—	64	5th/Adams	—	—		Scotty Bowman, Craig Ramsay
1987-88	37	32	11	—	85	3rd/Adams	2	4	Division semifinals	Ted Sator
1988-89	38	35	7	—	83	3rd/Adams	1	4	Division semifinals	Ted Sator
1989-90	45	27	8	—	98	2nd/Adams	2	4	Division semifinals	Rick Dudley
1990-91	31	30	19	—	81	3rd/Adams	2	4	Division semifinals	Rick Dudley Ted Sator
1991-92	31	37	12	—	74	3rd/Adams	3	4	Division semifinals	Rick Dudley, John Muckler
1992-93	38	36	10	—	86	4th/Adams	4	4	Division finals	John Muckler
1993-94	43	32	9	—	95	4th/Northeast	3	4	Conference quarterfinals	John Muckler
1994-95	22	19	7	—	51	4th/Northeast	1	4	Conference quarterfinals	John Muckler
1995-96	33	42	7	—	73	5th/Northeast	—	—		Ted Nolan
1996-97	40	30	12	—	92	1st/Northeast	5	7	Conference semifinals	Ted Nolan
1997-98	36	29	17	—	89	3rd/Northeast	10	5	Conference finals	Lindy Ruff
1998-99	37	28	17	—	91	4rd/Northeast	14	7	Stanley Cup finals	Lindy Ruff
1999-00	35	32	11	4	85	3rd/Northeast	1	4	Conference quarterfinals	Lindy Ruff
2000-01	46	30	5	1	98	2nd/Northeast	7	6	Conference semifinals	Lindy Ruff
2001-02	35	35	11	1	82	5th/Northeast	—	—		Lindy Ruff
2002-03	27	37	10	8	72	5th/Northeast	—	—		Lindy Ruff
2003-04	37	34	7	4	85	5th/Northeast	—	—		Lindy Ruff

FIRST-ROUND ENTRY DRAFT CHOICES

Year Player, Overall, Last amateur team (league)

1970—Gilbert Perreault, 1, Montreal (OHL)
1971—Rick Martin, 5, Montreal (OHL)
1972—Jim Schoenfeld, 5, Niagara Falls (OHL)
1973—Morris Titanic, 12, Sudbury (OHL)
1974—Lee Fogolin, 11, Oshawa (OHL)
1975—Robert Sauve, 17, Laval (QMJHL)
1976—No first-round selection
1977—Ric Seiling, 14, St. Catharines (OHL)
1978—Larry Playfair, 13, Portland (WHL)
1979—Mike Ramsey, 11, University of Minnesota
1980—Steve Patrick, 20, Brandon (WHL)
1981—Jiri Dudacek, 17, Kladno (Czechoslovakia)
1982—Phil Housley, 6, South St. Paul H.S. (Minn.)
Paul Cyr, 9, Victoria (WHL)
Dave Andreychuk, 16, Oshawa (OHL)
1983—Tom Barrasso, 5, Acton Boxboro H.S. (Mass.)
Norm Lacombe, 10, Univ. of New Hampshire
Adam Creighton, 11, Ottawa (OHL)
1984—Bo Andersson, 18, Vastra Frolunda, Sweden
1985—Carl Johansson, 14, Vastra Frolunda, Sweden
1986—Shawn Anderson, 5, Team Canada
1987—Pierre Turgeon, 1, Granby (QMJHL)

Year Player, Overall, Last amateur team (league)

1988—Joel Savage, 13, Victoria (WHL)
1989—Kevin Haller, 14, Regina (WHL)
1990—Brad May, 14, Niagara Falls (OHL)
1991—Philippe Boucher, 13, Granby (QMJHL)
1992—David Cooper, 11, Medicine Hat (WHL)
1993—No first-round selection
1994—Wayne Primeau, 17, Owen Sound (OHL)
1995—Jay McKee, 14, Niagara Falls (OHL)
Martin Biron, 16, Beauport (QMJHL)
1996—Erik Rasmussen, 7, University of Minnesota
1997—Mika Noronen, 21, Tappara Tampere, Finland
1998—Dimitri Kalinin, 18, Traktor Chelyabinsk, Russia
1999—Barrett Heisten, 20, Maine (H. East)
2000—Artem Kriukov, 15, Yaroslavl, Russia
2001—Jiri Novotny, 22, Budejovice, Czech Republic
2002—Keith Ballard, 11, University of Minnesota (WCHA)
Daniel Paille, 20, Guelph (OHL)
2003—Thomas Vanek, 5, Minnesota (WCHA)
2004—Drew Stafford, 13, North Dakota (WCHA)
2005—Marek Zagrapan, 13, Chicoutimi (QMJHL)

SINGLE-SEASON INDIVIDUAL RECORDS

FORWARDS/DEFENSEMEN

Most goals
76—Alexander Mogilny, 1992-93

Most assists
95—Pat LaFontaine, 1992-93

Most points
148—Pat LaFontaine, 1992-93

Most penalty minutes
354—Rob Ray, 1991-92

Most power play goals
28—Dave Andreychuk, 1991-92

Most shorthanded goals
8—Don Luce, 1974-75

Most games with three or more goals
7—Rick Martin, 1975-76
Alexander Mogilny, 1992-93

Most shots
360—Alexander Mogilny, 1992-93

GOALTENDERS

Most games
72—Don Edwards, 1977-78
Dominik Hasek, 1997-98
Martin Biron, 2001-02

Most minutes
4,220—Dominik Hasek, 1997-98

Most shots against
2,190—Roger Crozier, 1971-72

Most goals allowed
214—Roger Crozier, 1971-72
Tom Barrasso, 1985-86

Lowest goals-against average
1.87—Dominik Hasek, 1998-99

Most shutouts
13—Dominik Hasek, 1997-98

Most wins
38—Don Edwards, 1977-78

Most losses
34—Roger Crozier, 1971-72

Most ties
17—Don Edwards, 1977-78

CALGARY FLAMES

YEAR-BY-YEAR RECORDS

	REGULAR SEASON						PLAYOFFS			
Season	W	L	T	OTL	Pts.	Finish	W	L	Highest round	Coach
1972-73*	25	38	15	—	65	7th/West	—	—		Bernie Geoffrion
1973-74*	30	34	14	—	74	4th/West	0	4	Division semifinals	Bernie Geoffrion
1974-75*	34	31	15	—	83	4th/Patrick	—	—		Bernie Geoffrion, Fred Creighton
1975-76*	35	33	12	—	82	3rd/Patrick	0	2	Preliminaries	Fred Creighton
1976-77*	34	34	12	—	80	3rd/Patrick	1	2	Preliminaries	Fred Creighton
1977-78*	34	27	19	—	87	3rd/Patrick	0	2	Preliminaries	Fred Creighton
1978-79*	41	31	8	—	90	4th/Patrick	0	2	Preliminaries	Fred Creighton
1979-80*	35	32	13	—	83	4th/Patrick	1	3	Preliminaries	Al MacNeil
1980-81	39	27	14	—	92	3rd/Patrick	9	7	Semifinals	Al MacNeil
1981-82	29	34	17	—	75	3rd/Smythe	0	3	Division semifinals	Al MacNeil
1982-83	32	34	14	—	78	2nd/Smythe	4	5	Division finals	Bob Johnson
1983-84	34	32	14	—	82	2nd/Smythe	6	5	Division finals	Bob Johnson
1984-85	41	27	12	—	94	3rd/Smythe	1	3	Division semifinals	Bob Johnson
1985-86	40	31	9	—	89	2nd/Smythe	12	10	Stanley Cup finals	Bob Johnson
1986-87	46	31	3	—	95	2nd/Smythe	2	4	Division semifinals	Bob Johnson
1987-88	48	23	9	—	105	1st/Smythe	4	5	Division finals	Terry Crisp
1988-89	54	17	9	—	117	1st/Smythe	16	6	Stanley Cup champ	Terry Crisp
1989-90	42	23	15	—	99	1st/Smythe	2	4	Division semifinals	Terry Crisp
1990-91	46	26	8	—	100	2nd/Smythe	3	4	Division semifinals	Doug Risebrough
1991-92	31	37	12	—	74	5th/Smythe	—	—		Doug Risebrough, Guy Charron
1992-93	43	30	11	—	97	2nd/Smythe	2	4	Division semifinals	Dave King
1993-94	42	29	13	—	97	1st/Pacific	3	4	Conference quarterfinals	Dave King
1994-95	24	17	7	—	55	1st/Pacific	3	4	Conference quarterfinals	Dave King
1995-96	34	37	11	—	79	2nd/Pacific	0	4	Conference quarterfinals	Pierre Page
1996-97	32	41	9	—	73	5th/Pacific	—	—		Pierre Page
1997-98	26	41	15	—	67	5th/Pacific	—	—		Brian Sutter
1998-99	30	40	12	—	72	3rd/Northwest	—	—		Brian Sutter
1999-00	31	36	10	5	77	4th/Northwest	—	—		Brian Sutter
2000-01	27	36	15	4	73	4th/Northwest	—	—		Don Hay, Greg Gilbert
2001-02	32	35	12	3	79	4th/Northwest	—	—		Greg Gilbert
2002-03	29	36	13	4	75	5th/Northwest	—	—		G. Gilbert, A. MacNeil, D. Sutter
2003-04	42	30	7	3	94	3rd/Northwest	15	11	Stanley Cup finals	Darryl Sutter

*Atlanta Flames.

FIRST-ROUND ENTRY DRAFT CHOICES

Year Player, Overall, Last amateur team (league)
1972—Jacques Richard, 2, Quebec (QMJHL)
1973—Tom Lysiak, 2, Medicine Hat (WCHL)
Vic Mercredi, 16, New Westminster (WCHL)
1974—No first-round selection
1975—Richcard Mulhern, 8, Sherbrooke (QMJHL)
1976—Dave Shand, 8, Peterborough (OHL)
Harold Phillipoff, 10, New Westminster (WCHL)
1977—No first-round selection
1978—Brad Marsh, 11, London (OHL)
1979—Paul Reinhart, 12, Kitchener (OHL)
1980—Denis Cyr, 13, Montreal (OHL)
1981—Al MacInnis, 15, Kitchener (OHL)
1982—No first-round selection

Year Player, Overall, Last amateur team (league)
1983—Dan Quinn, 13, Belleville (OHL)
1984—Gary Roberts, 12, Ottawa (OHL)
1985—Chris Biotti, 17, Belmont Hill H.S. (Mass.)
1986—George Pelawa, 16, Bemidji H.S. (Minn.)
1987—Bryan Deasley, 19, University of Michigan
1988—Jason Muzzatti, 21, Michigan State University
1989—No first-round selection
1990—Trevor Kidd, 11, Brandon (WHL)
1991—Niklas Sundblad, 19, AIK, Sweden
1992—Cory Stillman, 6, Windsor (OHL)
1993—Jesper Mattsson, 18, Malmo, Sweden
1994—Chris Dingman, 19, Brandon (WHL)

Year	Player, Overall, Last amateur team (league)
1995	Denis Gauthier, 20, Drummondville (QMJHL)
1996	Derek Morris, 13, Regina (WHL)
1997	Daniel Tkaczuk, 6, Barrie (OHL)
1998	Rico Fata, 6, London (OHL)
1999	Oleg Saprykin, 11, Seattle (WHL)
2000	Brent Krahn, 9, Calgary (WHL)
2001	Chuck Kobasew, 14, Boston College
2002	Eric Nystrom, 10, University of Michigan (CCHA)
2003	Dion Phaneuf, 9, Red Deer (WHL)
2004	Kris Chucko, 24, Salmon Arm (BCHL)
2005	Matt Pelech, 26, Sarnia (OHL)

SINGLE-SEASON INDIVIDUAL RECORDS

FORWARDS/DEFENSEMEN

Most goals
66—Lanny McDonald, 1982-83

Most assists
82—Kent Nilsson, 1980-81

Most points
131—Kent Nilsson, 1980-81

Most penalty minutes
375—Tim Hunter, 1988-89

Most power play goals
31—Joe Nieuwendyk, 1987-88

Most shorthanded goals
9—Kent Nilsson, 1984-85

Most games with three or more goals
5—Hakan Loob, 1987-88
Theo Fleury, 1990-91

Most shots
353—Theo Fleury, 1995-96

GOALTENDERS

Most games
69—Roman Turek, 2001-02

Most minutes
4,081—Roman Turek, 2001-02

Most shots against
1,853—Mike Vernon, 1991-92

Most goals allowed
229—Rejean Lemelin, 1985-86

Lowest goals-against average
2.20—Jamie McLennan, 2003-04

Most shutouts
5—Dan Bouchard, 1973-74
Phil Myre, 1974-75
Fred Brathwaite, 1999-2000
Fred Brathwaite, 2000-01
Roman Turek, 2001-02

Most wins
39—Mike Vernon, 1987-88

Most losses
30—Mike Vernon, 1991-92

Most ties
19—Dan Bouchard, 1977-78

CAROLINA HURRICANES

YEAR-BY-YEAR RECORDS

	REGULAR SEASON						PLAYOFFS			
Season	W	L	T	OTL	Pts.	Finish	W	L	Highest round	Coach
1972-73*	46	30	2	—	94	1st	12	3	Avco World Cup champ	Jack Kelley
1973-74*	43	31	4	—	90	1st	3	4	League quarterfinals	Ron Ryan
1974-75*	43	30	5	—	91	1st	2	4	League quarterfinals	Ron Ryan, Jack Kelley
1975-76*	33	40	7	—	73	3rd	10	7	League semifinals	Jack Kelley, Don Blackburn, Harry Neale
1976-77*	35	40	6	—	76	4th	1	4	League quarterfinals	Harry Neale
1977-78*	44	31	5	—	93	2nd	8	6	Avco World Cup finals	Harry Neale
1978-79*	37	34	9	—	83	4th	5	5	League semifinals	Bill Dineen, Don Blackburn
1979-80†	27	34	19	—	73	4th/Norris	0	3	Preliminaries	Don Blackburn
1980-81†	21	41	18	—	60	4th/Norris	—	—		Don Blackburn, Larry Pleau
1981-82†	21	41	18	—	60	5th/Adams	—	—		Larry Pleau
1982-83†	19	54	7	—	45	5th/Adams	—	—		Larry Kish, Larry Pleau, John Cunniff
1983-84†	28	42	10	—	66	5th/Adams	—	—		Jack Evans
1984-85†	30	41	9	—	69	5th/Adams	—	—		Jack Evans
1985-86†	40	36	4	—	84	4th/Adams	6	4	Division finals	Jack Evans
1986-87†	43	30	7	—	93	1st/Adams	2	4	Division semifinals	Jack Evans
1987-88†	35	38	7	—	77	4th/Adams	2	4	Division semifinals	Jack Evans, Larry Pleau
1988-89†	37	38	5	—	79	4th/Adams	0	4	Division semifinals	Larry Pleau
1989-90†	38	33	9	—	85	4th/Adams	3	4	Division semifinals	Rick Ley
1990-91†	31	38	11	—	73	4th/Adams	2	4	Division semifinals	Rick Ley
1991-92†	26	41	13	—	65	4th/Adams	3	4	Division semifinals	Jim Roberts
1992-93†	26	52	6	—	58	5th/Adams	—	—		Paul Holmgren
1993-94†	27	48	9	—	63	6th/Northeast	—	—		Paul Holmgren, Pierre McGuire
1994-95†	19	24	5	—	43	5th/Northeast	—	—		Paul Holmgren
1995-96†	34	39	9	—	77	4th/Northeast	—	—		Paul Holmgren, Paul Maurice
1996-97†	32	39	11	—	75	5th/Northeast	—	—		Paul Maurice
1997-98	33	41	8	—	74	6th/Northeast	—	—		Paul Maurice
1998-99	34	30	18	—	86	1st/Southeast	2	4	Conference quarterfinals	Paul Maurice
1999-00	37	35	10	0	84	3rd/Southeast	—	—		Paul Maurice
2000-01	38	32	9	3	88	2nd/Southeast	2	4	Conference quarterfinals	Paul Maurice
2001-02	35	26	16	5	91	1st/Southeast	13	10	Stanley Cup finals	Paul Maurice
2002-03	22	43	11	6	61	5th/Southeast	—	—		Paul Maurice
2003-04	28	34	14	6	76	3rd/Southeast	—	—		Paul Maurice, Peter Laviolette

*New England Whalers, members of World Hockey Association.
†Hartford Whalers.

FIRST-ROUND ENTRY DRAFT CHOICES

Year Player, Overall, Last amateur team (league)
1979—Ray Allison, 18, Brandon (WHL)
1980—Fred Arthur, 8, Cornwall (QMJHL)
1981—Ron Francis, 4, Sault Ste. Marie (OHL)
1982—Paul Lawless, 14, Windsor (OHL)
1983—Sylvain Turgeon, 2, Hull (QMJHL)
David A. Jensen, 20, Lawrence Academy (Mass.)
1984—Sylvain Cote, 11, Quebec (QMJHL)
1985—Dana Murzyn, 5, Calgary (WHL)
1986—Scott Young, 11, Boston University
1987—Jody Hull, 18, Peterborough (OHL)
1988—Chris Govedaris, 11, Toronto (OHL)
1989—Robert Holik, 10, Jihlava, Czechoslovakia
1990—Mark Greig, 15, Lethbridge (WHL)
1991—Patrick Poulin, 9, St. Hyacinthe (QMJHL)
1992—Robert Petrovicky, 9, Dukla Trencin, Czech Republic

Year Player, Overall, Last amateur team (league)
1993—Chris Pronger, 2, Peterborough (OHL)
1994—Jeff O'Neill, 5, Guelph (OHL)
1995—Jean-Sebastien Giguere, 13, Halifax (QMJHL)
1996—No first-round selection
1997—Nikos Tselios, 22, Belleville (OHL)
1998—Jeff Heerema, 11, Sarnia (OHL)
1999—David Tanabe, 16, Wisconsin (WCHA)
2000—No first-round selection
2001—Igor Knyazev, 15, Spartak Jr., Russia
2002—Cam Ward, 25, Red Deer (WHL)
2003—Eric Staal, 2, Peterborough (OHL)
2004—Andrew Ladd, 4, Calgary (WHL)
2005—Jack Johnson, 3, U.S. National team
NOTE: Hartford chose Jordy Douglas, John Garrett and Mark Howe as priority selections before the 1979 expansion draft.

SINGLE-SEASON INDIVIDUAL RECORDS

FORWARDS/DEFENSEMEN

Most goals
56—Blaine Stoughton, 1979-80

Most assists
69—Ron Francis, 1989-90

Most points
105—Mike Rogers, 1979-80
Mike Rogers, 1980-81

Most penalty minutes
358—Torrie Robertson, 1985-86

Most power play goals
21—Geoff Sanderson, 1992-93

Most shorthanded goals
5—Kevyn Adams, 2003-04

Most games with three or more goals
3—Mike Rogers, 1980-81
Blaine Stoughton, 1981-82

Most shots
316—Jeff O'Neill, 2002-03

GOALTENDERS

Most games
77—Arturs Irbe, 2000-01

Most minutes
4,406—Arturs Irbe, 2000-01

Most shots against
1,947—Arturs Irbe, 2000-01

Most goals allowed
282—Greg Millen, 1982-83

Lowest goals-against average
2.17—Trevor Kidd, 1997-98

Most shutouts
6—Arturs Irbe, 1998-99
Arturs Irbe, 2000-01
Kevin Weekes, 2003-04

Most wins
37—Arturs Irbe, 2000-01

Most losses
38—Greg Millen, 1982-83

Most ties
12—John Garrett, 1980-81
Greg Millen, 1982-83
Arturs Irbe, 1998-99

CHICAGO BLACKHAWKS

YEAR-BY-YEAR RECORDS

	REGULAR SEASON						PLAYOFFS			
Season	W	L	T	OTL	Pts.	Finish	W	L	Highest round	Coach
1926-27	19	22	3	—	41	3rd/American	*0	1	Quarterfinals	Pete Muldoon
1927-28	7	34	3	—	17	5th/American	—	—		Barney Stanley, Hugh Lehman
1928-29	7	29	8	—	22	5th/American	—	—		Herb Gardiner
1929-30	21	18	5	—	47	2nd/American	*0	1	Quarterfinals	Tom Schaughnessy, Bill Tobin
1930-31	24	17	3	—	51	2nd/American	*5	3	Stanley Cup finals	Dick Irvin
1931-32	18	19	11	—	47	2nd/American	1	1	Quarterfinals	Dick Irvin, Bill Tobin
1932-33	16	20	12	—	44	4th/American	—	—		Godfrey Matheson, Emil Iverson
1933-34	20	17	11	—	51	2nd/American	*6	1	Stanley Cup champ	Tom Gorman
1934-35	26	17	5	—	57	2nd/American	*0	1	Quarterfinals	Clem Loughlin
1935-36	21	19	8	—	50	3rd/American	1	1	Quarterfinals	Clem Loughlin
1936-37	14	27	7	—	35	4th/American	—	—		Clem Loughlin
1937-38	14	25	9	—	37	3rd/American	7	3	Stanley Cup champ	Bill Stewart
1938-39	12	28	8	—	32	7th	—	—		Bill Stewart, Paul Thompson
1939-40	23	19	6	—	52	4th	0	2	Quarterfinals	Paul Thompson
1940-41	16	25	7	—	39	5th	2	3	Semifinals	Paul Thompson
1941-42	22	23	3	—	47	4th	1	2	Quarterfinals	Paul Thompson
1942-43	17	18	15	—	49	5th	—	—		Paul Thompson
1943-44	22	23	5	—	49	4th	4	5	Stanley Cup finals	Paul Thompson
1944-45	13	30	7	—	33	5th	—	—		Paul Thompson, John Gottselig
1945-46	23	20	7	—	53	3rd	0	4	League semifinals	John Gottselig
1946-47	19	37	4	—	42	6th	—	—		John Gottselig
1947-48	20	34	6	—	46	6th	—	—		John Gottselig, Charlie Conacher
1948-49	21	31	8	—	50	5th	—	—		Charlie Conacher
1949-50	22	38	10	—	54	6th	—	—		Charlie Conacher
1950-51	13	47	10	—	36	6th	—	—		Ebbie Goodfellow
1951-52	17	44	9	—	43	6th	—	—		Ebbie Goodfellow
1952-53	27	28	15	—	69	4th	3	4	League semifinals	Sid Abel

	REGULAR SEASON						PLAYOFFS			
Season	W	L	T	OTL	Pts.	Finish	W	L	Highest round	Coach
1953-54	12	51	7	—	31	6th	—	—		Sid Abel
1954-55	13	40	17	—	43	6th	—	—		Frank Eddolls
1955-56	19	39	12	—	50	6th	—	—		Dick Irvin
1956-57	16	39	15	—	47	6th	—	—		Tommy Ivan
1957-58	24	39	7	—	55	5th	—	—		Tommy Ivan, Rudy Pilous
1958-59	28	29	13	—	69	3rd	2	4	League semifinals	Rudy Pilous
1959-60	28	29	13	—	69	3rd	0	4	League semifinals	Rudy Pilous
1960-61	29	24	17	—	75	3rd	8	4	Stanley Cup champ	Rudy Pilous
1961-62	31	26	13	—	75	3rd	6	6	Stanley Cup finals	Rudy Pilous
1962-63	32	21	17	—	81	2nd	2	4	League semifinals	Rudy Pilous
1963-64	36	22	12	—	84	2nd	3	4	League semifinals	Billy Reay
1964-65	34	28	8	—	76	3rd	7	7	Stanley Cup finals	Billy Reay
1965-66	37	25	8	—	82	2nd	2	4	League semifinals	Billy Reay
1966-67	41	17	12	—	94	1st	2	4	League semifinals	Billy Reay
1967-68	32	26	16	—	80	4th/East	5	6	Division finals	Billy Reay
1968-69	34	33	9	—	77	6th/East	—	—		Billy Reay
1969-70	45	22	9	—	99	1st/East	4	4	Division finals	Billy Reay
1970-71	49	20	9	—	107	1st/West	11	7	Stanley Cup finals	Billy Reay
1971-72	46	17	15	—	107	1st/West	4	4	Division finals	Billy Reay
1972-73	42	27	9	—	93	1st/West	10	6	Stanley Cup finals	Billy Reay
1973-74	41	14	23	—	105	2nd/West	6	5	Division finals	Billy Reay
1974-75	37	35	8	—	82	3rd/Smythe	3	5	Quarterfinals	Billy Reay
1975-76	32	30	18	—	82	1st/Smythe	0	4	Quarterfinals	Billy Reay
1976-77	26	43	11	—	63	3rd/Smythe	0	2	Preliminaries	Billy Reay, Bill White
1977-78	32	29	19	—	83	1st/Smythe	0	4	Quarterfinals	Bob Pulford
1978-79	29	36	15	—	73	1st/Smythe	0	4	Quarterfinals	Bob Pulford
1979-80	34	27	19	—	87	1st/Smythe	3	4	Quarterfinals	Eddie Johnston
1980-81	31	33	16	—	78	2nd/Smythe	0	3	Preliminaries	Keith Magnuson
1981-82	30	38	12	—	72	4th/Norris	8	7	Conference finals	Keith Magnuson, Bob Pulford
1982-83	47	23	10	—	104	1st/Norris	7	6	Conference finals	Orval Tessier
1983-84	30	42	8	—	68	4th/Norris	2	3	Division semifinals	Orval Tessier
1984-85	38	35	7	—	83	2nd/Norris	9	6	Conference finals	Orval Tessier, Bob Pulford
1985-86	39	33	8	—	86	1st/Norris	0	3	Division semifinals	Bob Pulford
1986-87	29	37	14	—	72	3rd/Norris	0	4	Division semifinals	Bob Pulford
1987-88	30	41	9	—	69	3rd/Norris	1	4	Division semifinals	Bob Murdoch
1988-89	27	41	12	—	66	4th/Norris	9	7	Conference finals	Mike Keenan
1989-90	41	33	6	—	88	1st/Norris	10	10	Conference finals	Mike Keenan
1990-91	49	23	8	—	106	1st/Norris	2	4	Division semifinals	Mike Keenan
1991-92	36	29	15	—	87	2nd/Norris	12	6	Stanley Cup finals	Mike Keenan
1992-93	47	25	12	—	106	1st/Norris	0	4	Division semifinals	Darryl Sutter
1993-94	39	36	9	—	87	5th/Central	2	4	Conference quarterfinals	Darryl Sutter
1994-95	24	19	5	—	53	3rd/Central	9	7	Conference finals	Darryl Sutter
1995-96	40	28	14	—	94	2nd/Central	6	4	Conference semifinals	Craig Hartsburg
1996-97	34	35	13	—	81	5th/Central	2	4	Conference quarterfinals	Craig Hartsburg
1997-98	30	39	13	—	73	5th/Central	—	—		Craig Hartsburg
1998-99	29	41	12	—	70	3rd/Central	—	—		Dirk Graham, Lorne Molleken
1999-00	33	37	10	2	78	3rd/Central	—	—		Lorne Molleken, Bob Pulford
2000-01	29	40	8	5	71	4th/Central	—	—		Alpo Suhonen, Denis Savard, Al MacAdam
2001-02	41	27	13	1	96	3rd/Central	1	4	Conference quarterfinals	Brian Sutter
2002-03	30	33	13	6	79	3rd/Central	—	—		Brian Sutter
2003-04	20	43	11	8	59	5th/Central	—	—		Brian Sutter

*Won-lost record does not indicate tie(s) resulting from two-game, total-goals series that year (two-game, total-goals series were played from 1917-18 through 1935-36).

FIRST-ROUND ENTRY DRAFT CHOICES

Year Player, Overall, Last amateur team (league)

1969—J.P. Bordeleau, 13, Montreal (OHL)
1970—Dan Maloney, 14, London (OHL)
1971—Dan Spring, 12, Edmonton (WCHL)
1972—Phil Russell, 13, Edmonton (WCHL)
1973—Darcy Rota, 13, Edmonton (WCHL)
1974—Grant Mulvey, 16, Calgary (WCHL)
1975—Greg Vaydik, 7, Medicine Hat (WCHL)
1976—Real Cloutier, 9, Quebec (WHA)
1977—Doug Wilson, 6, Ottawa (OHL)
1978—Tim Higgins, 10, Ottawa (OHL)
1979—Keith Brown, 7, Portland (WHL)
1980—Denis Savard, 3, Montreal (QMJHL)
Jerome Dupont, 15, Toronto (OHL)

Year Player, Overall, Last amateur team (league)

1981—Tony Tanti, 12, Oshawa (OHL)
1982—Ken Yaremchuk, 7, Portland (WHL)
1983—Bruce Cassidy, 18, Ottawa (OHL)
1984—Ed Olczyk, 3, U.S. Olympic Team
1985—Dave Manson, 11, Prince Albert (WHL)
1986—Everett Sanipass, 14, Verdun (QMJHL)
1987—Jimmy Waite, 8, Chicoutimi (QMJHL)
1988—Jeremy Roenick, 8, Thayer Academy (Mass.)
1989—Adam Bennett, 6, Sudbury (OHL)
1990—Karl Dykhuis, 16, Hull (QMJHL)
1991—Dean McAmmond, 22, Prince Albert (WHL)
1992—Sergei Krivokrasov, 12, Central Red Army, CIS

Year	Player, Overall, Last amateur team (league)
1993	Eric Lecompte, 24, Hull (QMJHL)
1994	Ethan Moreau, 14, Niagara Falls (OHL)
1995	Dimitri Nabokov, 19, Krylja Sovetov, CIS
1996	No first-round selection
1997	Daniel Cleary, 13, Belleville (OHL)
	Ty Jones, 16, Spokane (WHL)
1998	Mark Bell, 8, Ottawa (OHL)
1999	Steve McCarthy, 23, Kootenay (WHL)
2000	Mikhail Yakubov, 10, Togliatta, Russia
	Pavel Vorobiev, 11, Yaroslavl, Russia
2001	Tuomo Ruutu, 9, Jokerit, Finland
	Adam Munro, 29, Erie (OHL)
2002	Anton Babchuk, 21, Elektrostal Jr., Russia
2003	Brent Seabrook, 14, Lethbridge (WHL)
2004	Cameron Barker, 3, Medicine Hat (WHL)
2005	Jack Skille, 7, U.S. National team

SINGLE-SEASON INDIVIDUAL RECORDS

FORWARDS/DEFENSEMEN

Most goals
58—Bobby Hull, 1968-69

Most assists
87—Denis Savard, 1981-82
Denis Savard, 1987-88

Most points
131—Denis Savard, 1987-88

Most penalty minutes
408—Mike Peluso, 1991-92

Most power play goals
24—Jeremy Roenick, 1993-94

Most shorthanded goals
10—Dirk Graham, 1988-89

Most games with three or more goals
4—Bobby Hull, 1959-60
Bobby Hull, 1965-66

Most shots
414—Bobby Hull, 1968-69

GOALTENDERS

Most games
74—Ed Belfour, 1990-91

Most minutes
4,219—Tony Esposito, 1974-75

Most goals allowed
246—Harry Lumley, 1950-51
Tony Esposito, 1980-81

Lowest goals-against average
1.73—Charles Gardiner, 1933-34

Most shutouts
15—Tony Esposito, 1969-70

Most wins
43—Ed Belfour, 1990-91

Most losses
47—Al Rollins, 1953-54

Most ties
21—Tony Esposito, 1973-74

CLEVELAND BARONS (DEFUNCT)

YEAR-BY-YEAR RECORDS

	REGULAR SEASON					PLAYOFFS			
Season	W	L	T	Pts.	Finish	W	L	Highest round	Coach
1967-68*	15	42	17	47	6th/West	—	—		Bert Olmstead, Gordie Fashoway
1968-69*	29	36	11	69	2nd/West	3	4	Division semifinals	Fred Glover
1969-70*	22	40	14	58	4th/West	0	4	Division semifinals	Fred Glover
1970-71†	20	53	5	45	7th/West	—	—		Fred Glover
1971-72†	21	39	18	60	6th/West	—	—		Fred Glover, Vic Stasiuk
1972-73†	16	46	16	48	8th/West	—	—		Garry Young, Fred Glover
1973-74†	13	55	10	36	8th/West	—	—		Fred Glover, Marsh Johnston
1974-75†	19	48	13	51	4th/Adams	—	—		Marsh Johnston
1975-76†	27	42	11	65	4th/Adams	—	—		Jack Evans
1976-77	25	42	13	63	4th/Adams	—	—		Jack Evans
1977-78	22	45	13	57	4th/Adams	—	—		Jack Evans

*Oakland Seals.
†California Golden Seals.
Barons disbanded after 1977-78 season. Owners merged with Minnesota franchise and a number of Cleveland players were awarded to North Stars; remaining players were dispersed to other clubs in draft.

COLORADO AVALANCHE

YEAR-BY-YEAR RECORDS

	REGULAR SEASON						PLAYOFFS			
Season	W	L	T	OTL	Pts.	Finish	W	L	Highest round	Coach
1972-73*	33	40	5	—	71	5th	—	—		Maurice Richard, Maurice Filion
1973-74*	38	36	4	—	80	5th	—	—		Jacques Plante
1974-75*	46	32	0	—	92	1st	8	7	Avco World Cup finals	Jean-Guy Gendron
1975-76*	50	27	4	—	104	2nd	1	4	League quarterfinals	Jean-Guy Gendron
1976-77*	47	31	3	—	97	1st	12	5	Avco World Cup champ	Marc Boileau
1977-78*	40	37	3	—	83	4th	5	6	League semifinals	Marc Boileau
1978-79*	41	34	5	—	87	2nd	0	4	League semifinals	Jacques Demers
1979-80†	25	44	11	—	61	5th/Adams	—	—		Jacques Demers
1980-81†	30	32	18	—	78	4th/Adams	2	3	Preliminaries	Maurice Filion, Michel Bergeron
1981-82†	33	31	16	—	82	4th/Adams	7	9	Conference finals	Michel Bergeron
1982-83†	34	34	12	—	80	4th/Adams	1	3	Division semifinals	Michel Bergeron
1983-84†	42	28	10	—	94	3rd/Adams	5	4	Division finals	Michel Bergeron
1984-85†	41	30	9	—	91	2nd/Adams	9	9	Conference finals	Michel Bergeron
1985-86†	43	31	6	—	92	1st/Adams	0	3	Division semifinals	Michel Bergeron
1986-87†	31	39	10	—	72	4th/Adams	7	6	Division finals	Michel Bergeron
1987-88†	32	43	5	—	69	5th/Adams	—	—		Andre Savard, Ron Lapointe
1988-89†	27	46	7	—	61	5th/Adams	—	—		Ron Lapointe, Jean Perron

Season	W	L	T	OTL	Pts.	Finish	W	L	Highest round	Coach
					REGULAR SEASON				PLAYOFFS	
1989-90†	12	61	7	—	31	5th/Adams	—	—		Michel Bergeron
1990-91†	16	50	14	—	46	5th/Adams	—	—		Dave Chambers
1991-92†	20	48	12	—	52	5th/Adams	—	—		Dave Chambers, Pierre Page
1992-93†	47	27	10	—	104	2nd/Adams	2	4	Division semifinals	Pierre Page
1993-94†	34	42	8	—	76	5th/Northeast	—	—		Pierre Page
1994-95†	30	13	5	—	65	1st/Northeast	2	4	Conference quarterfinals	Marc Crawford
1995-96	47	25	10	—	104	1st/Pacific	16	6	Stanley Cup champ	Marc Crawford
1996-97	49	24	9	—	107	1st/Pacific	10	7	Conference finals	Marc Crawford
1997-98	39	26	17	—	95	1st/Pacific	3	4	Conference quarterfinals	Marc Crawford
1998-99	44	28	10	—	98	1st/Northwest	11	8	Conference finals	Bob Hartley
1999-00	42	28	11	1	96	1st/Northwest	11	6	Conference finals	Bob Hartley
2000-01	52	16	10	4	118	1st/Northwest	16	7	Stanley Cup champ	Bob Hartley
2001-02	45	28	8	1	99	1st/Northwest	11	10	Conference finals	Bob Hartley
2002-03	42	19	13	8	105	1st/Northwest	3	4	Conference quarterfinals	Bob Hartley, Tony Granato
2003-04	40	22	13	7	100	2nd/Northwest	6	5	Conference semifinals	Tony Granato

*Quebec Nordiques, members of World Hockey Association.
†Quebec Nordiques.

FIRST-ROUND ENTRY DRAFT CHOICES

Year Player, Overall, Last amateur team (league)

1979—Michel Goulet, 20, Birmingham (WHA)
1980—No first-round selection
1981—Randy Moller, 11, Lethbridge (WHL)
1982—David Shaw, 13, Kitchener (OHL)
1983—No first-round selection
1984—Trevor Steinburg, 15, Guelph (OHL)
1985—Dave Latta, 15, Kitchener (OHL)
1986—Ken McRae, 18, Sudbury (OHL)
1987—Bryan Fogarty, 9, Kingston (OHL)
Joe Sakic, 15, Swift Current (WHL)
1988—Curtis Leschyshyn, 3, Saskatoon (WHL)
Daniel Dore, 5, Drummondville (QMJHL)
1989—Mats Sundin, 1, Nacka (Sweden)
1990—Owen Nolan, 1, Cornwall (OHL)
1991—Eric Lindros, 1, Oshawa (OHL)
1992—Todd Warriner, 4, Windsor (OHL)
1993—Jocelyn Thibault, 10, Sherbrooke (QMJHL)
Adam Deadmarsh, 14, Portland (WHL)

Year Player, Overall, Last amateur team (league)

1994—Wade Belak, 12, Saskatoon (WHL)
Jeffrey Kealty, 22, Catholic Memorial H.S.
1995—Marc Denis, 25, Chicoutimi (QMJHL)
1996—Peter Ratchuk, 25, Shattuck-St. Mary's H.S. (Min.)
1997—Kevin Grimes, 26, Kingston (OHL)
1998—Alex Tanguay, 12, Halifax (QMJHL)
Martin Skoula, 17, Barrie (OHL)
Robyn Regehr, 19, Kamloops (WHL)
Scott Parker, 20, Kelowna (WHL)
1999—Mihail Kuleshov, 25, Cherepovec, Russia
2000—Vaclav Nedorost, 14, Budejovice, Czech Republic
2001—No first-round selection
2002—Jonas Johansson, 28, HV 71, Sweden
2003—No first-round selection.
2004—Wojtek Wolski, 21, Brampton (OHL)
2005—No first-round selection.

NOTE: Quebec chose Paul Baxter, Richard Brodeur and Garry Larivierre as priority selections before the 1979 expansion draft.

SINGLE-SEASON INDIVIDUAL RECORDS

FORWARDS/DEFENSEMEN

Most goals
57—Michel Goulet, 1982-83

Most assists
93—Peter Stastny, 1981-82

Most points
139—Peter Stastny, 1981-82

Most penalty minutes
301—Gord Donnelly, 1987-88

Most power play goals
29—Michel Goulet, 1987-88

Most shorthanded goals
6—Michel Goulet, 1981-82
Scott Young, 1992-93
Joe Sakic, 1995-96

Most games with three or more goals
4—Miroslav Frycer, 1981-82
Peter Stastny, 1982-83

Most shots
332—Joe Sakic, 2000-01

GOALTENDERS

Most games
65—Patrick Roy, 1997-98

Most minutes
3,835—Patrick Roy, 1997-98

Most shots against
1,861—Patrick Roy, 1996-97

Most goals allowed
230—Dan Bouchard, 1981-82

Lowest goals-against average
1.94—Patrick Roy, 2001-02

Most shutouts
9—Patrick Roy, 2001-02

Most wins
40—Patrick Roy, 2000-01

Most losses
29—Ron Tugnutt, 1990-91

Most ties
13—Patrick Roy, 1997-98

COLUMBUS BLUE JACKETS

YEAR-BY-YEAR RECORDS

Season	W	L	T	OTL	Pts.	Finish	W	L	Highest round	Coach
					REGULAR SEASON				PLAYOFFS	
2000-01	28	39	9	6	71	5th/Central	—	—		Dave King
2001-02	22	47	8	5	57	5th/Central	—	—		Dave King
2002-03	29	42	8	3	69	5th/Central	—	—		Dave King, Doug MacLean
2003-04	25	45	8	4	62	4th/Central	—	—		Doug MacLean, Gerard Gallant

FIRST-ROUND ENTRY DRAFT CHOICES

Year Player, Overall, Last amateur team (league)
2000—Rostislav Klesla, 4, Brampton (OHL)
2001—Pascal LeClaire, 8, Halifax (QMJHL)
2002—Rick Nash, 1, London (OHL)
2003—Nikolai Zherdev, 4, Russia

Year Player, Overall, Last amateur team (league)
2004—Alexandre Picard, 8, Lewiston (QMJHL)
2005—Gilbert Brule, 6, Vancouver (WHL)

SINGLE-SEASON INDIVIDUAL RECORDS

FORWARDS/DEFENSEMEN

Most goals
41—Rick Nash, 2003-04

Most assists
52—Ray Whitney, 2002-03

Most points
76—Ray Whitney, 2002-03

Most penalty minutes
249—Jody Shelley, 2001-02

Most power play goals
19—Rick Nash, 2003-04

Most shorthanded goals
4—David Vyborny, 2003-04

Most games with three or more goals
1—Deron Quint, 2000-01
Geoff Sanderson, 2000-01
Tyler Wright, 2000-01
Espen Knutsen, 2001-02
David Vyborny, 2003-04

Most shots
286—Geoff Sanderson, 2002-03

GOALTENDERS

Most games
77—Marc Denis, 2002-03

Most minutes
3,129—Ron Tugnutt, 2000-01

Most shots against
2,404—Marc Denis, 2002-03

Most goals allowed
232—Marc Denis, 2002-03

Lowest goals-against average
2.44—Ron Tugnutt, 2000-01

Most shutouts
5—Marc Denis, 2002-03
Marc Denis, 2003-04

Most wins
27—Marc Denis, 2002-03

Most losses
41—Marc Denis, 2002-03

Most ties
8—Marc Denis, 2002-03

DALLAS STARS

YEAR-BY-YEAR RECORDS

	REGULAR SEASON						PLAYOFFS			
Season	W	L	T	OTL	Pts.	Finish	W	L	Highest round	Coach
1967-68*	27	32	15	—	69	4th/West	7	7	Division finals	Wren Blair
1968-69*	18	43	15	—	51	6th/West	—	—		Wren Blair, John Muckler
1969-70*	19	35	22	—	60	3rd/West	2	4	Division semifinals	Wren Blair, Charlie Burns
1970-71*	28	34	16	—	72	4th/West	6	6	Division finals	Jack Gordon
1971-72*	37	29	12	—	86	2nd/West	3	4	Division semifinals	Jack Gordon
1972-73*	37	30	11	—	85	3rd/West	2	4	Division semifinals	Jack Gordon
1973-74*	23	38	17	—	63	7th/West	—	—		Jack Gordon, Parker MacDonald
1974-75*	23	50	7	—	53	4th/Smythe	—	—		Jack Gordon, Charlie Burns
1975-76*	20	53	7	—	47	4th/Smythe	—	—		Ted Harris
1976-77*	23	39	18	—	64	2nd/Smythe	0	2	Preliminaries	Ted Harris
1977-78*	18	53	9	—	45	5th/Smythe	—	—		Ted Harris, Andre Beaulieu, Lou Nanne
1978-79*	28	40	12	—	68	4th/Adams	—	—		Harry Howell, Glen Sonmor
1979-80*	36	28	16	—	88	3rd/Adams	8	7	Semifinals	Glen Sonmor
1980-81*	35	28	17	—	87	3rd/Adams	12	7	Stanley Cup finals	Glen Sonmor
1981-82*	37	23	20	—	94	1st/Norris	1	3	Division semifinals	Glen Sonmor, Murray Oliver
1982-83*	40	24	16	—	96	2nd/Norris	4	5	Division finals	Glen Sonmor, Murray Oliver
1983-84*	39	31	10	—	88	1st/Norris	7	9	Conference finals	Bill Maloney
1984-85*	25	43	12	—	62	4th/Norris	5	4	Division finals	Bill Maloney, Glen Sonmor
1985-86*	38	33	9	—	85	2nd/Norris	2	3	Division semifinals	Lorne Henning
1986-87*	30	40	10	—	70	5th/Norris	—	—		Lorne Henning, Glen Sonmor
1987-88*	19	48	13	—	51	5th/Norris	—	—		Herb Brooks
1988-89*	27	37	16	—	70	3rd/Norris	1	4	Division semifinals	Pierre Page
1989-90*	36	40	4	—	76	4th/Norris	3	4	Division semifinals	Pierre Page
1990-91*	27	39	14	—	68	4th/Norris	14	9	Stanley Cup finals	Bob Gainey
1991-92*	32	42	6	—	70	4th/Norris	3	4	Division semifinals	Bob Gainey
1992-93*	36	38	10	—	82	5th/Norris	—	—		Bob Gainey
1993-94	42	29	13	—	97	3rd/Central	5	4	Conference semifinals	Bob Gainey
1994-95	17	23	8	—	42	5th/Central	1	4	Conference quarterfinals	Bob Gainey
1995-96	26	42	14	—	66	6th/Central	—	—		Bob Gainey, Ken Hitchcock
1996-97	48	26	8	—	104	1st/Central	3	4	Conference quarterfinals	Ken Hitchcock
1997-98	49	22	11	—	109	1st/Central	10	7	Conference finals	Ken Hitchcock
1998-99	51	19	12	—	114	1st/Pacific	16	7	Stanley Cup champ	Ken Hitchcock
1999-00	43	23	10	6	102	1st/Pacific	14	9	Stanley Cup finals	Ken Hitchcock
2000-01	48	24	8	2	106	1st/Pacific	4	6	Conference semifinals	Ken Hitchcock
2001-02	36	28	13	5	90	4th/Pacific	—	—		Ken Hitchcock, Rick Wilson
2002-03	46	17	15	4	111	1st/Pacific	6	6	Conference semifinals	Dave Tippett
2003-04	41	26	13	2	97	2nd/Pacific	1	4	Conference quarterfinals	Dave Tippett

*Minnesota North Stars.

FIRST-ROUND ENTRY DRAFT CHOICES

Year Player, Overall, Last amateur team (league)
1969—Dick Redmond, 5, St. Catharines (OHL)
Dennis O'Brien, 14, St. Catharines (OHL)
1970—No first-round selection
1971—No first-round selection
1972—Jerry Byers, 12, Kitchener (OHL)
1973—No first-round selection
1974—Doug Hicks, 6, Flin Flon (WCHL)
1975—Brian Maxwell, 4, Medicine Hat (WCHL)
1976—Glen Sharpley, 3, Hull (QMJHL)
1977—Brad Maxwell, 7, New Westminster (WCHL)
1978—Bobby Smith, 1, Ottawa (OHL)
1979—Craig Hartsburg, 6, Birmingham (WHA)
Tom McCarthy, 10, Oshawa (OHL)
1980—Brad Palmer, 16, Victoria (WHL)
1981—Ron Meighan, 13, Niagara Falls (OHL)
1982—Brian Bellows, 2, Kitchener (OHL)
1983—Brian Lawton, 1, Mount St. Charles H.S. (R.I.)
1984—David Quinn, 13, Kent H.S. (Ct.)
1985—No first-round selection
1986—Warren Babe, 12, Lethbridge (WHL)

Year Player, Overall, Last amateur team (league)
1987—Dave Archibald, 6, Portland (WHL)
1988—Mike Modano, 1, Prince Albert (WHL)
1989—Doug Zmolek, 7, John Marshall H.S. (Minn.)
1990—Derian Hatcher, 8, North Bay (OHL)
1991—Richard Matvichuk, 8, Saskatoon (WHL)
1992—No first-round selection
1993—Todd Harvey, 9, Detroit (OHL)
1994—Jason Botterill, 20, Michigan (CCHA)
1995—Jarome Iginla, 11, Kamloops (WHL)
1996—Richard Jackman, 5, Sault Ste. Marie (OHL)
1997—Brenden Morrow, 25, Portland (WHL)
1998—No first-round selection
1999—No first-round selection
2000—Steve Ott, 25, Windsor (OHL)
2001—Jason Bacashihua, 26, Chicago (NAHL)
2002—Martin Vagner, 26, Hull (QMJHL)
2003—No first-round selection
2004—Mark Fistric, 28, Vancouver (WHL)
2005—Matt Niskanen, 28, Virginia (USHSW)

SINGLE-SEASON INDIVIDUAL RECORDS

FORWARDS/DEFENSEMEN

Most goals
55—Dino Ciccarelli, 1981-82
Brian Bellows, 1989-90

Most assists
76—Neal Broten, 1985-86

Most points
114—Bobby Smith, 1981-82

Most penalty minutes
382—Basil McRae, 1987-88

Most power play goals
22—Dino Ciccarelli, 1986-87

Most shorthanded goals
6—Bill Collins, 1969-70

Most games with three or more goals
3—Bill Goldsworthy, 1973-74
Dino Ciccarelli, 1981-82
Dino Ciccarelli, 1983-84
Tom McCarthy, 1984-85
Scott Bjugstad, 1985-86
Dino Ciccarelli, 1985-86
Mike Modano, 1998-99

Most shots
321—Bill Goldsworthy, 1973-74

GOALTENDERS

Most games
73—Marty Turco, 2003-04

Most minutes
4,359—Marty Turco, 2003-04

Most shots against
1,648—Marty Turco, 2003-04

Most goals allowed
216—Pete LoPresti, 1977-78

Lowest goals-against average
1.88—Ed Belfour, 1997-98

Most shutouts
9—Ed Belfour, 1997-98
Marty Turco, 2003-04

Most wins
37—Ed Belfour, 1997-98
Marty Turco, 2003-04

Most losses
35—Pete LoPresti, 1977-78

Most ties
16—Cesare Maniago, 1969-70

DETROIT RED WINGS

YEAR-BY-YEAR RECORDS

	REGULAR SEASON						PLAYOFFS			
Season	W	L	T	OTL	Pts.	Finish	W	L	Highest round	Coach
1926-27†	12	28	4	—	28	5th/American	—	—		Art Duncan, Duke Keats
1927-28†	19	19	6	—	44	4th/American	—	—		Jack Adams
1928-29†	19	16	9	—	47	3rd/American	0	2	Quarterfinals	Jack Adams
1929-30†	14	24	6	—	34	4th/American	—	—		Jack Adams
1930-31‡	16	21	7	—	39	4th/American	—	—		Jack Adams
1931-32‡	18	20	10	—	46	3rd/American	*0	1	Quarterfinals	Jack Adams
1932-33	25	15	8	—	58	2nd/American	2	2	Semifinals	Jack Adams
1933-34	24	14	10	—	58	1st/American	4	5	Stanley Cup finals	Jack Adams
1934-35	19	22	7	—	45	4th/American	—	—		Jack Adams
1935-36	24	16	8	—	56	1st/American	6	1	Stanley Cup champ	Jack Adams
1936-37	25	14	9	—	59	1st/American	6	4	Stanley Cup champ	Jack Adams
1937-38	12	25	11	—	35	4th/American	—	—		Jack Adams
1938-39	18	24	6	—	42	5th	3	3	Semifinals	Jack Adams
1939-40	16	26	6	—	38	5th	2	3	Semifinals	Jack Adams
1940-41	21	16	11	—	53	3rd	4	5	Stanley Cup finals	Jack Adams
1941-42	19	25	4	—	42	5th	7	5	Stanley Cup finals	Jack Adams
1942-43	25	14	11	—	61	1st	8	2	Stanley Cup champ	Jack Adams
1943-44	26	18	6	—	58	2nd	1	4	League semifinals	Jack Adams
1944-45	31	14	5	—	67	2nd	7	7	Stanley Cup finals	Jack Adams
1945-46	20	20	10	—	50	4th	1	4	League semifinals	Jack Adams
1946-47	22	27	11	—	55	4th	1	4	League semifinals	Jack Adams
1947-48	30	18	12	—	72	2nd	4	6	Stanley Cup finals	Tommy Ivan

Season	W	L	T	OTL	Pts.	Finish	W	L	Highest round	Coach
	REGULAR SEASON						PLAYOFFS			
1948-49	34	19	7	—	75	1st	4	7	Stanley Cup finals	Tommy Ivan
1949-50	37	19	14	—	88	1st	8	6	Stanley Cup champ	Tommy Ivan
1950-51	44	13	13	—	101	1st	2	4	League semifinals	Tommy Ivan
1951-52	44	14	12	—	100	1st	8	0	Stanley Cup champ	Tommy Ivan
1952-53	36	16	18	—	90	1st	2	4	League semifinals	Tommy Ivan
1953-54	37	19	14	—	88	1st	8	4	Stanley Cup champ	Tommy Ivan
1954-55	42	17	11	—	95	1st	8	3	Stanley Cup champ	Jimmy Skinner
1955-56	30	24	16	—	76	2nd	5	5	Stanley Cup finals	Jimmy Skinner
1956-57	38	20	12	—	88	1st	1	4	League semifinals	Jimmy Skinner
1957-58	29	29	12	—	70	3rd	0	4	League semifinals	Jimmy Skinner, Sid Abel
1958-59	25	37	8	—	58	6th	—	—		Sid Abel
1959-60	26	29	15	—	67	4th	2	4	League semifinals	Sid Abel
1960-61	25	29	16	—	66	4th	6	5	Stanley Cup finals	Sid Abel
1961-62	23	33	14	—	60	5th	—	—		Sid Abel
1962-63	32	25	13	—	77	4th	5	6	Stanley Cup finals	Sid Abel
1963-64	30	29	11	—	71	4th	7	7	Stanley Cup finals	Sid Abel
1964-65	40	23	7	—	87	1st	3	4	League semifinals	Sid Abel
1965-66	31	27	12	—	74	4th	6	6	Stanley Cup finals	Sid Abel
1966-67	27	39	4	—	58	5th	—	—		Sid Abel
1967-68	27	35	12	—	66	6th/East	—	—		Sid Abel
1968-69	33	31	12	—	78	5th/East	—	—		Bill Gadsby
1969-70	40	21	15	—	95	3rd/East	0	4	Division semifinals	Bill Gadsby, Sid Abel
1970-71	22	45	11	—	55	7th/East	—	—		Ned Harkness, Doug Barkley
1971-72	33	35	10	—	76	5th/East	—	—		Doug Barkley, Johnny Wilson
1972-73	37	29	12	—	86	5th/East	—	—		Johnny Wilson
1973-74	29	39	10	—	68	6th/East	—	—		Ted Garvin, Alex Delvecchio
1974-75	23	45	12	—	58	4th/Norris	—	—		Alex Delvecchio
1975-76	26	44	10	—	62	4th/Norris	—	—		Ted Garvin, Alex Delvecchio
1976-77	16	55	9	—	41	5th/Norris	—	—		Alex Delvecchio, Larry Wilson
1977-78	32	34	14	—	78	2nd/Norris	3	4	Quarterfinals	Bobby Kromm
1978-79	23	41	16	—	62	5th/Norris	—	—		Bobby Kromm
1979-80	26	43	11	—	63	5th/Norris	—	—		Bobby Kromm, Ted Lindsay
1980-81	19	43	18	—	56	5th/Norris	—	—		Ted Lindsay, Wayne Maxner
1981-82	21	47	12	—	54	6th/Norris	—	—		Wayne Maxner, Billy Dea
1982-83	21	44	15	—	57	5th/Norris	—	—		Nick Polano
1983-84	31	42	7	—	69	3rd/Norris	1	3	Division semifinals	Nick Polano
1984-85	27	41	12	—	66	3rd/Norris	0	3	Division semifinals	Nick Polano
1985-86	17	57	6	—	40	5th/Norris	—	—		Harry Neale, Brad Park, Dan Belisle
1986-87	34	36	10	—	78	2nd/Norris	9	7	Conference finals	Jacques Demers
1987-88	41	28	11	—	93	1st/Norris	9	7	Conference finals	Jacques Demers
1988-89	34	34	12	—	80	1st/Norris	2	4	Division semifinals	Jacques Demers
1989-90	28	38	14	—	70	5th/Norris	—	—		Jacques Demers
1990-91	34	38	8	—	76	3rd/Norris	3	4	Division semifinals	Bryan Murray
1991-92	43	25	12	—	98	1st/Norris	4	7	Division finals	Bryan Murray
1992-93	47	28	9	—	103	2nd/Norris	3	4	Division semifinals	Bryan Murray
1993-94	46	30	8	—	100	1st/Central	3	4	Division semifinals	Scotty Bowman
1994-95	33	11	4	—	70	1st/Central	12	6	Stanley Cup finals	Scotty Bowman
1995-96	62	13	7	—	131	1st/Central	10	9	Conference finals	Scotty Bowman
1996-97	38	26	18	—	94	2nd/Central	16	4	Stanley Cup champ	Scotty Bowman
1997-98	44	23	15	—	103	2nd/Central	16	6	Stanley Cup champ	Scotty Bowman
1998-99	43	32	7	—	93	1st/Central	6	4	Conference semifinals	Dave Lewis, Barry Smith, Scotty Bowman
1999-00	48	22	10	2	108	2nd/Central	5	4	Conference semifinals	Scotty Bowman
2000-01	49	20	9	4	111	1st/Central	2	4	Conference quarterfinals	Scotty Bowman
2001-02	51	17	10	4	116	1st/Central	16	7	Stanley Cup champ	Scotty Bowman
2002-03	48	20	10	4	110	1st/Central	0	4	Conference quarterfinals	Dave Lewis
2003-04	48	21	11	2	109	2nd/Central	6	6	Conference semifinals	Dave Lewis

*Won-lost record does not indicate tie(s) resulting from two-game, total goals series that year (two-game, total-goals series were played from 1917-18 through 1935-36).

†Detroit Cougars.

‡Detroit Falcons.

FIRST-ROUND ENTRY DRAFT CHOICES

Year Player, Overall, Last amateur team (league)
1969—Jim Rutherford, 10, Hamilton (OHL)
1970—Serge Lajeunesse, 12, Montreal (OHL)
1971—Marcel Dionne, 2, St. Catharines (OHL)
1972—No first-round selection
1973—Terry Richardson, 11, New Westminster (WCHL)
1974—Bill Lochead, 9, Oshawa (OHL)
1975—Rick Lapointe, 5, Victoria (WCHL)

Year Player, Overall, Last amateur team (league)
1976—Fred Williams, 4, Saskatoon (WCHL)
1977—Dale McCourt, 1, St. Catharines (OHL)*
1978—Willie Huber, 9, Hamilton (OHL)
Brent Peterson, 12, Portland (WCHL)
1979—Mike Foligno, 3, Sudbury (OHL)
1980—Mike Blaisdell, 11, Regina (WHL)
1981—No first-round selection

Year	Player, Overall, Last amateur team (league)
1982	Murray Craven, 17, Medicine Hat (WHL)
1983	Steve Yzerman, 4, Peterborough (OHL)
1984	Shawn Burr, 7, Kitchener (OHL)
1985	Brent Fedyk, 8, Regina (WHL)
1986	Joe Murphy, 1, Michigan State University
1987	Yves Racine, 11, Longueuil (QMJHL)
1988	Kory Kocur, 17, Saskatoon (WHL)
1989	Mike Sillinger, 11, Regina (WHL)
1990	Keith Primeau, 3, Niagara Falls (OHL)
1991	Martin Lapointe, 10, Laval (QMJHL)
1992	Curtis Bowen, 22, Ottawa (OHL)
1993	Anders Eriksson, 22, MoDo, Sweden
1994	Yan Golvbovsky, 23, Dynamo Moscow, CIS
1995	Maxim Kuznetsov, 26, Dynamo Moscow, CIS
1996	Jesse Wallin, 26, Red Deer (WHL)
1997	No first-round selection
1998	Jiri Fischer, 25, Hull (QMJHL)
1999	No first-round selection
2000	Niklas Kronvall, 29, Djurgarden, Sweden
2001	No first-round selection
2002	No first-round selection
2003	No first-round selection
2004	No first-round selection
2005	Jakub Kindl, 19, Kitchener (OHL)

SINGLE-SEASON INDIVIDUAL RECORDS

FORWARDS/DEFENSEMEN

Most goals
65—Steve Yzerman, 1988-89

Most assists
90—Steve Yzerman, 1988-89

Most points
155—Steve Yzerman, 1988-89

Most penalty minutes
398—Bob Probert, 1987-88

Most power play goals
21—Mickey Redmond, 1973-74
Dino Ciccarelli, 1992-93

Most shorthanded goals
10—Marcel Dionne, 1974-75

Most games with three or more goals
4—Frank Mahovlich, 1968-69

Most shots
388—Steve Yzerman, 1988-89

GOALTENDERS

Most games
72—Tim Cheveldae, 1991-92

Most minutes
4,236—Tim Cheveldae, 1991-92

Most goals allowed
226—Tim Cheveldae, 1991-92

Lowest goals-against average
1.43—Dolly Dodson, 1928-29

Most shutouts
12—Terry Sawchuk, 1951-52
Terry Sawchuk, 1953-54
Terry Sawchuk, 1954-55
Glenn Hall, 1955-56

Most wins
44—Terry Sawchuk, 1950-51
Terry Sawchuk, 1951-52

EDMONTON OILERS

YEAR-BY-YEAR RECORDS

	REGULAR SEASON						PLAYOFFS			
Season	W	L	T	OTL	Pts.	Finish	W	L	Highest round	Coach
1972-73*	38	37	3	—	79	5th	—	—		Ray Kinasewich
1973-74†	38	37	3	—	79	3rd	1	4	League quarterfinals	Brian Shaw
1974-75†	36	38	4	—	76	5th	—	—		Brian Shaw, Bill Hunter
1975-76†	27	49	5	—	59	4th	0	4	League quarterfinals	Clare Drake, Bill Hunter
1976-77†	34	43	4	—	72	4th	1	4	League quarterfinals	Bep Guidolin, Glen Sather
1977-78†	38	39	3	—	79	5th	1	4	League quarterfinals	Glen Sather
1978-79†	48	30	2	—	98	1st	6	7	Avco World Cup finals	Glen Sather
1979-80	28	39	13	—	69	4th/Smythe	0	3	Preliminaries	Glen Sather
1980-81	29	35	16	—	74	4th/Smythe	5	4	Quarterfinals	Glen Sather
1981-82	48	17	15	—	111	1st/Smythe	2	3	Division semifinals	Glen Sather
1982-83	47	21	12	—	106	1st/Smythe	11	5	Stanley Cup finals	Glen Sather
1983-84	57	18	5	—	119	1st/Smythe	15	4	Stanley Cup champ	Glen Sather
1984-85	49	20	11	—	109	1st/Smythe	15	3	Stanley Cup champ	Glen Sather
1985-86	56	17	7	—	119	1st/Smythe	6	4	Division finals	Glen Sather
1986-87	50	24	6	—	106	1st/Smythe	16	5	Stanley Cup champ	Glen Sather
1987-88	44	25	11	—	99	2nd/Smythe	16	2	Stanley Cup champ	Glen Sather
1988-89	38	34	8	—	84	3rd/Smythe	3	4	Division semifinals	Glen Sather
1989-90	38	28	14	—	90	2nd/Smythe	16	6	Stanley Cup champ	John Muckler
1990-91	37	37	6	—	80	3rd/Smythe	9	9	Conference finals	John Muckler
1991-92	36	34	10	—	82	3rd/Smythe	8	8	Conference finals	Ted Green
1992-93	26	50	8	—	60	5th/Smythe	—	—		Ted Green
1993-94	25	45	14	—	64	6th/Pacific	—	—		Ted Green, Glen Sather
1994-95	17	27	4	—	38	5th/Pacific	—	—		George Burnett, Ron Low
1995-96	30	44	8	—	68	5th/Pacific	—	—		Ron Low
1996-97	36	37	9	—	81	3rd/Pacific	5	7	Conference semifinals	Ron Low
1997-98	35	37	10	—	80	3rd/Pacific	5	7	Conference semifinals	Ron Low
1998-99	33	37	12	—	78	2nd/Northwest	0	4	Conference quarterfinals	Ron Low
1999-00	32	26	16	8	88	2nd/Northwest	1	4	Conference quarterfinals	Kevin Lowe
2000-01	39	28	12	3	93	2nd/Northwest	2	4	Conference quarterfinals	Craig MacTavish
2001-02	38	28	12	4	92	3rd/Northwest	—	—		Craig MacTavish
2002-03	36	26	11	9	92	4th/Northwest	2	4	Conference quarterfinals	Craig MacTavish
2003-04	36	29	12	5	89	4th/Pacific	—	—		Craig MacTavish

*Alberta Oilers, members of World Hockey Association.
†Members of World Hockey Association.

FIRST-ROUND ENTRY DRAFT CHOICES

Year Player, Overall, Last amateur team (league)
1979—Kevin Lowe, 21, Quebec (QMJHL)
1980—Paul Coffey, 6, Kitchener (OHL)
1981—Grant Fuhr, 8, Victoria (WHL)
1982—Jim Playfair, 20, Portland (WHL)
1983—Jeff Beukeboom, 19, Sault Ste. Marie (OHL)
1984—Selmar Odelein, 21, Regina (WHL)
1985—Scott Metcalfe, 20, Kingston (OHL)
1986—Kim Issel, 21, Prince Albert (WHL)
1987—Peter Soberlak, 21, Swift Current (WHL)
1988—Francois Leroux, 19, St. Jean (QMJHL)
1989—Jason Soules, 15, Niagara Falls (OHL)
1990—Scott Allison, 17, Prince Albert (WHL)
1991—Tyler Wright, 12, Swift Current (WHL)
Martin Rucinsky, 20, Litvinov, Czechoslovakia
1992—Joe Hulbig, 13, St. Sebastian H.S. (Mass.)
1993—Jason Arnott, 7, Oshawa (OHL)
Nick Stajduhar, 16, London (OHL)

Year Player, Overall, Last amateur team (league)
1994—Jason Bonsignore, 4, Niagara Falls (OHL)
Ryan Smyth, 6, Moose Jaw (WHL)
1995—Steve Kelly, 6, Prince Albert (WHL)
1996—Boyd Devereaux, 6, Kitchener (OHL)
Matthieu Descoteaux, 19, Shawinigan (QMJHL)
1997—Michel Riessen, 14, HC Biel, Switzerland
1998—Michael Henrich, 13, Barrie (OHL)
1999—Jani Rita, 13, Jokerit Helsinki, Finland
2000—Alexei Mikhnov, 17, Yaroslavl, Russia
2001—Ales Hemsky, 13, Hull (QMJHL)
2002—Jesse Niinimaki, 15, Ilves, Finland
2003—Marc-Antoine Pouliot, 22, Rimouski (QMJHL)
2004—Devan Dubnyk, 14, Kamloops (WHL)
Rob Schremp, 25, London (OHL)
2005—Andrew Cogliano, C, St. Michael's Jr. A

NOTE: Edmonton chose Dave Dryden, Bengt Gustafsson and Ed Mio as priority selections before the 1979 expansion draft.

SINGLE-SEASON INDIVIDUAL RECORDS

FORWARDS/DEFENSEMEN

Most goals
92—Wayne Gretzky, 1981-82

Most assists
163—Wayne Gretzky, 1985-86

Most points
215—Wayne Gretzky, 1985-86

Most penalty minutes
286—Steve Smith, 1987-88

Most power play goals
20—Wayne Gretzky, 1983-84
Ryan Smyth, 1996-97

Most shorthanded goals
12—Wayne Gretzky, 1983-84

Most games with three or more goals
10—Wayne Gretzky, 1981-82
Wayne Gretzky, 1983-84

Most shots
369—Wayne Gretzky, 1981-82

GOALTENDERS

Most games
75—Grant Fuhr, 1987-88

Most minutes
4,364—Tommy Salo, 2000-01

Most goals allowed
246—Grant Fuhr, 1987-88

Lowest goals-against average
2.22—Tommy Salo, 2001-02

Most shutouts
8—Curtis Joseph, 1997-98
Tommy Salo, 2000-01

Most wins
40—Grant Fuhr, 1987-88

Most losses
38—Bill Ranford, 1992-93

Most ties
14—Grant Fuhr, 1981-82

FLORIDA PANTHERS

YEAR-BY-YEAR RECORDS

	REGULAR SEASON						PLAYOFFS			
Season	W	L	T	OTL	Pts.	Finish	W	L	Highest round	Coach
1993-94	33	34	17	—	83	5th/Atlantic	—	—		Roger Neilson
1994-95	20	22	6	—	46	5th/Atlantic	—	—		Roger Neilson
1995-96	41	31	10	—	92	3rd/Atlantic	12	10	Stanley Cup finals	Doug MacLean
1996-97	35	28	19	—	89	3rd/Atlantic	1	4	Conference quarterfinals	Doug MacLean
1997-98	24	43	15	—	63	6th/Atlantic	—	—		Doug MacLean, Bryan Murray
1998-99	30	34	18	—	78	2nd/Southeast	—	—		Terry Murray
1999-00	43	27	6	6	98	2nd/Southeast	0	4	Conference quarterfinals	Terry Murray
2000-01	22	38	13	9	66	3rd/Southeast	—	—		Terry Murray, Duane Sutter
2001-02	22	44	10	6	60	4th/Southeast	—	—		Duane Sutter, Mike Keenan
2002-03	24	36	13	9	70	4th/Southeast	—	—		Mike Keenan
2003-04	28	35	15	4	75	4th/Southeast	—	—		M.Keenan, R.Dudley, J.Torchetti

FIRST-ROUND ENTRY DRAFT CHOICES

Year Player, Overall, Last amateur team (league)
1993—Rob Niedermayer, 5, Medicine Hat (WHL)
1994—Ed Jovanovski, 1, Windsor (OHL)
1995—Radek Dvorak, 10, Budejovice, Czech Republic
1996—Marcus Nilson, 20, Djurgarden-Stockholm, Sweden
1997—Mike Brown, 20, Red Deer (WHL)
1998—No first-round selection
1999—Denis Shvidki, 12, Barrie (OHL)
2000—No first-round selection
2001—Stephen Weiss, 4, Plymouth (OHL)

Year Player, Overall, Last amateur team (league)
Lukas Krajicek, 24, Peterborough (OHL)
2002—Jay Bouwmeester, 3, Medicine Hat (WHL)
Petr Taticek, 9, Sault Ste. Marie (OHL)
2003—Nathan Horton, 3, Oshawa (OHL)
Anthony Stewart, 25, Kingston (OHL)
2004—Rostislav Olesz, 7, Vitkovic, Czech. Rep.
2005—Kenndal McArdle, 20, Moose Jaw (WHL)

SINGLE-SEASON INDIVIDUAL RECORDS

FORWARDS/DEFENSEMEN

Most goals
59—Pavel Bure, 2000-01

Most assists
53—Viktor Kozlov, 1999-2000

Most points
94—Pavel Bure, 1999-2000

Most penalty minutes
354—Peter Worrell, 2001-02

Most power play goals
19—Scott Mellanby, 1995-96
Pavel Bure, 2000-01

Most shorthanded goals
6—Tom Fitzgerald, 1995-96

Most games with three or more goals
4—Pavel Bure, 1999-2000
Pavel Bure, 2000-01

Most shots
384—Pavel Bure, 2000-01

GOALTENDERS

Most games
65—Roberto Longo, 2002-03

Most minutes
3,451—John Vanbiesbrouck, 1997-98

Most shots against
2,011—John Vanbiesbrouck, 1993-94

Most goals allowed
165—John Vanbiesbrouck, 1997-98

Lowest goals-against average
2.29—John Vanbiesbrouck, 1996-97

Most shutouts
5—Robert Luongo, 2000-01

Most wins
27—John Vanbiesbrouck, 1996-97

Most losses
33—Robert Luongo, 2001-02

Most ties
14—Sean Burke, 1998-99

LOS ANGELES KINGS

YEAR-BY-YEAR RECORDS

	REGULAR SEASON						PLAYOFFS			
Season	W	L	T	OTL	Pts.	Finish	W	L	Highest round	Coach
1967-68	31	33	10	—	72	2nd/West	3	4	Division semifinals	Red Kelly
1968-69	24	42	10	—	58	4th/West	4	7	Division finals	Red Kelly
1969-70	14	52	10	—	38	6th/West	—	—		Hal Laycoe, Johnny Wilson
1970-71	25	40	13	—	63	5th/West	—	—		Larry Regan
1971-72	20	49	9	—	49	7th/West	—	—		Larry Regan, Fred Glover
1972-73	31	36	11	—	73	6th/West	—	—		Bob Pulford
1973-74	33	33	12	—	78	3rd/West	1	4	Division semifinals	Bob Pulford
1974-75	42	17	21	—	105	2nd/Norris	1	2	Preliminaries	Bob Pulford
1975-76	38	33	9	—	85	2nd/Norris	5	4	Quarterfinals	Bob Pulford
1976-77	34	31	15	—	83	2nd/Norris	4	5	Quarterfinals	Bob Pulford
1977-78	31	34	15	—	77	3rd/Norris	0	2	Preliminaries	Ron Stewart
1978-79	34	34	12	—	80	3rd/Norris	0	2	Preliminaries	Bob Berry
1979-80	30	36	14	—	74	2nd/Norris	1	3	Preliminaries	Bob Berry
1980-81	43	24	13	—	99	2nd/Norris	1	3	Preliminaries	Bob Berry
1981-82	24	41	15	—	63	4th/Smythe	4	6	Division finals	Parker MacDonald, Don Perry,
1982-83	27	41	12	—	66	5th/Smythe	—	—		Don Perry
1983-84	23	44	13	—	59	5th/Smythe	—	—		Don Perry, Rogie Vachon, Roger Neilson
1984-85	34	32	14	—	82	4th/Smythe	0	3	Division semifinals	Pat Quinn
1985-86	23	49	8	—	54	5th/Smythe	—	—		Pat Quinn
1986-87	31	41	8	—	70	4th/Smythe	1	4	Division semifinals	Pat Quinn, Mike Murphy
1987-88	30	42	8	—	68	4th/Smythe	1	4	Division semifinals	Mike Murphy, Rogie Vachon, Robbie Ftorek
1988-89	42	31	7	—	91	2nd/Smythe	4	7	Division finals	Robbie Ftorek
1989-90	34	39	7	—	75	4th/Smythe	4	6	Division finals	Tom Webster
1990-91	46	24	10	—	102	1st/Smythe	6	6	Division finals	Tom Webster
1991-92	35	31	14	—	84	2nd/Smythe	2	4	Division semifinals	Tom Webster
1992-93	39	35	10	—	88	3rd/Smythe	13	11	Stanley Cup finals	Barry Melrose
1993-94	27	45	12	—	66	5th/Pacific	—	—		Barry Melrose
1994-95	16	23	9	—	41	4th/Pacific	—	—		Barry Melrose, Rogie Vachon
1995-96	24	40	18	—	66	6th/Pacific	—	—		Larry Robinson
1996-97	28	43	11	—	67	6th/Pacific	—	—		Larry Robinson
1997-98	38	33	11	—	87	2nd/Pacific	0	4	Conference quarterfinals	Larry Robinson
1998-99	32	45	5	—	69	5th/Pacific	—	—		Larry Robinson
1999-00	39	27	12	4	94	2nd/Pacific	0	4	Conference quarterfinals	Andy Murray
2000-01	38	28	13	3	92	3rd/Pacific	7	6	Conference semifinals	Andy Murray
2001-02	40	27	11	4	95	3rd/Pacific	3	4	Conference quarterfinals	Andy Murray
2002-03	33	37	6	6	78	3rd/Pacific	—	—		Andy Murray, Dave Tippett
2003-04	28	29	16	9	81	3rd/Pacific	—	—		Andy Murray

FIRST-ROUND ENTRY DRAFT CHOICES

Year Player, Overall, Last amateur team (league)
1969—No first-round selection
1970—No first-round selection
1971—No first-round selection
1972—No first-round selection
1973—No first-round selection
1974—No first-round selection
1975—Tim Young, 16, Ottawa (OHL)
1976—No first-round selection
1977—No first-round selection
1978—No first-round selection
1979—Jay Wells, 16, Kingston (OHL)
1980—Larry Murphy, 4, Peterborough (OHL)

Year	Player, Overall, Last amateur team (league)
	Jim Fox, 10, Ottawa (OHL)
1981—	Doug Smith, 2, Ottawa (OHL)
1982—	No first-round selection
1983—	No first-round selection
1984—	Craig Redmond, 6, Canadian Olympic Team
1985—	Craig Duncanson, 9, Sudbury (OHL)
	Dan Gratton, 10, Oshawa (OHL)
1986—	Jimmy Carson, 2, Verdun (QMJHL)
1987—	Wayne McBean, 4, Medicine Hat (WHL)
1988—	Martin Gelinas, 7, Hull (QMJHL)
1989—	No first-round selection
1990—	Darryl Sydor, 7, Kamloops (WHL)
1991—	No first-round selection
1992—	No first-round selection
1993—	No first-round selection
1994—	Jamie Storr, 7, Owen Sound (OHL)
1995—	Aki-Petteri Berg, 3, TPS Jrs., Finland
1996—	No first-round selection
1997—	Olli Jokinen, 3, IFK Helsinki, Finland
	Matt Zultek, 15, Ottawa (OHL)
1998—	Mathieu Biron, 21, Shawinigan (QMJHL)
1999—	No first-round selection
2000—	Alexander Frolov, 20, Yaroslavl, Russia
2001—	Jens Karlsson, 18, Frolunda, Sweden
	David Steckel, 30, Ohio State
2002—	Denis Grebeshkov, 18, Yaroslavl, Russia
2003—	Dustin Brown, 13, Guelph (OHL)
	Brian Boyle, 26, St. Sebastian's (U.S. high school)
	Jeff Tambellini, 27, Michigan (CCHA)
2004—	Lauri Tukonen, 11, Espoo, Finland
2005—	Anze Kopitar, 11, Sodertalje, Sweden

SINGLE-SEASON INDIVIDUAL RECORDS

FORWARDS/DEFENSEMEN

Most goals
70—Bernie Nicholls, 1988-89

Most assists
122—Wayne Gretzky, 1990-91

Most points
168—Wayne Gretzky, 1988-89

Most penalty minutes
399—Marty McSorley, 1992-93

Most power play goals
26—Luc Robitaille, 1991-92

Most shorthanded goals
8—Bernie Nicholls, 1988-89

Most games with three or more goals
5—Jimmy Carson, 1987-88

Most shots
385—Bernie Nicholls, 1988-89

GOALTENDERS

Most games
71—Felix Potvin, 2001-02

Most minutes
4,107—Rogie Vachon, 1977-78

Most shots against
2,219—Kelly Hrudey, 1993-94

Most goals allowed
228—Kelly Hrudey, 1993-94

Lowest goals-against average
2.24—Rogie Vachon, 1974-75

Most shutouts
8—Rogie Vachon, 1976-77

Most wins
35—Mario Lessard, 1980-81

Most losses
31—Kelly Hrudey, 1993-94

Most ties
13—Rogie Vachon, 1974-75
Rogie Vachon, 1977-78
Kelly Hrudey, 1991-92

MINNESOTA WILD

YEAR-BY-YEAR RECORDS

	REGULAR SEASON						PLAYOFFS			
Season	W	L	T	OTL	Pts.	Finish	W	L	Highest round	Coach
2000-01	25	39	13	5	68	5th/Northwest	—	—		Jacques Lemaire
2001-02	26	35	12	9	73	5th/Northwest	—	—		Jacques Lemaire
2002-03	42	29	10	1	95	3rd/Northwest	8	10	Conference finals	Jacques Lemaire
2003-04	30	29	20	3	83	5th/Northwest	—	—		Jacques Lemaire

FIRST-ROUND ENTRY DRAFT CHOICES

Year	Player, Overall, Last amateur team (league)
2000—	Marian Gaborik, 3, Trencin, Slovakia
2001—	Mikko Koivu, 6, TPS, Finland
2002—	Pierre-Marc Bouchard, 8, Chicoutimi
2003—	Brent Burns, 20, Brampton (OHL)
2004—	A.J. Thelen, 12, Michigan State (CCHA)
2005—	Benoit Pouliot, 4, Sudbury (OHL)

SINGLE-SEASON INDIVIDUAL RECORDS

FORWARDS/DEFENSEMEN

Most goals
30—Marian Gaborik, 2002-03

Most assists
48—Andrew Brunette, 2001-02

Most points
69—Andrew Brunette, 2001-02

Most penalty minutes
201—Matt Johnson, 2002-03

Most power play goals
10—Andrew Brunette, 2001-02
Marian Gaborik, 2001-02
Sergei Zholtok, 2001-02

Most shorthanded goals
7—Wes Walz, 2000-01

Most games with three or more goals
2—Marian Gaborik, 2001-02

Most shots
280—Marian Gaborik, 2002-03

GOALTENDERS

Most games
48—Dwayne Roloson, 2003-04

Most minutes
2,847—Dwayne Roloson, 2003-04

Most shots against
1,334—Dwayne Roloson, 2001-02

Most goals allowed
125—Manny Fernandez, 2001-02

Lowest goals-against average
1.88—Dwayne Roloson, 2003-04

Most shutouts
5—Dwayne Roloson, 2001-02
Dwayne Roloson, 2003-04

Most wins
23—Dwayne Roloson, 2002-03

Most losses
24—Manny Fernandez, 2001-02

Most ties
11—Dwayne Roloson, 2003-04

MONTREAL CANADIENS

YEAR-BY-YEAR RECORDS

	REGULAR SEASON						PLAYOFFS			
Season	W	L	T	OTL	Pts.	Finish	W	L	Highest round	Coach
1917-18	13	9	0	—	26	1st/3rd	1	1	Semifinals	George Kennedy
1918-19	10	8	0	—	20	1st/2nd	†*6	3	Stanley Cup finals	George Kennedy
1919-20	13	11	0	—	26	2nd/3rd	—	—		George Kennedy
1920-21	13	11	0	—	26	3rd/2nd	—	—		George Kennedy
1921-22	12	11	1	—	25	3rd	—	—		Leo Dandurand
1922-23	13	9	2	—	28	2nd	1	1	Quarterfinals	Leo Dandurand
1923-24	13	11	0	—	26	2nd	6	0	Stanley Cup champ	Leo Dandurand
1924-25	17	11	2	—	36	3rd	3	3	Stanley Cup finals	Leo Dandurand
1925-26	11	24	1	—	23	7th	—	—		Cecil Hart
1926-27	28	14	2	—	58	2nd/Canadian	*1	1	Semifinals	Cecil Hart
1927-28	26	11	7	—	59	1st/Canadian	*0	1	Semifinals	Cecil Hart
1928-29	22	7	15	—	59	1st/Canadian	0	3	Semifinals	Cecil Hart
1929-30	21	14	9	—	51	2nd/Canadian	*5	0	Stanley Cup champ	Cecil Hart
1930-31	26	10	8	—	60	1st/Canadian	6	4	Stanley Cup champ	Cecil Hart
1931-32	25	16	7	—	57	1st/Canadian	1	3	Semifinals	Cecil Hart
1932-33	18	25	5	—	41	3rd/Canadian	*0	1	Quarterfinals	Newsy Lalonde
1933-34	22	20	6	—	50	2nd/Canadian	*0	1	Quarterfinals	Newsy Lalonde
1934-35	19	23	6	—	44	3rd/Canadian	*0	1	Quarterfinals	Newsy Lalonde, Leo Dandurand
1935-36	11	26	11	—	33	4th/Canadian	—	—		Sylvio Mantha
1936-37	24	18	6	—	54	1st/Canadian	2	3	Semifinals	Cecil Hart
1937-38	18	17	13	—	49	3rd/Canadian	1	2	Quarterfinals	Cecil Hart
1938-39	15	24	9	—	39	6th	1	2	Quarterfinals	Cecil Hart, Jules Dugal
1939-40	10	33	5	—	25	7th	—	—		Pit Lepine
1940-41	16	26	6	—	38	6th	1	2	Quarterfinals	Dick Irvin
1941-42	18	27	3	—	39	6th	1	2	Quarterfinals	Dick Irvin
1942-43	19	19	12	—	50	4th	1	4	League semifinals	Dick Irvin
1943-44	38	5	7	—	83	1st	8	1	Stanley Cup champ	Dick Irvin
1944-45	38	8	4	—	80	1st	2	4	League semifinals	Dick Irvin
1945-46	28	17	5	—	61	1st	8	1	Stanley Cup champ	Dick Irvin
1946-47	34	16	10	—	78	1st	6	5	Stanley Cup finals	Dick Irvin
1947-48	20	29	11	—	51	5th	—	—		Dick Irvin
1948-49	28	23	9	—	65	3rd	3	4	League semifinals	Dick Irvin
1949-50	29	22	19	—	77	2nd	1	4	League semifinals	Dick Irvin
1950-51	25	30	15	—	65	3rd	5	6	Stanley Cup finals	Dick Irvin
1951-52	34	26	10	—	78	2nd	4	7	Stanley Cup finals	Dick Irvin
1952-53	28	23	19	—	75	2nd	8	4	Stanley Cup champ	Dick Irvin
1953-54	35	24	11	—	81	2nd	7	4	Stanley Cup finals	Dick Irvin
1954-55	41	18	11	—	93	2nd	7	5	Stanley Cup finals	Dick Irvin
1955-56	45	15	10	—	100	1st	8	2	Stanley Cup champ	Toe Blake
1956-57	35	23	12	—	82	2nd	8	2	Stanley Cup champ	Toe Blake
1957-58	43	17	10	—	96	1st	8	2	Stanley Cup champ	Toe Blake
1958-59	39	18	13	—	91	1st	8	3	Stanley Cup champ	Toe Blake
1959-60	40	18	12	—	92	1st	8	0	Stanley Cup champ	Toe Blake
1960-61	41	19	10	—	92	1st	2	4	League semifinals	Toe Blake
1961-62	42	14	14	—	98	1st	2	4	League semifinals	Toe Blake
1962-63	28	19	23	—	79	3rd	1	4	League semifinals	Toe Blake
1963-64	36	21	13	—	85	1st	3	4	League semifinals	Toe Blake
1964-65	36	23	11	—	83	2nd	8	5	Stanley Cup champ	Toe Blake
1965-66	41	21	8	—	90	1st	8	2	Stanley Cup champ	Toe Blake
1966-67	32	25	13	—	77	2nd	6	4	Stanley Cup finals	Toe Blake
1967-68	42	22	10	—	94	1st/East	12	1	Stanley Cup champ	Toe Blake
1968-69	46	19	11	—	103	1st/East	12	2	Stanley Cup champ	Claude Ruel
1969-70	38	22	16	—	92	5th/East	—	—		Claude Ruel
1970-71	42	23	13	—	97	3rd/East	12	8	Stanley Cup champ	Claude Ruel, Al MacNeil
1971-72	46	16	16	—	108	3rd/East	2	4	Division semifinals	Scotty Bowman
1972-73	52	10	16	—	120	1st/East	12	5	Stanley Cup champ	Scotty Bowman
1973-74	45	24	9	—	99	2nd/East	2	4	Division semifinals	Scotty Bowman
1974-75	47	14	19	—	113	1st/Norris	6	5	Semifinals	Scotty Bowman
1975-76	58	11	11	—	127	1st/Norris	12	1	Stanley Cup champ	Scotty Bowman
1976-77	60	8	12	—	132	1st/Norris	12	2	Stanley Cup champ	Scotty Bowman
1977-78	59	10	11	—	129	1st/Norris	12	3	Stanley Cup champ	Scotty Bowman
1978-79	52	17	11	—	115	1st/Norris	12	4	Stanley Cup champ	Scotty Bowman
1979-80	47	20	13	—	107	1st/Norris	6	4	Quarterfinals	Bernie Geoffrion, Claude Ruel
1980-81	45	22	13	—	103	1st/Norris	0	3	Preliminaries	Claude Ruel
1981-82	46	17	17	—	109	1st/Adams	2	3	Division semifinals	Bob Berry
1982-83	42	24	14	—	98	2nd/Adams	0	3	Division semifinals	Bob Berry
1983-84	35	40	5	—	75	4th/Adams	9	6	Conference finals	Bob Berry, Jacques Lemaire

Season	W	L	T	OTL	Pts.	Finish	W	L	Highest round	Coach
	REGULAR SEASON						PLAYOFFS			
1984-85	41	27	12	—	94	1st/Adams	6	6	Division finals	Jacques Lemaire
1985-86	40	33	7	—	87	2nd/Adams	15	5	Stanley Cup champ	Jean Perron
1986-87	41	29	10	—	92	2nd/Adams	10	7	Conference finals	Jean Perron
1987-88	45	22	13	—	103	1st/Adams	5	6	Division finals	Jean Perron
1988-89	53	18	9	—	115	1st/Adams	14	7	Stanley Cup finals	Pat Burns
1989-90	41	28	11	—	93	3rd/Adams	5	6	Division finals	Pat Burns
1990-91	39	30	11	—	89	2nd/Adams	7	6	Division finals	Pat Burns
1991-92	41	28	11	—	93	1st/Adams	4	7	Division finals	Pat Burns
1992-93	48	30	6	—	102	3rd/Adams	16	4	Stanley Cup champ	Jacques Demers
1993-94	41	29	14	—	96	3rd/Northeast	3	4	Conference quarterfinals	Jacques Demers
1994-95	18	23	7	—	43	6th/Northeast	—	—		Jacques Demers
1995-96	40	32	10	—	90	3rd/Northeast	2	4	Conference quarterfinals	Jacques Demers, Mario Tremblay
1996-97	31	36	15	—	77	4th/Northeast	1	4	Conference quarterfinals	Mario Tremblay
1997-98	37	32	13	—	87	4th/Northeast	4	6	Conference semifinals	Alain Vigneault
1998-99	32	39	11	—	75	5th/Northeast	—	—		Alain Vigneault
1999-00	35	34	9	4	83	4th/Northeast	—	—		Alain Vigneault
2000-01	28	40	8	6	70	5th/Northeast	—	—		Alain Vigneault, Michel Therrien
2001-02	36	31	12	3	87	4th/Northeast	6	6	Conference semifinals	Michel Therrien
2002-03	30	35	8	9	77	4th/Northeast	—	—		Michael Therrien, Claude Julien
2003-04	41	30	7	4	93	4th/Northeast	4	7	Conference semifinals	Claude Julien

*Won-lost record does not indicate tie(s) resulting from two-game, total-goals series that year (two-game, total-goals series were played from 1917-18 through 1935-36).

†1918-19 series abandoned with no Cup holder due to influenza epidemic.

FIRST-ROUND ENTRY DRAFT CHOICES

Year Player, Overall, Last amateur team (league)

1969—Rejean Houle, 1, Montreal (OHL)
Marc Tardif, 2, Montreal (OHL)
1970—Ray Martiniuk, 5, Flin Flon (WCHL)
Chuck Lefley, 6, Canadian Nationals
1971—Guy Lafleur, 1, Quebec (QMJHL)
Chuck Arnason, 7, Flin Flon (WCHL)
Murray Wilson, 11, Ottawa (OHL)
1972—Steve Shutt, 4, Toronto (OHL)
Michel Larocque, 6, Ottawa (OHL)
Dave Gardner, 8, Toronto (OHL)
John Van Boxmeer, 14, Guelph (SOJHL)
1973—Bob Gainey, 8, Peterborough (OHL)
1974—Cam Connor, 5, Flin Flon (WCHL)
Doug Risebrough, 7, Kitchener (OHL)
Rick Chartraw, 10, Kitchener (OHL)
Mario Tremblay, 12, Montreal (OHL)
Gord McTavish, 15, Sudbury (OHL)
1975—Robin Sadler, 9, Edmonton (WCHL)
Pierre Mondou, 15, Montreal (QMJHL)
1976—Peter Lee, 12, Ottawa (OHL)
Rod Schutt, 13, Sudbury (OHL)
Bruce Baker, 18, Ottawa (OHL)
1977—Mark Napier, 10, Birmingham (WHA)
Normand Dupont, 18, Montreal (QMJHL)
1978—Danny Geoffrion, 8, Cornwall (QMJHL)
Dave Hunter, 17, Sudbury (OHL)
1979—No first-round selection
1980—Doug Wickenheiser, 1, Regina (WHL)
1981—Mark Hunter, 7, Brantford (OHL)
Gilbert Delorme, 18, Chicoutimi (QMJHL)

Year Player, Overall, Last amateur team (league)

Jan Ingman, 19, Farjestads (Sweden)
1982—Alain Heroux, 19, Chicoutimi (QMJHL)
1983—Alfie Turcotte, 17, Portland (WHL)
1984—Petr Svoboda, 5, Czechoslovakia
Shayne Corson, 8, Brantford (OHL)
1985—Jose Charbonneau, 12, Drummondville (QMJHL)
Tom Chorske, 16, Minneapolis SW H.S. (Minn.)
1986—Mark Pederson, 15, Medicine Hat (WHL)
1987—Andrew Cassels, 17, Ottawa (OHL)
1988—Eric Charron, 20, Trois-Rivieres (QMJHL)
1989—Lindsay Vallis, 13, Seattle (WHL)
1990—Turner Stevenson, 12, Seattle (WHL)
1991—Brent Bilodeau, 17, Seattle (WHL)
1992—David Wilkie, 20, Kamloops (WHL)
1993—Saku Koivu, 21, TPS Turku (Finland)
1994—Brad Brown, 18, North Bay (OHL)
1995—Terry Ryan, 8, Tri-City (WHL)
1996—Matt Higgins, 18, Moose Jaw (WHL)
1997—Jason Ward, 11, Erie (OHL)
1998—Eric Chouinard, 16, Quebec (QMJHL)
1999—No first-round selection
2000—Ron Hainsey, 13, Univ. of Mass.-Lowell
Marcel Hossa, 16, Portland (WHL)
2001—Michael Komisarek, 7, Univ. of Michigan
Alexander Perezhogin, 25, OMSK, Russia
2002—Christopher Higgins, 14, Yale (ECAC)
2003—Andrei Kastsitsyn, 10, Belarus
2004—Kyle Chipchura, 18, Prince Albert (WHL)
2005—Carey Price, 5, Tri-City (WHL)

SINGLE-SEASON INDIVIDUAL RECORDS

FORWARDS/DEFENSEMEN

Most goals

60—Steve Shutt, 1976-77
Guy Lafleur, 1977-78

Most assists

82—Pete Mahovlich, 1974-75

Most points

136—Guy Lafleur, 1976-77

Most penalty minutes

358—Chris Nilan, 1984-85

Most power play goals

20—Yvan Cournoyer, 1966-67

Most shorthanded goals

8—Guy Carbonneau, 1983-84

Most games with three or more goals

7—Joe Malone, 1917-18

GOALTENDERS

Most games

70—Gerry McNeil, 1950-51
Gerry McNeil, 1951-52
Jacques Plante, 1961-62

Most minutes

4,200—Gerry McNeil, 1950-51
Gerry McNeil, 1951-52
Jacques Plante, 1961-62

Most goals allowed

192—Patrick Roy, 1992-93

Lowest goals-against average

0.92—George Hainsworth, 1928-29

Most shutouts

22—George Hainsworth, 1928-29

Most wins

42—Jacques Plante, 1955-56
Jacques Plante, 1961-62
Ken Dryden, 1975-76

Most losses

31—Jose Theodore, 2002-03

Most ties

19—Jacques Plante, 1962-63

MONTREAL MAROONS (DEFUNCT)

YEAR-BY-YEAR RECORDS

	REGULAR SEASON					PLAYOFFS			
Season	W	L	T	Pts.	Finish	W	L	Highest round	Coach
1924-25	9	19	2	20	5th	—	—		Eddie Gerard
1925-26	20	11	5	45	2nd	3	1	Stanley Cup champ	Eddie Gerard
1926-27	20	20	4	44	3rd/Canadian	*0	1	Quarterfinals	Eddie Gerard
1927-28	24	14	6	54	2nd/Canadian	*5	3	Stanley Cup finals	Eddie Gerard
1928-29	15	20	9	39	5th/Canadian	—	—		Eddie Gerard
1929-30	23	16	5	51	1st/Canadian	1	3	Semifinals	Dunc Munro
1930-31	20	18	6	46	3rd/Canadian	*0	2	Quarterfinals	Dunc Munro, George Boucher
1931-32	19	22	7	45	3rd/Canadian	*1	1	Semifinals	Sprague Cleghorn
1932-33	22	20	6	50	2nd/Canadian	0	2	Quarterfinals	Eddie Gerard
1933-34	19	18	11	49	3rd/Canadian	*1	2	Semifinals	Eddie Gerard
1934-35	24	19	5	53	2nd/Canadian	*5	0	Stanley Cup champ	Tommy Gorman
1935-36	22	16	10	54	1st/Canadian	0	3	Semifinals	Tommy Gorman
1936-37	22	17	9	53	2nd/Canadian	2	3	Semifinals	Tommy Gorman
1937-38	12	30	6	30	4th/Canadian	—	—		King Clancy, Tommy Gorman

*Won-lost record does not indicate tie(s) resulting from two-game, total goals series that year (two-game, total-goals series were played from 1917-18 through 1935-36).

MONTREAL WANDERERS (DEFUNCT)

YEAR-BY-YEAR RECORDS

	REGULAR SEASON					PLAYOFFS			
Season	W	L	T	Pts.	Finish	W	L	Highest round	Coach
1917-18*	1	5	0	2	4th	—	—		Art Ross

*Franchise disbanded after Montreal Arena burned down. Montreal Canadiens and Toronto each counted one win for defaulted games with Wanderers.

NASHVILLE PREDATORS

YEAR-BY-YEAR RECORDS

	REGULAR SEASON						PLAYOFFS			
Season	W	L	T	OTL	Pts.	Finish	W	L	Highest round	Coach
1998-99	28	47	7	—	63	4th/Central	—	—		Barry Trotz
1999-00	28	40	7	7	70	4th/Central	—	—		Barry Trotz
2000-01	34	36	9	3	80	3rd/Central	—	—		Barry Trotz
2001-02	28	41	13	0	69	4th/Central	—	—		Barry Trotz
2002-03	27	35	13	7	74	4th/Central	—	—		Barry Trotz
2003-04	38	29	11	4	91	3rd/Central	2	4	Conference quarterfinals	Barry Trotz

FIRST-ROUND ENTRY DRAFT CHOICES

Year Player, Overall, Last amateur team (league)
1998—David Legwand, 2, Plymouth (OHL)
1999—Brian Finley, 6, Barrie (OHL)
2000—Scott Hartnell, 6, Prince Albert (WHL)
2001—Dan Hamhuis, 12, Prince George (WHL)

Year Player, Overall, Last amateur team (league)
2002—Scottie Upshall, 6, Kamloops (WHL)
2003—Ryan Suter, 7, U.S. National under-18 (NTDP)
2004—Alexander Radulov, 15, Dynamo 2, Russia
2005—Ryan Parent, 18, Guelph (OHL)

SINGLE-SEASON INDIVIDUAL RECORDS

FORWARDS/DEFENSEMEN

Most goals
26—Cliff Ronning, 1999-2000

Most assists
49—Steve Sullivan, 2003-04

Most points
73—Steve Sullivan, 2003-04

Most penalty minutes
242—Patrick Cote, 1998-99

Most power play goals
14—Andy Delmore, 2002-03

Most shorthanded goals
4—Greg Johnson, 2003-04

Most games with three or more goals
1—Robert Valicevic, 1999-2000
Scott Walker, 2000-01
Petr Tenkrat, 2001-02
Vladimir Orszagh, 2003-04
Steve Sullivan, 2003-04
Scott Walker, 2003-04

Most shots
248—Cliff Ronning, 1999-2000

GOALTENDERS

Most games
73—Tomas Vokoun, 2003-04

Most minutes
4,221—Tomas Vokoun, 2003-04

Most shots against
1,958—Tomas Vokoun, 2003-04

Most goals allowed
178—Tomas Vokoun, 2003-04

Lowest goals-against average
2.20—Tomas Vokoun, 2002-03

Most shutouts
4—Mike Dunham, 2000-01

Most wins
34—Tomas Vokoun, 2003-04

Most losses
31—Tomas Vokoun, 2002-03

Most ties
11—Tomas Vokoun, 2002-03

NEW JERSEY DEVILS

YEAR-BY-YEAR RECORDS

	REGULAR SEASON						PLAYOFFS			
Season	W	L	T	OTL	Pts.	Finish	W	L	Highest round	Coach
1974-75*	15	54	11	—	41	5th/Smythe	—	—		Bep Guidolin
1975-76*	12	56	12	—	36	5th/Smythe	—	—		Bep Guidolin, Sid Abel, Eddie Bush
1976-77†	20	46	14	—	54	5th/Smythe	—	—		John Wilson
1977-78†	19	40	21	—	59	2nd/Smythe	0	2	Preliminaries	Pat Kelly
1978-79†	15	53	12	—	42	4th/Smythe	—	—		Pat Kelly, Bep Guidolin
1979-80†	19	48	13	—	51	6th/Smythe	—	—		Don Cherry
1980-81†	22	45	13	—	57	5th/Smythe	—	—		Billy MacMillan
1981-82†	18	49	13	—	49	5th/Smythe	—	—		Bert Marshall, Marshall Johnston
1982-83	17	49	14	—	48	5th/Patrick	—	—		Billy MacMillan
1983-84	17	56	7	—	41	5th/Patrick	—	—		Billy MacMillan, Tom McVie
1984-85	22	48	10	—	54	5th/Patrick	—	—		Doug Carpenter
1985-86	28	49	3	—	59	6th/Patrick	—	—		Doug Carpenter
1986-87	29	45	6	—	64	6th/Patrick	—	—		Doug Carpenter
1987-88	38	36	6	—	82	4th/Patrick	11	9	Conference finals	Doug Carpenter, Jim Schoenfeld
1988-89	27	41	12	—	66	5th/Patrick	—	—		Jim Schoenfeld
1989-90	37	34	9	—	83	2nd/Patrick	2	4	Division semifinals	Jim Schoenfeld, John Cunniff
1990-91	32	33	15	—	79	4th/Patrick	3	4	Division semifinals	John Cunniff, Tom McVie
1991-92	38	31	11	—	87	4th/Patrick	3	4	Division semifinals	Tom McVie
1992-93	40	37	7	—	87	4th/Patrick	1	4	Division semifinals	Herb Brooks
1993-94	47	25	12	—	106	2nd/Atlantic	11	9	Conference finals	Jacques Lemaire
1994-95	22	18	8	—	52	2nd/Atlantic	16	4	Stanley Cup champ	Jacques Lemaire
1995-96	37	33	12	—	86	6th/Atlantic	—	—		Jacques Lemaire
1996-97	45	23	14	—	104	1st/Atlantic	5	5	Conference semifinals	Jacques Lemaire
1997-98	48	23	11	—	107	1st/Atlantic	2	4	Conference quarterfinals	Jacques Lemaire
1998-99	47	24	11	—	105	1st/Atlantic	3	4	Conference quarterfinals	Robbie Ftorek
1999-00	45	24	8	5	103	2nd/Atlantic	16	7	Stanley Cup champ	Robbie Ftorek, Larry Robinson
2000-01	48	19	12	3	111	1st/Atlantic	15	10	Stanley Cup finals	Larry Robinson
2001-02	41	28	9	4	95	3rd/Atlantic	2	4	Conference quarterfinals	Larry Robinson, Kevin Constantine
2002-03	46	20	10	6	108	1st/Atlantic	16	8	Stanley Cup finals	Pat Burns
2003-04	43	25	12	2	100	2nd/Atlantic	1	4	Conference quarterfinals	Pat Burns

*Kansas City Scouts.
†Colorado Rockies.

FIRST-ROUND ENTRY DRAFT CHOICES

Year Player, Overall, Last amateur team (league)

1974—Wilf Paiement, 2, St. Catharines (OHL)
1975—Barry Dean, 2, Medicine Hat (WCHL)
1976—Paul Gardner, 11, Oshawa (OHL)
1977—Barry Beck, 2, New Westminster (WCHL)
1978—Mike Gillis, 5, Kingston (OHL)
1979—Rob Ramage, 1, Birmingham (WHA)
1980—Paul Gagne, 19, Windsor (OHL)
1981—Joe Cirella, 5, Oshawa (OHL)
1982—Rocky Trottier, 8, Billings (WHL)
Ken Daneyko, 18, Seattle (WHL)
1983—John MacLean, 6, Oshawa (OHL)
1984—Kirk Muller, 2, Guelph (OHL)
1985—Craig Wolanin, 3, Kitchener (OHL)
1986—Neil Brady, 3, Medicine Hat (WHL)
1987—Brendan Shanahan, 2, London (OHL)
1988—Corey Foster, 12, Peterborough (OHL)
1989—Bill Guerin, 5, Springfield (Mass.) Jr.
Jason Miller, 18, Medicine Hat (WHL)
1990—Martin Brodeur, 20, St. Hyacinthe (QMJHL)

Year Player, Overall, Last amateur team (league)

1991—Scott Niedermayer, 3, Kamloops (WHL)
Brian Rolston, 11, Detroit Compuware Jr.
1992—Jason Smith, 18, Regina (WHL)
1993—Denis Pederson, 13, Prince Albert (WHL)
1994—Vadim Sharifjanov, 25, Salavat (Russia)
1995—Petr Sykora, 18, Detroit (IHL)
1996—Lance Ward, 10, Red Deer (WHL)
1997—Jean-Francois Damphousse, 24, Moncton (QMJHL)
1998—Mike Van Ryn, 26, Michigan
Scott Gomez, 27, Tri-City (WHL)
1999—Ari Ahonen, 27, Jyvaskyla, Finland
2000—David Hale, 22, Sioux City (USHL)
2001—Adrian Foster, 28, Saskatoon (WHL)
2002—No first-round selection
2003—Zach Parise, 17, North Dakota (WCHA)
2004—Travis Zajac, 20, Salmon Arm (BCHL)
2005—Nicklas Bergfors, W, Sodertalje (Sweden Jr.)

SINGLE-SEASON INDIVIDUAL RECORDS

FORWARDS/DEFENSEMEN

Most goals
46—Pat Verbeek, 1987-88

Most assists
60—Scott Stevens, 1993-94

Most points
96—Patrik Elias, 2000-01

Most penalty minutes
295—Krzysztof Oliwa, 1997-98

Most power play goals
19—John MacLean, 1990-91

Most shorthanded goals
6—John Madden, 1999-2000

Most games with three or more goals
3—Kirk Muller, 1987-88
John MacLean, 1988-89
Patrik Elias, 2000-01

Most shots
322—John MacLean, 1989-90

GOALTENDERS

Most games
77—Martin Brodeur, 1995-96

Most minutes
4,555—Martin Brodeur, 2003-04

Most shots against
1,954—Martin Brodeur, 1995-96

Most goals allowed
243—Denis Herron, 1975-76

Lowest goals-against average
1.88—Martin Brodeur, 1996-97

Most shutouts
11—Martin Brodeur, 2003-04

Most wins
43—Martin Brodeur, 1997-98
Martin Brodeur, 1999-2000

Most losses
39—Denis Herron, 1975-76

Most ties
13—Martin Brodeur, 1996-97

NEW YORK AMERICANS (DEFUNCT)

YEAR-BY-YEAR RECORDS

	REGULAR SEASON					PLAYOFFS			
Season	W	L	T	Pts.	Finish	W	L	Highest round	Coach
1919-20	4	20	0	8	4th/4th	—	—		Mike Quinn
1920-21†	6	18	0	12	4th/4th	—	—		Percy Thompson
1921-22†	7	17	0	14	4th	—	—		Percy Thompson
1922-23†	6	18	0	12	4th	—	—		Art Ross
1923-24†	9	15	0	18	4th	—	—		Percy Lesueur
1924-25†	19	10	1	39	1st	‡—	—		Jimmy Gardner
1925-26	12	20	4	28	5th	—	—		Tommy Gorman
1926-27	17	25	2	36	4th/Canadian	—	—		Newsy Lalonde
1927-28	11	27	6	28	5th/Canadian	—	—		Wilf Green
1928-29	19	13	12	50	2nd/Canadian	§0	1	Semifinals	Tommy Gorman
1929-30	14	25	5	33	5th/Canadian	—	—		Lionel Conacher
1930-31	18	16	10	46	4th/Canadian	—	—		Eddie Gerard
1931-32	16	24	8	40	4th/Canadian	—	—		Eddie Gerard
1932-33	15	22	11	41	4th/Canadian	—	—		Joe Simpson
1933-34	15	23	10	40	4th/Canadian	—	—		Joe Simpson
1934-35	12	27	9	33	4th/Canadian	—	—		Joe Simpson
1935-36	16	25	7	39	3rd/Canadian	2	3	Semifinals	Red Dutton
1936-37	15	29	4	34	4th/Canadian	—	—		Red Dutton
1937-38	19	18	11	49	2nd/Canadian	3	3	Semifinals	Red Dutton
1938-39	17	21	10	44	4th	0	2	Quarterfinals	Red Dutton
1939-40	15	29	4	34	6th	1	2	Quarterfinals	Red Dutton
1940-41	8	29	11	27	7th	—	—		Red Dutton
1941-42∞	16	29	3	35	7th	—	—		Red Dutton

*Quebec Bulldogs.

†Hamilton Tigers.

∞Brooklyn Americans.

‡Refused to participate in playoffs—held out for more compensation.

§Won-lost record does not indicate tie(s) resulting from two-game, total goals series that year (two-game, total-goals series were played from 1917-18 through 1935-36).

NEW YORK ISLANDERS

YEAR-BY-YEAR RECORDS

	REGULAR SEASON						PLAYOFFS			
Season	W	L	T	OTL	Pts.	Finish	W	L	Highest round	Coach
1972-73	12	60	6	—	30	8th/East	—	—		Phil Goyette, Earl Ingarfield
1973-74	19	41	18	—	56	8th/East	—	—		Al Arbour
1974-75	33	25	22	—	88	3rd/Patrick	9	8	Semifinals	Al Arbour
1975-76	42	21	17	—	101	2nd/Patrick	7	6	Semifinals	Al Arbour
1976-77	47	21	12	—	106	2nd/Patrick	8	4	Semifinals	Al Arbour
1977-78	48	17	15	—	111	1st/Patrick	3	4	Quarterfinals	Al Arbour
1978-79	51	15	14	—	116	1st/Patrick	6	4	Semifinals	Al Arbour
1979-80	39	28	13	—	91	2nd/Patrick	15	6	Stanley Cup champ	Al Arbour
1980-81	48	18	14	—	110	1st/Patrick	15	3	Stanley Cup champ	Al Arbour
1981-82	54	16	10	—	118	1st/Patrick	15	4	Stanley Cup champ	Al Arbour
1982-83	42	26	12	—	96	2nd/Patrick	15	5	Stanley Cup champ	Al Arbour
1983-84	50	26	4	—	104	1st/Patrick	12	9	Stanley Cup finals	Al Arbour
1984-85	40	34	6	—	86	3rd/Patrick	4	6	Division finals	Al Arbour
1985-86	39	29	12	—	90	3rd/Patrick	0	3	Division semifinals	Al Arbour
1986-87	35	33	12	—	82	3rd/Patrick	7	7	Division finals	Terry Simpson
1987-88	39	31	10	—	88	1st/Patrick	2	4	Division semifinals	Terry Simpson
1988-89	28	47	5	—	61	6th/Patrick	—	—		Terry Simpson, Al Arbour
1989-90	31	38	11	—	73	4th/Patrick	1	4	Division semifinals	Al Arbour

Season	W	L	T	OTL	Pts.	Finish	W	L	Highest round	Coach
	REGULAR SEASON						PLAYOFFS			
1990-91	25	45	10	—	60	6th/Patrick	—	—		Al Arbour
1991-92	34	35	11	—	79	5th/Patrick	—	—		Al Arbour
1992-93	40	37	7	—	87	3rd/Patrick	9	9	Conference finals	Al Arbour
1993-94	36	36	12	—	84	4th/Atlantic	0	4	Conference quarterfinals	Al Arbour, Lorne Henning
1994-95	15	28	5	—	35	7th/Atlantic	—	—		Lorne Henning
1995-96	22	50	10	—	54	7th/Atlantic	—	—		Mike Milbury
1996-97	29	41	12	—	70	7th/Atlantic	—	—		Mike Milbury, Rick Bowness
1997-98	30	41	11	—	71	4th/Atlantic	—	—		Rick Bowness, Mike Milbury
1998-99	24	48	10	—	58	5th/Atlantic	—	—		Mike Milbury, Bill Stewart
1999-00	24	48	9	1	58	5th/Atlantic	—	—		Butch Goring
2000-01	21	51	7	3	52	5th/Atlantic	—	—		Butch Goring, Lorne Henning
2001-02	42	28	8	4	96	2nd/Atlantic	3	4	Conference quarterfinals	Peter Laviolette
2002-03	35	34	11	2	83	3rd/Atlantic	1	4	Conference quarterfinals	Peter Laviolette
2003-04	38	29	11	4	91	3rd/Atlantic	1	5	Conference quarterfinals	Steve Stirling

FIRST-ROUND ENTRY DRAFT CHOICES

Year Player, Overall, Last amateur team (league)

1972—Billy Harris, 1, Toronto (OHL)
1973—Denis Potvin, 1, Ottawa (OHL)
1974—Clark Gillies, 4, Regina (WCHL)
1975—Pat Price, 11, Vancouver (WHA)
1976—Alex McKendry, 14, Sudbury (OHL)
1977—Mike Bossy, 15, Laval (QMJHL)
1978—Steve Tambellini, 15, Lethbridge (WCHL)
1979—Duane Sutter, 17, Lethbridge (WHL)
1980—Brent Sutter, 17, Red Deer (AJHL)
1981—Paul Boutilier, 21, Sherbrooke (QMJHL)
1982—Pat Flatley, 21, University of Wisconsin
1983—Pat LaFontaine, 3, Verdun (QMJHL)
Gerald Diduck, 16, Lethbridge (WHL)
1984—Duncan MacPherson, 20, Saskatoon (WHL)
1985—Brad Dalgarno, 6, Hamilton (OHL)
Derek King, 13, Sault Ste. Marie (OHL)
1986—Tom Fitzgerald, 17, Austin Prep (Mass.)
1987—Dean Chynoweth, 13, Medicine Hat (WHL)
1988—Kevin Cheveldayoff, 16, Brandon (WHL)
1989—Dave Chyzowski, 2, Kamloops (WHL)
1990—Scott Scissons, 6, Saskatoon (WHL)

Year Player, Overall, Last amateur team (league)

1991—Scott Lachance, 4, Boston University
1992—Darius Kasparaitis, 5, Dynamo Moscow (CIS)
1993—Todd Bertuzzi, 23, Guelph (OHL)
1994—Brett Lindros, 9, Kingston (OHL)
1995—Wade Redden, 2, Brandon (WHL)
1996—Jean-Pierre Dumont, 3, Val-d'Or (QMJHL)
1997—Roberto Luongo, 4, Val d'Or (QMJHL)
Eric Brewer, 5, Prince George (WHL)
1998—Michael Rupp, 9, Erie (OHL)
1999—Tim Connolly, 5, Erie (OHL)
Taylor Pyatt, 8, Sudbury (OHL)
Branislav Mezei, 10, Belleville (OHL)
Kristian Kudroc, 28, Michalovce, Slovakia
2000—Rick DiPietro, 1, Boston University
Raffi Torres, 5, Brampton (OHL)
2001—No first-round selection
2002—Sean Bergenheim, 22, Jokerit, Finland
2003—Robert Nilsson, 15, Sweden
2004—Petteri Nokelainen, 16, Saipa, Finland
2005—Ryan O'Marra, 15, Erie (OHL)

SINGLE-SEASON INDIVIDUAL RECORDS

FORWARDS/DEFENSEMEN

Most goals
69—Mike Bossy, 1978-79

Most assists
87—Bryan Trottier, 1978-79

Most points
147—Mike Bossy, 1981-82

Most penalty minutes
356—Brian Curran, 1986-87

Most power play goals
28—Mike Bossy, 1980-81

Most shorthanded goals
7—Bob Bourne, 1980-81

Most games with three or more goals
9—Mike Bossy, 1980-81

Most shots
315—Mike Bossy, 1980-81

GOALTENDERS

Most games
66—Chris Osgood, 2001-02

Most minutes
3,743—Chris Osgood, 2001-02

Most shots against
1,801—Ron Hextall, 1993-94

Most goals allowed
195—Gerry Desjardins, 1972-73

Lowest goals-against average
2.07—Chico Resch, 1975-76

Most shutouts
7—Chico Resch, 1975-76

Most wins
32—Billy Smith, 1981-82
Chris Osgood, 2001-02

Most losses
35—Gerry Desjardins, 1972-73

Most ties
17—Billy Smith, 1974-75

NEW YORK RANGERS

YEAR-BY-YEAR RECORDS

Season	W	L	T	OTL	Pts.	Finish	W	L	Highest round	Coach
	REGULAR SEASON						PLAYOFFS			
1926-27	25	13	6	—	56	1st/American	*0	1	Semifinals	Lester Patrick
1927-28	19	16	9	—	47	2nd/American	*5	3	Stanley Cup champ	Lester Patrick
1928-29	21	13	10	—	52	2nd/American	*3	2	Stanley Cup finals	Lester Patrick
1929-30	17	17	10	—	44	3rd/American	*1	2	Semifinals	Lester Patrick
1930-31	19	16	9	—	47	3rd/American	2	2	Semifinals	Lester Patrick

	REGULAR SEASON						PLAYOFFS			
Season	W	L	T	OTL	Pts.	Finish	W	L	Highest round	Coach
1931-32	23	17	8	—	54	1st/American	3	4	Stanley Cup finals	Lester Patrick
1932-33	23	17	8	—	54	3rd/American	*6	1	Stanley Cup champ	Lester Patrick
1933-34	21	19	8	—	50	3rd/American	*0	1	Quarterfinals	Lester Patrick
1934-35	22	20	6	—	50	3rd/American	*1	1	Semifinals	Lester Patrick
1935-36	19	17	12	—	50	4th/American	—	—		Lester Patrick
1936-37	19	20	9	—	47	3rd/American	6	3	Stanley Cup finals	Lester Patrick
1937-38	27	15	6	—	60	2nd/American	1	2	Quarterfinals	Lester Patrick
1938-39	26	16	6	—	58	2nd	3	4	Semifinals	Lester Patrick
1939-40	27	11	10	—	64	2nd	8	4	Stanley Cup champ	Frank Boucher
1940-41	21	19	8	—	50	4th	1	2	Quarterfinals	Frank Boucher
1941-42	29	17	2	—	60	1st	2	4	Semifinals	Frank Boucher
1942-43	11	31	8	—	30	6th	—	—		Frank Boucher
1943-44	6	39	5	—	17	6th	—	—		Frank Boucher
1944-45	11	29	10	—	32	6th	—	—		Frank Boucher
1945-46	13	28	9	—	35	6th	—	—		Frank Boucher
1946-47	22	32	6	—	50	5th	—	—		Frank Boucher
1947-48	21	26	13	—	55	4th	2	4	League semifinals	Frank Boucher
1948-49	18	31	11	—	47	6th	—	—		Frank Boucher, Lynn Patrick
1949-50	28	31	11	—	67	4th	7	5	Stanley Cup finals	Lynn Patrick
1950-51	20	29	21	—	61	5th	—	—		Neil Colville
1951-52	23	34	13	—	59	5th	—	—		Neil Colville, Bill Cook
1952-53	17	37	16	—	50	6th	—	—		Bill Cook
1953-54	29	31	10	—	68	5th	—	—		Frank Boucher, Muzz Patrick
1954-55	17	35	18	—	52	5th	—	—		Muzz Patrick
1955-56	32	28	10	—	74	3rd	1	4	League semifinals	Phil Watson
1956-57	26	30	14	—	66	4th	1	4	League semifinals	Phil Watson
1957-58	32	25	13	—	77	2nd	2	4	League semifinals	Phil Watson
1958-59	26	32	12	—	64	5th	—	—		Phil Watson
1959-60	17	38	15	—	49	6th	—	—		Phil Watson, Alf Pike
1960-61	22	38	10	—	54	5th	—	—		Alf Pike
1961-62	26	32	12	—	64	4th	2	4	League semifinals	Doug Harvey
1962-63	22	36	12	—	56	5th	—	—		Muzz Patrick, Red Sullivan
1963-64	22	38	10	—	54	5th	—	—		Red Sullivan
1964-65	20	38	12	—	52	5th	—	—		Red Sullivan
1965-66	18	41	11	—	47	6th	—	—		Red Sullivan, Emile Francis
1966-67	30	28	12	—	72	4th	0	4	League semifinals	Emile Francis
1967-68	39	23	12	—	90	2nd/East	2	4	Division semifinals	Emile Francis
1968-69	41	26	9	—	91	3rd/East	0	4	Division semifinals	Bernie Geoffrion, Emile Francis
1969-70	38	22	16	—	92	4th/East	2	4	Division semifinals	Emile Francis
1970-71	49	18	11	—	109	2nd/East	7	6	Division finals	Emile Francis
1971-72	48	17	13	—	109	2nd/East	10	6	Stanley Cup finals	Emile Francis
1972-73	47	23	8	—	102	3rd/East	5	5	Division finals	Emile Francis
1973-74	40	24	14	—	94	3rd/East	7	6	Division finals	Larry Popein, Emile Francis
1974-75	37	29	14	—	88	2nd/Patrick	1	2	Preliminaries	Emile Francis
1975-76	29	42	9	—	67	4th/Patrick	—	—		Ron Stewart, John Ferguson
1976-77	29	37	14	—	72	4th/Patrick	—	—		John Ferguson
1977-78	30	37	13	—	73	4th/Patrick	1	2	Preliminaries	Jean-Guy Talbot
1978-79	40	29	11	—	91	3rd/Patrick	11	7	Stanley Cup finals	Fred Shero
1979-80	38	32	10	—	86	3rd/Patrick	4	5	Quarterfinals	Fred Shero
1980-81	30	36	14	—	74	4th/Patrick	7	7	Semifinals	Fred Shero, Craig Patrick
1981-82	39	27	14	—	92	2nd/Patrick	5	5	Division finals	Herb Brooks
1982-83	35	35	10	—	80	4th/Patrick	5	4	Division finals	Herb Brooks
1983-84	42	29	9	—	93	4th/Patrick	2	3	Division semifinals	Herb Brooks
1984-85	26	44	10	—	62	4th/Patrick	0	3	Division semifinals	Herb Brooks, Craig Patrick
1985-86	36	38	6	—	78	4th/Patrick	8	8	Conference finals	Ted Sator
1986-87	34	38	8	—	76	4th/Patrick	2	4	Division semifinals	T. Sator, T. Webster, P. Esposito
1987-88	36	34	10	—	82	5th/Patrick	—	—		Michel Bergeron
1988-89	37	35	8	—	82	3rd/Patrick	0	4	Division semifinals	Michel Bergeron, Phil Esposito
1989-90	36	31	13	—	85	1st/Patrick	5	5	Division finals	Roger Neilson
1990-91	36	31	13	—	85	2nd/Patrick	2	4	Division semifinals	Roger Neilson
1991-92	50	25	5	—	105	1st/Patrick	6	7	Division finals	Roger Neilson
1992-93	34	39	11	—	79	6th/Patrick	—	—		Roger Neilson, Ron Smith
1993-94	52	24	8	—	112	1st/Atlantic	16	7	Stanley Cup champ	Mike Keenan
1994-95	22	23	3	—	47	4th/Atlantic	4	6	Conference semifinals	Colin Campbell
1995-96	41	27	14	—	96	2nd/Atlantic	5	6	Conference semifinals	Colin Campbell
1996-97	38	34	10	—	86	4th/Atlantic	9	6	Conference finals	Colin Campbell
1997-98	25	39	18	—	68	5th/Atlantic	—	—		Colin Campbell, John Muckler
1998-99	33	38	11	—	77	4th/Atlantic	—	—		John Muckler
1999-00	29	38	12	3	73	4th/Atlantic	—	—		John Muckler, John Tortorella
2000-01	33	43	5	1	72	4th/Atlantic	—	—		Ron Low
2001-02	36	38	4	4	80	4th/Atlantic	—	—		Ron Low
2002-03	32	36	10	4	78	4th/Atlantic	—	—		Bryan Trottier, Glen Sather

Season	W	L	T	OTL	Pts.	Finish	W	L	Highest round	Coach
	REGULAR SEASON						PLAYOFFS			
2003-04	27	40	7	8	69	4th/Pacific	—	—		Glen Sather, Tom Renney

*Won-lost record does not indicate tie(s) resulting from two-game, total goals series that year (two-game, total-goals series were played from 1917-18 through 1935-36).

FIRST-ROUND ENTRY DRAFT CHOICES

Year Player, Overall, Last amateur team (league)
1969—Andre Dupont, 8, Montreal (OHL)
Pierre Jarry, 12, Ottawa (OHL)
1970—Normand Gratton, 11, Montreal (OHL)
1971—Steve Vickers, 10, Toronto (OHL)
Steve Durbano, 13, Toronto (OHL)
1972—Albert Blanchard, 10, Kitchener (OHL)
Bobby MacMillan, 15, St. Catharines (OHL)
1973—Rick Middleton, 14, Oshawa (OHL)
1974—Dave Maloney, 14, Kitchener (OHL)
1975—Wayne Dillon, 12, Toronto (WHA)
1976—Don Murdoch, 6, Medicine Hat (WCHL)
1977—Lucien DeBlois, 8, Sorel (QMJHL)
Ron Duguay, 13, Sudbury (OHL)
1978—No first-round selection
1979—Doug Sulliman, 13, Kitchener (OHL)
1980—Jim Malone, 14, Toronto (OHL)
1981—James Patrick, 9, Prince Albert (AJHL)
1982—Chris Kontos, 15, Toronto (OHL)
1983—Dave Gagner, 12, Brantford (OHL)
1984—Terry Carkner, 14, Peterborough (OHL)
1985—Ulf Dahlen, 7, Ostersund (Sweden)

Year Player, Overall, Last amateur team (league)
1986—Brian Leetch, 9, Avon Old Farms Prep (Ct.)
1987—Jayson More, 10, New Westminster (WCHL)
1988—No first-round selection
1989—Steven Rice, 20, Kitchener (OHL)
1990—Michael Stewart, 13, Michigan State University
1991—Alexei Kovalev, 15, Dynamo Moscow, USSR
1992—Peter Ferraro, 24, Waterloo (USHL)
1993—Niklas Sundstrom, 8, Ornskoldsvik, Sweden
1994—Dan Cloutier, 26, Sault Ste. Marie (OHL)
1995—No first-round selection
1996—Jeff Brown, 22, Sarnia (OHL)
1997—Stefan Cherneski, 19, Brandon (WHL)
1998—Manny Malhotra, 7, Guelph (OHL)
1999—Pavel Brendl, 4, Calgary (WHL)
Jamie Lundmark, 9, Moose Jaw (WHL)
2000—No first-round selection
2001—Daniel Blackburn, 10, Kootenay (WHL)
2002—No first-round selection
2003—Hugh Jessiman, 12, Dartmouth (ECAC)
2004—Al Montoya, 6, Michigan (CCHA)
Lauri Korpikoski, 19, TPS Jr., Finland
2005—Marc Staal, 12, Sudbury (OHL)

SINGLE-SEASON INDIVIDUAL RECORDS

FORWARDS/DEFENSEMEN

Most goals
52—Adam Graves, 1993-94

Most assists
80—Brian Leetch, 1991-92

Most points
109—Jean Ratelle, 1971-72

Most penalty minutes
305—Troy Mallette, 1989-90

Most power play goals
23—Vic Hadfield, 1971-72

Most shorthanded goals
7—Theo Fleury, 2000-01

Most games with three or more goals
4—Tomas Sandstrom, 1986-87

Most shots
344—Phil Esposito, 1976-77

GOALTENDERS

Most games
72—Mike Richter, 1997-98

Most minutes
4,200—Johnny Bower, 1953-54
Gump Worsley, 1955-56

Most goals allowed
310—Ken McAuley, 1943-44

Lowest goals-against average
1.48—John Ross Roach, 1928-29

Most shutouts
13—John Ross Roach, 1928-29

Most wins
42—Mike Richter, 1993-94

Most losses
39—Ken McAuley, 1943-44

Most ties
20—Chuck Rayner, 1950-51

OTTAWA SENATORS (MODERN ERA)

YEAR-BY-YEAR RECORDS

Season	W	L	T	OTL	Pts.	Finish	W	L	Highest round	Coach
	REGULAR SEASON						PLAYOFFS			
1992-93	10	70	4	—	24	6th/Adams	—	—		Rick Bowness
1993-94	14	61	9	—	37	7th/Northeast	—	—		Rick Bowness
1994-95	9	34	5	—	23	7th/Northeast	—	—		Rick Bowness
1995-96	18	59	5	—	41	6th/Northeast	—	—		Rick Bowness, Dave Allison, Jacques Martin
1996-97	31	36	15	—	77	3rd/Northeast	3	4	Conference quarterfinals	Jacques Martin
1997-98	34	33	15	—	83	5th/Northeast	5	6	Conference semifinals	Jacques Martin
1998-99	44	23	15	—	103	1st/Northeast	0	4	Conference quarterfinals	Jacques Martin
1999-00	41	28	11	2	95	2nd/Northeast	2	4	Conference quarterfinals	Jacques Martin
2000-01	48	21	9	4	109	1st/Northeast	0	4	Conference quarterfinals	Jacques Martin
2001-02	39	27	9	7	94	3rd/Northeast	7	5	Conference semifinals	Jacques Martin, Roger Neilson
2002-03	52	21	8	1	113	1st/Northeast	11	7	Conference finals	Jacques Martin
2003-04	43	23	10	6	102	3rd/Northeast	3	4	Conference quarterfinals	Jacques Martin

FIRST-ROUND ENTRY DRAFT CHOICES

Year Player, Overall, Last amateur team (league)
1992—Alexei Yashin, 2, Dynamo Moscow (CIS)
1993—Alexandre Daigle, 1, Victoriaville (QMJHL)
1994—Radek Bonk, 3, Las Vegas (IHL)
1995—Bryan Berard, 1, Detroit (OHL)

Year Player, Overall, Last amateur team (league)
1996—Chris Phillips, 1, Prince Albert (WHL)
1997—Marian Hossa, 12, Dukla Trencin, Czechoslovakia
1998—Mathieu Chouinard, 15, Shawinigan (QMJHL)
1999—Martin Havlat, 26, Trinec, Czech Republic

Year	Player, Overall, Last amateur team (league)
2000	Anton Volchenkov, 21, CSKA, Russia
2001	Jason Spezza, 2, Windsor (OHL)
	Tim Gleason, 23, Windsor (OHL)
2002	Jakub Klepis, 16, Portland (WHL)
2003	Patrick Eaves, 29, Boston College (HE)
2004	Andrej Meszaros, 23, Trencin (Slovakia)
2005	Brian Lee, 9, Moorhead (USHSW)

SINGLE-SEASON INDIVIDUAL RECORDS

FORWARDS/DEFENSEMEN

Most goals
45—Marian Hosson, 2002-03

Most assists
51—Daniel Alfredsson, 2002-03

Most points
94—Alexei Yashin, 1998-99

Most penalty minutes
318—Mike Peluso, 1992-93

Most power play goals
19—Alexei Yashin, 1998-99

Most shorthanded goals
4—Magnus Arvedson, 1998-99

Most games with three or more goals
2—Daniel Alfredsson, 2001-02

Most shots
337—Alexei Yashin, 1998-99

GOALTENDERS

Most games
67—Patrick Lalime, 2002-03

Most minutes
3,943—Patrick Lalime, 2002-03

Most shots against
1,801—Craig Billington, 1993-94

Most goals allowed
254—Craig Billington, 1993-94

Lowest goals-against average
1.79—Ron Tugnutt, 1998-99

Most shutouts
8—Patrick Lalime, 2002-03

Most wins
39—Patrick Lalime, 2002-03

Most losses
46—Peter Sidorkiewicz, 1992-93

Most ties
14—Damian Rhodes, 1996-97

PHILADELPHIA FLYERS

YEAR-BY-YEAR RECORDS

	REGULAR SEASON						PLAYOFFS			
Season	W	L	T	OTL	Pts.	Finish	W	L	Highest round	Coach
1967-68	31	32	11	—	73	1st/West	3	4	Division semifinals	Keith Allen
1968-69	20	35	21	—	61	3rd/West	0	4	Division semifinals	Keith Allen
1969-70	17	35	24	—	58	5th/West	—	—		Vic Stasiuk
1970-71	28	33	17	—	73	3rd/West	0	4	Division semifinals	Vic Stasiuk
1971-72	26	38	14	—	66	5th/West	—	—		Fred Shero
1972-73	37	30	11	—	85	2nd/West	5	6	Division finals	Fred Shero
1973-74	50	16	12	—	112	1st/West	12	5	Stanley Cup champ	Fred Shero
1974-75	51	18	11	—	113	1st/Patrick	12	5	Stanley Cup champ	Fred Shero
1975-76	51	13	16	—	118	1st/Patrick	8	8	Stanley Cup finals	Fred Shero
1976-77	48	16	16	—	112	1st/Patrick	4	6	Semifinals	Fred Shero
1977-78	45	20	15	—	105	2nd/Patrick	7	5	Semifinals	Fred Shero
1978-79	40	25	15	—	95	2nd/Patrick	3	5	Quarterfinals	Bob McCammon, Pat Quinn
1979-80	48	12	20	—	116	1st/Patrick	13	6	Stanley Cup finals	Pat Quinn
1980-81	41	24	15	—	97	2nd/Patrick	6	6	Quarterfinals	Pat Quinn
1981-82	38	31	11	—	87	3rd/Patrick	1	3	Division semifinals	Pat Quinn, Bob McCammon
1982-83	49	23	8	—	106	1st/Patrick	0	3	Division semifinals	Bob McCammon
1983-84	44	26	10	—	98	3rd/Patrick	0	3	Division semifinals	Bob McCammon
1984-85	53	20	7	—	113	1st/Patrick	12	7	Stanley Cup finals	Mike Keenan
1985-86	53	23	4	—	110	1st/Patrick	2	3	Division semifinals	Mike Keenan
1986-87	46	26	8	—	100	1st/Patrick	15	11	Stanley Cup finals	Mike Keenan
1987-88	38	33	9	—	85	3rd/Patrick	3	4	Division semifinals	Mike Keenan
1988-89	36	36	8	—	80	4th/Patrick	10	9	Conference finals	Paul Holmgren
1989-90	30	39	11	—	71	6th/Patrick	—	—		Paul Holmgren
1990-91	33	37	10	—	76	5th/Patrick	—	—		Paul Holmgren
1991-92	32	37	11	—	75	6th/Patrick	—	—		Paul Holmgren, Bill Dineen
1992-93	36	37	11	—	83	5th/Patrick	—	—		Bill Dineen
1993-94	35	39	10	—	80	6th/Atlantic	—	—		Terry Simpson
1994-95	28	16	4	—	60	1st/Atlantic	10	5	Conference finals	Terry Murray
1995-96	45	24	13	—	103	1st/Atlantic	6	6	Conference semifinals	Terry Murray
1996-97	45	24	13	—	103	2nd/Atlantic	12	7	Stanley Cup finals	Terry Murray
1997-98	42	29	11	—	95	2nd/Atlantic	1	4	Conference quarterfinals	Wayne Cashman, Roger Neilson
1998-99	37	26	19	—	93	2nd/Atlantic	2	4	Conference quarterfinals	Roger Neilson
1999-00	45	22	12	3	105	1st/Atlantic	11	7	Conference finals	Roger Neilson, Craig Ramsay
2000-01	43	25	11	3	100	2nd/Atlantic	2	4	Conference quarterfinals	Craig Ramsay, Bill Barber
2001-02	42	27	10	3	97	1st/Atlantic	1	4	Conference quarterfinals	Bill Barber
2002-03	45	20	13	4	107	2nd/Atlantic	6	7	Conference semifinals	Ken Hitchcock
2003-04	40	21	15	6	101	1st/Atlantic	11	7	Conference finals	Ken Hitchcock

FIRST-ROUND ENTRY DRAFT CHOICES

Year Player, Overall, Last amateur team (league)
1969—Bob Currier, 6, Cornwall (QMJHL)
1970—No first-round selection
1971—Larry Wright, 8, Regina (WCHL)
Pierre Plante, 9, Drummondville (QMJHL)
1972—Bill Barber, 7, Kitchener (OHL)
1973—No first-round selection
1974—No first-round selection
1975—Mel Bridgman, 1, Victoria (WCHL)
1976—Mark Suzor, 17, Kingston (OHL)
1977—Kevin McCarthy, 17, Winnipeg (WCHL)
1978—Behn Wilson, 6, Kingston (OHL)
Ken Linseman, 7, Birmingham (WHA)
Dan Lucas, 14, Sault Ste. Marie (OHL)
1979—Brian Propp, 14, Brandon (WHL)
1980—Mike Stothers, 21, Kingston (OHL)
1981—Steve Smith, 16, Sault Ste. Marie (OHL)
1982—Ron Sutter, 4, Lethbridge (WHL)
1983—No first-round selection
1984—No first-round selection
1985—Glen Seabrooke, 21, Peterborough (OHL)
1986—Kerry Huffman, 20, Guelph (OHL)

Year Player, Overall, Last amateur team (league)
1987—Darren Rumble, 20, Kitchener (OHL)
1988—Claude Boivin, 14, Drummondville (QMJHL)
1989—No first-round selection
1990—Mike Ricci, 4, Peterborough (OHL)
1991—Peter Forsberg, 6, Modo, Sweden
1992—Ryan Sittler, 7, Nichols H.S. (N.Y.)
Jason Bowen, 15, Tri-City (WHL)
1993—No first-round selection
1994—No first-round selection
1995—Brian Boucher, 22, Tri-City (WHL)
1996—Dainius Zubrus, 15, Pembroke, Tier II
1997—No first-round selection
1998—Simon Gagne, 22, Quebec (QMJHL)
1999—Maxime Ouellet, 22, Quebec (QMJHL)
2000—Justin Williams, 28, Plymouth (OHL)
2001—Jeff Woywitka, 27, Red Deer (WHL)
2002—Joni Pitkanen, 4, Karpat, Finland
2003—Jeff Carter, 11, Sault Ste. Marie (OHL)
Mike Richards, 24, Kitchener (OHL)
2004—No first-round selection
2005—Steve Downie, 29, Windsor (OHL)

SINGLE-SEASON INDIVIDUAL RECORDS

FORWARDS/DEFENSEMEN

Most goals
61—Reggie Leach, 1975-76

Most assists
89—Bobby Clarke, 1974-75
Bobby Clarke, 1975-76

Most points
123—Mark Recchi, 1992-93

Most penalty minutes
472—Dave Schultz, 1974-75

Most power play goals
34—Tim Kerr, 1985-86

Most shorthanded goals
7—Brian Propp, 1984-85
Mark Howe, 1985-86

Most games with three or more goals
5—Tim Kerr, 1984-85

Most shots
380—Bill Barber, 1975-76

GOALTENDERS

Most games
73—Bernie Parent, 1973-74

Most minutes
4,314—Bernie Parent, 1973-74

Most goals allowed
208—Ron Hextall, 1987-88

Lowest goals-against average
1.83—Roman Cechmanek, 2002-03

Most shutouts
12—Bernie Parent, 1973-74
Bernie Parent, 1974-75

Most wins
47—Bernie Parent, 1973-74

Most losses
29—Bernie Parent, 1969-70

Most ties
20—Bernie Parent, 1969-70

PHOENIX COYOTES

YEAR-BY-YEAR RECORDS

	REGULAR SEASON						PLAYOFFS			
Season	W	L	T	OTL	Pts.	Finish	W	L	Highest round	Coach
1972-73*	43	31	4	—	90	1st	9	5	Avco World Cup finals	Nick Mickoski, Bobby Hull
1973-74*	34	39	5	—	73	4th	0	4	League quarterfinals	Nick Mickoski, Bobby Hull
1974-75*	38	35	5	—	81	3rd	—	—		Rudy Pilous
1975-76*	52	27	2	—	106	1st	12	1	Avco World Cup champ	Bobby Kromm
1976-77*	46	32	2	—	94	2nd	11	9	Avco World Cup finals	Bobby Kromm
1977-78*	50	28	2	—	102	1st	8	1	Avco World Cup champ	Larry Hillman
1978-79*	39	35	6	—	84	3rd	8	2	Avco World Cup champ	Larry Hillman, Tom McVie
1979-80†	20	49	11	—	51	5th/Smythe	—	—		Tom McVie
1980-81†	9	57	14	—	32	6th/Smythe	—	—		T. McVie, Bill Sutherland, M. Smith
1981-82†	33	33	14	—	80	2nd/Norris	1	3	Division semifinals	Tom Watt
1982-83†	33	39	8	—	74	4th/Smythe	0	3	Division semifinals	Tom Watt
1983-84†	31	38	11	—	73	4th/Smythe	0	3	Division semifinals	Tom Watt, Barry Long
1984-85†	43	27	10	—	96	2nd/Smythe	3	5	Division finals	Barry Long
1985-86†	26	47	7	—	59	3rd/Smythe	0	3	Division semifinals	Barry Long, John Ferguson
1986-87†	40	32	8	—	88	3rd/Smythe	4	6	Division finals	Dan Maloney
1987-88†	33	36	11	—	77	3rd/Smythe	1	4	Division semifinals	Dan Maloney
1988-89†	26	42	12	—	64	5th/Smythe	—	—		Dan Maloney, Rick Bowness
1989-90†	37	32	11	—	85	3rd/Smythe	3	4	Division semifinals	Bob Murdoch
1990-91†	26	43	11	—	63	5th/Smythe	—	—		Bob Murdoch
1991-92†	33	32	15	—	81	4th/Smythe	3	4	Division semifinals	John Paddock
1992-93†	40	37	7	—	87	4th/Smythe	2	4	Division semifinals	John Paddock
1993-94†	24	51	9	—	57	6th/Central	—	—		John Paddock

Season	W	L	T	OTL	Pts.	Finish	W	L	Highest round	Coach
	REGULAR SEASON						PLAYOFFS			
1994-95†	16	25	7	—	39	6th/Central	—	—		John Paddock, Terry Simpson
1995-96†	36	40	6	—	78	5th/Central	—	—		Terry Simpson
1996-97	38	37	7	—	83	3rd/Central	3	4	Conference quarterfinals	Don Hay
1997-98	35	35	12	—	82	4th/Central	2	4	Conference quarterfinals	Jim Schoenfeld
1998-99	39	31	12	—	90	2nd/Pacific	3	4	Conference quarterfinals	Jim Schoenfeld
1999-00	39	31	8	4	90	3rd/Pacific	1	4	Conference quarterfinals	Bob Francis
2000-01	35	27	17	3	90	4th/Pacific	—	—		Bob Francis
2001-02	40	27	9	6	95	2nd/Pacific	1	4	Conference quarterfinals	Bob Francis
2002-03	31	35	11	5	78	4th/Pacific	—	—		Bob Francis
2003-04	22	36	18	6	68	5th/Pacific	—	—		Bob Francis, Rick Bowness

*Winnipeg Jets, members of World Hockey Association. †Winnipeg Jets.

FIRST-ROUND ENTRY DRAFT CHOICES

Year Player, Overall, Last amateur team (league)

1979—Jimmy Mann, 19, Sherbrooke (QMJHL)
1980—David Babych, 2, Portland (WHL)
1981—Dale Hawerchuk, 1, Cornwall (QMJHL)*
1982—Jim Kyte, 12, Cornwall (OHL)
1983—Andrew McBain, 8, North Bay (OHL)
Bobby Dollas, 14, Laval (QMJHL)
1984—No first-round selection
1985—Ryan Stewart, 18, Kamloops (WHL)
1986—Pat Elynuik, 8, Prince Albert (WHL)
1987—Bryan Marchment, 16, Belleville (OHL)
1988—Teemu Selanne, 10, Jokerit, Finland
1989—Stu Barnes, 4, Tri-City (WHL)
1990—Keith Tkachuk, 19, Malden Cath. H.S. (Mass.)
1991—Aaron Ward, 5, University of Michigan
1992—Sergei Bautin, 17, Dynamo Moscow (CIS)
1993—Mats Lindgren, 15, Skelleftea, Sweden
1994—No first-round selection

Year Player, Overall, Last amateur team (league)

1995—Shane Doan, 7, Kamloops (WHL)
1996—Dan Focht, 11, Tri-City (WHL)
Daniel Briere, 24, Drummondville (QMJHL)
1997—No first-round selection
1998—Patrick DesRochers, 14, Sarnia (OHL)
1999—Scott Kelman, 15, Seattle (WHL)
Kirill Safronov, 19, SKA St. Petersburg, Russia
2000—Krystofer Kolanos, 19, Boston College
2001—Fredrik Sjostrom, 11, Frolunda, Sweden
2002—Jakub Koreis, 19, Plzen, Czechoslovakia
Ben Eager, 23, Oshawa (OHL)
2003—No first-round selection
2004—Blake Wheeler, 5, Breck (USHSW)
2005—Martin Hanzal, 17, Budejovice (Czech Rep. Jr.)

NOTE: Winnipeg chose Scott Campbell, Morris Lukowich and Markus Mattsson as priority selections before the 1979 expansion draft.

SINGLE-SEASON INDIVIDUAL RECORDS

FORWARDS/DEFENSEMEN

Most goals
76—Teemu Selanne, 1992-93

Most assists
79—Phil Housley, 1992-93

Most points
132—Teemu Selanne, 1992-93

Most penalty minutes
347—Tie Domi, 1993-94

Most power play goals
24—Teemu Selanne, 1992-93

Most shorthanded goals
7—Dave McLlwain, 1989-90

Most games with three or more goals
5—Teemu Selanne, 1992-93

Most shots
387—Teemu Selanne, 1992-93

GOALTENDERS

Most games
72—Nikolai Khabibulin, 1996-97

Most minutes
4,091—Nikolai Khabibulin, 1996-97

Most shots against
2,119—Bob Essensa, 1992-93

Most goals allowed
227—Bob Essensa, 1992-93

Lowest goals-against average
2.13—Nikolai Khabibulin, 1998-99

Most shutouts
8—Nikolai Khabibulin, 1998-99

Most wins
33—Brian Hayward, 1984-85
Bob Essensa, 1992-93
Sean Burke, 2001-02

Most losses
33—Nikolai Khabibulin, 1996-97

Most ties
13—Sean Burke, 2000-01

PITTSBURGH PENGUINS

YEAR-BY-YEAR RECORDS

Season	W	L	T	OTL	Pts.	Finish	W	L	Highest round	Coach
	REGULAR SEASON						PLAYOFFS			
1967-68	27	34	13	—	67	5th/West	—	—		Red Sullivan
1968-69	20	45	11	—	51	5th/West	—	—		Red Sullivan
1969-70	26	38	12	—	64	2nd/West	6	4	Division finals	Red Kelly
1970-71	21	37	20	—	62	6th/West	—	—		Red Kelly
1971-72	26	38	14	—	66	4th/West	0	4	Division semifinals	Red Kelly
1972-73	32	37	9	—	73	5th/West	—	—		Red Kelly, Ken Schinkel
1973-74	28	41	9	—	65	5th/West	—	—		Ken Schinkel, Marc Boileau
1974-75	37	28	15	—	89	3rd/Norris	5	4	Quarterfinals	Marc Boileau
1975-76	35	33	12	—	82	3rd/Norris	1	2	Preliminaries	Marc Boileau, Ken Schinkel
1976-77	34	33	13	—	81	3rd/Norris	1	2	Preliminaries	Ken Schinkel
1977-78	25	37	18	—	68	4th/Norris	—	—		Johnny Wilson
1978-79	36	31	13	—	85	2nd/Norris	2	5	Quarterfinals	Johnny Wilson

Season	W	L	T	OTL	Pts.	Finish	W	L	Highest round	Coach
		REGULAR SEASON					PLAYOFFS			
1979-80	30	37	13	—	73	3rd/Norris	2	3	Preliminaries	Johnny Wilson
1980-81	30	37	13	—	73	3rd/Norris	2	3	Preliminaries	Eddie Johnston
1981-82	31	36	13	—	75	4th/Patrick	2	3	Division semifinals	Eddie Johnston
1982-83	18	53	9	—	45	6th/Patrick	—	—		Eddie Johnston
1983-84	16	58	6	—	38	6th/Patrick	—	—		Lou Angotti
1984-85	24	51	5	—	53	6th/Patrick	—	—		Bob Berry
1985-86	34	38	8	—	76	5th/Patrick	—	—		Bob Berry
1986-87	30	38	12	—	72	5th/Patrick	—	—		Bob Berry
1987-88	36	35	9	—	81	6th/Patrick	—	—		Pierre Creamer
1988-89	40	33	7	—	87	2nd/Patrick	7	4	Division finals	Gene Ubriaco
1989-90	32	40	8	—	72	5th/Patrick	—	—		Gene Ubriaco, Craig Patrick
1990-91	41	33	6	—	88	1st/Patrick	16	8	Stanley Cup champ	Bob Johnson
1991-92	39	32	9	—	87	3rd/Patrick	16	5	Stanley Cup champ	Scotty Bowman
1992-93	56	21	7	—	119	1st/Patrick	7	5	Division finals	Scotty Bowman
1993-94	44	27	13	—	101	1st/Northeast	2	4	Conference quarterfinals	Eddie Johnston
1994-95	29	16	3	—	61	2nd/Northeast	5	7	Conference semifinals	Eddie Johnston
1995-96	49	29	4	—	102	1st/Northeast	11	7	Conference finals	Eddie Johnston
1996-97	38	36	8	—	84	2nd/Northeast	1	4	Conference quarterfinals	Eddie Johnston, Craig Patrick
1997-98	40	24	18	—	98	1st/Northeast	2	4	Conference quarterfinals	Kevin Constantine
1998-99	38	30	14	—	90	3rd/Atlantic	6	7	Conference semifinals	Kevin Constantine
1999-00	37	31	8	6	88	3rd/Atlantic	6	5	Conference semifinals	Kevin Constantine, Herb Brooks
2000-01	42	28	9	3	96	3rd/Atlantic	9	9	Conference finals	Ivan Hlinka
2001-02	28	41	8	5	69	5th/Atlantic	—	—		Ivan Hlinka, Rick Kehoe
2002-03	27	44	6	5	65	5th/Atlantic	—	—		Rick Kehoe
2003-04	23	47	8	4	58	5th/Atlantic	—	—		Ed Olczyk

FIRST-ROUND ENTRY DRAFT CHOICES

Year Player, Overall, Last amateur team (league)

1969—No first-round selection
1970—Greg Polis, 7, Estevan (WCHL)
1971—No first-round selection
1972—No first-round selection
1973—Blaine Stoughton, 7, Flin Flon (WCHL)
1974—Pierre Larouche, 8, Sorel (QMJHL)
1975—Gord Laxton, 13, New Westminster (WCHL)
1976—Blair Chapman, 2, Saskatoon (WCHL)
1977—No first-round selection
1978—No first-round selection
1979—No first-round selection
1980—Mike Bullard, 9, Brantford (OHL)
1981—No first-round selection
1982—Rich Sutter, 10, Lethbridge (WHL)
1983—Bob Errey, 15, Peterborough (OHL)
1984—Mario Lemieux, 1, Laval (QMJHL)
Doug Bodger, 9, Kamloops (WHL)
Roger Belanger, 16, Kingston (OHL)
1985—Craig Simpson, 2, Michigan State University
1986—Zarley Zalapski, 4, Team Canada

Year Player, Overall, Last amateur team (league)

1987—Chris Joseph, 5, Seattle (WHL)
1988—Darrin Shannon, 4, Windsor (OHL)
1989—Jamie Heward, 16, Regina (WHL)
1990—Jaromir Jagr, 5, Poldi Kladno, Czech. Republic
1991—Markus Naslund, 16, MoDo, Sweden
1992—Martin Straka, 19, Skoda Plzen, Czech. Republic
1993—Stefan Bergqvist, 26, Leksand, Sweden
1994—Chris Wells, 24, Seattle (WHL)
1995—Alexei Morozov, 24, Krylja Sovetov, CIS
1996—Craig Hillier, 23, Ottawa (OHL)
1997—Robert Dome, 17, Las Vegas (IHL)
1998—Milan Kraft, 23, Plzen (Czech.)
1999—Konstantin Koltsov, 18, Cherepovec, Russia
2000—Brooks Orpik, 18, Boston College
2001—Colby Armstrong, 21, Red Deer (WHL)
2002—Ryan Whitney, Boston University (H. East)
2003—Marc-Andre Fleury, 1, Cape Breton (QMJHL)
2004—Evgeni Malkin, 2, Magnitogorsk, Russia
2005—Sidney Crosby, 1, Rimouski (QMJHL)

SINGLE-SEASON INDIVIDUAL RECORDS

FORWARDS/DEFENSEMEN

Most goals
85—Mario Lemieux, 1988-89

Most assists
114—Mario Lemieux, 1988-89

Most points
199—Mario Lemieux, 1988-89

Most penalty minutes
409—Paul Baxter, 1981-82

Most power play goals
31—Mario Lemieux, 1988-89
Mario Lemieux, 1995-96

Most shorthanded goals
13—Mario Lemieux, 1988-89

Most games with three or more goals
9—Mario Lemieux, 1988-89

Most shots
403—Jaromir Jagr, 1995-96

GOALTENDERS

Most games
66—Johan Hedberg, 2001-02

Most minutes
3,877—Johan Hedberg, 2001-02

Most shots against
1,885—Tom Barrasso, 1992-93

Most goals allowed
258—Greg Millen, 1980-81

Lowest goals-against average
2.07—Tom Barrasso, 1997-98

Most shutouts
7—Tom Barrasso, 1997-98

Most wins
43—Tom Barrasso, 1992-93

Most losses
34—Johan Hedberg, 2001-02

Most ties
15—Denis Herron, 1977-78

PITTSBURGH PIRATES (DEFUNCT)

YEAR-BY-YEAR RECORDS

	REGULAR SEASON					PLAYOFFS			
Season	W	L	T	Pts.	Finish	W	L	Highest round	Coach
1925-26	19	16	1	39	3rd	—	—		Odie Cleghorn
1926-27	15	26	3	33	4th/American	—	—		Odie Cleghorn
1927-28	19	17	8	46	3rd/American	1	1	Quarterfinals	Odie Cleghorn
1928-29	9	27	8	26	4th/American	—	—		Odie Cleghorn
1929-30	5	36	3	13	5th/American	—	—		Frank Fredrickson
1930-31*	4	36	4	12	5th/American	—	—		Cooper Smeaton

*Philadelphia Quakers.

ST. LOUIS BLUES

YEAR-BY-YEAR RECORDS

	REGULAR SEASON						PLAYOFFS			
Season	W	L	T	OTL	Pts.	Finish	W	L	Highest round	Coach
1967-68	27	31	16	—	70	3rd/West	8	10	Stanley Cup finals	Lynn Patrick, Scotty Bowman
1968-69	37	25	14	—	88	1st/West	8	4	Stanley Cup finals	Scotty Bowman
1969-70	37	27	12	—	86	1st/West	8	8	Stanley Cup finals	Scotty Bowman
1970-71	34	25	19	—	87	2nd/West	2	4	Division semifinals	Al Arbour, Scotty Bowman
1971-72	28	39	11	—	67	3rd/West	4	7	Division finals	Sid Abel, Bill McCreary, Al Arbour
1972-73	32	34	12	—	76	4th/West	1	4	Division semifinals	Al Arbour, Jean-Guy Talbot
1973-74	26	40	12	—	64	6th/West	—	—		Jean-Guy Talbot, Lou Angotti
1974-75	35	31	14	—	84	2nd/Smythe	0	2	Preliminaries	Lou Angotti, Lynn Patrick, Garry Young
1975-76	29	37	14	—	72	3rd/Smythe	1	2	Preliminaries	Garry Young, Lynn Patrick, Leo Boivin
1976-77	32	39	9	—	73	1st/Smythe	0	4	Quarterfinals	Emile Francis
1977-78	20	47	13	—	53	4th/Smythe	—	—		Leo Boivin, Barclay Plager
1978-79	18	50	12	—	48	3rd/Smythe	—	—		Barclay Plager
1979-80	34	34	12	—	80	2nd/Smythe	0	3	Preliminaries	Barclay Plager, Red Berenson
1980-81	45	18	17	—	107	1st/Smythe	5	6	Quarterfinals	Red Berenson
1981-82	32	40	8	—	72	3rd/Norris	5	5	Division finals	Red Berenson, Emile Francis
1982-83	25	40	15	—	65	4th/Norris	1	3	Division semifinals	Emile Francis, Barclay Plager
1983-84	32	41	7	—	71	2nd/Norris	6	5	Division finals	Jacques Demers
1984-85	37	31	12	—	86	1st/Norris	0	3	Division semifinals	Jacques Demers
1985-86	37	34	9	—	83	3rd/Norris	10	9	Conference finals	Jacques Demers
1986-87	32	33	15	—	79	1st/Norris	2	4	Division semifinals	Jacques Martin
1987-88	34	38	8	—	76	2nd/Norris	5	5	Division finals	Jacques Martin
1988-89	33	35	12	—	78	2nd/Norris	5	5	Division finals	Brian Sutter
1989-90	37	34	9	—	83	2nd/Norris	7	5	Division finals	Brian Sutter
1990-91	47	22	11	—	105	2nd/Norris	6	7	Division finals	Brian Sutter
1991-92	36	33	11	—	83	3rd/Norris	2	4	Division semifinals	Brian Sutter
1992-93	37	36	11	—	85	4th/Norris	7	4	Division finals	Bob Plager, Bob Berry
1993-94	40	33	11	—	91	4th/Central	0	4	Conference quarterfinals	Bob Berry
1994-95	28	15	5	—	61	2nd/Central	3	4	Conference quarterfinals	Mike Keenan
1995-96	32	34	16	—	80	4th/Central	7	6	Conference semifinals	Mike Keenan
1996-97	36	35	11	—	83	4th/Central	2	4	Conference quarterfinals	Mike Keenan, Jimmy Roberts, Joel Quenneville
1997-98	45	29	8	—	98	3rd/Central	6	4	Conference semifinals	Joel Quenneville
1998-99	37	32	13	—	87	2nd/Central	6	7	Conference semifinals	Joel Quenneville
1999-00	51	19	11	1	114	1st/Central	3	4	Conference quarterfinals	Joel Quenneville
2000-01	43	22	12	5	103	2nd/Central	9	6	Conference finals	Joel Quenneville
2001-02	43	27	8	4	98	2nd/Central	5	5	Conference semifinals	Joel Quenneville
2002-03	41	24	11	6	99	2nd/Central	3	4	Conference quarterfinals	Joel Quenneville
2003-04	39	30	11	2	91	2nd/Central	1	4	Conference quarterfinals	Joel Quenneville, Mike Kitchen

FIRST-ROUND ENTRY DRAFT CHOICES

Year Player, Overall, Last amateur team (league)

1969—No first-round selection
1970—No first-round selection
1971—Gene Carr, 4, Flin Flon (WCHL)
1972—Wayne Merrick, 9, Ottawa (OHL)
1973—John Davidson, 5, Calgary (WCHL)
1974—No first-round selection
1975—No first-round selection
1976—Bernie Federko, 7, Saskatoon (WCHL)
1977—Scott Campbell, 9, London (OHL)
1978—Wayne Babych, 3, Portland (WCHL)
1979—Perry Turnbull, 2, Portland (WHL)
1980—Rik Wilson, 12, Kingston (OHL)
1981—Marty Ruff, 20, Lethbridge (WHL)
1982—No first-round selection
1983—No first-round selection
1984—No first-round selection

Year	Player, Overall, Last amateur team (league)
1985	No first-round selection
1986	Jocelyn Lemieux, 10, Laval (QMJHL)
1987	Keith Osborne, 12, North Bay (OHL)
1988	Rod Brind'Amour, 9, Notre Dame Academy (Sask.)
1989	Jason Marshall, 9, Vernon (B.C.) Tier II
1990	No first-round selection
1991	No first-round selection
1992	No first-round selection
1993	No first-round selection
1994	No first-round selection
1995	No first-round selection
1996	Marty Reasoner, 14, Boston College
1997	No first-round selection
1998	Christian Backman, 24, Frolunda Goteborg, Sweden
1999	Barret Jackman, 17, Regina (WHL)
2000	Jeff Taffe, 30, University of Minnesota
2001	No first-round selection
2002	No first-round selection
2003	Shawn Belle, 30, Tri-City (WHL)
2004	Marek Schwarz, 17, Sparta Prague, Czech Republic
2005	T.J. Oshie, 24, Warroad (USHSW)

SINGLE-SEASON INDIVIDUAL RECORDS

FORWARDS/DEFENSEMEN

Most goals
86—Brett Hull, 1990-91

Most assists
90—Adam Oates, 1990-91

Most points
131—Brett Hull, 1990-91

Most penalty minutes
306—Bob Gassoff, 1975-76

Most power play goals
29—Brett Hull, 1990-91
Brett Hull, 1992-93

Most shorthanded goals
8—Chuck Lefley, 1975-76
Larry Patey, 1980-81

Most games with three or more goals
8—Brett Hull, 1991-92

Most shots
408—Brett Hull, 1991-92

GOALTENDERS

Most games
79—Grant Fuhr, 1995-96

Most minutes
4,365—Grant Fuhr, 1995-96

Most shots against
2,382—Curtis Joseph, 1993-94

Most goals allowed
250—Mike Liut, 1991-92

Lowest goals-against average
1.95—Roman Turek, 1999-2000

Most shutouts
8—Glenn Hall, 1968-69

Most wins
42—Roman Turek, 1999-2000

Most losses
29—Mike Liut, 1983-84

Most ties
16—Grant Fuhr, 1995-96

ST. LOUIS EAGLES (DEFUNCT)

YEAR-BY-YEAR RECORDS

	REGULAR SEASON					PLAYOFFS			
Season	W	L	T	Pts.	Finish	W	L	Highest round	Coach
1917-18*	9	13	0	18	3rd/2nd	—	—		Eddie Gerard
1918-19*	12	6	0	24	2nd/1st	1	4	Semifinals	Alf Smith
1919-20*	19	5	0	38	1st/1st	3	2	Stanley Cup champ	Pete Green
1920-21*	14	10	0	28	1st/3rd	†4	2	Stanley Cup champ	Pete Green
1921-22*	14	8	2	30	1st	†0	1	Semifinals	Pete Green
1922-23*	14	9	1	29	1st	6	2	Stanley Cup champ	Pete Green
1923-24*	16	8	0	32	1st	0	2	Semifinals	Pete Green
1924-25*	17	12	1	35	4th	—	—		Pete Green
1925-26*	24	8	4	52	1st	†0	1	Semifinals	Pete Green
1926-27*	30	10	4	64	1st/Canadian	†3	0	Stanley Cup champ	Dave Gill
1927-28*	20	14	10	50	3rd/Canadian	0	2	Quarterfinals	Dave Gill
1928-29*	14	17	13	41	4th/Canadian	—	—		Dave Gill
1929-30*	21	15	8	50	3rd/Canadian	†0	1	Semifinals	Newsy Lalonde
1930-31*	10	30	4	24	5th/Canadian	—	—		Newsy Lalonde
1931-32*					Club suspended operations for one season.				
1932-33*	11	27	10	32	5th/Canadian	—	—		Cy Denneny
1933-34*	13	29	6	32	5th/Canadian	—	—		George Boucher
1934-35	11	31	6	28	5th/Canadian	—	—		Eddie Gerard, George Boucher

*Ottawa Senators (first club).

†Won-lost record does not indicate tie(s) resulting from two-game, total goals series that year (two-game, total-goals series were played from 1917-18 through 1935-36).

SAN JOSE SHARKS

YEAR-BY-YEAR RECORDS

	REGULAR SEASON						PLAYOFFS			
Season	W	L	T	OTL	Pts.	Finish	W	L	Highest round	Coach
1991-92	17	58	5	—	39	6th/Smythe	—	—		George Kingston
1992-93	11	71	2	—	24	6th/Smythe	—	—		George Kingston
1993-94	33	35	16	—	82	3rd/Pacific	7	7	Conference semifinals	Kevin Constantine
1994-95	19	25	4	—	42	3rd/Pacific	4	7	Conference semifinals	Kevin Constantine
1995-96	20	55	7	—	47	7th/Pacific	—	—		Kevin Constantine, Jim Wiley
1996-97	27	47	8	—	62	7th/Pacific	—	—		Al Sims
1997-98	34	38	10	—	78	4th/Pacific	2	4	Conference quarterfinals	Darryl Sutter

Season	W	L	T	OTL	Pts.	Finish	W	L	Highest round	Coach
	REGULAR SEASON						PLAYOFFS			
1998-99	31	33	18	—	80	4th/Pacific	2	4	Conference quarterfinals	Darryl Sutter
1999-00	35	30	10	7	87	4th/Pacific	5	7	Conference semifinals	Darryl Sutter
2000-01	40	27	12	3	95	2nd/Pacific	2	4	Conference quarterfinals	Darryl Sutter
2001-02	44	27	8	3	99	1st/Pacific	7	5	Conference semifinals	Darryl Sutter
2002-03	28	37	9	8	73	5th/Pacific	—	—		Darryl Sutter, Doug Wilson, Cap Raeder, Ron Wilson
2003-04	43	21	12	6	104	1st/Pacific	10	7	Conference finals	Ron Wilson

FIRST-ROUND ENTRY DRAFT CHOICES

Year Player, Overall, Last amateur team (league)

1991—Pat Falloon, 2, Spokane (WHL)
1992—Mike Rathje, 3, Medicine Hat (WHL)
Andrei Nazarov, 10, Dynamo Moscow, CIS
1993—Viktor Kozlov, 6, Moscow, CIS
1994—Jeff Friesen, 11, Regina (WHL)
1995—Teemu Riihijarvi, 12, Espoo Jrs., Finland
1996—Andrei Zyuzin, 2, Salavat Yulayev UFA, CIS
Marco Sturm, 21, Landshut, Germany
1997—Patrick Marleau, 2, Seattle (WHL)
Scott Hannan, 23, Kelowna (WHL)

Year Player, Overall, Last amateur team (league)

1998—Brad Stuart, 3, Regina (WHL)
1999—Jeff Jillson, 14, University of Michigan
2000—No first-round selection
2001—Marcel Goc, 20, Schwennigen, Germany
2002—Mike Morris, 27, St. Sebastian's (USHSE)
2003—Milan Michalek, 6, Czech Republic
Steve Bernier, 16, Moncton (QMJHL)
2004—Lukas Kaspar, 22, Litvinov, Czech Republic
2005—Devin Setoguchi, 8, Saskatoon (WHL)

SINGLE-SEASON INDIVIDUAL RECORDS

FORWARDS/DEFENSEMEN

Most goals
44—Owen Nolan, 1999-2000

Most assists
52—Kelly Kisio, 1992-93

Most points
84—Owen Nolan, 1999-2000

Most penalty minutes
326—Link Gaetz, 1991-92

Most power play goals
18—Owen Nolan, 1999-2000

Most shorthanded goals
6—Jamie Baker, 1995-96
Jeff Friesen, 1997-98

Most games with three or more goals
2—Rob Gaudreau, 1992-93
Igor Larionov, 1993-94
Tony Granato, 1996-97

Most shots
261—Owen Nolan, 1999-2000

GOALTENDERS

Most games
74—Arturs Irbe, 1993-94

Most minutes
4,412—Arturs Irbe, 1993-94

Most shots against
2,064—Arturs Irbe, 1993-94

Most goals allowed
209—Arturs Irbe, 1993-94

Lowest goals-against average
2.06—Vesa Toskala, 2003-04

Most shutouts
7—Evgeni Nabokov, 2001-02

Most wins
37—Evgeni Nabokov, 2001-02

Most losses
30—Jeff Hackett, 1992-93
Steve Shields, 1999-2000

Most ties
16—Arturs Irbe, 1993-94

TAMPA BAY LIGHTNING

YEAR-BY-YEAR RECORDS

Season	W	L	T	OTL	Pts.	Finish	W	L	Highest round	Coach
	REGULAR SEASON						PLAYOFFS			
1992-93	23	54	7	—	53	6th/Norris	—	—		Terry Crisp
1993-94	30	43	11	—	71	7th/Atlantic	—	—		Terry Crisp
1994-95	17	28	3	—	37	6th/Atlantic	—	—		Terry Crisp
1995-96	38	32	12	—	88	5th/Atlantic	2	4	Conference quarterfinals	Terry Crisp
1996-97	32	40	10	—	74	6th/Atlantic	—	—		Terry Crisp
1997-98	17	55	10	—	44	7th/Atlantic	—	—		Terry Crisp, Rick Paterson, Jacques Demers
1998-99	19	54	9	—	47	4th/Southeast	—	—		Jacques Demers
1999-00	19	47	9	7	54	4th/Southeast	—	—		Steve Ludzik
2000-01	24	47	6	5	59	5th/Southeast	—	—		Steve Ludzik, John Tortorella
2001-02	27	40	11	4	69	3rd/Southeast	—	—		John Tortorella
2002-03	36	25	16	5	93	1st/Southeast	5	6	Conference semifinals	John Tortorella
2003-04	46	22	8	6	106	1st/Southeast	16	7	Stanley Cup champ	John Tortorella

FIRST-ROUND ENTRY DRAFT CHOICES

Year Player, Overall, Last amateur team (league)

1992—Roman Hamrlik, 1, Zlin, Czechoslovakia
1993—Chris Gratton, 3, Kingston (OHL)
1994—Jason Weimer, 8, Portland (WHL)
1995—Daymond Langkow, 5, Tri-City (WHL)
1996—Mario Larocque, 16, Hull (QMJHL)
1997—Paul Mara, 7, Sudbury (OHL)
1998—Vincent Lecavalier, 1, Rimouski (QMJHL)

Year Player, Overall, Last amateur team (league)

1999—No first-round selection
2000—Nikita Alexeev, 8, Erie (OHL)
2001—Alexander Svitov, 3, OMSK, Russia
2002—No first-round selection
2003—No first-round selection
2004—Andy Rogers, 30, Calgary (WHL)
2005—Vladimir Mihalik, 30, Presov (Slovakia 2)

SINGLE-SEASON INDIVIDUAL RECORDS

FORWARDS/DEFENSEMEN

Most goals
42—Brian Bradley, 1992-93

Most assists
57—Vaclav Prospal, 2002-03

Most points
94—Martin St. Louis, 2003-04

Most penalty minutes
258—Enrico Ciccone, 1995-96

Most power play goals
16—Brian Bradley, 1992-93

Most shorthanded goals
8—Martin St. Louis, 2003-04

Most games with three or more goals
3—Wendel Clark, 1998-99

Most shots
281—Roman Hamrlik, 1995-96

GOALTENDERS

Most games
70—Nikolai Khabibulin, 2001-02

Most minutes
3,896—Nikolai Khabibulin, 2001-02

Most shots against
1,914—Nikolai Khabibulin, 2001-02

Most goals allowed
177—Kevin Weekes, 2000-01

Lowest goals-against average
2.33—Nikolai Khabibulin, 2003-04

Most shutouts
7—Nikolai Khabibulin, 2001-02

Most wins
30—Nikolai Khabibulin, 2002-03

Most losses
33—Daren Puppa, 1993-94
Kevin Weekes, 2000-01

Most ties
11—Nikolai Khabibulin, 2002-03

TORONTO MAPLE LEAFS

YEAR-BY-YEAR RECORDS

	REGULAR SEASON						PLAYOFFS			
Season	W	L	T	OTL	Pts.	Finish	W	L	Highest round	Coach
1917-18‡	13	9	0	—	26	2nd/1st	4	3	Stanley Cup champ	Dick Carroll
1918-19‡	5	13	0	—	10	3rd/3rd	—	—		Dick Carroll
1919-20§	12	12	0	—	24	3rd/2nd	—	—		Frank Heffernan, Harry Sproule
1920-21§	15	9	0	—	30	2nd/1st	0	2	Semifinals	Dick Carroll
1921-22§	13	10	1	—	27	2nd	*4	2	Stanley Cup champ	Eddie Powers
1922-23§	13	10	1	—	27	3rd	—	—		Charlie Querrie, Jack Adams
1923-24§	10	14	0	—	20	3rd	—	—		Eddie Powers
1924-25§	19	11	0	—	38	2nd	0	2	Semifinals	Eddie Powers
1925-26§	12	21	3	—	27	6th	—	—		Eddie Powers
1926-27§	15	24	5	—	35	5th/Canadian	—	—		Conn Smythe
1927-28	18	18	8	—	44	4th/Canadian	—	—		Alex Roveril, Conn Smythe
1928-29	21	18	5	—	47	3rd/Canadian	2	2	Semifinals	Alex Roveril, Conn Smythe
1929-30	17	21	6	—	40	4th/Canadian	—	—		Alex Roveril, Conn Smythe
1930-31	22	13	9	—	53	2nd/Canadian	*0	1	Quarterfinals	Conn Smythe, Art Duncan
1931-32	23	18	7	—	53	2nd/Canadian	*5	1	Stanley Cup champ	Art Duncan, Dick Irvin
1932-33	24	18	6	—	54	1st/Canadian	4	5	Stanley Cup finals	Dick Irvin
1933-34	26	13	9	—	61	1st/Canadian	2	3	Semifinals	Dick Irvin
1934-35	30	14	4	—	64	1st/Canadian	3	4	Stanley Cup finals	Dick Irvin
1935-36	23	19	6	—	52	2nd/Canadian	4	5	Stanley Cup finals	Dick Irvin
1936-37	22	21	5	—	49	3rd/Canadian	0	2	Quarterfinals	Dick Irvin
1937-38	24	15	9	—	57	1st/Canadian			Stanley Cup finals	Dick Irvin
1938-39	19	20	9	—	47	3rd	5	5	Stanley Cup finals	Dick Irvin
1939-40	25	17	6	—	56	3rd	6	4	Stanley Cup finals	Dick Irvin
1940-41	28	14	6	—	62	2nd	3	4	Semifinals	Hap Day
1941-42	27	18	3	—	57	2nd	8	5	Stanley Cup champ	Hap Day
1942-43	22	19	9	—	53	3rd	2	4	League semifinals	Hap Day
1943-44	23	23	4	—	50	3rd	1	4	League semifinals	Hap Day
1944-45	24	22	4	—	52	3rd	8	5	Stanley Cup champ	Hap Day
1945-46	19	24	7	—	45	5th	—	—		Hap Day
1946-47	31	19	10	—	72	2nd	8	3	Stanley Cup champ	Hap Day
1947-48	32	15	13	—	77	1st	8	1	Stanley Cup champ	Hap Day
1948-49	22	25	13	—	57	4th	8	1	Stanley Cup champ	Hap Day
1949-50	31	27	12	—	74	3rd	3	4	League semifinals	Hap Day
1950-51	41	16	13	—	95	2nd	†8	2	Stanley Cup champ	Joe Primeau
1951-52	29	25	16	—	74	3rd	0	4	League semifinals	Joe Primeau
1952-53	27	30	13	—	67	5th	—	—		Joe Primeau
1953-54	32	24	14	—	78	3rd	1	4	League semifinals	King Clancy
1954-55	24	24	22	—	70	3rd	0	4	League semifinals	King Clancy
1955-56	24	33	13	—	61	4th	1	4	League semifinals	King Clancy
1956-57	21	34	15	—	57	5th	—	—		Howie Meeker
1957-58	21	38	11	—	53	6th	—	—		Billy Reay
1958-59	27	32	11	—	65	4th	5	7	Stanley Cup finals	Billy Reay, Punch Imlach
1959-60	35	26	9	—	79	2nd	4	6	Stanley Cup finals	Punch Imlach
1960-61	39	19	12	—	90	2nd	1	4	League semifinals	Punch Imlach
1961-62	37	22	11	—	85	2nd	8	4	Stanley Cup champ	Punch Imlach
1962-63	35	23	12	—	82	1st	8	2	Stanley Cup champ	Punch Imlach
1963-64	33	25	12	—	78	3rd	8	6	Stanley Cup champ	Punch Imlach

	REGULAR SEASON						PLAYOFFS			
Season	W	L	T	OTL	Pts.	Finish	W	L	Highest round	Coach
1964-65	30	26	14	—	74	4th	2	4	League semifinals	Punch Imlach
1965-66	34	25	11	—	79	3rd	0	4	League semifinals	Punch Imlach
1966-67	32	27	11	—	75	3rd	8	4	Stanley Cup champ	Punch Imlach
1967-68	33	31	10	—	76	5th/East	—	—		Punch Imlach
1968-69	35	26	15	—	85	4th/East	0	4	Division semifinals	Punch Imlach
1969-70	29	34	13	—	71	6th/East	—	—		John McLellan
1970-71	37	33	8	—	82	4th/East	2	4	Division semifinals	John McLellan
1971-72	33	31	14	—	80	4th/East	1	4	Division semifinals	John McLellan
1972-73	27	41	10	—	64	6th/East	—	—		John McLellan
1973-74	35	27	16	—	86	4th/East	0	4	Division semifinals	Red Kelly
1974-75	31	33	16	—	78	3rd/Adams	2	5	Quarterfinals	Red Kelly
1975-76	34	31	15	—	83	3rd/Adams	5	5	Quarterfinals	Red Kelly
1976-77	33	32	15	—	81	3rd/Adams	4	5	Quarterfinals	Red Kelly
1977-78	41	29	10	—	92	3rd/Adams	6	7	Semifinals	Roger Neilson
1978-79	34	33	13	—	81	3rd/Adams	2	4	Quarterfinals	Roger Neilson
1979-80	35	40	5	—	75	4th/Adams	0	3	Preliminaries	Floyd Smith
1980-81	28	37	15	—	71	5th/Adams	0	3	Preliminaries	Punch Imlach, Joe Crozier
1981-82	20	44	16	—	56	5th/Norris	—	—		Mike Nykoluk
1982-83	28	40	12	—	68	3rd/Norris	1	3	Division semifinals	Mike Nykoluk
1983-84	26	45	9	—	61	5th/Norris	—	—		Mike Nykoluk
1984-85	20	52	8	—	48	5th/Norris	—	—		Dan Maloney
1985-86	25	48	7	—	57	4th/Norris	6	4	Division finals	Dan Maloney
1986-87	32	42	6	—	70	4th/Norris	7	6	Division finals	John Brophy
1987-88	21	49	10	—	52	4th/Norris	2	4	Division semifinals	John Brophy
1988-89	28	46	6	—	62	5th/Norris	—	—		John Brophy, George Armstrong
1989-90	38	38	4	—	80	3rd/Norris	1	4	Division semifinals	Doug Carpenter
1990-91	23	46	11	—	57	5th/Norris	—	—		Doug Carpenter, Tom Watt
1991-92	30	43	7	—	67	5th/Norris	—	—		Tom Watt
1992-93	44	29	11	—	99	3rd/Norris	11	10	Conference finals	Pat Burns
1993-94	43	29	12	—	98	2nd/Central	9	9	Conference finals	Pat Burns
1994-95	21	19	8	—	50	4th/Central	3	4	Conference quarterfinals	Pat Burns
1995-96	34	36	12	—	80	3rd/Central	2	4	Conference quarterfinals	Pat Burns, Nick Beverley
1996-97	30	44	8	—	68	6th/Central	—	—		Mike Murphy
1997-98	30	43	9	—	69	6th/Central	—	—		Mike Murphy
1998-99	45	30	7	—	97	2nd/Northeast	9	8	Conference finals	Pat Quinn
1999-00	45	27	7	3	100	1st/Northeast	6	6	Conference semifinals	Pat Quinn
2000-01	37	29	11	5	90	3rd/Northeast	7	4	Conference semifinals	Pat Quinn
2001-02	43	25	10	4	100	2nd/Northeast	10	10	Conference finals	Pat Quinn
2002-03	44	28	7	3	98	2nd/Northeast	3	4	Conference quarterfinals	Pat Quinn
2003-04	43	24	10	3	104	2nd/Northeast	6	7	Conference semifinals	Pat Quinn

*Won-lost record does not indicate tie(s) resulting from two-game, total-goals series that year (two-game, total-goals series were played from 1917-18 through 1935-36).

†Game 2 semifinals vs. Boston tied 1-1 after one overtime (curfew law).

‡Toronto Arenas.

§Toronto St. Patricks (until April 14, 1927).

FIRST-ROUND ENTRY DRAFT CHOICES

Year Player, Overall, Last amateur team (league)

1969—Ernie Moser, 9, Esteven (WCHL)
1970—Darryl Sittler, 8, London (OHL)
1971—No first-round selection
1972—George Ferguson, 11, Toronto (OHL)
1973—Lanny McDonald, 4, Medicine Hat (WCHL)
Bob Neely, 10, Peterborough (OHL)
Ian Turnbull, 15, Ottawa (OHL)
1974—Jack Valiquette, 13, Sault Ste. Marie (OHL)
1975—Don Ashby, 6, Calgary (WCHL)
1976—No first-round selection
1977—John Anderson, 11, Toronto (OHA)
Trevor Johansen, 12, Toronto (OHA)
1978—No first-round selection
1979—Laurie Boschman, 9, Brandon (WHL)
1980—No first-round selection
1981—Jim Benning, 6, Portland (WHL)
1982—Gary Nylund, 3, Portland (WHL)
1983—Russ Courtnall, 7, Victoria (WHL)
1984—Al Iafrate, 4, U.S. Olympics/Belleville (OHL)
1985—Wendel Clark, 1, Saskatoon (WHL)
1986—Vincent Damphousse, 6, Laval (QMJHL)
1987—Luke Richardson, 7, Peterborough (OHL)
1988—Scott Pearson, 6, Kingston (OHL)

Year Player, Overall, Last amateur team (league)

1989—Scott Thornton, 3, Belleville (OHL)
Rob Pearson, 12, Belleville (OHL)
Steve Bancroft, 21, Belleville (OHL)
1990—Drake Berehowsky, 10, Kingston (OHL)
1991—No first-round selection
1992—Brandon Convery, 8, Sudbury (OHL)
Grant Marshall, 23, Ottawa (OHL)
1993—Kenny Jonsson, 12, Rogle (Sweden)
Landon Wilson, 19, Dubuque (USHL)
1994—Eric Fichaud, 16, Chicoutimi (QMJHL)
1995—Jeff Ware, 15, Oshawa (OHL)
1996—No first-round selection
1997—No first-round selection
1998—Nikolai Antropov, 10, Torpedo (Russia)
1999—Luca Cereda, 24, Ambri (Switzerland)
2000—Brad Boyes, 24, Erie (OHL)
2001—Carlo Colaiacovo, 17, Erie (OHL)
2002—Alexander Steen, 24, Frolunda (Sweden)
2003—No first-round selection
2004—No first-round selection
2005—Tuuka Rask, 21, Ilves (Finland Jr.)

SINGLE-SEASON INDIVIDUAL RECORDS

FORWARDS/DEFENSEMEN

Most goals
54—Rick Vaive, 1981-82

Most assists
95—Doug Gilmour, 1992-93

Most points
127—Doug Gilmour, 1992-93

Most penalty minutes
365—Tie Domi, 1997-98

Most power play goals
21—Dave Andreychuk, 1993-94
Wendell Clark, 1993-94

Most shorthanded goals
8—Dave Keon, 1970-71
Dave Reid, 1990-91

Most games with three or more goals
5—Darryl Sittler, 1980-81

Most shots
346—Darryl Sittler, 1975-76

GOALTENDERS

Most games
74—Felix Potvin, 1996-97

Most minutes
4,271—Felix Potvin, 1996-97

Most goals allowed
230—Grant Fuhr, 1991-92

Lowest goals-against average
1.61—Lorne Chabot, 1928-29

Most shutouts
13—Harry Lumley, 1953-54

Most wins
37—Ed Belfour, 2002-03

Most losses
38—Ed Chadwick, 1957-58

Most ties
22—Harry Lumley, 1954-55

VANCOUVER CANUCKS

YEAR-BY-YEAR RECORDS

	REGULAR SEASON						PLAYOFFS			
Season	W	L	T	OTL	Pts.	Finish	W	L	Highest round	Coach
1970-71	24	46	8	—	56	6th/East	—	—		Hal Laycoe
1971-72	20	50	8	—	48	7th/East	—	—		Hal Laycoe
1972-73	22	47	9	—	53	7th/East	—	—		Vic Stasiuk
1973-74	24	43	11	—	59	7th/East	—	—		Bill McCreary, Phil Maloney
1974-75	38	32	10	—	86	1st/Smythe	1	4	Quarterfinals	Phil Maloney
1975-76	33	32	15	—	81	2nd/Smythe	0	2	Preliminaries	Phil Maloney
1976-77	25	42	13	—	63	4th/Smythe	—	—		Phil Maloney, Orland Kurtenbach
1977-78	20	43	17	—	57	3rd/Smythe	—	—		Orland Kurtenbach
1978-79	25	42	13	—	63	2nd/Smythe	1	2	Preliminaries	Harry Neale
1979-80	27	37	16	—	70	3rd/Smythe	1	3	Preliminaries	Harry Neale
1980-81	28	32	20	—	76	3rd/Smythe	0	3	Preliminaries	Harry Neale
1981-82	30	33	17	—	77	2nd/Smythe	11	6	Stanley Cup finals	Harry Neale, Roger Neilson
1982-83	30	35	15	—	75	3rd/Smythe	1	3	Division semifinals	Roger Neilson
1983-84	32	39	9	—	73	3rd/Smythe	1	3	Division semifinals	Roger Neilson, Harry Neale
1984-85	25	46	9	—	59	5th/Smythe	—	—		Bill Laforge, Harry Neale
1985-86	23	44	13	—	59	4th/Smythe	0	3	Division semifinals	Tom Watt
1986-87	29	43	8	—	66	5th/Smythe	—	—		Tom Watt
1987-88	25	46	9	—	59	5th/Smythe	—	—		Bob McCammon
1988-89	33	39	8	—	74	4th/Smythe	3	4	Division semifinals	Bob McCammon
1989-90	25	41	14	—	64	5th/Smythe	—	—		Bob McCammon
1990-91	28	43	9	—	65	4th/Smythe	2	4	Division semifinals	Bob McCammon, Pat Quinn
1991-92	42	26	12	—	96	1st/Smythe	6	7	Division finals	Pat Quinn
1992-93	46	29	9	—	101	1st/Smythe	6	6	Division finals	Pat Quinn
1993-94	41	40	3	—	85	2nd/Pacific	15	9	Stanley Cup finals	Pat Quinn
1994-95	18	18	12	—	48	2nd/Pacific	4	7	Conference semifinals	Rick Ley
1995-96	32	35	15	—	79	3rd/Pacific	2	4	Conference quarterfinals	Rick Ley, Pat Quinn
1996-97	35	40	7	—	77	4th/Pacific	—	—		Tom Renney
1997-98	25	43	14	—	64	7th/Pacific	—	—		Tom Renney, Mike Keenan
1998-99	23	47	12	—	58	4th/Northwest	—	—		Mike Keenan, Marc Crawford
1999-00	30	29	15	8	83	3rd/Northwest	—	—		Marc Crawford
2000-01	36	28	11	7	90	3rd/Northwest	0	4	Conference quarterfinals	Marc Crawford
2001-02	42	30	7	3	94	2nd/Northwest	2	4	Conference quarterfinals	Marc Crawford
2002-03	45	23	13	1	104	2nd/Northwest	7	7	Conference semifinals	Marc Crawford
2003-04	43	24	10	5	101	1st/Northwest	3	4	Conference quarterfinals	Marc Crawford

FIRST-ROUND ENTRY DRAFT CHOICES

Year Player, Overall, Last amateur team (league)
1970—Dale Tallon, 2, Toronto (OHL)
1971—Jocelyn Guevremont, 3, Montreal (OHL)
1972—Don Lever, 3, Niagara Falls (OHL)
1973—Dennis Ververgaert, 3, London (OHL)
Bob Dailey, 9, Toronto (OHL)
1974—No first-round selection
1975—Rick Blight, 10, Brandon (WCHL)
1976—No first-round selection
1977—Jere Gillis, 4, Sherbrooke (QMJHL)
1978—Bill Derlago, 4, Brandon (WCHL)

Year Player, Overall, Last amateur team (league)
1979—Rick Vaive, 5, Birmingham (WHA)
1980—Rick Lanz, 7, Oshawa (OHL)
1981—Garth Butcher, 10, Regina (WHL)
1982—Michel Petit, 11, Sherbrooke (QMJHL)
1983—Cam Neely, 9, Portland (WHL)
1984—J.J. Daigneault, 10, Can. Ol./Longueuil (QMJHL)
1985—Jim Sandlak, 4, London (OHL)
1986—Dan Woodley, 7, Portland (WHL)
1987—No first-round selection
1988—Trevor Linden, 2, Medicine Hat (WHL)

Year	Player, Overall, Last amateur team (league)
1989	Jason Herter, 8, University of North Dakota
1990	Petr Nedved, 2, Seattle (WHL)
	Shawn Antoski, 18, North Bay (OHL)
1991	Alex Stojanov, 7, Hamilton (OHL)
1992	Libor Polasek, 21, TJ Vikovice (Czech.)
1993	Mike Wilson, 20, Sudbury (OHL)
1994	Mattias Ohlund, 13, Pitea Div. I (Sweden)
1995	No first-round selection
1996	Josh Holden, 12, Regina (WHL)
1997	Brad Ference, 10, Spokane (WHL)
1998	Bryan Allen, 4, Oshawa (OHL)
1999	Daniel Sedin, 2, Modo Ornskoldsvik, Sweden
	Henrik Sedin, 3, Modo Ornskoldsvik, Sweden
2000	Nathan Smith, 23, Swift Current (WHL)
2001	R.J. Umberger, 16, Ohio State
2002	No first-round selection
2003	Ryan Kesler, 23, Ohio State (CCHA)
2004	Cory Schneider, 26, Phillips-Andover (USHSE)
2005	Luc Bourdon, 10, Val d'Or (QMJHL)

SINGLE-SEASON INDIVIDUAL RECORDS

FORWARDS/DEFENSEMEN

Most goals
60—Pavel Bure, 1992-93
Pavel Bure, 1993-94

Most assists
62—Andre Boudrias, 1974-75

Most points
110—Pavel Bure, 1992-93

Most penalty minutes
372—Donald Brashear, 1997-98

Most power play goals
25—Pavel Bure, 1993-94
Todd Bertuzzi, 2002-03

Most shorthanded goals
7—Pavel Bure, 1992-93

Most games with three or more goals
4—Petri Skriko, 1986-87

Most shots
407—Pavel Bure, 1992-93

GOALTENDERS

Most games
72—Gary Smith, 1974-75

Most minutes
3,852—Kirk McLean, 1991-92

Most shots against
1,804—Kirk McLean, 1989-90

Most goals allowed
240—Richard Brodeur, 1985-86

Lowest goals-against average
2.27—Dan Cloutier, 2003-04

Most shutouts
7—Dan Cloutier, 2002-03

Most wins
38—Kirk McLean, 1991-92

Most losses
33—Gary Smith, 1973-74

Most ties
16—Richard Brodeur, 1980-81

WASHINGTON CAPITALS

YEAR-BY-YEAR RECORDS

	REGULAR SEASON						PLAYOFFS			
Season	W	L	T	OTL	Pts.	Finish	W	L	Highest round	Coach
1974-75	8	67	5	—	21	5th/Norris	—	—		Jim Anderson, Red Sullivan, Milt Schmidt
1975-76	11	59	10	—	32	5th/Norris	—	—		Milt Schmidt, Tom McVie
1976-77	24	42	14	—	62	4th/Norris	—	—		Tom McVie
1977-78	17	49	14	—	48	5th/Norris	—	—		Tom McVie
1978-79	24	41	15	—	63	4th/Norris	—	—		Dan Belisle
1979-80	27	40	13	—	67	5th/Patrick	—	—		Dan Belisle, Gary Green
1980-81	26	36	18	—	70	5th/Patrick	—	—		Gary Green
1981-82	26	41	13	—	65	5th/Patrick	—	—		Gary Green, Roger Crozier, Bryan Murray
1982-83	39	25	16	—	94	3rd/Patrick	1	3	Division semifinals	Bryan Murray
1983-84	48	27	5	—	101	2nd/Patrick	4	4	Division finals	Bryan Murray
1984-85	46	25	9	—	101	2nd/Patrick	2	3	Division semifinals	Bryan Murray
1985-86	50	23	7	—	107	2nd/Patrick	5	4	Division finals	Bryan Murray
1986-87	38	32	10	—	86	2nd/Patrick	3	4	Division semifinals	Bryan Murray
1987-88	38	33	9	—	85	2nd/Patrick	7	7	Division finals	Bryan Murray
1988-89	41	29	10	—	92	1st/Patrick	2	4	Division semifinals	Bryan Murray
1989-90	36	38	6	—	78	3rd/Patrick	8	7	Conference finals	Bryan Murray, Terry Murray
1990-91	37	36	7	—	81	3rd/Patrick	5	6	Division finals	Terry Murray
1991-92	45	27	8	—	98	2nd/Patrick	3	4	Division semifinals	Terry Murray
1992-93	43	34	7	—	93	2nd/Patrick	2	4	Division semifinals	Terry Murray
1993-94	39	35	10	—	88	3rd/Atlantic	5	6	Conference semifinals	Terry Murray, Jim Schoenfeld
1994-95	22	18	8	—	52	3rd/Atlantic	3	4	Conference quarterfinals	Jim Schoenfeld
1995-96	39	32	11	—	89	4th/Atlantic	2	4	Conference quarterfinals	Jim Schoenfeld
1996-97	33	40	9	—	75	5th/Atlantic	—	—		Jim Schoenfeld
1997-98	40	30	12	—	92	3rd/Atlantic	12	9	Stanley Cup finals	Ron Wilson
1998-99	31	45	6	—	68	3rd/Southeast	—	—		Ron Wilson
1999-00	44	24	12	2	102	1st/Southeast	1	4	Conference quarterfinals	Ron Wilson
2000-01	41	27	10	4	96	1st/Southeast	2	4	Conference quarterfinals	Ron Wilson
2001-02	36	33	11	2	85	2nd/Southeast	—	—		Ron Wilson
2002-03	39	29	8	6	92	2nd/Southeast	2	4	Conference quarterfinals	Bruce Cassidy
2003-04	23	46	10	3	59	5th/Southeast	—	—		Bruce Cassidy, Glen Hanlon

FIRST-ROUND ENTRY DRAFT CHOICES

Year Player, Overall, Last amateur team (league)
1974—Greg Joly, 1, Regina (WCHL)
1975—Alex Forsyth, 18, Kingston (OHA)
1976—Rick Green, 1, London (OHL)
Greg Carroll, 15, Medicine Hat (WCHL)
1977—Robert Picard, 3, Montreal (QMJHL)
1978—Ryan Walter, 2, Seattle (WCHL)
Tim Coulis, 18, Hamilton (OHL)
1979—Mike Gartner, 4, Cincinnati (WHA)
1980—Darren Veitch, 5, Regina (WHL)
1981—Bobby Carpenter, 3, St. John's H.S. (Mass.)
1982—Scott Stevens, 5, Kitchener (OHL)
1983—No first-round selection
1984—Kevin Hatcher, 17, North Bay (OHL)
1985—Yvon Corriveau, 19, Toronto (OHL)
1986—Jeff Greenlaw, 19, Team Canada
1987—No first-round selection
1988—Reggie Savage, 15, Victoriaville (QMJHL)
1989—Olaf Kolzig, 19, Tri-City (WHL)
1990—John Slaney, 9, Cornwall (OHL)
1991—Pat Peake, 14, Detroit (OHL)
Trevor Halverson, 21, North Bay (OHL)
1992—Sergei Gonchar, 14, Dynamo Moscow, CIS

Year Player, Overall, Last amateur team (league)
1993—Brendan Witt, 11, Seattle (WHL)
Jason Allison, 17, London (OHL)
1994—Nolan Baumgartner, 10, Kamloops (WHL)
Alexander Kharlamov, 15, CSKA Moscow, CIS
1995—Brad Church, 17, Prince Albert (WHL)
Miikka Elomo, 23, Kiekko-67, Finland
1996—Alexander Volchkov, 4, Barrie (OHL)
Jaroslav Svejkovsky, 17, Tri-City (WHL)
1997—Nick Boynton, 9, Ottawa (OHL)
1998—No first-round selection
1999—Kris Breech, 7, Calgary (WHL)
2000—Brian Sutherby, 26, Moose Jaw (WHL)
2001—No first-round selection
2002—Steve Eminger, 12, Kitchener (OHL)
Alexander Syemin, 13, Chelyabinsk, Russia
Boyd Gordon, 17, Red Deer (WHL)
2003—Eric Fehr, 18, Brandon (WHL)
2004—Alexander Ovechkin, 1, Dynamo Moscow, Russia
Jeff Schultz, 27, Calgary (WHL)
Mike Green, 29, Saskatoon (WHL)
2005—Sasha Pokulok, 14, Cornell (ECAC)
Joe Finley, 27, Sioux Falls (USHL)

SINGLE-SEASON INDIVIDUAL RECORDS

FORWARDS/DEFENSEMEN

Most goals
60—Dennis Maruk, 1981-82

Most assists
76—Dennis Maruk, 1981-82

Most points
136—Dennis Maruk, 1981-82

Most penalty minutes
339—Alan May, 1989-90

Most power play goals
22—Peter Bondra, 2000-01

Most shorthanded goals
6—Mike Gartner, 1986-87
Peter Bondra, 1994-95

Most games with three or more goals
4—Dennis Maruk, 1980-81
Dennis Maruk, 1981-82
Peter Bondra, 1995-96

Most shots
333—Peter Bondra, 2001-02

GOALTENDERS

Most games
73—Olaf Kolzig, 1999-2000

Most minutes
4,371—Olaf Kolzig, 1999-2000

Most shots against
1,977—Olaf Kolzig, 2001-02

Most goals allowed
235—Ron Low, 1974-75

Lowest goals-against average
2.13—Jim Carey, 1994-95

Most shutouts
9—Jim Carey, 1995-96

Most wins
41—Olaf Kolzig, 1999-2000

Most losses
36—Ron Low, 1974-75

Most ties
11—Olaf Kolzig, 1999-2000

Sporting News

BOOKS

PLAYER REGISTER

2005-2006 EDITION

VETERANS AND TOP PROSPECTS

ABDELKADER, JUSTIN — LW — RED WINGS

PERSONAL: Born February 25, 1987, in Muskegon, Mich. ... 6-1/195. ... Shoots left.

		REGULAR SEASON								PLAYOFFS				
Season Team	League	GP	G	A	Pts.	PIM	+/-	PP	SH	GP	G	A	Pts.	PIM
04-05—Cedar Rapids	USHL	60	27	25	52	86	...	...	...	—	—	—	—	—

ABID, RAMZI — LW — THRASHERS

PERSONAL: Born March 24, 1980, in Montreal. ... 6-2/210. ... Shoots left.
TRANSACTIONS/CAREER NOTES: Selected by Colorado Avalanche in 2nd round (5th Avalanche pick, 28th overall) of NHL draft (June 27, 1998). ... Returned to draft pool by Avalanche and selected by Phoenix Coyotes in 3rd round (3rd Coyotes pick, 86th overall) of NHL draft (June 24, 2000). ... Traded by Coyotes with D Dan Focht and LW Guillaume Lefebvre to Pittsburgh Penguins for C Jan Hrdina and D Francois Leroux (March 11, 2003). ... Injured knee (March 18, 2003); missed nine games. ... Injured knee (December 6, 2003); missed final 57 games of season. ... Signed as free agent by Atlanta Thrashers (Aug. 8, 2005).

		REGULAR SEASON								PLAYOFFS				
Season Team	League	GP	G	A	Pts.	PIM	+/-	PP	SH	GP	G	A	Pts.	PIM
96-97—Chicoutimi	QMJHL	65	13	24	37	151	...	...	...	—	—	—	—	—
97-98—Chicoutimi	QMJHL	68	50	*85	*135	266	...	...	...	6	3	4	7	10
98-99—Chicoutimi	QMJHL	21	11	15	26	97	-4	2	0	—	—	—	—	—
—Acadie-Bathurst	QMJHL	24	14	22	36	102	11	3	0	23	14	20	34	84
99-00—Acadie-Bathurst	QMJHL	13	10	11	21	61	10	0	0	—	—	—	—	—
—Halifax	QMJHL	59	57	80	137	148	29	18	5	10	10	13	23	18
00-01—Springfield	AHL	17	6	4	10	38	...	...	...	—	—	—	—	—
01-02—Springfield	AHL	66	18	25	43	214	-4	7	1	—	—	—	—	—
02-03—Springfield	AHL	27	15	10	25	50	-1	9	1	—	—	—	—	—
—Phoenix	NHL	30	10	8	18	30	1	4	0	—	—	—	—	—
—Pittsburgh	NHL	3	0	0	0	2	-5	0	0	—	—	—	—	—
03-04—Pittsburgh	NHL	16	3	2	5	27	-5	2	0	—	—	—	—	—
04-05—Wilkes-Barre/Scranton	AHL	78	26	29	55	119	1	10	0	7	0	2	2	18
NHL Totals (2 years)		49	13	10	23	59	-9	6	0					

ADAMS, CRAIG — RW — HURRICANES

PERSONAL: Born April 26, 1977, in Seria, Brunei. ... 6-0/200. ... Shoots right.
TRANSACTIONS/CAREER NOTES: Selected by Hartford Whalers in the ninth round (ninth Whalers pick, 223 overall) in the 1996 draft (June 22, 1996). ... Whalers franchise moved to North Carolina and renamed Carolina Hurricanes for 1997-98 season; NHL approved move on June 25, 1997. ... Bruised chest (November 30, 2000); missed four games. ... Suspended 10 games for leaving bench to fight (February 13, 2002).

		REGULAR SEASON								PLAYOFFS				
Season Team	League	GP	G	A	Pts.	PIM	+/-	PP	SH	GP	G	A	Pts.	PIM
95-96—Harvard	ECAC	34	8	9	17	56	...	...	...	—	—	—	—	—
96-97—Harvard	ECAC	32	6	4	10	36	...	0	0	—	—	—	—	—
97-98—Harvard	ECAC	23	6	6	12	12	...	...	...	—	—	—	—	—
98-99—Harvard	ECAC	31	9	14	23	53	...	...	...	—	—	—	—	—
99-00—Cincinnati	IHL	73	12	12	24	124	...	...	...	8	0	1	1	14
00-01—Carolina	NHL	44	1	0	1	20	-7	0	0	3	0	0	0	0
—Cincinnati	IHL	4	0	1	1	9	...	...	...	1	0	0	0	2
01-02—Carolina	NHL	33	0	1	1	38	2	0	0	1	0	0	0	0
—Lowell	AHL	22	5	4	9	51	2	0	1	—	—	—	—	—
02-03—Carolina	NHL	81	6	12	18	71	-11	1	0	—	—	—	—	—
03-04—Carolina	NHL	80	7	10	17	69	-5	0	1	—	—	—	—	—
04-05—Milano	Italy	30	15	14	29	82	...	...	...	—	—	—	—	—
NHL Totals (4 years)		238	14	23	37	198	-21	1	1	4	0	0	0	0

ADAMS, KEVYN — C — HURRICANES

PERSONAL: Born October 8, 1974, in Washington, D.C. ... 6-2/195. ... Shoots right.
TRANSACTIONS/CAREER NOTES: Selected by Boston Bruins in first round (first Bruins pick, 25th overall) of NHL draft (June 26, 1993). ... Signed as free agent by Toronto Maple Leafs (August 1, 1997). ... Selected by Columbus Blue Jackets in expansion draft (June 23, 2000). ... Strained gluteal muscle (December 13, 2000); missed two games. ... Traded by Blue Jackets with fourth-round pick (RW Michael Woodford) in 2001 draft to Florida Panthers for LW Ray Whitney and future considerations (March 13, 2001). ... Traded by Panthers with D Bret Hedican, D Tomas Malec and future considerations to Carolina Hurricanes for D Sandis Ozolinsh and C Byron Ritchie (January 16, 2002). ... Infected knee (January 21, 2004); missed one game. ... Injured left knee (January 30, 2004); missed eight games.

		REGULAR SEASON								PLAYOFFS				
Season Team	League	GP	G	A	Pts.	PIM	+/-	PP	SH	GP	G	A	Pts.	PIM
90-91—Niagara	NAJHL	55	17	20	37	24	...	...	...	—	—	—	—	—
91-92—Niagara	NAJHL	40	25	33	58	51	...	...	...	—	—	—	—	—
92-93—Miami (Ohio)	CCHA	41	17	16	33	18	...	2	0	—	—	—	—	—
93-94—Miami (Ohio)	CCHA	36	15	28	43	24	9	3	2	—	—	—	—	—
94-95—Miami (Ohio)	CCHA	38	20	29	49	30	5	5	1	—	—	—	—	—
95-96—Miami (Ohio)	CCHA	36	17	30	47	30	...	...	...	—	—	—	—	—
96-97—Grand Rapids	IHL	82	22	25	47	47	...	...	...	5	1	1	2	4

Season Team	League	REGULAR SEASON GP	G	A	Pts.	PIM	+/-	PP	SH	PLAYOFFS GP	G	A	Pts.	PIM
97-98—Toronto	NHL	5	0	0	0	7	0	0	0	—	—	—	—	—
—St. John's	AHL	58	17	21	38	99	-5	3	2	4	0	0	0	4
98-99—St. John's	AHL	80	15	35	50	85	-2	1	1	5	2	0	2	4
—Toronto	NHL	1	0	0	0	0	0	0	0	7	0	2	2	14
99-00—St. John's	AHL	23	6	11	17	24	...	...	...	—	—	—	—	—
—Toronto	NHL	52	5	8	13	39	-7	0	0	12	1	0	1	7
00-01—Columbus	NHL	66	8	12	20	52	-4	0	0	—	—	—	—	—
—Florida	NHL	12	3	6	9	2	7	0	0	—	—	—	—	—
01-02—Florida	NHL	44	4	8	12	28	-3	0	0	—	—	—	—	—
—Carolina	NHL	33	2	3	5	15	-2	0	0	23	1	0	1	4
02-03—Carolina	NHL	77	9	9	18	57	-8	0	0	—	—	—	—	—
03-04—Carolina	NHL	73	10	12	22	43	6	0	5	—	—	—	—	—
04-05—DEG Metro Stars	Germany	9	1	2	3	4	0	0	0	—	—	—	—	—
NHL Totals (7 years)		363	41	58	99	243	-11	0	5	42	2	2	4	25

AEBISCHER, DAVID G AVALANCHE

PERSONAL: Born February 7, 1978, in Fribourg, Switzerland. ... 6-1/190. ... Catches left. ... Name pronounced EH-bih-shuhr.
TRANSACTIONS/CAREER NOTES: Selected by Colorado Avalanche in sixth round (seventh Avalanche pick, 161st overall) of NHL draft (June 21, 1997). ... Pharyngitas (November 25, 2000); missed one game.

Season Team	League	REGULAR SEASON GP	Min.	W	L	T	GA	SO	GAA	SV%	PLAYOFFS GP	Min.	W	L	GA	SO	GAA	SV%
96-97—Fribourg-Gotteron	Switzerland	10	577	...	...	...	34	...	3.54	...	3	184	1	2	13	0	4.24	...
97-98—Fribourg-Gotteron	Switzerland	1	60	...	...	...	1	0	1.00	...	4	240	...	...	17	...	4.25	...
—Hershey	AHL	2	80	0	0	1	5	0	3.75	.853	—	—	—	—	—	—	—	—
—Chesapeake	ECHL	17	930	5	7	2	52	0	3.35	...	—	—	—	—	—	—	—	—
—Wheeling	ECHL	10	564	5	3	1	30	1	3.19	...	—	—	—	—	—	—	—	—
98-99—Hershey	AHL	38	1932	17	10	5	79	2	2.45	.920	3	152	1	2	6	0	2.37	.925
99-00—Hershey	AHL	58	3259	29	23	2	*180	1	3.31	...	14	788	7	6	40	2	3.05	...
00-01—Colorado	NHL	26	1393	12	7	3	52	3	2.24	.903	1	1	0	0	0	0	0.00	...
01-02—Colorado	NHL	21	1184	13	6	0	37	2	1.88	.931	1	34	0	0	1	0	1.76	.929
—Swiss Olympic team	Int'l	2	81	0	1	1	6	0	4.44	.806	—	—	—	—	—	—	—	—
02-03—Colorado	NHL	22	1235	7	12	0	50	1	2.43	.916	—	—	—	—	—	—	—	—
03-04—Colorado	NHL	62	3703	32	19	9	129	4	2.09	.924	11	662	6	5	23	1	2.08	.922
04-05—Lugano	Switzerland	18	1019	12	2	3	41	0	2.41	...	4	...	1	3	8	0	2.02	...
NHL Totals (4 years)		131	7515	64	44	12	268	10	2.14	.921	13	697	6	5	24	1	2.07	.922

AFANASENKOV, DIMITRY LW LIGHTNING

PERSONAL: Born May 12, 1980, in Arkhangelsk, U.S.S.R. ... 6-1/195. ... Shoots right. ... Name pronounced ah-fahn-ah-SEHN-kov.
TRANSACTIONS/CAREER NOTES: Selected by Tampa Bay Lightning in third round (3rd Lightning pick, 72nd overall) of draft (June 27, 1998).

Season Team	League	REGULAR SEASON GP	G	A	Pts.	PIM	+/-	PP	SH	PLAYOFFS GP	G	A	Pts.	PIM
95-96—Torpedo Yaroslavl	CIS Div. II	25	10	5	15	10	...	...	...	—	—	—	—	—
—Torpedo Yaroslavl	CIS Jr.	35	28	16	44	8	...	...	...	—	—	—	—	—
96-97—Torpedo Yaroslavl	Rus. Div	45	20	15	35	14	...	...	...	—	—	—	—	—
97-98—Torpedo-Yaroslavl	Russian	45	19	11	30	28	...	...	...	—	—	—	—	—
98-99—Moncton	QMJHL	15	5	5	10	12	...	...	...	—	—	—	—	—
—Sherbrooke	QMJHL	51	23	30	53	22	...	...	...	13	10	6	16	6
99-00—Sherbrooke	QMJHL	60	56	43	99	70	6	18	3	5	3	2	5	4
00-01—Detroit	IHL	65	15	22	37	26	...	...	...	—	—	—	—	—
—Tampa Bay	NHL	9	1	1	2	4	1	0	0	—	—	—	—	—
01-02—Springfield	AHL	28	4	5	9	4	-2	0	0	—	—	—	—	—
—Grand Rapids	AHL	18	1	2	3	2	2	0	0	—	—	—	—	—
—Tampa Bay	NHL	5	0	0	0	0	-1	0	0	—	—	—	—	—
02-03—Springfield	AHL	41	4	9	13	25	...	...	...	—	—	—	—	—
03-04—Tampa Bay	NHL	71	6	10	16	12	-4	0	0	23	1	2	3	6
04-05—Lada Togliatti	Russian	30	2	9	11	12	11	...	...	9	0	0	0	4
NHL Totals (3 years)		85	7	11	18	16	-4	0	0	23	1	2	3	6

AFINOGENOV, MAXIM RW SABRES

PERSONAL: Born September 4, 1979, in Moscow, U.S.S.R. ... 6-0/190. ... Shoots left. ... Name pronounced ah-FEEN-o-gin-ov.
TRANSACTIONS/CAREER NOTES: Selected by Buffalo Sabres in third round (third Sabres pick, 69th overall) of NHL draft (June 21, 1997). ... Flu (January 10, 2002); missed one game. ... Had concussion (September 5, 2002); missed first 46 games of season.
STATISTICAL PLATEAUS: Three-goal games: 2003-04 (1).

Season Team	League	REGULAR SEASON GP	G	A	Pts.	PIM	+/-	PP	SH	PLAYOFFS GP	G	A	Pts.	PIM
95-96—Dynamo Moscow	CIS	1	0	0	0	0	...	...	...	—	—	—	—	—
96-97—Dynamo Moscow	Russian	29	6	5	11	10	...	...	...	4	0	2	2	0
—Dynamo Moscow	Rus. Div.	14	9	2	11	10	...	...	...	—	—	—	—	—
97-98—Dynamo Moscow	Russian	35	10	5	15	53	...	...	...	—	—	—	—	—
98-99—Dynamo Moscow	Russian	38	8	13	21	24	15	...	...	16	*10	6	16	14
99-00—Rochester	AHL	15	6	12	18	8	...	...	...	8	3	1	4	4

Season Team	League	GP	G	A	Pts.	PIM	+/-	PP	SH		GP	G	A	Pts.	PIM
		REGULAR SEASON									PLAYOFFS				
—Buffalo	NHL	65	16	18	34	41	-4	2	0		5	0	1	1	2
00-01—Buffalo	NHL	78	14	22	36	40	1	3	0		11	2	3	5	4
01-02—Buffalo	NHL	81	21	19	40	69	-9	3	1		—	—	—	—	—
—Russian Oly. team	Int'l	6	2	2	4	4	...	...	...		—	—	—	—	—
02-03—Buffalo	NHL	35	5	6	11	21	-12	2	0		—	—	—	—	—
03-04—Buffalo	NHL	73	17	14	31	57	-4	3	0		—	—	—	—	—
04-05—Dynamo Moscow	Russian	36	13	14	27	91	7	...	...		10	4	4	8	8
NHL Totals (5 years)		332	73	79	152	228	-28	13	1		16	2	4	6	6

AHONEN, ARI — G — DEVILS

PERSONAL: Born February 6, 1981, in Jyvaskyla, Finland. ... 6-1/195. ... Catches left. ... Name pronounced AH-ree ah-HON-nuhn.

TRANSACTIONS/CAREER NOTES: Selected by New Jersey Devils in first round (first Devils pick, 27th overall) of NHL entry draft (June 26, 1999).

Season Team	League	GP	Min.	W	L	T	GA	SO	GAA	SV%		GP	Min.	W	L	GA	SO	GAA	SV%
		REGULAR SEASON										PLAYOFFS							
97-98—JyP HT Jyvaskyla	Finland Jr.	31	1853	...	...	...	64	...	2.07	...		—	—	—	—	—	—	—	—
98-99—JyP HT Jyvaskyla	Finland Jr.	24	1447	...	...	...	70	0	2.90	...		—	—	—	—	—	—	—	—
99-00—HIFK Helsinki	Finland	24	1347	11	7	1	70	1	3.12	...		2	119	0	2	7	0	3.53	...
—HIFK Helsinki	Finland Jr.	11	658	...	...	...	22	...	2.01	...		—	—	—	—	—	—	—	—
00-01—HIFK Helsinki	Finland Jr.	37	2101	18	13	4	97	2	2.77	...		5	395	2	3	9	1	1.37	...
01-02—Albany	AHL	36	2106	6	22	6	106	0	3.02	.906		—	—	—	—	—	—	—	—
02-03—Albany	AHL	38	2171	13	20	3	110	1	3.04	.898		—	—	—	—	—	—	—	—
03-04—Albany	AHL	50	3011	13	30	6	150	2	2.99	.891		—	—	—	—	—	—	—	—
04-05—Albany	AHL	38	2195	16	20	...	114	4	3.12	.910		—	—	—	—	—	—	—	—

AITKEN, JOHNATHAN — D — CANADIENS

PERSONAL: Born May 24, 1978, in Edmonton. ... 6-4/211. ... Shoots left. ... Name pronounced ATE-kin.

TRANSACTIONS/CAREER NOTES: Selected by Boston Bruins in first round (first Bruins pick, eighth overall) of NHL draft (June 22, 1996). ... Signed as free agent by Chicago Blackhawks (May 22, 2002). ... Signed as free agent by Vancouver Canucks (July 7, 2004).

Season Team	League	GP	G	A	Pts.	PIM	+/-	PP	SH		GP	G	A	Pts.	PIM
		REGULAR SEASON									PLAYOFFS				
94-95—Medicine Hat	WHL	53	0	5	5	71	...	...	...		—	—	—	—	—
95-96—Medicine Hat	WHL	71	6	14	20	131	...	...	...		5	1	0	1	6
96-97—Brandon	WHL	65	4	18	22	211	16	1	0		6	0	0	0	4
97-98—Brandon	WHL	69	9	25	34	183	25	6	1		18	0	8	8	67
98-99—Providence	AHL	65	2	9	11	92	-5	0	0		13	0	0	0	17
99-00—Providence	AHL	70	2	12	14	121	...	...	...		11	1	0	1	26
—Boston	NHL	3	0	0	0	0	-3	0	0		—	—	—	—	—
00-01—Sparta Praha	Czech Rep.	24	0	3	3	62	...	...	...		—	—	—	—	—
01-02—Jackson	ECHL	43	1	9	10	141	-1	0	0		—	—	—	—	—
—Norfolk	AHL	28	0	1	1	43	-2	0	0		4	0	0	0	2
02-03—Norfolk	AHL	80	1	7	8	207	-6	0	0		9	2	1	3	18
03-04—Norfolk	AHL	40	1	4	5	97	-11	0	0		8	1	4	5	27
—Chicago	NHL	41	0	1	1	70	-9	0	0		—	—	—	—	—
04-05—Manitoba	AHL	46	1	6	7	101	4	0	0		1	0	0	0	7
NHL Totals (2 years)		44	0	1	1	70	-12	0	0						

ALDRIDGE, KEITH — D/RW — ISLANDERS

PERSONAL: Born July 20, 1973, in Detroit. ... 5-11/185. ... Shoots right.

TRANSACTIONS/CAREER NOTES: Signed as free agent by Dallas Stars (September 1, 1999). ... Signed as free agent by New York Islanders (August 12, 2004).

Season Team	League	GP	G	A	Pts.	PIM	+/-	PP	SH		GP	G	A	Pts.	PIM
		REGULAR SEASON									PLAYOFFS				
92-93—Lake Superior St.	CCHA	37	3	11	14	30	...	...	...		—	—	—	—	—
93-94—Lake Superior St.	CCHA	45	10	24	34	86	...	...	...		—	—	—	—	—
94-95—Lake Superior St.	CCHA	40	10	31	41	89	...	...	...		—	—	—	—	—
95-96—Lake Superior St.	CCHA	38	14	36	50	88	...	...	...		—	—	—	—	—
—Baltimore	AHL	7	0	2	2	2	...	...	...		—	—	—	—	—
96-97—Baltimore	AHL	51	4	9	13	92	...	...	...		3	0	0	0	4
97-98—Detroit	IHL	79	13	21	34	89	...	...	...		23	1	9	10	67
98-99—Detroit	IHL	66	15	28	43	130	...	...	...		11	2	7	9	49
99-00—Michigan	IHL	55	2	10	12	55	...	...	...		—	—	—	—	—
—Dallas	NHL	4	0	0	0	0	1	0	0		—	—	—	—	—
00-01—Grand Rapids	IHL	36	3	8	11	99	...	...	...		10	0	2	2	8
01-02—Eisbaren Berlin	Germany	48	7	15	22	159	...	...	...		4	0	2	2	4
02-03—Eisbaren Berlin	Germany	50	12	23	35	99	...	...	...		9	0	2	2	22
03-04—Eisbaren Berlin	Germany	48	8	13	21	84	...	...	...		11	1	7	8	20
04-05—Bridgeport	AHL	32	1	9	10	35	6	1	0		—	—	—	—	—
NHL Totals (1 year)		4	0	0	0	0	1	0	0						

ALEN, JUHA — D — MIGHTY DUCKS

PERSONAL: Born October 25, 1981, in Tampere, Finland. ... 6-3/210. ... Shoots left.
TRANSACTIONS/CAREER NOTES: Selected by Anaheim Mighty Ducks in third round (fourth Mighty Ducks pick, 90th overall) in entry draft (June 20, 2003).

		REGULAR SEASON								PLAYOFFS				
Season Team	League	GP	G	A	Pts.	PIM	+/-	PP	SH	GP	G	A	Pts.	PIM
02-03—N. Michigan Univ.	WCHA	40	4	19	23	64	7	...	...	—	—	—	—	—
03-04—Cincinnati	AHL	59	2	3	5	64	-7	...	...	—	—	—	—	—
04-05—Cincinnati	AHL	0	0	0	0	0	0	0	0	—	—	—	—	—

ALEXEEV, NIKITA — RW/LW — LIGHTNING

PERSONAL: Born December 27, 1981, in Murmansk, U.S.S.R. ... 6-5/225. ... Shoots left. ... Name pronounced uh-LEX-ee-ehv.
TRANSACTIONS/CAREER NOTES: Selected by Tampa Bay Lightning in first round (first Lightning pick, eighth overall) of NHL entry draft (June 24, 2000). ... Injured left shoulder and had surgery (November 4, 2003); missed remainder of regular season. ... Signed as free agent by Springfield of the AHL (September 27, 2004).

		REGULAR SEASON								PLAYOFFS				
Season Team	League	GP	G	A	Pts.	PIM	+/-	PP	SH	GP	G	A	Pts.	PIM
97-98—Krylja Sov. Moscow	Rus. Div.	61	11	4	15	36	...	...	...	—	—	—	—	—
98-99—Erie	OHL	61	17	18	35	15	...	...	...	5	1	1	2	4
99-00—Erie	OHL	64	24	29	53	42	...	...	...	13	4	3	7	6
00-01—Erie	OHL	64	31	41	72	45	37	7	1	12	7	7	14	12
01-02—Tampa Bay	NHL	44	4	4	8	8	-9	1	0	—	—	—	—	—
—Springfield	AHL	35	5	9	14	16	-8	0	0	—	—	—	—	—
02-03—Springfield	AHL	36	7	5	12	8	-10	4	0	—	—	—	—	—
—Tampa Bay	NHL	37	4	2	6	8	-6	1	0	11	1	0	1	0
03-04—Hershey	AHL	14	0	1	1	8	-1	0	0	—	—	—	—	—
04-05—Springfield	AHL	72	13	9	22	16	-9	2	0	—	—	—	—	—
NHL Totals (2 years)		81	8	6	14	16	-15	2	0	11	1	0	1	0

ALFREDSSON, DANIEL — RW — SENATORS

PERSONAL: Born December 11, 1972, in Gothenburg, Sweden. ... 5-11/202. ... Shoots right.
TRANSACTIONS/CAREER NOTES: Selected by Ottawa Senators in sixth round (fifth Senators pick, 133rd overall) of NHL draft (June 29, 1994). ... Strained abdominal muscle (January 29, 1997); missed six games. ... Injured right ankle (November 3, 1997); missed eight games. ... Fractured right leg (December 11, 1997); missed 13 games. ... Tore left knee ligament (September 16, 1998); missed first nine games of season. ... Injured right eye (November 12, 1998); missed four games. ... Flu (December 30, 1998); missed one game. ... Sprained left knee (January 26, 1999); missed five games. ... Strained abdominal muscle (March 17, 1999); missed five games. ... Tore right knee ligament (October 21, 1999); missed 20 games. ... Sprained left knee (February 15, 2000); missed three games. ... Bruised left foot (March 31, 2000); missed one game. ... Strained hip flexor (October 19, 2001); missed 13 games. ... Injured right wrist (April 6, 2001); missed final game of regular season. ... Injured hip (December 8, 2001); missed four games. ... Strained lower back (December 4, 2002); missed three games. ... Injured hip flexor (March 21, 2003); missed one game. ... Sprained right knee (November 21, 2003); missed one game. ... Flu (January 15, 2004); missed one game. ... Bruised thigh (March 15, 2004); missed three games.
STATISTICAL PLATEAUS: Three-goal games: 1995-96 (1), 2000-01 (1), 2001-02 (2). Total: 4.

		REGULAR SEASON								PLAYOFFS				
Season Team	League	GP	G	A	Pts.	PIM	+/-	PP	SH	GP	G	A	Pts.	PIM
91-92—Molndal	Sweden Dv. 2	32	12	8	20	43	...	...	...	—	—	—	—	—
92-93—Vastra Frolunda	Sweden	20	1	5	6	8	...	...	...	—	—	—	—	—
93-94—Vastra Frolunda	Sweden	39	20	10	30	18	...	...	...	4	1	1	2	...
94-95—Vastra Frolunda	Sweden	22	7	11	18	22	...	...	...	—	—	—	—	—
95-96—Ottawa	NHL	82	26	35	61	28	-18	8	2	—	—	—	—	—
96-97—Ottawa	NHL	76	24	47	71	30	5	11	1	7	5	2	7	6
97-98—Ottawa	NHL	55	17	28	45	18	7	7	0	11	7	2	9	20
—Swedish Oly. team	Int'l	4	2	3	5	2	3	1	0	—	—	—	—	—
98-99—Ottawa	NHL	58	11	22	33	14	8	3	0	4	1	2	3	4
99-00—Ottawa	NHL	57	21	38	59	28	11	4	2	6	1	3	4	2
00-01—Ottawa	NHL	68	24	46	70	30	11	10	0	4	1	0	1	2
01-02—Ottawa	NHL	78	37	34	71	45	3	9	1	12	7	6	13	4
—Swedish Oly. team	Int'l	4	1	4	5	2	...	...	...	—	—	—	—	—
02-03—Ottawa	NHL	78	27	51	78	42	15	9	0	18	4	4	8	12
03-04—Ottawa	NHL	77	32	48	80	24	12	9	0	7	1	2	3	2
04-05—Vastra Frolunda	Sweden	15	8	9	17	10	9	1	0	14	12	6	18	8
NHL Totals (9 years)		629	219	349	568	259	54	70	6	69	27	21	48	52

ALLEN, BOBBY — D — DEVILS

PERSONAL: Born November 14, 1978, in Braintree, Mass. ... 6-1/205. ... Shoots left.
TRANSACTIONS/CAREER NOTES: Selected by Boston Bruins in second round (second Bruins pick, 52nd overall) of NHL draft (June 27, 1998). ... Traded by Bruins to Edmonton Oilers for D Sean Brown (March 19, 2002). ... Signed as free agent by New Jersey Devils (August 17, 2004).

		REGULAR SEASON								PLAYOFFS				
Season Team	League	GP	G	A	Pts.	PIM	+/-	PP	SH	GP	G	A	Pts.	PIM
96-97—Cushing Academy	Mass. H.S.	36	11	33	44	28	...	...	...	—	—	—	—	—
97-98—Boston College	Hockey East	37	7	19	26	34	...	...	...	—	—	—	—	—
98-99—Boston College	Hockey East	43	9	23	32	34	...	...	...	—	—	—	—	—

Season Team	League	REGULAR SEASON								PLAYOFFS				
		GP	G	A	Pts.	PIM	+/-	PP	SH	GP	G	A	Pts.	PIM
99-00—Boston College	Hockey East	42	4	23	27	40	...	...	...	—	—	—	—	—
00-01—Boston College	Hockey East	42	5	18	23	30	...	...	...	—	—	—	—	—
01-02—Providence	AHL	49	5	10	15	18	-12	4	0	—	—	—	—	—
—Hamilton	AHL	10	1	6	7	0	6	0	0	14	0	3	3	6
02-03—Hamilton	AHL	56	1	12	13	24	14	1	0	23	0	5	5	10
—Edmonton	NHL	1	0	0	0	0	0	0	0	—	—	—	—	—
03-04—Toronto	AHL	56	5	10	15	18	-2	...	...	3	0	2	2	4
04-05—Albany	AHL	66	5	11	16	20	-1	3	0	—	—	—	—	—
NHL Totals (1 year)		1	0	0	0	0	0	0	0					

ALLEN, BRYAN — D — CANUCKS

PERSONAL: Born August 21, 1980, in Kingston, Ont. ... 6-4/220. ... Shoots left.

TRANSACTIONS/CAREER NOTES: Selected by Vancouver Canucks in first round (first Canucks pick, fourth overall) of NHL entry draft (June 27, 1998). ... Injured knee (September 15, 1999); missed first 57 games of season. ... Suspended two games by NHL in slashing incident (November 5, 2003). ... Injured shoulder (March 27, 2004); missed final four games of regular season and three playoff games.

Season Team	League	REGULAR SEASON								PLAYOFFS				
		GP	G	A	Pts.	PIM	+/-	PP	SH	GP	G	A	Pts.	PIM
95-96—Ernestown	Jr. C	36	1	16	17	71	...	...	...	—	—	—	—	—
96-97—Oshawa	OHL	60	2	4	6	76	...	...	...	18	1	3	4	26
97-98—Oshawa	OHL	48	6	13	19	126	11	...	...	5	0	5	5	18
98-99—Oshawa	OHL	37	7	15	22	77	14	...	...	17	0	3	3	30
99-00—Oshawa	OHL	3	0	2	2	12	1	0	0	3	0	0	0	13
—Syracuse	AHL	9	1	1	2	11	...	...	...	2	0	0	0	2
00-01—Kansas City	IHL	75	5	20	25	99	...	...	...	—	—	—	—	—
—Vancouver	NHL	6	0	0	0	0	0	0	0	2	0	0	0	2
01-02—Vancouver	NHL	11	0	0	0	6	1	0	0	—	—	—	—	—
—Manitoba	AHL	68	7	18	25	121	1	2	0	5	0	1	1	8
02-03—Manitoba	AHL	7	0	1	1	4	3	0	0	—	—	—	—	—
—Vancouver	NHL	48	5	3	8	73	8	0	0	1	0	0	0	2
03-04—Vancouver	NHL	74	2	5	7	94	-10	0	0	4	0	0	0	2
04-05—Khimik Voskresensk	Russian	19	0	3	3	34	0	...	...	—	—	—	—	—
NHL Totals (4 years)		139	7	8	15	173	-1	0	0	7	0	0	0	6

ALLISON, JAMIE — D/LW — PREDATORS

PERSONAL: Born May 13, 1975, in Lindsay, Ont. ... 6-1/203. ... Shoots left.

TRANSACTIONS/CAREER NOTES: Selected by Calgary Flames in second round (second Flames pick, 44th overall) of NHL entry draft (June 26, 1993). ... Suffered concussion (December 20, 1996); missed three games. ... Fractured thumb (January 9, 1998); missed 11 games. ... Suffered concussion (March 28, 1998); missed 10 games. ... Traded by Flames with C/LW Marty McInnis and RW Erik Andersson to Chicago Blackhawks for C Jeff Shantz and C/LW Steve Dubinsky (October 27, 1998). ... Sprained wrist (November 17, 1998); missed 23 games. ... Strained groin (March 31, 1999); missed three games. ... Strained groin (December 26, 1999); missed four games. ... Injured rib cage muscle (February 23, 2000); missed eight games. ... Had stiff neck (March 26, 2000); missed one game. ... Bruised foot (December 21, 2000); missed one game. ... Sprained knee (February 10, 2001); missed 13 games. ... Claimed by Flames from Blackhawks in NHL waiver draft (September 28, 2001). ... Injured groin (November 3, 2001); missed three games. ... Traded by Flames to Columbus Blue Jackets for RW Blake Sloan (March 19, 2002). ... Strained back (March 25, 2002); missed one game. ... Injured neck (November 20, 2002); missed four games. ... Sprained hand (November 30, 2002); missed 14 games. ... Injured groin (March 13, 2003); missed two games. ... Signed as free agent by the Nashville Predators (September 10, 2003). ... Injured rib (October 9, 2003); missed seven games. ... Sprained thumb (November 8, 2003); missed one game. ... Injured groin (December 13, 2003); missed eight games. ... Suffered concussion (January 7, 2004); missed five games. ... Suspended one game by NHL for unsportsmanlike conduct (January 30, 2004).

Season Team	League	REGULAR SEASON								PLAYOFFS				
		GP	G	A	Pts.	PIM	+/-	PP	SH	GP	G	A	Pts.	PIM
90-91—Waterloo Jr. B	OHA	45	3	8	11	91	...	...	...	—	—	—	—	—
91-92—Windsor	OHL	59	4	8	12	52	...	...	...	4	1	1	2	2
92-93—Det. Jr. Red Wings	OHL	61	0	13	13	64	...	...	...	15	2	5	7	23
93-94—Det. Jr. Red Wings	OHL	40	2	22	24	69	...	0	0	17	2	9	11	35
94-95—Det. Jr. Red Wings	OHL	50	1	14	15	119	...	0	0	18	2	7	9	35
—Calgary	NHL	1	0	0	0	0	0	0	0	—	—	—	—	—
95-96—Saint John	AHL	71	3	16	19	223	...	...	...	14	0	2	2	16
96-97—Saint John	AHL	46	3	6	9	139	-10	1	0	5	0	1	1	4
—Calgary	NHL	20	0	0	0	35	-4	0	0	—	—	—	—	—
97-98—Saint John	AHL	16	0	5	5	49	3	0	0	—	—	—	—	—
—Calgary	NHL	43	3	8	11	104	3	0	0	—	—	—	—	—
98-99—Saint John	AHL	5	0	0	0	23	-1	0	0	—	—	—	—	—
—Chicago	NHL	39	2	2	4	62	0	0	0	—	—	—	—	—
—Indianapolis	IHL	3	1	0	1	10	1	0	0	—	—	—	—	—
99-00—Chicago	NHL	59	1	3	4	102	-5	0	0	—	—	—	—	—
00-01—Chicago	NHL	44	1	3	4	53	7	0	0	—	—	—	—	—
01-02—Calgary	NHL	37	0	2	2	24	-3	0	0	—	—	—	—	—
—Columbus	NHL	7	0	0	0	28	-4	0	0	—	—	—	—	—
02-03—Columbus	NHL	48	0	1	1	99	-15	0	0	—	—	—	—	—
03-04—Nashville	NHL	47	0	3	3	76	-7	0	0	—	—	—	—	—
NHL Totals (9 years)		345	7	22	29	583	-28	0	0					

ALLISON, JASON — C — MAPLE LEAFS

PERSONAL: Born May 29, 1975, in North York, Ont. ... 6-3/215. ... Shoots right.

TRANSACTIONS/CAREER NOTES: Selected by Washington Capitals in first round (second Capitals pick, 17th overall) of NHL draft (June 26, 1993). ... Injured ankle (February 15, 1997); missed one game. ... Traded by Capitals with G Jim Carey, C Anson Carter and 3rd-round pick (RW Lee Goren) in 1997 draft to Boston Bruins for C Adam Oates, RW Rick Tocchet and G Bill Ranford (March 1, 1997). ... Injured hip (March 1, 1998); missed one game. ... Injured wrist (October 30, 1999); missed two games. ... Injured wrist (December 23, 1999); missed three games. ... Injured ligaments in left thumb (January 8, 2000) and had surgery; missed 15 games. ... Injured wrist (February 12, 2000) and had surgery; missed final 25 games of season. ... Missed first nine games of 2001-02 season in contract dispute. ... Traded by Bruins with C/LW Mikko Eloranta to Los Angeles Kings for C Jozef Stumpel and RW Glen Murray (October 24, 2001). ... Sprained knee (October 29, 2002); missed 15 games. ... Reinjured knee (December 22, 2002); missed eight games. ... Injured hip, suffered concussion (January 25, 2003); missed 33 games. ... Missed 2003-04 season with postconcussion syndrome. ... Signed as free agent by Toronto Maple Leafs (Aug. 5, 2005).

STATISTICAL PLATEAUS: Three-goal games: 1997-98 (2), 1998-99 (1), 2000-01 (1). Total: 4.

		REGULAR SEASON								PLAYOFFS				
Season Team	**League**	**GP**	**G**	**A**	**Pts.**	**PIM**	**+/-**	**PP**	**SH**	**GP**	**G**	**A**	**Pts.**	**PIM**
91-92—London	OHL	65	11	18	29	15	...	...	...	7	0	0	0	0
92-93—London	OHL	66	42	76	118	50	...	...	...	12	7	13	20	8
93-94—London	OHL	56	55	87	*142	68	...	21	6	5	2	13	15	13
—Washington	NHL	2	0	1	1	0	1	0	0	—	—	—	—	—
—Portland	AHL	6	2	1	3	0	...	...	...	—	—	—	—	—
94-95—London	OHL	15	15	21	36	43	...	3	1	—	—	—	—	—
—Washington	NHL	12	2	1	3	6	-3	2	0	—	—	—	—	—
—Portland	AHL	8	5	4	9	2	-1	1	1	7	3	8	11	2
95-96—Washington	NHL	19	0	3	3	2	-3	0	0	—	—	—	—	—
—Portland	AHL	57	28	41	69	42	...	...	...	6	1	6	7	9
96-97—Washington	NHL	53	5	17	22	25	-3	1	0	—	—	—	—	—
—Boston	NHL	19	3	9	12	9	-3	1	0	—	—	—	—	—
97-98—Boston	NHL	81	33	50	83	60	33	5	0	6	2	6	8	4
98-99—Boston	NHL	82	23	53	76	68	5	5	1	12	2	9	11	6
99-00—Boston	NHL	37	10	18	28	20	5	3	0	—	—	—	—	—
00-01—Boston	NHL	82	36	59	95	85	-8	11	3	—	—	—	—	—
01-02—Los Angeles	NHL	73	19	55	74	68	2	5	0	7	3	3	6	4
02-03—Los Angeles	NHL	26	6	22	28	22	9	2	0	—	—	—	—	—
03-04—Los Angeles	NHL	Did not play — injured												
NHL Totals (11 years)		486	137	288	425	365	35	35	4	25	7	18	25	14

AMONTE, TONY — RW — FLAMES

PERSONAL: Born August 2, 1970, in Hingham, Mass. ... 6-0/200. ... Shoots left. ... Name pronounced ah-MAHN-tee.

TRANSACTIONS/CAREER NOTES: Selected by New York Rangers in 4th round (3rd Rangers pick, 68th overall) of NHL draft (June 11, 1988). ... Traded by Rangers with rights to LW Matt Oates to Chicago Blackhawks for LW Stephane Matteau and RW Brian Noonan (March 21, 1994). ... Injured groin (1993-94 season); missed three games. ... Signed as free agent by Phoenix Coyotes (July 12, 2002). ... Bruised ribs (January 11, 2003); missed eight games. ... Contract bought out by Flyers (July 23, 2005). ... Signed as free agent by Calgary Flames (Aug. 2, 2005).

STATISTICAL PLATEAUS: Three-goal games: 1991-92 (1), 1995-96 (1), 1996-97 (2), 1998-99 (2), 1999-00 (1). Total: 7.

		REGULAR SEASON								PLAYOFFS				
Season Team	**League**	**GP**	**G**	**A**	**Pts.**	**PIM**	**+/-**	**PP**	**SH**	**GP**	**G**	**A**	**Pts.**	**PIM**
86-87—Thayer Academy	Mass. H.S.	25	25	32	57	...	...	...	...	—	—	—	—	—
87-88—Thayer Academy	Mass. H.S.	28	30	38	68	...	...	...	...	—	—	—	—	—
88-89—Thayer Academy	Mass. H.S.	25	35	38	73	...	...	...	...	—	—	—	—	—
—Team USA Juniors	Int'l	7	1	3	4	...	...	...	...	—	—	—	—	—
89-90—Boston University	Hockey East	41	25	33	58	52	...	...	...	—	—	—	—	—
90-91—Boston University	Hockey East	38	31	37	68	82	...	...	...	—	—	—	—	—
—New York Rangers	NHL	...	...	...	...	...	...	...	...	2	0	2	2	2
91-92—New York Rangers	NHL	79	35	34	69	55	12	9	0	13	3	6	9	2
92-93—New York Rangers	NHL	83	33	43	76	49	0	13	0	—	—	—	—	—
93-94—New York Rangers	NHL	72	16	22	38	31	5	3	0	—	—	—	—	—
—Chicago	NHL	7	1	3	4	6	-5	1	0	6	4	2	6	4
94-95—Fassa	Italy	14	22	16	38	10	...	...	...	—	—	—	—	—
—Chicago	NHL	48	15	20	35	41	7	6	1	16	3	3	6	10
95-96—Chicago	NHL	81	31	32	63	62	10	5	4	7	2	4	6	6
96-97—Chicago	NHL	81	41	36	77	64	35	9	2	6	4	2	6	8
97-98—Chicago	NHL	82	31	42	73	66	21	7	3	—	—	—	—	—
—U.S. Olympic team	Int'l	4	0	1	1	4	-4	0	0	—	—	—	—	—
98-99—Chicago	NHL	82	44	31	75	60	0	14	3	—	—	—	—	—
99-00—Chicago	NHL	82	43	41	84	48	10	11	5	—	—	—	—	—
00-01—Chicago	NHL	82	35	29	64	54	-22	9	1	—	—	—	—	—
01-02—Chicago	NHL	82	27	39	66	67	11	6	1	5	0	1	1	4
—U.S. Olympic team	Int'l	6	2	2	4	0	...	...	...	—	—	—	—	—
02-03—Phoenix	NHL	59	13	23	36	26	-12	6	0	—	—	—	—	—
—Philadelphia	NHL	13	7	8	15	2	12	1	1	13	1	6	7	4
03-04—Philadelphia	NHL	80	20	33	53	38	13	4	0	18	3	5	8	6
NHL Totals (14 years)		1013	392	436	828	669	97	104	21	86	20	31	51	46

ANDERSON, CRAIG — G — BLACKHAWKS

PERSONAL: Born May 21, 1981, in Park Ridge, Ill. ... 6-2/174. ... Catches left. ... Also known as Craig Andersson.

TRANSACTIONS/CAREER NOTES: Selected by Calgary Flames in third round (third Flames pick, 77th overall) of NHL entry draft (June 26, 1999). ... Returned to draft pool by Flames and selected by Chicago Blackhawks in third round (fourth Blackhawks pick, 73th overall) of NHL entry draft (June 23, 2001).

Season Team	League	GP	Min.	W	L	T	GA	SO	GAA	SV%	GP	Min.	W	L	GA	SO	GAA	SV%
		REGULAR SEASON									PLAYOFFS							
98-99—Chicago	NAHL	14	821	11	3	0	35	0	2.56	...	—	—	—	—	—	—	—	—
—Guelph	OHL	21	1006	12	5	1	52	1	3.10	...	3	114	0	2	9	0	4.74	...
99-00—Guelph	OHL	38	1955	12	17	2	117	0	3.59	.903	3	110	0	1	5	0	2.73	.900
00-01—Guelph	OHL	59	3555	30	19	*9	156	3	2.63	.918	4	240	0	4	17	0	4.25	...
01-02—Norfolk	AHL	28	1567	9	13	4	77	2	2.95	.871	1	21	0	1	1	0	2.86	.938
02-03—Norfolk	AHL	32	1794	15	11	5	58	4	1.94	.923	5	344	2	3	15	0	2.61	...
—Chicago	NHL	6	270	0	3	2	18	0	4.00	.856	—	—	—	—	—	—	—	—
03-04—Chicago	NHL	21	1205	6	14	0	57	1	2.84	.905	—	—	—	—	—	—	—	—
—Norfolk	AHL	37	2108	17	20	0	74	3	2.11	.905	5	326	2	3	10	0	1.84	.929
04-05—Norfolk	AHL	15	885	9	4	...	27	2	1.83	.929	6	355	2	4	14	0	2.37	.925
NHL Totals (2 years)		27	1475	6	17	2	75	1	3.05	.897								

ANDREYCHUK, DAVE — LW

PERSONAL: Born September 29, 1963, in Hamilton, Ont. ... 6-4/220. ... Shoots right. ... Name pronounced AN-druh-chuhk.

TRANSACTIONS/CAREER NOTES: Selected by Buffalo Sabres in first round (third Sabres pick, 16th overall) of NHL draft (June 9, 1982). ... Sprained knee (March 1983). ... Fractured collarbone (March 1985). ... Twisted knee (September 1985). ... Injured right knee (September 1986). ... Strained left knee ligaments (November 27, 1988). ... Fractured left thumb (February 18, 1990). ... Suspended two off-days and fined $500 by NHL for cross-checking incident (November 16, 1992). ... Traded by Sabres with G Daren Puppa and first-round pick (D Kenny Jonsson) in 1993 entry draft to Toronto Maple Leafs for G Grant Fuhr and fifth-round pick (D Kevin Popp) in 1995 draft (February 2, 1993). ... Injured knee (December 27, 1993); missed one game. ... Separated shoulder (December 2, 1995); missed five games. ... Flu (December 27, 1995); missed one game. ... Thumb surgery (January 15, 1996); missed two games. ... Traded by Maple Leafs to New Jersey Devils for second-round pick (D Marek Posmyk) in 1996 draft and third-round pick (traded back to New Jersey) in 1999 draft (March 13, 1996). ... Bruised left foot (October 23, 1997); missed six games. ... Bruised sternum (November 7, 1998); missed six games. ... Fractured right ankle (January 5, 1999); missed 21 games. ... Signed as free agent by Boston Bruins (July 28, 1999). ... Injured knee (January 11, 2000); missed two games. ... Traded by Bruins with D Ray Bourque to Colorado Avalanche for LW Brian Rolston, D Martin Grenier, C Samuel Pahlsson and first-round pick (LW Martin Samuelsson) in 2000 entry draft (March 6, 2000). ... Signed as free agent by Sabres (July 13, 2000). ... Injured knee (February 13, 2001); missed two games. ... Signed as free agent by Tampa Bay Lightning (July 13, 2001). ... Fractured foot (December 5, 2002); missed nine games.

STATISTICAL PLATEAUS: Three-goal games: 1987-88 (3), 1988-89 (1), 1989-90 (1), 1991-92 (1), 1993-94 (1). Total: 7. ... Four-goal games: 1991-92 (1), 1992-93 (1), 1999-00 (1). Total: 3. ... Five-goal games: 1985-86 (1). ... Total hat tricks: 11.

Season Team	League	GP	G	A	Pts.	PIM	+/-	PP	SH	GP	G	A	Pts.	PIM
		REGULAR SEASON								PLAYOFFS				
80-81—Oshawa	OMJHL	67	22	22	44	80	...	...	...	10	3	2	5	20
81-82—Oshawa	OHL	67	58	43	101	71	...	...	...	3	1	4	5	16
82-83—Oshawa	OHL	14	8	24	32	6	...	...	...	—	—	—	—	—
—Buffalo	NHL	43	14	23	37	16	6	3	0	4	1	0	1	4
83-84—Buffalo	NHL	78	38	42	80	42	20	10	0	2	0	1	1	2
84-85—Buffalo	NHL	64	31	30	61	54	-4	14	0	5	4	2	6	4
85-86—Buffalo	NHL	80	36	51	87	61	3	12	0	—	—	—	—	—
86-87—Buffalo	NHL	77	25	48	73	46	2	13	0	—	—	—	—	—
87-88—Buffalo	NHL	80	30	48	78	112	1	15	0	6	2	4	6	0
88-89—Buffalo	NHL	56	28	24	52	40	0	7	0	5	0	3	3	0
89-90—Buffalo	NHL	73	40	42	82	42	6	18	0	6	2	5	7	2
90-91—Buffalo	NHL	80	36	33	69	32	11	13	0	6	2	2	4	8
91-92—Buffalo	NHL	80	41	50	91	71	-9	*28	0	7	1	3	4	12
92-93—Buffalo	NHL	52	29	32	61	48	-8	20	0	—	—	—	—	—
—Toronto	NHL	31	25	13	38	8	12	12	0	21	12	7	19	35
93-94—Toronto	NHL	83	53	46	99	98	22	21	5	18	5	5	10	16
94-95—Toronto	NHL	48	22	16	38	34	-7	8	0	7	3	2	5	25
95-96—Toronto	NHL	61	20	24	44	54	-11	12	2	—	—	—	—	—
—New Jersey	NHL	15	8	5	13	10	2	2	0	—	—	—	—	—
96-97—New Jersey	NHL	82	27	34	61	48	38	4	1	1	0	0	0	0
97-98—New Jersey	NHL	75	14	34	48	26	19	4	0	6	1	0	1	4
98-99—New Jersey	NHL	52	15	13	28	20	1	4	0	4	2	0	2	4
99-00—Boston	NHL	63	19	14	33	28	-11	7	0	—	—	—	—	—
—Colorado	NHL	14	1	2	3	2	-9	1	0	17	3	2	5	18
00-01—Buffalo	NHL	74	20	13	33	32	0	8	0	13	1	2	3	4
01-02—Tampa Bay	NHL	82	21	17	38	109	-12	9	1	—	—	—	—	—
02-03—Tampa Bay	NHL	72	20	14	34	34	-12	15	0	11	3	3	6	10
03-04—Tampa Bay	NHL	82	21	18	39	42	-9	10	0	23	1	13	14	14
NHL Totals (22 years)		1597	634	686	1320	1109	51	270	9	162	43	54	97	162

ANGELSTAD, MEL — LW — CAPITALS

PERSONAL: Born October 31, 1972, in Saskatoon, Sask. ... 6-2/214. ... Shoots left.

TRANSACTIONS/CAREER NOTES: Signed as free agent by Dallas Stars (July 29, 1998). ... Signed as free agent by Washington Capitals (April 3, 2004).

Season Team	League	GP	G	A	Pts.	PIM	+/-	PP	SH	GP	G	A	Pts.	PIM
		REGULAR SEASON								PLAYOFFS				
92-93—Thunder Bay	Col.HL	45	2	5	7	256	...	...	...	—	—	—	—	—
—Nashville	ECHL	1	0	0	0	14	...	...	...	—	—	—	—	—
93-94—Prince Edward	AHL	1	0	0	0	5	...	...	...	—	—	—	—	—
—Thunder Bay	Col.HL	58	1	20	21	374	...	...	...	9	1	2	3	65
94-95—Prince Edward	AHL	3	0	0	0	16	...	...	...	—	—	—	—	—
—Thunder Bay	Col.HL	46	0	8	8	317	...	...	...	7	0	3	3	62

Season Team	League	REGULAR SEASON								PLAYOFFS				
		GP	G	A	Pts.	PIM	+/-	PP	SH	GP	G	A	Pts.	PIM
95-96—Phoenix	IHL	5	0	0	0	43	...	...	...	—	—	—	—	—
—Thunder Bay	Col.HL	51	3	3	6	335	...	...	...	16	0	6	6	94
96-97—Thunder Bay	Col.HL	66	10	21	31	422	...	...	...	7	0	1	1	21
97-98—Las Vegas	IHL	3	0	0	0	5	...	...	...	—	—	—	—	—
—Orlando	IHL	63	1	3	4	321	...	...	...	8	0	0	0	29
—Fort Worth	WPHL	19	1	6	7	102	...	...	...	—	—	—	—	—
98-99—Michigan	IHL	78	3	5	8	*421	-7	1	0	5	1	0	1	16
99-00—Michigan	IHL	33	3	4	7	144	...	...	...	—	—	—	—	—
00-01—Manitoba	IHL	67	1	5	6	232	...	...	...	8	0	0	0	26
01-02—Portland	AHL	53	1	7	8	212	-9	1	0	—	—	—	—	—
02-03—Portland	AHL	57	5	2	7	139	-6	0	0	3	0	0	0	6
03-04—Portland	AHL	53	0	1	1	118	...	...	...	—	—	—	—	—
—Washington	NHL	2	0	0	0	2	0	0	0	—	—	—	—	—
NHL Totals (1 year)		2	0	0	0	2	0	0	0					

ANIKEYENKO, VITALY — D — SENATORS

PERSONAL: Born January 2, 1987, in Yaroslavl, Russia. ... 6-3/198.

Season Team	League	REGULAR SEASON								PLAYOFFS				
		GP	G	A	Pts.	PIM	+/-	PP	SH	GP	G	A	Pts.	PIM
04-05—Torpedo Yaroslavl	Rus. Div.	...	...	...	...	...	...	...	...	—	—	—	—	—

ANTROPOV, NIK — C — MAPLE LEAFS

PERSONAL: Born February 18, 1980, in Vost, U.S.S.R. ... 6-6/230. ... Shoots left.
TRANSACTIONS/CAREER NOTES: Selected by Toronto Maple Leafs in first round (first Maple Leafs pick, 10th overall) of NHL draft (June 27, 1998). ... Injured (November 27, 1999); missed seven games. ... Injured (January 5, 2000); missed two games. ... Injured (March 29, 2000); missed one game. ... Sprained knee (November 5, 2002); missed five games. ... Injured shoulder (January 3, 2003); missed three games. ... Injured groin (March 22, 2003); missed two games. ... Fractured foot (April 9, 2003); missed four playoff games. ... Injured shoulder (October 27, 2003); missed 20 games.
STATISTICAL PLATEAUS: Three-goal games: 1999-00 (1).

Season Team	League	REGULAR SEASON								PLAYOFFS				
		GP	G	A	Pts.	PIM	+/-	PP	SH	GP	G	A	Pts.	PIM
95-96—Torpedo Ust-Kam	CIS Jr.	20	18	20	38	30	...	...	...	—	—	—	—	—
96-97—Torpedo Ust-Kam	Rus. Div.	8	2	1	3	6	...	...	...	—	—	—	—	—
97-98—Torpedo Ust-Kam	Rus. Div.	42	15	24	39	62	...	...	...	—	—	—	—	—
98-99—Dynamo Moscow	Russian	30	5	9	14	30	...	...	...	11	0	1	1	4
99-00—St. John's	AHL	2	0	0	0	4	...	...	...	—	—	—	—	—
—Toronto	NHL	66	12	18	30	41	14	0	0	3	0	0	0	4
00-01—Toronto	NHL	52	6	11	17	30	5	0	0	9	2	1	3	12
01-02—Toronto	NHL	11	1	1	2	4	-1	0	0	—	—	—	—	—
—St. John's	AHL	34	11	24	35	47	9	2	0	—	—	—	—	—
02-03—Toronto	NHL	72	16	29	45	124	11	2	1	3	0	0	0	0
03-04—Toronto	NHL	62	13	18	31	62	7	1	1	13	0	2	2	18
04-05—Ak Bars Kazan	Russian	10	2	3	5	6	3	...	...	—	—	—	—	—
—Lokomotiv Yaroslavl	Russian	26	4	15	19	44	6	...	...	9	3	4	7	18
NHL Totals (5 years)		263	48	77	125	261	36	3	2	28	2	3	5	34

ARKHIPOV, DENIS — C — PREDATORS

PERSONAL: Born May 19, 1979, in Kazan, U.S.S.R. ... 6-3/214. ... Shoots left.
TRANSACTIONS/CAREER NOTES: Selected by Nashville Predators in third round (second Predators pick, 60th overall) of NHL draft (June 27, 1998). ... Bruised shoulder (February 25, 2003); missed one game.

Season Team	League	REGULAR SEASON								PLAYOFFS				
		GP	G	A	Pts.	PIM	+/-	PP	SH	GP	G	A	Pts.	PIM
94-95—Ak Bars Kazan	CIS Jr.	40	20	12	32	10	...	...	...	—	—	—	—	—
95-96—Ak Bars Kazan	CIS Jr.	40	15	8	23	30	...	...	...	—	—	—	—	—
—Ak Bars-2 Kazan	CIS Div. II	15	10	8	18	10	...	...	...	—	—	—	—	—
96-97—Ak Bars-2 Kazan	Rus. Div.	50	17	23	40	20	...	...	...	—	—	—	—	—
—Ak Bars Kazan	Russian	1	1	0	1	0	...	...	...	—	—	—	—	—
97-98—Ak Bars Kazan	Russian	29	2	2	4	2	...	...	...	—	—	—	—	—
98-99—Ak Bars Kazan	Russian	34	12	1	13	22	...	...	...	9	2	3	5	6
99-00—Ak Bars Kazan	Russian	32	7	9	16	14	...	...	...	18	5	5	10	6
00-01—Milwaukee	IHL	40	9	8	17	11	...	...	...	—	—	—	—	—
—Nashville	NHL	40	6	7	13	4	0	0	0	—	—	—	—	—
01-02—Nashville	NHL	82	20	22	42	16	-18	7	0	—	—	—	—	—
02-03—Nashville	NHL	79	11	24	35	32	-18	3	0	—	—	—	—	—
03-04—Nashville	NHL	72	9	12	21	22	-2	3	0	—	—	—	—	—
04-05—Ak Bars Kazan	Russian	45	9	8	17	28	12	...	...	4	0	0	0	0
NHL Totals (4 years)		273	46	65	111	74	-38	13	0					

ARMSTRONG, CHRIS — D

PERSONAL: Born June 26, 1975, in Regina, Sask. ... 6-0/203. ... Shoots left.
TRANSACTIONS/CAREER NOTES: Selected by Florida Panthers in third round (third Panthers pick, 57th overall) of NHL entry draft (June 26, 1993). ... Selected by Nashville Predators in NHL expansion draft (June 26, 1998). ... Signed as free agent by San Jose Sharks (August 30,

1999). ... Selected by Minnesota Wild in NHL expansion draft (June 23, 2000). ... Signed as free agent by New York Islanders (August 1, 2001). ... Signed as free agent by EV Zug of Swiss league (April 12, 2002). ... Signed as free agent by Anaheim Mighty Ducks (June 26, 2003). ... Signed as free agent by ERC Ingolstadt of German league (April 2, 2004).

		REGULAR SEASON								PLAYOFFS				
Season Team	**League**	**GP**	**G**	**A**	**Pts.**	**PIM**	**+/-**	**PP**	**SH**	**GP**	**G**	**A**	**Pts.**	**PIM**
91-92—Moose Jaw	WHL	43	2	7	9	19	...	...	...	4	0	0	0	0
92-93—Moose Jaw	WHL	67	9	35	44	104	...	...	...	—	—	—	—	—
93-94—Moose Jaw	WHL	64	13	55	68	54	-19	5	0	—	—	—	—	—
—Cincinnati	IHL	1	0	0	0	0	0	0	0	10	1	3	4	2
94-95—Moose Jaw	WHL	66	17	54	71	61	27	5	1	10	2	12	14	22
—Cincinnati	IHL	...	...	...	...	...	...	...	...	9	1	3	4	10
95-96—Carolina	AHL	78	9	33	42	65	...	...	...	—	—	—	—	—
96-97—Carolina	AHL	66	9	23	32	38	2	0	0	—	—	—	—	—
97-98—Fort Wayne	IHL	79	8	36	44	66	9	4	1	4	0	2	2	4
98-99—Milwaukee	IHL	5	0	3	3	4	1	0	0	—	—	—	—	—
—Hershey	AHL	65	12	32	44	30	8	9	0	5	0	1	1	0
99-00—Kentucky	AHL	78	9	48	57	77	...	...	...	9	1	5	6	4
00-01—Cleveland	IHL	77	9	32	41	42	...	...	...	4	0	2	2	2
—Minnesota	NHL	3	0	0	0	0	-3	0	0	—	—	—	—	—
01-02—Bridgeport	AHL	80	10	38	48	49	6	5	0	20	3	7	10	4
02-03—Zug	Switzerland	21	0	7	7	43	...	...	...	—	—	—	—	—
—Augsburg	Germany	22	3	16	19	32	...	...	...	—	—	—	—	—
03-04—Cincinnati	AHL	70	9	36	45	48	-13	3	0	9	1	3	4	2
—Anaheim	NHL	4	0	1	1	0	-1	0	0	—	—	—	—	—
04-05—Ingolstadt ERC	Germany	46	5	19	24	36	-1	2	0	11	2	6	8	18
NHL Totals (2 years)		7	0	1	1	0	-4	0	0					

ARMSTRONG, COLBY RW PENGUINS

PERSONAL: Born November 23, 1982, in Lloydminster, Sask. ... 6-1/180. ... Shoots right.

TRANSACTIONS/CAREER NOTES: Selected by Pittsburgh Penguins in first round (first Penguins pick, 21st overall) of NHL draft (June 23, 2001).

		REGULAR SEASON								PLAYOFFS				
Season Team	**League**	**GP**	**G**	**A**	**Pts.**	**PIM**	**+/-**	**PP**	**SH**	**GP**	**G**	**A**	**Pts.**	**PIM**
98-99—Red Deer	WHL	1	0	1	1	0	...	...	...	—	—	—	—	—
99-00—Red Deer	WHL	68	13	25	38	122	...	...	...	2	0	1	1	11
00-01—Red Deer	WHL	72	36	42	78	156	...	...	...	21	6	6	12	39
01-02—Red Deer	WHL	64	27	41	68	115	...	...	...	23	6	10	16	32
02-03—Wilkes-Barre/Scranton	AHL	73	7	11	18	76	...	...	...	3	0	0	0	4
03-04—Wilkes-Barre/Scranton	AHL	67	10	17	27	71	6	3	0	24	3	2	5	45
04-05—Wilkes-Barre/Scranton	AHL	80	18	37	55	89	9	6	3	10	4	2	6	14

ARMSTRONG, DEREK C KINGS

PERSONAL: Born April 23, 1973, in Ottawa. ... 6-0/195. ... Shoots right.

TRANSACTIONS/CAREER NOTES: Selected by New York Islanders in sixth round (fifth Islanders pick, 128th overall) of NHL draft (June 20, 1992). ... Food poisoning (January 28, 1997); missed one game. ... Signed as free agent by Ottawa Senators (July 10, 1997). ... Signed as free agent by New York Rangers (July 20, 1998). ... Traded by Rangers to Los Angeles Kings for sixth-round pick (G Chris Holt) in 2003 draft (July 16, 2002). ... Injured groin (December 11, 2002); missed six games. ... Injured knee (January 2, 2003); missed two games. ... Fractured finger (November 15, 2003); missed 22 games.

		REGULAR SEASON								PLAYOFFS				
Season Team	**League**	**GP**	**G**	**A**	**Pts.**	**PIM**	**+/-**	**PP**	**SH**	**GP**	**G**	**A**	**Pts.**	**PIM**
89-90—Hawkesbury	COJHL	48	8	10	18	30	...	...	...	—	—	—	—	—
90-91—Hawkesbury	COJHL	54	27	45	72	49	...	...	...	—	—	—	—	—
—Sudbury	OHL	2	0	2	2	0	...	...	...	—	—	—	—	—
91-92—Sudbury	OHL	66	31	54	85	22	...	...	...	9	2	2	4	2
92-93—Sudbury	OHL	66	44	62	106	56	...	...	...	14	9	10	19	26
93-94—Salt Lake City	IHL	76	23	35	58	61	-17	8	0	—	—	—	—	—
—New York Islanders	NHL	1	0	0	0	0	0	0	0	—	—	—	—	—
94-95—Denver	IHL	59	13	18	31	65	6	3	0	6	0	2	2	0
95-96—Worcester	AHL	51	11	15	26	33	...	...	...	4	2	1	3	0
—New York Islanders	NHL	19	1	3	4	14	-6	0	0	—	—	—	—	—
96-97—New York Islanders	NHL	50	6	7	13	33	-8	0	0	—	—	—	—	—
—Utah	IHL	17	4	8	12	10	...	...	...	6	0	4	4	4
97-98—Detroit	IHL	10	0	1	1	2	-1	0	0	—	—	—	—	—
—Hartford	AHL	54	16	30	46	40	15	1	0	15	2	6	8	22
—Ottawa	NHL	9	2	0	2	9	1	0	0	—	—	—	—	—
98-99—Hartford	AHL	59	29	51	80	73	16	6	2	7	5	4	9	10
—New York Rangers	NHL	3	0	0	0	0	0	0	0	—	—	—	—	—
99-00—Hartford	AHL	77	28	54	82	101	...	...	...	23	7	16	23	24
—New York Rangers	NHL	1	0	0	0	0	0	0	0	—	—	—	—	—
00-01—Hartford	AHL	75	32	*69	*101	73	...	...	...	5	0	6	6	6
—New York Rangers	NHL	3	0	0	0	0	0	0	0	—	—	—	—	—
01-02—Bern	Switzerland	44	17	36	53	62	...	...	...	6	3	5	8	8
02-03—Los Angeles	NHL	66	12	26	38	30	5	2	0	—	—	—	—	—
—Manchester	AHL	2	3	0	3	4	...	...	...	—	—	—	—	—
03-04—Los Angeles	NHL	57	14	21	35	33	4	5	0	—	—	—	—	—
04-05—Rapperswil	Switzerland	3	1	3	4	4	...	0	1	—	—	—	—	—
—Geneva	Switzerland	9	6	7	13	18	...	3	0	—	—	—	—	—
NHL Totals (9 years)		209	35	57	92	119	-4	7	0					

ARNASON, TYLER — C — BLACKHAWKS

PERSONAL: Born March 16, 1979, in Oklahoma City, Okla. ... 5-11/192. ... Shoots left. ... Son of Chuck Arnason, RW with eight NHL teams (1971-79).
TRANSACTIONS/CAREER NOTES: Selected by Chicago Blackhawks in sixth round (sixth Blackhawks pick, 183rd overall) of NHL draft (June 28, 1998).
STATISTICAL PLATEAUS: Three-goal games: 2002-03 (1), 2003-04 (1). Total: 2.

		REGULAR SEASON								PLAYOFFS				
Season Team	**League**	**GP**	**G**	**A**	**Pts.**	**PIM**	**+/-**	**PP**	**SH**	**GP**	**G**	**A**	**Pts.**	**PIM**
96-97—Winnipeg	MJHL	56	35	30	65	18	...	...	...	—	—	—	—	—
97-98—Fargo	USHL	52	37	45	82	16	...	...	...	—	—	—	—	—
98-99—St. Cloud State	WCHA	38	14	17	31	16	...	...	...	—	—	—	—	—
99-00—St. Cloud State	WCHA	39	19	30	49	18	...	...	...	—	—	—	—	—
00-01—St. Cloud State	WCHA	41	28	28	56	14	...	...	...	—	—	—	—	—
01-02—Norfolk	AHL	60	26	30	56	42	-2	11	0	—	—	—	—	—
—Chicago	NHL	21	3	1	4	4	-3	0	0	3	0	0	0	0
02-03—Chicago	NHL	82	19	20	39	20	7	3	0	—	—	—	—	—
03-04—Chicago	NHL	82	22	33	55	16	-13	6	0	—	—	—	—	—
04-05—Brynas IF	Sweden	4	0	0	0	0	-1	0	0	—	—	—	—	—
NHL Totals (3 years)		185	44	54	98	40	-9	9	0	3	0	0	0	0

ARNOTT, JASON — C — STARS

PERSONAL: Born October 11, 1974, in Collingwood, Ont. ... 6-4/225. ... Shoots right. ... Name pronounced AHR-niht.
TRANSACTIONS/CAREER NOTES: Selected by Edmonton Oilers in first round (first Oilers pick, seventh overall) of NHL draft (June 26, 1993). ... Tonsillitis (November 3, 1993); missed one game. ... Bruised sternum (November 27, 1993); missed one game. ... Sprained back (December 7, 1993); missed one game. ... Appendectomy (December 28, 1993); missed three games. ... Flu (February 22, 1995); missed one game. ... Suffered concussion (March 23, 1995); missed two games. ... Strained knee (April 19, 1995); missed two games. ... Suspended one game for game misconduct penalties (April 22, 1995). ... Suffered concussion and cut face (October 8, 1995); missed seven games. ... Sprained knee (February 11, 1996); missed nine games. ... Strained knee (March 19, 1996); missed one game. ... Inner ear infection (April 8, 1996); missed one game. ... Fractured ankle (December 27, 1996); missed seven games. ... Injured ankle (January 22, 1997); missed two games. ... Flu (February 12, 1997); missed two games. ... Strained lower back (March 23, 1997); missed four games. ... Separated right shoulder (December 10, 1997); missed five games. ... Reinjured shoulder (January 2, 1998); missed two games. ... Traded by Oilers with D Bryan Muir to New Jersey Devils for RW Bill Guerin and RW Valeri Zelepukin (January 4, 1998). ... Back spasms (March 21, 1998); missed one game. ... Bruised hip (April 8, 1998); missed three games. ... Reinjured hip (April 16, 1998); missed two games. ... Had offseason finger surgery; missed first game of 1998-99 season. ... Bruised thigh (December 28, 1998); missed one game. ... Had the flu (January 15, 1999); missed two games ... Bruised foot (January 20, 1999); missed one game ... Bruised hip (March 28, 1999); missed one game. ... Reinjured hip (April 4, 1999); missed two games. ... Injured mouth (October 23, 1999); missed three games. ... Flu (February 21, 2000); missed two games. ... Bruised ribs (March 17, 2000); missed one game. ... Missed first 18 games of 2000-01 season in contract dispute. ... Injured back (February 16, 2001); missed six games. ... Flu (December 20, 2001); missed two games. ... Injured back (March 10, 2002); missed five games. ... Traded by Devils with RW Randy McKay and first-round pick (traded to Columbus; traded to Buffalo; Sabres selected Dan Paille) in 2002 draft to Dallas Stars for C Joe Nieuwendyk and RW Jamie Langenbrunner (March 19, 2002). ... Strained groin (April 10, 2002); missed remainder of season. ... Sprained right ankle (October 10, 2002); missed nine games. ... Injured knee (March 16, 2003); missed one game. ... Injured groin (December 3, 2003); missed four games. ... Injured ankle (December 27, 2003); missed one game. ... Strained groin (March 24, 2004); missed one game. ... Injured groin (March 31, 2004); missed final three games of regular season.
STATISTICAL PLATEAUS: Three-goal games: 1994-95 (1), 1995-96 (1), 2001-02 (1), 2002-03 (1), 2003-04 (1). Total: 5.

		REGULAR SEASON								PLAYOFFS				
Season Team	**League**	**GP**	**G**	**A**	**Pts.**	**PIM**	**+/-**	**PP**	**SH**	**GP**	**G**	**A**	**Pts.**	**PIM**
89-90—Stayner	Jr. C	34	21	31	52	12	...	...	...	—	—	—	—	—
90-91—Lindsay Jr. B	OHA	42	17	44	61	10	...	...	...	—	—	—	—	—
91-92—Oshawa	OHL	57	9	15	24	12	...	...	...	—	—	—	—	—
92-93—Oshawa	OHL	56	41	57	98	74	...	...	...	13	9	9	18	20
93-94—Edmonton	NHL	78	33	35	68	104	1	10	0	—	—	—	—	—
94-95—Edmonton	NHL	42	15	22	37	128	-14	7	0	—	—	—	—	—
95-96—Edmonton	NHL	64	28	31	59	87	-6	8	0	—	—	—	—	—
96-97—Edmonton	NHL	67	19	38	57	92	-21	10	1	12	3	6	9	18
97-98—Edmonton	NHL	35	5	13	18	78	-16	1	0	—	—	—	—	—
—New Jersey	NHL	35	5	10	15	21	-8	3	0	5	0	2	2	0
98-99—New Jersey	NHL	74	27	27	54	79	10	8	0	7	2	2	4	4
99-00—New Jersey	NHL	76	22	34	56	51	22	7	0	23	8	12	20	18
00-01—New Jersey	NHL	54	21	34	55	75	23	8	0	23	8	7	15	16
01-02—New Jersey	NHL	63	22	19	41	59	3	8	0	—	—	—	—	—
—Dallas	NHL	10	3	1	4	6	-1	2	0	—	—	—	—	—
02-03—Dallas	NHL	72	23	24	47	51	9	7	0	11	3	2	5	6
03-04—Dallas	NHL	73	21	36	57	66	23	5	0	5	1	1	2	2
NHL Totals (11 years)		743	244	324	568	897	25	84	1	86	25	32	57	64

ARVEDSON, MAGNUS — LW

PERSONAL: Born November 25, 1971, in Karlstad, Sweden. ... 6-2/198. ... Shoots left. ... Name pronounced AHR-vihd-suhn.
TRANSACTIONS/CAREER NOTES: Selected by Ottawa Senators in fifth round (fourth Senators pick, 119th overall) of NHL draft (June 21, 1997). ... Strained groin (October 17, 1997); missed seven games. ... Strained groin (November 29, 1997); missed three games. ... Suffered concussion (December 16, 1997); missed five games. ... Strained left shoulder (January 11, 1998); missed one game. ... Strained groin (March 20, 1998); missed three games. ... Back spasms (October 20, 1998); missed two games. ... Bruised hip (October 14, 1999); missed one game. ... Injured abdomen (January 20, 2000) and had surgery; missed 34 games. ... Strained buttocks (November 2, 2000); missed one game. ... Fractured left foot (November 16, 2000); missed 19 games. ... Sprained right knee (January 10, 2001); missed 10 games. ... Strained groin (April 6, 2001); missed final game of regular season and two playoff games. ... Injured groin (October 3, 2001); missed first six games of season. ... Suffered concussion (December 26, 2001); missed two games. ... Injured knee (December 14, 2002); missed two games. ...

Signed as free agent by Vancouver Canucks (September 10, 2003). ... Injured groin (November 8, 2003); missed two games. ... Injured groin (November 18, 2003); missed four games. ... Back spasms (January 10, 2004); missed seven games. ... Tore knee ligament (January 31, 2004); missed remainder of season. ... Signed as free agent by Fjarstadt of the Swedish league (August 6, 2004).
STATISTICAL PLATEAUS: Three-goal games: 1998-99 (1).

		REGULAR SEASON								PLAYOFFS				
Season Team	**League**	**GP**	**G**	**A**	**Pts.**	**PIM**	**+/-**	**PP**	**SH**	**GP**	**G**	**A**	**Pts.**	**PIM**
91-92—Orebro	Sweden Dv. 2	32	12	21	33	30	...	...	...	7	4	4	8	4
92-93—Orebro	Sweden Dv. 2	36	11	18	29	34	...	...	...	6	2	1	3	0
93-94—Farjestad Karlstad	Sweden	16	1	7	8	10	...	...	...	—	—	—	—	—
94-95—Farjestad Karlstad	Sweden	36	1	7	8	45	...	...	...	4	0	0	0	6
95-96—Farjestad Karlstad	Sweden	39	10	14	24	42	...	...	...	8	0	3	3	10
96-97—Farjestad Karlstad	Sweden	48	13	11	24	36	...	...	...	14	4	7	11	8
97-98—Ottawa	NHL	61	11	15	26	36	2	0	1	11	0	1	1	6
98-99—Ottawa	NHL	80	21	26	47	50	33	0	4	3	0	1	1	2
99-00—Ottawa	NHL	47	15	13	28	36	4	1	1	6	0	0	0	6
00-01—Ottawa	NHL	51	17	16	33	24	23	1	2	2	0	0	0	0
01-02—Ottawa	NHL	74	12	27	39	35	27	0	0	12	2	1	3	4
—Swedish Oly. team	Int'l	4	0	0	0	0	...	...	...	—	—	—	—	—
02-03—Ottawa	NHL	80	16	21	37	48	13	2	0	18	1	5	6	16
03-04—Vancouver	NHL	41	8	7	15	12	7	2	0	—	—	—	—	—
NHL Totals (7 years)		434	100	125	225	241	109	6	8	52	3	8	11	34

ASHAM, ARRON RW ISLANDERS

PERSONAL: Born April 13, 1978, in Portage-La-Prairie, Man. ... 5-11/205. ... Shoots right.
TRANSACTIONS/CAREER NOTES: Selected by Montreal Canadiens in third round (third Canadiens pick, 71st overall) of NHL draft (June 22, 1996). ... Injured back (October 23, 1999); missed one game. ... Flu (December 27, 1999); missed one game. ... Strained groin (January 22, 2000); missed 23 games. ... Strained hip flexor (February 17, 2001); missed eight games. ... Flu (March 19, 2001); missed one game. ... Traded by Canadiens with fifth-round pick (W Markus Pahlsson) in 2002 draft to New York Islanders for RW Mariusz Czerkawski (June 22, 2002). ... Injured neck (November 3, 2003); missed three games.

		REGULAR SEASON								PLAYOFFS				
Season Team	**League**	**GP**	**G**	**A**	**Pts.**	**PIM**	**+/-**	**PP**	**SH**	**GP**	**G**	**A**	**Pts.**	**PIM**
94-95—Red Deer	WHL	62	11	16	27	126	...	...	...	—	—	—	—	—
95-96—Red Deer	WHL	70	32	45	77	174	...	...	...	10	6	3	9	20
96-97—Red Deer	WHL	67	45	51	96	149	12	14	7	16	12	14	26	36
97-98—Red Deer	WHL	67	43	49	92	153	-3	16	2	5	0	2	2	8
—Fredericton	AHL	2	1	1	2	0	0	0	0	2	0	1	1	0
98-99—Fredericton	AHL	60	16	18	34	118	-3	5	0	13	8	6	14	11
—Montreal	NHL	7	0	0	0	0	-4	0	0	—	—	—	—	—
99-00—Montreal	NHL	33	4	2	6	24	-7	0	1	—	—	—	—	—
—Quebec	AHL	13	4	5	9	32	...	...	...	2	0	0	0	2
00-01—Quebec	AHL	15	7	9	16	51	...	...	...	7	1	2	3	2
—Montreal	NHL	46	2	3	5	59	-9	0	0	—	—	—	—	—
01-02—Quebec	AHL	24	9	14	23	35	1	2	0	—	—	—	—	—
—Montreal	NHL	35	5	4	9	55	7	0	0	3	0	1	1	0
02-03—New York Islanders	NHL	78	15	19	34	57	1	4	0	5	0	0	0	16
03-04—New York Islanders	NHL	79	12	12	24	92	-12	1	0	5	0	1	1	4
04-05—Visp	Switzerland	5	2	4	6	6	...	0	0	4	1	2	3	8
NHL Totals (6 years)		278	38	40	78	287	-24	5	1	13	0	2	2	20

AUBIN, JEAN-SEBASTIEN G PENGUINS

PERSONAL: Born July 19, 1977, in Montreal. ... 5-11/180. ... Catches right. ... Name pronounced OH-ban.
TRANSACTIONS/CAREER NOTES: Selected by Pittsburgh Penguins in third round (second Penguins pick, 76th overall) of NHL entry draft (July 8, 1995). ... Strained hamstring (April 3, 1999); missed six games. ... Injured shoulder (November 23, 1999); missed two games. ... Sprained ankle (April 3, 2000); missed final three games of season. ... Injured knee and had surgery (December 3, 2000); missed 14 games. ... Bruised hand (February 8, 2003); missed nine games.

		REGULAR SEASON									PLAYOFFS							
Season Team	**League**	**GP**	**Min.**	**W**	**L**	**T**	**GA**	**SO**	**GAA**	**SV%**	**GP**	**Min.**	**W**	**L**	**GA**	**SO**	**GAA**	**SV%**
94-95—Sherbrooke	QMJHL	27	1287	13	10	1	73	1	3.40	...	3	185	1	2	11	0	3.57	.891
95-96—Sherbrooke	QMJHL	40	2084	18	14	2	127	0	3.66	...	4	174	1	3	16	0	5.52	...
96-97—Sherbrooke	QMJHL	4	249	3	1	0	8	0	1.93	...	—	—	—	—	—	—	—	—
—Moncton	QMJHL	23	1311	9	13	0	72	1	3.30	...	—	—	—	—	—	—	—	—
—Laval	QMJHL	11	532	2	6	1	41	0	4.62	...	2	128	0	2	10	0	4.69	.872
97-98—Syracuse	AHL	8	380	2	4	1	26	0	4.11	.855	—	—	—	—	—	—	—	—
—Dayton	ECHL	21	1177	15	2	2	59	1	3.01	...	3	142	1	1	4	0	1.69	...
98-99—Kansas City	IHL	13	751	5	7	1	41	0	3.28	.900	—	—	—	—	—	—	—	—
—Pittsburgh	NHL	17	756	4	3	6	28	2	2.22	.908	—	—	—	—	—	—	—	—
99-00—Wilkes-Barre/Scranton	AHL	11	538	2	8	0	39	0	4.35	...	—	—	—	—	—	—	—	—
—Pittsburgh	NHL	51	2789	23	21	3	120	2	2.58	.914	—	—	—	—	—	—	—	—
00-01—Pittsburgh	NHL	36	2050	20	14	1	107	0	3.13	.890	1	1	0	0	0	0	0.00	...
01-02—Pittsburgh	NHL	21	1094	3	12	1	65	0	3.56	.879	—	—	—	—	—	—	—	—
02-03—Pittsburgh	NHL	21	1132	6	13	0	59	1	3.13	.900	—	—	—	—	—	—	—	—
—Wilkes-Barre/Scranton	AHL	16	919	8	6	1	29	3	1.89	.937	6	355	3	3	12	0	2.03	.930
03-04—Pittsburgh	NHL	22	1067	7	9	0	53	1	2.98	.908	—	—	—	—	—	—	—	—
—Wilkes-Barre/Scranton	AHL	13	670	4	5	2	31	0	2.78	.890	—	—	—	—	—	—	—	—
04-05—St. John's	AHL	23	1335	12	9	...	64	3	2.88	.921	1	47	0	0	1	0	1.28	.957
NHL Totals (6 years)		168	8888	63	72	11	432	6	2.92	.901	1	1	0	0	0	0	0.00	...

AUBIN, SERGE LW THRASHERS

PERSONAL: Born February 15, 1975, in Val d'Or, Que. ... 6-1/200. ... Shoots left. ... Name pronounced AH-ban.

TRANSACTIONS/CAREER NOTES: Selected by Pittsburgh Penguins in seventh round (ninth Penguins pick, 161st overall) of NHL draft (June 29, 1994). ... Signed as free agent by Colorado Avalanche (December 18, 1998). ... Signed as free agent by Columbus Blue Jackets (July 11, 2000). ... Flu (January 15, 2001); missed one game. ... Cut knee (November 25, 2001); missed two games. ... Bruised thigh (December 8, 2001); missed two games. ... Had concussion (January 26, 2002); missed two games. ... Flu (March 14, 2002); missed one game. ... Injured mouth (March 26, 2002); missed two games. ... Signed as free agent by Avalanche (August 27, 2002). ... Injured ankle (December 26, 2002); missed three games. ... Injured ankle (January 4, 2003); missed two games. ... Bruised foot (January 23, 2003); missed one game. ... Claimed by Atlanta Thrashers in waiver draft (October 3, 2003). ... Had concussion and strained neck; (December 21, 2003); missed 16 games.

		REGULAR SEASON								PLAYOFFS				
Season Team	**League**	**GP**	**G**	**A**	**Pts.**	**PIM**	**+/-**	**PP**	**SH**	**GP**	**G**	**A**	**Pts.**	**PIM**
92-93—Drummondville	QMJHL	65	16	34	50	30	...	...	...	8	0	1	1	16
93-94—Granby	QMJHL	63	42	32	74	80	...	...	...	7	2	3	5	8
94-95—Granby	QMJHL	60	37	73	110	55	...	...	...	11	8	15	23	4
95-96—Cleveland	IHL	2	0	0	0	0	...	...	...	2	0	0	0	0
—Hampton Roads	ECHL	62	24	62	86	74	...	...	...	3	1	4	5	10
96-97—Cleveland	IHL	57	9	16	25	38	...	...	...	2	0	0	0	0
97-98—Syracuse	AHL	55	6	14	20	57	-11	2	0	—	—	—	—	—
—Hershey	AHL	5	2	1	3	0	0	1	0	7	1	3	4	6
98-99—Hershey	AHL	64	30	39	69	58	-2	13	1	3	0	1	1	2
—Colorado	NHL	1	0	0	0	0	0	0	0	—	—	—	—	—
99-00—Hershey	AHL	58	42	38	80	56	...	...	...	—	—	—	—	—
—Colorado	NHL	15	2	1	3	6	1	0	0	17	0	1	1	6
00-01—Columbus	NHL	81	13	17	30	107	-20	0	0	—	—	—	—	—
01-02—Columbus	NHL	71	8	8	16	32	-20	1	0	—	—	—	—	—
02-03—Colorado	NHL	66	4	6	10	64	-2	0	0	5	0	0	0	4
03-04—Atlanta	NHL	66	10	15	25	73	0	1	0	—	—	—	—	—
04-05—Geneva	Switzerland	6	2	1	3	8	...	0	0	3	1	2	3	2
NHL Totals (6 years)		300	37	47	84	282	-41	2	0	22	0	1	1	10

AUCOIN, ADRIAN D BLACKHAWKS

PERSONAL: Born July 3, 1973, in Ottawa. ... 6-2/215. ... Shoots right. ... Name pronounced oh-COYN.

TRANSACTIONS/CAREER NOTES: Selected by Vancouver Canucks in 5th round 7th Canucks pick, 117th overall) of NHL draft (June 20, 1992). ... Sprained shoulder (January 10, 1997); missed six games. ... Strained groin (October 30, 1997); missed five games. ... Reinjured groin (November 12, 1997); missed 10 games. ... Sprained ankle (December 13, 1997); missed seven games. ... Injured groin (December 4, 1999); missed four games. ... Fractured finger (February 9, 2000); missed 20 games. ... Strained groin (November 4, 2000); missed two games. ... Reinjured groin (November 9, 2000); missed three games. ... Traded by Canucks with 2nd-round pick (C/LW Alexander Polushin) in 2001 draft to Tampa Bay Lightning for G Dan Cloutier (February 7, 2001). ... Traded by Lightning with RW Alexander Kharitonov to New York Islanders for D Mathieu Biron and 2nd-round pick (traded to Washington; traded to Vancouver; Canucks selected Denis Grot) in 2002 draft (June 22, 2001). ... Injured heel (March 28, 2002); missed one game. ... Injured groin (January 15, 2003); missed eight games. ... Injured groin (April 1, 2003); missed one game. ... Signed as free agent by Chicago Blackhawks (Aug. 2, 2005).

		REGULAR SEASON								PLAYOFFS				
Season Team	**League**	**GP**	**G**	**A**	**Pts.**	**PIM**	**+/-**	**PP**	**SH**	**GP**	**G**	**A**	**Pts.**	**PIM**
91-92—Boston University	Hockey East	33	2	10	12	62	...	...	...	—	—	—	—	—
92-93—Canadian nat'l team	Int'l	42	8	10	18	71	...	...	...	—	—	—	—	—
93-94—Canadian nat'l team	Int'l	59	5	12	17	80	...	...	...	—	—	—	—	—
—Can. Olympic team	Int'l	4	0	0	0	2	4	0	0	—	—	—	—	—
—Hamilton	AHL	13	1	2	3	19	-6	1	0	4	0	2	2	6
94-95—Syracuse	AHL	71	13	18	31	52	-14	5	0	—	—	—	—	—
—Vancouver	NHL	1	1	0	1	0	1	0	0	4	1	0	1	0
95-96—Syracuse	AHL	29	5	13	18	47	...	...	...	—	—	—	—	—
—Vancouver	NHL	49	4	14	18	34	8	2	0	6	0	0	0	2
96-97—Vancouver	NHL	70	5	16	21	63	0	1	0	—	—	—	—	—
97-98—Vancouver	NHL	35	3	3	6	21	-4	1	0	—	—	—	—	—
98-99—Vancouver	NHL	82	23	11	34	77	-14	18	2	—	—	—	—	—
99-00—Vancouver	NHL	57	10	14	24	30	7	4	0	—	—	—	—	—
00-01—Vancouver	NHL	47	3	13	16	20	13	1	0	—	—	—	—	—
—Tampa Bay	NHL	26	1	11	12	25	-8	1	0	—	—	—	—	—
01-02—New York Islanders	NHL	81	12	22	34	62	23	7	0	7	2	5	7	4
02-03—New York Islanders	NHL	73	8	27	35	70	-5	5	0	5	1	2	3	4
03-04—New York Islanders	NHL	81	13	31	44	54	29	4	0	5	0	0	0	6
04-05—MoDo Ornskoldsvik	Sweden	14	2	4	6	32	3	1	0	6	1	0	1	16
NHL Totals (10 years)		602	83	162	245	456	50	44	2	27	4	7	11	16

AUDETTE, DONALD RW

PERSONAL: Born September 23, 1969, in Laval, Que. ... 5-8/191. ... Shoots right. ... Name pronounced aw-DEHT.

TRANSACTIONS/CAREER NOTES: Selected by Buffalo Sabres in ninth round (eighth Sabres pick, 183rd overall) of NHL draft (June 17, 1989). ... Fractured left hand (February 11, 1990); missed seven games. ... Bruised thigh (September 1990). ... Bruised thigh (October 1990); missed five games. ... Tore left knee ligaments (November 16, 1990); and had surgery. ... Sprained ankle (December 14, 1991); missed eight games. ... Injured knee (March 31, 1992). ... Knee surgery before 1992-93 season; missed first 22 games. ... Tore knee cartilage (September 23, 1995); missed 11 games. ... Fractured right thumb (November 8, 1995); missed two games. ... Injured right knee (December 1, 1995); missed seven games. ... Right knee surgery (January 26, 1996); missed remainder of season. ... Strained groin (October 26, 1996); missed five games. ... Suffered concussion (October 22, 1997); missed seven games. ... Missed first 25 games of 1998-99 season in contract dispute. ... Traded by Sabres to Los Angeles Kings for second-round pick (RW Milan Bartovic) in 1999 entry draft (December 18, 1998). ... Back spasms (April 8, 1999); missed one game. ... Flu (April 18, 1999); missed one game. ... Sprained left ankle (January 6, 2000); missed 15 games. ...

Traded by Kings with D Frantisek Kaberle to Atlanta Thrashers for RW Kelly Buchberger and RW Nelson Emerson (March 13, 2000). ... Strained groin (December 27, 2000); missed one game. ... Suspended four games for cross-checking incident (January 16, 2001). ... Suspended two games for illegal blow to the head (March 12, 2001). ... Traded by Thrashers to Sabres for C Kamil Piros and fourth-round pick (traded to St. Louis; Blues selected Igor Valeyev) in 2001 draft (March 13, 2001). ... Signed as free agent by Dallas Stars (July 2, 2001). ... Traded by Stars with C Shaun Van Allen to Montreal Canadiens for LW Martin Rucinsky and LW Benoit Brunet (November 21, 2001). ... Cut forearm (December 1, 2001); missed 49 games. ... Virus (January 15, 2003); missed one game. ... Separated shoulder (November 20, 2003); missed nine games. ... Released by Canadiens; signed as free agent by Florida Panthers (January 16, 2003). ... Suspended two games for kicking incident (March 18, 2004).

STATISTICAL PLATEAUS: Three-goal games: 1994-95 (1), 1995-96 (1), 2000-01 (2). Total: 4.

		REGULAR SEASON								PLAYOFFS				
Season Team	**League**	**GP**	**G**	**A**	**Pts.**	**PIM**	**+/-**	**PP**	**SH**	**GP**	**G**	**A**	**Pts.**	**PIM**
86-87—Laval	QMJHL	66	17	22	39	36	...	...	...	14	2	6	8	10
87-88—Laval	QMJHL	63	48	61	109	56	...	...	...	14	7	12	19	20
88-89—Laval	QMJHL	70	76	85	161	123	...	...	...	17	*17	12	29	43
89-90—Rochester	AHL	70	42	46	88	78	...	...	...	15	9	8	17	29
—Buffalo	NHL	0	0	0	0	0	0	0	0	2	0	0	0	0
90-91—Rochester	AHL	5	4	0	4	2	...	...	...	—	—	—	—	—
—Buffalo	NHL	8	4	3	7	4	-1	2	0	—	—	—	—	—
91-92—Buffalo	NHL	63	31	17	48	75	-1	5	0	—	—	—	—	—
92-93—Buffalo	NHL	44	12	7	19	51	-8	2	0	8	2	2	4	6
—Rochester	AHL	6	8	4	12	10	7	3	0	—	—	—	—	—
93-94—Buffalo	NHL	77	29	30	59	41	2	16	1	7	0	1	1	6
94-95—Buffalo	NHL	46	24	13	37	27	-3	13	0	5	1	1	2	4
95-96—Buffalo	NHL	23	12	13	25	18	0	8	0	—	—	—	—	—
96-97—Buffalo	NHL	73	28	22	50	48	-6	8	0	11	4	5	9	6
97-98—Buffalo	NHL	75	24	20	44	59	10	10	0	15	5	8	13	10
98-99—Los Angeles	NHL	49	18	18	36	51	7	6	0	—	—	—	—	—
99-00—Los Angeles	NHL	49	12	20	32	45	6	1	0	—	—	—	—	—
—Atlanta	NHL	14	7	4	11	12	-4	0	1	—	—	—	—	—
00-01—Atlanta	NHL	64	32	39	71	64	-3	13	1	—	—	—	—	—
—Buffalo	NHL	12	2	6	8	12	1	1	0	13	3	6	9	4
01-02—Dallas	NHL	20	4	8	12	12	2	3	0	—	—	—	—	—
—Montreal	NHL	13	1	5	6	8	1	0	0	12	6	4	10	10
02-03—Hamilton	AHL	11	5	5	10	8	1	2	0	—	—	—	—	—
—Montreal	NHL	54	11	12	23	19	-7	4	0	—	—	—	—	—
03-04—Montreal	NHL	23	3	5	8	16	-4	0	0	—	—	—	—	—
—Florida	NHL	28	6	7	13	22	-9	5	0	—	—	—	—	—
NHL Totals (15 years)		735	260	249	509	584	-17	97	3	73	21	27	48	46

AULD, ALEX G CANUCKS

PERSONAL: Born January 7, 1981, in Cold Lake, Alta. ... 6-4/200. ... Catches left.

TRANSACTIONS/CAREER NOTES: Selected by Florida Panthers in second round (second Panthers pick, 40th overall) of NHL draft (June 26, 1999). ... Traded by Panthers to Vancouver Canucks for second-round pick (traded to New Jersey; Devils selected Tuomas Pihlman) in 2001 draft and (traded to Atlanta; traded Buffalo; Sabres selected John Adams) in 2002 draft (May 31, 2001).

		REGULAR SEASON									PLAYOFFS							
Season Team	**League**	**GP**	**Min.**	**W**	**L**	**T**	**GA**	**SO**	**GAA**	**SV%**	**GP**	**Min.**	**W**	**L**	**GA**	**SO**	**GAA**	**SV%**
97-98—North Bay	OHL	6	206	0	4	0	17	0	4.95	...	—	—	—	—	—	—	—	—
98-99—North Bay	OHL	37	1894	9	20	1	106	1	3.36	.899	3	170	0	3	10	0	3.53	.905
99-00—North Bay	OHL	55	3047	21	26	6	167	2	3.29	.891	6	374	2	4	12	0	1.93	.950
00-01—North Bay	OHL	40	2319	22	11	5	98	1	2.54	.917	4	240	0	4	15	0	3.75	...
01-02 —Manitoba	AHL	21	1103	11	9	0	65	1	3.54	.865	1	20	0	0	0	0	0.00	1.00
—Columbia	ECHL	6	375	3	1	2	12	0	1.92	.921	—	—	—	—	—	—	—	—
—Vancouver	NHL	1	60	1	0	0	2	0	2.00	.909	—	—	—	—	—	—	—	—
02-03—Manitoba	AHL	37	2208	15	19	3	97	3	2.64	.908	—	—	—	—	—	—	—	—
—Vancouver	NHL	7	382	3	3	0	10	1	1.57	.939	1	20	0	0	1	0	3.00	.800
03-04—Manitoba	AHL	40	2329	18	16	4	99	4	2.55	.908	—	—	—	—	—	—	—	—
—Vancouver	NHL	6	349	2	2	2	12	0	2.06	.929	3	222	1	2	9	0	2.43	.898
04-05—Manitoba	AHL	50	2763	25	18	...	118	2	2.56	.909	3	127	0	2	7	0	3.31	.860
NHL Totals (3 years)		14	791	6	5	2	24	1	1.82	.932	4	242	1	2	10	0	2.48	.892

AULIN, JARED C CAPITALS

PERSONAL: Born March 15, 1982, in Calgary. ... 6-0/192. ... Shoots right. ... Name pronounced AW-lihn.

TRANSACTIONS/CAREER NOTES: Selected by Colorado Avalanche in second round (second Avalanche pick, 47th overall) of NHL draft (June 24, 2000). ... Traded by Avalanche to Los Angeles Kings (March 22, 2001); completing deal in which Kings traded D Rob Blake and C Steve Reinprecht to Colorado Avalanche for RW Adam Deadmarsh, D Aaron Miller, first-round pick (C David Steckel) in 2001 draft, a player to be named and first-round pick (C Brian Boyle) in 2003 draft (February 21, 2001). ... Injured elbow (February 11, 2003); missed two games. ... Missed 2003-04 season recovering from left shoulder surgery (September 10, 2003). ... Traded by Kings to Washington Capitals for RW Anson Carter (March 8, 2004).

		REGULAR SEASON								PLAYOFFS				
Season Team	**League**	**GP**	**G**	**A**	**Pts.**	**PIM**	**+/-**	**PP**	**SH**	**GP**	**G**	**A**	**Pts.**	**PIM**
97-98—Kamloops	WHL	2	0	0	0	0	...	...	...	0	0	0	0	0
98-99—Kamloops	WHL	55	7	19	26	23	...	...	...	13	1	3	4	2
99-00—Kamloops	WHL	57	17	38	55	70	...	...	...	4	0	1	1	6
00-01—Kamloops	WHL	70	31	77	108	62	...	...	...	4	0	2	2	0
01-02—Kamloops	WHL	46	33	34	67	80	...	...	...	4	1	2	3	2
02-03—Manchester	AHL	44	12	32	44	21	-2	2	0	3	0	4	4	0

Season Team	League	GP	G	A	Pts.	PIM	+/-	PP	SH	GP	G	A	Pts.	PIM
—Los Angeles	NHL	17	2	2	4	0	-3	1	0	—	—	—	—	—
03-04—Portland	AHL	10	2	1	3	4	0	2	0	6	1	1	2	4
—Los Angeles	NHL	Did not play; injured												
04-05—Portland	AHL	65	11	28	39	30	-9	1	0	—	—	—	—	—
NHL Totals (2 years)		17	2	2	4	0	-3	1	0					

AVERY, SEAN — C/LW — KINGS

PERSONAL: Born April 10, 1980, in Pickering, Ont. ... 5-9/196. ... Shoots left.

TRANSACTIONS/CAREER NOTES: Signed as free agent by Detroit Red Wings (September 21, 1999). ... Traded by Red Wings with D Maxim Kuznetsov, first-round pick (Jeff Tambellini) in 2003 draft and second-round pick (later traded to Boston Bruins) in 2004 draft to Los Angeles Kings for D Mathieu Schneider (March 11, 2003). ... Injured back (March 27, 2003); missed one game. ... Signed as free agent by Motor City of the UHL (February 11, 2005).

		REGULAR SEASON								PLAYOFFS				
Season Team	**League**	**GP**	**G**	**A**	**Pts.**	**PIM**	**+/-**	**PP**	**SH**	**GP**	**G**	**A**	**Pts.**	**PIM**
95-96—Markham Waxers	OJHL	1	0	0	0	4	...	...	...	—	—	—	—	—
96-97—Owen Sound	OHL	58	10	21	31	86	...	...	...	4	1	0	1	4
97-98—Owen Sound	OHL	47	13	41	54	105	...	...	...	—	—	—	—	—
98-99—Owen Sound	OHL	28	22	23	45	70	...	...	...	—	—	—	—	—
—Kingston	OHL	33	14	25	39	88	...	...	...	5	1	3	4	13
99-00—Kingston	OHL	55	28	56	84	215	...	...	...	5	2	2	4	26
00-01—Cincinnati	AHL	58	8	15	23	304	...	...	...	4	1	0	1	19
01-02—Cincinnati	AHL	36	14	7	21	106	-4	6	0	—	—	—	—	—
—Detroit	NHL	36	2	2	4	68	1	0	0	—	—	—	—	—
02-03—Detroit	NHL	39	5	6	11	120	7	0	0	—	—	—	—	—
—Grand Rapids	AHL	15	6	6	12	82	2	2	0	—	—	—	—	—
—Los Angeles	NHL	12	1	3	4	33	0	0	0	—	—	—	—	—
—Manchester	AHL	...	...	...	...	...	...	...	...	3	2	1	3	8
03-04—Los Angeles	NHL	76	9	19	28	261	2	0	0	—	—	—	—	—
04-05—Reipas Lahti	Finland	2	3	0	3	26	-3	...	...	—	—	—	—	—
—Motor City	UHL	16	15	11	26	149	19	4	2	—	—	—	—	—
NHL Totals (3 years)		163	17	30	47	482	10	0	0					

AXELSSON, P.J. — LW — BRUINS

PERSONAL: Born February 26, 1975, in Kungalv, Sweden. ... 6-1/184. ... Shoots left.

TRANSACTIONS/CAREER NOTES: Selected by Boston Bruins in seventh round (seventh Bruins pick, 177th overall) of NHL draft (June 8, 1995). ... Had concussion (October 28, 1998); missed one game. ... Had concussion (November 3, 1998); missed three games. ... Flu (April 17, 1999); missed one game. ... Charley horse (October 23, 1999); missed one game. ... Strained shoulder (December 15, 2001); missed three games. ... Injured knee (November 19, 2002); missed four games. ... Injured back (December 7, 2002); missed six games. ... Flu (January 3, 2003); missed two games. ... Injured back (January 23, 2003); missed four games. ... Injured collarbone (November 22, 2003); missed two games. ... Injured shoulder (November 30, 2003); missed 10 games. ... Sprained right knee (January 8, 2004); missed two games.

		REGULAR SEASON								PLAYOFFS				
Season Team	**League**	**GP**	**G**	**A**	**Pts.**	**PIM**	**+/-**	**PP**	**SH**	**GP**	**G**	**A**	**Pts.**	**PIM**
93-94—Frolunda	Sweden	11	0	0	0	4	...	...	...	4	0	0	0	0
94-95—Frolunda	Sweden	8	2	1	3	6	...	...	...	—	—	—	—	—
95-96—Frolunda	Sweden	36	15	5	20	10	...	...	...	13	3	0	3	10
96-97—Vastra Frolunda	Sweden	50	19	15	34	34	...	...	...	3	0	2	2	0
97-98—Boston	NHL	82	8	19	27	38	-14	2	0	6	1	0	1	0
98-99—Boston	NHL	77	7	10	17	18	-14	0	0	12	1	1	2	4
99-00—Boston	NHL	81	10	16	26	24	1	0	0	—	—	—	—	—
00-01—Boston	NHL	81	8	15	23	27	-12	0	0	—	—	—	—	—
01-02—Boston	NHL	78	7	17	24	16	6	0	2	6	2	1	3	6
—Swedish Oly. team	Int'l	4	0	0	0	2	...	...	...	—	—	—	—	—
02-03—Boston	NHL	66	17	19	36	24	8	2	2	5	0	0	0	6
03-04—Boston	NHL	68	6	14	20	42	2	0	0	7	0	0	0	4
04-05—Vastra Frolunda	Sweden	45	8	9	17	95	6	3	0	14	1	10	11	18
NHL Totals (7 years)		533	63	110	173	189	-23	4	4	36	4	2	6	20

BABCHUK, ANTON — D — BLACKHAWKS

PERSONAL: Born May 6, 1984, in Kiev, U.S.S.R. ... 6-5/202. ... Shoots right.

TRANSACTIONS/CAREER NOTES: Selected by Chicago Blackhawks in first round (first Blackhawks pick, 21st overall) of NHL draft (June 22, 2002).

		REGULAR SEASON								PLAYOFFS				
Season Team	**League**	**GP**	**G**	**A**	**Pts.**	**PIM**	**+/-**	**PP**	**SH**	**GP**	**G**	**A**	**Pts.**	**PIM**
01-02—Elektrostal	Russian Div. 1	40	7	8	15	90	...	...	...	—	—	—	—	—
02-03—Ak Bars Kazan	Russian	10	0	0	0	4	...	...	...	—	—	—	—	—
—St. Petersburg	Rus. Div.	20	3	0	3	10	...	...	...	—	—	—	—	—
03-04—Norfolk	AHL	73	8	14	22	89	9	3	0	8	0	2	2	6
—Chicago	NHL	5	0	2	2	2	-1	0	0	—	—	—	—	—
04-05—Norfolk	AHL	66	8	16	24	88	-15	3	0	2	0	0	0	2
NHL Totals (1 year)		5	0	2	2	2	-1	0	0					

BACASHIHUA, JASON — G — BLUES

PERSONAL: Born September 20, 1982, in Garden City, Mich. ... 5-11/167. ... Catches left. ... Name pronounced bak-ah-SHIH-hu-ah.

TRANSACTIONS/CAREER NOTES: Selected by Dallas Stars in first round (first Stars pick, 26th overall) of NHL draft (June 23, 2001). ... Traded by Stars to St. Louis Blues for D Shawn Belle (June 25, 2004).

		REGULAR SEASON									PLAYOFFS							
Season Team	League	GP	Min.	W	L	T	GA	SO	GAA	SV%	GP	Min.	W	L	GA	SO	GAA	SV%
99-00—Chicago	NAHL	41	2432	20	19	2	118	2	2.91	...	2	103	0	2	12	0	6.99	...
00-01—Chicago	NAHL	39	2246	24	14	0	121	1	3.23	...	3	190	1	2	12	0	3.79	...
01-02—Plymouth	OHL	46	2688	26	12	7	105	*5	2.34	...	6	360	2	4	15	0	2.50	...
—Utah	AHL	1	60	0	1	0	3	0	3.00	.925	—	—	—	—	—	—	—	—
02-03—Utah	AHL	39	2244	18	18	2	118	3	3.16	.907	1	58	0	1	2	0	2.07	.941
03-04—Utah	AHL	39	2234	13	19	5	99	3	2.66	.908	—	—	—	—	—	—	—	—
04-05—Worcester	AHL	35	1908	18	13	...	80	2	2.52	.902	—	—	—	—	—	—	—	—

BACKMAN, CHRISTIAN D BLUES

PERSONAL: Born April 28, 1980, in Alingsas, Sweden. ... 6-3/208. ... Shoots left. ... Name pronounced BEK-man.
TRANSACTIONS/CAREER NOTES: Selected by St. Louis Blues in first round (first Blues pick, 24th overall) of NHL draft (June 27, 1998). ... Bruised shoulder (December 31, 2003); missed 10 games. ... Flu (February 20, 2004); missed one game.

		REGULAR SEASON								PLAYOFFS				
Season Team	League	GP	G	A	Pts.	PIM	+/-	PP	SH	GP	G	A	Pts.	PIM
96-97—Vastra Frolunda	Sweden Jr.	26	2	5	7	16	...	...	...	—	—	—	—	—
97-98—Vastra Frolunda	Sweden Jr.	28	5	14	19	12	...	...	...	2	0	1	1	4
98-99—Vastra Frolunda	Sweden	49	0	4	4	4	...	...	...	4	0	0	0	0
99-00—Vastra Frolunda	Sweden	27	1	0	1	14	...	...	...	5	0	0	0	0
00-01—Vastra Frolunda	Sweden	50	1	10	11	32	...	...	...	3	0	2	2	2
01-02—Vastra Frolunda	Sweden	44	7	4	11	38	...	...	...	10	0	0	0	8
02-03—St. Louis	NHL	4	0	0	0	0	-3	0	0	—	—	—	—	—
—Worcester	AHL	72	8	19	27	66	-2	4	0	3	0	1	1	5
03-04—Worcester	AHL	4	1	2	3	2	3	1	0	—	—	—	—	—
—St. Louis	NHL	66	5	13	18	16	3	1	0	5	0	2	2	4
04-05—Vastra Frolunda	Sweden	—	—	—	—	—	—	—	—	14	2	7	9	10
—Vastra Frolunda	Sweden	50	4	15	19	40	29	2	0	—	—	—	—	—
NHL Totals (2 years)		70	5	13	18	16	0	1	0	5	0	2	2	4

BALA, CHRIS LW

PERSONAL: Born September 24, 1978, in Alexandria, Va. ... 6-1/180. ... Shoots left.
TRANSACTIONS/CAREER NOTES: Selected by Ottawa Senators in second round (third Senators pick, 58th overall) of NHL entry draft (June 27, 1998). ... Traded by Senators to Minnesota Wild (June 26, 2003) in three-way deal in which Nashville Predators traded D Peter Smrek to Senators and Wild traded D Curtis Murphy to the Nashville Predators. ... Traded by Wild to Colorado Avalanche for LW Jordan Krestanovich (March 9, 2004).

		REGULAR SEASON								PLAYOFFS				
Season Team	League	GP	G	A	Pts.	PIM	+/-	PP	SH	GP	G	A	Pts.	PIM
96-97—The Hill School	USHS (East)	23	28	33	61	36	...	...	...	—	—	—	—	—
97-98—Harvard	ECAC	33	16	14	30	23	...	...	...	—	—	—	—	—
98-99—Harvard	ECAC	28	5	10	15	16	...	...	...	—	—	—	—	—
99-00—Harvard	ECAC	30	10	14	24	18	...	...	...	—	—	—	—	—
00-01—Harvard	ECAC	32	14	16	30	24	...	...	...	—	—	—	—	—
01-02—Grand Rapids	AHL	70	21	16	37	9	11	2	2	4	0	1	1	0
—Ottawa	NHL	6	0	1	1	0	1	0	0	—	—	—	—	—
02-03—Binghamton	AHL	51	6	18	24	20	-1	2	1	14	2	5	7	4
03-04—Houston	AHL	61	11	7	18	18	-6	1	2	—	—	—	—	—
—Hershey	AHL	13	4	2	6	0	1	0	0	—	—	—	—	—
04-05—Hershey	AHL	58	9	5	14	17	-23	0	0	—	—	—	—	—
NHL Totals (1 year)		6	0	1	1	0	1	0	0					

BALEJ, JOZEF RW RANGERS

PERSONAL: Born February 22, 1982, in Myjava, Czechoslovakia. ... 6-1/187. ... Shoots right. ... Name pronounced BAH-lee.
TRANSACTIONS/CAREER NOTES: Selected by Montreal Canadiens in third round (third Canadiens pick, 78th overall) of NHL draft (June 24, 2000). ... Traded by Canadiens with second-round pick (C Bruce Graham) in 2004 draft to New York Rangers for RW Alexei Kovalev (March 2, 2004).

		REGULAR SEASON								PLAYOFFS				
Season Team	League	GP	G	A	Pts.	PIM	+/-	PP	SH	GP	G	A	Pts.	PIM
97-98—Dukla Trencin	Slovakia Jrs.	52	57	40	97	60	...	...	...	—	—	—	—	—
98-99—Thunder Bay Flyers	USHL	38	8	7	15	9	...	...	...	—	—	—	—	—
99-00—Portland	WHL	65	22	23	45	33	...	...	...	—	—	—	—	—
00-01—Portland	WHL	46	32	21	53	18	...	...	...	16	6	9	15	6
01-02—Portland	WHL	65	51	41	92	52	...	...	...	7	0	2	2	6
02-03—Hamilton	AHL	56	5	15	20	29	0	2	0	3	1	0	1	2
03-04—Hamilton	AHL	55	26	32	58	32	19	3	2	—	—	—	—	—
—Montreal	NHL	4	0	0	0	0	-1	0	0	—	—	—	—	—
—New York Rangers	NHL	13	1	4	5	4	0	0	0	—	—	—	—	—
—Hartford	AHL	5	1	3	4	21	0	0	0	16	9	7	16	10
04-05—Hartford	AHL	69	20	22	42	46	2	5	2	6	0	0	0	4
NHL Totals (1 year)		17	1	4	5	4	-1	0	0					

BALMOCHNYKH, MAXIM — LW — DEVILS

PERSONAL: Born March 7, 1979, in Lipetsk, U.S.S.R. ... 6-1/200. ... Shoots left. ... Name pronounced bal-MOTCH-nick.

TRANSACTIONS/CAREER NOTES: Selected by Anaheim Mighty Ducks in second round (second Mighty Ducks pick, 45th overall) of NHL entry draft (June 21, 1997). ... Traded by Mighty Ducks with D Oleg Tverdovsky and LW Jeff Friesen to New Jersey Devils for RW Petr Sykora, C Igor Pohanka, D Mike Commodore and G J.F. Damphousse (July 7, 2002). ... Suspended three games by the AHL for abuse of an official (March 22, 2004).

		REGULAR SEASON								PLAYOFFS				
Season Team	**League**	**GP**	**G**	**A**	**Pts.**	**PIM**	**+/-**	**PP**	**SH**	**GP**	**G**	**A**	**Pts.**	**PIM**
94-95—HC Lipetsk	CIS Div. II	3	0	1	1	4	...	...	...	—	—	—	—	—
95-96—HC Lipetsk	CIS Div. II	40	15	5	20	60	...	...	...	—	—	—	—	—
96-97—Lada Togliatti	Russian	18	6	1	7	22	...	...	...	—	—	—	—	—
97-98—Lada Togliatti	Russian	37	10	4	14	46	...	...	...	—	—	—	—	—
—Traktor Chelyabinsk	Russian	2	0	0	0	2	...	...	...	—	—	—	—	—
98-99—Lada Togliatti	Russian	15	2	1	3	10	...	...	...	4	0	1	1	8
—Quebec	QMJHL	21	9	27	36	38	...	...	...	—	—	—	—	—
99-00—Cincinnati	AHL	40	9	12	21	82	...	...	...	—	—	—	—	—
—Anaheim	NHL	6	0	1	1	2	2	0	0	—	—	—	—	—
00-01—Cincinnati	AHL	65	6	9	15	45	...	...	...	—	—	—	—	—
01-02—Cincinnati	AHL	23	6	4	10	33	-1	0	0	—	—	—	—	—
02-03—Cherepovets	Russian	12	1	2	3	31	...	...	...	—	—	—	—	—
03-04—Albany	AHL	42	5	9	14	54	-6	0	0	—	—	—	—	—
NHL Totals (1 year)		6	0	1	1	2	2	0	0					

B

BARINKA, MICHAL — D — BLACKHAWKS

PERSONAL: Born June 12, 1984, in Vyskov, Czechoslovakia. ... 6-3/217. ... Shoots left.

TRANSACTIONS/CAREER NOTES: Drafted by Chicago Blackhawks in second round (59th overall) of NHL entry draft (June 20, 2003).

		REGULAR SEASON								PLAYOFFS				
Season Team	**League**	**GP**	**G**	**A**	**Pts.**	**PIM**	**+/-**	**PP**	**SH**	**GP**	**G**	**A**	**Pts.**	**PIM**
01-02—HC Ceske Budejovice	Czech Rep.	3	0	0	0	0	0	...	...	—	—	—	—	—
02-03—HC Ceske Budejovice	Czech Rep.	31	0	1	1	14	...	...	...	4	0	0	0	2
03-04—Norfolk	AHL	40	4	2	6	80	-2	1	0	—	—	—	—	—
—Chicago	NHL	9	0	1	1	6	-5	0	0	—	—	—	—	—
04-05—Norfolk	AHL	59	1	10	11	77	-3	0	0	0	0	0	0	0
NHL Totals (1 year)		9	0	1	1	6	-5	0	0					

BARKER, CAM — D — BLACKHAWKS

PERSONAL: Born April 4, 1986, in Winnipeg. ... 6-3/214. ... Shoots left.

TRANSACTIONS/CAREER NOTES: Selected by Chicago Blackhawks in first round (first Blackhawks pick, third overall) of NHL entry draft (June 26, 2004). ... Signed by Blackhawks (July 26, 2005).

		REGULAR SEASON								PLAYOFFS				
Season Team	**League**	**GP**	**G**	**A**	**Pts.**	**PIM**	**+/-**	**PP**	**SH**	**GP**	**G**	**A**	**Pts.**	**PIM**
01-02—Medicine Hat	WHL	3	0	1	1	0	...	...	...	—	—	—	—	—
02-03—Medicine Hat	WHL	64	10	37	47	79	...	...	...	11	3	4	7	17
03-04—Medicine Hat	WHL	69	21	44	65	105	...	...	...	20	3	9	12	18
04-05—Medicine Hat	WHL	52	15	33	48	99	19	6	0	12	3	3	6	16

BARNABY, MATTHEW — RW — BLACKHAWKS

PERSONAL: Born May 4, 1973, in Ottawa. ... 6-1/190. ... Shoots left.

TRANSACTIONS/CAREER NOTES: Selected by Buffalo Sabres in fourth round (fifth Sabres pick, 83rd overall) of NHL draft (June 20, 1992). ... Had back spasms (March 28, 1995); missed one game. ... Suspended one game for accumulating three game misconduct penalties (March 31, 1996). ... Injured groin (April 3, 1996); missed five games. ... Sprained knee ligament (April 2, 1997); missed final six games of regular season and four playoff games. ... Injured sternum (October 10, 1997); missed five games. ... Strained shoulder (February 2, 1998); missed one game. ... Suspended four games and fined $1,000 for striking another player in the head (November 5, 1998). ... Back spasms (December 12, 1998); missed one game. ... Injured ankle (December 18, 1998); missed one game. ... Flu (January 11, 1999); missed one game. ... Traded by Sabres to Pittsburgh Penguins for C Stu Barnes (March 11, 1999). ... Strained knee (November 2, 1999); missed five games. ... Suffered concussion (December 15, 1999); missed seven games. ... Suffered concussion (January 13, 2000); missed one game. ... Suspended five games for fighting incident (February 13, 2000). ... Traded by Penguins to Tampa Bay Lightning for C Wayne Primeau (February 1, 2001). ... Injured elbow (October 14, 2001); missed one game. ... Traded by Lightning to New York Rangers for LW Zdeno Ciger (December 12, 2001). ... Injured knee (December 5, 2002); missed three games. ... Traded by Rangers with third-round pick (LW Denis Pershin) in 2004 entry draft to Colorado Avalanche for D Chris McAllister, D David Liffiton and future considerations (March 8, 2004). ... Signed as free agent by Chicago Blackhawks (July 2, 2004).

		REGULAR SEASON								PLAYOFFS				
Season Team	**League**	**GP**	**G**	**A**	**Pts.**	**PIM**	**+/-**	**PP**	**SH**	**GP**	**G**	**A**	**Pts.**	**PIM**
90-91—Beauport	QMJHL	52	9	5	14	262	...	...	...	—	—	—	—	—
91-92—Beauport	QMJHL	63	29	37	66	*476	...	...	...	—	—	—	—	—
92-93—Victoriaville	QMJHL	65	44	67	111	*448	...	...	...	6	2	4	6	44
—Buffalo	NHL	2	1	0	1	10	0	1	0	1	0	1	1	4
93-94—Buffalo	NHL	35	2	4	6	106	-7	1	0	3	0	0	0	17
—Rochester	AHL	42	10	32	42	153	-8	6	0	—	—	—	—	—
94-95—Rochester	AHL	56	21	29	50	274	7	6	0	—	—	—	—	—
—Buffalo	NHL	23	1	1	2	116	-2	0	0	—	—	—	—	—
95-96—Buffalo	NHL	73	15	16	31	*335	-2	0	0	—	—	—	—	—

Season Team	League	REGULAR SEASON GP	G	A	Pts.	PIM	+/-	PP	SH	PLAYOFFS GP	G	A	Pts.	PIM
96-97—Buffalo	NHL	68	19	24	43	249	16	2	0	8	0	4	4	36
97-98—Buffalo	NHL	72	5	20	25	289	8	0	0	15	7	6	13	22
98-99—Buffalo	NHL	44	4	14	18	143	-2	0	0	—	—	—	—	—
—Pittsburgh	NHL	18	2	2	4	34	-10	1	0	13	0	0	0	35
99-00—Pittsburgh	NHL	64	12	12	24	197	3	0	0	11	0	2	2	29
00-01—Pittsburgh	NHL	47	1	4	5	168	-7	0	0	—	—	—	—	—
—Tampa Bay	NHL	29	4	4	8	97	-3	1	0	—	—	—	—	—
01-02—Tampa Bay	NHL	29	0	0	0	70	-7	0	0	—	—	—	—	—
—New York Rangers	NHL	48	8	13	21	144	-3	0	0	—	—	—	—	—
02-03—New York Rangers	NHL	79	14	22	36	142	9	1	0	—	—	—	—	—
03-04—New York Rangers	NHL	69	12	20	32	120	15	0	0	—	—	—	—	—
—Colorado	NHL	13	4	5	9	37	3	1	0	11	0	2	2	27
NHL Totals (12 years)		713	104	161	265	2257	11	8	0	62	7	15	22	170

BARNES, RYAN — LW — RED WINGS

PERSONAL: Born January 30, 1980, in Dunnville, Ont. ... 6-1/201. ... Shoots left.
TRANSACTIONS/CAREER NOTES: Selected by Detroit Red Wings in second round (second Red Wings pick, 55th overall) of NHL draft (June 27, 1998).

Season Team	League	REGULAR SEASON GP	G	A	Pts.	PIM	+/-	PP	SH	PLAYOFFS GP	G	A	Pts.	PIM
96-97—Quinte	Tier II Jr. A	46	15	19	34	245	...	...	...	—	—	—	—	—
97-98—Sudbury	OHL	46	13	18	31	111	...	...	...	10	0	2	2	24
98-99—Sudbury	OHL	8	2	0	2	23	...	...	...	—	—	—	—	—
—Toronto St. Michael's	OHL	31	11	14	25	215	...	...	...	—	—	—	—	—
—Barrie	OHL	24	16	14	30	161	-1	...	...	12	2	4	6	40
99-00—Barrie	OHL	31	17	12	29	98	15	5	0	25	7	7	14	49
00-01—Cincinnati	AHL	1	0	0	0	7	...	...	...	—	—	—	—	—
—Toledo	ECHL	16	2	4	6	31	...	...	...	—	—	—	—	—
01-02—Cincinnati	AHL	46	2	3	5	152	-8	0	0	—	—	—	—	—
—Toledo	ECHL	1	1	0	1	0	-1	0	0	—	—	—	—	—
02-03—Grand Rapids	AHL	73	5	6	11	151	12	1	0	15	1	1	2	17
03-04—Detroit	NHL	2	0	0	0	0	0	0	0	—	—	—	—	—
—Grand Rapids	AHL	69	6	13	19	175	6	0	0	4	0	0	0	7
04-05—Grand Rapids	AHL	69	7	8	15	167	1	0	0	—	—	—	—	—
NHL Totals (1 year)		2	0	0	0	0	0	0	0					

BARNES, STU — C/RW — STARS

PERSONAL: Born December 25, 1970, in Spruce Grove, Alta. ... 5-11/180. ... Shoots right.
TRANSACTIONS/CAREER NOTES: Selected by Winnipeg Jets in first round (first Jets pick, fourth overall) of NHL draft (June 17, 1989). ... Traded by Jets to Florida Panthers for C Randy Gilhen (November 26, 1993). ... Strained left calf (January 1, 1994); missed one game. ... Cut and bruised in and around left eye (February 15, 1995); missed seven games. ... Sprained left knee (March 10, 1996); missed 10 games. ... Traded by Panthers with D Jason Woolley to Pittsburgh Penguins for C Chris Wells (November 19, 1996). ... Injured hip (April 11, 1997); missed one game. ... Back spasms (October 9, 1997); missed one game. ... Strained hip flexor (April 16, 1998); missed one game. ... Traded by Penguins to Buffalo Sabres for RW Matthew Barnaby (March 11, 1999). ... Injured groin (November 3, 2000); missed seven games. ... Suffered concussion (March 17, 2002); missed remainder of season. ... Traded by Sabres to Dallas Stars for C Mike Ryan and second-round pick (RW Branislav Fabry) in 2003 draft (March 10, 2003). ... Injured upper body (March 24, 2004); missed five games.
STATISTICAL PLATEAUS: Three-goal games: 1991-92 (1), 1997-98 (1), 1998-99 (1). Total: 3.

Season Team	League	REGULAR SEASON GP	G	A	Pts.	PIM	+/-	PP	SH	PLAYOFFS GP	G	A	Pts.	PIM
86-87—St. Albert	AJHL	57	43	32	75	80	...	...	...	—	—	—	—	—
87-88—New Westminster	WHL	71	37	64	101	88	...	...	...	5	2	3	5	6
88-89—Tri-City	WHL	70	59	82	141	117	...	...	...	7	6	5	11	10
89-90—Tri-City	WHL	63	52	92	144	165	...	...	...	7	1	5	6	26
90-91—Canadian nat'l team	Int'l	53	22	27	49	68	...	...	...	—	—	—	—	—
91-92—Winnipeg	NHL	46	8	9	17	26	-2	4	0	—	—	—	—	—
—Moncton	AHL	30	13	19	32	10	...	...	...	11	3	9	12	6
92-93—Moncton	AHL	42	23	31	54	58	3	4	0	—	—	—	—	—
—Winnipeg	NHL	38	12	10	22	10	-3	3	0	6	1	3	4	2
93-94—Winnipeg	NHL	18	5	4	9	8	-1	2	0	—	—	—	—	—
—Florida	NHL	59	18	20	38	30	5	6	1	—	—	—	—	—
94-95—Florida	NHL	41	10	19	29	8	7	1	0	—	—	—	—	—
95-96—Florida	NHL	72	19	25	44	46	-12	8	0	22	6	10	16	4
96-97—Florida	NHL	19	2	8	10	10	-3	1	0	—	—	—	—	—
—Pittsburgh	NHL	62	17	22	39	16	-20	4	0	5	0	1	1	0
97-98—Pittsburgh	NHL	78	30	35	65	30'	15	15	1	6	3	3	6	2
98-99—Pittsburgh	NHL	64	20	12	32	20	-12	13	0	—	—	—	—	—
—Buffalo	NHL	17	0	4	4	10	1	0	0	21	7	3	10	6
99-00—Buffalo	NHL	82	20	25	45	16	-3	8	2	5	3	0	3	2
00-01—Buffalo	NHL	75	19	24	43	26	-2	3	2	13	4	4	8	2
01-02—Buffalo	NHL	68	17	31	48	26	6	5	0	—	—	—	—	—
02-03—Buffalo	NHL	68	11	21	32	20	-13	2	1	—	—	—	—	—
—Dallas	NHL	13	2	5	7	8	2	2	0	12	2	3	5	0
03-04—Dallas	NHL	77	11	18	29	18	7	0	1	5	0	0	0	0
NHL Totals (13 years)		897	221	292	513	328	-28	77	8	95	26	27	53	18

BARNEY, SCOTT — RW — THRASHERS

PERSONAL: Born March 27, 1979, in Oshawa, Ont. ... 6-4/208. ... Shoots right.

TRANSACTIONS/CAREER NOTES: Selected by Los Angeles Kings in 2nd round (3rd Kings pick, 29th overall) of NHL draft (June 21, 1997). ... Missed 1999-2000, 2000-01 and 2001-02 seasons recovering from back injury suffered in training camp (September 28, 1999). ... Injured shoulder (February 14, 2004); missed 12 games. ... Missed entire 2004-05 season after undergoing abdominal surgery. ... Signed as free agent by Atlanta Thrashers (Aug. 8, 2005).

		REGULAR SEASON								PLAYOFFS				
Season Team	League	GP	G	A	Pts.	PIM	+/-	PP	SH	GP	G	A	Pts.	PIM
94-95—North York	MTHL	41	16	19	35	88	...	...	...	—	—	—	—	—
95-96—Peterborough	OHL	60	22	24	46	52	...	...	...	24	6	8	14	38
96-97—Peterborough	OHL	64	21	33	54	110	...	...	...	9	0	3	3	16
97-98—Peterborough	OHL	62	44	32	76	60	...	...	...	4	1	0	1	6
98-99—Peterborough	OHL	44	41	26	67	80	15	...	...	5	4	1	5	4
—Springfield	AHL	5	0	0	0	2	0	0	0	1	0	0	0	2
02-03—Manchester	AHL	57	13	5	18	74	-11	5	0	—	—	—	—	—
—Los Angeles	NHL	5	0	0	0	0	-1	0	0	—	—	—	—	—
03-04—Los Angeles	NHL	19	5	6	11	4	3	2	0	—	—	—	—	—
—Manchester	AHL	44	20	14	34	28	12	8	0	6	2	3	5	8
04-05—Manchester	AHL	Did not play — injured												
NHL Totals (2 years)		24	5	6	11	4	2	2	0					

BARON, MURRAY — D

PERSONAL: Born June 1, 1967, in Prince George, B.C. ... 6-3/236. ... Shoots left.

TRANSACTIONS/CAREER NOTES: Selected by Philadelphia Flyers in eighth round (seventh Flyers pick, 167th overall) of NHL draft (June 21, 1986). ... Separated left shoulder (October 5, 1989). ... Bone spur removed from foot (April 1990). ... Traded by Flyers with C Ron Sutter to St. Louis Blues for C Rod Brind'Amour and C Dan Quinn (September 22, 1991). ... Injured shoulder (December 3, 1991); missed seven games. ... Fractured foot (March 22, 1993); missed remainder of regular season. ... Injured groin (December 1, 1993); missed three games. ... Injured groin (December 11, 1993); missed three games. ... Injured knee (March 7, 1994); missed one game. ... Injured knee (April 18, 1995); missed final nine games of regular season. ... Traded by Blues with LW Shayne Corson and fifth-round pick (D Gennady Razin) in 1997 draft to Montreal Canadiens for C Pierre Turgeon, C Craig Conroy and D Rory Fitzpatrick (October 29, 1996). ... Bruised eye (November 21, 1996); missed one game. ... Traded by Canadiens with RW Chris Murray to Phoenix Coyotes for D Dave Manson (March 18, 1997). ... Fractured foot (April 6, 1997); missed remainder of regular season. ... Tore triceps muscle (November 17, 1997); missed 37 games. ... Signed as free agent by Vancouver Canucks (July 14, 1998). ... Fractured ankle (October 4, 2001); missed first 11 games of season. ... Flu (November 23, 2001); missed one game. ... Cut face (December 6, 2001); missed one game. ... Injured knee (December 22, 2001); missed three games. ... Injured hand (January 28, 2002); missed five games. ... Signed as free agent by Blues (September 5, 2003). ... Flu (March 9, 2004); missed two games.

		REGULAR SEASON								PLAYOFFS				
Season Team	League	GP	G	A	Pts.	PIM	+/-	PP	SH	GP	G	A	Pts.	PIM
84-85—Vernon	BCHL	37	5	9	14	93	...	...	...	—	—	—	—	—
85-86—Vernon	BCHL	49	15	32	47	176	...	...	...	7	1	2	3	13
86-87—North Dakota	WCHA	41	4	10	14	62	...	...	...	—	—	—	—	—
87-88—North Dakota	WCHA	41	1	10	11	95	...	...	...	—	—	—	—	—
88-89—North Dakota	WCHA	40	2	6	8	92	...	...	...	—	—	—	—	—
—Hershey	AHL	9	0	3	3	8	...	...	...	—	—	—	—	—
89-90—Hershey	AHL	50	0	10	10	101	...	...	...	—	—	—	—	—
—Philadelphia	NHL	16	2	2	4	12	1	0	0	—	—	—	—	—
90-91—Hershey	AHL	6	2	3	5	0	...	...	...	—	—	—	—	—
—Philadelphia	NHL	67	8	8	16	74	-3	3	0	—	—	—	—	—
91-92—St. Louis	NHL	67	3	8	11	94	-3	0	0	2	0	0	0	2
92-93—St. Louis	NHL	53	2	2	4	59	-5	0	0	11	0	0	0	12
93-94—St. Louis	NHL	77	5	9	14	123	-14	0	0	4	0	0	0	10
94-95—St. Louis	NHL	39	0	5	5	93	9	0	0	7	1	1	2	2
95-96—St. Louis	NHL	82	2	9	11	190	3	0	0	13	1	0	1	20
96-97—St. Louis	NHL	11	0	2	2	11	-4	0	0	—	—	—	—	—
—Montreal	NHL	60	1	5	6	107	-16	0	0	—	—	—	—	—
—Phoenix	NHL	8	0	0	0	4	0	0	0	1	0	0	0	0
97-98—Phoenix	NHL	45	1	5	6	106	-10	0	0	6	0	2	2	6
98-99—Vancouver	NHL	81	2	6	8	115	-23	0	0	—	—	—	—	—
99-00—Vancouver	NHL	81	2	10	12	67	8	0	0	—	—	—	—	—
00-01—Vancouver	NHL	82	3	8	11	63	-13	0	0	4	0	0	0	0
01-02—Vancouver	NHL	61	1	6	7	68	8	0	0	6	0	1	1	10
02-03—Vancouver	NHL	78	2	4	6	62	13	0	0	14	0	4	4	10
03-04—St. Louis	NHL	80	1	5	6	61	-6	0	0	5	0	0	0	6
NHL Totals (15 years)		988	35	94	129	1309	-57	3	0	73	2	8	10	78

BARTOVIC, MILAN — RW — SABRES

PERSONAL: Born April 9, 1981, in Trencin, Czechoslovakia. ... 5-11/191. ... Shoots left.

TRANSACTIONS/CAREER NOTES: Selected by Buffalo Sabres in second round (second Sabres pick, 35th overall) of NHL entry draft (June 26, 1999).

		REGULAR SEASON								PLAYOFFS				
Season Team	League	GP	G	A	Pts.	PIM	+/-	PP	SH	GP	G	A	Pts.	PIM
97-98—Dukla Trencin	Slovakia Jrs.	26	2	6	8	15	...	...	...	—	—	—	—	—
98-99—Dukla Trencin	Slovakia Jrs.	46	36	35	71	62	...	...	...	6	9	3	12	10
99-00—Tri-City	WHL	18	8	9	17	12	...	...	...	—	—	—	—	—
—Brandon	WHL	38	18	22	40	28	-7	9	3	—	—	—	—	—

Season Team	League	GP	G	A	Pts.	PIM	+/-	PP	SH	GP	G	A	Pts.	PIM
		REGULAR SEASON								PLAYOFFS				
00-01—Brandon	WHL	34	15	25	40	40	...	...	...	6	1	2	3	8
—Rochester	AHL	2	1	1	2	0	...	...	...	4	0	1	1	2
01-02—Rochester	AHL	73	15	11	26	56	10	0	3	2	0	0	0	0
02-03—Buffalo	NHL	3	1	0	1	0	0	0	0	—	—	—	—	—
—Rochester	AHL	74	18	10	28	84	-6	2	0	3	0	0	0	0
03-04—Rochester	AHL	52	18	11	29	52	1	4	1	2	0	0	0	2
—Buffalo	NHL	23	1	8	9	18	1	0	0	—	—	—	—	—
04-05—Rochester	AHL	69	10	18	28	83	8	1	1	9	0	3	3	22
NHL Totals (2 years)		26	2	8	10	18	1	0	0					

BATES, SHAWN — LW — ISLANDERS

B

PERSONAL: Born April 3, 1975, in Melrose, Mass. ... 6-0/210. ... Shoots right.

TRANSACTIONS/CAREER NOTES: Selected by Boston Bruins in fourth round (fourth Bruins pick, 103rd overall) of NHL entry draft (June 26, 1993). ... Involved in car accident (November 8, 1997); missed one game. ... Had the flu (December 1, 1998); missed one game. ... Injured hamstring (April 15, 1999); missed two games. ... Injured shoulder (October 30, 1999); missed four games. ... Sprained wrist (December 9, 1999); missed 25 games. ... Sprained wrist (March 25, 2000); missed seven games. ... Strained groin (December 16, 2000); missed three games. ... Reinjured groin (January 10, 2001); missed 16 games. ... Signed as free agent by New York Islanders (July 8, 2001). ... Injured groin (November 23, 2001); missed 10 games. ... Strained groin (March 28, 2002); missed one game. ... Injured groin (December 19, 2002); missed eight games. ... Injured groin (March 11, 2004); missed final 13 games of regular season.

Season Team	League	GP	G	A	Pts.	PIM	+/-	PP	SH	GP	G	A	Pts.	PIM
		REGULAR SEASON								PLAYOFFS				
90-91—Medford H.S.	Mass. H.S.	22	18	43	61	6	...	...	...	—	—	—	—	—
91-92—Medford H.S.	Mass. H.S.	22	38	41	79	10	...	...	...	—	—	—	—	—
92-93—Medford H.S.	Mass. H.S.	25	49	46	95	20	...	...	...	—	—	—	—	—
93-94—Boston University	Hockey East	41	10	19	29	24	25	1	1	—	—	—	—	—
94-95—Boston University	Hockey East	38	18	12	30	48	13	1	3	—	—	—	—	—
95-96—Boston University	Hockey East	40	28	22	50	54	...	...	...	—	—	—	—	—
96-97—Boston University	Hockey East	41	17	18	35	64	16	4	3	—	—	—	—	—
97-98—Boston	NHL	13	2	0	2	2	-3	0	0	—	—	—	—	—
—Providence	AHL	50	15	19	34	22	-24	5	4	—	—	—	—	—
98-99—Providence	AHL	37	25	21	46	39	8	10	5	—	—	—	—	—
—Boston	NHL	33	5	4	9	2	3	0	0	12	0	0	0	4
99-00—Boston	NHL	44	5	7	12	14	-17	0	0	—	—	—	—	—
00-01—Boston	NHL	45	2	3	5	26	-12	0	0	—	—	—	—	—
—Providence	AHL	11	5	8	13	12	...	...	...	8	2	6	8	8
01-02—New York Islanders	NHL	71	17	35	52	30	18	1	4	7	2	4	6	11
02-03—New York Islanders	NHL	74	13	29	42	52	-9	1	*6	5	1	0	1	0
03-04—New York Islanders	NHL	69	9	23	32	46	-8	0	1	5	0	0	0	4
NHL Totals (7 years)		349	53	101	154	172	-28	2	11	29	3	4	7	19

BATTAGLIA, BATES — LW

PERSONAL: Born December 13, 1975, in Chicago. ... 6-2/205. ... Shoots left. ... Name pronounced buh-TAG-lee-uh.

TRANSACTIONS/CAREER NOTES: Selected by Anaheim Mighty Ducks in sixth round (sixth Mighty Ducks pick, 132nd overall) of NHL draft (June 29, 1994). ... Traded by Mighty Ducks with fourth-round pick (C Josef Vasicek) in 1998 draft to Hartford Whalers for C Mark Janssens (March 18, 1997). ... Whalers franchise moved to North Carolina and renamed Carolina Hurricanes for 1997-98 season; NHL approved move on June 25, 1997. ... Injured shoulder (January 20, 2000); missed three games. ... Traded by Hurricanes to Colorado Avalanche for RW Radim Vrbata (March 11, 2003). ... Traded by Avalanche with RW Jonas Johansson to Washington Capitals for LW Steve Konowalchuk and a third-round pick (later traded to Carolina Hurricanes) in 2004 draft (October 22, 2003). ... Bruised foot (November 24, 2003); missed seven games.

STATISTICAL PLATEAUS: Three-goal games: 1999-00 (1).

Season Team	League	GP	G	A	Pts.	PIM	+/-	PP	SH	GP	G	A	Pts.	PIM
		REGULAR SEASON								PLAYOFFS				
93-94—Caledon	Jr. A	44	15	33	48	104	...	...	...	—	—	—	—	—
94-95—Lake Superior St.	CCHA	38	6	15	21	34	12	0	1	—	—	—	—	—
95-96—Lake Superior St.	CCHA	40	13	22	35	48	...	...	...	—	—	—	—	—
96-97—Lake Superior St.	CCHA	38	12	27	39	80	...	...	...	—	—	—	—	—
97-98—New Haven	AHL	48	15	21	36	48	-9	4	0	1	0	0	0	0
—Carolina	NHL	33	2	4	6	10	-1	0	0	—	—	—	—	—
98-99—Carolina	NHL	60	7	11	18	22	7	0	0	6	0	3	3	8
99-00—Carolina	NHL	77	16	18	34	39	20	3	0	—	—	—	—	—
00-01—Carolina	NHL	80	12	15	27	76	-14	2	0	6	0	2	2	2
01-02—Carolina	NHL	82	21	25	46	44	-6	5	1	23	5	9	14	14
02-03—Carolina	NHL	70	5	14	19	90	-17	0	1	—	—	—	—	—
—Colorado	NHL	13	1	5	6	10	-2	1	0	7	0	2	2	4
03-04—Colorado	NHL	4	0	1	1	4	-1	0	0	—	—	—	—	—
—Washington	NHL	66	4	6	10	38	-23	0	0	—	—	—	—	—
04-05—Mississippi	ECHL	25	6	11	17	24	7	2	...	4	0	0	0	10
NHL Totals (7 years)		485	68	99	167	333	-37	11	2	42	5	16	21	28

BAUMGARTNER, NOLAN — D — CANUCKS

PERSONAL: Born March 23, 1976, in Calgary. ... 6-1/200. ... Shoots right.

TRANSACTIONS/CAREER NOTES: Selected by Washington Capitals in first round (first Capitals pick, 10th overall) of NHL draft (June 28, 1994). ... Traded by Capitals to Chicago Blackhawks for D Remi Royer (July 21, 2000). ... Signed as free agent by Vancouver Canucks (July 11, 2002). ... Claimed by Pittsburgh Penguins from Canucks in waiver draft (October 3, 2003). ... Claimed by Canucks off waivers from Penguins (November 1, 2003).

		REGULAR SEASON								PLAYOFFS				
Season Team	**League**	**GP**	**G**	**A**	**Pts.**	**PIM**	**+/-**	**PP**	**SH**	**GP**	**G**	**A**	**Pts.**	**PIM**
92-93—Kamloops	WHL	43	0	5	5	30	...	...	...	11	1	1	2	0
93-94—Kamloops	WHL	69	13	42	55	109	62	5	1	19	3	14	17	33
94-95—Kamloops	WHL	62	8	36	44	71	50	3	0	21	4	13	17	16
95-96—Washington	NHL	1	0	0	0	0	-1	0	0	1	0	0	0	10
—Kamloops	WHL	28	13	15	28	45	...	...	...	16	1	9	10	26
96-97—Portland	AHL	8	2	2	4	4	-6	1	0	—	—	—	—	—
97-98—Portland	AHL	70	2	24	26	70	-12	1	0	10	1	4	5	10
—Washington	NHL	4	0	1	1	0	0	0	0	—	—	—	—	—
98-99—Portland	AHL	38	5	14	19	62	-16	2	0	—	—	—	—	—
—Washington	NHL	5	0	0	0	0	-3	0	0	—	—	—	—	—
99-00—Portland	AHL	71	5	18	23	56	...	...	...	4	1	2	3	10
—Washington	NHL	8	0	1	1	2	1	0	0	—	—	—	—	—
00-01—Norfolk	AHL	63	5	28	33	75	...	...	...	9	2	3	5	11
—Chicago	NHL	8	0	0	0	6	-4	0	0	—	—	—	—	—
01-02—Norfolk	AHL	76	10	24	34	72	1	4	0	4	0	1	1	2
02-03—Vancouver	NHL	8	1	2	3	4	4	1	0	2	0	0	0	0
—Manitoba	AHL	59	8	31	39	82	15	5	0	1	0	0	0	4
03-04—Manitoba	AHL	55	6	21	27	101	-2	1	0	—	—	—	—	—
—Pittsburgh	NHL	5	0	0	0	2	-7	0	0	—	—	—	—	—
—Vancouver	NHL	9	0	3	3	2	3	0	0	—	—	—	—	—
04-05—Manitoba	AHL	78	9	30	39	51	-5	7	0	14	0	4	4	10
NHL Totals (7 years)		48	1	7	8	16	-7	1	0	3	0	0	0	10

BAYDA, RYAN — LW — HURRICANES

PERSONAL: Born December 9, 1980, in Saskatoon, Sask. ... 5-11/185. ... Shoots left.
TRANSACTIONS/CAREER NOTES: Selected by Carolina Hurricanes in third round (second Hurricanes pick, 80th overall) of NHL draft (June 24, 2000).

		REGULAR SEASON								PLAYOFFS				
Season Team	**League**	**GP**	**G**	**A**	**Pts.**	**PIM**	**+/-**	**PP**	**SH**	**GP**	**G**	**A**	**Pts.**	**PIM**
98-99—Vernon	BCHL	45	24	58	82	15	...	...	...	—	—	—	—	—
99-00—Univ. of North Dakota	WCHA	36	14	14	28	32	...	...	...	—	—	—	—	—
00-01—Univ. of North Dakota	WCHA	46	25	34	59	48	...	...	...	—	—	—	—	—
01-02—Univ. of North Dakota	WCHA	37	19	28	47	52	...	...	...	—	—	—	—	—
—Lowell	AHL	3	1	1	2	0	3	0	0	5	3	0	3	0
02-03—Lowell	AHL	53	11	32	43	32	-9	2	0	—	—	—	—	—
—Carolina	NHL	25	4	10	14	16	-5	0	0	—	—	—	—	—
03-04—Carolina	NHL	44	3	3	6	22	-14	0	0	—	—	—	—	—
—Lowell	AHL	34	7	15	22	28	0	2	1	—	—	—	—	—
04-05—Lowell	AHL	80	13	27	40	91	-7	4	1	9	3	3	6	4
NHL Totals (2 years)		69	7	13	20	38	-19	0	0					

BEAUCHEMIN, FRANCOIS — D — BLUE JACKETS

PERSONAL: Born June 4, 1980, in Sorel, Que. ... 6-0/214. ... Shoots left. ... Name pronounced frahn-SWUH boh-sheh-MEH.
TRANSACTIONS/CAREER NOTES: Selected by Montreal Canadiens in 3rd round (3rd Canadiens pick, 75th overall) of entry draft (June 27, 1998). ... Claimed by Columbus Blue Jackets off waivers from Canadiens (September 14, 2004).

		REGULAR SEASON								PLAYOFFS				
Season Team	**League**	**GP**	**G**	**A**	**Pts.**	**PIM**	**+/-**	**PP**	**SH**	**GP**	**G**	**A**	**Pts.**	**PIM**
96-97—Laval	QMJHL	66	7	20	27	112	...	...	...	3	0	0	0	2
97-98—Laval	QMJHL	70	12	35	47	132	...	...	...	16	1	3	4	23
98-99—Acadie-Bathurst	QMJHL	31	4	17	21	53	27	1	1	23	2	16	18	55
99-00—Acadie-Bathurst	QMJHL	38	11	36	47	64	7	1	0	—	—	—	—	—
—Moncton	QMJHL	33	8	31	39	35	43	1	0	16	2	11	13	14
00-01—Quebec	AHL	56	3	6	9	44	...	...	...	—	—	—	—	—
01-02—Quebec	AHL	56	8	11	19	88	-11	3	0	3	0	1	1	0
—Mississippi	ECHL	7	1	3	4	2	-1	0	0	—	—	—	—	—
02-03—Montreal	NHL	1	0	0	0	0	-1	0	0	—	—	—	—	—
—Hamilton	AHL	75	7	21	28	92	25	3	0	23	1	9	10	16
04-05—Syracuse	AHL	72	3	27	30	55	17	1	0	—	—	—	—	—
NHL Totals (1 year)		1	0	0	0	0	-1	0	0					

BEAUDOIN, ERIC — LW — PANTHERS

PERSONAL: Born May 3, 1980, in Ottawa. ... 6-5/220. ... Shoots left. ... Name pronounced boh-DWEH.
TRANSACTIONS/CAREER NOTES: Selected by Tampa Bay Lightning in fourth round (fourth Lightning pick, 92nd overall) of NHL draft (June 27, 1998). ... Traded by Lightning to Florida Panthers for seventh-round pick (D Marek Priechodsky) in 2000 draft (June 2, 2000). ... Back spasms (October 17, 2002); missed two games.

		REGULAR SEASON								PLAYOFFS				
Season Team	**League**	**GP**	**G**	**A**	**Pts.**	**PIM**	**+/-**	**PP**	**SH**	**GP**	**G**	**A**	**Pts.**	**PIM**
96-97—Ottawa	Tier II Jr. A	54	12	19	31	55	...	...	...	—	—	—	—	—
97-98—Guelph	OHL	62	9	13	22	43	-3	...	...	12	3	2	5	4
98-99—Guelph	OHL	66	28	43	71	79	21	...	...	11	5	3	8	12
99-00—Guelph	OHL	68	38	34	72	126	1	14	5	6	3	0	3	2
00-01—Louisville	AHL	71	15	10	25	78	...	...	...	—	—	—	—	—

Season Team	League	GP	G	A	Pts.	PIM	+/-	PP	SH	GP	G	A	Pts.	PIM
		REGULAR SEASON								PLAYOFFS				
01-02—Utah	AHL	44	5	16	21	83	13	2	0	—	—	—	—	—
—Florida	NHL	8	1	3	4	4	-2	0	0	—	—	—	—	—
02-03—Florida	NHL	15	0	1	1	25	-7	0	0	—	—	—	—	—
—San Antonio	AHL	41	14	23	37	36	16	4	2	3	1	0	1	0
03-04—San Antonio	AHL	38	20	22	42	45	15	4	0	—	—	—	—	—
—Florida	NHL	30	2	4	6	12	-6	0	0	—	—	—	—	—
04-05—Edmonton	AHL	24	3	1	4	9	2	0	0	—	—	—	—	—
—San Antonio	AHL	32	6	4	10	21	-3	2	1	—	—	—	—	—
NHL Totals (3 years)		53	3	8	11	41	-15	0	0					

BEDNAR, JAROSLAV LW/RW

PERSONAL: Born November 9, 1976, in Prague, Czechoslovakia. ... 6-0/198. ... Shoots right. ... Name pronounced bed-NASH.

TRANSACTIONS/CAREER NOTES: Selected by Los Angeles Kings in second round (third Kings pick, 51st overall) of NHL draft (June 23, 2001). ... Traded by Kings with D Andreas Lilja to Florida Panthers for D Dmitry Yushkevich and fifth-round pick (Brady Murray) in 2003 draft (November 26, 2002). ... Flu (April 6, 2003); missed one game. ... Released by Panthers (December 1, 2003). ... Signed by the Avangard Omsk of the Russian league (May 9, 2004).

Season Team	League	GP	G	A	Pts.	PIM	+/-	PP	SH	GP	G	A	Pts.	PIM
		REGULAR SEASON								PLAYOFFS				
94-95—Slavia Praha	Czech Rep.	20	6	7	13	4	...	...	...	3	0	0	0	0
95-96—Slavia Praha	Czech Rep.	20	3	1	4	6	...	...	...	3	0	0	0	0
96-97—Slavia Praha	Czech Rep.	45	18	12	30	18	...	...	...	—	—	—	—	—
97-98—Slavia Praha	Czech Rep.	14	2	5	7	6	...	...	...	—	—	—	—	—
—HC Keramika Plzen	Czech Rep.	34	26	15	41	16	...	...	...	5	2	4	6	4
98-99—Sparta Praha	Czech Rep.	52	23	14	37	30	...	...	...	8	5	2	7	0
99-00—JyP Jyvaskyla	Finland	53	34	28	62	56	...	...	...	—	—	—	—	—
00-01—HIFK Helsinki	Finland	56	*32	28	60	51	...	...	...	5	3	1	4	0
01-02—Los Angeles	NHL	22	4	2	6	8	-4	1	0	3	0	0	0	0
—Manchester	AHL	48	16	21	37	16	16	3	0	—	—	—	—	—
02-03—Los Angeles	NHL	15	0	9	9	4	3	0	0	—	—	—	—	—
—Florida	NHL	52	5	13	18	14	-2	2	0	—	—	—	—	—
03-04—Florida	NHL	13	1	1	2	4	2	0	0	—	—	—	—	—
—San Antonio	AHL	2	2	1	3	0	1	0	0	—	—	—	—	—
—Avangard Omsk	Russian	29	10	5	15	34	7	...	...	11	2	0	2	2
04-05—Avangard Omsk	Russian	53	12	16	28	56	2	...	...	13	3	2	5	6
NHL Totals (3 years)		102	10	25	35	30	-1	3	0	3	0	0	0	0

BEECH, KRIS C PENGUINS

PERSONAL: Born February 5, 1981, in Salmon Arm, B.C. ... 6-2/209. ... Shoots left.

TRANSACTIONS/CAREER NOTES: Selected by Washington Capitals in first round (first Capitals pick, seventh overall) of NHL draft (June 26, 1999). ... Traded by Capitals with C Michal Sivek, D Ross Lupaschuk and future considerations to Pittsburgh Penguins for RW Jaromir Jagr and D Frantisek Kucera (July 11, 2001). ... Appendectomy (December 15, 2002); missed 15 games. ... Signed as free agent by Wilkes-Barre/Scranton of the AHL (September 26, 2004).

Season Team	League	GP	G	A	Pts.	PIM	+/-	PP	SH	GP	G	A	Pts.	PIM
		REGULAR SEASON								PLAYOFFS				
96-97—Sicamous	Jr. A	49	34	36	70	80	...	...	...	—	—	—	—	—
—Calgary	WHL	8	1	1	2	0	...	...	...	—	—	—	—	—
97-98—Calgary	WHL	68	26	41	67	103	...	...	...	—	—	—	—	—
98-99—Calgary	WHL	58	10	25	35	24	...	...	...	—	—	—	—	—
99-00—Calgary	WHL	66	32	54	86	99	25	15	2	5	3	5	8	16
00-01—Washington	NHL	4	0	0	0	2	-2	0	0	—	—	—	—	—
—Calgary	WHL	40	22	44	66	103	...	...	...	10	2	8	10	26
01-02—Pittsburgh	NHL	79	10	15	25	45	-25	2	0	—	—	—	—	—
02-03—Pittsburgh	NHL	12	0	1	1	6	-3	0	0	—	—	—	—	—
—Wilkes-Barre/Scranton	AHL	50	19	24	43	76	-4	10	1	5	1	1	2	0
03-04—Pittsburgh	NHL	4	0	1	1	6	0	0	0	—	—	—	—	—
—Wilkes-Barre/Scranton	AHL	53	20	26	46	97	15	9	0	22	9	5	14	22
04-05—Wilkes-Barre/Scranton	AHL	68	14	48	62	146	17	3	0	11	4	6	10	14
NHL Totals (4 years)		99	10	17	27	59	-30	2	0					

BEGIN, STEVE C/LW CANADIENS

PERSONAL: Born June 14, 1978, in Trois-Rivieres, Que. ... 5-11/195. ... Shoots left. ... Name pronounced BAY-zhin.

TRANSACTIONS/CAREER NOTES: Selected by Calgary Flames in second round (third Flames pick, 40th overall) of NHL draft (June 22, 1996). ... Injured shoulder (October 10, 1997); missed six games. ... Dislocated fibula (March 18, 2000); missed final 10 games of season. ... Injured shoulder (January 17, 2002); missed nine games. ... Injured head (April 2, 2002); missed remainder of season. ... Traded by Flames to Buffalo Sabres with C Chris Drury for D Rhett Warrener and C Steve Reinprecht (July 2, 2003). ... Claimed by Montreal Canadiens from Sabres in waiver draft (October 3, 2003). ... Injured shoulder (October 16, 2003); missed three games. ... Injured left shoulder (December 10, 2003) and had surgery (December 18, 2003); missed 23 games. ... Flu (March 16, 2004); missed one game.

Season Team	League	GP	G	A	Pts.	PIM	+/-	PP	SH	GP	G	A	Pts.	PIM
		REGULAR SEASON								PLAYOFFS				
95-96—Val-d'Or	QMJHL	64	13	23	36	218	...	...	...	13	1	3	4	33
96-97—Val-d'Or	QMJHL	58	13	33	46	207	...	...	...	10	0	3	3	8
—Saint John	AHL	...	...	...	...	...	...	...	...	4	0	2	2	6

Season Team	League	REGULAR SEASON GP	G	A	Pts.	PIM	+/-	PP	SH	PLAYOFFS GP	G	A	Pts.	PIM
97-98—Calgary	NHL	5	0	0	0	23	0	0	0	—	—	—	—	—
—Val-d'Or	QMJHL	35	18	17	35	73	...	...	...	15	2	12	14	34
98-99—Saint John	AHL	73	11	9	20	156	-16	3	0	7	2	0	2	18
99-00—Calgary	NHL	13	1	1	2	18	-3	0	0	—	—	—	—	—
—Saint John	AHL	47	13	12	25	99	...	...	...	—	—	—	—	—
00-01—Saint John	AHL	58	14	14	28	109	...	...	...	19	10	7	17	18
—Calgary	NHL	4	0	0	0	21	0	0	0	—	—	—	—	—
01-02—Calgary	NHL	51	7	5	12	79	-3	1	0	—	—	—	—	—
02-03—Calgary	NHL	50	3	1	4	51	-7	0	0	—	—	—	—	—
03-04—Montreal	NHL	52	10	5	15	41	6	0	1	9	0	1	1	10
04-05—Hamilton	AHL	21	10	3	13	20	6	0	2	4	0	2	2	8
NHL Totals (6 years)		175	21	12	33	233	-7	1	1	9	0	1	1	10

B

BEKAR DEREK — LW/C — ISLANDERS

PERSONAL: Born September 15, 1975, in Burnaby, B.C. ... 6-3/200. ... Shoots left. ... Name pronounced BEH-kahr.

TRANSACTIONS/CAREER NOTES: Selected by St. Louis Blues in eighth round (seventh Blues pick, 205th overall) of NHL draft (July 8, 1995). ... Traded by Blues to Washington Capitals for C Mike Peluso (November 29, 2000). ... Signed as free agent by Los Angeles Kings (September 25, 2001). ... Signed as free agent by New York Islanders (September 10, 2003). ... Signed as free agent by Springfield of the AHL (November 22, 2004).

Season Team	League	REGULAR SEASON GP	G	A	Pts.	PIM	+/-	PP	SH	PLAYOFFS GP	G	A	Pts.	PIM
94-95—Powell River	BCJHL	46	33	29	62	35	...	...	...	—	—	—	—	—
95-96—New Hampshire	Hockey East	34	15	18	33	4	...	...	...	—	—	—	—	—
96-97—New Hampshire	Hockey East	39	18	21	39	34	...	7	0	—	—	—	—	—
97-98—New Hampshire	Hockey East	35	32	28	60	46	...	...	...	—	—	—	—	—
98-99—Worcester	AHL	51	16	20	36	6	-3	4	1	4	0	0	0	0
99-00—Worcester	AHL	71	21	19	40	26	...	...	...	7	0	3	3	2
—St. Louis	NHL	1	0	0	0	0	0	0	0	—	—	—	—	—
00-01—Worcester	AHL	18	5	2	7	10	...	...	...	—	—	—	—	—
—Portland	AHL	58	19	16	35	49	...	...	...	3	0	0	0	0
01-02—Manchester	AHL	74	27	20	47	42	4	4	4	5	1	4	5	2
02-03—Los Angeles	NHL	6	0	0	0	4	-1	0	0	—	—	—	—	—
—Manchester	AHL	51	19	19	38	49	6	3	4	3	0	0	0	2
03-04—Bridgeport	AHL	76	24	11	35	57	4	5	0	3	2	2	4	0
—New York Islanders	NHL	4	0	0	0	2	0	0	0	—	—	—	—	—
04-05—Springfield	AHL	51	8	14	22	22	-16	1	0	—	—	—	—	—
NHL Totals (3 years)		11	0	0	0	6	-1	0	0					

BELAK WADE — D/RW — MAPLE LEAFS

PERSONAL: Born July 3, 1976, in Saskatoon, Sask. ... 6-5/221. ... Shoots right. ... Brother of Graham Belak, defenseman, Colorado Avalanche organization (1997-98 and 1998-99). ... Name pronounced BEE-lak.

TRANSACTIONS/CAREER NOTES: Selected by Quebec Nordiques in first round (first Nordiques pick, 12th overall) of NHL draft (June 28, 1994). ... Nordiques franchise moved to Colorado and renamed Avalanche for 1995-96 season (June 21, 1995). ... Injured abdominal muscle (March 5, 1998); missed six games. ... Strained groin (October 9, 1998); missed first two games of season. ... Strained groin (October 26, 1998); missed one game. ... Reinjured groin (November 2, 1998); missed 10 games. ... Traded by Avalanche with LW Rene Corbet and future considerations to Calgary Flames for RW Theo Fleury and LW Chris Dingman (February 28, 1999); Flames acquired D Robyn Regehr to complete deal (March 27, 1999). ... Had concussion (November 10, 1999); missed one game. ... Injured shoulder (February 10, 2000); missed 18 games. ... Injured groin (March 22, 2000); missed three games. ... Claimed off waivers by Toronto Maple Leafs (February 16, 2001). ... Injured (March 29, 2001); missed final four games of regular season. ... Flu (March 2, 2002); missed three games. ... Had concussion (October 15, 2002); missed seven games. ... Suspended two games for elbowing incident (November 27, 2002). ... Injured abdomen (November 21, 2003); missed 10 games. ... Injured left knee (January 7, 2004); missed 28 games. ... Suspended final six regular-season games and two playoff games for high-sticking incident (March 22, 2004).

Season Team	League	REGULAR SEASON GP	G	A	Pts.	PIM	+/-	PP	SH	PLAYOFFS GP	G	A	Pts.	PIM
91-92—North Battleford	SJHL	57	6	20	26	186	...	...	...	—	—	—	—	—
92-93—North Battleford	SJHL	32	3	13	16	142	...	...	...	—	—	—	—	—
93-94—Saskatoon	WHL	69	4	13	17	226	20	0	0	16	2	2	4	43
94-95—Saskatoon	WHL	72	4	14	18	290	12	0	0	9	0	0	0	36
—Cornwall	AHL	...	...	...	...	...	...	...	...	11	1	2	3	40
95-96—Saskatoon	WHL	63	3	15	18	207	...	...	...	4	0	0	0	9
—Cornwall	AHL	5	0	0	0	18	...	...	...	2	0	0	0	2
96-97—Colorado	NHL	5	0	0	0	11	-1	0	0	—	—	—	—	—
—Hershey	AHL	65	1	7	8	320	-1	0	0	16	0	1	1	61
97-98—Colorado	NHL	8	1	1	2	27	-3	0	0	—	—	—	—	—
—Hershey	AHL	11	0	0	0	30	-5	0	0	—	—	—	—	—
98-99—Colorado	NHL	22	0	0	0	71	-2	0	0	—	—	—	—	—
—Hershey	AHL	17	0	1	1	49	8	0	0	—	—	—	—	—
—Saint John	AHL	12	0	2	2	43	-3	0	0	6	0	1	1	23
—Calgary	NHL	9	0	1	1	23	3	0	0	—	—	—	—	—
99-00—Calgary	NHL	40	0	2	2	122	-4	0	0	—	—	—	—	—
00-01—Calgary	NHL	23	0	0	0	79	-2	0	0	—	—	—	—	—
—Toronto	NHL	16	1	1	2	31	-4	0	0	—	—	—	—	—
01-02—Toronto	NHL	63	1	3	4	142	2	0	0	16	1	0	1	18
02-03—Toronto	NHL	55	3	6	9	196	-2	0	0	2	0	0	0	4
03-04—Toronto	NHL	34	1	1	2	109	0	0	0	4	0	0	0	14
04-05—Coventry	England	34	6	9	15	170	...	...	...	8	1	1	2	16
NHL Totals (8 years)		275	7	15	22	811	-13	0	0	22	1	0	1	36

BELANGER, ERIC — C — KINGS

PERSONAL: Born December 16, 1977, in Sherbrooke, Que. ... 6-0/185. ... Shoots left. ... Name pronounced buh-LAH-zhay.
TRANSACTIONS/CAREER NOTES: Selected by Los Angeles Kings in 4th round (5th Kings pick, 96th overall) of NHL draft (June 22, 1996). ... Back spasms (February 25, 2001); missed two games. ... Left wrist surgery (January 15, 2002); missed 29 games. ... Injured back (December 29, 2002); missed six games. ... Reinjured back (January 13, 2003); missed 14 games.
STATISTICAL PLATEAUS: Three-goal games: 2002-03 (1).

		REGULAR SEASON								PLAYOFFS				
Season Team	**League**	**GP**	**G**	**A**	**Pts.**	**PIM**	**+/-**	**PP**	**SH**	**GP**	**G**	**A**	**Pts.**	**PIM**
94-95—Beauport	QMJHL	71	12	28	40	24	...	...	...	—	—	—	—	—
95-96—Beauport	QMJHL	59	35	48	83	18	...	...	...	20	13	14	27	6
96-97—Beauport	QMJHL	31	13	37	50	30	...	...	...	—	—	—	—	—
—Rimouski	QMJHL	31	26	41	67	36	...	...	...	4	2	3	5	10
97-98—Fredericton	AHL	56	17	34	51	28	-1	6	0	4	2	1	3	2
98-99—Springfield	AHL	33	8	18	26	10	8	1	0	3	0	1	1	2
—Long Beach	IHL	1	0	0	0	0	0	0	0	—	—	—	—	—
99-00—Lowell	AHL	65	15	25	40	20	...	...	...	7	3	3	6	2
00-01—Los Angeles	NHL	62	9	12	21	16	14	1	2	13	1	4	5	2
—Lowell	AHL	13	8	10	18	4	...	...	...	—	—	—	—	—
01-02—Los Angeles	NHL	53	8	16	24	21	2	2	1	7	0	0	0	4
02-03—Los Angeles	NHL	62	16	19	35	26	-5	0	3	—	—	—	—	—
03-04—Los Angeles	NHL	81	13	20	33	44	-16	0	1	—	—	—	—	—
04-05—Bolzano	Italy	12	13	10	23	20	...	...	...	—	—	—	—	—
NHL Totals (4 years)		258	46	67	113	107	-5	3	7	20	1	4	5	6

BELFOUR, ED — G — MAPLE LEAFS

PERSONAL: Born April 21, 1965, in Carman, Man. ... 5-11/202. ... Catches left.
TRANSACTIONS/CAREER NOTES: Signed as free agent by Chicago Blackhawks (June 18, 1987). ... Strained hip muscle (1993-94 season); missed four games. ... Sprained knee (January 31, 1996); missed one game. ... Injured back (February 19, 1996); missed three games. ... Traded by Blackhawks to San Jose Sharks for G Chris Terreri, D Michal Sykora and RW Ulf Dahlen (January 25, 1997). ... Injured knee ligament (February 1, 1997); missed 13 games. ... Bulging disc in back (March 1, 1997); missed seven games. ... Signed as free agent by Dallas Stars (July 2, 1997). ... Strained lower back (February 2, 1998); missed three games. ... Strained groin (November 10, 1999); missed one game. ... Injured back (March 23, 2001); missed one game. ... Injured back (March 29, 2002); missed two games. ... Traded by Stars with RW Cameron Mann to Nashville Predators for C David Gosselin and fifth-round pick (G Eero Kilpelainen) in 2003 entry draft (June 29, 2002). ... Signed as free agent by Toronto Maple Leafs (July 2, 2002). ... Infected thumb (October 13, 2002); missed four games. ... Back spasms (January 17, 2003); missed four games. ... Injured groin (January 4, 2004); missed three games. ... Injured back (February 3, 2004); missed three games. ... Reinjured back (February 14, 2004); missed eight games.

		REGULAR SEASON									PLAYOFFS							
Season Team	**League**	**GP**	**Min.**	**W**	**L**	**T**	**GA**	**SO**	**GAA**	**SV%**	**GP**	**Min.**	**W**	**L**	**GA**	**SO**	**GAA**	**SV%**
85-86—Winkler	MJHL	48	2880	...	...	...	124	1	2.58	...	—	—	—	—	—	—	—	—
86-87—North Dakota	WCHA	34	2049	29	4	0	81	3	2.37	...	—	—	—	—	—	—	—	—
87-88—Saginaw	IHL	61	*3446	32	25	0	183	3	3.19	...	9	561	4	5	33	0	3.53	...
88-89—Chicago	NHL	23	1148	4	12	3	74	0	3.87	.878	—	—	—	—	—	—	—	—
—Saginaw	IHL	29	1760	12	10	0	92	0	3.14	...	5	298	2	3	14	0	2.82	...
89-90—Canadian nat'l team	Int'l	33	1808	...	...	...	93	...	3.09	...	—	—	—	—	—	—	—	—
—Chicago	NHL	...	...	...	...	...	...	...	...	...	9	409	4	2	17	0	2.49	.915
90-91—Chicago	NHL	*74	*4127	*43	19	7	170	4	*2.47	*.910	6	295	2	4	20	0	4.07	.891
91-92—Chicago	NHL	52	2928	21	18	10	132	5	2.70	.894	18	949	12	4	39	1	*2.47	.902
92-93—Chicago	NHL	*71	*4106	41	18	11	177	*7	2.59	.906	4	249	0	4	13	0	3.13	.866
93-94—Chicago	NHL	70	3998	37	24	6	178	7	2.67	.906	6	360	2	4	15	0	2.50	.921
94-95—Chicago	NHL	42	2450	22	15	3	93	5	2.28	.906	16	1014	9	7	37	1	2.19	.923
95-96—Chicago	NHL	50	2956	22	17	10	135	1	2.74	.902	9	666	6	3	23	1	*2.07	.929
96-97—Chicago	NHL	33	1966	11	15	6	88	1	2.69	.907	—	—	—	—	—	—	—	—
—San Jose	NHL	13	757	3	9	0	43	1	3.41	.884	—	—	—	—	—	—	—	—
97-98—Dallas	NHL	61	3581	37	12	10	112	9	*1.88	.916	17	1039	10	7	31	1	1.79	.922
98-99—Dallas	NHL	61	3536	35	15	9	117	5	1.99	.915	*23	*1544	*16	7	43	*3	*1.67	.930
99-00—Dallas	NHL	62	3620	32	21	7	127	4	2.10	.919	23	1443	14	*9	*45	*4	1.87	.931
00-01—Dallas	NHL	63	3687	35	20	7	144	8	2.34	.905	10	671	4	6	25	0	2.24	.910
01-02—Dallas	NHL	60	3467	21	27	11	153	1	2.65	.895	—	—	—	—	—	—	—	—
—Can. Olympic team	Int'l		Did not play															
02-03—Toronto	NHL	62	3738	37	20	5	141	7	2.26	.922	7	532	3	4	24	0	2.71	.915
03-04—Toronto	NHL	59	3444	34	19	6	122	10	2.13	.918	13	774	6	7	27	3	2.09	.929
NHL Totals (16 years)		856	49509	435	281	111	2006	75	2.43	.908	161	9945	88	68	359	14	2.17	.920

BELL, BRENDAN — D — MAPLE LEAFS

PERSONAL: Born March 31, 1983, in Ottawa. ... 6-1/198. ... Shoots left.
TRANSACTIONS/CAREER NOTES: Selected by Toronto Maple Leafs in third round (third Maple Leafs pick, 65th overall) of NHL draft (June 23, 2001).

		REGULAR SEASON								PLAYOFFS				
Season Team	**League**	**GP**	**G**	**A**	**Pts.**	**PIM**	**+/-**	**PP**	**SH**	**GP**	**G**	**A**	**Pts.**	**PIM**
99-00—Ottawa	OHL	48	1	32	33	34	...	...	...	5	0	1	1	4
00-01—Ottawa	OHL	68	7	32	39	59	...	...	...	20	1	11	12	22
01-02—Ottawa	OHL	67	10	36	46	56	...	...	...	13	2	5	7	25
02-03—Ottawa	OHL	55	14	39	53	46	...	...	...	23	8	19	27	25
03-04—St. John's	AHL	74	7	19	26	62	-19	1	0	—	—	—	—	—
04-05—St. John's	AHL	75	6	25	31	57	-15	4	0	5	0	1	1	2

BELL, MARK — LW/C — BLACKHAWKS

PERSONAL: Born August 5, 1980, in St. Paul's, Ont. ... 6-4/205. ... Shoots left.
TRANSACTIONS/CAREER NOTES: Selected by Chicago Blackhawks in first round (first Blackhawks pick, eighth overall) of NHL draft (June 27, 1998). ... Bruised hip (March 18, 2002); missed two games.

		REGULAR SEASON								PLAYOFFS				
Season Team	League	GP	G	A	Pts.	PIM	+/-	PP	SH	GP	G	A	Pts.	PIM
95-96—Stratford Jr. B	OHA	47	8	15	23	32	...	...	...	—	—	—	—	—
96-97—Ottawa	OHL	65	8	12	20	40	...	...	...	24	4	7	11	13
97-98—Ottawa	OHL	55	34	26	60	87	...	...	...	13	6	5	11	14
98-99—Ottawa	OHL	44	29	26	55	69	28	...	...	9	6	5	11	8
99-00—Ottawa	OHL	48	34	38	72	95	11	12	7	2	0	1	1	0
00-01—Norfolk	AHL	61	15	27	42	126	...	...	...	9	4	3	7	10
—Chicago	NHL	13	0	1	1	4	0	0	0	—	—	—	—	—
01-02—Chicago	NHL	80	12	16	28	124	-6	1	0	5	0	0	0	8
02-03—Chicago	NHL	82	14	15	29	113	0	0	2	—	—	—	—	—
03-04—Chicago	NHL	82	21	24	45	106	-14	2	0	—	—	—	—	—
04-05—Trondheim	Norway	25	10	17	27	87	5	...	...	11	6	6	12	44
NHL Totals (4 years)		257	47	56	103	347	-20	3	2	5	0	0	0	8

BERARD, BRYAN — D — BLUE JACKETS

PERSONAL: Born March 5, 1977, in Woonsocket, R.I. ... 6-2/218. ... Shoots left. ... Name pronounced buh-RAHRD.
TRANSACTIONS/CAREER NOTES: Selected by Ottawa Senators in 1st round (1st Senators pick, 1st overall) of NHL draft (July 8, 1995). ... Traded by Senators with C Martin Straka to New York Islanders for D Wade Redden and G Damian Rhodes (January 23, 1996). ... Strained groin (October 16, 1997); missed one game. ... Reinjured groin (November 10, 1997); missed two games. ... Reinjured groin (November 15, 1997); missed three games. ... Bruised elbow (March 24, 1998); missed one game. ... Strained groin (December 18, 1998); missed nine games. ... Traded by Islanders with 6th-round pick (RW Jan Sochor) in 1999 draft to Toronto Maple Leafs for G Felix Potvin and 6th-round pick (C Fedor Fedorov) in 1999 draft (January 9, 1999). ... Strained groin (January 7, 1999); missed three games. ... Flu (March 28, 1999); missed two games. ... Suspended two games for illegal check (October 19, 1999). ... Injured (November 23, 1999); missed three games. ... Injured eye (March 11, 2000); missed remainder of season. ... Missed 2000-01 season recovering from eye injury. ... Signed as free agent by New York Rangers (October 4, 2001). ... Signed as free agent by Boston Bruins (August 13, 2002). ... Signed as free agent by Chicago Blackhawks (October 31, 2003). ... Injured groin (November 22, 2003); missed one game. ... Reinjured groin (December 12, 2003); missed 10 games. ... Signed as free agent by Columbus Blue Jackets (Aug. 3, 2005).

		REGULAR SEASON								PLAYOFFS				
Season Team	League	GP	G	A	Pts.	PIM	+/-	PP	SH	GP	G	A	Pts.	PIM
91-92—Mt. St. Charles H.S.	R.I.H.S.	32	3	15	18	10	...	...	...	—	—	—	—	—
92-93—Mt. St. Charles H.S.	R.I.H.S.	32	8	12	20	18	...	...	...	—	—	—	—	—
93-94—Mt. St. Charles H.S.	R.I.H.S.	32	11	36	47	5	...	...	...	—	—	—	—	—
94-95—Det. Jr. Red Wings	OHL	58	20	55	75	97	...	13	1	21	4	20	24	38
95-96—Det. Jr. Red Wings	OHL	56	31	58	89	116	...	...	...	17	7	18	25	41
96-97—New York Islanders	NHL	82	8	40	48	86	1	3	0	—	—	—	—	—
97-98—New York Islanders	NHL	75	14	32	46	59	-32	8	1	—	—	—	—	—
—U.S. Olympic team	Int'l	2	0	0	0	0	-1	0	0	—	—	—	—	—
98-99—New York Islanders	NHL	31	4	11	15	26	-6	2	0	—	—	—	—	—
—Toronto	NHL	38	5	14	19	22	7	2	0	17	1	8	9	8
99-00—Toronto	NHL	64	3	27	30	42	11	1	0	—	—	—	—	—
00-01—Toronto	NHL	Did not play — injured												
01-02—New York Rangers	NHL	82	2	21	23	60	-1	0	0	—	—	—	—	—
02-03—Boston	NHL	80	10	28	38	64	-4	4	0	3	1	0	1	2
03-04—Chicago	NHL	58	13	34	47	53	-24	6	0	—	—	—	—	—
NHL Totals (8 years)		510	59	207	266	412	-48	26	1	20	2	8	10	10

BEREHOWSKY, DRAKE — D

PERSONAL: Born January 3, 1972, in Toronto. ... 6-2/217. ... Shoots right. ... Name pronounced BAIR-ih-HOW-skee.
TRANSACTIONS/CAREER NOTES: Selected by Toronto Maple Leafs in first round (first Maple Leafs pick, 10th overall) of NHL draft (June 16, 1990). ... Sprained knee (April 15, 1993); missed remainder of season. ... Knee surgery before 1994-95 season; missed first four games of season. ... Traded by Maple Leafs to Pittsburgh Penguins for D Grant Jennings (April 7, 1995). ... Signed as free agent by Edmonton Oilers (September 29, 1997). ... Traded by Oilers with G Eric Fichaud and D Greg de Vries to Nashville Predators for F Jim Dowd and G Mikhail Shtalenkov (October 1, 1998). ... Sprained knee (February 4, 1999); missed two games. ... Injured neck (October 2, 1999); missed first game of season. ... Strained elbow (November 26, 2000); missed two games. ... Suspended one game by NHL for receiving match penalty (December 29, 2000). ... Traded by Predators to Vancouver Canucks for second-round pick (RW Timofei Shiskanov) in 2001 draft (March 9, 2001). ... Traded by Canucks with C Denis Pederson to Phoenix Coyotes for LW Todd Warriner, C Trevor Letowski, RW Tyler Bouck and third-round pick (C Dimitri Pestunov) in 2003 draft (December 28, 2001). ... Injured right knee (October 8, 2002) and had surgery; missed 59 games. ... Signed as free agent by Pittsburgh Penguins (August 29, 2003). ... Injured finger (December 27, 2003); missed five games. ... Traded by Penguins to Maple Leafs for D Ric Jackman (February 11, 2004).

		REGULAR SEASON								PLAYOFFS				
Season Team	League	GP	G	A	Pts.	PIM	+/-	PP	SH	GP	G	A	Pts.	PIM
87-88—Barrie Jr. B	OHA	40	10	36	46	81	...	...	...	—	—	—	—	—
88-89—Kingston	OHL	63	7	39	46	85	...	...	...	—	—	—	—	—
89-90—Kingston	OHL	9	3	11	14	28	...	...	...	—	—	—	—	—
90-91—Toronto	NHL	8	0	1	1	25	-6	0	0	—	—	—	—	—
—Kingston	OHL	13	5	13	18	28	...	...	...	—	—	—	—	—
—North Bay	OHL	26	7	23	30	51	...	...	...	10	2	7	9	21
91-92—North Bay	OHL	62	19	63	82	147	...	...	...	21	7	24	31	22
—Toronto	NHL	1	0	0	0	0	0	0	0	—	—	—	—	—
—St. John's	AHL	...	...	...	...	...	...	...	...	6	0	5	5	21

Season Team	League	GP	G	A	Pts.	PIM	+/-	PP	SH	GP	G	A	Pts.	PIM
		REGULAR SEASON								PLAYOFFS				
92-93—Toronto	NHL	41	4	15	19	61	1	1	0	—	—	—	—	—
—St. John's	AHL	28	10	17	27	38	18	5	0	—	—	—	—	—
93-94—Toronto	NHL	49	2	8	10	63	-3	2	0	—	—	—	—	—
—St. John's	AHL	18	3	12	15	40	2	3	0	—	—	—	—	—
94-95—Toronto	NHL	25	0	2	2	15	-10	0	0	—	—	—	—	—
—Pittsburgh	NHL	4	0	0	0	13	1	0	0	1	0	0	0	0
95-96—Cleveland	IHL	74	6	28	34	141	...	...	...	3	0	3	3	6
—Pittsburgh	NHL	1	0	0	0	0	1	0	0	—	—	—	—	—
96-97—San Antonio	IHL	16	3	4	7	36	...	...	...	—	—	—	—	—
—Carolina	AHL	49	2	15	17	55	-8	1	0	—	—	—	—	—
97-98—Edmonton	NHL	67	1	6	7	169	1	1	0	12	1	2	3	14
—Hamilton	AHL	8	2	0	2	21	0	1	0	—	—	—	—	—
98-99—Nashville	NHL	74	2	15	17	140	-9	0	0	—	—	—	—	—
99-00—Nashville	NHL	79	12	20	32	87	-4	5	0	—	—	—	—	—
00-01—Nashville	NHL	66	6	18	24	100	-9	3	0	—	—	—	—	—
—Vancouver	NHL	14	1	1	2	21	0	1	0	4	0	0	0	12
01-02—Vancouver	NHL	25	1	2	3	18	-5	0	0	—	—	—	—	—
—Phoenix	NHL	32	1	4	5	42	5	0	0	5	0	1	1	4
02-03—Springfield	AHL	2	0	0	0	0	0	0	0	—	—	—	—	—
—Phoenix	NHL	7	1	2	3	27	0	0	0	—	—	—	—	—
03-04—Pittsburgh	NHL	47	5	16	21	50	-16	3	0	—	—	—	—	—
—Toronto	NHL	9	1	2	3	17	5	0	0	—	—	—	—	—
04-05—Skelleftea AIK	Sweden	8	1	0	1	49	1	0	0	10	2	5	7	14
NHL Totals (13 years)		549	37	112	149	848	-48	16	0	22	1	3	4	30

BERENZWEIG, BUBBA D STARS

PERSONAL: Born August 8, 1977, in Arlington Heights, Ill. ... 6-1/217. ... Shoots left.

TRANSACTIONS/CAREER NOTES: Selected by New York Islanders in fifth round (fifth Islanders pick, 109th overall) of NHL draft (June 22, 1996). ... Traded by Islanders to Nashville Predators for fourth-round pick (D Johan Halvardsson) in 1999 draft (April 19, 1999). ... Sprained ankle (January 8, 2002); missed 13 games. ... Traded by Predators with future considerations to Dallas Stars for LW Jon Sim (February 17, 2003).

Season Team	League	GP	G	A	Pts.	PIM	+/-	PP	SH	GP	G	A	Pts.	PIM
		REGULAR SEASON								PLAYOFFS				
92-93—Loomis-Chaffee	Conn. H.S.	22	5	13	18	...	...	...	...	—	—	—	—	—
93-94—Loomis-Chaffee	Conn. H.S.	22	12	27	39	...	...	...	...	—	—	—	—	—
94-95—Loomis-Chaffee	Conn. H.S.	23	19	23	42	24	...	...	...	—	—	—	—	—
95-96—Univ. of Michigan	CCHA	42	4	8	12	4	...	...	...	—	—	—	—	—
96-97—Univ. of Michigan	CCHA	38	7	12	19	49	29	2	0	—	—	—	—	—
97-98—Univ. of Michigan	CCHA	43	6	10	16	28	...	...	...	—	—	—	—	—
98-99—Univ. of Michigan	CCHA	42	7	24	31	38	...	...	...	—	—	—	—	—
99-00—Milwaukee	IHL	79	4	23	27	48	...	...	...	3	1	2	3	0
—Nashville	NHL	2	0	0	0	0	-1	0	0	—	—	—	—	—
00-01—Milwaukee	IHL	72	10	26	36	38	...	...	...	5	0	4	4	4
—Nashville	NHL	5	0	0	0	0	0	0	0	—	—	—	—	—
01-02—Milwaukee	AHL	23	2	5	7	23	-4	1	0	—	—	—	—	—
—Nashville	NHL	26	3	7	10	14	-3	0	0	—	—	—	—	—
02-03—Milwaukee	AHL	48	6	11	17	26	-9	3	0	—	—	—	—	—
—Nashville	NHL	4	0	0	0	0	0	0	0	—	—	—	—	—
—Utah	AHL	26	6	11	17	4	3	1	1	1	0	0	0	0
03-04—Utah	AHL	21	4	3	7	2	-12	2	0	—	—	—	—	—
NHL Totals (4 years)		37	3	7	10	14	-4	0	0					

BERG, AKI D MAPLE LEAFS

PERSONAL: Born July 28, 1977, in Turku, Finland. ... 6-3/213. ... Shoots left. ... Name pronounced AH-kee BUHRG.

TRANSACTIONS/CAREER NOTES: Selected by Los Angeles Kings in 1st round (1st Kings pick, 3rd overall) of NHL draft (July 8, 1995). ... Charley horse (January 25, 1997); missed one game. ... Concussion (February 3, 1997); missed two games. ... Sprained left ankle (April 9, 1997); missed final two games of regular season. ... Bruised right foot (December 4, 1997); missed one game. ... Sprained right wrist (March 10, 1998); missed two games. ... Injured ribs (December 23, 1999); missed two games. ... Concussion (March 13, 2000); missed two games. ... Injured (January 4, 2001); missed three games. ... Traded by Kings to Toronto Maple Leafs for C Adam Mair and 2nd-round pick (C Mike Cammalleri) in 2001 draft (March 13, 2001). ... Injured (March 16, 2002); missed one game. ... Injured finger (February 8, 2003); missed two games. ... Reinjured finger (February 15, 2003); missed two games. ... Flu (December 19, 2003); missed three games.

Season Team	League	GP	G	A	Pts.	PIM	+/-	PP	SH	GP	G	A	Pts.	PIM
		REGULAR SEASON								PLAYOFFS				
92-93—TPS Turku	Finland Jr.	39	18	24	42	59	...	...	...	—	—	—	—	—
93-94—TPS Turku	Finland Jr.	21	3	11	14	24	...	...	...	7	0	0	0	10
—TPS Turku	Finland	6	0	3	3	4	...	...	...	—	—	—	—	—
94-95—Kiekko-67	Finland Div. 2	20	3	9	12	34	...	...	...	—	—	—	—	—
—TPS Turku	Finland Jr.	8	1	0	1	30	...	...	...	—	—	—	—	—
—TPS Turku	Finland	5	0	0	0	4	3	...	...	—	—	—	—	—
95-96—Los Angeles	NHL	51	0	7	7	29	-13	0	0	—	—	—	—	—
—Phoenix	IHL	20	0	3	3	18	...	...	...	2	0	0	0	4
96-97—Los Angeles	NHL	41	2	6	8	24	-9	2	0	—	—	—	—	—
—Phoenix	IHL	23	1	3	4	21	...	...	...	—	—	—	—	—
97-98—Los Angeles	NHL	72	0	8	8	61	3	0	0	4	0	3	3	0
—Fin. Olympic team	Int'l	6	0	0	0	6	2	0	0	—	—	—	—	—

Season Team	League	GP	G	A	Pts.	PIM	+/-	PP	SH	GP	G	A	Pts.	PIM
		REGULAR SEASON								PLAYOFFS				
98-99—TPS Turku	Finland	48	8	7	15	137	...	...	...	9	1	1	2	45
99-00—Los Angeles	NHL	70	3	13	16	45	-1	0	0	2	0	0	0	2
00-01—Los Angeles	NHL	47	0	4	4	43	3	0	0	—	—	—	—	—
—Toronto	NHL	12	3	0	3	2	-6	3	0	11	0	2	2	4
01-02—Toronto	NHL	81	1	10	11	46	14	0	0	20	0	1	1	37
—Fin. Olympic team	Int'l	4	1	0	1	2	...	...	...	—	—	—	—	—
02-03—Toronto	NHL	78	4	7	11	28	3	0	0	7	1	1	2	2
03-04—Toronto	NHL	79	2	7	9	40	-1	0	0	10	0	0	0	2
04-05—Timra	Sweden	47	6	14	20	46	11	2	1	7	0	0	0	6
NHL Totals (8 years)		531	15	62	77	318	-7	5	0	54	1	7	8	47

BERGENHEIM, SEAN — LW — ISLANDERS

PERSONAL: Born February 8, 1984, in Helsinki, Finland. ... 5-11/200. ... Shoots left.
TRANSACTIONS/CAREER NOTES: Selected by New York Islanders in first round (first Islanders pick, 22nd overall) of NHL draft (June 22, 2002).

Season Team	League	GP	G	A	Pts.	PIM	+/-	PP	SH	GP	G	A	Pts.	PIM
		REGULAR SEASON								PLAYOFFS				
01-02—Jokerit Helsinki	Finland	28	2	2	4	4	...	...	...	—	—	—	—	—
02-03—Jokerit Helsinki	Finland	38	3	3	6	4	...	...	...	—	—	—	—	—
03-04—Bridgeport	AHL	—	—	—	—	—	—	—	—	7	2	3	5	10
—New York Islanders	NHL	18	1	1	2	4	-4	0	1	—	—	—	—	—
04-05—Bridgeport	AHL	61	15	14	29	69	1	5	1	—	—	—	—	—
NHL Totals (1 year)		18	1	1	2	4	-4	0	1					

BERGERON, MARC-ANDRE — D — OILERS

PERSONAL: Born October 13, 1980, in St-Louis-de-France, Que. ... 5-10/190. ... Shoots left.
TRANSACTIONS/CAREER NOTES: Signed as free agent by Edmonton Oilers (July 20, 2001).

Season Team	League	GP	G	A	Pts.	PIM	+/-	PP	SH	GP	G	A	Pts.	PIM
		REGULAR SEASON								PLAYOFFS				
97-98—Baie-Comeau	QMJHL	40	6	14	20	48	...	...	...	—	—	—	—	—
98-99—Baie-Comeau	QMJHL	46	8	14	22	57	...	...	...	—	—	—	—	—
—Shawinigan	QMJHL	24	6	7	13	66	...	...	...	5	2	2	4	24
99-00—Shawinigan	QMJHL	70	24	50	74	173	...	...	...	13	4	7	11	45
00-01—Shawinigan	QMJHL	69	42	59	101	185	...	...	...	10	4	11	15	24
01-02—Hamilton	AHL	50	2	13	15	61	5	0	0	9	1	4	5	8
02-03—Edmonton	NHL	5	1	1	2	9	2	0	0	1	0	1	1	0
—Hamilton	AHL	66	8	31	39	73	34	3	0	20	0	7	7	25
03-04—Edmonton	NHL	54	9	17	26	26	13	3	0	—	—	—	—	—
—Toronto	AHL	17	4	3	7	23	4	2	0	—	—	—	—	—
04-05—Brynas IF	Sweden	10	3	2	5	72	-1	0	0	9	1	2	3	8
NHL Totals (2 years)		59	10	18	28	35	15	3	0	1	0	1	1	0

BERGERON, PATRICE — C — BRUINS

PERSONAL: Born July 24, 1985, in Ancienne-Lorette, Que. ... 6-0/178. ... Shoots right. ... Name pronounced BAIR-zhur-uhn.
TRANSACTIONS/CAREER NOTES: Selected by Boston Bruins in second round (second Bruins pick, 45th overall) of NHL entry draft (June 21, 2003). ... Injured shoulder (February 24, 2004); missed 11 games. ... Signed as free agent by Providence of the AHL (September 27, 2004).

Season Team	League	GP	G	A	Pts.	PIM	+/-	PP	SH	GP	G	A	Pts.	PIM
		REGULAR SEASON								PLAYOFFS				
01-02—Acadie-Bathurst	QMJHL	4	0	1	1	0	...	...	...	—	—	—	—	—
02-03—Acadie-Bathurst	QMJHL	70	23	50	73	62	...	...	...	11	6	9	15	6
03-04—Boston	NHL	71	16	23	39	22	5	7	0	7	1	3	4	0
04-05—Providence	AHL	68	21	40	61	59	2	6	1	16	5	7	12	4
NHL Totals (1 year)		71	16	23	39	22	5	7	0	7	1	3	4	0

BERGFORS, NIKLAS — RW — DEVILS

PERSONAL: Born March 7, 1987, in Sodertalje, Sweden. ... 5-11/192. ... Shoots right.
TRANSACTIONS/CAREER NOTES: Selected by New Jersey Devils in 1st round (1st Devils pick, 23rd overall) of entry draft (July 30, 2005).

Season Team	League	GP	G	A	Pts.	PIM	+/-	PP	SH	GP	G	A	Pts.	PIM
		REGULAR SEASON								PLAYOFFS				
03-04—Sodertalje	Sweden Jr.	31	13	17	30	22	...	...	...	—	—	—	—	—
04-05—Sodertalje	Sweden Jr.	21	18	16	34	25	...	...	...	—	—	—	—	—

BERGLUND, CHRISTIAN — LW — PANTHERS

PERSONAL: Born March 12, 1980, in Orebro, Sweden. ... 5-11/195. ... Shoots left.
TRANSACTIONS/CAREER NOTES: Selected by New Jersey Devils in second round (third Devils pick, 37th overall) of NHL draft (June 27, 1998). ... Bruised hip (December 13, 2003); missed seven games. ... Bruised hip (January 5, 2004); missed 30 games. ... Traded by Devils with D Victor Uchevatov to Florida Panthers for C Viktor Kozlov (March 1, 2004).

Season Team	League	GP	G	A	Pts.	PIM	+/-	PP	SH	GP	G	A	Pts.	PIM
		REGULAR SEASON								PLAYOFFS				
94-95—Karlskoga	Sweden Dv. 4	20	14	13	27	...	...	...	...	—	—	—	—	—
95-96—Kristinehamn	Sweden Dv. 3	23	8	8	16	12	...	...	...	—	—	—	—	—
96-97—Farjestad Karlstad	Sweden Jr.	21	2	3	5	24	...	...	...	—	—	—	—	—
97-98—Farjestad Karlstad	Sweden Jr.	29	23	19	42	88	...	...	...	2	0	0	0	0
—Farjestad Karlstad	Sweden	1	0	0	0	0	...	...	...	—	—	—	—	—
98-99—Farjestad Karlstad	Sweden Jr.	5	3	4	7	22	...	...	...	—	—	—	—	—
—Farjestad Karlstad	Sweden	37	2	4	6	37	4	...	...	4	1	0	1	4
99-00—Farjestad Karlstad	Sweden	43	8	6	14	44	...	...	...	7	2	1	3	10
—Bofors	Sweden Dv. 2	6	2	0	2	12	...	...	...	—	—	—	—	—
00-01—Farjestad Karlstad	Sweden	49	17	20	37	142	...	...	...	16	7	7	14	22
01-02—Albany	AHL	60	21	26	47	69	-16	7	1	—	—	—	—	—
—New Jersey	NHL	15	2	7	9	8	-3	0	0	3	0	0	0	2
02-03—Albany	AHL	26	6	14	20	57	7	2	0	—	—	—	—	—
—New Jersey	NHL	38	4	5	9	20	3	0	0	—	—	—	—	—
03-04—New Jersey	NHL	23	2	3	5	4	-4	0	0	—	—	—	—	—
—Florida	NHL	10	3	1	4	10	-2	0	0	—	—	—	—	—
04-05—Farjestad Karlstad	Sweden	48	7	13	20	97	-5	0	0	14	2	3	5	56
NHL Totals (3 years)		86	11	16	27	42	-6	0	0	3	0	0	0	2

BERNIER, STEVE RW SHARKS

PERSONAL: Born March 31, 1985, in Quebec City. ... 6-2/233. ... Shoots right.

TRANSACTIONS/CAREER NOTES: Selected by San Jose Sharks (2nd Sharks pick, 16th overall) in 2003 entry draft (June 23, 2003).

Season Team	League	GP	G	A	Pts.	PIM	+/-	PP	SH	GP	G	A	Pts.	PIM
		REGULAR SEASON								PLAYOFFS				
01-02—Moncton	QMJHL	66	31	28	59	51	...	...	...	—	—	—	—	—
02-03—Moncton	QMJHL	71	49	52	101	90	...	...	...	—	—	—	—	—
03-04—Moncton	QMJHL	66	36	46	82	80	...	...	...	20	7	10	17	17
04-05—Moncton	QMJHL	68	35	36	71	114	18	12	1	12	6	13	19	22

BERRY, RICK D COYOTES

PERSONAL: Born November 4, 1978, in Brandon, Man. ... 6-2/213. ... Shoots left.

TRANSACTIONS/CAREER NOTES: Selected by Colorado Avalanche in third round (third Avalanche pick, 55th overall) of NHL draft (June 21, 1997). ... Traded by Avalanche with LW Ville Nieminen to Pittsburgh Penguins for D Darius Kasparitis (March 19, 2002). ... Claimed by Washington Capitals from Penguins in waiver draft (October 4, 2002). ... Suspended one game for spearing incident (February 25, 2004). ... Signed as free agent by Phoenix Coyotes (September 2, 2004).

Season Team	League	GP	G	A	Pts.	PIM	+/-	PP	SH	GP	G	A	Pts.	PIM
		REGULAR SEASON								PLAYOFFS				
95-96—Seattle	WHL	59	4	9	13	103	...	...	...	1	0	0	0	0
96-97—Seattle	WHL	72	12	21	33	125	...	...	...	15	3	7	10	23
97-98—Spokane	WHL	59	9	21	30	131	11	1	1	17	1	4	5	26
—Seattle	WHL	37	5	12	17	100	...	...	...	—	—	—	—	—
98-99—Hershey	AHL	62	2	6	8	153	-12	0	0	—	—	—	—	—
99-00—Hershey	AHL	64	9	16	25	148	...	...	...	13	2	3	5	24
00-01—Hershey	AHL	48	6	17	23	87	...	...	...	12	2	2	4	18
—Colorado	NHL	19	0	4	4	38	5	0	0	—	—	—	—	—
01-02—Colorado	NHL	57	0	0	0	60	1	0	0	—	—	—	—	—
—Pittsburgh	NHL	13	0	2	2	21	-4	0	0	—	—	—	—	—
02-03—Washington	NHL	43	2	1	3	87	-3	0	0	—	—	—	—	—
03-04—Washington	NHL	65	0	6	6	108	-5	0	0	—	—	—	—	—
—Portland	AHL	10	2	1	3	12	-3	0	0	—	—	—	—	—
04-05—Utah	AHL	45	2	6	8	83	-20	1	0	—	—	—	—	—
NHL Totals (4 years)		197	2	13	15	314	-6	0	0					

BERTRAM, DAN RW BLACKHAWKS

PERSONAL: Born January 14, 1987, in Calgary, Alta. ... 5-11/175. ... Shoots right.

Season Team	League	GP	G	A	Pts.	PIM	+/-	PP	SH	GP	G	A	Pts.	PIM
		REGULAR SEASON								PLAYOFFS				
03-04—Camrose	AJHL	44	22	33	55	...	...	...	...	—	—	—	—	—
04-05—Boston College	Hockey East	38	9	8	17	58	...	...	...	—	—	—	—	—

BERTUZZI, TODD RW CANUCKS

PERSONAL: Born February 2, 1975, in Sudbury, Ont. ... 6-3/245. ... Shoots left. ... Name pronounced buhr-TOO-zee.

TRANSACTIONS/CAREER NOTES: Selected by New York Islanders in 1st round (1st Islanders pick, 23rd overall) of NHL draft (June 26, 1993). ... Injured eye (February 22, 1996); missed two games. ... Suspended three games for attempting to break free of a linesman (April 2, 1996). ... Bone chips in elbow (November 23, 1996); missed one game. ... Traded by Islanders with D Bryan McCabe and 3rd-round pick (LW Jarkko Ruutu) in 1998 entry draft to Vancouver Canucks for C Trevor Linden (February 6, 1998). ... Bruised thigh (March 17, 1998); missed four games. ... Fractured leg (November 1, 1998); missed 31 games. ... Tore knee ligament (March 5, 1999); missed remainder of season. ... Concussion (October 20, 1999); missed one game. ... Injured thumb (February 23, 2000); missed one game. ... Bruised shoulder (January 28, 2001); missed three games. ... Suspended 10 games for elbowing incident (October 15, 2001). ... Suspended indefinitely for match penalty for deliberate attempt to injure Colorado Avalanche C Steve Moore (March 8, 2004); missed remainder of season and playoffs. Reinstated

(Aug. 8, 2005); missed total of 13 regular season games and 7 playoff games.
STATISTICAL PLATEAUS: Three-goal games: 2000-01 (1), 2001-02 (1), 2002-03 (1). Total: 3.

		REGULAR SEASON								PLAYOFFS				
Season Team	**League**	**GP**	**G**	**A**	**Pts.**	**PIM**	**+/-**	**PP**	**SH**	**GP**	**G**	**A**	**Pts.**	**PIM**
91-92—Guelph	OHL	47	7	14	21	145	...	...	...	—	—	—	—	—
92-93—Guelph	OHL	59	27	32	59	164	...	...	...	5	2	2	4	6
93-94—Guelph	OHL	61	28	54	82	165	...	8	0	9	2	6	8	30
94-95—Guelph	OHL	62	54	65	119	58	...	15	0	14	*15	18	33	41
95-96—New York Islanders	NHL	76	18	21	39	83	-14	4	0	—	—	—	—	—
96-97—New York Islanders	NHL	64	10	13	23	68	-3	3	0	—	—	—	—	—
—Utah	IHL	13	5	5	10	16	...	...	...	—	—	—	—	—
97-98—New York Islanders	NHL	52	7	11	18	58	-19	1	0	—	—	—	—	—
—Vancouver	NHL	22	6	9	15	63	2	1	1	—	—	—	—	—
98-99—Vancouver	NHL	32	8	8	16	44	-6	1	0	—	—	—	—	—
99-00—Vancouver	NHL	80	25	25	50	126	-2	4	0	—	—	—	—	—
00-01—Vancouver	NHL	79	25	30	55	93	-18	14	0	4	2	2	4	8
01-02—Vancouver	NHL	72	36	49	85	110	21	14	0	6	2	2	4	14
02-03—Vancouver	NHL	82	46	51	97	144	2	*25	0	14	2	4	6	*60
03-04—Vancouver	NHL	69	17	43	60	122	21	8	0	—	—	—	—	—
NHL Totals (9 years)		628	198	260	458	911	-16	75	1	24	6	8	14	82

BETTS, BLAIR — C — RANGERS

PERSONAL: Born February 16, 1980, in Edmonton. ... 6-3/200. ... Shoots left.
TRANSACTIONS/CAREER NOTES: Selected by Calgary Flames in second round (second Flames pick, 33rd overall) of NHL draft (June 27, 1998). ... Injured shoulder (November 25, 2003); missed 15 games. ... Reinjured shoulder (December 31, 2003); missed final 46 games of season. ... Traded by Flames with G Jamie McLennan and RW Greg Moore to New York Rangers for LW Chris Simon and seventh-round pick (C Matt Schneider) in 2004 draft (March 6, 2004).

		REGULAR SEASON								PLAYOFFS				
Season Team	**League**	**GP**	**G**	**A**	**Pts.**	**PIM**	**+/-**	**PP**	**SH**	**GP**	**G**	**A**	**Pts.**	**PIM**
96-97—Prince George	WHL	58	12	18	30	19	...	...	...	15	2	2	4	6
97-98—Prince George	WHL	71	35	41	76	38	14	15	1	11	4	6	10	8
98-99—Prince George	WHL	42	20	22	42	39	2	8	1	7	3	2	5	8
99-00—Prince George	WHL	44	24	35	59	38	19	6	2	13	11	11	22	6
00-01—Saint John	AHL	75	13	15	28	28	...	...	...	19	2	3	5	4
01-02—Saint John	AHL	67	20	29	49	10	-3	10	0	—	—	—	—	—
—Calgary	NHL	6	1	0	1	2	-1	0	0	—	—	—	—	—
02-03—Saint John	AHL	19	6	7	13	6	2	0	0	—	—	—	—	—
—Calgary	NHL	9	1	3	4	0	3	0	0	—	—	—	—	—
03-04—Calgary	NHL	20	1	2	3	10	-1	1	0	—	—	—	—	—
04-05—Hartford	AHL	16	5	4	9	4	3	1	1	0	0	0	0	0
NHL Totals (3 years)		35	3	5	8	12	1	1	0					

BEZINA, GORAN — D — COYOTES

PERSONAL: Born March 21, 1980, in Split, Yugoslavia. ... 6-2/225. ... Shoots left.
TRANSACTIONS/CAREER NOTES: Selected by Phoenix Coyotes in eighth round (eighth Coyotes pick, 234th overall) of NHL draft (June 27, 1999).

		REGULAR SEASON								PLAYOFFS				
Season Team	**League**	**GP**	**G**	**A**	**Pts.**	**PIM**	**+/-**	**PP**	**SH**	**GP**	**G**	**A**	**Pts.**	**PIM**
98-99—Fribourg-Gotteron	Switz. Jr.	22	11	6	17	64	...	...	...	—	—	—	—	—
—Fribourg-Gotteron	Switzerland	38	0	0	0	14	...	...	...	4	0	0	0	2
99-00—Fribourg-Gotteron	Switz. Jr.	2	0	1	1	16	...	...	...	2	1	1	2	8
—Fribourg-Gotteron	Switzerland	44	3	6	9	10	...	...	...	4	0	0	0	6
00-01—Fribourg-Gotteron	Switzerland	44	10	10	20	44	...	...	...	5	1	1	2	12
01-02—Springfield	AHL	66	2	11	13	50	-17	1	0	—	—	—	—	—
02-03—Springfield	AHL	64	3	4	7	27	-10	1	0	—	—	—	—	—
03-04—Phoenix	NHL	3	0	0	0	2	-1	0	0	—	—	—	—	—
—Springfield	AHL	74	11	10	21	65	-22	4	1	—	—	—	—	—
04-05—Geneva	Switzerland	33	7	12	19	51	...	...	...	—	—	—	—	—
NHL Totals (1 year)		3	0	0	0	2	-1	0	0					

BICEK, JIRI — RW/LW

PERSONAL: Born December 3, 1978, in Kosice, Czechoslovakia. ... 5-10/190. ... Shoots left. ... Name pronounced YEH-ree bee-SEHK.
TRANSACTIONS/CAREER NOTES: Selected by New Jersey Devils in fifth round (fourth Devils pick, 131st overall) of NHL draft (June 21, 1997).

		REGULAR SEASON								PLAYOFFS				
Season Team	**League**	**GP**	**G**	**A**	**Pts.**	**PIM**	**+/-**	**PP**	**SH**	**GP**	**G**	**A**	**Pts.**	**PIM**
94-95—HC Kosice	Slovakia Jrs.	42	38	36	74	18	...	...	...	—	—	—	—	—
95-96—HC Kosice	Slovakia	30	10	15	25	16	...	...	...	9	2	4	6	0
96-97—HC Kosice	Slovakia	44	11	14	25	20	...	...	...	7	1	3	4	...
97-98—Albany	AHL	50	10	10	20	22	-3	1	0	13	1	6	7	4
98-99—Albany	AHL	79	15	45	60	102	23	4	0	5	2	2	4	2
99-00—Albany	AHL	80	7	36	43	51	...	...	...	4	0	2	2	0
00-01—Albany	AHL	73	12	29	41	73	...	...	...	—	—	—	—	—
—New Jersey	NHL	5	1	0	1	4	0	0	0	—	—	—	—	—
01-02—Albany	AHL	62	15	19	34	45	-30	4	0	—	—	—	—	—

Season Team	League	REGULAR SEASON GP	G	A	Pts.	PIM	+/-	PP	SH	PLAYOFFS GP	G	A	Pts.	PIM
—New Jersey	NHL	1	0	0	0	0	-1	0	0	—	—	—	—	—
02-03—Albany	AHL	24	4	10	14	28	-7	0	0	—	—	—	—	—
—New Jersey	NHL	44	5	6	11	25	7	1	0	5	0	0	0	0
03-04—Albany	AHL	55	12	18	30	39	-8	3	1	—	—	—	—	—
—New Jersey	NHL	12	0	1	1	0	0	0	0	2	0	0	0	0
04-05—HC Kosice	Slovakia	54	18	23	41	69	13	...	...	10	6	8	14	4
NHL Totals (4 years)		62	6	7	13	29	6	1	0	7	0	0	0	0

BIEKSA, KEVIN D CANUCKS

PERSONAL: Born June 3, 1981, in Grimsby, Ont. ... 6-1/180. ... Shoots right. ... Name pronounced BEEKS-ah.
TRANSACTIONS/CAREER NOTES: Selected by Vancouver Canucks in fifth round (fourth Canucks pick, 151th overall) of NHL entry draft (June 24, 2001).

Season Team	League	REGULAR SEASON GP	G	A	Pts.	PIM	+/-	PP	SH	PLAYOFFS GP	G	A	Pts.	PIM
00-01—Bowling Green	CCHA	35	4	9	13	90	...	...	...	—	—	—	—	—
01-02—Bowling Green	CCHA	40	5	10	15	68	...	...	...	—	—	—	—	—
02-03—Bowling Green	CCHA	34	8	17	25	92	...	...	...	—	—	—	—	—
03-04—Bowling Green	CCHA	38	7	15	22	66	...	...	...	—	—	—	—	—
—Manitoba	AHL	4	0	2	2	2	...	...	...	—	—	—	—	—
04-05—Manitoba	AHL	80	12	27	39	192	21	4	0	14	1	1	2	52

BIERK, ZAC G

PERSONAL: Born September 17, 1976, in Peterborough, Ont. ... 6-5/205. ... Catches left. ... Name pronounced BUHRK.
TRANSACTIONS/CAREER NOTES: Selected by Tampa Bay Lightning in ninth round (eighth Lightning pick, 212th overall) of NHL draft (July 8, 1995). ... Injured neck (April 6, 2000); missed final two games of season. ... Selected by Minnesota Wild in expansion draft (June 23, 2000). ... Signed as free agent by Phoenix Coyotes (August 30, 2001). ... Strained groin (February 15, 2003); missed 15 games. ... Injured hip flexor (November 12, 2003); missed 50 games. ... Strained groin (March 5, 2004); missed final 16 games of season.

Season Team	League	REGULAR SEASON GP	Min.	W	L	T	GA	SO	GAA	SV%	PLAYOFFS GP	Min.	W	L	GA	SO	GAA	SV%
93-94—Peterborough	Tier II Jr. A	4	205	...	...	...	17	0	4.98	...	—	—	—	—	—	—	—	—
—Peterborough	OHL	9	423	0	4	2	37	0	5.25	...	1	33	0	0	7	0	12.73	...
94-95—Peterborough	OHL	35	1798	12	15	5	118	0	3.94	.886	6	301	2	3	24	0	4.78	...
95-96—Peterborough	OHL	58	3292	31	16	6	174	2	3.17	...	*22	*1383	*14	7	*83	0	3.60	...
96-97—Peterborough	OHL	49	2744	*28	16	0	151	2	3.30	.916	11	666	6	5	35	0	3.15	.914
97-98—Adirondack	AHL	12	558	1	6	1	36	0	3.87	.891	—	—	—	—	—	—	—	—
—Tampa Bay	NHL	13	433	1	4	1	30	0	4.16	.857	—	—	—	—	—	—	—	—
98-99—Cleveland	IHL	27	1556	11	12	4	79	0	3.05	.914	—	—	—	—	—	—	—	—
—Tampa Bay	NHL	1	59	0	1	0	2	0	2.03	.905	—	—	—	—	—	—	—	—
99-00—Detroit	IHL	15	846	6	8	2	46	1	3.26	...	—	—	—	—	—	—	—	—
—Tampa Bay	NHL	12	509	4	4	1	31	0	3.65	.899	—	—	—	—	—	—	—	—
00-01—Cleveland	IHL	49	2785	24	18	5	134	6	2.89	...	4	182	0	3	10	0	3.30	...
—Minnesota	NHL	1	60	0	1	0	6	0	6.00	.778	—	—	—	—	—	—	—	—
01-02—Springfield	AHL	1	20	0	1	0	4	0	12.00	.714	—	—	—	—	—	—	—	—
—Augusta	ECHL	30	1747	16	9	3	68	1	2.34	.919	—	—	—	—	—	—	—	—
02-03—Springfield	AHL	13	685	6	4	1	33	0	2.89	.915	—	—	—	—	—	—	—	—
—Phoenix	NHL	16	884	4	9	1	32	1	2.17	.932	—	—	—	—	—	—	—	—
03-04—Phoenix	NHL	4	190	0	1	2	12	0	3.79	.889	—	—	—	—	—	—	—	—
—Springfield	AHL	2	106	0	1	1	6	0	3.40	.893	—	—	—	—	—	—	—	—
NHL Totals (6 years)		47	2135	9	20	5	113	1	3.18	.901								

BIRON, MARTIN G SABRES

PERSONAL: Born August 15, 1977, in Lac St. Charles, Que. ... 6-2/169. ... Catches left. ... Brother of Mathieu Biron, D, Florida Panthers.
TRANSACTIONS/CAREER NOTES: Selected by Buffalo Sabres in first round (second Sabres pick, 16th overall) of NHL draft (July 8, 1995). ... Missed first 12 games of 2000-01 season in contract dispute.

Season Team	League	REGULAR SEASON GP	Min.	W	L	T	GA	SO	GAA	SV%	PLAYOFFS GP	Min.	W	L	GA	SO	GAA	SV%
94-95—Beauport	QMJHL	56	3193	29	16	9	132	3	2.48	.898	16	902	8	7	37	4	2.46	.909
95-96—Beauport	QMJHL	55	3207	29	17	7	152	1	2.84	...	*19	1132	*12	8	64	0	3.39	...
—Buffalo	NHL	3	119	0	2	0	10	0	5.04	.844	—	—	—	—	—	—	—	—
96-97—Beauport	QMJHL	18	935	6	10	1	62	1	3.98	...	—	—	—	—	—	—	—	—
—Hull	QMJHL	16	972	11	4	1	43	2	2.65	...	6	326	3	1	19	0	3.50	.871
97-98—Rochester	AHL	41	2312	14	18	6	113	*5	2.93	.907	4	239	1	3	16	0	4.02	.885
—South Carolina	ECHL	2	86	0	1	1	3	0	2.09	...	—	—	—	—	—	—	—	—
98-99—Rochester	AHL	52	3129	36	13	3	108	*6	*2.07	.930	*20	1167	12	*8	42	1	*2.16	.934
—Buffalo	NHL	6	281	1	2	1	10	0	2.14	.917	—	—	—	—	—	—	—	—
99-00—Rochester	AHL	6	344	6	0	0	12	1	2.09	...	—	—	—	—	—	—	—	—
—Buffalo	NHL	41	2229	19	18	2	90	5	2.42	.909	—	—	—	—	—	—	—	—
00-01—Rochester	AHL	4	239	3	1	0	4	1	1.00	.955	—	—	—	—	—	—	—	—
—Buffalo	NHL	18	918	7	7	1	39	2	2.55	.909	—	—	—	—	—	—	—	—
01-02—Buffalo	NHL	72	4085	31	28	10	151	4	2.22	.915	—	—	—	—	—	—	—	—
02-03—Buffalo	NHL	54	3170	17	28	6	135	4	2.56	.908	—	—	—	—	—	—	—	—
03-04—Buffalo	NHL	52	2972	26	18	5	125	2	2.52	.913	—	—	—	—	—	—	—	—
NHL Totals (7 years)		246	13774	101	103	25	560	17	2.44	.911								

BIRON, MATHIEU — D — CAPITALS

PERSONAL: Born April 29, 1980, in Lac St. Charles, Que. ... 6-6/229. ... Shoots right. ... Brother of Martin Biron, G, Buffalo Sabres.
TRANSACTIONS/CAREER NOTES: Selected by Los Angeles Kings in 1st round (1st Kings pick, 21st overall) of NHL draft (June 27, 1998). ... Traded by Kings with C Olli Jokinen, LW Josh Green and 1st-round pick (LW Taylor Pyatt) in 1999 draft to New York Islanders for RW Zigmund Palffy, C Bryan Smolinski, G Marcel Cousineau and 4th-round pick (C Daniel Johansson) in 1999 draft (June 20, 1999). ... Traded by Islanders with 2nd-round pick (traded to Washington; traded to Vancouver; Canucks selected Denis Grot) in 2002 draft to Tampa Bay Lightning for RW Alexander Kharitonov and D Adrian Aucoin (June 22, 2001). ... Claimed by Columbus Blue Jackets from Lightning in waiver draft (October 4, 2002). ... Traded by Blue Jackets to Florida Panthers for RW Petr Tenkrat (October 4, 2002). ... Fractured thumb (October 3, 2003); missed 17 games. ... Contract bought out by Panthers (July 28, 2005). ... Signed as free agent by Washington Capitals (Aug. 10, 2005).

		REGULAR SEASON								PLAYOFFS				
Season Team	League	GP	G	A	Pts.	PIM	+/-	PP	SH	GP	G	A	Pts.	PIM
97-98—Shawinigan	QMJHL	59	8	28	36	60	...	...	...	6	0	1	1	10
98-99—Shawinigan	QMJHL	69	13	32	45	116	7	7	2	6	0	2	2	6
99-00—New York Islanders	NHL	60	4	4	8	38	-13	2	0	—	—	—	—	—
00-01—Lowell	AHL	22	1	3	4	17	...	...	...	—	—	—	—	—
—New York Islanders	NHL	14	0	1	1	12	2	0	0	—	—	—	—	—
—Springfield	AHL	34	0	6	6	18	...	...	...	—	—	—	—	—
01-02—Springfield	AHL	35	4	9	13	16	5	1	0	—	—	—	—	—
—Tampa Bay	NHL	36	0	0	0	12	-16	0	0	—	—	—	—	—
02-03—Florida	NHL	34	1	8	9	14	-18	0	1	—	—	—	—	—
—San Antonio	AHL	43	3	8	11	58	...	...	...	—	—	—	—	—
03-04—Florida	NHL	57	3	10	13	51	-13	0	0	—	—	—	—	—
NHL Totals (5 years)		201	8	23	31	127	-58	2	1					

BISHAI, MIKE — C

PERSONAL: Born May 30, 1979, in Edmonton. ... 5-11/185. ... Shoots left. ... Name pronounced BHISH-igh.
TRANSACTIONS/CAREER NOTES: Signed as free agent by Edmonton Oilers (April 4, 2002).

		REGULAR SEASON								PLAYOFFS				
Season Team	League	GP	G	A	Pts.	PIM	+/-	PP	SH	GP	G	A	Pts.	PIM
96-97—South Surrey	BCHL	38	6	13	19	10	...	...	...	—	—	—	—	—
97-98—South Surrey	BCHL	47	48	52	100	36	...	...	...	—	—	—	—	—
98-99—Western Michigan	CCHA	26	0	3	3	20	...	...	...	—	—	—	—	—
99-00—Western Michigan	CCHA	35	18	19	37	52	...	...	...	—	—	—	—	—
00-01—Western Michigan	CCHA	37	23	45	68	37	...	...	...	—	—	—	—	—
01-02—Western Michigan	CCHA	34	10	27	37	28	...	...	...	—	—	—	—	—
—Hamilton	AHL	3	0	0	0	0	...	...	...	—	—	—	—	—
02-03—Columbia	ECHL	25	12	17	29	24	...	...	...	—	—	—	—	—
—Hamilton	AHL	27	7	5	12	11	...	...	...	6	2	1	3	2
03-04—Toronto	AHL	48	11	22	33	18	6	1	1	3	0	0	0	4
—Edmonton	NHL	14	0	2	2	19	0	0	0	—	—	—	—	—
04-05—Edmonton	AHL	70	10	24	34	36	-6	3	0	—	—	—	—	—
NHL Totals (1 year)		14	0	2	2	19	0	0	0					

BLACKBURN, DAN — G

PERSONAL: Born May 20, 1983, In Montreal. ... 6-1/180. ... Catches left.
TRANSACTIONS/CAREER NOTES: Selected by New York Rangers in first round (first Rangers pick, 10th overall) of NHL draft (June 23, 2001). ... Injured groin (December 14, 2002); missed one game. ... Injured left shoulder (October 7, 2003) and had surgery (March 31, 2004); missed 2003-04 season.

		REGULAR SEASON									PLAYOFFS							
Season Team	League	GP	Min.	W	L	T	GA	SO	GAA	SV%	GP	Min.	W	L	GA	SO	GAA	SV%
99-00—Kootenay	WHL	51	3004	34	8	7	126	3	2.52	...	*21	*1272	*16	5	*43	2	2.03	...
00-01—Kootenay	WHL	50	2922	33	14	2	135	1	2.77	...	11	706	7	4	23	1	1.95	...
01-02—New York Rangers	NHL	31	1737	12	16	0	95	0	3.28	.898	—	—	—	—	—	—	—	—
—Hartford	AHL	4	243	2	1	1	11	0	2.72	.895	—	—	—	—	—	—	—	—
02-03—New York Rangers	NHL	32	1762	8	16	4	93	1	3.17	.890	—	—	—	—	—	—	—	—
03-04—New York Rangers	NHL	Did not play — injured.																
04-05—Victoria	ECHL	12	695	3	9	...	41	0	3.54	.892	—	—	—	—	—	—	—	—
NHL Totals (3 years)		63	3499	20	32	4	188	1	3.22	.894								

BLAKE, JASON — LW — ISLANDERS

PERSONAL: Born September 2, 1973, in Moorhead, Minn. ... 5-10/185. ... Shoots left.
TRANSACTIONS/CAREER NOTES: Signed as free agent by Los Angeles Kings (April 17, 1999). ... Had concussion (December 19, 1999); missed four games. ... Traded by Kings to New York Islanders for fifth-round pick (D Joel Andersen) in 2002 draft (January 3, 2001). ... Had concussion (February 9, 2001); missed one game. ... Granted personal leave for final 13 games of 2000-01 season. ... Sprained knee (November 4, 2003); missed two games. ... High ankle sprain (March 25, 2004); missed remainder of regular season.
STATISTICAL PLATEAUS: Three-goal games: 2002-03 (1), 2003-04 (1). Total: 2.

		REGULAR SEASON								PLAYOFFS				
Season Team	League	GP	G	A	Pts.	PIM	+/-	PP	SH	GP	G	A	Pts.	PIM
94-95—Ferris State	CCHA	36	16	16	32	46	...	...	...	—	—	—	—	—
96-97—Univ. of North Dakota	WCHA	43	19	32	51	44	17	4	2	—	—	—	—	—
97-98—Univ. of North Dakota	WCHA	38	24	27	51	62	...	...	...	—	—	—	—	—

Season Team	League	GP	G	A	Pts.	PIM	+/-	PP	SH	GP	G	A	Pts.	PIM
		REGULAR SEASON								PLAYOFFS				
98-99—North Dakota	WCHA	38	*28	41	*69	49	...	...	...	—	—	—	—	—
—Orlando	IHL	5	3	5	8	6	5	0	0	13	3	4	7	20
—Los Angeles	NHL	1	1	0	1	0	1	0	0	—	—	—	—	—
99-00—Los Angeles	NHL	64	5	18	23	26	4	0	0	3	0	0	0	0
—Long Beach	IHL	7	3	6	9	2	...	...	...	—	—	—	—	—
00-01—Los Angeles	NHL	17	1	3	4	10	-8	0	0	—	—	—	—	—
—Lowell	AHL	2	0	1	1	2	...	...	...	—	—	—	—	—
—New York Islanders	NHL	30	4	8	12	24	-12	1	1	—	—	—	—	—
01-02—New York Islanders	NHL	82	8	10	18	36	-11	0	0	7	0	1	1	13
02-03—New York Islanders	NHL	81	25	30	55	58	16	3	1	5	0	1	1	2
03-04—New York Islanders	NHL	75	22	25	47	56	11	1	4	4	2	0	2	2
04-05—Lugano	Switzerland	7	2	2	4	4	...	0	0	—	—	—	—	—
NHL Totals (6 years)		350	66	94	160	210	1	5	6	19	2	2	4	17

BLAKE, ROB — D — AVALANCHE

PERSONAL: Born December 10, 1969, in Simcoe, Ont. ... 6-4/225. ... Shoots right.

TRANSACTIONS/CAREER NOTES: Selected by Los Angeles Kings in fourth round (fourth Kings pick, 70th overall) of NHL draft (June 11, 1988). ... Sprained knee (April 1990). ... Injured knee (February 12, 1991); missed two games. ... Injured shoulder (October 8, 1991); missed 11 games. ... Sprained knee ligaments (November 28, 1991); missed six games. ... Flu (January 23, 1992); missed one game. ... Flu (February 13, 1992); missed one game. ... Strained shoulder (March 14, 1992); missed four games. ... Fractured rib (December 19, 1992); missed three games. ... Bruised lower back (April 3, 1993); missed final five games of regular season and one playoff game. ... Strained groin (January 23, 1995); missed 11 games. ... Strained groin (March 11, 1995); missed 12 games. ... Strained groin (April 7, 1995); missed one game. ... Tore left knee ligaments (October 20, 1995); missed 76 games. ... Fractured hand (December 26, 1996); missed 11 games. ... Suspended two games and fined $1,000 by NHL for high-sticking incident (February 5, 1997). ... Tendinitis in left knee (February 22, 1997); missed seven games. ... Fractured right foot (November 6, 1998); missed 15 games. ... Suspended three games and fined $1,000 for slashing incident (December 14, 1998). ... Suspended two games for cross-checking incident (April 9, 1999). ... Strained groin (December 8, 1999); missed two games. ... Bruised knee (April 1, 2000); missed three games. ... Fractured lumbar vertebrae (October 13, 2000); missed three games. ... Bruised shoulder (February 21, 2001); missed two games. ... Traded by Kings with C Steve Reinprecht to Colorado Avalanche for RW Adam Deadmarsh, D Aaron Miller, first-round pick (C David Steckel) in 2001 draft, C Jared Aulin and first-round pick (Brian Boyle) in 2003 draft (February 21, 2001). ... Sprained knee (March 20, 2001); missed eight games. ... Injured groin (November 27, 2001); missed three games. ... Flu (February 13, 2002); missed one game. ... Bruised knee (February 11, 2002); missed one game. ... Reinjured knee (February 26, 2002); missed two games. ... Injured groin (November 8, 2002); missed one game. ... Back spasms (January 2, 2003); missed two games. ... Fractured left leg (February 10, 2004); missed seven games.

STATISTICAL PLATEAUS: Three-goal games: 2000-01 (1).

Season Team	League	GP	G	A	Pts.	PIM	+/-	PP	SH	GP	G	A	Pts.	PIM
		REGULAR SEASON								PLAYOFFS				
86-87—Stratford Jr. B	OHA	31	11	20	31	115	...	...	...	—	—	—	—	—
87-88—Bowling Green	CCHA	36	5	8	13	72	...	...	...	—	—	—	—	—
88-89—Bowling Green	CCHA	46	11	21	32	140	...	...	...	—	—	—	—	—
89-90—Bowling Green	CCHA	42	23	36	59	140	...	...	...	—	—	—	—	—
—Los Angeles	NHL	4	0	0	0	4	0	0	0	8	1	3	4	4
90-91—Los Angeles	NHL	75	12	34	46	125	3	9	0	12	1	4	5	26
91-92—Los Angeles	NHL	57	7	13	20	102	-5	5	0	6	2	1	3	12
92-93—Los Angeles	NHL	76	16	43	59	152	18	10	0	23	4	6	10	46
93-94—Los Angeles	NHL	84	20	48	68	137	-7	7	0	—	—	—	—	—
94-95—Los Angeles	NHL	24	4	7	11	38	-16	4	0	—	—	—	—	—
95-96—Los Angeles	NHL	6	1	2	3	8	0	0	0	—	—	—	—	—
96-97—Los Angeles	NHL	62	8	23	31	82	-28	4	0	—	—	—	—	—
97-98—Los Angeles	NHL	81	23	27	50	94	-3	11	0	4	0	0	0	6
—Can. Olympic team	Int'l	6	1	1	2	2	8	0	0	—	—	—	—	—
98-99—Los Angeles	NHL	62	12	23	35	128	-7	5	1	—	—	—	—	—
99-00—Los Angeles	NHL	77	18	39	57	112	10	12	0	4	0	2	2	4
00-01—Los Angeles	NHL	54	17	32	49	69	-8	9	0	—	—	—	—	—
—Colorado	NHL	13	2	8	10	8	11	1	0	23	6	13	19	16
01-02—Colorado	NHL	75	16	40	56	58	16	10	0	20	6	6	12	16
—Can. Olympic team	Int'l	6	1	2	3	2	...	...	...	—	—	—	—	—
02-03—Colorado	NHL	79	17	28	45	57	20	8	2	7	1	2	3	8
03-04—Colorado	NHL	74	13	33	46	61	6	8	0	9	0	5	5	6
NHL Totals (15 years)		903	186	400	586	1235	10	103	3	116	21	42	63	144

BLATNY, ZDENEK — LW — THRASHERS

PERSONAL: Born January 14, 1981, in Brno, Czech. ... 6-1/195. ... Shoots left.

TRANSACTIONS/CAREER NOTES: Selected by Atlanta Thrashers in third round (third Thrashers pick, 68th overall) of NHL draft (June 26, 1999).

Season Team	League	GP	G	A	Pts.	PIM	+/-	PP	SH	GP	G	A	Pts.	PIM
		REGULAR SEASON								PLAYOFFS				
97-98—Kometa Brno	Czech. Jrs.	42	22	21	43	40	...	...	...	—	—	—	—	—
98-99—Seattle	WHL	44	18	15	33	25	7	6	0	11	4	0	4	24
99-00—Seattle	WHL	7	4	5	9	12	...	...	...	—	—	—	—	—
—Kootenay	WHL	61	43	39	82	119	42	20	5	21	10	*17	27	46
00-01—Kootenay	WHL	58	37	48	85	120	...	...	...	11	8	10	18	24
01-02—Chicago	AHL	41	4	3	7	30	-8	0	1	3	2	0	2	0
—Greenville	ECHL	12	5	5	10	17	1	2	0	9	2	8	10	14
02-03—Chicago	AHL	72	12	9	21	62	7	3	0	9	0	2	2	20
—Atlanta	NHL	4	0	0	0	0	-1	0	0	—	—	—	—	—

Season Team	League	GP	G	A	Pts.	PIM	+/-	PP	SH	GP	G	A	Pts.	PIM
		REGULAR SEASON								PLAYOFFS				
03-04—Chicago	AHL	61	11	23	34	115	5	2	0	10	0	4	4	24
—Atlanta	NHL	16	3	0	3	6	0	0	0	—	—	—	—	—
04-05—Reipas Lahti	Finland	9	1	1	2	22	-8	...	...	—	—	—	—	—
—HC Znojemsti Orli	Czech Rep.	15	3	4	7	28	-4	...	...	—	—	—	—	—
NHL Totals (2 years)		20	3	0	3	6	-1	0	0					

BLUNDEN, MICHAEL — RW — BLACKHAWKS

PERSONAL: Born December 15, 1986, in Toronto. ... 6-3/213. ... Shoots right.

Season Team	League	GP	G	A	Pts.	PIM	+/-	PP	SH	GP	G	A	Pts.	PIM
		REGULAR SEASON								PLAYOFFS				
02-03—Erie	OHL	63	10	7	17	55	...	...	...	—	—	—	—	—
03-04—Erie	OHL	52	22	17	39	53	...	...	...	—	—	—	—	—
04-05—Erie	OHL	61	22	19	41	75	-9	10	0	2	0	0	0	2

BOGUNIECKI, ERIC — RW — BLUES

PERSONAL: Born May 6, 1975, in New Haven, Conn. ... 5-8/192. ... Shoots right. ... Name pronounced BOH-guhn-in-kee.

TRANSACTIONS/CAREER NOTES: Selected by St. Louis Blues in eighth round (sixth Blues pick, 193rd overall) of NHL draft (June 29, 1993). ... Signed as free agent by Florida Panthers (July 20, 1999). ... Traded by Panthers to Blues for C Andrei Podkonicky (December 18, 2000). ... Injured shoulder (October 10, 2003); missed season's first 18 games. ... Reinjured shoulder (December 20, 2003); missed 14 games. ... Had concussion (February 29, 2004); missed 18 games. ... Signed as free agent by Worcester of the AHL (December 17, 2004).

Season Team	League	GP	G	A	Pts.	PIM	+/-	PP	SH	GP	G	A	Pts.	PIM
		REGULAR SEASON								PLAYOFFS				
92-93—Westminster School	Conn. H.S.	24	30	24	54	55	...	...	...	—	—	—	—	—
93-94—New Hampshire	Hockey East	40	17	16	33	66	...	3	0	—	—	—	—	—
94-95—New Hampshire	Hockey East	34	12	19	31	62	...	5	1	—	—	—	—	—
95-96—New Hampshire	Hockey East	32	23	28	51	46	...	...	...	—	—	—	—	—
96-97—New Hampshire	Hockey East	36	26	31	57	58	...	14	0	—	—	—	—	—
97-98—Dayton	ECHL	26	19	18	37	36	...	...	...	—	—	—	—	—
—Fort Wayne	IHL	35	4	8	12	29	-4	0	0	4	1	2	3	10
98-99—Fort Wayne	IHL	72	32	34	66	100	2	11	0	2	0	1	1	2
99-00—Louisville	AHL	57	33	42	75	148	...	...	...	4	3	2	5	20
—Florida	NHL	4	0	0	0	2	-1	0	0	—	—	—	—	—
00-01—Louisville	AHL	28	13	12	25	56	...	...	...	—	—	—	—	—
—Worcester	AHL	45	17	28	45	100	...	...	...	9	3	2	5	10
—St. Louis	NHL	1	0	0	0	0	-1	0	0	—	—	—	—	—
01-02—Worcester	AHL	63	38	46	84	181	22	9	3	3	2	0	2	4
—St. Louis	NHL	8	0	1	1	4	-2	0	0	1	0	1	1	0
02-03—St. Louis	NHL	80	22	27	49	38	22	3	1	7	1	2	3	2
03-04—Worcester	AHL	3	0	1	1	0	-2	0	0	—	—	—	—	—
—St. Louis	NHL	27	6	4	10	20	-1	2	0	1	0	0	0	0
04-05—Langenthal	Switzerland	10	5	3	8	47	...	3	1	—	—	—	—	—
—Worcester	AHL	30	14	11	25	46	-3	6	1	—	—	—	—	
NHL Totals (5 years)		120	28	32	60	64	17	5	1	9	1	3	4	2

BOILEAU, PATRICK — D — PENGUINS

PERSONAL: Born February 22, 1975, in Montreal. ... 6-0/202. ... Shoots right. ... Name pronounced BOY-loh.

TRANSACTIONS/CAREER NOTES: Selected by Washington Capitals in third round (third Capitals pick, 69th overall) of NHL draft (June 26, 1993). ... Signed as free agent by Detroit Red Wings (August 5, 2002). ... Signed as free agent by Pittsburgh Penguins (August 28, 2003).

Season Team	League	GP	G	A	Pts.	PIM	+/-	PP	SH	GP	G	A	Pts.	PIM
		REGULAR SEASON								PLAYOFFS				
92-93—Laval	QMJHL	69	4	19	23	73	...	...	...	13	1	2	3	10
93-94—Laval	QMJHL	64	13	57	70	56	27	12	1	21	1	7	8	24
94-95—Laval	QMJHL	38	8	25	33	46	17	5	0	20	4	16	20	24
95-96—Portland	AHL	78	10	28	38	41	...	...	...	19	1	3	4	12
96-97—Portland	AHL	67	16	28	44	63	7	7	1	5	1	1	2	4
—Washington	NHL	1	0	0	0	0	0	0	0	—	—	—	—	—
97-98—Portland	AHL	47	6	21	27	53	2	6	0	10	0	1	1	8
98-99—Portland	AHL	52	6	18	24	52	-23	5	0	—	—	—	—	—
—Indianapolis	IHL	29	8	13	21	27	6	4	0	4	0	1	1	2
—Washington	NHL	4	0	1	1	2	-4	0	0	—	—	—	—	—
99-00—Portland	AHL	63	2	15	17	61	...	...	...	4	0	0	0	4
00-01—Portland	AHL	77	6	14	20	50	...	...	...	3	0	0	0	8
01-02—Portland	AHL	75	17	19	36	43	7	5	0	—	—	—	—	—
—Washington	NHL	2	0	0	0	2	-1	0	0	—	—	—	—	—
02-03—Grand Rapids	AHL	23	2	11	13	39	2	0	0	—	—	—	—	—
—Detroit	NHL	25	2	6	8	14	8	0	0	—	—	—	—	—
03-04—Wilkes-Barre/Scranton	AHL	51	6	26	32	43	6	2	0	24	3	10	13	24
—Pittsburgh	NHL	16	3	4	7	8	-16	3	0	—	—	—	—	—
04-05—Lausanne HC	Switzerland	29	7	12	19	34	...	1	0	15	4	5	9	26
NHL Totals (5 years)		48	5	11	16	26	-13	3	0					

BOMBARDIR, BRAD — D

PERSONAL: Born May 5, 1972, in Powell River, B.C. ... 6-1/205. ... Shoots left. ... Name pronounced BAHM-bahr-deer.

TRANSACTIONS/CAREER NOTES: Selected by New Jersey Devils in third round (fifth Devils pick, 56th overall) of NHL draft (June 16, 1990). ... Bruised left knee (November 29, 1997); missed six games. ... Flu (April 14, 1999); missed three games. ... Injured throat (October 27, 1999); missed four games. ... Bruised left hand (December 9, 1999); missed six games. ... Traded by Devils to Minnesota Wild for G Chris Terreri (June 23, 2000). ... Strained groin (October 20, 2000); missed six games. ... Back spasms (March 19, 2001); missed two games. ... Fractured right ankle (October 14, 2001); missed 29 games. ... Bruised right ankle (December 26, 2001); missed one game. ... Reinjured ankle (January 9, 2002); missed 11 games. ... Reinjured ankle (February 10, 2002); missed two games. ... Reinjured ankle (March 10, 2002); missed four games. ... Reinjured ankle (April 5, 2002); missed remainder of season. ... Injured eye (October 27, 2002); missed one game. ... Suffered concussion (December 23, 2002); missed one game. ... Flu (January 4, 2003); missed two games. ... Back spasms (February 26, 2003); missed 20 games. ... Left team for personal reasons (November 7, 2003); missed four games. ... Injured gluteus muscle (January 17, 2004); missed eight games. ... Traded by Wild with F Sergei Zholtok for third- (D Clayton Stoner) and fourth-round (LW Patrick Bordeleau) picks in 2004 draft (March 5, 2004).

		REGULAR SEASON								PLAYOFFS				
Season Team	League	GP	G	A	Pts.	PIM	+/-	PP	SH	GP	G	A	Pts.	PIM
88-89—Powell River	BCJHL	30	6	5	11	24	...	...	...	6	0	0	0	0
89-90—Powell River	BCJHL	60	10	35	45	93	...	...	...	8	2	3	5	4
90-91—North Dakota	WCHA	33	3	6	9	18	...	...	...	—	—	—	—	—
91-92—North Dakota	WCHA	35	3	14	17	54	...	...	...	—	—	—	—	—
92-93—North Dakota	WCHA	38	8	15	23	34	...	...	...	—	—	—	—	—
93-94—North Dakota	WCHA	38	5	17	22	38	...	...	...	—	—	—	—	—
94-95—Albany	AHL	77	5	22	27	22	21	3	0	14	0	3	3	6
95-96—Albany	AHL	80	6	25	31	63	...	...	...	3	0	1	1	4
96-97—Albany	AHL	32	0	8	8	6	8	0	0	16	1	3	4	8
97-98—New Jersey	NHL	43	1	5	6	8	11	0	0	—	—	—	—	—
—Albany	AHL	5	0	0	0	0	5	0	0	—	—	—	—	—
98-99—New Jersey	NHL	56	1	7	8	16	-4	0	0	5	0	0	0	0
99-00—New Jersey	NHL	32	3	1	4	6	-6	0	0	1	0	0	0	0
00-01—Minnesota	NHL	70	0	15	15	42	-6	0	0	—	—	—	—	—
01-02—Minnesota	NHL	28	1	2	3	14	-6	1	0	—	—	—	—	—
02-03—Minnesota	NHL	58	1	14	15	16	15	1	0	4	0	0	0	0
03-04—Minnesota	NHL	56	1	2	3	21	-10	0	0	—	—	—	—	—
—Nashville	NHL	13	0	0	0	4	1	0	0	6	0	1	1	2
NHL Totals (7 years)		356	8	46	54	127	-5	2	0	16	0	1	1	2

BONDRA, PETER — RW

PERSONAL: Born February 7, 1968, in Luck, U.S.S.R. ... 6-1/202. ... Shoots left. ... Name pronounced BAHN-druh.

TRANSACTIONS/CAREER NOTES: Selected by Washington Capitals in eighth round (ninth Capitals pick, 156th overall) of NHL draft (June 16, 1990). ... Dislocated left shoulder (January 17, 1991). ... Recurring shoulder problems (February 13, 1991); missed 13 games. ... Injured throat (April 4, 1993); missed one game. ... Fractured left hand (November 26, 1993); missed 12 games. ... Flu (April 8, 1995); missed one game. ... Signed by Detroit of IHL during contract dispute (September 28, 1995); re-signed by Capitals (October 20, 1995). ... Separated shoulder (November 11, 1995); missed six games. ... Injured groin (February 24, 1996); missed four games. ... Strained groin (December 4, 1996); missed three games. ... Suspended one game and fined $1,000 for kneeing (February 4, 1997). ... Back spasms (April 1, 1997); missed one game. ... Injured foot (November 29, 1997); missed three games. ... Injured knee (April 8, 1998); missed two games. ... Injured hip (November 28, 1998); missed one game. ... Fractured hand (March 15, 1999); missed remainder of season. ... Knee surgery (December 5, 1999); missed eight games. ... Injured knee (January 4, 2000); missed seven games. ... Injured shoulder (March 30, 1999); missed five games. ... Flu (January 9, 2002); missed three games. ... Flu (February 26, 2002); missed one game. ... Flu (March 2, 2002); missed one game. ... Injured back (November 23, 2002); missed three games. ... Flu (January 1, 2003); missed three games. ... Injured groin (December 31, 2003); missed four games. ... Flu (January 17, 2004); missed one game. ... Traded by Capitals for LW/C Brooks Laich and second-round pick in 2005 draft (February 18, 2004).

STATISTICAL PLATEAUS: Three-goal games: 1990-91 (1), 1994-95 (1), 1995-96 (2), 1996-97 (1), 1997-98 (1), 1998-99 (2), 1999-00 (1), 2000-01 (2), 2001-02 (1), 2003-04 (1). Total: 13. ... Four-goal games: 1995-96 (2), 1996-97 (1), 1998-99 (1), 2000-01 (1). Total: 5. ... Five-goal games: 1993-94 (1). ... Total hat tricks: 19.

		REGULAR SEASON								PLAYOFFS				
Season Team	League	GP	G	A	Pts.	PIM	+/-	PP	SH	GP	G	A	Pts.	PIM
86-87—Kosice	Czech.	32	4	5	9	24	...	...	...	—	—	—	—	—
87-88—Kosice	Czech.	45	27	11	38	20	...	...	...	—	—	—	—	—
88-89—Kosice	Czech.	40	30	10	40	20	...	...	...	—	—	—	—	—
89-90—Kosice	Czech.	42	29	17	46	...	...	...	...	—	—	—	—	—
90-91—Washington	NHL	54	12	16	28	47	-10	4	0	4	0	1	1	2
91-92—Washington	NHL	71	28	28	56	42	16	4	0	7	6	2	8	4
92-93—Washington	NHL	83	37	48	85	70	8	10	0	6	0	6	6	0
93-94—Washington	NHL	69	24	19	43	40	22	4	0	9	2	4	6	4
94-95—HC Kosice	Slovakia	2	1	0	1	0	1	...	...	—	—	—	—	—
—Washington	NHL	47	*34	9	43	24	9	12	*6	7	5	3	8	10
95-96—Detroit	IHL	7	8	1	9	0	...	...	...	—	—	—	—	—
—Washington	NHL	67	52	28	80	40	18	11	4	6	3	2	5	8
96-97—Washington	NHL	77	46	31	77	72	7	10	4	—	—	—	—	—
97-98—Washington	NHL	76	52	26	78	44	14	11	5	17	7	5	12	12
—Slovakian Oly. team	Int'l	2	1	0	1	25	-1	1	0	—	—	—	—	—
98-99—Washington	NHL	66	31	24	55	56	-1	6	3	—	—	—	—	—
99-00—Washington	NHL	62	21	17	38	30	5	5	3	5	1	1	2	4
00-01—Washington	NHL	82	45	36	81	60	8	*22	4	6	2	0	2	2
01-02—Washington	NHL	77	39	31	70	80	-2	*17	1	—	—	—	—	—
02-03—Washington	NHL	76	30	26	56	52	-3	9	2	6	4	2	6	8
03-04—Washington	NHL	54	21	14	35	22	-17	12	0	—	—	—	—	—
—Ottawa	NHL	23	5	9	14	16	1	2	0	7	0	0	0	6
04-05—HC SKP Poprad	Slovakia	6	4	2	6	4	2	...	...	—	—	—	—	—
NHL Totals (14 years)		984	477	362	839	695	75	139	32	80	30	26	56	60

BONK, RADEK — C — CANADIENS

PERSONAL: Born January 9, 1976, in Krnov, Czechoslovakia. ... 6-3/212. ... Shoots left. ... Name pronounced BAHNK.
TRANSACTIONS/CAREER NOTES: Selected by Ottawa Senators in first round (first Senators pick, third overall) of NHL draft (June 28, 1994). ... Injured ankle (April 26, 1995); missed final five games of season. ... Injured hand (1995-96 season); missed one game. ... Strained abdomen (November 8, 1996); missed six games. ... Fractured left wrist (November 23, 1996); missed 23 games. ... Bruised knee (March 5, 1998); missed one game. ... Injured hip flexor (November 7, 1998); missed one game. ... Flu (January 4, 2000); missed two games. ... Flu (February 19, 2001); missed one game. ... Fractured left thumb (March 24, 2001); missed final seven games of regular season and two playoff games. ... Injured chest (October 23, 2002); missed five games. ... Injured shoulder, reinjured chest (November 9, 2002); missed three games. ... Injured back (February 12, 2003); missed two games. ... Bruised left leg (March 15, 2003); missed two games. ... Flu (December 30, 2003); missed two games. ... Fractured right foot (February 10, 2004); missed 14 games. ... Traded by Senators to Los Angeles Kings for third-round pick (LW Shawn Weller) in 2004 draft (June 26, 2004). ... Traded by Kings with G Cristobal Huet to Montreal Canadiens for G Mathieu Garon and third-round pick (D Paul Baier) in 2004 draft (June 26, 2004).
STATISTICAL PLATEAUS: Three-goal games: 2000-01 (1).

		REGULAR SEASON								PLAYOFFS				
Season Team	League	GP	G	A	Pts.	PIM	+/-	PP	SH	GP	G	A	Pts.	PIM
90-91—Opava	Czech.	35	47	42	89	25	...	...	...	—	—	—	—	—
91-92—ZPS Zlin	Czech Dv.I	45	47	36	83	30	...	...	...	—	—	—	—	—
92-93—ZPS Zlin	Czech.	30	5	5	10	10	...	...	...	—	—	—	—	—
93-94—Las Vegas	IHL	76	42	45	87	208	42	11	0	5	1	2	3	10
94-95—Las Vegas	IHL	33	7	13	20	62	-8	5	0	—	—	—	—	—
—Ottawa	NHL	42	3	8	11	28	-5	1	0	—	—	—	—	—
—Prince Edward	AHL	...	...	...	...	...	...	...	...	1	0	0	0	0
95-96—Ottawa	NHL	76	16	19	35	36	-5	5	0	—	—	—	—	—
96-97—Ottawa	NHL	53	5	13	18	14	-4	0	1	7	0	1	1	4
97-98—Ottawa	NHL	65	7	9	16	16	-13	1	0	5	0	0	0	2
98-99—Ottawa	NHL	81	16	16	32	48	15	0	1	4	0	0	0	6
99-00—HC Pardubice	Czech Rep.	3	1	0	1	4	...	...	...	—	—	—	—	—
—Ottawa	NHL	80	23	37	60	53	-2	10	0	6	0	0	0	8
00-01—Ottawa	NHL	74	23	36	59	52	27	5	2	2	0	0	0	2
01-02—Ottawa	NHL	82	25	45	70	52	3	6	2	12	3	7	10	6
02-03—Ottawa	NHL	70	22	32	54	36	6	11	0	18	6	5	11	10
03-04—Ottawa	NHL	66	12	32	44	66	2	6	0	7	0	2	2	0
04-05—Trinec	Czech Rep.	27	6	10	16	44	5	...	...	—	—	—	—	—
—Zlin	Czech Rep.	6	3	2	5	4	3	...	...	6	0	2	2	8
NHL Totals (10 years)		689	152	247	399	401	24	45	6	61	9	15	24	38

BONVIE, DENNIS — RW

PERSONAL: Born July 23, 1973, in Antigonish, Nova Scotia. ... 5-11/205. ... Shoots right. ... Name pronounced BAHN-vee.
TRANSACTIONS/CAREER NOTES: Signed as free agent by Edmonton Oilers (August 26, 1994). ... Selected by Chicago Blackhawks in waiver draft (October 5, 1998). ... Traded by Blackhawks to Philadelphia Flyers for D Frank Bialowas (January 8, 1999). ... Signed as free agent by Pittsburgh Penguins (September 20, 1999). ... Signed as free agent by Boston Bruins (October 5, 2001). ... Strained abdominal muscle (April 2, 2002); missed two games. ... Signed as free agent by Ottawa Senators (August 26, 2002). ... Traded by Senators to Colorado Avalanche for D Charlie Stephens (January 23, 2004).

		REGULAR SEASON								PLAYOFFS				
Season Team	League	GP	G	A	Pts.	PIM	+/-	PP	SH	GP	G	A	Pts.	PIM
91-92—Kitchener	OHL	7	1	1	2	23	...	...	...	—	—	—	—	—
—North Bay	OHL	49	0	12	12	261	...	...	...	21	0	1	1	91
92-93—North Bay	OHL	64	3	21	24	316	...	...	...	5	0	0	0	34
93-94—Cape Breton	AHL	63	1	10	11	278	...	...	...	4	0	0	0	11
94-95—Cape Breton	AHL	74	5	15	20	422	1	0	0	—	—	—	—	—
—Edmonton	NHL	2	0	0	0	0	0	0	0	—	—	—	—	—
95-96—Edmonton	NHL	8	0	0	0	47	-3	0	0	—	—	—	—	—
—Cape Breton	AHL	38	13	14	27	269	...	...	...	—	—	—	—	—
96-97—Hamilton	AHL	73	9	20	29	*522	-5	0	0	22	3	11	14	*91
97-98—Edmonton	NHL	4	0	0	0	27	0	0	0	—	—	—	—	—
—Hamilton	AHL	57	11	19	30	295	-4	4	0	9	0	5	5	18
98-99—Chicago	NHL	11	0	0	0	44	-4	0	0	—	—	—	—	—
—Portland	AHL	3	1	0	1	16	-1	0	0	—	—	—	—	—
—Philadelphia	AHL	37	4	10	14	158	1	0	0	14	3	3	6	26
99-00—Wilkes-Barre/Scranton	AHL	42	5	26	31	243	...	...	...	—	—	—	—	—
—Pittsburgh	NHL	28	0	0	0	80	-2	0	0	—	—	—	—	—
00-01—Pittsburgh	NHL	3	0	0	0	0	-1	0	0	—	—	—	—	—
—Wilkes-Barre/Scranton	AHL	65	5	18	23	221	...	...	...	21	0	4	4	35
01-02—Providence	AHL	55	8	8	16	290	-16	2	0	—	—	—	—	—
—Boston	NHL	23	1	2	3	84	3	0	0	1	0	0	0	0
02-03—Ottawa	NHL	12	0	0	0	29	-1	0	0	—	—	—	—	—
—Binghamton	AHL	51	7	3	10	311	3	0	0	14	2	4	6	85
03-04—Binghamton	AHL	29	2	4	6	137	2	0	0	—	—	—	—	—
—Colorado	NHL	1	0	0	0	0	0	0	0	—	—	—	—	—
—Hershey	AHL	30	3	6	9	154	-2	1	0	—	—	—	—	—
04-05—Hershey	AHL	76	4	14	18	357	-17	0	0	—	—	—	—	—
NHL Totals (9 years)		92	1	2	3	311	-8	0	0	1	0	0	0	0

BOOTLAND, DARRYL — RW — RED WINGS

PERSONAL: Born November 2, 1981, in Schomberg, Ont. ... 6-1/188. ... Shoots right.
TRANSACTIONS/CAREER NOTES: Selected by Colorado Avalanche in eighth round (11th Avalance pick, 252nd overall) in entry draft (June 24, 2000). ... Signed as free agent by Detroit Red Wings (August 20, 2003).

Season Team	League	GP	G	A	Pts.	PIM	+/-	PP	SH	GP	G	A	Pts.	PIM
		REGULAR SEASON								PLAYOFFS				
98-99—St. Michael's	OHL	28	12	6	18	80	...	...	...	—	—	—	—	—
—Barrie	OHL	38	18	11	29	89	...	...	...	—	—	—	—	—
99-00—St. Michael's	OHL	65	24	30	54	166	...	...	...	—	—	—	—	—
00-01—St. Michael's	OHL	56	32	33	65	136	...	...	...	11	3	1	4	20
01-02—St. Michael's	OHL	61	41	56	97	137	...	...	...	15	8	10	18	50
02-03—Toledo	ECHL	54	17	19	36	322	...	...	...	—	—	—	—	—
—Grand Rapids	AHL	16	1	4	5	41	...	...	...	15	3	2	5	46
03-04—Grand Rapids	AHL	54	12	2	14	175	-7	2	0	4	0	1	1	2
—Detroit	NHL	22	1	1	2	74	-3	0	0	—	—	—	—	—
04-05—Grand Rapids	AHL	78	14	20	34	336	5	1	1	—	—	—	—	—
NHL Totals (1 year)		22	1	1	2	74	-3	0	0					

BOTTERILL, JASON LW SABRES

PERSONAL: Born May 19, 1976, in Edmonton. ... 6-4/217. ... Shoots left. ... Name pronounced BAH-tuh-rihl.

TRANSACTIONS/CAREER NOTES: Selected by Dallas Stars in first round (first Stars pick, 20th overall) of NHL draft (June 28, 1994). ... Traded by Stars to Atlanta Thrashers for D Jamie Pushor (July 15, 1999). ... Traded by Thrashers with D Darryl Shannon to Calgary Flames for C Hnat Domenichelli and LW Dmitri Vlasenkov (February 11, 2000). ... Signed as free agent by Buffalo Sabres (August 12, 2002).

Season Team	League	GP	G	A	Pts.	PIM	+/-	PP	SH	GP	G	A	Pts.	PIM
		REGULAR SEASON								PLAYOFFS				
92-93—St. Paul's	USHL	22	22	26	48	...	...	...	...	—	—	—	—	—
93-94—Univ. of Michigan	CCHA	37	21	19	40	94	13	9	0	—	—	—	—	—
94-95—Univ. of Michigan	CCHA	34	14	14	28	117	7	7	0	—	—	—	—	—
95-96—Univ. of Michigan	CCHA	37	32	25	57	143	...	...	...	—	—	—	—	—
96-97—Univ. of Michigan	CCHA	42	37	24	61	129	27	20	2	—	—	—	—	—
97-98—Michigan	IHL	50	11	11	22	82	-13	2	0	4	0	0	0	5
—Dallas	NHL	4	0	0	0	19	-1	0	0	—	—	—	—	—
98-99—Michigan	IHL	56	13	25	38	106	-12	7	1	5	2	1	3	4
—Dallas	NHL	17	0	0	0	23	-2	0	0	—	—	—	—	—
99-00—Orlando	IHL	17	7	8	15	27	...	...	...	—	—	—	—	—
—Atlanta	NHL	25	1	4	5	17	-7	0	0	—	—	—	—	—
—Calgary	NHL	2	0	0	0	0	-4	0	0	—	—	—	—	—
—Saint John	AHL	21	3	4	7	39	...	...	...	3	0	0	0	19
00-01—Saint John	AHL	60	13	20	33	101	...	...	...	19	2	7	9	30
01-02—Saint John	AHL	71	21	21	42	121	-11	10	0	—	—	—	—	—
—Calgary	NHL	4	1	0	1	2	-3	1	0	—	—	—	—	—
02-03—Buffalo	NHL	17	1	4	5	14	1	1	0	—	—	—	—	—
—Rochester	AHL	64	37	22	59	105	0	13	2	3	1	1	2	21
03-04—Rochester	AHL	46	16	17	33	68	-1	5	1	16	5	10	15	19
—Buffalo	NHL	19	2	1	3	14	0	1	0	—	—	—	—	—
04-05—Rochester	AHL	8	6	2	8	9	-4	4	0	—	—	—	—	—
NHL Totals (6 years)		88	5	9	14	89	-16	3	0					

BOUCHARD, JOEL D

PERSONAL: Born January 23, 1974, in Montreal. ... 6-1/190. ... Shoots left.

TRANSACTIONS/CAREER NOTES: Selected by Calgary Flames in sixth round (sixth Flames pick, 129th overall) of NHL draft (June 20, 1992). ... Strained abdominal muscle (September 30, 1997); missed one game. ... Suffered concussion (January 24, 1998); missed six games. ... Selected by Nashville Predators in expansion draft (June 26, 1998). ... Sprained ankle (October 27, 1998); missed 11 games. ... Sprained ankle (December 19, 1998); missed seven games. ... Suffered concussion (December 15, 1999); missed nine games. ... Claimed on waivers by Dallas Stars (March 14, 2000). ... Signed as free agent by Phoenix Coyotes (August 31, 2000). ... Back spasms (December 30, 2000); missed two games. ... Signed as free agent by New Jersey Devils (October 25, 2001). ... Signed as free agent by New York Rangers (August 7, 2002). ... Traded by Rangers with RW Rico Fata, RW Mikael Samuelsson, D Richard Lintner and cash to Pittsburgh Penguins for RW Alexei Kovalev, LW Dan LaCouture, D Janne Laukkanen and D Mike Wilson (February 10, 2003). ... Fractured jaw (Febuary 22, 2003); missed 20 games. ... Signed as free agent by Buffalo Sabres (July 14, 2003). ... Acquired by Rangers in waiver draft (October 3, 2003). ... Injured hamstring (January 3, 2004); missed six games. ... Suffered concussion (February 14, 2004); missed final four games of season.

Season Team	League	GP	G	A	Pts.	PIM	+/-	PP	SH	GP	G	A	Pts.	PIM
		REGULAR SEASON								PLAYOFFS				
90-91—Longueuil	QMJHL	53	3	19	22	34	...	...	...	8	0	1	1	11
91-92—Verdun	QMJHL	70	9	37	46	55	...	...	...	19	1	7	8	20
92-93—Verdun	QMJHL	60	10	49	59	126	...	...	...	4	0	2	2	4
93-94—Verdun	QMJHL	60	15	55	70	62	37	6	2	4	1	0	1	6
—Saint John	AHL	1	0	0	0	0	0	0	0	2	0	0	0	0
94-95—Saint John	AHL	77	6	25	31	63	2	0	0	5	1	0	1	4
—Calgary	NHL	2	0	0	0	0	0	0	0	—	—	—	—	—
95-96—Saint John	AHL	74	8	25	33	104	...	...	...	16	1	4	5	10
—Calgary	NHL	4	0	0	0	4	0	0	0	—	—	—	—	—
96-97—Calgary	NHL	76	4	5	9	49	-23	0	1	—	—	—	—	—
97-98—Calgary	NHL	44	5	7	12	57	0	0	1	—	—	—	—	—
—Saint John	AHL	3	2	1	3	6	4	1	0	—	—	—	—	—
98-99—Nashville	NHL	64	4	11	15	60	-10	0	0	—	—	—	—	—
99-00—Nashville	NHL	52	1	4	5	23	-11	0	0	—	—	—	—	—
—Dallas	NHL	2	0	0	0	2	1	0	0	—	—	—	—	—
00-01—Grand Rapids	IHL	19	3	9	12	8	...	...	...	—	—	—	—	—
—Phoenix	NHL	32	1	2	3	22	-8	0	0	—	—	—	—	—
01-02—Albany	AHL	70	9	22	31	28	-30	4	1	—	—	—	—	—
—New Jersey	NHL	1	0	1	1	0	1	0	0	—	—	—	—	—

Season Team	League	REGULAR SEASON GP	G	A	Pts.	PIM	+/-	PP	SH	PLAYOFFS GP	G	A	Pts.	PIM
02-03—New York Rangers......	NHL	27	5	7	12	14	6	1	0	—	—	—	—	—
—Hartford......................	AHL	22	6	14	20	22	5	4	0	—	—	—	—	—
—Pittsburgh.....................	NHL	7	0	1	1	0	-6	0	0	—	—	—	—	—
03-04—New York Rangers......	NHL	28	1	7	8	10	2	0	0	—	—	—	—	—
04-05—Hartford......................	AHL	7	1	2	3	6	2	0	0	6	0	2	2	20
NHL Totals (10 years)..........		339	21	45	66	241	-48	1	2					

BOUCHARD, PIERRE-MARC LW WILD

PERSONAL: Born April 27, 1984, in Sherbrooke, Que. ... 5-10/162. ... Shoots left.
TRANSACTIONS/CAREER NOTES: Selected by Minnesota Wild in first round (first Wild pick, eighth overall) of NHL draft (June 22, 2002).

Season Team	League	REGULAR SEASON GP	G	A	Pts.	PIM	+/-	PP	SH	PLAYOFFS GP	G	A	Pts.	PIM
00-01—Chicoutimi..................	QMJHL	67	38	57	95	20	...	...	...	6	5	8	13	0
01-02—Chicoutimi..................	QMJHL	69	46	*94	*140	54	...	...	...	4	2	3	5	4
02-03—Minnesota..................	NHL	50	7	13	20	18	1	5	0	5	0	1	1	2
03-04—Minnesota..................	NHL	61	4	18	22	22	-7	2	0	—	—	—	—	—
04-05—Houston......................	AHL	67	12	42	54	46	-2	7	0	5	0	1	1	0
NHL Totals (2 years)...........		111	11	31	42	40	-6	7	0	5	0	1	1	2

BOUCHER, BRIAN G COYOTES

PERSONAL: Born January 2, 1977, in Woonsocket, R.I. ... 6-2/198. ... Catches left. ... Name pronounced boo-SHAY.
TRANSACTIONS/CAREER NOTES: Selected by Philadelphia Flyers in 1st round (1st Flyers pick, 22nd overall) of NHL draft (July 8, 1995). ... Throat infection (January 16, 2001); missed one game. ... Strained left hamstring (November 15, 2001); missed nine games. ... Traded by Flyers with third-round pick (D Joe Callahan) in 2002 draft to Phoenix Coyotes for G Robert Esche and C Michal Handzus (June 12, 2002). ... Bruised knee (January 3, 2003); missed five games. ... Signed as free agent by Coyotes (Aug. 2, 2005).

Season Team	League	REGULAR SEASON GP	Min.	W	L	T	GA	SO	GAA	SV%	PLAYOFFS GP	Min.	W	L	GA	SO	GAA	SV%
93-94—Mt. St. Charles H.S.	R.I.H.S.	23	1170	...	...	...	23	12	1.18	...	—	—	—	—	—	—	—	—
94-95—Wexford	Tier II Jr. A	8	425	...	...	...	23	0	3.25	...	—	—	—	—	—	—	—	—
—Tri-City	WHL	35	1969	17	11	2	108	1	3.29	.908	13	795	6	5	50	0	3.77	.904
95-96—Tri-City	WHL	55	3183	33	19	2	181	1	3.41	...	11	653	6	5	37	2	3.40	...
96-97—Tri-City	WHL	41	2458	10	24	6	149	1	3.64	.901	—	—	—	—	—	—	—	—
97-98—Philadelphia	AHL	34	1901	16	12	3	101	0	3.19	.888	2	31	0	0	1	0	1.94	.944
98-99—Philadelphia	AHL	36	2061	20	8	5	89	2	2.59	.911	16	947	9	7	45	0	2.85	.906
99-00—Philadelphia	NHL	35	2038	20	10	3	65	4	*1.91	.918	18	1183	11	7	40	1	2.03	.917
—Philadelphia	AHL	1	65	0	0	1	3	0	2.77	...	—	—	—	—	—	—	—	—
00-01—Philadelphia	NHL	27	1470	8	12	5	80	1	3.27	.876	1	37	0	0	3	0	4.86	.824
01-02—Philadelphia	NHL	41	2295	18	16	4	92	2	2.41	.905	2	88	0	1	2	0	1.36	.939
02-03—Phoenix........................	NHL	45	2544	15	20	8	128	0	3.02	.894	—	—	—	—	—	—	—	—
03-04—Phoenix........................	NHL	40	2364	10	19	10	108	5	2.74	.906	—	—	—	—	—	—	—	—
04-05—HV 71 Jonkoping..........	Sweden	4	235	...	...	...	13	0	3.32	.884	—	—	—	—	—	—	—	—
NHL Totals (5 years)............		188	10711	71	77	30	473	12	2.65	.901	21	1308	11	8	45	1	2.06	.016

BOUCHER, PHILIPPE D STARS

PERSONAL: Born March 24, 1973, in St. Apollinaire, Que. ... 6-2/221. ... Shoots right. ... Name pronounced fih-LEEP boo-SHAY.
TRANSACTIONS/CAREER NOTES: Selected by Buffalo Sabres in first round (first Sabres pick, 13th overall) of NHL draft (June 22, 1991). ... Traded by Sabres with G Grant Fuhr and D Denis Tsygurov to Los Angeles Kings for D Alexei Zhitnik, D Charlie Huddy, G Robb Stauber and fifth-round pick (D Marian Menhart) in 1995 entry draft (February 14, 1995). ... Sprained wrist (February 25, 1995); missed final 31 games of season. ... Tendinitis in right wrist (October 6, 1995); missed first 25 games of season. ... Injured left hand (February 19, 1996); missed four games. ... Sprained right shoulder (October 4, 1996); missed 10 games. ... Flu (December 18, 1997); missed two games. ... Injured (January 10, 1998); missed 12 games. ... Flu (March 3, 1999); missed two games. ... Foot surgery (April 27, 1999); missed first 71 games of 1999-2000 season. ... Flu (December 16, 2001); missed one game. ... Suffered concussion (January 17, 2002); missed one game. ... Signed as free agent by Dallas Stars (July 2, 2002). ... Injured groin (October 24, 2003); missed one game. ... Injured eye (November 29, 2003); missed nine games. ... Flu (January 5, 2004); missed two games.

Season Team	League	REGULAR SEASON GP	G	A	Pts.	PIM	+/-	PP	SH	PLAYOFFS GP	G	A	Pts.	PIM
90-91—Granby.........................	QMJHL	69	21	46	67	92	...	...	...	—	—	—	—	—
91-92—Granby.........................	QMJHL	49	22	37	59	47	...	...	...	—	—	—	—	—
—Laval..........................	QMJHL	16	7	11	18	36	...	...	...	10	5	6	11	8
92-93—Laval..........................	QMJHL	16	12	15	27	37	...	...	...	13	6	15	21	12
—Rochester	AHL	5	4	3	7	8	-1	1	0	3	0	1	1	2
—Buffalo	NHL	18	0	4	4	14	1	0	0	—	—	—	—	—
93-94—Buffalo	NHL	38	6	8	14	29	-1	4	0	7	1	1	2	2
—Rochester	AHL	31	10	22	32	51	-1	6	0	—	—	—	—	—
94-95—Rochester	AHL	43	14	27	41	26	-1	5	0	—	—	—	—	—
—Buffalo	NHL	9	1	4	5	0	6	0	0	—	—	—	—	—
—Los Angeles...............	NHL	6	1	0	1	4	-3	0	0	—	—	—	—	—
95-96—Los Angeles...............	NHL	53	7	16	23	31	-26	5	0	—	—	—	—	—
—Phoenix......................	IHL	10	4	3	7	4	...	...	...	—	—	—	—	—
96-97—Los Angeles...............	NHL	60	7	18	25	25	0	2	0	—	—	—	—	—
97-98—Los Angeles...............	NHL	45	6	10	16	49	6	1	0	—	—	—	—	—

Season Team	League	GP	G	A	Pts.	PIM	+/-	PP	SH	GP	G	A	Pts.	PIM
		REGULAR SEASON								PLAYOFFS				
—Long Beach	IHL	2	0	1	1	4	1	0	0	—	—	—	—	—
98-99—Los Angeles	NHL	45	2	6	8	32	-12	1	0	—	—	—	—	—
99-00—Long Beach	IHL	14	4	11	15	8	...	...	...	6	0	9	9	8
—Los Angeles	NHL	1	0	0	0	0	0	0	0	—	—	—	—	—
00-01—Manitoba	IHL	45	10	22	32	99	...	...	...	—	—	—	—	—
—Los Angeles	NHL	22	2	4	6	20	4	2	0	13	0	1	1	2
01-02—Los Angeles	NHL	80	7	23	30	94	0	4	0	5	0	1	1	2
02-03—Dallas	NHL	80	7	20	27	94	28	1	1	11	1	2	3	11
03-04—Dallas	NHL	70	8	16	24	64	15	2	0	5	1	0	1	6
NHL Totals (12 years)		527	54	129	183	456	18	22	1	41	3	5	8	23

B

BOUCK, TYLER — RW — CANUCKS

PERSONAL: Born January 13, 1980, in Camrose, Alta. ... 6-0/195. ... Shoots left.

TRANSACTIONS/CAREER NOTES: Selected by Dallas Stars in second round (second Stars pick, 57th overall) of NHL draft (June 27, 1998). ... Traded by Stars to Phoenix Coyotes for D Jyrki Lumme (June 23, 2001). ... Traded by Coyotes with LW Todd Warriner, C Trevor Letowski and third-round pick (traded back to Phoenix; Coyotes selected Dimitri Pestrunov) in 2003 draft to Vancouver Canucks for C Denis Pederson and D Drake Berehowsky (December 28, 2001).

Season Team	League	GP	G	A	Pts.	PIM	+/-	PP	SH	GP	G	A	Pts.	PIM
		REGULAR SEASON								PLAYOFFS				
96-97—Prince George	WHL	12	0	2	2	11	...	...	...	—	—	—	—	—
97-98—Prince George	WHL	65	11	26	37	90	...	...	...	11	1	0	1	21
98-99—Prince George	WHL	56	22	25	47	178	8	4	1	2	0	2	2	10
99-00—Prince George	WHL	57	30	33	63	183	17	9	5	13	6	13	19	36
00-01—Dallas	NHL	48	2	5	7	29	-3	0	0	1	0	0	0	0
—Utah	IHL	24	2	6	8	39	...	...	...	—	—	—	—	—
01-02—Phoenix	NHL	7	0	0	0	4	-1	0	0	—	—	—	—	—
—Springfield	AHL	21	1	2	3	33	-2	0	0	—	—	—	—	—
—Manitoba	AHL	41	5	6	11	58	-5	0	2	—	—	—	—	—
02-03—Manitoba	AHL	76	10	28	38	103	8	2	2	14	2	2	4	10
03-04—Vancouver	NHL	18	1	2	3	23	-4	0	1	1	0	0	0	0
—Manitoba	AHL	49	11	14	25	100	-3	2	0	—	—	—	—	—
04-05—TPS Turku	Finland	—	—	—	—	—	—	—	—	6	1	0	1	12
—TPS Turku	Finland	40	3	7	10	100	-2	...	...	—	—	—	—	—
NHL Totals (3 years)		73	3	7	10	56	-8	0	1	2	0	0	0	0

BOUGHNER, BOB — D — AVALANCHE

PERSONAL: Born March 8, 1971, in Windsor, Ont. ... 6-0/203. ... Shoots right. ... Name pronounced BOOG-nuhr.

TRANSACTIONS/CAREER NOTES: Selected by Detroit Red Wings in second round (second Red Wings pick, 32nd overall) of NHL draft (June 17, 1989). ... Signed as free agent by Florida Panthers (August 10, 1994). ... Traded by Panthers to Buffalo Sabres for third-round pick (D Chris Allen) in 1996 draft (February 1, 1996). ... Bruised left thigh (February 28, 1996); missed one game. ... Bruised shoulder (February 7, 1998); missed two games. ... Injured wrist (March 12, 1998); missed three games. ... Bruised foot (April 29, 1998); missed one game. ... Selected by Nashville Predators in expansion draft (June 26, 1998). ... Flu (October 27, 1998); missed one game. ... Flu (January 14, 1999); missed two games. ... Flu (November, 1999); missed two games. ... Sprained ankle (December, 1999); missed two games. ... Fractured finger (February 2, 2000); missed three games. ... Traded by Predators to Pittsburgh Penguins for D Pavel Skrbek (March 13, 2000). ... Fractured wrist (November 11, 2000); missed 23 games. ... Bruised chest (March 2, 2001); missed one game. ... Signed as free agent by Calgary Flames (July 2, 2001). ... Injured (November 10, 2001); missed one game. ... Injured (March 9, 2002); missed one game. ... Injured (March 16, 2002); missed one game. ... Traded by Flames to Carolina Hurricanes for fourth-round pick in 2004 draft and future considerations (July 16, 2003). ... Fractured left hand (October 4, 2003); missed seven games. ... Injured left knee (November 18, 2003); missed four games. ... Injured knee (February 3, 2004); missed five games. ... Traded by Hurricanes to Avalanche for D Chris Bahen and third-round pick (D Casey Borer) in 2004 draft (February 20, 2004). ... Reinjured knee (February 24, 2004) and had surgery (February 26, 2004); missed 11 games.

Season Team	League	GP	G	A	Pts.	PIM	+/-	PP	SH	GP	G	A	Pts.	PIM
		REGULAR SEASON								PLAYOFFS				
87-88—St. Mary's Jr. B	OHA	36	4	18	22	177	...	...	...	—	—	—	—	—
88-89—Sault Ste. Marie	OHL	64	6	15	21	182	...	...	...	—	—	—	—	—
89-90—Sault Ste. Marie	OHL	49	7	23	30	122	...	...	...	—	—	—	—	—
90-91—Sault Ste. Marie	OHL	64	13	33	46	156	...	...	...	14	2	9	11	35
91-92—Adirondack	AHL	1	0	0	0	7	...	...	...	—	—	—	—	—
—Toledo	ECHL	28	3	10	13	79	...	...	...	5	2	0	2	15
92-93—Adirondack	AHL	69	1	16	17	190	5	0	0	—	—	—	—	—
93-94—Adirondack	AHL	72	8	14	22	292	3	1	1	10	1	1	2	18
94-95—Cincinnati	IHL	81	2	14	16	192	10	0	0	10	0	0	0	18
95-96—Carolina	AHL	46	2	15	17	127	...	...	...	—	—	—	—	—
—Buffalo	NHL	31	0	1	1	104	3	0	0	—	—	—	—	—
96-97—Buffalo	NHL	77	1	7	8	225	12	0	0	11	0	1	1	9
97-98—Buffalo	NHL	69	1	3	4	165	5	0	0	14	0	4	4	15
98-99—Nashville	NHL	79	3	10	13	137	-6	0	0	—	—	—	—	—
99-00—Nashville	NHL	62	2	4	6	97	-13	0	0	—	—	—	—	—
—Pittsburgh	NHL	11	1	0	1	69	2	1	0	11	0	2	2	15
00-01—Pittsburgh	NHL	58	1	3	4	147	18	0	0	18	0	1	1	22
01-02—Calgary	NHL	79	2	4	6	170	9	0	0	—	—	—	—	—
02-03—Calgary	NHL	69	3	14	17	126	5	0	0	—	—	—	—	—
03-04—Carolina	NHL	43	0	5	5	80	-9	0	0	—	—	—	—	—
—Colorado	NHL	11	0	0	0	8	-1	0	0	11	0	4	4	6
NHL Totals (9 years)		589	14	51	65	1328	25	1	0	65	0	12	12	67

BOUILLON, FRANCIS — D — CANADIENS

PERSONAL: Born October 17, 1975, in New York City. ... 5-8/196. ... Shoots left.
TRANSACTIONS/CAREER NOTES: Signed as free agent by Montreal Canadiens (August 18, 1998). ... Fractured hand (November 14, 2000); missed 13 games. ... Sprained ankle (December 30, 2000); missed 23 games. ... Claimed by Nashville Predators in waiver draft (October 4, 2002). ... Claimed off waivers by Canadiens (October 25, 2002). ... Took personal leave (February 2, 2004); missed one game.

		REGULAR SEASON								PLAYOFFS				
Season Team	League	GP	G	A	Pts.	PIM	+/-	PP	SH	GP	G	A	Pts.	PIM
92-93—Laval	QMJHL	46	0	7	7	45	...	...	...	—	—	—	—	—
93-94—Laval	QMJHL	68	3	15	18	129	...	...	...	19	2	9	11	48
94-95—Laval	QMJHL	72	8	25	33	115	...	...	...	20	3	11	14	21
95-96—Granby	QMJHL	68	11	35	46	156	...	...	...	21	2	12	14	30
96-97—Wheeling	ECHL	69	10	32	42	77	...	...	...	3	0	2	2	10
97-98—Quebec	IHL	71	8	27	35	76	...	...	...	—	—	—	—	—
98-99—Fredericton	AHL	79	19	36	55	174	7	7	1	5	2	1	3	0
99-00—Montreal	NHL	74	3	13	16	38	-7	2	0	—	—	—	—	—
00-01—Montreal	NHL	29	0	6	6	26	3	0	0	—	—	—	—	—
—Quebec	AHL	4	0	0	0	0	...	...	...	—	—	—	—	—
01-02—Quebec	AHL	38	8	14	22	30	2	4	0	—	—	—	—	—
—Montreal	NHL	28	0	5	5	33	-5	0	0	—	—	—	—	—
02-03—Nashville	NHL	4	0	0	0	2	-1	0	0	—	—	—	—	—
—Montreal	NHL	20	3	1	4	2	-1	0	1	—	—	—	—	—
—Hamilton	AHL	29	1	12	13	31	9	0	0	—	—	—	—	—
03-04—Montreal	NHL	73	2	16	18	70	1	0	0	11	0	0	0	7
04-05—Leksand	Sweden Dv. 2	8	3	4	7	10	11	0	0	10	4	9	13	12
NHL Totals (5 years)		228	8	41	49	171	-10	2	1	11	0	0	0	7

BOULERICE, JESSE — RW/LW — HURRICANES

PERSONAL: Born August 10, 1978, in Plattsburgh, N.Y. ... 6-2/203. ... Shoots right.
TRANSACTIONS/CAREER NOTES: Selected by Philadelphia Flyers in fifth round (fourth Flyers pick, 133rd overall) of NHL draft (June 22, 1996). ... Traded by Flyers to Carolina Hurricanes for C Greg Koehler (February 13, 2002). ... Suffered concussion (February 11, 2003); missed 24 games.

		REGULAR SEASON								PLAYOFFS				
Season Team	League	GP	G	A	Pts.	PIM	+/-	PP	SH	GP	G	A	Pts.	PIM
95-96—Det. Jr. Red Wings	OHL	64	2	5	7	150	...	...	...	16	0	0	0	12
96-97—Detroit	OHL	33	10	14	24	209	-13	3	0	—	—	—	—	—
97-98—Plymouth	OHL	53	20	23	43	170	...	...	...	13	2	4	6	35
98-99—Philadelphia	AHL	24	1	2	3	82	-5	0	0	—	—	—	—	—
—New Orleans	ECHL	12	0	1	1	38	-2	0	0	—	—	—	—	—
99-00—Philadelphia	AHL	40	3	4	7	85	...	...	...	4	0	2	2	4
—Trenton	ECHL	25	8	8	16	90	...	...	...	—	—	—	—	—
00-01—Philadelphia	AHL	60	3	4	7	256	...	...	...	10	1	1	2	28
01-02—Philadelphia	NHL	3	0	0	0	5	-1	0	0	—	—	—	—	—
—Philadelphia	AHL	41	2	5	7	204	1	0	0	—	—	—	—	—
—Lowell	AHL	56	4	9	13	284	2	0	0	5	0	2	2	6
02-03—Carolina	NHL	48	2	1	3	108	-2	0	0	—	—	—	—	—
03-04—Carolina	NHL	76	6	1	7	127	-5	0	0	—	—	—	—	—
NHL Totals (3 years)		127	8	2	10	240	-8	0	0					

BOULTON, ERIC — LW — THRASHERS

PERSONAL: Born August 17, 1976, in Halifax, N.S. ... 6-0/224. ... Shoots left.
TRANSACTIONS/CAREER NOTES: Selected by New York Rangers in 9th round (12th Rangers pick, 234th overall) of NHL draft (June 29, 1994). ... Signed as free agent by Buffalo Sabres (August 20, 1999). ... Injured thumb (September 16, 2003); missed first 10 games of season. ... Signed as free agent by Atlanta Thrashers (Aug. 5, 2005).

		REGULAR SEASON								PLAYOFFS				
Season Team	League	GP	G	A	Pts.	PIM	+/-	PP	SH	GP	G	A	Pts.	PIM
93-94—Oshawa	OHL	45	4	3	7	149	...	...	...	5	0	0	0	16
94-95—Oshawa	OHL	27	7	5	12	125	...	2	0	—	—	—	—	—
—Sarnia	OHL	24	3	7	10	134	...	2	0	4	0	1	1	10
95-96—Sarnia	OHL	66	14	29	43	243	...	...	...	9	0	3	3	29
96-97—Binghamton	AHL	23	2	3	5	67	-5	0	0	3	0	0	0	4
—Charlotte	ECHL	44	14	11	25	325	...	...	...	3	0	1	1	6
97-98—Charlotte	ECHL	53	11	16	27	202	...	...	...	4	1	0	1	0
—Fort Wayne	IHL	8	0	2	2	42	...	...	...	—	—	—	—	—
98-99—Houston	IHL	7	1	0	1	41	1	0	0	—	—	—	—	—
—Florida	ECHL	26	9	13	22	143	5	1	0	—	—	—	—	—
—Kentucky	AHL	34	3	3	6	154	1	1	0	10	0	1	1	36
99-00—Rochester	AHL	76	2	2	4	276	...	...	...	18	2	1	3	53
00-01—Buffalo	NHL	35	1	2	3	94	-1	0	0	—	—	—	—	—
01-02—Buffalo	NHL	35	2	3	5	129	-1	0	0	—	—	—	—	—
02-03—Buffalo	NHL	58	1	5	6	178	1	0	0	—	—	—	—	—
03-04—Buffalo	NHL	44	1	2	3	110	-2	0	0	—	—	—	—	—
04-05—Columbia	ECHL	48	23	16	39	124	10	8	...	4	2	3	5	8
NHL Totals (4 years)		172	5	12	17	511	-3	0	0					

BOUMEDIENNE, JOSEF — D — CAPITALS

PERSONAL: Born January 12, 1978, in Stockholm, Sweden. ... 6-1/200. ... Shoots left. ... Name pronounced JOH-sehf BOO-mih-dyehn.
TRANSACTIONS/CAREER NOTES: Selected by New Jersey Devils in fourth round (seventh Devils pick, 91st overall) of NHL draft (June 22, 1996). ... Traded by Devils with D Sascha Goc and LW Anton But to Tampa Bay Lightning for D Andrei Zyuzin (November 9, 2001). ... Traded by Lightning to Ottawa Senators for seventh-round pick (G Fredrik Morrena) in 2002 draft (June 23, 2002). ... Traded by Senators to Washington Capitals for D Dean Melanson (December 16, 2002). ... Food poisoning (January 25, 2004); missed one game.

		REGULAR SEASON								PLAYOFFS				
Season Team	League	GP	G	A	Pts.	PIM	+/-	PP	SH	GP	G	A	Pts.	PIM
95-96—Huddinge	Sweden Jr.	25	2	4	6	66	...	...	...	—	—	—	—	—
—Huddinge	Sweden Dv. 2	7	0	0	0	14	...	...	...	—	—	—	—	—
96-97—Sodertalje SK	Sweden	32	1	1	2	32	...	...	...	—	—	—	—	—
97-98—Sodertalje SK	Sweden	26	3	3	6	28	...	...	...	—	—	—	—	—
98-99—Tappara Tampere	Finland	51	6	8	14	119	-5	...	...	—	—	—	—	—
99-00—Tappara Tampere	Finland	50	8	24	32	160	...	...	...	4	1	2	3	10
00-01—Albany	AHL	79	8	29	37	117	...	...	...	—	—	—	—	—
01-02—New Jersey	NHL	1	1	0	1	2	-1	0	0	—	—	—	—	—
—Albany	AHL	9	0	3	3	10	-7	0	0	—	—	—	—	—
—Springfield	AHL	62	7	28	35	67	-2	2	0	—	—	—	—	—
—Tampa Bay	NHL	3	0	0	0	4	-1	0	0	—	—	—	—	—
02-03—Binghamton	AHL	26	2	15	17	62	10	1	0	—	—	—	—	—
—Washington	NHL	6	1	0	1	0	-1	0	0	—	—	—	—	—
—Portland	AHL	44	8	22	30	77	9	4	0	—	—	—	—	—
03-04—Washington	NHL	37	2	12	14	30	-10	2	0	—	—	—	—	—
—Portland	AHL	13	1	8	9	10	5	1	0	—	—	—	—	—
04-05—Brynas IF	Sweden	13	6	0	6	43	-5	2	2	...	...	...	...	...
NHL Totals (3 years)		47	4	12	16	36	-13	2	0					

BOURDON, LUC — D — CANUCKS

PERSONAL: Born February 16, 1987, in Lameque, Quebec. ... 6-2/199. ... Shoots left.
TRANSACTIONS/CAREER NOTES: Selected by Vancouver Canucks in 1st round (1st Canucks pick, 10th overall) of entry draft (July 30, 2005).

		REGULAR SEASON								PLAYOFFS				
Season Team	League	GP	G	A	Pts.	PIM	+/-	PP	SH	GP	G	A	Pts.	PIM
03-04—Val-d'Or	QMJHL	64	2	6	8	58	...	...	...	—	—	—	—	—
04-05—Val-d'Or	QMJHL	70	13	19	32	117	-39	8	0	—	—	—	—	—

BOURRET, ALEX — RW — THRASHERS

PERSONAL: Born October 5, 1986, in Drummondville, Quebec. ... 5-9/209. ... Shoots left.
TRANSACTIONS/CAREER NOTES: Selected by Atlanta Thrashers in 1st round (1st Thrashers pick, 16th overall, obtained from New York Rangers) of entry draft (July 30, 2005).

		REGULAR SEASON								PLAYOFFS				
Season Team	League	GP	G	A	Pts.	PIM	+/-	PP	SH	GP	G	A	Pts.	PIM
02-03—Sherbrooke	QMJHL	61	13	15	28	73	...	...	...	—	—	—	—	—
03-04—Lewiston	QMJHL	65	22	41	63	94	...	...	...	—	—	—	—	—
04-05—Lewiston	QMJHL	65	31	55	86	172	27	7	5	8	6	8	14	25

BOUWMEESTER, JAY — D — PANTHERS

PERSONAL: Born September 27, 1983, in Edmonton. ... 6-4/218. ... Shoots left. ... Name pronounced boh-MEES-tuhr.
TRANSACTIONS/CAREER NOTES: Selected by Florida Panthers in first round (first Panthers pick, third overall) of NHL draft (June 22, 2002). ... Fractured left foot (January 19, 2004); missed 18 games.

		REGULAR SEASON								PLAYOFFS				
Season Team	League	GP	G	A	Pts.	PIM	+/-	PP	SH	GP	G	A	Pts.	PIM
98-99—Medicine Hat	WHL	8	2	1	3	2	...	...	...	—	—	—	—	—
99-00—Medicine Hat	WHL	34	13	21	34	26	...	...	...	—	—	—	—	—
00-01—Medicine Hat	WHL	61	14	39	53	44	...	...	...	—	—	—	—	—
01-02—Medicine Hat	WHL	61	12	49	61	42	...	...	...	—	—	—	—	—
02-03—Florida	NHL	82	4	12	16	14	-29	2	0	—	—	—	—	—
03-04—Florida	NHL	61	2	18	20	30	-15	0	0	—	—	—	—	—
—San Antonio	AHL	2	0	1	1	2	0	0	0	—	—	—	—	—
04-05—Chicago	AHL	18	6	3	9	12	4	3	0	18	0	0	0	14
—San Antonio	AHL	64	4	13	17	50	-22	1	1	—	—	—	—	—
NHL Totals (2 years)		143	6	30	36	44	-44	2	0					

BOYCHUK, JOHNNY — D — AVALANCHE

PERSONAL: Born January 19, 1984, in Edmonton. ... 6-2/209. ... Shoots right.
TRANSACTIONS/CAREER NOTES: Selected by Colorado Avalanche in second round (second Avalanche pick, 61st overall) of NHL draft (June 22, 2002).

		REGULAR SEASON								PLAYOFFS				
Season Team	League	GP	G	A	Pts.	PIM	+/-	PP	SH	GP	G	A	Pts.	PIM
00-01—Calgary	WHL	66	4	8	12	61	...	...	...	12	1	1	2	17

Season Team	League	REGULAR SEASON								PLAYOFFS				
		GP	G	A	Pts.	PIM	+/-	PP	SH	GP	G	A	Pts.	PIM
01-02—Calgary	WHL	70	8	32	40	85	...	...	...	7	1	1	2	6
02-03—Moose Jaw	WHL	67	13	35	48	90	...	...	...	13	2	6	8	29
03-04—Moose Jaw	WHL	62	13	20	33	71	...	...	...	10	1	9	10	9
04-05—Hershey	AHL	80	3	12	15	69	13	1	0	—	—	—	—	—

BOYES, BRAD — C — BRUINS

PERSONAL: Born April 17, 1982, in Mississauga, Ont. ... 6-1/195. ... Shoots right.

TRANSACTIONS/CAREER NOTES: Selected by Toronto Maple Leafs in first round (first Maple Leafs pick, 24th overall) of NHL draft (June 24, 2000). ... Traded by Maple Leafs with C Alyn McCauley and 2003 first-round pick (traded to Boston Bruins) to San Jose Sharks for RW Owen Nolan (March 5, 2003). ... Traded by Sharks to Bruins for D Jeff Jillson (March 9, 2004).

Season Team	League	REGULAR SEASON								PLAYOFFS				
		GP	G	A	Pts.	PIM	+/-	PP	SH	GP	G	A	Pts.	PIM
98-99—Erie	OHL	59	24	36	60	30	...	...	...	5	1	2	3	10
99-00—Erie	OHL	68	36	46	82	38	...	...	...	13	6	8	14	10
00-01—Erie	OHL	59	45	45	90	42	27	13	5	15	10	13	23	8
01-02—Erie	OHL	47	36	41	77	42	...	...	...	21	22	*19	41	27
02-03—St. John's	AHL	65	23	28	51	45	1	6	2	—	—	—	—	—
—Cleveland	AHL	15	7	6	13	21	-6	3	1	—	—	—	—	—
03-04—San Jose	NHL	1	0	0	0	2	-2	0	0	—	—	—	—	—
—Cleveland	AHL	61	25	35	60	38	9	7	0	—	—	—	—	—
—Providence	AHL	17	6	6	12	13	4	1	0	2	1	0	1	0
04-05—Providence	AHL	80	33	42	75	58	-6	20	2	16	8	7	15	23
NHL Totals (1 year)		1	0	0	0	2	-2	0	0					

BOYLE, DAN — D — LIGHTNING

PERSONAL: Born July 12, 1976, in Ottawa. ... 5-11/190. ... Shoots right.

TRANSACTIONS/CAREER NOTES: Signed as free agent by Florida Panthers (March 30, 1998). ... Traded by Panthers to Tampa Bay Lightning for fifth-round pick (D Martin Tuma) in 2003 draft (January 7, 2002). ... Fractured finger (January 7, 2003); missed four games. ... Had concussion (December 6, 2003); missed four games.

Season Team	League	REGULAR SEASON								PLAYOFFS				
		GP	G	A	Pts.	PIM	+/-	PP	SH	GP	G	A	Pts.	PIM
94-95—Miami (Ohio)	CCHA	35	8	18	26	24	...	...	...	—	—	—	—	—
95-96—Miami (Ohio)	CCHA	36	7	20	27	70	...	...	...	—	—	—	—	—
96-97—Miami (Ohio)	CCHA	40	11	43	54	52	...	...	...	—	—	—	—	—
97-98—Miami (Ohio)	CCHA	37	14	26	40	58	...	...	...	—	—	—	—	—
—Cincinnati	IHL	8	0	3	3	20	1	0	0	5	0	1	1	4
98-99—Kentucky	AHL	53	8	34	42	87	21	4	0	12	3	5	8	16
—Florida	NHL	22	3	5	8	6	0	1	0	—	—	—	—	—
99-00—Louisville	AHL	58	14	38	52	75	...	...	...	4	0	2	2	8
—Florida	NHL	13	0	3	3	4	-2	0	0	—	—	—	—	—
00-01—Florida	NHL	69	4	18	22	28	-14	1	0	—	—	—	—	—
—Louisville	AHL	6	0	5	5	12	...	...	...	—	—	—	—	—
01-02—Florida	NHL	25	3	3	6	12	-1	1	0	—	—	—	—	—
—Tampa Bay	NHL	41	5	15	20	27	-15	2	0	—	—	—	—	—
02-03—Tampa Bay	NHL	77	13	40	53	44	9	8	0	11	0	7	7	6
03-04—Tampa Bay	NHL	78	9	30	39	60	23	3	0	23	2	8	10	16
04-05—Djurgarden Stockholm	Sweden	32	9	9	18	47	4	3	1	12	2	3	5	26
NHL Totals (6 years)		325	37	114	151	181	0	16	0	34	2	15	17	22

BOYNTON, NICK — D — BRUINS

PERSONAL: Born January 14, 1979, in Nobleton, Ont. ... 6-2/211. ... Shoots right.

TRANSACTIONS/CAREER NOTES: Selected by Washington Capitals in first round (first Capitals pick, ninth overall) of NHL draft (June 21, 1997). ... Returned to draft pool by Capitals; selected by Boston Bruins in first round (first Bruins pick, 21st overall) of NHL draft (June 26, 1999). ... Food poisoning (December 12, 2001); missed two games. ... Injured hand (November 21, 2002); missed one game. ... Flu (December 21, 2002); missed two games. ... Injured shoulder (February 24, 2004); missed one game.

Season Team	League	REGULAR SEASON								PLAYOFFS				
		GP	G	A	Pts.	PIM	+/-	PP	SH	GP	G	A	Pts.	PIM
94-95—Caledon	Jr. A	44	10	35	45	139	...	...	...	—	—	—	—	—
95-96—Ottawa	OHL	64	10	14	24	90	...	...	...	4	0	3	3	10
96-97—Ottawa	OHL	63	13	51	64	143	81	6	0	24	4	24	28	38
97-98—Ottawa	OHL	40	7	31	38	94	...	...	...	13	0	4	4	24
98-99—Ottawa	OHL	51	11	48	59	83	53	...	...	9	1	9	10	18
99-00—Providence	AHL	53	5	14	19	66	...	...	...	12	1	0	1	6
—Boston	NHL	5	0	0	0	0	-5	0	0	—	—	—	—	—
00-01—Providence	AHL	78	6	27	33	105	...	...	...	17	0	2	2	35
—Boston	NHL	1	0	0	0	0	-1	0	0	—	—	—	—	—
01-02—Boston	NHL	80	4	14	18	107	18	0	0	6	1	2	3	8
02-03—Boston	NHL	78	7	17	24	99	8	0	1	5	0	1	1	4
03-04—Boston	NHL	81	6	24	30	98	17	1	1	7	0	2	2	2
04-05—Nottingham	England	13	2	3	5	10	...	...	...	6	1	2	3	22
NHL Totals (5 years)		245	17	55	72	304	37	1	2	18	1	5	6	14

BRADLEY, MATT — RW

PERSONAL: Born June 13, 1978, in Stittsville, Ont. ... 6-2/195. ... Shoots right.

TRANSACTIONS/CAREER NOTES: Selected by San Jose Sharks in fourth round (fourth Sharks pick, 102nd overall) of NHL draft (June 22, 1996). ... Injured shoulder (February 14, 2001); missed seven games. ... Injured back (March 3, 2002); missed one game. ... Injured wrist (April 10, 2002); missed final two games of season. ... Injured wrist (March 8, 2003); missed three games. ... Traded by Sharks to Pittsburgh Penguins for C Wayne Primeau (March 11, 2003); missed final 12 games of season because of wrist injury.

		REGULAR SEASON								PLAYOFFS				
Season Team	League	GP	G	A	Pts.	PIM	+/-	PP	SH	GP	G	A	Pts.	PIM
94-95—Cumberland	CJHL	49	13	20	33	18	...	...	...	—	—	—	—	—
95-96—Kingston	OHL	55	10	14	24	17	...	...	...	6	0	1	1	6
96-97—Kingston	OHL	65	24	24	48	41	17	5	0	5	0	4	4	2
—Kentucky	AHL	1	0	1	1	0	0	0	0	—	—	—	—	—
97-98—Kingston	OHL	55	33	50	83	24	13	...	...	8	3	4	7	7
—Kentucky	AHL	1	0	1	1	0	...	...	...	—	—	—	—	—
98-99—Kentucky	AHL	79	23	20	43	57	9	5	1	10	1	4	5	4
99-00—Kentucky	AHL	80	22	19	41	81	...	...	...	9	6	3	9	9
00-01—Kentucky	AHL	22	5	8	13	16	...	...	...	1	1	0	1	5
—San Jose	NHL	21	1	1	2	19	0	0	0	—	—	—	—	—
01-02—San Jose	NHL	54	9	13	22	43	22	0	0	10	0	0	0	0
02-03—San Jose	NHL	46	2	3	5	37	-1	0	0	—	—	—	—	—
03-04—Pittsburgh	NHL	82	7	9	16	65	-27	0	0	—	—	—	—	—
04-05—Dornbirner	Austria	6	5	2	7	18	...	...	...	—	—	—	—	—
NHL Totals (4 years)		203	19	26	45	164	-6	0	0	10	0	0	0	0

BRANDNER, CHRISTOPH — LW/RW

PERSONAL: Born May 7, 1975, in Bruck Mur, Austria. ... 6-4/224. ... Shoots left.

TRANSACTIONS/CAREER NOTES: Selected by Minnesota Wild in eighth round (eighth Wild pick, 237th overall) of NHL entryd draft (June 23, 2002). ... Flu (December 3, 2003); missed two games. ... Injured foot (December 13, 2003); missed one game. ... Reinjured foot (December 17, 2003); missed three games.

		REGULAR SEASON								PLAYOFFS				
Season Team	League	GP	G	A	Pts.	PIM	+/-	PP	SH	GP	G	A	Pts.	PIM
01-02—Krefeld Pinguine	Germany	50	30	25	55	20	...	...	...	3	1	0	1	4
02-03—Krefeld Pinguine	Germany	49	28	17	45	26	...	...	...	14	9	9	18	8
03-04—Minnesota	NHL	35	4	5	9	8	-2	1	0	—	—	—	—	—
—Houston	AHL	37	7	7	14	18	-2	3	0	2	1	0	1	0
04-05—Houston	AHL	26	5	3	8	15	-5	1	0	—	—	—	—	—
NHL Totals (1 year)		35	4	5	9	8	-2	1	0					

BRASHEAR, DONALD — LW — FLYERS

PERSONAL: Born January 7, 1972, in Bedford, Ind. ... 6-2/235. ... Shoots left. ... Name pronounced brah-SHEER.

TRANSACTIONS/CAREER NOTES: Signed as free agent by Montreal Canadiens (July 28, 1992). ... Bruised knee (November 23, 1993); missed one game. ... Injured shoulder (February 27, 1995); missed one game. ... Bruised hand (March 20, 1995); missed one game. ... Cut right thigh (December 30, 1995); missed seven games. ... Traded by Canadiens to Vancouver Canucks for D Jassen Cullimore (November 13, 1996). ... Strained back (February 8, 1997); missed three games. ... Suspended four games and fined $1,000 for fighting (February 25, 1997). ... Injured shoulder (March 11, 1998); missed two games. ... Suspended two games for illegal check (October 24, 1999). ... Suffered concussion (February 21, 2000); missed 20 games. ... Strained knee (October 18, 2000); missed one game. ... Strained back (November 21, 2000); missed two games. ... Injured leg (November 11, 2001); missed five games. ... Traded by Canucks with sixth-round pick (traded to Columbus; Blue Jackets selected Jaroslav Balastik) in 2002 draft to Philadelphia Flyers for LW Jan Hlavac and third-round pick (Brett Skinner) in 2002 (December 17, 2001). ... Bruised right hand (March 29, 2003); missed two games. ... Injured left knee (October 14, 2003); missed nine games. ... Sprained left knee (February 5, 2004); missed three games. ... Sprained left knee (February 17, 2004); missed six games.

		REGULAR SEASON								PLAYOFFS				
Season Team	League	GP	G	A	Pts.	PIM	+/-	PP	SH	GP	G	A	Pts.	PIM
89-90—Longueuil	QMJHL	64	12	14	26	169	...	...	...	7	0	0	0	11
90-91—Longueuil	QMJHL	68	12	26	38	195	...	...	...	8	0	3	3	33
91-92—Verdun	QMJHL	65	18	24	42	283	...	...	...	18	4	2	6	98
92-93—Fredericton	AHL	76	11	3	14	261	...	...	...	5	0	0	0	8
93-94—Fredericton	AHL	62	38	28	66	250	6	9	3	—	—	—	—	—
—Montreal	NHL	14	2	2	4	34	0	0	0	2	0	0	0	0
94-95—Montreal	NHL	20	1	1	2	63	-5	0	0	—	—	—	—	—
—Fredericton	AHL	29	10	9	19	182	1	3	0	17	7	5	12	77
95-96—Montreal	NHL	67	0	4	4	223	-10	0	0	6	0	0	0	2
96-97—Montreal	NHL	10	0	0	0	38	-2	0	0	—	—	—	—	—
—Vancouver	NHL	59	8	5	13	207	-6	0	0	—	—	—	—	—
97-98—Vancouver	NHL	77	9	9	18	*372	-9	0	0	—	—	—	—	—
98-99—Vancouver	NHL	82	8	10	18	209	-25	2	0	—	—	—	—	—
99-00—Vancouver	NHL	60	11	2	13	136	-9	1	0	—	—	—	—	—
00-01—Vancouver	NHL	79	9	19	28	145	0	0	0	4	0	0	0	0
01-02—Vancouver	NHL	31	5	8	13	90	-8	1	0	—	—	—	—	—
—Philadelphia	NHL	50	4	15	19	109	0	0	0	5	0	0	0	19
02-03—Philadelphia	NHL	80	8	17	25	161	5	0	0	13	1	2	3	21
03-04—Philadelphia	NHL	64	6	7	13	212	-1	0	0	18	1	3	4	61
NHL Totals (11 years)		693	71	99	170	1999	-70	4	0	48	2	5	7	103

BRATHWAITE, FRED — G

PERSONAL: Born November 24, 1972, in Ottawa. ... 5-8/178. ... Catches left. ... Name pronounced BRATH-wayt.

TRANSACTIONS/CAREER NOTES: Signed as free agent by Edmonton Oilers (October 6, 1993). ... Signed as free agent by Calgary Flames (January 7, 1999). ... Injured groin (November 7, 2000); missed two games. ... Traded by Flames with C Daniel Tkaczuk, RW Sergei Varlamov and ninth-round pick (C Grant Jacobsen) in 2001 draft to St. Louis Blues for G Roman Turek and fourth-round pick (LW Egor Shastin) in 2001 draft (June 23, 2001). ... Injured mouth (March 7, 2002); missed one game. ... Released by Blues (March 18, 2003). ... Signed as free agent by Columbus Blue Jackets (June 3, 2003). ... Injured groin (December 29, 2003); missed two games.

		REGULAR SEASON									PLAYOFFS							
Season Team	League	GP	Min.	W	L	T	GA	SO	GAA	SV%	GP	Min.	W	L	GA	SO	GAA	SV%
89-90—Oshawa	OHL	20	901	11	2	1	45	1	3.00	...	10	451	4	2	22	0	*2.93	...
90-91—Oshawa	OHL	39	1986	25	6	3	112	1	3.38	...	13	677	*9	2	43	0	3.81	...
91-92—Oshawa	OHL	24	1248	12	7	2	81	0	3.89	...	—	—	—	—	—	—	—	—
—London	OHL	23	1325	23	10	4	61	4	2.76	...	10	615	5	5	36	0	3.51	...
92-93—Det. Jr. Red Wings	OHL	37	2192	23	10	4	134	0	3.67	...	15	858	9	6	48	1	3.36	...
93-94—Cape Breton	AHL	2	119	1	1	0	6	0	3.03	.880	—	—	—	—	—	—	—	—
—Edmonton	NHL	19	982	3	10	3	58	0	3.54	.889	—	—	—	—	—	—	—	—
94-95—Edmonton	NHL	14	601	2	5	1	40	0	3.99	.863	—	—	—	—	—	—	—	—
95-96—Cape Breton	AHL	31	1699	12	16	0	110	1	3.88	...	—	—	—	—	—	—	—	—
—Edmonton	NHL	7	293	0	2	0	12	0	2.46	.914	—	—	—	—	—	—	—	—
96-97—Manitoba	IHL	58	2945	22	22	5	167	1	3.40	.901	—	—	—	—	—	—	—	—
97-98—Manitoba	IHL	51	2737	23	18	4	138	1	3.03	.908	2	73	0	1	4	0	3.29	.905
98-99—Canadian nat'l team	Int'l	24	989	6	8	3	47	...	2.85	...	—	—	—	—	—	—	—	—
—Calgary	NHL	28	1663	11	9	7	68	1	2.45	.915	—	—	—	—	—	—	—	—
99-00—Calgary	NHL	61	3448	25	25	7	158	5	2.75	.905	—	—	—	—	—	—	—	—
—Saint John	AHL	2	120	2	0	0	4	0	2.00	...	—	—	—	—	—	—	—	—
00-01—Calgary	NHL	49	2742	15	17	10	106	5	2.32	.910	—	—	—	—	—	—	—	—
01-02—St. Louis	NHL	25	1446	9	11	4	54	2	2.24	.901	1	1	0	0	0	0	0.00	...
02-03—St. Louis	NHL	30	1615	12	9	4	74	2	2.75	.883	—	—	—	—	—	—	—	—
03-04—Columbus	NHL	21	1050	4	11	1	59	0	3.37	.897	—	—	—	—	—	—	—	—
—Syracuse	AHL	3	188	0	2	1	7	1	2.23	.918	—	—	—	—	—	—	—	—
04-05—Ak Bars Kazan	Russian	35	...	...	...	...	...	...	1.87	...	2	...	...	...	...	...	0.94	...
NHL Totals (9 years)		254	13840	81	99	37	629	15	2.73	.901	1	1	0	0	0	0	0.00	...

BRENDL, PAVEL — RW — HURRICANES

PERSONAL: Born March 23, 1981, in Opocno, Czechoslovakia. ... 6-1/204. ... Shoots right.

TRANSACTIONS/CAREER NOTES: Selected by New York Rangers in first round (first Rangers pick, fourth overall) of NHL draft (June 26, 1999). ... Traded by Rangers with LW Jan Hlavac, D Kim Johnsson and third-round pick (LW Stefan Ruzicka) in 2003 draft to Philadelphia Flyers for rights to C Eric Lindros (August 20, 2001). ... Sprained right ankle (October 4, 2001); missed first seven games of season. ... Traded by Flyers with D Bruno St. Jacques to Carolina Hurricanes for RW Sami Kapanen and D Ryan Bast (February 7, 2003). ... Injured knee (February 25, 2003) and had surgery; missed 19 games. ... Fractured collarbone (February 25, 2004); missed final 21 games of season.

		REGULAR SEASON								PLAYOFFS				
Season Team	League	GP	G	A	Pts.	PIM	+/-	PP	SH	GP	G	A	Pts.	PIM
96-97—Olomouc	Czech. Jrs.	40	35	17	52	...	...	...	...	—	—	—	—	—
97-98—Olomouc	Czech. Jrs.	38	29	23	52	...	...	...	...	—	—	—	—	—
—Olomouc	Czech Dv.I	12	1	1	2	...	...	...	...	—	—	—	—	—
98-99—Calgary	WHL	68	*73	61	*134	40	68	20	10	20	*21	25	*46	18
99-00—Calgary	WHL	61	*59	52	111	94	41	16	8	10	7	12	19	8
—Hartford	AHL	...	...	...	...	...	...	...	...	2	0	0	0	0
00-01—Calgary	WHL	49	40	35	75	66	...	...	...	10	7	6	13	6
01-02—Philadelphia	NHL	8	1	0	1	2	-1	0	0	2	0	0	0	0
—Philadelphia	AHL	64	15	22	37	22	-15	7	0	5	4	1	5	0
02-03—Philadelphia	NHL	42	5	7	12	4	8	1	0	—	—	—	—	—
—Carolina	NHL	8	0	1	1	2	-3	0	0	—	—	—	—	—
03-04—Carolina	NHL	18	5	3	8	8	0	1	0	—	—	—	—	—
—Lowell	AHL	33	17	16	33	34	-6	3	0	—	—	—	—	—
04-05—Trinec	Czech Rep.	2	0	0	0	0	-1	0	0	—	—	—	—	—
—HC Olomouc	Czech Rep.	3	0	0	0	12	-4	...	...	—	—	—	—	—
—Thurgau	Switz. Div. 2	4	3	0	3	4	...	1	0	—	—	—	—	—
—Kiek.-Karhut Joensuu	Finland Div. 2	21	9	10	19	48	...	...	...	—	—	—	—	—
NHL Totals (3 years)		76	11	11	22	16	4	2	0	2	0	0	0	0

BRENNAN, KIP — LW — THRASHERS

PERSONAL: Born August 27, 1980, in Kingston, Ont. ... 6-4/228. ... Shoots left.

TRANSACTIONS/CAREER NOTES: Selected by Los Angeles Kings in fourth round (fourth Kings pick, 103rd overall) of NHL draft (June 27, 1998). ... Bruised foot, hip (January 4, 2003); missed three games. ... Strained left knee (January 16, 2003); missed eight games. ... Charley horse (December 2, 2003); missed 10 games. ... Suspended 10 games for returning to ice after being ejected (December 26, 2003). ... Traded by Kings to Atlanta Thrashers for LW Jeff Cowan (March 9, 2004). ... Injured hand (March 19, 2004); missed six games. ... Signed as free agent by Chicago of the AHL (September 27, 2004).

		REGULAR SEASON								PLAYOFFS				
Season Team	League	GP	G	A	Pts.	PIM	+/-	PP	SH	GP	G	A	Pts.	PIM
96-97—Windsor	OHL	42	0	10	10	156	...	...	...	5	0	1	1	16
97-98—Windsor	OHL	24	0	7	7	103	...	...	...	—	—	—	—	—
—Sudbury	OHL	24	0	3	3	85	...	...	...	—	—	—	—	—
98-99—Sudbury	OHL	38	9	12	21	160	-4	...	...	—	—	—	—	—

Season Team	League	GP	G	A	Pts.	PIM	+/-	PP	SH	GP	G	A	Pts.	PIM
		REGULAR SEASON								PLAYOFFS				
99-00—Sudbury	OHL	55	16	16	32	228	-2	4	1	12	3	3	6	67
00-01—Lowell	AHL	23	2	3	5	117	...	...	...	—	—	—	—	—
—Sudbury	OHL	27	7	14	21	94	12	3	0	12	5	6	11	*92
01-02—Manchester	AHL	44	4	1	5	269	-2	0	0	4	0	1	1	26
—Los Angeles	NHL	4	0	0	0	22	1	0	0	—	—	—	—	—
02-03—Los Angeles	NHL	19	0	0	0	57	0	0	0	—	—	—	—	—
—Manchester	AHL	35	3	2	5	195	-2	0	0	3	0	0	0	0
03-04—Manchester	AHL	2	0	0	0	6	0	0	0	2	0	1	1	2
—Los Angeles	NHL	18	1	0	1	79	-1	0	0	—	—	—	—	—
—Atlanta	NHL	5	0	0	0	17	0	0	0	—	—	—	—	—
04-05—Chicago	AHL	48	7	6	13	267	-4	3	0	18	1	1	2	105
NHL Totals (3 years)		46	1	0	1	175	0	0	0					

BRENNAN, RICH D

PERSONAL: Born November 26, 1972, in Schenectady, N.Y. ... 6-2/200. ... Shoots right.

TRANSACTIONS/CAREER NOTES: Selected by Quebec Nordiques in third round (third Nordiques pick, 56th overall) of NHL draft (June 22, 1991). ... Nordiques franchise moved to Colorado and renamed Avalanche for 1995-96 season (June 21, 1995). ... Signed as free agent by San Jose Sharks (July 9, 1997). ... Traded by Sharks to New York Rangers for G Jason Muzzatti (March 24, 1998). ... Signed as free agent by Nashville Predators (September 1999). ... Claimed by Los Angeles Kings in waiver draft (September 27, 1999). ... Signed as free agent by Predators (August 8, 2001). ... Traded by Predators to Kings for D Brett Hauer (December 18, 2001). ... Signed as free agent by Boston Bruins (July 18, 2002). ... Injured ankle (January 30, 2003); missed 27 games. ... Signed as free agent by Bern of the Swiss league (June 30, 2004).

Season Team	League	GP	G	A	Pts.	PIM	+/-	PP	SH	GP	G	A	Pts.	PIM
		REGULAR SEASON								PLAYOFFS				
88-89—Albany Academy	N.Y. H.S.	25	17	30	47	57	...	...	...	—	—	—	—	—
89-90—Tabor Academy	Mass. H.S.	33	12	14	26	68	...	...	...	—	—	—	—	—
90-91—Tabor Academy	Mass. H.S.	34	13	37	50	91	...	...	...	—	—	—	—	—
91-92—Boston University	Hockey East	31	4	13	17	54	...	...	...	—	—	—	—	—
92-93—Boston University	Hockey East	40	9	11	20	68	...	...	...	—	—	—	—	—
93-94—Boston University	Hockey East	41	8	27	35	82	26	3	0	—	—	—	—	—
94-95—Boston University	Hockey East	31	5	23	28	56	16	3	0	—	—	—	—	—
95-96—Brantford	Col.HL	5	1	2	3	2	...	...	...	—	—	—	—	—
96-97—Hershey	AHL	74	11	45	56	88	...	...	...	23	2	16	18	22
—Colorado	NHL	2	0	0	0	0	0	0	0	—	—	—	—	—
97-98—Kentucky	AHL	42	11	17	28	71	5	9	0	—	—	—	—	—
—San Jose	NHL	11	1	2	3	2	-4	1	0	—	—	—	—	—
—Hartford	AHL	9	2	4	6	12	0	1	0	—	—	—	—	—
98-99—Hartford	AHL	47	4	24	28	42	13	3	0	—	—	—	—	—
—New York Rangers	NHL	24	1	3	4	23	-4	0	0	—	—	—	—	—
99-00—Lowell	AHL	67	15	30	45	110	...	...	...	7	1	5	6	0
00-01—Lowell	AHL	69	10	31	41	146	...	...	...	—	—	—	—	—
—Los Angeles	NHL	2	0	0	0	0	-3	0	0	—	—	—	—	—
01-02—Milwaukee	AHL	23	4	8	12	27	-7	3	0	—	—	—	—	—
—Nashville	NHL	4	0	0	0	2	0	0	0	—	—	—	—	—
—Manchester	AHL	39	6	13	19	33	-10	5	0	5	1	1	2	16
02-03—Providence	AHL	41	3	29	32	51	1	2	1	—	—	—	—	—
—Boston	NHL	7	0	1	1	6	3	0	0	—	—	—	—	—
03-04—Providence	AHL	56	12	15	27	47	-1	8	0	2	0	1	1	2
04-05—Langenthal	Switzerland	1	0	2	2	0	...	0	0	—	—	—	—	—
—Bern	Switzerland	23	5	5	10	24	...	2	0	—	—	—	—	—
—Augsburger Panther	Germany	16	4	5	9	22	1	...	...	5	0	1	1	16
NHL Totals (6 years)		50	2	6	8	33	-8	1	0					

BRENT, TIM C MIGHTY DUCKS

PERSONAL: Born March 10, 1984, in Cambridge, Ont. ... 6-0/175. ... Shoots right.

TRANSACTIONS/CAREER NOTES: Selected by Mighty Ducks of Anaheim in second round (second Mighty Ducks pick, 37th overall) of NHL entry draft (June 22, 2002). ... Returned by Mighty Ducks to draft pool; selected by Mighty Ducks in third round (third Mighty Ducks pick, 75th overall) of NHL entry draft (June 27, 2004).

Season Team	League	GP	G	A	Pts.	PIM	+/-	PP	SH	GP	G	A	Pts.	PIM
		REGULAR SEASON								PLAYOFFS				
00-01—Toronto St. Michael's	OHL	64	9	19	28	31	...	...	...	18	2	8	10	6
01-02—Toronto St. Michael's	OHL	61	19	40	59	52	...	...	...	14	7	12	19	20
02-03—Toronto St. Michael's	OHL	60	24	42	66	74	...	...	...	19	7	17	24	14
03-04—Toronto St. Michael's	OHL	53	26	41	67	105	16	10	1	18	4	13	17	24
04-05—Cincinnati	AHL	46	5	13	18	42	7	0	0	12	0	1	1	6

BREWER, ERIC D BLUES

PERSONAL: Born April 17, 1979, in Vernon, B.C. ... 6-3/220. ... Shoots left.

TRANSACTIONS/CAREER NOTES: Selected by New York Islanders in 1st round (2nd Islanders pick, 5th overall) of NHL draft (June 21, 1997). ... Strained ankle tendon (April 8, 1999); missed four games. ... Injured toe (November 19, 1999); missed six games. ... Traded by Islanders with LW Josh Green and 2nd-round pick (LW Brad Winchester) in 2000 draft to Edmonton Oilers for D Roman Hamrlik (June 24, 2000). ... Strained buttocks (October 6, 2000); missed four games. ... Sprained left shoulder (January 21, 2002); missed one game. ... Sprained left shoulder (November 1, 2002); missed two games. ... Injured groin (November 26, 2003); missed 5 games. ... Traded by Oilers with D Jeff Woywitka and D Doug Lynch to St. Louis Blues for D Chris Pronger (Aug. 2, 2005).

Season Team	League	REGULAR SEASON								PLAYOFFS				
		GP	G	A	Pts.	PIM	+/-	PP	SH	GP	G	A	Pts.	PIM
95-96—Prince George	WHL	63	4	10	14	25	...	...	...	—	—	—	—	—
96-97—Prince George	WHL	71	5	24	29	81	...	...	...	15	2	4	6	16
97-98—Prince George	WHL	34	5	28	33	45	11	3	0	11	4	2	6	19
98-99—New York Islanders	NHL	63	5	6	11	32	-14	2	0	—	—	—	—	—
99-00—New York Islanders	NHL	26	0	2	2	20	-11	0	0	—	—	—	—	—
—Lowell	AHL	25	2	2	4	26	...	...	...	7	0	0	0	0
00-01—Edmonton	NHL	77	7	14	21	53	15	2	0	6	1	5	6	2
01-02—Edmonton	NHL	81	7	18	25	45	-5	6	0	—	—	—	—	—
—Can. Olympic team	Int'l	6	2	0	2	0	...	...	...	—	—	—	—	—
02-03—Edmonton	NHL	80	8	21	29	45	-11	1	0	6	1	3	4	6
03-04—Edmonton	NHL	77	7	18	25	67	-6	3	0	—	—	—	—	—
NHL Totals (6 years)		404	34	79	113	262	-32	14	0	12	2	8	10	8

BRIERE, DANIEL C SABRES

PERSONAL: Born October 6, 1977, in Gatineau, Que. ... 5-10/179. ... Shoots right.

TRANSACTIONS/CAREER NOTES: Selected by Phoenix Coyotes in first round (second Coyotes pick, 24th overall) of NHL draft (June 22, 1996). ... Separated shoulder (March 21, 1998); missed five games. ... Had concussion (October 6, 1998); missed first two games of season. ... Strained groin (September 25, 2000); missed first game of season. ... Strained groin (October 6, 2001); missed one game. ... Traded by Coyotes with third-round pick (D Andrej Sekera) in 2004 draft to Buffalo Sabres for C Chris Gratton and fourth-round pick (traded to Edmonton Oilers) in 2004 draft (March 10, 2003).

Season Team	League	REGULAR SEASON								PLAYOFFS				
		GP	G	A	Pts.	PIM	+/-	PP	SH	GP	G	A	Pts.	PIM
94-95—Drummondville	QMJHL	72	51	72	123	54	...	...	...	—	—	—	—	—
95-96—Drummondville	QMJHL	67	*67	*96	*163	84	...	...	...	6	6	12	18	8
96-97—Drummondville	QMJHL	59	52	78	130	86	...	...	...	8	7	7	14	14
97-98—Springfield	AHL	68	36	56	92	42	23	12	0	4	1	2	3	4
—Phoenix	NHL	5	1	0	1	2	1	0	0	—	—	—	—	—
98-99—Las Vegas	IHL	1	1	1	2	0	2	0	0	—	—	—	—	—
—Phoenix	NHL	64	8	14	22	30	-3	2	0	—	—	—	—	—
—Springfield	AHL	13	2	6	8	20	-2	0	0	3	0	1	1	2
99-00—Springfield	AHL	58	29	42	71	56	...	...	...	—	—	—	—	—
—Phoenix	NHL	13	1	1	2	0	0	0	0	1	0	0	0	0
00-01—Phoenix	NHL	30	11	4	15	12	-2	9	0	—	—	—	—	—
—Springfield	AHL	30	21	25	46	30	...	...	...	—	—	—	—	—
01-02—Phoenix	NHL	78	32	28	60	52	6	12	0	5	2	1	3	2
02-03—Phoenix	NHL	68	17	29	46	50	-21	4	0	—	—	—	—	—
—Buffalo	NHL	14	7	5	12	12	1	5	0	—	—	—	—	—
03-04—Buffalo	NHL	82	28	37	65	70	-7	11	0	—	—	—	—	—
04-05—Bern	Switzerland	36	17	29	46	26	...	5	0	11	1	6	7	2
NHL Totals (7 years)		354	105	118	223	228	-25	43	0	6	2	1	3	2

BRIGLEY, TRAVIS LW

PERSONAL: Born June 16, 1977, in Coronation, Alta. ... 6-0/205. ... Shoots left.

TRANSACTIONS/CAREER NOTES: Selected by Calgary Flames in second round (second Flames pick, 39th overall) of NHL draft (June 22, 1996). ... Traded by Flames with sixth-round pick (C Andrei Razin) in 2001 draft to Philadelphia Flyers for C/RW Marc Bureau (March 6, 2000). ... Signed as free agent by Anaheim Mighty Ducks (June 11, 2002). ... Traded by Mighty Ducks to Colorado Avalanche for future considerations (August 13, 2003). ... Injured back (November 20, 2003); missed two games. ... Reinjured back (December 20, 2003); missed 18 games. ... Bruised shoulder (February 11, 2004); missed eight games.

Season Team	League	REGULAR SEASON								PLAYOFFS				
		GP	G	A	Pts.	PIM	+/-	PP	SH	GP	G	A	Pts.	PIM
93-94—Lethbridge	WHL	1	0	0	0	0	...	...	...	—	—	—	—	—
94-95—Lethbridge	WHL	64	14	18	32	14	-25	4	0	—	—	—	—	—
95-96—Lethbridge	WHL	69	34	43	77	94	...	...	...	4	2	3	5	8
96-97—Lethbridge	WHL	71	43	47	90	56	17	11	5	19	9	9	18	31
97-98—Saint John	AHL	79	17	15	32	28	-8	1	1	8	0	0	0	0
—Calgary	NHL	2	0	0	0	2	0	0	0	—	—	—	—	—
98-99—Saint John	AHL	74	15	35	50	47	-13	2	1	7	3	1	4	2
99-00—Calgary	NHL	17	0	2	2	4	-6	0	0	—	—	—	—	—
—Saint John	AHL	9	3	1	4	4	...	...	...	—	—	—	—	—
—Detroit	IHL	29	6	10	16	24	...	...	...	—	—	—	—	—
—Philadelphia	AHL	15	2	2	4	15	...	...	...	5	1	0	1	4
00-01—Louisville	AHL	49	14	21	35	34	...	...	...	—	—	—	—	—
01-02—Cincinnati	AHL	70	22	21	43	40	-4	6	1	3	2	0	2	0
—Macon	ECHL	8	4	3	7	2	0	1	1	—	—	—	—	—
02-03—Cincinnati	AHL	64	18	27	45	58	-2	3	5	—	—	—	—	—
—Hershey	AHL	13	3	5	8	4	0	1	1	5	1	2	3	2
03-04—Colorado	NHL	36	3	4	7	10	0	1	0	—	—	—	—	—
—Hershey	AHL	18	6	6	12	8	-2	2	1	—	—	—	—	—
NHL Totals (3 years)		55	3	6	9	16	-6	1	0					

BRIMANIS, ARIS D BLUES

PERSONAL: Born March 14, 1972, in Cleveland. ... 6-3/212. ... Shoots right. ... Name pronounced AIR-ihz brih-MAN-ihz.

TRANSACTIONS/CAREER NOTES: Selected by Philadelphia Flyers in fourth round (third Flyers pick, 86th overall) of NHL draft (June 22, 1991).

... Signed as free agent by New York Islanders (August 12, 1999). ... Signed as free agent by Anaheim Mighty Ducks (August 1, 2001). ... Signed as free agent by St. Louis Blues (August 9, 2002).

		REGULAR SEASON								PLAYOFFS				
Season Team	**League**	**GP**	**G**	**A**	**Pts.**	**PIM**	**+/-**	**PP**	**SH**	**GP**	**G**	**A**	**Pts.**	**PIM**
88-89—Culver Military	Indiana H.S.	38	10	13	23	24	...	...	...	—	—	—	—	—
89-90—Culver Military	Indiana H.S.	37	15	10	25	52	...	...	...	—	—	—	—	—
90-91—Bowling Green	CCHA	38	3	6	9	42	...	...	...	—	—	—	—	—
91-92—Bowling Green	CCHA	32	2	9	11	38	...	...	...	—	—	—	—	—
92-93—Brandon	WHL	71	8	50	58	110	20	6	0	4	2	1	3	12
93-94—Philadelphia	NHL	1	0	0	0	0	-1	0	0	—	—	—	—	—
—Hershey	AHL	75	8	15	23	65	5	4	0	11	2	3	5	12
94-95—Hershey	AHL	76	8	17	25	68	3	3	0	6	1	1	2	14
95-96—Hershey	AHL	54	9	22	31	64	...	...	...	5	1	2	3	4
—Philadelphia	NHL	17	0	2	2	12	-1	0	0	—	—	—	—	—
96-97—Philadelphia	AHL	65	14	18	32	69	21	5	0	10	2	2	4	13
—Philadelphia	NHL	3	0	1	1	0	0	0	0	—	—	—	—	—
97-98—Philadelphia	AHL	30	1	11	12	26	7	0	1	—	—	—	—	—
—Michigan	IHL	35	3	9	12	24	-6	1	0	4	1	0	1	4
98-99—Grand Rapids	IHL	66	16	21	37	70	1	6	2	—	—	—	—	—
—Fredericton	AHL	8	2	4	6	6	-1	1	0	15	3	10	13	18
99-00—Kansas City	IHL	46	5	17	22	28	...	...	...	—	—	—	—	—
—New York Islanders	NHL	18	2	1	3	6	-5	2	0	—	—	—	—	—
00-01—Chicago	IHL	20	2	2	4	14	...	...	...	16	3	1	4	8
—New York Islanders	NHL	56	0	8	8	26	-12	0	0	—	—	—	—	—
01-02—Cincinnati	AHL	72	2	9	11	44	6	0	0	3	1	0	1	0
—Anaheim	NHL	5	0	0	0	9	-1	0	0	—	—	—	—	—
02-03—Worcester	AHL	38	8	13	21	51	19	1	0	3	0	0	0	2
03-04—St. Louis	NHL	13	0	0	0	4	0	0	0	—	—	—	—	—
—Worcester	AHL	65	4	15	19	56	-6	1	0	10	1	0	1	6
04-05—Worcester	AHL	69	4	13	17	44	5	0	1	—	—	—	—	—
NHL Totals (7 years)		113	2	12	14	57	-20	2	0					

BRIND'AMOUR, ROD C HURRICANES

PERSONAL: Born August 9, 1970, in Ottawa. ... 6-1/200. ... Shoots left. ... Name pronounced BRIHN-duh-MOHR.

TRANSACTIONS/CAREER NOTES: Selected by St. Louis Blues in first round (first Blues pick, ninth overall) of NHL draft (June 11, 1988). ... Traded by Blues with C Dan Quinn to Philadelphia Flyers for C Ron Sutter and D Murray Baron (September 22, 1991). ... Cut elbow (November 19, 1992); missed two games. ... Bruised right hand (February 20, 1993); missed one game. ... Fractured foot (September 25, 1999) and had surgery; missed first 34 games of season. ... Traded by Flyers with G Jean-Marc Pelletier and second-round pick (traded to Colorado; Avalanche selected Agris Saviels) in 2000 draft to Carolina Hurricanes for rights to C Keith Primeau and fifth-round pick (traded to New York Islanders; Islanders selected Kristofer Ottosson) in 2000 draft (January 23, 2000). ... Suffered concussion (April 3, 2000); missed one game. ... Injured groin (December 27, 2000); missed three games. ... Injured eye (February 8, 2002); missed one game. ... Injured hand (January 22, 2003) and had surgery; missed 34 games. ... Strained groin (January 23, 2004); missed three games. ... Injured elbow (February 14, 2004); missed one game.

STATISTICAL PLATEAUS: Three-goal games: 1992-93 (1), 2000-01 (1). Total: 2.

		REGULAR SEASON								PLAYOFFS				
Season Team	**League**	**GP**	**G**	**A**	**Pts.**	**PIM**	**+/-**	**PP**	**SH**	**GP**	**G**	**A**	**Pts.**	**PIM**
87-88—Notre Dame	SJHL	56	46	61	107	136	...	...	...	—	—	—	—	—
88-89—Michigan State	CCHA	42	27	32	59	63	...	...	...	—	—	—	—	—
—St. Louis	NHL	...	...	...	...	...	...	...	...	5	2	0	2	4
89-90—St. Louis	NHL	79	26	35	61	46	23	10	0	12	5	8	13	6
90-91—St. Louis	NHL	78	17	32	49	93	2	4	0	13	2	5	7	10
91-92—Philadelphia	NHL	80	33	44	77	100	-3	8	4	—	—	—	—	—
92-93—Philadelphia	NHL	81	37	49	86	89	-8	13	4	—	—	—	—	—
93-94—Philadelphia	NHL	84	35	62	97	85	-9	14	1	—	—	—	—	—
94-95—Philadelphia	NHL	48	12	27	39	33	-4	4	1	15	6	9	15	8
95-96—Philadelphia	NHL	82	26	61	87	110	20	4	4	12	2	5	7	6
96-97—Philadelphia	NHL	82	27	32	59	41	2	8	2	19	13	8	21	10
97-98—Philadelphia	NHL	82	36	38	74	54	-2	10	2	5	2	2	4	7
—Can. Olympic team	Int'l	6	1	2	3	0	3	0	0	—	—	—	—	—
98-99—Philadelphia	NHL	82	24	50	74	47	3	10	0	6	1	3	4	0
99-00—Philadelphia	NHL	12	5	3	8	4	-1	4	0	—	—	—	—	—
—Carolina	NHL	33	4	10	14	22	-12	0	1	—	—	—	—	—
00-01—Carolina	NHL	79	20	36	56	47	-7	5	1	6	1	3	4	6
01-02—Carolina	NHL	81	23	32	55	40	3	5	2	23	4	8	12	16
02-03—Carolina	NHL	48	14	23	37	37	-9	7	1	—	—	—	—	—
03-04—Carolina	NHL	78	12	26	38	28	0	1	0	—	—	—	—	—
04-05—Kloten	Switzerland	2	2	1	3	0	...	1	0	5	2	4	6	6
NHL Totals (16 years)		1109	351	560	911	876	-2	107	23	116	38	51	89	73

BRISEBOIS, PATRICE D AVALANCHE

PERSONAL: Born January 27, 1971, in Montreal. ... 6-2/202. ... Shoots right. ... Name pronounced pa-TREEZ BREES-bwah.

TRANSACTIONS/CAREER NOTES: Selected by Montreal Canadiens in 2nd round (2nd Canadiens pick, 30th overall) of NHL draft (June 17, 1989). ... Sprained right ankle (October 10, 1992); missed two games. ... Charley horse (December 16, 1992); missed two games. ... Injured knee (October 30, 1993); missed 10 games. ... Fractured ankle (December 1, 1993); missed 14 games. ... Sprained ankle (February 21, 1994); missed seven games. ... Acute herniated disc (April 3, 1995); missed 12 games. ... Injured rib cage (November 1, 1995). ... Sprained back (February 17, 1996); missed four games. ... Mild disc irritation (March 25, 1996); missed final nine games of regular season. ... Separated shoulder (January 4, 1997); missed 27 games. ... Strained shoulder (March 22, 1997); missed four games. ... Injured rib (April 10, 1997);

missed remainder of regular season and two playoff games. ... Sprained knee (April 15, 1998); missed three games. ... Injured back (October 2, 1998); missed first six games of season. ... Separated shoulder (December 23, 1998); missed nine games. ... Sprained knee (February 20, 1999); missed one game. ... Injured shoulder (March 11, 1999); missed 12 games. ... Injured back before start of 1999-2000 season; missed first 27 games. ... Injured back (January 28, 2001); missed five games. ... Fractured ankle (January 17, 2002); missed 10 games. ... Irregular heartbeat (Feburary 8, 2003); missed nine games. ... Injured groin (March 18, 2003); missed one game. ... Injured groin (December 11, 2003); missed seven games. ... Injured groin (March 19, 2004); missed four games. ... Contract bought out by Canadiens (July 25, 2005). ... Signed as free agent by Colorado Avalanche (Aug. 3, 2005).

		REGULAR SEASON								PLAYOFFS				
Season Team	**League**	**GP**	**G**	**A**	**Pts.**	**PIM**	**+/-**	**PP**	**SH**	**GP**	**G**	**A**	**Pts.**	**PIM**
87-88—Laval	QMJHL	48	10	34	44	95	...	...	...	6	0	2	2	2
88-89—Laval	QMJHL	50	20	45	65	95	...	...	...	17	8	14	22	45
89-90—Laval	QMJHL	56	18	70	88	108	...	...	...	13	7	9	16	26
90-91—Montreal	NHL	10	0	2	2	4	1	0	0	—	—	—	—	—
—Drummondville	QMJHL	54	17	44	61	72	...	...	...	14	6	18	24	49
91-92—Fredericton	AHL	53	12	27	39	51	...	...	...	—	—	—	—	—
—Montreal	NHL	26	2	8	10	20	9	0	0	11	2	4	6	6
92-93—Montreal	NHL	70	10	21	31	79	6	4	0	20	0	4	4	18
93-94—Montreal	NHL	53	2	21	23	63	5	1	0	7	0	4	4	6
94-95—Montreal	NHL	35	4	8	12	26	-2	0	0	—	—	—	—	—
95-96—Montreal	NHL	69	9	27	36	65	10	3	0	6	1	2	3	6
96-97—Montreal	NHL	49	2	13	15	24	-7	0	0	3	1	1	2	24
97-98—Montreal	NHL	79	10	27	37	67	16	5	0	10	1	0	1	0
98-99—Montreal	NHL	54	3	9	12	28	-8	1	0	—	—	—	—	—
99-00—Montreal	NHL	54	10	25	35	18	-1	5	0	—	—	—	—	—
00-01—Montreal	NHL	77	15	21	36	28	-31	11	0	—	—	—	—	—
01-02—Montreal	NHL	71	4	29	33	25	9	2	1	10	1	1	2	2
02-03—Montreal	NHL	73	4	25	29	32	-14	1	0	—	—	—	—	—
03-04—Montreal	NHL	71	4	27	31	22	17	2	0	11	2	1	3	4
04-05—Kloten	Switzerland	10	3	1	4	2	...	0	0	—	—	—	—	—
NHL Totals (14 years)		791	79	263	342	501	10	35	1	78	8	17	25	66

BROCHU, MARTIN G PENGUINS

PERSONAL: Born March 10, 1973, in Anjou, Que. ... 6-0/199. ... Catches left. ... Name pronounced MAHR-tan broh-SHOO.

TRANSACTIONS/CAREER NOTES: Signed as free agent by Montreal Canadiens (September 22, 1992). ... Traded by Canadiens to Washington Capitals for future considerations (March 15, 1996). ... Signed as free agent by Minnesota Wild (July 9, 2001). ... Claimed by Vancouver Canucks in waiver draft (September 28, 2001). ... Signed as free agent by Pittsburgh Penguins (August 22, 2003).

		REGULAR SEASON									PLAYOFFS							
Season Team	**League**	**GP**	**Min.**	**W**	**L**	**T**	**GA**	**SO**	**GAA**	**SV%**	**GP**	**Min.**	**W**	**L**	**GA**	**SO**	**GAA**	**SV%**
91-92—Granby	QMJHL	52	2772	15	29	2	218	0	4.72	...	—	—	—	—	—	—	—	—
92-93—Hull	QMJHL	29	1453	9	15	1	137	0	5.66	...	2	69	0	1	7	0	6.09	...
93-94—Fredericton	AHL	32	1506	10	11	3	76	2	3.03	.904	—	—	—	—	—	—	—	—
94-95—Fredericton	AHL	44	2475	18	18	4	145	0	3.52	.894	—	—	—	—	—	—	—	—
95-96—Fredericton	AHL	17	985	6	8	2	70	0	4.26	...	—	—	—	—	—	—	—	—
—Wheeling	ECHL	19	1060	10	6	2	51	1	2.89	...	—	—	—	—	—	—	—	—
—Portland	AHL	5	286	2	2	1	15	0	3.15	...	12	700	7	4	28	2	*2.40	...
96-97—Portland	AHL	55	2962	23	17	7	150	2	3.04	.903	5	324	2	3	13	0	2.41	.925
97-98—Portland	AHL	37	1926	16	14	1	96	2	2.99	.909	6	297	3	2	16	0	3.23	.901
98-99—Utah	IHL	5	298	1	3	1	13	0	2.62	.910	—	—	—	—	—	—	—	—
—Portland	AHL	20	1164	6	10	3	57	2	2.94	.917	—	—	—	—	—	—	—	—
—Washington	NHL	2	120	0	2	0	6	0	3.00	.891	—	—	—	—	—	—	—	—
99-00—Portland	AHL	54	3192	32	15	6	116	4	2.18	...	2	80	0	2	7	0	5.25	...
00-01—Saint John	AHL	55	3049	27	19	5	132	2	2.60	.899	19	1148	*14	4	39	*4	2.04	...
01-02—Vancouver	NHL	6	216	0	3	0	15	0	4.17	.856	—	—	—	—	—	—	—	—
—Manitoba	AHL	29	1625	10	14	3	91	1	3.36	.867	—	—	—	—	—	—	—	—
02-03—Cherepovets	Russian	8	480	...	...	...	15	2	1.88	...	—	—	—	—	—	—	—	—
03-04—Wheeling	ECHL	9	520	6	2	1	23	1	2.65	.889	—	—	—	—	—	—	—	—
—Pittsburgh	NHL	1	33	0	0	0	1	0	1.82	.947	—	—	—	—	—	—	—	—
—Wilkes-Barre/Scranton	AHL	15	730	4	9	1	31	1	2.55	.896	—	—	—	—	—	—	—	—
NHL Totals (3 years)		9	369	0	5	0	22	0	3.58	.876								

BRODEUR, MARTIN G DEVILS

PERSONAL: Born May 6, 1972, in Montreal. ... 6-2/210. ... Catches left. ... Son of Denis Brodeur, goaltender with bronze medal-winning Canadian Olympic team (1956). ... Name pronounced MAHR-tan broh-DOOR.

TRANSACTIONS/CAREER NOTES: Selected by New Jersey Devils in first round (first Devils pick, 20th overall) of NHL draft (June 16, 1990). ... Flu (December 30, 1997); missed two games.

		REGULAR SEASON									PLAYOFFS							
Season Team	**League**	**GP**	**Min.**	**W**	**L**	**T**	**GA**	**SO**	**GAA**	**SV%**	**GP**	**Min.**	**W**	**L**	**GA**	**SO**	**GAA**	**SV%**
89-90—St. Hyacinthe	QMJHL	42	2333	23	13	2	156	0	4.01	...	12	678	5	7	46	0	4.07	...
90-91—St. Hyacinthe	QMJHL	52	2946	22	24	4	162	2	3.30	...	4	232	0	4	16	0	4.14	...
91-92—St. Hyacinthe	QMJHL	48	2846	27	16	4	161	2	3.39	...	5	317	2	3	14	0	2.65	...
—New Jersey	NHL	4	179	2	1	0	10	0	3.35	.882	1	32	0	1	3	0	5.63	.800
92-93—Utica	AHL	32	1952	14	13	5	131	0	4.03	.884	4	258	1	3	18	0	4.19	.871
93-94—New Jersey	NHL	47	2625	27	11	8	105	3	2.40	.915	17	1171	8	9	38	1	1.95	.928
94-95—New Jersey	NHL	40	2184	19	11	6	89	3	2.45	.902	*20	*1222	*16	4	34	*3	*1.67	*.927
95-96—New Jersey	NHL	77	*4433	34	30	12	173	6	2.34	.911	—	—	—	—	—	—	—	—

Season Team	League	GP	Min.	W	L	T	GA	SO	GAA	SV%	GP	Min.	W	L	GA	SO	GAA	SV%
		REGULAR SEASON									PLAYOFFS							
96-97—New Jersey	NHL	67	3838	37	14	13	120	*10	*1.88	.927	10	659	5	5	19	2	1.73	.929
97-98—New Jersey	NHL	70	4128	*43	17	8	130	10	1.89	.917	6	366	2	4	12	0	1.97	.927
98-99—New Jersey	NHL	*70	*4239	*39	21	10	162	4	2.29	.906	7	425	3	4	20	0	2.82	.856
99-00—New Jersey	NHL	72	4312	*43	20	8	161	6	2.24	.910	23	*1450	*16	7	39	2	*1.61	.927
00-01—New Jersey	NHL	72	4297	*42	17	11	166	*9	2.32	.906	25	1505	15	10	52	4	2.07	.897
01-02—New Jersey	NHL	*73	*4347	38	26	9	156	4	2.15	.906	6	381	2	4	9	1	1.42	.938
—Can. Olympic team	Int'l	5	300	4	0	1	9	0	1.80	.917	—	—	—	—	—	—	—	—
02-03—New Jersey	NHL	73	4374	*41	23	9	147	*9	2.02	.914	*24	*1491	*16	8	41	*7	1.65	.934
03-04—New Jersey	NHL	75	4555	38	26	11	154	11	2.03	.917	5	298	1	4	13	0	2.62	.902
NHL Totals (12 years)		740	43511	403	217	105	1573	75	2.17	.912	144	9000	84	60	280	20	1.87	.921

BROOKBANK, SHELDON — D — PREDATORS

PERSONAL: Born October 3, 1980, in Lanigan, Sask. ... 6-2/200. ... Shoots right. ... Brother of Wade Brookbank, D, Vancouver Canucks.
TRANSACTIONS/CAREER NOTES: Signed as free agent by Anaheim Mighty Ducks (July 21, 2003). ... Signed as free agent by Nashville Predators (Aug. 4, 2005).

Season Team	League	GP	G	A	Pts.	PIM	+/-	PP	SH	GP	G	A	Pts.	PIM
		REGULAR SEASON								PLAYOFFS				
03-04—Milwaukee	AHL	6	0	0	0	6	-2	0	0	—	—	—	—	—
—Binghamton	AHL	4	0	0	0	31	0	0	0	—	—	—	—	—
—Manitoba	AHL	4	0	0	0	12	0	0	0	—	—	—	—	—
04-05—Cincinnati	AHL	60	1	11	12	181	4	0	0	11	0	0	0	40

BROOKBANK, WADE — D — CANUCKS

PERSONAL: Born September 29, 1977, in Lanigan, Sask. ... 6-4/221. ... Shoots left. ... Brother of Sheldon Brookbank, D, Anaheim Mighty Ducks organization.
TRANSACTIONS/CAREER NOTES: Signed as free agent by Ottawa Senators (July 27, 2001). ... Claimed by Nashville Predators in waiver draft (October 3, 2003). ... Traded by Senators to Vancouver Canucks for future considerations (December 17, 2003). ... Claimed by Senators off waivers from Canucks (December 19, 2003). ... Traded by Senators to Florida Panthers for future considerations (December 29, 2003). ... Claimed by Canucks off waivers from Panthers (January 3, 2004).

Season Team	League	GP	G	A	Pts.	PIM	+/-	PP	SH	GP	G	A	Pts.	PIM
		REGULAR SEASON								PLAYOFFS				
97-98—Anchorage	WCHL	7	0	0	0	46	...	...	...	4	0	0	0	20
98-99—Anchorage	WCHL	56	0	4	4	337	...	...	...	5	0	0	0	47
99-00—Oklahoma City	CHL	68	3	9	12	354	...	...	...	7	1	1	2	29
00-01—Oklahoma City	CHL	46	1	13	14	267	...	...	...	5	0	0	0	24
—Orlando	IHL	29	0	1	1	122	...	...	...	4	0	0	0	6
01-02—Grand Rapids	AHL	73	1	6	7	337	...	...	...	3	0	1	1	14
02-03—Binghamton	AHL	8	0	0	0	28	-4	0	0	—	—	—	—	—
03-04—Nashville	NHL	9	0	0	0	38	-4	0	0	—	—	—	—	—
—Milwaukee	AHL	6	0	0	0	6	-2	0	0	—	—	—	—	—
—Vancouver	NHL	20	2	0	2	95	3	0	0	—	—	—	—	—
—Binghamton	AHL	4	0	0	0	31	0	0	0	—	—	—	—	—
—Manitoba	AHL	4	0	0	0	12	0	0	0	—	—	—	—	—
04-05—Manitoba	AHL	68	0	10	10	285	2	0	0	9	0	0	0	10
NHL Totals (1 year)		29	2	0	2	133	-1	0	0					

BROWN, BRAD — D

PERSONAL: Born December 27, 1975, in Baie Verte, Newfoundland. ... 6-4/220. ... Shoots right.
TRANSACTIONS/CAREER NOTES: Selected by Montreal Canadiens in first round (first Canadiens pick, 18th overall) of NHL draft (June 28, 1994). ... Back spasms (October 17, 1998); missed three games. ... Traded by Canadiens with G Jocelyn Thibault and D Dave Manson to Chicago Blackhawks for G Jeff Hackett, D Eric Weinrich, D Alain Nasreddine and fourth-round pick (D Chris Dyment) in 1999 entry draft (November 16, 1998). ... Sore back (December 17, 1998); missed two games. ... Bruised foot (March 12, 1999); missed two games. ... Bruised wrist (October 4, 1999); missed three games. ... Cut hand (December 17, 1999); missed two games. ... Injured hand (December 26, 1999); missed 10 games. ... Bruised left hand (March 15, 2000); missed four games. ... Traded by Blackhawks with LW Michal Grosek to New York Rangers for future considerations (October 5, 2000). ... Injured shoulder (January 4, 2001); missed 10 games. ... Fractured right foot (February 23, 2001); missed remainder of season. ... Signed as free agent by Minnesota Wild (July 31, 2001). ... Bruised kidney (November 25, 2001); missed four games. ... Bruised left ankle (December 22, 2001); missed one game. ... Fractured left ankle (December 26, 2001); missed 12 games. ... Sprained right knee (January 24, 2002); missed six games. ... Bruised left foot (April 5, 2002); missed two games. ... Flu (December 15, 2002); missed one game. ... Fractured right wrist (December 15, 2003); missed two games. ... Reinjured right wrist (December 19, 2003); missed 23 games. ... Traded by Wild with sixth-round pick in 2005 draft to Buffalo Sabres for future considerations (March 8, 2004).

Season Team	League	GP	G	A	Pts.	PIM	+/-	PP	SH	GP	G	A	Pts.	PIM
		REGULAR SEASON								PLAYOFFS				
91-92—North Bay	OHL	49	2	9	11	170	...	...	...	18	0	6	6	43
92-93—North Bay	OHL	61	4	9	13	228	...	...	...	2	0	2	2	13
93-94—North Bay	OHL	66	8	24	32	196	...	3	...	18	3	12	15	33
94-95—North Bay	OHL	64	8	38	46	172	...	5	0	6	1	4	5	8
95-96—Barrie	OHL	27	3	13	16	82	...	...	...	—	—	—	—	—
—Fredericton	AHL	38	0	3	3	148	...	...	...	10	2	1	3	6
96-97—Fredericton	AHL	64	3	7	10	368	-23	2	0	—	—	—	—	—
—Montreal	NHL	8	0	0	0	22	-1	0	0	—	—	—	—	—
97-98—Fredericton	AHL	64	1	8	9	297	9	0	0	4	0	0	0	29

Season Team	League	GP	G	A	Pts.	PIM	+/-	PP	SH		GP	G	A	Pts.	PIM
		REGULAR SEASON									PLAYOFFS				
98-99—Montreal	NHL	5	0	0	0	21	0	0	0		—	—	—	—	—
—Chicago	NHL	61	1	7	8	184	-4	0	0		—	—	—	—	—
99-00—Chicago	NHL	57	0	9	9	134	-1	0	0		—	—	—	—	—
00-01—New York Rangers	NHL	48	1	3	4	107	0	0	0		—	—	—	—	—
01-02—Minnesota	NHL	51	0	4	4	123	-11	0	0		—	—	—	—	—
02-03—Minnesota	NHL	57	0	1	1	90	-1	0	0		11	0	0	0	16
03-04—Minnesota	NHL	30	0	1	1	54	-1	0	0		—	—	—	—	—
—Buffalo	NHL	13	0	2	2	12	3	0	0		—	—	—	—	—
NHL Totals (7 years)		330	2	27	29	747	-16	0	0		11	0	0	0	16

B

BROWN, CURTIS C BLACKHAWKS

PERSONAL: Born February 12, 1976, in Unity, Sask. ... 6-0/196. ... Shoots left.
TRANSACTIONS/CAREER NOTES: Selected by Buffalo Sabres in second round (second Sabres pick, 43rd overall) of NHL draft (June 28, 1994). ... Injured ankle before 1995-96 season; missed two games. ... Bruised knee (February 11, 1999); missed two games. ... Bruised knee (March 27, 1999); missed one game. ... Missed first game of 1999-2000 season in contract dispute. ... Suffered concussion (October 22, 1999); missed one game. ... Flu (February 10, 2000); missed five games. ... Injured knee (December 23, 2000); missed eight games. ... Back spasms (January 30, 2001); missed four games. ... Sprained right knee (March 12, 2003); missed two games. ... Injured ankle (March 29, 2003); missed five games. ... Traded by Sabres with D Andy Delmore to San Jose Sharks for D Jeff Jillson and ninth-round pick in 2005 draft (March 9, 2004). ... Signed as free agent by Chicago Blackhawks (July 2, 2004).
STATISTICAL PLATEAUS: Three-goal games: 2002-03 (1).

Season Team	League	GP	G	A	Pts.	PIM	+/-	PP	SH		GP	G	A	Pts.	PIM
		REGULAR SEASON									PLAYOFFS				
92-93—Moose Jaw	WHL	71	13	16	29	30	...	...	...		—	—	—	—	—
93-94—Moose Jaw	WHL	72	27	38	65	82	15	14	2		—	—	—	—	—
94-95—Moose Jaw	WHL	70	51	53	104	63	11	19	7		10	8	7	15	20
—Buffalo	NHL	1	1	1	2	2	2	0	0		—	—	—	—	—
95-96—Buffalo	NHL	4	0	0	0	0	0	0	0		—	—	—	—	—
—Moose Jaw	WHL	25	20	18	38	30	...	...	...		—	—	—	—	—
—Prince Albert	WHL	19	12	21	33	8	...	...	...		18	10	15	25	18
—Rochester	AHL	...	...	...	...	...	...	...	...		12	0	1	1	2
96-97—Buffalo	NHL	28	4	3	7	18	4	0	0		—	—	—	—	—
—Rochester	AHL	51	22	21	43	30	17	7	0		10	4	6	10	4
97-98—Buffalo	NHL	63	12	12	24	34	11	1	1		13	1	2	3	10
98-99—Buffalo	NHL	78	16	31	47	56	23	5	1		21	7	6	13	10
99-00—Buffalo	NHL	74	22	29	51	42	19	5	0		5	1	3	4	6
00-01—Buffalo	NHL	70	10	22	32	34	15	2	1		13	5	0	5	8
01-02—Buffalo	NHL	82	20	17	37	32	-4	4	1		—	—	—	—	—
02-03—Buffalo	NHL	74	15	16	31	40	4	3	4		—	—	—	—	—
03-04—Buffalo	NHL	68	9	12	21	30	2	2	1		—	—	—	—	—
—San Jose	NHL	12	2	2	4	6	1	0	0		17	0	2	2	18
04-05—San Diego	ECHL	47	9	29	38	24	5	3	2		—	—	—	—	—
NHL Totals (10 years)		554	111	145	256	294	77	22	9		69	14	13	27	52

BROWN, DUSTIN RW KINGS

PERSONAL: Born November 4, 1984, in Ithaca, N.Y. ... 6-0/200. ... Shoots right.
TRANSACTIONS/CAREER NOTES: Selected by Los Angeles Kings in first round (first Kings pick, 13th overall) of NHL entry draft (June 23, 2003). ... Sprained left ankle (November 30, 2003); missed 26 games. ... Sprained right ankle (January 31, 2004); missed 14 games.

Season Team	League	GP	G	A	Pts.	PIM	+/-	PP	SH		GP	G	A	Pts.	PIM
		REGULAR SEASON									PLAYOFFS				
00-01—Guelph	OHL	53	23	22	45	45	...	...	...		4	0	0	0	10
01-02—Guelph	OHL	63	41	32	73	56	...	...	...		9	8	5	13	14
02-03—Guelph	OHL	58	34	42	76	89	...	...	...		11	7	8	15	6
03-04—Los Angeles	NHL	31	1	4	5	16	0	0	0		—	—	—	—	—
04-05—Manchester	AHL	79	29	45	74	96	7	12	0		6	5	2	7	10
NHL Totals (1 year)		31	1	4	5	16	0	0	0						

BROWN, SEAN D/LW DEVILS

PERSONAL: Born November 5, 1976, in Oshawa, Ont. ... 6-3/215. ... Shoots left.
TRANSACTIONS/CAREER NOTES: Selected by Boston Bruins in first round (second Bruins pick, 21st overall) of NHL draft (July 8, 1995). ... Traded by Bruins with RW Mariusz Czerkawski and first-round pick (D Mattieu Descoteaux) in 1996 draft to Edmonton Oilers for G Bill Ranford (January 11, 1996). ... Suspended three games for high-sticking incident (November 13, 1998). ... Traded by Oilers to Bruins for D Bobby Allen (March 19, 2002). ... Suspended one game for cross-checking incident (November 11, 2002). ... Signed as free agent by New Jersey Devils (July 24, 2003).

Season Team	League	GP	G	A	Pts.	PIM	+/-	PP	SH		GP	G	A	Pts.	PIM
		REGULAR SEASON									PLAYOFFS				
92-93—Oshawa	Tier II Jr. A	15	0	1	1	9	...	...	...		—	—	—	—	—
93-94—Wellington	OJHL	32	5	14	19	165	...	...	...		—	—	—	—	—
—Belleville	OHL	28	1	2	3	53	...	...	...		8	0	0	0	17
94-95—Belleville	OHL	58	2	16	18	200	...	0	0		16	4	2	6	67
95-96—Belleville	OHL	37	10	23	33	150	...	...	...		—	—	—	—	—
—Sarnia	OHL	26	8	17	25	112	...	...	...		10	1	0	1	38
96-97—Hamilton	AHL	61	1	7	8	238	-8	1	0		19	1	0	1	47

Season Team	League	REGULAR SEASON GP	G	A	Pts.	PIM	+/-	PP	SH	PLAYOFFS GP	G	A	Pts.	PIM
—Edmonton	NHL	5	0	0	0	4	-1	0	0	—	—	—	—	—
97-98—Edmonton	NHL	18	0	1	1	43	-1	0	0	—	—	—	—	—
—Hamilton	AHL	43	4	6	10	166	-4	2	0	6	0	2	2	38
98-99—Edmonton	NHL	51	0	7	7	188	1	0	0	1	0	0	0	10
99-00—Edmonton	NHL	72	4	8	12	192	1	0	0	3	0	0	0	23
00-01—Edmonton	NHL	62	2	3	5	110	2	0	0	—	—	—	—	—
01-02—Edmonton	NHL	61	6	4	10	127	8	3	0	—	—	—	—	—
—Boston	NHL	12	0	1	1	47	-1	0	0	4	0	0	0	2
02-03—Boston	NHL	69	1	5	6	117	-6	0	0	—	—	—	—	—
03-04—New Jersey	NHL	39	0	3	3	44	5	0	0	1	0	0	0	2
—Albany	AHL	21	1	6	7	56	-5	1	0	—	—	—	—	—
NHL Totals (8 years)		389	13	32	45	872	8	3	0	9	0	0	0	37

BRULE, GILBERT — C — BLUE JACKETS

PERSONAL: Born January 1, 1987, in Edmonton. ... 5-10/175. ... Shoots right. ... Name pronounced broo-LAY.

TRANSACTIONS/CAREER NOTES: Selected by Columbus Blue Jackets in 1st round (1st Blue Jackets pick, 6th overall) of entry draft (July 30, 2005).

Season Team	League	REGULAR SEASON GP	G	A	Pts.	PIM	+/-	PP	SH	PLAYOFFS GP	G	A	Pts.	PIM
03-04—Vancouver	WHL	67	25	35	60	100	...	...	...	—	—	—	—	—
04-05—Vancouver	WHL	70	39	48	87	169	4	13	4	6	1	3	4	8

BRULE, STEVE — RW — AVALANCHE

PERSONAL: Born January 15, 1975, in Montreal. ... 6-0/200. ... Shoots right. ... Name pronounced broo-LAY.

TRANSACTIONS/CAREER NOTES: Selected by New Jersey Devils in sixth round (sixth Devils pick, 143rd overall) of NHL draft (June 26, 1993). ... Signed as free agent by Detroit Red Wings (July 20, 2000). ... Signed as free agent by Colorado Avalanche (July 22, 2002).

Season Team	League	REGULAR SEASON GP	G	A	Pts.	PIM	+/-	PP	SH	PLAYOFFS GP	G	A	Pts.	PIM
92-93—St. Jean	QMJHL	70	33	47	80	46	...	...	...	4	0	0	0	9
93-94—St. Jean	QMJHL	66	41	64	105	46	3	15	0	5	2	1	3	0
94-95—St. Jean	QMJHL	69	44	64	108	42	17	14	1	7	3	4	7	8
—Albany	AHL	3	1	4	5	0	2	0	0	14	9	5	14	4
95-96—Albany	AHL	80	30	21	51	37	...	...	...	4	0	0	0	17
96-97—Albany	AHL	79	28	48	76	27	21	7	0	16	7	7	14	12
97-98—Albany	AHL	80	34	43	77	34	14	20	3	13	8	3	11	4
98-99—Albany	AHL	78	32	52	84	35	17	12	1	5	3	1	4	4
99-00—Albany	AHL	75	30	46	76	18	...	...	...	5	1	2	3	0
—New Jersey	NHL	...	...	...	...	...	...	...	...	1	0	0	0	0
00-01—Manitoba	IHL	78	21	48	69	22	...	...	...	13	3	10	13	12
01-02—Cincinnati	AHL	77	21	42	63	50	-9	6	0	3	0	1	1	0
02-03—Colorado	NHL	2	0	0	0	0	0	0	0	—	—	—	—	—
—Hershey	AHL	49	18	19	37	30	7	5	0	5	4	0	4	8
03-04—Hershey	AHL	79	29	29	58	82	-8	9	0	—	—	—	—	—
04-05—Krefeld Pinguine	Germany	51	18	29	47	51	...	...	...	—	—	—	—	—
NHL Totals (2 years)		2	0	0	0	0	0	0	0	1	0	0	0	0

BRUNETTE, ANDREW — LW/RW — AVALANCHE

PERSONAL: Born August 24, 1973, in Sudbury, Ont. ... 6-1/210. ... Shoots left. ... Name pronounced broo-NEHT.

TRANSACTIONS/CAREER NOTES: Selected by Washington Capitals in 6th round (6th Capitals pick, 174th overall) of NHL draft (June 26, 1993). ... Selected by Nashville Predators in expansion draft (June 26, 1998). ... Traded by Predators to Atlanta Thrashers for 5th-round pick (C Matt Hendricks) in 2000 draft (June 21, 1999). ... Concussion (January 13, 2001); missed four games. ... Bruised thigh (February 15, 2001); missed one game. ... Signed as free agent by Minnesota Wild (July 6, 2001). ... Bruised shoulder (December 29, 2001); missed one game. ... Signed as free agent by Colorado Avalanche (Aug. 6, 2005).

Season Team	League	REGULAR SEASON GP	G	A	Pts.	PIM	+/-	PP	SH	PLAYOFFS GP	G	A	Pts.	PIM
90-91—Owen Sound	OHL	63	15	20	35	15	...	...	...	—	—	—	—	—
91-92—Owen Sound	OHL	66	51	47	98	42	...	...	...	5	5	0	5	8
92-93—Owen Sound	OHL	66	*62	*100	*162	91	...	...	...	8	8	6	14	16
93-94—Portland	AHL	23	9	11	20	10	...	...	...	2	0	1	1	0
—Hampton	ECHL	20	12	18	30	32	...	...	...	7	7	6	13	18
—Providence	AHL	3	0	0	0	0	...	...	...	—	—	—	—	—
94-95—Portland	AHL	79	30	50	80	53	...	...	...	7	3	3	6	10
95-96—Portland	AHL	69	28	66	94	125	...	...	...	20	11	18	29	15
—Washington	NHL	11	3	3	6	0	5	0	0	6	1	3	4	0
96-97—Portland	AHL	50	22	51	73	48	7	10	0	5	1	2	3	0
—Washington	NHL	23	4	7	11	12	-3	2	0	—	—	—	—	—
97-98—Portland	AHL	43	21	46	67	64	-17	12	1	10	1	11	12	12
—Washington	NHL	28	11	12	23	12	2	4	0	—	—	—	—	—
98-99—Nashville	NHL	77	11	20	31	26	-10	7	0	—	—	—	—	—
99-00—Atlanta	NHL	81	23	27	50	30	-32	9	0	—	—	—	—	—
00-01—Atlanta	NHL	77	15	44	59	26	-5	6	0	—	—	—	—	—
01-02—Minnesota	NHL	81	21	48	69	18	-4	10	0	—	—	—	—	—

Season Team	League	GP	G	A	Pts.	PIM	+/-	PP	SH	GP	G	A	Pts.	PIM
		REGULAR SEASON								PLAYOFFS				
02-03—Minnesota	NHL	82	18	28	46	30	-10	9	0	18	7	6	13	4
03-04—Minnesota	NHL	82	15	34	49	12	3	7	0	—	—	—	—	—
NHL Totals (9 years)		542	121	223	344	166	-54	54	0	24	8	9	17	4

BRYLIN, SERGEI — C/RW — DEVILS

PERSONAL: Born January 13, 1974, in Moscow, U.S.S.R. ... 5-10/190. ... Shoots left. ... Name pronounced BREE-lihn.

TRANSACTIONS/CAREER NOTES: Selected by New Jersey Devils in second round (second Devils pick, 42nd overall) of NHL draft (June 20, 1992). ... Tonsillitis (May 3, 1995); missed last game of season. ... Fractured hand (November 16, 1995); missed 13 games. ... Injured knee (September 19, 1997); missed 19 games. ... Injured knee (November 28, 2000); missed one game. ... Injured knee (February 22, 2001); missed five games. ... Bruised knee (November 13, 2001); missed five games. ... Fractured wrist (February 7, 2003); missed final 30 games of season and five playoff games.

Season Team	League	GP	G	A	Pts.	PIM	+/-	PP	SH	GP	G	A	Pts.	PIM
		REGULAR SEASON								PLAYOFFS				
91-92—CSKA Moscow	CIS	44	1	6	7	4	...	...	...	—	—	—	—	—
92-93—CSKA Moscow	CIS	42	5	4	9	36	...	...	...	—	—	—	—	—
93-94—CSKA Moscow	CIS	39	4	6	10	36	...	...	...	3	0	1	1	0
—Russian Penguins	IHL	13	4	5	9	18	-5	0	0	—	—	—	—	—
94-95—Albany	AHL	63	19	35	54	78	8	7	0	—	—	—	—	—
—New Jersey	NHL	26	6	8	14	8	12	0	0	12	1	2	3	4
95-96—New Jersey	NHL	50	4	5	9	26	-2	0	0	—	—	—	—	—
96-97—New Jersey	NHL	29	2	2	4	20	-13	0	0	—	—	—	—	—
—Albany	AHL	43	17	24	41	38	12	6	0	16	4	8	12	12
97-98—New Jersey	NHL	18	2	3	5	0	4	0	0	—	—	—	—	—
—Albany	AHL	44	21	22	43	60	25	4	1	—	—	—	—	—
98-99—New Jersey	NHL	47	5	10	15	28	8	3	0	5	3	1	4	4
99-00—New Jersey	NHL	64	9	11	20	20	0	1	0	17	3	5	8	0
00-01—New Jersey	NHL	75	23	29	52	24	25	3	1	20	3	4	7	6
01-02—New Jersey	NHL	76	16	28	44	10	21	5	0	6	0	2	2	2
02-03—New Jersey	NHL	52	11	8	19	16	-2	3	1	19	1	3	4	8
03-04—New Jersey	NHL	82	14	19	33	20	10	7	0	5	0	0	0	0
04-05—Khimik Voskresensk	Russian	35	8	19	27	40	-3	...	...	—	—	—	—	—
NHL Totals (10 years)		519	92	123	215	172	63	22	2	84	11	17	28	24

BRYZGALOV, ILYA — G — MIGHTY DUCKS

PERSONAL: Born June 22, 1980, in Togliatti, U.S.S.R. ... 6-3/203. ... Catches left. ... Name pronounced breez-GAH-lahf.

TRANSACTIONS/CAREER NOTES: Selected by Anaheim Mighty Ducks in second round (second Mighty Ducks pick, 44th overall) of NHL draft (June 24, 2000).

Season Team	League	GP	Min.	W	L	T	GA	SO	GAA	SV%	GP	Min.	W	L	GA	SO	GAA	SV%
		REGULAR SEASON									PLAYOFFS							
97-98—Lada-2 Togliatti	Rus. Div.	8	480	...	...	...	28	...	3.50	...	—	—	—	—	—	—	—	—
98-99—Lada-2 Togliatti	Rus.-4	20	1200	...	...	...	43	...	2.15	...	—	—	—	—	—	—	—	—
99-00—Spartak Moscow	Russian	9	500	...	...	...	21	...	2.52	...	—	—	—	—	—	—	—	—
—Lada Togliatti	Russian	14	796	...	...	...	18	3	1.36	...	7	407	...	...	10	1	1.47	...
00-01—Lada Togliatti	Russian	34	1992	...	...	...	61	*8	1.84	...	5	249	...	...	8	0	1.93	...
01-02—Anaheim	NHL	1	32	0	0	0	1	0	1.88	.917	—	—	—	—	—	—	—	—
—Cincinnati	AHL	45	2398	20	16	4	99	4	2.48	.909	—	—	—	—	—	—	—	—
02-03—Cincinnati	AHL	54	3019	12	26	9	142	1	2.82	.910	—	—	—	—	—	—	—	—
03-04—Anaheim	NHL	1	60	1	0	0	2	0	2.00	.929	—	—	—	—	—	—	—	—
—Cincinnati	AHL	64	3747	27	25	10	145	6	2.32	.912	9	535	5	4	27	1	3.03	.900
04-05—Cincinnati	AHL	36	2006	17	13	...	87	4	2.60	.902	7	314	3	3	13	0	2.48	.904
NHL Totals (2 years)		2	92	1	0	0	3	0	1.96	.925								

BUCHBERGER, KELLY — C

PERSONAL: Born December 2, 1966, in Langenburg, Sask. ... 6-2/210. ... Shoots left. ... Name pronounced BUK-buhr-guhr.

TRANSACTIONS/CAREER NOTES: Selected by Edmonton Oilers in ninth round (eighth Oilers pick, 188th overall) of NHL draft (June 15, 1985). ... Fractured right ankle (March 1989). ... Dislocated left shoulder (March 13, 1990). ... Reinjured shoulder (May 4, 1990). ... Strained shoulder (April 7, 1993); missed one game. ... Fractured right forearm (January 5, 1999); missed 30 games. ... Selected by Atlanta Thashers in expansion draft (June 25, 1999). ... Traded by Thrashers with RW Nelson Emerson to Los Angeles Kings for RW Donald Audette and D Frantisek Kaberle (March 13, 2000). ... Sprained right ankle (March 9, 2002); missed seven games. ... Signed as free agent by Phoenix Coyotes (July 7, 2002). ... Fractured toe (October 28, 2002); missed three games. ... Signed as free agent by Pittsburgh Penguins (July 31, 2003).

STATISTICAL PLATEAUS: Three-goal games: 1992-93 (1).

Season Team	League	GP	G	A	Pts.	PIM	+/-	PP	SH	GP	G	A	Pts.	PIM
		REGULAR SEASON								PLAYOFFS				
83-84—Melville	SAJHL	60	14	11	25	139	...	...	...	—	—	—	—	—
84-85—Moose Jaw	WHL	51	12	17	29	114	...	...	...	—	—	—	—	—
85-86—Moose Jaw	WHL	72	14	22	36	206	...	...	...	13	11	4	15	37
86-87—Nova Scotia	AHL	70	12	20	32	257	...	...	...	5	0	1	1	23
—Edmonton	NHL	...	...	...	...	...	...	...	...	3	0	1	1	5
87-88—Edmonton	NHL	19	1	0	1	81	-1	0	0	—	—	—	—	—
—Nova Scotia	AHL	49	21	23	44	206	...	...	...	2	0	0	0	11
88-89—Edmonton	NHL	66	5	9	14	234	-14	1	0	—	—	—	—	—

Season Team	League	GP	G	A	Pts.	PIM	+/-	PP	SH	GP	G	A	Pts.	PIM
		REGULAR SEASON								PLAYOFFS				
89-90—Edmonton	NHL	55	2	6	8	168	-8	0	0	19	0	5	5	13
90-91—Edmonton	NHL	64	3	1	4	160	-6	0	0	12	2	1	3	25
91-92—Edmonton	NHL	79	20	24	44	157	9	0	4	16	1	4	5	32
92-93—Edmonton	NHL	83	12	18	30	133	-27	1	2	—	—	—	—	—
93-94—Edmonton	NHL	84	3	18	21	199	-20	0	0	—	—	—	—	—
94-95—Edmonton	NHL	48	7	17	24	82	0	2	1	—	—	—	—	—
95-96—Edmonton	NHL	82	11	14	25	184	-20	0	2	—	—	—	—	—
96-97—Edmonton	NHL	81	8	30	38	159	4	0	0	12	5	2	7	16
97-98—Edmonton	NHL	82	6	17	23	122	-10	1	1	12	1	2	3	25
98-99—Edmonton	NHL	52	4	4	8	68	-6	0	2	4	0	0	0	0
99-00—Atlanta	NHL	68	5	12	17	139	-34	0	0	—	—	—	—	—
—Los Angeles	NHL	13	2	1	3	13	-2	0	0	4	0	0	0	4
00-01—Los Angeles	NHL	82	6	14	20	75	-10	0	0	8	1	0	1	2
01-02—Los Angeles	NHL	74	6	7	13	105	-13	0	0	7	0	0	0	7
02-03—Phoenix	NHL	79	3	9	12	109	0	0	1	—	—	—	—	—
03-04—Pittsburgh	NHL	71	1	3	4	109	-19	0	0	—	—	—	—	—
NHL Totals (18 years)		1182	105	204	309	2297	-177	5	13	97	10	15	25	129

BULIS, JAN — C — CANADIENS

PERSONAL: Born March 18, 1978, in Pardubice, Czechoslovakia. ... 6-1/208. ... Shoots left. ... Name pronounced YAHN BOO-lihsh.

TRANSACTIONS/CAREER NOTES: Selected by Washington Capitals in second round (third Capitals pick, 43rd overall) of NHL draft (June 22, 1996). ... Suffered concussion (November 11, 1997); missed one game. ... Sprained ankle before 1998-99 season; missed first 13 games of season. ... Sprained ankle (November 21, 1998); missed 15 games. ... Back spasms (November 11, 1999); missed one game. ... Bruised ribs (November 20, 1999); missed two games. ... Injured groin (December 15, 1999); missed three games. ... Separated shoulder (February 26, 2000); missed remainder of season. ... Fractured right thumb (November 22, 2000); missed 18 games. ... Traded by Capitals with RW Richard Zednik and first-round pick (C Alexander Perezhogin) in 2001 draft to Montreal Canadiens for C Trevor Linden, RW Dainius Zubrus and second-round pick (traded to Tampa Bay; Lightning selected D Andreas Holmqvist) in 2001 draft (March 13, 2001). ... Sprained knee (December 1, 2001); missed 20 games. ... Injured knee (February 24, 2004); missed 10 games.

Season Team	League	GP	G	A	Pts.	PIM	+/-	PP	SH	GP	G	A	Pts.	PIM
		REGULAR SEASON								PLAYOFFS				
94-95—Kelowna	BCJHL	51	23	25	48	36	...	...	...	17	7	9	16	...
95-96—Barrie	OHL	59	29	30	59	22	...	...	...	7	2	3	5	2
96-97—Barrie	OHL	64	42	61	103	42	17	13	1	9	3	7	10	10
97-98—Washington	NHL	48	5	11	16	18	-5	0	0	—	—	—	—	—
—Portland	AHL	3	1	4	5	12	1	1	0	—	—	—	—	—
—Kingston	OHL	2	0	1	1	0	-1	...	...	12	8	10	18	12
98-99—Washington	NHL	38	7	16	23	6	3	3	0	—	—	—	—	—
—Cincinnati	IHL	10	2	2	4	14	-5	0	0	—	—	—	—	—
99-00—Washington	NHL	56	9	22	31	30	7	0	0	—	—	—	—	—
00-01—Washington	NHL	39	5	13	18	26	0	1	0	—	—	—	—	—
—Portland	AHL	4	0	2	2	0	...	...	...	—	—	—	—	—
—Montreal	NHL	12	0	5	5	0	-1	0	0	—	—	—	—	—
01-02—Montreal	NHL	53	9	10	19	8	-2	1	0	6	0	0	0	6
02-03—Montreal	NHL	82	16	24	40	30	9	0	0	—	—	—	—	—
03-04—Montreal	NHL	72	13	17	30	30	-8	1	1	11	1	1	2	4
04-05—Pardubice	Czech Rep.	45	24	25	49	113	22	...	...	16	7	4	11	43
NHL Totals (7 years)		400	64	118	182	148	3	6	1	17	1	1	2	10

BURAVCHINKOV, VIACHESLAV — SABRES

PERSONAL: Born May 22, 1987, in Moscow, Russia.

Season Team	League	GP	G	A	Pts.	PIM	+/-	PP	SH	GP	G	A	Pts.	PIM
		REGULAR SEASON								PLAYOFFS				
04-05—Russian	Russian	26	4	1	5	14	...	...	...	—	—	—	—	—

BURE, VALERI — RW — KINGS

PERSONAL: Born June 13, 1974, in Moscow, U.S.S.R. ... 5-10/180. ... Shoots right. ... Brother of Pavel Bure, RW, 3 NHL teams (1991-2004). ... Name pronounced BOOR-ay.

TRANSACTIONS/CAREER NOTES: Selected by Montreal Canadiens in second round (second Canadiens pick, 33rd overall) of NHL draft (June 20, 1992). ... Bruised forearm (April 3, 1995); missed two games. ... Bruised kidney (October 19, 1996); missed 11 games. ... Bruised wrist (December 28, 1996); missed two games. ... Suffered concussion (January 4, 1997); missed five games. ... Bruised cheekbone (January 8, 1998); missed three games. ... Traded by Canadiens to Calgary Flames with fourth-round pick (C Shaun Sutter) in 1998 draft for D Zarley Zalapski and RW Jonas Hoglund (February 1, 1998). ... Suffered concussion (March 3, 1998); missed five games. ... Hyperextended shoulder (April 5, 1998); missed final seven games of season. ... Suffered concussion (January 10, 1999); missed two games. ... Traded by Flames with C Jason Wiemer to Florida Panthers for C Rob Niedermayer and second-round pick (G Andrei Medvedev) in 2001 draft (June 23, 2001). ... Injured right knee (October 16, 2001); missed 37 games. ... Injured knee (March 17, 2002); missed remainder of season. ... Fractured wrist (December 10, 2002); missed 12 games. ... Injured knee (February 15, 2003); missed 29 games. ... Traded by Panthers with fifth-round pick (D Nikita Nikitin) in 2004 draft to St. Louis Blues for D Mike Van Ryn (March 11, 2003). ... Claimed by Panthers off waivers from Blues (June 24, 2003). ... Injured groin (October 11, 2003); missed 11 games. ... Injured groin (February 14, 2004); missed three games. ... Traded by Panthers to Dallas Stars for D Drew Bagnall and future considerations (March 8, 2004).

STATISTICAL PLATEAUS: Three-goal games: 1997-98 (1).

Season Team	League	REGULAR SEASON GP	G	A	Pts.	PIM	+/-	PP	SH	PLAYOFFS GP	G	A	Pts.	PIM
90-91—CSKA Moscow	USSR	3	0	0	0	0	...	...	...	—	—	—	—	—
91-92—Spokane	WHL	53	27	22	49	78	...	...	...	10	11	6	17	10
92-93—Spokane	WHL	66	68	79	147	49	30	22	7	9	6	11	17	14
93-94—Spokane	WHL	59	40	62	102	48	1	14	7	3	5	3	8	2
94-95—Fredericton	AHL	45	23	25	48	32	-1	9	0	—	—	—	—	—
—Montreal	NHL	24	3	1	4	6	-1	0	0	—	—	—	—	—
95-96—Montreal	NHL	77	22	20	42	28	10	5	0	6	0	1	1	6
96-97—Montreal	NHL	64	14	21	35	6	4	4	0	5	0	1	1	2
97-98—Montreal	NHL	50	7	22	29	33	-5	2	0	—	—	—	—	—
—Calgary	NHL	16	5	4	9	2	0	0	0	—	—	—	—	—
—Russian Oly. team	Int'l	6	1	0	1	0	1	0	0	—	—	—	—	—
98-99—Calgary	NHL	80	26	27	53	22	0	7	0	—	—	—	—	—
99-00—Calgary	NHL	82	35	40	75	50	-7	13	0	—	—	—	—	—
00-01—Calgary	NHL	78	27	28	55	26	-21	16	0	—	—	—	—	—
01-02—Florida	NHL	31	8	10	18	12	-3	2	0	—	—	—	—	—
—Russian Oly. team	Int'l	6	1	0	1	2	...	...	...	—	—	—	—	—
02-03—Florida	NHL	46	5	21	26	10	-11	3	0	—	—	—	—	—
—St. Louis	NHL	5	0	2	2	0	-2	0	0	6	0	2	2	8
03-04—Florida	NHL	55	20	25	45	20	0	8	0	—	—	—	—	—
—Dallas	NHL	13	2	5	7	6	3	0	0	5	0	3	3	0
NHL Totals (10 years)		621	174	226	400	221	-33	60	0	22	0	7	7	16

BURKE, SEAN G LIGHTNING

PERSONAL: Born January 29, 1967, in Windsor, Ont. ... 6-4/209. ... Catches left. ... Name pronounced BUHRK.

TRANSACTIONS/CAREER NOTES: Selected by New Jersey Devils in 2nd round (2nd Devils pick, 24th overall) of NHL draft (June 15, 1985). ... Injured groin (December 1988). ... Arthroscopic right knee surgery (September 5, 1989). ... Traded by Devils with D Eric Weinrich to Hartford Whalers for RW Bobby Holik and 2nd-round pick (LW Jay Pandolfo) in 1993 draft (August 28, 1992). ... Sprained ankle (December 27, 1992); missed seven games. ... Back spasms (March 13, 1993); missed remainder of season. ... Injured hamstring (September 29, 1993); missed seven games. ... Reinjured hamstring (October 27, 1993); missed 14 games. ... Back spasms (December 23, 1993); missed one game. ... Strained groin (February 28, 1995); missed two games. ... Back spasms (November 19, 1995); missed two games. ... Back spasms (February 7, 1996); missed three games. ... Dislocated thumb (November 30, 1996); missed 19 games. ... Strained hip flexor (February 26, 1997); missed one game. ... Whalers franchise moved to North Carolina and renamed Carolina Hurricanes for 1997-98 season; NHL approved move on June 25, 1997. ... Traded by Hurricanes with LW Geoff Sanderson and D Enrico Ciccone to Vancouver Canucks for LW Martin Gelinas and G Kirk McLean (January 3, 1998). ... Traded by Canucks to Philadelphia Flyers for G Garth Snow (March 4, 1998). ... Lower back spasms (March 8, 1998); missed six games. ... Signed as free agent by Florida Panthers (September 11, 1998). ... Strained hip flexor (April 10, 1999); missed final three games of season. ... Traded by Panthers with 5th-round pick (D Nate Kiser) in 2000 draft to Phoenix Coyotes for G Mikhail Shtalenkov and 4th-round pick (D Chris Eade) in 2000 draft (November 19, 1999). ... Tore thumb ligament (November 26, 1999); missed 16 games. ... Strained hip flexor (January 12, 2000); missed one game. ... Injured groin (February 1, 2000); missed one game. ... Strained groin (March 1, 2000); missed one game. ... Injured elbow (November 30, 2000); missed one game. ... Bruised knee (February 11, 2001); missed two games. ... Strained groin (March 2, 2001); missed four games. ... Strained groin (November 17, 2001); missed three games. ... Strained groin (January 9, 2002); missed seven games. ... Flu (March 17, 2002); missed one game. ... High ankle sprain (October 22, 2002); missed 29 games. ... Sprained knee (January 3, 2003); missed 20 games. ... Strained groin (March 30, 2003); missed seven games. ... Traded by Coyotes with RW Branko Radivojevic and rights to LW Ben Eager to Phildelphia Flyers for C Mike Comrie (February 9, 2004). ... Signed as free agent by Tampa Bay Lightning (Aug. 9, 2005).

Season Team	League	REGULAR SEASON GP	Min.	W	L	T	GA	SO	GAA	SV%	PLAYOFFS GP	Min.	W	L	GA	SO	GAA	SV%
83-84—St. Michael's H.S.	MTHL	25	1482	...	...	...	120	0	4.86	...	—	—	—	—	—	—	—	—
84-85—Toronto	OHL	49	2987	25	21	3	211	0	4.24	...	5	266	1	3	25	0	5.64	...
85-86—Toronto	OHL	47	2840	16	27	3	233	0	4.92	...	4	238	0	4	24	0	6.05	...
—Canadian nat'l team	Int'l	5	284	...	...	...	22	0	4.65	...	—	—	—	—	—	—	—	—
86-87—Canadian nat'l team	Int'l	42	2550	27	13	2	130	0	3.06	...	—	—	—	—	—	—	—	—
87-88—Canadian nat'l team	Int'l	37	1962	19	9	2	92	1	2.81	...	—	—	—	—	—	—	—	—
—Can. Olympic team	Int'l	4	238	1	2	1	12	0	3.03	.893	—	—	—	—	—	—	—	—
—New Jersey	NHL	13	689	10	1	0	35	1	3.05	.883	17	1001	9	8	*57	1	3.42	.889
88-89—New Jersey	NHL	62	3590	22	31	9	230	3	3.84	.874	—	—	—	—	—	—	—	—
89-90—New Jersey	NHL	52	2914	22	22	6	175	0	3.60	.880	2	125	0	2	8	0	3.84	.860
90-91—New Jersey	NHL	35	1870	8	12	8	112	0	3.59	.872	—	—	—	—	—	—	—	—
91-92—Canadian nat'l team	Int'l	31	1721	18	6	4	75	1	2.61	...	—	—	—	—	—	—	—	—
—Can. Olympic team	Int'l	7	429	5	2	0	17	0	2.38	.928	—	—	—	—	—	—	—	—
—San Diego	IHL	7	424	4	2	1	17	0	2.41	...	3	160	0	3	13	0	4.88	...
92-93—Hartford	NHL	50	2656	16	27	3	184	0	4.16	.876	—	—	—	—	—	—	—	—
93-94—Hartford	NHL	47	2750	17	24	5	137	2	2.99	.906	—	—	—	—	—	—	—	—
94-95—Hartford	NHL	42	2418	17	19	4	108	0	2.68	.912	—	—	—	—	—	—	—	—
95-96—Hartford	NHL	66	3669	28	28	6	190	4	3.11	.907	—	—	—	—	—	—	—	—
96-97—Hartford	NHL	51	2985	22	22	6	134	4	2.69	.914	—	—	—	—	—	—	—	—
97-98—Carolina	NHL	25	1415	7	11	5	66	1	2.80	.899	—	—	—	—	—	—	—	—
—Vancouver	NHL	16	838	2	9	4	49	0	3.51	.876	—	—	—	—	—	—	—	—
—Philadelphia	NHL	11	632	7	3	0	27	1	2.56	.913	5	283	1	4	17	0	3.60	.860
98-99—Florida	NHL	59	3402	21	24	14	151	3	2.66	.907	—	—	—	—	—	—	—	—
99-00—Florida	NHL	7	418	2	5	0	18	0	2.58	.913	—	—	—	—	—	—	—	—
—Phoenix	NHL	35	2074	17	14	3	88	3	2.55	.914	5	296	1	4	16	0	3.24	.904
00-01—Phoenix	NHL	62	3644	25	22	*13	138	4	2.27	.922	—	—	—	—	—	—	—	—
01-02—Phoenix	NHL	60	3587	33	21	6	137	5	2.29	.920	5	297	1	4	13	0	2.63	.902
02-03—Phoenix	NHL	22	1248	12	6	2	44	2	2.12	.930	—	—	—	—	—	—	—	—
03-04—Phoenix	NHL	32	1795	10	15	5	84	1	2.81	.908	—	—	—	—	—	—	—	—
—Philadelphia	NHL	15	825	6	5	2	35	1	2.55	.910	1	40	0	0	1	0	1.50	.889
NHL Totals (16 years)		762	43419	304	321	101	2142	35	2.96	.902	35	2042	12	22	112	1	3.29	.888

BURNETT, GARRETT LW

PERSONAL: Born September 23, 1975, in Coquitlam, B.C. ... 6-3/230. ... Shoots left.
TRANSACTIONS/CAREER NOTES: Signed as free agent by San Jose Sharks (July 22, 1998). ... Signed as free agent by Anaheim Mighty Ducks (July 25, 2003).

		REGULAR SEASON								PLAYOFFS				
Season Team	League	GP	G	A	Pts.	PIM	+/-	PP	SH	GP	G	A	Pts.	PIM
94-95—S.S. Marie	OHL	14	0	1	1	78	...	...	...	—	—	—	—	—
—Kitchener	OHL	22	0	1	1	74	...	...	...	—	—	—	—	—
95-96—Utica	Col.HL	15	0	1	1	85	...	...	...	—	—	—	—	—
—Nashville	ECHL	3	0	0	0	22	...	...	...	—	—	—	—	—
—Oklahoma City	CHL	3	0	0	0	20	...	...	...	—	—	—	—	—
—Tulsa	CHL	6	1	0	1	94	...	...	...	—	—	—	—	—
—Jacksonville	ECHL	3	0	1	1	38	...	...	...	1	0	0	0	0
96-97—Knoxville	ECHL	50	5	11	16	321	...	...	...	—	—	—	—	—
97-98—Johnstown	ECHL	12	1	1	2	2	...	...	...	—	—	—	—	—
—Philadelphia	AHL	14	1	2	3	129	2	...	...	—	—	—	—	—
98-99—Kentucky	AHL	31	1	0	1	186	0	0	0	—	—	—	—	—
99-00—Kentucky	AHL	58	3	3	6	*506	...	...	...	4	0	0	0	31
00-01—Cleveland	IHL	54	2	4	6	250	...	...	...	—	—	—	—	—
01-02—Cincinnati	AHL	32	1	0	1	175	-3	0	0	—	—	—	—	—
02-03—Hartford	AHL	62	6	1	7	346	...	...	...	1	0	0	0	2
03-04—Anaheim	NHL	39	1	2	3	184	0	0	0	—	—	—	—	—
04-05—Danbury	UHL	7	0	1	1	48	-3	0	0	—	—	—	—	—
NHL Totals (1 year)		39	1	2	3	184	0	0	0					

BURNS, BRENT RW WILD

PERSONAL: Born March 9, 1985, in Ajax, Ont. ... 6-4/200. ... Shoots right.
TRANSACTIONS/CAREER NOTES: Selected by Minnesota Wild in first round (first Wild pick, 20th overall) in 2003 NHL entry draft (June 23, 2003). ... Separated shoulder (October 26, 2003); missed eight games. ... Injured neck (February 2, 2004); missed eight games.

		REGULAR SEASON								PLAYOFFS				
Season Team	League	GP	G	A	Pts.	PIM	+/-	PP	SH	GP	G	A	Pts.	PIM
02-03—Brampton	OHL	68	15	25	40	14	...	...	...	—	—	—	—	—
03-04—Minnesota	NHL	36	1	5	6	12	-10	0	0	—	—	—	—	—
—Houston	AHL	1	0	1	1	2	-1	0	0	—	—	—	—	—
04-05—Houston	AHL	73	11	16	27	57	-11	6	2	5	0	0	0	4
NHL Totals (1 year)		36	1	5	6	12	-10	0	0					

BUTENSCHON, SVEN D

PERSONAL: Born March 22, 1976, in Itzehoe, West Germany. ... 6-4/215. ... Shoots left. ... Name pronounced BOO-tihn-shohn.
TRANSACTIONS/CAREER NOTES: Selected by Pittsburgh Penguins in third round (third Penguins pick, 57th overall) of NHL draft (June 29, 1994). ... Flu (November 7, 1997); missed two games. ... Injured shoulder (March 3, 2001); missed four games. ... Traded by Penguins to Edmonton Oilers for LW Dan LaCouture (March 13, 2001). ... Signed as free agent by Florida Panthers (July 9, 2002). ... Traded by Panthers to New York Islanders for RW Juraj Kolnik and ninth-round pick (traded to San Jose; Sharks selected RW Carter Lee) in 2003 draft (October 11, 2002). ... Virus (December 21, 2003); missed four games.

		REGULAR SEASON								PLAYOFFS				
Season Team	League	GP	G	A	Pts.	PIM	+/-	PP	SH	GP	G	A	Pts.	PIM
93-94—Brandon	WHL	70	3	19	22	51	15	1	0	4	0	0	0	6
94-95—Brandon	WHL	21	1	5	6	44	15	0	0	18	1	2	3	11
95-96—Brandon	WHL	70	4	37	41	99	...	...	...	19	1	12	13	18
96-97—Cleveland	IHL	75	3	12	15	68	...	...	...	10	0	1	1	4
97-98—Syracuse	AHL	65	14	23	37	66	-7	7	0	5	1	2	3	0
—Pittsburgh	NHL	8	0	0	0	6	-1	0	0	—	—	—	—	—
98-99—Houston	IHL	57	1	4	5	81	15	0	0	—	—	—	—	—
—Pittsburgh	NHL	17	0	0	0	6	-7	0	0	—	—	—	—	—
99-00—Wilkes-Barre/Scranton	AHL	75	19	21	40	101	...	...	...	—	—	—	—	—
—Pittsburgh	NHL	3	0	0	0	0	3	0	0	—	—	—	—	—
00-01—Wilkes-Barre/Scranton	AHL	55	7	28	35	85	...	...	...	—	—	—	—	—
—Pittsburgh	NHL	5	0	1	1	2	1	0	0	—	—	—	—	—
—Edmonton	NHL	7	1	1	2	2	2	0	0	—	—	—	—	—
01-02—Hamilton	AHL	61	9	35	44	88	16	2	0	—	—	—	—	—
—Edmonton	NHL	14	0	0	0	4	0	0	0	—	—	—	—	—
02-03—New York Islanders	NHL	37	0	4	4	26	-6	0	0	—	—	—	—	—
—Bridgeport	AHL	36	3	13	16	58	-15	2	0	9	3	6	9	6
03-04—New York Islanders	NHL	41	1	6	7	30	-3	0	0	4	0	0	0	0
—Bridgeport	AHL	5	0	1	1	4	-1	0	0	—	—	—	—	—
04-05—Mannheim	Germany	50	1	5	6	54	1	0	0	14	0	1	1	16
NHL Totals (7 years)		132	2	12	14	76	-11	0	0	4	0	0	0	0

CAIRNS, ERIC D PANTHERS

PERSONAL: Born June 27, 1974, in Oakville, Ont. ... 6-6/232. ... Shoots left. ... Name pronounced KAIR-ihns.
TRANSACTIONS/CAREER NOTES: Selected by New York Rangers in third round (third Rangers pick, 72nd overall) of NHL draft (June 20, 1992). ... Claimed on waivers by New York Islanders (December 22, 1998). ... Strained back (January 6, 2000); missed one game. ... Suspended four

games for fighting incident (February 13, 2000). ... Fractured thumb (October 1, 2000); missed first 18 games of season. ... Hand surgery (December 8, 2000); missed 17 games. ... Sprained left wrist (February 18, 2001); missed two games. ... Strained oblique muscle (December 2, 2001); missed five games. ... Bruised ribs (January 24, 2002); missed one game. ... Suspended two games for unsportsmanlike conduct (March 28, 2002). ... Injured knee (December 21, 2002); missed one game. ... Injured shoulder (January 24, 2003); missed 20 games. ... Injured toe (December 9, 2003); missed two games. ... Back spasms (January 6, 2004); missed three games. ... Signed as free agent by Florida Panthers (July 5, 2004).

		REGULAR SEASON								PLAYOFFS				
Season Team	League	GP	G	A	Pts.	PIM	+/-	PP	SH	GP	G	A	Pts.	PIM
90-91—Burlington Jr. B	OHA	37	5	16	21	120	...	...	...	—	—	—	—	—
91-92—Det. Jr. Red Wings	OHL	64	1	11	12	237	...	...	...	7	0	0	0	31
92-93—Det. Jr. Red Wings	OHL	64	3	13	16	194	...	...	...	15	0	3	3	24
93-94—Det. Jr. Red Wings	OHL	59	7	35	42	204	...	3	0	17	0	4	4	46
94-95—Birmingham	ECHL	11	1	3	4	49	2	0	0	—	—	—	—	—
—Binghamton	AHL	27	0	3	3	134	5	0	0	9	1	1	2	28
95-96—Binghamton	AHL	46	1	13	14	192	...	...	...	4	0	0	0	37
—Charlotte	ECHL	6	0	1	1	34	...	...	...	—	—	—	—	—
96-97—New York Rangers	NHL	40	0	1	1	147	-7	0	0	3	0	0	0	0
—Binghamton	AHL	10	1	1	2	96	-1	1	0	—	—	—	—	—
97-98—New York Rangers	NHL	39	0	3	3	92	-3	0	0	—	—	—	—	—
—Hartford	AHL	7	1	2	3	43	10	0	0	—	—	—	—	—
98-99—Hartford	AHL	11	0	2	2	49	-2	0	0	—	—	—	—	—
—Lowell	AHL	24	0	0	0	91	7	0	0	3	1	0	1	32
—New York Islanders	NHL	9	0	3	3	23	1	0	0	—	—	—	—	—
99-00—Providence	AHL	4	1	1	2	14	...	...	...	—	—	—	—	—
—New York Islanders	NHL	67	2	7	9	196	-5	0	0	—	—	—	—	—
00-01—New York Islanders	NHL	45	2	2	4	106	-18	0	0	—	—	—	—	—
01-02—New York Islanders	NHL	74	2	5	7	176	-2	0	0	7	0	0	0	15
02-03—New York Islanders	NHL	60	1	4	5	124	-7	0	0	5	0	0	0	13
03-04—New York Islanders	NHL	72	2	6	8	189	-5	0	0	1	0	0	0	0
04-05—London	England	33	3	7	10	119	...	1	0	—	—	—	—	—
NHL Totals (8 years)		406	9	31	40	1053	-46	0	0	16	0	0	0	28

C

CAJANEK, PETR — C/LW — BLUES

PERSONAL: Born August 18, 1975, in Zlin, Czechoslovakia. ... 5-11/191. ... Shoots left. ... Name pronounced chuh-YA-nihk.
TRANSACTIONS/CAREER NOTES: Selected by St. Louis Blues in eighth round (sixth Blues pick, 253rd overall) of NHL draft (June 23, 2001). ... Fractured leg (Jan. 2, 2003); missed 24 games. ... Facial cuts (March 23, 2003); missed four games. ... Injured ribs (October 28, 2003); missed five games. ... Injured neck (December 20, 2003); missed seven games.

		REGULAR SEASON								PLAYOFFS				
Season Team	League	GP	G	A	Pts.	PIM	+/-	PP	SH	GP	G	A	Pts.	PIM
97-98—HC Continental Zlin	Czech Rep.	46	19	27	46	125	...	...	...	—	—	—	—	—
98-99—HC Continental Zlin	Czech Rep.	49	15	33	48	131	...	...	...	11	5	7	12	...
99-00—HC Continental Zlin	Czech Rep.	50	23	34	57	64	...	...	...	4	1	0	1	0
00-01—HC Continental Zlin	Czech Rep.	52	18	31	49	105	...	...	...	6	0	4	4	22
01-02—HC Continental Zlin	Czech Rep.	49	20	44	64	64	...	...	...	11	5	7	12	10
—Czech Rep. Oly. team	Int'l	4	0	0	0	0	...	...	...	—	—	—	—	—
02-03—St. Louis	NHL	51	9	29	38	20	16	2	2	2	0	0	0	2
03-04—St. Louis	NHL	70	12	14	26	16	12	3	0	5	0	2	2	2
04-05—Zlin	Czech Rep.	49	10	15	25	91	12	...	...	19	5	6	11	28
NHL Totals (2 years)		121	21	43	64	36	28	5	2	7	0	2	2	4

CALDER, KYLE — LW — BLACKHAWKS

PERSONAL: Born January 5, 1979, in Mannville, Alta. ... 5-11/176. ... Shoots left.
TRANSACTIONS/CAREER NOTES: Selected by Chicago Blackhawks in fifth round (seventh Blackhawks pick, 130th overall) of NHL draft (June 21, 1997). ... Had concussion (January 9, 2002); missed one game. ... Fractured leg (March 4, 2004); missed remainder of season.

		REGULAR SEASON								PLAYOFFS				
Season Team	League	GP	G	A	Pts.	PIM	+/-	PP	SH	GP	G	A	Pts.	PIM
95-96—Regina	WHL	27	1	8	9	10	...	...	...	11	0	0	0	0
96-97—Regina	WHL	62	25	34	59	17	...	...	...	5	3	0	3	6
97-98—Regina	WHL	62	27	50	77	58	...	...	...	2	0	1	1	0
98-99—Regina	WHL	34	23	28	51	29	...	...	...	—	—	—	—	—
—Kamloops	WHL	27	19	18	37	30	...	...	...	15	6	10	16	6
99-00—Cleveland	IHL	74	14	22	36	43	...	...	...	9	2	2	4	14
—Chicago	NHL	8	1	1	2	2	-3	0	0	—	—	—	—	—
00-01—Norfolk	AHL	37	12	15	27	21	...	...	...	9	2	6	8	2
—Chicago	NHL	43	5	10	15	14	-4	0	0	—	—	—	—	—
01-02—Chicago	NHL	81	17	36	53	47	8	6	0	5	2	0	2	2
02-03—Chicago	NHL	82	15	27	42	40	-6	7	0	—	—	—	—	—
03-04—Chicago	NHL	66	21	18	39	29	-18	10	0	—	—	—	—	—
04-05—Sodertalje	Sweden	12	5	1	6	6	-6	2	0	10	5	1	6	2
NHL Totals (5 years)		280	59	92	151	132	-23	23	0	5	2	0	2	2

CAMMALLERI, MIKE — C/RW — KINGS

PERSONAL: Born June 8, 1982, in Richmond Hill, Ont. ... 5-9/180. ... Shoots left.
TRANSACTIONS/CAREER NOTES: Selected by Los Angeles Kings in second round (third Kings pick, 49th overall) of NHL draft (June 23,

2001). ... Suffered concussion (January 28, 2003); missed 31 games. ... Sprained knee (September 22, 2003); missed first eight games of season.

		REGULAR SEASON								PLAYOFFS				
Season Team	League	GP	G	A	Pts.	PIM	+/-	PP	SH	GP	G	A	Pts.	PIM
99-00—Univ. of Michigan........	CCHA	39	13	13	26	32	...	...	...	—	—	—	—	—
00-01—Univ. of Michigan........	CCHA	42	*29	32	61	24	...	...	...	—	—	—	—	—
01-02—Univ. of Michigan........	CCHA	28	23	20	43	24	...	...	...	—	—	—	—	—
02-03—Manchester..................	AHL	13	5	15	20	12	-4	1	1	—	—	—	—	—
—Los Angeles...............	NHL	28	5	3	8	22	-4	2	0	—	—	—	—	—
03-04—Los Angeles................	NHL	31	9	6	15	20	1	2	0	—	—	—	—	—
—Manchester.................	AHL	41	20	18	38	28	13	4	0	1	0	1	1	0
04-05—Manchester..................	AHL	79	46	63	109	60	25	17	2	6	1	5	6	0
NHL Totals (2 years)............		59	14	9	23	42	-3	4	0					

CAMPBELL, BRIAN D SABRES

PERSONAL: Born May 23, 1979, in Strathroy, Ont. ... 6-0/191. ... Shoots left.
TRANSACTIONS/CAREER NOTES: Selected by Buffalo Sabres in sixth round (seventh Sabres pick, 156th overall) of NHL draft (June 21, 1997). ... Separated shoulder (April 1, 2002); missed remainder of season.

		REGULAR SEASON								PLAYOFFS				
Season Team	League	GP	G	A	Pts.	PIM	+/-	PP	SH	GP	G	A	Pts.	PIM
94-95—Petrolia......................	Jr. B	50	1	2	3	...	...	...	...	—	—	—	—	—
95-96—Ottawa........................	OHL	66	5	22	27	23	...	...	...	4	0	1	1	2
96-97—Ottawa........................	OHL	66	7	36	43	12	...	...	...	24	2	11	13	8
97-98—Ottawa........................	OHL	66	14	39	53	31	...	...	...	13	1	14	15	0
98-99—Ottawa........................	OHL	62	12	75	87	27	45	...	...	9	2	10	12	6
—Rochester.................	AHL	...	...	...	...	...	...	...	...	2	0	0	0	0
99-00—Buffalo.......................	NHL	12	1	4	5	4	-2	0	0	—	—	—	—	—
—Rochester.................	AHL	67	2	24	26	22	...	...	...	21	0	3	3	0
00-01—Rochester..................	AHL	65	7	25	32	24	...	...	...	4	0	1	1	0
—Buffalo.......................	NHL	8	0	0	0	2	-2	0	0	—	—	—	—	—
01-02—Rochester..................	AHL	45	2	35	37	13	9	1	0	—	—	—	—	—
—Buffalo.......................	NHL	29	3	3	6	12	0	0	0	—	—	—	—	—
02-03—Buffalo.......................	NHL	65	2	17	19	20	-8	0	0	—	—	—	—	—
03-04—Buffalo.......................	NHL	53	3	8	11	12	-8	0	0	—	—	—	—	—
04-05—Jokerit Helsinki...........	Finland	44	12	13	25	12	14	...	...	12	3	4	7	6
NHL Totals (5 years)............		167	9	32	41	50	-20	0	0					

CAMPBELL, GREG C PANTHERS

PERSONAL: Born December 17, 1983, in London, Ont. ... 6-0/191. ... Shoots left. ... Son of Colin Campbell, NHL director of hockey operations, who played for five NHL teams from 1970-85.
TRANSACTIONS/CAREER NOTES: Selected by Florida Panthers in third round (fourth Panthers pick, 67th overall) of NHL draft (June 22, 2002).

		REGULAR SEASON								PLAYOFFS				
Season Team	League	GP	G	A	Pts.	PIM	+/-	PP	SH	GP	G	A	Pts.	PIM
00-01—Plymouth....................	OHL	65	2	12	14	40	...	...	...	21	15	4	19	34
01-02—Plymouth....................	OHL	65	17	36	53	105	...	...	...	6	0	2	2	13
02-03—Kitchener....................	OHL	55	23	33	56	116	...	...	...	21	15	4	19	34
03-04—Florida........................	NHL	2	0	0	0	5	-1	0	0	—	—	—	—	—
—San Antonio..............	AHL	76	13	16	29	73	-13	1	0	—	—	—	—	—
04-05—San Antonio................	AHL	70	12	16	28	113	-17	3	1	—	—	—	—	—
NHL Totals (1 year).............		2	0	0	0	5	-1	0	0					

CAMPBELL, JIM RW ISLANDERS

PERSONAL: Born April 3, 1973, in Worcester, Mass. ... 6-2/205. ... Shoots right.
TRANSACTIONS/CAREER NOTES: Selected by Montreal Canadiens in second round (second Canadiens pick, 28th overall) of NHL entry draft (June 22, 1991). ... Traded by Canadiens to Anaheim Mighty Ducks for D Robert Dirk (January 21, 1996). ... Signed as free agent by St. Louis Blues (July 3, 1996). ... Strained thumb (February 25, 1997); missed 10 games. ... Reinjured thumb (April 6, 1997); missed remainder of regular season. ... Strained groin (December 6, 1997); missed one game. ... Injured left heel (January 20, 1998); missed five games. ... Bruised right shoulder (October 23, 1998); missed two games. ... Injured groin (February 9, 1999); missed three games. ... Injured abdominal muscle (March 18, 1999) and had surgery; missed remainder of season. ... Signed as free agent by Canadiens (August 22, 2000). ... Suffered concussion (October 17, 2000); missed one game. ... Strained groin (November 14, 2000); missed nine games. ... Signed as free agent by Chicago Blackhawks (November 19, 2001). ... Signed as free agent by Florida Panthers (July 19, 2002). ... Signed as free agent by Chicago of the AHL (December 10, 2003). ... Signed as free agent by New York Islanders (August 11, 2004).

		REGULAR SEASON								PLAYOFFS				
Season Team	League	GP	G	A	Pts.	PIM	+/-	PP	SH	GP	G	A	Pts.	PIM
88-89—Northwood School......	N.Y. H.S.	12	12	8	20	6	...	...	...	—	—	—	—	—
89-90—Northwood School......	N.Y. H.S.	8	14	7	21	8	...	...	...	—	—	—	—	—
90-91—Northwood School......	N.Y. H.S.	26	36	47	83	36	...	...	...	—	—	—	—	—
91-92—Hull............................	QMJHL	64	41	44	85	51	...	...	...	6	7	3	10	8
92-93—Hull............................	QMJHL	50	42	29	71	66	...	...	...	8	11	4	15	43
93-94—U.S. national team......	Int'l	56	24	33	57	59	...	0	0	—	—	—	—	—
—U.S. Olympic team......	Int'l	8	0	0	0	6	-5	0	0	—	—	—	—	—
—Fredericton.................	AHL	19	6	17	23	6	-9	2	0	—	—	—	—	—
94-95—Fredericton.................	AHL	77	27	24	51	103	-9	7	2	12	0	7	7	8

Season Team	League	GP	G	A	Pts.	PIM	+/-	PP	SH	GP	G	A	Pts.	PIM
95-96—Fredericton	AHL	44	28	23	51	24	...	...	...	—	—	—	—	—
—Baltimore	AHL	16	13	7	20	8	...	...	...	12	7	5	12	10
—Anaheim	NHL	16	2	3	5	36	0	1	0	—	—	—	—	—
96-97—St. Louis	NHL	68	23	20	43	68	3	5	0	4	1	0	1	6
97-98—St. Louis	NHL	76	22	19	41	55	0	7	0	10	7	3	10	12
98-99—St. Louis	NHL	55	4	21	25	41	-8	1	0	—	—	—	—	—
99-00—Manitoba	IHL	10	1	3	4	10	...	...	...	—	—	—	—	—
—Worcester	AHL	66	31	34	65	88	...	...	...	9	1	2	3	6
—St. Louis	NHL	2	0	0	0	9	0	0	0	—	—	—	—	—
00-01—Montreal	NHL	57	9	11	20	53	-3	6	0	—	—	—	—	—
—Quebec	AHL	3	5	0	5	6	...	...	...	—	—	—	—	—
01-02—Norfolk	AHL	44	11	14	25	26	6	5	0	4	3	1	4	2
—Chicago	NHL	9	1	1	2	4	-3	0	0	—	—	—	—	—
02-03—Florida	NHL	1	0	0	0	0	0	0	0	—	—	—	—	—
—San Antonio	AHL	64	16	37	53	55	-10	11	0	1	0	0	0	0
04-05—Bridgeport	AHL	46	8	12	20	64	-13	5	0	—	—	—	—	—
—Springfield	AHL	13	2	5	7	8	-7	2	0	—	—	—	—	—
NHL Totals (8 years)		284	61	75	136	266	-11	20	0	14	8	3	11	18

CARNEY, KEITH D MIGHTY DUCKS

PERSONAL: Born February 3, 1970, in Providence, R.I. ... 6-1/216. ... Shoots left.

TRANSACTIONS/CAREER NOTES: Selected by Buffalo Sabres in fourth round (third Sabres pick, 76th overall) of NHL draft (June 11, 1988). ... Traded by Sabres to Chicago Blackhawks for D Craig Muni (October 27, 1993). ... Traded by Blackhawks with RW Jim Cummins to Phoenix Coyotes for C Chad Kilger and D Jayson More (March 4, 1998). ... Traded by Coyotes to Anaheim Mighty Ducks for second-round pick (traded to New Jersey) in 2001 draft (June 19, 2001). ... Fractured right hand (November 7, 2001); missed 17 games. ... Had hip pointer and cut right elbow (March 30, 2002); missed one game. ... Reinjured elbow (April 3, 2002); missed four games. ... Stomach virus (December 19, 2002); missed one game. ... Fractured right foot (October 3, 2003); missed 11 games. ... Back spasms (December 13, 2003); missed 2 games.

		REGULAR SEASON								PLAYOFFS				
Season Team	**League**	**GP**	**G**	**A**	**Pts.**	**PIM**	**+/-**	**PP**	**SH**	**GP**	**G**	**A**	**Pts.**	**PIM**
88-89—Maine	Hockey East	40	4	22	26	24	...	...	...	—	—	—	—	—
89-90—Maine	Hockey East	41	3	41	44	43	...	...	...	—	—	—	—	—
90-91—Maine	Hockey East	40	7	49	56	38	...	...	...	—	—	—	—	—
91-92—U.S. national team	Int'l	49	2	17	19	16	...	...	...	—	—	—	—	—
—Rochester	AHL	24	1	10	11	2	...	...	...	2	0	2	2	0
—Buffalo	NHL	14	1	2	3	18	-3	1	0	7	0	3	3	0
92-93—Buffalo	NHL	30	2	4	6	55	3	0	0	8	0	3	3	6
—Rochester	AHL	41	5	21	26	32	8	0	1	—	—	—	—	—
93-94—Louisville	ECHL	15	1	4	5	14	-6	0	0	—	—	—	—	—
—Buffalo	NHL	7	1	3	4	4	-1	0	0	—	—	—	—	—
—Indianapolis	IHL	28	0	14	14	20	-13	0	0	—	—	—	—	—
—Chicago	NHL	30	3	5	8	35	15	0	0	6	0	1	1	4
94-95—Chicago	NHL	18	1	0	1	11	-1	0	0	4	0	1	1	0
95-96—Chicago	NHL	82	5	14	19	94	31	1	0	10	0	3	3	4
96-97—Chicago	NHL	81	3	15	18	62	26	0	0	6	1	1	2	2
97-98—Chicago	NHL	60	2	13	15	73	-7	0	1	—	—	—	—	—
—U.S. Olympic team	Int'l	4	0	0	0	2	0	0	0	—	—	—	—	—
—Phoenix	NHL	20	1	6	7	18	5	1	0	6	0	0	0	4
98-99—Phoenix	NHL	82	2	14	16	62	15	0	2	7	1	2	3	10
99-00—Phoenix	NHL	82	4	20	24	87	11	0	0	5	0	0	0	17
00-01—Phoenix	NHL	82	2	14	16	86	15	0	0	—	—	—	—	—
01-02—Anaheim	NHL	60	5	9	14	30	14	0	0	—	—	—	—	—
02-03—Anaheim	NHL	81	4	18	22	65	8	0	0	21	0	4	4	16
03-04—Anaheim	NHL	69	2	5	7	42	-5	1	0	—	—	—	—	—
NHL Totals (13 years)		798	38	142	180	742	126	4	3	80	2	18	20	63

CARON, SEBASTIEN G PENGUINS

PERSONAL: Born June 25, 1980, in Amqui, Que. ... 6-1/170. ... Catches left.

TRANSACTIONS/CAREER NOTES: Selected by Pittsburgh Penguins in third round (fourth Penguins pick, 86th overall) of NHL draft (June 26, 1999).

		REGULAR SEASON									PLAYOFFS							
Season Team	**League**	**GP**	**Min.**	**W**	**L**	**T**	**GA**	**SO**	**GAA**	**SV%**	**GP**	**Min.**	**W**	**L**	**GA**	**SO**	**GAA**	**SV%**
98-99—Rimouski	QMJHL	30	1570	13	10	3	85	0	3.25	...	2	68	1	0	0	0	0.00	...
99-00—Rimouski	QMJHL	54	3040	*38	11	3	179	1	3.53	.896	14	828	*12	2	50	0	3.62	.900
00-01—Wilkes-Barre/Scranton	AHL	30	1746	12	14	3	103	4	3.54	.882	—	—	—	—	—	—	—	—
01-02—Wilkes-Barre/Scranton	AHL	46	2670	14	22	8	139	1	3.12	.892	—	—	—	—	—	—	—	—
02-03—Wilkes-Barre/Scranton	AHL	27	1560	12	14	1	81	1	3.12	.904	—	—	—	—	—	—	—	—
—Pittsburgh	NHL	24	1408	7	14	2	62	2	2.64	.916	—	—	—	—	—	—	—	—
03-04—Pittsburgh	NHL	40	2213	9	24	5	138	1	3.74	.883	—	—	—	—	—	—	—	—
—Wilkes-Barre/Scranton	AHL	14	811	7	3	4	26	2	1.92	.924	7	394	3	4	23	0	3.50	.823
NHL Totals (2 years)		64	3621	16	38	7	200	3	3.31	.896								

CARTER, ANSON RW

PERSONAL: Born June 6, 1974, in Toronto. ... 6-1/200. ... Shoots right.

TRANSACTIONS/CAREER NOTES: Selected by Quebec Nordiques in 10th round (10th Nordiques pick, 220th overall) of NHL draft (June 20, 1992). ... Nordiques franchise moved to Colorado and renamed Avalanche for 1995-96 season (June 21, 1995). ... Traded by Avalanche to

Washington Capitals for fourth-round pick (D Ben Storey) in 1996 draft (April 3, 1996). ... Sprained thumb (February 7, 1997); missed five games. ... Traded by Capitals with G Jim Carey, C Jason Allison and third-round pick (RW Lee Goren) in 1997 draft to Boston Bruins for C Adam Oates, RW Rick Tocchet and G Bill Ranford (March 1, 1997). ... Strained hip flexor (October 7, 1997); missed two games. ... Upper respiratory infection (November 22, 1997); missed two games. ... Missed first 12 games of 1998-99 season in contract dispute. ... Sprained ankle (January 2, 1999); missed 15 games. ... Bruised shoulder (February 21, 2000); missed eight games. ... Wrist surgery (March 10, 2000); missed final 15 games of season. ... Traded by Bruins with second-round pick (D Doug Lynch) in 2001 draft and swap of first-round picks in 2001 to Edmonton Oilers for RW Bill Guerin (November 15, 2000); with first-round picks, Bruins selected D Shaonne Morrisonn and Oilers selected RW Ales Hemsky. ... Traded by Oilers with D Ales Pisa to New York Rangers for RW Radek Dvorak and D Cory Cross (March 11, 2003). ... Injured wrist (November 27, 2003); missed two games. ... Injured ribs (December 26, 2003); missed three games. ... Traded by Rangers to Capitals for RW Jaromir Jagr (January 23, 2004). ... Traded by Capitals to Los Angeles Kings for C Jared Aulin (March 8, 2004).
STATISTICAL PLATEAUS: Three-goal games: 1998-99 (1).

		REGULAR SEASON								PLAYOFFS				
Season Team	**League**	**GP**	**G**	**A**	**Pts.**	**PIM**	**+/-**	**PP**	**SH**	**GP**	**G**	**A**	**Pts.**	**PIM**
91-92—Wexford	OHA Jr. A	42	18	22	40	24	...	...	...	—	—	—	—	—
92-93—Michigan State	CCHA	36	19	11	30	20	...	...	...	—	—	—	—	—
93-94—Michigan State	CCHA	39	30	24	54	36	...	...	...	—	—	—	—	—
94-95—Michigan State	CCHA	39	34	17	51	40	11	13	7	—	—	—	—	—
95-96—Michigan State	CCHA	42	23	20	43	36	...	...	...	—	—	—	—	—
96-97—Washington	NHL	19	3	2	5	7	0	1	0	—	—	—	—	—
—Portland	AHL	27	19	19	38	11	15	5	4	—	—	—	—	—
—Boston	NHL	19	8	5	13	2	-7	1	1	—	—	—	—	—
97-98—Boston	NHL	78	16	27	43	31	7	6	0	6	1	1	2	0
98-99—Utah	IHL	6	1	1	2	0	-2	0	0	—	—	—	—	—
—Boston	NHL	55	24	16	40	22	7	6	0	12	4	3	7	0
99-00—Boston	NHL	59	22	25	47	14	8	4	0	—	—	—	—	—
00-01—Edmonton	NHL	61	16	26	42	23	1	7	1	6	3	1	4	4
01-02—Edmonton	NHL	82	28	32	60	25	3	12	0	—	—	—	—	—
02-03—Edmonton	NHL	68	25	30	55	20	-11	10	0	—	—	—	—	—
—New York Rangers	NHL	11	1	4	5	6	0	0	0	—	—	—	—	—
03-04—New York Rangers	NHL	43	10	7	17	14	-12	4	1	—	—	—	—	—
—Washington	NHL	19	5	5	10	6	2	2	0	—	—	—	—	—
—Los Angeles	NHL	15	0	1	1	0	-5	0	0	—	—	—	—	—
NHL Totals (8 years)		529	158	180	338	170	-7	53	3	24	8	5	13	4

CARTER, JEFF — C — FLYERS

PERSONAL: Born January 1, 1985, in London, Ont. ... 6-3/182. ... Shoots right.
TRANSACTIONS/CAREER NOTES: Selected by Philadelphia Flyers in first round (first Flyers pick, 11th overall) of NHL entry draft (June 23, 2003). ... Signed by Flyers (July 27, 2005).

		REGULAR SEASON								PLAYOFFS				
Season Team	**League**	**GP**	**G**	**A**	**Pts.**	**PIM**	**+/-**	**PP**	**SH**	**GP**	**G**	**A**	**Pts.**	**PIM**
01-02—Sault Ste. Marie	OHL	63	18	17	35	12	...	...	...	—	—	—	—	—
02-03—Sault Ste. Marie	OHL	61	35	36	71	55	...	...	...	—	—	—	—	—
03-04—Sault Ste. Marie	OHL	57	36	30	66	26	...	...	...	—	—	—	—	—
—Philadelphia	AHL	...	...	...	...	...	...	...	...	12	4	1	5	0
04-05—Philadelphia	AHL	3	0	1	1	4	-1	0	0	21	12	11	23	12
—Sault Ste. Marie	OHL	55	34	40	74	40	20	14	1	7	5	5	10	6

CASSELS, ANDREW — C — CAPITALS

PERSONAL: Born July 23, 1969, in Bramalea, Ont. ... 6-1/185. ... Shoots left. ... Name pronounced KAS-uhls.
TRANSACTIONS/CAREER NOTES: Selected by Montreal Canadiens in 1st round (1st Canadiens pick, 17th overall) of NHL draft (June 13, 1987). ... Separated right shoulder (November 22, 1989); missed 10 games. ... Traded by Canadiens to Hartford Whalers for 2nd-round pick (RW Valeri Bure) in 1992 draft (September 17, 1991). ... Bruised kneecap (December 4, 1993); missed one game. ... Facial injury (March 13, 1994); missed four games. ... Bruised forearm (December 2, 1995); missed one game. ... Charley horse (March 6, 1997); missed one game. ... Whalers franchise moved to North Carolina and renamed Carolina Hurricanes for 1997-98 season; NHL approved move on June 25, 1997. ... Traded by Hurricanes with G Jean-Sebastien Giguere to Calgary Flames for LW Gary Roberts and G Trevor Kidd (August 25, 1997). ... Strained rib cage (October 9, 1997); missed one game. ... Injured groin (February 1, 1999); missed 12 games. ... Signed as free agent by Vancouver Canucks (July 13, 1999). ... Sprained thumb (October 19, 1999); missed three games. ... Fractured toe (January 20, 2001); missed 10 games. ... Sprained ankle (March 25, 2001); missed remainder of season. ... Sprained knee (October 23, 2001); missed 20 games. ... Suffered concussion (March 9, 2002); missed eight games. ... Signed as free agent by Columbus Blue Jackets (August 15, 2002). ... Injured elbow (December 26, 2002); missed three games. ... Back spasms (October 18, 2003); missed three games. ... Fractured foot (January 8, 2004); missed 22 games. ... Contract bought out by Blue Jackets (July 29, 2005). ... Signed as free agent by Washington Capitals (Aug. 9, 2005).
STATISTICAL PLATEAUS: Three-goal games: 2000-01 (1).

		REGULAR SEASON								PLAYOFFS				
Season Team	**League**	**GP**	**G**	**A**	**Pts.**	**PIM**	**+/-**	**PP**	**SH**	**GP**	**G**	**A**	**Pts.**	**PIM**
85-86—Bramalea Jr. B	OHA	33	18	25	43	26	...	...	...	—	—	—	—	—
86-87—Ottawa	OHL	66	26	66	92	28	...	...	...	11	5	9	14	7
87-88—Ottawa	OHL	61	48	*103	*151	39	...	...	...	16	8	*24	32	13
88-89—Ottawa	OHL	56	37	97	134	66	...	...	...	12	5	10	15	10
89-90—Sherbrooke	AHL	55	22	45	67	25	...	...	...	12	2	11	13	6
—Montreal	NHL	6	2	0	2	2	1	0	0	—	—	—	—	—
90-91—Montreal	NHL	54	6	19	25	20	2	1	0	8	0	2	2	2
91-92—Hartford	NHL	67	11	30	41	18	3	2	2	7	2	4	6	6
92-93—Hartford	NHL	84	21	64	85	62	-11	8	3	—	—	—	—	—
93-94—Hartford	NHL	79	16	42	58	37	-21	8	1	—	—	—	—	—
94-95—Hartford	NHL	46	7	30	37	18	-3	1	0	—	—	—	—	—
95-96—Hartford	NHL	81	20	43	63	39	8	6	0	—	—	—	—	—

Season Team	League	GP	G	A	Pts.	PIM	+/-	PP	SH	GP	G	A	Pts.	PIM
96-97—Hartford	NHL	81	22	44	66	46	-16	8	0	—	—	—	—	—
97-98—Calgary	NHL	81	17	27	44	32	-7	6	1	—	—	—	—	—
98-99—Calgary	NHL	70	12	25	37	18	-12	4	1	—	—	—	—	—
99-00—Vancouver	NHL	79	17	45	62	16	8	6	0	—	—	—	—	—
00-01—Vancouver	NHL	66	12	44	56	10	1	2	0	—	—	—	—	—
01-02—Vancouver	NHL	53	11	39	50	22	5	7	0	6	2	1	3	0
02-03—Columbus	NHL	79	20	48	68	30	-4	9	1	—	—	—	—	—
03-04—Columbus	NHL	58	6	20	26	26	-24	2	0	—	—	—	—	—
NHL Totals (15 years)		984	200	520	720	396	-70	70	9	21	4	7	11	8

CECHMANEK, ROMAN G

PERSONAL: Born March 2, 1971, in Gottwaldov, Czechoslovakia. ... 6-3/211. ... Catches left. ... Name pronounced chehkh-MAN-ehk.
TRANSACTIONS/CAREER NOTES: Selected by Philadelphia Flyers in sixth round (third Flyers pick, 171st overall) of NHL draft (June 24, 2000). ... Sinus infection (January 26, 2002); missed one game. ... Sprained right ankle (March 2, 2002); missed 13 games. ... Injured groin (March 20, 2003); missed three games. ... Traded by Philadelphia to Los Angeles Kings for second-round pick (traded to Chicago Blackhawks) in 2004 draft (May 28, 2003). ... Bruised hip (December 11, 2003); missed two games. ... Reinjured hip (December 22, 2003); missed six games. ... Injured groin (February 20, 2004); missed 12 games.

		REGULAR SEASON									PLAYOFFS							
Season Team	**League**	**GP**	**Min.**	**W**	**L**	**T**	**GA**	**SO**	**GAA**	**SV%**	**GP**	**Min.**	**W**	**L**	**GA**	**SO**	**GAA**	**SV%**
94-95—HC Vsetin	Czech Rep.	52	3046	...	...	...	121	5	2.38	...	11	619	...	...	23	2	2.23	...
95-96—HC Vsetin	Czech Rep.	49	2925	...	...	...	94	4	1.93	...	13	783	...	...	17	2	1.30	...
96-97—HC Vsetin	Czech Rep.	58	3364	...	...	...	109	3	1.94	...	10	602	...	...	11	2	1.10	...
97-98—HC Vsetin	Czech Rep.	51	2906	...	...	...	92	...	1.90	...	10	600	...	...	16	1	1.60	...
98-99—HC Vsetin	Czech Rep.	46	2875	...	...	...	97	...	2.02	...	12	747	...	...	23	1	1.85	...
99-00—HC Vsetin	Czech Rep.	46	2875	...	...	...	97	...	2.47	...	9	545	...	...	15	...	1.65	...
00-01—Philadelphia	AHL	3	160	1	1	0	3	0	1.13	.969	—	—	—	—	—	—	—	—
—Philadelphia	NHL	59	3431	35	15	6	115	10	2.01	.921	6	347	2	4	18	0	3.11	.891
01-02—Philadelphia	NHL	46	2603	24	13	6	89	4	2.05	.921	4	227	1	3	7	1	1.85	.936
02-03—Philadelphia	NHL	58	3350	33	15	10	102	6	1.83	.925	13	867	6	7	31	2	2.15	.909
03-04—Los Angeles	NHL	49	2701	18	21	6	113	5	2.51	.906	—	—	—	—	—	—	—	—
04-05—HC Vsetin	Czech Rep.	35	1974	15	18	2	88	3	2.67	.922	—	—	—	—	—	—	—	—
NHL Totals (4 years)		212	12085	110	64	28	419	25	2.08	.919	23	1441	9	14	56	3	2.33	.909

CHARA, ZDENO D SENATORS

PERSONAL: Born March 18, 1977, in Trencin, Czechoslovakia. ... 6-9/261. ... Shoots left. ... Name pronounced zuh-DAY-noh CHAH-ruh.
TRANSACTIONS/CAREER NOTES: Selected by New York Islanders in third round (third Islanders pick, 56th overall) of NHL draft (June 22, 1996). ... Injured left shoulder (January 10, 2000); missed 16 games. ... Flu (April 9, 2000); missed one game. ... Traded by Islanders with RW Bill Muckalt and first-round pick (C Jason Spezza) in 2001 draft to Ottawa Senators for C Alexei Yashin (June 23, 2001). ... Injured left shoulder (January 12, 2002); missed three games. ... Flu (March 23, 2002); missed four games. ... Bruised chest (February 15, 2003); missed eight games. ... Injured upper body (February 3, 2004); missed two games. ... Bruised right foot (March 5, 2004); missed one game.

		REGULAR SEASON								PLAYOFFS				
Season Team	**League**	**GP**	**G**	**A**	**Pts.**	**PIM**	**+/-**	**PP**	**SH**	**GP**	**G**	**A**	**Pts.**	**PIM**
94-95—Dukla Trencin	Slovakia Jrs.	2	0	0	0	2	...	...	...	—	—	—	—	—
95-96—Dukla Trencin	Slovakia Jrs.	22	1	13	14	80	...	...	...	—	—	—	—	—
—HC Piestany	Slov. Div.	10	1	3	4	10	...	...	...	—	—	—	—	—
—Sparta Praha Jrs.	Czech Rep.	15	1	2	3	42	...	...	...	—	—	—	—	—
—Sparta Praha	Czech Rep.	1	0	0	0	0	...	...	...	—	—	—	—	—
96-97—Prince George	WHL	49	3	19	22	120	-5	0	1	15	1	7	8	45
97-98—Kentucky	AHL	48	4	9	13	125	0	0	0	1	0	0	0	4
—New York Islanders	NHL	25	0	1	1	50	1	0	0	—	—	—	—	—
98-99—Lowell	AHL	23	2	2	4	47	5	0	0	—	—	—	—	—
—New York Islanders	NHL	59	2	6	8	83	-8	0	1	—	—	—	—	—
99-00—New York Islanders	NHL	65	2	9	11	57	-27	0	0	—	—	—	—	—
00-01—New York Islanders	NHL	82	2	7	9	157	-27	0	1	—	—	—	—	—
01-02—Dukla Trencin	Slovakia	8	2	2	4	32	...	...	...	—	—	—	—	—
—Ottawa	NHL	75	10	13	23	156	30	4	1	10	0	1	1	12
02-03—Ottawa	NHL	74	9	30	39	116	29	3	0	18	1	6	7	14
03-04—Ottawa	NHL	79	16	25	41	147	33	7	0	7	1	1	2	8
04-05—Farjestad Karlstad	Sweden	33	10	15	25	132	24	5	0	13	3	5	8	82
NHL Totals (7 years)		459	41	91	132	766	31	14	3	35	2	8	10	34

CHARPENTIER, SEBASTIEN G

PERSONAL: Born April 18, 1977, in Drummondville, Que. ... 5-9/189. ... Catches left. ... Name pronounced SHAHR-pihnt-yay.
TRANSACTIONS/CAREER NOTES: Selected by Washington Capitals in fourth round (fourth Capitals pick, 93rd overall) of NHL draft (July 8, 1995). ... Injured leg (November 4, 2004); missed 48 games. ... Arthritic hip (March 16, 2004); missed final 10 games or season.

		REGULAR SEASON									PLAYOFFS							
Season Team	**League**	**GP**	**Min.**	**W**	**L**	**T**	**GA**	**SO**	**GAA**	**SV%**	**GP**	**Min.**	**W**	**L**	**GA**	**SO**	**GAA**	**SV%**
94-95—Laval	QMJHL	41	2152	25	12	1	99	2	2.76	...	16	886	9	4	45	0	3.05	.889
95-96—Laval	QMJHL	18	938	4	10	0	97	0	6.20	...	—	—	—	—	—	—	—	—
—Val-d'Or	QMJHL	33	1906	21	9	1	87	1	2.74	...	13	778	7	5	47	0	3.62	...
96-97—Shawinigan	QMJHL	*62	*3474	*37	17	4	176	1	3.04	...	4	195	2	1	13	0	4.00	.863
97-98—Hampton Roads	ECHL	43	2388	20	16	6	114	0	2.86	...	18	*1183	*14	4	38	1	*1.93	...
—Portland	AHL	4	230	1	3	0	10	0	2.61	.926	—	—	—	—	—	—	—	—

Season Team	League	REGULAR SEASON GP	Min.	W	L	T	GA	SO	GAA	SV%	PLAYOFFS GP	Min.	W	L	GA	SO	GAA	SV%
98-99—Portland	AHL	3	180	0	3	0	10	0	3.33	.891	—	—	—	—	—	—	—	—
—Quad City	UHL	6	4	0	0	0	0	0	0.00	1.00	—	—	—	—	—	—	—	—
99-00—Portland	AHL	18	1041	10	4	3	48	0	2.77	...	3	183	1	1	9	0	2.95	...
00-01—Portland	AHL	34	1978	16	16	1	113	1	3.43	.895	1	102	0	1	3	0	1.76	...
01-02—Portland	AHL	49	2941	20	18	10	131	3	2.67	.917	—	—	—	—	—	—	—	—
—Washington	NHL	2	122	1	1	0	5	0	2.46	.936	—	—	—	—	—	—	—	—
02-03—Portland	AHL	12	727	3	7	2	28	2	2.31	.925	—	—	—	—	—	—	—	—
—Washington	NHL	17	859	5	7	1	40	0	2.79	.906	—	—	—	—	—	—	—	—
03-04—Washington	NHL	7	369	0	6	0	21	0	3.41	.875	—	—	—	—	—	—	—	—
NHL Totals (3 years)		26	1350	6	14	1	66	0	2.93	.902								

CHARTRAND, BRAD — C/LW

PERSONAL: Born December 14, 1974, in Winnipeg. ... 5-11/191. ... Shoots left.

TRANSACTIONS/CAREER NOTES: Signed as free agent by Los Angeles Kings (July 21, 1999). ... Strained muscle in abdomen (December 8, 2001); missed nine games. ... Injured groin (January 23, 2003); missed five games. ... Injured back (February 21, 2003); missed 11 games.

Season Team	League	REGULAR SEASON GP	G	A	Pts.	PIM	+/-	PP	SH	PLAYOFFS GP	G	A	Pts.	PIM
88-89—Winnipeg	MAHA	24	30	50	80	40	...	...	...	—	—	—	—	—
89-90—Winnipeg	MAHA	24	26	55	81	40	...	...	...	—	—	—	—	—
90-91—Winnipeg	MAHA	34	26	45	71	40	...	...	...	—	—	—	—	—
91-92—St. James	MJHL	Statistics unavailable.												
92-93—Cornell	ECAC	26	10	6	16	16	...	...	...	—	—	—	—	—
93-94—Cornell	ECAC	30	4	14	18	48	...	...	...	—	—	—	—	—
94-95—Cornell	ECAC	28	9	9	18	10	...	...	...	—	—	—	—	—
95-96—Cornell	ECAC	34	24	19	43	16	...	...	...	—	—	—	—	—
96-97—Canadian nat'l team	Int'l	54	10	14	24	42	...	...	...	—	—	—	—	—
97-98—Canadian nat'l team	Int'l	60	24	30	54	47	...	...	...	—	—	—	—	—
—Rapperswil	Switzerland	8	2	3	5	4	...	...	...	—	—	—	—	—
98-99—St. John's	AHL	64	16	14	30	48	...	...	...	5	0	2	2	2
99-00—Los Angeles	NHL	50	6	6	12	17	4	0	1	4	0	0	0	6
—Long Beach	IHL	1	0	0	0	0	...	...	...	3	0	0	0	0
—Lowell	AHL	16	5	10	15	8	...	...	...	—	—	—	—	—
00-01—Lowell	AHL	72	17	34	51	44	...	...	...	4	0	1	1	8
—Los Angeles	NHL	4	1	0	1	2	-2	0	0	—	—	—	—	—
01-02—Manchester	AHL	22	10	12	22	31	2	2	3	—	—	—	—	—
—Los Angeles	NHL	46	7	9	16	40	5	0	0	7	1	1	2	2
02-03—Los Angeles	NHL	62	8	6	14	33	-10	0	1	—	—	—	—	—
03-04—Los Angeles	NHL	53	3	4	7	30	-3	0	1	—	—	—	—	—
NHL Totals (5 years)		215	25	25	50	122	-6	0	3	11	1	1	2	8

CHEECHOO, JONATHAN — RW — SHARKS

PERSONAL: Born July 15, 1980, in Moose Factory, Ont. ... 6-1/190. ... Shoots right.

TRANSACTIONS/CAREER NOTES: Selected by San Jose Sharks in second round (second Sharks pick, 29th overall) of NHL draft (June 27, 1998). ... Injured torso (January 10, 2004); missed two games.

Season Team	League	REGULAR SEASON GP	G	A	Pts.	PIM	+/-	PP	SH	PLAYOFFS GP	G	A	Pts.	PIM
96-97—Kitchener Jr. B	OHA	43	35	41	76	33	...	...	...	—	—	—	—	—
97-98—Belleville	OHL	64	31	45	76	62	...	...	...	10	4	2	6	10
98-99—Belleville	OHL	63	35	47	82	74	23	...	...	21	15	15	30	27
99-00—Belleville	OHL	66	45	46	91	102	25	13	3	16	5	12	17	16
00-01—Kentucky	AHL	75	32	34	66	63	...	...	...	3	0	0	0	0
01-02—Cleveland	AHL	53	21	25	46	54	-6	7	2	—	—	—	—	—
02-03—Cleveland	AHL	9	3	4	7	16	0	1	0	—	—	—	—	—
—San Jose	NHL	66	9	7	16	39	-5	0	0	—	—	—	—	—
03-04—San Jose	NHL	81	28	19	47	33	5	8	0	17	4	6	10	10
04-05—HV 71 Jonkoping	Sweden	20	5	0	5	10	-11	1	0	—	—	—	—	—
NHL Totals (2 years)		147	37	26	63	72	0	8	0	17	4	6	10	10

CHELIOS, CHRIS — D — RED WINGS

PERSONAL: Born January 25, 1962, in Chicago. ... 6-1/190. ... Shoots right. ... Cousin of Nikos Tselios, D, Carolina Hurricanes organization. ... Name pronounced CHEH-lee-ohz.

TRANSACTIONS/CAREER NOTES: Selected by Montreal Canadiens in 2nd round (5th Canadiens pick, 40th overall) of NHL draft (June 10, 1981). ... Sprained right ankle (January 1985). ... Injured left knee (April 1985). ... Sprained knee (December 19, 1985). ... Reinjured knee (January 20, 1986). ... Back spasms (October 1986). ... Fractured finger on left hand (December 1987). ... Bruised tailbone (February 7, 1988). ... Strained left knee ligaments (February 1990). ... Surgery for torn abdominal muscle (April 30, 1990). ... Traded by Canadiens with 2nd-round pick (C Michael Pomichter) in 1991 draft to Chicago Blackhawks for C Denis Savard (June 29, 1990). ... Cut left temple (February 9, 1991). ... Suspended four games (October 15, 1993). ... Suspended four games without pay and fined $500 for eye-scratching incident (February 5, 1994). ... Sprained knee (March 1, 1997); missed eight games. ... Sore back (April 6, 1997); missed one game. ... Strained groin (November 12, 1998); missed five games. ... Traded by Blackhawks to Detroit Red Wings for D Anders Eriksson, 1st-round pick (D Steve McCarthy) in 1999 draft and 1st-round pick (G Adam Munro) in 2001 draft (March 23, 1999). ... Strained groin (April 7, 1999); missed two games. ... Injured (April 7, 2000); missed one game. ... Injured knee and had surgery (October 18, 2000); missed five games. ... Knee surgery (November 20, 2000); missed 44 games. ... Fractured thumb (March 17, 2001); missed final seven games of regular season. ... Injured knee

(December 9, 2003); missed 10 games. ... Strained right shoulder (February 25, 2004); missed three games. ... Injured upper body (April 27, 2004); missed final four games of playoffs. ... Signed as free agent by Red Wings (Aug. 4, 2005).

		REGULAR SEASON								PLAYOFFS				
Season Team	**League**	**GP**	**G**	**A**	**Pts.**	**PIM**	**+/-**	**PP**	**SH**	**GP**	**G**	**A**	**Pts.**	**PIM**
79-80—Moose Jaw	SJHL	53	12	31	43	118	...	...	...	—	—	—	—	—
80-81—Moose Jaw	SJHL	54	23	64	87	175	...	...	...	—	—	—	—	—
81-82—Wisconsin	WCHA	43	6	43	49	50	...	...	...	—	—	—	—	—
82-83—Wisconsin	WCHA	45	16	32	48	62	...	...	...	—	—	—	—	—
83-84—U.S. national team	Int'l	60	14	35	49	58	...	...	...	—	—	—	—	—
—U.S. Olympic team	Int'l	6	0	3	3	8	...	...	...	—	—	—	—	—
—Montreal	NHL	12	0	2	2	12	-5	0	0	15	1	9	10	17
84-85—Montreal	NHL	74	9	55	64	87	11	2	1	9	2	8	10	17
85-86—Montreal	NHL	41	8	26	34	67	4	2	0	20	2	9	11	49
86-87—Montreal	NHL	71	11	33	44	124	-5	6	0	17	4	9	13	38
87-88—Montreal	NHL	71	20	41	61	172	14	10	1	11	3	1	4	29
88-89—Montreal	NHL	80	15	58	73	185	35	8	0	21	4	15	19	28
89-90—Montreal	NHL	53	9	22	31	136	20	1	2	5	0	1	1	8
90-91—Chicago	NHL	77	12	52	64	192	23	5	2	6	1	7	8	46
91-92—Chicago	NHL	80	9	47	56	245	24	2	2	18	6	15	21	37
92-93—Chicago	NHL	84	15	58	73	282	14	8	0	4	0	2	2	14
93-94—Chicago	NHL	76	16	44	60	212	12	7	1	6	1	1	2	8
94-95—Biel-Bienne	Switzerland	3	0	3	3	4	...	...	...	—	—	—	—	—
—Chicago	NHL	48	5	33	38	72	17	3	1	16	4	7	11	12
95-96—Chicago	NHL	81	14	58	72	140	25	7	0	9	0	3	3	8
96-97—Chicago	NHL	72	10	38	48	112	16	2	0	6	0	1	1	8
97-98—Chicago	NHL	81	3	39	42	151	-7	1	0	—	—	—	—	—
—U.S. Olympic team	Int'l	4	2	0	2	2	-2	1	0	—	—	—	—	—
98-99—Chicago	NHL	65	8	26	34	89	-4	2	1	—	—	—	—	—
—Detroit	NHL	10	1	1	2	4	5	1	0	10	0	4	4	14
99-00—Detroit	NHL	81	3	31	34	103	48	0	0	9	0	1	1	8
00-01—Detroit	NHL	24	0	3	3	45	4	0	0	5	1	0	1	2
01-02—Detroit	NHL	79	6	33	39	126	*40	1	0	23	1	13	14	44
—U.S. Olympic team	Int'l	6	1	0	1	4	...	...	...	—	—	—	—	—
02-03—Detroit	NHL	66	2	17	19	78	4	0	1	4	0	0	0	2
03-04—Detroit	NHL	69	2	19	21	61	12	0	0	8	0	1	1	4
04-05—Motor City	UHL	23	5	19	24	25	13	3	1	—	—	—	—	—
NHL Totals (21 years)		1395	178	736	914	2695	307	68	12	222	30	107	137	393

CHIMERA, JASON — LW/C — COYOTES

PERSONAL: Born May 2, 1979, in Edmonton. ... 6-2/204. ... Shoots left. ... Name pronounced chih-MAIR-uh.

TRANSACTIONS/CAREER NOTES: Selected by Edmonton Oilers in fifth round (fifth Oilers pick, 121st overall) of NHL draft (June 21, 1997). ... Traded by Oilers with third-round pick (traded to New York Rangers) in 2004 draft to Phoenix Coyotes for second- (LW Geoff Pankovich) and fourth-round (LW Liam Reddox) picks in 2004 draft (June 26, 2004).

		REGULAR SEASON								PLAYOFFS				
Season Team	**League**	**GP**	**G**	**A**	**Pts.**	**PIM**	**+/-**	**PP**	**SH**	**GP**	**G**	**A**	**Pts.**	**PIM**
96-97—Medicine Hat	WHL	71	16	23	39	64	...	...	...	4	0	1	1	4
97-98—Medicine Hat	WHL	72	34	32	66	93	-34	13	0	—	—	—	—	—
—Hamilton	AHL	4	0	0	0	8	-2	0	0	—	—	—	—	—
98-99—Medicine Hat	WHL	37	18	22	40	84	...	...	...	—	—	—	—	—
—Brandon	WHL	21	14	12	26	32	...	...	...	5	4	1	5	8
99-00—Hamilton	AHL	78	15	13	28	77	...	...	...	10	0	2	2	12
00-01—Hamilton	AHL	78	29	25	54	93	...	...	...	—	—	—	—	—
—Edmonton	NHL	1	0	0	0	0	0	0	0	—	—	—	—	—
01-02—Hamilton	AHL	77	26	51	77	158	28	7	3	15	4	6	10	10
—Edmonton	NHL	3	1	0	1	0	-3	0	0	—	—	—	—	—
02-03—Edmonton	NHL	66	14	9	23	36	-2	0	1	2	0	2	2	0
03-04—Edmonton	NHL	60	4	8	12	57	-1	0	0	—	—	—	—	—
04-05—Varese	Italy	15	6	3	9	34	...	...	...	5	2	1	3	31
NHL Totals (4 years)		130	19	17	36	93	-6	0	1	2	0	2	2	0

CHIODO, ANDY — G — PENGUINS

PERSONAL: Born April 25, 1983, in Toronto. ... 5-11/192. ... Catches left.

TRANSACTIONS/CAREER NOTES: Selected by New York Islanders in sixth round (third Islanders choice, 166th overall) of NHL entry draft (June 24, 2001). ... Returned to draft pool by Islanders; selected by Pittsburgh Penguins in seventh round (eighth Penguins pick, 199th overall) of NHL entry draft (June 21, 2003).

		REGULAR SEASON									PLAYOFFS							
Season Team	**League**	**GP**	**Min.**	**W**	**L**	**T**	**GA**	**SO**	**GAA**	**SV%**	**GP**	**Min.**	**W**	**L**	**GA**	**SO**	**GAA**	**SV%**
00-01—Toronto	OHL	38	2069	18	12	5	86	4	2.49	...	9	479	2	6	30	0	3.76	...
01-02—Toronto St. Michael's	OHL	33	1743	14	10	3	79	2	2.72	...	7	288	3	1	17	1	3.54	...
02-03—Toronto St. Michael's	OHL	57	3065	26	18	6	154	3	3.01	...	...	...	10	8	56	0	...	...
03-04—Wheeling	ECHL	2	86	0	2	0	9	0	6.28	.727	—	—	—	—	—	—	—	—
—Pittsburgh	NHL	8	486	3	4	1	28	0	3.46	.892	—	—	—	—	—	—	—	—
—Wilkes-Barre/Scranton	AHL	44	2449	18	19	2	98	4	2.40	.899	18	1047	9	7	38	3	2.18	.908
04-05—Wilkes-Barre/Scranton	AHL	14	788	5	7	...	43	2	3.27	.879	9	556	5	4	23	1	2.48	.906
—Wheeling	ECHL	22	1259	9	10	...	47	1	2.24	.926	—	—	—	—	—	—	—	—
NHL Totals (1 year)		8	486	3	4	1	28	0	3.46	.892								

CHIPCHURA, KYLE — C — CANADIENS

PERSONAL: Born February 19, 1986, in Westlock, Alta. ... 6-2/187. ... Shoots left.
TRANSACTIONS/CAREER NOTES: Selected by Montreal Canadiens in first round (first Canadiens pick, 18th overall) of NHL entry draft (June 26, 2004).

		REGULAR SEASON								PLAYOFFS				
Season Team	League	GP	G	A	Pts.	PIM	+/-	PP	SH	GP	G	A	Pts.	PIM
02-03—Prince Albert	WHL	63	9	21	30	89	...	...	...	—	—	—	—	—
03-04—Prince Albert	WHL	64	15	33	48	118	...	...	...	6	2	4	6	12
04-05—Prince Albert	WHL	28	14	18	32	32	8	5	1	14	4	7	11	25

CHISTOV, STANISLAV — LW — MIGHTY DUCKS

PERSONAL: Born April 17, 1983, in Chelyabinsk, U.S.S.R. ... 5-9/193. ... Shoots right. ... Name pronounced chihs-TOV.
TRANSACTIONS/CAREER NOTES: Selected by Anaheim Mighty Ducks in first round (first Mighty Ducks pick, fifth overall) of NHL draft (June 23, 2001). ... Injured hip (January 15, 2004); missed one game.

		REGULAR SEASON								PLAYOFFS				
Season Team	League	GP	G	A	Pts.	PIM	+/-	PP	SH	GP	G	A	Pts.	PIM
99-00—Avangard Omsk	Russian	3	1	0	1	2	...	...	...	—	—	—	—	—
00-01—Avangard Omsk	Russian	24	4	8	12	12	...	...	...	5	0	0	0	2
01-02—Avangard Omsk	Russian	9	0	0	0	4	...	...	...	—	—	—	—	—
02-03—Anaheim	NHL	79	12	18	30	54	4	3	0	21	4	2	6	8
03-04—Anaheim	NHL	56	2	16	18	26	-16	2	0	—	—	—	—	—
—Cincinnati	AHL	23	5	8	13	45	-1	2	0	9	5	2	7	4
04-05—Cincinnati	AHL	79	15	23	38	141	-6	8	0	9	2	1	3	6
NHL Totals (2 years)		135	14	34	48	80	-12	5	0	21	4	2	6	8

CHOUINARD, ERIC — RW — WILD

PERSONAL: Born July 8, 1980, in Atlanta. ... 6-3/215. ... Shoots left. ... Son of Guy Chouinard, C with Atlanta/Calgary Flames (1974-83) and St. Louis Blues (1983-84); and cousin of Marc Chouinard, C, Minnesota Wild. ... Name pronounced Shwee-NAHRD.
TRANSACTIONS/CAREER NOTES: Selected by Montreal Canadiens in first round (first Canadiens pick, 16th overall) of NHL draft (June 27, 1998). ... Traded by Canadiens to Philadelphia Flyers for second-round pick (C Maxime Lapierre) in 2003 draft (January 29, 2003). ... Traded by Flyers to Minnesota Wild for fifth-round pick in 2004 draft (December 17, 2003).

		REGULAR SEASON								PLAYOFFS				
Season Team	League	GP	G	A	Pts.	PIM	+/-	PP	SH	GP	G	A	Pts.	PIM
97-98—Quebec	QMJHL	68	41	42	83	18	...	...	...	14	7	10	17	6
98-99—Quebec	QMJHL	62	50	59	109	56	35	15	7	13	8	10	18	8
99-00—Quebec	QMJHL	50	57	47	104	105	23	16	6	11	14	4	18	8
—Fredericton	AHL	...	...	...	...	...	...	...	...	6	3	2	5	0
00-01—Quebec	AHL	48	12	21	33	6	...	...	...	9	2	0	2	2
—Montreal	NHL	13	1	3	4	0	0	1	0	—	—	—	—	—
01-02—Quebec	AHL	65	19	23	42	18	-7	1	0	2	0	0	0	0
02-03—Utah	AHL	32	12	12	24	16	2	4	0	—	—	—	—	—
—Philadelphia	NHL	28	4	4	8	8	2	1	0	—	—	—	—	—
03-04—Philadelphia	NHL	17	3	0	3	0	-3	0	0	—	—	—	—	—
—Philadelphia	AHL	1	0	0	0	0	...	0	0	—	—	—	—	—
—Minnesota	NHL	31	3	4	7	6	-7	0	0	—	—	—	—	—
04-05—Salzburg	Austria	16	5	5	10	42	-7	...	...	—	—	—	—	—
NHL Totals (3 years)		89	11	11	22	14	-8	2	0					

CHOUINARD, MARC — C — WILD

PERSONAL: Born May 6, 1977, in Charlesbourg, Que. ... 6-5/218. ... Shoots right. ... Cousin of Eric Chouinard, C, Minnesota Wild; and nephew of Guy Chouinard, C with Atlanta/Calgary Flames (1974-83) and St. Louis Blues (1983-84). ... Name pronounced shwee-NAHRD.
TRANSACTIONS/CAREER NOTES: Selected by Winnipeg Jets in second round (second Jets pick, 32nd overall) of NHL draft (July 8, 1995). ... Traded by Jets with RW Teemu Selanne and fourth-round pick (traded to Toronto; traded to Montreal; Canadiens picked C Kim Staal) in 1996 draft to Anaheim Mighty Ducks for C Chad Kilger, D Oleg Tverdovsky and third-round pick (D Per-Anton Lundstrom) in 1996 draft (February 7, 1996). ... Tore Achilles' tendon (October 31, 1997); missed remainder of season. ... Was injured (October 8, 2001); missed one game. ... Bruised right knee (October 14, 2001); missed one game. ... Strained left shoulder (February 27, 2002); missed remainder of season. ... Strained neck, had concussion (January 5, 2003); missed three games. ... Signed as free agent by Minnesota Wild (July 28, 2003). ... Fractured jaw (November 14, 2003); missed 32 games. ... Bruised left thumb (February 27, 2004); missed four games.

		REGULAR SEASON								PLAYOFFS				
Season Team	League	GP	G	A	Pts.	PIM	+/-	PP	SH	GP	G	A	Pts.	PIM
93-94—Beauport	QMJHL	62	11	19	30	23	...	...	...	13	2	5	7	2
94-95—Beauport	QMJHL	68	24	40	64	32	40	5	0	18	1	6	7	4
95-96—Beauport	QMJHL	30	14	21	35	19	...	...	...	—	—	—	—	—
—Halifax	QMJHL	24	6	12	18	17	...	...	...	6	2	1	3	2
96-97—Halifax	QMJHL	63	24	49	73	52	...	...	...	18	10	16	26	12
97-98—Cincinnati	AHL	8	1	2	3	4	0	0	0	—	—	—	—	—
98-99—Cincinnati	AHL	69	7	8	15	20	-11	2	0	3	0	0	0	4
99-00—Cincinnati	AHL	70	17	16	33	29	...	...	...	—	—	—	—	—
00-01—Cincinnati	AHL	32	10	9	19	4	...	...	...	—	—	—	—	—
—Anaheim	NHL	44	3	4	7	12	-5	0	0	—	—	—	—	—
01-02—Anaheim	NHL	45	4	5	9	10	2	0	0	—	—	—	—	—
02-03—Anaheim	NHL	70	3	4	7	40	-9	0	1	15	1	0	1	0
03-04—Minnesota	NHL	45	11	10	21	17	4	3	1	—	—	—	—	—
04-05—Frisk	Norway	16	9	8	17	26	5	...	...	3	5	2	7	24
NHL Totals (4 years)		204	21	23	44	79	-8	3	2	15	1	0	1	0

CHOUINARD, MATHIEU G

PERSONAL: Born April 11, 1980, in Laval, Que. ... 6-1/211. ... Catches left. ... Name pronounced SHWEE-nuhr.
TRANSACTIONS/CAREER NOTES: Selected by Ottawa Senators in first round (first Senators pick, 15th overall) of NHL entry draft (June 27, 1998). ... Returned to draft pool by Senators and selected by Senators in second round (second Senators pick, 45th overall) of NHL entry draft (June 24, 2000). ... Signed as free agent by Los Angeles Kings (July 7, 2003).

		REGULAR SEASON									PLAYOFFS							
Season Team	League	GP	Min.	W	L	T	GA	SO	GAA	SV%	GP	Min.	W	L	GA	SO	GAA	SV%
96-97—Shawinigan	QMJHL	17	793	4	7	1	51	0	3.86	...	4	264	1	3	15	0	3.41	...
97-98—Shawinigan	QMJHL	55	3055	*32	18	3	142	2	2.79	.906	6	348	2	4	24	0	4.14	.896
98-99—Shawinigan	QMJHL	56	3288	36	16	4	150	*5	2.74	...	6	392	2	4	27	0	4.13	...
99-00—Shawinigan	QMJHL	59	*3338	32	20	5	186	4	3.34	.897	13	769	7	6	41	0	3.20	.890
00-01—Grand Rapids	IHL	28	1567	17	7	1	69	1	2.64	...	3	135	1	1	4	0	*1.78	...
01-02—Grand Rapids	AHL	25	1403	11	12	1	58	2	2.48	.881	—	—	—	—	—	—	—	—
02-03—Binghamton	AHL	4	152	2	0	0	5	...	1.97	...	1	2	0	0	0	0	0.00	...
—Peoria	ECHL	15	820	12	2	0	29	3	2.12	...	—	—	—	—	—	—	—	—
03-04—Manchester	AHL	22	1093	10	6	0	41	4	2.25	.904	—	—	—	—	—	—	—	—
—Reading	ECHL	3	185	1	1	1	7	0	2.27	.916	—	—	—	—	—	—	—	—
—Los Angeles	NHL	1	3	0	0	0	0	0	0.00	1.00	—	—	—	—	—	—	—	—
04-05—Cincinnati	AHL	3	152	1	1	...	4	1	1.58	.947	—	—	—	—	—	—	—	—
—Peoria	ECHL	1	57	0	1	...	2	0	2.07	.900	—	—	—	—	—	—	—	—
—San Diego	ECHL	27	1452	11	9	...	73	1	3.01	.906	—	—	—	—	—	—	—	—
NHL Totals (1 year)		1	3	0	0	0	0	0	0.00	1.00								

C

CHUBAROV, ARTEM C CANUCKS

PERSONAL: Born December 12, 1979, in Gorky, U.S.S.R. ... 6-1/205. ... Shoots left. ... Name pronounced choo-BAH-rahf.
TRANSACTIONS/CAREER NOTES: Selected by Vancouver Canucks in second round (second Canucks pick, 31st overall) of NHL draft (June 27, 1998). ... Injured hip (February 19, 2000); missed nine games. ... Injured hand (February 28, 2002); missed two games. ... Strained abdominal muscle (February 27, 2003); missed 13 games. ... Injured shoulder (November 15, 2003); missed one game. ... Injured back (November 24, 2003); missed three games. ... Injured groin (January 9, 2004); missed two games. ... Reinjured groin (January 15, 2004); missed four games.

		REGULAR SEASON								PLAYOFFS				
Season Team	League	GP	G	A	Pts.	PIM	+/-	PP	SH	GP	G	A	Pts.	PIM
94-95—Tor. Nizhny Nov.	CIS Jr.	60	20	30	50	20	...	...	...	—	—	—	—	—
95-96—Tor. Nizhny Nov.	CIS Jr.	60	22	25	47	20	...	...	...	—	—	—	—	—
96-97—Tor. Nizhny Nov.	Rus. Div.	40	24	5	29	16	...	...	...	—	—	—	—	—
—Tor. Nizhny Nov.	Rus. Div.	15	1	1	2	8	...	...	...	—	—	—	—	—
97-98—Dynamo Moscow	Russian	30	1	4	5	4	...	...	...	—	—	—	—	—
98-99—Dynamo Moscow	Russian	34	8	2	10	10	...	...	...	12	0	0	0	4
99-00—Vancouver	NHL	49	1	8	9	10	-4	0	0	—	—	—	—	—
—Syracuse	AHL	14	7	6	13	4	...	...	...	1	0	0	0	0
00-01—Vancouver	NHL	1	0	0	0	0	-1	0	0	—	—	—	—	—
—Kansas City	IHL	10	7	4	11	12	...	...	...	—	—	—	—	—
01-02—Manitoba	AHL	19	7	12	19	4	8	3	1	—	—	—	—	—
—Vancouver	NHL	51	5	5	10	10	-3	0	0	6	0	1	1	0
02-03—Vancouver	NHl	62	7	13	20	6	4	1	0	14	0	2	2	4
03-04—Vancouver	NHL	65	12	7	19	14	1	1	1	7	0	1	1	0
04-05—Dynamo Moscow	Russian	27	4	9	13	10	-4	...	...	—	—	—	—	—
NHL Totals (5 years)		228	25	33	58	40	-3	2	1	27	0	4	4	4

CHUCKO, KRIS LW FLAMES

PERSONAL: Born March 13, 1986, in Burnaby, B.C. ... 6-2/190. ... Shoots right.
TRANSACTIONS/CAREER NOTES: Selected by Calgary Flames in first round (first Flames pick, 24th overall) of NHL entry draft (June 26, 2004).

		REGULAR SEASON								PLAYOFFS				
Season Team	League	GP	G	A	Pts.	PIM	+/-	PP	SH	GP	G	A	Pts.	PIM
03-04—Salmon Arm	BCHL	53	32	55	87	161	...	...	...	14	10	10	20	36
04-05—Minnesota	WCHA	43	10	11	21	59	...	...	...	—	—	—	—	—

CIBAK, MARTIN C/LW LIGHTNING

PERSONAL: Born May 17, 1980, in Liptovmikulas, Czechoslovakia. ... 6-1/196. ... Shoots left. ... Name pronounced SEE-back.
TRANSACTIONS/CAREER NOTES: Selected by Tampa Bay Lightning in eighth round (11th Lightning pick, 252nd overall) of NHL draft (June 28, 1998).

		REGULAR SEASON								PLAYOFFS				
Season Team	League	GP	G	A	Pts.	PIM	+/-	PP	SH	GP	G	A	Pts.	PIM
95-96—Liptovsky Mikulas	Slovakia Jrs.	48	38	35	73	...	...	...	...	—	—	—	—	—
96-97—Liptovsky Mikulas	Slovakia Jrs.	45	22	18	40	...	...	...	...	—	—	—	—	—
97-98—Liptovsky Mikulas	Slovakia Jrs.	42	31	21	52	...	...	...	...	—	—	—	—	—
—HK 32 Lip. Mikulas	Slovakia	28	1	3	4	10	...	...	...	—	—	—	—	—
98-99—Medicine Hat	WHL	66	21	26	47	72	-21	6	1	—	—	—	—	—
99-00—Medicine Hat	WHL	58	16	29	45	77	5	4	0	—	—	—	—	—
00-01—Detroit	IHL	79	10	28	38	88	...	...	...	—	—	—	—	—

Season Team	League	GP	G	A	Pts.	PIM	+/-	PP	SH	GP	G	A	Pts.	PIM
		REGULAR SEASON								PLAYOFFS				
01-02—Springfield	AHL	52	5	9	14	44	-10	0	0	—	—	—	—	—
—Tampa Bay	NHL	26	1	5	6	8	-6	0	0	—	—	—	—	—
02-03—Springfield	AHL	62	5	15	20	78	-6	0	0	—	—	—	—	—
03-04—Hershey	AHL	1	0	0	0	2	-1	0	0	—	—	—	—	—
—Tampa Bay	NHL	63	2	7	9	30	-1	0	0	6	0	1	1	0
04-05—HK 32 Lip. Mikulas	Slovakia	4	0	0	0	6	-3	...	...	—	—	—	—	—
—Plzen	Czech Rep.	30	4	11	15	52	5	...	...	—	—	—	—	—
—HC Kosice	Slovakia	6	1	3	4	8	2	...	...	10	2	5	7	36
NHL Totals (2 years)		89	3	12	15	38	-7	0	0	6	0	1	1	0

CIERNIK, IVAN — LW/RW — CAPITALS

PERSONAL: Born October 30, 1977, in Levice, Czech. ... 6-0/218. ... Shoots left. ... Name pronounced SEER-nihk.

TRANSACTIONS/CAREER NOTES: Selected by Ottawa Senators in ninth round (sixth Senators pick, 216th overall) of NHL draft (June 22, 1996). ... Injured shoulder (January 29, 2001); missed four games. ... Injured right ankle (January 2, 2002); missed six games. ... Claimed off waivers by Washington Capitals from Senators (January 19, 2002). ... Bruised foot (December 4, 2003); missed three games.

Season Team	League	GP	G	A	Pts.	PIM	+/-	PP	SH	GP	G	A	Pts.	PIM
		REGULAR SEASON								PLAYOFFS				
94-95—HC Nitra	Slovakia Jrs.	30	22	15	37	36	...	...	...	—	—	—	—	—
—HC Nitra	Slovakia	7	1	0	1	2	...	...	...	—	—	—	—	—
95-96—HC Nitra	Slovakia	35	9	7	16	36	...	...	...	—	—	—	—	—
96-97—HC Nitra	Slovakia	41	11	19	30	...	...	...	...	—	—	—	—	—
97-98—Worcester	AHL	53	9	12	21	38	4	1	0	1	0	0	0	2
—Ottawa	NHL	2	0	0	0	0	0	0	0	—	—	—	—	—
98-99—Adirondack	AHL	21	1	4	5	4	-7	0	0	—	—	—	—	—
—Cincinnati	AHL	32	10	3	13	10	4	0	0	2	0	0	0	2
99-00—Grand Rapids	IHL	66	13	12	25	64	...	...	...	6	0	6	6	2
00-01—Grand Rapids	IHL	66	27	38	65	53	...	...	...	—	—	—	—	—
—Ottawa	NHL	4	2	0	2	2	2	0	0	—	—	—	—	—
01-02—Ottawa	NHL	23	1	2	3	4	0	0	0	—	—	—	—	—
—Grand Rapids	AHL	2	2	1	3	0	1	1	0	—	—	—	—	—
—Washington	NHL	6	0	1	1	2	0	0	0	—	—	—	—	—
—Portland	AHL	26	10	5	15	28	...	...	...	—	—	—	—	—
02-03—Portland	AHL	13	4	6	10	6	-3	1	0	—	—	—	—	—
—Washington	NHL	47	8	10	18	24	6	0	0	2	0	1	1	6
03-04—Washington	NHL	7	1	1	2	0	1	0	0	—	—	—	—	—
—Portland	AHL	54	10	21	31	43	0	1	0	7	2	1	3	10
04-05—Wolfsburg	Ger. Div. II	57	30	24	54	113	8	...	...	—	—	—	—	—
NHL Totals (5 years)		89	12	14	26	32	9	0	0	2	0	1	1	6

CLARK, BRETT — D — AVALANCHE

PERSONAL: Born December 23, 1976, in Wapella, Sask. ... 6-0/195. ... Shoots left.

TRANSACTIONS/CAREER NOTES: Selected by Montreal Canadiens in sixth round (seventh Canadiens pick, 154th overall) of NHL draft (June 22, 1996). ... Suffered concussion (November 19, 1998); missed four games. ... Selected by Atlanta Thrashers in expansion draft (June 25, 1999). ... Traded by Thrashers to Colorado Avalanche for G Frederic Cassivi (January 24, 2002).

Season Team	League	GP	G	A	Pts.	PIM	+/-	PP	SH	GP	G	A	Pts.	PIM
		REGULAR SEASON								PLAYOFFS				
94-95—Melville	SJHL	62	19	32	51	77	...	...	...	—	—	—	—	—
95-96—Maine	Hockey East	39	7	31	38	22	...	...	...	—	—	—	—	—
96-97—Canadian nat'l team	Int'l	60	12	20	32	87	...	...	...	—	—	—	—	—
97-98—Montreal	NHL	41	1	0	1	20	-3	0	0	—	—	—	—	—
—Fredericton	AHL	20	0	6	6	6	1	0	0	4	0	1	1	17
98-99—Montreal	NHL	61	2	2	4	16	-3	0	0	—	—	—	—	—
—Fredericton	AHL	3	1	0	1	0	2	0	0	—	—	—	—	—
99-00—Orlando	IHL	63	9	17	26	31	...	...	...	6	0	1	1	0
—Atlanta	NHL	14	0	1	1	4	-12	0	0	—	—	—	—	—
00-01—Atlanta	NHL	28	1	2	3	14	-12	0	0	—	—	—	—	—
—Orlando	IHL	43	2	9	11	32	...	...	...	15	1	6	7	2
01-02—Chicago	AHL	42	3	17	20	18	15	1	1	—	—	—	—	—
—Atlanta	NHL	2	0	0	0	0	-3	0	0	—	—	—	—	—
—Hershey	AHL	32	7	9	16	12	...	...	...	8	0	2	2	6
02-03—Hershey	AHL	80	8	27	35	26	-1	5	0	5	0	4	4	4
03-04—Colorado	NHL	12	1	1	2	6	3	0	0	—	—	—	—	—
—Hershey	AHL	64	11	21	32	35	-7	6	0	—	—	—	—	—
04-05—Hershey	AHL	67	7	37	44	54	1	3	0	—	—	—	—	—
NHL Totals (6 years)		158	5	6	11	60	-30	0	0					

CLARK, CHRIS — RW — CAPITALS

PERSONAL: Born March 8, 1976, in South Windsor, Conn. ... 6-0/200. ... Shoots right.

TRANSACTIONS/CAREER NOTES: Selected by Calgary Flames in 3rd round (3rd Flames pick, 77th overall) of NHL draft (June 29, 1994). ... Injured shoulder (January 15, 2000); missed one game. ... Injured (March 31, 2000); missed remainder of season. ... Injured hip (November 7, 2001); missed two games. ... Injured (December 6, 2001); missed one game. ... Bruised thigh (December 19, 2001); missed two games. ... Injured knee (January 19, 2002); missed 10 games. ... Traded by Flames to Washington Capitals for conditional pick in 2006 (Aug. 4, 2005).

Season Team	League	GP	G	A	Pts.	PIM	+/-	PP	SH	GP	G	A	Pts.	PIM
		REGULAR SEASON								PLAYOFFS				
93-94—Springfield Jr. B	NEJHL	35	31	26	57	185	...	...	...	—	—	—	—	—
94-95—Clarkson	ECAC	32	12	11	23	92	...	5	0	—	—	—	—	—
95-96—Clarkson	ECAC	38	10	8	18	108	...	...	...	—	—	—	—	—
96-97—Clarkson	ECAC	37	23	25	48	86	...	8	0	—	—	—	—	—
97-98—Clarkson	ECAC	35	18	21	39	*106	...	...	...	—	—	—	—	—
98-99—Saint John	AHL	73	13	27	40	123	-10	2	0	7	2	4	6	15
99-00—Saint John	AHL	48	16	17	33	134	...	...	...	—	—	—	—	—
—Calgary	NHL	22	0	1	1	14	-3	0	0	—	—	—	—	—
00-01—Saint John	AHL	48	18	17	35	131	...	...	...	18	4	10	14	49
—Calgary	NHL	29	5	1	6	38	0	1	0	—	—	—	—	—
01-02—Calgary	NHL	64	10	7	17	79	-12	2	1	—	—	—	—	—
02-03—Calgary	NHL	81	10	12	22	126	-11	2	0	—	—	—	—	—
03-04—Calgary	NHL	82	10	15	25	106	-3	4	0	26	3	3	6	30
04-05—Bern	Switzerland	3	0	0	0	6	...	0	0	—	—	—	—	—
—Storhamar	Norway	15	10	4	14	86	6	...	...	7	4	4	8	14
NHL Totals (5 years)		278	35	36	71	363	-29	9	1	26	3	3	6	30

CLARKE, NOAH — LW — KINGS

PERSONAL: Born June 11, 1979, in LaVerne, Calif. ... 5-10/193. ... Shoots left.
TRANSACTIONS/CAREER NOTES: Selected by Los Angeles Kings in 10th round (10th Kings pick, 250th overall) in NHL entry draft (June 26, 1999).

Season Team	League	GP	G	A	Pts.	PIM	+/-	PP	SH	GP	G	A	Pts.	PIM
		REGULAR SEASON								PLAYOFFS				
99-00—Colorado College	WCHA	39	17	20	37	30	...	...	...	—	—	—	—	—
00-01—Colorado College	WCHA	41	12	20	32	22	...	...	...	—	—	—	—	—
01-02—Colorado College	WCHA	42	13	24	37	32	...	...	...	—	—	—	—	—
02-03—Colorado College	WCHA	42	21	*49	70	15	...	...	...	—	—	—	—	—
—Manchester	AHL	3	1	1	2	0	...	...	...	—	—	—	—	—
03-04—Manchester	AHL	71	25	26	51	24	20	6	0	6	3	1	4	4
—Los Angeles	NHL	2	0	1	1	0	1	0	0	—	—	—	—	—
04-05—Manchester	AHL	61	21	24	45	24	24	6	4	6	1	0	1	4
NHL Totals (1 year)		2	0	1	1	0	1	0	0					

CLEARY, DANIEL — RW

PERSONAL: Born December 18, 1978, in Carbonear, Nfld. ... 6-0/211. ... Shoots left.
TRANSACTIONS/CAREER NOTES: Selected by Chicago Blackhawks in first round (first Blackhawks pick, 13th overall) of NHL draft (June 21, 1997). ... Traded by Blackhawks with C Chad Kilger, LW Ethan Moreau and D Christian Laflamme to Edmonton Oilers for D Boris Mironov, LW Dean McAmmond and D Jonas Elofsson (March 20, 1999). ... Left knee surgery (December 8, 2001); missed 14 games. ... Signed as free agent by Phoenix Coyotes (July 15, 2003). ... Injured elbow (November 19, 2003); missed one game. ... Separated shoulder (December 12, 2003); missed six games.

Season Team	League	GP	G	A	Pts.	PIM	+/-	PP	SH	GP	G	A	Pts.	PIM
		REGULAR SEASON								PLAYOFFS				
93-94—Kingston	Tier II Jr. A	41	18	28	46	33	...	...	...	—	—	—	—	—
94-95—Belleville	OHL	62	26	55	81	62	...	...	...	16	7	10	17	23
95-96—Belleville	OHL	64	53	62	115	74	...	...	...	14	10	17	27	40
96-97—Belleville	OHL	64	32	48	80	88	-11	12	1	6	3	4	7	6
97-98—Chicago	NHL	6	0	0	0	0	-2	0	0	—	—	—	—	—
—Indianapolis	IHL	4	2	1	3	6	1	0	0	—	—	—	—	—
—Belleville	OHL	30	16	31	47	14	9	...	...	10	6	*17	*23	10
98-99—Chicago	NHL	35	4	5	9	24	-1	0	0	—	—	—	—	—
—Portland	AHL	30	9	17	26	74	-3	4	0	—	—	—	—	—
—Hamilton	AHL	9	0	1	1	7	-5	0	0	3	0	0	0	0
99-00—Hamilton	AHL	58	22	52	74	108	...	...	...	5	2	3	5	18
—Edmonton	NHL	17	3	2	5	8	-1	0	0	4	0	1	1	2
00-01—Edmonton	NHL	81	14	21	35	37	5	2	0	6	1	1	2	8
01-02—Edmonton	NHL	65	10	19	29	51	-1	2	1	—	—	—	—	—
02-03—Edmonton	NHL	57	4	13	17	31	5	0	0	—	—	—	—	—
03-04—Phoenix	NHL	68	6	11	17	42	-8	0	3	—	—	—	—	—
04-05—Mora	Sweden Dv. 2	47	11	26	37	138	-18	2	1	—	—	—	—	—
NHL Totals (7 years)		329	41	71	112	193	-3	4	4	10	1	2	3	10

CLEMMENSEN, SCOTT — G — DEVILS

PERSONAL: Born July 23, 1977, in Des Moines, Iowa. ... 6-3/205. ... Catches left.
TRANSACTIONS/CAREER NOTES: Selected by New Jersey Devils in eighth round (seventh Devils pick, 215th overall) of NHL draft (June 21, 1997).

Season Team	League	GP	Min.	W	L	T	GA	SO	GAA	SV%	GP	Min.	W	L	GA	SO	GAA	SV%
		REGULAR SEASON									PLAYOFFS							
96-97—Des Moines	USHL	36	2042	...	...	...	111	1	3.26	...	—	—	—	—	—	—	—	—
97-98—Boston College	Hockey East	37	2205	24	9	4	102	*4	2.78	...	—	—	—	—	—	—	—	—
98-99—Boston College	Hockey East	*42	*2507	26	12	*4	*120	1	2.87	...	—	—	—	—	—	—	—	—
99-00—Boston College	Hockey East	29	1610	19	7	0	59	3	2.20	...	—	—	—	—	—	—	—	—
00-01—Boston College	Hockey East	*39	*2312	*30	7	2	*82	3	2.13	...	—	—	—	—	—	—	—	—

Season Team	League	REGULAR SEASON GP	Min.	W	L	T	GA	SO	GAA	SV%	PLAYOFFS GP	Min.	W	L	GA	SO	GAA	SV%
01-02—New Jersey	NHL	2	20	0	0	0	1	0	3.00	.800	—	—	—	—	—	—	—	—
—Albany	AHL	29	1676	5	19	4	92	0	3.29	.899	—	—	—	—	—	—	—	—
02-03—Albany	AHL	47	2694	12	24	8	119	1	2.65	.910	—	—	—	—	—	—	—	—
03-04—New Jersey	NHL	4	238	3	1	0	4	2	1.01	.952	—	—	—	—	—	—	—	—
—Albany	AHL	22	1309	5	12	4	67	0	3.07	.891	—	—	—	—	—	—	—	—
04-05—Albany	AHL	46	2644	13	25	...	124	2	2.81	.916	—	—	—	—	—	—	—	—
NHL Totals (2 years)		6	258	3	1	0	5	2	1.16	.944								

CLOUTIER, DAN — G — CANUCKS

PERSONAL: Born April 22, 1976, in Mont-Laurier, Que. ... 6-1/195. ... Catches left. ... Brother of Sylvain Cloutier, C, New Jersey Devils organization (1999-2004). ... Name pronounced KLOO-tee-yay.

TRANSACTIONS/CAREER NOTES: Selected by New York Rangers in first round (first Rangers pick, 26th overall) of NHL draft (June 28, 1994). ... Traded by Rangers with LW Niklas Sundstrom and first- (RW Nikita Alexeev) and third-round (traded to San Jose) picks in 2000 draft to Tampa Bay Lightning for first-round pick (RW Pavel Brendl) in 1999 draft (June 26, 1999). ... Strained groin (November 18, 1999); missed two games. ... Suspended four games for kicking incident (January 14, 2000). ... Strained groin (February 21, 2000); missed three games. ... Injured neck (March 14, 2000); missed four games. ... Strained knee (March 28, 2000); missed five games. ... Strained biceps (October 22, 2000); missed nine games. ... Flu (December 8, 2000); missed one game. ... Traded by Lightning to Vancouver Canucks for D Adrian Aucoin and second-round pick (C/LW Alexander Polushin) in 2001 draft (February 7, 2001). ... Injured ankle (January 23, 2002); missed nine games. ... Injured knee (December 28, 2002); missed three games. ... Sprained knee (March 18, 2003); missed 10 games. ... Injured knee (March 27, 2003); missed two games. ... Injured knee (March 30, 2003); missed one game. ... Injured groin (December 9, 2003); missed three games. ... Injured hip flexor (March 18, 2004); missed two games.

Season Team	League	REGULAR SEASON GP	Min.	W	L	T	GA	SO	GAA	SV%	PLAYOFFS GP	Min.	W	L	GA	SO	GAA	SV%
91-92—St. Thomas	Jr. B	14	823	...	...	...	80	...	5.83	...	—	—	—	—	—	—	—	—
92-93—Sault Ste. Marie	OHL	12	572	4	6	0	44	0	4.62	...	4	231	1	2	12	0	3.12	...
93-94—Sault Ste. Marie	OHL	55	2934	28	14	6	174	2	3.56	.890	14	833	10	4	52	0	3.75	.887
94-95—Sault Ste. Marie	OHL	45	2517	15	25	2	184	1	4.39	.881	—	—	—	—	—	—	—	—
95-96—Sault Ste. Marie	OHL	13	641	9	3	0	43	0	4.02	...	—	—	—	—	—	—	—	—
—Guelph	OHL	17	1004	12	2	2	35	2	2.09	...	16	993	11	5	52	*2	3.14	...
96-97—Binghamton	AHL	60	3367	23	28	8	199	3	3.55	.892	4	236	1	3	13	0	3.31	.893
97-98—Hartford	AHL	24	1417	12	8	3	62	0	2.63	.917	8	479	5	3	24	0	3.01	.921
—New York Rangers	NHL	12	551	4	5	1	23	0	2.50	.907	—	—	—	—	—	—	—	—
98-99—New York Rangers	NHL	22	1097	6	8	3	49	0	2.68	.914	—	—	—	—	—	—	—	—
99-00—Tampa Bay	NHL	52	2492	9	30	3	145	0	3.49	.885	—	—	—	—	—	—	—	—
00-01—Detroit	IHL	1	59	0	1	0	3	0	3.05	...	—	—	—	—	—	—	—	—
—Tampa Bay	NHL	24	1005	3	13	3	59	1	3.52	.891	—	—	—	—	—	—	—	—
—Vancouver	NHL	16	914	4	6	5	37	0	2.43	.894	2	117	0	2	9	0	4.62	.842
01-02—Vancouver	NHL	62	3502	31	22	5	142	7	2.43	.901	6	273	2	3	16	0	3.52	.870
02-03—Vancouver	NHL	57	3376	33	16	7	136	2	2.42	.908	14	833	7	7	45	0	3.24	.868
03-04—Vancouver	NHL	60	3539	33	21	6	134	5	2.27	.914	3	138	1	1	5	0	2.17	.922
04-05—KAC	Austria	23	1362	13	5	4	52	2	2.29	.924	—	—	—	—	—	—	—	—
NHL Totals (7 years)		305	16476	123	121	33	725	15	2.64	.903	25	1361	10	13	75	0	3.31	.872

CLYMER, BEN — RW — CAPITALS

PERSONAL: Born April 11, 1978, in Edina, Minn. ... 6-1/198. ... Shoots right.

TRANSACTIONS/CAREER NOTES: Selected by Boston Bruins in 2nd round (3rd Bruins pick, 27th overall) of NHL draft (June 21, 1997). ... Signed as free agent by Tampa Bay Lightning (October 2, 1999). ... Bruised foot (November 2, 2002); missed one game. ... Strained groin (January 2, 2003); missed four games. ... Reinjured groin (January 17, 2003); missed five games. ... Reinjured groin (January 28, 2003); missed two games. ... Reinjured groin (March 20, 2003); missed four games. ... Concussion (December 7, 2003); missed four games. ... Signed as free agent by Washington Capitals (Aug. 8, 2005).

Season Team	League	REGULAR SEASON GP	G	A	Pts.	PIM	+/-	PP	SH	PLAYOFFS GP	G	A	Pts.	PIM
93-94—Thomas Jefferson	Minn. H.S.	23	3	7	10	6	...	...	...	—	—	—	—	—
94-95—Thomas Jefferson	Minn. H.S.	28	6	20	26	26	...	...	...	—	—	—	—	—
95-96—Thomas Jefferson	Minn. H.S.	19	12	28	40	38	...	...	...	—	—	—	—	—
96-97—Minnesota	WCHA	29	7	13	20	64	...	...	...	—	—	—	—	—
97-98—Minnesota	WCHA	1	0	0	0	2	...	...	...	—	—	—	—	—
98-99—Seattle	WHL	70	12	44	56	93	21	3	0	11	1	5	6	12
99-00—Detroit	IHL	19	1	9	10	30	...	...	...	—	—	—	—	—
—Tampa Bay	NHL	60	2	6	8	87	-26	2	0	—	—	—	—	—
00-01—Detroit	IHL	53	5	8	13	88	...	...	...	—	—	—	—	—
—Tampa Bay	NHL	23	5	1	6	21	-7	3	0	—	—	—	—	—
01-02—Tampa Bay	NHL	81	14	20	34	36	-10	4	0	—	—	—	—	—
02-03—Tampa Bay	NHL	65	6	12	18	57	-2	1	0	11	0	2	2	6
03-04—Tampa Bay	NHL	66	2	8	10	50	5	0	0	5	0	0	0	0
04-05—Biel-Bienne	Switz. Div. 2	19	12	13	25	30	...	4	1	11	6	11	17	24
NHL Totals (5 years)		295	29	47	76	251	-40	10	0	16	0	2	2	6

COBURN, BRAYDON — D — THRASHERS

PERSONAL: Born February 27, 1985, in Calgary. ... 6-5/205. ... Shoots left.

TRANSACTIONS/CAREER NOTES: Selected by Atlanta Thrashers in first round (first Thrashers pick, eighth overall) in 2003 NHL entry draft (June 23, 2003).

Season Team	League	GP	G	A	Pts.	PIM	+/-	PP	SH	GP	G	A	Pts.	PIM
		REGULAR SEASON								PLAYOFFS				
00-01—Portland	WHL	2	0	1	1	0	...	...	...	14	0	4	4	2
01-02—Portland	WHL	68	4	33	37	100	...	...	...	—	—	—	—	—
02-03—Portland	WHL	53	3	16	19	147	...	...	...	—	—	—	—	—
03-04—Portland	WHL	55	10	20	30	92	-19	7	0	5	0	1	1	10
04-05—Chicago	AHL	3	0	1	1	5	-1	0	0	18	0	1	1	36
—Portland	WHL	60	12	32	44	144	9	7	0	7	1	5	6	6

COGLIANO, ANDREW — C — OILERS

PERSONAL: Born June 14, 1987, in Toronto, Ont. ... 5-9/175. ... Shoots left.
TRANSACTIONS/CAREER NOTES: Selected by Edmonton Oilers in 1st round (1st Oilers pick, 25th overall) of entry draft (July 30, 2005).

Season Team	League	GP	G	A	Pts.	PIM	+/-	PP	SH	GP	G	A	Pts.	PIM
		REGULAR SEASON								PLAYOFFS				
03-04—St. Michael's H.S.	Jr. A	36	26	47	73	14	...	...	...	—	—	—	—	—
04-05—St. Michael's H.S.	Jr. A	49	36	66	102	33	...	...	...	—	—	—	—	—

COLAIACOVO, CARLO — D — MAPLE LEAFS

C

PERSONAL: Born January 27, 1983, in Toronto. ... 6-1/188. ... Shoots left. ... Name pronounced KOH-lee-ah-kovo.
TRANSACTIONS/CAREER NOTES: Selected by Toronto Maple Leafs in first round (first Maple Leafs pick, 17th overall) of NHL draft (June 23, 2001).

Season Team	League	GP	G	A	Pts.	PIM	+/-	PP	SH	GP	G	A	Pts.	PIM
		REGULAR SEASON								PLAYOFFS				
99-00—Erie	OHL	52	4	18	22	12	...	...	...	13	2	4	6	9
00-01—Erie	OHL	62	12	27	39	59	...	...	...	14	4	7	11	16
01-02—Erie	OHL	60	13	27	40	49	...	...	...	21	7	10	17	20
02-03—Toronto	NHL	2	0	1	1	0	0	0	0	—	—	—	—	—
—Erie	OHL	35	14	21	35	12	...	...	...	—	—	—	—	—
03-04—St. John's	AHL	62	6	25	31	50	-15	1	0	—	—	—	—	—
—Toronto	NHL	2	0	1	1	2	1	0	0	—	—	—	—	—
04-05—St. John's	AHL	49	4	20	24	59	9	2	0	5	0	1	1	2
NHL Totals (2 years)		4	0	2	2	2	1	0	0					

COLE, ERIK — LW — HURRICANES

PERSONAL: Born November 6, 1978, in Oswego, N.Y. ... 6-2/200. ... Shoots left.
TRANSACTIONS/CAREER NOTES: Selected by Carolina Hurricanes in third round (third Hurricanes pick, 71st overall) of NHL draft (June 27, 1998). ... Flu (November 8, 2001); missed one game. ... Fractured leg (February 5, 2003); missed 28 games. ... Injured elbow (November 8, 2003); missed one game. ... Injured hamstring (March 23, 2004); missed one game.
STATISTICAL PLATEAUS: Three-goal games: 2001-02 (1), 2002-03 (1). Total: 2.

Season Team	League	GP	G	A	Pts.	PIM	+/-	PP	SH	GP	G	A	Pts.	PIM
		REGULAR SEASON								PLAYOFFS				
96-97—Des Moines	USHL	48	30	34	64	185	...	...	...	—	—	—	—	—
97-98—Clarkson	ECAC	34	11	20	31	55	...	...	...	—	—	—	—	—
98-99—Clarkson	ECAC	36	22	20	42	50	...	...	...	—	—	—	—	—
99-00—Clarkson	ECAC	33	19	11	30	46	...	...	...	—	—	—	—	—
—Cincinnati	IHL	9	4	3	7	2	...	...	...	7	1	1	2	2
00-01—Cincinnati	IHL	69	23	20	43	28	...	...	...	5	1	0	1	2
01-02—Carolina	NHL	81	16	24	40	35	-10	3	0	23	6	3	9	30
02-03—Carolina	NHL	53	14	13	27	72	1	6	2	—	—	—	—	—
03-04—Carolina	NHL	80	18	24	42	93	-4	2	2	—	—	—	—	—
04-05—Eisbaren Berlin	Germany	39	6	21	27	76	7	2	0	8	5	1	6	37
NHL Totals (3 years)		214	48	61	109	200	-13	11	4	23	6	3	9	30

COLLINS, DAN — RW — PANTHERS

PERSONAL: Born February 26, 1987, in Syracuse, N.Y. ... 6-1/185. ... Shoots right.

Season Team	League	GP	G	A	Pts.	PIM	+/-	PP	SH	GP	G	A	Pts.	PIM
		REGULAR SEASON								PLAYOFFS				
04-05—Plymouth	OHL	68	25	21	46	60	-2	6	2	4	0	0	0	6

COMMODORE, MIKE — D — HURRICANES

PERSONAL: Born November 7, 1979, in Fort Saskatchewan, Alta. ... 6-4/230. ... Shoots right.
TRANSACTIONS/CAREER NOTES: Selected by New Jersey Devils in 2nd round (2nd Devils pick, 42nd overall) of NHL draft (June 26, 1999). ... Flu (March 20, 2002); missed two games. ... Traded by Devils with RW Petr Sykora, C Igor Pohanka and G J.F. Damphousse to Anaheim Mighty Ducks for D Oleg Tverdovsky, LW Jeff Friesen and RW Maxin Balmochnykh (July 7, 2002). ... Traded by Mighty Ducks with G J.F. Damphousse to Calgary Flames for C Rob Niedermayer (March 11, 2003). ... Injured shoulder (February 11, 2004); missed 19 games. ... Traded by Flames to Carolina Hurricanes for 3rd-round pick (obtained from Atlanta) in 2005 draft (July 29, 2005).

Season Team	League	GP	G	A	Pts.	PIM	+/-	PP	SH	GP	G	A	Pts.	PIM
		REGULAR SEASON								PLAYOFFS				
96-97—Fort Saskatchewan	Tier II Jr. A	51	3	8	11	244	...	...	...	—	—	—	—	—
97-98—Univ. of North Dakota	WCHA	29	0	5	5	74	...	...	...	—	—	—	—	—

Season Team	League	GP	G	A	Pts.	PIM	+/-	PP	SH	GP	G	A	Pts.	PIM
		REGULAR SEASON								PLAYOFFS				
98-99—Univ. of North Dakota.	WCHA	39	5	8	13	*154	...	...	...	—	—	—	—	—
99-00—Univ. of North Dakota.	WCHA	38	5	7	12	*154	...	...	...	—	—	—	—	—
00-01—Albany	AHL	41	2	5	7	59	...	...	...	—	—	—	—	—
—New Jersey	NHL	20	1	4	5	14	5	0	0	—	—	—	—	—
01-02—Albany	AHL	14	0	3	3	31	0	0	0	—	—	—	—	—
—New Jersey	NHL	37	0	1	1	30	-12	0	0	—	—	—	—	—
02-03—Cincinnati	AHL	61	2	9	11	210	-12	0	0	—	—	—	—	—
—Calgary	NHL	6	0	1	1	19	2	0	0	—	—	—	—	—
—Saint John	AHL	7	0	3	3	18	1	0	0	—	—	—	—	—
03-04—Calgary	NHL	12	0	0	0	25	-4	0	0	20	0	2	2	19
—Lowell	AHL	37	5	11	16	75	-1	1	1	—	—	—	—	—
04-05—Lowell	AHL	73	6	29	35	175	23	3	2	11	1	2	3	18
NHL Totals (4 years)		75	1	6	7	88	-9	0	0	20	0	2	2	19

COMRIE, MIKE — C — COYOTES

PERSONAL: Born November 11, 1980, in Edmonton. ... 5-9/175. ... Shoots left. ... Brother of Paul Comrie, C, Edmonton Oilers organization, 1998-2000.

TRANSACTIONS/CAREER NOTES: Selected by Edmonton Oilers in third round (fifth Oilers pick, 91st overall) on NHL draft (June 25, 1999). ... Fractured thumb (January 6, 2003); missed 13 games. ... Missed first 30 games of 2003-04 season in contract dispute. ... Traded by Oilers to Philadelphia Flyers for D Jeff Woywitka, Flyers' first-round pick (C Robbie Schremp) in 2004 draft and Flyers' third-round pick in 2005 draft (December 16, 2003). ... Traded by Flyers to Phoenix Coyotes for G Sean Burke, RW Branko Radivojevic and rights to LW Ben Eager (February 9, 2004).

Season Team	League	GP	G	A	Pts.	PIM	+/-	PP	SH	GP	G	A	Pts.	PIM
		REGULAR SEASON								PLAYOFFS				
98-99—Univ. of Michigan	CCHA	42	19	25	44	38	...	...	...	—	—	—	—	—
99-00—Univ. of Michigan	CCHA	40	24	35	59	95	...	...	...	—	—	—	—	—
00-01—Kootenay	WHL	37	39	40	79	79	...	...	...	—	—	—	—	—
—Edmonton	NHL	41	8	14	22	14	6	3	0	6	1	2	3	0
01-02—Edmonton	NHL	82	33	27	60	45	16	8	0	—	—	—	—	—
02-03—Edmonton	NHL	69	20	31	51	90	-18	8	0	6	1	0	1	10
03-04—Philadelphia	NHL	21	4	5	9	12	2	0	0	—	—	—	—	—
—Phoenix	NHL	28	8	7	15	16	-8	1	1	—	—	—	—	—
04-05—Farjestad Karlstad	Sweden	10	1	6	7	10	-5	0	0	—	—	—	—	—
NHL Totals (4 years)		241	73	84	157	177	-2	20	1	12	2	2	4	10

CONKLIN, TY — G — OILERS

PERSONAL: Born March 4, 1976, in Anchorage, Alaska. ... 6-0/180. ... Catches left.

TRANSACTIONS/CAREER NOTES: Signed as free agent by Edmonton Oilers (April 18, 2000). ... Injured groin (October 23, 2003); missed two games. ... Fractured right hand (February 14, 2004); missed 11 games.

Season Team	League	GP	Min.	W	L	T	GA	SO	GAA	SV%	GP	Min.	W	L	GA	SO	GAA	SV%
		REGULAR SEASON									PLAYOFFS							
98-99—New Hampshire	Hockey East	22	1338	18	3	1	41	0	*1.84	...	—	—	—	—	—	—	—	—
99-00—New Hampshire	Hockey East	*37	*2194	*22	8	*6	*91	1	2.49	...	—	—	—	—	—	—	—	—
00-01—New Hampshire	Hockey East	34	2048	17	12	*5	70	*4	*2.05	...	—	—	—	—	—	—	—	—
01-02—Hamilton	AHL	37	2043	13	12	8	89	1	2.61	.908	7	416	4	2	18	0	2.60	.917
—Edmonton	NHL	4	148	2	0	0	4	0	1.62	.939	—	—	—	—	—	—	—	—
02-03—Hamilton	AHL	38	2140	19	13	3	91	4	2.55	.914	17	1023	9	6	38	1	2.23	.933
03-04—Edmonton	NHL	38	2086	17	14	4	84	1	2.42	.912	—	—	—	—	—	—	—	—
04-05—Wolfsburg	Ger. Div. II	11	623	...	...	...	31	0	2.99	.920	7	414	...	...	11	2	1.59	.946
NHL Totals (2 years)		42	2234	19	14	4	88	1	2.36	.914								

CONNOLLY, TIM — C — SABRES

PERSONAL: Born May 7, 1981, in Syracuse, N.Y. ... 6-1/186. ... Shoots right.

TRANSACTIONS/CAREER NOTES: Selected by New York Islanders in first round (first Islanders pick, fifth overall) of NHL draft (June 26, 1999). ... Traded by Islanders with LW Taylor Pyatt to Buffalo Sabres for C Michael Peca (June 24, 2001). ... Suspended four games for high-sticking incident (April 3, 2003). ... Had concussion (October 9, 2003); missed 2003-04 season.

Season Team	League	GP	G	A	Pts.	PIM	+/-	PP	SH	GP	G	A	Pts.	PIM
		REGULAR SEASON								PLAYOFFS				
96-97—Syracuse	Jr. A	50	42	62	104	34	...	...	...	—	—	—	—	—
97-98—Erie	OHL	59	30	32	62	32	...	...	...	7	1	6	7	6
98-99—Erie	OHL	46	34	34	68	50	5	...	...	—	—	—	—	—
99-00—New York Islanders	NHL	81	14	20	34	44	-25	2	1	—	—	—	—	—
00-01—New York Islanders	NHL	82	10	31	41	42	-14	5	0	—	—	—	—	—
01-02—Buffalo	NHL	82	10	35	45	34	4	3	0	—	—	—	—	—
02-03—Buffalo	NHL	80	12	13	25	32	-28	6	0	—	—	—	—	—
03-04—Buffalo	NHL	Did not play; injured												
04-05—SC Langnau	Switzerland	16	8	3	11	14	...	2	2	—	—	—	—	—
NHL Totals (5 years)		325	46	99	145	152	-63	16	1					

CONROY, CRAIG — C — KINGS

PERSONAL: Born September 4, 1971, in Potsdam, N.Y. ... 6-2/197. ... Shoots right. ... Nickname: Connie.
TRANSACTIONS/CAREER NOTES: Selected by Montreal Canadiens in sixth round (seventh Canadiens pick, 123rd overall) of NHL draft (June 16, 1990). ... Traded by Canadiens with C Pierre Turgeon and D Rory Fitzpatrick to St. Louis Blues for LW Shayne Corson, D Murray Baron and fifth-round pick (D Gennady Razin) in 1997 entry draft (October 29, 1996). ... Sprained ankle (March 12, 1999); missed 11 games. ... Reinjured ankle (April 7, 1999); missed two games. ... Flu (October 2, 1999); missed one game. ... Traded by Blues with seventh-round pick (LW David Moss) in 2001 entry draft to Calgary Flames for LW Cory Stillman (March 13, 2001). ... Injured (November 20, 2001); missed one game. ... Bruised foot (November 4, 2002); missed two games. ... Injured right shoulder (December 21, 2002); missed one game. ... Injured knee (December 7, 2003); missed 19 games. ... Signed as free agent by Los Angeles Kings (July 6, 2004).
STATISTICAL PLATEAUS: Three-goal games: 1998-99 (1).

		REGULAR SEASON								PLAYOFFS				
Season Team	League	GP	G	A	Pts.	PIM	+/-	PP	SH	GP	G	A	Pts.	PIM
89-90—Northwood School	N.Y. H.S.	31	33	43	76	...	...	...	...	—	—	—	—	—
90-91—Clarkson	ECAC	40	8	21	29	24	...	...	...	—	—	—	—	—
91-92—Clarkson	ECAC	31	19	17	36	36	...	...	...	—	—	—	—	—
92-93—Clarkson	ECAC	35	10	23	33	26	...	...	...	—	—	—	—	—
93-94—Clarkson	ECAC	34	26	40	66	66	...	...	...	—	—	—	—	—
94-95—Fredericton	AHL	55	26	18	44	29	-5	11	0	11	7	3	10	6
—Montreal	NHL	6	1	0	1	0	-1	0	0	—	—	—	—	—
95-96—Fredericton	AHL	67	31	38	69	65	...	...	...	10	5	7	12	6
—Montreal	NHL	7	0	0	0	2	-4	0	0	—	—	—	—	—
96-97—Fredericton	AHL	9	10	6	16	10	2	3	0	—	—	—	—	—
—St. Louis	NHL	61	6	11	17	43	0	0	0	6	0	0	0	8
—Worcester	AHL	5	5	6	11	2	3	1	0	—	—	—	—	—
97-98—St. Louis	NHL	81	14	29	43	46	20	0	3	10	1	2	3	8
98-99—St. Louis	NHL	69	14	25	39	38	14	0	1	13	2	1	3	6
99-00—St. Louis	NHL	79	12	15	27	36	5	1	2	7	0	2	2	2
00-01—St. Louis	NHL	69	11	14	25	46	2	0	3	—	—	—	—	—
—Calgary	NHL	14	3	4	7	14	0	0	1	—	—	—	—	—
01-02—Calgary	NHL	81	27	48	75	32	24	7	2	—	—	—	—	—
02-03—Calgary	NHL	79	22	37	59	36	-4	5	0	—	—	—	—	—
03-04—Calgary	NHL	63	8	39	47	44	13	2	0	26	6	11	17	12
NHL Totals (10 years)		609	118	222	340	337	69	15	12	62	9	16	25	36

COOKE, MATT — C/RW — CANUCKS

PERSONAL: Born September 7, 1978, in Belleville, Ont. ... 5-11/205. ... Shoots left.
TRANSACTIONS/CAREER NOTES: Selected by Vancouver Canucks in sixth round (eighth Canucks pick, 144th overall) of NHL draft (June 21, 1997). ... Injured knee (March 2, 2001); missed one game. ... Injured shoulder (November 25, 2003); missed 13 games. ... Injured knee (January 10, 2004); missed 14 games. ... Suspended two games for spearing incident (February 21, 2004).

		REGULAR SEASON								PLAYOFFS				
Season Team	League	GP	G	A	Pts.	PIM	+/-	PP	SH	GP	G	A	Pts.	PIM
95-96—Windsor	OHL	61	8	11	19	102	...	...	...	7	1	3	4	6
96-97—Windsor	OHL	65	45	50	95	146	...	...	...	5	5	5	10	4
97-98—Windsor	OHL	23	14	19	33	50	1	...	...	—	—	—	—	—
—Kingston	OHL	25	8	13	21	49	-6	...	...	12	8	8	16	20
98-99—Vancouver	NHL	30	0	2	2	27	-12	0	0	—	—	—	—	—
—Syracuse	AHL	37	15	18	33	119	-28	8	0	—	—	—	—	—
99-00—Syracuse	AHL	18	5	8	13	27	...	...	...	—	—	—	—	—
—Vancouver	NHL	51	5	7	12	39	3	0	1	—	—	—	—	—
00-01—Vancouver	NHL	81	14	13	27	94	5	0	2	4	0	0	0	4
01-02—Vancouver	NHL	82	13	20	33	111	4	1	0	6	3	2	5	0
02-03—Vancouver	NHL	82	15	27	42	82	21	1	4	14	2	1	3	12
03-04—Vancouver	NHL	53	11	12	23	73	5	1	1	7	3	1	4	12
NHL Totals (6 years)		379	58	81	139	426	26	3	8	31	8	4	12	28

CORAZZINI, CARL — C — BRUINS

PERSONAL: Born April 21, 1979, in Framingham, Mass. ... 5-10/182. ... Shoots left.
TRANSACTIONS/CAREER NOTES: Signed as free agent by Boston Bruins (August 8, 2001). ... Signed as free agent by Providence of the AHL (October 1, 2004).

		REGULAR SEASON								PLAYOFFS				
Season Team	League	GP	G	A	Pts.	PIM	+/-	PP	SH	GP	G	A	Pts.	PIM
01-02—Providence	AHL	61	7	8	15	10	-4	2	1	—	—	—	—	—
02-03—Providence	AHL	33	7	6	13	4	9	0	0	—	—	—	—	—
—Atlantic City	ECHL	27	13	8	21	14	10	2	0	—	—	—	—	—
03-04—Boston	NHL	12	2	0	2	0	2	0	1	—	—	—	—	—
—Providence	AHL	62	16	9	25	6	11	5	4	2	1	0	1	2
04-05—Hershey	AHL	52	10	13	23	6	-1	4	0	—	—	—	—	—
—Providence	AHL	8	0	0	0	0	-3	0	0	—	—	—	—	—
NHL Totals (1 year)		12	2	0	2	0	2	0	1					

CORSO, DANIEL — C/RW — THRASHERS

PERSONAL: Born April 3, 1978, in Montreal. ... 5-9/187. ... Shoots left.
TRANSACTIONS/CAREER NOTES: Selected by St. Louis Blues in seventh round (fifth Blues pick, 169th overall) of NHL draft (June 22, 1996). ... Flu (November 29, 2001); missed one game. ... Dislocated shoulder (March 2, 2002); missed five games. ... Signed as free agent by Ottawa Senators (September 2, 2003). ... Traded by Senators to Atlanta Thrashers for RW Brad Tapper (January 6, 2003).

Season Team	League	REGULAR SEASON GP	G	A	Pts.	PIM	+/-	PP	SH	PLAYOFFS GP	G	A	Pts.	PIM
94-95—Victoriaville	QMJHL	65	27	26	53	6	...	...	...	4	2	5	7	2
95-96—Victoriaville	QMJHL	65	49	65	114	77	...	...	...	12	6	7	13	4
96-97—Victoriaville	QMJHL	54	51	68	119	50	...	...	...	—	—	—	—	—
97-98—Victoriaville	QMJHL	35	24	51	75	20	...	...	...	3	1	1	2	2
98-99—Worcester	AHL	63	14	14	28	26	-13	5	1	—	—	—	—	—
99-00—Worcester	AHL	71	21	34	55	19	...	...	...	9	2	3	5	10
00-01—Worcester	AHL	52	19	37	56	47	...	...	...	—	—	—	—	—
—St. Louis	NHL	28	10	3	13	14	0	5	0	12	0	1	1	0
01-02—St. Louis	NHL	41	4	7	11	6	3	1	0	2	0	0	0	0
02-03—Worcester	AHL	1	0	0	0	0	0	0	0	—	—	—	—	—
—St. Louis	NHL	1	0	0	0	0	-1	0	0	—	—	—	—	—
03-04—Binghamton	AHL	32	7	11	18	16	-3	3	0	—	—	—	—	—
—Atlanta	NHL	7	0	1	1	0	-2	0	0	—	—	—	—	—
—Chicago	AHL	29	8	18	26	15	-2	3	0	10	1	5	6	0
04-05—Kassel	Germany	45	8	30	38	32	...	...	...	—	—	—	—	—
NHL Totals (4 years)		77	14	11	25	20	0	6	0	14	0	1	1	0

CORSON, SHAYNE — LW/C

PERSONAL: Born August 13, 1966, in Barrie, Ont. ... 6-1/207. ... Shoots left.

TRANSACTIONS/CAREER NOTES: Selected by Montreal Canadiens in first round (second Canadiens pick, eighth overall) of NHL draft (June 9, 1984). ... Fractured jaw (January 24, 1987). ... Strained right knee (September 1987). ... Injured groin (March 1988). ... Injured knee (April 1988). ... Injured knee (April 1989). ... Bruised left shoulder (October 29, 1989). ... Fractured toe on right foot (December 1989). ... Had hip pointer (November 10, 1990); missed seven games. ... Injured groin (February 11, 1991). ... Traded by Canadiens with LW Vladimir Vujtek and C Brent Gilchrist to Edmonton Oilers for LW Vincent Damphousse and fourth-round pick (D Adam Wiesel) in 1993 draft (August 27, 1992). ... Fractured leg (February 18, 1994); missed 12 games. ... Injured leg (March 23, 1994); missed remainder of season. ... Signed by St. Louis Blues to an offer sheet (July 28, 1995); Oilers received Blues first-round picks in 1996 and 1997 drafts as compensation; Oilers then traded picks to Blues for rights to G Curtis Joseph and RW Michael Grier (August 4, 1995). ... Fractured jaw (March 26, 1996); missed five games. ... Traded by Blues with D Murray Baron and fifth-round pick (D Gennady Razin) in 1997 draft to Canadiens for C Pierre Turgeon, C Craig Conroy and D Rory Fitzpatrick (October 29, 1996). ... Injured knee (November 25, 1996) and had surgery; missed 10 games. ... Sprained ankle (December 26, 1996); missed 10 games. ... Strained hip flexor (February 3, 1997); missed five games. ... Strained hip flexor (January 21, 1998); missed six games. ... Strained abdominal muscle and groin (February 25, 1998); missed 13 games. ... Charley horse (April 18, 1998); missed one game. ... Injured ribs (October 16, 1998); missed six games. ... Irritated nerve in neck (November 19, 1998); missed four games. ... Sprained ankle (March 8, 1999); missed three games. ... Suspended six games for high-sticking incident (April 1, 1999). ... Colitis (October 6, 1999); missed 10 games. ... Injured eye (March 16, 2000); missed two games. ... Signed as free agent by Toronto Maple Leafs (July 4, 2000). ... Injured (February 15, 2000); missed one game. ... Suffered injury (March 21, 2001); missed four games. ... Sprained shoulder (December 29, 2001); missed five games. ... Injured knee (April 1, 2002); missed three games. ... Suspended one playoff game for kicking incident (April 29, 2002). ... Injured groin (November 23, 2002); missed seven games. ... Reinjured groin (December 7, 2002); missed 17 games. ... Injured finger (February 15, 2003); missed eight games. ... Colitis (March 29, 2003); missed four games. ... Announced retirement (April 15, 2003). ... Signed as free agent by Dallas Stars (February 17, 2004).

STATISTICAL PLATEAUS: Three-goal games: 1988-89 (2), 1993-94 (1). Total: 3.

Season Team	League	REGULAR SEASON GP	G	A	Pts.	PIM	+/-	PP	SH	PLAYOFFS GP	G	A	Pts.	PIM
82-83—Barrie	COJHL	23	13	29	42	87	...	...	...	—	—	—	—	—
83-84—Brantford	OHL	66	25	46	71	165	...	...	...	6	4	1	5	26
84-85—Hamilton	OHL	54	27	63	90	154	...	...	...	11	3	7	10	19
85-86—Hamilton	OHL	47	41	57	98	153	...	...	...	—	—	—	—	—
—Montreal	NHL	3	0	0	0	2	-3	0	0	—	—	—	—	—
86-87—Montreal	NHL	55	12	11	23	144	10	0	1	17	6	5	11	30
87-88—Montreal	NHL	71	12	27	39	152	22	2	0	3	1	0	1	12
88-89—Montreal	NHL	80	26	24	50	193	-1	10	0	21	4	5	9	65
89-90—Montreal	NHL	76	31	44	75	144	33	7	0	11	2	8	10	20
90-91—Montreal	NHL	71	23	24	47	138	9	7	0	13	9	6	15	36
91-92—Montreal	NHL	64	17	36	53	118	15	3	0	10	2	5	7	15
92-93—Edmonton	NHL	80	16	31	47	209	-19	9	2	—	—	—	—	—
93-94—Edmonton	NHL	64	25	29	54	118	-8	11	0	—	—	—	—	—
94-95—Edmonton	NHL	48	12	24	36	86	-17	2	0	—	—	—	—	—
95-96—St. Louis	NHL	77	18	28	46	192	3	13	0	13	8	6	14	22
96-97—St. Louis	NHL	11	2	1	3	24	-4	1	0	—	—	—	—	—
—Montreal	NHL	47	6	15	21	80	-5	2	0	5	1	0	1	4
97-98—Montreal	NHL	62	21	34	55	108	2	14	1	10	3	6	9	26
—Can. Olympic team	Int'l	6	1	1	2	2	3	0	0	—	—	—	—	—
98-99—Montreal	NHL	63	12	20	32	147	-10	7	0	—	—	—	—	—
99-00—Montreal	NHL	70	8	20	28	115	-2	2	0	—	—	—	—	—
00-01—Toronto	NHL	77	8	18	26	189	1	0	0	11	1	1	2	14
01-02—Toronto	NHL	74	12	21	33	120	11	0	1	19	1	6	7	33
02-03—Toronto	NHL	46	7	8	15	49	-5	0	0	2	0	0	0	2
03-04—Dallas	NHL	17	5	5	10	29	12	0	1	5	0	1	1	12
NHL Totals (19 years)		1156	273	420	693	2357	44	90	6	140	38	49	87	291

CORVO, JOE — D — KINGS

PERSONAL: Born June 20, 1977, in Oak Park, Ill. ... 6-1/205. ... Shoots right.

TRANSACTIONS/CAREER NOTES: Selected by Los Angeles Kings in fourth round (fourth Kings pick, 83rd overall) of NHL entry draft (June 21, 1997). ... Missed 1999-2000 season in contract dispute. ... Suspended three games by Kings for off-ice issues (October 30, 2003).

Season Team	League	REGULAR SEASON GP	G	A	Pts.	PIM	+/-	PP	SH	PLAYOFFS GP	G	A	Pts.	PIM
95-96—Western Michigan	CCHA	41	5	25	30	38	...	...	...	—	—	—	—	—
96-97—Western Michigan	CCHA	32	12	21	33	85	...	...	...	—	—	—	—	—
97-98—Western Michigan	CCHA	32	5	12	17	93	...	...	...	—	—	—	—	—
98-99—Springfield	AHL	50	5	15	20	32	9	4	0	—	—	—	—	—
—Hampton Roads	ECHL	5	0	0	0	15	-1	0	0	4	0	1	1	0
99-00—Springfield	AHL	Did not play.												
00-01—Lowell	AHL	77	10	23	33	31	...	...	...	4	3	1	4	0
01-02—Manchester	AHL	80	13	37	50	30	6	7	0	5	0	5	5	0
02-03—Los Angeles	NHL	50	5	7	12	14	2	2	0	—	—	—	—	—
—Manchester	AHL	26	8	18	26	8	7	4	0	3	0	0	0	0
03-04—Los Angeles	NHL	72	8	17	25	36	7	0	0	—	—	—	—	—
04-05—Chicago	AHL	23	7	7	14	14	7	3	1	18	4	5	9	12
NHL Totals (2 years)		122	13	24	37	50	9	2	0					

COTE, JEAN-PHILIPPE — D — CANADIENS

PERSONAL: Born April 22, 1982, in Quebec City. ... 6-1/193. ... Shoots left. ... Son of Alain Cote, defenseman, Quebec Nordiques (1979-80 through 1988-89).

TRANSACTIONS/CAREER NOTES: Selected by Toronto Maple Leafs in ninth round (10th Maple Leafs pick, 265th overall) of NHL entry draft (June 25, 2000). ... Signed as free agent by Hamilton of the AHL (September 16, 2003). ... Signed as free agent by Montreal Canadiens (August 19, 2004).

Season Team	League	REGULAR SEASON GP	G	A	Pts.	PIM	+/-	PP	SH	PLAYOFFS GP	G	A	Pts.	PIM
98-99—Quebec	QMJHL	8	0	0	0	2	...	...	...	—	—	—	—	—
99-00—Quebec	QMJHL	34	0	10	10	15	...	...	...	—	—	—	—	—
—Cape Breton	QMJHL	28	0	4	4	21	...	...	...	4	0	1	1	4
00-01—Cape Breton	QMJHL	71	6	29	35	90	...	...	...	12	0	0	0	18
01-02—Cape Breton	QMJHL	61	4	20	24	72	...	...	...	16	1	6	7	38
02-03—Cape Breton	QMJHL	16	1	3	4	12	...	...	...	—	—	—	—	—
—Acadie-Bathurst	QMJHL	48	8	18	26	87	...	...	...	11	2	3	5	20
03-04—Hamilton	AHL	75	2	7	9	79	...	...	...	10	0	4	4	24
04-05—Hamilton	AHL	51	1	8	9	58	14	0	0	4	0	1	1	0
—Drummondville	QMJHL	24	0	0	0	14	-3	0	0	5	0	0	0	2
—Rouyn-Noranda	QMJHL	31	5	4	9	29	3	1	0	—	—	—	—	—

COWAN, JEFF — LW/RW — KINGS

PERSONAL: Born September 27, 1976, in Scarborough, Ont. ... 6-2/205. ... Shoots left. ... Name pronounced KOW-ihn.

TRANSACTIONS/CAREER NOTES: Signed as free agent by Calgary Flames (October 2, 1995). ... Injured (March 3, 2000); missed one game. ... Flu (March 25, 2000); missed final six games of season. ... Injured knee (February 10, 2001); missed 19 games. ... Reinjured knee (March 28, 2001); missed three games. ... Traded by Flames with D Kurtis Foster to Atlanta Thrashers for D Petr Buzek (December 18, 2001). ... Fractured hand (January 19, 2002); missed 10 games. ... Strained knee (November 2, 2002); missed seven games. ... Injured groin (December 27, 2002); missed two games. ... Suffered concussion (January 21, 2003); missed one game. ... Injured ribs (February 15, 2003); missed two games. ... Suffered concussion (December 16, 2003); missed four games. ... Post-concussion syndrome (December 31, 2003); missed six games. ... Traded by Thrashers to Los Angeles Kings for LW Kip Brennan (March 9, 2004).

Season Team	League	REGULAR SEASON GP	G	A	Pts.	PIM	+/-	PP	SH	PLAYOFFS GP	G	A	Pts.	PIM
92-93—Guelph	Jr. B	45	8	8	16	22	...	...	...	—	—	—	—	—
93-94—Guelph	Jr. B	43	30	26	56	96	...	...	...	—	—	—	—	—
—Guelph	OHL	17	1	0	1	5	...	...	...	0	0	0	0	0
94-95—Guelph	OHL	51	10	7	17	14	...	0	1	14	1	1	2	0
95-96—Barrie	OHL	66	38	14	52	29	...	...	...	5	1	2	3	6
96-97—Saint John	AHL	22	5	5	10	8	-8	1	1	—	—	—	—	—
—Roanoke	ECHL	47	21	13	34	42	...	...	...	—	—	—	—	—
97-98—Saint John	AHL	69	15	13	28	23	9	5	0	13	4	1	5	14
98-99—Saint John	AHL	71	7	12	19	117	-18	0	0	4	0	1	1	10
99-00—Saint John	AHL	47	15	10	25	77	...	...	...	—	—	—	—	—
—Calgary	NHL	13	4	1	5	16	2	0	0	—	—	—	—	—
00-01—Calgary	NHL	51	9	4	13	74	-8	2	0	—	—	—	—	—
01-02—Calgary	NHL	19	1	0	1	40	-3	0	0	—	—	—	—	—
—Atlanta	NHL	38	4	1	5	50	-11	0	0	—	—	—	—	—
02-03—Atlanta	NHL	66	3	5	8	115	-15	0	0	—	—	—	—	—
03-04—Atlanta	NHL	58	9	15	24	68	2	1	0	—	—	—	—	—
—Los Angeles	NHL	13	2	1	3	24	-1	1	0	—	—	—	—	—
NHL Totals (5 years)		258	32	27	59	387	-34	4	0					

CROSBY, SIDNEY — C — PENGUINS

PERSONAL: Born August 7, 1987, in Dartmouth, Nova Scotia. ... 5-11/193. ... Shoots left.

TRANSACTIONS/CAREER NOTES: Selected by Pittsburgh Penguins in 1st round (1st Penguins pick, 1st overall) of entry draft (July 30, 2005).

Season Team	League	REGULAR SEASON GP	G	A	Pts.	PIM	+/-	PP	SH	PLAYOFFS GP	G	A	Pts.	PIM
03-04—Rimouski	QMJHL	59	54	81	135	74	...	...	...	—	—	—	—	—
04-05—Rimouski	QMJHL	62	66	102	168	84	78	15	7	13	14	17	31	16

CROSS, CORY — D — OILERS

PERSONAL: Born January 3, 1971, in Lloydminster, Alta. ... 6-5/220. ... Shoots left.

TRANSACTIONS/CAREER NOTES: Selected by Tampa Bay Lightning in NHL supplemental draft (June 19, 1992). ... Injured foot (November 3, 1995); missed one game. ... Bruised right foot (November 10, 1996); missed five games. ... Flu (March 28, 1998); missed one game. ... Injured ankle (January 4, 1999); missed two games. ... Had hip pointer (January 30, 1999); missed 12 games. ... Traded by Lightning with seventh-round pick (F Ivan Kolozvary) in 2001 draft to Toronto Maple Leafs for RW Fredrik Modin (October 1, 1999). ... Injured (November 15, 1999); missed two games. ... Injured (March 29, 2000); missed two games. ... Injured (November 10, 2000); missed five games. ... Injured hip (November 29, 2000); missed 14 games. ... Injured foot (February 10, 2001); missed 12 games. ... Injured (March 20, 2001); missed five games. ... Injured groin (December 29, 2001); missed 19 games. ... Injured (March 12, 2002); missed one game. ... Signed as free agent by New York Rangers (December 17, 2002). ... Flu (January 13, 2003); missed one game. ... Back spasms (January 18, 2003); missed one game. ... Strained abdomen (February 5, 2003); missed six games. ... Traded by Rangers with RW Radek Dvorak to Edmonton Oilers for RW Anson Carter and D Ales Pisa (March 11, 2003). ... Injured shoulder (October 18, 2003); missed two games. ... Back spasms (December 28, 2003); missed five games. ... Fractured nose (January 17, 2004); missed one game. ... Injured back (March 26, 2004); missed two games. ... Back spasms (March 31, 2004); missed final two games of season.

		REGULAR SEASON								PLAYOFFS				
Season Team	League	GP	G	A	Pts.	PIM	+/-	PP	SH	GP	G	A	Pts.	PIM
90-91—Alberta	CIS	20	2	5	7	16	...	...	...	—	—	—	—	—
91-92—Alberta	CIS	39	3	10	13	76	...	...	...	—	—	—	—	—
92-93—Alberta	CIS	43	11	28	39	105	...	...	...	—	—	—	—	—
—Atlanta	IHL	7	0	1	1	2	4	0	0	4	0	0	0	6
93-94—Atlanta	IHL	70	4	14	18	72	13	0	0	9	1	2	3	14
—Tampa Bay	NHL	5	0	0	0	6	-3	0	0	—	—	—	—	—
94-95—Atlanta	IHL	41	5	10	15	67	10	1	0	—	—	—	—	—
—Tampa Bay	NHL	43	1	5	6	41	-6	0	0	—	—	—	—	—
95-96—Tampa Bay	NHL	75	2	14	16	66	4	0	0	6	0	0	0	22
96-97—Tampa Bay	NHL	72	4	5	9	95	6	0	0	—	—	—	—	—
97-98—Tampa Bay	NHL	74	3	6	9	77	-24	0	1	—	—	—	—	—
98-99—Tampa Bay	NHL	67	2	16	18	92	-25	0	0	—	—	—	—	—
99-00—Toronto	NHL	71	4	11	15	64	13	0	0	12	0	2	2	2
00-01—Toronto	NHL	41	3	5	8	50	7	1	0	11	2	1	3	10
01-02—Toronto	NHL	50	3	9	12	54	11	0	0	12	0	0	0	8
02-03—Hartford	AHL	2	0	0	0	2	0	0	0	—	—	—	—	—
—New York Rangers	NHL	26	0	4	4	16	13	0	0	—	—	—	—	—
—Edmonton	NHL	11	2	3	5	8	3	1	0	6	0	1	1	20
03-04—Edmonton	NHL	68	7	14	21	56	9	1	0	—	—	—	—	—
NHL Totals (11 years)		603	31	92	123	625	8	3	1	47	2	4	6	62

CULLEN, DAVID — D — SABRES

PERSONAL: Born December 30, 1976, in St. Catharines, Ont. ... 6-1/195. ... Shoots right.

TRANSACTIONS/CAREER NOTES: Signed as free agent by Phoenix Coyotes (April 8, 1999). ... Traded by Coyotes to Minnesota Wild for C Sebastien Bordeleau (January 4, 2002). ... Signed as free agent by Buffalo Sabres (July 1, 2003).

		REGULAR SEASON								PLAYOFFS				
Season Team	League	GP	G	A	Pts.	PIM	+/-	PP	SH	GP	G	A	Pts.	PIM
95-96—Maine	Hockey East	34	2	4	6	22	...	...	...	—	—	—	—	—
96-97—Maine	Hockey East	35	5	25	30	8	9	4	0	—	—	—	—	—
97-98—Maine	Hockey East	36	10	27	37	24	...	...	...	—	—	—	—	—
98-99—Maine	Hockey East	41	11	33	44	24	...	...	...	—	—	—	—	—
99-00—Springfield	AHL	78	10	21	31	57	...	...	...	2	0	0	0	2
00-01—Springfield	AHL	69	13	29	42	40	...	...	...	—	—	—	—	—
—Phoenix	NHL	2	0	0	0	0	1	0	0	—	—	—	—	—
01-02—Springfield	AHL	15	1	4	5	4	-9	0	0	—	—	—	—	—
—Phoenix	NHL	14	0	0	0	6	-5	0	0	—	—	—	—	—
—Houston	AHL	38	5	15	20	4	...	...	...	13	0	6	6	6
—Minnesota	NHL	3	0	0	0	0	-3	0	0	—	—	—	—	—
02-03—Houston	AHL	72	2	27	29	42	10	0	0	—	—	—	—	—
03-04—Rochester	AHL	75	12	35	47	26	-15	9	0	16	1	4	5	6
04-05—Rochester	AHL	43	2	19	21	25	-11	1	0	9	2	3	5	4
NHL Totals (2 years)		19	0	0	0	6	-7	0	0					

CULLEN, MATT — C — HURRICANES

PERSONAL: Born November 2, 1976, in Virginia, Minn. ... 6-2/218. ... Shoots left.

TRANSACTIONS/CAREER NOTES: Selected by Anaheim Mighty Ducks in second round (second Mighty Ducks pick, 35th overall) of NHL draft (June 22, 1996). ... Sprained ankle (December 16, 1998); missed one game. ... Traded by Mighty Ducks with D Pavel Trnka and fourth-round pick (D James Pemberton) in 2003 draft to Florida Panthers for D Sandis Ozolinsh and D Lance Ward (January 30, 2003). ... Injured groin (October 14, 2003); missed 14 games. ... Signed as free agent by Carolina Hurricanes (August 5, 2004).

		REGULAR SEASON								PLAYOFFS				
Season Team	League	GP	G	A	Pts.	PIM	+/-	PP	SH	GP	G	A	Pts.	PIM
94-95—Moorhead Senior	Minn. H.S.	28	47	42	89	78	...	...	...	—	—	—	—	—
95-96—St. Cloud State	WCHA	39	12	29	41	28	...	...	...	—	—	—	—	—
96-97—St. Cloud State	WCHA	36	15	30	45	70	...	4	3	—	—	—	—	—
—Baltimore	AHL	6	3	3	6	7	-4	1	0	3	0	2	2	0
97-98—Anaheim	NHL	61	6	21	27	23	-4	2	0	—	—	—	—	—
—Cincinnati	AHL	18	15	12	27	2	12	3	1	—	—	—	—	—
98-99—Anaheim	NHL	75	11	14	25	47	-12	5	1	4	0	0	0	0
—Cincinnati	AHL	3	1	2	3	8	1	0	0	—	—	—	—	—

Season Team	League	GP	G	A	Pts.	PIM	+/-	PP	SH	GP	G	A	Pts.	PIM
		REGULAR SEASON								PLAYOFFS				
99-00—Anaheim	NHL	80	13	26	39	24	5	1	0	—	—	—	—	—
00-01—Anaheim	NHL	82	10	30	40	38	-23	4	0	—	—	—	—	—
01-02—Anaheim	NHL	79	18	30	48	24	-1	3	1	—	—	—	—	—
02-03—Anaheim	NHL	50	7	14	21	12	-4	1	0	—	—	—	—	—
—Florida	NHL	30	6	6	12	22	-4	2	1	—	—	—	—	—
03-04—Florida	NHL	56	6	13	19	24	-2	1	0	—	—	—	—	—
04-05—Cortina	Italy	36	27	34	61	58	...	...	...	—	—	—	—	—
NHL Totals (7 years)		513	77	154	231	214	-45	19	3	4	0	0	0	0

CULLIMORE, JASSEN — D — BLACKHAWKS

PERSONAL: Born December 4, 1972, in Simcoe, Ont. ... 6-5/244. ... Shoots left. ... Name pronounced KUHL-ih-MOHR.

TRANSACTIONS/CAREER NOTES: Selected by Vancouver Canucks in second round (second Canucks pick, 29th overall) of NHL draft (June 22, 1991). ... Injured knee (March 31, 1995); missed three games. ... Traded by Canucks to Montreal Canadiens for LW Donald Brashear (November 13, 1996). ... Bruised eye (March 1, 1997); missed one game. ... Claimed off waivers by Tampa Bay Lightning (January 22, 1998). ... Sprained knee (April 4, 1998); missed final seven games of season. ... Injured neck (October 14, 1998); missed two games. ... Injured wrist (December 11, 1998); missed one game. ... Injured knee (April 2, 2000); missed final four games of season. ... Bruised hand (November 27, 2000); missed one game. ... Injured knee (January 10, 2001); missed one game. ... Injured shin (February 10, 2001); missed one game. ... Strained muscle in abdomen (March 8, 2001); missed two games. ... Sprained left ankle (October 30, 2001); missed two games. ... Bruised right thigh (February 9, 2002); missed one game. ... Injured shoulder (November 27, 2002) and had surgery (December 9, 2002); missed 54 games. ... Injured shoulder (February 26, 2004); missed three games. ... Injured wrist (April 14, 2004); missed 12 playoff games. ... Signed as free agent by Chicago Blackhawks (July 21, 2004).

Season Team	League	GP	G	A	Pts.	PIM	+/-	PP	SH	GP	G	A	Pts.	PIM
		REGULAR SEASON								PLAYOFFS				
88-89—Peterborough	OHL	20	2	1	3	6	...	...	...	—	—	—	—	—
—Peterborough	Jr. B	29	11	17	28	88	...	...	...	—	—	—	—	—
89-90—Peterborough	OHL	59	2	6	8	61	...	...	...	11	0	2	2	8
90-91—Peterborough	OHL	62	8	16	24	74	...	...	...	4	1	0	1	7
91-92—Peterborough	OHL	54	9	37	46	65	...	...	...	10	3	6	9	8
92-93—Hamilton	AHL	56	5	7	12	60	-16	2	0	—	—	—	—	—
93-94—Hamilton	AHL	71	8	20	28	86	-1	0	1	3	0	1	1	2
94-95—Syracuse	AHL	33	2	7	9	66	4	0	0	—	—	—	—	—
—Vancouver	NHL	34	1	2	3	39	-2	0	0	11	0	0	0	12
95-96—Vancouver	NHL	27	1	1	2	21	4	0	0	—	—	—	—	—
96-97—Vancouver	NHL	3	0	0	0	2	-2	0	0	—	—	—	—	—
—Montreal	NHL	49	2	6	8	42	4	0	1	2	0	0	0	2
97-98—Montreal	NHL	3	0	0	0	4	0	0	0	—	—	—	—	—
—Fredericton	AHL	5	1	0	1	8	5	0	0	—	—	—	—	—
—Tampa Bay	NHL	25	1	2	3	22	-4	1	0	—	—	—	—	—
98-99—Tampa Bay	NHL	78	5	12	17	81	-22	1	1	—	—	—	—	—
99-00—Providence	AHL	16	5	10	15	31	...	...	...	—	—	—	—	—
—Tampa Bay	NHL	46	1	1	2	66	-12	0	0	—	—	—	—	—
00-01—Tampa Bay	NHL	74	1	6	7	80	-6	0	0	—	—	—	—	—
01-02—Tampa Bay	NHL	78	4	9	13	58	-1	0	0	—	—	—	—	—
02-03—Tampa Bay	NHL	28	1	3	4	31	3	0	0	11	1	1	2	4
03-04—Tampa Bay	NHL	79	2	5	7	58	8	0	0	11	0	2	2	6
NHL Totals (10 years)		524	19	47	66	504	-30	2	2	35	1	3	4	24

CUMMINS, JIM — RW

PERSONAL: Born May 17, 1970, in Dearborn, Mich. ... 6-2/210. ... Shoots right. ... Name pronounced KUH-mihns.

TRANSACTIONS/CAREER NOTES: Selected by New York Rangers in fourth round (fifth Rangers pick, 67th overall) of NHL draft (June 17, 1989). ... Traded by Rangers with LW Kevin Miller and D Dennis Vial to Detroit Red Wings for RW Joe Kocur and D Per Djoos (March 5, 1991). ... Suspended 11 games for leaving penalty box to join fight (January 23, 1993). ... Traded by Red Wings with fourth-round pick (traded to Boston) in 1993 entry draft to Philadelphia Flyers for rights to C Greg Johnson and fifth-round pick (G Frederic Deschene) in 1994 entry draft (June 20, 1993). ... Separated shoulder during 1993-94 season. ... Traded by Flyers with fourth-round pick in 1995 entry draft to Tampa Bay Lightning for C Rob DiMaio (March 18, 1994). ... Traded by Lightning with D Jeff Buchanan and D Tom Tilley to Chicago Blackhawks for LW Paul Ysebaert and RW Rich Sutter (February 22, 1995). ... Sprained triceps (March 16, 1995); missed five games. ... Fractured thumb (November 1, 1995); missed 16 games. ... Suspended eight games and fined $1,000 for cross-checking and punching another player (March 14, 1996). ... Bruised clavicle (December 9, 1996); missed 11 games. ... Suspended one game by NHL for third game misconduct of season (January 23, 1997). ... Flu (November 11, 1997); missed three games. ... Traded by Blackhawks with D Keith Carney to Phoenix Coyotes for C Chad Kilger and D Jayson More (March 4, 1998). ... Suspended five games for elbowing incident (February 8, 1999). ... Traded by Coyotes to Montreal Canadiens for sixth-round pick (D Erik Lewerstrom) in 1999 draft (June 26, 1999). ... Suffered concussion (September 12, 1999); missed first two games of season. ... Separated shoulder (December 20, 1999); missed three games. ... Sprained ankle (January 24, 2000); missed 22 games. ... Signed as free agent by Anaheim Mighty Ducks (July 5, 2000). ... Traded by Mighty Ducks to New York Islanders for LW Dave Roche (January 17, 2002). ... Did not play, 2002-03 season. ... Signed as free agent by Colorado Avalanche (September 17, 2003). ... Injured neck (January 7, 2004); missed five games.

Season Team	League	GP	G	A	Pts.	PIM	+/-	PP	SH	GP	G	A	Pts.	PIM
		REGULAR SEASON								PLAYOFFS				
87-88—Detroit	NAJHL	31	11	15	26	146	...	...	...	—	—	—	—	—
88-89—Michigan State	CCHA	36	3	9	12	100	...	...	...	—	—	—	—	—
89-90—Michigan State	CCHA	41	8	7	15	94	...	...	...	—	—	—	—	—
90-91—Michigan State	CCHA	34	9	6	15	110	...	...	...	—	—	—	—	—
91-92—Adirondack	AHL	65	7	13	20	338	...	...	...	5	0	0	0	19
—Detroit	NHL	1	0	0	0	7	0	0	0	—	—	—	—	—
92-93—Adirondack	AHL	43	16	4	20	179	-3	2	0	9	3	1	4	4
—Detroit	NHL	7	1	1	2	58	0	0	0	—	—	—	—	—

		REGULAR SEASON								PLAYOFFS				
Season Team	League	GP	G	A	Pts.	PIM	+/-	PP	SH	GP	G	A	Pts.	PIM
93-94—Philadelphia	NHL	22	1	2	3	71	0	0	0	—	—	—	—	—
—Hershey	AHL	17	6	6	12	70	-4	0	0	—	—	—	—	—
—Atlanta	IHL	7	4	5	9	14	-1	1	0	13	1	2	3	90
—Tampa Bay	NHL	4	0	0	0	13	-1	0	0	—	—	—	—	—
94-95—Tampa Bay	NHL	10	1	0	1	41	-3	0	0	—	—	—	—	—
—Chicago	NHL	27	3	1	4	117	-3	0	0	14	1	1	2	4
95-96—Chicago	NHL	52	2	4	6	180	-1	0	0	10	0	0	0	2
96-97—Chicago	NHL	65	6	6	12	199	4	0	0	6	0	0	0	24
97-98—Chicago	NHL	55	0	2	2	178	-9	0	0	—	—	—	—	—
—Phoenix	NHL	20	0	0	0	47	-7	0	0	3	0	0	0	4
98-99—Phoenix	NHL	55	1	7	8	190	3	0	0	3	0	1	1	0
99-00—Montreal	NHL	47	3	5	8	92	-5	0	0	—	—	—	—	—
00-01—Anaheim	NHL	79	5	6	11	167	-11	0	0	—	—	—	—	—
01-02—Anaheim	NHL	2	0	0	0	0	-1	0	0	—	—	—	—	—
—Cincinnati	AHL	11	1	4	5	39	5	0	0	—	—	—	—	—
—New York Islanders	NHL	10	0	0	0	31	-5	0	0	1	0	0	0	9
02-03—	Did not play													
03-04—Colorado	NHL	55	1	2	3	147	-5	0	0	—	—	—	—	—
NHL Totals (12 years)		511	24	36	60	1538	-44	0	0	37	1	2	3	43

CUTTA, JAKUB D CAPITALS

PERSONAL: Born December 29, 1981, in Jablonec nad Nisou, Czech. ... 6-3/208. ... Shoots left.
TRANSACTIONS/CAREER NOTES: Selected by Washington Capitals in second round (third Capitals pick, 61st overall) of NHL draft (June 24, 2000).

		REGULAR SEASON								PLAYOFFS				
Season Team	League	GP	G	A	Pts.	PIM	+/-	PP	SH	GP	G	A	Pts.	PIM
98-99—Swift Current	WHL	59	3	3	6	63	...	...	...	—	—	—	—	—
99-00—Swift Current	WHL	71	2	12	14	114	...	...	...	12	0	2	2	24
00-01—Washington	NHL	3	0	0	0	0	-1	0	0	—	—	—	—	—
—Swift Current	WHL	47	5	8	13	102	...	...	...	16	1	3	4	32
01-02—Portland	AHL	56	1	3	4	69	2	0	0	—	—	—	—	—
—Washington	NHL	2	0	0	0	0	-3	0	0	—	—	—	—	—
02-03—Portland	AHL	66	3	12	15	106	5	2	0	3	0	0	0	2
03-04—Washington	NHL	3	0	0	0	0	-1	0	0	—	—	—	—	—
—Portland	AHL	59	1	5	6	58	-11	0	0	7	2	0	2	7
04-05—Portland	AHL	63	0	5	5	100	-11	0	0	—	—	—	—	—
NHL Totals (3 years)		8	0	0	0	0	-5	0	0					

CZERKAWSKI, MARIUSZ RW

PERSONAL: Born April 13, 1972, in Radomsko, Poland. ... 6-0/200. ... Shoots right. ... Name pronounced MAIR-ee-uhz chuhr-KAW-skee.
TRANSACTIONS/CAREER NOTES: Selected by Boston Bruins (fifth Bruins pick, 106th overall) of NHL draft (June 22, 1991). ... Traded by Bruins with D Sean Brown and first-round pick (D Mathieu Descoteaux) in 1996 draft to Edmonton Oilers for G Bill Ranford (January 11, 1996). ... Injured finger (March 23, 1996); missed two games. ... Had hip pointer (January 11, 1997); missed two games. ... Traded by Oilers to New York Islanders for LW Dan LaCouture (August 25, 1997). ... Strained rib cage muscle (December 15, 1999); missed three games. ... Traded by Islanders to Montreal Canadiens for RW/C Aaron Asham and fifth-round pick (W Markus Pahlsson) in 2002 draft (June 22, 2002). ... Signed as free agent by New York Islanders (July 17, 2003). ... Irregular heartbeat (December 2, 2003); missed one game.
STATISTICAL PLATEAUS: Three-goal games: 1996-97 (2), 1999-00 (1), 2001-02 (1). Total: 4.

		REGULAR SEASON								PLAYOFFS				
Season Team	League	GP	G	A	Pts.	PIM	+/-	PP	SH	GP	G	A	Pts.	PIM
90-91—GKS Tychy	Poland	24	25	15	40	...	...	...	...	—	—	—	—	—
91-92—Djurgarden Stockholm	Sweden	39	8	5	13	4	...	...	...	3	0	0	0	2
—Polish Olympic Team	Int'l	5	0	1	1	4	-6	0	0	—	—	—	—	—
92-93—Hammarby	Sweden Dv. 2	32	39	30	69	74	...	...	...	—	—	—	—	—
93-94—Djurgarden Stockholm	Sweden	39	13	21	34	20	...	...	...	—	—	—	—	—
—Boston	NHL	4	2	1	3	0	-2	1	0	13	3	3	6	4
94-95—Kiekko-Espoo	Finland	7	9	3	12	10	-1	...	...	—	—	—	—	—
—Boston	NHL	47	12	14	26	31	4	1	0	5	1	0	1	0
95-96—Boston	NHL	33	5	6	11	10	-11	1	0	—	—	—	—	—
—Edmonton	NHL	37	12	17	29	8	7	2	0	—	—	—	—	—
96-97—Edmonton	NHL	76	26	21	47	16	0	4	0	12	2	1	3	10
97-98—New York Islanders	NHL	68	12	13	25	23	11	2	0	—	—	—	—	—
98-99—New York Islanders	NHL	78	21	17	38	14	-10	4	0	—	—	—	—	—
99-00—New York Islanders	NHL	79	35	35	70	34	-16	16	0	—	—	—	—	—
00-01—New York Islanders	NHL	82	30	32	62	48	-24	10	1	—	—	—	—	—
01-02—New York Islanders	NHL	82	22	29	51	48	-8	6	0	7	2	2	4	4
02-03—Montreal	NHL	43	5	9	14	16	-7	1	0	—	—	—	—	—
—Hamilton	AHL	20	8	12	20	12	0	3	0	6	1	3	4	6
03-04—New York Islanders	NHL	81	25	24	49	16	8	9	0	5	0	1	1	0
04-05—Djurgarden Stockholm	Sweden	46	15	9	24	20	-10	4	0	5	1	0	1	2
NHL Totals (11 years)		710	207	218	425	264	-48	57	1	42	8	7	15	18

DACKELL, ANDREAS RW

PERSONAL: Born December 29, 1972, in Gavle, Sweden. ... 5-11/192. ... Shoots right. ... Name pronounced AHN-dray-uhz DA-kuhl.
TRANSACTIONS/CAREER NOTES: Selected by Ottawa Senators in sixth round (third Senators pick, 136th overall) of NHL draft (June 22, 1996). ... Suffered concussion (October 29, 1998); missed four games. ... Injured knee (January 14, 1999); missed one game. ... Flu (November 18,

2000); missed one game. ... Traded by Senators to Montreal Canadiens for eighth-round pick (D Neil Petruic) in 2001 draft (June 24, 2001). ... Flu (January 4, 2002); missed one game. ... Injured knee (January 13, 2004); missed two games. ... Reinjured knee (January 23, 2004); missed 10 games. ... Signed as free agent by Brynas of Swedish league (May 14, 2004).

STATISTICAL PLATEAUS: Three-goal games: 2000-01 (1).

		REGULAR SEASON								PLAYOFFS				
Season Team	**League**	**GP**	**G**	**A**	**Pts.**	**PIM**	**+/-**	**PP**	**SH**	**GP**	**G**	**A**	**Pts.**	**PIM**
90-91—Brynas Gavle	Sweden	3	0	1	1	2	...	...	...	—	—	—	—	—
91-92—Brynas Gavle	Sweden	4	0	0	0	2	...	...	...	2	0	1	1	4
92-93—Brynas Gavle	Sweden	40	12	15	27	12	...	...	...	10	4	5	9	2
93-94—Brynas Gavle	Sweden	38	12	17	29	47	...	...	...	7	2	2	4	8
94-95—Brynas Gavle	Sweden	39	17	16	33	34	...	...	...	14	3	3	6	14
95-96—Brynas Gavle	Sweden	22	6	6	12	8	...	...	...	—	—	—	—	—
96-97—Ottawa	NHL	79	12	19	31	8	-6	2	0	7	1	0	1	0
97-98—Ottawa	NHL	82	15	18	33	24	-11	3	2	11	1	1	2	2
98-99—Ottawa	NHL	77	15	35	50	30	9	6	0	4	0	1	1	0
99-00—Ottawa	NHL	82	10	25	35	18	5	0	0	6	2	1	3	2
00-01—Ottawa	NHL	81	13	18	31	24	7	1	0	4	0	0	0	0
01-02—Montreal	NHL	79	15	18	33	24	-3	2	3	12	1	2	3	6
02-03—Montreal	NHL	73	7	18	25	24	-5	0	0	—	—	—	—	—
03-04—Montreal	NHL	60	4	8	12	10	8	0	0	—	—	—	—	—
04-05—Brynas IF	Sweden	40	9	13	22	48	-13	2	2	10	2	6	8	8
NHL Totals (8 years)		613	91	159	250	162	4	14	5	44	5	5	10	10

DAFOE, BYRON G THRASHERS

PERSONAL: Born February 25, 1971, in Sussex, England. ... 5-11/185. ... Catches left.

TRANSACTIONS/CAREER NOTES: Selected by Washington Capitals in second round (second Capitals pick, 35th overall) of NHL draft (June 17, 1989). ... Traded by Capitals with RW Dimitri Khristich to Los Angeles Kings for first-(C Alexander Volchkov) and fourth-round (RW Justin Davis) picks in 1996 draft (July 8, 1995). ... Strained thumb (February 1, 1997); missed two games. ... Traded by Kings with RW Dimitri Khristich to Boston Bruins for C Jozef Stumpel, RW Sandy Moger and fourth-round pick (traded to New Jersey) in 1998 draft (August 29, 1997). ... Injured knee (February 21, 2000) and had surgery; missed remainder of season. ... Injured hamstring (October 13, 2000); missed 11 games. ... Injured knee (November 22, 2000); missed 11 games. ... Strained hamstring (February 10, 2001); missed 13 games. ... Injured groin (December 23, 2002); missed four games. ... Reinjured groin (January 3, 2003); missed two games. ... Reinjured groin (January 15, 2003); missed six games. ... Reinjured groin (February 17, 2003); missed 25 games. ... Suffered concussion (January 31, 2004); missed two games. ... Injured back (February 19, 2004); missed final 21 games of season.

		REGULAR SEASON									PLAYOFFS							
Season Team	**League**	**GP**	**Min.**	**W**	**L**	**T**	**GA**	**SO**	**GAA**	**SV%**	**GP**	**Min.**	**W**	**L**	**GA**	**SO**	**GAA**	**SV%**
87-88—Juan de Fuca	BCJHL	32	1716	...	...	...	129	0	4.51	...	—	—	—	—	—	—	—	—
88-89—Portland	WHL	59	3279	29	24	3	*291	1	5.32	...	*18	*1091	10	8	*81	*1	4.45	...
89-90—Portland	WHL	40	2265	14	21	3	193	0	5.11	...	—	—	—	—	—	—	—	—
90-91—Portland	WHL	8	414	1	5	1	41	0	5.94	...	—	—	—	—	—	—	—	—
—Prince Albert	WHL	32	1839	13	12	4	124	0	4.05	...	—	—	—	—	—	—	—	—
91-92—New Haven	AHL	7	364	3	2	1	22	0	3.63	...	—	—	—	—	—	—	—	—
—Baltimore	AHL	33	1847	12	16	4	119	0	3.87	...	—	—	—	—	—	—	—	—
—Hampton Roads	ECHL	10	562	6	4	0	26	1	2.78	...	—	—	—	—	—	—	—	—
92-93—Baltimore	AHL	48	2617	16	*20	7	191	1	4.38	.865	5	241	2	3	22	0	5.48	.873
—Washington	NHL	1	1	0	0	0	0	0	0.00	...	—	—	—	—	—	—	—	—
93-94—Portland	AHL	47	2662	24	16	4	148	1	3.34	.891	1	9	0	0	1	0	6.67	.857
—Washington	NHL	5	230	2	2	0	13	0	3.39	.871	2	118	0	2	5	0	2.54	.872
94-95—Portland	AHL	6	330	5	0	0	16	0	2.91	.920	7	417	3	4	29	0	4.17	.877
—Phoenix	IHL	49	2744	25	16	6	169	2	3.70	.889	—	—	—	—	—	—	—	—
—Washington	NHL	4	187	1	1	1	11	0	3.53	.863	1	20	0	0	1	0	3.00	.667
95-96—Los Angeles	NHL	47	2666	14	24	8	172	1	3.87	.888	—	—	—	—	—	—	—	—
96-97—Los Angeles	NHL	40	2162	13	17	5	112	0	3.11	.905	—	—	—	—	—	—	—	—
97-98—Boston	NHL	65	3693	30	25	9	138	6	2.24	.914	6	422	2	4	14	1	1.99	.912
98-99—Boston	NHL	68	4001	32	23	11	133	*10	1.99	.926	12	768	6	6	26	2	2.03	.921
99-00—Boston	NHL	41	2307	13	16	10	114	3	2.96	.889	—	—	—	—	—	—	—	—
00-01—Boston	NHL	45	2536	22	14	7	101	2	2.39	.906	—	—	—	—	—	—	—	—
01-02—Boston	NHL	64	3827	35	26	3	141	4	2.21	.907	6	358	2	4	19	0	3.18	.865
02-03—Atlanta	NHL	17	895	5	11	1	65	0	4.36	.862	—	—	—	—	—	—	—	—
03-04—Atlanta	NHL	18	973	4	11	1	51	0	3.14	.898	—	—	—	—	—	—	—	—
NHL Totals (12 years)		415	23478	171	170	56	1051	26	2.69	.904	27	1686	10	16	65	3	2.31	.903

DAGENAIS, PIERRE RW/LW CANADIENS

PERSONAL: Born March 3, 1978, in Blainville, Que. ... 6-5/215. ... Shoots left. ... Name pronounced da-zhih-NAY.

TRANSACTIONS/CAREER NOTES: Selected by New Jersey Devils in second round (fourth Devils pick, 47th overall) of NHL draft (June 22, 1996). ... Returned to draft pool by Devils; selected by Devils in fourth round (sixth Devils pick, 105th overall) of draft (June 27, 1998). ... Claimed on waivers by Florida Panthers (January 12, 2002). ... Injured ankle (April 10, 2002); missed remainder of season. ... Signed as free agent by Montreal Canadiens (July 3, 2003). ... Suspended two games for high-sticking (January 24, 2004).

		REGULAR SEASON								PLAYOFFS				
Season Team	**League**	**GP**	**G**	**A**	**Pts.**	**PIM**	**+/-**	**PP**	**SH**	**GP**	**G**	**A**	**Pts.**	**PIM**
95-96—Moncton	QMJHL	67	43	25	68	59	...	...	...	—	—	—	—	—
96-97—Moncton	QMJHL	6	4	2	6	0	...	...	...	—	—	—	—	—
—Laval	QMJHL	37	16	14	30	40	...	...	...	—	—	—	—	—
—Rouyn-Noranda	QMJHL	27	21	8	29	22	...	...	...	—	—	—	—	—
97-98—Rouyn-Noranda	QMJHL	60	*66	67	133	50	...	...	...	6	6	2	8	2

Season Team	League	REGULAR SEASON GP	G	A	Pts.	PIM	+/-	PP	SH	PLAYOFFS GP	G	A	Pts.	PIM
98-99—Albany	AHL	69	17	13	30	37	-2	3	0	4	0	0	0	0
99-00—Albany	AHL	80	35	30	65	47	...	...	...	5	1	0	1	14
00-01—Albany	AHL	69	34	28	62	52	...	...	...	—	—	—	—	—
—New Jersey	NHL	9	3	2	5	6	1	1	0	—	—	—	—	—
01-02—New Jersey	NHL	16	3	3	6	4	-5	1	0	—	—	—	—	—
—Albany	AHL	6	0	2	2	2	0	0	0	—	—	—	—	—
—Florida	NHL	26	7	1	8	4	-5	2	0	—	—	—	—	—
—Utah	AHL	4	1	1	2	2	...	...	...	—	—	—	—	—
02-03—Florida	NHL	9	0	0	0	4	-1	0	0	—	—	—	—	—
—San Antonio	AHL	49	21	14	35	28	4	7	3	3	2	0	2	2
03-04—Montreal	NHL	50	17	10	27	24	15	4	0	8	0	1	1	6
—Hamilton	AHL	20	12	9	21	19	4	4	0	—	—	—	—	—
04-05—Ajoie	Switz. Div. 2	7	5	5	10	12	...	4	0	6	7	7	14	6
NHL Totals (4 years)		110	30	16	46	42	5	8	0	8	0	1	1	6

DAIGLE, ALEXANDRE RW/LW WILD

PERSONAL: Born February 7, 1975, in Montreal. ... 6-0/203. ... Shoots left. ... Name pronounced DAYG.

TRANSACTIONS/CAREER NOTES: Selected by Ottawa Senators in first round (first Senators pick, first overall) of NHL draft (June 26, 1993). ... Fractured left forearm (February 3, 1996); missed remainder of season. ... Traded by Senators to Flyers for C Vaclav Prospal, RW Pat Falloon and second round pick (LW Chris Bala) in 1998 draft (January 17, 1998). ... Had concussion (October 29, 1998); missed two games. ... Strained left groin (November 14, 1998); missed one game. ... Traded by Flyers to Edmonton Oilers for RW Andrei Kovalenko (January 29, 1999). ... Traded by Oilers to Tampa Bay Lightning for RW Alexander Selivanov (January 29, 1999). ... Injured wrist (March 19, 1999); missed one game. ... Reinjured wrist (March 31, 1999); missed one game. ... Traded by Lightning to New York Rangers for cash (October 3, 1999). ... Did not play in 2000-01 and 2001-02 seasons. ... Signed as free agent by Pittsburgh Penguins (October 4, 2002). ... Signed as free agent by Minnesota Wild (September 30, 2003). ... Flu (December 9, 2003); missed one game.

STATISTICAL PLATEAUS: Three-goal games: 1994-95 (1), 1997-98 (1). Total: 2.

Season Team	League	REGULAR SEASON GP	G	A	Pts.	PIM	+/-	PP	SH	PLAYOFFS GP	G	A	Pts.	PIM
91-92—Victoriaville	QMJHL	66	35	75	110	63	...	...	...	—	—	—	—	—
92-93—Victoriaville	QMJHL	53	45	92	137	85	...	...	...	6	5	6	11	4
93-94—Ottawa	NHL	84	20	31	51	40	-45	4	0	—	—	—	—	—
94-95—Victoriaville	QMJHL	18	14	20	34	16	...	...	...	—	—	—	—	—
—Ottawa	NHL	47	16	21	37	14	-22	4	1	—	—	—	—	—
95-96—Ottawa	NHL	50	5	12	17	24	-30	1	0	—	—	—	—	—
96-97—Ottawa	NHL	82	26	25	51	33	-33	4	0	7	0	0	0	2
97-98—Ottawa	NHL	38	7	9	16	8	-7	4	0	—	—	—	—	—
—Philadelphia	NHL	37	9	17	26	6	-1	4	0	5	0	2	2	0
98-99—Philadelphia	NHL	31	3	2	5	2	-1	1	0	—	—	—	—	—
—Tampa Bay	NHL	32	6	6	12	2	-12	3	0	—	—	—	—	—
99-00—Hartford	AHL	16	6	13	19	4	...	...	...	—	—	—	—	—
—New York Rangers	NHL	58	8	18	26	23	-5	1	0	—	—	—	—	—
02-03—Wilkes-Barre/Scranton	AHL	40	9	29	38	18	-10	3	2	4	0	1	1	0
—Pittsburgh	NHL	33	4	3	7	8	-10	1	0	—	—	—	—	—
03-04—Minnesota	NHL	78	20	31	51	14	-4	6	0	—	—	—	—	—
04-05—Morges	Switzerland	—	—	—	—	—	—	—	—	2	1	1	2	0
NHL Totals (9 years)		570	124	175	299	174	-170	33	1	12	0	2	2	2

DAIGNEAULT, MAXIME G CAPITALS

PERSONAL: Born January 23, 1984, in St-Jacques-Le-Mineur, Que. ... 6-1/194. ... Catches left. ... Name pronounced DAYN-yoh.

TRANSACTIONS/CAREER NOTES: Selected by Washington Capitals in second round (fourth Capitals pick, 59th overall) of NHL entry draft (June 22, 2002).

Season Team	League	REGULAR SEASON GP	Min.	W	L	T	GA	SO	GAA	SV%	PLAYOFFS GP	Min.	W	L	GA	SO	GAA	SV%
00-01—Val-d'Or	QMJHL	28	1386	14	8	1	82	0	3.55	...	10	504	8	1	21	0	2.50	...
01-02—Val-d'Or	QMJHL	61	3270	25	27	5	184	3	3.38	...	7	431	3	4	23	0	3.20	...
02-03—Val-d'Or	QMJHL	67	2694	23	18	3	138	2	3.07	...	—	—	—	—	—	—	—	—
03-04—Val-d'Or	QMJHL	57	3249	23	22	9	158	2	2.92	...	—	—	—	—	—	—	—	—
04-05—Portland	AHL	11	473	3	2	...	23	0	2.92	.906	—	—	—	—	—	—	—	—
—South Carolina	ECHL	21	1172	11	6	...	59	1	3.02	.904	—	—	—	—	—	—	—	—

DALEY, TREVOR D STARS

PERSONAL: Born October 9, 1983, in Toronto. ... 5-9/197. ... Shoots left.

TRANSACTIONS/CAREER NOTES: Selected by Dallas Stars in second round (fifth Stars pick, 43rd overall) of NHL entry draft (June 22, 2002).

Season Team	League	REGULAR SEASON GP	G	A	Pts.	PIM	+/-	PP	SH	PLAYOFFS GP	G	A	Pts.	PIM
99-00—Sault Ste. Marie	OHL	54	16	30	46	77	...	...	...	15	3	7	10	12
00-01—Sault Ste. Marie	OHL	58	14	27	41	105	...	...	...	—	—	—	—	—
01-02—Sault Ste. Marie	OHL	47	9	39	48	38	...	...	...	6	2	2	4	4
02-03—Sault Ste. Marie	OHL	57	20	33	53	128	...	...	...	1	0	0	0	2
03-04—Dallas	NHL	27	1	5	6	14	-6	1	0	1	0	0	0	0
—Utah	AHL	40	8	6	14	76	-22	3	0	—	—	—	—	—
04-05—Hamilton	AHL	78	7	27	34	109	-4	4	0	4	0	1	1	2
NHL Totals (1 year)		27	1	5	6	14	-6	1	0	1	0	0	0	0

DAMPHOUSSE, J.F. — G — CANADIENS

PERSONAL: Born July 21, 1979, in St. Alexis-des-Monts, Que. ... 6-0/175. ... Catches left. ... Name pronounced dahm-FOOZ.

TRANSACTIONS/CAREER NOTES: Selected by New Jersey Devils in first round (first Devils pick, 24th overall) of NHL entry draft (June 21, 1997). ... Traded by Devils with RW Petr Sykora, C Igor Pohanka and D Mike Commodore to Anaheim Mighty Ducks for D Oleg Tverdovsky, LW Jeff Friesen and RW Maxin Balmochnykh (July 7, 2002). ... Traded by Mighty Ducks with D Mike Commodore to Calgary Flames for C Rob Niedermayer (March 11, 2003). ... Signed as free agent by Montreal Canadiens (July 3, 2003).

		REGULAR SEASON									PLAYOFFS							
Season Team	League	GP	Min.	W	L	T	GA	SO	GAA	SV%	GP	Min.	W	L	GA	SO	GAA	SV%
96-97—Moncton	QMJHL	39	2063	6	25	2	190	0	5.53	...	—	—	—	—	—	—	—	—
97-98—Moncton	QMJHL	59	3400	24	26	*6	174	1	3.07	.893	10	595	5	5	28	0	2.82	.897
98-99—Moncton	QMJHL	40	2163	19	17	2	121	1	3.36	...	4	200	0	4	12	0	3.60	...
—Albany	AHL	1	59	0	1	0	3	0	3.05	.893	—	—	—	—	—	—	—	—
99-00—Albany	AHL	26	1326	9	11	2	62	0	2.81	...	2	62	0	1	4	0	3.87	...
—Augusta	ECHL	14	676	6	7	0	49	0	4.35	...	—	—	—	—	—	—	—	—
00-01—Albany	AHL	55	2963	24	23	3	141	1	2.86	.914	—	—	—	—	—	—	—	—
01-02—Albany	AHL	18	1000	3	11	2	57	0	3.42	.892	—	—	—	—	—	—	—	—
—New Jersey	NHL	6	294	1	3	0	12	0	2.45	.896	—	—	—	—	—	—	—	—
02-03—Cincinnati	AHL	31	1668	12	14	4	87	0	3.13	.902	—	—	—	—	—	—	—	—
—Saint John	AHL	10	591	5	5	0	23	0	2.34	.911	—	—	—	—	—	—	—	—
03-04—Hamilton	AHL	35	2009	19	11	4	77	2	2.30	.904	10	591	4	6	25	1	2.54	.905
NHL Totals (1 year)		6	294	1	3	0	12	0	2.45	.896								

DAMPHOUSSE, VINCENT — C/LW — AVALANCHE

PERSONAL: Born December 17, 1967, in Montreal. ... 6-1/205. ... Shoots left. ... Name pronounced dahm-FOOZ.

TRANSACTIONS/CAREER NOTES: Selected by Toronto Maple Leafs in first round (first Maple Leafs pick, sixth overall) of NHL draft (June 21, 1986). ... Traded by Maple Leafs with D Luke Richardson, G Peter Ing, C Scott Thornton to Edmonton Oilers for G Grant Fuhr, LW//RW Glenn Anderson and LW Craig Berube (September 19, 1991). ... Traded by Oilers with fourth-round pick (D Adam Wiesel) in 1993 draft to Montreal Canadiens for LW Shayne Corson, LW Vladimir Vujtek and C Brent Gilchrist (August 27, 1992). ... Suspended two games and fined $1,000 for cross-checking incident (March 30, 1996). ... Partially dislocated left shoulder (March 11, 1998); missed six games. ... Back spasms (November 27, 1998); missed five games. ... Traded by Canadiens to San Jose Sharks for fifth-round pick (RW Marc-Andre Thinel) in 1999 draft and first-round pick (C Marcel Hossa) in 2000 draft (March 23, 1999). ... Injured shoulder (January 15, 2001); missed 36 games. ... Signed as free agent by Colorado Avalanche (August 18, 2004).

STATISTICAL PLATEAUS: Three-goal games: 1988-89 (1), 1989-90 (2), 1992-93 (2), 1993-94 (2), 1996-97 (1), 1997-98 (2), 1998-99 (1). Total: 11. ... Four-goal games: 1991-92 (1). ... Total hat tricks: 12.

		REGULAR SEASON								PLAYOFFS				
Season Team	League	GP	G	A	Pts.	PIM	+/-	PP	SH	GP	G	A	Pts.	PIM
83-84—Laval	QMJHL	66	29	36	65	25	...	...	...	—	—	—	—	—
84-85—Laval	QMJHL	68	35	68	103	62	...	...	...	—	—	—	—	—
85-86—Laval	QMJHL	69	45	110	155	70	...	...	...	14	9	27	36	12
86-87—Toronto	NHL	80	21	25	46	26	-6	4	0	12	1	5	6	8
87-88—Toronto	NHL	75	12	36	48	40	2	1	0	6	0	1	1	10
88-89—Toronto	NHL	80	26	42	68	75	-8	6	0	—	—	—	—	—
89-90—Toronto	NHL	80	33	61	94	56	2	9	0	5	0	2	2	2
90-91—Toronto	NHL	79	26	47	73	65	-31	10	1	—	—	—	—	—
91-92—Edmonton	NHL	80	38	51	89	53	10	12	1	16	6	8	14	8
92-93—Montreal	NHL	84	39	58	97	98	5	9	3	20	11	12	23	16
93-94—Montreal	NHL	84	40	51	91	75	0	13	0	7	1	2	3	8
94-95—Ratingen	Germany	11	5	6	11	24	...	...	...	—	—	—	—	—
—Montreal	NHL	48	10	30	40	42	15	4	0	—	—	—	—	—
95-96—Montreal	NHL	80	38	56	94	158	5	11	4	6	4	4	8	0
96-97—Montreal	NHL	82	27	54	81	82	-6	7	2	5	0	0	0	2
97-98—Montreal	NHL	76	18	41	59	58	14	2	1	10	3	6	9	22
98-99—Montreal	NHL	65	12	24	36	46	-7	3	2	—	—	—	—	—
—San Jose	NHL	12	7	6	13	4	3	3	0	6	3	2	5	6
99-00—San Jose	NHL	82	21	49	70	58	4	3	1	12	1	7	8	16
00-01—San Jose	NHL	45	9	37	46	62	17	4	0	6	2	1	3	14
01-02—San Jose	NHL	82	20	38	58	60	8	7	2	12	2	6	8	12
02-03—San Jose	NHL	82	23	38	61	66	-13	15	0	—	—	—	—	—
03-04—San Jose	NHL	82	12	29	41	66	-5	7	0	17	7	7	14	20
NHL Totals (18 years)		1378	432	773	1205	1190	9	130	17	140	41	63	104	144

DANDENAULT, MATHIEU — D/LW — CANADIENS

PERSONAL: Born February 3, 1976, in Sherbrooke, Que. ... 6-1/200. ... Shoots right. ... Cousin of Eric Dandenault, D with Philadelphia Flyers organization (1991-94). ... Name pronounced DAN-dih-noh.

TRANSACTIONS/CAREER NOTES: Selected by Detroit Red Wings in 2nd round (2nd Red Wings pick, 49th overall) of entry draft (June 28, 1994). ... Flu (November 11, 1995); missed one game. ... Bruised ribs (March 10, 1997); missed four games. ... Injured eye (December 14, 2002); missed eight games. ... Injured groin (November 5, 2003); missed one game. ... Flu (December 15, 2003); missed one game. ... Fractured right foot (March 3, 2004); missed 15 games. ... Signed as free agent by Montreal Canadiens (Aug. 3, 2005).

		REGULAR SEASON								PLAYOFFS				
Season Team	League	GP	G	A	Pts.	PIM	+/-	PP	SH	GP	G	A	Pts.	PIM
91-92—Gloucester	OPJHL	6	3	4	7	0	...	...	...	—	—	—	—	—
92-93—Gloucester	OPJHL	55	11	26	37	64	...	...	...	—	—	—	—	—
93-94—Sherbrooke	QMJHL	67	17	36	53	67	...	...	...	12	4	10	14	12
94-95—Sherbrooke	QMJHL	67	37	70	107	76	41	12	1	7	1	7	8	10

Season Team	League	REGULAR SEASON GP	G	A	Pts.	PIM	+/-	PP	SH	PLAYOFFS GP	G	A	Pts.	PIM
95-96—Detroit	NHL	34	5	7	12	6	6	1	0	—	—	—	—	—
—Adirondack	AHL	4	0	0	0	0	...	...	...	—	—	—	—	—
96-97—Detroit	NHL	65	3	9	12	28	-10	0	0	—	—	—	—	—
97-98—Detroit	NHL	68	5	12	17	43	5	0	0	3	1	0	1	0
98-99—Detroit	NHL	75	4	10	14	59	17	0	0	10	0	1	1	0
99-00—Detroit	NHL	81	6	12	18	20	-12	0	0	6	0	0	0	2
00-01—Detroit	NHL	73	10	15	25	38	11	2	0	6	0	1	1	0
01-02—Detroit	NHL	81	8	12	20	44	-5	2	0	23	1	2	3	8
02-03—Detroit	NHL	74	4	15	19	64	25	1	0	4	0	0	0	2
03-04—Detroit	NHL	65	3	9	12	40	9	0	1	12	1	1	2	6
04-05—Asiago	Italy	10	0	2	2	2	...	...	...	9	1	5	6	4
NHL Totals (9 years)		616	48	101	149	342	46	6	1	64	3	5	8	18

DARBY, CRAIG — C — LIGHTNING

PERSONAL: Born September 26, 1972, in Oneida, N.Y. ... 6-3/205. ... Shoots right.

TRANSACTIONS/CAREER NOTES: Selected by Montreal Canadiens in second round (third Canadiens pick, 43rd overall) of NHL draft (June 22, 1991). ... Traded by Canadiens with LW Kirk Muller and D Mathieu Schneider to New York Islanders for D Vladimir Malakhov and C Pierre Turgeon (April 5, 1995). ... Claimed off waivers by Philadelphia Flyers (June 4, 1996). ... Selected by Nashville Predators in expansion draft (June 26, 1998). ... Signed as free agent by Canadiens (July 9, 1999). ... Separated shoulder (January 10, 2001); missed four games. ... Signed as free agent by New Jersey Devils (July 12, 2002). ... Signed as free agent by Tampa Bay Lightning (July 19, 2004). ... Signed as free agent by Springfield of the AHL (September 27, 2004).

Season Team	League	REGULAR SEASON GP	G	A	Pts.	PIM	+/-	PP	SH	PLAYOFFS GP	G	A	Pts.	PIM
89-90—Albany Academy	N.Y. H.S.	29	32	53	85	...	...	...	...	—	—	—	—	—
90-91—Albany Academy	N.Y. H.S.	27	33	61	94	53	...	...	...	—	—	—	—	—
91-92—Providence College	Hockey East	35	17	24	41	47	...	...	...	—	—	—	—	—
92-93—Providence College	Hockey East	35	11	21	32	62	...	...	...	—	—	—	—	—
93-94—Fredericton	AHL	66	23	33	56	51	-5	8	0	—	—	—	—	—
94-95—Fredericton	AHL	64	21	47	68	82	-14	4	0	—	—	—	—	—
—Montreal	NHL	10	0	2	2	0	-5	0	0	—	—	—	—	—
—New York Islanders	NHL	3	0	0	0	0	-1	0	0	—	—	—	—	—
95-96—Worcester	AHL	68	22	28	50	47	...	...	...	4	1	1	2	2
—New York Islanders	NHL	10	0	2	2	0	-1	0	0	—	—	—	—	—
96-97—Philadelphia	AHL	59	26	33	59	24	25	8	1	10	3	6	9	0
—Philadelphia	NHL	9	1	4	5	2	2	0	1	—	—	—	—	—
97-98—Philadelphia	NHL	3	1	0	1	0	0	0	0	—	—	—	—	—
—Philadelphia	AHL	77	42	45	87	34	8	20	2	20	5	9	14	4
98-99—Milwaukee	IHL	81	32	22	54	33	-11	10	2	2	3	0	3	0
99-00—Montreal	NHL	76	7	10	17	14	-14	0	1	—	—	—	—	—
00-01—Montreal	NHL	78	12	16	28	16	-17	0	1	—	—	—	—	—
01-02—Quebec	AHL	66	16	55	71	18	21	4	0	3	2	1	3	0
—Montreal	NHL	2	0	0	0	0	0	0	0	—	—	—	—	—
02-03—Albany	AHL	76	23	51	74	42	-12	11	1	—	—	—	—	—
—New Jersey	NHL	3	0	1	1	0	-1	0	0	—	—	—	—	—
03-04—New Jersey	NHL	2	0	0	0	0	-1	0	0	—	—	—	—	—
—Albany	AHL	77	21	48	69	46	-15	6	2	—	—	—	—	—
04-05—Springfield	AHL	70	8	26	34	28	-5	1	0	—	—	—	—	—
NHL Totals (9 years)		196	21	35	56	32	-38	0	3					

DARBY, REGAN — D — SENATORS

PERSONAL: Born July 17, 1980, in Estevan, Sask. ... 6-2/200. ... Shoots left.

TRANSACTIONS/CAREER NOTES: Selected by Vancouver Canucks in fourth round (fifth Canucks pick, 90th overall) of NHL entry draft (June 27, 1998). ... Signed as free agent by Utah of the AHL (Sept 10, 2003). ... Signed as free agent by Las Vegas of the ECHL (September 16, 2004).

Season Team	League	REGULAR SEASON GP	G	A	Pts.	PIM	+/-	PP	SH	PLAYOFFS GP	G	A	Pts.	PIM
97-98—Spokane	WHL	7	0	1	1	28	...	...	...	—	—	—	—	—
—Tri-City	WHL	32	1	2	3	125	...	...	...	—	—	—	—	—
98-99—Tri-City	WHL	38	2	4	6	152	...	...	...	—	—	—	—	—
—Red Deer	WHL	19	1	6	7	90	...	...	...	9	0	1	1	18
99-00—Red Deer	WHL	18	3	6	9	79	...	...	...	—	—	—	—	—
—Prince Albert	WHL	44	1	9	10	143	3	1	0	6	0	1	1	23
00-01—Kansas City	IHL	55	1	5	6	164	...	...	...	—	—	—	—	—
01-02—Manitoba	AHL	39	0	1	1	196	-2	0	0	—	—	—	—	—
—Columbia	ECHL	7	0	2	2	14	-1	0	0	3	0	0	0	0
02-03—Manitoba	AHL	10	0	0	0	30	-7	0	0	—	—	—	—	—
—Columbia	ECHL	48	1	7	8	170	1	0	0	17	0	1	1	20
04-05—Binghamton	AHL	3	0	0	0	5	-1	0	0	—	—	—	—	—
—Las Vegas	ECHL	41	1	2	3	155	-2	0	...	—	—	—	—	—
—Augusta	ECHL	11	1	4	5	61	-5	0	...	—	—	—	—	—
—Charlotte	ECHL	7	0	1	1	34	1	0	...	12	1	0	1	22

DARCHE, MATHIEU LW

PERSONAL: Born November 26, 1976, in St. Laurent, Que. ... 6-1/211. ... Shoots left. ... Brother of Jean-Phillipe Darche, tight end, Seattle Seahawks.

TRANSACTIONS/CAREER NOTES: Signed as free agent by Columbus Blue Jackets (May 8, 2000). ... Signed as free agent by Nashville Predators (September 9, 2003). ... Signed as free agent by Colorado Avalanche (July 26, 2004).

		REGULAR SEASON								PLAYOFFS				
Season Team	**League**	**GP**	**G**	**A**	**Pts.**	**PIM**	**+/-**	**PP**	**SH**	**GP**	**G**	**A**	**Pts.**	**PIM**
96-97—McGill University	CIAU	23	1	2	3	27	...	...	...	—	—	—	—	—
97-98—McGill University	CIAU	40	28	17	45	69	...	...	...	—	—	—	—	—
98-99—McGill University	CIAU	32	16	24	40	60	...	...	...	—	—	—	—	—
99-00—McGill University	CIAU	38	33	49	82	54	...	...	...	—	—	—	—	—
00-01—Syracuse	AHL	66	16	24	40	21	...	...	...	5	0	1	1	4
—Columbus	NHL	9	0	0	0	0	-4	0	0	—	—	—	—	—
01-02—Syracuse	AHL	63	22	23	45	26	5	8	0	10	2	5	7	2
—Columbus	NHL	14	1	1	2	6	-5	0	0	—	—	—	—	—
02-03—Syracuse	AHL	76	32	32	64	38	-14	10	3	—	—	—	—	—
—Columbus	NHL	1	0	0	0	0	-1	0	0	—	—	—	—	—
03-04—Nashville	NHL	2	0	0	0	0	-1	0	0	—	—	—	—	—
—Milwaukee	AHL	76	28	31	59	41	11	10	1	22	6	8	14	8
04-05—Hershey	AHL	79	29	25	54	49	4	10	2	—	—	—	—	—
NHL Totals (4 years)		26	1	1	2	6	-11	0	0					

DATSYUK, PAVEL C RED WINGS

PERSONAL: Born July 20, 1978, in Sverdolvsk, U.S.S.R. ... 5-11/185. ... Shoots left.

TRANSACTIONS/CAREER NOTES: Selected by Detroit Red Wings in sixth round (eighth Red Wings pick, 171st overall) of NHL draft (June 27, 1998). ... Flu (February 26, 2002); missed one game. ... Injured knee (December 1, 2002); missed 28 games.

		REGULAR SEASON								PLAYOFFS				
Season Team	**League**	**GP**	**G**	**A**	**Pts.**	**PIM**	**+/-**	**PP**	**SH**	**GP**	**G**	**A**	**Pts.**	**PIM**
96-97—Spartak Yekaterinburg	Russian	18	2	2	4	4	...	...	...	—	—	—	—	—
—Spartak Yekaterinburg	Rus. Div.	36	12	10	22	12	...	...	...	—	—	—	—	—
97-98—Dynamo-Energiya	Russian	24	3	5	8	4	...	...	...	—	—	—	—	—
—Dynamo-Energiya	Rus. Div.	22	7	8	15	4	...	...	...	—	—	—	—	—
99-00—Dyn.-Energiya Yek.	Russian	15	1	3	4	4	...	...	...	—	—	—	—	—
00-01—Ak Bars Kazan	Russian	42	9	18	27	10	...	...	...	4	0	1	1	2
01-02—Detroit	NHL	70	11	24	35	4	4	2	0	21	3	3	6	2
—Russian Oly. team	Int'l	6	1	2	3	0	...	...	...	—	—	—	—	—
02-03—Detroit	NHL	64	12	39	51	16	20	1	0	4	0	0	0	0
03-04—Detroit	NHL	75	30	38	68	35	-2	8	1	12	0	6	6	2
04-05—Dynamo Moscow	Russian	47	15	17	32	16	22	...	...	10	6	3	9	4
NHL Totals (3 years)		209	53	101	154	55	22	11	1	37	3	9	12	4

DAVIDSON, MATT RW FLAMES

PERSONAL: Born August 9, 1977, in Flin Flon, Man. ... 6-3/196. ... Shoots right.

TRANSACTIONS/CAREER NOTES: Selected by Buffalo Sabres in fourth round (fifth Sabres pick, 94th overall) of NHL draft (July 8, 1995). ... Traded by Sabres with D Jean-Luc Grand-Pierre, fifth-round pick (C Tyler Kolarik) in 2000 draft and fifth-round pick (traded to Calgary; traded to Detroit; Red Wings selected Andreas Jamtin) in 2001 draft to Columbus Blue Jackets complete expansion draft agreement in which Columbus selected Geoff Sanderson and Dwayne Roloson from Buffalo (June 23, 2000). ... Signed as free agent by Calgary Flames (July 15, 2003).

		REGULAR SEASON								PLAYOFFS				
Season Team	**League**	**GP**	**G**	**A**	**Pts.**	**PIM**	**+/-**	**PP**	**SH**	**GP**	**G**	**A**	**Pts.**	**PIM**
93-94—Portland	WHL	59	4	12	16	18	...	...	...	10	0	0	0	4
94-95—Portland	WHL	72	17	20	37	51	-23	2	0	9	1	3	4	0
95-96—Portland	WHL	70	24	26	50	96	...	...	...	7	2	2	4	2
96-97—Portland	WHL	72	44	27	71	47	34	15	3	6	0	1	1	2
97-98—Rochester	AHL	72	15	12	27	12	-18	6	0	3	1	0	1	2
98-99—Rochester	AHL	80	26	15	41	42	27	1	2	18	2	1	3	6
99-00—Rochester	AHL	80	12	20	32	30	...	...	...	19	4	2	6	8
00-01—Syracuse	AHL	72	14	11	25	24	...	...	...	5	1	2	3	2
—Columbus	NHL	5	0	0	0	0	2	0	0	—	—	—	—	—
01-02—Syracuse	AHL	47	9	11	20	64	2	3	0	8	1	3	4	4
—Columbus	NHL	17	1	2	3	10	-11	0	0	—	—	—	—	—
02-03—Syracuse	AHL	48	18	16	34	26	-12	8	4	—	—	—	—	—
—Columbus	NHL	34	4	5	9	18	-12	0	0	—	—	—	—	—
03-04—Lowell	AHL	66	14	28	42	36	-4	7	0	—	—	—	—	—
NHL Totals (3 years)		56	5	7	12	28	-21	0	0					

DAVIS, PATRICK LW

PERSONAL: Born December 28, 1986, in Sterling, Mich. ... 6-2/188. ... Shoots right.

		REGULAR SEASON								PLAYOFFS				
Season Team	**League**	**GP**	**G**	**A**	**Pts.**	**PIM**	**+/-**	**PP**	**SH**	**GP**	**G**	**A**	**Pts.**	**PIM**
03-04—Kitchener	OHL	27	8	10	18	21	...	...	...	—	—	—	—	—
04-05—Kitchener	OHL	59	20	30	50	41	2	8	1	14	3	4	7	20

DAVISON, ROB — D — SHARKS

PERSONAL: Born May 1, 1980, in St. Catharines, Ont. ... 6-3/220. ... Shoots left.
TRANSACTIONS/CAREER NOTES: Selected by San Jose Sharks in fourth round (fourth Sharks pick, 98th overall) of NHL draft (June 27, 1998).

		REGULAR SEASON								PLAYOFFS				
Season Team	League	GP	G	A	Pts.	PIM	+/-	PP	SH	GP	G	A	Pts.	PIM
96-97—St. Michael's	Tier II Jr. A	45	2	6	8	93	...	...	...	—	—	—	—	—
97-98—North Bay	OHL	59	0	11	11	200	-28	...	...	—	—	—	—	—
98-99—North Bay	OHL	59	2	17	19	150	-1	...	...	4	0	1	1	12
99-00—North Bay	OHL	67	4	6	10	194	-15	1	0	6	0	1	1	8
00-01—Kentucky	AHL	72	0	4	4	230	...	...	...	3	0	0	0	0
01-02—Cleveland	AHL	70	1	3	4	206	-12	0	1	—	—	—	—	—
02-03—Cleveland	AHL	42	1	3	4	82	-8	0	0	—	—	—	—	—
—San Jose	NHL	15	1	2	3	22	4	0	0	—	—	—	—	—
03-04—San Jose	NHL	55	0	3	3	92	-3	0	0	5	0	2	2	4
04-05—Cardiff	England	42	7	7	14	148	...	...	...	8	0	1	1	12
NHL Totals (2 years)		70	1	5	6	114	1	0	0	5	0	2	2	4

DAWES, NIGEL — LW — RANGERS

PERSONAL: Born February 9, 1985, in Winnipeg. ... 5-8/170. ... Shoots left.
TRANSACTIONS/CAREER NOTES: Selected by New York Rangers in fifth round (fifth Rangers pick, 149th overall) of NHL entry draft (June 21, 2003).

		REGULAR SEASON								PLAYOFFS				
Season Team	League	GP	G	A	Pts.	PIM	+/-	PP	SH	GP	G	A	Pts.	PIM
01-02—Kootenay	WHL	54	15	19	34	14	-1	5	0	22	9	6	15	8
02-03—Kootenay	WHL	72	47	45	92	54	2	22	0	11	4	8	12	6
03-04—Kootenay	WHL	56	47	23	70	31	2	15	3	4	1	2	3	10
—Hartford	AHL	4	0	0	0	0	...	...	...	—	—	—	—	—
04-05—Kootenay	WHL	63	50	26	76	30	26	18	2	12	5	10	15	5

DAZE, ERIC — LW/RW — BLACKHAWKS

PERSONAL: Born July 2, 1975, in Montreal. ... 6-6/235. ... Shoots left. ... Name pronounced dah-ZAY.
TRANSACTIONS/CAREER NOTES: Selected by Chicago Blackhawks in fourth round (fifth Blackhawks pick, 90th overall) of NHL draft (June 26, 1993). ... Sprained left ankle before 1996-97 season; missed eight games. ... Flu (January 20, 1997); missed one game. ... Injured back (March 27, 1998); missed two games. ... Bruised ankle (October 22, 1998); missed three games. ... Back spasms (October 27, 1999); missed three games. ... Flu (January 2, 2000); missed one game. ... Migraine headache (February 16, 2000); missed one game. ... Back spasms (March 3, 2000) and surgery; missed final 18 games of season. ... Disk surgery (September 25, 2002); missed 15 games. ... Injured back (January 5, 2003); missed three games ... Injured groin (January 30, 2003); missed five games. ... Infected ankle (Feburary 27, 2003); missed five games. ... Injured back (October 16, 2003) and had surgery; missed 63 games.
STATISTICAL PLATEAUS: Three-goal games: 1996-97 (1), 2001-02 (2), 2002-03 (2). Total: 5. ... Four-goal games: 1997-98 (1). ... Total hat tricks: 6.

		REGULAR SEASON								PLAYOFFS				
Season Team	League	GP	G	A	Pts.	PIM	+/-	PP	SH	GP	G	A	Pts.	PIM
92-93—Beauport	QMJHL	68	19	36	55	24	...	...	...	—	—	—	—	—
93-94—Beauport	QMJHL	66	59	48	107	31	22	17	3	15	16	8	24	2
94-95—Beauport	QMJHL	57	54	45	99	20	42	14	3	16	9	12	21	23
—Chicago	NHL	4	1	1	2	2	2	0	0	16	0	1	1	4
95-96—Chicago	NHL	80	30	23	53	18	16	2	0	10	3	5	8	0
96-97—Chicago	NHL	71	22	19	41	16	-4	11	0	6	2	1	3	2
97-98—Chicago	NHL	80	31	11	42	22	4	10	0	—	—	—	—	—
98-99—Chicago	NHL	72	22	20	42	22	-13	8	0	—	—	—	—	—
99-00—Chicago	NHL	59	23	13	36	28	-16	6	0	—	—	—	—	—
00-01—Chicago	NHL	79	33	24	57	16	1	9	1	—	—	—	—	—
01-02—Chicago	NHL	82	38	32	70	36	17	12	0	5	0	0	0	2
02-03—Chicago	NHL	54	22	22	44	14	10	3	0	—	—	—	—	—
03-04—Chicago	NHL	19	4	7	11	0	-7	1	0	—	—	—	—	—
NHL Totals (10 years)		600	226	172	398	174	10	62	1	37	5	7	12	8

DE VRIES, GREG — D — SENATORS

PERSONAL: Born January 4, 1973, in Sundridge, Ont. ... 6-2/209. ... Shoots left. ... Name pronounced duh-VREES.
TRANSACTIONS/CAREER NOTES: Signed as free agent by Edmonton Oilers (March 28, 1994). ... Sprained ankle (January 26, 1997); missed four games. ... Traded by Oilers with G Eric Fichaud and D Drake Berehowsky to Nashville Predators for C Jim Dowd and G Mikhail Shtalenkov (October 1, 1998). ... Traded by Predators to Colorado Avalanche for third-round pick (RW Branko Radivojevic) in 1999 entry draft (October 25, 1998). ... Had the flu (December 27, 1999); missed two games. ... Separated shoulder (February 19, 2001); missed three games. ... Signed as free agent by New York Rangers (July 14, 2003). ... Sprained right knee (January 8, 2004); missed 15 games. ... Had the flu (February 16, 2004); missed one game. ... Traded by Rangers to Ottawa Senators for D Karel Rachunek and C/LW Alexandre Giroux (March 9, 2004).

		REGULAR SEASON								PLAYOFFS				
Season Team	League	GP	G	A	Pts.	PIM	+/-	PP	SH	GP	G	A	Pts.	PIM
91-92—Bowling Green	CCHA	24	0	3	3	20	...	...	...	—	—	—	—	—
92-93—Niagara Falls	OHL	62	3	23	26	86	...	...	...	4	0	1	1	6
93-94—Niagara Falls	OHL	64	5	40	45	135	...	...	...	—	—	—	—	—
—Cape Breton	AHL	9	0	0	0	11	...	...	...	1	0	0	0	0

Season Team	League	GP	G	A	Pts.	PIM	+/-	PP	SH		GP	G	A	Pts.	PIM
		REGULAR SEASON									PLAYOFFS				
94-95—Cape Breton	AHL	77	5	19	24	68	-13	1	1		—	—	—	—	—
95-96—Edmonton	NHL	13	1	1	2	12	-2	0	0		—	—	—	—	—
—Cape Breton	AHL	58	9	30	39	174	...	...	...		—	—	—	—	—
96-97—Hamilton	AHL	34	4	14	18	26	-1	2	0		—	—	—	—	—
—Edmonton	NHL	37	0	4	4	52	-2	0	0		12	0	1	1	8
97-98—Edmonton	NHL	65	7	4	11	80	-17	1	0		7	0	0	0	21
98-99—Nashville	NHL	6	0	0	0	4	-4	0	0		—	—	—	—	—
—Colorado	NHL	67	1	3	4	60	-3	0	0		19	0	2	2	22
99-00—Colorado	NHL	69	2	7	9	73	-7	0	0		5	0	0	0	4
00-01—Colorado	NHL	79	5	12	17	51	23	0	0		23	0	1	1	20
01-02—Colorado	NHL	82	8	12	20	57	18	1	1		21	4	9	13	2
02-03—Colorado	NHL	82	6	26	32	70	15	0	0		7	2	0	2	0
03-04—New York Rangers	NHL	53	3	12	15	37	12	0	0		—	—	—	—	—
—Ottawa	NHL	13	0	1	1	6	0	0	0		7	0	1	1	8
NHL Totals (9 years)		566	33	82	115	502	33	2	1		101	6	14	20	85

DEADMARSH, ADAM RW/LW

PERSONAL: Born May 10, 1975, in Trail, B.C. ... 6-0/210. ... Shoots right. ... Cousin of Butch Deadmarsh, LW with three NHL teams (1970-75); and brother of Jake Deadmarsh, LW with San Jose Sharks organization (1996-98).

TRANSACTIONS/CAREER NOTES: Selected by Quebec Nordiques in first round (second Nordiques pick, 14th overall) of NHL draft (June 26, 1993). ... Nordiques franchise moved to Colorado and renamed Avalanche for 1995-96 season (June 21, 1995). ... Strained groin (April 3, 1996); missed four games. ... Strained shoulder (December 13, 1997); missed one game. ... Flu (January 14, 1998); missed one game. ... Strained hip flexor (March 19, 1998); missed one game. ... Injured shoulder (April 1, 1998); missed two games. ... Bruised thigh (April 11, 1998); missed two games. ... Bruised ribs (October 9, 1998); missed first two games of season. ... Infected left elbow (October 24, 1998); missed three games. ... Back spasms (March 16, 1999); missed five games. ... Injured eye (April 3, 1999); missed final six games of season. ... Hip pointer; missed first two games of 1999-2000 season. ... Bruised toe (December 12, 1999); missed one game. ... Sprained knee (January 13, 2000); missed three games. ... Injured rib (February 15, 2000); missed five games. ... Injured eye (October 18, 2000); missed one game. ... Concussion (November 1, 2000); missed 14 games. ... Injured knee (January 18, 2001); missed five games. ... Traded by Avalanche with D Aaron Miller, first-round pick (C David Steckel) in 2001 draft, player to be named and future considerations to Los Angeles Kings for C Steve Reinprecht and D Rob Blake (February 21, 2001); Kings acquired C Jared Aulin to complete deal (March 22, 2001). ... Bruised hand (March 5, 2001); missed three games. ... Strained groin (October 2, 2001); missed first game of season. ... Injured (October 28, 2001); missed one game. ... Injured (November 17, 2001); missed four games. ... Injured hand (October 31, 2002); missed one game. ... Concussion (November 12, 2002); missed nine games. ... Concussion (December 23, 2002); missed final 48 games of season. ... Missed 2003-04 season recovering from concussion.

STATISTICAL PLATEAUS: Three-goal games: 1999-00 (1), 2002-03 (1). Total: 2.

Season Team	League	GP	G	A	Pts.	PIM	+/-	PP	SH		GP	G	A	Pts.	PIM
		REGULAR SEASON									PLAYOFFS				
91-92—Portland	WHL	68	30	30	60	81	...	...	...		6	3	3	6	13
92-93—Portland	WHL	58	33	36	69	126	...	...	...		16	7	8	15	29
93-94—Portland	WHL	65	43	56	99	212	52	11	3		10	9	8	17	33
94-95—Portland	WHL	29	28	20	48	129	-1	8	3		—	—	—	—	—
—Quebec	NHL	48	9	8	17	56	16	0	0		6	0	1	1	0
95-96—Colorado	NHL	78	21	27	48	142	20	3	0		22	5	12	17	25
96-97—Colorado	NHL	78	33	27	60	136	8	10	3		17	3	6	9	24
97-98—Colorado	NHL	73	22	21	43	125	0	10	0		7	2	0	2	4
—U.S. Olympic team	Int'l	4	1	0	1	2	-3	0	0		—	—	—	—	—
98-99—Colorado	NHL	66	22	27	49	99	-2	10	0		19	8	4	12	20
99-00—Colorado	NHL	71	18	27	45	106	-10	5	0		17	4	11	15	21
00-01—Colorado	NHL	39	13	13	26	59	-2	7	0		—	—	—	—	—
—Los Angeles	NHL	18	4	2	6	4	3	0	0		13	3	3	6	4
01-02—Los Angeles	NHL	76	29	33	62	71	8	12	0		4	1	3	4	2
—U.S. Olympic team	Int'l	6	1	1	2	2	...	...	...		—	—	—	—	—
02-03—Los Angeles	NHL	20	13	4	17	21	2	4	0		—	—	—	—	—
03-04—Los Angeles	NHL	Did not play; injured													
NHL Totals (10 years)		567	184	189	373	819	43	61	3		105	26	40	66	100

DELMORE, ANDY D RED WINGS

PERSONAL: Born December 26, 1976, in LaSalle, Ont. ... 6-0/201. ... Shoots right.

TRANSACTIONS/CAREER NOTES: Signed as free agent by Philadelphia Flyers (July 9, 1997). ... Sprained right knee (March 5, 2000); missed nine games. ... Traded by Flyers to Nashville Predators for third-round pick (traded to Phoenix) in 2002 entry draft (July 31, 2001). ... Strained hamstring (December 17, 2001); missed one game. ... Reinjured hamstring (December 23, 2001); missed eight games. ... Injured shoulder (November 7, 2002); missed five games. ... Injured wrist (March 12, 2003); missed two games. ... Reinjured wrist (March 20, 2003); missed one game. ... Traded by Predators to the Buffalo Sabres for a third-round pick (later traded to Minnesota Wild) in 2004 entry draft (June 27, 2003). ... Injured groin (December 9, 2003); missed 11 games. ... Traded by Sabres with C Curtis Brown to San Jose Sharks for D Jeff Jillson and ninth-round pick in 2005 entry draft; then traded by Sharks to Boston Bruins for future considerations (March 9, 2004).

Season Team	League	GP	G	A	Pts.	PIM	+/-	PP	SH		GP	G	A	Pts.	PIM
		REGULAR SEASON									PLAYOFFS				
92-93—Chatham Jr. B	OHA	47	4	21	25	38	...	...	...		—	—	—	—	—
93-94—North Bay	OHL	45	2	7	9	33	...	...	...		17	0	0	0	2
94-95—North Bay	OHL	40	2	14	16	21	...	0	0		—	—	—	—	—
—Sarnia	OHL	27	5	13	18	27	...	3	0		3	0	0	0	2
95-96—Sarnia	OHL	64	21	38	59	45	...	...	...		10	3	7	10	2
96-97—Sarnia	OHL	63	18	60	78	39	21	11	1		12	2	10	12	10
—Fredericton	AHL	4	0	1	1	0	2	0	0		—	—	—	—	—
97-98—Philadelphia	AHL	73	9	30	39	46	-4	5	0		18	4	4	8	21

Season Team	League	REGULAR SEASON								PLAYOFFS				
		GP	G	A	Pts.	PIM	+/-	PP	SH	GP	G	A	Pts.	PIM
98-99—Philadelphia	AHL	70	5	18	23	51	1	1	1	15	1	4	5	6
—Philadelphia	NHL	2	0	1	1	0	-1	0	0	—	—	—	—	—
99-00—Philadelphia	AHL	39	12	14	26	31	...	...	...	—	—	—	—	—
—Philadelphia	NHL	27	2	5	7	8	-1	0	0	18	5	2	7	14
00-01—Philadelphia	NHL	66	5	9	14	16	2	2	0	2	1	0	1	2
01-02—Nashville	NHL	73	16	22	38	22	-13	11	0	—	—	—	—	—
02-03—Nashville	NHL	71	18	16	34	28	-17	14	0	—	—	—	—	—
03-04—Buffalo	NHL	37	2	5	7	29	-5	2	0	—	—	—	—	—
—Rochester	AHL	8	0	2	2	2	-3	0	0	—	—	—	—	—
04-05—Mannheim	Germany	50	7	16	23	59	-2	4	0	14	1	6	7	12
NHL Totals (6 years)		276	43	58	101	103	-35	29	0	20	6	2	8	16

DEMITRA, PAVOL — C/RW — KINGS

PERSONAL: Born November 29, 1974, in Dubnica, Czech. ... 6-0/206. ... Shoots left. ... Name pronounced PA-vuhl dih-MEE-truh.

TRANSACTIONS/CAREER NOTES: Selected by Ottawa Senators in 9th round (9th Senators pick, 227th overall) of NHL draft (June 26, 1993). ... Fractured ankle (October 14, 1993); missed 23 games. ... Traded by Senators to St. Louis Blues for D Christer Olsson (November 27, 1996). ... Back spasms and bruised tailbone (December 8, 1997); missed 10 games. ... Fractured jaw (March 7, 1998); missed 11 games. ... Injured triceps (December 26, 1999); missed three games. ... Concussion (March 24, 2000); missed remainder of season. ... Injured eye (December 30, 2000); missed 17 games. ... Injured hamstring (February 10, 2001); missed 14 games. ... Reinjured hamstring (March 14, 2001); missed seven games. ... Chicken pox (December 8, 2002); missed four games. ... Flu (November 1, 2003); missed one game. ... Injured neck (December 29, 2003); missed four games. ... Injured hip (January 28, 2004); missed nine games. ... Signed as free agent by Los Angeles Kings (Aug. 2, 2005).

STATISTICAL PLATEAUS: Three-goal games: 1999-00 (1), 2000-01 (1), 2002-03 (1). Total: 3.

Season Team	League	REGULAR SEASON								PLAYOFFS				
		GP	G	A	Pts.	PIM	+/-	PP	SH	GP	G	A	Pts.	PIM
91-92—Sparta Dubnica	Czech Dv.I	28	13	10	23	12	...	...	...	—	—	—	—	—
92-93—Dukla Trencin	Czech.	46	11	17	28	0	...	...	...	—	—	—	—	—
—CAPEH Dubnica	Czech Dv.I	4	3	0	3	...	...	...	...	—	—	—	—	—
93-94—Ottawa	NHL	12	1	1	2	4	-7	1	0	—	—	—	—	—
—Prince Edward	AHL	41	18	23	41	8	-13	4	0	—	—	—	—	—
94-95—Prince Edward	AHL	61	26	48	74	23	20	4	0	5	0	7	7	0
—Ottawa	NHL	16	4	3	7	0	-4	1	0	—	—	—	—	—
95-96—Prince Edward	AHL	48	28	53	81	44	...	...	...	—	—	—	—	—
—Ottawa	NHL	31	7	10	17	6	-3	2	0	—	—	—	—	—
96-97—Las Vegas	IHL	22	8	13	21	10	...	...	...	—	—	—	—	—
—Grand Rapids	IHL	42	20	30	50	24	...	...	...	—	—	—	—	—
—Dukla Trencin	Slovakia	1	1	1	2	...	...	...	...	—	—	—	—	—
—St. Louis	NHL	8	3	0	3	2	0	2	0	6	1	3	4	6
97-98—St. Louis	NHL	61	22	30	52	22	11	4	4	10	3	3	6	2
98-99—St. Louis	NHL	82	37	52	89	16	13	14	0	13	5	4	9	4
99-00—St. Louis	NHL	71	28	47	75	8	34	8	0	—	—	—	—	—
00-01—St. Louis	NHL	44	20	25	45	16	27	5	0	15	2	4	6	2
01-02—St. Louis	NHL	82	35	43	78	46	13	11	0	10	4	7	11	6
—Slovakian Oly. team	Int'l	2	1	2	3	2	...	...	...	—	—	—	—	—
02-03—St. Louis	NHL	78	36	57	93	32	0	11	0	7	2	4	6	2
03-04—St. Louis	NHL	68	23	35	58	18	1	8	0	5	1	0	1	4
04-05—Dukla Trencin	Slovakia	54	28	54	82	39	49	...	...	12	4	13	17	14
NHL Totals (11 years)		553	216	303	519	170	85	67	4	66	18	25	43	26

DEMPSEY, NATHAN — D — KINGS

PERSONAL: Born July 14, 1974, in Spruce Grove, Alta. ... 6-0/191. ... Shoots left.

TRANSACTIONS/CAREER NOTES: Selected by Toronto Maple Leafs in 11th round (11th Leafs pick, 245th overall) of NHL draft (June 20, 1992). ... Signed as free agent by Chicago Blackhawks (July 12, 2002). ... Injured elbow (January 8, 2004); missed four games. ... Concussion (February 24, 2004); missed three games. ... Traded by Blackhawks to Los Angeles Kings for 4th-round pick in 2005 draft and future considerations (March 2, 2004).

Season Team	League	REGULAR SEASON								PLAYOFFS				
		GP	G	A	Pts.	PIM	+/-	PP	SH	GP	G	A	Pts.	PIM
91-92—Regina	WHL	70	4	22	26	72	...	...	...	—	—	—	—	—
92-93—Regina	WHL	72	12	29	41	95	...	...	...	13	3	8	11	14
—St. John's	AHL	0	0	0	0	0	...	...	...	2	0	0	0	0
93-94—Regina	WHL	56	14	36	50	100	...	...	...	4	0	0	0	4
94-95—St. John's	AHL	74	7	30	37	91	19	1	1	5	1	0	1	11
95-96—St. John's	AHL	73	5	15	20	103	...	...	...	4	1	0	1	9
96-97—St. John's	AHL	52	8	18	26	108	-5	2	0	6	1	0	1	4
—Toronto	NHL	14	1	1	2	2	-2	0	0	—	—	—	—	—
97-98—St. John's	AHL	68	12	16	28	85	-12	5	0	4	0	0	0	0
98-99—St. John's	AHL	67	2	29	31	70	-12	0	0	5	0	1	1	2
99-00—St. John's	AHL	44	15	12	27	40	...	...	...	—	—	—	—	—
—Toronto	NHL	6	0	2	2	2	2	0	0	—	—	—	—	—
00-01—St. John's	AHL	55	11	28	39	60	...	...	...	4	0	4	4	8
—Toronto	NHL	25	1	9	10	4	13	1	0	—	—	—	—	—
01-02—St. John's	AHL	75	13	48	61	66	4	6	1	11	1	5	6	8
—Toronto	NHL	3	0	0	0	0	1	0	0	6	0	2	2	0
02-03—Chicago	NHL	67	5	23	28	26	-7	1	0	—	—	—	—	—
03-04—Chicago	NHL	58	8	17	25	30	-5	2	0	—	—	—	—	—
—Los Angeles	NHL	17	4	3	7	2	-7	1	0	—	—	—	—	—
04-05—Eisbaren Berlin	Germany	10	2	3	5	26	2	1	0	12	0	3	3	14
NHL Totals (6 years)		190	19	55	74	66	-5	5	0	6	0	2	2	0

DENIS, MARC — G — BLUE JACKETS

PERSONAL: Born August 1, 1977, in Montreal. ... 6-1/193. ... Catches left. ... Name pronounced deh-NEE.

TRANSACTIONS/CAREER NOTES: Selected by Colorado Avalanche in first round (first Avalanche pick, 25th overall) of NHL entry draft (July 8, 1995). ... Traded by Avalanche to Columbus Blue Jackets for second-round pick (traded to Carolina) in 2000 entry draft (June 7, 2000). ... Strained groin (March 6, 2002); missed four games. ... Had the flu (November 22, 2003); missed one game.

		REGULAR SEASON									PLAYOFFS							
Season Team	League	GP	Min.	W	L	T	GA	SO	GAA	SV%	GP	Min.	W	L	GA	SO	GAA	SV%
94-95 —Chicoutimi	QMJHL	32	1688	17	9	1	98	0	3.48	.891	6	374	4	2	19	1	3.05	.915
95-96 —Chicoutimi	QMJHL	51	2895	23	21	4	157	2	3.25	...	16	917	8	8	66	0	4.32	...
96-97 —Chicoutimi	QMJHL	41	2317	22	15	2	104	4	*2.69	...	*21	*1226	*11	*10	*70	*1	3.43	.883
—Colorado	NHL	1	60	0	1	0	3	0	3.00	.885	—	—	—	—	—	—	—	—
—Hershey	AHL	...	...	...	...	...	...	...	...	...	4	56	1	0	1	0	*1.07	.960
97-98 —Hershey	AHL	47	2589	17	23	4	125	1	2.90	.899	6	347	3	3	15	0	2.59	.894
98-99 —Hershey	AHL	52	2908	20	23	5	137	4	2.83	.914	3	143	1	1	7	0	2.94	.909
—Colorado	NHL	4	217	1	1	1	9	0	2.49	.918	—	—	—	—	—	—	—	—
99-00 —Colorado	NHL	23	1203	9	8	3	51	3	2.54	.917	—	—	—	—	—	—	—	—
00-01 —Columbus	NHL	32	1830	6	20	4	99	0	3.25	.895	—	—	—	—	—	—	—	—
01-02 —Columbus	NHL	42	2335	9	24	5	121	1	3.11	.899	—	—	—	—	—	—	—	—
02-03 —Columbus	NHL	*77	*4511	27	41	8	232	5	3.09	.903	—	—	—	—	—	—	—	—
03-04 —Columbus	NHL	66	3796	21	36	7	162	5	2.56	.918	—	—	—	—	—	—	—	—
NHL Totals (7 years)		245	13952	73	131	28	677	14	2.91	.907								

DESJARDINS, ERIC — D — FLYERS

PERSONAL: Born June 14, 1969, in Rouyn, Que. ... 6-1/205. ... Shoots right. ... Name pronounced day-zhar-DAN.

TRANSACTIONS/CAREER NOTES: Selected by Montreal Canadiens in 2nd round (3rd Canadiens pick, 38th overall) of NHL draft (June 13, 1987). ... Flu (January 1989). ... Injured groin (November 2, 1989); missed seven games. ... Sprained left ankle (January 26, 1991); missed 16 games. ... Fractured right thumb (December 8, 1991); missed two games. ... Traded by Canadiens with LW Gilbert Dionne and C John LeClair to Philadelphia Flyers for RW Mark Recchi and 3rd-round pick (C Martin Hohenberger) in 1995 draft (February 9, 1995). ... Strained groin (March 28, 1995); missed one game. ... Reinjured groin (April 1, 1995); missed three games. ... Flu (December 26, 1995); missed one game. ... Inflamed pelvic bone (October 1, 1997); missed five games. ... Strained groin (October 27, 1998); missed four games. ... Stomach virus (March 6, 1999); missed three games. ... Sprained left knee (March 21, 1999); missed seven games. ... Injured head; missed first game of 1999-2000 season. ... Stromach virus (December 21, 2000); missed one game. ... Concussion (March 8, 2001); missed two games. ... Strained lower back and injured left elbow (October 27, 2001); missed three games. ... Fractured finger (December 10, 2001); missed 12 games. ... Strained lower back (April 4, 2002); missed two games. ... Injured back (December 4, 2002); missed two games. ... Bruised left knee (March 31, 2003); missed one game. ... Fractured foot (April 19, 2003); missed final eight playoff games. ... Back spasms (November 5, 2003); missed two games. ... Fractured right forearm (January 17, 2004); missed 32 games. ... Reinjured right forearm (April 6, 2004); missed remainder of season and all of playoffs.

		REGULAR SEASON								PLAYOFFS				
Season Team	League	GP	G	A	Pts.	PIM	+/-	PP	SH	GP	G	A	Pts.	PIM
86-87 —Granby	QMJHL	66	14	24	38	75	...	...	...	8	3	2	5	10
87-88 —Granby	QMJHL	62	18	49	67	138	...	...	...	5	0	3	3	10
—Sherbrooke	AHL	3	0	0	0	6	...	...	...	4	0	2	2	2
88-89 —Montreal	NHL	36	2	12	14	26	9	1	0	14	1	1	2	6
89-90 —Montreal	NHL	55	3	13	16	51	1	1	0	6	0	0	0	10
90-91 —Montreal	NHL	62	7	18	25	27	7	0	0	13	1	4	5	8
91-92 —Montreal	NHL	77	6	32	38	50	17	4	0	11	3	3	6	4
92-93 —Montreal	NHL	82	13	32	45	98	20	7	0	20	4	10	14	23
93-94 —Montreal	NHL	84	12	23	35	97	-1	6	1	7	0	2	2	4
94-95 —Montreal	NHL	9	0	6	6	2	2	0	0	—	—	—	—	—
—Philadelphia	NHL	34	5	18	23	12	10	1	0	15	4	4	8	10
95-96 —Philadelphia	NHL	80	7	40	47	45	19	5	0	12	0	6	6	2
96-97 —Philadelphia	NHL	82	12	34	46	50	25	5	1	19	2	8	10	12
97-98 —Philadelphia	NHL	77	6	27	33	36	11	2	1	5	0	1	1	0
—Can. Olympic team	Int'l	6	0	0	0	2	1	0	0	—	—	—	—	—
98-99 —Philadelphia	NHL	68	15	36	51	38	18	6	0	6	2	2	4	4
99-00 —Philadelphia	NHL	81	14	41	55	32	20	8	0	18	2	10	12	2
00-01 —Philadelphia	NHL	79	15	33	48	50	-3	6	1	6	1	1	2	0
01-02 —Philadelphia	NHL	65	6	19	25	24	-1	2	1	5	0	1	1	2
02-03 —Philadelphia	NHL	79	8	24	32	35	30	1	0	5	2	1	3	0
03-04 —Philadelphia	NHL	48	1	11	12	28	11	0	0	—	—	—	—	—
NHL Totals (16 years)		1098	132	419	551	701	195	55	5	162	22	54	76	87

DESROCHERS, PATRICK — G

PERSONAL: Born October 27, 1979, in Penetanguishene, Ont. ... 6-4/205. ... Catches left.

TRANSACTIONS/CAREER NOTES: Selected by Phoenix Coyotes in first round (first Coyotes pick, 14th overall) of NHL entry draft (June 27, 1998). ... Traded by Coyotes to Carolina Hurricanes for G Jean-Marc Pelletier and future considerations (December 31, 2002). ... Fractured elbow (March 22, 2003); missed eight games. ... Signed as free agent by Florida Panthers (August 25, 2004). ... Signed as free agent by San Antonio of the AHL (September 26, 2004).

		REGULAR SEASON									PLAYOFFS							
Season Team	League	GP	Min.	W	L	T	GA	SO	GAA	SV%	GP	Min.	W	L	GA	SO	GAA	SV%
95-96 —Sarnia	OHL	29	1265	12	6	2	96	0	4.55	...	3	71	0	1	5	0	4.23	...
96-97 —Sarnia	OHL	50	2667	22	17	4	154	4	3.46	...	11	576	6	5	42	0	4.38	...
97-98 —Sarnia	OHL	56	3205	26	17	11	179	1	3.35	.901	4	160	1	2	12	0	4.50	.874
98-99 —Sarnia	OHL	8	425	3	5	0	26	0	3.67	.878	—	—	—	—	—	—	—	—

Season Team	League	GP	Min.	W	L	T	GA	SO	GAA	SV%	GP	Min.	W	L	GA	SO	GAA	SV%
		REGULAR SEASON									PLAYOFFS							
—Kingston	OHL	44	2389	14	22	3	177	1	4.45	.893	5	323	1	4	21	0	3.90	.908
—Canadian nat'l team	Int'l	6	60	1	0	0	4	...	4.00	.917	—	—	—	—	—	—	—	—
99-00—Springfield	AHL	52	2710	21	17	7	137	1	3.03	...	2	120	1	1	7	1	3.50	...
00-01—Springfield	AHL	50	2807	17	24	5	156	0	3.33	.893	—	—	—	—	—	—	—	—
01-02—Springfield	AHL	34	1864	12	18	1	94	2	3.03	.895	—	—	—	—	—	—	—	—
—Phoenix	NHL	5	243	1	2	1	15	0	3.70	.848	—	—	—	—	—	—	—	—
02-03—Phoenix	NHL	4	175	0	3	0	11	0	3.77	.875	—	—	—	—	—	—	—	—
—Springfield	AHL	8	454	2	4	1	20	0	2.64	.917	—	—	—	—	—	—	—	—
—Carolina	NHL	2	122	1	1	0	7	0	3.44	.901	—	—	—	—	—	—	—	—
—Lowell	AHL	17	1029	4	12	1	48	0	2.80	.912	—	—	—	—	—	—	—	—
03-04—Lowell	AHL	50	2837	23	25	1	138	0	2.92	.898	—	—	—	—	—	—	—	—
04-05—San Antonio	AHL	34	1487	8	19	...	79	2	3.19	.885	—	—	—	—	—	—	—	—
—Texas	ECHL	2	120	0	2	...	10	0	5.00	.884	—	—	—	—	—	—	—	—
NHL Totals (2 years)		11	540	2	6	1	33	0	3.67	.872								

DEVEREAUX, BOYD — C — COYOTES

PERSONAL: Born April 16, 1978, in Seaforth, Ont,. ... 6-2/195. ... Shoots left. ... Name pronounced DEH-vuh-roh.

TRANSACTIONS/CAREER NOTES: Selected by Edmonton Oilers in first round (first Oilers pick, sixth overall) of NHL draft (June 22, 1996). ... Suffered concussion (April 1, 2000); missed remainder of season. ... Signed as free agent by Detroit Red Wings (August 23, 2000). ... Fractured thumb (October 10, 2002); missed three games. ... Injured face (February 23, 2004); missed five games. ... Signed as free agent by Phoenix Coyotes (July 5, 2004).

STATISTICAL PLATEAUS: Three-goal games: 1999-00 (1).

Season Team	League	GP	G	A	Pts.	PIM	+/-	PP	SH	GP	G	A	Pts.	PIM
		REGULAR SEASON								PLAYOFFS				
93-94—Stratford	OPJHL	46	12	27	39	8	...	...	...	—	—	—	—	—
94-95—Stratford	OPJHL	45	31	74	105	21	...	...	...	—	—	—	—	—
95-96—Kitchener	OHL	66	20	38	58	35	...	...	...	12	3	7	10	4
96-97—Kitchener	OHL	54	28	41	69	37	15	8	3	13	4	11	15	8
—Hamilton	AHL	...	...	...	...	...	...	...	...	1	0	1	1	0
97-98—Edmonton	NHL	38	1	4	5	6	-5	0	0	—	—	—	—	—
—Hamilton	AHL	14	5	6	11	6	0	1	0	9	1	1	2	8
98-99—Edmonton	NHL	61	6	8	14	23	2	0	1	1	0	0	0	0
—Hamilton	AHL	7	4	6	10	2	3	2	0	8	0	3	3	4
99-00—Edmonton	NHL	76	8	19	27	20	7	0	1	—	—	—	—	—
00-01—Detroit	NHL	55	5	6	11	14	1	0	0	2	0	0	0	0
01-02—Detroit	NHL	79	9	16	25	24	9	0	0	21	2	4	6	4
02-03—Detroit	NHL	61	3	9	12	16	4	0	0	—	—	—	—	—
03-04—Detroit	NHL	61	6	9	15	20	-1	0	0	3	1	0	1	0
NHL Totals (7 years)		431	38	71	109	123	17	0	2	27	3	4	7	4

DIMAIO, ROB — RW — LIGHTNING

PERSONAL: Born February 19, 1968, in Calgary. ... 5-10/190. ... Shoots right. ... Name pronounced duh-MIGH-oh.

TRANSACTIONS/CAREER NOTES: Selected by New York Islanders in sixth round (sixth Islanders pick, 118th overall) of NHL draft (June 13, 1987). ... Bruised left hand (February 1989). ... Sprained clavicle (November 1989). ... Sprained wrist (February 20, 1992); missed four games. ... Reinjured wrist (February 29, 1992); missed remainder of season. ... Selected by Tampa Bay Lightning in expansion draft (June 18, 1992). ... Bruised wrist (November 28, 1992); missed four games. ... Sprained ankle (February 14, 1993); missed nine games. ... Reinjured right ankle (March 20, 1993); missed three games. ... Reinjured right ankle (April 1, 1993); missed remainder of season. ... Fractured left leg (October 16, 1993); missed 27 games. ... Traded by Lightning to Philadelphia Flyers for RW Jim Cummins and fourth-round pick (traded back to Flyers) in 1995 draft (March 18, 1994). ... Bruised foot (February 28, 1995); missed two games. ... Flu (April 16, 1995); missed one game. ... Bruised bone in left leg (December 16, 1995); missed 14 games. ... Sprained right knee (March 29, 1996); missed final eight games of regular season. ... Selected by San Jose Sharks from Flyers in waiver draft (September 30, 1996). ... Traded by Sharks to Boston Bruins for fifth-round pick (RW Adam Nittel) in 1997 draft (September 30, 1996). ... Strained knee (November 6, 1996); missed five games. ... Flu (December 17, 1996); missed one game. ... Sprained knee (March 8, 1997); missed two games. ... Injured hip (April 5, 1997); missed two games. ... Strained groin (January 12, 1998); missed one game. ... Suffered concussion (February 26, 1998); missed one game. ... Injured ankle (November 3, 1998); missed one game. ... Had viral meningitis (December 26, 1998); missed five games. ... Strained elbow (April 1, 1999); missed one game. ... Reinjured elbow (April 7, 1999); missed two games. ... Injured hip (October 20, 1999); missed one game. ... Bruised foot (November 10, 1999); missed two games. ... Fractured foot (November 17, 1999); missed eight games. ... Injured wrist (February 25, 2000); missed seven games. ... Traded by Bruins to New York Rangers for RW Mike Knuble (March 10, 2000). ... Suffered concussion (March 19, 2000); missed one game. ... Traded by Rangers with LW Darren Langdon to Carolina Hurricanes for RW Sandy McCarthy and fourth-round (D Bryce Lampman) in 2001 draft (August 4, 2000). ... Back spasms (November 4, 2000); missed three games. ... Strained shoulder (March 21, 2001); missed two games. ... Bruised sternum (March 30, 2001); missed three games. ... Signed as free agent by Dallas Stars (July 1, 2001). ... Strained back (December 13, 2002); missed one game. ... Injured neck (January 29, 2003); missed one game. ... Bruised chest (February 27, 2003); missed nine games. ... Injured hip flexor (November 8, 2003); missed one game. ... Injured ankle (January 13, 2004); missed 11 games. ... Signed as free agent by Tampa Bay Lightning (Aug. 9, 2005).

Season Team	League	GP	G	A	Pts.	PIM	+/-	PP	SH	GP	G	A	Pts.	PIM
		REGULAR SEASON								PLAYOFFS				
84-85—Kamloops	WHL	55	9	18	27	29	...	...	...	—	—	—	—	—
85-86—Kamloops	WHL	6	1	0	1	0	...	...	...	—	—	—	—	—
—Medicine Hat	WHL	55	20	30	50	82	...	...	...	—	—	—	—	—
86-87—Medicine Hat	WHL	70	27	43	70	130	...	...	...	20	7	11	18	46
87-88—Medicine Hat	WHL	54	47	43	90	120	...	...	...	14	12	19	31	59
88-89—New York Islanders	NHL	16	1	0	1	30	-6	0	0	—	—	—	—	—
—Springfield	AHL	40	13	18	31	67	...	...	...	—	—	—	—	—
89-90—New York Islanders	NHL	7	0	0	0	2	0	0	0	1	1	0	1	4

Season Team	League	GP	G	A	Pts.	PIM	+/-	PP	SH	GP	G	A	Pts.	PIM
		REGULAR SEASON								PLAYOFFS				
—Springfield	AHL	54	25	27	52	69	...	...	...	16	4	7	11	45
90-91—New York Islanders	NHL	1	0	0	0	0	0	0	0	—	—	—	—	—
—Capital District	AHL	12	3	4	7	22	...	...	...	—	—	—	—	—
91-92—New York Islanders	NHL	50	5	2	7	43	-23	0	2	—	—	—	—	—
92-93—Tampa Bay	NHL	54	9	15	24	62	0	2	0	—	—	—	—	—
93-94—Tampa Bay	NHL	39	8	7	15	40	-5	2	0	—	—	—	—	—
—Philadelphia	NHL	14	3	5	8	6	1	0	0	—	—	—	—	—
94-95—Philadelphia	NHL	36	3	1	4	53	8	0	0	15	2	4	6	4
95-96—Philadelphia	NHL	59	6	15	21	58	0	1	1	3	0	0	0	0
96-97—Boston	NHL	72	13	15	28	82	-21	0	3	—	—	—	—	—
97-98—Boston	NHL	79	10	17	27	82	-13	0	0	6	1	0	1	8
98-99—Boston	NHL	71	7	14	21	95	-14	1	0	12	2	0	2	8
99-00—Boston	NHL	50	5	16	21	42	-1	0	0	—	—	—	—	—
—New York Rangers	NHL	12	1	3	4	8	-8	0	0	—	—	—	—	—
00-01—Carolina	NHL	74	6	18	24	54	-14	0	2	6	0	0	0	4
01-02—Dallas	NHL	61	6	6	12	25	-2	0	2	—	—	—	—	—
—Utah	AHL	3	1	1	2	0	0	1	0	—	—	—	—	—
02-03—Dallas	NHL	69	10	9	19	76	18	0	0	12	1	4	5	10
03-04—Dallas	NHL	69	9	15	24	52	2	0	1	5	0	1	1	2
04-05—Milano	Italy	9	4	8	12	4	...	...	...	15	9	10	19	16
—SC Langnau	Switzerland	9	2	3	5	8	...	0	0	—	—	—	—	—
NHL Totals (16 years)		833	102	158	260	810	-78	6	11	60	7	9	16	40

DIMITRAKOS, NIKO — RW — SHARKS

PERSONAL: Born May 21, 1979, in Somersville, Mass. ... 5-10/205. ... Shoots right. ... Name pronounced NIK-oh DIH-mih-tra-kohs.
TRANSACTIONS/CAREER NOTES: Selected by San Jose Sharks in fifth round (fourth Sharks pick, 155th overall) of NHL draft (June 26, 1999).

Season Team	League	GP	G	A	Pts.	PIM	+/-	PP	SH	GP	G	A	Pts.	PIM
		REGULAR SEASON								PLAYOFFS				
98-99—Maine	Hockey East	35	8	19	27	33	...	1	0	—	—	—	—	—
99-00—Maine	Hockey East	32	11	16	27	16	...	...	...	—	—	—	—	—
00-01—Maine	Hockey East	29	11	14	25	43	...	...	...	—	—	—	—	—
01-02—Maine	Hockey East	43	20	31	51	44	...	...	...	—	—	—	—	—
02-03—Cleveland	AHL	55	15	29	44	30	-18	10	0	—	—	—	—	—
—San Jose	NHL	21	6	7	13	8	-7	3	0	—	—	—	—	—
03-04—Cleveland	AHL	7	4	4	8	4	7	1	0	—	—	—	—	—
—San Jose	NHL	68	9	15	24	49	6	2	0	15	1	8	9	8
04-05—SC Langnau	Switzerland	3	0	1	1	2	...	0	0	6	3	3	6	16
NHL Totals (2 years)		89	15	22	37	57	-1	5	0	15	1	8	9	8

DINGMAN, CHRIS — LW — LIGHTNING

PERSONAL: Born July 6, 1976, in Edmonton. ... 6-4/235. ... Shoots left.
TRANSACTIONS/CAREER NOTES: Selected by Calgary Flames in first round (first Flames pick, 19th overall) of NHL draft (June 28, 1994). ... Traded by Flames with RW Theo Fleury to Colorado Avalanche for LW Rene Corbet, D Wade Belak and future considerations (February 28, 1999); Flames acquired D Robyn Regehr to complete deal (March 27, 1999). ... Partially dislocated right shoulder (November 15, 1999); missed six games. ... Sprained knee (November 13, 2000); missed 13 games. ... Traded by Avalanche to Carolina Hurricanes for fifth-round pick (D Mikko Viitanen) in 2001 draft (June 24, 2001). ... Strained groin (September 26, 2001); missed first eight games of season. ... Injured groin (November 9, 2001); missed two games. ... Injured knee (December 12, 2001); missed 16 games. ... Traded by Hurricanes with RW Shane Willis to Tampa Bay Lightning for G Kevin Weekes (March 5, 2002). ... Back spasms (March 30, 2002); missed five games. ... Suspended two games for high-sticking incident (October 16, 2002). ... Injured shoulder (December 27, 2003); missed four games.

Season Team	League	GP	G	A	Pts.	PIM	+/-	PP	SH	GP	G	A	Pts.	PIM
		REGULAR SEASON								PLAYOFFS				
92-93—Brandon	WHL	50	10	17	27	64	...	...	...	4	0	0	0	0
93-94—Brandon	WHL	45	21	20	41	77	10	5	0	13	1	7	8	39
94-95—Brandon	WHL	66	40	43	83	201	40	11	1	3	1	0	1	9
95-96—Brandon	WHL	40	16	29	45	109	...	...	...	19	12	11	23	60
—Saint John	AHL	...	...	...	...	...	...	...	...	1	0	0	0	0
96-97—Saint John	AHL	71	5	6	11	195	-9	0	0	—	—	—	—	—
97-98—Calgary	NHL	70	3	3	6	149	-11	1	0	—	—	—	—	—
98-99—Saint John	AHL	50	5	7	12	140	-12	0	0	—	—	—	—	—
—Calgary	NHL	2	0	0	0	17	-2	0	0	—	—	—	—	—
—Hershey	AHL	17	1	3	4	102	-8	0	0	5	0	2	2	6
—Colorado	NHL	1	0	0	0	7	0	0	0	—	—	—	—	—
99-00—Colorado	NHL	68	8	3	11	132	-2	2	0	—	—	—	—	—
00-01—Colorado	NHL	41	1	1	2	108	-3	0	0	16	0	4	4	14
01-02—Carolina	NHL	30	0	1	1	77	-2	0	0	—	—	—	—	—
—Tampa Bay	NHL	14	0	4	4	26	-8	0	0	—	—	—	—	—
02-03—Tampa Bay	NHL	51	2	1	3	91	-11	0	0	10	1	0	1	4
03-04—Tampa Bay	NHL	74	1	5	6	140	-9	0	0	23	1	1	2	63
NHL Totals (7 years)		351	15	18	33	747	-48	3	0	49	2	5	7	81

DIPIETRO, RICK — G — ISLANDERS

PERSONAL: Born September 19, 1981, in Winthrop, Mass. ... 6-0/190. ... Catches right.
TRANSACTIONS/CAREER NOTES: Selected by New York Islanders in first round (first Islanders pick, first overall) of NHL entry draft (June 24, 2000).

Season Team	League	GP	Min.	W	L	T	GA	SO	GAA	SV%	GP	Min.	W	L	GA	SO	GAA	SV%
		REGULAR SEASON									PLAYOFFS							
97-98—U.S. Jr. national team....	Int'l	46	2526	21	19	0	131	2	3.11	.893	—	—	—	—	—	—	—	—
98-99—U.S. Jr. national team....	Int'l	30	1733	22	6	2	67	3	2.32	.907	—	—	—	—	—	—	—	—
99-00—Boston University..........	Hockey East	30	1791	18	5	5	73	2	2.45	.913	—	—	—	—	—	—	—	—
00-01—Chicago........................	IHL	14	778	4	5	2	44	0	3.39	...	—	—	—	—	—	—	—	—
—New York Islanders.......	NHL	20	1083	3	15	1	63	0	3.49	.878	—	—	—	—	—	—	—	—
01-02—Bridgeport....................	AHL	59	3471	*30	22	7	134	4	2.32	.905	20	*1270	12	*8	*45	*3	2.13	.906
02-03—New York Islanders.......	NHL	10	585	2	5	2	29	0	2.97	.894	1	15	0	0	0	0	0.00	1.00
—Bridgeport....................	AHL	34	2044	16	10	8	73	3	2.14	.924	5	298	2	3	10	1	2.01	.925
03-04—New York Islanders.......	NHL	50	2844	23	18	5	112	5	2.36	.911	5	303	1	4	11	1	2.18	.908
—Bridgeport....................	AHL	2	119	0	2	0	3	0	1.51	.942	—	—	—	—	—	—	—	—
NHL Totals (3 years)............		80	4512	28	38	8	204	5	2.71	.900	6	318	1	4	11	1	2.08	.911

DIVIS, REINHARD — G — BLUES

PERSONAL: Born July 4, 1975, in Vienna, Austria. ... 6-0/192. ... Catches left.

TRANSACTIONS/CAREER NOTES: Selected by St. Louis Blues in eighth round (eighth Blues pick, 261st overall) of NHL entry draft (June 25, 2000).

Season Team	League	GP	Min.	W	L	T	GA	SO	GAA	SV%	GP	Min.	W	L	GA	SO	GAA	SV%
		REGULAR SEASON									PLAYOFFS							
95-96—VEU Feldkirch...............	Austria	37	2200	...	...	...	85	0	2.32	...	—	—	—	—	—	—	—	—
96-97—VEU Feldkirch...............	Alpenliga	45	2792	...	...	...	105	0	2.26	...	—	—	—	—	—	—	—	—
—VEU Feldkirch...............	Austria	...	...	...	...	...	27	0	...	...	11	620	...	...	...	...	...	...
97-98—VEU Feldkirch...............	Austria	13	779	...	...	...	22	0	1.69	...	—	—	—	—	—	—	—	—
—VEU Feldkirch...............	Alpenliga	27	1620	...	...	...	55	0	2.04	...	—	—	—	—	—	—	—	—
98-99—VEU Feldkirch...............	Austria	15	900	...	...	...	58	0	3.87	...	—	—	—	—	—	—	—	—
99-00—Leksand	Sweden Dv. 2	48	2839	...	...	...	160	3	3.38	...	—	—	—	—	—	—	—	—
00-01—Leksand	Sweden Dv. 2	41	2451	...	...	...	141	3	3.45	...	—	—	—	—	—	—	—	—
01-02—Worcester	AHL	55	3173	28	20	5	137	3	2.59	.892	3	204	1	2	8	0	2.35	.930
—Austrian Olympic team..	Int'l	4	238	1	3	0	12	0	3.03	.875	—	—	—	—	—	—	—	—
—St. Louis	NHL	1	25	0	0	0	0	0	0.00	1.00	—	—	—	—	—	—	—	—
02-03—Worcester	AHL	9	452	6	1	0	17	0	2.26	.923	—	—	—	—	—	—	—	—
—St. Louis	NHL	2	83	2	0	0	1	0	0.72	.971	—	—	—	—	—	—	—	—
03-04—St. Louis......................	NHL	13	629	4	4	2	29	0	2.77	.900	1	18	0	0	0	0	0.00	1.00
—Worcester	AHL	31	1710	12	10	8	63	3	2.21	.911	—	—	—	—	—	—	—	—
04-05—VSV.............................	Austria	29	1651	10	13	4	73	2	2.65	.920	—	—	—	—	—	—	—	—
NHL Totals (3 years)............		16	737	6	4	2	30	0	2.44	.909	1	18	0	0	0	0	0.00	1.00

D

DOAN, SHANE — LW — COYOTES

PERSONAL: Born October 10, 1976, in Halkirk, Alta. ... 6-2/216. ... Shoots right. ... Name pronounced DOHN.

TRANSACTIONS/CAREER NOTES: Selected by Winnipeg Jets in first round (first Jets pick, seventh overall) of NHL draft (July 8, 1995). ... Flu (January 8, 1996); missed one game. ... Bruised ribs (January 14, 1996); missed two games. ... Strained back (February 23, 1996); missed two games. ... Jets franchise moved to Phoenix and renamed Coyotes for 1996-97 season; NHL approved move on January 18, 1996. ... Sprained ankle (October 14, 1996); missed two games. ... Strained ligament in foot (November 8, 1996); missed eight games. ... Bruised hand (February 22, 1997); missed four games. ... Injured eye (February 20, 1999); missed one game. ... Injured forearm (March 15, 1999); missed one game. ... Injured knee (December 10, 2000); missed one game. ... Strained muscle in abdomen (January 24, 2001); missed five games. ... Sprained ankle (March 17, 2002); missed one game. ... Charley horse (March 12, 2004); missed two games. ... Injured knee (April 2, 2004); missed final game of season.

Season Team	League	GP	G	A	Pts.	PIM	+/-	PP	SH	GP	G	A	Pts.	PIM
		REGULAR SEASON								PLAYOFFS				
92-93—Kamloops	WHL	51	7	12	19	55	...	...	...	13	0	1	1	8
93-94—Kamloops	WHL	52	24	24	48	88	...	...	...	—	—	—	—	—
94-95—Kamloops	WHL	71	37	57	94	106	47	12	1	21	6	10	16	16
95-96—Winnipeg	NHL	74	7	10	17	101	-9	1	0	6	0	0	0	6
96-97—Phoenix......................	NHL	63	4	8	12	49	-3	0	0	4	0	0	0	2
97-98—Phoenix......................	NHL	33	5	6	11	35	-3	0	0	6	1	0	1	6
—Springfield	AHL	39	21	21	42	64	20	6	0	—	—	—	—	—
98-99—Phoenix......................	NHL	79	6	16	22	54	-5	0	0	7	2	2	4	6
99-00—Phoenix......................	NHL	81	26	25	51	66	6	1	1	4	1	2	3	8
00-01—Phoenix......................	NHL	76	26	37	63	89	0	6	1	—	—	—	—	—
01-02—Phoenix......................	NHL	81	20	29	49	61	11	6	0	5	2	2	4	6
02-03—Phoenix......................	NHL	82	21	37	58	86	3	7	0	—	—	—	—	—
03-04—Phoenix......................	NHL	79	27	41	68	47	-11	9	2	—	—	—	—	—
NHL Totals (9 years)...........		648	142	209	351	588	-11	30	4	32	6	6	12	34

DOIG, JASON — D

PERSONAL: Born January 29, 1977, in Montreal. ... 6-3/223. ... Shoots right. ... Name pronounced DOYG.

TRANSACTIONS/CAREER NOTES: Selected by Winnipeg Jets in second round (third Jets pick, 34th overall) of NHL draft (July 8, 1995). ... Had irregular heart beat (November 17, 1995); missed four games. ... Jets franchise moved to Phoenix and renamed Coyotes for 1996-97 season; NHL approved move on January 18, 1996. ... Hyperextended elbow; missed first five games of 1996-97 season. ... Sprained knee (November 20, 1997); missed 26 games. ... Tore pectoral muscle; missed first 18 games of 1998-99 season. ... Traded by Coyotes with sixth-round pick (C Jay Dardis) in 1999 entry draft to New York Rangers for D Stan Neckar (March 23, 1999). ... Sprained knee (February 8, 2000); missed five games. ... Traded by Rangers with RW Jeff Ulmer to Ottawa Senators for D Sean Gagnon (June 29, 2001). ... Signed as free agent by Washington Capitals (September 13, 2002). ... Suspended two games for kneeing incident (January 30, 2004). ... Sprained wrist (March 6, 2004); missed final 15 games of season.

		REGULAR SEASON								PLAYOFFS				
Season Team	League	GP	G	A	Pts.	PIM	+/-	PP	SH	GP	G	A	Pts.	PIM
93-94—St. Jean	QMJHL	63	8	17	25	65	...	...	...	5	0	2	2	2
94-95—Laval	QMJHL	55	13	42	55	259	23	6	1	20	4	13	17	39
95-96—Winnipeg	NHL	15	1	1	2	28	-2	0	0	—	—	—	—	—
—Springfield	AHL	5	0	0	0	28	...	...	...	—	—	—	—	—
—Laval	QMJHL	2	1	1	2	6	...	...	...	—	—	—	—	—
—Granby	QMJHL	27	6	35	41	*105	...	...	...	20	10	22	32	110
96-97—Las Vegas	IHL	6	0	1	1	19	...	...	...	—	—	—	—	—
—Granby	QMJHL	39	14	33	47	197	...	...	...	5	0	4	4	27
—Springfield	AHL	5	0	3	3	2	0	0	0	17	1	4	5	37
97-98—Springfield	AHL	46	2	25	27	153	20	1	0	3	0	0	0	2
—Phoenix	NHL	4	0	1	1	12	-4	0	0	—	—	—	—	—
98-99—Phoenix	NHL	9	0	1	1	10	2	0	0	—	—	—	—	—
—Springfield	AHL	32	3	5	8	67	-2	0	0	—	—	—	—	—
—Hartford	AHL	8	1	4	5	40	-2	1	0	7	1	1	2	39
99-00—New York Rangers	NHL	7	0	1	1	22	-2	0	0	—	—	—	—	—
—Hartford	AHL	27	3	11	14	70	...	...	...	21	1	5	6	20
00-01—New York Rangers	NHL	3	0	0	0	0	0	0	0	—	—	—	—	—
—Hartford	AHL	52	4	20	24	178	...	...	...	5	0	1	1	4
01-02—Grand Rapids	AHL	57	1	17	18	103	13	0	0	5	0	0	0	18
02-03—Portland	AHL	21	1	4	5	66	2	0	0	—	—	—	—	—
—Washington	NHL	55	3	5	8	108	-3	0	0	6	0	1	1	6
03-04—Washington	NHL	65	2	9	11	105	-12	0	0	—	—	—	—	—
NHL Totals (7 years)		158	6	18	24	285	-21	0	0	6	0	1	1	6

DOMI, TIE — RW — MAPLE LEAFS

PERSONAL: Born November 1, 1969, in Windsor, Ont. ... 5-10/213. ... Shoots right. ... Name pronounced TIGH DOH-mee.

TRANSACTIONS/CAREER NOTES: Selected by Toronto Maple Leafs in 2nd round (2nd Maple Leafs pick, 27th overall) of NHL draft (June 11, 1988). ... Traded by Maple Leafs with G Mark Laforest to New York Rangers for RW Greg Johnston (June 28, 1990). ... Sprained right knee (March 11, 1992); missed eight games. ... Traded by Rangers with LW Kris King to Winnipeg Jets for C Ed Olczyk (December 28, 1992). ... Fined $500 for premeditated fight (January 4, 1993). ... Sprained knee (January 25, 1994); missed three games. ... Traded by Jets to Maple Leafs for C Mike Eastwood and third-round pick (RW Brad Isbister) in 1995 draft (April 7, 1995). ... Strained groin (April 8, 1995); missed two games. ... Flu (April 19, 1995); missed one game. ... Suspended eight games for fighting (October 17, 1995). ... Sprained knee (December 2, 1995); missed two games. ... Fined $1,000 for fighting (November 13, 1996). ... Sprained ankle (April 2, 1997); missed two games. ... Strained abdominal muscle (October 25, 1997); missed two games. ... Sprained knee (January 7, 1999); missed 10 games. ... Injured (October 30, 1999); missed five games. ... Injured (January 14, 2000); missed seven games. ... Suspended remainder of playoffs and first eight games of 2001-02 season game for elbowing incident (May 4, 2001). ... Traded by Maple Leafs to Nashville Predators for eighth-round pick (C Shaun Landolt) in 2003 draft (June 30, 2002). ... Signed as free agent by Maple Leafs (July 12, 2002). ... Suspended two games for unsportsmanlike conduct (March 5, 2003). ... Signed as free agent by Maple Leafs (Aug. 4, 2005).

		REGULAR SEASON								PLAYOFFS				
Season Team	League	GP	G	A	Pts.	PIM	+/-	PP	SH	GP	G	A	Pts.	PIM
85-86—Windsor Jr. B	OHA	32	8	17	25	346	...	...	...	—	—	—	—	—
86-87—Peterborough	OHL	18	1	1	2	79	...	...	...	—	—	—	—	—
87-88—Peterborough	OHL	60	22	21	43	*292	...	...	...	12	3	9	12	24
88-89—Peterborough	OHL	43	14	16	30	175	...	...	...	17	10	9	19	*70
89-90—Newmarket	AHL	57	14	11	25	285	...	...	...	—	—	—	—	—
—Toronto	NHL	2	0	0	0	42	0	0	0	—	—	—	—	—
90-91—New York Rangers	NHL	28	1	0	1	185	-5	0	0	—	—	—	—	—
—Binghamton	AHL	25	11	6	17	219	...	...	...	7	3	2	5	16
91-92—New York Rangers	NHL	42	2	4	6	246	-4	0	0	6	1	1	2	32
92-93—New York Rangers	NHL	12	2	0	2	95	-1	0	0	—	—	—	—	—
—Winnipeg	NHL	49	3	10	13	249	2	0	0	6	1	0	1	23
93-94—Winnipeg	NHL	81	8	11	19	*347	-8	0	0	—	—	—	—	—
94-95—Winnipeg	NHL	31	4	4	8	128	-6	0	0	—	—	—	—	—
—Toronto	NHL	9	0	1	1	31	1	0	0	7	1	0	1	0
95-96—Toronto	NHL	72	7	6	13	297	-3	0	0	6	0	2	2	4
96-97—Toronto	NHL	80	11	17	28	275	-17	2	0	—	—	—	—	—
97-98—Toronto	NHL	80	4	10	14	365	-5	0	0	—	—	—	—	—
98-99—Toronto	NHL	72	8	14	22	198	5	0	0	14	0	2	2	24
99-00—Toronto	NHL	70	5	9	14	198	-5	0	0	12	0	1	1	20
00-01—Toronto	NHL	82	13	7	20	214	2	1	0	8	0	1	1	20
01-02—Toronto	NHL	74	9	10	19	157	3	0	0	19	1	3	4	61
02-03—Toronto	NHL	79	15	14	29	171	-1	4	0	7	1	0	1	13
03-04—Toronto	NHL	80	7	13	20	208	-2	1	0	13	2	2	4	41
NHL Totals (15 years)		943	99	130	229	3406	-44	8	0	98	7	12	19	238

DONOVAN, SHEAN — RW — FLAMES

PERSONAL: Born January 22, 1975, in Timmins, Ont. ... 6-2/205. ... Shoots right. ... Name pronounced SHAWN DAHN-ih-vihn.

TRANSACTIONS/CAREER NOTES: Selected by San Jose Sharks in second round (second Sharks pick, 28th overall) of NHL entry draft (June 26, 1993). ... Suffered concussion (October 5, 1996); missed two games. ... Injured knee (December 21, 1996); missed two games. ... Traded by Sharks with first-round pick (C Alex Tanguay) in 1998 entry draft to Colorado Avalanche for C Mike Ricci and second-round pick (RW Jonathan Cheechoo) in 1998 entry draft (November 20, 1997). ... Bruised knee (January 3, 1998); missed one game. ... Bruised knee (January 21, 1998); missed three games. ... Suffered concussion (October 24, 1998); missed one game. ... Injured shoulder and jaw (February 5, 1999); missed one game. ... Injured hip (March 20, 1999); missed two games. ... Traded by Avalanche to Atlanta Thrashers for G Rick Tabaracci

(December 8, 1999). ... Strained abdominal muscle (January 1, 2000); missed three games. ... Fractured right foot (January 27, 2000); missed 20 games. ... Sprained knee (December 9, 2000); missed 13 games. ... Bruised heel (January 22, 2002); missed one game. ... Claimed on waivers by Pittsburgh Penguins (March 15, 2002). ... Cut elbow (April 8, 2002); missed two games. ... Injured knee (November 2, 2002); missed seven games. ... Fractured foot (November 30, 2002); missed 11 games. ... Traded by Penguins to Calgary Flames for D Micki Dupont and C Mathias Johansson (March 11, 2003).

STATISTICAL PLATEAUS: Three-goal games: 2000-01 (1), 2003-04 (1). Total: 2.

		REGULAR SEASON								PLAYOFFS				
Season Team	**League**	**GP**	**G**	**A**	**Pts.**	**PIM**	**+/-**	**PP**	**SH**	**GP**	**G**	**A**	**Pts.**	**PIM**
91-92—Ottawa	OHL	58	11	8	19	14	...	...	...	11	1	0	1	5
92-93—Ottawa	OHL	66	29	23	52	33	...	...	...	—	—	—	—	—
93-94—Ottawa	OHL	62	35	49	84	63	...	8	4	17	10	11	21	14
94-95—Ottawa	OHL	29	22	19	41	41	...	4	1	—	—	—	—	—
—San Jose	NHL	14	0	0	0	6	-6	0	0	7	0	1	1	6
—Kansas City	IHL	5	0	2	2	7	-2	0	0	14	5	3	8	23
95-96—Kansas City	IHL	4	0	0	0	8	...	...	...	5	0	0	0	8
—San Jose	NHL	74	13	8	21	39	-17	0	1	—	—	—	—	—
96-97—San Jose	NHL	73	9	6	15	42	-18	0	1	—	—	—	—	—
—Kentucky	AHL	3	1	3	4	18	2	0	0	—	—	—	—	—
—Canadian nat'l team	Int'l	10	0	1	1	31	...	...	...	—	—	—	—	—
97-98—San Jose	NHL	20	3	3	6	22	3	0	0	—	—	—	—	—
—Colorado	NHL	47	5	7	12	48	3	0	0	—	—	—	—	—
98-99—Colorado	NHL	68	7	12	19	37	4	1	0	5	0	0	0	2
99-00—Colorado	NHL	18	1	0	1	8	-4	0	0	—	—	—	—	—
—Atlanta	NHL	33	4	7	11	18	-13	1	0	—	—	—	—	—
00-01—Atlanta	NHL	63	12	11	23	47	-14	1	3	—	—	—	—	—
01-02—Atlanta	NHL	48	6	6	12	40	-16	1	0	—	—	—	—	—
—Pittsburgh	NHL	13	2	1	3	4	-5	0	0	—	—	—	—	—
02-03—Pittsburgh	NHL	52	4	5	9	30	-6	0	1	—	—	—	—	—
—Calgary	NHL	13	1	2	3	7	-2	0	0	—	—	—	—	—
03-04—Calgary	NHL	82	18	24	42	72	14	3	3	24	5	5	10	23
04-05—Geneva	Switzerland	12	5	3	8	30	...	1	1	—	—	—	—	—
NHL Totals (10 years)		618	85	92	177	420	-77	7	9	36	5	6	11	31

D

DOULL, DOUG — LW — COYOTES

PERSONAL: Born May 31, 1974, in Glace Bay, N.S. ... 6-2/216. ... Shoots left.

TRANSACTIONS/CAREER NOTES: Signed as free agent by Toronto Maple Leafs (July 25, 2001). ... Signed as free agent by Boston Bruins (July 28, 2003). ... Flu (January 7, 2004); missed one game. ... Suspended one game for charging incident (January 20, 2004). ... Signed as free agent by Phoenix Coyotes (September 2, 2004).

		REGULAR SEASON								PLAYOFFS				
Season Team	**League**	**GP**	**G**	**A**	**Pts.**	**PIM**	**+/-**	**PP**	**SH**	**GP**	**G**	**A**	**Pts.**	**PIM**
91-92—Belleville	OHL	62	6	11	17	123	...	...	...	—	—	—	—	—
92-93—Belleville	OHL	65	19	37	56	143	...	...	...	—	—	—	—	—
93-94—Belleville	OHL	62	13	24	37	143	...	...	...	—	—	—	—	—
94-95—Belleville	OHL	29	7	12	19	71	...	...	...	16	2	13	15	39
95-96—St. Mary's University	AUAA	11	4	4	8	54	...	...	...	—	—	—	—	—
96-97—St. Mary's University	AUAA	18	3	10	13	138	...	...	...	—	—	—	—	—
97-98—St. Mary's University	AUAA	25	4	11	15	227	...	...	...	—	—	—	—	—
98-99—Michigan	IHL	55	4	11	15	227	...	...	...	3	1	1	2	4
99-00—Manitoba	AHL	45	4	4	8	184	...	...	...	2	0	0	0	2
—Detroit	IHL	17	0	2	2	69	...	...	...	—	—	—	—	—
00-01—Manchester	England	15	1	6	7	51	...	...	...	—	—	—	—	—
—Saint John	AHL	49	3	10	13	167	...	...	...	16	0	1	1	32
01-02—St. John's	AHL	36	5	8	13	166	...	...	...	9	0	1	1	17
02-03—St. John's	AHL	70	15	10	25	257	...	...	...	—	—	—	—	—
03-04—Providence	AHL	22	1	0	1	98	-7	0	0	—	—	—	—	—
—Boston	NHL	35	0	1	1	132	2	0	0	—	—	—	—	—
04-05—Utah	AHL	40	1	1	2	232	-11	0	0	—	—	—	—	—
NHL Totals (1 year)		35	0	1	1	132	2	0	0					

DOWD, JIM — C — BLACKHAWKS

PERSONAL: Born December 25, 1968, in Brick, N.J. ... 6-1/190. ... Shoots right.

TRANSACTIONS/CAREER NOTES: Selected by New Jersey Devils in 8th round (7th Devils pick, 149th overall) of NHL draft (June 13, 1987). ... Injured shoulder (February 2, 1995) and had shoulder surgery; missed 35 games. ... Traded by Devils with 2nd-round pick (traded to Calgary; Flames selected Dmitri Kokorev) in 1997 draft to Hartford Whalers for RW Jocelyn Lemieux and second-round pick (traded to Dallas; Stars picked D John Erskine) in 1998 draft (December 19, 1995). ... Traded by Whalers with D Frantisek Kucera and 2nd-round pick (D Ryan Bonni) in 1997 draft to Vancouver Canucks for D Jeff Brown and 3rd-round pick (traded to Dallas; Stars picked D Paul Manning) in 1998 draft (December 19, 1995). ... Selected by New York Islanders from Canucks in waiver draft (September 30, 1996). ... Signed as free agent by Calgary Flames (July 10, 1997). ... Traded by Flames to Nashville Predators for future considerations (June 27, 1998). ... Traded by Predators with G Mikhail Shtalenkov to Edmonton Oilers for G Eric Fichaud, D Drake Berehowsky and D Greg de Vries (October 1, 1998). ... Selected by Minnesota Wild in expansion draft (June 23, 2000). ... Injured ribs (January 6, 2001); missed 10 games. ... Strained neck (March 31, 2001); missed four games. ... Flu (December 14, 2002); missed one game. ... Injured groin (February 10, 2004); missed 10 games. ... Traded by Wild to Montreal Canadiens for 4th-round pick (W Julien Sprunger) in 2004 draft (March 4, 2004). ... Signed as free agent by Chicago Blackhawks (Aug. 5, 2005).

		REGULAR SEASON								PLAYOFFS				
Season Team	**League**	**GP**	**G**	**A**	**Pts.**	**PIM**	**+/-**	**PP**	**SH**	**GP**	**G**	**A**	**Pts.**	**PIM**
83-84—Brick Township	N.J. H.S.	...	19	30	49	...	...	...	...	—	—	—	—	—
84-85—Brick Township	N.J. H.S.	...	58	55	113	...	...	...	...	—	—	—	—	—
85-86—Brick Township	N.J. H.S.	...	47	51	98	...	...	...	...	—	—	—	—	—

Season Team	League	GP	G	A	Pts.	PIM	+/-	PP	SH	GP	G	A	Pts.	PIM
		REGULAR SEASON								PLAYOFFS				
86-87—Brick Township	N.J. H.S.	24	22	33	55	...	...	...	...	—	—	—	—	—
87-88—Lake Superior St.	CCHA	45	18	27	45	16	...	...	...	—	—	—	—	—
88-89—Lake Superior St.	CCHA	46	24	35	59	40	...	...	...	—	—	—	—	—
89-90—Lake Superior St.	CCHA	46	25	67	92	30	...	...	...	—	—	—	—	—
90-91—Lake Superior St.	CCHA	44	24	54	78	53	...	...	...	—	—	—	—	—
91-92—Utica	AHL	78	17	42	59	47	...	...	...	4	2	2	4	4
—New Jersey	NHL	1	0	0	0	0	0	0	0	—	—	—	—	—
92-93—Utica	AHL	78	27	45	72	62	-6	3	2	5	1	7	8	10
—New Jersey	NHL	1	0	0	0	0	-1	0	0	—	—	—	—	—
93-94—Albany	AHL	58	26	37	63	76	15	3	3	—	—	—	—	—
—New Jersey	NHL	15	5	10	15	0	8	2	0	19	2	6	8	8
94-95—New Jersey	NHL	10	1	4	5	0	-5	1	0	11	2	1	3	8
95-96—New Jersey	NHL	28	4	9	13	17	-1	0	0	—	—	—	—	—
—Vancouver	NHL	38	1	6	7	6	-8	0	0	1	0	0	0	0
96-97—New York Islanders	NHL	3	0	0	0	0	-1	0	0	—	—	—	—	—
—Utah	IHL	48	10	21	31	27	...	...	...	—	—	—	—	—
—Saint John	AHL	24	5	11	16	18	-5	2	0	5	1	2	3	0
97-98—Saint John	AHL	35	8	30	38	20	5	1	1	19	3	13	16	10
—Calgary	NHL	48	6	8	14	12	10	0	1	—	—	—	—	—
98-99—Hamilton	AHL	51	15	29	44	82	3	5	2	11	3	6	9	8
—Edmonton	NHL	1	0	0	0	0	0	0	0	—	—	—	—	—
99-00—Edmonton	NHL	69	5	18	23	45	10	2	0	5	2	1	3	4
00-01—Minnesota	NHL	68	7	22	29	80	-6	0	0	—	—	—	—	—
01-02—Minnesota	NHL	82	13	30	43	54	-14	5	0	—	—	—	—	—
02-03—Minnesota	NHL	78	8	17	25	31	-1	3	1	15	0	2	2	0
03-04—Minnesota	NHL	55	4	20	24	38	6	2	0	—	—	—	—	—
—Montreal	NHL	14	3	2	5	6	6	0	1	11	0	2	2	2
04-05—Hamburg	Germany	20	4	9	13	12	1	1	1	...	...	...	...	...
NHL Totals (13 years)		511	57	146	203	289	3	15	3	62	6	12	18	22

DOWNEY, AARON RW BLUES

PERSONAL: Born August 27, 1974, in Shelburne, Ont. ... 6-1/216. ... Shoots right.

TRANSACTIONS/CAREER NOTES: Signed as free agent by Boston Bruins (January 20, 1998). ... Signed as free agent by Chicago Blackhawks (August 8, 2000). ... Signed as free agent by Dallas Stars (July 3, 2002). ... Injured hip flexor (November 11, 2003); missed 17 games. ... Signed as free agent by St. Louis Blues (Aug. 1, 2005).

Season Team	League	GP	G	A	Pts.	PIM	+/-	PP	SH	GP	G	A	Pts.	PIM
		REGULAR SEASON								PLAYOFFS				
92-93—Guelph	OHL	53	3	3	6	88	...	...	...	5	1	0	1	0
93-94—Cole Harbor	MWJHL	35	8	20	28	210	...	...	...	—	—	—	—	—
94-95—Cole Harbor	MWJHL	40	10	31	41	320	...	...	...	—	—	—	—	—
95-96—Hampton	ECHL	65	12	11	23	354	...	...	...	—	—	—	—	—
96-97—Hampton	ECHL	64	8	8	16	338	...	...	...	9	0	3	3	26
—Portland	AHL	3	0	0	0	19	...	...	...	—	—	—	—	—
—Manitoba	IHL	2	0	0	0	17	...	...	...	—	—	—	—	—
97-98—Providence	AHL	78	5	10	15	*407	-8	0	0	—	—	—	—	—
98-99—Providence	AHL	75	10	12	22	*401	3	1	0	19	1	1	2	46
99-00—Providence	AHL	47	6	4	10	221	...	...	...	14	1	0	1	24
—Boston	NHL	1	0	0	0	0	0	0	0	—	—	—	—	—
00-01—Norfolk	AHL	67	6	15	21	234	...	...	...	9	0	0	0	4
—Chicago	NHL	3	0	0	0	6	-1	0	0	—	—	—	—	—
01-02—Chicago	NHL	36	1	0	1	76	-2	0	0	4	0	0	0	8
—Norfolk	AHL	12	0	2	2	21	1	0	0	—	—	—	—	—
02-03—Dallas	NHL	43	1	1	2	69	1	0	0	—	—	—	—	—
03-04—Dallas	NHL	37	1	1	2	77	2	0	0	—	—	—	—	—
NHL Totals (5 years)		120	3	2	5	228	0	0	0	4	0	0	0	8

DOWNIE, STEVE RW FLYERS

PERSONAL: Born April 3, 1987, in Newmarket, Ont. ... 5-10/192. ... Shoots right.

TRANSACTIONS/CAREER NOTES: Selected by Philadelphia Flyers in 1st round (1st Flyers pick, 29th overall) of entry draft (July 30, 2005).

Season Team	League	GP	G	A	Pts.	PIM	+/-	PP	SH	GP	G	A	Pts.	PIM
		REGULAR SEASON								PLAYOFFS				
04-05—Windsor	OHL	61	21	52	73	179	1	9	0	11	4	5	9	49

DRAKE, DALLAS RW BLUES

PERSONAL: Born February 4, 1969, in Trail, B.C. ... 6-0/195. ... Shoots left.

TRANSACTIONS/CAREER NOTES: Selected by Detroit Red Wings in sixth round (sixth Red Wings pick, 116th overall) of NHL draft (June 17, 1989). ... Bruised left leg (November 27, 1992); missed three games. ... Back spasms (December 28, 1992); missed one game. ... Bruised kneecap (January 23, 1993); missed three games. ... Suffered concussion (February 13, 1993); missed one game. ... Injured right wrist (October 16, 1993); missed three games. ... Injured tendon in right hand (December 14, 1993); missed 16 games. ... Traded by Red Wings with G Tim Cheveldae to Winnipeg Jets for G Bob Essensa and D Sergei Bautin (March 8, 1994). ... Back spasms (March 17, 1995); missed four games. ... Bruised right shoulder (October 22, 1995); missed seven games. ... Ear infection (November 21, 1995); missed two games. ... Strained Achilles' tendon (December 28, 1995); missed two games. ... Jets franchise moved to Phoenix and renamed Coyotes for 1996-97 season; NHL approved move on January 18, 1996. ... Sprained ankle (November 16, 1996); missed eight games. ... Sprained knee (January

29, 1997); missed 10 games. ... Flu (October 19, 1997); missed one game. ... Injured knee (December 3, 1997); missed 12 games. ... Bruised knee (March 2, 1998); missed one game. ... Injured wrist (March 18, 1998); missed five games. ... Bruised ankle (October 21, 1998); missed one game. ... Suffered concussion (November 6, 1998); missed two games. ... Bruised elbow (December 28, 1998); missed one game. ... Suspended four games by NHL for illegal hit (December 29, 1998). ... Separated shoulder (January 29, 1999); missed 13 games. ... Strained shoulder (March 15, 1999); missed two games. ... Bruised shoulder (March 23, 1999); missed five games. ... Sprained shoulder (October 30, 1999); missed three games. ... Selected by Columbus Blue Jackets in expansion draft (June 23, 2000). ... Signed as free agent by St. Louis Blues (July 1, 2000). ... Injured knee (November 6, 2001); missed one game. ... Injured ankle (November 20, 2002); missed one game. ... Flu (December 20, 2002); missed one game. ... Fractured cheekbone (October 9, 2003); missed two games.

		REGULAR SEASON								PLAYOFFS				
Season Team	League	GP	G	A	Pts.	PIM	+/-	PP	SH	GP	G	A	Pts.	PIM
84-85—Rossland	KIJHL	30	13	37	50	...	...	...	...	—	—	—	—	—
85-86—Rossland	KIJHL	41	53	73	126	...	...	...	...	—	—	—	—	—
86-87—Rossland	KIJHL	40	55	80	135	...	...	...	...	—	—	—	—	—
87-88—Vernon	BCHL	47	39	85	124	50	...	...	...	11	9	17	26	30
88-89—N. Michigan Univ.	WCHA	45	18	24	42	26	...	...	...	—	—	—	—	—
89-90—N. Michigan Univ.	WCHA	36	13	24	37	42	...	...	...	—	—	—	—	—
90-91—N. Michigan Univ.	WCHA	44	22	36	58	89	...	...	...	—	—	—	—	—
91-92—N. Michigan Univ.	WCHA	40	*39	44	83	58	...	...	...	—	—	—	—	—
92-93—Detroit	NHL	72	18	26	44	93	15	3	2	7	3	3	6	6
93-94—Detroit	NHL	47	10	22	32	37	5	0	1	—	—	—	—	—
—Adirondack	AHL	1	2	0	2	0	2	0	0	—	—	—	—	—
—Winnipeg	NHL	15	3	5	8	12	-6	1	1	—	—	—	—	—
94-95—Winnipeg	NHL	43	8	18	26	30	-6	0	0	—	—	—	—	—
95-96—Winnipeg	NHL	69	19	20	39	36	-7	4	4	3	0	0	0	0
96-97—Phoenix	NHL	63	17	19	36	52	-11	5	1	7	0	1	1	2
97-98—Phoenix	NHL	60	11	29	40	71	17	3	0	4	0	1	1	2
98-99—Phoenix	NHL	53	9	22	31	65	17	0	0	7	4	3	7	4
99-00—Phoenix	NHL	79	15	30	45	62	11	0	2	5	0	1	1	4
00-01—St. Louis	NHL	82	12	29	41	71	18	2	0	15	4	2	6	16
01-02—St. Louis	NHL	80	11	15	26	87	8	1	3	8	0	0	0	8
02-03—St. Louis	NHL	80	20	10	30	66	-7	4	1	7	1	4	5	23
03-04—St. Louis	NHL	79	13	22	35	65	10	3	2	5	1	1	2	2
NHL Totals (12 years)		822	166	267	433	747	64	26	17	68	13	16	29	67

DRAPER, KRIS C RED WINGS

PERSONAL: Born May 24, 1971, in Toronto. ... 5-10/190. ... Shoots left.

TRANSACTIONS/CAREER NOTES: Selected by Winnipeg Jets in third round (fourth Jets pick, 62nd overall) of NHL draft (June 17, 1989). ... Traded by Jets to Detroit Red Wings for future considerations (June 30, 1993). ... Sprained right knee (February 4, 1995); missed eight games. ... Flu (January 5, 1996); missed one game. ... Injured right knee (February 15, 1996); missed 12 games. ... Reinjured right knee (March 25, 1996); missed three games. ... Dislocated thumb (December 17, 1997) and had surgery; missed 18 games. ... Suspended two games for slashing (January 29, 1999). ... Cut face (November 15, 1999); missed three games. ... Fractured wrist (November 24, 1999); missed 25 games. ... Injured rotator cuff (March 3, 2004); missed 14 games.

		REGULAR SEASON								PLAYOFFS				
Season Team	League	GP	G	A	Pts.	PIM	+/-	PP	SH	GP	G	A	Pts.	PIM
88-89—Canadian nat'l team	Int'l	60	11	15	26	16	...	...	...	—	—	—	—	—
89-90—Canadian nat'l team	Int'l	61	12	22	34	44	...	...	...	—	—	—	—	—
90-91—Winnipeg	NHL	3	1	0	1	5	0	0	0	—	—	—	—	—
—Moncton	AHL	7	2	1	3	2	...	...	...	—	—	—	—	—
—Ottawa	OHL	39	19	42	61	35	...	...	...	17	8	11	19	20
91-92—Moncton	AHL	61	11	18	29	113	...	...	...	4	0	1	1	6
—Winnipeg	NHL	10	2	0	2	2	0	0	0	2	0	0	0	0
92-93—Winnipeg	NHL	7	0	0	0	2	-6	0	0	—	—	—	—	—
—Moncton	AHL	67	12	23	35	40	-13	0	4	5	2	2	4	18
93-94—Adirondack	AHL	46	20	23	43	49	10	1	2	—	—	—	—	—
—Detroit	NHL	39	5	8	13	31	11	0	1	7	2	2	4	4
94-95—Detroit	NHL	36	2	6	8	22	1	0	0	18	4	1	5	12
95-96—Detroit	NHL	52	7	9	16	32	2	0	1	18	4	2	6	18
96-97—Detroit	NHL	76	8	5	13	73	-11	1	0	20	2	4	6	12
97-98—Detroit	NHL	64	13	10	23	45	5	1	0	19	1	3	4	12
98-99—Detroit	NHL	80	4	14	18	79	2	0	1	10	0	1	1	6
99-00—Detroit	NHL	51	5	7	12	28	3	0	0	9	2	0	2	6
00-01—Detroit	NHL	75	8	17	25	38	17	0	1	6	0	1	1	2
01-02—Detroit	NHL	82	15	15	30	56	26	0	2	23	2	3	5	20
02-03—Detroit	NHL	82	14	21	35	82	6	0	1	4	0	0	0	4
03-04—Detroit	NHL	67	24	16	40	31	22	2	5	12	1	3	4	6
NHL Totals (14 years)		724	108	128	236	526	78	4	12	148	18	20	38	102

DRUKEN, HAROLD C

PERSONAL: Born January 26, 1979, in St. John's, Newfoundland. ... 6-0/215. ... Shoots left. ... Name pronounced DROO-kihn.

TRANSACTIONS/CAREER NOTES: Selected by Vancouver Canucks in second round (third Canucks pick, 36th overall) of NHL draft (June 21, 1997). ... Sprained ankle (November 30, 2001); missed 11 games. ... Traded by Canucks with LW Jan Hlavac to Carolina Hurricanes for D Marek Malik and LW Darren Langdon (November 1, 2002). ... Claimed off waivers by Toronto Maple Leafs (December 11, 2002). ... Claimed off waivers by Hurricanes (January 17, 2003). ... Traded by Hurricanes to Maple Leafs for D Allan Rourke (May 30, 2003).

STATISTICAL PLATEAUS: Three-goal games: 2000-01 (1).

		REGULAR SEASON								PLAYOFFS				
Season Team	League	GP	G	A	Pts.	PIM	+/-	PP	SH	GP	G	A	Pts.	PIM
95-96—Noble & Greenough	Mass. H.S.	30	37	28	65	28	...	...	...	—	—	—	—	—
96-97—Detroit	OHL	63	27	31	58	14	-1	12	2	5	3	2	5	0

Season Team	League	GP	G	A	Pts.	PIM	+/-	PP	SH		GP	G	A	Pts.	PIM
		REGULAR SEASON									PLAYOFFS				
97-98—Plymouth	OHL	64	38	44	82	12	...	...	...		15	9	11	20	4
98-99—Plymouth	OHL	60	*58	45	103	34	53	...	...		11	9	12	21	14
99-00—Syracuse	AHL	47	20	25	45	32	...	...	...		4	1	2	3	6
—Vancouver	NHL	33	7	9	16	10	14	2	0		—	—	—	—	—
00-01—Kansas City	IHL	15	5	9	14	20	...	...	...		—	—	—	—	—
—Vancouver	NHL	55	15	15	30	14	2	6	0		4	0	1	1	0
01-02—Vancouver	NHL	27	4	4	8	6	-1	1	0		—	—	—	—	—
—Manitoba	AHL	11	2	9	11	4	-5	0	0		—	—	—	—	—
02-03—Vancouver	NHL	3	1	1	2	0	-1	0	0		—	—	—	—	—
—Carolina	NHL	14	0	1	1	2	-1	0	0		—	—	—	—	—
—Toronto	NHL	5	0	2	2	2	1	0	0		—	—	—	—	—
—St. John's	AHL	6	0	3	3	2	-4	0	0		—	—	—	—	—
—Lowell	AHL	24	8	10	18	8	-10	2	0		—	—	—	—	—
03-04—Toronto	NHL	9	0	4	4	2	4	0	0		—	—	—	—	—
—St. John's	AHL	57	26	25	51	31	-18	8	0		—	—	—	—	—
04-05—St. John's	AHL	48	18	20	38	28	-12	7	0		0	0	0	0	0
NHL Totals (5 years)		146	27	36	63	36	18	9	0		4	0	1	1	0

DRURY, CHRIS C/LW SABRES

PERSONAL: Born August 20, 1976, in Trumbull, Conn. ... 5-10/202. ... Shoots right. ... Brother of Ted Drury, C, played for six NHL teams (1993-2001).

TRANSACTIONS/CAREER NOTES: Selected by Quebec Nordiques in third round (fifth Nordiques pick, 72nd overall) of NHL entry draft (June 29, 1994). ... Nordiques franchise moved to Colorado and renamed Avalanche for 1995-96 season (June 21, 1995). ... Had hip pointer (October 29, 1998); missed two games. ... Sprained knee (November 1, 2000); missed 11 games. ... Traded by Avalanche with C Stephane Yelle to Calgary Flames for D Derek Morris, LW Deam McAmmond and C Jeff Shantz (October 1, 2002). ... Traded by Flames with C Steve Begin to Buffalo Sabres for D Rhett Warrener and C Steve Reinprecht (July 2, 2003). ... Separated shoulder (December 16, 2003); missed four games. ... Suffered concussion (March 15, 2004); missed two games.

Season Team	League	GP	G	A	Pts.	PIM	+/-	PP	SH		GP	G	A	Pts.	PIM
		REGULAR SEASON									PLAYOFFS				
92-93—Fairfield College Prep..	Conn. H.S.	24	25	32	57	15	...	...	...		—	—	—	—	—
93-94—Fairfield College Prep..	Conn. H.S.	24	37	18	55	...	...	...	...		—	—	—	—	—
94-95—Boston University	Hockey East	39	12	15	27	38	15	1	0		—	—	—	—	—
95-96—Boston University	Hockey East	37	35	33	68	46	...	...	...		—	—	—	—	—
96-97—Boston University	Hockey East	41	38	24	62	64	29	10	4		—	—	—	—	—
97-98—Boston University	Hockey East	38	28	29	57	88	...	...	...		—	—	—	—	—
98-99—Colorado	NHL	79	20	24	44	62	9	6	0		19	6	2	8	4
99-00—Colorado	NHL	82	20	47	67	42	8	7	0		17	4	10	14	4
00-01—Colorado	NHL	71	24	41	65	47	6	11	0		23	11	5	16	4
01-02—Colorado	NHL	82	21	25	46	38	1	5	0		21	5	7	12	10
02-03—Calgary	NHL	80	23	30	53	33	-9	5	1		—	—	—	—	—
03-04—Buffalo	NHL	76	18	35	53	68	8	5	1		—	—	—	—	—
NHL Totals (6 years)		470	126	202	328	290	23	39	2		80	26	24	50	22

DUBIELEWICZ, WADE G ISLANDERS

PERSONAL: Born January 30, 1979, in Invermere, B.C. ... 5-10/180. ... Catches left.

TRANSACTIONS/CAREER NOTES: Signed as free agent by New York Islanders (July 2, 2003).

Season Team	League	GP	Min.	W	L	T	GA	SO	GAA	SV%		GP	Min.	W	L	GA	SO	GAA	SV%
		REGULAR SEASON										PLAYOFFS							
99-00—Denver	WCHA	13	596	3	5	1	27	1	2.72	.902		—	—	—	—	—	—	—	—
00-01—Denver	WCHA	29	1542	12	9	3	59	2	2.30	.921		—	—	—	—	—	—	—	—
01-02—Denver	WCHA	24	1431	20	4	0	41	2	1.72	.943		—	—	—	—	—	—	—	—
02-03—Denver	WCHA	19	1060	9	8	2	43	3	2.43	.912		—	—	—	—	—	—	—	—
03-04—New York Islanders	NHL	2	105	1	0	1	3	0	1.71	.940		—	—	—	—	—	—	—	—
—Bridgeport	AHL	33	1959	20	8	5	45	9	1.38	.943		3	181	2	1	11	0	3.65	.864
04-05—Bridgeport	AHL	43	2538	18	23	...	113	1	2.67	.911		—	—	—	—	—	—	—	—
NHL Totals (1 year)		2	105	1	0	1	3	0	1.71	.940									

DUBNYK, DEVAN G OILERS

PERSONAL: Born May 4, 1986, in Regina, Sask. ... 6-5/194. ... Catches left.

TRANSACTIONS/CAREER NOTES: Selected by Edmonton Oilers in first round (first Oilers pick, 14th overall) of NHL entry draft (June 26, 2004).

Season Team	League	GP	Min.	W	L	T	GA	SO	GAA	SV%		GP	Min.	W	L	GA	SO	GAA	SV%
		REGULAR SEASON										PLAYOFFS							
01-02—Kamloops	WHL	3	143	1	1	0	13	0	5.45	.838		—	—	—	—	—	—	—	—
02-03—Kamloops	WHL	26	1279	12	8	1	66	1	3.10	.907		—	—	—	—	—	—	—	—
03-04—Kamloops	WHL	44	2533	20	18	5	106	6	2.51	.917		—	—	—	—	—	—	—	—
04-05—Kamloops	WHL	65	3699	23	34	7	166	6	2.69	.910		6	363	2	4	22	0	3.64	.890

DUMONT, J.P. RW SABRES

PERSONAL: Born April 1, 1978, in Montreal. ... 6-1/203. ... Shoots left.

TRANSACTIONS/CAREER NOTES: Selected by New York Islanders in first round (first Islanders pick, third overall) of NHL draft (June 22, 1996). ... Traded by Islanders with fifth-round pick (traded to Philadelphia) in 1998 draft to Chicago Blackhawks for C/LW Dmitri Nabokov (May 30, 1998). ... Injured back (April 8, 1999); missed two games. ... Traded by Blackhawks with C Doug Gilmour to Buffalo Sabres for LW Michal Grosek (March 10, 2000). ... Injured rib (February 13, 2001); missed two games. ... Injured shoulder (April 1, 2002); missed remainder of season. ... Flu (December 13, 2002); missed two games. ... Injured hip (December 26, 2003); missed five games.

STATISTICAL PLATEAUS: Three-goal games: 1998-99 (1), 2000-01 (1), 2001-02 (1). Total: 3.

		REGULAR SEASON								PLAYOFFS				
Season Team	League	GP	G	A	Pts.	PIM	+/-	PP	SH	GP	G	A	Pts.	PIM
93-94—Val-d'Or	QMJHL	25	9	11	20	10	...	...	...	—	—	—	—	—
94-95—Val-d'Or	QMJHL	48	5	14	19	24	...	...	...	—	—	—	—	—
95-96—Val-d'Or	QMJHL	66	48	57	105	109	...	...	...	13	12	8	20	22
96-97—Val-d'Or	QMJHL	62	44	64	108	88	...	...	...	13	9	7	16	12
97-98—Val-d'Or	QMJHL	55	57	42	99	63	...	...	...	19	*31	15	*46	18
98-99—Portland	AHL	50	32	14	46	39	-2	12	0	—	—	—	—	—
—Chicago	NHL	25	9	6	15	10	7	0	0	—	—	—	—	—
99-00—Chicago	NHL	47	10	8	18	18	-6	0	0	—	—	—	—	—
—Cleveland	IHL	7	5	2	7	8	...	...	...	—	—	—	—	—
—Rochester	AHL	13	7	10	17	18	...	...	...	21	*14	7	21	32
00-01—Buffalo	NHL	79	23	28	51	54	1	9	0	13	4	3	7	8
01-02—Buffalo	NHL	76	23	21	44	42	-10	7	0	—	—	—	—	—
02-03—Buffalo	NHL	76	14	21	35	44	-14	2	0	—	—	—	—	—
03-04—Buffalo	NHL	77	22	31	53	40	-9	10	0	—	—	—	—	—
04-05—Bern	Switzerland	3	2	2	4	6	...	0	0	10	4	1	5	14
NHL Totals (6 years)		380	101	115	216	208	-31	28	0	13	4	3	7	8

DUNHAM, MIKE G

PERSONAL: Born June 1, 1972, in Johnson City, N.Y. ... 6-2/190. ... Catches left.

TRANSACTIONS/CAREER NOTES: Selected by New Jersey Devils in third round (fourth Devils pick, 53rd overall) of NHL draft (June 16, 1990). ... Injured hand (January 1, 1998); missed three games. ... Injured knee and had surgery (March 5, 1998); missed 18 games. ... Selected by Nashville Predators in expansion draft (June 26, 1998). ... Strained right groin (November 29, 1998); missed seven games. ... Reinjured groin (December 19, 1998); missed 13 games. ... Strained groin (March 27, 1999); missed six games. ... Flu (December 26, 1999); missed one game. ... Sprained right thumb (February 3, 2000); missed four games. ... Sprained left knee (October 27, 2000); missed 15 games. ... Injured knee (December 4, 2000); missed two games. ... Strained neck (February 20, 2001); missed one game. ... Had concussion (April 6, 2002); missed remainder of season. ... Strained groin (December 5, 2002); missed three games. ... Traded by Predators to New York Rangers for LW Rem Murray, D Tomas Kloucek and D Marek Zidlicky (December 12, 2002). ... Injured groin (February 5, 2003); missed two games. ... Injured hamstring (March 22, 2003); missed one game. ... Injured hip (November 18, 2003); missed three games. ... Suffered concussion (January 22, 2004); missed two games. ... Flu (February 16, 2004); missed one game. ... Bruised shoulder (March 27, 2004); missed two games.

		REGULAR SEASON									PLAYOFFS							
Season Team	League	GP	Min.	W	L	T	GA	SO	GAA	SV%	GP	Min.	W	L	GA	SO	GAA	SV%
87-88—Canterbury School	Conn. H.S.	29	1740	...	...	...	69	4	2.38	...	—	—	—	—	—	—	—	—
88-89—Canterbury School	Conn. H.S.	25	1500	...	...	...	63	2	2.52	...	—	—	—	—	—	—	—	—
89-90—Canterbury School	Conn. H.S.	32	1558	...	...	...	55	3	2.12	...	—	—	—	—	—	—	—	—
90-91—Maine	Hockey East	23	1275	14	5	2	63	2	*2.96	...	—	—	—	—	—	—	—	—
91-92—Maine	Hockey East	7	382	6	0	0	14	1	2.20	...	—	—	—	—	—	—	—	—
—U.S. national team	Int'l	3	157	0	1	1	10	0	3.82	...	—	—	—	—	—	—	—	—
92-93—Maine	Hockey East	25	1429	21	1	1	63	0	2.65	...	—	—	—	—	—	—	—	—
—U.S. national team	Int'l	1	60	0	0	1	1	0	1.00	...	—	—	—	—	—	—	—	—
93-94—U.S. national team	Int'l	33	1983	22	9	2	125	2	3.78	...	—	—	—	—	—	—	—	—
—U.S. Olympic team	Int'l	3	180	0	1	2	15	0	5.00	.826	—	—	—	—	—	—	—	—
—Albany	AHL	5	305	2	2	1	26	0	5.11	.858	—	—	—	—	—	—	—	—
94-95—Albany	AHL	35	2120	20	7	8	99	1	2.80	.898	7	420	6	1	20	1	2.86	.895
95-96—Albany	AHL	44	2591	30	10	2	109	1	2.52	...	3	181	1	2	5	1	1.66	...
96-97—Albany	AHL	3	184	1	1	1	12	0	3.91	.871	—	—	—	—	—	—	—	—
—New Jersey	NHL	26	1013	8	7	1	43	2	2.55	.906	—	—	—	—	—	—	—	—
97-98—New Jersey	NHL	15	773	5	5	3	29	1	2.25	.913	—	—	—	—	—	—	—	—
98-99—Nashville	NHL	44	2472	16	23	3	127	1	3.08	.908	—	—	—	—	—	—	—	—
99-00—Milwaukee	IHL	1	60	2	0	0	1	0	1.00	...	—	—	—	—	—	—	—	—
—Nashville	NHL	52	3077	19	27	6	146	0	2.85	.908	—	—	—	—	—	—	—	—
00-01—Nashville	NHL	48	2810	21	21	4	107	4	2.28	.923	—	—	—	—	—	—	—	—
01-02—Nashville	NHL	58	3316	23	24	9	144	3	2.61	.906	—	—	—	—	—	—	—	—
—U.S. Olympic team	Int'l	1	60	1	0	0	0	1	0.00	1.00	—	—	—	—	—	—	—	—
02-03—Nashville	NHL	15	819	2	9	2	43	0	3.15	.892	—	—	—	—	—	—	—	—
—New York Rangers	NHL	43	2467	19	17	5	94	5	2.29	.924	—	—	—	—	—	—	—	—
03-04—New York Rangers	NHL	57	3148	16	30	6	159	2	3.03	.896	—	—	—	—	—	—	—	—
04-05—Skelleftea	Sweden Dv. 2	3	176	...	...	...	4	1	1.36	.945	10	550	...	...	32	3	3.49	.879
NHL Totals (8 years)		358	19895	129	163	39	892	18	2.69	.909								

DUPUIS, PASCAL LW/RW WILD

PERSONAL: Born April 7, 1979, in Laval, Que. ... 6-0/196. ... Shoots left.

TRANSACTIONS/CAREER NOTES: Signed as free agent by Minnesota Wild (September 18, 2000). ... Injured leg (October 18, 2002); missed one game. ... Missed 2003-04 season's first nine games in holdout. ... Left team for personal reasons (December 20, 2003); missed two games. ... Sprained ankle (January 9, 2004); missed one game. ... Sprained ankle (March 7, 2004); missed nine games.

Season Team	League	GP	G	A	Pts.	PIM	+/-	PP	SH	GP	G	A	Pts.	PIM
		REGULAR SEASON								PLAYOFFS				
96-97—Rouyn-Noranda	QMJHL	44	9	15	24	20	...	...	...	—	—	—	—	—
97-98—Rouyn-Noranda	QMJHL	39	9	17	26	36	...	...	...	—	—	—	—	—
—Shawinigan	QMJHL	28	7	13	20	10	...	...	...	6	2	0	2	4
98-99—Shawinigan	QMJHL	57	30	42	72	118	...	...	...	6	1	8	9	18
99-00—Shawinigan	QMJHL	61	50	55	105	164	31	17	7	13	15	7	22	4
00-01—Cleveland	IHL	70	19	24	43	37	...	...	...	4	0	0	0	0
—Minnesota	NHL	4	1	0	1	4	0	1	0	—	—	—	—	—
01-02—Minnesota	NHL	76	15	12	27	16	-10	3	2	—	—	—	—	—
02-03—Minnesota	NHL	80	20	28	48	44	17	6	0	16	4	4	8	8
03-04—Minnesota	NHL	59	11	15	26	20	5	2	0	—	—	—	—	—
04-05—Ajoie	Switz. Div. 2	8	5	5	10	26	...	1	3	6	6	8	14	8
NHL Totals (4 years)		219	47	55	102	84	12	12	2	16	4	4	8	8

DURAND, CHRIS — C — AVALANCHE

PERSONAL: Born January 21, 1987, in Saskatoon, Saskatchewan. ... 6-1/186. ... Shoots right.

Season Team	League	GP	G	A	Pts.	PIM	+/-	PP	SH	GP	G	A	Pts.	PIM
		REGULAR SEASON								PLAYOFFS				
03-04—Seattle	WHL	60	17	26	43	71	...	...	...	—	—	—	—	—
04-05—Seattle	WHL	66	19	34	53	76	30	3	3	12	0	1	1	14

DUSABLON, BENOIT — C

PERSONAL: Born August 1, 1979, in Ste. Anne de la Perad, Que. ... 6-1/207. ... Shoots left.
TRANSACTIONS/CAREER NOTES: Signed as free agent by New York Rangers (October 1, 2001). ... Signed as free agent by Montreal Canadiens (August 24, 2004).

Season Team	League	GP	G	A	Pts.	PIM	+/-	PP	SH	GP	G	A	Pts.	PIM
		REGULAR SEASON								PLAYOFFS				
00-01—Johnstown	ECHL	11	2	3	5	4	...	...	...	—	—	—	—	—
—Tallahassee	ECHL	49	21	29	50	33	...	...	...	—	—	—	—	—
01-02—Charlotte	ECHL	19	12	13	25	2	...	...	...	—	—	—	—	—
—Hartford	AHL	38	8	15	23	16	...	...	...	9	1	2	3	4
02-03—Hartford	AHL	50	8	16	24	41	...	...	...	1	0	0	0	0
03-04—Charlotte	ECHL	19	10	10	20	10	1	2	0	—	—	—	—	—
—New York Rangers	NHL	3	0	0	0	2	-1	0	0	—	—	—	—	—
—Hartford	AHL	35	10	14	24	18	17	2	0	16	2	5	7	6
NHL Totals (1 year)		3	0	0	0	2	-1	0	0					

DVORAK, RADEK — RW — OILERS

PERSONAL: Born March 9, 1977, in Tabor, Czech. ... 6-2/200. ... Shoots right. ... Name pronounced RA-dihk duh-VOHR-ak.
TRANSACTIONS/CAREER NOTES: Selected by Florida Panthers in first round (first Panthers pick, 10th overall) of NHL entry draft (July 8, 1995). ... Fractured left wrist (October 30, 1997); missed 15 games. ... Traded by Panthers to San Jose Sharks for G Mike Vernon and third-round pick (RW Sean O'Connor) in 2000 entry draft (December 30, 1999). ... Traded by Sharks to New York Rangers for RW Todd Harvey and fourth-round pick (G Dimitri Patzold) in 2001 entry draft (December 30, 1999). ... Sprained left knee (November 23, 2001); missed three games. ... Tore right knee ligament (March 13, 2002); missed remainder of season. ... Injured knee (October 15, 2002); missed four games. ... Had back spasms (November 28, 2002); missed one game. ... Suffered concussion (January 21, 2003); missed three games. ... Traded by Rangers with D Cory Cross to Edmonton Oilers for RW Anson Carter and D Ales Pisa (March 11, 2003). ... Injured groin (February 16, 2004); missed four games.
STATISTICAL PLATEAUS: Three-goal games: 1999-00 (1). ... Four-goal games: 2000-01 (1). ... Total hat tricks: 2.

Season Team	League	GP	G	A	Pts.	PIM	+/-	PP	SH	GP	G	A	Pts.	PIM
		REGULAR SEASON								PLAYOFFS				
92-93—Motor-Ceske Bude.	Czech.	35	44	46	90	...	...	...	...	—	—	—	—	—
93-94—HC Ceske Budejovice	Czech Rep.	8	0	0	0	...	...	...	...	—	—	—	—	—
—Motor-Ceske Bude.	Czech Rep.	20	17	18	35	...	...	...	...	—	—	—	—	—
94-95—HC Ceske Budejovice	Czech Rep.	10	3	5	8	...	...	...	...	9	5	1	6	...
95-96—Florida	NHL	77	13	14	27	20	5	0	0	16	1	3	4	0
96-97—Florida	NHL	78	18	21	39	30	-2	2	0	3	0	0	0	0
97-98—Florida	NHL	64	12	24	36	33	-1	2	3	—	—	—	—	—
98-99—Florida	NHL	82	19	24	43	29	7	0	4	—	—	—	—	—
99-00—Florida	NHL	35	7	10	17	6	5	0	0	—	—	—	—	—
—New York Rangers	NHL	46	11	22	33	10	0	2	1	—	—	—	—	—
00-01—New York Rangers	NHL	82	31	36	67	20	9	5	2	—	—	—	—	—
01-02—New York Rangers	NHL	65	17	20	37	14	-20	3	3	—	—	—	—	—
—Czech Rep. Oly. team	Int'l	4	0	0	0	0	...	...	...	—	—	—	—	—
02-03—New York Rangers	NHL	63	6	21	27	16	-3	2	0	—	—	—	—	—
—Edmonton	NHL	12	4	4	8	14	-3	1	0	4	1	0	1	0
03-04—Edmonton	NHL	78	15	35	50	26	18	6	0	—	—	—	—	—
04-05—Budejovice	Czech Dv.I	32	23	35	58	18	50	...	...	16	5	13	18	20
NHL Totals (9 years)		682	153	231	384	218	15	23	13	23	2	3	5	0

DWYER, GORDIE — LW — HURRICANES

PERSONAL: Born January 25, 1978, in Dalhousie, N.B. ... 6-3/202. ... Shoots left.
TRANSACTIONS/CAREER NOTES: Selected by St. Louis Blues in third round (second Blues pick, 67th overall) of NHL draft (June 22, 1996). ... Returned to draft pool by Blues; selected by Montreal Canadiens in sixth round (fifth Canadiens pick, 152nd overall) of draft (June 27, 1998).

... Traded by Canadiens to Tampa Bay Lightning for D Mike McBain (November 26, 1999). ... Injured finger (April 8, 2000); missed final game of season. ... Suspended 23 games for abuse of an official (September 28, 2000). ... Shoulder surgery (February 26, 2002); missed remainder of season. ... Traded by Lightning to New York Rangers for LW Boyd Kane (October 10, 2002). ... Concussion (March 13, 2003); missed three games. ... Injured ankle (March 31, 2003); missed three games. ... Signed as free agent by Carolina Hurricanes (August 11, 2004).

		REGULAR SEASON								PLAYOFFS				
Season Team	League	GP	G	A	Pts.	PIM	+/-	PP	SH	GP	G	A	Pts.	PIM
94-95—Hull	QMJHL	57	3	7	10	204	...	...	...	17	1	3	4	54
95-96—Hull	QMJHL	25	5	9	14	199	...	...	...	—	—	—	—	—
—Laval	QMJHL	22	5	17	22	72	...	...	...	—	—	—	—	—
—Beauport	QMJHL	22	4	9	13	87	...	...	...	20	3	5	8	104
96-97—Drummondville	QMJHL	66	21	48	69	391	...	...	...	8	6	1	7	39
97-98—Quebec	QMJHL	59	18	27	45	365	...	...	...	14	4	9	13	67
98-99—Fredericton	AHL	14	0	0	0	46	-1	0	0	—	—	—	—	—
—New Orleans	ECHL	36	1	3	4	163	-8	1	0	11	0	0	0	27
99-00—Quebec	AHL	7	0	0	0	37	...	...	...	—	—	—	—	—
—Detroit	IHL	27	0	2	2	147	...	...	...	—	—	—	—	—
—Tampa Bay	NHL	24	0	1	1	135	-6	0	0	—	—	—	—	—
00-01—Tampa Bay	NHL	28	0	1	1	96	-7	0	0	—	—	—	—	—
—Detroit	IHL	24	2	3	5	169	...	...	...	—	—	—	—	—
01-02—Springfield	AHL	17	1	3	4	80	-4	0	0	—	—	—	—	—
—Tampa Bay	NHL	26	0	2	2	60	-4	0	0	—	—	—	—	—
02-03—New York Rangers	NHL	17	0	1	1	50	-1	0	0	—	—	—	—	—
—Hartford	AHL	15	3	2	5	117	3	1	0	—	—	—	—	—
—Montreal	NHL	11	0	0	0	46	-2	0	0	—	—	—	—	—
03-04—Montreal	NHL	2	0	0	0	7	0	0	0	—	—	—	—	—
—Hamilton	AHL	55	6	6	12	110	0	1	1	6	0	0	0	15
04-05—Lowell	AHL	56	2	7	9	183	-1	0	0	11	1	0	1	54
NHL Totals (5 years)		108	0	5	5	394	-20	0	0					

DYKHUIS, KARL — D

PERSONAL: Born July 8, 1972, in Sept-Iles, Que. ... 6-3/209. ... Shoots left. ... Name pronounced DIGH-kowz.

TRANSACTIONS/CAREER NOTES: Selected by Chicago Blackhawks in first round (first Blackhawks pick, 16th overall) of NHL draft (June 16, 1990). ... Traded by Blackhawks to Philadelphia Flyers for D Bob Wilkie (February 16, 1995). ... Sprained knee (November 26, 1996); missed two games. ... Cut face (December 31, 1996); missed two games. ... Dislocated shoulder (January 28, 1997); missed 13 games. ... Traded by Flyers with RW Mikael Renberg to Tampa Bay Lightning for C Chris Gratton (August 20, 1997). ... Flu (November 14, 1997); missed one game. ... Flu (January 31, 1998); missed one game. ... Traded by Lightning to Flyers for D Petr Svoboda (December 28, 1998). ... Fractured cheekbone (December 29, 1998); missed one game. ... Traded by Flyers to Montreal Canadiens for future considerations (October 20, 1999). ... Injured knee (March 6, 2000); missed one game. ... Injured groin (March 18, 2000); missed five games. ... Had abdominal surgery (October 6, 2000); missed first 11 games of 2000-01 season.

		REGULAR SEASON								PLAYOFFS				
Season Team	League	GP	G	A	Pts.	PIM	+/-	PP	SH	GP	G	A	Pts.	PIM
88-89—Hull	QMJHL	63	2	29	31	59	...	...	...	9	1	9	10	6
89-90—Hull	QMJHL	69	10	45	55	119	...	...	...	11	2	5	7	2
90-91—Longueuil	QMJHL	3	1	4	5	6	...	...	...	—	—	—	—	—
—Canadian nat'l team	Int'l	37	2	9	11	16	...	...	...	—	—	—	—	—
91-92—Longueuil	QMJHL	29	5	19	24	55	...	...	...	17	0	12	12	14
—Chicago	NHL	6	1	3	4	4	-1	1	0	—	—	—	—	—
92-93—Indianapolis	IHL	59	5	18	23	76	7	2	0	5	1	1	2	8
—Chicago	NHL	12	0	5	5	0	2	0	0	—	—	—	—	—
93-94—Indianapolis	IHL	73	7	25	32	132	-25	1	1	—	—	—	—	—
94-95—Indianapolis	IHL	52	2	21	23	63	-17	1	0	—	—	—	—	—
—Hershey	AHL	1	0	0	0	0	2	0	0	—	—	—	—	—
—Philadelphia	NHL	33	2	6	8	37	7	1	0	15	4	4	8	14
95-96—Philadelphia	NHL	82	5	15	20	101	12	1	0	12	2	2	4	22
96-97—Philadelphia	NHL	62	4	15	19	35	6	2	0	18	0	3	3	2
97-98—Tampa Bay	NHL	78	5	9	14	110	-8	0	1	—	—	—	—	—
98-99—Tampa Bay	NHL	33	2	1	3	18	-21	0	0	—	—	—	—	—
—Philadelphia	NHL	45	2	4	6	32	-2	1	0	5	1	0	1	4
99-00—Philadelphia	NHL	5	0	1	1	6	-2	0	0	—	—	—	—	—
—Montreal	NHL	67	7	12	19	40	-3	3	1	—	—	—	—	—
00-01—Montreal	NHL	67	8	9	17	44	9	2	0	—	—	—	—	—
01-02—Montreal	NHL	80	5	7	12	32	16	0	0	12	1	1	2	8
02-03—Montreal	NHL	65	1	4	5	34	-5	0	0	—	—	—	—	—
03-04—Montreal	NHL	9	0	0	0	2	-2	0	0	—	—	—	—	—
—Hamilton	AHL	54	5	17	22	61	4	3	0	5	1	0	1	8
04-05—Amsterdam	Netherlands	6	1	1	2	36	...	...	...	7	1	3	4	39
NHL Totals (12 years)		644	42	91	133	495	8	11	2	62	8	10	18	50

EAGER, BEN — LW — FLYERS

PERSONAL: Born January 22, 1984, in Ottawa. ... 6-2/215. ... Shoots left.

TRANSACTIONS/CAREER NOTES: Selected by Phoenix Coyotes in first round (second Coyotes pick, 23rd overall) of NHL entry draft (June 22, 2002). ... Traded by Coyotes with G Sean Burke and RW Branko Radivojevic to Philadelphia Flyers for C Mike Comrie (February 9, 2004).

		REGULAR SEASON								PLAYOFFS				
Season Team	League	GP	G	A	Pts.	PIM	+/-	PP	SH	GP	G	A	Pts.	PIM
00-01—Oshawa	OHL	61	4	6	10	120	...	...	...	—	—	—	—	—
01-02—Oshawa	OHL	63	14	23	37	255	...	...	...	5	0	1	1	13
02-03—Oshawa	OHL	58	16	24	40	216	...	...	...	8	0	4	4	8

Season Team	League	REGULAR SEASON								PLAYOFFS				
		GP	G	A	Pts.	PIM	+/-	PP	SH	GP	G	A	Pts.	PIM
03-04—Oshawa	OHL	61	25	27	52	204	...	...	...	7	2	3	5	31
—Philadelphia	AHL	5	0	0	0	0	0	0	0	3	0	1	1	8
04-05—Philadelphia	AHL	66	7	10	17	232	12	2	0	16	1	1	2	71

EASTWOOD, MIKE C

PERSONAL: Born July 1, 1967, in Ottawa. ... 6-3/216. ... Shoots right.

TRANSACTIONS/CAREER NOTES: Selected by Toronto Maple Leafs in fifth round (fifth Maple Leafs pick, 91st overall) of NHL draft (June 13, 1987). ... Traded by Maple Leafs with third-round pick (RW Brad Isbister) in 1995 draft to Winnipeg Jets for RW Tie Domi (April 7, 1995). ... Jets franchise moved to Phoenix and renamed Coyotes for 1996-97 season; NHL approved move on January 18, 1996. ... Fractured wrist (October 28, 1996); missed eight games. ... Traded by Coyotes with D Dallas Eakins to New York Rangers for D Jay More (February 6, 1997). ... Traded by Rangers to St. Louis Blues for C Harry York (March 24, 1998). ... Sore wrist (April 18, 1998); missed two games. ... Sprained ankle (October 8, 2000); missed three games. ... Flu (March 10, 2001); missed one game. ... Claimed off waivers by Chicago Blackhawks (December 11, 2002). ... Signed as free agent by Pittsburgh Penguins (July 31, 2003).

STATISTICAL PLATEAUS: Three-goal games: 1999-00 (1).

Season Team	League	REGULAR SEASON								PLAYOFFS				
		GP	G	A	Pts.	PIM	+/-	PP	SH	GP	G	A	Pts.	PIM
87-88—Western Michigan	CCHA	42	5	8	13	14	...	...	...	—	—	—	—	—
88-89—Western Michigan	CCHA	40	10	13	23	87	...	...	...	—	—	—	—	—
89-90—Western Michigan	CCHA	40	25	27	52	36	...	...	...	—	—	—	—	—
90-91—Western Michigan	CCHA	42	29	32	61	84	...	...	...	—	—	—	—	—
91-92—St. John's	AHL	61	18	25	43	28	...	...	...	16	9	10	19	16
—Toronto	NHL	9	0	2	2	4	-4	0	0	—	—	—	—	—
92-93—St. John's	AHL	60	24	35	59	32	20	4	0	—	—	—	—	—
—Toronto	NHL	12	1	6	7	21	-2	0	0	10	1	2	3	8
93-94—Toronto	NHL	54	8	10	18	28	2	1	0	18	3	2	5	12
94-95—Toronto	NHL	36	5	5	10	32	-12	0	0	—	—	—	—	—
—Winnipeg	NHL	13	3	6	9	4	3	0	0	—	—	—	—	—
95-96—Winnipeg	NHL	80	14	14	28	20	-14	2	0	6	0	1	1	2
96-97—Phoenix	NHL	33	1	3	4	4	-3	0	0	—	—	—	—	—
—New York Rangers	NHL	27	1	7	8	10	2	0	0	15	1	2	3	22
97-98—New York Rangers	NHL	48	5	5	10	16	-2	0	0	—	—	—	—	—
—St. Louis	NHL	10	1	0	1	6	0	0	0	3	1	0	1	0
98-99—St. Louis	NHL	82	9	21	30	36	6	0	0	13	1	1	2	6
99-00—St. Louis	NHL	79	19	15	34	32	5	1	3	7	1	1	2	6
00-01—St. Louis	NHL	77	6	17	23	28	4	0	2	15	0	2	2	2
01-02—St. Louis	NHL	71	7	10	17	41	-2	0	0	10	0	0	0	6
02-03—St. Louis	NHL	17	1	3	4	8	1	1	0	—	—	—	—	—
—Chicago	NHL	53	2	10	12	24	-6	0	0	—	—	—	—	—
03-04—Pittsburgh	NHL	82	4	15	19	40	-18	0	0	—	—	—	—	—
NHL Totals (13 years)		783	87	149	236	354	-40	5	5	97	8	11	19	64

EATON, MARK D PREDATORS

PERSONAL: Born May 6, 1977, in Wilmington, Del. ... 6-2/208. ... Shoots left.

TRANSACTIONS/CAREER NOTES: Signed as free agent by Philadelphia Flyers (July 28, 1998). ... Stomach virus (March 26, 2000); missed one game. ... Traded by Flyers to Nashville Predators for 3rd-round pick (C Patrick Sharp) in 2001 draft (September 29, 2000). ... Strained back (October 18, 2001); missed seven games. ... Separated shoulder (December 20, 2001); missed two games. ... Injured knee and shoulder (December 3, 2002); missed five games. ... Strained groin (October 18, 2003); missed two games. ... Back spasms (March 13, 2004); missed four games. ... Signed as free agent by Nashville Predators (Aug. 4, 2005).

Season Team	League	REGULAR SEASON								PLAYOFFS				
		GP	G	A	Pts.	PIM	+/-	PP	SH	GP	G	A	Pts.	PIM
97-98—Notre Dame	CCHA	41	12	17	29	32	...	...	...	—	—	—	—	—
98-99—Philadelphia	AHL	74	9	27	36	38	13	7	0	16	4	8	12	0
99-00—Philadelphia	NHL	27	1	1	2	8	1	0	0	7	0	0	0	0
—Philadelphia	AHL	47	9	17	26	6	...	...	...	—	—	—	—	—
00-01—Milwaukee	IHL	34	3	12	15	27	...	...	...	—	—	—	—	—
—Nashville	NHL	34	3	8	11	14	7	1	0	—	—	—	—	—
01-02—Nashville	NHL	58	3	5	8	24	-12	0	0	—	—	—	—	—
02-03—Milwaukee	AHL	3	1	0	1	2	3	1	0	—	—	—	—	—
—Nashville	NHL	50	2	7	9	22	1	0	0	—	—	—	—	—
03-04—Nashville	NHL	75	4	9	13	26	16	0	0	6	0	0	0	2
04-05—Grand Rapids	AHL	29	3	3	6	21	2	1	1	—	—	—	—	—
NHL Totals (5 years)		244	13	30	43	94	13	1	0	13	0	0	0	2

EAVES, PATRICK RW SENATORS

PERSONAL: Born May 1, 1984, in Calgary. ... 5-11/174. ... Shoots right. ... Son of Mike Eaves, RW with two NHL teams (1976-86).

TRANSACTIONS/CAREER NOTES: Selected by Ottawa Senators in first round (Senators' first pick, ninth overall) in NHL entry draft (June 21, 2003).

Season Team	League	REGULAR SEASON								PLAYOFFS				
		GP	G	A	Pts.	PIM	+/-	PP	SH	GP	G	A	Pts.	PIM
02-03—Boston College	Hockey East	14	10	8	18	61	...	...	...	—	—	—	—	—
03-04—Boston College	Hockey East	34	18	23	41	66	...	...	...	—	—	—	—	—
04-05—Boston College	ECAC	36	19	29	48	36	...	...	...	—	—	—	—	—

EHRHOFF, CHRISTIAN — D — SHARKS

PERSONAL: Born July 6, 1982, in Moers, West Germany. ... 6-2/195. ... Shoots left.
TRANSACTIONS/CAREER NOTES: Selected by San Jose Sharks in fourth round (second Sharks pick, 106th overall) of NHL entry draft (June 23, 2001).

		REGULAR SEASON								PLAYOFFS				
Season Team	**League**	**GP**	**G**	**A**	**Pts.**	**PIM**	**+/-**	**PP**	**SH**	**GP**	**G**	**A**	**Pts.**	**PIM**
00-01—Krefeld Pinguine	Germany	58	3	11	14	73	...	...	...	—	—	—	—	—
01-02—Krefeld Pinguine	Germany	46	7	17	24	81	...	...	...	3	0	0	0	2
—German Oly. team	Int'l	7	0	0	0	8	...	...	...	—	—	—	—	—
02-03—Krefeld Pinguine	Germany	48	10	17	27	54	...	...	...	14	3	6	9	24
03-04—San Jose	NHL	41	1	11	12	14	4	0	0	—	—	—	—	—
—Cleveland	AHL	27	4	10	14	43	14	2	0	9	2	6	8	11
04-05—Cleveland	AHL	79	12	23	35	103	-12	7	0	—	—	—	—	—
NHL Totals (1 year)		41	1	11	12	14	4	0	0					

EKMAN, NILS — LW — SHARKS

PERSONAL: Born March 11, 1976, in Stockholm, Sweden. ... 6-0/185. ... Shoots left.
TRANSACTIONS/CAREER NOTES: Selected by Calgary Flames in fifth round (sixth Flames pick, 107th overall) of NHL draft (June 29, 1994). ... Rights traded by Flames with fourth-round pick (traded to New York Islanders; Islanders selected RW Vladimir Gorbunov) in 2000 draft to Tampa Bay Lightning for C/LW Andreas Johansson (November 20, 1999). ... Injured hip (January 20, 2000); missed one game. ... Traded by Lightning with LW Kyle Freadrich to New York Rangers for C Tim Taylor (July 1, 2001). ... Traded by Rangers to San Jose Sharks for LW Chad Wiseman (August 12, 2003).

		REGULAR SEASON								PLAYOFFS				
Season Team	**League**	**GP**	**G**	**A**	**Pts.**	**PIM**	**+/-**	**PP**	**SH**	**GP**	**G**	**A**	**Pts.**	**PIM**
93-94—Hammarby	Sweden Dv. 2	18	7	2	9	4	...	...	...	—	—	—	—	—
94-95—Hammarby	Sweden Dv. 2	29	10	7	17	18	...	...	...	—	—	—	—	—
95-96—Hammarby	Sweden Dv. 2	22	9	7	16	20	...	...	...	—	—	—	—	—
96-97—Kiekko-Espoo	Finland	50	24	19	43	60	...	...	...	4	2	0	2	4
97-98—Kiekko-Espoo	Finland	43	14	14	28	86	...	...	...	7	2	2	4	27
—Saint John	AHL	...	...	...	...	...	...	...	...	1	0	0	0	2
98-99—Blues Espoo	Finland	52	20	14	34	96	...	...	...	3	1	1	2	6
99-00—Tampa Bay	NHL	28	2	2	4	36	-8	1	0	—	—	—	—	—
—Detroit	IHL	10	7	2	9	8	...	...	...	—	—	—	—	—
—Long Beach	IHL	27	11	12	23	26	...	...	...	5	3	3	6	4
00-01—Detroit	IHL	33	22	14	36	63	...	...	...	—	—	—	—	—
—Tampa Bay	NHL	43	9	11	20	40	-15	2	1	—	—	—	—	—
01-02—Djurgarden Stockholm	Sweden	38	16	15	31	57	...	...	...	4	1	0	1	32
02-03—Hartford	AHL	57	30	36	66	73	6	9	3	2	0	2	2	4
03-04—San Jose	NHL	82	22	33	55	34	30	1	4	16	0	3	3	8
04-05—Djurgarden Stockholm	Sweden	44	18	27	45	106	2	7	1	12	4	5	9	20
NHL Totals (3 years)		153	33	46	79	110	7	4	5	16	0	3	3	8

ELIAS, PATRIK — LW — DEVILS

PERSONAL: Born April 13, 1976, in Trebic, Czechoslovakia. ... 6-1/195. ... Shoots left. ... Name pronounced EH-lee-ahsh.
TRANSACTIONS/CAREER NOTES: Selected by New Jersey Devils in second round (second Devils pick, 51st overall) of NHL draft (June 28, 1994). ... Flu (January 14, 1999); missed five games. ... Missed first nine games of 1999-2000 season in contract dispute. ... Infected finger (January 3, 2002); missed five games. ... Flu (March 20, 2002); missed two games. ... Back spasms (January 17, 2003); missed one game. ... Contracted hepatitis-A while playing in Russia (2004); sidelined for start of 2005-06 season.
STATISTICAL PLATEAUS: Three-goal games: 2000-01 (3), 2001-02 (2). Total: 5. ... Four-goal games: 2002-03 (1). ... Total hat tricks: 6.

		REGULAR SEASON								PLAYOFFS				
Season Team	**League**	**GP**	**G**	**A**	**Pts.**	**PIM**	**+/-**	**PP**	**SH**	**GP**	**G**	**A**	**Pts.**	**PIM**
92-93—HC Kladno	Czech.	2	0	0	0	0	...	...	...	—	—	—	—	—
93-94—HC Kladno	Czech Rep.	15	1	2	3	...	...	...	...	11	2	2	4	...
—Czech Rep. Oly. team	Int'l	5	2	5	7	...	...	...	...	—	—	—	—	—
94-95—HC Kladno	Czech Rep.	28	4	3	7	...	...	...	...	7	1	2	3	...
95-96—Albany	AHL	74	27	36	63	83	...	...	...	4	1	1	2	2
—New Jersey	NHL	1	0	0	0	0	-1	0	0	—	—	—	—	—
96-97—Albany	AHL	57	24	43	67	76	22	6	0	6	1	2	3	8
—New Jersey	NHL	17	2	3	5	2	-4	0	0	8	2	3	5	4
97-98—New Jersey	NHL	74	18	19	37	28	18	5	0	4	0	1	1	0
—Albany	AHL	3	3	0	3	2	-2	1	1	—	—	—	—	—
98-99—New Jersey	NHL	74	17	33	50	34	19	3	0	7	0	5	5	6
99-00—SK Trebic	Czech Dv.I	2	2	1	3	2	...	...	...	—	—	—	—	—
—HC Pardubice	Czech Rep.	5	1	4	5	6	...	...	...	—	—	—	—	—
—New Jersey	NHL	72	35	37	72	58	16	9	0	23	7	13	20	9
00-01—New Jersey	NHL	82	40	56	96	51	45	8	3	25	9	14	23	10
01-02—New Jersey	NHL	75	29	32	61	36	4	8	1	6	2	4	6	6
—Czech Rep. Oly. team	Int'l	4	1	1	2	0	...	...	...	—	—	—	—	—
02-03—New Jersey	NHL	81	28	29	57	22	17	6	0	24	5	8	13	26
03-04—New Jersey	NHL	82	38	43	81	44	26	9	3	5	3	2	5	2
04-05—HC Znojemsti Orli	Czech Rep.	28	8	20	28	65	7	...	...	—	—	—	—	—
—Metal. Magnitogorsk	Russian	17	5	9	14	28	10	...	...	—	—	—	—	—
NHL Totals (9 years)		558	207	252	459	275	140	48	7	102	28	50	78	63

ELLIS, DAN — G — STARS

PERSONAL: Born June 19, 1980, in Saskatoon, Sask. ... 6-0/185. ... Catches left.
TRANSACTIONS/CAREER NOTES: Selected by Dallas Stars in second round (second Stars pick, 60th overall) of NHL draft (June 24, 2000).

		REGULAR SEASON									PLAYOFFS							
Season Team	League	GP	Min.	W	L	T	GA	SO	GAA	SV%	GP	Min.	W	L	GA	SO	GAA	SV%
98-99—Newmarket	OPJHL	30	...	...	...	...	...	3	2.35	...	—	—	—	—	—	—	—	—
99-00—Omaha	USHL	55	...	34	16	4	...	11	2.25	...	—	—	—	—	—	—	—	—
00-01—U. of Neb.-Omaha	NCAA	40	2285	21	14	3	95	1	2.49	...	—	—	—	—	—	—	—	—
01-02—U. of Neb.-Omaha	NCAA	40	2405	20	15	4	97	3	2.42	...	—	—	—	—	—	—	—	—
02-03—U. of Neb.-Omaha	NCAA	39	2210	12	21	5	117	0	3.18	...	—	—	—	—	—	—	—	—
03-04—Utah	AHL	20	1129	5	14	0	55	2	2.92	.899	—	—	—	—	—	—	—	—
—Dallas	NHL	1	60	1	0	0	3	0	3.00	.893	—	—	—	—	—	—	—	—
—Idaho	ECHL	22	1334	13	8	1	57	2	2.56	.900	16	966	13	3	30	3	1.86	.934
04-05—Hamilton	AHL	31	1773	10	19	...	82	1	2.77	.908	0	0	0	0	0	0	...	...
NHL Totals (1 year)		1	60	1	0	0	3	0	3.00	.893								

ELLISON, MATT — RW — BLACKHAWKS

PERSONAL: Born December 8, 1983, in Duncan, B.C. ... 6-0/192. ... Shoots right.
TRANSACTIONS/CAREER NOTES: Selected by Chicago Blackhawks in fourth round (fourth Blackhawks pick, 128th overall) of NHL entry draft (June 23, 2002).

		REGULAR SEASON								PLAYOFFS				
Season Team	League	GP	G	A	Pts.	PIM	+/-	PP	SH	GP	G	A	Pts.	PIM
99-00—Cowichan	BCJHL	60	11	23	34	95	...	...	...	—	—	—	—	—
00-01—Cowichan	BCJHL	60	22	44	66	102	...	...	...	—	—	—	—	—
02-03—Red Deer	WHL	72	40	56	96	80	...	...	...	22	7	13	20	28
03-04—Norfolk	AHL	71	14	21	35	115	-10	6	0	7	0	1	1	4
—Chicago	NHL	10	0	1	1	0	-3	0	0	—	—	—	—	—
04-05—Norfolk	AHL	71	14	37	51	44	8	5	1	5	0	1	1	2
NHL Totals (1 year)		10	0	1	1	0	-3	0	0					

EMERY, RAY — G — SENATORS

PERSONAL: Born September 28, 1982, in Cayuga, Ont. ... 6-2/203. ... Catches left.
TRANSACTIONS/CAREER NOTES: Selected by Ottawa Senators in fourth round (fourth Senators pick, 99th overall) of NHL entry draft (June 23, 2001).

		REGULAR SEASON									PLAYOFFS							
Season Team	League	GP	Min.	W	L	T	GA	SO	GAA	SV%	GP	Min.	W	L	GA	SO	GAA	SV%
99-00—Sault Ste. Marie	OHL	16	716	9	3	0	36	1	3.02	...	15	883	8	7	33	*3	*2.24	...
00-01—Sault Ste. Marie	OHL	52	2938	18	29	2	174	1	3.55	.904	—	—	—	—	—	—	—	—
01-02—Sault Ste. Marie	OHL	*59	*3477	*33	17	*9	158	4	2.73	...	6	360	2	4	19	1	3.17	...
02-03—Ottawa	NHL	3	85	1	0	0	2	0	1.41	.923	—	—	—	—	—	—	—	—
—Binghamton	AHL	50	2923	27	17	6	118	7	2.42	.924	14	848	8	6	40	2	2.83	.912
03-04—Binghamton	AHL	53	3108	21	23	7	128	3	2.47	.916	2	119	0	2	6	0	3.03	.903
—Ottawa	NHL	3	126	2	0	0	5	0	2.38	.904	—	—	—	—	—	—	—	—
04-05—Binghamton	AHL	51	2992	28	18	...	132	0	2.65	.910	6	409	2	4	14	0	2.05	.925
NHL Totals (2 years)		6	211	3	0	0	7	0	1.99	.910								

E

EMINGER, STEVE — D — CAPITALS

PERSONAL: Born October 31, 1983, in Woodbridge, Ont. ... 6-1/197. ... Shoots right.
TRANSACTIONS/CAREER NOTES: Selected by Washington Capitals in first round (first Capitals pick, 12th overall) of NHL entry draft (June 22, 2002). ... Suffered concussion (November 8, 2003); missed two games. ... Bruised thigh (December 29, 2003); missed four games.

		REGULAR SEASON								PLAYOFFS				
Season Team	League	GP	G	A	Pts.	PIM	+/-	PP	SH	GP	G	A	Pts.	PIM
99-00—Kitchener	OHL	50	2	14	16	74	...	...	...	5	0	0	0	0
00-01—Kitchener	OHL	54	6	26	32	66	...	...	...	—	—	—	—	—
01-02—Kitchener	OHL	64	19	39	58	93	...	...	...	4	0	2	2	10
02-03—Washington	NHL	17	0	2	2	24	-3	0	0	—	—	—	—	—
—Kitchener	OHL	23	2	27	29	40	...	...	...	21	3	8	11	44
03-04—Washington	NHL	41	0	4	4	45	-11	0	0	—	—	—	—	—
—Portland	AHL	41	0	4	4	40	-5	0	0	7	0	1	1	2
04-05—Portland	AHL	62	3	17	20	40	-8	1	0	—	—	—	—	—
NHL Totals (2 years)		58	0	6	6	69	-14	0	0					

ENDICOTT, SHANE — C — PENGUINS

PERSONAL: Born December 21, 1981, in Saskatoon, Sask. ... 6-4/214. ... Shoots left.
TRANSACTIONS/CAREER NOTES: Selected by Pittsburgh Penguins in second round (second Penguins pick, 52nd overall) of NHL entry draft (June 24, 2000). ... Signed as free agent by Wilkes-Barre/Scranton of the AHL (September 26, 2004).

Season Team	League	REGULAR SEASON GP	G	A	Pts.	PIM	+/-	PP	SH	PLAYOFFS GP	G	A	Pts.	PIM
97-98—Seattle	WHL	5	0	0	0	0	...	...	...	5	0	0	0	0
98-99—Seattle	WHL	72	13	26	39	27	...	...	...	11	0	1	1	0
99-00—Seattle	WHL	70	23	32	55	62	...	...	...	7	1	6	7	6
00-01—Seattle	WHL	72	36	43	79	86	...	...	...	9	4	5	9	12
01-02—Wilkes-Barre/Scranton	AHL	63	19	20	39	46	-12	8	1	—	—	—	—	—
—Pittsburgh	NHL	4	0	1	1	4	-1	0	0	—	—	—	—	—
02-03—Wilkes-Barre/Scranton	AHL	74	13	26	39	68	-7	3	0	6	0	2	2	4
03-04—Wilkes-Barre/Scranton	AHL	79	17	22	39	68	-2	6	2	24	8	4	12	26
04-05—Wilkes-Barre/Scranton	AHL	68	24	23	47	89	3	7	2	11	2	2	4	31
NHL Totals (1 year)		4	0	1	1	4	-1	0	0					

ERAT, MARTIN — LW — PREDATORS

PERSONAL: Born August 28, 1981, in Trebic, Czechoslovakia. ... 6-0/195. ... Shoots left.

TRANSACTIONS/CAREER NOTES: Selected by Nashville Predators in seventh round (12th Predators pick, 191st overall) of NHL draft (June 26, 1999). ... Injured shoulder (March 6, 2004); missed one game.

Season Team	League	REGULAR SEASON GP	G	A	Pts.	PIM	+/-	PP	SH	PLAYOFFS GP	G	A	Pts.	PIM
97-98—ZPS Zlin	Czech. Jrs.	46	35	30	65	...	...	...	...	—	—	—	—	—
98-99—ZPS Zlin	Czech. Jrs.	35	21	23	44	...	...	...	...	—	—	—	—	—
—ZPS Zlin	Czech.	5	0	0	0	2	...	...	...	—	—	—	—	—
99-00—Saskatoon	WHL	66	27	26	53	82	...	...	...	11	4	8	12	16
00-01—Saskatoon	WHL	31	19	35	54	48	...	...	...	—	—	—	—	—
—Red Deer	WHL	17	4	24	28	24	...	...	...	22	*15	*21	*36	32
01-02—Nashville	NHL	80	9	24	33	32	-11	2	0	—	—	—	—	—
02-03—Milwaukee	AHL	45	10	22	32	41	-3	0	2	—	—	—	—	—
—Nashville	NHL	27	1	7	8	14	-9	1	0	—	—	—	—	—
03-04—Nashville	NHL	76	16	33	49	38	10	4	0	6	0	1	1	6
04-05—Zlin	Czech Rep.	48	20	23	43	129	7	...	...	18	8	6	14	12
NHL Totals (3 years)		183	26	64	90	84	-10	7	0	6	0	1	1	6

ERIKSSON, ANDERS — D

PERSONAL: Born January 9, 1975, in Bollnas, Sweden. ... 6-3/215. ... Shoots left.

TRANSACTIONS/CAREER NOTES: Selected by Detroit Red Wings in first round (first Red Wings pick, 22nd overall) of NHL draft (June 26, 1993). ... Traded by Red Wings with first-round pick (D Steve McCarthy) in 1999 draft and first-round pick (G Adam Munro) in 2001 draft to Chicago Blackhawks for D Chris Chelios (March 23, 1999). ... Traded by Blackhawks to Florida Panthers for D Jaroslav Spacek (November 6, 2000). ... Injured knee (November 10, 2000); missed one game. ... Sprained knee (February 22, 2001); missed nine games. ... Signed as free agent by Toronto Maple Leafs (July 4, 2001). ... Signed as free agent by Columbus Blue Jackets (October 10, 2003). ... Signed as free agent by Calgary Flames (September 15, 2004).

E

Season Team	League	REGULAR SEASON GP	G	A	Pts.	PIM	+/-	PP	SH	PLAYOFFS GP	G	A	Pts.	PIM
92-93—MoDo Ornskoldsvik	Sweden	20	0	2	2	2	...	...	...	—	—	—	—	—
93-94—MoDo Ornskoldsvik	Sweden	38	2	8	10	42	...	...	...	11	0	0	0	8
94-95—MoDo Ornskoldsvik	Sweden	39	3	6	9	54	...	...	...	—	—	—	—	—
95-96—Adirondack	AHL	75	6	36	42	64	...	...	...	3	0	0	0	0
—Detroit	NHL	1	0	0	0	2	1	0	0	3	0	0	0	0
96-97—Detroit	NHL	23	0	6	6	10	5	0	0	—	—	—	—	—
—Adirondack	AHL	44	3	25	28	36	10	0	0	4	0	1	1	4
97-98—Detroit	NHL	66	7	14	21	32	21	1	0	18	0	5	5	16
98-99—Detroit	NHL	61	2	10	12	34	5	0	0	—	—	—	—	—
—Chicago	NHL	11	0	8	8	0	6	0	0	—	—	—	—	—
99-00—Chicago	NHL	73	3	25	28	20	4	0	0	—	—	—	—	—
00-01—Chicago	NHL	13	2	3	5	2	-4	1	0	—	—	—	—	—
—Florida	NHL	60	0	21	21	28	2	0	0	—	—	—	—	—
01-02—Toronto	NHL	34	0	2	2	12	-1	0	0	10	0	0	0	0
—St. John's	AHL	25	4	6	10	14	3	3	0	11	0	5	5	6
02-03—St. John's	AHL	72	5	34	39	133	-9	2	0	—	—	—	—	—
—Toronto	NHL	4	0	0	0	0	1	0	0	—	—	—	—	—
03-04—Columbus	NHL	66	7	20	27	18	-6	2	0	—	—	—	—	—
—Syracuse	AHL	9	1	3	4	12	-5	1	0	—	—	—	—	—
04-05—HV 71 Jonkoping	Sweden	32	1	9	10	54	-13	1	0	—	—	—	—	—
NHL Totals (9 years)		412	21	109	130	158	34	4	0	31	0	5	5	16

ERSKINE, JOHN — D — STARS

PERSONAL: Born June 26, 1980, in Kingston, Ont. ... 6-4/215. ... Shoots left.

TRANSACTIONS/CAREER NOTES: Selected by Dallas Stars in second round (first Stars pick, 39th overall) of NHL entry draft (June 27, 1998). ... Fractured foot (March 8, 2002); missed 13 games. ... Injured ankle (December 29, 2003); missed 7 games. ... Injured calf (January 16, 2004); missed four games. ... Had hernia (March 3, 2004); missed final 15 games of regular season and playoffs. ... Signed as a free agent by Houston of the AHL (September 27, 2004).

Season Team	League	REGULAR SEASON GP	G	A	Pts.	PIM	+/-	PP	SH	PLAYOFFS GP	G	A	Pts.	PIM
96-97—Quinte	Tier II Jr. A	48	4	16	20	241	...	...	...	—	—	—	—	—
97-98—London	OHL	55	0	9	9	205	...	...	...	16	0	5	5	25

Season Team	League	REGULAR SEASON GP	G	A	Pts.	PIM	+/-	PP	SH	PLAYOFFS GP	G	A	Pts.	PIM
98-99—London	OHL	57	8	12	20	208	21	...	...	25	5	10	15	38
99-00—London	OHL	58	12	31	43	177	-17	6	1	—	—	—	—	—
00-01—Utah	IHL	77	1	8	9	284	...	...	...	—	—	—	—	—
01-02—Utah	AHL	39	2	6	8	118	1	1	0	3	0	0	0	10
—Dallas	NHL	33	0	1	1	62	-8	0	0	—	—	—	—	—
02-03—Dallas	NHL	16	2	0	2	29	1	0	0	—	—	—	—	—
—Utah	AHL	52	2	8	10	274	2	0	0	1	0	1	1	15
03-04—Dallas	NHL	32	0	1	1	84	-9	0	0	—	—	—	—	—
—Utah	AHL	5	0	0	0	18	0	0	0	—	—	—	—	—
04-05—Houston	AHL	61	3	7	10	238	-5	0	0	5	0	1	1	20
NHL Totals (3 years)		81	2	2	4	175	-16	0	0					

ESCHE, ROBERT — G — FLYERS

PERSONAL: Born January 22, 1978, in Whitesboro, N.Y. ... 6-1/210. ... Catches left. ... Name pronounced EHSH.

TRANSACTIONS/CAREER NOTES: Selected by Phoenix Coyotes in sixth round (fifth Coyotes pick, 139th overall) of NHL entry draft (June 22, 1996). ... Strained hamstring (April 12, 2002); missed final game of season. ... Traded by Coyotes with C Michal Handzus to Philadelphia Flyers for G Brian Boucher and third-round pick (D Joe Callahan) in 2002 entry draft (June 12, 2002). ... Injured groin (December 8, 2003); missed six games. ... Reinjured groin (December 23, 2003): missed one game. ... Sprained left knee (February 4, 2004); missed 10 games.

Season Team	League	REGULAR SEASON GP	Min.	W	L	T	GA	SO	GAA	SV%	PLAYOFFS GP	Min.	W	L	GA	SO	GAA	SV%
95-96—Det. Jr. Red Wings	OHL	23	1219	13	6	0	76	1	3.74	...	3	105	0	2	4	0	2.29	...
96-97—Det. Jr. Red Wings	OHL	58	3241	24	28	2	206	2	3.81	.878	5	317	1	4	19	0	3.60	.907
97-98—Plymouth	OHL	48	2810	29	13	4	135	3	2.88	.896	15	869	8	7	45	0	3.11	.914
98-99—Springfield	AHL	55	2957	24	20	6	138	1	2.80	.905	1	60	0	1	4	0	4.00	.867
—Phoenix	NHL	3	130	0	1	0	7	0	3.23	.860	—	—	—	—	—	—	—	—
99-00—Houston	IHL	7	419	4	2	1	16	2	2.29	...	—	—	—	—	—	—	—	—
—Phoenix	NHL	8	408	2	5	0	23	0	3.38	.893	—	—	—	—	—	—	—	—
—Springfield	AHL	21	1207	9	9	2	61	2	3.03	...	3	180	1	2	12	0	4.00	...
00-01—Phoenix	NHL	25	1350	10	8	4	68	2	3.02	.896	—	—	—	—	—	—	—	—
01-02—Phoenix	NHL	22	1145	6	10	2	52	1	2.72	.902	—	—	—	—	—	—	—	—
—Springfield	AHL	1	60	1	0	0	0	1	0.00	1.00	—	—	—	—	—	—	—	—
02-03—Philadelphia	NHL	30	1638	12	9	3	60	2	2.20	.907	1	30	0	0	1	0	2.00	.929
03-04—Philadelphia	NHL	40	2322	21	11	7	79	3	2.04	.915	18	1061	11	7	41	1	2.32	.918
NHL Totals (6 years)		128	6993	51	44	16	289	8	2.48	.905	19	1091	11	7	42	1	2.31	.918

EVANS, BRENNAN — D

PERSONAL: Born January 16, 1982, in Camrose, Alta. ... 6-3/200. ... Shoots left.

TRANSACTIONS/CAREER NOTES: Signed as free agent by Calgary Flames (September 9, 2003).

Season Team	League	REGULAR SEASON GP	G	A	Pts.	PIM	+/-	PP	SH	PLAYOFFS GP	G	A	Pts.	PIM
98-99—Seattle	WHL	...	...	...	...	...	...	...	...	1	0	0	0	0
99-00—Seattle	WHL	52	1	2	3	40	0	...	...	1	0	0	0	0
00-01—Seattle	WHL	10	1	0	1	25	-5	...	...	—	—	—	—	—
—Kootenay	WHL	55	2	7	9	105	7	...	...	11	0	0	0	0
01-02—Kootenay	WHL	72	2	3	5	121	6	0	0	22	0	6	6	38
02-03—Kootenay	WHL	6	182	2	184	2	0	...	...	11	1	1	2	24
03-04—Lowell	AHL	64	1	9	10	65	3	...	...	—	—	—	—	—
—Calgary	NHL	...	...	...	...	...	...	...	...	2	0	0	0	0
04-05—Lowell	AHL	51	0	7	7	79	1	0	0	5	0	0	0	2
NHL Totals (1 year)		0	...	...	...	...	...	...	...	2	0	0	0	0

EXELBY, GARNET — D — THRASHERS

PERSONAL: Born August 16, 1981, in Craik, Sask. ... 6-1/215. ... Shoots left.

TRANSACTIONS/CAREER NOTES: Selected by Atlanta Thrashers in eighth round (ninth Thrashers pick, 217th overall) of NHL entry draft (June 27, 1999). ... Injured hip (January 22, 2004); missed six games. ... Injured ankle (February 5, 2004); missed two games. ... Had the flu (March 29, 2004); missed final three games of season.

Season Team	League	REGULAR SEASON GP	G	A	Pts.	PIM	+/-	PP	SH	PLAYOFFS GP	G	A	Pts.	PIM
01-02—Chicago	AHL	75	3	4	7	257	-8	0	0	25	0	4	4	49
02-03—Chicago	AHL	53	3	6	9	140	11	0	0	—	—	—	—	—
—Atlanta	NHL	15	0	2	2	41	0	0	0	—	—	—	—	—
03-04—Atlanta	NHL	71	1	9	10	134	-10	0	0	—	—	—	—	—
NHL Totals (2 years)		86	1	11	12	175	-10	0	0					

FAHEY, JIM — D — SHARKS

PERSONAL: Born May 11, 1979, in Boston. ... 6-0/205. ... Shoots right.

TRANSACTIONS/CAREER NOTES: Selected by San Jose Sharks in eighth round (ninth Sharks pick, 212th overall) of NHL draft (June 27, 1998). ... Suffered concussion (March 1, 2003); missed three games.

Season Team	League	GP	G	A	Pts.	PIM	+/-	PP	SH	GP	G	A	Pts.	PIM
		REGULAR SEASON								PLAYOFFS				
97-98—Catholic Memorial.....	Mass. H.S.	24	12	12	24	28	...	...	...	—	—	—	—	—
98-99—Northeastern Univ.....	Hockey East	32	5	13	18	34	...	...	...	—	—	—	—	—
99-00—Northeastern Univ.....	Hockey East	36	3	17	20	62	...	...	...	—	—	—	—	—
00-01—Northeastern Univ.....	Hockey East	36	4	23	27	48	...	...	...	—	—	—	—	—
01-02—Northeastern Univ.....	Hockey East	39	14	32	46	50	...	...	...	—	—	—	—	—
02-03—Cleveland..................	AHL	25	3	14	17	42	-2	2	0	—	—	—	—	—
—San Jose..................	NHL	43	1	19	20	33	-3	0	0	—	—	—	—	—
03-04—San Jose..................	NHL	15	0	2	2	18	-2	0	0	2	0	0	0	0
—Cleveland..................	AHL	32	1	18	19	64	-2	0	0	—	—	—	—	—
04-05—Cleveland..................	AHL	69	4	22	26	146	-6	1	1	—	—	—	—	—
NHL Totals (2 years)		58	1	21	22	51	-5	0	0	2	0	0	0	0

FARRELL, MIKE — D — PREDATORS

PERSONAL: Born October 20, 1978, in Edina, Minn. ... 6-0/222. ... Shoots right.

TRANSACTIONS/CAREER NOTES: Selected by Washington Capitals in eighth round (ninth Capitals pick, 220th overall) of NHL draft (June 27, 1998). ... Traded by Capitals to Nashville Predators for D Alexander Riazantsev (July 14, 2003).

Season Team	League	GP	G	A	Pts.	PIM	+/-	PP	SH	GP	G	A	Pts.	PIM
		REGULAR SEASON								PLAYOFFS				
97-98—Providence College.....	Hockey East	33	5	8	13	32	...	...	...	—	—	—	—	—
98-99—Providence College.....	Hockey East	29	3	12	15	51	...	...	...	—	—	—	—	—
99-00—Providence College.....	Hockey East	36	3	6	9	71	...	...	...	—	—	—	—	—
—Portland.....................	AHL	7	2	0	2	0	...	...	...	4	0	1	1	0
00-01—Portland.....................	AHL	79	6	18	24	61	...	...	...	3	0	2	2	2
01-02—Portland.....................	AHL	61	12	15	27	62	-4	2	0	—	—	—	—	—
—Washington	NHL	8	0	0	0	0	-1	0	0	—	—	—	—	—
02-03—Portland.....................	AHL	68	12	12	24	107	5	2	0	3	0	1	1	0
—Washington	NHL	4	0	0	0	2	1	0	0	—	—	—	—	—
03-04—Nashville.....................	NHL	1	0	0	0	0	0	0	0	—	—	—	—	—
—Milwaukee..................	AHL	49	10	8	18	66	3	0	1	19	1	1	2	13
NHL Totals (3 years)...........		13	0	0	0	2	0	0	0					

FAST, BRAD — D — HURRICANES

PERSONAL: Born February 21, 1980, in Fort St. John, B.C. ... 6-0/185. ... Shoots left.

TRANSACTIONS/CAREER NOTES: Selected by Carolina Hurricanes in third round (third Hurricanes pick, 84th overall) of NHL entry draft (June 26, 1999).

Season Team	League	GP	G	A	Pts.	PIM	+/-	PP	SH	GP	G	A	Pts.	PIM
		REGULAR SEASON								PLAYOFFS				
98-99—Prince George............	BCJHL	59	27	46	73	31	...	...	...	—	—	—	—	—
99-00—Michigan State...........	CCHA	41	5	9	14	20	...	...	...	—	—	—	—	—
00-01—Michigan State...........	CCHA	42	4	24	28	16	...	...	...	—	—	—	—	—
01-02—Michigan State...........	CCHA	41	10	16	26	26	...	...	...	—	—	—	—	—
02-03—Lowell.........................	AHL	7	0	1	1	12	-4	0	0	—	—	—	—	—
—Michigan State...........	CCHA	39	11	35	46	28	...	...	...	—	—	—	—	—
03-04—Carolina	NHL	1	1	0	1	0	1	0	0	—	—	—	—	—
—Lowell.........................	AHL	79	10	25	35	35	-20	4	0	—	—	—	—	—
04-05—Lowell.........................	AHL	32	1	5	6	23	-4	1	0	0	0	0	0	0
—Florida.........................	ECHL	14	2	5	7	0	7	0	0	18	1	3	4	6
NHL Totals (1 year).............		1	1	0	1	0	1	0	0					

FATA, RICO — RW/LW — PENGUINS

PERSONAL: Born February 12, 1980, in Sault Ste. Marie, Ont. ... 6-0/200. ... Shoots left. ... Brother of Drew Fata, D, Pittsburgh Penguins organization.

TRANSACTIONS/CAREER NOTES: Selected by Calgary Flames in first round (first Flames pick, sixth overall) of NHL draft (June 27, 1998). ... Claimed off waivers by New York Rangers (October 3, 2001). ... Had concussion (January 4, 2003); missed one game. ... Traded by Rangers with RW Mikael Samuelsson, D Joel Bouchard, D Richard Lintner and cash to Pittsburgh Penguins for RW Alexei Kovalev, LW Dan LaCouture, D Janne Laukkanen and D Mike Wilson (February 10, 2003). ... Injured hamstring (November 12, 2003); missed three games. ... Injured knee (November 29, 2003); missed five games.

Season Team	League	GP	G	A	Pts.	PIM	+/-	PP	SH	GP	G	A	Pts.	PIM
		REGULAR SEASON								PLAYOFFS				
95-96—Sault Ste. Marie..........	OMJHL	62	11	15	26	52	...	...	...	—	—	—	—	—
96-97—London	OHL	59	19	34	53	76	...	...	...	—	—	—	—	—
97-98—London	OHL	64	43	33	76	110	...	...	...	16	9	5	14	*49
98-99—Calgary	NHL	20	0	1	1	4	0	0	0	—	—	—	—	—
—London	OHL	23	15	18	33	41	3	...	...	25	10	12	22	42
99-00—Calgary	NHL	2	0	0	0	0	-1	0	0	—	—	—	—	—
—Saint John	AHL	76	29	29	58	65	...	...	...	3	0	0	0	4
00-01—Saint John	AHL	70	23	29	52	129	...	...	...	19	2	3	5	22
—Calgary	NHL	5	0	0	0	6	-3	0	0	—	—	—	—	—
01-02—New York Rangers......	NHL	10	0	0	0	0	-2	0	0	—	—	—	—	—
—Hartford	AHL	61	35	36	71	36	27	8	2	10	2	5	7	4
02-03—New York Rangers......	NHL	36	2	4	6	6	-1	0	0	—	—	—	—	—
—Hartford	AHL	9	8	6	14	6	4	1	1	—	—	—	—	—

Season Team	League	GP	G	A	Pts.	PIM	+/-	PP	SH	GP	G	A	Pts.	PIM
		REGULAR SEASON								PLAYOFFS				
—Pittsburgh	NHL	27	5	8	13	10	-6	0	0	—	—	—	—	—
03-04—Pittsburgh	NHL	73	16	18	34	54	-46	6	2	—	—	—	—	—
04-05—Asiago	Italy	35	18	20	38	36	...	...	...	—	—	—	—	—
NHL Totals (6 years)		173	23	31	54	80	-59	6	2					

FEDOROV, FEDOR — C — CANUCKS

PERSONAL: Born June 11, 1981, in Moscow, U.S.S.R. ... 6-3/230. ... Shoots left. ... Brother of Sergei Fedorov, C, Anaheim Mighty Ducks. ... Name pronounced feh-DUHR FEH-duhr-rahf.

TRANSACTIONS/CAREER NOTES: Selected by Tampa Bay Lightning in sixth round (seventh Lightning pick, 182nd overall) of NHL draft (June 26, 1999). ... Returned to draft pool by Lightning; selected by Vancouver Canucks in third round (second Canucks pick, 66th overall) of NHL draft (June 23, 2001).

Season Team	League	GP	G	A	Pts.	PIM	+/-	PP	SH	GP	G	A	Pts.	PIM
		REGULAR SEASON								PLAYOFFS				
97-98—Detroit Little Caesars	MNHL	13	3	7	10	18	...	...	...	—	—	—	—	—
98-99—Port Huron	UHL	42	2	5	7	20	...	...	...	—	—	—	—	—
99-00—Windsor	OHL	60	7	10	17	115	-5	0	0	12	1	0	1	4
00-01—Sudbury	OHL	37	33	45	78	88	25	11	1	12	4	6	10	36
01-02—Manitoba	AHL	8	2	1	3	6	3	1	0	—	—	—	—	—
—Columbia	ECHL	2	0	2	2	0	2	0	0	—	—	—	—	—
02-03—Vancouver	NHL	7	0	1	1	4	0	0	0	—	—	—	—	—
—Manitoba	AHL	50	10	13	23	61	-4	3	1	3	1	2	3	0
03-04—Manitoba	AHL	58	23	16	39	52	-8	10	0	—	—	—	—	—
—Vancouver	NHL	8	0	1	1	4	0	0	0	—	—	—	—	—
04-05—Spartak Moscow	Russian	19	4	7	11	52	0	...	...	—	—	—	—	—
—Metal. Magnitogorsk	Russian	10	3	0	3	22	-1	...	...	5	2	0	2	30
NHL Totals (2 years)		15	0	2	2	8	0	0	0					

FEDOROV, SERGEI — C — MIGHTY DUCKS

PERSONAL: Born December 13, 1969, in Pskov, USSR. ... 6-2/205. ... Shoots left. ... Brother of Fedor Fedorov, C, Vancouver Canucks organization. ... Name pronounced SAIR-gay FEH-duh-rahf.

TRANSACTIONS/CAREER NOTES: Selected by Detroit Red Wings in fourth round (fourth Red Wings pick, 74th overall) of NHL draft (June 17, 1989). ... Bruised left shoulder (October 1990). ... Reinjured left shoulder (January 16, 1991). ... Sprained left shoulder (November 27, 1992); missed seven games. ... Flu (January 30, 1993); missed two games. ... Charley horse (February 11, 1993); missed one game. ... Suffered concussion (April 5, 1994); missed two games. ... Suspended four games without pay and fined $500 for high-sticking incident in playoff game (May 17, 1994); suspension reduced to three games due to abbreviated 1994-95 season. ... Flu (February 7, 1995); missed one game. ... Bruised right hamstring (April 9, 1995); missed one game. ... Tonsillitis (October 6, 1995); missed three games. ... Sprained left wrist (December 15, 1995); missed one game. ... Strained groin (January 9, 1997); missed two games. ... Reinjured groin (January 20, 1997); missed six games. ... Missed first 59 games of 1997-98 season in contract dispute. ... Tendered offer sheet by Carolina Hurricanes (February 19, 1998). ... Offer matched by Red Wings (February 26, 1998). ... Suspended two games and fined $1,000 for illegal check (March 31, 1998). ... Suspended five games for slashing incident (March 3, 1999). ... Injured head (November 20, 1999); missed six games. ... Injured neck (January 16, 2000); missed three games. ... Injured wrist (February 18, 2000); missed five games. ... Fractured nose (February 23, 2001); missed six games. ... Signed as free agent by Anaheim Mighty Ducks (July 20, 2003). ... Stomach virus (January 21, 2004); missed one game. ... Flu (March 8, 2004); missed one game.

STATISTICAL PLATEAUS: Three-goal games: 1993-94 (1), 2000-01 (1), 2002-03 (2). Total: 4. ... Four-goal games: 1994-95 (1). ... Five-goal games: 1996-97 (1). ... Total hat tricks: 6.

Season Team	League	GP	G	A	Pts.	PIM	+/-	PP	SH	GP	G	A	Pts.	PIM
		REGULAR SEASON								PLAYOFFS				
85-86—Dynamo Minsk	USSR	15	6	1	7	10	...	...	...	—	—	—	—	—
86-87—CSKA Moscow	USSR	29	6	6	12	12	...	...	...	—	—	—	—	—
87-88—CSKA Moscow	USSR	48	7	9	16	20	...	...	...	—	—	—	—	—
88-89—CSKA Moscow	USSR	44	9	8	17	35	...	...	...	—	—	—	—	—
89-90—CSKA Moscow	USSR	48	19	10	29	20	...	...	...	—	—	—	—	—
90-91—Detroit	NHL	77	31	48	79	66	11	11	3	7	1	5	6	4
91-92—Detroit	NHL	80	32	54	86	72	26	7	2	11	5	5	10	8
92-93—Detroit	NHL	73	34	53	87	72	33	13	4	7	3	6	9	23
93-94—Detroit	NHL	82	56	64	120	34	48	13	4	7	1	7	8	6
94-95—Detroit	NHL	42	20	30	50	24	6	7	3	17	7	*17	*24	6
95-96—Detroit	NHL	78	39	68	107	48	49	11	3	19	2	*18	20	10
96-97—Detroit	NHL	74	30	33	63	30	29	9	2	20	8	12	20	12
97-98—Russian Oly. team	Int'l	6	1	5	6	8	6	0	0	—	—	—	—	—
—Detroit	NHL	21	6	11	17	25	10	2	0	22	*10	10	20	12
98-99—Detroit	NHL	77	26	37	63	66	9	6	2	10	1	8	9	8
99-00—Detroit	NHL	68	27	35	62	22	8	4	4	9	4	4	8	4
00-01—Detroit	NHL	75	32	37	69	40	12	14	2	6	2	5	7	0
01-02—Detroit	NHL	81	31	37	68	36	20	10	0	23	5	14	19	20
—Russian Oly. team	Int'l	6	2	2	4	4	...	...	...	—	—	—	—	—
02-03—Detroit	NHL	80	36	47	83	52	15	10	2	4	1	2	3	0
03-04—Anaheim	NHL	80	31	34	65	42	-5	9	2	—	—	—	—	—
04-05—Spartak Moscow	Russian	...	...	...	...	...	...	...	...	—	—	—	—	—
NHL Totals (14 years)		988	431	588	1019	629	271	126	33	162	50	113	163	113

FEDORUK, TODD — LW — MIGHTY DUCKS

PERSONAL: Born February 13, 1979, in Redwater, Alta. ... 6-2/235. ... Shoots left.

TRANSACTIONS/CAREER NOTES: Selected by Philadelphia Flyers in 7th round (6th Flyers pick, 16th overall) of entry draft (June 21, 1997). ... Strained elbow (January 13, 2001); missed two games. ... Cut eyelid (January 31, 2001); missed one game. ... Strained right thumb

(October 24, 2002); missed three games. ... Facial cuts and headaches (December 21, 2002); missed two games. ... Sprained right thumb (February 25, 2003); missed three games. ... Bruised left tight (March 18, 2003); missed four games. ... Injured cheekbone (November 12, 2003); missed six games. ... Fractured cheekbone (December 1, 2003); missed eight games. ... Injured knee (Februrary 18, 2004); missed four games. ... Traded by Flyers to Anaheim Mighty Ducks for 2nd-round pick in 2005 (July 29, 2005).

		REGULAR SEASON								PLAYOFFS				
Season Team	League	GP	G	A	Pts.	PIM	+/-	PP	SH	GP	G	A	Pts.	PIM
96-97—Kelowna	WHL	31	1	5	6	87	...	...	...	6	0	0	0	13
97-98—Kelowna	WHL	31	3	5	8	120	...	...	...	—	—	—	—	—
—Regina	WHL	21	4	3	7	80	...	...	...	9	1	2	3	23
98-99—Regina	WHL	39	12	12	24	107	...	...	...	—	—	—	—	—
—Prince Albert	WHL	28	6	4	10	75	...	...	...	—	—	—	—	—
99-00—Philadelphia	AHL	19	1	2	3	40	...	...	...	5	0	1	1	2
—Trenton	ECHL	18	2	5	7	118	...	...	...	—	—	—	—	—
00-01—Philadelphia	AHL	14	0	1	1	49	...	...	...	—	—	—	—	—
—Philadelphia	NHL	53	5	5	10	109	0	0	0	2	0	0	0	20
01-02—Philadelphia	NHL	55	3	4	7	141	-2	0	0	3	0	0	0	0
—Philadelphia	AHL	7	0	1	1	54	-3	0	0	—	—	—	—	—
02-03—Philadelphia	NHL	63	1	5	6	105	1	0	0	1	0	0	0	0
03-04—Philadelphia	AHL	2	0	2	2	2	2	0	0	—	—	—	—	—
—Philadelphia	NHL	49	1	4	5	136	-4	0	0	1	0	0	0	2
04-05—Philadelphia	AHL	42	4	12	16	142	8	0	0	16	2	2	4	33
NHL Totals (4 years)		220	10	18	28	491	-5	0	0	7	0	0	0	22

FEDOTENKO, RUSLAN RW LIGHTNING

PERSONAL: Born January 18, 1979, in Kiev, U.S.S.R. ... 6-2/195. ... Shoots left.

TRANSACTIONS/CAREER NOTES: Signed as free agent by Philadelphia Flyers (August 3, 1999). ... Sprained right knee (February 27, 2002); missed four games. ... Traded by Flyers with two second-round picks (traded to Ottawa [Tobias Stephan] and traded to Phoenix [Dan Spang]) in 2002 draft to Tampa Bay Lightning for first-round pick (D Joni Pitkanen) in 2002 draft (June 21, 2002). ... Injured shoulder (November 21, 2002); missed one game. ... Fractured finger (February 25, 2003); missed five games. ... Facial injury (May 29, 2004); missed one playoff game.

		REGULAR SEASON								PLAYOFFS				
Season Team	League	GP	G	A	Pts.	PIM	+/-	PP	SH	GP	G	A	Pts.	PIM
97-98—Melfort	SJHL	68	35	31	66	...	...	...	...	—	—	—	—	—
98-99—Sioux City	USHL	55	43	34	77	139	...	...	...	5	5	1	6	9
99-00—Philadelphia	AHL	67	16	34	50	42	...	...	...	2	0	0	0	0
—Trenton	ECHL	8	5	3	8	9	...	...	...	—	—	—	—	—
00-01—Philadelphia	AHL	8	1	0	1	8	...	...	...	—	—	—	—	—
—Philadelphia	NHL	74	16	20	36	72	8	3	0	6	0	1	1	4
01-02—Philadelphia	NHL	78	17	9	26	43	15	0	1	5	1	0	1	2
—Ukranian Oly. team	Int'l	1	1	0	1	4	...	...	...	—	—	—	—	—
02-03—Tampa Bay	NHL	76	19	13	32	44	-7	6	0	11	0	1	1	2
03-04—Tampa Bay	NHL	77	17	22	39	30	14	0	0	22	12	2	14	14
NHL Totals (4 years)		305	69	64	133	189	30	9	1	44	13	4	17	22

FEHR, ERIC RW CAPITALS

PERSONAL: Born September 7, 1985, in Winkler, Man. ... 6-3/187. ... Shoots right.

TRANSACTIONS/CAREER NOTES: Selected by Washington Capitals in first round (first Capitals pick, 18th overall) in 2003 NHL entry draft (June 23, 2003).

		REGULAR SEASON								PLAYOFFS				
Season Team	League	GP	G	A	Pts.	PIM	+/-	PP	SH	GP	G	A	Pts.	PIM
01-02—Brandon	WHL	63	11	16	27	29	...	...	...	—	—	—	—	—
02-03—Brandon	WHL	70	26	29	55	76	...	...	...	—	—	—	—	—
03-04—Brandon	WHL	71	50	34	84	129	...	...	...	7	5	0	5	16
04-05—Brandon	WHL	71	59	52	111	91	26	31	2	24	16	16	32	47

FERENCE, ANDREW D FLAMES

PERSONAL: Born March 17, 1979, in Edmonton. ... 5-10/196. ... Shoots left.

TRANSACTIONS/CAREER NOTES: Selected by Pittsburgh Penguins in eighth round (eighth Penguins pick, 208th overall) of 1997 NHL entry draft (June 21, 2004). ... Flu (December 9, 1999); missed four games. ... Flu (December 26, 2001); missed one game. ... Hernia (October 10, 2002); missed 21 games. ... Traded by Penguins to Calgary Flames for 3rd-round pick (C Brian Gifford) in 2004 entry draft (February 10, 2003). ... Injured ankle (March 18, 2003); missed season's final nine games. ... Injured groin (December 2, 2003); missed two games. ... Injured right shoulder (January 8, 2004); missed two games.

		REGULAR SEASON								PLAYOFFS				
Season Team	League	GP	G	A	Pts.	PIM	+/-	PP	SH	GP	G	A	Pts.	PIM
95-96—Portland	WHL	72	9	31	40	159	...	...	...	7	1	3	4	12
96-97—Portland	WHL	72	12	32	44	163	...	...	...	—	—	—	—	—
97-98—Portland	WHL	72	11	57	68	142	75	5	1	16	2	18	20	28
98-99—Portland	WHL	40	11	21	32	104	13	6	1	4	1	4	5	10
—Kansas City	IHL	5	1	2	3	4	-5	0	0	3	0	0	0	9
99-00—Pittsburgh	NHL	30	2	4	6	20	3	0	0	—	—	—	—	—
—Wilkes-Barre/Scranton	AHL	44	8	20	28	58	...	...	...	—	—	—	—	—
00-01—Wilkes-Barre/Scranton	AHL	43	6	18	24	95	...	...	...	3	1	0	1	12
—Pittsburgh	NHL	36	4	11	15	28	6	1	0	18	3	7	10	16
01-02—Pittsburgh	NHL	75	4	7	11	73	-12	1	0	—	—	—	—	—

Season Team	League	GP	G	A	Pts.	PIM	+/-	PP	SH	GP	G	A	Pts.	PIM
		REGULAR SEASON								PLAYOFFS				
02-03—Pittsburgh	NHL	22	1	3	4	36	-16	1	0	—	—	—	—	—
—Wilkes-Barre/Scranton	AHL	1	0	0	0	2	1	0	0	—	—	—	—	—
—Calgary	NHL	16	0	4	4	6	1	0	0	—	—	—	—	—
03-04—Calgary	NHL	72	4	12	16	53	5	1	0	26	0	3	3	25
04-05—Budejovice	Czech Dv.I	19	5	6	11	45	16	...	...	12	2	7	9	10
NHL Totals (5 years)		251	15	41	56	216	-13	4	0	44	3	10	13	41

FERENCE, BRAD — D — COYOTES

PERSONAL: Born April 2, 1979, in Calgary. ... 6-3/218. ... Shoots right.

TRANSACTIONS/CAREER NOTES: Selected by Vancouver Canucks in first round (first Canucks pick, 10th overall) of NHL draft (June 21, 1997). ... Traded by Canucks with RW Pavel Bure, D Bret Hedican and third-round pick (RW Robert Fried) in 2000 draft to Florida Panthers for D Ed Jovanovski, G Kevin Weekes, C Dave Gagner, C Mike Brown and first-round pick (C Nathan Smith) in 2000 draft (January 17, 1999). ... Fractured jaw (September 4, 2000); missed first nine games of season. ... Suspended two games for receiving three instigator penalties in one season (April 1, 2002). ... Injured shoulder (December 10, 2002); missed five games. ... Reinjured shoulder (December 28, 2002); missed two games. ... Traded by Panthers to Phoenix Coyotes for LW Darcy Hordichuk and second-round pick (later traded to Tampa Bay; Lightning selected D Matt Smaby) in 2003 draft (March 9, 2003). ... Fined by NHL for punching at opponent (March 27, 2004).

Season Team	League	GP	G	A	Pts.	PIM	+/-	PP	SH	GP	G	A	Pts.	PIM
		REGULAR SEASON								PLAYOFFS				
95-96—Spokane	WHL	5	0	2	2	18	...	...	...	—	—	—	—	—
96-97—Spokane	WHL	67	6	20	26	324	-4	3	0	9	0	4	4	21
97-98—Spokane	WHL	54	9	29	38	213	16	5	0	18	0	7	7	59
98-99—Spokane	WHL	31	3	22	25	125	...	...	...	—	—	—	—	—
—Tri-City	WHL	20	6	15	21	116	...	...	...	12	1	9	10	63
99-00—Louisville	AHL	58	2	7	9	231	...	...	...	2	0	0	0	2
—Florida	NHL	13	0	2	2	46	2	0	0	—	—	—	—	—
00-01—Florida	NHL	14	0	1	1	14	-10	0	0	—	—	—	—	—
—Louisville	AHL	52	3	21	24	200	...	...	...	—	—	—	—	—
01-02—Florida	NHL	80	2	15	17	254	-13	0	0	—	—	—	—	—
02-03—Florida	NHL	60	2	6	8	118	2	0	0	—	—	—	—	—
—Phoenix	NHL	15	0	1	1	28	-5	0	0	—	—	—	—	—
03-04—Phoenix	NHL	63	0	5	5	103	-19	0	0	—	—	—	—	—
04-05—Morzine-Avoriaz	France	17	2	10	12	138	...	...	...	4	1	4	5	10
NHL Totals (5 years)		245	4	30	34	563	-43	0	0					

FERGUSON, SCOTT — D — WILD

PERSONAL: Born January 6, 1973, in Camrose, Alta. ... 6-1/195. ... Shoots left.

TRANSACTIONS/CAREER NOTES: Signed as free agent by Edmonton Oilers (June 2, 1994). ... Traded by Oilers to Ottawa Senators for D Frank Musil (March 9, 1998). ... Signed as free agent by Anaheim Mighty Ducks (July 22, 1998). ... Signed as free agent by Oilers (July 5, 2000). ... Stomach virus (February 27, 2003); missed one game. ... Signed as free agent by Minnesota Wild (Aug. 4, 2005).

Season Team	League	GP	G	A	Pts.	PIM	+/-	PP	SH	GP	G	A	Pts.	PIM
		REGULAR SEASON								PLAYOFFS				
90-91—Kamloops	WHL	4	0	0	0	0	...	...	...	—	—	—	—	—
91-92—Kamloops	WHL	62	4	10	14	148	...	...	...	12	0	2	2	21
92-93—Kamloops	WHL	71	4	19	23	206	...	...	...	13	0	2	2	24
93-94—Kamloops	WHL	68	5	49	54	180	...	3	1	19	5	11	16	48
94-95—Wheeling	ECHL	5	1	5	6	16	5	0	0	—	—	—	—	—
—Cape Breton	AHL	58	4	6	10	103	-7	2	0	—	—	—	—	—
95-96—Cape Breton	AHL	80	5	16	21	196	...	...	...	—	—	—	—	—
96-97—Hamilton	AHL	74	6	14	20	115	4	2	1	21	5	7	12	59
97-98—Hamilton	AHL	77	7	17	24	150	6	2	1	9	0	3	3	16
—Edmonton	NHL	1	0	0	0	0	1	0	0	—	—	—	—	—
98-99—Cincinnati	AHL	78	4	31	35	144	4	3	0	3	0	0	0	4
—Anaheim	NHL	2	0	1	1	0	0	0	0	—	—	—	—	—
99-00—Cincinnati	AHL	77	7	25	32	166	...	...	...	—	—	—	—	—
00-01—Hamilton	AHL	42	3	18	21	79	...	...	...	—	—	—	—	—
—Edmonton	NHL	20	0	1	1	13	2	0	0	6	0	0	0	0
01-02—Edmonton	NHL	50	3	2	5	75	11	0	0	—	—	—	—	—
02-03—Edmonton	NHL	78	3	5	8	120	11	0	0	5	0	0	0	8
03-04—Edmonton	NHL	52	1	5	6	80	-5	0	0	—	—	—	—	—
04-05—Skovde	Sweden	10	0	2	2	57	3	0	0	—	—	—	—	—
NHL Totals (6 years)		203	7	14	21	288	20	0	0	11	0	0	0	8

FERNANDEZ, MANNY — G — WILD

PERSONAL: Born August 27, 1974, in Etobicoke, Ont. ... 6-0/180. ... Catches left. ... Nephew of Jacques Lemaire, coach, Minnesota Wild, and Hall of Fame center with Montreal Canadiens (1967-68 through 1978-79).

TRANSACTIONS/CAREER NOTES: Selected by Quebec Nordiques in third round (fourth Nordiques pick, 52nd overall) of NHL entry draft (June 20, 1992). ... Traded by Nordiques to Dallas Stars for D Tommy Sjodin and third-round pick (C Chris Drury) in 1994 entry draft (February 13, 1994). ... Traded by Stars with D Brad Lukowich to Minnesota Wild for third-round pick (C Joel Lundqvist) in 2000 entry draft and fourth-round pick (traded back to Minnesota) in 2002 entry draft (June 12, 2000). ... Injured right ankle (October 14, 2000); missed five games. ... Sprained right knee (March 6, 2001); missed two games. ... Sprained left ankle (March 15, 2001); missed remainder of season. ... Sprained ankle (April 10, 2002); missed remainder of season. ... Strained knee (January 6, 2003); missed 10 games.

Season	Team	League	GP	Min.	W	L	T	GA	SO	GAA	SV%	GP	Min.	W	L	GA	SO	GAA	SV%
			REGULAR SEASON									PLAYOFFS							
91-92	—Laval	QMJHL	31	1593	14	13	2	99	1	3.73	...	9	468	3	5	39	0	5.00	...
92-93	—Laval	QMJHL	43	2348	26	14	2	141	1	3.60	.887	13	818	12	1	42	0	3.08	...
93-94	—Laval	QMJHL	51	2776	29	14	1	143	*5	3.09	.906	19	1116	14	5	49	1	*2.63	.914
94-95	—Kalamazoo	IHL	46	2470	21	10	9	115	2	2.79	.905	12	655	9	1	30	1	2.75	.901
	—Dallas	NHL	1	59	0	1	0	3	0	3.05	.889	—	—	—	—	—	—	—	—
95-96	—Michigan	IHL	47	2663	22	15	9	133	4	3.00	...	6	372	5	1	14	0	*2.26	...
	—Dallas	NHL	5	249	0	1	1	19	0	4.58	.843	—	—	—	—	—	—	—	—
96-97	—Michigan	IHL	48	2721	20	24	2	142	2	3.13	...	4	277	1	3	15	0	3.25	...
97-98	—Michigan	IHL	55	3023	27	17	5	139	5	2.76	.916	2	89	0	2	7	0	4.72	.860
	—Dallas	NHL	2	69	1	0	0	2	0	1.74	.943	1	2	0	0	0	0	0.00	...
98-99	—Houston	IHL	50	2949	34	6	9	116	2	2.36	.916	*19	*1126	*11	*8	49	1	2.61	.904
	—Dallas	NHL	1	60	0	1	0	2	0	2.00	.931	—	—	—	—	—	—	—	—
99-00	—Dallas	NHL	24	1353	11	8	3	48	1	2.13	.920	1	17	0	0	1	0	3.53	.875
00-01	—Minnesota	NHL	42	2461	19	17	4	92	4	2.24	.920	—	—	—	—	—	—	—	—
01-02	—Minnesota	NHL	44	2463	12	24	5	125	1	3.05	.892	—	—	—	—	—	—	—	—
02-03	—Minnesota	NHL	35	1979	19	13	2	74	2	2.24	.924	9	552	3	4	18	0	1.96	.929
03-04	—Minnesota	NHL	37	2166	11	14	9	90	2	2.49	.915	—	—	—	—	—	—	—	—
04-05	—Lulea	Sweden	19	1083	...	...	...	50	2	2.77	.895	3	159	...	...	13	0	4.90	.849
NHL Totals (9 years)			191	10859	73	79	24	455	10	2.51	.912	11	571	3	4	19	0	2.00	.927

FIBIGER, JESSE — D — SENATORS

PERSONAL: Born April 4, 1978, in Victoria, B.C. ... 6-3/220. ... Shoots left.

TRANSACTIONS/CAREER NOTES: Signed as free agent by San Jose Sharks (August 15, 2001). ... Signed as free agent by Ottawa Senators (August 11, 2004).

Season	Team	League	GP	G	A	Pts.	PIM	+/-	PP	SH	GP	G	A	Pts.	PIM
			REGULAR SEASON								PLAYOFFS				
96-97	—Victoria	BCJHL	53	6	18	24	...	...	...	...	—	—	—	—	—
97-98	—Minnesota-Duluth	WCHA	40	3	6	9	82	...	...	...	—	—	—	—	—
98-99	—Minnesota-Duluth	WCHA	36	4	16	20	61	...	...	...	—	—	—	—	—
99-00	—Minnesota-Duluth	WCHA	37	4	6	10	83	...	...	...	—	—	—	—	—
00-01	—Minnesota-Duluth	WCHA	37	0	8	8	56	...	...	...	—	—	—	—	—
01-02	—Cleveland	AHL	79	6	12	18	94	-4	4	0	—	—	—	—	—
02-03	—Cleveland	AHL	59	3	11	14	63	-10	2	0	—	—	—	—	—
	—San Jose	NHL	16	0	0	0	2	-5	0	0	—	—	—	—	—
03-04	—Cleveland	AHL	55	5	12	17	39	6	1	0	9	0	2	2	8
04-05	—Binghamton	AHL	79	3	19	22	79	23	0	0	6	1	0	1	6
NHL Totals (1 year)			16	0	0	0	2	-5	0	0					

FICHAUD, ERIC — G — CANADIENS

PERSONAL: Born November 4, 1975, in Anjou, Que. ... 5-11/171. ... Catches left. ... Name pronounced FEE-shoh.

TRANSACTIONS/CAREER NOTES: Selected by Toronto Maple Leafs in first round (first Maple Leafs pick, 16th overall) of NHL entry draft (June 28, 1994). ... Traded by Maple Leafs to New York Islanders for C Benoit Hogue, 3rd-round pick (RW Ryan Pepperall) in 1995 draft and 5th-round pick (D Brandon Sugden) in 1996 draft (April 6, 1995). ... Strained abdominal muscle (October 12, 1996); missed two games. ... Partially dislocated left shoulder (December 2, 1997); missed seven games. ... Had shoulder surgery while assigned to Utah of the IHL (January 20, 1998); missed remainder of season. ... Traded by Islanders to Edmonton Oilers for LW Mike Watt (June 18, 1998). ... Traded by Oilers with D Drake Berehowsky and D Greg de Vries to Nashville Predators for F Jim Dowd and G Mikhail Shtalenkov (October 1, 1998). ... Partially dislocated left shoulder (December 8, 1998); missed five games. ... Reinjured shoulder (January 4, 1999) and had surgery; missed remainder of season. ... Traded by Predators to Carolina Hurricanes for 4th-round pick (C/RW Yevgeny Pavlov) in 1999 draft and future considerations (June 26, 1999). ... Claimed off waivers by Montreal Canadiens (February 11, 2000). ... Injured shoulder (February 11, 2000); missed 14 games. ... Announced retirement (October 28, 2001). ... Signed as free agent by Canadiens (September 10, 2002).

Season	Team	League	GP	Min.	W	L	T	GA	SO	GAA	SV%	GP	Min.	W	L	GA	SO	GAA	SV%
			REGULAR SEASON									PLAYOFFS							
92-93	—Chicoutimi	QMJHL	43	2040	18	13	1	149	0	4.38	...	—	—	—	—	—	—	—	—
93-94	—Chicoutimi	QMJHL	63	3493	37	21	3	192	4	3.30	.899	26	1560	16	10	86	1	3.31	.892
94-95	—Chicoutimi	QMJHL	46	2637	21	19	4	151	4	3.44	.898	7	430	2	5	20	0	2.79	.910
95-96	—Worcester	AHL	34	1988	13	15	6	97	1	2.93	...	2	127	1	1	7	0	3.31	...
	—New York Islanders	NHL	24	1234	7	12	2	68	1	3.31	.897	—	—	—	—	—	—	—	—
96-97	—New York Islanders	NHL	34	1759	9	14	4	91	0	3.10	.899	—	—	—	—	—	—	—	—
97-98	—New York Islanders	NHL	17	807	3	8	3	40	0	2.97	.905	—	—	—	—	—	—	—	—
	—Utah	IHL	1	40	0	0	0	3	0	4.50	.870	—	—	—	—	—	—	—	—
98-99	—Milwaukee	IHL	8	480	5	2	1	25	0	3.13	.905	—	—	—	—	—	—	—	—
	—Nashville	NHL	9	447	0	6	0	24	0	3.22	.895	—	—	—	—	—	—	—	—
99-00	—Carolina	NHL	9	490	3	5	1	24	1	2.94	.883	—	—	—	—	—	—	—	—
	—Quebec	AHL	6	368	4	1	1	17	0	2.77	...	3	177	0	3	10	0	3.39	...
00-01	—Quebec	AHL	42	2441	19	19	2	127	1	3.12	.913	2	98	0	1	3	0	1.84	...
	—Montreal	NHL	2	62	0	2	0	4	0	3.87	.875	—	—	—	—	—	—	—	—
01-02	—Manitoba	AHL	5	278	2	3	0	13	1	2.81	.893	—	—	—	—	—	—	—	—
	—Krefeld Pinguine	Germany	9	401	...	...	...	11	0	1.65	...	3	197	...	...	8	0	2.44	...
02-03	—Hamilton	AHL	27	1446	14	7	3	55	4	2.28	.925	8	472	5	3	17	0	2.16	.917
03-04	—Hamilton	AHL	31	1835	16	11	3	70	1	2.29	.910	—	—	—	—	—	—	—	—
NHL Totals (6 years)			95	4799	22	47	10	251	2	3.14	.897								

F

FIDDLER, VERNON — C — PREDATORS

PERSONAL: Born May 9, 1980, in Edmonton. ... 5-11/197. ... Shoots left.
TRANSACTIONS/CAREER NOTES: Signed as free agent by Nashville Predators (May 6, 2002).

		REGULAR SEASON								PLAYOFFS				
Season Team	League	GP	G	A	Pts.	PIM	+/-	PP	SH	GP	G	A	Pts.	PIM
97-98—Kelowna	WHL	65	10	11	21	31	...	...	...	7	0	1	1	4
98-99—Kelowna	WHL	68	22	21	43	82	...	...	...	6	2	0	2	8
99-00—Kelowna	WHL	64	20	28	48	60	...	...	...	5	1	3	4	4
00-01—Arkansas	ECHL	3	0	1	1	2	...	...	...	5	3	0	3	5
—Kelowna	WHL	3	0	2	2	0	...	...	...	—	—	—	—	—
—Medicine Hat	WHL	67	33	38	71	100	...	...	...	—	—	—	—	—
01-02—Roanoke	ECHL	44	27	28	55	71	...	...	...	—	—	—	—	—
—Norfolk	AHL	38	8	5	13	28	...	...	...	4	1	3	4	2
02-03—Nashville	NHL	19	4	2	6	14	2	0	0	—	—	—	—	—
—Milwaukee	AHL	54	8	16	24	70	9	0	0	6	1	2	3	14
03-04—Nashville	NHL	17	0	0	0	23	-6	0	0	—	—	—	—	—
—Milwaukee	AHL	47	9	15	24	72	13	0	0	22	5	3	8	36
04-05—Milwaukee	AHL	73	20	22	42	70	19	1	2	7	0	0	0	18
NHL Totals (2 years)		36	4	2	6	37	-4	0	0					

FINLEY, BRIAN — G — PREDATORS

PERSONAL: Born July 3, 1981, in Sault Ste. Marie, Ont. ... 6-3/205. ... Catches right.
TRANSACTIONS/CAREER NOTES: Selected by Nashville Predators in 1st round (1st Predators pick, 6th overall) of draft (June 26, 1999). ... Groin injury; Did not play in 2001-02.

		REGULAR SEASON									PLAYOFFS							
Season Team	League	GP	Min.	W	L	T	GA	SO	GAA	SV%	GP	Min.	W	L	GA	SO	GAA	SV%
97-98—Barrie	OHL	41	2154	23	14	1	105	3	2.92	.909	5	260	1	3	13	0	3.00	.911
98-99—Barrie	OHL	52	3063	*36	10	4	136	3	2.66	.913	5	323	4	1	15	0	2.79	.910
99-00—Barrie	OHL	47	2540	24	12	6	130	2	3.07	.908	*23	1353	14	8	*58	1	1.00	.917
00-01—Barrie	OHL	16	818	5	8	0	42	0	3.08	.904	—	—	—	—	—	—	—	—
—Brampton	OHL	11	631	7	3	1	31	0	2.95	.889	9	503	5	4	26	1	3.10	...
02-03—Milwaukee	AHL	22	1207	7	11	2	59	2	2.93	.898	—	—	—	—	—	—	—	—
—Nashville	NHL	1	47	0	0	0	3	0	3.83	.769	—	—	—	—	—	—	—	—
—Toledo	ECHL	7	305	4	2	0	12	0	2.36	.918	1	60	0	1	4	0	4.00	.889
03-04—Milwaukee	AHL	43	2562	23	15	4	100	2	2.34	.911	1	58	0	1	2	0	2.07	.909
04-05—Milwaukee	AHL	64	3642	36	22	...	139	7	2.29	.921	7	457	3	4	20	1	2.63	.913
NHL Totals (1 year)		1	47	0	0	0	3	0	3.83	.769								

FINLEY, JEFF — D

PERSONAL: Born April 14, 1967, in Edmonton. ... 6-2/203. ... Shoots left.
TRANSACTIONS/CAREER NOTES: Selected by New York Islanders in third round (fourth Islanders pick, 55th overall) of NHL draft (June 15, 1985). ... Swollen left knee (September 1988). ... Traded by Islanders to Ottawa Senators for D Chris Luongo (June 30, 1993). ... Signed as free agent by Philadelphia Flyers (August 2, 1993). ... Traded by Flyers to Winnipeg Jets for LW Russ Romaniuk (June 26, 1995). ... Separated shoulder (December 10, 1995); missed one game. ... Jets franchise moved to Phoenix and renamed Coyotes for 1996-97 season; NHL approved move on January 18, 1996. ... Flu (December 7, 1996); missed two games. ... Strained hip flexor (December 30, 1996); missed one game. ... Sprained ankle (March 27, 1997); missed remainder of season and first six games of playoffs. ... Signed as free agent by New York Rangers (July 16, 1997). ... Traded by Rangers with D Geoff Smith to St. Louis Blues for future considerations (February 13, 1999); Rangers acquired RW Chris Kenady to complete deal (February 22, 1999). ... Injured back (December 21, 1999); missed two games. ... Injured groin (March 12, 2000); missed one game. ... Back spasms (March 30, 2000); missed final five games of season. ... Flu (November 16, 2000); missed one game. ... Suffered concussion (March 25, 2001); missed final six games of season. ... Sprained hip (October 20, 2001); missed three games. ... Bruised hip (March 2, 2002); missed one game. ... Flu (December 10, 2002); missed one game. ... Suspended four games for leaving penalty box to fight (March 24, 2003). ... Injured shoulder (January 12, 2004); missed 10 games. ... Injured hip (February 14, 2004); missed three games. ... Injured hip (February 22, 2004); missed three games. ... Injured shoulder (April 8, 2004); missed four playoff games.

		REGULAR SEASON								PLAYOFFS				
Season Team	League	GP	G	A	Pts.	PIM	+/-	PP	SH	GP	G	A	Pts.	PIM
83-84—Portland	WHL	5	0	0	0	0	...	...	...	5	0	1	1	4
—Summerland	BCJHL	49	0	21	21	14	...	...	...	—	—	—	—	—
84-85—Portland	WHL	69	6	44	50	57	...	...	...	6	1	2	3	2
85-86—Portland	WHL	70	11	59	70	83	...	...	...	15	1	7	8	16
86-87—Portland	WHL	72	13	53	66	113	...	...	...	20	1	21	22	27
87-88—Springfield	AHL	52	5	18	23	50	...	...	...	—	—	—	—	—
—New York Islanders	NHL	10	0	5	5	15	5	0	0	1	0	0	0	2
88-89—New York Islanders	NHL	4	0	0	0	6	1	0	0	—	—	—	—	—
—Springfield	AHL	65	3	16	19	55	...	...	...	—	—	—	—	—
89-90—New York Islanders	NHL	11	0	1	1	0	0	0	0	5	0	2	2	2
—Springfield	AHL	57	1	15	16	41	...	...	...	13	1	4	5	23
90-91—Capital District	AHL	67	10	34	44	34	...	...	...	—	—	—	—	—
—New York Islanders	NHL	11	0	0	0	4	-1	0	0	—	—	—	—	—
91-92—Capital District	AHL	20	1	9	10	6	...	...	...	—	—	—	—	—
—New York Islanders	NHL	51	1	10	11	26	-6	0	0	—	—	—	—	—
92-93—Capital District	AHL	61	6	29	35	34	5	4	0	4	0	1	1	0
93-94—Philadelphia	NHL	55	1	8	9	24	16	0	0	—	—	—	—	—
94-95—Hershey	AHL	36	2	9	11	33	-6	1	0	6	0	1	1	8
95-96—Springfield	AHL	14	3	12	15	22	...	...	...	—	—	—	—	—

Season Team	League	REGULAR SEASON GP	G	A	Pts.	PIM	+/-	PP	SH	PLAYOFFS GP	G	A	Pts.	PIM
—Winnipeg	NHL	65	1	5	6	81	-2	0	0	6	0	0	0	4
96-97—Phoenix	NHL	65	3	7	10	40	-8	1	0	1	0	0	0	2
97-98—New York Rangers	NHL	63	1	6	7	55	-3	0	0	—	—	—	—	—
98-99—Hartford	AHL	42	2	10	12	28	16	1	0	—	—	—	—	—
—New York Rangers	NHL	2	0	0	0	0	-1	0	0	—	—	—	—	—
—St. Louis	NHL	30	1	2	3	20	12	0	0	13	1	2	3	8
99-00—St. Louis	NHL	74	2	8	10	38	26	0	0	7	0	2	2	4
00-01—St. Louis	NHL	72	2	8	10	38	7	0	0	2	0	0	0	0
01-02—St. Louis	NHL	78	0	6	6	30	12	0	0	10	0	0	0	8
02-03—St. Louis	NHL	64	1	3	4	46	-2	0	0	6	0	0	0	6
03-04—St. Louis	NHL	53	0	1	1	34	-9	0	0	1	0	0	0	2
NHL Totals (15 years)		708	13	70	83	457	47	1	0	52	1	6	7	38

FINLEY, JOE — D — CAPITALS

PERSONAL: Born June 29, 1987, in Edina, Minn. ... 6-7/235. ... Shoots left.

TRANSACTIONS/CAREER NOTES: Selected in the 1st round by Washington Capitals (1st Capitals pick, 27th overall) of entry draft (July 30, 2005).

Season Team	League	REGULAR SEASON GP	G	A	Pts.	PIM	+/-	PP	SH	PLAYOFFS GP	G	A	Pts.	PIM
04-05—Sioux Falls	USHL	55	3	10	13	181	...	...	...	—	—	—	—	—

FISCHER, JIRI — D — RED WINGS

PERSONAL: Born July 31, 1980, in Horovice, Czech. ... 6-5/235. ... Shoots left.

TRANSACTIONS/CAREER NOTES: Selected by Detroit Red Wings in first round (first Red Wings pick, 25th overall) of NHL draft (June 27, 1998). ... Sprained ankle (December 2, 2000); missed eight games. ... Suspended one playoff game for cross-checking incident (June 11, 2002). ... Injured knee (November 15, 2002); missed remainer of season (67 games). ... Suspended for one game for head-butting incident (January 24, 2004).

Season Team	League	REGULAR SEASON GP	G	A	Pts.	PIM	+/-	PP	SH	PLAYOFFS GP	G	A	Pts.	PIM
95-96—Poldi Kladno	Czech Rep.	39	6	10	16	...	...	...	...	—	—	—	—	—
96-97—Poldi Kladno	Czech Rep.	38	11	16	27	...	...	...	...	—	—	—	—	—
97-98—Hull	QMJHL	70	3	19	22	112	-18	2	0	11	1	4	5	16
98-99—Hull	QMJHL	65	22	56	78	141	11	15	2	23	6	17	23	44
99-00—Detroit	NHL	52	0	8	8	45	1	0	0	—	—	—	—	—
—Cincinnati	AHL	7	0	2	2	10	...	...	...	—	—	—	—	—
00-01—Detroit	NHL	55	1	8	9	59	3	0	0	5	0	0	0	9
—Cincinnati	AHL	18	2	6	8	22	...	...	...	—	—	—	—	—
01-02—Detroit	NHL	80	2	8	10	67	17	0	0	22	3	3	6	30
02-03—Detroit	NHL	15	1	5	6	16	0	0	0	—	—	—	—	—
03-04—Detroit	NHL	81	4	15	19	75	0	1	0	—	—	—	—	—
04-05—Liberec	Czech Rep.	27	6	12	18	52	15	...	...	11	1	4	5	22
NHL Totals (5 years)		283	8	44	52	262	21	1	0	27	3	3	6	39

FISHER, MIKE — C/LW — SENATORS

F

PERSONAL: Born June 5, 1980, in Peterborough, Ont. ... 6-0/203. ... Shoots right.

TRANSACTIONS/CAREER NOTES: Selected by Ottawa Senators in second round (second Senators pick, 44th overall) of NHL draft (June 27, 1998). ... Had hip pointer (October 5, 1999); missed three games. ... Tore right knee ligament (December 30, 1999); missed remainder of season. ... Injured left shoulder (November 2, 2000); missed 22 games. ... Injured left shoulder (February 8, 2002); missed five games. ... Injured right shoulder (March 7, 2002); missed final 19 games of season. ... Had the flu (December 17, 2002); missed one game. ... Bruised right knee (January 2, 2003); missed two games. ... Separated left shoulder (March 25, 2003); missed four games. ... Injured left elbow (October 4, 2003); missed 33 games. ... Injured left elbow (December 30, 2003); missed 25 games.

Season Team	League	REGULAR SEASON GP	G	A	Pts.	PIM	+/-	PP	SH	PLAYOFFS GP	G	A	Pts.	PIM
96-97—Peterborough	Tier II Jr. A	51	26	30	56	33	...	...	...	—	—	—	—	—
97-98—Sudbury	OHL	66	24	25	49	65	...	...	...	9	2	2	4	13
98-99—Sudbury	OHL	68	41	65	106	55	10	...	...	4	2	1	3	4
99-00—Ottawa	NHL	32	4	5	9	15	-6	0	0	—	—	—	—	—
00-01—Ottawa	NHL	60	7	12	19	46	-1	0	0	4	0	1	1	4
01-02—Ottawa	NHL	58	15	9	24	55	8	0	3	10	2	1	3	0
02-03—Ottawa	NHL	74	18	20	38	54	13	5	1	18	2	2	4	16
03-04—Ottawa	NHL	24	4	6	10	39	-3	1	0	7	1	0	1	4
04-05—Zug	Switzerland	21	9	17	26	32	11	4	2	9	2	3	5	10
NHL Totals (5 years)		248	48	52	100	209	11	6	4	39	5	4	9	24

FISTRIC, MARK — D — STARS

PERSONAL: Born June 1, 1986, in Edmonton. ... 6-2/232. ... Shoots left.

TRANSACTIONS/CAREER NOTES: Selected by Dallas Stars in first round (first Stars pick, 28th overall) of NHL entry draft (June 26, 2004).

Season Team	League	GP	G	A	Pts.	PIM	+/-	PP	SH	GP	G	A	Pts.	PIM
		REGULAR SEASON								PLAYOFFS				
01-02—Vancouver	WHL	4	0	1	1	0	...	...	...	—	—	—	—	—
02-03—Vancouver	WHL	63	2	7	9	81	...	...	...	4	0	0	0	8
03-04—Vancouver	WHL	72	1	11	12	192	...	...	...	11	0	2	2	10
04-05—Vancouver	WHL	15	1	5	6	32	7	0	0	6	1	1	2	16

FITZGERALD, TOM — RW — BRUINS

PERSONAL: Born August 28, 1968, in Billerica, Mass. ... 6-0/190. ... Shoots right. ... Cousin of Keith Tkachuk, LW, St. Louis Blues.

TRANSACTIONS/CAREER NOTES: Selected by New York Islanders in first round (first Islanders pick, 17th overall) of NHL draft (June 21, 1986). ... Bruised left knee (November 7, 1990). ... Strained abdominal muscle (October 22, 1991); missed 16 games. ... Tore rib cage muscle (October 24, 1992); missed four games. ... Selected by Florida Panthers in expansion draft (June 24, 1993). ... Sore hip (March 18, 1994); missed one game. ... Bruised eye (November 13, 1996); missed one game. ... Flu (December 29, 1996); missed one game. ... Strained abdominal muscle (January 25, 1997); missed three games. ... Reinjured abdominal muscle (February 22, 1997); missed five games. ... Traded by Panthers to Colorado Avalanche for rights to LW Mark Parrish and third-round pick (D Lance Ward) in 1998 entry draft (March 24, 1998). ... Signed as free agent by Nashville Predators (July 6, 1998). ... Strained neck (December 8, 1998); missed one game. ... Injured ribs (December 15, 2001); missed three games. ... Traded by Predators to Chicago Blackhawks for fourth-round pick (traded to Anaheim Mighty Ducks) in 2003 draft (March 13, 2002). ... Signed as free agent by Toronto Maple Leafs (July 17, 2002). ... Injured upper body (January 13, 2003); missed four games. ... Injured left leg (March 3, 2003); missed six games. ... Injured shoulder (October 8, 2003); missed two games. ... Injured foot (January 21, 2004); missed nine games. ... Signed as free agent by Boston Bruins (July 28, 2004).

Season Team	League	GP	G	A	Pts.	PIM	+/-	PP	SH	GP	G	A	Pts.	PIM
		REGULAR SEASON								PLAYOFFS				
84-85—Austin Prep	Mass. H.S.	18	20	21	41	...	...	...	...	—	—	—	—	—
85-86—Austin Prep	Mass. H.S.	24	35	38	73	...	...	...	...	—	—	—	—	—
86-87—Providence College	Hockey East	27	8	14	22	22	...	...	...	—	—	—	—	—
87-88—Providence College	Hockey East	36	19	15	34	50	...	...	...	—	—	—	—	—
88-89—Springfield	AHL	61	24	18	42	43	...	...	...	—	—	—	—	—
—New York Islanders	NHL	23	3	5	8	10	1	0	0	—	—	—	—	—
89-90—Springfield	AHL	53	30	23	53	32	...	...	...	14	2	9	11	13
—New York Islanders	NHL	19	2	5	7	4	-3	0	0	4	1	0	1	4
90-91—New York Islanders	NHL	41	5	5	10	24	-9	0	0	—	—	—	—	—
—Capital District	AHL	27	7	7	14	50	...	...	...	—	—	—	—	—
91-92—New York Islanders	NHL	45	6	11	17	28	-3	0	2	—	—	—	—	—
—Capital District	AHL	4	1	1	2	4	...	...	...	—	—	—	—	—
92-93—New York Islanders	NHL	77	9	18	27	34	-2	0	3	18	2	5	7	18
93-94—Florida	NHL	83	18	14	32	54	-3	0	3	—	—	—	—	—
94-95—Florida	NHL	48	3	13	16	31	-3	0	0	—	—	—	—	—
95-96—Florida	NHL	82	13	21	34	75	-3	1	6	22	4	4	8	34
96-97—Florida	NHL	71	10	14	24	64	7	0	2	5	0	1	1	0
97-98—Florida	NHL	69	10	5	15	57	-4	0	1	—	—	—	—	—
—Colorado	NHL	11	2	1	3	22	0	0	1	7	0	1	1	20
98-99—Nashville	NHL	80	13	19	32	48	-18	0	0	—	—	—	—	—
99-00—Nashville	NHL	82	13	9	22	66	-18	0	3	—	—	—	—	—
00-01—Nashville	NHL	82	9	9	18	71	-5	0	2	—	—	—	—	—
01-02—Nashville	NHL	63	7	9	16	33	-4	0	1	—	—	—	—	—
—Chicago	NHL	15	1	3	4	6	-3	0	1	5	0	0	0	4
02-03—Toronto	NHL	66	4	13	17	57	10	0	0	7	0	1	1	4
03-04—Toronto	NHL	69	7	10	17	52	-2	1	0	10	0	0	0	6
NHL Totals (16 years)		1026	135	184	319	736	-62	2	25	78	7	12	19	90

FITZPATRICK, RORY — D — SABRES

F

PERSONAL: Born January 11, 1975, in Rochester, N.Y. ... 6-2/208. ... Shoots right.

TRANSACTIONS/CAREER NOTES: Selected by Montreal Canadiens in second round (second Canadiens pick, 47th overall) of NHL entry draft (June 26, 1993). ... Traded by Canadiens with C Pierre Turgeon and C Craig Conroy to St. Louis Blues for LW Shayne Corson, D Murray Baron and fifth-round pick (D Gennady Razin) in 1997 entry draft (October 29, 1996). ... Selected by Boston Bruins in NHL waiver draft (October 5, 1998). ... Claimed on waivers by Blues (October 7, 1998). ... Traded by Blues to Nashville Predators for D Dan Keczmer (February 9, 2000). ... Traded by Predators to Edmonton Oilers for future considerations (January 12, 2001). ... Signed as free agent by Buffalo Sabres (August 14, 2001). ... Suffered concussion (December 14, 2002); missed five games. ... Injured thigh (March 31, 2003); missed one game. ... Bruised knee (November 19, 2003); missed one game. ... Fractured nose (February 16, 2004); missed two games. ... Injured knee (February 28, 2004); mised final 17 games of season.

Season Team	League	GP	G	A	Pts.	PIM	+/-	PP	SH	GP	G	A	Pts.	PIM
		REGULAR SEASON								PLAYOFFS				
90-91—Rochester Jr. B	OHA	40	0	5	5	...	...	...	...	—	—	—	—	—
91-92—Rochester Jr. B	OHA	28	8	28	36	141	...	...	...	—	—	—	—	—
92-93—Sudbury	OHL	58	4	20	24	68	...	...	...	14	0	0	0	17
93-94—Sudbury	OHL	65	12	34	46	112	...	8	0	10	2	5	7	10
94-95—Sudbury	OHL	56	12	36	48	72	...	9	0	18	3	15	18	21
—Fredericton	AHL	...	...	...	...	...	...	...	...	10	1	2	3	5
95-96—Fredericton	AHL	18	4	6	10	36	...	...	...	—	—	—	—	—
—Montreal	NHL	42	0	2	2	18	-7	0	0	6	1	1	2	0
96-97—Montreal	NHL	6	0	1	1	6	-2	0	0	—	—	—	—	—
—Worcester	AHL	49	4	13	17	78	8	2	0	5	1	2	3	0
—St. Louis	NHL	2	0	0	0	2	-2	0	0	—	—	—	—	—
97-98—Worcester	AHL	62	8	22	30	111	-3	6	0	11	0	3	3	26
98-99—Worcester	AHL	53	5	16	21	82	-11	4	0	4	0	1	1	17
—St. Louis	NHL	1	0	0	0	2	-3	0	0	—	—	—	—	—
99-00—Worcester	AHL	28	0	5	5	48	...	...	...	—	—	—	—	—

Season Team	League	REGULAR SEASON GP	G	A	Pts.	PIM	+/-	PP	SH	PLAYOFFS GP	G	A	Pts.	PIM
—Milwaukee	IHL	27	2	1	3	27	...	...	...	3	0	2	2	2
00-01—Hamilton	AHL	34	3	17	20	29	...	...	...	—	—	—	—	—
—Nashville	NHL	2	0	0	0	2	-2	0	0	—	—	—	—	—
—Milwaukee	IHL	22	0	2	2	32	...	...	...	—	—	—	—	—
01-02—Rochester	AHL	60	4	8	12	83	12	1	0	2	0	1	1	0
—Buffalo	NHL	5	0	0	0	4	-2	0	0	—	—	—	—	—
02-03—Rochester	AHL	41	5	11	16	65	-2	2	0	—	—	—	—	—
—Buffalo	NHL	36	1	3	4	16	-7	0	0	—	—	—	—	—
03-04—Buffalo	NHL	60	4	7	11	44	-5	2	0	—	—	—	—	—
04-05—Rochester	AHL	20	1	1	2	18	-8	0	1	9	0	1	1	12
NHL Totals (7 years)		154	5	13	18	94	-30	2	0	6	1	1	2	0

FLAHERTY, WADE — G — CANUCKS

PERSONAL: Born January 11, 1968, in Terrace, B.C. ... 6-0/170. ... Catches left.

TRANSACTIONS/CAREER NOTES: Selected by Buffalo Sabres in ninth round (10th Sabres pick, 181st overall) of NHL draft (June 11, 1988). ... Signed as free agent by San Jose Sharks (September 3, 1991). ... Injured ribs (February 28, 1995); missed three games. ... Strained groin (February 1, 1996); missed two games. ... Back spasms (March 8, 1996); missed six games. ... Back spasms (March 31, 1996); missed seven games. ... Fractured collarbone (September 12, 1996); missed 23 games. ... Signed as free agent by New York Islanders (July 1, 1997). ... Sprained shoulder (November 21, 1999) and had surgery; missed remainder of season. ... Traded by Islanders to Tampa Bay Lightning for conditional ninth-round pick (February 16, 2001). ... Signed as free agent by Florida Panthers (August 2, 2001). ... Traded by Panthers to Nashville Predators for D Pascal Trepanier (March 9, 2003). ... Injured groin (March 31, 2003); missed final three games of season. ... Signed as free agent by Vancouver Canucks (July 7, 2004).

Season Team	League	REGULAR SEASON GP	Min.	W	L	T	GA	SO	GAA	SV%	PLAYOFFS GP	Min.	W	L	GA	SO	GAA	SV%
84-85—Kelowna	WHL	1	55	0	0	0	5	0	5.45	...	—	—	—	—	—	—	—	—
85-86—Seattle	WHL	9	271	1	3	0	36	0	7.97	...	—	—	—	—	—	—	—	—
—Spokane	WHL	5	161	0	3	0	21	0	7.83	...	—	—	—	—	—	—	—	—
86-87—Nanaimo	BCHL	15	830	...	...	...	53	0	3.83	...	—	—	—	—	—	—	—	—
—Victoria	WHL	3	127	0	2	0	16	0	7.56	...	—	—	—	—	—	—	—	—
87-88—Victoria	WHL	36	2052	20	15	0	135	0	3.95	...	5	300	2	3	18	0	3.60	...
88-89—Victoria	WHL	42	2408	21	19	0	180	0	4.49	...	8	480	3	5	35	0	4.38	...
89-90—Kalamazoo	IHL	1	13	0	0	0	0	0	0.00	...	—	—	—	—	—	—	—	—
—Greensboro	ECHL	27	1308	12	10	0	96	...	4.40	...	9	567	*8	1	21	0	*2.22	...
90-91—Kansas City	IHL	56	2990	16	31	4	*224	0	4.49	...	—	—	—	—	—	—	—	—
91-92—Kansas City	IHL	43	2603	26	14	3	140	1	3.23	...	1	1	0	0	0	0	0.00	...
—San Jose	NHL	3	178	0	3	0	13	0	4.38	.892	—	—	—	—	—	—	—	—
92-93—Kansas City	IHL	61	*3642	*34	19	0	*195	2	3.21	.888	12	*733	6	*5	34	*1	2.78	...
—San Jose	NHL	1	60	0	1	0	5	0	5.00	.891	—	—	—	—	—	—	—	—
93-94—Kansas City	IHL	60	*3564	32	19	9	202	0	3.40	.896	—	—	—	—	—	—	—	—
94-95—San Jose	NHL	18	852	5	6	1	44	1	3.10	.903	7	377	2	3	31	0	4.93	.860
95-96—San Jose	NHL	24	1137	3	12	1	92	0	4.85	.866	—	—	—	—	—	—	—	—
96-97—Kentucky	AHL	19	1032	8	6	2	54	1	3.14	.910	3	200	1	2	11	0	3.30	.884
—San Jose	NHL	7	359	2	4	0	31	0	5.18	.847	—	—	—	—	—	—	—	—
97-98—Utah	IHL	24	1341	16	5	3	40	3	1.79	.936	—	—	—	—	—	—	—	—
—New York Islanders	NHL	16	694	4	4	3	23	3	1.99	.926	—	—	—	—	—	—	—	—
98-99—New York Islanders	NHL	20	1048	5	11	2	53	0	3.03	.892	—	—	—	—	—	—	—	—
—Lowell	AHL	5	305	1	3	1	16	0	3.15	.903	—	—	—	—	—	—	—	—
99-00—New York Islanders	NHL	4	182	0	1	1	7	0	2.31	.914	—	—	—	—	—	—	—	—
00-01—New York Islanders	NHL	20	1017	6	10	0	56	1	3.30	.881	—	—	—	—	—	—	—	—
—Tampa Bay	NHL	2	118	0	2	0	8	0	4.07	.855	—	—	—	—	—	—	—	—
01-02—Utah	AHL	45	2351	22	13	5	92	2	2.35	.922	5	311	2	3	11	0	2.12	.935
—Florida	NHL	4	245	2	1	1	12	0	2.94	.919	—	—	—	—	—	—	—	—
02-03—Nashville	NHL	1	51	0	1	0	4	0	4.71	.852	—	—	—	—	—	—	—	—
—San Antonio	AHL	30	1791	11	13	5	86	1	2.88	.914	—	—	—	—	—	—	—	—
03-04—Milwaukee	AHL	36	2146	21	12	3	78	3	2.18	.915	21	1370	16	5	44	1	1.93	.927
04-05—Manitoba	AHL	36	2009	19	10	...	78	4	2.33	.918	12	719	8	4	29	2	2.42	.912
NHL Totals (11 years)		120	5941	27	56	9	348	5	3.51	.887	7	377	2	3	31	0	4.93	.860

FLEURY, MARC-ANDRE — G — PENGUINS

PERSONAL: Born November 28, 1984, in Sorel, Que. ... 6-2/172. ... Catches left.

TRANSACTIONS/CAREER NOTES: Selected by Pittsburgh Penguins in first round (first Penguins pick, 1st overall) in 2003 NHL draft June 23, 2003).

Season Team	League	REGULAR SEASON GP	Min.	W	L	T	GA	SO	GAA	SV%	PLAYOFFS GP	Min.	W	L	GA	SO	GAA	SV%
00-01—Cape Breton	QMJHL	35	1705	12	13	2	115	0	4.05	...	2	32	0	1	4	0	7.50	...
01-02—Cape Breton	QMJHL	55	3043	26	14	8	141	2	2.78	...	16	1003	9	7	55	0	3.29	...
02-03—Cape Breton	QMJHL	51	2889	17	24	6	162	2	3.36	...	—	—	—	—	—	—	—	—
03-04—Pittsburgh	NHL	21	1154	4	14	2	70	1	3.64	.896	—	—	—	—	—	—	—	—
—Cape Breton	QMJHL	10	606	8	1	1	20	0	1.98	.933	—	—	—	—	—	—	—	—
—Wilkes-Barre/Scranton	AHL	...	...	...	...	...	...	...	...	...	2	92	0	1	6	0	3.91	.750
04-05—Wilkes-Barre/Scranton	AHL	54	3029	26	19	...	127	5	2.52	.901	4	151	0	2	11	0	4.37	.843
NHL Totals (1 year)		21	1154	4	14	2	70	1	3.64	.896								

F

FLINN, RYAN — LW

PERSONAL: Born April 20, 1980, in Halifax, N.S. ... 6-5/248. ... Shoots left.

TRANSACTIONS/CAREER NOTES: Selected by New Jersey Devils in fifth round (eighth Devils pick, 143rd overall) of NHL entry draft (June 27, 1998). ... Signed as free agent by Los Angeles Kings (January 9, 2002). ... Signed as free agent by Manchester of the AHL (September 27, 2004).

		REGULAR SEASON								PLAYOFFS				
Season Team	League	GP	G	A	Pts.	PIM	+/-	PP	SH	GP	G	A	Pts.	PIM
96-97—Laval	QMJHL	23	3	2	5	66	...	...	...	2	0	0	0	0
97-98—Laval	QMJHL	59	4	12	16	217	...	...	...	15	1	0	1	63
98-99—Acadie-Bathurst	QMJHL	44	3	4	7	195	-9	1	0	23	2	0	2	37
99-00—Halifax	QMJHL	67	14	19	33	365	4	5	0	—	—	—	—	—
00-01—Cape Breton	QMJHL	57	16	17	33	280	5	4	0	9	1	1	2	43
01-02—Reading	ECHL	20	1	3	4	130	-10	0	0	—	—	—	—	—
—Manchester	AHL	37	0	1	1	113	-6	0	0	1	0	0	0	0
—Los Angeles	NHL	10	0	0	0	51	0	0	0	—	—	—	—	—
02-03—Manchester	AHL	27	2	2	4	95	0	0	0	—	—	—	—	—
—Los Angeles	NHL	19	1	0	1	28	0	0	0	—	—	—	—	—
03-04—Manchester	AHL	59	3	5	8	164	-7	0	0	6	0	0	0	4
04-05—Manchester	AHL	14	1	1	2	112	-1	1	0	0	0	0	0	0
NHL Totals (2 years)		29	1	0	1	79	0	0	0					

FOCHT DAN — D

PERSONAL: Born December 31, 1977, in Regina, Sask. ... 6-6/234. ... Shoots left. ... Name pronounced FOHKT.

TRANSACTIONS/CAREER NOTES: Selected by Phoenix Coyotes in first round (first Coyotes pick, 11th overall) of NHL entry draft (June 22, 1996). ... Traded by Coyotes with LW Ramzi Abid and LW Guillaume Lefebvre to Pittsburgh Penguins for C Jan Hrdina and D Francois Leroux (March 11, 2003). ... Fractured finger (November 15, 2003); missed 13 games. ... Suffered concussion (January 3, 2004); missed nine games.

		REGULAR SEASON								PLAYOFFS				
Season Team	League	GP	G	A	Pts.	PIM	+/-	PP	SH	GP	G	A	Pts.	PIM
95-96—Tri-City	WHL	63	6	12	18	161	...	...	...	11	1	1	2	23
96-97—Tri-City	WHL	28	0	5	5	92	-16	0	0	—	—	—	—	—
—Regina	WHL	22	2	2	4	59	6	0	0	5	0	2	2	8
—Springfield	AHL	1	0	0	0	2	1	0	0	—	—	—	—	—
97-98—Springfield	AHL	61	2	5	7	125	5	0	0	3	0	0	0	4
98-99—Springfield	AHL	30	0	2	2	58	-2	0	0	3	1	0	1	10
—Mississippi	ECHL	2	0	0	0	6	-2	0	0	—	—	—	—	—
99-00—Jokerit Helsinki	Finland	2	0	0	0	0	...	...	...	—	—	—	—	—
—Springfield	AHL	44	2	9	11	86	...	...	...	5	0	1	1	2
—Mississippi	ECHL	4	0	1	1	0	...	...	...	—	—	—	—	—
00-01—Springfield	AHL	69	0	6	6	156	...	...	...	—	—	—	—	—
01-02—Springfield	AHL	56	2	8	10	134	14	0	0	—	—	—	—	—
—Phoenix	NHL	8	0	0	0	11	0	0	0	1	0	1	1	0
02-03—Phoenix	NHL	10	0	0	0	10	-2	0	0	—	—	—	—	—
—Springfield	AHL	37	2	7	9	80	-12	1	0	—	—	—	—	—
—Pittsburgh	NHL	12	0	3	3	19	-7	0	0	—	—	—	—	—
03-04—Pittsburgh	NHL	52	2	3	5	105	-23	0	0	—	—	—	—	—
04-05—Hamilton	AHL	26	2	3	5	84	-3	1	0	—	—	—	—	—
NHL Totals (3 years)		82	2	6	8	145	-32	0	0	1	0	1	1	0

FOOT ADAM — D — BLUE JACKETS

PERSONAL: Born July 10, 1971, in Toronto. ... 6-2/215. ... Shoots right.

TRANSACTIONS/CAREER NOTES: Selected by Quebec Nordiques in 2nd round (2nd Nordiques pick, 22nd overall) of NHL draft (June 17, 1989). ... Fractured right thumb (February 1992); missed remainder of season. ... Injured knee (October 21, 1992); missed one game. ... Flu (January 28, 1993); missed two games. ... Injured groin (January 18, 1994); missed eight games. ... Herniated disc (February 11, 1994) and had surgery; missed remainder of season. ... Injured back (February 9, 1995); missed two games. ... Injured groin (February 28, 1995); missed two games. ... Injured groin (March 26, 1995); missed four games. ... Reinjured groin (April 6, 1995); missed five games. ... Nordiques franchise moved to Colorado and renamed Avalanche for 1995-96 season (June 21, 1995). ... Fractured wrist before 1995-96 season; missed season's first two games. ... Separated left shoulder (January 6, 1996); missed five games. ... Bruised left knee (February 8, 1997); missed two games. ... Bruised knee (January 2, 1998); missed one game. ... Bruised knee (January 10, 1998); missed three games. ... Injured elbow (October 24, 1998); missed 15 games. ... Suffered concussion (December 4, 1998); missed three games. ... Injured shoulder (October 10, 1999); missed one game. ... Reinjured shoulder (October 21, 1999); missed six games. ... Reinjured shoulder (November 17, 1999); missed eight games. ... Injured groin (January 9, 2000); missed one game. ... Injured groin (February 10, 2000); missed six games. ... Stress fracture in heel (November 9, 2000); missed 12 games. ... Separated right shoulder (January 4, 2001); missed 35 games. ... Had shoulder surgery before start of 2000-01 season; missed first 16 games of season. ... Injured knee (December 27, 2001); missed six games. ... Injured finger (March 14, 2002); missed two games. ... Suspended two games for cross-checking incident (April 1, 2002). ... Injured groin (April 12, 2002); missed final game of season. ... Strained groin (December 2, 2002); missed two games. ... Injured hamstring (March 5, 2003); missed two games. ... Injured hamstring (November 5, 2003); missed four games. ... Flu (December 4, 2003); missed one game. ... Headache (January 30, 2004); missed two games. ... Injured groin (February 20, 2004); missed two games. ... Signed as free agent by Columbus Blue Jackets (Aug. 1, 2005).

		REGULAR SEASON								PLAYOFFS				
Season Team	League	GP	G	A	Pts.	PIM	+/-	PP	SH	GP	G	A	Pts.	PIM
88-89—Sault Ste. Marie	OHL	66	7	32	39	120	...	...	...	—	—	—	—	—
89-90—Sault Ste. Marie	OHL	61	12	43	55	199	...	...	...	—	—	—	—	—
90-91—Sault Ste. Marie	OHL	59	18	51	69	93	...	...	...	14	5	12	17	28
91-92—Quebec	NHL	46	2	5	7	44	-4	0	0	—	—	—	—	—
—Halifax	AHL	6	0	1	1	2	...	...	...	—	—	—	—	—

F

Season Team	League	GP	G	A	Pts.	PIM	+/-	PP	SH	GP	G	A	Pts.	PIM
		REGULAR SEASON								PLAYOFFS				
92-93—Quebec	NHL	81	4	12	16	168	6	0	1	6	0	1	1	2
93-94—Quebec	NHL	45	2	6	8	67	3	0	0	—	—	—	—	—
94-95—Quebec	NHL	35	0	7	7	52	17	0	0	6	0	1	1	14
95-96—Colorado	NHL	73	5	11	16	88	27	1	0	22	1	3	4	36
96-97—Colorado	NHL	78	2	19	21	135	16	0	0	17	0	4	4	62
97-98—Colorado	NHL	77	3	14	17	124	-3	0	0	7	0	0	0	23
—Can. Olympic team	Int'l	6	0	1	1	4	-2	0	0	—	—	—	—	—
98-99—Colorado	NHL	64	5	16	21	92	20	3	0	19	2	3	5	24
99-00—Colorado	NHL	59	5	13	18	98	5	1	0	16	0	7	7	28
00-01—Colorado	NHL	35	3	12	15	42	6	1	1	23	3	4	7	*47
01-02—Colorado	NHL	55	5	22	27	55	7	1	1	21	1	6	7	28
—Can. Olympic team	Int'l	6	1	0	1	2	...	...	...	—	—	—	—	—
02-03—Colorado	NHL	78	11	20	31	88	30	3	0	6	0	1	1	8
03-04—Colorado	NHL	73	8	22	30	87	13	5	0	11	0	4	4	10
NHL Totals (13 years)		799	55	179	234	1140	143	15	3	154	7	34	41	282

FORBES, COLIN — C/RW — HURRICANES

PERSONAL: Born February 16, 1976, in New Westminster, B.C. ... 6-3/220. ... Shoots left.

TRANSACTIONS/CAREER NOTES: Selected by Philadelphia Flyers in seventh round (fifth Flyers pick, 166th overall) of NHL draft (June 29, 1994). ... Bruised thumb (November 7, 1998); missed one game. ... Stomach virus (January 7, 1999); missed one game. ... Traded by Flyers with fifth-round pick (G Michal Lanicek) in 1999 draft to Tampa Bay Lightning for RW Mikael Andersson and RW Sandy McCarthy (March 20, 1999). ... Traded by Lightning to Ottawa Senators for C Bruce Gardiner (November 11, 1999). ... Traded by Senators to New York Rangers for LW Eric Lacroix (March 1, 2001). ... Signed as free agent by Washington Capitals (January 8, 2002). ... Signed as free agent by Colorado Avalanche (September 11, 2003). ... Signed as free agent by Capitals (December 20, 2003). ... Signed as free agent by Carolina Hurricanes (August 11, 2004).

Season Team	League	GP	G	A	Pts.	PIM	+/-	PP	SH	GP	G	A	Pts.	PIM
		REGULAR SEASON								PLAYOFFS				
93-94—Sherwood Park	AJHL	47	18	22	40	76	...	...	...	—	—	—	—	—
94-95—Portland	WHL	72	24	31	55	108	-17	7	0	9	1	3	4	10
95-96—Portland	WHL	72	33	44	77	137	...	...	...	7	2	5	7	14
—Hershey	AHL	2	1	0	1	2	...	...	...	4	0	2	2	2
96-97—Philadelphia	AHL	74	21	28	49	108	4	1	1	10	5	5	10	33
—Philadelphia	NHL	3	1	0	1	0	0	0	0	3	0	0	0	0
97-98—Philadelphia	AHL	13	7	4	11	22	-4	2	0	—	—	—	—	—
—Philadelphia	NHL	63	12	7	19	59	2	2	0	5	0	0	0	2
98-99—Philadelphia	NHL	66	9	7	16	51	0	0	0	—	—	—	—	—
—Tampa Bay	NHL	14	3	1	4	10	-5	0	1	—	—	—	—	—
99-00—Tampa Bay	NHL	8	0	0	0	18	-4	0	0	—	—	—	—	—
—Ottawa	NHL	45	2	5	7	12	-1	0	0	5	1	0	1	14
00-01—Ottawa	NHL	39	0	1	1	31	-3	0	0	—	—	—	—	—
—New York Rangers	NHL	19	1	4	5	15	-3	0	0	—	—	—	—	—
01-02—Utah	AHL	4	0	0	0	21	-1	0	0	—	—	—	—	—
—Portland	AHL	14	4	5	9	18	...	1	0	—	—	—	—	—
—Washington	NHL	38	5	3	8	15	-2	0	1	—	—	—	—	—
02-03—Washington	NHL	5	0	0	0	0	-2	0	0	—	—	—	—	—
—Portland	AHL	69	22	38	60	73	10	7	2	3	2	2	4	4
03-04—Washington	NHL	2	0	0	0	0	0	0	0	—	—	—	—	—
—Portland	AHL	69	16	32	48	59	-10	5	0	7	0	6	6	16
04-05—Lowell	AHL	76	27	37	64	80	32	7	0	11	3	1	4	20
NHL Totals (8 years)		302	33	28	61	211	-18	2	2	13	1	0	1	16

FORSBERG, PETER — C/LW — FLYERS

PERSONAL: Born July 20, 1973, in Ornskoldsvik, Sweden. ... 6-1/205. ... Shoots left. ... Son of Kent Forsberg, head coach, Swedish Olympic team and Swedish National team (1995-98).

TRANSACTIONS/CAREER NOTES: Selected by Philadelphia Flyers in 1st round (1st Flyers pick, 6th overall) of NHL draft (June 22, 1991). ... Traded by Flyers with G Ron Hextall, C Mike Ricci, D Steve Duchesne, D Kerry Huffman, 1st-round pick (G Jocelyn Thibault) in 1993 draft, cash and future considerations to Quebec Nordiques for C Eric Lindros (June 20, 1992); Nordiques acquired LW Chris Simon and 1st-round pick (traded to Toronto; traded to Washington; Capitals selected D Nolan Baumgartner) in 1994 draft to complete deal (July 21, 1992). ... Flu (March 1, 1995); missed one game. ... Nordiques franchise moved to Colorado and renamed Avalanche for 1995-96 season (June 21, 1995). ... Bruised thigh (December 14, 1996); missed 17 games. ... Bruised shoulder (November 8, 1997); missed three games. ... Injured groin (March 26, 1998); missed seven games. ... Concussion (May 7, 1998); missed two playoff games. ... Charley horse (May 22, 1998); missed one playoff game. ... Injured groin (December 14, 1998); missed one game. ... Injured elbow (March 4, 1999); missed three games. ... Shoulder surgery before start of 1999-2000 season; missed first 23 games of season. ... Hip pointer (November 30, 1999); missed two games. ... Concussion (February 1, 2000); missed five games. ... Bruised shoulder (March 26, 2000); missed two games. ... Separated shoulder (April 7, 2000); missed final game of season. ... Injured ribs (November 11, 2000); missed eight games. ... Spleen removed (May 10, 2001); missed remainder of playoffs. ... Missed 2001-02 regular season because of spleen, shoulder and ankle surgery. ... Injured wrist and groin (November 30, 2002); missed two games. ... Stiff neck (December 13, 2002); missed three games. ... Flu (December 26, 2002); missed one game. ... Charley horse (March 15, 2003); missed two games. ... Injured groin (November 1, 2003); missed three games. ... Injured groin (November 11, 2003); missed 19 games. ... Injured groin (January 17, 2004); missed four games. ... Strained groin (February 18, 2004); missed 17 games. ... Signed as free agent by Flyers (Aug. 3, 2005).

STATISTICAL PLATEAUS: Three-goal games: 1995-96 (2), 1996-97 (1), 1998-99 (1), 2002-03 (2), 2003-04 (1). Total: 7.

Season Team	League	GP	G	A	Pts.	PIM	+/-	PP	SH	GP	G	A	Pts.	PIM
		REGULAR SEASON								PLAYOFFS				
89-90—MoDo Hockey	Sweden Jr.	30	15	12	27	42	...	...	...	—	—	—	—	—
90-91—MoDo Ornskoldsvik	Sweden	23	7	10	17	22	...	...	...	—	—	—	—	—

Season Team	League	REGULAR SEASON GP	G	A	Pts.	PIM	+/-	PP	SH	PLAYOFFS GP	G	A	Pts.	PIM
91-92—MoDo Ornskoldsvik....	Sweden	39	9	19	28	78	...	...	...	—	—	—	—	—
92-93—MoDo Ornskoldsvik....	Sweden	39	23	24	47	92	...	...	...	3	4	1	5	...
93-94—MoDo Ornskoldsvik....	Sweden	39	18	26	44	82	...	...	...	11	9	7	16	14
—Swedish Oly. team......	Int'l	8	2	6	8	6	4	0	0	—	—	—	—	—
94-95—MoDo Ornskoldsvik....	Sweden	11	5	9	14	20	...	...	...	—	—	—	—	—
—Quebec....................	NHL	47	15	35	50	16	17	3	0	6	2	4	6	4
95-96—Colorado....................	NHL	82	30	86	116	47	26	7	3	22	10	11	21	18
96-97—Colorado....................	NHL	65	28	58	86	73	31	5	4	14	5	12	17	10
97-98—Colorado....................	NHL	72	25	66	91	94	6	7	3	7	6	5	11	12
—Swedish Oly. team......	Int'l	4	1	4	5	6	5	0	0	—	—	—	—	—
98-99—Colorado....................	NHL	78	30	67	97	108	27	9	2	19	8	16	*24	31
99-00—Colorado....................	NHL	49	14	37	51	52	9	3	0	16	7	8	15	12
00-01—Colorado....................	NHL	73	27	62	89	54	23	12	2	11	4	10	14	6
01-02—Colorado....................	NHL	...	...	...	...	...	...	...	...	20	9	*18	*27	20
02-03—Colorado....................	NHL	75	29	*77	*106	70	52	8	0	7	2	6	8	6
03-04—Colorado....................	NHL	39	18	37	55	30	16	3	1	11	4	7	11	12
04-05—MoDo Ornskoldsvik....	Sweden	33	13	26	39	88	14	1	0	1	0	0	0	2
NHL Totals (10 years)..........		580	216	525	741	544	207	57	15	133	57	97	154	131

FORTIN, J.F. — D — CAPITALS

PERSONAL: Born March 15, 1979, in Laval, Que. ... 6-3/214. ... Shoots right.

TRANSACTIONS/CAREER NOTES: Selected by Washington Capitals in second round (second Capitals pick, 35th overall) of NHL entry draft (June 21, 1997). ... Injured leg (January 22, 2002); missed two games. ... Had back spasms (February 20, 2003); missed 10 games.

Season Team	League	REGULAR SEASON GP	G	A	Pts.	PIM	+/-	PP	SH	PLAYOFFS GP	G	A	Pts.	PIM
95-96—Sherbrooke................	QMJHL	69	7	15	22	40	...	...	...	7	2	6	8	2
96-97—Sherbrooke................	QMJHL	59	7	30	37	89	...	...	...	2	0	1	1	14
97-98—Sherbrooke................	QMJHL	55	12	25	37	37	-3	7	0	—	—	—	—	—
98-99—Sherbrooke................	QMJHL	64	17	33	50	78	24	7	0	12	5	13	18	20
99-00—Portland.....................	AHL	43	3	5	8	44	...	...	...	2	0	0	0	0
—Hampton Roads..........	ECHL	7	0	2	2	0	...	...	...	—	—	—	—	—
00-01—Portland.....................	AHL	32	1	7	8	22	...	...	...	1	0	0	0	0
—Richmond..................	ECHL	15	0	4	4	2	...	...	...	—	—	—	—	—
01-02—Portland.....................	AHL	44	4	9	13	20	4	2	0	—	—	—	—	—
—Washington................	NHL	36	1	3	4	20	-1	0	0	—	—	—	—	—
02-03—Portland.....................	AHL	10	2	1	3	17	4	0	0	—	—	—	—	—
—Washington................	NHL	33	0	1	1	22	-3	0	0	—	—	—	—	—
03-04—Washington................	NHL	2	0	0	0	0	0	0	0	—	—	—	—	—
—Portland.....................	AHL	4	0	1	1	6	-2	0	0	—	—	—	—	—
04-05—Portland.....................	AHL	39	1	8	9	50	-9	1	0	—	—	—	—	—
NHL Totals (3 years)...........		71	1	4	5	42	-4	0	0					

FOSTER, ADRIAN — LW/C — DEVILS

PERSONAL: Born January 15, 1982, in Lethbridge, Alta. ... 6-1/205. ... Shoots left.

TRANSACTIONS/CAREER NOTES: Selected by New Jersey Devils in first round (first Devils pick, 28th overall) of NHL entry draft (June 23, 2001). ... Injured groin (October 2, 2001); missed first 15 games of season.

Season Team	League	REGULAR SEASON GP	G	A	Pts.	PIM	+/-	PP	SH	PLAYOFFS GP	G	A	Pts.	PIM
99-00—Saskatoon..................	WHL	7	1	2	3	6	...	...	...	—	—	—	—	—
00-01—Saskatoon..................	WHL	5	0	5	5	4	...	...	...	—	—	—	—	—
01-02—Saskatoon..................	WHL	13	9	3	12	18	...	...	...	—	—	—	—	—
—Brandon...................	WHL	14	5	10	15	23	...	...	...	15	4	11	15	14
02-03—Albany........................	AHL	9	3	0	3	4	-5	1	0	—	—	—	—	—
03-04—Albany........................	AHL	44	8	13	21	25	-9	2	2	—	—	—	—	—
04-05—Albany........................	AHL	51	6	11	17	27	-10	2	1	—	—	—	—	—

FOSTER, KURTIS — D — WILD

PERSONAL: Born November 24, 1981, in Carp, Ontario. ... 6-5/225. ... Shoots right.

TRANSACTIONS/CAREER NOTES: Selected by Calgary Flames in 2nd round (2nd Flames pick, 40th overall) of entry draft (June 24, 2000). ... Traded by Flames with LW Jeff Cowan to Atlanta Thrashers for D Petr Buzek and future considerations (December 18, 2001). ... Traded by Thrashers to Anaheim Mighty Ducks for D Niclas Havelid (June 26, 2004). ... Signed as free agent by Minnesota Wild (Aug. 4, 2005).

Season Team	League	REGULAR SEASON GP	G	A	Pts.	PIM	+/-	PP	SH	PLAYOFFS GP	G	A	Pts.	PIM
97-98—Peterborough.............	OHL	39	1	1	2	45	...	...	...	4	0	0	0	2
98-99—Peterborough.............	OHL	54	2	13	15	59	...	...	...	5	0	0	0	6
99-00—Peterborough.............	OHL	68	6	18	24	116	...	...	...	5	1	2	3	4
00-01—Peterborough.............	OHL	62	17	24	41	78	19	8	0	7	1	1	2	10
01-02—Peterborough.............	OHL	33	10	4	14	58	...	...	...	—	—	—	—	—
—Chicago.....................	AHL	39	6	9	15	59	6	1	0	14	1	1	2	21
02-03—Atlanta.......................	NHL	2	0	0	0	0	-2	0	0	—	—	—	—	—
—Chicago.....................	AHL	75	15	27	42	159	-15	9	0	9	1	3	4	14
03-04—Chicago.......................	AHL	67	11	19	30	95	-2	7	0	10	0	3	3	12

Season Team	League	GP	G	A	Pts.	PIM	+/-	PP	SH	GP	G	A	Pts.	PIM
		REGULAR SEASON								PLAYOFFS				
—Atlanta	NHL	3	0	1	1	0	0	0	0	—	—	—	—	—
04-05—Cincinnati	AHL	78	17	25	42	71	16	8	0	9	2	3	5	28
NHL Totals (2 years)		5	0	1	1	0	-2	0	0					

FRANCIS, RON — C

PERSONAL: Born March 1, 1963, in Sault Ste. Marie, Ont. ... 6-3/200. ... Shoots left. ... Cousin of Mike Liut, G with three NHL teams (1979-92) and Cincinnati of the WHA (1977-79).

TRANSACTIONS/CAREER NOTES: Selected by Hartford Whalers in 1st round (1st Whalers pick, 4th overall) of entry draft (June 10, 1981). ... Injured eye (January 27, 1982); missed three weeks. ... Strained right knee (November 30, 1983). ... Fractured left ankle (January 18, 1986); missed 27 games. ... Fractured left index finger (January 28, 1989); missed 11 games. ... Fractured nose (November 24, 1990). ... Traded by Whalers with D Ulf Samuelsson and D Grant Jennings to Pittsburgh Penguins for C John Cullen, D Zarley Zalapski and RW Jeff Parker (March 4, 1991). ... Flu (February 19, 1995); missed one game. ... Back spasms (February 21, 1995); missed three games. ... Strained hip flexor (January 5, 1996); missed two games. ... Suspended two games and fined $1,000 for checking player from behind (February 27, 1996). ... Fractured left foot (May 11, 1996); missed remainder of playoffs. ... Injured groin (February 22, 1997); missed one game. ... Injured hamstring (April 16, 1998); missed one game. ... Signed as free agent by Carolina Hurricanes (July 13, 1998). ... Vertigo (November 26, 1999); missed two games. ... Injured back (January 27, 2000); missed two games. ... Traded by Hurricanes to Toronto Maple Leafs for 4th-round pick in 2005 entry draft (March 9, 2004).

STATISTICAL PLATEAUS: Three-goal games: 1982-83 (1), 1984-85 (1), 1985-86 (2), 1987-88 (1), 1988-89 (1), 1989-90 (1), 1990-91 (1), 1995-96 (1), 1997-98 (1). Total: 10. ... Four-goal games: 1983-84 (1). ... Total hat tricks: 11.

Season Team	League	GP	G	A	Pts.	PIM	+/-	PP	SH	GP	G	A	Pts.	PIM
		REGULAR SEASON								PLAYOFFS				
80-81—Sault Ste. Marie	OMJHL	64	26	43	69	33	...	...	...	19	7	8	15	34
81-82—Sault Ste. Marie	OHL	25	18	30	48	46	...	...	...	—	—	—	—	—
—Hartford	NHL	59	25	43	68	51	-13	12	0	—	—	—	—	—
82-83—Hartford	NHL	79	31	59	90	60	-25	4	2	—	—	—	—	—
83-84—Hartford	NHL	72	23	60	83	45	-10	5	0	—	—	—	—	—
84-85—Hartford	NHL	80	24	57	81	66	-23	4	0	—	—	—	—	—
85-86—Hartford	NHL	53	24	53	77	24	8	7	1	10	1	2	3	4
86-87—Hartford	NHL	75	30	63	93	45	10	7	0	6	2	2	4	6
87-88—Hartford	NHL	80	25	50	75	87	-8	11	1	6	2	5	7	2
88-89—Hartford	NHL	69	29	48	77	36	4	8	0	4	0	2	2	0
89-90—Hartford	NHL	80	32	69	101	73	13	15	1	7	3	3	6	8
90-91—Hartford	NHL	67	21	55	76	51	-2	10	1	—	—	—	—	—
—Pittsburgh	NHL	14	2	9	11	21	0	0	0	24	7	10	17	24
91-92—Pittsburgh	NHL	70	21	33	54	30	-7	5	1	21	8	*19	27	6
92-93—Pittsburgh	NHL	84	24	76	100	68	6	9	2	12	6	11	17	19
93-94—Pittsburgh	NHL	82	27	66	93	62	-3	8	0	6	0	2	2	6
94-95—Pittsburgh	NHL	44	11	*48	59	18	*30	3	0	12	6	13	19	4
95-96—Pittsburgh	NHL	77	27	*92	119	56	25	12	1	11	3	6	9	4
96-97—Pittsburgh	NHL	81	27	63	90	20	7	10	1	5	1	2	3	2
97-98—Pittsburgh	NHL	81	25	62	87	20	12	7	0	6	1	5	6	2
98-99—Carolina	NHL	82	21	31	52	34	-2	8	0	3	0	1	1	0
99-00—Carolina	NHL	78	23	50	73	18	10	7	0	—	—	—	—	—
00-01—Carolina	NHL	82	15	50	65	32	-15	7	0	3	0	0	0	0
01-02—Carolina	NHL	80	27	50	77	18	4	14	0	23	6	10	16	6
02-03—Carolina	NHL	82	22	35	57	30	-22	8	1	—	—	—	—	—
03-04—Carolina	NHL	68	10	20	30	14	-12	5	0	—	—	—	—	—
—Toronto	NHL	12	3	7	10	0	3	2	0	12	0	4	4	2
NHL Totals (23 years)		1731	549	1249	1798	979	-10	188	12	171	46	97	143	95

F

FRAZEE, JEFF — G — DEVILS

PERSONAL: Born May 13, 1987, in Burnsville, Minn.

Season Team	League	GP	G	A	Pts.	PIM	+/-	PP	SH	GP	G	A	Pts.	PIM
		REGULAR SEASON								PLAYOFFS				
03-04—U.S. National	USHL	...	...	...	...	...	...	...	...	—	—	—	—	—
04-05—U.S. National	USHL	...	...	...	...	...	...	...	...	—	—	—	—	—

FRIESEN, JEFF — LW — DEVILS

PERSONAL: Born August 5, 1976, in Meadow Lake, Sask. ... 6-1/205. ... Shoots left. ... Name pronounced FREE-sihn.

TRANSACTIONS/CAREER NOTES: Selected by San Jose Sharks in first round (first Sharks pick, 11th overall) of NHL draft (June 28, 1994). ... Injured hand (October 18, 1996); missed two games. ... Missed first two games of 1997-98 season due to contract dispute. ... Injured shoulder (December 26, 1998); missed two games. ... Traded by Sharks with G Steve Shields and second-round pick (traded to Dallas Stars) in 2004 draft to Anaheim Mighty Ducks for RW Teemu Selanne (March 5, 2001). ... Sprained left ankle (January 12, 2002); missed one game. ... Traded by Mighty Ducks with D Oleg Tverdovsky and RW Maxim Balmochnykh to New Jersey Devils for RW Petr Sykora, C Igor Pohanka, D Mike Commodore and G J.F. Damphousse (July 7, 2002). ... Flu (January 25, 2003); missed one game. ... Pinched nerve (March 30, 2004); missed one game.

STATISTICAL PLATEAUS: Three-goal games: 1995-96 (1), 1999-00 (1). Total: 2.

Season Team	League	GP	G	A	Pts.	PIM	+/-	PP	SH	GP	G	A	Pts.	PIM
		REGULAR SEASON								PLAYOFFS				
91-92—Regina	WHL	4	3	1	4	2	...	...	...	—	—	—	—	—
92-93—Regina	WHL	70	45	38	83	23	...	...	...	13	7	10	17	8
93-94—Regina	WHL	66	51	67	118	48	3	20	5	4	3	2	5	2

		REGULAR SEASON								PLAYOFFS				
Season Team	League	GP	G	A	Pts.	PIM	+/-	PP	SH	GP	G	A	Pts.	PIM
94-95—Regina	WHL	25	21	23	44	22	6	5	1	—	—	—	—	—
—San Jose	NHL	48	15	10	25	14	-8	5	1	11	1	5	6	4
95-96—San Jose	NHL	79	15	31	46	42	-19	2	0	—	—	—	—	—
96-97—San Jose	NHL	82	28	34	62	75	-8	6	2	—	—	—	—	—
97-98—San Jose	NHL	79	31	32	63	40	8	7	6	6	0	1	1	2
98-99—San Jose	NHL	78	22	35	57	42	3	10	1	6	2	2	4	14
99-00—San Jose	NHL	82	26	35	61	47	-2	11	3	11	2	2	4	10
00-01—San Jose	NHL	64	12	24	36	56	7	2	0	—	—	—	—	—
—Anaheim	NHL	15	2	10	12	10	-2	2	0	—	—	—	—	—
01-02—Anaheim	NHL	81	17	26	43	44	-1	1	1	—	—	—	—	—
02-03—New Jersey	NHL	81	23	28	51	26	23	3	0	24	10	4	14	6
03-04—New Jersey	NHL	81	17	20	37	26	8	5	0	5	0	0	0	4
NHL Totals (10 years)		770	208	285	493	422	9	54	14	63	15	14	29	40

FRITSCHE, DAN — C — BLUE JACKETS

PERSONAL: Born July 13, 1985, in Parma, Ohio. ... 6-1/198.

TRANSACTIONS/CAREER NOTES: Selected by Columbus Blue Jackets in the second round (second Blue Jackets selection, 46th overall) of NHL draft (June 21, 2003).

		REGULAR SEASON								PLAYOFFS				
Season Team	League	GP	G	A	Pts.	PIM	+/-	PP	SH	GP	G	A	Pts.	PIM
01-02—Sarnia	OHL	17	5	13	18	20	...	...	...	—	—	—	—	—
02-03—Sarnia	OHL	61	32	39	71	79	...	...	...	5	2	2	4	4
03-04—Columbus	NHL	19	1	0	1	12	-5	0	0	—	—	—	—	—
—Sarnia	OHL	27	16	13	29	26	...	...	...	5	1	5	6	0
—Syracuse	AHL	4	2	0	2	0	2	0	0	4	0	1	1	4
04-05—Sarnia	OHL	2	1	1	2	0	-1	0	0	—	—	—	—	—
—London	OHL	28	17	18	35	18	27	5	0	17	9	13	22	12
NHL Totals (1 year)		19	1	0	1	12	-5	0	0					

FROLOV, ALEXANDER — LW — KINGS

PERSONAL: Born July 26, 1982, in Moscow, U.S.S.R. ... 6-2/210. ... Shoots right.

TRANSACTIONS/CAREER NOTES: Selected by Los Angeles Kings in first round (first Kings pick, 20th overall) of NHL draft (June 24, 2000). ... Cut face (December 29, 2002); missed two games. ... Injured leg (March 27, 2004); missed final five games of season.

		REGULAR SEASON								PLAYOFFS				
Season Team	League	GP	G	A	Pts.	PIM	+/-	PP	SH	GP	G	A	Pts.	PIM
99-00—Torpedo Yaroslavl	Rus. Div.	36	27	13	40	30	...	...	...	—	—	—	—	—
00-01—Krylja Sovetov	Rus. Div.	44	20	19	39	8	...	...	...	—	—	—	—	—
01-02—Kryla Sov. Moscow	Russian	43	18	12	30	16	...	...	...	3	1	0	1	0
02-03—Los Angeles	NHL	79	14	17	31	34	12	1	0	—	—	—	—	—
03-04—Los Angeles	NHL	77	24	24	48	24	8	5	2	—	—	—	—	—
04-05—CSKA Moscow	Russian	42	20	17	37	10	16	...	...	—	—	—	—	—
—Dynamo Moscow	Russian	6	2	1	3	2	2	...	...	6	2	1	3	0
NHL Totals (2 years)		156	38	41	79	58	20	6	2					

FUSSEY, OWEN — RW — CAPITALS

PERSONAL: Born April 2, 1983, in Winnipeg. ... 6-0/185. ... Shoots left.

TRANSACTIONS/CAREER NOTES: Selected by Washington Capitals in third round (second Capitals pick, 90th overall) of NHL entry draft (June 23, 2001).

		REGULAR SEASON								PLAYOFFS				
Season Team	League	GP	G	A	Pts.	PIM	+/-	PP	SH	GP	G	A	Pts.	PIM
99-00—Calgary	WHL	51	7	6	13	35	...	...	...	12	3	4	7	2
00-01—Calgary	WHL	48	15	10	25	33	...	...	...	12	2	1	3	6
01-02—Calgary	WHL	72	43	27	70	61	...	...	...	7	3	1	4	4
02-03—Calgary	WHL	39	17	18	35	31	...	...	...	—	—	—	—	—
—Moose Jaw	WHL	66	41	30	71	51	...	...	...	13	6	6	12	10
03-04—Washington	NHL	4	0	1	1	0	-1	0	0	—	—	—	—	—
—Portland	AHL	69	6	7	13	23	-11	0	0	7	0	0	0	5
04-05—Portland	AHL	71	14	12	26	26	6	0	1	—	—	—	—	—
NHL Totals (1 year)		4	0	1	1	0	-1	0	0					

GABORIK, MARIAN — RW/LW — WILD

PERSONAL: Born February 14, 1982, in Trencin, Czechoslovakia. ... 6-1/190. ... Shoots left.

TRANSACTIONS/CAREER NOTES: Selected by Minnesota Wild in first round (first Wild pick, third overall) of NHL draft (June 24, 2000). ... Bruised leg (November 15, 2000); missed six games. ... Strained abdominal muscle (March 31, 2001); missed four games. ... Had hernia surgery before 2001-02 season; missed season's first game. ... Strained right quadriceps (December 20, 2001); missed three games. ... Flu (December 15, 2002); missed one game. ... Missed 2003-04 season's first 12 games in contract dispute. ... Injured hip flexor (January 22, 2004); missed five games.

STATISTICAL PLATEAUS: Three-goal games: 2001-02 (2), 2002-03 (3), 2003-04 (2). Total: 7.

Season Team	League	GP	G	A	Pts.	PIM	+/-	PP	SH	GP	G	A	Pts.	PIM
		REGULAR SEASON								PLAYOFFS				
98-99—Dukla Trencin	Slovakia	33	11	9	20	6	...	...	...	3	1	0	1	2
99-00—Dukla Trencin	Slovakia	50	25	21	46	34	...	...	...	5	1	2	3	2
00-01—Minnesota	NHL	71	18	18	36	32	-6	6	0	—	—	—	—	—
01-02—Minnesota	NHL	78	30	37	67	34	0	10	0	—	—	—	—	—
02-03—Minnesota	NHL	81	30	35	65	46	12	5	1	18	9	8	17	6
03-04—Minnesota	NHL	65	18	22	40	20	10	3	0	—	—	—	—	—
04-05—Dukla Trencin	Slovakia	29	25	27	52	46	43	...	...	12	8	9	17	26
—Farjestad Karlstad	Sweden	12	6	4	10	45	8	0	0	—	—	—	—	—
NHL Totals (4 years)		295	96	112	208	132	16	24	1	18	9	8	17	6

GAGNE, SIMON — LW — FLYERS

PERSONAL: Born February 29, 1980, in Ste-Foy, Que. ... 6-0/195. ... Shoots left. ... Name pronounced see-MONE gahn-YAY.
TRANSACTIONS/CAREER NOTES: Selected by Philadelphia Flyers in first round (first Flyers pick, 22nd overall) of NHL draft (June 27, 1998). ... Flu (January 2, 2000); missed one game. ... Flu (March 23, 2000); missed one game. ... Strained lower back (February 19, 2001); missed one game. ... Separated shoulder (February 24, 2001); missed 12 games. ... Bruised left shoulder (December 31, 2001); missed two games. ... Injured (April 13, 2002); missed final game of regular season. ... Suffered concussion (December 28, 2002); missed five games. ... Strained groin (January 25, 2003); missed three games. ... Reinjured groin (February 4, 2003); missed 13 games. ... Reinjured groin (March 8, 2003); missed 13 games. ... Bruised right shoulder (October 21, 2003); missed two games.
STATISTICAL PLATEAUS: Three-goal games: 2001-02 (1).

Season Team	League	GP	G	A	Pts.	PIM	+/-	PP	SH	GP	G	A	Pts.	PIM
		REGULAR SEASON								PLAYOFFS				
96-97—Beauport	QMJHL	51	9	22	31	39	...	...	...	—	—	—	—	—
97-98—Quebec	QMJHL	53	30	39	69	26	...	...	...	12	11	5	16	23
98-99—Quebec	QMJHL	61	50	70	120	42	51	15	5	13	9	8	17	4
99-00—Philadelphia	NHL	80	20	28	48	22	11	8	1	17	5	5	10	2
00-01—Philadelphia	NHL	69	27	32	59	18	24	6	0	6	3	0	3	0
01-02—Philadelphia	NHL	79	33	33	66	32	31	4	1	5	0	0	0	2
—Can. Olympic team	Int'l	6	1	3	4	0	...	...	...	—	—	—	—	—
02-03—Philadelphia	NHL	46	9	18	27	16	20	1	1	13	4	1	5	6
03-04—Philadelphia	NHL	80	24	21	45	29	12	6	0	18	5	4	9	12
NHL Totals (5 years)		354	113	132	245	117	98	25	3	59	17	10	27	22

GAINEY, STEVE — LW/C — FLYERS

PERSONAL: Born January 26, 1979, in Montreal. ... 6-1/192. ... Shoots left. ... Son of Bob Gainey, coach of Minnesotaallas Stars (1990-91 through January 8, 1996), G.M. of Stars (1992-93 through January 25, 2002), G.M. of Montreal Canadiens (June 2, 2003 to present) and Hall of Fame C with Montreal Canadiens (1973-74 through 1988-89).
TRANSACTIONS/CAREER NOTES: Selected by Dallas Stars in 3rd round (3rd Stars pick, 77th overall) of NHL draft (June 21, 1997). ... Traded by Stars to Philadelphia Flyers for F Mike Siklenka (February 16, 2004).

Season Team	League	GP	G	A	Pts.	PIM	+/-	PP	SH	GP	G	A	Pts.	PIM
		REGULAR SEASON								PLAYOFFS				
95-96—Kamloops	WHL	49	1	4	5	40	...	...	...	3	0	0	0	0
96-97—Kamloops	WHL	60	9	18	27	60	...	...	...	2	0	0	0	9
97-98—Kamloops	WHL	68	21	34	55	93	1	6	3	7	1	7	8	15
98-99—Kamloops	WHL	68	30	34	64	155	37	11	4	15	5	4	9	38
99-00—Michigan	IHL	58	8	10	18	41	...	...	...	—	—	—	—	—
—Fort Wayne	UHL	1	0	0	0	0	...	...	...	—	—	—	—	—
00-01—Utah	IHL	61	7	7	14	167	...	...	...	—	—	—	—	—
—Dallas	NHL	1	0	0	0	0	0	0	0	—	—	—	—	—
01-02—Utah	AHL	58	16	18	34	87	4	4	1	—	—	—	—	—
—Dallas	NHL	5	0	1	1	7	-1	0	0	—	—	—	—	—
02-03—Utah	AHL	68	9	17	26	106	-4	4	1	2	0	0	0	11
03-04—Dallas	NHL	7	0	0	0	7	1	0	0	—	—	—	—	—
—Utah	AHL	45	7	8	15	74	-15	1	2	—	—	—	—	—
—Philadelphia	AHL	27	2	7	9	27	-3	1	0	11	0	1	1	14
04-05—Epinal	France	30	10	13	23	97	-7	1	1	4	1	3	4	6
NHL Totals (3 years)		13	0	1	1	14	0	0	0					

G

GAMACHE, SIMON — LW/C — PREDATORS

PERSONAL: Born January 3, 1981, in Thetford Mines, Que. ... 5-9/180. ... Shoots left.
TRANSACTIONS/CAREER NOTES: Selected by Atlanta Thrashers in ninth round (14th Thrashers pick, 290th overall) of NHL entry draft (June 25, 2000). ... Traded by Thrashers with D Kirill Safronov to Nashville Predators for D Tomas Kloucek and C Ben Simon (December 2, 2003).

Season Team	League	GP	G	A	Pts.	PIM	+/-	PP	SH	GP	G	A	Pts.	PIM
		REGULAR SEASON								PLAYOFFS				
98-99—Val-d'Or	QMJHL	70	19	43	62	54	...	...	...	—	—	—	—	—
99-00—Val-d'Or	QMJHL	72	64	79	143	74	...	...	...	—	—	—	—	—
00-01—Val-d'Or	QMJHL	72	*74	*110	*184	70	64	16	8	21	*22	*35	*57	18
01-02—Chicago	AHL	26	2	4	6	11	-7	1	0	—	—	—	—	—
—Greenville	ECHL	31	19	19	38	35	4	7	2	17	*15	9	*24	22
02-03—Atlanta	NHL	2	0	0	0	2	-1	0	0	—	—	—	—	—
—Chicago	AHL	76	35	42	77	37	15	16	0	9	7	2	9	4
03-04—Chicago	AHL	16	5	6	11	4	5	2	0	—	—	—	—	—
—Atlanta	NHL	2	0	1	1	0	0	0	0	—	—	—	—	—

Season Team	League	GP	G	A	Pts.	PIM	+/-	PP	SH		GP	G	A	Pts.	PIM
		REGULAR SEASON									PLAYOFFS				
—Nashville	NHL	7	1	0	1	0	-3	1	0		—	—	—	—	—
—Milwaukee	AHL	52	19	27	46	26	-2	4	0		22	6	18	24	14
04-05—Milwaukee	AHL	80	29	57	86	93	11	16	0		7	6	4	10	18
NHL Totals (2 years)		11	1	1	2	2	-4	1	0						

GARON, MATHIEU — G — KINGS

PERSONAL: Born January 9, 1978, in Chandler, Que. ... 6-2/202. ... Catches right.
TRANSACTIONS/CAREER NOTES: Selected by Montreal Canadiens in second round (second Canadiens pick, 44th overall) of NHL entry draft (June 22, 1996). ... Traded by Canadiens with C Radek Bonk to Los Angeles Kings for G Cristobal Huet and third-round pick (D Paul Baier) in 2004 entry draft (June 27, 2004). ... Signed as free agent by Manchester of the AHL (September 27, 2004).

Season Team	League	GP	Min.	W	L	T	GA	SO	GAA	SV%		GP	Min.	W	L	GA	SO	GAA	SV%
		REGULAR SEASON										PLAYOFFS							
95-96—Victoriaville	QMJHL	51	2709	18	27	0	189	1	4.00	...		12	676	7	4	38	1	3.37	...
96-97—Victoriaville	QMJHL	53	3026	29	18	3	148	*6	2.93	...		6	330	2	4	23	0	4.18	.903
97-98—Victoriaville	QMJHL	47	2802	27	18	2	125	5	2.68	.909		6	345	2	4	22	0	3.83	.851
98-99—Fredericton	AHL	40	2222	14	22	2	114	3	3.08	.904		6	208	1	1	12	0	3.46	.911
99-00—Quebec	AHL	53	2884	17	28	3	149	2	3.10	...		1	20	0	0	3	0	9.00	...
00-01—Montreal	NHL	11	589	4	5	1	24	2	2.44	.897		—	—	—	—	—	—	—	—
—Quebec	AHL	31	1768	16	13	1	86	1	2.92	.920		8	459	4	4	22	1	2.88	...
01-02—Quebec	AHL	50	2987	21	15	12	136	2	2.73	.911		3	198	0	3	12	0	3.64	.874
—Montreal	NHL	5	261	1	4	0	19	0	4.37	.871		—	—	—	—	—	—	—	—
02-03—Hamilton	AHL	20	1150	15	2	2	34	4	1.77	.937		—	—	—	—	—	—	—	—
—Montreal	NHL	8	482	3	5	0	16	2	1.99	.940		—	—	—	—	—	—	—	—
03-04—Montreal	NHL	19	1003	8	6	2	38	0	2.27	.921		1	12	0	0	0	0	0.00	1.00
04-05—Manchester	AHL	52	2969	32	14	...	105	8	2.12	.927		6	284	2	4	17	0	3.59	.893
NHL Totals (4 years)		43	2335	16	20	3	97	4	2.49	.914		1	12	0	0	0	0	0.00	1.00

GAUTHIER, DENIS — D — COYOTES

PERSONAL: Born October 1, 1976, in Montreal. ... 6-2/224. ... Shoots left. ... Name pronounced GO-tee-ay.
TRANSACTIONS/CAREER NOTES: Selected by Calgary Flames in first round (first Flames pick, 20th overall) of NHL draft (July 8, 1995). ... Suffered concussion (September 27, 1997); missed two games. ... Suffered concussion (January 10, 1999); missed two games. ... Injured groin (March 25, 1999); missed two games. ... Injured shoulder (October 26, 1999); missed 11 games. ... Suspended two games for elbowing incident (December 7, 1999). ... Had hip pointer (February 1, 2000); missed remainder of season. ... Injured wrist (October 15, 2000); missed 17 games. ... Injured shoulder (March 16, 2001); missed two games. ... Strained oblique muscle (October 22, 2001); missed five games. ... Suffered facial injury (December 31, 2001); missed five games. ... Injured shoulder (April 2, 2002); missed remainder of season. ... Suspended one game for illegal checking incident (November 16, 2002). ... Strained left shoulder (February 4, 2003); missed four games. ... Suffered concussion (March 29, 2003); missed season's final four games. ... Suspended two games for kneeing incident (December 26, 2003). ... Injured leg (April 17, 2004); missed remainder of playoffs. ... Traded by Flames with LW Oleg Saprykin to Phoenix Coyotes for C Daymond Langkow (August 26, 2004).

Season Team	League	GP	G	A	Pts.	PIM	+/-	PP	SH		GP	G	A	Pts.	PIM
		REGULAR SEASON									PLAYOFFS				
92-93—Drummondville	QMJHL	61	1	7	8	136	...	...	...		10	0	5	5	40
93-94—Drummondville	QMJHL	60	0	7	7	176	...	...	...		9	2	0	2	41
94-95—Drummondville	QMJHL	64	9	31	40	190	...	...	...		4	0	5	5	12
95-96—Drummondville	QMJHL	53	25	49	74	140	...	...	...		6	4	4	8	32
—Saint John	AHL	5	2	0	2	8	...	...	...		16	1	6	7	20
96-97—Saint John	AHL	73	3	28	31	74	2	2	0		5	0	0	0	6
97-98—Calgary	NHL	10	0	0	0	16	-5	0	0		—	—	—	—	—
—Saint John	AHL	68	4	20	24	154	-5	2	0		21	0	4	4	83
98-99—Saint John	AHL	16	0	3	3	31	-3	0	0		—	—	—	—	—
—Calgary	NHL	55	3	4	7	68	3	0	0		—	—	—	—	—
99-00—Calgary	NHL	39	1	1	2	50	-4	0	0		—	—	—	—	—
00-01—Calgary	NHL	62	2	6	8	78	3	0	0		—	—	—	—	—
01-02—Calgary	NHL	66	5	8	13	91	9	0	1		—	—	—	—	—
02-03—Calgary	NHL	72	1	11	12	99	5	0	0		—	—	—	—	—
03-04—Calgary	NHL	80	1	15	16	113	4	0	0		6	0	1	1	4
NHL Totals (7 years)		384	13	45	58	515	15	0	1		6	0	1	1	4

GELINAS, MARTIN — LW — PANTHERS

PERSONAL: Born June 5, 1970, in Shawinigan, Que. ... 5-11/196. ... Shoots left. ... Name pronounced MAHR-tahn ZHEHL-ih-nuh.
TRANSACTIONS/CAREER NOTES: Selected by Los Angeles Kings in 1st round (1st Kings pick, 7th overall) of NHL draft (June 11, 1988). ... Traded by Kings with C Jimmy Carson, first-round picks in 1989 (traded to New Jersey), 1991 (LW Martin Rucinsky) and 1993 (D Nick Stajduhar) drafts and cash to Edmonton Oilers for C Wayne Gretzky, RW Marty McSorley and LW/C Mike Krushelnyski (August 9, 1988). ... Suspended five games (March 9, 1990). ... Shoulder surgery (June 1990). ... Traded by Oilers with sixth-round pick (C Nicholas Checco) in 1993 draft to Quebec Nordiques for LW Scott Pearson (June 20, 1993). ... Injured thigh (October 20, 1993); missed one game. ... Separated left shoulder (November 25, 1993); missed 10 games. ... Claimed off waivers by Vancouver Canucks (January 15, 1994). ... Charley horse (March 27, 1994); missed six games. ... Injured knee (April 30, 1995); missed last game of season and eight playoff games. ... Fractured rib (November 2, 1996); missed eight games. ... Sprained knee (October 13, 1997); missed 16 games. ... Traded by Canucks with G Kirk McLean to Carolina Hurricanes for LW Geoff Sanderson, D Enrico Ciccone and G Sean Burke (January 3, 1998). ... Strained quadriceps (October 27, 1998); missed two games. ... Bruised thigh (April 3, 1999); missed four games. ... Injured knee (February 8, 2001); missed three games. ... Injured ankle (October 11, 2001); missed three games. ... Concussion (January 25, 2002); missed seven games. ... Signed as free agent by Calgary Flames (July 2, 2002). ... Injured thumb (January 23, 2003); missed one game. ... Injured ankle (November 15, 2003); missed two

games. ... Injured neck (March 4, 2004); missed four games. ... Signed as free agent by Florida Panthers (Aug. 2, 2005).
STATISTICAL PLATEAUS: Three-goal games: 1989-90 (1), 1996-97 (1). Total: 2. ... Four-goal games: 1996-97 (1). ... Total hat tricks: 3.

		REGULAR SEASON								PLAYOFFS				
Season Team	**League**	**GP**	**G**	**A**	**Pts.**	**PIM**	**+/-**	**PP**	**SH**	**GP**	**G**	**A**	**Pts.**	**PIM**
87-88—Hull	QMJHL	65	63	68	131	74	...	...	...	17	15	18	33	32
88-89—Edmonton	NHL	6	1	2	3	0	-1	0	0	—	—	—	—	—
—Hull	QMJHL	41	38	39	77	31	...	...	...	9	5	4	9	14
89-90—Edmonton	NHL	46	17	8	25	30	0	5	0	20	2	3	5	6
90-91—Edmonton	NHL	73	20	20	40	34	-7	4	0	18	3	6	9	25
91-92—Edmonton	NHL	68	11	18	29	62	14	1	0	15	1	3	4	10
92-93—Edmonton	NHL	65	11	12	23	30	3	0	0	—	—	—	—	—
93-94—Quebec	NHL	31	6	6	12	8	-2	0	0	—	—	—	—	—
—Vancouver	NHL	33	8	8	16	26	-6	3	0	24	5	4	9	14
94-95—Vancouver	NHL	46	13	10	23	36	8	1	0	3	0	1	1	0
95-96—Vancouver	NHL	81	30	26	56	59	8	3	4	6	1	1	2	12
96-97—Vancouver	NHL	74	35	33	68	42	6	6	1	—	—	—	—	—
97-98—Vancouver	NHL	24	4	4	8	10	-6	1	1	—	—	—	—	—
—Carolina	NHL	40	12	14	26	30	1	2	1	—	—	—	—	—
98-99—Carolina	NHL	76	13	15	28	67	3	0	0	6	0	3	3	2
99-00—Carolina	NHL	81	14	16	30	40	-10	3	0	—	—	—	—	—
00-01—Carolina	NHL	79	23	29	52	59	-4	6	1	6	0	1	1	6
01-02—Carolina	NHL	72	13	16	29	30	-1	3	0	23	3	4	7	10
02-03—Calgary	NHL	81	21	31	52	51	-3	6	0	—	—	—	—	—
03-04—Calgary	NHL	76	17	18	35	70	10	5	0	26	8	7	15	35
04-05—Lugano	Switzerland	1	0	0	0	0	...	0	0	5	0	1	1	2
—Morges	Switzerland	41	38	23	61	81	...	9	2	4	2	2	4	24
NHL Totals (16 years)		1052	269	286	555	684	13	49	8	147	23	33	56	120

GERBER, MARTIN — G — HURRICANES

PERSONAL: Born September 3, 1974, in Burgdorf, Switzerland. ... 5-11/200. ... Catches left.
TRANSACTIONS/CAREER NOTES: Selected by Anaheim Mighty Ducks in eighth round (10th Mighty Ducks pick, 232nd overall) of NHL draft (June 24, 2001). ... Traded by Mighty Ducks to Carolina Hurricanes for D Tomas Malec and third-round pick (D Kyle Klubertanz) in 2004 draft (June 18, 2004).

		REGULAR SEASON									PLAYOFFS							
Season Team	**League**	**GP**	**Min.**	**W**	**L**	**T**	**GA**	**SO**	**GAA**	**SV%**	**GP**	**Min.**	**W**	**L**	**GA**	**SO**	**GAA**	**SV%**
01-02—Farjestad Karlstad	Sweden	44	2664	...	...	...	87	*4	*1.96	...	10	*657	...	...	18	2	*1.64	...
02-03—Cincinnati	AHL	1	60	1	0	0	2	0	2.00	.951	—	—	—	—	—	—	—	—
—Anaheim	NHL	22	1203	6	11	3	39	1	1.95	.929	2	20	0	0	1	0	3.00	.833
03-04—Anaheim	NHL	32	1698	11	12	4	64	2	2.26	.918	—	—	—	—	—	—	—	—
04-05—SC Langnau	Switzerland	20	1217	6	10	4	57	0	2.87	...	—	—	—	—	—	—	—	—
—Farjestad Karlstad	Sweden	30	1828	...	...	...	58	4	1.90	.929	15	901	...	...	36	1	2.41	.925
NHL Totals (2 years)		54	2901	17	23	7	103	3	2.13	.923	2	20	0	0	1	0	3.00	.833

GERNANDER, KEN — C/LW — RANGERS

PERSONAL: Born June 30, 1969, in Coleraine, Minn. ... 5-11/180. ... Shoots left. ... Name pronounced juhr-NAN-duhr.
TRANSACTIONS/CAREER NOTES: Selected by Winnipeg Jets in fifth round (fourth Jets pick, 96th overall) of NHL draft (June 13, 1987). ... Signed as free agent by New York Rangers (September 9, 1994).

		REGULAR SEASON								PLAYOFFS				
Season Team	**League**	**GP**	**G**	**A**	**Pts.**	**PIM**	**+/-**	**PP**	**SH**	**GP**	**G**	**A**	**Pts.**	**PIM**
85-86—Greenway H.S.	USHS (West)	23	14	23	37	...	...	...	...	—	—	—	—	—
86-87—Greenway H.S.	USHS (West)	26	35	34	69	...	...	...	...	—	—	—	—	—
87-88—Minnesota	WCHA	44	14	14	28	14	...	...	...	—	—	—	—	—
88-89—Minnesota	WCHA	44	9	11	20	2	...	...	...	—	—	—	—	—
89-90—Minnesota	WCHA	44	32	17	49	24	...	...	...	—	—	—	—	—
90-91—Minnesota	WCHA	44	23	20	43	24	...	...	...	—	—	—	—	—
91-92—Moncton	AHL	43	8	18	26	9	...	...	...	8	1	1	2	2
—Fort Wayne	IHL	13	7	6	13	2	...	...	...	—	—	—	—	—
92-93—Moncton	AHL	71	18	29	47	20	-13	5	0	5	1	4	5	0
93-94—Moncton	AHL	71	22	25	47	12	1	6	1	19	6	1	7	0
94-95—Binghamton	AHL	80	28	25	53	24	34	8	0	11	2	2	4	6
95-96—Binghamton	AHL	63	44	29	73	38	...	...	...	—	—	—	—	—
—New York Rangers	NHL	10	2	3	5	4	-3	2	0	6	0	0	0	0
96-97—Binghamton	AHL	46	13	18	31	30	-11	2	0	2	0	1	1	0
—New York Rangers	NHL	...	...	...	...	...	...	...	...	9	0	0	0	0
97-98—Hartford	AHL	80	35	28	63	26	22	9	5	12	5	6	11	4
98-99—U.S. national team	Int'l	3	0	1	1	0	...	...	...	—	—	—	—	—
—Hartford	AHL	70	23	26	49	32	-1	9	1	7	1	2	3	2
99-00—Hartford	AHL	79	28	29	57	24	...	...	...	23	5	5	10	0
00-01—Hartford	AHL	80	22	27	49	39	...	...	...	2	0	0	0	0
01-02—Hartford	AHL	75	18	31	49	19	13	8	0	10	1	3	4	4
02-03—Hartford	AHL	72	17	19	36	22	14	2	3	2	0	0	0	0
03-04—Hartford	AHL	77	12	19	31	28	13	2	0	16	3	4	7	2
—New York Rangers	NHL	2	0	0	0	2	-1	0	0	—	—	—	—	—
04-05—Hartford	AHL	66	5	8	13	18	4	0	0	6	1	0	1	0
NHL Totals (3 years)		12	2	3	5	6	-4	2	0	15	0	0	0	0

GETZLAF, RYAN — C — MIGHTY DUCKS

PERSONAL: Born May 10, 1985, in Regina, Sask. ... 6-2/195. ... Shoots right.
TRANSACTIONS/CAREER NOTES: Selected by Anaheim Mighty Ducks in first round (first Mighty Ducks pick, 19th overall) in 2003 NHL entry draft (June 23, 2003).

		REGULAR SEASON								PLAYOFFS				
Season Team	League	GP	G	A	Pts.	PIM	+/-	PP	SH	GP	G	A	Pts.	PIM
01-02—Calgary	WHL	63	9	9	18	34	...	...	...	7	2	1	3	4
02-03—Calgary	WHL	70	29	39	68	121	...	...	...	5	1	1	2	6
03-04—Calgary	WHL	49	28	47	75	97	...	...	...	7	5	1	6	12
04-05—Cincinnati	AHL	—	—	—	—	—	—	—	—	10	1	4	5	4
—Calgary	WHL	51	29	25	54	102	22	7	2	12	4	13	17	18

GIGUERE, JEAN-SEBASTIEN — G — MIGHTY DUCKS

PERSONAL: Born May 16, 1977, in Montreal. ... 6-1/200. ... Catches left. ... Name pronounced zhee-GAIR.
TRANSACTIONS/CAREER NOTES: Selected by Hartford Whalers in first round (first Whalers pick, 13th overall) of NHL draft (July 8, 1995). ... Whalers franchise moved to North Carolina and renamed Carolina Hurricanes for 1997-98 season; NHL approved move on June 25, 1997. ... Traded by Hurricanes with C Andrew Cassels to Calgary Flames for LW Gary Roberts and G Trevor Kidd (August 25, 1997). ... Strained hamstring (December 27, 1998); missed seven games. ... Traded by Flames to Anaheim Mighty Ducks for second-round pick (later traded to Washington; Capitals selected LW Matt Pettinger) in 2000 draft (June 10, 2000). ... Strained groin; missed first five games of 2001-02 season. ... Injured neck (January 3, 2003); missed three games.

		REGULAR SEASON									PLAYOFFS							
Season Team	League	GP	Min.	W	L	T	GA	SO	GAA	SV%	GP	Min.	W	L	GA	SO	GAA	SV%
93-94—Verdun	QMJHL	25	1234	13	5	2	66	0	3.21	...	—	—	—	—	—	—	—	—
94-95—Halifax	QMJHL	47	2755	14	27	5	181	2	3.94	.889	7	417	3	4	17	1	2.45	.934
95-96—Verdun	QMJHL	55	3228	26	23	2	185	1	3.44	...	6	356	1	5	24	0	4.04	...
96-97—Halifax	QMJHL	50	3009	28	19	3	169	2	3.37	...	16	954	9	7	58	0	3.65	.899
—Hartford	NHL	8	394	1	4	0	24	0	3.65	.881	—	—	—	—	—	—	—	—
97-98—Saint John	AHL	31	1758	16	10	3	72	2	2.46	.926	10	537	5	3	27	0	3.02	.897
98-99—Saint John	AHL	39	2145	18	16	3	123	3	3.44	.905	7	304	3	2	21	0	4.14	.859
—Calgary	NHL	15	860	6	7	1	46	0	3.21	.897	—	—	—	—	—	—	—	—
99-00—Saint John	AHL	41	2243	17	17	3	114	0	3.05	...	3	178	0	3	9	0	3.03	...
—Calgary	NHL	7	330	1	3	1	15	0	2.73	.914	—	—	—	—	—	—	—	—
00-01—Cincinnati	AHL	23	1306	12	7	2	53	0	2.43	.917	—	—	—	—	—	—	—	—
—Anaheim	NHL	34	2031	11	17	5	87	4	2.57	.911	—	—	—	—	—	—	—	—
01-02—Anaheim	NHL	53	3127	20	25	6	111	4	2.13	.920	—	—	—	—	—	—	—	—
02-03—Anaheim	NHL	65	3775	34	22	6	145	8	2.30	.920	21	1407	15	6	38	5	*1.62	.945
03-04—Anaheim	NHL	55	3210	17	31	6	140	3	2.62	.914	—	—	—	—	—	—	—	—
04-05—Hamburg	Germany	6	301	...	...	...	12	0	2.39	.925	2	100	...	...	7	0	4.20	.881
NHL Totals (7 years)		237	13727	90	109	25	568	19	2.48	.914	21	1407	15	6	38	5	1.62	.945

GILL, HAL — D — BRUINS

PERSONAL: Born April 6, 1975, in Concord, Mass. ... 6-7/250. ... Shoots left.
TRANSACTIONS/CAREER NOTES: Selected by Boston Bruins in eighth round (eighth Bruins pick, 207th overall) of NHL draft (June 26, 1993). ... Flu (January 21, 1998); missed one game. ... Strained hip flexor (April 7, 1999); missed two games. ... Flu (January 11, 2000); missed one game. ... Tendinitis in shoulder (December 4, 2001); missed two games. ... Bruised foot (April 6, 2002); missed one game. ... Injured finger (Feburary 15, 2003); missed six games.

		REGULAR SEASON								PLAYOFFS				
Season Team	League	GP	G	A	Pts.	PIM	+/-	PP	SH	GP	G	A	Pts.	PIM
93-94—Providence College	Hockey East	31	1	2	3	26	...	...	...	—	—	—	—	—
94-95—Providence College	Hockey East	26	1	3	4	22	7	0	1	—	—	—	—	—
95-96—Providence College	Hockey East	39	5	12	17	54	...	...	...	—	—	—	—	—
96-97—Providence College	Hockey East	35	5	16	21	52	-3	1	1	—	—	—	—	—
97-98—Boston	NHL	68	2	4	6	47	4	0	0	6	0	0	0	4
—Providence	AHL	4	1	0	1	23	-2	0	0	—	—	—	—	—
98-99—Boston	NHL	80	3	7	10	63	-10	0	0	12	0	0	0	14
99-00—Boston	NHL	81	3	9	12	51	0	0	0	—	—	—	—	—
00-01—Boston	NHL	80	1	10	11	71	-2	0	0	—	—	—	—	—
01-02—Boston	NHL	79	4	18	22	77	16	0	0	6	0	1	1	2
02-03—Boston	NHL	76	4	13	17	56	21	0	0	5	0	0	0	4
03-04—Boston	NHL	82	2	7	9	99	16	0	0	7	0	1	1	4
04-05—Lukko Rauma	Finland	31	2	8	10	110	-2	...	...	8	0	0	0	57
NHL Totals (7 years)		546	19	68	87	464	45	0	0	36	0	2	2	28

GIONTA, BRIAN — RW — DEVILS

PERSONAL: Born January 18, 1979, in Rochester, N.Y. ... 5-7/175. ... Shoots right.
TRANSACTIONS/CAREER NOTES: Selected by New Jersey Devils in third round (fourth Devils pick, 82nd overall) of NHL draft (June 27, 1998). ... Injured ankle (December 14, 2002); missed two games. ... Fractured leg (January 4, 2003); missed 19 games. ... Injured ankle (February 18, 2003); missed three games. ... Cut face (March 5, 2004); missed seven games.

		REGULAR SEASON								PLAYOFFS				
Season Team	League	GP	G	A	Pts.	PIM	+/-	PP	SH	GP	G	A	Pts.	PIM
97-98—Boston College	Hockey East	40	30	32	62	44	...	...	...	—	—	—	—	—
98-99—Boston College	Hockey East	39	27	33	60	46	...	...	...	—	—	—	—	—
99-00—Boston College	Hockey East	42	*33	23	56	66	...	...	...	—	—	—	—	—

G

		REGULAR SEASON								PLAYOFFS				
Season Team	League	GP	G	A	Pts.	PIM	+/-	PP	SH	GP	G	A	Pts.	PIM
00-01—Boston College	Hockey East	43	*33	21	*54	47	...	...	...	—	—	—	—	—
01-02—Albany	AHL	37	9	16	25	18	0	1	0	—	—	—	—	—
—New Jersey	NHL	33	4	7	11	8	10	0	0	6	2	2	4	0
02-03—New Jersey	NHL	58	12	13	25	23	5	2	0	24	1	8	9	6
03-04—New Jersey	NHL	75	21	8	29	36	19	0	0	5	2	3	5	0
04-05—Albany	AHL	15	5	7	12	10	0	2	0	—	—	—	—	—
NHL Totals (3 years)		166	37	28	65	67	34	2	0	35	5	13	18	6

GIRARD, JONATHAN D BRUINS

PERSONAL: Born May 27, 1980, in Joliette, Que. ... 5-11/192. ... Shoots right.
TRANSACTIONS/CAREER NOTES: Selected by Boston Bruins in second round (first Bruins pick, 48th overall) of NHL entry draft (June 27, 1998). ... Fractured pelvis in auto accident (September 10, 2003); missed 2003-04 season. ... Missed 2004-05 season while recovering from pelvis injury; insurance prevented him from playing with Providence (AHL).

		REGULAR SEASON								PLAYOFFS				
Season Team	League	GP	G	A	Pts.	PIM	+/-	PP	SH	GP	G	A	Pts.	PIM
96-97—Laval	QMJHL	38	11	21	32	23	...	...	...	3	0	3	3	0
97-98—Laval	QMJHL	64	20	47	67	44	...	...	...	16	2	16	18	13
98-99—Acadie-Bathurst	QMJHL	50	9	58	67	60	21	4	0	23	13	18	31	22
—Boston	NHL	3	0	0	0	0	1	0	0	—	—	—	—	—
99-00—Boston	NHL	23	1	2	3	2	-1	0	0	—	—	—	—	—
—Providence	AHL	5	0	1	1	0	...	...	...	—	—	—	—	—
—Moncton	QMJHL	26	10	25	35	36	33	2	1	16	3	15	18	36
00-01—Boston	NHL	31	3	13	16	14	2	2	0	—	—	—	—	—
—Providence	AHL	39	3	21	24	6	...	...	...	17	0	5	5	4
01-02—Providence	AHL	59	6	31	37	36	-13	3	1	—	—	—	—	—
—Boston	NHL	20	0	3	3	9	0	0	0	1	0	0	0	2
02-03—Boston	NHL	73	6	16	22	21	4	2	0	2	0	1	1	0
NHL Totals (5 years)		150	10	34	44	46	6	4	0	3	0	1	1	2

GIROUX, ALEXANDRE C RANGERS

PERSONAL: Born June 16, 1981, in Quebec City. ... 6-2/165. ... Shoots left. ... Name pronounced zhih-ROO.
TRANSACTIONS/CAREER NOTES: Selected by Ottawa Senators in seventh round (ninth Senators pick, 213th overall) of NHL entry draft (June 26, 1999). ... Traded by Senators with D Karel Rachunek to New York Rangers for D Greg de Vries (March 9, 2004).

		REGULAR SEASON								PLAYOFFS				
Season Team	League	GP	G	A	Pts.	PIM	+/-	PP	SH	GP	G	A	Pts.	PIM
98-99—Hull	QMJHL	67	15	22	37	124	...	...	...	22	2	2	4	8
99-00—Hull	QMJHL	72	52	47	99	117	...	...	...	15	12	6	18	30
00-01—Hull	QMJHL	38	31	32	63	62	...	...	...	—	—	—	—	—
—Rouyn-Noranda	QMJHL	25	13	14	27	56	...	...	...	9	2	6	8	22
01-02—Grand Rapids	AHL	70	11	16	27	74	5	2	0	—	—	—	—	—
02-03—Binghamton	AHL	67	19	16	35	101	-4	9	0	10	1	0	1	10
03-04—Binghamton	AHL	60	19	23	42	79	15	6	1	—	—	—	—	—
—Hartford	AHL	16	6	3	9	13	-2	2	0	16	3	4	7	28
04-05—Hartford	AHL	78	32	22	54	128	15	13	0	6	3	3	6	23

GIROUX, RAYMOND D

PERSONAL: Born July 20, 1976, in North Bay, Ont. ... 6-1/190. ... Shoots left. ... Name pronounced zhih-ROO.
TRANSACTIONS/CAREER NOTES: Selected by Philadelphia Flyers in eighth round (seventh Flyers pick, 202nd overall) of NHL draft (June 29, 1994). ... Rights traded by Flyers to New York Islanders for sixth-round pick (later traded to Montreal; Canadiens selected Scott Selig) in 2000 draft (August 25, 1998). ... Fractured finger (February 10, 2000); missed 12 games. ... Signed as free agent by New Jersey Devils (July 12, 2002). ... Signed as free agent by Minnesota Wild (July 7, 2004).

		REGULAR SEASON								PLAYOFFS				
Season Team	League	GP	G	A	Pts.	PIM	+/-	PP	SH	GP	G	A	Pts.	PIM
93-94—Powasson	Jr. A	36	10	40	50	42	...	...	...	—	—	—	—	—
94-95—Yale	ECAC	31	1	9	10	20	...	0	0	—	—	—	—	—
95-96—Yale	ECAC	30	3	17	20	36	...	...	...	—	—	—	—	—
96-97—Yale	ECAC	32	9	12	21	38	...	5	0	—	—	—	—	—
97-98—Yale	ECAC	35	9	30	39	62	...	...	...	—	—	—	—	—
98-99—Lowell	AHL	59	13	19	32	92	-6	9	0	3	1	1	2	0
99-00—Lowell	AHL	49	12	21	33	34	...	...	...	7	0	0	0	2
—New York Islanders	NHL	14	0	9	9	10	0	0	0	—	—	—	—	—
00-01—AIK Solna	Sweden	9	0	1	1	16	...	...	...	—	—	—	—	—
—HIFK Helsinki	Finland	22	3	9	12	34	...	...	...	—	—	—	—	—
—Jokerit Helsinki	Finland	24	4	9	13	16	...	...	...	5	0	0	0	0
01-02—Bridgeport	AHL	79	13	40	53	73	13	7	0	19	1	7	8	20
—New York Islanders	NHL	2	0	0	0	2	-1	0	0	—	—	—	—	—
02-03—Albany	AHL	67	11	38	49	49	-10	6	0	—	—	—	—	—
—New Jersey	NHL	11	0	1	1	6	-2	0	0	—	—	—	—	—
03-04—Albany	AHL	65	11	17	28	34	-20	4	0	—	—	—	—	—
—New Jersey	NHL	11	0	3	3	4	-3	0	0	4	0	0	0	0
04-05—Houston	AHL	70	13	20	33	54	10	5	0	5	0	0	0	13
NHL Totals (4 years)		38	0	13	13	22	-6	0	0	4	0	0	0	0

GLEASON, TIM — D — KINGS

PERSONAL: Born January 29, 1983, in Southfield, Mich. ... 6-1/214. ... Shoots left.
TRANSACTIONS/CAREER NOTES: Selected by Ottawa Senators in first round (second Senators pick, 23rd overall) of NHL entry draft (June 23, 2001). ... Traded by Senators to Los Angeles Kings for C Bryan Smolinski (March 11, 2003).

		REGULAR SEASON								PLAYOFFS				
Season Team	**League**	**GP**	**G**	**A**	**Pts.**	**PIM**	**+/-**	**PP**	**SH**	**GP**	**G**	**A**	**Pts.**	**PIM**
99-00—Windsor	OHL	55	5	13	18	101	...	...	...	12	2	4	6	14
00-01—Windsor	OHL	47	8	26	34	124	...	...	...	9	1	2	3	23
01-02—Windsor	OHL	67	17	42	59	109	...	...	...	16	7	13	20	40
02-03—Windsor	OHL	45	7	31	38	75	...	...	...	7	5	2	7	17
03-04—Los Angeles	NHL	47	0	7	7	21	1	0	0	—	—	—	—	—
—Manchester	AHL	22	0	8	8	19	10	0	0	6	0	1	1	4
04-05—Manchester	AHL	67	10	14	24	112	17	2	1	5	0	0	0	4
NHL Totals (1 year)		47	0	7	7	21	1	0	0					

GOC, MARCEL — C — SHARKS

PERSONAL: Born August 24, 1983, in Calw, West Germany. ... 6-1/187. ... Shoots left. ... Brother of Sascha Goc, D, New Jersey Devils (1998-2001) and Tampa Bay Lightning (2001-02).
TRANSACTIONS/CAREER NOTES: Selected by San Jose Sharks in first round (first Sharks pick, 20th overall) of NHL entry draft (June 23, 2001).

		REGULAR SEASON								PLAYOFFS				
Season Team	**League**	**GP**	**G**	**A**	**Pts.**	**PIM**	**+/-**	**PP**	**SH**	**GP**	**G**	**A**	**Pts.**	**PIM**
99-00—Schwenningen	Germany	62	1	4	5	6	...	...	...	—	—	—	—	—
00-01—Schwenningen	Germany	58	13	28	41	12	...	...	...	—	—	—	—	—
01-02—Schwenningen	Germany	45	8	9	17	24	...	...	...	—	—	—	—	—
—Mannheim	Germany	8	0	2	2	0	...	...	...	—	—	—	—	—
02-03—Mannheim	Germany	36	6	14	20	16	...	...	...	8	1	2	3	0
03-04—Cleveland	AHL	78	16	21	37	24	3	0	1	—	—	—	—	—
—San Jose	NHL	...	...	...	...	...	...	...	...	5	1	1	2	0
04-05—Cleveland	AHL	76	16	34	50	28	6	5	3	—	—	—	—	—
NHL Totals (1 year)		0	...	...	...	...	...	...	...	5	1	1	2	0

GODARD, ERIC — RW — ISLANDERS

PERSONAL: Born March 7, 1980, in Vernon, B.C. ... 6-4/235. ... Shoots right.
TRANSACTIONS/CAREER NOTES: Signed as free agent by Florida Panthers (September 24, 1999). ... Traded by Panthers to New York Islanders for third-round pick (C/LW Gregory Campbell) in 2002 draft (June 22, 2002). ... Suspended one playoff game for high-sticking incident (April 10, 2003). ... Injured shoulder (November 28, 2003); missed three games.

		REGULAR SEASON								PLAYOFFS				
Season Team	**League**	**GP**	**G**	**A**	**Pts.**	**PIM**	**+/-**	**PP**	**SH**	**GP**	**G**	**A**	**Pts.**	**PIM**
97-98—Lethbridge	WHL	7	0	0	0	26	...	0	0	2	0	0	0	0
98-99—Lethbridge	WHL	66	2	5	7	213	...	...	...	4	0	0	0	14
99-00—Lethbridge	WHL	60	3	5	8	*310	...	...	...	—	—	—	—	—
—Louisville	AHL	4	0	1	1	16	...	...	...	—	—	—	—	—
00-01—Louisville	AHL	45	0	0	0	132	...	...	...	—	—	—	—	—
01-02—Bridgeport	AHL	67	1	4	5	198	1	0	0	20	0	4	4	30
02-03—Bridgeport	AHL	46	2	2	4	199	-10	2	0	6	0	0	0	16
—New York Islanders	NHL	19	0	0	0	48	-3	0	0	2	0	1	1	4
03-04—New York Islanders	NHL	31	0	1	1	97	-2	0	0	—	—	—	—	—
—Bridgeport	AHL	7	0	0	0	13	-2	0	0	—	—	—	—	—
04-05—Bridgeport	AHL	75	7	11	18	295	-10	2	0	—	—	—	—	—
NHL Totals (2 years)		50	0	1	1	145	-5	0	0	2	0	1	1	4

GOMEZ, SCOTT — C/LW — DEVILS

PERSONAL: Born December 23, 1979, in Anchorage, Alaska. ... 5-11/200. ... Shoots left.
TRANSACTIONS/CAREER NOTES: Selected by New Jersey Devils in first round (second Devils pick, 27th overall) of NHL draft (June 27, 1998). ... Injured back (February 17, 2001); missed six games. ... Fractured left hand (April 1, 2002); missed remainder of season. ... Bruised ribs (December 2, 2003); missed two games.
STATISTICAL PLATEAUS: Three-goal games: 1999-00 (1).

		REGULAR SEASON								PLAYOFFS				
Season Team	**League**	**GP**	**G**	**A**	**Pts.**	**PIM**	**+/-**	**PP**	**SH**	**GP**	**G**	**A**	**Pts.**	**PIM**
96-97—Surrey Jr. A	BCJHL	56	48	76	124	94	...	...	...	—	—	—	—	—
97-98—Tri-City	WHL	45	12	37	49	57	-11	6	0	—	—	—	—	—
98-99—Tri-City	WHL	58	30	*78	108	55	43	9	1	10	6	13	19	31
99-00—New Jersey	NHL	82	19	51	70	78	14	7	0	23	4	6	10	4
00-01—New Jersey	NHL	76	14	49	63	46	-1	2	0	25	5	9	14	24
01-02—New Jersey	NHL	76	10	38	48	36	-4	1	0	—	—	—	—	—
02-03—New Jersey	NHL	80	13	42	55	48	17	2	0	24	3	9	12	2
03-04—New Jersey	NHL	80	14	56	70	70	18	3	0	5	0	6	6	0
04-05—Alaska	ECHL	61	13	73	86	69	26	1	1	4	1	3	4	4
NHL Totals (5 years)		394	70	236	306	278	44	15	0	77	12	30	42	30

G

GONCHAR, SERGEI D PENGUINS

PERSONAL: Born April 13, 1974, in Chelyabinsk, U.S.S.R. ... 6-1/212. ... Shoots left. ... Name pronounced GAHN-shahr.
TRANSACTIONS/CAREER NOTES: Selected by Washington Capitals in 1st round (1st Capitals pick, 14th overall) of NHL draft (June 20, 1992). ... Injured groin (November 30, 1995); missed two games. ... Flu (December 13, 1995); missed one game. ... Flu (November 7, 1996); missed one game. ... Hyperextended elbow (November 18, 1996); missed one game. ... Back spasms (December 28, 1996); missed eight games. ... Bruised knee (January 29, 1997); missed two games. ... Sprained knee (February 26, 1997); missed 12 games. ... Sprained knee (October 23, 1998); missed 10 games. ... Strained groin (January 1, 1999); missed one game. ... Sprained wrist (January 30, 1999); missed eight games. ... Sprained ankle (March 13, 1999); missed two games. ... Reinjured ankle (April 7, 1999); missed remainder of season. ... Injured (November 11, 1999); missed five games. ... Injured neck (February 28, 2000); missed two games. ... Reinjured neck (March 5, 2000); missed two games. ... Missed first two games of 2000-01 season in contract dispute. ... Injured neck (December 21, 2000); missed one game. ... Bruised shoulder (January 18, 2001); missed three games. ... Injured (November 27, 2001); missed one game. ... Concussion (March 21, 2002); missed five games. ... Injured shoulder (January 14, 2004); missed seven games. ... Flu (February 27, 2004); missed three games. ... Traded by Capitals to Boston Bruins for D Shaone Morrisonn and 1st- (D Jeff Schultz) and 2nd-round (C/W Mihail Yunkov) picks in 2004 draft (March 3, 2004). ... Signed as free agent by Pittsburgh Penguins (Aug. 3, 2005).
STATISTICAL PLATEAUS: Three-goal games: 1999-00 (1).

		REGULAR SEASON								PLAYOFFS				
Season Team	**League**	**GP**	**G**	**A**	**Pts.**	**PIM**	**+/-**	**PP**	**SH**	**GP**	**G**	**A**	**Pts.**	**PIM**
90-91—Mechel Chelyabinsk....	USSR	2	0	0	0	0	...	...	...	—	—	—	—	—
91-92—Traktor Chelyabinsk....	CIS	31	1	0	1	6	...	...	...	—	—	—	—	—
92-93—Dynamo Moscow........	CIS	31	1	3	4	70	...	...	...	10	0	0	0	12
93-94—Dynamo Moscow........	CIS	44	4	5	9	36	...	...	...	10	0	3	3	14
—Portland.....................	AHL	...	...	...	...	...	...	...	...	2	0	0	0	0
94-95—Portland.....................	AHL	61	10	32	42	67	39	1	0	—	—	—	—	—
—Washington	NHL	31	2	5	7	22	4	0	0	7	2	2	4	2
95-96—Washington	NHL	78	15	26	41	60	25	4	0	6	2	4	6	4
96-97—Washington	NHL	57	13	17	30	36	-11	3	0	—	—	—	—	—
97-98—Washington	NHL	72	5	16	21	66	2	2	0	21	7	4	11	30
—Russian Oly. team.......	Int'l	6	0	2	2	0	0	0	0	—	—	—	—	—
98-99—Washington	NHL	53	21	10	31	57	1	13	1	—	—	—	—	—
99-00—Washington	NHL	73	18	36	54	52	26	5	0	5	1	0	1	6
00-01—Washington	NHL	76	19	38	57	70	12	8	0	6	1	3	4	2
01-02—Washington	NHL	76	26	33	59	58	-1	7	0	—	—	—	—	—
—Russian Oly. team.......	Int'l	6	0	0	0	2	...	...	...	—	—	—	—	—
02-03—Washington	NHL	82	18	49	67	52	13	7	0	6	0	5	5	4
03-04—Washington	NHL	56	7	42	49	44	-20	4	0	—	—	—	—	—
—Boston	NHL	15	4	5	9	12	6	2	0	7	1	4	5	4
04-05—Metal. Magnitogorsk...	Russian	40	2	17	19	54	11	...	...	4	1	1	2	6
NHL Totals (10 years).........		669	148	277	425	529	57	55	1	58	14	22	36	52

GORDON, BOYD RW/C CAPITALS

PERSONAL: Born October 19, 1983, in Unity, Sask. ... 6-0/191. ... Shoots right.
TRANSACTIONS/CAREER NOTES: Selected by Washington Capitals in first round (third Capitals pick, 17th overall) of NHL entry draft (June 22, 2002).

		REGULAR SEASON								PLAYOFFS				
Season Team	**League**	**GP**	**G**	**A**	**Pts.**	**PIM**	**+/-**	**PP**	**SH**	**GP**	**G**	**A**	**Pts.**	**PIM**
99-00—Red Deer.....................	WHL	66	10	26	36	24	...	...	...	4	0	1	1	2
00-01—Red Deer.....................	WHL	72	12	27	39	39	...	...	...	22	3	6	9	2
01-02—Red Deer.....................	WHL	66	22	29	51	19	...	...	...	23	10	12	22	8
02-03—Red Deer.....................	WHL	56	33	48	81	28	...	...	...	23	8	12	20	14
03-04—Washington	NHL	41	1	5	6	8	-9	0	0	—	—	—	—	—
—Portland.....................	AHL	43	5	17	22	16	-1	0	0	7	2	1	3	0
04-05—Portland.....................	AHL	80	17	22	39	35	-20	7	1	—	—	—	—	—
NHL Totals (1 year).............		41	1	5	6	8	-9	0	0					

GOREN, LEE RW CANUCKS

PERSONAL: Born December 26, 1977, in Winnipeg. ... 6-3/215. ... Shoots right.
TRANSACTIONS/CAREER NOTES: Selected by Boston Bruins in third round (fifth Bruins pick, 63rd overall) of NHL draft (June 21, 1997). ... Signed as free agent by Florida Panthers (July 24, 2003). ... Signed as free agent by Vancouver Canucks (July 7, 2004).

		REGULAR SEASON								PLAYOFFS				
Season Team	**League**	**GP**	**G**	**A**	**Pts.**	**PIM**	**+/-**	**PP**	**SH**	**GP**	**G**	**A**	**Pts.**	**PIM**
95-96—Minote	Jr. A	64	31	55	86	...	...	...	...	—	—	—	—	—
96-97—Univ. of North Dakota .	WCHA	Did not play												
97-98—Univ. of North Dakota .	WCHA	29	3	13	16	26	...	...	...	—	—	—	—	—
98-99—Univ. of North Dakota .	WCHA	38	26	19	45	20	...	...	...	—	—	—	—	—
99-00—Univ. of North Dakota .	WCHA	44	*34	29	63	42	...	...	...	—	—	—	—	—
00-01—Providence..................	AHL	54	15	18	33	72	...	...	...	17	5	2	7	11
—Boston	NHL	21	2	0	2	7	-3	1	0	—	—	—	—	—
01-02—Providence..................	AHL	71	11	26	37	121	-19	6	0	—	—	—	—	—
02-03—Providence..................	AHL	65	32	37	69	106	9	17	0	—	—	—	—	—
—Boston	NHL	14	2	1	3	7	-2	2	0	5	0	0	0	5
03-04—Florida........................	NHL	2	0	1	1	0	-4	0	0	—	—	—	—	—
—San Antonio................	AHL	65	27	22	49	72	-4	9	3	—	—	—	—	—
04-05—Manitoba.....................	AHL	79	32	30	62	117	24	16	1	14	10	3	13	23
NHL Totals (3 years)...........		37	4	2	6	14	-9	3	0	5	0	0	0	5

GRAHAME, JOHN G LIGHTNING

PERSONAL: Born August 31, 1975, in Denver. ... 6-2/220. ... Catches left. ... Son of Ron Grahame, goaltender with three NHL teams (1977-78 through 1980-81). ... Name pronounced GRAY-ihm.

TRANSACTIONS/CAREER NOTES: Selected by Boston Bruins in ninth round (seventh Bruins pick, 229th overall) of NHL draft (June 29, 1994). ... Injured ankle (December 19, 2000) and had surgery; missed seven games. ... Injured shoulder (October 17, 2002); missed seven games. ... Traded by Bruins to Tampa Bay Lightning for fourth-round pick (later traded to San Jose Sharks) in 2004 draft (January 13, 2003).

		REGULAR SEASON									PLAYOFFS							
Season Team	**League**	**GP**	**Min.**	**W**	**L**	**T**	**GA**	**SO**	**GAA**	**SV%**	**GP**	**Min.**	**W**	**L**	**GA**	**SO**	**GAA**	**SV%**
93-94—Sioux City	USHL	20	1136	...	...	...	72	0	3.80	...	—	—	—	—	—	—	—	—
94-95—Lake Superior St.	CCHA	28	1616	16	7	3	75	1	2.78	.887	—	—	—	—	—	—	—	—
95-96—Lake Superior St.	CCHA	29	1658	21	4	2	67	2	2.42	...	—	—	—	—	—	—	—	—
96-97—Lake Superior St.	CCHA	37	2197	19	13	4	134	3	3.66	.876	—	—	—	—	—	—	—	—
97-98—Providence	AHL	55	3054	15	*31	4	164	3	3.22	.898	—	—	—	—	—	—	—	—
98-99—Providence	AHL	48	2771	*37	9	1	134	3	2.90	.896	19	*1209	*15	4	*48	1	2.38	.912
99-00—Boston	NHL	24	1344	7	10	5	55	2	2.46	.910	—	—	—	—	—	—	—	—
—Providence	AHL	27	1528	11	13	2	86	1	3.38	...	13	839	10	3	35	0	2.50	...
00-01—Boston	NHL	10	471	3	4	0	28	0	3.57	.867	—	—	—	—	—	—	—	—
—Providence	AHL	16	893	4	7	3	47	0	3.16	.899	17	1043	8	*9	46	2	2.65	...
01-02—Boston	NHL	19	1079	8	7	2	52	1	2.89	.897	—	—	—	—	—	—	—	—
02-03—Boston	NHL	23	1352	11	9	2	61	1	2.71	.902	1	111	0	1	2	0	1.08	.958
—Tampa Bay	NHL	17	914	6	5	4	34	2	2.23	.920	...	...	...	...	...	...	...	...
03-04—Tampa Bay	NHL	29	1688	18	9	1	58	1	2.06	.913	1	34	0	0	2	0	3.53	.882
NHL Totals (5 years)		122	6848	53	44	14	288	7	2.52	.905	2	145	0	1	4	0	1.66	.938

GRAND-PIERRE, JEAN-LUC RW

PERSONAL: Born February 2, 1977, in Montreal. ... 6-3/228. ... Shoots right. ... Name pronounced zhah-LOOK GRAHN-pee-AIR.

TRANSACTIONS/CAREER NOTES: Selected by St. Louis Blues in 7th round (6th Blues pick, 179th overall) of NHL draft (July 8, 1995). ... Traded by Blues with 2nd-round pick (D Cory Sarich) in 1996 entry draft and 3rd-round pick (RW Maxim Afinogenov) in 1997 draft to Buffalo Sabres for LW Yuri Khmylev and 8th-round pick (C Andrei Podkonicky) in 1996 draft (March 20, 1996). ... Suspended one game for tripping incident (April 10, 1999). ... Flu (March 12, 2000); missed one game. ... Traded by Sabres with RW Matt Davidson, 5th-round pick (C Tyler Kolarik) in 2000 draft and 5th-round pick (traded to Detroit Red Wings) in 2001 draft to Columbus Blue Jackets to complete expansion draft agreement in which Columbus selected LW Geoff Sanderson and G Dwayne Roloson. (June 23, 2000). ... Bruised foot (October 21, 2000); missed two games. ... Concussion (December 26, 2000); missed three games. ... Bruised foot (March 7, 2001); missed six games. ... Injured knee (November 30, 2002); missed seven games. ... Injured knee (December 26, 2002); missed one game. ... Traded by Blue Jackets to Atlanta Thrashers for future considerations (December 31, 2003). ... Claimed off waivers from Thrashers by Washington Capitals (March 9, 2004).

		REGULAR SEASON								PLAYOFFS				
Season Team	**League**	**GP**	**G**	**A**	**Pts.**	**PIM**	**+/-**	**PP**	**SH**	**GP**	**G**	**A**	**Pts.**	**PIM**
93-94—Beauport	QMJHL	46	1	4	5	27	...	...	...	1	0	0	0	0
94-95—Val-d'Or	QMJHL	59	10	13	23	126	-42	9	0	—	—	—	—	—
95-96—Val-d'Or	QMJHL	67	13	21	34	209	...	...	...	13	1	4	5	47
96-97—Val-d'Or	QMJHL	58	9	24	33	196	...	...	...	13	5	8	13	46
97-98—Rochester	AHL	75	4	6	10	211	-7	1	0	4	0	0	0	2
98-99—Rochester	AHL	56	5	4	9	90	10	1	0	—	—	—	—	—
—Buffalo	NHL	16	0	1	1	17	0	0	0	—	—	—	—	—
99-00—Buffalo	NHL	11	0	0	0	15	-1	0	0	4	0	0	0	4
—Rochester	AHL	62	5	8	13	124	...	...	...	17	0	1	1	40
00-01—Columbus	NHL	64	1	4	5	73	-6	0	0	—	—	—	—	—
01-02—Columbus	NHL	81	2	6	8	90	-28	0	0	—	—	—	—	—
02-03—Columbus	NHL	41	1	0	1	64	-6	0	0	—	—	—	—	—
—Syracuse	AHL	2	1	0	1	6	...	...	...	—	—	—	—	—
03-04—Columbus	NHL	16	0	0	0	12	-3	0	0	—	—	—	—	—
—Syracuse	AHL	4	0	1	1	8	-2	0	0	—	—	—	—	—
—Atlanta	NHL	27	2	2	4	26	-7	0	1	—	—	—	—	—
—Washington	NHL	13	1	0	1	14	-2	0	0	—	—	—	—	—
04-05—Troja-Ljungby	Sweden Dv. 2	—	—	—	—	—	—	—	—	10	1	2	3	24
—Troja-Ljungby	Sweden Dv. 2	11	1	1	2	45	-2	...	...	—	—	—	—	—
NHL Totals (6 years)		269	7	13	20	311	-53	0	1	4	0	0	0	4

GRATTON, BENOIT C CANADIENS

PERSONAL: Born December 28, 1976, in Montreal. ... 5-11/180. ... Shoots left. ... Name pronounced BEHN-wah grah-TOHN.

TRANSACTIONS/CAREER NOTES: Selected by Washington Capitals in fifth round (sixth Capitals pick, 105th overall) of NHL draft (July 8, 1995). ... Injured groin (December 20, 1997); missed one game. ... Traded by Capitals to Calgary Flames for D Steve Shirreffs (August 18, 1999). ... Injured head (February 13, 2001). ... Claimed off waivers by Montreal Canadiens from Flames (April 11, 2001). ... Sprained ankle (January 5, 2002); missed 26 games. ... Suffered concussion (December 29, 2003); missed 17 games.

		REGULAR SEASON								PLAYOFFS				
Season Team	**League**	**GP**	**G**	**A**	**Pts.**	**PIM**	**+/-**	**PP**	**SH**	**GP**	**G**	**A**	**Pts.**	**PIM**
93-94—Laval	QMJHL	51	9	14	23	70	...	...	...	20	2	1	3	19
94-95—Laval	QMJHL	71	30	58	88	199	32	11	2	20	8	21	29	42
95-96—Laval	QMJHL	38	21	39	60	130	...	...	...	—	—	—	—	—
—Granby	QMJHL	27	12	46	58	97	...	...	...	21	13	26	39	68
96-97—Portland	AHL	76	6	40	46	140	-4	1	0	5	2	1	3	14
97-98—Portland	AHL	58	19	31	50	137	11	5	1	8	4	2	6	24
—Washington	NHL	6	0	1	1	6	1	0	0	—	—	—	—	—
98-99—Portland	AHL	64	18	42	60	135	-1	5	0	—	—	—	—	—

Season Team	League	GP	G	A	Pts.	PIM	+/-	PP	SH	GP	G	A	Pts.	PIM
		REGULAR SEASON								PLAYOFFS				
—Washington	NHL	16	4	3	7	16	-1	0	0	—	—	—	—	—
99-00—Saint John	AHL	65	17	49	66	137	...	...	...	3	0	1	1	4
—Calgary	NHL	10	0	2	2	10	1	0	0	—	—	—	—	—
00-01—Saint John	AHL	53	10	36	46	153	...	...	...	—	—	—	—	—
—Calgary	NHL	14	1	3	4	14	0	0	0	—	—	—	—	—
01-02—Quebec	AHL	35	10	19	29	70	-5	2	0	3	2	3	5	10
—Montreal	NHL	8	1	0	1	8	-1	0	0	—	—	—	—	—
02-03—Hamilton	AHL	43	21	39	60	78	22	7	1	22	2	15	17	73
03-04—Montreal	NHL	4	0	1	1	4	0	0	0	—	—	—	—	—
—Hamilton	AHL	50	17	34	51	119	9	6	0	10	1	2	3	67
04-05—Lugano	Switzerland	31	6	12	18	81	...	2	0	—	—	—	—	—
NHL Totals (6 years)		58	6	10	16	58	0	0	0					

GRATTON, CHRIS C/LW PANTHERS

PERSONAL: Born July 5, 1975, in Brantford, Ont. ... 6-4/221. ... Shoots left. ... Name pronounced GRA-tuhn.

TRANSACTIONS/CAREER NOTES: Selected by Tampa Bay Lightning in 1st round (1st Lightning pick, 3rd overall) of NHL draft (June 26, 1993). ... Bruised shoulder (April 2, 1995); missed two games. ... Traded by Lightning to Philadelphia Flyers for RW Mikael Renberg and D Karl Dykhuis (August 20, 1997). ... Traded by Flyers with C/RW Mike Sillinger to Lightning for RW Mikael Renberg and C Daymond Langkow (December 12, 1998). ... Suspended three games for spitting at referee (December 25, 1998). ... Bruised right foot (February 17, 2000); missed seven games. ... Traded by Lightning with 2nd-round pick (C Derek Roy) in 2001 draft to Buffalo Sabres for C/RW Brian Holzinger, C Wayne Primeau, D Cory Sarich and 3rd-round pick (RW Alexandre Kharitonov) in 2000 draft (March 9, 2000). ... Suffered concussion (January 30, 2003); missed two games. ... Traded by Sabres with 4th-round pick (later traded to Edmonton Oilers) in 2004 draft to Phoenix Coyotes for C Daniel Briere and 3rd-round pick (D Andrej Sekera) in 2004 entry draft (March 10, 2003). ... Traded by Coyotes with D Ossi Vaananen and 2nd-round pick in 2005 draft to Colorado Avalanche for D Derek Morris and D Keith Ballard (March 9, 2004). ... Placed on waivers by Avalanche (July 28, 2005).

STATISTICAL PLATEAUS: Three-goal games: 1996-97 (1).

Season Team	League	GP	G	A	Pts.	PIM	+/-	PP	SH	GP	G	A	Pts.	PIM
		REGULAR SEASON								PLAYOFFS				
90-91—Brantford Jr. B	OHA	31	30	30	60	28	...	...	...	—	—	—	—	—
91-92—Kingston	OHL	62	27	39	66	35	...	...	...	—	—	—	—	—
92-93—Kingston	OHL	58	55	54	109	125	...	...	...	16	11	18	29	42
93-94—Tampa Bay	NHL	84	13	29	42	123	-25	5	1	—	—	—	—	—
94-95—Tampa Bay	NHL	46	7	20	27	89	-2	2	0	—	—	—	—	—
95-96—Tampa Bay	NHL	82	17	21	38	105	-13	7	0	6	0	2	2	27
96-97—Tampa Bay	NHL	82	30	32	62	201	-28	9	0	—	—	—	—	—
97-98—Philadelphia	NHL	82	22	40	62	159	11	5	0	5	2	0	2	10
98-99—Philadelphia	NHL	26	1	7	8	41	-8	0	0	—	—	—	—	—
—Tampa Bay	NHL	52	7	19	26	102	-20	1	0	—	—	—	—	—
99-00—Tampa Bay	NHL	58	14	27	41	121	-24	4	0	—	—	—	—	—
—Buffalo	NHL	14	1	7	8	15	1	0	0	5	0	1	1	4
00-01—Buffalo	NHL	82	19	21	40	102	0	5	0	13	6	4	10	14
01-02—Buffalo	NHL	82	15	24	39	75	0	1	0	—	—	—	—	—
02-03—Buffalo	NHL	66	15	29	44	86	-5	4	0	—	—	—	—	—
—Phoenix	NHL	14	0	1	1	21	-11	0	0	—	—	—	—	—
03-04—Phoenix	NHL	68	11	18	29	93	-19	3	0	—	—	—	—	—
—Colorado	NHL	13	2	1	3	18	1	0	0	11	0	0	0	27
NHL Totals (11 years)		851	174	296	470	1351	-142	46	1	40	8	7	15	82

GREBESHKOV, DENIS D KINGS

PERSONAL: Born October 11, 1983, in Yaroslavl, U.S.S.R. ... 6-1/195. ... Shoots left.

TRANSACTIONS/CAREER NOTES: Selected by Los Angeles Kings in first round (first Kings pick, 18th overall) of NHL entry draft (June 22, 2002).

Season Team	League	GP	G	A	Pts.	PIM	+/-	PP	SH	GP	G	A	Pts.	PIM
		REGULAR SEASON								PLAYOFFS				
01-02—Lokomotiv Yaroslavl	Russian	27	1	2	3	10	...	...	...	—	—	—	—	—
02-03—Lokomotiv Yaroslavl	Russian	48	0	7	7	26	...	...	...	—	—	—	—	—
03-04—Los Angeles	NHL	4	0	1	1	0	-4	0	0	—	—	—	—	—
—Manchester	AHL	43	2	7	9	34	6	0	0	6	0	1	1	6
04-05—Manchester	AHL	75	5	44	49	87	21	3	0	6	0	4	4	2
NHL Totals (1 year)		4	0	1	1	0	-4	0	0					

G

GREEN, JOSH LW

PERSONAL: Born November 16, 1977, in Camrose, Alta. ... 6-4/225. ... Shoots left.

TRANSACTIONS/CAREER NOTES: Selected by Los Angeles Kings in second round (first Kings pick, 30th overall) of NHL entry draft (June 22, 1996). ... Strained shoulder (October 18, 1998); missed three games. ... Traded by Kings with C Olli Jokinen, D Mathieu Biron and first-round pick (LW Taylor Pyatt) in 1999 entry draft to New York Islanders for RW Zigmund Palffy, C Bryan Smolinski, G Marcel Cousineau and fourth-round pick (C Daniel Johansson) in 1999 entry draft (June 20, 1999). ... Injured shoulder (March 21, 2000); missed remainder of season. ... Traded by Islanders with D Eric Brewer and second-round pick (LW Brad Winchester) in 2000 entry draft to Edmonton Oilers for D Roman Hamrlik (June 24, 2000). ... Dislocated shoulder (September 11, 2000); missed first 39 games of season. ... Reinjured shoulder (December 30, 2000); missed final 42 games of season. ... Bruised right hand (January 21, 2002); missed one game. ... Injured back (October 8, 2002); missed seven games. ... Traded by Oilers to New York Rangers for future considerations (December 12, 2002). ... Sprained wrist (December 19, 2002); missed seven games. ... Claimed off waivers by Washington Capitals (January 15, 2003). ... Signed as free agent by Calgary Flames (July 17, 2003). ... Claimed off waivers by Rangers (March 6, 2004).

Season Team	League	REGULAR SEASON GP	G	A	Pts.	PIM	+/-	PP	SH	PLAYOFFS GP	G	A	Pts.	PIM
93-94—Medicine Hat	WHL	63	22	22	44	43	...	...	...	3	0	0	0	4
94-95—Medicine Hat	WHL	68	32	23	55	64	...	...	...	5	5	1	6	2
95-96—Medicine Hat	WHL	46	18	25	43	55	...	...	...	5	2	2	4	4
96-97—Medicine Hat	WHL	51	25	32	57	61	17	5	1	—	—	—	—	—
—Swift Current	WHL	23	10	15	25	33	9	1	1	10	9	7	16	19
97-98—Swift Current	WHL	5	9	1	10	9	...	...	...	—	—	—	—	—
—Portland	WHL	31	35	19	54	36	22	14	1	—	—	—	—	—
—Fredericton	AHL	43	16	15	31	14	7	8	0	4	1	3	4	6
98-99—Los Angeles	NHL	27	1	3	4	8	-5	1	0	—	—	—	—	—
—Springfield	AHL	41	15	15	30	29	1	7	0	—	—	—	—	—
99-00—Lowell	AHL	17	6	2	8	19	...	...	...	—	—	—	—	—
—New York Islanders	NHL	49	12	14	26	41	-7	2	0	—	—	—	—	—
00-01—Hamilton	AHL	2	2	0	2	2	...	...	...	—	—	—	—	—
—Edmonton	NHL	...	...	...	...	...	...	...	...	3	0	0	0	0
01-02—Edmonton	NHL	61	10	5	15	52	9	1	0	—	—	—	—	—
02-03—Edmonton	NHL	20	0	2	2	12	-3	0	0	—	—	—	—	—
—New York Rangers	NHL	4	0	0	0	2	-1	0	0	—	—	—	—	—
—Washington	NHL	21	1	2	3	7	1	0	0	—	—	—	—	—
03-04—Calgary	NHL	36	2	4	6	24	-3	0	0	—	—	—	—	—
—Lowell	AHL	22	6	9	15	46	1	3	0	—	—	—	—	—
—New York Rangers	NHL	14	3	2	5	8	0	0	0	—	—	—	—	—
04-05—Manitoba	AHL	67	21	19	40	72	6	5	0	14	9	5	14	26
NHL Totals (6 years)		232	29	32	61	154	-9	4	0	3	0	0	0	0

GREEN, MIKE — D — CAPITALS

PERSONAL: Born October 12, 1985, in Calgary. ... 6-1/198. ... Shoots right.
TRANSACTIONS/CAREER NOTES: Selected by Washington Capitals in first round (third Capitals pick, 29th overall) of NHL entry draft (June 26, 2004).

Season Team	League	REGULAR SEASON GP	G	A	Pts.	PIM	+/-	PP	SH	PLAYOFFS GP	G	A	Pts.	PIM
00-01—Saskatoon	WHL	7	0	2	2	0	...	...	...	—	—	—	—	—
01-02—Saskatoon	WHL	62	3	20	23	57	...	...	...	7	0	1	1	2
02-03—Saskatoon	WHL	72	6	36	42	70	...	...	...	6	0	2	2	6
03-04—Saskatoon	WHL	59	14	25	39	92	...	...	...	—	—	—	—	—
04-05—Saskatoon	WHL	67	14	52	66	105	36	6	2	4	0	0	0	6

GREEN, MIKE — C — RANGERS

PERSONAL: Born August 23, 1979, in Calgary. ... 5-11/195. ... Shoots right.
TRANSACTIONS/CAREER NOTES: Signed as free agent by Florida Panthers (March 29, 2000). ... Claimed off waivers by New York Rangers (March 9, 2004).

Season Team	League	REGULAR SEASON GP	G	A	Pts.	PIM	+/-	PP	SH	PLAYOFFS GP	G	A	Pts.	PIM
96-97—Edmonton	WHL	7	0	2	2	0	...	...	...	—	—	—	—	—
97-98—Edmonton	WHL	71	15	26	41	16	...	...	...	—	—	—	—	—
98-99—Kootenay	WHL	73	35	45	80	37	...	...	...	7	2	2	4	4
99-00—Kootenay	WHL	69	42	48	90	63	...	...	...	21	9	16	25	20
00-01—Saskatoon	WHL	7	0	2	2	0	...	...	...	—	—	—	—	—
—Port Huron	UHL	11	1	5	6	6	...	...	...	—	—	—	—	—
—Louisville	AHL	24	2	1	3	4	...	...	...	—	—	—	—	—
—Knoxville	UHL	48	18	24	42	35	...	...	...	1	0	0	0	0
01-02—Macon	ECHL	54	27	35	62	18	22	4	2	—	—	—	—	—
—Cincinnati	AHL	22	2	9	11	4	0	0	0	3	0	0	0	0
02-03—San Antonio	AHL	80	26	34	60	25	10	6	2	3	0	2	2	0
03-04—Florida	NHL	11	0	1	1	2	0	0	0	—	—	—	—	—
—San Antonio	AHL	45	12	23	35	16	6	1	1	—	—	—	—	—
—New York Rangers	NHL	13	1	2	3	2	0	0	0	—	—	—	—	—
04-05—Nurnberg	Germany	44	11	17	28	38	-5	4	1	6	1	3	4	0
NHL Totals (1 year)		24	1	3	4	4	0	0	0					

GREEN, TRAVIS — C

PERSONAL: Born December 20, 1970, in Castlegar, B.C. ... 6-2/200. ... Shoots right.
TRANSACTIONS/CAREER NOTES: Selected by New York Islanders in second round (second Islanders pick, 23rd overall) of NHL draft (June 17, 1989). ... Sore groin (November 30, 1995); missed four games. ... Sprained knee (February 8, 1996); missed nine games. ... Traded by Islanders with D Doug Houda and RW Tony Tuzzolino to Anaheim Mighty Ducks for D J.J. Daigneault, C Mark Janssens and RW Joe Sacco (February 6, 1998). ... Strained groin (February 7, 1998); missed five games. ... Sprained right knee (November 20, 1998); missed three games. ... Traded by Mighty Ducks with first-round pick (C Scott Kelman) in 1999 draft to Phoenix Coyotes for D Oleg Tverdovsky (June 26, 1999). ... Infected knee (November 25, 1999); missed three games. ... Suffered concussion (March 21, 2000); missed one game. ... Strained knee (January 6, 2001); missed nine games. ... Bruised knee (March 4, 2001); missed three games. ... Traded by Coyotes with C Robert Reichel and RW Craig Mills to Toronto Maple Leafs for D Danny Markov (June 12, 2001). ... Bruised ribs (March 25, 2003); missed six games. ... Claimed by Columbus Blue Jackets in waiver draft (October 3, 2003). ... Traded by Blue Jackets to Boston Bruins for sixth-round pick (C/W Lennart Petrell) in 2004 draft (October 3, 2003). ... Injured ribs (January 13, 2004); missed eight games. ... Reinjured ribs (February 3, 2004); missed 10 games.
STATISTICAL PLATEAUS: Three-goal games: 1993-94 (1).

G

Season Team	League	REGULAR SEASON GP	G	A	Pts.	PIM	+/-	PP	SH	PLAYOFFS GP	G	A	Pts.	PIM
85-86—Castlegar	KIJHL	35	30	40	70	41	...	...	...	—	—	—	—	—
86-87—Spokane	WHL	64	8	17	25	27	...	...	...	3	0	0	0	0
87-88—Spokane	WHL	72	33	53	86	42	...	...	...	15	10	10	20	13
88-89—Spokane	WHL	72	51	51	102	79	...	...	...	—	—	—	—	—
89-90—Spokane	WHL	50	45	44	89	80	...	...	...	—	—	—	—	—
—Medicine Hat	WHL	25	15	24	39	19	...	...	...	3	0	0	0	2
90-91—Capital District	AHL	73	21	34	55	26	...	...	...	—	—	—	—	—
91-92—Capital District	AHL	71	23	27	50	10	...	...	...	7	0	4	4	21
92-93—Capital District	AHL	20	12	11	23	39	4	2	0	—	—	—	—	—
—New York Islanders	NHL	61	7	18	25	43	4	1	0	12	3	1	4	6
93-94—New York Islanders	NHL	83	18	22	40	44	16	1	0	4	0	0	0	2
94-95—New York Islanders	NHL	42	5	7	12	25	-10	0	0	—	—	—	—	—
95-96—New York Islanders	NHL	69	25	45	70	42	-20	14	1	—	—	—	—	—
96-97—New York Islanders	NHL	79	23	41	64	38	-5	10	0	—	—	—	—	—
97-98—New York Islanders	NHL	54	14	12	26	66	-19	8	0	—	—	—	—	—
—Anaheim	NHL	22	5	11	16	16	-10	1	0	—	—	—	—	—
98-99—Anaheim	NHL	79	13	17	30	81	-7	3	1	4	0	1	1	4
99-00—Phoenix	NHL	78	25	21	46	45	-4	6	0	5	2	1	3	2
00-01—Phoenix	NHL	69	13	15	28	63	-11	3	0	—	—	—	—	—
01-02—Toronto	NHL	82	11	23	34	61	13	3	0	20	3	6	9	34
02-03—Toronto	NHL	75	12	12	24	67	2	2	1	4	2	1	3	4
03-04—Boston	NHL	64	11	5	16	67	-6	2	0	7	0	1	1	8
NHL Totals (12 years)		857	182	249	431	658	-57	54	3	56	10	11	21	60

GRENIER, MARTIN — D — RANGERS

PERSONAL: Born November 2, 1980, in Laval, Que. ... 6-5/245. ... Shoots left.

TRANSACTIONS/CAREER NOTES: Selected by Colorado Avalanche in second round (second Avalanche pick, 45th overall) of NHL entry draft (June 26, 1999). ... Traded by Avalanche with LW Brian Rolston, C Samual Pahlsson and first-round pick (Martin Samuelsson) in 2000 entry draft to Boston Bruins for D Ray Bourque and LW Dave Andreychuk (March 6, 2000). ... Signed as free agent by Phoenix Coyotes (June 5, 2001). ... Traded by Coyotes to Vancouver Canucks for D Bryan Helmer (July 25, 2003). ... Traded by Canucks with C R.J. Umberger to New York Rangers for LW Martin Rucinsky (March 9, 2004).

Season Team	League	REGULAR SEASON GP	G	A	Pts.	PIM	+/-	PP	SH	PLAYOFFS GP	G	A	Pts.	PIM
97-98—Quebec	QMJHL	61	4	11	15	202	...	...	...	14	0	2	2	36
98-99—Quebec	QMJHL	60	7	18	25	*479	15	4	0	13	0	4	4	29
99-00—Quebec	QMJHL	67	11	35	46	302	32	2	1	7	1	4	5	27
00-01—Quebec	QMJHL	26	5	16	21	82	4	3	0	—	—	—	—	—
—Victoriaville	QMJHL	28	9	19	28	108	29	2	0	13	2	8	10	51
01-02—Phoenix	NHL	5	0	0	0	5	0	0	0	—	—	—	—	—
—Springfield	AHL	69	2	6	8	241	-16	0	0	—	—	—	—	—
02-03—Springfield	AHL	73	2	10	12	232	-6	0	0	—	—	—	—	—
—Phoenix	NHL	3	0	0	0	0	-1	0	0	—	—	—	—	—
03-04—Vancouver	NHL	7	1	0	1	9	3	0	0	—	—	—	—	—
—Manitoba	AHL	38	5	4	9	145	6	0	0	—	—	—	—	—
—Hartford	AHL	12	0	2	2	95	3	0	0	9	0	1	1	32
04-05—Charlotte	ECHL	4	0	2	2	10	7	0	0	—	—	—	—	—
—Hartford	AHL	23	2	5	7	136	0	0	0	5	0	0	0	32
NHL Totals (3 years)		15	1	0	1	14	2	0	0					

GRIER, MIKE — RW — SABRES

PERSONAL: Born January 5, 1975, in Detroit. ... 6-1/227. ... Shoots right.

TRANSACTIONS/CAREER NOTES: Selected by St. Louis Blues in ninth round (seventh Blues pick, 219th overall) of NHL draft (June 26, 1993). ... Rights traded by Blues with rights to G Curtis Joseph to Edmonton Oilers for first-round picks in 1996 (C Marty Reasoner) and 1997 (later traded to Los Angeles) drafts (August 4, 1995). ... Strained left knee (November 19, 1997); missed 14 games. ... Fractured clavicle (November 24, 1999); missed four games. ... Tore triceps (March 13, 2000) and had surgery; missed remainder of season. ... Dislocated right shoulder (December 3, 2000); missed eight games. ... Traded by Oilers to Washington Capitals for second- (later traded to New York Islanders) and third-round (RW Zachary Stortini) picks in 2003 draft (October 7, 2002). ... Suspended one game for elbowing incident (October 14, 2003). ... Traded by Capitals to Buffalo Sabres for C Jakub Klepis (March 9, 2004).

STATISTICAL PLATEAUS: Three-goal games: 1998-99 (1).

Season Team	League	REGULAR SEASON GP	G	A	Pts.	PIM	+/-	PP	SH	PLAYOFFS GP	G	A	Pts.	PIM
92-93—St. Sebastian's	USHS (East)	22	16	27	43	32	...	...	...	—	—	—	—	—
93-94—Boston University	Hockey East	39	9	9	18	56	...	...	...	—	—	—	—	—
94-95—Boston University	Hockey East	37	29	26	55	85	24	13	3	—	—	—	—	—
95-96—Boston University	Hockey East	38	21	25	46	82	...	...	...	—	—	—	—	—
96-97—Edmonton	NHL	79	15	17	32	45	7	4	0	12	3	1	4	4
97-98—Edmonton	NHL	66	9	6	15	73	-3	1	0	12	2	2	4	13
98-99—Edmonton	NHL	82	20	24	44	54	5	3	2	4	1	1	2	6
99-00—Edmonton	NHL	65	9	22	31	68	9	0	3	—	—	—	—	—
00-01—Edmonton	NHL	74	20	16	36	20	11	2	3	6	0	0	0	8
01-02—Edmonton	NHL	82	8	17	25	32	1	0	2	—	—	—	—	—
02-03—Washington	NHL	82	15	17	32	36	-14	2	2	6	1	1	2	2
03-04—Washington	NHL	68	8	12	20	32	-19	1	1	—	—	—	—	—
—Buffalo	NHL	14	1	8	9	4	10	0	0	—	—	—	—	—
NHL Totals (8 years)		612	105	139	244	364	7	13	13	40	7	5	12	33

G

GROSEK, MICHAL — LW/RW — BRUINS

PERSONAL: Born June 1, 1975, in Vyskov, Czech. ... 6-2/207. ... Shoots right. ... Name pronounced GROH-shehk.

TRANSACTIONS/CAREER NOTES: Selected by Winnipeg Jets in sixth round (seventh Jets pick, 145th overall) of NHL draft (June 26, 1993). ... Sprained knee ligaments (February 15, 1995); missed four games. ... Fractured foot (April 5, 1995); missed remainder of season. ... Traded by Jets with D Darryl Shannon to Buffalo Sabres for D Craig Muni (February 15, 1996). ... Back spasms (April 9, 1999); missed five games. ... Traded by Sabres to Chicago Blackhawks for C Doug Gilmour and RW J.P. Dumont (March 10, 2000). ... Traded by Blackhawks with D Brad Brown to New York Rangers for future considerations (October 5, 2000). ... Flu (December 20, 2000); missed one game. ... Injured jaw and had the flu (March 7, 2002); missed three games. ... Signed as free agent by Boston Bruins (July 16, 2002). ... Injured oblique muscle (December 14, 2002); missed five games. ... Injured ankle (January 17, 2003); missed three games. ... Charley horse (April 3, 2003); missed two games. ... Injured shoulder (December 6, 2003); missed two games. ... Suffered concussion (January 10, 2004); missed 37 games.

STATISTICAL PLATEAUS: Three-goal games: 1996-97 (1).

		REGULAR SEASON								PLAYOFFS				
Season Team	League	GP	G	A	Pts.	PIM	+/-	PP	SH	GP	G	A	Pts.	PIM
92-93—ZPS Zlin	Czech.	17	1	3	4	0	...	...	...	—	—	—	—	—
93-94—Moncton	AHL	20	1	2	3	47	-9	0	0	2	0	0	0	0
—Tacoma	WHL	30	25	20	45	106	4	10	0	7	2	2	4	30
—Winnipeg	NHL	3	1	0	1	0	-1	0	0	—	—	—	—	—
94-95—Springfield	AHL	45	10	22	32	98	-1	0	0	—	—	—	—	—
—Winnipeg	NHL	24	2	2	4	21	-3	0	0	—	—	—	—	—
95-96—Springfield	AHL	39	16	19	35	68	...	...	...	—	—	—	—	—
—Winnipeg	NHL	1	0	0	0	0	-1	0	0	—	—	—	—	—
—Buffalo	NHL	22	6	4	10	31	0	2	0	—	—	—	—	—
96-97—Buffalo	NHL	82	15	21	36	71	25	1	0	12	3	3	6	8
97-98—Buffalo	NHL	67	10	20	30	60	9	2	0	15	6	4	10	28
98-99—Buffalo	NHL	76	20	30	50	102	21	4	0	13	0	4	4	28
99-00—Buffalo	NHL	61	11	23	34	35	12	2	0	—	—	—	—	—
—Chicago	NHL	14	2	4	6	12	-1	1	0	—	—	—	—	—
00-01—New York Rangers	NHL	65	9	11	20	61	-10	2	0	—	—	—	—	—
—Hartford	AHL	12	8	7	15	12	...	...	...	—	—	—	—	—
01-02—New York Rangers	NHL	15	3	2	5	12	-3	0	0	—	—	—	—	—
—Hartford	AHL	48	14	30	44	167	13	2	1	—	—	—	—	—
02-03—Boston	NHL	63	2	18	20	71	2	0	0	5	0	0	0	13
03-04—Boston	NHL	33	3	2	5	33	1	0	0	—	—	—	—	—
04-05—Geneva	Switzerland	41	15	21	36	141	...	6	2	—	—	—	—	—
NHL Totals (11 years)		526	84	137	221	509	51	14	0	45	9	11	20	77

GUERIN, BILL — RW — STARS

PERSONAL: Born November 9, 1970, in Worcester, Mass. ... 6-2/210. ... Shoots right. ... Name pronounced GAIR-ihn.

TRANSACTIONS/CAREER NOTES: Selected by New Jersey Devils in first round (first Devils pick, fifth overall) of NHL draft (June 17, 1989). ... Flu (February 1992); missed three games. ... Sore leg (March 19, 1994); missed two games. ... Flu (December 6, 1995); missed two games. ... Missed first 21 games of 1997-98 season in contract dispute. ... Traded by Devils with RW Valeri Zelepukin to Edmonton Oilers for C Jason Arnott and D Bryan Muir (January 4, 1998). ... Sprained left knee (April 12, 1999); missed final two games of regular season and one playoff game. ... Flu (December 9, 1999); missed one game. ... Traded by Oilers to Boston Bruins for C Anson Carter, second-round pick (D Doug Lynch) in 2001 draft and swap of first-round picks in 2001 draft; Oilers selected RW Ales Hemsky; Bruins selected D Shaone Morrisonn) (November 15, 2000). ... Suspended three games for high-sticking incident (October 8, 2001). ... Charley horse (December 13, 2001); missed one game. ... Signed as free agent by Dallas Stars (July 3, 2002). ... Bruised thigh (February 28, 2003); missed 16 games.

STATISTICAL PLATEAUS: Three-goal games: 1996-97 (1), 2003-04 (3). Total: 4.

		REGULAR SEASON								PLAYOFFS				
Season Team	League	GP	G	A	Pts.	PIM	+/-	PP	SH	GP	G	A	Pts.	PIM
85-86—Springfield Jr. B	NEJHL	48	26	19	45	71	...	...	...	—	—	—	—	—
86-87—Springfield Jr. B	NEJHL	32	34	20	54	40	...	...	...	—	—	—	—	—
87-88—Springfield Jr. B	NEJHL	38	31	44	75	146	...	...	...	—	—	—	—	—
88-89—Springfield Jr. B	NEJHL	31	32	37	69	90	...	...	...	—	—	—	—	—
89-90—Boston College	Hockey East	39	14	11	25	64	...	...	...	—	—	—	—	—
90-91—Boston College	Hockey East	38	26	19	45	102	...	...	...	—	—	—	—	—
91-92—U.S. national team	Int'l	46	12	15	27	67	...	...	...	—	—	—	—	—
—Utica	AHL	22	13	10	23	6	...	...	...	4	1	3	4	14
—New Jersey	NHL	5	0	1	1	9	1	0	0	6	3	0	3	4
92-93—New Jersey	NHL	65	14	20	34	63	14	0	0	5	1	1	2	4
—Utica	AHL	18	10	7	17	47	-4	0	0	—	—	—	—	—
93-94—New Jersey	NHL	81	25	19	44	101	14	2	0	17	2	1	3	35
94-95—New Jersey	NHL	48	12	13	25	72	6	4	0	20	3	8	11	30
95-96—New Jersey	NHL	80	23	30	53	116	7	8	0	—	—	—	—	—
96-97—New Jersey	NHL	82	29	18	47	95	-2	7	0	8	2	1	3	18
97-98—New Jersey	NHL	19	5	5	10	13	0	1	0	—	—	—	—	—
—Edmonton	NHL	40	13	16	29	80	1	8	0	12	7	1	8	17
—U.S. Olympic team	Int'l	4	0	3	3	2	2	0	0	—	—	—	—	—
98-99—Edmonton	NHL	80	30	34	64	133	7	13	0	3	0	2	2	2
99-00—Edmonton	NHL	70	24	22	46	123	4	11	0	5	3	2	5	9
00-01—Edmonton	NHL	21	12	10	22	18	11	4	0	—	—	—	—	—
—Boston	NHL	64	28	35	63	122	-4	7	1	—	—	—	—	—
01-02—Boston	NHL	78	41	25	66	91	-1	10	1	6	4	2	6	6
—U.S. Olympic team	Int'l	6	4	0	4	4	...	...	...	—	—	—	—	—
02-03—Dallas	NHL	64	25	25	50	113	5	11	0	4	0	0	0	4
03-04—Dallas	NHL	82	34	35	69	109	14	9	0	5	0	1	1	4
NHL Totals (13 years)		879	315	308	623	1258	77	95	2	91	25	19	44	133

HAGMAN, NIKLAS — LW/RW — PANTHERS

PERSONAL: Born December 5, 1979, in Espoo, Finland. ... 6-0/205. ... Shoots left.

TRANSACTIONS/CAREER NOTES: Selected by Florida Panthers in third round (third Panthers pick, 70th overall) of NHL entry draft (June 26, 1999).

		REGULAR SEASON								PLAYOFFS				
Season Team	**League**	**GP**	**G**	**A**	**Pts.**	**PIM**	**+/-**	**PP**	**SH**	**GP**	**G**	**A**	**Pts.**	**PIM**
96-97—HIFK Helsinki	Finland Jr.	30	13	12	25	30	...	...	...	4	1	1	2	0
97-98—HIFK Helsinki	Finland	8	1	0	1	0	...	...	...	—	—	—	—	—
—HIFK Helsinki	Finland Jr.	26	9	5	14	16	...	...	...	—	—	—	—	—
98-99—HIFK Helsinki	Finland	17	1	1	2	14	...	...	...	—	—	—	—	—
—HIFK Helsinki	Finland Jr.	14	4	9	13	43	...	...	...	—	—	—	—	—
99-00—Espoo	Finland	14	1	1	2	2	...	...	...	—	—	—	—	—
—Karpat Oulu	Finland	41	17	18	35	12	...	...	...	7	4	2	6	...
00-01—Karpat Oulu	Finland	56	28	18	46	32	...	...	...	8	3	1	4	0
01-02—Florida	NHL	78	10	18	28	8	-6	0	1	—	—	—	—	—
—Fin. Olympic team	Int'l	4	1	2	3	0	...	...	...	—	—	—	—	—
02-03—Florida	NHL	80	8	15	23	20	-8	2	0	—	—	—	—	—
03-04—Florida	NHL	75	10	13	23	22	-5	0	1	—	—	—	—	—
04-05—Davos	Switzerland	44	17	22	39	20	...	2	3	15	10	7	17	6
NHL Totals (3 years)		233	28	46	74	50	-19	2	2					

HAHL, RIKU — C/LW — AVALANCHE

PERSONAL: Born November 1, 1980, in Hameenlinna, Finland. ... 6-1/205. ... Shoots left.

TRANSACTIONS/CAREER NOTES: Selected by Colorado Avalanche in sixth round (eighth Avalanche pick, 183rd overall) of NHL draft (June 26, 1999). ... Injured rib (October 8, 2002); missed two games. ... Injured shoulder (October 25, 2003); missed 53 games.

		REGULAR SEASON								PLAYOFFS				
Season Team	**League**	**GP**	**G**	**A**	**Pts.**	**PIM**	**+/-**	**PP**	**SH**	**GP**	**G**	**A**	**Pts.**	**PIM**
97-98—HPK Hameenlinna	Finland Jr.	35	13	6	19	12	...	...	...	—	—	—	—	—
98-99—HPK Hameenlinna	Finland Jr.	6	0	2	2	6	...	...	...	—	—	—	—	—
—HPK Hameenlinna	Finland	28	0	1	1	0	...	...	...	—	—	—	—	—
99-00—HPK Hameenlinna	Finland	50	4	3	7	18	...	...	...	8	0	0	0	2
00-01—HPK Hameenlinna	Finland	55	3	9	12	32	...	...	...	8	0	0	0	2
01-02—Hershey	AHL	52	6	17	23	16	16	1	0	—	—	—	—	—
—Colorado	NHL	22	2	3	5	14	1	0	0	21	1	2	3	0
02-03—Hershey	AHL	28	7	7	14	17	-1	2	0	—	—	—	—	—
—Colorado	NHL	42	3	4	7	12	3	0	0	6	0	2	2	2
03-04—Colorado	NHL	28	0	1	1	12	-7	0	0	7	1	0	1	2
04-05—HPK Hameenlinna	Finland	44	8	13	21	12	12	...	...	10	2	6	8	2
NHL Totals (3 years)		92	5	8	13	38	-3	0	0	34	2	4	6	4

HAINSEY, RON — D — CANADIENS

PERSONAL: Born March 24, 1981, in Bolton, Conn. ... 6-3/211. ... Shoots left.

TRANSACTIONS/CAREER NOTES: Selected by Montreal Canadiens in first round (first Canadiens pick, 13th overall) of NHL entry draft (June 24, 2000).

		REGULAR SEASON								PLAYOFFS				
Season Team	**League**	**GP**	**G**	**A**	**Pts.**	**PIM**	**+/-**	**PP**	**SH**	**GP**	**G**	**A**	**Pts.**	**PIM**
98-99—U.S. National	USHL	48	5	12	17	45	...	...	...	—	—	—	—	—
99-00—Mass.-Lowell	Hockey East	30	3	8	11	20	...	...	...	—	—	—	—	—
00-01—Mass.-Lowell	Hockey East	33	10	26	36	51	...	...	...	—	—	—	—	—
—Quebec	AHL	4	1	0	1	0	...	...	...	1	0	0	0	0
01-02—Quebec	AHL	63	7	24	31	26	16	4	0	3	0	0	0	0
02-03—Montreal	NHL	21	0	0	0	2	-1	0	0	—	—	—	—	—
—Hamilton	AHL	33	2	11	13	26	-2	1	0	23	1	10	11	20
03-04—Hamilton	AHL	54	7	24	31	35	14	3	0	10	0	5	5	6
—Montreal	NHL	11	1	1	2	4	3	0	0	—	—	—	—	—
04-05—Hamilton	AHL	68	9	14	23	45	-3	8	0	4	1	1	2	0
NHL Totals (2 years)		32	1	1	2	6	2	0	0					

HAJT, CHRIS — D — CAPITALS

PERSONAL: Born July 5, 1978, in Saskatoon, Sask. ... 6-3/204. ... Shoots left. ... Son of Bill Hajt, defenseman with Buffalo Sabres (1973-74 through 1986-87). ... Name pronounced HIGHT.

TRANSACTIONS/CAREER NOTES: Selected by Edmonton Oilers in second round (third Oilers pick, 32nd overall) of NHL entry draft (June 22, 1996). ... Signed as free agent by Washington Capitals (July 23, 2002). ... Signed as free agent by Augusta of the ECHL (September 27, 2004).

		REGULAR SEASON								PLAYOFFS				
Season Team	**League**	**GP**	**G**	**A**	**Pts.**	**PIM**	**+/-**	**PP**	**SH**	**GP**	**G**	**A**	**Pts.**	**PIM**
94-95—Guelph	OHL	57	1	7	8	35	...	...	...	14	0	2	2	9
95-96—Guelph	OHL	63	8	27	35	69	...	...	...	16	0	6	6	13
96-97—Guelph	OHL	58	11	15	26	62	34	3	0	18	0	8	8	25
97-98—Guelph	OHL	44	2	21	23	42	4	...	...	12	1	5	6	11
98-99—Hamilton	AHL	64	0	4	4	36	6	0	0	—	—	—	—	—
99-00—Hamilton	AHL	54	0	8	8	30	...	...	...	10	0	2	2	0
00-01—Hamilton	AHL	70	0	10	10	48	...	...	...	—	—	—	—	—

Season Team	League	REGULAR SEASON GP	G	A	Pts.	PIM	+/-	PP	SH	PLAYOFFS GP	G	A	Pts.	PIM
—Edmonton	NHL	1	0	0	0	0	-1	0	0	—	—	—	—	—
01-02—Hamilton	AHL	39	2	3	5	34	3	0	0	15	1	2	3	8
02-03—Portland	AHL	71	11	15	26	61	3	7	0	1	0	0	0	2
03-04—Portland	AHL	66	3	13	16	53	-9	3	0	7	1	2	3	8
—Washington	NHL	5	0	0	0	2	0	0	0	—	—	—	—	—
04-05—Portland	AHL	53	3	6	9	16	5	0	0	—	—	—	—	—
NHL Totals (2 years)		6	0	0	0	2	-1	0	0					

HALE, DAVID — D — DEVILS

PERSONAL: Born June 18, 1981, in Colorado Springs, Colo. ... 6-1/215. ... Shoots left.

TRANSACTIONS/CAREER NOTES: Selected by New Jersey Devils in first round (first Devils pick, 22nd overall) of NHL entry draft (June 24, 2000). ... Injured groin (October 24, 2003); missed four games. ... Flu (December 18, 2003); missed three games. ... Sprained knee (February 5, 2004); missed five games.

Season Team	League	REGULAR SEASON GP	G	A	Pts.	PIM	+/-	PP	SH	PLAYOFFS GP	G	A	Pts.	PIM
98-99—Sioux City	USHL	56	3	15	18	127	...	...	...	—	—	—	—	—
99-00—Sioux City	USHL	54	6	18	24	187	...	...	...	—	—	—	—	—
00-01—Univ. of North Dakota	WCHA	44	4	5	9	79	...	...	...	—	—	—	—	—
01-02—Univ. of North Dakota	WCHA	34	4	5	9	63	...	...	...	—	—	—	—	—
02-03—Univ. of North Dakota	WCHA	26	2	6	8	49	...	...	...	—	—	—	—	—
03-04—New Jersey	NHL	65	0	4	4	72	12	0	0	1	0	0	0	0
04-05—Albany	AHL	30	2	3	5	39	-3	0	0	—	—	—	—	—
NHL Totals (1 year)		65	0	4	4	72	12	0	0	1	0	0	0	0

HALL, ADAM — RW — PREDATORS

PERSONAL: Born August 14, 1980, in Kalamazoo, Mich. ... 6-3/205. ... Shoots right.

TRANSACTIONS/CAREER NOTES: Selected by Nashville Predators in second round (third Predators pick, 52nd overall) of NHL draft (June 26, 1999). ... Flu (February 13, 2004); missed three games.

Season Team	League	REGULAR SEASON GP	G	A	Pts.	PIM	+/-	PP	SH	PLAYOFFS GP	G	A	Pts.	PIM
97-98—U.S. National	NAHL	72	43	23	66	63	...	12	0	—	—	—	—	—
98-99—Michigan State	CCHA	36	16	7	23	74	...	...	...	—	—	—	—	—
99-00—Michigan State	CCHA	39	*25	13	38	36	...	...	...	—	—	—	—	—
00-01—Michigan State	CCHA	42	18	12	30	42	...	...	...	—	—	—	—	—
01-02—Michigan State	CCHA	41	19	15	34	36	...	...	...	—	—	—	—	—
—Milwaukee	AHL	6	2	2	4	4	4	0	0	—	—	—	—	—
—Nashville	NHL	1	0	1	1	0	0	0	0	—	—	—	—	—
02-03—Milwaukee	AHL	1	0	0	0	2	0	0	0	—	—	—	—	—
—Nashville	NHL	79	16	12	28	31	-8	8	0	—	—	—	—	—
03-04—Nashville	NHL	79	13	14	27	37	-8	6	0	6	2	1	3	2
04-05—KalPa Kuopio	Finland	36	23	17	40	28	22	...	...	9	2	3	5	4
NHL Totals (3 years)		159	29	27	56	68	-16	14	0	6	2	1	3	2

HALPERN, JEFF — C — CAPITALS

PERSONAL: Born May 3, 1976, in Potomac, Md. ... 6-0/202. ... Shoots right.

TRANSACTIONS/CAREER NOTES: Signed as free agent by Washington Capitals (March 29, 1999). ... Back spasms (February 19, 2000); missed three games. ... Strained groin (January 8, 2001); missed two games. ... Tore left knee ligament (January 18, 2002); missed remainder of season.

Season Team	League	REGULAR SEASON GP	G	A	Pts.	PIM	+/-	PP	SH	PLAYOFFS GP	G	A	Pts.	PIM
95-96—Princeton	ECAC	29	3	11	14	30	...	...	...	—	—	—	—	—
96-97—Princeton	ECAC	33	7	24	31	35	...	...	...	—	—	—	—	—
97-98—Princeton	ECAC	36	*28	25	*53	46	...	...	...	—	—	—	—	—
98-99—Princeton	ECAC	33	22	22	44	32	...	...	...	—	—	—	—	—
—Portland	AHL	6	2	1	3	4	-1	1	0	—	—	—	—	—
99-00—Washington	NHL	79	18	11	29	39	21	4	4	5	2	1	3	0
00-01—Washington	NHL	80	21	21	42	60	13	2	1	6	2	3	5	17
01-02—Washington	NHL	48	5	14	19	29	-9	0	0	—	—	—	—	—
02-03—Washington	NHL	82	13	21	34	88	6	1	2	6	0	1	1	2
03-04—Washington	NHL	79	19	27	46	56	-21	7	0	—	—	—	—	—
04-05—Kloten	Switzerland	9	7	4	11	6	...	4	0	—	—	—	—	—
—Ajoie	Switz. Div. 2	15	5	12	17	54	...	0	1	—	—	—	—	—
NHL Totals (5 years)		368	76	94	170	272	10	14	7	17	4	5	9	19

HAMEL, DENIS — LW/C — SENATORS

PERSONAL: Born May 10, 1977, in Lachute, Que. ... 6-2/203. ... Shoots left. ... Name pronounced uh-MEHL.

TRANSACTIONS/CAREER NOTES: Selected by St. Louis Blues in sixth round (fifth Blues pick, 153rd overall) of NHL entry draft (July 8, 1995). ... Traded by Blues to Buffalo Sabres for D Charlie Huddy and seventh-round pick (C Daniel Corso) in 1996 entry draft (March 19, 1996). ... Tore knee ligament (January 27, 2001); missed remainder of season. ... Claimed by Washington Capitals in waiver draft (October 3, 2003). ... Traded by Capitals to Senators for future considerations (October 5, 2003).

Season Team	League	GP	G	A	Pts.	PIM	+/-	PP	SH	GP	G	A	Pts.	PIM
		REGULAR SEASON								PLAYOFFS				
94-95—Chicoutimi	QMJHL	66	15	12	27	155	-3	4	0	13	2	0	2	29
95-96—Chicoutimi	QMJHL	65	40	49	89	199	...	...	...	17	10	14	24	64
96-97—Chicoutimi	QMJHL	70	50	50	100	339	...	...	...	20	15	10	25	65
97-98—Rochester	AHL	74	10	15	25	98	-1	4	1	4	1	2	3	0
98-99—Rochester	AHL	74	16	17	33	121	20	2	1	20	3	4	7	10
99-00—Rochester	AHL	76	34	24	58	122	...	...	...	21	6	7	13	49
—Buffalo	NHL	3	1	0	1	0	-1	0	0	—	—	—	—	—
00-01—Buffalo	NHL	41	8	3	11	22	-2	1	1	—	—	—	—	—
01-02—Buffalo	NHL	61	2	6	8	28	-1	0	0	—	—	—	—	—
02-03—Buffalo	NHL	25	2	0	2	17	-4	0	0	—	—	—	—	—
—Rochester	AHL	48	27	20	47	64	15	7	4	3	3	2	5	4
03-04—Ottawa	NHL	5	0	0	0	0	-3	0	0	—	—	—	—	—
—Binghamton	AHL	78	29	38	67	116	2	5	4	2	0	0	0	2
04-05—Binghamton	AHL	80	39	39	78	75	10	17	2	5	1	0	1	4
NHL Totals (5 years)		135	13	9	22	67	-11	1	1					

HAMHUIS, DAN D PREDATORS

PERSONAL: Born December 13, 1982, in Smithers, B.C. ... 6-0/205. ... Shoots left. ... Name pronounced HAM-hoos.

TRANSACTIONS/CAREER NOTES: Selected by Nashville Predators in first round (first Predators pick, 12th overall) of NHL entry draft (June 23, 2001).

Season Team	League	GP	G	A	Pts.	PIM	+/-	PP	SH	GP	G	A	Pts.	PIM
		REGULAR SEASON								PLAYOFFS				
98-99—Prince George	WHL	56	1	3	4	45	...	...	...	7	1	2	3	8
99-00—Prince George	WHL	70	10	23	33	140	...	...	...	13	2	3	5	35
00-01—Prince George	WHL	62	13	46	59	125	...	...	...	6	2	3	5	15
01-02—Prince George	WHL	72	10	50	60	135	...	...	...	7	0	5	5	16
02-03—Milwaukee	AHL	68	6	21	27	81	-3	2	0	6	0	3	3	2
03-04—Nashville	NHL	80	7	19	26	57	-12	2	0	6	0	2	2	6
04-05—Milwaukee	AHL	76	13	38	51	85	10	8	0	7	0	2	2	10
NHL Totals (1 year)		80	7	19	26	57	-12	2	0	6	0	2	2	6

HAMILTON, JEFF C ISLANDERS

PERSONAL: Born September 4, 1977, in Englewood, Ohio. ... 5-10/185. ... Shoots right.

TRANSACTIONS/CAREER NOTES: Signed as free agent by New York Islanders (August 6, 2002).

Season Team	League	GP	G	A	Pts.	PIM	+/-	PP	SH	GP	G	A	Pts.	PIM
		REGULAR SEASON								PLAYOFFS				
96-97—Yale	ECAC	31	10	13	23	26	...	...	...	—	—	—	—	—
97-98—Yale	ECAC	33	27	20	47	28	...	...	...	—	—	—	—	—
98-99—Yale	ECAC	30	20	28	48	51	...	...	...	—	—	—	—	—
99-00—Yale	ECAC	2	0	1	1	0	...	...	...	—	—	—	—	—
00-01—Yale	ECAC	31	23	32	55	39	...	...	...	—	—	—	—	—
01-02—Karpat Oulu	Finland	39	18	15	33	16	...	...	...	3	0	0	0	0
02-03—Bridgeport	AHL	67	22	16	38	35	8	7	0	9	3	3	6	0
03-04—Bridgeport	AHL	67	43	25	68	26	16	20	0	7	4	0	4	4
—New York Islanders	NHL	1	0	0	0	0	0	0	0	—	—	—	—	—
04-05—Hartford	AHL	60	23	30	53	32	15	6	0	6	4	3	7	0
NHL Totals (1 year)		1	0	0	0	0	0	0	0					

HAMRLIK, ROMAN D FLAMES

PERSONAL: Born April 12, 1974, in Ziln, Czechoslovakia. ... 6-2/210. ... Shoots left. ... Brother of Martin Hamrlik, defenseman with Hartford Whalers (1991-92 through 1993-94) and St. Louis Blues (1993-94 and 1994-95) organizations. ... Name pronounced ROH-muhn HAM-uhr-lihk.

TRANSACTIONS/CAREER NOTES: Selected by Tampa Bay Lightning in first round (first Lightning pick, first overall) of NHL draft (June 20, 1992). ... Bruised shoulder (November 3, 1993); missed six games. ... Bruised shoulder (March 1, 1994); missed seven games. ... Back spasms (January 9, 1997); missed two games. ... Traded by Lightning with C Paul Comrie to Edmonton Oilers for C Steve Kelly, D Bryan Marchment and C Jason Bonsignore (December 30, 1997). ... Fractured toe (January 5, 1999); missed six games. ... Bruised finger (December 1, 1999); missed two games. ... Traded by Oilers to New York Islanders for D Eric Brewer, LW Josh Green and second-round pick (LW Brad Winchester) in 2000 draft (June 24, 2000). ... Strained groin (December 21, 2000); missed five games. ... Strained hip flexor (January 31, 2001); missed one game. ... Sprained knee (November 27, 2001); missed one game. ... Injured right knee (December 29, 2001); missed 11 games. ... Injured shoulder (December 13, 2002); missed six games. ... Injured hip (March 6, 2003); missed two games. ... Sinus ailment (April 6, 2003); missed one game. ... Flu (December 23, 2003); missed one game. ... Signed as free agent by Calgary Flames (Aug. 14, 2005).

Season Team	League	GP	G	A	Pts.	PIM	+/-	PP	SH	GP	G	A	Pts.	PIM
		REGULAR SEASON								PLAYOFFS				
90-91—TJ Zlin	Czech.	14	2	2	4	18	...	...	...	—	—	—	—	—
91-92—ZPS Zlin	Czech.	34	5	5	10	34	...	...	...	—	—	—	—	—
92-93—Tampa Bay	NHL	67	6	15	21	71	-21	1	0	—	—	—	—	—
—Atlanta	IHL	2	1	1	2	2	2	0	0	—	—	—	—	—
93-94—Tampa Bay	NHL	64	3	18	21	135	-14	0	0	—	—	—	—	—
94-95—ZPS Zlin	Czech Rep.	2	1	0	1	10	...	...	...	—	—	—	—	—
—Tampa Bay	NHL	48	12	11	23	86	-18	7	1	—	—	—	—	—
95-96—Tampa Bay	NHL	82	16	49	65	103	-24	12	0	5	0	1	1	4
96-97—Tampa Bay	NHL	79	12	28	40	57	-29	6	0	—	—	—	—	—

Season Team	League	GP	G	A	Pts.	PIM	+/-	PP	SH	GP	G	A	Pts.	PIM
		REGULAR SEASON								PLAYOFFS				
97-98—Tampa Bay	NHL	37	3	12	15	22	-18	1	0	—	—	—	—	—
—Edmonton	NHL	41	6	20	26	48	3	4	1	12	0	6	6	12
—Czech Rep. Oly. team	Int'l	6	1	0	1	2	4	0	0	—	—	—	—	—
98-99—Edmonton	NHL	75	8	24	32	70	9	3	0	3	0	0	0	2
99-00—Edmonton	NHL	80	8	37	45	68	1	5	0	5	0	1	1	4
00-01—New York Islanders	NHL	76	16	30	46	92	-20	5	1	—	—	—	—	—
01-02—New York Islanders	NHL	70	11	26	37	78	7	4	1	7	1	6	7	6
—Czech Rep. Oly. team	Int'l	4	0	1	1	2	...	...	...	—	—	—	—	—
02-03—New York Islanders	NHL	73	9	32	41	87	21	3	0	5	0	2	2	2
03-04—New York Islanders	NHL	81	7	22	29	68	2	2	0	5	0	1	1	2
04-05—Zlin	Czech Rep.	45	2	14	16	70	16	...	...	19	1	4	5	28
NHL Totals (12 years)		873	117	324	441	985	-101	53	4	42	1	17	18	32

HANDZUS, MICHAL — C — FLYERS

PERSONAL: Born March 11, 1977, in Banska Bystrica, Czechoslovakia. ... 6-5/217. ... Shoots left. ... Name pronounced han-ZOOZ.
TRANSACTIONS/CAREER NOTES: Selected by St. Louis Blues in fourth round (third Blues pick, 101st overall) of NHL draft (July 8, 1995). ... Bruised shoulder (February 26, 1999); missed five games. ... Bruised shoulder (March 25, 1999); missed final 11 games of regular season and two playoffs games. ... Injured groin (October 1, 2000); missed first five games of season. ... Strained abdominal muscle (January 11, 2001) and had surgery; missed 33 games. ... Traded by Blues with RW Ladislav Nagy, C Jeff Taffe and first-round pick (LW Ben Eager) in 2002 draft to Phoenix Coyotes for LW Keith Tkachuk (March 13, 2001). ... Strained groin (January 17, 2002); missed three games. ... Traded by Coyotes with G Robert Esche to Philadelphia Flyers for G Brian Boucher and third-round pick (D Joe Callahan) in 2002 draft (June 12, 2002).
STATISTICAL PLATEAUS: Three-goal games: 2000-01 (1).

Season Team	League	GP	G	A	Pts.	PIM	+/-	PP	SH	GP	G	A	Pts.	PIM
		REGULAR SEASON								PLAYOFFS				
93-94—IS Banska Byst.	Slovakia Jrs.	40	23	36	59	...	...	...	...	—	—	—	—	—
94-95—IS Banska Bystrica	Slov. Div.	22	15	14	29	10	...	...	...	—	—	—	—	—
95-96—IS Banska Bystrica	Slov. Div.	19	3	1	4	8	...	...	...	—	—	—	—	—
96-97—Poprad	Slovakia	44	15	18	33	...	...	...	...	—	—	—	—	—
97-98—Worcester	AHL	69	27	36	63	54	-8	6	1	11	2	6	8	10
98-99—St. Louis	NHL	66	4	12	16	30	-9	0	0	11	0	2	2	8
99-00—St. Louis	NHL	81	25	28	53	44	19	3	4	7	0	3	3	6
00-01—St. Louis	NHL	36	10	14	24	12	11	3	2	—	—	—	—	—
—Phoenix	NHL	10	4	4	8	21	5	0	1	—	—	—	—	—
01-02—Phoenix	NHL	79	15	30	45	34	-8	3	1	5	0	0	0	2
—Slovakian Oly. team	Int'l	2	1	0	1	6	...	...	...	—	—	—	—	—
02-03—Philadelphia	NHL	82	23	21	44	46	13	1	1	13	2	6	8	6
03-04—Philadelphia	NHL	82	20	38	58	82	18	7	1	18	5	5	10	10
04-05—Zvolen	Slovakia	34	14	25	39	34	33	...	...	17	5	10	15	6
NHL Totals (6 years)		436	101	147	248	269	49	17	10	54	7	16	23	32

HANKINSON, CASEY — LW — MIGHTY DUCKS

PERSONAL: Born May 8, 1976, in Edina, Minn. ... 6-1/196. ... Shoots left. ... Brother of Ben Hankinson, RW with New Jersey Devils (1992-95) and Tampa Bay Lightning (1994-95); and brother of Peter Hankinson, C with Winnipeg Jets organization (1989-92).
TRANSACTIONS/CAREER NOTES: Selected by Chicago Blackhawks in eighth round (ninth Blackhawks pick, 201st overall) of NHL entry draft (July 8, 1995). ... Signed as free agent by Anaheim Mighty Ducks (July 25, 2003).

Season Team	League	GP	G	A	Pts.	PIM	+/-	PP	SH	GP	G	A	Pts.	PIM
		REGULAR SEASON								PLAYOFFS				
92-93—Edina High School	Minn. H.S.	25	20	26	46	...	...	...	...	—	—	—	—	—
93-94—Edina High School	Minn. H.S.	24	21	20	41	50	...	...	...	—	—	—	—	—
94-95—Minnesota	WCHA	33	7	1	8	86	...	2	0	—	—	—	—	—
95-96—Minnesota	WCHA	39	16	19	35	101	...	...	...	—	—	—	—	—
96-97—Minnesota	WCHA	42	17	24	41	79	8	7	0	—	—	—	—	—
97-98—Minnesota	WCHA	35	10	12	22	81	...	...	...	—	—	—	—	—
98-99—Portland	AHL	72	10	13	23	106	-6	2	0	—	—	—	—	—
99-00—Cleveland	IHL	82	7	22	29	140	...	...	...	2	0	0	0	2
00-01—Norfolk	AHL	69	30	21	51	74	...	...	...	9	5	4	9	2
—Chicago	NHL	11	0	1	1	9	-3	0	0	—	—	—	—	—
01-02—Norfolk	AHL	72	19	30	49	85	1	6	2	4	1	2	3	0
—Chicago	NHL	3	0	0	0	0	-2	0	0	—	—	—	—	—
02-03—Norfolk	AHL	78	27	28	55	59	-11	10	2	9	4	3	7	10
03-04—Anaheim	NHL	4	0	0	0	4	0	0	0	—	—	—	—	—
—Cincinnati	AHL	78	15	24	39	123	-10	4	2	9	4	1	5	10
04-05—La Chaux-de-Fonds	Switzerland	4	2	1	3	6	...	0	0	—	—	—	—	—
—Cincinnati	AHL	54	4	7	11	92	-2	0	0	12	2	4	6	36
NHL Totals (3 years)		18	0	1	1	13	-5	0	0					

HANNAN, SCOTT — D — SHARKS

PERSONAL: Born January 23, 1979, in Richmond, B.C. ... 6-1/220. ... Shoots left.
TRANSACTIONS/CAREER NOTES: Selected by San Jose Sharks in first round (second Sharks pick, 23rd overall) of NHL entry draft (June 21, 1997). ... Injured ankle (October 24, 2000); missed three games. ... Injured knee (March 3, 2002); missed six games. ... Had the flu (February 14, 2003); missed two games.

Season Team	League	GP	G	A	Pts.	PIM	+/-	PP	SH	GP	G	A	Pts.	PIM
		REGULAR SEASON								PLAYOFFS				
94-95—Tacoma	WHL	2	0	0	0	0	...	...	...	—	—	—	—	—
95-96—Kelowna	WHL	69	4	5	9	76	...	...	...	6	0	1	1	4
96-97—Kelowna	WHL	70	17	26	43	101	...	...	...	6	0	0	0	8
97-98—Kelowna	WHL	47	10	30	40	70	...	...	...	—	—	—	—	—
98-99—San Jose	NHL	5	0	2	2	6	0	0	0	—	—	—	—	—
—Kelowna	WHL	47	15	30	45	92	-7	9	0	6	1	2	3	14
—Kentucky	AHL	2	0	0	0	2	0	0	0	12	0	2	2	10
99-00—Kentucky	AHL	41	5	12	17	40	...	...	...	—	—	—	—	—
—San Jose	NHL	30	1	2	3	10	7	0	0	1	0	1	1	0
00-01—San Jose	NHL	75	3	14	17	51	10	0	0	6	0	1	1	6
01-02—San Jose	NHL	75	2	12	14	57	10	0	0	12	0	2	2	12
02-03—San Jose	NHL	81	3	19	22	61	0	1	0	—	—	—	—	—
03-04—San Jose	NHL	82	6	15	21	48	10	0	0	17	1	5	6	22
NHL Totals (6 years)		348	15	64	79	233	37	1	0	36	1	9	10	40

HANZAL, MARTIN — COYOTES

PERSONAL: Born February 20, 1987, in Tabor, Czech.

TRANSACTIONS/CAREER NOTES: Selected by Phoenix Coyotes in 1st round (Coyotes 1st pick, 17th overall) of entry draft (July 30, 2005).

Season Team	League	GP	G	A	Pts.	PIM	+/-	PP	SH	GP	G	A	Pts.	PIM
		REGULAR SEASON								PLAYOFFS				
03-04—Budejovice	Czech Rep.	53	15	7	22	32	...	...	...	—	—	—	—	—
04-05—Budejovice	Czech Rep.	37	22	22	44	80	...	...	...	—	—	—	—	—

HARTIGAN, MARK — C — BLUE JACKETS

PERSONAL: Born October 15, 1977, in Fort St. John, B.C. ... 6-0/205.

TRANSACTIONS/CAREER NOTES: Signed as free agent by Atlanta Thrashers (March 27, 2002). ... Tore hamstring (April 3, 2002); missed remainder of season. ... Signed as free agent by Columbus Blue Jackets (July 15, 2003).

Season Team	League	GP	G	A	Pts.	PIM	+/-	PP	SH	GP	G	A	Pts.	PIM
		REGULAR SEASON								PLAYOFFS				
99-00—St. Cloud State	WCHA	37	22	20	42	24	...	...	...	—	—	—	—	—
00-01—St. Cloud State	WCHA	40	27	21	48	20	...	...	...	—	—	—	—	—
01-02—St. Cloud State	WCHA	42	*37	38	75	42	...	...	...	—	—	—	—	—
—Atlanta	NHL	2	0	0	0	2	-2	0	0	—	—	—	—	—
02-03—Atlanta	NHL	23	5	2	7	6	-8	1	0	—	—	—	—	—
—Chicago	AHL	55	15	31	46	43	6	5	0	9	1	2	3	10
03-04—Syracuse	AHL	69	23	23	46	81	-5	4	0	7	1	4	5	8
—Columbus	NHL	9	1	3	4	6	-2	1	0	—	—	—	—	—
04-05—Syracuse	AHL	69	31	28	59	105	2	15	0	—	—	—	—	—
NHL Totals (3 years)		34	6	5	11	14	-12	2	0					

HARTNELL, SCOTT — LW/RW — PREDATORS

PERSONAL: Born April 18, 1982, in Regina, Sask. ... 6-2/205. ... Shoots left. ... Cousin of Mark Deyell, C, Toronto Maple Leafs organization (1996-99).

TRANSACTIONS/CAREER NOTES: Selected by Nashville Predators in first round (first Predators pick, sixth overall) of NHL draft (June 24, 2000). ... Had concussion (November 26, 2000); missed six games. ... Bruised left eye (October 27, 2001); missed five games. ... Had concussion (April 9, 2002); missed remainder of season. ... Injured right ankle (December 17, 2003); missed 13 games. ... Had concussion (February 21, 2004); missed 10 games.

Season Team	League	GP	G	A	Pts.	PIM	+/-	PP	SH	GP	G	A	Pts.	PIM
		REGULAR SEASON								PLAYOFFS				
97-98—Lloydminster	Jr. A	56	9	16	25	82	...	...	...	4	2	1	3	8
—Prince Albert	WHL	1	0	1	1	2	...	...	...	—	—	—	—	—
98-99—Prince Albert	WHL	65	10	34	44	104	...	...	...	14	0	5	5	22
99-00—Prince Albert	WHL	62	27	55	82	124	...	...	...	6	3	2	5	6
00-01—Nashville	NHL	75	2	14	16	48	-8	0	0	—	—	—	—	—
01-02—Nashville	NHL	75	14	27	41	111	5	3	0	—	—	—	—	—
02-03—Nashville	NHL	82	12	22	34	101	-3	2	0	—	—	—	—	—
03-04—Nashville	NHL	59	18	15	33	87	-5	5	0	6	1	2	3	2
04-05—Valerengen	Norway	28	17	12	29	103	26	...	...	11	12	7	19	24
NHL Totals (4 years)		291	46	78	124	347	-11	10	0	6	1	2	3	2

HARVEY, TODD — RW/C — SHARKS

PERSONAL: Born February 17, 1975, in Hamilton, Ont. ... 6-0/210. ... Shoots right.

TRANSACTIONS/CAREER NOTES: Selected by Dallas Stars in first round (first Stars pick, ninth overall) of NHL draft (June 26, 1993). ... Strained back (March 13, 1995); missed one game. ... Sprained knee (October 30, 1995); missed two games. ... Strained groin (November 3, 1996); missed one game. ... Sprained knee (November 19, 1996); missed five games. ... Flu (December 29, 1996); missed one game. ... Suspended two games and fined $1,000 for elbowing incident (February 2, 1997). ... Bruised hand (April 4, 1997); missed one game. ... Suffered concussion (November 16, 1997); missed one game. ... Strained hip flexor (December 20, 1997); missed one game. ... Sprained knee (January 7, 1998); missed five games. ... Injured hand (February 4, 1998); missed one game. ... Strained lower back (March 13, 1998); missed one game. ... Right knee surgery (March 22, 1998); missed 12 games. ... Traded by Stars with LW Bob Errey and fourth-round pick (LW Boyd Kane) in 1998 draft to New York Rangers for RW Mike Keane, C Brian Skrudland and sixth-round pick (RW Pavel Patera) in 1998

draft (March 24, 1998). ... Strained hip flexor (October 9, 1998); missed first two games of season. ... Suspended one game and fined $1,000 for roughing incident (December 13, 1998). ... Bruised right thumb (December 11, 1998); missed two games. ... Sprained knee (January 13, 1999); missed 10 games. ... Fractured thumb (February 17, 1999); missed final 27 games of season. ... Sprained knee (November 18, 1999); missed three games. ... Traded by Rangers with fourth-round pick (G Dimitri Patzold) in 2001 draft to San Jose Sharks for RW Radek Dvorak (December 30, 1999). ... Suffered concussion and whiplash (January 1, 2001); missed 10 games. ... Injured knee (November 27, 2001); missed three games. ... Injured shoulder (March 10, 2002); missed 10 games. ... Injured shoulder (November 23, 2002); missed four games.
STATISTICAL PLATEAUS: Three-goal games: 1994-95 (1), 2000-01 (1). Total: 2.

		REGULAR SEASON								PLAYOFFS				
Season Team	League	GP	G	A	Pts.	PIM	+/-	PP	SH	GP	G	A	Pts.	PIM
89-90—Cambridge Jr. B	OHA	41	35	27	62	213	...	...	...	—	—	—	—	—
90-91—Cambridge Jr. B	OHA	35	32	39	71	174	...	...	...	—	—	—	—	—
91-92—Det. Jr. Red Wings	OHL	58	21	43	64	141	...	...	...	7	3	5	8	32
92-93—Det. Jr. Red Wings	OHL	55	50	50	100	83	...	...	...	15	9	12	21	39
93-94—Det. Jr. Red Wings	OHL	49	34	51	85	75	...	13	2	17	10	12	22	26
94-95—Det. Jr. Red Wings	OHL	11	8	14	22	12	...	3	0	—	—	—	—	—
—Dallas	NHL	40	11	9	20	67	-3	2	0	5	0	0	0	8
95-96—Dallas	NHL	69	9	20	29	136	-13	3	0	—	—	—	—	—
—Michigan	IHL	5	1	3	4	8	...	...	...	—	—	—	—	—
96-97—Dallas	NHL	71	9	22	31	142	19	1	0	7	0	1	1	10
97-98—Dallas	NHL	59	9	10	19	104	5	0	0	—	—	—	—	—
98-99—New York Rangers	NHL	37	11	17	28	72	-1	6	0	—	—	—	—	—
99-00—New York Rangers	NHL	31	3	3	6	62	-9	0	0	—	—	—	—	—
—San Jose	NHL	40	8	4	12	78	-2	2	0	12	1	0	1	8
00-01—San Jose	NHL	69	10	11	21	72	6	1	0	6	0	0	0	8
01-02—San Jose	NHL	69	9	13	22	73	16	0	0	12	0	2	2	12
02-03—San Jose	NHL	76	3	16	19	74	5	0	0	—	—	—	—	—
03-04—San Jose	NHL	47	4	5	9	38	3	0	0	16	1	2	3	2
—Cleveland	AHL	13	6	1	7	29	2	1	0	—	—	—	—	—
NHL Totals (10 years)		608	86	130	216	918	26	15	0	58	2	5	7	48

HASEK, DOMINIK G SENATORS

PERSONAL: Born January 29, 1965, in Pardubice, Czechoslovakia. ... 5-11/180. ... Catches left. ... Name pronounced HA-shehk.
TRANSACTIONS/CAREER NOTES: Selected by Chicago Blackhawks in 10th round (11th Blackhawks pick, 199th overall) of NHL draft (June 8, 1983). ... Traded by Blackhawks to Buffalo Sabres for G Stephane Beauregard and fourth-round pick (LW Eric Daze) in 1993 entry draft (August 7, 1992). ... Injured groin (November 25, 1992); missed three games. ... Strained abdominal muscle (January 6, 1993); missed six games. ... Strained rotator cuff (March 16, 1995); missed three games. ... Injured abdominal muscle (December 15, 1995); missed 10 games. ... Sprained left knee (April 6, 1996); missed last two games of season. ... Fractured rib (March 19, 1997); missed five games. ... Sprained knee (April 21, 1997); missed six playoff games. ... Suspended three playoff games and fined $10,000 for assaulting a journalist (May 1, 1997). ... Ear infection (April 15, 1998); missed one game. ... Strained groin (February 17, 1999); missed 12 games. ... Strained back (March 23, 1999); missed one game. ... Tore groin muscle (October 29, 1999); missed 40 games. ... Injured knee (October 5, 2000); missed one game. ... Traded by Sabres to Detroit Red Wings for LW Slava Kozlov, first-round pick (traded to Columbus; traded to Atlanta; Thrashers selected Jim Slater) in 2002 draft and future considerations (July 1, 2001). ... Announced retirement (June 25, 2002). ... Announced return from retirement (July 8, 2003). ... Injured groin (October 30, 2003); missed five games. ... Reinjured groin (November 19, 2003); missed seven games. ... Reinjured groin (December 10, 2003); missed remainer of season and playoffs. ... Signed as free agent by Ottawa Senators (July 6, 2004).

		REGULAR SEASON									PLAYOFFS							
Season Team	League	GP	Min.	W	L	T	GA	SO	GAA	SV%	GP	Min.	W	L	GA	SO	GAA	SV%
81-82—Pardubice	Czech Rep.	12	661	...	...	...	34	...	3.09	...	—	—	—	—	—	—	—	—
82-83—Pardubice	Czech Rep.	42	2358	...	...	...	105	...	2.67	...	—	—	—	—	—	—	—	—
83-84—Pardubice	Czech Rep.	40	2304	...	...	...	108	...	2.81	...	—	—	—	—	—	—	—	—
84-85—Pardubice	Czech Rep.	42	2419	...	...	...	131	...	3.25	...	—	—	—	—	—	—	—	—
85-86—Pardubice	Czech Rep.	45	2689	...	...	...	138	...	3.08	...	—	—	—	—	—	—	—	—
86-87—Pardubice	Czech Rep.	23	2515	...	...	...	103	...	2.46	...	—	—	—	—	—	—	—	—
87-88—Pardubice	Czech Rep.	31	1863	...	...	...	93	...	3.00	...	—	—	—	—	—	—	—	—
—Czech. Olympic Team	Int'l	5	217	3	2	0	18	1	4.98	.833	—	—	—	—	—	—	—	—
88-89—Pardubice	Czech Rep.	42	2507	...	...	...	114	...	2.73	...	—	—	—	—	—	—	—	—
89-90—Dukla Jihlava	Czech.	40	2251	...	...	...	80	...	2.13	...	—	—	—	—	—	—	—	—
90-91—Chicago	NHL	5	195	3	0	1	8	0	2.46	.914	3	69	0	0	3	0	2.61	.923
—Indianapolis	IHL	33	1903	20	11	4	80	*5	*2.52	...	1	60	1	0	3	0	3.00	...
91-92—Indianapolis	IHL	20	1162	7	10	3	69	1	3.56	...	—	—	—	—	—	—	—	—
—Chicago	NHL	20	1014	10	4	1	44	1	2.60	.893	3	158	0	2	8	0	3.04	.886
92-93—Buffalo	NHL	28	1429	11	10	4	75	0	3.15	.896	1	45	1	0	1	0	1.33	.958
93-94—Buffalo	NHL	58	3358	30	20	6	109	7	*1.95	*.930	7	484	3	4	13	2	*1.61	*.950
94-95—HC Pardubice	Czech Rep.	2	125	...	...	...	6	...	2.88	...	—	—	—	—	—	—	—	—
—Buffalo	NHL	41	2416	19	14	7	85	5	*2.11	*.930	5	309	1	4	18	0	3.50	.863
95-96—Buffalo	NHL	59	3417	22	30	6	161	2	2.83	*.920	—	—	—	—	—	—	—	—
96-97—Buffalo	NHL	67	4037	37	20	10	153	5	2.27	*.930	3	153	1	1	5	0	1.96	.926
97-98—Buffalo	NHL	*72	*4220	33	23	13	147	*13	2.09	.932	15	948	10	5	32	1	2.03	.938
—Czech Rep. Oly. team	Int'l	6	369	5	1	0	6	2	0.98	.961	—	—	—	—	—	—	—	—
98-99—Buffalo	NHL	64	3817	30	18	14	119	9	1.87	*.937	19	1217	13	6	36	2	1.77	.939
99-00—Buffalo	NHL	35	2066	15	11	6	76	3	2.21	.919	5	301	1	4	12	0	2.39	.918
00-01—Buffalo	NHL	67	3904	37	24	4	137	*11	2.11	.921	13	833	7	6	29	1	2.09	.916
01-02—Detroit	NHL	65	3872	*41	15	8	140	5	2.17	.915	*23	*1455	*16	7	45	*6	1.86	.920
—Czech Rep. Oly. team	Int'l	4	239	1	2	1	8	0	2.01	.924	—	—	—	—	—	—	—	—
02-03—Detroit	NHL	Did not play																
03-04—Detroit	NHL	14	817	8	3	2	30	2	2.20	.907	—	—	—	—	—	—	—	—
NHL Totals (14 years)		595	34562	296	192	82	1284	63	2.23	.924	97	5972	53	39	202	12	2.03	.927

H

HATCHER, DERIAN — D — FLYERS

PERSONAL: Born June 4, 1972, in Sterling Heights, Mich. ... 6-5/235. ... Shoots left. ... Brother of Kevin Hatcher, D with five NHL teams (1984-01).

TRANSACTIONS/CAREER NOTES: Selected by Minnesota North Stars in 1st round (1st North Stars pick, 8th overall) of NHL draft (June 16, 1990). ... Suspended 10 games (December 1991). ... Fractured ankle in off ice incident (January 19, 1992); missed 21 games. ... Sprained knee (January 6, 1993); missed 14 games. ... Suspended one game for game misconduct penalties (March 9, 1993). ... North Stars franchise moved from Minnesota to Dallas and renamed Stars for 1993-94 season. ... Sprained ankle (February 2, 1995); missed one game. ... Staph infection on finger (February 14, 1995); missed four games. ... Injured right knee (May 1, 1995); missed playoffs. ... Injured shoulder (November 14, 1995); missed three games. ... Strained knee (December 8, 1996); missed 14 games. ... Knee surgery (March 19, 1997); missed five games. ... Injured knee (March 8, 1998); missed seven games. ... Suspended four preseason games and fined $1,000 for injuring another player (September 23, 1998). ... Suspended seven games for illegal check (April 17, 1999); missed final two games of season and first five playoff games. ... Lacerated calf (December 17, 1999); missed 24 games. ... Strained Achilles' tendon (March 8, 2000); missed one game. ... Suspended two games for elbowing incident (March 27, 2001). ... Strained hamstring (November 21, 2001); missed two games. ... Suspended one playoff game for receiving second game misconduct during the playoffs (April 12, 2003). ... Signed as free agent by Detroit Red Wings (July 2, 2003). ... Torn knee ligament (October 16, 2003); missed 64 games. ... Bruised shoulder (March 16, 2004); missed three games. ... Suspended three games (to be served in 2005-06 season) for elbowing incident (May 11, 2004). ... Placed on waivers by Red Wings (July 25, 2005). ... Signed as free agent by the Philadelphia Flyers (Aug. 2, 2005).

		REGULAR SEASON								PLAYOFFS				
Season Team	League	GP	G	A	Pts.	PIM	+/-	PP	SH	GP	G	A	Pts.	PIM
88-89—Detroit G.P.D.	MNHL	51	19	35	54	100	...	...	...	—	—	—	—	—
89-90—North Bay	OHL	64	14	38	52	81	...	...	...	5	2	3	5	8
90-91—North Bay	OHL	64	13	50	63	163	...	...	...	10	2	10	12	28
91-92—Minnesota	NHL	43	8	4	12	88	7	0	0	5	0	2	2	8
92-93—Minnesota	NHL	67	4	15	19	178	-27	0	0	—	—	—	—	—
—Kalamazoo	IHL	2	1	2	3	21	-3	0	0	—	—	—	—	—
93-94—Dallas	NHL	83	12	19	31	211	19	2	1	9	0	2	2	14
94-95—Dallas	NHL	43	5	11	16	105	3	2	0	—	—	—	—	—
95-96—Dallas	NHL	79	8	23	31	129	-12	2	0	—	—	—	—	—
96-97—Dallas	NHL	63	3	19	22	97	8	0	0	7	0	2	2	20
97-98—Dallas	NHL	70	6	25	31	132	9	3	0	17	3	3	6	39
—U.S. Olympic team	Int'l	4	0	0	0	0	-1	0	0	—	—	—	—	—
98-99—Dallas	NHL	80	9	21	30	102	21	3	0	18	1	6	7	24
99-00—Dallas	NHL	57	2	22	24	68	6	0	0	23	1	3	4	29
00-01—Dallas	NHL	80	2	21	23	77	5	1	0	10	0	1	1	16
01-02—Dallas	NHL	80	4	21	25	87	12	1	0	—	—	—	—	—
02-03—Dallas	NHL	82	8	22	30	106	37	1	1	11	1	2	3	33
03-04—Detroit	NHL	15	0	4	4	8	4	0	0	12	0	1	1	15
04-05—Motor City	UHL	24	5	12	17	27	9	4	0	—	—	—	—	—
NHL Totals (13 years)		842	71	227	298	1388	92	15	2	112	6	22	28	198

HAVELID, NICLAS — D — THRASHERS

PERSONAL: Born April 12, 1973, in Stockholm, Sweden. ... 6-0/200. ... Shoots left.

TRANSACTIONS/CAREER NOTES: Selected by Anaheim Mighty Ducks in third round (second Mighty Ducks pick, 83rd overall) of NHL draft (June 26, 1999). ... Fractured finger (January 15, 2000); missed 23 games. ... Tore knee ligament (January 15, 2001); missed remainder of season. ... Traded by Mighty Ducks to Atlanta Thrashers for D Kurtis Foster (June 26, 2004).

		REGULAR SEASON								PLAYOFFS				
Season Team	League	GP	G	A	Pts.	PIM	+/-	PP	SH	GP	G	A	Pts.	PIM
91-92—AIK Solna	Sweden	10	0	0	0	2	...	...	...	—	—	—	—	—
92-93—AIK Solna	Sweden	22	1	0	1	16	...	...	...	—	—	—	—	—
93-94—AIK Solna	Sweden	Statistics unavailable												
94-95—AIK Solna	Sweden	40	3	7	10	38	...	...	...	—	—	—	—	—
95-96—AIK Solna	Sweden	40	5	6	11	30	...	...	...	—	—	—	—	—
96-97—AIK Solna	Sweden	49	3	6	9	42	...	...	...	7	1	2	3	8
97-98—AIK Solna	Sweden	43	8	4	12	42	...	...	...	—	—	—	—	—
98-99—Malmo	Sweden	50	10	12	22	42	...	...	...	8	0	4	4	10
99-00—Anaheim	NHL	50	2	7	9	20	0	0	0	—	—	—	—	—
—Cincinnati	AHL	2	0	0	0	0	...	...	...	—	—	—	—	—
00-01—Anaheim	NHL	47	4	10	14	34	-6	2	0	—	—	—	—	—
01-02—Anaheim	NHL	52	1	2	3	40	-13	0	0	—	—	—	—	—
02-03—Anaheim	NHL	82	11	22	33	30	5	4	0	21	0	4	4	2
03-04—Anaheim	NHL	79	6	20	26	28	-28	5	0	—	—	—	—	—
04-05—Sodertalje	Sweden Dv. 2	46	2	2	4	60	-5	1	0	10	1	1	2	18
NHL Totals (5 years)		310	24	61	85	152	-42	11	0	21	0	4	4	2

HAVLAT, MARTIN — RW/LW — SENATORS

PERSONAL: Born April 19, 1981, in Mlada Boleslav, Czechoslovakia. ... 6-1/194. ... Shoots left.

TRANSACTIONS/CAREER NOTES: Selected by Ottawa Senators in first round (first Senators pick, 26th pick overall) of NHL draft (June 26, 1999). ... Injured shoulder (November 23, 2000); missed eight games. ... Strained groin (April 6, 2001); missed final game of regular season. ... Injured groin (January 30, 2002); missed one game. ... Strained groin (March 17, 2002); missed two games. ... Reinjured groin (March 28, 2002); missed final seven games of regular season. ... Injured groin (October 29, 2002); missed six games. ... Bruised right elbow (January 20, 2003); missed two games. ... Injured groin (February 19, 2003); missed four games. ... Injured groin (March 4, 2003); missed two games. ... Missed first two games of 2003-04 season in contract dispute. ... Injured hamstring (November 22, 2003); missed 3 games. ... Suspended for two games for kicking incident (January 1, 2004). ... Injured groin (January 29, 2004); missed two games. ... Suspended two games for high-sticking incident (February 27, 2004).

STATISTICAL PLATEAUS: Three-goal games: 2000-01 (1), 2001-02 (1), 2002-03 (1), 2003-04 (1). Total: 4.

Season Team	League	GP	G	A	Pts.	PIM	+/-	PP	SH	GP	G	A	Pts.	PIM
		REGULAR SEASON								PLAYOFFS				
96-97—Ytong Brno	Czech. Jrs.	34	43	27	70	...	...	...	...	—	—	—	—	—
97-98—Ytong Brno	Czech. Jrs.	32	38	29	67	...	...	...	...	—	—	—	—	—
98-99—Zelezarny Trinec	Czech. Jrs.	31	28	23	51	...	...	...	...	—	—	—	—	—
—Zelezarny Trinec	Czech Rep.	24	2	3	5	4	...	...	...	8	0	0	0	...
99-00—Zelezarny Trinec	Czech Rep.	46	13	29	42	42	...	...	...	4	0	2	2	8
00-01—Ottawa	NHL	73	19	23	42	20	8	7	0	4	0	0	0	2
01-02—Ottawa	NHL	72	22	28	50	66	-7	9	0	12	2	5	7	14
—Czech Rep. Oly. team	Int'l	4	3	1	4	27	...	...	...	—	—	—	—	—
02-03—Ottawa	NHL	67	24	35	59	30	20	9	0	18	5	6	11	14
03-04—Ottawa	NHL	68	31	37	68	46	12	13	0	7	0	3	3	2
04-05—HC Znojemsti Orli	Czech Rep.	12	10	4	14	16	5	...	...	—	—	—	—	—
—Dynamo Moscow	Russian	10	2	0	2	14	1	...	...	—	—	—	—	—
—Sparta Praha	Czech Rep.	9	5	4	9	37	4	...	...	5	0	0	0	20
NHL Totals (4 years)		280	96	123	219	162	33	38	0	41	7	14	21	32

HEALEY, PAUL RW

PERSONAL: Born March 20, 1975, in Edmonton. ... 6-2/207. ... Shoots right.

TRANSACTIONS/CAREER NOTES: Selected by Philadelphia Flyers in eighth round (seventh Flyers pick, 192nd overall) of NHL entry draft (June 26, 1993). ... Traded by Flyers to Nashville Predators for RW Matt Henderson (September 27, 1999). ... Signed as free agent by Edmonton Oilers (August 31, 2000). ... Signed as free agent by Toronto Maple Leafs (July 24, 2001). ... Signed as free agent by New York Rangers (July 28, 2003). ... Injured ribs (November 6, 2003); missed four games. ... Traded by Rangers to Atlanta Thrashers for D Jeff Paul (March 9, 2004).

Season Team	League	GP	G	A	Pts.	PIM	+/-	PP	SH	GP	G	A	Pts.	PIM
		REGULAR SEASON								PLAYOFFS				
92-93—Prince Albert	WHL	72	12	20	32	66	...	...	...	—	—	—	—	—
93-94—Prince Albert	WHL	63	23	26	49	70	...	...	...	—	—	—	—	—
94-95—Prince Albert	WHL	71	43	50	93	67	25	6	8	12	3	4	7	2
95-96—Hershey	AHL	61	7	15	22	35	...	...	...	—	—	—	—	—
96-97—Philadelphia	AHL	64	21	19	40	56	9	5	1	10	4	1	5	10
—Philadelphia	NHL	2	0	0	0	0	0	0	0	—	—	—	—	—
97-98—Philadelphia	AHL	71	34	18	52	48	8	8	2	20	6	2	8	4
—Philadelphia	NHL	4	0	0	0	12	0	0	0	—	—	—	—	—
98-99—Philadelphia	AHL	72	26	20	46	39	-2	10	3	15	4	6	10	11
99-00—Milwaukee	IHL	76	21	18	39	28	...	...	...	3	1	2	3	0
00-01—Hamilton	AHL	79	39	32	71	34	...	...	...	—	—	—	—	—
01-02—St. John's	AHL	58	27	29	56	30	20	6	2	2	1	1	2	8
—Toronto	NHL	21	3	7	10	2	7	0	0	18	0	1	1	2
02-03—St. John's	AHL	17	6	10	16	12	-6	3	0	—	—	—	—	—
—Toronto	NHL	44	3	7	10	16	8	1	0	4	0	1	1	2
03-04—New York Rangers	NHL	4	0	0	0	0	0	0	0	—	—	—	—	—
—Hartford	AHL	50	11	10	21	37	2	2	2	—	—	—	—	—
—San Antonio	AHL	18	5	5	10	20	-1	2	1	—	—	—	—	—
04-05—Edmonton	AHL	17	3	6	9	29	-3	1	0	—	—	—	—	—
—San Antonio	AHL	62	6	17	23	50	-9	0	0	—	—	—	—	—
NHL Totals (5 years)		75	6	14	20	30	15	1	0	22	0	2	2	4

HEATLEY, DANY RW THRASHERS

PERSONAL: Born January 21, 1981, in Freiburg, West Germany. ... 6-3/215. ... Shoots left.

TRANSACTIONS/CAREER NOTES: Selected by Atlanta Thrashers in first round (first Thrashers pick, second overall) of NHL entry draft (June 24, 2000). ... Injured knee (December 14, 2002); missed five games. ... Injured knees and fractured jaw in offseason auto accident (September 29, 2003); missed 51 games.

STATISTICAL PLATEAUS: Three-goal games: 2002-03 (2).

Season Team	League	GP	G	A	Pts.	PIM	+/-	PP	SH	GP	G	A	Pts.	PIM
		REGULAR SEASON								PLAYOFFS				
98-99—Calgary Royals	AJHL	60	*70	56	*126	91	...	...	...	13	*22	13	*35	6
99-00—Wisconsin	WCHA	38	28	28	56	32	...	...	...	—	—	—	—	—
00-01—Wisconsin	WCHA	39	24	33	57	74	...	...	...	—	—	—	—	—
01-02—Atlanta	NHL	82	26	41	67	56	-19	7	0	—	—	—	—	—
02-03—Atlanta	NHL	77	41	48	89	58	-8	19	1	—	—	—	—	—
03-04—Atlanta	NHL	31	13	12	25	18	-8	5	0	—	—	—	—	—
04-05—Bern	Switzerland	16	14	10	24	58	...	7	0	—	—	—	—	—
—Ak Bars Kazan	Russian	11	3	1	4	22	1	...	...	4	2	1	3	4
NHL Totals (3 years)		190	80	101	181	132	-35	31	1					

HECHT, JOCHEN LW/RW SABRES

PERSONAL: Born June 21, 1977, in Mannheim, West Germany. ... 6-1/191. ... Shoots left.

TRANSACTIONS/CAREER NOTES: Selected by St. Louis Blues in second round (first Blues pick, 49th overall) of NHL draft (July 8, 1995). ... Sprained ankle (January 13, 2000); missed 13 games. ... Reinjured ankle (February 23, 2000); missed six games. ... Strained oblique muscle (January 27, 2001); missed one game. ... Strained oblique muscle (February 1, 2001); missed two games. ... Strained oblique muscle (March 24, 2001); missed seven games. ... Traded by Blues with C Marty Reasoner and D Jan Horacek to Edmonton Oilers for C Doug Weight and LW Michel Riesen (July 1, 2001). ... Traded by Oilers to Buffalo Sabres for two second-round (G Jeff Deslauriers and C Jarrett Stoll) picks in 2002 draft (June 22, 2002). ... Bruised right knee (October 22, 2002); missed two games. ... Had concussion, injured ear (December 7, 2002); missed 20 games. ... Injured wrist (February 11, 2003); missed two games. ... Bruised right wrist (February 19, 2003); missed nine games. ... Had concussion (March 14, 2003); missed two games. ... Fractured left arm (October 4, 2003); missed 17 games. ... Bruised left shoulder (January 30, 2004); missed one game.

Season Team	League	REGULAR SEASON GP	G	A	Pts.	PIM	+/-	PP	SH	PLAYOFFS GP	G	A	Pts.	PIM
94-95—Mannheim	Germany	43	11	12	23	68	...	...	...	10	5	4	9	12
95-96—Mannheim	Germany	44	12	16	28	68	...	...	...	8	3	2	5	6
96-97—Mannheim	Germany	46	21	21	42	36	...	...	...	—	—	—	—	—
97-98—Mannheim	Germany	44	7	19	26	42	...	...	...	10	1	1	2	14
—German Oly. team	Int'l	4	1	0	1	6	-1	0	0	—	—	—	—	—
98-99—Worcester	AHL	74	21	35	56	48	-2	9	3	4	1	1	2	2
—St. Louis	NHL	3	0	0	0	0	-2	0	0	5	2	0	2	0
99-00—St. Louis	NHL	63	13	21	34	28	20	5	0	7	4	6	10	2
00-01—St. Louis	NHL	72	19	25	44	48	11	8	3	15	2	4	6	4
01-02—Edmonton	NHL	82	16	24	40	60	4	5	0	—	—	—	—	—
—German Oly. team	Int'l	4	1	1	2	2	...	...	...	—	—	—	—	—
02-03—Buffalo	NHL	49	10	16	26	30	4	2	0	—	—	—	—	—
03-04—Buffalo	NHL	64	15	37	52	49	17	2	1	—	—	—	—	—
04-05—Mannheim	Germany	48	16	34	50	151	11	6	1	14	10	10	20	14
NHL Totals (6 years)		333	73	123	196	215	54	22	4	27	8	10	18	6

HEDBERG, JOHAN G STARS

PERSONAL: Born May 3, 1973, in Leksand, Sweden. ... 6-0/190. ... Catches left.

TRANSACTIONS/CAREER NOTES: Selected by Philadelphia Flyers in 9th round (8th Flyers pick, 218th overall) of NHL draft (June 29, 1994). ... Traded by Flyers to San Jose Sharks for 7th-round pick (C Pavel Kasparik) in 1999 draft (July 6, 1998). ... Traded by Sharks with D Bobby Dollas to Pittsburgh Penguins for D Jeff Norton (March 12, 2001). ... Fractured collarbone (February 8, 2003); missed 14 games. ... Traded by Penguins to Vancouver Canucks for a 2nd-round pick (D Alex Goligoski) in 2004 draft (August 25, 2003). ... Injured foot (November 11, 2003); missed one game. ... Fractured wrist (December 16, 2003); missed 16 games. ... Signed as free agent by Dallas Stars (Aug. 5, 2005).

Season Team	League	REGULAR SEASON GP	Min.	W	L	T	GA	SO	GAA	SV%	PLAYOFFS GP	Min.	W	L	GA	SO	GAA	SV%
92-93—Leksand	Sweden Dv. 2	10	600	...	...	...	24	...	2.40	...	—	—	—	—	—	—	—	—
93-94—Leksand	Sweden Dv. 2	17	1020	...	...	...	48	0	2.82	...	—	—	—	—	—	—	—	—
94-95—Leksand	Sweden Dv. 2	17	986	...	...	...	58	1	3.53	...	—	—	—	—	—	—	—	—
95-96—Leksand	Sweden Dv. 2	34	2013	...	...	...	95	...	2.83	...	4	240	...	...	13	...	3.25	...
96-97—Leksand	Sweden Dv. 2	38	2260	...	...	...	95	3	2.52	...	4	581	...	...	18	1	1.86	...
97-98—Baton Rouge	ECHL	2	100	1	1	0	7	0	4.20	...	—	—	—	—	—	—	—	—
—Detroit	IHL	16	726	7	2	2	32	1	2.64	.899	—	—	—	—	—	—	—	—
—Manitoba	IHL	14	745	8	4	1	32	1	2.58	.922	2	106	0	2	6	0	3.40	.905
98-99—Leksand	Sweden Dv. 2	48	2940	...	...	...	140	0	2.86	...	4	255	...	...	15	0	3.53	...
99-00—Kentucky	AHL	33	1973	18	9	5	88	3	2.68	...	5	311	3	2	10	1	1.93	...
00-01—Manitoba	IHL	46	2697	23	13	7	115	1	2.56	...	—	—	—	—	—	—	—	—
—Pittsburgh	NHL	9	545	7	1	1	24	0	2.64	.905	18	1123	9	9	43	2	2.30	.911
01-02—Pittsburgh	NHL	66	3877	25	*34	7	178	6	2.75	.904	—	—	—	—	—	—	—	—
—Swedish Oly. team	Int'l	1	60	1	0	0	1	0	1.00	.950	—	—	—	—	—	—	—	—
02-03—Pittsburgh	NHL	41	2410	14	22	4	126	1	3.14	.895	—	—	—	—	—	—	—	—
03-04—Vancouver	NHL	21	1098	8	6	2	46	3	2.51	.900	2	98	1	1	4	0	2.45	.922
—Manitoba	AHL	2	124	0	2	0	9	0	4.35	.868	—	—	—	—	—	—	—	—
04-05—Leksand	Sweden Dv. 2	12	724	...	...	...	26	0	2.15	.909	9	550	...	...	19	1	2.07	.918
NHL Totals (4 years)		137	7930	54	63	14	374	10	2.83	.901	20	1221	10	10	47	2	2.31	.912

HEDICAN, BRET D HURRICANES

PERSONAL: Born August 10, 1970, in St. Paul, Minn. ... 6-2/205. ... Shoots left. ... Name pronounced HEHD-ih-kihn.

TRANSACTIONS/CAREER NOTES: Selected by St. Louis Blues in 10th round (10th Blues pick, 198th overall) of NHL draft (June 11, 1988). ... Strained knee ligaments (September 27, 1992); missed first 15 games of season. ... Injured shoulder (October 24, 1993); missed three games. ... Injured groin (January 18, 1994); missed six games. ... Traded by Blues with D Jeff Brown and C Nathan LaFayette to Vancouver Canucks for C Craig Janney (March 21, 1994). ... Strained groin (March 27, 1994); missed three games. ... Injured back (February 1, 1996); missed three games. ... Strained back (October 5, 1996); missed six games. ... Strained groin (December 4, 1996); missed five games. ... Strained groin (December 26, 1996); missed four games. ... Missed one game for personal reasons (December 13, 1997). ... Strained back (January 21, 1998); missed one game. ... Strained abdominal muscle (February 17, 1998); missed six games. ... Sprained ankle (September 23, 1998); missed first game of season. ... Traded by Canucks with RW Pavel Bure, D Brad Ference and third-round pick (RW Robert Fried) in 2000 draft to Florida Panthers for D Ed Jovanovski, G Kevin Weekes, C Dave Gagner, C Mike Brown and first-round pick (C Nathan Smith) in 2000 draft (January 17, 1999). ... Injured eye (February 11, 1999); missed eight games. ... Strained groin (March 31, 1999); missed eight games. ... Suspended three games for slashing incident (November 3, 1999). ... Strained groin (October 22, 1999); missed two games. ... Strained groin (February 26, 2000); missed one game. ... Suffered concussion (December 4, 2000); missed three games. ... Sprained left ankle (December 29, 2000); missed nine games. ... Fractured jaw (September 29, 2001); missed first 14 games of season. ... Traded by Panthers with C Kevyn Adams, D Tomas Malec and future considerations to Carolina Hurricanes for D Sandis Ozolinsh and C Byron Ritchie (January 16, 2002). ... Strained back (January 25, 2002); missed seven games. ... Suffered concussion (December 15, 2002); missed five games. ... Suffered concussion (January 3, 2003); missed five games. ... Injured knee (February 4, 2004); missed one game.

Season Team	League	REGULAR SEASON GP	G	A	Pts.	PIM	+/-	PP	SH	PLAYOFFS GP	G	A	Pts.	PIM
88-89—St. Cloud State	WCHA	28	5	3	8	28	...	...	...	—	—	—	—	—
89-90—St. Cloud State	WCHA	36	4	17	21	37	...	...	...	—	—	—	—	—
90-91—St. Cloud State	WCHA	41	18	30	48	52	...	...	...	—	—	—	—	—
91-92—U.S. national team	Int'l	54	1	8	9	59	...	...	...	—	—	—	—	—
—U.S. Olympic team	Int'l	8	0	0	0	4	...	...	...	—	—	—	—	—
—St. Louis	NHL	4	1	0	1	0	1	0	0	5	0	0	0	0
92-93—Peoria	IHL	19	0	8	8	10	-2	0	0	—	—	—	—	—
—St. Louis	NHL	42	0	8	8	30	-2	0	0	10	0	0	0	14
93-94—St. Louis	NHL	61	0	11	11	64	-8	0	0	—	—	—	—	—

Season Team	League	GP	G	A	Pts.	PIM	+/-	PP	SH	GP	G	A	Pts.	PIM
		REGULAR SEASON								PLAYOFFS				
—Vancouver	NHL	8	0	1	1	0	1	0	0	24	1	6	7	16
94-95—Vancouver	NHL	45	2	11	13	34	-3	0	0	11	0	2	2	6
95-96—Vancouver	NHL	77	6	23	29	83	8	1	0	6	0	1	1	10
96-97—Vancouver	NHL	67	4	15	19	51	-3	2	0	—	—	—	—	—
97-98—Vancouver	NHL	71	3	24	27	79	3	1	0	—	—	—	—	—
98-99—Vancouver	NHL	42	2	11	13	34	7	0	2	—	—	—	—	—
—Florida	NHL	25	3	7	10	17	-2	0	0	—	—	—	—	—
99-00—Florida	NHL	76	6	19	25	68	4	2	0	4	0	0	0	0
00-01—Florida	NHL	70	5	15	20	72	-7	4	0	—	—	—	—	—
01-02—Florida	NHL	31	3	7	10	12	-4	0	0	—	—	—	—	—
—Carolina	NHL	26	2	4	6	10	3	0	0	23	1	4	5	20
02-03—Carolina	NHL	72	3	14	17	75	-24	1	0	—	—	—	—	—
03-04—Carolina	NHL	81	7	17	24	64	-10	2	0	—	—	—	—	—
NHL Totals (13 years)		798	47	187	234	693	-36	13	2	83	2	13	15	66

HEDIN, PIERRE — D — MAPLE LEAFS

PERSONAL: Born February 19, 1978, in Ornskoldsvik, Sweden. ... 6-1/198. ... Shoots left.

TRANSACTIONS/CAREER NOTES: Selected by Toronto Maple Leafs in the eighth round (eighth Maple Leafs pick, 239th overall) in the 1999 draft (June 24, 1999).

Season Team	League	GP	G	A	Pts.	PIM	+/-	PP	SH	GP	G	A	Pts.	PIM
		REGULAR SEASON								PLAYOFFS				
96-97—MoDo Ornskoldsvik	Sweden	19	1	2	3	6	...	...	...	—	—	—	—	—
97-98—MoDo Ornskoldsvik	Sweden	29	2	1	3	26	...	...	...	—	—	—	—	—
98-99—MoDo Ornskoldsvik	Sweden	41	6	5	11	28	...	...	...	13	1	1	2	12
99-00—MoDo Ornskoldsvik	Sweden	48	9	5	14	36	...	...	...	—	—	—	—	—
00-01—MoDo Ornskoldsvik	Sweden	46	5	8	13	59	...	...	...	7	3	0	3	4
01-02—MoDo Ornskoldsvik	Sweden	39	7	9	16	20	...	...	...	14	8	2	10	10
02-03—MoDo Ornskoldsvik	Sweden	46	8	14	22	32	...	...	...	6	0	1	1	4
03-04—St. John's	AHL	62	5	19	24	52	7	2	0	—	—	—	—	—
—Toronto	NHL	3	0	1	1	0	-1	0	0	—	—	—	—	—
04-05—MoDo Ornskoldsvik	Sweden	31	3	4	7	28	-3	1	0	6	1	0	1	6
NHL Totals (1 year)		3	0	1	1	0	-1	0	0					

HEEREMA, JEFF — RW

PERSONAL: Born January 17, 1980, in Thunder Bay, Ontario. ... 6-1/190. ... Shoots right.

TRANSACTIONS/CAREER NOTES: Selected by Carolina Hurricanes in first round (first Hurricanes pick, 11th overall) of NHL entry draft (June 27, 1998). ... Fractured wrist (February 7, 2003); missed 27 games. ... Claimed off waivers by New York Rangers (September 30, 2003). ... Claimed by St. Louis Blues in NHL waiver draft (October 3, 2003). ... Claimed off waivers by Rangers (January 10, 2004). ... Signed as free agent by Vancouver Canucks (August 19, 2004).

Season Team	League	GP	G	A	Pts.	PIM	+/-	PP	SH	GP	G	A	Pts.	PIM
		REGULAR SEASON								PLAYOFFS				
97-98—Sarnia	OHL	63	32	40	72	88	...	...	...	5	4	1	5	10
98-99—Sarnia	OHL	62	31	39	70	113	24	...	...	6	5	1	6	0
99-00—Sarnia	OHL	67	36	41	77	62	11	14	3	7	4	2	6	10
00-01—Cincinnati	IHL	73	17	16	33	42	...	...	...	4	0	0	0	0
01-02—Lowell	AHL	76	33	37	70	90	20	11	0	5	2	3	5	2
02-03—Lowell	AHL	36	15	17	32	25	-10	8	0	—	—	—	—	—
—Carolina	NHL	10	3	0	3	2	-2	1	0	—	—	—	—	—
03-04—St. Louis	NHL	22	1	2	3	4	-5	0	0	—	—	—	—	—
—Worcester	AHL	1	0	0	0	2	0	0	0	—	—	—	—	—
—Hartford	AHL	41	12	15	27	25	11	4	0	4	0	0	0	9
04-05—Manitoba	AHL	80	14	31	45	67	9	3	0	14	4	6	10	12
NHL Totals (2 years)		32	4	2	6	6	-7	1	0					

HEINS, SHAWN — D — THRASHERS

PERSONAL: Born December 24, 1973, in Eganville, Ontario. ... 6-4/210. ... Shoots left.

TRANSACTIONS/CAREER NOTES: Signed as free agent by San Jose Sharks (January 5, 1998). ... Injured finger (February 29, 2000); missed five games. ... Injured knee (November 24, 2001); missed 18 games. ... Injured jaw (January 17, 2002); missed 14 games. ... Traded by Sharks to Pittsburgh Penguins for 5th-round pick (G Patrick Ehelechner) in 2003 draft (February 8, 2003). ... Signed as free agent by Atlanta Thrashers (September 10, 2003). ... Claimed by New York Rangers off waivers from Thrashers (September 30, 2003). ... Claimed by Thrashers from Rangers in waiver draft (October 3, 2003).

Season Team	League	GP	G	A	Pts.	PIM	+/-	PP	SH	GP	G	A	Pts.	PIM
		REGULAR SEASON								PLAYOFFS				
91-92—Peterborough	OHL	49	1	1	2	73	...	...	...	—	—	—	—	—
92-93—Peterborough	OHL	5	0	0	0	10	...	...	...	—	—	—	—	—
—Windsor	OHL	53	7	10	17	107	...	...	...	—	—	—	—	—
93-94—Renfrew	EOGHL	32	16	34	50	250	...	...	...	—	—	—	—	—
94-95—Renfrew	EOGHL	49	40	90	130	175	...	...	...	—	—	—	—	—
95-96—Cape Breton	AHL	1	0	0	0	0	...	...	...	—	—	—	—	—
—Mobile	ECHL	62	7	20	27	152	...	...	...	—	—	—	—	—
96-97—Mobile	ECHL	56	6	17	23	253	...	...	...	3	0	2	2	2
—Kansas City	IHL	6	0	0	0	9	...	...	...	—	—	—	—	—

Season Team	League	REGULAR SEASON								PLAYOFFS				
		GP	G	A	Pts.	PIM	+/-	PP	SH	GP	G	A	Pts.	PIM
97-98—Kansas City	IHL	82	22	28	50	303	-2	4	2	11	1	0	1	49
98-99—Canadian nat'l team	Int'l	36	5	16	21	66	...	...	...	—	—	—	—	—
—San Jose	NHL	5	0	0	0	13	0	0	0	—	—	—	—	—
—Kentucky	AHL	18	2	2	4	108	3	2	0	12	2	7	9	10
99-00—Kentucky	AHL	69	11	52	63	238	...	...	...	9	3	3	6	44
—San Jose	NHL	1	0	0	0	2	-1	0	0	—	—	—	—	—
00-01—San Jose	NHL	38	3	4	7	57	2	2	0	2	0	0	0	0
01-02—San Jose	NHL	17	0	2	2	24	1	0	0	—	—	—	—	—
02-03—San Jose	NHL	20	0	1	1	9	-2	0	0	—	—	—	—	—
—Pittsburgh	NHL	27	1	1	2	33	-2	0	0	—	—	—	—	—
03-04—Atlanta	NHL	17	0	4	4	16	-1	0	0	—	—	—	—	—
—Chicago	AHL	58	12	19	31	120	-2	6	0	10	1	5	6	44
04-05—Eisbaren Berlin	Germany	49	6	21	27	142	21	1	0	11	3	4	7	24
NHL Totals (6 years)		125	4	12	16	154	-3	2	0	2	0	0	0	0

HEISTEN, BARRETT — LW — ISLANDERS

PERSONAL: Born March 19, 1980, in Anchorage, Alaska. ... 6-1/189. ... Shoots left.
TRANSACTIONS/CAREER NOTES: Selected by Buffalo Sabres in first round (first Sabres pick, 20th overall) of NHL entry draft (June 26, 1999). ... Signed as free agent by New York Rangers (June 12, 2001). ... Traded by Rangers with C Manny Malhotra to Dallas Stars C Roman Lyashenko and LW Martin Rucinsky (March 12, 2002). ... Signed as free agent by New York Islanders (August 25, 2004).

Season Team	League	REGULAR SEASON								PLAYOFFS				
		GP	G	A	Pts.	PIM	+/-	PP	SH	GP	G	A	Pts.	PIM
97-98—U.S. National	NAHL	50	11	26	37	245	...	4	0	—	—	—	—	—
98-99—Maine	Hockey East	34	12	16	28	72	...	...	...	—	—	—	—	—
99-00—Maine	Hockey East	37	13	24	37	86	...	...	...	—	—	—	—	—
00-01—Seattle	WHL	58	20	57	77	61	...	...	...	9	2	6	8	20
01-02—New York Rangers	NHL	10	0	0	0	2	-4	0	0	—	—	—	—	—
—Hartford	AHL	49	9	9	18	60	0	0	1	—	—	—	—	—
—Utah	AHL	12	5	1	6	14	...	...	...	5	1	0	1	4
02-03—Utah	AHL	58	10	10	20	47	-3	3	1	2	0	0	0	4
03-04—Utah	AHL	73	4	13	17	98	-6	0	1	—	—	—	—	—
04-05—Bridgeport	AHL	64	7	13	20	59	-1	1	0	—	—	—	—	—
NHL Totals (1 year)		10	0	0	0	2	-4	0	0					

HEJDUK, MILAN — RW — AVALANCHE

PERSONAL: Born February 14, 1976, in Usti-nad-Labem, Czech. ... 6-0/190. ... Shoots right. ... Name pronounced MEE-lan HAY-dook.
TRANSACTIONS/CAREER NOTES: Selected by Quebec Nordiques in 4th round (6th Nordiques pick, 72nd overall) of NHL draft (June 29, 1994). ... Nordiques franchise moved to Colorado and renamed Avalanche for 1995-96 season (June 21, 1995). ... Strained back (January 7, 2000); missed one game. ... Strained abdominal muscle (February 28, 2002); missed final 20 games of season.
STATISTICAL PLATEAUS: Three-goal games: 2002-03 (1), 2003-04 (1). Total: 2.

Season Team	League	REGULAR SEASON								PLAYOFFS				
		GP	G	A	Pts.	PIM	+/-	PP	SH	GP	G	A	Pts.	PIM
93-94—HC Pardubice	Czech Rep.	22	6	3	9	...	...	...	...	10	5	1	6	...
94-95—HC Pardubice	Czech Rep.	Did not play												
95-96—HC Pardubice	Czech Rep.	37	13	7	20	...	...	...	...	—	—	—	—	—
96-97—HC Pardubice	Czech Rep.	51	27	11	38	10	...	...	...	10	6	0	6	27
97-98—Pojistovna Pardubice	Czech Rep.	48	26	19	45	20	...	...	...	3	0	0	0	2
—Czech Rep. Oly. team	Int'l	4	0	0	0	2	2	0	0	—	—	—	—	—
98-99—Colorado	NHL	82	14	34	48	26	8	4	0	16	6	6	12	4
99-00—Colorado	NHL	82	36	36	72	16	14	13	0	17	5	4	9	6
00-01—Colorado	NHL	80	41	38	79	36	32	12	1	23	7	*16	23	6
01-02—Colorado	NHL	62	21	23	44	24	0	7	1	16	3	3	6	4
—Czech Rep. Oly. team	Int'l	4	1	0	1	0	...	...	...	—	—	—	—	—
02-03—Colorado	NHL	82	*50	48	98	32	52	18	0	7	2	2	4	2
03-04—Colorado	NHL	82	35	40	75	20	19	16	0	11	5	2	7	0
04-05—Pardubice	Czech Rep.	48	25	26	51	14	12	...	...	16	6	2	8	6
NHL Totals (6 years)		470	197	219	416	154	125	70	2	90	28	33	61	22

HELMER, BRYAN — D — RED WINGS

PERSONAL: Born July 15, 1972, in Sault Ste. Marie, Ont. ... 6-2/208. ... Shoots right.
TRANSACTIONS/CAREER NOTES: Signed as free agent by New Jersey Devils (October 1, 1993). ... Signed as free agent by Phoenix Coyotes (July 22, 1998). ... Claimed off waivers by St. Louis Blues (December 19, 1998). ... Signed as free agent by Vancouver Canucks (August 21, 2000). ... Traded by Canucks to Phoenix Coyotes for D Martin Grenier (July 27, 2003). ... Injured left shoulder (October 7, 2003); missed 53 games. ... Signed as free agent by Detroit Red Wings (July 20, 2004).

Season Team	League	REGULAR SEASON								PLAYOFFS				
		GP	G	A	Pts.	PIM	+/-	PP	SH	GP	G	A	Pts.	PIM
89-90—Wellington	OJHL	51	6	22	28	204	...	...	...	—	—	—	—	—
—Belleville	OHL	6	0	1	1	0	...	...	...	—	—	—	—	—
90-91—Wellington	OJHL	50	11	14	25	109	...	...	...	—	—	—	—	—
91-92—Wellington	OJHL	45	19	32	51	66	...	...	...	—	—	—	—	—
92-93—Wellington	OJHL	57	25	62	87	62	...	...	...	—	—	—	—	—
93-94—Albany	AHL	65	4	19	23	79	...	...	...	5	0	0	0	9

Season Team	League	GP	G	A	Pts.	PIM	+/-	PP	SH	GP	G	A	Pts.	PIM
		REGULAR SEASON								PLAYOFFS				
94-95—Albany	AHL	77	7	36	43	101	17	4	0	7	1	0	1	0
95-96—Albany	AHL	80	14	30	44	107	...	...	...	4	2	0	2	6
96-97—Albany	AHL	77	12	27	39	113	22	5	0	16	1	7	8	10
97-98—Albany	AHL	80	14	49	63	101	15	8	0	13	4	9	13	18
98-99—Phoenix	NHL	11	0	0	0	23	2	0	0	—	—	—	—	—
—Las Vegas	IHL	8	1	3	4	28	-4	1	0	—	—	—	—	—
—St. Louis	NHL	29	0	4	4	19	3	0	0	—	—	—	—	—
—Worcester	AHL	16	7	8	15	18	0	4	0	4	0	0	0	12
99-00—Worcester	AHL	54	10	25	35	124	...	...	...	9	1	4	5	10
—St. Louis	NHL	15	1	1	2	10	-3	1	0	—	—	—	—	—
00-01—Kansas City	IHL	42	4	15	19	76	...	...	...	—	—	—	—	—
—Vancouver	NHL	20	2	4	6	18	0	0	0	—	—	—	—	—
01-02—Manitoba	AHL	34	6	18	24	69	18	1	1	—	—	—	—	—
—Vancouver	NHL	40	5	5	10	53	10	2	0	6	0	0	0	0
02-03—Vancouver	NHL	2	0	0	0	0	1	0	0	—	—	—	—	—
—Manitoba	AHL	60	7	24	31	82	-10	5	0	14	0	4	4	20
03-04—Phoenix	NHL	17	0	1	1	10	-5	0	0	—	—	—	—	—
—Springfield	AHL	9	1	6	7	6	5	1	0	—	—	—	—	—
04-05—Grand Rapids	AHL	80	7	18	25	64	11	5	1	—	—	—	—	—
NHL Totals (6 years)		134	8	15	23	133	8	3	0	6	0	0	0	0

HEMSKY, ALES — RW — OILERS

PERSONAL: Born August 13, 1983, in Pardubice, Czechoslovakia. ... 6-0/192. ... Shoots right.

TRANSACTIONS/CAREER NOTES: Selected by Edmonton Oilers in first round (first Oilers pick, 13th overall) of NHL draft (June 23, 2001). ... Flu and abdominal soreness (January 22, 2003); missed one game. ... Strained abdomen (January 29, 2003); missed two games. ... Flu and abdominal soreness (February 18, 2003); missed four games.

Season Team	League	GP	G	A	Pts.	PIM	+/-	PP	SH	GP	G	A	Pts.	PIM
		REGULAR SEASON								PLAYOFFS				
99-00—Pardubice	Czech. Jrs.	52	24	50	74	90	...	...	...	—	—	—	—	—
—HC Pardubice	Czech Rep.	4	0	1	1	0	...	...	...	—	—	—	—	—
00-01—Hull	QMJHL	68	36	64	100	67	...	...	...	5	2	3	5	2
01-02—Hull	QMJHL	53	27	70	97	86	...	...	...	10	6	10	16	6
02-03—Edmonton	NHL	59	6	24	30	14	5	0	0	6	0	0	0	0
03-04—Edmonton	NHL	71	12	22	34	14	-7	4	0	—	—	—	—	—
04-05—Pardubice	Czech Rep.	47	13	18	31	28	5	...	...	16	4	10	14	26
NHL Totals (2 years)		130	18	46	64	28	-2	4	0	6	0	0	0	0

HENDRICKSON, DARBY — C

PERSONAL: Born August 28, 1972, in Richfield, Minn. ... 6-1/195. ... Shoots left.

TRANSACTIONS/CAREER NOTES: Selected by Toronto Maple Leafs in fourth round (third Maple Leafs pick, 73rd overall) of NHL draft (June 16, 1990). ... Suspended three games for kneeing incident (October 26, 1995). ... Flu (December 30, 1995); missed one game. ... Traded by Maple Leafs with LW Sean Haggerty, D Kenny Jonsson and first-round pick (G Roberto Luongo) in 1997 draft to New York Islanders for LW Wendel Clark, D Mathieu Schneider and D D.J. Smith (March 13, 1996). ... Traded by Islanders to Maple Leafs for fifth-round pick (C Jiri Dopita) in 1998 draft (October 11, 1996). ... Strained back (January 27, 1997); missed five games. ... Back spasms (November 4, 1997); missed two games. ... Back spasms (November 3, 1998); missed six games. ... Traded by Maple Leafs to Vancouver Canucks for D/LW Chris McAllister (February 16, 1999). ... Injured ankle (September 11, 1999); missed four games. ... Selected by Minnesota Wild in expansion draft (June 23, 2000). ... Had concussion (November 22, 2000); missed six games. ... Injured head (February 14, 2001); missed three games. ... Strained groin (October 16, 2001); missed one game. ... Back spasms (November 8, 2001); missed four games. ... Sinus infection (November 24, 2001); missed three games. ... Injured left eye (April 2, 2002); missed remainder of season. ... Fractured arm (September 23, 2002); missed 45 games. ... Had concussion (February 9, 2003); missed two games. ... Traded by Wild with eighth-round pick (RW Brandon Yip) in 2004 draft to Colorado Avalanche for fourth-round pick in 2005 draft (February 25, 2004).

Season Team	League	GP	G	A	Pts.	PIM	+/-	PP	SH	GP	G	A	Pts.	PIM
		REGULAR SEASON								PLAYOFFS				
87-88—Richfield H.S.	Minn. H.S.	22	12	9	21	10	...	...	...	—	—	—	—	—
88-89—Richfield H.S.	Minn. H.S.	22	22	20	42	12	...	...	...	—	—	—	—	—
89-90—Richfield H.S.	Minn. H.S.	24	23	27	50	49	...	...	...	—	—	—	—	—
90-91—Richfield H.S.	Minn. H.S.	27	32	29	61	...	...	...	...	—	—	—	—	—
91-92—Minnesota	WCHA	41	25	28	53	61	...	...	...	—	—	—	—	—
92-93—Minnesota	WCHA	31	12	15	27	35	...	...	...	—	—	—	—	—
93-94—U.S. national team	Int'l	59	12	16	28	30	...	0	1	—	—	—	—	—
—U.S. Olympic team	Int'l	8	0	0	0	6	-2	0	0	—	—	—	—	—
—St. John's	AHL	6	4	1	5	4	2	0	1	3	1	1	2	0
—Toronto	NHL	...	...	...	...	...	...	...	...	2	0	0	0	0
94-95—St. John's	AHL	59	16	20	36	48	10	3	3	—	—	—	—	—
—Toronto	NHL	8	0	1	1	4	0	0	0	—	—	—	—	—
95-96—Toronto	NHL	46	6	6	12	47	-2	0	0	—	—	—	—	—
—New York Islanders	NHL	16	1	4	5	33	-6	0	0	—	—	—	—	—
96-97—St. John's	AHL	12	5	4	9	21	-3	2	0	—	—	—	—	—
—Toronto	NHL	64	11	6	17	47	-20	0	1	—	—	—	—	—
—U.S. national team	Int'l	8	0	1	1	8	...	...	...	—	—	—	—	—
97-98—Toronto	NHL	80	8	4	12	67	-20	0	0	—	—	—	—	—
98-99—Toronto	NHL	35	2	3	5	30	-4	0	0	—	—	—	—	—
—Vancouver	NHL	27	2	2	4	22	-15	1	0	—	—	—	—	—
99-00—Vancouver	NHL	40	5	4	9	14	-3	0	1	—	—	—	—	—
—Syracuse	AHL	20	5	8	13	16	...	...	...	—	—	—	—	—

Season Team	League	REGULAR SEASON GP	G	A	Pts.	PIM	+/-	PP	SH	PLAYOFFS GP	G	A	Pts.	PIM
00-01—Minnesota	NHL	72	18	11	29	36	1	3	1	—	—	—	—	—
01-02—Minnesota	NHL	68	9	15	24	50	-22	2	2	—	—	—	—	—
02-03—Minnesota	NHL	28	1	5	6	8	-3	0	0	17	2	3	5	4
03-04—Houston	AHL	31	4	5	9	19	-14	2	0	—	—	—	—	—
—Minnesota	NHL	14	1	0	1	6	-7	0	0	—	—	—	—	—
—Colorado	NHL	20	1	3	4	6	-8	0	0	6	1	0	1	2
04-05—Riga	Belarus	6	2	2	4	26	...	...	...	—	—	—	—	—
—Riga	Latvia	1	1	1	2	0	...	...	...	—	—	—	—	—
NHL Totals (11 years)		518	65	64	129	370	-109	6	5	25	3	3	6	6

HENRY, ALEX — D — WILD

PERSONAL: Born October 18, 1979, in Elliot Lake, Ont. ... 6-5/220. ... Shoots left.

TRANSACTIONS/CAREER NOTES: Selected by Edmonton Oilers in third round (second Oilers pick, 67th overall) of NHL draft (June 27, 1998). ... Claimed off waivers by Washington Capitals (October 24, 2002). ... Flu (January 25, 2003); missed four games. ... Had concussion (October 3, 2003); missed five games. ... Claimed off waivers by Minnesota Wild (October 9, 2003). ... Injured groin (November 19, 2003); missed three games.

Season Team	League	REGULAR SEASON GP	G	A	Pts.	PIM	+/-	PP	SH	PLAYOFFS GP	G	A	Pts.	PIM
96-97—London	OHL	61	1	10	11	65	...	...	...	—	—	—	—	—
97-98—London	OHL	62	5	9	14	97	...	...	...	16	0	3	3	14
98-99—London	OHL	68	5	23	28	105	33	...	...	25	3	10	13	22
99-00—Hamilton	AHL	60	1	0	1	69	...	...	...	—	—	—	—	—
00-01—Hamilton	AHL	56	2	3	5	87	...	...	...	—	—	—	—	—
01-02—Hamilton	AHL	69	4	8	12	143	12	0	0	15	1	2	3	16
02-03—Edmonton	NHL	3	0	0	0	0	-1	0	0	—	—	—	—	—
—Washington	NHL	38	0	0	0	80	-4	0	0	—	—	—	—	—
—Portland	AHL	3	0	1	1	0	1	0	0	—	—	—	—	—
03-04—Minnesota	NHL	71	2	4	6	106	4	0	0	—	—	—	—	—
04-05—Kaufbeuren	Germany	16	4	4	8	20	...	...	...	—	—	—	—	—
NHL Totals (2 years)		112	2	4	6	186	-1	0	0					

HENRY, BURKE — D — PANTHERS

PERSONAL: Born January 21, 1979, in Ste. Rose, Man. ... 6-3/200. ... Shoots left.

TRANSACTIONS/CAREER NOTES: Selected by New York Rangers in third round (third Rangers pick, 73rd overall) of NHL entry draft (June 21, 1997). ... Traded by Rangers to Calgary Flames for D Chris St. Croix (June 24, 2001). ... Signed as free agent by Chicago Blackhawks (December 11, 2002). ... Signed as free agent by Florida Panthers (July 23, 2004).

Season Team	League	REGULAR SEASON GP	G	A	Pts.	PIM	+/-	PP	SH	PLAYOFFS GP	G	A	Pts.	PIM
95-96—Brandon	WHL	50	6	11	17	58	...	...	...	19	0	4	4	19
96-97—Brandon	WHL	55	6	25	31	81	...	...	...	6	1	3	4	4
97-98—Brandon	WHL	72	18	65	83	153	35	6	1	18	3	16	19	37
98-99—Brandon	WHL	68	18	58	76	151	...	...	...	5	1	6	7	9
99-00—Hartford	AHL	64	3	12	15	47	...	...	...	5	0	0	0	2
00-01—Hartford	AHL	80	8	30	38	133	...	...	...	5	0	0	0	2
01-02—Saint John	AHL	58	0	17	17	92	-16	0	0	—	—	—	—	—
02-03—Chicago	NHL	16	0	2	2	9	-13	0	0	—	—	—	—	—
—Norfolk	AHL	60	6	22	28	121	-11	4	0	9	1	2	3	9
03-04—Norfolk	AHL	53	1	8	9	70	-15	0	0	8	0	1	1	4
—Chicago	NHL	23	2	4	6	24	0	0	0	—	—	—	—	—
04-05—Milwaukee	AHL	16	0	3	3	28	6	0	0	1	0	0	0	0
—San Antonio	AHL	24	0	2	2	44	2	0	0	—	—	—	—	—
NHL Totals (2 years)		39	2	6	8	33	-13	0	0					

HIGGINS, CHRIS — C — CANADIENS

PERSONAL: Born June 2, 1983, in Smithtown, N.Y. ... 5-11/188. ... Shoots left.

TRANSACTIONS/CAREER NOTES: Selected by Montreal Canadiens in 1st round (1st Canadiens pick, 14th overall) of NHL draft (June 22, 2002).

Season Team	League	REGULAR SEASON GP	G	A	Pts.	PIM	+/-	PP	SH	PLAYOFFS GP	G	A	Pts.	PIM
00-01—Avon Old Farms	USHS (East)	24	22	14	36	29	...	...	...	—	—	—	—	—
01-02—Yale	ECAC	25	13	16	29	32	...	...	...	—	—	—	—	—
02-03—Yale	ECAC	28	20	21	41	41	...	...	...	—	—	—	—	—
03-04—Montreal	NHL	2	0	0	0	0	0	0	0	—	—	—	—	—
—Hamilton	AHL	67	21	27	48	18	16	4	1	10	3	2	5	0
04-05—Hamilton	AHL	76	28	23	51	33	9	8	4	4	3	3	6	4
NHL Totals (1 year)		2	0	0	0	0	0	0	0					

HILBERT, ANDY — C/LW — BRUINS

PERSONAL: Born February 6, 1981, in Lansing, Mich. ... 5-11/194. ... Shoots left.

TRANSACTIONS/CAREER NOTES: Selected by Boston Bruins in second round (third Bruins pick, 37th overall) of NHL draft (June 24, 2000). ... Signed as free agent by Providence of the AHL (September 27, 2004).

Season Team	League	REGULAR SEASON GP	G	A	Pts.	PIM	+/-	PP	SH	PLAYOFFS GP	G	A	Pts.	PIM
98-99—U.S. National	USHL	46	23	35	58	140	...	...	...	—	—	—	—	—
99-00—Univ. of Michigan	CCHA	35	17	15	32	39	...	...	...	—	—	—	—	—
00-01—Univ. of Michigan	CCHA	42	26	38	64	72	...	...	...	—	—	—	—	—
01-02—Providence	AHL	72	26	27	53	74	-2	10	2	—	—	—	—	—
—Boston	NHL	6	1	0	1	2	-2	0	0	—	—	—	—	—
02-03—Providence	AHL	64	35	35	70	119	0	11	2	—	—	—	—	—
—Boston	NHL	14	0	3	3	7	-1	0	0	—	—	—	—	—
03-04—Providence	AHL	19	3	5	8	20	2	1	1	—	—	—	—	—
—Boston	NHL	18	2	0	2	9	1	0	0	5	1	0	1	0
04-05—Providence	AHL	79	37	42	79	83	11	16	3	17	7	14	21	27
NHL Totals (3 years)		38	3	3	6	18	-2	0	0	5	1	0	1	0

HILL, SEAN — D — PANTHERS

PERSONAL: Born February 14, 1970, in Duluth, Minn. ... 6-0/205. ... Shoots right.

TRANSACTIONS/CAREER NOTES: Selected by Montreal Canadiens in eighth round (ninth Canadiens pick, 167th overall) of NHL draft (June 11, 1988). ... Strained abdominal muscle (October 13, 1992); missed 14 games. ... Selected by Anaheim Mighty Ducks in expansion draft (June 24, 1993). ... Sprained shoulder (January 6, 1994); missed nine games. ... Traded by Mighty Ducks with ninth-round pick (G Frederic Cassivi) in 1994 entry draft to Ottawa Senators for third-round pick (traded to Tampa Bay) in 1994 entry draft (June 29, 1994). ... Strained abdominal muscle during 1995-96 season; missed two games. ... Tore left knee ligament (October 18, 1996); missed remainder of season. ... Traded by Senators to Carolina Hurricanes for RW Chris Murray (November 18, 1997). ... Strained hip flexor (December 1, 1997); missed three games. ... Fractured leg (March 26, 1998); missed final 11 games of season. ... Fractured ankle and strained abdominal muscle (December 21, 1998); missed 20 games. ... Strained abdominal muscle (February 13, 1999); missed one game. ... Sprained ankle (March 21, 1999); missed four games. ... Fractured cheekbone (April 14, 1999); missed final two games of season. ... Strained groin (December 22, 1999); missed 18 games. ... Reinjured groin (April 3, 2000); missed final two games of season. ... Signed as free agent by St. Louis Blues (July 1, 2000). ... Strained muscle in abdomen (November 29, 2000); missed 32 games. ... Strained groin (October 31, 2001); missed two games. ... Traded by Blues to Hurricanes for D Steve Halko and fourth-round pick (later traded to Atlanta; Thrashers selected Lane Manson) in 2002 draft (December 5, 2001). ... Strained groin (October 28, 2003); missed two games. ... Signed as free agent by Florida Panthers (July 15, 2004).

Season Team	League	REGULAR SEASON GP	G	A	Pts.	PIM	+/-	PP	SH	PLAYOFFS GP	G	A	Pts.	PIM
88-89—Wisconsin	WCHA	45	2	23	25	69	...	...	...	—	—	—	—	—
89-90—Wisconsin	WCHA	42	14	39	53	78	...	...	...	—	—	—	—	—
90-91—Wisconsin	WCHA	37	19	32	51	122	...	...	...	—	—	—	—	—
—Fredericton	AHL	...	...	...	...	...	...	...	...	3	0	2	2	2
—Montreal	NHL	...	...	...	...	...	...	...	...	1	0	0	0	0
91-92—Fredericton	AHL	42	7	20	27	65	...	...	...	7	1	3	4	6
—U.S. national team	Int'l	12	4	3	7	16	...	...	...	—	—	—	—	—
—U.S. Olympic team	Int'l	8	2	0	2	6	...	...	...	—	—	—	—	—
—Montreal	NHL	...	...	...	...	...	...	...	...	4	1	0	1	2
92-93—Montreal	NHL	31	2	6	8	54	-5	1	0	3	0	0	0	4
—Fredericton	AHL	6	1	3	4	10	3	1	0	—	—	—	—	—
93-94—Anaheim	NHL	68	7	20	27	78	-12	2	1	—	—	—	—	—
94-95—Ottawa	NHL	45	1	14	15	30	-11	0	0	—	—	—	—	—
95-96—Ottawa	NHL	80	7	14	21	94	-26	2	0	—	—	—	—	—
96-97—Ottawa	NHL	5	0	0	0	4	1	0	0	—	—	—	—	—
97-98—Ottawa	NHL	13	1	1	2	6	-3	0	0	—	—	—	—	—
—Carolina	NHL	42	0	5	5	48	-2	0	0	—	—	—	—	—
98-99—Carolina	NHL	54	0	10	10	48	9	0	0	—	—	—	—	—
99-00—Carolina	NHL	62	13	31	44	59	3	8	0	—	—	—	—	—
00-01—St. Louis	NHL	48	1	10	11	51	5	0	0	15	0	1	1	12
01-02—St. Louis	NHL	23	0	3	3	28	1	0	0	—	—	—	—	—
—Carolina	NHL	49	7	23	30	61	-1	4	0	23	4	4	8	20
02-03—Carolina	NHL	82	5	24	29	141	4	1	0	—	—	—	—	—
03-04—Carolina	NHL	80	13	26	39	84	-2	6	0	—	—	—	—	—
NHL Totals (14 years)		682	57	187	244	786	-39	24	1	46	5	5	10	38

HINOTE, DAN — RW/C — AVALANCHE

PERSONAL: Born January 30, 1977, in Leesburg, Fla. ... 6-0/195. ... Shoots right.

TRANSACTIONS/CAREER NOTES: Selected by Colorado Avalanche in 7th round (9th Avalanche pick, 167th overall) of NHL draft (June 22, 1996). ... Sprained knee (February 19, 2001); missed one game. ... Injured finger (November 10, 2001); missed one game. ... Injured knee (December 12, 2001); missed one game. ... Injured heel (January 5, 2002); missed 11 games. ... Injured shoulder (March 6, 2002); missed 11 games. ... Fractured leg (October 8, 2002); missed nine games. ... Injured head, leg (February 2, 2003); missed 12 games. ... Concussion (January 30, 2003); missed 14 games. ... Dislocated shoulder (March 14, 2004); missed nine games.

Season Team	League	REGULAR SEASON GP	G	A	Pts.	PIM	+/-	PP	SH	PLAYOFFS GP	G	A	Pts.	PIM
95-96—Army	AH	33	20	24	44	20	...	...	...	—	—	—	—	—
96-97—Oshawa	OHL	60	15	13	28	58	...	...	...	18	4	5	9	8
97-98—Hershey	AHL	24	1	4	5	25	-6	0	0	—	—	—	—	—
—Oshawa	OHL	35	12	15	27	39	7	...	...	5	2	2	4	7
98-99—Hershey	AHL	65	4	16	20	95	3	0	0	5	3	1	4	6
99-00—Colorado	NHL	27	1	3	4	10	0	0	0	—	—	—	—	—
—Hershey	AHL	55	28	31	59	96	...	...	...	14	4	5	9	19
00-01—Colorado	NHL	76	5	10	15	51	1	1	0	23	2	4	6	21
01-02—Colorado	NHL	58	6	6	12	39	8	0	1	19	1	2	3	9
02-03—Colorado	NHL	60	6	4	10	49	4	0	0	7	1	2	3	2

Season Team	League	REGULAR SEASON GP	G	A	Pts.	PIM	+/-	PP	SH	PLAYOFFS GP	G	A	Pts.	PIM
03-04—Colorado	NHL	59	4	7	11	57	-6	0	2	11	1	0	1	0
04-05—MoDo Ornskoldsvik	Sweden	18	2	1	3	106	-1	1	0	5	0	0	0	56
NHL Totals (5 years)		280	22	30	52	206	7	1	3	60	5	8	13	32

HLAVAC, JAN — LW

PERSONAL: Born September 20, 1976, in Prague, Czechoslovakia. ... 6-0/197. ... Shoots left. ... Name pronounced YAHN luh-VAHCH.
TRANSACTIONS/CAREER NOTES: Selected by New York Islanders in second round (second Islanders pick, 28th overall) of NHL draft (July 8, 1995). ... Traded by Islanders to Calgary Flames for LW Jorgen Jonsson (July 14, 1998). ... Traded by Flames with first- (C Jamie Lundmark) and third-round (D Pat Aufiero) picks in 1999 draft to New York Rangers for C Marc Savard and first-round pick (C/LW Oleg Saprykin) in 1999 draft (June 26, 1999). ... Strained hip flexor (March 15, 2000); missed two games. ... Bruised foot (April 4, 2000); missed one game. ... Injured shoulder (January 14, 2001); missed one game. ... Injured left knee (April 4, 2001); missed final two games of season. ... Traded by Rangers with D Kim Johnsson, RW Pavel Brendl and third-round pick (RW Stefan Ruzicka) in 2003 draft to Philadelphia Flyers for rights to C Eric Lindros (August 20, 2001). ... Traded by Flyers with third-round pick (D Brett Skinner) in 2002 draft to Vancouver Canucks for LW Donald Brashear and sixth-round pick (traded to Colorado; Avalanche selected RW Jaroslav Balastik) in 2002 draft (December 17, 2001). ... Traded by Canucks with C Harold Druken to Carolina Hurricanes for D Marek Malik and LW Darren Langdon (November 1, 2002). ... Fractured finger (March 4, 2003); missed 17 games. ... Signed as free agent by New York Rangers (August 28, 2003). ... Flu (March 4, 2004); missed two games.
STATISTICAL PLATEAUS: Three-goal games: 1999-00 (1), 2000-01 (1), 2002-03 (1). Total: 3.

Season Team	League	REGULAR SEASON GP	G	A	Pts.	PIM	+/-	PP	SH	PLAYOFFS GP	G	A	Pts.	PIM
93-94—Sparta Prague	Czech. Jrs.	27	12	15	27	...	...	...	...	—	—	—	—	—
—Sparta Prague	Czech Rep.	9	1	1	2	...	...	...	...	—	—	—	—	—
94-95—Sparta Prague	Czech Rep.	38	7	6	13	...	...	...	...	5	0	2	2	...
95-96—Sparta Prague	Czech Rep.	34	8	5	13	...	...	...	...	12	1	2	3	...
96-97—Sparta Praha	Czech Rep.	38	8	13	21	24	...	...	...	10	5	2	7	2
97-98—Sparta Praha	Czech Rep.	48	17	30	47	40	...	...	...	5	1	0	1	2
98-99—Sparta Praha	Czech Rep.	49	*33	20	53	52	...	...	...	6	1	3	4	...
99-00—New York Rangers	NHL	67	19	23	42	16	3	6	0	—	—	—	—	—
—Hartford	AHL	3	1	0	1	0	...	...	...	—	—	—	—	—
00-01—New York Rangers	NHL	79	28	36	64	20	3	5	0	—	—	—	—	—
01-02—Philadelphia	NHL	31	7	3	10	8	5	0	0	—	—	—	—	—
—Vancouver	NHL	46	9	12	21	10	4	1	0	5	0	1	1	0
02-03—Vancouver	NHL	9	1	1	2	6	-1	0	0	...	...	...	...	...
—Carolina	NHL	52	9	15	24	22	-9	6	0	—	—	—	—	—
03-04—New York Rangers	NHL	72	5	21	26	16	-8	2	0	—	—	—	—	—
04-05—Sparta Praha	Czech Rep.	48	10	28	38	34	14	...	...	5	2	0	2	6
NHL Totals (5 years)		356	78	111	189	98	-3	20	0	5	0	1	1	0

HNIDY, SHANE — D — THRASHERS

PERSONAL: Born November 8, 1975, in Neepawa, Man. ... 6-1/207. ... Shoots right. ... Name pronounced NIGH-dee.
TRANSACTIONS/CAREER NOTES: Selected by Buffalo Sabres in 7th round (Sabres 7th pick, 173rd overall) of NHL draft (June 28, 1994). ... Signed as free agent by Detroit Red Wings (August 6, 1998). ... Traded by Red Wings to Ottawa Senators for 8th-round pick (RW Todd Jackson) in 2000 draft (June 25, 2000). ... Bruised left foot (December 14, 2000); missed four games. ... Strained groin (March 26, 2001); missed final six game of regular season. ... Injured left ankle (December 23, 2001); missed 11 games. ... Injured left eye (November 21, 2002); missed eight games. ... Fractured finger (January 9, 2003); missed three games. ... Bruised neck (April 1, 2003); missed 1 game. ... Bruised right foot (November 8, 2003); missed 11 games. ... Bruised leg (January 17, 2004); missed two games. ... Flu (February 10, 2004); missed one game. ... Traded by Senators to Nashville Predators for 3rd-round pick (C/W Peter Regin) in 2004 draft (March 9, 2004). ... Left team for personal reasons (March 23, 2004); missed one game. ... Traded by the Predators to the Atlanta Thrashers for 4th-round pick in 2006 (July 30, 2005)

Season Team	League	REGULAR SEASON GP	G	A	Pts.	PIM	+/-	PP	SH	PLAYOFFS GP	G	A	Pts.	PIM
91-92—Swift Current	WHL	56	1	3	4	11	...	...	...	—	—	—	—	—
92-93—Swift Current	WHL	72	7	22	29	105	...	...	...	—	—	—	—	—
93-94—Prince Albert	WHL	69	7	26	33	113	18	2	1	—	—	—	—	—
94-95—Prince Albert	WHL	72	5	29	34	169	18	0	0	15	4	7	11	29
95-96—Prince Albert	WHL	58	11	42	53	100	...	...	...	18	4	11	15	34
96-97—Baton Rouge	ECHL	21	3	10	13	50	...	...	...	—	—	—	—	—
—Saint John	AHL	44	2	12	14	112	-16	0	0	—	—	—	—	—
97-98—Grand Rapids	IHL	77	6	12	18	210	2	0	0	3	0	2	2	23
98-99—Adirondack	AHL	68	9	20	29	121	-29	4	0	3	0	1	1	0
99-00—Cincinnati	AHL	68	9	19	28	153	...	...	...	—	—	—	—	—
00-01—Ottawa	NHL	52	3	2	5	84	8	0	0	1	0	0	0	0
—Grand Rapids	IHL	2	0	0	0	2	...	...	...	—	—	—	—	—
01-02—Ottawa	NHL	33	1	1	2	57	-10	0	0	12	1	1	2	12
02-03—Ottawa	NHL	67	0	8	8	130	-1	0	0	1	0	0	0	0
03-04—Ottawa	NHL	37	0	5	5	72	2	0	0	—	—	—	—	—
—Nashville	NHL	9	0	2	2	10	3	0	0	5	0	0	0	6
04-05—Florida	ECHL	19	1	4	5	56	7	0	...	17	0	4	4	6
NHL Totals (4 years)		198	4	18	22	353	2	0	0	19	1	1	2	18

HNILICKA, MILAN — G

PERSONAL: Born June 24, 1973, in Kladno, Czechoslovakia. ... 6-1/190. ... Catches left. ... Name pronounced MEE-lahn nun-LEECH-kuh.
TRANSACTIONS/CAREER NOTES: Selected by New York Islanders in fourth round (fourth Islanders pick, 70th overall) of NHL entry draft (June

22, 1991). ... Signed as free agent by New York Rangers (July 22, 1999). ... Signed as free agent by Atlanta Thrashers (July 28, 2000). ... Traded by Thrashers to Los Angeles Kings for future considerations (September 15, 2003). ... Fractured finger (January 3, 2004); missed 21 games. ... Signed by HC Liberec of Czech league (May 18, 2004).

		REGULAR SEASON									PLAYOFFS							
Season Team	League	GP	Min.	W	L	T	GA	SO	GAA	SV%	GP	Min.	W	L	GA	SO	GAA	SV%
89-90—Poldi Kladno	Czech Rep.	24	1113	...	...	...	70	...	3.77	...	—	—	—	—	—	—	—	—
90-91—Poldi Kladno	Czech Rep.	35	2122	...	...	...	98	...	2.77	...	—	—	—	—	—	—	—	—
91-92—Poldi Kladno	Czech Rep.	30	1788	...	...	...	107	...	3.59	...	—	—	—	—	—	—	—	—
92-93—Swift Current	WHL	65	3679	*46	12	2	206	2	3.36	.896	17	1017	12	5	54	*2	3.19	.911
93-94—Salt Lake City	IHL	9	381	5	1	0	25	0	3.94	.892	—	—	—	—	—	—	—	—
—Richmond	ECHL	43	2299	18	16	5	155	0	4.05	.883	—	—	—	—	—	—	—	—
94-95—Denver	IHL	15	798	9	4	1	47	1	3.53	.890	—	—	—	—	—	—	—	—
95-96—Poldi Kladno	Czech Rep.	33	1959	...	...	...	93	1	2.85	...	8	493	...	...	24	...	2.92	...
96-97—Poldi Kladno	Czech Rep.	48	2736	...	...	...	120	4	2.63	...	3	151	...	...	14	0	5.56	...
97-98—Sparta Praha	Czech Rep.	49	2847	...	...	...	99	...	2.09	...	11	632	...	...	31	...	2.94	...
98-99—Sparta Praha	Czech Rep.	50	2877	...	...	...	109	...	2.27	...	8	507	...	...	13	...	1.54	...
99-00—New York Rangers	NHL	2	86	0	1	0	5	0	3.49	.886	—	—	—	—	—	—	—	—
—Hartford	AHL	36	1979	22	11	0	71	5	2.15	...	3	99	0	1	6	0	3.64	...
00-01—Atlanta	NHL	36	1879	12	19	2	105	2	3.35	.890	—	—	—	—	—	—	—	—
01-02—Atlanta	NHL	60	3367	13	33	10	179	3	3.19	.908	—	—	—	—	—	—	—	—
02-03—Chicago	AHL	15	838	11	2	1	33	1	2.36	.922	—	—	—	—	—	—	—	—
—Atlanta	NHL	21	1097	4	13	1	65	0	3.56	.893	—	—	—	—	—	—	—	—
03-04—Los Angeles	NHL	2	80	0	1	0	5	0	3.75	.881	—	—	—	—	—	—	—	—
—Manchester	AHL	20	1021	8	10	0	44	1	2.59	.899	2	126	0	2	5	0	2.38	.906
04-05—Liberec	Czech Rep.	46	2740	28	16	2	106	5	2.32	.928	12	702	5	7	32	0	2.74	.927
NHL Totals (5 years)		121	6509	29	67	13	359	5	3.31	.900								

HOGEBOOM, GREG RW KINGS

PERSONAL: Born September 26, 1982, in Toronto. ... 6-0/190. ... Shoots right.

TRANSACTIONS/CAREER NOTES: Selected by Los Angeles Kings in fifth round (sixth Kings pick,152nd overall) of NHL entry draft (June 23, 2002). ... Signed to amateur tryout contract by Manchester of the AHL (March 30, 2004).

		REGULAR SEASON								PLAYOFFS				
Season Team	League	GP	G	A	Pts.	PIM	+/-	PP	SH	GP	G	A	Pts.	PIM
00-01—Miami (Ohio)	CCHA	38	8	5	13	20	...	...	...	—	—	—	—	—
01-02—Miami (Ohio)	CCHA	36	14	9	23	22	...	...	...	—	—	—	—	—
02-03—Miami (Ohio)	CCHA	41	24	18	42	16	...	...	...	—	—	—	—	—
03-04—Miami (Ohio)	CCHA	41	19	23	42	16	...	...	...	—	—	—	—	—
—Manchester	AHL	3	0	1	1	0	...	...	...	—	—	—	—	—
04-05—Manchester	AHL	14	1	0	1	10	-2	0	0	0	0	0	0	0

HOLDEN, JOSH C/RW MAPLE LEAFS

PERSONAL: Born January 18, 1978, in Calgary. ... 6-0/189. ... Shoots left.

TRANSACTIONS/CAREER NOTES: Selected by Vancouver Canucks in 1st round (1st Canucks pick, 12th overall) of NHL draft (June 22, 1996). ... Hernia; missed first 22 games of 1999-2000 season. ... Claimed by Carolina Hurricanes in waiver draft (September 28, 2001). ... Claimed off waivers by Canucks (October 25, 2001). ... Traded by Canucks to Toronto Maple Leafs for C Jeff Farkas (June 22, 2002).

		REGULAR SEASON								PLAYOFFS				
Season Team	League	GP	G	A	Pts.	PIM	+/-	PP	SH	GP	G	A	Pts.	PIM
94-95—Regina	WHL	62	20	23	43	45	...	...	...	4	3	1	4	0
95-96—Regina	WHL	70	57	55	112	105	...	...	...	11	4	5	9	23
96-97—Regina	WHL	58	49	49	98	148	14	17	2	5	3	2	5	10
97-98—Regina	WHL	56	41	58	99	134	45	12	6	2	2	2	4	10
98-99—Syracuse	AHL	38	14	15	29	48	-19	7	1	—	—	—	—	—
—Vancouver	NHL	30	2	4	6	10	-10	1	0	—	—	—	—	—
99-00—Syracuse	AHL	45	19	32	51	113	...	...	...	4	1	0	1	10
—Vancouver	NHL	6	1	5	6	2	2	0	0	—	—	—	—	—
00-01—Kansas City	IHL	60	27	26	53	136	...	...	...	—	—	—	—	—
—Vancouver	NHL	10	1	0	1	0	0	0	0	—	—	—	—	—
01-02—Carolina	NHL	8	0	0	0	2	0	0	0	—	—	—	—	—
—Manitoba	AHL	68	16	17	33	187	-1	6	2	7	1	1	2	4
02-03—St. John's	AHL	65	24	29	53	123	0	3	1	—	—	—	—	—
—Toronto	NHL	5	1	0	1	2	-2	0	0	—	—	—	—	—
03-04—Toronto	NHL	1	0	0	0	0	0	0	0	—	—	—	—	—
—St. John's	AHL	52	22	33	55	106	1	8	3	—	—	—	—	—
04-05—HPK Hameenlinna	Finland	51	21	15	36	94	9	...	...	10	6	1	7	12
NHL Totals (6 years)		60	5	9	14	16	-10	1	0					

HOLIK, BOBBY C THRASHERS

PERSONAL: Born January 1, 1971, in Jihlava, Czech. ... 6-4/235. ... Shoots right. ... Name pronounced hoh-LEEK.

TRANSACTIONS/CAREER NOTES: Selected by Hartford Whalers in 1st round (1st Whalers pick, 10th overall) of NHL draft (June 17, 1989). ... Traded by Whalers with 2nd-round pick (LW Jay Pandolfo) in 1993 draft to New Jersey Devils for G Sean Burke and D Eric Weinrich (August 28, 1992). ... Bruised left shoulder (December 8, 1993); missed 11 games. ... Fractured left index finger (October 7, 1995); missed 13 games. ... Sprained left ankle (February 28, 1996); missed six games. ... Suspended two games and fined $1,000 for tripping incident (November 8, 1998). ... Suspended two games for slashing incident (March 23, 1999). ... Suspended three games for slashing incident (November 25,

1999). ... Injured knee (February 15, 2001); missed two games. ... Suspended one game for high-sticking incident (March 24, 2002). ... Signed as free agent by New York Rangers (July 1, 2002). ... Injured hip flexor (October 16, 2002); missed 18 games. ... Contract bought out by Rangers (July 29, 2005). ... Signed as a free agent by the Atlanta Thrashers (Aug. 2, 2005).
STATISTICAL PLATEAUS: Three-goal games: 1992-93 (2), 1998-99 (1). Total: 3.

		REGULAR SEASON								PLAYOFFS				
Season Team	**League**	**GP**	**G**	**A**	**Pts.**	**PIM**	**+/-**	**PP**	**SH**	**GP**	**G**	**A**	**Pts.**	**PIM**
87-88—Dukla Jihlava	Czech.	31	5	9	14	...	...	...	...	—	—	—	—	—
88-89—Dukla Jihlava	Czech.	24	7	10	17	...	...	...	...	—	—	—	—	—
89-90—Dukla Jihlava	Czech.	42	15	26	41	...	...	...	...	—	—	—	—	—
—Czech. national team	Int'l	10	1	5	6	0	...	...	...	—	—	—	—	—
90-91—Hartford	NHL	78	21	22	43	113	-3	8	0	6	0	0	0	7
91-92—Hartford	NHL	76	21	24	45	44	4	1	0	7	0	1	1	6
92-93—Utica	AHL	1	0	0	0	2	-1	0	0	—	—	—	—	—
—New Jersey	NHL	61	20	19	39	76	-6	7	0	5	1	1	2	6
93-94—New Jersey	NHL	70	13	20	33	72	28	2	0	20	0	3	3	6
94-95—New Jersey	NHL	48	10	10	20	18	9	0	0	20	4	4	8	22
95-96—New Jersey	NHL	63	13	17	30	58	9	1	0	—	—	—	—	—
96-97—New Jersey	NHL	82	23	39	62	54	24	5	0	10	2	3	5	4
97-98—New Jersey	NHL	82	29	36	65	100	23	8	0	5	0	0	0	8
98-99—New Jersey	NHL	78	27	37	64	119	16	5	0	7	0	7	7	6
99-00—New Jersey	NHL	79	23	23	46	106	7	7	0	23	3	7	10	14
00-01—New Jersey	NHL	80	15	35	50	97	19	3	0	25	6	10	16	37
01-02—New Jersey	NHL	81	25	29	54	97	7	6	0	6	4	1	5	2
02-03—New York Rangers	NHL	64	16	19	35	50	-1	3	0	—	—	—	—	—
03-04—New York Rangers	NHL	82	25	31	56	96	4	8	0	—	—	—	—	—
NHL Totals (14 years)		1024	281	361	642	1100	140	64	0	134	20	37	57	118

HOLLAND, JASON — D

PERSONAL: Born April 30, 1976, in Morinville, Alta. ... 6-3/210. ... Shoots right.
TRANSACTIONS/CAREER NOTES: Selected by New York Islanders in second round (second Islanders pick, 38th overall) of NHL entry draft (June 28, 1994). ... Traded by Islanders with LW Paul Kruse to Buffalo Sabres for RW Jason Dawe (March 24, 1998). ... Injured shoulder (October 2, 1999); missed two games. ... Signed as free agent by Los Angeles Kings (August 23, 2001). ... Bruised thigh (February 26, 2004); missed five games.

		REGULAR SEASON								PLAYOFFS				
Season Team	**League**	**GP**	**G**	**A**	**Pts.**	**PIM**	**+/-**	**PP**	**SH**	**GP**	**G**	**A**	**Pts.**	**PIM**
92-93—Kamloops	WHL	4	0	0	0	2	...	...	...	—	—	—	—	—
93-94—Kamloops	WHL	59	14	15	29	80	...	...	...	18	2	3	5	4
94-95—Kamloops	WHL	71	9	32	41	65	51	5	0	21	2	7	9	9
95-96—Kamloops	WHL	63	24	33	57	98	...	...	...	16	4	9	13	22
96-97—Kentucky	AHL	72	14	25	39	46	14	6	1	4	0	2	2	0
—New York Islanders	NHL	4	1	0	1	0	1	0	0	—	—	—	—	—
97-98—Kentucky	AHL	50	10	16	26	29	-12	5	0	—	—	—	—	—
—New York Islanders	NHL	8	0	0	0	4	-4	0	0	—	—	—	—	—
—Rochester	AHL	9	0	4	4	10	5	0	0	4	0	3	3	4
98-99—Buffalo	NHL	3	0	0	0	8	-1	0	0	—	—	—	—	—
—Rochester	AHL	74	4	25	29	36	30	3	0	20	2	5	7	8
99-00—Buffalo	NHL	9	0	1	1	0	0	0	0	1	0	0	0	0
—Rochester	AHL	54	3	15	18	24	...	...	...	12	1	0	1	2
00-01—Rochester	AHL	63	4	19	23	45	...	...	...	4	1	0	1	0
01-02—Manchester	AHL	65	9	18	27	39	2	2	1	5	1	0	1	5
—Los Angeles	NHL	3	0	0	0	0	-1	0	0	—	—	—	—	—
02-03—Manchester	AHL	67	4	27	31	53	0	3	0	3	0	0	0	0
—Los Angeles	NHL	2	0	1	1	0	1	0	0	—	—	—	—	—
03-04—Los Angeles	NHL	52	3	3	6	24	5	0	0	—	—	—	—	—
04-05—Alleghe	Italy	13	3	4	7	6	...	...	...	—	—	—	—	—
—Manchester	AHL	53	1	9	10	64	10	0	1	6	1	1	2	0
NHL Totals (7 years)		81	4	5	9	36	1	0	0	1	0	0	0	0

HOLMQVIST, ANDREAS — D — LIGHTNING

PERSONAL: Born July 23, 1981, in Stockholm, Sweden. ... 6-3/187. ... Shoots right.
TRANSACTIONS/CAREER NOTES: Selected by Tampa Bay Lightning in second round (third Lightning pick, 61st overall) of NHL entry draft (June 23, 2001).

		REGULAR SEASON								PLAYOFFS				
Season Team	**League**	**GP**	**G**	**A**	**Pts.**	**PIM**	**+/-**	**PP**	**SH**	**GP**	**G**	**A**	**Pts.**	**PIM**
99-00—Hammarby	Sweden Jr.	38	8	12	20	16	...	...	...	6	1	2	3	4
00-01—Hammarby	Sweden Jr.	47	6	15	21	40	...	...	...	—	—	—	—	—
01-02—Hammarby	Sweden Dv. 2	42	11	13	24	97	...	...	...	—	—	—	—	—
02-03—Linkopings	Sweden	43	4	9	13	...	28	...	...	—	—	—	—	—
03-04—Hamilton	AHL	4	0	0	0	0	1	0	0	—	—	—	—	—
—Pensacola	ECHL	63	4	33	37	16	...	...	...	5	0	4	4	0
04-05—Springfield	AHL	42	3	9	12	22	-15	0	0	—	—	—	—	—

HOLMQVIST, JOHAN — G — WILD

PERSONAL: Born May 24, 1978, in Tolfta, Sweden. ... 6-3/195. ... Catches left.
TRANSACTIONS/CAREER NOTES: Selected by New York Rangers in seventh round (ninth Rangers pick, 182nd overall) of NHL entry draft

(June 21, 1997). ... Traded by Rangers to Minnesota Wild for D Lawrence Nycholat (March 11, 2003). ... Signed as free agent by Brynas of the Swedish league (July 29, 2004).

		REGULAR SEASON									PLAYOFFS							
Season Team	**League**	**GP**	**Min.**	**W**	**L**	**T**	**GA**	**SO**	**GAA**	**SV%**	**GP**	**Min.**	**W**	**L**	**GA**	**SO**	**GAA**	**SV%**
96-97—Brynas Gavle	Sweden	2	80	0	0	0	4	...	3.00	...	—	—	—	—	—	—	—	—
97-98—Brynas Gavle	Sweden	33	1897	...	...	...	82	...	2.59	...	3	180	0	3	14	...	4.67	...
98-99—Brynas Gavle	Sweden	41	2383	...	...	...	111	4	2.79	...	14	855	9	5	34	0	2.39	...
99-00—Brynas Gavle	Sweden	41	2402	...	...	...	104	4	2.60	...	11	671	...	...	30	1	2.68	...
00-01—Hartford	AHL	43	2305	19	14	4	111	2	2.89	.906	5	314	2	3	13	0	2.48	...
—New York Rangers	NHL	2	119	0	2	0	10	0	5.04	.859	—	—	—	—	—	—	—	—
01-02—Hartford	AHL	48	2733	26	12	6	140	1	3.07	.888	4	163	1	2	12	0	4.42	.815
—New York Rangers	NHL	1	9	0	0	0	0	0	0.00	1.00	—	—	—	—	—	—	—	—
02-03—Hartford	AHL	35	1904	14	13	5	84	2	2.65	.910	—	—	—	—	—	—	—	—
—Charlotte	ECHL	1	60	1	0	0	2	0	2.00	.956	—	—	—	—	—	—	—	—
—New York Rangers	NHL	1	39	0	1	0	2	0	3.08	.889	—	—	—	—	—	—	—	—
—Houston	AHL	8	479	5	3	0	23	1	2.88	.900	23	1498	15	8	50	1	2.00	.928
03-04—Houston	AHL	59	3469	23	27	7	148	4	2.56	.899	—	—	—	—	—	—	—	—
NHL Totals (3 years)		4	167	0	3	0	12	0	4.31	.868								

HOLMQVIST, MIKAEL C MIGHTY DUCKS

PERSONAL: Born June 8, 1979, in Stockholm, Sweden. ... 6-3/202. ... Shoots left.

TRANSACTIONS/CAREER NOTES: Selected by Mighty Ducks of Anaheim in first round (first Mighty Ducks pick, 18th overall) of NHL entry draft (June 21, 1997). ... Injured stomach muscle (January 18, 2004); missed 22 games.

		REGULAR SEASON								PLAYOFFS				
Season Team	**League**	**GP**	**G**	**A**	**Pts.**	**PIM**	**+/-**	**PP**	**SH**	**GP**	**G**	**A**	**Pts.**	**PIM**
95-96—Djurgarden Stockholm	Sweden Jr.	24	7	2	9	4	...	...	...	—	—	—	—	—
96-97—Sweden	Int'l	6	1	3	4	4	...	...	...	—	—	—	—	—
—Djurgarden Stockholm	Sweden Jr.	39	29	35	64	110	...	...	...	—	—	—	—	—
—Djurgarden Stockholm	Sweden	9	0	0	0	0	...	...	...	—	—	—	—	—
97-98—Farjestad Karlstad	Sweden	41	2	3	5	6	...	...	...	7	0	0	0	0
—Swedish nat. Jr.	Sweden	7	0	1	1	28	...	...	...	—	—	—	—	—
98-99—Farjestad Karlstad	Sweden	15	0	0	0	6	-1	...	...	—	—	—	—	—
99-00—TPS Turku	Finland	54	12	3	15	14	...	...	...	11	2	3	5	4
00-01—TPS Turku	Finland	46	4	5	9	8	...	...	...	10	1	3	4	2
01-02—TPS Turku	Finland	56	9	13	22	16	...	...	...	8	1	0	1	12
02-03—TPS Turku	Finland	56	15	25	40	36	...	...	...	7	0	0	0	4
03-04—Anaheim	NHL	21	2	0	2	25	-6	0	0	—	—	—	—	—
—Cincinnati	AHL	24	7	7	14	20	0	1	2	—	—	—	—	—
04-05—Cincinnati	AHL	79	14	32	46	111	-2	6	0	11	2	2	4	10
NHL Totals (1 year)		21	2	0	2	25	-6	0	0					

HOLMSTROM, TOMAS LW RED WINGS

PERSONAL: Born January 23, 1973, in Pieta, Sweden. ... 6-0/200. ... Shoots left.

TRANSACTIONS/CAREER NOTES: Selected by Detroit Red Wings in 10th round (ninth Red Wings pick, 257th overall) of NHL draft (June 29, 1994). ... Sprained knee (October 30, 1996); missed seven games. ... Bruised shoulder (March 28, 1997); missed one game. ... Sprained knee (November 17, 1999); missed five games. ... Injured (March 3, 2000); missed one game. ... Cut face (March 29, 2000); missed two games. ... Charley horse (November 12, 2000); missed one game. ... Back spasms (December 31, 2000); missed three games. ... Injured (October 16, 2001); missed two games. ... Injured wrist (November 2, 2001); missed five games. ... Flu (January 4, 2002); missed three games. ... Injured sternum (October 29, 2002); missed three games. ... Flu (December 8, 2002); missed one game. ... Injured sternum (January 28, 2003); missed two games. ... Flu (March 22, 2003); missed two games. ... Separated right shoulder (November 27, 2003); missed 15 games.

STATISTICAL PLATEAUS: Three-goal games: 2000-01 (1).

		REGULAR SEASON								PLAYOFFS				
Season Team	**League**	**GP**	**G**	**A**	**Pts.**	**PIM**	**+/-**	**PP**	**SH**	**GP**	**G**	**A**	**Pts.**	**PIM**
94-95—Lulea	Sweden	40	14	14	28	56	...	...	...	8	1	2	3	20
95-96—Lulea	Sweden	34	12	11	23	78	...	...	...	11	6	2	8	22
96-97—Detroit	NHL	47	6	3	9	33	-10	3	0	1	0	0	0	0
—Adirondack	AHL	6	3	1	4	7	-1	1	0	—	—	—	—	—
97-98—Detroit	NHL	57	5	17	22	44	6	1	0	22	7	12	19	16
98-99—Detroit	NHL	82	13	21	34	69	-11	5	0	10	4	3	7	4
99-00—Detroit	NHL	72	13	22	35	43	4	4	0	9	3	1	4	16
00-01—Detroit	NHL	73	16	24	40	40	-12	9	0	6	1	3	4	8
01-02—Detroit	NHL	69	8	18	26	58	-12	6	0	23	8	3	11	8
—Swedish Oly. team	Int'l	4	1	0	1	2	...	...	...	—	—	—	—	—
02-03—Detroit	NHL	74	20	20	40	62	11	12	0	4	1	1	2	4
03-04—Detroit	NHL	67	15	15	30	38	8	6	0	12	2	2	4	10
04-05—Lulea	Sweden	47	14	16	30	50	-10	6	0	4	0	0	0	18
NHL Totals (8 years)		541	96	140	236	387	-16	46	0	87	26	25	51	66

HOLZINGER, BRIAN C/RW

PERSONAL: Born October 10, 1972, in Parma, Ohio. ... 5-11/186. ... Shoots right. ... Name pronounced HOHL-zihng-uhr.

TRANSACTIONS/CAREER NOTES: Selected by Buffalo Sabres in sixth round (seventh Sabres pick, 124th overall) of NHL draft (June 22, 1991). ... Bruised heel (November 10, 1997); missed three games. ... Sprained ankle (March 1, 1998); missed seven games. ... Flu (January 7, 1999); missed one game. ... Injured shoulder (October 17, 1999); missed three games. ... Injured shoulder (January 6, 2000); missed three games.

... Traded by Sabres with C Wayne Primeau, D Cory Sarich and third-round pick (RW Alexandre Kharitonov) in 2000 draft to Tampa Bay Lightning for C Chris Gratton and second-round pick (C Derek Roy) in 2001 draft (March 9, 2000). ... Strained muscle in abdomen (March 12, 2000); missed three games. ... Fractured finger (December 2, 2000); missed five games. ... Injured foot (March 24, 2001); missed two games. ... Fractured right ankle (April 1, 2001); missed final two games of season. ... Injured left shoulder (November 25, 2001); missed three games. ... Reinjured shoulder (December 6, 2001); missed 10 games. ... Injured left shoulder (January 4, 2002); missed remainder of season. ... Fractured leg (October 10, 2002); missed 18 games. ... Traded by Lightning to Pittsburgh Penguins for D Marc Bergevin (March 11, 2003). ... Injured knee (March 31, 2003); missed three games. ... Traded by Penguins to Columbus Blue Jackets for LW Lasse Pirjeta (March 9, 2004).

		REGULAR SEASON								PLAYOFFS				
Season Team	**League**	**GP**	**G**	**A**	**Pts.**	**PIM**	**+/-**	**PP**	**SH**	**GP**	**G**	**A**	**Pts.**	**PIM**
90-91—Det. Jr. Red Wings	NAJHL	37	45	41	86	16	...	...	...	—	—	—	—	—
91-92—Bowling Green	CCHA	30	14	8	22	36	...	6	1	—	—	—	—	—
92-93—Bowling Green	CCHA	41	31	26	57	44	...	8	0	—	—	—	—	—
93-94—Bowling Green	CCHA	38	22	15	37	24	...	4	3	—	—	—	—	—
94-95—Bowling Green	CCHA	38	35	34	69	42	19	9	4	—	—	—	—	—
—Buffalo	NHL	4	0	3	3	0	2	0	0	4	2	1	3	2
95-96—Buffalo	NHL	58	10	10	20	37	-21	5	0	—	—	—	—	—
—Rochester	AHL	17	10	11	21	14	...	...	...	19	10	14	24	10
96-97—Buffalo	NHL	81	22	29	51	54	9	2	2	12	2	5	7	8
97-98—Buffalo	NHL	69	14	21	35	36	-2	4	2	15	4	7	11	18
98-99—Buffalo	NHL	81	17	17	34	45	2	5	0	21	3	5	8	33
99-00—Buffalo	NHL	59	7	17	24	30	4	0	1	—	—	—	—	—
—Tampa Bay	NHL	14	3	3	6	21	-7	1	1	—	—	—	—	—
00-01—Tampa Bay	NHL	70	11	25	36	64	-9	3	0	—	—	—	—	—
01-02—Tampa Bay	NHL	23	1	2	3	4	-4	0	0	—	—	—	—	—
02-03—Tampa Bay	NHL	5	0	1	1	2	1	0	0	—	—	—	—	—
—Springfield	AHL	28	6	20	26	16	3	0	0	—	—	—	—	—
—Pittsburgh	NHL	9	1	2	3	6	-6	0	0	—	—	—	—	—
03-04—Pittsburgh	NHL	61	6	15	21	38	-27	1	1	—	—	—	—	—
—Columbus	NHL	13	1	0	1	2	-4	0	0	—	—	—	—	—
NHL Totals (10 years)		547	93	145	238	339	-62	21	7	52	11	18	29	61

HORCOFF, SHAWN C/LW OILERS

PERSONAL: Born September 17, 1978, in Trail, B.C. ... 6-1/204. ... Shoots left.

TRANSACTIONS/CAREER NOTES: Selected by Edmonton Oilers in 4th round (3rd Oilers pick, 99th overall) of NHL draft (June 27, 1998). ... Back spasms (November 20, 2003); missed one game.

		REGULAR SEASON								PLAYOFFS				
Season Team	**League**	**GP**	**G**	**A**	**Pts.**	**PIM**	**+/-**	**PP**	**SH**	**GP**	**G**	**A**	**Pts.**	**PIM**
95-96—Chilliwack	BCJHL	58	49	96	*145	44	...	...	...	—	—	—	—	—
96-97—Michigan State	CCHA	40	10	13	23	20	...	...	...	—	—	—	—	—
97-98—Michigan State	CCHA	34	14	13	27	50	...	...	...	—	—	—	—	—
98-99—Michigan State	CCHA	39	12	25	37	70	...	...	...	—	—	—	—	—
99-00—Michigan State	CCHA	41	14	*48	*62	46	...	...	...	—	—	—	—	—
00-01—Hamilton	AHL	24	10	18	28	19	...	...	...	—	—	—	—	—
—Edmonton	NHL	49	9	7	16	10	8	0	0	5	0	0	0	0
01-02—Edmonton	NHL	61	8	14	22	18	3	0	0	—	—	—	—	—
—Hamilton	AHL	2	1	2	3	6	2	0	0	—	—	—	—	—
02-03—Edmonton	NHL	78	12	21	33	55	10	2	0	6	3	1	4	6
03-04—Edmonton	NHL	80	15	25	40	73	0	0	2	—	—	—	—	—
04-05—Mora	Sweden Dv. 1	50	19	27	46	117	-11	6	1	—	—	—	—	—
NHL Totals (4 years)		268	44	67	111	156	21	2	2	11	3	1	4	6

HORDICHUK, DARCY LW PREDATORS

PERSONAL: Born August 10, 1980, in Kamsack, Sask. ... 6-1/215. ... Shoots left.

TRANSACTIONS/CAREER NOTES: Selected by Atlanta Thrashers in 6th round (8th Thrashers pick, 180th overall) of NHL draft (June 24, 2000). ... Traded by Thrashers with 4th- (RW Lance Monych) and 5th-round (RW John Zeiler) picks in 2002 draft to Phoenix Coyotes for D Kirill Safronov, RW Ruslan Zainullin and 4th-round pick (RW Patrick Dwyer) in 2002 draft (March 19, 2002). ... Suspended 10 games for abuse of an official (November 1, 2002). ... Injured ankle (March 15, 2003); missed 10 games. ... Traded by Coyotes with 2nd-round pick (Matt Smaby) in 2003 draft to Florida Panthers for D Brad Ference (March 9, 2003). ... Fractured foot (November 13, 2003); missed 21 games. ... Fractured left hand (March 27, 2004) and had surgery; missed remainer of season. ... Traded by Panthers to Nashville Predators for 4th-round pick in 2005 draft (July 27, 2005).

		REGULAR SEASON								PLAYOFFS				
Season Team	**League**	**GP**	**G**	**A**	**Pts.**	**PIM**	**+/-**	**PP**	**SH**	**GP**	**G**	**A**	**Pts.**	**PIM**
96-97—Calgary	WHL	3	0	0	0	2	...	...	...	—	—	—	—	—
98-99—Saskatoon	WHL	66	3	2	5	246	...	...	...	—	—	—	—	—
99-00—Saskatoon	WHL	63	6	8	14	269	...	...	...	—	—	—	—	—
00-01—Orlando	IHL	69	7	3	10	*369	...	...	...	16	3	3	6	*41
—Atlanta	NHL	11	0	0	0	38	-3	0	0	—	—	—	—	—
01-02—Chicago	AHL	34	5	4	9	127	2	0	0	—	—	—	—	—
—Atlanta	NHL	33	1	1	2	127	-5	0	0	—	—	—	—	—
—Phoenix	NHL	1	0	0	0	14	0	0	0	—	—	—	—	—
02-03—Phoenix	NHL	25	0	0	0	82	-1	0	0	—	—	—	—	—
—Springfield	AHL	22	1	3	4	38	-3	0	0	—	—	—	—	—
—Florida	NHL	3	0	0	0	15	-1	0	0	—	—	—	—	—
03-04—Florida	NHL	57	3	1	4	158	-10	0	0	—	—	—	—	—
NHL Totals (4 years)		130	4	2	6	434	-20	0	0					

HORTON, NATHAN — C — PANTHERS

PERSONAL: Born May 29, 1985, in Welland, Ont. ... 6-2/201. ... Shoots right.

TRANSACTIONS/CAREER NOTES: Selected by Florida Panthers in first round (first Panthers pick, third overall) in 2003 NHL entry draft (June 23, 2003). ... Injured left shoulder (January 13, 2004) and had surgery (January 16, 2004); missed 21 games.. ... Had sore shoulder (March 9, 2004); missed one game. ... Injured shoulder (March 29, 2004) and had surgery; missed remainder of season.

		REGULAR SEASON								PLAYOFFS				
Season Team	**League**	**GP**	**G**	**A**	**Pts.**	**PIM**	**+/-**	**PP**	**SH**	**GP**	**G**	**A**	**Pts.**	**PIM**
01-02—Oshawa	OHL	64	31	36	67	84	...	...	...	—	—	—	—	—
02-03—Oshawa	OHL	54	33	35	68	111	...	...	...	—	—	—	—	—
03-04—Florida	NHL	55	14	8	22	57	-5	6	1	—	—	—	—	—
04-05—San Antonio	AHL	21	5	4	9	21	1	1	0	—	—	—	—	—
NHL Totals (1 year)		55	14	8	22	57	-5	6	1					

HOSSA, MARCEL — LW — CANADIENS

PERSONAL: Born October 12, 1981, in Ilava, Czechoslovakia. ... 6-2/215. ... Shoots left. ... Brother of Marian Hossa, LW, Ottawa Senators. ... Name pronounced HOH-suh.

TRANSACTIONS/CAREER NOTES: Selected by Montreal Canadiens in first round (second Canadiens pick, 16th overall) of NHL draft (June 24, 2000). ... Injured wrist (January 14, 2002); missed two games. ... Reinjured wrist (January 19, 2002); missed five games.

		REGULAR SEASON								PLAYOFFS				
Season Team	**League**	**GP**	**G**	**A**	**Pts.**	**PIM**	**+/-**	**PP**	**SH**	**GP**	**G**	**A**	**Pts.**	**PIM**
96-97—Dukla Trencin	Slovakia Jrs.	45	30	21	51	30	...	...	...	—	—	—	—	—
97-98—Dukla Trencin	Slovakia Jrs.	39	11	38	49	44	...	...	...	—	—	—	—	—
98-99—Portland	WHL	70	7	14	21	66	...	...	...	2	0	0	0	0
99-00—Portland	WHL	60	24	29	53	58	...	...	...	—	—	—	—	—
00-01—Portland	WHL	58	34	56	90	58	...	...	...	16	5	7	12	14
01-02—Quebec	AHL	50	17	15	32	24	-5	4	0	3	0	0	0	4
—Montreal	NHL	10	3	1	4	2	2	0	0	—	—	—	—	—
02-03—Montreal	NHL	34	6	7	13	14	3	2	0	—	—	—	—	—
—Hamilton	AHL	37	19	13	32	18	22	7	0	21	4	7	11	12
03-04—Montreal	NHL	15	1	1	2	8	-3	0	0	—	—	—	—	—
—Hamilton	AHL	57	18	22	40	45	7	6	0	10	2	3	5	8
04-05—Mora	Sweden Dv. 1	48	18	6	24	69	-6	8	1	—	—	—	—	—
NHL Totals (3 years)		59	10	9	19	24	2	2	0					

HOSSA, MARIAN — RW — SENATORS

PERSONAL: Born January 12, 1979, in Stara Lubovna, Czechoslovakia. ... 6-1/207. ... Shoots left. ... Brother of Marcel Hossa, C, Montreal Canadiens organization. ... Name pronounced HOH-suh.

TRANSACTIONS/CAREER NOTES: Selected by Ottawa Senators in first round (first Senators pick, 12th overall) of NHL draft (June 21, 1997). ... Tore knee ligaments (May 21, 1998); missed first 22 games of season. ... Had concussion (November 18, 1999); missed one game. ... Bruised left wrist (January 6, 2000); missed two games. ... Flu (February 1, 2000); missed one game. ... Bruised calf (February 18, 2001); missed one game. ... Injured left knee (February 4, 2002); missed one game. ... Flu (April 13, 2002); missed one game. ... Flu (February 4, 2003); missed two games. ... Injured foot (November 11, 2003); missed one game.

STATISTICAL PLATEAUS: Three-goal games: 2000-01 (1), 2002-03 (2). Total: 3. ... Four-goal games: 2002-03 (1). ... Total hat tricks: 4.

		REGULAR SEASON								PLAYOFFS				
Season Team	**League**	**GP**	**G**	**A**	**Pts.**	**PIM**	**+/-**	**PP**	**SH**	**GP**	**G**	**A**	**Pts.**	**PIM**
95-96—Dukla Trencin	Slovakia Jrs.	53	42	49	91	26	...	...	...	—	—	—	—	—
96-97—Dukla Trencin	Slovakia	46	25	19	44	33	...	...	...	7	5	5	10	...
97-98—Ottawa	NHL	7	0	1	1	0	-1	0	0	—	—	—	—	—
—Portland	WHL	53	45	40	85	50	41	11	1	16	13	6	19	6
98-99—Ottawa	NHL	60	15	15	30	37	18	1	0	4	0	2	2	4
99-00—Ottawa	NHL	78	29	27	56	32	5	5	0	6	0	0	0	2
00-01—Ottawa	NHL	81	32	43	75	44	19	11	2	4	1	1	2	4
01-02—Dukla Trencin	Slovakia	8	3	4	7	16	...	...	...	—	—	—	—	—
—Ottawa	NHL	80	31	35	66	50	11	9	1	12	4	6	10	2
—Slovakian Oly. team	Int'l	2	4	2	6	0	...	...	...	—	—	—	—	—
02-03—Ottawa	NHL	80	45	35	80	34	8	14	0	18	5	11	16	6
03-04—Ottawa	NHL	81	36	46	82	46	4	14	1	7	3	1	4	0
04-05—Mora	Sweden Dv. 1	24	18	14	32	22	8	3	1	—	—	—	—	—
—Dukla Trencin	Slovakia	25	22	20	42	38	34	...	...	5	4	5	9	14
NHL Totals (7 years)		467	188	202	390	243	64	54	4	51	13	21	34	18

HRDEL, ZBYNEK — LW — LIGHTNING

PERSONAL: Born August 19, 1985, in Pisek, Czechoslovakia. ... 6-4/195. ... Shoots right.

TRANSACTIONS/CAREER NOTES: Selected by Tampa Bay Lightning in ninth round (10th Lightning pick, 286th overall) of NHL entry draft (June 21, 2003).

		REGULAR SEASON								PLAYOFFS				
Season Team	**League**	**GP**	**G**	**A**	**Pts.**	**PIM**	**+/-**	**PP**	**SH**	**GP**	**G**	**A**	**Pts.**	**PIM**
02-03—Rimouski	QMJHL	65	10	14	24	131	...	...	...	—	—	—	—	—
03-04—Rimouski	QMJHL	54	15	31	46	41	19	3	1	9	4	6	10	4
04-05—Rimouski	QMJHL	56	23	35	58	47	25	7	2	13	8	7	15	10

HRDINA, JAN — C/LW — BLUE JACKETS

PERSONAL: Born February 5, 1976, in Hradec Kralove, Czech. ... 6-0/206. ... Shoots right. ... Name pronounced YAHN huhr-DEE-nuh.

TRANSACTIONS/CAREER NOTES: Selected by Pittsburgh Penguins in 5th round (4th Penguins pick, 128th overall) of NHL draft (July 8, 1995). ... Sprained ankle (October 14, 1999); missed 12 games. ... Strained groin (December 5, 2000); missed three games. ... Bruised hip (January 12, 2001); missed one game. ... Strained back (January 23, 2002); missed two games. ... Flu (April 3, 2002); missed one game. ... Back spasms (January 7, 2003); missed two games. ... Injured hip (February 14, 2003); missed four games. ... Aggravated hip injury (February 27, 2003); missed seven games. ... Traded by Penguins with D Francois Leroux to Phoenix Coyotes for LW Ramzi Abid, D Dan Focht and LW Guillaume Lefebvre (March 11, 2003). ... Injured hip flexor (March 14, 2003); missed 10 games. ... Fractured toe (November 17, 2003); missed 11 games. ... Traded by Coyotes to New Jersey Devils for C Mike Rupp and 2nd-round pick (traded to Edmonton Oilers) in 2004 draft (March 5, 2004). ... Signed as free agent by Columbus Blue Jackets (Aug. 10, 2005).

		REGULAR SEASON								PLAYOFFS				
Season Team	**League**	**GP**	**G**	**A**	**Pts.**	**PIM**	**+/-**	**PP**	**SH**	**GP**	**G**	**A**	**Pts.**	**PIM**
93-94—Std.Hradec Kralove	Czech Rep.	21	1	5	6	...	...	...	...	—	—	—	—	—
94-95—Seattle	WHL	69	41	59	100	79	24	12	4	4	0	1	1	8
95-96—Seattle	WHL	30	19	28	47	37	...	...	...	—	—	—	—	—
—Spokane	WHL	18	10	16	26	25	...	...	...	18	5	14	19	49
96-97—Cleveland	IHL	68	23	31	54	82	...	...	...	13	1	2	3	8
97-98—Syracuse	AHL	72	20	24	44	82	-3	3	0	5	1	3	4	10
98-99—Pittsburgh	NHL	82	13	29	42	40	-2	3	0	13	4	1	5	12
99-00—Pittsburgh	NHL	70	13	33	46	43	13	3	0	9	4	8	12	2
00-01—Pittsburgh	NHL	78	15	28	43	48	19	3	0	18	2	5	7	8
01-02—Pittsburgh	NHL	79	24	33	57	50	-7	6	0	—	—	—	—	—
—Czech Rep. Oly. team	Int'l	4	0	0	0	0	...	...	...	—	—	—	—	—
02-03—Pittsburgh	NHL	57	14	25	39	34	1	11	0	—	—	—	—	—
—Phoenix	NHL	4	0	4	4	8	3	0	0	—	—	—	—	—
03-04—Phoenix	NHL	55	11	15	26	30	-10	5	0	—	—	—	—	—
—New Jersey	NHL	13	1	6	7	10	4	0	0	5	2	0	2	2
04-05—HC Kladno	Czech Rep.	23	4	3	7	38	-7	...	...	7	3	3	6	4
NHL Totals (6 years)		438	91	173	264	263	21	31	0	45	12	14	26	24

HRKAC, TONY — C

PERSONAL: Born July 7, 1966, in Thunder Bay, Ont. ... 5-11/190. ... Shoots left. ... Name pronounced HUHR-kuhz.

TRANSACTIONS/CAREER NOTES: Selected by St. Louis Blues in second round (second Blues pick, 32nd overall) of NHL draft (June 9, 1984). ... Bruised left leg (January 1987). ... Sprained shoulder (January 12, 1988). ... Cut ankle (March 1988). ... Bruised left shoulder (November 28, 1989). ... Traded by Blues with G Greg Millen to Quebec Nordiques for D Jeff Brown (December 13, 1989). ... Traded by Nordiques to San Jose Sharks for RW Greg Paslawski (May 30, 1991). ... Injured wrist during preseason (September 1991); missed first 27 games of season. ... Traded by Sharks to Chicago Blackhawks for future considerations (February 7, 1992). ... Signed as free agent by Blues (July 30, 1993). ... Signed as free agent by Dallas Stars (July 25, 1997). ... Claimed on waivers by Edmonton Oilers (January 6, 1998). ... Traded by Oilers with D Bobby Dollas to Pittsburgh Penguins for LW Josef Beranek (June 16, 1998). ... Selected by Nashville Predators in expansion draft (June 26, 1998). ... Traded by Predators to Stars for future considerations (July 9, 1998). ... Signed as free agent by New York Islanders (July 29, 1999). ... Traded by Islanders with D Dean Malkoc to Anaheim Mighty Ducks for C/LW Ted Drury (October 29, 1999). ... Signed as free agent by Atlanta Thrashers (July 16, 2001). ... Injured knee (January 7, 2003); missed two games. ... Signed as free agent by Nashville Predators (July 9, 2004).

		REGULAR SEASON								PLAYOFFS				
Season Team	**League**	**GP**	**G**	**A**	**Pts.**	**PIM**	**+/-**	**PP**	**SH**	**GP**	**G**	**A**	**Pts.**	**PIM**
83-84—Orillia	OHA	42	*52	54	*106	20	...	...	...	—	—	—	—	—
84-85—North Dakota	WCHA	36	18	36	54	16	...	...	...	—	—	—	—	—
85-86—Canadian nat'l team	Int'l	62	19	30	49	36	...	...	...	—	—	—	—	—
86-87—North Dakota	WCHA	48	46	*70	*116	48	...	...	...	—	—	—	—	—
—St. Louis	NHL	...	...	...	...	...	...	...	...	3	0	0	0	0
87-88—St. Louis	NHL	67	11	37	48	22	5	2	1	10	6	1	7	4
88-89—St. Louis	NHL	70	17	28	45	8	-10	5	0	4	1	1	2	0
89-90—St. Louis	NHL	28	5	12	17	8	1	1	0	—	—	—	—	—
—Quebec	NHL	22	4	8	12	2	-5	2	0	—	—	—	—	—
—Halifax	AHL	20	12	21	33	4	...	...	...	6	5	9	14	4
90-91—Halifax	AHL	3	4	1	5	2	...	...	...	—	—	—	—	—
—Quebec	NHL	70	16	32	48	16	-22	6	0	—	—	—	—	—
91-92—San Jose	NHL	22	2	10	12	4	-2	0	0	—	—	—	—	—
—Chicago	NHL	18	1	2	3	6	4	0	0	3	0	0	0	2
92-93—Indianapolis	IHL	80	45	*87	*132	70	15	14	5	5	0	2	2	2
93-94—St. Louis	NHL	36	6	5	11	8	-11	1	1	4	0	0	0	0
—Peoria	IHL	45	30	51	81	25	19	6	4	1	1	2	3	0
94-95—Milwaukee	IHL	71	24	67	91	26	11	3	1	15	4	9	13	16
95-96—Milwaukee	IHL	43	14	28	42	18	...	...	...	5	1	3	4	4
96-97—Milwaukee	IHL	81	27	61	88	20	...	...	...	3	1	1	2	2
97-98—Michigan	IHL	20	7	15	22	6	-4	1	0	—	—	—	—	—
—Dallas	NHL	13	5	3	8	0	0	3	0	—	—	—	—	—
—Edmonton	NHL	36	8	11	19	10	3	4	0	12	0	3	3	2
98-99—Dallas	NHL	69	13	14	27	26	2	2	0	5	0	2	2	4
99-00—New York Islanders	NHL	7	0	2	2	0	-1	0	0	—	—	—	—	—
—Anaheim	NHL	60	4	7	11	8	-2	1	0	—	—	—	—	—
00-01—Anaheim	NHL	80	13	25	38	29	0	0	0	—	—	—	—	—
01-02—Atlanta	NHL	80	18	26	44	12	-12	5	1	—	—	—	—	—
02-03—Atlanta	NHL	80	9	17	26	14	-16	2	0	—	—	—	—	—
03-04—Milwaukee	AHL	68	20	39	59	20	9	6	3	22	8	12	20	8
04-05—Milwaukee	AHL	77	12	28	40	14	-5	5	0	6	0	1	1	8
NHL Totals (13 years)		758	132	239	371	173	-66	34	3	41	7	7	14	12

HUDLER, JIRI — C — RED WINGS

PERSONAL: Born January 4, 1984, in Olomouc, Czechoslovakia. ... 5-9/154. ... Shoots left.

TRANSACTIONS/CAREER NOTES: Selected by Detroit Red Wings in second round (first Red Wings pick, 58th overall) of NHL draft (June 22, 2002).

Season Team	League	GP	G	A	Pts.	PIM	+/-	PP	SH		GP	G	A	Pts.	PIM
		REGULAR SEASON									PLAYOFFS				
01-02—HC Vsetin	Czech Rep.	46	15	31	46	54	...	...	...		—	—	—	—	—
02-03—Kazan	Rus. Div.	11	1	5	6	12	...	...	...		—	—	—	—	—
—HC Vsetin	Czech Rep.	11	1	5	6	12	...	...	...		1	0	0	0	0
03-04—Grand Rapids	AHL	57	17	32	49	46	15	4	0		4	1	5	6	2
—Detroit	NHL	12	1	2	3	10	-1	1	0		—	—	—	—	—
04-05—HC Vsetin	Czech Rep.	7	5	2	7	10	-1	...	...		—	—	—	—	—
—Grand Rapids	AHL	52	12	22	34	10	1	4	0		—	—	—	—	—
NHL Totals (1 year)		12	1	2	3	10	-1	1	0						

HUET, CRISTOBAL — G — CANADIENS

PERSONAL: Born September 3, 1975, in St. Martin D'Heres, France. ... 6-0/194. ... Name pronounced oo-AY.

TRANSACTIONS/CAREER NOTES: Selected by Los Angeles Kings in 7th round (9th Kings pick, 214th overall) of NHL draft (June 24, 2001). ... Traded by Kings with C Radek Bonk to Montreal Canadiens for G Mathieu Garon and 3rd-round pick (D Paul Baier) in 2004 draft (June 26, 2004). ... Torn ACL (June 2005); out indefinitely.

Season Team	League	GP	Min.	W	L	T	GA	SO	GAA	SV%		GP	Min.	W	L	GA	SO	GAA	SV%
		REGULAR SEASON										PLAYOFFS							
97-98—French Olympic Team	Int'l	2	120	1	1	0	5	0	2.50	...		—	—	—	—	—	—	—	—
98-99—Lugano	Switzerland	21	1275	...	...	...	58	1	2.73	...		...	...	...	...	18	1	...	...
99-00—Lugano	Switzerland	31	1886	...	...	...	50	8	1.59	...		...	...	...	...	29	0	...	...
00-01—Lugano	Switzerland	39	2365	...	...	...	77	6	1.95	...		...	...	...	...	39	2	...	...
01-02—Lugano	Switzerland	39	2313	...	...	...	107	4	2.78	...		...	...	...	...	3	0	...	...
—French Olympic Team	Int'l	3	179	0	2	1	10	0	3.35	...		—	—	—	—	—	—	—	—
02-03—Los Angeles	NHL	12	541	4	4	1	21	1	2.33	.913		—	—	—	—	—	—	—	—
—Manchester	AHL	30	1784	16	8	5	68	1	2.29	...		1	29	0	1	4	0	8.28	...
03-04—Los Angeles	NHL	41	2199	10	16	10	89	3	2.43	.907		—	—	—	—	—	—	—	—
04-05—Mannheim	Germany	36	2001	...	...	...	93	1	2.79	.915		14	850	...	...	40	2	2.82	.919
NHL Totals (2 years)		53	2740	14	20	11	110	4	2.41	.908									

HULL, BRETT — RW — COYOTES

PERSONAL: Born August 9, 1964, in Belleville, Ont. ... 5-11/203. ... Shoots right. ... Son of Bobby Hull, Hall of Fame LW with three NHL teams (1957-72 and 1979-80) and Winnipeg Jets of WHA (1972-79); and nephew of Dennis Hull, LW with two NHL teams (1964-78).

TRANSACTIONS/CAREER NOTES: Selected by Calgary Flames in 6th round (6th Flames pick, 117th overall) of NHL draft (June 9, 1984). ... Traded by Flames with LW Steve Bozek to St. Louis Blues for D Rob Ramage and G Rick Wamsley (March 7, 1988). ... Sprained left ankle (January 15, 1991); missed two regular-season games and All-Star Game. ... Back spasms (March 12, 1992); missed seven games. ... Sore wrist (March 20, 1993); missed four games. ... Injured abdominal muscle (October 7, 1993); missed three games. ... Strained groin (November 1, 1995); missed two games. ... Reinjured groin (November 10, 1995); missed five games. ... Injured hamstring (March 28, 1996); missed four games. ... Strained groin (March 30, 1997); missed four games. ... Strained buttocks (December 8, 1997); missed two games. ... Fractured left hand (December 27, 1997); missed 13 games. ... Signed as free agent by Dallas Stars (July 3, 1998). ... Bruised kidney (November 20, 1998); missed two games. ... Strained groin (November 25, 1998); missed one game. ... Reinjured groin (December 2, 1998); missed six games. ... Strained back (January 10, 1999); missed one game. ... Strained hamstring (February 24, 1999); missed 11 games. ... Injured groin (January 12, 2000); missed one game. ... Fractured nose (February 9, 2000); missed one game. ... Strained hip flexor (March 8, 2000); missed one game. ... Strained lower back (December 23, 2000); missed three games. ... Signed as free agent by Detroit Red Wings (August 22, 2001). ... Sore back (October 16, 2003); missed one game. ... Signed as a free agent by Phoenix Coyotes (Aug. 6, 2004).

STATISTICAL PLATEAUS: Three-goal games: 1987-88 (1), 1989-90 (5), 1990-91 (4), 1991-92 (8), 1993-94 (3), 1994-95 (1), 1995-96 (1), 1996-97 (2), 1997-98 (1), 2000-01 (1), 2001-02 (1), 2002-03 (2). Total: 30. ... Four-goal games: 1994-95 (1), 1995-96 (1), 2000-01 (1). Total: 3. ... Total hat tricks: 33.

Season Team	League	GP	G	A	Pts.	PIM	+/-	PP	SH		GP	G	A	Pts.	PIM
		REGULAR SEASON									PLAYOFFS				
82-83—Penticton	BCJHL	50	48	56	104	27	...	...	...		—	—	—	—	—
83-84—Penticton	BCJHL	56	*105	83	*188	20	...	...	...		—	—	—	—	—
84-85—Minnesota-Duluth	WCHA	48	32	28	60	24	...	...	...		—	—	—	—	—
85-86—Minnesota-Duluth	WCHA	42	*52	32	84	46	...	...	...		—	—	—	—	—
—Calgary	NHL	...	...	...	...	...	...	...	...		2	0	0	0	0
86-87—Moncton	AHL	67	50	42	92	16	...	...	...		3	2	2	4	2
—Calgary	NHL	5	1	0	1	0	-1	0	0		4	2	1	3	0
87-88—Calgary	NHL	52	26	24	50	12	10	4	0		—	—	—	—	—
—St. Louis	NHL	13	6	8	14	4	4	2	0		10	7	2	9	4
88-89—St. Louis	NHL	78	41	43	84	33	-17	16	0		10	5	5	10	6
89-90—St. Louis	NHL	80	*72	41	113	24	-1	*27	0		12	13	8	21	17
90-91—St. Louis	NHL	78	*86	45	131	22	23	*29	0		13	11	8	19	4
91-92—St. Louis	NHL	73	*70	39	109	48	-2	20	5		6	4	4	8	4
92-93—St. Louis	NHL	80	54	47	101	41	-27	29	0		11	8	5	13	2
93-94—St. Louis	NHL	81	57	40	97	38	-3	25	3		4	2	1	3	0
94-95—St. Louis	NHL	48	29	21	50	10	13	9	3		7	6	2	8	0
95-96—St. Louis	NHL	70	43	40	83	30	4	16	5		13	6	5	11	10
96-97—St. Louis	NHL	77	42	40	82	10	-9	12	2		6	2	7	9	2
97-98—St. Louis	NHL	66	27	45	72	26	-1	10	0		10	3	3	6	2
—U.S. Olympic team	Int'l	4	2	1	3	0	-1	1	0		—	—	—	—	—

H

Season Team	League	GP	G	A	Pts.	PIM	+/-	PP	SH	GP	G	A	Pts.	PIM
		REGULAR SEASON								PLAYOFFS				
98-99—Dallas	NHL	60	32	26	58	30	19	15	0	22	8	7	15	4
99-00—Dallas	NHL	79	24	35	59	43	-21	11	0	23	*11	13	*24	4
00-01—Dallas	NHL	79	39	40	79	18	10	11	0	10	2	5	7	6
01-02—Detroit	NHL	82	30	33	63	35	18	7	1	23	*10	8	18	4
—U.S. Olympic team	Int'l	6	3	5	8	6	...	...	...	—	—	—	—	—
02-03—Detroit	NHL	82	37	39	76	22	11	12	1	4	0	1	1	0
03-04—Detroit	NHL	81	25	43	68	12	-4	10	0	12	3	2	5	4
NHL Totals (19 years)		1264	741	649	1390	458	26	265	20	202	103	87	190	73

HULSE, CALE — D — COYOTES

PERSONAL: Born November 10, 1973, in Edmonton. ... 6-3/220. ... Shoots right. ... Name pronounced HUHLZ.

TRANSACTIONS/CAREER NOTES: Selected by New Jersey Devils in third round (third Devils pick, 66th overall) of NHL draft (June 20, 1992). ... Traded by Devils with D Tommy Albelin and RW Jocelyn Lemieux to Calgary Flames for D Phil Housley and D Dan Keczmer (February 26, 1996). ... Bruised ankle (February 28, 1997); missed four games. ... Reinjured ankle (March 7, 1997); missed one game. ... Reinjured ankle (March 21, 1997); missed one game. ... Bruised ribs (April 1, 1999); missed six games. ... Fractured hand (September 18, 1999); missed first four games of season. ... Sprained ankle (February 23, 2000); missed nine games. ... Traded by Flames with third-round pick (C/LW Denis Platonov) in 2001 entry draft to Nashville Predators for RW Sergei Krivokrasov (March 14, 2000); missed Predators final 12 games with sprained ankle. ... Fractured right hand (September 29, 2001); missed first 18 games of season. ... Strained right knee (March 10, 2002); missed one game. ... Suspended one game for cross-checking incident (February 23, 2003). ... Signed by Phoenix Coyotes as free agent (July 9, 2003).

Season Team	League	GP	G	A	Pts.	PIM	+/-	PP	SH	GP	G	A	Pts.	PIM
		REGULAR SEASON								PLAYOFFS				
90-91—Calgary Royals	AJHL	49	3	23	26	220	...	...	...	—	—	—	—	—
91-92—Portland	WHL	70	4	18	22	250	...	...	...	6	0	2	2	27
92-93—Portland	WHL	72	10	26	36	284	38	0	0	16	4	4	8	*65
93-94—Albany	AHL	79	7	14	21	186	-3	0	1	5	0	3	3	11
94-95—Albany	AHL	77	5	13	18	215	5	1	0	12	1	1	2	17
95-96—Albany	AHL	42	4	23	27	107	...	...	...	—	—	—	—	—
—New Jersey	NHL	8	0	0	0	15	-2	0	0	—	—	—	—	—
—Saint John	AHL	13	2	7	9	39	...	...	...	—	—	—	—	—
—Calgary	NHL	3	0	0	0	5	3	0	0	1	0	0	0	0
96-97—Calgary	NHL	63	1	6	7	91	-2	0	1	—	—	—	—	—
97-98—Calgary	NHL	79	5	22	27	169	1	1	1	—	—	—	—	—
98-99—Calgary	NHL	73	3	9	12	117	-8	0	0	—	—	—	—	—
99-00—Calgary	NHL	47	1	6	7	47	-11	0	0	—	—	—	—	—
00-01—Nashville	NHL	82	1	7	8	128	-5	0	0	—	—	—	—	—
01-02—Nashville	NHL	63	0	2	2	121	-18	0	0	—	—	—	—	—
02-03—Nashville	NHL	80	2	6	8	121	-11	0	0	—	—	—	—	—
03-04—Phoenix	NHL	82	3	17	20	123	-4	1	0	—	—	—	—	—
NHL Totals (9 years)		580	16	75	91	937	-57	2	2	1	0	0	0	0

HUML, IVAN — LW/RW — BRUINS

PERSONAL: Born September 6, 1981, in Kladno, Czech. ... 6-2/194. ... Shoots left.

TRANSACTIONS/CAREER NOTES: Selected by Boston Bruins in second round (fourth Bruins pick, 59th overall) of NHL draft (June 24, 2000).

Season Team	League	GP	G	A	Pts.	PIM	+/-	PP	SH	GP	G	A	Pts.	PIM
		REGULAR SEASON								PLAYOFFS				
98-99—Langley	BCHL	33	23	17	40	41	...	...	...	—	—	—	—	—
99-00—Langley	BCHL	49	53	51	104	72	...	...	...	—	—	—	—	—
00-01—Providence	AHL	79	13	6	19	28	...	...	...	17	0	0	0	2
01-02—Providence	AHL	76	28	19	47	75	-15	5	3	—	—	—	—	—
—Boston	NHL	1	0	1	1	0	2	0	0	—	—	—	—	—
02-03—Providence	AHL	30	10	16	26	42	6	1	0	—	—	—	—	—
—Boston	NHL	41	6	11	17	30	3	0	0	—	—	—	—	—
03-04—Boston	NHL	7	0	0	0	6	-3	0	0	—	—	—	—	—
—Providence	AHL	62	15	16	31	53	-5	9	0	1	0	0	0	0
04-05—HC Kladno	Czech Rep.	3	0	0	0	2	-2	...	...	1	0	0	0	0
NHL Totals (3 years)		49	6	12	18	36	2	0	0					

HUNTER, TRENT — RW — ISLANDERS

PERSONAL: Born July 5, 1980, in Red Deer, Alta. ... 6-3/210. ... Shoots right.

TRANSACTIONS/CAREER NOTES: Selected by Anaheim Mighty Ducks in sixth round (fourth Mighty Ducks pick, 150th overall) of NHL draft (June 27, 1998). ... Traded by Mighty Ducks to New York Islanders for fourth-round pick (RW/LW Jonas Ronnqvist) in 2000 draft (May 23, 2000).

Season Team	League	GP	G	A	Pts.	PIM	+/-	PP	SH	GP	G	A	Pts.	PIM
		REGULAR SEASON								PLAYOFFS				
96-97—Red Deer	AMHL	42	30	25	55	50	...	...	...	—	—	—	—	—
97-98—Prince George	WHL	60	13	14	27	34	...	...	...	8	1	0	1	4
98-99—Prince George	WHL	50	18	20	38	34	13	2	0	7	2	5	7	2
99-00—Prince George	WHL	67	46	49	95	47	21	16	4	13	7	15	22	6
00-01—Springfield	AHL	57	18	17	35	14	...	...	...	—	—	—	—	—
01-02—Bridgeport	AHL	80	30	35	65	30	27	8	0	17	8	11	19	6
—New York Islanders	NHL	...	...	...	...	...	...	...	...	4	1	1	2	2

H

Season Team	League	GP	G	A	Pts.	PIM	+/-	PP	SH	GP	G	A	Pts.	PIM
02-03—New York Islanders.....	NHL	8	0	4	4	4	5	0	0	—	—	—	—	—
—Bridgeport..................	AHL	70	30	41	71	39	0	13	1	9	7	4	11	10
03-04—New York Islanders.....	NHL	77	25	26	51	16	23	4	0	5	0	0	0	4
04-05—Nykoping	Sweden	24	9	6	15	53	0	5	0	14	5	3	8	24
NHL Totals (3 years)...........		85	25	30	55	20	28	4	0	9	1	1	2	6

HURME, JANI — G — THRASHERS

PERSONAL: Born January 7, 1975, in Turku, Finland. ... 6-0/197. ... Catches left. ... Name pronounced hoor-MAY.

TRANSACTIONS/CAREER NOTES: Selected by Ottawa Senators in third round (second Senators pick, 58th overall) of NHL draft (June 21, 1997). ... Injured right knee (February 27, 2001); missed six games. ... Strained groin (March 4, 2002); missed three games. ... Flu (March 23, 2002); missed two games. ... Traded by Senators to Florida Panthers for C Greg Watson and G Billy Thompson (October 1, 2002). ... Injured knee (December 7, 2002); missed two games. ... Injured foot (January 7, 2003); missed one game. ... Claimed by Carolina Hurricanes from Panthers in waiver draft, then traded by Hurricanes to Atlanta Thrashers for a fourth-round pick (LW Chad Painchaud) in 2004 draft (October 3, 2003). ... Injured back (October 9, 2003); missed 2003-04 season.

		REGULAR SEASON									PLAYOFFS							
Season Team	League	GP	Min.	W	L	T	GA	SO	GAA	SV%	GP	Min.	W	L	GA	SO	GAA	SV%
92-93—TPS Turku	Finland Jr.	12	669	...	...	...	47	0	4.22	...	1	60	...	...	...	1	...	...
93-94—TPS Turku	Finland	1	2	...	...	...	0	0	0.00	...	—	—	—	—	—	—	—	—
—Kiekko-67 Turku...........	Finland Div. 2	3	190	...	...	...	7	0	2.21	...	—	—	—	—	—	—	—	—
—Kiekko-67 Turku...........	Finland Jr.	18	...	...	...	...	...	...	3.00	...	—	—	—	—	—	—	—	—
94-95—Kiekko-67 Turku...........	Finland Div. 2	19	1049	...	...	...	53	...	3.03	...	3	180	...	...	6	...	2.00	...
—TPS Turku	Finland Jr.	2	125	...	...	...	5	0	2.40	...	—	—	—	—	—	—	—	—
—Kiekko-67 Turku...........	Finland Jr.	9	540	...	...	...	47	...	5.22	...	—	—	—	—	—	—	—	—
95-96—TPS Turku	Finland	16	945	...	...	...	34	2	2.16	...	10	545	...	...	22	2	2.42	...
—Kiekko-67 Turku...........	Finland Div. 2	16	968	...	...	...	39	1	2.42	...	—	—	—	—	—	—	—	—
—TPS Turku	Finland Jr.	13	777	...	...	...	34	1	2.63	...	—	—	—	—	—	—	—	—
96-97—TPS Turku	Finland	48	2917	31	11	6	101	6	2.08	...	12	722	...	...	39	0	3.24	...
97-98—Detroit..........................	IHL	6	290	2	2	2	20	0	4.14	.859	—	—	—	—	—	—	—	—
—Indianapolis	IHL	29	1506	11	11	3	83	...	3.31	.902	3	130	1	0	10	0	4.62	.851
98-99—Detroit..........................	IHL	12	643	7	3	1	26	1	2.43	.898	—	—	—	—	—	—	—	—
—Cincinnati	IHL	26	1428	14	9	2	81	0	3.40	.895	—	—	—	—	—	—	—	—
99-00—Grand Rapids...............	IHL	52	2948	35	15	4	107	4	2.18	...	*17	*1028	*10	*7	*37	1	2.16	...
—Ottawa.........................	NHL	1	60	1	0	0	2	0	2.00	.895	—	—	—	—	—	—	—	—
00-01—Ottawa..........................	NHL	22	1296	12	5	4	54	2	2.50	.904	—	—	—	—	—	—	—	—
01-02—Ottawa..........................	NHL	25	1309	12	9	1	54	3	2.48	.907	—	—	—	—	—	—	—	—
—Fin. Olympic team	Int'l	3	179	1	2	0	9	0	3.02	.909	—	—	—	—	—	—	—	—
02-03—Florida..........................	NHL	28	1376	4	11	6	66	1	2.88	.907	—	—	—	—	—	—	—	—
03-04—Atlanta..........................	NHL	Did not play; injured																
NHL Totals (5 years)............		76	4041	29	25	11	176	6	2.61	.906								

HUSELIUS, KRISTIAN — LW — PANTHERS

PERSONAL: Born October 10, 1978, in Stockholm, Sweden. ... 6-1/190. ... Shoots left. ... Name pronounced hoo-say-LE-US.

TRANSACTIONS/CAREER NOTES: Selected by Florida Panthers in second round (second Panthers pick, 47th overall) of NHL draft (June 21, 1997). ... Intestinal infection (December 15, 2001); missed three games. ... Injured knee (September 12, 2002); missed three games.

		REGULAR SEASON								PLAYOFFS				
Season Team	League	GP	G	A	Pts.	PIM	+/-	PP	SH	GP	G	A	Pts.	PIM
94-95—Hammarby..................	Sweden Jr.	17	6	2	8	2	...	...	...	—	—	—	—	—
95-96—Hammarby..................	Sweden Jr.	25	13	8	21	14	...	...	...	—	—	—	—	—
—Hammarby..................	Sweden Dv. 2	6	1	0	1	0	...	...	...	—	—	—	—	—
96-97—Farjestad Karlstad	Sweden	13	2	0	2	4	...	...	...	5	1	0	1	0
97-98—Farjestad Karlstad	Sweden	34	2	1	3	2	...	...	...	11	0	0	0	0
98-99—Farjestad Karlstad	Sweden	28	4	4	8	4	...	...	...	—	—	—	—	—
—Vastra Frolunda	Sweden	20	2	2	4	2	...	...	...	4	1	0	1	0
99-00—Vastra Frolunda	Sweden	50	21	23	44	20	...	...	...	5	2	2	4	8
00-01—Vastra Frolunda	Sweden	49	*32	*35	*67	26	...	...	...	5	4	5	9	14
01-02—Florida..........................	NHL	79	23	22	45	14	-4	6	1	—	—	—	—	—
02-03—Florida..........................	NHL	78	20	23	43	20	-6	3	0	—	—	—	—	—
03-04—Florida..........................	NHL	76	10	21	31	24	-6	2	0	—	—	—	—	—
04-05—Rapperswil.................	Switzerland	—	—	—	—	—	—	—	—	4	1	3	4	2
—Linkopings..................	Sweden	34	14	35	49	10	20	5	2	—	—	—	—	—
NHL Totals (3 years)...........		233	53	66	119	58	-16	11	1					

HUSSEY, MATT — C — PENGUINS

PERSONAL: Born May 28, 1979, in New Haven, Conn. ... 6-2/212. ... Shoots left.

TRANSACTIONS/CAREER NOTES: Selected by Pittsburgh Penguins in ninth round (Penguins' 10th pick, 254th overall) of NHL entry draft (June 27, 1998).

		REGULAR SEASON								PLAYOFFS				
Season Team	League	GP	G	A	Pts.	PIM	+/-	PP	SH	GP	G	A	Pts.	PIM
98-99—Wisconsin..................	WCHA	37	10	5	15	18	...	...	...	—	—	—	—	—
99-00—Wisconsin..................	WCHA	35	5	11	16	8	...	...	...	—	—	—	—	—
00-01—Wisconsin..................	WCHA	40	9	11	20	24	...	...	...	—	—	—	—	—
01-02—Wisconsin..................	WCHA	39	18	15	33	16	...	...	...	—	—	—	—	—
02-03—Wilkes-Barre/Scranton	AHL	69	12	11	23	28	...	...	...	2	0	0	0	0

Season Team	League	GP	G	A	Pts.	PIM	+/-	PP	SH	GP	G	A	Pts.	PIM
		REGULAR SEASON								PLAYOFFS				
03-04—Pittsburgh	NHL	3	2	1	3	0	-1	2	0	—	—	—	—	—
—Wilkes-Barre/Scranton	AHL	55	2	1	3	6	-3	1	0	6	2	2	4	0
04-05—Wilkes-Barre/Scranton	AHL	80	16	14	30	19	3	3	2	10	1	2	3	2
NHL Totals (1 year)		3	2	1	3	0	-1	2	0					

HUTCHINSON, ANDREW D HURRICANES

PERSONAL: Born March 24, 1980, in Evanston, Ill. ... 6-2/204. ... Shoots right.

TRANSACTIONS/CAREER NOTES: Selected by Nashville Predators in 2nd round (4th Predators pick, 54th overall) of entry draft (June 26, 1999). ... Traded by Predators to Carolina Hurricanes for 3rd-round pick (acquired from Phoenix) in 2005 draft (July 29, 2005).

Season Team	League	GP	G	A	Pts.	PIM	+/-	PP	SH	GP	G	A	Pts.	PIM
		REGULAR SEASON								PLAYOFFS				
97-98—U.S. National	NAHL	60	7	22	29	63	...	2	0	—	—	—	—	—
98-99—Michigan State	CCHA	37	3	12	15	26	...	...	...	—	—	—	—	—
99-00—Michigan State	CCHA	41	4	11	15	62	...	...	...	—	—	—	—	—
00-01—Michigan State	CCHA	42	5	19	24	46	...	...	...	—	—	—	—	—
01-02—Michigan State	CCHA	39	6	16	22	24	...	...	...	—	—	—	—	—
—Milwaukee	AHL	5	0	1	1	0	-2	0	0	—	—	—	—	—
02-03—Toledo	ECHL	10	2	5	7	4	8	1	0	—	—	—	—	—
—Milwaukee	AHL	63	9	17	26	40	-10	4	0	3	1	0	1	0
03-04—Milwaukee	AHL	46	12	12	24	39	7	4	0	22	5	11	16	33
—Nashville	NHL	18	4	4	8	4	1	2	0	—	—	—	—	—
04-05—Milwaukee	AHL	76	10	35	45	79	1	4	1	7	1	3	4	8
NHL Totals (1 year)		18	4	4	8	4	1	2	0					

IGINLA, JAROME RW FLAMES

PERSONAL: Born July 1, 1977, in Edmonton. ... 6-1/208. ... Shoots right. ... Name pronounced ih-GIHN-luh.

TRANSACTIONS/CAREER NOTES: Selected by Dallas Stars in first round (first Stars pick, 11th overall) of NHL draft (July 8, 1995). ... Traded by Stars with C Corey Millen to Calgary Flames for C Joe Nieuwendyk (December 19, 1995). ... Fractured right hand (January 21, 1998); missed 10 games. ... Missed first three games of 1999-2000 season in contract dispute. ... Bruised knee (March 22, 2000); missed two games. ... Injured knee (December 13, 2000); missed one game. ... Fractured wrist (March 31, 2001); missed remainder of season. ... Injured hip, groin (December 21, 2002); missed five games. ... Injured shoulder (March 21, 2003); missed two games. ... Sprained knee (January 18, 2004); missed one game.

STATISTICAL PLATEAUS: Three-goal games: 2001-02 (1), 2002-03 (1), 2003-04 (1). Total: 3. ... Four-goal games: 2002-03 (1). ... Total hat tricks: 4.

Season Team	League	GP	G	A	Pts.	PIM	+/-	PP	SH	GP	G	A	Pts.	PIM
		REGULAR SEASON								PLAYOFFS				
93-94—Kamloops	WHL	48	6	23	29	33	...	...	...	19	3	6	9	10
94-95—Kamloops	WHL	72	33	38	71	111	29	8	0	21	7	11	18	34
95-96—Kamloops	WHL	63	63	73	136	120	...	...	...	16	16	13	29	44
—Calgary	NHL	...	...	...	...	...	...	...	...	2	1	1	2	0
96-97—Calgary	NHL	82	21	29	50	37	-4	8	1	—	—	—	—	—
97-98—Calgary	NHL	70	13	19	32	29	-10	0	2	—	—	—	—	—
98-99—Calgary	NHL	82	28	23	51	58	1	7	0	—	—	—	—	—
99-00—Calgary	NHL	77	29	34	63	26	0	12	0	—	—	—	—	—
00-01—Calgary	NHL	77	31	40	71	62	-2	10	0	—	—	—	—	—
01-02—Calgary	NHL	82	*52	44	*96	77	27	16	1	—	—	—	—	—
—Can. Olympic team	Int'l	6	3	1	4	0	...	...	...	—	—	—	—	—
02-03—Calgary	NHL	75	35	32	67	49	-10	11	3	—	—	—	—	—
03-04—Calgary	NHL	81	41	32	73	84	21	8	4	26	13	9	22	45
NHL Totals (9 years)		626	250	253	503	422	23	72	11	28	14	10	24	45

IRBE, ARTURS G

PERSONAL: Born February 2, 1967, in Riga, U.S.S.R. ... 5-8/190. ... Catches left. ... Name pronounced AHR-tuhrs UHR-bay.

TRANSACTIONS/CAREER NOTES: Selected by Minnesota North Stars in 10th round (11th North Stars pick, 196th overall) of NHL draft (June 17, 1989). ... Selected by San Jose Sharks in dispersal draft (May 30, 1991). ... Sprained knee (November 27, 1992); missed 19 games. ... Injured foot (February 15, 1995); missed one game. ... Injured knee (January 17, 1996); remainder of season. ... Signed as free agent by Dallas Stars (July 22, 1996). ... Strained groin (November 8, 1996); missed six games. ... Signed as free agent by Vancouver Canucks (August 5, 1997). ... Signed as free agent by Carolina Hurricanes (September 10, 1998). ... Traded by Hurricanes to Columbus Blue Jackets for further considerations (June 16, 2004).

Season Team	League	GP	Min.	W	L	T	GA	SO	GAA	SV%	GP	Min.	W	L	GA	SO	GAA	SV%
		REGULAR SEASON									PLAYOFFS							
86-87—Dynamo Riga	USSR	2	27	...	...	...	1	0	2.22	...	—	—	—	—	—	—	—	—
87-88—Dynamo Riga	USSR	34	1870	...	...	...	84	0	2.70	...	—	—	—	—	—	—	—	—
88-89—Dynamo Riga	USSR	41	2460	...	...	...	117	0	2.85	...	—	—	—	—	—	—	—	—
89-90—Dynamo Riga	USSR	48	2880	...	...	...	116	0	2.42	...	—	—	—	—	—	—	—	—
90-91—Dynamo Riga	USSR	46	2713	...	...	...	133	0	2.94	...	—	—	—	—	—	—	—	—
91-92—Kansas City	IHL	32	1955	24	7	1	80	0	*2.46	...	15	914	12	3	44	0	2.89	...
—San Jose	NHL	13	645	2	6	3	48	0	4.47	.868	—	—	—	—	—	—	—	—
92-93—Kansas City	IHL	6	364	3	3	0	20	0	3.30	.877	—	—	—	—	—	—	—	—
—San Jose	NHL	36	2074	7	26	0	142	1	4.11	.886	—	—	—	—	—	—	—	—
93-94—San Jose	NHL	*74	*4412	30	28	*16	209	3	2.84	.899	14	806	7	7	50	0	3.72	.875

Season Team	League	GP	Min.	W	L	T	GA	SO	GAA	SV%		GP	Min.	W	L	GA	SO	GAA	SV%
		REGULAR SEASON										PLAYOFFS							
94-95—San Jose	NHL	38	2043	14	19	3	111	4	3.26	.895		6	316	2	4	27	0	5.13	.853
95-96—San Jose	NHL	22	1112	4	12	4	85	0	4.59	.860		—	—	—	—	—	—	—	—
—Kansas City	IHL	4	226	1	2	1	16	0	4.25	...		—	—	—	—	—	—	—	—
96-97—Dallas	NHL	35	1965	17	12	3	88	3	2.69	.893		1	13	0	0	0	0	0.00	1.00
97-98—Vancouver	NHL	41	1999	14	11	6	91	2	2.73	.907		—	—	—	—	—	—	—	—
98-99—Carolina	NHL	62	3643	27	20	12	135	6	2.22	.923		6	408	2	4	15	0	2.21	.917
99-00—Carolina	NHL	*75	4345	34	28	9	*175	5	2.42	.906		—	—	—	—	—	—	—	—
00-01—Carolina	NHL	*77	*4406	37	29	9	180	6	2.45	.908		6	360	2	4	20	0	3.33	.900
01-02—Carolina	NHL	51	2974	20	19	11	126	3	2.54	.902		18	1078	10	8	30	1	1.67	.938
—Latvian Olympic team	Int'l	1	60	0	1	0	4	0	4.00	.862		—	—	—	—	—	—	—	—
02-03—Carolina	NHL	34	1884	7	24	2	100	0	3.18	.877		—	—	—	—	—	—	—	—
—Lowell	AHL	7	426	3	3	1	21	0	2.96	.908		—	—	—	—	—	—	—	—
03-04—Carolina	NHL	10	564	5	2	1	23	0	2.45	.899		--	—	—	—	—	—	—	—
—Johnstown	ECHL	14	847	10	3	1	30	1	2.13	.921		—	—	—	—	—	—	—	—
NHL Totals (13 years)		568	32066	218	236	79	1513	33	2.83	.899		51	2981	23	27	142	1	2.86	.902

ISBISTER, BRAD — LW — BRUINS

PERSONAL: Born May 7, 1977, in Edmonton. ... 6-4/220. ... Shoots right. ... Name pronounced ihs-BIH-stuhr.

TRANSACTIONS/CAREER NOTES: Selected by Winnipeg Jets in 3rd round (4th Jets pick, 67th overall) of NHL draft (July 8, 1995). ... Jets franchise moved to Phoenix and renamed Coyotes for 1996-97 season; NHL approved move on January 18, 1996. ... Strained abdominal muscle (November 22, 1997); missed six games. ... Strained groin (January 8, 1999); missed six games. ... Hernia (January 27, 1999); missed 19 games. ... Strained groin (March 11, 1999); missed remainder of season. ... Traded by Coyotes with 3d-round pick (C Brian Collins) in 1999 entry draft to New York Islanders for C Robert Reichel and third- (C/LW Jason Jaspers) and 4th-round (C Preston Mizzi) picks in 1999 entry draft (March 20, 1999). ... Sprained ankle (January 26, 2000); missed 18 games. ... Fractured jaw (December 12, 2000); missed 15 games. ... Flu (February 1, 2001); missed one game. ... Sprained right knee (March 3, 2001); missed remainder of season. ... Injured back (February 26, 2002); missed three games. ... Injured ankle (December 23, 2002); missed one game. ... Reinjured ankle (January 7, 2003); missed seven games). ... Reinjured ankle (January 28, 2003); missed six games). ... Traded by Islanders with LW Raffi Torres to Edmonton Oilers for D Janne Niinimaa and 2nd-round pick (C Evgeni Tunik) in 2003 draft (March 11, 2003). ... Injured neck (November 8, 2003); missed five games. ... Back spasms (November 30, 2003); missed four games. ... Back spasms (January 11, 2004); missed one game. ... Injured right leg (January 31, 2004); missed four games. ... Injured ankle (February 16, 2004); missed 12 games. ... Traded by Oilers to Boston Bruins for 4th-round pick in 2006 (Aug. 1, 2005).

Season Team	League	GP	G	A	Pts.	PIM	+/-	PP	SH		GP	G	A	Pts.	PIM
		REGULAR SEASON									PLAYOFFS				
93-94—Portland	WHL	64	7	10	17	45	...	...	...		10	0	2	2	0
94-95—Portland	WHL	67	16	20	36	123	-13	3	1		—	—	—	—	—
95-96—Portland	WHL	71	45	44	89	184	...	...	...		7	2	4	6	20
96-97—Springfield	AHL	7	3	1	4	14	-1	1	0		9	1	2	3	10
—Portland	WHL	24	15	18	33	45	18	3	3		6	2	1	3	16
97-98—Phoenix	NHL	66	9	8	17	102	4	1	0		5	0	0	0	2
—Springfield	AHL	9	8	2	10	36	8	0	0		—	—	—	—	—
98-99—Las Vegas	IHL	2	0	0	0	9	1	0	0		—	—	—	—	—
—Springfield	AHL	4	1	1	2	12	1	0	0		—	—	—	—	—
—Phoenix	NHL	32	4	4	8	46	1	0	0		—	—	—	—	—
99-00—New York Islanders	NHL	64	22	20	42	100	-18	9	0		—	—	—	—	—
00-01—New York Islanders	NHL	51	18	14	32	59	-19	7	1		—	—	—	—	—
01-02—New York Islanders	NHL	79	17	21	38	113	1	4	0		3	1	1	2	17
02-03—New York Islanders	NHL	53	10	13	23	34	-9	2	0		—	—	—	—	—
—Edmonton	NHL	13	3	2	5	9	0	0	0		6	0	1	1	12
03-04—Edmonton	NHL	51	10	8	18	54	-2	1	0		—	—	—	—	—
04-05—Innsbruck	Austria	11	7	4	11	41	-1	...	...		5	3	1	4	6
NHL Totals (7 years)		409	93	90	183	517	-42	24	1		14	1	2	3	31

ISTOMIN, DENIS — RW — BLACKHAWKS

PERSONAL: Born January 12, 1987, in Magnitogorsk, Russia.

Season Team	League	GP	G	A	Pts.	PIM	+/-	PP	SH		GP	G	A	Pts.	PIM
		REGULAR SEASON									PLAYOFFS				
04-05—Chelyabinsk	Russian Div. 1	42	11	5	16	24	...	...	...		—	—	—	—	—

JACKMAN, BARRET — D — BLUES

PERSONAL: Born March 5, 1981, in Trail, B.C. ... 6-0/209. ... Shoots left.

TRANSACTIONS/CAREER NOTES: Selected by St. Louis Blues in first round (first Blues pick, 17th overall) of NHL entry draft (June 26, 1999). ... Dislocated shoulder (October 22, 2003); missed six games. ... Shoulder injury (November 26, 2003); missed 17 games. ... Reinjured shoulder (January 5, 2004) and had surgery; missed remainder of the season.

Season Team	League	GP	G	A	Pts.	PIM	+/-	PP	SH		GP	G	A	Pts.	PIM
		REGULAR SEASON									PLAYOFFS				
97-98—Regina	WHL	68	2	11	13	224	...	...	...		9	0	3	3	32
98-99—Regina	WHL	70	8	36	44	259	-9	4	0		—	—	—	—	—
99-00—Regina	WHL	53	9	37	46	175	-10	3	0		6	1	1	2	19
—Worcester	AHL	...	...	...	...	...	...	...	...		2	0	0	0	13
00-01—Regina	WHL	43	9	27	36	138	...	...	...		6	0	3	3	8

Season Team	League	GP	G	A	Pts.	PIM	+/-	PP	SH	GP	G	A	Pts.	PIM
		REGULAR SEASON								PLAYOFFS				
01-02—Worcester	AHL	75	2	12	14	266	16	1	0	3	0	1	1	4
—St. Louis	NHL	1	0	0	0	0	0	0	0	1	0	0	0	2
02-03—St. Louis	NHL	82	3	16	19	190	23	0	0	7	0	0	0	14
03-04—St. Louis	NHL	15	1	2	3	41	-1	0	0	—	—	—	—	—
04-05—Missouri	UHL	28	3	17	20	61	10	2	0	—	—	—	—	—
NHL Totals (3 years)		98	4	18	22	231	22	0	0	8	0	0	0	16

JACKMAN, RIC — D — PENGUINS

PERSONAL: Born June 28, 1978, in Toronto. ... 6-2/197. ... Shoots right.
TRANSACTIONS/CAREER NOTES: Selected by Dallas Stars in first round (first Stars pick, fifth overall) of NHL draft (June 22, 1996). ... Traded by Stars to Boston Bruins for RW Cameron Mann (June 24, 2001). ... Separated shoulder (September 20, 2001); missed first four games of season. ... Traded by Bruins to Toronto Maple Leafs for C Kris Vernarsky (May 13, 2002). ... Traded by Maple Leafs to Pittsburgh Penguins for D Drake Berehowsky (February 11, 2004). ... Had the flu (March 2, 2004); missed one game.

Season Team	League	GP	G	A	Pts.	PIM	+/-	PP	SH	GP	G	A	Pts.	PIM
		REGULAR SEASON								PLAYOFFS				
95-96—Sault Ste. Marie	OHL	66	13	29	42	97	...	...	...	4	1	0	1	15
96-97—Sault Ste. Marie	OHL	53	13	34	47	116	12	9	0	10	2	6	8	24
97-98—Sault Ste. Marie	OHL	60	33	40	73	111	...	...	...	—	—	—	—	—
—Michigan	IHL	14	1	5	6	10	-1	0	0	4	0	0	0	10
98-99—Michigan	IHL	71	13	17	30	106	-12	8	0	5	0	4	4	6
99-00—Michigan	IHL	50	3	16	19	51	...	...	...	—	—	—	—	—
—Dallas	NHL	22	1	2	3	6	-1	1	0	—	—	—	—	—
00-01—Dallas	NHL	16	0	0	0	18	-6	0	0	—	—	—	—	—
—Utah	IHL	57	9	19	28	24	...	...	...	—	—	—	—	—
01-02—Boston	NHL	2	0	0	0	2	-1	0	0	—	—	—	—	—
—Providence	AHL	9	0	1	1	8	-1	0	0	—	—	—	—	—
02-03—St. John's	AHL	8	2	6	8	24	-4	1	0	—	—	—	—	—
—Toronto	NHL	42	0	2	2	41	-10	0	0	—	—	—	—	—
03-04—Toronto	NHL	29	2	4	6	13	-11	1	0	—	—	—	—	—
—St. John's	AHL	3	2	1	3	0	3	1	0	—	—	—	—	—
—Pittsburgh	NHL	25	7	17	24	14	-5	6	0	—	—	—	—	—
04-05—Bjorkloven	Sweden	32	13	19	32	148	6	5	0	—	—	—	—	—
NHL Totals (5 years)		136	10	25	35	94	-34	8	0					

JACKMAN, TIM — RW — BLUE JACKETS

PERSONAL: Born November 14, 1981, in Minot, N.D. ... 6-4/210. ... Shoots right.
TRANSACTIONS/CAREER NOTES: Selected by Columbus Blue Jackets in second round (second Blue Jackets pick, 38th overall) of NHL entry draft (June 23, 2001).

Season Team	League	GP	G	A	Pts.	PIM	+/-	PP	SH	GP	G	A	Pts.	PIM
		REGULAR SEASON								PLAYOFFS				
99-00—Park Center	USHS (West)	19	34	22	56	...	...	...	...	—	—	—	—	—
00-01—Minnesota-Mankato	WCHA	35	11	14	25	82	...	...	...	—	—	—	—	—
01-02—Minnesota-Mankato	WCHA	36	14	14	28	86	...	...	...	—	—	—	—	—
02-03—Syracuse	AHL	77	9	7	16	48	-13	3	0	—	—	—	—	—
03-04—Columbus	NHL	19	1	2	3	16	-7	0	0	—	—	—	—	—
—Syracuse	AHL	65	23	13	36	61	12	5	0	7	2	3	5	12
04-05—Syracuse	AHL	73	14	21	35	98	0	4	1	—	—	—	—	—
NHL Totals (1 year)		19	1	2	3	16	-7	0	0					

JACKSON, SCOTT — D — BLUES

PERSONAL: Born February 5, 1987, in Salmon Arm, B.C. ... 6-4/200. ... Shoots left.

Season Team	League	GP	G	A	Pts.	PIM	+/-	PP	SH	GP	G	A	Pts.	PIM
		REGULAR SEASON								PLAYOFFS				
02-03—Seattle	WHL	2	0	0	0	2	...	...	...	—	—	—	—	—
03-04—Seattle	WHL	66	4	9	13	17	...	...	...	—	—	—	—	—
04-05—Seattle	WHL	72	6	16	22	46	26	3	0	12	1	2	3	4

JAGR, JAROMIR — RW — RANGERS

PERSONAL: Born February 15, 1972, in Kladno, Czechoslovakia. ... 6-2/233. ... Shoots left. ... Name pronounced YAHR-oh-meer YAH-gihr.
TRANSACTIONS/CAREER NOTES: Selected by Pittsburgh Penguins in first round (Penguins' first pick, fifth overall) of NHL draft (June 16, 1990). ... Separated shoulder (February 23, 1993); missed three games. ... Strained groin (January 21, 1994); missed four games. ... Flu (January 11, 1997); missed one game. ... Strained groin (February 16, 1997); missed three games. ... Injured groin (February 27, 1997); missed 13 games. ... Strained groin (April 10, 1997); missed two games. ... Strained hip flexor and groin (November 14, 1997); missed four games. ... Injured groin (April 16, 1998); missed one game. ... Injured groin (April 5, 1999); missed one game. ... Bruised thigh (November 18, 1999); missed one game. ... Strained abdominal muscle (January 15, 2000); missed four games. ... Injured hamstring (February 21, 2000); missed 12 games. ... Bruised upper back (March 26, 2000); missed two games. ... Bruised finger (April 7, 2001); missed one game. ... Traded by Penguins with D Frantisek Kucera to Washington Capitals for C Kris Beech, C Michal Sivek, D Ross Lupaschuk and future considerations (July 11, 2001). ... Injured knee (October 10, 2001); missed three games. ... Strained knee (November 2, 2001); missed four games. ... Strained groin (January 11, 2002); missed six games. ... Injured groin (November 27, 2002); missed one game. ... Fractured wrist (March 10, 2003); missed six games. ... Injured thumb (December 16, 2003); missed two games. ... Traded by Capitals to New York Rangers for RW

Anson Carter (January 23, 2004). ... Strained groin (February 14, 2004); missed two games. ... Injured hip flexor (April 3, 2004); missed final game of season.
STATISTICAL PLATEAUS: Three-goal games: 1990-91 (1), 1994-95 (1), 1996-97 (2), 1999-00 (2), 2000-01 (2), 2002-03 (2). Total: 10. ... Four-goal games: 2000-01 (1). ... Total hat tricks: 11.

		REGULAR SEASON								PLAYOFFS				
Season Team	League	GP	G	A	Pts.	PIM	+/-	PP	SH	GP	G	A	Pts.	PIM
88-89—Poldi Kladno	Czech.	39	8	10	18	...	...	...	...	—	—	—	—	—
89-90—Poldi Kladno	Czech.	51	30	30	60	...	...	...	...	—	—	—	—	—
90-91—Pittsburgh	NHL	80	27	30	57	42	-4	7	0	24	3	10	13	6
91-92—Pittsburgh	NHL	70	32	37	69	34	12	4	0	21	11	13	24	6
92-93—Pittsburgh	NHL	81	34	60	94	61	30	10	1	12	5	4	9	23
93-94—Pittsburgh	NHL	80	32	67	99	61	15	9	0	6	2	4	6	16
94-95—HC Kladno	Czech Rep.	11	8	14	22	10	...	...	...	—	—	—	—	—
—HC Bolzano	Euro	5	8	8	16	4	...	...	...	—	—	—	—	—
—HC Bolzano	Italy	1	0	0	0	0	...	...	...	—	—	—	—	—
—Schalker Haie	Ger. Div. II	1	1	10	11	0	...	...	...	—	—	—	—	—
—Pittsburgh	NHL	48	32	38	70	37	23	8	3	12	10	5	15	6
95-96—Pittsburgh	NHL	82	62	87	149	96	31	20	1	18	11	12	23	18
96-97—Pittsburgh	NHL	63	47	48	95	40	22	11	2	5	4	4	8	4
97-98—Pittsburgh	NHL	77	35	67	*102	64	17	7	0	6	4	5	9	2
—Czech Rep. Oly. team	Int'l	6	1	4	5	2	3	0	0	—	—	—	—	—
98-99—Pittsburgh	NHL	81	44	*83	*127	66	17	10	1	9	5	7	12	16
99-00—Pittsburgh	NHL	63	42	54	*96	50	25	10	0	11	8	8	16	6
00-01—Pittsburgh	NHL	81	52	69	*121	42	19	14	1	16	2	10	12	18
01-02—Washington	NHL	69	31	48	79	30	0	10	0	—	—	—	—	—
—Czech Rep. Oly. team	Int'l	4	2	3	5	4	...	...	...	—	—	—	—	—
02-03—Washington	NHL	75	36	41	77	38	5	13	2	6	2	5	7	2
03-04—Washington	NHL	46	16	29	45	26	-4	6	0	—	—	—	—	—
—New York Rangers	NHL	31	15	14	29	12	-1	4	0	—	—	—	—	—
04-05—HC Kladno	Czech Rep.	17	11	17	28	16	7	...	...	—	—	—	—	—
—Avangard Omsk	Russian	32	16	22	38	63	1	...	...	14	6	11	17	32
NHL Totals (14 years)		1027	537	772	1309	699	207	143	11	146	67	87	154	123

JANIK, DOUG — D — SABRES

PERSONAL: Born March 26, 1980, in Agawam, Mass. ... 6-2/209. ... Shoots left.
TRANSACTIONS/CAREER NOTES: Selected by Buffalo Sabres in second round (third Sabres pick, 55th overall) of NHL entry draft (June 26, 1999).

		REGULAR SEASON								PLAYOFFS				
Season Team	League	GP	G	A	Pts.	PIM	+/-	PP	SH	GP	G	A	Pts.	PIM
97-98—U.S. National	NAHL	65	8	26	34	105	...	4	0	—	—	—	—	—
98-99—Maine	Hockey East	35	3	13	16	44	...	...	...	—	—	—	—	—
99-00—Maine	Hockey East	36	6	13	19	54	...	...	...	—	—	—	—	—
00-01—Maine	Hockey East	39	3	15	18	52	...	...	...	—	—	—	—	—
01-02—Rochester	AHL	80	6	17	23	100	10	1	0	2	0	0	0	0
02-03—Buffalo	NHL	6	0	0	0	2	1	0	0	—	—	—	—	—
—Rochester	AHL	75	3	13	16	120	-11	1	0	3	0	0	0	6
03-04—Rochester	AHL	74	2	14	16	109	-8	0	0	16	1	2	3	22
—Buffalo	NHL	4	0	0	0	19	0	0	0	—	—	—	—	—
04-05—Rochester	AHL	76	2	10	12	196	18	0	0	9	0	2	2	10
NHL Totals (2 years)		10	0	0	0	21	1	0	0					

JASPERS, JASON — C — COYOTES

PERSONAL: Born April 8, 1981, in Thunder Bay, Ont. ... 5-11/207. ... Shoots left.
TRANSACTIONS/CAREER NOTES: Selected by Phoenix Coyotes in third round (fourth Coyotes pick, 71st overall) of NHL entry draft (June 26, 1999).

		REGULAR SEASON								PLAYOFFS				
Season Team	League	GP	G	A	Pts.	PIM	+/-	PP	SH	GP	G	A	Pts.	PIM
97-98—Thunder Bay	NOHA	72	45	75	120	90	...	...	...	—	—	—	—	—
98-99—Sudbury	OHL	68	28	33	61	81	...	...	...	4	2	1	3	13
99-00—Sudbury	OHL	68	46	61	107	107	47	9	1	12	4	6	10	27
00-01—Sudbury	OHL	63	42	42	84	77	26	17	2	12	3	16	19	18
01-02—Springfield	AHL	71	25	23	48	55	-1	7	3	—	—	—	—	—
—Phoenix	NHL	4	0	1	1	4	-1	0	0	—	—	—	—	—
02-03—Springfield	AHL	63	4	15	19	57	-15	1	1	—	—	—	—	—
—Phoenix	NHL	2	0	0	0	0	-1	0	0	—	—	—	—	—
—Springfield	AHL	6	0	0	0	4	...	...	...	—	—	—	—	—
03-04—Springfield	AHL	58	16	22	38	56	-4	5	0	—	—	—	—	—
—Phoenix	NHL	3	0	0	0	2	-1	0	0	—	—	—	—	—
04-05—Springfield	AHL	48	12	17	29	45	0	3	0	—	—	—	—	—
—Utah	AHL	11	0	3	3	6	-4	0	0	—	—	—	—	—
NHL Totals (3 years)		9	0	1	1	6	-3	0	0					

JESSIMAN, HUGH — LW/RW — RANGERS

PERSONAL: Born March 28, 1984, in New York City. ... 6-4/200. ... Shoots right.
TRANSACTIONS/CAREER NOTES: Selected by New York Rangers in first round (first Rangers pick,12th overall) in 2003 NHL entry draft.

Season Team	League	REGULAR SEASON								PLAYOFFS				
		GP	G	A	Pts.	PIM	+/-	PP	SH	GP	G	A	Pts.	PIM
02-03—Dartmouth	ECAC	34	23	24	47	48	...	...	...	—	—	—	—	—
03-04—Dartmouth	ECAC	34	16	17	33	71	...	...	...	—	—	—	—	—
04-05—Dartmouth	ECAC	12	1	1	2	18	...	...	...	—	—	—	—	—

JILLSON, JEFF D SABRES

PERSONAL: Born July 24, 1980, in North Smithfield, R.I. ... 6-3/220. ... Shoots right.

TRANSACTIONS/CAREER NOTES: Selected by San Jose Sharks in first round (first Sharks pick, 14th overall) of NHL entry draft (June 26, 1999). ... Traded by Sharks with G Jeff Hackett to Boston Bruins for D Kyle McLaren and fourth-round pick (G Jason Churchill) in 2004 entry draft (January 23, 2003). ... Traded by Bruins to Sharks for C Brad Boyes; then traded by Sharks with ninth-round pick in 2005 entry draft to Buffalo Sabres for C Curtis Brown and D Andy Delmore (March 9, 2004).

Season Team	League	REGULAR SEASON								PLAYOFFS				
		GP	G	A	Pts.	PIM	+/-	PP	SH	GP	G	A	Pts.	PIM
96-97—Mount St. Charles	USHS (East)	15	16	14	30	20	...	...	...	—	—	—	—	—
97-98—Mount St. Charles	USHS (East)	15	10	13	23	32	...	...	...	—	—	—	—	—
98-99—Univ. of Michigan	CCHA	38	5	19	24	71	...	...	...	—	—	—	—	—
99-00—Univ. of Michigan	CCHA	36	8	26	34	111	...	...	...	—	—	—	—	—
00-01—Univ. of Michigan	CCHA	43	10	20	30	74	...	...	...	—	—	—	—	—
01-02—San Jose	NHL	48	5	13	18	29	2	3	0	4	0	0	0	0
—Cleveland	AHL	27	2	13	15	45	-10	1	0	—	—	—	—	—
02-03—Cleveland	AHL	19	3	5	8	12	-13	1	0	—	—	—	—	—
—San Jose	NHL	26	0	6	6	9	-7	0	0	—	—	—	—	—
—Providence	AHL	30	4	11	15	26	4	2	0	—	—	—	—	—
03-04—Boston	NHL	50	4	10	14	35	-1	1	0	—	—	—	—	—
—Buffalo	NHL	14	0	3	3	19	-3	0	0	—	—	—	—	—
04-05—Rochester	AHL	78	12	17	29	46	6	8	0	9	1	1	2	12
NHL Totals (3 years)		138	9	32	41	92	-9	4	0	4	0	0	0	0

JOHANSSON, ANDREAS LW

PERSONAL: Born May 19, 1973, in Hofors, Sweden. ... 6-0/205. ... Shoots left. ... Name pronounced yoh-HAN-suhn.

TRANSACTIONS/CAREER NOTES: Selected by New York Islanders in seventh round (seventh Islanders pick, 136th overall) of NHL entry draft (June 22, 1991). ... Injured back (April 5, 1996); missed three games. ... Traded by Islanders with D Darius Kasparaitis to Pittsburgh Penguins for C Bryan Smolinski (November 17, 1996). ... Bruised shoulder (December 10, 1996); missed 12 games. ... Had the flu (January 26, 1997); missed one game. ... Had back spasms (February 15, 1997); missed one game. ... Bruised ribs (November 15, 1997); missed six games. ... Sprained knee (March 8, 1998); missed 10 games. ... Signed as free agent by Ottawa Senators (September 29, 1998). ... Injured left knee (January 18, 1999); missed two games. ... Reinjured left knee (February 25, 1999); missed three games. ... Strained hamstring (March 8, 1999); missed two games. ... Injured knee (April 5, 1999); missed two games. ... Had back spasms (April 15, 1999); missed one game. ... Traded by Senators to Tampa Bay Lightning for LW Rob Zamuner and second-round pick in 2002 entry draft (later traded to Philadelphia Flyers) to complete deal that allowed Lightning to sign general manager Rick Dudley (June 30, 1999). ... Suffered concussion (October 7, 1999); missed one game. ... Bruised foot (November 2, 1999); missed four games. ... Traded by Lightning to Calgary Flames for rights to LW Nils Ekman and fourth-round pick (traded to New York Islanders) in 2000 entry draft (November 20, 1999). ... Suffered injury (December 21, 1999); missed three games. ... Had the flu (January 5, 2000); missed three games. ... Had back spasms (January 12, 2000); missed 15 games. ... Injured back (March 11, 2000); missed remainder of season. ... Claimed by New York Rangers from Flames in NHL waiver draft (September 29, 2000). ... Fractured left wrist (January 14, 2002); missed 11 games. ... Had the flu (March 16, 2002); missed one game. ... Signed as free agent by Nashville Predators (September 6, 2002). ... Separated shoulder (November 29, 2002); missed three games. ... Had the flu (January 21, 2003); missed one game. ... Bruised hip and strained groin (February 15, 2003); missed 13 games. ... Injured wrist and had back spasms (March 23, 2003); missed four games. ... Injured hip (April 4, 2003); missed season's final two games. ... Suffered concussion (October 25, 2003); missed 34 games.

STATISTICAL PLATEAUS: Three-goal games: 2002-03 (1).

Season Team	League	REGULAR SEASON								PLAYOFFS				
		GP	G	A	Pts.	PIM	+/-	PP	SH	GP	G	A	Pts.	PIM
90-91—Falun	Sweden	31	12	10	22	38	...	...	...	—	—	—	—	—
91-92—Farjestad Karlstad	Sweden	30	3	1	4	4	...	...	...	6	0	0	0	4
92-93—Farjestad Karlstad	Sweden	38	4	7	11	38	...	...	...	2	0	0	0	0
93-94—Farjestad Karlstad	Sweden	20	3	6	9	6	...	...	...	—	—	—	—	—
94-95—Farjestad Karlstad	Sweden	36	9	10	19	42	...	...	...	4	0	0	0	10
95-96—Worcester	AHL	29	5	5	10	32	...	...	...	—	—	—	—	—
—Utah	IHL	22	4	13	17	28	...	...	...	12	0	5	5	6
—New York Islanders	NHL	3	0	1	1	0	1	0	0	—	—	—	—	—
96-97—New York Islanders	NHL	15	2	2	4	0	-6	1	0	—	—	—	—	—
—Pittsburgh	NHL	27	2	7	9	20	-6	0	0	—	—	—	—	—
—Cleveland	IHL	10	2	4	6	42	...	...	...	11	1	5	6	8
97-98—Pittsburgh	NHL	50	5	10	15	20	4	0	1	1	0	0	0	0
—Swedish Oly. team	Int'l	3	0	0	0	2	0	0	0	—	—	—	—	—
98-99—Ottawa	NHL	69	21	16	37	34	1	7	0	2	0	0	0	0
99-00—Tampa Bay	NHL	12	2	3	5	8	1	0	0	—	—	—	—	—
—Calgary	NHL	28	3	7	10	14	-3	1	0	—	—	—	—	—
00-01—Bern	Switzerland	40	15	29	44	94	...	...	...	7	5	4	9	0
01-02—New York Rangers	NHL	70	14	10	24	46	6	3	0	—	—	—	—	—
02-03—Nashville	NHL	56	20	17	37	22	-4	10	0	—	—	—	—	—
03-04—Nashville	NHL	47	12	15	27	26	-2	3	1	6	0	0	0	0
—Milwaukee	AHL	1	0	0	0	2	0	0	0	—	—	—	—	—
04-05—Geneva	Switzerland	40	12	26	38	60	...	5	0	4	0	6	6	24
NHL Totals (8 years)		377	81	88	169	190	-8	25	2	9	0	0	0	0

JOHANSSON, JONAS — RW/LW — CAPITALS

PERSONAL: Born March 18, 1984, in Jönkoping, Sweden. ... 6-1/180. ... Shoots right.
TRANSACTIONS/CAREER NOTES: Selected by Colorado Avalanche in first round (first Avalanche pick, 28th overall) of NHL entry draft (June 22, 2002). ... Traded to Washington Capitals with LW Bates Battaglia for LW Steve Konowalchuk and a third-round pick (later traded to Carolina Hurricanes) in the 2004 entry draft (October 22, 2003).

		REGULAR SEASON								PLAYOFFS				
Season Team	League	GP	G	A	Pts.	PIM	+/-	PP	SH	GP	G	A	Pts.	PIM
01-02—HV 71 Jonkoping	Sweden Jr.	26	15	19	34	20	...	...	...	—	—	—	—	—
—HV 71 Jonkoping	Sweden	5	0	0	0	0	...	...	...	2	0	0	0	0
02-03—Kamloops	WHL	26	10	25	35	8	...	...	...	6	1	2	3	4
03-04—Kamloops	WHL	72	18	19	37	70	...	...	...	5	2	2	4	4
04-05—Portland	AHL	50	3	6	9	8	-10	1	0	—	—	—	—	—
—South Carolina	ECHL	5	4	2	6	10	4	1	0	—	—	—	—	—

JOHNSON, AARON — D — BLUE JACKETS

PERSONAL: Born April 30, 1983, in Point Hawkesbury, N.S. ... 6-0/186. ... Shoots left.
TRANSACTIONS/CAREER NOTES: Selected by Columbus Blue Jackets in third round (fourth Blue Jackets pick, 85th overall) of NHL entry draft (June 23, 2001).

		REGULAR SEASON								PLAYOFFS				
Season Team	League	GP	G	A	Pts.	PIM	+/-	PP	SH	GP	G	A	Pts.	PIM
00-01—Rimouski	QMJHL	64	12	41	53	128	...	...	...	11	2	4	6	35
01-02—Rimouski	QMJHL	68	17	49	66	172	...	...	...	7	1	2	3	12
02-03—Rimouski	QMJHL	25	6	31	37	41	...	...	...	—	—	—	—	—
—Quebec	QMJHL	32	6	31	37	41	...	...	...	11	4	4	8	25
03-04—Syracuse	AHL	49	6	15	21	83	0	4	0	7	2	3	5	27
—Columbus	NHL	29	2	6	8	32	-2	0	0	—	—	—	—	—
04-05—Syracuse	AHL	77	6	17	23	140	-13	2	0	—	—	—	—	—
NHL Totals (1 year)		29	2	6	8	32	-2	0	0					

JOHNSON, BRENT — G

PERSONAL: Born March 12, 1977, in Farmington, Mich. ... 6-2/196. ... Catches left. ... Son of Bob Johnson, G with two NHL teams (1972-75). Grandson of Hall of Fame member Sid Abel, F with two NHL teams (1938-54) and coach and general manager.
TRANSACTIONS/CAREER NOTES: Selected by Colorado Avalanche in fifth round (fifth Avalanche pick, 129th overall) of NHL draft (July 8, 1995). ... Traded by Avalanche to St. Louis Blues for third-round pick (D Rick Berry) in 1997 draft (May 30, 1997). ... Injured knee (January 23, 2001); missed three games. ... Flu (November 23, 2001); missed one game. ... Strained hip flexor (April 7, 2002); missed one game. ... Injured ankle before 2002 training camp; missed first 27 games of season. ... Groin injury (February 27, 2003); missed five games. ... Traded by Blues to Phoenix Coyotes for C Mike Sillinger (March 4, 2004).

		REGULAR SEASON									PLAYOFFS							
Season Team	League	GP	Min.	W	L	T	GA	SO	GAA	SV%	GP	Min.	W	L	GA	SO	GAA	SV%
94-95—Owen Sound	OHL	18	904	3	9	1	75	0	4.98	...	4	253	0	4	24	0	5.69	.865
95-96—Owen Sound	OHL	58	3211	24	28	1	243	1	4.54	...	6	371	2	4	29	0	4.69	...
96-97—Owen Sound	OHL	50	2798	20	28	1	201	1	4.31	.891	4	253	0	4	24	0	5.69	.865
97-98—Worcester	AHL	42	2241	14	15	7	119	0	3.19	.899	6	332	3	2	19	0	3.43	.885
98-99—Worcester	AHL	49	2925	22	22	4	146	2	2.99	.896	4	238	1	3	12	0	3.03	.916
—St. Louis	NHL	6	286	3	2	0	10	0	2.10	.921	—	—	—	—	—	—	—	—
99-00—Worcester	AHL	58	3319	24	27	5	161	3	2.91	...	9	561	4	5	23	1	2.46	...
00-01—St. Louis	NHL	31	1744	19	9	2	63	4	2.17	.907	2	62	0	1	2	0	1.94	.944
01-02—St. Louis	NHL	58	3491	34	20	4	127	5	2.18	.902	10	590	5	5	18	3	1.83	.929
02-03—Worcester	AHL	2	125	0	1	1	8	0	3.84	.881	—	—	—	—	—	—	—	—
—St. Louis	NHL	38	2042	16	13	5	84	2	2.47	.900	—	—	—	—	—	—	—	—
03-04—St. Louis	NHL	10	493	4	3	1	20	1	2.43	.901	—	—	—	—	—	—	—	—
—Phoenix	NHL	8	486	1	6	1	21	0	2.59	.914	—	—	—	—	—	—	—	—
—Worcester	AHL	8	365	2	2	2	14	0	2.30	.901	—	—	—	—	—	—	—	—
NHL Totals (5 years)		151	8542	77	53	13	325	12	2.28	.904	12	652	5	6	20	3	1.84	.931

JOHNSON, CRAIG — LW/C

PERSONAL: Born March 18, 1972, in St. Paul, Minn. ... 6-2/198. ... Shoots left.
TRANSACTIONS/CAREER NOTES: Selected by St. Louis Blues in second round (first Blues pick, 33rd overall) of NHL draft (June 16, 1990). ... Traded by Blues with C Patrice Tardiff, C Roman Vopat, fifth-round pick (D Peter Hogan) in 1996 draft and first-round pick (LW Matt Zultek) in 1997 draft to Los Angeles Kings for C Wayne Gretzky (February 27, 1996). ... Sprained left shoulder (March 13, 1996); missed seven games. ... Strained abdominal muscle; missed first seven games of 1996-97 season. ... Strained groin (November 2, 1996); missed one game. ... Strained abdominal muscle (November 30, 1996); missed 36 games. ... Strained groin (March 29, 1997); missed six games. ... Flu (December 18, 1997); missed two games. ... Bruised abdomen (February 2, 1998); missed three games. ... Injured ribs (January 14, 1999); missed four games. ... Cut finger (February 16, 2000); missed three games. ... Cut tendon in right leg (December 26, 2000); missed remainder of season. ... Injured eye (January 21, 2002); missed two games. ... Eye surgery (March 19, 2002); missed eight games. ... Signed as free agent by Anaheim Mighty Ducks (September 9, 2003). ... Claimed by Toronto Maple Leafs off waivers from Mighty Ducks (January 10, 2004). ... Injured shoulder (February 26, 2004); missed five games. ... Claimed by Washington Capitals off waivers from Maple Leafs (March 5, 2004).

		REGULAR SEASON								PLAYOFFS				
Season Team	League	GP	G	A	Pts.	PIM	+/-	PP	SH	GP	G	A	Pts.	PIM
87-88—Hill-Murray H.S.	Minn. H.S.	28	14	20	34	4	...	...	...	—	—	—	—	—
88-89—Hill-Murray H.S.	Minn. H.S.	24	22	30	52	10	...	...	...	—	—	—	—	—

Season Team	League	GP	G	A	Pts.	PIM	+/-	PP	SH	GP	G	A	Pts.	PIM
		REGULAR SEASON								PLAYOFFS				
89-90—Hill-Murray H.S.	Minn. H.S.	23	15	36	51	...	...	...	...	—	—	—	—	—
90-91—Minnesota	WCHA	33	13	18	31	34	...	...	...	—	—	—	—	—
91-92—Minnesota	WCHA	44	19	39	58	70	...	...	...	—	—	—	—	—
92-93—Minnesota	WCHA	42	22	24	46	70	...	...	...	—	—	—	—	—
93-94—U.S. national team	Int'l	54	25	26	51	64	...	4	2	—	—	—	—	—
—U.S. Olympic team	Int'l	8	0	4	4	4	-1	0	0	—	—	—	—	—
94-95—Peoria	IHL	16	2	6	8	25	0	0	0	9	0	4	4	10
—St. Louis	NHL	15	3	3	6	6	4	0	0	1	0	0	0	2
95-96—Worcester	AHL	5	3	0	3	2	...	...	...	—	—	—	—	—
—St. Louis	NHL	49	8	7	15	30	-4	1	0	—	—	—	—	—
—Los Angeles	NHL	11	5	4	9	6	-4	3	0	—	—	—	—	—
96-97—Mobile	ECHL	4	0	0	0	74	...	...	...	—	—	—	—	—
—Los Angeles	NHL	31	4	3	7	26	-7	1	0	—	—	—	—	—
—Oklahoma City	CHL	36	6	11	17	134	...	...	...	—	—	—	—	—
—Michigan	IHL	2	0	0	0	2	...	...	...	—	—	—	—	—
—Manitoba	IHL	16	2	2	4	38	...	...	...	—	—	—	—	—
97-98—Los Angeles	NHL	74	17	21	38	42	9	6	0	4	1	0	1	4
98-99—Los Angeles	NHL	69	7	12	19	32	-12	2	0	—	—	—	—	—
—Houston	IHL	1	0	0	0	0	1	0	0	—	—	—	—	—
99-00—Los Angeles	NHL	76	9	14	23	28	-10	1	0	4	1	0	1	2
00-01—Los Angeles	NHL	26	4	5	9	16	0	0	0	—	—	—	—	—
01-02—Los Angeles	NHL	72	13	14	27	24	14	4	1	7	1	2	3	2
02-03—Los Angeles	NHL	70	3	6	9	22	-13	0	0	—	—	—	—	—
03-04—Anaheim	NHL	39	1	2	3	14	-4	0	0	—	—	—	—	—
—Toronto	NHL	10	1	1	2	6	0	0	0	—	—	—	—	—
—Washington	NHL	15	0	6	6	8	-6	0	0	—	—	—	—	—
04-05—Hamburg	Germany	42	19	25	44	56	8	5	1	...	...	...	...	...
NHL Totals (10 years)		557	75	98	173	260	-33	18	1	16	3	2	5	10

JOHNSON, GREG — C — PREDATORS

PERSONAL: Born March 16, 1971, in Thunder Bay, Ont. ... 5-11/202. ... Shoots left. ... Brother of Ryan Johnson, C, St. Louis Blues.

TRANSACTIONS/CAREER NOTES: Selected by Philadelphia Flyers in second round (first Flyers pick, 33rd overall) of NHL draft (June 17, 1989). ... Separated right shoulder (November 24, 1990). ... Rights traded by Flyers with fifth-round pick (G Frederic Deschenes) in 1994 draft to Detroit Red Wings for RW Jim Cummins and fourth-round pick (traded to Boston) in 1993 entry draft (June 20, 1993). ... Loaned to Canadian Olympic Team (January 19, 1994). ... Returned to Red Wings (March 1, 1994). ... Sprained left ankle (April 14, 1995); missed final nine games of season. ... Injured left hand (October 8, 1995); missed two games. ... Injured knee (March 19, 1996); missed 12 games. ... Traded by Red Wings to Pittsburgh Penguins for RW Tomas Sandstrom (January 27, 1997). ... Bruised shoulder (April 3, 1997); missed one game. ... Strained groin (October 3, 1997); missed five games. ... Traded by Penguins to Chicago Blackhawks for D Tuomas Gronman (October 27, 1997). ... Strained groin (October 31, 1997); missed three games. ... Selected by Nashville Predators in expansion draft (June 26, 1998). ... Suffered concussion (December 10, 1998); missed four games. ... Strained groin (February 20, 1999); missed five games. ... Stress fracture in ankle (April 7, 1999); missed final five games of season. ... Concussion (October 22, 2002); missed 44 games.

Season Team	League	GP	G	A	Pts.	PIM	+/-	PP	SH	GP	G	A	Pts.	PIM
		REGULAR SEASON								PLAYOFFS				
88-89—Thunder Bay Jrs.	USHL	47	32	64	96	4	...	...	...	12	5	13	18	...
89-90—North Dakota	WCHA	44	17	38	55	11	...	...	...	—	—	—	—	—
90-91—North Dakota	WCHA	38	18	*61	79	6	...	...	...	—	—	—	—	—
91-92—North Dakota	WCHA	39	20	54	74	8	...	...	...	—	—	—	—	—
92-93—Canadian nat'l team	Int'l	23	6	14	20	2	...	...	...	—	—	—	—	—
—North Dakota	WCHA	34	19	45	64	18	...	...	...	—	—	—	—	—
93-94—Detroit	NHL	52	6	11	17	22	-7	1	1	7	2	2	4	2
—Canadian nat'l team	Int'l	6	2	6	8	4	...	...	...	—	—	—	—	—
—Can. Olympic team	Int'l	8	0	3	3	0	0	0	0	—	—	—	—	—
—Adirondack	AHL	3	2	4	6	0	3	1	0	4	0	4	4	2
94-95—Detroit	NHL	22	3	5	8	14	1	2	0	1	0	0	0	0
95-96—Detroit	NHL	60	18	22	40	30	6	5	0	13	3	1	4	8
96-97—Detroit	NHL	43	6	10	16	12	-5	0	0	—	—	—	—	—
—Pittsburgh	NHL	32	7	9	16	14	-13	1	0	5	1	0	1	2
97-98—Pittsburgh	NHL	5	1	0	1	2	0	0	0	—	—	—	—	—
—Chicago	NHL	69	11	22	33	38	-2	4	0	—	—	—	—	—
98-99—Nashville	NHL	68	16	34	50	24	-8	2	3	—	—	—	—	—
99-00—Nashville	NHL	82	11	33	44	40	-15	2	0	—	—	—	—	—
00-01—Nashville	NHL	82	15	17	32	46	-6	1	0	—	—	—	—	—
01-02—Nashville	NHL	82	18	*26	44	38	-14	3	0	—	—	—	—	—
02-03—Nashville	NHL	38	8	9	17	22	7	0	0	—	—	—	—	—
03-04—Nashville	NHL	82	14	18	32	33	-21	1	4	6	1	2	3	0
04-05—Pee Dee	ECHL	70	27	36	63	46	1	5	2	—	—	—	—	—
NHL Totals (11 years)		717	134	216	350	335	-77	22	8	32	7	5	12	12

JOHNSON, JACK — D — HURRICANES

PERSONAL: Born January 13, 1987, in Indianapolis, Ind. ... 6-1/201.

TRANSACTIONS/CAREER NOTES: Selected by Carolina Hurricanes in 1st round (1st Hurricanes pick, 3rd overall) of entry draft (July 30, 2005).

Season Team	League	GP	G	A	Pts.	PIM	+/-	PP	SH	GP	G	A	Pts.	PIM
		REGULAR SEASON								PLAYOFFS				
03-04—U.S. National	USHL	60	15	21	36	171	...	...	...	—	—	—	—	—
04-05—U.S. National	USHL	42	14	27	41	170	...	...	...	—	—	—	—	—

JOHNSON, MATT — LW

PERSONAL: Born November 23, 1975, in Welland, Ont. ... 6-5/235. ... Shoots left.

TRANSACTIONS/CAREER NOTES: Selected by Los Angeles Kings in 2nd round (2nd Kings pick, 33rd overall) of NHL draft (June 28, 1994). ... Flu (February 25, 1995); missed one game. ... Bruised right hand (April 3, 1995); missed four games. ... Strained shoulder (December 18, 1996); missed six games. ... Concussion (February 1, 1997); missed one game. ... Suspended four games and fined $1,000 for elbowing incident (February 5, 1997). ... Strained back (March 10, 1997); missed final 13 games of season. ... Suspended four games and fined $1,000 for slashing incident (September 29, 1997). ... Strained groin (December 23, 1997); missed one game. ... Strained left biceps (March 21, 1998); missed three games. ... Suspended 12 games for deliberately injuring another player (November 23, 1998). ... Selected by Atlanta Thrashers in expansion draft (June 25, 1999). ... Injured groin (October 7, 1999); missed two games. ... Strained hip flexor (November 25, 1999); missed two games. ... Injured eye (December 13, 1999); missed nine games. ... Sprained knee (March 28, 2000); missed two games. ... Traded by Thrashers to Minnesota Wild for 3rd-round pick (traded to Pittsburgh) in 2001 draft (September 29, 2000). ... Sprained finger (November 7, 2000); missed four games. ... Concussion (November 26, 2000); missed eight games. ... Concussion, bruised hand (January 14, 2001); missed seven games. ... Dizziness (March 1, 2001); missed 10 games. ... Bruised right foot (February 8, 2002); missed three games. ... Suspended five games for unsportsmanlike conduct (March 10, 2002). ... Back spasms (October 12, 2002); missed four games. ... Flu (January 7, 2003: missed one game. ... Flu (January 15, 2003); missed one game. ... Back spasms (February 4, 2003); missed three games. ... Back spasms (February 13, 2003); missed four games. ... Separated right shoulder (November 12, 2003); missed eight games. ... Suspended five games for slashing incident (February 19, 2004). ... Contract bought out by Wild (July 29, 2005).

		REGULAR SEASON								PLAYOFFS				
Season Team	League	GP	G	A	Pts.	PIM	+/-	PP	SH	GP	G	A	Pts.	PIM
91-92—Welland	Jr. B	38	6	19	25	214	...	...	...	—	—	—	—	—
92-93—Peterborough	OHL	66	8	17	25	211	...	...	...	16	1	1	2	54
93-94—Peterborough	OHL	50	13	24	37	233	...	5	...	—	—	—	—	—
94-95—Peterborough	OHL	14	1	2	3	43	...	0	0	—	—	—	—	—
—Los Angeles	NHL	14	1	0	1	102	0	0	0	—	—	—	—	—
95-96—Los Angeles	NHL	1	0	0	0	5	0	0	0	—	—	—	—	—
—Phoenix	IHL	29	4	4	8	87	...	...	...	—	—	—	—	—
96-97—Los Angeles	NHL	52	1	3	4	194	-4	0	0	—	—	—	—	—
97-98—Los Angeles	NHL	66	2	4	6	249	-8	0	0	4	0	0	0	6
98-99—Los Angeles	NHL	49	2	1	3	131	-5	0	0	—	—	—	—	—
99-00—Atlanta	NHL	64	2	5	7	144	-11	0	0	—	—	—	—	—
00-01—Minnesota	NHL	50	1	1	2	137	-6	0	0	—	—	—	—	—
01-02—Minnesota	NHL	60	4	0	4	183	-13	0	0	—	—	—	—	—
02-03—Minnesota	NHL	60	3	5	8	201	-8	0	0	12	0	0	0	25
03-04—Minnesota	NHL	57	7	1	8	177	4	0	0	—	—	—	—	—
NHL Totals (10 years)		473	23	20	43	1523	-51	0	0	16	0	0	0	31

JOHNSON, MIKE — RW — COYOTES

PERSONAL: Born October 3, 1974, in Scarborough, Ont. ... 6-2/201. ... Shoots right.

TRANSACTIONS/CAREER NOTES: Signed as free agent by Toronto Maple Leafs (March 16, 1997). ... Suspended two games for elbowing (April 8, 1999). ... Traded by Maple Leafs with D Marek Posmyk and fifth- (F Pavel Sedov) and sixth-round (D Aaron Gionet) picks in 2000 draft to Tampa Bay Lightning for C Darcy Tucker and fourth-round pick (RW Miguel Delisle) in 2000 draft (February 9, 2000). ... Injured (November 27, 1999); missed two games. ... Fractured facial bone (March 17, 2000); missed one game. ... Injured ribs (December 2, 2000); missed two games. ... Traded by Lightning with D Paul Mara, RW Ruslan Zainullin and second-round pick (D Matthew Spiller) in 2001 draft to Phoenix Coyotes for G Nikolai Khabibulin and D Stan Neckar (March 5, 2001). ... Injured shoulder (March 8, 2001); missed four games. ... Injured neck (November 23, 2001); missed one game. ... Sprained knee (November 29, 2001); missed 11 games. ... Reinjured knee (December 28, 2001); missed 11 games. ... Injured shoulder (November 6, 2003) and had surgery; missed remainder of season.

		REGULAR SEASON								PLAYOFFS				
Season Team	League	GP	G	A	Pts.	PIM	+/-	PP	SH	GP	G	A	Pts.	PIM
92-93—Aurora	OPJHL	48	25	40	65	18	...	...	...	—	—	—	—	—
93-94—Bowling Green	CCHA	38	6	14	20	18	...	...	...	—	—	—	—	—
94-95—Bowling Green	CCHA	37	16	33	49	35	...	...	...	—	—	—	—	—
95-96—Bowling Green	CCHA	30	12	19	31	22	...	...	...	—	—	—	—	—
96-97—Bowling Green	CCHA	38	30	32	62	46	8	...	...	—	—	—	—	—
—Toronto	NHL	13	2	2	4	4	-2	0	1	—	—	—	—	—
97-98—Toronto	NHL	82	15	32	47	24	-4	5	0	—	—	—	—	—
98-99—Toronto	NHL	79	20	24	44	35	13	5	3	17	3	2	5	4
99-00—Toronto	NHL	52	11	14	25	23	8	2	1	—	—	—	—	—
—Tampa Bay	NHL	28	10	12	22	4	-2	4	0	—	—	—	—	—
00-01—Tampa Bay	NHL	64	11	27	38	38	-10	3	1	—	—	—	—	—
—Phoenix	NHL	12	2	3	5	4	0	1	0	—	—	—	—	—
01-02—Phoenix	NHL	57	5	22	27	28	14	1	2	5	1	1	2	6
02-03—Phoenix	NHL	82	23	40	63	47	9	8	0	—	—	—	—	—
03-04—Phoenix	NHL	11	1	9	10	10	-1	1	0	—	—	—	—	—
04-05—Farjestad Karlstad	Sweden	8	1	2	3	4	2	0	0	6	0	2	2	4
NHL Totals (8 years)		480	100	185	285	217	25	30	8	22	4	3	7	10

JOHNSON, RYAN — C/LW — BLUES

PERSONAL: Born June 14, 1976, in Thunder Bay, Ont. ... 6-1/205. ... Shoots left. ... Brother of Greg Johnson, C, Nashville Predators.

TRANSACTIONS/CAREER NOTES: Selected by Florida Panthers in second round (fourth Panthers pick, 36th overall) of NHL draft (June 28, 1994). ... Loaned to Canadian national team before 1995-96 season. ... Bruised left ankle (October 16, 1999); missed two games. ... Flu (January 6, 2000); missed one game. ... Traded by Panthers with LW Dwayne Hay to Tampa Bay Lightning for C Mike Sillinger (March 14, 2000). ... Virus (December 2, 2000); missed two games. ... Traded by Lightning with sixth-round pick (later traded back to Lightning, who selected D Doug O'Brien) in 2003 draft to Florida Panthers for C Vaclav Prospal (July 10, 2001). ... Fractured left foot (November 24, 2001); missed five games. ... Suffered concussion (December 22, 2001); missed remainder of season. ... Claimed off waivers by St. Louis Blues from Panthers (February 19, 2003). ... Injured lower body (April 15, 2004); missed final two games of playoffs.

Season Team	League	GP	G	A	Pts.	PIM	+/-	PP	SH	GP	G	A	Pts.	PIM
		REGULAR SEASON								PLAYOFFS				
93-94—Thunder Bay Jrs.	USHL	48	14	36	50	28	...	...	...	—	—	—	—	—
94-95—North Dakota	WCHA	38	6	22	28	39	...	2	1	—	—	—	—	—
95-96—Canadian nat'l team	Int'l	28	5	12	17	14	...	...	...	—	—	—	—	—
—North Dakota	WCHA	21	2	17	19	14	...	...	...	—	—	—	—	—
96-97—Carolina	AHL	79	18	24	42	28	-25	0	1	—	—	—	—	—
97-98—New Haven	AHL	64	19	48	67	12	10	5	5	3	0	1	1	0
—Florida	NHL	10	0	2	2	0	-4	0	0	—	—	—	—	—
98-99—New Haven	AHL	37	8	19	27	18	-15	4	0	—	—	—	—	—
—Florida	NHL	1	1	0	1	0	0	0	0	—	—	—	—	—
99-00—Florida	NHL	66	4	12	16	14	1	0	0	—	—	—	—	—
—Tampa Bay	NHL	14	0	2	2	2	-9	0	0	—	—	—	—	—
00-01—Tampa Bay	NHL	80	7	14	21	44	-20	1	0	—	—	—	—	—
01-02—Florida	NHL	29	1	3	4	10	-5	0	0	—	—	—	—	—
02-03—Florida	NHL	58	2	5	7	26	-13	0	0	—	—	—	—	—
—St. Louis	NHL	17	0	0	0	12	0	0	0	6	0	2	2	6
03-04—St. Louis	NHL	69	4	7	11	8	-2	0	1	3	0	0	0	0
04-05—Missouri	UHL	29	7	14	21	12	8	1	0	—	—	—	—	—
NHL Totals (7 years)		344	19	45	64	116	-52	1	1	9	0	2	2	6

JOHNSSON, KIM — D — FLYERS

PERSONAL: Born March 16, 1976, in Malmo, Sweden. ... 6-1/205. ... Shoots left.

TRANSACTIONS/CAREER NOTES: Selected by New York Rangers in 11th round (15th Rangers pick, 286th overall) of NHL draft (June 29, 1994). ... Injured eye (February 8, 2000); missed one game. ... Fractured hand (November 2, 2000); missed five games. ... Traded by Rangers with LW Jan Hlavac, RW Pavel Brendl and third-round pick (LW Stefan Ruzicka) in 2003 draft to Philadelphia Flyers for rights to C Eric Lindros (August 20, 2001). ... Flu (December 3, 2003); missed two games. ... Fractured hand (April 30, 2004); missed three playoff games.

Season Team	League	GP	G	A	Pts.	PIM	+/-	PP	SH	GP	G	A	Pts.	PIM
		REGULAR SEASON								PLAYOFFS				
94-95—Malmo	Sweden	13	0	0	0	4	...	...	...	1	0	0	0	0
95-96—Malmo	Sweden	38	2	0	2	30	...	...	...	4	0	1	1	8
96-97—Malmo	Sweden	49	4	9	13	42	...	...	...	4	0	0	0	2
97-98—Malmo	Sweden	45	5	9	14	29	...	...	...	—	—	—	—	—
98-99—Malmo	Sweden	49	9	8	17	76	...	...	...	8	2	3	5	12
99-00—New York Rangers	NHL	76	6	15	21	46	-13	1	0	—	—	—	—	—
00-01—New York Rangers	NHL	75	5	21	26	40	-3	4	0	—	—	—	—	—
01-02—Philadelphia	NHL	82	11	30	41	42	12	5	0	5	0	0	0	2
—Swedish Oly. team	Int'l	4	1	1	2	0	...	...	...	—	—	—	—	—
02-03—Philadelphia	NHL	82	10	29	39	38	11	5	0	13	0	3	3	8
03-04—Philadelphia	NHL	80	13	29	42	26	16	4	0	15	2	6	8	8
04-05—Ambri-Piotta	Switzerland	24	4	10	14	61	...	3	0	—	—	—	—	—
NHL Totals (5 years)		395	45	124	169	192	23	19	0	33	2	9	11	18

JOKINEN, OLLI — C — PANTHERS

PERSONAL: Born December 5, 1978, in Kuopio, Finland. ... 6-3/215. ... Shoots left. ... Name pronounced OH-lee YOH-kih-nehn.

TRANSACTIONS/CAREER NOTES: Selected by Los Angeles Kings in first round (first Kings pick, third overall) of NHL draft (June 21, 1997). ... Traded by Kings with LW Josh Green, D Mathieu Biron and first-round pick (LW Taylor Pyatt) in 1999 draft to New York Islanders for RW Zigmund Palffy, C Bryan Smolinski, G Marcel Cousineau and fourth-round pick (C Daniel Johansson) in 1999 draft (June 20, 1999). ... Traded by Islanders with G Roberto Luongo to Florida Panthers for RW Mark Parrish and LW Oleg Kvasha (June 24, 2000). ... Flu (December 23, 2002); missed one game.

Season Team	League	GP	G	A	Pts.	PIM	+/-	PP	SH	GP	G	A	Pts.	PIM
		REGULAR SEASON								PLAYOFFS				
94-95—KalPa Kuopio	Finland Jr.	6	0	1	1	6	...	...	...	—	—	—	—	—
95-96—KalPa Kuopio	Finland Jr.	15	1	1	2	2	...	...	...	—	—	—	—	—
—KalPa Kuopio	Finland	15	1	1	2	2	...	...	...	—	—	—	—	—
96-97—HIFK Helsinki	Finland	50	14	27	41	88	...	...	...	—	—	—	—	—
97-98—Los Angeles	NHL	8	0	0	0	6	-5	0	0	—	—	—	—	—
—HIFK Helsinki	Finland	30	11	28	39	8	...	...	...	9	7	2	9	2
98-99—Springfield	AHL	9	3	6	9	6	-1	1	0	—	—	—	—	—
—Los Angeles	NHL	66	9	12	21	44	-10	3	1	—	—	—	—	—
99-00—New York Islanders	NHL	82	11	10	21	80	0	1	2	—	—	—	—	—
00-01—Florida	NHL	78	6	10	16	106	-22	0	0	—	—	—	—	—
01-02—Florida	NHL	80	9	20	29	98	-16	3	1	—	—	—	—	—
—Fin. Olympic team	Int'l	4	2	1	3	0	...	...	...	—	—	—	—	—
02-03—Florida	NHL	81	36	29	65	79	-17	13	3	—	—	—	—	—
03-04—Florida	NHL	82	26	32	58	81	-16	8	2	—	—	—	—	—
04-05—Kloten	Switzerland	8	6	1	7	14	1	1	1	—	—	—	—	—
—Sodertalje SK	Sweden	23	13	9	22	52	-5	4	0	—	—	—	—	—
—HIFK Helsinki	Finland	14	9	8	17	10	8	...	...	5	2	0	2	24
NHL Totals (7 years)		477	97	113	210	494	-86	28	9					

JONES, RANDY — D — FLYERS

PERSONAL: Born July 23, 1981, in Quispamsis, New Brunswick. ... 6-2/195. ... Shoots left.

TRANSACTIONS/CAREER NOTES: Signed as free agent by Philadelphia Flyers (July 24, 2003).

Season Team	League	GP	G	A	Pts.	PIM	+/-	PP	SH	GP	G	A	Pts.	PIM
		REGULAR SEASON								PLAYOFFS				
01-02—Clarkson	ECAC	34	9	11	20	32	...	...	...	—	—	—	—	—
02-03—Clarkson	ECAC	33	13	20	33	65	...	...	...	—	—	—	—	—
03-04—Philadelphia	AHL	55	8	24	32	63	0	2	0	12	0	1	1	17
—Philadelphia	NHL	5	0	0	0	0	1	0	0	—	—	—	—	—
04-05—Philadelphia	AHL	69	5	19	24	32	1	2	0	18	0	5	5	10
NHL Totals (1 year)		5	0	0	0	0	1	0	0					

JONES, TY — RW — PANTHERS

PERSONAL: Born May 24, 1978, in Richland, Wash. ... 6-3/218. ... Shoots right.
TRANSACTIONS/CAREER NOTES: Selected by Chicago Blackhawks in first round (second Blackhawks pick, 16th overall) of NHL entry draft (June 21, 1997). ... Traded by Blackhawks to Florida Panthers for future considerations (March 2, 2004).

Season Team	League	GP	G	A	Pts.	PIM	+/-	PP	SH	GP	G	A	Pts.	PIM
		REGULAR SEASON								PLAYOFFS				
95-96—Spokane	WHL	34	1	0	1	77	...	...	...	3	0	0	0	6
96-97—Spokane	WHL	67	20	34	54	202	...	...	...	9	2	4	6	...
97-98—Spokane	WHL	60	36	48	84	161	24	16	0	18	2	14	16	35
98-99—Spokane	WHL	26	15	12	27	98	...	...	...	—	—	—	—	—
—Kamloops	WHL	20	3	16	19	84	...	...	...	14	5	3	8	22
—Chicago	NHL	8	0	0	0	12	-1	0	0	—	—	—	—	—
99-00—Cleveland	IHL	10	1	1	2	34	...	...	...	—	—	—	—	—
—Florida	ECHL	48	11	26	37	81	...	...	...	5	1	1	2	7
00-01—Norfolk	AHL	64	11	17	28	114	...	...	...	—	—	—	—	—
01-02—Norfolk	AHL	55	6	14	20	172	4	1	0	4	0	0	0	2
02-03—Anchorage	WCHL	12	1	7	8	49	5	...	...	—	—	—	—	—
03-04—Norfolk	AHL	37	4	5	9	93	-4	1	0	—	—	—	—	—
—San Antonio	AHL	2	0	0	0	2	0	0	0	—	—	—	—	—
—Florida	NHL	6	0	0	0	7	0	0	0	—	—	—	—	—
04-05—San Antonio	AHL	0	0	0	0	0	0	0	0	—	—	—	—	—
NHL Totals (2 years)		14	0	0	0	19	-1	0	0					

JONSSON, KENNY — D — ISLANDERS

PERSONAL: Born October 6, 1974, in Angelholm, Sweden. ... 6-3/205. ... Shoots left. ... Brother of Jorgen Jonsson, LW with New York Islanders (1999-2000) and Mighty Ducks of Anaheim (1999-2000). ... Name pronounced YAHN-suhn.
TRANSACTIONS/CAREER NOTES: Selected by Toronto Maple Leafs in first round (first Maple Leafs pick, 12th overall) of NHL draft (June 26, 1993). ... Flu (February 13, 1995); missed two games. ... Strained hip flexor (February 27, 1995); missed one game. ... Had hip pointer (April 7, 1995); missed one game. ... Flu (April 19, 1995); missed one game. ... Strained back (December 9, 1995); missed one game. ... Separated shoulder (January 30, 1996); missed 17 games. ... Traded by Maple Leafs with C Darby Hendrickson, LW Sean Haggerty and first-round pick (G Robert Luongo) in 1997 draft to New York Islanders for LW Wendel Clark, D Mathieu Schneider and D D.J. Smith (March 13, 1996). ... Flu (December 23, 1996); missed one game. ... Sprained knee (February 4, 1998); missed one game. ... Suffered concussion (November 17, 1998); missed eight games. ... Sprained knee (January 16, 1999); missed nine games. ... Fractured finger (April 17, 1999); missed final game of season. ... Flu (December 30, 1999); missed four games. ... Suffered concussion (January 19, 2000); missed 11 games. ... Sprained left wrist (March 26, 2000); missed one game. ... Headaches (April 1, 2000); missed final five games of regular season. ... Injured neck (December 3, 2000); missed one game. ... Sprained left knee (December 19, 2000); missed 13 games. ... Injured knee (January 23, 2001); missed one game. ... Suffered concussion (December 22, 2001); missed two games. ... Flu (January 23, 2002); missed two games. ... Strained neck (January 30, 2002); missed one game. ... Injured quadricep (April 15, 2002); missed final game of season. ... Virus (November 8, 2002); missed three games. ... Injured knee (November 30, 2002); missed one game. ... Injured knee (March 1, 2003); missed four games. ... Migraine headaches (April 1, 2003); missed three games. ... Virus (February 11, 2004); missed one game.

Season Team	League	GP	G	A	Pts.	PIM	+/-	PP	SH	GP	G	A	Pts.	PIM
		REGULAR SEASON								PLAYOFFS				
91-92—Rogle Angelholm	Sweden	30	4	11	15	24	...	...	...	—	—	—	—	—
92-93—Rogle Angelholm	Sweden	39	3	10	13	42	...	...	...	—	—	—	—	—
93-94—Rogle Angelholm	Sweden	36	4	13	17	40	...	...	...	3	1	1	2	...
—Swedish Oly. team	Int'l	3	1	0	1	0	-2	0	0	—	—	—	—	—
94-95—Rogle Angelholm	Sweden	8	3	1	4	20	...	...	...	—	—	—	—	—
—St. John's	AHL	10	2	5	7	2	-4	2	0	—	—	—	—	—
—Toronto	NHL	39	2	7	9	16	-8	0	0	4	0	0	0	0
95-96—Toronto	NHL	50	4	22	26	22	12	3	0	—	—	—	—	—
—New York Islanders	NHL	16	0	4	4	10	-5	0	0	—	—	—	—	—
96-97—New York Islanders	NHL	81	3	18	21	24	10	1	0	—	—	—	—	—
97-98—New York Islanders	NHL	81	14	26	40	58	-2	6	0	—	—	—	—	—
98-99—New York Islanders	NHL	63	8	18	26	34	-18	6	0	—	—	—	—	—
99-00—New York Islanders	NHL	65	1	24	25	32	-15	1	0	—	—	—	—	—
00-01—New York Islanders	NHL	65	8	21	29	30	-22	5	0	—	—	—	—	—
01-02—New York Islanders	NHL	76	10	22	32	26	15	2	1	5	1	2	3	4
—Swedish Oly. team	Int'l	3	1	0	1	2	...	...	...	—	—	—	—	—
02-03—New York Islanders	NHL	71	8	18	26	24	-8	3	1	5	0	1	1	0
03-04—New York Islanders	NHL	79	5	24	29	22	25	3	0	5	0	0	0	2
04-05—Rogle	Sweden Dv. 2	11	3	7	10	12	2	3	0	—	—	—	—	—
NHL Totals (10 years)		686	63	204	267	298	-16	30	2	19	1	3	4	6

JOSEPH, CURTIS — G — COYOTES

PERSONAL: Born April 29, 1967, in Keswick, Ontario. ... 5-11/190. ... Catches left.
TRANSACTIONS/CAREER NOTES: Signed as free agent by St. Louis Blues (June 16, 1989). ... Dislocated left shoulder (April 11, 1990). ... Left shoulder surgery (May 10, 1990). ... Sprained right knee (February 26, 1991); missed remainder of season. ... Injured ankle (March 12, 1992);

missed seven games. ... Sore knee (January 2, 1993); missed three games. ... Flu (February 9, 1993); missed one game. ... Strained groin (January 26, 1995); missed three games. ... Injured hamstring (April 16, 1995); missed four games. ... Traded by Blues with rights to RW Michael Grier to Edmonton Oilers for first-round picks in 1996 (C Marty Reasoner) and 1997 (traded to Los Angeles) drafts (August 4, 1995); picks had been awarded to Oilers as compensation for Blues signing free agent LW Shayne Corson (July 28, 1995). ... Injured right knee (March 30, 1996); missed three games. ... Strained groin (December 18, 1996); missed seven games. ... Signed as free agent by Toronto Maple Leafs (July 15, 1998). ... Strained groin (January 21, 1999); missed one game. ... Fractured hand (February 26, 2002); missed 20 games. ... Traded by Maple Leafs to Calgary Flames for third-round pick (traded to Minnesota; Wild selected Danny Irmen) in 2003 draft and future considerations (June 30, 2002). ... Signed as free agent by Detroit Red Wings (July 2, 2002). ... Injured ankle (September 10, 2003); missed first four games of season. ... Injured ankle (February 11, 2004); missed 10 games. ... Reinjured ankle (March 23, 2004); missed final 11 games of regular season.

		REGULAR SEASON									PLAYOFFS							
Season Team	League	GP	Min.	W	L	T	GA	SO	GAA	SV%	GP	Min.	W	L	GA	SO	GAA	SV%
87-88—Notre Dame	SCMHL	36	2174	25	4	7	94	1	2.59	...	—	—	—	—	—	—	—	—
88-89—Wisconsin	WCHA	38	2267	21	11	5	94	1	2.49	...	—	—	—	—	—	—	—	—
89-90—Peoria	IHL	23	1241	10	8	2	80	0	3.87	...	—	—	—	—	—	—	—	—
—St. Louis	NHL	15	852	9	5	1	48	0	3.38	.890	6	327	4	1	18	0	3.30	.892
90-91—St. Louis	NHL	30	1710	16	10	2	89	0	3.12	.898	—	—	—	—	—	—	—	—
91-92—St. Louis	NHL	60	3494	27	20	10	175	2	3.01	.910	6	379	2	4	23	0	3.64	.894
92-93—St. Louis	NHL	68	3890	29	28	9	196	1	3.02	*.911	11	715	7	4	27	2	2.27	.938
93-94—St. Louis	NHL	71	4127	36	23	11	213	1	3.10	.911	4	246	0	4	15	0	3.66	.905
94-95—St. Louis	NHL	36	1914	20	10	1	89	1	2.79	.902	7	392	3	3	24	0	3.67	.865
95-96—Las Vegas	IHL	15	873	12	2	1	29	1	1.99	...	—	—	—	—	—	—	—	—
—Edmonton	NHL	34	1936	15	16	2	111	0	3.44	.886	—	—	—	—	—	—	—	—
96-97—Edmonton	NHL	72	4100	32	29	9	200	6	2.93	.907	12	767	5	7	36	2	2.82	.911
97-98—Edmonton	NHL	71	4132	29	31	9	181	8	2.63	.905	12	716	5	7	23	3	1.93	.928
98-99—Toronto	NHL	67	4001	35	24	7	171	3	2.56	.910	17	1011	9	8	41	1	2.43	.907
99-00—Toronto	NHL	63	3801	36	20	7	158	4	2.49	.915	12	729	6	6	25	1	2.06	.932
00-01—Toronto	NHL	68	4100	33	27	8	163	6	2.39	.915	11	685	7	4	24	3	2.10	.927
01-02—Toronto	NHL	51	3065	29	17	5	114	4	2.23	.906	20	1253	10	10	48	3	2.30	.914
—Can. Olympic team	Int'l	1	60	0	1	0	5	0	5.00	.800	—	—	—	—	—	—	—	—
02-03—Detroit	NHL	61	3566	34	19	6	148	5	2.49	.912	4	289	0	4	10	0	2.08	.917
03-04—Detroit	NHL	31	1708	16	10	3	68	2	2.39	.909	9	518	4	4	12	1	1.39	.939
—Grand Rapids	AHL	1	60	1	0	0	1	0	1.00	.950	—	—	—	—	—	—	—	—
NHL Totals (15 years)		798	46396	396	289	90	2124	43	2.75	.908	131	8027	62	66	326	16	2.44	.916

JOVANOVSKI, ED D CANUCKS

PERSONAL: Born June 26, 1976, in Windsor, Ont. ... 6-2/210. ... Shoots left. ... Name pronounced joh-vuh-NAHV-skee.

TRANSACTIONS/CAREER NOTES: Selected by Florida Panthers in first round (first Panthers pick, first overall) of NHL draft (June 28, 1994). ... Fractured right index finger (September 29, 1995); missed first 11 games of season. ... Sprained knee (January 15, 1997); missed 16 games. ... Traded by Panthers with G Kevin Weekes, C Dave Gagner, C Mike Brown and first-round pick (C Nathan Smith) in 2000 draft to Vancouver Canucks for RW Pavel Bure, D Bret Hedican, D Brad Ference and third-round pick (RW Robert Fried) in 2000 draft (January 17, 1999). ... Fractured foot (February 9, 1999); missed eight games. ... Injured groin (January 12, 2000); missed six games. ... Injured hip (March 13, 2000); missed one game. ... Strained oblique muscle (October 27, 2000); missed one game. ... Fractured foot/heel (December 28, 2002); missed 14 games. ... Injured quadriceps muscle (November 11, 2003); missed one game. ... Sprained right shoulder (January 26, 2004); missed 25 games.

		REGULAR SEASON								PLAYOFFS				
Season Team	League	GP	G	A	Pts.	PIM	+/-	PP	SH	GP	G	A	Pts.	PIM
92-93—Windsor	OHL Jr. B	48	7	46	53	88	...	...	...	—	—	—	—	—
93-94—Windsor	OHL	62	15	35	50	221	...	7	...	4	0	0	0	15
94-95—Windsor	OHL	50	23	42	65	198	...	9	1	9	2	7	9	39
95-96—Florida	NHL	70	10	11	21	137	-3	2	0	22	1	8	9	52
96-97—Florida	NHL	61	7	16	23	172	-1	3	0	5	0	0	0	4
97-98—Florida	NHL	81	9	14	23	158	-12	2	1	—	—	—	—	—
98-99—Florida	NHL	41	3	13	16	82	-4	1	0	—	—	—	—	—
—Vancouver	NHL	31	2	9	11	44	-5	0	0	—	—	—	—	—
99-00—Vancouver	NHL	75	5	21	26	54	-3	1	0	—	—	—	—	—
00-01—Vancouver	NHL	79	12	35	47	102	-1	4	0	4	1	1	2	0
01-02—Vancouver	NHL	82	17	31	48	101	-7	7	1	6	1	4	5	8
—Can. Olympic team	Int'l	6	0	3	3	4	...	...	...	—	—	—	—	—
02-03—Vancouver	NHL	67	6	40	46	113	19	2	0	14	7	1	8	22
03-04—Vancouver	NHL	56	7	16	23	64	2	2	0	7	0	4	4	6
NHL Totals (9 years)		643	78	206	284	1027	-15	24	2	58	10	18	28	92

JUNTUNEN, HENRIK RW KINGS

PERSONAL: Born April 24, 1983, in Goteburg, Sweden. ... 6-2/185. ... Shoots right.

TRANSACTIONS/CAREER NOTES: Selected by Los Angeles Kings in third round (fourth Kings pick, 83rd overall) of NHL entry draft (June 23, 2001).

		REGULAR SEASON								PLAYOFFS				
Season Team	League	GP	G	A	Pts.	PIM	+/-	PP	SH	GP	G	A	Pts.	PIM
00-01—Karpat Oulu	Finland Jr.	17	4	4	8	12	...	...	...	—	—	—	—	—
—Karpat Oulu	Finland	...	...	...	...	...	...	...	...	2	0	0	0	0
01-02—Karpat Oulu	Finland	13	0	0	0	2	...	...	...	—	—	—	—	—
02-03—Karpat Oulu	Finland	50	5	4	9	30	...	...	...	—	—	—	—	—
03-04—Karpat Oulu	Finland	50	4	8	12	30	...	...	...	13	0	1	1	25
04-05—Karpat Oulu	Finland	52	6	4	10	20	...	...	...	—	—	—	—	—
—KalPa Kuopio	Finland	10	0	0	0	2	...	...	...	—	—	—	—	—

JURCINA, MILAN — D — BRUINS

PERSONAL: Born June 7, 1983, in Liptovsky Mikulas, Czech. ... 6-4/198. ... Shoots right.
TRANSACTIONS/CAREER NOTES: Selected by Boston Bruins in eighth round (seventh Bruins pick, 241st overall) of NHL entry draft (June 24, 2001).

		REGULAR SEASON								PLAYOFFS				
Season Team	League	GP	G	A	Pts.	PIM	+/-	PP	SH	GP	G	A	Pts.	PIM
00-01—Halifax	QMJHL	68	0	5	5	56	...	...	...	6	0	2	2	12
01-02—Halifax	QMJHL	61	4	16	20	58	...	...	...	13	5	3	8	10
02-03—Halifax	QMJHL	51	15	13	28	102	...	...	...	25	6	6	12	40
03-04—Providence	AHL	73	5	12	17	52	-1	1	0	2	0	1	1	2
04-05—Providence	AHL	79	6	17	23	92	6	4	0	17	1	3	4	30

KABERLE, FRANTISEK — D — HURRICANES

PERSONAL: Born November 8, 1973, in Kladno, Czechoslovakia. ... 6-0/190. ... Shoots left. ... Brother of Tomas Kaberle, D, Toronto Maple Leafs. ... Name pronounced KA-buhr-lay.
TRANSACTIONS/CAREER NOTES: Selected by Los Angeles Kings in third round (third Kings pick, 76th overall) of NHL draft (June 26, 1999). ... Traded by Kings with RW Donald Audette to Atlanta Thrashers for RW Kelly Buchberger and RW Nelson Emerson (March 13, 2000). ... Bruised foot (October 15, 2000); missed one game. ... Flu (January 25, 2001); missed one game. ... Fractured foot (February 1, 2001); missed 25 games. ... Strained groin (April 1, 2001); missed final three games of season. ... Strained right shoulder (November 23, 2001); missed four games. ... Strained groin and hamstring (March 1, 2002); missed 17 games. ... Injured foot (December 11, 2002); missed three games. ... Sprained right knee (February 19, 2004); missed 12 games. ... Signed as free agent by Carolina Hurricanes (July 15, 2004).

		REGULAR SEASON								PLAYOFFS				
Season Team	League	GP	G	A	Pts.	PIM	+/-	PP	SH	GP	G	A	Pts.	PIM
91-92—Poldi Kladno	Czech.	37	1	4	5	8	...	...	...	8	0	1	1	0
92-93—Poldi Kladno	Czech.	49	6	9	15	...	...	...	...	—	—	—	—	—
93-94—HC Kladno	Czech Rep.	40	4	15	19	...	...	...	...	9	1	2	3	...
94-95—HC Kladno	Czech Rep.	40	7	17	24	...	...	...	...	8	0	3	3	...
95-96—MoDo Ornskoldsvik	Sweden	40	5	7	12	34	...	...	...	8	0	1	1	0
96-97—MoDo Ornskoldsvik	Sweden	50	3	11	14	28	...	...	...	—	—	—	—	—
97-98—MoDo Ornskoldsvik	Sweden	46	5	4	9	22	...	...	...	9	1	1	2	4
98-99—MoDo Ornskoldsvik	Sweden	45	15	18	33	4	...	...	...	13	2	5	7	8
99-00—Los Angeles	NHL	37	0	9	9	4	3	0	0	—	—	—	—	—
—Long Beach	IHL	18	2	8	10	8	...	...	...	—	—	—	—	—
—Lowell	AHL	4	0	2	2	0	...	...	...	—	—	—	—	—
—Atlanta	NHL	14	1	6	7	6	-13	0	1	—	—	—	—	—
00-01—Atlanta	NHL	51	4	11	15	18	11	1	0	—	—	—	—	—
01-02—Atlanta	NHL	61	5	20	25	24	-11	1	0	—	—	—	—	—
02-03—Atlanta	NHL	79	7	19	26	32	-19	3	1	—	—	—	—	—
03-04—Atlanta	NHL	67	3	26	29	30	2	2	0	—	—	—	—	—
04-05—HC Kladno	Czech Rep.	22	5	11	16	34	6	...	...	—	—	—	—	—
—MoDo Ornskoldsvik	Sweden	8	2	2	4	0	-6	2	0	6	1	0	1	27
NHL Totals (5 years)		309	20	91	111	114	-27	7	2					

KABERLE, TOMAS — D — MAPLE LEAFS

PERSONAL: Born March 2, 1978, in Rakovnik, Czechoslovakia. ... 6-1/198. ... Shoots left. ... Brother of Frantisek Kaberle, D, Carolina Hurricanes.
TRANSACTIONS/CAREER NOTES: Selected by Toronto Maple Leafs in eighth round (13th Maple Leafs pick, 204th overall) of NHL draft (June 22, 1996). ... Missed first 12 games of 2001-02 season in contract dispute. ... Injured shoulder (December 19, 2003); missed five games. ... Injured shoulder (January 7, 2004); missed five games.

		REGULAR SEASON								PLAYOFFS				
Season Team	League	GP	G	A	Pts.	PIM	+/-	PP	SH	GP	G	A	Pts.	PIM
94-95—Kladno	Czech. Jrs.	38	7	10	17	...	...	...	...	—	—	—	—	—
—Poldi Kladno	Czech Rep.	1	0	1	1	0	...	0	0	3	0	0	0	2
95-96—Poldi Kladno	Czech. Jrs.	23	6	13	19	19	...	...	...	—	—	—	—	—
—Poldi Kladno	Czech Rep.	23	0	1	1	2	...	...	...	2	0	0	0	0
96-97—Poldi Kladno	Czech Rep.	49	0	5	5	26	...	...	...	3	0	0	0	0
97-98—Poldi Kladno	Czech Rep.	47	4	19	23	12	...	...	...	—	—	—	—	—
—St. John's	AHL	2	0	0	0	0	0	0	0	—	—	—	—	—
98-99—Toronto	NHL	57	4	18	22	12	3	0	0	14	0	3	3	2
99-00—Toronto	NHL	82	7	33	40	24	3	2	0	12	1	4	5	0
00-01—Toronto	NHL	82	6	39	45	24	10	0	0	11	1	3	4	0
01-02—HC Kladno	Czech Rep.	9	1	7	8	4	...	...	...	—	—	—	—	—
—Toronto	NHL	69	10	29	39	2	5	5	0	20	2	8	10	16
—Czech Rep. Oly. team	Int'l	4	0	1	1	2	...	...	...	—	—	—	—	—
02-03—Toronto	NHL	82	11	36	47	30	20	4	1	7	2	1	3	0
03-04—Toronto	NHL	71	3	28	31	18	16	0	0	13	0	3	3	6
04-05—HC Kladno	Czech Rep.	49	8	31	39	38	11	...	...	7	1	0	1	0
NHL Totals (6 years)		443	41	183	224	110	57	11	1	77	6	22	28	24

KADEYKIN, ANTON — D — DEVILS

PERSONAL: Born April 17, 1984, in Elektrostal, U.S.S.R. ... 6-2/180.
TRANSACTIONS/CAREER NOTES: Selected by New Jersey Devils in second round (first Devils pick, 51st overall) of NHL entry draft (June 22, 2002).

Season Team	League	GP	G	A	Pts.	PIM	+/-	PP	SH	GP	G	A	Pts.	PIM
		REGULAR SEASON								PLAYOFFS				
01-02—Elektrostal	Russian Div. 1	20	0	0	0	...	...	...	...	—	—	—	—	—
02-03—Sarnia	OHL	55	2	8	10	34	...	...	...	6	0	1	1	0
03-04—Sarnia	OHL	40	0	2	2	38	...	...	...	3	0	0	0	0

KALININ, DMITRI D SABRES

PERSONAL: Born July 22, 1980, in Cheljabinsk, U.S.S.R. ... 6-3/206. ... Shoots left.
TRANSACTIONS/CAREER NOTES: Selected by Buffalo Sabres in first round (first Sabres pick, 18th overall) of NHL draft (June 27, 1998). ... Fractured thumb (October 26, 2001); missed 18 games. ... Flu (April 5, 2002); missed one game. ... Separated left shoulder (March 12, 2003); missed seven games. ... Flu (March 28, 2003); missed one game.

Season Team	League	GP	G	A	Pts.	PIM	+/-	PP	SH	GP	G	A	Pts.	PIM
		REGULAR SEASON								PLAYOFFS				
95-96—Traktor Chelyabinsk	CIS Jr.	30	10	10	20	60	...	...	...	—	—	—	—	—
—Nadezhda Chelyabinsk	CIS Div. II	20	0	3	3	10	...	...	...	—	—	—	—	—
96-97—Traktor Chelyabinsk	Russian	2	0	0	0	0	...	...	...	0	...	...	...	...
—Traktor-2 Chelyabinsk	Rus. Div.	20	0	0	0	10	...	...	...	—	—	—	—	—
97-98—Traktor Chelyabinsk	Russian	26	0	2	2	24	...	...	...	—	—	—	—	—
98-99—Moncton	QMJHL	39	7	18	25	44	-8	4	0	4	1	1	2	0
—Rochester	AHL	3	0	1	1	14	2	0	0	7	0	0	0	6
99-00—Rochester	AHL	75	2	19	21	52	...	...	...	21	2	9	11	8
—Buffalo	NHL	4	0	0	0	4	0	0	0	—	—	—	—	—
00-01—Buffalo	NHL	79	4	18	22	38	-2	2	0	13	0	2	2	4
01-02—Buffalo	NHL	58	2	11	13	26	-6	0	0	—	—	—	—	—
02-03—Rochester	AHL	1	0	0	0	0	0	0	0	—	—	—	—	—
—Buffalo	NHL	65	8	13	21	57	-7	3	1	—	—	—	—	—
03-04—Buffalo	NHL	77	10	24	34	42	0	2	1	—	—	—	—	—
04-05—Metal. Magnitogorsk	Russian	—	—	—	—	—	—	—	—	5	0	0	0	2
—Metal. Magnitogorsk	Russian	48	2	8	10	14	3	...	...	48	2	8	10	14
NHL Totals (5 years)		283	24	66	90	167	-15	7	2	13	0	2	2	4

KANE, BOYD LW

PERSONAL: Born April 18, 1978, in Swift Current, Sask. ... 6-2/222. ... Shoots left.
TRANSACTIONS/CAREER NOTES: Selected by Pittsburgh Penguins in third round (third Penguins pick, 72nd overall) of NHL entry draft (June 22, 1996). ... Returned to draft pool by Penguins and selected by New York Rangers in fourth round (fourth Rangers pick, 114th overall) of NHL entry draft (June 27, 1998). ... Traded by Rangers to Tampa Bay Lightning for LW Gordie Dwyer (October 10, 2002). ... Signed as free agent by Philadelphia Flyers (July 14, 2003).

Season Team	League	GP	G	A	Pts.	PIM	+/-	PP	SH	GP	G	A	Pts.	PIM
		REGULAR SEASON								PLAYOFFS				
94-95—Regina	WHL	25	6	5	11	6	...	...	...	4	0	0	0	0
95-96—Regina	WHL	72	21	42	63	155	...	...	...	11	5	7	12	12
96-97—Regina	WHL	66	25	50	75	154	25	11	1	5	1	1	2	15
97-98—Regina	WHL	68	48	45	93	133	38	20	2	9	5	7	12	29
98-99—Hartford	AHL	56	3	5	8	23	-8	0	0	—	—	—	—	—
—Charlotte	ECHL	12	5	6	11	14	-6	2	0	—	—	—	—	—
99-00—Hartford	AHL	8	0	0	0	9	...	...	...	—	—	—	—	—
—B.C.	UHL	3	0	2	2	4	...	...	...	—	—	—	—	—
—Charlotte	ECHL	47	10	19	29	110	...	...	...	—	—	—	—	—
00-01—Hartford	AHL	56	11	17	28	81	...	...	...	5	2	0	2	2
—Charlotte	ECHL	12	9	8	17	6	...	...	...	—	—	—	—	—
01-02—Hartford	AHL	78	17	22	39	193	2	7	1	10	1	2	3	50
02-03—Springfield	AHL	72	15	22	37	121	-2	4	0	—	—	—	—	—
03-04—Philadelphia	NHL	7	0	0	0	7	-4	0	0	—	—	—	—	—
—Philadelphia	AHL	73	13	22	35	177	12	6	2	12	0	1	1	39
04-05—Philadelphia	AHL	58	9	15	24	112	-5	0	1	21	0	7	7	28
NHL Totals (1 year)		7	0	0	0	7	-4	0	0					

KAPANEN, NIKO C STARS

PERSONAL: Born April 29, 1978, in Hattula, Finland. ... 5-9/180. ... Shoots left. ... Name pronounced KAP-ih-nehn.
TRANSACTIONS/CAREER NOTES: Selected by Dallas Stars in sixth round (fifth Stars pick, 173rd overall) of NHL draft (June 27, 1998).

Season Team	League	GP	G	A	Pts.	PIM	+/-	PP	SH	GP	G	A	Pts.	PIM
		REGULAR SEASON								PLAYOFFS				
93-94—HPK Hameenlinna	Finland Jr.	31	17	33	50	34	...	...	...	—	—	—	—	—
94-95—HPK Hameenlinna	Finland Jr.	37	19	44	63	40	...	...	...	—	—	—	—	—
95-96—HPK Hameenlinna	Finland Jr.	26	15	22	37	34	...	...	...	—	—	—	—	—
—HPK Hameenlinna	Finland	7	1	0	1	0	...	...	...	—	—	—	—	—
96-97—HPK Hameenlinna	Finland	41	6	9	15	12	...	...	...	10	4	5	9	2
—HPK Hameenlinna	Finland Jr.	5	1	7	8	2	...	...	...	2	0	1	1	2
97-98—HPK Hameenlinna	Finland	48	8	18	26	44	...	...	...	—	—	—	—	—
—HPK Hameenlinna	Finland Jr.	2	1	1	2	0	...	...	...	—	—	—	—	—
98-99—HPK Hameenlinna	Finland	53	14	29	43	49	13	...	...	8	3	4	7	4
99-00—HPK Hameenlinna	Finland	53	20	28	48	40	...	...	...	8	1	9	10	4
00-01—TPS Turku	Finland	56	11	21	32	20	...	...	...	10	2	1	3	4
01-02—Dallas	NHL	9	0	1	1	2	-1	0	0	—	—	—	—	—

Season Team	League	GP	G	A	Pts.	PIM	+/-	PP	SH	GP	G	A	Pts.	PIM
		REGULAR SEASON								PLAYOFFS				
—Utah	AHL	59	13	28	41	40	-3	2	3	5	2	1	3	0
02-03—Dallas	NHL	82	5	29	34	44	25	0	1	12	4	3	7	12
03-04—Dallas	NHL	67	1	5	6	16	-15	0	0	1	1	0	1	0
04-05—Zug	Switzerland	44	10	34	44	24	8	4	0	9	2	5	7	35
NHL Totals (3 years)		158	6	35	41	62	9	0	1	13	5	3	8	12

KAPANEN, SAMI — RW/LW — FLYERS

PERSONAL: Born June 14, 1973, in Vantaa, Finland. ... 5-10/185. ... Shoots left. ... Name pronounced KAP-ih-nehn.

TRANSACTIONS/CAREER NOTES: Selected by Hartford Whalers in fourth round (fourth Whalers pick, 87th overall) of NHL draft (July 8, 1995). ... Flu (October 20, 1996); missed two games. ... Sprained knee (November 30, 1996); missed 16 games. ... Sprained knee (January 10, 1997); missed nine games. ... Sprained knee (February 26, 1997); missed three games. ... Sprained knee (March 15, 1997); missed six games. ... Flu (April 5, 1997); missed one game. ... Whalers franchise moved to North Carolina and renamed Carolina Hurricanes for 1997-98 season; NHL approved move on June 25, 1997. ... Flu (March 12, 1998); missed one game. ... Bruised knee (October 24, 1998); missed one game. ... Bruised shoulder (February 19, 2000); missed two games. ... Had concussion (March 29, 2000); missed four games. ... Injured back (October 18, 2001); missed two games. ... Cut hand (February 8, 2002); missed one game. ... Strained groin (November 15, 2002); missed 11 games. ... Traded by Hurricanes with D Ryan Bast to Philadelphia Flyers for RW Pavel Brendl and D Bruno St. Jacques (February 7, 2003). ... Bruised kidney (December 27, 2003); missed four games. ... Bruised ribs (January 25, 2004); missed two games. ... Flu (January 28, 2004); missed one game.

STATISTICAL PLATEAUS: Three-goal games: 1997-98 (2), 2001-02 (1). Total: 3.

Season Team	League	GP	G	A	Pts.	PIM	+/-	PP	SH	GP	G	A	Pts.	PIM
		REGULAR SEASON								PLAYOFFS				
90-91—KalPa Kuopio	Finland	14	1	2	3	2	...	...	...	8	2	1	3	2
91-92—KalPa Kuopio	Finland	42	15	10	25	8	...	...	...	—	—	—	—	—
92-93—KalPa Kuopio	Finland	37	4	17	21	12	...	...	...	—	—	—	—	—
93-94—KalPa Kuopio	Finland	48	23	32	55	16	...	...	...	—	—	—	—	—
94-95—HIFK Helsinki	Finland	49	14	28	42	42	...	...	...	3	0	0	0	0
95-96—Springfield	AHL	28	14	17	31	4	...	...	...	3	1	2	3	0
—Hartford	NHL	35	5	4	9	6	0	0	0	—	—	—	—	—
96-97—Hartford	NHL	45	13	12	25	2	6	3	0	—	—	—	—	—
97-98—Carolina	NHL	81	26	37	63	16	9	4	0	—	—	—	—	—
—Fin. Olympic team	Int'l	6	0	1	1	0	-4	0	0	—	—	—	—	—
98-99—Carolina	NHL	81	24	35	59	10	-1	5	0	5	1	1	2	0
99-00—Carolina	NHL	76	24	24	48	12	10	7	0	—	—	—	—	—
00-01—Carolina	NHL	82	20	37	57	24	-12	7	0	6	2	3	5	0
01-02—Carolina	NHL	77	27	42	69	23	9	11	0	23	1	8	9	6
—Fin. Olympic team	Int'l	4	1	2	3	4	...	...	...	—	—	—	—	—
02-03—Carolina	NHL	43	6	12	18	12	-17	3	0	—	—	—	—	—
—Philadelphia	NHL	28	4	9	13	6	-1	2	0	13	4	3	7	6
03-04—Philadelphia	NHL	74	12	18	30	14	9	0	1	18	3	7	10	6
04-05—KalPa Kuopio	Finland	10	6	3	9	2	4	...	...	9	5	3	8	4
NHL Totals (9 years)		622	161	230	391	125	12	42	1	65	11	22	33	18

KARIYA, PAUL — LW — PREDATORS

PERSONAL: Born October 16, 1974, in Vancouver. ... 5-10/175. ... Shoots left. ... Brother of Steve Kariya, LW, New Jersey Devils organization. Brother of Martin Kariya, LW, New York Islanders organization. ... Name pronounced kuh-REE-uh.

TRANSACTIONS/CAREER NOTES: Selected by Anaheim Mighty Ducks in 1st round (1st Mighty Ducks pick, 4th overall) of NHL draft (June 26, 1993). ... Lower back spasms (February 12, 1995); missed one game. ... Strained abdominal muscle; missed first 11 games of 1996-97 season. ... Suffered mild concussion (November 13, 1996); missed two games. ... Missed first 32 games of 1997-98 season in contract dispute. ... Concussion (February 1, 1998); missed remainder of season. ... Injured hip; missed first game of 1999-2000 season. ... Fractured right foot (February 18, 2000); missed seven games. ... Fractured right foot (December 20, 2000); missed 16 games. ... Signed as free agent by Colorado Avalanche (July 2, 2003). ... Sprained right wrist (Oct. 22, 2003); missed 10 games. ... Reinjured wrist (Nov. 15, 2003); missed 21 games. ... Sprained left ankle (April 4, 2004); missed 10 playoff games. ... Signed as free agent by Nashville Predators (Aug. 5, 2005).

STATISTICAL PLATEAUS: Three-goal games: 1996-97 (2), 1997-98 (1), 2000-01 (2), 2001-02 (2), 2002-03 (1). Total: 8.

Season Team	League	GP	G	A	Pts.	PIM	+/-	PP	SH	GP	G	A	Pts.	PIM
		REGULAR SEASON								PLAYOFFS				
90-91—Penticton	BCJHL	54	45	67	112	8	...	...	...	—	—	—	—	—
91-92—Penticton	BCJHL	40	46	86	132	16	...	...	...	—	—	—	—	—
92-93—Maine	Hockey East	39	25	*75	*100	12	...	...	...	—	—	—	—	—
93-94—Canadian nat'l team	Int'l	23	7	34	41	2	...	...	...	—	—	—	—	—
—Can. Olympic team	Int'l	8	3	4	7	2	6	1	0	—	—	—	—	—
—Maine	Hockey East	12	8	16	24	4	8	1	0	—	—	—	—	—
94-95—Anaheim	NHL	47	18	21	39	4	-17	7	1	—	—	—	—	—
95-96—Anaheim	NHL	82	50	58	108	20	9	20	3	—	—	—	—	—
96-97—Anaheim	NHL	69	44	55	99	6	36	15	3	11	7	6	13	4
97-98—Anaheim	NHL	22	17	14	31	23	12	3	0	—	—	—	—	—
98-99—Anaheim	NHL	82	39	62	101	40	17	11	2	3	1	3	4	0
99-00—Anaheim	NHL	74	42	44	86	24	22	11	3	—	—	—	—	—
00-01—Anaheim	NHL	66	33	34	67	20	-9	18	3	—	—	—	—	—
01-02—Anaheim	NHL	82	32	25	57	28	-15	11	0	—	—	—	—	—
—Can. Olympic team	Int'l	6	3	1	4	0	...	...	...	—	—	—	—	—
02-03—Anaheim	NHL	82	25	56	81	48	-3	11	1	21	6	6	12	6
03-04—Colorado	NHL	51	11	25	36	22	-5	5	1	1	0	1	1	0
NHL Totals (10 years)		657	311	394	705	235	47	112	17	36	14	16	30	10

KARPOVTSEV, ALEXANDER — D — PANTHERS

PERSONAL: Born April 7, 1970, in Moscow, U.S.S.R. ... 6-3/221. ... Shoots right. ... Name pronounced KAHR-puht-sehf.

TRANSACTIONS/CAREER NOTES: Selected by Quebec Nordiques in seventh round (seventh Nordiques pick, 158th overall) of NHL draft (June 16, 1990). ... Traded by Nordiques to New York Rangers for D Mike Hurlbut (September 9, 1993). ... Bruised buttocks (October 9, 1993); missed one game. ... Bruised hip (November 3, 1993); missed six games. ... Reinjured hip (November 23, 1993); missed one game. ... Injured face (February 28, 1994); missed two games. ... Injured (March 14, 1994); missed two games. ... Played in Europe during 1994-95 lockout. ... Sore ankle (April 14, 1995); missed one game. ... Hyperextended elbow (October 29, 1995); missed one game. ... Back spasms (February 10, 1996); missed one game. ... Back spasms (February 18, 1996); missed two games. ... Bruised thumb (March 13, 1996); missed two games. ... Back spasms (March 27, 1996); missed six games. ... Bruised toe (April 3, 1997); missed one game. ... Hyperextended elbow (April 10, 1997); missed one game. ... Throat infection (October 10, 1997); missed one game. ... Sprained wrist (January 19, 1998); missed one game. ... Had wrist surgery (February 2, 1998); missed 28 games. ... Bruised knee (October 13, 1998); missed two games. ... Traded by Rangers with fourth-round pick (LW Mirko Murovic) in 1999 draft to Toronto Maple Leafs for D Mathieu Schneider (October 14, 1998). ... Fractured thumb (November 14, 1998); missed 12 games. ... Sprained wrist (January 2, 1999); missed three games ... Strained wrist (February 2, 1999); missed three games. ... Fractured finger (March 17, 1999); missed three games. ... Strained shoulder (April 26, 1999); missed three playoff games. ... Injured (November 5, 1999); missed one game. ... Sprained shoulder (November 26, 1999); missed five games. ... Fractured hand (January 11, 2000); missed four games. ... Injured (March 16, 2000); missed one game. ... Injured (March 23, 2000); missed one game. ... Traded by Maple Leafs with fourth-round pick (D Vladimir Gusev) in 2001 draft to Chicago Blackhawks for D Bryan McCabe (October 2, 2000). ... Bruised ankle (November 2, 2000); missed one game. ... Reinjured ankle (November 5, 2000); missed two games. ... Injured knee (December 3, 2000); missed one game. ... Had knee surgery (December 10, 2000); missed 11 games. ... Cut arm (January 7, 2001); missed one game. ... Suspended two games by NHL for elbowing (February 10, 2001). ... Bruised knee (February 27, 2001); missed three games. ... Injured elbow (March 24, 2001); missed remainder of season. ... Sprained ankle (October 23, 2001); missed one game. ... Sprained knee (November 9, 2001); missed two games. ... Strained groin (November 19, 2001); missed three games. ... Bruised ribs (Janaury 10, 2002); missed three games. ... Had knee surgery (March 3, 2002); missed final seven games of season. ... Fractured ankle (November 5, 2002); missed 18 games. ... Bruised foot (January 15, 2003); missed seven games. ... Bruised ankle (February 5, 2003); missed three games. ... Fractured facial bones (February 20, 2003); missed 13 games. ... Injured back (November 9, 2003); missed four games. ... Injured ankle (November 28, 2003); missed 36 games. ... Injured shoulder (February 29, 2004); missed three games. ... Traded by Blackhawks to New York Islanders for fourth-round pick in 2005 draft (March 9, 2004). ... Bruised lower left leg (March 17, 2004); missed final 10 games of season and playoffs. ... Signed as free agent by Florida Panthers (July 14, 2004).

		REGULAR SEASON								PLAYOFFS				
Season Team	League	GP	G	A	Pts.	PIM	+/-	PP	SH	GP	G	A	Pts.	PIM
89-90—Dynamo Moscow	USSR	35	1	1	2	27	...	...	...	—	—	—	—	—
90-91—Dynamo Moscow	USSR	40	0	5	5	15	...	...	...	—	—	—	—	—
91-92—Dynamo Moscow	CIS	28	3	2	5	22	...	...	...	—	—	—	—	—
92-93—Dynamo Moscow	CIS	40	3	11	14	100	...	...	...	—	—	—	—	—
93-94—New York Rangers	NHL	67	3	15	18	58	12	1	0	17	0	4	4	12
94-95—Dynamo Moscow	CIS	13	0	2	2	10	...	...	...	—	—	—	—	—
—New York Rangers	NHL	47	4	8	12	30	-4	1	0	8	1	0	1	0
95-96—New York Rangers	NHL	40	2	16	18	26	12	1	0	6	0	1	1	4
96-97—New York Rangers	NHL	77	9	29	38	59	1	6	1	13	1	3	4	20
97-98—New York Rangers	NHL	47	3	7	10	38	-1	1	0	—	—	—	—	—
98-99—New York Rangers	NHL	2	1	0	1	0	1	0	0	—	—	—	—	—
—Toronto	NHL	56	2	25	27	52	38	1	0	14	1	3	4	12
99-00—Toronto	NHL	69	3	14	17	54	9	3	0	11	0	3	3	4
00-01—Dynamo Moscow	Russian	5	0	1	1	0	...	...	...	—	—	—	—	—
—Chicago	NHL	53	2	13	15	39	-4	1	0	—	—	—	—	—
01-02—Chicago	NHL	65	1	9	10	40	10	0	1	5	1	0	1	0
02-03—Chicago	NHL	40	4	10	14	12	-8	3	0	—	—	—	—	—
03-04—Chicago	NHL	24	0	7	7	14	-17	0	0	—	—	—	—	—
—New York Islanders	NHL	3	0	1	1	4	1	0	0	—	—	—	—	—
04-05—Sibir Novosibirsk	Russian	5	0	1	1	16	-3	...	...	—	—	—	—	—
—Lokomotiv Yaroslavl	Russian	33	2	5	7	45	-2	...	...	9	0	0	0	0
NHL Totals (11 years)		590	34	154	188	426	50	18	2	74	4	14	18	52

KASPAR, LUKAS — RW — SHARKS

PERSONAL: Born September 23, 1985, in Most, Czech. ... 6-2/202. ... Shoots right.

TRANSACTIONS/CAREER NOTES: Selected by San Jose Sharks in first round (first Sharks pick, 22nd overall) of NHL entry draft (June 26, 2004).

		REGULAR SEASON								PLAYOFFS				
Season Team	League	GP	G	A	Pts.	PIM	+/-	PP	SH	GP	G	A	Pts.	PIM
02-03—Litvinov	Czech Rep.	9	1	1	2	2	...	...	...	—	—	—	—	—
03-04—Litvinov	Czech Rep.	37	4	2	6	10	...	...	...	—	—	—	—	—
04-05—Ottawa	OHL	59	21	30	51	45	3	6	0	21	6	14	20	8

KASPARAITIS, DARIUS — D — RANGERS

PERSONAL: Born October 16, 1972, in Elektrenai, U.S.S.R. ... 6-0/215. ... Shoots left. ... Name pronounced kas-puhr-IGH-tihz.

TRANSACTIONS/CAREER NOTES: Selected by New York Islanders in first round (first Islanders pick, fifth overall) of NHL draft (June 20, 1992). ... Back spasms (February 12, 1993); missed two games. ... Strained back (April 15, 1993); missed one game. ... Strained lower back (November 10, 1993); missed two games. ... Jammed wrist (March 5, 1994); missed four games. ... Tore knee ligament (February 20, 1995); missed remainder of season and first 15 games of 1995-96 season. ... Flu (December 2, 1995); missed two games. ... Severed two tendons in right hand (December 9, 1995); missed 16 games. ... Injured groin (February 8, 1996); missed two games. ... Traded by Islanders with C Andreas Johansson to Pittsburgh Penguins for C Bryan Smolinski (November 17, 1996). ... Suffered concussion (December 23, 1996); missed two games. ... Cut face (January 2, 1997); missed one game. ... Twisted ankle (January 23, 1997); missed one game. ... Suffered concussion (March 18, 1997); missed three games. ... Flu (March 29, 1998); missed one game. ... Injured knee (September 20, 1998); missed first eight games of season. ... Strained knee (December 21, 1998); missed one game. ... Strained groin (February 24, 1999); missed two games. ... Strained knee (March 5, 1999) and had surgery; missed remainder of season. ... Injured knee; missed first four games of 1999-2000 season.

... Suspended two games for elbowing incident (October 20, 1999). ... Headaches (December 30, 1999); missed two games. ... Suspended one game for second major penalty and game misconduct in season (January 19, 2000). ... Bruised foot (December 16, 2000); missed three games. ... Injured (April 4, 2001); missed final two games of season. ... Traded by Penguins to Colorado Avalanche for LW Ville Nieminen and D Rick Berry (March 19, 2002). ... Signed as free agent by New York Rangers (July 2, 2002). ... Injured rib muscle (December 1, 2002); missed one game. ... Flu (January 27, 2003); missed one game. ... Strained ribs (December 30, 2003); missed two games. ... Injured left knee (January 19, 2004) and had right shoulder surgery (March 24, 2004); missed final 36 games of season.

		REGULAR SEASON								PLAYOFFS				
Season Team	**League**	**GP**	**G**	**A**	**Pts.**	**PIM**	**+/-**	**PP**	**SH**	**GP**	**G**	**A**	**Pts.**	**PIM**
88-89—Dynamo Moscow	USSR	3	0	0	0	0	...	...	...	—	—	—	—	—
89-90—Dynamo Moscow	USSR	1	0	0	0	0	...	...	...	—	—	—	—	—
90-91—Dynamo Moscow	USSR	17	0	1	1	10	...	...	...	—	—	—	—	—
91-92—Dynamo Moscow	CIS	31	2	10	12	14	...	...	...	—	—	—	—	—
—Unif. Olympic team	Int'l	8	0	2	2	2	4	0	0	—	—	—	—	—
92-93—Dynamo Moscow	CIS	7	1	3	4	8	...	...	...	—	—	—	—	—
—New York Islanders	NHL	79	4	17	21	166	15	0	0	18	0	5	5	31
93-94—New York Islanders	NHL	76	1	10	11	142	-6	0	0	4	0	0	0	8
94-95—New York Islanders	NHL	13	0	1	1	22	-11	0	0	—	—	—	—	—
95-96—New York Islanders	NHL	46	1	7	8	93	-12	0	0	—	—	—	—	—
96-97—New York Islanders	NHL	18	0	5	5	16	-7	0	0	—	—	—	—	—
—Pittsburgh	NHL	57	2	16	18	84	24	0	0	5	0	0	0	6
97-98—Pittsburgh	NHL	81	4	8	12	127	3	0	2	5	0	0	0	8
—Russian Oly. team	Int'l	6	0	2	2	6	8	0	0	—	—	—	—	—
98-99—Pittsburgh	NHL	48	1	4	5	70	12	0	0	—	—	—	—	—
99-00—Pittsburgh	NHL	73	3	12	15	146	-12	1	0	11	1	1	2	10
00-01—Pittsburgh	NHL	77	3	16	19	111	11	1	0	17	1	1	2	26
01-02—Pittsburgh	NHL	69	2	12	14	123	-1	0	0	—	—	—	—	—
—Russian Oly. team	Int'l	6	1	0	1	4	...	...	...	—	—	—	—	—
—Colorado	NHL	11	0	0	0	19	1	0	0	21	0	3	3	18
02-03—New York Rangers	NHL	80	3	11	14	85	5	0	0	—	—	—	—	—
03-04—New York Rangers	NHL	44	1	9	10	48	11	0	0	—	—	—	—	—
04-05—Ak Bars Kazan	Russian	29	1	3	4	118	8	...	...	3	0	0	0	6
NHL Totals (12 years)		772	25	128	153	1252	33	2	2	81	2	10	12	107

KAVANAGH, PAT — RW — SENATORS

PERSONAL: Born March 14, 1979, in Ottawa. ... 6-3/205. ... Shoots right.

TRANSACTIONS/CAREER NOTES: Selected by Philadelphia Flyers in second round (second Flyers pick, 50th overall) of NHL entry draft (June 21, 1997). ... Traded by Flyers to Vancouver Canucks for sixth-round pick (F Konstantin Rudenko) in 1999 entry draft (June 1, 1999). ... Signed as free agent by Ottawa Senators (July 27, 2004).

		REGULAR SEASON								PLAYOFFS				
Season Team	**League**	**GP**	**G**	**A**	**Pts.**	**PIM**	**+/-**	**PP**	**SH**	**GP**	**G**	**A**	**Pts.**	**PIM**
96-97—Peterborough	OHL	43	6	8	14	53	...	...	...	11	1	1	2	12
97-98—Peterborough	OHL	66	10	16	26	85	...	...	...	4	1	0	1	6
98-99—Peterborough	OHL	68	26	43	69	118	14	...	...	5	0	5	5	10
99-00—Syracuse	AHL	68	12	8	20	56	...	...	...	4	0	0	0	0
00-01—Kansas City	IHL	78	26	15	41	86	...	...	...	—	—	—	—	—
—Vancouver	NHL	...	...	...	...	...	...	...	...	3	0	0	0	2
01-02—Manitoba	AHL	70	13	19	32	100	4	1	1	7	1	0	1	6
02-03—Vancouver	NHL	3	1	0	1	2	2	0	0	—	—	—	—	—
—Manitoba	AHL	63	15	15	30	96	7	3	3	14	7	4	11	20
03-04—Manitoba	AHL	73	23	22	45	69	3	6	4	—	—	—	—	—
—Vancouver	NHL	3	1	0	1	0	0	0	0	—	—	—	—	—
04-05—Binghamton	AHL	80	14	17	31	87	7	0	3	6	0	1	1	10
NHL Totals (3 years)		6	2	0	2	2	2	0	0	3	0	0	0	2

KEEFE, SHELDON — RW/C — COYOTES

PERSONAL: Born September 17, 1980, in Brampton, Ont. ... 5-11/184. ... Shoots right.

TRANSACTIONS/CAREER NOTES: Selected by Tampa Bay Lightning in second round (first Lightning pick, 47th overall) of NHL entry draft (June 26, 1999). ... Sprained right knee (January 13, 2002); missed 14 games. ... Claimed by New York Rangers in NHL waiver draft (October 3, 2003). ... Claimed off waivers by Lightning (October 24, 2003). ... Signed as free agent by Phoenix Coyotes (July 12, 2004).

		REGULAR SEASON								PLAYOFFS				
Season Team	**League**	**GP**	**G**	**A**	**Pts.**	**PIM**	**+/-**	**PP**	**SH**	**GP**	**G**	**A**	**Pts.**	**PIM**
96-97—Quinte	Tier II Jr. A	44	21	23	44	...	...	...	...	—	—	—	—	—
97-98—Caledon	Jr. A	51	52	51	103	117	...	...	...	—	—	—	—	—
98-99—Toronto St. Michael's	OHL	38	37	37	74	80	...	...	...	—	—	—	—	—
—Barrie	OHL	28	14	28	42	60	...	...	...	10	5	5	10	31
99-00—Barrie	OHL	66	48	*73	*121	95	23	17	2	25	10	13	23	41
00-01—Detroit	IHL	13	7	5	12	23	...	...	...	—	—	—	—	—
—Tampa Bay	NHL	49	4	0	4	38	-13	0	0	—	—	—	—	—
01-02—Springfield	AHL	24	9	9	18	26	-9	3	0	—	—	—	—	—
—Tampa Bay	NHL	39	6	7	13	16	-11	0	0	—	—	—	—	—
02-03—Springfield	AHL	33	16	15	31	28	6	6	1	—	—	—	—	—
—Tampa Bay	NHL	37	2	5	7	24	-1	0	0	—	—	—	—	—
03-04—Hershey	AHL	59	16	16	32	82	-10	5	0	—	—	—	—	—
04-05—Utah	AHL	4	0	1	1	0	-3	0	0	—	—	—	—	—
NHL Totals (3 years)		125	12	12	24	78	-25	0	0					

KEITH, MATT — RW — BLACKHAWKS

PERSONAL: Born April 11, 1983, in Edmonton. ... 6-2/200. ... Shoots right.

TRANSACTIONS/CAREER NOTES: Selected by Chicago Blackhawks in second round (third Blackhawks pick, 59th overall) of NHL entry draft (June 23, 2001).

		REGULAR SEASON								PLAYOFFS				
Season Team	League	GP	G	A	Pts.	PIM	+/-	PP	SH	GP	G	A	Pts.	PIM
98-99—Spokane	WHL	7	1	0	1	4	...	...	...	—	—	—	—	—
99-00—Spokane	WHL	39	1	3	4	37	...	...	...	15	1	2	3	11
00-01—Spokane	WHL	33	13	14	27	63	...	...	...	12	1	3	4	14
01-02—Spokane	WHL	68	34	33	67	71	...	...	...	11	5	5	10	16
02-03—Spokane	WHL	7	2	2	4	11	...	...	...	—	—	—	—	—
—Red Deer	WHL	49	25	26	51	32	...	...	...	23	6	7	13	30
03-04—Chicago	NHL	20	2	3	5	10	-5	1	0	—	—	—	—	—
—Norfolk	AHL	66	13	13	26	57	-4	5	0	8	1	2	3	10
04-05—Norfolk	AHL	80	18	31	49	74	10	9	0	6	0	1	1	0
NHL Totals (1 year)		20	2	3	5	10	-5	1	0					

KELLY, CHRIS — C — SENATORS

PERSONAL: Born November 11, 1980, in Toronto. ... 6-0/191. ... Shoots left.

TRANSACTIONS/CAREER NOTES: Selected by Ottawa Senators in third round (fourth Senators pick, 94th overall) of NHL entry draft (June 26, 1999). ... Injured knee (February 14, 2004); missed 12 games.

		REGULAR SEASON								PLAYOFFS				
Season Team	League	GP	G	A	Pts.	PIM	+/-	PP	SH	GP	G	A	Pts.	PIM
96-97—Aurora	OPJHL	49	14	20	34	11	...	...	...	—	—	—	—	—
97-98—London	OHL	54	15	14	29	4	...	...	...	16	4	5	9	12
98-99—London	OHL	68	36	41	77	60	17	...	...	25	9	17	26	22
99-00—London	OHL	63	29	43	72	57	-6	7	1	—	—	—	—	—
00-01—London	OHL	31	21	34	55	46	...	...	...	—	—	—	—	—
—Sudbury	OHL	19	5	16	21	17	...	...	...	12	11	5	16	14
01-02—Grand Rapids	AHL	31	3	3	6	20	0	0	1	5	1	1	2	5
02-03—Binghamton	AHL	77	17	14	31	73	7	5	3	14	2	3	5	8
03-04—Ottawa	NHL	4	0	0	0	0	-2	0	0	—	—	—	—	—
—Binghamton	AHL	54	15	19	34	40	5	3	1	2	0	0	0	4
04-05—Binghamton	AHL	77	24	36	60	57	30	4	4	6	1	2	3	11
NHL Totals (1 year)		4	0	0	0	0	-2	0	0					

KELLY, STEVE — C — KINGS

PERSONAL: Born October 26, 1976, in Vancouver. ... 6-2/200. ... Shoots left.

TRANSACTIONS/CAREER NOTES: Selected by Edmonton Oilers in first round (first Oilers pick, sixth overall) of NHL entry draft (July 8, 1995). ... Traded by Oilers to Tampa Bay Lightning with C Jason Bonsignore and D Bryan Marchment for D Roman Hamrlik and C Paul Comrie (December 30, 1997). ... Had the flu (January 21, 1998); missed two games. ... Had the flu (January 31, 1998); missed one game. ... Suffered concussion (October 10, 1998); missed eight games. ... Traded by Lightning to New Jersey Devils for 7th-round pick (G Brian Eklund) in 2000 draft (October 7, 1999). ... Traded by Devils to Los Angeles Kings for C Bob Corkum (February 27, 2001). ... Strained lower back (March 19, 2001); missed two games. ... Abdominal surgery (September 18, 2001); missed first 16 games of season. ... Injured knee (April 6, 2003); missed one game.

		REGULAR SEASON								PLAYOFFS				
Season Team	League	GP	G	A	Pts.	PIM	+/-	PP	SH	GP	G	A	Pts.	PIM
92-93—Prince Albert	WHL	65	11	9	20	75	...	...	...	—	—	—	—	—
93-94—Prince Albert	WHL	65	19	42	61	106	...	...	...	—	—	—	—	—
94-95—Prince Albert	WHL	68	31	41	72	153	24	10	0	15	7	9	16	35
95-96—Prince Albert	WHL	70	27	74	101	203	...	...	...	18	13	18	31	47
96-97—Hamilton	AHL	48	9	29	38	111	2	4	1	11	3	3	6	24
—Edmonton	NHL	8	1	0	1	6	-1	0	0	6	0	0	0	2
97-98—Edmonton	NHL	19	0	2	2	8	-4	0	0	—	—	—	—	—
—Hamilton	AHL	11	2	8	10	18	6	1	0	—	—	—	—	—
—Tampa Bay	NHL	24	2	1	3	15	-9	1	0	—	—	—	—	—
—Milwaukee	IHL	5	0	1	1	19	-3	0	0	—	—	—	—	—
—Cleveland	IHL	5	1	1	2	29	1	1	0	1	0	1	1	0
98-99—Tampa Bay	NHL	34	1	3	4	27	-15	0	0	—	—	—	—	—
—Cleveland	IHL	18	6	7	13	36	1	2	1	—	—	—	—	—
99-00—Detroit	IHL	1	0	0	0	4	...	...	...	—	—	—	—	—
—Albany	AHL	76	21	36	57	131	...	...	...	3	1	1	2	2
—New Jersey	NHL	1	0	0	0	0	0	0	0	10	0	0	0	4
00-01—New Jersey	NHL	24	2	2	4	21	0	0	0	—	—	—	—	—
—Los Angeles	NHL	11	1	0	1	4	0	0	0	8	0	0	0	2
01-02—Manchester	AHL	49	10	21	31	88	-1	2	3	5	1	8	9	4
—Los Angeles	NHL	8	0	1	1	2	-1	0	0	1	0	0	0	0
02-03—Los Angeles	NHL	15	2	3	5	0	-6	0	0	—	—	—	—	—
—Manchester	AHL	54	19	44	63	144	9	8	1	3	0	1	1	0
03-04—Los Angeles	NHL	3	0	0	0	0	0	0	0	—	—	—	—	—
—Manchester	AHL	59	21	49	70	117	32	5	0	1	0	0	0	2
04-05—Mannheim	Germany	46	11	22	33	210	9	1	2	12	1	4	5	72
NHL Totals (8 years)		147	9	12	21	83	-36	1	0	25	0	0	0	8

KESLER, RYAN — C/LW — CANUCKS

PERSONAL: Born August 31, 1984, in Detroit. ... 6-2/195.
TRANSACTIONS/CAREER NOTES: Selected by Vancouver Canucks in first round (23rd overall) of NHL entry draft (June 21, 2003).

		REGULAR SEASON								PLAYOFFS				
Season Team	League	GP	G	A	Pts.	PIM	+/-	PP	SH	GP	G	A	Pts.	PIM
02-03—Ohio State	CCHA	40	11	20	31	44	...	...	...	—	—	—	—	—
03-04—Manitoba	AHL	33	3	8	11	29	-4	0	1	—	—	—	—	—
—Vancouver	NHL	28	2	3	5	16	-2	0	0	—	—	—	—	—
04-05—Manitoba	AHL	78	30	27	57	105	22	8	1	14	4	5	9	8
NHL Totals (1 year)		28	2	3	5	16	-2	0	0					

KHABIBULIN, NIKOLAI — G — BLACKHAWKS

PERSONAL: Born January 13, 1973, in Sverdlovsk, U.S.S.R. ... 6-1/203. ... Catches left. ... Name pronounced hah-bee-BOO-lihn.
TRANSACTIONS/CAREER NOTES: Selected by Winnipeg Jets in 9th round (8th Jets pick, 204th overall) of NHL draft (June 20, 1992). ... Sprained knee (November 30, 1995); missed 20 games. ... Jets franchise moved to Phoenix and renamed Coyotes for 1996-97 season; NHL approved move on January 18, 1996. ... Bruised hand (November 6, 1998); missed two games. ... Strained groin (March 2, 1999); missed one game. ... Traded by Coyotes with D Stan Neckar to Tampa Bay Lightning for D Paul Mara, RW Mike Johnson, RW Ruslan Zainullin and 2nd-round pick (D Matthew Spiller) in 2001 draft (March 5, 2001). ... Signed as free agent by Chicago Blackhawks (Aug. 5, 2005).

		REGULAR SEASON									PLAYOFFS							
Season Team	League	GP	Min.	W	L	T	GA	SO	GAA	SV%	GP	Min.	W	L	GA	SO	GAA	SV%
91-92—CSKA Moscow	CIS	2	34	...	...	...	2	...	3.53	...	—	—	—	—	—	—	—	—
92-93—CSKA Moscow	CIS	13	491	...	...	...	27	...	3.30	...	—	—	—	—	—	—	—	—
93-94—Russian Penguins	IHL	12	639	2	7	2	47	0	4.41	.873	—	—	—	—	—	—	—	—
—CSKA Moscow	CIS	46	2625	...	...	...	116	5	2.65	...	3	193	1	2	11	0	3.42	...
94-95—Springfield	AHL	23	1240	9	9	3	80	0	3.87	.874	—	—	—	—	—	—	—	—
—Winnipeg	NHL	26	1339	8	9	4	76	0	3.41	.895	—	—	—	—	—	—	—	—
95-96—Winnipeg	NHL	53	2914	26	20	3	152	2	3.13	.908	6	359	2	4	19	0	3.18	.911
96-97—Phoenix	NHL	72	4091	30	33	6	193	7	2.83	.908	7	426	3	4	15	1	2.11	.932
97-98—Phoenix	NHL	70	4026	30	28	10	184	4	2.74	.900	4	185	2	1	13	0	4.22	.877
98-99—Phoenix	NHL	63	3657	32	23	7	130	8	2.13	.923	7	449	3	4	18	0	2.41	.924
99-00—Long Beach	IHL	33	1936	26	11	1	59	5	*1.83	...	5	321	2	3	15	0	2.80	...
00-01—Tampa Bay	NHL	2	123	1	1	0	6	0	2.93	.913	—	—	—	—	—	—	—	—
01-02—Tampa Bay	NHL	70	3896	24	32	10	153	7	2.36	.920	—	—	—	—	—	—	—	—
—Russian Oly. team	Int'l	6	359	3	2	1	14	1	2.34	.930	—	—	—	—	—	—	—	—
02-03—Tampa Bay	NHL	65	3787	30	22	11	156	4	2.47	.911	10	644	5	5	26	0	2.42	.913
03-04—Tampa Bay	NHL	55	3274	28	19	7	127	3	2.33	.910	23	1401	16	7	40	5	1.71	.933
04-05—Ak Bars Kazan	Russian	24	1457	...	...	...	40	5	1.65	...	2	118	...	...	6	0	3.04	...
NHL Totals (9 years)		476	27107	209	187	58	1177	35	2.61	.910	57	3464	31	25	131	6	2.27	.922

KHAVANOV, ALEXANDER — D — MAPLE LEAFS

PERSONAL: Born January 30, 1972, in Moscow, U.S.S.R. ... 6-2/192.
TRANSACTIONS/CAREER NOTES: Selected by St. Louis Blues in 8th round (8th Blues pick, 232nd overall) of NHL draft (June 24, 2000). ... Fractured toe (October 12, 2003); missed five games. ... Bruised foot (January 31, 2003); missed 15 games. ... Fractured foot (March 20, 2004); missed final eight games of regular season and five playoff games. ... Signed as free agent by Toronto Maple Leafs (Aug. 9, 2005).

		REGULAR SEASON								PLAYOFFS				
Season Team	League	GP	G	A	Pts.	PIM	+/-	PP	SH	GP	G	A	Pts.	PIM
92-93—Birmingham	ECHL	19	0	3	3	14	...	...	...	—	—	—	—	—
—Raleigh	ECHL	17	0	6	6	8	...	...	...	—	—	—	—	—
93-94—St. Petersburg	CIS	41	1	2	3	24	...	...	...	—	—	—	—	—
94-95—St. Petersburg	CIS	49	7	0	7	32	...	...	...	3	0	0	0	0
95-96—St. Petersburg	CIS	32	1	5	6	41	...	...	...	—	—	—	—	—
—HPK Hameenlinna	Finland	16	0	2	2	4	...	...	...	9	0	0	0	0
96-97—Cherepovets	Russian	39	3	8	11	56	...	...	...	3	1	0	1	4
97-98—Cherepovets	Russian	44	3	5	8	46	...	...	...	—	—	—	—	—
98-99—Dynamo	Russian	40	2	7	9	14	...	...	...	16	1	5	6	35
99-00—Dynamo	Russian	38	5	12	17	49	...	...	...	17	0	3	3	4
00-01—St. Louis	NHL	74	7	16	23	52	16	2	0	15	3	2	5	14
01-02—St. Louis	NHL	81	3	21	24	55	9	0	0	4	0	0	0	2
02-03—St. Louis	NHL	81	8	25	33	48	-1	2	1	7	2	3	5	2
03-04—St. Louis	NHL	48	3	7	10	18	2	2	0	—	—	—	—	—
04-05—SKA St. Petersburg	Russian	3	0	0	0	27	...	...	...	—	—	—	—	—
NHL Totals (4 years)		284	21	69	90	173	26	6	1	26	5	5	10	18

KIDD, TREVOR — G

PERSONAL: Born March 26, 1972, in Dugald, Man. ... 6-2/213. ... Catches left.
TRANSACTIONS/CAREER NOTES: Selected by Calgary Flames in first round (first Flames pick, 11th overall) of NHL draft (June 16, 1990). ... Sprained left ankle (October 18, 1993); missed one game. ... Traded by Flames with LW Gary Roberts to Carolina Hurricanes for G Jean-Sebastien Giguere and C Andrew Cassels (August 25, 1997). ... Strained groin (November 9, 1997); missed seven games. ... Fractured finger on right hand (December 20, 1997); missed seven games. ... Injured groin (April 16, 1998); missed three games. ... Selected by Atlanta Thrashers in expansion draft (June 25, 1999). ... Traded by Thrashers to Florida Panthers for D Gord Murphy, C Herbert Vasiljevs, D Daniel Tjarnqvist and sixth-round pick (later traded to Dallas; Stars selected RW Justin Cox) in 1999 draft (June 25, 1999). ... Separated shoulder

(December 13, 1999); missed 29 games. ... Released by Panthers (August 23, 2002). ... Signed as free agent by Toronto Maple Leafs (August 26, 2002). ... Strained groin (January 21, 2003); missed six games. ... Injured shoulder (September 10, 2003); missed 22 games. ... Injured groin (December 27, 2003); missed one game.

		REGULAR SEASON									PLAYOFFS							
Season Team	**League**	**GP**	**Min.**	**W**	**L**	**T**	**GA**	**SO**	**GAA**	**SV%**	**GP**	**Min.**	**W**	**L**	**GA**	**SO**	**GAA**	**SV%**
88-89—Brandon	WHL	32	1509	11	13	1	102	0	4.06	...	—	—	—	—	—	—	—	—
89-90—Brandon	WHL	*63	*3676	24	32	2	254	2	4.15	...	—	—	—	—	—	—	—	—
90-91—Brandon	WHL	30	1730	10	19	1	117	0	4.06	...	—	—	—	—	—	—	—	—
—Spokane	WHL	14	749	8	3	0	44	0	3.52	...	15	926	*14	1	32	*2	*2.07	...
91-92—Canadian nat'l team	Int'l	28	1349	18	4	4	79	2	3.51	...	—	—	—	—	—	—	—	—
—Can. Olympic team	Int'l	1	60	1	0	0	0	1	0.00	1.00	—	—	—	—	—	—	—	—
—Calgary	NHL	2	120	1	1	0	8	0	4.00	.857	—	—	—	—	—	—	—	—
92-93—Salt Lake City	IHL	30	1696	10	16	0	111	1	3.93	.887	—	—	—	—	—	—	—	—
93-94—Calgary	NHL	31	1614	13	7	6	85	0	3.16	.887	—	—	—	—	—	—	—	—
94-95—Calgary	NHL	*43	*2463	22	14	6	107	3	2.61	.909	7	434	3	4	26	1	3.59	.856
95-96—Calgary	NHL	47	2570	15	21	8	119	3	2.78	.895	2	83	0	1	9	0	6.51	.775
96-97—Calgary	NHL	55	2979	21	23	6	141	4	2.84	.900	—	—	—	—	—	—	—	—
97-98—Carolina	NHL	47	2685	21	21	3	97	3	2.17	.922	—	—	—	—	—	—	—	—
98-99—Carolina	NHL	25	1358	7	10	6	61	2	2.70	.905	—	—	—	—	—	—	—	—
99-00—Florida	NHL	28	1574	14	11	2	69	1	2.63	.915	—	—	—	—	—	—	—	—
—Louisville	AHL	1	60	0	1	0	5	0	5.00	...	—	—	—	—	—	—	—	—
00-01—Florida	NHL	42	2354	10	23	6	130	1	3.31	.893	—	—	—	—	—	—	—	—
01-02—Florida	NHL	33	1683	4	16	5	90	1	3.21	.895	—	—	—	—	—	—	—	—
02-03—Toronto	NHL	19	1143	6	10	2	59	0	3.10	.896	—	—	—	—	—	—	—	—
03-04—Toronto	NHL	15	883	6	5	2	48	1	3.26	.876	1	33	0	0	1	0	1.82	.909
—St. John's	AHL	1	60	1	0	0	1	0	1.00	.964	—	—	—	—	—	—	—	—
04-05—Orebro	Sweden Dv. 2	8	480	...	...	...	19	2	2.37	...	—	—	—	—	—	—	—	—
NHL Totals (12 years)		387	21426	140	162	52	1014	19	2.84	.901	10	550	3	5	36	1	3.93	.845

KILGER, CHAD — LW/C — MAPLE LEAFS

PERSONAL: Born November 27, 1976, in Cornwall, Ont. ... 6-4/223. ... Shoots left. ... Son of Bob Kilger, NHL referee (1970-80).

TRANSACTIONS/CAREER NOTES: Selected by Mighty Ducks of Anaheim in first round (first Mighty Ducks pick, fourth overall) of NHL entry draft (July 8, 1995). ... Traded by Mighty Ducks with D Oleg Tverdovsky and third-round pick (D Per-Anton Lundstrom) in 1996 entry draft to Winnipeg Jets for C Marc Chouinard, RW Teemu Selanne and fourth-round pick (traded to Toronto) in 1996 entry draft (February 7, 1996). ... Had the flu (February 21, 1996); missed one game. ... Jets franchise moved to Phoenix and renamed Coyotes for 1996-97 season; NHL approved move on January 18, 1996. ... Bruised thigh (October 7, 1996); missed one game. ... Traded by Coyotes with D Jayson More to Chicago Blackhawks for D Keith Carney and RW Jim Cummins (March 4, 1998). ... Suffered concussion (February 19, 1999); missed three games. ... Traded by Blackhawks with LW Daniel Cleary, LW Ethan Moreau and D Christian Laflamme to Edmonton Oilers for D Boris Mironov, LW Dean McAmmond and D Jonas Elofsson (March 20, 1999). ... Had hip pointer (December 30, 1999); missed five games. ... Had hip pointer (February 23, 2000); missed two games. ... Traded by Oilers to Montreal Canadiens for C Sergei Zholtok (December 18, 2000). ... Suffered concussion (March 3, 2001); missed five games. ... Strained groin (April 2, 2001); missed one game. ... Strained neck (January 8, 2002); missed seven games. ... Injured knee (January 17, 2003); missed five games. ... Injured finger (March 31, 2003); missed two games. ... Injured eye (September 16, 2003); missed 10 games. ... Claimed off waivers by Toronto Maple Leafs (March 9, 2004).

		REGULAR SEASON								PLAYOFFS				
Season Team	**League**	**GP**	**G**	**A**	**Pts.**	**PIM**	**+/-**	**PP**	**SH**	**GP**	**G**	**A**	**Pts.**	**PIM**
92-93—Cornwall	CJHL	55	30	36	66	26	...	...	...	6	0	0	0	0
93-94—Kingston	OHL	66	17	35	52	23	...	...	...	6	7	2	9	8
94-95—Kingston	OHL	65	42	53	95	95	...	12	1	6	5	2	7	10
95-96—Anaheim	NHL	45	5	7	12	22	-2	0	0	—	—	—	—	—
—Winnipeg	NHL	29	2	3	5	12	-2	0	0	4	1	0	1	0
96-97—Phoenix	NHL	24	4	3	7	13	-5	1	0	—	—	—	—	—
—Springfield	AHL	52	17	28	45	36	7	5	0	16	5	7	12	56
97-98—Springfield	AHL	35	14	14	28	33	-8	3	0	—	—	—	—	—
—Phoenix	NHL	10	0	1	1	4	-2	0	0	—	—	—	—	—
—Chicago	NHL	22	3	8	11	6	2	2	0	—	—	—	—	—
98-99—Chicago	NHL	64	14	11	25	30	-1	2	1	—	—	—	—	—
—Edmonton	NHL	13	1	1	2	4	-3	0	0	4	0	0	0	4
99-00—Edmonton	NHL	40	3	2	5	18	-6	0	0	3	0	0	0	0
—Hamilton	AHL	3	3	3	6	0	...	...	...	—	—	—	—	—
00-01—Edmonton	NHL	34	5	2	7	17	-7	1	0	—	—	—	—	—
—Montreal	NHL	43	9	16	25	34	-1	1	1	—	—	—	—	—
01-02—Montreal	NHL	75	8	15	23	27	-7	0	1	12	0	1	1	9
02-03—Montreal	NHL	60	9	7	16	21	-4	0	0	—	—	—	—	—
03-04—Montreal	NHL	36	2	2	4	14	2	0	0	—	—	—	—	—
—Hamilton	AHL	2	1	0	1	0	-1	1	0	—	—	—	—	—
—Toronto	NHL	5	1	1	2	2	2	0	0	13	2	1	3	0
NHL Totals (9 years)		500	66	79	145	224	-34	7	3	36	3	2	5	13

KINDL, JAKUB — D — RED WINGS

PERSONAL: Born February 10, 1987, in Sumperk, Czech Republic. ... 6-2/200. ... Shoots left.

TRANSACTIONS/CAREER NOTES: Selected by Detroit Red Wings in 1st round (1st Red Wings pick, 19th overall) of entry draft (July 30, 2005).

		REGULAR SEASON								PLAYOFFS				
Season Team	**League**	**GP**	**G**	**A**	**Pts.**	**PIM**	**+/-**	**PP**	**SH**	**GP**	**G**	**A**	**Pts.**	**PIM**
03-04—Pardubice	Czech. Jrs.	48	4	14	18	108	...	...	...	—	—	—	—	—
04-05—Kitchener	OHL	62	3	11	14	92	12	1	0	12	0	0	0	22

KING, JASON — RW — CANUCKS

PERSONAL: Born September 14, 1981, in Corner Brook, Nfld. ... 6-1/195. ... Shoots left.
TRANSACTIONS/CAREER NOTES: Selected by Vancouver Canucks in the seventh round (212nd overall) of NHL entry draft (June 24, 2001). ... Injured hand (January 21, 2004); missed one game.

		REGULAR SEASON								PLAYOFFS				
Season Team	League	GP	G	A	Pts.	PIM	+/-	PP	SH	GP	G	A	Pts.	PIM
99-00—Halifax	QMJHL	53	3	7	10	8	...	...	...	10	0	0	0	2
00-01—Halifax	QMJHL	72	48	41	89	78	...	...	...	6	3	2	5	16
01-02—Halifax	QMJHL	61	63	36	99	39	...	...	...	13	9	8	17	13
02-03—Vancouver	NHL	8	0	2	2	0	0	0	0	—	—	—	—	—
—Manitoba	AHL	67	20	20	40	15	3	5	0	14	4	3	7	14
03-04—Manitoba	AHL	29	12	11	23	6	-2	4	0	—	—	—	—	—
—Vancouver	NHL	47	12	9	21	8	0	6	0	1	0	0	0	0
04-05—Manitoba	AHL	59	26	27	53	22	1	10	2	0	0	0	0	0
NHL Totals (2 years)		55	12	11	23	8	0	6	0	1	0	0	0	0

KIPRUSOFF, MIIKKA — G — FLAMES

PERSONAL: Born October 26, 1976, in Turku, Finland. ... 6-1/195. ... Catches left. ... Brother of Marko Kiprusoff, defenseman, Montreal Canadiens (1995-96) and New York Islanders (2001-02).
TRANSACTIONS/CAREER NOTES: Selected by San Jose Sharks in fifth round (fifth Sharks pick, 115th overall) of NHL draft (July 8, 1995). ... Injured knee (March 22, 2003); missed nine games. ... Traded by Sharks to Calgary Flames for second-round pick in 2005 draft (November 16, 2003). ... Injured left knee (December 31, 2003); missed 19 games.

		REGULAR SEASON									PLAYOFFS							
Season Team	League	GP	Min.	W	L	T	GA	SO	GAA	SV%	GP	Min.	W	L	GA	SO	GAA	SV%
93-94—TPS Turku	Finland Jr.	35	...	...	...	...	...	...	3.00	...	6	...	...	...	...	...	4.00	...
94-95—TPS Turku	Finland Jr.	31	1880	...	...	...	93	...	2.97	...	—	—	—	—	—	—	—	—
—TPS Turku	Finland	4	240	...	...	...	12	0	3.00	...	2	120	...	...	7	...	3.50	...
95-96—TPS Turku	Finland	12	550	...	...	...	38	...	4.15	...	—	—	—	—	—	—	—	—
—Kiekko	Finland	5	300	...	...	...	7	...	1.40	...	—	—	—	—	—	—	—	—
96-97—AIK	Sweden	42	2466	...	...	...	104	3	2.53	...	7	420	...	...	23	0	3.29	...
97-98—AIK Solna	Sweden	42	2457	...	...	...	110	...	2.69	...	—	—	—	—	—	—	—	—
98-99—TPS Turku	Finland	39	2259	*26	6	6	70	4	1.86	...	10	580	*9	1	15	*3	*1.55	...
99-00—Kentucky	AHL	47	2759	23	19	4	114	3	2.48	...	5	239	1	3	13	0	3.26	...
00-01—Kentucky	AHL	36	2038	19	9	6	76	2	2.24	.926	—	—	—	—	—	—	—	—
—San Jose	NHL	5	154	2	1	0	5	0	1.95	.902	3	149	1	1	5	0	2.01	.937
01-02—San Jose	NHL	20	1037	7	6	3	43	2	2.49	.915	1	8	0	0	0	0	0.00	1.00
—Cleveland	AHL	4	242	4	0	0	7	0	1.74	.946	—	—	—	—	—	—	—	—
02-03—San Jose	NHL	22	1199	5	14	0	65	1	3.25	.879	—	—	—	—	—	—	—	—
03-04—Calgary	NHL	38	2301	24	10	4	65	4	1.69	.933	26	1655	15	11	51	5	1.85	.928
04-05—Timra	Sweden Dv. 2	46	2719	...	...	...	97	5	2.14	.916	6	356	...	...	13	0	2.19	.890
NHL Totals (4 years)		85	4691	38	31	7	178	7	2.28	.914	30	1812	16	12	56	5	1.85	.929

KLATT, TRENT — RW — KINGS

PERSONAL: Born January 30, 1971, in Robbinsdale, Minn. ... 6-0/225. ... Shoots right.
TRANSACTIONS/CAREER NOTES: Selected by Washington Capitals in fourth round (fifth Capitals pick, 82nd overall) of NHL draft (June 17, 1989). ... Rights traded by Capitals with LW Steve Maltais to Minnesota North Stars for D Sean Chambers (June 21, 1991). ... Injured finger (January 7, 1993); missed three games. ... North Stars franchise moved from Minnesota to Dallas and renamed Stars for 1993-94 season. ... Strained back (November 7, 1993); missed one game. ... Sprained knee (November 11, 1993); missed two games. ... Sprained knee (February 6, 1994); missed three games. ... Traded by Stars to Philadelphia Flyers for LW Brent Fedyk (December 13, 1995). ... Suffered concussion (March 9, 1997); missed two games. ... Traded by Flyers to Vancouver Canucks for sixth-round pick (traded to Atlanta Thrashers) in 2000 draft (October 19, 1998). ... Had rash (February 14, 2001); missed five games. ... Strained abdominal muscle (November 20, 2001); missed 25 games. ... Strained abdominal muscle (February 12, 2002); missed remainder of season. ... Signed as free agent by Los Angeles Kings (July 7, 2003).
STATISTICAL PLATEAUS: Three-goal games: 1996-97 (1).

		REGULAR SEASON								PLAYOFFS				
Season Team	League	GP	G	A	Pts.	PIM	+/-	PP	SH	GP	G	A	Pts.	PIM
87-88—Osseo H.S.	Minn. H.S.	22	19	17	36	...	...	...	...	—	—	—	—	—
88-89—Osseo H.S.	Minn. H.S.	22	24	39	63	...	...	...	...	—	—	—	—	—
89-90—Minnesota	WCHA	38	22	14	36	16	...	...	...	—	—	—	—	—
90-91—Minnesota	WCHA	39	16	28	44	58	...	...	...	—	—	—	—	—
91-92—Minnesota	WCHA	44	30	36	66	78	...	...	...	—	—	—	—	—
—Minnesota	NHL	1	0	0	0	0	0	0	0	6	0	0	0	2
92-93—Kalamazoo	IHL	31	8	11	19	18	-6	1	1	—	—	—	—	—
—Minnesota	NHL	47	4	19	23	38	2	1	0	—	—	—	—	—
93-94—Dallas	NHL	61	14	24	38	30	13	3	0	9	2	1	3	4
—Kalamazoo	IHL	6	3	2	5	4	4	0	0	—	—	—	—	—
94-95—Dallas	NHL	47	12	10	22	26	-2	5	0	5	1	0	1	0
95-96—Dallas	NHL	22	4	4	8	23	0	0	0	—	—	—	—	—
—Michigan	IHL	2	1	2	3	5	...	...	...	—	—	—	—	—
—Philadelphia	NHL	49	3	8	11	21	2	0	0	12	4	1	5	0
96-97—Philadelphia	NHL	76	24	21	45	20	9	5	5	19	4	3	7	12
97-98—Philadelphia	NHL	82	14	28	42	16	2	5	0	5	0	0	0	0
98-99—Philadelphia	NHL	2	0	0	0	0	0	0	0	—	—	—	—	—

Season Team	League	GP	G	A	Pts.	PIM	+/-	PP	SH	GP	G	A	Pts.	PIM
		REGULAR SEASON								PLAYOFFS				
—Vancouver	NHL	73	4	10	14	12	-3	0	0	—	—	—	—	—
99-00—Syracuse	AHL	24	13	10	23	6	...	...	...	—	—	—	—	—
—Vancouver	NHL	47	10	10	20	26	-8	8	0	—	—	—	—	—
00-01—Vancouver	NHL	77	13	20	33	31	8	3	0	4	3	0	3	0
01-02—Vancouver	NHL	34	8	7	15	10	9	2	1	—	—	—	—	—
02-03—Vancouver	NHL	82	16	13	29	8	10	3	0	14	2	4	6	2
03-04—Los Angeles	NHL	82	17	26	43	46	2	6	0	—	—	—	—	—
NHL Totals (13 years)		782	143	200	343	307	44	41	6	74	16	9	25	20

KLEE, KEN D MAPLE LEAFS

PERSONAL: Born April 24, 1971, in Indianapolis, Ind. ... 6-0/214. ... Shoots right.

TRANSACTIONS/CAREER NOTES: Selected by Washington Capitals in ninth round (11th Capitals pick, 177th overall) of NHL draft (June 16, 1990). ... Injured foot (January 27, 1995); missed six games. ... Injured groin (March 12, 1996); missed 13 games. ... Sprained knee (April 10, 1996); missed two games. ... Fractured facial bone (March 28, 1998); missed eight games. ... Bruised foot (February 12, 2000); missed one game. ... Injured wrist (October 19, 2000); missed six games. ... Strained left knee (December 12, 2000); missed one game. ... Strained back (February 13, 2001); missed six games. ... Suffered concussion (March 7, 2001); missed two games. ... Injured ribs (November 8, 2001); missed three games. ... Injured groin (January 18, 2002); missed four games. ... Injured foot (March 29, 2002); missed five games. ... Signed as free agent by Toronto Maple Leafs (September 27, 2003). ... Strained abdominal muscle (January 13, 2004); missed five games. ... Reinjured abdominal muscle (March 13, 2004); missed four games. ... Injured shoulder (March 20, 2004); missed final seven games of regular season and one playoff game. ... Had knee surgery (Mary 4, 2004); missed final playoff game.

K

Season Team	League	GP	G	A	Pts.	PIM	+/-	PP	SH	GP	G	A	Pts.	PIM
		REGULAR SEASON								PLAYOFFS				
89-90—Bowling Green	CCHA	39	0	5	5	52	...	...	...	—	—	—	—	—
90-91—Bowling Green	CCHA	37	7	28	35	50	...	...	...	—	—	—	—	—
91-92—Bowling Green	CCHA	10	0	1	1	14	...	...	...	—	—	—	—	—
92-93—Baltimore	AHL	77	4	14	18	68	...	...	...	7	0	1	1	15
93-94—Portland	AHL	65	2	9	11	87	0	0	0	17	1	2	3	14
94-95—Portland	AHL	49	5	7	12	89	12	0	0	—	—	—	—	—
—Washington	NHL	23	3	1	4	41	2	0	0	7	0	0	0	4
95-96—Washington	NHL	66	8	3	11	60	-1	0	1	1	0	0	0	0
96-97—Washington	NHL	80	3	8	11	115	-5	0	0	—	—	—	—	—
97-98—Washington	NHL	51	4	2	6	46	-3	0	0	9	1	0	1	10
98-99—Washington	NHL	78	7	13	20	80	-9	0	0	—	—	—	—	—
99-00—Washington	NHL	80	7	13	20	79	8	0	0	5	0	1	1	10
00-01—Washington	NHL	54	2	4	6	60	-5	0	0	6	0	1	1	8
01-02—Washington	NHL	68	8	8	16	38	4	2	0	—	—	—	—	—
02-03—Washington	NHL	70	1	16	17	89	22	0	0	6	0	0	0	6
03-04—Toronto	NHL	66	4	25	29	36	-1	3	0	11	0	0	0	6
NHL Totals (10 years)		636	47	93	140	644	12	5	1	45	1	2	3	44

KLEMM, JON D STARS

PERSONAL: Born January 8, 1970, in Cranbrook, B.C. ... 6-2/200. ... Shoots right.

TRANSACTIONS/CAREER NOTES: Signed as non-drafted free agent by Quebec Nordiques (May 14, 1991). ... Injured abdomen (March 28, 1995); missed five games. ... Reinjured abdomen (April 8, 1995); missed remainder of season. ... Nordiques franchise moved to Colorado and renamed Avalanche for 1995-96 season (June 21, 1995). ... Injured groin (January 27, 1996); missed one game. ... Sprained thumb (October 30, 1997) and had surgery; missed 11 games. ... Strained groin (December 27, 1997); missed one game. ... Injured knee (November 15, 1998); missed 29 games. ... Had appendicitis (March 25, 1999); missed six games. ... Injured groin (October 20, 1999); missed seven games. ... Had back spasms (February 25, 2000); missed one game. ... Injured hamstring (December 5, 2000); missed three games. ... Signed as free agent by Chicago Blackhawks (July 1, 2001). ... Fractured finger (December 20, 2002); missed 12 games. ... Traded by Blackhawks to Dallas Stars with fourth-round pick (RW Fredrik Naslund) in 2004 entry draft for D Stephane Robidas and second-round pick (C Jakub Sindel) in 2004 entry draft (November 17, 2003). ... Injured groin (January 10, 2004); missed one game. ... Injured groin (March 24, 2004); missed five games. ... Reinjured groin (April 7, 2004); missed playoffs.

Season Team	League	GP	G	A	Pts.	PIM	+/-	PP	SH	GP	G	A	Pts.	PIM
		REGULAR SEASON								PLAYOFFS				
87-88—Seattle	WHL	68	6	7	13	24	...	...	...	—	—	—	—	—
88-89—Seattle	WHL	2	1	1	2	0	...	...	...	—	—	—	—	—
—Spokane	WHL	66	6	34	40	42	...	...	...	—	—	—	—	—
89-90—Spokane	WHL	66	3	28	31	100	...	...	...	6	1	1	2	5
90-91—Spokane	WHL	72	7	58	65	65	...	...	...	15	3	6	9	8
91-92—Halifax	AHL	70	6	13	19	40	...	...	...	—	—	—	—	—
—Quebec	NHL	4	0	1	1	0	2	0	0	—	—	—	—	—
92-93—Halifax	AHL	80	3	20	23	32	-2	0	0	—	—	—	—	—
93-94—Cornwall	AHL	66	4	26	30	78	15	1	0	13	1	2	3	6
—Quebec	NHL	7	0	0	0	4	-1	0	0	—	—	—	—	—
94-95—Cornwall	AHL	65	6	13	19	84	-12	1	0	—	—	—	—	—
—Quebec	NHL	4	1	0	1	2	3	0	0	—	—	—	—	—
95-96—Colorado	NHL	56	3	12	15	20	12	0	1	15	2	1	3	0
96-97—Colorado	NHL	80	9	15	24	37	12	1	2	17	1	1	2	6
97-98—Colorado	NHL	67	6	8	14	30	-3	0	0	4	0	0	0	0
98-99—Colorado	NHL	39	1	2	3	31	4	0	0	19	0	1	1	10
99-00—Colorado	NHL	73	5	7	12	34	26	0	0	17	2	1	3	9
00-01—Colorado	NHL	78	4	11	15	54	22	2	0	22	1	2	3	16
01-02—Chicago	NHL	82	4	16	20	42	-3	2	0	5	0	1	1	4
02-03—Chicago	NHL	70	2	14	16	44	-9	1	0	—	—	—	—	—
03-04—Chicago	NHL	19	0	1	1	20	6	0	0	—	—	—	—	—
—Dallas	NHL	58	2	4	6	24	10	0	0	—	—	—	—	—
NHL Totals (12 years)		637	37	91	128	342	81	6	3	99	6	7	13	45

KLEPIS, JAKUB — C — CAPITALS

PERSONAL: Born June 5, 1984, in Prague, Czechoslovakia. ... 6-0/200. ... Shoots right. ... Name pronounced KLEH-pihsh.
TRANSACTIONS/CAREER NOTES: Selected by Ottawa Senators in first round (first Senators pick, 16th pick overall) of NHL entry draft (June 22, 2002). ... Traded by Senators to Buffalo Sabres for RW Vaclav Varada and fifth-round pick (Tim Cook) in 2003 entry draft (February 25, 2003). ... Traded by Sabres to Washington Capitals for RW Mike Grier (March 9, 2004).

		REGULAR SEASON								PLAYOFFS				
Season Team	League	GP	G	A	Pts.	PIM	+/-	PP	SH	GP	G	A	Pts.	PIM
01-02—Portland	WHL	70	14	50	64	111	...	...	...	7	0	3	3	22
02-03—Slavia Praha	Czech. Jrs.	38	2	6	8	22	...	...	...	—	—	—	—	—
03-04—Slavia Praha	Czech Rep.	44	4	9	13	43	...	...	...	17	5	3	8	10
04-05—Portland	AHL	78	13	14	27	76	-26	5	0	—	—	—	—	—

KLESLA, ROSTISLAV — D — BLUE JACKETS

PERSONAL: Born March 21, 1982, in Novy Jicin, Czechoslovakia. ... 6-3/208. ... Shoots left. ... Nickname: Rusty.
TRANSACTIONS/CAREER NOTES: Selected by Columbus Blue Jackets in first round (first Blue Jackets pick, fourth overall) of NHL draft (June 24, 2000). ... Strained shoulder (January 24, 2002); missed seven games. ... Injured shoulder (January 10, 2003); missed eight games. ... Flu (February 15, 2003); missed one game. ... Had hip pointer (October 25, 2003); missed five games. ... Sprained knee (November 29, 2003); missed 13 games. ... Sprained wrist (February 25, 2004); missed 15 games. ... Charley horse (March 31, 2004); missed final two games of season.

		REGULAR SEASON								PLAYOFFS				
Season Team	League	GP	G	A	Pts.	PIM	+/-	PP	SH	GP	G	A	Pts.	PIM
97-98—Opava	Czech. Jrs.	40	11	16	27	...	...	...	...	—	—	—	—	—
98-99—Sioux City	USHL	54	4	12	16	100	...	...	...	—	—	—	—	—
99-00—Brampton	OHL	67	16	29	45	174	...	...	...	6	1	1	2	21
00-01—Columbus	NHL	8	2	0	2	6	-1	0	0	—	—	—	—	—
—Brampton	OHL	45	18	36	54	59	22	7	1	9	2	9	11	26
01-02—Columbus	NHL	75	8	8	16	74	-6	1	0	—	—	—	—	—
02-03—Columbus	NHL	72	2	14	16	71	-22	0	0	—	—	—	—	—
03-04—Columbus	NHL	47	2	11	13	27	-16	0	0	—	—	—	—	—
04-05—HPK Hameenlinna	Finland	9	1	2	3	12	0	...	...	10	0	2	2	12
—HC Vsetin	Czech Rep.	34	6	15	21	134	3	...	...	—	—	—	—	—
—HC Ceske Budejovice	Czech Rep.	7	1	2	3	2	0	...	...	—	—	—	—	—
NHL Totals (4 years)		202	14	33	47	178	-45	1	0					

KLOUCEK, TOMAS — D — THRASHERS

PERSONAL: Born March 7, 1980, in Prague, Czechoslovakia. ... 6-3/225. ... Shoots left.
TRANSACTIONS/CAREER NOTES: Selected by New York Rangers in fifth round (sixth Rangers pick, 131st overall) of NHL draft (June 27, 1998). ... Bruised ankle (February 19, 2001); missed one game. ... Bruised shoulder (March 10, 2001): mised two games. ... Bruised heel (March 25, 2001); missed two games. ... Injured knee (April 1, 2001); missed final three games of season. ... Had knee surgery; missed first five games of 2001-02 season. ... Reinjured knee (October 19, 2001); missed one game. ... Had back spasms (November 18, 2001); missed two games. ... Traded with LW Rem Murray and D Marek Zidlicky to Nashville Predators for G Mike Dunham (December 12, 2002). ... Injured knee (October 9, 2003); missed five games. ... Traded with C Ben Simon to Atlanta Thrashers for C Simon Gamache and D Kirill Safronov (December 2, 2003). ... Bruised shoulder (December 5, 2003); missed nine games. ... Bruised shoulder (December 21, 2003); missed nine games. ... Suffered concussion (February 22, 2004); missed six games.

		REGULAR SEASON								PLAYOFFS				
Season Team	League	GP	G	A	Pts.	PIM	+/-	PP	SH	GP	G	A	Pts.	PIM
95-96—Slavia Praha	Czech. Jrs.	40	2	8	10	...	...	...	...	—	—	—	—	—
96-97—Slavia Praha	Czech. Jrs.	43	4	14	18	44	...	...	...	—	—	—	—	—
97-98—Slavia Praha	Czech. Jrs.	43	1	9	10	...	...	...	...	—	—	—	—	—
98-99—Cape Breton	QMJHL	59	4	17	21	162	10	1	0	2	0	0	0	4
99-00—Hartford	AHL	73	2	8	10	113	...	...	...	23	0	4	4	18
00-01—Hartford	AHL	21	0	2	2	44	...	...	...	—	—	—	—	—
—New York Rangers	NHL	43	1	4	5	74	-3	0	0	—	—	—	—	—
01-02—New York Rangers	NHL	52	1	3	4	137	-2	0	0	—	—	—	—	—
—Hartford	AHL	9	0	2	2	27	1	0	0	10	1	1	2	8
02-03—Hartford	AHL	20	3	4	7	102	5	2	0	—	—	—	—	—
—Nashville	NHL	3	0	0	0	2	1	0	0	—	—	—	—	—
—Milwaukee	AHL	34	0	6	6	80	1	0	0	—	—	—	—	—
03-04—Nashville	NHL	5	0	1	1	10	3	0	0	—	—	—	—	—
—Atlanta	NHL	37	0	0	0	25	-8	0	0	—	—	—	—	—
04-05—Slavia Praha	Czech Rep.	29	1	1	2	28	4	...	...	—	—	—	—	—
—Trinec	Czech Rep.	11	1	2	3	24	-2	...	...	—	—	—	—	—
—Liberec	Czech Rep.	8	0	1	1	12	8	...	...	9	0	1	1	35
NHL Totals (4 years)		140	2	8	10	248	-9	0	0					

KNUBLE, MIKE — LW — FLYERS

PERSONAL: Born July 4, 1972, in Toronto. ... 6-3/228. ... Shoots right. ... Name pronounced kuh-NOO-buhl.
TRANSACTIONS/CAREER NOTES: Selected by Detroit Red Wings in fourth round (fourth Red Wings pick, 76th overall) of NHL draft (June 22, 1991). ... Traded by Red Wings to New York Rangers for third-round pick (traded back to Rangers; Rangers selected Tomas Kopecky) in 2000 draft (October 1, 1998). ... Traded by Rangers to Boston Bruins for LW Rob DiMaio (March 10, 2000). ... Fractured vetebra (November 20, 2001); missed nine games. ... Injured back (March 1, 2002); missed four games. ... Injured back (November 27, 2002); missed nine games. ... Had concussion (November 14, 2002); missed three games. ... Flu (December 27, 2002); missed two games. ... Signed as free agent by Philadelphia Flyers (July 3, 2004).

Season Team	League	REGULAR SEASON								PLAYOFFS				
		GP	G	A	Pts.	PIM	+/-	PP	SH	GP	G	A	Pts.	PIM
88-89—East Kentwood H.S.	Mich. H.S.	28	52	37	89	60	...	...	...	—	—	—	—	—
89-90—East Kentwood H.S.	Mich. H.S.	29	63	40	103	40	...	...	...	—	—	—	—	—
90-91—Kalamazoo	NAJHL	36	18	24	42	30	...	...	...	—	—	—	—	—
91-92—Univ. of Michigan	CCHA	43	7	8	15	48	...	...	...	—	—	—	—	—
92-93—Univ. of Michigan	CCHA	39	26	16	42	57	...	...	...	—	—	—	—	—
93-94—Univ. of Michigan	CCHA	41	32	26	58	71	6	21	0	—	—	—	—	—
94-95—Univ. of Michigan	CCHA	34	38	22	60	62	26	15	0	—	—	—	—	—
95-96—Adirondack	AHL	80	22	23	45	59	...	...	...	3	1	0	1	0
96-97—Adirondack	AHL	68	28	35	63	54	...	...	...	—	—	—	—	—
—Detroit	NHL	9	1	0	1	0	-1	0	0	—	—	—	—	—
97-98—Detroit	NHL	53	7	6	13	16	2	0	0	3	0	1	1	0
98-99—New York Rangers	NHL	82	15	20	35	26	-7	3	0	—	—	—	—	—
99-00—New York Rangers	NHL	59	9	5	14	18	-5	1	0	—	—	—	—	—
—Boston	NHL	14	3	3	6	8	-2	1	0	—	—	—	—	—
00-01—Boston	NHL	82	7	13	20	37	0	0	1	—	—	—	—	—
01-02—Boston	NHL	54	8	6	14	42	9	0	0	2	0	0	0	0
02-03—Boston	NHL	75	30	29	59	45	18	9	0	5	0	2	2	2
03-04—Boston	NHL	82	21	25	46	32	19	4	0	7	2	0	2	0
04-05—Linkopings	Sweden	49	26	13	39	40	24	5	0	6	0	1	1	2
NHL Totals (8 years)		510	101	107	208	224	33	18	1	17	2	3	5	2

KNYAZEV, IGOR — D — COYOTES

PERSONAL: Born January 27, 1983, in Elektrosal, U.S.S.R. ... 6-0/183. ... Shoots left.

TRANSACTIONS/CAREER NOTES: Selected by Carolina Hurricanes in 1st round (1st Hurricanes pick, 15th overall) of NHL draft (June 23, 2001). ... Traded by Hurricanes with D David Tanabe to the Phoenix Coyotes for D Danny Markov and future considerations (June 21, 2003).

Season Team	League	REGULAR SEASON								PLAYOFFS				
		GP	G	A	Pts.	PIM	+/-	PP	SH	GP	G	A	Pts.	PIM
00-01—Spartak	Russian Div. 1	43	6	3	9	66	...	...	...	—	—	—	—	—
01-02—Spartak Moscow	Russian	3	0	0	0	8	...	...	...	—	—	—	—	—
—Ak Bars Kazan	Russian	14	0	1	1	4	...	...	...	3	0	0	0	0
02-03—Lowell	AHL	68	2	5	7	68	-22	1	0	—	—	—	—	—
03-04—Springfield	AHL	72	1	6	7	61	-10	0	0	—	—	—	—	—
04-05—Voskresensk	Russian	29	0	1	1	59	...	...	...	—	—	—	—	—

KOBASEW, CHUCK — RW — FLAMES

PERSONAL: Born April 17, 1982, in Osoyoos, B.C. ... 6-1/190. ... Shoots right.

TRANSACTIONS/CAREER NOTES: Selected by Calgary Flames in first round (first Flames pick, 14th overall) of NHL entry draft (June 23, 2001). ... Injured right shoulder (January 3, 2004); missed eight games.

Season Team	League	REGULAR SEASON								PLAYOFFS				
		GP	G	A	Pts.	PIM	+/-	PP	SH	GP	G	A	Pts.	PIM
98-99—Penticton	BCHL	30	11	17	28	18	...	...	...	—	—	—	—	—
99-00—Penticton	BCHL	58	54	52	106	83	...	...	...	—	—	—	—	—
00-01—Boston College	Hockey East	43	27	22	49	38	...	...	...	—	—	—	—	—
01-02—Kelowna	WHL	55	41	21	62	114	...	...	...	15	10	5	15	22
02-03—Calgary	NHL	23	4	2	6	8	-3	1	0	—	—	—	—	—
—Saint John	AHL	48	21	12	33	61	-5	9	1	—	—	—	—	—
03-04—Calgary	NHL	70	6	11	17	51	-12	3	0	26	0	1	1	24
04-05—Lowell	AHL	79	38	37	75	110	37	9	1	11	6	3	9	27
NHL Totals (2 years)		93	10	13	23	59	-15	4	0	26	0	1	1	24

KOCHAN, DIETER — G

PERSONAL: Born May 11, 1974, in Saskatoon, Sask. ... 6-1/180. ... Catches left.

TRANSACTIONS/CAREER NOTES: Selected by Vancouver Canucks in fourth round (third Canucks pick, 98th overall) of NHL entry draft (June 26, 1993). ... Signed as free agent by Tampa Bay Lightning (March 27, 2000). ... Signed as free agent by Minnesota Wild (August 5, 2002). ... Signed as free agent by New York Islanders (August 12, 2003).

Season Team	League	REGULAR SEASON									PLAYOFFS							
		GP	Min.	W	L	T	GA	SO	GAA	SV%	GP	Min.	W	L	GA	SO	GAA	SV%
91-92—Sioux City	USHL	23	1131	7	10	0	100	...	5.31	.875	—	—	—	—	—	—	—	—
92-93—Kelowna	BCJHL	44	2582	34	8	0	137	1	*3.18	.887	—	—	—	—	—	—	—	—
93-94—N. Michigan Univ.	WCHA	16	984	9	7	0	57	2	3.48	.875	—	—	—	—	—	—	—	—
94-95—N. Michigan Univ.	WCHA	29	1512	8	17	3	107	0	4.25	.880	—	—	—	—	—	—	—	—
95-96—N. Michigan Univ.	WCHA	31	1627	7	21	2	123	0	4.54	...	—	—	—	—	—	—	—	—
96-97—N. Michigan Univ.	WCHA	26	1528	8	15	2	99	0	3.89	.888	—	—	—	—	—	—	—	—
97-98—Louisville Riverfrogs	ECHL	18	980	7	9	2	61	1	3.73	...	—	—	—	—	—	—	—	—
98-99—Binghamton	UHL	40	2321	18	16	5	115	2	2.97	...	4	207	1	2	9	0	2.61	...
99-00—Binghamton	UHL	43	2544	29	11	3	110	4	2.59	...	—	—	—	—	—	—	—	—
—Orlando	IHL	4	240	4	0	0	4	1	1.00	...	—	—	—	—	—	—	—	—
—Grand Rapids	IHL	2	93	1	0	1	1	0	0.65	...	—	—	—	—	—	—	—	—
—Springfield	AHL	2	120	1	1	0	5	1	2.50	...	—	—	—	—	—	—	—	—
—Tampa Bay	NHL	5	238	1	4	0	17	0	4.29	.847	—	—	—	—	—	—	—	—
00-01—Detroit	IHL	49	2606	13	*28	3	*154	0	3.55	...	—	—	—	—	—	—	—	—
—Tampa Bay	NHL	10	314	0	3	0	18	0	3.44	.870	—	—	—	—	—	—	—	—

Season Team	League	GP	Min.	W	L	T	GA	SO	GAA	SV%	GP	Min.	W	L	GA	SO	GAA	SV%
		REGULAR SEASON									PLAYOFFS							
01-02—Springfield	AHL	45	2518	21	20	1	112	2	2.67	.901	—	—	—	—	—	—	—	—
—Tampa Bay	NHL	5	237	0	3	1	16	0	4.05	.876	—	—	—	—	—	—	—	—
02-03—Minnesota	NHL	1	60	0	1	0	5	0	5.00	.821	—	—	—	—	—	—	—	—
—Houston	AHL	25	1446	15	6	3	61	1	2.53	.907	2	20	0	0	0	0	0.00	1.00
03-04—Bridgeport	AHL	45	2728	20	17	7	85	6	1.87	.929	4	280	1	3	12	0	2.57	.910
04-05—Bridgeport	AHL	39	2302	19	19	...	102	1	2.66	.914	—	—	—	—	—	—	—	—
NHL Totals (4 years)		21	849	1	11	1	56	0	3.96	.862								

KOHN, DUSTIN — D — ISLANDERS

PERSONAL: Born February 2, 1987, in Edmonton, Alta. ... 6-1/180. ... Shoots left.

Season Team	League	GP	G	A	Pts.	PIM	+/-	PP	SH	GP	G	A	Pts.	PIM
		REGULAR SEASON								PLAYOFFS				
04-05—Calgary	WHL	71	8	35	43	61	18	3	0	12	0	4	4	6

KOIVU, MIKKO — C — WILD

PERSONAL: Born March 12, 1983, in Turku, Finland. ... 6-2/183. ... Shoots left. ... Brother of Saku Koivu, C, Montreal Canadiens.
TRANSACTIONS/CAREER NOTES: Selected by Minnesota Wild in first round (first Wild pick, sixth overall) of NHL entry draft (June 23, 2001).

Season Team	League	GP	G	A	Pts.	PIM	+/-	PP	SH	GP	G	A	Pts.	PIM
		REGULAR SEASON								PLAYOFFS				
99-00—TPS Turku	Finland Jr.	30	4	8	12	22	...	...	...	—	—	—	—	—
00-01—TPS Turku	Finland Jr.	30	11	38	49	34	...	...	...	—	—	—	—	—
—TPS Turku	Finland	21	0	1	1	2	...	...	...	—	—	—	—	—
01-02—TPS Turku	Finland	48	4	3	7	34	...	...	...	8	0	3	3	4
02-03—TPS Turku	Finland	37	7	13	20	20	...	...	...	—	—	—	—	—
03-04—TPS Turku	Finland	45	6	24	30	36	...	...	...	13	1	7	8	8
04-05—Houston	AHL	67	20	28	48	47	-1	4	1	5	1	0	1	2

KOIVU, SAKU — C — CANADIENS

PERSONAL: Born November 23, 1974, in Turku, Finland. ... 5-10/181. ... Shoots left. ... Brother of Mikko Koivu, C, Minnesota Wild organization. ... Name pronounced SAK-oo KOY-voo.
TRANSACTIONS/CAREER NOTES: Selected by Montreal Canadiens in first round (first Canadiens pick, 21st overall) of NHL draft (June 26, 1993). ... Tore knee ligament (December 7, 1996); missed 26 games. ... Sprained shoulder (March 10, 1997); missed five games. ... Had tonsillitis (March 29, 1997); missed one game. ... Strained ribcage (January 8, 1998); missed seven games. ... Fractured hand (April 7, 1998); missed six games. ... Strained abdominal muscle (October 24, 1998); missed 12 games. ... Had infected elbow (January 18, 1999); missed three games. ... Injured knee (March 24, 1999); missed two games. ... Injured (October 30, 1999); missed five games. ... Separated shoulder (November 2, 1999); missed 40 games. ... Tore knee ligament (March 11, 2000); missed remainder of season. ... Tore knee ligament (October 11, 2000) and had surgery; missed 28 games. ... Diagnosed with non-Hodgkin's lymphoma; missed first 79 games of 2001-02 season. ... Injured right knee (September 22, 2003); missed first 13 games of 2003-04 season. ... Had concussion (December 30, 2003); missed one game.
STATISTICAL PLATEAUS: Three-goal games: 2002-03 (1).

Season Team	League	GP	G	A	Pts.	PIM	+/-	PP	SH	GP	G	A	Pts.	PIM
		REGULAR SEASON								PLAYOFFS				
90-91—TPS Turku	Finland Jr.	24	20	28	48	26	...	...	...	—	—	—	—	—
91-92—TPS Turku	Finland Jr.	42	30	37	67	63	...	...	...	—	—	—	—	—
92-93—TPS Turku	Finland	46	3	7	10	28	...	...	...	—	—	—	—	—
93-94—TPS Turku	Finland	47	23	30	53	42	...	...	...	11	4	8	12	16
—Fin. Olympic team	Int'l	8	4	3	7	12	3	2	0	—	—	—	—	—
94-95—TPS Turku	Finland	45	27	47	74	73	...	...	...	13	7	10	17	16
95-96—Montreal	NHL	82	20	25	45	40	-7	8	3	6	3	1	4	8
96-97—Montreal	NHL	50	17	39	56	38	7	5	0	5	1	3	4	10
97-98—Montreal	NHL	69	14	43	57	48	8	2	2	6	2	3	5	2
—Fin. Olympic team	Int'l	6	2	8	10	4	1	1	0	—	—	—	—	—
98-99—Montreal	NHL	65	14	30	44	38	-7	4	2	—	—	—	—	—
99-00—Montreal	NHL	24	3	18	21	14	7	1	0	—	—	—	—	—
00-01—Montreal	NHL	54	17	30	47	40	2	7	0	—	—	—	—	—
01-02—Montreal	NHL	3	0	2	2	0	0	0	0	12	4	6	10	4
02-03—Montreal	NHL	82	21	50	71	72	5	5	1	—	—	—	—	—
03-04—Montreal	NHL	68	14	41	55	52	-5	5	0	11	3	8	11	10
04-05—TPS Turku	Finland	20	8	8	16	28	11	...	...	6	3	2	5	30
NHL Totals (9 years)		497	120	278	398	342	10	37	8	40	13	21	34	34

KOLANOS, KRYSTOFER — C — COYOTES

PERSONAL: Born July 27, 1981, in Calgary. ... 6-3/206. ... Shoots right.
TRANSACTIONS/CAREER NOTES: Selected by Phoenix Coyotes in first round (first Coyotes pick, 19th overall) of NHL draft (June 24, 2000). ... Suffered concussion (January 19, 2002); missed 22 games. ... Had post-concussion syndrome; missed first 80 games of 2002-03 season.

Season Team	League	GP	G	A	Pts.	PIM	+/-	PP	SH	GP	G	A	Pts.	PIM
		REGULAR SEASON								PLAYOFFS				
98-99—Calgary Royals	AJHL	58	43	67	110	98	...	...	...	—	—	—	—	—
99-00—Boston College	Hockey East	34	14	13	27	44	...	...	...	—	—	—	—	—

Season Team	League	REGULAR SEASON GP	G	A	Pts.	PIM	+/-	PP	SH	PLAYOFFS GP	G	A	Pts.	PIM
00-01—Boston College	Hockey East	41	25	25	50	54	...	...	...	—	—	—	—	—
01-02—Phoenix	NHL	57	11	11	22	48	6	0	0	2	0	0	0	6
02-03—Phoenix	NHL	2	0	0	0	0	0	0	0	—	—	—	—	—
03-04—Phoenix	NHL	41	4	6	10	24	-9	1	0	—	—	—	—	—
—Springfield	AHL	32	10	11	21	38	-2	1	0	—	—	—	—	—
04-05—Krefeld Pinguine	Germany	7	3	2	5	16	2	1	0	—	—	—	—	—
—Blues Espoo	Finland	15	7	9	16	40	4	...	...	—	—	—	—	—
NHL Totals (3 years)		100	15	17	32	72	-3	1	0	2	0	0	0	6

KOLNIK, JURAJ — RW — PANTHERS

PERSONAL: Born November 13, 1980, in Nitra, Czechoslovakia. ... 5-10/190. ... Shoots right.
TRANSACTIONS/CAREER NOTES: Selected by New York Islanders in fourth round (seventh Islanders pick, 101st overall) of NHL entry draft (June 26, 1999). ... Traded by Islanders with ninth-round pick (later traded to San Jose Sharks) in 2003 entry draft to Florida Panthers for D Sven Butenschon (October 11, 2002). ... Injured ankle (December 31, 2003); missed seven games. ... Had the flu (March 17, 2004); missed one game.

Season Team	League	REGULAR SEASON GP	G	A	Pts.	PIM	+/-	PP	SH	PLAYOFFS GP	G	A	Pts.	PIM
97-98—Plastika Nitra	Slovakia	28	1	3	4	6	...	...	...	—	—	—	—	—
98-99—Quebec	QMJHL	12	6	5	11	6	...	...	...	—	—	—	—	—
—Rimouski	QMJHL	50	36	37	73	34	...	...	...	11	9	6	15	6
99-00—Rimouski	QMJHL	47	53	53	106	53	48	11	2	14	10	17	27	16
00-01—Lowell	AHL	25	2	6	8	18	...	...	...	—	—	—	—	—
—Springfield	AHL	29	15	20	35	20	...	...	...	—	—	—	—	—
—New York Islanders	NHL	29	4	3	7	12	-8	0	0	—	—	—	—	—
01-02—Bridgeport	AHL	67	18	30	48	40	4	1	1	20	7	14	21	17
—New York Islanders	NHL	7	2	0	2	0	-2	1	0	—	—	—	—	—
02-03—Florida	NHL	10	0	1	1	0	1	0	0	—	—	—	—	—
—San Antonio	AHL	65	25	15	40	36	5	4	2	3	0	1	1	4
03-04—San Antonio	AHL	15	2	14	16	21	1	0	0	—	—	—	—	—
—Florida	NHL	53	14	11	25	14	-7	2	0	—	—	—	—	—
04-05—San Antonio	AHL	74	13	16	29	24	-1	6	0	—	—	—	—	—
NHL Totals (4 years)		99	20	15	35	26	-16	3	0					

KOLTSOV, KIRILL — D — CANUCKS

PERSONAL: Born February 1, 1983, in Chelyabinsk, U.S.S.R. ... 5-11/183. ... Shoots left.
TRANSACTIONS/CAREER NOTES: Selected by Vancouver Canucks in second round (first Canucks pick, 49th overall) of NHL entry draft (June 22, 2002).

Season Team	League	REGULAR SEASON GP	G	A	Pts.	PIM	+/-	PP	SH	PLAYOFFS GP	G	A	Pts.	PIM
00-01—Avangard Omsk	Russian	39	0	1	1	20	...	...	...	16	1	3	4	12
01-02—Avangard Omsk	Russian	41	1	5	6	34	...	...	...	11	1	0	1	18
02-03—Avangard Omsk	Russian	45	4	8	12	54	...	...	...	—	—	—	—	—
03-04—Manitoba	AHL	74	7	25	32	62	-15	4	0	—	—	—	—	—
04-05—Avangard Omsk	Russian	22	2	2	4	46	18	...	...	10	0	1	1	18
—Manitoba	AHL	28	3	14	17	42	3	2	0	—	—	—	—	—

KOLTSOV, KONSTANTIN — LW — PENGUINS

PERSONAL: Born April 17, 1981, in Minsk, U.S.S.R. ... 6-0/190. ... Shoots left.
TRANSACTIONS/CAREER NOTES: Selected by Pittsburgh Penguins in 1st round (1st Penguins pick, 18th overall) of entry draft (June 26, 1999).

Season Team	League	REGULAR SEASON GP	G	A	Pts.	PIM	+/-	PP	SH	PLAYOFFS GP	G	A	Pts.	PIM
97-98—Minsk	Belarus	52	15	18	33	60	...	...	...	—	—	—	—	—
—Severstal Cherepovets	Russian	2	0	0	0	2	...	...	...	—	—	—	—	—
—Severstal-2 Cherep.	Rus. Div.	44	11	12	23	16	...	...	...	—	—	—	—	—
98-99—Severstal Cherepovets	Russian	33	3	0	3	8	...	...	...	1	0	0	0	2
99-00—Metal. Novokuznetsk	Russian	30	3	4	7	28	...	...	...	14	1	1	2	8
00-01—Ak Bars Kazan	Russian	24	7	8	15	10	...	...	...	2	0	0	0	4
01-02—Ak Bars Kazan	Russian	10	1	2	3	2	...	...	...	—	—	—	—	—
—Spartak Moscow	Russian	23	1	0	1	12	...	...	...	—	—	—	—	—
—Belarus Oly. team	Int'l	2	0	0	0	0	...	...	...	—	—	—	—	—
02-03—Pittsburgh	NHL	2	0	0	0	0	-2	0	0	—	—	—	—	—
—Wilkes-Barre/Scranton	AHL	65	9	21	30	41	-8	1	0	6	2	4	6	4
03-04—Pittsburgh	NHL	82	9	20	29	30	-30	2	0	—	—	—	—	—
—Wilkes-Barre/Scranton	AHL	3	0	4	4	4	3	0	0	24	6	11	17	18
04-05—Dynamo Minsk	Belarus	11	6	2	8	38	...	...	...	—	—	—	—	—
—Spartak Moscow	Russian	31	6	10	16	48	3	...	...	—	—	—	—	—
NHL Totals (2 years)		84	9	20	29	30	-32	2	0					

KOLZIG, OLAF — G — CAPITALS

PERSONAL: Born April 9, 1970, in Johannesburg, South Africa. ... 6-3/225. ... Catches left. ... Name pronounced OH-lahf KOHL-zihg.

TRANSACTIONS/CAREER NOTES: Selected by Washington Capitals in first round (first Capitals pick, 19th overall) of NHL draft (June 17, 1989). ... Dislocated kneecap (October 13, 1993); missed 14 games. ... Had mononucleosis (October 8, 1996); missed three games. ... Had knee surgery (September 26, 2000); missed first two games of regular season. ... Sprained ankle (December 14, 2001); missed one game. ... Injured knee (February 8, 2002); missed two games. ... Injured hand (October 30, 2002); missed four games. ... Injured groin (December 7, 2002); missed four games.

		REGULAR SEASON									PLAYOFFS							
Season Team	**League**	**GP**	**Min.**	**W**	**L**	**T**	**GA**	**SO**	**GAA**	**SV%**	**GP**	**Min.**	**W**	**L**	**GA**	**SO**	**GAA**	**SV%**
87-88—New Westminster	WHL	15	650	6	5	0	48	1	4.43	...	3	149	0	0	11	0	4.43	...
88-89—Tri-City	WHL	30	1671	16	10	2	97	1	*3.48	...	—	—	—	—	—	—	—	—
89-90—Washington	NHL	2	120	0	2	0	12	0	6.00	.810	—	—	—	—	—	—	—	—
—Tri-City	WHL	48	2504	27	27	3	187	1	4.48	...	6	318	4	0	27	0	5.09	...
90-91—Baltimore	AHL	26	1367	10	12	1	72	0	3.16	...	—	—	—	—	—	—	—	—
—Hampton Roads	ECHL	21	1248	11	9	1	71	2	3.41	...	3	180	1	2	14	0	4.67	...
91-92—Baltimore	AHL	28	1503	5	17	2	105	1	4.19	...	—	—	—	—	—	—	—	—
—Hampton Roads	ECHL	14	847	11	3	0	41	0	2.90	...	—	—	—	—	—	—	—	—
92-93—Rochester	AHL	49	2737	25	16	4	168	0	3.68	.882	17	*1040	9	8	61	0	3.52	.911
—Washington	NHL	1	20	0	0	0	2	0	6.00	.714	—	—	—	—	—	—	—	—
93-94—Portland	AHL	29	1726	16	8	5	88	3	3.06	.906	17	1035	12	5	44	0	2.55	.918
—Washington	NHL	7	224	0	3	0	20	0	5.36	.844	—	—	—	—	—	—	—	—
94-95—Washington	NHL	14	724	2	8	2	30	0	2.49	.902	2	44	1	0	1	0	1.36	.952
—Portland	AHL	2	125	1	0	1	3	0	1.44	.952	—	—	—	—	—	—	—	—
95-96—Washington	NHL	18	897	4	8	2	46	0	3.08	.887	5	341	2	3	11	0	*1.94	.934
—Portland	AHL	5	300	5	0	0	7	1	1.40	...	—	—	—	—	—	—	—	—
96-97—Washington	NHL	29	1645	8	15	4	71	2	2.59	.906	—	—	—	—	—	—	—	—
97-98—Washington	NHL	64	3788	33	18	10	139	5	2.20	.920	21	1351	12	9	44	*4	1.95	.941
—German Oly. team	Int'l	2	120	2	0	0	2	1	1.00	.966	—	—	—	—	—	—	—	—
98-99—Washington	NHL	64	3586	26	31	3	154	4	2.58	.900	—	—	—	—	—	—	—	—
99-00—Washington	NHL	73	*4371	41	20	11	163	5	2.24	.917	5	284	1	4	16	0	3.38	.845
00-01—Washington	NHL	72	4279	37	26	8	177	5	2.48	.909	6	375	2	4	14	1	2.24	.908
01-02—Washington	NHL	71	4131	31	29	8	*192	6	2.79	.903	—	—	—	—	—	—	—	—
02-03—Washington	NHL	66	3894	33	25	6	156	4	2.40	.919	6	404	2	4	14	1	2.08	.927
03-04—Washington	NHL	63	3738	19	35	9	180	2	2.89	.908	—	—	—	—	—	—	—	—
04-05—Eisbaren Berlin	Germany	8	452	...	...	...	19	2	2.52	.905	3	178	...	...	7	1	2.36	.879
NHL Totals (13 years)		544	31417	234	220	63	1342	33	2.56	.909	45	2799	20	24	100	6	2.14	.927

KOMADOSKI, NEIL — D — SENATORS

PERSONAL: Born February 10, 1982, in St. Louis. ... 6-1/212. ... Shoots left. ... Son of Neil Komadoski Sr., D with Los Angeles Kings (1972-78) and St. Louis Blues (1977-80).

TRANSACTIONS/CAREER NOTES: Selected by Ottawa Senators in third round (third Senators pick, 81st overall) of NHL draft (June 23, 2001).

		REGULAR SEASON								PLAYOFFS				
Season Team	**League**	**GP**	**G**	**A**	**Pts.**	**PIM**	**+/-**	**PP**	**SH**	**GP**	**G**	**A**	**Pts.**	**PIM**
00-01— Notre Dame	CCHA	30	2	5	7	106	...	...	...	—	—	—	—	—
01-02— Notre Dame	CCHA	37	2	9	11	100	...	...	...	—	—	—	—	—
02-03— Notre Dame	CCHA	40	1	23	24	46	...	...	...	—	—	—	—	—
03-04— Notre Dame	CCHA	39	5	15	20	48	...	...	...	—	—	—	—	—
—Binghamton	AHL	3	0	0	0	2	-1	0	0	1	0	0	0	0
04-05—Binghamton	AHL	36	2	1	3	68	-1	0	0	0	0	0	0	0

KOMARNISKI, ZENITH — D — BLUE JACKETS

PERSONAL: Born August 13, 1978, in Vegreville, Alta. ... 6-0/200. ... Shoots left. ... Name pronounced ZEH-nihth koh-mahr-NIH-skee.

TRANSACTIONS/CAREER NOTES: Selected by Vancouver Canucks in third round (second Canucks pick, 75th overall) of NHL entry draft (June 22, 1996). ... Injured shoulder (November 26, 1999); missed four games. ... Traded by Canucks to Columbus Blue Jackets for C Sean Pronger (October 30, 2003).

		REGULAR SEASON								PLAYOFFS				
Season Team	**League**	**GP**	**G**	**A**	**Pts.**	**PIM**	**+/-**	**PP**	**SH**	**GP**	**G**	**A**	**Pts.**	**PIM**
94-95—Tri-City	WHL	66	5	19	24	110	...	...	...	17	1	2	3	47
95-96—Tri-City	WHL	42	5	21	26	85	...	...	...	—	—	—	—	—
96-97—Tri-City	WHL	58	12	44	56	112	-13	8	0	—	—	—	—	—
97-98—Tri-City	WHL	3	0	4	4	18	...	...	...	—	—	—	—	—
—Spokane	WHL	43	7	20	27	90	...	...	...	18	4	6	10	49
98-99—Syracuse	AHL	58	9	19	28	89	-14	2	0	—	—	—	—	—
99-00—Syracuse	AHL	42	4	12	16	130	...	...	...	4	2	0	2	6
—Vancouver	NHL	18	1	1	2	8	-1	0	0	—	—	—	—	—
00-01—Kansas City	IHL	70	7	22	29	191	...	...	...	—	—	—	—	—
01-02—Manitoba	AHL	77	5	20	25	153	0	0	1	7	0	2	2	13
02-03—Vancouver	NHL	1	0	0	0	2	0	0	0	—	—	—	—	—
—Manitoba	AHL	53	15	8	23	94	-6	2	1	13	2	2	4	30
03-04—Manitoba	AHL	10	0	0	0	35	-2	0	0	—	—	—	—	—
—Columbus	NHL	2	0	0	0	0	0	0	0	—	—	—	—	—
—Syracuse	AHL	54	2	22	24	94	16	1	0	7	0	1	1	4
04-05—Syracuse	AHL	62	3	11	14	99	0	2	0	—	—	—	—	—
NHL Totals (3 years)		21	1	1	2	10	-1	0	0					

KOMISAREK, MIKE — D — CANADIENS

PERSONAL: Born January 19, 1982, in West Islip, N.Y. ... 6-4/237. ... Shoots right.
TRANSACTIONS/CAREER NOTES: Selected by Montreal Canadiens in first round (first Canadiens pick, seventh overall) of NHL entry draft (June 23, 2001).

		REGULAR SEASON								PLAYOFFS				
Season Team	League	GP	G	A	Pts.	PIM	+/-	PP	SH	GP	G	A	Pts.	PIM
99-00—U.S. National	USHL	51	5	8	13	124	...	...	...	—	—	—	—	—
00-01—Univ. of Michigan	CCHA	41	4	12	16	77	...	...	...	—	—	—	—	—
01-02—Univ. of Michigan	CCHA	39	11	19	30	68	...	...	...	—	—	—	—	—
02-03—Montreal	NHL	21	0	1	1	28	-6	0	0	—	—	—	—	—
—Hamilton	AHL	56	5	25	30	79	27	3	0	23	1	5	6	60
03-04—Hamilton	AHL	18	2	7	9	47	0	0	0	—	—	—	—	—
—Montreal	NHL	46	0	4	4	34	4	0	0	7	0	0	0	8
04-05—Hamilton	AHL	20	1	4	5	49	6	1	0	4	0	1	1	8
NHL Totals (2 years)		67	0	5	5	62	-2	0	0	7	0	0	0	8

KONDRATIEV, MAXIM — D — RANGERS

PERSONAL: Born January 20, 1983, in Togliatti, U.S.S.R. ... 6-1/176. ... Shoots left.
TRANSACTIONS/CAREER NOTES: Selected by Toronto Maple Leafs in sixth round (seventh Leafs pick, 168th overall) of NHL draft (June 24, 2001). ... Traded by Maple Leafs with C Jarkko Immonen, first-round pick in 2004 draft (traded to Calgary; Flames selected RW Kris Chucko) and second-round pick in 2005 draft to New York Rangers for D Brian Leetch and future considerations (March 3, 2004).

		REGULAR SEASON								PLAYOFFS				
Season Team	League	GP	G	A	Pts.	PIM	+/-	PP	SH	GP	G	A	Pts.	PIM
01-02—Lada Togliatti	Russian	43	3	3	6	32	...	...	...	4	0	0	0	0
02-03—Lada Togliatti	Russian	47	2	3	5	56	...	...	...	10	0	0	0	6
03-04—Toronto	NHL	7	0	0	0	2	0	0	0	—	—	—	—	—
—St. John's	AHL	18	3	5	8	10	4	1	0	—	—	—	—	—
04-05—Lada Togliatti	Russian	32	2	4	6	65	12	...	...	5	0	2	2	0
—Hartford	AHL	13	1	4	5	8	-1	1	0	—	—	—	—	—
NHL Totals (1 year)		7	0	0	0	2	0	0	0					

KONOWALCHUK, STEVE — LW — AVALANCHE

PERSONAL: Born November 11, 1972, in Salt Lake City, Utah. ... 6-2/204. ... Shoots left. ... Name pronounced kah-nah-WAHL-chuhk.
TRANSACTIONS/CAREER NOTES: Selected by Washington Capitals in third round (fifth Capitals pick, 58th overall) of NHL draft (June 22, 1991). ... Separated shoulder (October 13, 1995); missed four games. ... Injured left hand (March 26, 1996); missed eight games. ... Separated rib cartilage; missed four games of 1996-97 season. ... Strained groin (January 28, 1998); missed two games. ... Sprained ankle (October 10, 1998); missed 15 games. ... Suffered concussion (March 2, 1999); missed remainder of season. ... Injured shoulder (October 13, 2001) and had surgery; missed 54 games. ... Injured groin (January 25, 2003); missed three games. ... Injured foot (March 22, 2003); missed one game. ... Injured foot (April 5, 2003); missed one game. ... Traded by Capitals with a third-round pick (later traded to Carolina Hurricanes) in 2004 draft to Colorado Avalanche for LW Bates Battaglia and RW Jonas Johansson (October 22, 2003).
STATISTICAL PLATEAUS: Three-goal games: 1995-96 (2), 2000-01 (1). Total: 3.

		REGULAR SEASON								PLAYOFFS				
Season Team	League	GP	G	A	Pts.	PIM	+/-	PP	SH	GP	G	A	Pts.	PIM
90-91—Portland	WHL	72	43	49	92	78	...	...	...	—	—	—	—	—
91-92—Portland	WHL	64	51	53	104	95	...	...	...	6	3	6	9	12
—Baltimore	AHL	3	1	1	2	0	...	...	...	—	—	—	—	—
—Washington	NHL	1	0	0	0	0	0	0	0	—	—	—	—	—
92-93—Baltimore	AHL	37	18	28	46	74	2	4	1	—	—	—	—	—
—Washington	NHL	36	4	7	11	16	4	1	0	2	0	1	1	0
93-94—Portland	AHL	8	11	4	15	4	6	3	1	—	—	—	—	—
—Washington	NHL	62	12	14	26	33	9	0	0	11	0	1	1	10
94-95—Washington	NHL	46	11	14	25	44	7	3	3	7	2	5	7	12
95-96—Washington	NHL	70	23	22	45	92	13	7	1	2	0	2	2	0
96-97—Washington	NHL	78	17	25	42	67	-3	2	1	—	—	—	—	—
97-98—Washington	NHL	80	10	24	34	80	9	2	0	—	—	—	—	—
98-99—Washington	NHL	45	12	12	24	26	0	4	1	—	—	—	—	—
99-00—Washington	NHL	82	16	27	43	80	19	3	0	5	1	0	1	2
00-01—Washington	NHL	82	24	23	47	87	8	6	0	6	2	3	5	14
01-02—Washington	NHL	28	2	12	14	23	-2	0	0	—	—	—	—	—
02-03—Washington	NHL	77	15	15	30	71	3	2	0	6	0	0	0	6
03-04—Washington	NHL	6	0	1	1	0	-5	0	0	—	—	—	—	—
—Colorado	NHL	76	19	20	39	70	2	3	0	11	4	0	4	12
NHL Totals (13 years)		769	165	216	381	689	64	33	6	50	9	12	21	56

KOPECKY, TOMAS — C — RED WINGS

PERSONAL: Born February 5, 1982, in Ilava, Czech. ... 6-3/187. ... Shoots left.
TRANSACTIONS/CAREER NOTES: Selected by Detroit Red Wings in second round (second Red Wings pick, 38th overall) of NHL draft (June 24, 2000).

		REGULAR SEASON								PLAYOFFS				
Season Team	League	GP	G	A	Pts.	PIM	+/-	PP	SH	GP	G	A	Pts.	PIM
98-99—Dukla Trencin	Slovakia Jrs.	44	13	16	29	...	...	...	...	—	—	—	—	—
99-00—Dukla Trencin	Slovakia	52	3	4	7	24	...	...	...	5	0	0	0	0
—Dukla Trencin	Slovakia Jrs.	12	11	13	24	10	...	...	...	—	—	—	—	—

Season Team	League	GP	G	A	Pts.	PIM	+/-	PP	SH	GP	G	A	Pts.	PIM
		REGULAR SEASON								PLAYOFFS				
00-01—Lethbridge	WHL	49	22	28	50	52	...	...	...	5	1	1	2	6
—Cincinnati	AHL	1	0	0	0	0	...	...	...	—	—	—	—	—
01-02—Lethbridge	WHL	60	34	42	76	94	...	...	...	4	2	1	3	15
—Cincinnati	AHL	2	1	1	2	6	1	0	0	2	0	0	0	0
02-03—Grand Rapids	AHL	70	17	21	38	32	18	3	0	14	0	0	0	6
03-04—Grand Rapids	AHL	48	6	6	12	28	-3	2	0	1	0	0	0	2
04-05—Grand Rapids	AHL	48	8	8	16	35	1	2	0	—	—	—	—	—

KOPITAR, ANZE C KINGS

PERSONAL: Born August 24, 1987, in Jesenice, Slovenia. ... 6-3/202. ... Shoots left.
TRANSACTIONS/CAREER NOTES: Selected by Los Angeles Kings in 1st round (1st Kings pick, 11th overall) of entry draft (July 30, 2005).

Season Team	League	GP	G	A	Pts.	PIM	+/-	PP	SH	GP	G	A	Pts.	PIM
		REGULAR SEASON								PLAYOFFS				
04-05—Sodertalje	Sweden Dv. 2	30	28	21	49	26	...	...	...	—	—	—	—	—

KORHONEN, RISTO D HURRICANES

PERSONAL: Born November 27, 1986, in Kajaani, Finland. ... 6-3/202. ... Shoots left.

Season Team	League	GP	G	A	Pts.	PIM	+/-	PP	SH	GP	G	A	Pts.	PIM
		REGULAR SEASON								PLAYOFFS				
03-04—Karpat Oulu	Finland Div. 2	36	1	3	4	30	...	...	...	—	—	—	—	—
04-05—Karpat Oulu	Finland Div. 2	36	5	12	17	73	...	...	...	—	—	—	—	—

KOROLEV, IGOR C/LW

PERSONAL: Born September 6, 1970, in Moscow, U.S.S.R. ... 6-1/196. ... Shoots left. ... Name pronounced EE-gohr KOHR-ih-lehv.
TRANSACTIONS/CAREER NOTES: Selected by St. Louis Blues in second round (first Blues pick, 38th overall) of NHL draft (June 20, 1992). ... Flu (March 3, 1994); missed one game. ... Injured hip (March 12, 1994); missed three games. ... Selected by Winnipeg Jets in waiver draft (January 18, 1995). ... Played in Europe during 1994-95 NHL lockout. ... Fractured wrist (December 10, 1995); missed two games. ... Had hip pointer (February 1, 1996); missed three games. ... Jets franchise moved to Phoenix and renamed Coyotes for 1996-97 season; NHL approved move on January 18, 1996. ... Signed as free agent by Toronto Maple Leafs (September 28, 1997). ... Sprained shoulder (October 28, 1997); missed one game. ... Strained back (January 6, 1998); missed one game. ... Back spasms (January 9, 1999); missed three games. ... Fractured finger (March 20, 1999); missed 13 games. ... Fractured leg (April 22, 1999); missed remainder of playoffs. ... Injured (October 13, 1999); missed two games. ... Injured (February 8, 2001); missed five games. ... Traded by Maple Leafs to Chicago Blackhawks for third-round pick (C Nicolas Corbeil) in 2001 draft (June 23, 2001). ... Injured groin (November 20, 2002); missed four games.
STATISTICAL PLATEAUS: Three-goal games: 1995-96 (1).

Season Team	League	GP	G	A	Pts.	PIM	+/-	PP	SH	GP	G	A	Pts.	PIM
		REGULAR SEASON								PLAYOFFS				
88-89—Dynamo Moscow	USSR	1	0	0	0	2	...	...	...	—	—	—	—	—
89-90—Dynamo Moscow	USSR	17	3	2	5	2	...	...	...	—	—	—	—	—
90-91—Dynamo Moscow	USSR	38	12	4	16	12	...	...	...	—	—	—	—	—
91-92—Dynamo Moscow	CIS	39	15	12	27	16	...	...	...	—	—	—	—	—
92-93—Dynamo Moscow	CIS	5	1	2	3	4	...	...	...	—	—	—	—	—
—St. Louis	NHL	74	4	23	27	20	-1	2	0	3	0	0	0	0
93-94—St. Louis	NHL	73	6	10	16	40	-12	0	0	2	0	0	0	0
94-95—Dynamo Moscow	CIS	13	4	6	10	18	...	...	...	—	—	—	—	—
—Winnipeg	NHL	45	8	22	30	10	1	1	0	—	—	—	—	—
95-96—Winnipeg	NHL	73	22	29	51	42	1	8	0	6	0	3	3	0
96-97—Michigan	IHL	4	2	2	4	0	...	...	...	—	—	—	—	—
—Phoenix	IHL	4	2	6	8	4	...	...	...	—	—	—	—	—
—Phoenix	NHL	41	3	7	10	28	-5	2	0	1	0	0	0	0
97-98—Toronto	NHL	78	17	22	39	22	-18	6	3	—	—	—	—	—
98-99—Toronto	NHL	66	13	34	47	46	11	1	0	1	0	0	0	0
99-00—Toronto	NHL	80	20	26	46	22	12	5	3	12	0	4	4	6
00-01—Toronto	NHL	73	10	19	29	28	3	2	0	11	0	0	0	0
01-02—Chicago	NHL	82	9	20	29	20	-5	0	1	5	0	1	1	0
02-03—Chicago	NHL	48	4	5	9	30	-1	1	0	—	—	—	—	—
—Norfolk	AHL	14	4	3	7	0	0	1	0	9	2	4	6	4
03-04—Chicago	NHL	62	3	10	13	22	-15	0	0	—	—	—	—	—
—Norfolk	AHL	10	1	4	5	4	-1	1	0	—	—	—	—	—
04-05—Lokomotiv Yaroslavl	Russian	60	8	20	28	28	6	...	...	9	1	6	7	2
NHL Totals (12 years)		795	119	227	346	330	-29	28	7	41	0	8	8	6

KOROLYUK, ALEXANDER LW SHARKS

PERSONAL: Born January 15, 1976, in Moscow, U.S.S.R. ... 5-9/195. ... Shoots left. ... Name pronounced KOH-rohl-yook.
TRANSACTIONS/CAREER NOTES: Selected by San Jose Sharks in sixth round (sixth Sharks pick, 141st overall) of NHL draft (June 29, 1994). ... Injured eye (December 2, 1999); missed three games. ... Injured back (January 19, 2000); missed eight games. ... Reinjured back (February 11, 2000); missed four games. ... Signed as free agent by AK Bars Kazan of Russian league (July 9, 2002). ... Signed as free agent by Sharks (June 21, 2003). ... Injured leg (November 6, 2003); missed three games. ... Injured leg (November 21, 2003); misssed six games.

Season Team	League	GP	G	A	Pts.	PIM	+/-	PP	SH	GP	G	A	Pts.	PIM
		REGULAR SEASON								PLAYOFFS				
93-94—Soviet Wings	CIS	22	4	4	8	20	...	...	...	3	1	0	1	4
94-95—Soviet Wings	CIS	52	16	13	29	62	...	...	...	4	1	2	3	4

Season Team	League	GP	G	A	Pts.	PIM	+/-	PP	SH	GP	G	A	Pts.	PIM
		REGULAR SEASON								PLAYOFFS				
95-96—Soviet Wings	CIS	50	30	19	49	77	...	...	...	—	—	—	—	—
96-97—Soviet Wings	CIS	17	8	5	13	46	...	...	...	—	—	—	—	—
—Manitoba	IHL	42	20	16	36	71	...	...	...	—	—	—	—	—
97-98—San Jose	NHL	19	2	3	5	6	-5	1	0	—	—	—	—	—
—Kentucky	AHL	44	16	23	39	96	-2	3	0	3	0	0	0	0
98-99—Kentucky	AHL	23	9	13	22	16	2	2	0	—	—	—	—	—
—San Jose	NHL	55	12	18	30	26	3	2	0	6	1	3	4	2
99-00—San Jose	NHL	57	14	21	35	35	4	3	0	9	0	3	3	6
00-01—Ak Bars Kazan	Russian	6	0	5	5	4	...	...	...	—	—	—	—	—
—San Jose	NHL	70	12	13	25	41	2	3	0	2	0	0	0	0
01-02—San Jose	NHL	32	3	7	10	14	2	0	0	—	—	—	—	—
02-03—Kazan	Rus. Div.	46	14	17	31	122	...	...	...	17	1	6	7	8
03-04—San Jose	NHL	63	19	18	37	18	20	4	0	17	5	2	7	10
04-05—Vityaz Podolsk	Russian	42	24	28	52	54	10	...	...	—	—	—	—	—
—Khimik Voskresensk	Russian	10	4	3	7	14	0	...	...	—	—	—	—	—
NHL Totals (6 years)		296	62	80	142	140	26	13	0	34	6	8	14	18

KORPIKOSKI, LAURI — LW — RANGERS

PERSONAL: Born July 28, 1986, in Turku, Finland. ... 6-1/183. ... Shoots left.

TRANSACTIONS/CAREER NOTES: Selected by New York Rangers in first round (second Rangers pick, 19th overall) of NHL entry draft (June 26, 2004).

Season Team	League	GP	G	A	Pts.	PIM	+/-	PP	SH	GP	G	A	Pts.	PIM
		REGULAR SEASON								PLAYOFFS				
03-04—TPS Turku	Finland Jr.	36	12	8	20	26	...	...	...	—	—	—	—	—
04-05—TPS Turku	Finland Jr.	41	0	6	6	12	...	...	...	6	1	0	1	0

KOSTOPOULOS, TOM — RW — KINGS

PERSONAL: Born January 24, 1979, in Mississauga, Ont. ... 6-0/200. ... Shoots right.

TRANSACTIONS/CAREER NOTES: Selected by Pittsburgh Penguins in 9th round (9th Penguins pick, 204th overall) of entry draft (June 26, 1999). ... Signed as free agent by Manchester of the AHL (July 12, 2004). ... Signed as free agent by Los Angeles Kings (Aug. 1, 2005).

Season Team	League	GP	G	A	Pts.	PIM	+/-	PP	SH	GP	G	A	Pts.	PIM
		REGULAR SEASON								PLAYOFFS				
96-97—London	OHL	64	13	12	25	67	...	...	...	—	—	—	—	—
97-98—London	OHL	66	24	26	50	108	...	...	...	16	6	4	10	26
98-99—London	OHL	66	27	60	87	114	...	...	...	25	19	16	35	32
99-00—Wilkes-Barre/Scranton	AHL	76	26	32	58	121	...	...	...	—	—	—	—	—
00-01—Wilkes-Barre/Scranton	AHL	80	16	36	52	120	...	...	...	21	3	9	12	6
01-02—Wilkes-Barre/Scranton	AHL	70	27	26	53	112	-1	10	2	—	—	—	—	—
—Pittsburgh	NHL	11	1	2	3	9	-1	0	0	—	—	—	—	—
02-03—Pittsburgh	NHL	8	0	1	1	0	-4	0	0	—	—	—	—	—
—Wilkes-Barre/Scranton	AHL	71	21	42	63	131	-4	9	0	6	1	2	3	7
03-04—Pittsburgh	NHL	60	9	13	22	67	-14	2	1	—	—	—	—	—
—Wilkes-Barre/Scranton	AHL	21	7	13	20	43	13	1	0	24	7	16	23	32
04-05—Manchester	AHL	64	25	46	71	99	30	9	2	6	0	7	7	10
NHL Totals (3 years)		79	10	16	26	76	-19	2	1					

KOTALIK, ALES — RW/LW — SABRES

PERSONAL: Born December 23, 1978, in Jindrichuv Hradec, Czechoslovakia. ... 6-1/227. ... Shoots right.

TRANSACTIONS/CAREER NOTES: Selected by Buffalo Sabres in sixth round (seventh Sabres pick, 164th overall) of NHL entry draft (June 27, 1998). ... Flu (March 28, 2003); missed three games. ... Injured shoulder (February 27, 2004); missed final 19 games of season.

Season Team	League	GP	G	A	Pts.	PIM	+/-	PP	SH	GP	G	A	Pts.	PIM
		REGULAR SEASON								PLAYOFFS				
93-94—HC Ceske Budejovice	Czech. Jrs.	28	12	12	24	...	...	...	...	—	—	—	—	—
94-95—HC Ceske Budejovice	Czech. Jrs.	36	26	17	43	...	...	...	...	—	—	—	—	—
95-96—HC Ceske Budejovice	Czech. Jrs.	28	6	7	13	...	...	...	...	—	—	—	—	—
96-97—HC Ceske Budejovice	Czech. Jrs.	36	15	16	31	24	...	...	...	—	—	—	—	—
97-98—ZPS Zlin	Czech.	47	9	7	16	14	...	...	...	—	—	—	—	—
98-99—HC Ceske Budejovice	Czech Rep.	41	8	13	21	16	4	...	...	3	0	0	0	0
99-00—HC Ceske Budejovice	Czech Rep.	43	7	12	19	34	...	...	...	3	0	1	1	6
00-01—HC Ceske Budejovice	Czech Rep.	52	19	29	48	54	...	...	...	—	—	—	—	—
01-02—Rochester	AHL	68	18	25	43	55	-2	5	0	1	0	0	0	0
—Buffalo	NHL	13	1	3	4	2	-1	0	0	—	—	—	—	—
02-03—Rochester	AHL	8	0	2	2	4	-5	0	0	—	—	—	—	—
—Buffalo	NHL	68	21	14	35	30	-2	4	0	—	—	—	—	—
03-04—Buffalo	NHL	62	15	11	26	41	-1	2	0	—	—	—	—	—
04-05—Liberec	Czech Rep.	25	8	8	16	46	10	...	...	12	2	5	7	12
NHL Totals (3 years)		143	37	28	65	73	-4	6	0					

KOVALCHUK, ILYA — LW — THRASHERS

PERSONAL: Born April 15, 1983, in Tver, U.S.S.R. ... 6-1/220. ... Shoots right.

TRANSACTIONS/CAREER NOTES: Selected by Atlanta Thrashers in first round (first Thrashers pick, first overall) of NHL draft (June 23, 2001). ... Injured shoulder (March 10, 2002); missed remainder of season.

STATISTICAL PLATEAUS: Three-goal games: 2002-03 (1), 2003-04 (2). Total: 3.

		REGULAR SEASON								PLAYOFFS				
Season Team	**League**	**GP**	**G**	**A**	**Pts.**	**PIM**	**+/-**	**PP**	**SH**	**GP**	**G**	**A**	**Pts.**	**PIM**
00-01—Spartak	Russian Div. 1	40	28	18	46	78	...	...	...	—	—	—	—	—
01-02—Atlanta	NHL	65	29	22	51	28	-19	7	0	—	—	—	—	—
—Russian Oly. team	Int'l	6	1	2	3	14	...	...	...	—	—	—	—	—
02-03—Atlanta	NHL	81	38	29	67	57	-24	9	0	—	—	—	—	—
03-04—Atlanta	NHL	81	41	46	87	63	-10	16	1	—	—	—	—	—
04-05—Ak Bars Kazan	Russian	53	19	23	42	72	16	...	...	4	0	1	1	0
NHL Totals (3 years)		227	108	97	205	148	-53	32	1					

KOVALEV, ALEXEI — RW — CANADIENS

PERSONAL: Born February 24, 1973, in Togliatti, U.S.S.R. ... 6-2/220. ... Shoots left. ... Name pronounced KOH-vuh-lahf.

TRANSACTIONS/CAREER NOTES: Selected by New York Rangers in 1st round (1st Rangers pick, 15th overall) of entry draft (June 22, 1991). ... Back spasms (January 16, 1993); missed one game. ... Suspended one game (November 10, 1993). ... Suspended five games for tripping (November 30, 1993). ... Suspended two games (February 12, 1994). ... Flu (December 2, 1995); missed one game. ... Torn knee ligament (January 8, 1997); missed remainder of season. ... Sprained knee and had arthroscopic surgery (January 22, 1998); missed eight games. ... Separated shoulder (October 27, 1998); missed five games. ... Bruised shoulder (November 21, 1998); missed one game. ... Traded by Rangers with C Harry York and future considerations to Pittsburgh Penguins for C Petr Nedved, C Sean Pronger and D Chris Tamer (November 25, 1998). ... Bruised shoulder (November 21, 1998); missed one game. ... Suspended three games for unsportsmanlike conduct (March 24, 2001). ... Knee surgery (October 16, 2001); missed 13 games. ... Injured hip (April 6, 2002); missed one game. ... Reinjured hip (April 12, 2002); missed remainder of season. ... Bruised arm (December 7, 2003); missed one game. ... Traded by Penguins with LW Dan LaCouture, D Janne Laukkanen and D Mike Wilson to Rangers for RW Rico Fata, RW Mikael Samuelsson, D Joel Bouchard, D Richard Lintner and cash (February 10, 2003). ... Traded by Rangers to Montreal Canadiens for RW Jozef Balej and 2nd-round pick (C Bruce Graham) in 2004 draft (March 2, 2004). ... Signed as free agent by Canadiens (Aug. 3, 2005).

STATISTICAL PLATEAUS: Three-goal games: 1992-93 (1), 1996-97 (1), 2000-01 (4), 2001-02 (3), 2002-03 (1). Total: 10.

		REGULAR SEASON								PLAYOFFS				
Season Team	**League**	**GP**	**G**	**A**	**Pts.**	**PIM**	**+/-**	**PP**	**SH**	**GP**	**G**	**A**	**Pts.**	**PIM**
89-90—Dynamo Moscow	USSR	1	0	0	0	0	...	...	...	—	—	—	—	—
90-91—Dynamo Moscow	USSR	18	1	2	3	4	...	...	...	—	—	—	—	—
91-92—Dynamo Moscow	CIS	33	16	9	25	20	...	...	...	—	—	—	—	—
—Unif. Olympic team	Int'l	8	1	2	3	14	4	0	0	—	—	—	—	—
92-93—New York Rangers	NHL	65	20	18	38	79	-10	3	0	—	—	—	—	—
—Binghamton	AHL	13	13	11	24	35	12	8	0	9	3	5	8	14
93-94—New York Rangers	NHL	76	23	33	56	154	18	7	0	23	9	12	21	18
94-95—Lada Togliatti	CIS	12	8	8	16	49	...	...	...	—	—	—	—	—
—New York Rangers	NHL	48	13	15	28	30	-6	1	1	10	4	7	11	10
95-96—New York Rangers	NHL	81	24	34	58	98	5	8	1	11	3	4	7	14
96-97—New York Rangers	NHL	45	13	22	35	42	11	1	0	—	—	—	—	—
97-98—New York Rangers	NHL	73	23	30	53	44	-22	8	0	—	—	—	—	—
98-99—New York Rangers	NHL	14	3	4	7	12	-6	1	0	—	—	—	—	—
—Pittsburgh	NHL	63	20	26	46	37	8	5	1	10	5	7	12	14
99-00—Pittsburgh	NHL	82	26	40	66	94	-3	9	2	11	1	5	6	10
00-01—Pittsburgh	NHL	79	44	51	95	96	12	12	2	18	5	5	10	16
01-02—Pittsburgh	NHL	67	32	44	76	80	2	8	1	—	—	—	—	—
—Russian Oly. team	Int'l	6	3	1	4	4	...	...	...	—	—	—	—	—
02-03—Pittsburgh	NHL	54	27	37	64	50	-11	8	0	...	...	...	...	...
—New York Rangers	NHL	24	10	3	13	20	2	3	0	—	—	—	—	—
03-04—New York Rangers	NHL	66	13	29	42	54	-5	3	0	—	—	—	—	—
—Montreal	NHL	12	1	2	3	12	-4	0	0	11	6	4	10	8
04-05—Ak Bars Kazan	Russian	35	10	11	21	80	-1	...	...	4	0	0	0	8
NHL Totals (12 years)		849	292	388	680	902	-9	77	8	94	33	44	77	90

KOZLOV, VIKTOR — RW/C — DEVILS

PERSONAL: Born February 14, 1975, in Togliatti, U.S.S.R. ... 6-5/233. ... Shoots right. ... Name pronounced KAHZ-lahf.

TRANSACTIONS/CAREER NOTES: Selected by San Jose Sharks in first round (first Sharks pick, sixth overall) of NHL draft (June 26, 1993). ... Fractured ankle (November 27, 1994); missed 13 games. ... Played in Europe during 1994-95 NHL lockout. ... Bruised ankle (March 26, 1997); missed four games. ... Traded by Sharks with fifth-round pick (D Jaroslav Spacek) in 1998 draft to Florida Panthers for LW Dave Lowry and first-round pick (traded to Tampa Bay; Lightning selected C Vincent Lecavalier) in 1998 draft (November 13, 1997). ... Separated right shoulder (November 18, 1997); missed 16 games. ... Had concussion (April 1, 1998); missed three games. ... Separated shoulder (October 30, 1998); missed six games. ... Reinjured shoulder (January 8, 1999); missed one game. ... Strained shoulder (January 20, 1999); missed three games. ... Fractured finger (April 3, 1999); missed final seven games of season. ... Sprained shoulder (March 8, 2000); missed two games. ... Injured shoulder (October 25, 2000); missed six games. ... Injured left shoulder (December 13, 2000); missed nine games. ... Injured groin (March 14, 2001); missed five games. ... Reinjured groin (March 28, 2001); missed final five games of season. ... Injured groin and hip (December 6, 2001); missed seven games. ... Strained muscle in abdomen (February 9, 2002); missed remainder of season. ... Injured groin (October 15, 2002); missed eight games. ... Injured face (November 11, 2003); missed four games. ... Injured toe (January 17, 2004); missed two games. ... Injured thumb (January 28, 2004); missed four games. ... Had concussion (February 18, 2004); missed 15 games. ... Traded by Panthers to New Jersey Devils for F Christian Berglund and D Victor Uchevatov (March 1, 2004). ... Injured (April 10, 2004); missed one playoff game.

STATISTICAL PLATEAUS: Three-goal games: 1999-00 (1).

		REGULAR SEASON								PLAYOFFS				
Season Team	**League**	**GP**	**G**	**A**	**Pts.**	**PIM**	**+/-**	**PP**	**SH**	**GP**	**G**	**A**	**Pts.**	**PIM**
90-91—Lada Togliatti	USSR Div.	2	2	0	2	0	...	...	...	—	—	—	—	—
91-92—Lada Togliatti	CIS	3	0	0	0	0	...	...	...	—	—	—	—	—
92-93—Dynamo Moscow	CIS	30	6	5	11	4	...	...	...	10	3	0	3	0
93-94—Dynamo Moscow	CIS	42	16	9	25	14	...	...	...	7	3	2	5	0

Season Team	League	GP	G	A	Pts.	PIM	+/-	PP	SH	GP	G	A	Pts.	PIM
		REGULAR SEASON								PLAYOFFS				
94-95—Dynamo Moscow	CIS	3	1	1	2	2	...	...	...	—	—	—	—	—
—San Jose	NHL	16	2	0	2	2	-5	0	0	—	—	—	—	—
—Kansas City	IHL	...	...	...	...	...	...	...	...	13	4	5	9	12
95-96—Kansas City	IHL	15	4	7	11	12	...	...	...	—	—	—	—	—
—San Jose	NHL	62	6	13	19	6	-15	1	0	—	—	—	—	—
96-97—San Jose	NHL	78	16	25	41	40	-16	4	0	—	—	—	—	—
97-98—San Jose	NHL	18	5	2	7	2	-2	2	0	—	—	—	—	—
—Florida	NHL	46	12	11	23	14	-1	3	2	—	—	—	—	—
98-99—Florida	NHL	65	16	35	51	24	13	5	1	—	—	—	—	—
99-00—Florida	NHL	80	17	53	70	16	24	6	0	4	0	1	1	0
00-01—Florida	NHL	51	14	23	37	10	-4	6	0	—	—	—	—	—
01-02—Florida	NHL	50	9	18	27	20	-16	6	0	—	—	—	—	—
02-03—Florida	NHL	74	22	34	56	18	-8	7	1	—	—	—	—	—
03-04—Florida	NHL	48	11	16	27	16	-4	3	1	—	—	—	—	—
—New Jersey	NHL	11	2	4	6	2	0	0	0	2	0	0	0	0
04-05—Lada Togliatti	Russian	52	15	22	37	22	19	...	...	10	3	3	6	6
NHL Totals (10 years)		599	132	234	366	170	-34	43	5	6	0	1	1	0

KOZLOV, SLAVA — LW — THRASHERS

PERSONAL: Born May 3, 1972, in Voskresensk, U.S.S.R. ... 5-10/185. ... Shoots left. ... Name pronounced VYACH-ih-slav KAHS-lahf.

TRANSACTIONS/CAREER NOTES: Selected by Detroit Red Wings in third round (second Red Wings pick, 45th overall) of NHL draft (June 16, 1990). ... Played in Europe during 1994-95 NHL lockout. ... Bruised left foot (April 16, 1995); missed one game. ... Sprained knee (April 15, 1998); missed two games. ... Suspended three games by NHL for elbowing incident (December 18, 1998). ... Injured ankle (December 22, 1999); missed three games. ... Reinjured ankle (January 4, 2000); missed four games. ... Had concussion (March 29, 2000); missed two games. ... Traded by Red Wings with first-round pick (traded to Columbus; traded to Atlanta; Thrashers selected C Jim Slater) in 2002 draft and future considerations to Buffalo Sabres for G Dominik Hasek (July 1, 2001). ... Injured Achilles' tendon (December 29, 2001); missed remainder of season. ... Traded by Sabres with second-round pick (traded to Nashville; Predators selected LW Konstantin Glazachev) in 2002 draft to Atlanta Thrashers for second-(traded to Florida; Panthers selected C Kamil Kreps) and third-round (traded to Phoenix; Coyotes selected C Tyler Redenbach) picks in 2002 draft (June 22, 2002). ... Suspended three games by NHL for abuse of official (January 3, 2003). ... Injured shoulder (February 16, 2004); missed six games.

STATISTICAL PLATEAUS: Three-goal games: 1993-94 (1), 1998-99 (1). Total: 2. ... Four-goal games: 1995-96 (1). ... Total hat tricks: 3.

Season Team	League	GP	G	A	Pts.	PIM	+/-	PP	SH	GP	G	A	Pts.	PIM
		REGULAR SEASON								PLAYOFFS				
87-88—Khimik	USSR	2	0	1	1	0	...	...	...	—	—	—	—	—
88-89—Khimik	USSR	13	0	1	1	2	...	...	...	—	—	—	—	—
89-90—Khimik	USSR	45	14	12	26	38	...	...	...	—	—	—	—	—
90-91—Khimik	USSR	45	11	13	24	46	...	...	...	—	—	—	—	—
91-92—Khimik	USSR	11	6	5	11	12	...	...	...	—	—	—	—	—
—Detroit	NHL	7	0	2	2	2	-2	0	0	—	—	—	—	—
92-93—Detroit	NHL	17	4	1	5	14	-1	0	0	4	0	2	2	2
—Adirondack	AHL	45	23	36	59	54	10	1	2	4	1	1	2	4
93-94—Detroit	NHL	77	34	39	73	50	27	8	2	7	2	5	7	12
—Adirondack	AHL	3	0	1	1	15	-1	0	0	—	—	—	—	—
94-95—CSKA Moscow	CIS	10	3	4	7	14	...	...	...	—	—	—	—	—
—Detroit	NHL	46	13	20	33	45	12	5	0	18	9	7	16	10
95-96—Detroit	NHL	82	36	37	73	70	33	9	0	19	5	7	12	10
96-97—Detroit	NHL	75	23	22	45	46	21	3	0	20	8	5	13	14
97-98—Detroit	NHL	80	25	27	52	46	14	6	0	22	6	8	14	10
98-99—Detroit	NHL	79	29	29	58	45	10	6	1	10	6	1	7	4
99-00—Detroit	NHL	72	18	18	36	28	11	4	0	8	2	1	3	12
00-01—Detroit	NHL	72	20	18	38	30	9	4	0	6	4	1	5	2
01-02—Buffalo	NHL	38	9	13	22	16	0	3	0	—	—	—	—	—
02-03—Atlanta	NHL	79	21	49	70	66	-10	9	1	—	—	—	—	—
03-04—Atlanta	NHL	76	20	32	52	74	-12	6	0	—	—	—	—	—
04-05—Khimik Voskresensk	Russian	38	12	18	30	69	1	...	...	—	—	—	—	—
—Ak Bars Kazan	Russian	8	2	4	6	0	0	...	...	4	1	0	1	8
NHL Totals (13 years)		800	252	307	559	532	112	63	4	114	42	37	79	76

KRAFT, MILAN — C — PENGUINS

PERSONAL: Born January 17, 1980, in Plzen, Czechoslovakia. ... 6-3/214. ... Shoots right.

TRANSACTIONS/CAREER NOTES: Selected by Pittsburgh Penguins in first round (first Penguins pick, 23rd overall) of NHL draft (June 27, 1998). ... Injured groin (February 15, 2003); missed five games.

Season Team	League	GP	G	A	Pts.	PIM	+/-	PP	SH	GP	G	A	Pts.	PIM
		REGULAR SEASON								PLAYOFFS				
96-97—Plzen	Czech. Jrs.	36	26	17	43	...	...	...	...	—	—	—	—	—
—ZKZ Plzen	Czech Rep.	9	0	1	1	2	...	...	...	—	—	—	—	—
97-98—Plzen	Czech. Jrs.	24	22	23	45	12	...	...	...	—	—	—	—	—
—ZKZ Plzen	Czech Rep.	16	0	5	5	0	...	...	...	—	—	—	—	—
98-99—Prince Albert	WHL	68	40	46	86	32	25	14	1	14	7	13	20	6
99-00—Prince Albert	WHL	56	34	35	69	42	-5	12	0	6	4	1	5	4
00-01—Pittsburgh	NHL	42	7	7	14	8	-6	1	1	8	0	0	0	2
—Wilkes-Barre/Scranton	AHL	40	21	23	44	27	...	...	...	14	12	7	19	6
01-02—Pittsburgh	NHL	68	8	8	16	16	-9	1	0	—	—	—	—	—
—Wilkes-Barre/Scranton	AHL	8	4	4	8	10	8	0	0	—	—	—	—	—
02-03—Pittsburgh	NHL	31	7	5	12	10	-8	0	0	—	—	—	—	—

Season Team	League	REGULAR SEASON GP	G	A	Pts.	PIM	+/-	PP	SH	PLAYOFFS GP	G	A	Pts.	PIM
—Wilkes-Barre/Scranton	AHL	40	13	24	37	28	-16	4	0	6	2	4	6	4
03-04—Pittsburgh	NHL	66	19	21	40	18	-22	6	0	—	—	—	—	—
04-05—Plzen	Czech Rep.	17	2	4	6	6	2	...	...	—	—	—	—	—
—Karlovy Vary	Czech Rep.	35	9	10	19	20	-6	...	...	—	—	—	—	—
NHL Totals (4 years)		207	41	41	82	52	-45	8	1	8	0	0	0	2

KRAFT, RYAN C

PERSONAL: Born November 7, 1975, in Bottineau, N.D. ... 5-9/185. ... Shoots left.
TRANSACTIONS/CAREER NOTES: Selected by San Jose Sharks in eighth round (11th Sharks pick, 194th overall) of NHL entry draft (July 8, 1995). ... Signed as free agent by New York Islanders (July 13, 2003).

Season Team	League	REGULAR SEASON GP	G	A	Pts.	PIM	+/-	PP	SH	PLAYOFFS GP	G	A	Pts.	PIM
93-94—Moorhead Senior	Minn. H.S.	27	44	40	84	40	...	...	...	—	—	—	—	—
94-95—Minnesota	WCHA	44	13	33	46	40	...	7	0	—	—	—	—	—
95-96—Minnesota	WCHA	41	13	24	37	24	...	...	...	—	—	—	—	—
96-97—Minnesota	WCHA	42	25	21	46	37	9	11	0	—	—	—	—	—
97-98—Minnesota	WCHA	32	11	26	37	16	...	...	...	—	—	—	—	—
98-99—Richmond	ECHL	63	28	36	64	35	0	10	4	18	10	10	20	4
99-00—Richmond	ECHL	44	32	35	67	32	...	...	...	—	—	—	—	—
—Kentucky	AHL	15	7	6	13	2	...	...	...	5	3	1	4	0
—Cleveland	IHL	1	0	1	1	0	...	...	...	—	—	—	—	—
00-01—Kentucky	AHL	77	38	50	88	36	...	...	...	3	2	0	2	0
01-02—Cleveland	AHL	63	19	41	60	42	-23	9	3	—	—	—	—	—
02-03—Cleveland	AHL	53	14	27	41	12	-21	4	1	—	—	—	—	—
—San Jose	NHL	7	0	1	1	0	2	0	0	—	—	—	—	—
03-04—Bridgeport	AHL	74	15	20	35	20	6	2	2	6	2	2	4	0
04-05—Bridgeport	AHL	38	9	9	18	12	0	3	1	—	—	—	—	—
NHL Totals (1 year)		7	0	1	1	0	2	0	0					

KRAHN, BRENT G FLAMES

PERSONAL: Born April 2, 1982, in Winnipeg. ... 6-4/200. ... Catches right.
TRANSACTIONS/CAREER NOTES: Selected by Calgary Flames in first round (first Flames pick, ninth overall) of NHL entry draft (June 24, 2000).

Season Team	League	REGULAR SEASON GP	Min.	W	L	T	GA	SO	GAA	SV%	PLAYOFFS GP	Min.	W	L	GA	SO	GAA	SV%
99-00—Calgary	WHL	39	2315	33	6	0	92	4	2.38	...	5	266	2	2	13	0	2.93	...
00-01—Calgary	WHL	37	2087	22	10	3	104	1	2.99	...	—	—	—	—	—	—	—	—
01-02—Calgary	WHL	18	1033	8	6	2	61	0	3.54	...	2	119	1	1	6	0	3.03	...
02-03—Calgary	WHL	23	1343	11	10	2	72	2	3.22	...	—	—	—	—	—	—	—	—
—Seattle	WHL	5	302	5	0	0	9	2	1.79	...	15	960	9	6	38	2	2.38	...
03-04—Lowell	AHL	7	344	2	3	0	15	0	2.62	.918	—	—	—	—	—	—	—	—
—Las Vegas	ECHL	14	827	7	5	2	36	0	2.61	.919	—	—	—	—	—	—	—	—
—San Antonio	AHL	14	714	3	7	1	41	0	3.45	.869	—	—	—	—	—	—	—	—
04-05—Lowell	AHL	35	1998	20	11		83	6	2.49	.923	1	0	0	0	0	0	...	...

KRAJICEK, LUKAS D PANTHERS

PERSONAL: Born March 11, 1983, in Prostejov, Czechoslovakia. ... 6-2/185. ... Shoots left. ... Name pronounced LOO-kahsh KRIGH-ee-chehk.
TRANSACTIONS/CAREER NOTES: Selected by Florida Panthers in first round (second Panthers pick, 24th overall) of NHL entry draft (June 23, 2001).

Season Team	League	REGULAR SEASON GP	G	A	Pts.	PIM	+/-	PP	SH	PLAYOFFS GP	G	A	Pts.	PIM
99-00—Detroit	NAHL	53	5	22	27	61	...	...	...	—	—	—	—	—
00-01—Peterborough	OHL	61	8	27	35	53	...	...	...	7	0	5	5	0
01-02—Peterborough	OHL	55	10	32	42	56	...	...	...	6	0	5	5	6
—Florida	NHL	5	0	0	0	0	0	0	0	—	—	—	—	—
02-03—Peterborough	OHL	52	11	42	53	42	...	...	...	7	0	3	3	0
—San Antonio	AHL	3	0	1	1	0	-1	0	0	3	0	0	0	0
03-04—San Antonio	AHL	54	5	12	17	24	-7	3	0	—	—	—	—	—
—Florida	NHL	18	1	6	7	12	-2	1	0	—	—	—	—	—
04-05—San Antonio	AHL	78	2	22	24	57	-20	0	0	—	—	—	—	—
NHL Totals (2 years)		23	1	6	7	12	-2	1	0					

KRESTANOVICH, JORDAN LW

PERSONAL: Born June 14, 1981, in Langley, B.C. ... 6-1/180. ... Shoots left. ... Brother of Derek Krestanovich, Washington Capitals organization.
TRANSACTIONS/CAREER NOTES: Selected by Colorado Avalanche in fifth round (sixth Avalanche pick, 152nd overall) of NHL entry draft (June 26, 1999). ... Traded by Avalanche to Minnesota Wild for LW Chris Bala (March 9, 2004).

Season Team	League	GP	G	A	Pts.	PIM	+/-	PP	SH	GP	G	A	Pts.	PIM
		REGULAR SEASON								PLAYOFFS				
97-98—Calgary	WHL	22	1	0	1	0	...	...	...	13	0	0	0	0
98-99—Calgary	WHL	62	6	13	19	10	6	2	0	20	3	8	11	4
99-00—Calgary	WHL	72	19	24	43	22	35	4	4	13	7	7	14	4
—Hershey	AHL	...	...	...	...	...	...	...	...	1	0	0	0	0
00-01—Calgary	WHL	70	40	60	100	32	...	...	...	12	8	4	12	8
—Hershey	AHL	...	...	...	...	...	...	...	...	2	0	0	0	0
01-02—Hershey	AHL	68	12	22	34	18	0	3	1	8	1	0	1	0
—Colorado	NHL	8	0	2	2	0	1	0	0	—	—	—	—	—
02-03—Hershey	AHL	70	13	21	34	24	-5	3	1	4	0	1	1	2
03-04—Hershey	AHL	38	4	15	19	11	0	1	1	—	—	—	—	—
—Colorado	NHL	14	0	0	0	6	0	0	0	—	—	—	—	—
—Houston	AHL	12	2	1	3	0	-3	0	0	2	0	0	0	0
04-05—Pensacola	ECHL	69	27	41	68	22	11	7	...	3	1	1	2	0
NHL Totals (2 years)		22	0	2	2	6	1	0	0					

KROG, JASON C

PERSONAL: Born October 9, 1975, in Fernie, B.C. ... 5-11/192. ... Shoots right.

TRANSACTIONS/CAREER NOTES: Signed as free agent by New York Islanders (April 10, 1999). ... Sprained right ankle (March 27, 2000); missed final six games of season. ... Dislocated left shoulder (December 15, 2000); missed 20 games. ... Signed as free agent by Anaheim Mighty Ducks (July 17, 2002).

Season Team	League	GP	G	A	Pts.	PIM	+/-	PP	SH	GP	G	A	Pts.	PIM
		REGULAR SEASON								PLAYOFFS				
95-96—New Hampshire	Hockey East	34	4	16	20	20	...	...	...	—	—	—	—	—
96-97—New Hampshire	Hockey East	39	23	44	67	28	...	...	...	—	—	—	—	—
97-98—New Hampshire	Hockey East	38	33	33	66	44	...	...	...	—	—	—	—	—
98-99—New Hampshire	Hockey East	41	*34	*51	*85	38	...	...	...	—	—	—	—	—
99-00—Lowell	AHL	45	6	21	27	22	...	...	...	—	—	—	—	—
—New York Islanders	NHL	17	2	4	6	6	-1	1	0	—	—	—	—	—
—Providence	AHL	11	9	8	17	4	...	...	...	6	2	2	4	0
00-01—Lowell	AHL	26	11	16	27	6	...	...	...	—	—	—	—	—
—Springfield	AHL	24	7	23	30	4	...	...	...	—	—	—	—	—
—New York Islanders	NHL	9	0	3	3	0	4	0	0	—	—	—	—	—
01-02—Bridgeport	AHL	64	26	36	62	13	-8	9	0	20	10	13	23	8
—New York Islanders	NHL	2	0	0	0	0	0	0	0	—	—	—	—	—
02-03—Cincinnati	AHL	9	3	4	7	6	-3	1	1	—	—	—	—	—
—Anaheim	NHL	67	10	15	25	12	1	0	1	21	3	1	4	4
03-04—Anaheim	NHL	80	6	12	18	16	-4	1	0	—	—	—	—	—
04-05—VSV	Austria	48	27	33	60	38	8	9	2	3	0	1	1	4
NHL Totals (5 years)		175	18	34	52	34	0	2	1	21	3	1	4	4

KRONWALL, NIKLAS D RED WINGS

PERSONAL: Born January 12, 1981, in Stockholm, Sweden. ... 6-0/158. ... Shoots left. ... Brother of Staffan Kronwall, Toronto Maple Leafs organization.

TRANSACTIONS/CAREER NOTES: Selected by Detroit Red Wings in first round (first Red Wings pick, 29th overall) of NHL entry draft (June 24, 2000). ... Fractured right leg (January 22, 2004); missed final 33 games of regular season and playoffs.

Season Team	League	GP	G	A	Pts.	PIM	+/-	PP	SH	GP	G	A	Pts.	PIM
		REGULAR SEASON								PLAYOFFS				
98-99—Huddinge	Sweden	14	0	1	1	10	...	...	...	—	—	—	—	—
99-00—Djurgarden Stockholm	Sweden	37	1	4	5	16	...	...	...	8	0	0	0	8
00-01—Djurgarden Stockholm	Sweden	31	1	9	10	32	...	...	...	15	0	1	1	8
01-02—Djurgarden Stockholm	Sweden	48	5	7	12	34	...	...	...	5	0	0	0	0
02-03—Djurgarden Stockholm	Sweden	50	5	13	18	46	...	...	...	12	3	2	5	18
03-04—Detroit	NHL	20	1	4	5	16	5	0	0	—	—	—	—	—
—Grand Rapids	AHL	25	2	11	13	20	6	1	0	—	—	—	—	—
04-05—Grand Rapids	AHL	76	13	40	53	53	6	3	0	—	—	—	—	—
NHL Totals (1 year)		20	1	4	5	16	5	0	0					

KUBA, FILIP D WILD

PERSONAL: Born December 29, 1976, in Ostrava, Czechoslovakia. ... 6-3/205. ... Shoots left. ... Name pronounced KOO-buh.

TRANSACTIONS/CAREER NOTES: Selected by Florida Panthers in eighth round (eighth Panthers pick, 192nd overall) of NHL entry draft (July 8, 1995). ... Traded by Panthers to Calgary Flames for RW Rocky Thompson (March 16, 2000). ... Selected by Minnesota Wild in NHL expansion draft (June 23, 2000). ... Bruised ribs (November 15, 2000); missed five games. ... Bruised knee (January 19, 2001); missed one game. ... Fractured right hand (February 10, 2002); missed 20 games. ... Fractured finger (March 27, 2004); missed remainder of season.

Season Team	League	GP	G	A	Pts.	PIM	+/-	PP	SH	GP	G	A	Pts.	PIM
		REGULAR SEASON								PLAYOFFS				
94-95—Vitkovice	Czech. Jrs.	35	10	15	25	...	...	...	...	—	—	—	—	—
—Vitkovice	Czech Rep.	...	...	...	...	...	...	...	...	4	0	0	0	2
95-96—Vitkovice	Czech Rep.	19	0	1	1	...	...	...	...	—	—	—	—	—
96-97—Carolina	AHL	51	0	12	12	38	...	...	...	—	—	—	—	—
97-98—New Haven	AHL	77	4	13	17	58	11	2	0	3	1	1	2	0
98-99—Kentucky	AHL	45	2	8	10	33	13	1	0	10	0	1	1	4
—Florida	NHL	5	0	1	1	0	2	0	0	—	—	—	—	—

Season Team	League	GP	G	A	Pts.	PIM	+/-	PP	SH	GP	G	A	Pts.	PIM
		REGULAR SEASON								PLAYOFFS				
99-00—Florida	NHL	13	1	5	6	2	-3	1	0	—	—	—	—	—
—Houston	IHL	27	3	6	9	13	...	...	...	11	1	2	3	4
00-01—Minnesota	NHL	75	9	21	30	28	-6	4	0	—	—	—	—	—
01-02—Minnesota	NHL	62	5	19	24	32	-6	3	0	—	—	—	—	—
02-03—Minnesota	NHL	78	8	21	29	29	0	4	2	18	3	5	8	24
03-04—Minnesota	NHL	77	5	19	24	28	-7	2	1	—	—	—	—	—
NHL Totals (6 years)		310	28	86	114	119	-20	14	3	18	3	5	8	24

KUBINA, PAVEL D LIGHTNING

PERSONAL: Born April 15, 1977, in Caledna, Czechoslovakia. ... 6-4/230. ... Shoots right. ... Name pronounced koo-BEE-nuh.

TRANSACTIONS/CAREER NOTES: Selected by Tampa Bay Lightning in seventh round (sixth Lightning pick, 179th overall) of NHL draft (June 22, 1996). ... Injured knee (November 8, 1998); missed two games. ... Injured shoulder (November 29, 1998); missed three games. ... Bruised rib (January 5, 2000); missed two games. ... Bruised hand (March 1, 2000); missed one game. ... Injured ankle (March 21, 2000); missed final nine games of season. ... Had concussion (November 3, 2000); missed two games. ... Cut finger (December 30, 2000); missed two games. ... Injured leg (Feburary 24, 2001); missed eight games. ... Bruised foot (December 12, 2002); missed one game. ... Injured neck (February 19, 2003); missed three games.

Season Team	League	GP	G	A	Pts.	PIM	+/-	PP	SH	GP	G	A	Pts.	PIM
		REGULAR SEASON								PLAYOFFS				
93-94—HC Vitkovice	Czech Rep.	1	0	0	0	0	...	...	...	—	—	—	—	—
94-95—HC Vitkovice	Czech Rep.	8	2	0	2	0	...	...	...	4	0	0	0	0
95-96—HC Vitkovice	Czech Rep.	32	3	4	7	0	...	...	...	4	0	0	0	0
96-97—Moose Jaw	WHL	61	12	32	44	116	...	...	...	11	2	5	7	27
—HC Vitkovice	Czech Rep.	1	0	0	0	0	...	...	...	—	—	—	—	—
97-98—Adirondack	AHL	55	4	8	12	86	20	0	0	1	1	0	1	14
—Tampa Bay	NHL	10	1	2	3	22	-1	0	0	—	—	—	—	—
98-99—Tampa Bay	NHL	68	9	12	21	80	-33	3	1	—	—	—	—	—
—Cleveland	IHL	6	2	2	4	16	-1	1	0	—	—	—	—	—
99-00—Tampa Bay	NHL	69	8	18	26	93	-19	6	0	—	—	—	—	—
00-01—Tampa Bay	NHL	70	11	19	30	103	-14	6	1	—	—	—	—	—
01-02—Tampa Bay	NHL	82	11	23	34	106	-22	5	2	—	—	—	—	—
—Czech Rep. Oly. team	Int'l	4	0	1	1	0	...	...	...	—	—	—	—	—
02-03—Tampa Bay	NHL	75	3	19	22	78	-7	0	0	11	0	0	0	12
03-04—Tampa Bay	NHL	81	17	18	35	85	9	8	1	22	0	4	4	50
04-05—Vitkovice	Czech Rep.	28	6	5	11	46	2	...	...	12	4	6	10	34
NHL Totals (7 years)		455	60	111	171	567	-87	28	5	33	0	4	4	62

KUDELKA, TOMAS D SENATORS

PERSONAL: Born March 10, 1987, in Zlin, Czech Republic. ... 6-1/176. ... Shoots left.

Season Team	League	GP	G	A	Pts.	PIM	+/-	PP	SH	GP	G	A	Pts.	PIM
		REGULAR SEASON								PLAYOFFS				
03-04—Zlin	Czech Rep.	51	1	12	13	97	...	...	...	—	—	—	—	—
04-05—Zlin	Czech Rep.	38	9	8	17	38	...	...	...	—	—	—	—	—

KUDROC, KRISTIAN D PANTHERS

PERSONAL: Born May 21, 1981, In Michalovce, Czechoslovakia. ... 6-7/255. ... Shoots right.

TRANSACTIONS/CAREER NOTES: Selected by New York Islanders in first round (fourth Islanders pick, 28th overall) of NHL entry draft (June 26, 1999). ... Traded by Islanders with G Kevin Weekes and second-round pick (later traded to Phoenix Coyotes) in 2001 entry draft to Tampa Bay Lightning for first-(LW Raffi Torres), fourth-(RW/LW Vladimir Gorbunov) and seventh-round (D Ryan Caldwell) picks in 2000 entry draft (June 24, 2000). ... Signed as free agent by Florida Panthers (July 3, 2003). ... Injured ankle (October 8, 2003); missed 38 games.

Season Team	League	GP	G	A	Pts.	PIM	+/-	PP	SH	GP	G	A	Pts.	PIM
		REGULAR SEASON								PLAYOFFS				
97-98—Michalovce	Slovakia Jrs.	47	7	4	11	...	...	...	...	—	—	—	—	—
—HK Michalovce	Slov. Div.	4	0	0	0	0	...	0	0	—	—	—	—	—
98-99—Michalovce	Slovakia	17	0	3	3	12	...	...	...	—	—	—	—	—
99-00—Quebec	QMJHL	57	9	22	31	172	38	3	1	11	2	5	7	29
00-01—Detroit	IHL	44	4	3	7	80	...	...	...	—	—	—	—	—
—Tampa Bay	NHL	22	2	2	4	36	0	0	0	—	—	—	—	—
01-02—Tampa Bay	NHL	2	0	0	0	0	0	0	0	—	—	—	—	—
—Springfield	AHL	55	0	8	8	126	1	0	0	—	—	—	—	—
—Philadelphia	AHL	10	0	3	3	14	-5	0	0	5	1	1	2	21
02-03—Springfield	AHL	35	0	4	4	58	7	0	0	—	—	—	—	—
03-04—Florida	NHL	2	0	0	0	2	0	0	0	—	—	—	—	—
—San Antonio	AHL	47	1	4	5	120	-4	0	0	—	—	—	—	—
04-05—Hammarby	Sweden Dv. 2	6	0	2	2	65	-1	0	0	—	—	—	—	—
NHL Totals (3 years)		26	2	2	4	38	0	0	0					

KUKKONEN, LASSE D BLACKHAWKS

PERSONAL: Born September 18, 1981, in Oulu, Finland. ... 6-1/187. ... Shoots left.

TRANSACTIONS/CAREER NOTES: Selected by Chicago Blackhawks in fifth round (fourth Blackhawks pick, 151st overall) of NHL entry draft (June 21, 2003).

		REGULAR SEASON								PLAYOFFS				
Season Team	League	GP	G	A	Pts.	PIM	+/-	PP	SH	GP	G	A	Pts.	PIM
00-01—Karpat Oulu	Finland	47	1	5	6	46	...	...	...	9	0	2	2	4
01-02—Karpat Oulu	Finland Jr.	...	...	...	...	...	...	...	...	1	1	0	1	0
—Karpat Oulu	Finland	55	2	6	8	42	...	...	...	4	0	3	3	4
02-03—Karpat Oulu	Finland	56	6	12	18	67	...	...	...	15	1	4	5	16
03-04—Norfolk	AHL	58	3	11	14	58	4	1	0	8	0	0	0	8
—Chicago	NHL	10	0	1	1	4	-2	0	0	—	—	—	—	—
04-05—Karpat Oulu	Finland	55	5	13	18	68	8	...	...	15	1	2	3	10
NHL Totals (1 year)		10	0	1	1	4	-2	0	0					

KULESHOV, MIKHAIL — LW — AVALANCHE

PERSONAL: Born January 7, 1981, in Perm, U.S.S.R. ... 6-3/220. ... Shoots right.

TRANSACTIONS/CAREER NOTES: Selected by Colorado Avalanche in first round (first Avalanche pick, 25th overall) of NHL draft (June 26, 1999).

		REGULAR SEASON								PLAYOFFS				
Season Team	League	GP	G	A	Pts.	PIM	+/-	PP	SH	GP	G	A	Pts.	PIM
97-98—Avangard Omsk	Russian	4	1	0	1	4	...	...	...	—	—	—	—	—
—Avangard-VDV Omsk	Rus. Div.	12	12	3	15	12	...	...	...	—	—	—	—	—
98-99—Severstal Cherepovets	Russian	15	2	0	2	8	...	...	...	3	0	0	0	4
99-00—Severstal Cherepovets	Russian	8	0	0	0	4	...	...	...	3	0	0	0	2
00-01—SKA St. Petersburg	Russian	7	0	0	0	8	...	...	...	—	—	—	—	—
—Hershey	AHL	3	0	0	0	4	...	...	...	11	1	0	1	0
01-02—Hershey	AHL	60	8	11	19	43	-11	1	0	7	0	1	1	4
02-03—Hershey	AHL	77	7	13	20	76	-1	1	0	5	0	0	0	6
03-04—Colorado	NHL	3	0	0	0	0	-1	0	0	—	—	—	—	—
—Hershey	AHL	55	4	6	10	40	-8	0	0	—	—	—	—	—
04-05—SKA St. Petersburg	Russian	11	0	0	0	6	...	...	...	—	—	—	—	—
—Molot Perm	Russian	23	0	3	3	16	...	...	...	—	—	—	—	—
NHL Totals (1 year)		3	0	0	0	0	-1	0	0					

KUNITZ, CHRIS — LW — MIGHTY DUCKS

PERSONAL: Born September 26, 1979, in Regina, Sask. ... 5-11/198. ... Shoots left.

TRANSACTIONS/CAREER NOTES: Signed as free agent by Anaheim Mighty Ducks (April 1, 2003).

		REGULAR SEASON								PLAYOFFS				
Season Team	League	GP	G	A	Pts.	PIM	+/-	PP	SH	GP	G	A	Pts.	PIM
99-00—Ferris State	CCHA	38	20	9	29	70	...	...	...	—	—	—	—	—
00-01—Ferris State	CCHA	37	16	13	29	81	...	...	...	—	—	—	—	—
01-02—Ferris State	CCHA	35	28	10	38	68	...	...	...	—	—	—	—	—
02-03—Ferris State	CCHA	42	35	44	79	56	...	...	...	—	—	—	—	—
03-04—Anaheim	NHL	21	0	6	6	12	1	0	0	—	—	—	—	—
—Cincinnati	AHL	59	19	25	44	101	4	5	1	9	4	2	6	24
04-05—Cincinnati	AHL	54	22	17	39	71	13	10	2	12	1	7	8	20
NHL Totals (1 year)		21	0	6	6	12	1	0	0					

KURKA, TOMAS — LW — HURRICANES

PERSONAL: Born December 14, 1981, in Most, Czechoslovakia. ... 5-11/190. ... Shoots left.

TRANSACTIONS/CAREER NOTES: Selected by Carolina Hurricanes in second round (first Hurricanes pick, 32nd overall) of NHL entry draft (June 24, 2000). ... Injured hip (March 31, 2003); missed two games.

		REGULAR SEASON								PLAYOFFS				
Season Team	League	GP	G	A	Pts.	PIM	+/-	PP	SH	GP	G	A	Pts.	PIM
97-98—Litvinov	Czech. Jrs.	44	38	23	61	...	...	...	...	—	—	—	—	—
98-99—Litvinov	Czech. Jrs.	48	60	42	102	38	...	...	...	—	—	—	—	—
—Litvinov	Czech.	6	0	0	0	0	...	...	...	—	—	—	—	—
99-00—Plymouth	OHL	64	36	28	64	37	...	...	...	17	7	6	13	6
00-01—Plymouth	OHL	47	15	29	44	20	7	7	0	16	8	13	21	13
01-02—Lowell	AHL	71	13	15	28	24	13	4	0	5	1	1	2	2
02-03—Lowell	AHL	61	17	12	29	10	-32	8	1	—	—	—	—	—
—Carolina	NHL	14	3	2	5	2	1	0	0	—	—	—	—	—
03-04—Carolina	NHL	3	0	0	0	0	0	0	0	—	—	—	—	—
—Lowell	AHL	55	6	26	32	14	-7	2	0	—	—	—	—	—
04-05—Chem. Litvinov	Czech Rep.	29	1	5	6	6	-2	...	...	—	—	—	—	—
—Providence	AHL	40	8	3	11	4	0	0	0	17	4	4	8	13
NHL Totals (2 years)		17	3	2	5	2	1	0	0					

KUTLAK, ZDENEK — D — BRUINS

PERSONAL: Born February 13, 1980, in Ceske Budejovice, Czechoslovakia. ... 6-3/221. ... Shoots left.

TRANSACTIONS/CAREER NOTES: Selected by Boston Bruins in eighth round (10th Bruins pick, 237th overall) of NHL entry draft (June 24, 2000). ... Signed as free agent by Karlovy Vary of Czech league with Bruins retaining NHL rights (May 16, 2004).

Season Team	League	GP	G	A	Pts.	PIM	+/-	PP	SH	GP	G	A	Pts.	PIM
		REGULAR SEASON								PLAYOFFS				
98-99—HC Ceske Budejovice..	Czech. Jrs.	2	1	3	4	4	...	...	...	3	0	0	0	0
99-00—HC Ceske Budejovice..	Czech. Jrs.	28	1	0	1	2	...	...	...	1	0	0	0	0
00-01—Providence	AHL	62	4	5	9	16	...	...	...	—	—	—	—	—
—Boston	NHL	10	0	2	2	4	-3	0	0	—	—	—	—	—
01-02—Providence	AHL	80	5	15	20	73	-19	4	0	—	—	—	—	—
02-03—Providence	AHL	68	4	12	16	52	0	0	0	—	—	—	—	—
—Boston	NHL	4	1	0	1	0	0	0	0	—	—	—	—	—
03-04—Boston	NHL	2	0	0	0	0	-1	0	0	—	—	—	—	—
—Providence	AHL	47	7	12	19	22	10	1	0	2	0	0	0	2
04-05—Karlovy Vary	Czech Rep.	52	5	9	14	26	8	...	...	—	—	—	—	—
NHL Totals (3 years)		16	1	2	3	4	-4	0	0					

KUZNETSOV, MAXIM — D — KINGS

PERSONAL: Born March 24, 1977, in Pavlodar, U.S.S.R. ... 6-5/235. ... Shoots left. ... Name pronounced koos-NEHT-sahf.

TRANSACTIONS/CAREER NOTES: Selected by Detroit Red Wings in first round (first Red Wings pick, 26th overall) of NHL entry draft (July 8, 1995). ... Sprained knee (November 22, 2000); missed nine games. ... Strained rib muscle (December 22, 2000); missed 18 games. ... Injured back (March 11, 2001); missed one game. ... Strained hip flexor (November 7, 2001); missed nine games. ... Traded by Red Wings with C Sean Avery, first-round pick (Jeff Tambellini) in 2003 entry draft and second-round pick (later traded to Boston Bruins) in 2004 entry draft to Los Angeles Kings for D Mathieu Schneider (March 11, 2003). ... Fractured foot (March 18, 2003); missed 10 games. ... Suspended by Kings for not reporting to camp (October 7, 2003). ... Signed as free agent by Dynamo Moscow of Russian league (June 7, 2004).

Season Team	League	GP	G	A	Pts.	PIM	+/-	PP	SH	GP	G	A	Pts.	PIM
		REGULAR SEASON								PLAYOFFS				
94-95—Dynamo Moscow	CIS	11	0	0	0	8	...	...	...	—	—	—	—	—
95-96—Dynamo Moscow	CIS	9	1	1	2	22	...	...	...	4	0	0	0	0
96-97—Dynamo Moscow	CIS	23	0	2	2	16	...	...	...	—	—	—	—	—
—Adirondack	AHL	2	0	1	1	6	1	0	0	2	0	0	0	0
97-98—Adirondack	AHL	51	5	5	10	43	-4	0	0	3	0	1	1	4
98-99—Adirondack	AHL	60	0	4	4	30	-23	0	0	3	0	0	0	0
99-00—Cincinnati	AHL	47	2	9	11	36	...	...	...	—	—	—	—	—
00-01—Detroit	NHL	25	1	2	3	23	-1	0	0	—	—	—	—	—
01-02—Detroit	NHL	39	1	2	3	40	0	0	0	—	—	—	—	—
—Cincinnati	AHL	7	1	0	1	4	2	0	0	—	—	—	—	—
02-03—Detroit	NHL	53	0	3	3	54	0	0	0	—	—	—	—	—
—Los Angeles	NHL	3	0	0	0	0	1	0	0	—	—	—	—	—
03-04—Manchester	AHL	39	2	8	10	57	10	0	0	2	0	0	0	4
—Los Angeles	NHL	16	0	1	1	20	-5	0	0	—	—	—	—	—
04-05—Dynamo Moscow	Russian	10	0	0	0	24	0	...	...	—	—	—	—	—
—SKA St. Petersburg	Russian	34	4	6	10	72	6	...	...	—	—	—	—	—
NHL Totals (4 years)		136	2	8	10	137	-5	0	0					

KVASHA, OLEG — LW/C — ISLANDERS

PERSONAL: Born July 26, 1978, in Moscow, U.S.S.R. ... 6-5/230. ... Shoots right. ... Name pronounced kuh-VA-shuh.

TRANSACTIONS/CAREER NOTES: Selected by Florida Panthers in third round (third Panthers pick, 65th overall) of NHL draft (June 22, 1996). ... Bruised right ankle (December 16, 1998); missed one game. ... Bruised shoulder (February 27, 1999); missed one game. ... Separated left shoulder (March 31, 1999); missed final nine games of season. ... Sprained knee (March 7, 2000); missed two games. ... Traded by Panthers with RW Mark Parrish to New York Islanders for C Olli Jokinen and G Roberto Luongo (June 24, 2000). ... Strained back (December 6, 2000); missed two games. ... Sprained right knee (January 12, 2001); missed 10 games. ... Injured left knee (February 10, 2001); missed eight games. ... Injured shoulder (November 21, 2001); missed two games. ... Flu (December 18, 2001); missed one game. ... Injured knee and had surgery (February 28, 2002); missed five games. ... Fractured ankle (October 24, 2002); missed seven games. ... Reinjured ankle (November 20, 2002); missed three games. ... Fractured nose (December 10, 2003); missed one game.

Season Team	League	GP	G	A	Pts.	PIM	+/-	PP	SH	GP	G	A	Pts.	PIM
		REGULAR SEASON								PLAYOFFS				
94-95—CSKA	CIS Jr.	Statistics unavailable												
95-96—CSKA Moscow	CIS	38	2	3	5	14	...	...	...	2	0	0	0	0
96-97—CSKA Moscow	USSR	44	20	22	42	115	...	...	...	—	—	—	—	—
97-98—New Haven	AHL	57	13	16	29	46	11	4	0	3	2	1	3	0
98-99—Florida	NHL	68	12	13	25	45	5	4	0	—	—	—	—	—
99-00—Florida	NHL	78	5	20	25	34	3	2	0	4	0	0	0	0
00-01—New York Islanders	NHL	62	11	9	20	46	-15	0	0	—	—	—	—	—
01-02—New York Islanders	NHL	71	13	25	38	80	-4	2	0	7	0	1	1	6
—Russian Oly. team	Int'l	5	0	0	0	0	...	...	...	—	—	—	—	—
02-03—New York Islanders	NHL	69	12	14	26	44	4	0	1	5	0	1	1	2
03-04—New York Islanders	NHL	81	15	36	51	48	4	5	3	5	1	0	1	0
04-05—Severstal Cherepovets	Russian	22	6	5	11	24	3	...	...	—	—	—	—	—
—CSKA Moscow	Russian	26	3	6	9	20	-7	...	...	—	—	—	—	—
NHL Totals (6 years)		429	68	117	185	297	-3	13	4	21	1	2	3	8

KWIATKOWSKI, JOEL — D — PANTHERS

PERSONAL: Born March 22, 1977, in Kindersley, Sask. ... 5-11/201. ... Shoots left. ... Name pronounced kwee-iht-KOW-skee.

TRANSACTIONS/CAREER NOTES: Signed as free agent by Anaheim Mighty Ducks (June 18, 1998). ... Traded by Mighty Ducks to Ottawa Senators for D Patrick Traverse (June 12, 2000). ... Injured ankle (December 31, 2002); missed three games. ... Traded by Senators to Washington Capitals for ninth-round pick (F Mark Olafson) in 2003 draft (January 15, 2003). ... Signed as free agent by Florida Panthers (July 16, 2004). ... Signed as free agent by San Antonio of the AHL (September 26, 2004). ... Signed as free agent by Florida Panthers (Aug. 2, 2005).

K

Season Team	League	REGULAR SEASON GP	G	A	Pts.	PIM	+/-	PP	SH	PLAYOFFS GP	G	A	Pts.	PIM
94-95—Tacoma	WHL	70	4	13	17	66	...	...	...	4	0	0	0	2
95-96—Prince George	WHL	72	12	28	40	133	...	...	...	—	—	—	—	—
96-97—Prince George	WHL	72	16	36	52	94	...	...	...	4	4	2	6	24
97-98—Prince George	WHL	62	21	43	64	65	16	8	0	11	3	6	9	6
98-99—Cincinnati	AHL	80	12	21	33	48	7	2	0	3	2	0	2	0
99-00—Cincinnati	AHL	70	4	22	26	28	...	...	...	—	—	—	—	—
00-01—Grand Rapids	IHL	77	4	17	21	58	...	...	...	10	1	0	1	4
—Ottawa	NHL	4	1	0	1	0	1	0	0	—	—	—	—	—
01-02—Grand Rapids	AHL	65	8	21	29	94	21	1	0	5	1	2	3	12
—Ottawa	NHL	11	0	0	0	12	5	0	0	—	—	—	—	—
02-03—Ottawa	NHL	20	0	2	2	6	2	0	0	—	—	—	—	—
—Binghamton	AHL	1	0	0	0	2	...	...	...	—	—	—	—	—
—Washington	NHL	34	0	3	3	12	1	0	0	6	0	0	0	2
03-04—Washington	NHL	80	6	6	12	89	-28	2	0	—	—	—	—	—
04-05—San Antonio	AHL	64	13	19	32	76	-1	5	0	—	—	—	—	—
—St. John's	AHL	17	7	6	13	16	8	4	0	5	0	4	4	23
NHL Totals (4 years)		149	7	11	18	119	-19	2	0	6	0	0	0	2

LAAKSONEN, ANTTI LW/RW AVALANCHE

PERSONAL: Born October 3, 1973, in Tammela, Finland. ... 6-0/180. ... Shoots left. ... Name pronounced AHN-tee lah-AHK-soh-nehn.
TRANSACTIONS/CAREER NOTES: Selected by Boston Bruins in eighth round (10th Bruins pick, 191st overall) of NHL draft (July 21, 1997). ... Signed as free agent by Minnesota Wild (July 20, 2000). ... Signed as free agent by Colorado Avalanche (July 2, 2004).
STATISTICAL PLATEAUS: Three-goal games: 2000-01 (1).

Season Team	League	REGULAR SEASON GP	G	A	Pts.	PIM	+/-	PP	SH	PLAYOFFS GP	G	A	Pts.	PIM
92-93—HPK Hameenlinna	Finland	2	0	0	0	0	...	0	0	—	—	—	—	—
93-94—Denver	WCHA	36	12	9	21	38	...	...	...	—	—	—	—	—
94-95—Denver	WCHA	40	17	18	35	42	...	...	...	—	—	—	—	—
95-96—Denver	WCHA	39	25	28	53	71	...	...	...	—	—	—	—	—
96-97—Denver	WCHA	39	21	17	38	63	...	...	...	—	—	—	—	—
97-98—Providence	AHL	38	3	2	5	14	-13	0	0	—	—	—	—	—
—Charlotte	ECHL	15	4	3	7	12	...	...	...	6	0	3	3	0
98-99—Boston	NHL	11	1	2	3	2	-1	0	0	—	—	—	—	—
—Providence	AHL	66	25	33	58	52	40	5	1	19	7	2	9	28
99-00—Providence	AHL	40	10	12	22	57	...	...	...	14	5	4	9	4
—Boston	NHL	27	6	3	9	2	3	0	0	—	—	—	—	—
00-01—Minnesota	NHL	82	12	16	28	24	-7	0	2	—	—	—	—	—
01-02—Minnesota	NHL	82	16	17	33	22	-5	0	0	—	—	—	—	—
02-03—Minnesota	NHL	82	15	16	31	26	4	1	2	16	1	3	4	4
03-04—Minnesota	NHL	77	12	14	26	20	0	0	1	—	—	—	—	—
NHL Totals (6 years)		361	62	68	130	96	-6	1	5	16	1	3	4	4

LABARBERA, JASON G KINGS

PERSONAL: Born January 18, 1980, in Prince George, B.C. ... 6-3/224. ... Catches left.
TRANSACTIONS/CAREER NOTES: Selected by New York Rangers in 3rd round (3rd Rangers pick, 66th overall) of entry draft (June 27, 1998). ... Signed as free agent by Los Angeles Kings (Aug. 2, 2005).

Season Team	League	REGULAR SEASON GP	Min.	W	L	T	GA	SO	GAA	SV%	PLAYOFFS GP	Min.	W	L	GA	SO	GAA	SV%
96-97—Tri-City	WHL	2	...	1	0	0	...	...	3.81	...	—	—	—	—	—	—	—	—
—Portland	WHL	9	443	5	1	1	18	0	2.44	...	—	—	—	—	—	—	—	—
97-98—Portland	WHL	23	1305	18	4	0	72	1	3.31	...	—	—	—	—	—	—	—	—
98-99—Portland	WHL	51	2991	18	23	9	170	4	3.41	.904	4	252	0	4	19	0	4.52	.899
99-00—Portland	WHL	34	2005	8	24	2	123	1	3.68	.903	—	—	—	—	—	—	—	—
—Spokane	WHL	21	1146	12	6	2	50	0	2.62	.900	9	435	6	1	18	1	2.48	.890
00-01—Hartford	AHL	4	156	1	1	0	12	0	4.62	.871	—	—	—	—	—	—	—	—
—New York Rangers	NHL	1	10	0	0	0	0	0	0.00	1.00	—	—	—	—	—	—	—	—
—Charlotte	ECHL	35	2100	18	10	7	112	1	3.20	...	2	143	1	1	5	0	2.10	...
01-02—Hartford	AHL	20	1057	7	11	1	55	0	3.12	.904	—	—	—	—	—	—	—	—
—Charlotte	ECHL	13	743	9	3	1	29	0	2.34	.918	4	212	2	2	12	0	3.40	.910
02-03—Hartford	AHL	46	2451	18	17	6	105	2	2.57	.915	2	117	0	2	6	0	3.08	.867
03-04—Hartford	AHL	59	3393	34	9	9	90	13	1.59	.932	16	1042	11	5	30	3	1.73	.930
—New York Rangers	NHL	4	198	1	2	0	16	0	4.85	.824	—	—	—	—	—	—	—	—
04-05—Hartford	AHL	53	2937	31	16	...	90	6	1.84	.934	4	237	1	3	9	0	2.28	.940
NHL Totals (2 years)		5	208	1	2	0	16	0	4.62	.828								

LACHANCE, SCOTT D

PERSONAL: Born October 22, 1972, in Charlottesville, Va. ... 6-2/215. ... Shoots left. ... Brother of Bob Lachance, RW with two NHL organizations (1992-2000).
TRANSACTIONS/CAREER NOTES: Selected by New York Islanders in 1st round (1st Islanders pick, 4th overall) of entry draft (June 22, 1991). ... Sprained wrist (April 13, 1993); missed remainder of season. ... Wrist surgery (April 30, 1993). ... Separated right shoulder (October 8, 1993); missed four games. ... Fractured ankle (February 25, 1995); missed 22 games. ... Injured groin (October 31, 1995); missed 27 games. ... Fractured finger (November 1, 1997); missed two games. ... Strained abdominal muscle (March 14, 1998); missed five games. ... Reinjured

abdomen (March 28, 1998); missed 11 games. ... Charley horse (November 21, 1998); missed one game. ... Flu (December 22, 1998); missed one game. ... Sprained knee (January 5, 1999); missed one game. ... Traded by Islanders to Montreal Canadiens for 3rd-round pick (RW Mattias Weinhandl) in 1999 entry draft (March 9, 1999). ... Injured back (November 23, 1999); missed 12 games. ... Signed as free agent by Vancouver Canucks (August 14, 2000). ... Flu (December 8, 2000); missed one game. ... Sprained knee (January 28, 2001); missed five games. ... Injured knee (December 22, 2001); missed one game. ... Signed as free agent by Columbus Blue Jackets (July 4, 2002). ... Strained back (November 9, 2002); missed one game. ... High ankle sprain (January 4, 2003); missed 12 games. ... Injured back (March 22, 2003); missed 8 games. ... Back spasms (November 19, 2003); missed three games. ... Contract bought out by Blue Jackets (July 29, 2005).

		REGULAR SEASON								PLAYOFFS				
Season Team	League	GP	G	A	Pts.	PIM	+/-	PP	SH	GP	G	A	Pts.	PIM
88-89—Springfield Jr. B	NEJHL	36	8	28	36	20	...	...	...	—	—	—	—	—
89-90—Springfield Jr. B	NEJHL	34	25	41	66	62	...	...	...	—	—	—	—	—
90-91—Boston University	Hockey East	31	5	19	24	48	...	...	...	—	—	—	—	—
91-92—U.S. national team	Int'l	36	1	10	11	34	...	...	...	—	—	—	—	—
—U.S. Olympic team	Int'l	8	0	1	1	6	...	...	...	—	—	—	—	—
—New York Islanders	NHL	17	1	4	5	9	13	0	0	—	—	—	—	—
92-93—New York Islanders	NHL	75	7	17	24	67	-1	0	1	—	—	—	—	—
93-94—New York Islanders	NHL	74	3	11	14	70	-5	0	0	3	0	0	0	0
94-95—New York Islanders	NHL	26	6	7	13	26	2	3	0	—	—	—	—	—
95-96—New York Islanders	NHL	55	3	10	13	54	-19	1	0	—	—	—	—	—
96-97—New York Islanders	NHL	81	3	11	14	47	-7	1	0	—	—	—	—	—
97-98—New York Islanders	NHL	63	2	11	13	45	-11	1	0	—	—	—	—	—
98-99—New York Islanders	NHL	59	1	8	9	30	-19	1	0	—	—	—	—	—
—Montreal	NHL	17	1	1	2	11	-2	0	0	—	—	—	—	—
99-00—Montreal	NHL	57	0	6	6	22	-4	0	0	—	—	—	—	—
00-01—Vancouver	NHL	76	3	11	14	46	5	0	0	2	0	1	1	2
01-02—Vancouver	NHL	81	1	10	11	50	15	0	0	6	1	1	2	4
02-03—Columbus	NHL	61	0	1	1	46	-20	0	0	—	—	—	—	—
03-04—Columbus	NHL	77	0	4	4	44	-23	0	0	—	—	—	—	—
NHL Totals (13 years)		819	31	112	143	567	-76	7	1	11	1	2	3	6

LACOUTURE, DAN LW

PERSONAL: Born April 18, 1977, in Hyannis, Mass. ... 6-3/215. ... Shoots left. ... Name pronounced LA-kuh-toor.
TRANSACTIONS/CAREER NOTES: Selected by New York Islanders in second round (second Islanders pick, 29th overall) of NHL draft (June 22, 1996). ... Traded by Islanders to Edmonton Oilers for RW Mariusz Czerkawski (August 25, 1997). ... Traded by Oilers to Pittsburgh Penguins for D Steve Butenschon (March 13, 2001). ... Suffered concussion (December 7, 2002); missed four games. ... Traded by Penguins with RW Alexei Kovalev, D Janne Laukkanen and D Mike Wilson to New York Rangers for RW Rico Fata, RW Mikael Samuelsson, D Joel Bouchard, D Richard Lintner and cash (February 10, 2003). ... Separated shoulder (November 24, 2003); missed six games. ... Suffered concussion (January 6, 2004); missed seven games. ... Post-concussion syndrome (January 24, 2004); missed eight games.

		REGULAR SEASON								PLAYOFFS				
Season Team	League	GP	G	A	Pts.	PIM	+/-	PP	SH	GP	G	A	Pts.	PIM
94-95—Springfield Jr. B	EJHL	49	37	39	76	100	...	...	...	—	—	—	—	—
95-96—Jr. Whalers	EJHL	42	36	48	84	102	...	9	8	—	—	—	—	—
96-97—Boston University	Hockey East	31	13	12	25	18	13	6	0	—	—	—	—	—
97-98—Hamilton	AHL	77	15	10	25	31	-2	4	0	5	1	0	1	0
98-99—Hamilton	AHL	72	17	14	31	73	-5	1	4	9	2	1	3	2
—Edmonton	NHL	3	0	0	0	0	1	0	0	—	—	—	—	—
99-00—Hamilton	AHL	70	23	17	40	85	...	...	...	6	2	1	3	0
—Edmonton	NHL	5	0	0	0	10	0	0	0	1	0	0	0	0
00-01—Edmonton	NHL	37	2	4	6	29	-2	0	0	—	—	—	—	—
—Pittsburgh	NHL	11	0	0	0	14	0	0	0	5	0	0	0	2
01-02—Pittsburgh	NHL	82	6	11	17	71	-19	0	1	—	—	—	—	—
02-03—Pittsburgh	NHL	44	2	2	4	72	-8	0	0	—	—	—	—	—
—New York Rangers	NHL	24	1	4	5	0	4	0	0	—	—	—	—	—
03-04—New York Rangers	NHL	59	5	2	7	82	-13	1	0	—	—	—	—	—
04-05—Providence	AHL	64	12	15	27	52	9	3	2	6	1	1	2	4
NHL Totals (6 years)		265	16	23	39	278	-37	1	1	6	0	0	0	2

LADD, ANDREW LW HURRICANES

PERSONAL: Born December 12, 1985, in Maple Ridge,B.C. ... 6-2/200. ... Shoots left.
TRANSACTIONS/CAREER NOTES: Selected by Carolina Hurricanes in first round (first Hurricanes pick, fourth overall) of NHL entry draft (June 26, 2004).

		REGULAR SEASON								PLAYOFFS				
Season Team	League	GP	G	A	Pts.	PIM	+/-	PP	SH	GP	G	A	Pts.	PIM
02-03—Vancouver	WHL	1	0	0	0	0	...	...	...	—	—	—	—	—
03-04—Calgary	WHL	71	30	45	75	119	...	...	...	7	1	6	7	10
04-05—Calgary	WHL	65	19	26	45	167	16	6	2	12	7	4	11	18

LAFLAMME, CHRISTIAN D

PERSONAL: Born November 24, 1976, in St. Charles, Que. ... 6-1/208. ... Shoots right. ... Name pronounced lah-FLAHM.
TRANSACTIONS/CAREER NOTES: Selected by Chicago Blackhawks in 2nd round (2nd Blackhawks pick, 45th overall) of ntry draft (July 8, 1995). ... Fractured left foot (October 1, 1997); missed six games. ... Fractured right cheekbone (January 24, 1998); missed four games. ... Traded by Blackhawks with C Chad Kilger, LW Daniel Cleary and LW Ethan Moreau to Edmonton Oilers for D Boris Mironov, LW Dean McAmmond and D Jonas Elofsson (March 20, 1999). ... Had concussion (March 28, 1999); missed one game. ... Bruised shoulder (January 11, 2000); missed one game. ... Traded by Oilers with D Mathieu Descoteaux to Montreal Canadiens for D Igor Ulanov and D Alain Nasreddine

(March 9, 2000). ... Concussion (October 24, 2000); missed six games. ... Strained groin (December 11, 2000); missed 10 games. ... Signed as free agent by St. Louis Blues (August 21, 2001). ... Flu (November 30, 2002); missed two games. ... Injured knee (December 18, 2002); missed two games. ... Injured wrist (March 27, 2003); missed five games. ... Fractured foot (October 12, 2003); missed 17 games.

		REGULAR SEASON								PLAYOFFS				
Season Team	League	GP	G	A	Pts.	PIM	+/-	PP	SH	GP	G	A	Pts.	PIM
92-93—Verdun	QMJHL	69	2	17	19	70	...	...	...	3	0	2	2	6
93-94—Verdun	QMJHL	72	4	34	38	85	...	...	...	4	0	3	3	4
94-95—Beauport	QMJHL	67	6	41	47	82	...	...	...	8	1	4	5	6
95-96—Beauport	QMJHL	41	13	23	36	63	...	...	...	20	7	17	24	32
96-97—Indianapolis	IHL	62	5	15	20	60	...	...	...	4	1	1	2	16
—Chicago	NHL	4	0	1	1	2	3	0	0	—	—	—	—	—
97-98—Chicago	NHL	72	0	11	11	59	14	0	0	—	—	—	—	—
98-99—Chicago	NHL	62	2	11	13	70	0	0	0	—	—	—	—	—
—Portland	AHL	2	0	1	1	2	-1	0	0	—	—	—	—	—
—Edmonton	NHL	11	0	1	1	0	-3	0	0	4	0	1	1	2
99-00—Edmonton	NHL	50	0	5	5	32	-4	0	0	—	—	—	—	—
—Montreal	NHL	15	0	2	2	8	-5	0	0	—	—	—	—	—
00-01—Montreal	NHL	39	0	3	3	42	-11	0	0	—	—	—	—	—
01-02—Worcester	AHL	62	2	17	19	52	13	0	0	—	—	—	—	—
—St. Louis	NHL	8	0	1	1	4	3	0	0	—	—	—	—	—
02-03—Worcester	AHL	8	0	4	4	6	2	0	0	—	—	—	—	—
—St. Louis	NHL	47	0	9	9	45	1	0	0	5	0	0	0	4
03-04—St. Louis	NHL	16	0	1	1	20	-3	0	0	—	—	—	—	—
—Worcester	AHL	28	1	4	5	25	-9	0	0	7	0	0	0	6
04-05—Kassel	Germany	43	4	12	16	96	-12	2	0	7	0	1	1	12
NHL Totals (8 years)		324	2	45	47	282	-5	0	0	9	0	1	1	6

LAICH, BROOKS — C — CAPITALS

PERSONAL: Born June 23, 1983, in Wawota, Alta. ... 6-2/205. ... Shoots left.
TRANSACTIONS/CAREER NOTES: Selected by Ottawa Senators in sixth round (193rd overall) in NHL draft (June 24, 2001). ... Traded by Senators with second-round pick in 2005 draft to Washington for RW Peter Bondra (February 18, 2004).

		REGULAR SEASON								PLAYOFFS				
Season Team	League	GP	G	A	Pts.	PIM	+/-	PP	SH	GP	G	A	Pts.	PIM
00-01—Moose Jaw	WHL	71	9	21	30	28	...	...	...	4	0	0	0	5
01-02—Moose Jaw	WHL	28	6	14	20	12	...	...	...	—	—	—	—	—
—Seattle	WHL	47	22	36	58	42	...	...	...	11	5	3	8	11
02-03—Seattle	WHL	60	41	53	94	65	...	...	...	15	5	14	19	24
03-04—Binghamton	AHL	44	15	18	33	16	3	7	1	—	—	—	—	—
—Ottawa	NHL	1	0	0	0	2	0	0	0	—	—	—	—	—
—Portland	AHL	22	1	3	4	12	-9	0	0	6	0	0	0	0
—Washington	NHL	4	0	1	1	0	-1	0	0	—	—	—	—	—
04-05—Portland	AHL	68	16	10	26	33	-20	8	1	—	—	—	—	—
NHL Totals (1 year)		5	0	1	1	2	-1	0	0					

LAINE, TEEMU — RW — DEVILS

PERSONAL: Born August 9, 1982, in Helsinki, Finland. ... 6-0/194. ... Shoots left.
TRANSACTIONS/CAREER NOTES: Selected by New Jersey Devils in 2nd round (2nd Devils pick, 39th overall) of entry draft (June 24, 2000).

		REGULAR SEASON								PLAYOFFS				
Season Team	League	GP	G	A	Pts.	PIM	+/-	PP	SH	GP	G	A	Pts.	PIM
98-99—Jokerit Helsinki	Finland Jr. B	34	20	19	39	87	...	...	...	—	—	—	—	—
99-00—Jokerit Helsinki	Finland	14	1	1	2	8	...	...	...	—	—	—	—	—
—Jokerit Helsinki	Finland Jr.	23	5	9	14	14	...	...	...	—	—	—	—	—
00-01—Jokerit Helsinki	Finland	25	3	2	5	10	...	...	...	5	1	0	1	2
01-02—Jokerit Helsinki	Finland	38	0	1	1	45	...	...	...	7	0	0	0	2
02-03—Jokerit Helsinki	Finland	53	7	5	12	52	...	...	...	—	—	—	—	—
03-04—Jokerit Helsinki	Finland	56	5	8	13	50	...	...	...	8	1	1	2	2
04-05—Tappara Tampere	Finland	53	7	10	17	60	-2	...	...	5	0	1	1	14

LAING, QUINTIN — LW — BLACKHAWKS

PERSONAL: Born June 8, 1979, in Harris, Sask. ... 6-2/208. ... Shoots left.
TRANSACTIONS/CAREER NOTES: Selected by Detroit Red Wings in fourth round (third Red Wings pick, 102nd overall) of NHL entry draft (June 21, 1997). ... Signed as free agent by Chicago Blackhawks (June 4, 2003).

		REGULAR SEASON								PLAYOFFS				
Season Team	League	GP	G	A	Pts.	PIM	+/-	PP	SH	GP	G	A	Pts.	PIM
96-97—Kelowna	WHL	63	13	24	37	54	...	...	...	1	0	0	0	0
97-98—Kelowna	WHL	59	11	24	35	47	1	1	1	7	0	1	1	8
98-99—Kelowna	WHL	70	11	10	21	107	-12	1	1	6	3	0	3	0
99-00—Kelowna	WHL	68	22	30	52	61	-6	4	3	5	1	1	2	8
00-01—Norfolk	AHL	10	0	1	1	10	...	...	...	—	—	—	—	—
—Jackson	ECHL	60	13	24	37	39	...	...	...	5	0	0	0	0
01-02—Jackson	ECHL	16	4	6	10	12	0	1	1	—	—	—	—	—
—Norfolk	AHL	61	6	15	21	32	-2	1	0	4	0	0	0	2
02-03—Norfolk	AHL	69	5	12	17	33	2	0	1	8	2	2	4	0
03-04—Chicago	NHL	3	0	1	1	0	1	0	0	—	—	—	—	—
—Norfolk	AHL	78	12	10	22	74	3	1	0	8	5	1	6	4
04-05—Norfolk	AHL	66	10	13	23	54	-3	1	3	4	0	0	0	0
NHL Totals (1 year)		3	0	1	1	0	1	0	0					

LALIME, PATRICK G BLUES

PERSONAL: Born July 7, 1974, in St. Bonaventure, Que. ... 6-3/192. ... Catches left. ... Name pronounced luh-LEEM.

TRANSACTIONS/CAREER NOTES: Selected by Pittsburgh Penguins in sixth round (sixth Penguins pick, 156th overall) of NHL entry draft (June 26, 1993). ... Rights traded by Penguins to Anaheim Mighty Ducks for C Sean Pronger (March 24, 1998). ... Traded by Mighty Ducks to Ottawa Senators for LW Ted Donato and D Antti-Jussi Niemi (June 18, 1999). ... Flu (February 1, 2000); missed one game. ... Sprained left knee (October 14, 2000); missed 10 games. ... Flu (February 6, 2003); missed two games. ... Flu (December 2, 2003); missed two games. ... Sprained left knee (March 27, 2004); missed remainder of regular season. ... Traded by Senators to St. Louis Blues for fourth-round pick in 2005 entry draft (June 27, 2004).

		REGULAR SEASON									PLAYOFFS							
Season Team	**League**	**GP**	**Min.**	**W**	**L**	**T**	**GA**	**SO**	**GAA**	**SV%**	**GP**	**Min.**	**W**	**L**	**GA**	**SO**	**GAA**	**SV%**
92-93—Shawinigan	QMJHL	44	2467	10	24	4	192	0	4.67	.863	—	—	—	—	—	—	—	—
93-94—Shawinigan	QMJHL	48	2733	22	20	2	192	1	4.22	.874	5	223	1	3	25	0	6.73	.793
94-95—Hampton Roads	ECHL	26	1471	15	7	3	82	2	3.34	.894	—	—	—	—	—	—	—	—
—Cleveland	IHL	23	1230	7	10	4	91	0	4.44	.882	—	—	—	—	—	—	—	—
95-96—Cleveland	IHL	41	2314	20	12	7	149	0	3.86	...	—	—	—	—	—	—	—	—
96-97—Cleveland	IHL	14	834	6	6	2	45	1	3.24	...	—	—	—	—	—	—	—	—
—Pittsburgh	NHL	39	2058	21	12	2	101	3	2.94	.913	—	—	—	—	—	—	—	—
97-98—Grand Rapids	IHL	31	1749	10	10	9	76	2	2.61	.918	1	77	0	1	4	0	3.12	.892
98-99—Kansas City	IHL	*66	*3789	*39	20	4	*190	2	3.01	.900	3	179	1	2	6	1	2.01	.942
99-00—Ottawa	NHL	38	2038	19	14	3	79	3	2.33	.905	—	—	—	—	—	—	—	—
00-01—Ottawa	NHL	60	3607	36	19	5	141	7	2.35	.914	4	251	0	4	10	0	2.39	.899
01-02—Ottawa	NHL	61	3583	27	24	8	148	7	2.48	.903	12	778	7	5	18	4	*1.39	.946
02-03—Ottawa	NHL	67	3943	39	20	7	142	8	2.16	.911	18	1122	11	7	34	1	1.82	.924
03-04—Ottawa	NHL	57	3324	25	23	7	127	5	2.29	.905	7	398	3	4	13	0	1.96	.906
NHL Totals (6 years)		322	18553	167	112	32	738	33	2.39	.909	41	2549	21	20	75	5	1.77	.926

LAMOTHE, MARC G

PERSONAL: Born February 27, 1974, in New Liskeard, Ont. ... 6-0/215. ... Catches left. ... Name pronounced luh-MAHTH.

TRANSACTIONS/CAREER NOTES: Selected by Montreal Canadiens in fourth round (sixth Canadiens pick, 92nd overall) of NHL entry draft (June 20, 1992). ... Signed as free agent by Chicago Blackhawks (August 21, 1996). ... Signed as free agent by Columbus Blue Jackets (September 1, 2000). ... Signed as free agent by Detroit Red Wings (August 6, 2002).

		REGULAR SEASON									PLAYOFFS							
Season Team	**League**	**GP**	**Min.**	**W**	**L**	**T**	**GA**	**SO**	**GAA**	**SV%**	**GP**	**Min.**	**W**	**L**	**GA**	**SO**	**GAA**	**SV%**
90-91—Ottawa	OHA Mj. Jr	25	1220	...	...	...	82	1	4.03	...	—	—	—	—	—	—	—	—
91-92—Kingston	OHL	42	2378	10	25	2	189	1	4.77	...	—	—	—	—	—	—	—	—
92-93—Kingston	OHL	45	2489	23	12	6	162	1	3.91	.889	15	733	8	5	46	1	3.77	.896
93-94—Kingston	OHL	48	2828	23	20	5	177	2	3.76	.888	6	224	2	2	12	0	3.21	*.922
94-95—Fredericton	AHL	9	428	2	5	0	32	0	4.49	.873	—	—	—	—	—	—	—	—
—Wheeling	ECHL	13	737	9	2	1	38	0	3.09	.892	—	—	—	—	—	—	—	—
95-96—Fredericton	AHL	23	1165	5	9	3	73	1	3.76	...	3	160	1	2	9	0	3.38	...
96-97—Indianapolis	IHL	38	2271	20	14	4	100	1	2.64	.918	1	20	0	0	1	0	3.00	...
97-98—Indianapolis	IHL	31	1773	18	10	2	72	3	2.44	.920	4	178	1	3	10	0	3.37	.896
98-99—Indianapolis	IHL	32	1823	9	16	6	115	1	3.78	.881	6	330	3	3	10	*2	1.78	.948
—Detroit	IHL	...	...	...	...	...	...	...	...	...	1	80	0	1	5	0	3.75	...
99-00—Cleveland	IHL	44	2455	23	18	4	112	2	2.74	...	4	325	2	2	12	0	2.22	...
—Chicago	NHL	2	116	1	1	0	10	0	5.17	.800	—	—	—	—	—	—	—	—
00-01—Syracuse	AHL	42	2323	17	15	*7	112	2	2.89	.921	—	—	—	—	—	—	—	—
01-02—Hamilton	AHL	45	2569	22	19	2	102	3	2.38	.911	9	550	6	3	18	0	1.96	.933
02-03—Grand Rapids	AHL	60	3438	33	18	8	122	6	2.13	.923	15	944	10	5	29	1	1.84	.935
03-04—Grand Rapids	AHL	43	2534	21	16	5	87	4	2.06	.918	4	199	0	3	12	0	3.62	.876
—Detroit	NHL	2	125	1	0	1	3	0	1.44	.948	—	—	—	—	—	—	—	—
04-05—Lokomotiv Yaroslavl	Russian	55	3357	...	...	...	90	6	1.61	...	9	521	...	...	21	0	2.42	...
NHL Totals (2 years)		4	241	2	1	1	13	0	3.24	.880								

LAMPMAN, BRYCE D RANGERS

PERSONAL: Born August 31, 1982, in Rochester, Minn. ... 6-2/201. ... Shoots left.

TRANSACTIONS/CAREER NOTES: Selected by New York Rangers in fourth round (fourth Rangers pick, 113th overall) of NHL entry draft (June 23, 2001).

		REGULAR SEASON								PLAYOFFS				
Season Team	**League**	**GP**	**G**	**A**	**Pts.**	**PIM**	**+/-**	**PP**	**SH**	**GP**	**G**	**A**	**Pts.**	**PIM**
00-01—Omaha	USHL	55	10	11	21	77	...	...	...	—	—	—	—	—
01-02—U. of Neb.-Omaha	CCHA	26	0	4	4	28	...	...	...	—	—	—	—	—
02-03—Kamloops	WHL	29	1	17	18	32	...	...	...	—	—	—	—	—
—Hartford	AHL	45	0	6	6	32	11	0	0	2	0	1	1	0
03-04—Hartford	AHL	68	4	11	15	52	12	2	0	16	1	3	4	14
—New York Rangers	NHL	8	0	0	0	0	-4	0	0	—	—	—	—	—
04-05—Hartford	AHL	74	7	18	25	74	19	2	0	4	0	0	0	4
NHL Totals (1 year)		8	0	0	0	0	-4	0	0					

LANG, ROBERT — C — RED WINGS

PERSONAL: Born December 19, 1970, in Teplice, Czechoslovakia. ... 6-2/217. ... Shoots right.

TRANSACTIONS/CAREER NOTES: Selected by Los Angeles Kings in 7nth round (6th Kings pick, 133rd overall) of entry draft (June 16, 1990). ... Dislocated shoulder (April 3, 1994); missed remainder of season. ... Strained left shoulder (March 26, 1995); missed one game. ... Strained back (November 20, 1995); missed seven games. ... Signed as free agent by Edmonton Oilers (October 19, 1996). ... Loaned by Oilers to Sparta Praha of Czech league (October 19, 1996). ... Signed as free agent by Pittsburgh Penguins (September 2, 1997). ... Claimed by Boston Bruins from Penguins in waiver draft (September 28, 1997). ... Claimed off waivers by Penguins (October 25, 1997). ... Fractured thumb (March 21, 1998); missed nine games. ... Bruised ankle (March 23, 1999); missed 10 games. ... Back spasms (October 16, 1999); missed one game. ... Injured thumb (December 14, 1999); missed one game. ... Injured face (March 9, 2000); missed two games. ... Oral surgery (January 26, 2002); missed two games. ... Fractured hand (March 5, 2002); missed seven games. ... Reinjured hand (March 23, 2002); missed remainder of season. ... Signed as free agent by Washington Capitals (July 1, 2002). ... Traded by Capitals to Detroit Red Wings for C Tomas Fleischmann, a 1st-round pick (D Mike Green) in 2004 entry draft and a 4th-round pick in 2006 entry draft. ... Cracked ribs (March 9, 2004); missed 11 games. ... Reinjured ribs (April 1, 2004); missed 1 game.

STATISTICAL PLATEAUS: Three-goal games: 2003-04 (1).

		REGULAR SEASON								PLAYOFFS				
Season Team	**League**	**GP**	**G**	**A**	**Pts.**	**PIM**	**+/-**	**PP**	**SH**	**GP**	**G**	**A**	**Pts.**	**PIM**
88-89—Litvinov	Czech.	7	3	2	5	0	...	...	...	—	—	—	—	—
89-90—Litvinov	Czech.	39	11	10	21	20	...	...	...	—	—	—	—	—
90-91—Litvinov	Czech.	56	26	26	52	38	...	...	...	—	—	—	—	—
91-92—Litvinov	Czech.	43	12	31	43	34	...	...	...	—	—	—	—	—
—Czech. national team	Int'l	8	5	8	13	8	...	...	...	—	—	—	—	—
—Czech. Olympic Team	Int'l	8	5	8	13	8	8	2	0	—	—	—	—	—
92-93—Los Angeles	NHL	11	0	5	5	2	-3	0	0	—	—	—	—	—
—Phoenix	IHL	38	9	21	30	20	-2	4	0	—	—	—	—	—
93-94—Phoenix	IHL	44	11	24	35	34	-14	4	0	—	—	—	—	—
—Los Angeles	NHL	32	9	10	19	10	7	0	0	—	—	—	—	—
94-95—Chem. Litvinov	Czech Rep.	16	4	19	23	28	...	...	...	—	—	—	—	—
—Los Angeles	NHL	36	4	8	12	4	-7	0	0	—	—	—	—	—
95-96—Los Angeles	NHL	68	6	16	22	10	-15	0	2	—	—	—	—	—
96-97—Sparta Praha	Czech Rep.	38	14	27	41	30	...	...	...	5	1	2	3	4
97-98—Boston	NHL	3	0	0	0	2	1	0	0	—	—	—	—	—
—Houston	IHL	9	1	7	8	4	1	0	0	—	—	—	—	—
—Pittsburgh	NHL	51	9	13	22	14	6	1	1	6	0	3	3	2
—Czech Rep. Oly. team	Int'l	6	0	3	3	0	4	0	0	—	—	—	—	—
98-99—Pittsburgh	NHL	72	21	23	44	24	-10	7	0	12	0	2	2	0
99-00—Pittsburgh	NHL	78	23	42	65	14	-9	13	0	11	3	3	6	0
00-01—Pittsburgh	NHL	82	32	48	80	28	20	10	0	16	4	4	8	4
01-02—Pittsburgh	NHL	62	18	32	50	16	9	5	1	—	—	—	—	—
—Czech Rep. Oly. team	Int'l	4	1	2	3	2	...	...	...	—	—	—	—	—
02-03—Washington	NHL	82	22	47	69	22	12	10	0	6	2	1	3	2
03-04—Washington	NHL	63	29	45	74	24	2	10	0	—	—	—	—	—
—Detroit	NHL	6	1	4	5	0	2	0	0	12	4	5	9	6
NHL Totals (11 years)		646	174	293	467	170	15	56	4	63	13	18	31	14

LANGDON, DARREN — LW — DEVILS

PERSONAL: Born January 8, 1971, in Deer Lake, Nfld. ... 6-1/205. ... Shoots left.

TRANSACTIONS/CAREER NOTES: Signed as free agent by New York Rangers (August 16, 1993). ... Suspended three games for abuse of an official in preseason game (September 23, 1995). ... Sprained right knee (December 13, 1996); missed 13 games. ... Suspended two games for initiating altercation (March 7, 1997). ... Sprained knee (November 21, 1997); missed six games. ... Bruised sternum (March 4, 1998); missed three games. ... Strained groin (January 2, 2000); missed remainder of season. ... Traded by Rangers with RW Rob DiMaio to Carolina Hurricanes for RW Sandy McCarthy and fourth-round pick (D Bryce Lampman) in 2001 entry draft (August 4, 2000). ... Injured groin (February 7, 2001); missed nine games. ... Injured shoulder (March 26, 2002); missed four games. ... Injured knee (October 16, 2002); missed two games. ... Traded by Hurricanes with D Marek Malik to Vancouver Canucks for LW Jan Hlavac and C Harold Druken (November 1, 2002). ... Injured hand (March 3, 2003); missed 17 games. ... Claimed by Montreal Canadiens in waiver draft (October 3, 2003). ... Injured groin (October 14, 2003); missed nine games. ... Signed as free agent by New Jersey Devils (July 3, 2004).

		REGULAR SEASON								PLAYOFFS				
Season Team	**League**	**GP**	**G**	**A**	**Pts.**	**PIM**	**+/-**	**PP**	**SH**	**GP**	**G**	**A**	**Pts.**	**PIM**
91-92—Summerside	MJHL	44	34	49	83	441	...	...	...	—	—	—	—	—
92-93—Binghamton	AHL	18	3	4	7	115	...	...	...	8	0	1	1	14
—Dayton	ECHL	54	23	22	45	429	...	...	...	3	0	1	1	40
93-94—Binghamton	AHL	54	2	7	9	327	...	...	...	...	...	...	...	...
94-95—Binghamton	AHL	55	6	14	20	296	5	1	0	11	1	3	4	84
—New York Rangers	NHL	18	1	1	2	62	0	0	0	—	—	—	—	—
95-96—New York Rangers	NHL	64	7	4	11	175	2	0	0	2	0	0	0	0
—Binghamton	AHL	1	0	0	0	12	...	...	...	—	—	—	—	—
96-97—New York Rangers	NHL	60	3	6	9	195	-1	0	0	10	0	0	0	2
97-98—New York Rangers	NHL	70	3	3	6	197	0	0	0	—	—	—	—	—
98-99—New York Rangers	NHL	44	0	0	0	80	-3	0	0	—	—	—	—	—
99-00—New York Rangers	NHL	21	0	1	1	26	-2	0	0	—	—	—	—	—
00-01—Carolina	NHL	54	0	2	2	94	-4	0	0	4	0	0	0	12
01-02—Carolina	NHL	58	2	1	3	106	2	0	0	—	—	—	—	—
02-03—Carolina	NHL	9	0	0	0	16	0	0	0	—	—	—	—	—
—Vancouver	NHL	45	0	1	1	143	-2	0	0	—	—	—	—	—
03-04—Montreal	NHL	64	0	3	3	135	-2	0	0	9	1	0	1	6
NHL Totals (10 years)		507	16	22	38	1229	-10	0	0	25	1	0	1	20

LANGENBRUNNER, JAMIE RW/LW DEVILS

PERSONAL: Born July 24, 1975, in Duluth, Minn. ... 6-1/200. ... Shoots right. ... Name pronounced LANG-ihn-BRUH-nuhr.

TRANSACTIONS/CAREER NOTES: Selected by Dallas Stars in second round (second Stars pick, 35th overall) of NHL draft (June 26, 1993). ... Had back spasms (February 21, 1997); missed one game. ... Had whiplash (January 12, 1998); missed one game. ... Injured shoulder (January 6, 1999); missed five games. ... Strained abdominal muscle (March 26, 1999); missed one game. ... Had concussion (November 30, 1999); missed one game. ... Sprained shoulder (December 17, 1999); missed one game. ... Pinched nerve in neck (January 7, 2000); missed 11 games. ... Strained neck (February 16, 2000); missed three games. ... Strained abdominal muscle (December 20, 2000); missed 22 games. ... Reinjured abdominal muscle (March 4, 2001); missed five games. ... Strained back (March 31, 2001); missed one game. ... Traded by Stars with C Joe Nieuwendyk to New Jersey Devils for C Jason Arnott, RW Randy McKay and 1st-round pick (later traded to Columbus; Blue Jackets selected LW Dan Paille) in 2002 draft (March 19, 2002). ... Viral infection (November 19, 2002); missed four games. ... Injured knee (November 29, 2003) and had surgery (January 19, 2004); missed 28 games.

		REGULAR SEASON								PLAYOFFS				
Season Team	**League**	**GP**	**G**	**A**	**Pts.**	**PIM**	**+/-**	**PP**	**SH**	**GP**	**G**	**A**	**Pts.**	**PIM**
90-91—Cloquet H.S.	Minn. H.S.	20	6	16	22	8	...	...	...	—	—	—	—	—
91-92—Cloquet H.S.	Minn. H.S.	23	16	23	39	24	...	...	...	—	—	—	—	—
92-93—Cloquet H.S.	Minn. H.S.	27	27	62	89	18	...	...	...	—	—	—	—	—
93-94—Peterborough	OHL	62	33	58	91	53	...	10	0	7	4	6	10	2
94-95—Peterborough	OHL	62	42	57	99	84	...	19	1	11	8	14	22	12
—Dallas	NHL	2	0	0	0	2	0	0	0	—	—	—	—	—
—Kalamazoo	IHL	...	...	...	...	...	...	...	...	11	1	3	4	2
95-96—Michigan	IHL	59	25	40	65	129	...	...	...	10	3	10	13	8
—Dallas	NHL	12	2	2	4	6	-2	1	0	—	—	—	—	—
96-97—Dallas	NHL	76	13	26	39	51	-2	3	0	5	1	1	2	14
97-98—Dallas	NHL	81	23	29	52	61	9	8	0	16	1	4	5	14
—U.S. Olympic team	Int'l	3	0	0	0	4	-2	0	0	—	—	—	—	—
98-99—Dallas	NHL	75	12	33	45	62	10	4	0	23	10	7	17	16
99-00—Dallas	NHL	65	18	21	39	68	16	4	2	15	1	7	8	18
00-01—Dallas	NHL	53	12	18	30	57	4	3	2	10	2	2	4	6
01-02—Dallas	NHL	68	10	16	26	54	-11	0	1	—	—	—	—	—
—New Jersey	NHL	14	3	3	6	23	2	0	0	5	0	1	1	8
02-03—New Jersey	NHL	78	22	33	55	65	17	5	1	24	11	7	18	16
03-04—New Jersey	NHL	53	10	16	26	43	9	1	2	5	0	2	2	2
04-05—Ingolstadt ERC	Germany	11	2	2	4	22	-3	1	0	11	2	6	8	6
NHL Totals (10 years)		577	125	197	322	492	52	29	8	103	26	31	57	94

LANGFELD, JOSH RW SENATORS

PERSONAL: Born July 17, 1977, in Fridley, Minn. ... 6-3/214. ... Shoots right.

TRANSACTIONS/CAREER NOTES: Selected by Ottawa Senators in 3rd round (3rd Senators pick, 66th overall) of entry draft (June 21, 1997). ... Concussion (March 30, 2002); missed two games.

		REGULAR SEASON								PLAYOFFS				
Season Team	**League**	**GP**	**G**	**A**	**Pts.**	**PIM**	**+/-**	**PP**	**SH**	**GP**	**G**	**A**	**Pts.**	**PIM**
96-97—Lincoln	Jr. A	38	35	23	58	100	...	...	...	—	—	—	—	—
97-98—Univ. of Michigan	CCHA	46	19	17	36	66	...	...	...	—	—	—	—	—
98-99—Univ. of Michigan	CCHA	41	21	14	35	84	...	...	...	—	—	—	—	—
99-00—Univ. of Michigan	CCHA	37	9	20	29	56	...	...	...	—	—	—	—	—
00-01—Univ. of Michigan	CCHA	42	16	12	28	44	...	...	...	—	—	—	—	—
01-02—Grand Rapids	AHL	68	21	16	37	29	1	8	1	5	2	0	2	0
—Ottawa	NHL	1	0	0	0	2	0	0	0	—	—	—	—	—
02-03—Ottawa	NHL	12	0	1	1	4	2	0	0	—	—	—	—	—
—Binghamton	AHL	59	14	21	35	38	-4	4	0	13	5	3	8	8
03-04—Ottawa	NHL	38	7	10	17	16	6	2	0	—	—	—	—	—
—Binghamton	AHL	30	13	14	27	25	12	4	0	2	0	0	0	0
04-05—Binghamton	AHL	74	32	25	57	75	17	9	6	6	2	2	4	2
NHL Totals (3 years)		51	7	11	18	22	8	2	0					

LANGKOW, DAYMOND C FLAMES

PERSONAL: Born September 27, 1976, in Edmonton. ... 5-11/185. ... Shoots left. ... Brother of Scott Langkow, G with three NHL teams (1995-2000).

TRANSACTIONS/CAREER NOTES: Selected by Tampa Bay Lightning in first round (first Lightning pick, fifth overall) of NHL entry draft (July 8, 1995). ... Had the flu (October 1, 1997); missed one game. ... Suffered concussion (January 7, 1998); missed two games. ... Had the flu (January 31, 1998); missed three games ... Traded by Lightning with RW Mikael Renberg to Philadelphia Flyers for C Chris Gratton and C/RW Mike Sillinger (December 12, 1998). ... Fractured right foot (February 25, 2001); missed 11 games. ... Traded by Flyers to Phoenix Coyotes for second-round pick (later traded to Tampa Bay Lightning) in 2002 entry draft and first-round pick (C Jeff Carter) in 2003 entry draft (July 2, 2001). ... Fractured toe (January 3, 2002); missed two games. ... Traded by Coyotes to Calgary Flames for D Denis Gauthier and LW Oleg Saprykin (August 26, 2004).

STATISTICAL PLATEAUS: Three-goal games: 2001-02 (1), 2002-03 (1). Total: 2.

		REGULAR SEASON								PLAYOFFS				
Season Team	**League**	**GP**	**G**	**A**	**Pts.**	**PIM**	**+/-**	**PP**	**SH**	**GP**	**G**	**A**	**Pts.**	**PIM**
91-92—Tri-City	WHL	1	0	0	0	0	...	...	...	4	2	2	4	15
92-93—Tri-City	WHL	65	22	42	64	96	...	...	...	4	1	0	1	4
93-94—Tri-City	WHL	61	40	43	83	174	...	...	...	4	2	2	4	15
94-95—Tri-City	WHL	72	67	73	140	142	32	26	5	17	12	15	27	52
95-96—Tampa Bay	NHL	4	0	1	1	0	-1	0	0	—	—	—	—	—
—Tri-City	WHL	48	30	61	91	103	...	...	...	11	14	13	27	20
96-97—Adirondack	AHL	2	1	1	2	0	-1	0	0	—	—	—	—	—

Season Team	League	REGULAR SEASON GP	G	A	Pts.	PIM	+/-	PP	SH	PLAYOFFS GP	G	A	Pts.	PIM
—Tampa Bay	NHL	79	15	13	28	35	1	3	1	—	—	—	—	—
97-98—Tampa Bay	NHL	68	8	14	22	62	-9	2	0	—	—	—	—	—
98-99—Cleveland	IHL	4	1	1	2	18	-4	1	0	—	—	—	—	—
—Tampa Bay	NHL	22	4	6	10	15	0	1	0	—	—	—	—	—
—Philadelphia	NHL	56	10	13	23	24	-8	3	1	6	0	2	2	2
99-00—Philadelphia	NHL	82	18	32	50	56	1	5	0	16	5	5	10	23
00-01—Philadelphia	NHL	71	13	41	54	50	12	3	0	6	2	4	6	2
01-02—Phoenix	NHL	80	27	35	62	36	18	6	3	5	1	0	1	0
02-03—Phoenix	NHL	82	20	32	52	56	20	4	2	—	—	—	—	—
03-04—Phoenix	NHL	81	21	31	52	40	4	4	1	—	—	—	—	—
NHL Totals (9 years)		625	136	218	354	374	38	31	8	33	8	11	19	27

LAPERRIERE, IAN — RW/C — AVALANCHE

PERSONAL: Born January 19, 1974, in Montreal. ... 6-1/201. ... Shoots right. ... Name pronounced EE-ihn luh-PAIR-ee-AIR.
TRANSACTIONS/CAREER NOTES: Selected by St. Louis Blues in 7th round (6th Blues pick, 158th overall) of NHL draft (June 20, 1992). ... Concussion (March 26, 1995); missed three games. ... Traded by Blues to New York Rangers for LW Stephane Matteau (December 28, 1995). ... Traded by Rangers with C Ray Ferraro, C Nathan LaFayette, D Mattias Norstrom and 4th-round pick (D Sean Blanchard) in 1997 entry draft to Los Angeles Kings for RW Shane Churla, LW Jari Kurri and D/RW Marty McSorley (March 14, 1996). ... Sprained left shoulder (March 16, 1996); missed two games. ... Strained shoulder (October 29, 1996); missed three games. ... Strained hip flexor (February 1, 1997); missed three games. ... Concussion (February 25, 1997); missed two games. ... Shoulder surgery (March 17, 1997); missed final 11 games of regular season. ... Blurred vision (December 31, 1997); missed three games. ... Tore knee ligament (October 12, 1998); missed nine games. ... Inflamed left knee (January 2, 1999); missed one game. ... Sprained knee (December 30, 1999); missed three games. ... Strained hip flexor (October 15, 2000); missed one game. ... Concussion (April 3, 2001); missed two games. ... Cervical strain (November 27, 2002); missed four games. ... Injured back (January 18, 2003); missed one game. ... Injured right knee and had surgery (February 3, 2003); missed three games. ... Concussion (November 27, 2003); missed 19 games. ... Signed as free agent by Colorado Avalanche (July 2, 2004).
STATISTICAL PLATEAUS: Three-goal games: 2000-01 (1).

Season Team	League	REGULAR SEASON GP	G	A	Pts.	PIM	+/-	PP	SH	PLAYOFFS GP	G	A	Pts.	PIM
90-91—Drummondville	QMJHL	65	19	29	48	117	...	...	...	—	—	—	—	—
91-92—Drummondville	QMJHL	70	28	49	77	160	...	...	...	—	—	—	—	—
92-93—Drummondville	QMJHL	60	44	96	140	188	...	...	...	10	6	13	19	20
93-94—Drummondville	QMJHL	62	41	72	113	150	17	13	1	9	4	6	10	35
—St. Louis	NHL	1	0	0	0	0	0	0	0	—	—	—	—	—
—Peoria	IHL	...	...	...	...	...	...	...	...	5	1	3	4	2
94-95—Peoria	IHL	51	16	32	48	111	11	5	1	—	—	—	—	—
—St. Louis	NHL	37	13	14	27	85	12	1	0	7	0	4	4	21
95-96—St. Louis	NHL	33	3	6	9	87	-4	1	0	—	—	—	—	—
—Worcester	AHL	3	2	1	3	22	...	...	...	—	—	—	—	—
—New York Rangers	NHL	28	1	2	3	53	-5	0	0	—	—	—	—	—
—Los Angeles	NHL	10	2	3	5	15	-2	0	0	—	—	—	—	—
96-97—Los Angeles	NHL	62	8	15	23	102	-25	0	1	—	—	—	—	—
97-98—Los Angeles	NHL	77	6	15	21	131	0	0	1	4	1	0	1	6
98-99—Los Angeles	NHL	72	3	10	13	138	-5	0	0	—	—	—	—	—
99-00—Los Angeles	NHL	79	9	13	22	185	-14	0	0	4	0	0	0	2
00-01—Los Angeles	NHL	79	8	10	18	141	5	0	0	13	1	2	3	12
01-02—Los Angeles	NHL	81	8	14	22	125	5	0	0	7	0	1	1	9
02-03—Los Angeles	NHL	73	7	12	19	122	-9	1	1	—	—	—	—	—
03-04—Los Angeles	NHL	62	10	12	22	58	-4	1	0	—	—	—	—	—
NHL Totals (11 years)		694	78	126	204	1242	-46	4	3	35	2	7	9	50

LAPOINTE, CLAUDE — C

PERSONAL: Born October 11, 1968, in Lachine, Que. ... 5-9/188. ... Shoots left. ... Name pronounced KLOHD luh-pwah.
TRANSACTIONS/CAREER NOTES: Selected by Quebec Nordiques in 12th round (12th Nordiques pick, 234th overall) of NHL entry draft (June 11, 1988). ... Tore groin muscle (February 9, 1991). ... Injured groin (October 23, 1991); missed one game. ... Injured back in training camp (September 1992); missed first five games of season. ... Bruised hip (April 6, 1993); missed two games. ... Sprained left knee (October 18, 1993); missed 13 games. ... Sprained back (February 1, 1994); missed nine games. ... Injured back (March 19, 1994); missed three games. ... Had lower back pain (January 21, 1995); missed 16 games. ... Had the flu (April 16, 1995); missed one game. ... Injured hip (April 30, 1995); missed one game. ... Nordiques franchise moved to Colorado and renamed Avalanche for 1995-96 season (June 21, 1995). ... Traded by Avalanche to Calgary Flames for seventh-round pick (C Samuel Pahlsson) in 1996 entry draft (November 1, 1995). ... Injured groin (December 20, 1995); missed one game. ... Reinjured groin (December 27, 1995); missed three games. ... Reinjured groin (January 5, 1996); missed three games. ... Injured hip (January 26, 1996); missed 17 games. ... Signed as free agent by New York Islanders (August 22, 1996). ... Hyperextended ankle (January 2, 1997); missed one game. ... Had sore ankle (January 25, 1997); missed one game. ... Bruised foot (January 22, 1998); missed one game. ... Fractured toe (February 1, 1998); missed three games. ... Injured foot (October 16, 1999); missed one game. ... Sprained knee (October 30, 1999); missed two games. ... Cut face (December 29, 1999); missed one game. ... Had the flu (April 6, 2000); missed two games. ... Injured toe (February 25, 2001); missed one game. ... Bruised foot (March 28, 2001); missed one game. ... Had the flu (December 12, 2001); missed one game. ... Had the flu (January 3, 2002); missed one game. ... Sprained ankle (November 23, 2002); missed two games. ... Traded by Islanders to Philadelphia Flyers for fifth-round pick (later traded to Pittsburgh Penguins) in 2003 entry draft (March 9, 2003). ... Had the flu (March 27, 2003); missed one game. ... Was ill (October 18, 2003); missed one game. ... Suffered from depression (November 6, 2003); missed two games. ... Entered NHL behavioral health program (December 3, 2003); missed 31 games. ... Had the flu (March 27, 2004); missed three games. ... Suspended by NHL for violating behavioral health policy (April 9, 2004).

Season Team	League	REGULAR SEASON GP	G	A	Pts.	PIM	+/-	PP	SH	PLAYOFFS GP	G	A	Pts.	PIM
85-86—Trois-Rivieres	QMJHL	72	19	38	57	74	...	...	...	—	—	—	—	—
86-87—Trois-Rivieres	QMJHL	70	47	57	104	123	...	...	...	—	—	—	—	—
87-88—Laval	QMJHL	69	37	83	120	143	...	...	...	13	2	17	19	53

Season Team	League	GP	G	A	Pts.	PIM	+/-	PP	SH		GP	G	A	Pts.	PIM
		REGULAR SEASON									PLAYOFFS				
88-89—Laval	QMJHL	63	32	72	104	158	...	...	...		17	5	14	19	66
89-90—Halifax	AHL	63	18	19	37	51	...	...	...		6	1	1	2	34
90-91—Quebec	NHL	13	2	2	4	4	3	0	0		—	—	—	—	—
—Halifax	AHL	43	17	17	34	46	...	...	...		—	—	—	—	—
91-92—Quebec	NHL	78	13	20	33	86	-8	0	2		—	—	—	—	—
92-93—Quebec	NHL	74	10	26	36	98	5	0	0		6	2	4	6	8
93-94—Quebec	NHL	59	11	17	28	70	2	1	1		—	—	—	—	—
94-95—Quebec	NHL	29	4	8	12	41	5	0	0		5	0	0	0	8
95-96—Colorado	NHL	3	0	0	0	0	-1	0	0		—	—	—	—	—
—Calgary	NHL	32	4	5	9	20	2	0	2		2	0	0	0	0
—Saint John	AHL	12	5	3	8	10	...	...	...		—	—	—	—	—
96-97—Utah	IHL	9	7	6	13	14	...	...	...		—	—	—	—	—
—New York Islanders	NHL	73	13	5	18	49	-12	0	3		—	—	—	—	—
97-98—New York Islanders	NHL	78	10	10	20	47	-9	0	1		—	—	—	—	—
98-99—New York Islanders	NHL	82	14	23	37	62	-19	2	2		—	—	—	—	—
99-00—New York Islanders	NHL	76	15	16	31	60	-22	2	1		—	—	—	—	—
00-01—New York Islanders	NHL	80	9	23	32	56	-2	1	1		—	—	—	—	—
01-02—New York Islanders	NHL	80	9	12	21	60	-9	0	3		7	0	0	0	14
02-03—New York Islanders	NHL	66	6	6	12	20	-3	0	0		—	—	—	—	—
—Philadelphia	NHL	14	2	2	4	16	5	0	0		13	2	3	5	14
03-04—Philadelphia	NHL	42	5	3	8	32	2	0	1		1	0	0	0	0
—Philadelphia	AHL	2	1	1	2	0	-1	1	0		—	—	—	—	—
NHL Totals (14 years)		879	127	178	305	721	-61	6	17		34	4	7	11	44

LAPOINTE, MARTIN RW BLACKHAWKS

PERSONAL: Born September 12, 1973, in Ville Ste-Pierre, Que. ... 5-11/215. ... Shoots right. ... Name pronounced MAHR-tahn luh-POYNT.
TRANSACTIONS/CAREER NOTES: Selected by Detroit Red Wings in 1st round (1st Red Wings pick, 10th overall) of entry draft (June 22, 1991). ... Fractured wrist (October 9, 1991); missed 22 games. ... Injured left knee (February 29, 1996); missed eight games. ... Injured leg (April 10, 1996); missed two games. ... Fractured finger (December 1, 1996); missed four games. ... Strained hamstring (February 25, 1998); missed one game. ... Suspended two games and fined $1,000 for cross-checking incident (March 18, 1998). ... Back spasms (December 22, 1998); missed one game. ... Bruised knee (February 12, 1999); missed three games. ... Signed as free agent by Boston Bruins (July 2, 2001). ... Strained hamstring (January 30, 2002); missed seven games. ... Reinjured hamstring (March 6, 2002); missed five games. ... Injured hamstring (February 5, 2003); missed seven games. ... Injured hamstring (March 8, 2003); missed five games. ... Had offseason knee surgery; missed first three games of 2003-04 season. ... Suspended one game for high-sticking incident (December 29, 2003). ... Signed as free agent by Chicago Blackhawks (Aug. 4, 2005).
STATISTICAL PLATEAUS: Three-goal games: 1999-00 (1), 2002-03 (1). Total: 2.

Season Team	League	GP	G	A	Pts.	PIM	+/-	PP	SH		GP	G	A	Pts.	PIM
		REGULAR SEASON									PLAYOFFS				
89-90—Laval	QMJHL	65	42	54	96	77	...	...	...		14	8	17	25	54
90-91—Laval	QMJHL	64	44	54	98	66	...	...	...		13	7	14	21	26
91-92—Detroit	NHL	4	0	1	1	5	2	0	0		3	0	1	1	4
—Laval	QMJHL	31	25	30	55	84	...	...	...		10	4	10	14	32
—Adirondack	AHL	...	...	...	...	...	...	...	...		8	2	2	4	4
92-93—Adirondack	AHL	8	1	2	3	9	1	0	0		—	—	—	—	—
—Detroit	NHL	3	0	0	0	0	-2	0	0		—	—	—	—	—
—Laval	QMJHL	35	38	51	89	41	...	...	...		13	*13	*17	*30	22
93-94—Adirondack	AHL	28	25	21	46	47	13	14	0		4	1	1	2	8
—Detroit	NHL	50	8	8	16	55	7	2	0		4	0	0	0	6
94-95—Adirondack	AHL	39	29	16	45	80	12	10	5		—	—	—	—	—
—Detroit	NHL	39	4	6	10	73	1	0	0		2	0	1	1	8
95-96—Detroit	NHL	58	6	3	9	93	0	1	0		11	1	2	3	12
96-97—Detroit	NHL	78	16	17	33	167	-14	5	1		20	4	8	12	60
97-98—Detroit	NHL	79	15	19	34	106	0	4	0		21	9	6	15	20
98-99—Detroit	NHL	77	16	13	29	141	7	7	1		10	0	2	2	20
99-00—Detroit	NHL	82	16	25	41	121	17	1	1		9	3	1	4	20
00-01—Detroit	NHL	82	27	30	57	127	3	13	0		6	0	1	1	8
01-02—Boston	NHL	68	17	23	40	101	12	4	0		6	1	2	3	12
02-03—Boston	NHL	59	8	10	18	87	-19	1	0		5	1	0	1	14
03-04—Boston	NHL	78	15	10	25	67	-5	9	0		7	0	0	0	14
NHL Totals (13 years)		757	148	165	313	1143	9	47	3		104	19	24	43	198

LARAQUE, GEORGES RW OILERS

PERSONAL: Born December 7, 1976, in Montreal. ... 6-3/245. ... Shoots right. ... Name pronounced zhawrzh la-RAHK.
TRANSACTIONS/CAREER NOTES: Selected by Edmonton Oilers in second round (second Oilers pick, 31st overall) of NHL draft (July 8, 1995). ... Fractured left foot (November 17, 1997); missed five games. ... Tore cartilige in right knee (December 5, 1997); missed seven games. ... Suspended two games by AHL for checking from behind (October 21, 1998). ... Bruised sternum (January 17, 1999); missed two games. ... Sprained ankle (March 24, 1999); missed three games. ... Had concussion (April 1, 1999); missed three games. ... Injured eye (December 19, 1999); missed two games. ... Sprained knee (March 27, 2000); missed one game. ... Had tendinitis in right forearm (January 18, 2002); missed two games. ... Sprained left wrist (November 8, 2002); missed five games. ... Injured elbow (November 30, 2002); missed five games. ... Injured knee (January 18, 2003); missed six games. ... Injured shoulder (February 22, 2003); missed one game. ... Injured thumb (October 30, 2003); missed 1 game. ... Reinjured thumb (November 4, 2003); missed two games.
STATISTICAL PLATEAUS: Three-goal games: 1999-00 (1).

Season Team	League	GP	G	A	Pts.	PIM	+/-	PP	SH		GP	G	A	Pts.	PIM
		REGULAR SEASON									PLAYOFFS				
93-94—St. Jean	QMJHL	70	11	11	22	142	...	...	...		4	0	0	0	7
94-95—St. Jean	QMJHL	62	19	22	41	259	-1	8	0		7	1	1	2	42

Season Team	League	GP	G	A	Pts.	PIM	+/-	PP	SH	GP	G	A	Pts.	PIM
		REGULAR SEASON								PLAYOFFS				
95-96—Laval	QMJHL	11	8	13	21	76	...	...	...	—	—	—	—	—
—St. Hyacinthe	QMJHL	8	3	4	7	59	...	...	...	—	—	—	—	—
—Granby	QMJHL	22	9	7	16	125	...	...	...	18	7	6	13	104
96-97—Hamilton	AHL	73	14	20	34	179	-11	6	0	15	1	3	4	12
97-98—Hamilton	AHL	46	10	20	30	154	6	2	0	3	0	0	0	11
—Edmonton	NHL	11	0	0	0	59	-4	0	0	—	—	—	—	—
98-99—Hamilton	AHL	25	6	8	14	93	-2	0	0	—	—	—	—	—
—Edmonton	NHL	39	3	2	5	57	-1	0	0	4	0	0	0	2
99-00—Edmonton	NHL	76	8	8	16	123	5	0	0	5	0	1	1	6
00-01—Edmonton	NHL	82	13	16	29	148	5	1	0	6	1	1	2	8
01-02—Edmonton	NHL	80	5	14	19	157	6	1	0	—	—	—	—	—
02-03—Edmonton	NHL	64	6	7	13	110	-4	0	0	6	1	3	4	4
03-04—Edmonton	NHL	66	6	11	17	99	7	1	0	—	—	—	—	—
04-05—AIK Solna	Sweden Dv. 2	16	11	5	16	24	...	...	...	—	—	—	—	—
NHL Totals (7 years)		418	41	58	99	753	14	3	0	21	2	5	7	20

LAROSE, CORY — C — THRASHERS

PERSONAL: Born May 14, 1975, in Campbellton, N.B. ... 6-0/191. ... Shoots left.

TRANSACTIONS/CAREER NOTES: Signed as free agent by Minnesota Wild. ... Traded by Wild to New York Rangers for LW Jay Henderson (February 20, 2003). ... Signed as free agent by Atlanta Thrashers (July 14, 2004).

Season Team	League	GP	G	A	Pts.	PIM	+/-	PP	SH	GP	G	A	Pts.	PIM
		REGULAR SEASON								PLAYOFFS				
96-97—Maine	Hockey East	35	10	27	37	32	...	...	...	—	—	—	—	—
97-98—Maine	Hockey East	34	15	25	40	22	...	...	...	—	—	—	—	—
98-99—Maine	Hockey East	38	21	31	52	34	...	...	...	—	—	—	—	—
99-00—Maine	Hockey East	39	15	36	51	45	...	...	...	—	—	—	—	—
00-01—Cleveland	IHL	4	1	1	2	6	...	...	...	—	—	—	—	—
—Jackson	ECHL	63	21	32	53	73	...	...	...	5	2	2	4	12
01-02—Houston	AHL	78	32	32	64	73	23	6	2	14	6	8	14	15
02-03—Houston	AHL	58	18	38	56	57	4	5	2	—	—	—	—	—
—Hartford	AHL	24	9	10	19	20	0	4	0	2	0	1	1	0
03-04—New York Rangers	NHL	7	0	1	1	4	-2	0	0	—	—	—	—	—
—Hartford	AHL	69	13	36	49	66	12	4	3	14	4	6	10	24
04-05—Chicago	AHL	80	26	37	63	44	6	12	0	18	6	6	12	29
NHL Totals (1 year)		7	0	1	1	4	-2	0	0					

LARSEN, BRAD — LW — THRASHERS

PERSONAL: Born January 28, 1977, in Nakusp, B.C. ... 6-1/200. ... Shoots left.

TRANSACTIONS/CAREER NOTES: Selected by Ottawa Senators in third round (third Senators pick, 53rd overall) of NHL entry draft (July 8, 1995). ... Rights traded by Senators to Colorado Avalanche for D Janne Laukkanen (January 25, 1996); did not sign. ... Returned to draft pool by Avalanche; selected by Avalanche in fourth round (fifth Avalanche pick, 87th overall) of NHL entry draft (June 21, 1997). ... Injured ribs (December 27, 2001); missed 11 games. ... Strained back (April 1, 2002); missed four games. ... Injured groin (October 27, 2002); missed 18 games. ... Injured back (December 10, 2002); missed 28 games. ... Injured groin (October 26, 2003); missed four games. ... Reinjured groin (November 11, 2003); missed six games. ... Reinjured groin (February 14, 2004); missed seven games. ... Claimed on waivers by Atlanta Thrashers (February 25, 2004). ... Bruised ribs (March 5, 2004); missed 12 games.

Season Team	League	GP	G	A	Pts.	PIM	+/-	PP	SH	GP	G	A	Pts.	PIM
		REGULAR SEASON								PLAYOFFS				
92-93—Nelson	Tier II Jr. A	42	31	37	68	164	...	...	...	—	—	—	—	—
93-94—Swift Current	WHL	64	15	18	33	37	...	...	...	7	1	2	3	4
94-95—Swift Current	WHL	62	24	33	57	73	-18	7	0	6	0	1	1	2
95-96—Swift Current	WHL	51	30	47	77	67	...	...	...	6	3	2	5	13
96-97—Swift Current	WHL	61	36	46	82	61	27	11	2	—	—	—	—	—
97-98—Hershey	AHL	65	12	10	22	80	-6	3	0	7	3	2	5	2
—Colorado	NHL	1	0	0	0	0	0	0	0	—	—	—	—	—
98-99—Hershey	AHL	18	3	4	7	11	-4	1	0	5	1	0	1	6
99-00—Hershey	AHL	52	13	26	39	66	...	...	...	14	5	2	7	29
00-01—Hershey	AHL	67	21	25	46	93	...	...	...	10	1	3	4	6
—Colorado	NHL	9	0	0	0	0	1	0	0	—	—	—	—	—
01-02—Colorado	NHL	50	2	7	9	47	4	1	0	21	1	1	2	13
02-03—Colorado	NHL	6	0	3	3	2	3	0	0	—	—	—	—	—
—Hershey	AHL	25	3	6	9	25	-5	1	0	4	1	1	2	8
03-04—Colorado	NHL	26	2	2	4	11	2	0	0	—	—	—	—	—
—Hershey	AHL	21	4	13	17	40	9	2	0	—	—	—	—	—
—Atlanta	NHL	6	0	0	0	2	-2	0	0	—	—	—	—	—
04-05—Chicago	AHL	75	26	23	49	112	9	10	1	18	4	7	11	22
NHL Totals (5 years)		98	4	12	16	62	8	1	0	21	1	1	2	13

LASHOFF, MATT — D — BRUINS

PERSONAL: Born September 29, 1986, in East Greenbush, N.Y. ... 6-1/201. ... Shoots left.

TRANSACTIONS/CAREER NOTES: Selected by Boston Bruins in 1st round (1st Bruins pick, 23rd overall) of entry draft (July 30, 2005).

Season Team	League	GP	G	A	Pts.	PIM	+/-	PP	SH	GP	G	A	Pts.	PIM
		REGULAR SEASON								PLAYOFFS				
03-04—Kitchener	OHL	62	5	19	24	94	...	...	...	—	—	—	—	—
04-05—Kitchener	OHL	44	4	18	22	44	16	3	0	13	0	3	3	18

LATENDRESSE, GUILLAUME RW CANADIENS

PERSONAL: Born May 24, 1987, in Ste-Catherine, Que. ... 6-2/220. ... Shoots left.

		REGULAR SEASON								PLAYOFFS				
Season Team	League	GP	G	A	Pts.	PIM	+/-	PP	SH	GP	G	A	Pts.	PIM
04-05—Drummondville	QMJHL	65	29	49	78	76	7	16	1	6	6	4	10	7

LAW, KIRBY RW WILD

PERSONAL: Born March 11, 1977, in McCreary, Man. ... 6-1/190. ... Shoots right.
TRANSACTIONS/CAREER NOTES: Signed as free agent by Atlanta Thrashers (July 6, 1999). ... Traded by Thrashers to Philadelphia Flyers for sixth-round pick (D Jeff Dwyer) in 2000 draft and conditional sixth-round pick (G Pasi Nurminen) in 2001 draft (March 14, 2000). ... Signed as free agent by Minnesota Wild (July 6, 2004).

		REGULAR SEASON								PLAYOFFS				
Season Team	League	GP	G	A	Pts.	PIM	+/-	PP	SH	GP	G	A	Pts.	PIM
93-94—Saskatoon	WHL	66	9	11	20	39	...	...	...	16	0	0	0	6
94-95—Saskatoon	WHL	46	10	15	25	44	8	1	0	—	—	—	—	—
—Lethbridge	WHL	24	4	10	14	38	-7	0	1	—	—	—	—	—
95-96—Lethbridge	WHL	71	17	45	62	133	...	...	...	4	0	0	0	12
96-97—Lethbridge	WHL	72	39	52	91	200	20	15	0	19	4	14	18	60
98-99—Orlando	IHL	67	18	13	31	136	-17	8	0	—	—	—	—	—
—Adirondack	AHL	11	2	3	5	40	-3	0	0	3	1	0	1	2
99-00—Orlando	IHL	1	1	0	1	0	...	...	...	—	—	—	—	—
—Louisville	AHL	66	31	21	52	173	...	...	...	—	—	—	—	—
—Philadelphia	AHL	12	1	4	5	6	...	...	...	5	2	0	2	2
00-01—Philadelphia	AHL	78	27	34	61	150	...	...	...	10	1	6	7	16
—Philadelphia	NHL	1	0	0	0	0	-1	0	0	—	—	—	—	—
01-02—Philadelphia	AHL	71	18	24	42	102	-14	8	0	5	0	0	0	0
02-03—Philadelphia	AHL	74	22	19	41	166	5	7	2	—	—	—	—	—
—Philadelphia	NHL	2	0	0	0	2	0	0	0	—	—	—	—	—
03-04—Philadelphia	NHL	6	0	1	1	2	0	0	0	—	—	—	—	—
—Philadelphia	AHL	74	32	41	73	139	16	9	0	12	0	5	5	12
04-05—Houston	AHL	80	25	24	49	134	3	5	1	5	0	1	1	4
NHL Totals (3 years)		9	0	1	1	4	-1	0	0					

LAWRENCE, CHRIS C LIGHTNING

PERSONAL: Born February 5, 1987, in Toronto. ... 6-4/199. ... Shoots right.

		REGULAR SEASON								PLAYOFFS				
Season Team	League	GP	G	A	Pts.	PIM	+/-	PP	SH	GP	G	A	Pts.	PIM
03-04—S.S. Marie	OHL	62	7	6	13	34	...	...	...	—	—	—	—	—
04-05—Sault Ste. Marie	OHL	68	11	40	51	57	16	5	0	7	3	3	6	4

LEAHY, PAT RW BRUINS

PERSONAL: Born June 9, 1979, in Brighton, Mass. ... 6-3/200. ... Shoots right.
TRANSACTIONS/CAREER NOTES: Selected by New York Rangers in fifth round (fifth Rangers pick, 122nd overall) of NHL entry draft (June 27, 1998). ... Signed as free agent by Boston Bruins (July 28, 2003). ... Signed as free agent by Providence of the AHL (October 1, 2004).

		REGULAR SEASON								PLAYOFFS				
Season Team	League	GP	G	A	Pts.	PIM	+/-	PP	SH	GP	G	A	Pts.	PIM
97-98—Miami (Ohio)	CCHA	28	0	1	1	24	...	...	...	—	—	—	—	—
98-99—Miami (Ohio)	CCHA	34	10	20	30	40	...	...	...	—	—	—	—	—
99-00—Miami (Ohio)	CCHA	36	16	22	38	89	...	...	...	—	—	—	—	—
00-01—Miami (Ohio)	CCHA	37	13	19	32	52	...	...	...	—	—	—	—	—
01-02—Trenton	ECHL	41	20	21	41	64	9	7	2	—	—	—	—	—
—Hershey	AHL	9	1	2	3	8	-1	0	0	—	—	—	—	—
—Portland	AHL	9	1	1	2	8	2	0	0	—	—	—	—	—
—Bridgeport	AHL	14	2	2	4	2	4	0	0	20	3	4	7	4
02-03—Providence	AHL	66	20	23	43	63	14	5	1	—	—	—	—	—
03-04—Boston	NHL	6	0	0	0	0	1	0	0	—	—	—	—	—
—Providence	AHL	55	14	16	30	37	3	6	2	2	0	0	0	0
04-05—Providence	AHL	38	1	14	15	18	2	0	0	17	4	6	10	20
NHL Totals (1 year)		6	0	0	0	0	1	0	0					

LECAVALIER, VINCENT C LIGHTNING

PERSONAL: Born April 21, 1980, in Ile-Bizard, Que. ... 6-4/207. ... Shoots left.
TRANSACTIONS/CAREER NOTES: Selected by Tampa Bay Lightning in first round (first Lightning pick, first overall) of NHL draft (June 27, 1998). ... Injured ankle (April 6, 2000); missed final two games of season. ... Fractured left foot (January 12, 2001); missed 14 games. ... Fractured left ankle (February 9, 2002); missed four games. ... Sprained knee (October 21, 2002); missed two games. ... Suspended one game by NHL for kicking incident (January 11, 2004).
STATISTICAL PLATEAUS: Three-goal games: 2002-03 (2), 2003-04 (1). Total: 3.

Season Team	League	GP	G	A	Pts.	PIM	+/-	PP	SH	GP	G	A	Pts.	PIM
		REGULAR SEASON								PLAYOFFS				
95-96—Notre Dame	SJHL	22	52	52	104	...	...	...	...	—	—	—	—	—
96-97—Rimouski	QMJHL	64	42	60	102	36	...	...	...	4	4	3	7	2
97-98—Rimouski	QMJHL	58	44	71	115	117	...	...	...	18	15	26	41	46
98-99—Tampa Bay	NHL	82	13	15	28	23	-19	2	0	—	—	—	—	—
99-00—Tampa Bay	NHL	80	25	42	67	43	-25	6	0	—	—	—	—	—
00-01—Tampa Bay	NHL	68	23	28	51	66	-26	7	0	—	—	—	—	—
01-02—Tampa Bay	NHL	76	20	17	37	61	-18	5	0	—	—	—	—	—
02-03—Tampa Bay	NHL	80	33	45	78	39	0	11	2	11	3	3	6	22
03-04—Tampa Bay	NHL	81	32	34	66	52	23	5	2	23	9	7	16	25
04-05—Ak Bars Kazan	Russian	30	7	9	16	78	4	...	...	4	1	0	1	6
NHL Totals (6 years)		467	146	181	327	284	-65	36	4	34	12	10	22	47

LECLAIR, JOHN — LW — PENGUINS

PERSONAL: Born July 5, 1969, in St. Albans, Vt. ... 6-3/225. ... Shoots left.

TRANSACTIONS/CAREER NOTES: Selected by Montreal Canadiens in second round (2nd Canadiens pick, 33rd overall) of entry draft (June 13, 1987). ... Injured shoulder (January 15, 1992); missed four games. ... Charley horse (January 20, 1993); missed four games. ... Sprained knee (October 2, 1993); missed eight games. ... Bruised sternum (March 28, 1994); missed two games. ... Traded by Canadiens with LW Gilbert Dionne and D Eric Desjardins to Philadelphia Flyers for RW Mark Recchi and third-round pick (C Martin Hohenberger) in 1995 entry draft (February 9, 1995). ... Strained right hip (April 18, 1995); missed one playoff game. ... Strained hip flexor (March 9, 1999); missed four games. ... Back spasms (April 1, 1999); missed two games. ... Injured back (October 9, 2000); missed 20 games. ... Strained lower back (December 9, 2000); missed 46 games. ... Dislocated right shoulder (November 29, 2002), required surgery; missed 47 games. ... Fractured left foot (October 8, 2003); missed seven games. ... Contract bought out by Flyers (July 23, 2005).

STATISTICAL PLATEAUS: Three-goal games: 1994-95 (2), 1995-96 (2), 1996-97 (1), 1997-98 (1), 1998-99 (1), 2000-01 (1). Total: 8. ... Four-goal games: 1996-97 (1), 1998-99 (1), 2002-03 (1). Total: 3. ... Total hat tricks: 11.

Season Team	League	GP	G	A	Pts.	PIM	+/-	PP	SH	GP	G	A	Pts.	PIM
		REGULAR SEASON								PLAYOFFS				
85-86—Bellows Free Acad.	VT. H.S.	22	41	28	69	14	...	...	...	—	—	—	—	—
86-87—Bellows Free Acad.	VT. H.S.	23	44	40	84	25	...	...	...	—	—	—	—	—
87-88—Vermont	ECAC	31	12	22	34	62	...	...	...	—	—	—	—	—
88-89—Vermont	ECAC	19	9	12	21	40	...	...	...	—	—	—	—	—
89-90—Vermont	ECAC	10	10	6	16	38	...	...	...	—	—	—	—	—
90-91—Vermont	ECAC	33	25	20	45	58	...	...	...	—	—	—	—	—
—Montreal	NHL	10	2	5	7	2	1	0	0	3	0	0	0	0
91-92—Montreal	NHL	59	8	11	19	14	5	3	0	8	1	1	2	4
—Fredericton	AHL	8	7	7	14	10	...	...	...	2	0	0	0	4
92-93—Montreal	NHL	72	19	25	44	33	11	2	0	20	4	6	10	14
93-94—Montreal	NHL	74	19	24	43	32	17	1	0	7	2	1	3	8
94-95—Montreal	NHL	9	1	4	5	10	-1	1	0	—	—	—	—	—
—Philadelphia	NHL	37	25	24	49	20	21	5	0	15	5	7	12	4
95-96—Philadelphia	NHL	82	51	46	97	64	21	19	0	11	6	5	11	6
96-97—Philadelphia	NHL	82	50	47	97	58	*44	10	0	19	9	12	21	10
97-98—Philadelphia	NHL	82	51	36	87	32	30	16	0	5	1	1	2	8
—U.S. Olympic team	Int'l	4	0	1	1	0	-2	0	0	—	—	—	—	—
98-99—Philadelphia	NHL	76	43	47	90	30	36	16	0	6	3	0	3	12
99-00—Philadelphia	NHL	82	40	37	77	36	8	13	0	18	6	7	13	6
00-01—Philadelphia	NHL	16	7	5	12	0	2	3	0	6	1	2	3	2
01-02—Philadelphia	NHL	82	25	26	51	30	5	4	0	5	0	0	0	2
—U.S. Olympic team	Int'l	6	6	1	7	2	...	...	...	—	—	—	—	—
02-03—Philadelphia	NHL	35	18	10	28	16	10	8	0	13	2	3	5	10
03-04—Philadelphia	NHL	75	23	32	55	51	20	8	0	18	2	2	4	8
NHL Totals (14 years)		873	382	379	761	428	230	109	0	154	42	47	89	94

LECLAIRE, PASCAL — G — BLUE JACKETS

PERSONAL: Born November 7, 1982, in Repentigny, Que. ... 6-2/190. ... Catches left.

TRANSACTIONS/CAREER NOTES: Selected by Columbus Blue Jackets in 1st round (1st Blue Jackets pick, 8th overall) of entry draft (June 23, 2001).

Season Team	League	GP	Min.	W	L	T	GA	SO	GAA	SV%	GP	Min.	W	L	GA	SO	GAA	SV%
		REGULAR SEASON									PLAYOFFS							
98-99—Halifax	QMJHL	33	1828	19	11	1	96	2	3.15	...	1	17	0	0	2	0	7.06	...
99-00—Halifax	QMJHL	31	1729	16	8	4	103	1	3.57	...	5	198	1	2	12	0	3.64	...
00-01—Halifax	QMJHL	33	2111	14	16	5	126	1	3.58	...	2	109	0	2	10	0	5.50	...
01-02—Montreal	QMJHL	45	2513	15	23	4	138	1	3.29	...	—	—	—	—	—	—	—	—
02-03—Syracuse	AHL	36	1886	8	21	3	112	0	3.56	.890	—	—	—	—	—	—	—	—
03-04—Syracuse	AHL	44	2446	21	16	3	125	2	3.07	.907	3	142	1	2	12	0	5.07	.842
—Columbus	NHL	2	119	0	2	0	7	0	3.53	.899	—	—	—	—	—	—	—	—
04-05—Syracuse	AHL	14	844	5	6	...	33	2	2.35	.926	—	—	—	—	—	—	—	—
NHL Totals (1 year)		2	119	0	2	0	7	0	3.53	.899								

LECLERC, MIKE — LW/RW — MIGHTY DUCKS

PERSONAL: Born November 10, 1976, in Winnipeg. ... 6-2/212. ... Shoots left. ... Name pronounced luh-KLAIR.

TRANSACTIONS/CAREER NOTES: Selected by Anaheim Mighty Ducks in third round (third Mighty Ducks pick, 55th overall) of NHL entry draft (July 8, 1995). ... Elbow surgery (October 29, 1999); missed 11 games. ... Injured elbow (December 17, 1999); missed two games. ... Injured knee (December 28, 2000); missed 15 games. ... Strained abdominal muscle (March 11, 2001); missed remainder of season. ... Injured right elbow (November 12, 2002); missed two games. ... Injured left knee (November 15, 2002) and had surgery; missed 11 games. ... Sore knee (January 3, 2003); missed 10 games. ... Sore knee (February 25, 2003); missed one game. ... Knee surgery (September 10, 2003); missed first 55 games of 2003-04 season. ... Reinjured knee (February 29, 2004); missed final 17 games of season.

		REGULAR SEASON								PLAYOFFS				
Season Team	League	GP	G	A	Pts.	PIM	+/-	PP	SH	GP	G	A	Pts.	PIM
91-92—St. Boniface	Tier II Jr. A	43	16	12	28	25	...	...	...	—	—	—	—	—
—Victoria	WHL	2	0	0	0	0	...	...	...	—	—	—	—	—
92-93—Victoria	WHL	70	4	11	15	118	...	...	...	—	—	—	—	—
93-94—Victoria	WHL	68	29	11	40	112	...	...	...	—	—	—	—	—
94-95—Prince George	WHL	43	20	36	56	78	-13	6	1	—	—	—	—	—
—Brandon	WHL	23	5	8	13	50	3	1	0	18	10	6	16	33
95-96—Brandon	WHL	71	58	53	111	161	...	...	...	19	6	19	25	25
96-97—Baltimore	AHL	71	29	27	56	134	-10	11	0	—	—	—	—	—
—Anaheim	NHL	5	1	1	2	0	2	0	0	1	0	0	0	0
97-98—Cincinnati	AHL	48	18	22	40	83	-1	7	0	—	—	—	—	—
—Anaheim	NHL	7	0	0	0	6	-6	0	0	—	—	—	—	—
98-99—Cincinnati	AHL	65	25	28	53	153	12	13	0	3	0	1	1	19
—Anaheim	NHL	7	0	0	0	4	-2	0	0	1	0	0	0	0
99-00—Anaheim	NHL	69	8	11	19	70	-15	0	0	—	—	—	—	—
00-01—Anaheim	NHL	54	15	20	35	26	-1	3	0	—	—	—	—	—
01-02—Anaheim	NHL	82	20	24	44	107	-12	8	0	—	—	—	—	—
02-03—Anaheim	NHL	57	9	19	28	34	-8	1	0	21	2	9	11	12
03-04—Anaheim	NHL	10	1	3	4	4	-1	0	0	—	—	—	—	—
NHL Totals (8 years)		291	54	78	132	251	-43	12	0	23	2	9	11	12

LEE, BRIAN — D — SENATORS

PERSONAL: Born March 26, 1987, in Fargo, N.D. ... 6-2/202. ... Shoots right.
TRANSACTIONS/CAREER NOTES: Selected by Ottawa Senators in 1st round (1st Senators pick, 9th overall) of entry draft (July 30, 2005).

		REGULAR SEASON								PLAYOFFS				
Season Team	League	GP	G	A	Pts.	PIM	+/-	PP	SH	GP	G	A	Pts.	PIM
04-05—Lincoln	USHL	12	0	3	3	4	...	...	...	—	—	—	—	—

LEEB, BRAD — RW — MAPLE LEAFS

PERSONAL: Born August 29, 1979, in Red Deer, Alta. ... 5-11/187. ... Shoots right.
TRANSACTIONS/CAREER NOTES: Signed as free agent by Vancouver Canucks (October 8, 1999). ... Traded by Canucks to Toronto Maple Leafs for D Tomas Mojzis (September 4, 2002).

		REGULAR SEASON								PLAYOFFS				
Season Team	League	GP	G	A	Pts.	PIM	+/-	PP	SH	GP	G	A	Pts.	PIM
94-95—Red Deer	WHL	3	0	0	0	4	...	...	...	—	—	—	—	—
95-96—Red Deer	WHL	38	3	6	9	30	...	...	...	10	2	0	2	11
96-97—Red Deer	WHL	70	15	20	35	76	...	...	...	16	3	3	6	6
97-98—Red Deer	WHL	63	23	23	46	88	...	...	...	3	2	0	2	2
98-99—Red Deer	WHL	64	32	47	79	84	...	...	...	9	5	9	14	10
99-00—Syracuse	AHL	61	19	18	37	50	...	...	...	4	0	0	0	6
—Vancouver	NHL	2	0	0	0	2	-2	0	0	—	—	—	—	—
00-01—Kansas City	IHL	53	18	16	34	53	...	...	...	—	—	—	—	—
01-02—Manitoba	AHL	60	17	15	32	45	-6	3	1	—	—	—	—	—
—Vancouver	NHL	2	0	0	0	0	1	0	0	—	—	—	—	—
02-03—St. John's	AHL	79	35	26	61	78	-7	15	0	—	—	—	—	—
03-04—Toronto	NHL	1	0	0	0	0	-1	0	0	—	—	—	—	—
—St. John's	AHL	77	24	25	49	116	-9	6	1	—	—	—	—	—
04-05—St. John's	AHL	48	16	13	29	43	7	3	0	3	2	1	3	0
NHL Totals (3 years)		5	0	0	0	2	-2	0	0					

LEETCH, BRIAN — D — BRUINS

PERSONAL: Born March 3, 1968, in Corpus Christi, Texas. ... 6-0/185. ... Shoots left.
TRANSACTIONS/CAREER NOTES: Selected by New York Rangers in 1st round (1st Rangers pick, 9th overall) of entry draft (June 21, 1986). ... Fractured left foot (December 1988). ... Hip pointer (March 15, 1989). ... Fractured left ankle (March 14, 1990). ... Injured ankle (November 21, 1992); missed one game. ... Stretched nerve in neck (December 17, 1992); missed 34 games. ... Fractured ankle (March 19, 1993) and underwent ankle surgery; missed remainder of season. ... Nerve compression in right leg (January 4, 1998); missed two games. ... Injured head (April 5, 1998); missed four games. ... Fractured arm (November 24, 1999); missed 32 games. ... Injured ankle (December 3, 2002); missed 31 games. ... Traded by Rangers to Edmonton Oilers for G Jussi Markkanen and a 4th-round pick (later traded to Toronto Maple Leafs) in 2004 enty draft (June 30, 2003). ... Signed as free agent by Rangers (July 30, 2003). ... Injured ankle (September 10, 2003); missed nine games. ... Traded by Rangers to Toronto Maple Leafs for D Maxim Kondratiev, F Jarkko Immonen, 1st-round pick (later traded to Calgary Flames) in 2004 entry draft and second-round pick of 2005 entry draft (March 3, 2004). ... Signed as free agent by Boston Bruins (Aug. 3, 2005).

		REGULAR SEASON								PLAYOFFS				
Season Team	League	GP	G	A	Pts.	PIM	+/-	PP	SH	GP	G	A	Pts.	PIM
84-85—Avon Old Farms H.S.	Conn. H.S.	26	30	46	76	15	...	...	...	—	—	—	—	—
85-86—Avon Old Farms H.S.	Conn. H.S.	28	40	44	84	18	...	...	...	—	—	—	—	—
86-87—Boston College	Hockey East	37	9	38	47	10	...	...	...	—	—	—	—	—
87-88—U.S. national team	Int'l	60	13	61	74	38	...	...	...	—	—	—	—	—
—U.S. Olympic team	Int'l	6	1	5	6	4	2	...	...	—	—	—	—	—

Season	Team	League	GP	G	A	Pts.	PIM	+/-	PP	SH	GP	G	A	Pts.	PIM
			REGULAR SEASON								PLAYOFFS				
	—New York Rangers	NHL	17	2	12	14	0	5	1	0	—	—	—	—	—
88-89	—New York Rangers	NHL	68	23	48	71	50	8	8	3	4	3	2	5	2
89-90	—New York Rangers	NHL	72	11	45	56	26	-18	5	0	—	—	—	—	—
90-91	—New York Rangers	NHL	80	10	72	88	42	2	6	0	6	1	3	4	0
91-92	—New York Rangers	NHL	80	22	80	102	26	25	10	1	13	4	11	15	4
92-93	—New York Rangers	NHL	36	6	30	36	26	2	2	1	—	—	—	—	—
93-94	—New York Rangers	NHL	84	23	56	79	67	28	17	1	23	11	*23	*34	6
94-95	—New York Rangers	NHL	48	9	32	41	18	0	3	0	10	6	8	14	8
95-96	—New York Rangers	NHL	82	15	70	85	30	12	7	0	11	1	6	7	4
96-97	—New York Rangers	NHL	82	20	58	78	40	31	9	0	15	2	8	10	6
97-98	—New York Rangers	NHL	76	17	33	50	32	-36	11	0	—	—	—	—	—
	—U.S. Olympic team	Int'l	4	1	1	2	0	-4	1	0	—	—	—	—	—
98-99	—New York Rangers	NHL	82	13	42	55	42	-7	4	0	—	—	—	—	—
99-00	—New York Rangers	NHL	50	7	19	26	20	-16	3	0	—	—	—	—	—
00-01	—New York Rangers	NHL	82	21	58	79	34	-18	10	1	—	—	—	—	—
01-02	—New York Rangers	NHL	82	10	45	55	28	14	1	0	—	—	—	—	—
	—U.S. Olympic team	Int'l	6	0	5	5	0	...	...	...	—	—	—	—	—
02-03	—New York Rangers	NHL	51	12	18	30	20	-3	5	0	—	—	—	—	—
03-04	—New York Rangers	NHL	57	13	23	36	24	-5	4	1	—	—	—	—	—
	—Toronto	NHL	15	2	13	15	10	11	1	0	13	0	8	8	6
	NHL Totals (17 years)		1144	242	754	996	535	35	107	8	95	28	69	97	36

LEFEBVRE, GUILLAUME — C — PENGUINS

PERSONAL: Born May 7, 1981, in Amos, Que. ... 6-1/200. ... Shoots left.

TRANSACTIONS/CAREER NOTES: Selected by Philadelphia Flyers in eighth round (sixth Flyers pick, 227th overall) of NHL entry draft (June 25, 2000). ... Traded by Flyers with third-round pick (C Tyler Redenbach) in 2003 entry draft and second-round pick (later traded to New York Rangers) in 2004 entry draft to Phoenix Coyotes for RW Tony Amonte (March 10, 2003). ... Traded by Coyotes with LW Ramzi Abid and D Dan Focht to Pittsburgh Penguins for C Jan Hrdina and D Francois Leroux (March 11, 2003). ... Signed as free agent by Wilkes-Barre/Scranton of the AHL (September 26, 2004).

Season	Team	League	GP	G	A	Pts.	PIM	+/-	PP	SH	GP	G	A	Pts.	PIM
			REGULAR SEASON								PLAYOFFS				
98-99	—Shawinigan	QMJHL	40	3	1	4	49	...	...	...	—	—	—	—	—
	—Cape Breton	QMJHL	24	2	7	9	13	...	...	...	5	0	1	1	0
99-00	—Cape Breton	QMJHL	44	26	28	54	82	...	...	...	—	—	—	—	—
	—Quebec	QMJHL	2	3	1	4	0	...	...	...	—	—	—	—	—
	—Rouyn-Noranda	QMJHL	25	4	11	15	39	...	...	...	11	4	0	4	25
00-01	—Rouyn-Noranda	QMJHL	61	24	43	67	160	...	...	...	9	3	1	4	22
01-02	—Philadelphia	AHL	78	19	15	34	111	12	1	3	5	0	0	0	4
	—Philadelphia	NHL	3	0	0	0	0	-1	0	0	—	—	—	—	—
02-03	—Philadelphia	NHL	14	0	0	0	4	1	0	0	—	—	—	—	—
	—Philadelphia	AHL	47	7	6	13	113	9	0	0	—	—	—	—	—
	—Pittsburgh	NHL	12	2	4	6	0	1	0	0	—	—	—	—	—
	—Wilkes-Barre/Scranton	AHL	1	1	0	1	0	2	0	0	5	0	0	0	6
03-04	—Wilkes-Barre/Scranton	AHL	64	4	12	16	78	-4	0	0	14	1	0	1	19
04-05	—Wilkes-Barre/Scranton	AHL	34	3	3	6	76	-5	0	0	11	1	0	1	23
	NHL Totals (2 years)		29	2	4	6	4	1	0	0					

LEGACE, MANNY — G — RED WINGS

PERSONAL: Born February 4, 1973, in Toronto. ... 5-9/162. ... Catches left. ... Name pronounced LEH-guh-see.

TRANSACTIONS/CAREER NOTES: Selected by Hartford Whalers in 8th round (5th Whalers pick, 188th overall) of NHL draft (June 26, 1993). ... Whalers franchise moved to North Carolina and renamed Carolina Hurricanes for 1997-98 season; NHL approved move on June 25, 1997. ... Traded by Hurricanes to Los Angeles Kings for conditional considerations (July 31, 1998); Legace did not meet conditions for the pick and it was forfeited. ... Signed as free agent by Detroit Red Wings (July 15, 1999). ... Claimed off waivers by Vancouver Canucks (September 30, 1999). ... Claimed off waivers by Red Wings (October 13, 1999). ... Injured (November 27, 2000); missed two games. ... Injured elbow (March 31, 2001); missed one game. ... Strained hip flexor (February 11, 2002); missed one game. ... Injured knee (December 9, 2003); missed two games.

Season	Team	League	GP	Min.	W	L	T	GA	SO	GAA	SV%	GP	Min.	W	L	GA	SO	GAA	SV%
			REGULAR SEASON									PLAYOFFS							
89-90	—Vaughan-Thornhill Jr. B	OHA	29	1660	...	...	...	119	1	4.30	...	—	—	—	—	—	—	—	—
90-91	—Niagara Falls	OHL	30	1515	13	11	2	107	0	4.24	...	4	119	...	...	10	0	5.04	...
91-92	—Niagara Falls	OHL	43	2384	21	16	3	143	0	3.60	...	14	791	...	...	56	0	4.25	...
92-93	—Niagara Falls	OHL	48	*2630	22	19	3	*170	0	3.88	.897	4	240	0	4	18	0	4.50	.851
93-94	—Canadian nat'l team	Int'l	16	859	8	6	0	36	2	2.51	...	—	—	—	—	—	—	—	—
94-95	—Springfield	AHL	39	2169	12	17	6	128	2	3.54	.887	—	—	—	—	—	—	—	—
95-96	—Springfield	AHL	37	2196	20	12	4	83	*5	*2.27	...	4	220	1	3	18	0	4.91	...
96-97	—Springfield	AHL	36	2119	17	14	5	107	1	3.03	.897	12	746	9	3	25	2	2.01	.931
	—Richmond	ECHL	3	157	2	1	0	8	0	3.06	...	—	—	—	—	—	—	—	—
97-98	—Las Vegas	IHL	41	2107	18	16	4	111	1	3.16	.911	4	237	1	3	16	0	4.05	.887
	—Springfield	AHL	6	345	4	2	0	16	0	2.78	.889	—	—	—	—	—	—	—	—
98-99	—Long Beach	IHL	33	1796	22	8	1	67	2	2.24	.912	6	338	4	2	9	0	1.60	.944
	—Los Angeles	NHL	17	899	2	9	2	39	0	2.60	.911	—	—	—	—	—	—	—	—
99-00	—Manitoba	IHL	42	2409	20	18	5	104	2	2.59	...	2	141	0	2	7	0	2.98	...
	—Detroit	NHL	4	240	4	0	0	11	0	2.75	.906	—	—	—	—	—	—	—	—
00-01	—Detroit	NHL	39	2136	24	5	5	73	2	2.05	.920	—	—	—	—	—	—	—	—

Season Team	League	GP	Min.	W	L	T	GA	SO	GAA	SV%	GP	Min.	W	L	GA	SO	GAA	SV%
		REGULAR SEASON									PLAYOFFS							
01-02—Detroit	NHL	20	1117	10	6	2	45	1	2.42	.911	1	11	0	0	1	0	5.45	.500
02-03—Detroit	NHL	25	1406	14	5	4	51	0	2.18	.925	—	—	—	—	—	—	—	—
03-04—Detroit	NHL	41	2325	23	10	5	82	3	2.12	.920	4	220	2	2	8	0	2.18	.905
04-05—Khimik Voskresensk	Russian	2	89	...	...	...	10	0	6.73	...	—	—	—	—	—	—	—	—
NHL Totals (6 years)		146	8123	77	35	18	301	6	2.22	.918	5	231	2	2	9	0	2.34	.895

LEGWAND, DAVID — C — PREDATORS

PERSONAL: Born August 17, 1980, in Detroit. ... 6-2/190. ... Shoots left.

TRANSACTIONS/CAREER NOTES: Selected by Nashville Predators in first round (first Predators pick, second overall) of NHL draft (June 27, 1998). ... Fractured left foot (January 13, 2000); missed 11 games. ... Injured back (January 30, 2002); missed 12 games. ... Strained back (March 30, 2002); missed remainder of season. ... Fractured collarbone (March 31, 2003); missed season's final 18 games.

Season Team	League	GP	G	A	Pts.	PIM	+/-	PP	SH	GP	G	A	Pts.	PIM
		REGULAR SEASON								PLAYOFFS				
96-97—Detroit	Jr. A	44	21	41	62	58	...	...	...	—	—	—	—	—
97-98—Plymouth	OHL	59	54	51	105	56	...	...	...	15	8	12	20	24
98-99—Plymouth	OHL	55	31	49	80	65	32	...	...	11	3	8	11	8
—Nashville	NHL	1	0	0	0	0	0	0	0	—	—	—	—	—
99-00—Nashville	NHL	71	13	15	28	30	-6	4	0	—	—	—	—	—
00-01—Nashville	NHL	81	13	28	41	38	1	3	0	—	—	—	—	—
01-02—Nashville	NHL	63	11	19	30	54	1	1	1	—	—	—	—	—
02-03—Nashville	NHL	64	17	31	48	34	-2	3	1	—	—	—	—	—
03-04—Nashville	NHL	82	18	29	47	46	9	5	1	6	1	0	1	8
04-05—Basel	Switzerland	3	6	2	8	2	...	1	0	12	11	19	30	10
NHL Totals (6 years)		362	72	122	194	202	3	16	3	6	1	0	1	8

LEHOUX, YANICK — C — KINGS

PERSONAL: Born April 8, 1982, in Montreal. ... 5-11/170. ... Shoots right.

TRANSACTIONS/CAREER NOTES: Selected by Los Angeles Kings in third round (third Kings pick, 86th overall) of NHL draft (June 24, 2000).

Season Team	League	GP	G	A	Pts.	PIM	+/-	PP	SH	GP	G	A	Pts.	PIM
		REGULAR SEASON								PLAYOFFS				
99-00—Baie-Comeau	QMJHL	67	31	61	92	14	...	...	...	—	—	—	—	—
00-01—Baie-Comeau	QMJHL	70	67	68	135	62	26	15	13	11	8	16	24	0
01-02—Baie-Comeau	QMJHL	66	56	69	125	63	...	...	...	5	5	4	9	0
—Manchester	AHL	0	0	0	0	0	0	0	0	1	0	0	0	0
02-03—Manchester	AHL	78	16	21	37	26	...	...	...	1	0	0	0	0
03-04—Manchester	AHL	66	14	28	42	22	...	...	...	5	2	3	5	16
04-05—Manchester	AHL	38	23	31	54	16	13	8	0	0	0	0	0	0

LEHTINEN, JERE — RW/LW — STARS

PERSONAL: Born June 24, 1973, in Espoo, Finland. ... 6-0/200. ... Shoots right. ... Name pronounced YAIR-ee LEH-tih-nehn.

TRANSACTIONS/CAREER NOTES: Selected by Minnesota North Stars in fourth round (third North Stars pick, 88th overall) of NHL draft (June 20, 1992). ... North Stars franchise moved from Minnesota to Dallas and renamed Stars for 1993-94 season. ... Strained groin (December 21, 1995); missed six games. ... Reinjured groin (January 10, 1996); missed one game. ... Sprained ankle (March 20, 1996); missed remainder of season. ... Sprained knee (January 31, 1997); missed 13 games. ... Sprained knee (March 5, 1997); missed five games. ... Separated shoulder (October 19, 1997); missed 10 games. ... Fractured thumb (November 14, 1998); missed five games. ... Sprained ankle (March 25, 1999); missed two games. ... Fractured ankle (October 16, 1999); missed 30 games. ... Injured ankle (January 19, 2000); missed 35 games. ... Flu (November 14, 2000); missed one game. ... Sprained ankle (December 6, 2000); missed five games. ... Injured hip flexor (February 15, 2001); missed two games. ... Injured knee (January 29, 2002) and had surgery; missed one game. ... Bruised ankle (March 20, 2002); missed eight games. ... Injured hip (February 9, 2003); missed two games. ... Back spasms (October 13, 2003); missed 16 games. ... Flu (December 26, 2003); missed two games. ... Back spasms (March 22, 2004); missed six games.

STATISTICAL PLATEAUS: Three-goal games: 2000-01 (1), 2002-03 (1). Total: 2.

Season Team	League	GP	G	A	Pts.	PIM	+/-	PP	SH	GP	G	A	Pts.	PIM
		REGULAR SEASON								PLAYOFFS				
90-91—Kiekko-Espoo	Finland	32	15	9	24	12	...	...	...	—	—	—	—	—
91-92—Kiekko-Espoo	Finland	43	32	17	49	6	...	...	...	—	—	—	—	—
92-93—Kiekko-Espoo	Finland	45	13	14	27	6	...	...	...	—	—	—	—	—
93-94—TPS Turku	Finland	42	19	20	39	6	...	...	...	11	11	2	13	2
—Fin. Olympic team	Int'l	8	3	0	3	11	5	1	0	—	—	—	—	—
94-95—TPS Turku	Finland	39	19	23	42	33	26	...	...	13	8	6	14	4
95-96—Dallas	NHL	57	6	22	28	16	5	0	0	—	—	—	—	—
—Michigan	IHL	1	1	0	1	0	...	...	...	—	—	—	—	—
96-97—Dallas	NHL	63	16	27	43	2	26	3	1	7	2	2	4	0
97-98—Dallas	NHL	72	23	19	42	20	19	7	2	12	3	5	8	2
—Fin. Olympic team	Int'l	6	4	2	6	2	1	1	0	—	—	—	—	—
98-99—Dallas	NHL	74	20	32	52	18	29	7	1	23	10	3	13	2
99-00—Dallas	NHL	17	3	5	8	0	1	0	0	13	1	5	6	2
00-01—Dallas	NHL	74	20	25	45	24	14	7	0	10	1	0	1	2
01-02—Dallas	NHL	73	25	24	49	14	27	7	1	—	—	—	—	—
—Fin. Olympic team	Int'l	4	1	2	3	2	...	...	...	—	—	—	—	—
02-03—Dallas	NHL	80	31	17	48	20	39	5	0	12	3	2	5	0
03-04—Dallas	NHL	58	13	13	26	20	0	4	1	5	0	0	0	0
NHL Totals (9 years)		568	157	184	341	134	160	40	6	82	20	17	37	8

LEHTONEN, KARI — G — THRASHERS

PERSONAL: Born November 16, 1983, in Helsinki, Finland. ... 6-3/200. ... Catches left.
TRANSACTIONS/CAREER NOTES: Selected by Atlanta Thrashers in first round (first Thrashers pick, second overall) of NHL entry draft (June 22, 2002).

		REGULAR SEASON									PLAYOFFS							
Season Team	League	GP	Min.	W	L	T	GA	SO	GAA	SV%	GP	Min.	W	L	GA	SO	GAA	SV%
99-00—Jokerit Helsinki	Finland	2	...	...	...	...	...	...	...	...	—	—	—	—	—	—	—	—
00-01—Jokerit Helsinki	Finland	4	189	3	0	0	6	0	1.90	...	—	—	—	—	—	—	—	—
01-02—Jokerit Helsinki	Finland	23	1242	13	5	3	37	4	1.79	...	*11	*623	*8	3	18	*3	1.73	...
02-03—Jokerit Helsinki	Finland	49	...	...	...	...	...	...	...	...	—	—	—	—	—	—	—	—
03-04—Atlanta	NHL	4	240	4	0	0	5	1	1.25	.953	—	—	—	—	—	—	—	—
—Chicago	AHL	39	2192	20	14	2	88	3	2.41	.920	10	663	6	4	23	1	2.08	.939
04-05—Chicago	AHL	57	3378	38	17	...	128	5	2.27	.929	16	982	10	6	28	2	1.71	.939
NHL Totals (1 year)		4	240	4	0	0	5	1	1.25	.953								

LEHTONEN, MIKKO — RW — BRUINS

PERSONAL: Born April 1, 1987, in Espoo, Finland. ... 6-3/191. ... Shoots right.

		REGULAR SEASON								PLAYOFFS				
Season Team	League	GP	G	A	Pts.	PIM	+/-	PP	SH	GP	G	A	Pts.	PIM
02-03—Espoo	Finland Jr.	13	9	9	18	28	...	...	...	—	—	—	—	—
03-04—Espoo	Finland Jr.	19	3	0	3	0	...	...	...	—	—	—	—	—
04-05—Espoo	Finland Jr.	37	6	9	15	38	...	...	...	—	—	—	—	—

LEIGHTON, MICHAEL — G — BLACKHAWKS

PERSONAL: Born May 19, 1981, in Petrolia, Ont. ... 6-3/186. ... Catches left.
TRANSACTIONS/CAREER NOTES: Selected by Chicago Blackhawks in sixth round (fifth Blackhawks pick, 165th overall) of NHL entry draft (June 26, 1999).

		REGULAR SEASON									PLAYOFFS							
Season Team	League	GP	Min.	W	L	T	GA	SO	GAA	SV%	GP	Min.	W	L	GA	SO	GAA	SV%
97-98—Petrolia	Jr. B	30	...	...	...	...	...	...	...	...	—	—	—	—	—	—	—	—
98-99—Windsor	OHL	28	1389	4	17	2	112	0	4.84	...	3	80	0	1	10	0	7.50	...
99-00—Windsor	OHL	42	2272	17	17	2	118	1	3.12	.889	12	616	5	6	32	0	3.12	.915
00-01—Windsor	OHL	54	3035	32	13	5	138	2	2.73	.910	—	—	—	—	—	—	—	—
01-02—Norfolk	AHL	52	3114	27	16	8	111	6	2.14	.913	4	237	1	2	8	0	2.03	.927
02-03—Chicago	NHL	8	447	2	3	2	21	1	2.82	.913	—	—	—	—	—	—	—	—
—Norfolk	AHL	36	2183	18	13	5	91	4	2.50	.912	4	240	3	1	7	1	1.75	.931
03-04—Chicago	NHL	34	1988	6	18	8	99	2	2.99	.900	—	—	—	—	—	—	—	—
—Norfolk	AHL	18	1080	10	7	1	33	1	1.83	.920	4	211	2	1	2	2	0.57	.978
04-05—Norfolk	AHL	41	2318	20	16	...	78	7	2.02	.921	...	...	...	...	...	...	...	...
NHL Totals (2 years)		42	2435	8	21	10	120	3	2.96	.902								

LEMIEUX, MARIO — C/LW — PENGUINS

PERSONAL: Born October 5, 1965, in Montreal. ... 6-4/230. ... Shoots right. ... Brother of Alain Lemieux, C for three NHL teams (1981-82 through 1986-87). ... Name pronounced luh-MYOO.
TRANSACTIONS/CAREER NOTES: Selected by Pittsburgh Penguins in 1st round (1st Penguins pick, 1st overall) of entry draft (June 9, 1984). ... Sprained left knee (September 1984). ... Reinjured knee (December 2, 1984). ... Sprained right knee (December 20, 1986). ... Bruised right shoulder (November 1987). ... Sprained right wrist (November 3, 1988). ... Herniated disk (February 14, 1990); missed 21 games. ... Disc removed from back (July 11, 1990); missed first 50 games of 1990-91 season. ... Back spasms (October 1991); missed three games. ... Back spasms (January 4, 1992); missed three games. ... Injured back (January 29, 1992); missed six games. ... Flu (February 1992); missed one game. ... Fractured hand (May 5, 1992). ... Injured heel (December 1992); missed one game. ... Injured back (January 5, 1993); missed three games. ... Diagnosed with Hodgkin's disease (January 12, 1993) and had radiation treatment (February 1-March 2); missed 20 games. ... Injured back; missed first 10 games of 1993-94 season. ... Injured back (October 28, 1993); missed one game. ... Injured back (November 2, 1993); missed one game. ... Flu (November 9, 1993); missed one game. ... Injured back (November 11, 1993); missed 38 games. ... Injured back (February 13, 1994); missed two games. ... Injured back (February 19, 1994); missed two games. ... Injured back (March 12, 1994); missed four games. ... Fined $500 for charging referee (April 6, 1994). ... On medical leave; missed 1994-95 season. ... Back spasms (November 9, 1996); missed one game. ... Back spasms (January 21, 1997); missed one game. ... Back spasms (February 4, 1997); missed one game. ... Strained hip flexor (March 4, 1997); missed one game. ... Strained hip flexor (March 14, 1997); missed two games. ... Announced retirement (April 6, 1997). ... Inducted into Hockey Hall of Fame (November 17, 1997). ... Strained hip flexor (October 3, 2001); missed two games. ... Hip surgery (October 28, 2001); missed six games. ... Injured hip (November 17, 2001); missed 23 games. ... Reinjured hip (February 27, 2002); missed remainder of season. ... Injured groin (January 7, 2003); missed two games. ... Aggravated groin injury (Jan. 13, 2003); missed eight games. ... Back spasms (March 25, 2003); missed two games. ... Injured hip (October 25, 2003) and had surgery; missed remainder of season.
STATISTICAL PLATEAUS: Three-goal games: 1986-87 (5), 1987-88 (3), 1988-89 (7), 1989-90 (3), 1990-91 (1), 1991-92 (1), 1992-93 (1), 1995-96 (4), 1996-97 (1), 2000-01 (1). Total: 27. ... Four-goal games: 1985-86 (1), 1986-87 (1), 1987-88 (2), 1988-89 (1), 1989-90 (1), 1992-93 (2), 1995-96 (1), 1996-97 (1). Total: 10. ... Five-goal games: 1988-89 (1), 1992-93 (1), 1995-96 (1). Total: 3. ... Total hat tricks: 40.

		REGULAR SEASON								PLAYOFFS				
Season Team	League	GP	G	A	Pts.	PIM	+/-	PP	SH	GP	G	A	Pts.	PIM
81-82—Laval	QMJHL	64	30	66	96	22	...	...	...	18	5	9	14	31
82-83—Laval	QMJHL	66	84	100	184	76	...	...	...	12	14	18	32	18
83-84—Laval	QMJHL	70	*133	*149	*282	92	...	...	...	14	*29	*23	*52	29
84-85—Pittsburgh	NHL	73	43	57	100	54	-35	11	0	—	—	—	—	—

Season Team	League	REGULAR SEASON GP	G	A	Pts.	PIM	+/-	PP	SH	PLAYOFFS GP	G	A	Pts.	PIM
85-86—Pittsburgh	NHL	79	48	93	141	43	-6	17	0	—	—	—	—	—
86-87—Pittsburgh	NHL	63	54	53	107	57	13	19	0	—	—	—	—	—
87-88—Pittsburgh	NHL	77	*70	98	*168	92	23	22	*10	—	—	—	—	—
88-89—Pittsburgh	NHL	76	*85	114	*199	100	41	*31	*13	11	12	7	19	16
89-90—Pittsburgh	NHL	59	45	78	123	78	-18	14	3	—	—	—	—	—
90-91—Pittsburgh	NHL	26	19	26	45	30	8	6	1	23	16	*28	*44	16
91-92—Pittsburgh	NHL	64	44	87	*131	94	27	12	4	15	*16	18	*34	2
92-93—Pittsburgh	NHL	60	69	91	*160	38	*55	16	6	11	8	10	18	10
93-94—Pittsburgh	NHL	22	17	20	37	32	-2	7	0	6	4	3	7	2
94-95—Pittsburgh	NHL	Did not play												
95-96—Pittsburgh	NHL	70	*69	92	*161	54	10	*31	*8	18	11	16	27	33
96-97—Pittsburgh	NHL	76	50	72	*122	65	27	15	3	5	3	3	6	4
97-98—Pittsburgh	NHL	Did not play												
98-99—Pittsburgh	NHL	Did not play												
99-00—Pittsburgh	NHL	Did not play												
00-01—Pittsburgh	NHL	43	35	41	76	18	15	16	1	18	6	11	17	4
01-02—Pittsburgh	NHL	24	6	25	31	14	0	2	0	—	—	—	—	—
—Can. Olympic team	Int'l	5	2	4	6	0	...	...	...	—	—	—	—	—
02-03—Pittsburgh	NHL	67	28	63	91	43	-25	14	0	—	—	—	—	—
03-04—Pittsburgh	NHL	10	1	8	9	6	-2	0	0	—	—	—	—	—
NHL Totals (20 years)		889	683	1018	1701	818	131	233	49	107	76	96	172	87

LENEVEU, DAVID — G — COYOTES

PERSONAL: Born May 23, 1983, in Fernie, B.C. ... 6-1/170. ... Catches left.
TRANSACTIONS/CAREER NOTES: Selected by Phoenix Coyotes in second round (third Coyotes pick, 46th overall) of NHL entry draft (June 22, 2002).

Season Team	League	REGULAR SEASON GP	Min.	W	L	T	GA	SO	GAA	SV%	PLAYOFFS GP	Min.	W	L	GA	SO	GAA	SV%
01-02—Cornell	ECAC	14	842	11	2	1	21	2	*1.50	...	—	—	—	—	—	—	—	—
02-03—Cornell	ECAC	32	1946	28	3	1	39	9	1.20	.940	—	—	—	—	—	—	—	—
03-04—Springfield	AHL	38	2219	16	19	3	102	1	2.76	.909	—	—	—	—	—	—	—	—
04-05—Utah	AHL	48	2702	11	32	...	132	0	2.93	.909	—	—	—	—	—	—	—	—

LEOPOLD, JORDAN — D — FLAMES

PERSONAL: Born August 3, 1980, in Golden Valley, Minn. ... 6-0/210. ... Shoots left.
TRANSACTIONS/CAREER NOTES: Selected by Anaheim Mighty Ducks in second round (first Mighty Ducks pick, 44th overall) of NHL entry draft (June 26, 1999). ... Traded by Mighty Ducks to Calgary Flames for LW Andrei Nazarov and second-round pick (traded back to Calgary) in 2001 entry draft (September 26, 2000). ... Suffered concussion (October 4, 2002); missed season's first four games. ... Injured shoulder (November 27, 2002); missed six games.

Season Team	League	REGULAR SEASON GP	G	A	Pts.	PIM	+/-	PP	SH	PLAYOFFS GP	G	A	Pts.	PIM
97-98—U.S. National	NAHL	60	11	12	23	16	...	4	0	—	—	—	—	—
98-99—Minnesota	WCHA	39	7	16	23	20	...	...	...	—	—	—	—	—
99-00—Minnesota	WCHA	39	6	18	24	20	...	...	...	—	—	—	—	—
00-01—Minnesota	WCHA	42	12	37	49	38	...	...	...	—	—	—	—	—
01-02—Minnesota	WCHA	44	20	28	48	28	...	...	...	—	—	—	—	—
02-03—Saint John	AHL	3	1	2	3	0	-3	1	0	—	—	—	—	—
—Calgary	NHL	58	4	10	14	12	-15	3	0	—	—	—	—	—
03-04—Calgary	NHL	82	9	24	33	24	8	6	0	26	0	10	10	6
NHL Totals (2 years)		140	13	34	47	36	-7	9	0	26	0	10	10	6

LESCHYSHYN, CURTIS — D

PERSONAL: Born September 21, 1969, in Thompson, Man. ... 6-1/208. ... Shoots left. ... Name pronounced luh-SIH-shihn.
TRANSACTIONS/CAREER NOTES: Selected by Quebec Nordiques in first round (first Nordiques pick, third overall) of NHL entry draft (June 11, 1988). ... Separated shoulder (January 10, 1989). ... Sprained left knee (November 1989). ... Damaged knee ligaments (February 18, 1991) and had surgery; missed final 19 games of 1990-91 season and first 30 games of 1991-92 season. ... Strained back (October 13, 1992); missed two games. ... Injured right collarbone (December 30, 1994); missed two games. ... Injured thigh (March 19, 1994); missed two games. ... Injured groin (March 31, 1994); missed remainder of season. ... Cut groin (April 22, 1995); missed final four games of season. ... Nordiques franchise moved to Colorado and renamed Avalanche for 1995-96 season (June 21, 1995). ... Injured hip flexor (January 17, 1996); missed three games. ... Traded by Avalanche with LW Chris Simon to Washington Capitals for RW Keith Jones and first- (D Scott Parker) and fourth-round (traded back to Washington) picks in 1998 entry draft (November 2, 1996). ... Traded by Capitals to Hartford Whalers for C Andrei Nikolishin (November 9, 1996). ... Injured abdominal muscle (March 7, 1997); missed five games. ... Whalers franchise moved to North Carolina and renamed Carolina Hurricanes for 1997-98 season; NHL approved move on June 25, 1997. ... Strained groin (September 25, 1997); missed four games. ... Strained groin (November 13, 1997); missed one game. ... Had back spasms (February 28, 1998); missed one game. ... Had back spasms (December 5, 1998); missed three games. ... Bruised sternum (December 19, 1998); missed one game. ... Strained groin (January 4, 1999); missed six games. ... Strained groin (March 24, 1999); missed six games. ... Strained groin (January 27, 2000); missed 20 games. ... Reinjured groin (March 17, 2000); missed nine games. ... Selected by Minnesota Wild in NHL expansion draft (June 23, 2000). ... Strained groin (October 20, 2000); missed one game. ... Reinjured groin (November 3, 2000); missed three games. ... Reinjured groin (November 28, 2000); missed 10 games. ... Traded by Wild to Ottawa Senators for third-round pick (C Stephane Veilleux) in 2001 entry draft and future considerations (March 13, 2001). ... Suffered concussion (April 3, 2001); missed final two games of regular season. ... Injured back (December 1, 2001); missed one game. ... Had the flu (February 6, 2002); missed two games. ... Injured right leg and knee (December 18, 2002); missed five games. ... Injured left shoulder (January 6, 2003); missed two games. ... Strained groin (January 22, 2003); missed four games. ... Strained groin (February 6, 2003); missed six games. ... Sprained right ankle (March 11, 2003); missed 10 games. ... Cut forehead (January 29, 2004); missed one game. ... Injured groin (March 3, 2004); missed seven games.

Season Team	League	GP	G	A	Pts.	PIM	+/-	PP	SH	GP	G	A	Pts.	PIM
		REGULAR SEASON								PLAYOFFS				
85-86—Saskatoon	WHL	1	0	0	0	0	...	...	...	—	—	—	—	—
86-87—Saskatoon	WHL	70	14	26	40	107	...	...	...	11	1	5	6	14
87-88—Saskatoon	WHL	56	14	41	55	86	...	...	...	10	2	5	7	16
88-89—Quebec	NHL	71	4	9	13	71	-32	1	1	—	—	—	—	—
89-90—Quebec	NHL	68	2	6	8	44	-41	1	0	—	—	—	—	—
90-91—Quebec	NHL	55	3	7	10	49	-19	2	0	—	—	—	—	—
91-92—Quebec	NHL	42	5	12	17	42	-28	3	0	—	—	—	—	—
—Halifax	AHL	6	0	2	2	4	...	...	...	—	—	—	—	—
92-93—Quebec	NHL	82	9	23	32	61	25	4	0	6	1	1	2	6
93-94—Quebec	NHL	72	5	17	22	65	-2	3	0	—	—	—	—	—
94-95—Quebec	NHL	44	2	13	15	20	29	0	0	3	0	1	1	4
95-96—Colorado	NHL	77	4	15	19	73	32	0	0	17	1	2	3	8
96-97—Colorado	NHL	11	0	5	5	6	1	0	0	—	—	—	—	—
—Washington	NHL	2	0	0	0	2	0	0	0	—	—	—	—	—
—Hartford	NHL	64	4	13	17	30	-19	1	1	—	—	—	—	—
97-98—Carolina	NHL	73	2	10	12	45	-2	1	0	—	—	—	—	—
98-99—Carolina	NHL	65	2	7	9	50	-1	0	0	6	0	0	0	6
99-00—Carolina	NHL	53	0	2	2	14	-19	0	0	—	—	—	—	—
00-01—Minnesota	NHL	54	2	3	5	19	-2	1	0	—	—	—	—	—
—Ottawa	NHL	11	0	4	4	0	7	0	0	4	0	0	0	0
01-02—Ottawa	NHL	79	1	9	10	44	-5	0	0	12	0	1	1	0
02-03—Ottawa	NHL	54	1	6	7	18	11	0	0	18	0	1	1	10
03-04—Ottawa	NHL	56	1	4	5	16	13	0	0	2	0	0	0	0
NHL Totals (16 years)		1033	47	165	212	669	-52	17	2	68	2	6	8	34

LESSARD, FRANCIS — RW — THRASHERS

PERSONAL: Born May 30, 1979, in Montreal. ... 6-3/225. ... Shoots right. ... Name pronounced luh-SAHRD.

TRANSACTIONS/CAREER NOTES: Selected by Carolina Hurricanes in third round (third Hurricanes pick, 80th overall) of NHL entry draft (June 21, 1997). ... Traded by Hurricanes to Philadelphia Flyers for eighth-round pick (G Antti Jokela) in 1999 entry draft (May 25, 1999). ... Traded by Flyers to Atlanta Thrashers for D David Harlock, third- (later traded to Phoenix Coyotes) and seventh-round (later traded to San Jose Sharks) picks in 2003 entry draft (March 15, 2002). ... Had back spasms (November 23, 2002); missed seven games. ... Suspended one game by NHL in spearing incident (November 14, 2003). ... Injured shoulder (March 15, 2004); missed one game.

Season Team	League	GP	G	A	Pts.	PIM	+/-	PP	SH	GP	G	A	Pts.	PIM
		REGULAR SEASON								PLAYOFFS				
96-97—Val-d'Or	QMJHL	66	1	9	10	287	...	...	...	—	—	—	—	—
97-98—Val-d'Or	QMJHL	63	3	20	23	338	...	...	...	19	1	6	7	*101
98-99—Drummondville	QMJHL	53	12	36	48	295	-24	5	2	—	—	—	—	—
99-00—Philadelphia	AHL	78	4	8	12	416	...	...	...	5	0	1	1	7
00-01—Philadelphia	AHL	64	3	7	10	330	...	...	...	10	0	0	0	33
01-02—Philadelphia	AHL	60	0	6	6	251	-6	0	0	—	—	—	—	—
—Chicago	AHL	7	2	1	3	34	4	0	0	15	0	1	1	40
—Atlanta	NHL	5	0	0	0	26	0	0	0	—	—	—	—	—
02-03—Atlanta	NHL	18	0	2	2	61	1	0	0	—	—	—	—	—
—Chicago	AHL	50	2	5	7	194	3	0	0	1	0	0	0	0
03-04—Atlanta	NHL	62	1	1	2	181	-5	0	0	—	—	—	—	—
NHL Totals (3 years)		85	1	3	4	268	-4	0	0					

LETOWSKI, TREVOR — RW/LW — BLUE JACKETS

PERSONAL: Born April 5, 1977, in Thunder Bay, Ont. ... 5-10/180. ... Shoots right.

TRANSACTIONS/CAREER NOTES: Selected by Phoenix Coyotes in seventh round (sixth Coyotes pick, 174th overall) of NHL draft (June 22, 1996). ... Traded by Coyotes with LW Todd Warriner, RW Tyler Bouck and third-round pick (returned to Phoenix; Coyotes selected C Dimitri Pestunov) in 2003 draft to Vancouver Canucks for C Denis Pederson and D Drake Berehowsky (December 28, 2001). ... Signed as free agent by Columbus Blue Jackets (July 3, 2003). ... Fractured finger (October 11, 2003); missed seven games.

Season Team	League	GP	G	A	Pts.	PIM	+/-	PP	SH	GP	G	A	Pts.	PIM
		REGULAR SEASON								PLAYOFFS				
94-95—Sarnia	OHL	66	22	19	41	33	...	...	...	4	0	1	1	9
95-96—Sarnia	OHL	66	36	63	99	66	...	...	...	10	9	5	14	10
96-97—Sarnia	OHL	55	35	73	108	51	...	...	...	12	9	12	21	20
97-98—Springfield	AHL	75	11	20	31	26	...	...	...	4	1	2	3	18
98-99—Springfield	AHL	67	32	35	67	46	16	11	3	3	1	0	1	2
—Phoenix	NHL	14	2	2	4	2	1	0	0	—	—	—	—	—
99-00—Phoenix	NHL	82	19	20	39	20	2	3	4	5	1	1	2	4
00-01—Phoenix	NHL	77	7	15	22	32	-2	0	1	—	—	—	—	—
01-02—Phoenix	NHL	33	2	6	8	4	2	0	0	—	—	—	—	—
—Vancouver	NHL	42	7	10	17	15	2	1	0	6	0	1	1	8
02-03—Vancouver	NHL	78	11	14	25	36	8	1	1	6	0	1	1	0
03-04—Columbus	NHL	73	15	17	32	16	-12	4	0	—	—	—	—	—
04-05—Fribourg	Switzerland	9	4	5	9	6	...	2	2	—	—	—	—	—
NHL Totals (6 years)		399	63	84	147	125	1	9	6	17	1	3	4	12

LEVASSEUR, JEAN-PHILIPPE — G — MIGHTY DUCKS

PERSONAL: Born January 15, 1987, in Victoriaville, Que. ... 6-0/190. ... Catches right.

Season Team	League	GP	Min.	W	L	T	GA	SO	GAA	SV%	GP	Min.	W	L	GA	SO	GAA	SV%
		REGULAR SEASON									PLAYOFFS							
03-04—Rouyn-Noranda	QMJHL	...	...	0	2	1	...	...	4.57	.874	—	—	—	—	—	—	—	—
04-05—Rouyn-Noranda	QMJHL	29	1393	8	14	3	89	0	3.83	.882	3	48	0	0	3	0	3.76	.893

LIDSTROM, NICKLAS — D — RED WINGS

PERSONAL: Born April 28, 1970, in Vasteras, Sweden. ... 6-2/190. ... Shoots left. ... Name pronounced NIHK-luhs LIHD-struhm.
TRANSACTIONS/CAREER NOTES: Selected by Detroit Red Wings in third round (third Red Wings pick, 53rd overall) of NHL entry draft (June 17, 1989). ... Played in Europe during 1994-95 NHL lockout. ... Had back spasms (April 9, 1995); missed five games. ... Had the flu (April 14, 1996); missed one game. ... Had the flu (January 20, 1997); missed one game.

		REGULAR SEASON								PLAYOFFS				
Season Team	League	GP	G	A	Pts.	PIM	+/-	PP	SH	GP	G	A	Pts.	PIM
87-88—Vasteras	Sweden	3	0	0	0	0	...	...	...	—	—	—	—	—
88-89—Vasteras	Sweden	19	0	2	2	4	...	...	...	—	—	—	—	—
89-90—Vasteras	Sweden	39	8	8	16	14	...	...	...	—	—	—	—	—
90-91—Vasteras	Sweden	20	2	12	14	14	...	...	...	—	—	—	—	—
91-92—Detroit	NHL	80	11	49	60	22	36	5	0	11	1	2	3	0
92-93—Detroit	NHL	84	7	34	41	28	7	3	0	7	1	0	1	0
93-94—Detroit	NHL	84	10	46	56	26	43	4	0	7	3	2	5	0
94-95—Vasteras	Sweden	13	2	10	12	4	...	...	...	—	—	—	—	—
—Detroit	NHL	43	10	16	26	6	15	7	0	18	4	12	16	8
95-96—Vasteras	Sweden	13	2	10	12	4	...	...	...	—	—	—	—	—
—Detroit	NHL	81	17	50	67	20	29	8	1	19	5	9	14	10
96-97—Detroit	NHL	79	15	42	57	30	11	8	0	20	2	6	8	2
97-98—Detroit	NHL	80	17	42	59	18	22	7	1	22	6	13	19	8
—Swedish Oly. team	Int'l	4	1	1	2	2	4	1	0	—	—	—	—	—
98-99—Detroit	NHL	81	14	43	57	14	14	6	2	10	2	9	11	4
99-00—Detroit	NHL	81	20	53	73	18	19	9	4	9	2	4	6	4
00-01—Detroit	NHL	82	15	56	71	18	9	8	0	6	1	7	8	0
01-02—Detroit	NHL	78	9	50	59	20	13	6	0	23	5	11	16	2
—Swedish Oly. team	Int'l	4	1	5	6	0	...	...	...	—	—	—	—	—
02-03—Detroit	NHL	82	18	44	62	38	40	8	1	4	0	2	2	0
03-04—Detroit	NHL	81	10	28	38	18	19	3	1	12	2	5	7	4
NHL Totals (13 years)		1016	173	553	726	276	277	82	10	168	34	82	116	42

LILES, JOHN-MICHAEL — D — AVALANCHE

PERSONAL: Born November 25, 1980, in Zionsville, Ind. ... 5-10/185. ... Shoots left.
TRANSACTIONS/CAREER NOTES: Selected by Colorado Avalanche in fifth round (eighth Avalanche pick, 159th overall) of NHL entry draft (June 24, 2000). ... Bruised right knee (March 23, 2004); missed three games. ... Fractured foot (summer 2004).

		REGULAR SEASON								PLAYOFFS				
Season Team	League	GP	G	A	Pts.	PIM	+/-	PP	SH	GP	G	A	Pts.	PIM
99-00—Michigan State	CCHA	37	7	19	26	26	...	...	...	—	—	—	—	—
00-01—Michigan State	CCHA	42	7	18	25	28	...	...	...	—	—	—	—	—
01-02—Michigan State	CCHA	41	13	22	35	18	...	...	...	—	—	—	—	—
02-03—Michigan State	CCHA	39	16	34	50	46	...	...	...	—	—	—	—	—
—Hershey	AHL	5	0	1	1	4	-2	0	0	5	0	0	0	2
03-04—Colorado	NHL	79	10	24	34	28	7	2	0	11	0	1	1	4
04-05—Iserlohn	Germany	17	5	6	11	24	-3	3	1	...	...	...	...	...
NHL Totals (1 year)		79	10	24	34	28	7	2	0	11	0	1	1	4

LILJA, ANDREAS — D

PERSONAL: Born July 13, 1975, in Landskrona, Sweden. ... 6-3/228. ... Shoots left. ... Name pronounced LIHL-yuh.
TRANSACTIONS/CAREER NOTES: Selected by Los Angeles Kings in 2nd round (2nd Kings pick, 54th overall) of entry draft (June 24, 2000). ... Sprained left knee (October 13, 2001); missed 19 games. ... Traded by Kings with RW Jaroslav Bednar to Florida Panthers for D Dmitry Yushkevich and 5th-round pick (C Brady Murray) in 2003 draft (November 26, 2002). ... Injured foot (January 1, 2003); missed one game. ... Injured hand (January 25, 2003); missed two games. ... Shoulder injury (November 13, 2003); missed three games. ... Signed as free agent by Nashville Predators (July 25, 2004).

		REGULAR SEASON								PLAYOFFS				
Season Team	League	GP	G	A	Pts.	PIM	+/-	PP	SH	GP	G	A	Pts.	PIM
95-96—Malmo	Sweden	40	1	5	6	63	...	...	...	5	0	1	1	2
96-97—Malmo	Sweden	47	1	0	1	22	...	...	...	4	0	0	0	10
97-98—Malmo	Sweden	10	0	0	0	0	...	...	...	—	—	—	—	—
98-99—Malmo	Sweden	41	0	3	3	14	...	...	...	1	0	0	0	4
99-00—Malmo	Sweden	49	8	11	19	88	...	...	...	6	0	0	0	8
00-01—Lowell	AHL	61	7	29	36	149	...	...	...	4	0	6	6	6
—Los Angeles	NHL	2	0	0	0	4	-2	0	0	1	0	0	0	0
01-02—Los Angeles	NHL	26	1	4	5	22	3	1	0	5	0	0	0	6
—Manchester	AHL	4	0	1	1	4	1	0	0	—	—	—	—	—
02-03—Los Angeles	NHL	17	0	3	3	14	5	0	0	—	—	—	—	—
—Florida	NHL	56	4	8	12	56	8	0	0	—	—	—	—	—
03-04—Florida	NHL	79	3	4	7	90	-8	0	0	—	—	—	—	—
04-05—Mora	Sweden Dv. 1	44	3	8	11	67	-8	0	1	—	—	—	—	—
NHL Totals (4 years)		180	8	19	27	186	6	1	0	6	0	0	0	6

LINDEN, TREVOR — C — CANUCKS

PERSONAL: Born April 11, 1970, in Medicine Hat, Alta. ... 6-4/220. ... Shoots right. ... Brother of Jamie Linden, RW with Florida Panthers organization (1993-97). ... President, NHLPA.

TRANSACTIONS/CAREER NOTES: Selected by Vancouver Canucks in 1st round (1st Canucks pick, 2nd overall) of entry draft (June 11, 1988). ... Hyperextended elbow (October 1989). ... Separated shoulder (March 17, 1990). ... Sprained knee (December 1, 1996); missed 24 games. ... Bruised ribs (March 8, 1997); missed eight games. ... Injured knee (April 5, 1997); missed one game. ... Strained groin (November 16, 1997); missed eight games. ... Sprained knee (January 26, 1998); missed six games. ... Traded by Canucks to New York Islanders for D Bryan McCabe, LW Todd Bertuzzi and third-round pick (LW Jarkko Ruutu) in 1998 entry draft (February 6, 1998). ... Traded by Islanders to Montreal Canadiens for first-round pick (D Branislav Mezei) in 1999 entry draft (May 29, 1999). ... Sprained ankle (December 1, 1999); missed 14 games. ... Reinjured ankle (January 6, 2000); missed six games. ... Fractured ribs (March 14, 2000); missed final 12 games of regular season. ... Bruised foot (December 8, 2000); missed one game. ... Bruised foot (December 30, 2000); missed 12 games. ... Traded by Canadiens with RW Dainius Zubrus and second-round pick (traded to Tampa Bay) in 2001 entry draft to Washington Capitals for F Jan Bulis, F Richard Zednik and first-round pick (C Alexander Perezhogin) in 2001 entry draft (March 13, 2001). ... Traded by Capitals with second-round pick (D Denis Grot) in 2003 entry draft to Canucks for first-round pick (RW Boyd Gordon) in 2002 entry draft and third-round pick (later traded to Edmonton Oilers) in 2003 entry draft (November 10, 2001). ... Sprained knee (October 10, 2002); missed six games. ... Cut above eye (December 15, 2002); mised five games.

STATISTICAL PLATEAUS: Three-goal games: 1988-89 (2), 1990-91 (1), 1995-96 (1), 1999-00 (1). Total: 5.

		REGULAR SEASON								PLAYOFFS				
Season Team	**League**	**GP**	**G**	**A**	**Pts.**	**PIM**	**+/-**	**PP**	**SH**	**GP**	**G**	**A**	**Pts.**	**PIM**
85-86—Medicine Hat	WHL	5	2	0	2	0	...	...	...	—	—	—	—	—
86-87—Medicine Hat	WHL	72	14	22	36	59	...	...	...	20	5	4	9	17
87-88—Medicine Hat	WHL	67	46	64	110	76	...	...	...	16	13	12	25	19
88-89—Vancouver	NHL	80	30	29	59	41	-10	10	1	7	3	4	7	8
89-90—Vancouver	NHL	73	21	30	51	43	-17	6	2	—	—	—	—	—
90-91—Vancouver	NHL	80	33	37	70	65	-25	16	2	6	0	7	7	2
91-92—Vancouver	NHL	80	31	44	75	101	3	6	1	13	4	8	12	6
92-93—Vancouver	NHL	84	33	39	72	64	19	8	0	12	5	8	13	16
93-94—Vancouver	NHL	84	32	29	61	73	6	10	2	24	12	13	25	18
94-95—Vancouver	NHL	48	18	22	40	40	-5	9	0	11	2	6	8	12
95-96—Vancouver	NHL	82	33	47	80	42	6	12	1	6	4	4	8	6
96-97—Vancouver	NHL	49	9	31	40	27	5	2	2	—	—	—	—	—
97-98—Vancouver	NHL	42	7	14	21	49	-13	2	0	—	—	—	—	—
—New York Islanders	NHL	25	10	7	17	33	-1	3	2	—	—	—	—	—
—Can. Olympic team	Int'l	6	1	0	1	10	2	0	0	—	—	—	—	—
98-99—New York Islanders	NHL	82	18	29	47	32	-14	8	1	—	—	—	—	—
99-00—Montreal	NHL	50	13	17	30	34	-3	4	0	—	—	—	—	—
00-01—Montreal	NHL	57	12	21	33	52	-2	6	0	—	—	—	—	—
—Washington	NHL	12	3	1	4	8	2	0	0	6	0	4	4	14
01-02—Washington	NHL	16	1	2	3	6	-2	1	0	—	—	—	—	—
—Vancouver	NHL	64	12	22	34	65	-3	2	0	6	1	4	5	0
02-03—Vancouver	NHL	71	19	22	41	30	-1	4	1	14	1	2	3	10
03-04—Vancouver	NHL	82	14	22	36	26	-6	4	0	7	0	0	0	6
NHL Totals (16 years)		1161	349	465	814	831	-61	113	15	112	32	60	92	98

LINDROS, ERIC C MAPLE LEAFS

PERSONAL: Born February 28, 1973, in London, Ont. ... 6-5/237. ... Shoots right. ... Brother of Brett Lindros, RW with New York Islanders (1994-96). ... Name pronounced LIHND-rahz.

TRANSACTIONS/CAREER NOTES: Selected by Quebec Nordiques in first round (first Nordiques pick, first overall) of NHL entry draft (June 22, 1991); refused to report. ... Traded by Nordiques to Philadelphia Flyers for G Ron Hextall, C Mike Ricci, C Peter Forsberg, D Steve Duchesne, D Kerry Huffman, first-round pick (G Jocelyn Thibault) in 1993 draft, cash and future considerations (June 20, 1992); Nordiques aquired LW Chris Simon and first-round pick (traded to Toronto Maple Leafs) in 1994 entry draft to complete deal (July 21, 1992). ... Sprained knee ligament (November 22, 1992); missed nine games. ... Injured knee (December 29, 1992); missed two games. ... Reinjured knee (January 10, 1993); missed 12 games. ... Tore right knee ligament (November 12, 1993); missed 14 games. ... Back spasms (March 6, 1994); missed one game. ... Sprained shoulder (April 4, 1994); missed remainder of season. ... Flu (January 29, 1995); missed one game. ... Bruised eye (April 30, 1995); missed final game of season and first three playoff games. ... Bruised left knee (November 2, 1995); missed seven games. ... Injured knee (April 5, 1996); missed two games. ... Injured right groin (October 1, 1996); missed 23 games. ... Bruised bone in back (February 13, 1997); missed two games. ... Charley horse (March 2, 1997); missed one game. ... Bruised calf (March 22, 1997); missed two games. ... Suspended two games and fined $2,000 by NHL for two high-sticking incidents (April 9, 1997). ... Bruised ribs (November 6, 1997); missed one game. ... Suffered concussion (March 8, 1998); missed 18 games. ... Fined $1,000 for slashing incident (December 5, 1998). ... Concussion (December 29, 1998); missed two games. ... Suspended two games by NHL for high-sticking incident (March 28, 1999). ... Collapsed lung (April 1, 1999); missed remainder of season. ... Ill (October 28, 1999); missed two games. ... Bruised left hand (December 11, 1999); missed two games. ... Concussion (January 14, 2000); missed four games. ... Back spasms (February 20, 2000); missed five games. ... Concussion (March 13, 2000); missed final 14 games of regular season and 16 playoff games. ... Missed 2000-01 season in contract dispute. ... Rights traded by Flyers with future considerations to New York Rangers for LW Jan Hlavac, D Kim Johnsson, RW Pavel Brendl and 3rd-round pick (LW Stefan Ruzicka) in 2003 entry draft (August 20, 2001). ... Sprained right knee (December 12, 2001); missed three games. ... Suffered concussion (December 28, 2001); missed four games. ... Sprained right knee (January 28, 2002); missed one game. ... Bruised foot (March 9, 2002); missed two games. ... Suspended one game for high-sticking incident (October 12, 2002). ... Sprained left shoulder (October 20, 2003); missed seven games. ... Injured left eye (November 12, 2003); missed four games. ... Flu (January 22, 2004); missed one game. ... Concussion (January 29, 2004) and had shoulder surgery (March 25, 2004); missed final 31 games of season. ... Signed as free agent by Toronto Maple Leafs (Aug. 11, 2005).

STATISTICAL PLATEAUS: Three-goal games: 1992-93 (3), 1993-94 (1), 1994-95 (3), 1995-96 (1), 1997-98 (1), 1999-00 (1), 2001-02 (2). Total: 12. ... Four-goal games: 1996-97 (1). ... Total hat tricks: 13.

		REGULAR SEASON								PLAYOFFS				
Season Team	**League**	**GP**	**G**	**A**	**Pts.**	**PIM**	**+/-**	**PP**	**SH**	**GP**	**G**	**A**	**Pts.**	**PIM**
88-89—St. Michaels	MTHL	37	24	43	67	193	...	...	...	—	—	—	—	—
89-90—Detroit	NAJHL	14	23	29	52	123	...	...	...	—	—	—	—	—
—Oshawa	OHL	25	17	19	36	61	...	...	...	17	*18	18	36	*76
90-91—Oshawa	OHL	57	*71	78	*149	189	...	...	...	16	*18	20	*38	*93
91-92—Oshawa	OHL	13	9	22	31	54	...	...	...	—	—	—	—	—
—Canadian nat'l team	Int'l	24	19	16	35	34	...	...	...	—	—	—	—	—
—Can. Olympic team	Int'l	8	5	6	11	6	...	...	...	—	—	—	—	—
92-93—Philadelphia	NHL	61	41	34	75	147	28	8	1	—	—	—	—	—

Season Team	League	GP	G	A	Pts.	PIM	+/-	PP	SH		Playoffs GP	G	A	Pts.	PIM
		REGULAR SEASON									PLAYOFFS				
93-94—Philadelphia	NHL	65	44	53	97	103	16	13	2		—	—	—	—	—
94-95—Philadelphia	NHL	46	29	41	70	60	27	7	0		12	4	11	15	18
95-96—Philadelphia	NHL	73	47	68	115	163	26	15	0		12	6	6	12	43
96-97—Philadelphia	NHL	52	32	47	79	136	31	9	0		19	12	14	26	40
97-98—Philadelphia	NHL	63	30	41	71	134	14	10	1		5	1	2	3	17
—Can. Olympic team	Int'l	6	2	3	5	2	6	0	0		—	—	—	—	—
98-99—Philadelphia	NHL	71	40	53	93	120	35	10	1		—	—	—	—	—
99-00—Philadelphia	NHL	55	27	32	59	83	11	10	1		2	1	0	1	0
00-01—Philadelphia	NHL	Did not play — holdout													
01-02—New York Rangers	NHL	72	37	36	73	138	19	12	1		—	—	—	—	—
—Can. Olympic team	Int'l	6	1	0	1	8	...	...	...		—	—	—	—	—
02-03—New York Rangers	NHL	81	19	34	53	141	5	9	0		—	—	—	—	—
03-04—New York Rangers	NHL	39	10	22	32	60	7	3	0		—	—	—	—	—
NHL Totals (12 years)		678	356	461	817	1285	219	106	7		50	24	33	57	118

LINDSAY, BILL — LW/RW

PERSONAL: Born May 17, 1971, in Fernie, B.C. ... 6-1/210. ... Shoots left.

TRANSACTIONS/CAREER NOTES: Selected by Quebec Nordiques in 5th round (6th Nordiques pick, 103rd overall) of entry draft (June 22, 1991). ... Separated right shoulder (December 26, 1992); missed four games. ... Selected by Florida Panthers in NHL expansion draft (June 24, 1993). ... Lacerated left hand (February 22, 1996); missed seven games. ... Strained hip flexor (April 1, 1996); missed three games. ... Sprained knee (March 26, 1999); missed one game. ... Reinjured knee (April 7, 1999); missed final six games of season. ... Traded by Panthers to Calgary Flames for D Todd Simpson (September 30, 1999). ... Suffered injury (March 7, 2000); missed one game. ... Suffered injury (March 15, 2000); missed one game. ... Suspended two games for elbowing incident (December 14, 2000). ... Traded by Flames to San Jose Sharks for 8th-round pick (D Joe Campbell) in 2001 entry draft (March 6, 2001). ... Signed as free agent by Panthers (August 23, 2001). ... Claimed off waivers by Montreal Canadiens (March 19, 2002). ... Signed as free agent by Atlanta Thrashers (August 25, 2003). ... Fractured larynx (January 3, 2004) and had surgery; missed remainder of season ... Claimed off waivers by Washington Capitals (March 9, 2004); claim rescinded because of injury.

Season Team	League	GP	G	A	Pts.	PIM	+/-	PP	SH		Playoffs GP	G	A	Pts.	PIM
		REGULAR SEASON									PLAYOFFS				
88-89—Vernon	BCHL	56	24	29	53	166	...	...	...		—	—	—	—	—
89-90—Tri-City	WHL	72	40	45	85	84	...	...	...		—	—	—	—	—
90-91—Tri-City	WHL	63	46	47	93	151	...	...	...		—	—	—	—	—
91-92—Tri-City	WHL	42	34	59	93	111	...	...	...		3	2	3	5	16
—Quebec	NHL	23	2	4	6	14	-6	0	0		—	—	—	—	—
92-93—Quebec	NHL	44	4	9	13	16	0	0	0		—	—	—	—	—
—Halifax	AHL	20	11	13	24	18	3	1	1		—	—	—	—	—
93-94—Florida	NHL	84	6	6	12	97	-2	0	0		—	—	—	—	—
94-95—Florida	NHL	48	10	9	19	46	1	0	1		—	—	—	—	—
95-96—Florida	NHL	73	12	22	34	57	13	0	3		22	5	5	10	18
96-97—Florida	NHL	81	11	23	34	120	1	0	1		3	0	1	1	8
97-98—Florida	NHL	82	12	16	28	80	-2	0	2		—	—	—	—	—
98-99—Florida	NHL	75	12	15	27	92	-1	0	1		—	—	—	—	—
99-00—Calgary	NHL	80	8	12	20	86	-7	0	0		—	—	—	—	—
00-01—Calgary	NHL	52	1	9	10	97	-8	0	0		—	—	—	—	—
—San Jose	NHL	16	0	4	4	29	2	0	0		6	0	0	0	16
01-02—Florida	NHL	63	4	7	11	117	-11	0	0		—	—	—	—	—
—Montreal	NHL	13	1	3	4	23	0	0	0		11	2	2	4	2
02-03—Hamilton	AHL	28	6	12	18	89	3	1	1		—	—	—	—	—
—Montreal	NHL	19	0	2	2	23	-1	0	0		—	—	—	—	—
03-04—Atlanta	NHL	24	0	0	0	25	-6	0	0		—	—	—	—	—
—Chicago	AHL	13	3	5	8	8	-1	0	0		—	—	—	—	—
04-05—Long Beach	ECHL	32	9	14	23	78	-8	0	...		7	2	2	4	12
NHL Totals (13 years)		777	83	141	224	922	-27	0	8		42	7	8	15	44

LING, DAVID — RW — BLUE JACKETS

PERSONAL: Born January 9, 1975, in Halifax, N.S. ... 5-10/197. ... Shoots right.

TRANSACTIONS/CAREER NOTES: Selected by Quebec Nordiques in seventh round (ninth Nordiques pick, 179th overall) of NHL entry draft (June 29, 1993). ... Nordiques franchise moved to Colorado and renamed Avalanche for 1995-96 season (June 21, 1995). ... Traded by Avalanche with ninth-round pick (D Steve Shirreffs) in 1995 entry draft to Calgary Flames for ninth-round pick (RW Chris George) in 1995 entry draft (July 7, 1995). ... Traded by Flames with sixth-round pick (LW Gordie Dwyer) in 1998 entry draft to Montreal Canadiens for C Scott Fraser (October 24, 1996). ... Traded by Canadiens to Chicago Blackhawks for RW Martin Gendron (March 14, 1998). ... Traded by Blackhawks to Dallas Stars for future considerations (August 11, 2000). ... Signed as free agent by Columbus Blue Jackets (July 10, 2001). ... Injured neck (February 23, 2004); missed two games.

Season Team	League	GP	G	A	Pts.	PIM	+/-	PP	SH		Playoffs GP	G	A	Pts.	PIM
		REGULAR SEASON									PLAYOFFS				
92-93—Kingston	OHL	64	17	46	63	275	...	...	...		16	3	12	15	72
93-94—Kingston	OHL	61	37	40	77	254	...	...	...		6	4	2	6	16
94-95—Kingston	OHL	62	*61	74	135	136	...	*24	1		6	7	8	15	12
95-96—Saint John	AHL	75	24	32	56	179	...	...	...		9	0	5	5	12
96-97—Fredericton	AHL	48	22	36	58	229	5	4	0		—	—	—	—	—
—Montreal	NHL	2	0	0	0	0	0	0	0		—	—	—	—	—
—Saint John	AHL	5	0	2	2	19	-3	0	0		—	—	—	—	—
97-98—Fredericton	AHL	67	25	41	66	148	6	12	0		—	—	—	—	—
—Montreal	NHL	1	0	0	0	0	-1	0	0		—	—	—	—	—
—Indianapolis	IHL	12	8	6	14	30	-2	3	0		5	4	1	5	31

Season Team	League	GP	G	A	Pts.	PIM	+/-	PP	SH	GP	G	A	Pts.	PIM
		REGULAR SEASON								PLAYOFFS				
98-99—Kansas City	IHL	82	30	42	72	112	-8	9	1	3	1	0	1	20
99-00—Kansas City	IHL	82	35	48	83	210	...	...	...	—	—	—	—	—
00-01—Utah	IHL	79	15	28	43	202	...	...	...	—	—	—	—	—
01-02—Syracuse	AHL	71	19	41	60	240	-8	9	0	10	5	5	10	16
—Columbus	NHL	5	0	0	0	7	-1	0	0	—	—	—	—	—
02-03—Syracuse	AHL	46	7	34	41	129	-13	4	0	—	—	—	—	—
—Columbus	NHL	35	3	2	5	86	-6	0	0	—	—	—	—	—
03-04—Columbus	NHL	50	1	2	3	98	-3	0	0	—	—	—	—	—
—Syracuse	AHL	14	7	10	17	25	-2	3	0	7	0	1	1	36
04-05—St. John's	AHL	80	28	60	88	152	-1	12	0	5	1	1	2	43
NHL Totals (5 years)		93	4	4	8	191	-11	0	0					

LITTLE, NEIL — G — FLYERS

PERSONAL: Born December 18, 1971, in Medicine Hat, Alta. ... 6-1/190. ... Catches left.
TRANSACTIONS/CAREER NOTES: Selected by Philadelphia Flyers in 11th round (10th Flyers pick, 226th overall) of NHL entry draft (June 22, 1991).

Season Team	League	GP	Min.	W	L	T	GA	SO	GAA	SV%	GP	Min.	W	L	GA	SO	GAA	SV%
		REGULAR SEASON									PLAYOFFS							
89-90—Estevan	SJHL	46	2707	21	19	4	150	1	3.32	...	—	—	—	—	—	—	—	—
90-91—Rensselaer Poly. Inst.	ECAC	18	1032	9	8	0	71	0	4.13	...	—	—	—	—	—	—	—	—
91-92—Rensselaer Poly. Inst.	ECAC	28	1532	11	11	3	96	0	3.76	...	—	—	—	—	—	—	—	—
92-93—Rensselaer Poly. Inst.	ECAC	31	1801	19	9	3	88	0	2.93	...	—	—	—	—	—	—	—	—
93-94—Rensselaer Poly. Inst.	ECAC	27	1570	16	7	4	88	0	3.36	...	—	—	—	—	—	—	—	—
—Hershey	AHL	1	18	0	0	0	1	0	3.33	.889	—	—	—	—	—	—	—	—
94-95—Hershey	AHL	19	919	5	7	3	60	0	3.92	.868	—	—	—	—	—	—	—	—
—Johnstown	ECHL	16	897	7	6	1	55	0	3.68	.896	3	145	0	2	11	0	4.55	.864
95-96—Hershey	AHL	48	2679	21	18	6	149	0	3.34	...	1	59	0	1	4	0	4.07	...
96-97—Philadelphia	AHL	54	3007	31	12	7	145	0	2.89	.909	10	620	6	4	20	1	1.94	.935
97-98—Philadelphia	AHL	51	2961	*31	11	7	145	0	2.94	.903	*20	*1193	*15	5	*48	*3	2.41	.927
98-99—Grand Rapids	IHL	50	2740	18	21	5	144	3	3.15	.894	—	—	—	—	—	—	—	—
99-00—Philadelphia	AHL	51	2830	26	18	2	143	1	3.03	...	5	298	2	3	15	0	3.02	...
00-01—Philadelphia	AHL	*58	*3117	22	27	4	148	2	2.85	.909	10	631	5	5	23	1	2.19	...
01-02—Philadelphia	AHL	35	2078	13	15	7	70	2	2.02	.920	5	298	2	3	13	0	2.62	.917
—Philadelphia	NHL	1	60	0	1	0	4	0	4.00	.862	—	—	—	—	—	—	—	—
02-03—Philadelphia	AHL	42	2478	18	19	4	103	4	2.49	.907	—	—	—	—	—	—	—	—
03-04—Philadelphia	NHL	1	33	0	1	0	2	0	3.64	.750	—	—	—	—	—	—	—	—
—Philadelphia	AHL	34	1899	21	12	1	62	6	1.96	.913	—	—	—	—	—	—	—	—
04-05—Philadelphia	AHL	26	1382	15	7	...	54	3	2.34	.921	2	24	1	0	0	0	0.00	1.00
NHL Totals (2 years)		2	93	0	2	0	6	0	3.87	.838								

LOMBARDI, MATTHEW — C — FLAMES

PERSONAL: Born March 18, 1982, in Montreal. ... 6-0/190. ... Shoots left.
TRANSACTIONS/CAREER NOTES: Selected by Calgary Flames in 3rd round (3rd pick of Flames, 90th overall) in 2002 entry draft (June 22, 2002). ... Injured head (May 9, 2004); missed final 13 playoff games.
STATISTICAL PLATEAUS: Three-goal games: 2003-04 (1).

Season Team	League	GP	G	A	Pts.	PIM	+/-	PP	SH	GP	G	A	Pts.	PIM
		REGULAR SEASON								PLAYOFFS				
00-01—Victoriaville	QMJHL	72	28	39	67	66	...	...	...	13	12	6	18	10
01-02—Victoriaville	QMJHL	66	57	73	130	70	...	...	...	22	*17	18	35	18
02-03—Saint John	AHL	76	25	21	46	41	-6	7	1	—	—	—	—	—
03-04—Calgary	NHL	79	16	13	29	32	4	3	2	13	1	5	6	4
04-05—Lowell	AHL	9	3	1	4	9	0	0	1	11	0	3	3	16
NHL Totals (1 year)		79	16	13	29	32	4	3	2	13	1	5	6	4

LOW, REED — RW — BLUES

PERSONAL: Born June 21, 1976, in Moose Jaw, Sask. ... 6-4/227. ... Shoots right.
TRANSACTIONS/CAREER NOTES: Selected by St. Louis Blues in seventh round (seventh Blues pick, 177th overall) of NHL entry draft (June 22, 1996). ... Injured thumb (January 29, 2001); missed three games. ... Injured knee (October 22, 2001); missed two games. ... Suspended one game by NHL (January 2, 2003) for infractions in a December 31, 2002, game. ... Suspended two games by NHL for receiving third instigator penalty in one season (March 24, 2003). ... Fractured ribs (December 11, 2003); missed 22 games.

Season Team	League	GP	G	A	Pts.	PIM	+/-	PP	SH	GP	G	A	Pts.	PIM
		REGULAR SEASON								PLAYOFFS				
94-95—Regina	WHL	2	0	0	0	5	...	...	...	—	—	—	—	—
95-96—Moose Jaw	WHL	61	12	7	19	221	...	...	...	—	—	—	—	—
96-97—Moose Jaw	WHL	62	16	11	27	228	...	...	...	12	2	1	3	50
97-98—Baton Rouge	ECHL	39	4	2	6	145	...	...	...	—	—	—	—	—
—Worcester	AHL	17	1	1	2	75	-3	1	0	3	0	0	0	0
98-99—Worcester	AHL	77	5	6	11	239	-15	1	0	4	0	0	0	2
99-00—Worcester	AHL	80	12	16	28	203	...	...	...	9	1	3	4	16
00-01—St. Louis	NHL	56	1	5	6	159	4	0	0	—	—	—	—	—

Season Team	League	REGULAR SEASON GP	G	A	Pts.	PIM	+/-	PP	SH	PLAYOFFS GP	G	A	Pts.	PIM
01-02—St. Louis	NHL	58	0	5	5	160	-3	0	0	—	—	—	—	—
02-03—St. Louis	NHL	79	2	4	6	234	3	0	0	—	—	—	—	—
03-04—St. Louis	NHL	57	0	2	2	141	-6	0	0	—	—	—	—	—
NHL Totals (4 years)		250	3	16	19	694	-2	0	0					

LOYNS, LYNN — LW — FLAMES

PERSONAL: Born February 22, 1981, in Naicam, Sask. ... 5-11/205.

TRANSACTIONS/CAREER NOTES: Signed as free agent by San Jose Sharks (September 22, 2001). ... Traded by Sharks to Calgary Flames (January 9, 2004) for future considerations. ... Injured ankle (April 26, 2004); missed remainder of playoffs.

Season Team	League	REGULAR SEASON GP	G	A	Pts.	PIM	+/-	PP	SH	PLAYOFFS GP	G	A	Pts.	PIM
97-98—Spokane	WHL	49	1	12	13	8	...	...	...	13	1	4	5	2
98-99—Spokane	WHL	72	20	30	50	43	...	...	...	—	—	—	—	—
99-00—Spokane	WHL	71	20	29	49	47	...	...	...	14	3	2	5	12
00-01—Spokane	WHL	66	31	42	73	81	...	...	...	12	6	12	18	18
01-02—Cleveland	AHL	76	9	9	18	81	...	...	...	—	—	—	—	—
02-03—San Jose	NHL	19	3	0	3	19	-4	0	0	—	—	—	—	—
—Cleveland	AHL	36	7	8	15	39	...	...	...	—	—	—	—	—
03-04—San Jose	NHL	2	0	0	0	0	-1	0	0	—	—	—	—	—
—Cleveland	AHL	30	5	9	14	40	9	0	1	—	—	—	—	—
—Calgary	NHL	12	0	2	2	2	-2	0	0	—	—	—	—	—
—Lowell	AHL	18	6	6	12	9	1	0	0	—	—	—	—	—
04-05—Lowell	AHL	77	7	8	15	42	4	1	0	11	0	0	0	0
NHL Totals (2 years)		33	3	2	5	21	-7	0	0					

LUKOWICH, BRAD — D — ISLANDERS

PERSONAL: Born August 12, 1976, in Cranbrook, B.C. ... 6-1/200. ... Shoots left. ... Name pronounced LOO-kih-wihch.

TRANSACTIONS/CAREER NOTES: Selected by New York Islanders in 4th round (4th Islanders pick, 90th overall) of entry draft (June 29, 1994). ... Traded by Islanders to Dallas Stars for 3rd-round pick (D Robert Schnabel) in 1997 entry draft (June 1, 1996). ... Back spasms (December 6, 1999); missed one game. ... Traded by Stars with G Manny Fernandez to Minnesota Wild for third-round pick (C Joel Lundqvist) in 2000 entry draft and 4th-round pick (later traded back to Wild) in 2002 entry draft (June 12, 2000). ... Traded by Wild with 3rd- (C Yared Hagos) and 9th-round (RW Dale Sullivan) picks in 2001 entry draft to Stars for C Aaron Gavey, C Pavel Patera, 8th-round pick (C Eric Johansson) in 2000 entry draft and 4th-round pick (later traded to Los Angeles Kings) in 2002 entry draft (June 25, 2000). ... Fractured finger (January 2, 2002); missed five games. ... Traded by Stars with 7th-round pick (D Jay Rosehill) in 2003 entry draft to Tampa Bay Lightning for 2nd-round pick (G Tobias Stephan) in 2002 entry draft (June 22, 2002). ... Fractured facial bone (March 27, 2003); missed six games. ... Flu (March 16, 2004); missed two games. ... Injured upper body (May 13, 2004); missed two playoff games.

Season Team	League	REGULAR SEASON GP	G	A	Pts.	PIM	+/-	PP	SH	PLAYOFFS GP	G	A	Pts.	PIM
92-93—Cranbook	Tier II Jr. A	54	21	41	62	162	...	...	...	—	—	—	—	—
—Kamloops	WHL	1	0	0	0	0	...	...	...	—	—	—	—	—
93-94—Kamloops	WHL	42	5	11	16	166	...	0	0	16	0	1	1	35
94-95—Kamloops	WHL	63	10	35	45	125	53	2	0	18	0	7	7	21
95-96—Kamloops	WHL	65	14	55	69	114	...	...	...	13	2	10	12	29
96-97—Michigan	IHL	69	2	6	8	77	...	...	...	4	0	1	1	2
97-98—Michigan	IHL	60	6	27	33	104	-7	2	0	4	0	4	4	14
—Dallas	NHL	4	0	1	1	2	-2	0	0	—	—	—	—	—
98-99—Michigan	IHL	67	8	21	29	95	1	3	0	—	—	—	—	—
—Dallas	NHL	14	1	2	3	19	3	0	0	8	0	1	1	4
99-00—Dallas	NHL	60	3	1	4	50	-14	0	0	—	—	—	—	—
00-01—Dallas	NHL	80	4	10	14	76	28	0	0	10	1	0	1	4
01-02—Dallas	NHL	66	1	6	7	40	-1	0	0	—	—	—	—	—
02-03—Tampa Bay	NHL	70	1	14	15	46	4	0	0	9	0	1	1	2
03-04—Tampa Bay	NHL	79	5	14	19	24	29	0	0	18	0	2	2	6
04-05—Fort Worth	CHL	16	3	5	8	33	...	...	...	—	—	—	—	—
NHL Totals (7 years)		373	15	48	63	257	47	0	0	45	1	4	5	16

LUNDMARK, JAMIE — RW/LW — RANGERS

PERSONAL: Born January 16, 1981, in Edmonton. ... 6-0/195. ... Shoots right.

TRANSACTIONS/CAREER NOTES: Selected by New York Rangers in first round (second Rangers pick, ninth overall) of NHL draft (June 26, 1999). ... Flu (January 15, 2003); missed one game. ... Sprained right knee (December 4, 2003); missed 23 games.

Season Team	League	REGULAR SEASON GP	G	A	Pts.	PIM	+/-	PP	SH	PLAYOFFS GP	G	A	Pts.	PIM
97-98—St. Albert	Jr. A	53	33	58	91	176	...	...	...	—	—	—	—	—
98-99—Moose Jaw	WHL	70	40	51	91	121	-11	21	2	11	5	4	9	24
99-00—Moose Jaw	WHL	37	21	27	48	33	-7	8	1	—	—	—	—	—
00-01—Seattle	WHL	52	35	42	77	49	...	...	...	9	4	4	8	16
01-02—Hartford	AHL	79	27	32	59	56	-17	10	1	10	3	4	7	16
02-03—Hartford	AHL	22	9	9	18	18	2	2	1	—	—	—	—	—
—New York Rangers	NHL	55	8	11	19	16	-3	0	0	—	—	—	—	—
03-04—New York Rangers	NHL	56	2	8	10	33	-8	0	0	—	—	—	—	—
04-05—Bolzano	Italy	14	10	10	20	22	...	...	...	—	—	—	—	—
—Hartford	AHL	64	14	27	41	146	-1	5	2	6	2	4	6	8
NHL Totals (2 years)		111	10	19	29	49	-11	0	0					

LUOMA, MIKKO — D — OILERS

PERSONAL: Born June 22, 1976, in Jyvaskyla, Finland. ... 6-3/207. ... Shoots left.

TRANSACTIONS/CAREER NOTES: Selected by Edmonton Oilers in 6th round (10th Oilers pick, 181st overall) of entry draft (June 23, 2002).

		REGULAR SEASON								PLAYOFFS				
Season Team	**League**	**GP**	**G**	**A**	**Pts.**	**PIM**	**+/-**	**PP**	**SH**	**GP**	**G**	**A**	**Pts.**	**PIM**
98-99—Jyvaskyla	Finland Jr.	53	2	8	10	...	...	...	...	3	0	0	0	...
99-00—Jyvaskyla	Finland Jr.	51	2	6	8	...	...	...	...	—	—	—	—	—
00-01—Tappara Tampere	Finland	56	10	11	21	...	...	...	...	10	0	2	2	...
01-02—Tappara Tampere	Finland	56	11	18	29	...	...	...	...	10	1	2	3	...
02-03—Tappara Tampere	Finland	55	4	13	17	...	...	...	...	14	2	1	3	...
03-04—Edmonton	NHL	3	0	1	1	0	0	0	0	—	—	—	—	—
—Toronto	AHL	65	4	22	26	54	7	1	0	3	1	0	1	8
04-05—Malmo	Sweden	50	9	9	18	72	-4	3	1	10	1	4	5	12
NHL Totals (1 year)		3	0	1	1	0	0	0	0					

LUONGO, ROBERTO — G — PANTHERS

PERSONAL: Born April 4, 1979, in Montreal. ... 6-3/205. ... Catches left. ... Name pronounced luh-WAHN-goh.

TRANSACTIONS/CAREER NOTES: Selected by New York Islanders in first round (first Islanders pick, fourth overall) of NHL draft (June 21, 1997). ... Traded by Islanders with C Olli Jokinen to Florida Panthers for RW Mark Parrish and LW Oleg Kvasha (June 24, 2000). ... Cut forearm (October 10, 2001); missed four games. ... Sprained right ankle (March 20, 2002); missed remainder of season. ... Back spasms (November 7, 2002); missed three games. ... Injured knee (March 26, 2003); missed one game.

		REGULAR SEASON									PLAYOFFS							
Season Team	**League**	**GP**	**Min.**	**W**	**L**	**T**	**GA**	**SO**	**GAA**	**SV%**	**GP**	**Min.**	**W**	**L**	**GA**	**SO**	**GAA**	**SV%**
95-96—Val-d'Or	QMJHL	23	1199	6	11	4	74	0	3.70	.878	3	68	0	1	5	0	4.41	...
96-97—Val-d'Or	QMJHL	60	3305	32	21	2	171	2	3.10	...	13	777	8	5	44	0	3.40	.904
97-98—Val-d'Or	QMJHL	54	3046	27	20	5	157	*7	3.09	.899	*17	*1019	*14	3	37	*2	*2.18	.933
98-99—Val-d'Or	QMJHL	21	1177	6	10	2	77	1	3.93	...	—	—	—	—	—	—	—	—
—Acadie-Bathurst	QMJHL	22	1341	14	7	1	74	0	3.31	...	*23	*1400	*16	6	64	0	2.74	...
99-00—Lowell	AHL	26	1517	10	12	4	74	1	2.93	...	6	359	3	3	18	0	3.01	...
—New York Islanders	NHL	24	1292	7	14	1	70	1	3.25	.904	—	—	—	—	—	—	—	—
00-01—Florida	NHL	47	2628	12	24	7	107	5	2.44	.920	—	—	—	—	—	—	—	—
—Louisville	AHL	3	178	1	2	0	10	0	3.37	.917	—	—	—	—	—	—	—	—
01-02—Florida	NHL	58	3030	16	33	4	140	4	2.77	.915	—	—	—	—	—	—	—	—
02-03—Florida	NHL	65	3627	20	34	7	164	6	2.71	.918	—	—	—	—	—	—	—	—
03-04—Florida	NHL	72	4252	25	33	14	172	7	2.43	.931	—	—	—	—	—	—	—	—
NHL Totals (5 years)		266	14829	80	138	33	653	23	2.64	.920								

LUPASCHUK, ROSS — D — PENGUINS

PERSONAL: Born January 19, 1981, in Edmonton. ... 6-1/211. ... Shoots right.

TRANSACTIONS/CAREER NOTES: Selected by Washington Capitals in second round (fourth Capitals pick, 34th overall) of NHL entry draft (June 26, 1999). ... Traded by Capitals with C Michal Sivek, C Kris Beech and future considerations to Pittsburgh Penguins for RW Jaromir Jagr and D Frantisek Kucera (July 11, 2001). ... Signed as free agent by Wilkes-Barre/Scranton of the AHL (September 26, 2004).

		REGULAR SEASON								PLAYOFFS				
Season Team	**League**	**GP**	**G**	**A**	**Pts.**	**PIM**	**+/-**	**PP**	**SH**	**GP**	**G**	**A**	**Pts.**	**PIM**
97-98—Prince Albert	WHL	67	6	12	18	170	...	...	...	—	—	—	—	—
98-99—Prince Albert	WHL	67	8	19	27	127	24	3	0	14	4	9	13	16
99-00—Prince Albert	WHL	22	8	8	16	42	...	...	...	—	—	—	—	—
—Red Deer	WHL	46	13	27	40	116	17	11	1	4	0	1	1	10
00-01—Red Deer	WHL	65	28	37	65	135	...	...	...	22	5	10	15	54
01-02—Wilkes-Barre/Scranton	AHL	72	9	20	29	91	-10	3	0	—	—	—	—	—
02-03—Pittsburgh	NHL	3	0	0	0	4	-3	0	0	—	—	—	—	—
—Wilkes-Barre/Scranton	AHL	74	18	18	36	101	1	8	1	4	0	2	2	20
03-04—Wilkes-Barre/Scranton	AHL	58	4	17	21	96	7	1	0	—	—	—	—	—
04-05—Wilkes-Barre/Scranton	AHL	67	11	19	30	145	9	7	0	5	0	0	0	2
NHL Totals (1 year)		3	0	0	0	4	-3	0	0					

LUPUL, JOFFREY — C — MIGHTY DUCKS

PERSONAL: Born September 23, 1983, in Edmonton. ... 6-1/200. ... Shoots right.

TRANSACTIONS/CAREER NOTES: Selected by Anaheim Mighty Ducks in first round (first Mighty Ducks pick, seventh overall) of NHL entry draft (June 22, 2002).

		REGULAR SEASON								PLAYOFFS				
Season Team	**League**	**GP**	**G**	**A**	**Pts.**	**PIM**	**+/-**	**PP**	**SH**	**GP**	**G**	**A**	**Pts.**	**PIM**
00-01—Medicine Hat	WHL	69	30	26	56	39	...	...	...	—	—	—	—	—
01-02—Medicine Hat	WHL	72	*56	50	106	95	...	...	...	—	—	—	—	—
02-03—Medicine Hat	WHL	50	41	37	78	82	...	...	...	11	4	11	15	20
03-04—Anaheim	NHL	75	13	21	34	28	-6	4	0	—	—	—	—	—
—Cincinnati	AHL	3	3	2	5	2	4	0	0	—	—	—	—	—
04-05—Cincinnati	AHL	65	30	26	56	58	10	10	1	12	3	9	12	27
NHL Totals (1 year)		75	13	21	34	28	-6	4	0					

LYDMAN, TONI — D — FLAMES

PERSONAL: Born September 25, 1977, in Lahti, Finland. ... 6-1/202. ... Shoots left.

TRANSACTIONS/CAREER NOTES: Selected by Calgary Flames in fourth round (fifth Flames pick, 89th overall) of NHL draft (June 22, 1996). ... Suffered concussion (January 5, 2001); missed 12 games. ... Ill (December 26, 2001); missed two games. ... Ill (March 28, 2002); missed one game. ... Had the flu (December 27, 2002); missed one game. ... Injured shoulder (December 5, 2003); missed five games. ... Had concussion (March 16, 2004); missed 10 games. ... Injured upper body (April 13, 2004); missed 20 playoff games.

		REGULAR SEASON								PLAYOFFS				
Season Team	League	GP	G	A	Pts.	PIM	+/-	PP	SH	GP	G	A	Pts.	PIM
93-94—Reipas Lahti	Finland Jr.	1	0	0	0	0	...	...	...	—	—	—	—	—
94-95—Reipas Lahti	Finland Jr.	26	6	4	10	10	...	...	...	—	—	—	—	—
95-96—Reipas Lahti	Finland Jr.	1	0	0	0	0	...	...	...	—	—	—	—	—
—Reipas Lahti	Finland	39	5	2	7	30	...	...	...	—	—	—	—	—
96-97—Tappara	Finland	49	1	2	3	65	...	...	...	3	0	0	0	6
97-98—Tappara Tampere	Finland	48	4	10	14	48	...	...	...	4	0	2	2	0
98-99—HIFK Helsinki	Finland	42	4	7	11	36	...	...	...	11	0	3	3	2
99-00—HIFK Helsinki	Finland	46	4	18	22	36	...	...	...	9	0	4	4	6
00-01—Calgary	NHL	62	3	16	19	30	-7	1	0	—	—	—	—	—
01-02—Calgary	NHL	79	6	22	28	52	-8	1	0	—	—	—	—	—
02-03—Calgary	NHL	81	6	20	26	28	-7	3	0	—	—	—	—	—
03-04—Calgary	NHL	67	4	16	20	30	6	2	0	6	0	1	1	2
04-05—HIFK Helsinki	Finland	8	1	2	3	2	6	...	...	5	0	3	3	0
NHL Totals (4 years)		289	19	74	93	140	-16	7	0	6	0	1	1	2

LYNCH, DOUG — D — BLUES

PERSONAL: Born April 4, 1983, in North Vancouver, B.C. ... 6-3/214. ... Shoots left.

TRANSACTIONS/CAREER NOTES: Selected by Edmonton Oilers in 2nd round (2nd Oilers pick, 43rd overall) of entry draft (June 23, 2001). ... Traded by Oilers with D Eric Brewer and D Jeff Woywitka to St. Louis Blues for D Chris Pronger (Aug. 2, 2005).

		REGULAR SEASON								PLAYOFFS				
Season Team	League	GP	G	A	Pts.	PIM	+/-	PP	SH	GP	G	A	Pts.	PIM
98-99—Red Deer	WHL	2	0	1	1	2	...	...	...	—	—	—	—	—
99-00—Red Deer	WHL	65	9	5	14	57	...	...	...	4	0	0	0	5
00-01—Red Deer	WHL	72	12	37	49	181	...	...	...	21	1	9	10	30
01-02—Red Deer	WHL	71	21	27	48	202	...	...	...	22	5	4	9	12
02-03—Spokane	WHL	55	13	17	30	156	...	...	...	4	1	0	1	16
—Red Deer	WHL	13	7	5	12	27	...	...	...	—	—	—	—	—
03-04—Edmonton	NHL	2	0	0	0	0	0	0	0	—	—	—	—	—
—Toronto	AHL	74	11	25	36	77	11	5	0	3	0	1	1	2
04-05—Edmonton	AHL	74	1	13	14	109	-7	0	1	—	—	—	—	—
NHL Totals (1 year)		2	0	0	0	0	0	0	0					

LYSAK, BRETT — C — HURRICANES

PERSONAL: Born December 30, 1980, in Edmonton. ... 6-0/190. ... Shoots left.

TRANSACTIONS/CAREER NOTES: Selected by Carolina Hurricanes in 2nd round (2nd Hurricanes pick, 49th overall) of entry draft (June 26, 1999).

		REGULAR SEASON								PLAYOFFS				
Season Team	League	GP	G	A	Pts.	PIM	+/-	PP	SH	GP	G	A	Pts.	PIM
96-97—Regina	WHL	66	11	14	25	41	...	...	...	5	0	1	1	5
97-98—Regina	WHL	70	22	38	60	82	...	...	...	9	6	2	8	8
98-99—Regina	WHL	61	39	49	88	84	-3	17	4	—	—	—	—	—
99-00—Regina	WHL	70	38	40	78	24	-8	22	0	7	5	4	9	2
00-01—Regina	WHL	64	35	48	83	44	...	...	...	6	5	1	6	4
01-02—Lowell	AHL	53	6	8	14	26	-6	2	0	3	0	0	0	0
—Florida	ECHL	16	2	7	9	14	3	1	0	6	3	1	4	6
02-03—Lowell	AHL	49	6	9	15	59	-16	3	0	—	—	—	—	—
03-04—Carolina	NHL	2	0	0	0	2	0	0	0	—	—	—	—	—
—Lowell	AHL	71	17	18	35	104	-14	5	2	—	—	—	—	—
04-05—Iserlohn	Germany	49	9	9	18	151	-8	...	...	—	—	—	—	—
NHL Totals (1 year)		2	0	0	0	2	0	0	0					

MACDONALD, CRAIG — C/LW — BRUINS

PERSONAL: Born April 7, 1977, in Antigonish, N.S. ... 6-1/200. ... Shoots left.

TRANSACTIONS/CAREER NOTES: Selected by Hartford Whalers in fourth round (third Whalers pick, 88th overall) of NHL entry draft (June 22, 1996). ... Whalers franchise moved to North Carolina and renamed Carolina Hurricanes for 1997-98 season; NHL approved move on June 25, 1997. ... Signed as free agent by Florida Panthers (August 14, 2003). ... Injured groin (November 18, 2003); missed five games. ... Claimed off waivers by Boston Bruins (January 20, 2004).

		REGULAR SEASON								PLAYOFFS				
Season Team	League	GP	G	A	Pts.	PIM	+/-	PP	SH	GP	G	A	Pts.	PIM
94-95—Lawrence Academy	Mass. H.S.	30	25	52	77	10	...	...	...	—	—	—	—	—
95-96—Harvard	ECAC	34	7	10	17	10	...	...	...	—	—	—	—	—
96-97—Harvard	ECAC	32	6	10	16	20	...	2	1	—	—	—	—	—
97-98—Canadian nat'l team	Int'l	51	15	20	35	133	...	...	...	—	—	—	—	—
98-99—New Haven	AHL	62	17	31	48	77	1	5	0	—	—	—	—	—

Season Team	League	GP	G	A	Pts.	PIM	+/-	PP	SH	GP	G	A	Pts.	PIM
		REGULAR SEASON								PLAYOFFS				
—Carolina	NHL	11	0	0	0	0	0	0	0	1	0	0	0	0
99-00—Cincinnati	IHL	78	12	24	36	76	...	...	...	11	4	1	5	8
00-01—Cincinnati	IHL	82	20	28	48	104	...	...	...	5	0	1	1	6
01-02—Lowell	AHL	64	19	22	41	61	1	2	1	—	—	—	—	—
—Carolina	NHL	12	1	1	2	0	-1	0	0	4	0	0	0	2
02-03—Lowell	AHL	27	7	20	27	38	-3	1	0	—	—	—	—	—
—Carolina	NHL	35	1	3	4	20	-3	0	0	—	—	—	—	—
03-04—San Antonio	AHL	2	0	0	0	4	0	0	0	—	—	—	—	—
—Florida	NHL	34	0	3	3	25	-5	0	0	—	—	—	—	—
—Boston	NHL	18	0	3	3	8	0	0	0	1	0	0	0	0
04-05—Lowell	AHL	71	10	18	28	104	-3	3	0	2	0	0	0	0
NHL Totals (4 years)		110	2	10	12	53	-9	0	0	6	0	0	0	2

MACDONALD, JASON — RW — RANGERS

PERSONAL: Born April 1, 1974, in Charlottetown, P.E.I. ... 5-11/205. ... Shoots right.

TRANSACTIONS/CAREER NOTES: Selected by Detroit Red Wings in sixth round (fifth Red Wings pick, 142nd overall) of NHL entry draft (June 20, 1992). ... Traded by Red Wings to Montreal Canadiens for cash (November 8, 1996). ... Signed as free agent by Pittsburgh Penguins (September 29, 2000). ... Signed as free agent by New York Rangers (September 10, 2003).

Season Team	League	GP	G	A	Pts.	PIM	+/-	PP	SH	GP	G	A	Pts.	PIM
		REGULAR SEASON								PLAYOFFS				
89-90—Charlottetown	PEIJHL	25	11	29	40	206	...	...	...	—	—	—	—	—
90-91—North Bay	OHL	57	12	15	27	126	...	...	...	10	3	3	6	15
91-92—North Bay	OHL	17	5	8	13	50	...	...	...	—	—	—	—	—
—Owen Sound	OHL	42	17	19	36	129	...	...	...	5	0	2	2	8
92-93—Owen Sound	OHL	55	46	43	89	197	...	...	...	8	6	5	11	28
93-94—Owen Sound	OHL	66	55	61	116	177	...	19	2	9	7	11	18	36
—Adirondack	AHL	...	...	...	...	...	...	...	...	1	0	0	0	0
94-95—Adirondack	AHL	68	14	21	35	238	-18	2	1	4	0	0	0	2
95-96—Adirondack	AHL	43	9	13	22	99	...	...	...	—	—	—	—	—
—Toledo	ECHL	9	5	5	10	26	...	...	...	9	3	1	4	39
96-97—Adirondack	AHL	1	0	0	0	2	-2	0	0	—	—	—	—	—
—Fredericton	AHL	63	22	25	47	189	2	5	0	—	—	—	—	—
97-98—Saint John	AHL	6	2	0	2	27	1	0	0	11	1	3	4	17
98-99—Manitoba	IHL	82	25	27	52	283	-7	8	0	5	2	2	4	13
99-00—Manitoba	IHL	30	5	10	15	77	...	...	...	—	—	—	—	—
—Orlando	IHL	29	7	7	14	113	...	...	...	4	0	0	0	19
00-01—Wilkes-Barre/Scranton	AHL	74	17	16	33	290	...	...	...	17	1	3	4	66
01-02—Wilkes-Barre/Scranton	AHL	57	8	13	21	330	-15	1	0	—	—	—	—	—
02-03—Wilkes-Barre/Scranton	AHL	56	4	7	11	137	1	1	0	1	0	0	0	0
03-04—Hartford	AHL	41	11	11	22	101	10	3	1	10	4	0	4	50
—New York Rangers	NHL	4	0	0	0	19	-1	0	0	—	—	—	—	—
04-05—St. John's	AHL	29	4	8	12	152	-10	3	0	5	2	0	2	27
—Regina	WHL	5	0	0	0	0	-2	0	0	—	—	—	—	—
NHL Totals (1 year)		4	0	0	0	19	-1	0	0					

M

MACINNIS, AL — D — BLUES

PERSONAL: Born July 11, 1963, in Inverness, N.S. ... 6-1/204. ... Shoots right. ... Name pronounced muh-KIHN-ihz.

TRANSACTIONS/CAREER NOTES: Selected by Calgary Flames in 1st round (1st Flames pick, 15th overall) of entry draft (June 10, 1981). ... Twisted knee (February 1985). ... Cut hand (March 23, 1986). ... Stretched knee ligaments (April 8, 1990). ... Separated shoulder (November 22, 1991); missed eight games. ... Dislocated left hip (November 12, 1992); missed 34 games. ... Strained shoulder (December 22, 1993); missed one game. ... Strained shoulder (January 2, 1994); missed four games. ... Bruised knee (February 24, 1994); missed four games. ... Traded by Flames with 4th-round pick (D Didier Tremblay) in 1997 entry draft to St. Louis Blues for D Phil Housley and 2nd-round picks in 1996 (C Steve Begin) and 1997 (RW John Tripp) entry drafts (July 4, 1994). ... Injured shoulder (January 31, 1995); missed eight games. ... Flu (April 9, 1995); missed three games. ... Injured shoulder (April 25, 1995); missed final five games of season. ... Dislocated shoulder (February 4, 1997); missed nine games. ... Dislocated shoulder (December 13, 1997); missed nine games. ... Cut around left eye (April 12, 1998); missed one game. ... Fractured leg (October 9, 1999); missed 11 games. ... Injured rib (January 14, 2000); missed one game. ... Collapsed lung (January 21, 2000); missed five games. ... Back spasms (February 10, 2000); missed three games. ... Injured eye (January 29, 2001); missed 23 games. ... Bruised ankle (November 17, 2001); missed four games. ... Back spasms (January 5, 2002); missed three games. ... Bruised foot (January 28, 2002); missed three games. ... Back spasms (December 11, 2002); missed one game. ... Injured shoulder (April 12, 2003); missed four playoff games. ... Eye surgeries (October 17, 2003); missed remainder of season.

STATISTICAL PLATEAUS: Three-goal games: 1991-92 (1), 1996-97 (1), 1998-99 (1). Total: 3.

Season Team	League	GP	G	A	Pts.	PIM	+/-	PP	SH	GP	G	A	Pts.	PIM
		REGULAR SEASON								PLAYOFFS				
79-80—Regina Blues	SJHL	59	20	28	48	110	...	...	...	—	—	—	—	—
80-81—Kitchener	OMJHL	47	11	28	39	59	...	...	...	18	4	12	16	20
81-82—Kitchener	OHL	59	25	50	75	145	...	...	...	15	5	10	15	44
—Calgary	NHL	2	0	0	0	0	0	0	0	—	—	—	—	—
82-83—Kitchener	OHL	51	38	46	84	67	...	...	...	8	3	8	11	9
—Calgary	NHL	14	1	3	4	9	0	0	0	—	—	—	—	—
83-84—Colorado	CHL	19	5	14	19	22	1	7	0	—	—	—	—	—
—Calgary	NHL	51	11	34	45	42	0	7	0	11	2	12	14	13
84-85—Calgary	NHL	67	14	52	66	75	7	8	0	4	1	2	3	8
85-86—Calgary	NHL	77	11	57	68	76	38	4	0	21	4	*15	19	30
86-87—Calgary	NHL	79	20	56	76	97	20	7	0	4	1	0	1	0
87-88—Calgary	NHL	80	25	58	83	114	13	7	2	7	3	6	9	18
88-89—Calgary	NHL	79	16	58	74	126	38	8	0	22	7	*24	*31	46
89-90—Calgary	NHL	79	28	62	90	82	20	14	1	6	2	3	5	8

		REGULAR SEASON								PLAYOFFS				
Season Team	**League**	**GP**	**G**	**A**	**Pts.**	**PIM**	**+/-**	**PP**	**SH**	**GP**	**G**	**A**	**Pts.**	**PIM**
90-91—Calgary	NHL	78	28	75	103	90	42	17	0	7	2	3	5	8
91-92—Calgary	NHL	72	20	57	77	83	13	11	0	—	—	—	—	—
92-93—Calgary	NHL	50	11	43	54	61	15	7	0	6	1	6	7	10
93-94—Calgary	NHL	75	28	54	82	95	35	12	1	7	2	6	8	12
94-95—St. Louis	NHL	32	8	20	28	43	19	2	0	7	1	5	6	10
95-96—St. Louis	NHL	82	17	44	61	88	5	9	1	13	3	4	7	20
96-97—St. Louis	NHL	72	13	30	43	65	2	6	1	6	1	2	3	4
97-98—St. Louis	NHL	71	19	30	49	80	6	9	1	8	2	6	8	12
—Can. Olympic team	Int'l	6	2	0	2	2	2	2	0	—	—	—	—	—
98-99—St. Louis	NHL	82	20	42	62	70	33	11	1	13	4	8	12	20
99-00—St. Louis	NHL	61	11	28	39	34	20	6	0	7	1	3	4	14
00-01—St. Louis	NHL	59	12	42	54	52	23	6	1	15	2	8	10	18
01-02—Can. Olympic team	Int'l	6	0	0	0	8	...	...	...	—	—	—	—	—
—St. Louis	NHL	71	11	35	46	52	3	6	0	10	0	7	7	4
02-03—St. Louis	NHL	80	16	52	68	61	22	9	1	3	0	1	1	0
03-04—St. Louis	NHL	3	0	2	2	6	-1	0	0	—	—	—	—	—
NHL Totals (23 years)		1416	340	934	1274	1501	373	166	10	177	39	121	160	255

MACKENZIE, DEREK — C — THRASHERS

PERSONAL: Born June 11, 1981, in Sudbury, Ont. ... 5-11/180. ... Shoots left.
TRANSACTIONS/CAREER NOTES: Selected by Atlanta Thrashers in fifth round (sixth Thrashers pick, 128th overall) of NHL entry draft (June 26, 1999). ... Signed as free agent by Chicago of the AHL (September 30, 2004).

		REGULAR SEASON								PLAYOFFS				
Season Team	**League**	**GP**	**G**	**A**	**Pts.**	**PIM**	**+/-**	**PP**	**SH**	**GP**	**G**	**A**	**Pts.**	**PIM**
97-98—Sudbury	OHL	59	9	11	20	26	...	...	...	10	0	1	1	6
98-99—Sudbury	OHL	68	22	65	87	74	...	...	...	4	2	4	6	2
99-00—Sudbury	OHL	68	24	33	57	110	1	5	4	12	5	9	14	16
00-01—Sudbury	OHL	62	40	49	89	89	25	8	5	12	6	8	14	16
01-02—Chicago	AHL	68	13	12	25	80	0	0	3	25	4	2	6	20
—Atlanta	NHL	1	0	0	0	2	-1	0	0	—	—	—	—	—
02-03—Chicago	AHL	80	14	18	32	97	14	0	4	9	0	0	0	4
03-04—Atlanta	NHL	12	0	1	1	10	0	0	0	—	—	—	—	—
—Chicago	AHL	63	19	16	35	67	8	0	2	10	7	1	8	13
04-05—Chicago	AHL	78	13	20	33	87	5	0	6	18	5	6	11	33
NHL Totals (2 years)		13	0	1	1	12	-1	0	0					

MACMILLAN, JEFF — D — BLUE JACKETS

PERSONAL: Born March 30, 1979, in Durham, Ont. ... 6-3/206. ... Shoots left.
TRANSACTIONS/CAREER NOTES: Selected by Dallas Stars in seventh round (eighth Star pick, 215th overall) of NHL entry draft (June 26, 1999). ... Signed as free agent by New York Rangers (July 22, 2004). ... Signed as free agent by Columbus Blue Jackets (Aug. 12, 2005).

		REGULAR SEASON								PLAYOFFS				
Season Team	**League**	**GP**	**G**	**A**	**Pts.**	**PIM**	**+/-**	**PP**	**SH**	**GP**	**G**	**A**	**Pts.**	**PIM**
95-96—Hanover	OJHL	29	7	13	20	26	...	...	...	—	—	—	—	—
96-97—Oshawa	OHL	39	0	4	4	15	...	...	...	15	0	0	0	4
97-98—Oshawa	OHL	64	3	12	15	72	...	...	...	7	0	3	3	11
98-99—Oshawa	OHL	65	3	18	21	109	...	...	...	15	3	6	9	28
99-00—Michigan	IHL	53	0	3	3	54	...	...	...	—	—	—	—	—
—Fort Wayne	UHL	7	1	1	2	25	...	...	...	9	0	2	2	10
00-01—Utah	IHL	81	5	15	20	105	...	...	...	—	—	—	—	—
01-02—Utah	AHL	77	6	9	15	146	12	0	0	5	1	0	1	17
02-03—Utah	AHL	78	8	7	15	132	-9	1	0	2	0	0	0	6
03-04—Dallas	NHL	4	0	0	0	0	-2	0	0	—	—	—	—	—
—Utah	AHL	73	4	6	10	108	-14	2	0	—	—	—	—	—
04-05—Hartford	AHL	71	2	5	7	136	18	0	0	6	0	0	0	4
NHL Totals (1 year)		4	0	0	0	0	-2	0	0					

MADDEN, JOHN — C — DEVILS

PERSONAL: Born May 4, 1973, in Barrie, Ont. ... 5-11/190. ... Shoots left.
TRANSACTIONS/CAREER NOTES: Signed as free agent by New Jersey Devils (June 26, 1997). ... Injured toe (January 20, 2001); missed one game. ... Injured groin (March 27, 2003); missed two games. ... Injured face (December 12, 2003); missed two games.
STATISTICAL PLATEAUS: Three-goal games: 2002-03 (1). ... Four-goal games: 2000-01 (1). ... Total hat tricks: 2.

		REGULAR SEASON								PLAYOFFS				
Season Team	**League**	**GP**	**G**	**A**	**Pts.**	**PIM**	**+/-**	**PP**	**SH**	**GP**	**G**	**A**	**Pts.**	**PIM**
92-93—Barrie	COJHL	43	49	75	124	62	...	...	...	—	—	—	—	—
93-94—Univ. of Michigan	CCHA	36	6	11	17	14	...	...	...	—	—	—	—	—
94-95—Univ. of Michigan	CCHA	39	21	22	43	8	...	...	...	—	—	—	—	—
95-96—Univ. of Michigan	CCHA	43	27	30	57	45	...	...	...	—	—	—	—	—
96-97—Univ. of Michigan	CCHA	42	26	37	63	56	...	...	...	—	—	—	—	—
97-98—Albany	AHL	74	20	36	56	40	35	3	2	13	3	13	16	14
98-99—Albany	AHL	75	38	60	98	44	24	8	6	5	2	2	4	6
—New Jersey	NHL	4	0	1	1	0	-2	0	0	—	—	—	—	—
99-00—New Jersey	NHL	74	16	9	25	6	7	0	*6	20	3	4	7	0

Season Team	League	REGULAR SEASON GP	G	A	Pts.	PIM	+/-	PP	SH	PLAYOFFS GP	G	A	Pts.	PIM
00-01—New Jersey	NHL	80	23	15	38	12	24	0	3	25	4	3	7	6
01-02—New Jersey	NHL	82	15	8	23	25	6	0	0	6	0	0	0	0
02-03—New Jersey	NHL	80	19	22	41	26	13	2	2	24	6	10	16	2
03-04—New Jersey	NHL	80	12	23	35	22	7	1	1	5	0	0	0	0
04-05—HIFK Helsinki	Finland	3	0	0	0	0	0	0	0	—	—	—	—	—
NHL Totals (6 years)		400	85	78	163	91	55	3	12	80	13	17	30	8

MAIR, ADAM C SABRES

PERSONAL: Born February 15, 1979, in Hamilton, Ont. ... 6-1/208. ... Shoots right.

TRANSACTIONS/CAREER NOTES: Selected by Toronto Maple Leafs in fourth round (second Maple Leafs pick, 84th overall) of NHL entry draft (June 21, 1997). ... Traded by Maple Leafs with second-round pick (C Mike Cammalleri) in 2001 entry draft to Los Angeles Kings for D Aki Berg (March 13, 2001). ... Suspended 10 games by NHL for leaving bench to fight (December 21, 2001). ... Traded by Kings with fifth-round pick (D Thomas Morrow) in 2003 entry draft to Buffalo Sabres for LW Erik Rasmussen (July 24, 2002). ... Bruised right foot (March 19, 2003); missed three games. ... Suspended one game by NHL for cross-checking incident (December 13, 2003).

Season Team	League	REGULAR SEASON GP	G	A	Pts.	PIM	+/-	PP	SH	PLAYOFFS GP	G	A	Pts.	PIM
94-95—Ohsweken	Jr. B	39	21	23	44	91	...	...	...	—	—	—	—	—
95-96—Owen Sound	OHL	62	12	15	27	63	...	...	...	6	0	0	0	2
96-97—Owen Sound	OHL	65	16	35	51	113	-17	5	1	4	1	0	1	2
97-98—Owen Sound	OHL	56	25	27	52	179	...	...	...	11	6	3	9	31
98-99—Owen Sound	OHL	43	23	41	64	109	21	...	...	16	10	10	20	47
—Saint John	AHL	24	5	12	17	31	...	...	...	3	1	0	1	6
—Toronto	NHL	...	...	...	...	...	...	...	...	5	1	0	1	14
99-00—St. John's	AHL	66	22	27	49	124	...	...	...	—	—	—	—	—
—Toronto	NHL	8	1	0	1	6	-1	0	0	5	0	0	0	8
00-01—St. John's	AHL	47	18	27	45	69	...	...	...	—	—	—	—	—
—Toronto	NHL	16	0	2	2	14	3	0	0	—	—	—	—	—
—Los Angeles	NHL	10	0	0	0	6	-3	0	0	—	—	—	—	—
01-02—Manchester	AHL	27	10	9	19	48	3	4	1	5	5	1	6	10
—Los Angeles	NHL	18	1	1	2	57	1	0	0	—	—	—	—	—
02-03—Buffalo	NHL	79	6	11	17	146	-4	0	1	—	—	—	—	—
03-04—Buffalo	NHL	81	6	14	20	146	-3	1	0	—	—	—	—	—
NHL Totals (6 years)		212	14	28	42	375	-7	1	1	10	1	0	1	22

MAJESKY, IVAN D CAPITALS

PERSONAL: Born September 2, 1976, in Banska Bystrica, Czech. ... 6-5/230.

TRANSACTIONS/CAREER NOTES: Selected by Florida Panthers in 9th round (12th Panthers pick, 267th overall) of NHL draft (June 24, 2001). ... Traded by Panthers to Atlanta Thrashers for second-round pick (C Kamil Kreps) in 2003 draft (June 20, 2003). ... Sprained left knee (November 29, 2003); missed five games. ... Reinjured left knee (December 13, 2003); missed nine games. ... Signed as free agent by Washington Capitals (Aug. 10, 2005).

Season Team	League	REGULAR SEASON GP	G	A	Pts.	PIM	+/-	PP	SH	PLAYOFFS GP	G	A	Pts.	PIM
95-96—Banska Bystrica	Slovakia	17	0	0	0	18	...	...	...	—	—	—	—	—
96-97—Banska Bystrica	Slovakia	49	2	4	6	...	...	...	...	—	—	—	—	—
97-98—Banska Bystrica	Slov. Div.	...	...	...	...	...	...	...	...	—	—	—	—	—
98-99—Hkm Zvolen	Slovakia	...	...	...	...	...	...	...	...	6	0	2	2	2
—Banska Bystrica	Slovakia	48	7	7	14	68	...	...	...	—	—	—	—	—
99-00—Hkm Zvolen	Slovakia	51	7	9	16	68	...	...	...	10	0	4	4	2
00-01—Ilves Tampere	Finland	54	2	14	16	99	...	...	...	9	0	1	1	6
01-02—Slovakian Oly. team	Int'l	2	0	1	1	2	...	...	...	—	—	—	—	—
—Ilves Tampere	Finland	44	6	6	12	84	...	...	...	—	—	—	—	—
02-03—Florida	NHL	82	4	8	12	92	-18	0	0	—	—	—	—	—
03-04—Atlanta	NHL	63	3	7	10	76	-7	0	0	—	—	—	—	—
04-05—Sparta Praha	Czech Rep.	28	2	6	8	40	12	...	...	5	2	1	3	6
NHL Totals (2 years)		145	7	15	22	168	-25	0	0					

MALAKHOV, VLADIMIR D DEVILS

PERSONAL: Born August 30, 1968, in Ekaterinburg, U.S.S.R. ... 6-5/230. ... Shoots left. ... Name pronounced MAL-uh-kahf.

TRANSACTIONS/CAREER NOTES: Selected by New York Islanders in 10th round (12th Islanders pick, 191st overall) of entry draft (June 17, 1989). ... Sore groin; missed first two games of 1992-93 season. ... Injured right shoulder (January 16, 1993); missed eight games. ... Sprained shoulder (March 14, 1993); missed five games. ... Concussion (December 7, 1993); missed one game. ... Strained lower back (December 28, 1993); missed six games. ... Strained hip flexor (February 9, 1995); missed five games. ... Charley horse (March 14, 1995); missed two games. ... Traded by Islanders with C Pierre Turgeon to Montreal Canadiens for LW Kirk Muller, D Mathieu Schneider and C Craig Darby (April 5, 1995). ... Strained hip flexor (April 24, 1995); missed one game. ... Flu (October 25, 1995); missed two games. ... Bruised right leg (December 12, 1995); missed two games. ... Bruised ribs (October 24, 1996); missed one game. ... Fractured thumb (December 23, 1996); missed 16 games. ... Bruised lower back (October 29, 1997); missed one game. ... Sprained knee (December 10, 1997); missed four games. ... Shoulder tendinitis (February 28, 1998); missed three games. ... Back spasms (November 9, 1998); missed two games. ... Back spasms (December 5, 1998); missed six games. ... Back spasms (January 31, 1999); missed two games. ... Sprained knee (March 28, 1999); missed six games. ... Reinjured knee (April 10, 1999); missed final three games of season. ... Injured knee (September 17, 1999); missed first 53 games of 1999-2000 season. ... Injured knee (February 14, 2000); missed two games. ... Traded by Canadiens to New Jersey Devils for D Sheldon Souray, D Josh DeWolf and 2nd-round draft pick (later traded to Washington Capitals) in 2001 entry draft (March 1, 2000). ... Signed as free agent by New York Rangers (July 10, 2000). ... Sprained knee (October 7, 2000); missed 14 games. ... Reinjured knee (November 15, 2000); missed remainder of season. ... Flu (February 6, 2002); missed one game. ... Back spasms (January 30, 2003); missed two games. ...

Back spasms (February 8, 2003); missed two games. ... Injured shoulder (March 3, 2003); missed two games. ... Reinjured shoulder (March 26, 2003); missed five games. ... Injured wrist (January 26, 2004); missed 13 games. ... Traded by Rangers to Philadelphia Flyers for RW Rick Kozak and 2nd-round pick in 2005 entry draft (March 8, 2004). ... Fractured jaw (March 18, 2004); missed six games. ... Concussion (May 2, 2004); missed final playoff game. ... Signed as free agent by Devils (Aug. 4, 2005).

STATISTICAL PLATEAUS: Three-goal games: 1997-98 (1).

		REGULAR SEASON								PLAYOFFS				
Season Team	**League**	**GP**	**G**	**A**	**Pts.**	**PIM**	**+/-**	**PP**	**SH**	**GP**	**G**	**A**	**Pts.**	**PIM**
86-87—Spartak Moscow	USSR	22	0	1	1	12	...	...	...	—	—	—	—	—
87-88—Spartak Moscow	USSR	28	2	2	4	26	...	...	...	—	—	—	—	—
88-89—CSKA Moscow	USSR	34	6	2	8	16	...	...	...	—	—	—	—	—
89-90—CSKA Moscow	USSR	48	2	10	12	34	...	...	...	—	—	—	—	—
90-91—CSKA Moscow	USSR	46	5	13	18	22	...	...	...	—	—	—	—	—
91-92—CSKA Moscow	CIS	40	1	9	10	12	...	...	...	—	—	—	—	—
—Unif. Olympic team	Int'l	8	3	0	3	4	...	...	...	—	—	—	—	—
92-93—Capital District	AHL	3	2	1	3	11	6	0	0	—	—	—	—	—
—New York Islanders	NHL	64	14	38	52	59	14	7	0	17	3	6	9	12
93-94—New York Islanders	NHL	76	10	47	57	80	29	4	0	4	0	0	0	6
94-95—New York Islanders	NHL	26	3	13	16	32	-1	1	0	—	—	—	—	—
—Montreal	NHL	14	1	4	5	14	-2	0	0	—	—	—	—	—
95-96—Montreal	NHL	61	5	23	28	79	7	2	0	—	—	—	—	—
96-97—Montreal	NHL	65	10	20	30	43	3	5	0	5	0	0	0	6
97-98—Montreal	NHL	74	13	31	44	70	16	8	0	9	3	4	7	10
98-99—Montreal	NHL	62	13	21	34	77	-7	8	0	—	—	—	—	—
99-00—Montreal	NHL	7	0	0	0	4	0	0	0	—	—	—	—	—
—New Jersey	NHL	17	1	4	5	19	1	1	0	23	1	4	5	18
00-01—New York Rangers	NHL	3	0	2	2	4	0	0	0	—	—	—	—	—
01-02—New York Rangers	NHL	81	6	22	28	83	10	1	0	—	—	—	—	—
—Russian Oly. team	Int'l	6	1	3	4	4	...	...	...	—	—	—	—	—
02-03—New York Rangers	NHL	71	3	14	17	52	-7	1	0	—	—	—	—	—
03-04—New York Rangers	NHL	56	3	15	18	53	-5	1	0	—	—	—	—	—
—Philadelphia	NHL	6	0	1	1	2	-1	0	0	17	1	5	6	12
NHL Totals (12 years)		683	82	255	337	671	57	39	0	75	8	19	27	64

MALEC, TOMAS D

PERSONAL: Born May 13, 1982, in Skalica, Czechoslovakia. ... 6-2/193. ... Shoots left.

TRANSACTIONS/CAREER NOTES: Selected by Florida Panthers in third round (fourth Panthers pick, 64th overall) of NHL entry draft (June 23, 2001). ... Traded by Panthers with D Bret Hedican, C Kevyn Adams and future considerations to Carolina Hurricanes for D Sandis Ozolinsh and C Byron Ritchie (January 16, 2002). ... Traded by Hurricanes with third-round pick (D Kyle Klubertanz) in 2004 entry draft to Anaheim Mighty Ducks for G Martin Gerber (June 18, 2004).

		REGULAR SEASON								PLAYOFFS				
Season Team	**League**	**GP**	**G**	**A**	**Pts.**	**PIM**	**+/-**	**PP**	**SH**	**GP**	**G**	**A**	**Pts.**	**PIM**
00-01—Rimouski	QMJHL	64	13	50	63	198	...	...	...	11	0	11	11	26
01-02—Rimouski	QMJHL	51	14	32	46	164	...	...	...	7	3	1	4	10
—Lowell	AHL	...	...	...	...	...	...	...	...	4	0	0	0	4
02-03—Lowell	AHL	30	0	4	4	50	-6	0	0	—	—	—	—	—
—Carolina	NHL	41	0	2	2	43	-5	0	0	—	—	—	—	—
03-04—Carolina	NHL	2	0	0	0	2	-1	0	0	—	—	—	—	—
—Lowell	AHL	74	7	13	20	101	-11	0	1	—	—	—	—	—
04-05—Cincinnati	AHL	66	4	14	18	104	-17	1	0	6	0	2	2	10
NHL Totals (2 years)		43	0	2	2	45	-6	0	0					

MALHOTRA, MANNY C/LW BLUE JACKETS

PERSONAL: Born May 18, 1980, in Mississauga, Ont. ... 6-2/215. ... Shoots left.

TRANSACTIONS/CAREER NOTES: Selected by New York Rangers in first round (first Rangers pick, seventh overall) of NHL draft (June 27, 1998). ... Sprained ankle (November 18, 1999); missed four games. ... Sprained ankle (November 6, 2001); missed three games. ... Traded by Rangers with LW Barrett Heisten to Dallas Stars for C Roman Lyashenko and LW Martin Rucinsky (March 12, 2002). ... Had the flu (April 14, 2002); missed one game. ... Claimed off waivers by Columbus Blue Jackets (November 21, 2003). ... Bruised ankle (March 26, 2004); missed remainder of regular season.

		REGULAR SEASON								PLAYOFFS				
Season Team	**League**	**GP**	**G**	**A**	**Pts.**	**PIM**	**+/-**	**PP**	**SH**	**GP**	**G**	**A**	**Pts.**	**PIM**
96-97—Guelph	OHL	61	16	28	44	26	...	...	...	18	7	7	14	11
97-98—Guelph	OHL	57	16	35	51	29	...	...	...	12	7	6	13	8
98-99—New York Rangers	NHL	73	8	8	16	13	-2	1	0	—	—	—	—	—
99-00—New York Rangers	NHL	27	0	0	0	4	-6	0	0	—	—	—	—	—
—Hartford	AHL	12	1	5	6	2	...	...	...	23	1	2	3	10
—Guelph	OHL	5	2	2	4	4	3	0	0	6	0	2	2	4
00-01—Hartford	AHL	28	5	6	11	69	...	...	...	5	0	0	0	0
—New York Rangers	NHL	50	4	8	12	31	-10	0	0	—	—	—	—	—
01-02—New York Rangers	NHL	56	7	6	13	42	-1	0	1	—	—	—	—	—
—Dallas	NHL	16	1	0	1	5	-3	0	0	—	—	—	—	—
02-03—Dallas	NHL	59	3	7	10	42	-2	0	0	5	1	0	1	0
03-04—Dallas	NHL	9	0	0	0	4	-2	0	0	—	—	—	—	—
—Columbus	NHL	56	12	13	25	24	-5	1	0	—	—	—	—	—
04-05—HV 71 Jonkoping	Sweden	20	5	2	7	16	-6	1	1	—	—	—	—	—
—Olimpija	Slovenia	26	13	14	27	36	...	...	...	—	—	—	—	—
NHL Totals (6 years)		346	35	42	77	165	-31	2	1	5	1	0	1	0

MALIK, MAREK — D — RANGERS

PERSONAL: Born June 24, 1975, in Ostrava, Czechoslovakia. ... 6-5/235. ... Shoots left. ... Name pronounced muh-REHK muh-LEEK.
TRANSACTIONS/CAREER NOTES: Selected by Hartford Whalers in 3rd round (2nd Whalers pick, 72nd overall) of entry draft (June 26, 1993). ... Flu (January 20, 1997); missed three games. ... Bruised shin (March 20, 1997); missed four games. ... Whalers franchise moved to North Carolina and renamed Carolina Hurricanes for 1997-98 season; NHL approved move on June 25, 1997. ... Injured knee (April 7, 1999); missed one game. ... Whiplash (September 30, 2000); missed first six games of season. ... Cut face (December 15, 2002); missed one game. ... Traded by Hurricanes with LW Darren Langdon to Vancouver Canucks for LW Jan Hlavac and C Harold Druken (November 1, 2002). ... Sore back (March 8, 2004); missed two games. ... Signed as free agent by New York Rangers (Aug. 2, 2005).

		REGULAR SEASON								PLAYOFFS				
Season Team	**League**	**GP**	**G**	**A**	**Pts.**	**PIM**	**+/-**	**PP**	**SH**	**GP**	**G**	**A**	**Pts.**	**PIM**
91-92—TJ Vitkovice	Czech. Jrs.Statistics unavailable													
92-93—TJ Vitkovice	Czech.	20	5	10	15	16	...	...	...	—	—	—	—	—
93-94—HC Vitkovice	Czech Rep.	38	3	3	6	...	...	...	...	3	0	1	1	...
94-95—Springfield	AHL	58	11	30	41	91	-1	5	1	—	—	—	—	—
—Hartford	NHL	1	0	1	1	0	1	0	0	—	—	—	—	—
95-96—Springfield	AHL	68	8	14	22	135	...	...	...	8	1	3	4	20
—Hartford	NHL	7	0	0	0	4	-3	0	0	—	—	—	—	—
96-97—Springfield	AHL	3	0	3	3	4	0	0	0	—	—	—	—	—
—Hartford	NHL	47	1	5	6	50	5	0	0	—	—	—	—	—
97-98—Malmoif	Sweden	37	1	5	6	21	...	...	...	—	—	—	—	—
98-99—HC Vitkovice	Czech Rep.	1	1	0	1	6	...	...	...	—	—	—	—	—
—New Haven	AHL	21	2	8	10	28	-7	1	0	—	—	—	—	—
—Carolina	NHL	52	2	9	11	36	-6	1	0	4	0	0	0	4
99-00—Carolina	NHL	57	4	10	14	63	13	0	0	—	—	—	—	—
00-01—Carolina	NHL	61	6	14	20	34	-4	1	0	3	0	0	0	6
01-02—Carolina	NHL	82	4	19	23	88	8	0	0	23	0	3	3	18
02-03—Carolina	NHL	10	0	2	2	16	-3	0	0	—	—	—	—	—
—Vancouver	NHL	69	7	11	18	52	23	1	1	14	1	1	2	10
03-04—Vancouver	NHL	78	3	16	19	45	35	0	0	7	0	0	0	10
04-05—Vitkovice	Czech Rep.	42	1	9	10	50	10	...	...	7	0	0	0	37
NHL Totals (9 years)		464	27	87	114	388	69	3	1	51	1	4	5	48

MALKIN, EVGENY — C/RW — PENGUINS

PERSONAL: Born July 31, 1986, in Magnitogorsk, U.S.S.R. ... 6-3/186. ... Shoots left.
TRANSACTIONS/CAREER NOTES: Selected by Pittsburgh Penguins in first round (first Penguins pick, second overall) of NHL entry draft (June 26, 2004).

		REGULAR SEASON								PLAYOFFS				
Season Team	**League**	**GP**	**G**	**A**	**Pts.**	**PIM**	**+/-**	**PP**	**SH**	**GP**	**G**	**A**	**Pts.**	**PIM**
03-04—Metal. Magnitogorsk	Russian	34	3	9	12	12	...	...	...	—	—	—	—	—
04-05—Metal. Magnitogorsk	Russian	52	12	20	32	24	21	...	...	5	0	4	4	0

MALONE, RYAN — LW — PENGUINS

PERSONAL: Born December 1, 1979, in Pittsburgh. ... 6-4/215. ... Shoots left. ... Son of Greg Malone, player for Penguins (1976-77 through 1982-83), Hartford Whalers (1983-84 through 1985-86) and Quebec Nordiques (1985-86 through 1986-87).
TRANSACTIONS/CAREER NOTES: Selected by Pittsburgh Penguins in fourth round (fifth Penguins pick, 115th overall) of NHL draft (June 26, 1999).

		REGULAR SEASON								PLAYOFFS				
Season Team	**League**	**GP**	**G**	**A**	**Pts.**	**PIM**	**+/-**	**PP**	**SH**	**GP**	**G**	**A**	**Pts.**	**PIM**
97-98—Shattuck	USHS (West)	50	41	44	85	69	...	...	...	—	—	—	—	—
98-99—Omaha	USHL	51	14	22	36	81	...	...	...	—	—	—	—	—
99-00—St. Cloud State	WCHA	38	9	21	30	68	...	...	...	—	—	—	—	—
00-01—St. Cloud State	WCHA	36	7	18	25	52	...	...	...	—	—	—	—	—
01-02—St. Cloud State	WCHA	41	24	25	49	76	...	...	...	—	—	—	—	—
02-03—St. Cloud State	WCHA	27	16	20	36	85	...	...	...	—	—	—	—	—
—Wilkes-Barre/Scranton	AHL	3	0	1	1	2	-1	0	0	—	—	—	—	—
03-04—Pittsburgh	NHL	81	22	21	43	64	-23	5	3	—	—	—	—	—
04-05—Ambri-Piotta	Switzerland	—	—	—	—	—	—	—	—	1	0	0	0	2
—Blues Espoo	Finland	9	2	1	3	36	-2	...	...	—	—	—	—	—
—SV Renon	Italy	10	6	1	7	20	...	...	...	6	4	4	8	32
NHL Totals (1 year)		81	22	21	43	64	-23	5	3					

MALTBY, KIRK — LW/RW — RED WINGS

PERSONAL: Born December 22, 1972, in Guelph, Ont. ... 6-0/190. ... Shoots right.
TRANSACTIONS/CAREER NOTES: Selected by Edmonton Oilers in 3rd round (4th Oilers pick, 65th overall) of entry draft (June 20, 1992). ... Chipped ankle bone (February 2, 1994); missed 13 games. ... Cut right eye (March 1, 1995); missed last game of season. ... Scratched left cornea (February 1, 1996); missed 16 games. ... Traded by Oilers to Detroit Red Wings for D Dan McGillis (March 20, 1996). ... Separated shoulder (September 24, 1997); missed 16 games. ... Abdominal pain (November 14, 1998); missed 19 games. ... Sprained knee (December 31, 1998); missed five games. ... Injured ankle (March 31, 1999); missed one game. ... Suspended four games for slashing incident (March 17, 1999). ... Hernia (October 5, 1999); missed 41 games.
STATISTICAL PLATEAUS: Three-goal games: 1997-98 (1).

Season Team	League	GP	G	A	Pts.	PIM	+/-	PP	SH	GP	G	A	Pts.	PIM
		REGULAR SEASON								PLAYOFFS				
88-89—Cambridge Jr. B	OHA	48	28	18	46	138	...	...	...	—	—	—	—	—
89-90—Owen Sound	OHL	61	12	15	27	90	...	...	...	12	1	6	7	15
90-91—Owen Sound	OHL	66	34	32	66	100	...	...	...	—	—	—	—	—
91-92—Owen Sound	OHL	64	50	41	91	99	...	...	...	5	3	3	6	18
92-93—Cape Breton	AHL	73	22	23	45	130	9	3	4	16	3	3	6	45
93-94—Edmonton	NHL	68	11	8	19	74	-2	0	1	—	—	—	—	—
94-95—Edmonton	NHL	47	8	3	11	49	-11	0	2	—	—	—	—	—
95-96—Edmonton	NHL	49	2	6	8	61	-16	0	0	—	—	—	—	—
—Cape Breton	AHL	4	1	2	3	6	...	...	...	—	—	—	—	—
—Detroit	NHL	6	1	0	1	6	0	0	0	8	0	1	1	4
96-97—Detroit	NHL	66	3	5	8	75	3	0	0	20	5	2	7	24
97-98—Detroit	NHL	65	14	9	23	89	11	2	1	22	3	1	4	30
98-99—Detroit	NHL	53	8	6	14	34	-6	0	1	10	1	0	1	8
99-00—Detroit	NHL	41	6	8	14	24	1	0	2	8	0	1	1	4
00-01—Detroit	NHL	79	12	7	19	22	16	1	3	6	0	0	0	6
01-02—Detroit	NHL	82	9	15	24	40	15	0	1	23	3	3	6	32
02-03—Detroit	NHL	82	14	23	37	91	17	0	4	4	0	0	0	4
03-04—Detroit	NHL	79	14	19	33	80	24	1	4	12	1	3	4	11
NHL Totals (11 years)		717	102	109	211	645	52	4	19	113	13	11	24	123

MANLOW, ERIC — C — RED WINGS

PERSONAL: Born April 7, 1975, in Belleville, Ont. ... 6-0/205. ... Shoots left.

TRANSACTIONS/CAREER NOTES: Selected by Chicago Blackhawks in second round (second Blackhawks pick, 50th overall) of NHL entry draft (June 26, 1993). ... Released by Blackhawks (June 18, 1998). ... Signed as free agent by Boston Bruins (July 11, 2000). ... Signed as free agent by New York Islanders (July 19, 2002). ... Signed as free agent by Detroit Red Wings (July 20, 2004).

Season Team	League	GP	G	A	Pts.	PIM	+/-	PP	SH	GP	G	A	Pts.	PIM
		REGULAR SEASON								PLAYOFFS				
91-92—Kitchener	OHL	59	12	20	32	17	...	...	...	14	2	5	7	8
92-93—Kitchener	OHL	53	26	21	47	31	...	...	...	4	0	1	1	2
93-94—Kitchener	OHL	49	28	32	60	25	...	11	1	3	0	1	1	4
94-95—Kitchener	OHL	44	25	29	54	26	...	7	1	—	—	—	—	—
—Det. Jr. Red Wings	OHL	16	4	16	20	11	...	2	0	21	11	10	21	18
95-96—Indianapolis	IHL	75	6	11	17	32	...	...	...	4	0	1	1	4
96-97—Columbus	ECHL	32	18	18	36	20	...	...	...	—	—	—	—	—
—Baltimore	AHL	36	6	6	12	13	-4	0	0	3	0	0	0	0
97-98—Indianapolis	IHL	60	8	11	19	25	-3	0	2	3	1	0	1	0
98-99—Florida	ECHL	18	8	15	23	11	13	1	0	—	—	—	—	—
—Long Beach	IHL	51	9	19	28	30	-1	2	2	8	0	0	0	8
99-00—Florida	ECHL	26	14	24	38	24	...	...	...	—	—	—	—	—
—Providence	AHL	46	17	16	33	14	...	...	...	14	6	8	14	8
00-01—Providence	AHL	60	16	51	67	18	...	...	...	17	6	7	13	6
—Boston	NHL	8	0	1	1	2	0	0	0	—	—	—	—	—
01-02—Providence	AHL	70	13	35	48	30	-10	3	1	—	—	—	—	—
—Boston	NHL	3	0	0	0	0	0	0	0	—	—	—	—	—
02-03—New York Islanders	NHL	8	2	1	3	4	2	1	0	—	—	—	—	—
—Bridgeport	AHL	62	19	40	59	58	3	4	1	9	0	6	6	2
03-04—New York Islanders	NHL	18	0	2	2	2	-2	0	0	—	—	—	—	—
—Bridgeport	AHL	40	8	26	34	16	15	2	0	1	0	0	0	2
04-05—Grand Rapids	AHL	61	21	20	41	24	-4	10	0	—	—	—	—	—
NHL Totals (4 years)		37	2	4	6	8	0	1	0					

MAPLETOFT, JUSTIN — C — ISLANDERS

PERSONAL: Born January 11, 1981, in Lloydminster, Sask. ... 6-1/200. ... Shoots left.

TRANSACTIONS/CAREER NOTES: Selected by New York Islanders in fifth round (ninth Islanders pick, 130th overall) of NHL entry draft (June 26, 1999).

Season Team	League	GP	G	A	Pts.	PIM	+/-	PP	SH	GP	G	A	Pts.	PIM
		REGULAR SEASON								PLAYOFFS				
97-98—Red Deer	WHL	65	9	4	13	41	...	...	...	5	1	0	1	0
98-99—Red Deer	WHL	72	24	22	46	81	...	...	...	9	2	3	5	12
99-00—Red Deer	WHL	72	39	57	96	135	26	6	5	4	2	1	3	28
00-01—Red Deer	WHL	70	43	77	*120	111	...	...	...	22	13	21	34	59
01-02—Bridgeport	AHL	80	13	20	33	60	11	3	0	20	7	10	17	23
02-03—New York Islanders	NHL	11	2	2	4	2	-1	1	0	2	0	0	0	0
—Bridgeport	AHL	63	13	26	39	47	9	4	0	7	1	2	3	6
03-04—Bridgeport	AHL	36	10	13	23	59	-1	4	1	—	—	—	—	—
—New York Islanders	NHL	27	1	4	5	6	-1	0	0	—	—	—	—	—
04-05—Bridgeport	AHL	61	11	24	35	51	-9	2	1	—	—	—	—	—
NHL Totals (2 years)		38	3	6	9	8	-2	1	0	2	0	0	0	0

MARA, PAUL — D — COYOTES

PERSONAL: Born September 7, 1979, in Ridgewood, N.J. ... 6-4/219. ... Shoots left.

TRANSACTIONS/CAREER NOTES: Selected by Tampa Bay Lightning in first round (first Lightning pick, seventh overall) of NHL draft (June 21, 1997). ... Fractured jaw (November 9, 1999); missed 13 games. ... Strained hip flexor (November 14, 2000); missed six games. ... Strained abdominal muscle (December 2, 2000); missed four games. ... Traded by Lightning with RW Mike Johnson, RW Ruslan Zainullin and second-round pick (D Matthew Spiller) in 2001 draft to Phoenix Coyotes for G Nikolai Khabibulin and D Stan Neckar (March 5, 2001). ... Bruised wrist (October 30, 2001); missed two games. ... Bruised foot (March 3, 2002); missed five games. ... Sprained shoulder (February 28, 2003); missed nine games. ... Flu (December 12, 2003); missed one game.

		REGULAR SEASON								PLAYOFFS				
Season Team	League	GP	G	A	Pts.	PIM	+/-	PP	SH	GP	G	A	Pts.	PIM
94-95—Belmont Hill	Mass. H.S.	29	19	24	43	24	...	...	...	—	—	—	—	—
95-96—Belmont Hill	Mass. H.S.	28	18	20	38	40	...	...	...	—	—	—	—	—
96-97—Sudbury	OHL	44	9	34	43	61	-11	2	0	—	—	—	—	—
97-98—Sudbury	OHL	25	8	18	26	79	...	...	...	—	—	—	—	—
—Plymouth	OHL	25	8	15	23	30	...	...	...	15	3	14	17	30
98-99—Plymouth	OHL	52	13	41	54	95	25	...	...	11	5	7	12	28
—Tampa Bay	NHL	1	1	1	2	0	-3	1	0	—	—	—	—	—
99-00—Detroit	IHL	15	3	5	8	22	...	...	...	—	—	—	—	—
—Tampa Bay	NHL	54	7	11	18	73	-27	4	0	—	—	—	—	—
00-01—Tampa Bay	NHL	46	6	10	16	40	-17	2	0	—	—	—	—	—
—Detroit	IHL	10	3	3	6	22	...	...	...	—	—	—	—	—
—Phoenix	NHL	16	0	4	4	14	1	0	0	—	—	—	—	—
01-02—Phoenix	NHL	75	7	17	24	58	-6	2	0	5	0	0	0	4
02-03—Phoenix	NHL	73	10	15	25	78	-7	1	0	—	—	—	—	—
03-04—Phoenix	NHL	81	6	36	42	48	-11	1	0	—	—	—	—	—
04-05—Hannover	Germany	35	5	13	18	89	-6	3	0	...	...	...	...	...
NHL Totals (6 years)		346	37	94	131	311	-70	11	0	5	0	0	0	4

MARCHANT, TODD — C — BLUE JACKETS

PERSONAL: Born August 12, 1973, in Buffalo. ... 5-10/180. ... Shoots left. ... Brother of Terry Marchant, LW with Edmonton Oilers organization (1994-99). ... Name pronounced MAHR-shahnt.

TRANSACTIONS/CAREER NOTES: Selected by New York Rangers in 7th round (8th Rangers pick, 164th overall) of entry draft (June 26, 1993). ... Traded by Rangers to Edmonton Oilers for C Craig MacTavish (March 21, 1994). ... Suffered concussion (March 9, 1997); missed three games. ... Strained groin (November 10, 1997); missed four games. ... Scratched left eye (February 4, 1998); missed two games. ... Separated left shoulder (January 10, 2001); missed 10 games. ... Sprained right knee (February 12, 2001); missed one game. ... Virus (March 15, 2003); missed four games. ... Signed as free agent by Columbus Blue Jackets (July 2, 2003). ... Flu (November 14, 2003); missed one game. ... Injured groin (March 29, 2004); missed remainder of regular season.

		REGULAR SEASON								PLAYOFFS				
Season Team	League	GP	G	A	Pts.	PIM	+/-	PP	SH	GP	G	A	Pts.	PIM
91-92—Clarkson	ECAC	33	20	12	32	32	...	...	...	—	—	—	—	—
92-93—Clarkson	ECAC	33	18	28	46	38	...	...	...	—	—	—	—	—
93-94—U.S. national team	Int'l	59	28	39	67	48	...	9	1	—	—	—	—	—
—U.S. Olympic team	Int'l	8	1	1	2	6	1	1	0	—	—	—	—	—
—Binghamton	AHL	8	2	7	9	6	-3	0	0	—	—	—	—	—
—New York Rangers	NHL	1	0	0	0	0	-1	0	0	—	—	—	—	—
—Edmonton	NHL	3	0	1	1	2	-1	0	0	—	—	—	—	—
—Cape Breton	AHL	3	1	4	5	2	4	0	0	5	1	1	2	0
94-95—Cape Breton	AHL	38	22	25	47	25	8	5	2	—	—	—	—	—
—Edmonton	NHL	45	13	14	27	32	-3	3	2	—	—	—	—	—
95-96—Edmonton	NHL	81	19	19	38	66	-19	2	3	—	—	—	—	—
96-97—Edmonton	NHL	79	14	19	33	44	11	0	4	12	4	2	6	12
97-98—Edmonton	NHL	76	14	21	35	71	9	2	1	12	1	1	2	10
98-99—Edmonton	NHL	82	14	22	36	65	3	3	1	4	1	1	2	12
99-00—Edmonton	NHL	82	17	23	40	70	7	0	1	3	1	0	1	2
00-01—Edmonton	NHL	71	13	26	39	51	1	0	4	6	0	0	0	4
01-02—Edmonton	NHL	82	12	22	34	41	7	0	3	—	—	—	—	—
02-03—Edmonton	NHL	77	20	40	60	48	13	7	1	6	0	2	2	2
03-04—Columbus	NHL	77	9	25	34	34	-17	4	0	—	—	—	—	—
NHL Totals (11 years)		756	145	232	377	524	10	21	20	43	7	6	13	42

MARCHMENT, BRYAN — D

PERSONAL: Born May 1, 1969, in Scarborough, Ont. ... 6-1/200. ... Shoots left.

TRANSACTIONS/CAREER NOTES: Selected by Winnipeg Jets in first round (first Jets pick, 16th overall) of NHL entry draft (June 13, 1987). ... Sprained shoulder (March 1990). ... Had back spasms (March 13, 1991). ... Traded by Jets with D Chris Norton to Chicago Blackhawks for C Troy Murray and LW Warren Rychel (July 22, 1991). ... Fractured cheekbone (December 12, 1991); missed 12 games. ... Suspended one preseason game and fined $500 by NHL for headbutting (September 30, 1993). ... Traded by Blackhawks with RW Steve Larmer to Hartford Whalers for LW Patrick Poulin and D Eric Weinrich (November 2, 1993). ... Suspended two games and fined $500 by NHL for illegal check (December 21, 1993). ... Sprained ankle (January 14, 1994); missed three games. ... Sprained ankle (February 19, 1994); missed remainder of season. ... Awarded to Edmonton Oilers as compensation for Whalers signing free agent RW Steven Rice (August 30, 1994). ... Suspended one game by NHL for game misconduct penalties (March 22, 1995). ... Suspended two games by NHL for game misconduct penalties (March 27, 1995). ... Strained lower back (April 15, 1995); missed two games. ... Suspended three games and fined $500 by NHL for leaving bench to fight (April 29, 1995). ... Suspended five games by NHL for kneeing player in preseason game (September 25, 1995). ... Injured ribs (October 22, 1996); missed two games. ... Had the flu (January 28, 1997); missed one game. ... Cracked ribs (February 13, 1997); missed eight games. ... Suffered concussion (April 18, 1997); missed remainder of season. ... Suspended three games and fined $1,000 by NHL for hitting another player (December 5, 1997). ... Traded by Oilers to Tampa Bay Lightning with C Steve Kelly and C Jason Bonsignore for D Roman Hamrlik and C Paul Comrie (December 30, 1997). ... Suspended three games by NHL for kneeing incident (February 6, 1998). ... Suspended eight games and fined $1,000 by NHL for kneeing incident (February 25, 1998). ... Traded by Lightning with D David Shaw and first-round pick (traded to Nashville) in 1998 draft to San Jose Sharks for LW Andrei Nazarov, first-round pick (C Vincent Lecavalier) in 1998 draft and future considerations (March 24, 1998). ... Injured shoulder (January 7, 1999); missed 20 games. ... Suspended one game by NHL for unsportsmanlike conduct (April 6, 1999). ... Injured knee (October 2, 1999); missed nine games. ... Had the flu (December 8, 1999); missed one game. ... Injured ankle (January 5, 2000); missed 14 games. ... Injured groin (March 2, 2000); missed five games. ... Suspended three games by NHL for spearing incident (March 19, 2000). ... Injured neck (April 3, 2000); missed one game. ... Suspended three games by NHL for kneeing incident (March 13, 2001). ... Suspended six games by NHL for elbowing incident (Novmeber 10, 2001). ... Injured back (April 6, 2002); missed final four games of season. ... Traded by Sharks to Colorado Avalanche for third- (later traded to Calgary Flames) and fifth-round (later returned to Avalanche) picks in 2003 entry draft (March 9, 2003). ... Signed as free agent by Toronto Maple Leafs (July 10, 2003). ... Injured groin (February 26, 2004); missed five games.

		REGULAR SEASON								PLAYOFFS				
Season Team	**League**	**GP**	**G**	**A**	**Pts.**	**PIM**	**+/-**	**PP**	**SH**	**GP**	**G**	**A**	**Pts.**	**PIM**
84-85—Toronto Nationals	MTHL	...	14	35	49	229	...	...	...	—	—	—	—	—
85-86—Belleville	OHL	57	5	15	20	225	...	...	...	21	0	7	7	*83
86-87—Belleville	OHL	52	6	38	44	238	...	...	...	6	0	4	4	17
87-88—Belleville	OHL	56	7	51	58	200	...	...	...	6	1	3	4	19
88-89—Belleville	OHL	43	14	36	50	198	...	...	...	5	0	1	1	12
—Winnipeg	NHL	2	0	0	0	2	0	0	0	—	—	—	—	—
89-90—Winnipeg	NHL	7	0	2	2	28	0	0	0	—	—	—	—	—
—Moncton	AHL	56	4	19	23	217	...	...	...	—	—	—	—	—
90-91—Winnipeg	NHL	28	2	2	4	91	-5	0	0	—	—	—	—	—
—Moncton	AHL	33	2	11	13	101	...	...	...	—	—	—	—	—
91-92—Chicago	NHL	58	5	10	15	168	-4	2	0	16	1	0	1	36
92-93—Chicago	NHL	78	5	15	20	313	15	1	0	4	0	0	0	12
93-94—Chicago	NHL	13	1	4	5	42	-2	0	0	—	—	—	—	—
—Hartford	NHL	42	3	7	10	124	-12	0	1	—	—	—	—	—
94-95—Edmonton	NHL	40	1	5	6	184	-11	0	0	—	—	—	—	—
95-96—Edmonton	NHL	78	3	15	18	202	-7	0	0	—	—	—	—	—
96-97—Edmonton	NHL	71	3	13	16	132	13	1	0	3	0	0	0	4
97-98—Edmonton	NHL	27	0	4	4	58	-2	0	0	—	—	—	—	—
—Tampa Bay	NHL	22	2	4	6	43	-3	0	0	—	—	—	—	—
—San Jose	NHL	12	0	3	3	43	2	0	0	6	0	0	0	10
98-99—San Jose	NHL	59	2	6	8	101	-7	0	0	6	0	0	0	4
99-00—San Jose	NHL	49	0	4	4	72	3	0	0	11	2	1	3	12
00-01—San Jose	NHL	75	7	11	18	204	15	0	1	5	0	1	1	2
01-02—San Jose	NHL	72	2	20	22	178	22	0	0	12	1	1	2	10
02-03—San Jose	NHL	67	2	9	11	108	-2	0	0	—	—	—	—	—
—Colorado	NHL	14	0	3	3	33	4	0	0	7	0	0	0	4
03-04—Toronto	NHL	75	1	3	4	106	4	0	0	13	0	0	0	8
NHL Totals (16 years)		889	39	140	179	2232	23	4	2	83	4	3	7	102

MARKKANEN, JUSSI G OILERS

PERSONAL: Born May 8, 1975, in Imatra, Finland. ... 6-0/182. ... Catches left.

TRANSACTIONS/CAREER NOTES: Selected by Edmonton Oilers in 5th round (5th Oilers pick, 133rd overall) of entry draft (June 23, 2001). ... Traded by Oilers with 4th-round pick (traded to Toronto; Maple Leafs selected RW Roman Kukumberg) in 2004 draft to New York Rangers for D Brian Leetch (June 30, 2003). ... Traded by Rangers with C Petr Nedved to Oilers for F Dwight Helminen, G Stephen Valiquette and 2nd-round pick (LW Dane Byers) in 2004 draft (March 3, 2004). ... Signed as free agent by Oilers (Aug. 5, 2005).

		REGULAR SEASON									PLAYOFFS							
Season Team	**League**	**GP**	**Min.**	**W**	**L**	**T**	**GA**	**SO**	**GAA**	**SV%**	**GP**	**Min.**	**W**	**L**	**GA**	**SO**	**GAA**	**SV%**
91-92—SaiPa	Finland Jr.	2	120	...	...	...	11	0	5.50	...	—	—	—	—	—	—	—	—
92-93—SaiPa	Finland Jr.	7	367	...	...	...	28	...	4.58	...	—	—	—	—	—	—	—	—
—SaiPa	Finland Div. 2	16	798	...	...	...	60	...	4.51	...	—	—	—	—	—	—	—	—
93-94—SaiPa	Finland Div. 2	30	1726	...	...	...	97	...	3.37	...	—	—	—	—	—	—	—	—
94-95—SaiPa	Finland Div. 2	43	2493	...	...	...	122	...	2.94	...	3	179	...	...	5	...	1.68	...
95-96—Tappara Tampere	Finland Jr.	5	298	...	...	...	21	...	4.23	...	—	—	—	—	—	—	—	—
—Tappara Tampere	Finland	23	1238	11	8	2	59	1	2.86	...	—	—	—	—	—	—	—	—
96-97—SaiPa	Finland	41	2340	9	24	7	132	0	3.38	...	—	—	—	—	—	—	—	—
97-98—SaiPa	Finland	48	2870	21	20	5	138	4	2.89	...	3	164	0	3	11	0	4.02	...
98-99—SaiPa	Finland	45	2633	21	19	4	105	4	2.39	...	7	366	3	3	21	0	3.44	...
99-00—SaiPa	Finland	48	2794	4	23	9	150	2	3.22	...	—	—	—	—	—	—	—	—
00-01—Tappara Tampere	Finland	52	3076	*30	17	5	107	*9	2.09	...	10	*608	7	3	18	1	1.78	...
01-02—Edmonton	NHL	14	784	6	4	2	24	2	1.84	.929	—	—	—	—	—	—	—	—
—Hamilton	AHL	4	239	2	2	0	9	0	2.26	.914	—	—	—	—	—	—	—	—
02-03—Edmonton	NHL	22	1180	7	8	3	51	3	2.59	.904	1	14	0	0	1	0	4.29	.917
03-04—New York Rangers	NHL	26	1244	8	12	1	53	2	2.56	.913	—	—	—	—	—	—	—	—
—Edmonton	NHL	7	394	2	2	2	12	0	1.83	.934	—	—	—	—	—	—	—	—
04-05—Lada Togliatti	Russian	54	...	...	...	...	...	...	1.20	...	10	...	...	...	...	...	1.44	...
NHL Totals (3 years)		69	3602	23	26	8	140	7	2.33	.916	1	14	0	0	1	0	4.29	.917

MARKOV, ANDREI D CANADIENS

PERSONAL: Born December 20, 1978, in Voskresensk, U.S.S.R. ... 6-0/203. ... Shoots left.

TRANSACTIONS/CAREER NOTES: Selected by Montreal Canadiens in sixth round (sixth Canadiens pick, 162nd overall) of NHL draft (June 27, 1998). ... Injured thigh (December 21, 2002); missed one game. ... Injured knee (March 31, 2003); missed two games. ... Injured ankle (November 29, 2003); missed one game. ... Had infected foot and sore hip (January 3, 2004); missed nine games. ... Left team for personal reasons (February 20, 2004); missed three games.

		REGULAR SEASON								PLAYOFFS				
Season Team	**League**	**GP**	**G**	**A**	**Pts.**	**PIM**	**+/-**	**PP**	**SH**	**GP**	**G**	**A**	**Pts.**	**PIM**
95-96—Khimik Voskresensk	CIS	36	0	0	0	14	...	...	...	—	—	—	—	—
96-97—Khimik Voskresensk	Russian	43	8	4	12	32	...	...	...	2	1	1	2	0
97-98—Khimik Voskresensk	Russian	43	10	5	15	83	...	...	...	—	—	—	—	—
98-99—Dynamo Moscow	Russian	38	10	11	21	32	...	...	...	16	3	6	9	6

Season Team	League	GP	G	A	Pts.	PIM	+/-	PP	SH	GP	G	A	Pts.	PIM
		REGULAR SEASON								PLAYOFFS				
99-00—Dynamo Moscow	Russian	29	11	12	23	28	...	...	...	17	4	3	7	8
00-01—Montreal	NHL	63	6	17	23	18	-6	2	0	—	—	—	—	—
—Quebec	AHL	14	0	5	5	4	...	...	...	7	1	1	2	2
01-02—Quebec	AHL	12	4	6	10	7	14	1	0	—	—	—	—	—
—Montreal	NHL	56	5	19	24	24	-1	2	0	12	1	3	4	8
02-03—Montreal	NHL	79	13	24	37	34	13	3	0	—	—	—	—	—
03-04—Montreal	NHL	69	6	22	28	20	-2	2	0	11	1	4	5	8
04-05—Dynamo Moscow	Russian	42	7	16	23	76	27	...	...	10	2	0	2	22
NHL Totals (4 years)		267	30	82	112	96	4	9	0	23	2	7	9	16

MARKOV, DANNY — D — PREDATORS

PERSONAL: Born July 30, 1976, in Moscow, U.S.S.R. ... 6-1/190. ... Shoots left.

TRANSACTIONS/CAREER NOTES: Selected by Toronto Maple Leafs in ninth round (seventh Maple Leafs pick, 223rd overall) of entry draft (July 8, 1995). ... Had concussion (October 16, 1998); missed one game. ... Fractured foot (November 11, 1998); missed two games. ... Injured throat (November 23, 1998); missed two games. ... Back spasms (December 7, 1998); missed two games. ... Separated shoulder (December 16, 1998); missed 11 games. ... Injured (December 15, 1999); missed three games. ... Injured ankle (January 5, 2000); missed 10 games. ... Injured (March 15, 2000); missed one game. ... Injured foot (March 23, 2000); missed final eight games of season. ... Injured (January 6, 2001); missed one game. ... Injured back (January 31, 2001); missed 22 games. ... Traded by Maple Leafs to Phoenix Coyotes for C Robert Reichel, C Travis Green and RW Craig Mills (June 12, 2001). ... Fractured foot (March 24, 2002); missed remainder of season. ... Fractured forearm (December 28, 2002); missed 17 games. ... Traded by Coyotes with future considerations to Carolina Hurricanes for D DavidTanabe and D Igor Knyazev (June 22, 2003). ... Injured shoulder (January 9, 2004); missed two games. ... Traded by Hurricanes to Philadelphia Flyers for F Justin Williams (January 20, 2004). ... Suspended one game for receiving third game misconduct penalty of season (March 16, 2004). ... Traded by the Flyers to the Nashville Predators for a 3rd-round pick in 2006 (Aug. 2, 2005).

Season Team	League	GP	G	A	Pts.	PIM	+/-	PP	SH	GP	G	A	Pts.	PIM
		REGULAR SEASON								PLAYOFFS				
93-94—Spartak Moscow	Russian	13	1	0	1	6	...	...	...	1	0	0	0	0
94-95—Spartak Moscow	Russian	39	0	1	1	36	...	...	...	—	—	—	—	—
95-96—Spartak Moscow	Russian	38	2	0	2	12	...	...	...	2	0	0	0	2
96-97—Spartak Moscow	Russian	36	3	6	9	41	...	...	...	—	—	—	—	—
—St. John's	AHL	10	2	4	6	18	...	...	...	11	2	6	8	14
97-98—St. John's	AHL	52	3	23	26	124	11	0	0	2	0	1	1	0
—Toronto	NHL	25	2	5	7	28	0	1	0	—	—	—	—	—
98-99—Toronto	NHL	57	4	8	12	47	5	0	0	17	0	6	6	18
99-00—Toronto	NHL	59	0	10	10	28	13	0	0	12	0	3	3	10
00-01—Toronto	NHL	59	3	13	16	34	6	1	0	11	1	1	2	12
01-02—Phoenix	NHL	72	6	30	36	67	-7	4	0	—	—	—	—	—
—Russian Oly. team	Int'l	5	0	1	1	0	...	...	...	—	—	—	—	—
02-03—Phoenix	NHL	64	4	16	20	36	2	2	0	—	—	—	—	—
03-04—Carolina	NHL	44	4	10	14	37	-6	2	0	—	—	—	—	—
—Philadelphia	NHL	34	2	3	5	58	0	1	0	18	1	2	3	25
04-05—Vityaz Podolsk	Russian	26	5	7	12	16	7	...	...	12	0	3	3	6
NHL Totals (7 years)		414	25	95	120	335	13	11	0	58	2	12	14	65

M

MARLEAU, PATRICK — C — SHARKS

PERSONAL: Born September 15, 1979, in Aneroid, Sask. ... 6-2/220. ... Shoots left. ... Name pronounced MAHR-loh.

TRANSACTIONS/CAREER NOTES: Selected by San Jose Sharks in first round (first Sharks pick, second overall) of NHL entry draft (June 21, 1997). ... Injured ankle (January 17, 2004); missed one game. ... Injured knee (January 21, 2004); missed one game.

STATISTICAL PLATEAUS: Three-goal games: 2001-02 (1).

Season Team	League	GP	G	A	Pts.	PIM	+/-	PP	SH	GP	G	A	Pts.	PIM
		REGULAR SEASON								PLAYOFFS				
93-94—Swift Current	Jr. A	53	72	95	167	...	...	...	...	—	—	—	—	—
94-95—Swift Current	Jr. A	30	30	22	52	20	...	...	...	—	—	—	—	—
95-96—Seattle	WHL	72	32	42	74	22	...	...	...	5	3	4	7	4
96-97—Seattle	WHL	71	51	74	125	37	14	7	9	15	7	16	23	12
97-98—San Jose	NHL	74	13	19	32	14	5	1	0	5	0	1	1	0
98-99—San Jose	NHL	81	21	24	45	24	10	4	0	6	2	1	3	4
99-00—San Jose	NHL	81	17	23	40	36	-9	3	0	5	1	1	2	2
00-01—San Jose	NHL	81	25	27	52	22	7	5	0	6	2	0	2	4
01-02—San Jose	NHL	79	21	23	44	40	9	3	0	12	6	5	11	6
02-03—San Jose	NHL	82	28	29	57	33	-10	8	1	—	—	—	—	—
03-04—San Jose	NHL	80	28	29	57	24	-5	9	0	17	8	4	12	6
NHL Totals (7 years)		558	153	174	327	193	7	33	1	51	19	12	31	22

MARSHALL, GRANT — RW — DEVILS

PERSONAL: Born June 9, 1973, in Mississauga, Ont. ... 6-1/200. ... Shoots right.

TRANSACTIONS/CAREER NOTES: Selected by Toronto Maple Leafs in first round (second Maple Leafs pick, 23rd overall) of NHL entry draft (June 20, 1992). ... Awarded to Dallas Stars with C Peter Zezel as compensation for Maple Leafs signing free-agent RW Mike Craig (August 10, 1994). ... Strained muscle (November 15, 1996); missed four games. ... Sprained shoulder (December 8, 1996); missed four games. ... Suffered concussion (January 4, 1997); missed two games. ... Strained groin (November 21, 1997); missed five games. ... Strained groin (April 16, 1998); missed one game. ... Fined $1,000 by NHL for elbowing incident (May 8, 1998). ... Injured groin; missed first four games of 1999-2000 season. ... Reinjured groin (October 13, 1999); missed 22 games. ... Reinjured groin (December 15, 1999); missed two games. ... Reinjured groin (December 27, 1999); missed five games. ... Reinjured groin (March 13, 2000); missed three games. ... Strained thigh (December 17, 2000); missed five games. ... Traded by Stars to Columbus Blue Jackets for second-round pick (LW Loui Eriksson) in 2003 entry draft (August 29, 2001). ... Injured foot (November 14, 2002); missed one game. ... Traded by Blue Jackets to New Jersey Devils for fourth-round pick (later traded to Carolina Hurricanes and Calgary Flames; Flames picked LW Kris Hogg) in 2004 draft (March 10, 2003). ... Injured back (October 28, 2003); missed 11 games. ... Bruised knee (March 21, 2003); missed five games. ... Injured back (October 28, 2003); missed 11 games. ... Injured groin (December 18, 2003); missed two games. ... Fractured right hand (March 28, 2004); missed final three games of regular season and playoffs.

		REGULAR SEASON								PLAYOFFS				
Season Team	League	GP	G	A	Pts.	PIM	+/-	PP	SH	GP	G	A	Pts.	PIM
90-91—Ottawa	OHL	26	6	11	17	25	...	...	...	1	0	0	0	0
91-92—Ottawa	OHL	61	32	51	83	132	...	...	...	11	6	11	17	11
92-93—Newmarket	OHL	31	12	25	37	85	...	...	...	7	4	7	11	20
—Ottawa	OHL	30	14	28	42	83	...	...	...	—	—	—	—	—
—St. John's	AHL	2	0	0	0	0	-4	0	0	2	0	0	0	2
93-94—St. John's	AHL	67	11	29	40	155	1	1	1	11	1	5	6	17
94-95—Kalamazoo	IHL	61	17	29	46	96	24	3	5	16	9	3	12	27
—Dallas	NHL	2	0	1	1	0	1	0	0	—	—	—	—	—
95-96—Dallas	NHL	70	9	19	28	111	0	0	0	—	—	—	—	—
96-97—Dallas	NHL	56	6	4	10	98	5	0	0	5	0	2	2	8
97-98—Dallas	NHL	72	9	10	19	96	-2	3	0	17	0	2	2	*47
98-99—Dallas	NHL	82	13	18	31	85	1	2	0	14	0	3	3	20
99-00—Dallas	NHL	45	2	6	8	38	-5	1	0	14	0	1	1	4
00-01—Dallas	NHL	75	13	24	37	64	1	4	0	9	0	0	0	0
01-02—Columbus	NHL	81	15	18	33	86	-20	6	0	—	—	—	—	—
02-03—Columbus	NHL	66	8	20	28	71	-8	3	0	—	—	—	—	—
—New Jersey	NHL	10	1	3	4	7	-3	0	0	24	6	2	8	8
03-04—New Jersey	NHL	65	8	7	15	67	-9	5	0	—	—	—	—	—
NHL Totals (10 years)		624	84	130	214	723	-39	24	0	83	6	10	16	87

MARSHALL, JASON — D/LW — MIGHTY DUCKS

PERSONAL: Born February 22, 1971, in Cranbrook, B.C. ... 6-2/196. ... Shoots right.

TRANSACTIONS/CAREER NOTES: Selected by St. Louis Blues in 1st round (1st Blues pick, 9th overall) of entry draft (June 17, 1989). ... Traded by Blues to Anaheim Mighty Ducks for D Bill Houlder (August 29, 1994). ... Cut finger (November 24, 1996); missed two games. ... Bruised hand (March 19, 1997); missed five games. ... Separated right shoulder (December 19, 1997); missed eight games. ... Strained left hamstring (December 18, 1998); missed six games. ... Ill (March 17, 1999); missed one game. ... Traded by Mighty Ducks to Washington Capitals for D Alexei Tezikov and 4th-round pick (D Brandon Rogers) in 2001 draft (March 13, 2001). ... Signed as free agent by Minnesota Wild (July 2, 2001). ... Injured eye (November 21, 2002); missed three games. ... Concussion (December 7, 2002); missed 14 games. ... Traded by Wild to San Jose Sharks for 5th-round pick (D Jean-Claude Sawyer) in 2004 draft (March 3, 2004). ... Signed as free agent by New York Rangers (Aug. 25, 2004). ... Signed as free agent by Anaheim Mighty Ducks (Aug. 8, 2005).

		REGULAR SEASON								PLAYOFFS				
Season Team	League	GP	G	A	Pts.	PIM	+/-	PP	SH	GP	G	A	Pts.	PIM
87-88—Columbia Valley	KIJHL	40	4	28	32	150	...	...	...	—	—	—	—	—
88-89—Vernon	BCHL	48	10	30	40	197	...	...	...	31	6	6	12	141
—Canadian nat'l team	Int'l	2	0	1	1	0	...	...	...	—	—	—	—	—
89-90—Canadian nat'l team	Int'l	72	1	11	12	57	...	...	...	—	—	—	—	—
90-91—Tri-City	WHL	59	10	34	44	236	...	...	...	7	1	2	3	20
—Peoria	IHL	...	...	...	...	...	...	...	...	18	0	1	1	48
91-92—Peoria	IHL	78	4	18	22	178	...	...	...	10	0	1	1	16
—St. Louis	NHL	2	1	0	1	4	0	0	0	—	—	—	—	—
92-93—Peoria	IHL	77	4	16	20	229	2	0	0	4	0	0	0	20
93-94—Peoria	IHL	20	1	1	2	72	-5	0	0	3	2	0	2	2
—Canadian nat'l team	Int'l	41	3	10	13	60	...	...	...	—	—	—	—	—
94-95—San Diego	IHL	80	7	18	25	218	-9	0	0	5	0	1	1	8
—Anaheim	NHL	1	0	0	0	0	-2	0	0	—	—	—	—	—
95-96—Baltimore	AHL	57	1	13	14	150	...	...	...	—	—	—	—	—
—Anaheim	NHL	24	0	1	1	42	3	0	0	—	—	—	—	—
96-97—Anaheim	NHL	73	1	9	10	140	6	0	0	7	0	1	1	4
97-98—Anaheim	NHL	72	3	6	9	189	-8	1	0	—	—	—	—	—
98-99—Anaheim	NHL	72	1	7	8	142	-5	0	0	4	1	0	1	10
99-00—Anaheim	NHL	55	0	3	3	88	-10	0	0	—	—	—	—	—
00-01—Anaheim	NHL	50	3	4	7	105	-12	2	1	—	—	—	—	—
—Washington	NHL	5	0	0	0	17	-1	0	0	—	—	—	—	—
01-02—Minnesota	NHL	80	5	6	11	148	-8	1	0	—	—	—	—	—
02-03—Minnesota	NHL	45	1	5	6	69	4	0	0	15	1	1	2	16
03-04—Houston	AHL	49	7	12	19	87	0	3	0	—	—	—	—	—
—Minnesota	NHL	12	1	4	5	18	-1	1	0	—	—	—	—	—
—San Jose	NHL	12	0	2	2	8	-2	0	0	17	0	1	1	25
04-05—Plzen	Czech Rep.	11	1	3	4	53	4	...	...	—	—	—	—	—
NHL Totals (11 years)		503	16	47	63	970	-36	5	1	43	2	3	5	55

MARTENSSON, TONY — C — MIGHTY DUCKS

PERSONAL: Born June 23, 1980, in Upplands Vasby, Sweden. ... 6-0/192.

TRANSACTIONS/CAREER NOTES: Selected by Anaheim Mighty Ducks in seventh round (224th overall) of NHL entry draft (June 24, 2001). ... Signed as free agent by Linkopings of Swedish league (May 17, 2004), with Mighty Ducks retaining NHL rights.

		REGULAR SEASON								PLAYOFFS				
Season Team	League	GP	G	A	Pts.	PIM	+/-	PP	SH	GP	G	A	Pts.	PIM
00-01—Brynas IF	Sweden	50	15	11	26	20	...	...	...	4	0	1	1	2
01-02—Brynas IF	Sweden	50	9	17	26	14	-14	...	...	4	1	3	4	2
02-03—Cincinnati	AHL	79	17	36	53	20	-3	...	...	—	—	—	—	—

Season Team	League	GP	G	A	Pts.	PIM	+/-	PP	SH		GP	G	A	Pts.	PIM
		REGULAR SEASON									PLAYOFFS				
03-04—Cincinnati	AHL	67	16	34	50	20	12	4	2		9	3	11	14	4
—Anaheim	NHL	6	1	1	2	0	-2	0	0		—	—	—	—	—
04-05—Linkopings	Sweden	50	13	21	34	12	15	1	0		5	0	1	1	0
NHL Totals (1 year)		6	1	1	2	0	-2	0	0						

MARTIN, PAUL — D — DEVILS

PERSONAL: Born March 5, 1981, in Minneapolis, Minn. ... 6-1/190. ... Shoots left.

TRANSACTIONS/CAREER NOTES: Selected by New Jersey Devils in second round (fifth Devils pick, 62nd overall) of NHL draft (June 24, 2000). ... Flu (January 27, 2004); missed two games.

Season Team	League	GP	G	A	Pts.	PIM	+/-	PP	SH		GP	G	A	Pts.	PIM
		REGULAR SEASON									PLAYOFFS				
98-99—Elk River	USHS (West)	25	9	21	30	28	...	...	...		—	—	—	—	—
99-00—Elk River	USHS (West)	24	15	35	50	26	...	...	...		—	—	—	—	—
00-01—Minnesota	WCHA	38	3	17	20	8	...	...	...		—	—	—	—	—
01-02—Minnesota	WCHA	44	8	30	38	22	...	...	...		—	—	—	—	—
02-03—Minnesota	WCHA	45	9	30	39	32	...	...	...		—	—	—	—	—
03-04—New Jersey	NHL	70	6	18	24	4	12	2	0		—	—	—	—	—
04-05—Fribourg	Switzerland	11	3	4	7	2	...	0	0		—	—	—	—	—
NHL Totals (1 year)		70	6	18	24	4	12	2	0						

MARTINEK, RADEK — D — ISLANDERS

PERSONAL: Born August 31, 1976, in Havlicko Brod, Czechoslovakia. ... 6-1/210. ... Shoots left.

TRANSACTIONS/CAREER NOTES: Selected by New York Islanders in eighth round (12th Islanders pick, 228th overall) of NHL entry draft (June 27, 1999). ... Sprained knee (November 8, 2001); missed seven games. ... Reinjured knee (December 11, 2001); missed remainder of season. ... Strained ribs (October 10, 2002); missed four games. ... Suffered concussion (November 18, 2003); missed three games. ... Fractured left ankle (February 21, 2004); missed 20 games.

Season Team	League	GP	G	A	Pts.	PIM	+/-	PP	SH		GP	G	A	Pts.	PIM
		REGULAR SEASON									PLAYOFFS				
96-97—HC Ceske Budejovice	Czech Rep.	52	3	5	8	40	...	...	...		5	0	1	1	2
97-98—HC Ceske Budejovice	Czech Rep.	42	2	7	9	36	...	...	...		—	—	—	—	—
98-99—HC Ceske Budejovice	Czech Rep.	52	12	13	25	50	...	...	...		3	0	2	2	...
99-00—HC Ceske Budejovice	Czech Rep.	45	5	18	23	24	...	...	...		3	0	0	0	6
00-01—HC Ceske Budejovice	Czech.	44	8	10	18	45	...	...	...		—	—	—	—	—
01-02—New York Islanders	NHL	23	1	4	5	16	5	0	0		—	—	—	—	—
02-03—Bridgeport	AHL	3	0	3	3	2	3	0	0		—	—	—	—	—
—New York Islanders	NHL	66	2	11	13	26	15	0	0		4	0	0	0	4
03-04—New York Islanders	NHL	47	4	3	7	43	-9	0	0		5	0	1	1	0
04-05—Budejovice	Czech Dv.I	30	12	18	30	80	36	...	...		12	2	3	5	6
NHL Totals (3 years)		136	7	18	25	85	11	0	0		9	0	1	1	4

M

MARTINS, STEVE — C

PERSONAL: Born April 13, 1972, in Gatineau, Que. ... 5-7/187. ... Shoots left.

TRANSACTIONS/CAREER NOTES: Selected by Hartford Whalers in 1st round (1st Whalers pick, fifth overall) of supplemental draft (June 24, 1994). ... Whalers franchise moved to North Carolina and renamed Carolina Hurricanes for 1997-98 season; NHL approved move on June 25, 1997. ... Signed as free agent by Ottawa Senators (July 22, 1998). ... Back spasms (December 4, 1998); missed four games. ... Injured hip flexor (February 13, 1999); missed three games. ... Reinjured hip flexor (February 23, 1999); missed four games. ... Flu (March 24, 1999); missed four games. ... Claimed off waivers by Tampa Bay Lightning (October 29, 1999). ... Strained groin (November 13, 1999); missed one game. ... Sprained ankle (December 4, 1999); missed 12 games. ... Strained groin (November 14, 2000); missed three games. ... Traded by Lightning to New York Islanders for future considerations (January 4, 2001). ... Sprained chest muscle (January 16, 2001); missed one game. ... Signed as free agent by Senators (August 30, 2001). ... Injured right knee (March 2, 2002); missed final 21 games of regular season. ... Claimed off waivers by St. Louis Blues (January 15, 2003).

Season Team	League	GP	G	A	Pts.	PIM	+/-	PP	SH		GP	G	A	Pts.	PIM
		REGULAR SEASON									PLAYOFFS				
91-92—Harvard	ECAC	20	13	14	27	26	...	...	...		—	—	—	—	—
92-93—Harvard	ECAC	18	6	8	14	40	...	...	...		—	—	—	—	—
93-94—Harvard	ECAC	32	25	35	60	93	...	...	...		—	—	—	—	—
94-95—Harvard	ECAC	28	15	23	38	93	...	7	2		—	—	—	—	—
95-96—Springfield	AHL	30	9	20	29	10	...	...	...		—	—	—	—	—
—Hartford	NHL	23	1	3	4	8	-3	0	0		—	—	—	—	—
96-97—Springfield	AHL	63	12	31	43	78	11	5	0		17	1	3	4	26
—Hartford	NHL	2	0	1	1	0	0	0	0		—	—	—	—	—
97-98—Chicago	IHL	78	20	41	61	122	14	6	0		21	6	14	20	28
—Carolina	NHL	3	0	0	0	0	0	0	0		—	—	—	—	—
98-99—Detroit	IHL	4	1	6	7	16	2	0	0		—	—	—	—	—
—Ottawa	NHL	36	4	3	7	10	4	1	0		—	—	—	—	—
99-00—Ottawa	NHL	2	1	0	1	0	-1	0	0		—	—	—	—	—
—Tampa Bay	NHL	57	5	7	12	37	-11	0	1		—	—	—	—	—
00-01—Tampa Bay	NHL	20	1	1	2	13	-9	0	0		—	—	—	—	—
—Detroit	IHL	8	5	4	9	4	...	...	...		—	—	—	—	—
—New York Islanders	NHL	39	1	3	4	20	-7	0	1		—	—	—	—	—
—Chicago	IHL	5	1	2	3	0	...	...	...		16	1	6	7	22
01-02—Ottawa	NHL	14	1	0	1	4	1	0	0		2	0	0	0	0

Season Team	League	REGULAR SEASON GP	G	A	Pts.	PIM	+/-	PP	SH	PLAYOFFS GP	G	A	Pts.	PIM
—Grand Rapids	AHL	51	10	21	31	66	4	4	2	3	0	0	0	0
02-03—Binghamton	AHL	26	5	11	16	31	9	0	1	—	—	—	—	—
—Ottawa	NHL	14	2	3	5	10	3	0	0	—	—	—	—	—
—St. Louis	NHL	28	3	3	6	18	-8	0	1	2	0	1	1	0
03-04—Worcester	AHL	22	4	9	13	16	0	1	0	—	—	—	—	—
—St. Louis	NHL	25	1	0	1	22	-7	0	1	1	0	0	0	0
04-05—JyP Jyvaskyla	Finland	54	13	12	25	66	4	...	...	3	0	0	0	4
NHL Totals (9 years)		263	20	24	44	142	-38	1	4	5	0	1	1	0

MASON, CHRIS — G — PREDATORS

PERSONAL: Born April 20, 1976, in Red Deer, Alta. ... 6-0/195. ... Catches left.

TRANSACTIONS/CAREER NOTES: Selected by New Jersey Devils in fifth round (seventh Devils pick, 122nd overall) of NHL draft (July 8, 1995). ... Signed as free agent by Anaheim Mighty Ducks (May 31, 1996). ... Traded by Mighty Ducks with D Marc Moro to Nashville Predators for G Dominic Roussel (October 5, 1998). ... Signed as free agent by Florida Panthers (August 16, 2002). ... Claimed by Predators in waiver draft (October 3, 2003).

Season Team	League	REGULAR SEASON GP	Min.	W	L	T	GA	SO	GAA	SV%	PLAYOFFS GP	Min.	W	L	GA	SO	GAA	SV%
93-94—Victoria	WHL	3	129	0	3	0	16	...	7.44	...	—	—	—	—	—	—	—	—
94-95—Prince George	WHL	44	2288	8	30	1	192	1	5.03	...	—	—	—	—	—	—	—	—
95-96—Prince George	WHL	59	3289	16	37	1	236	1	4.31	...	—	—	—	—	—	—	—	—
96-97—Prince George	WHL	50	2851	19	24	4	172	2	3.62	.900	15	938	9	6	44	1	2.81	.914
97-98—Cincinnati	AHL	47	2368	13	19	7	136	0	3.45	.903	—	—	—	—	—	—	—	—
98-99—Milwaukee	IHL	34	1901	15	12	6	92	1	2.90	.906	—	—	—	—	—	—	—	—
—Nashville	NHL	3	69	0	0	0	6	0	5.22	.864	—	—	—	—	—	—	—	—
99-00—Milwaukee	IHL	53	2952	27	21	8	137	2	2.78	...	3	252	1	2	11	0	2.62	...
00-01—Nashville	NHL	1	59	0	1	0	2	0	2.03	.900	—	—	—	—	—	—	—	—
—Milwaukee	IHL	37	2226	17	14	5	87	5	2.35	...	4	239	1	3	12	0	3.01	...
01-02—Milwaukee	AHL	48	2755	17	21	7	116	2	2.53	.910	—	—	—	—	—	—	—	—
02-03—San Antonio	AHL	50	2914	25	18	6	122	1	2.51	.921	3	194	0	3	9	0	2.78	.926
03-04—Nashville	NHL	17	744	4	4	1	27	1	2.18	.926	—	—	—	—	—	—	—	—
—Milwaukee	AHL	1	60	1	0	0	2	0	2.00	.929	—	—	—	—	—	—	—	—
04-05—Valerengen	Norway	20	1204	...	...	...	36	1	1.79	.934	11	657	...	...	22	1	2.01	.936
NHL Totals (3 years)		21	872	4	5	1	35	1	2.41	.918								

MATVICHUK, RICHARD — D — DEVILS

PERSONAL: Born February 5, 1973, in Edmonton. ... 6-2/215. ... Shoots left. ... Name pronounced MAT-vih-chuhk.

TRANSACTIONS/CAREER NOTES: Selected by Minnesota North Stars in first round (first North Stars pick, eighth overall) of 1991 NHL draft (June 22, 1991). ... Strained lower back (November 9, 1992); missed two games. ... Sprained ankle (December 27, 1992); missed 10 games. ... North Stars franchise moved from Minnesota to Dallas and renamed Stars for 1993-94 season. ... Bruised shoulder (April 5, 1994); missed one game. ... Tore knee ligaments (September 20, 1994) and had surgery; missed first 16 games of season. ... Had concussion (March 13, 1996); missed five games. ... Bruised shoulder (October 26, 1996); missed two games. ... Strained groin (February 18, 1997); missed 19 games. ... Tore knee ligament (January 21, 1998); missed eight games. ... Bruised thigh (December 31, 1998); missed one game. ... Has headaches (January 8, 1999); missed one game. ... Strained groin (March 14, 1999); missed two games. ... Reinjured groin (March 19, 1999); missed final 14 games of regular season and one playoff game. ... Injured knee (October 16, 1999); missed three games. ... Injured knee (November 10, 1999); missed three games. ... Flu (January 23, 2000); missed one game. ... Sprained thumb (February 2, 2000); missed one game. ... Sprained knee (March 1, 2000); missed one game. ... Fractured jaw (January 24, 2001); missed four games. ... Fractured left leg (January 11, 2003); missed 14 games. ... Injured knee (November 8, 2003); missed one game. ... Flu (November 29, 2003); missed one game. ... Injured knee (December 7, 2003); missed four games. ... Left team for personal reasons (April 4, 2004); missed one game. ... Signed as free agent by New Jersey Devils (July 12, 2004).

Season Team	League	REGULAR SEASON GP	G	A	Pts.	PIM	+/-	PP	SH	PLAYOFFS GP	G	A	Pts.	PIM
88-89—Fort Saskatchewan	AJHL	58	7	36	43	147	...	...	...	—	—	—	—	—
89-90—Saskatoon	WHL	56	8	24	32	126	...	...	...	10	2	8	10	16
90-91—Saskatoon	WHL	68	13	36	49	117	...	...	...	—	—	—	—	—
91-92—Saskatoon	WHL	58	14	40	54	126	...	...	...	22	1	9	10	61
92-93—Minnesota	NHL	53	2	3	5	26	-8	1	0	—	—	—	—	—
—Kalamazoo	IHL	3	0	1	1	6	1	0	0	—	—	—	—	—
93-94—Kalamazoo	IHL	43	8	17	25	84	0	4	0	—	—	—	—	—
—Dallas	NHL	25	0	3	3	22	1	0	0	7	1	1	2	12
94-95—Dallas	NHL	14	0	2	2	14	-7	0	0	5	0	2	2	4
—Kalamazoo	IHL	17	0	6	6	16	-9	0	0	—	—	—	—	—
95-96—Dallas	NHL	73	6	16	22	71	4	0	0	—	—	—	—	—
96-97—Dallas	NHL	57	5	7	12	87	1	0	2	7	0	1	1	20
97-98—Dallas	NHL	74	3	15	18	63	7	0	0	16	1	1	2	14
98-99—Dallas	NHL	64	3	9	12	51	23	1	0	22	1	5	6	20
99-00—Dallas	NHL	70	4	21	25	42	7	0	0	23	2	5	7	14
00-01—Dallas	NHL	78	4	16	20	62	5	2	0	10	0	0	0	14
01-02—Dallas	NHL	82	9	12	21	52	11	4	0	—	—	—	—	—
02-03—Dallas	NHL	68	1	5	6	58	1	0	0	12	0	3	3	8
03-04—Dallas	NHL	75	1	20	21	36	0	0	0	5	0	1	1	8
NHL Totals (12 years)		733	38	129	167	584	45	8	2	107	5	19	24	114

MAULDIN, GREG — C — BLUE JACKETS

PERSONAL: Born June 10, 1982, in Boston. ... 5-11/180.

TRANSACTIONS/CAREER NOTES: Selected by Columbus Blue Jackets in seventh round (10th Blue Jackets pick, 199th overall) of NHL entry draft (June 23, 2002).

		REGULAR SEASON								PLAYOFFS				
Season Team	League	GP	G	A	Pts.	PIM	+/-	PP	SH	GP	G	A	Pts.	PIM
01-02—Massachusetts	Hockey East	33	12	12	24	10	...	...	...	—	—	—	—	—
02-03—Massachusetts	Hockey East	36	21	21	42	26	...	...	...	—	—	—	—	—
03-04—Massachusetts	Hockey East	29	15	14	29	15	...	...	...	—	—	—	—	—
—Columbus	NHL	6	0	0	0	4	-2	0	0	—	—	—	—	—
—Syracuse	AHL	2	0	0	0	0	-1	0	0	1	0	0	0	0
04-05—Syracuse	AHL	66	7	20	27	49	9	2	0	—	—	—	—	—
NHL Totals (1 year)		6	0	0	0	4	-2	0	0					

MAY, BRAD — LW — AVALANCHE

PERSONAL: Born November 29, 1971, in Toronto. ... 6-1/213. ... Shoots left.

TRANSACTIONS/CAREER NOTES: Selected by Buffalo Sabres in 1st round (1st Sabres pick, 14th overall) of entry draft (June 16, 1990). ... Fractured hand (March 11, 1995); missed 15 games. ... Injured left arm (March 3, 1996); missed one game. ... Suspended one game for accumulating three game misconduct penalties (March 31, 1996). ... Right shoulder surgery (October 14, 1996); missed 27 games. ... Fractured right hand (December 20, 1996); missed nine games. ... Fractured thumb (March 1, 1997); missed four games. ... Strained shoulder (September 27, 1997); missed first six games of season. ... Sprained knee (December 29, 1997); missed 11 games. ... Traded by Sabres with 3rd-round pick (later traded to Tampa Bay; Lightning picked RW Jimmie Olvestad) in 1999 entry draft to Vancouver Canucks for LW Geoff Sanderson (February 4, 1998). ... Strained groin (October 30, 1998); missed five games. ... Fractured hand (March 26, 1999); missed final 10 games of season. ... Sprained knee (December 10, 1999); missed 13 games. ... Traded by Canucks to Phoenix Coyotes for future considerations (June 25, 2000). ... Suspended 20 games for slashing incident (November 15, 2000). ... Fractured rib (January 3, 2002); missed 10 games. ... Torn shoulder muscle (October 1, 2002) and had surgery; missed first 44 games. ... Injured groin (January 23, 2003); missed four games. ... Traded by Coyotes to Canucks for 3rd-round pick (C/RW Dimitri Pestunov) in 2003 entry draft (March 11, 2003). ... Concussion (March 15, 2003); missed nine games. ... Suspended one game for fighting incident (October 21, 2003). ... Flu (November 29, 2003); missed one game. ... Injured foot (March 13, 2004); missed three games. ... Injured knee (March 27, 2004); missed two games. ... Signed as free agent by Colorado Avalanche (Aug. 5, 2005).

		REGULAR SEASON								PLAYOFFS				
Season Team	League	GP	G	A	Pts.	PIM	+/-	PP	SH	GP	G	A	Pts.	PIM
87-88—Markham Jr. B	OHA	6	1	1	2	21	...	...	...	—	—	—	—	—
88-89—Niagara Falls	OHL	65	8	14	22	304	...	...	...	17	0	1	1	55
89-90—Niagara Falls	OHL	61	33	58	91	223	...	...	...	16	9	13	22	64
90-91—Niagara Falls	OHL	34	37	32	69	93	...	...	...	14	11	14	25	53
91-92—Buffalo	NHL	69	11	6	17	309	-12	1	0	7	1	4	5	2
92-93—Buffalo	NHL	82	13	13	26	242	3	0	0	8	1	1	2	14
93-94—Buffalo	NHL	84	18	27	45	171	-6	3	0	7	0	2	2	9
94-95—Buffalo	NHL	33	3	3	6	87	5	1	0	4	0	0	0	2
95-96—Buffalo	NHL	79	15	29	44	295	6	3	0	—	—	—	—	—
96-97—Buffalo	NHL	42	3	4	7	106	-8	1	0	10	1	1	2	32
97-98—Buffalo	NHL	36	4	7	11	113	2	0	0	—	—	—	—	—
—Vancouver	NHL	27	9	3	12	41	0	4	0	—	—	—	—	—
98-99—Vancouver	NHL	66	6	11	17	102	-14	1	0	—	—	—	—	—
99-00—Vancouver	NHL	59	9	7	16	90	-2	0	0	—	—	—	—	—
00-01—Phoenix	NHL	62	11	14	25	107	10	0	0	—	—	—	—	—
01-02—Phoenix	NHL	72	10	12	22	95	11	1	0	5	0	0	0	0
02-03—Phoenix	NHL	20	3	4	7	32	3	0	0	—	—	—	—	—
—Vancouver	NHL	3	0	0	0	10	1	0	0	14	0	0	0	15
03-04—Vancouver	NHL	70	5	6	11	137	-2	0	0	6	1	0	1	6
NHL Totals (13 years)		804	120	146	266	1937	-3	15	0	61	4	8	12	80

MAYERS, JAMAL — RW — BLUES

PERSONAL: Born October 24, 1974, in Toronto. ... 6-1/212. ... Shoots right.

TRANSACTIONS/CAREER NOTES: Selected by St. Louis Blues in 4th round (3rd Blues pick, 89th overall) of entry draft (June 26, 1993). ... Suspended one playoff game for slashing (May 7, 1999). ... Flu (March 24, 2001); missed one game. ... Strained groin (October 3, 2001); missed first four games of season. ... Bruised left foot (January 17, 2002); missed one game. ... Injured knee (November 15, 2002); missed final 67 games of regular season and playoffs. ... Injured wrist (January 10, 2004); missed one game.

		REGULAR SEASON								PLAYOFFS				
Season Team	League	GP	G	A	Pts.	PIM	+/-	PP	SH	GP	G	A	Pts.	PIM
90-91—Thornhill	Jr. A	44	12	24	36	78	...	...	...	—	—	—	—	—
91-92—Thornhill	Jr. A	56	38	69	107	36	...	...	...	—	—	—	—	—
92-93—Western Michigan	CCHA	38	8	17	25	26	...	...	...	—	—	—	—	—
93-94—Western Michigan	CCHA	40	17	32	49	40	12	4	1	—	—	—	—	—
94-95—Western Michigan	CCHA	39	13	33	46	40	18	4	1	—	—	—	—	—
95-96—Western Michigan	CCHA	38	17	22	39	75	...	...	...	—	—	—	—	—
96-97—Worcester	AHL	62	12	14	26	104	-12	2	0	5	4	4	8	4
—St. Louis	NHL	6	0	1	1	2	-3	0	0	—	—	—	—	—
97-98—Worcester	AHL	61	19	24	43	117	-5	8	1	11	3	4	7	10
98-99—Worcester	AHL	20	9	7	16	34	-3	3	0	—	—	—	—	—
—St. Louis	NHL	34	4	5	9	40	-3	0	0	11	0	1	1	8
99-00—St. Louis	NHL	79	7	10	17	90	0	0	0	7	0	4	4	2
00-01—St. Louis	NHL	77	8	13	21	117	-3	0	0	15	2	3	5	8
01-02—St. Louis	NHL	77	9	8	17	99	9	0	1	10	3	0	3	2

Season Team	League	REGULAR SEASON GP	G	A	Pts.	PIM	+/-	PP	SH	PLAYOFFS GP	G	A	Pts.	PIM
02-03—St. Louis	NHL	15	2	5	7	8	1	0	0	—	—	—	—	—
03-04—St. Louis	NHL	80	6	5	11	91	-19	0	1	5	0	0	0	0
04-05—Hammarby	Sweden Dv. 2	10	7	8	15	10	10	1	0	9	2	5	7	26
—Missouri	UHL	13	5	2	7	68	-3	2	1	—	—	—	—	—
NHL Totals (7 years)		368	36	47	83	447	-18	0	2	48	5	8	13	20

MCALLISTER, CHRIS D/LW

PERSONAL: Born June 16, 1975, in Saskatoon, Sask. ... 6-8/240. ... Shoots left.

TRANSACTIONS/CAREER NOTES: Selected by Vancouver Canucks in second round (first Canucks pick, 40th overall) of NHL draft (July 8, 1995). ... Had heel spur (December 13, 1997); missed three games. ... Traded by Canucks to Toronto Maple Leafs for C Darby Hendrickson (February 16, 1999). ... Suspended two games by NHL for leaving bench during altercation (February 26, 1999). ... Injured (October 20, 1999); missed six games. ... Injured (January 22, 2000); missed one game. ... Injured foot (March 30, 2000); missed final five games of season. ... Traded by Maple Leafs to Philadelphia Flyers for D Regan Kelly (September 26, 2000). ... Sprained wrist (December 21, 2000); missed two games. ... Reinjured wrist (December 30, 2000); missed five games. ... Fractured left wrist (April 6, 2002); missed remainder of season. ... Traded by Flyers to Colorado Avalanche for sixth-round pick (G Ville Hostikka) in 2003 draft (February 5, 2003). ... Injured shoulder (February 13, 2003); missed two games. ... Fractured foot (March 8, 2003); missed 13 games. ... Injured knee (October 5, 2003); missed six games. ... Injured foot (November 24, 2003); missed one game. ... Injured ribs (December 29, 2003); missed seven games. ... Traded by Avalanche with D David Liffiton and future considerations to New York Rangers for F Matthew Barnaby and third-round pick (LW Denis Parshin) in 2004 draft (March 8, 2004).

Season Team	League	REGULAR SEASON GP	G	A	Pts.	PIM	+/-	PP	SH	PLAYOFFS GP	G	A	Pts.	PIM
93-94—Humboldt	SJHL	50	3	5	8	150	...	...	...	—	—	—	—	—
—Saskatoon	WHL	2	0	0	0	5	...	...	...	—	—	—	—	—
94-95—Saskatoon	WHL	65	2	8	10	134	15	2	0	10	0	0	0	28
95-96—Syracuse	AHL	68	0	2	2	142	...	...	...	16	0	0	0	34
96-97—Syracuse	AHL	43	3	1	4	108	-5	0	0	3	0	0	0	6
97-98—Syracuse	AHL	23	0	1	1	71	-5	0	0	5	0	0	0	21
—Vancouver	NHL	36	1	2	3	106	-12	0	0	—	—	—	—	—
98-99—Vancouver	NHL	28	1	1	2	63	-7	0	0	—	—	—	—	—
—Syracuse	AHL	5	0	0	0	24	-3	0	0	—	—	—	—	—
—Toronto	NHL	20	0	2	2	39	4	0	0	6	0	1	1	4
99-00—Toronto	NHL	36	0	3	3	68	-4	0	0	—	—	—	—	—
00-01—Philadelphia	NHL	60	2	2	4	124	1	0	0	2	0	0	0	0
01-02—Philadelphia	NHL	42	0	5	5	113	-7	0	0	—	—	—	—	—
02-03—Philadelphia	NHL	19	0	0	0	21	-2	0	0	—	—	—	—	—
—Philadelphia	AHL	4	0	0	0	12	-3	0	0	—	—	—	—	—
—Colorado	NHL	14	0	1	1	26	6	0	0	1	0	0	0	0
03-04—Colorado	NHL	34	0	0	0	62	-2	0	0	—	—	—	—	—
—New York Rangers	NHL	12	0	1	1	12	-4	0	0	—	—	—	—	—
04-05—Newcastle	England	23	0	6	6	54	...	0	0	—	—	—	—	—
NHL Totals (7 years)		301	4	17	21	634	-27	0	0	9	0	1	1	4

MCAMMOND, DEAN C BLUES

PERSONAL: Born June 15, 1973, in Grand Cache, Alta. ... 5-11/200. ... Shoots left.

TRANSACTIONS/CAREER NOTES: Selected by Chicago Blackhawks in 1st round (1st Blackhawks pick, 22nd overall) of entry draft (June 22, 1991). ... Traded by Blackhawks with D Igor Kravchuk to Edmonton Oilers for RW Joe Murphy (February 25, 1993). ... Severed left Achilles' tendon (February 1, 1995); missed final 41 games of season. ... Fractured nose (November 11, 1996); missed two games. ... Flu (January 21, 1997); missed two games. ... Back spasms (March 1, 1997); missed remainder of season. ... Traded by Oilers with D Boris Mironov and D Jonas Elofsson to Blackhawks for C Chad Kilger, LW Daniel Cleary, LW Ethan Moreau and D Christian Laflamme (March 20, 1999). ... Bruised ribs (October 4, 1999); missed five games. ... Sore wrist (December 9, 1999); missed one game. ... Traded by Blackhawks to Philadelphia Flyers for 3rd-round pick (later traded to Toronto Maple Leafs) in 2001 entry draft (March 13, 2001). ... Traded by Flyers to Calgary Flames for 4th-round pick (D Rosario Ruggeri) in 2002 entry draft (June 24, 2001). ... Injured back (January 19, 2002); missed one game. ... Injured ribs (January 24, 2002); missed eight games. ... Traded by Flames with D Derek Morris and C Jeff Shantz to Colorado Avalanche for LW Chris Drury and C Stephane Yelle (October 1, 2002). ... Injured back (October 18, 2002); missed 23 games. ... Traded by Avalanche to Flames for 5th-round pick (C Mark McCutheon) in 2003 entry draft (March 11, 2003). ... Ruled ineligible to play remainder of the 2002-03 season because of transaction violation by Flames (March 15, 2003). ... Concussion (October 25, 2003); missed five games. ... Sore back (March 11, 2004); missed final 13 games of regular season and playoffs. ... Signed as free agent by Albany of the AHL (October 5, 2004). ... Signed as free agent by St. Louis Blues (Aug. 9, 2005).

Season Team	League	REGULAR SEASON GP	G	A	Pts.	PIM	+/-	PP	SH	PLAYOFFS GP	G	A	Pts.	PIM
89-90—Prince Albert	WHL	53	11	11	22	49	...	...	...	14	2	3	5	18
90-91—Prince Albert	WHL	71	33	35	68	108	...	...	...	2	0	1	1	6
91-92—Prince Albert	WHL	63	37	54	91	189	...	...	...	10	12	11	23	26
—Chicago	NHL	5	0	2	2	0	-2	0	0	3	0	0	0	2
92-93—Prince Albert	WHL	30	19	29	48	44	-1	5	2	—	—	—	—	—
—Swift Current	WHL	18	10	13	23	29	-4	2	1	17	*16	19	35	20
93-94—Edmonton	NHL	45	6	21	27	16	12	2	0	—	—	—	—	—
—Cape Breton	AHL	28	9	12	21	38	-3	3	0	—	—	—	—	—
94-95—Edmonton	NHL	6	0	0	0	0	-1	0	0	—	—	—	—	—
95-96—Edmonton	NHL	53	15	15	30	23	6	4	0	—	—	—	—	—
—Cape Breton	AHL	22	9	15	24	55	...	...	...	—	—	—	—	—
96-97—Edmonton	NHL	57	12	17	29	28	-15	4	0	—	—	—	—	—
97-98—Edmonton	NHL	77	19	31	50	46	9	8	0	12	1	4	5	12
98-99—Edmonton	NHL	65	9	16	25	36	5	1	0	—	—	—	—	—
—Chicago	NHL	12	1	4	5	2	3	0	0	—	—	—	—	—

Season Team	League	GP	G	A	Pts.	PIM	+/-	PP	SH	GP	G	A	Pts.	PIM
		REGULAR SEASON								PLAYOFFS				
99-00—Chicago	NHL	76	14	18	32	72	11	1	0	—	—	—	—	—
00-01—Chicago	NHL	61	10	16	26	43	4	1	0	—	—	—	—	—
—Philadelphia	NHL	10	1	1	2	0	-1	1	0	4	0	0	0	2
01 02—Calgary	NHL	73	21	30	51	60	2	7	0	—	—	—	—	—
02-03—Colorado	NHL	41	10	8	18	10	1	2	0	—	—	—	—	—
03-04—Calgary	NHL	64	17	13	30	18	9	4	1	—	—	—	—	—
04-05—Albany	AHL	79	19	42	61	72	-1	5	1	—	—	—	—	—
NHL Totals (12 years)		645	135	192	327	354	43	35	1	19	1	4	5	16

MCARDLE, KENNDAL — LW — PANTHERS

PERSONAL: Born January 4, 1987, in Toronto. ... 5-11/195. ... Shoots left.
TRANSACTIONS/CAREER NOTES: Selected by Florida Panthers in 1st round (1st Panthers pick, 20th overall, obtained from Philadelphia) of entry draft (July 30, 2005).

Season Team	League	GP	G	A	Pts.	PIM	+/-	PP	SH	GP	G	A	Pts.	PIM
		REGULAR SEASON								PLAYOFFS				
02-03—Moose Jaw	WHL	2	0	0	0	0	...	...	...	—	—	—	—	—
03-04—Moose Jaw	WHL	54	8	8	16	57	...	...	...	10	3	2	5	6
04-05—Moose Jaw	WHL	70	37	37	74	122	-4	17	2	5	1	0	1	16

MCCABE, BRYAN — D — MAPLE LEAFS

PERSONAL: Born June 8, 1975, in St. Catharines, Ont. ... 6-2/220. ... Shoots left.
TRANSACTIONS/CAREER NOTES: Selected by New York Islanders in second round (second Islanders pick, 40th overall) of NHL entry draft (June 26, 1993). ... Traded by Islanders with LW Todd Bertuzzi and third-round pick (LW Jarkko Ruutu) in 1998 entry draft to Vancouver Canucks for C Trevor Linden (February 6, 1998). ... Missed first 13 games of 1998-99 season in contract dispute. ... Traded by Canucks with first-round pick (RW Pavel Vorobiev) in 2000 entry draft to Chicago Blackhawks for first-round pick (later traded to Tampa Bay Lightning) in 1999 entry draft (June 26, 1999). ... Fractured facial bone (March 11, 2000); missed two games. ... Traded by Blackhawks to Toronto Maple Leafs for D Alexander Karpovtsev and fourth-round pick (D Vladimir Gusev) in 2001 entry draft (October 2, 2000). ... Bruised left hand (October 14, 2002); missed one game. ... Fractured right foot (November 19, 2002); missed six games. ... Injured knee (October 4, 2003) and had surgery; missed season's first seven games.

Season Team	League	GP	G	A	Pts.	PIM	+/-	PP	SH	GP	G	A	Pts.	PIM
		REGULAR SEASON								PLAYOFFS				
91-92—Medicine Hat	WHL	68	6	24	30	157	...	...	...	4	0	0	0	6
92-93—Medicine Hat	WHL	14	0	13	13	83	-10	0	0	—	—	—	—	—
—Spokane	WHL	46	3	44	47	134	-13	1	0	10	1	5	6	28
93-94—Spokane	WHL	64	22	62	84	218	13	6	3	3	0	4	4	4
94-95—Spokane	WHL	42	14	39	53	115	-6	3	1	—	—	—	—	—
—Brandon	WHL	20	6	10	16	38	4	0	3	18	4	13	17	59
95-96—New York Islanders	NHL	82	7	16	23	156	-24	3	0	—	—	—	—	—
96-97—New York Islanders	NHL	82	8	20	28	165	-2	2	1	—	—	—	—	—
97-98—New York Islanders	NHL	56	3	9	12	145	9	1	0	—	—	—	—	—
—Vancouver	NHL	26	1	11	12	64	10	0	1	—	—	—	—	—
98-99—Vancouver	NHL	69	7	14	21	120	-11	1	2	—	—	—	—	—
99-00—Chicago	NHL	79	6	19	25	139	-8	2	0	—	—	—	—	—
00-01—Toronto	NHL	82	5	24	29	123	16	3	0	11	2	3	5	16
01-02—Toronto	NHL	82	17	26	43	129	16	8	0	20	5	5	10	30
02-03—Toronto	NHL	75	6	18	24	135	9	3	0	7	0	3	3	10
03-04—Toronto	NHL	75	16	37	53	86	22	8	0	13	3	5	8	14
04-05—HV 71 Jonkoping	Sweden	10	1	0	1	30	-12	1	0	—	—	—	—	—
NHL Totals (9 years)		708	76	194	270	1262	37	31	4	51	10	16	26	70

MCCARTHY, SANDY — RW

PERSONAL: Born June 15, 1972, in Toronto. ... 6-3/222. ... Shoots right.
TRANSACTIONS/CAREER NOTES: Selected by Calgary Flames in third round (third Flames pick, 52nd overall) of NHL draft (June 22, 1991). ... Strained right shoulder (December 18, 1993); missed two games. ... Strained shoulder (December 27, 1993); missed one game. ... Strained right knee (January 20, 1995); missed five games. ... Hernia (February 3, 1995); missed six games. ... Injured ribs (December 16, 1995); missed seven games. ... Fractured ankle (October 9, 1996); missed 25 games. ... Reinjured left ankle (January 9, 1997) and had surgery; missed 23 games. ... Bruised shoulder (November 13, 1997); missed six games. ... Injured groin (December 9, 1997); missed two games. ... Had hip pointer (December 22, 1997); missed four games. ... Charley horse (January 24, 1998); missed one game. ... Traded by Flames with third- (LW Brad Richards) and fifth-round (D Curtis Rich) picks in 1998 entry draft to Tampa Bay Lightning for C Jason Wiemer (March 24, 1998). ... Traded by Lightning with RW Mikael Andersson to Philadelphia Flyers for LW Colin Forbes and fifth-round pick (G Michal Lanicek) in 1999 entry draft (March 20, 1999). ... Sprained right knee (November 5, 1999); missed one game. ... Injured groin (February 19, 2000); missed four games. ... Traded by Flyers to Carolina Hurricanes for C Kent Manderville (March 14, 2000). ... Traded by Hurricanes with fourth-round pick (D Bryce Lampman) in 2001 draft to New York Rangers for RW Rob DiMaio and LW Darren Langdon (August 4, 2000). ... Signed as free agent by Boston Bruins (August 12, 2003). ... Injured groin (December 8, 2003); missed five games. ... Injured jaw and suffered concussion (January 15, 2004); missed 25 games. ... Claimed off waivers by Rangers from Bruins (March 9, 2004).

Season Team	League	GP	G	A	Pts.	PIM	+/-	PP	SH	GP	G	A	Pts.	PIM
		REGULAR SEASON								PLAYOFFS				
89-90—Laval	QMJHL	65	10	11	21	269	...	...	...	—	—	—	—	—
90-91—Laval	QMJHL	68	21	19	40	297	...	...	...	—	—	—	—	—
91-92—Laval	QMJHL	62	39	51	90	326	...	...	...	8	4	5	9	81
92-93—Salt Lake City	IHL	77	18	20	38	220	-14	7	0	—	—	—	—	—
93-94—Calgary	NHL	79	5	5	10	173	-3	0	0	7	0	0	0	34

Season Team	League	GP	G	A	Pts.	PIM	+/-	PP	SH	GP	G	A	Pts.	PIM
		REGULAR SEASON								PLAYOFFS				
94-95—Calgary	NHL	37	5	3	8	101	1	0	0	6	0	1	1	17
95-96—Calgary	NHL	75	9	7	16	173	-8	3	0	4	0	0	0	10
96-97—Calgary	NHL	33	3	5	8	113	-8	1	0	—	—	—	—	—
97-98—Calgary	NHL	52	8	5	13	170	-18	1	0	—	—	—	—	—
—Tampa Bay	NHL	14	0	5	5	71	-1	0	0	—	—	—	—	—
98-99—Tampa Bay	NHL	67	5	7	12	135	-22	1	0	—	—	—	—	—
—Philadelphia	NHL	13	0	1	1	25	-2	0	0	6	0	1	1	0
99-00—Philadelphia	NHL	58	6	5	11	111	-5	1	0	—	—	—	—	—
—Carolina	NHL	13	0	0	0	9	2	0	0	—	—	—	—	—
00-01—New York Rangers	NHL	81	11	10	21	171	3	0	0	—	—	—	—	—
01-02—New York Rangers	NHL	82	10	13	23	171	-8	1	0	—	—	—	—	—
02-03—New York Rangers	NHL	82	6	9	15	81	-4	0	0	—	—	—	—	—
03-04—Boston	NHL	37	3	1	4	28	0	0	0	—	—	—	—	—
—New York Rangers	NHL	13	1	0	1	2	-8	1	0	—	—	—	—	—
NHL Totals (11 years)		736	72	76	148	1534	-81	9	0	23	0	2	2	61

MCCARTHY, STEVE — D — BLACKHAWKS

PERSONAL: Born February 3, 1981, in Trail, B.C. ... 6-1/198. ... Shoots left.

TRANSACTIONS/CAREER NOTES: Selected by Chicago Blackhawks in first round (first Blackhawks pick, 23rd overall) of NHL entry draft (June 26, 1999). ... Injured groin (November 26, 2003); missed 54 games.

Season Team	League	GP	G	A	Pts.	PIM	+/-	PP	SH	GP	G	A	Pts.	PIM
		REGULAR SEASON								PLAYOFFS				
96-97—Edmonton	WHL	2	0	0	0	0	...	...	...	—	—	—	—	—
97-98—Edmonton	WHL	58	11	29	40	59	...	...	...	—	—	—	—	—
98-99—Kootenay	WHL	57	19	33	52	79	6	11	0	6	0	5	5	8
99-00—Chicago	NHL	5	1	1	2	4	0	1	0	—	—	—	—	—
—Kootenay	WHL	37	13	23	36	36	18	11	0	—	—	—	—	—
00-01—Chicago	NHL	44	0	5	5	8	-7	0	0	—	—	—	—	—
—Norfolk	AHL	7	0	4	4	2	...	...	...	—	—	—	—	—
01-02—Chicago	NHL	3	0	0	0	2	-1	0	0	—	—	—	—	—
—Norfolk	AHL	77	7	21	28	37	-16	2	0	2	0	3	3	2
02-03—Chicago	NHL	57	1	4	5	23	-1	0	0	—	—	—	—	—
—Norfolk	AHL	19	1	6	7	14	4	0	0	9	0	4	4	0
03-04—Chicago	NHL	25	1	3	4	8	-9	0	0	—	—	—	—	—
NHL Totals (5 years)		134	3	13	16	45	-18	1	0					

MCCARTY, DARREN — RW — FLAMES

PERSONAL: Born April 1, 1972, in Burnaby, B.C. ... 6-1/215. ... Shoots right.

TRANSACTIONS/CAREER NOTES: Selected by Detroit Red Wings in 2nd round (2nd Red Wings pick, 46th overall) of entry draft (June 20, 1992). ... Injured groin (January 29, 1994); missed five games. ... Injured shoulder (March 23, 1994); missed five games. ... Separated right shoulder (February 7, 1995); missed eight games. ... Injured right hand (March 30, 1995); missed two games. ... Injured left knee (April 9, 1995); missed five games. ... Injured right heel (November 7, 1995); missed one game ... Separated shoulder (December 2, 1995); missed six games. ... Cut right forearm (January 12, 1996); missed three games. ... Injured left hand (February 15, 1996); missed seven games. ... Injured hand (January 3, 1997); missed seven games. ... Bruised thigh (January 29, 1997); missed four games. ... Injured groin (April 5, 1997); missed two games. ... Fractured foot (January 11, 1998); missed eight games. ... Vertigo (April 4, 1998); missed three games. ... Strained groin (March 12, 1999); missed 10 games. ... Reinjured groin (April 5, 1999); missed three games. ... Strained groin (November 12, 1999); missed 39 games. ... Injured leg (March 5, 2000); missed final 17 games of regular season. ... Back spasms (December 1, 2000); missed one game. ... Sprained ankle (March 18, 2001); missed remainder of regular season. ... Injured shoulder (September 21, 2001); missed first two games of season. ... Sprained knee (October 13, 2001); missed 11 games. ... Infected finger (March 2, 2002); missed six games. ... Injured elbow (February 6, 2003); missed nine games. ... Back spasms (November 8, 2003); missed 39 games. ... Placed on waivers by Red Wings (July 25, 2005). ... Signed as free agent by Calgary Flames (Aug. 2, 2005).

Season Team	League	GP	G	A	Pts.	PIM	+/-	PP	SH	GP	G	A	Pts.	PIM
		REGULAR SEASON								PLAYOFFS				
88-89—Peterborough Jr. B	OHA	34	18	17	35	135	...	...	...	—	—	—	—	—
89-90—Belleville	OHL	63	12	15	27	142	...	...	...	11	1	1	2	21
90-91—Belleville	OHL	60	30	37	67	151	...	...	...	6	2	2	4	13
91-92—Belleville	OHL	65	*55	72	127	177	...	...	...	5	1	4	5	13
92-93—Adirondack	AHL	73	17	19	36	278	16	1	0	11	0	1	1	33
93-94—Detroit	NHL	67	9	17	26	181	12	0	0	7	2	2	4	8
94-95—Detroit	NHL	31	5	8	13	88	5	1	0	18	3	2	5	14
95-96—Detroit	NHL	63	15	14	29	158	14	8	0	19	3	2	5	20
96-97—Detroit	NHL	68	19	30	49	126	14	5	0	20	3	4	7	34
97-98—Detroit	NHL	71	15	22	37	157	0	5	1	22	3	8	11	34
98-99—Detroit	NHL	69	14	26	40	108	10	6	0	10	1	1	2	23
99-00—Detroit	NHL	24	6	6	12	48	1	0	0	9	0	1	1	12
00-01—Detroit	NHL	72	12	10	22	123	-5	1	1	6	1	0	1	2
01-02—Detroit	NHL	62	5	7	12	98	2	0	0	23	4	4	8	34
02-03—Detroit	NHL	73	13	9	22	138	10	1	0	4	0	0	0	6
03-04—Detroit	NHL	43	6	5	11	50	2	1	0	12	0	1	1	7
NHL Totals (11 years)		643	119	154	273	1275	65	28	2	150	20	25	45	194

MCCAULEY, ALYN — C/LW — SHARKS

PERSONAL: Born May 29, 1977, in Brockville, Ont. ... 6-0/192. ... Shoots left.

TRANSACTIONS/CAREER NOTES: Selected by New Jersey Devils in fourth round (fifth Devils pick, 79th overall) of NHL entry draft (July 8, 1995). ... Traded by Devils with D Jason Smith and C Steve Sullivan to Toronto Maple Leafs for C Doug Gilmour, D Dave Ellett and third-round

pick (D Andre Lakos) in 1999 entry draft (February 25, 1997). ... Fractured ankle (December 31, 1997); missed 17 games. ... Strained shoulder (February 26, 1998); missed three games. ... Sprained left knee (December 30, 1998); missed 22 games. ... Concussion (March 3, 1999); missed remainder of season. ... Injured (October 9, 1999); missed one game. ... Flu (December 4, 1999); missed six games. ... Ill (January 11, 2000); missed one game. ... Sprained wrist (October 11, 2000); missed four games. ... Traded by Maple Leafs with C Brad Boyes and 1st-round pick (later traded to Boston; Bruins selected D Mark Stuart) in 2003 entry draft to San Jose Sharks for RW Owen Nolan (March 5, 2003).
STATISTICAL PLATEAUS: Three-goal games: 2003-04 (1).

		REGULAR SEASON								PLAYOFFS				
Season Team	**League**	**GP**	**G**	**A**	**Pts.**	**PIM**	**+/-**	**PP**	**SH**	**GP**	**G**	**A**	**Pts.**	**PIM**
92-93—Kingston Jr. A	MTHL	38	31	29	60	18	...	...	...	—	—	—	—	—
93-94—Ottawa	OHL	38	13	23	36	10	...	...	...	13	5	14	19	4
94-95—Ottawa	OHL	65	16	38	54	20	...	3	0	—	—	—	—	—
95-96—Ottawa	OHL	55	34	48	82	24	...	...	...	2	0	0	0	0
96-97—Ottawa	OHL	50	56	56	112	16	47	18	3	22	14	22	36	14
—St. John's	AHL	...	...	...	...	...	...	...	...	3	0	1	1	0
97-98—Toronto	NHL	60	6	10	16	6	-7	0	0	—	—	—	—	—
98-99—Toronto	NHL	39	9	15	24	2	7	1	0	—	—	—	—	—
99-00—Toronto	NHL	45	5	5	10	10	-6	1	0	5	0	0	0	6
—St. John's	AHL	5	1	1	2	0	...	...	...	—	—	—	—	—
00-01—Toronto	NHL	14	1	0	1	0	0	0	0	10	0	0	0	2
—St. John's	AHL	47	16	28	44	12	...	...	...	—	—	—	—	—
01-02—Toronto	NHL	82	6	10	16	18	10	0	1	20	5	10	15	4
02-03—Toronto	NHL	64	6	9	15	16	3	0	0	—	—	—	—	—
—San Jose	NHL	16	3	7	10	4	-2	3	0	—	—	—	—	—
03-04—San Jose	NHL	82	20	27	47	28	23	5	0	11	2	1	3	2
NHL Totals (7 years)		402	56	83	139	84	28	10	1	46	7	11	18	14

MCCORMICK, CODY C/RW AVALANCHE

PERSONAL: Born April 18, 1983, in London, Ont. ... 6-2/200. ... Shoots right.
TRANSACTIONS/CAREER NOTES: Selected by Colorado Avalanche in fifth round (fourth Avalanche pick, 144th overall) of NHL entry draft (June 23, 2001). ... Fractured finger (November 30, 2003); missed one game.

		REGULAR SEASON								PLAYOFFS				
Season Team	**League**	**GP**	**G**	**A**	**Pts.**	**PIM**	**+/-**	**PP**	**SH**	**GP**	**G**	**A**	**Pts.**	**PIM**
00-01—Belleville	OHL	66	7	16	23	135	...	...	...	10	1	1	2	23
01-02—Belleville	OHL	63	10	17	27	118	...	...	...	11	2	4	6	24
02-03—Belleville	OHL	61	36	33	69	166	...	...	...	7	4	7	11	11
03-04—Hershey	AHL	32	3	6	9	60	-9	0	1	—	—	—	—	—
—Colorado	NHL	44	2	3	5	73	-4	0	0	—	—	—	—	—
04-05—Hershey	AHL	40	5	6	11	68	-8	2	1	—	—	—	—	—
NHL Totals (1 year)		44	2	3	5	73	-4	0	0					

MCDONALD, ANDY LW/RW MIGHTY DUCKS

PERSONAL: Born August 25, 1977, in Strathroy, Ont. ... 5-10/174. ... Shoots left.
TRANSACTIONS/CAREER NOTES: Signed as free agent by Anaheim Mighty Ducks (April 3, 2000). ... Concussion (January 12, 2001); missed seven games. ... Concussion (February 27, 2002); missed three games. ... Concussion (January 9, 2003); missed seven games. ... Concussion (February 7, 2003); missed 29 games. ... Concussion (October 6, 2003); missed three games.

		REGULAR SEASON								PLAYOFFS				
Season Team	**League**	**GP**	**G**	**A**	**Pts.**	**PIM**	**+/-**	**PP**	**SH**	**GP**	**G**	**A**	**Pts.**	**PIM**
96-97—Colgate	ECAC	33	9	10	19	19	...	...	...	—	—	—	—	—
97-98—Colgate	ECAC	35	13	19	32	26	...	...	...	—	—	—	—	—
98-99—Colgate	ECAC	35	20	26	46	42	...	...	...	—	—	—	—	—
99-00—Colgate	ECAC	34	25	*33	*58	49	...	...	...	—	—	—	—	—
00-01—Cincinnati	AHL	46	15	25	40	21	...	...	...	3	0	1	1	2
—Anaheim	NHL	16	1	0	1	6	0	0	0	—	—	—	—	—
01-02—Cincinnati	AHL	21	7	25	32	6	13	1	0	—	—	—	—	—
—Anaheim	NHL	53	7	21	28	10	2	2	0	—	—	—	—	—
02-03—Anaheim	NHL	46	10	11	21	14	-1	3	0	—	—	—	—	—
03-04—Anaheim	NHL	79	9	21	30	24	-13	2	1	—	—	—	—	—
04-05—Ingolstadt ERC	Germany	36	13	17	30	26	15	3	1	10	5	2	7	35
NHL Totals (4 years)		194	27	53	80	54	-12	7	1					

MCDONELL, KENT RW RED WINGS

PERSONAL: Born March 1, 1979, in Williamstown, Ont. ... 6-2/206. ... Shoots right.
TRANSACTIONS/CAREER NOTES: Selected by Carolina Hurricanes in 9th round (9th Hurricanes pick, 225th overall) of entry draft (June 21, 1997). ... Returned to draft pool by Hurricanes; selected by Detroit Red Wings in 6th round (3rd Red Wings pick, 181st overall) of entry draft (June 26, 1999). ... Traded by Red Wings to Columbus Blue Jackets for 6th-round pick (LW Andreas Sundin) in 2003 entry draft (August 17, 2000). ... Signed by Red Wings as free agent (Aug. 12, 2005).

		REGULAR SEASON								PLAYOFFS				
Season Team	**League**	**GP**	**G**	**A**	**Pts.**	**PIM**	**+/-**	**PP**	**SH**	**GP**	**G**	**A**	**Pts.**	**PIM**
96-97—Guelph	OHL	56	7	5	12	57	...	...	...	16	0	2	2	4
97-98—Guelph	OHL	57	28	23	51	76	2	...	...	12	7	4	11	18
98-99—Guelph	OHL	60	31	38	69	110	32	...	...	11	4	3	7	36
99-00—Guelph	OHL	56	35	35	70	100	7	10	4	6	1	4	5	6
00-01—Syracuse	AHL	32	3	3	6	36	...	...	...	3	1	0	1	0
—Dayton	ECHL	28	16	9	25	94	...	...	...	3	0	0	0	4

Season Team	League	REGULAR SEASON GP	G	A	Pts.	PIM	+/-	PP	SH	PLAYOFFS GP	G	A	Pts.	PIM
01-02—Syracuse	AHL	72	18	13	31	122	9	3	1	3	0	2	2	0
02-03—Syracuse	AHL	72	14	24	38	93	-1	6	3	—	—	—	—	—
—Columbus	NHL	3	0	0	0	0	-1	0	0	—	—	—	—	—
03-04—Columbus	NHL	29	1	2	3	36	-7	0	0	—	—	—	—	—
—Syracuse	AHL	51	17	31	48	102	1	6	0	5	0	1	1	10
NHL Totals (2 years)		32	1	2	3	36	-8	0	0					

MCEACHERN, SHAWN RW BRUINS

PERSONAL: Born February 28, 1969, in Waltham, Mass. ... 5-11/200. ... Shoots left. ... Name pronounced muh-KEH-kuhrn.

TRANSACTIONS/CAREER NOTES: Selected by Pittsburgh Penguins in sixth round (sixth Penguins pick, 110th overall) of NHL draft (June 13, 1987). ... Traded by Penguins to Los Angeles Kings for D Marty McSorley (August 27, 1993). ... Traded by Kings to Penguins for D Marty McSorley and D Jim Paek (February 15, 1994). ... Suspended for first three games of 1994-95 season and fined $500 by NHL for slashing incident (September 21, 1994); suspension reduced to two games because of abbreviated 1994-95 season. ... Traded by Penguins with LW Kevin Stevens to Boston Bruins for C Bryan Smolinski and RW Glen Murray (August 2, 1995). ... Traded by Bruins to Ottawa Senators for RW Trent McCleary and third-round pick (LW Eric Naud) in 1996 draft (June 22, 1996). ... Fractured jaw (December 6, 1996); missed 17 games. ... Back spasms (February 7, 1998); missed one game. ... Injured wrist (April 3, 1999); missed one game. ... Injured groin (April 8, 1999); missed four games. ... Ill (February 1, 2000); missed one game. ... Bruised shoulder (February 26, 2000); missed four games. ... Fractured left thumb (March 25, 2000); missed final eight games of season. ... Injured groin (April 9, 2002); missed final two games of regular season. ... Traded by Senators with sixth-round pick (G Dan Turple) in 2004 draft to Atlanta Thrashers for D Brian Pothier (June 30, 2002). ... Injured groin (January 21, 2003: missed six games. ... Injured back (February 7, 2003); missed 30 games. ... Signed as a free agent by the Boston Bruins (Aug. 2, 2005).

STATISTICAL PLATEAUS: Three-goal games: 1997-98 (1), 2002-03 (1). Total: 2.

Season Team	League	REGULAR SEASON GP	G	A	Pts.	PIM	+/-	PP	SH	PLAYOFFS GP	G	A	Pts.	PIM
85-86—Matignon	Mass. H.S.	20	32	20	52	...	...	...	...	—	—	—	—	—
86-87—Matignon	Mass. H.S.	16	29	28	57	...	...	...	...	—	—	—	—	—
87-88—Matignon	Mass. H.S.	22	52	40	92	...	...	...	...	—	—	—	—	—
88-89—Boston University	Hockey East	36	20	28	48	32	...	...	...	—	—	—	—	—
89-90—Boston University	Hockey East	43	25	31	56	78	...	...	...	—	—	—	—	—
90-91—Boston University	Hockey East	41	34	48	82	43	...	...	...	—	—	—	—	—
91-92—U.S. national team	Int'l	57	26	23	49	38	...	...	...	—	—	—	—	—
—U.S. Olympic team	Int'l	8	1	0	1	10	...	...	...	—	—	—	—	—
—Pittsburgh	NHL	15	0	4	4	0	1	0	0	19	2	7	9	4
92-93—Pittsburgh	NHL	84	28	33	61	46	21	7	0	12	3	2	5	10
93-94—Los Angeles	NHL	49	8	13	21	24	1	0	3	—	—	—	—	—
—Pittsburgh	NHL	27	12	9	21	10	13	0	2	6	1	0	1	2
94-95—Kiekko-Espoo	Finland	8	1	3	4	6	-2	...	...	—	—	—	—	—
—Pittsburgh	NHL	44	13	13	26	22	4	1	2	11	0	2	2	8
95-96—Boston	NHL	82	24	29	53	34	-5	3	2	5	2	1	3	8
96-97—Ottawa	NHL	65	11	20	31	18	-5	0	1	7	2	0	2	8
97-98—Ottawa	NHL	81	24	24	48	42	1	8	2	11	0	4	4	8
98-99—Ottawa	NHL	77	31	25	56	46	8	7	0	4	2	0	2	6
99-00—Ottawa	NHL	69	29	22	51	24	2	10	0	6	0	3	3	4
00-01—Ottawa	NHL	82	32	40	72	62	10	9	0	4	0	2	2	2
01-02—Ottawa	NHL	80	15	31	46	52	9	5	0	12	0	4	4	2
02-03—Atlanta	NHL	46	10	16	26	28	-27	4	1	—	—	—	—	—
03-04—Atlanta	NHL	82	17	38	55	76	5	5	1	—	—	—	—	—
04-05—Malmo	Sweden	6	0	1	1	14	-4	0	0	10	1	1	2	12
NHL Totals (13 years)		803	254	317	571	484	38	59	14	97	12	25	37	62

MCGILLIS, DAN D DEVILS

PERSONAL: Born July 1, 1972, in Hawkesbury, Ont. ... 6-2/230. ... Shoots left.

TRANSACTIONS/CAREER NOTES: Selected by Detroit Red Wings in 10th round (10th Red Wings pick, 238th overall) of entry draft (June 20, 1992). ... Signed as free agent by Edmonton Oilers (September 6, 1996). ... Traded by Oilers with 2nd-round pick (D Jason Beckett) in 1998 entry draft to Philadelphia Flyers for D Janne Niinimaa (March 24, 1998). ... Neck spasms (February 21, 1999); missed two games. ... Injured left knee (March 30, 1999); missed one game. ... Fractured right foot (November 28, 1999); missed four games. ... Strained groin (February 22, 2000); missed 10 games. ... Strained groin (November 3, 2001); missed one game. ... Strained lower back (January 19, 2002); missed six games. ... Traded by Flyers to San Jose Sharks for D Marcus Ragnarsson (December 6, 2002). ... Concussion (January 25, 2003); missed four games. ... Concussion (March 9, 2003); missed one game. ... Traded by Sharks to Boston Bruins for 2nd-round pick (later traded to New York Rangers; Rangers selected D Ivan Baranka) in 2003 entry draft (March 11, 2003). ... Injured hip (February 3, 2004); missed two games. ... Signed as free agent by New Jersey Devils (Aug. 4, 2005).

Season Team	League	REGULAR SEASON GP	G	A	Pts.	PIM	+/-	PP	SH	PLAYOFFS GP	G	A	Pts.	PIM
91-92—Hawkesbury	Tier II Jr. A	36	5	19	24	106	...	...	...	—	—	—	—	—
92-93—Northeastern Univ.	Hockey East	35	5	12	17	42	...	...	...	—	—	—	—	—
93-94—Northeastern Univ.	Hockey East	38	4	25	29	82	...	...	...	—	—	—	—	—
94-95—Northeastern Univ.	Hockey East	34	9	22	31	70	...	6	...	—	—	—	—	—
95-96—Northeastern Univ.	Hockey East	34	12	24	36	50	...	...	...	—	—	—	—	—
96-97—Edmonton	NHL	73	6	16	22	52	2	2	1	12	0	5	5	24
97-98—Edmonton	NHL	67	10	15	25	74	-17	5	0	—	—	—	—	—
—Philadelphia	NHL	13	1	5	6	35	-4	1	0	5	1	2	3	10
98-99—Philadelphia	NHL	78	8	37	45	61	16	6	0	6	0	1	1	12
99-00—Philadelphia	NHL	68	4	14	18	55	16	3	0	18	2	6	8	12
00-01—Philadelphia	NHL	82	14	35	49	86	13	4	0	6	1	0	1	6
01-02—Philadelphia	NHL	75	5	14	19	46	17	2	0	5	1	0	1	8

Season Team	League	GP	G	A	Pts.	PIM	+/-	PP	SH	GP	G	A	Pts.	PIM
		REGULAR SEASON								PLAYOFFS				
02-03—Philadelphia	NHL	24	0	3	3	20	7	0	0	—	—	—	—	—
—San Jose	NHL	37	3	13	16	30	-6	2	0	—	—	—	—	—
—Boston	NHL	10	0	1	1	10	2	0	0	5	3	0	3	2
03-04—Boston	NHL	80	5	23	28	65	-1	1	0	7	0	0	0	2
NHL Totals (8 years)		607	56	176	232	534	45	26	1	64	8	14	22	76

MCKEE, JAY — D — SABRES

PERSONAL: Born September 8, 1977, in Kingston, Ont. ... 6-3/199. ... Shoots left.

TRANSACTIONS/CAREER NOTES: Selected by Buffalo Sabres in first round (first Sabres pick, 14th overall) of NHL entry draft (July 8, 1995). ... Bruised stomach (March 29, 1998); missed two games. ... Bruised hand (October 30, 1998); missed one game. ... Bruised foot (February 13, 1999); missed six games. ... Had the flu (March 13, 1999); missed two games. ... Injured (November 25, 2000); missed five games. ... Injured hand (March 16, 2001); missed three games. ... Had the flu (January 23, 2002); missed one game. ... Injured knee (November 30, 2002); missed one game. ... Injured leg (December 21, 2002); missed one game. ... Had the flu (December 31, 2002); missed one game. ... Injured knee (February 15, 2003); missed 20 games. ... Injured knee (November 20, 2003); missed 13 games. ... Reinjured knee (January 9, 2004); missed six games. ... Reinjured knee (January 24, 2004); missed 18 games.

Season Team	League	GP	G	A	Pts.	PIM	+/-	PP	SH	GP	G	A	Pts.	PIM
		REGULAR SEASON								PLAYOFFS				
92-93—Ernestown	Jr. C	36	0	17	17	37	...	...	...	—	—	—	—	—
93-94—Sudbury	OHL	51	0	1	1	51	...	...	...	3	0	0	0	0
94-95—Sudbury	OHL	39	6	6	12	91	...	0	0	—	—	—	—	—
—Niagara Falls	OHL	26	3	13	16	60	...	2	0	6	2	3	5	10
95-96—Niagara Falls	OHL	64	5	41	46	129	...	...	...	10	1	5	6	16
—Rochester	AHL	4	0	1	1	15	...	...	...	—	—	—	—	—
—Buffalo	NHL	1	0	1	1	2	1	0	0	—	—	—	—	—
96-97—Buffalo	NHL	43	1	9	10	35	3	0	0	3	0	0	0	0
—Rochester	AHL	7	2	5	7	4	0	1	0	—	—	—	—	—
97-98—Buffalo	NHL	56	1	13	14	42	-1	0	0	1	0	0	0	0
—Rochester	AHL	13	1	7	8	11	6	0	0	—	—	—	—	—
98-99—Buffalo	NHL	72	0	6	6	75	20	0	0	21	0	3	3	24
99-00—Buffalo	NHL	78	5	12	17	50	5	1	0	1	0	0	0	0
00-01—Buffalo	NHL	74	1	10	11	76	9	0	0	8	1	0	1	6
01-02—Buffalo	NHL	81	2	11	13	43	18	0	0	—	—	—	—	—
02-03—Buffalo	NHL	59	0	5	5	49	-16	0	0	—	—	—	—	—
03-04—Buffalo	NHL	43	2	3	5	41	6	0	0	—	—	—	—	—
NHL Totals (9 years)		507	12	70	82	413	45	1	0	34	1	3	4	30

MCKENNA, STEVE — LW

PERSONAL: Born August 21, 1973, in Toronto. ... 6-8/252. ... Shoots left.

TRANSACTIONS/CAREER NOTES: Signed as free agent by Los Angeles Kings (May 17, 1996). ... Strained abdominal muscle (November 9, 1998); missed 14 games. ... Reinjured abdominal muscle (December 9, 1998); missed 42 games. ... Cut eye (October 4, 1999); missed six games. ... Selected by Minnesota Wild in expansion draft (June 23, 2000). ... Had back spasms (September 8, 2000); missed 12 games. ... Traded by Wild to Pittsburgh Penguins for C Roman Simicek (January 13, 2001). ... Signed as free agent by New York Rangers (August 28, 2001). ... Signed as free agent by Penguins (July 12, 2002). ... Had elbow infection (December 10, 2002); missed one game. ... Flu (February 4, 2003); missed one game. ... Injured eye (October 5, 2003); missed four games. ... Tore chest muscle (February 10, 2004); missed final 27 games of season.

Season Team	League	GP	G	A	Pts.	PIM	+/-	PP	SH	GP	G	A	Pts.	PIM
		REGULAR SEASON								PLAYOFFS				
93-94—Merrimack	Hockey East	37	1	2	3	74	...	...	...	—	—	—	—	—
94-95—Merrimack	Hockey East	37	1	9	10	74	...	...	...	—	—	—	—	—
95-96—Merrimack	Hockey East	33	3	11	14	67	...	...	...	—	—	—	—	—
96-97—Phoenix	IHL	66	6	5	11	187	...	...	...	—	—	—	—	—
—Los Angeles	NHL	9	0	0	0	37	1	0	0	—	—	—	—	—
97-98—Fredericton	AHL	6	2	1	3	48	-2	1	0	—	—	—	—	—
—Los Angeles	NHL	62	4	4	8	150	-9	1	0	3	0	1	1	8
98-99—Los Angeles	NHL	20	1	0	1	36	-3	0	0	—	—	—	—	—
99-00—Los Angeles	NHL	46	0	5	5	125	3	0	0	—	—	—	—	—
00-01—Minnesota	NHL	20	1	1	2	19	0	0	0	—	—	—	—	—
—Pittsburgh	NHL	34	0	0	0	100	-4	0	0	—	—	—	—	—
01-02—New York Rangers	NHL	54	2	1	3	144	0	1	0	—	—	—	—	—
—Hartford	AHL	3	0	0	0	11	-2	0	0	—	—	—	—	—
02-03—Pittsburgh	NHL	79	9	1	10	128	-18	5	0	—	—	—	—	—
03-04—Pittsburgh	NHL	49	1	2	3	85	-10	0	0	—	—	—	—	—
04-05—Nottingham	England	41	6	12	18	26	...	...	...	—	—	—	—	—
NHL Totals (8 years)		373	18	14	32	824	-40	7	0	3	0	1	1	8

MCKENZIE, JIM — LW/RW

PERSONAL: Born November 3, 1969, in Gull Lake, Sask. ... 6-4/230. ... Shoots left.

TRANSACTIONS/CAREER NOTES: Selected by Hartford Whalers in 4th round (3rd Whalers pick, 73rd overall) of entry draft (June 17, 1989). ... Injured elbow (January 31, 1992); missed two games. ... Injured hip flexor (November 11, 1992); missed three games. ... Injured hip flexor (December 5, 1992); missed four games. ... Back spasms (January 24, 1993); missed three games. ... Suspended two games for game misconduct penalties (April 3, 1993). ... Suspended three games for game misconduct penalties (April 10, 1993). ... Traded by Whalers to Florida Panthers for D Alexander Godynyuk (December 16, 1993). ... Traded by Panthers to Dallas Stars for 4th-round pick (LW Jamie Wright) in 1994 draft (December 16, 1993). ... Traded by Stars to Pittsburgh Penguins for RW Mike Needham (March 21, 1994). ... Fractured toe (November

M

24, 1993); missed four games. ... Bruised hand (March 11, 1995); missed one game. ... Sprained wrist (April 5, 1995); missed seven games. ... Signed as free agent by New York Islanders (July 31, 1995). ... Claimed by Winnipeg Jets in waiver draft (October 2, 1995). ... Jets franchise moved to Phoenix and renamed Coyotes for 1996-97 season; NHL approved move on January 18, 1996. ... Fractured leg (November 8, 1996); missed five games. ... Flu (January 27, 1997); missed one game. ... Fractured leg (December 23, 1997); missed 11 games. ... Traded by Coyotes to Mighty Ducks of Anaheim for C J.F. Jomphe (June 18, 1998). ... Cut below right eye (January 10, 1999); missed five games. ... Injured ankle (February 3, 1999); missed two games. ... Suspended four games for fighting incident (October 5, 1999). ... Fractured right hand (November 9, 1999); missed 10 games. ... Claimed off waivers by Washington Capitals (January 18, 2000). ... Signed as free agent by New Jersey Devils (July 3, 2000). ... Flu (March 20, 2002); missed one game. ... Bruised foot (February 11, 2003) missed one game. ... Signed as free agent by Nashville Predators (July 22, 2003). ... Injured knee (October 3, 2003); missed 10 games. ... Bruised throat (January 25, 2004); missed four games. ... Reinjured throat (February 13, 2004); missed two games.

STATISTICAL PLATEAUS: Three-goal games: 1996-97 (1).

		REGULAR SEASON								PLAYOFFS				
Season Team	League	GP	G	A	Pts.	PIM	+/-	PP	SH	GP	G	A	Pts.	PIM
85-86—Moose Jaw	WHL	3	0	2	2	0	...	...	...	—	—	—	—	—
86-87—Moose Jaw	WHL	65	5	3	8	125	...	...	...	9	0	0	0	7
87-88—Moose Jaw	WHL	62	1	17	18	134	...	...	...	—	—	—	—	—
88-89—Victoria	WHL	67	15	27	42	176	...	...	...	8	1	4	5	30
89-90—Binghamton	AHL	56	4	12	16	149	...	...	...	—	—	—	—	—
—Hartford	NHL	5	0	0	0	4	0	0	0	—	—	—	—	—
90-91—Springfield	AHL	24	3	4	7	102	...	...	...	—	—	—	—	—
—Hartford	NHL	41	4	3	7	108	-7	0	0	6	0	0	0	8
91-92—Hartford	NHL	67	5	1	6	87	-6	0	0	—	—	—	—	—
92-93—Hartford	NHL	64	3	6	9	202	-10	0	0	—	—	—	—	—
93-94—Hartford	NHL	26	1	2	3	67	-6	0	0	—	—	—	—	—
—Dallas	NHL	34	2	3	5	63	4	0	0	—	—	—	—	—
—Pittsburgh	NHL	11	0	0	0	16	-5	0	0	3	0	0	0	0
94-95—Pittsburgh	NHL	39	2	1	3	63	-7	0	0	5	0	0	0	4
95-96—Winnipeg	NHL	73	4	2	6	202	-4	0	0	1	0	0	0	2
96-97—Phoenix	NHL	65	5	3	8	200	-5	0	0	7	0	0	0	2
97-98—Phoenix	NHL	64	3	4	7	146	-7	0	0	1	0	0	0	0
98-99—Anaheim	NHL	73	5	4	9	99	-18	1	0	4	0	0	0	4
99-00—Anaheim	NHL	31	3	3	6	48	-5	0	0	—	—	—	—	—
—Washington	NHL	30	1	2	3	16	0	0	0	1	0	0	0	0
00-01—New Jersey	NHL	53	2	2	4	119	0	0	0	3	0	0	0	2
01-02—New Jersey	NHL	67	3	5	8	123	0	1	0	6	0	0	0	2
02-03—New Jersey	NHL	76	4	8	12	88	3	0	0	13	0	0	0	14
03-04—Nashville	NHL	61	1	3	4	88	-13	0	0	1	0	0	0	0
NHL Totals (15 years)		880	48	52	100	1739	-86	2	0	51	0	0	0	38

MCLAREN, KYLE D SHARKS

PERSONAL: Born June 18, 1977, in Humboldt, Sask. ... 6-4/225. ... Shoots left.

TRANSACTIONS/CAREER NOTES: Selected by Boston Bruins in first round (first Bruins pick, ninth overall) of NHL entry draft (July 8, 1995). ... Injured back (November 21, 1995); missed one game. ... Injured knee (November 25, 1995); missed five games. ... Had the flu (January 3, 1996); missed one game. ... Suffered concussion (March 10, 1996); missed one game. ... Had charley horse (October 26, 1996); missed two games. ... Strained shoulder (February 2, 1997); missed 13 games. ... Injured foot (March 15, 1997); missed one game. ... Sprained thumb (March 27, 1997); missed remainder of season. ... Had hip pointer (November 1, 1997); missed five games. ... Injured knee (December 17, 1997); missed one game. ... Fractured foot (March 19, 1998); missed seven games. ... Strained groin (April 7, 1998); missed three games. ... Missed first 15 games of 1998-99 season in contract dispute. ... Separated shoulder (January 15, 1999); missed 14 games. ... Injured foot (April 10, 1999); missed one game. ... Strained thumb (November 18, 1999); missed seven games. ... Tore knee cartilage (April 1, 2000); missed final four games of season. ... Injured knee (October 20, 2000); missed 24 games. ... Sprained chest muscle (October 8, 2001); missed 12 games. ... Bruised right knee (November 17, 2001); missed one game. ... Tore right wrist ligament (December 22, 2001) and had surgery; missed 31 games. ... Suspended three playoff games by NHL for elbowing incident (April 26, 2002). ... Traded by Bruins with fourth-round pick (C Torrey Mitchell) in 2004 entry draft to San Jose Sharks as part of three-team trade in which Bruins acquired G Jeff Hackett and D Jeff Jillson and Montreal Canadiens acquired LW Niklas Sundstrom and third-round pick in 2004 draft (January 23, 2003); Canadiens later traded third-round pick to Los Angeles Kings (selected D Paul Baier). ... Injured foot (November 11, 2003); missed one game. ... Injured knee (November 26, 2003); missed two games. ... Injured knee (December 11, 2003); missed two games. ... Injured ribs (January 3, 2004); missed seven games. ... Had severe facial cuts (February 27, 2004); missed six games. ... Injured upper body (May 12, 2004); missed one playoff game.

		REGULAR SEASON								PLAYOFFS				
Season Team	League	GP	G	A	Pts.	PIM	+/-	PP	SH	GP	G	A	Pts.	PIM
93-94—Tacoma	WHL	62	1	9	10	53	...	...	...	6	1	4	5	6
94-95—Tacoma	WHL	47	13	19	32	68	29	5	0	4	1	1	2	4
95-96—Boston	NHL	74	5	12	17	73	16	0	0	5	0	0	0	14
96-97—Boston	NHL	58	5	9	14	54	-9	0	0	—	—	—	—	—
97-98—Boston	NHL	66	5	20	25	56	13	2	0	6	1	0	1	4
98-99—Boston	NHL	52	6	18	24	48	1	3	0	12	0	3	3	10
99-00—Boston	NHL	71	8	11	19	67	-4	2	0	—	—	—	—	—
00-01—Boston	NHL	58	5	12	17	53	-5	2	0	—	—	—	—	—
01-02—Boston	NHL	38	0	8	8	19	-4	0	0	4	0	0	0	20
02-03—San Jose	NHL	33	0	8	8	30	-10	0	0	—	—	—	—	—
03-04—San Jose	NHL	64	2	22	24	60	10	0	1	16	0	3	3	10
NHL Totals (9 years)		514	36	120	156	460	8	9	1	43	1	6	7	58

MCLAREN, STEVE LW LIGHTNING

PERSONAL: Born February 3, 1975, in Owen Sound, Ont. ... 6-0/225. ... Shoots left.

TRANSACTIONS/CAREER NOTES: Selected by Chicago Blackhawks in fourth round (third Blackhawks pick, 85th overall) of NHL draft (June 29, 1994). ... Signed as free agent by Philadelphia Flyers (August 17, 1998). ... Signed as free agent by St. Louis Blues (July 1, 2001). ...

Bruised head (December 30, 2003); missed 28 games. ... Signed as free agent by Tampa Bay Lightning (July 28, 2004). ... Signed as free agent by Springfield of the AHL (September 27, 2004).

		REGULAR SEASON								PLAYOFFS				
Season Team	**League**	**GP**	**G**	**A**	**Pts.**	**PIM**	**+/-**	**PP**	**SH**	**GP**	**G**	**A**	**Pts.**	**PIM**
93-94—North Bay	OHL	55	2	15	17	130	...	0	...	18	0	3	3	50
94-95—North Bay	OHL	27	3	10	13	119	...	2	0	6	2	1	3	23
95-96—Indianapolis	IHL	54	1	2	3	170	...	...	...	3	0	0	0	2
96-97—Indianapolis	IHL	63	2	5	7	309	...	...	...	4	0	0	0	10
97-98—Indianapolis	IHL	61	3	5	8	208	-14	0	0	5	0	0	0	24
98-99—Philadelphia	AHL	52	4	3	7	216	3	0	0	7	0	0	0	2
99-00—Philadelphia	AHL	64	1	2	3	247	...	...	...	—	—	—	—	—
00-01—Philadelphia	AHL	48	3	1	4	177	...	...	...	8	0	0	0	38
01-02—Worcester	AHL	58	0	4	4	251	0	0	0	1	0	0	0	2
02-03—Worcester	AHL	40	0	0	0	80	-8	0	0	3	0	0	0	4
03-04—Worcester	AHL	35	2	1	3	146	-8	0	0	6	0	0	0	2
—St. Louis	NHL	6	0	0	0	25	0	0	0	—	—	—	—	—
04-05—Springfield	AHL	26	1	0	1	78	-3	0	0	—	—	—	—	—
NHL Totals (1 year)		6	0	0	0	25	0	0	0					

MCLEAN, BRETT — C — AVALANCHE

PERSONAL: Born August 14, 1978, in Comox, B.C. ... 5-11/185. ... Shoots left.

TRANSACTIONS/CAREER NOTES: Selected by Dallas Stars in 9th round (9th Stars pick, 242nd overall) of entry draft (June 21, 1997). ... Signed as free agent by Calgary Flames (September 1, 1999). ... Signed as free agent by Minnesota Wild (July 13, 2000). ... Signed as free agent by Chicago Blackhawks (July 23, 2002). ... Concussion (February 29, 2004); missed three games. ... Signed as free agent by Colorado Avalanche (July 21, 2004).

		REGULAR SEASON								PLAYOFFS				
Season Team	**League**	**GP**	**G**	**A**	**Pts.**	**PIM**	**+/-**	**PP**	**SH**	**GP**	**G**	**A**	**Pts.**	**PIM**
94-95—Tacoma	WHL	67	11	23	34	33	...	...	...	4	0	1	1	0
95-96—Kelowna	WHL	71	37	42	79	60	...	...	...	6	2	2	4	6
96-97—Kelowna	WHL	72	44	60	104	96	...	...	...	4	4	2	6	12
97-98—Kelowna	WHL	54	42	46	88	91	25	10	6	7	4	5	9	17
98-99—Kelowna	WHL	44	32	38	70	46	...	...	...	—	—	—	—	—
—Brandon	WHL	21	15	16	31	20	...	...	...	5	1	6	7	8
—Cincinnati	AHL	7	0	3	3	6	-3	0	0	—	—	—	—	—
99-00—Saint John	AHL	72	15	23	38	115	...	...	...	3	0	1	1	2
—Johnstown	ECHL	8	4	7	11	6	...	...	...	—	—	—	—	—
00-01—Cleveland	IHL	74	20	24	44	54	...	...	...	4	0	0	0	18
01-02—Houston	AHL	78	24	21	45	71	-19	10	0	14	1	6	7	12
02-03—Chicago	NHL	2	0	0	0	0	-1	0	0	—	—	—	—	—
—Norfolk	AHL	77	23	38	61	60	14	4	3	9	2	6	8	9
03-04—Norfolk	AHL	4	3	3	6	6	-2	2	0	—	—	—	—	—
—Chicago	NHL	76	11	20	31	54	-11	5	1	—	—	—	—	—
04-05—Malmo	Sweden	38	7	6	13	102	0	1	0	9	1	1	2	16
NHL Totals (2 years)		78	11	20	31	54	-12	5	1					

MCLENNAN, JAMIE — G — PANTHERS

PERSONAL: Born June 30, 1971, in Edmonton. ... 6-0/190. ... Catches left.

TRANSACTIONS/CAREER NOTES: Selected by New York Islanders in third round (third Islanders pick, 48th overall) of NHL draft (June 22, 1991). ... Signed as free agent by St. Louis Blues (July 3, 1996). ... Strained groin (October 29, 1997); missed two games. ... Strained groin (March 22, 1998); missed one game. ... Strained hip flexor (January 19, 1999); missed one game. ... Had the flu (March 11, 1999); missed two games. ... Selected by Minnesota Wild in expansion draft (June 23, 2000). ... Bruised forearm (November 11, 2000); missed one game. ... Ill (March 5, 2001); missed four games. ... Traded by Wild to Calgary Flames for ninth-round pick (F Mika Hannula) in 2002 draft (June 22, 2002). ... Injured back (November 29, 2002); missed two games. ... Fractured sternum (February 26, 2004); missed eight games. ... Traded by Flames with C Blair Betts and RW Greg Moore to New York Rangers for LW Chris Simon and seventh-round pick (C Matt Schneider) in 2004 draft (March 6, 2004). ... Signed as free agent by Florida Panthers (July 2, 2004).

		REGULAR SEASON									PLAYOFFS							
Season Team	**League**	**GP**	**Min.**	**W**	**L**	**T**	**GA**	**SO**	**GAA**	**SV%**	**GP**	**Min.**	**W**	**L**	**GA**	**SO**	**GAA**	**SV%**
88-89—Spokane	WHL	11	578	...	...	...	63	0	6.54	...	—	—	—	—	—	—	—	—
—Lethbridge	WHL	7	368	...	...	...	22	0	3.59	...	—	—	—	—	—	—	—	—
89-90—Lethbridge	WHL	34	1690	20	4	2	110	1	3.91	...	13	677	6	5	44	0	3.90	...
90-91—Lethbridge	WHL	56	3230	32	18	4	205	0	3.81	...	*16	*970	8	8	*56	0	3.46	...
91-92—Capital District	AHL	18	952	4	10	2	60	1	3.78	...	—	—	—	—	—	—	—	—
—Richmond	ECHL	32	1837	16	12	2	114	0	3.72	...	—	—	—	—	—	—	—	—
92-93—Capital District	AHL	38	2171	17	14	6	117	1	3.23	.893	1	20	0	1	5	0	15.00	.583
93-94—Salt Lake City	IHL	24	1320	8	12	2	80	0	3.64	.889	—	—	—	—	—	—	—	—
—New York Islanders	NHL	22	1287	8	7	6	61	0	2.84	.905	2	82	0	1	6	0	4.39	.872
94-95—New York Islanders	NHL	21	1185	6	11	2	67	0	3.39	.876	—	—	—	—	—	—	—	—
—Denver	IHL	4	240	3	0	1	12	0	3.00	.906	11	641	8	2	23	1	*2.15	.929
95-96—Utah	IHL	14	728	9	2	2	29	0	2.39	...	—	—	—	—	—	—	—	—
—New York Islanders	NHL	13	636	3	9	1	39	0	3.68	.886	—	—	—	—	—	—	—	—
—Worcester	AHL	22	1215	14	7	1	57	0	2.81	...	2	118	0	2	8	0	4.07	...
96-97—Worcester	AHL	39	2152	18	13	4	100	2	2.79	.903	4	262	2	2	16	0	3.66	.894
97-98—St. Louis	NHL	30	1658	16	8	2	60	2	2.17	.903	1	14	0	0	1	0	4.29	.750
98-99—St. Louis	NHL	33	1763	13	14	4	70	3	2.38	.891	1	37	0	1	0	0	0.00	1.00
99-00—St. Louis	NHL	19	1009	9	5	2	33	2	1.96	.903	—	—	—	—	—	—	—	—

Season Team	League	REGULAR SEASON GP	Min.	W	L	T	GA	SO	GAA	SV%	PLAYOFFS GP	Min.	W	L	GA	SO	GAA	SV%
00-01—Minnesota	NHL	38	2230	5	23	9	98	2	2.64	.905	—	—	—	—	—	—	—	—
01-02—Houston	AHL	51	2851	25	18	4	130	3	2.74	.895	14	879	8	6	31	2	2.12	.929
02-03—Calgary	NHL	22	1165	2	11	4	58	0	2.99	.892	—	—	—	—	—	—	—	—
03-04—Calgary	NHL	26	1446	12	9	3	53	4	2.20	.910	—	—	—	—	—	—	—	—
—New York Rangers	NHL	4	244	1	3	0	12	0	2.95	.876	—	—	—	—	—	—	—	—
04-05—Guildford	England	3	185	2	1	0	8	0	2.59	.927	7	385	4	3	13	0	2.02	.932
NHL Totals (9 years)		228	12623	75	100	33	551	13	2.62	.897	4	133	0	2	7	0	3.16	.879

MCNEILL, GRANT — D — PANTHERS

PERSONAL: Born June 8, 1983, in Vermillion, Alta. ... 6-2/214. ... Shoots left.
TRANSACTIONS/CAREER NOTES: Selected by Florida Panthers in third round (fifth Panthers pick, 68th overall) of NHL entry draft (June 23, 2001).

Season Team	League	REGULAR SEASON GP	G	A	Pts.	PIM	+/-	PP	SH	PLAYOFFS GP	G	A	Pts.	PIM
99-00—Prince Albert	WHL	58	1	1	2	43	...	...	...	6	0	1	1	0
00-01—Prince Albert	WHL	61	2	6	8	280	...	...	...	—	—	—	—	—
01-02—Prince Albert	WHL	70	7	6	13	*326	...	...	...	—	—	—	—	—
02-03—Prince Albert	WHL	71	1	8	9	280	...	...	...	—	—	—	—	—
03-04—Florida	NHL	3	0	0	0	5	0	0	0	—	—	—	—	—
—San Antonio	AHL	34	0	0	0	110	-1	0	0	—	—	—	—	—
04-05—San Antonio	AHL	40	0	2	2	231	-15	0	0	—	—	—	—	—
—Texas	ECHL	24	0	3	3	111	-21	0	...	—	—	—	—	—
NHL Totals (1 year)		3	0	0	0	5	0	0	0					

MELICHAR, JOSEF — D — PENGUINS

PERSONAL: Born January 20, 1979, in Ceske Budejovice, Czechoslovakia. ... 6-2/222. ... Shoots left. ... Name pronounced YOU-sehf mehl-ee-KHAHR.
TRANSACTIONS/CAREER NOTES: Selected by Pittsburgh Penguins in third round (third Penguins pick, 71st overall) of NHL draft (June 21, 1997). ... Bruised hip (December 6, 2001); missed one game. ... Dislocated shoulder (February 12, 2002); missed 15 games. ... Reinjured shoulder (April 4, 2002); missed remainder of season. ... Reinjured should (October 14, 2002); missed nine games. ... Reinjured shoulder (November 20, 2003); missed final 65 games of season.

Season Team	League	REGULAR SEASON GP	G	A	Pts.	PIM	+/-	PP	SH	PLAYOFFS GP	G	A	Pts.	PIM
95-96—HC Ceske Budejovice..	Czech. Jrs.	38	3	4	7	...	...	...	...	—	—	—	—	—
96-97—HC Ceske Budejovice..	Czech. Jrs.	41	2	3	5	10	...	...	...	—	—	—	—	—
97-98—Tri-City	WHL	67	9	24	33	152	-42	5	0	—	—	—	—	—
98-99—Tri-City	WHL	65	8	28	36	125	30	4	0	11	1	0	1	15
99-00—Wilkes-Barre/Scranton	AHL	80	3	9	12	126	...	...	...	—	—	—	—	—
00-01—Wilkes-Barre/Scranton	AHL	46	2	5	7	69	...	...	...	21	0	5	5	6
—Pittsburgh	NHL	18	0	2	2	21	-5	0	0	—	—	—	—	—
01-02—Pittsburgh	NHL	60	0	3	3	68	-1	0	0	—	—	—	—	—
02-03—Pittsburgh	NHL	8	0	0	0	2	-2	0	0	—	—	—	—	—
03-04—Pittsburgh	NHL	82	3	5	8	62	-17	0	0	—	—	—	—	—
04-05—Sparta Praha	Czech Rep.	13	0	4	4	8	4	...	...	5	0	0	0	6
NHL Totals (4 years)		168	3	10	13	153	-25	0	0					

MELLANBY, SCOTT — RW — THRASHERS

PERSONAL: Born June 11, 1966, in Montreal. ... 6-1/208. ... Shoots right.
TRANSACTIONS/CAREER NOTES: Selected by Philadelphia Flyers in second round (first Flyers pick, 27th overall) of NHL entry draft (June 9, 1984). ... Cut right index finger (October 1987). ... Severed nerve and damaged tendon in left forearm (August 1989); missed first 20 games of season. ... Had virus (November 1989). ... Traded by Flyers with LW Craig Berube and C Craig Fisher to Edmonton Oilers for RW Dave Brown, D Corey Foster and rights to RW Jari Kurri (May 30, 1991). ... Injured shoulder (February 14, 1993); missed 15 games. ... Selected by Florida Panthers in NHL expansion draft (June 24, 1993). ... Fractured nose and cut face (February 1, 1994); missed four games. ... Fractured finger (March 7, 1996); missed three games. ... Sprained left knee (January 9, 1998); missed three games. ... Strained groin (September 29, 1998); missed first nine games of season. ... Injured neck (January 16, 1999); missed one game. ... Reinjured neck (January 21, 1999); missed three games. ... Suspended one game by NHL for cross-checking incident (March 21, 1999). ... Suffered slight concussion (April 5, 1999); missed one game. ... Suffered concussion (October 12, 1999); missed three games. ... Had the flu (March 3, 2000); missed one game. ... Strained neck (October 28, 2000). ... Strained back (November 13, 2000); missed 12 games. ... Traded by Panthers to St. Louis Blues for RW David Morisset and fifth-round pick (C Vince Bellissimo) in 2002 entry draft (February 9, 2001). ... Fractured jaw (September 28, 2001); missed first 12 games of season. ... Had the flu (December 10, 2002); missed one game. ... Injured ribs (October 9, 2003); missed seven games. ... Suffered concussion (October 29, 2003); missed four games. ... Had the flu (February 20, 2004); missed one game. ... Signed as free agent by Atlanta Thrashers (July 26, 2004).
STATISTICAL PLATEAUS: Four-goal games: 2002-03 (1).

Season Team	League	REGULAR SEASON GP	G	A	Pts.	PIM	+/-	PP	SH	PLAYOFFS GP	G	A	Pts.	PIM
83-84—Henry Carr H.S.	MTHL	39	37	37	74	97	...	...	...	—	—	—	—	—
84-85—Wisconsin	WCHA	40	14	24	38	60	...	...	...	—	—	—	—	—
85-86—Wisconsin	WCHA	32	21	23	44	89	...	...	...	—	—	—	—	—
—Philadelphia	NHL	2	0	0	0	0	-1	0	0	—	—	—	—	—
86-87—Philadelphia	NHL	71	11	21	32	94	8	1	0	24	5	5	10	46
87-88—Philadelphia	NHL	75	25	26	51	185	-7	7	0	7	0	1	1	16
88-89—Philadelphia	NHL	76	21	29	50	183	-13	11	0	19	4	5	9	28

Season Team	League	GP	G	A	Pts.	PIM	+/-	PP	SH	GP	G	A	Pts.	PIM
		REGULAR SEASON								PLAYOFFS				
89-90—Philadelphia	NHL	57	6	17	23	77	-4	0	0	—	—	—	—	—
90-91—Philadelphia	NHL	74	20	21	41	155	8	5	0	—	—	—	—	—
91-92—Edmonton	NHL	80	23	27	50	197	5	7	0	16	2	1	3	29
92-93—Edmonton	NHL	69	15	17	32	147	-4	6	0	—	—	—	—	—
93-94—Florida	NHL	80	30	30	60	149	0	17	0	—	—	—	—	—
94-95—Florida	NHL	48	13	12	25	90	-16	4	0	—	—	—	—	—
95-96—Florida	NHL	79	32	38	70	160	4	19	0	22	3	6	9	44
96-97—Florida	NHL	82	27	29	56	170	7	9	1	5	0	2	2	4
97-98—Florida	NHL	79	15	24	39	127	-14	6	0	—	—	—	—	—
98-99—Florida	NHL	67	18	27	45	85	5	4	0	—	—	—	—	—
99-00—Florida	NHL	77	18	28	46	126	14	6	0	4	0	1	1	2
00-01—Florida	NHL	40	4	9	13	46	-13	1	0	—	—	—	—	—
—St. Louis	NHL	23	7	1	8	25	0	2	0	15	3	3	6	17
01-02—St. Louis	NHL	64	15	26	41	93	-5	8	0	10	7	3	10	18
02-03—St. Louis	NHL	80	26	31	57	176	1	13	0	6	0	1	1	10
03-04—St. Louis	NHL	68	14	17	31	76	-7	6	0	4	0	1	1	2
NHL Totals (19 years)		1291	340	430	770	2361	-32	132	1	132	24	29	53	216

MELOCHE, ERIC — RW — FLYERS

PERSONAL: Born May 1, 1976, in Montreal. ... 5-10/197. ... Shoots right.

TRANSACTIONS/CAREER NOTES: Selected by Pittsburgh Penguins in seventh round (seventh Penguins pick, 186th overall) of NHL draft (June 22, 1996). ... Signed as free agent by Philadelphia Flyers (July 14, 2004).

Season Team	League	GP	G	A	Pts.	PIM	+/-	PP	SH	GP	G	A	Pts.	PIM
		REGULAR SEASON								PLAYOFFS				
95-96—Cornwall	Tier II	64	68	53	121	162	...	...	...	—	—	—	—	—
96-97—Ohio State	CCHA	39	12	11	23	78	...	...	...	—	—	—	—	—
97-98—Ohio State	CCHA	42	26	22	48	86	...	...	...	—	—	—	—	—
98-99—Ohio State	CCHA	35	11	16	27	87	...	...	...	—	—	—	—	—
99-00—Ohio State	CCHA	35	20	11	31	*136	...	...	...	—	—	—	—	—
00-01—Wilkes-Barre/Scranton	AHL	79	20	20	40	72	...	...	...	21	6	10	16	17
01-02—Wilkes-Barre/Scranton	AHL	55	13	14	27	91	-4	4	1	—	—	—	—	—
—Pittsburgh	NHL	23	0	1	1	8	-7	0	0	—	—	—	—	—
02-03—Pittsburgh	NHL	13	5	1	6	4	-2	2	0	—	—	—	—	—
—Wilkes-Barre/Scranton	AHL	59	12	17	29	95	0	2	2	6	1	0	1	20
03-04—Pittsburgh	NHL	25	3	7	10	20	-6	0	0	—	—	—	—	—
—Wilkes-Barre/Scranton	AHL	56	16	26	42	49	6	4	0	23	9	6	15	14
04-05—Philadelphia	AHL	63	6	11	17	102	-1	1	1	17	3	2	5	18
NHL Totals (3 years)		61	8	9	17	32	-15	2	0					

MESSIER, ERIC — LW/RW

PERSONAL: Born October 29, 1973, in Drummondville, Que. ... 6-2/195. ... Shoots left. ... Name pronounced MEHZ-yay.

TRANSACTIONS/CAREER NOTES: Signed as free agent by Colorado Avalanche (June 14, 1995). ... Sprained ankle (October 28, 1997); missed three games. ... Fractured left elbow (October 10, 1998); missed 27 games. ... Injured eye (December 19, 1998); missed two games. ... Suffered injury (November 26, 1999); missed one game. ... Fractured lower leg (February 19, 2001); missed 17 games. ... Injured knee (January 15, 2002); missed eight games. ... Injured elbow (March 23, 2003); missed three games. ... Traded by Avalanche to Florida Panthers with C Vaclav Nedorost for W Peter Worrell and 2nd-round pick (traded to New York Rangers; traded to Florida; Panthers selected G David Shantz) in 2004 draft (July 20, 2003). ... Injured wrist (November 22, 2003); missed final 61 games of season.

Season Team	League	GP	G	A	Pts.	PIM	+/-	PP	SH	GP	G	A	Pts.	PIM
		REGULAR SEASON								PLAYOFFS				
91-92—Trois-Rivieres	QMJHL	58	2	10	12	28	...	...	...	15	2	2	4	13
92-93—Sherbrooke	QMJHL	51	4	17	21	82	...	...	...	15	0	4	4	18
93-94—Sherbrooke	QMJHL	67	4	24	28	69	...	...	...	12	1	7	8	14
94-95—Quebec	OUAA	13	8	5	13	20	...	...	...	4	0	3	3	8
95-96—Cornwall	AHL	72	5	9	14	111	...	...	...	8	1	1	2	20
96-97—Hershey	AHL	55	16	26	42	69	...	...	...	9	3	8	11	14
—Colorado	NHL	21	0	0	0	4	7	0	0	6	0	0	0	4
97-98—Colorado	NHL	62	4	12	16	20	4	0	0	—	—	—	—	—
98-99—Colorado	NHL	31	4	2	6	14	0	1	0	3	0	0	0	0
—Hershey	AHL	6	1	3	4	4	1	1	0	—	—	—	—	—
99-00—Colorado	NHL	61	3	6	9	24	0	1	0	14	0	1	1	4
00-01—Colorado	NHL	64	5	7	12	26	-3	0	0	23	2	2	4	14
01-02—Colorado	NHL	74	5	10	15	26	-5	0	0	21	1	2	3	0
02-03—Colorado	NHL	72	4	10	14	16	-2	0	1	5	0	0	0	0
03-04—Florida	NHL	21	0	3	3	16	-2	0	0	—	—	—	—	—
NHL Totals (8 years)		406	25	50	75	146	-1	2	1	72	3	5	8	22

MESSIER, MARK — C

PERSONAL: Born January 18, 1961, in Edmonton. ... 6-2/211. ... Shoots left. ... Brother of Paul Messier, C with Colorado Rockies (1978-79); cousin of Mitch Messier, C/RW with Minnesota North Stars (1987-91); cousin of Joby Messier, D with New York Rangers (1992-95); and brother-in-law of John Blum, defenseman with four NHL teams (1982-90). ... Name pronounced MEHZ-yay.

TRANSACTIONS/CAREER NOTES: Signed 10-game trial with Indianapolis Racers (November 5, 1978). ... Signed as free agent by Cincinnati of WHA (December 1978). ... Selected by Edmonton Oilers in 3rd round (2nd Oilers pick, 48th overall) of entry draft (August 9, 1979). ... Injured ankle (November 7, 1981). ... Fractured wrist (March 1983). ... Suspended six games for hitting player with stick (January 18, 1984).

... Sprained knee ligaments (November 1984). ... Suspended 10 games for injuring player (December 26, 1984). ... Bruised left foot (December 3, 1985); missed 17 games. ... Suspended six games for injuring player with stick (October 23, 1988). ... Twisted left knee (January 28, 1989). ... Strained right knee (February 3, 1989). ... Bruised left knee (February 12, 1989). ... Sprained left knee (October 16, 1990); missed 10 games. ... Reinjured left knee (December 12, 1990); missed three games. ... Reinjured knee (December 22, 1990); missed nine games. ... Fractured left thumb (February 11, 1991); missed eight games. ... Missed one game in contract dispute (October 1991). ... Traded by Oilers with future considerations to New York Rangers for C Bernie Nicholls, LW Louie DeBrusk, RW Steven Rice and future considerations (October 4, 1991); Oilers traded D Jeff Beukeboom to Rangers for D David Shaw to complete deal (November 12, 1991). ... Sprained wrist (January 19, 1993); missed six games. ... Strained rib cage muscle (February 27, 1993); missed two games. ... Strained rib cage muscle (March 11, 1993); missed one game. ... Suspended three off-days and fined $500 for stick-swinging incident (March 18, 1993). ... Sprained wrist (December 22, 1993); missed six games. ... Bruised thigh (March 16, 1994); missed two games. ... Back spasms (April 30, 1995); missed two games. ... Bruised shoulder (February 27, 1996); missed two games. ... Bruised ribs (April 4, 1996); missed six games. ... Suspended two games and fined $1,000 for checking opponent from behind (October 8, 1996). ... Hyperextended elbow (December 7, 1996); missed four games. ... Back spasms (February 23, 1997); missed two games. ... Charley horse (March 27, 1997); missed two games. ... Signed as free agent by Vancouver Canucks (July 28, 1997). ... Concussion (December 22, 1998); missed one game. ... Sprained knee (February 11, 1999); missed 18 games. ... Injured groin (March 31, 1999); missed four games. ... Sprained knee (November 9, 1999); missed 15 games. ... Injured knee (December 29, 2000); missed one game. ... Signed as free agent by Rangers (July 13, 2000). ... Strained rib muscle (October 13, 2001); missed two games. ... Strained shoulder and had back spasms (December 6, 2001); missed one game. ... Back spasms, reinjured shoulder (December 17, 2001); missed four games. ... Reinjured shoulder (January 2, 2002); missed 11 games. ... Reinjured shoulder (February 13, 2002); missed remainder of season. ... Neck spasms (December 8, 2002); missed one game. ... Bruised foot (December 29, 2002); missed one game. ... Bruised arm (January 28, 2003); missed one game. ... Strained ribs (April 4, 2003); missed one game. ... Traded by Rangers to San Jose Sharks for future considerations (June 30, 2003). ... Signed as free agent by Rangers (September 5, 2003). ... Charley horse (December 3, 2003); missed one game. ... Suspended two games for spearing incident (March 22, 2004). ... Bruised right elbow (March 27, 2004); missed two games.

STATISTICAL PLATEAUS: Three-goal games: 1980-81 (1), 1981-82 (2), 1982-83 (1), 1983-84 (2), 1985-86 (1), 1987-88 (1), 1989-90 (2), 1991-92 (2), 1995-96 (1), 1996-97 (2). Total: 15. ... Four-goal games: 1982-83 (1), 1988-89 (1), 1989-90 (1), 1991-92 (1). Total: 4. ... Total hat tricks: 19.

		REGULAR SEASON								PLAYOFFS				
Season Team	**League**	**GP**	**G**	**A**	**Pts.**	**PIM**	**+/-**	**PP**	**SH**	**GP**	**G**	**A**	**Pts.**	**PIM**
76-77—Spruce Grove	AJHL	57	27	39	66	91	...	...	...	—	—	—	—	—
77-78—St. Albert	AJHL	Statistics unavailable												
—Portland	WHL	...	...	...	...	...	...	...	...	7	4	1	5	2
78-79—Indianapolis	WHA	5	0	0	0	0	...	...	...	—	—	—	—	—
—Cincinnati	WHA	47	1	10	11	58	...	...	...	—	—	—	—	—
79-80—Houston	CHL	4	0	3	3	4	...	...	...	—	—	—	—	—
—Edmonton	NHL	75	12	21	33	120	-10	1	1	3	1	2	3	2
80-81—Edmonton	NHL	72	23	40	63	102	-12	4	0	9	2	5	7	13
81-82—Edmonton	NHL	78	50	38	88	119	21	10	0	5	1	2	3	8
82-83—Edmonton	NHL	77	48	58	106	72	19	12	1	15	15	6	21	14
83-84—Edmonton	NHL	73	37	64	101	165	40	7	4	19	8	18	26	19
84-85—Edmonton	NHL	55	23	31	54	57	8	4	5	18	12	13	25	12
85-86—Edmonton	NHL	63	35	49	84	68	36	10	5	10	4	6	10	18
86-87—Edmonton	NHL	77	37	70	107	73	21	7	4	21	12	16	28	16
87-88—Edmonton	NHL	77	37	74	111	103	21	12	3	19	11	23	34	29
88-89—Edmonton	NHL	72	33	61	94	130	-5	6	6	7	1	11	12	8
89-90—Edmonton	NHL	79	45	84	129	79	19	13	6	22	9	*22	31	20
90-91—Edmonton	NHL	53	12	52	64	34	15	3	1	18	4	11	15	16
91-92—New York Rangers	NHL	79	35	72	107	76	31	12	4	11	7	7	14	6
92-93—New York Rangers	NHL	75	25	66	91	72	-6	7	2	—	—	—	—	—
93-94—New York Rangers	NHL	76	26	58	84	76	25	6	2	23	12	18	30	33
94-95—New York Rangers	NHL	46	14	39	53	40	8	3	3	10	3	10	13	8
95-96—New York Rangers	NHL	74	47	52	99	122	29	14	1	11	4	7	11	16
96-97—New York Rangers	NHL	71	36	48	84	88	12	7	5	15	3	9	12	6
97-98—Vancouver	NHL	82	22	38	60	58	-10	8	2	—	—	—	—	—
98-99—Vancouver	NHL	59	13	35	48	33	-12	4	2	—	—	—	—	—
99-00—Vancouver	NHL	66	17	37	54	30	-15	6	0	—	—	—	—	—
00-01—New York Rangers	NHL	82	24	43	67	89	-25	12	3	—	—	—	—	—
01-02—New York Rangers	NHL	41	7	16	23	32	-1	2	0	—	—	—	—	—
02-03—New York Rangers	NHL	78	18	22	40	30	-2	8	1	—	—	—	—	—
03-04—New York Rangers	NHL	76	18	25	43	42	3	1	2	—	—	—	—	—
NHL Totals (25 years)		1756	694	1193	1887	1910	210	179	63	236	109	186	295	244

M

MESZAROS, ANDREJ — D — SENATORS

PERSONAL: Born October 13, 1985, in Povazska Bystrica, Czech. ... 6-0/198. ... Shoots right.

TRANSACTIONS/CAREER NOTES: Selected by Ottawa Senators in first round (first Senators pick, 23rd overall) of NHL entry draft (June 26, 2004).

		REGULAR SEASON								PLAYOFFS				
Season Team	**League**	**GP**	**G**	**A**	**Pts.**	**PIM**	**+/-**	**PP**	**SH**	**GP**	**G**	**A**	**Pts.**	**PIM**
02-03—Trencin	Slovakia	23	0	1	1	4	...	...	...	—	—	—	—	—
03-04—Trencin	Slovakia	44	3	3	6	8	...	...	...	14	3	1	4	2
04-05—Vancouver	WHL	59	11	30	41	94	7	5	1	6	1	3	4	14

MEYER, FREDDY — D — FLYERS

PERSONAL: Born January 4, 1981, in Sanbornville, N.H. ... 5-11/190. ... Shoots left.

TRANSACTIONS/CAREER NOTES: Signed as free agent by Philadelphia Flyers (May 21, 2003).

		REGULAR SEASON								PLAYOFFS				
Season Team	**League**	**GP**	**G**	**A**	**Pts.**	**PIM**	**+/-**	**PP**	**SH**	**GP**	**G**	**A**	**Pts.**	**PIM**
99-00—Boston University	ECAC	25	1	11	12	52	...	...	...	—	—	—	—	—
00-01—Boston University	ECAC	28	6	13	19	82	...	...	...	—	—	—	—	—
01-02—Boston University	ECAC	37	5	15	20	78	...	...	...	—	—	—	—	—

Season Team	League	GP	G	A	Pts.	PIM	+/-	PP	SH	GP	G	A	Pts.	PIM
		REGULAR SEASON								PLAYOFFS				
02-03—Boston University	ECAC	36	5	16	21	76	...	...	...	—	—	—	—	—
03-04—Philadelphia	NHL	1	0	0	0	0	0	0	0	—	—	—	—	—
—Philadelphia	AHL	59	14	14	28	50	13	6	0	12	0	3	3	8
04-05—Philadelphia	AHL	59	6	9	15	71	15	2	0	21	3	9	12	34
NHL Totals (1 year)		1	0	0	0	0	0	0	0					

MEZEI, BRANISLAV D PANTHERS

PERSONAL: Born October 8, 1980, in Nitra, Czechoslovakia. ... 6-5/235. ... Shoots left. ... Name pronounced MEE-zy.

TRANSACTIONS/CAREER NOTES: Selected by New York Islanders in 1st round (3rd Islanders pick, 10th overall) of entry draft (June 26, 1999). ... Separated left shoulder (January 16, 2001); missed 13 games. ... Traded by Islanders to Florida Panthers for C Jason Wiemer (July 3, 2002). ... Fractured ankle (October 12, 2002); missed 27 games. ... Fractured foot (January 1, 2003); missed 43 games. ... Injured eye (November 24, 2003); missed 37 games.

Season Team	League	GP	G	A	Pts.	PIM	+/-	PP	SH	GP	G	A	Pts.	PIM
		REGULAR SEASON								PLAYOFFS				
96-97—Plastika Nitra	Slovakia Jrs.	40	8	17	25	42	...	...	...	—	—	—	—	—
97-98—Belleville	OHL	53	3	5	8	58	...	...	...	8	0	2	2	8
98-99—Belleville	OHL	60	5	18	23	90	44	...	...	18	0	4	4	29
99-00—Belleville	OHL	58	7	21	28	99	30	5	0	6	0	3	3	10
00-01—Lowell	AHL	20	0	3	3	28	...	...	...	—	—	—	—	—
—New York Islanders	NHL	42	1	4	5	53	-5	0	0	—	—	—	—	—
01-02—Bridgeport	AHL	59	1	9	10	137	12	0	0	20	0	3	3	48
—New York Islanders	NHL	24	0	2	2	12	2	0	0	—	—	—	—	—
02-03—San Antonio	AHL	1	0	0	0	0	1	0	0	—	—	—	—	—
—Florida	NHL	11	2	0	2	10	-2	0	0	—	—	—	—	—
03-04—Florida	NHL	45	0	7	7	80	-4	0	0	—	—	—	—	—
04-05—Dukla Trencin	Slovakia	—	—	—	—	—	—	—	—	12	1	2	3	38
—Trinec	Czech Rep.	41	1	2	3	68	-15	...	...	—	—	—	—	—
—Dukla Trencin	Slovakia	10	1	1	2	16	4	...	...	—	—	—	—	—
NHL Totals (4 years)		122	3	13	16	155	-9	0	0					

MICHALEK, MILAN RW SHARKS

PERSONAL: Born December 7, 1984, in Jindrichuv Hradec, Czechoslovakia. ... 6-2/220. ... Shoots left.

TRANSACTIONS/CAREER NOTES: Selected by San Jose Sharks in first round (first Sharks pick, sixth overall) in 2003 NHL entry draft (June 23, 2003). ... Injured right knee (October 12, 2003); missed 46 games.

Season Team	League	GP	G	A	Pts.	PIM	+/-	PP	SH	GP	G	A	Pts.	PIM
		REGULAR SEASON								PLAYOFFS				
00-01—Budejovice	Czech. Jrs.	30	10	13	23	30	...	...	...	—	—	—	—	—
01-02—Budejovice	Czech.	47	6	11	17	12	...	...	...	—	—	—	—	—
02-03—Budejovice	Czech.	46	3	5	8	14	...	...	...	—	—	—	—	—
03-04—San Jose	NHL	2	1	0	1	4	1	0	0	—	—	—	—	—
—Cleveland	AHL	7	2	2	4	4	1	1	0	—	—	—	—	—
04-05—Cleveland	AHL	0	0	0	0	0	0	0	0	—	—	—	—	—
NHL Totals (1 year)		2	1	0	1	4	1	0	0					

MICHALEK, ZBYNEK D WILD

PERSONAL: Born December 23, 1982, in Jindrchuv, Czech. ... 6-1/176. ... Shoots right.

TRANSACTIONS/CAREER NOTES: Signed as free agent by Minnesota Wild (September 29, 2001).

Season Team	League	GP	G	A	Pts.	PIM	+/-	PP	SH	GP	G	A	Pts.	PIM
		REGULAR SEASON								PLAYOFFS				
00-01—Shawinigan	QMJHL	69	10	29	39	52	...	...	...	3	0	0	0	0
01-02—Shawinigan	QMJHL	68	16	35	51	54	...	...	...	10	8	7	15	10
03-04—Minnesota	NHL	22	1	1	2	4	-7	0	0	—	—	—	—	—
—Houston	AHL	55	5	16	21	32	-5	3	0	2	1	0	1	0
04-05—Houston	AHL	76	7	17	24	48	-10	5	0	5	1	2	3	4
NHL Totals (1 year)		22	1	1	2	4	-7	0	0					

MICHAUD, OLIVIER G CANADIENS

PERSONAL: Born September 14, 1983, in Beloeil, Que. ... 5-11/160. ... Catches left.

TRANSACTIONS/CAREER NOTES: Signed as free agent by Montreal Canadiens (September 18, 2001).

Season Team	League	GP	Min.	W	L	T	GA	SO	GAA	SV%	GP	Min.	W	L	GA	SO	GAA	SV%
		REGULAR SEASON									PLAYOFFS							
99-00—Shawinigan	QMJHL	1	49	0	1	0	2	0	2.45	...	—	—	—	—	—	—	—	—
00-01—Shawinigan	QMJHL	21	1096	12	4	4	54	1	2.96	...	3	150	1	2	6	0	2.40	...
01-02—Shawinigan	QMJHL	46	2650	29	11	3	108	3	*2.45	...	12	744	7	5	36	0	2.90	...
—Montreal	NHL	1	18	0	0	0	0	0	0.00	1.00	—	—	—	—	—	—	—	—
02-03—Shawinigan	QMJHL	27	1497	8	13	3	82	1	3.29	...	—	—	—	—	—	—	—	—
—Baie-Comeau	QMJHL	31	1775	23	5	2	90	3	3.04	...	12	748	7	5	38	0	3.05	...
03-04—Hamilton	AHL	16	900	4	7	3	38	2	2.53	.895	—	—	—	—	—	—	—	—
—Columbus	ECHL	22	1234	8	10	2	62	1	3.01	.884	—	—	—	—	—	—	—	—
04-05—Long Beach	ECHL	42	2314	18	14	...	98	1	2.54	.918	1	58	0	1	4	...	4.10	.840
NHL Totals (1 year)		1	18	0	0	0	0	0	0.00	1.00								

MIETTINEN, ANTTI — LW/C — STARS

PERSONAL: Born July 3, 1980, in Hameenlinna, Finland. ... 5-11/180. ... Shoots left.
TRANSACTIONS/CAREER NOTES: Selected by Dallas Stars in seventh round (224th overall) of NHL entry draft (June 24, 2000). ... Had back spasms (October 27, 2003); missed two games.

		REGULAR SEASON								PLAYOFFS				
Season Team	**League**	**GP**	**G**	**A**	**Pts.**	**PIM**	**+/-**	**PP**	**SH**	**GP**	**G**	**A**	**Pts.**	**PIM**
99-00—HPK Hameenlinna	Finland	39	2	1	3	8	...	...	...	7	1	0	1	0
00-01—HPK Hameenlinna	Finland	55	13	11	24	28	...	...	...	—	—	—	—	—
01-02—HPK Hameenlinna	Finland	56	19	37	56	50	...	...	...	8	2	4	6	8
02-03—HPK Hameenlinna	Finland	53	25	25	50	54	...	...	...	10	1	7	8	29
03-04—Dallas	NHL	16	1	0	1	0	-9	0	0	—	—	—	—	—
—Utah	AHL	48	7	23	30	20	-17	4	1	—	—	—	—	—
04-05—Ilves Tampere	Finland	25	0	1	1	10	...	...	...	—	—	—	—	—
—Hamilton	AHL	35	8	20	28	21	11	3	0	4	1	1	2	6
NHL Totals (1 year)		16	1	0	1	0	-9	0	0					

MIHALIK, VLADIMIR — D — LIGHTNING

PERSONAL: Born January 29, 1987, in Presov, Slovakia. ... 6-7/225. ... Shoots left.
TRANSACTIONS/CAREER NOTES: Selected by Tampa Bay Lightning in 1st round (1st Lightning pick, 30th overall) of entry draft (July 30, 2005).

		REGULAR SEASON								PLAYOFFS				
Season Team	**League**	**GP**	**G**	**A**	**Pts.**	**PIM**	**+/-**	**PP**	**SH**	**GP**	**G**	**A**	**Pts.**	**PIM**
04-05—Presov	Slovakia Jrs.	...	...	...	...	...	...	...	...	—	—	—	—	—

MIKKELSON, BRENDAN — D — MIGHTY DUCKS

PERSONAL: Born June 22, 1987, in Regina, Saskatchewan. ... 6-2/180. ... Shoots left.
TRANSACTIONS/CAREER NOTES: Selected by Anaheim Might Ducks in 1st round (2nd Ducks pick, 31st overall, obtained from Tampa Bay) of entry draft (July 30, 2005).

		REGULAR SEASON								PLAYOFFS				
Season Team	**League**	**GP**	**G**	**A**	**Pts.**	**PIM**	**+/-**	**PP**	**SH**	**GP**	**G**	**A**	**Pts.**	**PIM**
03-04—Portland	WHL	65	3	12	15	43	...	...	...	5	1	0	1	0
04-05—Portland	WHL	70	5	10	15	60	-10	4	0	7	1	2	3	0

MILLER, AARON — D — KINGS

PERSONAL: Born August 11, 1971, in Buffalo. ... 6-4/210. ... Shoots right.
TRANSACTIONS/CAREER NOTES: Selected by New York Rangers in fifth round (sixth Rangers pick, 88th overall) of NHL entry draft (June 17, 1989). ... Traded by Rangers with fifth-round pick (LW Bill Lindsay) in 1991 entry draft to Quebec Nordiques for D Joe Cirella (January 17, 1991). ... Nordiques franchise moved to Colorado and renamed Avalanche for 1995-96 season (June 21, 1995). ... Suffered concussion (October 24, 1998); missed one game. ... Bruised knee (November 8, 1998); missed one game. ... Had back spasms (March 17, 1999); missed three games. ... Bruised sternum (November 17, 1999); missed 27 games. ... Bruised right hand (November 22, 2000); missed five games. ... Traded by Avalanche with RW Adam Deadmarsh, first-round pick (C David Steckel) in 2001 entry draft, a player to be named and first-round pick (C Brian Boyle) in 2003 entry draft to Los Angeles Kings for C Steve Reinprecht and D Rob Blake (February 21, 2001); Kings acquired C Jared Aulin to complete deal (March 22, 2001). ... Sprained wrist (March 19, 2001); missed final nine games of season. ... Had back spasms (October 20, 2001); missed eight games. ... Had hernia (September 13, 2002) and had surgery; missed 13 games. ... Fractured foot (December 11, 2002); missed 18 games. ... Strained back (April 4, 2003); missed two games. ... Injured wrist (October 5, 2003); missed eight games. ... Had cervical strain (December 11, 2003); missed 29 games.

		REGULAR SEASON								PLAYOFFS				
Season Team	**League**	**GP**	**G**	**A**	**Pts.**	**PIM**	**+/-**	**PP**	**SH**	**GP**	**G**	**A**	**Pts.**	**PIM**
87-88—Niagara	NAJHL	30	4	9	13	2	...	...	...	—	—	—	—	—
88-89—Niagara	NAJHL	59	24	38	62	60	...	...	...	—	—	—	—	—
89-90—Vermont	ECAC	31	1	15	16	24	...	...	...	—	—	—	—	—
90-91—Vermont	ECAC	30	3	7	10	22	...	...	...	—	—	—	—	—
91-92—Vermont	ECAC	31	3	16	19	36	...	...	...	—	—	—	—	—
92-93—Vermont	ECAC	30	4	13	17	16	...	...	...	—	—	—	—	—
93-94—Cornwall	AHL	64	4	10	14	49	2	0	0	13	0	2	2	10
—Quebec	NHL	1	0	0	0	0	-1	0	0	—	—	—	—	—
94-95—Cornwall	AHL	76	4	18	22	69	-8	2	0	—	—	—	—	—
—Quebec	NHL	9	0	3	3	6	2	0	0	—	—	—	—	—
95-96—Cornwall	AHL	62	4	23	27	77	...	...	...	8	0	1	1	6
—Colorado	NHL	5	0	0	0	0	0	0	0	—	—	—	—	—
96-97—Colorado	NHL	56	5	12	17	15	15	0	0	17	1	2	3	10
97-98—Colorado	NHL	55	2	2	4	51	0	0	0	7	0	0	0	8
98-99—Colorado	NHL	76	5	13	18	42	3	1	0	19	1	5	6	10
99-00—Colorado	NHL	53	1	7	8	36	3	0	0	17	1	1	2	6
00-01—Colorado	NHL	56	4	9	13	29	19	0	0	—	—	—	—	—
—Los Angeles	NHL	13	0	5	5	14	3	0	0	13	0	1	1	6
01-02—Los Angeles	NHL	74	5	12	17	54	14	0	1	7	0	0	0	0
—U.S. Olympic team	Int'l	6	0	0	0	4	...	...	...	—	—	—	—	—
02-03—Los Angeles	NHL	49	1	5	6	24	-7	0	0	—	—	—	—	—
03-04—Los Angeles	NHL	35	1	2	3	32	-3	0	0	—	—	—	—	—
NHL Totals (11 years)		482	24	70	94	303	48	1	1	80	3	9	12	40

MILLER, KEVIN — C — RED WINGS

PERSONAL: Born September 9, 1965, in Lansing, Mich. ... 5-11/190. ... Shoots right. ... Brother of Kelly Miller, RW with New York Rangers (1984-87) and Washington Capitals (1986-99); and brother of Kip Miller, C with eight NHL teams (1988-89 through 2003-04).

TRANSACTIONS/CAREER NOTES: Selected by New York Rangers in 10th round (10th Rangers pick, 202nd overall) of NHL entry draft (June 9, 1984). ... Injured groin (September 1990). ... Sprained shoulder (December 1990). ... Traded by Rangers with D Dennis Vial and RW Jim Cummings to Detroit Red Wings for RW Joe Kocur and D Per Djoos (March 5, 1991). ... Traded by Red Wings to Washington Capitals for RW Dino Ciccarelli (June 20, 1992). ... Traded by Capitals to St. Louis Blues for D Paul Cavallini (November 1, 1992). ... Had sore knee (November 3, 1993); missed two games. ... Injured knee (November 24, 1993); missed two games. ... Injured hip (March 30, 1994); missed one game. ... Had sore groin (April 8, 1994); missed three games. ... Traded by Blues to San Jose Sharks for C Todd Elik (March 23, 1995). ... Injured knee (March 15, 1996); missed two games. ... Traded by Sharks to Pittsburgh Penguins for fifth-round pick (later traded to Boston; Bruins picked D Elias Abrahamsson) in 1996 entry draft (March 20, 1996). ... Signed as free agent by Chicago Blackhawks (July 17, 1996). ... Had the flu (November 22, 1996); missed one game. ... Injured groin (January 10, 1997); missed two games. ... Strained groin (December 20, 1997); missed one game. ... Signed as free agent by New York Islanders (October 9, 1998). ... Signed as free agent by Ottawa Senators (August 24, 1999). ... Separated right shoulder (March 30, 2000); missed four games. ... Signed as free agent by Detroit Red Wings (August 27, 2003).

STATISTICAL PLATEAUS: Three-goal games: 1991-92 (1), 1992-93 (1), 1993-94 (1), 1995-96 (1). Total: 4.

		REGULAR SEASON								PLAYOFFS				
Season Team	**League**	**GP**	**G**	**A**	**Pts.**	**PIM**	**+/-**	**PP**	**SH**	**GP**	**G**	**A**	**Pts.**	**PIM**
84-85—Michigan State	CCHA	44	11	29	40	84	...	...	...	—	—	—	—	—
85-86—Michigan State	CCHA	45	19	52	71	112	...	...	...	—	—	—	—	—
86-87—Michigan State	CCHA	42	25	56	81	63	...	...	...	—	—	—	—	—
87-88—Michigan State	CCHA	9	6	3	9	18	...	...	...	—	—	—	—	—
—U.S. Olympic team	Int'l	50	32	34	66	...	...	...	...	—	—	—	—	—
88-89—New York Rangers	NHL	24	3	5	8	2	-1	0	0	—	—	—	—	—
—Denver	IHL	55	29	47	76	19	...	...	...	4	2	1	3	2
89-90—New York Rangers	NHL	16	0	5	5	2	-1	0	0	1	0	0	0	0
—Flint	IHL	48	19	23	42	41	...	...	...	—	—	—	—	—
90-91—New York Rangers	NHL	63	17	27	44	63	1	1	2	—	—	—	—	—
—Detroit	NHL	11	5	2	7	4	-4	0	1	7	3	2	5	20
91-92—Detroit	NHL	80	20	26	46	53	6	3	1	9	0	2	2	4
92-93—Washington	NHL	10	0	3	3	35	-4	0	0	—	—	—	—	—
—St. Louis	NHL	72	24	22	46	65	6	8	3	10	0	3	3	11
93-94—St. Louis	NHL	75	23	25	48	83	6	6	3	3	1	0	1	4
94-95—St. Louis	NHL	15	2	5	7	0	4	0	0	—	—	—	—	—
—San Jose	NHL	21	6	7	13	13	0	1	1	6	0	0	0	2
95-96—San Jose	NHL	68	22	20	42	41	-8	2	2	—	—	—	—	—
—Pittsburgh	NHL	13	6	5	11	4	4	1	0	18	3	2	5	8
96-97—Chicago	NHL	69	14	17	31	41	-10	5	1	6	0	1	1	0
97-98—Indianapolis	IHL	26	11	11	22	41	-3	4	1	2	1	1	2	0
—Chicago	NHL	37	4	7	11	8	-4	0	0	—	—	—	—	—
98-99—New York Islanders	NHL	33	1	5	6	13	-5	0	0	—	—	—	—	—
—Chicago	IHL	30	11	20	31	8	14	2	1	10	2	7	9	22
99-00—Grand Rapids	IHL	63	20	34	54	51	...	...	...	17	*11	7	18	30
—Ottawa	NHL	9	3	2	5	2	1	1	0	1	0	0	0	0
00-01—Davos	Switzerland	36	*29	27	56	61	...	...	...	4	3	0	3	2
01-02—Davos	Switzerland	43	23	18	41	78	...	...	...	16	4	10	14	12
03-04—Detroit	NHL	4	0	2	2	0	2	0	0	—	—	—	—	—
—Grand Rapids	AHL	74	27	21	48	22	0	11	2	4	3	0	3	5
04-05—UHL	UHL	7	1	4	5	10	0	0	0	—	—	—	—	—
NHL Totals (13 years)		620	150	185	335	429	-7	28	14	61	7	10	17	49

MILLER, KIP — LW/RW/C

PERSONAL: Born June 11, 1969, in Lansing, Mich. ... 5-10/188. ... Shoots left. ... Brother of Kelly Miller, RW with New York Rangers (1984-87) and Washington Capitals (1986-99); and brother of Kevin Miller, LW with 10 NHL teams (1988-89 through 2003-04).

TRANSACTIONS/CAREER NOTES: Selected by Quebec Nordiques in fourth round (fourth Nordiques pick, 72nd overall) of NHL entry draft (June 13, 1987). ... Traded by Nordiques to Minnesota North Stars for LW Steve Maltais (March 8, 1992). ... North Stars franchise moved from Minnesota to Dallas and renamed Stars for 1993-94 season. ... Signed as free agent by San Jose Sharks (August 10, 1993). ... Signed as free agent by New York Islanders (August 2, 1994). ... Signed as free agent by Chicago Blackhawks (August 10, 1995). ... Signed as free agent by Islanders (November 26, 1997). ... Selected by Pittsburgh Penguins in NHL waiver draft (October 5, 1998). ... Injured eye (March 20, 1999); missed one game. ... Sprained knee (October 30, 1999); missed one game. ... Traded by Penguins to Anaheim Mighty Ducks for future considerations (January 30, 2000). ... Signed as free agent by Penguins (September 24, 2000). ... Strained groin (November 28, 2000); missed four games. ... Signed as free agent by Islanders (January 17, 2002). ... Signed as free agent by Washington Capitals (July 9, 2002). ... Bruised hand (March 4, 2003); missed seven games.

		REGULAR SEASON								PLAYOFFS				
Season Team	**League**	**GP**	**G**	**A**	**Pts.**	**PIM**	**+/-**	**PP**	**SH**	**GP**	**G**	**A**	**Pts.**	**PIM**
86-87—Michigan State	CCHA	41	20	19	39	92	...	...	...	—	—	—	—	—
87-88—Michigan State	CCHA	39	16	25	41	51	...	...	...	—	—	—	—	—
88-89—Michigan State	CCHA	47	32	45	77	94	...	...	...	—	—	—	—	—
89-90—Michigan State	CCHA	45	*48	53	*101	60	...	...	...	—	—	—	—	—
90-91—Quebec	NHL	13	4	3	7	7	-1	0	0	—	—	—	—	—
—Halifax	AHL	66	36	33	69	40	...	...	...	—	—	—	—	—
91-92—Quebec	NHL	36	5	10	15	12	-21	1	0	—	—	—	—	—
—Halifax	AHL	24	9	17	26	8	...	...	...	—	—	—	—	—
—Minnesota	NHL	3	1	2	3	2	-1	1	0	—	—	—	—	—
—Kalamazoo	IHL	6	1	8	9	4	...	...	...	12	3	9	12	12
92-93—Kalamazoo	IHL	61	17	39	56	59	-24	8	0	—	—	—	—	—
93-94—San Jose	NHL	11	2	2	4	6	-1	0	0	—	—	—	—	—
—Kansas City	IHL	71	38	54	92	51	0	9	6	—	—	—	—	—
94-95—Denver	IHL	71	46	60	106	54	26	12	1	17	*15	14	29	8

Season Team	League	REGULAR SEASON GP	G	A	Pts.	PIM	+/-	PP	SH	PLAYOFFS GP	G	A	Pts.	PIM
—New York Islanders	NHL	8	0	1	1	0	1	0	0	—	—	—	—	—
95-96—Indianapolis	IHL	73	32	59	91	46	...	...	...	5	2	6	8	2
—Chicago	NHL	10	1	4	5	2	1	0	0	—	—	—	—	—
96-97—Chicago	IHL	43	11	41	52	32	...	...	...	—	—	—	—	—
—Indianapolis	IHL	37	17	24	41	18	...	...	...	4	2	2	4	2
97-98—Utah	IHL	72	38	59	97	30	14	11	3	4	3	2	5	10
—New York Islanders	NHL	9	1	3	4	2	-2	0	0	—	—	—	—	—
98-99—Pittsburgh	NHL	77	19	23	42	22	1	1	0	13	2	7	9	19
99-00—Pittsburgh	NHL	44	4	15	19	10	-1	0	0	—	—	—	—	—
—Anaheim	NHL	30	6	17	23	4	1	2	0	—	—	—	—	—
00-01—Pittsburgh	NHL	33	3	8	11	6	0	1	0	—	—	—	—	—
—Grand Rapids	IHL	34	16	19	35	12	...	...	...	10	5	8	13	2
01-02—Grand Rapids	AHL	41	21	35	56	27	13	5	3	—	—	—	—	—
—New York Islanders	NHL	37	7	17	24	6	2	2	0	7	4	2	6	2
02-03—Washington	NHL	72	12	38	50	18	-1	3	0	5	0	2	2	2
03-04—Washington	NHL	66	9	22	31	8	-10	6	0	—	—	—	—	—
04-05—Grand Rapids	AHL	50	13	32	45	17	-3	7	0	—	—	—	—	—
NHL Totals (12 years)		449	74	165	239	105	-32	17	0	25	6	11	17	23

MILLER, RYAN G SABRES

PERSONAL: Born July 17, 1980, in East Lansing, Mich. ... 6-2/166. ... Catches left.
TRANSACTIONS/CAREER NOTES: Selected by Buffalo Sabres in fifth round (seventh Sabres pick, 138th overall) of NHL entry draft (June 26, 1999).

Season Team	League	REGULAR SEASON GP	Min.	W	L	T	GA	SO	GAA	SV%	PLAYOFFS GP	Min.	W	L	GA	SO	GAA	SV%
98-99—Soo	NAHL	47	2711	31	14	1	104	8	2.30	.921	4	218	2	2	10	1	2.75	...
99-00—Michigan State	CCHA	26	1525	16	4	3	39	*8	*1.53	...	—	—	—	—	—	—	—	—
00-01—Michigan State	CCHA	40	2447	*31	5	4	54	*10	*1.32	...	—	—	—	—	—	—	—	—
01-02—Michigan State	CCHA	40	2411	26	9	5	71	*8	*1.77	...	—	—	—	—	—	—	—	—
02-03—Buffalo	NHL	15	912	6	8	1	40	1	2.63	.902	—	—	—	—	—	—	—	—
—Rochester	AHL	47	2816	23	18	5	110	2	2.34	.920	3	189	1	2	13	0	4.13	.856
03-04—Rochester	AHL	60	3578	27	25	7	132	5	2.21	.919	14	856	7	7	26	2	1.82	.929
—Buffalo	NHL	3	178	0	3	0	15	0	5.06	.795	—	—	—	—	—	—	—	—
04-05—Rochester	AHL	63	3740	41	17	...	153	8	2.45	.922	9	547	5	4	24	0	2.63	.909
NHL Totals (2 years)		18	1090	6	11	1	55	1	3.03	.886								

MILLEY, NORM RW SABRES

PERSONAL: Born February 14, 1980, in Toronto. ... 6-0/211. ... Shoots right.
TRANSACTIONS/CAREER NOTES: Selected by Buffalo Sabres in second round (third Sabres pick, 47th overall) of NHL entry draft (June 27, 1998).

Season Team	League	REGULAR SEASON GP	G	A	Pts.	PIM	+/-	PP	SH	PLAYOFFS GP	G	A	Pts.	PIM
95-96—Toronto Red Wings	MTHL	42	42	36	78	109	...	...	...	—	—	—	—	—
96-97—Sudbury	OHL	61	30	32	62	15	...	...	...	—	—	—	—	—
97-98—Sudbury	OHL	62	33	41	74	48	...	...	...	10	0	1	1	4
98-99—Sudbury	OHL	68	52	68	120	47	9	...	...	4	2	3	5	4
99-00—Sudbury	OHL	68	*52	60	112	47	39	13	2	12	8	11	19	6
00-01—Rochester	AHL	77	20	27	47	56	...	...	...	4	0	0	0	2
01-02—Rochester	AHL	74	20	18	38	20	11	5	1	2	0	3	3	6
—Buffalo	NHL	5	0	1	1	0	0	0	0	—	—	—	—	—
02-03—Buffalo	NHL	8	0	2	2	6	-2	0	0	—	—	—	—	—
—Rochester	AHL	67	16	32	48	39	...	...	...	3	2	0	2	2
03-04—Rochester	AHL	77	18	19	37	60	2	2	0	16	7	6	13	10
—Buffalo	NHL	2	0	0	0	2	0	0	0	—	—	—	—	—
04-05—Rochester	AHL	72	12	21	33	46	1	1	0	9	1	2	3	4
NHL Totals (3 years)		15	0	3	3	8	-2	0	0					

MINK, GRAHAM LW CAPITALS

PERSONAL: Born May 21, 1979, in Stowe, Vt. ... 6-3/220. ... Shoots right.
TRANSACTIONS/CAREER NOTES: Signed as free agent by Washington Capitals (April 11, 2002).

Season Team	League	REGULAR SEASON GP	G	A	Pts.	PIM	+/-	PP	SH	PLAYOFFS GP	G	A	Pts.	PIM
98-99—Vermont	ECAC	27	4	2	6	34	...	...	...	—	—	—	—	—
99-00—Vermont	ECAC	17	7	4	11	18	...	...	...	—	—	—	—	—
00-01—Vermont	ECAC	32	17	12	29	52	...	...	...	—	—	—	—	—
01-02—Richmond	ECHL	29	8	9	17	78	-2	...	...	—	—	—	—	—
—Portland	AHL	56	17	17	34	50	...	...	...	—	—	—	—	—
02-03—Portland	AHL	71	22	15	37	115	...	...	...	—	—	—	—	—
03-04—Portland	AHL	68	18	19	37	74	6	3	0	3	0	1	1	4
—Washington	NHL	2	0	0	0	2	-1	0	0	—	—	—	—	—
04-05—Portland	AHL	63	18	21	39	86	-10	7	1	—	—	—	—	—
NHL Totals (1 year)		2	0	0	0	2	-1	0	0					

M

MIRONOV, BORIS D

PERSONAL: Born March 21, 1972, in Moscow, U.S.S.R. ... 6-4/223. ... Shoots right. ... Brother of Dmitri Mironov, D with five NHL teams (1991-2001). ... Name pronounced MIHR-ih-nahf.

TRANSACTIONS/CAREER NOTES: Selected by Winnipeg Jets in 2nd round (2nd Jets pick, 27th overall) of entry draft (June 20, 1992). ... Bruised back (February 2, 1994); missed three games. ... Traded by Jets with C Mats Lindgren and 1st- (C Jason Bonsignore) and 4th-round (RW Adam Copeland) picks in 1994 entry draft to Edmonton Oilers for D Dave Manson and 6th-round pick (D Chris Kibermanis) in 1994 entry draft (March 15, 1994). ... Bruised ankle (April 3, 1995); missed one game. ... Strained lower back (April 13, 1995); missed 10 games. ... Strained abdominal muscle (January 21, 1997); missed 12 games. ... Strained groin (February 19, 1997); missed five games. ... Strained groin (March 7, 1997); missed five games. ... Bruised right shoulder (February 3, 1999); missed two games. ... Traded by Oilers with LW Dean McAmmond and D Jonas Elofsson to Chicago Blackhawks for C Chad Kilger, LW Daniel Cleary, LW Ethan Moreau and D Christian Laflamme (March 20, 1999). ... Charley horse (March 25, 1999); missed one game. ... Hip pointer (December 4, 1999); missed one game. ... Sprained knee (March 26, 2000); missed final seven games of season. ... Torn wrist ligament (January 25, 2001); missed 15 games. ... Strained side muscle (December 31, 2001); missed three games. ... Dislocated shoulder (March 11, 2002); missed nine games. ... Strained groin (April 3, 2002); missed final five games of season. ... Traded by Blackhawks to New York Rangers for 4th-round pick (later traded to Florida; Panthers selected D Evan Schafer) in 2004 entry draft (January 8, 2003). ... Injured shoulder (February 19, 2003); missed two games. ... Back spasms (March 10, 2003); missed one game. ... Suspended two games by NHL (December 13, 2003) for cross-checking incident. ... Flu (January 17, 2004); missed two games.

		REGULAR SEASON								PLAYOFFS				
Season Team	League	GP	G	A	Pts.	PIM	+/-	PP	SH	GP	G	A	Pts.	PIM
88-89—CSKA Moscow	USSR	1	0	0	0	0	...	...	...	—	—	—	—	—
89-90—CSKA Moscow	USSR	7	0	0	0	0	...	...	...	—	—	—	—	—
90-91—CSKA Moscow	USSR	36	1	5	6	16	...	...	...	—	—	—	—	—
91-92—CSKA Moscow	CIS	36	2	1	3	22	...	...	...	—	—	—	—	—
92-93—CSKA Moscow	CIS	19	0	5	5	20	...	...	...	—	—	—	—	—
93-94—Winnipeg	NHL	65	7	22	29	96	-29	5	0	—	—	—	—	—
—Edmonton	NHL	14	0	2	2	14	-4	0	0	—	—	—	—	—
94-95—Cape Breton	AHL	4	2	5	7	23	-2	2	0	—	—	—	—	—
—Edmonton	NHL	29	1	7	8	40	-9	0	0	—	—	—	—	—
95-96—Edmonton	NHL	78	8	24	32	101	-23	7	0	—	—	—	—	—
96-97—Edmonton	NHL	55	6	26	32	85	2	2	0	12	2	8	10	16
97-98—Edmonton	NHL	81	16	30	46	100	-8	10	1	12	3	3	6	27
—Russian Oly. team	Int'l	6	0	2	2	2	7	0	0	—	—	—	—	—
98-99—Edmonton	NHL	63	11	29	40	104	6	5	0	—	—	—	—	—
—Chicago	NHL	12	0	9	9	27	7	0	0	—	—	—	—	—
99-00—Chicago	NHL	58	9	28	37	72	-3	4	2	—	—	—	—	—
00-01—Chicago	NHL	66	5	17	22	42	-14	3	0	—	—	—	—	—
01-02—Chicago	NHL	64	4	14	18	68	15	0	0	1	0	0	0	2
—Russian Oly. team	Int'l	6	1	0	1	2	...	...	...	—	—	—	—	—
02-03—Chicago	NHL	20	3	1	4	22	-1	1	0	—	—	—	—	—
—New York Rangers	NHL	36	3	9	12	34	3	1	0	—	—	—	—	—
03-04—New York Rangers	NHL	75	3	13	16	86	1	1	0	—	—	—	—	—
NHL Totals (11 years)		716	76	231	307	891	-57	39	3	25	5	11	16	45

MITCHELL, WILLIE D WILD

PERSONAL: Born April 23, 1977, in Port McNeill, B.C. ... 6-3/205. ... Shoots left.

TRANSACTIONS/CAREER NOTES: Selected by New Jersey Devils in eighth round (12th Devils pick, 199th overall) of NHL entry draft (June 22, 1996). ... Traded by Devils with future considerations to Minnesota Wild for D Sean O'Donnell (March 4, 2001). ... Bruised right shoulder (October 16, 2001); missed five games. ... Strained groin (December 10, 2001); missed three games. ... Bruised left wrist (January 19, 2002); missed five games. ... Injured ribs (November 19, 2002); missed five games. ... Suffered concussion (December 12, 2002); missed eight games. ... Injured knee (October 20, 2003); missed one game. ... Injured knee (November 21, 2003); missed 10 games. ... Had the flu (March 10, 2004); missed one game.

		REGULAR SEASON								PLAYOFFS				
Season Team	League	GP	G	A	Pts.	PIM	+/-	PP	SH	GP	G	A	Pts.	PIM
95-96—Melfort	Jr. A	19	2	6	8	0	...	...	...	14	0	2	2	12
96-97—Melfort	Jr. A	64	14	42	56	227	...	...	...	4	0	1	1	23
97-98—Clarkson	ECAC	34	9	17	26	105	...	...	...	—	—	—	—	—
98-99—Clarkson	ECAC	34	10	19	29	40	...	...	...	—	—	—	—	—
—Albany	AHL	6	1	3	4	29	3	1	0	—	—	—	—	—
99-00—Albany	AHL	63	5	14	19	71	...	...	...	5	1	2	3	4
—New Jersey	NHL	2	0	0	0	0	1	0	0	—	—	—	—	—
00-01—Albany	AHL	41	3	13	16	94	...	...	...	—	—	—	—	—
—New Jersey	NHL	16	0	2	2	29	0	0	0	—	—	—	—	—
—Minnesota	NHL	17	1	7	8	11	4	0	0	—	—	—	—	—
01-02—Minnesota	NHL	68	3	10	13	68	-16	0	0	—	—	—	—	—
02-03—Minnesota	NHL	69	2	12	14	84	13	0	1	18	1	3	4	14
03-04—Minnesota	NHL	70	1	13	14	83	12	0	0	—	—	—	—	—
NHL Totals (5 years)		242	7	44	51	275	14	0	1	18	1	3	4	14

MODANO, MIKE C STARS

PERSONAL: Born June 7, 1970, in Livonia, Mich. ... 6-3/205. ... Shoots left. ... Name pronounced muh-DAH-noh.

TRANSACTIONS/CAREER NOTES: Selected by Minnesota North Stars in first round (first North Stars pick, first overall) of NHL entry draft (June 11, 1988). ... Fractured nose (March 4, 1990). ... Injured groin (November 30, 1992); missed two games. ... North Stars franchise moved from Minnesota to Dallas and renamed Stars for 1993-94 season. ... Strained knee (January 6, 1994); missed six games. ... Suffered concussion (February 26, 1994); missed two games. ... Bruised ankle (March 12, 1995); missed four games. ... Ruptured ankle tendons (April 4, 1995) and had surgery; missed remainder of season. ... Injured stomach muscle (November 9, 1995); missed four games. ... Had the flu

(February 9, 1997); missed one game. ... Bruised ankle (November 12, 1997); missed one game. ... Tore knee ligament (December 5, 1997); missed 10 games. ... Reinjured knee (January 2, 1998); missed two games. ... Separated shoulder (March 13, 1998); missed 17 games. ... Strained groin (March 31, 1999); missed four games. ... Strained neck ligaments, suffered concussion, fractured nose (October 2, 1999); missed three games. ... Suffered concussion (January 12, 2000); missed one game. ... Strained hip flexor (March 28, 2000); missed one game. ... Strained back (October 10, 2000); missed one game. ... Bruised thigh (October 20, 2001); missed one game. ... Strained lower back (November 7, 2001); missed two games. ... Suffered concussion (December 17, 2002); missed three games. ... Injured groin (January 2, 2004); missed six games.

STATISTICAL PLATEAUS: Three-goal games: 1989-90 (1), 1993-94 (1), 1997-98 (1), 1998-99 (3). Total: 6. ... Four-goal games: 1995-96 (1). ... Total hat tricks: 7.

		REGULAR SEASON								PLAYOFFS				
Season Team	**League**	**GP**	**G**	**A**	**Pts.**	**PIM**	**+/-**	**PP**	**SH**	**GP**	**G**	**A**	**Pts.**	**PIM**
86-87—Prince Albert	WHL	70	32	30	62	96	...	...	...	8	1	4	5	4
87-88—Prince Albert	WHL	65	47	80	127	80	...	...	...	9	7	11	18	18
88-89—Prince Albert	WHL	41	39	66	105	74	...	...	...	—	—	—	—	—
—Minnesota	NHL	...	...	...	...	...	...	...	...	2	0	0	0	0
89-90—Minnesota	NHL	80	29	46	75	63	-7	12	0	7	1	1	2	12
90-91—Minnesota	NHL	79	28	36	64	65	2	9	0	23	8	12	20	16
91-92—Minnesota	NHL	76	33	44	77	46	-9	5	0	7	3	2	5	4
92-93—Minnesota	NHL	82	33	60	93	83	-7	9	0	—	—	—	—	—
93-94—Dallas	NHL	76	50	43	93	54	-8	18	0	9	7	3	10	16
94-95—Dallas	NHL	30	12	17	29	8	7	4	1	—	—	—	—	—
95-96—Dallas	NHL	78	36	45	81	63	-12	8	4	—	—	—	—	—
96-97—Dallas	NHL	80	35	48	83	42	43	9	5	7	4	1	5	0
97-98—Dallas	NHL	52	21	38	59	32	25	7	5	17	4	10	14	12
—U.S. Olympic team	Int'l	4	2	0	2	0	-2	0	0	—	—	—	—	—
98-99—Dallas	NHL	77	34	47	81	44	29	6	4	23	5	*18	23	16
99-00—Dallas	NHL	77	38	43	81	48	0	11	1	23	10	13	23	10
00-01—Dallas	NHL	81	33	51	84	52	26	8	3	9	3	4	7	0
01-02—Dallas	NHL	78	34	43	77	38	14	6	2	—	—	—	—	—
—U.S. Olympic team	Int'l	6	0	6	6	4	...	...	...	—	—	—	—	—
02-03—Dallas	NHL	79	28	57	85	30	34	5	2	12	5	10	15	4
03-04—Dallas	NHL	76	14	30	44	46	-21	6	0	5	1	2	3	8
NHL Totals (16 years)		1101	458	648	1106	714	116	123	27	144	51	76	127	98

MODIN, FREDRIK — LW — LIGHTNING

PERSONAL: Born October 8, 1974, in Sundsvall, Sweden. ... 6-4/220. ... Shoots left. ... Name pronounced moh-DEEN.

TRANSACTIONS/CAREER NOTES: Selected by Toronto Maple Leafs in 3rd round (3rd Maple Leafs pick, 64th overall) of entry draft (June 29, 1994). ... Concussion (October 22, 1996); missed three games. ... Flu (March 10, 1997); missed one game. ... Strained groin (December 2, 1997); missed two games. ... Fractured collarbone (February 13, 1999); missed 15 games. ... Traded by Maple Leafs to Tampa Bay Lightning for D Cory Cross and 7th-round pick (F Ivan Kolozvary) in 2001 draft (October 1, 1999). ... Bruised thigh (December 8, 2000); missed one game. ... Flu (January 4, 2001); missed one game. ... Bruised hip (March 4, 2001); missed two games. ... Charley horse (November 29, 2001); missed two games. ... Injured right wrist (January 26, 2002); missed 26 games. ... Strained groin (October 10, 2002); missed two games. ... Injured back and ribs (November 17, 2002); missed four games.

STATISTICAL PLATEAUS: Three-goal games: 2000-01 (1), 2003-04 (1). Total: 2.

		REGULAR SEASON								PLAYOFFS				
Season Team	**League**	**GP**	**G**	**A**	**Pts.**	**PIM**	**+/-**	**PP**	**SH**	**GP**	**G**	**A**	**Pts.**	**PIM**
91-92—Sundsvall Timra	Sweden Dv. 2	11	1	0	1	0	...	...	...	—	—	—	—	—
92-93—Sundsvall Timra	Sweden Dv. 2	30	5	7	12	12	...	...	...	—	—	—	—	—
93-94—Sundsvall Timra	Sweden Dv. 2	30	16	15	31	36	...	...	...	—	—	—	—	—
94-95—Brynas Gavle	Sweden	38	9	10	19	33	...	...	...	14	4	4	8	6
95-96—Brynas Gavle	Sweden	22	4	8	12	22	...	...	...	—	—	—	—	—
96-97—Toronto	NHL	76	6	7	13	24	-14	0	0	—	—	—	—	—
97-98—Toronto	NHL	74	16	16	32	32	-5	1	0	—	—	—	—	—
98-99—Toronto	NHL	67	16	15	31	35	14	1	0	8	0	0	0	6
99-00—Tampa Bay	NHL	80	22	26	48	18	-26	3	0	—	—	—	—	—
00-01—Tampa Bay	NHL	76	32	24	56	48	-1	8	0	—	—	—	—	—
01-02—Tampa Bay	NHL	54	14	17	31	27	0	2	0	—	—	—	—	—
02-03—Tampa Bay	NHL	76	17	23	40	43	7	2	1	11	2	0	2	18
03-04—Tampa Bay	NHL	82	29	28	57	32	31	5	1	23	8	11	19	10
04-05—Timra	Sweden	43	12	24	36	58	3	6	0	7	1	1	2	8
NHL Totals (8 years)		585	152	156	308	259	6	22	2	42	10	11	21	34

MODRY, JAROSLAV — D — THRASHERS

PERSONAL: Born February 27, 1971, in Ceske Budejovice, Czech. ... 6-2/219. ... Shoots left. ... Name pronounced MOH-dree.

TRANSACTIONS/CAREER NOTES: Selected by New Jersey Devils in ninth round (10th Devils pick, 179th overall) of NHL draft (June 16, 1990). ... Injured ankle (January 31, 1995); missed two games. ... Reinjured ankle (February 18, 1995); missed three games. ... Traded by Devils to Ottawa Senators for fourth-round pick (C Alyn McCauley) in 1995 entry draft (July 8, 1995). ... Ruptured eardrum (December 27, 1995). ... Traded by Senators to Los Angeles Kings for RW Kevin Brown (March 20, 1996). ... Sprained left knee (January 14, 1997); missed one game. ... Strained hip flexor (January 5, 2002); missed one game. ... Had the flu (April 14, 2002); missed one game. ... Left team for personal reasons (February 16, 2004); missed one game. ... Signed as free agent by Atlanta Thrashers (July 1, 2004).

		REGULAR SEASON								PLAYOFFS				
Season Team	**League**	**GP**	**G**	**A**	**Pts.**	**PIM**	**+/-**	**PP**	**SH**	**GP**	**G**	**A**	**Pts.**	**PIM**
88-89—Budejovice	Czech.	28	0	1	1	...	...	...	...	—	—	—	—	—
89-90—Budejovice	Czech.	41	2	2	4	...	...	...	...	—	—	—	—	—
90-91—Dukla Trencin	Czech.	33	1	9	10	6	...	...	...	—	—	—	—	—
91-92—Dukla Trencin	Czech.	18	0	4	4	...	...	...	...	—	—	—	—	—

M

Season Team	League	REGULAR SEASON GP	G	A	Pts.	PIM	+/-	PP	SH	PLAYOFFS GP	G	A	Pts.	PIM
—Budejovice	Czech Dv.I	14	4	10	14	...	...	...	...	—	—	—	—	—
92-93—Utica	AHL	80	7	35	42	62	-17	3	0	5	0	2	2	2
93-94—New Jersey	NHL	41	2	15	17	18	10	2	0	—	—	—	—	—
—Albany	AHL	19	1	5	6	25	3	0	0	—	—	—	—	—
94-95—HC Ceske Budejovice	Czech Rep.	19	1	3	4	30	...	...	...	—	—	—	—	—
—New Jersey	NHL	11	0	0	0	0	-1	0	0	—	—	—	—	—
—Albany	AHL	18	5	6	11	14	11	1	0	14	3	3	6	4
95-96—Ottawa	NHL	64	4	14	18	38	-17	1	0	—	—	—	—	—
—Los Angeles	NHL	9	0	3	3	6	-4	0	0	—	—	—	—	—
96-97—Los Angeles	NHL	30	3	3	6	25	-13	1	1	—	—	—	—	—
—Phoenix	IHL	23	3	12	15	17	...	...	...	—	—	—	—	—
—Utah	IHL	11	1	4	5	20	...	...	...	7	0	1	1	6
97-98—Utah	IHL	74	12	21	33	72	13	4	0	4	0	2	2	6
98-99—Long Beach	IHL	64	6	29	35	44	16	1	0	8	4	2	6	4
—Los Angeles	NHL	5	0	1	1	0	1	0	0	—	—	—	—	—
99-00—Los Angeles	NHL	26	5	4	9	18	-2	5	0	2	0	0	0	2
—Long Beach	IHL	11	2	4	6	8	...	...	...	—	—	—	—	—
00-01—Los Angeles	NHL	63	4	15	19	48	16	0	0	10	1	0	1	4
01-02—Los Angeles	NHL	80	4	38	42	65	-4	4	0	7	0	2	2	0
02-03—Los Angeles	NHL	82	13	25	38	68	-13	8	0	—	—	—	—	—
03-04—Los Angeles	NHL	79	5	27	32	44	11	1	0	—	—	—	—	—
04-05—Liberec	Czech Rep.	19	3	7	10	24	12	...	...	12	0	4	4	22
NHL Totals (10 years)		490	40	145	185	330	-16	22	1	19	1	2	3	6

MOEN, TRAVIS — LW — MIGHTY DUCKS

PERSONAL: Born April 6, 1982, in Swift Current, Sask. ... 6-3/210. ... Shoots left.

TRANSACTIONS/CAREER NOTES: Selected by Calgary Flames in 5th round (6th Flames pick, 141st overall) of entry draft (June 24, 2000). ... Signed as free agent by Chicago Blackhawks (October 21, 2002). ... Traded by Blackhawks to the Anaheim Mighty Ducks for RW Michael Holmqvist (July 30, 2005).

Season Team	League	REGULAR SEASON GP	G	A	Pts.	PIM	+/-	PP	SH	PLAYOFFS GP	G	A	Pts.	PIM
98-99—Kelowna	WHL	4	0	0	0	0	...	...	...	—	—	—	—	—
99-00—Kelowna	WHL	66	9	6	15	96	...	...	...	—	—	—	—	—
00-01—Kelowna	WHL	40	8	8	16	106	...	...	...	—	—	—	—	—
01-02—Kelowna	WHL	71	10	17	27	197	...	...	...	13	1	0	1	28
02-03—Norfolk	AHL	42	1	2	3	62	-12	0	0	9	0	0	0	20
03-04—Chicago	NHL	82	4	2	6	142	-17	0	0	—	—	—	—	—
04-05—Norfolk	AHL	79	8	12	20	187	5	1	0	6	0	1	1	6
NHL Totals (1 year)		82	4	2	6	142	-17	0	0					

MOGILNY, ALEXANDER — RW — DEVILS

PERSONAL: Born February 18, 1969, in Khabarovsk, U.S.S.R. ... 6-0/209. ... Shoots left. ... Name pronounced moh-GIHL-nee.

TRANSACTIONS/CAREER NOTES: Selected by Buffalo Sabres in 5th round (4th Sabres pick, 89th overall) of entry draft (June 11, 1988). ... Flu (November 26, 1989). ... Missed games because of fear of flying (January 22, 1990); spent remainder of season using ground travel. ... Separated shoulder (February 8, 1991); missed six games. ... Flu (November 1991); missed two games. ... Flu (December 18, 1991); missed one game. ... Bruised shoulder (October 10, 1992); missed six games. ... Fractured leg and tore ankle ligaments (May 6, 1993); missed remainder of 1992-93 playoffs and first nine games of 1993-94 season. ... Sore ankle (February 2, 1994); missed four games. ... Inflamed ankle tendon (February 15, 1994); missed four games. ... Pinched nerve in neck (April 9, 1995); missed three games. ... Traded by Sabres with 5th-round pick (LW Todd Norman) in 1995 entry draft to Vancouver Canucks for C Michael Peca, D Mike Wilson and 1st-round pick (D Jay McKee) in 1995 entry draft (July 8, 1995). ... Injured hamstring (October 28, 1995); missed three games. ... Flu (December 3, 1996); missed two games. ... Strained groin (April 4, 1997); missed remainder of season. ... Missed first 16 games of 1997-98 season in contract dispute. ... Injured groin (December 15, 1997); missed 11 games. ... Strained back (February 24, 1998); missed four games. ... Sprained knee ligament (November 21, 1998); missed 17 games. ... Bruised kidney (January 4, 1999); missed two games. ... Strained abdominal muscle (February 20, 1999); missed four games. ... Injured back (November 26, 1999); missed eight games. ... Injured hip (January 12, 2000); missed seven games. ... Injured shoulder (February 12, 2000); missed eight games. ... Traded by Canucks to New Jersey Devils for C Brendan Morrison and C Denis Pederson (March 14, 2000). ... Injured neck (February 10, 2000); missed one game. ... Bruised abdomen (February 14, 2001); missed four games. ... Strained groin (April 4, 2001); missed one game. ... Signed as free agent by Toronto Maple Leafs (July 3, 2001). ... Back spasms (January 12, 2002); missed three games. ... Injured back (January 29, 2002); missed 13 games. ... Injured neck (November 19, 2002); missed one game. ... Injured foot (January 17, 2003); missed two games. ... Injured back (January 24, 2003); missed two games. ... Concussion (April 14, 2003); missed one playoff game. ... Injured groin (October 14, 2003); missed five games. ... Injured hip (November 22, 2003); missed 40 games. ... Hip surgery (September 27, 2004).

STATISTICAL PLATEAUS: Three-goal games: 1990-91 (1), 1991-92 (1), 1992-93 (5), 1993-94 (1), 1995-96 (3), 1996-97 (1), 2000-01 (1), 2002-03 (2). Total: 15. ... Four-goal games: 1992-93 (2). ... Total hat tricks: 17.

Season Team	League	REGULAR SEASON GP	G	A	Pts.	PIM	+/-	PP	SH	PLAYOFFS GP	G	A	Pts.	PIM
86-87—CSKA Moscow	USSR	28	15	1	16	4	...	...	...	—	—	—	—	—
87-88—CSKA Moscow	USSR	39	12	8	20	20	...	...	...	—	—	—	—	—
88-89—CSKA Moscow	USSR	31	11	11	22	24	...	...	...	—	—	—	—	—
89-90—Buffalo	NHL	65	15	28	43	16	8	4	0	4	0	1	1	2
90-91—Buffalo	NHL	62	30	34	64	16	14	3	3	6	0	6	6	2
91-92—Buffalo	NHL	67	39	45	84	73	7	15	0	2	0	2	2	0
92-93—Buffalo	NHL	77	76	51	127	40	7	27	0	7	7	3	10	6
93-94—Buffalo	NHL	66	32	47	79	22	8	17	0	7	4	2	6	6
94-95—Spartak Moscow	Russian	1	0	1	1	0	...	...	...	—	—	—	—	—
—Buffalo	NHL	44	19	28	47	36	0	12	0	5	3	2	5	2

Season Team	League	GP	G	A	Pts.	PIM	+/-	PP	SH	GP	G	A	Pts.	PIM
		REGULAR SEASON								PLAYOFFS				
95-96—Vancouver	NHL	79	55	52	107	16	14	10	5	6	1	8	9	8
96-97—Vancouver	NHL	76	31	42	73	18	9	7	1	—	—	—	—	—
97-98—Vancouver	NHL	51	18	27	45	36	-6	5	4	—	—	—	—	—
98-99—Vancouver	NHL	59	14	31	45	58	0	3	2	—	—	—	—	—
99-00—Vancouver	NHL	47	21	17	38	16	7	3	1	—	—	—	—	—
—New Jersey	NHL	12	3	3	6	4	-4	2	0	23	4	3	7	4
00-01—New Jersey	NHL	75	43	40	83	43	10	12	0	25	5	11	16	8
01-02—Toronto	NHL	66	24	33	57	8	1	5	0	20	8	3	11	8
02-03—Toronto	NHL	73	33	46	79	12	4	5	3	6	5	2	7	4
03-04—Toronto	NHL	37	8	22	30	12	9	4	1	13	2	4	6	8
NHL Totals (15 years)		956	461	546	1007	426	88	134	20	124	39	47	86	58

MONTADOR, STEVE — D — FLAMES

PERSONAL: Born December 21, 1979, in Vancouver. ... 6-0/210. ... Shoots right.
TRANSACTIONS/CAREER NOTES: Signed as free agent by Calgary Flames (September 5, 2000). ... Injured upper body (March 22, 2004); missed six games.

Season Team	League	GP	G	A	Pts.	PIM	+/-	PP	SH	GP	G	A	Pts.	PIM
		REGULAR SEASON								PLAYOFFS				
96-97—North Bay	OHL	63	7	28	35	129	...	...	...	—	—	—	—	—
97-98—North Bay	OHL	37	5	16	21	54	...	...	...	—	—	—	—	—
—Erie	OHL	26	3	17	20	35	...	...	...	7	1	1	2	8
98-99—Erie	OHL	61	9	33	42	114	...	...	...	5	0	2	2	9
99-00—Peterborough	OHL	64	14	42	56	97	...	...	...	5	0	2	2	4
00-01—Saint John	AHL	58	1	6	7	95	...	...	...	19	0	8	8	13
01-02—Saint John	AHL	67	9	16	25	107	-11	0	0	—	—	—	—	—
—Calgary	NHL	11	1	2	3	26	-2	0	0	—	—	—	—	—
02-03—Saint John	AHL	11	1	7	8	20	-4	0	0	—	—	—	—	—
—Calgary	NHL	50	1	1	2	114	-9	0	0	—	—	—	—	—
03-04—Calgary	NHL	26	1	2	3	50	-1	0	0	20	1	2	3	6
04-05—Mulhouse	France	15	1	7	8	69	...	...	...	—	—	—	—	—
NHL Totals (3 years)		87	3	5	8	190	-12	0	0	20	1	2	3	6

MONTOYA, AL — G — RANGERS

PERSONAL: Born February 13, 1985, in Chicago. ... 6-1/190. ... Catches left.
COLLEGE: Michigan.
TRANSACTIONS/CAREER NOTES: Selected by New York Rangers in 1st round (1st Rangers pick, 6th overall) of entry draft (June 26, 2004).

Season Team	League	GP	Min.	W	L	T	GA	SO	GAA	SV%	GP	Min.	W	L	GA	SO	GAA	SV%
		REGULAR SEASON									PLAYOFFS							
02-03—Univ. of Michigan	CCHA	43	2547	30	10	3	99	0	2.33	.911	—	—	—	—	—	—	—	—
03-04—Univ. of Michigan	CCHA	40	2340	26	12	2	87	6	2.23	.917	—	—	—	—	—	—	—	—
04-05—Univ. of Michigan	CCHA	40	...	30	7	3	99	3	2.52	.895	—	—	—	—	—	—	—	—

MOORE, DOMINIC — C — RANGERS

PERSONAL: Born August 3, 1980, in Thornhill, Ont. ... 6-0/194. ... Shoots left. ... Brother of Steve Moore, C, Colorado Avalanche. Brother of Mark Moore, Pittsburgh Penguins organization.
TRANSACTIONS/CAREER NOTES: Selected by New York Rangers in third round (second Rangers pick, 95th overall) of NHL entry draft (June 24, 2000).

Season Team	League	GP	G	A	Pts.	PIM	+/-	PP	SH	GP	G	A	Pts.	PIM
		REGULAR SEASON								PLAYOFFS				
98-99—Aurora	OPJHL	51	34	53	87	70	...	...	...	—	—	—	—	—
99-00—Harvard	ECAC	28	12	8	20	28	...	...	...	—	—	—	—	—
00-01—Harvard	ECAC	32	15	28	43	40	...	...	...	—	—	—	—	—
01-02—Harvard	ECAC	32	13	16	29	37	...	...	...	—	—	—	—	—
02-03—Harvard	ECAC	34	24	27	51	30	...	...	...	—	—	—	—	—
03-04—New York Rangers	NHL	5	0	3	3	0	0	0	0	—	—	—	—	—
—Hartford	AHL	70	14	25	39	60	3	3	0	16	3	3	6	8
04-05—Hartford	AHL	78	19	31	50	78	14	8	2	6	1	1	2	4
NHL Totals (1 year)		5	0	3	3	0	0	0	0					

MOORE, STEVE — C

PERSONAL: Born September 22, 1978, in Windsor, Ont. ... 6-1/210. ... Shoots right. ... Brother of Dominic Moore, C, New York Rangers organization. Brother of Mark Moore, D, Pittsburgh Penguins organization.
TRANSACTIONS/CAREER NOTES: Selected by Colorado Avalanche in 2nd round (7th Avalanche pick, 53rd overall) of entry draft (June 27, 1998). ... Fractured neck, suffered concussion and cut face (March 8, 2004); missed remainder of season.

Season Team	League	GP	G	A	Pts.	PIM	+/-	PP	SH	GP	G	A	Pts.	PIM
		REGULAR SEASON								PLAYOFFS				
95-96—Thornhill	OHA Jr. A	77	30	43	73	90	...	...	...	—	—	—	—	—
96-97—Thornhill	OHA Jr. A	50	34	52	86	52	...	...	...	—	—	—	—	—
97-98—Harvard	ECAC	33	10	23	33	46	...	...	...	—	—	—	—	—

M

Season Team	League	REGULAR SEASON GP	G	A	Pts.	PIM	+/-	PP	SH	PLAYOFFS GP	G	A	Pts.	PIM
98-99—Harvard	ECAC	30	18	13	31	34	...	...	...	—	—	—	—	—
99-00—Harvard	ECAC	27	10	16	26	53	...	...	...	—	—	—	—	—
—Kansas City	IHL	1	0	0	0	2	...	...	...	—	—	—	—	—
00-01—Kansas City	IHL	32	7	26	33	43	...	...	...	—	—	—	—	—
01-02—Hershey	AHL	68	10	17	27	31	-3	0	1	8	0	1	1	6
—Colorado	NHL	8	0	0	0	4	-4	0	0	—	—	—	—	—
02-03—Colorado	NHL	4	0	0	0	0	0	0	0	—	—	—	—	—
—Hershey	AHL	58	10	13	23	41	-14	0	0	5	0	1	1	4
03-04—Hershey	AHL	13	4	4	8	6	10	1	0	—	—	—	—	—
—Colorado	NHL	57	5	7	12	37	-5	0	0	—	—	—	—	—
NHL Totals (3 years)		69	5	7	12	41	-9	0	0					

MORAN, BRAD — C

PERSONAL: Born March 20, 1979, in Abbotsford, B.C. ... 5-11/186. ... Shoots left.

TRANSACTIONS/CAREER NOTES: Selected by Buffalo Sabres in 7th round (8th Sabres pick, 191st pick overall) of entry draft (June 27, 1998). ... Signed as free agent by Columbus Blue Jackets (June 5, 2000).

Season Team	League	REGULAR SEASON GP	G	A	Pts.	PIM	+/-	PP	SH	PLAYOFFS GP	G	A	Pts.	PIM
95-96—Calgary	WHL	70	13	31	44	28	...	...	...	—	—	—	—	—
96-97—Calgary	WHL	72	30	36	66	61	...	...	...	—	—	—	—	—
97-98—Calgary	WHL	72	53	49	102	64	...	...	...	18	10	8	18	20
98-99—Calgary	WHL	71	60	58	118	96	55	24	8	21	17	25	42	26
99-00—Calgary	WHL	72	48	*72	*120	84	53	21	7	13	7	15	22	18
00-01—Syracuse	AHL	71	11	19	30	30	...	...	...	5	3	4	7	3
01-02—Syracuse	AHL	64	25	24	49	51	4	8	3	10	5	8	13	2
—Columbus	NHL	3	0	0	0	0	0	0	0	—	—	—	—	—
02-03—Syracuse	AHL	47	12	19	31	22	-4	5	2	—	—	—	—	—
03-04—Columbus	NHL	2	1	1	2	2	-1	0	0	—	—	—	—	—
—Syracuse	AHL	72	24	35	59	44	1	10	1	7	5	3	8	2
04-05—Syracuse	AHL	80	26	46	72	70	0	13	1	—	—	—	—	—
NHL Totals (2 years)		5	1	1	2	2	-1	0	0					

MORAN, IAN — D/RW — BRUINS

PERSONAL: Born August 24, 1972, in Cleveland. ... 6-0/200. ... Shoots right. ... Name pronounced muh-RAN.

TRANSACTIONS/CAREER NOTES: Selected by Pittsburgh Penguins in 6th round (5th Penguins pick, 107th overall) of entry draft (June 16, 1990). ... Bruised shoulder (November 22, 1995); missed nine games. ... Injured shoulder (February 21, 1996); missed one game. ... Shoulder surgery (March 21, 1996); missed remainder of season. ... Injured back and neck (April 10, 1997); missed two games. ... Bruised kneecap and had surgery (September 30, 1997); missed 34 games. ... Concussion (February 2, 1998); missed four games. ... Injured knee (March 21, 1998); missed five games. ... Injured ankle (October 26, 1998); missed five games. ... Reinjured ankle (November 7, 1998); missed nine games. ... Bruised ankle (January 5, 1999); missed two games. ... Bruised right testicle (February 5, 1999); missed three games. ... Injured ankle (April 3, 1999); missed one game. ... Fractured foot (December 2, 1999); missed two games. ... Flu (January 2, 2000); missed one game. ... Bruised ankle (April 7, 2000); missed final game of season. ... Injured knee (October 18, 2000); missed seven games. ... Fractured hand (November 10, 2000); missed 15 games. ... Flu (February 16, 2001); missed one game. ... Fractured thumb (February 19, 2001); missed 18 games. ... Fractured foot (December 8, 2001); missed 12 games. ... Injured hip (April 3, 2002); missed remainder of season. ... Traded by Penguins to Boston Bruins for 4th-round pick (D Paul Bissonette) in 2003 draft (March 11, 2003). ... Injured back (March 22, 2003); missed four games. ... Sprained ankle (December 23, 2003); missed final 47 games of regular season and playoffs.

Season Team	League	REGULAR SEASON GP	G	A	Pts.	PIM	+/-	PP	SH	PLAYOFFS GP	G	A	Pts.	PIM
87-88—Belmont Hill	Mass. H.S.	25	3	13	16	15	...	...	...	—	—	—	—	—
88-89—Belmont Hill	Mass. H.S.	23	7	25	32	8	...	...	...	—	—	—	—	—
89-90—Belmont Hill	Mass. H.S.	...	10	36	46	0	...	...	...	—	—	—	—	—
90-91—Belmont Hill	Mass. H.S.	23	7	44	51	12	...	...	...	—	—	—	—	—
91-92—Boston College	Hockey East	30	2	16	18	44	...	...	...	—	—	—	—	—
92-93—Boston College	Hockey East	31	8	12	20	32	...	...	...	—	—	—	—	—
93-94—U.S. national team	Int'l	50	8	15	23	69	...	0	0	—	—	—	—	—
—Cleveland	IHL	33	5	13	18	39	-4	3	0	—	—	—	—	—
94-95—Cleveland	IHL	64	7	31	38	94	3	2	0	4	0	1	1	2
—Pittsburgh	NHL	...	...	...	...	...	...	...	...	8	0	0	0	0
95-96—Pittsburgh	NHL	51	1	1	2	47	-1	0	0	—	—	—	—	—
96-97—Cleveland	IHL	36	6	23	29	26	...	...	...	—	—	—	—	—
—Pittsburgh	NHL	36	4	5	9	22	-11	0	0	5	1	2	3	4
97-98—Pittsburgh	NHL	37	1	6	7	19	0	0	0	6	0	0	0	2
98-99—Pittsburgh	NHL	62	4	5	9	37	1	0	1	13	0	2	2	8
99-00—Pittsburgh	NHL	73	4	8	12	28	-10	0	0	11	0	1	1	2
00-01—Pittsburgh	NHL	40	3	4	7	28	5	0	0	18	0	1	1	4
01-02—Pittsburgh	NHL	64	2	8	10	54	-11	0	0	—	—	—	—	—
02-03—Pittsburgh	NHL	70	0	7	7	46	-17	0	0	—	—	—	—	—
—Boston	NHL	8	0	1	1	2	-1	0	0	5	0	1	1	4
03-04—Boston	NHL	35	1	4	5	28	3	0	0	—	—	—	—	—
04-05—Bofors	Sweden Dv. 1	7	0	4	4	22	-3	0	0	—	—	—	—	—
—Bofors	Sweden Dv. 2	7	0	4	4	22	-3	0	0	—	—	—	—	—
—Nottingham	England	14	2	6	8	8	...	...	...	5	0	1	1	2
NHL Totals (10 years)		476	20	49	69	311	-42	0	1	66	1	7	8	24

MOREAU, ETHAN — LW — OILERS

PERSONAL: Born September 22, 1975, in Huntsville, Ont. ... 6-2/209. ... Shoots left. ... Name pronounced MOHR-oh.

TRANSACTIONS/CAREER NOTES: Selected by Chicago Blackhawks in 1st round (1st Blackhawks pick, 14th overall) of entry draft (June 28, 1994). ... Fractured knuckle (November 16, 1997); missed seven games. ... Fractured ankle (December 14, 1997); missed 20 games. ... Traded by Blackhawks with LW Daniel Cleary, C Chad Kilger and D Christian Laflamme to Edmonton Oilers for D Boris Mironov, LW Dean McAmmond and D Jonas Elofsson (March 20, 1999). ... Injured ribs (November 24, 1999); missed eight games. ... Flu (December 27, 1999); missed one game. ... Shoulder surgery (May 24, 2000); missed first 14 games of season. ... Bruised ankle (December 16, 2001); missed one game. ... Flu (December 11, 2002); missed two games. ... Injured shoulder (December 23, 2003); missed one game.

		REGULAR SEASON								PLAYOFFS				
Season Team	**League**	**GP**	**G**	**A**	**Pts.**	**PIM**	**+/-**	**PP**	**SH**	**GP**	**G**	**A**	**Pts.**	**PIM**
90-91—Orillia	OHA	42	17	22	39	26	...	...	...	—	—	—	—	—
91-92—Niagara Falls	OHL	62	20	35	55	39	...	...	...	17	4	6	10	4
92-93—Niagara Falls	OHL	65	32	41	73	69	...	...	...	4	0	3	3	4
93-94—Niagara Falls	OHL	59	44	54	98	100	...	11	...	—	—	—	—	—
94-95—Niagara Falls	OHL	39	25	41	66	69	...	11	1	—	—	—	—	—
—Sudbury	OHL	23	13	17	30	22	...	2	0	18	6	12	18	26
95-96—Indianapolis	IHL	71	21	20	41	126	...	...	...	5	4	0	4	8
—Chicago	NHL	8	0	1	1	4	1	0	0	—	—	—	—	—
96-97—Chicago	NHL	82	15	16	31	123	13	0	0	6	1	0	1	9
97-98—Chicago	NHL	54	9	9	18	73	0	2	0	—	—	—	—	—
98-99—Chicago	NHL	66	9	6	15	84	-5	0	0	—	—	—	—	—
—Edmonton	NHL	14	1	5	6	8	2	0	0	4	0	3	3	6
99-00—Edmonton	NHL	73	17	10	27	62	8	1	0	5	0	1	1	0
00-01—Edmonton	NHL	68	9	10	19	90	-6	0	1	4	0	0	0	2
01-02—Edmonton	NHL	80	11	5	16	81	4	0	2	—	—	—	—	—
02-03—Edmonton	NHL	78	14	17	31	112	-7	2	3	6	0	1	1	16
03-04—Edmonton	NHL	81	20	12	32	96	7	0	3	—	—	—	—	—
04-05—VSV	Austria	16	10	6	16	73	-8	4	1	3	4	0	4	0
NHL Totals (9 years)		604	105	91	196	733	17	5	9	25	1	5	6	33

MORGAN, GAVIN — C

PERSONAL: Born July 9, 1976, in Scarborough, Ont. ... 5-11/191. ... Shoots right.

TRANSACTIONS/CAREER NOTES: Signed as free agent by Idaho of the ECHL (August 25, 1999). ... Signed as free agent by Utah of the AHL (July 26, 2000). ... Signed as free agent by Dallas Stars (July 17, 2001). ... Signed as free agent by Montreal Canadiens (July 23, 2004). ... Contract not renewed (July 25, 2005).

		REGULAR SEASON								PLAYOFFS				
Season Team	**League**	**GP**	**G**	**A**	**Pts.**	**PIM**	**+/-**	**PP**	**SH**	**GP**	**G**	**A**	**Pts.**	**PIM**
95-96—Denver	WCHA	28	2	9	11	47	...	...	...	—	—	—	—	—
96-97—Denver	WCHA	41	8	15	23	46	...	...	...	—	—	—	—	—
97-98—Denver	WCHA	37	9	8	17	42	...	...	...	—	—	—	—	—
98-99—Denver	WCHA	40	13	16	29	85	...	...	...	—	—	—	—	—
99-00—Long Beach	IHL	7	0	1	1	10	2	...	...	—	—	—	—	—
—Utah	IHL	10	0	2	2	4	2	...	...	2	0	2	2	2
—Idaho	WCHL	54	17	33	50	150	...	...	...	3	0	3	3	4
00-01—Utah	IHL	79	7	14	21	187	2	...	...	—	—	—	—	—
01-02—Utah	AHL	76	8	24	32	249	0	...	...	5	0	1	1	2
02-03—Utah	AHL	73	15	24	39	244	-27	...	...	2	0	1	1	17
03-04—Hershey	AHL	67	10	23	33	152	-3	2	2	—	—	—	—	—
—Dallas	NHL	6	0	0	0	21	0	0	0	—	—	—	—	—
04-05—Hamilton	AHL	76	10	23	33	147	-4	0	2	4	0	0	0	6
NHL Totals (1 year)		6	0	0	0	21	0	0	0					

MORGAN, JASON — C — BLACKHAWKS

PERSONAL: Born October 9, 1976, in St. John's, Newfoundland. ... 6-1/194. ... Shoots left.

TRANSACTIONS/CAREER NOTES: Selected by Los Angeles Kings in 5th round (5th Kings pick, 118th overall) of entry draft (July 8, 1995). ... Signed as free agent by Calgary Flames (July 11, 2002). ... Claimed off waivers by Nashville Predators (December 31, 2003). ... Separated shoulder (January 7, 2004); missed 10 games. ... Claimed off waivers by Flames (February 19, 2004). ... Traded by Flames with future considerations to Chicago Blackhawks for LW Ville Nieminen (February 24, 2004).

		REGULAR SEASON								PLAYOFFS				
Season Team	**League**	**GP**	**G**	**A**	**Pts.**	**PIM**	**+/-**	**PP**	**SH**	**GP**	**G**	**A**	**Pts.**	**PIM**
93-94—Kitchener	OHL	65	6	15	21	16	...	...	...	5	1	0	1	0
94-95—Kitchener	OHL	35	3	15	18	25	...	0	0	—	—	—	—	—
—Kingston	OHL	20	0	3	3	14	...	0	0	6	0	2	2	0
95-96—Kingston	OHL	66	16	38	54	50	...	...	...	6	1	2	3	0
96-97—Phoenix	IHL	57	3	6	9	29	...	...	...	—	—	—	—	—
—Mississippi	ECHL	6	3	0	3	0	...	...	...	3	1	1	2	6
—Los Angeles	NHL	3	0	0	0	0	-3	0	0	—	—	—	—	—
97-98—Springfield	AHL	58	13	22	35	66	13	4	1	3	1	0	1	18
—Los Angeles	NHL	11	1	0	1	4	-7	0	0	—	—	—	—	—
98-99—Long Beach	IHL	13	4	6	10	18	-2	0	0	—	—	—	—	—
—Springfield	AHL	46	6	16	22	51	-5	1	0	3	0	0	0	6
99-00—Florida	ECHL	48	14	25	39	79	...	...	...	5	2	2	4	16
—Cincinnati	IHL	15	1	3	4	14	...	...	...	—	—	—	—	—
00-01—Hamilton	AHL	11	2	0	2	10	...	...	...	—	—	—	—	—
—Springfield	AHL	16	1	4	5	19	...	...	...	6	0	1	1	2

Season Team	League	GP	G	A	Pts.	PIM	+/-	PP	SH	GP	G	A	Pts.	PIM
		REGULAR SEASON								PLAYOFFS				
—Florida	ECHL	37	15	22	37	41	...	...	...	5	2	3	5	17
01-02—Saint John	AHL	76	17	20	37	69	-19	10	1	—	—	—	—	—
02-03—Saint John	AHL	80	13	40	53	63	-2	3	2	—	—	—	—	—
03-04—Calgary	NHL	13	0	2	2	2	1	0	0	—	—	—	—	—
—Lowell	AHL	21	6	13	19	16	2	1	0	8	0	1	1	10
—Nashville	NHL	6	0	2	2	2	0	0	0	—	—	—	—	—
—Norfolk	AHL	19	6	8	14	16	-4	4	0	—	—	—	—	—
04-05—Norfolk	AHL	71	9	20	29	116	-8	2	0	6	2	2	4	8
NHL Totals (3 years)		33	1	4	5	8	-9	0	0					

MOROZOV, ALEKSEY — RW/LW — PENGUINS

PERSONAL: Born February 16, 1977, in Moscow. ... 6-1/204. ... Shoots left. ... Name pronounced muh-ROH-sahf.

TRANSACTIONS/CAREER NOTES: Selected by Pittsburgh Penguins in 1st round (1st Penguins pick, 24th overall) of entry draft (July 8, 1995). ... Fractured toe (December 27, 1997); missed one game. ... Concussion (November 14, 1998); missed three games. ... Concussion (December 21, 1998); missed 12 games. ... Charley horse (October 30, 1999); missed eight games. ... Bruised back (January 25, 2000); missed two games. ... Charley horse (March 16, 2000); missed four games. ... Bruised shoulder (December 12, 2001); missed five games. ... Injured shoulder (January 3, 2002); missed four games. ... Fractured wrist (December 12, 2002); missed final 55 games of season. ... Injured shoulder (December 31, 2003); missed three games. ... Injured back (March 16, 2004); missed two games.

STATISTICAL PLATEAUS: Three-goal games: 1999-00 (1), 2001-02 (1). Total: 2.

Season Team	League	GP	G	A	Pts.	PIM	+/-	PP	SH	GP	G	A	Pts.	PIM
		REGULAR SEASON								PLAYOFFS				
93-94—Soviet Wings	CIS	7	0	0	0	0	...	...	...	3	0	0	0	2
94-95—Soviet Wings	CIS	48	15	12	27	53	...	...	...	4	0	3	3	0
95-96—Soviet Wings	CIS	47	12	9	21	26	...	...	...	—	—	—	—	—
96-97—Kryla Sov. Moscow	Russian	44	21	11	32	32	...	...	...	2	0	1	1	2
97-98—Pittsburgh	NHL	76	13	13	26	8	-4	2	0	6	0	1	1	2
—Russian Oly. team	Int'l	6	2	2	4	0	1	0	0	—	—	—	—	—
98-99—Pittsburgh	NHL	67	9	10	19	14	5	0	0	10	1	1	2	0
99-00—Pittsburgh	NHL	68	12	19	31	14	12	0	1	5	0	0	0	0
00-01—Pittsburgh	NHL	66	5	14	19	6	-8	0	0	18	3	3	6	6
01-02—Pittsburgh	NHL	72	20	29	49	16	-7	7	0	—	—	—	—	—
02-03—Pittsburgh	NHL	27	9	16	25	16	-3	6	0	—	—	—	—	—
03-04—Pittsburgh	NHL	75	16	34	50	24	-24	8	0	—	—	—	—	—
04-05—Ak Bars Kazan	Russian	58	20	26	46	30	19	...	...	4	0	1	1	2
NHL Totals (7 years)		451	84	135	219	98	-29	23	1	39	4	5	9	8

MORRIS, DEREK — D — COYOTES

PERSONAL: Born August 24, 1978, in Edmonton. ... 5-11/200. ... Shoots right.

TRANSACTIONS/CAREER NOTES: Selected by Calgary Flames in first round (first Flames pick, 13th overall) of NHL entry draft (June 22, 1996). ... Separated shoulder (February 22, 1999); missed 10 games. ... Suffered concussion (December 14, 1999); missed three games. ... Missed first 27 games of 2000-01 season in contract dispute. ... Injured (November 8, 2001); missed one game. ... Injured wrist (November 29, 2001); missed 20 games. ... Traded by Flames with LW Dean McAmmond and C Jeff Shantz to Colorado Avalanche for LW Chris Drury and C Stephane Yelle (October 1, 2002). ... Injured eye (January 23, 2003); missed seven games. ... Traded by Avalanche with D Keith Ballard to Phoenix Coyotes for F Chris Gratton, D Ossi Vaananen and second-round pick in 2005 entry draft (March 9, 2004).

Season Team	League	GP	G	A	Pts.	PIM	+/-	PP	SH	GP	G	A	Pts.	PIM
		REGULAR SEASON								PLAYOFFS				
95-96—Regina	WHL	67	8	44	52	70	...	...	...	11	1	7	8	26
96-97—Regina	WHL	67	18	57	75	180	10	8	0	5	0	3	3	9
—Saint John	AHL	7	0	3	3	7	-1	0	0	5	0	3	3	7
97-98—Calgary	NHL	82	9	20	29	88	1	5	1	—	—	—	—	—
98-99—Calgary	NHL	71	7	27	34	73	4	3	0	—	—	—	—	—
99-00—Calgary	NHL	78	9	29	38	80	2	3	0	—	—	—	—	—
00-01—Saint John	AHL	3	1	2	3	2	...	...	...	—	—	—	—	—
—Calgary	NHL	51	5	23	28	56	-15	3	1	—	—	—	—	—
01-02—Calgary	NHL	61	4	30	34	88	-4	2	0	—	—	—	—	—
02-03—Colorado	NHL	75	11	37	48	68	16	9	0	7	0	3	3	6
03-04—Colorado	NHL	69	6	22	28	47	4	2	0	—	—	—	—	—
—Phoenix	NHL	14	0	4	4	2	-5	0	0	—	—	—	—	—
NHL Totals (7 years)		501	51	192	243	502	3	27	2	7	0	3	3	6

MORRIS, MIKE — RW — SHARKS

PERSONAL: Born July 14, 1983, in Dorchester, Mass. ... 6-0/182. ... Shoots right.

TRANSACTIONS/CAREER NOTES: Selected by San Jose Sharks in 1st round (1st Sharks pick, 27th overall) of entry draft (June 22, 2002).

Season Team	League	GP	G	A	Pts.	PIM	+/-	PP	SH	GP	G	A	Pts.	PIM
		REGULAR SEASON								PLAYOFFS				
00-01—St. Sebastian's	USHS (East)	28	20	28	48	18	...	...	...	—	—	—	—	—
01-02—St. Sebastian's	USHS (East)	31	29	29	58	26	...	...	...	—	—	—	—	—
02-03—Northeastern	ECAC	26	9	12	21	16	...	...	...	—	—	—	—	—
03-04—Northeastern	ECAC	34	10	20	30	14	...	...	...	—	—	—	—	—
04-05—Northeastern	ECAC	34	19	20	39	24	...	...	...	—	—	—	—	—

MORRISON, BRENDAN C CANUCKS

PERSONAL: Born August 15, 1975, in Pitt Meadows, B.C. ... 5-11/185. ... Shoots left.
TRANSACTIONS/CAREER NOTES: Selected by New Jersey Devils in 2nd round (3rd Devils pick, 39th overall) of NHL draft (June 26, 1993). ... Missed first nine games of 1999-2000 season in contract dispute. ... Injured (October 29, 1999); missed two games. ... Traded by Devils with C Denis Pederson to Vancouver Canucks for RW Alexander Mogilny (March 14, 2000).
STATISTICAL PLATEAUS: Three-goal games: 2003-04 (1).

		REGULAR SEASON								PLAYOFFS				
Season Team	League	GP	G	A	Pts.	PIM	+/-	PP	SH	GP	G	A	Pts.	PIM
92-93—Penticton	BCJHL	56	35	59	94	45	...	...	...	—	—	—	—	—
93-94—Univ. of Michigan	CCHA	38	20	28	48	24	8	10	1	—	—	—	—	—
94-95—Univ. of Michigan	CCHA	39	23	53	76	42	28	5	1	—	—	—	—	—
95-96—Univ. of Michigan	CCHA	35	28	44	72	41	...	...	...	—	—	—	—	—
96-97—Univ. of Michigan	CCHA	43	31	57	88	52	39	14	0	—	—	—	—	—
97-98—Albany	AHL	72	35	49	84	44	11	8	4	8	3	4	7	19
—New Jersey	NHL	11	5	4	9	0	3	0	0	3	0	1	1	0
98-99—New Jersey	NHL	76	13	33	46	18	-4	5	0	7	0	2	2	0
99-00—HC Pardubice	Czech Rep.	6	5	2	7	2	...	...	...	—	—	—	—	—
—New Jersey	NHL	44	5	21	26	8	8	2	0	—	—	—	—	—
—Vancouver	NHL	12	2	7	9	10	4	0	0	—	—	—	—	—
00-01—Vancouver	NHL	82	16	38	54	42	2	3	2	4	1	2	3	0
01-02—Vancouver	NHL	82	23	44	67	26	18	6	0	6	0	2	2	6
02-03—Vancouver	NHL	82	25	46	71	36	18	6	2	14	4	7	11	18
03-04—Vancouver	NHL	82	22	38	60	50	16	5	1	7	2	3	5	8
04-05—Linkopings	Sweden	45	16	28	44	50	30	4	3	6	0	2	2	10
NHL Totals (7 years)		471	111	231	342	190	65	27	5	41	7	17	24	32

MORRISON, JUSTIN RW CANUCKS

PERSONAL: Born August 10, 1979, in Los Angeles. ... 6-3/200. ... Shoots right.
TRANSACTIONS/CAREER NOTES: Selected by Vancouver Canucks in third round (fourth Canucks pick, 81st overall) of NHL entry draft (June 27, 1998).

		REGULAR SEASON								PLAYOFFS				
Season Team	League	GP	G	A	Pts.	PIM	+/-	PP	SH	GP	G	A	Pts.	PIM
96-97—Omaha	USHL	62	12	24	36	44	...	...	...	—	—	—	—	—
97-98—Colorado College	WCHA	42	4	9	13	8	...	...	...	—	—	—	—	—
98-99—Colorado College	WCHA	38	13	15	28	33	...	...	...	—	—	—	—	—
99-00—Colorado College	WCHA	38	7	19	26	28	...	...	...	—	—	—	—	—
00-01—Colorado College	WCHA	41	21	14	35	42	...	...	...	—	—	—	—	—
02-03—Manitoba	AHL	30	10	6	16	13	...	...	...	14	2	3	5	4
—Columbia	ECHL	40	20	35	55	39	...	...	...	2	0	0	0	4
03-04—Manitoba	AHL	66	18	18	36	27	3	4	0	—	—	—	—	—
04-05—Manitoba	AHL	71	11	10	21	33	1	2	0	14	1	5	6	10

M

MORRISONN, SHAONE D CAPITALS

PERSONAL: Born December 23, 1982, in Vancouver. ... 6-3/205. ... Shoots left.
TRANSACTIONS/CAREER NOTES: Selected by Boston Bruins in first round (first Bruins pick, 19th overall) of NHL entry draft (June 23, 2001). ... Traded by Bruins with first- (D Jeff Schultz) and second-round (D Mikhail Yunkov) picks in 2004 entry draft to Washington Capitals for D Sergei Gonchar (March 3, 2004).

		REGULAR SEASON								PLAYOFFS				
Season Team	League	GP	G	A	Pts.	PIM	+/-	PP	SH	GP	G	A	Pts.	PIM
99-00—Kamloops	WHL	57	1	6	7	80	...	...	...	4	0	0	0	6
00-01—Kamloops	WHL	61	13	25	38	132	...	...	...	4	0	0	0	6
01-02—Kamloops	WHL	61	11	26	37	106	...	...	...	4	0	2	2	2
02-03—Providence	AHL	60	5	16	21	103	5	1	0	—	—	—	—	—
—Boston	NHL	11	0	0	0	8	0	0	0	—	—	—	—	—
03-04—Boston	NHL	30	1	7	8	10	10	0	0	—	—	—	—	—
—Providence	AHL	18	0	2	2	16	1	0	0	—	—	—	—	—
—Washington	NHL	3	0	0	0	0	0	0	0	—	—	—	—	—
—Portland	AHL	13	1	4	5	10	8	0	0	7	0	1	1	4
04-05—Portland	AHL	71	4	14	18	63	-17	3	0	—	—	—	—	—
NHL Totals (2 years)		44	1	7	8	18	10	0	0					

MORROW, BRENDEN LW STARS

PERSONAL: Born January 16, 1979, in Carlyle, Sask. ... 5-11/200. ... Shoots left.
TRANSACTIONS/CAREER NOTES: Selected by Dallas Stars in first round (first Stars pick, 25th overall) of NHL entry draft (June 21, 1997). ... Injured knee (December 1, 2001); missed 10 games. ... Strained groin (December 19, 2002); missed one game. ... Injured groin, had charley horse (January 5, 2003); missed one game. ... Bruised chest (February 13, 2003); missed nine games. ... Injured shoulder (January 7, 2004); missed one game.
STATISTICAL PLATEAUS: Three-goal games: 2003-04 (1).

		REGULAR SEASON								PLAYOFFS				
Season Team	League	GP	G	A	Pts.	PIM	+/-	PP	SH	GP	G	A	Pts.	PIM
95-96—Portland	WHL	65	13	12	25	61	...	...	...	7	0	0	0	8
96-97—Portland	WHL	71	39	49	88	178	...	...	...	6	2	1	3	4

		REGULAR SEASON								PLAYOFFS				
Season Team	League	GP	G	A	Pts.	PIM	+/-	PP	SH	GP	G	A	Pts.	PIM
97-98—Portland	WHL	68	34	52	86	184	51	11	2	16	10	8	18	65
98-99—Portland	WHL	61	41	44	85	248	-1	19	1	4	0	4	4	18
99-00—Michigan	IHL	9	2	0	2	18	...	...	...	—	—	—	—	—
—Dallas	NHL	64	14	19	33	81	8	3	0	21	2	4	6	22
00-01—Dallas	NHL	82	20	24	44	128	10	7	0	10	0	3	3	12
01-02—Dallas	NHL	72	17	18	35	109	12	4	0	—	—	—	—	—
02-03—Dallas	NHL	71	21	22	43	134	20	2	3	12	3	5	8	16
03-04—Dallas	NHL	81	25	24	49	121	10	9	0	5	0	1	1	4
04-05—Oklahoma City	CHL	—	—	—	—	—	—	—	—	19	8	14	22	31
NHL Totals (5 years)		370	97	107	204	573	68	25	3	48	5	13	18	54

MOSS, TYLER G

PERSONAL: Born June 29, 1975, in Ottawa. ... 6-0/185. ... Catches right.

TRANSACTIONS/CAREER NOTES: Selected by Tampa Bay Lightning in second round (second Lightning pick, 29th overall) of NHL entry draft (June 26, 1993). ... Traded by Lightning to Calgary Flames for D Jamie Huscroft (March 18, 1997). ... Injured groin (December 12, 1998); missed 18 games. ... Traded by Flames with LW Rene Corbet to Pittsburgh Penguins for D Brad Werenka (March 14, 2000). ... Signed as free agent by Carolina Hurricanes (August 9, 2000). ... Signed as free agent by Vancouver Canucks (July 5, 2002). ... Traded by Canucks to Edmonton Oilers for C Peter Sarno (February 16, 2004).

		REGULAR SEASON									PLAYOFFS							
Season Team	League	GP	Min.	W	L	T	GA	SO	GAA	SV%	GP	Min.	W	L	GA	SO	GAA	SV%
91-92—Nepean	COJHL	26	1335	7	12	1	109	0	4.90	...	—	—	—	—	—	—	—	—
92-93—Kingston	OHL	31	1537	13	7	5	97	0	3.79	.896	6	228	1	2	19	0	5.00	.866
93-94—Kingston	OHL	13	795	6	4	3	42	1	3.17	.909	3	136	0	2	8	0	3.53	.905
94-95—Kingston	OHL	57	3249	33	17	5	164	1	3.03	.903	6	333	2	4	27	0	4.86	...
95-96—Atlanta	IHL	40	2030	11	19	4	138	1	4.08	...	3	213	0	3	11	0	3.10	...
96-97—Adirondack	AHL	11	507	1	5	2	42	1	4.97	.860	—	—	—	—	—	—	—	—
—Grand Rapids	IHL	15	715	5	6	1	35	0	2.94	...	—	—	—	—	—	—	—	—
—Saint John	AHL	9	534	6	1	1	17	0	1.91	.940	5	242	2	3	15	0	3.72	.872
—Muskegon	Col.HL	2	119	1	1	0	5	0	2.52	.906	—	—	—	—	—	—	—	—
97-98—Saint John	AHL	39	2194	19	10	7	91	0	2.49	.923	15	762	8	5	37	0	2.91	.906
—Calgary	NHL	6	367	2	3	1	20	0	3.27	.892	—	—	—	—	—	—	—	—
98-99—Calgary	NHL	11	550	3	7	0	23	0	2.51	.922	—	—	—	—	—	—	—	—
—Saint John	AHL	9	475	2	5	1	25	0	3.16	.897	—	—	—	—	—	—	—	—
—Orlando	IHL	9	515	6	2	1	21	1	2.45	.909	17	1017	10	7	*53	0	3.13	.896
99-00—Kansas City	IHL	36	2116	21	12	5	105	3	2.98	...	—	—	—	—	—	—	—	—
—Wilkes-Barre/Scranton	AHL	4	188	1	1	1	11	0	3.51	...	—	—	—	—	—	—	—	—
00-01—Carolina	NHL	12	557	1	6	0	37	0	3.99	.853	—	—	—	—	—	—	—	—
—Cincinnati	IHL	9	506	5	3	1	24	2	2.85	...	—	—	—	—	—	—	—	—
01-02—Lowell	AHL	43	2571	20	16	7	106	1	2.47	.924	—	—	—	—	—	—	—	—
02-03—Vancouver	NHL	1	22	0	0	0	1	0	2.73	.929	—	—	—	—	—	—	—	—
—Manitoba	AHL	42	2502	21	15	5	117	3	2.81	.909	10	617	6	4	23	0	2.24	.922
03-04—Manitoba	AHL	32	1882	10	16	5	91	3	2.90	.885	—	—	—	—	—	—	—	—
—Toronto	AHL	16	932	7	9	0	41	3	2.64	.922	—	—	—	—	—	—	—	—
04-05—Edmonton	AHL	50	2870	24	19	...	126	5	2.63	.906	—	—	—	—	—	—	—	—
NHL Totals (4 years)		30	1496	6	16	1	81	0	3.25	.891								

MOTTAU, MIKE D

PERSONAL: Born March 19, 1978, in Quincy, Mass. ... 6-0/193. ... Shoots left.

TRANSACTIONS/CAREER NOTES: Selected by New York Rangers in 7th round (10th pick, 182nd overall) of entry draft (June 1997). ... Traded by Rangers to Calgary Flames for 6th-round pick (C Ivan Dornic) in 2003 entry draft and future considerations (January 22, 2003). ... Signed as free agent by Anaheim Mighty Ducks (July 25, 2003). ... Signed as free agent by Worcester of the AHL (September 10, 2004).

		REGULAR SEASON								PLAYOFFS				
Season Team	League	GP	G	A	Pts.	PIM	+/-	PP	SH	GP	G	A	Pts.	PIM
96-97—Boston College	Hockey East	38	5	18	23	77	...	...	...	—	—	—	—	—
97-98—Boston College	Hockey East	40	13	36	49	50	...	...	...	—	—	—	—	—
98-99—Boston College	Hockey East	43	3	39	42	44	...	...	...	—	—	—	—	—
99-00—Boston College	Hockey East	42	6	*37	43	57	...	...	...	—	—	—	—	—
00-01—Hartford	AHL	61	10	33	43	45	...	...	...	5	0	1	1	19
—New York Rangers	NHL	18	0	3	3	13	-6	0	0	—	—	—	—	—
01-02—Hartford	AHL	80	9	42	51	56	16	3	1	10	0	5	5	4
—New York Rangers	NHL	1	0	0	0	0	0	0	0	—	—	—	—	—
02-03—Hartford	AHL	29	1	18	19	24	9	0	0	—	—	—	—	—
—Calgary	NHL	4	0	0	0	0	-1	0	0	—	—	—	—	—
—Saint John	AHL	32	5	12	17	14	-6	2	0	—	—	—	—	—
03-04—Cincinnati	AHL	69	9	22	31	79	-11	2	0	—	—	—	—	—
04-05—Worcester	AHL	73	4	31	35	23	-18	4	0	—	—	—	—	—
NHL Totals (3 years)		23	0	3	3	13	-7	0	0					

MOTZKO, JOE RW BLUE JACKETS

PERSONAL: Born March 14, 1980, in Bemidji, Minn. ... 6-0/190.

TRANSACTIONS/CAREER NOTES: Signed as free agent by Columbus Blue Jackets (May 15, 2003).

Season Team	League	REGULAR SEASON GP	G	A	Pts.	PIM	+/-	PP	SH	PLAYOFFS GP	G	A	Pts.	PIM
99-00—St. Cloud State	WCHA	36	9	15	24	52	...	...	...	—	—	—	—	—
00-01—St. Cloud State	WCHA	41	17	20	37	56	...	...	...	—	—	—	—	—
01-02—St. Cloud State	WCHA	39	9	30	39	34	...	...	...	—	—	—	—	—
02-03—St. Cloud State	WCHA	38	17	25	42	59	...	...	...	—	—	—	—	—
—Syracuse	AHL	...	0	0	0	0	0	...	...	—	—	—	—	—
03-04—Syracuse	AHL	70	17	24	41	38	0	6	2	7	2	2	4	6
—Columbus	NHL	2	0	0	0	0	0	0	0	—	—	—	—	—
04-05—Syracuse	AHL	79	28	38	66	72	-8	9	2	—	—	—	—	—
NHL Totals (1 year)		2	0	0	0	0	0	0	0					

MOWERS, MARK — RW/C — RED WINGS

PERSONAL: Born February 16, 1974, in Whitesboro, N.Y. ... 5-11/190. ... Shoots right.

TRANSACTIONS/CAREER NOTES: Signed as free agent by Nashville Predators (June 11, 1998). ... Injured knee (March 19, 2000); missed final nine games of season. ... Signed as free agent by Detroit Red Wings (August 5, 2002). ... Injured foot (March 29, 2004); missed final 10 games of regular season and playoffs.

Season Team	League	REGULAR SEASON GP	G	A	Pts.	PIM	+/-	PP	SH	PLAYOFFS GP	G	A	Pts.	PIM
94-95—New Hampshire	Hockey East	36	13	23	36	16	...	...	...	—	—	—	—	—
95-96—New Hampshire	Hockey East	34	21	26	47	18	...	...	...	—	—	—	—	—
96-97—New Hampshire	Hockey East	39	26	32	58	52	...	...	...	—	—	—	—	—
97-98—New Hampshire	Hockey East	35	25	31	56	32	...	...	...	—	—	—	—	—
98-99—Milwaukee	IHL	51	14	22	36	24	6	0	2	1	0	0	0	0
—Nashville	NHL	30	0	6	6	4	-4	0	0	—	—	—	—	—
99-00—Milwaukee	IHL	23	11	15	26	34	...	...	...	—	—	—	—	—
—Nashville	NHL	41	4	5	9	10	0	0	0	—	—	—	—	—
00-01—Milwaukee	IHL	63	25	25	50	54	...	...	...	58	1	2	3	2
01-02—Milwaukee	AHL	45	19	20	39	34	4	6	1	—	—	—	—	—
—Nashville	NHL	14	1	2	3	2	-2	0	0	—	—	—	—	—
02-03—Grand Rapids	AHL	78	34	47	81	47	26	9	2	15	3	4	7	4
03-04—Grand Rapids	AHL	16	8	6	14	4	5	3	1	—	—	—	—	—
—Detroit	NHL	52	3	8	11	4	3	1	0	11	1	0	1	16
04-05—Malmo	Sweden	9	2	0	2	0	-1	0	0	—	—	—	—	—
—Fribourg-Gotteron	Switzerland	3	2	0	2	0	...	...	...	9	9	8	17	12
NHL Totals (4 years)		137	8	21	29	20	-3	1	0	11	1	0	1	16

MUIR, BRYAN — D — CAPITALS

PERSONAL: Born June 8, 1973, in Winnipeg. ... 6-3/215. ... Shoots left. ... Name pronounced MYOOR.

TRANSACTIONS/CAREER NOTES: Signed as free agent by Edmonton Oilers (April 30, 1996). ... Traded by Oilers with C Jason Arnott to New Jersey Devils for RW Bill Guerin and RW Valeri Zelepukin (Jan. 4, 1998). ... Traded by Devils to Chicago Blackhawks for future considerations (Nov. 13, 1998). ... Injured back (April 5, 1999); missed three games. ... Traded by Blackhawks with LW Reid Simpson to Tampa Bay Lightning for C Michael Nylander (Nov. 12, 1999). ... Fractured ankle (Nov. 17, 1999); missed 18 games. ... Injured ankle (March 12, 2000); missed 11 games. ... Traded by Lightning to Colorado Avalanche for 8th-round pick (LW Dimitri Bezrukov) in 2001 draft (Jan. 23, 2001). ... Signed as free agent by Los Angeles Kings (July 31, 2003). ... Traded by Kings to Washington Capitals for future considerations (Aug. 12, 2005).

Season Team	League	REGULAR SEASON GP	G	A	Pts.	PIM	+/-	PP	SH	PLAYOFFS GP	G	A	Pts.	PIM
91-92—Wexford	OJHL	50	11	35	46	...	...	...	...	—	—	—	—	—
92-93—New Hampshire	Hockey East	26	1	2	3	24	...	...	...	—	—	—	—	—
93-94—New Hampshire	Hockey East	36	0	4	4	48	...	...	...	—	—	—	—	—
94-95—New Hampshire	Hockey East	28	9	9	18	48	...	...	...	—	—	—	—	—
95-96—Canadian nat'l team	Int'l	42	6	12	18	36	...	...	...	—	—	—	—	—
—Edmonton	NHL	5	0	0	0	6	-4	0	0	—	—	—	—	—
96-97—Hamilton	AHL	75	8	16	24	80	-16	3	0	14	0	5	5	12
—Edmonton	NHL	...	...	...	...	...	...	...	...	5	0	0	0	4
97-98—Hamilton	AHL	28	3	10	13	62	9	2	0	—	—	—	—	—
—Edmonton	NHL	7	0	0	0	17	0	0	0	—	—	—	—	—
—Albany	AHL	41	3	10	13	67	6	0	0	13	3	0	3	12
98-99—New Jersey	NHL	1	0	0	0	0	0	0	0	—	—	—	—	—
—Albany	AHL	10	0	0	0	29	-7	0	0	—	—	—	—	—
—Chicago	NHL	53	1	4	5	50	1	0	0	—	—	—	—	—
—Portland	AHL	2	1	1	2	2	0	1	0	—	—	—	—	—
99-00—Chicago	NHL	11	2	3	5	13	-1	0	1	—	—	—	—	—
—Tampa Bay	NHL	30	1	1	2	32	-8	0	0	—	—	—	—	—
00-01—Tampa Bay	NHL	10	0	3	3	15	-7	0	0	—	—	—	—	—
—Detroit	IHL	21	5	7	12	36	...	...	...	—	—	—	—	—
—Hershey	AHL	26	5	8	13	50	...	...	...	—	—	—	—	—
—Colorado	NHL	8	0	0	0	4	0	0	0	3	0	0	0	0
01-02—Hershey	AHL	59	10	16	26	133	-6	6	0	—	—	—	—	—
—Colorado	NHL	22	1	1	2	9	1	0	0	21	0	0	0	2
02-03—Colorado	NHL	32	0	2	2	19	3	0	0	—	—	—	—	—
—Hershey	AHL	36	9	12	21	75	...	...	...	5	2	6	8	6
03-04—Los Angeles	NHL	2	0	1	1	2	1	0	0	—	—	—	—	—
—Manchester	AHL	73	13	36	49	141	24	5	0	6	2	3	5	12
04-05—MoDo Hockey	Sweden Jr.	26	1	5	6	36	4	0	0	—	—	—	—	—
NHL Totals (9 years)		181	5	15	20	167	-14	0	1	29	0	0	0	6

MUNRO, ADAM — G — BLACKHAWKS

PERSONAL: Born November 12, 1982, in St. George, Ont. ... 6-1/194. ... Catches left.

TRANSACTIONS/CAREER NOTES: Selected by Chicago Blackhawks in 1st round (2nd Blackhawks pick, 29th overall) of entry draft (June 23, 2001). ... Signed as free agent by Blackhawks (February 18, 2004). ... Concussion (March 4, 2004); missed three games.

		REGULAR SEASON									PLAYOFFS							
Season Team	League	GP	Min.	W	L	T	GA	SO	GAA	SV%	GP	Min.	W	L	GA	SO	GAA	SV%
99-00—Erie	OHL	22	948	8	7	1	48	1	3.04	...	1	5	0	0	1	0	12.00	...
00-01—Erie	OHL	41	2283	26	6	6	88	4	2.31	...	10	509	6	2	27	1	3.18	...
01-02—Erie	OHL	43	2277	24	13	1	128	3	3.37	...	6	361	4	2	17	0	2.83	...
03-04—Chicago	NHL	7	426	1	5	1	26	0	3.66	.880	—	—	—	—	—	—	—	—
—Norfolk	AHL	12	695	5	4	1	26	0	2.24	.891	—	—	—	—	—	—	—	—
04-05—Norfolk	AHL	30	1594	14	10	...	66	4	2.48	.905	...	...	...	...	...	...	...	...
—Atlantic City	ECHL	5	271	2	2	...	9	0	1.99	.937	—	—	—	—	—	—	—	—
NHL Totals (1 year)		7	426	1	5	1	26	0	3.66	.880								

MURLEY, MATT — LW — PENGUINS

PERSONAL: Born December 17, 1979, in Troy, N.Y. ... 6-1/192. ... Shoots left.

TRANSACTIONS/CAREER NOTES: Selected by Pittsburgh Penguins in second round (second Penguins pick, 51st overall) of NHL entry draft (June 26, 1999).

		REGULAR SEASON								PLAYOFFS				
Season Team	League	GP	G	A	Pts.	PIM	+/-	PP	SH	GP	G	A	Pts.	PIM
97-98—Syracuse	Jr. A	49	56	70	126	203	...	...	...	—	—	—	—	—
98-99—Rensselaer Poly. Inst.	ECAC	36	17	32	49	32	...	...	...	—	—	—	—	—
99-00—Rensselaer Poly. Inst.	ECAC	35	9	29	38	42	...	...	...	—	—	—	—	—
00-01—Rensselaer Poly. Inst.	ECAC	34	*24	18	42	34	...	...	...	—	—	—	—	—
01-02—Rensselaer Poly. Inst.	ECAC	32	*24	22	46	26	...	...	...	—	—	—	—	—
02-03—Wilkes-Barre/Scranton	AHL	73	21	37	58	45	-4	10	1	6	0	2	2	15
03-04—Wilkes-Barre/Scranton	AHL	63	10	27	37	69	2	5	0	24	7	6	13	17
—Pittsburgh	NHL	18	1	1	2	14	-6	0	0	—	—	—	—	—
04-05—Wilkes-Barre/Scranton	AHL	80	17	24	41	55	16	3	2	11	3	0	3	0
NHL Totals (1 year)		18	1	1	2	14	-6	0	0					

MURRAY, GARTH — C/LW — RANGERS

PERSONAL: Born September 17, 1982, in Regina, Sask. ... 6-1/207. ... Shoots left.

TRANSACTIONS/CAREER NOTES: Selected by New York Rangers in third round (third Rangers pick, 79th overall) of NHL entry draft (June 23, 2001).

		REGULAR SEASON								PLAYOFFS				
Season Team	League	GP	G	A	Pts.	PIM	+/-	PP	SH	GP	G	A	Pts.	PIM
97-98—Regina	WHL	4	0	0	0	2	...	...	...	2	0	0	0	0
98-99—Regina	WHL	60	3	5	8	101	...	...	...	—	—	—	—	—
99-00—Regina	WHL	68	14	26	40	155	...	...	...	7	1	1	2	7
00-01—Regina	WHL	72	28	16	44	183	...	...	...	6	1	1	2	10
01-02—Regina	WHL	62	33	30	63	154	...	...	...	6	2	3	5	9
—Hartford	AHL	4	0	0	0	0	-5	0	0	9	1	3	4	6
02-03—Hartford	AHL	64	10	14	24	121	2	4	0	2	0	0	0	6
03-04—Hartford	AHL	63	11	11	22	161	4	0	1	16	0	4	4	29
—New York Rangers	NHL	20	1	0	1	24	-5	0	0	—	—	—	—	—
04-05—Hartford	AHL	55	4	5	9	182	0	0	0	5	1	0	1	8
NHL Totals (1 year)		20	1	0	1	24	-5	0	0					

MURRAY, GLEN — RW — BRUINS

PERSONAL: Born November 1, 1972, in Halifax, N.S. ... 6-3/225. ... Shoots right.

TRANSACTIONS/CAREER NOTES: Selected by Boston Bruins in first round (first Bruins pick, 18th overall) of NHL draft (June 22, 1991). ... Injured elbow (December 15, 1993); missed two games. ... Traded by Bruins with C Bryan Smolinski to Pittsburgh Penguins for LW Kevin Stevens and LW Shawn McEachern (August 2, 1995). ... Separated shoulder (January 1, 1996); missed 10 games. ... Suffered concussion (April 11, 1996); missed one game. ... Traded by Penguins to Los Angeles Kings for C Ed Olczyk (March 18, 1997). ... Flu (November 13, 1997); missed one game. ... Tore knee ligament (January 2, 1999); missed 19 games. ... Strained groin (March 28, 1999); missed two games. ... Bruised chest (January 13, 2000); missed three games. ... Strained quadriceps (November 18, 2000); missed 18 games. ... Traded by Kings with C Jozef Stumpel to Bruins for C Jason Allison and C/LW Mikko Eloranta (October 24, 2001). ... Flu (February 10, 2004); missed one game.

STATISTICAL PLATEAUS: Three-goal games: 1997-98 (1), 1999-00 (1), 2001-02 (1), 2002-03 (1), 2003-04 (1). Total: 5.

		REGULAR SEASON								PLAYOFFS				
Season Team	League	GP	G	A	Pts.	PIM	+/-	PP	SH	GP	G	A	Pts.	PIM
89-90—Sudbury	OHL	62	8	28	36	17	...	...	...	7	0	0	0	4
90-91—Sudbury	OHL	66	27	38	65	82	...	...	...	5	8	4	12	10
91-92—Sudbury	OHL	54	37	47	84	93	...	...	...	11	7	4	11	18
—Boston	NHL	5	3	1	4	0	2	1	0	15	4	2	6	10
92-93—Providence	AHL	48	30	26	56	42	15	3	0	6	1	4	5	4
—Boston	NHL	27	3	4	7	8	-6	2	0	—	—	—	—	—
93-94—Boston	NHL	81	18	13	31	48	-1	0	0	13	4	5	9	14
94-95—Boston	NHL	35	5	2	7	46	-11	0	0	2	0	0	0	2
95-96—Pittsburgh	NHL	69	14	15	29	57	4	0	0	18	2	6	8	10

Season Team	League	REGULAR SEASON GP	G	A	Pts.	PIM	+/-	PP	SH	PLAYOFFS GP	G	A	Pts.	PIM
96-97—Pittsburgh	NHL	66	11	11	22	24	-19	3	0	—	—	—	—	—
—Los Angeles	NHL	11	5	3	8	8	-2	0	0	—	—	—	—	—
97-98—Los Angeles	NHL	81	29	31	60	54	6	7	3	4	2	0	2	6
98-99—Los Angeles	NHL	61	16	15	31	36	-14	3	3	—	—	—	—	—
99-00—Los Angeles	NHL	78	29	33	62	60	13	10	1	4	0	0	0	2
00-01—Los Angeles	NHL	64	18	21	39	32	9	3	1	13	4	3	7	4
01-02—Los Angeles	NHL	9	6	5	11	0	5	4	0	—	—	—	—	—
—Boston	NHL	73	35	25	60	40	26	5	0	6	1	4	5	4
02-03—Boston	NHL	82	44	48	92	64	9	12	0	5	1	1	2	4
03-04—Boston	NHL	81	32	28	60	56	17	11	0	7	2	1	3	8
NHL Totals (13 years)		823	268	255	523	533	38	61	8	87	20	22	42	64

MURRAY, MARTY — C/LW

PERSONAL: Born February 16, 1975, in Deloraine, Man. ... 5-9/180. ... Shoots left.

TRANSACTIONS/CAREER NOTES: Selected by Calgary Flames in fourth round (fifth Flames pick, 96th overall) of NHL entry draft (June 26, 1993). ... Bruised foot (April 8, 1996); missed three games. ... Strained hip flexor (October 12, 2000); missed nine games. ... Signed as free agent by Philadelphia Flyers (July 9, 2001). ... Strained rib cage muscle (March 28, 2002); missed five games. ... Traded by Flyers to Carolina Hurricanes for sixth-round pick (C/LW Frederik Cabana) in 2004 entry draft (June 22, 2003). ... Fractured hand (March 10, 2004); missed remainder of season.

Season Team	League	REGULAR SEASON GP	G	A	Pts.	PIM	+/-	PP	SH	PLAYOFFS GP	G	A	Pts.	PIM
91-92—Brandon	WHL	68	20	36	56	12	...	...	...	—	—	—	—	—
92-93—Brandon	WHL	67	29	65	94	50	...	...	...	4	1	3	4	0
93-94—Brandon	WHL	64	43	71	114	33	24	16	3	14	6	14	20	14
94-95—Brandon	WHL	65	40	88	128	53	57	10	5	18	9	20	29	16
95-96—Calgary	NHL	15	3	3	6	0	-4	2	0	—	—	—	—	—
—Saint John	AHL	58	25	31	56	20	...	...	...	14	2	4	6	4
96-97—Saint John	AHL	67	19	39	58	40	-9	5	1	5	2	3	5	4
—Calgary	NHL	2	0	0	0	4	0	0	0	—	—	—	—	—
97-98—Calgary	NHL	2	0	0	0	2	1	0	0	—	—	—	—	—
—Saint John	AHL	41	10	30	40	16	7	3	0	21	10	10	20	12
99-00—Kolner Haie	Germany	56	12	47	59	28	...	...	...	10	4	3	7	2
00-01—Calgary	NHL	7	0	0	0	0	-2	0	0	—	—	—	—	—
—Saint John	AHL	56	24	52	76	36	...	...	...	19	4	16	20	18
01-02—Philadelphia	AHL	3	0	3	3	2	-1	0	0	—	—	—	—	—
—Philadelphia	NHL	74	12	15	27	10	10	1	1	5	0	1	1	0
02-03—Philadelphia	NHL	76	11	15	26	13	-1	1	1	4	0	0	0	4
03-04—Carolina	NHL	66	5	7	12	8	6	0	0	—	—	—	—	—
NHL Totals (7 years)		242	31	40	71	37	10	4	2	9	0	1	1	4

MURRAY, REM — C/LW

PERSONAL: Born October 9, 1972, in Stratford, Ont. ... 6-2/200. ... Shoots left.

TRANSACTIONS/CAREER NOTES: Selected by Los Angeles Kings in sixth round (fifth Kings pick, 135th overall) of NHL entry draft (June 20, 1992). ... Signed as free agent by Edmonton Oilers (August 17, 1995). ... Missed first five games of 1997-98 season recovering from wrist injury and offseason appendectomy. ... Strained neck (March 17, 1998); missed one game. ... Had the flu (April 6, 1998); missed three games. ... Separated shoulder (October 7, 1999); missed seven games. ... Sprained knee (November 3, 1999); missed 28 games. ... Traded by Oilers with D Tom Poti to New York Rangers for C Mike York and fourth-round pick (D Ivan Koltsov) in 2002 entry draft (March 19, 2002). ... Traded by Rangers with D Tomas Kloucek and D Marek Zidlicky to Nashville Predators for G Mike Dunham (December 12, 2002). ... Strained neck (January 6, 2004); missed final 43 games of regular season and playoffs.

STATISTICAL PLATEAUS: Three-goal games: 1996-97 (1).

Season Team	League	REGULAR SEASON GP	G	A	Pts.	PIM	+/-	PP	SH	PLAYOFFS GP	G	A	Pts.	PIM
90-91—Stratford Jr. B	OHA	48	39	59	98	22	...	...	...	—	—	—	—	—
91-92—Michigan State	CCHA	44	12	36	48	16	...	...	...	—	—	—	—	—
92-93—Michigan State	CCHA	40	22	35	57	24	...	...	...	—	—	—	—	—
93-94—Michigan State	CCHA	41	16	38	54	18	7	7	1	—	—	—	—	—
94-95—Michigan State	CCHA	40	20	36	56	21	18	4	0	—	—	—	—	—
95-96—Cape Breton	AHL	79	31	59	90	40	...	...	...	—	—	—	—	—
96-97—Edmonton	NHL	82	11	20	31	16	9	1	0	12	1	2	3	4
97-98—Edmonton	NHL	61	9	9	18	39	-9	2	2	11	1	4	5	2
98-99—Edmonton	NHL	78	21	18	39	20	4	4	1	4	1	1	2	2
99-00—Edmonton	NHL	44	9	5	14	8	-2	2	0	5	0	1	1	2
00-01—Edmonton	NHL	82	15	21	36	24	5	1	3	6	2	0	2	6
01-02—Edmonton	NHL	69	7	17	24	14	5	0	2	—	—	—	—	—
—New York Rangers	NHL	11	1	2	3	4	-9	0	0	—	—	—	—	—
02-03—New York Rangers	NHL	32	6	6	12	4	-3	1	1	—	—	—	—	—
—Nashville	NHL	53	6	13	19	18	1	1	0	—	—	—	—	—
03-04—Nashville	NHL	39	8	9	17	12	-1	0	2	—	—	—	—	—
NHL Totals (8 years)		551	93	120	213	159	0	12	11	38	5	8	13	16

MYRVOLD, ANDERS — D — RED WINGS

PERSONAL: Born August 12, 1975, in Lorenskog, Norway. ... 6-2/203. ... Shoots left. ... Name pronounced MUHR-vohld.

TRANSACTIONS/CAREER NOTES: Selected by Quebec Nordiques in 5th round (6th Nordiques pick, 127th overall) of entry draft (June 26,

1993). ... Nordiques franchise moved to Colorado and renamed Avalanche for 1995-96 season (June 21, 1995). ... Traded by Avalanche with RW Landon Wilson to Boston Bruins for first-round pick (D Robyn Regehr) in 1998 draft (November 22, 1996). ... Signed as free agent by New York Islanders (August 28, 2000). ... Signed as free agent by New York Rangers (July 27, 2001). ... Signed as free agent by Detroit Red Wings (September 1, 2003).

		REGULAR SEASON								PLAYOFFS				
Season Team	League	GP	G	A	Pts.	PIM	+/-	PP	SH	GP	G	A	Pts.	PIM
92-93—Farjestad Karlstad	Sweden	2	0	0	0	0	...	...	...	—	—	—	—	—
93-94—Grums	Sweden Dv. 2	24	1	0	1	59	...	...	...	—	—	—	—	—
94-95—Laval	QMJHL	64	14	50	64	173	29	7	0	20	4	10	14	68
—Cornwall	AHL	...	...	...	...	...	...	...	...	3	0	1	1	2
95-96—Colorado	NHL	4	0	1	1	6	-2	0	0	—	—	—	—	—
—Cornwall	AHL	70	5	24	29	125	...	...	...	5	1	0	1	19
96-97—Hershey	AHL	20	0	3	3	16	-3	0	0	—	—	—	—	—
—Providence	AHL	53	6	15	21	107	11	1	1	10	0	1	1	6
—Boston	NHL	9	0	2	2	4	-1	0	0	—	—	—	—	—
97-98—Providence	AHL	75	4	21	25	91	-39	1	0	—	—	—	—	—
98-99—AIK	Sweden	19	1	3	4	24	...	...	...	—	—	—	—	—
—Djurgarden Stockholm	Sweden	29	3	4	7	52	...	...	...	—	—	—	—	—
99-00—AIK Solna	Sweden	49	1	3	4	87	...	...	...	—	—	—	—	—
00-01—Springfield	AHL	69	5	25	30	129	...	...	...	—	—	—	—	—
—New York Islanders	NHL	12	0	1	1	0	-2	0	0	—	—	—	—	—
01-02—Hartford	AHL	19	3	3	6	28	0	1	0	—	—	—	—	—
—Fribourg-Gotteron	Switzerland	6	0	0	0	16	...	...	...	4	0	1	1	6
03-04—Detroit	NHL	8	0	1	1	2	-1	0	0	—	—	—	—	—
—Grand Rapids	AHL	71	0	21	21	94	3	0	0	4	0	1	1	2
04-05—Valerengen	Norway	40	8	24	32	108	...	...	...	11	2	1	3	24
NHL Totals (4 years)		33	0	5	5	12	-6	0	0					

NABOKOV, EVGENI G SHARKS

PERSONAL: Born July 25, 1975, in Kamenogorsk, U.S.S.R. ... 6-0/200. ... Catches left. ... Name pronounced ehv-GEH-nee nuh-BAH-kahf.
TRANSACTIONS/CAREER NOTES: Selected by San Jose Sharks in 9th round (ninth Sharks pick, 219th overall) of entry draft (June 29, 1994). ... Injured chest (March 13, 2003); missed four games. ... Injured groin (November 21, 2003); missed six games. ... Left team for personal reasons (January 5, 2004); missed one game. ... Left team for personal reasons (January 19, 2004); missed one game.

		REGULAR SEASON									PLAYOFFS							
Season Team	League	GP	Min.	W	L	T	GA	SO	GAA	SV%	GP	Min.	W	L	GA	SO	GAA	SV%
92-93—Torpedo Ust-Kam.	CIS	4	109	...	...	...	5	...	2.75	...	—	—	—	—	—	—	—	—
93-94—Torpedo Ust-Kam.	CIS	11	539	...	...	...	29	0	3.23	...	—	—	—	—	—	—	—	—
94-95—Dynamo Moscow	CIS	37	2075	...	...	...	70	...	2.02	...	—	—	—	—	—	—	—	—
95-96—Dynamo Moscow	CIS	37	1948	...	...	...	70	...	2.16	...	6	298	...	...	7	...	1.41	...
96-97—Dynamo Moscow	Russian	27	1588	...	...	...	56	2	2.12	...	4	255	...	...	12	0	2.82	...
97-98—Kentucky	AHL	33	1867	10	21	2	122	0	3.92	.872	1	23	0	0	1	0	2.61	.923
98-99—Kentucky	AHL	43	2429	26	14	1	106	5	2.62	.909	11	599	6	5	30	2	3.01	.907
99-00—Cleveland	IHL	20	1164	16	4	3	52	0	2.68	...	—	—	—	—	—	—	—	—
—San Jose	NHL	11	414	2	2	1	15	1	2.17	.910	1	20	0	0	0	0	0.00	1.00
—Kentucky	AHL	2	120	1	1	0	3	1	1.50	...	—	—	—	—	—	—	—	—
00-01—San Jose	NHL	66	3700	32	21	7	135	6	2.19	.915	4	218	1	3	10	1	2.75	.903
01-02—San Jose	NHL	67	3901	37	24	5	149	7	2.29	.918	12	712	7	5	31	0	2.61	.904
02-03—San Jose	NHL	55	3227	19	28	8	146	3	2.71	.906	—	—	—	—	—	—	—	—
03-04—San Jose	NHL	59	3456	31	19	8	127	9	2.20	.921	17	1052	10	7	30	3	1.71	.935
04-05—Metal. Magnitogorsk	Russian	14	808	...	...	...	27	3	2.00	...	5	307	...	...	13	0	2.53	...
NHL Totals (5 years)		258	14698	121	94	29	572	26	2.34	.915	34	2002	18	15	71	4	2.13	.921

NAGY, LADISLAV LW COYOTES

PERSONAL: Born June 1, 1979, in Saca, Czechoslovakia. ... 5-11/192. ... Shoots left.
TRANSACTIONS/CAREER NOTES: Selected by St. Louis Blues in seventh round (sixth Blues pick, 177th overall) of NHL draft (June 21, 1997). ... Traded by Blues with C Michal Handzus, C Jeff Taffe and first-round pick (LW Ben Eager) in 2002 draft to Phoenix Coyotes for LW Keith Tkachuk (March 13, 2001). ... Bruised knee (October 24, 2001); missed seven games. ... Bruised shoulder (November 10, 2001); missed one game. ... Injured groin (October 16, 2003); missed one game. ... Bruised eye (January 14, 2004); missed two games. ... Fractured left wrist (February 17, 2004) and had surgery (February 21, 2004); missed remainder of season.
STATISTICAL PLATEAUS: Three-goal games: 2003-04 (1).

		REGULAR SEASON								PLAYOFFS				
Season Team	League	GP	G	A	Pts.	PIM	+/-	PP	SH	GP	G	A	Pts.	PIM
96-97—Dragon Presov	Slov. Div.	11	6	5	11	...	...	...	...	—	—	—	—	—
97-98—HC Kosice	Slovakia	29	19	15	34	41	...	...	...	—	—	—	—	—
98-99—Halifax	QMJHL	63	*71	55	126	148	55	14	13	5	3	3	6	18
—Worcester	AHL	...	...	...	...	...	...	...	...	3	2	2	4	0
99-00—Worcester	AHL	69	23	28	51	67	...	...	...	2	1	0	1	0
—St. Louis	NHL	11	2	4	6	2	2	1	0	6	1	1	2	0
00-01—St. Louis	NHL	40	8	8	16	20	-2	2	0	—	—	—	—	—
—Worcester	AHL	20	6	14	20	36	...	...	...	—	—	—	—	—
—Phoenix	NHL	6	0	1	1	2	0	0	0	—	—	—	—	—
01-02—Phoenix	NHL	74	23	19	42	50	6	5	0	5	0	0	0	21
02-03—Phoenix	NHL	80	22	35	57	92	17	8	0	—	—	—	—	—
03-04—Phoenix	NHL	55	24	28	52	46	11	11	0	—	—	—	—	—
04-05—HC Kosice	Slovakia	18	9	7	16	40	...	...	...	—	—	—	—	—
—Mora	Sweden Dv. 1	19	4	4	8	22	-12	0	0	—	—	—	—	—
NHL Totals (5 years)		266	79	95	174	212	34	27	0	11	1	1	2	21

NASH, RICK — LW — BLUE JACKETS

PERSONAL: Born June 16, 1984, in Brampton, Ont. ... 6-4/206. ... Shoots left.
TRANSACTIONS/CAREER NOTES: Selected by Columbus Blue Jackets in 1st round (1st Blue Jackets pick, 1st overall) of entry draft (June 22, 2002). ... Concussion and eye injury (October 14, 2003); missed one game. ... Bruised tailbone (December 9, 2002); missed four games. ... Hip pointer (January 23, 2003); missed three games. ... Bruised foot (January 31, 2004); missed two games.

		REGULAR SEASON								PLAYOFFS				
Season Team	League	GP	G	A	Pts.	PIM	+/-	PP	SH	GP	G	A	Pts.	PIM
00-01—London	OHL	58	31	35	66	56	...	...	...	4	3	3	6	8
01-02—London	OHL	54	32	40	72	88	...	...	...	12	10	9	19	21
02-03—Columbus	NHL	74	17	22	39	78	-27	6	0	—	—	—	—	—
03-04—Columbus	NHL	80	41	16	57	87	-35	19	0	—	—	—	—	—
04-05—Davos	Switzerland	44	26	20	46	81	...	10	1	15	9	2	11	26
NHL Totals (2 years)		154	58	38	96	165	-62	25	0					

NASH, TYSON — LW — COYOTES

PERSONAL: Born March 11, 1975, in Edmonton. ... 5-11/191. ... Shoots left.
TRANSACTIONS/CAREER NOTES: Selected by Vancouver Canucks in 10th round (eighth Canucks pick, 247th overall) of NHL entry draft (June 29, 1994). ... Signed as free agent by St. Louis Blues (July 24, 1998). ... Suffered concussion (December 5, 1999); missed three games. ... Injured shoulder (March 11, 2000); missed final 13 games of regular season. ... Injured shoulder (December 5, 2000); missed one game. ... Torn anterior cruciate ligament in knee (February 11, 2001); missed 16 games. ... Reinjured knee (March 22, 2001); missed remainder of season. ... Knee and abdominal surgery before start of 2001-02 season; missed first four games of season. ... Injured elbow (November 13, 2001); missed two games. ... Suffered hip pointer (December 28, 2001); missed six games. ... Fractured nose (January 26, 2002); missed one game. ... Traded by Blues for fifth-round draft pick in 2003 (RW Lee Stempniak) to Phoenix Coyotes (June 22, 2003). ... Sprained right knee (January 16, 2004); missed four games. ... Suspended two games for slashing incident (February 10, 2004).

		REGULAR SEASON								PLAYOFFS				
Season Team	League	GP	G	A	Pts.	PIM	+/-	PP	SH	GP	G	A	Pts.	PIM
90-91—Kamloops	WHL	3	0	0	0	0	...	...	...	—	—	—	—	—
91-92—Kamloops	WHL	33	1	6	7	32	...	...	...	4	0	0	0	0
92-93—Kamloops	WHL	61	10	16	26	78	...	...	...	13	3	2	5	32
93-94—Kamloops	WHL	65	20	36	56	137	...	...	...	16	3	3	6	12
94-95—Kamloops	WHL	63	34	41	75	70	39	9	0	21	10	7	17	30
95-96—Syracuse	AHL	50	4	7	11	58	...	...	...	4	0	0	0	11
—Raleigh	ECHL	6	1	1	2	8	...	...	...	—	—	—	—	—
96-97—Syracuse	AHL	77	17	17	34	105	-17	2	1	3	0	2	2	0
97-98—Syracuse	AHL	74	20	20	40	184	-5	3	0	5	0	2	2	28
98-99—Worcester	AHL	55	14	22	36	143	-2	4	4	4	4	1	5	27
—St. Louis	NHL	2	0	0	0	5	-1	0	0	1	0	0	0	2
99-00—St. Louis	NHL	66	4	9	13	150	6	0	1	6	1	0	1	24
00-01—St. Louis	NHL	57	8	7	15	110	8	0	1	—	—	—	—	—
01-02—St. Louis	NHL	64	6	7	13	100	2	0	0	9	0	1	1	20
02-03—St. Louis	NHL	66	6	3	9	114	0	1	0	7	2	1	3	6
03-04—Phoenix	NHL	69	3	5	8	110	-6	0	0	—	—	—	—	—
NHL Totals (6 years)		324	27	31	58	589	9	1	2	23	3	2	5	52

NASLUND, MARKUS — LW/RW — CANUCKS

PERSONAL: Born July 30, 1973, in Ornskoldsvik, Sweden. ... 5-11/195. ... Shoots left. ... Name pronounced NAZ-luhnd.
TRANSACTIONS/CAREER NOTES: Selected by Pittsburgh Penguins in 1st round (1st Penguins pick, 16th overall) of NHL draft (June 22, 1991). ... Traded by Penguins to Vancouver Canucks for LW Alex Stojanov (March 20, 1996). ... Flu (November 26, 1996); missed one game. ... Fractured leg (March 16, 2001); missed remainder of season. ... Injured groin (December 6, 2003); missed one game. ... Concussion (February 17, 2004); missed three games.
STATISTICAL PLATEAUS: Three-goal games: 1995-96 (1), 1998-99 (1), 2000-01 (1), 2001-02 (3), 2002-03 (1). Total: 7. ... Four-goal games: 2002-03 (1), 2003-04 (1). Total: 2. ... Total hat tricks: 9.

		REGULAR SEASON								PLAYOFFS				
Season Team	League	GP	G	A	Pts.	PIM	+/-	PP	SH	GP	G	A	Pts.	PIM
89-90—MoDo Hockey	Sweden Jr.	33	43	35	78	20	...	...	...	—	—	—	—	—
90-91—MoDo Ornskoldsvik	Sweden	32	10	9	19	14	...	...	...	—	—	—	—	—
91-92—MoDo Ornskoldsvik	Sweden	39	22	18	40	54	...	...	...	—	—	—	—	—
92-93—MoDo Ornskoldsvik	Sweden	39	22	17	39	67	...	...	...	3	3	2	5	...
93-94—Pittsburgh	NHL	71	4	7	11	27	-3	1	0	—	—	—	—	—
—Cleveland	IHL	5	1	6	7	4	0	0	0	—	—	—	—	—
94-95—Pittsburgh	NHL	14	2	2	4	2	0	0	0	—	—	—	—	—
—Cleveland	IHL	7	3	4	7	6	4	0	0	4	1	3	4	8
95-96—Pittsburgh	NHL	66	19	33	52	36	17	3	0	—	—	—	—	—
—Vancouver	NHL	10	3	0	3	6	3	1	0	6	1	2	3	8
96-97—Vancouver	NHL	78	21	20	41	30	-15	4	0	—	—	—	—	—
97-98—Vancouver	NHL	76	14	20	34	56	5	2	1	—	—	—	—	—
98-99—Vancouver	NHL	80	36	30	66	74	-13	15	2	—	—	—	—	—
99-00—Vancouver	NHL	82	27	38	65	64	-5	6	2	—	—	—	—	—
00-01—Vancouver	NHL	72	41	34	75	58	-2	18	1	—	—	—	—	—
01-02—Vancouver	NHL	81	40	50	90	50	22	8	0	6	1	1	2	2
—Swedish Oly. team	Int'l	4	2	1	3	0	...	...	...	—	—	—	—	—
02-03—Vancouver	NHL	82	48	56	104	52	6	24	0	14	5	9	14	18
03-04—Vancouver	NHL	78	35	49	84	58	24	5	0	7	2	7	9	2
04-05—MoDo Ornskoldsvik	Sweden	13	8	9	17	8	1	3	0	6	0	1	1	10
NHL Totals (11 years)		790	290	339	629	513	39	87	6	33	9	19	28	30

NAZAROV, ANDREI — LW/RW — WILD

PERSONAL: Born May 22, 1974, in Chelyabinsk, U.S.S.R. ... 6-5/242. ... Shoots right. ... Name pronounced nuh-ZAH-rahf.

TRANSACTIONS/CAREER NOTES: Selected by San Jose Sharks in 1st round (2nd Sharks pick, 10th overall) of NHL draft (June 20, 1992). ... Suspended four games and fined $500 for head-butting (March 8, 1995). ... Fractured facial bones (February 5, 1997); missed 14 games. ... Suspended 13 games for physical abuse of officials (March 25, 1997). ... Injured knee (October 13, 1997); missed seven games. ... Traded by Sharks with 1st-round pick (C Vincent Lecavalier) in 1998 draft to Tampa Bay Lightning for D Bryan Marchment, D David Shaw and 1st-round pick (traded to Nashville; Predators selected C David Legwand) in 1998 draft (March 24, 1998). ... Injured finger (November 8, 1998); missed one game. ... Suspended seven games and fined $1,000 by NHL in cross-checking incident (November 19, 1998). ... Traded by Lightning to Calgary Flames for C Michael Nylander (January 19, 1999). ... Traded by Flames with second-round pick (returned to Calgary; Flames selected C Andrei Taratukhin) in 2001 draft to Anaheim Mighty Ducks for D Jordan Leopold (September 26, 2000). ... Traded by Mighty Ducks with D Patrick Traverse to Boston Bruins for C Samuel Pahlsson (November 18, 2000). ... Traded by Bruins to Phoenix Coyotes for fifth-round pick (G Peter Hamerlik) in 2002 draft (January 25, 2002). ... Suspended four games for receiving match penalty in game (March 10, 2003). ... Suspended two games for receiving match penalty in game (February 26, 2004). ... Signed as free agent by Minnesota Wild (Aug. 1, 2005).

		REGULAR SEASON								PLAYOFFS				
Season Team	League	GP	G	A	Pts.	PIM	+/-	PP	SH	GP	G	A	Pts.	PIM
90-91—Mechel Chelyabinsk	USSR	2	0	0	0	0	...	...	...	—	—	—	—	—
91-92—Dynamo Moscow	CIS	2	1	0	1	2	...	...	...	—	—	—	—	—
92-93—Dynamo Moscow	CIS	42	8	2	10	79	...	...	...	10	1	1	2	8
93-94—Kansas City	IHL	71	15	18	33	64	-15	6	0	—	—	—	—	—
—San Jose	NHL	1	0	0	0	0	0	0	0	—	—	—	—	—
94-95—Kansas City	IHL	43	15	10	25	55	3	2	0	—	—	—	—	—
—San Jose	NHL	26	3	5	8	94	-1	0	0	6	0	0	0	9
95-96—San Jose	NHL	42	7	7	14	62	-15	2	0	—	—	—	—	—
—Kansas City	IHL	27	4	6	10	118	...	...	...	2	0	0	0	2
96-97—San Jose	NHL	60	12	15	27	222	-4	1	0	—	—	—	—	—
—Kentucky	AHL	3	1	2	3	4	-2	0	0	—	—	—	—	—
97-98—San Jose	NHL	40	1	1	2	112	-4	0	0	—	—	—	—	—
—Tampa Bay	NHL	14	1	1	2	58	-9	0	0	—	—	—	—	—
98-99—Tampa Bay	NHL	26	2	0	2	43	-5	0	0	—	—	—	—	—
—Calgary	NHL	36	5	9	14	30	1	0	0	—	—	—	—	—
99-00—Calgary	NHL	76	10	22	32	78	3	1	0	—	—	—	—	—
00-01—Anaheim	NHL	16	1	0	1	29	-9	0	0	—	—	—	—	—
—Boston	NHL	63	1	4	5	200	-14	0	0	—	—	—	—	—
01-02—Boston	NHL	47	0	2	2	164	-2	0	0	—	—	—	—	—
—Phoenix	NHL	30	6	3	9	51	7	0	0	3	0	0	0	2
02-03—Phoenix	NHL	59	3	0	3	135	-9	2	0	—	—	—	—	—
03-04—Phoenix	NHL	33	1	2	3	125	-7	0	0	—	—	—	—	—
04-05—Metallurg Novokuznetsk	Russian	9	0	0	0	20	-6	...	...	...	—	—	—	—
—														
—Avangard Omsk	Russian	23	0	2	2	153	-4	...	...	10	0	0	0	10
NHL Totals (11 years)		569	53	71	124	1403	-68	6	0	9	0	0	0	11

NEAL, JAMES — LW — STARS

PERSONAL: Born September 3, 1987, in Whitby, Ont. ... 6-2/185. ... Shoots left.

		REGULAR SEASON								PLAYOFFS				
Season Team	League	GP	G	A	Pts.	PIM	+/-	PP	SH	GP	G	A	Pts.	PIM
03-04—Plymouth	OHL	9	2	4	6	0	...	...	...	—	—	—	—	—
04-05—Plymouth	OHL	67	18	26	44	32	-5	7	0	4	1	1	2	6

NECKAR, STAN — D

PERSONAL: Born December 22, 1975, in Ceske Budejovice, Czechoslovakia. ... 6-1/209. ... Shoots left. ... Name pronounced NEHTS-kash.

TRANSACTIONS/CAREER NOTES: Selected by Ottawa Senators in second round (second Senators pick, 29th overall) of NHL entry draft (June 28, 1994). ... Suffered torn knee ligament (October 18, 1996); missed remainder of the season. ... Injured right knee (January 24, 1998); missed two games. ... Reinjured knee (April 3, 1998) and had surgery; missed final nine games of season. ... Fractured right foot (October 22, 1998); missed 16 games. ... Traded by Senators to New York Rangers for LW Bill Berg and second-round pick (traded to Anaheim) in 1999 draft (November 27, 1998). ... Traded by Rangers to Phoenix Coyotes for D Jason Doig and sixth-round pick (C Jay Dardis) in 1999 draft (March 23, 1999). ... Strained knee (October 18, 1999); missed 13 games. ... Injured ankle (November 21, 2000); missed 12 games. ... Traded by Coyotes with G Nikolai Khabibulin to Tampa Bay Lightning for D Paul Mara, RW Mike Johnson, RW Ruslan Zainullin and second-round pick (D Matthew Spiller) in 2001 (March 5, 2001). ... Strained groin (January 24, 2003); missed four games. ... Reinjured groin (February 6, 2003); missed seven games. ... Signed as free agent by the Nashville Predators (November 26, 2003). ... Injured groin (December 3, 2003); missed 35 games. ... Reinjured groin (February 28, 2004); missed remainder of season. ... Traded by Predators to Lightning for sixth-round pick in 2004 entry draft (March 9, 2004).

		REGULAR SEASON								PLAYOFFS				
Season Team	League	GP	G	A	Pts.	PIM	+/-	PP	SH	GP	G	A	Pts.	PIM
91-92—Budejovice	Czech Dv.I	18	1	3	4	...	...	...	...	—	—	—	—	—
92-93—Motor-Ceske Bude.	Czech.	42	2	9	11	12	...	...	...	—	—	—	—	—
93-94—HC Ceske Budejovice	Czech Rep.	12	3	2	5	2	...	...	...	3	0	0	0	0
94-95—Detroit	IHL	15	2	2	4	15	1	0	0	—	—	—	—	—
—Ottawa	NHL	48	1	3	4	37	-20	0	0	—	—	—	—	—
95-96—Ottawa	NHL	82	3	9	12	54	-16	1	0	—	—	—	—	—
96-97—Ottawa	NHL	5	0	0	0	2	2	0	0	—	—	—	—	—
97-98—Ottawa	NHL	60	2	2	4	31	-14	0	0	9	0	0	0	2
98-99—Ottawa	NHL	3	0	2	2	0	-1	0	0	—	—	—	—	—
—New York Rangers	NHL	18	0	0	0	8	-1	0	0	—	—	—	—	—
—Phoenix	NHL	11	0	1	1	10	3	0	0	6	0	1	1	4

		REGULAR SEASON								PLAYOFFS				
Season Team	**League**	**GP**	**G**	**A**	**Pts.**	**PIM**	**+/-**	**PP**	**SH**	**GP**	**G**	**A**	**Pts.**	**PIM**
99-00—Phoenix	NHL	66	2	8	10	36	1	0	0	5	0	0	0	0
00-01—Phoenix	NHL	53	2	2	4	63	-2	0	0	—	—	—	—	—
—Tampa Bay	NHL	16	0	2	2	8	-1	0	0	—	—	—	—	—
01-02—Tampa Bay	NHL	77	1	7	8	24	-18	0	1	—	—	—	—	—
02-03—Tampa Bay	NHL	70	1	4	5	43	-6	0	0	7	0	2	2	2
03-04—Tampa Bay	NHL	—	—	—	—	—	—	—	—	2	0	0	0	0
—Milwaukee	AHL	3	0	3	3	2	2	0	0	—	—	—	—	—
—Nashville	NHL	1	0	1	1	0	2	0	0	—	—	—	—	—
04-05—Budejovice	Czech Dv.I	16	2	6	8	8	10	...	...	16	0	1	1	18
NHL Totals (10 years)		510	12	41	53	316	-71	1	1	29	0	3	3	8

NEDOROST, VACLAV C PANTHERS

PERSONAL: Born March 16, 1982, in Ceske Budejovice, Czechoslovakia. ... 6-1/190. ... Shoots left.
TRANSACTIONS/CAREER NOTES: Selected by Colorado Avalanche in first round (first Avalanche pick, 14th overall) of NHL entry draft (June 24, 2000). ... Had hip pointer (November 18, 2001); missed two games. ... Charley horse (November 15, 2002); missed two games. ... Injured shoulder (November 23, 2002); missed two games. ... Fractured hand (December 29, 2002); missed 15 games. ... Injured head (February 21, 2003); missed one game. ... Traded to Florida Panthers with LW Eric Messier for F Peter Worrell and second-round pick (D David Booth) in 2004 draft (July 20, 2003). ... Suffered concussion (February 27, 2004); missed seven games.

		REGULAR SEASON								PLAYOFFS				
Season Team	**League**	**GP**	**G**	**A**	**Pts.**	**PIM**	**+/-**	**PP**	**SH**	**GP**	**G**	**A**	**Pts.**	**PIM**
98-99—Budejovice	Czech. Jrs.	35	5	13	18	10	...	...	...	—	—	—	—	—
99-00—Budejovice	Czech Rep.	38	8	6	14	6	...	...	...	3	0	0	0	0
—Budejovice	Czech. Jrs.	7	2	5	7	6	...	...	...	—	—	—	—	—
00-01—HC Ceske Budejovice	Czech Rep.	36	3	12	15	22	...	...	...	—	—	—	—	—
01-02—Colorado	NHL	25	2	2	4	2	-4	1	0	—	—	—	—	—
—Hershey	AHL	49	12	22	34	16	10	2	0	7	2	3	5	2
02-03—Colorado	NHL	42	4	5	9	20	8	1	0	—	—	—	—	—
—Hershey	AHL	5	3	2	5	0	5	0	0	5	2	2	4	0
03-04—San Antonio	AHL	21	9	6	15	2	3	5	0	—	—	—	—	—
—Florida	NHL	32	4	3	7	12	-6	2	0	—	—	—	—	—
04-05—Liberec	Czech Rep.	48	15	18	33	20	20	...	...	6	0	1	1	12
NHL Totals (3 years)		99	10	10	20	34	-2	4	0					

NEDVED, PETR C/LW COYOTES

PERSONAL: Born December 9, 1971, in Liberec, Czechoslovakia. ... 6-3/196. ... Shoots left. ... Name pronounced NEHD-vehd.
TRANSACTIONS/CAREER NOTES: Selected by Vancouver Canucks in first round (first Canucks pick, second overall) of NHL draft (June 16, 1990). ... Signed to offer sheet by St. Louis Blues (March 4, 1994); C Craig Janney and second-round pick (C Dave Scatchard) in 1994 draft awarded to Canucks as compensation (March 14, 1994). ... Traded by Blues to New York Rangers for LW Esa Tikkanen and D Doug Lidster (July 24, 1994); trade arranged as compensation for Blues signing coach Mike Keenan. ... Strained abdomen (February 27, 1995); missed two games. ... Traded by Rangers with D Sergei Zubov to Pittsburgh Penguins for LW Luc Robitaille and D Ulf Samuelsson (August 31, 1995). ... Bruised thigh (November 18, 1995); missed two games. ... Bruised tailbone (December 19, 1996); missed two games. ... Sprained wrist (January 14, 1997); missed two games. ... Charley horse (February 8, 1997); missed one game. ... Sprained wrist (March 20, 1997); missed three games. ... Missed all of 1997-98 season and first 18 games of 1998-99 season in contract dispute. ... Traded by Penguins with C Sean Pronger and D Chris Tamer to Rangers for RW Alexei Kovalev and C Harry York (November 25, 1998). ... Strained ribcage muscle (April 2, 1999); missed final seven games of season. ... Strained groin (December 2, 1999); missed four games. ... Bruised ribs (March 15, 2000); missed two games. ... Suspended three games for high-sticking incident (December 12, 2000). ... Suffered concussion (October 31, 2001); missed four games. ... Hip pointer (December 21, 2002); missed four games. ... Strained lower back (November 2, 2003); missed one game. ... Traded by Rangers with G Jussi Markkanen to Edmonton Oilers for G Stephen Valiquette, C Dwight Helminen and a second-round pick (C Brandon Dubinsky) in 2004 draft (March 3, 2004). ... Signed as free agent by Phoenix Coyotes (August 26, 2004).
STATISTICAL PLATEAUS: Three-goal games: 1998-99 (1), 1999-00 (3), 2000-01 (1), 2002-03 (1). Total: 6. ... Four-goal games: 1995-96 (1). ... Total hat tricks: 7.

		REGULAR SEASON								PLAYOFFS				
Season Team	**League**	**GP**	**G**	**A**	**Pts.**	**PIM**	**+/-**	**PP**	**SH**	**GP**	**G**	**A**	**Pts.**	**PIM**
88-89—Litvinov	Czech. Jrs.	20	32	19	51	12	...	...	...	—	—	—	—	—
89-90—Seattle	WHL	71	65	80	145	80	...	...	...	11	4	9	13	2
90-91—Vancouver	NHL	61	10	6	16	20	-21	1	0	6	0	1	1	0
91-92—Vancouver	NHL	77	15	22	37	36	-3	5	0	10	1	4	5	16
92-93—Vancouver	NHL	84	38	33	71	96	20	2	1	12	2	3	5	2
93-94—Canadian nat'l team	Int'l	17	19	12	31	16	...	...	...	—	—	—	—	—
—Can. Olympic team	Int'l	8	5	1	6	6	4	2	0	—	—	—	—	—
—St. Louis	NHL	19	6	14	20	8	2	2	0	4	0	1	1	4
94-95—New York Rangers	NHL	46	11	12	23	26	-1	1	0	10	3	2	5	6
95-96—Pittsburgh	NHL	80	45	54	99	68	37	8	1	18	10	10	20	16
96-97—Pittsburgh	NHL	74	33	38	71	66	-2	12	3	5	1	2	3	12
97-98—Sparta Praha	Czech Rep.	5	2	3	5	8	...	...	...	6	0	2	2	52
—Las Vegas	IHL	3	3	3	6	4	-4	2	0	—	—	—	—	—
98-99—Las Vegas	IHL	13	8	10	18	32	6	2	0	—	—	—	—	—
—New York Rangers	NHL	56	20	27	47	50	-6	9	1	—	—	—	—	—
99-00—New York Rangers	NHL	76	24	44	68	40	2	6	2	—	—	—	—	—
00-01—New York Rangers	NHL	79	32	46	78	54	10	9	1	—	—	—	—	—
01-02—New York Rangers	NHL	78	21	25	46	36	-8	6	1	—	—	—	—	—
02-03—New York Rangers	NHL	78	27	31	58	64	-4	8	3	—	—	—	—	—
03-04—New York Rangers	NHL	65	14	17	31	42	-9	5	0	—	—	—	—	—
—Edmonton	NHL	16	5	10	15	4	1	2	0	—	—	—	—	—
04-05—Sparta Praha	Czech Rep.	46	22	13	35	44	11	...	...	5	2	3	5	10
NHL Totals (13 years)		889	301	379	680	610	18	76	13	65	17	23	40	56

N

NEIL, CHRIS — RW — SENATORS

PERSONAL: Born June 18, 1979, in Markdale, Ont. ... 6-0/215. ... Shoots right.
TRANSACTIONS/CAREER NOTES: Selected by Ottawa Senators in sixth round (seventh Senators pick, 161st overall) of NHL entry draft (June 27, 1998). ... Injured hip (March 19, 2002); missed one game. ... Reinjured hip (March 24, 2002); missed three games. ... Fractured left leg (September 21, 2002); missed 12 games.

		REGULAR SEASON								PLAYOFFS				
Season Team	**League**	**GP**	**G**	**A**	**Pts.**	**PIM**	**+/-**	**PP**	**SH**	**GP**	**G**	**A**	**Pts.**	**PIM**
96-97—North Bay	OHL	65	13	16	29	150	...	...	...	—	—	—	—	—
97-98—North Bay	OHL	59	26	29	55	231	-8	...	...	—	—	—	—	—
98-99—North Bay	OHL	66	26	46	72	215	2	...	...	4	1	0	1	15
99-00—Grand Rapids	IHL	51	9	10	19	*301	...	...	...	8	0	2	2	24
—Mobile	ECHL	4	0	2	2	39	...	...	...	—	—	—	—	—
00-01—Grand Rapids	IHL	78	15	21	36	354	...	...	...	10	2	2	4	22
01-02—Ottawa	NHL	72	10	7	17	231	5	1	0	12	0	0	0	12
02-03—Ottawa	NHL	68	6	4	10	147	8	0	0	15	1	0	1	24
03-04—Ottawa	NHL	82	8	8	16	194	13	0	0	7	0	1	1	19
04-05—Binghamton	AHL	22	4	6	10	132	10	1	0	6	1	1	2	26
NHL Totals (3 years)		222	24	19	43	572	26	1	0	34	1	1	2	55

NICHOL, SCOTT — C/RW — PREDATORS

PERSONAL: Born December 31, 1974, in Edmonton. ... 5-8/173. ... Shoots right.
TRANSACTIONS/CAREER NOTES: Selected by Buffalo Sabres in 11th round (9th Sabres pick, 272nd overall) of entry draft (June 26, 1993). ... Signed as free agent by Calgary Flames (August 2, 2001). ... Hand injury (October 10, 2001); missed one game. ... Hip injury (October 25, 2001); missed one game. ... Suspended two games for unsportsmanlike conduct (December 10, 2001). ... Hip injury (January 5, 2002); missed three games. ... Knee injury (February 26, 2002); missed 14 games. ... Suspended five games for butt-ending (December 20, 2002). ... Signed by Chicago Blackhawks as free agent (July 1, 2003). ... Injured groin (January 27, 2004); missed five games. ... Suspended two games for slashing incident (March 27, 2004). ... Signed as free agent by Nashville Predators (Aug. 6, 2005).

		REGULAR SEASON								PLAYOFFS				
Season Team	**League**	**GP**	**G**	**A**	**Pts.**	**PIM**	**+/-**	**PP**	**SH**	**GP**	**G**	**A**	**Pts.**	**PIM**
92-93—Portland	WHL	67	31	33	64	146	...	...	...	—	—	—	—	—
93-94—Portland	WHL	65	40	53	93	144	...	...	...	—	—	—	—	—
94-95—Rochester	AHL	71	11	16	27	136	-12	1	4	5	0	3	3	14
95-96—Rochester	AHL	62	14	17	31	170	...	...	...	19	7	6	13	36
—Buffalo	NHL	2	0	0	0	10	0	0	0	—	—	—	—	—
96-97—Rochester	AHL	68	22	21	43	133	9	1	4	10	2	1	3	26
97-98—Rochester	AHL	35	13	7	20	113	-10	1	1	—	—	—	—	—
—Buffalo	NHL	3	0	0	0	4	0	0	0	—	—	—	—	—
98-99—Rochester	AHL	53	13	20	33	120	19	1	0	—	—	—	—	—
99-00—Rochester	AHL	37	7	11	18	141	...	...	...	—	—	—	—	—
00-01—Detroit	IHL	67	7	24	31	198	...	...	...	—	—	—	—	—
01-02—Calgary	NHL	60	8	9	17	107	-9	2	1	—	—	—	—	—
02-03—Calgary	NHL	68	5	5	10	149	-7	0	1	—	—	—	—	—
03-04—Chicago	NHL	75	7	11	18	145	-16	0	0	—	—	—	—	—
04-05—London	England	15	7	12	19	86	...	1	0	—	—	—	—	—
NHL Totals (5 years)		208	20	25	45	415	-32	2	2					

NICKULAS, ERIC — RW

PERSONAL: Born March 25, 1975, in Hyannis, Mass. ... 5-11/206. ... Shoots right. ... Name pronounced NICK-luhs.
TRANSACTIONS/CAREER NOTES: Selected by Boston Bruins in fourth round (third Bruins pick, 99th overall) of NHL draft (June 29, 1994). ... Charley horse (September 22, 2000); missed first three games of season. ... Bruised ribs (October 14, 2000); missed two games. ... Signed as free agent by St. Louis Blues (July 16, 2002). ... Claimed by Chicago Blackhawks off waivers from Blues (February 24, 2004).

		REGULAR SEASON								PLAYOFFS				
Season Team	**League**	**GP**	**G**	**A**	**Pts.**	**PIM**	**+/-**	**PP**	**SH**	**GP**	**G**	**A**	**Pts.**	**PIM**
91-92—Barnstable H.S.	Mass. Jr.	24	30	25	55	...	...	...	...	—	—	—	—	—
92-93—Tabor Academy	Mass. H.S.	28	25	25	50	...	...	...	...	—	—	—	—	—
93-94—Cushing Academy	Mass. H.S.	25	46	36	82	...	...	...	...	—	—	—	—	—
94-95—New Hampshire	Hockey East	33	15	9	24	32	...	1	1	—	—	—	—	—
95-96—New Hampshire	Hockey East	34	26	12	38	66	...	...	...	—	—	—	—	—
96-97—New Hampshire	Hockey East	39	29	22	51	80	...	7	1	—	—	—	—	—
97-98—Orlando	IHL	76	22	9	31	77	5	3	1	6	0	0	0	10
98-99—Providence	AHL	75	31	27	58	83	13	15	0	18	8	12	20	33
—Boston	NHL	2	0	0	0	0	0	0	0	1	0	0	0	2
99-00—Providence	AHL	40	6	6	12	37	...	...	...	12	2	3	5	20
—Boston	NHL	20	5	6	11	12	-1	1	0	—	—	—	—	—
00-01—Boston	NHL	7	0	0	0	4	-2	0	0	—	—	—	—	—
—Providence	AHL	62	20	23	43	100	...	...	...	12	4	4	8	24
01-02—Worcester	AHL	54	11	25	36	48	19	2	1	3	0	1	1	2
02-03—St. Louis	NHL	8	0	1	1	6	-2	0	0	—	—	—	—	—
—Worcester	AHL	39	17	16	33	40	7	7	2	3	0	0	0	2
03-04—St. Louis	NHL	44	7	11	18	44	-2	1	0	—	—	—	—	—
—Chicago	NHL	21	1	1	2	8	-6	0	0	—	—	—	—	—
04-05—Norfolk	AHL	53	11	11	22	32	-7	4	1	6	0	3	3	8
NHL Totals (5 years)		102	13	19	32	74	-13	2	0	1	0	0	0	2

NIEDERMAYER, ROB — C — MIGHTY DUCKS

PERSONAL: Born December 28, 1974, in Cassiar, B.C. ... 6-2/209. ... Shoots left. ... Brother of Scott Niedermayer, D, New Jersey Devils. ... Name pronounced NEE-duhr-MIGH-uhr.

TRANSACTIONS/CAREER NOTES: Selected by Florida Panthers in 1st round (1st Panthers pick, 5th overall) of NHL draft (June 26, 1993). ... Separated right shoulder (November 18, 1993); missed 17 games. ... Sprained knee ligament (November 22, 1996); missed 17 games. ... Strained groin (March 5, 1997); missed two games. ... Sprained wrist (March 20, 1997); missed three games. ... Concussion (October 1, 1997); missed 10 games. ... Dislocated right thumb (November 18, 1997); missed 15 games. ... Knee surgery during 1997-98 All-Star break; missed eight games. ... Postconcussion syndrome (March 19, 1998); missed remainder of season. ... Injured head (March 3, 2000); missed one game. ... Concussion (February 21, 2001); missed 15 games. ... Traded by Panthers with 2nd-round pick (G Andrei Medvedev) in 2001 draft to Calgary Flames for RW Valeri Bure and C Jason Wiemer (June 23, 2001). ... Bruised hip (October 13, 2001); missed four games. ... Injured (November 17, 2001); missed one game. ... Sprained knee and ankle (January 8, 2002); missed 18 games. ... Injured (March 6, 2002); missed two games. ... Traded by Flames to Anaheim Mighty Ducks for D Mike Commodore and G J.F. Damphousse (March 11, 2003). ... Injured groin (December 2, 2003); missed 12 games. ... Reinjured groin (January 29, 2004); missed 14 games.

		REGULAR SEASON								PLAYOFFS				
Season Team	League	GP	G	A	Pts.	PIM	+/-	PP	SH	GP	G	A	Pts.	PIM
90-91—Medicine Hat	WHL	71	24	26	50	8	...	...	...	12	3	7	10	2
91-92—Medicine Hat	WHL	71	32	46	78	77	...	...	...	4	2	3	5	2
92-93—Medicine Hat	WHL	52	43	34	77	67	...	...	...	—	—	—	—	—
93-94—Florida	NHL	65	9	17	26	51	-11	3	0	—	—	—	—	—
94-95—Medicine Hat	WHL	13	9	15	24	14	-5	4	1	—	—	—	—	—
—Florida	NHL	48	4	6	10	36	-13	1	0	—	—	—	—	—
95-96—Florida	NHL	82	26	35	61	107	1	11	0	22	5	3	8	12
96-97—Florida	NHL	60	14	24	38	54	4	3	0	5	2	1	3	6
97-98—Florida	NHL	33	8	7	15	41	-9	5	0	—	—	—	—	—
98-99—Florida	NHL	82	18	33	51	50	-13	6	1	—	—	—	—	—
99-00—Florida	NHL	81	10	23	33	46	-5	1	0	4	1	0	1	6
00-01—Florida	NHL	67	12	20	32	50	-12	3	1	—	—	—	—	—
01-02—Calgary	NHL	57	6	14	20	49	-15	1	2	—	—	—	—	—
02-03—Calgary	NHL	54	8	10	18	42	-13	2	0	—	—	—	—	—
—Anaheim	NHL	12	2	2	4	15	3	1	0	21	3	7	10	18
03-04—Anaheim	NHL	55	12	16	28	34	-6	6	0	—	—	—	—	—
04-05—Ferencvaros	Hungary	5	2	1	3	14	...	...	...	—	—	—	—	—
NHL Totals (11 years)		696	129	207	336	575	-89	43	4	52	11	11	22	42

NIEDERMAYER, SCOTT — D — MIGHTY DUCKS

PERSONAL: Born August 31, 1973, in Edmonton. ... 6-1/200. ... Shoots left. ... Brother of Rob Niedermayer, C, Anaheim Mighty Ducks. ... Name pronounced NEE-duhr-MIGH-uhr.

TRANSACTIONS/CAREER NOTES: Selected by New Jersey Devils in 1st round (1st Devils pick, 3rd overall) of NHL draft (June 22, 1991). ... Sore back (December 9, 1992); missed four games. ... Injured knee (December 19, 1995); missed three games. ... Strained groin (February 12, 1997); missed one game. ... Flu (February 4, 1998); missed one game. ... Missed first nine games of 1998-99 season in contact dispute. ... Strained hip flexor (January 15, 2000); missed one game. ... Flu (January 26, 2000); missed one game. ... Suspended final nine games of regular season and one playoff game for high-sticking incident (March 21, 2000). ... Missed first 19 games of 2000-01 season due to contract dispute. ... Injured knee (January 20, 2001); missed one game. ... Injured knee (February 8, 2001); missed five games. ... Strained lower back (October 5, 2001); missed first two games of season. ... Pinched nerve in neck (February 27, 2002); missed three games. ... Sore back (October 18, 2003); missed one game. ... Signed as free agent by Anaheim Mighty Ducks (Aug. 4, 2005).

		REGULAR SEASON								PLAYOFFS				
Season Team	League	GP	G	A	Pts.	PIM	+/-	PP	SH	GP	G	A	Pts.	PIM
89-90—Kamloops	WHL	64	14	55	69	64	...	...	...	17	2	14	16	35
90-91—Kamloops	WHL	57	26	56	82	52	...	...	...	—	—	—	—	—
91-92—New Jersey	NHL	4	0	1	1	2	1	0	0	—	—	—	—	—
—Kamloops	WHL	35	7	32	39	61	...	...	...	17	9	14	23	28
92-93—New Jersey	NHL	80	11	29	40	47	8	5	0	5	0	3	3	2
93-94—New Jersey	NHL	81	10	36	46	42	34	5	0	20	2	2	4	8
94-95—New Jersey	NHL	48	4	15	19	18	19	4	0	20	4	7	11	10
95-96—New Jersey	NHL	79	8	25	33	46	5	6	0	—	—	—	—	—
96-97—New Jersey	NHL	81	5	30	35	64	-4	3	0	10	2	4	6	6
97-98—New Jersey	NHL	81	14	43	57	27	5	11	0	6	0	2	2	4
98-99—Utah	IHL	5	0	2	2	0	-5	0	0	—	—	—	—	—
—New Jersey	NHL	72	11	35	46	26	16	1	1	7	1	3	4	18
99-00—New Jersey	NHL	71	7	31	38	48	19	1	0	22	5	2	7	10
00-01—New Jersey	NHL	57	6	29	35	22	14	1	0	21	0	6	6	14
01-02—New Jersey	NHL	76	11	22	33	30	12	2	0	6	0	2	2	6
—Can. Olympic team	Int'l	6	1	1	2	4	...	...	...	—	—	—	—	—
02-03—New Jersey	NHL	81	11	28	39	62	23	3	0	24	2	*16	*18	16
03-04—New Jersey	NHL	81	14	40	54	44	20	9	0	5	1	0	1	6
NHL Totals (13 years)		892	112	364	476	478	172	51	1	146	17	47	64	100

NIEMINEN, VILLE — LW — RANGERS

PERSONAL: Born April 6, 1977, in Tampere, Finland. ... 6-0/200. ... Shoots left.

TRANSACTIONS/CAREER NOTES: Selected by Colorado Avalanche in 3rd round (4th Avalanche pick, 78th overall) of NHL draft (June 21, 1997). ... Concussion (October 13, 2001); missed six games. ... Traded by Avalanche with D Rick Berry to Pittsburgh Penguins for D Darius Kasparitis (March 19, 2002). ... Signed as free agent by Chicago Blackhawks (July 29, 2003). ... Traded by Blackhawks to Calgary Flames for C Jason Morgan and a conditional pick (February 24, 2004). ... Signed as free agent by New York Rangers (Aug. 4, 2005).

Season Team	League	GP	G	A	Pts.	PIM	+/-	PP	SH	GP	G	A	Pts.	PIM
		REGULAR SEASON								PLAYOFFS				
94-95—Tappara Tampere	Finland Jr.	16	11	21	32	47	...	...	...	—	—	—	—	—
—Tappara Tampere	Finland	16	0	0	0	0	...	...	...	—	—	—	—	—
95-96—Tappara Tampere	Finland Jr.	20	20	23	43	63	...	...	...	—	—	—	—	—
—Tappara Tampere	Finland	4	0	1	1	8	...	...	...	—	—	—	—	—
—KooVee Tampere	Finland	7	2	1	3	4	...	...	...	—	—	—	—	—
96-97—Tappara Tampere	Finland	49	10	13	23	120	...	...	...	3	1	0	1	8
97-98—Hershey	AHL	74	14	22	36	85	6	2	0	—	—	—	—	—
98-99—Hershey	AHL	67	24	19	43	127	1	7	0	3	0	1	1	0
99-00—Hershey	AHL	74	21	30	51	54	...	...	...	9	2	4	6	6
—Colorado	NHL	1	0	0	0	0	0	0	0	—	—	—	—	—
00-01—Hershey	AHL	28	10	11	21	48	...	...	...	—	—	—	—	—
—Colorado	NHL	50	14	8	22	38	8	2	0	23	4	6	10	20
01-02—Colorado	NHL	53	10	14	24	30	1	1	0	—	—	—	—	—
—Fin. Olympic team	Int'l	4	0	1	1	2	...	...	...	—	—	—	—	—
—Pittsburgh	NHL	13	1	2	3	8	-2	0	0	—	—	—	—	—
02-03—Pittsburgh	NHL	75	9	12	21	93	-25	0	2	—	—	—	—	—
03-04—Chicago	NHL	60	2	11	13	40	-15	1	0	—	—	—	—	—
—Calgary	NHL	19	3	5	8	18	6	0	0	24	4	4	8	55
04-05—Tappara Tampere	Finland	26	14	13	27	32	3	...	...	8	2	4	6	12
NHL Totals (5 years)		271	39	52	91	227	-27	4	2	47	8	10	18	75

NIEUWENDYK, JOE — C — PANTHERS

PERSONAL: Born September 10, 1966, in Oshawa, Ont. ... 6-2/205. ... Shoots left. ... Nephew of Ed Kea, D with two NHL teams (1973-83); and cousin of Jeff Beukeboom, D with two NHL teams (1985-99). ... Name pronounced NOO-ihn-dighk.

TRANSACTIONS/CAREER NOTES: Selected by Calgary Flames in 2nd round (2nd Flames pick, 27th overall) of NHL draft (June 15, 1985). ... Concussion (November 1987). ... Bruised ribs (May 25, 1989). ... Torn left knee ligament (April 17, 1990). ... Arthroscopic knee surgery (September 28, 1991); missed 12 games. ... Flu (November 19, 1992); missed one game. ... Strained right knee (March 26, 1993); missed four games. ... Charley horse (November 13, 1993); missed three games. ... Strained right knee ligaments (February 24, 1994); missed 17 games. ... Strained back (April 29, 1995); missed two games. ... Traded by Flames to Dallas Stars for C Corey Millen and rights to C/RW Jarome Iginla (December 19, 1995). ... Bruised chest (October 5, 1996); missed 12 games. ... Sprained knee (December 18, 1997); missed eight games. ... Reinjured knee (January 9, 1998); missed one game. ... Suffered inflammed knee (January 10, 1999); missed five games. ... Sprained ankle (February 23, 1999); missed one game. ... Back spasms (March 16, 1999); missed one game. ... Injured knee (March 31, 1999); missed one game. ... Back spasms (October 20, 1999); missed three games. ... Bruised chest (December 17, 1999); missed 10 games. ... Separated shoulder (January 19, 2000); missed 21 games. ... Flu (January 4, 2001); missed two games. ... Strained groin (February 28, 2001); missed 11 games. ... Flu (February 10, 2002); missed one game. ... Traded by Stars with RW Jamie Langenbrunner to New Jersey Devils for C Jason Arnott, RW Randy McKay and 1st-round pick (traded to Columbus; traded to Buffalo; Sabres selected LW Dan Paille) in 2002 draft (March 19, 2002). ... Ill (March 13, 2003); missed one game. ... Injured hip (May 27, 2003); missed seven playoff games. ... Signed as free agent by Toronto Maple Leafs (September 9, 2003). ... Back spasms (November 2, 2003); missed seven games. ... Back spasms (November 20, 2003); missed four games. ... Injured ankle (December 13, 2003); missed one game. ... Injured rib cage (February 3, 2004); missed five games. ... Signed as free agent by Florida Panthers (Aug. 1, 2005).

STATISTICAL PLATEAUS: Three-goal games: 1987-88 (2), 1988-89 (1), 1989-90 (1), 1992-93 (1), 1993-94 (1), 1994-95 (1), 1997-98 (1), 2000-01 (1). Total: 9. ... Four-goal games: 1987-88 (2), 1997-98 (1). Total: 3. ... Five-goal games: 1988-89 (1). ... Total hat tricks: 13.

Season Team	League	GP	G	A	Pts.	PIM	+/-	PP	SH	GP	G	A	Pts.	PIM
		REGULAR SEASON								PLAYOFFS				
83-84—Pickering Jr. B	MTHL	38	30	28	58	35	...	...	...	—	—	—	—	—
84-85—Cornell	ECAC	23	18	21	39	20	...	...	...	—	—	—	—	—
85-86—Cornell	ECAC	21	21	21	42	45	...	...	...	—	—	—	—	—
86-87—Cornell	ECAC	23	26	26	52	26	...	...	...	—	—	—	—	—
—Canadian nat'l team	Int'l	5	2	0	2	0	...	...	...	—	—	—	—	—
—Calgary	NHL	9	5	1	6	0	0	2	0	6	2	2	4	0
87-88—Calgary	NHL	75	51	41	92	23	20	*31	3	8	3	4	7	2
88-89—Calgary	NHL	77	51	31	82	40	26	19	3	22	10	4	14	10
89-90—Calgary	NHL	79	45	50	95	40	32	18	0	6	4	6	10	4
90-91—Calgary	NHL	79	45	40	85	36	19	22	4	7	4	1	5	10
91-92—Calgary	NHL	69	22	34	56	55	-1	7	0	—	—	—	—	—
92-93—Calgary	NHL	79	38	37	75	52	9	14	0	6	3	6	9	10
93-94—Calgary	NHL	64	36	39	75	51	19	14	1	6	2	2	4	0
94-95—Calgary	NHL	46	21	29	50	33	11	3	0	5	4	3	7	0
95-96—Dallas	NHL	52	14	18	32	41	-17	8	0	—	—	—	—	—
96-97—Dallas	NHL	66	30	21	51	32	-5	8	0	7	2	2	4	6
97-98—Dallas	NHL	73	39	30	69	30	16	14	0	1	1	0	1	0
—Can. Olympic team	Int'l	6	2	3	5	2	0	0	0	—	—	—	—	—
98-99—Dallas	NHL	67	28	27	55	34	11	8	0	23	*11	10	21	19
99-00—Dallas	NHL	48	15	19	34	26	-1	7	0	23	7	3	10	18
00-01—Dallas	NHL	69	29	23	52	30	5	12	0	7	4	0	4	4
01-02—Dallas	NHL	67	23	24	47	18	-2	6	0	—	—	—	—	—
—Can. Olympic team	Int'l	6	1	1	2	0	...	...	...	—	—	—	—	—
—New Jersey	NHL	14	2	9	11	4	2	0	0	5	0	1	1	0
02-03—New Jersey	NHL	80	17	28	45	56	10	3	0	17	3	6	9	4
03-04—Toronto	NHL	64	22	28	50	26	7	10	1	9	6	0	6	4
NHL Totals (18 years)		1177	533	529	1062	627	161	206	12	158	66	50	116	91

NIINIMAA, JANNE — D — ISLANDERS

PERSONAL: Born May 22, 1975, in Raahe, Finland. ... 6-1/220. ... Shoots left. ... Name pronounced YAH-nee NEE-nuh-muh.

TRANSACTIONS/CAREER NOTES: Selected by Philadelphia Flyers in second round (first Flyers pick, 36th overall) of NHL draft (June 26, 1993). ... Traded by Flyers to Edmonton Oilers for D Dan McGillis and second-round pick (D Jason Beckett) in 1998 draft (March 24, 1998).

... Back spasms (November 4, 1998); missed one game. ... Back spasms (November 24, 1999); missed one game. ... Sprained knee (December 28, 2002); missed two games. ... Injured left knee and had flu (January 13, 2003); missed three games. ... Traded by Oilers with second-round pick (C Evgeni Tunik) in 2003 draft to New York Islanders for LW Brad Isbister and LW Raffi Torres (March 11, 2003).

		REGULAR SEASON								PLAYOFFS				
Season Team	**League**	**GP**	**G**	**A**	**Pts.**	**PIM**	**+/-**	**PP**	**SH**	**GP**	**G**	**A**	**Pts.**	**PIM**
91-92—Karpat Oulu	Finland Div. 2	41	2	11	13	49	...	...	...	—	—	—	—	—
92-93—Karpat Oulu	Finland Div. 2	29	2	3	5	14	...	...	...	—	—	—	—	—
—Karpat	Finland Jr.	10	3	9	12	16	...	...	...	—	—	—	—	—
93-94—Jokerit Helsinki	Finland	45	3	8	11	24	...	...	...	12	1	1	2	4
94-95—Jokerit Helsinki	Finland	42	7	10	17	36	4	...	...	10	1	4	5	35
95-96—Jokerit Helsinki	Finland	49	5	15	20	79	...	...	...	11	0	2	2	12
96-97—Philadelphia	NHL	77	4	40	44	58	12	1	0	19	1	12	13	16
97-98—Philadelphia	NHL	66	3	31	34	56	6	2	0	—	—	—	—	—
—Fin. Olympic team	Int'l	6	0	3	3	8	1	0	0	—	—	—	—	—
—Edmonton	NHL	11	1	8	9	6	7	1	0	11	1	1	2	12
98-99—Edmonton	NHL	81	4	24	28	88	7	2	0	4	0	0	0	2
99-00—Edmonton	NHL	81	8	25	33	89	14	2	2	5	0	2	2	2
00-01—Edmonton	NHL	82	12	34	46	90	6	8	0	6	0	2	2	6
01-02—Edmonton	NHL	81	5	39	44	80	13	1	0	—	—	—	—	—
—Fin. Olympic team	Int'l	4	0	3	3	2	...	...	...	—	—	—	—	—
02-03—Edmonton	NHL	63	4	24	28	66	-7	2	0	—	—	—	—	—
—New York Islanders	NHL	13	1	5	6	14	-2	1	0	5	0	1	1	12
03-04—New York Islanders	NHL	82	9	19	28	64	12	4	0	5	1	2	3	2
04-05—Malmo	Sweden	10	0	3	3	34	-2	0	0	—	—	—	—	—
—Karpat Oulu	Finland	26	3	10	13	30	14	...	...	12	0	5	5	8
NHL Totals (8 years)		637	51	249	300	611	68	24	2	55	3	20	23	52

NIINIMAKI, JESSE — C — OILERS

PERSONAL: Born August 19, 1983, in Tampere, Finland. ... 6-2/183. ... Shoots left.
TRANSACTIONS/CAREER NOTES: Selected by Edmonton Oilers in first round (first Oilers pick, 15th overall) of NHL draft (June 22, 2002).

		REGULAR SEASON								PLAYOFFS				
Season Team	**League**	**GP**	**G**	**A**	**Pts.**	**PIM**	**+/-**	**PP**	**SH**	**GP**	**G**	**A**	**Pts.**	**PIM**
01-02—Ilves Tampere	Finland	16	2	4	6	4	...	...	...	3	0	0	0	0
02-03—Ilves Tampere	Finland	41	4	13	17	12	...	...	...	—	—	—	—	—
03-04—Ilves Tampere	Finland	10	3	3	6	2	...	...	...	—	—	—	—	—
04-05—Ilves Tampere	Finland	18	4	4	8	8	...	...	...	—	—	—	—	—
—Edmonton	AHL	24	1	0	1	2	-6	0	0	—	—	—	—	—

NIITTYMAKI, ANTERO — G — FLYERS

PERSONAL: Born June 18, 1980, in Turku, Finland. ... 6-1/183. ... Catches left.
TRANSACTIONS/CAREER NOTES: Selected by Philadelphia Flyers in sixth round (seventh Flyers pick, 168th overall) of NHL entry draft (June 27, 1998).

		REGULAR SEASON									PLAYOFFS							
Season Team	**League**	**GP**	**Min.**	**W**	**L**	**T**	**GA**	**SO**	**GAA**	**SV%**	**GP**	**Min.**	**W**	**L**	**GA**	**SO**	**GAA**	**SV%**
96-97—TPS Turku	Finland Jr.	22	...	...	...	...	...	...	...	...	6	...	...	...	...	...	...	...
97-98—TPS Turku	Finland Jr.	33	...	...	...	...	...	...	...	...	—	—	—	—	—	—	—	—
99-00—TPS Turku	Finland	32	1899	23	6	2	68	3	2.15	...	8	453	6	1	13	0	*1.72	...
00-01—TPS Turku	Finland	21	1112	10	6	1	46	2	2.48	...	—	—	—	—	—	—	—	—
01-02—TPS Turku	Finland	27	1498	16	8	1	46	3	1.84	...	4	295	2	2	11	0	2.24	...
02-03—Philadelphia	AHL	40	2283	14	21	2	98	0	2.58	.903	—	—	—	—	—	—	—	—
03-04—Philadelphia	NHL	3	180	3	0	0	3	0	1.00	.961	—	—	—	—	—	—	—	—
—Philadelphia	AHL	49	2730	24	13	6	92	7	2.02	.917	12	795	6	6	24	0	1.81	.920
04-05—Philadelphia	AHL	58	3452	33	21	...	119	6	2.07	.924	21	1269	15	5	37	3	1.75	.943
NHL Totals (1 year)		3	180	3	0	0	3	0	1.00	.961								

NIKOLISHIN, ANDREI — C

PERSONAL: Born March 25, 1973, in Vorkuta, U.S.S.R. ... 6-0/215. ... Shoots left. ... Name pronounced nih-koh-LEE-shihn.
TRANSACTIONS/CAREER NOTES: Selected by Hartford Whalers in second round (second Whalers pick, 47th overall) of NHL draft (June 20, 1992). ... Sprained ankle (October 21, 1995); missed one game. ... Injured back (November 15, 1995); missed five games. ... Strained back (December 2, 1995); missed 15 games. ... Traded by Whalers to Washington Capitals for D Curtis Leschyshyn (November 9, 1996). ... Bulging disc in back (February 2, 1997); missed eight games. ... Injured knee before 1997-98 season; missed first 42 games. ... Missed first nine games of 1998-99 season in contract dispute. ... Strained abdominal muscle (March 28, 2000); missed four games. ... Bruised leg (December 11, 2001); missed two games. ... Traded by Capitals with LW Chris Simon to Chicago Blackhawks for C Michael Nylander and a third-round pick (RW Stephen Werner) in 2004 (November 1, 2002). ... Traded by Blackhawks to Colorado Avalanche for future considerations (June 22, 2003). ... Injured knee (November 22, 2003); missed three games. ... Injured abdomen (January 24, 2004); missed 20 games. ... Back spasms (March 14, 2004); missed nine games.

		REGULAR SEASON								PLAYOFFS				
Season Team	**League**	**GP**	**G**	**A**	**Pts.**	**PIM**	**+/-**	**PP**	**SH**	**GP**	**G**	**A**	**Pts.**	**PIM**
90-91—Dynamo Moscow	USSR	2	0	0	0	0	...	...	...	—	—	—	—	—
91-92—Dynamo Moscow	CIS	18	1	0	1	4	...	...	...	—	—	—	—	—
92-93—Dynamo Moscow	CIS	42	5	7	12	30	...	...	...	10	2	1	3	8
93-94—Dynamo Moscow	CIS	41	8	12	20	30	...	...	...	9	1	3	4	4
—Russian Oly. team	Int'l	8	2	5	7	6	1	2	0	—	—	—	—	—

Season Team	League	GP	G	A	Pts.	PIM	+/-	PP	SH	GP	G	A	Pts.	PIM
		REGULAR SEASON								PLAYOFFS				
94-95—Dynamo Moscow	CIS	12	7	2	9	6	...	...	...	—	—	—	—	—
—Hartford	NHL	39	8	10	18	10	7	1	1	—	—	—	—	—
95-96—Hartford	NHL	61	14	37	51	34	-2	4	1	—	—	—	—	—
96-97—Hartford	NHL	12	2	5	7	2	-2	0	0	—	—	—	—	—
—Washington	NHL	59	7	14	21	30	5	1	0	—	—	—	—	—
97-98—Portland	AHL	2	0	0	0	2	-3	0	0	—	—	—	—	—
—Washington	NHL	38	6	10	16	14	1	1	0	21	1	13	14	12
98-99—Dynamo Moscow	Russian	4	0	0	0	0	...	...	...	—	—	—	—	—
—Washington	NHL	73	8	27	35	28	0	0	1	—	—	—	—	—
99-00—Washington	NHL	76	11	14	25	28	6	0	2	5	0	2	2	4
00-01—Washington	NHL	81	13	25	38	34	9	4	0	6	0	0	0	2
01-02—Washington	NHL	80	13	23	36	40	-1	1	0	—	—	—	—	—
—Russian Oly. team	Int'l	6	0	1	1	6	...	...	...	—	—	—	—	—
02-03—Chicago	NHL	60	6	15	21	26	-3	0	1	—	—	—	—	—
03-04—Colorado	NHL	49	5	7	12	24	3	1	0	11	0	2	2	4
04-05—CSKA Moscow	Russian	55	7	20	27	64	0	...	...	—	—	—	—	—
NHL Totals (10 years)		628	93	187	280	270	23	13	6	43	1	17	18	22

NILSON, MARCUS — LW/RW — FLAMES

PERSONAL: Born March 1, 1978, in Balsta, Sweden. ... 6-2/195. ... Shoots right.
TRANSACTIONS/CAREER NOTES: Selected by Florida Panthers in first round (first Panthers pick, 20th overall) of NHL draft (June 22, 1996). ... Suspended one game by NHL for slashing (March 16, 2002). ... Traded by Panthers to Calgary Flames for second-round pick (LW David Booth) in 2004 entry draft (March 8, 2004).

Season Team	League	GP	G	A	Pts.	PIM	+/-	PP	SH	GP	G	A	Pts.	PIM
		REGULAR SEASON								PLAYOFFS				
94-95—Djurgarden	Sweden Jr.	24	7	8	15	22	...	...	...	—	—	—	—	—
95-96—Djurgarden	Sweden Jr.	25	19	17	36	46	...	...	...	2	1	1	2	12
—Djurgarden Stockholm	Sweden	12	0	0	0	0	...	...	...	1	0	0	0	0
96-97—Djurgarden Stockholm	Sweden	37	0	3	3	33	...	...	...	4	0	0	0	0
97-98—Djurgarden Stockholm	Sweden	41	4	7	11	18	...	...	...	15	2	1	3	16
98-99—New Haven	AHL	69	8	25	33	10	-14	4	0	—	—	—	—	—
—Florida	NHL	8	1	1	2	5	2	0	0	—	—	—	—	—
99-00—Louisville	AHL	64	9	23	32	52	...	...	...	4	0	0	0	2
—Florida	NHL	9	0	2	2	2	2	0	0	—	—	—	—	—
00-01—Florida	NHL	78	12	24	36	74	-3	0	0	—	—	—	—	—
01-02—Florida	NHL	81	14	19	33	55	-14	6	1	—	—	—	—	—
02-03—Florida	NHL	82	15	19	34	31	2	7	1	—	—	—	—	—
03-04—Florida	NHL	69	6	13	19	26	-9	1	1	—	—	—	—	—
—Calgary	NHL	14	5	0	5	14	3	1	0	26	4	7	11	12
04-05—Djurgarden Stockholm	Sweden	48	17	22	39	110	11	7	2	7	1	2	3	10
NHL Totals (6 years)		341	53	78	131	207	-17	15	3	26	4	7	11	12

NILSSON, ROBERT — RW — ISLANDERS

PERSONAL: Born January 10, 1985, in Calgary. ... 5-11/176. ... Shoots left. ... Son of Kent Nilsson, player with four NHL teams (1979-1987 and 1994-95).
TRANSACTIONS/CAREER NOTES: Selected by New York Islanders in first round (first Islanders pick, 15th overall) in 2003 NHL entry draft (June 23, 2003).

Season Team	League	GP	G	A	Pts.	PIM	+/-	PP	SH	GP	G	A	Pts.	PIM
		REGULAR SEASON								PLAYOFFS				
01-02—Leksand	Sweden Jr.	21	13	18	31	24	...	...	...	—	—	—	—	—
02-03—Leksand	Sweden Dv. 2	41	8	13	21	10	...	...	...	—	—	—	—	—
03-04—Leksand	Sweden Dv. 2	34	2	4	6	6	...	...	...	—	—	—	—	—
—Fribourg	Switzerland	7	1	3	4	2	...	...	...	4	1	0	1	2
04-05—Djurgarden	Sweden Jr.	8	8	4	12	12	4	3	0	—	—	—	—	—
—Djurgarden Stockholm	Sweden	23	2	4	6	6	0	1	0	3	0	0	0	0
—Hammarby	Sweden Dv. 2	7	0	4	4	4	2	0	0	—	—	—	—	—

NISKANEN, MATTHEW — D — STARS

PERSONAL: Born December 6, 1986, in Virginia, Minn. ... 6-0/195. ... Shoots right.
TRANSACTIONS/CAREER NOTES: Selected by Dallas Stars in 1st round (1st Stars pick, 28th overall) of entry draft (July 30, 2005).

Season Team	League	GP	G	A	Pts.	PIM	+/-	PP	SH	GP	G	A	Pts.	PIM
		REGULAR SEASON								PLAYOFFS				
04-05—Virginia	USHS (West)	29	27	38	65	34	...	...	...	—	—	—	—	—

NOKELAINEN, PETTERI — C/RW — ISLANDERS

PERSONAL: Born January 16, 1986, in Imatra, Finland. ... 6-1/190. ... Shoots right.
TRANSACTIONS/CAREER NOTES: Selected by New York Islanders in first round (first Islanders pick, 16th overall) of NHL entry draft (June 26, 2004).

Season Team	League	GP	G	A	Pts.	PIM	+/-	PP	SH		GP	G	A	Pts.	PIM
		REGULAR SEASON									PLAYOFFS				
02-03—SaiPa	Finland	2	1	0	1	2	...	...	...		—	—	—	—	—
03-04—SaiPa	Finland	40	4	4	8	16	...	...	...		—	—	—	—	—
04-05—SaiPa	Finland	52	15	5	20	34	-12	...	...		—	—	—	—	—

NOLAN, BRANDON C/LW CANUCKS

PERSONAL: Born July 18, 1983, in Sault Ste. Marie, Ont. ... 6-0/177. ... Shoots left. ... Son of Ted Nolan, former coach of Buffalo Sabres (1995-97) and C with Detroit Red Wings (1981-84) and Pittsburgh Penguins (1985-86).

TRANSACTIONS/CAREER NOTES: Selected by New Jersey Devils in third round (sixth Devils pick, 72nd overall) of NHL entry draft (June 23, 2001). ... Returned to draft pool; selected by Vancouver Canucks in fourth round (third Canucks pick, 111th overall) of NHL draft (June 21, 2003).

Season Team	League	GP	G	A	Pts.	PIM	+/-	PP	SH		GP	G	A	Pts.	PIM
		REGULAR SEASON									PLAYOFFS				
00-01—Oshawa	OHL	52	15	23	38	21	...	...	...		—	—	—	—	—
01-02—Oshawa	OHL	57	30	28	58	78	...	...	...		5	2	4	6	4
02-03—Oshawa	OHL	68	36	52	88	57	...	...	...		13	10	7	17	17
03-04—Manitoba	AHL	48	7	10	17	18	-6	3	0		—	—	—	—	—
—Columbia	ECHL	19	5	10	15	38	2	1	0		3	0	1	1	17
04-05—Manitoba	AHL	48	4	8	12	16	8	1	0		0	0	0	0	0

NOLAN, OWEN RW

PERSONAL: Born February 12, 1972, in Belfast, Northern Ireland. ... 6-1/215. ... Shoots right.

TRANSACTIONS/CAREER NOTES: Selected by Quebec Nordiques in first round (first Nordiques pick, first overall) of NHL draft (June 16, 1990). ... Suffered concussion, sore knee and sore back (October 1990). ... Suspended four off-days by NHL for cross-checking incident (December 7, 1992). ... Bruised hand (March 2, 1993); missed three games. ... Bruised shoulder (March 15, 1993); eight games. ... Injured right shoulder (October 19, 1993); missed 11 games. ... Dislocated left shoulder (November 12, 1993); missed remainder of season. ... Bruised shoulder (April 16, 1995); missed two games. ... Nordiques franchise moved to Colorado and renamed Avalanche for 1995-96 season (June 21, 1995). ... Traded by Avalanche to San Jose Sharks for D Sandis Ozolinsh (October 26, 1995). ... Flu (March 5, 1996); missed two games. ... Flu (November 27, 1996); missed one game. ... Bruised shoulder (January 9, 1997); missed two games. ... Sore ankle (March 20, 1997); missed four games. ... Strained groin (April 7, 1997); missed three games. ... Strained shoulder (March 26, 1998); missed six games. ... Missed first two games of 1998-99 season in contract dispute. ... Injured back (January 26, 1999); missed one game. ... Reinjured back (February 4, 1999); missed one game. ... Injured shoulder (March 29, 2000); missed four games. ... Hernia surgery (August 19, 2000); missed first four games of season. ... Strained muscle in abdomen (October 24, 2000); missed 10 games. ... Suspended 11 games by NHL for illegal check (February 2, 2001). ... Injured groin (November 3, 2001); missed one game. ... Injured back (December 26, 2001); missed one game. ... Injured back (January 21, 2002); missed three games. ... Injured leg (March 21, 2002); missed one game. ... Cut head (December 3, 2002); missed one game. ... Injured groin (January 11, 2003); missed two games. ... Injured back (March 4, 2003); missed two games. ... Traded by Sharks to Toronto Maple Leafs for C Alyn McCauley, C Brad Boyes and first-round pick in 2003 draft (later traded to Boston; Bruins picked D Mark Stuart) (March 5, 2003). ... Injured hip (December 9, 2003); missed two games. ... Injured left eye (January 3, 2004) and had surgery; missed 12 games. ... Injured right knee (March 27, 2004); missed remainder of season. ... Knee surgery (July 26, 2005); out indefinitely.

STATISTICAL PLATEAUS: Three-goal games: 1991-92 (2), 1992-93 (2), 1994-95 (3), 1996-97 (1), 1999-00 (1). Total: 9. ... Four-goal games: 1995-96 (1). ... Total hat tricks: 10.

Season Team	League	GP	G	A	Pts.	PIM	+/-	PP	SH		GP	G	A	Pts.	PIM
		REGULAR SEASON									PLAYOFFS				
88-89—Cornwall	OHL	62	34	25	59	213	...	...	...		18	5	11	16	41
89-90—Cornwall	OHL	58	51	59	110	240	...	...	...		6	7	5	12	26
90-91—Quebec	NHL	59	3	10	13	109	-19	0	0		—	—	—	—	—
—Halifax	AHL	6	4	4	8	11	...	...	...		—	—	—	—	—
91-92—Quebec	NHL	75	42	31	73	183	-9	17	0		—	—	—	—	—
92-93—Quebec	NHL	73	36	41	77	185	-1	15	0		5	1	0	1	2
93-94—Quebec	NHL	6	2	2	4	8	2	0	0		—	—	—	—	—
94-95—Quebec	NHL	46	30	19	49	46	21	13	2		6	2	3	5	6
95-96—Colorado	NHL	9	4	4	8	9	-3	4	0		—	—	—	—	—
—San Jose	NHL	72	29	32	61	137	-30	12	1		—	—	—	—	—
96-97—San Jose	NHL	72	31	32	63	155	-19	10	0		—	—	—	—	—
97-98—San Jose	NHL	75	14	27	41	144	-2	3	1		6	2	2	4	26
98-99—San Jose	NHL	78	19	26	45	129	16	6	2		6	1	1	2	6
99-00—San Jose	NHL	78	44	40	84	110	-1	*18	4		10	8	2	10	6
00-01—San Jose	NHL	57	24	25	49	75	0	10	1		6	1	1	2	8
01-02—San Jose	NHL	75	23	43	66	93	7	8	2		12	3	6	9	8
—Can. Olympic team	Int'l	6	0	3	3	2	...	...	...		—	—	—	—	—
02-03—San Jose	NHL	61	22	20	42	91	-5	8	3		—	—	—	—	—
—Toronto	NHL	14	7	5	12	16	2	5	0		7	0	2	2	2
03-04—Toronto	NHL	65	19	29	48	110	4	7	2		—	—	—	—	—
NHL Totals (14 years)		915	349	386	735	1600	-37	136	18		58	18	17	35	64

NORONEN, MIKA G SABRES

PERSONAL: Born June 17, 1979, in Tampere, Finland. ... 6-2/200. ... Catches left. ... Name pronounced NO-rah-nehn.

TRANSACTIONS/CAREER NOTES: Selected by Buffalo Sabres in first round (first Sabres pick, 21st overall) of NHL entry draft (June 21, 1997). ... Injured neck (December 9, 2003); missed one game. ... Injured groin (December 30, 2003); missed six games.

Season Team	League	GP	Min.	W	L	T	GA	SO	GAA	SV%		GP	Min.	W	L	GA	SO	GAA	SV%
		REGULAR SEASON										PLAYOFFS							
95-96—Tappara Tampere	Finland Jr.	16	962	...	...	...	37	2	2.31	...		—	—	—	—	—	—	—	—
96-97—Tappara Tampere	Finland	5	215	...	...	...	17	0	4.74	...		—	—	—	—	—	—	—	—

Season Team	League	GP	Min.	W	L	T	GA	SO	GAA	SV%	GP	Min.	W	L	GA	SO	GAA	SV%
		REGULAR SEASON									PLAYOFFS							
97-98—Tappara Tampere	Finland	47	1703	14	12	3	83	1	2.92	...	4	196	1	2	12	0	3.67	...
98-99—Tappara Tampere	Finland	43	2494	18	20	5	*135	2	3.25	...	—	—	—	—	—	—	—	—
99-00—Rochester	AHL	54	3089	*33	13	4	112	6	*2.18	...	21	1235	13	*8	37	*6	*1.80	...
00-01—Buffalo	NHL	2	108	2	0	0	5	0	2.78	.872	—	—	—	—	—	—	—	—
—Rochester	AHL	47	2753	26	15	5	100	4	2.18	.913	4	250	1	3	11	0	2.64	...
01-02—Rochester	AHL	45	2763	16	17	12	115	3	2.50	.896	1	58	0	1	3	0	3.10	.870
—Buffalo	NHL	10	518	4	3	1	23	0	2.66	.894	—	—	—	—	—	—	—	—
02-03—Buffalo	NHL	16	891	4	9	3	36	1	2.42	.912	—	—	—	—	—	—	—	—
—Rochester	AHL	19	1168	5	9	5	55	2	2.83	.903	—	—	—	—	—	—	—	—
03-04—Buffalo	NHL	35	1796	11	17	2	77	2	2.57	.906	—	—	—	—	—	—	—	—
04-05—HPK Hameenlinna	Finland	27	1614	14	8	4	54	1	2.01	.927	9	482	4	4	21	1	2.61	.918
NHL Totals (4 years)		63	3313	21	29	6	141	3	2.55	.905								

NORSTROM, MATTIAS D KINGS

PERSONAL: Born January 2, 1972, in Stockholm, Sweden. ... 6-2/222. ... Shoots left. ... Name pronounced muh-TEE-uhz NOHR-struhm.

TRANSACTIONS/CAREER NOTES: Selected by New York Rangers in second round (second Rangers pick, 48th overall) of NHL draft (June 20, 1992). ... Flu (April 28, 1995); missed two games. ... Separated shoulder (December 30, 1995); missed six games. ... Traded by Rangers with C Ray Ferraro, C Ian Laperriere, C Nathan Lafayette and fourth-round pick (D Sean Blanchard) in 1997 draft to Los Angeles Kings for RW Shane Churla, LW Jari Kurri and D Marty McSorley (March 14, 1996). ... Bruised left wrist (November 7, 1996); missed one game. ... Suspended one game by NHL for illegal check (January 12, 1998). ... Bruised ribs (April 11, 1999); missed four games. ... Bruised ribs (October 13, 2001); missed three games. ... Bruised chest (October 11, 2003); missed seven games. ... Left team for personal reasons (February 29, 2004); missed one game. ... Offseason left elbow surgery (April 6, 2004).

Season Team	League	GP	G	A	Pts.	PIM	+/-	PP	SH	GP	G	A	Pts.	PIM
		REGULAR SEASON								PLAYOFFS				
91-92—AIK Solna	Sweden	39	4	4	8	28	...	...	...	—	—	—	—	—
92-93—AIK Solna	Sweden	22	0	1	1	16	...	...	...	—	—	—	—	—
93-94—New York Rangers	NHL	9	0	2	2	6	0	0	0	—	—	—	—	—
—Binghamton	AHL	55	1	9	10	70	-7	0	0	—	—	—	—	—
94-95—Binghamton	AHL	63	9	10	19	91	-1	0	1	—	—	—	—	—
—New York Rangers	NHL	9	0	3	3	2	2	0	0	3	0	0	0	0
95-96—New York Rangers	NHL	25	2	1	3	22	5	0	0	—	—	—	—	—
—Los Angeles	NHL	11	0	1	1	18	-8	0	0	—	—	—	—	—
96-97—Los Angeles	NHL	80	1	21	22	84	-4	0	0	—	—	—	—	—
97-98—Los Angeles	NHL	73	1	12	13	90	14	0	0	4	0	0	0	2
—Swedish Oly. team	Int'l	4	0	1	1	2	3	0	0	—	—	—	—	—
98-99—Los Angeles	NHL	78	2	5	7	36	-10	0	1	—	—	—	—	—
99-00—Los Angeles	NHL	82	1	13	14	66	22	0	0	4	0	0	0	6
00-01—Los Angeles	NHL	82	0	18	18	60	10	0	0	13	0	2	2	18
01-02—Los Angeles	NHL	79	2	9	11	38	-2	0	0	7	0	0	0	4
—Swedish Oly. team	Int'l	4	0	0	0	0	...	...	...	—	—	—	—	—
02-03—Los Angeles	NHL	82	0	6	6	49	0	0	0	—	—	—	—	—
03-04—Los Angeles	NHL	74	1	13	14	44	-3	0	0	—	—	—	—	—
04-05—AIK Solna	Sweden Dv. 2	8	1	0	1	4	...	...	...	—	—	—	—	—
NHL Totals (11 years)		684	10	104	114	515	26	0	1	31	0	2	2	30

NORTON, BRAD D/LW

PERSONAL: Born February 13, 1975, in Cambridge, Mass. ... 6-4/242. ... Shoots left. ... Brother of Jeff Norton, D with eight NHL teams (1987-2002).

TRANSACTIONS/CAREER NOTES: Selected by Edmonton Oilers in ninth round (ninth Oilers pick, 215th overall) of NHL entry draft (June 26, 1993). ... Suspended three games by NHL for unsportsmanlike conduct (October 4, 2000). ... Strained hip flexor (October 11, 2000); missed 10 games. ... Signed as free agent by Florida Panthers (July 27, 2001). ... Suffered illness (February 11, 2002); missed one game. ... Signed as free agent by Los Angeles Kings (October 8, 2002). ... Suffered concussion (February 9, 2003); missed five games. ... Suffered cervical injury (March 8, 2003); missed 14 games. ... Injured right arm (October 1, 2003); missed 37 games. ... Claimed by Washington Capitals on waivers from Kings (March 4, 2004). ... Injured hand (March 24, 2004); out indefinitely.

Season Team	League	GP	G	A	Pts.	PIM	+/-	PP	SH	GP	G	A	Pts.	PIM
		REGULAR SEASON								PLAYOFFS				
94-95—Massachusetts	Hockey East	30	0	6	6	89	-7	0	0	—	—	—	—	—
95-96—Massachusetts	Hockey East	34	4	12	16	99	...	...	...	—	—	—	—	—
96-97—Massachusetts	Hockey East	35	2	16	18	88	1	0	1	—	—	—	—	—
97-98—Massachusetts	Hockey East	20	2	13	15	28	...	...	...	—	—	—	—	—
—Detroit	IHL	33	1	4	5	56	1	0	0	22	0	2	2	87
98-99—Hamilton	AHL	58	1	8	9	134	8	0	0	11	0	1	1	6
99-00—Hamilton	AHL	40	5	12	17	104	...	...	...	10	1	4	5	26
00-01—Hamilton	AHL	46	3	15	18	114	...	...	...	—	—	—	—	—
01-02—Hershey	AHL	40	0	10	10	62	-8	0	0	2	0	0	0	6
—Florida	NHL	22	0	2	2	45	-2	0	0	—	—	—	—	—
02-03—Los Angeles	NHL	53	3	3	6	97	1	0	0	—	—	—	—	—
03-04—Los Angeles	NHL	20	0	1	1	77	-1	0	0	—	—	—	—	—
—Washington	NHL	16	0	1	1	17	-4	0	0	—	—	—	—	—
NHL Totals (3 years)		111	3	7	10	236	-6	0	0					

NOVAK, FILIP — D — PANTHERS

PERSONAL: Born May 7, 1982, in Ceske Budejovice, Czechoslovakia. ... 6-1/174. ... Shoots left.
TRANSACTIONS/CAREER NOTES: Selected by New York Rangers in second round (first Rangers pick, 64th overall) of NHL entry draft (June 24, 2000). ... Traded by Rangers with D Igor Ulanov, first- (later traded to Calgary; Flames picked LW Eric Nystrom) and second-round picks (C/RW Rob Globke) in 2002 draft and fourth-round pick (later traded to Atlanta; Thrashers picked RW Guillaume Desbiens) in 2003 draft to Florida Panthers for RW Pavel Bure and second-round pick (C Lee Falardeau) in 2002 draft (March 18, 2002). ... Injured ankle (October 8, 2003); missed entire season.

		REGULAR SEASON								PLAYOFFS				
Season Team	League	GP	G	A	Pts.	PIM	+/-	PP	SH	GP	G	A	Pts.	PIM
98-99—Budejovice	Czech. Jrs.	68	8	10	18	34	...	...	...	—	—	—	—	—
99-00—Regina	WHL	47	7	32	39	70	...	...	...	7	1	4	5	5
00-01—Regina	WHL	64	17	50	67	75	...	...	...	6	1	4	5	6
01-02—Regina	WHL	60	12	46	58	125	...	...	...	6	2	2	4	19
02-03—San Antonio	AHL	57	10	17	27	79	5	4	0	1	0	0	0	0
03-04—San Antonio	AHL	Did not play — injured												
04-05—San Antonio	AHL	71	1	12	13	84	-8	1	0	—	—	—	—	—

NOVOSELTSEV, IVAN — RW/LW

PERSONAL: Born January 23, 1979, in Golitsino, U.S.S.R. ... 6-1/215. ... Shoots left. ... Name pronounced noh-vuh-SEHLT-sehf.
TRANSACTIONS/CAREER NOTES: Selected by Florida Panthers in fourth round (fifth Panthers pick, 95th overall) of NHL draft (June 21, 1997). ... Back spasms (February 9, 2002); missed two games. ... Injured back (March 30, 2002); missed three games. ... Injured face (October 26, 2002); missed one game. ... Injured thumb (October 8, 2003); missed one game. ... Traded by Panthers to Phoenix Coyotes for future considerations (December 30, 2003). ... Had concussion (January 21, 2004); missed 19 games.

		REGULAR SEASON								PLAYOFFS				
Season Team	League	GP	G	A	Pts.	PIM	+/-	PP	SH	GP	G	A	Pts.	PIM
95-96—Krylja Sov. Moscow	CIS	1	0	0	0	0	...	...	...	—	—	—	—	—
96-97—Kryla Sov. Moscow	Russian	30	0	3	3	18	...	...	...	2	0	0	0	4
—Krylja Sov. Moscow	Rus. Div.	19	5	3	8	39	...	...	...	—	—	—	—	—
97-98—Sarnia	OHL	53	26	22	48	41	...	...	...	5	1	1	2	8
98-99—Sarnia	OHL	68	57	39	96	45	26	...	...	5	2	4	6	6
99-00—Louisville	AHL	47	14	21	35	22	...	...	...	4	1	0	1	6
—Florida	NHL	14	2	1	3	8	-3	2	0	—	—	—	—	—
00-01—Louisville	AHL	34	2	10	12	8	...	...	...	—	—	—	—	—
—Florida	NHL	38	3	6	9	16	-5	0	0	—	—	—	—	—
01-02—Florida	NHL	70	13	16	29	44	-10	1	1	—	—	—	—	—
02-03—Florida	NHL	78	10	17	27	30	-16	1	0	—	—	—	—	—
03-04—Florida	NHL	17	1	4	5	8	-6	0	0	—	—	—	—	—
—Springfield	AHL	2	1	0	1	2	-1	0	0	—	—	—	—	—
—Phoenix	NHL	17	2	0	2	6	-7	0	0	—	—	—	—	—
04-05—Lada Togliatti	Russian	13	0	2	2	8	1	...	...	—	—	—	—	—
—Spartak Moscow	Russian	26	5	1	6	47	-12	...	...	—	—	—	—	—
NHL Totals (5 years)		234	31	44	75	112	-47	4	1					

NOVOTNY, JIRI — C — SABRES

PERSONAL: Born August 12, 1983, in Pelhrimov, Czechoslovakia. ... 6-2/187. ... Shoots right.
TRANSACTIONS/CAREER NOTES: Selected by Buffalo Sabres in first round (first Sabres pick, 22nd overall) of NHL entry draft (June 23, 2001).

		REGULAR SEASON								PLAYOFFS				
Season Team	League	GP	G	A	Pts.	PIM	+/-	PP	SH	GP	G	A	Pts.	PIM
99-00—Budejovice	Czech. Jrs.	39	11	12	23	14	...	...	...	—	—	—	—	—
00-01—Budejovice	Czech. Jrs.	33	10	10	20	...	...	...	...	—	—	—	—	—
—HC Ceske Budejovice	Czech Rep.	19	0	4	4	2	...	...	...	—	—	—	—	—
01-02—HC Ceske Budejovice	Czech Rep.	41	8	6	14	6	...	...	...	—	—	—	—	—
02-03—Rochester	AHL	43	2	9	11	14	-12	0	0	3	0	1	1	10
03-04—Rochester	AHL	48	1	14	15	16	-14	0	0	13	0	1	1	10
04-05—Rochester	AHL	61	5	20	25	36	8	1	0	9	2	2	4	4

NOWAK, BRETT — C/LW — BRUINS

PERSONAL: Born May 20, 1981, in New Haven, Conn. ... 6-2/192. ... Shoots left.
TRANSACTIONS/CAREER NOTES: Selected by Boston Bruins in fourth round (seventh Bruins pick, 103rd overall) of NHL entry draft (June 24, 2000).

		REGULAR SEASON								PLAYOFFS				
Season Team	League	GP	G	A	Pts.	PIM	+/-	PP	SH	GP	G	A	Pts.	PIM
98-99—Hotchkiss	Conn. H.S.	21	24	42	66	42	...	...	...	—	—	—	—	—
99-00—Harvard	ECAC	24	5	10	15	20	...	...	...	—	—	—	—	—
00-01—Harvard	ECAC	33	7	14	21	8	...	...	...	—	—	—	—	—
01-02—Harvard	ECAC	33	14	17	31	50	...	...	...	—	—	—	—	—
02-03—Harvard	ECAC	33	12	29	41	57	...	...	...	—	—	—	—	—
03-04—Providence	AHL	55	3	10	13	37	-7	0	0	1	1	0	1	2
04-05—Bridgeport	AHL	13	0	0	0	5	-5	0	0	—	—	—	—	—
—Dayton	ECHL	24	8	11	19	39	4	2	1	—	—	—	—	—

NUMMINEN, TEPPO D SABRES

PERSONAL: Born July 3, 1968, in Tampere, Finland. ... 6-2/199. ... Shoots right. ... Name pronounced TEH-poh NOO-mih-nehn.

TRANSACTIONS/CAREER NOTES: Selected by Winnipeg Jets in 2nd round (2nd Jets pick, 29th overall) of NHL draft (June 21, 1986). ... Separated shoulder (March 5, 1989). ... Fractured thumb (April 14, 1990). ... Fractured foot (January 28, 1993); missed 17 games. ... Dislocated thumb (February 9, 1994); missed remainder of season. ... Flu (January 23, 1995); missed one game. ... Stress fracture in right knee (February 22, 1995); missed five games. ... Separated shoulder (November 28, 1995); missed eight games. ... Jets franchise moved to Phoenix and renamed Coyotes for 1996-97 season; NHL approved move on January 18, 1996. ... Strained hip flexor (March 1, 2000); missed two games. ... Sprained ankle (December 30, 2000); missed one game. ... Bruised foot (November 14, 2000); missed two games. ... Bruised foot (November 29, 2000); missed three games. ... Brused foot (March 6, 2001); missed one game. ... Strained hip flexor (March 15, 2001); missed two games. ... Bruised foot (April 6, 2001); missed one game. ... Fractured foot (November 4, 2001); missed six games. ... Bruised ankle (November 11, 2002); missed four games. ... Traded by Coyotes to Dallas Stars for C Mike Sillinger (July 22, 2003). ... Injured groin (November 8, 2003); missed two games. ... Fractured right foot (November 20, 2003); missed 12 games. ... Aggravated foot injury (December 20, 2003); missed one game. ... Heart ailment (March 20, 2004); missed five games. ... Signed as free agent by Buffalo Sabres (Aug. 4, 2005).

		REGULAR SEASON								PLAYOFFS				
Season Team	**League**	**GP**	**G**	**A**	**Pts.**	**PIM**	**+/-**	**PP**	**SH**	**GP**	**G**	**A**	**Pts.**	**PIM**
84-85—Tappara	Finland	30	14	17	31	10	...	...	...	—	—	—	—	—
85-86—Tappara	Finland	39	2	4	6	6	...	...	...	8	0	0	0	0
86-87—Tappara	Finland	44	9	9	18	16	...	...	...	9	4	1	5	4
87-88—Tappara	Finland	44	10	10	20	29	...	...	...	10	6	6	12	6
—Fin. Olympic team	Int'l	6	1	4	5	0	2	...	...	—	—	—	—	—
88-89—Winnipeg	NHL	69	1	14	15	36	-11	0	1	—	—	—	—	—
89-90—Winnipeg	NHL	79	11	32	43	20	-4	1	0	7	1	2	3	10
90-91—Winnipeg	NHL	80	8	25	33	28	-15	3	0	—	—	—	—	—
91-92—Winnipeg	NHL	80	5	34	39	32	15	4	0	7	0	0	0	0
92-93—Winnipeg	NHL	66	7	30	37	33	4	3	1	6	1	1	2	2
93-94—Winnipeg	NHL	57	5	18	23	28	-23	4	0	—	—	—	—	—
94-95—TuTu Turku	Finland	12	3	8	11	4	4	...	...	—	—	—	—	—
—Winnipeg	NHL	42	5	16	21	16	12	2	0	—	—	—	—	—
95-96—Winnipeg	NHL	74	11	43	54	22	-4	6	0	6	0	0	0	2
96-97—Phoenix	NHL	82	2	25	27	28	-3	0	0	7	3	3	6	0
97-98—Phoenix	NHL	82	11	40	51	30	25	6	0	1	0	0	0	0
—Fin. Olympic team	Int'l	6	1	1	2	2	-1	1	0	—	—	—	—	—
98-99—Phoenix	NHL	82	10	30	40	30	3	1	0	7	2	1	3	4
99-00—Phoenix	NHL	79	8	34	42	16	21	2	0	5	1	1	2	0
00-01—Phoenix	NHL	72	5	26	31	36	9	1	0	—	—	—	—	—
01-02—Phoenix	NHL	76	13	35	48	20	13	4	0	4	0	0	0	2
—Fin. Olympic team	Int'l	4	0	1	1	0	...	...	...	—	—	—	—	—
02-03—Phoenix	NHL	78	6	24	30	30	0	2	0	—	—	—	—	—
03-04—Dallas	NHL	62	3	14	17	18	-5	0	0	4	0	1	1	0
NHL Totals (16 years)		1160	111	440	551	423	37	39	2	54	8	9	17	20

NURMINEN, PASI G THRASHERS

PERSONAL: Born December 17, 1975, in Lahti, Finland. ... 5-10/215. ... Catches left. ... Name pronounced PAS-ee NUR-muh-nehn.

TRANSACTIONS/CAREER NOTES: Selected by Atlanta Thrashers in sixth round (sixth Thrashers pick, 189th overall) of NHL draft (June 24, 2001). ... Injured knee (October 1, 2001); missed first 10 games of season. ... Injured groin (February 17, 2003); missed seven games.

		REGULAR SEASON									PLAYOFFS							
Season Team	**League**	**GP**	**Min.**	**W**	**L**	**T**	**GA**	**SO**	**GAA**	**SV%**	**GP**	**Min.**	**W**	**L**	**GA**	**SO**	**GAA**	**SV%**
93-94—Reipas Lahti	Finland Jr.	14	847	...	...	...	58	0	4.11	...	—	—	—	—	—	—	—	—
—Reipas Lahti	Finland	1	30	...	...	...	2	0	4.00	...	—	—	—	—	—	—	—	—
94-95—Reipas Lahti	Finland Jr.	9	542	...	...	...	22	...	2.44	...	—	—	—	—	—	—	—	—
—Reipas Lahti	Finland Div. 2	9	423	...	...	...	44	0	6.24	...	—	—	—	—	—	—	—	—
95-96—Kettera Imatra	Finland Div. 2	38	2204	...	...	...	146	0	3.97	...	—	—	—	—	—	—	—	—
96-97—Pelicans Lahti	Finland Div. 2	30	1726	...	...	...	69	0	2.40	...	3	204	...	...	8	...	2.35	...
97-98—Pelicans Lahti	Finland Div. 2	35	2044	...	...	...	59	...	1.73	...	3	180	...	...	4	...	1.33	...
98-99—HPK Hameenlinna	Finland	48	2810	24	17	6	127	2	2.71	...	7	425	3	4	24	1	3.39	...
99-00—Jokerit Helsinki	Finland	48	2770	24	15	8	104	6	2.25	...	11	719	7	4	22	2	1.84	...
00-01—Jokerit Helsinki	Finland	52	2971	30	13	7	107	5	2.16	...	5	308	2	3	11	1	2.14	...
01-02—Chicago	AHL	20	1165	9	9	1	57	2	2.94	.893	*21	1267	*15	5	41	2	1.94	.935
—Atlanta	NHL	9	465	2	5	0	28	0	3.61	.898	—	—	—	—	—	—	—	—
—Fin. Olympic team	Int'l	1	60	1	0	0	1	0	1.00	.952	—	—	—	—	—	—	—	—
02-03—Atlanta	NHL	52	2856	21	19	5	137	2	2.88	.906	—	—	—	—	—	—	—	—
03-04—Atlanta	NHL	64	3738	25	30	7	173	3	2.78	.903	—	—	—	—	—	—	—	—
04-05—Pelicans-Lahti	Finland	17	965	2	7	6	48	0	2.98	.921	—	—	—	—	—	—	—	—
—Malmo	Sweden	30	1766	...	...	...	86	3	2.94	.900	10	578	...	...	20	0	2.08	.915
NHL Totals (3 years)		125	7059	48	54	12	338	5	2.87	.904								

NYCHOLAT, LAWRENCE D CAPITALS

PERSONAL: Born May 7, 1979, in Calgary. ... 6-0/194. ... Shoots left. ... Name pronounced NIH-coh-lat.

TRANSACTIONS/CAREER NOTES: Signed as free agent by Minnesota Wild (August 31, 2000). ... Traded by Wild to New York Rangers for G Johan Holmqvist (March 11, 2003). ... Signed as free agent by Washington Capitals (Aug. 9, 2005).

		REGULAR SEASON								PLAYOFFS				
Season Team	**League**	**GP**	**G**	**A**	**Pts.**	**PIM**	**+/-**	**PP**	**SH**	**GP**	**G**	**A**	**Pts.**	**PIM**
00-01—Jackson	ECHL	5	1	2	3	5	...	...	...	—	—	—	—	—
—Cleveland	IHL	42	3	7	10	69	...	...	...	4	0	0	0	2

Season Team	League	GP	G	A	Pts.	PIM	+/-	PP	SH	GP	G	A	Pts.	PIM
		REGULAR SEASON								PLAYOFFS				
01-02—Houston	AHL	72	3	11	14	92	12	1	0	14	1	0	1	23
02-03—Houston	AHL	66	11	28	39	155	21	7	1	—	—	—	—	—
—Hartford	AHL	15	2	9	11	6	6	0	0	2	2	0	2	0
03-04—Hartford	AHL	72	6	26	32	128	19	3	0	16	0	5	5	28
—New York Rangers	NHL	9	0	0	0	6	-2	0	0	—	—	—	—	—
04-05—Hartford	AHL	79	5	38	43	132	12	2	0	6	0	3	3	11
NHL Totals (1 year)		9	0	0	0	6	-2	0	0					

NYLANDER, MICHAEL — C — RANGERS

PERSONAL: Born October 3, 1972, in Stockholm, Sweden. ... 6-1/189. ... Shoots left. ... Name pronounced NEE-lan-duhr.

TRANSACTIONS/CAREER NOTES: Selected by Hartford Whalers in third round (fourth Whalers pick, 59th overall) of NHL draft (June 22, 1991). ... Fractured jaw (January 23, 1993); missed 15 games. ... Traded by Whalers with D Zarley Zalapski and D James Patrick to Calgary Flames for D Gary Suter, LW Paul Ranheim and C Ted Drury (March 10, 1994). ... Fractured left wrist and forearm (January 24, 1995); missed 42 games. ... Injured wrist (January 16, 1996); missed three games. ... Injured left knee (March 26, 1998); missed final 11 games of season and first 23 games of 1998-99 season. ... Traded by Flames to Tampa Bay Lightning for RW Andrei Nazarov (January 19, 1999). ... Had concussion (April 8, 1999); missed final five games of season. ... Traded by Lightning to Chicago Blackhawks for D Bryan Muir and LW Reid Simpson (November 12, 1999). ... Traded by Blackhawks with third-round pick (RW Stephen Werner) in 2003 draft and future considerations to Washington Capitals for C Andrei Nikolishin and LW Chris Simon (November 1, 2002). ... Fractured right leg (October 3, 2003); missed first 63 games of the season. ... Traded by Capitals to Boston Bruins for second-round pick in 2006 draft and future considerations (March 4, 2004). ... Signed as free agent by New York Rangers (August 10, 2004).

STATISTICAL PLATEAUS: Three-goal games: 1992-93 (1). ... Four-goal games: 1999-00 (1). ... Total hat tricks: 2.

Season Team	League	GP	G	A	Pts.	PIM	+/-	PP	SH	GP	G	A	Pts.	PIM
		REGULAR SEASON								PLAYOFFS				
89-90—Huddinge	Sweden	31	7	15	22	4	...	...	...	—	—	—	—	—
90-91—Huddinge	Sweden	33	14	20	34	10	...	...	...	—	—	—	—	—
91-92—AIK Solna	Sweden	40	11	17	28	30	...	...	...	—	—	—	—	—
—Swedish Oly. team	Int'l	6	0	1	1	0	...	...	...	—	—	—	—	—
92-93—Hartford	NHL	59	11	22	33	36	-7	3	0	—	—	—	—	—
—Springfield	AHL	59	11	22	33	36	...	...	...	—	—	—	—	—
93-94—Hartford	NHL	58	11	33	44	24	-2	4	0	—	—	—	—	—
—Springfield	AHL	4	0	9	9	0	0	0	0	—	—	—	—	—
—Calgary	NHL	15	2	9	11	6	10	0	0	3	0	0	0	0
94-95—JyP HT	Finland	16	11	19	30	63	18	...	...	—	—	—	—	—
—Calgary	NHL	6	0	1	1	2	1	0	0	6	0	6	6	2
95-96—Calgary	NHL	73	17	38	55	20	0	4	0	4	0	0	0	0
96-97—Lugano	Switzerland	36	12	43	55	...	...	...	...	—	—	—	—	—
97-98—Calgary	NHL	65	13	23	36	24	10	0	0	—	—	—	—	—
—Swedish Oly. team	Int'l	4	0	0	0	6	1	0	0	—	—	—	—	—
98-99—Calgary	NHL	9	2	3	5	2	1	1	0	—	—	—	—	—
—Tampa Bay	NHL	24	2	7	9	6	-10	0	0	—	—	—	—	—
99-00—Tampa Bay	NHL	11	1	2	3	4	-3	1	0	—	—	—	—	—
—Chicago	NHL	66	23	28	51	26	9	4	0	—	—	—	—	—
00-01—Chicago	NHL	82	25	39	64	32	7	4	0	—	—	—	—	—
01-02—Chicago	NHL	82	15	46	61	50	28	6	0	5	0	3	3	2
—Swedish Oly. team	Int'l	4	1	2	3	0	...	...	...	—	—	—	—	—
02-03—Chicago	NHL	9	0	4	4	4	0	0	0	—	—	—	—	—
—Washington	NHL	71	17	39	56	36	3	7	0	6	3	2	5	8
03-04—Washington	NHL	3	0	2	2	8	1	0	0	—	—	—	—	—
—Boston	NHL	15	1	11	12	14	3	0	0	6	3	3	6	0
04-05—Karpat Oulu	Finland	23	5	15	20	22	9	...	...	—	—	—	—	—
—SKA St. Petersburg	Russian	8	2	5	7	0	-9	...	...	—	—	—	—	—
—Ak Bars Kazan	Russian	5	0	1	1	2	-1	...	...	—	—	—	—	—
NHL Totals (11 years)		648	140	307	447	294	51	34	0	30	6	14	20	12

NYSTROM, ERIC — LW — FLAMES

PERSONAL: Born February 14, 1983, in Syosset, N.Y. ... 6-1/195. ... Shoots left. ... Son of Bobby Nystrom, RW with New York Islanders (1972-86).

TRANSACTIONS/CAREER NOTES: Selected by Calgary Flames in first round (first Flames pick, 10th overall) of NHL entry draft (June 22, 2002).

Season Team	League	GP	G	A	Pts.	PIM	+/-	PP	SH	GP	G	A	Pts.	PIM
		REGULAR SEASON								PLAYOFFS				
00-01—U.S. National	USHL	66	15	17	32	102	...	...	...	—	—	—	—	—
01-02—Univ. of Michigan	CCHA	32	15	9	24	32	...	...	...	—	—	—	—	—
02-03—Univ. of Michigan	CCHA	39	15	11	26	24	...	...	...	—	—	—	—	—
03-04—Univ. of Michigan	CCHA	43	10	12	22	50	8	6	0	—	—	—	—	—
04-05—Univ. of Michigan	CCHA	38	13	19	32	33	...	...	...	—	—	—	—	—

O'BRIEN, SHANE — D — MIGHTY DUCKS

PERSONAL: Born August 9, 1983, in Port Hope, Ont. ... 6-2/224. ... Shoots left.

TRANSACTIONS/CAREER NOTES: Selected by Anaheim Mighty Ducks in eighth round (eighth Mighty Ducks pick, 250th overall) of NHL entry draft (June 21, 2003).

		REGULAR SEASON								PLAYOFFS				
Season Team	League	GP	G	A	Pts.	PIM	+/-	PP	SH	GP	G	A	Pts.	PIM
00-01—Kingston	OHL	61	2	12	14	89	...	...	...	4	0	1	1	6
01-02—Kingston	OHL	67	10	23	33	130	...	...	...	1	0	0	0	2
02-03—Toronto St. Michael's	OHL	61	16	26	42	208	...	...	...	19	4	10	14	79
03-04—Cincinnati	AHL	60	2	8	10	163	2	2	0	—	—	—	—	—
04-05—Cincinnati	AHL	77	5	20	25	319	...	...	...	12	1	3	4	57

O'CONNOR, SEAN — RW — PANTHERS

PERSONAL: Born October 19, 1981, in Victoria, B.C. ... 6-2/211. ... Shoots right.
TRANSACTIONS/CAREER NOTES: Selected by Florida Panthers in third round (third Panthers pick, 82nd overall) of NHL entry draft (June 24, 2000).

		REGULAR SEASON								PLAYOFFS				
Season Team	League	GP	G	A	Pts.	PIM	+/-	PP	SH	GP	G	A	Pts.	PIM
97-98—Victoria	BCJHL	50	9	17	26	145	...	...	...	—	—	—	—	—
98-99—Victoria	BCJHL	53	17	18	35	197	...	...	...	—	—	—	—	—
99-00—Moose Jaw	WHL	51	5	8	13	166	...	...	...	2	0	0	0	2
00-01—Moose Jaw	WHL	71	34	15	49	192	...	...	...	4	0	1	1	15
01-02—Moose Jaw	WHL	62	15	19	34	135	...	...	...	12	0	3	3	4
02-03—San Antonio	AHL	8	0	0	0	4	-2	0	0	1	0	0	0	0
—Jackson	ECHL	49	12	11	23	149	5	3	0	1	0	0	0	0
03-04—San Antonio	AHL	28	1	0	1	88	-17	1	0	—	—	—	—	—
—Augusta	ECHL	19	3	4	7	79	-1	0	1	—	—	—	—	—
04-05—San Diego	ECHL	46	20	10	30	142	...	...	...	—	—	—	—	—
—Cincinnati	AHL	15	0	1	1	28	...	...	...	—	—	—	—	—

O'DONNELL, SEAN — D — COYOTES

PERSONAL: Born October 13, 1971, in Ottawa. ... 6-3/228. ... Shoots left.
TRANSACTIONS/CAREER NOTES: Selected by Buffalo Sabres in sixth round (sixth Sabres pick, 123rd overall) of NHL draft (June 22, 1991). ... Traded by Sabres to Los Angeles Kings for D Doug Houda (July 26, 1994). ... Bruised sternum (February 4, 1995); missed two games. ... Sprained left wrist (January 27, 1996); missed eight games. ... Sprained wrist (December 26, 1996); missed nine games. ... Suspended one game for an altercation while on the bench (January 30, 1997). ... Strained back (March 1, 1997); missed two games. ... Suspended two games for cross-checking and spearing incidents (April 14, 1999). ... Selected by Minnesota Wild in expansion draft (June 23, 2000). ... Flu (February 11, 2001); missed one game. ... Traded by Wild to New Jersey Devils for D Willie Mitchell (March 4, 2001). ... Signed as free agent by Boston Bruins (July 2, 2001). ... Back spasms (March 21, 2002); missed two games. ... Injured knee (February 6, 2003); missed 11 games. ... Signed as free agent by Phoenix Coyotes (July 6, 2004).

		REGULAR SEASON								PLAYOFFS				
Season Team	League	GP	G	A	Pts.	PIM	+/-	PP	SH	GP	G	A	Pts.	PIM
88-89—Sudbury	OHL	56	1	9	10	49	...	...	...	—	—	—	—	—
89-90—Sudbury	OHL	64	7	19	26	84	...	...	...	—	—	—	—	—
90-91—Sudbury	OHL	66	8	23	31	114	...	...	...	5	1	4	5	10
91-92—Rochester	AHL	73	4	9	13	193	...	...	...	16	1	2	3	21
92-93—Rochester	AHL	74	3	18	21	203	...	...	...	17	1	6	7	38
93-94—Rochester	AHL	64	2	10	12	242	...	...	...	4	0	1	1	21
94-95—Phoenix	IHL	61	2	18	20	132	13	0	0	9	0	1	1	21
—Los Angeles	NHL	15	0	2	2	49	-2	0	0	—	—	—	—	—
95-96—Los Angeles	NHL	71	2	5	7	127	3	0	0	—	—	—	—	—
96-97—Los Angeles	NHL	55	5	12	17	144	-13	2	0	—	—	—	—	—
97-98—Los Angeles	NHL	80	2	15	17	179	7	0	0	4	1	0	1	36
98-99—Los Angeles	NHL	80	1	13	14	186	1	0	0	—	—	—	—	—
99-00—Los Angeles	NHL	80	2	12	14	114	4	0	0	4	1	0	1	4
00-01—Minnesota	NHL	63	4	12	16	128	-2	1	0	—	—	—	—	—
—New Jersey	NHL	17	0	1	1	33	2	0	0	23	1	2	3	41
01-02—Boston	NHL	80	3	22	25	89	27	1	0	6	0	2	2	4
02-03—Boston	NHL	70	1	15	16	76	8	0	0	—	—	—	—	—
03-04—Boston	NHL	82	1	10	11	110	10	0	0	7	0	0	0	0
NHL Totals (10 years)		693	21	119	140	1235	45	4	0	44	3	4	7	85

O'MARRA, RYAN — C — ISLANDERS

PERSONAL: Born June 9, 1987, in Tokyo, Japan. ... 6-1/203. ... Shoots right.
TRANSACTIONS/CAREER NOTES: Selected by New York Islanders in 1st round (1st Islanders pick, 15th overall) of entry draft (July 30, 2005).

		REGULAR SEASON								PLAYOFFS				
Season Team	League	GP	G	A	Pts.	PIM	+/-	PP	SH	GP	G	A	Pts.	PIM
03-04—Mississauga	OHL	63	16	16	32	33	...	...	...	—	—	—	—	—
04-05—Erie	OHL	64	25	38	63	60	-4	8	1	6	4	1	5	0

O'NEILL, JEFF — RW/LW — MAPLE LEAFS

PERSONAL: Born February 23, 1976, in Richmond Hill, Ont. ... 6-1/195. ... Shoots right.
TRANSACTIONS/CAREER NOTES: Selected by Hartford Whalers in 1st round (1st Whalers pick, fifth overall) of NHL draft (June 28, 1994). ... Bruised foot (December 30, 1995); missed four games. ... Reinjured foot (January 10, 1996); missed four games. ... Injured shoulder (February 17, 1996); missed four games. ... Injured groin (January 2, 1997); missed one game. ... Sprained wrist (April 2, 1997); missed four games. ... Whalers franchise moved to North Carolina and renamed Carolina Hurricanes for 1997-98 season; NHL approved move on June

25, 1997. ... Suffered concussion (December 20, 1997); missed one game. ... Fractured kneecap (April 13, 1998); missed three games. ... Strained neck (February 3, 1999); missed seven games. ... Back spasms (November 24, 1999); missed two games. ... Injured back (December 31, 2001); missed four games. ... Suspended one playoff game by NHL for checking from behind (May 4, 2002). ... Injured right shoulder (March 6, 2004) and had surgery (March 12, 2004); missed remainder of season. ... Traded by Hurricanes to Toronto Maple Leafs for a conditional pick in the 2006 entry draft (July 30, 2005).

STATISTICAL PLATEAUS: Three-goal games: 1996-97 (1), 2003-04 (1). Total: 2.

		REGULAR SEASON								PLAYOFFS				
Season Team	**League**	**GP**	**G**	**A**	**Pts.**	**PIM**	**+/-**	**PP**	**SH**	**GP**	**G**	**A**	**Pts.**	**PIM**
91-92—Thornhill	Tier II Jr. A	43	27	53	80	48	...	...	...	—	—	—	—	—
92-93—Guelph	OHL	65	32	47	79	88	...	...	...	5	2	2	4	6
93-94—Guelph	OHL	66	45	81	126	95	...	8	...	9	2	11	13	31
94-95—Guelph	OHL	57	43	81	124	56	...	6	1	14	8	18	26	34
95-96—Hartford	NHL	65	8	19	27	40	-3	1	0	—	—	—	—	—
96-97—Hartford	NHL	72	14	16	30	40	-24	2	1	—	—	—	—	—
—Springfield	AHL	1	0	0	0	0	0	0	0	—	—	—	—	—
97-98—Carolina	NHL	74	19	20	39	67	-8	7	1	—	—	—	—	—
98-99—Carolina	NHL	75	16	15	31	66	3	4	0	6	0	1	1	0
99-00—Carolina	NHL	80	25	38	63	72	-9	4	0	—	—	—	—	—
00-01—Carolina	NHL	82	41	26	67	106	-18	17	0	6	1	2	3	10
01-02—Carolina	NHL	76	31	33	64	63	-5	11	0	22	8	5	13	27
02-03—Carolina	NHL	82	30	31	61	38	-21	11	0	—	—	—	—	—
03-04—Carolina	NHL	67	14	20	34	60	-12	7	0	—	—	—	—	—
NHL Totals (9 years)		673	198	218	416	552	-97	64	2	34	9	8	17	37

ODELEIN, LYLE D

PERSONAL: Born July 21, 1968, in Quill Lake, Sask. ... 6-0/206. ... Shoots right. ... Brother of Selmar Odelein, defenseman with Edmonton Oilers (1985-86 through 1988-89). ... Name pronounced OH-duh-lighn.

TRANSACTIONS/CAREER NOTES: Selected by Montreal Canadiens in seventh round (eighth Canadiens pick, 141st overall) of NHL raft (June 21, 1986). ... Bruised right ankle (January 22, 1991); missed five games. ... Twisted right ankle (February 9, 1991). ... Suspended one game by NHL for game misconduct penalties (March 1, 1993). ... Bruised shoulder (January 24, 1994); missed three games. ... Suspended two games without pay and fined $1,000 by NHL for shooting puck into the opposing team's bench (April 3, 1996). ... Traded by Canadiens to New Jersey Devils for RW Stephane Richer (August 22, 1996). ... Bruised knee (January 21, 1997); missed three games. ... Bruised shoulder (November 12, 1997); missed one game. ... Flu (January 11, 1999); missed two games. ... Bruised right knee (March 22, 1999); missed nine games. ... Injured back (November 5, 1999); missed three games. ... Flu (January 14, 2000); missed three games. ... Traded by Devils to Phoenix Coyotes for D Deron Quint and third-round pick (traded back to Phoenix; Coyotes selected D Beat Forster) in 2001 draft (March 7, 2000). ... Selected by Columbus Blue Jackets in NHL expansion draft (June 23, 2000). ... Bruised knee (March 15, 2001); missed one game. ... Back spasms (January 16, 2002); missed three games. ... Traded by Blue Jackets to Chicago Blackhawks for D Jaroslav Spacek and second-round pick (C Dan Fritsche) in 2003 draft (March 19, 2002). ... Suspended one playoff game by NHL for cross-checking incident (April 22, 2002). ... Traded by Blackhawks to Dallas Stars for D Sami Helenius and seventh-round pick in 2004 entry draft (March 10, 2003). ... Injured foot (March 15, 2003); missed eight games. ... Signed as free agent by Florida Panthers (September 9, 2003).

STATISTICAL PLATEAUS: Three-goal games: 1993-94 (1).

		REGULAR SEASON								PLAYOFFS				
Season Team	**League**	**GP**	**G**	**A**	**Pts.**	**PIM**	**+/-**	**PP**	**SH**	**GP**	**G**	**A**	**Pts.**	**PIM**
85-86—Moose Jaw	WHL	67	9	37	46	117	...	...	...	13	1	6	7	34
86-87—Moose Jaw	WHL	59	9	50	59	70	...	...	...	9	2	5	7	26
87-88—Moose Jaw	WHL	63	15	43	58	166	...	...	...	—	—	—	—	—
88-89—Sherbrooke	AHL	33	3	4	7	120	...	...	...	3	0	2	2	5
—Peoria	IHL	36	2	8	10	116	...	...	...	—	—	—	—	—
89-90—Sherbrooke	AHL	68	7	24	31	265	...	...	...	12	6	5	11	79
—Montreal	NHL	8	0	2	2	33	-1	0	0	—	—	—	—	—
90-91—Montreal	NHL	52	0	2	2	259	7	0	0	12	0	0	0	54
91-92—Montreal	NHL	71	1	7	8	212	15	0	0	7	0	0	0	11
92-93—Montreal	NHL	83	2	14	16	205	35	0	0	20	1	5	6	30
93-94—Montreal	NHL	79	11	29	40	276	8	6	0	7	0	0	0	17
94-95—Montreal	NHL	48	3	7	10	152	-13	0	0	—	—	—	—	—
95-96—Montreal	NHL	79	3	14	17	230	8	0	1	6	1	1	2	6
96-97—New Jersey	NHL	79	3	13	16	110	16	1	0	10	2	2	4	19
97-98—New Jersey	NHL	79	4	19	23	171	11	1	0	6	1	1	2	21
98-99—New Jersey	NHL	70	5	26	31	114	6	1	0	7	0	3	3	10
99-00—New Jersey	NHL	57	1	15	16	104	-10	0	0	—	—	—	—	—
—Phoenix	NHL	16	1	7	8	19	1	1	0	5	0	0	0	16
00-01—Columbus	NHL	81	3	14	17	118	-16	1	0	—	—	—	—	—
01-02—Columbus	NHL	65	2	14	16	89	-28	0	0	—	—	—	—	—
—Chicago	NHL	12	0	2	2	4	0	0	0	4	0	1	1	25
02-03—Chicago	NHL	65	7	4	11	76	7	0	0	—	—	—	—	—
—Dallas	NHL	3	0	0	0	6	0	0	0	2	0	0	0	0
03-04—Florida	NHL	82	4	12	16	88	-7	2	0	—	—	—	—	—
NHL Totals (15 years)		1029	50	201	251	2266	39	13	1	86	5	13	18	209

O

OHLUND, MATTIAS D CANUCKS

PERSONAL: Born September 9, 1976, in Pitea, Sweden. ... 6-2/220. ... Shoots left. ... Name pronounced MAT-tee-uhz OH-luhnd.

TRANSACTIONS/CAREER NOTES: Selected by Vancouver Canucks in first round (first Canucks pick, 13th overall) of NHL draft (June 28, 1994). ... Suffered concussion (March 26, 1998); missed four games. ... Sprained shoulder (February 23, 1999); missed three games. ... Suffered concussion (April 3, 1999); missed final five games of season. ... Injured eye (September 12, 1999); missed first 38 games of season. ... Injured groin (March 8, 2000); missed two games. ... Eye surgery (October 20, 2000); missed 17 games. ... Flu (October 6, 2001); missed one game. ... Sprained left knee (October 6, 2002); missed five games. ... Flu (December 28, 2002); missed one game. ... Injured knee (February 27, 2003); missed last 18 games of season and one playoff game.

Season Team	League	GP	G	A	Pts.	PIM	+/-	PP	SH	GP	G	A	Pts.	PIM
		REGULAR SEASON								PLAYOFFS				
92-93—Pitea	Sweden Dv. 2	22	0	6	6	16	...	...	...	—	—	—	—	—
93-94—Pitea	Sweden Dv. 2	28	7	10	17	62	...	...	...	—	—	—	—	—
94-95—Lulea	Sweden	34	6	10	16	34	...	...	...	9	4	0	4	16
95-96—Lulea	Sweden	30	4	10	14	26	...	...	...	13	0	1	1	47
96-97—Lulea	Sweden	47	7	9	16	38	...	...	...	10	1	2	3	8
97-98—Vancouver	NHL	77	7	23	30	76	3	1	0	—	—	—	—	—
—Swedish Oly. team	Int'l	4	0	1	1	4	-1	0	0	—	—	—	—	—
98-99—Vancouver	NHL	74	9	26	35	83	-19	2	1	—	—	—	—	—
99-00—Vancouver	NHL	42	4	16	20	24	6	2	1	—	—	—	—	—
00-01—Vancouver	NHL	65	8	20	28	46	-16	1	1	4	1	3	4	6
01-02—Vancouver	NHL	81	10	26	36	56	16	4	1	6	1	1	2	6
—Swedish Oly. team	Int'l	4	0	2	2	2	...	...	...	—	—	—	—	—
02-03—Vancouver	NHL	59	2	27	29	42	1	0	0	13	3	4	7	12
03-04—Vancouver	NHL	82	14	20	34	73	14	5	0	7	1	4	5	13
04-05—Lulea	Sweden	2	1	0	1	4	-1	1	0	...	...	...	...	...
NHL Totals (7 years)		480	54	158	212	400	5	15	4	30	6	12	18	37

OLESZ, ROSTISLAV — C — PANTHERS

PERSONAL: Born October 10, 1985, in Bolivec, Czech. ... 6-1/202. ... Shoots left.
TRANSACTIONS/CAREER NOTES: Selected by Florida Panthers in 1st round (1st Panthers pick, 7th overall) of entry draft (June 26, 2004).

Season Team	League	GP	G	A	Pts.	PIM	+/-	PP	SH	GP	G	A	Pts.	PIM
		REGULAR SEASON								PLAYOFFS				
00-01—Vitkovice	Czech Rep.	3	0	1	1	0	...	...	...	—	—	—	—	—
01-02—Vitkovice	Czech Rep.	11	1	2	3	0	...	...	...	—	—	—	—	—
02-03—Vitkovice	Czech Rep.	40	6	3	9	41	...	...	...	5	0	0	0	2
03-04—Vitkovice	Czech Rep.	35	1	11	12	10	...	...	...	6	2	1	3	4
04-05—Sparta Praha	Czech Rep.	47	6	7	13	12	...	...	...	—	—	—	—	—

OLIVER, DAVID — RW

PERSONAL: Born April 17, 1971, in Sechelt, B.C. ... 6-0/190. ... Shoots right.
TRANSACTIONS/CAREER NOTES: Selected by Edmonton Oilers in seventh round (seventh Oilers pick, 144th overall) of NHL draft (June 22, 1991). ... Had hip pointer (January 24, 1997); missed one game. ... Claimed off waivers by New York Rangers (February 22, 1997). ... Signed as free agent by Ottawa Senators (July 2, 1998). ... Signed as free agent by Phoenix Coyotes (July 16, 1999). ... Signed as free agent by Ottawa Senators (August 2, 2000). ... Had hip pointer (November 11, 2000); missed two games. ... Strained groin (November 19, 2000); missed five games. ... Signed as free agent by Dallas Stars (July 30, 2002). ... Injured throat (January 19, 2004); missed one game. ... Sore back (February 25, 2004); missed one game.
STATISTICAL PLATEAUS: Three-goal games: 1994-95 (1).

Season Team	League	GP	G	A	Pts.	PIM	+/-	PP	SH	GP	G	A	Pts.	PIM
		REGULAR SEASON								PLAYOFFS				
90-91—Univ. of Michigan	CCHA	27	13	11	24	34	...	...	...	—	—	—	—	—
91-92—Univ. of Michigan	CCHA	44	31	27	58	32	...	...	...	—	—	—	—	—
92-93—Univ. of Michigan	CCHA	40	35	20	55	18	...	...	...	—	—	—	—	—
93-94—Univ. of Michigan	CCHA	41	28	40	68	16	...	16	0	—	—	—	—	—
94-95—Cape Breton	AHL	32	11	18	29	8	-2	4	1	—	—	—	—	—
—Edmonton	NHL	44	16	14	30	20	-11	10	0	—	—	—	—	—
95-96—Edmonton	NHL	80	20	19	39	34	-22	14	0	—	—	—	—	—
96-97—Edmonton	NHL	17	1	2	3	4	-8	0	0	—	—	—	—	—
—New York Rangers	NHL	14	2	1	3	4	3	0	0	3	0	0	0	0
97-98—Houston	IHL	78	38	27	65	60	-5	18	1	4	3	0	3	4
98-99—Ottawa	NHL	17	2	5	7	4	1	0	0	—	—	—	—	—
—Houston	IHL	37	18	17	35	30	-1	4	0	19	10	6	16	22
99-00—Phoenix	NHL	9	1	0	1	2	0	1	0	—	—	—	—	—
—Houston	IHL	45	16	11	27	40	...	...	...	11	3	4	7	8
00-01—Grand Rapids	IHL	51	14	17	31	35	...	...	...	10	6	2	8	8
—Ottawa	NHL	7	0	0	0	2	0	0	0	—	—	—	—	—
01-02—Munich	Germany	59	20	14	34	30	...	...	...	9	2	2	4	6
02-03—Utah	AHL	37	11	14	25	14	-8	4	0	—	—	—	—	—
—Dallas	NHL	6	0	3	3	2	1	0	0	6	0	0	0	2
03-04—Utah	AHL	31	5	12	17	12	-2	2	1	—	—	—	—	—
—Dallas	NHL	36	7	5	12	12	6	3	0	1	0	0	0	0
04-05—Guildford	England	16	8	14	22	4	...	3	0	15	3	5	8	31
NHL Totals (8 years)		230	49	49	98	84	-30	28	0	10	0	0	0	2

OLIWA, KRZYSZTOF — LW/RW — DEVILS

PERSONAL: Born April 12, 1973, in Tychy, Poland. ... 6-5/245. ... Shoots left. ... Name pronounced KRIH-stahf OH-lee-vuh.
TRANSACTIONS/CAREER NOTES: Selected by New Jersey Devils in third round (fourth Devils pick, 65th overall) of NHL draft (June 26, 1993). ... Injured foot (November 10, 1997); missed two games. ... Strained groin (November 28, 1998); missed one game. ... Sprained left knee (October 30, 1999); missed six games. ... Flu (January 11, 2000); missed one game. ... Injured left knee (April 2, 2000); missed final three games of season. ... Traded by Devils with future considerations (D Deron Quint) to Columbus Blue Jackets for third-round pick (C/LW Brandon Nolan) in 2001 draft and future considerations (June 12, 2000); Devils acquired RW Turner Stevenson to complete deal (June 23, 2000). ... Fractured arm (October 28, 2000); missed 23 games. ... Traded by Blue Jackets to Pittsburgh Penguins for third-round pick (D Aaron Johnson) in 2001 draft (January 14, 2001). ... Injured hamstring (March 20, 2001); missed five games. ... Traded by Penguins to New York Rangers for ninth-round pick (traded to Tampa Bay; Lightning selected RW Albert Vishnayako) in 2003 draft (June 22, 2002). ... Suspended

five games for unsportsmanlike conduct (November 11, 2002). ... Traded by Rangers to Boston Bruins for future considerations (January 6, 2003). ... Signed as free agent by Calgary Flames (July 30, 2003). ... Suspended two games for high-sticking incident (November 21, 2003). ... Suspended three games for abuse of officials (March 21, 2004). ... Signed as free agent by Devils (July 15, 2004).

		REGULAR SEASON								PLAYOFFS				
Season Team	**League**	**GP**	**G**	**A**	**Pts.**	**PIM**	**+/-**	**PP**	**SH**	**GP**	**G**	**A**	**Pts.**	**PIM**
90-91—GKS Katowice	Poland Jrs	5	4	4	8	10	...	...	...	—	—	—	—	—
91-92—GKS Tychy	Poland	10	3	7	10	6	...	...	...	—	—	—	—	—
92-93—Welland Jr. B	OHA	30	13	21	34	127	...	...	...	—	—	—	—	—
93-94—Albany	AHL	33	2	4	6	151	-6	0	0	—	—	—	—	—
—Raleigh	ECHL	15	0	2	2	65	-1	0	0	9	0	0	0	35
94-95—Albany	AHL	20	1	1	2	77	-2	0	0	—	—	—	—	—
—Detroit	IHL	4	0	1	1	24	-5	0	0	—	—	—	—	—
—Saint John	AHL	14	1	4	5	79	-4	0	0	—	—	—	—	—
—Raleigh	ECHL	5	0	2	2	32	-2	0	0	—	—	—	—	—
95-96—Albany	AHL	51	5	11	16	217	...	...	...	—	—	—	—	—
—Raleigh	ECHL	9	1	0	1	53	...	...	...	—	—	—	—	—
96-97—Albany	AHL	60	13	14	27	322	13	3	0	15	7	1	8	49
—New Jersey	NHL	1	0	0	0	5	-1	0	0	—	—	—	—	—
97-98—New Jersey	NHL	73	2	3	5	295	3	0	0	6	0	0	0	23
98-99—New Jersey	NHL	64	5	7	12	240	4	0	0	1	0	0	0	2
99-00—New Jersey	NHL	69	6	10	16	184	-2	1	0	—	—	—	—	—
00-01—Columbus	NHL	10	0	2	2	34	1	0	0	—	—	—	—	—
—Pittsburgh	NHL	26	1	2	3	131	-4	0	0	5	0	0	0	16
01-02—Pittsburgh	NHL	57	0	2	2	150	-5	0	0	—	—	—	—	—
02-03—New York Rangers	NHL	9	0	0	0	51	1	0	0	—	—	—	—	—
—Hartford	AHL	15	0	1	1	30	-7	0	0	—	—	—	—	—
—Boston	NHL	33	0	0	0	110	-4	0	0	—	—	—	—	—
03-04—Calgary	NHL	65	3	2	5	247	-8	0	0	20	2	0	2	6
04-05—Podhale Nowy Targ	Poland	...	...	...	...	...	...	...	...	2	0	0	0	12
NHL Totals (8 years)		407	17	28	45	1447	-15	1	0	32	2	0	2	47

OLSON, JOSH LW

PERSONAL: Born July 13, 1981, in Grand Forks, N.D. ... 6-5/236. ... Shoots left.
TRANSACTIONS/CAREER NOTES: Selected by Florida Panthers in sixth round (sixth Panthers pick, 190th overall) of NHL entry draft (June 24, 2000). ... Signed as free agent by San Antonio of the AHL (September 26, 2004).

		REGULAR SEASON								PLAYOFFS				
Season Team	**League**	**GP**	**G**	**A**	**Pts.**	**PIM**	**+/-**	**PP**	**SH**	**GP**	**G**	**A**	**Pts.**	**PIM**
99-00—Fargo	USHL	18	2	5	7	37	...	...	...	—	—	—	—	—
—Omaha	USHL	61	8	12	20	81	...	...	...	4	0	0	0	4
00-01—Portland	WHL	72	22	38	60	86	...	...	...	16	5	4	9	17
01-02—Portland	WHL	72	40	48	88	85	...	...	...	7	4	3	7	8
—Utah	AHL	1	0	0	0	0	-1	0	0	1	0	0	0	0
02-03—San Antonio	AHL	23	0	1	1	14	-6	0	0	—	—	—	—	—
—Jackson	ECHL	39	10	17	27	13	3	3	0	1	0	1	1	0
03-04—Florida	NHL	5	1	0	1	0	1	0	0	—	—	—	—	—
—San Antonio	AHL	73	22	16	38	33	1	4	0	—	—	—	—	—
04-05—Hershey	AHL	23	1	2	3	4	-2	0	0	—	—	—	—	—
—San Antonio	AHL	53	9	7	16	17	3	1	0	—	—	—	—	—
NHL Totals (1 year)		5	1	0	1	0	1	0	0					

OLVESTAD, JIMMIE LW/RW

PERSONAL: Born February 16, 1980, in Stockholm, Sweden. ... 6-1/194. ... Shoots left.
TRANSACTIONS/CAREER NOTES: Selected by Tampa Bay Lightning in 3rd round (4th Lightning pick, 88th overall) of NHL draft (June 26, 1999). ... Sprained right shoulder (October 30, 2001); missed three games. ... Concussion (January 13, 2002); missed four games. ... Flu (December 12, 2002); missed two games.

		REGULAR SEASON								PLAYOFFS				
Season Team	**League**	**GP**	**G**	**A**	**Pts.**	**PIM**	**+/-**	**PP**	**SH**	**GP**	**G**	**A**	**Pts.**	**PIM**
96-97—Huddinge	Sweden Jr.	40	15	16	31	...	...	...	...	—	—	—	—	—
97-98—Huddinge	Sweden Dv. 2	11	0	0	0	6	...	...	...	—	—	—	—	—
—Djurgarden Stockholm	Sweden Jr.	15	6	4	10	...	...	...	...	—	—	—	—	—
98-99—Djurgarden Stockholm	Sweden	44	2	4	6	18	...	...	...	4	0	0	0	8
99-00—Djurgarden Stockholm	Sweden	50	6	3	9	34	...	...	...	13	1	2	3	12
00-01—Djurgarden Stockholm	Sweden	50	7	8	15	79	...	...	...	16	7	2	9	14
01-02—Tampa Bay	NHL	74	3	11	14	24	3	0	0	—	—	—	—	—
02-03—Springfield	AHL	6	0	1	1	13	-4	0	0	—	—	—	—	—
—Tampa Bay	NHL	37	0	3	3	16	-2	0	0	—	—	—	—	—
03-04—Hamilton	AHL	75	7	14	21	56	-8	0	2	4	2	0	2	4
04-05—Djurgarden Stockholm	Sweden	46	4	8	12	89	-4	0	0	12	0	1	1	47
NHL Totals (2 years)		111	3	14	17	40	1	0	0					

O

ORPIK, BROOKS D PENGUINS

PERSONAL: Born September 26, 1980, in San Francisco. ... 6-2/224. ... Shoots left.
TRANSACTIONS/CAREER NOTES: Selected by Pittsburgh Penguins in first round (first Penguins pick, 18th overall) of NHL draft (June 24, 2000). ... Suspended one game for kneeing incident (October 11, 2003).

Season Team	League	GP	G	A	Pts.	PIM	+/-	PP	SH	GP	G	A	Pts.	PIM
		REGULAR SEASON								PLAYOFFS				
97-98—Thayer Academy.........	Mass. H.S.	22	0	7	7	...	...	...	...	—	—	—	—	—
98-99—Boston College..........	Hockey East	41	1	10	11	96	...	...	...	—	—	—	—	—
99-00—Boston College..........	Hockey East	38	1	9	10	100	...	...	...	—	—	—	—	—
00-01—Boston College..........	Hockey East	40	0	20	20	*124	...	...	...	—	—	—	—	—
01-02—Wilkes-Barre/Scranton	AHL	78	2	18	20	99	2	1	0	—	—	—	—	—
02-03—Pittsburgh..................	NHL	6	0	0	0	2	-5	0	0	—	—	—	—	—
—Wilkes-Barre/Scranton	AHL	71	4	14	18	105	5	0	0	6	0	0	0	14
03-04—Wilkes-Barre/Scranton	AHL	3	0	0	0	2	1	0	0	24	0	4	4	53
—Pittsburgh..................	NHL	79	1	9	10	127	-36	0	0	—	—	—	—	—
NHL Totals (2 years)...........		85	1	9	10	129	-41	0	0					

ORR, COLTON — RW — BRUINS

PERSONAL: Born March 3, 1982, in Winnipeg, Manitoba. ... 6-3/210. ... Shoots right.
TRANSACTIONS/CAREER NOTES: Signed as free agent by Boston Bruins (September 19, 2001).

Season Team	League	GP	G	A	Pts.	PIM	+/-	PP	SH	GP	G	A	Pts.	PIM
		REGULAR SEASON								PLAYOFFS				
98-99—Swift Current.............	WHL	2	0	0	0	2	...	...	...	1	0	0	0	0
99-00—Swift Current.............	WHL	61	3	2	5	130	...	...	...	—	—	—	—	—
00-01—Swift Current.............	WHL	19	0	4	4	67	...	...	...	—	—	—	—	—
—Kamloops..................	WHL	41	8	1	9	179	...	...	...	3	0	0	0	20
01-02—Kamloops..................	WHL	1	0	0	0	7	...	...	...	2	0	0	0	2
02-03—Kamloops..................	WHL	3	2	0	2	17	...	...	...	—	—	—	—	—
—Regina.......................	WHL	37	6	2	8	170	...	...	...	3	0	0	0	19
—Providence.................	AHL	1	0	0	0	7	0	0	0	—	—	—	—	—
03-04—Providence.................	AHL	64	1	4	5	257	-6	0	0	2	0	0	0	9
—Boston.......................	NHL	1	0	0	0	0	-1	0	0	—	—	—	—	—
04-05—Providence.................	AHL	61	1	6	7	279	-6	0	0	17	1	0	1	44
NHL Totals (1 year).............		1	0	0	0	0	-1	0	0					

ORSZAGH, VLADIMIR — RW

PERSONAL: Born May 24, 1977, in Banska Bystrica, Czechoslovakia. ... 5-11/195. ... Shoots left. ... Name pronounced OHR-sahg.
TRANSACTIONS/CAREER NOTES: Selected by New York Islanders in 5th round (4th Islanders pick, 106th overall) of NHL draft (July 8, 1995). ... Tendinitis (December 14, 1999); missed one game. ... Signed as free agent by Nashville Predators (June 1, 2001). ... Charley horse (March 2, 2002); missed two games. ... Injured rib muscle (December 23, 2002); missed three games. ... Bruised shoulder (March 31, 2003); missed one game. ... Torn ACL and MCL in right knee at world championships (May 2005); out indefinitely.
STATISTICAL PLATEAUS: Three-goal games: 2003-04 (1).

Season Team	League	GP	G	A	Pts.	PIM	+/-	PP	SH	GP	G	A	Pts.	PIM
		REGULAR SEASON								PLAYOFFS				
93-94—IS Banska Byst.	Slovakia Jrs.	...	38	27	65	...	...	...	...	—	—	—	—	—
94-95—Banska Bystrica..........	Slov. Div.	38	18	12	30	...	...	...	...	—	—	—	—	—
—Martimex ZTS Martin..	Slovakia	1	0	0	0	0	...	...	...	—	—	—	—	—
95-96—Banska Bystrica..........	Slovakia	31	9	5	14	22	...	...	...	—	—	—	—	—
96-97—Utah..........................	IHL	68	12	15	27	30	...	...	...	3	0	1	1	4
97-98—Utah..........................	IHL	62	13	10	23	60	0	1	0	4	2	0	2	0
—New York Islanders.....	NHL	11	0	1	1	2	-3	0	0	—	—	—	—	—
98-99—Lowell.......................	AHL	68	18	23	41	57	-6	7	2	3	2	2	4	2
—New York Islanders.....	NHL	12	1	0	1	6	2	0	0	—	—	—	—	—
99-00—Lowell.......................	AHL	55	8	12	20	22	...	...	...	7	3	3	6	2
—New York Islanders.....	NHL	11	2	1	3	4	1	0	0	—	—	—	—	—
00-01—Djurgarden Stockholm	Sweden	50	23	13	36	62	...	...	...	16	7	3	10	20
01-02—Nashville.....................	NHL	79	15	21	36	56	-15	5	0	—	—	—	—	—
02-03—Nashville.....................	NHL	78	16	16	32	38	-1	3	0	—	—	—	—	—
03-04—Nashville.....................	NHL	82	16	21	37	74	-4	2	2	6	2	0	2	4
04-05—Zvolen........................	Slovakia	38	16	14	30	50	40	...	...	17	5	2	7	24
—Banska Bystrica..........	Slov. Div.	2	2	0	2	4	1	...	...	—	—	—	—	—
NHL Totals (6 years)...........		273	50	60	110	180	-20	10	2	6	2	0	2	4

ORTMEYER, JED — RW — RANGERS

PERSONAL: Born September 3, 1978, in Omaha, Neb. ... 6-1/189. ... Shoots right.
TRANSACTIONS/CAREER NOTES: Signed as free agent by New York Rangers (May 10, 2003). ... Injured leg (March 20, 2004); missed remainder of season.

Season Team	League	GP	G	A	Pts.	PIM	+/-	PP	SH	GP	G	A	Pts.	PIM
		REGULAR SEASON								PLAYOFFS				
99-00—Univ. of Michigan........	CCHA	41	8	16	24	24	40	...	...	—	—	—	—	—
00-01—Univ. of Michigan........	CCHA	27	10	11	21	52	...	...	...	—	—	—	—	—
01-02—Univ. of Michigan........	CCHA	41	15	23	38	40	...	...	...	—	—	—	—	—
02-03—Univ. of Michigan........	CCHA	36	18	16	34	48	...	...	...	—	—	—	—	—
03-04—Hartford.....................	AHL	13	2	8	10	4	8	0	0	16	5	2	7	6
—New York Rangers......	NHL	58	2	4	6	16	-10	0	0	—	—	—	—	—
04-05—Hartford.....................	AHL	61	7	20	27	63	11	1	0	6	0	1	1	4
NHL Totals (1 year).............		58	2	4	6	16	-10	0	0					

OSGOOD, CHRIS — G — RED WINGS

PERSONAL: Born November 26, 1972, in Peace River, Alta. ... 5-11/178. ... Catches left. ... Nickname: Ozzie.

TRANSACTIONS/CAREER NOTES: Selected by Detroit Red Wings in 3rd round (3rd Red Wings pick, 54th overall) of NHL draft (June 22, 1991). ... Strained hamstring (January 14, 1997); missed five games. ... Strained groin (March 14, 1998); missed four games. ... Strained hip flexor (November 19, 1998); missed six games. ... Injured right knee (April 27, 1999); missed four playoff games. ... Injured hand (November 24, 1999); missed 15 games. ... Claimed by New York Islanders from Red Wings in waiver draft (September 28, 2001). ... Tendinitis in wrist (January 22, 2002); missed three games. ... Sprained ankle (January 24, 2002); missed 18 games. ... Traded by Islanders with 3rd-round pick (G Konstantin Barulin) in 2003 draft to St. Louis Blues for C Justin Papineau and 2nd-round pick (C Jeremy Colliton) in 2003 draft (March 11, 2003). ... Injured leg (December 30, 2003); missed two games. ... Sore hand (March 7, 2004); missed one game. ... Signed as free agent by Red Wings (Aug. 8, 2005).

		REGULAR SEASON									PLAYOFFS							
Season Team	**League**	**GP**	**Min.**	**W**	**L**	**T**	**GA**	**SO**	**GAA**	**SV%**	**GP**	**Min.**	**W**	**L**	**GA**	**SO**	**GAA**	**SV%**
89-90—Medicine Hat	WHL	57	3094	24	28	2	228	0	4.42	...	3	173	3	4	17	0	5.90	...
90-91—Medicine Hat	WHL	46	2630	23	18	3	173	2	3.95	...	12	714	7	5	42	0	3.53	...
91-92—Medicine Hat	WHL	15	819	10	3	0	44	0	3.22	...	—	—	—	—	—	—	—	—
—Brandon	WHL	16	890	3	10	1	60	1	4.04	...	—	—	—	—	—	—	—	—
—Seattle	WHL	21	1217	12	7	1	65	1	3.20	...	15	904	9	6	51	0	3.38	...
92-93—Adirondack	AHL	45	2438	19	19	2	159	0	3.91	.881	1	59	0	1	2	0	2.03	.920
93-94—Adirondack	AHL	4	240	3	1	0	13	0	3.25	.893	—	—	—	—	—	—	—	—
—Detroit	NHL	41	2206	23	8	5	105	2	2.86	.895	6	307	3	2	12	1	2.35	.891
94-95—Adirondack	AHL	2	120	1	1	0	6	0	3.00	.908	—	—	—	—	—	—	—	—
—Detroit	NHL	19	1087	14	5	0	41	1	2.26	.917	2	68	0	0	2	0	1.76	.920
95-96—Detroit	NHL	50	2933	*39	6	5	106	5	2.17	.911	15	936	8	7	33	2	2.12	.898
96-97—Detroit	NHL	47	2769	23	13	9	106	6	2.30	.910	2	47	0	0	2	0	2.55	.905
97-98—Detroit	NHL	64	3807	33	20	11	140	6	2.21	.913	*22	*1361	*16	6	48	2	2.12	.918
98-99—Detroit	NHL	63	3691	34	25	4	149	3	2.42	.910	6	358	4	2	14	1	2.35	.919
99-00—Detroit	NHL	53	3148	30	14	8	126	6	2.40	.907	9	547	5	4	18	2	1.97	.924
00-01—Detroit	NHL	52	2834	25	19	4	127	1	2.69	.903	6	365	2	4	15	1	2.47	.905
01-02—New York Islanders	NHL	66	3743	32	25	6	156	4	2.50	.910	7	392	3	4	17	0	2.60	.912
02-03—New York Islanders	NHL	37	1993	17	14	4	97	2	2.92	.894	7	417	3	4	17	1	2.45	.907
—St. Louis	NHL	9	532	4	3	2	27	2	3.05	.888	...	...	...	...	...	...	...	...
03-04—St. Louis	NHL	67	3861	31	25	8	144	3	2.24	.910	5	287	1	4	12	0	2.51	.890
NHL Totals (11 years)		568	32604	305	177	66	1324	41	2.44	.907	87	5085	45	37	190	10	2.24	.910

OSHIE, T.J. — C — BLUES

PERSONAL: Born December 23, 1986, in Mount Vernon, Wash. ... 5-10/170. ... Shoots left.

TRANSACTIONS/CAREER NOTES: Selected by St. Louis in 1st round (1st Blues pick, 24th overall) of entry draft (July 30, 2005).

		REGULAR SEASON								PLAYOFFS				
Season Team	**League**	**GP**	**G**	**A**	**Pts.**	**PIM**	**+/-**	**PP**	**SH**	**GP**	**G**	**A**	**Pts.**	**PIM**
04-05—Warroad	USHS (West)	31	37	62	99	22	...	...	...	—	—	—	—	—

OTT, STEVE — C/LW — STARS

PERSONAL: Born August 19, 1982, in Summerside, Prince Edward Island. ... 6-0/180. ... Shoots left.

TRANSACTIONS/CAREER NOTES: Selected by Dallas Stars in first round (first Stars pick, 25th overall) of NHL draft (June 24, 2000). ... Sprained back (December 7, 2003); missed seven games. ... Fined $1,000 for penalties in game against Ottawa Senators (January 28, 2004).

		REGULAR SEASON								PLAYOFFS				
Season Team	**League**	**GP**	**G**	**A**	**Pts.**	**PIM**	**+/-**	**PP**	**SH**	**GP**	**G**	**A**	**Pts.**	**PIM**
98-99—Leamington	Jr. B	48	14	30	44	110	...	...	...	—	—	—	—	—
99-00—Windsor	OHL	66	23	39	62	131	...	...	...	12	3	5	8	21
00-01—Windsor	OHL	55	50	37	87	164	40	11	4	9	3	8	11	27
01-02—Windsor	OHL	53	43	45	88	178	...	...	...	14	6	10	16	49
02-03—Utah	AHL	40	9	11	20	98	-1	5	0	—	—	—	—	—
—Dallas	NHL	26	3	4	7	31	6	0	0	1	0	0	0	0
03-04—Dallas	NHL	73	2	10	12	152	-2	0	0	4	1	0	1	0
04-05—Hamilton	AHL	67	18	21	39	279	-1	1	0	4	0	0	0	20
NHL Totals (2 years)		99	5	14	19	183	4	0	0	5	1	0	1	0

OUELLET, MAXIME — G — CAPITALS

PERSONAL: Born June 17, 1981, in Beauport, Que. ... 6-2/196. ... Catches left.

TRANSACTIONS/CAREER NOTES: Selected by Philadelphia Flyers in first round (first Flyers pick, 22nd overall) of NHL draft (June 26, 1999). ... Traded by Flyers with first- (traded to Dallas; Stars selected D Martin Vagner), second-(G Maxime Daigneault) and third-round (C Derek Krestanovich) picks in 2002 draft to Washington Capitals for C Adam Oates (March 19, 2002).

		REGULAR SEASON									PLAYOFFS							
Season Team	**League**	**GP**	**Min.**	**W**	**L**	**T**	**GA**	**SO**	**GAA**	**SV%**	**GP**	**Min.**	**W**	**L**	**GA**	**SO**	**GAA**	**SV%**
97-98—Quebec	QMJHL	24	1199	12	7	1	66	0	3.30	...	7	305	3	1	16	0	3.15	...
98-99—Quebec	QMJHL	*58	*3447	*40	12	*6	155	3	*2.70	...	13	803	6	7	41	1	3.06	...
99-00—Quebec	QMJHL	53	2984	31	16	4	133	2	2.67	.916	11	638	7	4	28	*2	*2.63	.912
00-01—Philadelphia	NHL	2	76	0	1	0	3	0	2.37	.889	—	—	—	—	—	—	—	—
—Philadelphia	AHL	2	86	1	0	0	4	0	2.79	.926	—	—	—	—	—	—	—	—
—Rouyn-Noranda	QMJHL	25	1471	18	6	1	65	3	2.65	.913	8	490	4	4	25	0	3.06	.894

Season Team	League	GP	Min.	W	L	T	GA	SO	GAA	SV%		GP	Min.	W	L	GA	SO	GAA	SV%
		REGULAR SEASON										PLAYOFFS							
01-02—Philadelphia	AHL	41	2294	16	13	8	104	1	2.72	.902		—	—	—	—	—	—	—	—
—Portland	AHL	6	358	3	3	0	17	0	2.85	.917		—	—	—	—	—	—	—	—
02-03—Portland	AHL	48	2773	22	16	7	111	7	2.40	.929		2	120	1	1	8	0	4.00	.889
03-04—Washington	NHL	6	365	2	3	1	19	1	3.12	.910		—	—	—	—	—	—	—	—
—Portland	AHL	52	3051	15	29	8	101	10	1.99	.925		5	302	2	2	8	0	1.59	.938
04-05—Portland	AHL	40	2304	15	20	...	111	0	2.89	.911		—	—	—	—	—	—	—	—
NHL Totals (2 years)		8	441	2	4	1	22	1	2.99	.907									

OUELLET, MICHEL — RW — PENGUINS

PERSONAL: Born March 5, 1982, in Rimouski, Que. ... 6-1/182. ... Shoots right.
TRANSACTIONS/CAREER NOTES: Selected by Pittsburgh Penguins in fourth round (fourth Penguins pick, 124th overall) of NHL entry draft (June 24, 2000).

Season Team	League	GP	G	A	Pts.	PIM	+/-	PP	SH		GP	G	A	Pts.	PIM
		REGULAR SEASON									PLAYOFFS				
98-99—Rimouski	QMJHL	28	7	13	20	10	...	...	...		—	—	—	—	—
99-00—Rimouski	QMJHL	72	36	53	89	38	...	...	...		—	—	—	—	—
00-01—Rimouski	QMJHL	63	42	50	92	50	-12	28	1		11	6	7	13	8
01-02—Rimouski	QMJHL	61	40	58	98	66	...	...	...		7	3	6	9	4
02-03—Wilkes-Barre/Scranton	AHL	4	0	2	2	0	1	0	0		—	—	—	—	—
—Wheeling	ECHL	55	20	26	46	40	-1	7	0		—	—	—	—	—
03-04—Wilkes-Barre/Scranton	AHL	79	30	19	49	34	0	12	0		22	2	10	12	6
04-05—Wilkes-Barre/Scranton	AHL	80	31	32	63	56	15	6	0		11	2	3	5	6

OVECHKIN, ALEXANDER — LW — CAPITALS

PERSONAL: Born September 17, 1985, in Moscow, U.S.S.R. ... 6-2/212. ... Shoots right.
TRANSACTIONS/CAREER NOTES: Selected by Washington Capitals in first round (first Capitals pick, first overall) of NHL entry draft (June 26, 2004).

Season Team	League	GP	G	A	Pts.	PIM	+/-	PP	SH		GP	G	A	Pts.	PIM
		REGULAR SEASON									PLAYOFFS				
01-02—Dynamo	Russian	21	2	2	4	4	...	...	...		—	—	—	—	—
02-03—Dynamo	Russian	40	8	7	15	28	...	...	...		5	0	0	0	2
03-04—Dynamo	Russian	53	13	10	23	42	...	...	...		3	0	0	0	2
04-05—Dynamo	Russian	37	13	14	27	32	...	...	...		—	—	—	—	—

OZOLINSH, SANDIS — D — MIGHTY DUCKS

PERSONAL: Born August 3, 1972, in Riga, USSR. ... 6-3/217. ... Shoots left. ... Name pronounced SAN-dihz OH-zoh-lihnsh.
TRANSACTIONS/CAREER NOTES: Selected by San Jose Sharks in second round (third Sharks pick, 30th overall) of NHL entry draft (June 22, 1991). ... Strained back (November 7, 1992); missed one game. ... Tore anterior cruciate ligament in knee (December 30, 1992); missed remainder of season. ... Injured knee (December 11, 1993); missed one game. ... Traded by Sharks to Colorado Avalanche for RW Owen Nolan (October 26, 1995). ... Separated left shoulder (December 7, 1995); missed four games. ... Fractured finger (February 23, 1996); missed two games. ... Back spasms (March 9, 1997); missed two games. ... Separated shoulder (October 7, 1997); missed two games. ... Injured knee (October 17, 1997) and underwent arthroscopic surgery; missed 13 games. ... Missed first 38 games of 1998-99 season due to contract dispute. ... Bruised sternum (February 9, 1999); missed two games. ... Traded by Avalanche with second-round pick (LW Tomas Kurka) in 2000 draft to Carolina Hurricanes for D Nolan Pratt, first- (C Vaclav Nedorost) and two second-round (C Jared Aulin and D Argis Saviels) picks in 2000 draft (June 24, 2000). ... Injured knee (December 29, 2000) and underwent surgery; missed 10 games. ... Sprained knee (October 18, 2001); missed three games. ... Traded by Hurricanes with C Byron Ritchie to Florida Panthers for D Bret Hedican, C Kevyn Adams and D Tomas Malec (January 16, 2002). ... Traded by Panthers with D Lance Ward to Mighty Ducks of Anaheim for C Matt Cullen, D Pavel Trnka and fourth-round pick (D James Pemberton) in 2003 (January 30, 2003). ... Injured ribs (December 5, 2003); missed four games. ... Strained shoulder (December 21, 2003) and had surgery (December 30, 2003); missed remainder of season.
STATISTICAL PLATEAUS: Three-goal games: 1999-00 (1), 2000-01 (1). Total: 2.

Season Team	League	GP	G	A	Pts.	PIM	+/-	PP	SH		GP	G	A	Pts.	PIM
		REGULAR SEASON									PLAYOFFS				
90-91—Dynamo Riga	USSR	44	0	3	3	49	...	...	...		—	—	—	—	—
91-92—HC Riga	CIS	30	5	0	5	42	...	...	...		—	—	—	—	—
—Kansas City	IHL	34	6	9	15	20	...	...	...		15	2	5	7	22
92-93—San Jose	NHL	37	7	16	23	40	-9	2	0		—	—	—	—	—
93-94—San Jose	NHL	81	26	38	64	24	16	4	0		14	0	10	10	8
94-95—San Jose	NHL	48	9	16	25	30	-6	3	1		11	3	2	5	6
95-96—San Francisco	IHL	2	1	0	1	0	...	...	...		—	—	—	—	—
—San Jose	NHL	7	1	3	4	4	2	1	0		—	—	—	—	—
—Colorado	NHL	66	13	37	50	50	0	7	1		22	5	14	19	16
96-97—Colorado	NHL	80	23	45	68	88	4	13	0		17	4	13	17	24
97-98—Colorado	NHL	66	13	38	51	65	-12	9	0		7	0	7	7	14
98-99—Colorado	NHL	39	7	25	32	22	10	4	0		19	4	8	12	22
99-00—Colorado	NHL	82	16	36	52	46	17	6	0		17	5	5	10	20
00-01—Carolina	NHL	72	12	32	44	71	-25	4	2		6	0	2	2	5
01-02—Carolina	NHL	46	4	19	23	34	-4	1	0		—	—	—	—	—
—Florida	NHL	37	10	19	29	24	-3	2	0		—	—	—	—	—
—Latvian Olympic team	Int'l	1	0	4	4	0	...	...	...		—	—	—	—	—
02-03—Florida	NHL	51	7	19	26	40	-16	5	0		—	—	—	—	—
—Anaheim	NHL	31	5	13	18	16	10	1	0		21	2	6	8	10
03-04—Anaheim	NHL	36	5	11	16	24	-7	1	0		—	—	—	—	—
NHL Totals (12 years)		779	158	367	525	578	-23	63	4		134	23	67	90	125

PAETSCH, NATHAN — D — SABRES

PERSONAL: Born March 30, 1983, in Humboldt, Sask. ... 6-0/195. ... Shoots left.

TRANSACTIONS/CAREER NOTES: Selected by Washington Capitals in second round (first Capitals pick, 58th overall) of NHL entry draft (June 23, 2001). ... Returned to draft pool by Capitals; selected by Buffalo Sabres in seventh round (eighth Sabres pick, 202nd overall) of NHL entry draft (June 21, 2003).

		REGULAR SEASON								PLAYOFFS				
Season Team	League	GP	G	A	Pts.	PIM	+/-	PP	SH	GP	G	A	Pts.	PIM
98-99—Moose Jaw	WHL	2	0	0	0	0	...	...	...	—	—	—	—	—
99-00—Moose Jaw	WHL	68	9	35	44	48	...	...	...	4	0	1	1	0
00-01—Moose Jaw	WHL	70	8	54	62	118	...	...	...	4	1	2	3	6
01-02—Moose Jaw	WHL	59	16	36	52	86	...	...	...	12	0	4	4	16
02-03—Moose Jaw	WHL	59	15	39	54	81	...	...	...	13	3	10	13	6
03-04—Rochester	AHL	54	5	5	10	49	2	0	1	16	1	1	2	28
04-05—Rochester	AHL	80	4	19	23	150	15	1	0	9	1	1	2	16

PAHLSSON, SAMUEL — C/LW — MIGHTY DUCKS

PERSONAL: Born December 17, 1977, in Ornskoldsvik, Sweden. ... 6-0/212. ... Shoots left.

TRANSACTIONS/CAREER NOTES: Selected by Colorado Avalanche in seventh round (10th Avalanche pick, 176th overall) of NHL draft (June 22, 1996). ... Traded by Avalanche with LW Brian Rolston, D Martin Grenier and first-round pick (LW Martin Samuelsson) in 2000 draft to Boston Bruins for D Ray Bourque and LW Dave Andreychuk (March 6, 2000). ... Traded by Bruins to Anaheim Mighty Ducks for LW Andrei Nazarov and D Patrick Traverse (November 18, 2000).

		REGULAR SEASON								PLAYOFFS				
Season Team	League	GP	G	A	Pts.	PIM	+/-	PP	SH	GP	G	A	Pts.	PIM
94-95—MoDo Ornskoldsvik	Sweden Jr.	30	10	11	21	26	...	...	...	—	—	—	—	—
95-96—MoDo Ornskoldsvik	Sweden	36	1	3	4	8	...	...	...	—	—	—	—	—
—MoDo Ornskoldsvik	Sweden Jr.	5	2	6	8	2	...	...	...	—	—	—	—	—
96-97—MoDo Ornskoldsvik	Sweden	49	8	9	17	83	...	...	...	—	—	—	—	—
97-98—MoDo Ornskoldsvik	Sweden	23	6	11	17	24	...	...	...	9	3	0	3	6
98-99—MoDo Ornskoldsvik	Sweden	50	17	17	34	44	...	...	...	13	3	3	6	10
99-00—MoDo Ornskoldsvik	Sweden	47	16	11	27	67	...	...	...	13	3	3	6	8
00-01—Boston	NHL	17	1	1	2	6	-5	0	0	—	—	—	—	—
—Anaheim	NHL	59	3	4	7	14	-9	1	1	—	—	—	—	—
01-02—Anaheim	NHL	80	6	14	20	26	-16	1	1	—	—	—	—	—
02-03—Cincinnati	AHL	13	1	7	8	24	7	0	0	—	—	—	—	—
—Anaheim	NHL	34	4	11	15	18	10	0	1	21	2	4	6	12
03-04—Anaheim	NHL	82	8	14	22	52	-2	1	0	—	—	—	—	—
04-05—Vastra Frolunda	Sweden	48	6	18	24	56	13	1	2	14	4	7	11	24
NHL Totals (4 years)		272	22	44	66	116	-22	3	3	21	2	4	6	12

PAILLE, DAN — LW — SABRES

PERSONAL: Born April 15, 1984, in Welland, Ont. ... 6-0/200. ... Shoots left.

TRANSACTIONS/CAREER NOTES: Selected by Buffalo Sabres in first round (second Sabres pick, 20th overall) of NHL entry draft (June 22, 2002).

		REGULAR SEASON								PLAYOFFS				
Season Team	League	GP	G	A	Pts.	PIM	+/-	PP	SH	GP	G	A	Pts.	PIM
00-01—Guelph	OHL	64	22	31	53	57	...	...	...	4	2	0	2	2
01-02—Guelph	OHL	62	27	30	57	54	...	...	...	9	5	2	7	9
02-03—Guelph	OHL	54	30	27	57	57	...	...	...	11	8	6	14	6
03-04—Guelph	OHL	59	37	43	80	63	...	...	...	22	9	9	18	14
04-05—Rochester	AHL	79	14	15	29	54	4	0	3	9	2	2	4	6

PALFFY, ZIGGY — RW — PENGUINS

PERSONAL: Born May 5, 1972, in Skalica, Czech. ... 5-10/180. ... Shoots left. ... Name pronounced PAL-fee.

TRANSACTIONS/CAREER NOTES: Selected by New York Islanders in 2nd round (2nd Islanders pick, 26th overall) of NHL draft (June 22, 1991). ... Concussion (February 17, 1996); missed one game. ... Sprained shoulder (January 13, 1997); missed two games. ... Missed first 32 games of 1998-99 season in contract dispute. ... Traded by Islanders with C Bryan Smolinski, G Marcel Cousineau and 4th-round pick (C Daniel Johansson) in 1999 draft to Los Angeles Kings for C Olli Jokinen, LW Josh Green, D Mathieu Biron and 1st-round pick (LW Taylor Pyatt) in 1999 draft (June 20, 1999). ... Back spasms (December 4, 1999); missed four games. ... Back spasms (January 4, 2000); missed one game. ... Strained right shoulder (March 15, 2000); missed final 12 games of regular season. ... Strained hamstring (December 16, 2000); missed eight games. ... Flu (January 8, 2001); missed one game. ... Back spasms (October 26, 2001); missed five games. ... Fractured rib (December 1, 2001); missed 14 games. ... Strained groin (October 13, 2002); missed three games. ... Reinjured groin (October 25, 2002); missed three games. ... Suffered facial injury (November 25, 2003); missed five games. ... Dislocated right shoulder (January 8, 2004) and had surgery; missed remainder of season. ... Signed as free agent by Pittsburgh Penguins (Aug. 6, 2005).

STATISTICAL PLATEAUS: Three-goal games: 1995-96 (2), 1996-97 (1), 1997-98 (2), 1998-99 (1), 2000-01 (1), 2001-02 (1). Total: 8.

		REGULAR SEASON								PLAYOFFS				
Season Team	League	GP	G	A	Pts.	PIM	+/-	PP	SH	GP	G	A	Pts.	PIM
90-91—Nitra	Slovakia	50	34	16	50	18	...	...	...	—	—	—	—	—
91-92—Dukla Trencin	Czech.	32	23	25	*48	...	...	...	...	—	—	—	—	—
92-93—Dukla Trencin	Czech.	43	38	41	79	...	...	...	...	—	—	—	—	—
93-94—Salt Lake City	IHL	57	25	32	57	83	1	6	2	—	—	—	—	—
—Slovakian Oly. team	Int'l	8	3	7	10	8	3	0	2	—	—	—	—	—

Season Team	League	REGULAR SEASON GP	G	A	Pts.	PIM	+/-	PP	SH	PLAYOFFS GP	G	A	Pts.	PIM
—New York Islanders	NHL	5	0	0	0	0	-6	0	0	—	—	—	—	—
94-95—Denver	IHL	33	20	23	43	40	8	4	0	—	—	—	—	—
—New York Islanders	NHL	33	10	7	17	6	3	1	0	—	—	—	—	—
95-96—New York Islanders	NHL	81	43	44	87	56	-17	17	1	—	—	—	—	—
96-97—New York Islanders	NHL	80	48	42	90	43	21	6	1	—	—	—	—	—
97-98—New York Islanders	NHL	82	45	42	87	34	-2	*17	2	—	—	—	—	—
98-99—HK 36 Skalica	Slovakia	9	11	8	19	6	...	...	...	—	—	—	—	—
—New York Islanders	NHL	50	22	28	50	34	-6	5	2	—	—	—	—	—
99-00—Los Angeles	NHL	64	27	39	66	32	18	4	0	4	2	0	2	0
00-01—Los Angeles	NHL	73	38	51	89	20	22	12	4	13	3	5	8	8
01-02—Los Angeles	NHL	63	32	27	59	26	5	15	1	7	4	5	9	0
—Slovakian Oly. team	Int'l	1	0	0	0	0	...	...	...	—	—	—	—	—
02-03—Los Angeles	NHL	76	37	48	85	47	22	10	2	—	—	—	—	—
03-04—Los Angeles	NHL	35	16	25	41	12	18	3	3	—	—	—	—	—
04-05—Skalica	Slovakia	8	10	3	13	6	5	...	...	—	—	—	—	—
—Praha	Czech.	41	21	19	40	30	8	...	...	7	5	2	7	2
NHL Totals (11 years)		642	318	353	671	310	78	90	19	24	9	10	19	8

PANDOLFO, JAY — LW — DEVILS

PERSONAL: Born December 27, 1974, in Winchester, Mass. ... 6-1/190. ... Shoots left. ... Brother of Mike Pandolfo, LW, Columbus Blue Jackets.

TRANSACTIONS/CAREER NOTES: Selected by New Jersey Devils in second round (second Devils pick, 32nd overall) of NHL draft (June 26, 1993). ... Flu (January 14, 1999); missed two games. ... Bruised shoulder (March 17, 1999); missed 10 games. ... Facial lacerations (January 29, 2000); missed three games. ... Bruised shoulder (October 14, 2000); missed 13 games. ... Bruised ribs (December 19, 2001); missed six games. ... Bruised hip (January 21, 2002); missed 10 games. ... Injured groin (October 25, 2002); missed three games. ... Aggravated groin injury (November 9, 2003); missed seven games. ... Suffered concussion (January 13, 2003); missed four games.

Season Team	League	REGULAR SEASON GP	G	A	Pts.	PIM	+/-	PP	SH	PLAYOFFS GP	G	A	Pts.	PIM
89-90—Burlington H.S.	Mass. H.S.	23	33	30	63	18	...	...	...	—	—	—	—	—
90-91—Burlington H.S.	Mass. H.S.	20	19	27	46	10	...	...	...	—	—	—	—	—
91-92—Burlington H.S.	Mass. H.S.	20	35	34	69	14	...	...	...	—	—	—	—	—
92-93—Boston University	Hockey East	37	16	22	38	16	...	...	...	—	—	—	—	—
93-94—Boston University	Hockey East	37	17	25	42	27	24	6	1	—	—	—	—	—
94-95—Boston University	Hockey East	20	7	13	20	6	13	1	0	—	—	—	—	—
95-96—Boston University	Hockey East	39	38	29	67	6	...	...	...	—	—	—	—	—
—Albany	AHL	5	3	1	4	0	...	...	...	3	0	0	0	0
96-97—Albany	AHL	12	3	9	12	0	6	0	0	—	—	—	—	—
—New Jersey	NHL	46	6	8	14	6	-1	0	0	6	0	1	1	0
97-98—New Jersey	NHL	23	1	3	4	4	-4	0	0	3	0	2	2	0
—Albany	AHL	51	18	19	37	24	9	3	4	—	—	—	—	—
98-99—New Jersey	NHL	70	14	13	27	10	3	1	1	7	1	0	1	0
99-00—New Jersey	NHL	71	7	8	15	4	0	0	0	23	0	5	5	0
00-01—New Jersey	NHL	63	4	12	16	16	3	0	0	25	1	4	5	4
01-02—New Jersey	NHL	65	4	10	14	15	12	0	1	6	0	0	0	0
02-03—New Jersey	NHL	68	6	11	17	23	12	0	1	24	6	6	12	2
03-04—New Jersey	NHL	82	13	13	26	14	5	1	2	5	0	0	0	0
04-05—Salzburg	Austria	19	5	7	12	0	-9	2	1	—	—	—	—	—
NHL Totals (8 years)		488	55	78	133	92	30	2	5	99	8	18	26	6

PANDOLFO, MIKE — LW — BLUE JACKETS

PERSONAL: Born September 15, 1979, in Winchester, Mass. ... 6-3/218. ... Shoots left. ... Brother of Jay Pandolfo, LW, New Jersey Devils.

TRANSACTIONS/CAREER NOTES: Selected by Buffalo Sabres in third round (fifth Sabres pick, 77th overall) of NHL entry draft (June 27, 1998). ... Traded by Sabres with first-round pick (traded to Atlanta; Thrasher selected C Jim Slater) in 2002 draft to Columbus Blue Jackets for first-round pick (LW Dan Paille) in 2002 draft (June 22, 2002).

Season Team	League	REGULAR SEASON GP	G	A	Pts.	PIM	+/-	PP	SH	PLAYOFFS GP	G	A	Pts.	PIM
96-97—St. Sebastian's	USHS (East)	32	27	28	55	30	...	...	...	—	—	—	—	—
97-98—St. Sebastian's	USHS (East)	28	29	23	52	18	...	...	...	—	—	—	—	—
98-99—Boston University	Hockey East	34	13	4	17	26	...	...	...	—	—	—	—	—
99-00—Boston University	Hockey East	41	13	10	23	37	...	...	...	—	—	—	—	—
00-01—Boston University	Hockey East	37	16	13	29	30	...	...	...	—	—	—	—	—
01-02—Boston University	Hockey East	38	22	18	40	22	...	...	...	—	—	—	—	—
02-03—Syracuse	AHL	74	9	9	18	31	-1	0	1	—	—	—	—	—
03-04—Columbus	NHL	3	0	0	0	0	-2	0	0	—	—	—	—	—
—Syracuse	AHL	77	18	19	37	29	...	...	...	7	1	0	1	2
04-05—Syracuse	AHL	62	8	8	16	18	8	2	1	—	—	—	—	—
NHL Totals (1 year)		3	0	0	0	0	-2	0	0					

PAPINEAU, JUSTIN — C/LW — ISLANDERS

PERSONAL: Born January 15, 1980, in Ottawa. ... 5-11/180. ... Shoots left.

TRANSACTIONS/CAREER NOTES: Selected by Los Angeles Kings in second round (second Kings pick, 46th overall) of NHL draft (June 27, 1998). ... Returned to draft pool by Kings and selected by St. Louis Blues in third round (third Blues pick, 75th overall) of NHL entry draft (June 24, 2000). ... Traded by Blues with second-round pick (C Jeremy Colliton) in 2003 draft to New York Islanders for G Chris Osgood and third-round pick (G Konstantin Barulin) in 2003 draft (March 11, 2003).

P

Season Team	League	GP	G	A	Pts.	PIM	+/-	PP	SH	GP	G	A	Pts.	PIM
		REGULAR SEASON								PLAYOFFS				
95-96—Ottawa	OHA Jr. A	52	31	19	50	51	...	...	...	—	—	—	—	—
96-97—Belleville	OHL	40	10	32	42	32	...	...	...	—	—	—	—	—
97-98—Belleville	OHL	66	41	53	94	34	...	...	...	10	5	9	14	6
98-99—Belleville	OHL	68	52	47	99	28	40	...	...	21	*21	*30	*51	20
99-00—Belleville	OHL	60	40	36	76	52	18	11	4	16	4	12	16	16
00-01—Worcester	AHL	43	7	22	29	33	...	...	...	11	7	3	10	8
01-02—Worcester	AHL	75	38	38	76	86	6	14	3	3	1	2	3	4
—St. Louis	NHL	1	0	0	0	0	-2	0	0	—	—	—	—	—
02-03—St. Louis	NHL	11	2	1	3	0	-1	0	0	—	—	—	—	—
—Worcester	AHL	44	21	17	38	42	2	9	0	—	—	—	—	—
—New York Islanders	NHL	5	1	2	3	4	1	0	0	1	0	0	0	0
—Bridgeport	AHL	5	7	1	8	4	2	3	0	7	1	3	4	7
03-04—New York Islanders	NHL	64	8	5	13	8	4	5	0	—	—	—	—	—
04-05—Bridgeport	AHL	59	18	15	33	52	-5	7	1	—	—	—	—	—
NHL Totals (3 years)		81	11	8	19	12	2	5	0	1	0	0	0	0

PARENT, RYAN — D — PREDATORS

PERSONAL: Born March 19, 1987, in Prince Albert, Saskatchewan. ... 6-2/183. ... Shoots left.
TRANSACTIONS/CAREER NOTES: Selected by Nashville Predators in 1st round (1st Predators pick, 18th overall) of entry draft (July 30, 2005).

Season Team	League	GP	G	A	Pts.	PIM	+/-	PP	SH	GP	G	A	Pts.	PIM
		REGULAR SEASON								PLAYOFFS				
03-04—Guelph	OHL	58	1	5	6	18	...	...	...	—	—	—	—	—
04-05—Guelph	OHL	66	2	17	19	36	5	0	0	4	0	1	1	4

PARENTEAU, PIERRE — C/RW — MIGHTY DUCKS

PERSONAL: Born March 24, 1983, in Hull, Que. ... 5-11/156. ... Shoots right.
TRANSACTIONS/CAREER NOTES: Selected by Anaheim Mighty Ducks in 9th round (11th Ducks pick, 264th overall) of entry draft (June 24, 2001).

Season Team	League	GP	G	A	Pts.	PIM	+/-	PP	SH	GP	G	A	Pts.	PIM
		REGULAR SEASON								PLAYOFFS				
01-02—Chicoutimi	QMJHL	68	51	67	118	120	...	...	...	4	3	1	4	10
02-03—Sherbrooke	QMJHL	28	13	35	48	84	...	...	...	12	8	11	19	6
03-04—Cincinnati	AHL	66	14	16	30	20	...	...	...	7	1	2	3	6
04-05—Cincinnati	AHL	76	17	24	41	58	-1	8	0	9	2	0	2	8

PARISE, ZACH — C — DEVILS

PERSONAL: Born July 28, 1984, in Minneapolis, Minn. ... 5-11/186. ... Shoots left.
TRANSACTIONS/CAREER NOTES: Selected by New Jersey Devils in first round (first Devils pick, 17th overall) in 2003 NHL entry draft (June 23, 2003).

Season Team	League	GP	G	A	Pts.	PIM	+/-	PP	SH	GP	G	A	Pts.	PIM
		REGULAR SEASON								PLAYOFFS				
02-03—Univ. of North Dakota	WCHA	39	26	35	61	34	...	...	...	—	—	—	—	—
03-04—Univ. of North Dakota	WCHA	37	23	32	55	24	...	...	...	—	—	—	—	—
04-05—Albany	AHL	73	18	40	58	56	-11	5	2	—	—	—	—	—

PARK, RICHARD — RW/LW — CANUCKS

PERSONAL: Born May 27, 1976, in Seoul, S. Korea. ... 5-11/190. ... Shoots right.
TRANSACTIONS/CAREER NOTES: Selected by Pittsburgh Penguins in 2nd round (2nd Penguins pick, 50th overall) of NHL draft (June 28, 1994). ... Traded by Penguins to Anaheim Mighty Ducks for RW Roman Oksiuta (March 18, 1997). ... Signed as free agent by Philadelphia Flyers (August 24, 1998). ... Signed as free agent by Minnesota Wild (June 6, 2000). ... Injured knee (October 5, 2003); missed five games. ... Injured elbow (December 18, 2003); missed two games. ... Signed as free agent by Vancouver Canucks (Aug. 8, 2005).

Season Team	League	GP	G	A	Pts.	PIM	+/-	PP	SH	GP	G	A	Pts.	PIM
		REGULAR SEASON								PLAYOFFS				
91-92—Williams Lake	PCJHL	76	49	58	107	91	...	...	...	—	—	—	—	—
92-93—Belleville	OHL	66	23	38	61	38	...	...	...	5	0	0	0	14
93-94—Belleville	OHL	59	27	49	76	70	...	10	...	12	3	5	8	18
94-95—Belleville	OHL	45	28	51	79	35	...	6	2	16	9	18	27	12
—Pittsburgh	NHL	1	0	1	1	2	1	0	0	3	0	0	0	2
95-96—Belleville	OHL	6	7	6	13	2	...	...	...	14	18	12	30	10
—Pittsburgh	NHL	56	4	6	10	36	3	0	1	1	0	0	0	0
96-97—Cleveland	IHL	50	12	15	27	30	...	...	...	—	—	—	—	—
—Pittsburgh	NHL	1	0	0	0	0	-1	0	0	—	—	—	—	—
—Anaheim	NHL	11	1	1	2	10	0	0	0	11	0	1	1	2
97-98—Cincinnati	AHL	56	17	26	43	36	-10	4	3	—	—	—	—	—
—Anaheim	NHL	15	0	2	2	8	-3	0	0	—	—	—	—	—
98-99—Philadelphia	AHL	75	41	42	83	33	32	11	8	16	9	6	15	4
—Philadelphia	NHL	7	0	0	0	0	-1	0	0	—	—	—	—	—
99-00—Utah	IHL	82	28	32	60	36	...	...	...	5	1	0	1	0
00-01—Cleveland	IHL	75	27	21	48	29	...	...	...	4	0	2	2	4
01-02—Houston	AHL	13	4	10	14	6	7	1	1	—	—	—	—	—

Season Team	League	GP	G	A	Pts.	PIM	+/-	PP	SH	GP	G	A	Pts.	PIM
		REGULAR SEASON								PLAYOFFS				
—Minnesota	NHL	63	10	15	25	10	-1	2	1	—	—	—	—	—
02-03—Minnesota	NHL	81	14	10	24	16	-3	2	2	18	3	3	6	4
03-04—Minnesota	NHL	73	13	12	25	28	0	4	0	—	—	—	—	—
04-05—Malmo	Sweden	9	1	3	4	4	2	0	0	—	—	—	—	—
—SC Langnau	Switzerland	10	3	0	3	8	...	1	0	6	4	1	5	6
NHL Totals (8 years)		308	42	47	89	110	-5	8	4	33	3	4	7	8

PARKER, SCOTT — RW — SHARKS

PERSONAL: Born January 29, 1978, in Hanford, Calif. ... 6-5/230. ... Shoots right.

TRANSACTIONS/CAREER NOTES: Selected by New Jersey Devils in third round (sixth Devils pick, 63rd overall) of NHL entry draft (June 22, 1996). ... Returned to draft pool by Devils; selected by Colorado Avalanche in first round (fourth Avalanche pick, 20th overall) of NHL entry draft (June 27, 1998). ... Bruised shoulder (December 11, 2000); missed four games. ... Bruised foot (February 17, 2001); missed three games. ... Suspended two games by NHL for unsportsmanlike conduct (October 15, 2001). ... Injured thumb and fractured nose (January 28, 2002); missed one game. ... Injured hand (November 25, 2002); missed two games. ... Fractured foot (December 23, 2002); missed 16 games. ... Injured arm (February 23, 2003); missed one game. ... Traded by Avalanche to San Jose Sharks for 2003 fifth-round pick (C Brad Richardson); (June 21, 2003). ... Flu (December 6, 2003); missed one game. ... Injured hip (December 26, 2003); missed three games. ... Reinjured hip (January 2, 2004); missed three games. ... Fractured forearm (January 15, 2004); missed one game. ... Reinjured hip (January 22, 2004); missed five games. ... Injured hand (March 20, 2004); missed remainder of season.

Season Team	League	GP	G	A	Pts.	PIM	+/-	PP	SH	GP	G	A	Pts.	PIM
		REGULAR SEASON								PLAYOFFS				
94-95—Spokane	KIJHL	43	7	21	28	128	...	...	...	—	—	—	—	—
95-96—Kelowna	WHL	64	3	4	7	159	...	...	...	6	0	0	0	12
96-97—Kelowna	WHL	68	18	8	26	*330	-14	6	0	6	0	2	2	4
97-98—Kelowna	WHL	71	30	22	52	243	-4	12	0	7	6	0	6	23
98-99—Hershey	AHL	32	4	3	7	143	-7	0	0	4	0	0	0	6
—Colorado	NHL	27	0	0	0	71	-3	0	0	—	—	—	—	—
99-00—Hershey	AHL	68	12	7	19	206	...	...	...	11	1	1	2	56
00-01—Colorado	NHL	69	2	3	5	155	-2	0	0	4	0	0	0	2
01-02—Colorado	NHL	63	1	4	5	154	0	0	0	—	—	—	—	—
02-03—Colorado	NHL	43	1	3	4	82	6	0	0	1	0	0	0	2
03-04—San Jose	NHL	50	1	3	4	101	0	0	0	—	—	—	—	—
NHL Totals (5 years)		252	5	13	18	563	1	0	0	5	0	0	0	4

PARRISH, MARK — RW — ISLANDERS

PERSONAL: Born February 2, 1977, in Edina, Minn. ... 6-0/200. ... Shoots right.

TRANSACTIONS/CAREER NOTES: Selected by Colorado Avalanche in third round (third Avalanche pick, 79th overall) of NHL entry draft (June 22, 1996). ... Rights traded by Avalanche with third-round pick (D Lance Ward) in 1998 draft to Florida Panthers for RW/C Tom Fitzgerald (March 24, 1998). ... Strained back (February 14, 2000); missed one game. ... Traded by Panthers with LW Oleg Kvasha to New York Islanders for C Olli Jokinen and G Roberto Luongo (June 24, 2000). ... Sprained medial collateral ligament in right knee (February 9, 2001); missed 12 games. ... Injured ribs (January 15, 2002); missed four games. ... Flu (November 27, 2002); missed one game. ... Sprained ankle (January 1, 2004); missed 23 games.

STATISTICAL PLATEAUS: Three-goal games: 2001-02 (2), 2002-03 (1). Total: 3. ... Four-goal games: 1998-99 (1). ... Total hat tricks: 4.

Season Team	League	GP	G	A	Pts.	PIM	+/-	PP	SH	GP	G	A	Pts.	PIM
		REGULAR SEASON								PLAYOFFS				
94-95—Thomas Jefferson	Minn. H.S.	27	40	20	60	42	...	...	...	—	—	—	—	—
95-96—St. Cloud State	WCHA	38	15	14	29	28	...	...	...	—	—	—	—	—
96-97—St. Cloud State	WCHA	35	27	15	42	60	...	11	2	—	—	—	—	—
97-98—Seattle	WHL	54	54	38	92	29	...	...	...	5	2	3	5	2
—New Haven	AHL	1	1	0	1	2	-1	0	0	—	—	—	—	—
98-99—Florida	NHL	73	24	13	37	25	-6	5	0	—	—	—	—	—
—New Haven	AHL	2	1	0	1	0	1	0	0	—	—	—	—	—
99-00—Florida	NHL	81	26	18	44	39	1	6	0	4	0	1	1	0
00-01—New York Islanders	NHL	70	17	13	30	28	-27	6	0	—	—	—	—	—
01-02—New York Islanders	NHL	78	30	30	60	32	10	9	1	7	2	1	3	6
02-03—New York Islanders	NHL	81	23	25	48	28	-11	9	0	5	1	0	1	4
03-04—New York Islanders	NHL	59	24	11	35	18	8	6	0	5	1	2	3	0
NHL Totals (6 years)		442	144	110	254	170	-25	41	1	21	4	4	8	10

PARROS, GEORGE — RW — KINGS

PERSONAL: Born December 29, 1979, in Washington, Pa. ... 6-4/210. ... Shoots right.

TRANSACTIONS/CAREER NOTES: Selected by Los Angeles Kings in eighth round (ninth Kings pick, 222nd overall) of NHL entry draft (June 24, 1999).

Season Team	League	GP	G	A	Pts.	PIM	+/-	PP	SH	GP	G	A	Pts.	PIM
		REGULAR SEASON								PLAYOFFS				
99-00—Princeton	ECAC	27	4	2	6	14	...	...	...	—	—	—	—	—
00-01—Princeton	ECAC	31	7	10	17	38	...	...	...	—	—	—	—	—
01-02—Princeton	ECAC	31	9	13	22	38	...	...	...	—	—	—	—	—
02-03—Princeton	ECAC	22	0	7	7	29	...	...	...	—	—	—	—	—
—Manchester	AHL	9	0	1	1	7	...	...	...	—	—	—	—	—
03-04—Manchester	AHL	57	3	6	9	126	...	...	...	5	0	0	0	4
04-05—Manchester	AHL	—	—	—	—	—	—	—	—	...	...	...	...	...
—Manchester	AHL	67	14	8	22	247	2	2	4	6	1	1	2	27
—Reading	ECHL	3	0	0	0	9	-2	0	0	—	—	—	—	—

PASSMORE, STEVE — G — BLACKHAWKS

PERSONAL: Born January 29, 1973, in Thunder Bay, Ont. ... 5-9/165. ... Catches left.

TRANSACTIONS/CAREER NOTES: Selected by Quebec Nordiques in ninth round (10th Nordiques pick, 196th overall) of NHL entry draft (June 20, 1992). ... Traded by Nordiques to Edmonton Oilers for D Brad Werenka (March 21, 1994). ... Signed as free agent by Chicago Blackhawks (July 7, 1999). ... Traded by Blackhawks to Los Angeles Kings for fourth-round pick (D Olli Malmivaara) in 2000 draft (May 1, 2000). ... Traded by Kings to Blackhawks for eighth-round pick (D Mike Gabinet) in 2001 draft (February 28, 2001). ... Sprained knee (November 2, 2001); missed two games. ... Had hip surgery (February 17, 2004); missed remainder of season. ... Signed as free agent by Adler Mannheim of the German league (August 30, 2004).

		REGULAR SEASON									PLAYOFFS							
Season Team	League	GP	Min.	W	L	T	GA	SO	GAA	SV%	GP	Min.	W	L	GA	SO	GAA	SV%
88-89—Tri-City	WHL	1	60	0	1	0	6	0	6.00	...	—	—	—	—	—	—	—	—
89-90—Tri-City	WHL	4	215	...	...	...	17	0	4.74	...	—	—	—	—	—	—	—	—
90-91—Victoria	WHL	35	1838	3	25	1	190	0	6.20	...	—	—	—	—	—	—	—	—
91-92—Victoria	WHL	*71	*4228	15	50	7	347	0	4.92	...	—	—	—	—	—	—	—	—
92-93—Victoria	WHL	43	2402	14	24	2	150	1	3.75	...	—	—	—	—	—	—	—	—
—Kamloops	WHL	25	1479	19	6	0	69	1	2.80	...	7	401	4	2	22	1	3.29	...
93-94—Kamloops	WHL	36	1927	22	9	2	88	1	*2.74	.909	18	1099	11	7	60	0	3.28	.900
94-95—Cape Breton	AHL	25	1455	8	13	3	93	0	3.84	.890	—	—	—	—	—	—	—	—
95-96—Cape Breton	AHL	2	90	1	0	0	2	0	1.33	...	—	—	—	—	—	—	—	—
96-97—Raleigh	ECHL	2	118	1	1	0	13	0	6.61	...	—	—	—	—	—	—	—	—
—Hamilton	AHL	27	1568	12	12	3	70	1	2.68	.901	22	1325	12	*10	*61	2	2.76	.911
97-98—Hamilton	AHL	27	1656	11	10	6	87	2	3.15	.900	3	133	0	2	14	0	6.32	.803
—San Antonio	IHL	14	737	3	8	2	56	0	4.56	.878	—	—	—	—	—	—	—	—
98-99—Hamilton	AHL	54	3148	24	21	7	117	4	2.23	.929	11	680	5	6	31	0	2.74	.919
—Edmonton	NHL	6	362	1	4	1	17	0	2.82	.907	—	—	—	—	—	—	—	—
99-00—Chicago	NHL	24	1388	7	12	3	63	1	2.72	.904	—	—	—	—	—	—	—	—
—Cleveland	IHL	2	120	1	0	1	3	1	1.50	...	—	—	—	—	—	—	—	—
00-01—Lowell	AHL	6	333	2	4	0	24	0	4.32	.848	—	—	—	—	—	—	—	—
—Los Angeles	NHL	14	718	3	8	1	37	1	3.09	.881	—	—	—	—	—	—	—	—
—Chicago	IHL	6	340	2	2	2	22	0	3.88	...	—	—	—	—	—	—	—	—
—Chicago	NHL	6	340	0	4	1	14	0	2.47	.905	—	—	—	—	—	—	—	—
01-02—Chicago	NHL	23	1142	8	5	4	43	0	2.26	.904	3	138	0	2	6	0	2.61	.903
—Norfolk	AHL	2	120	2	0	0	6	0	3.00	.908	—	—	—	—	—	—	—	—
02-03—Norfolk	AHL	14	831	4	7	2	33	2	2.38	.906	—	—	—	—	—	—	—	—
—Chicago	NHL	11	617	2	5	2	38	0	3.70	.866	—	—	—	—	—	—	—	—
03-04—Chicago	NHL	9	478	2	6	0	23	0	2.89	.896	—	—	—	—	—	—	—	—
—Norfolk	AHL	15	889	3	10	2	39	2	2.63	.888	—	—	—	—	—	—	—	—
04-05—Mannheim	Germany	21	1109	...	...	...	48	0	2.59	.916	0	0	...	...	0	0	0.00	...
NHL Totals (6 years)		93	5045	23	44	12	235	2	2.79	.895	3	138	0	2	6	0	2.61	.903

PATRICK, JAMES — D — SABRES

PERSONAL: Born June 14, 1963, in Winnipeg, Man. ... 6-2/198. ... Shoots right. ... Brother of Steve Patrick, RW with three NHL teams (1980-86).

TRANSACTIONS/CAREER NOTES: Selected by New York Rangers in first round (first Rangers pick, ninth overall) of NHL entry draft (June 10, 1981). ... Injured groin (October 1984). ... Pinched nerve (December 15, 1985). ... Strained left knee ligaments (March 1988). ... Bruised shoulder and chest (December 1988). ... Pulled groin (March 13, 1989). ... Sprained shoulder (November 4, 1992); missed three games. ... Bruised right shoulder (November 27, 1992); missed three games. ... Sprained left knee (January 27, 1993); missed four games. ... Herniated disc (February 24, 1993); missed two games. ... Herniated disc (March 28, 1993); missed remainder of season. ... Traded by Rangers with C Darren Turcotte to Hartford Whalers for RW Steve Larmer, LW Nick Kypreos and sixth-round pick (C Yuri Litvinov) in 1994 draft (November 2, 1993). ... Herniated disc (December 7, 1993); missed five games. ... Traded by Whalers with C Michael Nylander and D Zarley Zalapski to Calgary Flames for D Gary Suter, LW Paul Ranheim and C Ted Drury (March 10, 1994). ... Strained left hip (March 10, 1995); missed five games. ... Suffered concussion (April 9, 1996); missed two games. ... Injured back (October 16, 1996); missed one game. ... Strained knee (October 24, 1996); missed five games. ... Suffered concussion (November 20, 1996); missed two games. ... Knee surgery (December 12, 1996); missed remainder of season. ... Strained neck (October 22, 1997); missed six games. ... Reinjured neck (November 13, 1997); missed nine games. ... Charley horse (January 5, 1998); missed one game. ... Signed as free agent by Buffalo Sabres (October 7, 1998). ... Suffered pinched nerve in neck (October 10, 1998); missed three games. ... Suffered concussion (February 24, 1999); missed one game. ... Back spasms (February 17, 2000); missed two games. ... Injured shoulder (September 23, 2000); missed first five games of season. ... Injured head (November 27, 2001); missed one game. ... Back spasms (December 10, 2002); missed four games. ... Back spasms (February 28, 2003); missed six games. ... Injured groin (December 30, 2003); missed two games. ... Facial cuts and infection (January 6, 2004); missed four games. ... Injured neck (January 25, 2004); missed 15 games.

		REGULAR SEASON								PLAYOFFS				
Season Team	League	GP	G	A	Pts.	PIM	+/-	PP	SH	GP	G	A	Pts.	PIM
80-81—Prince Albert	SJHL	59	21	61	82	162	...	...	...	4	1	6	7	0
81-82—North Dakota	WCHA	42	5	24	29	26	...	...	...	—	—	—	—	—
82-83—North Dakota	WCHA	36	12	36	48	29	...	...	...	—	—	—	—	—
83-84—Can. Olympic team	Int'l	63	7	24	31	52	...	...	...	—	—	—	—	—
—New York Rangers	NHL	12	1	7	8	2	6	0	0	5	0	3	3	2
84-85—New York Rangers	NHL	75	8	28	36	71	-17	4	1	3	0	0	0	4
85-86—New York Rangers	NHL	75	14	29	43	88	14	2	1	16	1	5	6	34
86-87—New York Rangers	NHL	78	10	45	55	62	13	5	0	6	1	2	3	2
87-88—New York Rangers	NHL	70	17	45	62	52	16	9	0	—	—	—	—	—
88-89—New York Rangers	NHL	68	11	36	47	41	3	6	0	4	0	1	1	2
89-90—New York Rangers	NHL	73	14	43	57	50	4	9	0	10	3	8	11	0
90-91—New York Rangers	NHL	74	10	49	59	58	-5	6	0	6	0	0	0	6
91-92—New York Rangers	NHL	80	14	57	71	54	34	6	0	13	0	7	7	12
92-93—New York Rangers	NHL	60	5	21	26	61	1	3	0	—	—	—	—	—

Season Team	League	REGULAR SEASON GP	G	A	Pts.	PIM	+/-	PP	SH	PLAYOFFS GP	G	A	Pts.	PIM
93-94—New York Rangers	NHL	6	0	3	3	2	1	0	0	—	—	—	—	—
—Hartford	NHL	47	8	20	28	32	-12	4	1	—	—	—	—	—
—Calgary	NHL	15	2	2	4	6	6	1	0	7	0	1	1	6
94-95—Calgary	NHL	43	0	10	10	14	-3	0	0	5	0	1	1	0
95-96—Calgary	NHL	80	3	32	35	30	3	1	0	4	0	0	0	2
96-97—Calgary	NHL	19	3	1	4	6	2	1	0	—	—	—	—	—
97-98—Calgary	NHL	60	6	11	17	26	-2	1	0	—	—	—	—	—
98-99—Buffalo	NHL	45	1	7	8	16	12	0	0	20	0	1	1	12
99-00—Buffalo	NHL	66	5	8	13	22	8	0	0	5	0	1	1	2
00-01—Buffalo	NHL	54	4	9	13	12	9	1	0	13	1	2	3	2
01-02—Buffalo	NHL	56	5	8	13	16	3	1	0	—	—	—	—	—
02-03—Buffalo	NHL	69	4	12	16	26	-3	2	0	—	—	—	—	—
03-04—Buffalo	NHL	55	4	7	11	12	11	0	0	—	—	—	—	—
NHL Totals (21 years)		1280	149	490	639	759	104	62	3	117	6	32	38	86

PATZOLD, DIMITRI — G — SHARKS

PERSONAL: Born February 3, 1983, in Ust-Kamenogorsk, U.S.S.R. ... 6-0/183. ... Catches left.
TRANSACTIONS/CAREER NOTES: Selected by San Jose Sharks in first round (third Sharks pick, 107th overall) of NHL draft (June 23, 2001).

Season Team	League	REGULAR SEASON GP	Min.	W	L	T	GA	SO	GAA	SV%	PLAYOFFS GP	Min.	W	L	GA	SO	GAA	SV%
00-01—Erding	German Jr.	23	1311	...	...	...	85	...	3.89	...	—	—	—	—	—	—	—	—
01-02—Kolner Haie	Germany	7	260	...	...	...	16	0	3.69	...	—	—	—	—	—	—	—	—
02-03—Mannheim	Germany	15	817	...	...	...	35	...	2.57	...	2	34	...	...	2	0	3.53	...
03-04—Cleveland	AHL	27	1458	10	15	0	70	3	2.88	.907	—	—	—	—	—	—	—	—
—Johnstown	ECHL	8	442	7	0	0	20	0	2.71	.898	1	59	0	1	2	0	2.03	.933
04-05—Cleveland	AHL	41	2418	18	16	...	104	1	2.58	.911	—	—	—	—	—	—	—	—

PAUL, JEFF — D — CAPITALS

PERSONAL: Born March 1, 1978, in London, Ont. ... 6-4/225. ... Shoots right.
TRANSACTIONS/CAREER NOTES: Selected by Chicago Blackhawks in second round (second Blackhawks pick, 42nd overall) of NHL entry draft (June 22, 1996). ... Signed as free agent by Colorado Avalanche (August 8, 2002). ... Injured ribs (October 22, 2002); missed five games. ... Signed as free agent by Florida Panthers (August 19, 2003). ... Traded by Panthers to New York Rangers for LW Jeff Healey (March 9, 2004). ... Signed as free agent by Washington Capitals (August 2, 2004).

Season Team	League	REGULAR SEASON GP	G	A	Pts.	PIM	+/-	PP	SH	PLAYOFFS GP	G	A	Pts.	PIM
94-95—Niagara Falls	OHL	57	3	10	13	64	...	...	...	6	0	2	2	0
95-96—Niagara Falls	OHL	48	1	7	8	81	...	...	...	10	0	4	4	37
96-97—Erie	OHL	60	4	23	27	152	-9	1	0	5	2	0	2	12
97-98—Erie	OHL	48	3	17	20	108	3	...	...	7	0	2	2	13
98-99—Portland	AHL	6	0	0	0	4	-1	0	0	—	—	—	—	—
—Indianapolis	IHL	55	0	7	7	120	3	0	0	7	0	2	2	12
99-00—Cleveland	IHL	69	6	6	12	210	...	...	...	9	1	0	1	12
00-01—Norfolk	AHL	59	5	6	11	171	...	...	...	9	0	2	2	12
01-02—Hershey	AHL	58	1	13	14	201	-5	0	0	7	0	1	1	6
02-03—Hershey	AHL	50	2	3	5	123	-9	1	0	—	—	—	—	—
—Colorado	NHL	2	0	0	0	7	0	0	0	—	—	—	—	—
03-04—San Antonio	AHL	57	2	6	8	174	2	0	0	—	—	—	—	—
—Hartford	AHL	17	0	5	5	38	6	0	0	15	1	2	3	31
04-05—Portland	AHL	54	1	2	3	137	-13	0	0	—	—	—	—	—
NHL Totals (1 year)		2	0	0	0	7	0	0	0					

PAVELEC, ONDREJ — G — THRASHERS

PERSONAL: Born August 31, 1987, in Czech Republic. ... 6-2/180. ... Catches left.

Season Team	League	REGULAR SEASON GP	Min.	W	L	T	GA	SO	GAA	SV%	PLAYOFFS GP	Min.	W	L	GA	SO	GAA	SV%
03-04—HC Kladno	Czech Rep.	38	...	...	...	...	...	...	2.22	.922	—	—	—	—	—	—	—	—
04-05—HC Kladno	Czech Rep.	39	...	...	...	...	...	...	2.30	.930	—	—	—	—	—	—	—	—

PAYER, SERGE — C

PERSONAL: Born May 9, 1979, in Rockland, Ont. ... 6-0/191. ... Shoots left.
TRANSACTIONS/CAREER NOTES: Signed as free agent by Florida Panthers (October 2, 1997). ... Traded by Panthers to Ottawa Senators for a ninth-round pick (D Luke Beaverson) in 2004 draft (September 10, 2003). ... Signed as free agent by Panthers (July 23, 2004). ... Signed as free agent by San Antonio of the AHL (September 26, 2004).

Season Team	League	REGULAR SEASON GP	G	A	Pts.	PIM	+/-	PP	SH	PLAYOFFS GP	G	A	Pts.	PIM
95-96—Kitchener	OHL	66	8	16	24	18	...	...	...	12	0	2	2	2
96-97—Kitchener	OHL	63	7	16	23	27	...	...	...	13	1	3	4	2
97-98—Kitchener	OHL	44	20	21	41	51	...	...	...	6	3	0	3	7
98-99—Kitchener	OHL	40	18	19	37	22	10	...	...	—	—	—	—	—

Season Team	League	REGULAR SEASON GP	G	A	Pts.	PIM	+/-	PP	SH	PLAYOFFS GP	G	A	Pts.	PIM
99-00—Kitchener	OHL	44	10	26	36	53	-11	2	0	5	0	3	3	6
00-01—Louisville	AHL	32	6	6	12	15	...	...	...	—	—	—	—	—
—Florida	NHL	43	5	1	6	21	0	0	1	—	—	—	—	—
01-02—Utah	AHL	20	6	2	8	9	-2	3	0	—	—	—	—	—
02-03—San Antonio	AHL	78	10	31	41	30	9	2	3	1	0	0	0	2
03-04—Ottawa	NHL	5	0	1	1	2	1	0	0	—	—	—	—	—
—Binghamton	AHL	67	14	21	35	91	-6	4	3	2	0	0	0	0
04-05—San Antonio	AHL	3	1	1	2	4	0	0	0	—	—	—	—	—
NHL Totals (2 years)		48	5	2	7	23	1	0	1					

PEAT STEPHEN RW CAPITALS

PERSONAL: Born March 10, 1980, in Princeton, B.C. ... 6-2/226. ... Shoots right.

TRANSACTIONS/CAREER NOTES: Selected by Mighty Ducks of Anaheim in second round (second Mighty Ducks pick, 32nd overall) of NHL entry draft (June 27, 1998). ... Traded by Mighty Ducks to Washington Capitals for fourth-round pick (RW Michel Ouellet) in 2000 draft (June 1, 2000). ... Strained groin (January 30, 2002); missed six games. ... Injured hand (November 9, 2002); missed 21 games. ... Injured foot (October 9, 2003); missed two games. ... Flu (January 23, 2004); missed one game.

Season Team	League	REGULAR SEASON GP	G	A	Pts.	PIM	+/-	PP	SH	PLAYOFFS GP	G	A	Pts.	PIM
95-96—Red Deer	WHL	1	0	0	0	0	...	...	...	—	—	—	—	—
96-97—Red Deer	WHL	68	3	14	17	161	...	...	...	16	0	2	2	22
97-98—Red Deer	WHL	63	6	12	18	189	...	...	...	5	0	0	0	8
98-99—Red Deer	WHL	31	2	6	8	98	...	...	...	—	—	—	—	—
—Tri-City	WHL	5	0	0	0	19	...	...	...	—	—	—	—	—
99-00—Tri-City	WHL	12	0	2	2	48	...	...	...	—	—	—	—	—
—Calgary	WHL	23	0	8	8	100	19	0	0	13	0	1	1	33
00-01—Portland	AHL	6	0	0	0	16	...	...	...	—	—	—	—	—
01-02—Washington	NHL	38	2	2	4	85	-1	0	0	—	—	—	—	—
—Portland	AHL	17	2	2	4	57	-2	0	0	—	—	—	—	—
02-03—Portland	AHL	18	0	0	0	52	-5	0	0	—	—	—	—	—
—Washington	NHL	27	1	0	1	57	-3	0	0	—	—	—	—	—
03-04—Washington	NHL	64	5	0	5	90	-10	0	0	—	—	—	—	—
04-05—Danbury	UHL	7	0	1	1	45	-1	0	0	—	—	—	—	—
NHL Totals (3 years)		129	8	2	10	232	-14	0	0					

PECA MICHAEL C OILERS

PERSONAL: Born March 26, 1974, in Toronto. ... 5-11/183. ... Shoots right. ... Name pronounced PEH-kuh.

TRANSACTIONS/CAREER NOTES: Selected by Vancouver Canucks in 2nd round (2nd Canucks pick, 40th overall) of NHL draft (June 20, 1992). ... Fractured cheekbone (February 9, 1995); missed 12 games. ... Injured wrist (April 26, 1995); missed one game. ... Traded by Canucks with D Mike Wilson and 1st-round pick (D Jay McKee) in 1995 draft to Buffalo Sabres for RW Alexander Mogilny and 5th-round pick (LW Todd Norman) in 1995 draft (July 8, 1995). ... Strained back (October 29, 1995); missed six games. ... Bruised sternum (December 2, 1995); missed one game. ... Sprained right knee (March 18, 1996); missed seven games. ... Injured shoulder (November 27, 1996); missed three games. ... Missed first 11 games of 1997-98 season in contract dispute. ... Injured hip (November 6, 1997); missed three games. ... Suspended three games and fined $1,000 for elbowing incident (March 27, 1998). ... Reinjured hip (April 8, 1998); missed two games. ... Sprained knee (April 15, 1998); missed final two games of season and two playoff games. ... Dislocated shoulder (March 5, 2000); missed seven games. ... Suspended two games for elbowing incident (March 25, 2000). ... Missed 2000-01 season in contract dispute. ... Traded by Sabres to New York Islanders for C Tim Connolly and LW Taylor Pyatt (June 24, 2001). ... Concussion (October 11, 2001); missed two games. ... Injured shoulder (October 19, 2002); missed 10 games. ... Injured knee (November 4, 2002); missed five games. ... Strained groin (December 31, 2003); missed one game. ... Injured left leg (February 27, 2004); missed two games. ... Traded by Islanders to Edmonton Oilers for C Mike York and conditional pick in 2006 (Aug. 3, 2005).

STATISTICAL PLATEAUS: Three-goal games: 1999-00 (1).

Season Team	League	REGULAR SEASON GP	G	A	Pts.	PIM	+/-	PP	SH	PLAYOFFS GP	G	A	Pts.	PIM
90-91—Sudbury	OHL	62	14	27	41	24	...	...	...	5	1	0	1	7
91-92—Sudbury	OHL	39	16	34	50	61	...	...	...	—	—	—	—	—
—Ottawa	OHL	27	8	17	25	32	...	...	...	11	6	10	16	6
92-93—Ottawa	OHL	55	38	64	102	80	...	...	...	—	—	—	—	—
—Hamilton	AHL	9	6	3	9	11	3	1	0	—	—	—	—	—
93-94—Ottawa	OHL	55	50	63	113	101	...	14	3	17	7	22	29	30
—Vancouver	NHL	4	0	0	0	2	-1	0	0	—	—	—	—	—
94-95—Syracuse	AHL	35	10	24	34	75	5	4	0	—	—	—	—	—
—Vancouver	NHL	33	6	6	12	30	-6	2	0	5	0	1	1	8
95-96—Buffalo	NHL	68	11	20	31	67	-1	4	3	—	—	—	—	—
96-97—Buffalo	NHL	79	20	29	49	80	26	5	*6	10	0	2	2	8
97-98—Buffalo	NHL	61	18	22	40	57	12	6	5	13	3	2	5	8
98-99—Buffalo	NHL	82	27	29	56	81	7	10	0	21	5	8	13	18
99-00—Buffalo	NHL	73	20	21	41	67	6	2	0	5	0	1	1	4
00-01—Buffalo	NHL	Did not play												
01-02—New York Islanders	NHL	80	25	35	60	62	19	3	6	5	1	0	1	2
—Can. Olympic team	Int'l	6	0	2	2	2	...	...	...	—	—	—	—	—
02-03—New York Islanders	NHL	66	13	29	42	43	-4	4	2	5	0	0	0	4
03-04—New York Islanders	NHL	76	11	29	40	71	17	0	1	5	0	0	0	6
NHL Totals (11 years)		622	151	220	371	560	75	36	23	69	9	14	23	58

P

PECKER, CORY — C

PERSONAL: Born March 20, 1981, in Montreal. ... 6-0/190. ... Shoots right.
TRANSACTIONS/CAREER NOTES: Selected by Calgary Flames in sixth round (seventh Flames pick, 166th overall) of NHL entry draft (June 26, 1999). ... Signed as free agent by Mighty Ducks of Anaheim (July 8, 2002).

		REGULAR SEASON								PLAYOFFS				
Season Team	**League**	**GP**	**G**	**A**	**Pts.**	**PIM**	**+/-**	**PP**	**SH**	**GP**	**G**	**A**	**Pts.**	**PIM**
97-98—Sault Ste. Marie	OHL	29	3	4	7	15	...	...	...	—	—	—	—	—
98-99—Sault Ste. Marie	OHL	68	25	34	59	24	...	...	...	5	1	2	3	2
99-00—Sault Ste. Marie	OHL	65	33	36	69	38	4	8	3	12	6	8	14	8
00-01—Sault Ste. Marie	OHL	31	24	16	40	37	...	...	...	—	—	—	—	—
—Erie	OHL	30	17	22	39	32	...	...	...	15	*14	9	23	16
01-02—Erie	OHL	56	53	46	99	108	...	...	...	21	*25	17	*42	36
02-03—Cincinnati	AHL	77	20	13	33	66	-5	3	0	—	—	—	—	—
03-04—Cincinnati	AHL	54	6	10	16	32	-14	1	0	—	—	—	—	—
—Binghamton	AHL	14	3	5	8	27	-5	3	0	1	0	0	0	0
04-05—Cincinnati	AHL	49	4	8	12	51	-2	0	0	—	—	—	—	—
—Manitoba	AHL	12	1	1	2	8	-2	1	0	5	1	0	1	4
—San Diego	ECHL	3	1	0	1	0	-2	0	...	—	—	—	—	—

PELECH, MATT — D — FLAMES

PERSONAL: Born September 4, 1987, in Toronto. ... 6-3/220. ... Shoots right.
TRANSACTIONS/CAREER NOTES: Selected by the Calgary Flames in the 1st round (1st Flames pick, 26th overall) of entry draft (July 20, 2005).

		REGULAR SEASON								PLAYOFFS				
Season Team	**League**	**GP**	**G**	**A**	**Pts.**	**PIM**	**+/-**	**PP**	**SH**	**GP**	**G**	**A**	**Pts.**	**PIM**
03-04—Sarnia	OHL	62	4	6	10	39	...	...	...	5	0	1	1	12
04-05—Sarnia	OHL	31	1	5	6	74	-4	0	0	—	—	—	—	—

PELLERIN, SCOTT — LW — BLUES

PERSONAL: Born January 9, 1970, in Shediac, N.B. ... 5-11/190. ... Shoots left. ... Name pronounced PEHL-ih-rihn.
TRANSACTIONS/CAREER NOTES: Selected by New Jersey Devils in third round (fourth Devils pick, 47th overall) of NHL entry draft (June 17, 1989). ... Signed as free agent by St. Louis Blues (July 3, 1996). ... Sore ankle (March 9, 1998); missed one game. ... Suffered concussion (November 28, 1998); missed one game. ... Flu (February 3, 2000); missed one game. ... Selected by Minnesota Wild in NHL expansion draft (June 23, 2000). ... Bruised shoulder (November 10, 2000); missed three games. ... Flu (January 14, 2001); missed one game. ... Traded by Wild to Carolina Hurricanes for LW Askhat Rakhmatullin, third-round pick (traded to New York Rangers; Rangers selected C Garth Murray) in 2001 draft and fifth-round pick (C Armands Berzins) in 2002 draft (March 1, 2001). ... Signed as free agent by Boston Bruins (July 26, 2001). ... Injured eye (November 15, 2001); missed four games. ... Traded by Bruins to Dallas Stars for C Benoit Hogue (January 13, 2002). ... Traded by Stars with conditional pick in 2004 draft to Phoenix Coyotes for RW Claude Lemieux (January 16, 2003). ... Signed as free agent by Washington Capitals (October 8, 2003); released (November 4, 2003). ... Signed by Blues as free agent (December 22, 2003).

		REGULAR SEASON								PLAYOFFS				
Season Team	**League**	**GP**	**G**	**A**	**Pts.**	**PIM**	**+/-**	**PP**	**SH**	**GP**	**G**	**A**	**Pts.**	**PIM**
86-87—Notre Dame H.S.	SASK. H.S.	72	62	68	130	98	...	...	...	—	—	—	—	—
87-88—Notre Dame	SJHL	57	37	49	86	139	...	...	...	—	—	—	—	—
88-89—Maine	Hockey East	45	29	33	62	92	...	...	...	—	—	—	—	—
89-90—Maine	Hockey East	42	22	34	56	68	...	...	...	—	—	—	—	—
90-91—Maine	Hockey East	43	23	25	48	60	...	...	...	—	—	—	—	—
91-92—Maine	Hockey East	37	32	25	57	54	...	...	...	—	—	—	—	—
—Utica	AHL	...	...	...	...	...	...	...	...	3	1	0	1	0
92-93—Utica	AHL	27	15	18	33	33	2	4	0	2	0	1	1	0
—New Jersey	NHL	45	10	11	21	41	-1	1	2	—	—	—	—	—
93-94—Albany	IHL	73	28	46	74	84	...	...	...	5	2	1	3	11
—New Jersey	NHL	1	0	0	0	2	0	0	0	—	—	—	—	—
94-95—Albany	AHL	74	23	33	56	95	14	5	3	14	6	4	10	8
95-96—Albany	AHL	75	35	47	82	142	...	...	...	4	0	3	3	10
—New Jersey	NHL	6	2	1	3	0	1	0	0	—	—	—	—	—
96-97—Worcester	AHL	24	10	16	26	37	3	5	0	—	—	—	—	—
—St. Louis	NHL	54	8	10	18	35	12	0	2	6	0	0	0	6
97-98—St. Louis	NHL	80	8	21	29	62	14	1	1	10	0	2	2	10
98-99—St. Louis	NHL	80	20	21	41	42	1	0	5	8	1	0	1	4
99-00—St. Louis	NHL	80	8	15	23	48	8	0	2	7	0	0	0	2
00-01—Minnesota	NHL	58	11	28	39	45	6	2	2	—	—	—	—	—
—Carolina	NHL	19	0	5	5	6	-4	0	0	6	0	0	0	4
01-02—Boston	NHL	35	1	5	6	6	-6	0	0	—	—	—	—	—
—Dallas	NHL	33	3	5	8	15	-5	0	0	—	—	—	—	—
02-03—Dallas	NHL	20	1	3	4	8	-3	1	0	—	—	—	—	—
—Phoenix	NHL	23	0	1	1	8	-5	0	0	—	—	—	—	—
03-04—St. Louis	NHL	2	0	0	0	2	-3	0	0	—	—	—	—	—
—Portland	AHL	6	0	3	3	0	3	0	0	—	—	—	—	—
—Worcester	AHL	49	9	21	30	38	4	4	0	10	3	1	4	19
NHL Totals (11 years)		536	72	126	198	320	15	5	14	37	1	2	3	26

PELLETIER, JEAN-MARC — G

PERSONAL: Born March 4, 1978, in Atlanta. ... 6-3/209. ... Catches left. ... Name pronounced PEHL-tyay.
TRANSACTIONS/CAREER NOTES: Selected by Philadelphia Flyers in second round (first Flyers pick, 30th overall) of NHL entry draft (June 21, 1997). ... Traded by Flyers with C Rod Brind'Amour and second-round pick (traded to Colorado; Avalanche selected D Argis Saviels) in 2000

draft to Carolina Hurricanes for rights to C Keith Primeau and fifth-round pick (traded to New York Islanders; Islanders selected RW Kristofer Ottosson) in 2000 draft (January 23, 2000). ... Traded by Hurricanes with conditional draft pick to Phoenix Coyotes for G Patrick DesRochers (December 31, 2002).

		REGULAR SEASON									PLAYOFFS							
Season Team	League	GP	Min.	W	L	T	GA	SO	GAA	SV%	GP	Min.	W	L	GA	SO	GAA	SV%
95-96—Cornell	ECAC	5	179	1	2	0	15	0	5.00	.860	—	—	—	—	—	—	—	—
96-97—Cornell	ECAC	11	678	5	2	3	28	1	2.48	...	—	—	—	—	—	—	—	—
97-98—Rimouski	QMJHL	34	1913	17	11	3	118	0	3.70	.888	16	895	11	3	51	1	3.42	.899
98-99—Philadelphia	AHL	47	2636	25	16	4	122	2	2.78	...	1	27	0	0	0	0	0.00	...
—Philadelphia	NHL	1	60	0	1	0	5	0	5.00	.828	—	—	—	—	—	—	—	—
99-00—Philadelphia	AHL	24	1405	14	10	0	58	3	2.48	...	—	—	—	—	—	—	—	—
—Cincinnati	IHL	22	1278	16	4	2	52	2	2.44	...	3	160	1	1	8	1	3.00	...
00-01—Cincinnati	IHL	39	2261	18	14	5	119	2	3.16	...	5	518	1	3	15	0	1.74	...
01-02—Lowell	AHL	40	2284	21	12	4	98	2	2.57	.915	5	298	2	3	13	0	2.62	.908
02-03—Phoenix	NHL	2	119	0	2	0	6	0	3.03	.875	—	—	—	—	—	—	—	—
—Lowell	AHL	17	861	6	10	0	51	1	3.55	.898	—	—	—	—	—	—	—	—
—Springfield	AHL	24	1390	12	7	4	55	2	2.37	.926	6	368	3	3	16	1	2.61	.924
03-04—Phoenix	NHL	4	175	1	1	0	12	0	4.11	.857	—	—	—	—	—	—	—	—
—Springfield	AHL	43	2434	10	24	5	109	2	2.69	.916	—	—	—	—	—	—	—	—
04-05—Springfield	AHL	13	714	2	10	...	35	0	2.94	.904	—	—	—	—	—	—	—	—
—Utah	AHL	23	1231	6	12	...	77	0	3.75	.891	—	—	—	—	—	—	—	—
NHL Totals (3 years)		7	354	1	4	0	23	0	3.90	.857								

PELUSO, MIKE — LW — FLYERS

PERSONAL: Born September 2, 1974, in Bismarck, N.D. ... 6-1/194. ... Shoots right. ... Cousin of Mike Peluso, LW for five NHL teams (1989-98).
TRANSACTIONS/CAREER NOTES: Selected by Calgary Flames in 10th round (11th Flames pick, 253rd overall) of NHL entry draft (June 29, 1994). ... Signed as free agent by Washington Capitals (February 10, 1999). ... Traded by Capitals to St. Louis Blues for LW/C Derek Bekar (November 29, 2000). ... Signed as free agent by Chicago Blackhawks (August 1, 2001). ... Signed as free agent by Philadelphia Flyers (July 24, 2003).

		REGULAR SEASON								PLAYOFFS				
Season Team	League	GP	G	A	Pts.	PIM	+/-	PP	SH	GP	G	A	Pts.	PIM
93-94—Omaha	USHL	48	36	29	65	77	...	...	...	—	—	—	—	—
94-95—Minnesota-Duluth	WCHA	38	11	23	34	38	...	4	1	—	—	—	—	—
95-96—Minnesota-Duluth	WCHA	38	25	19	44	64	...	...	...	—	—	—	—	—
96-97—Minnesota-Duluth	WCHA	37	20	20	40	53	...	11	0	—	—	—	—	—
97-98—Minnesota-Duluth	WCHA	40	24	21	45	100	...	...	...	—	—	—	—	—
98-99—Portland	AHL	26	7	6	13	6	-8	2	0	—	—	—	—	—
99-00—Portland	AHL	71	25	29	54	86	...	...	...	4	2	0	2	0
00-01—Portland	AHL	19	12	10	22	17	...	...	...	—	—	—	—	—
—Worcester	AHL	44	17	23	40	22	...	...	...	11	3	3	6	4
01-02—Norfolk	AHL	29	18	9	27	4	3	6	0	4	1	0	1	0
—Chicago	NHL	37	4	2	6	19	-3	0	0	—	—	—	—	—
02-03—Norfolk	AHL	74	24	31	55	35	2	12	0	9	1	2	3	4
03-04—Philadelphia	NHL	1	0	0	0	0	0	0	0	—	—	—	—	—
—Philadelphia	AHL	72	13	18	31	87	7	3	0	5	0	1	1	4
NHL Totals (2 years)		38	4	2	6	19	-3	0	0					

PENNER, DUSTIN — LW/RW — MIGHTY DUCKS

PERSONAL: Born September 28, 1982, in Winkler, Man. ... 6-4/218. ... Shoots left.
TRANSACTIONS/CAREER NOTES: Signed as free agent by Anaheim Mighty Ducks (May 12, 2004).

		REGULAR SEASON								PLAYOFFS				
Season Team	League	GP	G	A	Pts.	PIM	+/-	PP	SH	GP	G	A	Pts.	PIM
03-04—University of Maine	ECAC	43	11	12	23	52	...	...	...	—	—	—	—	—
04-05—Cincinnati	AHL	77	10	18	28	82	10	4	0	9	2	3	5	13

PEREZHOGIN, ALEXANDER — RW/C — CANADIENS

PERSONAL: Born August 10, 1983, in Ust-Kamenogorsk, U.S.S.R. ... 5-11/185. ... Shoots left.
TRANSACTIONS/CAREER NOTES: Selected by Montreal Canadiens in first round (second Canadiens pick, 25th overall) of NHL entry draft (June 23, 2001). ... Suspended indefinitely by AHL for stick-swinging incident (April 30, 2004).

		REGULAR SEASON								PLAYOFFS				
Season Team	League	GP	G	A	Pts.	PIM	+/-	PP	SH	GP	G	A	Pts.	PIM
00-01—Avangard	Rus. Div.	41	47	24	71	40	...	...	...	—	—	—	—	—
01-02—Avangard Omsk	Russian	4	1	0	1	4	...	...	...	—	—	—	—	—
02-03—Avangard Omsk	Russian	48	15	6	21	28	...	...	...	—	—	—	—	—
03-04—Hamilton	AHL	77	23	27	50	52	19	6	0	5	3	3	6	16
04-05—Omsk	Russian	43	15	18	33	18	...	...	...	—	—	—	—	—

PERRAULT, JOEL — C/RW — MIGHTY DUCKS

PERSONAL: Born April 6, 1983, in Montreal. ... 6-2/165. ... Shoots right. ... Name pronounced PAIR-oh.
TRANSACTIONS/CAREER NOTES: Selected by Mighty Ducks of Anaheim in fifth round (seventh Mighty Ducks pick, 137th overall) of NHL entry draft (June 23, 2001).

P

Season Team	League	REGULAR SEASON GP	G	A	Pts.	PIM	+/-	PP	SH	PLAYOFFS GP	G	A	Pts.	PIM
00-01—Baie-Comeau	QMJHL	68	10	14	24	46	...	...	...	11	1	1	2	10
01-02—Baie-Comeau	QMJHL	57	18	44	62	96	...	...	...	5	2	0	2	6
02-03—Baie-Comeau	QMJHL	70	51	65	116	93	...	...	...	12	3	7	10	14
03-04—Cincinnati	AHL	65	14	14	28	38	0	3	1	9	1	1	2	2
04-05—Cincinnati	AHL	51	9	19	28	40	-6	3	0	—	—	—	—	—

PERREAULT, YANIC — C

PERSONAL: Born April 4, 1971, in Sherbrooke, Que. ... 5-11/184. ... Shoots left. ... Name pronounced YAH-nihk puh-ROH.

TRANSACTIONS/CAREER NOTES: Selected by Toronto Maple Leafs in third round (first Maple Leafs pick, 47th overall) of NHL entry draft (June 22, 1991). ... Signed as free agent by Los Angeles Kings (July 14, 1994). ... Strained abdominal muscle (December 13, 1996); missed 11 games. ... Kidney surgery (February 3, 1997); missed remainder of season. ... Traded by Kings to Maple Leafs for C/RW Jason Podollan and third-round pick (G Cory Campbell) in 1999 draft (March 23, 1999). ... Fractured arm (December 4, 1999); missed 23 games. ... Signed as free agent by Montreal Canadiens (July 4, 2001). ... Injured groin (January 25, 2003); missed eight games. ... Injured groin (December 18, 2003); missed four games. ... Injured ankle (January 4, 2004); missed one game.

STATISTICAL PLATEAUS: Three-goal games: 1997-98 (2), 2001-02 (1). Total: 3. ... Four-goal games: 1998-99 (1). ... Total hat tricks: 4.

Season Team	League	REGULAR SEASON GP	G	A	Pts.	PIM	+/-	PP	SH	PLAYOFFS GP	G	A	Pts.	PIM
88-89—Trois-Rivieres	QMJHL	70	53	55	108	48	...	...	...	—	—	—	—	—
89-90—Trois-Rivieres	QMJHL	63	51	63	114	75	...	...	...	7	6	5	11	19
90-91—Trois-Rivieres	QMJHL	67	*87	98	*185	103	...	...	...	6	4	7	11	6
91-92—St. John's	AHL	62	38	38	76	19	...	...	...	16	7	8	15	4
92-93—St. John's	AHL	79	49	46	95	56	-19	20	0	9	4	5	9	2
93-94—St. John's	AHL	62	45	60	105	38	25	19	2	11	*12	6	18	14
—Toronto	NHL	13	3	3	6	0	1	2	0	—	—	—	—	—
94-95—Phoenix	IHL	68	51	48	99	52	-18	*19	1	—	—	—	—	—
—Los Angeles	NHL	26	2	5	7	20	3	0	0	—	—	—	—	—
95-96—Los Angeles	NHL	78	25	24	49	16	-11	8	3	—	—	—	—	—
96-97—Los Angeles	NHL	41	11	14	25	20	0	1	1	—	—	—	—	—
97-98—Los Angeles	NHL	79	28	20	48	32	6	3	2	4	1	2	3	6
98-99—Los Angeles	NHL	64	10	17	27	30	-3	2	2	—	—	—	—	—
—Toronto	NHL	12	7	8	15	12	10	2	1	17	3	6	9	6
99-00—Toronto	NHL	58	18	27	45	22	3	5	0	1	0	1	1	0
00-01—Toronto	NHL	76	24	28	52	52	0	5	0	11	2	3	5	4
01-02—Montreal	NHL	82	27	29	56	40	-3	6	0	11	3	5	8	0
02-03—Montreal	NHL	73	24	22	46	30	-11	7	0	—	—	—	—	—
03-04—Montreal	NHL	69	16	15	31	40	-10	5	0	9	2	2	4	0
NHL Totals (11 years)		671	195	212	407	314	-15	46	9	53	11	19	30	16

PERRIN, ERIC — C — LIGHTNING

PERSONAL: Born November 1, 1975, in Laval, Que. ... 5-9/176. ... Shoots left. ... Name pronounced peh-REHN.

TRANSACTIONS/CAREER NOTES: Signed as free agent by Tampa Bay Lightning (June 19, 2003). ... Signed as free agent by Hershey of the AHL (September 27, 2004).

Season Team	League	REGULAR SEASON GP	G	A	Pts.	PIM	+/-	PP	SH	PLAYOFFS GP	G	A	Pts.	PIM
98-99—Kansas City	IHL	82	24	37	61	71	-7	8	0	3	0	0	0	0
99-00—Kansas City	IHL	21	3	15	18	16	...	...	...	—	—	—	—	—
00-01—Jokerit Helsinki	Finland	6	1	1	2	2	...	...	...	—	—	—	—	—
—Assat Pori	Finland	43	15	23	38	70	...	...	...	—	—	—	—	—
01-02—Assat Pori	Finland	45	13	13	26	16	...	...	...	—	—	—	—	—
—HPK Hameenlinna	Finland	12	5	10	15	4	...	...	...	8	2	4	6	6
02-03—JyP Jyvaskyla	Finland	56	18	28	46	36	...	...	...	7	4	6	10	8
03-04—Tampa Bay	NHL	4	0	0	0	0	-1	0	0	12	0	1	1	6
—Hershey	AHL	71	21	54	75	49	-5	9	1	—	—	—	—	—
04-05—Hershey	AHL	80	24	49	73	46	-2	6	0	—	—	—	—	—
NHL Totals (1 year)		4	0	0	0	0	-1	0	0	12	0	1	1	6

PERROTT, NATHAN — RW — MAPLE LEAFS

PERSONAL: Born December 8, 1976, in Owen Sound, Ont. ... 6-0/225. ... Shoots right. ... Name pronounced PAIR-iht.

TRANSACTIONS/CAREER NOTES: Selected by New Jersey Devils in second round (second Devils pick, 44th overall) of NHL entry draft (July 8, 1995). ... Signed as free agent by Chicago Blackhawks (August 27, 1997). ... Traded by Blackhawks to Nashville Predators for pick in 2003 draft (October 9, 2001). ... Traded by Predators to Toronto Maple Leafs for C Bob Wren (December 31, 2002).

Season Team	League	REGULAR SEASON GP	G	A	Pts.	PIM	+/-	PP	SH	PLAYOFFS GP	G	A	Pts.	PIM
93-94—St. Mary's Jr. B	OHA	41	11	26	37	249	...	...	...	—	—	—	—	—
94-95—Oshawa	OHL	63	18	28	46	233	...	9	0	2	1	1	2	9
95-96—Oshawa	OHL	59	30	32	62	158	...	...	...	5	2	3	5	8
96-97—Sault Ste. Marie	OHL	42	19	23	42	137	10	8	0	11	5	5	10	*60
97-98—Indianapolis	IHL	31	4	3	7	76	2	0	1	—	—	—	—	—
—Jacksonville	ECHL	30	6	8	14	135	...	...	...	—	—	—	—	—
98-99—Indianapolis	IHL	72	14	11	25	307	7	3	0	7	3	1	4	45
99-00—Cleveland	IHL	65	12	9	21	248	...	...	...	9	2	1	3	19
00-01—Norfolk	AHL	73	11	17	28	268	...	...	...	9	2	0	2	18

Season Team	League	GP	G	A	Pts.	PIM	+/-	PP	SH	GP	G	A	Pts.	PIM
		REGULAR SEASON								PLAYOFFS				
01-02—Norfolk........................	AHL	2	0	0	0	5	0	0	0	—	—	—	—	—
—Milwaukee..................	AHL	56	6	10	16	190	-5	0	0	—	—	—	—	—
—Nashville....................	NHL	22	1	2	3	74	-1	0	0	—	—	—	—	—
02-03—Milwaukee..................	AHL	27	1	2	3	106	1	0	0	—	—	—	—	—
—Nashville....................	NHL	1	0	0	0	5	0	0	0	—	—	—	—	—
—St. John's....................	AHL	36	7	8	15	97	-12	0	0	—	—	—	—	—
03-04—Toronto........................	NHL	40	1	2	3	116	-1	0	0	—	—	—	—	—
04-05—St. John's....................	AHL	60	16	12	28	276	6	1	0	2	0	0	0	6
NHL Totals (3 years)...........		63	2	4	6	195	-2	0	0					

PERRY, COREY — RW — MIGHTY DUCKS

PERSONAL: Born May 16, 1985, in Peterborough, Ont. ... 6-2/184. ... Shoots right.
TRANSACTIONS/CAREER NOTES: Selected by Anaheim Mighty Ducks in 1st round (2nd Mighty Ducks pick, 28th overall) of entry draft (June 20, 2003).

Season Team	League	GP	G	A	Pts.	PIM	+/-	PP	SH	GP	G	A	Pts.	PIM
		REGULAR SEASON								PLAYOFFS				
01-02—London........................	OHL	60	28	31	59	56	...	...	...	12	2	3	5	30
02-03—London........................	OHL	67	25	53	78	145	...	...	...	14	7	16	23	27
03-04—London........................	OHL	66	40	73	113	98	...	...	...	15	7	15	22	20
—Cincinnati....................	AHL	3	1	1	2	4	...	...	...	—	—	—	—	—
04-05—London........................	OHL	60	47	83	130	117	66	18	4	18	11	27	38	46

PETERS, ANDREW — LW — SABRES

PERSONAL: Born May 5, 1980, in St. Catharines, Ont. ... 6-4/247. ... Shoots left.
TRANSACTIONS/CAREER NOTES: Selected by Buffalo Sabres in second round (second Sabres pick, 34th overall) of NHL draft (June 27, 1998).

Season Team	League	GP	G	A	Pts.	PIM	+/-	PP	SH	GP	G	A	Pts.	PIM
		REGULAR SEASON								PLAYOFFS				
96-97—Georgetown................	Tier II Jr. A	46	11	16	27	105	...	...	...	—	—	—	—	—
97-98—Oshawa........................	OHL	60	11	7	18	220	...	...	...	7	2	0	2	19
98-99—Oshawa........................	OHL	54	14	10	24	137	2	...	...	15	2	7	9	36
99-00—Kitchener.....................	OHL	42	6	13	19	95	-1	2	0	4	0	1	1	14
00-01—Rochester.....................	AHL	49	0	4	4	118	...	...	...	—	—	—	—	—
01-02—Rochester.....................	AHL	67	4	1	5	*388	-2	0	0	—	—	—	—	—
02-03—Rochester.....................	AHL	57	3	0	3	223	-16	0	0	3	0	0	0	24
03-04—Buffalo........................	NHL	42	2	0	2	151	-3	0	0	—	—	—	—	—
04-05—Boden..........................	Sweden Dv. 2	9	1	2	3	101	-2	1	0	13	1	2	3	95
NHL Totals (1 year).............		42	2	0	2	151	-3	0	0					

PETROVICKY, RONALD — RW — THRASHERS

PERSONAL: Born February 15, 1977, in Zilina, Czechoslovakia. ... 6-1/188. ... Shoots right.
TRANSACTIONS/CAREER NOTES: Signed as free agent by Calgary Flames (June 1, 1998). ... Injured wrist (October 5, 2000); missed 49 games. ... Claimed by New York Rangers in waiver draft (October 4, 2002). ... Injured ankle (January 6, 2003); missed 11 games. ... Claimed by Atlanta Thrashers in waiver draft (October 3, 2003). ... Suspended one game for kneeing (March 18, 2004).

Season Team	League	GP	G	A	Pts.	PIM	+/-	PP	SH	GP	G	A	Pts.	PIM
		REGULAR SEASON								PLAYOFFS				
93-94—Dukla Trencin.............	Slovakia	36	28	27	55	42	...	...	...	—	—	—	—	—
94-95—Tri-City........................	WHL	39	4	11	15	86	-1	1	0	—	—	—	—	—
—Prince George............	WHL	21	4	6	10	37	-14	2	0	—	—	—	—	—
95-96—Prince George............	WHL	39	19	21	40	61	...	...	...	—	—	—	—	—
96-97—Prince George............	WHL	72	32	37	69	119	-20	9	0	15	4	9	13	31
97-98—Regina........................	WHL	71	64	49	113	45	168	19	3	9	2	4	6	11
98-99—Saint John..................	AHL	78	12	21	33	114	-16	6	0	7	1	2	3	19
99-00—Saint John..................	AHL	67	23	33	56	131	...	...	...	3	1	1	2	6
00-01—Calgary........................	NHL	30	4	5	9	54	0	1	0	—	—	—	—	—
01-02—Calgary........................	NHL	77	5	7	12	85	0	1	0	—	—	—	—	—
02-03—New York Rangers......	NHL	66	5	9	14	77	-12	2	1	—	—	—	—	—
03-04—Atlanta........................	NHL	78	16	15	31	123	-9	0	0	—	—	—	—	—
04-05—Brynas IF....................	Sweden	10	0	5	5	27	-5	0	0	9	0	2	2	0
—HK SKP PChZ Zilina....	Slovakia	34	10	9	19	34	5	...	...	—	—	—	—	—
NHL Totals (4 years)...........		251	30	36	66	339	-21	4	1					

PETTINEN, TOMI — D — ISLANDERS

PERSONAL: Born June 17, 1977, in Ylojarvi, Finland. ... 6-4/220. ... Shoots left.
TRANSACTIONS/CAREER NOTES: Selected by New York Islanders in ninth round (ninth Islanders choice, 267th overall) of NHL draft (June 25, 2000).

Season Team	League	GP	G	A	Pts.	PIM	+/-	PP	SH	GP	G	A	Pts.	PIM
		REGULAR SEASON								PLAYOFFS				
96-97—Ilves Tampere............	Finland	16	1	0	1	12	...	...	...	—	—	—	—	—
97-98—Ilves Tampere............	Finland	3	0	0	0	0	...	...	...	—	—	—	—	—
—Lukko Rauma............	Finland	27	0	2	2	16	...	...	...	—	—	—	—	—

P

Season Team	League	REGULAR SEASON GP	G	A	Pts.	PIM	+/-	PP	SH	PLAYOFFS GP	G	A	Pts.	PIM
98-99—HIFK Helsinki	Finland	4	0	0	0	2	...	...	...	—	—	—	—	—
99-00—Ilves Tampere	Finland	51	1	6	7	78	...	...	...	3	1	2	3	2
00-01—Ilves Tampere	Finland	56	2	2	4	...	86	...	...	9	0	0	0	4
01-02—Bridgeport	AHL	...	...	...	...	...	...	...	...	9	0	1	1	0
—Ilves Tampere	Finland	48	5	4	9	51	...	...	...	3	0	0	0	4
02-03—Bridgeport	AHL	75	1	8	9	56	6	0	0	9	0	0	0	17
—New York Islanders	NHL	2	0	0	0	0	1	0	0	—	—	—	—	—
03-04—New York Islanders	NHL	4	0	0	0	2	-2	0	0	—	—	—	—	—
—Bridgeport	AHL	71	1	8	9	37	15	0	0	7	1	0	1	0
04-05—Lukko Rauma	Finland	56	6	14	20	49	10	...	...	9	0	2	2	33
NHL Totals (2 years)		6	0	0	0	2	-1	0	0					

PETTINGER, MATT — LW — CAPITALS

PERSONAL: Born October 22, 1980, in Edmonton. ... 6-1/210. ... Shoots left. ... Nephew of Gord Pettinger, C with three NHL teams (1932-40).
TRANSACTIONS/CAREER NOTES: Selected by Washington Capitals in second round (second Capitals pick, 43rd overall) of NHL draft (June 24, 2000). ... Flu (January 14, 2002); missed two games. ... Had concussion (November 1, 2003); missed 11 games.

Season Team	League	REGULAR SEASON GP	G	A	Pts.	PIM	+/-	PP	SH	PLAYOFFS GP	G	A	Pts.	PIM
98-99—Denver	WCHA	38	14	6	20	52	...	...	...	—	—	—	—	—
99-00—Denver	WCHA	19	2	6	8	...	...	...	...	—	—	—	—	—
—Calgary	WHL	27	14	6	20	41	...	...	...	11	2	6	8	30
00-01—Portland	AHL	64	19	17	36	92	...	...	...	2	0	0	0	4
—Washington	NHL	10	0	0	0	2	-1	0	0	—	—	—	—	—
01-02—Portland	AHL	9	3	3	6	24	-1	2	0	—	—	—	—	—
—Washington	NHL	61	7	3	10	44	-8	1	0	—	—	—	—	—
02-03—Washington	NHL	1	0	0	0	0	0	0	0	—	—	—	—	—
—Portland	AHL	69	14	13	27	72	-6	4	0	3	0	2	2	2
03-04—Washington	NHL	71	7	5	12	37	-9	1	0	—	—	—	—	—
04-05—Olimpija	Slovenia	8	2	5	7	41	...	...	...	—	—	—	—	—
NHL Totals (4 years)		143	14	8	22	83	-18	2	0					

PHANEUF, DION — D — FLAMES

PERSONAL: Born April 10, 1985, in Edmonton. ... 6-2/205. ... Shoots left.
TRANSACTIONS/CAREER NOTES: Selected by Calgary Flames in first round (first Flames pick, ninth overall) of NHL entry draft (June 20, 2003).

Season Team	League	REGULAR SEASON GP	G	A	Pts.	PIM	+/-	PP	SH	PLAYOFFS GP	G	A	Pts.	PIM
01-02—Red Deer	WHL	66	5	11	16	168	...	...	...	—	—	—	—	—
02-03—Red Deer	WHL	71	16	14	30	185	...	...	...	—	—	—	—	—
03-04—Red Deer	WHL	62	19	24	43	126	11	8	0	19	2	11	13	30
04-05—Red Deer	WHL	55	24	32	56	73	15	12	0	7	1	4	5	12

PHILLIPS, CHRIS — D — SENATORS

PERSONAL: Born March 9, 1978, in Calgary. ... 6-3/216. ... Shoots left. ... Nephew of Rod Phillips, Edmonton Oilers play-by-play announcer.
TRANSACTIONS/CAREER NOTES: Selected by Ottawa Senators in first round (first Senators pick, first overall) of NHL entry draft (June 22, 1996). ... Bruised knee (November 13, 1997); missed two games. ... Bruised eye (February 25, 1998); missed five games. ... Back spasms (November 18, 1998); missed three games. ... Sprained right ankle (January 1, 1999); missed 21 games. ... Reinjured right ankle (February 20, 1999); missed 23 games. ... Injured right ankle (December 9, 1999) and underwent surgery; missed 17 games. ... Back spasms (November 2, 2000); missed three games. ... Back spasms (December 2, 2000); missed two games. ... Injured left shoulder (April 1, 2001); missed final three games of season. ... Injured shoulder (September 19, 2001); missed first three games of season. ... Injured left elbow (December 18, 2001); missed 15 games. ... Injured right knee (December 7, 2002); missed three games.

Season Team	League	REGULAR SEASON GP	G	A	Pts.	PIM	+/-	PP	SH	PLAYOFFS GP	G	A	Pts.	PIM
93-94—Fort McMurray	AJHL	56	6	16	22	72	...	...	...	—	—	—	—	—
94-95—Fort McMurray	AJHL	48	16	32	48	127	...	...	...	—	—	—	—	—
95-96—Prince Albert	WHL	61	10	30	40	97	...	...	...	18	2	12	14	30
96-97—Prince Albert	WHL	32	3	23	26	58	-8	1	0	—	—	—	—	—
—Lethbridge	WHL	26	4	18	22	28	16	1	0	19	4	*21	25	20
97-98—Ottawa	NHL	72	5	11	16	38	2	2	0	11	0	2	2	2
98-99—Ottawa	NHL	34	3	3	6	32	-5	2	0	3	0	0	0	0
99-00—Ottawa	NHL	65	5	14	19	39	12	0	0	6	0	1	1	4
00-01—Ottawa	NHL	73	2	12	14	31	8	2	0	1	1	0	1	0
01-02—Ottawa	NHL	63	6	16	22	29	5	1	0	12	0	0	0	12
02-03—Ottawa	NHL	78	3	16	19	71	7	2	0	18	2	4	6	12
03-04—Ottawa	NHL	82	7	16	23	46	15	0	0	7	1	0	1	12
04-05—Brynas IF	Sweden	27	5	3	8	45	-15	2	0	9	1	2	3	2
NHL Totals (7 years)		467	31	88	119	286	44	9	0	58	4	7	11	42

P

PICARD, ALEXANDRE — LW — BLUE JACKETS

PERSONAL: Born October 9, 1985, in Les Saules, Que. ... 6-2/190. ... Shoots left.
TRANSACTIONS/CAREER NOTES: Selected by Columbus Blue Jackets in first round (first Blue Jackets pick, eighth overall) of NHL entry draft (June 26, 2004).

Season Team	League	GP	G	A	Pts.	PIM	+/-	PP	SH	GP	G	A	Pts.	PIM
		REGULAR SEASON								PLAYOFFS				
01-02—Sherbrooke	QMJHL	6	0	3	3	0	...	...	...	—	—	—	—	—
02-03—Sherbrooke	QMJHL	66	14	15	29	41	...	...	...	12	4	0	4	10
03-04—Lewiston	QMJHL	69	39	41	80	88	...	...	...	7	7	4	11	6
04-05—Lewiston	QMJHL	65	40	45	85	160	20	15	6	8	5	2	7	18

PIHLMAN, TUOMAS LW/RW DEVILS

PERSONAL: Born November 13, 1982, in Espoo, Finland. ... 6-2/205. ... Shoots left.
TRANSACTIONS/CAREER NOTES: Selected by New Jersey Devils in second round (third Devils pick, 48th overall) of NHL entry draft (June 23, 2001).

Season Team	League	GP	G	A	Pts.	PIM	+/-	PP	SH	GP	G	A	Pts.	PIM
		REGULAR SEASON								PLAYOFFS				
00-01—JyP Jyvaskyla	Finland	47	3	6	9	59	...	...	...	—	—	—	—	—
01-02—JyP Jyvaskyla	Finland	44	9	2	11	93	...	...	...	—	—	—	—	—
02-03—JyP Jyvaskyla	Finland	53	19	15	34	58	...	...	...	1	0	0	0	0
03-04—New Jersey	NHL	2	0	0	0	2	0	0	0	—	—	—	—	—
—Albany	AHL	73	10	19	29	59	-11	2	1	—	—	—	—	—
04-05—Albany	AHL	68	9	13	22	48	-16	1	0	—	—	—	—	—
NHL Totals (1 year)		2	0	0	0	2	0	0	0					

PILAR, KAREL D MAPLE LEAFS

PERSONAL: Born December 23, 1977, in Prague, Czechoslovakia. ... 6-3/207. ... Shoots right. ... Name pronounced pee-LAHSH.
TRANSACTIONS/CAREER NOTES: Selected by Toronto Maple Leafs in second round (second Maple Leafs pick, 39th overall) of NHL draft (June 23, 2001). ... Viral infection (December 31, 2002); missed 45 games. ... Fractured thumb (April 16, 2003); missed three playoff games. ... Viral infection (October 10, 2003); missed nine games.

Season Team	League	GP	G	A	Pts.	PIM	+/-	PP	SH	GP	G	A	Pts.	PIM
		REGULAR SEASON								PLAYOFFS				
99-00—Litvinov	Czech Rep.	49	2	12	14	53	...	...	...	7	0	0	0	4
00-01—Litvinov	Czech Rep.	52	12	26	38	52	...	...	...	4	1	1	2	25
01-02—St. John's	AHL	52	10	14	24	26	2	6	1	—	—	—	—	—
—Toronto	NHL	23	1	3	4	8	3	0	0	11	0	4	4	12
02-03—St. John's	AHL	7	2	5	7	28	-7	2	0	—	—	—	—	—
—Toronto	NHL	17	3	4	7	12	-7	1	0	—	—	—	—	—
03-04—Toronto	NHL	50	2	17	19	22	2	1	0	1	1	0	1	0
—St. John's	AHL	6	3	3	6	6	0	2	0	—	—	—	—	—
04-05—Sparta Praha	Czech Rep.	52	13	15	28	70	15	...	...	—	—	—	—	—
NHL Totals (3 years)		90	6	24	30	42	-2	2	0	12	1	4	5	12

PIRJETA, LASSE C/RW PENGUINS

PERSONAL: Born April 4, 1974, in Oulu, Finland. ... 6-4/225. ... Shoots left. ... Name pronounced PEER-yeh-tuh.
TRANSACTIONS/CAREER NOTES: Selected by Columbus Blue Jackets in fifth round (seventh Blue Jackets pick, 133rd overall) in NHL draft (June 23, 2002). ... Separated shoulder (October 15, 2003); missed 16 games. ... Had concussion (January 4, 2003); missed four games. ... Injured throat (January 21, 2004); missed one game. ... Traded by Blue Jackets to Pittsburgh Penguins for C Brian Holzinger (March 9, 2004).

Season Team	League	GP	G	A	Pts.	PIM	+/-	PP	SH	GP	G	A	Pts.	PIM
		REGULAR SEASON								PLAYOFFS				
91-92—Tacoma	WHL	16	5	2	7	4	...	...	...	—	—	—	—	—
93-94—TPS Turku	Finland	43	9	9	18	14	...	...	...	11	4	0	4	2
94-95—TPS Turku	Finland	49	7	13	20	64	...	...	...	8	0	1	1	29
95-96—TPS Turku	Finland	45	13	14	27	34	...	...	...	11	6	3	9	4
96-97—Vastra Frolunda	Sweden	50	14	8	22	36	...	...	...	3	0	1	1	4
97-98—Tappara	Finland	48	24	22	46	20	...	...	...	4	1	1	2	2
98-99—Tappara	Finland	54	22	19	41	32	...	...	...	—	—	—	—	—
99-00—HIFK Helsinki	Finland	54	18	25	43	24	...	...	...	9	2	3	5	10
00-01—HIFK Helsinki	Finland	55	15	18	33	24	...	...	...	—	—	—	—	—
01-02—Karpat Oulu	Finland	55	15	26	41	24	...	...	...	4	2	2	4	4
02-03—Columbus	NHL	51	11	10	21	12	-4	2	0	—	—	—	—	—
03-04—Columbus	NHL	57	2	8	10	20	-6	0	0	—	—	—	—	—
—Syracuse	AHL	5	1	2	3	2	2	0	0	—	—	—	—	—
—Pittsburgh	NHL	13	6	6	12	0	3	1	0	—	—	—	—	—
04-05—HIFK Helsinki	Finland	45	16	20	36	26	13	...	...	5	2	0	2	2
NHL Totals (2 years)		121	19	24	43	32	-7	3	0					

PIRNES, ESA C

PERSONAL: Born April 1, 1977, in Oulu, Finland. ... 6-0/190. ... Shoots left. ... Name pronounced PEER-nehz.
TRANSACTIONS/CAREER NOTES: Selected by Los Angeles Kings in the sixth round (seventh Kings pick, 174th overall) in NHL draft (June 21, 2003). ... Had cervical strain (November 29, 2003); missed 18 games.

Season Team	League	GP	G	A	Pts.	PIM	+/-	PP	SH	GP	G	A	Pts.	PIM
		REGULAR SEASON								PLAYOFFS				
99-00—Espoo	Finland	51	15	24	39	12	...	...	...	4	0	1	1	2
00-01—Espoo	Finland	54	10	8	18	51	...	...	...	—	—	—	—	—

Season Team	League	REGULAR SEASON GP	G	A	Pts.	PIM	+/-	PP	SH	PLAYOFFS GP	G	A	Pts.	PIM
01-02—Tappara Tampere	Finland	49	8	16	24	30	...	...	...	10	0	1	1	2
02-03—Tappara Tampere	Finland	56	23	14	37	6	...	...	...	15	5	9	14	2
03-04—Los Angeles	NHL	57	3	8	11	12	-9	0	1	—	—	—	—	—
—Manchester	AHL	4	3	1	4	2	2	0	0	—	—	—	—	—
04-05—Lukko Rauma	Finland	47	9	29	38	31	16	...	...	9	1	3	4	2
NHL Totals (1 year)		57	3	8	11	12	-9	0	1					

PIROS, KAMIL — RW

PERSONAL: Born November 20, 1978, in Most, Czechoslovakia. ... 6-0/195. ... Shoots left. ... Name pronounced KA-mihl PIH-ruhsh.
TRANSACTIONS/CAREER NOTES: Selected by Buffalo Sabres in eighth round (ninth Sabres pick, 212th overall) of NHL draft (June 21, 1997). ... Traded by Sabres with fourth-round pick (traded to St. Louis; Blues selected Igor Valeev) in 2001 draft to Atlanta Thrashers for RW Donald Audette (March 13, 2001). ... Bruised knee (March 23, 2002); missed three games. ... Traded by Thrashers to Florida Panthers for D Kyle Rossiter (March 8, 2004).
STATISTICAL PLATEAUS: Three-goal games: 2002-03 (1).

Season Team	League	REGULAR SEASON GP	G	A	Pts.	PIM	+/-	PP	SH	PLAYOFFS GP	G	A	Pts.	PIM
93-94—Most Jrs.	Czech. Jrs.	16	12	10	22	...	...	...	...	—	—	—	—	—
—Chemopetrol Litvinov	Czech. Jrs.	22	6	13	19	...	...	...	...	—	—	—	—	—
94-95—Chemopetrol Litvinov	Czech. Jrs.	40	27	16	43	...	...	...	...	—	—	—	—	—
95-96—Chemopetrol Litvinov	Czech. Jrs.	42	16	13	29	...	...	...	...	—	—	—	—	—
96-97—Litvinov	Czech Rep.	38	4	19	23	0	...	...	...	—	—	—	—	—
97-98—Chem. Litvinov	Czech Rep.	14	0	1	1	2	...	...	...	—	—	—	—	—
—HC Vitkovice	Czech Rep.	26	2	9	11	14	...	...	...	—	—	—	—	—
98-99—Chem. Litvinov	Czech Rep.	41	7	9	16	10	...	...	...	—	—	—	—	—
99-00—Chem. Litvinov	Czech Rep.	40	8	8	16	18	...	...	...	7	0	3	3	2
00-01—Chem. Litvinov	Czech Rep.	48	11	13	24	28	...	...	...	6	1	1	2	2
01-02—Atlanta	NHL	8	0	1	1	4	-2	0	0	—	—	—	—	—
—Chicago	AHL	64	19	30	49	16	3	7	0	25	6	11	17	6
02-03—Chicago	AHL	51	10	9	19	16	-8	3	0	9	1	0	1	4
—Atlanta	NHL	3	3	2	5	2	4	0	0	—	—	—	—	—
03-04—Atlanta	NHL	14	0	1	1	4	-3	0	0	—	—	—	—	—
—Chicago	AHL	51	10	20	30	20	4	4	0	—	—	—	—	—
—Florida	NHL	3	1	0	1	0	-1	1	0	—	—	—	—	—
—San Antonio	AHL	14	2	5	7	6	-3	0	0	—	—	—	—	—
04-05—Khimik Voskresensk	Russian	27	2	6	8	8	-2	...	...	—	—	—	—	—
NHL Totals (3 years)		28	4	4	8	10	-2	1	0					

PISANI, FERNANDO — RW/LW — OILERS

PERSONAL: Born December 27, 1976, in Edmonton. ... 6-1/203. ... Shoots left. ... Name pronounced pih-ZAN-ee.
TRANSACTIONS/CAREER NOTES: Selected by Edmonton Oilers in eighth round (ninth Oilers pick, 195th overall) of NHL entry draft (June 22, 1996). ... Strained right shoulder (December 16, 2003); missed three games. ... Bruised ribs (January 20, 2004); missed two games.
STATISTICAL PLATEAUS: Three-goal games: 2002-03 (1).

Season Team	League	REGULAR SEASON GP	G	A	Pts.	PIM	+/-	PP	SH	PLAYOFFS GP	G	A	Pts.	PIM
95-96—St. Albert	AJHL	58	40	63	103	134	...	...	...	18	7	22	29	28
96-97—Providence College	Hockey East	35	12	18	30	36	...	...	...	—	—	—	—	—
97-98—Providence College	Hockey East	36	16	18	34	20	...	...	...	—	—	—	—	—
98-99—Providence College	Hockey East	38	14	37	51	42	...	...	...	—	—	—	—	—
99-00—Providence College	Hockey East	38	14	24	38	56	...	...	...	—	—	—	—	—
00-01—Hamilton	AHL	52	12	13	25	28	...	...	...	—	—	—	—	—
01-02—Hamilton	AHL	79	26	34	60	60	24	11	0	15	4	6	10	4
02-03—Hamilton	AHL	41	17	15	32	24	14	7	0	—	—	—	—	—
—Edmonton	NHL	35	8	5	13	10	9	0	1	6	1	0	1	2
03-04—Edmonton	NHL	76	16	14	30	46	14	4	1	—	—	—	—	—
04-05—SC Langnau	Switzerland	7	1	3	4	0	...	0	0	—	—	—	—	—
—Asiago	Italy	12	1	5	6	6	...	...	...	9	4	6	10	0
NHL Totals (2 years)		111	24	19	43	56	23	4	2	6	1	0	1	2

PITKANEN, JONI — D — FLYERS

PERSONAL: Born September 19, 1983, in Oulu, Finland. ... 6-3/200. ... Shoots left.
TRANSACTIONS/CAREER NOTES: Selected by Philadelphia Flyers in first round (first Flyers pick, fourth overall) of NHL entry draft (June 22, 2002). ... Stomach virus (December 18, 2003); missed four games. ... Suffered concussion (January 8, 2004); missed two games. ... Suffered concussion (March 6, 2004); missed two games.

Season Team	League	REGULAR SEASON GP	G	A	Pts.	PIM	+/-	PP	SH	PLAYOFFS GP	G	A	Pts.	PIM
00-01—Karpat Oulu	Finland	21	0	0	0	10	...	...	...	2	0	0	0	2
01-02—Karpat Oulu	Finland	49	4	15	19	65	...	...	...	4	0	0	0	12
02-03—Karpat Oulu	Finland	35	5	15	20	38	...	...	...	—	—	—	—	—
03-04—Philadelphia	NHL	71	8	19	27	44	15	5	0	15	0	3	3	6
04-05—Philadelphia	AHL	76	6	35	41	105	9	3	0	21	3	4	7	16
NHL Totals (1 year)		71	8	19	27	44	15	5	0	15	0	3	3	6

P

PITTIS, DOMENIC — C/LW — SABRES

PERSONAL: Born October 1, 1974, in Calgary. ... 5-11/190. ... Shoots left. ... Name pronounced PIHT-ihz.

TRANSACTIONS/CAREER NOTES: Selected by Pittsburgh Penguins in second round (second Penguins pick, 52nd overall) of NHL entry draft (June 26, 1993). ... Signed as free agent by Buffalo Sabres (July 30, 1998). ... Flu (October 27, 1999); missed one game. ... Injured ankle (November 9, 1999); missed three games. ... Signed as free agent by Edmonton Oilers (July 26, 2000). ... Strained groin (January 23, 2002); missed four games. ... Suffered concussion (February 22, 2002); missed 20 games. ... Signed as free agent by Nashville Predators (July 24, 2002). ... Suffered concussion (November 10, 2002); missed 45 games. ... Signed as free agent by Buffalo Sabres (July 26, 2003).

		REGULAR SEASON								PLAYOFFS				
Season Team	League	GP	G	A	Pts.	PIM	+/-	PP	SH	GP	G	A	Pts.	PIM
91-92—Lethbridge	WHL	65	6	17	23	48	...	...	...	5	0	2	2	4
92-93—Lethbridge	WHL	66	46	73	119	69	...	...	...	4	3	3	6	8
93-94—Lethbridge	WHL	72	58	69	127	93	18	25	5	8	4	11	15	16
94-95—Cleveland	IHL	62	18	32	50	66	-12	4	0	3	0	2	2	2
95-96—Cleveland	IHL	74	10	28	38	100	...	...	...	3	0	0	0	2
96-97—Pittsburgh	NHL	1	0	0	0	0	-1	0	0	—	—	—	—	—
—Long Beach	IHL	65	23	43	66	91	...	...	...	18	5	9	14	26
97-98—Syracuse	AHL	75	23	41	64	90	-18	4	2	5	1	3	4	4
98-99—Rochester	AHL	76	38	66	*104	108	24	12	1	20	7	14	*21	40
—Buffalo	NHL	3	0	0	0	2	0	0	0	—	—	—	—	—
99-00—Buffalo	NHL	7	1	0	1	6	1	0	0	—	—	—	—	—
—Rochester	AHL	53	17	48	65	85	...	...	...	21	4	*26	*30	28
00-01—Edmonton	NHL	47	4	5	9	49	-5	0	0	3	0	0	0	2
01-02—Edmonton	NHL	22	0	6	6	8	-2	0	0	—	—	—	—	—
02-03—Nashville	NHL	2	0	0	0	2	0	0	0	—	—	—	—	—
—Milwaukee	AHL	30	11	21	32	65	3	3	0	6	2	4	6	8
03-04—Rochester	AHL	75	20	57	77	137	9	8	2	16	5	14	19	30
—Buffalo	NHL	4	0	0	0	4	-1	0	0	—	—	—	—	—
04-05—Kloten	Switzerland	43	17	28	45	110	...	4	0	3	2	2	4	4
NHL Totals (7 years)		86	5	11	16	71	-8	0	0	3	0	0	0	2

PIVKO, LIBOR — LW — PREDATORS

PERSONAL: Born March 29, 1980, in Novy Vicin, Czechoslovakia. ... 6-2/195. ... Shoots left.

TRANSACTIONS/CAREER NOTES: Selected by Nashville Predators in third round (fourth Predators pick, 89th overall) of NHL entry draft (June 24, 2000).

		REGULAR SEASON								PLAYOFFS				
Season Team	League	GP	G	A	Pts.	PIM	+/-	PP	SH	GP	G	A	Pts.	PIM
98-99—Opava	Czech.	5	0	1	1	0	...	0	0	—	—	—	—	—
99-00—Havirov	Czech Rep.	40	11	11	22	41	...	...	...	—	—	—	—	—
00-01—Havirov	Czech Rep.	37	4	15	19	28	...	...	...	—	—	—	—	—
01-02—HC Continental Zlin	Czech Rep.	46	8	20	28	36	...	...	...	9	5	3	8	8
02-03—HC Continental Zlin	Czech Rep.	52	13	12	25	60	...	...	...	—	—	—	—	—
03-04—Nashville	NHL	1	0	0	0	0	0	0	0	—	—	—	—	—
—Milwaukee	AHL	67	11	20	31	50	17	3	0	21	7	6	13	22
04-05—Milwaukee	AHL	56	5	15	20	59	2	1	2	6	0	1	1	2
NHL Totals (1 year)		1	0	0	0	0	0	0	0					

PLEKANEC, TOMAS — C — CANADIENS

PERSONAL: Born October 31, 1982, in Kladno, Czechoslovakia. ... 5-10/200. ... Shoots left. ... Name pronounced pleh-KA-nyehts.

TRANSACTIONS/CAREER NOTES: Selected by Montreal Canadiens in third round (fourth Canadiens pick, 71st overall) of NHL entry draft (June 23, 2001).

		REGULAR SEASON								PLAYOFFS				
Season Team	League	GP	G	A	Pts.	PIM	+/-	PP	SH	GP	G	A	Pts.	PIM
00-01—HC Kladno	Czech Rep.	47	9	9	18	24	...	...	...	—	—	—	—	—
01-02—HC Kladno	Czech Rep.	48	7	16	23	28	...	...	...	—	—	—	—	—
02-03—Hamilton	AHL	77	19	27	46	74	5	6	0	13	3	2	5	8
03-04—Hamilton	AHL	74	23	43	66	90	21	5	3	10	2	5	7	6
—Montreal	NHL	2	0	0	0	0	0	0	0	—	—	—	—	—
04-05—Hamilton	AHL	80	29	35	64	68	4	11	1	4	2	4	6	6
NHL Totals (1 year)		2	0	0	0	0	0	0	0					

PLIHAL, TOMAS — LW/RW — SHARKS

PERSONAL: Born March 28, 1983, in Frydlant v Cechach, Czechoslovakia. ... 6-1/180. ... Shoots left.

TRANSACTIONS/CAREER NOTES: Selected by San Jose Sharks in fifth round (fourth Sharks pick, 140th overall) of NHL entry draft (June 23, 2001).

		REGULAR SEASON								PLAYOFFS				
Season Team	League	GP	G	A	Pts.	PIM	+/-	PP	SH	GP	G	A	Pts.	PIM
00-01—Liberic	Czech. Jrs.	33	16	12	28	0	...	...	...					
01-02—Kootenay	WHL	72	32	54	86	28	...	...	...	22	4	10	14	14
02-03—Kootenay	WHL	67	35	42	77	113	...	...	...	11	2	4	6	18
03-04—Cleveland	AHL	51	4	12	16	16	8	1	0	6	0	3	3	2
04-05—Cleveland	AHL	62	17	11	28	26	-18	5	0	—	—	—	—	—

POAPST, STEVE — D

PERSONAL: Born January 3, 1969, in Cornwall, Ont. ... 6-0/199. ... Shoots left. ... Name pronounced POHPST.

TRANSACTIONS/CAREER NOTES: Signed as free agent by Washington Capitals (February 4, 1995). ... Signed as free agent by Chicago Blackhawks (July 27, 2000). ... Strained groin (April 1, 2001); missed three games. ... Suffered concussion (January 8, 2004); missed 29 games.

		REGULAR SEASON								PLAYOFFS				
Season Team	League	GP	G	A	Pts.	PIM	+/-	PP	SH	GP	G	A	Pts.	PIM
86-87—Smith Falls	OJHL	54	10	27	37	94	...	...	...	—	—	—	—	—
87-88—Colgate	ECAC	32	3	13	16	22	...	...	...	—	—	—	—	—
88-89—Colgate	ECAC	30	0	5	5	38	...	...	...	—	—	—	—	—
89-90—Colgate	ECAC	38	4	15	19	54	...	...	...	—	—	—	—	—
90-91—Colgate	ECAC	32	6	15	21	43	...	...	...	—	—	—	—	—
91-92—Hampton Roads	ECHL	55	8	20	28	29	...	...	...	14	1	4	5	12
92-93—Hampton Roads	ECHL	63	10	35	45	57	...	...	...	4	0	1	1	4
—Baltimore	AHL	7	0	1	1	4	...	...	...	7	0	3	3	6
93-94—Portland	AHL	78	14	21	35	47	...	...	...	12	0	3	3	8
94-95—Portland	AHL	71	8	22	30	60	41	4	0	7	0	1	1	16
95-96—Portland	AHL	70	10	24	34	79	...	...	...	20	2	6	8	16
—Washington	NHL	3	1	0	1	0	-1	0	0	6	0	0	0	0
96-97—Portland	AHL	47	1	20	21	34	0	0	0	5	0	1	1	6
97-98—Portland	AHL	76	8	29	37	46	17	5	0	10	2	3	5	8
98-99—Portland	AHL	54	3	21	24	36	3	2	0	—	—	—	—	—
—Washington	NHL	22	0	0	0	8	-8	0	0	—	—	—	—	—
99-00—Portland	AHL	56	0	14	14	20	...	...	...	3	1	0	1	2
00-01—Norfolk	AHL	37	1	8	9	14	...	...	...	—	—	—	—	—
—Chicago	NHL	36	2	3	5	12	3	0	0	—	—	—	—	—
01-02—Chicago	NHL	56	1	7	8	30	6	0	0	5	0	0	0	0
02-03—Chicago	NHL	75	2	11	13	50	14	0	0	—	—	—	—	—
03-04—Chicago	NHL	53	2	2	4	26	-16	0	0	—	—	—	—	—
NHL Totals (6 years)		245	8	23	31	126	-2	0	0	11	0	0	0	0

POCK, THOMAS — D — RANGERS

PERSONAL: Born December 2, 1981, in Klagenfurt, Austria. ... 6-1/208. ... Shoots left.

TRANSACTIONS/CAREER NOTES: Signed as free agent by New York Rangers (March 23, 2004).

		REGULAR SEASON								PLAYOFFS				
Season Team	League	GP	G	A	Pts.	PIM	+/-	PP	SH	GP	G	A	Pts.	PIM
00-01—Massachusetts	Hockey East	33	6	6	12	59	...	...	...	—	—	—	—	—
01-02—Massachusetts	Hockey East	23	5	7	12	26	...	...	...	—	—	—	—	—
02-03—Massachusetts	Hockey East	37	17	20	37	46	...	...	...	—	—	—	—	—
03-04—Massachusetts	Hockey East	37	16	25	41	48	...	...	...	—	—	—	—	—
—New York Rangers	NHL	6	2	2	4	0	-4	0	0	—	—	—	—	—
04-05—Hartford	AHL	50	1	5	6	55	9	1	0	6	0	1	1	8
—Charlotte	ECHL	3	0	2	2	2	1	0	0	—	—	—	—	—
NHL Totals (1 year)		6	2	2	4	0	-4	0	0					

PODKONICKY, ANDREJ — C — CAPITALS

PERSONAL: Born May 9, 1978, in Zypien, Czechoslovakia. ... 6-0/206. ... Shoots left. ... Name pronounced pahd-kah-NIH-kee.

TRANSACTIONS/CAREER NOTES: Selected by St. Louis Blues in 8th round (8th Blues pick, 196th overall) of entry draft (June 22, 1996). ... Traded by Blues to Florida Panthers for C Eric Boguniecki (December 18, 2000). ... Signed as free agent by Washington Capitals (July 14, 2003).

		REGULAR SEASON								PLAYOFFS				
Season Team	League	GP	G	A	Pts.	PIM	+/-	PP	SH	GP	G	A	Pts.	PIM
94-95—Zvolen	Czech Rep.	17	0	4	4	6	...	...	...	—	—	—	—	—
95-96—ZTK Zvolen	Slov. Div.	38	18	12	30	18	...	...	...	—	—	—	—	—
96-97—Portland	WHL	71	25	46	71	127	...	...	...	6	1	1	2	8
97-98—Portland	WHL	64	30	44	74	81	52	8	2	16	4	12	16	20
98-99—Worcester	AHL	61	19	24	43	52	1	4	0	4	0	0	0	4
99-00—Worcester	AHL	77	16	25	41	68	...	...	...	9	2	5	7	6
00-01—Worcester	AHL	16	2	3	5	15	...	...	...	—	—	—	—	—
—Louisville	AHL	41	6	10	16	31	...	...	...	—	—	—	—	—
—Florida	NHL	6	1	0	1	2	0	0	0	—	—	—	—	—
01-02—HIFK Helsinki	Finland	23	3	6	9	41	...	...	...	—	—	—	—	—
—Slovan Bratislava	Slovakia	16	11	2	13	2	...	...	...	19	4	7	11	49
02-03—Iserlohn	Germany	52	18	15	33	54	...	...	...	—	—	—	—	—
03-04—Washington	NHL	2	0	0	0	0	-1	0	0	—	—	—	—	—
—Portland	AHL	56	12	14	26	31	3	1	0	7	0	2	2	16
04-05—Liberec	Czech Rep.	24	9	4	13	16	...	...	...	6	0	1	1	8
NHL Totals (2 years)		8	1	0	1	2	-1	0	0					

P

POHANKA, IGOR — C — MIGHTY DUCKS

PERSONAL: Born July 5, 1983, in Plestany, Czechoslovakia. ... 6-3/185. ... Shoots left.

TRANSACTIONS/CAREER NOTES: Selected by New Jersey Devils in second round (second Devils pick, 44th overall) of NHL entry draft (June

23, 2001). ... Traded by Devils with RW Petr Sykora, D Mike Commodore and G J.F. Damphousse to Mighty Ducks of Anaheim for D Oleg Tverdovsky, LW Jeff Friesen and RW Maxin Balmochnykh (July 7, 2002).

		REGULAR SEASON								PLAYOFFS				
Season Team	League	GP	G	A	Pts.	PIM	+/-	PP	SH	GP	G	A	Pts.	PIM
99-00—Bratislava	Slov. Jr.	32	12	18	30	29	...	...	...	—	—	—	—	—
00-01—Prince Albert	WHL	70	16	33	49	24	...	...	...	—	—	—	—	—
01-02—Prince Albert	WHL	58	25	43	68	18	...	...	...	—	—	—	—	—
02-03—Prince Albert	WHL	56	25	31	56	28	...	...	...	—	—	—	—	—
03-04—Cincinnati	AHL	42	5	6	11	6	-3	0	0	4	0	0	0	0
—San Diego	ECHL	11	1	5	6	10	-1	0	0	3	0	2	2	0
04-05—Cincinnati	AHL	35	5	3	8	18	-1	1	0	0	0	0	0	0

POHL, JOHNNY — C — BLUES

PERSONAL: Born June 29, 1979, in Rochester, Minn. ... 6-1/194. ... Shoots right.
TRANSACTIONS/CAREER NOTES: Selected by St. Louis Blues in ninth round (eighth Blues pick, 255th overall) of NHL entry draft (June 27, 1998).

		REGULAR SEASON								PLAYOFFS				
Season Team	League	GP	G	A	Pts.	PIM	+/-	PP	SH	GP	G	A	Pts.	PIM
97-98—Red Wing H.S.	Minn. H.S.	28	30	77	107	18	...	...	...	—	—	—	—	—
—Twin Cities	USHL	10	5	3	8	10	...	...	...	—	—	—	—	—
98-99—Minnesota	WCHA	42	7	10	17	18	...	...	...	—	—	—	—	—
99-00—Minnesota	WCHA	41	18	49	67	26	...	...	...	—	—	—	—	—
00-01—Minnesota	WCHA	38	19	26	45	24	...	...	...	—	—	—	—	—
01-02—Minnesota	WCHA	44	27	*52	*79	26	...	...	...	—	—	—	—	—
02-03—Worcester	AHL	58	26	32	58	34	11	6	0	3	0	1	1	6
03-04—Worcester	AHL	65	16	25	41	65	-2	7	0	3	0	1	1	2
—St. Louis	NHL	1	0	0	0	0	-2	0	0	—	—	—	—	—
04-05—Worcester	AHL	13	3	6	9	2	-3	1	0	—	—	—	—	—
NHL Totals (1 year)		1	0	0	0	0	-2	0	0					

POKULOK, SASHA — D — CAPITALS

PERSONAL: Born May 25, 1986, in Montreal. ... 6-5/220. ... Shoots right.
TRANSACTIONS/CAREER NOTES: Selected by Washington Capitals in 1st round (1st Capitals pick, 14th overall) of entry draft (July 30, 2005).

		REGULAR SEASON								PLAYOFFS				
Season Team	League	GP	G	A	Pts.	PIM	+/-	PP	SH	GP	G	A	Pts.	PIM
03-04—Notre Dame	SJHL	39	7	16	23	34	...	...	...	—	—	—	—	—
04-05—Cornell	ECAC	26	3	7	10	33	...	...	...	—	—	—	—	—

POLLOCK, JAME — D

PERSONAL: Born June 16, 1979, in Quebec City. ... 6-1/209. ... Shoots right.
TRANSACTIONS/CAREER NOTES: Selected by St. Louis Blues in 4th round (4th Blues pick, 106th overall) of entry draft (June 21, 1997).

		REGULAR SEASON								PLAYOFFS				
Season Team	League	GP	G	A	Pts.	PIM	+/-	PP	SH	GP	G	A	Pts.	PIM
95-96—Seattle	WHL	32	0	1	1	15	...	...	...	—	—	—	—	—
96-97—Seattle	WHL	66	15	19	34	94	...	...	...	15	3	5	8	16
97-98—Seattle	WHL	66	11	36	47	78	22	6	1	5	0	1	1	17
98-99—Seattle	WHL	59	10	32	42	78	2	7	1	11	3	4	7	8
99-00—Worcester	AHL	56	12	12	24	50	...	...	...	9	5	3	8	6
00-01—Worcester	AHL	55	15	8	23	36	...	...	...	11	1	7	8	10
01-02—Worcester	AHL	71	23	43	66	89	-4	12	0	3	1	0	1	2
02-03—Worcester	AHL	44	5	17	22	50	-6	3	0	3	1	0	1	2
03-04—St. Louis	NHL	9	0	0	0	6	-1	0	0	—	—	—	—	—
—Worcester	AHL	44	8	24	32	52	1	5	0	7	1	4	5	14
04-05—Lugano	Switzerland	—	—	—	—	—	—	—	—	2	0	1	1	8
—Kloten	Switzerland	26	4	8	12	34	...	1	0	—	—	—	—	—
NHL Totals (1 year)		9	0	0	0	6	-1	0	0					

POMINVILLE, JASON — RW — SABRES

PERSONAL: Born November 30, 1982, in Repentigny, Que. ... 6-0/186. ... Shoots right.
TRANSACTIONS/CAREER NOTES: Selected by Buffalo Sabres in second round (fourth Sabres pick, 55th overall) of NHL entry draft (June 23, 2001).

		REGULAR SEASON								PLAYOFFS				
Season Team	League	GP	G	A	Pts.	PIM	+/-	PP	SH	GP	G	A	Pts.	PIM
98-99—Shawinigan	QMJHL	2	0	0	0	0	...	...	...	—	—	—	—	—
99-00—Shawinigan	QMJHL	60	4	17	21	12	...	...	...	13	2	3	5	0
00-01—Shawinigan	QMJHL	71	46	61	107	24	...	...	...	10	6	6	12	0
01-02—Shawinigan	QMJHL	66	57	64	121	32	...	...	...	2	0	0	0	0
02-03—Rochester	AHL	73	13	21	34	16	5	3	0	3	1	1	2	0
03-04—Rochester	AHL	66	34	30	64	30	1	22	0	16	9	10	19	6
—Buffalo	NHL	1	0	0	0	0	0	0	0	—	—	—	—	—
04-05—Rochester	AHL	78	30	38	68	43	1	11	0	0	0	0	0	0
NHL Totals (1 year)		1	0	0	0	0	0	0	0					

PONIKAROVSKY, ALEXEI — LW — MAPLE LEAFS

PERSONAL: Born April 9, 1980, in Kiev, U.S.S.R. ... 6-4/220. ... Shoots left.
TRANSACTIONS/CAREER NOTES: Selected by Toronto Maple Leafs in fourth round (fourth Maple Leafs pick, 87th overall) of NHL draft (June 27, 1998).

		REGULAR SEASON								PLAYOFFS				
Season Team	**League**	**GP**	**G**	**A**	**Pts.**	**PIM**	**+/-**	**PP**	**SH**	**GP**	**G**	**A**	**Pts.**	**PIM**
95-96—Dynamo Moscow........	CIS Jr.	70	14	10	24	20	...	...	...	—	—	—	—	—
96-97—Dynamo Moscow........	Russian Jr.	60	12	15	27	30	...	...	...	—	—	—	—	—
—Dynamo Moscow........	Rus. Div.	2	0	0	0	2	...	...	...	—	—	—	—	—
97-98—Dynamo Moscow........	Rus. Div.	24	1	2	3	30	...	...	...	—	—	—	—	—
98-99—Dynamo Moscow........	Russian	...	...	...	...	...	...	...	...	3	0	0	0	2
99-00—Dynamo Moscow........	Russian	19	1	0	1	8	...	...	...	1	0	0	0	0
00-01—St. John's..................	AHL	49	12	24	36	44	...	...	...	4	0	0	0	4
—Toronto......................	NHL	22	1	3	4	14	-1	0	0	—	—	—	—	—
01-02—St. John's..................	AHL	72	21	27	48	74	4	4	1	5	2	1	3	8
—Toronto......................	NHL	8	2	0	2	0	2	0	0	10	0	0	0	4
02-03—St. John's..................	AHL	63	24	22	46	68	18	5	2	—	—	—	—	—
—Toronto......................	NHL	13	0	3	3	11	4	0	0	—	—	—	—	—
03-04—Toronto......................	NHL	73	9	19	28	44	14	1	0	13	1	3	4	8
04-05—Khimik Voskresensk ...	Russian	19	1	5	6	16	4	...	...	—	—	—	—	—
NHL Totals (4 years)...........		116	12	25	37	69	19	1	0	23	1	3	4	12

POPOVIC, MARK — D — MIGHTY DUCKS

PERSONAL: Born October 11, 1982, in Stoney Creek, Ontario. ... 6-1/207. ... Shoots left.
TRANSACTIONS/CAREER NOTES: Selected by Mighty Ducks of Anaheim in second round (second Mighty Ducks pick, 35th overall) of NHL entry draft (June 23, 2001).

		REGULAR SEASON								PLAYOFFS				
Season Team	**League**	**GP**	**G**	**A**	**Pts.**	**PIM**	**+/-**	**PP**	**SH**	**GP**	**G**	**A**	**Pts.**	**PIM**
98-99—Toronto St. Michael's..	OHL	60	6	26	32	46	...	...	...	—	—	—	—	—
99-00—Toronto St. Michael's..	OHL	68	11	29	40	68	...	...	...	—	—	—	—	—
00-01—Toronto St. Michael's..	OHL	61	7	35	42	54	...	...	...	18	3	5	8	22
01-02—Toronto St. Michael's..	OHL	58	12	29	41	42	...	...	...	15	1	11	12	10
02-03—Cincinnati...................	AHL	73	3	21	24	46	8	2	0	—	—	—	—	—
03-04—Anaheim	NHL	1	0	0	0	0	0	0	0	—	—	—	—	—
—Cincinnati...................	AHL	74	4	11	15	63	0	0	0	9	1	2	3	4
04-05—Cincinnati...................	AHL	74	1	17	18	47	16	0	0	11	2	3	5	6
NHL Totals (1 year).............		1	0	0	0	0	0	0	0					

POSPISIL, TOMAS — RW — THRASHERS

PERSONAL: Born August 26, 1987, in Czech Republic. ... 5-11/175. ... Shoots right.

		REGULAR SEASON								PLAYOFFS				
Season Team	**League**	**GP**	**G**	**A**	**Pts.**	**PIM**	**+/-**	**PP**	**SH**	**GP**	**G**	**A**	**Pts.**	**PIM**
02-03—Trinec.........................	Czech. Jrs.	1	0	0	0	0	...	...	...	2	0	0	0	0
03-04—Trinec.........................	Czech. Jrs.	45	14	11	25	40	8	...	...	2	1	1	2	0
04-05—Trinec.........................	Czech. Jrs.	38	19	18	37	44	-1	...	...	5	4	1	5	27
—Trinec.........................	Czech Rep.	14	0	0	0	0	-6	...	...	—	—	—	—	—

POTHIER, BRIAN — D — SENATORS

PERSONAL: Born April 15, 1977, in New Bedford, Mass. ... 6-0/198. ... Shoots right. ... Name pronounced POH-thee-uhr.
TRANSACTIONS/CAREER NOTES: Signed as free agent by Atlanta Thrashers (April 8, 2000). ... Suffered concussion (March 22, 2002); missed remainder of season. ... Traded by Thrashers to Ottawa Senators for LW Shawn McEachern and sixth-round pick (G Dan Turple) in 2004 entry draft (June 30, 2002). ... Suffered concussion (December 14, 2003); missed 11 games.

		REGULAR SEASON								PLAYOFFS				
Season Team	**League**	**GP**	**G**	**A**	**Pts.**	**PIM**	**+/-**	**PP**	**SH**	**GP**	**G**	**A**	**Pts.**	**PIM**
96-97—R.P.I...........................	ECAC	34	1	11	12	42	...	...	...	—	—	—	—	—
97-98—R.P.I...........................	ECAC	35	2	9	11	28	...	...	...	—	—	—	—	—
98-99—R.P.I...........................	ECAC	37	5	13	18	36	...	...	...	—	—	—	—	—
99-00—R.P.I...........................	ECAC	36	9	24	33	44	...	...	...	—	—	—	—	—
00-01—Orlando.......................	IHL	76	12	29	41	69	...	...	...	16	3	5	8	11
—Atlanta	NHL	3	0	0	0	2	4	0	0	—	—	—	—	—
01-02—Atlanta	NHL	33	3	6	9	22	-19	1	0	—	—	—	—	—
—Chicago.......................	AHL	39	6	13	19	30	2	1	0	—	—	—	—	—
02-03—Ottawa	NHL	14	2	4	6	6	11	0	0	1	0	0	0	2
—Binghamton	AHL	68	7	40	47	58	5	6	0	8	2	8	10	4
03-04—Ottawa	NHL	55	2	6	8	24	6	1	0	7	0	0	0	6
04-05—Binghamton	AHL	77	12	36	48	64	13	11	0	6	0	1	1	6
NHL Totals (4 years)...........		105	7	16	23	54	2	2	0	8	0	0	0	8

POTI, TOM — D — RANGERS

PERSONAL: Born March 22, 1977, in Worcester, Mass. ... 6-3/208. ... Shoots left.
TRANSACTIONS/CAREER NOTES: Selected by Edmonton Oilers in third round (fourth Oilers pick, 59th overall) of NHL entry draft (June 22,

1996). ... Bruised right knee (November 10, 1999); missed one game. ... Strained neck (December 4, 1999); missed two games. ... Bruised thumb (January 14, 2000); missed one game. ... Bruised ankle (February 13, 2000); missed one game. ... Reinjured ankle (February 29, 2000); missed one game. ... Fractured finger (December 21, 2001); missed seven games. ... Traded by Oilers with LW Rem Murray to New York Rangers for C Mike York and fourth-round pick (D Ivan Koltsov) in 2002 draft (March 19, 2002). ... Flu (December 21, 2002); missed one game. ... Injured neck (January 11, 2003); missed one game. ... Flu (November 4, 2003); missed two games. ... Injured thumb (November 20, 2003); missed one game. ... Back spasms (December 13, 2003); missed one game. ... Injured hip flexor (January 3, 2004); missed one game. ... Injured back (January 20, 2004); missed two games. ... Reinjured back (February 2, 2004); missed two games.

		REGULAR SEASON								PLAYOFFS				
Season Team	League	GP	G	A	Pts.	PIM	+/-	PP	SH	GP	G	A	Pts.	PIM
94-95—Cushing Academy	Mass. H.S.	36	16	47	63	35	...	...	...	—	—	—	—	—
95-96—Cushing Academy	Mass. H.S.	29	14	59	73	18	...	...	...	—	—	—	—	—
96-97—Boston University	Hockey East	38	4	17	21	54	10	1	0	—	—	—	—	—
97-98—Boston University	Hockey East	38	13	29	42	60	...	...	...	—	—	—	—	—
98-99—Edmonton	NHL	73	5	16	21	42	10	2	0	4	0	1	1	2
99-00—Edmonton	NHL	76	9	26	35	65	8	2	1	5	0	1	1	0
00-01—Edmonton	NHL	81	12	20	32	60	-4	6	0	6	0	2	2	2
01-02—Edmonton	NHL	55	1	16	17	42	-6	1	0	—	—	—	—	—
—U.S. Olympic team	Int'l	6	0	1	1	4	...	...	...	—	—	—	—	—
—New York Rangers	NHL	11	1	7	8	2	-4	1	0	—	—	—	—	—
02-03—New York Rangers	NHL	80	11	37	48	60	-6	3	0	—	—	—	—	—
03-04—New York Rangers	NHL	67	10	14	24	47	-1	4	0	—	—	—	—	—
NHL Totals (6 years)		443	49	136	185	318	-3	19	1	15	0	4	4	4

POTVIN, FELIX G

PERSONAL: Born June 23, 1971, in Anjou, Que. ... 6-1/190. ... Catches left. ... Name pronounced PAHT-vihn. ... Nickname: The Cat.

TRANSACTIONS/CAREER NOTES: Selected by Toronto Maple Leafs in second round (second Maple Leafs pick, 31st overall) of NHL entry draft (June 16, 1990). ... Traded by Maple Leafs with sixth-round pick (traded to Tampa Bay; Lightning selected C Fedor Fedorov) in 1999 draft to New York Islanders for D Bryan Berard and sixth-round pick (RW Jan Sochor) in 1999 draft (January 9, 1999). ... Strained groin (February 13, 1999); missed 22 games. ... Traded by Islanders with second- (traded to New Jersey; Devils selected RW Teemu Laine) and third-round (C Thatcher Bell) picks in 2000 draft to Vancouver Canucks for G Kevin Weekes, C Dave Scatchard and RW Bill Muckalt (December 19, 1999). ... Injured knee (January 23, 2000); missed five games. ... Traded by Canucks to Los Angeles Kings for future considerations (February 15, 2001). ... Signed by Boston Bruins as an unrestricted free agent (September 3, 2003). ... Injured knee (February 5, 2004); missed one game.

		REGULAR SEASON										PLAYOFFS							
Season Team	League	GP	Min.	W	L	T	GA	SO	GAA	SV%	GP	Min.	W	L	GA	SO	GAA	SV%
88-89—Chicoutimi	QMJHL	*65	*3489	25	31	1	*271	2	4.66	...	—	—	—	—	—	—	—	—
89-90—Chicoutimi	QMJHL	*62	*3478	31	26	2	231	2	3.99	...	—	—	—	—	—	—	—	—
90-91—Chicoutimi	QMJHL	54	3216	33	15	4	145	*6	2.71	...	*16	*992	*11	5	46	0	*2.78	...
91-92—St. John's	AHL	35	2070	18	10	6	101	2	2.93	...	11	642	7	4	41	0	3.83	...
—Toronto	NHL	4	210	0	2	1	8	0	2.29	.933	—	—	—	—	—	—	—	—
92-93—Toronto	NHL	48	2781	25	15	7	116	2	*2.50	.910	*21	*1308	11	10	62	1	2.84	.903
—St. John's	AHL	5	309	3	0	2	18	0	3.50	.894	—	—	—	—	—	—	—	—
93-94—Toronto	NHL	66	3883	34	22	9	187	3	2.89	.907	18	1124	9	9	46	3	2.46	.912
94-95—Toronto	NHL	36	2144	15	13	7	104	0	2.91	.907	7	424	3	4	20	1	2.83	.921
95-96—Toronto	NHL	69	4009	30	26	11	192	2	2.87	.910	6	350	2	4	19	0	3.26	.904
96-97—Toronto	NHL	*74	*4271	27	*36	7	*224	0	3.15	.908	—	—	—	—	—	—	—	—
97-98—Toronto	NHL	67	3864	26	*33	7	176	5	2.73	.906	—	—	—	—	—	—	—	—
98-99—Toronto	NHL	5	299	3	2	0	19	0	3.81	.866	—	—	—	—	—	—	—	—
—New York Islanders	NHL	11	606	2	7	1	37	0	3.66	.893	—	—	—	—	—	—	—	—
99-00—New York Islanders	NHL	22	1273	5	14	3	68	1	3.21	.892	—	—	—	—	—	—	—	—
—Vancouver	NHL	34	1966	12	13	7	85	0	2.59	.906	—	—	—	—	—	—	—	—
00-01—Vancouver	NHL	35	2006	14	17	3	103	1	3.08	.887	—	—	—	—	—	—	—	—
—Los Angeles	NHL	23	1410	13	5	5	46	5	1.96	.919	13	812	7	6	33	2	2.44	.909
01-02—Los Angeles	NHL	71	4071	31	27	8	157	6	2.31	.907	7	417	3	4	15	1	2.16	.925
02-03—Los Angeles	NHL	42	2367	17	20	3	105	3	2.66	.894	—	—	—	—	—	—	—	—
03-04—Boston	NHL	28	1605	12	8	6	67	4	2.50	.903	—	—	—	—	—	—	—	—
NHL Totals (13 years)		635	36765	266	260	85	1694	32	2.76	.905	72	4435	35	37	195	8	2.64	.910

POULIOT, BENOIT LW WILD

PERSONAL: Born September 29, 1986, in Alfred, Ont. ... 6-3/179. ... Shoots left.

TRANSACTIONS/CAREER NOTES: Selected by Minnesota Wild in the 1st round (1st Wild pick, 4th overall) of entry draft (July 30, 2005).

		REGULAR SEASON								PLAYOFFS				
Season Team	League	GP	G	A	Pts.	PIM	+/-	PP	SH	GP	G	A	Pts.	PIM
03-04—Hawkesbury	OJHL	45	21	21	42	85	...	...	...	—	—	—	—	—
—Sudbury	OHL	4	2	2	4	0	...	...	...	—	—	—	—	—
04-05—Sudbury	OHL	67	29	38	67	102	7	8	0	—	—	—	—	—

PRATT, NOLAN D LIGHTNING

PERSONAL: Born August 14, 1975, in Fort McMurray, Alta. ... 6-3/203. ... Shoots left. ... Brother of Harlan Pratt, D, in Pittsburgh and Carolina organizations (1997-2003).

TRANSACTIONS/CAREER NOTES: Selected by Hartford Whalers in fifth round (fourth Whalers pick, 115th overall) of NHL entry draft (June 26, 1993). ... Whalers franchise moved to North Carolina and renamed Carolina Hurricanes for 1997-98 season; NHL approved move on June 25, 1997. ... Back spasms (December 21, 1998); missed eight games. ... Injured hip (December 20, 1999); missed two games. ... Injured hand (April 3, 2000); missed final two games of season. ... Traded by Hurricanes with first-(C Vaclav Nedorost) and two second-round (C Jared

Aulin and D Argis Saviels) picks in 2000 draft to Colorado Avalanche for D Sandis Ozolinsh and second-round pick (LW Tomas Kurka) in 2000 draft (June 24, 2000). ... Injured wrist (October 4, 2000); missed two games. ... Traded by Avalanche to Tampa Bay Lightning for sixth-round pick (RW Scott Horvath) in 2001 draft (June 24, 2001). ... Fractured foot (September 29, 2001); missed first 11 games of season. ... Fractured right leg (December 31, 2001); missed 25 games. ... Dizziness (December 8, 2002); missed one game.

		REGULAR SEASON								PLAYOFFS				
Season Team	**League**	**GP**	**G**	**A**	**Pts.**	**PIM**	**+/-**	**PP**	**SH**	**GP**	**G**	**A**	**Pts.**	**PIM**
91-92—Portland	WHL	22	2	9	11	13	...	...	...	6	1	3	4	12
92-93—Portland	WHL	70	4	19	23	97	...	...	...	16	2	7	9	31
93-94—Portland	WHL	72	4	32	36	105	36	0	0	10	1	2	3	14
94-95—Portland	WHL	72	6	37	43	196	-22	3	0	9	1	6	7	10
95-96—Richmond	ECHL	4	1	0	1	2	...	...	...	—	—	—	—	—
—Springfield	AHL	62	2	6	8	72	...	...	...	2	0	0	0	0
96-97—Hartford	NHL	9	0	2	2	6	0	0	0	—	—	—	—	—
—Springfield	AHL	66	1	18	19	127	7	0	0	17	0	3	3	18
97-98—New Haven	AHL	54	3	15	18	135	-5	1	0	—	—	—	—	—
—Carolina	NHL	23	0	2	2	44	-2	0	0	—	—	—	—	—
98-99—Carolina	NHL	61	1	14	15	95	15	0	0	3	0	0	0	2
99-00—Carolina	NHL	64	3	1	4	90	-22	0	0	—	—	—	—	—
00-01—Colorado	NHL	46	1	2	3	40	2	0	0	—	—	—	—	—
01-02—Tampa Bay	NHL	46	0	3	3	51	-4	0	0	—	—	—	—	—
02-03—Tampa Bay	NHL	67	1	7	8	35	-6	0	0	4	0	1	1	0
03-04—Tampa Bay	NHL	58	1	3	4	42	11	0	0	20	0	0	0	8
NHL Totals (8 years)		374	7	34	41	403	-6	0	0	27	0	1	1	10

PREISSING, TOM — D — SHARKS

PERSONAL: Born December 3, 1978, in Rosemount, Minn. ... 6-0/205. ... Shoots right. ... Name pronounced PREH-sihng.
TRANSACTIONS/CAREER NOTES: Signed as free agent by San Jose Sharks (April 4, 2003). ... Injured upper body (February 23, 2004); missed two games.

		REGULAR SEASON								PLAYOFFS				
Season Team	**League**	**GP**	**G**	**A**	**Pts.**	**PIM**	**+/-**	**PP**	**SH**	**GP**	**G**	**A**	**Pts.**	**PIM**
99-00—Colorado College	WCHA	36	4	14	18	20	...	...	...	—	—	—	—	—
00-01—Colorado College	WCHA	33	6	18	24	26	...	...	...	—	—	—	—	—
01-02—Colorado College	WCHA	43	6	26	32	42	...	...	...	—	—	—	—	—
02-03—Colorado College	WCHA	42	23	29	52	16	...	...	...	—	—	—	—	—
03-04—San Jose	NHL	69	2	17	19	12	8	2	0	11	0	1	1	0
04-05—Krefeld Pinguine	Germany	33	1	6	7	32	6	1	0	—	—	—	—	—
NHL Totals (1 year)		69	2	17	19	12	8	2	0	11	0	1	1	0

PRICE, CAREY — G — CANADIENS

PERSONAL: Born August 16, 1987, in Williams, B.C. ... 6-2/175. ... Catches left.
TRANSACTIONS/CAREER NOTES: Selected by the Montreal Canadiens in the 1st round (1st Canadiens pick, fifth overall) of entry draft (July 30, 2005).

		REGULAR SEASON									PLAYOFFS							
Season Team	**League**	**GP**	**Min.**	**W**	**L**	**T**	**GA**	**SO**	**GAA**	**SV%**	**GP**	**Min.**	**W**	**L**	**GA**	**SO**	**GAA**	**SV%**
02-03—Tri-City	WHL	1	...	0	0	0	2	0	6.00	.857	—	—	—	—	—	—	—	—
03-04—Tri-City	WHL	28	...	8	9	3	54	1	2.38	.915	—	—	—	—	—	—	—	—
04-05—Tri-City	WHL	63	...	...	...	...	...	...	...	...	5	...	...	...	...	...	...	...

PRIMEAU, KEITH — C — FLYERS

PERSONAL: Born November 24, 1971, in Toronto. ... 6-5/220. ... Shoots left. ... Brother of Wayne Primeau, C, San Jose Sharks. ... Name pronounced PREE-moh.
TRANSACTIONS/CAREER NOTES: Selected by Detroit Red Wings in first round (first Red Wings pick, third overall) of NHL draft (June 16, 1990). ... Flu (January 13, 1993); missed two games. ... Sprained right shoulder (February 9, 1993); missed one game. ... Sprained right knee (March 2, 1993); missed two games. ... Sprained right knee (April 1, 1993); missed four games. ... Injured right thumb (February 10, 1995); missed one game. ... Flu (February 25, 1995); missed one game. ... Reinjured thumb (March 2, 1995); missed one game. ... Injured ribs (November 1, 1995); missed eight games. ... Injured left knee (January 13, 1996); missed one game. ... Traded by Red Wings with D Paul Coffey and first-round pick (D Nikos Tselios) in 1997 draft to Hartford Whalers for LW Brendan Shanahan and D Brian Glynn (October 9, 1996). ... Flu (December 3, 1996); missed one game. ... Suffered concussion (December 21, 1996); missed one game. ... Suspended two games by NHL for slashing incident (January 3, 1997). ... Asthma (February 12, 1997); missed one game. ... Whalers franchise moved to North Carolina and renamed Carolina Hurricanes for 1997-98 season; NHL approved move on June 25, 1997. ... Strained hip flexor (November 13, 1997); missed one game. ... Injured wrist (February 13, 1999); missed one game. ... Strained lower back (April 10, 1999); missed three games. ... Missed first 47 games of 1999-2000 season in contract dispute. ... Rights traded by Hurricanes with fifth-round pick (traded to New York Islanders; Islanders selected RW Kristofer Ottosson) in 2000 draft to Philadelphia Flyers for C Rod Brind'Amour, G Jean-Marc Pelletier and second-round pick (traded to Colorado; Avalanche selected D Agris Saviels) in 2000 draft (January 23, 2000). ... Fractured rib (February 12, 2000); missed nine games. ... Reinjured ribs (March 4, 2000); missed three games. ... Headaches (October 29, 2000); missed two games. ... Bruised shoulder (December 27, 2000); missed three games. ... Sprained left knee (March 26, 2001); missed final six games of season and two playoff games. ... Sprained right ankle (October 13, 2001); missed three games. ... Strained muscle in ribs (March 4, 2002); missed two games. ... Reinjured ribs (March 18, 2002); missed two games. ... Bruised right ankle (October 12, 2002); missed two games. ... Injured wrist (December 10, 2003); missed one game. ... Fractured thumb (January 2, 2004); missed six games. ... Suffered concussion (February 13, 2004); missed 21 games.
STATISTICAL PLATEAUS: Three-goal games: 2000-01 (1).

Season Team	League	GP	G	A	Pts.	PIM	+/-	PP	SH	GP	G	A	Pts.	PIM
		REGULAR SEASON								PLAYOFFS				
87-88—Hamilton	OHL	47	6	6	12	69	...	...	...	11	0	2	2	2
88-89—Niagara Falls	OHL	48	20	35	55	56	...	...	...	17	9	6	15	12
89-90—Niagara Falls	OHL	65	*57	70	*127	97	...	...	...	16	*16	17	*33	49
90-91—Detroit	NHL	58	3	12	15	106	-12	0	0	5	1	1	2	25
—Adirondack	AHL	6	3	5	8	8	...	...	...	—	—	—	—	—
91-92—Detroit	NHL	35	6	10	16	83	9	0	0	11	0	0	0	14
—Adirondack	AHL	42	21	24	45	89	...	...	...	9	1	7	8	27
92-93—Detroit	NHL	73	15	17	32	152	-6	4	1	7	0	2	2	26
93-94—Detroit	NHL	78	31	42	73	173	34	7	3	7	0	2	2	6
94-95—Detroit	NHL	45	15	27	42	99	17	1	0	17	4	5	9	45
95-96—Detroit	NHL	74	27	25	52	168	19	6	2	17	1	4	5	28
96-97—Hartford	NHL	75	26	25	51	161	-3	6	3	—	—	—	—	—
97-98—Carolina	NHL	81	26	37	63	110	19	7	3	—	—	—	—	—
—Can. Olympic team	Int'l	6	2	1	3	4	3	0	1	—	—	—	—	—
98-99—Carolina	NHL	78	30	32	62	75	8	9	1	6	0	3	3	6
99-00—Philadelphia	NHL	23	7	10	17	31	10	1	0	18	2	11	13	13
00-01—Philadelphia	NHL	71	34	39	73	76	17	11	0	4	0	3	3	8
01-02—Philadelphia	NHL	75	19	29	48	128	-3	5	0	5	0	0	0	6
02-03—Philadelphia	NHL	80	19	27	46	93	4	6	0	13	1	1	2	14
03-04—Philadelphia	NHL	54	7	15	22	80	11	0	1	18	9	7	16	22
NHL Totals (14 years)		900	265	347	612	1535	124	63	14	128	18	39	57	213

PRIMEAU, WAYNE C/LW SHARKS

PERSONAL: Born June 4, 1976, in Scarborough, Ont. ... 6-4/230. ... Shoots left. ... Brother of Keith Primeau, C, Philadelphia Flyers. ... Name pronounced PREE-moh.

TRANSACTIONS/CAREER NOTES: Selected by Buffalo Sabres in first round (first Sabres pick, 17th overall) of NHL draft (June 28, 1994). ... Bruised shoulder (November 4, 1998); missed four games. ... Reinjured shoulder (December 5, 1998); missed four games. ... Reinjured shoulder (January 11, 1999); missed one game. ... Strained groin (March 7, 1999); missed one game. ... Injured hip (January 1, 2000); missed 20 games. ... Traded by Sabres with C/RW Brian Holzinger, D Cory Sarich and third-round pick (RW Alexandre Kharitonov) in 2000 draft to Tampa Bay Lightning for C Chris Gratton and second-round pick (C Derek Roy) in 2001 draft (March 9, 2000). ... Suspended by NHL two games for slashing incident (January 23, 2001). ... Traded by Lightning to Pittsburgh Penguins for LW Matthew Barnaby (February 1, 2001). ... Injured neck (Feburary 14, 2001); missed one game. ... Suffered injury (March 14, 2001); missed one game. ... Injured heel before start of 2001-02 season; missed first eight games of season. ... Knee surgery (January 6, 2002); missed remainder of season. ... Traded by Penguins to San Jose Sharks for RW Matt Bradley (March 11, 2003). ... Injured back (March 21, 2003); missed five games. ... Injured groin (October 18, 2003); missed three games. ... Injured hip flexor (November 13, 2003); missed two games. ... Reinjured hip flexor (November 21, 2003); missed two games.

Season Team	League	GP	G	A	Pts.	PIM	+/-	PP	SH	GP	G	A	Pts.	PIM
		REGULAR SEASON								PLAYOFFS				
92-93—Owen Sound	OHL	66	10	27	37	110	...	...	...	8	1	4	5	0
93-94—Owen Sound	OHL	65	25	50	75	75	...	7	...	9	1	6	7	8
94-95—Owen Sound	OHL	66	34	62	96	84	...	10	1	10	4	9	13	15
—Buffalo	NHL	1	1	0	1	0	-2	0	0	—	—	—	—	—
95-96—Buffalo	NHL	2	0	0	0	0	0	0	0	—	—	—	—	—
—Owen Sound	OHL	28	15	29	44	52	...	...	...	—	—	—	—	—
—Oshawa	OHL	24	12	13	25	33	...	...	...	3	2	3	5	2
—Rochester	AHL	8	2	3	5	6	...	...	...	17	3	1	4	11
96-97—Rochester	AHL	24	9	5	14	27	-3	1	0	1	0	0	0	0
—Buffalo	NHL	45	2	4	6	64	-2	1	0	9	0	0	0	6
97-98—Buffalo	NHL	69	6	6	12	87	9	2	0	14	1	3	4	6
98-99—Buffalo	NHL	67	5	8	13	38	-6	0	0	19	3	4	7	6
99-00—Buffalo	NHL	41	5	7	12	38	-8	2	0	—	—	—	—	—
—Tampa Bay	NHL	17	2	3	5	25	-4	0	0	—	—	—	—	—
00-01—Tampa Bay	NHL	47	2	13	15	77	-17	0	0	—	—	—	—	—
—Pittsburgh	NHL	28	1	6	7	54	0	0	0	18	1	3	4	2
01-02—Pittsburgh	NHL	33	3	7	10	18	-1	0	1	—	—	—	—	—
02-03—Pittsburgh	NHL	70	5	11	16	55	-30	1	0	—	—	—	—	—
—San Jose	NHL	7	1	1	2	0	2	0	0	—	—	—	—	—
03-04—San Jose	NHL	72	9	20	29	90	4	0	1	17	1	2	3	4
NHL Totals (10 years)		499	42	86	128	546	-55	6	2	77	6	12	18	24

PRONGER, CHRIS D OILERS

PERSONAL: Born October 10, 1974, in Dryden, Ont. ... 6-6/218. ... Shoots left. ... Brother of Sean Pronger, C, Vancouver Canucks.

TRANSACTIONS/CAREER NOTES: Selected by Hartford Whalers in 1st round (1st Whalers pick, 2nd overall) of NHL draft (June 26, 1993). ... Bruised left wrist (March 29, 1994); missed three games. ... Injured left shoulder (January 21, 1995); missed five games. ... Traded by Whalers to St. Louis Blues for LW Brendan Shanahan (July 27, 1995). ... Suspended four games for slashing incident (November 1, 1995). ... Injured hand (February 15, 1997); missed one game. ... Suspended four games for slashing incident (December 19, 1998). ... Bruised ankle (February 11, 1999); missed 11 games. ... Back spasms (March 12, 2000); missed one game. ... Suspended one game for fighting incident (October 13, 2000). ... Knee surgery (January 21, 2001); missed 15 games. ... Fractured forearm (February 26, 2001); missed 15 games. ... Injured wrist (November 13, 2001); missed one game. ... Suspended two games for cross-checking incident (April 4, 2002). ... Offseason knee and wrist surgery; missed first 77 games of 2002-03 season. ... Suspended one game for kicking incident (March 16, 2004). ... Traded by Blues to the Edmonton Oilers for D Eric Brewer, D Jeff Woywitka and D Doug Lynch.

Season Team	League	GP	G	A	Pts.	PIM	+/-	PP	SH	GP	G	A	Pts.	PIM
		REGULAR SEASON								PLAYOFFS				
90-91—Stratford	OPJHL	48	15	37	52	132	...	...	...	—	—	—	—	—
91-92—Peterborough	OHL	63	17	45	62	90	...	...	...	10	1	8	9	28

P

Season Team	League	GP	G	A	Pts.	PIM	+/-	PP	SH	GP	G	A	Pts.	PIM
		REGULAR SEASON								PLAYOFFS				
92-93—Peterborough	OHL	61	15	62	77	108	...	...	...	21	15	25	40	51
93-94—Hartford	NHL	81	5	25	30	113	-3	2	0	—	—	—	—	—
94-95—Hartford	NHL	43	5	9	14	54	-12	3	0	—	—	—	—	—
95-96—St. Louis	NHL	78	7	18	25	110	-18	3	1	13	1	5	6	16
96-97—St. Louis	NHL	79	11	24	35	143	15	4	0	6	1	1	2	22
97-98—St. Louis	NHL	81	9	27	36	180	*47	1	0	10	1	9	10	26
—Can. Olympic team	Int'l	6	0	0	0	4	0	0	0	—	—	—	—	—
98-99—St. Louis	NHL	67	13	33	46	113	3	8	0	13	1	4	5	28
99-00—St. Louis	NHL	79	14	48	62	92	*52	8	0	7	3	4	7	32
00-01—St. Louis	NHL	51	8	39	47	75	21	4	0	15	1	7	8	32
01-02—St. Louis	NHL	78	7	40	47	120	23	4	1	9	1	7	8	24
—Can. Olympic team	Int'l	6	0	1	1	2	...	...	...	—	—	—	—	—
02-03—St. Louis	NHL	5	1	3	4	10	-2	0	0	7	1	3	4	14
03-04—St. Louis	NHL	80	14	40	54	88	-1	7	0	5	0	1	1	16
NHL Totals (11 years)		722	94	306	400	1098	125	44	2	85	10	41	51	210

PRONGER, SEAN — C/LW — CANUCKS

PERSONAL: Born November 30, 1972, in Dryden, Ont. ... 6-3/205. ... Shoots left. ... Brother of Chris Pronger, D, St. Louis Blues.

TRANSACTIONS/CAREER NOTES: Selected by Vancouver Canucks in third round (third Canucks pick, 51st overall) of NHL draft (June 22, 1991). ... Signed as free agent by Mighty Ducks of Anaheim (February 14, 1995). ... Strained abdominal muscle (February 17, 1997); missed two games. ... Traded by Mighty Ducks to Pittsburgh Penguins for rights to G Patrick Lalime (March 24, 1998). ... Fractured foot (April 4, 1998); missed seven games. ... Traded by Penguins with C Petr Nedved and D Chris Tamer to New York Rangers for RW Alexei Kovalev and C Harry York (November 25, 1998). ... Traded by Rangers to Los Angeles Kings for LW Eric Lacroix (February 12, 1999). ... Tore medial collateral ligament in left knee (March 18, 1999); missed final 14 games of season. ... Signed as free agent by Boston Bruins (August 25, 1999). ... Traded by Bruins to New York Islanders for future considerations (December 5, 2000). ... Claimed off waivers from Islanders by Columbus Blue Jackets (May 18, 2001). ... Traded by Blue Jackets to Vancouver Canucks for D Zenith Komarniski (October 20, 2003).

Season Team	League	GP	G	A	Pts.	PIM	+/-	PP	SH	GP	G	A	Pts.	PIM
		REGULAR SEASON								PLAYOFFS				
89-90—Thunder Bay Flyers	USHL	48	18	34	52	61	...	...	...	—	—	—	—	—
90-91—Bowling Green	CCHA	40	3	7	10	30	...	...	...	—	—	—	—	—
91-92—Bowling Green	CCHA	34	9	7	16	28	...	...	...	—	—	—	—	—
92-93—Bowling Green	CCHA	39	23	23	46	35	...	...	...	—	—	—	—	—
93-94—Bowling Green	CCHA	38	17	17	34	38	8	5	2	—	—	—	—	—
94-95—Knoxville	ECHL	34	18	23	41	55	-9	5	0	—	—	—	—	—
—Greensboro	ECHL	2	0	2	2	0	1	0	0	—	—	—	—	—
—San Diego	IHL	8	0	0	0	2	-4	0	0	—	—	—	—	—
95-96—Baltimore	AHL	72	16	17	33	61	...	...	...	12	3	7	10	16
—Anaheim	NHL	7	0	1	1	6	0	0	0	—	—	—	—	—
96-97—Baltimore	AHL	41	26	17	43	17	-13	5	2	—	—	—	—	—
—Anaheim	NHL	39	7	7	14	20	6	1	0	9	0	2	2	4
97-98—Anaheim	NHL	62	5	15	20	30	-9	1	0	—	—	—	—	—
—Pittsburgh	NHL	5	1	0	1	2	-1	0	0	5	0	0	0	4
98-99—Houston	IHL	16	11	7	18	32	2	5	0	—	—	—	—	—
—Pittsburgh	NHL	2	0	0	0	0	0	0	0	—	—	—	—	—
—New York Rangers	NHL	14	0	3	3	4	-3	0	0	—	—	—	—	—
—Los Angeles	NHL	13	0	1	1	4	2	0	0	—	—	—	—	—
99-00—Providence	AHL	51	11	18	29	26	...	...	...	—	—	—	—	—
—Boston	NHL	11	0	1	1	13	-4	0	0	—	—	—	—	—
—Manitoba	IHL	14	3	5	8	21	...	...	...	2	0	1	1	2
00-01—Manitoba	IHL	82	18	21	39	85	...	...	...	13	3	6	9	2
01-02—Syracuse	AHL	54	23	26	49	53	8	7	1	8	4	1	5	10
—Columbus	NHL	26	3	1	4	4	-4	0	0	—	—	—	—	—
02-03—Columbus	NHL	78	7	6	13	72	-26	1	0	—	—	—	—	—
03-04—Vancouver	NHL	3	0	1	1	4	-1	0	0	—	—	—	—	—
—Syracuse	AHL	7	2	0	2	7	-1	1	0	—	—	—	—	—
—Manitoba	AHL	68	17	15	32	68	-1	5	2	—	—	—	—	—
04-05—Frankfurt	Germany	51	6	10	16	78	...	...	...	4	0	0	0	6
NHL Totals (8 years)		260	23	36	59	159	-40	3	0	14	0	2	2	8

PROSPAL, VACLAV — LW — LIGHTNING

PERSONAL: Born February 17, 1975, in Ceske-Budejovice, Czech. ... 6-1/194. ... Shoots left. ... Name pronounced PRAHS-puhl. ... Nickname: Vinny.

TRANSACTIONS/CAREER NOTES: Selected by Philadelphia Flyers in third round (second Flyers pick, 71st overall) of NHL draft (June 26, 1993). ... Fractured left leg (January 3, 1998); missed 18 games. ... Traded by Flyers with RW Pat Falloon and second-round pick (LW Chris Bala) in 1998 draft to Ottawa Senators for RW Alexandre Daigle (January 17, 1998). ... Bruised thumb (April 2, 1998); missed two games. ... Bruised mouth (April 7, 1998); missed four games. ... Flu (November 29, 1998); missed one game. ... Traded by Senators to Florida Panthers for fourth-round pick (G Ray Emery) in 2001 draft and third-round pick (traded back to Ottawa) in 2002 draft (January 21, 2001). ... Traded by Panthers to Tampa Bay Lightning for C Ryan Johnson and sixth-round pick (traded back to Tampa Bay; Lightning selected D Doug O'Brien) in 2003 draft (July 10, 2001). ... Flu (December 26, 2001); missed one game. ... Suspended two games by NHL for cross-checking incident (January 21, 2003). ... Signed as free agent by Anaheim Mighty Ducks (July 17, 2003). ... Traded by Mighty Ducks to Lightning for second-round pick in 2005 draft (August 16, 2004).

STATISTICAL PLATEAUS: Three-goal games: 2003-04 (1).

Season Team	League	GP	G	A	Pts.	PIM	+/-	PP	SH	GP	G	A	Pts.	PIM
		REGULAR SEASON								PLAYOFFS				
91-92—Motor-Ceske Bude.	Czech. Jrs.	36	16	16	32	12	...	...	...	—	—	—	—	—
92-93—Motor-Ceske Bude.	Czech. Jrs.	36	26	31	57	24	...	...	...	—	—	—	—	—

P

Season Team	League	REGULAR SEASON GP	G	A	Pts.	PIM	+/-	PP	SH	PLAYOFFS GP	G	A	Pts.	PIM
93-94—Hershey	AHL	55	14	21	35	38	-2	4	0	2	0	0	0	2
94-95—Hershey	AHL	69	13	32	45	36	-16	3	0	2	1	0	1	4
95-96—Hershey	AHL	68	15	36	51	59	...	...	...	5	2	4	6	2
96-97—Philadelphia	AHL	63	32	63	95	70	32	6	4	—	—	—	—	—
—Philadelphia	NHL	18	5	10	15	4	3	0	0	5	1	3	4	4
97-98—Philadelphia	NHL	41	5	13	18	17	-10	4	0	—	—	—	—	—
—Ottawa	NHL	15	1	6	7	4	-1	0	0	6	0	0	0	0
98-99—Ottawa	NHL	79	10	26	36	58	8	2	0	4	0	0	0	0
99-00—Ottawa	NHL	79	22	33	55	40	-2	5	0	6	0	4	4	4
00-01—Ottawa	NHL	40	1	12	13	12	1	0	0	—	—	—	—	—
—Florida	NHL	34	4	12	16	10	-2	1	0	—	—	—	—	—
01-02—Tampa Bay	NHL	81	18	37	55	38	-11	7	0	—	—	—	—	—
02-03—Tampa Bay	NHL	80	22	57	79	53	9	9	0	11	4	2	6	8
03-04—Anaheim	NHL	82	19	35	54	54	-9	7	0	—	—	—	—	—
04-05—Budejovice	Czech Dv.I	39	28	60	88	82	57	...	...	16	15	15	30	32
NHL Totals (8 years)		549	107	241	348	290	-14	35	0	32	5	9	14	16

PRUSEK, MARTIN G BLUE JACKETS

PERSONAL: Born December 11, 1975, in Ostrava, Czechoslovakia. ... 6-1/188. ... Catches left. ... Name pronounced PREW-sehk.

TRANSACTIONS/CAREER NOTES: Selected by Ottawa Senators in 6th round (6th Senators pick, 164th overall) of NHL draft (June 26, 1999). ... Injured groin (January 2, 2003); missed five games. ... Concussion (March 15, 2003); missed four games. ... Back spasms (December 9, 2003); missed four games. ... Strained left knee (February 24, 2004); missed one game. ... Back spasms (March 17, 2004); missed three games. ... Signed as free agent by Columbus Blue Jackets (Aug. 4, 2005).

Season Team	League	REGULAR SEASON GP	Min.	W	L	T	GA	SO	GAA	SV%	PLAYOFFS GP	Min.	W	L	GA	SO	GAA	SV%
94-95—HC Vitkovice	Czech Rep.	4	232	...	...	...	18	...	4.66	...	—	—	—	—	—	—	—	—
95-96—HC Vitkovice	Czech Rep.	40	...	...	...	...	114	1	...	...	4	...	...	...	10	...	...	...
96-97—HC Vitkovice	Czech Rep.	49	...	...	...	...	109	8	...	...	9	...	...	...	19	1	...	...
97-98—HC Vitkovice	Czech Rep.	50	...	...	...	...	129	...	...	...	9	...	...	...	26	...	...	...
98-99—HC Vitkovice	Czech Rep.	37	1905	...	...	...	85	...	2.68	...	4	250	...	...	12	...	2.88	...
99-00—HC Vitkovice	Czech Rep.	50	2647	...	...	...	132	...	2.99	...	—	—	—	—	—	—	—	—
00-01—HC Vitkovice	Czech Rep.	30	1679	...	...	...	64	...	2.29	...	9	460	...	...	25	...	3.26	...
01-02—Grand Rapids	AHL	33	1903	18	8	5	58	4	*1.83	.925	5	277	2	3	10	0	2.17	.896
—Ottawa	NHL	1	62	0	1	0	3	0	2.90	.800	—	—	—	—	—	—	—	—
02-03—Binghamton	AHL	4	242	1	2	1	7	1	1.74	.925	—	—	—	—	—	—	—	—
—Ottawa	NHL	18	935	12	2	1	37	0	2.37	.911	—	—	—	—	—	—	—	—
03-04—Ottawa	NHL	29	1528	16	6	3	54	3	2.12	.917	1	40	0	0	1	0	1.50	.933
04-05—Vitkovice	Czech Rep.	14	672	...	...	...	28	0	2.50	.931	—	—	—	—	—	—	—	—
—HC Znojemsti Orli	Czech Rep.	8	453	...	...	...	18	0	2.38	.933	—	—	—	—	—	—	—	—
NHL Totals (3 years)		48	2525	28	9	4	94	3	2.23	.913	1	40	0	0	1	0	1.50	.933

PURINTON, DALE D RANGERS

PERSONAL: Born October 11, 1976, in Fort Wayne, Ind. ... 6-2/220. ... Shoots left.

TRANSACTIONS/CAREER NOTES: Selected by New York Rangers in fifth round (fourth Ranger pick, 117th overall) of NHL entry draft (July 8, 1995). ... Injured ribs (December 15, 2000); missed five games. ... Injured arm (January 16, 2001); missed four games. ... Suspended seven games by NHL for cross-checking incident (October 12, 2001). ... Bruised wrist (November 17, 2001); missed two games. ... Suspended three games by NHL for fighting incident (February 5, 2002). ... Strained muscle in ribs (January 3, 2002); missed two games. ... Fractured foot (December 14, 2002); missed 15 games.

Season Team	League	REGULAR SEASON GP	G	A	Pts.	PIM	+/-	PP	SH	PLAYOFFS GP	G	A	Pts.	PIM
93-94—Vernon	Tier II Jr. A	42	1	6	7	194	...	...	...	—	—	—	—	—
94-95—Tacoma	WHL	65	0	8	8	291	6	0	0	3	0	0	0	13
95-96—Kelowna	WHL	22	1	4	5	88	...	...	...	—	—	—	—	—
—Lethbridge	WHL	37	3	6	9	144	...	...	...	4	1	1	2	25
96-97—Lethbridge	WHL	51	6	26	32	254	...	...	...	18	3	5	8	*88
97-98—Charlotte	ECHL	34	3	5	8	186	...	...	...	—	—	—	—	—
—Hartford	AHL	17	0	0	0	95	0	0	0	—	—	—	—	—
98-99—Hartford	AHL	45	1	3	4	306	5	0	0	7	0	2	2	24
99-00—Hartford	AHL	62	4	4	8	415	...	...	...	23	0	3	3	*87
—New York Rangers	NHL	1	0	0	0	7	-1	0	0	—	—	—	—	—
00-01—Hartford	AHL	11	0	1	1	75	...	...	...	—	—	—	—	—
—New York Rangers	NHL	42	0	2	2	180	5	0	0	—	—	—	—	—
01-02—New York Rangers	NHL	40	0	4	4	113	4	0	0	—	—	—	—	—
02-03—New York Rangers	NHL	58	3	9	12	161	-2	0	0	—	—	—	—	—
03-04—New York Rangers	NHL	40	1	1	2	117	-9	0	0	—	—	—	—	—
04-05—Victoria	ECHL	25	3	9	12	192	-4	0	...	—	—	—	—	—
NHL Totals (5 years)		181	4	16	20	578	-3	0	0					

PUSHOR, JAMIE D

PERSONAL: Born February 11, 1973, in Lethbridge, Alta. ... 6-4/223. ... Shoots right.

TRANSACTIONS/CAREER NOTES: Selected by Detroit Red Wings in second round (second Wings pick, 32nd overall) of NHL entry draft (June 22, 1991). ... Strained groin (November 21, 1997); missed three games. ... Traded by Red Wings with fourth-round pick (C Viktor Wallin) in

1998 draft to Mighty Ducks of Anaheim for D Dmitri Mironov (March 24, 1998). ... Fractured right finger (April 15, 1998); missed remainder of season. ... Suffered eye injury (January 6, 1999); missed two games. ... Bruised left shoulder and chest (February 14, 1999); missed four games. ... Selected by Atlanta Thrashers in NHL expansion draft (June 25, 1999). ... Traded by Thrashers to Dallas Stars for LW Jason Botterill (July 15, 1999). ... Selected by Columbus Blue Jackets in NHL expansion draft (June 23, 2000). ... Sprained knee (March 26, 2001); missed seven games. ... Traded by Blue Jackets to Pittsburgh Penguins for fourth-round pick (LW Kevin Jarman) in 2003 draft (March 15, 2002). ... Signed as free agent by the Columbus Blue Jackets (December 10, 2003) ... Traded by Blue Jackets to New York Rangers for eighth-round pick in 2004 draft (January 23, 2004) .

		REGULAR SEASON								PLAYOFFS				
Season Team	League	GP	G	A	Pts.	PIM	+/-	PP	SH	GP	G	A	Pts.	PIM
88-89—Lethbridge	WHL	2	0	0	0	0	...	0	0	—	—	—	—	—
89-90—Lethbridge	WHL	10	0	2	2	2	...	...	...	—	—	—	—	—
90-91—Lethbridge	WHL	71	1	13	14	193	...	...	...	—	—	—	—	—
91-92—Lethbridge	WHL	49	2	15	17	232	...	...	...	5	0	0	0	33
92-93—Lethbridge	WHL	72	6	22	28	200	...	...	...	4	0	1	1	9
93-94—Adirondack	AHL	73	1	17	18	124	32	0	0	12	0	0	0	22
94-95—Adirondack	AHL	58	2	11	13	129	-12	0	0	4	0	1	1	0
95-96—Detroit	NHL	5	0	1	1	17	2	0	0	—	—	—	—	—
—Adirondack	AHL	65	2	16	18	126	...	...	...	3	0	0	0	5
96-97—Detroit	NHL	75	4	7	11	129	1	0	0	5	0	1	1	5
97-98—Detroit	NHL	54	2	5	7	71	2	0	0	—	—	—	—	—
—Anaheim	NHL	10	0	2	2	10	1	0	0	—	—	—	—	—
98-99—Anaheim	NHL	70	1	2	3	112	-20	0	0	4	0	0	0	6
99-00—Dallas	NHL	62	0	8	8	53	0	0	0	5	0	0	0	5
00-01—Columbus	NHL	75	3	10	13	94	7	0	1	—	—	—	—	—
01-02—Columbus	NHL	61	0	6	6	54	-10	0	0	—	—	—	—	—
—Pittsburgh	NHL	15	0	2	2	30	-3	0	0	—	—	—	—	—
02-03—Pittsburgh	NHL	76	3	1	4	76	-28	0	0	—	—	—	—	—
03-04—Columbus	NHL	7	0	0	0	2	-2	0	0	—	—	—	—	—
—Syracuse	AHL	17	1	4	5	24	1	0	0	...	...	...	...	...
—New York Rangers	NHL	7	0	0	0	0	-3	0	0	—	—	—	—	—
—Hartford	AHL	14	0	2	2	21	10	0	0	16	1	1	2	18
04-05—Syracuse	AHL	68	1	9	10	85	12	0	0	—	—	—	—	—
NHL Totals (9 years)		517	13	44	57	648	-53	0	1	14	0	1	1	16

PYATT, TAYLOR — LW — SABRES

PERSONAL: Born August 19, 1981, in Thunder Bay, Ont. ... 6-4/227. ... Shoots left. ... Son of Nelson Pyatt, C/LW with three NHL teams (1973-74 through 1979-80).

TRANSACTIONS/CAREER NOTES: Selected by New York Islanders in first round (second Islanders pick, eighth overall) of NHL draft (June 26, 1999). ... Traded by Islanders with C Tim Connolly to Buffalo Sabres for C Michael Peca (June 24, 2001). ... Had concussion (March 18, 2003); missed four games. ... Injured knee (January 7, 2004); missed 11 games. ... Separated collarbone (March 17, 2004); missed eight games.

STATISTICAL PLATEAUS: Three-goal games: 2002-03 (1).

		REGULAR SEASON								PLAYOFFS				
Season Team	League	GP	G	A	Pts.	PIM	+/-	PP	SH	GP	G	A	Pts.	PIM
97-98—Sudbury	OHL	58	14	17	31	104	...	...	...	10	3	1	4	6
98-99—Sudbury	OHL	68	37	38	75	95	-9	...	...	4	0	4	4	6
99-00—Sudbury	OHL	68	40	49	89	98	47	9	5	12	8	7	15	25
00-01—New York Islanders	NHL	78	4	14	18	39	-17	1	0	—	—	—	—	—
01-02—Rochester	AHL	27	6	4	10	36	-2	0	0	—	—	—	—	—
—Buffalo	NHL	48	10	10	20	35	4	0	0	—	—	—	—	—
02-03—Buffalo	NHL	78	14	14	28	38	-8	2	0	—	—	—	—	—
03-04—Buffalo	NHL	63	8	12	20	25	-7	1	2	—	—	—	—	—
04-05—Hammarby	Sweden Dv. 2	10	7	4	11	...	12	1	1	14	4	5	9	12
NHL Totals (4 years)		267	36	50	86	137	-28	4	2					

QUINT, DERON — D

PERSONAL: Born March 12, 1976, in Durham, N.H. ... 6-2/192. ... Shoots left.

TRANSACTIONS/CAREER NOTES: Selected by Winnipeg Jets in second round (first Jets pick, 30th overall) of NHL entry draft (June 28, 1994). ... Flu (January 29, 1996); missed two games. ... Jets franchise moved to Phoenix and renamed Coyotes for 1996-97 season; NHL approved move on January 18, 1996. ... Separated shoulder (November 27, 1997); missed six games. ... Suffered concussion (January 30, 1998); missed one game. ... Hernia surgery (March 8, 1998); missed 11 games. ... Suffered concussion (October 6, 1998); missed first nine games of season. ... Separated shoulder (January 31, 1999); missed three games. ... Suffered concussion (March 30, 1999); missed final seven games of season. ... Traded by Coyotes with third-round pick (traded back to Phoenix; Coyotes selected D Beat Forster) in 2001 draft to New Jersey Devils for D Lyle Odelein (March 7, 2000). ... Traded by Devils to Columbus Blue Jackets to complete earlier trade (Krzysztof Oliwa-Turner Stevenson) (June 25, 2000). ... Flu (January 3, 2001); missed one game. ... Bruised thigh (February 8, 2002); missed one game. ... Signed by Phoenix Coyotes as unrestricted free agent (October 26, 2002). ... Sprained knee (December 9, 2002); missed three games. ... Injured groin (January 11, 2003); missed two games. ... Bruised shoulder (March 27, 2003); missed five games. ... Signed by Chicago Blackhawks as free agent (August 5, 2003). ... Sprained knee (January 24, 2004); missed 15 games.

STATISTICAL PLATEAUS: Three-goal games: 2000-01 (1).

		REGULAR SEASON								PLAYOFFS				
Season Team	League	GP	G	A	Pts.	PIM	+/-	PP	SH	GP	G	A	Pts.	PIM
90-91 —Cardigan Prep School	USHS (East)	31	67	54	121	...	...	...	...	—	—	—	—	—
91-92 —Cardigan Prep School	USHS (East)	32	111	68	179	...	...	...	...	—	—	—	—	—
92-93—Tabor Academy	Mass. H.S.	28	15	26	41	30	...	...	...	1	0	2	2	0
93-94—Seattle	WHL	63	15	29	44	47	14	9	0	9	4	12	16	8
94-95—Seattle	WHL	65	29	60	89	82	39	14	0	3	1	2	3	6
95-96—Winnipeg	NHL	51	5	13	18	22	-2	2	0	—	—	—	—	—

Season Team	League	REGULAR SEASON GP	G	A	Pts.	PIM	+/-	PP	SH	PLAYOFFS GP	G	A	Pts.	PIM
—Springfield	AHL	11	2	3	5	4	...	...	...	10	2	3	5	6
—Seattle	WHL	...	...	...	...	...	...	...	...	5	4	1	5	6
96-97—Springfield	AHL	43	6	18	24	20	5	2	0	12	2	7	9	4
—Phoenix	NHL	27	3	11	14	4	-4	1	0	7	0	2	2	0
97-98—Phoenix	NHL	32	4	7	11	16	-6	1	0	—	—	—	—	—
—Springfield	AHL	8	1	7	8	10	3	0	0	1	0	0	0	0
98-99—Phoenix	NHL	60	5	8	13	20	-10	2	0	—	—	—	—	—
99-00—Phoenix	NHL	50	3	7	10	22	0	0	0	—	—	—	—	—
—New Jersey	NHL	4	1	0	1	2	-2	0	0	—	—	—	—	—
00-01—Syracuse	AHL	21	5	15	20	30	...	...	...	—	—	—	—	—
—Columbus	NHL	57	7	16	23	16	-19	3	0	—	—	—	—	—
01-02—Columbus	NHL	75	7	18	25	26	-34	3	0	—	—	—	—	—
02-03—Springfield	AHL	4	1	2	3	4	-2	0	1	—	—	—	—	—
—Phoenix	NHL	51	7	10	17	20	-5	2	0	—	—	—	—	—
03-04—Chicago	NHL	51	4	7	11	18	-26	2	0	—	—	—	—	—
04-05—Bolzano	Italy	14	5	11	16	12	...	...	...	9	4	5	9	12
NHL Totals (9 years)		458	46	97	143	166	-108	16	0	7	0	2	2	0

QUINTAL, STEPHANE — D

PERSONAL: Born October 22, 1968, in Boucherville, Que. ... 6-3/233. ... Shoots right. ... Name pronounced steh-FAN kahn-TAHL.

TRANSACTIONS/CAREER NOTES: Selected by Boston Bruins in first round (second Bruins pick, 14th overall) of NHL draft (June 13, 1987). ... Fractured bone near eye (October 1988). ... Injured knee (January 1989). ... Sprained right knee (October 17, 1989); missed eight games. ... Fractured left ankle (April 9, 1991); missed remainder of playoffs. ... Traded by Bruins with C Craig Janney to St. Louis Blues for C Adam Oates (February 7, 1992). ... Traded by Blues with RW Nelson Emerson to Winnipeg Jets for D Phil Housley (September 24, 1993). ... Sprained wrist (January 16, 1994); missed two games. ... Sprained neck (April 6, 1994); missed one game. ... Sprained ankle (February 6, 1995); missed five games. ... Traded by Jets to Montreal Canadiens for second-round pick (D Jason Doig) in 1995 draft (July 8, 1995). ... Suffered concussion (November 11, 1995); missed one game. ... Sprained right knee (February 7, 1996); missed seven games. ... Knee surgery (March 19, 1996); missed five games. ... Bruised foot (December 21, 1996); missed two games. ... Injured collarbone (January 1, 1997); missed two games. ... Sprained left knee (February 6, 1997); missed seven games. ... Suffered concussion (November 8, 1997); missed one game. ... Strained hip flexor (February 7, 1998); missed one game. ... Sprained ankle (April 1, 1998); missed nine games. ... Signed as free agent by New York Rangers (July 6, 1999). ... Suffered concussion (November 24, 1999); missed one game. ... Neck spasms (January 4, 2000); missed one game. ... Claimed on waivers by Chicago Blackhawks (October 5, 2000). ... Strained groin (January 21, 2001); missed two games. ... Sinus infection (April 4, 2001); missed three games. ... Traded by Blackhawks to Canadiens for fourth-round pick (D Brent MacLellan) in 2001 draft (June 23, 2001). ... Separated shoulder (November 3, 2001); missed three games. ... Injured jaw (December 8, 2001); missed one game. ... Injured finger (October 19, 2002); missed two games. ... Virus (January 28, 2003); missed two games. ... Injured hamstring (February 24, 2003); missed nine games. ... Irregular heartbeat (November 7, 2003); missed four games. ... Suspended one game for a match penalty (December 7, 2003). ... Traded by Canadiens to Los Angeles Kings for future considerations (June 27, 2004).

Season Team	League	REGULAR SEASON GP	G	A	Pts.	PIM	+/-	PP	SH	PLAYOFFS GP	G	A	Pts.	PIM
85-86—Granby	QMJHL	67	2	17	19	144	...	...	...	—	—	—	—	—
86-87—Granby	QMJHL	67	13	41	54	178	...	...	...	8	0	9	9	10
87-88—Hull	QMJHL	38	13	23	36	138	...	...	...	19	7	12	19	30
88-89—Maine	AHL	16	4	10	14	28	...	...	...	—	—	—	—	—
—Boston	NHL	26	0	1	1	29	-5	0	0	—	—	—	—	—
89-90—Boston	NHL	38	2	2	4	22	-11	0	0	—	—	—	—	—
—Maine	AHL	37	4	16	20	27	...	...	...	—	—	—	—	—
90-91—Maine	AHL	23	1	5	6	30	...	...	...	—	—	—	—	—
—Boston	NHL	45	2	6	8	89	2	1	0	3	0	1	1	7
91-92—Boston	NHL	49	4	10	14	77	-8	0	0	—	—	—	—	—
—St. Louis	NHL	26	0	6	6	32	-3	0	0	4	1	2	3	6
92-93—St. Louis	NHL	75	1	10	11	100	-6	0	1	9	0	0	0	8
93-94—Winnipeg	NHL	81	8	18	26	119	-25	1	1	—	—	—	—	—
94-95—Winnipeg	NHL	43	6	17	23	78	0	3	0	—	—	—	—	—
95-96—Montreal	NHL	68	2	14	16	117	-4	0	1	6	0	1	1	6
96-97—Montreal	NHL	71	7	15	22	100	1	1	0	5	0	1	1	6
97-98—Montreal	NHL	71	6	10	16	97	13	0	0	9	0	2	2	4
98-99—Montreal	NHL	82	8	19	27	84	-23	1	1	—	—	—	—	—
99-00—New York Rangers	NHL	75	2	14	16	77	-10	0	0	—	—	—	—	—
00-01—Chicago	NHL	72	1	18	19	60	-9	0	0	—	—	—	—	—
01-02—Montreal	NHL	75	6	10	16	87	-7	1	0	12	1	3	4	12
02-03—Montreal	NHL	67	5	5	10	70	-4	0	0	—	—	—	—	—
03-04—Montreal	NHL	73	3	5	8	82	10	0	0	4	0	0	0	2
04-05—Asiago	Italy	10	1	2	3	8	...	...	...	5	2	0	2	4
NHL Totals (16 years)		1037	63	180	243	1320	-89	8	4	52	2	10	12	51

RACINE, JEAN-FRANCOIS — G — MAPLE LEAFS

PERSONAL: Born April 27, 1982, in St-Hyacinthe, Que. ... 6-3/175. ... Catches left.

TRANSACTIONS/CAREER NOTES: Selected by Toronto Maple Leafs in third round (fourth Maple Leafs pick, 90th overall) of NHL entry draft (June 24, 2000).

Season Team	League	REGULAR SEASON GP	Min.	W	L	T	GA	SO	GAA	SV%	PLAYOFFS GP	Min.	W	L	GA	SO	GAA	SV%
99-00—Drummondville	QMJHL	30	1562	...	...	...	...	1	3.49	.878	—	—	—	—	—	—	—	—
00-01—Drummondville	QMJHL	61	3362	27	26	3	189	4	3.37	.894	5	302	2	3	20	0	3.97	.896
01-02—Drummondville	QMJHL	65	3640	29	30	3	*208	2	3.43	...	12	720	5	7	42	1	3.50	...
02-03—Memphis	CHL	35	2050	22	9	3	94	0	2.75	.907	1	58	0	1	5	0	5.14	...

Season Team	League	GP	Min.	W	L	T	GA	SO	GAA	SV%	GP	Min.	W	L	GA	SO	GAA	SV%
		REGULAR SEASON									PLAYOFFS							
03-04—Memphis	CHL	35	2050	22	9	3	94	0	2.75	.907	—	—	—	—	—	—	—	—
—St. John's	AHL	9	496	4	5	0	24	1	2.90	.915	—	—	—	—	—	—	—	—
04-05—St. John's	AHL	17	892	10	4	...	41	0	2.76	.921	0	0	0	0	0	0	...	...
—Memphis	CHL	19	951	9	6	1	57	0	3.60	.904	—	—	—	—	—	—	—	—

RADIVOJEVIC, BRANKO RW FLYERS

PERSONAL: Born November 24, 1980, in Piestany, Czechoslovakia. ... 6-2/207. ... Shoots right. ... Name pronounced rah-dih-VOI-uh-vich.
TRANSACTIONS/CAREER NOTES: Selected by Colorado Avalanche in third round (third Avalanche pick, 93rd overall) of NHL draft (June 26, 1999). ... Signed as free agent by Phoenix Coyotes (June 19, 2001). ... Traded by Coyotes with G Sean Burke and rights to LW Ben Eager to Philadelphia Flyers for C Mike Comrie (February 9, 2004).

Season Team	League	GP	G	A	Pts.	PIM	+/-	PP	SH	GP	G	A	Pts.	PIM
		REGULAR SEASON								PLAYOFFS				
97-98—Dukla Trencin	Slovakia Jrs.	52	30	33	63	50	...	...	...	—	—	—	—	—
98-99—Belleville	OHL	68	20	38	58	61	...	...	...	21	7	17	24	18
99-00—Belleville	OHL	59	23	49	72	86	27	7	1	16	5	8	13	32
00-01—Belleville	OHL	61	34	70	104	77	45	6	1	10	6	10	16	18
01-02—Springfield	AHL	62	18	21	39	64	-2	3	1	—	—	—	—	—
—Phoenix	NHL	18	4	2	6	4	1	0	0	1	0	0	0	2
02-03—Phoenix	NHL	79	12	15	27	63	-2	1	0	—	—	—	—	—
03-04—Phoenix	NHL	53	9	14	23	36	-5	2	1	—	—	—	—	—
—Philadelphia	NHL	24	1	8	9	36	0	0	0	18	1	1	2	32
04-05—HC Vsetin	Czech Rep.	31	7	11	18	114	4	...	...	—	—	—	—	—
—Lulea	Sweden	10	6	5	11	8	3	0	0	4	0	0	0	44
NHL Totals (3 years)		174	26	39	65	139	-6	3	1	19	1	1	2	34

RADULOV, ALEXANDER RW PREDATORS

PERSONAL: Born July 5, 1986, in Nizhi Tagli, U.S.S.R. ... 6-1/178. ... Shoots left.
TRANSACTIONS/CAREER NOTES: Selected by Nashville Predators in first round (first Predators pick, 15th overall) of NHL entry draft (June 26, 2004).

Season Team	League	GP	G	A	Pts.	PIM	+/-	PP	SH	GP	G	A	Pts.	PIM
		REGULAR SEASON								PLAYOFFS				
03-04—Dynamo	Russian	1	0	0	0	2	...	...	...	—	—	—	—	—
—Tver	Russian	42	15	16	31	102	...	...	...	—	—	—	—	—
04-05—Quebec	QMJHL	65	32	43	75	64	30	10	2	13	6	5	11	15

RADULOV, IGOR LW

PERSONAL: Born August 23, 1982, in Nizhny Tagil, U.S.S.R. ... 6-1/186. ... Shoots left.
TRANSACTIONS/CAREER NOTES: Selected by Chicago Blackhawks in third round (fourth Blackhawks pick, 74th overall) of NHL entry draft (June 24, 2000).

Season Team	League	GP	G	A	Pts.	PIM	+/-	PP	SH	GP	G	A	Pts.	PIM
		REGULAR SEASON								PLAYOFFS				
99-00—Yaroslavl	CIS	45	20	7	27	36	...	...	...	—	—	—	—	—
00-01—SKA St. Petersburg	Russian	8	1	0	1	6	...	...	...	—	—	—	—	—
01-02—Mississauga	OHL	62	33	30	63	30	...	...	...	—	—	—	—	—
02-03—Chicago	NHL	7	5	0	5	4	-3	3	0	—	—	—	—	—
—Norfolk	AHL	62	18	9	27	26	1	4	0	9	2	2	4	8
03-04—Chicago	NHL	36	4	7	11	18	-2	0	0	—	—	—	—	—
—Norfolk	AHL	38	9	14	23	26	5	1	0	8	0	1	1	4
04-05—Norfolk	AHL	16	0	0	0	16	-2	0	0	—	—	—	—	—
—Spartak Moscow	Russian	25	2	2	4	22	-11	...	...	—	—	—	—	—
NHL Totals (2 years)		43	9	7	16	22	-5	3	0					

RAFALSKI, BRIAN D DEVILS

PERSONAL: Born September 28, 1973, in Dearborn, Mich. ... 5-10/190. ... Shoots right.
TRANSACTIONS/CAREER NOTES: Signed as free agent by New Jersey Devils (June 18, 1999). ... Suffered illness (January 3, 2000); missed one game. ... Bruised ribs (March 17, 2000); missed five games. ... Bruised left shoulder (February 8, 2001); missed three games. ... Sprained knee (January 24, 2002); missed four games. ... Bruised ribs (December 10, 2002); missed three games. ... Flu (April 24, 2003); missed one playoff game. ... Bruised knee (February 28, 2004); missed one game. ... Fractured right leg (March 9, 2004); missed 12 games. ... Signed as free agent by Devils (Aug. 4, 2005).

Season Team	League	GP	G	A	Pts.	PIM	+/-	PP	SH	GP	G	A	Pts.	PIM
		REGULAR SEASON								PLAYOFFS				
91-92—Wisconsin	WCHA	34	3	14	17	34	...	...	...	—	—	—	—	—
92-93—Wisconsin	WCHA	32	0	13	13	10	...	...	...	—	—	—	—	—
93-94—Wisconsin	WCHA	37	6	17	23	26	...	...	...	—	—	—	—	—
94-95—Wisconsin	WCHA	43	11	34	45	48	...	...	...	—	—	—	—	—
95-96—Brynas Gavle	Sweden Dv. 2	18	3	6	9	12	...	...	...	9	0	1	1	2
—Brynas Gavle	Sweden	22	1	8	9	14	...	...	...	—	—	—	—	—
96-97—HPK Hameenlinna	Finland	49	11	24	35	26	...	...	...	10	6	5	11	4
97-98—HIFK Helsinki	Finland	40	13	10	23	24	...	...	...	9	5	6	11	0

Season Team	League	GP	G	A	Pts.	PIM	+/-	PP	SH	GP	G	A	Pts.	PIM
		REGULAR SEASON								PLAYOFFS				
98-99—HIFK Helsinki	Finland	53	19	34	53	18	...	...	...	11	5	9	14	4
99-00—New Jersey	NHL	75	5	27	32	28	21	1	0	23	2	6	8	8
00-01—New Jersey	NHL	78	9	43	52	26	36	6	0	25	7	11	18	7
01-02—New Jersey	NHL	76	7	40	47	18	15	2	0	6	3	2	5	4
—U.S. Olympic team	Int'l	6	1	2	3	2	...	...	...	—	—	—	—	—
02-03—New Jersey	NHL	79	3	37	40	14	18	2	0	23	2	9	11	8
03-04—New Jersey	NHL	69	6	30	36	24	6	2	0	5	0	1	1	0
NHL Totals (5 years)		377	30	177	207	110	96	13	0	82	14	29	43	27

RAGNARSSON, MARCUS D

PERSONAL: Born August 13, 1971, in Ostervala, Sweden. ... 6-1/215. ... Shoots left. ... Name pronounced RAG-nuhr-suhn.

TRANSACTIONS/CAREER NOTES: Selected by San Jose Sharks in fifth round (fifth Sharks pick, 99th overall) of NHL draft (June 20, 1992). ... Injured foot (November 8, 1995); missed two games. ... Injured head (December 5, 1995); missed two games. ... Injured knee (January 10, 1996); missed one game. ... Flu (January 16, 1996); missed one game. ... Injured hamstring (February 10, 1996); missed four games. ... Injured back (March 22, 1996); missed one game. ... Injured leg (November 1, 1996); missed two games. ... Fractured toe (December 9, 1996); missed two games. ... Suspended one game by NHL for high-sticking (November 3, 1997). ... Injured thumb (October 3, 1998); missed first eight games of season. ... Injured foot (October 19, 1999); missed 16 games. ... Had concussion (February 22, 2000); missed three games. ... Injured knee (November 1, 2000); missed seven games. ... Injured shoulder (February 16, 2001); missed five games. ... Injured finger (January 5, 2002); missed 12 games. ... Traded by Sharks to Philadelphia Flyers for D Dan McGillis (December 6, 2002). ... Pinched nerve in back (January 2, 2003); missed 13 games. ... Flu (November 18, 2003); missed two games. ... Sprained left shoulder (January 19, 2004); missed five games. ... Injured shoulder (February 29, 2004); missed three games.

Season Team	League	GP	G	A	Pts.	PIM	+/-	PP	SH	GP	G	A	Pts.	PIM
		REGULAR SEASON								PLAYOFFS				
89-90—Djurgarden Stockholm	Sweden	13	0	2	2	0	...	...	...	1	0	0	0	0
90-91—Djurgarden Stockholm	Sweden	35	4	1	5	12	...	...	...	7	0	0	0	6
91-92—Djurgarden Stockholm	Sweden	40	8	5	13	14	...	...	...	—	—	—	—	—
92-93—Djurgarden Stockholm	Sweden	35	3	3	6	53	...	...	...	6	0	2	2	...
93-94—Djurgarden Stockholm	Sweden	19	0	4	4	24	...	...	...	—	—	—	—	—
94-95—Djurgarden Stockholm	Sweden	38	7	9	16	20	...	...	...	3	0	0	0	4
95-96—San Jose	NHL	71	8	31	39	42	-24	4	0	—	—	—	—	—
96-97—San Jose	NHL	69	3	14	17	63	-18	2	0	—	—	—	—	—
97-98—San Jose	NHL	79	5	20	25	65	-11	3	0	6	0	0	0	4
—Swedish Oly. team	Int'l	3	0	1	1	0	1	0	0	—	—	—	—	—
98-99—San Jose	NHL	74	0	13	13	66	7	0	0	6	0	1	1	6
99-00—San Jose	NHL	63	3	13	16	38	13	0	0	12	0	3	3	10
00-01—San Jose	NHL	68	3	12	15	44	2	1	0	5	0	1	1	8
01-02—San Jose	NHL	70	5	15	20	44	4	2	0	12	1	3	4	12
—Swedish Oly. team	Int'l	4	0	2	2	2	...	...	...	—	—	—	—	—
02-03—San Jose	NHL	25	1	7	8	30	2	0	0	—	—	—	—	—
—Philadelphia	NHL	43	2	6	8	32	5	1	0	13	0	1	1	6
03-04—Philadelphia	NHL	70	7	9	16	58	12	2	0	14	1	4	5	14
04-05—Uppsala	Sweden Dv. 2	—	—	—	—	—	—	—	—	1	1	0	1	0
NHL Totals (9 years)		632	37	140	177	482	-8	15	0	68	2	13	15	60

RASK, TUUKKA G MAPLE LEAFS

PERSONAL: Born March 10, 1987, in Savonlinna, Finland. ... 6-1/190. ... Catches left.

TRANSACTIONS/CAREER NOTES: Selected by Toronto Maple Leafs in 1st round (1st Leafs pick, 21st overall) of entry draft (July 30, 2005).

Season Team	League	GP	Min.	W	L	T	GA	SO	GAA	SV%	GP	Min.	W	L	GA	SO	GAA	SV%
		REGULAR SEASON									PLAYOFFS							
03-04—Ilves Tampere	Finland Jr.	26	...	...	...	...	...	...	2.24	.936	—	—	—	—	—	—	—	—
04-05—Ilves Tampere	Finland Div. 2	4	...	...	...	...	...	...	4.46	.875	—	—	—	—	—	—	—	—

RASMUSSEN, ERIK C DEVILS

PERSONAL: Born March 28, 1977, in Minneapolis, Minn. ... 6-1/210. ... Shoots left. ... Name pronounced RAS-muh-suhn.

TRANSACTIONS/CAREER NOTES: Selected by Buffalo Sabres in first round (first Sabres pick, seventh overall) of NHL draft (June 22, 1996). ... Injured shoulder (October 26, 1997); missed one game. ... Injured foot (April 13, 1999); missed one game. ... Bruised hand (December 4, 1999); missed five games. ... Back spasms (March 23, 2000); missed one game. ... Injured knee (October 6, 2001); missed one game. ... Bruised knee (December 12, 2001); missed seven games. ... Injured shoulder (January 23, 2002); missed three games. ... Traded by Sabres to Los Angeles Kings for C Adam Mair and fifth-round (D Thomas Morrow) pick in 2003 draft (July 24, 2002). ... Signed as free agent by New Jersey Devils (July 27, 2003). ... Flu (December 13, 2003); missed one game. ... Injured shoulder (January 1, 2004); missed three games.

Season Team	League	GP	G	A	Pts.	PIM	+/-	PP	SH	GP	G	A	Pts.	PIM
		REGULAR SEASON								PLAYOFFS				
92-93—Saint Louis Park	Minn. H.S.	23	16	24	40	50	...	...	...	—	—	—	—	—
93-94—Saint Louis Park	Minn. H.S.	18	25	18	43	60	...	...	...	—	—	—	—	—
94-95—Saint Louis Park	Minn. H.S.	23	19	33	52	80	...	...	...	—	—	—	—	—
95-96—Minnesota	WCHA	40	16	32	48	55	...	...	...	—	—	—	—	—
96-97—Minnesota	WCHA	34	15	12	27	123	1	6	1	—	—	—	—	—
97-98—Buffalo	NHL	21	2	3	5	14	2	0	0	—	—	—	—	—
—Rochester	AHL	53	9	14	23	83	-11	5	0	1	0	0	0	5
98-99—Rochester	AHL	37	12	14	26	47	13	4	0	—	—	—	—	—
—Buffalo	NHL	42	3	7	10	37	6	0	0	21	2	4	6	18
99-00—Buffalo	NHL	67	8	6	14	43	1	0	0	3	0	0	0	4

Season Team	League	REGULAR SEASON GP	G	A	Pts.	PIM	+/-	PP	SH	PLAYOFFS GP	G	A	Pts.	PIM
00-01—Buffalo	NHL	82	12	19	31	51	0	1	0	3	0	1	1	0
01-02—Buffalo	NHL	69	8	11	19	34	-1	0	0	—	—	—	—	—
02-03—Los Angeles	NHL	57	4	12	16	28	-1	0	0	—	—	—	—	—
03-04—New Jersey	NHL	69	7	6	13	41	5	0	0	5	0	2	2	2
NHL Totals (7 years)		407	44	64	108	240	12	1	0	32	2	7	9	24

RATHJE, MIKE — D — FLYERS

PERSONAL: Born May 11, 1974, in Mannville, Alta. ... 6-5/235. ... Shoots left. ... Name pronounced RATH-jee. ... Nickname: Rat.

TRANSACTIONS/CAREER NOTES: Selected by San Jose Sharks in first round (first Sharks pick, third overall) of NHL entry draft (June 20, 1992). ... Strained abdominal muscle (February 19, 1994); missed three games. ... Sprained knee (February 26, 1994); missed four games. ... Sprained knee (February 2, 1995); missed three games. ... Injured foot (February 15, 1995); missed one game. ... Injured hip flexor (April 25, 1995); missed two games. ... Strained abdominal muscle (October 6, 1995); missed first two games of season. ... Injured shoulder (November 14, 1995); missed 12 games. ... Strained groin (November 8, 1996); missed 50 games. ... Injured groin (November 12, 1999); missed 16 games. ... Missed first 28 games of 2001-02 season due to contract dispute. ... Injured knee (January 23, 2002); missed two games. ... Injured wrist (November 13, 2003); missed one game. ... Injured eye (November 30, 2003); missed one game. ... Signed as free agent by the Philadelphia Flyers (Aug. 2, 2005).

Season Team	League	REGULAR SEASON GP	G	A	Pts.	PIM	+/-	PP	SH	PLAYOFFS GP	G	A	Pts.	PIM
90-91—Medicine Hat	WHL	64	1	16	17	28	...	...	...	12	0	4	4	2
91-92—Medicine Hat	WHL	67	11	23	34	109	...	...	...	4	0	1	1	2
92-93—Medicine Hat	WHL	57	12	37	49	103	-1	7	0	10	3	3	6	12
—Kansas City	IHL	...	...	...	...	...	...	...	...	5	0	0	0	12
93-94—San Jose	NHL	47	1	9	10	59	-9	1	0	1	0	0	0	0
—Kansas City	IHL	6	0	2	2	0	-4	0	0	—	—	—	—	—
94-95—Kansas City	IHL	6	0	1	1	7	-3	0	0	—	—	—	—	—
—San Jose	NHL	42	2	7	9	29	-1	0	0	11	5	2	7	4
95-96—Kansas City	IHL	36	6	11	17	34	...	...	...	—	—	—	—	—
—San Jose	NHL	27	0	7	7	14	-16	0	0	—	—	—	—	—
96-97—San Jose	NHL	31	0	8	8	21	-1	0	0	—	—	—	—	—
97-98—San Jose	NHL	81	3	12	15	59	-4	1	0	6	1	0	1	6
98-99—San Jose	NHL	82	5	9	14	36	15	2	0	6	0	0	0	4
99-00—San Jose	NHL	66	2	14	16	31	-2	0	0	12	1	3	4	8
00-01—San Jose	NHL	81	0	11	11	48	7	0	0	6	0	1	1	4
01-02—San Jose	NHL	52	5	12	17	48	23	4	0	12	1	3	4	6
02-03—San Jose	NHL	82	7	22	29	48	-19	3	0	—	—	—	—	—
03-04—San Jose	NHL	80	2	17	19	46	18	0	1	17	1	5	6	13
NHL Totals (11 years)		671	27	128	155	439	11	11	1	71	9	14	23	45

RAY, ROB — RW

PERSONAL: Born June 8, 1968, in Stirling, Ont. ... 6-0/222. ... Shoots left.

TRANSACTIONS/CAREER NOTES: Selected by Buffalo Sabres in fifth round (fifth Sabres pick, 97th overall) of NHL entry draft (June 11, 1988). ... Tore right knee ligament (April 11, 1993); missed remainder of season. ... Flu (March 11, 1995); missed one game. ... Fractured right cheekbone (November 27, 1995); missed eight games. ... Fractured thumb (November 22, 1997); missed 19 games. ... Suspended one playoff game by NHL for verbally abusing officials (April 26, 1998). ... Suspended four games by NHL for slew-footing incident (November 29, 1998). ... Bruised knee (February 6, 1999); missed one game. ... Injured shoulder (November 13, 2000); missed seven games. ... Suspended seven games by NHL for abusing an official (January 11, 2001). ... Suspended five games by NHL for delivering a blow to the head of opponent (April 1, 2002). ... Traded by Sabres to Ottawa Senators for future considerations (March 10, 2003). ... Missed 2003-04 season's first 64 games as unsigned free agent (re-signed February 13, 2004).

Season Team	League	REGULAR SEASON GP	G	A	Pts.	PIM	+/-	PP	SH	PLAYOFFS GP	G	A	Pts.	PIM
84-85—Whitby Lawmen	OPJHL	35	5	10	15	318	...	...	...	—	—	—	—	—
85-86—Cornwall	OHL	53	6	13	19	253	...	...	...	6	0	0	0	26
86-87—Cornwall	OHL	46	17	20	37	158	...	...	...	5	1	1	2	16
87-88—Cornwall	OHL	61	11	41	52	179	...	...	...	11	2	3	5	33
88-89—Rochester	AHL	74	11	18	29	*446	...	...	...	—	—	—	—	—
89-90—Buffalo	NHL	27	2	1	3	99	-2	0	0	—	—	—	—	—
—Rochester	AHL	43	2	13	15	335	...	...	...	17	1	3	4	*115
90-91—Rochester	AHL	8	1	1	2	15	...	...	...	—	—	—	—	—
—Buffalo	NHL	66	8	8	16	*350	-11	0	0	6	1	1	2	56
91-92—Buffalo	NHL	63	5	3	8	354	-9	0	0	7	0	0	0	2
92-93—Buffalo	NHL	68	3	2	5	211	-3	1	0	—	—	—	—	—
93-94—Buffalo	NHL	82	3	4	7	274	2	0	0	7	1	0	1	43
94-95—Buffalo	NHL	47	0	3	3	173	-4	0	0	5	0	0	0	14
95-96—Buffalo	NHL	71	3	6	9	287	-8	0	0	—	—	—	—	—
96-97—Buffalo	NHL	82	7	3	10	286	3	0	0	12	0	1	1	28
97-98—Buffalo	NHL	63	2	4	6	234	2	1	0	10	0	0	0	24
98-99—Buffalo	NHL	76	0	4	4	*261	-2	0	0	5	1	0	1	0
99-00—Buffalo	NHL	69	1	3	4	158	0	0	0	—	—	—	—	—
00-01—Buffalo	NHL	63	4	6	10	210	2	0	0	3	0	0	0	2
01-02—Buffalo	NHL	71	2	3	5	200	-3	0	0	—	—	—	—	—
02-03—Buffalo	NHL	41	0	0	0	92	-5	0	0	—	—	—	—	—
—Ottawa	NHL	5	0	0	0	4	0	0	0	—	—	—	—	—
03-04—Ottawa	NHL	6	1	0	1	14	0	0	0	—	—	—	—	—
—Binghamton	AHL	5	2	0	2	11	-1	2	0	—	—	—	—	—
NHL Totals (15 years)		900	41	50	91	3207	-38	2	0	55	3	2	5	169

RAYCROFT, ANDREW — G — BRUINS

PERSONAL: Born May 4, 1980, in Belleville, Ont. ... 6-0/180. ... Catches left.
TRANSACTIONS/CAREER NOTES: Selected by Boston Bruins in fifth round (fourth Bruins pick, 135th overall) of NHL draft (June 27, 1998). ... Injured groin (March 22, 2003); missed six games.

		REGULAR SEASON									PLAYOFFS							
Season Team	League	GP	Min.	W	L	T	GA	SO	GAA	SV%	GP	Min.	W	L	GA	SO	GAA	SV%
96-97—Wellington	Tier II Jr. A	27	1402	...	...	...	92	0	3.94	...	—	—	—	—	—	—	—	—
97-98—Sudbury	OHL	33	1802	8	16	5	125	0	4.16	.898	2	89	0	1	8	0	5.39	.830
98-99—Sudbury	OHL	45	2528	17	22	5	173	1	4.11	.897	3	96	0	2	13	0	8.13	.812
99-00—Kingston	OHL	*61	3340	33	20	5	191	0	3.43	.918	5	300	1	4	21	0	4.20	.897
00-01—Boston	NHL	15	649	4	6	0	32	0	2.96	.890	—	—	—	—	—	—	—	—
—Providence	AHL	26	1459	8	14	4	82	1	3.37	.891	—	—	—	—	—	—	—	—
01-02—Providence	AHL	56	3317	25	24	6	142	4	2.57	.908	—	—	—	—	—	—	—	—
—Boston	NHL	1	65	0	0	1	3	0	2.77	.897	—	—	—	—	—	—	—	—
02-03—Boston	NHL	5	300	2	3	0	12	0	2.40	.918	—	—	—	—	—	—	—	—
—Providence	AHL	39	2255	23	10	3	94	1	2.50	.917	4	264	1	3	6	1	1.36	.955
03-04—Boston	NHL	57	3420	29	18	9	117	3	2.05	.926	7	447	3	4	16	1	2.15	.924
04-05—Tappara Tampere	Finland	11	658	4	5	2	32	1	2.92	.912	3	104	0	2	11	0	6.36	.847
NHL Totals (4 years)		78	4434	35	27	10	164	3	2.22	.920	7	447	3	4	16	1	2.15	.924

READY, RYAN — LW

PERSONAL: Born November 7, 1978, in Peterborough, Ont. ... 6-0/195. ... Shoots left.
TRANSACTIONS/CAREER NOTES: Selected by Calgary Flames in fourth round (eighth Flames pick, 100th overall) of NHL entry draft (June 21, 1997). ... Signed as free agent by Vancouver Canucks (June 16, 1999). ... Traded by Canucks to St. Louis Blues for LW Sergei Varlamov (March 9, 2004). ... Signed as free agent by Philadelphia Flyers (August 23, 2004).

		REGULAR SEASON								PLAYOFFS				
Season Team	League	GP	G	A	Pts.	PIM	+/-	PP	SH	GP	G	A	Pts.	PIM
95-96—Peterborough	Jr. B	48	20	33	53	56	...	...	...	—	—	—	—	—
—Belleville	OHL	63	5	13	18	54	...	...	...	10	0	2	2	2
96-97—Belleville	OHL	66	23	24	47	102	-8	8	0	6	1	3	4	4
97-98—Belleville	OHL	66	33	39	72	80	1	...	...	10	5	2	7	12
98-99—Belleville	OHL	63	33	59	92	73	40	...	...	21	10	28	38	22
99-00—Syracuse	AHL	70	4	12	16	59	...	...	...	2	0	0	0	0
00-01—Kansas City	IHL	67	10	15	25	75	...	...	...	—	—	—	—	—
01-02—Manitoba	AHL	72	23	32	55	73	0	9	0	7	5	1	6	4
02-03—Manitoba	AHL	68	24	26	50	52	1	11	1	14	2	5	7	2
03-04—Manitoba	AHL	64	7	18	25	55	-16	2	1	—	—	—	—	—
—Worcester	AHL	16	2	5	7	10	-1	0	0	10	1	2	3	10
04-05—Philadelphia	AHL	72	7	18	25	104	8	2	1	19	2	11	13	6

REASONER, MARTY — C — OILERS

PERSONAL: Born February 26, 1977, in Rochester, N.Y. ... 6-1/191. ... Shoots left.
TRANSACTIONS/CAREER NOTES: Selected by St. Louis Blues in first round (first Blues pick, 14th overall) of NHL entry draft (June 22, 1996). ... Traded by Blues with C Jochen Hecht and D Jan Horacek to Edmonton Oilers for C Doug Weight and LW Michel Riesen (July 1, 2001). ... Sprained left knee (January 23, 2002); missed four games. ... Fractured left ankle (November 10, 2003); missed 27 games. ... Injured right knee (January 15, 2004) and had arthroscopic surgery (January 21, 2004); missed remainder of season.

		REGULAR SEASON								PLAYOFFS				
Season Team	League	GP	G	A	Pts.	PIM	+/-	PP	SH	GP	G	A	Pts.	PIM
93-94—Deerfield Academy	Mass. H.S.	22	27	24	51	...	...	...	...	—	—	—	—	—
94-95—Deerfield Academy	Mass. H.S.	26	25	32	57	14	...	...	...	—	—	—	—	—
95-96—Boston College	Hockey East	34	16	29	45	32	...	...	...	—	—	—	—	—
96-97—Boston College	Hockey East	35	20	24	44	31	...	5	0	—	—	—	—	—
97-98—Boston College	Hockey East	42	33	40	*73	56	...	...	...	—	—	—	—	—
98-99—St. Louis	NHL	22	3	7	10	8	2	1	0	—	—	—	—	—
—Worcester	AHL	44	17	22	39	24	-4	9	0	4	2	1	3	6
99-00—Worcester	AHL	44	23	28	51	39	...	...	...	—	—	—	—	—
—St. Louis	NHL	32	10	14	24	20	9	3	0	7	2	1	3	4
00-01—St. Louis	NHL	41	4	9	13	14	-5	0	0	10	3	1	4	0
—Worcester	AHL	34	17	18	35	25	...	...	...	—	—	—	—	—
01-02—Edmonton	NHL	52	6	5	11	41	0	3	0	—	—	—	—	—
02-03—Hamilton	AHL	2	0	2	2	2	0	0	0	—	—	—	—	—
—Edmonton	NHL	70	11	20	31	28	19	2	2	6	1	0	1	2
03-04—Edmonton	NHL	17	2	6	8	10	5	0	1	—	—	—	—	—
04-05—Salzburg	Austria	11	5	4	9	12	-6	1	0	—	—	—	—	—
NHL Totals (6 years)		234	36	61	97	121	30	9	3	23	6	2	8	6

RECCHI, MARK — LW — PENGUINS

PERSONAL: Born February 1, 1968, in Kamloops, B.C. ... 5-10/190. ... Shoots left. ... Name pronounced REH-kee.
TRANSACTIONS/CAREER NOTES: Selected by Pittsburgh Penguins in fourth round (fourth Penguins pick, 67th overall) of NHL draft (June 11, 1988). ... Injured left shoulder (December 23, 1990). ... Sprained right knee (March 30, 1991). ... Traded by Penguins with D Brian Benning and first-round pick (LW Jason Bowen) in 1992 draft to Philadelphia Flyers for RW Rick Tocchet, D Kjell Samuelsson, G Ken Wregget and third-round pick (C Dave Roche) in 1993 draft (February 19, 1992). ... Traded by Flyers with third-round pick (C Martin Hohenberger) in 1995

draft to Montreal Canadiens for D Eric Desjardins, LW Gilbert Dionne and LW John LeClair (February 9, 1995). ... Pneumonia (December 12, 1998); missed four games. ... Traded by Canadiens to Flyers for RW Dainius Zubrus and second-round pick (D Matt Carkner) in 1999 draft (March 10, 1999). ... Concussion (March 22, 1999); missed three games. ... Headaches (April 1, 1999); missed two games. ... Concussion (April 13, 1999); missed two games. ... Headaches (October 11, 2000); missed four games. ... Fatigue (October 24, 2000); missed nine games. ... Suspended two games for elbowing (March 8, 2002). ... Signed as free agent by Pittsburgh Penguins (July 9, 2004).

STATISTICAL PLATEAUS: Three-goal games: 1991-92 (1), 1996-97 (1), 1997-98 (1), 2001-02 (1), 2002-03 (1). Total: 5.

		REGULAR SEASON								PLAYOFFS				
Season Team	**League**	**GP**	**G**	**A**	**Pts.**	**PIM**	**+/-**	**PP**	**SH**	**GP**	**G**	**A**	**Pts.**	**PIM**
84-85—Langley Eagles	BCJHL	51	26	39	65	39	...	...	...	—	—	—	—	—
85-86—New Westminster	WHL	72	21	40	61	55	...	...	...	—	—	—	—	—
86-87—Kamloops	WHL	40	26	50	76	63	...	...	...	13	3	16	19	17
87-88—Kamloops	WHL	62	61	*93	154	75	...	...	...	17	10	*21	31	18
88-89—Pittsburgh	NHL	15	1	1	2	0	-2	0	0	—	—	—	—	—
—Muskegon	IHL	63	50	49	99	86	...	...	...	14	7	*14	21	28
89-90—Muskegon	IHL	4	7	4	11	2	...	...	...	—	—	—	—	—
—Pittsburgh	NHL	74	30	37	67	44	6	6	2	—	—	—	—	—
90-91—Pittsburgh	NHL	78	40	73	113	48	0	12	0	24	10	24	34	33
91-92—Pittsburgh	NHL	58	33	37	70	78	-16	16	1	—	—	—	—	—
—Philadelphia	NHL	22	10	17	27	18	-5	4	0	—	—	—	—	—
92-93—Philadelphia	NHL	84	53	70	123	95	1	15	4	—	—	—	—	—
93-94—Philadelphia	NHL	84	40	67	107	46	-2	11	0	—	—	—	—	—
94-95—Philadelphia	NHL	10	2	3	5	12	-6	1	0	—	—	—	—	—
—Montreal	NHL	39	14	29	43	16	-3	8	0	—	—	—	—	—
95-96—Montreal	NHL	82	28	50	78	69	20	11	2	6	3	3	6	0
96-97—Montreal	NHL	82	34	46	80	58	-1	7	2	5	4	2	6	2
97-98—Montreal	NHL	82	32	42	74	51	11	9	1	10	4	8	12	6
—Can. Olympic team	Int'l	5	0	2	2	0	1	0	0	—	—	—	—	—
98-99—Montreal	NHL	61	12	35	47	28	-4	3	0	—	—	—	—	—
—Philadelphia	NHL	10	4	2	6	6	-3	0	0	6	0	1	1	2
99-00—Philadelphia	NHL	82	28	*63	91	50	20	7	1	18	6	12	18	6
00-01—Philadelphia	NHL	69	27	50	77	33	15	7	1	6	2	2	4	2
01-02—Philadelphia	NHL	80	22	42	64	46	5	7	2	4	0	0	0	2
02-03—Philadelphia	NHL	79	20	32	52	35	0	8	1	13	7	3	10	2
03-04—Philadelphia	NHL	82	26	49	75	47	18	14	1	18	4	2	6	4
NHL Totals (16 years)		1173	456	745	1201	780	54	146	18	110	40	57	97	59

REDDEN, WADE — D — SENATORS

PERSONAL: Born June 12, 1977, in Lloydminster, Sask. ... 6-2/212. ... Shoots left.

TRANSACTIONS/CAREER NOTES: Selected by New York Islanders in first round (first Islanders pick, second overall) of NHL entry draft (July 8, 1995). ... Traded by Islanders with G Damian Rhodes to Ottawa Senators for G Don Beaupre, D Bryan Berard and C Martin Straka (January 23, 1996). ... Bruised left foot (January 29, 1998); missed one game. ... Back spasms (December 22, 1998); missed two games. ... Injured shoulder (March 4, 1999); missed eight games. ... Suffered illness (February 1, 2000); missed one game. ... Bruised hand (September 25, 2000); missed first four games of regular season. ... Flu (April 8, 2002); missed final three games of regular season. ... Injured right hip flexor (November 8, 2002); missed three games. ... Flu (January 27, 2003); missed two games. ... Flu (February 5, 2004); missed one game.

		REGULAR SEASON								PLAYOFFS				
Season Team	**League**	**GP**	**G**	**A**	**Pts.**	**PIM**	**+/-**	**PP**	**SH**	**GP**	**G**	**A**	**Pts.**	**PIM**
92-93—Lloydminster	SJHL	34	4	11	15	64	...	...	...	—	—	—	—	—
93-94—Brandon	WHL	64	4	35	39	98	...	...	...	14	2	4	6	10
94-95—Brandon	WHL	64	14	46	60	83	49	4	0	18	5	10	15	8
95-96—Brandon	WHL	51	9	45	54	55	...	...	...	19	5	10	15	19
96-97—Ottawa	NHL	82	6	24	30	41	1	2	0	7	1	3	4	2
97-98—Ottawa	NHL	80	8	14	22	27	17	3	0	9	0	2	2	2
98-99—Ottawa	NHL	72	8	21	29	54	7	3	0	4	1	2	3	2
99-00—Ottawa	NHL	81	10	26	36	49	-1	3	0	—	—	—	—	—
00-01—Ottawa	NHL	78	10	37	47	49	22	4	0	4	0	0	0	0
01-02—Ottawa	NHL	79	9	25	34	48	22	4	1	12	3	2	5	6
02-03—Ottawa	NHL	76	10	35	45	70	23	4	0	18	1	8	9	10
03-04—Ottawa	NHL	81	17	26	43	65	21	12	0	7	1	0	1	2
NHL Totals (8 years)		629	78	208	286	403	112	35	1	61	7	17	24	24

REDLIHS, KRISJANIS — D — DEVILS

PERSONAL: Born January 15, 1981, in Riga, U.S.S.R. ... 6-2/190.

TRANSACTIONS/CAREER NOTES: Selected by New Jersey Devils in fifth round (seventh Devils pick, 154th overall) of NHL entry draft (June 23, 2002).

		REGULAR SEASON								PLAYOFFS				
Season Team	**League**	**GP**	**G**	**A**	**Pts.**	**PIM**	**+/-**	**PP**	**SH**	**GP**	**G**	**A**	**Pts.**	**PIM**
02-03—Albany	AHL	61	1	9	10	20	...	...	...	—	—	—	—	—
03-04—Albany	AHL	66	9	10	19	16	...	...	...	—	—	—	—	—
04-05—Albany	AHL	46	0	10	10	12	-7	0	0	—	—	—	—	—

REGEHR, ROBYN — D — FLAMES

PERSONAL: Born April 19, 1980, in Recife, Brazil. ... 6-3/226. ... Shoots left. ... Brother of Richie Regehr, Calgary Flames organization. ... Name pronounced ruh-ZHEER.

TRANSACTIONS/CAREER NOTES: Selected by Colorado Avalanche in first round (third Avalanche pick, 19th overall) of NHL entry draft (June

27, 1998). ... Traded by Avalanche to Calgary Flames (March 27, 1999); completing deal in which Flames traded RW Theo Fleury and LW Chris Dingman to Avalanche for LW Rene Corbet, D Wade Belak and future considerations (February 28, 1999). ... Fractured legs before 1999-2000 season; missed first five games of season. ... Suffered concussion (January 11, 2000); missed 11 games. ... Injured knee (November 4, 2000); missed six games. ... Injured knee (December 22, 2000); missed two games. ... Injured wrist (November 7, 2001); missed one game. ... Injured ribs, strained oblique muscle (February 4, 2003); missed six games.

		REGULAR SEASON								PLAYOFFS				
Season Team	League	GP	G	A	Pts.	PIM	+/-	PP	SH	GP	G	A	Pts.	PIM
96-97—Kamloops	WHL	64	4	19	23	96	...	...	...	5	0	1	1	18
97-98—Kamloops	WHL	65	4	10	14	120	...	...	...	5	0	3	3	8
98-99—Kamloops	WHL	54	12	20	32	130	37	6	1	12	1	4	5	21
99-00—Saint John	AHL	5	0	0	0	0	...	...	...	—	—	—	—	—
—Calgary	NHL	57	5	7	12	46	-2	2	0	—	—	—	—	—
00-01—Calgary	NHL	71	1	3	4	70	-7	0	0	—	—	—	—	—
01-02—Calgary	NHL	77	2	6	8	93	-24	0	0	—	—	—	—	—
02-03—Calgary	NHL	76	0	12	12	87	-9	0	0	—	—	—	—	—
03-04—Calgary	NHL	82	4	14	18	74	14	2	0	26	2	7	9	20
NHL Totals (5 years)		363	12	42	54	370	-28	4	0	26	2	7	9	20

REICH, JEREMY LW

PERSONAL: Born February 11, 1979, in Craik, Sask. ... 6-1/204. ... Shoots left. ... Nephew of Jim Archibald, RW with Minnesota North Stars (1984-85 through 1986-87). ... Name pronounced REECH.

TRANSACTIONS/CAREER NOTES: Selected by Chicago Blackhawks in second round (third Blackhawks pick, 39th overall) of NHL entry draft (June 21, 1997). ... Signed as free agent by Columbus Blue Jackets (May 16, 2000).

		REGULAR SEASON								PLAYOFFS				
Season Team	League	GP	G	A	Pts.	PIM	+/-	PP	SH	GP	G	A	Pts.	PIM
94-95—Saskatoon	SJHL	35	13	20	33	81	...	...	...	—	—	—	—	—
95-96—Seattle	WHL	65	11	11	22	88	...	...	...	5	0	1	1	10
96-97—Seattle	WHL	62	19	31	50	134	...	...	...	15	2	5	7	36
97-98—Seattle	WHL	43	24	23	47	121	...	...	...	—	—	—	—	—
—Swift Current	WHL	35	32	31	63	168	14	8	3	12	5	6	11	37
98-99—Swift Current	WHL	67	21	28	49	220	0	5	3	6	0	3	3	26
99-00—Swift Current	WHL	72	33	58	91	167	32	13	0	12	2	10	12	19
00-01—Syracuse	AHL	56	6	9	15	108	...	...	...	5	0	0	0	6
01-02—Syracuse	AHL	59	9	7	16	178	-6	1	0	10	4	0	4	16
02-03—Syracuse	AHL	78	14	13	27	195	-21	2	2	—	—	—	—	—
03-04—Columbus	NHL	9	0	1	1	20	-3	0	0	—	—	—	—	—
—Syracuse	AHL	72	14	37	51	145	8	3	0	6	1	1	2	13
04-05—Houston	AHL	18	3	4	7	34	3	1	0	5	0	1	1	28
—Syracuse	AHL	50	4	5	9	189	-8	2	1	—	—	—	—	—
NHL Totals (1 year)		9	0	1	1	20	-3	0	0					

REID, BRANDON C/RW CANUCKS

PERSONAL: Born March 9, 1981, in Kirkland, Que. ... 5-9/190. ... Shoots right.

TRANSACTIONS/CAREER NOTES: Selected by Vancouver Canucks in seventh round (fifth Canucks pick, 208th overall) of NHL entry draft (June 24, 2000).

		REGULAR SEASON								PLAYOFFS				
Season Team	League	GP	G	A	Pts.	PIM	+/-	PP	SH	GP	G	A	Pts.	PIM
98-99—Halifax	QMJHL	70	32	25	57	33	...	...	...	5	2	2	4	...
99-00—Halifax	QMJHL	62	44	80	124	10	...	...	...	10	7	11	18	...
00-01—Val-d'Or	QMJHL	57	45	81	126	18	47	15	7	21	13	29	42	14
01-02—Manitoba	AHL	60	18	19	37	6	2	3	1	7	0	3	3	0
02-03—Vancouver	NHL	7	2	3	5	0	4	0	0	9	0	1	1	0
—Manitoba	AHL	73	18	36	54	18	1	7	1	1	1	1	2	0
03-04—Vancouver	NHL	3	0	1	1	0	1	0	0	—	—	—	—	—
—Manitoba	AHL	73	19	39	58	20	2	4	0	—	—	—	—	—
04-05—Hamburg	Germany	45	18	29	47	41	10	5	0	6	0	3	3	4
NHL Totals (2 years)		10	2	4	6	0	5	0	0	9	0	1	1	0

REID, DARREN RW LIGHTNING

PERSONAL: Born May 8, 1983, in Lac La Biche, Alta. ... 6-2/185. ... Shoots right.

TRANSACTIONS/CAREER NOTES: Selected by Tampa Bay Lightning in eighth round (11th Lightning pick, 256th overall) of NHL entry draft (June 23, 2002).

		REGULAR SEASON								PLAYOFFS				
Season Team	League	GP	G	A	Pts.	PIM	+/-	PP	SH	GP	G	A	Pts.	PIM
01-02—Medicine Hat	WHL	37	8	9	17	70	...	...	...	—	—	—	—	—
02-03—Medicine Hat	WHL	63	14	30	44	163	...	...	...	11	5	0	5	19
03-04—Medicine Hat	WHL	67	33	48	81	194	...	...	...	20	13	8	21	31
04-05—Springfield	AHL	56	3	19	22	99	-10	0	1	—	—	—	—	—

REINPRECHT, STEVEN C/RW FLAMES

PERSONAL: Born May 7, 1976, in Edmonton. ... 6-0/190. ... Shoots left.

TRANSACTIONS/CAREER NOTES: Signed as free agent by Los Angeles Kings (March 31, 2000). ... Traded by Kings with D Rob Blake to

Colorado Avalanche for RW Adam Deadmarsh, D Aaron Miller, first-round pick (C David Steckel) in 2001 draft, a player to be named and future considerations (February 21, 2001); Kings acquired C Jared Aulin to complete deal (March 22, 2001). ... Injured knee (January 15, 2002); missed 13 games. ... Injured foot (March 21, 2002); missed one game. ... Shoulder injury (November 22, 2002); missed five games. ... Traded by Avalanche to Buffalo Sabres for D Keith Ballard (July 2, 2003). ... Traded by Sabres with D Rhett Warrener to Calgary Flames for C/LW Chris Drury and C Steve Begin (July 3, 2003). ... Bruised shoulder (October 5, 2003); missed five games. ... Fractured left leg (December 2, 2003); missed 17 games. ... Flu (February 26, 2004); missed one game. ... Injured shoulder (March 2, 2004); misssed two games. ... Reinjured shoulder (March 9, 2004); missed remainder of season.

STATISTICAL PLATEAUS: Three-goal games: 2001-02 (1), 2002-03 (1). Total: 2.

		REGULAR SEASON								PLAYOFFS				
Season Team	League	GP	G	A	Pts.	PIM	+/-	PP	SH	GP	G	A	Pts.	PIM
96-97—Wisconsin	WCHA	38	11	9	20	12	...	...	...	—	—	—	—	—
97-98—Wisconsin	WCHA	41	19	24	43	18	...	...	...	—	—	—	—	—
98-99—Wisconsin	WCHA	38	16	17	33	14	...	...	...	—	—	—	—	—
99-00—Wisconsin	WCHA	37	26	40	*66	14	...	...	...	—	—	—	—	—
—Los Angeles	NHL	1	0	0	0	2	0	0	0	—	—	—	—	—
00-01—Los Angeles	NHL	59	12	17	29	12	11	3	2	—	—	—	—	—
—Colorado	NHL	21	3	4	7	2	-1	0	0	22	2	3	5	2
01-02—Colorado	NHL	67	19	27	46	18	14	4	0	21	7	5	12	8
02-03—Colorado	NHL	77	18	33	51	18	-6	2	1	7	1	2	3	0
03-04—Calgary	NHL	44	7	22	29	4	1	3	0	—	—	—	—	—
04-05—Mulhouse	France	22	20	27	47	6	...	...	...	10	7	6	13	2
NHL Totals (5 years)		269	59	103	162	56	19	12	3	50	10	10	20	10

REIRDEN, TODD D

PERSONAL: Born June 25, 1971, in Deerfield, Ill. ... 6-4/214. ... Shoots left.

TRANSACTIONS/CAREER NOTES: Selected by New Jersey Devils in 12th round (14th Devils pick, 242nd overall) of NHL entry draft (June 16, 1990). ... Signed as free agent by Edmonton Oilers (May 31, 1998). ... Claimed off waivers by St. Louis Blues (September 30, 1999). ... Strained shoulder (December 4, 1999); missed three games. ... Fractured foot (January 28, 2000); missed 18 games. ... Foot surgery (July 2000); missed first 25 games of season. ... Strained oblique muscle (January 23, 2001); missed one game. ... Signed as free agent by Atlanta Thrashers (July 16, 2001). ... Strained groin (September 25, 2001); missed first five games of season. ... Injured elbow (December 31, 2001); missed three games. ... Signed as free agent by Anaheim Mighty Ducks (July 17, 2002). ... Traded by Mighty Ducks to Phoenix Coyotes for future considerations (January 17, 2004). ... Signed as free agent by Houston of the AHL (September 22, 2004).

		REGULAR SEASON								PLAYOFFS				
Season Team	League	GP	G	A	Pts.	PIM	+/-	PP	SH	GP	G	A	Pts.	PIM
90-91—Bowling Green	CCHA	28	1	5	6	22	...	...	...	—	—	—	—	—
91-92—Bowling Green	CCHA	33	8	7	15	34	...	...	...	—	—	—	—	—
92-93—Bowling Green	CCHA	41	8	17	25	48	...	...	...	—	—	—	—	—
93-94—Bowling Green	CCHA	38	7	23	30	56	...	...	...	—	—	—	—	—
94-95—Albany	AHL	2	0	1	1	2	0	0	0	—	—	—	—	—
—Raleigh	ECHL	26	2	13	15	33	-7	2	0	—	—	—	—	—
—Tallahassee	ECHL	43	5	25	30	61	12	2	0	13	2	5	7	10
95-96—Chicago	IHL	31	0	2	2	39	...	...	...	9	0	2	2	16
—Tallahassee	ECHL	7	1	3	4	10	...	...	...	—	—	—	—	—
—Jacksonville	ECHL	15	1	10	11	41	...	...	...	1	0	2	2	4
96-97—Chicago	IHL	57	3	10	13	108	...	...	...	—	—	—	—	—
—San Antonio	IHL	23	2	5	7	51	...	...	...	9	0	1	1	17
97-98—San Antonio	IHL	70	5	14	19	132	-4	1	0	—	—	—	—	—
—Fort Wayne	IHL	11	2	2	4	16	-10	1	0	4	0	2	2	4
98-99—Hamilton	AHL	58	9	25	34	84	4	5	0	11	0	5	5	6
—Edmonton	NHL	17	2	3	5	20	-1	0	0	—	—	—	—	—
99-00—St. Louis	NHL	56	4	21	25	32	18	0	0	4	0	1	1	0
00-01—Worcester	AHL	7	2	6	8	20	...	...	...	—	—	—	—	—
—St. Louis	NHL	38	2	4	6	43	-2	1	0	1	0	0	0	0
01-02—Atlanta	NHL	65	3	5	8	82	-25	1	0	—	—	—	—	—
02-03—Cincinnati	AHL	58	7	13	20	97	-5	2	1	—	—	—	—	—
03-04—Phoenix	NHL	7	0	2	2	4	-4	0	0	—	—	—	—	—
—Cincinnati	AHL	39	3	8	11	42	-9	1	1	—	—	—	—	—
—Springfield	AHL	34	6	7	13	42	-14	0	1	—	—	—	—	—
04-05—Houston	AHL	52	3	5	8	56	3	0	0	5	0	0	0	6
NHL Totals (5 years)		183	11	35	46	181	-14	2	0	5	0	1	1	0

REITZ, ERIK D WILD

PERSONAL: Born August 29, 1982, in Detroit. ... 6-0/192. ... Shoots right. ... Name pronounced RIGHTZ.

TRANSACTIONS/CAREER NOTES: Selected by Minnesota Wild in sixth round (fifth Wild pick, 170th overall) of NHL entry draft (June 24, 2000).

		REGULAR SEASON								PLAYOFFS				
Season Team	League	GP	G	A	Pts.	PIM	+/-	PP	SH	GP	G	A	Pts.	PIM
99-00—Barrie	OHL	63	2	10	12	85	...	...	...	—	—	—	—	—
00-01—Barrie	OHL	68	5	21	26	178	6	0	0	5	1	0	1	21
01-02—Barrie	OHL	61	13	27	40	153	...	...	...	20	4	16	20	40
02-03—Houston	AHL	62	6	13	19	112	-6	2	0	11	0	3	3	31
03-04—Houston	AHL	69	5	19	24	148	-6	2	0	2	0	0	0	0
04-05—Houston	AHL	38	2	12	14	91	-1	1	0	—	—	—	—	—

RENBERG, MIKAEL RW MAPLE LEAFS

PERSONAL: Born May 5, 1972, in Pitea, Sweden. ... 6-2/235. ... Shoots left.

TRANSACTIONS/CAREER NOTES: Selected by Philadelphia Flyers in second round (third Flyers pick, 40th overall) of NHL entry draft (June 16, 1990). ... Had sore shoulder (March 25, 1995); missed one game. ... Strained abdominal muscles (December 30, 1995); missed one game. ... Strained lower abdominal muscles (January 22, 1996); missed 17 games. ... Reinjured lower abdominal muscles (March 12, 1996); missed one game. ... Reinjured lower abdominal muscles (March 16, 1996); missed one game. ... Reinjured lower abdominal muscles (March 19, 1996); missed 11 games. ... Abdominal surgery (May 1996). ... Strained groin (March 8, 1997); missed one game. ... Cut face (April 6, 1997); missed remainder of season. ... Traded by Flyers with D Karl Dykhuis to Tampa Bay Lightning for C Chris Gratton (August 20, 1997). ... Flu (October 15, 1997); missed one game. ... Fractured wrist (December 13, 1997); missed 13 games. ... Fractured left thumb (November 10, 1998); missed seven games. ... Traded by Lightning with C Daymond Langkow to Flyers for C Chris Gratton and C/RW Mike Sillinger (December 12, 1998). ... Separated shoulder (December 23, 1998); missed nine games. ... Flu (February 9, 2000); missed two games. ... Traded by Flyers to Phoenix Coyotes for RW Rick Tocchet (March 8, 2000). ... Strained hip flexor (March 15, 2000); missed six games. ... Flu (February 9, 2000); missed two games. ... Signed by Lulea of Swedish league (June 13, 2000). ... Traded by Coyotes to Toronto Maple Leafs for LW Sergei Berezin (June 22, 2001). ... Suffered injury (December 18, 2001); missed two games. ... Suffered injury (March 6, 2002); missed four games. ... Strained hamstring (March 23, 2002); missed four games. ... Sprained right ankle (December 18, 2002); missed two games. ... Flu (December 27, 2002); missed one game. ... Infected hand (January 3, 2003); missed six games. ... Strained hamstring (March 28, 2003); missed three games. ... Injured chest (October 20, 2003); missed eight games. ... Left team for personal reasons (December 26, 2003); missed three games. ... Injured hamstring (January 29, 2004); missed two games. ... Suffered concussion (March 9, 2004); missed three games. ... Injured hamstring (March 16, 2004); missed seven games.

STATISTICAL PLATEAUS: Three-goal games: 1993-94 (1), 1997-98 (1). Total: 2.

		REGULAR SEASON								PLAYOFFS				
Season Team	**League**	**GP**	**G**	**A**	**Pts.**	**PIM**	**+/-**	**PP**	**SH**	**GP**	**G**	**A**	**Pts.**	**PIM**
88-89—Pitea	Sweden	12	6	3	9	...	...	...	...	—	—	—	—	—
89-90—Pitea	Sweden	29	15	19	34	...	...	...	...	—	—	—	—	—
90-91—Lulea	Sweden	29	11	6	17	12	...	...	...	5	1	1	2	4
91-92—Lulea	Sweden	38	8	15	23	20	...	...	...	2	0	0	0	0
92-93—Lulea	Sweden	39	19	13	32	61	...	...	...	11	4	4	8	...
93-94—Philadelphia	NHL	83	38	44	82	36	8	9	0	—	—	—	—	—
94-95—Lulea	Sweden	10	9	4	13	16	...	...	...	—	—	—	—	—
—Philadelphia	NHL	47	26	31	57	20	20	8	0	15	6	7	13	6
95-96—Philadelphia	NHL	51	23	20	43	45	8	9	0	11	3	6	9	14
96-97—Philadelphia	NHL	77	22	37	59	65	36	1	0	18	5	6	11	4
97-98—Tampa Bay	NHL	68	16	22	38	34	-37	6	3	—	—	—	—	—
—Swedish Oly. team	Int'l	4	1	2	3	4	2	0	0	—	—	—	—	—
98-99—Tampa Bay	NHL	20	4	8	12	4	-2	2	0	—	—	—	—	—
—Philadelphia	NHL	46	11	15	26	14	7	4	0	6	0	1	1	0
99-00—Philadelphia	NHL	62	8	21	29	30	-1	3	0	—	—	—	—	—
—Phoenix	NHL	10	2	4	6	2	0	0	0	5	1	2	3	4
00-01—Lulea	Sweden	48	22	32	54	36	...	...	...	11	6	5	11	35
01-02—Toronto	NHL	71	14	38	52	36	11	4	0	3	0	0	0	2
—Swedish Oly. team	Int'l	4	1	0	1	4	...	...	...	—	—	—	—	—
02-03—Toronto	NHL	67	14	21	35	36	5	7	0	7	1	0	1	8
03-04—Toronto	NHL	59	12	13	25	50	-1	2	0	2	0	0	0	4
04-05—Lulea	Sweden	22	6	5	11	16	-7	4	0	—	—	—	—	—
NHL Totals (10 years)		661	190	274	464	372	54	55	3	67	16	22	38	42

RHEAUME, PASCAL C/LW DEVILS

PERSONAL: Born June 21, 1973, in Quebec City. ... 6-1/220. ... Shoots left. ... Name pronounced ray-OHM.

TRANSACTIONS/CAREER NOTES: Signed as free agent by New Jersey Devils (October 1, 1992). ... Claimed by St. Louis Blues from Devils in NHL waiver draft (September 28, 1997). ... Suffered concussion (February 28, 1999); missed 10 games. ... Shoulder surgery before 1999-2000 season; missed first 62 games of season. ... Signed as free agent by Chicago Blackhawks (July 31, 2001). ... Claimed off waivers by Atlanta Thrashers (November 14, 2001). ... Strained hamstring (December 3, 2001); missed 21 games. ... Pneumonia (April 7, 2002); missed two games. ... Flu (January 15, 2003); missed one game. ... Traded by Thrashers to Devils for conditional pick in 2004 entry draft (February 24, 2003). ... Signed as free agent by New York Rangers (October 22, 2003). ... Injured left knee (October 29, 2003); missed 24 games. ... Claimed by Blues off waivers from Rangers (January 29, 2004). ... Injured hip flexor (March 16, 2004); missed three games. ... Signed as free agent by New Jersey Devils (August 13, 2004).

STATISTICAL PLATEAUS: Four-goal games: 2001-02 (1).

		REGULAR SEASON								PLAYOFFS				
Season Team	**League**	**GP**	**G**	**A**	**Pts.**	**PIM**	**+/-**	**PP**	**SH**	**GP**	**G**	**A**	**Pts.**	**PIM**
91-92—Trois-Rivieres	QMJHL	65	17	20	37	84	...	...	...	14	5	4	9	23
92-93—Sherbrooke	QMJHL	65	28	34	62	88	...	...	...	14	6	5	11	31
93-94—Albany	AHL	55	17	18	35	43	...	...	...	5	0	1	1	0
94-95—Albany	AHL	78	19	25	44	46	17	5	0	14	3	6	9	19
95-96—Albany	AHL	68	26	42	68	50	...	...	...	4	1	2	3	2
96-97—Albany	AHL	51	22	23	45	40	15	4	3	16	2	8	10	16
—New Jersey	NHL	2	1	0	1	0	1	0	0	—	—	—	—	—
97-98—St. Louis	NHL	48	6	9	15	35	4	1	0	10	1	3	4	8
98-99—St. Louis	NHL	60	9	18	27	24	10	2	0	5	1	0	1	4
99-00—St. Louis	NHL	7	1	1	2	6	-2	0	0	—	—	—	—	—
—Worcester	AHL	7	1	1	2	4	...	...	...	—	—	—	—	—
00-01—Worcester	AHL	56	23	36	59	63	...	...	...	11	2	4	6	2
—St. Louis	NHL	8	2	0	2	5	-1	2	0	3	0	1	1	0
01-02—Chicago	NHL	19	0	2	2	4	-1	0	0	—	—	—	—	—
—Atlanta	NHL	42	11	9	20	25	-3	6	0	—	—	—	—	—
02-03—Atlanta	NHL	56	4	9	13	24	-8	0	2	—	—	—	—	—
—New Jersey	NHL	21	4	1	5	8	3	0	1	24	1	2	3	13
03-04—New York Rangers	NHL	17	0	0	0	5	-3	0	0	—	—	—	—	—

Season Team	League	REGULAR SEASON GP	G	A	Pts.	PIM	+/-	PP	SH	PLAYOFFS GP	G	A	Pts.	PIM
—Hartford	AHL	3	1	0	1	0	0	0	0	—	—	—	—	—
—St. Louis	NHL	25	1	3	4	4	-3	0	0	3	0	0	0	2
04-05—Albany	AHL	78	24	25	49	85	-1	6	1	—	—	—	—	—
NHL Totals (8 years)		305	39	52	91	140	-3	11	3	45	3	6	9	27

RIBEIRO, MIKE — C — CANADIENS

PERSONAL: Born February 10, 1980, in Montreal. ... 6-0/176. ... Shoots left. ... Name pronounced rih-bee-AIR-roh.
TRANSACTIONS/CAREER NOTES: Selected by Montreal Canadiens in second round (second Canadiens pick, 45th overall) of NHL entry draft (June 27, 1998). ... Injured collarbone (September 27, 2002); missed 13 games. ... Injured knee (Febuary 21, 2003); missed four games.

Season Team	League	REGULAR SEASON GP	G	A	Pts.	PIM	+/-	PP	SH	PLAYOFFS GP	G	A	Pts.	PIM
97-98—Rouyn-Noranda	QMJHL	67	40	85	125	55	...	...	...	—	—	—	—	—
98-99—Rouyn-Noranda	QMJHL	69	67	*100	*167	137	50	24	8	11	5	11	16	12
—Fredericton	AHL	...	...	...	...	...	...	...	...	5	0	1	1	2
99-00—Montreal	NHL	19	1	1	2	2	-6	1	0	—	—	—	—	—
—Quebec	AHL	3	0	0	0	2	...	...	...	—	—	—	—	—
—Rouyn-Noranda	QMJHL	2	1	3	4	0	2	0	0	—	—	—	—	—
—Quebec	QMJHL	21	17	28	45	30	17	4	2	11	3	20	23	38
00-01—Quebec	AHL	74	26	40	66	44	...	...	...	9	1	5	6	23
—Montreal	NHL	2	0	0	0	2	0	0	0	—	—	—	—	—
01-02—Montreal	NHL	43	8	10	18	12	-11	3	0	—	—	—	—	—
—Quebec	AHL	23	9	14	23	36	7	2	2	3	0	3	3	0
02-03—Hamilton	AHL	3	0	1	1	0	1	0	0	—	—	—	—	—
—Montreal	NHL	52	5	12	17	6	-3	2	0	—	—	—	—	—
03-04—Montreal	NHL	81	20	45	65	34	15	7	0	11	2	1	3	18
04-05—Blues Espoo	Finland	17	8	9	17	4	7	...	...	—	—	—	—	—
NHL Totals (5 years)		197	34	68	102	56	-5	13	0	11	2	1	3	18

RICCI, MIKE — C — COYOTES

PERSONAL: Born October 27, 1971, in Scarborough, Ont. ... 6-0/200. ... Shoots left. ... Name pronounced REE-chee.
TRANSACTIONS/CAREER NOTES: Selected by Philadelphia Flyers in first round (first Flyers pick, fourth overall) of NHL draft (June 16, 1990). ... Fractured right index finger and thumb (October 4, 1990); missed nine games. ... Traded by Flyers with G Ron Hextall, C Peter Forsberg, D Steve Duchesne, D Kerry Huffman, first-round pick (G Jocelyn Thibault) in 1993 draft, cash and future considerations to Quebec Nordiques for C Eric Lindros (June 20, 1992); Nordiques acquired LW Chris Simon and first-round pick (traded to Toronto; traded to Washington; Capitals selected D Nolan Baumgartner) in 1994 draft to complete deal (July 21, 1992). ... Sprained left wrist (November 3, 1992); missed four games. ... Flu (January 5, 1993); missed two games. ... Nordiques franchise moved to Colorado and renamed Avalanche for 1995-96 season (July 21, 1995). ... Sinus surgery (October 15, 1995); missed one game. ... Injured ankle (November 5, 1995); missed one game. ... Sprained left ankle (December 11, 1995); missed two games. ... Back spasms (January 4, 1996); missed 16 games. ... Strained shoulder (October 30, 1996); missed 11 games. ... Fractured thumb (January 6, 1997); missed four games. ... Shoulder surgery before 1997-98 season; missed first 16 games of season. ... Traded by Avalanche with second-round pick (RW Jonathan Cheechoo) in 1998 draft to San Jose Sharks for RW Shean Donovan and first-round pick (C Alex Tanguay) in 1998 draft (November 20, 1997). ... Injured back (March 3, 2002); missed one game. ... Injured shoulder (March 10, 2002); missed two games. ... Cut face (March 1, 2003); missed three games. ... Injured back (March 24, 2003); missed five games. ... Injured back (April 6, 2003); missed one game. ... Strained right shoulder (February 26, 2004); missed 11 games. ... Signed as free agent by Phoenix Coyotes (July 9, 2004).
STATISTICAL PLATEAUS: Three-goal games: 2000-01 (1). ... Five-goal games: 1993-94 (1). ... Total hat tricks: 2.

Season Team	League	REGULAR SEASON GP	G	A	Pts.	PIM	+/-	PP	SH	PLAYOFFS GP	G	A	Pts.	PIM
87-88—Peterborough	OHL	41	24	37	61	20	...	...	...	8	5	5	10	4
88-89—Peterborough	OHL	60	54	52	106	43	...	...	...	17	19	16	35	18
89-90—Peterborough	OHL	60	52	64	116	39	...	...	...	12	5	7	12	26
90-91—Philadelphia	NHL	68	21	20	41	64	-8	9	0	—	—	—	—	—
91-92—Philadelphia	NHL	78	20	36	56	93	-10	11	2	—	—	—	—	—
92-93—Quebec	NHL	77	27	51	78	123	8	12	1	6	0	6	6	8
93-94—Quebec	NHL	83	30	21	51	113	-9	13	3	—	—	—	—	—
94-95—Quebec	NHL	48	15	21	36	40	5	9	0	6	1	3	4	8
95-96—Colorado	NHL	62	6	21	27	52	1	3	0	22	6	11	17	18
96-97—Colorado	NHL	63	13	19	32	59	-3	5	0	17	2	4	6	17
97-98—Colorado	NHL	6	0	4	4	2	0	0	0	—	—	—	—	—
—San Jose	NHL	59	9	14	23	30	-4	5	0	6	1	3	4	6
98-99—San Jose	NHL	82	13	26	39	68	1	2	1	6	2	3	5	10
99-00—San Jose	NHL	82	20	24	44	60	14	10	0	12	5	1	6	2
00-01—San Jose	NHL	81	22	22	44	60	3	9	2	6	0	3	3	0
01-02—San Jose	NHL	79	19	34	53	44	9	5	2	12	4	6	10	4
02-03—San Jose	NHL	75	11	23	34	53	-12	5	1	—	—	—	—	—
03-04—San Jose	NHL	71	7	19	26	40	8	2	0	17	2	3	5	4
NHL Totals (14 years)		1014	233	355	588	901	3	100	12	110	23	43	66	77

RICHARDS, BRAD — C — LIGHTNING

PERSONAL: Born May 2, 1980, in Montague, Prince Edward Island. ... 6-1/198. ... Shoots left.
TRANSACTIONS/CAREER NOTES: Selected by Tampa Bay Lightning in third round (second Lightning pick, 64th overall) of NHL draft (June 27, 1998).

Season Team	League	REGULAR SEASON GP	G	A	Pts.	PIM	+/-	PP	SH	PLAYOFFS GP	G	A	Pts.	PIM
96-97—Notre Dame	SJHL	63	39	48	87	73	...	...	...	—	—	—	—	—
97-98—Rimouski	QMJHL	68	33	82	115	44	...	...	...	19	8	24	32	2
98-99—Rimouski	QMJHL	59	39	92	131	55	18	10	8	11	9	12	21	6
99-00—Rimouski	QMJHL	63	*71	*115	*186	69	80	18	6	12	13	*24	*37	16
00-01—Tampa Bay	NHL	82	21	41	62	14	-10	7	0	—	—	—	—	—
01-02—Tampa Bay	NHL	82	20	42	62	13	-18	5	0	—	—	—	—	—
02-03—Tampa Bay	NHL	80	17	57	74	24	3	4	0	11	0	5	5	12
03-04—Tampa Bay	NHL	82	26	53	79	12	14	5	1	23	12	14	26	4
04-05—Ak Bars Kazan	Russian	6	2	5	7	16	2	...	...	—	—	—	—	—
NHL Totals (4 years)		326	84	193	277	63	-11	21	1	34	12	19	31	16

RICHARDSON, LUKE — D — BLUE JACKETS

PERSONAL: Born March 26, 1969, in Ottawa. ... 6-4/215. ... Shoots left.

TRANSACTIONS/CAREER NOTES: Selected by Toronto Maple Leafs in first round (first Maple Leafs pick, seventh overall) of NHL draft (June 13, 1987). ... Traded by Maple Leafs with LW Vincent Damphousse, G Peter Ing and C Scott Thornton to Edmonton Oilers for G Grant Fuhr, LW Glenn Anderson and LW Craig Berube (September 19, 1991). ... Strained clavicular joint (February 11, 1992); missed three games. ... Flu (March 1993); missed one game. ... Fractured cheekbone (January 7, 1994); missed 15 games. ... Flu (February 28, 1995); missed two games. ... Signed as free agent by Philadelphia Flyers (July 14, 1997). ... Suspended two games by NHL for fighting incident (January 30, 2000). ... Bruised shoulder (February 24, 2000); missed five games. ... Fractured right foot (November 10, 2001); missed 10 games. ... Signed as free agent by Columbus Blue Jackets (July 4, 2002). ... Fractured finger (November 16, 2003); missed 17 games.

Season Team	League	REGULAR SEASON GP	G	A	Pts.	PIM	+/-	PP	SH	PLAYOFFS GP	G	A	Pts.	PIM
84-85—Ottawa Jr. B	ODHA	35	5	26	31	72	...	...	...	—	—	—	—	—
85-86—Peterborough	OHL	63	6	18	24	57	...	...	...	16	2	1	3	50
86-87—Peterborough	OHL	59	13	32	45	70	...	...	...	12	0	5	5	24
87-88—Toronto	NHL	78	4	6	10	90	-25	0	0	2	0	0	0	0
88-89—Toronto	NHL	55	2	7	9	106	-15	0	0	—	—	—	—	—
89-90—Toronto	NHL	67	4	14	18	122	-1	0	0	5	0	0	0	22
90-91—Toronto	NHL	78	1	9	10	238	-28	0	0	—	—	—	—	—
91-92—Edmonton	NHL	75	2	19	21	118	-9	0	0	16	0	5	5	45
92-93—Edmonton	NHL	82	3	10	13	142	-18	0	2	—	—	—	—	—
93-94—Edmonton	NHL	69	2	6	8	131	-13	0	0	—	—	—	—	—
94-95—Edmonton	NHL	46	3	10	13	40	-6	1	1	—	—	—	—	—
95-96—Edmonton	NHL	82	2	9	11	108	-27	0	0	—	—	—	—	—
96-97—Edmonton	NHL	82	1	11	12	91	9	0	0	12	0	2	2	14
97-98—Philadelphia	NHL	81	2	3	5	139	7	2	0	5	0	0	0	0
98-99—Philadelphia	NHL	78	0	6	6	106	-3	0	0	—	—	—	—	—
99-00—Philadelphia	NHL	74	2	5	7	140	14	0	0	18	0	1	1	41
00-01—Philadelphia	NHL	82	2	6	8	131	23	0	1	6	0	0	0	4
01-02—Philadelphia	NHL	72	1	8	9	102	18	0	0	5	0	0	0	4
02-03—Columbus	NHL	82	0	13	13	73	-16	0	0	—	—	—	—	—
03-04—Columbus	NHL	64	1	5	6	48	-11	0	0	—	—	—	—	—
NHL Totals (17 years)		1247	32	147	179	1925	-101	3	4	69	0	8	8	130

RISSMILLER, PAT — C — SHARKS

PERSONAL: Born October 26, 1978, in Belmont, Mass. ... 6-4/210. ... Shoots left. ... Name pronounced RIGHZ-mih-luhr.

TRANSACTIONS/CAREER NOTES: Signed as free agent by San Jose Sharks (June 30, 2003).

Season Team	League	REGULAR SEASON GP	G	A	Pts.	PIM	+/-	PP	SH	PLAYOFFS GP	G	A	Pts.	PIM
02-03—Cincinnati	ECHL	2	2	2	4	0	...	...	...	—	—	—	—	—
—Cleveland	AHL	72	14	26	40	24	...	...	...	—	—	—	—	—
03-04—San Jose	NHL	4	0	0	0	0	0	0	0	—	—	—	—	—
—Cleveland	AHL	75	14	31	45	66	-7	3	1	9	0	1	1	8
04-05—Cleveland	AHL	69	21	23	44	50	-12	8	0	—	—	—	—	—
NHL Totals (1 year)		4	0	0	0	0	0	0	0					

RITA, JANI — LW — OILERS

PERSONAL: Born July 25, 1981, in Helsinki, Finland. ... 6-1/206. ... Shoots right. ... Name pronounced YAH-nee REE-tah.

TRANSACTIONS/CAREER NOTES: Selected by Edmonton Oilers in first round (first Oilers pick, 13th overall) of NHL draft (June 26, 1999). ... Injured shoulder (March 6, 2002); missed one game.

Season Team	League	REGULAR SEASON GP	G	A	Pts.	PIM	+/-	PP	SH	PLAYOFFS GP	G	A	Pts.	PIM
96-97—Jokerit Helsinki	Finland Jr.	3	0	0	0	0	...	...	...	—	—	—	—	—
97-98—Jokerit Helsinki	Finland Jr.	36	15	9	24	2	...	...	...	8	4	1	5	0
—Jokerit Helsinki	Finland	...	...	...	...	...	...	...	...	1	0	0	0	0
98-99—Jokerit Helsinki	Finland	41	3	2	5	39	...	...	...	—	—	—	—	—
—Jokerit Helsinki	Finland Jr.	20	9	13	22	8	...	...	...	—	—	—	—	—
99-00—Jokerit Helsinki	Finland	49	6	3	9	10	...	...	...	11	1	0	1	0
00-01—Jokerit Helsinki	Finland	50	5	10	15	18	...	...	...	5	0	0	0	2
01-02—Hamilton	AHL	76	25	17	42	32	-10	4	1	15	8	4	12	0
—Edmonton	NHL	1	0	0	0	0	0	0	0	—	—	—	—	—
02-03—Hamilton	AHL	64	21	27	48	18	12	4	0	23	3	4	7	2

Season Team	League	REGULAR SEASON GP	G	A	Pts.	PIM	+/-	PP	SH	PLAYOFFS GP	G	A	Pts.	PIM
—Edmonton	NHL	12	3	1	4	0	2	0	0	—	—	—	—	—
03-04—Edmonton	NHL	2	0	0	0	0	0	0	0	—	—	—	—	—
—Toronto	AHL	64	17	24	41	18	7	4	0	1	1	0	1	0
04-05—HPK Hameenlinna	Finland	56	21	18	39	12	27	...	...	10	7	4	11	4
NHL Totals (3 years)		15	3	1	4	0	2	0	0					

RITCHIE, BYRON — C — FLAMES

PERSONAL: Born April 24, 1977, in Burnaby, British Columbia. ... 5-10/200. ... Shoots left.

TRANSACTIONS/CAREER NOTES: Selected by Hartford Whalers in 7th round (6th Whalers pick, 165th overall) of NHL draft (July 8, 1995). ... Whalers franchise moved to North Carolina and renamed Carolina Hurricanes for 1997-98 season; NHL approved move on June 25, 1997. ... Traded by Hurricanes with D Sandis Ozolinsh to Florida Panthers for D Bret Hedican, C Kevyn Adams, D Tomas Malec and conditional 2nd-round draft pick in 2003 (January 16, 2002). ... Injured left knee (November 4, 2003); missed 15 games. ... Fractured collarbone (March 10, 2004); missed remainder of season. ... Signed as free agent by Calgary Flames (July 2, 2004).

Season Team	League	REGULAR SEASON GP	G	A	Pts.	PIM	+/-	PP	SH	PLAYOFFS GP	G	A	Pts.	PIM
93-94—Lethbridge	WHL	44	4	11	15	44	...	...	...	6	0	0	0	14
94-95—Lethbridge	WHL	58	22	28	50	132	-23	5	0	—	—	—	—	—
95-96—Lethbridge	WHL	66	55	51	106	163	...	...	...	4	0	2	2	4
—Springfield	AHL	6	2	1	3	4	...	...	...	8	0	3	3	0
96-97—Lethbridge	WHL	63	50	76	126	115	33	15	6	18	16	12	*28	28
97-98—New Haven	AHL	65	13	18	31	97	-12	2	0	—	—	—	—	—
98-99—New Haven	AHL	66	24	33	57	139	-21	9	1	—	—	—	—	—
—Carolina	NHL	3	0	0	0	0	0	0	0	—	—	—	—	—
99-00—Carolina	NHL	26	0	2	2	17	-10	0	0	—	—	—	—	—
—Cincinnati	IHL	34	8	13	21	81	...	...	...	10	1	6	7	32
00-01—Cincinnati	IHL	77	31	35	66	166	...	...	...	5	3	2	5	10
01-02—Lowell	AHL	43	25	30	55	38	13	8	4	—	—	—	—	—
—Carolina	NHL	4	0	0	0	2	0	0	0	—	—	—	—	—
—Florida	NHL	31	5	6	11	34	-2	2	0	—	—	—	—	—
02-03—San Antonio	AHL	26	3	14	17	68	-8	0	1	3	1	0	1	0
—Florida	NHL	30	0	3	3	19	-4	0	0	—	—	—	—	—
03-04—Florida	NHL	50	5	6	11	84	-10	0	0	—	—	—	—	—
04-05—Rogle	Sweden Dv. 2	16	10	11	21	83	8	3	0	16	7	5	12	32
NHL Totals (5 years)		144	10	17	27	156	-26	2	0					

RIVERS, JAMIE — D/LW — RED WINGS

PERSONAL: Born March 16, 1975, in Ottawa. ... 6-0/190. ... Shoots left. ... Brother of Shawn Rivers, defenseman with Tampa Bay Lightning (1992-93).

TRANSACTIONS/CAREER NOTES: Selected by St. Louis Blues in third round (second Blues pick, 63rd overall) of NHL draft (June 26, 1993). ... Claimed by New York Islanders from Blues in waiver draft (September 27, 1999). ... Bruised ankle (February 26, 2000); missed three games. ... Signed as free agent by Ottawa Senators (November 10, 2000). ... Claimed off waivers by Boston Bruins (October 13, 2001). ... Signed as free agent by Florida Panthers (December 16, 2002). ... Signed as free agent by Detroit Red Wings (July 29, 2003).

Season Team	League	REGULAR SEASON GP	G	A	Pts.	PIM	+/-	PP	SH	PLAYOFFS GP	G	A	Pts.	PIM
90-91—Ottawa	OHA Jr. A	55	4	30	34	74	...	...	...	—	—	—	—	—
91-92—Sudbury	OHL	55	3	13	16	20	...	...	...	8	0	0	0	0
92-93—Sudbury	OHL	62	12	43	55	20	...	...	...	14	7	19	26	4
93-94—Sudbury	OHL	65	32	*89	121	58	...	22	1	10	1	9	10	14
94-95—Sudbury	OHL	46	9	56	65	30	...	6	0	18	7	26	33	22
95-96—St. Louis	NHL	3	0	0	0	2	-1	0	0	—	—	—	—	—
—Worcester	AHL	75	7	45	52	130	...	...	...	4	0	1	1	4
96-97—Worcester	AHL	63	8	35	43	83	-4	5	0	5	1	2	3	14
—St. Louis	NHL	15	2	5	7	6	-4	1	0	—	—	—	—	—
97-98—St. Louis	NHL	59	2	4	6	36	5	1	0	—	—	—	—	—
98-99—St. Louis	NHL	76	2	5	7	47	-3	1	0	9	1	1	2	2
99-00—New York Islanders	NHL	75	1	16	17	84	-4	1	0	—	—	—	—	—
00-01—Grand Rapids	IHL	2	0	0	0	2	...	...	...	—	—	—	—	—
—Ottawa	NHL	45	2	4	6	44	6	0	0	1	0	0	0	4
01-02—Ottawa	NHL	2	0	0	0	4	-3	0	0	—	—	—	—	—
—Boston	NHL	64	4	2	6	45	6	1	0	3	0	0	0	0
02-03—Florida	NHL	1	0	0	0	2	-2	0	0	—	—	—	—	—
—San Antonio	AHL	50	6	19	25	68	3	4	0	3	0	1	1	10
03-04—Detroit	NHL	50	3	4	7	41	9	0	0	2	0	0	0	2
—Grand Rapids	AHL	2	0	0	0	4	-1	0	0	—	—	—	—	—
04-05—Hershey	AHL	50	7	13	20	46	-13	5	0	—	—	—	—	—
NHL Totals (9 years)		390	16	40	56	311	9	5	0	15	1	1	2	8

RIVET, CRAIG — D — CANADIENS

PERSONAL: Born September 13, 1974, in North Bay, Ont. ... 6-2/201. ... Shoots right. ... Name pronounced REE-vay.

TRANSACTIONS/CAREER NOTES: Selected by Montreal Canadiens in third round (fourth Canadiens pick, 68th overall) of NHL draft (June 20, 1992). ... Separated shoulder (January 20, 1997); missed six games. ... Bruised back (November 1, 1997); missed one game. ... Had concussion (December 19, 1997); missed seven games. ... Sprained shoulder (November 9, 1998); missed five games. ... Back spasms and flu (January 18, 1999); missed three games. ... Strained groin (March 13, 1999); missed three games. ... Reinjured groin (March 24, 1999);

missed five games. ... Fractured cheekbone (October 8, 1999); missed nine games. ... Flu (November 3, 1999); missed four games. ... Strained groin (January 4, 2000); missed eight games. ... Injured shoulder (November 29, 2000); missed five games. ... Reinjured shoulder (December 15, 2000) and had surgery; missed remainder of season. ... Injured ankle (February 5, 2004); missed two games.

		REGULAR SEASON								PLAYOFFS				
Season Team	**League**	**GP**	**G**	**A**	**Pts.**	**PIM**	**+/-**	**PP**	**SH**	**GP**	**G**	**A**	**Pts.**	**PIM**
90-91—Barrie Jr. B	OHA	42	9	17	26	55	...	...	...	—	—	—	—	—
91-92—Kingston	OHL	66	5	21	26	97	...	...	...	—	—	—	—	—
92-93—Kingston	OHL	64	19	55	74	117	...	...	...	16	5	7	12	39
93-94—Fredericton	AHL	4	0	2	2	2	-2	0	0	—	—	—	—	—
—Kingston	OHL	61	12	52	64	100	...	5	0	6	0	3	3	6
94-95—Fredericton	AHL	78	5	27	32	126	-5	1	0	12	0	4	4	17
—Montreal	NHL	5	0	1	1	5	2	0	0	—	—	—	—	—
95-96—Fredericton	AHL	49	5	18	23	189	...	...	...	6	0	0	0	12
—Montreal	NHL	19	1	4	5	54	4	0	0	—	—	—	—	—
96-97—Montreal	NHL	35	0	4	4	54	7	0	0	5	0	1	1	14
—Fredericton	AHL	23	3	12	15	99	6	1	0	—	—	—	—	—
97-98—Montreal	NHL	61	0	2	2	93	-3	0	0	5	0	0	0	2
98-99—Montreal	NHL	66	2	8	10	66	-3	0	0	—	—	—	—	—
99-00—Montreal	NHL	61	3	14	17	76	11	0	0	—	—	—	—	—
00-01—Montreal	NHL	26	1	2	3	36	-8	0	0	—	—	—	—	—
01-02—Montreal	NHL	82	8	17	25	76	1	0	0	12	0	3	3	4
02-03—Montreal	NHL	82	7	15	22	71	1	3	0	—	—	—	—	—
03-04—Montreal	NHL	80	4	8	12	98	-1	2	0	11	1	4	5	2
04-05—TPS Turku	Finland	18	3	1	4	28	3	...	...	6	0	0	0	39
NHL Totals (10 years)		517	26	75	101	629	11	5	0	33	1	8	9	22

ROBERTS, GARY — LW — PANTHERS

PERSONAL: Born May 23, 1966, in North York, Ont. ... 6-2/215. ... Shoots left.

TRANSACTIONS/CAREER NOTES: Selected by Calgary Flames in 1st round (1st Flames pick, 12th overall) of entry draft (June 9, 1984). ... Injured back (January 1989). ... Whiplash (November 9, 1991); missed one game. ... Flu (January 19, 1993); missed one game. ... Left quadricep hematoma (February 16, 1993); missed 25 games. ... Suspended one game for high-sticking (November 19, 1993). ... Suspended four games and fined $500 for two slashing incidents and fined $500 for high-sticking (January 7, 1994). ... Fractured thumb (March 20, 1994); missed one game. ... Fractured thumb (April 3, 1994); missed last five games of season. ... Neck and spinal injury (February 4, 1995); had surgery and missed last 40 games of 1994-95 season and first 42 games of 1995-96 season. ... Injured neck (April 3, 1996); missed five games. ... Retired (June 17, 1996); Did not play during 1996-97 season. ... Traded by Flames with G Trevor Kidd to Carolina Hurricanes for G Jean-Sebastien Giguere and C Andrew Cassels (August 25, 1997). ... Strained abdominal muscle (November 12, 1997); missed six games. ... Strained rib muscle (January 11, 1998); missed 10 games. ... Flu (March 31, 1998); missed one game. ... Injured groin (April 13, 1998); missed final three games of season. ... Sprained wrist (December 2, 1998); missed four games. ... Strained neck (April 14, 1999); missed one game. ... Strained shoulder (October 7, 1999); missed one game. ... Injured groin (October 23, 1999); missed four game. ... Flu (January 18, 2000); missed one game. ... Injured groin (February 12, 2000); missed seven games. ... Signed as free agent by Toronto Maple Leafs (July 4, 2000). ... Suffered injury (January 11, 2002); missed one game. ... Back spasms (January 24, 2002); missed two games. ... Strained rib muscle (March 25, 2002); missed final 10 games of season. ... Injured shoulder (October 10, 2002) and had surgery; missed 57 games. ... Injured groin (March 13, 2003); missed 11 games. ... Strained muscle (December 2, 2003); missed two games. ... Strained groin (February 16, 2004); missed eight games. ... Signed as free agent by Florida Panthers (Aug. 1, 2005).

STATISTICAL PLATEAUS: Three-goal games: 1989-90 (1), 1991-92 (2), 1992-93 (2), 1993-94 (1), 1995-96 (3), 1997-98 (1), 2001-02 (1). Total: 11. ... Four-goal games: 1993-94 (1). ... Total hat tricks: 12.

		REGULAR SEASON								PLAYOFFS				
Season Team	**League**	**GP**	**G**	**A**	**Pts.**	**PIM**	**+/-**	**PP**	**SH**	**GP**	**G**	**A**	**Pts.**	**PIM**
82-83—Ottawa	OHL	53	12	8	20	83	...	...	...	5	1	0	1	19
83-84—Ottawa	OHL	48	27	30	57	144	...	...	...	13	10	7	17	*62
84-85—Ottawa	OHL	59	44	62	106	186	...	...	...	5	2	8	10	10
—Moncton	AHL	7	4	2	6	7	...	...	...	—	—	—	—	—
85-86—Ottawa	OHL	24	26	25	51	83	...	...	...	—	—	—	—	—
—Guelph	OHL	23	18	15	33	65	...	...	...	20	18	13	31	43
86-87—Moncton	AHL	38	20	18	38	72	...	...	...	—	—	—	—	—
—Calgary	NHL	32	5	10	15	85	6	0	0	2	0	0	0	4
87-88—Calgary	NHL	74	13	15	28	282	24	0	0	9	2	3	5	29
88-89—Calgary	NHL	71	22	16	38	250	32	0	1	22	5	7	12	57
89-90—Calgary	NHL	78	39	33	72	222	31	5	0	6	2	5	7	41
90-91—Calgary	NHL	80	22	31	53	252	15	0	0	7	1	3	4	18
91-92—Calgary	NHL	76	53	37	90	207	32	15	0	—	—	—	—	—
92-93—Calgary	NHL	58	38	41	79	172	32	8	3	5	1	6	7	43
93-94—Calgary	NHL	73	41	43	84	145	37	12	3	7	2	6	8	24
94-95—Calgary	NHL	8	2	2	4	43	1	2	0	—	—	—	—	—
95-96—Calgary	NHL	35	22	20	42	78	15	9	0	—	—	—	—	—
96-97—Calgary	NHL	Did not play												
97-98—Carolina	NHL	61	20	29	49	103	3	4	0	—	—	—	—	—
98-99—Carolina	NHL	77	14	28	42	178	2	1	1	6	1	1	2	8
99-00—Carolina	NHL	69	23	30	53	62	-10	12	0	—	—	—	—	—
00-01—Toronto	NHL	82	29	24	53	109	16	8	2	11	2	9	11	0
01-02—Toronto	NHL	69	21	27	48	63	-4	6	2	19	7	12	19	*56
02-03—Toronto	NHL	14	5	3	8	10	-2	3	0	7	1	1	2	8
03-04—Toronto	NHL	72	28	20	48	84	9	11	1	13	4	4	8	10
NHL Totals (18 years)		1029	397	409	806	2345	239	96	13	114	28	57	85	298

ROBIDAS, STEPHANE — D — STARS

PERSONAL: Born March 3, 1977, in Sherbrooke, Que. ... 5-11/189. ... Shoots right. ... Name pronounced ROE-bee-daw.

TRANSACTIONS/CAREER NOTES: Selected by Montreal Canadiens in 7th round (7th Canadiens pick, 164th overall) of NHL draft (June 26,

1995). ... Bruised shoulder (December 16, 2000); missed two games. ... Claimed by Atlanta Thrashers from Canadiens in waiver draft (October 4, 2002). ... Traded by Thrashers to Dallas Stars for 6th-round pick in 2003 (October 4, 2002). ... Traded by Stars with 2nd-round pick in 2004 to Chicago Blackhawks for D Jon Klemm and 4th-round pick in 2004 (November 17, 2003). ... Fractured left cheekbone (February 29, 2004); missed remainder of season. ... Signed as free agent by Stars (Aug. 5, 2005).

		REGULAR SEASON								PLAYOFFS				
Season Team	**League**	**GP**	**G**	**A**	**Pts.**	**PIM**	**+/-**	**PP**	**SH**	**GP**	**G**	**A**	**Pts.**	**PIM**
93-94—Shawinigan	QMJHL	67	3	18	21	33	...	...	...	1	0	0	0	0
94-95—Shawinigan	QMJHL	71	13	56	69	44	...	...	...	15	7	12	19	4
95-96—Shawinigan	QMJHL	67	23	56	79	53	...	...	...	6	1	5	6	10
96-97—Shawinigan	QMJHL	67	24	51	75	59	...	...	...	7	4	6	10	14
97-98—Fredericton	AHL	79	10	21	31	50	0	6	0	4	0	2	2	0
98-99—Fredericton	AHL	79	8	33	41	59	20	2	1	15	1	5	6	10
99-00—Quebec	AHL	76	14	31	45	36	...	...	...	3	0	1	1	0
—Montreal	NHL	1	0	0	0	0	0	0	0	—	—	—	—	—
00-01—Montreal	NHL	65	6	6	12	14	0	1	0	—	—	—	—	—
01-02—Montreal	NHL	56	1	10	11	14	-25	1	0	2	0	0	0	4
02-03—Dallas	NHL	76	3	7	10	35	15	0	0	12	0	1	1	20
03-04—Dallas	NHL	14	1	0	1	8	-2	1	0	—	—	—	—	—
—Chicago	NHL	45	2	10	12	33	6	0	1	—	—	—	—	—
04-05—Frankfurt	Germany	51	15	32	47	64	14	12	0	6	1	2	3	6
NHL Totals (5 years)		257	13	33	46	104	-6	3	1	14	0	1	1	24

ROBINSON, NATHAN LW

PERSONAL: Born December 31, 1981, in Scarborough, Ont. ... 5-9/180. ... Shoots left.
TRANSACTIONS/CAREER NOTES: Signed by Detroit Red Wings as free agent (October 12, 2002).

		REGULAR SEASON								PLAYOFFS				
Season Team	**League**	**GP**	**G**	**A**	**Pts.**	**PIM**	**+/-**	**PP**	**SH**	**GP**	**G**	**A**	**Pts.**	**PIM**
98-99—Belleville	OHL	50	11	8	19	23	...	...	...	21	4	4	8	14
99-00—Belleville	OHL	61	19	18	37	45	...	...	...	15	3	4	7	10
00-01—Belleville	OHL	66	32	37	69	57	...	...	...	10	6	10	16	7
01-02—Belleville	OHL	67	47	63	110	74	...	...	...	11	8	6	14	10
02-03—Toledo	ECHL	9	5	9	14	29	...	...	...	—	—	—	—	—
—Grand Rapids	AHL	53	3	14	17	24	...	...	...	8	0	3	3	0
03-04—Detroit	NHL	5	0	0	0	2	-1	0	0	—	—	—	—	—
—Grand Rapids	AHL	69	24	26	50	41	8	11	2	3	0	0	0	2
04-05—Grand Rapids	AHL	50	8	16	24	10	-5	3	0	—	—	—	—	—
—Syracuse	AHL	19	6	14	20	18	9	1	0	—	—	—	—	—
NHL Totals (1 year)		5	0	0	0	2	-1	0	0					

ROBITAILLE, LUC LW KINGS

PERSONAL: Born February 17, 1966, in Montreal. ... 6-1/207. ... Shoots left. ... Name pronounced ROH-bih-tigh. ... Nickname: Lucky.
TRANSACTIONS/CAREER NOTES: Selected by Los Angeles Kings in 9th round (ninth Kings pick, 171st overall) of NHL draft (June 9, 1984). ... Suspended four games for cross-checking from behind (November 10, 1990). ... Surgery to repair slight fracture of right ankle (June 15, 1994). ... Traded by Kings to Pittsburgh Penguins for RW Rick Tocchet and 2nd-round pick (RW Pavel Rosa) in 1995 draft (July 29, 1994). ... Suspended for two games for high-sticking (February 7, 1995). ... Traded by Penguins with D Ulf Samuelsson to New York Rangers for D Sergei Zubov and C Petr Nedved (August 31, 1995). ... Stress fracture in ankle (December 15, 1995); missed five games. ... Fractured foot (March 12, 1997); missed final 13 games of regular season. ... Traded by Rangers to Kings for LW Kevin Stevens (August 28, 1997). ... Injured right groin and abdomen (February 25, 1998) and had surgery; missed final 25 games of season. ... Fractured foot (November 3, 1999); missed 10 games. ... Signed as free agent by Detroit Red Wings (July 2, 2001). ... Signed as free agent by Los Angeles Kings (July 24, 2003).
STATISTICAL PLATEAUS: Three-goal games: 1986-87 (1), 1987-88 (3), 1988-89 (1), 1989-90 (2), 1992-93 (2), 1998-99 (1), 1999-00 (1). Total: 11. ... Four-goal games: 1991-92 (1), 1993-94 (1), 1994-95 (1). Total: 3. ... Total hat tricks: 14.

		REGULAR SEASON								PLAYOFFS				
Season Team	**League**	**GP**	**G**	**A**	**Pts.**	**PIM**	**+/-**	**PP**	**SH**	**GP**	**G**	**A**	**Pts.**	**PIM**
83-84—Hull	QMJHL	70	32	53	85	48	...	...	...	—	—	—	—	—
84-85—Hull	QMJHL	64	55	94	149	115	...	...	...	5	4	2	6	27
85-86—Hull	QMJHL	63	68	*123	191	93	...	...	...	15	17	27	*44	28
86-87—Los Angeles	NHL	79	45	39	84	28	-18	18	0	5	1	4	5	2
87-88—Los Angeles	NHL	80	53	58	111	82	-9	17	0	5	2	5	7	18
88-89—Los Angeles	NHL	78	46	52	98	65	5	10	0	11	2	6	8	10
89-90—Los Angeles	NHL	80	52	49	101	38	8	20	0	10	5	5	10	12
90-91—Los Angeles	NHL	76	45	46	91	68	28	11	0	12	12	4	16	22
91-92—Los Angeles	NHL	80	44	63	107	95	-4	26	0	6	3	4	7	12
92-93—Los Angeles	NHL	84	63	62	125	100	18	24	2	24	9	13	22	28
93-94—Los Angeles	NHL	83	44	42	86	86	-20	24	0	—	—	—	—	—
94-95—Pittsburgh	NHL	46	23	19	42	37	10	5	0	12	7	4	11	26
95-96—New York Rangers	NHL	77	23	46	69	80	13	11	0	11	1	5	6	8
96-97—New York Rangers	NHL	69	24	24	48	48	16	5	0	15	4	7	11	4
97-98—Los Angeles	NHL	57	16	24	40	66	5	5	0	4	1	2	3	6
98-99—Los Angeles	NHL	82	39	35	74	54	-1	11	0	—	—	—	—	—
99-00—Los Angeles	NHL	71	36	38	74	68	11	13	0	4	2	2	4	6
00-01—Los Angeles	NHL	82	37	51	88	66	10	16	1	13	4	3	7	10
01-02—Detroit	NHL	81	30	20	50	38	-2	13	0	23	4	5	9	10
02-03—Detroit	NHL	81	11	20	31	50	4	3	0	4	1	0	1	0
03-04—Los Angeles	NHL	80	22	29	51	56	4	12	0	—	—	—	—	—
NHL Totals (18 years)		1366	653	717	1370	1125	78	244	3	159	58	69	127	174

ROBITAILLE, RANDY C/LW THRASHERS

PERSONAL: Born October 12, 1975, in Ottawa. ... 5-11/200. ... Shoots left. ... Name pronounced ROH-bih-tigh.

TRANSACTIONS/CAREER NOTES: Signed as free agent by Boston Bruins (March 27, 1997). ... Injured shoulder (March 27, 1997); missed remainder of season. ... Traded by Bruins to Atlanta Thrashers for RW Peter Ferraro (June 25, 1999). ... Traded by Thrashers to Nashville Predators for LW Denny Lambert (August 16, 1999). ... Signed as free agent by Los Angeles Kings (July 6, 2001). ... Separated shoulder (December 3, 2001); missed 12 games. ... Claimed off waivers by Pittsburgh Penguins (January 4, 2002). ... Fractured foot (October 22, 2002); missed 10 games. ... Traded by Penguins to New York Islanders for fifth-round pick (RW Yevgeny Isakov) in 2003 draft (March 9, 2003). ... Signed as free agent by Atlanta Thrashers (August 12, 2003). ... Injured knee (January 24, 2004); missed seven games.

		REGULAR SEASON								PLAYOFFS				
Season Team	League	GP	G	A	Pts.	PIM	+/-	PP	SH	GP	G	A	Pts.	PIM
94-95—Ottawa	CJHL	54	48	77	125	111	...	...	...	—	—	—	—	—
95-96—Miami (Ohio)	CCHA	36	14	31	45	26	...	...	...	—	—	—	—	—
96-97—Miami (Ohio)	CCHA	39	27	34	61	44	18	5	7	—	—	—	—	—
—Boston	NHL	1	0	0	0	0	0	0	0	—	—	—	—	—
97-98—Providence	AHL	48	15	29	44	16	-12	4	2	—	—	—	—	—
—Boston	NHL	4	0	0	0	0	-2	0	0	—	—	—	—	—
98-99—Providence	AHL	74	28	*74	102	34	15	7	2	19	6	14	20	20
—Boston	NHL	4	0	2	2	0	-1	0	0	1	0	0	0	0
99-00—Nashville	NHL	69	11	14	25	10	-13	2	0	—	—	—	—	—
00-01—Milwaukee	IHL	19	10	23	33	4	...	...	...	—	—	—	—	—
—Nashville	NHL	62	9	17	26	12	-11	5	0	—	—	—	—	—
01-02—Los Angeles	NHL	18	4	3	7	17	-9	2	0	—	—	—	—	—
—Manchester	AHL	6	7	3	10	0	1	2	0	—	—	—	—	—
—Pittsburgh	NHL	40	10	20	30	16	-14	3	0	—	—	—	—	—
02-03—Pittsburgh	NHL	41	5	12	17	8	5	1	0	—	—	—	—	—
—New York Islanders	NHL	10	1	2	3	2	0	1	0	5	1	1	2	0
03-04—Atlanta	NHL	69	11	26	37	20	-12	5	0	—	—	—	—	—
04-05—ZSC Lions Zurich	Switzerland	36	22	45	67	56	...	10	1	15	2	17	19	10
NHL Totals (8 years)		318	51	96	147	85	-57	19	0	6	1	1	2	0

ROCHE, TRAVIS D THRASHERS

PERSONAL: Born June 17, 1978, in Grand Cache, Alta. ... 6-1/190. ... Shoots right.

TRANSACTIONS/CAREER NOTES: Signed as free agent by Minnesota Wild (April 8, 2001). ... Signed as free agent by Atlanta Thrashers (July 14, 2004). ... Signed as free agent by Chicago of the AHL (September 29, 2004).

		REGULAR SEASON								PLAYOFFS				
Season Team	League	GP	G	A	Pts.	PIM	+/-	PP	SH	GP	G	A	Pts.	PIM
99-00—North Dakota	WCHA	42	6	22	28	60	...	...	...	—	—	—	—	—
00-01—North Dakota	WCHA	41	10	35	45	40	...	...	...	—	—	—	—	—
—Minnesota	NHL	1	0	0	0	0	0	0	0	—	—	—	—	—
01-02—Houston	AHL	60	13	21	34	107	2	6	0	12	2	3	5	6
—Minnesota	NHL	4	0	0	0	2	-1	0	0	—	—	—	—	—
02-03—Houston	AHL	65	14	34	48	42	12	7	0	23	3	5	8	26
03-04—Houston	AHL	60	8	30	38	18	0	2	1	2	0	0	0	2
—Minnesota	NHL	5	0	1	1	0	-3	0	0	—	—	—	—	—
04-05—Chicago	AHL	73	12	38	50	59	25	3	0	18	1	6	7	18
NHL Totals (3 years)		10	0	1	1	2	-4	0	0					

ROENICK, JEREMY C KINGS

PERSONAL: Born January 17, 1970, in Boston. ... 6-1/196. ... Shoots right. ... Brother of Trevor Roenick, center with Hartford Whalers/Carolina Hurricanes organization (1993-94 through 1996-97). ... Name pronounced ROH-nihk.

TRANSACTIONS/CAREER NOTES: Selected by Chicago Blackhawks in 1st round (1st Blackhawks pick, 8th overall) of NHL draft (June 11, 1988). ... Sprained knee ligaments (January 9, 1989); missed one month. ... Sprained knee ligament (April 2, 1995); missed remainder of regular season and first eight games of playoffs. ... Pulled thigh muscle (March 4, 1996); missed three games. ... Sprained ankle (March 17, 1996); missed 12 games. ... Traded by Blackhawks to Phoenix Coyotes for C Alexei Zhamnov, RW Craig Mills and 1st-round pick (RW Ty Jones) in 1997 draft (August 16, 1996). ... Missed first four games of 1996-97 season due to contract dispute. ... Sprained knee (November 23, 1996); missed six games. ... Mild concussion (December 5, 1997); missed one game. ... Concussion (December 28, 1998); missed two games. ... Fractured jaw (April 14, 1999); missed final two games of regular season and six playoff games. ... Suspended five games for slashing incident (October 11, 1999). ... Suffered injury (March 3, 2000); missed one game. ... Concussion (November 14, 2000); missed one game. ... Signed as free agent by Philadelphia Flyers (July 2, 2001). ... Sprained right knee (March 18, 2002); missed seven games. ... Suspended two games for checking from behind (December 18, 2002). ... Suspended one game for misconduct incident involving a referee (January 13, 2004). ... Fractured jaw and concussion (February 12, 2004); missed 19 games. ... Traded by Flyers with 3rd-round pick in 2006 to Los Angeles Kings for future considerations (Aug. 4, 2005).

STATISTICAL PLATEAUS: Three-goal games: 1989-90 (1), 1990-91 (2), 1992-93 (1), 1999-00 (2), 2000-01 (1). Total: 7. ... Four-goal games: 1991-92 (1), 1993-94 (1). Total: 2. ... Total hat tricks: 9.

		REGULAR SEASON								PLAYOFFS				
Season Team	League	GP	G	A	Pts.	PIM	+/-	PP	SH	GP	G	A	Pts.	PIM
86-87—Thayer Academy	Mass. H.S.	24	31	34	65	...	...	...	...	—	—	—	—	—
87-88—Thayer Academy	Mass. H.S.	24	34	50	84	...	...	...	...	—	—	—	—	—
88-89—U.S. national team	Int'l	11	8	8	16	0	...	...	...	—	—	—	—	—
—Chicago	NHL	20	9	9	18	4	4	2	0	10	1	3	4	7
—Hull	QMJHL	28	34	36	70	14	...	...	...	—	—	—	—	—
89-90—Chicago	NHL	78	26	40	66	54	2	6	0	20	11	7	18	8
90-91—Chicago	NHL	79	41	53	94	80	38	15	4	6	3	5	8	4
91-92—Chicago	NHL	80	53	50	103	98	23	22	3	18	12	10	22	12
92-93—Chicago	NHL	84	50	57	107	86	15	22	3	4	1	2	3	2

Season Team	League	REGULAR SEASON GP	G	A	Pts.	PIM	+/-	PP	SH	PLAYOFFS GP	G	A	Pts.	PIM
93-94—Chicago	NHL	84	46	61	107	125	21	24	5	6	1	6	7	2
94-95—Koln	Germany	3	3	1	4	2	...	...	...	—	—	—	—	—
—Chicago	NHL	33	10	24	34	14	5	5	0	8	1	2	3	16
95-96—Chicago	NHL	66	32	35	67	109	9	12	4	10	5	7	12	2
96-97—Phoenix	NHL	72	29	40	69	115	-7	10	3	6	2	4	6	4
97-98—Phoenix	NHL	79	24	32	56	103	5	6	1	6	5	3	8	4
—U.S. Olympic team	Int'l	4	0	1	1	6	-1	0	0	—	—	—	—	—
98-99—Phoenix	NHL	78	24	48	72	130	7	4	0	1	0	0	0	0
99-00—Phoenix	NHL	75	34	44	78	102	11	6	3	5	2	2	4	10
00-01—Phoenix	NHL	80	30	46	76	114	-1	13	0	—	—	—	—	—
01-02—Philadelphia	NHL	75	21	46	67	74	32	5	0	5	0	0	0	14
—U.S. Olympic team	Int'l	6	1	4	5	2	...	...	...	—	—	—	—	—
02-03—Philadelphia	NHL	79	27	32	59	75	20	8	1	13	3	5	8	8
03-04—Philadelphia	NHL	62	19	28	47	62	1	10	1	18	4	9	13	8
NHL Totals (16 years)		1124	475	645	1120	1345	185	170	28	136	51	65	116	101

ROGERS, ANDY — D — LIGHTNING

PERSONAL: Born August 25, 1986, in Calgary. ... 6-5/206. ... Shoots left.
TRANSACTIONS/CAREER NOTES: Selected by Tampa Bay Lightning in first round (first Lightning pick, 30th overall) of NHL entry draft (June 26, 2004).

Season Team	League	REGULAR SEASON GP	G	A	Pts.	PIM	+/-	PP	SH	PLAYOFFS GP	G	A	Pts.	PIM
02-03—Calgary	WHL	25	0	3	3	17	...	...	...	—	—	—	—	—
03-04—Calgary	WHL	64	1	3	4	89	...	...	...	7	0	0	0	11
04-05—Prince George	WHL	30	1	5	6	49	-9	0	0	—	—	—	—	—
—Calgary	WHL	18	1	4	5	36	...	...	...	—	—	—	—	—

ROHLOFF, TODD — D

PERSONAL: Born January 16, 1974, in Grand Rapids, Minn. ... 6-2/218. ... Shoots left.
TRANSACTIONS/CAREER NOTES: Signed as free agent by Chicago Blackhawks (March 24, 1998). ... Signed as free agent by Washington Capitals (July 21, 2000). ... Signed as free agent by Columbus Blue Jackets (September 5, 2003). ... Claimed by Capitals off waivers from Blue Jackets (January 9, 2004). ... Signed as free agent by Rochester of the AHL (September 13, 2004).

Season Team	League	REGULAR SEASON GP	G	A	Pts.	PIM	+/-	PP	SH	PLAYOFFS GP	G	A	Pts.	PIM
94-95—Miami (Ohio)	CCHA	38	1	6	7	22	...	...	...	—	—	—	—	—
95-96—Miami (Ohio)	CCHA	23	2	4	6	24	...	...	...	—	—	—	—	—
96-97—Miami (Ohio)	CCHA	38	2	12	14	48	...	...	...	—	—	—	—	—
97-98—Miami (Ohio)	CCHA	17	2	5	7	38	...	...	...	—	—	—	—	—
—Indianapolis	IHL	5	0	1	1	6	...	...	...	—	—	—	—	—
98-99—Portland	AHL	58	1	6	7	59	-14	0	0	—	—	—	—	—
—Indianapolis	IHL	12	2	0	2	8	0	0	1	5	1	1	2	6
99-00—Cleveland	IHL	77	1	13	14	88	...	...	...	9	0	0	0	6
00-01—Portland	AHL	58	3	8	11	59	...	...	...	3	0	0	0	2
01-02—Portland	AHL	17	1	3	4	22	5	0	0	—	—	—	—	—
—Washington	NHL	16	0	1	1	14	-2	0	0	—	—	—	—	—
02-03—Portland	AHL	64	2	10	12	65	19	0	1	3	0	0	0	2
03-04—Columbus	NHL	24	0	2	2	8	-12	0	0	—	—	—	—	—
—Syracuse	AHL	14	1	5	6	16	-1	1	0	—	—	—	—	—
—Washington	NHL	35	0	3	3	18	-5	0	0	—	—	—	—	—
04-05—Rochester	AHL	12	0	1	1	4	-7	0	0	0	0	0	0	0
NHL Totals (2 years)		75	0	6	6	40	-19	0	0					

ROLOSON, DWAYNE — G — WILD

PERSONAL: Born October 12, 1969, in Simcoe, Ont. ... 6-1/178. ... Catches left. ... Name pronounced ROH-luh-suhn.
TRANSACTIONS/CAREER NOTES: Signed as free agent by Calgary Flames (July 4, 1994). ... Signed as free agent by Buffalo Sabres (July 9, 1998). ... Selected by Columbus Blue Jackets in expansion draft (June 23, 2000). ... Signed as free agent by St. Louis Blues (July 14, 2000). ... Signed as free agent by Minnesota Wild (July 2, 2001). ... Injured ankle (February 12, 2003); missed two games. ... Left team for personal reasons (February 25, 2004); missed two games.

Season Team	League	REGULAR SEASON GP	Min.	W	L	T	GA	SO	GAA	SV%	PLAYOFFS GP	Min.	W	L	GA	SO	GAA	SV%
90-91—Mass.-Lowell	Hockey East	15	823	5	9	0	63	0	4.59	...	—	—	—	—	—	—	—	—
91-92—Mass.-Lowell	Hockey East	12	660	3	8	0	52	0	4.73	...	—	—	—	—	—	—	—	—
92-93—Mass.-Lowell	Hockey East	39	2342	20	17	2	150	0	3.84	...	—	—	—	—	—	—	—	—
93-94—Mass.-Lowell	Hockey East	40	2305	23	10	7	106	0	2.76	...	—	—	—	—	—	—	—	—
94-95—Saint John	AHL	46	2734	16	21	8	156	1	3.42	.900	5	299	1	4	13	0	2.61	.897
95-96—Saint John	AHL	67	4026	33	22	11	190	1	2.83	...	16	1027	10	6	49	1	2.86	...
96-97—Calgary	NHL	31	1618	9	14	3	78	1	2.89	.897	—	—	—	—	—	—	—	—
—Saint John	AHL	8	481	6	2	0	22	1	2.74	.910	—	—	—	—	—	—	—	—
97-98—Saint John	AHL	4	245	3	0	1	8	0	1.96	.939	—	—	—	—	—	—	—	—
—Calgary	NHL	39	2205	11	16	8	110	0	2.99	.890	—	—	—	—	—	—	—	—
98-99—Buffalo	NHL	18	911	6	8	2	42	1	2.77	.909	4	139	1	1	10	0	4.32	.851
—Rochester	AHL	2	120	2	0	0	4	0	2.00	.922	—	—	—	—	—	—	—	—

Season Team	League	REGULAR SEASON GP	Min.	W	L	T	GA	SO	GAA	SV%	PLAYOFFS GP	Min.	W	L	GA	SO	GAA	SV%
99-00—Buffalo	NHL	14	677	1	7	3	32	0	2.84	.884	—	—	—	—	—	—	—	—
00-01—Worcester	AHL	52	3127	*32	15	5	113	*6	*2.17	.929	11	697	6	5	23	1	1.98	...
01-02—Minnesota	NHL	45	2506	14	20	7	112	5	2.68	.901	—	—	—	—	—	—	—	—
02-03—Minnesota	NHL	50	2945	23	16	8	98	4	2.00	.927	11	579	5	6	25	0	2.59	.903
03-04—Minnesota	NHL	48	2847	19	18	11	89	5	1.88	.933	—	—	—	—	—	—	—	—
04-05—Lukko Rauma	Finland	34	2049	20	10	4	70	4	2.05	.931	9	512	4	5	18	2	2.11	.941
NHL Totals (7 years)		245	13709	83	99	42	561	16	2.46	.911	15	718	6	7	35	0	2.92	.892

ROLSTON, BRIAN — C/RW — WILD

PERSONAL: Born February 21, 1973, in Flint, Mich. ... 6-2/210. ... Shoots left.

TRANSACTIONS/CAREER NOTES: Selected by New Jersey Devils in first round (second Devils pick, 11th overall) of NHL draft (June 22, 1991). ... Loaned by Devils to U.S. Olympic Team (November 2, 1993). ... Fractured foot (October 17, 1995); missed 11 games. ... Injured hamstring (January 12, 1998); missed one game. ... Flu (January 28, 1998); missed one game. ... Traded by Devils with a conditional third-round pick in the 2001 draft to Colorado Avalanche for RW Claude Lemieux, second-round pick (D Matt DeMarchi) in 2000 draft and swap of first-round picks in 2000 draft (November 3, 1999). ... Bruised ankle (January 27, 2000); missed three games. ... Traded by Avalanche with D Martin Grenier, C Samual Pahlsson and first-round pick (LW Martin Samuelsson) in 2000 draft to Boston Bruins for D Ray Bourque and LW Dave Andreychuk (March 6, 2000). ... Injured ribs (October 28, 2000); missed five games. ... Headaches (March 8, 2003); missed one game. ... Signed as free agent by Minnesota Wild (July 8, 2004).

STATISTICAL PLATEAUS: Three-goal games: 1996-97 (1).

Season Team	League	REGULAR SEASON GP	G	A	Pts.	PIM	+/-	PP	SH	PLAYOFFS GP	G	A	Pts.	PIM
89-90—Detroit	NAJHL	40	36	37	73	57	...	...	...	—	—	—	—	—
90-91—Detroit	NAJHL	36	49	46	95	14	...	...	...	—	—	—	—	—
91-92—Lake Superior St.	CCHA	41	18	28	46	16	...	...	...	—	—	—	—	—
92-93—Lake Superior St.	CCHA	39	33	31	64	20	...	...	...	—	—	—	—	—
—U.S. Jr. national team	Int'l	7	6	2	8	2	...	...	...	—	—	—	—	—
93-94—U.S. national team	Int'l	41	20	28	48	36	...	4	2	—	—	—	—	—
—U.S. Olympic team	Int'l	8	7	0	7	8	1	2	0	—	—	—	—	—
—Albany	AHL	17	5	5	10	8	-3	0	0	5	1	2	3	0
94-95—Albany	AHL	18	9	11	20	10	-3	3	0	—	—	—	—	—
—New Jersey	NHL	40	7	11	18	17	5	2	0	6	2	1	3	4
95-96—New Jersey	NHL	58	13	11	24	8	9	3	1	—	—	—	—	—
96-97—New Jersey	NHL	81	18	27	45	20	6	2	2	10	4	1	5	6
97-98—New Jersey	NHL	76	16	14	30	16	7	0	2	6	1	0	1	2
98-99—New Jersey	NHL	82	24	33	57	14	11	5	5	7	1	0	1	2
99-00—New Jersey	NHL	11	3	1	4	0	-2	1	0	—	—	—	—	—
—Colorado	NHL	50	8	10	18	12	-6	1	0	—	—	—	—	—
—Boston	NHL	16	5	4	9	6	-4	3	0	—	—	—	—	—
00-01—Boston	NHL	77	19	39	58	28	6	5	0	—	—	—	—	—
01-02—Boston	NHL	82	31	31	62	30	11	6	*9	6	4	1	5	0
—U.S. Olympic team	Int'l	6	0	3	3	0	...	...	...	—	—	—	—	—
02-03—Boston	NHL	81	27	32	59	32	1	6	5	5	0	2	2	0
03-04—Boston	NHL	82	19	29	48	40	9	3	2	7	1	0	1	8
NHL Totals (10 years)		736	190	242	432	223	53	37	26	47	13	5	18	22

ROSA, PAVEL — RW — KINGS

PERSONAL: Born June 7, 1977, in Most, Czechoslovakia. ... 5-11/188. ... Shoots right.

TRANSACTIONS/CAREER NOTES: Selected by Los Angeles Kings in second round (third Kings pick, 50th overall) of NHL entry draft (July 8, 1995).

Season Team	League	REGULAR SEASON GP	G	A	Pts.	PIM	+/-	PP	SH	PLAYOFFS GP	G	A	Pts.	PIM
94-95—Chemopetrol Litvinov	Czech. Jrs.	40	56	42	98	...	...	...	...	—	—	—	—	—
—Chem. Litvinov	Czech Rep.	2	0	0	0	0	...	...	...	1	0	0	0	0
95-96—Hull	QMJHL	61	46	70	116	39	...	...	...	18	14	22	36	25
96-97—Hull	QMJHL	68	*63	*89	*152	56	...	...	...	14	18	13	31	16
97-98—Fredericton	AHL	1	0	0	0	0	1	0	0	—	—	—	—	—
—Long Beach	IHL	2	0	1	1	0	0	0	0	1	1	1	2	0
98-99—Long Beach	IHL	31	17	13	30	28	2	9	0	6	1	2	3	0
—Los Angeles	NHL	29	4	12	16	6	0	0	0	—	—	—	—	—
99-00—Long Beach	IHL	74	22	31	53	76	...	...	...	6	2	2	4	4
—Los Angeles	NHL	3	0	0	0	0	-1	0	0	—	—	—	—	—
00-01—HPK Hameenlinna	Finland	54	25	25	50	53	...	...	...	—	—	—	—	—
01-02—Jokerit Helsinki	Finland	46	21	22	43	37	...	...	...	12	3	5	8	18
02-03—Los Angeles	NHL	2	0	0	0	0	-1	0	0	—	—	—	—	—
—Manchester	AHL	61	28	35	63	20	10	11	3	3	3	1	4	4
03-04—Manchester	AHL	77	39	49	88	34	38	8	0	6	3	6	9	6
—Los Angeles	NHL	2	1	1	2	0	1	0	0	—	—	—	—	—
04-05—Dynamo Moscow	Russian	54	21	23	44	14	30	...	...	8	3	2	5	2
NHL Totals (4 years)		36	5	13	18	6	-1	0	0					

ROSSITER, KYLE — D — THRASHERS

PERSONAL: Born June 9, 1980, in Edmonton. ... 6-3/217. ... Shoots left.

TRANSACTIONS/CAREER NOTES: Selected by Florida Panthers in second round (first Panthers pick, 30th overall) of NHL entry draft (June

27, 1998). ... Suffered concussion (February 26, 2003); missed four games. ... Traded by Panthers to Atlanta Thrashers for C Kamil Piros (March 8, 2004). ... Signed as free agent by Chicago of the AHL (September 30, 2004).

		REGULAR SEASON								PLAYOFFS				
Season Team	League	GP	G	A	Pts.	PIM	+/-	PP	SH	GP	G	A	Pts.	PIM
96-97—Spokane	WHL	50	0	2	2	65	...	...	...	9	0	0	0	6
97-98—Spokane	WHL	61	6	16	22	190	...	...	...	15	0	3	3	28
98-99—Spokane	WHL	71	4	17	21	206	-29	2	0	—	—	—	—	—
99-00—Spokane	WHL	63	11	22	33	155	11	3	0	14	1	4	5	21
00-01—Louisville	AHL	78	2	5	7	110	...	...	...	—	—	—	—	—
01-02—Utah	AHL	74	3	7	10	88	-7	0	0	5	0	1	1	0
—Florida	NHL	2	0	0	0	2	-1	0	0	—	—	—	—	—
02-03—Florida	NHL	3	0	0	0	0	-2	0	0	—	—	—	—	—
—San Antonio	AHL	67	0	7	7	107	10	0	0	3	0	0	0	0
03-04—Florida	NHL	4	0	0	0	7	-1	0	0	—	—	—	—	—
—San Antonio	AHL	51	5	7	12	70	-6	1	0	—	—	—	—	—
—Atlanta	NHL	2	0	1	1	0	1	0	0	—	—	—	—	—
—Chicago	AHL	12	0	1	1	25	2	0	0	6	0	0	0	19
04-05—Chicago	AHL	33	1	5	6	43	-3	0	0	—	—	—	—	—
—Wilkes-Barre/Scranton	AHL	9	0	1	1	5	-4	0	0	1	0	0	0	0
NHL Totals (3 years)		11	0	1	1	9	-3	0	0					

ROURKE, ALLAN — D — ISLANDERS

PERSONAL: Born March 6, 1980, in Mississauga, Ont. ... 6-2/215. ... Shoots left.

TRANSACTIONS/CAREER NOTES: Selected by Toronto Maple Leafs in 6th round (6th Maple Leafs pick, 154th overall) of entry draft (June 27, 1998). ... Traded by Toronto to Carolina Hurricanes for C Harold Druken (May 30, 2003). ... Signed as free agent by Islanders (Aug. 12, 2005).

		REGULAR SEASON								PLAYOFFS				
Season Team	League	GP	G	A	Pts.	PIM	+/-	PP	SH	GP	G	A	Pts.	PIM
96-97—Kitchener	OHL	25	1	1	2	12	...	...	...	6	0	0	0	0
97-98—Kitchener	OHL	48	5	17	22	59	-8	...	...	6	1	1	2	6
98-99—Kitchener	OHL	66	11	28	39	79	-27	...	...	1	0	0	0	2
99-00—Kitchener	OHL	67	31	43	74	57	-9	13	1	5	0	6	6	13
00-01—St. John's	AHL	64	9	19	28	36	...	...	...	—	—	—	—	—
01-02—St. John's	AHL	62	2	9	11	48	-1	1	0	10	0	2	2	6
02-03—St. John's	AHL	65	12	19	31	49	5	3	1	—	—	—	—	—
03-04—Carolina	NHL	25	1	2	3	22	4	0	0	—	—	—	—	—
—Lowell	AHL	45	5	9	14	45	5	3	0	—	—	—	—	—
04-05—Lowell	AHL	60	7	9	16	75	11	2	2	11	1	2	3	40
NHL Totals (1 year)		25	1	2	3	22	4	0	0					

ROY, ANDRE — LW/RW — PENGUINS

PERSONAL: Born February 8, 1975, in Port Chester, N.Y. ... 6-3/221. ... Shoots left. ... Name pronounced WAH.

TRANSACTIONS/CAREER NOTES: Selected by Boston Bruins in 6th round (5th Bruins pick, 151st overall) of NHL draft (June 29, 1994). ... Signed as free agent by Ottawa Senators (March 19, 1999). ... Injured right knee (November 18, 1999); missed one game. ... Back spasms (November 6, 2000); missed two games. ... Flu (January 13, 2001); missed two games. ... Suspended two games for unsportsmanlike conduct (February 26, 2001). ... Strained groin (March 30, 2001); missed one game. ... Injured left ankle (February 6, 2002); missed 11 games. ... Traded by Senators with 6th-round pick (D Paul Ranger) in 2002 draft to Tampa Bay Lightning for C Juha Ylonen (March 15, 2002). ... Suspended 13 games for leaving penalty box to fight (April 2, 2002); missed seven games at end of 2001-02 season and six games at start of 2002-03 season. ... Injured eye (December 29, 2002); missed one game. ... Suspended three games for abuse of official (February 9, 2003). ... Sprained knee (December 4, 2003); missed five games. ... Injured left knee (February 20, 2004); missed five games. ... Signed as free agent by Pittsburgh Penguins (Aug. 4, 2005).

		REGULAR SEASON								PLAYOFFS				
Season Team	League	GP	G	A	Pts.	PIM	+/-	PP	SH	GP	G	A	Pts.	PIM
93-94—Beauport	QMJHL	33	6	7	13	125	...	...	...	—	—	—	—	—
—Chicoutimi	QMJHL	32	4	14	18	152	...	...	...	25	3	6	9	94
94-95—Chicoutimi	QMJHL	20	15	8	23	90	...	...	...	—	—	—	—	—
—Drummondville	QMJHL	34	18	13	31	233	...	...	...	4	2	0	2	34
95-96—Providence	AHL	58	7	8	15	167	...	...	...	1	0	0	0	10
—Boston	NHL	3	0	0	0	0	0	0	0	—	—	—	—	—
96-97—Providence	AHL	50	17	11	28	234	11	0	0	—	—	—	—	—
—Boston	NHL	10	0	2	2	12	-5	0	0	—	—	—	—	—
97-98—Providence	AHL	36	3	11	14	154	-7	0	0	—	—	—	—	—
—Charlotte	ECHL	27	10	8	18	132	...	...	...	7	2	3	5	34
98-99—Fort Wayne	IHL	65	15	6	21	395	0	1	0	2	0	0	0	11
99-00—Ottawa	NHL	73	4	3	7	145	3	0	0	5	0	0	0	2
00-01—Ottawa	NHL	64	3	5	8	169	1	0	0	2	0	0	0	16
01-02—Ottawa	NHL	56	6	8	14	148	3	0	0	—	—	—	—	—
—Tampa Bay	NHL	9	1	1	2	63	-5	0	0	—	—	—	—	—
02-03—Tampa Bay	NHL	62	10	7	17	119	0	0	0	5	0	1	1	2
03-04—Tampa Bay	NHL	33	1	1	2	78	-5	0	0	21	1	2	3	61
NHL Totals (7 years)		310	25	27	52	734	-8	0	0	33	1	3	4	81

ROY, DEREK — C — SABRES

PERSONAL: Born May 4, 1983, in Ottawa, Ont. ... 5-9/188. ... Shoots left.

TRANSACTIONS/CAREER NOTES: Selected by Buffalo Sabres in second round (second Sabres pick, 32nd overall) of NHL entry draft (June 23, 2001).

Season Team	League	GP	G	A	Pts.	PIM	+/-	PP	SH	GP	G	A	Pts.	PIM
		REGULAR SEASON								PLAYOFFS				
99-00—Kitchener	OHL	66	34	53	87	44	...	...	...	5	4	1	5	6
00-01—Kitchener	OHL	65	42	39	81	114	-20	22	6	—	—	—	—	—
01-02—Kitchener	OHL	62	43	46	89	92	...	...	...	4	1	2	3	2
02-03—Kitchener	OHL	49	28	50	78	73	...	...	...	21	9	23	32	14
03-04—Buffalo	NHL	49	9	10	19	12	-8	1	0	—	—	—	—	—
—Rochester	AHL	26	10	16	26	20	6	2	0	16	6	8	14	18
04-05—Rochester	AHL	67	16	45	61	60	-4	7	0	9	6	5	11	6
NHL Totals (1 year)		49	9	10	19	12	-8	1	0					

ROZSIVAL, MICHAL D

PERSONAL: Born September 3, 1978, in Vlasim, Czechoslovakia. ... 6-2/212. ... Shoots right. ... Name pronounced roh-ZIH-vahl.

TRANSACTIONS/CAREER NOTES: Selected by Pittsburgh Penguins in fourth round (fifth Penguins pick, 105th overall) of NHL draft (June 22, 1996). ... Strained hip flexor (March 21, 2000); missed two games. ... Injured groin (April 4, 2002); missed two games. ... Sore groin (October 19, 2002); missed one game. ... Separated shoulder (November 18, 2002); missed 15 games. ... Injured head (February 23, 2003); missed three games. ... Bruised thumb (March 4, 2003); missed seven games. ... Aggravated thumb injury (March 31, 2003); missed three games. ... Injured right knee (October 3, 2003); missed 30 games. ... Reinjured right knee (December 24, 2003); missed remainder of season.

Season Team	League	GP	G	A	Pts.	PIM	+/-	PP	SH	GP	G	A	Pts.	PIM
		REGULAR SEASON								PLAYOFFS				
94-95—Czech Rep.	Czech Rep.	31	8	13	21	...	...	...	...	—	—	—	—	—
95-96—Czech Rep.	Czech Rep.	36	3	4	7	...	...	...	...	—	—	—	—	—
96-97—Swift Current	WHL	63	8	31	39	80	23	4	0	10	0	6	6	15
97-98—Swift Current	WHL	71	14	55	69	122	24	8	1	12	0	5	5	33
98-99—Syracuse	AHL	49	3	22	25	72	-12	2	0	—	—	—	—	—
99-00—Pittsburgh	NHL	75	4	17	21	48	11	1	0	2	0	0	0	4
00-01—Pittsburgh	NHL	30	1	4	5	26	3	0	0	—	—	—	—	—
—Wilkes-Barre/Scranton	AHL	29	8	8	16	32	...	...	...	21	3	*19	22	23
01-02—Pittsburgh	NHL	79	9	20	29	47	-6	4	0	—	—	—	—	—
02-03—Pittsburgh	NHL	53	4	6	10	40	-5	1	0	—	—	—	—	—
03-04—Wilkes-Barre/Scranton	AHL	1	0	0	0	2	0	0	0	—	—	—	—	—
04-05—Pardubice	Czech Rep.	16	1	3	4	30	6	...	...	16	1	2	3	34
—Trinec	Czech Rep.	35	1	10	11	40	-10	...	...	—	—	—	—	—
NHL Totals (4 years)		237	18	47	65	161	3	6	0	2	0	0	0	4

RUCCHIN, STEVE C MIGHTY DUCKS

PERSONAL: Born July 4, 1971, in Thunder Bay, Ontario. ... 6-2/215. ... Shoots left. ... Name pronounced ROO-chihn.

TRANSACTIONS/CAREER NOTES: Selected by Mighty Ducks of Anaheim in first round (first Mighty Ducks pick, second overall) of NHL supplemental draft (June 28, 1994). ... Flu (March 7, 1995); missed two games. ... Sprained left knee (November 27, 1995); missed 18 games. ... Strained groin (October 3, 1997); missed eight games. ... Strained left knee (April 9, 1998); missed two games. ... Injured groin (March 18, 1999); missed three games. ... Reinjured groin (March 31, 1999); missed seven games. ... Infected left ankle (December 28, 1999); missed 11 games. ... Fractured hand (September 22, 2000); missed six games. ... Fractured nose and cheek bone (November 15, 2000) and underwent surgery; missed 10 games. ... Suffered from concussion (December 13, 2001); missed remainder of season. ... Suffered stress fracture in leg (November 11, 2001); missed 44 games.

Season Team	League	GP	G	A	Pts.	PIM	+/-	PP	SH	GP	G	A	Pts.	PIM
		REGULAR SEASON								PLAYOFFS				
90-91—Univ. of W. Ontario	OUAA	34	13	16	29	14	...	...	...	—	—	—	—	—
91-92—Univ. of W. Ontario	OUAA	37	28	34	62	36	...	...	...	—	—	—	—	—
92-93—Univ. of W. Ontario	OUAA	34	22	26	48	16	...	...	...	—	—	—	—	—
93-94—Univ. of W. Ontario	OUAA	35	30	23	53	30	...	...	...	—	—	—	—	—
94-95—San Diego	IHL	41	11	15	26	14	-2	4	0	—	—	—	—	—
—Anaheim	NHL	43	6	11	17	23	7	0	0	—	—	—	—	—
95-96—Anaheim	NHL	64	19	25	44	12	3	8	1	—	—	—	—	—
96-97—Anaheim	NHL	79	19	48	67	24	26	6	1	8	1	2	3	10
97-98—Anaheim	NHL	72	17	36	53	13	8	8	1	—	—	—	—	—
98-99—Anaheim	NHL	69	23	39	62	22	11	5	1	4	0	3	3	0
99-00—Anaheim	NHL	71	19	38	57	16	9	10	0	—	—	—	—	—
00-01—Anaheim	NHL	16	3	5	8	0	-5	2	0	—	—	—	—	—
01-02—Anaheim	NHL	38	7	16	23	6	-3	4	0	—	—	—	—	—
02-03—Anaheim	NHL	82	20	38	58	12	-14	6	1	21	7	3	10	2
03-04—Anaheim	NHL	82	20	23	43	12	-14	9	1	—	—	—	—	—
NHL Totals (10 years)		616	153	279	432	140	28	58	6	33	8	8	16	12

RUCINSKY, MARTIN LW RANGERS

PERSONAL: Born March 11, 1971, in Most, Czech. ... 6-2/207. ... Shoots left. ... Name pronounced roo-SHIHN-skee.

TRANSACTIONS/CAREER NOTES: Selected by Edmonton Oilers in 1st round (2nd Oilers pick, 20th overall) of entry draft (June 22, 1991). ... Traded by Oilers to Quebec Nordiques for G Ron Tugnutt and LW Brad Zavisha (March 10, 1992). ... Flu (February 28, 1993); missed one game. ... Bruised buttocks (December 3, 1994); missed one game. ... Sprained right wrist (January 11, 1994); missed one game. ... Fractured left cheekbone (January 30, 1994); missed four games. ... Fractured right wrist (March 7, 1994); missed one game. ... Reinjured right wrist (March 21, 1994); missed six games. ... Reinjured right wrist (April 5, 1994); missed one game. ... Separated shoulder (February 25, 1995); missed 17 games. ... Reinjured shoulder (April 6, 1995); missed remainder of season. ... Nordiques franchise moved to Colorado and renamed Avalanche for 1995-96 season (June 21, 1995). ... Injured groin (November 28, 1995); missed one game. ... Traded by Avalanche with G Jocelyn Thibault and RW Andrei Kovalenko to Montreal Canadiens for G Patrick Roy and RW Mike Keane (December 6, 1995). ... Sprained right knee (April 6, 1996); missed two games. ... Injured hand (October 19, 1996); missed one game. ... Strained knee (November 25, 1996); missed one game. ... Separated shoulder (December 28, 1996); missed 10 games. ... Bruised foot (October 17, 1997); missed one game. ...

Sprained ankle (April 4, 1998); missed three games. ... Injured shoulder (March 6, 1999); missed three games. ... Concussion (November 16, 1999); missed one game. ... Back spasms (March 25, 2000); missed one game. ... Sprained medial collateral ligament in knee (December 18, 2000); missed 21 games. ... Bruised left thigh (March 12, 2001); missed four games. ... Injured eye (November 3, 2001); missed two games. ... Traded by Canadiens with LW Benoit Brunet to Dallas Stars for RW Donald Audette and C Shaun Van Allen (November 21, 2001). ... Traded by Stars with C Roman Lyashenko to New York Rangers for C Manny Malhotra and LW Barrett Heisten (March 12, 2002). ... Signed as free agent by St. Louis Blues (October 24, 2002). ... Signed as free agent by Rangers (August 28, 2003). ... Traded by Rangers to Vancouver Canucks for C R.J. Umberger and D Martin Grenier (March 9, 2004). ... Signed as free agent by New York Rangers (Aug. 3, 2005).
STATISTICAL PLATEAUS: Three-goal games: 1995-96 (1), 1996-97 (1). Total: 2.

		REGULAR SEASON								PLAYOFFS				
Season Team	**League**	**GP**	**G**	**A**	**Pts.**	**PIM**	**+/-**	**PP**	**SH**	**GP**	**G**	**A**	**Pts.**	**PIM**
88-89—CHZ Litvinov	Czech.	3	1	0	1	2	...	...	...	—	—	—	—	—
89-90—CHZ Litvinov	Czech.	47	12	6	18	...	...	...	...	—	—	—	—	—
90-91—CHZ Litvinov	Czech.	49	23	18	41	79	...	...	...	—	—	—	—	—
—Czechoslovakia Jr.	Czech.	7	9	5	14	2	...	...	...	—	—	—	—	—
91-92—Cape Breton	AHL	35	11	12	23	34	...	...	...	—	—	—	—	—
—Edmonton	NHL	2	0	0	0	0	-3	0	0	—	—	—	—	—
—Halifax	AHL	7	1	1	2	6	...	...	...	—	—	—	—	—
—Quebec	NHL	4	1	1	2	2	1	0	0	—	—	—	—	—
92-93—Quebec	NHL	77	18	30	48	51	16	4	0	6	1	1	2	4
93-94—Quebec	NHL	60	9	23	32	58	4	4	0	—	—	—	—	—
94-95—Chem. Litvinov	Czech Rep.	13	12	10	22	34	...	...	...	—	—	—	—	—
—Quebec	NHL	20	3	6	9	14	5	0	0	—	—	—	—	—
95-96—HC Vsetin	Czech Rep.	1	1	1	2	0	...	...	...	—	—	—	—	—
—Colorado	NHL	22	4	11	15	14	10	0	0	—	—	—	—	—
—Montreal	NHL	56	25	35	60	54	8	9	2	—	—	—	—	—
96-97—Montreal	NHL	70	28	27	55	62	1	6	3	5	0	0	0	4
97-98—Montreal	NHL	78	21	32	53	84	13	5	3	10	3	0	3	4
—Czech Rep. Oly. team	Int'l	6	3	1	4	4	3	0	0	—	—	—	—	—
98-99—Montreal	NHL	73	17	17	34	50	-25	5	0	—	—	—	—	—
99-00—Montreal	NHL	80	25	24	49	70	1	7	1	—	—	—	—	—
00-01—Montreal	NHL	57	16	22	38	66	-5	5	1	—	—	—	—	—
01-02—Montreal	NHL	18	2	6	8	12	-1	1	0	—	—	—	—	—
—Dallas	NHL	42	6	11	17	24	3	2	0	—	—	—	—	—
—Czech Rep. Oly. team	Int'l	4	0	3	3	2	...	...	...	—	—	—	—	—
—New York Rangers	NHL	15	3	10	13	6	6	0	0	—	—	—	—	—
02-03—Litvinov	Czech Rep.	2	0	1	1	2	...	...	...	—	—	—	—	—
—St. Louis	NHL	61	16	14	30	38	-1	4	4	7	4	2	6	4
03-04—New York Rangers	NHL	69	13	29	42	62	13	0	1	—	—	—	—	—
—Vancouver	NHL	13	1	2	3	10	2	0	0	7	1	1	2	6
04-05—Chem. Litvinov	Czech Rep.	38	15	26	41	87	-1	...	...	—	—	—	—	—
NHL Totals (13 years)		817	208	300	508	677	48	52	15	35	9	4	13	22

RUMBLE, DARREN D

PERSONAL: Born January 23, 1969, in Barrie, Ont. ... 6-1/200. ... Shoots left.
TRANSACTIONS/CAREER NOTES: Selected by Philadelphia Flyers in first round (first Flyers pick, 20th overall) of NHL draft (June 13, 1987). ... Stretched knee ligaments (November 27, 1988). ... Selected by Ottawa Senators in NHL expansion draft (June 18, 1992). ... Bruised thigh (November 29, 1993); missed four games. ... Injured thumb (March 5, 1994); missed one game. ... Signed as free agent by Flyers (July 31, 1995). ... Signed as free agent by St. Louis Blues (January 31, 2001). ... Injured hip (February 15, 2001); missed two games. ... Suspended two games by NHL for kneeing incident (February 28, 2001). ... Injured hip (March 10, 2001); missed one game. ... Signed as free agent by Tampa Bay Lightning (September 11, 2002).

		REGULAR SEASON								PLAYOFFS				
Season Team	**League**	**GP**	**G**	**A**	**Pts.**	**PIM**	**+/-**	**PP**	**SH**	**GP**	**G**	**A**	**Pts.**	**PIM**
85-86—Barrie Jr. B	OHA	46	14	32	46	91	...	...	...	—	—	—	—	—
86-87—Kitchener	OHL	64	11	32	43	44	...	...	...	4	0	1	1	9
87-88—Kitchener	OHL	55	15	50	65	64	...	...	...	—	—	—	—	—
88-89—Kitchener	OHL	46	11	28	39	25	...	...	...	5	1	0	1	2
89-90—Hershey	AHL	57	2	13	15	31	...	...	...	—	—	—	—	—
90-91—Philadelphia	NHL	3	1	0	1	0	1	0	0	—	—	—	—	—
—Hershey	AHL	73	6	35	41	48	...	...	...	3	0	5	5	2
91-92—Hershey	AHL	79	12	54	66	118	...	...	...	6	0	3	3	2
92-93—Ottawa	NHL	69	3	13	16	61	-24	0	0	—	—	—	—	—
—New Haven	AHL	2	1	0	1	0	-1	1	0	—	—	—	—	—
93-94—Ottawa	NHL	70	6	9	15	116	-50	0	0	—	—	—	—	—
—Prince Edward	AHL	3	2	0	2	0	4	0	0	—	—	—	—	—
94-95—Prince Edward	AHL	70	7	46	53	77	*45	2	0	11	0	6	6	4
95-96—Philadelphia	NHL	5	0	0	0	4	0	0	0	—	—	—	—	—
—Hershey	AHL	58	13	37	50	83	...	...	...	5	0	0	0	6
96-97—Philadelphia	AHL	72	18	44	62	83	24	10	0	7	0	3	3	19
—Philadelphia	NHL	10	0	0	0	0	-2	0	0	—	—	—	—	—
97-98—San Antonio	IHL	46	7	22	29	47	-17	6	0	—	—	—	—	—
98-99—Grand Rapids	IHL	53	6	22	28	44	3	2	2	—	—	—	—	—
—Utah	IHL	10	1	4	5	10	-7	0	0	—	—	—	—	—
99-00—Grand Rapids	IHL	29	3	10	13	20	...	...	...	—	—	—	—	—
—Worcester	AHL	39	0	17	17	31	...	...	...	9	0	2	2	6
00-01—Worcester	AHL	53	6	24	30	65	...	...	...	8	0	1	1	10
—St. Louis	NHL	12	0	4	4	27	7	0	0	—	—	—	—	—
01-02—Worcester	AHL	60	3	29	32	48	4	2	0	3	0	4	4	2
02-03—Springfield	AHL	33	5	17	22	18	-18	2	0	—	—	—	—	—
—Tampa Bay	NHL	19	0	0	0	6	-2	0	0	—	—	—	—	—
03-04—Tampa Bay	NHL	5	0	0	0	2	-2	0	0	—	—	—	—	—
—Hershey	AHL	5	2	0	2	6	1	1	1	—	—	—	—	—
04-05—Springfield	AHL	10	0	1	1	4	-1	0	0	—	—	—	—	—
NHL Totals (8 years)		193	10	26	36	216	-72	0	0					

RUPP, MIKE — RW/LW — COYOTES

PERSONAL: Born January 13, 1980, in Cleveland. ... 6-5/230. ... Shoots left.

TRANSACTIONS/CAREER NOTES: Selected by New York Islanders in first round (first Islanders pick, ninth overall) of NHL draft (June 27, 1998). ... Returned to draft pool; selected by New Jersey Devils in third round (seventh Devils pick, 76th overall) of NHL entry draft (June 24, 2000). ... Flu (February 5, 2003); missed three games. ... Traded by Devils with second-round pick in 2004 draft to Phoenix Coyotes for C Jan Hrdina (March 5, 2004). ... Injured shoulder (March 10, 2004); missed nine games.

		REGULAR SEASON								PLAYOFFS				
Season Team	League	GP	G	A	Pts.	PIM	+/-	PP	SH	GP	G	A	Pts.	PIM
96-97—St. Edward's	USHS (East)	20	26	24	50	...	...	...	...	—	—	—	—	—
97-98—Windsor	OHL	38	9	8	17	60	...	...	...	—	—	—	—	—
—Erie	OHL	26	7	3	10	57	...	...	...	7	3	1	4	6
98-99—Erie	OHL	63	22	25	47	102	-2	...	...	5	0	2	2	25
99-00—Erie	OHL	58	32	21	53	134	4	10	0	13	5	5	10	22
00-01—Albany	AHL	71	10	10	20	63	...	...	...	—	—	—	—	—
01-02—Albany	AHL	78	13	17	30	90	-27	3	0	—	—	—	—	—
02-03—Albany	AHL	47	8	11	19	74	1	1	0	—	—	—	—	—
—New Jersey	NHL	26	5	3	8	21	0	2	0	4	1	3	4	0
03-04—New Jersey	NHL	51	6	5	11	41	-1	1	0	—	—	—	—	—
—Phoenix	NHL	6	0	1	1	6	-3	0	0	—	—	—	—	—
04-05—Danbury	UHL	14	5	5	10	30	4	1	0	—	—	—	—	—
NHL Totals (2 years)		83	11	9	20	68	-4	3	0	4	1	3	4	0

RUUTU, JARKKO — LW/RW — CANUCKS

PERSONAL: Born August 23, 1975, in Helsinki, Finland. ... 6-2/200. ... Shoots left. ... Brother of Tuomo Ruutu, C/RW, Chicago Blackhawks organization; brother of Mikko Ruutu, LW, Ottawa Senators organization. ... Name pronounced ROO-too.

TRANSACTIONS/CAREER NOTES: Selected by Vancouver Canucks in third round (third Canucks pick, 68th overall) of NHL draft (June 27, 1998). ... Injured knee (March 19, 2004); missed 11 games.

		REGULAR SEASON								PLAYOFFS				
Season Team	League	GP	G	A	Pts.	PIM	+/-	PP	SH	GP	G	A	Pts.	PIM
91-92—HIFK Helsinki	Finland Jr.	1	0	0	0	0	...	...	...	—	—	—	—	—
92-93—HIFK Helsinki	Finland Jr.	34	26	21	47	53	...	...	...	—	—	—	—	—
93-94—HIFK Helsinki	Finland Jr.	19	9	12	21	44	...	...	...	—	—	—	—	—
94-95—HIFK Helsinki	Finland Jr.	35	26	22	48	117	...	...	...	—	—	—	—	—
95-96—Michigan Tech	WCHA	39	12	10	22	96	...	...	...	—	—	—	—	—
96-97—HIFK Helsinki	Finland	48	11	10	21	155	...	...	...	—	—	—	—	—
97-98—HIFK Helsinki	Finland	37	10	10	20	87	...	...	...	8	7	4	11	10
98-99—HIFK Helsinki	Finland	25	10	4	14	136	...	...	...	9	0	2	2	43
99-00—Syracuse	AHL	65	26	32	58	164	...	...	...	4	3	1	4	8
—Vancouver	NHL	8	0	1	1	6	-1	0	0	—	—	—	—	—
00-01—Kansas City	IHL	46	11	18	29	111	...	...	...	—	—	—	—	—
—Vancouver	NHL	21	3	3	6	32	1	0	1	4	0	1	1	8
01-02—Vancouver	NHL	49	2	7	9	74	-1	0	0	1	0	0	0	0
—Fin. Olympic team	Int'l	4	0	0	0	4	...	...	...	—	—	—	—	—
02-03—Vancouver	NHL	36	2	2	4	66	-7	0	0	13	0	2	2	14
03-04—Vancouver	NHL	71	6	8	14	133	-13	1	0	6	1	0	1	10
04-05—HIFK Helsinki	Finland	50	10	18	28	215	22	...	...	3	0	0	0	41
NHL Totals (5 years)		185	13	21	34	311	21	1	1	24	1	3	4	32

RUUTU, TUOMO — C/LW — BLACKHAWKS

PERSONAL: Born February 16, 1983, in Vantaa, Finland. ... 6-0/208. ... Shoots left. ... Brother of Jarkko Ruutu, RW, Vancouver Canucks; brother of Mikko Ruutu, LW, Ottawa Senators organization. ... Name pronounced ROO-too.

TRANSACTIONS/CAREER NOTES: Selected by Chicago Blackhawks in first round (first Blackhawks pick, ninth overall) of NHL entry draft (June 23, 2001). ... Had shoulder surgery (October 1, 2004); out indefinitely.

		REGULAR SEASON								PLAYOFFS				
Season Team	League	GP	G	A	Pts.	PIM	+/-	PP	SH	GP	G	A	Pts.	PIM
99-00—HIFK Helsinki	Finland Jr.	35	11	16	27	32	...	...	...	—	—	—	—	—
00-01—Jokerit Helsinki	Finland	47	11	11	22	86	...	...	...	5	0	0	0	4
01-02—Jokerit Helsinki	Finland	51	7	16	23	69	...	...	...	10	0	6	6	29
02-03—HIFK Helsinki	Finland	30	12	15	27	24	...	...	...	—	—	—	—	—
03-04—Chicago	NHL	82	23	21	44	58	-31	10	0	—	—	—	—	—
NHL Totals (1 year)		82	23	21	44	58	-31	10	0					

RYAN, BOBBY — RW — MIGHTY DUCKS

PERSONAL: Born March 17, 1987, in Camden, N.J. ... 6-1/213. ... Shoots right.

TRANSACTIONS/CAREER NOTES: Selected by Anaheim Mighty Ducks in 1st round (1st Ducks pick, 2nd overall) of entry draft (July 30, 2005).

		REGULAR SEASON								PLAYOFFS				
Season Team	League	GP	G	A	Pts.	PIM	+/-	PP	SH	GP	G	A	Pts.	PIM
03-04—Owen Sound	OHL	65	22	17	39	52	...	...	...	—	—	—	—	—
04-05—Owen Sound	OHL	62	37	52	89	51	30	11	4	8	2	7	9	8

RYAN, MIKE — C — SABRES

PERSONAL: Born May 16, 1980, in Boston. ... 6-1/188. ... Shoots left.
TRANSACTIONS/CAREER NOTES: Selected by Dallas Stars in second round (first Stars pick, 32nd overall) of NHL entry draft (June 26, 1999). ... Traded by Stars with second-round pick (RW Branislav Fabry) in 2003 draft to Buffalo Sabres for C Stu Barnes (March 10, 2003).

		REGULAR SEASON								PLAYOFFS				
Season Team	League	GP	G	A	Pts.	PIM	+/-	PP	SH	GP	G	A	Pts.	PIM
97-98—Boston College H.S.	USHS (East)	24	22	14	36	12	...	...	...	—	—	—	—	—
98-99—Boston College H.S.	USHS (East)	21	20	24	44	22	...	...	...	—	—	—	—	—
99-00—Northeastern Univ.	Hockey East	32	4	9	13	47	...	...	...	—	—	—	—	—
00-01—Northeastern Univ.	Hockey East	33	17	12	29	52	...	...	...	—	—	—	—	—
01-02—Northeastern Univ.	Hockey East	36	24	15	39	54	...	...	...	—	—	—	—	—
02-03—Northeastern Univ.	Hockey East	34	18	14	32	30	...	...	...	—	—	—	—	—
03-04—Rochester	AHL	45	3	9	12	31	-4	0	0	—	—	—	—	—
04-05—Rochester	AHL	59	11	11	22	20	4	2	0	5	0	1	1	4

RYCROFT, MARK — RW — BLUES

S

PERSONAL: Born July 12, 1978, in Penticton, B.C. ... 6-0/194. ... Shoots right. ... Son of Al Rycroft, player for Cleveland of WHA. ... Brother of Travis Rycroft, St. Louis Blues organization.
TRANSACTIONS/CAREER NOTES: Signed as free agent by St. Louis Blues (May 15, 2000). ... Charley horse (March 11, 2004); missed 11 games.

		REGULAR SEASON								PLAYOFFS				
Season Team	League	GP	G	A	Pts.	PIM	+/-	PP	SH	GP	G	A	Pts.	PIM
97-98—Denver	WCHA	35	15	17	32	28	...	...	...	—	—	—	—	—
98-99—Denver	WCHA	41	19	18	37	36	...	...	...	—	—	—	—	—
99-00—Denver	WCHA	41	17	17	34	87	...	5	0	—	—	—	—	—
00-01—Worcester	AHL	71	24	26	50	68	...	...	...	11	2	5	7	4
01-02—St. Louis	NHL	9	0	3	3	4	0	0	0	—	—	—	—	—
—Worcester	AHL	66	12	19	31	68	-2	5	0	3	0	1	1	0
02-03—Worcester	AHL	45	8	18	26	35	1	1	0	1	0	0	0	0
03-04—St. Louis	NHL	71	9	12	21	32	2	0	0	3	0	0	0	2
04-05—Briancon	France	13	8	8	16	18	...	...	...	4	2	1	3	0
NHL Totals (2 years)		80	9	15	24	36	2	0	0	3	0	0	0	2

RYDER, MICHAEL — RW/LW/C — CANADIENS

PERSONAL: Born March 31, 1980, in St. John's, Newfoundland. ... 6-0/196. ... Shoots right.
TRANSACTIONS/CAREER NOTES: Selected by Montreal Canadiens in ninth round (ninth Canadiens pick, 216th overall) of NHL draft (June 27, 1998).

		REGULAR SEASON								PLAYOFFS				
Season Team	League	GP	G	A	Pts.	PIM	+/-	PP	SH	GP	G	A	Pts.	PIM
97-98—Hull	QMJHL	69	34	28	62	41	...	...	...	10	4	2	6	4
98-99—Hull	QMJHL	69	44	43	87	41	...	...	...	23	20	16	36	39
99-00—Hull	QMJHL	63	50	58	108	50	26	18	5	15	11	17	28	28
00-01—Quebec	AHL	61	6	9	15	14	...	...	...	—	—	—	—	—
—Tallahassee	ECHL	5	4	5	9	6	...	...	...	—	—	—	—	—
01-02—Quebec	AHL	50	11	17	28	9	17	0	0	3	0	1	1	2
—Mississippi	ECHL	20	14	13	27	2	0	2	2	—	—	—	—	—
02-03—Hamilton	AHL	69	34	33	67	43	15	10	1	23	11	6	17	8
03-04—Montreal	NHL	81	25	38	63	26	10	10	0	11	1	2	3	4
04-05—Leksand	Sweden Dv. 2	18	14	12	26	24	21	5	0	10	7	6	13	0
NHL Totals (1 year)		81	25	38	63	26	10	10	0	11	1	2	3	4

SABOURIN, DANY — G — FLAMES

PERSONAL: Born September 2, 1980, in Val d'Or, Que. ... 6-2/185. ... Catches left. ... Name pronounced SA-boo-rihn.
TRANSACTIONS/CAREER NOTES: Selected by Calgary Flames in fourth round (fifth Flames pick, 108th overall) of NHL draft (June 27, 1998). ... Signed as free agent by Wilkes-Barre/Scranton of the AHL (September 26, 2004).

		REGULAR SEASON									PLAYOFFS							
Season Team	League	GP	Min.	W	L	T	GA	SO	GAA	SV%	GP	Min.	W	L	GA	SO	GAA	SV%
97-98—Sherbrooke	QMJHL	37	1906	15	15	2	128	1	4.03	.877	—	—	—	—	—	—	—	—
98-99—Sherbrooke	QMJHL	30	1477	8	13	2	102	1	4.14	...	1	49	0	1	2	0	2.45	...
99-00—Sherbrooke	QMJHL	55	3066	25	22	5	181	1	3.54	.889	5	324	1	4	18	0	3.33	.888
00-01—Saint John	AHL	1	40	1	0	0	0	0	0.00	1.00	—	—	—	—	—	—	—	—
—Johnstown	ECHL	19	903	4	9	1	56	0	3.72	...	1	40	0	0	2	0	3.00	...
01-02—Johnstown	ECHL	27	1538	14	10	1	84	0	3.28	.879	3	137	0	2	5	0	2.19	.936
—Saint John	AHL	10	447	4	4	0	18	1	2.42	.899	—	—	—	—	—	—	—	—
02-03—Saint John	AHL	41	2219	15	17	4	100	4	2.70	.905	—	—	—	—	—	—	—	—
03-04—Calgary	NHL	4	169	0	3	0	10	0	3.55	.848	—	—	—	—	—	—	—	—
—Las Vegas	ECHL	10	613	6	3	1	24	0	2.35	.933	1	57	0	1	2	0	2.11	.941
—Lowell	AHL	14	820	5	7	2	39	0	2.85	.894	—	—	—	—	—	—	—	—
04-05—Wilkes-Barre/Scranton	AHL	20	1028	8	8	...	38	1	2.22	.921	0	0	0	0	0	0	...	...
—Wheeling	ECHL	27	1578	19	6	...	44	5	1.67	.942	—	—	—	—	—	—	—	—
NHL Totals (1 year)		4	169	0	3	0	10	0	3.55	.848								

SAFRONOV, KIRILL D PREDATORS

PERSONAL: Born February 26, 1981, in Leningrad, U.S.S.R. ... 6-2/215. ... Shoots left.

TRANSACTIONS/CAREER NOTES: Selected by Phoenix Coyotes in first round (second Coyotes pick, 19th overall) of NHL draft (June 26, 1999). ... Traded by Coyotes with RW Ruslan Zainullin and fourth-round pick (RW Patrick Dwyer) in 2002 draft to Atlanta Thrashers for LW Darcy Hordichuk, fourth- (RW Lance Monych) and fifth-round (RW Josh Zeiler) picks in 2002 draft (March 19, 2002). ... Traded by Thrashers with C Simon Gamache to Nashville Predators for D Tomas Kloucek and C Ben Simon (December 2, 2003).

		REGULAR SEASON								PLAYOFFS				
Season Team	League	GP	G	A	Pts.	PIM	+/-	PP	SH	GP	G	A	Pts.	PIM
96-97—SKA St. Petersburg	Russian	1	0	0	0	0	...	...	...	—	—	—	—	—
97-98—SKA St. Petersburg	Russian	9	0	1	1	4	...	...	...	—	—	—	—	—
—SKA-2 St. Petersburg	Rus. Div.	34	4	3	7	36	...	...	...	—	—	—	—	—
98-99—SKA St. Petersburg	Russian	35	1	1	2	26	...	...	...	—	—	—	—	—
99-00—Quebec	QMJHL	55	11	32	43	95	28	6	0	11	2	4	6	14
00-01—Springfield	AHL	66	5	13	18	77	...	...	...	—	—	—	—	—
01-02—Springfield	AHL	68	3	19	22	26	8	0	0	—	—	—	—	—
—Phoenix	NHL	1	0	0	0	0	-2	0	0	—	—	—	—	—
—Chicago	AHL	8	0	2	2	2	-3	0	0	25	2	6	8	8
—Atlanta	NHL	2	0	0	0	2	-3	0	0	—	—	—	—	—
02-03—Atlanta	NHL	32	2	2	4	14	-10	0	0	—	—	—	—	—
—Chicago	AHL	44	4	15	19	29	8	2	0	9	1	2	3	4
03-04—Chicago	AHL	21	1	4	5	8	-4	1	0	—	—	—	—	—
—Milwaukee	AHL	59	4	16	20	41	16	2	0	21	0	6	6	20
04-05—Lokomotiv Yaroslavl	Russian	19	0	1	1	49	-1	...	...	—	—	—	—	—
—Khimik Voskresensk	Russian	35	5	8	13	34	-6	...	...	—	—	—	—	—
NHL Totals (2 years)		35	2	2	4	16	-15	0	0					

SAKIC, JOE C AVALANCHE

PERSONAL: Born July 7, 1969, in Burnaby, B.C. ... 5-11/190. ... Shoots left. ... Brother of Brian Sakic, LW with Washington Capitals (1990-91 and 1991-92) and New York Rangers organizations (1992-93 through 1994-95). ... Name pronounced SAK-ihk.

TRANSACTIONS/CAREER NOTES: Selected by Quebec Nordiques in first round (second Nordiques pick, 15th overall) of NHL draft (June 13, 1987). ... Sprained right ankle (November 28, 1988). ... Developed bursitis in left ankle (January 21, 1992); missed three games. ... Recurrence of bursitis in left ankle (January 30, 1992); missed eight games. ... Injured eye (January 2, 1993); missed six games. ... Nordiques franchise moved to Colorado and renamed Avalanche for 1995-96 season (June 21, 1995). ... Lacerated calf (January 4, 1997); missed 17 games. ... Injured knee (February 18, 1998); missed 18 games. ... Suspended one game and fined $1,000 by NHL for kneeing incident (April 21, 1998). ... Sprained right shoulder (December 17, 1998); missed seven games. ... Injured rib cartilage (November 8, 1999); missed six games. ... Reinjured rib cartilage (November 26, 1999); missed 13 games. ... Flu (January 18, 2000); missed one game. ... Injured groin (January 25, 2000); missed two games. ... Sprained ankle (December 13, 2002); missed nine games. ... Fractured foot (January 20, 2003); missed 15 games. ... Fractured jaw (January 4, 2004); missed 1 game.

STATISTICAL PLATEAUS: Three-goal games: 1988-89 (2), 1989-90 (1), 1990-91 (1), 1996-97 (1), 1998-99 (1), 1999-00 (2), 2000-01 (2), 2002-03 (1), 2003-04 (2). Total: 13. ... Four-goal games: 1991-92 (1). ... Total hat tricks: 14.

		REGULAR SEASON								PLAYOFFS				
Season Team	League	GP	G	A	Pts.	PIM	+/-	PP	SH	GP	G	A	Pts.	PIM
86-87—Swift Current	WHL	72	60	73	133	31	...	...	...	4	0	1	1	0
87-88—Swift Current	WHL	64	78	82	160	64	...	...	...	10	11	13	24	12
88-89—Quebec	NHL	70	23	39	62	24	-36	10	0	—	—	—	—	—
89-90—Quebec	NHL	80	39	63	102	27	-40	8	1	—	—	—	—	—
90-91—Quebec	NHL	80	48	61	109	24	-26	12	3	—	—	—	—	—
91-92—Quebec	NHL	69	29	65	94	20	5	6	3	—	—	—	—	—
92-93—Quebec	NHL	78	48	57	105	40	-3	20	2	6	3	3	6	2
93-94—Quebec	NHL	84	28	64	92	18	-8	10	1	—	—	—	—	—
94-95—Quebec	NHL	47	19	43	62	30	7	3	2	6	4	1	5	0
95-96—Colorado	NHL	82	51	69	120	44	14	17	6	22	*18	16	*34	14
96-97—Colorado	NHL	65	22	52	74	34	-10	10	2	17	8	*17	25	14
97-98—Colorado	NHL	64	27	36	63	50	0	12	1	6	2	3	5	6
—Can. Olympic team	Int'l	4	1	2	3	4	2	0	0	—	—	—	—	—
98-99—Colorado	NHL	73	41	55	96	29	23	12	5	19	6	13	19	8
99-00—Colorado	NHL	60	28	53	81	28	30	5	1	17	2	7	9	8
00-01—Colorado	NHL	82	54	64	118	30	45	19	3	21	*13	13	*26	6
01-02—Colorado	NHL	82	26	53	79	18	12	9	1	21	9	10	19	4
—Can. Olympic team	Int'l	6	4	3	7	0	...	...	...	—	—	—	—	—
02-03—Colorado	NHL	58	26	32	58	24	4	8	0	7	6	3	9	2
03-04—Colorado	NHL	81	33	54	87	42	11	13	1	11	7	5	12	8
NHL Totals (16 years)		1155	542	860	1402	482	28	174	32	153	78	91	169	72

SALEI, RUSLAN D MIGHTY DUCKS

PERSONAL: Born November 2, 1974, in Minsk, USSR. ... 6-1/213. ... Shoots left. ... Name pronounced ROO-slahn suh-LAY.

TRANSACTIONS/CAREER NOTES: Selected by Mighty Ducks of Anaheim in first round (first Mighty Ducks pick, ninth overall) of NHL draft (June 22, 1996). ... Charley horse (November 22, 1997); missed one game. ... Fractured left foot (December 10, 1997); missed one game. ... Suspended two games and fined $1,000 by NHL for head-butting incident (February 4, 1998). ... Suspended five games and fined $1,000 by NHL for illegal hit in preseason game (October 9, 1998). ... Injured shoulder (March 17, 1999); missed two games. ... Suspended 10 games by NHL for checking from behind incident (October 5, 1999). ... Injured foot (October 20, 2000); missed two games. ... Reinjured foot (October 23, 2000); missed six games. ... Injured back (December 17, 2000); missed one game. ... Headaches (January 21, 2001); missed 23 games. ... Bruised elbow, suffered back spasms (November 27, 2002); missed two games. ... Back spasms (December 4, 2002); missed seven games. ... Injured back (March 7, 2003); missed 11 games.

Season Team	League	REGULAR SEASON								PLAYOFFS				
		GP	G	A	Pts.	PIM	+/-	PP	SH	GP	G	A	Pts.	PIM
92-93—Tivali Minsk	CIS	9	1	0	1	10	...	...	...	—	—	—	—	—
93-94—Tivali Minsk	CIS	39	2	3	5	50	...	...	...	—	—	—	—	—
94-95—Tivali Minsk	CIS	51	4	2	6	44	...	...	...	—	—	—	—	—
95-96—Las Vegas	IHL	76	7	23	30	123	...	...	...	15	3	7	10	18
96-97—Anaheim	NHL	30	0	1	1	37	-8	0	0	—	—	—	—	—
—Baltimore	AHL	12	1	4	5	12	-1	1	0	—	—	—	—	—
—Las Vegas	IHL	8	0	2	2	24	...	...	...	3	2	1	3	6
97-98—Anaheim	NHL	66	5	10	15	70	7	1	0	—	—	—	—	—
—Cincinnati	AHL	6	3	6	9	14	1	2	0	—	—	—	—	—
—Belarus Oly. team	Int'l	7	1	0	1	4	-2	1	0	—	—	—	—	—
98-99—Anaheim	NHL	74	2	14	16	65	1	1	0	3	0	0	0	4
99-00—Anaheim	NHL	71	5	5	10	94	3	1	0	—	—	—	—	—
00-01—Anaheim	NHL	50	1	5	6	70	-14	0	0	—	—	—	—	—
01-02—Anaheim	NHL	82	4	7	11	97	-10	0	0	—	—	—	—	—
—Belarus Oly. team	Int'l	6	2	1	3	4	...	...	...	—	—	—	—	—
02-03—Anaheim	NHL	61	4	8	12	78	2	0	0	21	2	3	5	26
03-04—Anaheim	NHL	82	4	11	15	110	-1	0	1	—	—	—	—	—
04-05—Ak Bars Kazan	Russian	35	8	12	20	36	15	...	...	4	0	0	0	2
NHL Totals (8 years)		516	25	61	86	621	-20	3	1	24	2	3	5	30

SALMELAINEN, TONY — LW — OILERS

PERSONAL: Born August 8, 1981, in Espoo, Finland. ... 5-9/185. ... Shoots right.

TRANSACTIONS/CAREER NOTES: Selected by Edmonton Oilers in second round (third Oilers pick, 41st overall) of NHL entry draft (June 26, 1999).

Season Team	League	REGULAR SEASON								PLAYOFFS				
		GP	G	A	Pts.	PIM	+/-	PP	SH	GP	G	A	Pts.	PIM
97-98—HIFK Helsinki	Finland Jr.	33	23	16	39	30	...	...	...	—	—	—	—	—
98-99—HIFK Helsinki	Finland Jr.	30	21	17	38	53	...	...	...	—	—	—	—	—
99-00—HIFK Helsinki	Finland Jr.	1	1	0	1	0	...	...	...	—	—	—	—	—
00-01—HIFK Helsinki	Finland	19	1	0	1	6	...	...	...	—	—	—	—	—
—Ilves Tampere	Finland	26	3	10	13	4	...	...	...	3	0	0	0	0
01-02—Ilves Tampere	Finland	49	10	9	19	30	...	...	...	3	0	0	0	2
02-03—Hamilton	AHL	67	14	19	33	14	17	5	0	17	6	8	14	0
03-04—Edmonton	NHL	13	0	1	1	4	-1	0	0	—	—	—	—	—
—Toronto	AHL	58	19	25	44	27	9	8	0	3	0	1	1	0
04-05—Edmonton	AHL	76	22	24	46	26	9	4	0	—	—	—	—	—
NHL Totals (1 year)		13	0	1	1	4	-1	0	0					

SALO, SAMI — D — CANUCKS

PERSONAL: Born September 2, 1974, in Turku, Finland. ... 6-3/215. ... Shoots right.

TRANSACTIONS/CAREER NOTES: Selected by Ottawa Senators in ninth round (seventh Senators pick, 239th overall) of NHL draft (June 22, 1996). ... Strained groin (October 17, 1998); missed five games. ... Strained groin (November 28, 1998); missed six games. ... Bruised thigh (February 18, 1999); missed one game. ... Strained shoulder (April 14, 1999); missed two games. ... Bruised chest (October 2, 1999); missed one game. ... Fractured left wrist (October 30, 1999); missed 23 games. ... Reinjured left wrist (December 29, 1999); missed 19 games. ... Sprained right knee ligament (February 29, 2000); missed one game. ... Flu (September 30, 2000); missed first two games of season. ... Injured left shoulder (November 16, 2000); missed six games. ... Reinjured left shoulder (December 9, 2000) and had surgery; missed 38 games. ... Bruised right foot (March 21, 2001); missed one game. ... Had concussion (March 26, 2001); missed one game. ... Injured right knee (April 1, 2001); missed final three games of season. ... Injured groin (September 23, 2001); missed first three games of season. ... Flu (October 18, 2001); missed one game. ... Injured right hand (December 27, 2001); missed six games. ... Back spasms (March 9, 2002); missed five games. ... Injured back (March 23, 2002); missed one game. ... Traded by Senators to Vancouver Canucks for LW Peter Schaefer (September 21, 2002). ... Injured groin (December 7, 2002); missed one game ... Injured shoulder (February 18, 2003); missed two games. ... Injured leg (December 26, 2003); missed eight games.

STATISTICAL PLATEAUS: Three-goal games: 1998-99 (1).

Season Team	League	REGULAR SEASON								PLAYOFFS				
		GP	G	A	Pts.	PIM	+/-	PP	SH	GP	G	A	Pts.	PIM
94-95—TPS Turku	Finland	7	1	2	3	6	...	...	...	—	—	—	—	—
—Kiekko-67	Finland Div. 2	19	4	2	6	4	...	...	...	—	—	—	—	—
95-96—TPS Turku	Finland	47	7	14	21	32	...	...	...	11	1	3	4	8
96-97—TPS Turku	Finland	48	9	6	15	10	...	...	...	10	2	3	5	4
97-98—Jokerit Helsinki	Finland	35	3	5	8	10	...	...	...	8	0	1	1	2
98-99—Ottawa	NHL	61	7	12	19	24	20	2	0	4	0	0	0	0
—Detroit	IHL	5	0	2	2	0	1	0	0	—	—	—	—	—
99-00—Ottawa	NHL	37	6	8	14	2	6	3	0	6	1	1	2	0
00-01—Ottawa	NHL	31	2	16	18	10	9	1	0	4	0	0	0	0
01-02—Ottawa	NHL	66	4	14	18	14	1	1	1	12	2	1	3	4
—Fin. Olympic team	Int'l	4	0	0	0	0	...	...	...	—	—	—	—	—
02-03—Vancouver	NHL	79	9	21	30	10	9	4	0	12	1	3	4	0
03-04—Vancouver	NHL	74	7	19	26	22	8	5	0	7	1	2	3	2
04-05—Vastra Frolunda	Sweden	41	6	8	14	18	10	1	1	14	1	6	7	2
NHL Totals (6 years)		348	35	90	125	82	53	16	1	45	5	7	12	6

SALVADOR, BRYCE — D — BLUES

PERSONAL: Born February 11, 1976, in Brandon, Man. ... 6-2/214. ... Shoots left.

TRANSACTIONS/CAREER NOTES: Selected by Tampa Bay Lightning in sixth round (sixth Lightning pick, 138th overall) of NHL entry draft

(June 29, 1994). ... Signed as free agent by St. Louis Blues (December 16, 1996). ... Strained hamstring (February 8, 2001); missed four games. ... Injured foot (March 6, 2001); missed one game. ... Injured wrist (March 20, 2001); missed one game. ... Strained rib muscle (October 10, 2001); missed seven games. ... Injured chest (February 7, 2002); missed one game. ... Suffered concussion (March 28, 2002); missed eight games. ... Injured hamstring (December 7, 2002); missed two games. ... Injured in auto accident (January 2, 2003); missed two games. ... Bruised shoulder (February 22, 2003); missed two games. ... Injured wrist (October 2, 2003); missed eight games. ... Injured wrist (December 9, 2003); missed one game. ... Injured wrist (January 10, 2004); missed one game.

		REGULAR SEASON								PLAYOFFS				
Season Team	League	GP	G	A	Pts.	PIM	+/-	PP	SH	GP	G	A	Pts.	PIM
92-93—Lethbridge	WHL	64	1	4	5	29	...	...	...	4	0	0	0	0
93-94—Lethbridge	WHL	61	4	14	18	36	-6	0	0	9	0	1	1	2
94-95—Lethbridge	WHL	67	1	9	10	88	-33	0	0	—	—	—	—	—
95-96—Lethbridge	WHL	56	4	12	16	75	...	...	...	3	0	1	1	2
96-97—Lethbridge	WHL	63	8	32	40	81	19	6	0	19	0	7	7	14
97-98—Worcester	AHL	46	2	8	10	74	13	0	1	11	0	1	1	45
98-99—Worcester	AHL	69	5	13	18	129	-13	2	0	4	0	1	1	2
99-00—Worcester	AHL	55	0	13	13	53	...	...	...	9	0	1	1	2
00-01—St. Louis	NHL	75	2	8	10	69	-4	0	0	14	2	0	2	18
01-02—St. Louis	NHL	66	5	7	12	78	3	1	0	10	0	1	1	4
02-03—St. Louis	NHL	71	2	8	10	95	7	1	0	7	0	0	0	2
03-04—St. Louis	NHL	69	3	5	8	47	-4	0	0	5	0	0	0	2
—Worcester	AHL	2	0	1	1	0	0	0	0	—	—	—	—	—
04-05—Missouri	UHL	7	0	0	0	16	-8	0	0	—	—	—	—	—
NHL Totals (4 years)		281	12	28	40	289	2	2	0	36	2	1	3	26

S

SAMSONOV, SERGEI — LW — BRUINS

PERSONAL: Born October 27, 1978, in Moscow, U.S.S.R. ... 5-8/194. ... Shoots right. ... Name pronounced sam-SAH-nahf.

TRANSACTIONS/CAREER NOTES: Selected by Boston Bruins in first round (second Bruins pick, eighth overall) of NHL draft (June 21, 1997). ... Flu (December 20, 1997); missed one game. ... Bruised thigh (February 12, 1998); missed one game. ... Sinus infection (February 23, 1999); missed two games. ... Strained knee (January 4, 2000); missed five games. ... Sprained knee (December 4, 2001); missed six games. ... Flu (December 28, 2001); missed two games. ... Injured wrist (October 19, 2002); missed 18 games. ... Injured groin (December 2, 2002); missed two games. ... Injured groin (December 8, 2002); missed four games. ... Injured wrist (December 19, 2002); missed last 50 games of season. ... Sprained knee (December 12, 2003); missed nine games. ... Injured ribs (February 11, 2004); missed four games. ... Reinjured ribs (February 23, 2004); missed 11 games. ... Sore ribs (March 16, 2004); missed two games.

STATISTICAL PLATEAUS: Three-goal games: 1997-98 (1).

		REGULAR SEASON								PLAYOFFS				
Season Team	League	GP	G	A	Pts.	PIM	+/-	PP	SH	GP	G	A	Pts.	PIM
94-95—CSKA Moscow	CIS	13	2	2	4	14	...	...	...	2	0	0	0	0
—CSKA Moscow Jrs.	CIS	50	110	72	182	...	...	...	...	—	—	—	—	—
95-96—CSKA Moscow	CIS	51	21	17	38	12	...	...	...	3	1	1	2	4
96-97—Detroit	IHL	73	29	35	64	18	...	...	...	19	8	4	12	12
97-98—Boston	NHL	81	22	25	47	8	9	7	0	6	2	5	7	0
98-99—Boston	NHL	79	25	26	51	18	-6	6	0	11	3	1	4	0
99-00—Boston	NHL	77	19	26	45	4	-6	6	0	—	—	—	—	—
00-01—Boston	NHL	82	29	46	75	18	6	3	0	—	—	—	—	—
01-02—Boston	NHL	74	29	41	70	27	21	3	0	6	2	2	4	0
—Russian Oly. team	Int'l	6	1	2	3	4	...	...	...	—	—	—	—	—
02-03—Boston	NHL	8	5	6	11	2	8	1	0	5	0	2	2	0
03-04—Boston	NHL	58	17	23	40	4	12	3	0	7	2	5	7	0
04-05—Dynamo Moscow	Russian	3	1	0	1	0	1	...	...	3	1	2	3	0
NHL Totals (7 years)		459	146	193	339	81	44	29	0	35	9	15	24	0

SAMUELSSON, MARTIN — RW — BRUINS

PERSONAL: Born January 25, 1982, in Upplands-Vasby, Sweden. ... 6-2/200. ... Shoots left.

TRANSACTIONS/CAREER NOTES: Selected by Boston Bruins in first round (second Bruins pick, 27th overall) of NHL entry draft (June 24, 2000).

		REGULAR SEASON								PLAYOFFS				
Season Team	League	GP	G	A	Pts.	PIM	+/-	PP	SH	GP	G	A	Pts.	PIM
98-99—MoDo Ornskoldsvik	Sweden Jr.Statistics unavailable.													
99-00—MoDo Ornskoldsvik	Sweden Jr.	19	9	8	17	18	...	...	...	2	1	0	1	2
00-01—Hammarby	Sweden Jr.	1	0	1	1	0	...	...	...	—	—	—	—	—
—Hammarby	Sweden Dv. 2	38	15	6	21	28	...	...	...	—	—	—	—	—
01-02—Hammarby	Sweden Dv. 2	30	7	6	13	18	...	...	...	—	—	—	—	—
—MoDo Ornskoldsvik	Sweden Jr.	2	5	2	7	2	...	...	...	—	—	—	—	—
02-03—Providence	AHL	64	24	15	39	34	-5	11	0	4	0	0	0	0
—Boston	NHL	8	0	1	1	2	-1	0	0	—	—	—	—	—
03-04—Boston	NHL	6	0	0	0	0	-1	0	0	—	—	—	—	—
—Providence	AHL	56	1	9	10	15	-5	0	0	1	0	0	0	0
04-05—Providence	AHL	64	7	10	17	35	6	0	0	10	1	0	1	6
NHL Totals (2 years)		14	0	1	1	2	-2	0	0					

SAMUELSSON, MIKAEL — RW — PANTHERS

PERSONAL: Born December 23, 1976, in Mariefred, Sweden. ... 6-2/211. ... Shoots left.

TRANSACTIONS/CAREER NOTES: Selected by San Jose Sharks in fifth round (seventh Sharks pick, 145th overall) of NHL draft (June 27, 1998). ... Traded by Sharks with D Christian Gosselin to New York Rangers for LW Adam Graves (June 24, 2001). ... Traded by Rangers with

RW Rico Fata, D Joel Bouchard, D Richard Lintner and cash to Pittsburgh Penguins for RW Alexei Kovalev, LW Dan LaCouture, D Janne Laukkanen and D Mike Wilson (February 10, 2003). ... Traded by Penguins with first-round pick (F Nathan Horton) in 2003 entry draft to Florida Panthers for first-round pick (D Marc-Andre Fleury) in 2003 draft (June 22, 2003). ... Fractured jaw (November 14, 2003); missed 22 games. ... Injured right hand (January 23, 2004); missed 21 games.

		REGULAR SEASON								PLAYOFFS				
Season Team	League	GP	G	A	Pts.	PIM	+/-	PP	SH	GP	G	A	Pts.	PIM
94-95—Sodertalje	Sweden Jr.	30	8	6	14	12	...	...	...	—	—	—	—	—
95-96—Sodertalje	Sweden Dv. 2	18	5	1	6	0	...	...	...	4	0	0	0	0
—Sodertalje	Sweden Jr.	22	13	12	25	20	...	...	...	—	—	—	—	—
96-97—Sodertalje	Sweden	29	3	2	5	10	...	...	...	—	—	—	—	—
—Sodertalje	Sweden Jr.	2	2	1	3	...	...	...	...	—	—	—	—	—
97-98—Sodertalje	Sweden	31	8	8	16	47	...	...	...	—	—	—	—	—
98-99—Sodertalje	Sweden	12	7	9	16	20	4	...	...	—	—	—	—	—
—Vastra Frolunda	Sweden	27	0	5	5	10	...	...	...	—	—	—	—	—
99-00—Brynas Gavle	Sweden	40	4	3	7	76	...	...	...	11	7	2	9	6
00-01—Kentucky	AHL	66	32	46	78	58	...	...	...	3	1	0	1	0
—San Jose	NHL	4	0	0	0	0	0	0	0	—	—	—	—	—
01-02—Hartford	AHL	8	3	6	9	12	0	1	0	—	—	—	—	—
—New York Rangers	NHL	67	6	10	16	23	10	1	2	—	—	—	—	—
02-03—New York Rangers	NHL	58	8	14	22	32	0	1	1	—	—	—	—	—
—Pittsburgh	NHL	22	2	0	2	8	-21	1	0	—	—	—	—	—
03-04—Florida	NHL	37	3	6	9	35	0	0	0	—	—	—	—	—
04-05—Geneva	Switzerland	12	2	4	6	14	...	2	0	—	—	—	—	—
—Sodertalje	Sweden	29	7	13	20	45	1	2	0	10	3	3	6	24
NHL Totals (4 years)		188	19	30	49	98	-11	3	3					

SANDERSON, GEOFF — LW — BLUE JACKETS

PERSONAL: Born February 1, 1972, in Hay River, Northwest Territories. ... 6-0/190. ... Shoots left.

TRANSACTIONS/CAREER NOTES: Selected by Hartford Whalers in second round (second Whalers pick, 36th overall) of NHL draft (June 16, 1990). ... Bruised shoulder (October 14, 1991); missed one game. ... Injured groin (November 13, 1991); missed three games. ... Bruised knee (December 7, 1991); missed five games. ... Flu (February 1, 1994). ... Whalers franchise moved to North Carolina and renamed Carolina Hurricanes for 1997-98 season; NHL approved move on June 25, 1997. ... Traded by Hurricanes to Vancouver Canucks with D Enrico Ciccone and G Sean Burke for LW Martin Gelinas and G Kirk McLean (January 3, 1998). ... Injured shoulder (January 21, 1998); missed eight games. ... Traded by Canucks to Buffalo Sabres for LW Brad May and third-round pick (traded to Tampa Bay; Lightning selected LW Jimmie Olvestad) in 1999 draft (February 4, 1998). ... Bruised hip (April 13, 1998); missed one game. ... Injured back (January 18, 1999); missed one game. ... Injured hip (February 19, 1999); missed one game. ... Injured knee (March 1, 2000); missed five games. ... Selected by Columbus Blue Jackets in expansion draft (June 23, 2000). ... Fractured finger (February 25, 2001); missed one game. ... Sprained knee (March 14, 2001); missed 13 games. ... Bruised back (November 1, 2001); missed 10 games. ... Had hernia (December 6, 2001) and had surgery; missed 24 games. ... Had concussion (April 1, 2002); missed remainder of season. ... Injured shoulder (October 7, 2003); missed one game. ... Injured hip (October 25, 2003); missed one game. ... Traded by Blue Jackets to Canucks for third-round pick (G Daniel LaCosta) in 2004 draft (March 9, 2004). ... Claimed off waivers by Blue Jackets (June 28, 2004).

STATISTICAL PLATEAUS: Three-goal games: 1992-93 (2), 1994-95 (1), 1995-96 (2), 1998-99 (1), 2000-01 (1). Total: 7. ... Four-goal games: 2002-03 (1). ... Total hat tricks: 8.

		REGULAR SEASON								PLAYOFFS				
Season Team	League	GP	G	A	Pts.	PIM	+/-	PP	SH	GP	G	A	Pts.	PIM
88-89—Swift Current	WHL	58	17	11	28	16	...	...	...	12	3	5	8	6
89-90—Swift Current	WHL	70	32	62	94	56	...	...	...	4	1	4	5	8
90-91—Swift Current	WHL	70	62	50	112	57	...	...	...	3	1	2	3	4
—Hartford	NHL	2	1	0	1	0	-2	0	0	3	0	0	0	0
—Springfield	AHL	...	...	...	...	...	...	...	...	1	0	0	0	2
91-92—Hartford	NHL	64	13	18	31	18	5	2	0	7	1	0	1	2
92-93—Hartford	NHL	82	46	43	89	28	-21	21	2	—	—	—	—	—
93-94—Hartford	NHL	82	41	26	67	42	-13	15	1	—	—	—	—	—
94-95—HPK Hameenlinna	Finland	12	6	4	10	24	-4	...	...	—	—	—	—	—
—Hartford	NHL	46	18	14	32	24	-10	4	0	—	—	—	—	—
95-96—Hartford	NHL	81	34	31	65	40	0	6	0	—	—	—	—	—
96-97—Hartford	NHL	82	36	31	67	29	-9	12	1	—	—	—	—	—
97-98—Carolina	NHL	40	7	10	17	14	-4	2	0	—	—	—	—	—
—Vancouver	NHL	9	0	3	3	4	-1	0	0	—	—	—	—	—
—Buffalo	NHL	26	4	5	9	20	6	0	0	14	3	1	4	4
98-99—Buffalo	NHL	75	12	18	30	22	8	1	0	19	4	6	10	14
99-00—Buffalo	NHL	67	13	13	26	22	4	4	0	5	0	2	2	8
00-01—Columbus	NHL	68	30	26	56	46	4	9	0	—	—	—	—	—
01-02—Columbus	NHL	42	11	5	16	12	-15	5	0	—	—	—	—	—
02-03—Columbus	NHL	82	34	33	67	34	-4	15	2	—	—	—	—	—
03-04—Columbus	NHL	67	13	16	29	34	-9	5	0	—	—	—	—	—
—Vancouver	NHL	13	3	4	7	4	-1	1	0	7	1	1	2	4
04-05—Geneva	Switzerland	9	4	1	5	29	...	0	0	—	—	—	—	—
NHL Totals (14 years)		928	316	296	612	393	-62	102	6	55	9	10	19	32

SANTALA, TOMMI — C — THRASHERS

PERSONAL: Born June 27, 1979, in Helsinki, Finland. ... 6-2/210. ... Shoots right.

TRANSACTIONS/CAREER NOTES: Selected by Atlanta Thrashers in the ninth round (245th overall) in the NHL entry draft (June 26, 1999). ... Signed by HIFK Helsinki of the Finnish league (June 2, 2004).

		REGULAR SEASON								PLAYOFFS				
Season Team	League	GP	G	A	Pts.	PIM	+/-	PP	SH	GP	G	A	Pts.	PIM
00-01—HPK Hameenlinna	Finland	56	16	24	40	90	...	...	...	—	—	—	—	—
01-02—HPK Hameenlinna	Finland	17	6	16	22	14	...	...	...	—	—	—	—	—

		REGULAR SEASON								PLAYOFFS				
Season Team	League	GP	G	A	Pts.	PIM	+/-	PP	SH	GP	G	A	Pts.	PIM
02-03—HPK Hameenlinna	Finland	50	13	38	51	92	...	...	...	—	—	—	—	—
03-04—Atlanta	NHL	33	1	2	3	22	-7	0	0	—	—	—	—	—
—Chicago	AHL	50	15	22	37	34	1	6	0	10	1	6	7	31
04-05—Chicago	AHL	67	8	40	48	83	12	3	0	18	5	6	11	42
NHL Totals (1 year)		33	1	2	3	22	-7	0	0					

SAPRYKIN, OLEG LW COYOTES

PERSONAL: Born February 12, 1981, in Moscow, U.S.S.R. ... 6-1/195. ... Shoots left.

TRANSACTIONS/CAREER NOTES: Selected by Calgary Flames in 1st round (1st Flames pick, 11th overall) of entry draft (June 26, 1999). ... Concussion (January 5, 2001); missed 11 games. ... Injured neck (September 16, 2001); missed first 12 games of season. ... Sprained left knee (January 18, 2003); missed five games. ... Traded by Flames with D Denis Gauthier to Phoenix Coyotes for C Daymond Langkow (August 26, 2004).

		REGULAR SEASON								PLAYOFFS				
Season Team	League	GP	G	A	Pts.	PIM	+/-	PP	SH	GP	G	A	Pts.	PIM
97-98—HC CSKA	Rus. Div.	15	0	3	3	6	...	...	...	—	—	—	—	—
—CSKA Moscow	Russian	20	0	2	2	8	...	...	...	—	—	—	—	—
98-99—Seattle	WHL	66	47	46	93	107	31	15	5	11	5	11	16	36
99-00—Calgary	NHL	4	0	1	1	2	-4	0	0	—	—	—	—	—
—Seattle	WHL	48	30	36	66	89	17	8	2	6	3	3	6	37
00-01—Calgary	NHL	59	9	14	23	43	4	2	0	—	—	—	—	—
01-02—Calgary	NHL	3	0	0	0	0	-2	0	0	—	—	—	—	—
—Saint John	AHL	52	5	19	24	53	-8	2	0	—	—	—	—	—
02-03—Saint John	AHL	21	12	9	21	22	-2	3	1	—	—	—	—	—
—Calgary	NHL	52	8	15	23	46	5	1	0	—	—	—	—	—
03-04—Calgary	NHL	69	12	17	29	41	1	4	0	26	3	3	6	14
04-05—CSKA Moscow	Russian	40	15	8	23	105	-7	...	...	—	—	—	—	—
NHL Totals (5 years)		187	29	47	76	132	4	7	0	26	3	3	6	14

SARICH, CORY D LIGHTNING

PERSONAL: Born August 16, 1978, in Saskatoon, Sask. ... 6-3/204. ... Shoots right. ... Name pronounced SAIR-ich.

TRANSACTIONS/CAREER NOTES: Selected by Buffalo Sabres in second round (second Sabres pick, 27th overall) of NHL entry draft (June 22, 1996). ... Traded by Sabres with C Wayne Primeau, C/RW Brian Holzinger and third-round pick (RW Alexandre Kharitonov) in 2000 draft to Tampa Bay Lightning for C Chris Gratton and second-round pick (C Derek Roy) in 2001 draft (March 9, 2000). ... Bruised right knee (October 13, 2001); missed two games. ... Suffered concussion (October 27, 2001); missed one game. ... Bruised right shoulder (November 6, 2001); missed four games.

		REGULAR SEASON								PLAYOFFS				
Season Team	League	GP	G	A	Pts.	PIM	+/-	PP	SH	GP	G	A	Pts.	PIM
94-95—Saskatoon	WHL	6	0	0	0	4	...	...	...	3	0	1	1	0
95-96—Saskatoon	WHL	59	5	18	23	54	...	...	...	3	0	0	0	4
96-97—Saskatoon	WHL	58	6	27	33	158	-31	4	0	—	—	—	—	—
97-98—Seattle	WHL	46	8	40	48	137	-6	5	0	—	—	—	—	—
98-99—Rochester	AHL	77	3	26	29	82	30	3	0	20	2	4	6	14
—Buffalo	NHL	4	0	0	0	0	3	0	0	—	—	—	—	—
99-00—Buffalo	NHL	42	0	4	4	35	2	0	0	—	—	—	—	—
—Rochester	AHL	15	0	6	6	44	...	...	...	—	—	—	—	—
—Tampa Bay	NHL	17	0	2	2	42	-8	0	0	—	—	—	—	—
00-01—Tampa Bay	NHL	73	1	8	9	106	-25	0	0	—	—	—	—	—
—Detroit	IHL	3	0	2	2	2	...	...	...	—	—	—	—	—
01-02—Tampa Bay	NHL	72	0	11	11	105	-4	0	0	—	—	—	—	—
—Springfield	AHL	2	0	0	0	0	0	0	0	—	—	—	—	—
02-03—Tampa Bay	NHL	82	5	9	14	63	-3	0	0	11	0	2	2	6
03-04—Tampa Bay	NHL	82	3	16	19	89	5	0	1	23	0	2	2	25
NHL Totals (6 years)		372	9	50	59	440	-30	0	1	34	0	4	4	31

SARNO, PETER C

PERSONAL: Born July 26, 1979, in Toronto. ... 5-11/185. ... Shoots left.

TRANSACTIONS/CAREER NOTES: Selected by Edmonton Oilers in sixth round (sixth Oilers pick, 141st overall) of NHL entry draft (June 21, 1997). ... Traded by Oilers to Vancouver Canucks for G Tyler Moss (February 16, 2004).

		REGULAR SEASON								PLAYOFFS				
Season Team	League	GP	G	A	Pts.	PIM	+/-	PP	SH	GP	G	A	Pts.	PIM
95-96—North York Flames	OPJHL	52	39	57	96	27	...	...	...	—	—	—	—	—
96-97—Windsor	OHL	66	20	63	83	59	14	5	0	5	0	3	3	6
97-98—Windsor	OHL	64	33	*88	*121	18	...	...	...	—	—	—	—	—
—Hamilton	AHL	8	1	1	2	2	2	0	0	—	—	—	—	—
98-99—Sarnia	OHL	68	37	*93	*130	49	32	...	...	6	1	7	8	2
99-00—Hamilton	AHL	67	10	36	46	31	...	...	...	—	—	—	—	—
00-01—Hamilton	AHL	79	19	46	65	64	...	...	...	—	—	—	—	—
01-02—Hamilton	AHL	76	12	40	52	38	6	2	0	15	6	7	13	4
02-03—Blues Espoo	Finland	45	17	23	40	34	...	...	...	7	2	1	3	2
03-04—Edmonton	NHL	6	1	0	1	2	2	0	0	—	—	—	—	—
—Toronto	AHL	31	6	12	18	29	3	0	0	—	—	—	—	—
—Manitoba	AHL	23	5	9	14	6	-8	2	0	—	—	—	—	—
04-05—Manitoba	AHL	80	16	66	82	53	11	6	0	14	1	8	9	4
NHL Totals (1 year)		6	1	0	1	2	2	0	0					

SATAN, MIROSLAV — RW — ISLANDERS

PERSONAL: Born October 22, 1974, in Topolcany, Czech. ... 6-3/192. ... Shoots left. ... Name pronounced shuh-TAN.
TRANSACTIONS/CAREER NOTES: Selected by Edmonton Oilers in 5th round (6th Oilers pick, 111th overall) of NHL draft (June 26, 1993). ... Collapsed lung (October 1, 1995); missed two games. ... Separated right shoulder (January 13, 1996); missed four games. ... Flu (March 9, 1997); missed one game. ... Traded by Oilers to Buffalo Sabres for D Craig Millar and LW Barrie Moore (March 18, 1997). ... Flu (November 28, 1998); missed one game. ... Injured foot (April 25, 1999); missed nine playoff games. ... Bruised hip, back (November 3, 2002); missed three games. ... Signed as free agent by New York Islanders (Aug.3, 2005).
STATISTICAL PLATEAUS: Three-goal games: 1996-97 (1), 1997-98 (1), 1999-00 (1), 2002-03 (1), 2003-04 (1). Total: 5. ... Four-goal games: 2003-04 (1). ... Total hat tricks: 6.

		REGULAR SEASON								PLAYOFFS				
Season Team	League	GP	G	A	Pts.	PIM	+/-	PP	SH	GP	G	A	Pts.	PIM
91-92—VTJ Topolcany	Czech Dv.I	9	2	1	3	6	...	...	...	—	—	—	—	—
—VTJ Topolcany Jrs	Czech. Jrs.	31	30	22	52	...	...	...	...	—	—	—	—	—
92-93—Dukla Trencin	Czech.	38	11	6	17	...	...	...	...	—	—	—	—	—
93-94—Dukla Trencin	Slovakia	30	32	16	48	16	...	...	...	—	—	—	—	—
—Slovakian Oly. team	Int'l	8	9	0	9	0	-5	2	1	—	—	—	—	—
94-95—Detroit	IHL	8	1	3	4	4	-5	0	0	—	—	—	—	—
—San Diego	IHL	6	0	2	2	6	2	0	0	—	—	—	—	—
—Cape Breton	AHL	25	24	16	40	15	6	10	0	—	—	—	—	—
95-96—Edmonton	NHL	62	18	17	35	22	0	6	0	—	—	—	—	—
96-97—Edmonton	NHL	64	17	11	28	22	-4	5	0	—	—	—	—	—
—Buffalo	NHL	12	8	2	10	4	1	2	0	7	0	0	0	0
97-98—Buffalo	NHL	79	22	24	46	34	2	9	0	14	5	4	9	4
98-99—Buffalo	NHL	81	40	26	66	44	24	13	3	12	3	5	8	2
99-00—Dukla Trencin	Slovakia	3	2	8	10	2	...	...	...	—	—	—	—	—
—Buffalo	NHL	81	33	34	67	32	16	5	3	5	3	2	5	0
00-01—Buffalo	NHL	82	29	33	62	36	5	8	2	13	3	10	13	8
01-02—Buffalo	NHL	82	37	36	73	33	14	15	5	—	—	—	—	—
—Slovakian Oly. team	Int'l	2	0	1	1	0	...	...	...	—	—	—	—	—
02-03—Buffalo	NHL	79	26	49	75	20	-3	11	1	—	—	—	—	—
03-04—Buffalo	NHL	82	29	28	57	30	-15	11	1	—	—	—	—	—
04-05—Bratislava	Slovakia	18	11	9	20	14	8	4	1	18	15	7	22	16
NHL Totals (9 years)		704	259	260	519	277	40	85	15	51	14	21	35	14

SAUER, KURT — D — AVALANCHE

PERSONAL: Born January 16, 1981, in St. Cloud, Minn. ... 6-3/217. ... Shoots left. ... Name pronounced SAW-uhr.
TRANSACTIONS/CAREER NOTES: Selected by Colorado Avalanche in third round (fifth Avalanche pick, 88th overall) of NHL entry draft (June 24, 2000). ... Signed as free agent by Anaheim Mighty Ducks (June 6, 2002). ... Sprained left ankle (November 9, 2003); missed six games. ... Traded by Mighty Ducks with fifth-round pick in 2005 entry draft to Avalanche for D Martin Skoula (February 21, 2004).

		REGULAR SEASON								PLAYOFFS				
Season Team	League	GP	G	A	Pts.	PIM	+/-	PP	SH	GP	G	A	Pts.	PIM
99-00—Spokane	WHL	71	3	12	15	48	...	...	...	—	—	—	—	—
00-01—Spokane	WHL	48	5	10	15	85	...	...	...	3	1	0	1	2
01-02—Spokane	WHL	61	4	20	24	73	...	...	...	11	0	3	3	12
02-03—Anaheim	NHL	80	1	2	3	74	-23	0	0	21	1	1	2	6
03-04—Anaheim	NHL	55	1	4	5	32	-8	0	0	—	—	—	—	—
—Colorado	NHL	14	0	1	1	19	-3	0	0	3	0	0	0	0
NHL Totals (2 years)		149	2	7	9	125	-34	0	0	24	1	1	2	6

SAUER, MICHAEL — D — RANGERS

PERSONAL: Born August 7, 1987, in St. Cloud, Minn. ... 6-2/198. ... Shoots right.

		REGULAR SEASON								PLAYOFFS				
Season Team	League	GP	G	A	Pts.	PIM	+/-	PP	SH	GP	G	A	Pts.	PIM
04-05—Portland	WHL	32	2	11	13	10	6	1	0	—	—	—	—	—

SAUVE, PHILIPPE — G — FLAMES

PERSONAL: Born February 27, 1980, in Buffalo, N.Y. ... 6-0/180. ... Catches left.
TRANSACTIONS/CAREER NOTES: Selected by Colorado Avalanche in 2nd round (6th Avalanche pick, 38th overall) of entry draft (June 27, 1998). ... Traded by Avalanche for a conditional 7th-round pick in 2006 draft (Aug. 9, 2005).

		REGULAR SEASON									PLAYOFFS							
Season Team	League	GP	Min.	W	L	T	GA	SO	GAA	SV%	GP	Min.	W	L	GA	SO	GAA	SV%
96-97—Rimouski	QMJHL	26	1332	11	9	2	84	0	3.78	...	1	14	0	0	3	0	12.86	...
97-98—Rimouski	QMJHL	40	2326	23	16	0	131	1	3.38	...	7	262	0	5	33	0	7.56	...
98-99—Rimouski	QMJHL	44	2401	16	19	4	155	0	3.87	...	11	595	6	4	30	1	3.03	...
99-00—Drummondville	QMJHL	28	1526	12	12	2	106	0	4.17	.864	—	—	—	—	—	—	—	—
—Hull	QMJHL	17	992	9	7	1	57	0	3.45	.903	12	735	6	6	47	0	3.84	.890
00-01—Hershey	AHL	42	2182	17	18	1	100	3	2.75	.914	3	218	0	3	10	0	2.75	...
01-02—Hershey	AHL	55	3129	25	20	6	111	6	2.13	.922	8	486	3	5	21	0	2.59	.915
02-03—Hershey	AHL	60	3394	26	20	12	134	5	2.37	.917	5	294	2	3	14	0	2.86	.914
03-04—Colorado	NHL	17	986	7	7	3	50	0	3.04	.896	—	—	—	—	—	—	—	—
—Hershey	AHL	10	578	3	7	0	25	2	2.60	.901	—	—	—	—	—	—	—	—
04-05—Mississippi	ECHL	21	1297	13	4	...	56	2	2.59	.923	4	226	1	3	16	...	4.23	.904
NHL Totals (1 year)		17	986	7	7	3	50	0	3.04	.896								

SAVAGE, ANDRE — C

PERSONAL: Born May 27, 1975, in Ottawa. ... 6-0/186. ... Shoots right. ... Name pronounced suh-VAHJ.

TRANSACTIONS/CAREER NOTES: Signed as free agent by Boston Bruins (June 12, 1998). ... Bruised sternum (March 8, 2000); missed two games. ... Strained trapezius muscle (April 1, 2000); missed final four games of season. ... Dislocated shoulder (September 21, 2000) and had surgery; missed first 39 games of season. ... Signed as free agent by Vancouver Canucks (August 2, 2001). ... Signed as free agent by Philadelphia Flyers (July 14, 2002). ... Signed as free agent by Colorado Avalanche (July 21, 2004).

		REGULAR SEASON								PLAYOFFS				
Season Team	League	GP	G	A	Pts.	PIM	+/-	PP	SH	GP	G	A	Pts.	PIM
94-95—Michigan Tech	WCHA	39	7	17	24	56	...	2	0	—	—	—	—	—
95-96—Michigan Tech	WCHA	40	13	27	40	42	...	...	...	—	—	—	—	—
96-97—Michigan Tech	WCHA	37	18	20	38	34	-1	7	0	—	—	—	—	—
97-98—Michigan Tech	WCHA	33	14	27	41	34	...	...	...	—	—	—	—	—
98-99—Providence	AHL	63	27	42	69	54	30	8	0	5	0	1	1	0
—Boston	NHL	6	1	0	1	0	2	0	0	—	—	—	—	—
99-00—Providence	AHL	30	15	17	32	22	...	...	...	14	6	7	13	22
—Boston	NHL	43	7	13	20	10	-8	2	0	—	—	—	—	—
00-01—Providence	AHL	35	13	15	28	47	...	...	...	17	3	4	7	18
—Boston	NHL	1	0	0	0	0	0	0	0	—	—	—	—	—
01-02—Manitoba	AHL	76	35	26	61	115	14	12	0	6	2	3	5	16
02-03—Philadelphia	AHL	64	11	31	42	66	-3	5	0	—	—	—	—	—
—Philadelphia	NHL	16	2	1	3	4	2	0	0	—	—	—	—	—
03-04—Philadelphia	AHL	8	1	0	1	12	-1	1	0	—	—	—	—	—
—Providence	AHL	63	16	30	46	94	5	6	0	1	0	0	0	2
04-05—Hershey	AHL	53	7	23	30	36	-4	3	0	—	—	—	—	—
—San Antonio	AHL	20	1	4	5	12	-6	0	0	—	—	—	—	—
NHL Totals (4 years)		66	10	14	24	14	-4	2	0					

S

SAVAGE, BRIAN — LW

PERSONAL: Born February 24, 1971, in Sudbury, Ont. ... 6-1/200. ... Shoots left. ... Name pronounced SA-vuhj.

TRANSACTIONS/CAREER NOTES: Selected by Montreal Canadiens in eighth round (11th Canadiens pick, 171st overall) of NHL entry draft (June 22, 1991). ... Bruised knee (February 4, 1995); missed 10 games. ... Bruised knee (April 5, 1995); missed one game. ... Suffered hip pointer (February 17, 1996); missed six games. ... Flu (April 1, 1996); missed one game. ... Injured groin (October 26, 1996); missed one game. ... Fractured hand (October 1, 1997); missed seven games. ... Bruised thigh (November 26, 1997); missed one game. ... Fractured thumb (March 21, 1998); missed 10 games. ... Strained groin (November 4, 1998); missed one game. ... Reinjured groin (December 9, 1998); missed 11 games. ... Tore muscle in rib cage (January 21, 1999); missed 11 games. ... Fractured vertebrae in neck (November 20, 1999); missed 44 games. ... Fractured thumb (January 20, 2001); missed 20 games. ... Injured wrist (January 14, 2002); missed four games. ... Traded by Canadiens with 3rd-round pick (D Matt Jones) in 2002 and future considerations to Phoenix Coyotes for LW Sergei Berezin (January 25, 2002). ... Strained hip flexor (April 10, 2002); missed final two games of season. ... Injured groin (October 14, 2002); missed four games. ... Fractured thumb (November 17, 2002); missed five games. ... Suffered concussion (December 15, 2002); missed 21 games. ... Fractured collarbone (March 24, 2003); missed last seven games of season. ... Fractured thumb (October 25, 2003); missed five games. ... Traded by Coyotes to St. Louis Blues for future considerations (March 9, 2004); returned to Coyotes to complete deal. ... Contract bought out by Coyotes (July 29, 2005).

STATISTICAL PLATEAUS: Three-goal games: 1995-96 (1), 1996-97 (1), 1999-00 (2), 2000-01 (1), 2001-02 (1). Total: 6. ... Four-goal games: 1997-98 (1). ... Total hat tricks: 7.

		REGULAR SEASON								PLAYOFFS				
Season Team	League	GP	G	A	Pts.	PIM	+/-	PP	SH	GP	G	A	Pts.	PIM
89-90—Sudbury	OHA Mj. Jr	32	45	40	85	61	...	...	...	—	—	—	—	—
90-91—Miami (Ohio)	CCHA	28	5	6	11	26	...	...	...	—	—	—	—	—
91-92—Miami (Ohio)	CCHA	40	24	16	40	43	...	...	...	—	—	—	—	—
92-93—Miami (Ohio)	CCHA	38	37	21	58	44	23	10	2	—	—	—	—	—
—Canadian nat'l team	Int'l	9	3	0	3	12	...	...	...	—	—	—	—	—
93-94—Canadian nat'l team	Int'l	51	20	26	46	38	...	...	...	—	—	—	—	—
—Can. Olympic team	Int'l	8	2	2	4	6	2	0	0	—	—	—	—	—
—Fredericton	AHL	17	12	15	27	4	-7	4	0	—	—	—	—	—
—Montreal	NHL	3	1	0	1	0	0	0	0	3	0	2	2	0
94-95—Montreal	NHL	37	12	7	19	27	5	0	0	—	—	—	—	—
95-96—Montreal	NHL	75	25	8	33	28	-8	4	0	6	0	2	2	2
96-97—Montreal	NHL	81	23	37	60	39	-14	5	0	5	1	1	2	0
97-98—Montreal	NHL	64	26	17	43	36	11	8	0	9	0	2	2	6
98-99—Montreal	NHL	54	16	10	26	20	-14	5	0	—	—	—	—	—
99-00—Montreal	NHL	38	17	12	29	19	-4	6	1	—	—	—	—	—
00-01—Montreal	NHL	62	21	24	45	26	-13	12	0	—	—	—	—	—
01-02—Montreal	NHL	47	14	15	29	30	-14	7	0	—	—	—	—	—
—Phoenix	NHL	30	6	6	12	8	1	2	0	5	0	0	0	0
02-03—Phoenix	NHL	43	6	10	16	22	-4	1	0	—	—	—	—	—
03-04—Phoenix	NHL	61	12	13	25	36	-5	3	0	—	—	—	—	—
—St. Louis	NHL	13	4	3	7	2	-3	1	0	5	1	1	2	0
NHL Totals (11 years)		608	183	162	345	293	-62	54	1	33	2	8	10	8

SAVARD, MARC — C — THRASHERS

PERSONAL: Born July 17, 1977, in Ottawa. ... 5-10/195. ... Shoots left. ... Name pronounced suh-VAHRD.

TRANSACTIONS/CAREER NOTES: Selected by New York Rangers in fourth round (third Rangers pick, 91st overall) of NHL draft (July 8, 1995). ... Traded by Rangers with first-round pick (C/LW Oleg Saprykin) in 1999 draft to Calgary Flames for rights to LW Jan Hlavac and first- (C Jamie Lundmark) and third-round (D Pat Aufiero) picks in 1999 draft (June 26, 1999). ... Suffered concussion (January 8, 2000); missed two games. ... Missed first two games of 2000-01 season in contract dispute. ... Suffered concussion (December 31, 2000); missed three games.

... Injured knee (October 10, 2001); missed 15 games. ... Injured head (March 23, 2002); missed remainder of season. ... Traded by Flames to Atlanta Thrashers for RW Ruslan Zainullan (November 15, 2002). ... Injured groin (November 28, 2002); missed five games. ... Injured hamstring (January 28, 2003); missed one game. ... Flu (March 13, 2003); missed one game. ... Injured left ankle and had surgery (November 4, 2003); missed nine games. ... Suspended one game for match penalty incident (November 28, 2003). ... Suffered concussion (January 4, 2004); missed three games. ... Sprained right knee (January 15, 2004); missed seven games. ... Injured knee (February 27, 2004); missed remainder of season. ... Signed as free agent by Thurgau of Swiss league (October 11, 2004). ... Signed as free agent by Bern of Swiss league (November 23, 2004).

STATISTICAL PLATEAUS: Three-goal games: 2001-02 (1). ... Four-goal games: 1999-00 (1). ... Total hat tricks: 2.

		REGULAR SEASON								PLAYOFFS				
Season Team	League	GP	G	A	Pts.	PIM	+/-	PP	SH	GP	G	A	Pts.	PIM
92-93—Metcalfe	Jr. B	31	46	53	99	26	...	...	...	—	—	—	—	—
93-94—Oshawa	OHL	61	18	39	57	24	...	...	...	5	4	3	7	8
94-95—Oshawa	OHL	66	43	96	*139	78	...	12	3	7	5	6	11	8
95-96—Oshawa	OHL	48	28	59	87	77	...	...	...	5	4	5	9	6
96-97—Oshawa	OHL	64	43	*87	*130	94	22	10	3	18	13	24	*37	20
97-98—New York Rangers	NHL	28	1	5	6	4	-4	0	0	—	—	—	—	—
—Hartford	AHL	58	21	53	74	66	16	5	0	15	8	19	27	24
98-99—Hartford	AHL	9	3	10	13	16	1	1	0	7	1	12	13	16
—New York Rangers	NHL	70	9	36	45	38	-7	4	0	—	—	—	—	—
99-00—Calgary	NHL	78	22	31	53	56	-2	4	0	—	—	—	—	—
00-01—Calgary	NHL	77	23	42	65	46	-12	10	1	—	—	—	—	—
01-02—Calgary	NHL	56	14	19	33	48	-18	7	0	—	—	—	—	—
02-03—Calgary	NHL	10	1	2	3	8	-3	0	0	—	—	—	—	—
—Atlanta	NHL	57	16	31	47	77	-11	6	0	—	—	—	—	—
03-04—Atlanta	NHL	45	19	33	52	85	-8	6	1	—	—	—	—	—
04-05—Bern	Switzerland	5	1	2	3	0	...	0	0	—	—	—	—	—
—Thurgau	Switz. Div. 2	13	9	19	28	10	...	3	0	—	—	—	—	—
NHL Totals (7 years)		421	105	199	304	362	-65	37	2					

SCATCHARD, DAVE — C — BRUINS

PERSONAL: Born February 20, 1976, in Hinton, Alta. ... 6-3/220. ... Shoots right. ... Name pronounced SKATCH-uhrd.

TRANSACTIONS/CAREER NOTES: Selected by Vancouver Canucks in 2nd round (3rd Canucks pick, 42nd overall) of entry draft (June 28, 1994). ... Hip pointer (December 15, 1997); missed two games. ... Bruised ankle (October 13, 1999); missed five games. ... Traded by Canucks with G Kevin Weekes and RW Bill Muckalt to New York Islanders for G Felix Potvin, 2nd- (traded to New Jersey; Devils selected RW Teemu Laine) and 3rd-round (C Thatcher Bell) picks in 2000 draft (December 19, 1999). ... Concussion (March 22, 2000); missed final eight games of season. ... Strained neck (November 9, 2000); missed one game. ... Injured shoulder (October 20, 2003); missed 20 games. ... Signed as free agent by Boston Bruins (Aug. 2, 2005).

STATISTICAL PLATEAUS: Three-goal games: 2002-03 (2).

		REGULAR SEASON								PLAYOFFS				
Season Team	League	GP	G	A	Pts.	PIM	+/-	PP	SH	GP	G	A	Pts.	PIM
92-93—Kimberley	RMJHL	51	20	23	43	61	...	...	...	—	—	—	—	—
93-94—Portland	WHL	47	9	11	20	46	3	0	0	10	2	1	3	4
94-95—Portland	WHL	71	20	30	50	148	-23	5	1	8	0	3	3	21
95-96—Portland	WHL	59	19	28	47	146	...	...	...	7	1	8	9	14
—Syracuse	AHL	1	0	0	0	0	...	...	...	15	2	5	7	29
96-97—Syracuse	AHL	26	8	7	15	65	-1	4	0	—	—	—	—	—
97-98—Vancouver	NHL	76	13	11	24	165	-4	0	0	—	—	—	—	—
98-99—Vancouver	NHL	82	13	13	26	140	-12	0	2	—	—	—	—	—
99-00—Vancouver	NHL	21	0	4	4	24	-3	0	0	—	—	—	—	—
—New York Islanders	NHL	44	12	14	26	93	0	0	1	—	—	—	—	—
00-01—New York Islanders	NHL	81	21	24	45	114	-9	4	0	—	—	—	—	—
01-02—New York Islanders	NHL	80	12	15	27	111	-4	3	1	7	1	1	2	22
02-03—New York Islanders	NHL	81	27	18	45	108	9	5	0	5	1	0	1	6
03-04—New York Islanders	NHL	61	9	16	25	78	12	1	1	5	0	1	1	6
NHL Totals (7 years)		526	107	115	222	833	-11	13	5	17	2	2	4	34

SCHAEFER, NOLAN — G — SHARKS

PERSONAL: Born January 15, 1980, in Yellow Grass, Sask. ... 6-1/175. ... Catches left. ... Name pronounced SHAY-fuhr.

TRANSACTIONS/CAREER NOTES: Selected by San Jose Sharks in fifth round (fourth Sharks pick, 166th overall) of NHL entry draft (June 24, 2000).

		REGULAR SEASON									PLAYOFFS							
Season Team	League	GP	Min.	W	L	T	GA	SO	GAA	SV%	GP	Min.	W	L	GA	SO	GAA	SV%
99-00—Providence College	Hockey East	14	778	6	5	1	42	0	3.24	.904	—	—	—	—	—	—	—	—
00-01—Providence College	Hockey East	25	1529	15	8	2	63	3	2.47	...	—	—	—	—	—	—	—	—
01-02—Providence College	Hockey East	*35	*2062	11	18	*5	*113	0	3.29	...	—	—	—	—	—	—	—	—
02-03—Providence College	Hockey East	25	1440	13	8	2	71	0	2.96	...	—	—	—	—	—	—	—	—
03-04—Cleveland	AHL	27	1591	14	9	3	62	2	2.34	.919	9	572	4	5	24	0	2.52	.922
04-05—Cleveland	AHL	43	2417	17	23	...	110	3	2.73	.907	—	—	—	—	—	—	—	—

SCHAEFER, PETER — LW — SENATORS

PERSONAL: Born July 12, 1977, in Yellow Grass, Sask. ... 6-0/190. ... Shoots left. ... Name pronounced SHAY-fuhr.

TRANSACTIONS/CAREER NOTES: Selected by Vancouver Canucks in third round (third Canucks pick, 66th overall) of NHL draft (July 8, 1995). ... Sprained shoulder (April 2, 1999); missed final six games of season. ... Flu (November 20, 1999); missed one game. ... Injured knee (February 14, 2000); missed three games. ... Reinjured knee (February 23, 2000); missed four games. ... Flu (April 2, 2000); missed one game.

... Missed 2001-02 season in contract dispute. ... Traded by Canucks to Ottawa Senators for D Sami Salo (September 21, 2002). ... Injured right knee (December 4, 2002); missed two games. ... Injured lower left leg (February 8, 2003); missed three games. ... Injured lower back (March 21, 2003); missed two games. ... Bruised foot (November 1, 2003); missed one game.

		REGULAR SEASON								PLAYOFFS				
Season Team	League	GP	G	A	Pts.	PIM	+/-	PP	SH	GP	G	A	Pts.	PIM
93-94—Brandon	WHL	2	1	0	1	0	...	...	...	—	—	—	—	—
94-95—Brandon	WHL	68	27	32	59	34	20	6	0	18	5	3	8	18
95-96—Brandon	WHL	69	47	61	108	53	...	...	...	19	10	13	23	5
96-97—Brandon	WHL	61	49	74	123	85	57	15	6	6	1	4	5	4
—Syracuse	AHL	5	0	3	3	0	2	0	0	3	1	3	4	14
97-98—Syracuse	AHL	73	19	44	63	41	-8	6	0	5	2	1	3	2
98-99—Syracuse	AHL	41	10	19	29	66	-17	5	1	—	—	—	—	—
—Vancouver	NHL	25	4	4	8	8	-1	1	0	—	—	—	—	—
99-00—Vancouver	NHL	71	16	15	31	20	0	2	2	—	—	—	—	—
—Syracuse	AHL	2	0	0	0	2	...	...	...	—	—	—	—	—
00-01—Vancouver	NHL	82	16	20	36	22	4	3	4	3	0	0	0	0
01-02—TPS Turku	Finland	33	16	15	31	93	...	...	...	8	1	2	3	2
02-03—Ottawa	NHL	75	6	17	23	32	11	0	0	16	2	3	5	6
03-04—Ottawa	NHL	81	15	24	39	26	22	2	2	7	0	2	2	4
04-05—Bolzano	Italy	15	11	14	25	10	...	...	...	10	1	7	8	12
NHL Totals (5 years)		334	57	80	137	108	36	8	8	26	2	5	7	10

SCHASTLIVY, PETR — LW — MIGHTY DUCKS

PERSONAL: Born April 18, 1979, in Angarsk, U.S.S.R. ... 6-1/204. ... Shoots left.

TRANSACTIONS/CAREER NOTES: Selected by Ottawa Senators in fourth round (fifth Senators pick, 101st overall) of NHL draft (June 27, 1998). ... Tore right knee ligament (December 29, 2001); missed remainder of season. ... Injured groin (November 4, 2002); missed five games. ... Injured groin (November 27, 2002); missed two games. ... Injured groin (December 9, 2002); missed four games. ... Injured groin (December 18, 2002); missed eight games. ... Strained lower abdomen (January 29, 2003) and had surgery; missed remainder of season. ... Traded by Senators to Anaheim Mighty Ducks for D Todd Simpson (February 4, 2004). ... Visa problems (February 11, 2004); missed one game.

		REGULAR SEASON								PLAYOFFS				
Season Team	League	GP	G	A	Pts.	PIM	+/-	PP	SH	GP	G	A	Pts.	PIM
97-98—Torpedo Yaroslavl	Rus. Div.	47	15	9	24	34	...	...	...	—	—	—	—	—
—Torpedo Yaroslavl	Russian	4	0	0	0	0	...	...	...	—	—	—	—	—
98-99—Torpedo Yaroslavl	Russian	40	6	1	7	28	...	...	...	6	0	0	0	2
99-00—Grand Rapids	IHL	46	16	12	28	10	...	...	...	17	8	7	15	6
—Ottawa	NHL	13	2	5	7	2	4	1	0	1	0	0	0	0
00-01—Grand Rapids	IHL	43	10	14	24	10	...	...	...	7	4	4	8	0
—Ottawa	NHL	17	3	2	5	6	-1	0	0	—	—	—	—	—
01-02—Grand Rapids	AHL	31	22	13	35	10	14	6	0	—	—	—	—	—
—Ottawa	NHL	1	0	1	1	0	1	0	0	—	—	—	—	—
02-03—Ottawa	NHL	33	9	10	19	4	3	5	0	—	—	—	—	—
03-04—Ottawa	NHL	43	2	4	6	14	-1	1	0	—	—	—	—	—
—Anaheim	NHL	22	2	0	2	4	-3	0	0	—	—	—	—	—
04-05—Lokomotiv Yaroslavl	Russian	59	15	15	30	28	14	...	...	9	1	3	4	2
NHL Totals (5 years)		129	18	22	40	30	3	7	0	1	0	0	0	0

SCHNABEL, ROBERT — D — PREDATORS

PERSONAL: Born November 10, 1978, in Prague, Czechoslovakia. ... 6-5/230. ... Shoots left. ... Name pronounced SHNAY-buhl.

TRANSACTIONS/CAREER NOTES: Selected by New York Islanders in third round (fifth Islanders pick, 79th overall) of NHL draft (June 21, 1997). ... Returned to draft pool by Islanders and selected by Phoenix Coyotes in sixth round (seventh Coyotes pick, 129th overall) of NHL entry draft (June 27, 1998). ... Claimed off waivers by Atlanta Thrashers (January 2, 2001). ... Signed as free agent by Nashville Predators (July 13, 2001). ... Injured wrist (October 19, 2003); missed 25 games.

		REGULAR SEASON								PLAYOFFS				
Season Team	League	GP	G	A	Pts.	PIM	+/-	PP	SH	GP	G	A	Pts.	PIM
94-95—Slavia Praha	Czech. Jrs.	35	11	6	17	14	...	...	...	—	—	—	—	—
95-96—Slavia Praha	Czech. Jrs.	38	3	5	8	...	...	...	...	—	—	—	—	—
96-97—Slavia Praha	Czech. Jrs.	36	5	2	7	...	...	...	...	—	—	—	—	—
—Slavia Praha	Czech Rep.	4	0	0	0	4	...	...	...	1	0	0	0	0
97-98—Red Deer	WHL	61	1	22	23	143	...	...	...	5	0	0	0	16
98-99—Red Deer	WHL	1	0	0	0	2	...	0	0	—	—	—	—	—
—Springfield	AHL	77	1	7	8	155	9	0	0	3	1	0	1	4
99-00—Springfield	AHL	40	2	8	10	133	...	...	...	5	0	0	0	4
00-01—Timra	Sweden	16	0	2	2	72	...	...	...	—	—	—	—	—
—Springfield	AHL	22	1	2	3	38	...	...	...	—	—	—	—	—
01-02—Milwaukee	AHL	67	2	7	9	130	10	1	0	—	—	—	—	—
—Nashville	NHL	1	0	0	0	0	0	0	0	—	—	—	—	—
02-03—Nashville	NHL	1	0	0	0	0	0	0	0	—	—	—	—	—
—Milwaukee	AHL	62	3	6	9	178	9	0	0	6	0	0	0	34
03-04—Milwaukee	AHL	11	1	0	1	27	-2	0	0	—	—	—	—	—
—Nashville	NHL	20	0	3	3	34	6	0	0	—	—	—	—	—
04-05—Sparta Praha	Czech Rep.	47	1	4	5	85	8	...	...	4	0	0	0	12
NHL Totals (3 years)		22	0	3	3	34	6	0	0					

SCHNEIDER, CORY — G — CANUCKS

PERSONAL: Born March 18, 1986, in Salem, Mass. ... 6-2/195. ... Catches left.

TRANSACTIONS/CAREER NOTES: Selected by Vancouver Canucks in 1st round (1st Canucks pick, 26th overall) of entry draft (June 26, 2004).

		REGULAR SEASON									PLAYOFFS							
Season Team	League	GP	Min.	W	L	T	GA	SO	GAA	SV%	GP	Min.	W	L	GA	SO	GAA	SV%
03-04—Phillips Academy	Mass. H.S.	24	1336	...	...	...	...	6	...	...	—	—	—	—	—	—	—	—
04-05—Boston College	Hockey East	18	1102	13	1	4	35	1	1.90	.916	—	—	—	—	—	—	—	—

SCHNEIDER, MATHIEU — D — RED WINGS

PERSONAL: Born June 12, 1969, in New York City. ... 6-0/191. ... Shoots left.

TRANSACTIONS/CAREER NOTES: Selected by Montreal Canadiens in 3rd round (4th Canadiens pick, 44th overall) of NHL draft (June 13, 1987). ... Bruised left shoulder (February 1990). ... Sprained left ankle (January 26, 1991); missed nine games. ... Sprained ankle (January 27, 1993); missed 24 games. ... Separated shoulder (April 18, 1993); missed seven playoff games. ... Injured ankle (December 6, 1993); missed two games. ... Elbow surgery (March 29, 1994); missed five games. ... Flu (February 27, 1995); missed one game. ... Traded by Canadiens with LW Kirk Muller and C Craig Darby to New York Islanders for D Vladimir Malakhov and C Pierre Turgeon (April 5, 1995). ... Bruised ribs (October 28, 1995); missed one game. ... Traded by Islanders with LW Wendel Clark and D D.J. Smith to Toronto Maple Leafs for LW Sean Haggerty, C Darby Hendrickson, D Kenny Jonsson and first-round pick (G Roberto Luongo) in 1997 draft (March 13, 1996). ... Suspended three games for elbowing incident (November 14, 1996). ... Strained groin (December 12, 1996); missed 27 games. ... Reinjured groin (February 12, 1997) and had surgery; and missed final 26 games of season. ... Concussion and facial cuts (December 2, 1997); missed two games. ... Bruised shoulder (January 6, 1998); missed two games. ... Strained upper abdominal muscle (February 2, 1998); missed one game. ... Strained groin (April 6, 1998); missed one game. ... Traded by Maple Leafs to New York Rangers for D Alexander Karpovtsev and fourth-round pick (LW Mirko Murovic) in 1999 draft (October 14, 1998). ... Flu (January 27, 2000); missed one game. ... Flu (March 26, 2000); missed one game. ... Selected by Columbus Blue Jackets in expansion draft (June 23, 2000). ... Signed as free agent by Los Angeles Kings (August 13, 2000). ... Strained back (November 16, 2000); missed one game. ... Strained groin (February 23, 2001); missed eight games. ... Hernia (November 9, 2001); missed 23 games. ... Strained left shoulder (January 28, 2002); missed two games. ... Traded by Kings to Detroit Red Wings for C Sean Avery, D Maxim Kuznetsov, first-round pick (RW Jeff Tambellini) in 2003 draft and second-round pick in 2004 draft (March 11, 2003). ... Suspended two games for high-sticking incident (January 10, 2004). ... Strained groin (March 21, 2004); missed two games. ... Signed as free agent by Red Wings (Aug. 3, 2005).

		REGULAR SEASON								PLAYOFFS				
Season Team	League	GP	G	A	Pts.	PIM	+/-	PP	SH	GP	G	A	Pts.	PIM
85-86—Mt. St. Charles H.S.	R.I.H.S.	19	3	27	30	...	...	...	...	—	—	—	—	—
86-87—Cornwall	OHL	63	7	29	36	75	...	...	...	5	0	0	0	22
87-88—Montreal	NHL	4	0	0	0	2	-2	0	0	—	—	—	—	—
—Cornwall	OHL	48	21	40	61	85	...	...	...	11	2	6	8	14
—Sherbrooke	AHL	...	...	...	...	...	...	...	...	3	0	3	3	12
88-89—Cornwall	OHL	59	16	57	73	96	...	...	...	18	7	20	27	30
89-90—Sherbrooke	AHL	28	6	13	19	20	...	...	...	—	—	—	—	—
—Montreal	NHL	44	7	14	21	25	2	5	0	9	1	3	4	31
90-91—Montreal	NHL	69	10	20	30	63	7	5	0	13	2	7	9	18
91-92—Montreal	NHL	78	8	24	32	72	10	2	0	10	1	4	5	6
92-93—Montreal	NHL	60	13	31	44	91	8	3	0	11	1	2	3	16
93-94—Montreal	NHL	75	20	32	52	62	15	11	0	1	0	0	0	0
94-95—Montreal	NHL	30	5	15	20	49	-3	2	0	—	—	—	—	—
—New York Islanders	NHL	13	3	6	9	30	-5	1	0	—	—	—	—	—
95-96—New York Islanders	NHL	65	11	36	47	93	-18	7	0	—	—	—	—	—
—Toronto	NHL	13	2	5	7	10	-2	0	0	6	0	4	4	8
96-97—Toronto	NHL	26	5	7	12	20	3	1	0	—	—	—	—	—
97-98—Toronto	NHL	76	11	26	37	44	-12	4	1	—	—	—	—	—
—U.S. Olympic team	Int'l	4	0	0	0	6	-1	0	0	—	—	—	—	—
98-99—New York Rangers	NHL	75	10	24	34	71	-19	5	0	—	—	—	—	—
99-00—New York Rangers	NHL	80	10	20	30	78	-6	3	0	—	—	—	—	—
00-01—Los Angeles	NHL	73	16	35	51	56	0	7	1	13	0	9	9	10
01-02—Los Angeles	NHL	55	7	23	30	68	3	4	0	7	0	1	1	18
02-03—Los Angeles	NHL	65	14	29	43	57	0	10	0	—	—	—	—	—
—Detroit	NHL	13	2	5	7	16	2	1	0	4	0	0	0	6
03-04—Detroit	NHL	78	14	32	46	56	22	4	1	12	1	2	3	8
NHL Totals (16 years)		992	168	384	552	963	5	75	3	86	6	32	38	121

SCHREMP, ROB — C — OILERS

PERSONAL: Born July 1, 1986, in Syracuse, N.Y. ... 5-11/197. ... Shoots left.

TRANSACTIONS/CAREER NOTES: Selected by Edmonton Oilers in first round (second Oilers pick, 25th overall) of NHL entry draft (June 26, 2004).

		REGULAR SEASON								PLAYOFFS				
Season Team	League	GP	G	A	Pts.	PIM	+/-	PP	SH	GP	G	A	Pts.	PIM
02-03—Mississauga	OHL	65	26	48	74	25	...	...	...	2	1	0	1	0
03-04—Mississauga	OHL	3	2	4	6	0	...	...	...	—	—	—	—	—
—London	OHL	60	28	41	69	18	...	...	...	15	7	6	13	2
04-05—London	OHL	41	41	49	90	54	36	23	0	18	13	16	29	16

SCHUBERT, CHRISTOPH — D — SENATORS

PERSONAL: Born February 5, 1982, in Munich, West Germany. ... 6-1/186. ... Shoots left. ... Name pronounced SHOO-buhrt.

TRANSACTIONS/CAREER NOTES: Selected by Ottawa Senators in fourth round (fifth Senators pick, 127th overall) of NHL entry draft (June 23, 2001).

Season Team	League	REGULAR SEASON								PLAYOFFS				
		GP	G	A	Pts.	PIM	+/-	PP	SH	GP	G	A	Pts.	PIM
00-01—Munchen	Ger. Div. II	55	6	3	9	80	...	...	...	—	—	—	—	—
01-02—Munich	Germany	50	5	11	16	125	...	...	...	9	3	4	7	32
—German Oly. team	Int'l	7	0	1	1	6	...	...	...	—	—	—	—	—
02-03—Binghamton	AHL	70	2	8	10	102	18	0	0	8	0	1	1	2
03-04—Binghamton	AHL	70	2	10	12	69	-9	0	0	1	0	0	0	0
04-05—Binghamton	AHL	76	10	22	32	110	24	2	1	6	2	2	4	20

SCHULTZ, JEFF D CAPITALS

PERSONAL: Born February 25, 1986, in Calgary. ... 6-6/212. ... Shoots left.
TRANSACTIONS/CAREER NOTES: Selected by Washington Capitals in first round (second Capitals pick, 27th overall) of NHL entry draft (June 26, 2004).

Season Team	League	REGULAR SEASON								PLAYOFFS				
		GP	G	A	Pts.	PIM	+/-	PP	SH	GP	G	A	Pts.	PIM
02-03—Calgary	WHL	50	2	1	3	4	...	...	...	4	0	0	0	0
03-04—Calgary	WHL	72	11	24	35	33	...	...	...	7	1	1	2	0
04-05—Calgary	WHL	72	2	27	29	31	-7	1	1	12	2	1	3	6

SCHULTZ, NICK D WILD

PERSONAL: Born August 25, 1982, in Strasbourg, Sask. ... 6-1/207. ... Shoots left.
TRANSACTIONS/CAREER NOTES: Bruised shoulder (February 6, 2002); missed one game.

Season Team	League	REGULAR SEASON								PLAYOFFS				
		GP	G	A	Pts.	PIM	+/-	PP	SH	GP	G	A	Pts.	PIM
98-99—Prince Albert	WHL	58	5	10	15	37	...	...	...	—	—	—	—	—
99-00—Prince Albert	WHL	72	11	33	44	38	...	...	...	6	0	3	3	2
00-01—Prince Albert	WHL	59	17	30	47	120	...	...	...	—	—	—	—	—
—Cleveland	IHL	4	1	1	2	2	...	...	...	3	0	1	1	0
01-02—Minnesota	NHL	52	4	6	10	14	0	1	0	—	—	—	—	—
—Houston	AHL	0	0	0	0	0	0	0	0	14	1	5	6	2
02-03—Minnesota	NHL	75	3	7	10	23	11	0	0	18	0	1	1	10
03-04—Minnesota	NHL	79	6	10	16	16	12	1	0	—	—	—	—	—
04-05—Kassel	Germany	46	7	15	22	26	-15	3	0	7	0	4	4	6
NHL Totals (3 years)		206	13	23	36	53	23	2	0	18	0	1	1	10

SCHULTZ, RAY D DEVILS

PERSONAL: Born November 14, 1976, in Red Deer, Alta. ... 6-2/208. ... Shoots left. ... Cousin of Rene Chapdelaine, D with Los Angeles Kings (1990-91 through 1992-93).
TRANSACTIONS/CAREER NOTES: Selected by Ottawa Senators in eighth round (eighth Senators pick, 184th overall) of NHL entry draft (July 8, 1995). ... Signed as free agent by New York Islanders (June 17, 1997). ... Signed as free agent by Nashville Predators (July 17, 2003). ... Signed as free agent by New Jersey Devils (August 17, 2004).

Season Team	League	REGULAR SEASON								PLAYOFFS				
		GP	G	A	Pts.	PIM	+/-	PP	SH	GP	G	A	Pts.	PIM
93-94—Tri-City	WHL	3	0	0	0	11	...	...	...	—	—	—	—	—
94-95—Tri-City	WHL	63	1	8	9	209	16	1	0	11	0	0	0	16
95-96—Calgary	WHL	66	3	17	20	282	...	...	...	—	—	—	—	—
96-97—Calgary	WHL	32	3	17	20	141	-8	2	0	—	—	—	—	—
—Kelowna	WHL	23	3	11	14	63	24	1	0	6	0	2	2	12
97-98—Kentucky	AHL	51	2	4	6	179	6	1	0	1	0	0	0	25
—New York Islanders	NHL	13	0	1	1	45	3	0	0	—	—	—	—	—
98-99—Lowell	AHL	54	0	3	3	184	-3	0	0	1	0	0	0	4
—New York Islanders	NHL	4	0	0	0	7	-2	0	0	—	—	—	—	—
99-00—Kansas City	IHL	65	5	5	10	208	...	...	...	—	—	—	—	—
—New York Islanders	NHL	9	0	1	1	30	1	0	0	—	—	—	—	—
00-01—Lowell	AHL	13	0	1	1	33	...	...	...	—	—	—	—	—
—Cleveland	IHL	44	3	5	8	127	...	...	...	3	1	0	1	16
—New York Islanders	NHL	13	0	2	2	40	-1	0	0	—	—	—	—	—
01-02—Bridgeport	AHL	69	0	15	15	205	21	0	0	19	1	3	4	18
—New York Islanders	NHL	2	0	0	0	5	-1	0	0	2	0	0	0	2
02-03—New York Islanders	NHL	4	0	0	0	28	-1	0	0	—	—	—	—	—
—Bridgeport	AHL	51	2	8	10	105	7	0	0	9	1	0	1	14
03-04—Milwaukee	AHL	73	2	10	12	153	24	1	0	22	1	2	3	31
04-05—Albany	AHL	77	5	14	19	227	-3	0	0	—	—	—	—	—
NHL Totals (6 years)		45	0	4	4	155	-1	0	0	2	0	0	0	2

SCHWAB, COREY G

PERSONAL: Born November 4, 1970, in North Battleford, Sask. ... 6-0/180. ... Catches left. ... Name pronounced SHWAHB.
TRANSACTIONS/CAREER NOTES: Selected by New Jersey Devils in 10th round (12th Devils pick, 200th overall) of NHL draft (June 16, 1990). ... Injured groin (October 12, 1995); missed six games. ... Traded by Devils to Tampa Bay Lightning for G Jeff Reese and second-(LW Pierre Dagenais) and eighth-(RW Jason Bertsch) round picks in 1996 draft (June 22, 1996). ... Injured groin (January 9, 1997); missed one game. ... Injured groin (December 23, 1997); missed one game. ... Injured ankle (December 31, 1997); missed remainder of season. ... Selected by Atlanta Thrashers in NHL expansion draft (June 25, 1999). ... Traded by Thrashers to Vancouver Canucks for fourth-round pick (Carl Mallette)

in 2000 draft (October 29, 1999). ... Signed as free agent by Toronto Maple Leafs (October 1, 2001). ... Signed as free agent by Devils (July 8, 2002). ... Viral infection (December 10, 2002); missed two games. ... Bruised shoulder (March 27, 2003); missed four games. ... Injured groin (November 19, 2003); missed seven games. ... Aggravated groin injury (December 10, 2003); missed three games. ... Reinjured groin (December 29, 2003); missed seven games. ... Reinjured groin (January 20, 2004) and had surgery; missed remainder of regular season.

		REGULAR SEASON									PLAYOFFS							
Season Team	**League**	**GP**	**Min.**	**W**	**L**	**T**	**GA**	**SO**	**GAA**	**SV%**	**GP**	**Min.**	**W**	**L**	**GA**	**SO**	**GAA**	**SV%**
88-89—Seattle	WHL	10	386	2	2	0	31	0	4.82	...	—	—	—	—	—	—	—	—
89-90—Seattle	WHL	27	1150	15	2	1	69	0	3.60	...	3	49	0	0	2	0	2.45	...
90-91—Seattle	WHL	58	3289	32	18	3	224	1	4.09	...	6	382	1	5	25	0	3.93	...
91-92—Utica	AHL	24	1322	9	12	1	95	1	4.31	...	—	—	—	—	—	—	—	—
—Cincinnati	AHL	8	450	6	0	1	31	0	4.13	...	9	540	6	3	29	0	3.22	...
92-93—Cincinnati	IHL	3	185	1	2	0	17	0	5.51	...	—	—	—	—	—	—	—	—
—Utica	AHL	40	2387	18	16	5	169	2	4.25	...	1	59	0	1	6	0	6.10	...
93-94—Albany	AHL	51	3059	27	21	3	184	0	3.61	.887	5	298	1	4	20	0	4.03	.880
94-95—Albany	AHL	45	2711	25	10	9	117	3	*2.59	.906	7	425	6	1	19	0	2.68	.904
95-96—Albany	AHL	5	298	3	2	0	13	0	2.62	...	—	—	—	—	—	—	—	—
—New Jersey	NHL	10	331	0	3	0	12	0	2.18	.899	—	—	—	—	—	—	—	—
96-97—Tampa Bay	NHL	31	1462	11	12	1	74	2	3.04	.897	—	—	—	—	—	—	—	—
97-98—Tampa Bay	NHL	16	821	2	9	1	40	1	2.92	.892	—	—	—	—	—	—	—	—
98-99—Cleveland	IHL	8	477	1	6	1	31	0	3.90	.885	—	—	—	—	—	—	—	—
—Tampa Bay	NHL	40	2146	8	25	3	126	0	3.52	.891	—	—	—	—	—	—	—	—
99-00—Orlando	IHL	16	868	13	4	2	31	1	2.14	...	—	—	—	—	—	—	—	—
—Vancouver	NHL	6	269	2	1	1	16	0	3.57	.861	—	—	—	—	—	—	—	—
—Syracuse	AHL	12	720	7	5	0	42	0	3.50	...	4	246	1	3	11	1	2.68	...
00-01—Kansas City	IHL	50	2866	22	24	1	150	2	3.14	...	—	—	—	—	—	—	—	—
01-02—Toronto	NHL	30	1646	12	10	5	75	1	2.73	.894	1	12	0	0	0	0	0.00	1.00
02-03—New Jersey	NHL	11	614	5	3	1	15	1	1.47	.933	2	28	0	0	0	0	0.00	1.00
03-04—New Jersey	NHL	3	187	2	0	1	2	1	0.64	.971	—	—	—	—	—	—	—	—
NHL Totals (8 years)		147	7476	42	63	13	360	6	2.89	.896	3	40	0	0	0	0	0.00	1.00

SCHWARZ, MAREK G BLUES

PERSONAL: Born April 1, 1986, in Boleslav, Czech. ... 6-0/180. ... Catches right.
TRANSACTIONS/CAREER NOTES: Selected by St. Louis Blues in first round (first Blues pick, 17th overall) of NHL entry draft (June 26, 2004).

		REGULAR SEASON									PLAYOFFS							
Season Team	**League**	**GP**	**Min.**	**W**	**L**	**T**	**GA**	**SO**	**GAA**	**SV%**	**GP**	**Min.**	**W**	**L**	**GA**	**SO**	**GAA**	**SV%**
03-04—Trinec	Czech Rep.	5	280	3	2	0	12	0	2.57	.931	—	—	—	—	—	—	—	—
—Plzen	Czech Rep.	10	603	4	5	1	33	0	3.28	.922	—	—	—	—	—	—	—	—
—Sparta Praha	Czech Rep.	8	335	1	6	1	20	0	3.58	.896	—	—	—	—	—	—	—	—
04-05—Vancouver	WHL	56	3304	26	24	4	147	2	2.67	.900	6	378	2	4	18	0	2.86	.900

SCOTT, RICHARD RW

PERSONAL: Born August 1, 1978, in Orillia, Ontario. ... 6-2/210. ... Shoots right.
TRANSACTIONS/CAREER NOTES: Signed as free agent by New York Rangers (May 8, 2001). ... Suffered concussion (December 7, 2003); missed remainder of season.

		REGULAR SEASON								PLAYOFFS				
Season Team	**League**	**GP**	**G**	**A**	**Pts.**	**PIM**	**+/-**	**PP**	**SH**	**GP**	**G**	**A**	**Pts.**	**PIM**
96-97—Orillia	OPJHL	10	0	0	0	23	...	...	...	—	—	—	—	—
97-98—Couchiching	OPJHL	45	13	19	32	166	...	...	...	—	—	—	—	—
98-99—Oshawa	OHL	54	12	12	24	193	...	...	...	—	—	—	—	—
99-00—Charlotte	ECHL	55	1	5	6	317	...	...	...	—	—	—	—	—
00-01—Hartford	AHL	64	2	5	7	320	...	...	...	1	0	0	0	0
—Charlotte	ECHL	4	1	1	2	22	...	...	...	—	—	—	—	—
01-02—Hartford	AHL	39	2	3	5	211	0	0	0	—	—	—	—	—
—New York Rangers	NHL	5	0	0	0	5	0	0	0	—	—	—	—	—
02-03—Charlotte	ECHL	3	0	1	1	4	-2	0	0	—	—	—	—	—
—Hartford	AHL	32	0	5	5	150	-1	0	0	2	0	0	0	16
03-04—New York Rangers	NHL	5	0	0	0	23	0	0	0	—	—	—	—	—
—Hartford	AHL	15	2	2	4	79	1	1	1	—	—	—	—	—
NHL Totals (2 years)		10	0	0	0	28	0	0	0					

SCOTT, TRAVIS G PANTHERS

PERSONAL: Born September 14, 1975, in Kanata, Ont. ... 6-2/185. ... Catches left.
TRANSACTIONS/CAREER NOTES: Signed as free agent by St. Louis Blues (December 30, 1996). ... Signed as free agent by Los Angeles Kings (February 18, 2000). ... Signed as free agent by Florida Panthers (August 12, 2003). ... Signed as free agent by San Antonio of the AHL (September 26, 2004).

		REGULAR SEASON									PLAYOFFS							
Season Team	**League**	**GP**	**Min.**	**W**	**L**	**T**	**GA**	**SO**	**GAA**	**SV%**	**GP**	**Min.**	**W**	**L**	**GA**	**SO**	**GAA**	**SV%**
91-92—Smiths Falls-Nepean	Jr. A	22	1151	...	...	...	90	1	4.69	...	—	—	—	—	—	—	—	—
92-93—Nepean	COJHL	36	1968	...	...	...	133	0	4.05	...	—	—	—	—	—	—	—	—
93-94—Windsor	OHL	45	2312	20	18	0	158	1	4.10	...	4	240	0	4	16	0	4.00	...
94-95—Windsor	OHL	48	2644	26	14	3	147	*3	3.34	...	3	94	0	1	6	1	3.83	...
95-96—Oshawa	OHL	31	1763	15	9	4	78	3	*2.65	...	5	315	1	4	23	0	4.38	...

Season Team	League	REGULAR SEASON GP	Min.	W	L	T	GA	SO	GAA	SV%	PLAYOFFS GP	Min.	W	L	GA	SO	GAA	SV%
96-97—Baton Rouge	ECHL	10	501	5	2	1	22	0	2.63	...	—	—	—	—	—	—	—	—
—Worcester	AHL	29	1482	14	10	1	75	1	3.04	.911	—	—	—	—	—	—	—	—
97-98—Baton Rouge	ECHL	36	1949	14	11	6	96	1	2.96	...	—	—	—	—	—	—	—	—
98-99—Mississippi	ECHL	44	2337	22	12	5	112	1	2.88	.908	18	*1252	*14	4	42	3	2.01	.934
99-00—Lowell	AHL	46	2595	15	23	3	126	3	2.91	...	1	60	0	1	2	0	2.00	...
00-01—Lowell	AHL	34	1977	16	15	1	83	2	2.52	.921	4	209	1	2	7	1	2.01	...
—Los Angeles	NHL	1	25	0	0	0	3	0	7.20	.700	—	—	—	—	—	—	—	—
01-02—Manchester	AHL	39	2169	21	12	3	83	6	2.30	.924	5	326	2	3	15	0	2.76	.911
02-03—Manchester	AHL	50	2829	23	19	5	116	4	2.46	.921	3	147	0	2	9	0	3.67	.886
03-04—San Antonio	AHL	64	3746	26	31	6	156	4	2.50	.918	—	—	—	—	—	—	—	—
04-05—San Antonio	AHL	59	3211	18	28	...	126	3	2.35	.931	—	—	—	—	—	—	—	—
NHL Totals (1 year)		1	25	0	0	0	3	0	7.20	.700								

SCOVILLE, DARREL — D — BLUE JACKETS

PERSONAL: Born October 13, 1975, in Swift Current, Sask. ... 6-3/208. ... Shoots left.
TRANSACTIONS/CAREER NOTES: Signed as free agent by Calgary Flames (June 12, 1998). ... Signed as free agent by Columbus Blue Jackets (July 10, 2001).

Season Team	League	REGULAR SEASON GP	G	A	Pts.	PIM	+/-	PP	SH	PLAYOFFS GP	G	A	Pts.	PIM
95-96—Merrimack	Hockey East	34	6	20	26	54	...	...	...	—	—	—	—	—
96-97—Merrimack	Hockey East	35	7	16	23	71	...	...	...	—	—	—	—	—
97-98—Merrimack	Hockey East	38	4	26	30	84	...	...	...	—	—	—	—	—
98-99—Saint John	AHL	61	1	7	8	66	...	...	...	7	1	2	3	13
99-00—Saint John	AHL	64	11	25	36	99	...	...	...	3	1	2	3	0
—Calgary	NHL	6	0	0	0	2	1	0	0	—	—	—	—	—
00-01—Saint John	AHL	76	17	32	49	125	...	...	...	19	3	7	10	12
01-02—Syracuse	AHL	51	5	16	21	60	11	2	1	10	0	0	0	6
02-03—Syracuse	AHL	24	4	9	13	26	-9	0	0	—	—	—	—	—
—Columbus	NHL	2	0	0	0	4	0	0	0	—	—	—	—	—
03-04—Columbus	NHL	8	0	1	1	6	-4	0	0	—	—	—	—	—
—Syracuse	AHL	70	10	32	42	73	-11	4	0	6	0	2	2	4
04-05—Hershey	AHL	7	0	0	0	11	-7	0	0	—	—	—	—	—
—Providence	AHL	43	1	6	7	26	1	0	0	0	0	0	0	0
NHL Totals (3 years)		16	0	1	1	12	-3	0	0					

SCUDERI, ROBERT — D — PENGUINS

PERSONAL: Born December 30, 1978, in Syosset, N.Y. ... 6-0/214. ... Shoots left. ... Name pronounced SKUD-uhree.
TRANSACTIONS/CAREER NOTES: Selected by Pittsburgh Penguins in fifth round (fifth Penguins pick, 134th overall) of NHL entry draft (June 27, 1998). ... Signed as free agent by Wilkes-Barre/Scranton of the AHL (September 26, 2004).

Season Team	League	REGULAR SEASON GP	G	A	Pts.	PIM	+/-	PP	SH	PLAYOFFS GP	G	A	Pts.	PIM
96-97—NY AppleCore	Jr. B	80	42	70	112	52	...	...	...	—	—	—	—	—
97-98—Boston College	Hockey East	42	0	24	24	12	...	...	...	—	—	—	—	—
98-99—Boston College	Hockey East	41	2	8	10	20	...	...	...	—	—	—	—	—
99-00—Boston College	Hockey East	42	1	13	14	24	...	...	...	—	—	—	—	—
00-01—Boston College	Hockey East	43	4	19	23	42	...	...	...	—	—	—	—	—
01-02—Wilkes-Barre/Scranton	AHL	75	1	22	23	66	-4	1	0	—	—	—	—	—
02-03—Wilkes-Barre/Scranton	AHL	74	4	17	21	44	5	2	0	6	0	1	1	4
03-04—Pittsburgh	NHL	13	1	2	3	4	2	0	0	6	0	1	1	4
—Wilkes-Barre/Scranton	AHL	64	1	15	16	44	1	0	0	24	0	3	3	14
04-05—Wilkes-Barre/Scranton	AHL	79	2	18	20	34	15	0	0	11	2	1	3	2
NHL Totals (1 year)		13	1	2	3	4	2	0	0	6	0	1	1	4

SEABROOK, BRENT — D — BLACKHAWKS

PERSONAL: Born April 20, 1985, in Richmond, B.C. ... 6-3/220. ... Shoots right.
TRANSACTIONS/CAREER NOTES: Selected by Chicago Blackhawks in first round (first Blackhawks pick, 14th overall) in 2003 NHL entry draft (June 23, 2003).

Season Team	League	REGULAR SEASON GP	G	A	Pts.	PIM	+/-	PP	SH	PLAYOFFS GP	G	A	Pts.	PIM
00-01—Lethbridge	WHL	4	0	0	0	0	...	...	...	—	—	—	—	—
01-02—Lethbridge	WHL	67	6	33	39	70	...	...	...	4	1	1	2	2
02-03—Lethbridge	WHL	69	9	33	42	113	...	...	...	—	—	—	—	—
03-04—Lethbridge	WHL	61	12	29	41	107	...	...	...	—	—	—	—	—
04-05—Norfolk	AHL	3	0	0	0	2	-3	0	0	6	0	1	1	6
—Lethbridge	WHL	63	12	42	54	107	25	7	0	5	1	2	3	10

SEDIN, DANIEL — LW — CANUCKS

PERSONAL: Born September 26, 1980, in Ornskoldsvik, Sweden. ... 6-1/190. ... Shoots left. ... Twin brother of Henrik Sedin, C, Vancouver Canucks.
TRANSACTIONS/CAREER NOTES: Selected by Vancouver Canucks in first round (first Canucks pick, second overall) of NHL draft (June 26,

1999). ... Strained shoulder (November 30, 2000); missed four games. ... Injured back (March 25, 2001); missed two games. ... Reinjured back (April 2, 2001); missed one game. ... Sprained knee (December 19, 2001); missed two games.
STATISTICAL PLATEAUS: Four-goal games: 2003-04 (1).

		REGULAR SEASON								PLAYOFFS				
Season Team	**League**	**GP**	**G**	**A**	**Pts.**	**PIM**	**+/-**	**PP**	**SH**	**GP**	**G**	**A**	**Pts.**	**PIM**
96-97—MoDo Ornskoldsvik....	Sweden Jr.	26	26	14	40	...	...	...	...	—	—	—	—	—
97-98—MoDo Ornskoldsvik....	Sweden	45	4	8	12	26	...	...	...	9	0	0	0	2
—MoDo Ornskoldsvik....	Sweden Jr.	4	3	3	6	4	...	...	...	—	—	—	—	—
98-99—MoDo Ornskoldsvik....	Sweden	50	21	21	42	20	...	...	...	13	4	8	12	14
99-00—MoDo Ornskoldsvik....	Sweden	50	19	26	45	28	...	...	...	13	8	6	14	18
00-01—Vancouver..................	NHL	75	20	14	34	24	-3	10	0	4	1	2	3	0
01-02—Vancouver..................	NHL	79	9	23	32	32	1	4	0	6	0	1	1	0
02-03—Vancouver..................	NHL	79	14	17	31	34	8	4	0	14	1	5	6	8
03-04—Vancouver..................	NHL	82	18	36	54	18	18	1	0	7	1	2	3	0
04-05—MoDo Ornskoldsvik....	Sweden	49	13	20	33	40	5	4	1	6	0	3	3	6
NHL Totals (4 years)...........		315	61	90	151	108	24	19	0	31	3	10	13	8

SEDIN, HENRIK — C — CANUCKS

PERSONAL: Born September 26, 1980, in Ornskoldsvik, Sweden. ... 6-2/192. ... Shoots left. ... Twin brother of Daniel Sedin, LW, Vancouver Canucks.
TRANSACTIONS/CAREER NOTES: Selected by Vancouver Canucks in first round (second Canucks pick, third overall) of NHL draft (June 26, 1999). ... Injured shoulder (December 12, 2002); missed three games. ... Injured hand (February 25, 2003); missed one game. ... Strained abdominal muscle (March 13, 2004); missed four games.

		REGULAR SEASON								PLAYOFFS				
Season Team	**League**	**GP**	**G**	**A**	**Pts.**	**PIM**	**+/-**	**PP**	**SH**	**GP**	**G**	**A**	**Pts.**	**PIM**
96-97—MoDo Ornskoldsvik....	Sweden Jr.	26	14	22	36	...	...	...	...	—	—	—	—	—
97-98—MoDo Ornskoldsvik....	Sweden Jr.	8	4	7	11	6	...	...	...	—	—	—	—	—
—MoDo Ornskoldsvik....	Sweden	39	1	4	5	8	...	...	...	7	0	0	0	0
98-99—MoDo Ornskoldsvik....	Sweden	49	12	22	34	32	...	...	...	13	2	8	10	6
99-00—MoDo Ornskoldsvik....	Sweden	50	9	38	47	22	...	...	...	13	5	9	14	2
00-01—Vancouver..................	NHL	82	9	20	29	38	-2	2	0	4	0	4	4	0
01-02—Vancouver..................	NHL	82	16	20	36	36	9	3	0	6	3	0	3	0
02-03—Vancouver..................	NHL	78	8	31	39	38	9	4	1	14	3	2	5	8
03-04—Vancouver..................	NHL	76	11	31	42	32	23	2	0	7	2	2	4	2
04-05—MoDo Ornskoldsvik....	Sweden	44	14	22	36	50	9	4	1	6	1	3	4	6
NHL Totals (4 years)...........		318	44	102	146	144	39	11	1	31	8	8	16	10

SEELEY, RICHARD — D — ISLANDERS

PERSONAL: Born April 30, 1979, in Powell River, B.C. ... 6-2/205. ... Shoots left.
TRANSACTIONS/CAREER NOTES: Selected by Los Angeles Kings in sixth round (sixth Kings pick, 137th overall) of NHL entry draft (June 21, 1997). ... Signed as free agent by New York Islanders (August 12, 2004).

		REGULAR SEASON								PLAYOFFS				
Season Team	**League**	**GP**	**G**	**A**	**Pts.**	**PIM**	**+/-**	**PP**	**SH**	**GP**	**G**	**A**	**Pts.**	**PIM**
95-96—Powell River	BCJHL	44	1	8	9	42	...	...	...	—	—	—	—	—
96-97—Lethbridge	WHL	3	0	0	0	11	...	...	...	—	—	—	—	—
—Prince Albert..............	WHL	18	0	1	1	9	...	...	...	4	0	0	0	2
97-98—Prince Albert..............	WHL	65	8	21	29	114	-3	2	0	—	—	—	—	—
98-99—Prince Albert..............	WHL	61	10	48	58	110	34	3	1	14	1	11	12	14
99-00—Lowell	AHL	36	5	1	6	37	...	...	...	—	—	—	—	—
00-01—Lowell	AHL	55	2	8	10	102	...	...	...	—	—	—	—	—
—Trenton	ECHL	9	0	2	2	18	...	...	...	—	—	—	—	—
01-02—Manchester................	AHL	61	2	10	12	78	5	0	0	5	0	0	0	6
02-03—Manchester................	AHL	69	4	14	18	127	9	2	0	3	0	1	1	0
04-05—Bridgeport..................	AHL	47	2	6	8	108	6	0	0	—	—	—	—	—
—Norfolk.......................	AHL	12	0	0	0	17	1	0	0	6	1	0	1	8

SEIDENBERG, DENNIS — D — FLYERS

PERSONAL: Born July 18, 1981, in Schwenningen, West Germany. ... 6-0/200. ... Shoots left. ... Name pronounced ZIGH-dehn-buhrg.
TRANSACTIONS/CAREER NOTES: Selected by Philadelphia Flyers in sixth round (sixth Flyers pick, 172nd overall) of NHL entry draft (June 24, 2001). ... Fractured leg (January 15, 2004); missed remained of regular season.

		REGULAR SEASON								PLAYOFFS				
Season Team	**League**	**GP**	**G**	**A**	**Pts.**	**PIM**	**+/-**	**PP**	**SH**	**GP**	**G**	**A**	**Pts.**	**PIM**
01-02—Mannheim..................	Germany	55	7	13	20	56	...	...	...	8	0	0	0	2
02-03—Philadelphia	AHL	19	5	6	11	17	-7	1	0	—	—	—	—	—
—Philadelphia	NHL	58	4	9	13	20	8	1	0	—	—	—	—	—
03-04—Philadelphia	NHL	5	0	0	0	2	-4	0	0	3	0	0	0	0
—Philadelphia	AHL	33	7	12	19	31	11	2	0	9	2	2	4	4
04-05—Philadelphia	AHL	79	13	28	41	47	18	6	0	18	2	8	10	19
NHL Totals (2 years)...........		63	4	9	13	22	4	1	0	3	0	0	0	0

SEJNA, PETER — LW — BLUES

PERSONAL: Born October 5, 1979, in Liptovsky Mikulas, Czech. ... 5-10/197. ... Shoots left. ... Name pronounced SHAY-nah.
TRANSACTIONS/CAREER NOTES: Signed as free agent by St. Louis Blues (April 6, 2003).

		REGULAR SEASON								PLAYOFFS				
Season Team	League	GP	G	A	Pts.	PIM	+/-	PP	SH	GP	G	A	Pts.	PIM
98-99—Des Moines	USHL	52	40	23	63	26	...	...	...	14	11	6	17	8
99-00—Des Moines	USHL	58	41	53	94	36	...	...	...	9	4	5	9	4
00-01—Colorado College	WCHA	41	29	29	58	10	...	...	...	—	—	—	—	—
01-02—Colorado College	WCHA	43	26	24	50	16	...	...	...	—	—	—	—	—
02-03—St. Louis	NHL	1	1	0	1	0	0	1	0	—	—	—	—	—
—Colorado College	WCHA	42	36	46	82	12	...	...	...	—	—	—	—	—
03-04—St. Louis	NHL	20	2	2	4	4	-9	2	0	—	—	—	—	—
—Worcester	AHL	59	12	29	41	13	8	5	1	10	3	3	6	10
04-05—Worcester	AHL	64	17	21	38	24	3	1	5	—	—	—	—	—
NHL Totals (2 years)		21	3	2	5	4	-9	3	0					

SEKERAS, LUBOMIR — D

PERSONAL: Born November 18, 1968, in Trencin, Czechoslovakia. ... 6-0/183. ... Shoots left. ... Name pronounced SEH-kuhr-ahsh.
TRANSACTIONS/CAREER NOTES: Selected by Minnesota Wild in 8th round (8th Wild pick, 232nd overall) of NHL draft (June 24, 2000). ... Bruised foot (January 10, 2001); missed one game. ... Flu (April 4, 2001); missed one game. ... Sprained right knee (October 30, 2001); missed seven games. ... Flu (April 8, 2002); missed remainder of season. ... Injured shoulder (November 4, 2002); missed four games. ... Signed as free agent by Dallas Stars (March 9, 2004).

		REGULAR SEASON								PLAYOFFS				
Season Team	League	GP	G	A	Pts.	PIM	+/-	PP	SH	GP	G	A	Pts.	PIM
88-89—Dukla Trencin	Czech.	16	2	5	7	22	...	...	...	11	0	4	4	0
89-90—Dukla Trencin	Czech.	44	6	8	14	...	...	...	...	9	0	2	2	...
90-91—Dukla Trencin	Czech.	52	6	16	22	...	...	...	...	6	0	1	1	...
91-92—Dukla Trencin	Czech.	30	2	6	8	32	...	...	...	13	1	1	2	0
92-93—Dukla Trencin	Czech.	40	5	19	24	48	...	...	...	11	4	9	13	0
93-94—Dukla Trencin	Slovakia	36	9	12	21	46	...	...	...	9	2	4	6	10
94-95—Dukla Trencin	Slovakia	36	11	11	22	24	...	...	...	9	2	7	9	8
95-96—Trinec	Czech Rep.	40	11	13	24	44	...	...	...	3	0	0	0	0
96-97—Trinec	Czech Rep.	52	14	21	35	56	...	...	...	4	1	0	1	2
97-98—Trinec	Czech Rep.	50	11	33	44	42	...	...	...	13	2	10	12	4
98-99—Trinec	Czech Rep.	50	8	15	23	38	...	...	...	10	2	6	8	...
99-00—Trinec	Czech Rep.	52	7	24	31	36	...	...	...	4	0	2	2	2
00-01—Minnesota	NHL	80	11	23	34	52	-8	4	0	—	—	—	—	—
01-02—Minnesota	NHL	69	4	20	24	38	-7	4	0	—	—	—	—	—
02-03—Minnesota	NHL	60	2	9	11	30	-12	1	0	15	1	1	2	6
03-04—Dallas	NHL	4	1	1	2	2	0	0	0	—	—	—	—	—
04-05—Nurnberg	Germany	52	4	27	31	48	15	2	0	6	0	1	1	4
NHL Totals (4 years)		213	18	53	71	122	-27	9	0	15	1	1	2	6

SELANNE, TEEMU — RW

PERSONAL: Born July 3, 1970, in Helsinki, Finland. ... 6-0/205. ... Shoots right. ... Name pronounced TAY-moo suh-LAH-nay. ... Nickname: The Finnish Flash.
TRANSACTIONS/CAREER NOTES: Selected by Winnipeg Jets in first round (first Jets pick, 10th overall) of NHL draft (June 11, 1988). ... Severed ankle tendon (January 26, 1994); missed 33 games. ... Patella tendonitis (February 28, 1995); missed one game. ... Suspended two games and fined $500 by NHL (March 28, 1995). ... Traded by Jets with C Marc Chouinard and fourth-round pick (traded to Toronto; traded to Montreal; Canadiens selected C Kim Staal) in 1996 draft to Anaheim Mighty Ducks for C Chad Kilger, D Oleg Tverdovsky and third-round pick (D Per-Anton Lundstrom) in 1996 draft (Febraury 7, 1996). ... Strained abdominal muscle (March 23, 1997); missed four games. ... Strained abdominal muscle (February 7, 1998); missed five games. ... Strained groin (April 9, 1998); missed final four games of season. ... Strained thigh muscle (November 11,1998); missed six games. ... Reinjured thigh muscle (December 3, 1998); missed one game. ... Strained groin (November 14, 1999); missed three games. ... Strained groin (December 13, 2000); missed two games. ... Strained groin (December 22, 2000); missed two games. ... Injured knee (March 1, 2001) and had surgery; missed five games. ... Traded by Mighty Ducks to San Jose Sharks for LW Jeff Friesen, G Steve Shields and second-round pick (LW Vojtech Polak) in 2003 draft (March 5, 2001). ... Signed as free agent by Colorado Avalanche (July 3, 2003). ... Injured knee (October 28, 2003); missed one game. ... Injured neck (January 11, 2004); missed one game.
STATISTICAL PLATEAUS: Three-goal games: 1992-93 (4), 1993-94 (2), 1995-96 (2), 1996-97 (1), 1997-98 (3), 1998-99 (1), 1999-00 (1), 2000-01 (2). Total: 16. ... Four-goal games: 1992-93 (1), 1995-96 (1). Total: 2. ... Total hat tricks: 18.

		REGULAR SEASON								PLAYOFFS				
Season Team	League	GP	G	A	Pts.	PIM	+/-	PP	SH	GP	G	A	Pts.	PIM
87-88—Jokerit Helsinki	Finland Jr.	33	43	23	66	18	...	...	...	5	4	3	7	2
—Jokerit Helsinki	Finland	5	1	1	2	0	...	...	...	—	—	—	—	—
88-89—Jokerit Helsinki	Finland	34	35	33	68	12	...	...	...	5	7	3	10	4
89-90—Jokerit Helsinki	Finland	11	4	8	12	0	...	...	...	—	—	—	—	—
90-91—Jokerit Helsinki	Finland	42	*33	25	58	12	...	...	...	—	—	—	—	—
91-92—Fin. Olympic team	Int'l	8	7	4	11	...	...	...	...	—	—	—	—	—
—Jokerit Helsinki	Finland	44	39	23	62	20	...	...	...	—	—	—	—	—
92-93—Winnipeg	NHL	84	76	56	132	45	8	24	0	6	4	2	6	2
93-94—Winnipeg	NHL	51	25	29	54	22	-23	11	0	—	—	—	—	—
94-95—Jokerit Helsinki	Finland	20	7	12	19	6	3	...	...	—	—	—	—	—
—Winnipeg	NHL	45	22	26	48	2	1	8	2	—	—	—	—	—
95-96—Winnipeg	NHL	51	24	48	72	18	3	6	1	—	—	—	—	—
—Anaheim	NHL	28	16	20	36	4	2	3	0	—	—	—	—	—

Season Team	League	REGULAR SEASON GP	G	A	Pts.	PIM	+/-	PP	SH	PLAYOFFS GP	G	A	Pts.	PIM
96-97—Anaheim	NHL	78	51	58	109	34	28	11	1	11	7	3	10	4
97-98—Anaheim	NHL	73	52	34	86	30	12	10	1	—	—	—	—	—
—Fin. Olympic team	Int'l	5	4	6	10	8	0	3	0	—	—	—	—	—
98-99—Anaheim	NHL	75	*47	60	107	30	18	*25	0	4	2	2	4	2
99-00—Anaheim	NHL	79	33	52	85	12	6	8	0	—	—	—	—	—
00-01—Anaheim	NHL	61	26	33	59	36	-8	10	0	—	—	—	—	—
—San Jose	NHL	12	7	6	13	0	1	2	0	6	0	2	2	2
01-02—San Jose	NHL	82	29	25	54	40	-11	9	1	12	5	3	8	2
—Fin. Olympic team	Int'l	4	3	0	3	2	...	...	...	—	—	—	—	—
02-03—San Jose	NHL	82	28	36	64	30	-6	7	0	—	—	—	—	—
03-04—Colorado	NHL	78	16	16	32	32	2	6	1	10	0	3	3	2
NHL Totals (12 years)		879	452	499	951	335	33	140	7	49	18	15	33	14

SEMENOV, ALEXEI — D — OILERS

PERSONAL: Born April 10, 1981, in Murmansk, U.S.S.R. ... 6-6/236. ... Shoots left. ... Name pronounced seh-MEH-nahv.

TRANSACTIONS/CAREER NOTES: Selected by Edmonton Oilers in second round (second Oilers pick, 36th overall) of entry draft (June 26, 1999). ... Injured shoulder (February 16, 2004); missed eight games.

Season Team	League	REGULAR SEASON GP	G	A	Pts.	PIM	+/-	PP	SH	PLAYOFFS GP	G	A	Pts.	PIM
97-98—Krylja Sovetov-2 Mos.	Rus. Div.	52	1	2	3	48	...	...	...	—	—	—	—	—
98-99—Sudbury	OHL	28	0	3	3	28	-11	0	0	2	0	0	0	4
99-00—Sudbury	OHL	65	9	35	44	135	21	6	1	12	1	3	4	23
—Hamilton	AHL	...	...	...	...	...	...	...	...	3	0	0	0	0
00-01—Sudbury	OHL	65	21	42	63	106	28	15	0	12	4	13	17	17
01-02—Hamilton	AHL	78	5	11	16	67	7	2	0	—	—	—	—	—
02-03—Hamilton	AHL	37	4	3	7	45	6	2	0	—	—	—	—	—
—Edmonton	NHL	46	1	6	7	58	-7	0	0	6	0	0	0	0
03-04—Edmonton	NHL	46	2	3	5	32	8	1	0	—	—	—	—	—
04-05—SKA St. Petersburg	Russian	50	0	8	8	26	-16	...	...	—	—	—	—	—
NHL Totals (2 years)		92	3	9	12	90	1	1	0	6	0	0	0	0

SEMIN, ALEXANDER — LW — CAPITALS

PERSONAL: Born March 3, 1984, in Krasjonarsk, U.S.S.R. ... 6-0/174. ... Shoots left. ... Name pronounced SEH-min.

TRANSACTIONS/CAREER NOTES: Selected by Washington Capitals in first round (second Capitals pick, 13th overall) of NHL draft (June 22, 2002). ... Suspended by Capitals for failing to report to Portland of the AHL (September 28, 2004).

Season Team	League	REGULAR SEASON GP	G	A	Pts.	PIM	+/-	PP	SH	PLAYOFFS GP	G	A	Pts.	PIM
01-02—Chelyabinsk	Russian Div. 1	46	13	8	21	52	...	...	...	—	—	—	—	—
02-03—Lada Togliatti	Russian	47	10	7	17	36	...	...	...	10	5	3	8	10
03-04—Washington	NHL	52	10	12	22	36	-2	4	0	—	—	—	—	—
—Portland	AHL	4	3	1	4	6	0	2	0	7	4	7	11	19
04-05—Lada Togliatti	Russian	50	19	11	30	56	15	...	...	10	1	1	2	0
NHL Totals (1 year)		52	10	12	22	36	-2	4	0					

SETOGUCHI, DEVIN — RW — SHARKS

PERSONAL: Born January 1, 1987, in Taber, Alta. ... 5-11/186. ... Shoots right.

TRANSACTIONS/CAREER NOTES: Selected by San Jose Sharks in 1st round (1st Sharks pick, 8th overall, obtained from Atlanta for 12th, 49th and 207th overall picks) of entry draft (July 30, 2005).

Season Team	League	REGULAR SEASON GP	G	A	Pts.	PIM	+/-	PP	SH	PLAYOFFS GP	G	A	Pts.	PIM
03-04—Saskatoon	WHL	66	13	18	31	53	...	...	...	—	—	—	—	—
04-05—Saskatoon	WHL	69	33	31	64	34	20	8	2	4	0	1	1	0

SEVERSON, CAM — LW — PREDATORS

PERSONAL: Born August 15, 1978, in Canora, Saskatchewan. ... 6-2/220. ... Shoots left.

TRANSACTIONS/CAREER NOTES: Selected by San Jose Sharks in eighth round (192nd overall) of NHL draft (June 21, 1997). ... Signed as free agent by Hartford of the AHL (September 24, 2001). ... Signed as free agent by Anaheim Mighty Ducks (August 22, 2002). ... Signed as free agent by Nashville Predators (July 22, 2004).

Season Team	League	REGULAR SEASON GP	G	A	Pts.	PIM	+/-	PP	SH	PLAYOFFS GP	G	A	Pts.	PIM
98-99—Spokane	WHL	46	16	17	33	190	-25	4	0	—	—	—	—	—
—Oklahoma City	CHL	5	6	3	9	4	...	...	...	10	4	0	4	26
99-00—Louisiana	ECHL	7	0	2	2	22	...	...	...	—	—	—	—	—
—Peoria	ECHL	56	19	8	27	138	...	...	...	18	3	4	7	41
00-01—Portland	AHL	8	0	0	0	11	...	...	...	—	—	—	—	—
—Cincinnati	AHL	20	4	7	11	60	...	...	...	3	1	1	2	0
01-02—Hartford	AHL	65	11	10	21	116	-3	2	0	5	0	0	0	7
02-03—Cincinnati	AHL	71	12	9	21	156	-2	0	0	—	—	—	—	—
—Anaheim	NHL	2	0	0	0	8	0	0	0	1	0	0	0	0

		REGULAR SEASON								PLAYOFFS				
Season Team	League	GP	G	A	Pts.	PIM	+/-	PP	SH	GP	G	A	Pts.	PIM
03-04—Anaheim	NHL	31	3	0	3	50	-3	1	0	—	—	—	—	—
—Cincinnati	AHL	38	7	7	14	143	-2	1	0	—	—	—	—	—
04-05—Milwaukee	AHL	63	6	8	14	255	-12	1	0	4	0	0	0	12
NHL Totals (2 years)		33	3	0	3	58	-3	1	0	1	0	0	0	0

SHANAHAN, BRENDAN — LW — RED WINGS

PERSONAL: Born January 23, 1969, in Mimico, Ont. ... 6-3/220. ... Shoots right.

TRANSACTIONS/CAREER NOTES: Selected by New Jersey Devils in first round (first Devils pick, second overall) of NHL draft (June 13, 1987). ... Fractured nose (December 1987). ... Back spasms (March 1989). ... Suspended five games for stick-swinging incident (January 13, 1990). ... Lower abdominal strain (February 1990). ... Facial lacerations (January 8, 1991), underwent surgery; missed five games. ... Signed as free agent by St. Louis Blues (July 25, 1991); D Scott Stevens awarded to Devils as compensation (September 3, 1991). ... Pulled groin (October 24, 1992); missed 12 games. ... Suspended six off-days and fined $500 for hitting another player in face with his stick (January 7, 1993). ... Suspended one game for high-sticking incident (February 23, 1993). ... Viral infection (November 18, 1993); missed one game. ... Injured hamstring (March 22, 1994); missed two games. ... Viral infection (January 20, 1995); missed three games. ... Fractured ankle (May 15, 1995); missed last two games of playoffs. ... Traded by Blues to Hartford Whalers for D Chris Pronger (July 27, 1995). ... Sprained wrist (November 11, 1995); missed eight games. ... Traded by Whalers with D Brian Glynn to Detroit Red Wings for C Keith Primeau, D Paul Coffey and first-round pick (D Nikos Tselios) in 1997 draft (October 9, 1996). ... Suspended one game and fined $1,000 for cross-checking incident (October 11, 1996). ... Strained groin (October 30, 1996); missed one game. ... Stiff neck (October 12, 1997); missed four games. ... Back spasms (April 15, 1998); missed final game of season and two playoff games. ... Suspended two games for stick-swinging incident (November 9, 1999).

STATISTICAL PLATEAUS: Three-goal games: 1988-89 (1), 1992-93 (1), 1993-94 (4), 1995-96 (1), 1996-97 (3), 1998-99 (2), 2001-02 (1), 2002-03 (1), 2003-04 (1). Total: 15. ... Four-goal games: 2000-01 (1). ... Total hat tricks: 16.

		REGULAR SEASON								PLAYOFFS				
Season Team	League	GP	G	A	Pts.	PIM	+/-	PP	SH	GP	G	A	Pts.	PIM
84-85—Mississauga	MTHL	36	20	21	41	26	...	...	...	—	—	—	—	—
85-86—London	OHL	59	28	34	62	70	...	...	...	5	5	5	10	5
86-87—London	OHL	56	39	53	92	128	...	...	...	—	—	—	—	—
87-88—New Jersey	NHL	65	7	19	26	131	-20	2	0	12	2	1	3	44
88-89—New Jersey	NHL	68	22	28	50	115	2	9	0	—	—	—	—	—
89-90—New Jersey	NHL	73	30	42	72	137	15	8	0	6	3	3	6	20
90-91—New Jersey	NHL	75	29	37	66	141	4	7	0	7	3	5	8	12
91-92—St. Louis	NHL	80	33	36	69	171	-3	13	0	6	2	3	5	14
92-93—St. Louis	NHL	71	51	43	94	174	10	18	0	11	4	3	7	18
93-94—St. Louis	NHL	81	52	50	102	211	-9	15	*7	4	2	5	7	4
94-95—Dusseldorf	Germany	3	5	3	8	4	...	...	...	—	—	—	—	—
—St. Louis	NHL	45	20	21	41	136	7	6	2	5	4	5	9	14
95-96—Hartford	NHL	74	44	34	78	125	2	17	2	—	—	—	—	—
96-97—Hartford	NHL	2	1	0	1	0	1	0	1	—	—	—	—	—
—Detroit	NHL	79	46	41	87	131	31	20	2	20	9	8	17	43
97-98—Detroit	NHL	75	28	29	57	154	6	15	1	20	5	4	9	22
—Can. Olympic team	Int'l	6	2	0	2	0	3	1	0	—	—	—	—	—
98-99—Detroit	NHL	81	31	27	58	123	2	5	0	10	3	7	10	6
99-00—Detroit	NHL	78	41	37	78	105	24	13	1	9	3	2	5	10
00-01—Detroit	NHL	81	31	45	76	81	9	15	1	2	2	2	4	0
01-02—Detroit	NHL	80	37	38	75	118	23	12	3	23	8	11	19	20
—Can. Olympic team	Int'l	6	0	1	1	0	...	...	...	—	—	—	—	—
02-03—Detroit	NHL	78	30	38	68	103	5	13	0	4	1	1	2	4
03-04—Detroit	NHL	82	25	28	53	117	15	8	0	12	1	5	6	20
NHL Totals (17 years)		1268	558	593	1151	2273	124	196	20	151	52	65	117	251

SHARP, PATRICK — C — FLYERS

PERSONAL: Born December 27, 1981, in Thunder Bay, Ont. ... 6-0/188. ... Shoots right.

TRANSACTIONS/CAREER NOTES: Selected by Philadelphia Flyers in third round (second Flyers pick, 95th overall) of NHL entry draft (June 23, 2001).

		REGULAR SEASON								PLAYOFFS				
Season Team	League	GP	G	A	Pts.	PIM	+/-	PP	SH	GP	G	A	Pts.	PIM
98-99—Thunder Bay Flyers	USHL	55	19	24	43	48	...	...	...	3	1	1	2	0
99-00—Thunder Bay Flyers	USHL	56	20	35	55	41	...	...	...	—	—	—	—	—
00-01—Vermont	ECAC	30	11	13	24	34	...	...	...	—	—	—	—	—
01-02—Vermont	ECAC	31	13	13	26	50	...	...	...	—	—	—	—	—
02-03—Philadelphia	AHL	53	14	19	33	39	-5	6	0	—	—	—	—	—
—Philadelphia	NHL	3	0	0	0	2	0	0	0	—	—	—	—	—
03-04—Philadelphia	AHL	35	15	14	29	45	5	7	0	1	2	0	2	0
—Philadelphia	NHL	41	5	2	7	55	-3	0	0	12	1	0	1	2
04-05—Philadelphia	AHL	75	23	29	52	80	3	8	0	21	8	13	21	20
NHL Totals (2 years)		44	5	2	7	57	-3	0	0	12	1	0	1	2

SHELLEY, JODY — LW — BLUE JACKETS

PERSONAL: Born February 7, 1976, in Thompson, Man. ... 6-4/225. ... Shoots left.

TRANSACTIONS/CAREER NOTES: Signed as free agent by Calgary Flames (September 1, 1998). ... Signed as free agent by Columbus Blue Jackets (February 1, 2001). ... Suspended one game for fighting (December 5, 2002). ... Injured nose (November 20, 2003); missed one game. ... Injured throat (January 15, 2003); missed one game. ... Injured groin (March 1, 2003); missed two games. ... Injured abdomen (March 22, 2003) missed six games. ... Suspended three games for fighting incident (March 25, 2004).

Season	Team	League	GP	G	A	Pts.	PIM	+/-	PP	SH	Playoffs GP	G	A	Pts.	PIM
			REGULAR SEASON								PLAYOFFS				
94-95	—Halifax	QMJHL	72	10	12	22	194	...	...	...	7	0	1	1	12
95-96	—Halifax	QMJHL	50	13	19	32	319	...	...	...	6	0	2	2	36
96-97	—Halifax	QMJHL	58	25	19	44	448	...	...	...	17	6	6	12	123
97-98	—Dalhousie University	AUAA	19	6	11	17	145	...	...	...	—	—	—	—	—
	—Saint John	AHL	18	1	1	2	50	...	...	...	—	—	—	—	—
98-99	—Saint John	AHL	8	0	0	0	46	-1	0	0	—	—	—	—	—
	—Johnstown	ECHL	52	12	17	29	325	-4	3	0	—	—	—	—	—
99-00	—Johnstown	ECHL	36	9	17	26	256	...	...	...	—	—	—	—	—
	—Saint John	AHL	22	1	4	5	93	...	...	...	3	0	0	0	2
00-01	—Syracuse	AHL	69	1	7	8	*357	...	...	...	5	0	0	0	21
	—Columbus	NHL	1	0	0	0	10	0	0	0	—	—	—	—	—
01-02	—Columbus	NHL	52	3	3	6	206	1	0	0	—	—	—	—	—
	—Syracuse	AHL	22	3	5	8	165	4	1	0	—	—	—	—	—
02-03	—Columbus	NHL	68	1	4	5	*249	-5	0	0	—	—	—	—	—
03-04	—Columbus	NHL	76	3	3	6	228	-10	1	0	—	—	—	—	—
04-05	—JyP Jyvaskyla	Finland	11	0	1	1	20	-3	...	...	3	0	0	0	25
NHL Totals (4 years)			197	7	10	17	693	-14	1	0					

SHIELDS, STEVE — G

PERSONAL: Born July 19, 1972, in Toronto. ... 6-3/215. ... Catches left.

TRANSACTIONS/CAREER NOTES: Selected by Buffalo Sabres in fifth round (fifth Sabres pick, 101st overall) of NHL draft (June 22, 1991). ... Traded by Sabres with fourth-round pick (RW Miroslav Zalesak) in 1998 draft to San Jose Sharks for G Kay Whitmore, second-round pick (RW Jaroslav Kristek) in 1998 draft and fifth-round pick (traded to Columbus; Blue Jackets selected C Tyler Kolarik) in 2000 draft (June 18, 1998). ... Sprained ankle (October 12, 2000); missed eight games. ... Traded by Sharks with LW Jeff Friesen and second-round pick (traded to Dallas; Stars selected LW Vojtech Polak) in 2003 draft to Mighty Ducks of Anaheim for RW Teemu Selanne (March 5, 2001). ... Injured ligaments in left shoulder and had surgery (March 7, 2001); missed remainder of season. ... Lacerated face and bruised jaw (April 3, 2002); missed remainder of season. ... Traded by Mighty Ducks to Boston Bruins for third-round pick (RW Shane Hynes) in 2003 draft (June 25, 2002). ... Traded by Bruins to Florida Panthers for a sixth-round pick in 2004 entry draft (October 5, 2003). ... Injured foot (February 12, 2004); missed one game.

Season	Team	League	GP	Min.	W	L	T	GA	SO	GAA	SV%	Playoffs GP	Min.	W	L	GA	SO	GAA	SV%
			REGULAR SEASON									PLAYOFFS							
90-91	—Univ. of Michigan	CCHA	37	1963	26	6	3	106	0	3.24	...	—	—	—	—	—	—	—	—
91-92	—Univ. of Michigan	CCHA	*37	*2091	*27	7	2	98	1	2.81	...	—	—	—	—	—	—	—	—
92-93	—Univ. of Michigan	CCHA	*39	*2027	*30	6	2	75	2	2.22	...	—	—	—	—	—	—	—	—
93-94	—Univ. of Michigan	CCHA	36	1961	*28	6	1	87	0	2.66	...	—	—	—	—	—	—	—	—
94-95	—South Carolina	ECHL	21	1158	11	5	2	52	2	2.69	.912	3	144	0	2	11	0	4.58	.874
	—Rochester	AHL	13	673	3	8	0	53	0	4.73	.830	1	20	0	0	3	0	9.00	.824
95-96	—Rochester	AHL	43	2356	20	17	2	140	1	3.57	...	*19	*1126	*15	3	47	1	2.50	...
	—Buffalo	NHL	2	75	1	0	0	4	0	3.20	.875	—	—	—	—	—	—	—	—
96-97	—Rochester	AHL	23	1331	14	6	2	60	1	2.70	.914	—	—	—	—	—	—	—	—
	—Buffalo	NHL	13	789	3	8	2	39	0	2.97	.913	10	570	4	6	26	1	2.74	.922
97-98	—Buffalo	NHL	16	785	3	6	4	37	0	2.83	.909	—	—	—	—	—	—	—	—
	—Rochester	AHL	1	59	0	1	0	3	0	3.05	.885	—	—	—	—	—	—	—	—
98-99	—San Jose	NHL	37	2162	15	11	8	80	4	2.22	.921	1	60	0	1	6	0	6.00	.833
99-00	—San Jose	NHL	67	3797	27	30	8	162	4	2.56	.911	12	696	5	7	36	0	3.10	.889
00-01	—San Jose	NHL	21	1135	6	8	5	47	2	2.48	.911	—	—	—	—	—	—	—	—
01-02	—Anaheim	NHL	33	1777	9	20	2	79	0	2.67	.907	—	—	—	—	—	—	—	—
02-03	—Boston	NHL	36	2112	12	13	9	97	0	2.76	.896	2	119	0	2	6	0	3.03	.897
03-04	—Florida	NHL	16	732	3	6	1	42	0	3.44	.879	—	—	—	—	—	—	—	—
NHL Totals (9 years)			241	13364	79	102	39	587	10	2.64	.908	25	1445	9	16	74	1	3.07	.901

SHIROKOV, SERGEI — LW

PERSONAL: Born March 10, 1987, in Moscow, Russia. ... 5-10/170. ... Shoots right.

Season	Team	League	GP	G	A	Pts.	PIM	+/-	PP	SH	Playoffs GP	G	A	Pts.	PIM
			REGULAR SEASON								PLAYOFFS				
04-05	—CSKA Moscow	Russian	8	0	0	0	0	...	...	...	—	—	—	—	—

SHISHKANOV, TIMOFEI — LW — PREDATORS

PERSONAL: Born June 10, 1983, in Moscow, U.S.S.R. ... 6-1/213. ... Shoots right.

TRANSACTIONS/CAREER NOTES: Selected by Nashville Predators in second round (second Predators pick, 33rd overall) of NHL entry draft (June 23, 2001).

Season	Team	League	GP	G	A	Pts.	PIM	+/-	PP	SH	Playoffs GP	G	A	Pts.	PIM
			REGULAR SEASON								PLAYOFFS				
00-01	—Spartak	Russian Jr.	12	0	0	0	2	...	...	...	—	—	—	—	—
01-02	—HC CSKA Moscow	Rus. Div.	23	7	6	13	8	...	...	...	—	—	—	—	—
02-03	—Quebec	QMJHL	51	36	46	82	60	...	...	...	11	5	12	17	14
03-04	—Nashville	NHL	2	0	0	0	0	-1	0	0	—	—	—	—	—
	—Milwaukee	AHL	63	23	20	43	46	23	3	0	22	2	6	8	17
04-05	—Milwaukee	AHL	70	20	15	35	31	-3	6	0	6	1	0	1	2
NHL Totals (1 year)			2	0	0	0	0	-1	0	0					

SHVIDKI, DENIS — RW — PANTHERS

PERSONAL: Born November 21, 1980, in Kharkov, U.S.S.R. ... 6-2/210. ... Shoots left. ... Name pronounced SHVID-kee.
TRANSACTIONS/CAREER NOTES: Selected by Florida Panthers in first round (first Panthers pick, 12th overall) of NHL draft (June 26, 1999). ... Strained tendon in foot (February 28, 2001); missed three games. ... Had concussion (September 12, 2001); missed first 24 games of season. ... Injured knee (April 6, 2003); missed one game.

		REGULAR SEASON								PLAYOFFS				
Season Team	League	GP	G	A	Pts.	PIM	+/-	PP	SH	GP	G	A	Pts.	PIM
96-97—Torpedo-Yaroslavl	Russian	17	3	2	5	6	...	...	...	—	—	—	—	—
97-98—Torpedo-Yaroslavl	Russian	15	1	1	2	2	...	...	...	—	—	—	—	—
—Torpedo Yaroslavl	Rus. Div.	32	20	13	33	20	...	...	...	—	—	—	—	—
98-99—Barrie	OHL	61	35	59	94	8	57	...	...	12	7	9	16	2
99-00—Barrie	OHL	61	41	65	106	55	46	11	0	9	3	1	4	2
00-01—Florida	NHL	43	6	10	16	16	6	0	0	—	—	—	—	—
—Louisville	AHL	34	15	11	26	20	...	...	...	—	—	—	—	—
01-02—Florida	NHL	8	1	2	3	2	-4	0	0	—	—	—	—	—
—Utah	AHL	8	2	4	6	2	3	1	0	—	—	—	—	—
02-03—San Antonio	AHL	54	8	18	26	28	-11	2	0	—	—	—	—	—
—Florida	NHL	23	4	2	6	12	-7	2	0	—	—	—	—	—
03-04—Florida	NHL	2	0	0	0	0	0	0	0	—	—	—	—	—
—San Antonio	AHL	77	15	39	54	30	0	2	0	—	—	—	—	—
04-05—Lokomotiv Yaroslavl	Russian	52	7	11	18	24	11	...	...	4	0	0	0	8
NHL Totals (4 years)		76	11	14	25	30	-5	2	0					

SIKLENKA, MIKE — RW — STARS

PERSONAL: Born December 18, 1979, in Meadow Lake, Saskatchewan. ... 6-5/225. ... Shoots right. ... Name pronounced sih-KLEHN-kuh.
TRANSACTIONS/CAREER NOTES: Selected by Washington Capitals in fifth round (fifth Capitals pick, 118th overall) of NHL entry draft (June 27, 1998). ... Signed as free agent by Philadelphia Flyers (January 27, 2003). ... Claimed by New York Rangers from Flyers in waiver draft (October 3, 2003). ... Claimed by Flyers off waivers from Rangers (November 5, 2003). ... Traded by Flyers to Dallas Stars for LW Steve Gainey (February 16, 2004).

		REGULAR SEASON								PLAYOFFS				
Season Team	League	GP	G	A	Pts.	PIM	+/-	PP	SH	GP	G	A	Pts.	PIM
97-98—Olds	AJHL	54	10	17	27	120	...	...	...	—	—	—	—	—
—Seattle	WHL	1	0	0	0	0	...	...	...	5	0	0	0	6
98-99—Seattle	WHL	68	19	13	32	115	14	4	1	11	6	6	12	24
99-00—Portland	AHL	9	0	0	0	14	...	...	...	—	—	—	—	—
—Hampton Roads	ECHL	58	7	4	11	62	...	...	...	8	1	0	1	15
00-01—Portland	AHL	3	0	0	0	0	...	...	...	—	—	—	—	—
—Richmond	ECHL	65	19	18	37	117	...	...	...	4	0	0	0	34
01-02—Richmond	ECHL	55	13	21	34	111	-4	5	0	—	—	—	—	—
—Portland	AHL	8	1	0	1	2	1	0	0	—	—	—	—	—
02-03—Philadelphia	AHL	64	6	6	12	169	-5	2	0	—	—	—	—	—
—Philadelphia	NHL	1	0	0	0	0	0	0	0	—	—	—	—	—
03-04—New York Rangers	NHL	1	0	0	0	0	0	0	0	—	—	—	—	—
—Trenton	ECHL	1	1	0	1	0	0	0	0	—	—	—	—	—
—Philadelphia	AHL	18	1	5	6	29	-4	0	0	—	—	—	—	—
—Utah	AHL	26	3	6	9	74	3	2	0	—	—	—	—	—
04-05—Klagenfurt	Austria	39	16	18	34	156	...	...	...	12	6	1	7	44
NHL Totals (2 years)		2	0	0	0	0	0	0	0					

SILLINGER, MIKE — C — BLUES

PERSONAL: Born June 29, 1971, in Regina, Sask. ... 5-11/195. ... Shoots right. ... Name pronounced SIHL-in-juhr.
TRANSACTIONS/CAREER NOTES: Selected by Detroit Red Wings in first round (first Red Wings pick, 11th overall) of NHL draft (June 17, 1989). ... Fractured rib in training camp (September 1990). ... Flu (March 5, 1993); missed three games. ... Strained rotator cuff (October 9, 1993); missed four games. ... Injured eye (January 17, 1995); missed four games. ... Traded by Red Wings with D Jason York to Mighty Ducks of Anaheim for LW Stu Grimson, D Mark Ferner and sixth-round pick (LW Magnus Nilsson) in 1996 draft (April 4, 1995). ... Traded by Mighty Ducks to Vancouver Canucks for RW Roman Oksiuta (March 15, 1996). ... Suffered concussion (March 26, 1997); missed two games. ... Traded by Canucks to Flyers for sixth-round pick (traded back to Philadelphia; Flyers selected Garrett Prosofsky) in 1998 draft (February 5, 1998). ... Sprained left knee (October 22, 1998); missed one game. ... Traded by Flyers with C Chris Gratton to Tampa Bay Lightning for RW Mikael Renberg and C Daymond Langkow (December 12, 1998). ... Traded by Lightning to Florida Panthers for C Ryan Johnson and LW Dwayne Hay (March 14, 2000). ... Fractured foot (November 8, 2000); missed 12 games. ... Strained groin (January 24, 2001); missed three games. ... Traded by Panthers to Ottawa Senators for third-round pick (traded to New York Rangers) in 2002 draft and future considerations (March 13, 2001). ... Signed as free agent by Columbus Blue Jackets (July 5, 2001). ... Suffered concussion (November 1, 2001); missed one game. ... Sprained knee (December 31, 2001); missed one game. ... Injured shoulder (December 9, 2002); missed two games. ... Groin strain (March 15, 2003); missed five games. ... Traded by Blue Jackets with second-round pick (D Johan Fransson) in 2004 entry draft for D Darryl Sydor; then traded by Stars to Phoenix Coyotes for D Teppo Numminen (July 22, 2003). ... Hernia surgery (October 10, 2003); missed five games. ... Traded by Coyotes to St. Louis Blues for G Brent Johnson (March 4, 2004).

		REGULAR SEASON								PLAYOFFS				
Season Team	League	GP	G	A	Pts.	PIM	+/-	PP	SH	GP	G	A	Pts.	PIM
87-88—Regina	WHL	67	18	25	43	17	...	...	...	4	2	2	4	0
88-89—Regina	WHL	72	53	78	131	52	...	...	...	—	—	—	—	—
89-90—Regina	WHL	70	57	72	129	41	...	...	...	11	12	10	22	2
—Adirondack	AHL	...	...	...	...	...	...	...	...	1	0	0	0	0
90-91—Regina	WHL	57	50	66	116	42	...	...	...	8	6	9	15	4
—Detroit	NHL	3	0	1	1	0	-2	0	0	3	0	1	1	0
91-92—Adirondack	AHL	64	25	41	66	26	...	...	...	15	9	*19	*28	12

Season Team	League	GP	G	A	Pts.	PIM	+/-	PP	SH	GP	G	A	Pts.	PIM
		REGULAR SEASON								PLAYOFFS				
—Detroit	NHL	...	...	...	...	...	...	...	...	8	2	2	4	2
92-93—Detroit	NHL	51	4	17	21	16	0	0	0	—	—	—	—	—
—Adirondack	AHL	15	10	20	30	31	18	2	3	11	5	13	18	10
93-94—Detroit	NHL	62	8	21	29	10	2	0	1	—	—	—	—	—
94-95—Wien	Austria	13	13	14	27	10	...	...	...	—	—	—	—	—
—Detroit	NHL	13	2	6	8	2	3	0	0	—	—	—	—	—
—Anaheim	NHL	15	2	5	7	6	1	2	0	—	—	—	—	—
95-96—Anaheim	NHL	62	13	21	34	32	-20	7	0	—	—	—	—	—
—Vancouver	NHL	12	1	3	4	6	2	0	1	6	0	0	0	2
96-97—Vancouver	NHL	78	17	20	37	25	-3	3	3	—	—	—	—	—
97-98—Vancouver	NHL	48	10	9	19	34	-14	1	2	—	—	—	—	—
—Philadelphia	NHL	27	11	11	22	16	3	1	2	3	1	0	1	0
98-99—Philadelphia	NHL	25	0	3	3	8	-9	0	0	—	—	—	—	—
—Tampa Bay	NHL	54	8	2	10	28	-20	0	2	—	—	—	—	—
99-00—Tampa Bay	NHL	67	19	25	44	86	-29	6	3	—	—	—	—	—
—Florida	NHL	13	4	4	8	16	-1	2	0	4	2	1	3	2
00-01—Florida	NHL	55	13	21	34	44	-12	1	0	—	—	—	—	—
—Ottawa	NHL	13	3	4	7	4	1	0	0	4	0	0	0	2
01-02—Columbus	NHL	80	20	23	43	54	-35	8	0	—	—	—	—	—
02-03—Columbus	NHL	75	18	25	43	52	-21	9	3	—	—	—	—	—
03-04—Phoenix	NHL	60	8	6	14	54	-14	0	1	—	—	—	—	—
—St. Louis	NHL	16	5	5	10	14	4	0	1	5	3	1	4	6
NHL Totals (14 years)		829	166	232	398	507	-164	40	19	33	8	5	13	14

SIM, JON — LW/RW — FLYERS

PERSONAL: Born September 29, 1977, in New Glasgow, N.S. ... 5-10/190. ... Shoots left.

TRANSACTIONS/CAREER NOTES: Selected by Dallas Stars in third round (second Stars pick, 70th overall) of NHL draft (June 22, 1996). ... Fractured shoulder blade (September 16, 2000); missed first six games of season. ... Traded by Stars to Nashville Predators for D Bubba Berenzweig and conditional pick in 2003 draft (February 17, 2003). ... Claimed by Los Angeles Kings off waivers from Predators (March 9, 2003). ... Claimed by Pittsburgh Penguins off waivers from Kings (March 4, 2004). ... Signed as free agent by Phoenix Coyotes (September 2, 2004). ... Signed as free agent by Philadelphia Flyers (Aug. 2, 2005).

Season Team	League	GP	G	A	Pts.	PIM	+/-	PP	SH	GP	G	A	Pts.	PIM
		REGULAR SEASON								PLAYOFFS				
94-95—Laval	QMJHL	9	0	1	1	6	...	...	...	—	—	—	—	—
—Sarnia	OHL	25	9	12	21	19	...	...	...	4	3	2	5	2
95-96—Sarnia	OHL	63	56	46	102	130	...	...	...	10	8	7	15	26
96-97—Sarnia	OHL	64	56	39	95	109	0	29	2	12	9	5	14	32
97-98—Sarnia	OHL	59	44	50	94	95	...	...	...	5	1	4	5	14
98-99—Michigan	IHL	68	24	27	51	91	-19	12	1	5	3	1	4	18
—Dallas	NHL	7	1	0	1	12	1	0	0	4	0	0	0	0
99-00—Michigan	IHL	35	14	16	30	65	...	...	...	—	—	—	—	—
—Dallas	NHL	25	5	3	8	10	4	2	0	7	1	0	1	6
00-01—Dallas	NHL	15	0	3	3	6	-2	0	0	—	—	—	—	—
—Utah	IHL	39	16	13	29	44	...	...	...	—	—	—	—	—
01-02—Utah	AHL	31	21	6	27	63	-3	5	1	—	—	—	—	—
—Dallas	NHL	26	3	0	3	10	-3	1	0	—	—	—	—	—
02-03—Dallas	NHL	4	0	0	0	0	-1	0	0	—	—	—	—	—
—Utah	AHL	42	16	31	47	85	11	10	1	—	—	—	—	—
—Nashville	NHL	4	1	0	1	0	0	0	0	—	—	—	—	—
—Los Angeles	NHL	14	0	2	2	19	-3	0	0	—	—	—	—	—
03-04—Los Angeles	NHL	48	6	7	13	27	0	0	0	—	—	—	—	—
—Pittsburgh	NHL	15	2	3	5	6	-4	0	0	—	—	—	—	—
04-05—Philadelphia	AHL	63	35	26	61	66	29	7	3	21	10	7	17	44
—Utah	AHL	10	2	2	4	12	-8	2	0	—	—	—	—	—
NHL Totals (6 years)		158	18	18	36	90	-8	3	0	11	1	0	1	6

SIMON, BEN — LW — BLUE JACKETS

PERSONAL: Born June 14, 1978, in Shaker Heights, Ohio. ... 6-0/195. ... Shoots left.

TRANSACTIONS/CAREER NOTES: Selected by Chicago Blackhawks in 5th round (5th Blackhawks pick, 110th overall) of entry draft (June 21, 1997). ... Rights traded by Blackhawks to Atlanta Thrashers for 9th-round pick (C Peter Flache) in 2000 draft (June 25, 2000). ... Signed as free agent by Nashville Predators (July 14, 2003). ... Traded to Thrashers with D Tomas Kloucek for C Simon Gamache and D Kirill Safronov (December 2, 2003). ... Signed as free agent by Chicago of the AHL (September 27, 2004). ... Signed as free agent by Columbus Blue Jackets (Aug. 11, 2005).

Season Team	League	GP	G	A	Pts.	PIM	+/-	PP	SH	GP	G	A	Pts.	PIM
		REGULAR SEASON								PLAYOFFS				
92-93—Shaker Heights	Ohio H.S.	...	15	21	36	...	...	...	...	—	—	—	—	—
93-94—Shaker Heights	Ohio H.S.	...	45	41	86	...	...	...	...	—	—	—	—	—
94-95—Shaker Heights	Ohio H.S.	...	61	68	129	...	...	...	...	—	—	—	—	—
95-96—Cleveland	NAHL	50	45	46	91	...	...	...	...	—	—	—	—	—
96-97— Notre Dame	CCHA	30	4	15	19	79	...	...	...	—	—	—	—	—
97-98— Notre Dame	CCHA	37	9	28	37	91	...	...	...	—	—	—	—	—
98-99— Notre Dame	CCHA	37	18	24	42	65	...	...	...	—	—	—	—	—
99-00— Notre Dame	CCHA	40	13	19	32	53	...	...	...	—	—	—	—	—
00-01—Orlando	IHL	77	8	12	20	47	...	...	...	16	6	5	11	20
01-02—Chicago	AHL	74	11	23	34	56	3	0	1	25	2	3	5	24

Season Team	League	GP	G	A	Pts.	PIM	+/-	PP	SH	GP	G	A	Pts.	PIM
		REGULAR SEASON								PLAYOFFS				
—Atlanta	NHL	6	0	0	0	6	1	0	0	—	—	—	—	—
02-03—Atlanta	NHL	10	0	1	1	9	0	0	0	—	—	—	—	—
—Chicago	AHL	69	15	17	32	78	18	0	7	9	0	0	0	6
03-04—Milwaukee	AHL	18	1	3	4	6	-2	0	0	—	—	—	—	—
—Atlanta	NHL	52	3	0	3	28	-10	0	0	—	—	—	—	—
04-05—Chicago	AHL	53	11	10	21	58	2	3	0	18	1	5	6	44
NHL Totals (3 years)		68	3	1	4	43	-9	0	0					

SIMON, CHRIS — LW — FLAMES

PERSONAL: Born January 30, 1972, in Wawa, Ont. ... 6-3/232. ... Shoots left.

TRANSACTIONS/CAREER NOTES: Selected by Philadelphia Flyers in second round (second Flyers pick, 25th overall) of NHL entry draft (June 16, 1990). ... Traded by Flyers with first-round pick (traded to Toronto; traded to Washington; Capitals selected D Nolan Baumgartner) in 1994 draft to Quebec Nordiques (July 21, 1992) completing deal in which Flyers sent G Ron Hextall, C Mike Ricci, C Peter Forsberg, D Steve Duchesne, first-round pick (G Jocelyn Thibault) in 1993 draft and cash to Nordiques for C Eric Lindros (June 20, 1992). ... Flu (March 13, 1993); missed one game. ... Injured back (December 1, 1993); missed 31 games. ... Injured back (February 16, 1994); missed one game. ... Injured back (March 6, 1994); missed one game. ... Injured back (March 18, 1994); missed remainder of season. ... Injured back (January 31, 1995); missed six games. ... Injured shoulder (March 22, 1995); missed 13 games. ... Nordiques franchise moved to Colorado and renamed Avalanche for 1995-96 season (June 21, 1995). ... Back spasms (January 6, 1996); missed two games. ... Injured shoulder (February 5, 1996); missed four games. ... Traded by Avalanche with D Curtis Leschyshyn to Washington Capitals for RW Keith Jones and first- (D Scott Parker) and fourth-round (traded back to Washington; Capitals selected Krys Barch) picks in 1998 draft (November 2, 1996). ... Injured arm (December 20, 1996); missed two games. ... Back spasms (January 24, 1997); missed 17 games. ... Back spasms (March 22, 1997); missed one game. ... Strained shoulder (March 29, 1997); missed six games. ... Suspended three games for alleged racial remarks (November 9, 1997). ... Bruised shoulder (October 25, 1997); missed five games. ... Reinjured shoulder (December 20, 1997) and had shoulder surgery; missed remainder of season. ... Strained shoulder (December 5, 1998) and had shoulder surgery; missed remainder of season. ... Strained neck (November 27, 1999); missed six games. ... Reinjured neck (December 21, 1999); missed one game. ... Suspended one playoff game by NHL for cross-checking incident (April 14, 2000). ... Missed first nine games of 2000-01 season due to contract dispute. ... Injured shoulder (March 1, 2001); missed five games. ... Reinjured shoulder (March 19, 2001); missed five games. ... Suspended two games for elbowing incident (April 6, 2001). ... Traded by Capitals with C Andrei Nikolishin to Chicago Blackhawks for C Michael Nylander and conditional third-round pick in 2004 draft (November 1, 2002). ... Signed as free agent by New York Rangers (July 27, 2003). ... Suspended two games for cross-checking incident (January 11, 2004). ... Flu (February 23, 2004); missed one game. ... Traded by Rangers with seventh-round pick in 2004 draft to Calgary Flames for G Jamie McLennan, C Blair Betts and RW Greg Moore (March 6, 2004). ... Suspended two games for kneeing incident (March 23, 2004).

Season Team	League	GP	G	A	Pts.	PIM	+/-	PP	SH	GP	G	A	Pts.	PIM
		REGULAR SEASON								PLAYOFFS				
87-88—Sault Ste. Marie	OHA	55	42	36	78	172	...	...	...	—	—	—	—	—
88-89—Ottawa	OHL	36	4	2	6	31	...	...	...	—	—	—	—	—
89-90—Ottawa	OHL	57	36	38	74	146	...	...	...	3	2	1	3	4
90-91—Ottawa	OHL	20	16	6	22	69	...	...	...	17	5	9	14	59
91-92—Ottawa	OHL	2	1	1	2	24	...	...	...	—	—	—	—	—
—Sault Ste. Marie	OHL	31	19	25	44	143	...	...	...	11	5	8	13	49
92-93—Halifax	AHL	36	12	6	18	131	-9	1	0	—	—	—	—	—
—Quebec	NHL	16	1	1	2	67	-2	0	0	5	0	0	0	26
93-94—Quebec	NHL	37	4	4	8	132	-2	0	0	—	—	—	—	—
94-95—Quebec	NHL	29	3	9	12	106	14	0	0	6	1	1	2	19
95-96—Colorado	NHL	64	16	18	34	250	10	4	0	12	1	2	3	11
96-97—Washington	NHL	42	9	13	22	165	-1	3	0	—	—	—	—	—
97-98—Washington	NHL	28	7	10	17	38	-1	4	0	18	1	0	1	26
98-99—Washington	NHL	23	3	7	10	48	-4	0	0	—	—	—	—	—
99-00—Washington	NHL	75	29	20	49	146	11	7	0	4	2	0	2	24
00-01—Washington	NHL	60	10	10	20	109	-12	4	0	6	0	1	1	4
01-02—Washington	NHL	82	14	17	31	137	-8	1	0	—	—	—	—	—
02-03—Washington	NHL	10	0	2	2	23	-3	0	0	—	—	—	—	—
—Chicago	NHL	61	12	6	18	125	-4	2	0	—	—	—	—	—
03-04—New York Rangers	NHL	65	14	9	23	225	14	3	0	—	—	—	—	—
—Calgary	NHL	13	3	2	5	25	1	1	0	16	5	2	7	74
NHL Totals (12 years)		605	125	128	253	1596	13	29	0	67	10	6	16	184

SIMPSON, REID — LW

PERSONAL: Born May 21, 1969, in Flin Flon, Man. ... 6-2/217. ... Shoots left.

TRANSACTIONS/CAREER NOTES: Selected by Philadelphia Flyers in fourth round (third Flyers pick, 72nd overall) of NHL draft (June 17, 1989). ... Signed as free agent by Minnesota North Stars (December 13, 1992). ... North Stars franchise moved from Minnesota to Dallas and renamed Stars for 1993-94 season. ... Traded by Stars with D Roy Mitchell to New Jersey Devils for future considerations (March 21, 1994). ... Bruised right shoulder (November 27, 1995); missed six games. ... Strained groin (September 9, 1996); missed first two games of season. ... Reinjured groin (October 16, 1996); underwent groin surgery (November 22, 1996) and missed 38 games. ... Injured hamstring (November 8, 1997); missed 13 games. ... Traded by Devils to Chicago Blackhawks for fourth-round pick (D Mikko Jokela) in 1998 draft and future considerations (January 8, 1998). ... Strained hip flexor (March 12, 1998); missed two games. ... Fractured hand (September 20, 1998); missed first eight games of season. ... Suspended two games and fined $1,000 for actions toward a spectator (November 14, 1998). ... Traded by Blackhawks with D Bryan Muir to Tampa Bay Lightning for C Michael Nylander (November 12, 1999). ... Fractured jaw (January 13, 2000); missed final 40 games of season. ... Signed as free agent by St. Louis Blues (August 24, 2000). ... Injured groin (November 21, 2000); missed five games. ... Injured groin (February 1, 2001); missed seven games. ... Signed as free agent by Montreal Canadiens (September 10, 2001). ... Claimed off waivers by Nashville Predators (January 30, 2002). ... Back spasms, shoulder, head and knee injuries (March 6, 2003); missed 12 games. ... Signed as free agent by Pittsburgh Penguins (August 29, 2003).

Season Team	League	GP	G	A	Pts.	PIM	+/-	PP	SH	GP	G	A	Pts.	PIM
		REGULAR SEASON								PLAYOFFS				
85-86—Flin Flon	MJHL	40	20	21	41	200	...	...	...	—	—	—	—	—
—New Westminster	WHL	2	0	0	0	0	...	...	...	—	—	—	—	—
86-87—Prince Albert	WHL	47	3	8	11	105	...	...	...	—	—	—	—	—

S

Season Team	League	REGULAR SEASON GP	G	A	Pts.	PIM	+/-	PP	SH	PLAYOFFS GP	G	A	Pts.	PIM
87-88—Prince Albert	WHL	72	13	14	27	164	...	...	...	10	1	0	1	43
88-89—Prince Albert	WHL	59	26	29	55	264	...	...	...	4	2	1	3	30
89-90—Prince Albert	WHL	29	15	17	32	121	...	...	...	14	4	7	11	34
—Hershey	AHL	28	2	2	4	175	...	...	...	—	—	—	—	—
90-91—Hershey	AHL	54	9	15	24	183	...	...	...	1	0	0	0	0
91-92—Hershey	AHL	60	11	7	18	145	...	...	...	—	—	—	—	—
—Philadelphia	NHL	1	0	0	0	0	0	0	0	—	—	—	—	—
92-93—Kalamazoo	IHL	45	5	5	10	193	-12	2	0	—	—	—	—	—
—Minnesota	NHL	1	0	0	0	5	0	0	0	—	—	—	—	—
93-94—Kalamazoo	IHL	5	0	0	0	16	0	0	0	—	—	—	—	—
—Albany	AHL	37	9	5	14	135	7	0	0	5	1	1	2	18
94-95—Albany	AHL	70	18	25	43	268	12	4	0	14	1	8	9	13
—New Jersey	NHL	9	0	0	0	27	-1	0	0	—	—	—	—	—
95-96—New Jersey	NHL	23	1	5	6	79	2	0	0	—	—	—	—	—
—Albany	AHL	6	1	3	4	17	...	...	...	—	—	—	—	—
96-97—Albany	AHL	3	0	0	0	10	-1	0	0	—	—	—	—	—
—New Jersey	NHL	27	0	4	4	60	0	0	0	5	0	0	0	29
97-98—New Jersey	NHL	6	0	0	0	16	-2	0	0	—	—	—	—	—
—Chicago	NHL	38	3	2	5	102	-1	1	0	—	—	—	—	—
98-99—Chicago	NHL	53	5	4	9	145	2	1	0	—	—	—	—	—
99-00—Cleveland	IHL	12	2	2	4	56	...	...	...	—	—	—	—	—
—Tampa Bay	NHL	26	1	0	1	103	-3	0	0	—	—	—	—	—
00-01—St. Louis	NHL	38	2	1	3	96	-3	0	0	5	0	0	0	2
01-02—Montreal	NHL	25	1	1	2	63	0	0	0	—	—	—	—	—
—Milwaukee	AHL	2	1	0	1	37	-2	1	0	—	—	—	—	—
—Nashville	NHL	26	5	0	5	69	-1	0	0	—	—	—	—	—
02-03—Milwaukee	AHL	17	6	6	12	40	4	4	0	—	—	—	—	—
—Nashville	NHL	26	0	1	1	56	-4	0	0	—	—	—	—	—
03-04—Pittsburgh	NHL	2	0	0	0	17	0	0	0	—	—	—	—	—
—Wilkes-Barre/Scranton	AHL	51	6	11	17	168	-1	2	0	2	0	0	0	0
04-05—Rockford	UHL	15	1	3	4	46	-3	0	0	—	—	—	—	—
NHL Totals (12 years)		301	18	18	36	838	-11	2	0	10	0	0	0	31

SIMPSON, TODD — D

PERSONAL: Born May 28, 1973, in North Vancouver, B.C. ... 6-3/227. ... Shoots left.

TRANSACTIONS/CAREER NOTES: Signed as free agent by Calgary Flames (July 6, 1994). ... Injured knee (October 1, 1997) and underwent surgery; missed 10 games. ... Injured shoulder (November 15, 1997); missed four games. ... Suffered concussion (March 19, 1998); missed final 15 games of season. ... Facial injury (March 13, 1999); missed nine games. ... Traded by Flames to Florida Panthers for LW Bill Lindsay (September 30, 1999). ... Fractured toe (October 9, 2000); missed five games. ... Suffered concussion (December 4, 2000); missed 40 games. ... Traded by Panthers to Phoenix Coyotes for second-round draft pick (traded to New Jersey; Devils selected LW Tuomas Pihlman) in 2001 draft (March 13, 2001). ... Fractured foot (November 20, 2001); missed 15 games. ... Fractured right hand (October 12, 2002); missed 11 games. ... Suspended three games by NHL for high-sticking incident (November 27, 2002). ... Suspended two games by NHL for high-sticking incident (December 28, 2002). ... Claimed by Anaheim Mighty Ducks in NHL waiver draft (October 3, 2003). ... Injured shoulder (January 30, 2004); missed three games. ... Traded by Mighty Ducks to Ottawa Senators for LW Petr Schastlivy (February 4, 2004). ... Injured shoulder (February 21, 2004); missed five games.

Season Team	League	REGULAR SEASON GP	G	A	Pts.	PIM	+/-	PP	SH	PLAYOFFS GP	G	A	Pts.	PIM
91-92—Brown	ECAC	14	1	3	4	18	...	...	...	—	—	—	—	—
92-93—Tri-City	WHL	69	5	18	23	196	...	...	...	4	0	0	0	13
93-94—Tri-City	WHL	12	2	3	5	32	...	...	...	—	—	—	—	—
—Saskatoon	WHL	51	7	19	26	175	...	...	...	16	1	5	6	42
94-95—Saint John	AHL	80	3	10	13	321	-13	0	0	5	0	0	0	4
95-96—Calgary	NHL	6	0	0	0	32	0	0	0	—	—	—	—	—
—Saint John	AHL	66	4	13	17	277	...	...	...	16	2	3	5	32
96-97—Calgary	NHL	82	1	13	14	208	-14	0	0	—	—	—	—	—
97-98—Calgary	NHL	53	1	5	6	109	-10	0	0	—	—	—	—	—
98-99—Calgary	NHL	73	2	8	10	151	18	0	0	—	—	—	—	—
99-00—Florida	NHL	82	1	6	7	202	5	0	0	4	0	0	0	4
00-01—Florida	NHL	25	1	3	4	74	0	0	0	—	—	—	—	—
—Phoenix	NHL	13	0	1	1	12	-4	0	0	—	—	—	—	—
01-02—Phoenix	NHL	67	2	13	15	152	20	0	0	5	0	2	2	6
02-03—Phoenix	NHL	66	2	7	9	135	7	0	0	—	—	—	—	—
03-04—Anaheim	NHL	46	4	3	7	105	-6	0	0	—	—	—	—	—
—Ottawa	NHL	16	0	1	1	47	-1	0	0	—	—	—	—	—
04-05—Herning	Denmark	7	2	3	5	46	...	...	...	16	3	5	8	82
NHL Totals (9 years)		529	14	60	74	1227	15	0	0	9	0	2	2	10

SIPOTZ, BRIAN — D — THRASHERS

PERSONAL: Born September 16, 1981, in South Bend, Ind. ... 6-7/245. ... Shoots right.

TRANSACTIONS/CAREER NOTES: Selected by Atlanta Thrashers in fourth round (second Thrashers pick, 100th overall) of NHL entry draft (June 23, 2001).

Season Team	League	REGULAR SEASON GP	G	A	Pts.	PIM	+/-	PP	SH	PLAYOFFS GP	G	A	Pts.	PIM
00-01—Miami (Ohio)	CCHA	32	0	1	1	48	...	...	...	—	—	—	—	—
01-02—Miami (Ohio)	CCHA	25	0	1	1	28	...	...	...	—	—	—	—	—

Season Team	League	GP	G	A	Pts.	PIM	+/-	PP	SH	GP	G	A	Pts.	PIM
		REGULAR SEASON								PLAYOFFS				
02-03—Miami (Ohio)	CCHA	26	0	0	0	24	...	...	...	—	—	—	—	—
03-04—Miami (Ohio)	CCHA	36	0	3	3	39	...	...	...	—	—	—	—	—
04-05—Chicago	AHL	75	2	6	8	31	6	0	0	18	1	2	3	6

SIVEK, MICHAL — LW/C — PENGUINS

PERSONAL: Born January 21, 1981, in Nachod, Czech. ... 6-3/213. ... Shoots left.

TRANSACTIONS/CAREER NOTES: Selected by Washington Capitals in second round (second Capitals pick, 29th overall) of NHL entry draft (June 26, 1999). ... Traded by Capitals with C Kris Beech, D Ross Lupaschuk and future considerations to Pittsburgh Penguins for RW Jaromir Jagr and D Frantisek Kucera (July 11, 2001). ... Injured thigh (February 14, 2003); missed one game.

Season Team	League	GP	G	A	Pts.	PIM	+/-	PP	SH	GP	G	A	Pts.	PIM
		REGULAR SEASON								PLAYOFFS				
96-97—Sparta Praha Jrs.	Czech Rep.	38	18	11	29	...	...	...	...	—	—	—	—	—
97-98—Sparta Praha	Czech Rep.	25	1	1	2	10	...	...	...	5	1	0	1	0
—Sparta Praha Jrs.	Czech Rep.	31	13	8	21	...	...	...	...	—	—	—	—	—
98-99—Sparta Praha	Czech Rep.	1	1	0	1	2	...	...	...	—	—	—	—	—
—Velvana Kladno	Czech Rep.	34	3	8	11	24	...	...	...	—	—	—	—	—
99-00—Prince Albert	WHL	53	23	37	60	65	-6	8	0	6	1	4	5	10
00-01—Sparta Praha	Czech Rep.	32	6	7	13	28	...	...	...	13	4	2	6	8
01-02—Wilkes-Barre/Scranton	AHL	25	4	8	12	30	-12	3	0	—	—	—	—	—
—Sparta Praha	Czech Rep.	17	5	3	8	20	...	...	...	12	0	1	1	10
02-03—Pittsburgh	NHL	38	3	3	6	14	-5	1	0	—	—	—	—	—
—Wilkes-Barre/Scranton	AHL	40	10	17	27	33	-11	2	2	6	3	2	5	20
03-04—Wilkes-Barre/Scranton	AHL	22	4	7	11	6	0	0	0	—	—	—	—	—
04-05—Sparta Praha	Czech Rep.	37	1	5	6	48	...	...	...	—	—	—	—	—
NHL Totals (1 year)		38	3	3	6	14	-5	1	0					

S

SJOSTROM, FREDRIK — RW — COYOTES

PERSONAL: Born May 6, 1983, in Fargelanda, Sweden. ... 6-1/217. ... Shoots left.

TRANSACTIONS/CAREER NOTES: Selected by Phoenix Coyotes in first round (first Coyotes pick, 11th overall) of NHL entry draft (June 23, 2001).

Season Team	League	GP	G	A	Pts.	PIM	+/-	PP	SH	GP	G	A	Pts.	PIM
		REGULAR SEASON								PLAYOFFS				
99-00—MoDo Ornskoldsvik	Sweden Jr.	14	4	4	8	2	...	...	...	—	—	—	—	—
00-01—Vastra Frolunda	Sweden Jr.	7	2	5	7	6	...	...	...	—	—	—	—	—
—Vastra Frolunda	Sweden	31	2	3	5	6	...	...	...	5	0	0	0	2
01-02—Calgary	WHL	58	19	31	50	51	...	...	...	4	1	1	2	8
02-03—Springfield	AHL	2	1	0	1	0	-1	0	0	—	—	—	—	—
—Calgary	WHL	63	34	43	77	95	...	...	...	5	1	3	4	4
03-04—Phoenix	NHL	57	7	6	13	22	-7	0	0	—	—	—	—	—
—Springfield	AHL	17	0	7	7	8	-3	0	0	—	—	—	—	—
04-05—Utah	AHL	80	14	24	38	57	-14	3	1	—	—	—	—	—
NHL Totals (1 year)		57	7	6	13	22	-7	0	0					

SKILLE, JACK — RW — BLACKHAWKS

PERSONAL: Born May 19, 1987, in Madison, Wisc. ... 6-1/189. ... Shoots right.

TRANSACTIONS/CAREER NOTES: Selected by Chicago Blackhawks in 1st round (1st Blackhawks pick, 7th overall) of entry draft (July 30, 2005).

Season Team	League	GP	G	A	Pts.	PIM	+/-	PP	SH	GP	G	A	Pts.	PIM
		REGULAR SEASON								PLAYOFFS				
03-04—U.S. National	USHL	61	25	19	44	61	...	...	...	—	—	—	—	—
04-05—U.S. National	USHL	54	24	31	55	76	...	...	...	—	—	—	—	—

SKOULA, MARTIN — D — STARS

PERSONAL: Born October 28, 1979, in Litomerice, Czech. ... 6-3/220. ... Shoots left.

TRANSACTIONS/CAREER NOTES: Selected by Colorado Avalanche in 1st round (2nd Avalanche pick, 17th overall) of entry draft (June 27, 1998). ... Injured shoulder (January 5, 2000); missed two games. ... Injured shoulder (April 6, 2003); missed one game. ... Bruised foot (October 18, 2003); missed two games. ... Traded by Avalanche to Anaheim Mighty Ducks for D Kurt Sauer and 4th-round pick in 2005 draft (February 21, 2004). ... Signed as free agent by Dallas Stars (Aug. 3, 2005).

Season Team	League	GP	G	A	Pts.	PIM	+/-	PP	SH	GP	G	A	Pts.	PIM
		REGULAR SEASON								PLAYOFFS				
95-96—Litvinov	Czech. Jrs.	38	0	4	4	...	...	...	...	—	—	—	—	—
—Litvinov	Czech Rep.	...	...	...	...	...	...	...	...	1	0	0	0	0
96-97—Litvinov	Czech. Jrs.	38	2	9	11	...	...	...	...	—	—	—	—	—
—Litvinov	Czech Rep.	1	0	0	0	0	...	...	...	—	—	—	—	—
97-98—Barrie	COJHL	66	8	36	44	36	...	...	...	6	1	3	4	4
98-99—Barrie	OHL	67	13	46	59	46	58	...	...	12	3	10	13	13
—Hershey	AHL	...	...	...	...	...	...	...	...	1	0	0	0	0
99-00—Colorado	NHL	80	3	13	16	20	5	2	0	17	0	2	2	4
00-01—Colorado	NHL	82	8	17	25	38	8	3	0	23	1	4	5	8

Season Team	League	REGULAR SEASON GP	G	A	Pts.	PIM	+/-	PP	SH	PLAYOFFS GP	G	A	Pts.	PIM
01-02—Colorado	NHL	82	10	21	31	42	-3	5	0	21	0	6	6	2
—Czech Rep. Oly. team..	Int'l	4	0	0	0	0	...	...	...	—	—	—	—	—
02-03—Colorado	NHL	81	4	21	25	68	11	2	0	7	0	1	1	4
03-04—Colorado	NHL	58	2	14	16	30	2	0	0	—	—	—	—	—
—Anaheim	NHL	21	2	7	9	2	3	1	0	—	—	—	—	—
04-05—Chem. Litvinov	Czech Rep.	47	4	15	19	101	-8	...	...	6	0	0	0	6
NHL Totals (5 years)		404	29	93	122	200	26	13	0	68	1	13	14	18

SKRASTINS, KARLIS — D — AVALANCHE

PERSONAL: Born July 9, 1974, in Riga, U.S.S.R. ... 6-1/212. ... Shoots left. ... Name pronounced SKRAS-tinsh.

TRANSACTIONS/CAREER NOTES: Selected by Nashville Predators in ninth round (eighth Predators pick, 230th overall) of 1998 draft (June 27, 1998). ... Traded by Predators to Colorado Avalanche for third-round pick (later traded to Ottawa; Senators picked D Peter Regin) in 2004 draft (June 30, 2003).

Season Team	League	REGULAR SEASON GP	G	A	Pts.	PIM	+/-	PP	SH	PLAYOFFS GP	G	A	Pts.	PIM
92-93—Riga Stars	CIS	40	3	5	8	16	...	...	...	2	0	0	0	0
93-94—Riga Stars	CIS	42	7	5	12	18	...	...	...	2	1	0	1	4
94-95—Riga Stars	CIS	52	4	14	18	69	...	...	...	—	—	—	—	—
95-96—TPS Turku	Finland	50	4	11	15	32	...	...	...	11	2	2	4	10
96-97—TPS Turku	Finland	50	2	8	10	20	...	...	...	—	—	—	—	—
97-98—TPS Turku	Finland	48	4	15	19	67	...	...	...	—	—	—	—	—
98-99—Milwaukee	IHL	75	8	36	44	47	...	...	...	2	0	1	1	2
—Nashville	NHL	2	0	1	1	0	0	0	0	—	—	—	—	—
99-00—Milwaukee	IHL	19	3	8	11	10	...	...	...	—	—	—	—	—
—Nashville	NHL	59	5	6	11	20	-7	1	0	—	—	—	—	—
00-01—Nashville	NHL	82	1	11	12	30	-12	0	0	—	—	—	—	—
01-02—Nashville	NHL	82	4	13	17	36	-12	0	0	—	—	—	—	—
—Latvian Olympic team	Int'l	1	0	0	0	0	...	...	...	—	—	—	—	—
02-03—Nashville	NHL	82	3	10	13	44	-18	0	1	—	—	—	—	—
03-04—Colorado	NHL	82	5	8	13	26	18	0	1	11	0	2	2	2
04-05—Riga	Belarus	34	8	17	25	30	...	...	...	3	0	0	0	25
—Riga	Latvia	4	0	4	4	0	...	...	...	9	3	10	13	33
NHL Totals (6 years)		389	18	49	67	156	-31	1	2	11	0	2	2	2

SLANEY, JOHN — D

PERSONAL: Born February 7, 1972, in St. John's, Newfoundland. ... 6-0/190. ... Shoots left.

TRANSACTIONS/CAREER NOTES: Selected by Washington Capitals in first round (first Capitals pick, ninth overall) of NHL draft (June 16, 1990). ... Sprained right ankle (March 9, 1994); missed six games. ... Traded by Capitals to Colorado Avalanche for third-round pick (C Shawn McNeil) in 1996 draft (July 12, 1995). ... Traded by Avalanche to Los Angeles Kings for sixth-round pick (RW Brian Willsie) in 1996 draft (December 28, 1995). ... Fractured right hand (March 6, 1996); missed 12 games. ... Suffered concussion (November 17, 1996); missed one game. ... Signed as free agent by Phoenix Coyotes (August 18, 1997). ... Bruised thigh (October 30, 1997); missed one game. ... Flu (December 10, 1997); missed one game. ... Fractured thumb (January 24, 1998); missed seven games. ... Injured hamstring (April 18, 1998); missed one game. ... Selected by Nashville Predators in expansion draft (June 26, 1998). ... Bruised thumb (January 28, 1999); missed two games. ... Sprained wrist (February 5, 1999); missed three games. ... Injured rib (March 28, 1999); missed final nine games of season. ... Signed as free agent by Pittsburgh Penguins (September 30, 1999). ... Traded by Penguins to Philadelphia Flyers for LW Kevin Stevens (January 14, 2001).

Season Team	League	REGULAR SEASON GP	G	A	Pts.	PIM	+/-	PP	SH	PLAYOFFS GP	G	A	Pts.	PIM
88-89—Cornwall	OHL	66	16	43	59	23	...	...	...	18	8	16	24	10
89-90—Cornwall	OHL	64	38	59	97	60	...	...	...	6	0	8	8	11
90-91—Cornwall	OHL	34	21	25	46	28	...	...	...	—	—	—	—	—
91-92—Cornwall	OHL	34	19	41	60	43	...	...	...	6	3	8	11	0
—Baltimore	AHL	6	2	4	6	0	...	...	...	—	—	—	—	—
92-93—Baltimore	AHL	79	20	46	66	60	-12	10	1	7	0	7	7	8
93-94—Portland	AHL	29	14	13	27	17	4	6	0	—	—	—	—	—
—Washington	NHL	47	7	9	16	27	3	3	0	11	1	1	2	2
94-95—Washington	NHL	16	0	3	3	6	-3	0	0	—	—	—	—	—
—Portland	AHL	8	3	10	13	4	8	3	0	7	1	3	4	4
95-96—Colorado	NHL	7	0	3	3	4	2	0	0	—	—	—	—	—
—Cornwall	AHL	5	0	4	4	2	...	...	...	—	—	—	—	—
—Los Angeles	NHL	31	6	11	17	10	5	3	1	—	—	—	—	—
96-97—Los Angeles	NHL	32	3	11	14	4	-10	1	0	—	—	—	—	—
—Phoenix	IHL	35	9	25	34	8	...	...	...	—	—	—	—	—
97-98—Las Vegas	IHL	5	2	2	4	10	-4	1	0	—	—	—	—	—
—Phoenix	NHL	55	3	14	17	24	-3	1	0	—	—	—	—	—
98-99—Nashville	NHL	46	2	12	14	14	-12	0	0	—	—	—	—	—
—Milwaukee	IHL	7	0	1	1	0	5	0	0	—	—	—	—	—
99-00—Pittsburgh	NHL	29	1	4	5	10	-10	1	0	2	1	0	1	2
—Wilkes-Barre/Scranton	AHL	49	30	30	60	25	...	...	...	—	—	—	—	—
00-01—Wilkes-Barre/Scranton	AHL	40	12	38	50	4	...	...	...	—	—	—	—	—
—Philadelphia	AHL	25	6	11	17	10	...	...	...	10	2	6	8	6
01-02—Philadelphia	AHL	64	20	39	59	26	12	9	1	5	2	1	3	0
—Philadelphia	NHL	1	0	0	0	0	2	0	0	1	0	0	0	0
02-03—Philadelphia	AHL	55	9	33	42	36	2	3	0	—	—	—	—	—
03-04—Philadelphia	NHL	4	0	2	2	0	0	0	0	—	—	—	—	—
—Philadelphia	AHL	59	19	29	48	31	20	11	2	12	3	3	6	6
04-05—Philadelphia	AHL	78	14	30	44	39	12	7	0	21	3	7	10	12
NHL Totals (9 years)		268	22	69	91	99	-26	9	1	14	2	1	3	4

SLATER, JIM — C — THRASHERS

PERSONAL: Born December 9, 1982, in Petoskey, Mich. ... 6-0/190. ... Shoots left.

TRANSACTIONS/CAREER NOTES: Selected by Atlanta Thrashers in first round (second Thrashers pick, 30th overall) of NHL entry draft (June 22, 2002).

		REGULAR SEASON								PLAYOFFS				
Season Team	**League**	**GP**	**G**	**A**	**Pts.**	**PIM**	**+/-**	**PP**	**SH**	**GP**	**G**	**A**	**Pts.**	**PIM**
00-01—Cleveland	NAHL	48	27	37	64	122	...	...	...	—	—	—	—	—
01-02—Michigan State	CCHA	32	9	18	27	48	...	...	...	—	—	—	—	—
02-03—Michigan State	CCHA	37	18	26	44	26	...	...	...	—	—	—	—	—
03-04—Michigan State	CCHA	42	19	29	48	38	...	...	...	—	—	—	—	—
04-05—Michigan State	CCHA	41	16	32	48	30	...	...	...	—	—	—	—	—

SLEGR, JIRI — D — BRUINS

PERSONAL: Born May 30, 1971, in Jihlava, Czechoslovakia. ... 6-1/210. ... Shoots left. ... Son of Jiri Bubla, defenseman with Vancouver Canucks (1981-82 through 1985-86). ... Name pronounced YIH-ree SLAY-guhr.

TRANSACTIONS/CAREER NOTES: Selected by Vancouver Canucks in second round (third Canucks pick, 23rd overall) of NHL draft (June 16, 1990). ... Traded by Canucks to Edmonton Oilers for RW Roman Oksiuta (April 7, 1995). ... Sprained left knee ligaments (December 27, 1995); missed 19 games. ... Traded by Oilers to Pittsburgh Penguins for third-round pick (traded to New Jersey; Devils selected RW Brian Gionta) in 1998 draft (August 12, 1997). ... Had hip pointer (November 14, 1997); missed four games. ... Flu (December 16, 1997); missed one game. ... Injured shoulder (March 2, 1998); missed one game. ... Fractured hand (November 5, 1998); missed 13 games. ... Bruised knee (April 1, 1999); missed one game. ... Sprained ankle (October 8, 1999); missed five games. ... Flu (November 20, 1999); missed one game. ... Sprained knee (November 26, 1999); missed two games. ... Traded by Penguins to Atlanta Thrashers for third-round pick (traded to Columbus; Blue Jackets selected D Aaron Johnson) in 2001 draft (January 14, 2001). ... Strained groin (March 28, 2001); missed five games. ... Strained hip (November 3, 2001). ... Had herniated disk in back (November 19, 2001); missed 11 games. ... Strained knee (December 14, 2001); missed 15 games. ... Traded by Thrashers to Detroit Red Wings for C Yuri Butsayev and third-round pick (traded to Columbus; Blue Jackets selected LW Jeff Genovy) in 2002 draft (March 19, 2002). ... Signed as free agent by Vancouver Canucks (September 3, 2003). ... Traded by Canucks to Boston Bruins for future considerations (January 17, 2004).

		REGULAR SEASON								PLAYOFFS				
Season Team	**League**	**GP**	**G**	**A**	**Pts.**	**PIM**	**+/-**	**PP**	**SH**	**GP**	**G**	**A**	**Pts.**	**PIM**
87-88—Litvinov	Czech Rep.	4	1	1	2	0	...	...	...	—	—	—	—	—
88-89—Litvinov	Czech.	8	0	0	0	0	...	...	...	—	—	—	—	—
89-90—Litvinov	Czech.	51	4	15	19	...	...	...	...	—	—	—	—	—
90-91—Litvinov	Czech.	39	10	33	43	26	...	...	...	—	—	—	—	—
91-92—Litvinov	Czech.	38	7	22	29	30	...	...	...	—	—	—	—	—
—Czech. Olympic Team	Int'l	8	1	1	2	...	...	...	...	—	—	—	—	—
92-93—Vancouver	NHL	41	4	22	26	109	16	2	0	5	0	3	3	4
—Hamilton	AHL	21	4	14	18	42	-12	2	0	—	—	—	—	—
93-94—Vancouver	NHL	78	5	33	38	86	0	1	0	—	—	—	—	—
94-95—Chem. Litvinov	Czech Rep.	11	3	10	13	43	...	...	...	—	—	—	—	—
—Vancouver	NHL	19	1	5	6	32	0	0	0	—	—	—	—	—
—Edmonton	NHL	12	1	5	6	14	-5	1	0	—	—	—	—	—
95-96—Edmonton	NHL	57	4	13	17	74	-1	0	1	—	—	—	—	—
—Cape Breton	AHL	4	1	2	3	4	...	...	...	—	—	—	—	—
96-97—Chem. Litvinov	Czech Rep.	1	0	0	0	0	...	...	...	—	—	—	—	—
—Sodertalje SK	Sweden	30	4	14	18	62	...	...	...	—	—	—	—	—
97-98—Pittsburgh	NHL	73	5	12	17	109	10	1	1	6	0	4	4	2
—Czech Rep. Oly. team	Int'l	6	1	0	1	8	2	0	0	—	—	—	—	—
98-99—Pittsburgh	NHL	63	3	20	23	86	13	1	0	13	1	3	4	12
99-00—Pittsburgh	NHL	74	11	20	31	82	20	0	0	10	2	3	5	19
00-01—Pittsburgh	NHL	42	5	10	15	60	-9	0	1	—	—	—	—	—
—Atlanta	NHL	33	3	16	19	36	-1	2	0	—	—	—	—	—
01-02—Atlanta	NHL	38	3	5	8	51	-21	1	0	—	—	—	—	—
—Detroit	NHL	8	0	1	1	8	1	0	0	1	0	0	0	2
02-03—Litvinov	Czech Rep.	10	2	3	5	14	...	...	...	—	—	—	—	—
—Avangard Omsk	Russian	6	1	2	3	8	...	...	...	9	0	3	3	*45
03-04—Vancouver	NHL	16	2	5	7	8	6	1	1	—	—	—	—	—
—Boston	NHL	36	4	15	19	27	5	0	0	7	1	1	2	0
04-05—Chem. Litvinov	Czech Rep.	46	6	23	29	135	7	...	...	6	1	2	3	30
NHL Totals (10 years)		590	51	182	233	782	34	10	4	42	4	14	18	39

SLOAN, BLAKE — RW

PERSONAL: Born July 27, 1975, in Park Ridge, Ill. ... 5-10/196. ... Shoots right.

TRANSACTIONS/CAREER NOTES: Signed as free agent by Dallas Stars (March 10, 1999). ... Sprained ankle (February 21, 2000); missed 15 games. ... Claimed off waivers by Columbus Blue Jackets (March 13, 2001). ... Traded by Blue Jackets to Calgary Flames for D Jamie Allison (March 19, 2002). ... Signed as free agent by Detroit Red Wings (December 1, 2003). ... Claimed off waivers by Stars (December 3, 2003). ... Signed as free agent by Grand Rapids of the AHL (September 9, 2004).

		REGULAR SEASON								PLAYOFFS				
Season Team	**League**	**GP**	**G**	**A**	**Pts.**	**PIM**	**+/-**	**PP**	**SH**	**GP**	**G**	**A**	**Pts.**	**PIM**
93-94—Univ. of Michigan	CCHA	38	2	4	6	48	...	...	...	—	—	—	—	—
94-95—Univ. of Michigan	CCHA	39	2	15	17	60	...	...	...	—	—	—	—	—
95-96—Univ. of Michigan	CCHA	41	6	24	30	57	...	...	...	—	—	—	—	—
96-97—Univ. of Michigan	CCHA	41	2	15	17	52	...	...	...	—	—	—	—	—
97-98—Houston	IHL	70	2	13	15	86	...	...	...	2	0	0	0	0
98-99—Houston	IHL	62	8	10	18	76	...	...	...	—	—	—	—	—
—Dallas	NHL	14	0	0	0	10	-1	0	0	19	0	2	2	8

Season Team	League	REGULAR SEASON GP	G	A	Pts.	PIM	+/-	PP	SH	PLAYOFFS GP	G	A	Pts.	PIM
99-00—Dallas	NHL	67	4	13	17	50	11	0	0	16	0	0	0	12
00-01—Dallas	NHL	33	2	2	4	4	-2	0	0	—	—	—	—	—
—Houston	IHL	20	7	4	11	18	...	...	...	—	—	—	—	—
—Columbus	NHL	14	1	0	1	13	-2	0	0	—	—	—	—	—
01-02—Columbus	NHL	60	2	7	9	46	-18	0	0	—	—	—	—	—
—Calgary	NHL	7	0	2	2	4	1	0	0	—	—	—	—	—
02-03—Calgary	NHL	67	2	8	10	28	-5	0	0	—	—	—	—	—
03-04—Dallas	NHL	28	0	0	0	7	-1	0	0	—	—	—	—	—
—Grand Rapids	AHL	7	4	2	6	4	4	0	0	—	—	—	—	—
04-05—Grand Rapids	AHL	78	15	11	26	68	-3	4	1	—	—	—	—	—
NHL Totals (6 years)		290	11	32	43	162	-17	0	0	35	0	2	2	20

SLOVAK, TOMAS — D — AVALANCHE

PERSONAL: Born April 5, 1983, in Kosice, Czechoslovakia. ... 6-1/191. ... Shoots right.
TRANSACTIONS/CAREER NOTES: Selected by Nashville Predators in second round (third Predators pick, 42nd overall) of NHL draft (June 23, 2001). ... Traded by Predators to Colorado Avalanche for C/LW Sergei Soin (June 22, 2003).

Season Team	League	REGULAR SEASON GP	G	A	Pts.	PIM	+/-	PP	SH	PLAYOFFS GP	G	A	Pts.	PIM
99-00—VSZ Kosice	Slovakia	2	0	0	0	0	...	...	...	—	—	—	—	—
00-01—HC Kosice	Slovakia	43	5	5	10	28	...	...	...	3	1	0	1	2
01-02—Kelowna	WHL	53	2	24	26	41	...	...	...	15	0	0	0	8
02-03—Kelowna	WHL	65	18	53	71	86	...	...	...	19	2	20	22	26
03-04—Hershey	AHL	42	3	8	11	16	8	0	0	—	—	—	—	—
—Reading	ECHL	20	3	7	10	32	3	2	0	—	—	—	—	—
04-05—Hershey	AHL	1	0	0	0	2	0	0	0	—	—	—	—	—
—HC Kosice	Slovakia	33	3	11	14	42	...	...	...	—	—	—	—	—

SMID, LADISLAV — D — MIGHTY DUCKS

PERSONAL: Born February 1, 1986, in Frydlant, Czech. ... 6-3/202. ... Shoots left.
TRANSACTIONS/CAREER NOTES: Selected by Anaheim Mighty Ducks in first round (first Mighty Ducks pick, ninth overall) of NHL entry draft (June 26, 2004).

Season Team	League	REGULAR SEASON GP	G	A	Pts.	PIM	+/-	PP	SH	PLAYOFFS GP	G	A	Pts.	PIM
02-03—Liberec	Czech Rep.	4	0	0	0	0	...	...	...	—	—	—	—	—
03-04—Liberec	Czech Rep.	45	1	1	2	51	...	...	...	—	—	—	—	—
04-05—Liberec	Czech Rep.	39	1	3	4	14	...	...	...	—	—	—	—	—

SMIRNOV, ALEXEI — LW

PERSONAL: Born January 28, 1982, in Tver, USSR. ... 6-3/215. ... Shoots left.
TRANSACTIONS/CAREER NOTES: Selected by Might Ducks of Anaheim in first round (first Mighty Ducks pick, 12th overall) of NHL draft (June 24, 2000). ... Suffered concussion (February 8, 2003); missed two games.

Season Team	League	REGULAR SEASON GP	G	A	Pts.	PIM	+/-	PP	SH	PLAYOFFS GP	G	A	Pts.	PIM
97-98—Dynamo Moscow	Rus. Div.	11	1	1	2	4	...	...	...	—	—	—	—	—
98-99—Dynamo Moscow	Rus. Div.	27	9	3	12	24	...	...	...	—	—	—	—	—
—Dynamo Moscow	Russian	1	0	0	0	0	...	...	...	—	—	—	—	—
99-00—Dynamo Moscow	Russian	1	0	0	0	0	...	...	...	—	—	—	—	—
—Dynamo Moscow	Rus. Div.	12	5	3	8	34	...	...	...	—	—	—	—	—
—Tver	Russian	35	3	5	8	24	...	...	...	—	—	—	—	—
00-01—Dynamo Moscow	Russian	29	2	0	2	16	...	...	...	—	—	—	—	—
01-02—CSKA Moscow	Russian	51	5	11	16	42	...	...	...	—	—	—	—	—
02-03—Cincinnati	AHL	19	7	3	10	12	-1	0	1	—	—	—	—	—
—Anaheim	NHL	44	3	2	5	18	-1	0	0	4	0	0	0	2
03-04—Anaheim	NHL	8	0	1	1	2	0	0	0	—	—	—	—	—
—Cincinnati	AHL	51	9	10	19	34	-13	3	0	2	0	0	0	2
04-05—Cincinnati	AHL	65	9	9	18	53	4	1	1	4	0	0	0	0
NHL Totals (2 years)		52	3	3	6	20	-1	0	0	4	0	0	0	2

SMITH, BRANDON — D

PERSONAL: Born February 25, 1973, in Hazelton, B.C. ... 6-1/196. ... Shoots left.
TRANSACTIONS/CAREER NOTES: Signed as free agent by Detroit Red Wings (July 28, 1997). ... Signed as free agent by Boston Bruins (July 22, 1998). ... Separated shoulder (January 10, 2001); missed nine games. ... Signed as free agent by San Jose Sharks (July 23, 2001). ... Signed as free agent by New York Islanders (August 3, 2002). ... Signed as free agent by Rochester of the AHL (September 13, 2004).

Season Team	League	REGULAR SEASON GP	G	A	Pts.	PIM	+/-	PP	SH	PLAYOFFS GP	G	A	Pts.	PIM
89-90—Portland	WHL	59	2	17	19	16	...	...	...	—	—	—	—	—
90-91—Portland	WHL	17	8	5	13	8	...	...	...	—	—	—	—	—
91-92—Portland	WHL	70	12	32	44	63	...	...	...	—	—	—	—	—
92-93—Portland	WHL	72	20	54	74	38	...	...	...	16	4	9	13	6

Season Team	League	GP	G	A	Pts.	PIM	+/-	PP	SH	GP	G	A	Pts.	PIM
		REGULAR SEASON								PLAYOFFS				
93-94—Portland	WHL	72	19	63	82	47	...	...	...	10	2	10	12	8
94-95—Dayton	ECHL	60	16	49	65	57	...	...	...	4	2	3	5	0
—Adirondack	AHL	14	1	2	3	7	...	...	...	3	0	0	0	2
95-96—Adirondack	AHL	48	4	13	17	22	...	...	...	3	0	1	1	2
96-97—Adirondack	AHL	80	8	26	34	30	...	...	...	4	0	0	0	0
97-98—Adirondack	AHL	64	9	27	36	26	...	...	...	1	0	1	1	0
98-99—Providence	AHL	72	16	46	62	32	36	8	0	19	1	9	10	12
—Boston	NHL	5	0	0	0	0	2	0	0	—	—	—	—	—
99-00—Providence	AHL	55	8	30	38	20	...	...	...	14	1	11	12	2
—Boston	NHL	22	2	4	6	10	-4	0	0	—	—	—	—	—
00-01—Providence	AHL	63	11	28	39	30	...	...	...	17	0	5	5	6
—Boston	NHL	3	1	0	1	0	-1	1	0	—	—	—	—	—
01-02—Cleveland	AHL	59	6	29	35	26	-24	4	0	—	—	—	—	—
02-03—New York Islanders	NHL	3	0	0	0	0	-2	0	0	—	—	—	—	—
—Bridgeport	AHL	63	9	32	41	37	10	7	0	9	1	3	4	5
03-04—Bridgeport	AHL	74	5	23	28	39	-4	3	1	7	1	3	4	9
04-05—Rochester	AHL	67	4	14	18	32	-1	1	0	8	1	1	2	4
NHL Totals (4 years)		33	3	4	7	10	-5	1	0					

SMITH, JASON — D — OILERS

PERSONAL: Born November 2, 1973, in Calgary. ... 6-3/212. ... Shoots right.

TRANSACTIONS/CAREER NOTES: Selected by New Jersey Devils in first round (first Devils pick, 18th overall) of NHL draft (June 20, 1992). ... Injured right knee (November 5, 1994); missed 37 games. ... Bruised hand (November 5, 1995); missed 15 games. ... Traded by Devils with C Steve Sullivan and C Alyn McCauley to Toronto Maple Leafs for C Doug Gilmour, D Dave Ellett and third-round pick (D Andre Lakos) in 1999 draft (February 25, 1997). ... Fractured toe (March 30, 1998); missed one game. ... Traded by Maple Leafs to Edmonton Oilers for fourth-round pick (D Jonathan Zion) in 1999 draft and second-round pick (C Kris Vernarsky) in 2000 (March 23, 1999). ... Bruised shoulder (February 23, 2000); missed one game. ... Injured elbow (November 2, 2001); missed two games. ... Strained lower back (December 5, 2001); missed six games. ... Injured leg (January 29, 2003); missed two games. ... Injured shoulder (February 11, 2003); missed 12 games. ... Sprained left ankle (December 30, 2003); missed 14 games.

Season Team	League	GP	G	A	Pts.	PIM	+/-	PP	SH	GP	G	A	Pts.	PIM
		REGULAR SEASON								PLAYOFFS				
90-91—Calgary Canucks	AJHL	45	3	15	18	69	...	...	...	—	—	—	—	—
—Regina	WHL	2	0	0	0	7	...	...	...	—	—	—	—	—
91-92—Regina	WHL	62	9	29	38	168	...	...	...	—	—	—	—	—
92-93—Regina	WHL	64	14	52	66	175	-19	6	2	13	4	8	12	39
—Utica	AHL	...	...	...	...	...	...	...	...	1	0	0	0	2
93-94—New Jersey	NHL	41	0	5	5	43	7	0	0	6	0	0	0	7
—Albany	AHL	20	6	3	9	31	7	4	0	—	—	—	—	—
94-95—Albany	AHL	7	0	2	2	15	5	0	0	11	2	2	4	19
—New Jersey	NHL	2	0	0	0	0	-3	0	0	—	—	—	—	—
95-96—New Jersey	NHL	64	2	1	3	86	5	0	0	—	—	—	—	—
96-97—New Jersey	NHL	57	1	2	3	38	-8	0	0	—	—	—	—	—
—Toronto	NHL	21	0	5	5	16	-4	0	0	—	—	—	—	—
97-98—Toronto	NHL	81	3	13	16	100	-5	0	0	—	—	—	—	—
98-99—Toronto	NHL	60	2	11	13	40	-9	0	0	—	—	—	—	—
—Edmonton	NHL	12	1	1	2	11	0	0	0	4	0	1	1	4
99-00—Edmonton	NHL	80	3	11	14	60	16	0	0	5	0	1	1	4
00-01—Edmonton	NHL	82	5	15	20	120	14	1	1	6	0	2	2	6
01-02—Edmonton	NHL	74	5	13	18	103	14	0	1	—	—	—	—	—
02-03—Edmonton	NHL	68	4	8	12	64	5	0	0	6	0	0	0	19
03-04—Edmonton	NHL	68	7	12	19	98	13	0	1	—	—	—	—	—
NHL Totals (11 years)		710	33	97	130	779	45	1	3	27	0	4	4	40

SMITH, MARK — C/LW — SHARKS

PERSONAL: Born October 24, 1977, in Edmonton. ... 5-10/215. ... Shoots left.

TRANSACTIONS/CAREER NOTES: Selected by San Jose Sharks in ninth round (seventh Sharks pick, 219th overall) in NHL draft (June 21, 1997). ... Suffered concussion (November 5, 2000); missed seven games. ... Injured knee (February 26, 2001); missed three games. ... Flu (April 13, 2002); missed one game. ... Injured chest (November 15, 2003); missed 15 games.

Season Team	League	GP	G	A	Pts.	PIM	+/-	PP	SH	GP	G	A	Pts.	PIM
		REGULAR SEASON								PLAYOFFS				
94-95—Lethbridge	WHL	49	3	4	7	25	...	...	...	—	—	—	—	—
95-96—Lethbridge	WHL	71	11	24	35	59	...	...	...	19	7	13	20	51
96-97—Lethbridge	WHL	62	19	38	57	125	...	...	...	19	7	13	20	51
97-98—Lethbridge	WHL	70	42	67	109	206	28	19	5	3	0	2	2	18
98-99—Kentucky	AHL	78	18	21	39	101	8	4	0	12	2	7	9	16
99-00—Kentucky	AHL	79	21	45	66	153	...	...	...	9	0	5	5	22
00-01—San Jose	NHL	42	2	2	4	51	2	0	0	—	—	—	—	—
—Kentucky	AHL	6	2	6	8	23	...	...	...	—	—	—	—	—
01-02—San Jose	NHL	49	3	3	6	72	-1	0	0	—	—	—	—	—
02-03—San Jose	NHL	75	4	11	15	64	1	0	0	—	—	—	—	—
03-04—San Jose	NHL	36	1	3	4	72	-5	0	0	10	1	0	1	11
04-05—Victoria	ECHL	20	6	9	15	41	-13	3	0	—	—	—	—	—
NHL Totals (4 years)		202	10	19	29	259	-3	0	0	10	1	0	1	11

SMITH, MIKE — G — STARS

PERSONAL: Born March 22, 1982, in Kingston, Ont. ... 6-3/189. ... Catches left.

TRANSACTIONS/CAREER NOTES: Selected by Dallas Stars in fifth round (fifth Stars pick, 70th overall) of NHL entry draft (June 23, 2001).

		REGULAR SEASON									PLAYOFFS							
Season Team	League	GP	Min.	W	L	T	GA	SO	GAA	SV%	GP	Min.	W	L	GA	SO	GAA	SV%
00-01—Sudbury	OHL	43	2571	22	13	7	108	3	2.52	...	12	735	7	5	26	2	*2.12	...
01-02—Sudbury	OHL	53	3082	19	28	5	157	3	3.06	...	5	302	1	4	15	0	2.98	...
02-03—Utah	AHL	11	613	5	5	0	33	0	3.23	.906	—	—	—	—	—	—	—	—
—Lexington	ECHL	27	1553	11	10	4	66	1	2.55	.910	2	93	0	1	8	0	5.16	.822
03-04—Utah	AHL	21	1185	8	11	0	56	2	2.84	.899	—	—	—	—	—	—	—	—
04-05—Houston	AHL	45	2408	19	17	...	97	5	2.42	.915	3	180	1	2	4	0	1.33	.957

SMITH, NATHAN — C — CANUCKS

PERSONAL: Born February 9, 1982, in Strathcona, Alta. ... 6-2/200. ... Shoots left. ... Brother of Jarrett Smith, center, Mighty Ducks of Anaheim organization.

TRANSACTIONS/CAREER NOTES: Selected by Vancouver Canucks in first round (first Canucks pick, 23rd overall) of NHL entry draft (June 24, 2000).

		REGULAR SEASON								PLAYOFFS				
Season Team	League	GP	G	A	Pts.	PIM	+/-	PP	SH	GP	G	A	Pts.	PIM
98-99—Swift Current	WHL	47	5	8	13	26	...	...	...	—	—	—	—	—
99-00—Swift Current	WHL	70	21	28	49	72	...	...	...	12	1	6	7	4
00-01—Swift Current	WHL	67	28	62	90	78	...	...	...	19	4	3	7	20
01-02—Swift Current	WHL	47	22	38	60	52	...	...	...	12	3	6	9	18
02-03—Manitoba	AHL	53	9	8	17	30	6	3	0	14	1	3	4	25
03-04—Vancouver	NHL	2	0	0	0	0	-1	0	0	—	—	—	—	—
—Manitoba	AHL	76	4	16	20	71	-13	1	1	—	—	—	—	—
04-05—Manitoba	AHL	72	7	9	16	67	-11	0	0	14	2	4	6	20
NHL Totals (1 year)		2	0	0	0	0	-1	0	0					

SMITH, WYATT — C — PREDATORS

PERSONAL: Born February 13, 1977, in Thief River Falls, Minn. ... 5-11/200. ... Shoots left.

TRANSACTIONS/CAREER NOTES: Selected by Phoenix Coyotes in ninth round (sixth Coyotes pick, 233rd overall) of NHL entry draft (June 21, 1997). ... Signed as free agent by Nashville Predators (July 15, 2002). ... Bruised shoulder (November 16, 2002); missed five games.

		REGULAR SEASON								PLAYOFFS				
Season Team	League	GP	G	A	Pts.	PIM	+/-	PP	SH	GP	G	A	Pts.	PIM
95-96—Minnesota	WCHA	32	4	5	9	32	...	...	...	—	—	—	—	—
96-97—Minnesota	WCHA	39	24	23	47	62	...	...	...	—	—	—	—	—
97-98—Minnesota	WCHA	39	24	23	47	62	...	...	...	—	—	—	—	—
98-99—Minnesota	WCHA	43	23	20	43	37	...	...	...	—	—	—	—	—
99-00—Springfield	AHL	60	14	26	40	26	...	...	...	5	2	3	5	13
—Phoenix	NHL	2	0	0	0	0	-2	0	0	—	—	—	—	—
00-01—Phoenix	NHL	42	3	7	10	13	7	0	1	—	—	—	—	—
—Springfield	AHL	18	5	7	12	11	...	...	...	—	—	—	—	—
01-02—Springfield	AHL	69	23	32	55	69	-5	9	0	—	—	—	—	—
—Phoenix	NHL	10	0	0	0	0	-5	0	0	—	—	—	—	—
02-03—Nashville	NHL	11	1	0	1	0	-1	0	0	—	—	—	—	—
—Milwaukee	AHL	56	24	27	51	89	6	6	2	4	1	0	1	2
03-04—Nashville	NHL	18	3	1	4	2	2	0	1	—	—	—	—	—
—Milwaukee	AHL	40	9	7	16	40	5	2	2	22	5	7	12	25
04-05—Milwaukee	AHL	69	19	28	47	89	4	11	0	7	1	4	5	10
NHL Totals (5 years)		83	7	8	15	15	1	0	2					

SMITHSON, JERRED — C

PERSONAL: Born February 4, 1979, in Vernon, B.C. ... 6-2/200. ... Shoots right.

TRANSACTIONS/CAREER NOTES: Signed as free agent by Los Angeles Kings (February 18, 2000). ... Signed as free agent by Nashville Predators (July 22, 2004).

		REGULAR SEASON								PLAYOFFS				
Season Team	League	GP	G	A	Pts.	PIM	+/-	PP	SH	GP	G	A	Pts.	PIM
00-01—Trenton	ECHL	3	0	1	1	2	...	...	...	0	0	0	0	0
—Lowell	AHL	24	1	1	2	10	...	...	...	0	0	0	0	0
01-02—Manchester	AHL	78	5	13	18	45	...	...	...	0	0	0	0	0
02-03—Manchester	AHL	38	4	21	25	60	...	...	...	3	0	0	0	4
—Los Angeles	NHL	22	0	2	2	21	-5	0	0	—	—	—	—	—
03-04—Manchester	AHL	66	7	13	20	51	-2	1	1	6	0	1	1	10
—Los Angeles	NHL	8	0	1	1	4	0	0	0	—	—	—	—	—
04-05—Milwaukee	AHL	80	11	11	22	92	3	1	1	5	0	0	0	4
NHL Totals (2 years)		30	0	3	3	25	-5	0	0					

SMOLENAK, RADEK — LW — LIGHTNING

PERSONAL: Born December 3, 1986, in Prague, Czech. ... 6-2/190. ... Shoots left.

		REGULAR SEASON								PLAYOFFS				
Season Team	League	GP	G	A	Pts.	PIM	+/-	PP	SH	GP	G	A	Pts.	PIM
02-03—Kladno	Czech. Jrs.	33	31	18	49	38	...	...	...	—	—	—	—	—
03-04—Kladno	Czech. Jrs.	54	27	25	52	53	...	...	...	—	—	—	—	—
04-05—Kingston	OHL	67	32	28	60	58	-14	11	0	—	—	—	—	—

SMOLINSKI, BRYAN — C — SENATORS

PERSONAL: Born December 27, 1971, in Toledo, Ohio. ... 6-1/210. ... Shoots right.

TRANSACTIONS/CAREER NOTES: Selected by Boston Bruins in first round (first Bruins pick, 21st overall) of NHL entry draft (June 16, 1990). ... Injured knee (April 14, 1994); missed one game. ... Charley horse (April 1995); missed four games. ... Traded by Bruins with RW Glen Murray to Pittsburgh Penguins for LW Kevin Stevens and C Shawn McEachern (August 2, 1995). ... Bruised knee (January 16, 1996); missed one game. ... Traded by Penguins to New York Islanders for D Darius Kasparaitis and C Andreas Johansson (November 17, 1996). ... Traded by Islanders with RW Zigmund Palffy, G Marcel Cousineau and fourth-round pick (C Daniel Johansson) in 1999 draft to Los Angeles Kings for C Olli Jokinen, LW Josh Green, D Mathieu Biron and first-round pick (LW Taylor Pyatt) in 1999 draft (June 20, 1999). ... Sprained knee (April 3, 1999); missed final three games of season. ... Back spasms (April 3, 2001); missed final two games of season. ... Back spasms (October 26, 2001); missed one game. ... Flu (January 24, 2002); missed one game. ... Traded by Kings to Ottawa Senators for D Tim Gleason (March 11, 2003). ... Separated shoulder (November 23, 2003); missed two games.

STATISTICAL PLATEAUS: Three-goal games: 1994-95 (1), 2000-01 (1), 2002-03 (1). Total: 3.

		REGULAR SEASON								PLAYOFFS				
Season Team	League	GP	G	A	Pts.	PIM	+/-	PP	SH	GP	G	A	Pts.	PIM
87-88—Detroit Little Caesars	MNHL	80	43	77	120	...	...	...	...	—	—	—	—	—
88-89—Stratford Jr. B	OHA	46	32	62	94	132	...	...	...	—	—	—	—	—
89-90—Michigan State	CCHA	39	10	17	27	45	...	...	...	—	—	—	—	—
90-91—Michigan State	CCHA	35	9	12	21	24	...	...	...	—	—	—	—	—
91-92—Michigan State	CCHA	44	30	35	65	59	...	...	...	—	—	—	—	—
92-93—Michigan State	CCHA	40	31	37	68	93	...	...	...	—	—	—	—	—
—Boston	NHL	9	1	3	4	0	3	0	0	4	1	0	1	2
93-94—Boston	NHL	83	31	20	51	82	4	4	3	13	5	4	9	4
94-95—Boston	NHL	44	18	13	31	31	-3	6	0	5	0	1	1	4
95-96—Pittsburgh	NHL	81	24	40	64	69	6	8	2	18	5	4	9	10
96-97—Detroit	IHL	6	5	7	12	10	...	...	...	—	—	—	—	—
—New York Islanders	NHL	64	28	28	56	25	9	9	0	—	—	—	—	—
97-98—New York Islanders	NHL	81	13	30	43	34	-16	3	0	—	—	—	—	—
98-99—New York Islanders	NHL	82	16	24	40	49	-7	7	0	—	—	—	—	—
99-00—Los Angeles	NHL	79	20	36	56	48	2	2	0	4	0	0	0	2
00-01—Los Angeles	NHL	78	27	32	59	40	10	5	3	13	1	5	6	14
01-02—Los Angeles	NHL	80	13	25	38	56	7	4	1	7	2	0	2	2
02-03—Los Angeles	NHL	58	18	20	38	18	-1	6	1	...	...	...	...	...
—Ottawa	NHL	10	3	5	8	2	1	0	0	18	2	7	9	6
03-04—Ottawa	NHL	80	19	27	46	49	22	4	0	7	1	1	2	4
04-05—Motor City	UHL	21	9	23	32	18	20	1	1	—	—	—	—	—
NHL Totals (12 years)		829	231	303	534	503	37	58	10	89	17	22	39	48

SMYTH, RYAN — LW — OILERS

PERSONAL: Born February 21, 1976, in Banff, Alta. ... 6-1/190. ... Shoots left. ... Brother of Kevin Smyth, LW with Hartford Whalers (1993-94 through 1995-96). ... Name pronounced SMIHTH.

TRANSACTIONS/CAREER NOTES: Selected by Edmonton Oilers in first round (second Oilers pick, sixth overall) of NHL entry draft (June 28, 1994). ... Tore medial collateral ligament in knee (January 20, 1998); missed 15 games. ... Bruised thigh (December 27, 1998); missed one game. ... Fractured jaw (March 10, 1999); missed seven games. ... Fractured right ankle (November 16, 2001); missed 21 games. ... Injured shoulder (January 16, 2003); missed six games ... Injured shoulder (February 11, 2003); missed nine games.

STATISTICAL PLATEAUS: Three-goal games: 1996-97 (1), 1999-00 (1), 2000-01 (2). Total: 4.

		REGULAR SEASON								PLAYOFFS				
Season Team	League	GP	G	A	Pts.	PIM	+/-	PP	SH	GP	G	A	Pts.	PIM
91-92—Moose Jaw	WHL	2	0	0	0	0	...	...	...	—	—	—	—	—
92-93—Moose Jaw	WHL	64	19	14	33	59	...	...	...	—	—	—	—	—
93-94—Moose Jaw	WHL	72	50	55	105	88	-30	22	0	—	—	—	—	—
94-95—Moose Jaw	WHL	50	41	45	86	66	21	14	5	10	6	9	15	22
—Edmonton	NHL	3	0	0	0	0	-1	0	0	—	—	—	—	—
95-96—Edmonton	NHL	48	2	9	11	28	-10	1	0	—	—	—	—	—
—Cape Breton	AHL	9	6	5	11	4	...	...	...	—	—	—	—	—
96-97—Edmonton	NHL	82	39	22	61	76	-7	20	0	12	5	5	10	12
97-98—Edmonton	NHL	65	20	13	33	44	-24	10	0	12	1	3	4	16
98-99—Edmonton	NHL	71	13	18	31	62	0	6	0	3	3	0	3	0
99-00—Edmonton	NHL	82	28	26	54	58	-2	11	0	5	1	0	1	6
00-01—Edmonton	NHL	82	31	39	70	58	10	11	0	6	3	4	7	4
01-02—Edmonton	NHL	61	15	35	50	48	7	7	1	—	—	—	—	—
—Can. Olympic team	Int'l	6	0	1	1	0	...	...	...	—	—	—	—	—
02-03—Edmonton	NHL	66	27	34	61	67	5	10	0	6	2	0	2	16
03-04—Edmonton	NHL	82	23	36	59	70	11	8	2	—	—	—	—	—
NHL Totals (10 years)		642	198	232	430	511	-11	84	3	44	15	12	27	54

SNOW, GARTH — G — ISLANDERS

PERSONAL: Born July 28, 1969, in Wrentham, Mass. ... 6-3/210. ... Catches left.

TRANSACTIONS/CAREER NOTES: Selected by Quebec Nordiques in sixth round (sixth Nordiques pick, 114th overall) of NHL draft (June 13, 1987). ... Nordiques franchise moved to Colorado and renamed Avalanche for 1995-96 season (June 21, 1995). ... Rights traded by Avalanche to Philadelphia Flyers for third- (traded to Washington; Capitals selected C Shawn McNeil) and sixth-round (G Kai Fischer) picks in 1996 draft (July 12, 1995). ... Injured groin (March 27, 1997); missed three games. ... Traded by Flyers to Vancouver Canucks for G Sean Burke (March 4, 1998). ... Strained hip flexor (March 18, 1998); missed three games. ... Strained hip flexor (October 31, 1998); missed two games. ... Injured finger (September 21, 1999); missed two games. ... Fractured finger (October 13, 1999); missed 15 games. ... Signed as free agent by Pittsburgh Penguins (October 10, 2000). ... Suspended two games by NHL for fighting (December 16, 2000). ... Strained groin (February 7, 2001); missed 25 games. ... Signed as free agent by New York Islanders (July 1, 2001). ... Suspended two games for attempting to injure a player (November 22, 2002). ... Injured groin (March 25, 2004); missed five games.

		REGULAR SEASON									PLAYOFFS							
Season Team	League	GP	Min.	W	L	T	GA	SO	GAA	SV%	GP	Min.	W	L	GA	SO	GAA	SV%
88-89—Maine	Hockey East	5	241	2	2	0	14	1	3.49	...	—	—	—	—	—	—	—	—
89-90—Maine	Hockey East	Did not play																
90-91—Maine	Hockey East	25	1290	18	4	0	64	0	2.98	...	—	—	—	—	—	—	—	—
91-92—Maine	Hockey East	31	1792	25	4	2	73	2	2.44	...	—	—	—	—	—	—	—	—
92-93—Maine	Hockey East	23	1210	21	0	1	42	1	2.08	...	—	—	—	—	—	—	—	—
93-94—U.S. national team	Int'l	23	1324	13	5	3	71	1	3.22	...	—	—	—	—	—	—	—	—
—Quebec	NHL	5	279	3	2	0	16	0	3.44	.874	—	—	—	—	—	—	—	—
—U.S. Olympic team	Int'l	5	299	1	2	2	17	0	3.41	.881	—	—	—	—	—	—	—	—
—Cornwall	AHL	16	927	6	5	3	51	0	3.30	.891	13	790	8	5	42	0	3.19	.894
94-95—Cornwall	AHL	62	3558	*32	20	7	162	3	2.73	.900	8	402	4	3	14	2	*2.09	.944
—Quebec	NHL	2	119	1	1	0	11	0	5.55	.825	1	9	0	0	1	0	6.67	.667
95-96—Philadelphia	NHL	26	1437	12	8	4	69	0	2.88	.894	1	1	0	0	0	0	0.00	...
96-97—Philadelphia	NHL	35	1884	14	8	8	79	2	2.52	.903	12	699	8	4	33	0	2.83	.892
97-98—Philadelphia	NHL	29	1651	14	9	4	67	1	2.43	.902	—	—	—	—	—	—	—	—
—Vancouver	NHL	12	504	3	6	0	26	0	3.10	.901	—	—	—	—	—	—	—	—
98-99—Vancouver	NHL	65	3501	20	31	8	171	6	2.93	.900	—	—	—	—	—	—	—	—
99-00—Vancouver	NHL	32	1712	10	15	3	76	0	2.66	.902	—	—	—	—	—	—	—	—
00-01—Wilkes-Barre/Scranton	AHL	3	178	2	1	0	7	0	2.36	.920	—	—	—	—	—	—	—	—
—Pittsburgh	NHL	35	2032	14	15	4	101	3	2.98	.900	—	—	—	—	—	—	—	—
01-02—New York Islanders	NHL	25	1217	10	7	2	55	2	2.71	.900	1	26	0	0	2	0	4.62	.895
02-03—New York Islanders	NHL	43	2390	16	17	5	92	1	2.31	.918	5	305	1	4	12	1	2.36	.910
03-04—New York Islanders	NHL	39	2015	14	15	5	94	1	2.80	.899	—	—	—	—	—	—	—	—
04-05—SKA St. Petersburg	Russian	16	893	...	...	...	41	1	2.75	...	—	—	—	—	—	—	—	—
NHL Totals (11 years)		348	18741	131	134	43	857	16	2.74	.902	20	1040	9	8	48	1	2.77	.896

SOMIK, RADOVAN — RW

PERSONAL: Born May 5, 1977, in Martin, Czechoslovakia. ... 6-2/195. ... Shoots right.

TRANSACTIONS/CAREER NOTES: Selected by Philadelphia Flyers in fourth round (third Flyers pick, 100th overall) of NHL draft (July 8, 1995). ... Strained groin (October 2, 2002); missed two games. ... Reinjured groin (October 19, 2002); missed four games. ... Reinjured groin (November 7, 2002); missed seven games. ... Strained back (March 17, 2003); missed nine games. ... Injured knee (October 14, 2003); missed 14 games. ... Fractured cheekbone (March 12, 2004); missed six games. ... Injured hand (May 20, 2004); missed two playoff games.

		REGULAR SEASON								PLAYOFFS				
Season Team	League	GP	G	A	Pts.	PIM	+/-	PP	SH	GP	G	A	Pts.	PIM
93-94—Martimex ZTS Martin	Slovakia	1	0	0	0	0	...	...	...	—	—	—	—	—
94-95—Martimex ZTS Martin	Slovakia	28	4	0	4	31	...	...	...	3	1	0	1	2
95-96—Martimex ZTS Martin	Slovakia	25	3	6	9	8	...	...	...	9	1	0	1	...
96-97—Martimex ZTS Martin	Slovakia	35	3	5	8	...	...	...	...	3	0	0	0	...
97-98—Martimex ZTS Martin	Slovakia	26	6	9	15	10	...	...	...	3	0	0	0	0
98-99—Dulka Trencin	Slovakia	26	1	4	5	6	...	...	...	—	—	—	—	—
99-00—Martimex ZTS Martin	Slovakia	40	38	28	66	32	...	...	...	—	—	—	—	—
00-01—HC Continental Zlin	Czech Rep.	46	15	10	25	22	...	...	...	6	1	0	1	0
01-02—HC Continental Zlin	Czech Rep.	37	14	14	28	22	...	...	...	11	4	3	7	37
02-03—Philadelphia	NHL	60	8	10	18	10	9	0	1	5	1	1	2	6
03-04—Philadelphia	NHL	53	4	10	14	17	-2	0	0	10	1	1	2	4
—Philadelphia	AHL	1	0	0	0	2	0	0	0	—	—	—	—	—
04-05—Martimex ZTS Martin	Slovakia	2	1	0	1	0	2	...	...	—	—	—	—	—
—HC Vsetin	Czech Rep.	31	7	16	23	24	6	...	...	—	—	—	—	—
—Malmo	Sweden	8	1	0	1	6	0	0	0	10	1	3	4	2
NHL Totals (2 years)		113	12	20	32	27	7	0	1	15	2	2	4	10

SONNENBERG, MARTIN — LW — FLAMES

PERSONAL: Born January 23, 1978, in Wetaskiwin, Alta. ... 6-0/197. ... Shoots left.

TRANSACTIONS/CAREER NOTES: Signed as free agent by Pittsburgh Penguins (October 9, 1998). ... Signed as free agent by Calgary Flames (July 9, 2002).

		REGULAR SEASON								PLAYOFFS				
Season Team	League	GP	G	A	Pts.	PIM	+/-	PP	SH	GP	G	A	Pts.	PIM
95-96—Saskatoon	WHL	58	8	7	15	24	...	...	...	3	0	0	0	2
96-97—Saskatoon	WHL	72	38	26	64	79	...	...	...	—	—	—	—	—
97-98—Saskatoon	WHL	72	40	52	92	87	...	...	...	6	1	3	4	9
98-99—Syracuse	AHL	37	16	9	25	31	-26	10	0	—	—	—	—	—

Season Team	League	GP	G	A	Pts.	PIM	+/-	PP	SH		GP	G	A	Pts.	PIM
		REGULAR SEASON									PLAYOFFS				
—Pittsburgh	NHL	44	1	1	2	19	-2	0	0		7	0	0	0	0
99-00—Pittsburgh	NHL	14	1	2	3	0	0	1	0		—	—	—	—	—
—Wilkes-Barre/Scranton	AHL	62	20	33	53	109	...	...	...		—	—	—	—	—
00-01—Wilkes-Barre/Scranton	AHL	73	14	18	32	89	...	...	...		21	4	3	7	6
01-02—Wilkes-Barre/Scranton	AHL	78	20	30	50	127	-4	7	1		—	—	—	—	—
02-03—Saint John	AHL	54	11	10	21	63	0	5	1		—	—	—	—	—
03-04—Calgary	NHL	5	0	0	0	2	-2	0	0		—	—	—	—	—
—Lowell	AHL	48	20	22	42	46	15	7	0		—	—	—	—	—
04-05—Utah	AHL	65	13	13	26	94	-24	5	0		—	—	—	—	—
NHL Totals (3 years)		63	2	3	5	21	-4	1	0		7	0	0	0	0

SOPEL, BRENT — D — ISLANDERS

PERSONAL: Born January 7, 1977, in Calgary. ... 6-1/205. ... Shoots right. ... Name pronounced SOH-puhl.

TRANSACTIONS/CAREER NOTES: Selected by Vancouver Canucks in 6th round (6th Canucks pick, 144th overall) of entry draft (July 8, 1995). ... Injured ankle (January 21, 2003); missed one game. ... Injured groin (October 30, 2003); missed two games. ... Traded by Canucks to New York Islanders for conditional 2006 pick (Aug. 3, 2005).

Season Team	League	GP	G	A	Pts.	PIM	+/-	PP	SH		GP	G	A	Pts.	PIM
		REGULAR SEASON									PLAYOFFS				
93-94—Saskatoon	WHL	11	2	2	4	2	...	...	...		—	—	—	—	—
94-95—Saskatoon	WHL	22	1	10	11	31	12	0	0		—	—	—	—	—
—Swift Current	WHL	41	4	19	23	50	3	3	0		3	0	3	3	0
95-96—Swift Current	WHL	71	13	48	61	87	...	...	...		6	1	2	3	4
—Syracuse	AHL	1	0	0	0	0	...	...	...		—	—	—	—	—
96-97—Swift Current	WHL	62	15	41	56	109	39	6	0		10	5	11	16	32
—Syracuse	AHL	2	0	0	0	0	0	0	0		3	0	0	0	0
97-98—Syracuse	AHL	76	10	33	43	70	-4	6	0		5	0	7	7	12
98-99—Syracuse	AHL	53	10	21	31	59	-33	6	1		—	—	—	—	—
—Vancouver	NHL	5	1	0	1	4	-1	1	0		—	—	—	—	—
99-00—Syracuse	AHL	50	6	25	31	67	...	...	...		4	0	2	2	8
—Vancouver	NHL	18	2	4	6	12	9	0	0		—	—	—	—	—
00-01—Vancouver	NHL	52	4	10	14	10	4	0	0		4	0	0	0	2
—Kansas City	IHL	4	0	1	1	0	...	...	...		—	—	—	—	—
01-02—Vancouver	NHL	66	8	17	25	44	21	1	0		6	0	2	2	2
02-03—Vancouver	NHL	81	7	30	37	23	-15	6	0		14	2	6	8	4
03-04—Vancouver	NHL	80	10	32	42	36	11	6	0		7	0	1	1	0
NHL Totals (6 years)		302	32	93	125	129	29	14	0		31	2	9	11	8

SOURAY, SHELDON — D — CANADIENS

PERSONAL: Born July 13, 1976, in Elk Point, Alta. ... 6-4/227. ... Shoots left. ... Name pronounced SOOR-ay.

TRANSACTIONS/CAREER NOTES: Selected by New Jersey Devils in third round (third Devils pick, 71st overall) of NHL draft (June 29, 1994). ... Injured head (September 27, 1997); missed five games. ... Bruised right wrist (October 17, 1997); missed four games. ... Flu (December 18, 1997); missed one game. ... Flu (January 30, 1998); missed one game. ... Traded by Devils with D Josh DeWolf and second-round pick (traded to Washington; traded to Tampa Bay; Lightning selected D Andreas Holmqvist) in 2001 draft to Montreal Canadiens for D Vladimir Malakhov (March 1, 2000). ... Strained abdominal muscle (September 23, 2000) and had surgery; missed first 29 games of season. ... Bruised ankle (February 10, 2001); missed one game. ... Strained groin (September 27, 2001); missed first three games of season. ... Bruised hip (November 6, 2001); missed one game. ... Sprained wrist (November 17, 2001); missed two games. ... Fractured left wrist (December 17, 2001); missed 41 games. ... Missed 2002-03 season recovering from wrist surgery. ... Injured left knee (February 10, 2004); missed 17 games. ... Injured shoulder (March 24, 2004); missed two games.

STATISTICAL PLATEAUS: Three-goal games: 2003-04 (1).

Season Team	League	GP	G	A	Pts.	PIM	+/-	PP	SH		GP	G	A	Pts.	PIM
		REGULAR SEASON									PLAYOFFS				
92-93—Fort Saskatchewan	AJHL	35	0	12	12	125	...	...	...		—	—	—	—	—
—Tri-City	WHL	2	0	0	0	0	...	...	...		—	—	—	—	—
93-94—Tri-City	WHL	42	3	6	9	122	-4	1	1		—	—	—	—	—
94-95—Tri-City	WHL	40	2	24	26	140	-5	0	0		—	—	—	—	—
—Prince George	WHL	11	2	3	5	23	-12	1	0		—	—	—	—	—
—Albany	AHL	7	0	2	2	8	-5	0	0		—	—	—	—	—
95-96—Prince George	WHL	32	9	18	27	91	...	...	...		—	—	—	—	—
—Kelowna	WHL	27	7	20	27	94	...	...	...		6	0	5	5	2
—Albany	AHL	6	0	2	2	12	...	...	...		4	0	1	1	4
96-97—Albany	AHL	70	2	11	13	160	11	0	1		16	2	3	5	47
97-98—New Jersey	NHL	60	3	7	10	85	18	0	0		3	0	1	1	2
—Albany	AHL	6	0	0	0	8	-2	0	0		—	—	—	—	—
98-99—New Jersey	NHL	70	1	7	8	110	5	0	0		2	0	1	1	0
99-00—New Jersey	NHL	52	0	8	8	70	-6	0	0		—	—	—	—	—
—Montreal	NHL	19	3	0	3	44	7	0	0		—	—	—	—	—
00-01—Montreal	NHL	52	3	8	11	95	-11	0	0		—	—	—	—	—
01-02—Montreal	NHL	34	3	5	8	62	-5	1	0		12	0	1	1	16
03-04—Montreal	NHL	63	15	20	35	104	4	6	1		11	0	2	2	39
04-05—Farjestad Karlstad	Sweden	39	9	8	17	117	9	4	0		15	1	6	7	77
NHL Totals (6 years)		350	28	55	83	570	12	7	1		28	0	5	5	57

SPACEK, JAROSLAV — D — BLACKHAWKS

PERSONAL: Born February 11, 1974, in Rokycany, Czechoslovakia. ... 5-11/204. ... Shoots left.

TRANSACTIONS/CAREER NOTES: Selected by Florida Panthers in 5th round (5th Panthers pick, 117th overall) of entry draft (June 27, 1998). ... Flu (April 7, 1999); missed three games. ... Traded by Panthers to Chicago Blackhawks for D Anders Eriksson (November 6, 2000). ... Fractured left shoulder (January 14, 2001); missed 18 games. ... Suffered injury (November 13, 2001); missed two games. ... Fractured finger (November 25, 2001); missed eight games. ... Traded by Blackhawks with 2nd-round pick (C Dan Fritsche) in 2003 draft to Columbus Blue Jackets for D Lyle Odelein (March 19, 2002). ... Injured hand (March 8, 2003); missed two games. ... Injured groin (November 29, 2003); missed 24 games. ... Signed as free agent by Chicago Blackhawks (Aug. 4, 2005).

		REGULAR SEASON								PLAYOFFS				
Season Team	League	GP	G	A	Pts.	PIM	+/-	PP	SH	GP	G	A	Pts.	PIM
92-93—Skoda Plzen	Czech.	16	1	3	4	...	...	...	...	—	—	—	—	—
93-94—Skoda Plzen	Czech Rep.	34	2	10	12	...	...	...	...	—	—	—	—	—
94-95—Interconex Plzen	Czech Rep.	38	4	8	12	14	...	...	...	3	1	0	1	2
95-96—ZKZ Plzen	Czech Rep.	40	3	10	13	42	...	...	...	3	0	1	1	4
96-97—ZKZ Plzen	Czech Rep.	52	9	29	38	44	...	...	...	—	—	—	—	—
97-98—Farjestad Karlstad	Sweden	45	10	16	26	63	...	...	...	12	2	5	7	14
98-99—Florida	NHL	63	3	12	15	28	15	2	1	—	—	—	—	—
—New Haven	AHL	14	4	8	12	15	-1	3	0	—	—	—	—	—
99-00—Florida	NHL	82	10	26	36	53	7	4	0	4	0	0	0	0
00-01—Florida	NHL	12	2	1	3	8	-4	1	0	—	—	—	—	—
—Chicago	NHL	50	5	18	23	20	7	2	0	—	—	—	—	—
01-02—Chicago	NHL	60	3	10	13	29	5	0	0	—	—	—	—	—
—Czech Rep. Oly. team	Int'l	4	0	0	0	0	...	...	...	—	—	—	—	—
—Columbus	NHL	14	2	3	5	24	-9	1	1	—	—	—	—	—
02-03—Columbus	NHL	81	9	36	45	70	-23	5	0	—	—	—	—	—
03-04—Columbus	NHL	58	5	17	22	45	-13	2	1	—	—	—	—	—
04-05—Plzen	Czech Rep.	30	3	8	11	26	-9	...	...	—	—	—	—	—
—Slavia Praha	Czech Rep.	17	4	9	13	29	12	...	...	7	0	2	2	8
NHL Totals (6 years)		420	39	123	162	277	-15	17	3	4	0	0	0	0

SPEZZA, JASON — C — SENATORS

PERSONAL: Born June 13, 1983, in Mississauga, Ont. ... 6-2/205. ... Shoots right. ... Name pronounced SPEHT-zah.

TRANSACTIONS/CAREER NOTES: Selected by Ottawa Senators in first round (first Senators pick, second overall) of NHL entry draft (June 23, 2001). ... Injured left knee (January 31, 2003); missed two games.

		REGULAR SEASON								PLAYOFFS				
Season Team	League	GP	G	A	Pts.	PIM	+/-	PP	SH	GP	G	A	Pts.	PIM
98-99—Brampton	OHL	67	22	49	71	18	...	...	...	—	—	—	—	—
99-00—Mississauga	OHL	52	24	37	61	33	...	...	...	—	—	—	—	—
00-01—Mississauga	OHL	15	7	23	30	11	...	...	...	—	—	—	—	—
—Windsor	OHL	41	36	50	86	32	...	...	...	9	4	5	9	10
01-02—Windsor	OHL	27	19	26	45	16	...	...	...	—	—	—	—	—
—Belleville	OHL	26	23	37	60	26	...	...	...	11	5	6	11	18
—Grand Rapids	AHL	...	...	...	...	...	...	...	...	3	1	0	1	2
02-03—Ottawa	NHL	33	7	14	21	8	-3	3	0	3	1	1	2	0
—Binghamton	AHL	43	22	32	54	71	-5	5	0	2	1	2	3	4
03-04—Ottawa	NHL	78	22	33	55	71	22	5	0	3	0	0	0	2
04-05—Binghamton	AHL	80	32	85	117	50	18	10	3	6	1	3	4	6
NHL Totals (2 years)		111	29	47	76	79	19	8	0	6	1	1	2	2

SPILLER, MATTHEW — D — COYOTES

PERSONAL: Born February 7, 1983, in Daysland, Alta. ... 6-5/233. ... Shoots left.

TRANSACTIONS/CAREER NOTES: Selected by Phoenix Coyotes in second round (second Coyotes pick, 31st overall) of NHL entry draft (June 23, 2001).

		REGULAR SEASON								PLAYOFFS				
Season Team	League	GP	G	A	Pts.	PIM	+/-	PP	SH	GP	G	A	Pts.	PIM
99-00—Seattle	WHL	60	1	10	11	108	...	...	...	7	0	0	0	25
00-01—Seattle	WHL	71	4	7	11	174	...	...	...	9	1	0	1	22
01-02—Seattle	WHL	72	8	23	31	168	...	...	...	1	0	0	0	4
02-03—Seattle	WHL	68	11	24	35	198	...	...	...	15	2	7	9	36
03-04—Phoenix	NHL	51	0	0	0	54	-11	0	0	—	—	—	—	—
—Springfield	AHL	21	1	2	3	32	-8	0	0	—	—	—	—	—
04-05—Utah	AHL	79	4	7	11	160	-26	2	0	—	—	—	—	—
NHL Totals (1 year)		51	0	0	0	54	-11	0	0					

ST. JACQUES, BRUNO — D — HURRICANES

PERSONAL: Born August 22, 1980, in Montreal. ... 6-2/204. ... Shoots left.

TRANSACTIONS/CAREER NOTES: Selected by Philadelphia Flyers in ninth round (12th Flyers pick, 253rd overall) of NHL draft (June 27, 1998). ... Traded by Flyers with RW Pavel Brendl to Carolina Hurricanes for RW Sami Kapanen and D Ryan Bast (February 7, 2003). ... Injured shoulder (October 28, 2003); missed one game. ... Injured shoulder (November 1, 2003); missed nine games. ... Injured abdomen (November 29, 2003); missed 14 games. ... Strained abdomen (March 12, 2004); missed last 13 games of season.

Season Team	League	REGULAR SEASON GP	G	A	Pts.	PIM	+/-	PP	SH	PLAYOFFS GP	G	A	Pts.	PIM
97-98—Baie-Comeau	QMJHL	63	13	29	42	253	...	...	...	—	—	—	—	—
98-99—Baie-Comeau	QMJHL	49	1	21	22	138	...	...	...	—	—	—	—	—
99-00—Baie-Comeau	QMJHL	60	8	28	36	120	...	...	...	—	—	—	—	—
—Philadelphia	AHL	3	0	1	1	0	...	...	...	1	0	0	0	0
00-01—Philadelphia	AHL	45	1	16	17	83	...	...	...	10	1	0	1	16
01-02—Philadelphia	AHL	55	3	11	14	59	2	1	0	4	0	0	0	0
—Philadelphia	NHL	7	0	0	0	2	4	0	0	—	—	—	—	—
02-03—Philadelphia	NHL	6	0	0	0	2	-1	0	0	—	—	—	—	—
—Philadelphia	AHL	30	0	7	7	46	1	0	0	—	—	—	—	—
—Carolina	NHL	18	2	5	7	12	-3	0	0	—	—	—	—	—
—Lowell	AHL	8	1	1	2	8	-3	0	1	—	—	—	—	—
03-04—Carolina	NHL	35	0	2	2	31	-7	0	0	—	—	—	—	—
—Lowell	AHL	6	0	0	0	8	-4	0	0	—	—	—	—	—
04-05—Lowell	AHL	68	2	12	14	60	24	0	0	11	1	4	5	4
NHL Totals (3 years)		66	2	7	9	47	-7	0	0					

ST. LOUIS, MARTIN — RW — LIGHTNING

PERSONAL: Born June 18, 1975, in Laval, Que. ... 5-9/181. ... Shoots left.
TRANSACTIONS/CAREER NOTES: Signed as free agent by Calgary Flames (February 18, 1998). ... Had concussion (March 15, 2000); missed two games. ... Signed as free agent by Tampa Bay Lightning (July 31, 2000). ... Bruised heel (November 6, 2001); missed one game. ... Fractured right leg (January 23, 2002); missed 26 games.
STATISTICAL PLATEAUS: Three-goal games: 2002-03 (1), 2003-04 (2). Total: 3.

Season Team	League	REGULAR SEASON GP	G	A	Pts.	PIM	+/-	PP	SH	PLAYOFFS GP	G	A	Pts.	PIM
93-94—Vermont	ECAC	33	15	36	51	24	...	...	...	—	—	—	—	—
94-95—Vermont	ECAC	35	23	48	71	36	...	...	...	—	—	—	—	—
95-96—Vermont	ECAC	35	29	56	85	36	...	...	...	—	—	—	—	—
96-97—Vermont	ECAC	35	24	26	50	65	...	...	...	—	—	—	—	—
97-98—Cleveland	IHL	56	16	34	50	24	-1	5	0	—	—	—	—	—
—Saint John	AHL	25	15	11	26	20	3	6	0	20	5	15	20	16
98-99—Calgary	NHL	13	1	1	2	10	-2	0	0	—	—	—	—	—
—Saint John	AHL	53	28	34	62	30	-2	4	4	7	4	4	8	2
99-00—Saint John	AHL	17	15	11	26	14	...	...	...	—	—	—	—	—
—Calgary	NHL	56	3	15	18	22	-5	0	0	—	—	—	—	—
00-01—Tampa Bay	NHL	78	18	22	40	12	-4	3	3	—	—	—	—	—
01-02—Tampa Bay	NHL	53	16	19	35	20	4	6	1	—	—	—	—	—
02-03—Tampa Bay	NHL	82	33	37	70	32	10	12	3	11	7	5	12	0
03-04—Tampa Bay	NHL	82	38	56	94	24	35	8	8	23	9	15	24	14
04-05—Lausanne HC	Switzerland	23	9	16	25	16	...	4	1	—	—	—	—	—
NHL Totals (6 years)		364	109	150	259	120	38	29	15	34	16	20	36	14

STAAL, ERIC — C — HURRICANES

PERSONAL: Born October 29, 1984, in Thunder Bay, Ont. ... 6-3/189. ... Shoots left.
TRANSACTIONS/CAREER NOTES: Selected by Carolina Hurricanes in first round (first Hurricanes pick, second overall) in 2003 NHL entry draft (June 23, 2003).

Season Team	League	REGULAR SEASON GP	G	A	Pts.	PIM	+/-	PP	SH	PLAYOFFS GP	G	A	Pts.	PIM
00-01—Peterborough	OHL	63	19	30	49	23	...	...	...	7	2	5	7	4
01-02—Peterborough	OHL	56	23	39	62	40	...	...	...	6	3	6	9	10
02-03—Peterborough	OHL	66	39	59	98	36	...	...	...	7	9	5	14	6
03-04—Carolina	NHL	81	11	20	31	40	-6	2	1	—	—	—	—	—
04-05—Lowell	AHL	77	26	51	77	88	37	2	7	11	2	8	10	12
NHL Totals (1 year)		81	11	20	31	40	-6	2	1					

STAAL, MARC — D — RANGERS

PERSONAL: Born January 13, 1987, in Thunder Bay, Ont. ... 6-3/196. ... Shoots left.
TRANSACTIONS/CAREER NOTES: Selected by New York Rangers in 1st round (Rangers 1st pick, 12th overall, obtained from Atlanta for 16th and 41st overall picks) of entry draft (July 30, 2005).

Season Team	League	REGULAR SEASON GP	G	A	Pts.	PIM	+/-	PP	SH	PLAYOFFS GP	G	A	Pts.	PIM
03-04—Sudbury	OHL	61	1	13	14	34	...	...	...	—	—	—	—	—
04-05—Sudbury	OHL	65	6	20	26	53	22	4	0	12	0	4	4	15

STAFFORD, DREW — RW — SABRES

PERSONAL: Born October 30, 1985, in Milwaukee, Wis. ... 6-1/202. ... Shoots right.
TRANSACTIONS/CAREER NOTES: Selected in first round by Buffalo Sabres (first Sabres pick, 13th overall) of NHL entry draft (June 26, 2004).

Season Team	League	REGULAR SEASON GP	G	A	Pts.	PIM	+/-	PP	SH	PLAYOFFS GP	G	A	Pts.	PIM
03-04—Univ. of North Dakota	WCHA	36	11	21	32	30	...	...	...	—	—	—	—	—
04-05—Univ. of North Dakota	WCHA	40	13	22	35	34	...	...	...	—	—	—	—	—

STAIOS, STEVE — D — OILERS

PERSONAL: Born July 28, 1973, in Hamilton, Ont. ... 6-1/200. ... Shoots right. ... Name pronounced STAY-ohz.

TRANSACTIONS/CAREER NOTES: Selected by St. Louis Blues in second round (first Blues pick, 27th overall) of NHL draft (June 22, 1991). ... Traded by Blues with LW Kevin Sawyer to Boston Bruins for RW Steve Leach (March 8, 1996). ... Strained groin (November 6, 1996); missed 13 games. ... Claimed off waivers by Vancouver Canucks (March 18, 1997). ... Injured knee (February 24, 1999); missed 16 games. ... Selected by Atlanta Thrashers in expansion draft (June 25, 1999). ... Sprained right knee (November 20, 1999); missed four games. ... Injured groin (December 30, 1999); missed 16 games. ... Reinjured groin (February 15, 2000); missed final 27 games of season. ... Traded by Thrashers to New Jersey Devils for ninth-round pick (C Simon Gamache) in 2000 draft (June 12, 2000). ... Traded by Devils to Thrashers for future considerations (July 10, 2000). ... Had concussion (November 27, 2000); missed five games. ... Bruised foot (December 22, 2000); missed two games. ... Strained hamstring (January 23, 2001); missed two games. ... Strained groin (February 7, 2001); missed three games. ... Signed as free agent by Edmonton Oilers (July 12, 2001). ... Bruised foot (October 20, 2001); missed one game. ... Strained groin (February 5, 2002); missed four games. ... Injured thumb and had concussion (December 30, 2002); missed six games.

		REGULAR SEASON								PLAYOFFS				
Season Team	League	GP	G	A	Pts.	PIM	+/-	PP	SH	GP	G	A	Pts.	PIM
89-90—Hamilton Jr. B	OHA	40	9	27	36	66	...	...	...	—	—	—	—	—
90-91—Niagara Falls	OHL	66	17	29	46	115	...	...	...	12	2	3	5	10
91-92—Niagara Falls	OHL	65	11	42	53	122	...	...	...	17	7	8	15	27
92-93—Niagara Falls	OHL	12	4	14	18	30	...	...	...	—	—	—	—	—
—Sudbury	OHL	53	13	44	57	67	...	...	...	11	5	6	11	22
93-94—Peoria	IHL	38	3	9	12	42	-9	1	0	—	—	—	—	—
94-95—Peoria	IHL	60	3	13	16	64	-3	1	0	6	0	0	0	10
95-96—Peoria	IHL	6	0	1	1	14	...	...	...	—	—	—	—	—
—Worcester	AHL	57	1	11	12	114	...	...	...	—	—	—	—	—
—Providence	AHL	7	1	4	5	8	...	...	...	—	—	—	—	—
—Boston	NHL	12	0	0	0	4	-5	0	0	3	0	0	0	0
96-97—Boston	NHL	54	3	8	11	71	-26	0	0	—	—	—	—	—
—Vancouver	NHL	9	0	6	6	20	2	0	0	—	—	—	—	—
97-98—Vancouver	NHL	77	3	4	7	134	-3	0	0	—	—	—	—	—
98-99—Vancouver	NHL	57	0	2	2	54	-12	0	0	—	—	—	—	—
99-00—Atlanta	NHL	27	2	3	5	66	-5	0	0	—	—	—	—	—
00-01—Atlanta	NHL	70	9	13	22	137	-23	4	0	—	—	—	—	—
01-02—Edmonton	NHL	73	5	5	10	108	10	0	0	—	—	—	—	—
02-03—Edmonton	NHL	76	5	21	26	96	13	1	3	6	0	0	0	4
03-04—Edmonton	NHL	82	6	22	28	86	17	1	0	—	—	—	—	—
04-05—Lulea	Sweden	7	2	1	3	12	3	0	0	—	—	—	—	—
NHL Totals (9 years)		537	33	84	117	776	-32	6	3	9	0	0	0	4

STAJAN, MATT — C/LW — MAPLE LEAFS

PERSONAL: Born December 19, 1983, in Mississauga, Ont. ... 6-1/180. ... Shoots left. ... Name pronounced STAY-juhn.

TRANSACTIONS/CAREER NOTES: Selected by Toronto Maple Leafs in second round (second Maple Leafs pick, 57th overall) of NHL draft (June 22, 2002).

		REGULAR SEASON								PLAYOFFS				
Season Team	League	GP	G	A	Pts.	PIM	+/-	PP	SH	GP	G	A	Pts.	PIM
00-01—Belleville	OHL	57	9	18	27	27	...	...	...	7	1	6	7	5
01-02—Belleville	OHL	68	33	52	85	50	...	...	...	11	3	8	11	14
02-03—St. John's	AHL	1	0	1	1	0	1	0	0	—	—	—	—	—
—Toronto	NHL	1	1	0	1	0	1	0	0	—	—	—	—	—
03-04—Toronto	NHL	69	14	13	27	22	7	0	0	3	0	0	0	2
04-05—St. John's	AHL	80	23	43	66	43	0	6	2	5	2	2	4	6
NHL Totals (2 years)		70	15	13	28	22	8	0	0	3	0	0	0	2

STANA, RASTISLAV — G — CAPITALS

PERSONAL: Born January 10, 1980, in Kosice, Czechoslovakia. ... 6-2/185. ... Catches left.

TRANSACTIONS/CAREER NOTES: Selected by Washington Capitals in 7th round (193rd overall) in entry draft (June 27, 1998).

		REGULAR SEASON									PLAYOFFS							
Season Team	League	GP	Min.	W	L	T	GA	SO	GAA	SV%	GP	Min.	W	L	GA	SO	GAA	SV%
97-98—Kosice Jr.	Czech Rep.	32	1920	...	...	...	56	2	1.75	...	—	—	—	—	—	—	—	—
98-99—Moose Jaw	WHL	36	2131	21	14	1	123	2	3.46	.898	9	544	4	5	30	0	3.31	.914
99-00—Moose Jaw	WHL	14	730	4	9	0	48	0	3.95	.899	—	—	—	—	—	—	—	—
—Calgary	WHL	16	971	13	2	1	37	1	2.29	.918	9	526	7	2	21	1	2.40	.911
00-01—Portland	AHL	3	161	0	2	1	11	0	4.10	.883	—	—	—	—	—	—	—	—
—Richmond	ECHL	38	2111	15	16	2	90	1	2.56	...	3	178	1	2	7	1	2.36	...
01-02—Richmond	ECHL	36	2097	20	12	3	95	1	2.72	.917	—	—	—	—	—	—	—	—
—Portland	AHL	3	180	1	2	0	11	0	3.67	.880	—	—	—	—	—	—	—	—
—Slovakian Oly. team	Int'l	1	60	1	0	0	1	0	1.00	.947	—	—	—	—	—	—	—	—
02-03—Portland	AHL	24	1354	8	11	4	49	2	2.17	.933	1	58	0	1	3	0	3.10	.917
03-04—Portland	AHL	24	1429	14	5	4	40	5	1.68	.937	3	138	1	2	7	0	3.04	.897
—Washington	NHL	6	211	1	2	0	11	0	3.13	.890	—	—	—	—	—	—	—	—
04-05—Sodertalje	Sweden	45	2562	...	...	...	116	3	2.72	.914	10	605	...	...	22	1	2.18	.920
NHL Totals (1 year)		6	211	1	2	0	11	0	3.13	.890								

STECKEL, DAVID — C — KINGS

PERSONAL: Born March 15, 1982, in Milwaukee. ... 6-5/200. ... Shoots left.
TRANSACTIONS/CAREER NOTES: Selected by Los Angeles Kings in first round (second Kings pick, 30th overall) of NHL entry draft (June 23, 2001).

		REGULAR SEASON								PLAYOFFS				
Season Team	League	GP	G	A	Pts.	PIM	+/-	PP	SH	GP	G	A	Pts.	PIM
99-00—U.S. National	USHL	52	13	13	26	94	...	...	...	—	—	—	—	—
00-01—Ohio State	CCHA	33	17	18	35	80	...	...	...	—	—	—	—	—
01-02—Ohio State	CCHA	36	6	16	22	75	...	...	...	—	—	—	—	—
02-03—Ohio State	CCHA	36	10	8	18	50	...	...	...	—	—	—	—	—
03-04—Ohio State	CCHA	41	17	13	30	44	...	...	...	—	—	—	—	—
04-05—Manchester	AHL	63	10	7	17	26	4	2	0	6	1	1	2	4

STEEN, ALEXANDER — C — MAPLE LEAFS

PERSONAL: Born March 1, 1984, in Winnipeg. ... 6-1/183. ... Shoots left. ... Son of Thomas Steen, center with Winnipeg Jets (1981-82 through 1994-95).
TRANSACTIONS/CAREER NOTES: Selected by Toronto Maple Leafs in 1st round (1st Maple Leafs pick, 24th overall) of entry draft (June 22, 2002).

		REGULAR SEASON								PLAYOFFS				
Season Team	League	GP	G	A	Pts.	PIM	+/-	PP	SH	GP	G	A	Pts.	PIM
01-02—Vastra Frolunda	Sweden	26	0	3	3	14	...	...	...	10	1	2	3	0
02-03—Vastra Frolunda	Sweden	45	5	10	15	18	...	...	...	16	2	3	5	4
03-04—Vastra Frolunda	Sweden	48	10	14	24	50	...	...	...	10	4	6	10	14
04-05—MoDo Ornskoldsvik	Sweden	50	9	8	17	26	-2	1	0	6	1	0	1	4

S

STEFAN, PATRIK — C/LW — THRASHERS

PERSONAL: Born September 16, 1980, in Pribram, Czechoslovakia. ... 6-2/205. ... Shoots left.
TRANSACTIONS/CAREER NOTES: Selected by Atlanta Thrashers in first round (first Thrashers pick, first overall) of NHL draft (June 26, 1999). ... Suffered concussion (November 19, 1999); missed two games. ... Back spasms (February 29, 2000); missed three games. ... Flu (March 22, 2000); missed two games. ... Injured groin (September 26, 2000); missed first five games of season. ... Flu (November 17, 2000); missed one game. ... Suffered concussion (November 22, 2000); missed three games. ... Injured head (December 29, 2000); missed one game. ... Strained groin (January 29, 2001); missed one games. ... Strained groin (February 7, 2001); missed three games. ... Flu (February 23, 2001); missed one game. ... Fractured jaw (October 6, 2001); missed eight games. ... Injured elbow (November 4, 2001); missed nine games. ... Injured ankle (March 19, 2003); missed 11 games.

		REGULAR SEASON								PLAYOFFS				
Season Team	League	GP	G	A	Pts.	PIM	+/-	PP	SH	GP	G	A	Pts.	PIM
96-97—Sparta Praha	Czech Rep.	5	0	1	1	2	...	...	...	7	1	0	1	0
97-98—Sparta Praha	Czech Rep.	27	2	6	8	16	...	...	...	—	—	—	—	—
—Long Beach	IHL	25	5	15	20	10	...	...	...	10	1	1	2	2
98-99—Long Beach	IHL	33	11	24	35	26	...	...	...	—	—	—	—	—
99-00—Atlanta	NHL	72	5	20	25	30	-20	1	0	—	—	—	—	—
00-01—Atlanta	NHL	66	10	21	31	22	-3	0	0	—	—	—	—	—
01-02—Atlanta	NHL	59	7	16	23	22	-4	0	1	—	—	—	—	—
—Chicago	AHL	5	3	0	3	0	3	1	0	—	—	—	—	—
02-03—Atlanta	NHL	71	13	21	34	12	-10	3	0	—	—	—	—	—
03-04—Atlanta	NHL	82	14	26	40	26	-7	3	2	—	—	—	—	—
04-05—Ilves Tampere	Finland	37	13	28	41	47	13	...	...	7	1	6	7	4
NHL Totals (5 years)		350	49	104	153	112	-44	7	3					

STEPHENS, CHARLIE — C/RW

PERSONAL: Born April 5, 1981, in London, Ont. ... 6-3/220. ... Shoots right.
TRANSACTIONS/CAREER NOTES: Selected by Washington Capitals in second round (third Capitals pick, 31st overall) of NHL draft (June 26, 1999). ... Returned to draft pool by Capitals and selected by Colorado Avalanche in sixth round (ninth Avalanche pick, 196th overall) of NHL entry draft (June 23, 2001). ... Traded by Avalanche to Ottawa Senators for RW Dennis Bonvie (January 23, 2004).

		REGULAR SEASON								PLAYOFFS				
Season Team	League	GP	G	A	Pts.	PIM	+/-	PP	SH	GP	G	A	Pts.	PIM
97-98—Toronto St. Michael's	OHL	58	9	21	30	38	...	...	...	—	—	—	—	—
98-99—Toronto St. Michael's	OHL	7	2	4	6	8	...	...	...	—	—	—	—	—
—Guelph	OHL	61	24	28	52	72	...	...	...	11	3	5	8	19
99-00—Guelph	OHL	56	16	34	50	87	3	3	2	6	1	3	4	15
00-01—Guelph	OHL	67	38	38	76	53	-1	15	3	4	0	2	2	2
01-02—Guelph	OHL	4	1	2	3	2	...	...	...	—	—	—	—	—
—London	OHL	56	23	33	56	55	...	...	...	12	6	10	16	18
—Hershey	AHL	...	...	...	...	...	...	...	...	1	0	0	0	0
02-03—Colorado	NHL	2	0	0	0	0	0	0	0	—	—	—	—	—
—Hershey	AHL	74	17	33	50	38	1	5	1	5	1	1	2	2
03-04—Colorado	NHL	6	0	2	2	4	-1	0	0	—	—	—	—	—
—Hershey	AHL	32	5	9	14	21	-2	0	1	—	—	—	—	—
—Binghamton	AHL	37	15	17	32	43	1	3	0	2	0	0	0	0
—Quad City	UHL	7	0	1	1	0	...	...	...	—	—	—	—	—
04-05—Binghamton	AHL	80	7	21	28	64	3	0	0	6	3	0	3	19
NHL Totals (2 years)		8	0	2	2	4	-1	0	0					

STEPP, JOEL — C/LW — MIGHTY DUCKS

PERSONAL: Born February 11, 1983, in Estevan, Sask. ... 6-1/185. ... Shoots left.

TRANSACTIONS/CAREER NOTES: Selected by Mighty Ducks of Anaheim in third round (third Mighty Ducks pick, 69th overall) of NHL entry draft (June 23, 2001).

		REGULAR SEASON								PLAYOFFS				
Season Team	League	GP	G	A	Pts.	PIM	+/-	PP	SH	GP	G	A	Pts.	PIM
99-00—Red Deer	WHL	65	11	13	24	59	...	...	...	4	1	0	1	8
00-01—Red Deer	WHL	70	24	13	37	89	...	...	...	22	6	3	9	24
01-02—Red Deer	WHL	70	27	26	53	59	...	...	...	23	11	11	22	24
02-03—Red Deer	WHL	24	4	11	15	18	...	...	...	23	6	7	13	26
03-04—Cincinnati	AHL	65	7	7	14	28	-8	0	0	9	1	1	2	2
04-05—Cincinnati	AHL	63	3	9	12	23	-5	0	0	12	1	0	1	8
—San Diego	ECHL	12	7	0	7	10	4	1	...	—	—	—	—	—

STEVENS, SCOTT — D — DEVILS

PERSONAL: Born April 1, 1964, in Kitchener, Ont. ... 6-2/215. ... Shoots left. ... Brother of Mike Stevens, C/LW with four NHL teams (1984-85 and 1987-88 through 1989-90).

TRANSACTIONS/CAREER NOTES: Selected by Washington Capitals in first round (first Capitals pick, fifth overall) of NHL draft (June 9, 1982). ... Bruised right knee (November 6, 1985); missed seven games. ... Fractured right index finger (December 14, 1986). ... Bruised shoulder (April 1988). ... Poison oak (November 1988). ... Fractured left foot (December 29, 1989); missed 17 games. ... Suspended three games by NHL for scratching (February 27, 1990). ... Bruised left shoulder (March 27, 1990). ... Dislocated left shoulder (May 3, 1990). ... Signed as free agent by St. Louis Blues (July 9, 1990); Blues owed Capitals two first-round draft picks among the top seven over next two years and $100,000 cash; upon failing to get a pick in the top seven in 1991, Blues forfeited first-round picks in 1991 (LW Trevor Halverson), 1992 (D Sergei Gonchar), 1993 (D Brendan Witt), 1994 (traded to Toronto) and 1995 (LW Miikka Elomo) to Capitals (July 9, 1990). ... Awarded to New Jersey Devils as compensation for Blues signing free agent RW/LW Brendan Shanahan (September 3, 1991). ... Strained right knee (February 20, 1992); missed 12 games. ... Suffered concussion (December 27, 1992); missed three games. ... Strained knee (November 19, 1993); missed one game. ... Suspended one game for high-sticking incident (October 7, 1996). ... Flu (December 23, 1996); missed one game. ... Had hip pointer (February 28, 1998); missed one game. ... Flu (December 8, 1998); missed one game. ... Back spasms (December 19, 1998); missed one game. ... Strained groin (March 15, 1999); missed five games. ... Flu (January 8, 2000); missed two games. ... Flu (March 24, 2000); missed one game. ... Left team for personal reasons (November 7, 2003); missed one game. ... Suffered concussion (January 16, 2004); missed remainder of season.

		REGULAR SEASON								PLAYOFFS				
Season Team	League	GP	G	A	Pts.	PIM	+/-	PP	SH	GP	G	A	Pts.	PIM
80-81—Kitchener Jr. B	OHA	39	7	33	40	82	...	...	...	—	—	—	—	—
—Kitchener	OHL	1	0	0	0	0	...	...	...	—	—	—	—	—
81-82—Kitchener	OHL	68	6	36	42	158	...	...	...	15	1	10	11	71
82-83—Washington	NHL	77	9	16	25	195	14	0	0	4	1	0	1	26
83-84—Washington	NHL	78	13	32	45	201	26	7	0	8	1	8	9	21
84-85—Washington	NHL	80	21	44	65	221	19	16	0	5	0	1	1	20
85-86—Washington	NHL	73	15	38	53	165	0	3	0	9	3	8	11	12
86-87—Washington	NHL	77	10	51	61	283	13	2	0	7	0	5	5	19
87-88—Washington	NHL	80	12	60	72	184	14	5	1	13	1	11	12	46
88-89—Washington	NHL	80	7	61	68	225	1	6	0	6	1	4	5	11
89-90—Washington	NHL	56	11	29	40	154	1	7	0	15	2	7	9	25
90-91—St. Louis	NHL	78	5	44	49	150	23	1	0	13	0	3	3	36
91-92—New Jersey	NHL	68	17	42	59	124	24	7	1	7	2	1	3	29
92-93—New Jersey	NHL	81	12	45	57	120	14	8	0	5	2	2	4	10
93-94—New Jersey	NHL	83	18	60	78	112	*53	5	1	20	2	9	11	42
94-95—New Jersey	NHL	48	2	20	22	56	4	1	0	20	1	7	8	24
95-96—New Jersey	NHL	82	5	23	28	100	7	2	1	—	—	—	—	—
96-97—New Jersey	NHL	79	5	19	24	70	26	0	0	10	0	4	4	2
97-98—New Jersey	NHL	80	4	22	26	80	19	1	0	6	1	0	1	8
—Can. Olympic team	Int'l	6	0	0	0	2	5	0	0	—	—	—	—	—
98-99—New Jersey	NHL	75	5	22	27	64	29	0	0	7	2	1	3	10
99-00—New Jersey	NHL	78	8	21	29	103	30	0	1	23	3	8	11	6
00-01—New Jersey	NHL	81	9	22	31	71	40	3	0	25	1	7	8	37
01-02—New Jersey	NHL	82	1	16	17	44	15	0	0	6	0	0	0	4
02-03—New Jersey	NHL	81	4	16	20	41	18	0	0	24	3	6	9	14
03-04—New Jersey	NHL	38	3	9	12	22	3	1	0	—	—	—	—	—
NHL Totals (22 years)		1635	196	712	908	2785	393	75	5	233	26	92	118	402

STEVENSON, JEREMY — LW — PREDATORS

PERSONAL: Born July 28, 1974, in San Bernardino, Calif. ... 6-1/215. ... Shoots left.

TRANSACTIONS/CAREER NOTES: Selected by Winnipeg Jets in third round (third Jets pick, 60th overall) of NHL entry draft (June 20, 1992). ... Returned to draft pool by Jets and selected by Mighty Ducks of Anaheim in 11th round (10th Mighty Ducks pick, 262nd overall) of NHL entry draft (June 28, 1994). ... Fractured ankle (October 24, 1996); missed 33 games. ... Suffered concussion before 1997-98 season; missed first four games of season. ... Signed as free agent by Nashville Predators (September 25, 2000). ... Signed as free agent by Minnesota Wild (November 26, 2002). ... Fractured cheekbone (November 2, 2003); missed 5 games. ... Injured shoulder (January 28, 2003); missed eight games. ... Claimed by Nashville Predators off waivers from Wild (October 22, 2003). ... Injured checkbone (November 4, 2003); missed five games. ... Injured shoulder (January 5, 2004); missed two games. ... Injured shoulder (January 24, 2004); missed five games.

		REGULAR SEASON								PLAYOFFS				
Season Team	League	GP	G	A	Pts.	PIM	+/-	PP	SH	GP	G	A	Pts.	PIM
90-91—Cornwall	OHL	58	13	20	33	124	...	...	...	—	—	—	—	—
91-92—Cornwall	OHL	63	15	23	38	176	...	...	...	6	3	1	4	4
92-93—Newmarket	OHL	54	28	28	56	144	...	...	...	5	5	1	6	28

Season Team	League	GP	G	A	Pts.	PIM	+/-	PP	SH	GP	G	A	Pts.	PIM
		REGULAR SEASON								PLAYOFFS				
93-94—Newmarket	OHL	9	2	4	6	27	...	1	0	—	—	—	—	—
—Sault Ste. Marie	OHL	48	18	19	37	183	...	7	0	14	1	1	2	23
94-95—Greensboro	ECHL	43	14	13	27	231	3	4	0	17	6	11	17	64
95-96—Baltimore	AHL	60	11	10	21	295	...	...	...	12	4	2	6	23
—Anaheim	NHL	3	0	1	1	12	1	0	0	—	—	—	—	—
96-97—Baltimore	AHL	25	8	8	16	125	5	1	0	3	0	0	0	8
—Anaheim	NHL	5	0	0	0	14	-1	0	0	—	—	—	—	—
97-98—Anaheim	NHL	45	3	5	8	101	-4	0	0	—	—	—	—	—
—Cincinnati	AHL	10	5	0	5	34	-1	2	0	—	—	—	—	—
98-99—Cincinnati	AHL	22	4	4	8	83	-7	2	0	3	1	0	1	2
99-00—Cincinnati	AHL	41	11	14	25	100	...	...	...	—	—	—	—	—
—Anaheim	NHL	3	0	0	0	7	-1	0	0	—	—	—	—	—
00-01—Milwaukee	IHL	60	16	13	29	262	...	...	...	5	2	1	3	12
—Nashville	NHL	8	1	0	1	39	-1	0	0	—	—	—	—	—
01-02—Milwaukee	AHL	53	12	7	19	192	8	1	0	—	—	—	—	—
—Nashville	NHL	4	0	0	0	9	0	0	0	—	—	—	—	—
02-03—Houston	AHL	18	6	7	13	77	8	2	0	—	—	—	—	—
—Minnesota	NHL	32	5	6	11	69	6	1	0	14	0	5	5	12
03-04—Minnesota	NHL	3	0	0	0	2	-1	0	0	—	—	—	—	—
—Nashville	NHL	53	5	4	9	103	-2	3	0	6	0	0	0	8
04-05—South Carolina	ECHL	42	9	20	29	140	3	4	1	3	1	0	1	2
NHL Totals (8 years)		156	14	16	30	356	-3	4	0	20	0	5	5	20

STEVENSON, TURNER RW FLYERS

PERSONAL: Born May 18, 1972, in Prince George, British Columbia. ... 6-3/220. ... Shoots right.

TRANSACTIONS/CAREER NOTES: Selected by Montreal Canadiens in first round (first Canadiens pick, 12th overall) of NHL draft (June 16, 1990). ... Flu (October 21, 1995); missed two games. ... Sprained knee (October 7, 1996); missed five games. ... Sprained knee (October 26, 1996); missed four games. ... Sprained knee (November 11, 1996); missed seven games. ... Sprained left shoulder (November 12, 1997); missed eight games. ... Tore cartilage in ribs (December 19, 1997); missed five games. ... Strained hamstring (April 15, 1998); missed three games. ... Suspended two games and fined $1,000 for elbowing incident (October 19, 1998). ... Back spasms (December 29, 1998); missed one game. ... Sprained ankle (December 31, 1998); missed 10 games. ... Back spasms (October 9, 1999); missed two games. ... Strained back (November 16, 1999); missed 13 games. ... Flu (January 11, 2000); missed three games. ... Selected by Columbus Blue Jackets in expansion draft (June 23, 2000). ... Traded by Blue Jackets to New Jersey Devils (June 23, 2000), completing deal in which Devils traded RW Krzysztof Oliwa to Blue Jackets for third-round pick (C/LW Brandon Nolan) in 2001 draft and future considerations (June 12, 2000). ... Sprained ankle (March 21, 2001); missed nine games. ... Injured right knee (October 17, 2001); missed 12 games. ... Reinjured knee (December 29, 2001); missed remainder of season. ... Bruised ankle (January 15, 2003); missed one game. ... Injured knee (February 15, 2003); missed four games. ... Injured groin (April 30, 2003); missed two playoff games. ... Reinjured groin (May 15, 2003); missed three playoff games. ... Reinjured groin (May 23, 2003); missed five playoff games. ... Injured groin (October 3, 2003); missed eight games. ... Injured groin (December 10, 2003); missed 12 games. ... Signed as free agent by Philadelphia Flyers (July 3, 2004).

Season Team	League	GP	G	A	Pts.	PIM	+/-	PP	SH	GP	G	A	Pts.	PIM
		REGULAR SEASON								PLAYOFFS				
88-89—Seattle	WHL	69	15	12	27	84	...	...	...	—	—	—	—	—
89-90—Seattle	WHL	62	29	32	61	276	...	...	...	13	3	2	5	35
90-91—Seattle	WHL	57	36	27	63	222	...	...	...	6	1	5	6	15
—Fredericton	AHL	...	...	...	...	...	...	...	...	4	0	0	0	5
91-92—Seattle	WHL	58	20	32	52	264	...	...	...	15	9	3	12	55
92-93—Fredericton	AHL	79	25	34	59	102	15	6	2	5	2	3	5	11
—Montreal	NHL	1	0	0	0	0	-1	0	0	—	—	—	—	—
93-94—Fredericton	AHL	66	19	28	47	155	-2	5	2	—	—	—	—	—
—Montreal	NHL	2	0	0	0	2	-2	0	0	3	0	2	2	0
94-95—Fredericton	AHL	37	12	12	24	109	-2	2	0	—	—	—	—	—
—Montreal	NHL	41	6	1	7	86	0	0	0	—	—	—	—	—
95-96—Montreal	NHL	80	9	16	25	167	-2	0	0	6	0	1	1	2
96-97—Montreal	NHL	65	8	13	21	97	-14	1	0	5	1	1	2	2
97-98—Montreal	NHL	63	4	6	10	110	-8	1	0	10	3	4	7	12
98-99—Montreal	NHL	69	10	17	27	88	6	0	0	—	—	—	—	—
99-00—Montreal	NHL	64	8	13	21	61	-1	0	0	—	—	—	—	—
00-01—New Jersey	NHL	69	8	18	26	97	11	2	0	23	1	3	4	20
01-02—New Jersey	NHL	21	0	2	2	25	-3	0	0	1	0	0	0	4
02-03—New Jersey	NHL	77	7	13	20	115	7	0	0	14	1	1	2	26
03-04—New Jersey	NHL	61	14	13	27	76	0	4	0	5	0	0	0	0
NHL Totals (12 years)		613	74	112	186	924	-7	8	0	67	6	12	18	66

STEWART, ANTHONY C PANTHERS

PERSONAL: Born January 5, 1985, in LaSalle, Que. ... 6-1/225. ... Shoots right.

TRANSACTIONS/CAREER NOTES: Selected by Florida Panthers in first round (second Panthers selection, 25th overall) of NHL entry draft (June 20, 2003).

Season Team	League	GP	G	A	Pts.	PIM	+/-	PP	SH	GP	G	A	Pts.	PIM
		REGULAR SEASON								PLAYOFFS				
01-02—Kingston	OHL	65	19	24	43	43	...	...	...	1	0	0	0	0
02-03—Kingston	OHL	68	32	38	70	47	...	...	...	—	—	—	—	—
03-04—Kingston	OHL	53	35	23	58	76	...	...	...	5	3	4	7	7
04-05—San Antonio	AHL	10	1	2	3	14	1	0	0	—	—	—	—	—
—Kingston	OHL	62	32	35	67	70	-3	5	0	—	—	—	—	—

STEWART, KARL — LW/C — THRASHERS

PERSONAL: Born June 30, 1983, in Aurora, Ontario. ... 5-10/175. ... Shoots left.
TRANSACTIONS/CAREER NOTES: Signed as undrafted free agent by Atlanta Thrashers (September 21, 2001).

		REGULAR SEASON								PLAYOFFS				
Season Team	**League**	**GP**	**G**	**A**	**Pts.**	**PIM**	**+/-**	**PP**	**SH**	**GP**	**G**	**A**	**Pts.**	**PIM**
00-01—Plymouth	OHL	68	9	14	23	67	...	...	...	19	3	4	7	14
01-02—Plymouth	OHL	65	20	23	43	104	...	...	...	6	0	2	2	21
02-03—Plymouth	OHL	68	35	50	85	120	...	...	...	17	7	10	17	31
03-04—Atlanta	NHL	5	0	1	1	4	0	0	0	—	—	—	—	—
—Chicago	AHL	72	10	32	42	188	24	1	1	10	2	3	5	29
04-05—Chicago	AHL	77	16	8	24	226	1	0	1	12	4	2	6	32
NHL Totals (1 year)		5	0	1	1	4	0	0	0					

STILLMAN, CORY — LW — HURRICANES

PERSONAL: Born December 20, 1973, in Peterborough, Ont. ... 6-0/197. ... Shoots left. ... Second cousin of Cory Stillman, center, New York Islanders organization.
TRANSACTIONS/CAREER NOTES: Selected by Calgary Flames in 1st round (1st Flames pick, 6th overall) of NHL draft (June 20, 1992). ... Flu (October 8, 1995); missed one game. ... Bruised knee (January 14, 1996); missed two games. ... Injured shoulder (December 16, 1996); missed five games. ... Bruised ribs (October 11, 1997); missed six games. ... Strained knee (December 27, 1998); missed five games. ... Injured shoulder (December 27, 1999); missed final 45 games of season. ... Injured shoulder (October 30, 2000); missed one game. ... Traded by Flames to St. Louis Blues for C Craig Conroy and seventh-round pick (LW David Moss) in 2001 draft (March 13, 2001). ... Injured knee (November 8, 2001); missed two games. ... Injured knee (December 20, 2002); missed three games. ... Traded by Blues to Tampa Bay Lightning for second-round draft pick (C David Backes) in 2003 (June 22, 2003). ... Flu (December 20, 2003); missed one game. ... Signed as free agent by Carolina Hurricanes (Aug. 2, 2005).
STATISTICAL PLATEAUS: Three-goal games: 1997-98 (1), 2000-01 (1), 2001-02 (1). Total: 3.

		REGULAR SEASON								PLAYOFFS				
Season Team	**League**	**GP**	**G**	**A**	**Pts.**	**PIM**	**+/-**	**PP**	**SH**	**GP**	**G**	**A**	**Pts.**	**PIM**
89-90—Peterborough Jr. B	OHA	41	30	54	84	76	...	...	...	—	—	—	—	—
90-91—Windsor	OHL	64	31	70	101	31	...	...	...	11	3	6	9	8
91-92—Windsor	OHL	53	29	61	90	59	...	...	...	7	2	4	6	8
92-93—Peterborough	OHL	61	25	55	80	55	...	...	...	18	3	8	11	18
—Canadian nat'l team	Int'l	1	0	0	0	0	...	...	...	—	—	—	—	—
93-94—Saint John	AHL	79	35	48	83	52	-14	13	2	7	2	4	6	16
94-95—Saint John	AHL	63	28	53	81	70	-21	12	0	5	0	2	2	2
—Calgary	NHL	10	0	2	2	2	1	0	0	—	—	—	—	—
95-96—Calgary	NHL	74	16	19	35	41	-5	4	1	2	1	1	2	0
96-97—Calgary	NHL	58	6	20	26	14	-6	2	0	—	—	—	—	—
97-98—Calgary	NHL	72	27	22	49	40	-9	9	4	—	—	—	—	—
98-99—Calgary	NHL	76	27	30	57	38	7	9	3	—	—	—	—	—
99-00—Calgary	NHL	37	12	9	21	12	-9	6	0	—	—	—	—	—
00-01—Calgary	NHL	66	21	24	45	45	-6	7	0	—	—	—	—	—
—St. Louis	NHL	12	3	4	7	6	-2	3	0	15	3	5	8	8
01-02—St. Louis	NHL	80	23	22	45	36	8	6	0	9	0	2	2	2
02-03—St. Louis	NHL	79	24	43	67	56	12	6	0	6	2	2	4	2
03-04—Tampa Bay	NHL	81	25	55	80	36	18	11	1	21	2	5	7	15
NHL Totals (10 years)		645	184	250	434	326	9	63	9	53	8	15	23	27

STOA, RYAN — C — AVALANCHE

PERSONAL: Born April 13, 1987, in Bloomington, Minn. ... 6-3/200. ... Shoots left.

		REGULAR SEASON								PLAYOFFS				
Season Team	**League**	**GP**	**G**	**A**	**Pts.**	**PIM**	**+/-**	**PP**	**SH**	**GP**	**G**	**A**	**Pts.**	**PIM**
03-04—U.S. National	USHL	67	26	21	47	32	...	...	...	—	—	—	—	—
04-05—U.S. National	USHL	49	19	35	54	52	...	...	...	—	—	—	—	—

STOCK, P.J. — C/LW

PERSONAL: Born May 26, 1975, in Montreal. ... 5-10/197. ... Shoots left.
TRANSACTIONS/CAREER NOTES: Signed as free agent by New York Rangers (September 2, 1997). ... Signed as free agent by Montreal Canadiens (July 7, 2000). ... Traded by Canadiens with sixth-round pick (D Dennis Seidenberg) in 2001 draft to Philadelphia Flyers for LW Gino Odjick (December 7, 2000). ... Strained neck (April 7, 2001); missed final game of regular season. ... Signed as free agent by Rangers (August 23, 2001). ... Claimed by Boston Bruins from Rangers in waiver draft (September 28, 2001). ... Sprained ankle (November 8, 2001); missed 12 games. ... Underwent facial surgery (February 5, 2002); missed six games.

		REGULAR SEASON								PLAYOFFS				
Season Team	**League**	**GP**	**G**	**A**	**Pts.**	**PIM**	**+/-**	**PP**	**SH**	**GP**	**G**	**A**	**Pts.**	**PIM**
94-95—Victoriaville	QMJHL	70	9	46	55	386	...	...	...	4	0	0	0	60
95-96—Victoriaville	QMJHL	67	19	43	62	432	...	...	...	12	5	4	9	79
96-97—St. Francis Xavier	CIAU	27	11	20	31	110	...	...	...	3	0	4	4	14
97-98—Hartford	AHL	41	8	8	16	202	7	1	0	11	1	3	4	79
—New York Rangers	NHL	38	2	3	5	114	4	0	0	—	—	—	—	—
98-99—New York Rangers	NHL	5	0	0	0	6	-1	0	0	—	—	—	—	—
—Hartford	AHL	55	4	14	18	250	-9	2	1	6	0	1	1	35
99-00—Hartford	AHL	64	13	23	36	290	...	...	...	23	1	11	12	69
—New York Rangers	NHL	11	0	1	1	11	1	0	0	—	—	—	—	—

Season Team	League	GP	G	A	Pts.	PIM	+/-	PP	SH	GP	G	A	Pts.	PIM
		REGULAR SEASON								PLAYOFFS				
00-01—Montreal	NHL	20	1	2	3	32	-1	0	0	—	—	—	—	—
—Philadelphia	NHL	31	1	3	4	78	-2	0	0	2	0	0	0	0
—Philadelphia	AHL	9	1	2	3	37	...	...	...	—	—	—	—	—
01-02—Boston	NHL	58	0	3	3	122	-2	0	0	6	1	0	1	19
02-03—Boston	NHL	71	1	9	10	160	-5	1	0	—	—	—	—	—
03-04—Boston	NHL	1	0	0	0	0	0	0	0	—	—	—	—	—
—Providence	AHL	4	1	0	1	2	0	0	0	—	—	—	—	—
—Philadelphia	AHL	66	5	18	23	207	5	1	0	12	0	2	2	34
NHL Totals (7 years)		235	5	21	26	523	-6	1	0	8	1	0	1	19

STOLL, JARRET — C — OILERS

PERSONAL: Born June 24, 1982, in Melville, Sask. ... 6-1/200. ... Shoots right.

TRANSACTIONS/CAREER NOTES: Selected by Calgary Flames in second round (third Flames pick, 46th overall) of NHL entry draft (June 24, 2000). ... Returned to draft pool and selected by Edmonton Oilers in second round (third Oilers pick, 36th overall) of NHL entry draft (June 22, 2002). ... Tonsillitis (October 30, 2003); missed five games. ... Tonsillitis (February 25, 2004); missed one game.

Season Team	League	GP	G	A	Pts.	PIM	+/-	PP	SH	GP	G	A	Pts.	PIM
		REGULAR SEASON								PLAYOFFS				
0-1 —Hamilton	AHL	76	21	33	54	86	...	...	...	23	5	8	13	25
98-99—Kootenay	WHL	57	13	21	34	40	...	...	...	4	0	0	0	2
99-00—Kootenay	WHL	71	37	38	75	64	...	...	...	20	7	9	16	24
00-01—Kootenay	WHL	62	40	66	106	105	...	...	...	11	5	9	14	22
01-02—Kootenay	WHL	47	32	34	66	64	...	...	...	22	6	13	19	35
02-03—Hamilton	AHL	76	21	33	54	86	...	...	...	23	5	8	13	25
—Edmonton	NHL	4	0	1	1	0	-3	0	0	—	—	—	—	—
03-04—Edmonton	NHL	68	10	11	21	42	8	1	1	—	—	—	—	—
04-05—Edmonton	AHL	66	21	17	38	92	13	7	0	—	—	—	—	—
NHL Totals (2 years)		72	10	12	22	42	5	1	1					

STORR, JAMIE — G — HURRICANES

PERSONAL: Born December 28, 1975, in Brampton, Ont. ... 6-2/203. ... Catches left. ... Name pronounced STOHR.

TRANSACTIONS/CAREER NOTES: Selected by Los Angeles Kings in first round (first Kings pick, seventh overall) of NHL entry draft (June 28, 1994). ... Strained right groin (October 1, 1997); missed 12 games. ... Strained left groin (October 18, 1998); missed 16 games. ... Sprained ankle (April 2, 1999); missed final eight games of season. ... Strained right groin (November 23, 1999); missed one game. ... Suffered concussion (December 16, 1999); missed 10 games. ... Signed as free agent by Carolina Hurricanes (October 3, 2003). ... Signed as free agent by Springfield of the AHL (September 29, 2004).

Season Team	League	GP	Min.	W	L	T	GA	SO	GAA	SV%	GP	Min.	W	L	GA	SO	GAA	SV%
		REGULAR SEASON									PLAYOFFS							
90-91—Brampton	Jr. B	24	1145	...	...	...	91	0	4.77	...	—	—	—	—	—	—	—	—
91-92—Owen Sound	OHL	34	1733	11	16	1	128	0	4.43	...	5	299	1	4	28	0	5.62	...
92-93—Owen Sound	OHL	41	2362	20	17	3	180	0	4.57	...	8	454	4	4	35	0	4.63	...
93-94—Owen Sound	OHL	35	2004	21	11	1	120	1	3.59	*.915	9	547	4	5	44	0	4.83	.895
94-95—Owen Sound	OHL	17	977	5	9	2	64	0	3.93	.894	—	—	—	—	—	—	—	—
—Los Angeles	NHL	5	263	1	3	1	17	0	3.88	.888	—	—	—	—	—	—	—	—
—Windsor	OHL	4	241	3	1	0	8	1	1.99	.930	10	520	6	3	34	1	3.92	...
95-96—Los Angeles	NHL	5	262	3	1	0	12	0	2.75	.918	—	—	—	—	—	—	—	—
—Phoenix	IHL	48	2711	22	20	4	139	2	3.08	...	2	118	1	1	4	1	2.03	...
96-97—Phoenix	IHL	44	2441	16	22	4	147	0	3.61	...	—	—	—	—	—	—	—	—
—Los Angeles	NHL	5	265	2	1	1	11	0	2.49	.925	—	—	—	—	—	—	—	—
97-98—Los Angeles	NHL	17	920	9	5	1	34	2	2.22	.929	3	145	0	2	9	0	3.72	.883
—Long Beach	IHL	11	629	7	2	1	31	0	2.96	.897	—	—	—	—	—	—	—	—
98-99—Los Angeles	NHL	28	1525	12	12	2	61	4	2.40	.916	—	—	—	—	—	—	—	—
99-00—Los Angeles	NHL	42	2206	18	15	5	93	1	2.53	.908	1	36	0	1	2	0	3.33	.920
00-01—Los Angeles	NHL	45	2498	19	18	6	114	4	2.74	.899	—	—	—	—	—	—	—	—
01-02—Los Angeles	NHL	19	886	9	4	3	28	2	1.90	.922	1	1	0	0	0	0	0.00	...
02-03—Los Angeles	NHL	39	2027	12	19	2	86	3	2.55	.905	—	—	—	—	—	—	—	—
03-04—Carolina	NHL	14	660	0	8	2	32	0	2.91	.878	—	—	—	—	—	—	—	—
—Lowell	AHL	13	712	2	6	2	38	0	3.20	.864	—	—	—	—	—	—	—	—
04-05—Springfield	AHL	30	1696	8	20	...	91	0	3.22	.905	—	—	—	—	—	—	—	—
—Utah	AHL	16	885	6	7	...	36	1	2.44	.928	—	—	—	—	—	—	—	—
NHL Totals (10 years)		219	11512	85	86	23	488	16	2.54	.908	5	182	0	3	11	0	3.63	.892

STRAKA, MARTIN — C/LW — RANGERS

PERSONAL: Born September 3, 1972, in Plzen, Czech. ... 5-9/178. ... Shoots left. ... Name pronounced STRAH-kuh.

TRANSACTIONS/CAREER NOTES: Selected by Pittsburgh Penguins in 1st round (1st Penguins pick, 19th overall) of entry draft (June 20, 1992). ... Flu (February 14, 1995); missed four games. ... Traded by Penguins to Ottawa Senators for D Norm Maciver and C Troy Murray (April 7, 1995). ... Strained knee (April 19, 1995); missed remainder of season. ... Injured hamstring (November 11, 1995); missed one game. ... Traded by Senators with D Bryan Berard to New York Islanders for D Wade Redden and G Damian Rhodes (January 23, 1996). ... Claimed off waivers by Florida Panthers (March 15, 1996). ... Bruised buttocks (April 10, 1996); missed final two games of season. ... Strained groin (January 1, 1997); missed one game. ... Strained groin (January 8, 1997); missed two games. ... Strained groin (January 22, 1997); missed four games. ... Strained groin (March 5, 1997); missed nine games. ... Signed as free agent by Penguins (August 7, 1997). ... Fractured foot (December 29, 1997); missed seven games. ... Bruised shoulder (March 3, 1999); missed one game. ... Bruised shoulder (April 8, 1999);

missed one game. ... Bruised knee (October 16, 1999); missed one game. ... Reinjured knee (October 27, 1999); missed two games. ... Bruised ribs (December 15, 1999); missed seven games. ... Bruised shin (April 5, 2000); missed one game. ... Fractured leg (October 28, 2001); missed 47 games. ... Fractured orbital and sinus bones (February 27, 2002); missed four games. ... Reinjured leg (March 7, 2002); missed remainder of season. ... Back injury (October 10, 2002); missed 11 games. ... Injured hamstring (November 29, 2002); missed two games. ... Reinjured hamstring (December 10, 2002); missed four games. ... Reinjured hamstring (February 12, 2003); missed five games. ... Traded to Los Angeles Kings for D Martin Strbak and F Sergei Anshakov (November 30, 2003). ... Sprained knee (January 11, 2004) and had surgery (February 13, 2004); missed 23 games. ... Signed as free agent by New York Rangers (Aug. 2, 2005).
STATISTICAL PLATEAUS: Three-goal games: 1993-94 (1), 1997-98 (1), 1998-99 (1), 2000-01 (1). Total: 4.

		REGULAR SEASON								PLAYOFFS				
Season Team	**League**	**GP**	**G**	**A**	**Pts.**	**PIM**	**+/-**	**PP**	**SH**	**GP**	**G**	**A**	**Pts.**	**PIM**
89-90—Skoda Plzen	Czech.	1	0	3	3	...	...	...	...	—	—	—	—	—
90-91—Skoda Plzen	Czech.	47	7	24	31	6	...	...	...	—	—	—	—	—
91-92—Skoda Plzen	Czech.	50	27	28	55	20	...	...	...	—	—	—	—	—
92-93—Pittsburgh	NHL	42	3	13	16	29	2	0	0	11	2	1	3	2
—Cleveland	IHL	4	4	3	7	0	2	1	1	—	—	—	—	—
93-94—Pittsburgh	NHL	84	30	34	64	24	24	2	0	6	1	0	1	2
94-95—Interconex Plzen	Czech Rep.	19	10	11	21	18	...	...	...	—	—	—	—	—
—Pittsburgh	NHL	31	4	12	16	16	0	0	0	—	—	—	—	—
—Ottawa	NHL	6	1	1	2	0	-1	0	0	—	—	—	—	—
95-96—Ottawa	NHL	43	9	16	25	29	-14	5	0	—	—	—	—	—
—New York Islanders	NHL	22	2	10	12	6	-6	0	0	—	—	—	—	—
—Florida	NHL	12	2	4	6	6	1	1	0	13	2	2	4	2
96-97—Florida	NHL	55	7	22	29	12	9	2	0	4	0	0	0	0
97-98—Pittsburgh	NHL	75	19	23	42	28	-1	4	3	6	2	0	2	2
—Czech Rep. Oly. team	Int'l	6	1	2	3	0	1	0	0	—	—	—	—	—
98-99—Pittsburgh	NHL	80	35	48	83	26	12	5	4	13	6	9	15	6
99-00—Pittsburgh	NHL	71	20	39	59	26	24	3	1	11	3	9	12	10
00-01—Pittsburgh	NHL	82	27	68	95	38	19	7	1	18	5	8	13	8
01-02—Pittsburgh	NHL	13	5	4	9	0	3	1	0	—	—	—	—	—
02-03—Pittsburgh	NHL	60	18	28	46	12	-18	7	0	—	—	—	—	—
03-04—Pittsburgh	NHL	22	4	8	12	16	-16	1	0	—	—	—	—	—
—Los Angeles	NHL	32	6	8	14	4	-9	1	1	—	—	—	—	—
04-05—Plzen	Czech Rep.	45	16	18	34	76	5	...	...	—	—	—	—	—
NHL Totals (12 years)		730	192	338	530	272	29	39	10	82	21	29	50	32

STRBAK, MARTIN — D — PENGUINS

PERSONAL: Born January 15, 1975, in Presov, Czechoslovakia. ... 6-3/210. ... Shoots left. ... Name pronounced STUHR-bahk.
TRANSACTIONS/CAREER NOTES: Selected by Los Angeles Kings in ninth round (10th Kings pick, 224th overall) of NHL draft (June 26, 1993). ... Signed as free agent by the Los Angeles Kings (July 15, 2003). ... Traded with LW Sergei Anshakov to Pittsburgh Penguins for C Martin Straka (November 30, 2003). ... Fractured foot (February 10, 2004); missed 13 games.

		REGULAR SEASON								PLAYOFFS				
Season Team	**League**	**GP**	**G**	**A**	**Pts.**	**PIM**	**+/-**	**PP**	**SH**	**GP**	**G**	**A**	**Pts.**	**PIM**
93-94—Notre Dame	SJHL	54	8	18	26	157	...	...	...	—	—	—	—	—
94-95—HK Presov	Slovakia	10	1	0	1	6	...	...	...	—	—	—	—	—
—Slovan Bratislava	Slovakia	5	0	3	3	0	...	...	...	9	2	1	3	8
95-96—Slovan Bratislava	Slovakia	31	2	3	5	14	...	...	...	—	—	—	—	—
96-97—Slovan Bratislava	Slovakia	37	3	2	5	...	...	...	...	1	0	0	0	...
97-98—Spisska Nova Ves	Slovakia	31	1	1	2	18	...	...	...	2	0	0	0	0
98-99—Slovan Bratislava	Slovakia	18	0	0	0	41	...	...	...	—	—	—	—	—
—Bratislava B	Slovakia	13	2	5	7	12	...	...	...	—	—	—	—	—
99-00—Litvinov	Czech Rep.	50	3	6	9	22	...	...	...	7	0	2	2	12
00-01—HC Vsetin	Czech Rep.	49	2	6	8	46	...	...	...	14	2	1	3	35
01-02—HC Vsetin	Czech Rep.	33	8	9	17	46	...	...	...	—	—	—	—	—
—Lokomotiv Yaroslavl	Russian	19	1	1	2	10	...	...	...	9	1	2	3	8
02-03—HPK Hameenlinna	Finland	20	4	9	13	68	...	...	...	13	2	3	5	8
—Lokomotiv Yaroslavl	Russian	27	0	6	6	28	...	...	...	—	—	—	—	—
03-04—Los Angeles	NHL	5	2	0	2	8	1	0	0	—	—	—	—	—
—Manchester	AHL	12	0	1	1	25	-1	0	0	—	—	—	—	—
—Pittsburgh	NHL	44	3	11	14	38	-11	0	0	—	—	—	—	—
04-05—HC Kosice	Slovakia	14	1	4	5	14	1	...	...	—	—	—	—	—
—CSKA Moscow	Russian	36	2	11	13	34	-4	...	...	—	—	—	—	—
NHL Totals (1 year)		49	5	11	16	46	-10	0	0					

STRUDWICK, JASON — D/RW — RANGERS

PERSONAL: Born July 17, 1975, in Edmonton. ... 6-3/225. ... Shoots left. ... Name pronounced STRUHD-wihk.
TRANSACTIONS/CAREER NOTES: Selected by New York Islanders in third round (third Islanders pick, 63rd overall) of NHL draft (June 29, 1994). ... Traded by Islanders to Vancouver Canucks for LW Gino Odjick (March 23, 1998). ... Injured back (November 17, 1999); missed 10 games. ... Strained knee (February 24, 2001); missed 11 games. ... Signed as free agent by Chicago Blackhawks (July 15, 2002). ... Injured wrist (November 1, 2003); missed 13 games. ... Injured shoulder (December 19, 2003); missed 10 games. ... Signed as free agent by New York Rangers (July 20, 2004).

		REGULAR SEASON								PLAYOFFS				
Season Team	**League**	**GP**	**G**	**A**	**Pts.**	**PIM**	**+/-**	**PP**	**SH**	**GP**	**G**	**A**	**Pts.**	**PIM**
93-94—Kamloops	WHL	61	6	8	14	118	11	1	0	19	0	4	4	24
94-95—Kamloops	WHL	72	3	11	14	183	36	0	0	21	1	1	2	39
95-96—Worcester	AHL	60	2	7	9	119	...	...	...	4	0	1	1	0
—New York Islanders	NHL	1	0	0	0	7	0	0	0	—	—	—	—	—
96-97—Kentucky	AHL	80	1	9	10	198	-9	0	0	4	0	0	0	0

Season Team	League	REGULAR SEASON GP	G	A	Pts.	PIM	+/-	PP	SH	PLAYOFFS GP	G	A	Pts.	PIM
97-98—Kentucky	AHL	39	3	1	4	87	-12	0	0	—	—	—	—	—
—New York Islanders	NHL	17	0	1	1	36	1	0	0	—	—	—	—	—
—Vancouver	NHL	11	0	1	1	29	-3	0	0	—	—	—	—	—
—Syracuse	AHL	...	...	...	...	...	...	...	...	3	0	0	0	6
98-99—Vancouver	NHL	65	0	3	3	114	-19	0	0	—	—	—	—	—
99-00—Vancouver	NHL	63	1	3	4	64	-13	0	0	—	—	—	—	—
00-01—Vancouver	NHL	60	1	4	5	64	16	0	0	2	0	0	0	0
01-02—Vancouver	NHL	44	2	4	6	96	4	0	0	—	—	—	—	—
02-03—Chicago	NHL	48	2	3	5	87	-4	0	0	—	—	—	—	—
03-04—Chicago	NHL	54	1	3	4	73	-16	0	0	—	—	—	—	—
04-05—Ferencvaros	Hungary	6	1	2	3	8	...	...	...	—	—	—	—	—
NHL Totals (8 years)		363	7	22	29	570	-34	0	0	2	0	0	0	0

STUART, BRAD — D — SHARKS

PERSONAL: Born November 6, 1979, in Rocky Mountain House, Alta. ... 6-2/220. ... Shoots left.

TRANSACTIONS/CAREER NOTES: Selected by San Jose Sharks in first round (first Sharks pick, third overall) of NHL entry draft (June 27, 1998). ... Suspended two games by NHL for cross-checking incident (March 9, 2001). ... Injured ankle (January 6, 2003); missed eight games. ... Suffered concussion (February 24, 2003); missed 21 games. ... Separated shoulder (October 3, 2003); missed five games.

Season Team	League	REGULAR SEASON GP	G	A	Pts.	PIM	+/-	PP	SH	PLAYOFFS GP	G	A	Pts.	PIM
96-97—Regina	WHL	57	7	36	43	58	...	...	...	5	0	4	4	14
97-98—Regina	WHL	72	20	45	65	82	...	...	...	9	3	4	7	10
98-99—Regina	WHL	29	10	19	29	43	...	...	...	—	—	—	—	—
—Calgary	WHL	30	11	22	33	26	...	...	...	21	8	15	23	59
99-00—San Jose	NHL	82	10	26	36	32	3	5	1	12	1	0	1	6
00-01—San Jose	NHL	77	5	18	23	56	10	1	0	5	1	0	1	0
01-02—San Jose	NHL	82	6	23	29	39	13	2	0	12	0	3	3	8
02-03—San Jose	NHL	36	4	10	14	46	-6	2	0	—	—	—	—	—
03-04—San Jose	NHL	77	9	30	39	34	9	5	0	17	1	5	6	13
NHL Totals (5 years)		354	34	107	141	207	29	15	1	46	3	8	11	27

STUART, COLIN — C — THRASHERS

PERSONAL: Born July 8, 1982, in Rochester, Minn. ... 6-1/195. ... Shoots left. ... Brother of Mark Stuart (Boston Bruins organization) and Mike Stuart (St. Louis Blues organization).

TRANSACTIONS/CAREER NOTES: Selected by Atlanta Thrashers in fifth round (fifth Thrashers pick, 135th overall) of NHL entry draft (June 23, 2001).

Season Team	League	REGULAR SEASON GP	G	A	Pts.	PIM	+/-	PP	SH	PLAYOFFS GP	G	A	Pts.	PIM
00-01—Colorado College	WCHA	33	2	7	9	24	...	...	...	—	—	—	—	—
01-02—Colorado College	WCHA	43	13	9	22	34	...	...	...	—	—	—	—	—
02-03—Colorado College	WCHA	42	13	11	24	56	...	...	...	—	—	—	—	—
03-04—Colorado College	WCHA	30	10	12	22	38	...	...	...	—	—	—	—	—
04-05—Chicago	AHL	39	3	2	5	12	-3	0	1	0	0	0	0	0

STUART, MIKE — D — BLUES

PERSONAL: Born August 31, 1980, in Rochester, Minn. ... 6-0/195. ... Shoots right. ... Brother of Mark Stuart (Boston Bruins organization) and Colin Stuart (Atlanta Thrashers organization).

TRANSACTIONS/CAREER NOTES: Selected by Nashville Predators in fifth round (sixth Predators pick, 137th overall) of NHL entry draft (June 24, 2000). ... Signed as free agent by St. Louis Blues (October 7, 2002).

Season Team	League	REGULAR SEASON GP	G	A	Pts.	PIM	+/-	PP	SH	PLAYOFFS GP	G	A	Pts.	PIM
98-99—Colorado College	WCHA	40	2	12	14	44	...	...	...	—	—	—	—	—
99-00—Colorado College	WCHA	32	2	5	7	26	...	...	...	—	—	—	—	—
00-01—Colorado College	WCHA	33	1	13	14	36	...	...	...	—	—	—	—	—
01-02—Colorado College	WCHA	35	3	9	12	46	...	...	...	—	—	—	—	—
02-03—Worcester	AHL	41	1	5	6	19	-2	0	0	3	0	0	0	2
—Peoria	ECHL	19	2	7	9	12	3	0	0	—	—	—	—	—
03-04—Worcester	AHL	30	0	4	4	20	-3	0	0	—	—	—	—	—
—St. Louis	NHL	2	0	0	0	0	0	0	0	—	—	—	—	—
04-05—Worcester	AHL	70	1	10	11	26	5	0	0	—	—	—	—	—
NHL Totals (1 year)		2	0	0	0	0	0	0	0					

STUMPEL, JOZEF — C

PERSONAL: Born July 20, 1972, in Nitra, Czechoslovakia. ... 6-3/225. ... Shoots right. ... Name pronounced JOH-sehf STUHM-puhl.

TRANSACTIONS/CAREER NOTES: Selected by Boston Bruins in second round (second Bruins pick, 40th overall) of NHL draft (June 22, 1991). ... Injured shoulder (December 1992); missed nine games. ... Injured knee (March 17, 1994); missed nine games. ... Injured knee (April 1995). ... Fractured cheekbone (February 27, 1996); missed three games. ... Back spasms (January 4, 1997); missed one game. ... Back spasms (February 1, 1997); missed three games. ... Traded by Bruins with RW Sandy Moger and fourth-round pick (traded to New Jersey; Devils selected RW Pierre Dagenais) in 1998 draft to Los Angeles Kings for LW Dimitri Khristich and G Byron Dafoe (August 29, 1997). ... Flu (February 7, 1998); missed one game. ... Bruised kidney (March 5, 1998); missed four games. ... Strained hip flexor and abdominal muscle

(October 18, 1998); missed 10 games. ... Sprained right ankle (November 16, 1998); missed three games. ... Sprained right knee (April 8, 1999); missed final five games of season. ... Hernia (November 3, 1999); missed 18 games. ... Bruised left knee (January 3, 2000); missed seven games. ... Missed first seven games of 2000-01 season in contract dispute. ... Fractured toe (December 14, 2000); missed two games. ... Strained right hamstring (February 10, 2001); missed two games. ... Fractured rib (March 4, 2001); missed seven games. ... Traded by Kings with RW Glen Murray to Bruins for C Jason Allison and C/LW Mikko Eloranta (October 24, 2001). ... Strained groin (March 26, 2002); missed one game. ... Injured wrist (November 19, 2002); missed three games. ... Injured hip (April 1, 2003); missed one game. ... Traded by Bruins with seventh-round pick in 2003 draft (traded to Nashville; Predators selected G Miroslav Hanulak) to Los Angeles Kings for fourth-round pick (C Patrick Valcak) in 2003 draft and second-round pick (RW Martins Karsums) in 2004 draft (June 22, 2003). ... Injured chest (October 26, 2003); missed 14 games.

STATISTICAL PLATEAUS: Three-goal games: 1995-96 (1), 1997-98 (1). Total: 2.

		REGULAR SEASON								PLAYOFFS				
Season Team	**League**	**GP**	**G**	**A**	**Pts.**	**PIM**	**+/-**	**PP**	**SH**	**GP**	**G**	**A**	**Pts.**	**PIM**
89-90—Nitra	Slovakia	38	12	11	23	0	...	...	...	—	—	—	—	—
90-91—Nitra	Slovakia	49	23	22	45	14	...	...	...	—	—	—	—	—
91-92—Boston	NHL	4	1	0	1	0	1	0	0	—	—	—	—	—
—Koln	Germany	33	19	18	37	35	...	...	...	—	—	—	—	—
92-93—Providence	AHL	56	31	61	92	26	28	14	0	6	4	4	8	0
—Boston	NHL	13	1	3	4	4	-3	0	0	—	—	—	—	—
93-94—Boston	NHL	59	8	15	23	14	4	0	0	13	1	7	8	4
—Providence	AHL	17	5	12	17	4	0	2	0	—	—	—	—	—
94-95—Koln	Germany	25	16	23	39	18	...	...	...	—	—	—	—	—
—Boston	NHL	44	5	13	18	8	4	1	0	5	0	0	0	0
95-96—Boston	NHL	76	18	36	54	14	-8	5	0	5	1	2	3	0
96-97—Boston	NHL	78	21	55	76	14	-22	6	0	—	—	—	—	—
97-98—Los Angeles	NHL	77	21	58	79	53	17	4	0	4	1	2	3	2
98-99—Los Angeles	NHL	64	13	21	34	10	-18	1	0	—	—	—	—	—
99-00—Los Angeles	NHL	57	17	41	58	10	23	3	0	4	0	4	4	8
00-01—Slovan Bratislava	Slovakia	9	2	4	6	16	...	...	...	—	—	—	—	—
—Los Angeles	NHL	63	16	39	55	14	20	9	0	13	3	5	8	10
01-02—Los Angeles	NHL	9	1	3	4	4	1	0	0	—	—	—	—	—
—Boston	NHL	72	7	47	54	14	21	1	0	6	0	2	2	0
—Slovakian Oly. team	Int'l	2	2	1	3	0	...	...	...	—	—	—	—	—
02-03—Boston	NHL	78	14	37	51	12	0	4	0	5	0	2	2	0
03-04—Los Angeles	NHL	64	8	29	37	16	5	4	0	—	—	—	—	—
04-05—Slavia Praha	Czech Rep.	52	13	26	39	41	6	...	...	7	4	2	6	10
NHL Totals (13 years)		758	151	397	548	187	45	38	0	55	6	24	30	24

STURM, MARCO — LW/RW — SHARKS

PERSONAL: Born September 8, 1978, in Dingolfing, West Germany. ... 6-0/195. ... Shoots left.

TRANSACTIONS/CAREER NOTES: Selected by San Jose Sharks in first round (second Sharks pick, 21st overall) of NHL draft (June 22, 1996). ... Sprained wrist (April 1, 1998); missed six games. ... Injured foot (March 3, 1999); missed two games. ... Had concussion (December 2, 1999); missed four games. ... Injured elbow (January 4, 2002); missed two games. ... Flu (January 27, 2002); missed one game. ... Injured hand (March 20, 2002); missed two games. ... Injured chest (January 15, 2004); missed two games. ... Left team for personal reasons (January 21, 2004); missed one game. ... Fractured left leg and dislocated ankle (March 5, 2004); missed remainder of season and playoffs.

STATISTICAL PLATEAUS: Three-goal games: 1998-99 (1).

		REGULAR SEASON								PLAYOFFS				
Season Team	**League**	**GP**	**G**	**A**	**Pts.**	**PIM**	**+/-**	**PP**	**SH**	**GP**	**G**	**A**	**Pts.**	**PIM**
95-96—Landshut	Germany	47	12	20	32	50	...	...	...	—	—	—	—	—
96-97—Landshut	Germany	46	16	27	43	40	...	...	...	7	1	4	5	6
97-98—San Jose	NHL	74	10	20	30	40	-2	2	0	2	0	0	0	0
—German Oly. team	Int'l	2	0	0	0	0	0	0	0	—	—	—	—	—
98-99—San Jose	NHL	78	16	22	38	52	7	3	2	6	2	2	4	4
99-00—San Jose	NHL	74	12	15	27	22	4	2	4	12	1	3	4	6
00-01—San Jose	NHL	81	14	18	32	28	9	2	3	6	0	2	2	0
01-02—San Jose	NHL	77	21	20	41	32	23	4	3	12	3	2	5	2
—German Oly. team	Int'l	5	0	1	1	0	...	...	...	—	—	—	—	—
02-03—San Jose	NHL	82	28	20	48	16	9	6	0	—	—	—	—	—
03-04—San Jose	NHL	64	21	20	41	36	0	10	2	—	—	—	—	—
04-05—Ingolstadt ERC	Germany	45	22	16	38	56	14	6	1	11	3	4	7	12
NHL Totals (7 years)		530	122	135	257	226	50	29	14	38	6	9	15	12

STUTZEL, MIKE — LW

PERSONAL: Born February 28, 1979, in Victoria, B.C. ... 6-2/216. ... Shoots left.

TRANSACTIONS/CAREER NOTES: Signed as free agent by Phoenix Coyotes (April 10, 2003).

		REGULAR SEASON								PLAYOFFS				
Season Team	**League**	**GP**	**G**	**A**	**Pts.**	**PIM**	**+/-**	**PP**	**SH**	**GP**	**G**	**A**	**Pts.**	**PIM**
99-00—Northern Michigan	CCHA	29	3	6	9	44	...	...	...	—	—	—	—	—
00-01—Northern Michigan	CCHA	16	3	5	8	6	...	...	...	—	—	—	—	—
01-02—Northern Michigan	CCHA	40	16	17	33	20	...	...	...	—	—	—	—	—
02-03—Northern Michigan	CCHA	41	27	15	42	50	...	...	...	—	—	—	—	—
03-04—Phoenix	NHL	9	0	0	0	0	-4	0	0	—	—	—	—	—
—Springfield	AHL	62	12	12	24	39	-7	5	0	—	—	—	—	—
04-05—Utah	AHL	52	0	2	2	16	-7	0	0	—	—	—	—	—
—Idaho	ECHL	14	8	7	15	8	5	3	...	4	1	0	1	6
NHL Totals (1 year)		9	0	0	0	0	-4	0	0					

SUCHY, RADOSLAV — D — BLUE JACKETS

PERSONAL: Born April 7, 1976, in Kezmarok, Czechoslovakia. ... 6-2/196. ... Shoots left. ... Name pronounced soo-KHEE.
TRANSACTIONS/CAREER NOTES: Signed as free agent by Phoenix Coyotes (September 25, 1997). ... Bruised finger (December 21, 2001); missed one game. ... Traded by Coyotes with sixth-round pick in 2005 raft to Columbus Blue Jackets for fourth-round pick in 2005 draft (July 6, 2004).

		REGULAR SEASON								PLAYOFFS				
Season Team	League	GP	G	A	Pts.	PIM	+/-	PP	SH	GP	G	A	Pts.	PIM
94-95—Sherbrooke	QMJHL	69	12	32	44	30	...	...	...	7	0	3	3	2
95-96—Sherbrooke	QMJHL	68	15	53	68	68	...	...	...	7	0	3	3	2
96-97—Sherbrooke	QMJHL	32	6	34	40	14	...	...	...	—	—	—	—	—
—Chicoutimi	QMJHL	28	5	24	29	24	...	...	...	19	6	15	21	12
97-98—Las Vegas	IHL	26	1	4	5	10	0	0	0	—	—	—	—	—
—Springfield	AHL	41	6	15	21	16	13	0	1	4	0	1	1	2
98-99—Springfield	AHL	69	4	32	36	10	3	2	0	3	0	1	1	0
99-00—Springfield	AHL	2	0	1	1	0	...	...	...	—	—	—	—	—
—Phoenix	NHL	60	0	6	6	16	2	0	0	5	0	1	1	0
00-01—Phoenix	NHL	72	0	10	10	22	1	0	0	—	—	—	—	—
01-02—Phoenix	NHL	81	4	13	17	10	25	1	0	5	1	0	1	0
02-03—Phoenix	NHL	77	1	8	9	18	2	1	0	—	—	—	—	—
03-04—Phoenix	NHL	82	7	14	21	8	1	2	0	—	—	—	—	—
04-05—HC SKP Poprad	Slovakia	34	5	10	15	24	-1	...	...	5	0	0	0	2
NHL Totals (5 years)		372	12	51	63	74	31	4	0	10	1	1	2	0

SUGLOBOV, ALEKSANDER — RW — DEVILS

PERSONAL: Born January 15, 1982, in Elektrostal, U.S.S.R. ... 6-0/200. ... Shoots left. ... Name pronounced suh-GLOH-bahf.
TRANSACTIONS/CAREER NOTES: Selected by New Jersey Devils in second round (third Devils pick, 56th overall) of NHL draft (June 24, 2000).

		REGULAR SEASON								PLAYOFFS				
Season Team	League	GP	G	A	Pts.	PIM	+/-	PP	SH	GP	G	A	Pts.	PIM
98-99—Spartak Yekaterinburg	Russian	1	0	0	0	0	...	0	0	—	—	—	—	—
99-00—Torpedo Yaroslavl	Rus. Div.	38	23	10	33	...	...	...	...	—	—	—	—	—
—Torpedo Yaroslavl	Rus. Div.	2	0	0	0	0	...	0	0	—	—	—	—	—
00-01—Salavat Yulayev Ufa	Russian	6	0	0	0	4	...	...	...	—	—	—	—	—
—SKA St. Petersburg	Russian	8	1	0	1	6	...	...	...	—	—	—	—	—
—Lokomotiv Yaroslavl	Russian	4	0	0	0	2	...	...	...	11	1	2	3	6
01-02—Lokomotiv Yaroslavl	Russian	25	4	2	6	26	...	...	...	5	1	1	2	18
02-03—Yaroslavl	CIS	17	4	2	6	12	...	...	...	5	1	0	1	2
03-04—Albany	AHL	35	11	11	22	54	-9	4	0	—	—	—	—	—
—New Jersey	NHL	1	0	0	0	0	0	0	0	...	...	...	...	...
04-05—Albany	AHL	72	25	21	46	77	-15	7	0	—	—	—	—	—
NHL Totals (1 year)		1	0	0	0	0	0	0	0					

SULLIVAN, STEVE — RW/LW — PREDATORS

PERSONAL: Born July 6, 1974, in Timmins, Ont. ... 5-8/155. ... Shoots right.
TRANSACTIONS/CAREER NOTES: Selected by New Jersey Devils in ninth round (10th Devils pick, 233rd overall) of NHL draft (June 29, 1994). ... Traded by Devils with D Jason Smith and C Alyn McCauley to Toronto Maple Leafs for C Doug Gilmour, D Dave Ellett and third-round pick (D Andre Lakos) in 1999 draft (February 25, 1997). ... Flu (March 7, 1998); missed three games. ... Back spasms (May 11, 1999); missed one playoff game. ... Claimed off waivers by Chicago Blackhawks (October 23, 1999). ... Flu (February 18, 2000); missed one game. ... Flu (December 13, 2000); missed one game. ... Separated shoulder (March 20, 2002); missed four games. ... Injured back (November 28, 2003); missed two games. ... Traded by Blackhawks to Nashville Predators for a 2004 second-round pick and a 2005 second-round pick (February 16, 2004).
STATISTICAL PLATEAUS: Three-goal games: 2000-01 (1), 2002-03 (1), 2003-04 (1). Total: 3. ... Four-goal games: 1998-99 (1). ... Total hat tricks: 4.

		REGULAR SEASON								PLAYOFFS				
Season Team	League	GP	G	A	Pts.	PIM	+/-	PP	SH	GP	G	A	Pts.	PIM
91-92—Timmins	OJHL	47	66	55	121	141	...	...	...	—	—	—	—	—
92-93—Sault Ste. Marie	OHL	62	36	27	63	44	...	...	...	16	3	8	11	18
93-94—Sault Ste. Marie	OHL	63	51	62	113	82	...	...	...	14	9	16	25	22
94-95—Albany	AHL	75	31	50	81	124	41	8	0	14	4	7	11	10
95-96—Albany	AHL	53	33	42	75	127	...	...	...	4	3	0	3	6
—New Jersey	NHL	16	5	4	9	8	3	2	0	—	—	—	—	—
96-97—Albany	AHL	15	8	7	15	16	2	2	0	—	—	—	—	—
—New Jersey	NHL	33	8	14	22	14	9	2	0	—	—	—	—	—
—Toronto	NHL	21	5	11	16	23	5	1	0	—	—	—	—	—
97-98—Toronto	NHL	63	10	18	28	40	-8	1	0	—	—	—	—	—
98-99—Toronto	NHL	63	20	20	40	28	12	4	0	13	3	3	6	14
99-00—Toronto	NHL	7	0	1	1	4	-1	0	0	—	—	—	—	—
—Chicago	NHL	73	22	42	64	52	20	2	1	—	—	—	—	—
00-01—Chicago	NHL	81	34	41	75	54	3	6	*8	—	—	—	—	—
01-02—Chicago	NHL	78	21	39	60	67	23	3	0	5	1	0	1	2
02-03—Chicago	NHL	82	26	35	61	42	15	4	2	—	—	—	—	—
03-04—Chicago	NHL	56	15	28	43	36	-7	4	2	—	—	—	—	—
—Nashville	NHL	24	9	21	30	12	8	7	0	6	1	1	2	6
NHL Totals (9 years)		597	175	274	449	380	82	36	13	24	5	4	9	22

SUNDIN, MATS — C — MAPLE LEAFS

PERSONAL: Born February 13, 1971, in Bromma, Sweden. ... 6-5/231. ... Shoots right. ... Name pronounced suhn-DEEN.

TRANSACTIONS/CAREER NOTES: Selected by Quebec Nordiques in 1st round (1st Nordiques pick,1st overall) of NHL draft (June 17, 1989). ... Separated right shoulder (January 2, 1993); missed three games. ... Suspended one game for second stick-related infraction (March 2, 1993). ... Traded by Nordiques with D Garth Butcher, LW Todd Warriner and first-round pick (traded to Washington; Capitals selected D Nolan Baumgartner) in 1994 draft to Toronto Maple Leafs for LW Wendel Clark, D Sylvain Lefebvre, RW Landon Wilson and first-round pick (D Jeffrey Kealty) in 1994 draft (June 28, 1994). ... Sprained shoulder (March 25, 1995); missed one game. ... Slightly tore knee cartilage (October 24, 1995); missed four games. ... Fractured ankle (October 9, 1999); missed nine games. ... Bruised left shoulder (December 27, 2002); missed six games. ... Facial cut (April 9, 2003); missed one game. ... Suspended one game for throwing stick into stands (January 6, 2004).

STATISTICAL PLATEAUS: Three-goal games: 1990-91 (2), 1992-93 (1), 1996-97 (1), 1998-99 (1). Total: 5. ... Five-goal games: 1991-92 (1). ... Total hat tricks: 6.

		REGULAR SEASON								PLAYOFFS				
Season Team	League	GP	G	A	Pts.	PIM	+/-	PP	SH	GP	G	A	Pts.	PIM
88-89—Nacka	Sweden	25	10	8	18	18	...	...	...	—	—	—	—	—
89-90—Djurgarden Stockholm	Sweden	34	10	8	18	16	...	...	...	8	7	0	7	4
90-91—Quebec	NHL	80	23	36	59	58	-24	4	0	—	—	—	—	—
91-92—Quebec	NHL	80	33	43	76	103	-19	8	2	—	—	—	—	—
92-93—Quebec	NHL	80	47	67	114	96	21	13	4	6	3	1	4	6
93-94—Quebec	NHL	84	32	53	85	60	1	6	2	—	—	—	—	—
94-95—Djurgarden Stockholm	Sweden	12	7	2	9	14	...	...	...	—	—	—	—	—
—Toronto	NHL	47	23	24	47	14	-5	9	0	7	5	4	9	4
95-96—Toronto	NHL	76	33	50	83	46	8	7	6	6	3	1	4	4
96-97—Toronto	NHL	82	41	53	94	59	6	7	4	—	—	—	—	—
97-98—Toronto	NHL	82	33	41	74	49	-3	9	1	—	—	—	—	—
—Swedish Oly. team	Int'l	4	3	0	3	4	1	0	0	—	—	—	—	—
98-99—Toronto	NHL	82	31	52	83	58	22	4	0	17	8	8	16	16
99-00—Toronto	NHL	73	32	41	73	46	16	10	2	12	3	5	8	10
00-01—Toronto	NHL	82	28	46	74	76	15	9	0	11	6	7	13	14
01-02—Toronto	NHL	82	41	39	80	94	6	10	2	8	2	5	7	4
—Swedish Oly. team	Int'l	4	5	4	9	10	...	...	...	—	—	—	—	—
02-03—Toronto	NHL	75	37	35	72	58	1	16	3	7	1	3	4	6
03-04—Toronto	NHL	81	31	44	75	52	11	11	1	9	4	5	9	8
NHL Totals (14 years)		1086	465	624	1089	869	56	123	27	83	35	39	74	72

SUNDSTROM, NIKLAS — RW/LW — CANADIENS

PERSONAL: Born June 6, 1975, in Ornskoldsvik, Sweden. ... 6-0/191. ... Shoots left.

TRANSACTIONS/CAREER NOTES: Selected by New York Rangers in first round (first Rangers pick, eighth overall) of NHL draft (June 26, 1993). ... Fractured finger and sprained knee (December 5, 1997); missed 10 games. ... Traded by Rangers with G Dan Cloutier and first- (RW Nikita Alexeev) and third-round (traded to San Jose; traded to Chicago; Blackhawks selected LW Igor Radulov) picks in 2000 draft to Tampa Bay Lightning for first-round pick (RW Pavel Brendl) in 1999 draft (June 26, 1999). ... Traded by Lightning with third-round pick (traded to Chicago; Blackhawks selected LW Igor Radulov) in 2000 draft to San Jose Sharks for D Andrei Zyuzin, D Bill Houlder, LW Shawn Burr and C Steve Guolla (August 4, 1999). ... Injured knee (November 29, 2001); missed one game. ... Injured knee (March 21, 2002); missed eight games. ... Traded by Sharks with third-round pick (later traded to Los Angeles; Kings picked D Paul Baier) in 2004 draft to Montreal Canadiens for G Jeff Hackett. (January 23, 2003). ... Injured shoulder (October 11, 2003); missed one game. ... Injured abdomen (January 4, 2004); missed four games. ... Had concussion (February 29, 2004); missed seven games.

		REGULAR SEASON								PLAYOFFS				
Season Team	League	GP	G	A	Pts.	PIM	+/-	PP	SH	GP	G	A	Pts.	PIM
91-92—MoDo Ornskoldsvik	Sweden	9	1	3	4	0	...	...	...	—	—	—	—	—
92-93—MoDo Ornskoldsvik	Sweden	40	7	11	18	18	...	...	...	—	—	—	—	—
93-94—MoDo Ornskoldsvik	Sweden	37	7	12	19	28	...	...	...	11	4	3	7	2
94-95—MoDo Ornskoldsvik	Sweden	33	8	13	21	30	...	...	...	—	—	—	—	—
95-96—New York Rangers	NHL	82	9	12	21	14	2	1	1	11	4	3	7	4
96-97—New York Rangers	NHL	82	24	28	52	20	23	5	1	9	0	5	5	2
97-98—New York Rangers	NHL	70	19	28	47	24	0	4	0	—	—	—	—	—
—Swedish Oly. team	Int'l	4	1	1	2	2	3	0	0	—	—	—	—	—
98-99—New York Rangers	NHL	81	13	30	43	20	-2	1	2	—	—	—	—	—
99-00—San Jose	NHL	79	12	25	37	22	9	2	1	12	0	2	2	2
00-01—San Jose	NHL	82	10	39	49	28	10	4	1	6	0	3	3	2
01-02—San Jose	NHL	73	9	30	39	50	7	0	1	12	1	6	7	6
—Swedish Oly. team	Int'l	4	1	3	4	0	...	...	...	—	—	—	—	—
02-03—San Jose	NHL	47	2	10	12	22	-4	0	0	—	—	—	—	—
—Montreal	NHL	33	5	9	14	8	3	0	0	—	—	—	—	—
03-04—Montreal	NHL	66	8	12	20	18	3	0	0	4	1	0	1	2
04-05—Milano	Italy	33	9	27	36	40	...	...	...	—	—	—	—	—
NHL Totals (9 years)		695	111	223	334	226	51	17	7	54	6	19	25	18

SURMA, DAMIAN — C — HURRICANES

PERSONAL: Born January 22, 1981, in Lincoln Park, Mich. ... 5-10/200. ... Shoots left.

TRANSACTIONS/CAREER NOTES: Selected by Carolina Hurricanes in sixth round (fifth Hurricanes pick, 174th overall) of NHL entry draft (June 26, 1999). ... Injured shoulder (March 22, 2003); missed four games.

		REGULAR SEASON								PLAYOFFS				
Season Team	League	GP	G	A	Pts.	PIM	+/-	PP	SH	GP	G	A	Pts.	PIM
98-99—Plymouth	OHL	65	17	15	32	62	...	...	...	11	3	6	9	15
99-00—Plymouth	OHL	66	34	44	78	114	28	7	1	20	9	8	17	10

Season Team	League	GP	G	A	Pts.	PIM	+/-	PP	SH	GP	G	A	Pts.	PIM
		REGULAR SEASON								PLAYOFFS				
00-01—Plymouth	OHL	55	26	34	60	62	34	6	1	19	8	9	17	25
01-02—Plymouth	OHL	55	28	27	55	68	...	...	...	6	3	0	3	10
—Lowell	AHL	1	0	0	0	0	-1	0	0	4	0	0	0	0
02-03—Lowell	AHL	68	11	11	22	46	-15	0	2	—	—	—	—	—
—Carolina	NHL	1	1	0	1	0	0	0	0	—	—	—	—	—
03-04—Carolina	NHL	1	0	1	1	0	1	0	0	—	—	—	—	—
—Florida	ECHL	18	6	9	15	20	-1	1	1	16	5	4	9	20
—Lowell	AHL	48	3	5	8	21	-5	0	0	—	—	—	—	—
04-05—Florida	ECHL	72	32	28	60	74	22	9	...	19	7	6	13	14
NHL Totals (2 years)		2	1	1	2	0	1	0	0					

SUROVY, TOMAS LW/C PENGUINS

PERSONAL: Born September 24, 1981, in Banska Bystrica, Czechoslovakia. ... 6-0/191. ... Shoots left.

TRANSACTIONS/CAREER NOTES: Selected by Pittsburgh Penguins in fourth round (fifth Penguins pick, 120th overall) of NHL entry draft (June 23, 2001).

Season Team	League	GP	G	A	Pts.	PIM	+/-	PP	SH	GP	G	A	Pts.	PIM
		REGULAR SEASON								PLAYOFFS				
00-01—HC SKP Poprad	Slovakia	53	22	28	50	30	...	...	...	6	2	1	3	14
01-02—Wilkes-Barre/Scranton	AHL	65	23	10	33	37	-9	4	0	—	—	—	—	—
02-03—Pittsburgh	NHL	26	4	7	11	10	0	1	0	—	—	—	—	—
—Wilkes-Barre/Scranton	AHL	39	19	20	39	18	3	7	0	6	2	3	5	2
03-04—Pittsburgh	NHL	47	11	12	23	16	-8	3	0	—	—	—	—	—
—Wilkes-Barre/Scranton	AHL	30	14	13	27	14	13	4	0	24	6	11	17	8
04-05—Wilkes-Barre/Scranton	AHL	80	17	32	49	43	-10	3	0	11	2	6	8	9
NHL Totals (2 years)		73	15	19	34	26	-8	4	0					

S

SUTER, RYAN D PREDATORS

PERSONAL: Born January 21, 1985, in Madison, Wis. ... 6-1/183. ... Shoots left.

TRANSACTIONS/CAREER NOTES: Selected by Nashville Predators in first round (first Predators pick, seventh overall) in 2003 NHL entry draft (June 23, 2003).

Season Team	League	GP	G	A	Pts.	PIM	+/-	PP	SH	GP	G	A	Pts.	PIM
		REGULAR SEASON								PLAYOFFS				
01-02—U.S. national team	Int'l	39	3	16	19	93	...	1	0	—	—	—	—	—
02-03—U.S. national team	Int'l	47	8	19	27	114	...	...	...	—	—	—	—	—
03-04—Wisconsin	WCHA	39	3	16	19	93	...	...	...	—	—	—	—	—
04-05—Milwaukee	AHL	63	7	16	23	70	10	4	0	7	1	5	6	16

SUTHERBY, BRIAN C CAPITALS

PERSONAL: Born March 1, 1982, in Edmonton. ... 6-3/205. ... Shoots left.

TRANSACTIONS/CAREER NOTES: Selected by Washington Capitals in first round (first Capitals pick, 26th overall) of NHL entry draft (June 24, 2000). ... Strained lower back (November 18, 2004); missed five games.

Season Team	League	GP	G	A	Pts.	PIM	+/-	PP	SH	GP	G	A	Pts.	PIM
		REGULAR SEASON								PLAYOFFS				
98-99—Moose Jaw	WHL	66	9	12	21	47	...	...	...	11	0	1	1	0
99-00—Moose Jaw	WHL	47	18	17	35	102	...	...	...	4	1	1	2	12
00-01—Moose Jaw	WHL	59	34	43	77	138	...	...	...	4	2	1	3	10
01-02—Washington	NHL	7	0	0	0	2	-3	0	0	—	—	—	—	—
—Moose Jaw	WHL	36	18	27	45	75	...	...	...	12	7	5	12	33
02-03—Portland	AHL	5	0	5	5	11	1	0	0	—	—	—	—	—
—Washington	NHL	72	2	9	11	93	7	0	0	5	0	0	0	10
03-04—Washington	NHL	30	2	0	2	28	-5	0	0	—	—	—	—	—
—Portland	AHL	6	2	4	6	16	2	0	0	—	—	—	—	—
04-05—Portland	AHL	53	10	19	29	115	-3	3	1	—	—	—	—	—
NHL Totals (3 years)		109	4	9	13	123	-1	0	0	5	0	0	0	10

SUTTON, ANDY D THRASHERS

PERSONAL: Born March 10, 1975, in Kingston, Ontario. ... 6-6/245. ... Shoots left.

TRANSACTIONS/CAREER NOTES: Signed as free agent by San Jose Sharks (March 20, 1998). ... Injured wrist (November 27, 1999); missed three games. ... Reinjured wrist (December 8, 1999); missed three games. ... Reinjured wrist (December 20, 1999); missed seven games. ... Reinjured wrist (January 12, 2000); missed 10 games. ... Traded by Sharks with seventh-round pick (RW/LW Peter Bartos) in 2000 draft and third-round pick (traded to Atlanta; traded to Pittsburgh; traded to Columbus; Blue Jackets selected D Aaron Johnson) in 2001 draft to Minnesota Wild for eighth-round pick (traded to Calgary; Flames selected D Joe Campbell) in 2001 draft and future considerations (June 12, 2000). ... Bruised knee (November 8, 2000); missed two games. ... Dislocated shoulder (March 6, 2001); missed one game. ... Separated right shoulder (October 30, 2001); missed 12 games. ... Strained groin (January 9, 2002); missed four games. ... Traded by Wild to Atlanta Thrashers for LW Hnat Domenichelli (January 22, 2002). ... Had concussion (April 2, 2002); missed two games. ... Injured ankle (February 14, 2003); missed 27 games. ... Fractured left foot (January 1, 2004); missed 16 games.

Season Team	League	GP	G	A	Pts.	PIM	+/-	PP	SH	GP	G	A	Pts.	PIM
		REGULAR SEASON								PLAYOFFS				
94-95—Michigan Tech	WCHA	19	2	1	3	42	...	1	0	—	—	—	—	—
95-96—Michigan Tech	WCHA	32	2	2	4	38	...	...	...	—	—	—	—	—
96-97—Michigan Tech	WCHA	32	2	7	9	73	...	...	...	—	—	—	—	—

		REGULAR SEASON								PLAYOFFS				
Season Team	**League**	**GP**	**G**	**A**	**Pts.**	**PIM**	**+/-**	**PP**	**SH**	**GP**	**G**	**A**	**Pts.**	**PIM**
97-98—Michigan Tech	WCHA	38	16	24	40	97	...	...	...	—	—	—	—	—
—Kentucky	AHL	7	0	0	0	33	-4	0	0	—	—	—	—	—
98-99—San Jose	NHL	31	0	3	3	65	-4	0	0	—	—	—	—	—
—Kentucky	AHL	21	5	10	15	53	9	3	0	5	0	0	0	23
99-00—San Jose	NHL	40	1	1	2	80	-5	0	0	—	—	—	—	—
—Kentucky	AHL	3	0	1	1	0	...	...	...	—	—	—	—	—
00-01—Minnesota	NHL	69	3	4	7	131	-11	2	0	—	—	—	—	—
01-02—Minnesota	NHL	19	2	4	6	35	-4	1	0	—	—	—	—	—
—Atlanta	NHL	24	0	4	4	46	0	0	0	—	—	—	—	—
02-03—Atlanta	NHL	53	3	18	21	114	-8	1	1	—	—	—	—	—
03-04—Atlanta	NHL	65	8	13	21	94	0	7	1	—	—	—	—	—
04-05—Zurich	Switz. Div. 2	18	8	18	26	58	...	2	1	6	2	4	6	16
—ZSC Lions Zurich	Switzerland	8	2	2	4	32	...	0	0	1	0	1	1	2
NHL Totals (6 years)		301	17	47	64	565	-32	11	2					

SVATOS, MAREK — RW — AVALANCHE

PERSONAL: Born June 17, 1982, in Kosice, Czechoslovakia. ... 5-11/175. ... Shoots right.
TRANSACTIONS/CAREER NOTES: Selected by Avalanche in seventh round (10th Avalanche pick, 227th overall) of NHL entry draft (June 24, 2001). ... Injured left shoulder and had surgery (October 14, 2003); missed 72 games.

		REGULAR SEASON								PLAYOFFS				
Season Team	**League**	**GP**	**G**	**A**	**Pts.**	**PIM**	**+/-**	**PP**	**SH**	**GP**	**G**	**A**	**Pts.**	**PIM**
99-00—HC Kosice	Slovakia Jrs.	39	43	30	73	28	...	...	...	—	—	—	—	—
—HC Kosice	Slovakia	19	2	2	4	0	...	...	...	—	—	—	—	—
00-01—Kootenay	WHL	39	23	18	41	47	...	...	...	11	7	2	9	26
01-02—Kootenay	WHL	53	38	39	77	58	...	...	...	21	12	6	18	40
02-03—Hershey	AHL	30	9	4	13	10	...	...	...	—	—	—	—	—
03-04—Colorado	NHL	4	2	0	2	0	1	1	0	11	1	5	6	2
04-05—Hershey	AHL	72	18	28	46	69	9	3	0	—	—	—	—	—
NHL Totals (1 year)		4	2	0	2	0	1	1	0	11	1	5	6	2

SVITOV, ALEXANDER — C — BLUE JACKETS

PERSONAL: Born November 3, 1982, in Omsk, U.S.S.R. ... 6-3/217. ... Shoots left.
TRANSACTIONS/CAREER NOTES: Selected by Tampa Bay Lightning in first round (first Lightning pick, third overall) of NHL entry draft (June 23, 2001). ... Traded by Lightning with third-round pick (later traded to Calgary Flames) in 2004 entry draft to Columbus Blue Jackets for D Darryl Sydor and fourth-round pick (D Mike Lundin) in 2004 entry draft (January 27, 2004). ... Fractured right foot (March 30, 2004); missed remainder of season.

		REGULAR SEASON								PLAYOFFS				
Season Team	**League**	**GP**	**G**	**A**	**Pts.**	**PIM**	**+/-**	**PP**	**SH**	**GP**	**G**	**A**	**Pts.**	**PIM**
99-00—Avangard Omsk	Russian	18	3	3	6	45	...	...	...	6	1	0	1	16
00-01—Avangard Omsk	Russian	39	8	6	14	115	...	...	...	14	2	1	3	34
01-02—Avangard Omsk	Russian	2	0	1	1	2	...	...	...	—	—	—	—	—
02-03—Springfield	AHL	11	4	5	9	17	4	2	0	—	—	—	—	—
—Tampa Bay	NHL	63	4	4	8	58	-4	1	0	7	0	0	0	6
03-04—Tampa Bay	NHL	11	0	3	3	4	0	0	0	—	—	—	—	—
—Hamilton	AHL	30	9	9	18	79	5	3	1	—	—	—	—	—
—Columbus	NHL	29	2	6	8	16	-8	0	0	—	—	—	—	—
04-05—Syracuse	AHL	69	19	23	42	200	-9	6	2	—	—	—	—	—
NHL Totals (2 years)		103	6	13	19	78	-12	1	0	7	0	0	0	6

SVOBODA, JAROSLAV — LW — STARS

PERSONAL: Born June 1, 1980, in Cervenka, Czechoslovakia. ... 6-2/190. ... Shoots left. ... Name pronounced svah-BOH-duh.
TRANSACTIONS/CAREER NOTES: Selected by Carolina Hurricanes in eighth round (eighth Hurricanes pick, 208th overall) of NHL draft (June 21, 1997). ... Dislocated shoulder (February 11, 2003); missed 25 games. ... Strained abdomal muscle (February 21, 2004); missed eight games. ... Injured torso (April 2, 2004); missed remainder of season. ... Traded by Hurricanes to Dallas Stars for fourth-round pick in 2005 entry draft (June 29, 2004).

		REGULAR SEASON								PLAYOFFS				
Season Team	**League**	**GP**	**G**	**A**	**Pts.**	**PIM**	**+/-**	**PP**	**SH**	**GP**	**G**	**A**	**Pts.**	**PIM**
97-98—Olomouc	Czech. Jrs.	43	15	18	33	0	...	...	...	—	—	—	—	—
98-99—Kootenay	WHL	54	26	33	59	46	...	...	...	7	2	2	4	11
99-00—Kootenay	WHL	56	23	43	66	97	38	5	2	21	*15	13	*28	51
00-01—Cincinnati	IHL	52	4	10	14	25	...	...	...	—	—	—	—	—
01-02—Lowell	AHL	66	12	16	28	58	10	2	1	—	—	—	—	—
—Carolina	NHL	10	2	2	4	2	0	0	0	23	1	4	5	28
02-03—Lowell	AHL	9	1	1	2	10	-4	0	0	—	—	—	—	—
—Carolina	NHL	48	3	11	14	32	-5	1	0	—	—	—	—	—
03-04—Carolina	NHL	33	3	1	4	6	3	0	0	—	—	—	—	—
—Lowell	AHL	9	2	2	4	4	0	1	0	—	—	—	—	—
04-05—HC Trinec	Czech Rep.	9	0	2	2	14	-3	...	...	—	—	—	—	—
—Olomouc	Czech Dv.I	18	7	6	13	67	0	...	...	—	—	—	—	—
NHL Totals (3 years)		91	8	14	22	40	-2	1	0	23	1	4	5	28

SWANSON, BRIAN — C — THRASHERS

PERSONAL: Born March 24, 1976, in Eagle River, Alaska. ... 5-10/185. ... Shoots left.
TRANSACTIONS/CAREER NOTES: Selected by San Jose Sharks in fifth round (fifth Sharks pick, 115th overall) of NHL entry draft (June 29, 1994). ... Traded by Sharks with D Jayson More and fourth-round pick (D Tomi Kallarsson) in 1997 draft to New York Rangers for D Marty McSorley (August 20, 1996). ... Signed as free agent by Edmonton Oilers (August 20, 1999). ... Signed as free agent by Atlanta Thrashers (July 24, 2003).

		REGULAR SEASON								PLAYOFFS				
Season Team	**League**	**GP**	**G**	**A**	**Pts.**	**PIM**	**+/-**	**PP**	**SH**	**GP**	**G**	**A**	**Pts.**	**PIM**
93-94—Omaha	USHL	47	38	42	80	40	...	...	...	—	—	—	—	—
94-95—Portland	WHL	65	3	18	21	91	...	...	...	9	2	1	3	18
95-96—Colorado College	WCHA	40	26	33	59	24	...	...	...	—	—	—	—	—
96-97—Colorado College	WCHA	43	19	32	51	47	...	5	2	—	—	—	—	—
97-98—Colorado College	WCHA	42	18	*38	*56	26	...	...	...	—	—	—	—	—
98-99—Colorado College	WCHA	42	25	41	66	28	...	...	...	—	—	—	—	—
—Hartford	AHL	4	0	0	0	4	0	0	0	—	—	—	—	—
99-00—Hamilton	AHL	69	19	40	59	18	...	...	...	10	2	5	7	6
00-01—Edmonton	NHL	16	1	1	2	6	-1	0	0	—	—	—	—	—
—Hamilton	AHL	49	18	29	47	20	...	...	...	—	—	—	—	—
01-02—Hamilton	AHL	65	34	39	73	26	28	8	2	15	7	6	13	6
—Edmonton	NHL	8	1	1	2	0	-1	0	0	—	—	—	—	—
02-03—Edmonton	NHL	44	2	10	12	10	-7	1	0	—	—	—	—	—
03-04—Atlanta	NHL	2	0	1	1	0	0	0	0	—	—	—	—	—
—Chicago	AHL	70	13	34	47	30	-6	4	2	10	4	4	8	6
04-05—Kassel	Germany	37	14	19	33	16	...	...	...	5	2	2	4	4
NHL Totals (4 years)		70	4	13	17	16	-9	1	0					

SWEENEY, DON — D

PERSONAL: Born August 17, 1966, in St. Stephen, New Brunswick. ... 5-10/185. ... Shoots left.
TRANSACTIONS/CAREER NOTES: Selected by Boston Bruins in eighth round (eighth Bruins pick, 166th overall) of NHL entry draft (June 9, 1984). ... Bruised left heel (February 22, 1990). ... Injured knee (October 12, 1991); missed four games. ... Sprained knee (October 5, 1993); missed six games. ... Injured ribs (December 15, 1993); missed three games. ... Injured shoulder (October 17, 1995); missed three games. ... Injured shoulder (October 31, 1995); missed two games. ... Fractured shoulder (March 1, 1998); missed remainder of season. ... Flu (January 13, 2000); missed one game. ... Knee surgery (December 13, 2000); missed eight games. ... Injured knee (January 27, 2001); missed two games. ... Flu (January 12, 2002); missed one game. ... Signed as free agent by Dallas Stars (July 14, 2003).

		REGULAR SEASON								PLAYOFFS				
Season Team	**League**	**GP**	**G**	**A**	**Pts.**	**PIM**	**+/-**	**PP**	**SH**	**GP**	**G**	**A**	**Pts.**	**PIM**
83-84—St. Paul N.B. H.S.	N.B. H.S.	22	33	26	59	...	...	...	...	—	—	—	—	—
84-85—Harvard	ECAC	29	3	7	10	30	...	...	...	—	—	—	—	—
85-86—Harvard	ECAC	31	4	5	9	29	...	...	...	—	—	—	—	—
86-87—Harvard	ECAC	34	7	14	21	22	...	...	...	—	—	—	—	—
87-88—Harvard	ECAC	30	6	23	29	37	...	...	...	—	—	—	—	—
—Maine	AHL	...	...	...	...	...	...	...	...	6	1	3	4	0
88-89—Maine	AHL	42	8	17	25	24	...	...	...	—	—	—	—	—
—Boston	NHL	36	3	5	8	20	-6	0	0	—	—	—	—	—
89-90—Boston	NHL	58	3	5	8	58	11	0	0	21	1	5	6	18
—Maine	AHL	11	0	8	8	8	...	...	...	—	—	—	—	—
90-91—Boston	NHL	77	8	13	21	67	2	0	1	19	3	0	3	25
91-92—Boston	NHL	75	3	11	14	74	-9	0	0	15	0	0	0	10
92-93—Boston	NHL	84	7	27	34	68	34	0	1	4	0	0	0	4
93-94—Boston	NHL	75	6	15	21	50	29	1	2	12	2	1	3	4
94-95—Boston	NHL	47	3	19	22	24	6	1	0	5	0	0	0	4
95-96—Boston	NHL	77	4	24	28	42	-4	2	0	5	0	2	2	6
96-97—Boston	NHL	82	3	23	26	39	-5	0	0	—	—	—	—	—
97-98—Boston	NHL	59	1	15	16	24	12	0	0	—	—	—	—	—
98-99—Boston	NHL	81	2	10	12	64	14	0	0	11	3	0	3	6
99-00—Boston	NHL	81	1	13	14	48	-14	0	0	—	—	—	—	—
00-01—Boston	NHL	72	2	10	12	26	-1	1	0	—	—	—	—	—
01-02—Boston	NHL	81	3	15	18	35	22	1	0	6	0	1	1	2
02-03—Boston	NHL	67	3	5	8	24	-1	0	0	5	0	1	1	0
03-04—Dallas	NHL	63	0	11	11	18	22	0	0	5	0	0	0	2
NHL Totals (16 years)		1115	52	221	273	681	112	6	4	108	9	10	19	81

SYDOR, DARRYL — D — LIGHTNING

PERSONAL: Born May 13, 1972, in Edmonton. ... 6-1/211. ... Shoots left. ... Name pronounced sih-DOHR.
TRANSACTIONS/CAREER NOTES: Selected by Los Angeles Kings in first round (first Kings pick, seventh overall) of NHL entry draft (June 16, 1990). ... Bruised hip (November 27, 1992); missed two games. ... Sprained right shoulder (March 15, 1993); missed two games. ... Traded by Kings with seventh-round pick (G Eoin McInerney) in 1996 draft to Dallas Stars for RW Shane Churla and D Doug Zmolek (February 17, 1996). ... Sprained knee (February 21, 1999); missed three games. ... Reinjured knee (March 7, 1999); missed five games. ... Fractured eye socket (October 2, 1999); missed three games. ... Injured groin (October 20, 1999); missed three games. ... Injured neck (March 26, 2000); missed two games. ... Flu (December 31, 2000); missed one game. ... Injured ankle (November 17, 2001); missed one game. ... Suffered concussion (December 14, 2001); missed three games. ... Injured shoulder (February 21, 2003); missed one game. ... Traded by Stars to Columbus Blue Jackets for C Mike Sillinger and second round pick (D Johan Fransson) in 2004 entry draft (July 22, 2003). ... Traded by Blue Jackets with fourth-round pick (D Mike Lundin) in 2004 entry draft to Tampa Bay Lightning for C Alexander Svitov and third-round pick (later traded to Calgary Flames) in 2004 entry draft (January 27, 2004).
STATISTICAL PLATEAUS: Three-goal games: 1997-98 (1).

Season Team	League	REGULAR SEASON GP	G	A	Pts.	PIM	+/-	PP	SH	PLAYOFFS GP	G	A	Pts.	PIM
88-89—Kamloops	WHL	65	12	14	26	86	...	...	...	15	1	4	5	19
89-90—Kamloops	WHL	67	29	66	95	129	...	...	...	17	2	9	11	28
90-91—Kamloops	WHL	66	27	78	105	88	...	...	...	12	3	*22	25	10
91-92—Kamloops	WHL	29	9	39	48	43	...	...	...	17	3	15	18	18
—Los Angeles	NHL	18	1	5	6	22	-3	0	0	—	—	—	—	—
92-93—Los Angeles	NHL	80	6	23	29	63	-2	0	0	24	3	8	11	16
93-94—Los Angeles	NHL	84	8	27	35	94	-9	1	0	—	—	—	—	—
94-95—Los Angeles	NHL	48	4	19	23	36	-2	3	0	—	—	—	—	—
95-96—Los Angeles	NHL	58	1	11	12	34	-11	1	0	—	—	—	—	—
—Dallas	NHL	26	2	6	8	41	-1	1	0	—	—	—	—	—
96-97—Dallas	NHL	82	8	40	48	51	37	2	0	7	0	2	2	0
97-98—Dallas	NHL	79	11	35	46	51	17	4	1	17	0	5	5	14
98-99—Dallas	NHL	74	14	34	48	50	-1	9	0	23	3	9	12	16
99-00—Dallas	NHL	74	8	26	34	32	6	5	0	23	1	6	7	6
00-01—Dallas	NHL	81	10	37	47	34	5	8	0	10	1	3	4	0
01-02—Dallas	NHL	78	4	29	33	50	3	2	0	—	—	—	—	—
02-03—Dallas	NHL	81	5	31	36	40	22	2	0	12	0	6	6	6
03-04—Columbus	NHL	49	2	13	15	26	-19	1	0	—	—	—	—	—
—Tampa Bay	NHL	31	1	6	7	6	3	0	0	23	0	6	6	9
NHL Totals (13 years)		943	85	342	427	630	45	39	1	139	8	45	53	67

SYKORA, PETR — RW — MIGHTY DUCKS

PERSONAL: Born November 19, 1976, in Plzen, Czechoslovakia. ... 5-11/190. ... Shoots left. ... Name pronounced sih-KOHR-uh.

TRANSACTIONS/CAREER NOTES: Selected by New Jersey Devils in first round (first Devils pick, 18th overall) of NHL draft (July 8, 1995). ... Injured back (February 21, 1996); missed two games. ... Injured groin (October 5, 1996); missed two games. ... Reinjured groin (November 9, 1996); missed four games. ... Reinjured groin (November 30, 1996); missed three games. ... Bruised shoulder (November 5, 1997); missed two games. ... Sprained left ankle (November 29, 1997); missed 20 games. ... Food poisoning (January 2, 1999); missed two games ... Flu (March 2, 2000); missed three games. ... Injured groin (October 26, 2000); missed three games. ... Reinjured groin (November 4, 2000); missed one game. ... Bruised shoulder (February 17, 2001); missed five games. ... Flu (December 26, 2001); missed three games. ... Bruised ribs (February 9, 2002); missed one game. ... Flu (March 20, 2002); missed five games. ... Traded by Devils with C Igor Pohanka, D Mike Commodore and G J.F. Damphousse to Anaheim Mighty Ducks for D Oleg Tverdovsky, LW Jeff Friesen and RW Maxin Balmochnykh (July 7, 2002).

Season Team	League	REGULAR SEASON GP	G	A	Pts.	PIM	+/-	PP	SH	PLAYOFFS GP	G	A	Pts.	PIM
91-92—Skoda Plzen	Czech.	30	50	50	100	...	...	...	...	—	—	—	—	—
92-93—Skoda Plzen	Czech.	19	12	5	17	...	...	...	...	—	—	—	—	—
93-94—Skoda Plzen	Czech Rep.	37	10	16	26	...	...	...	...	4	0	1	1	...
—Cleveland	IHL	13	4	5	9	8	...	...	...	—	—	—	—	—
94-95—Detroit	IHL	29	12	17	29	16	10	3	0	—	—	—	—	—
95-96—Albany	AHL	5	4	1	5	0	...	...	...	—	—	—	—	—
—New Jersey	NHL	63	18	24	42	32	7	8	0	—	—	—	—	—
96-97—New Jersey	NHL	19	1	2	3	4	-8	0	0	2	0	0	0	2
—Albany	AHL	43	20	25	45	48	19	2	1	4	1	4	5	2
97-98—New Jersey	NHL	58	16	20	36	22	0	3	1	2	0	0	0	0
—Albany	AHL	2	4	1	5	0	...	...	...	—	—	—	—	—
98-99—New Jersey	NHL	80	29	43	72	22	16	15	0	7	3	3	6	4
99-00—New Jersey	NHL	79	25	43	68	26	24	5	1	23	9	8	17	10
00-01—New Jersey	NHL	73	35	46	81	32	36	9	2	25	10	12	22	12
01-02—New Jersey	NHL	73	21	27	48	44	12	4	0	4	0	1	1	0
—Czech Rep. Oly. team	Int'l	4	1	0	1	0	...	...	...	—	—	—	—	—
02-03—Anaheim	NHL	82	34	25	59	24	-7	15	1	21	4	9	13	12
03-04—Anaheim	NHL	81	23	29	52	34	-9	6	0	—	—	—	—	—
04-05—Metal. Magnitogorsk	Russian	45	18	13	31	46	20	...	...	5	2	3	5	8
NHL Totals (9 years)		608	202	259	461	240	71	65	5	84	26	33	59	40

TAFFE, JEFF — C — COYOTES

PERSONAL: Born February 19, 1981, in Hastings, Minn. ... 6-3/201. ... Shoots left. ... Name pronounced TAYFE.

TRANSACTIONS/CAREER NOTES: Selected by St. Louis Blues in first round (first Blues pick, 30th overall) of NHL entry draft (June 24, 2000). ... Traded by Blues with C Michal Handzus, RW Ladislav Nagy and first-round pick (LW Ben Eager) in 2002 draft to Phoenix Coyotes for LW Keith Tkachuk (March 13, 2001).

Season Team	League	REGULAR SEASON GP	G	A	Pts.	PIM	+/-	PP	SH	PLAYOFFS GP	G	A	Pts.	PIM
98-99—Hastings H.S.	USHS (West)	25	38	48	86	26	...	...	...	—	—	—	—	—
99-00—Minnesota	WCHA	34	9	10	19	16	...	...	...	—	—	—	—	—
00-01—Minnesota	WCHA	38	12	23	35	56	...	...	...	—	—	—	—	—
01-02—Minnesota	WCHA	43	*34	24	58	86	...	...	...	—	—	—	—	—
02-03—Phoenix	NHL	20	3	1	4	4	-4	1	0	—	—	—	—	—
—Springfield	AHL	57	23	26	49	44	-13	11	0	5	0	3	3	8
03-04—Phoenix	NHL	59	8	10	18	20	-8	5	0	—	—	—	—	—
—Springfield	AHL	15	10	6	16	19	-3	3	0	—	—	—	—	—
04-05—Utah	AHL	27	9	10	19	35	-19	4	0	—	—	—	—	—
NHL Totals (2 years)		79	11	11	22	24	-12	6	0					

TALLINDER, HENRIK D SABRES

PERSONAL: Born January 10, 1979, in Stockholm, Sweden. ... 6-3/214. ... Shoots left.
TRANSACTIONS/CAREER NOTES: Selected by Buffalo Sabres in second round (second Sabres pick, 48th overall) of NHL draft (June 21, 1997). ... Bruised shoulder (November 1, 2002); missed one game. ... Had concussion, separated shoulder (November 7, 2002); missed 19 games. ... Sprained right ankle (February 8, 2003); missed 24 games.

		REGULAR SEASON								PLAYOFFS				
Season Team	League	GP	G	A	Pts.	PIM	+/-	PP	SH	GP	G	A	Pts.	PIM
96-97—AIK Solna Jrs.	Sweden	Statistics unavailable.												
—AIK Solna	Sweden	1	0	0	0	0	...	...	...	—	—	—	—	—
97-98—AIK Solna	Sweden	34	0	0	0	26	...	...	...	—	—	—	—	—
98-99—AIK Solna	Sweden	36	0	0	0	30	-5	...	...	—	—	—	—	—
99-00—AIK Solna	Sweden	50	0	2	2	59	...	...	...	—	—	—	—	—
00-01—TPS Turku	Finland	56	5	9	14	62	...	...	...	10	2	1	3	8
01-02—Rochester	AHL	73	6	14	20	26	11	1	0	2	0	0	0	0
—Buffalo	NHL	2	0	0	0	0	-1	0	0	—	—	—	—	—
02-03—Buffalo	NHL	46	3	10	13	28	-3	1	0	—	—	—	—	—
03-04—Buffalo	NHL	72	1	9	10	26	5	0	0	—	—	—	—	—
04-05—Bern	Switzerland	—	—	—	—	—	—	—	—	10	1	1	2	4
—Linkopings	Sweden	44	6	10	16	63	30	1	0	—	—	—	—	—
—Linkoping	Sweden Dv. 2	44	6	10	16	63	30	1	0	—	—	—	—	—
NHL Totals (3 years)		120	4	19	23	54	1	1	0					

TAMBELLINI, JEFF LW KINGS

PERSONAL: Born April 13, 1984, in Calgary. ... 5-1/186. ... Shoots left. ... Son of Steve Tambellini, former NHL player.
TRANSACTIONS/CAREER NOTES: Selected by Los Angeles Kings in 1st round (3rd Kings pick, 27th overall) of entry draft (June 20, 2003). ... Son of Steve Tambellini, C, five NHL teams (1978-88) and current Canucks V.P. player personnel.

		REGULAR SEASON								PLAYOFFS				
Season Team	League	GP	G	A	Pts.	PIM	+/-	PP	SH	GP	G	A	Pts.	PIM
00-01—Chilliwack	BCJHL	54	21	30	51	13	...	...	...	—	—	—	—	—
01-02—Chilliwack	BCJHL	34	46	71	117	23	...	...	...	29	27	27	54	54
02-03—Univ. of Michigan	CCHA	43	26	19	45	24	...	...	...	—	—	—	—	—
03-04—Univ. of Michigan	CCHA	39	15	12	27	18	...	...	...	—	—	—	—	—
04-05—Univ. of Michigan	CCHA	42	24	33	57	32	...	...	...	—	—	—	—	—

T

TAMER, CHRIS D

PERSONAL: Born November 17, 1970, in Dearborn, Mich. ... 6-2/200. ... Shoots left. ... Name pronounced TAY-muhr.
TRANSACTIONS/CAREER NOTES: Selected by Pittsburgh Penguins in fourth round (third Penguins pick, 68th overall) of NHL draft (June 16, 1990). ... Injured shoulder (March 27, 1994); missed four games. ... Fractured ankle (May 6, 1995); missed eight playoff games. ... Pulled abdominal muscle (December 17, 1995); missed five games. ... Sprained wrist (December 30, 1995); missed five games. ... Fractured jaw (January 17, 1996); missed two games. ... Pulled abdominal muscle (November 22, 1996); missed 20 games. ... Strained hip flexor (January 4, 1997); missed 13 games. ... Strained hip flexor (March 4, 1997); missed four games. ... Traded by Penguins with C Petr Nedved and C Sean Pronger to New York Rangers for RW Alexei Kovalev and C Harry York (November 25, 1998). ... Selected by Atlanta Thrashers in expansion draft (June 25, 1999). ... Sprained knee (February 29, 2000); missed six games. ... Injured back (October 11, 2002); missed three games. ... Suspended two games for cross-checking incident (April 1, 2003). ... Injured back (January 14, 2004); missed eight games. ... Reinjured back (January 31, 2004) and had surgery (February 24, 2004); missed remainder of season.

		REGULAR SEASON								PLAYOFFS				
Season Team	League	GP	G	A	Pts.	PIM	+/-	PP	SH	GP	G	A	Pts.	PIM
87-88—Redford	NAJHL	40	10	20	30	217	...	...	...	—	—	—	—	—
88-89—Redford	NAJHL	31	6	13	19	79	...	...	...	—	—	—	—	—
89-90—Univ. of Michigan	CCHA	42	2	7	9	147	...	...	...	—	—	—	—	—
90-91—Univ. of Michigan	CCHA	45	8	19	27	130	...	...	...	—	—	—	—	—
91-92—Univ. of Michigan	CCHA	43	4	15	19	125	...	...	...	—	—	—	—	—
92-93—Univ. of Michigan	CCHA	39	5	18	23	113	...	...	...	—	—	—	—	—
93-94—Cleveland	IHL	53	1	2	3	160	-1	0	0	—	—	—	—	—
—Pittsburgh	NHL	12	0	0	0	9	3	0	0	5	0	0	0	2
94-95—Cleveland	IHL	48	4	10	14	204	-7	0	0	—	—	—	—	—
—Pittsburgh	NHL	36	2	0	2	82	0	0	0	4	0	0	0	18
95-96—Pittsburgh	NHL	70	4	10	14	153	20	0	0	18	0	7	7	24
96-97—Pittsburgh	NHL	45	2	4	6	131	-25	0	1	4	0	0	0	4
97-98—Pittsburgh	NHL	79	0	7	7	181	4	0	0	6	0	1	1	4
98-99—Pittsburgh	NHL	11	0	0	0	32	-2	0	0	—	—	—	—	—
—New York Rangers	NHL	52	1	5	6	92	-12	0	0	—	—	—	—	—
99-00—Atlanta	NHL	69	2	8	10	91	-32	0	0	—	—	—	—	—
00-01—Atlanta	NHL	82	4	13	17	128	-1	0	1	—	—	—	—	—
01-02—Atlanta	NHL	78	3	3	6	111	-11	0	1	—	—	—	—	—
02-03—Atlanta	NHL	72	1	9	10	118	-10	0	0	—	—	—	—	—
03-04—Atlanta	NHL	38	2	5	7	55	-9	0	0	—	—	—	—	—
NHL Totals (11 years)		644	21	64	85	1183	-75	0	3	37	0	8	8	52

TANABE, DAVID D COYOTES

PERSONAL: Born July 19, 1980, in White Bear Lake, Minn. ... 6-1/212. ... Shoots right. ... Name pronounced tuh-nah-BEE.
TRANSACTIONS/CAREER NOTES: Selected by Carolina Hurricanes in first round (first Hurricanes pick, 16th overall) of NHL draft (June 26,

1999). ... Had concussion (October 18, 2000); missed five games. ... Had hip pointer (March 2, 2001); missed three games. ... Flu (October 13, 2001); missed one game. ... Injured oblique muscle (October 23, 2002); missed two games. ... Injured shoulder (November 15, 2002); missed seven games. ... Reinjured shoulder (December 4, 2002); missed five games. ... Traded by Hurricanes to Phoenix Coyotes with D Igor Knyazev for D Danny Markov and conditional fourth-round pick (RW Roman Tumanek) in 2004 entry draft (June 21, 2003). ... Injured knee (January 18, 2004) and had surgery (January 28, 2004); missed remainder of season.

		REGULAR SEASON								PLAYOFFS				
Season Team	**League**	**GP**	**G**	**A**	**Pts.**	**PIM**	**+/-**	**PP**	**SH**	**GP**	**G**	**A**	**Pts.**	**PIM**
97-98—U.S. National	NAHL	73	8	21	29	96	...	1	0	—	—	—	—	—
98-99—Wisconsin	WCHA	35	10	12	22	44	...	...	...	—	—	—	—	—
99-00—Carolina	NHL	31	4	0	4	14	-4	3	0	—	—	—	—	—
—Cincinnati	IHL	32	0	13	13	14	...	...	...	11	1	4	5	6
00-01—Carolina	NHL	74	7	22	29	42	-9	5	0	6	2	0	2	12
01-02—Carolina	NHL	78	1	15	16	35	-13	0	0	1	0	1	1	0
02-03—Carolina	NHL	68	3	10	13	24	-27	2	0	—	—	—	—	—
03-04—Phoenix	NHL	45	5	7	12	22	4	2	0	—	—	—	—	—
04-05—Rapperswil	Switzerland	8	4	5	9	4	...	3	0	—	—	—	—	—
—Kloten	Switzerland	20	3	7	10	18	...	1	0	5	1	4	5	8
NHL Totals (5 years)		296	20	54	74	137	-49	12	0	7	2	1	3	12

TANGUAY, ALEX — LW — AVALANCHE

PERSONAL: Born November 21, 1979, in Ste-Justine, Que. ... 6-1/190. ... Shoots left. ... Name pronounced tan-GAY.

TRANSACTIONS/CAREER NOTES: Selected by Colorado Avalanche in first round (first Avalanche pick, 12th overall) of NHL draft (June 27, 1998). ... Strained neck (March 14, 2000); missed six games. ... Sinus infection (November 10, 2001); missed six games. ... Bruised ankle (December 23, 2001); missed one game. ... Reinjured ankle (December 27, 2001); missed three games. ... Bruised hip (January 29, 2002); missed two games. ... Injured groin (December 19, 2003); missed two games. ... Injured knee (March 12, 2004); missed 11 games.

STATISTICAL PLATEAUS: Three-goal games: 2002-03 (1), 2003-04 (1). Total: 2.

		REGULAR SEASON								PLAYOFFS				
Season Team	**League**	**GP**	**G**	**A**	**Pts.**	**PIM**	**+/-**	**PP**	**SH**	**GP**	**G**	**A**	**Pts.**	**PIM**
96-97—Halifax	QMJHL	70	27	41	68	50	...	...	...	12	4	8	12	8
97-98—Halifax	QMJHL	51	47	38	85	32	-6	13	3	5	7	6	13	4
98-99—Halifax	QMJHL	31	27	34	61	30	28	10	2	5	1	2	3	2
—Hershey	AHL	5	1	2	3	2	-2	0	0	5	0	2	2	0
99-00—Colorado	NHL	76	17	34	51	22	6	5	0	17	2	1	3	2
00-01—Colorado	NHL	82	27	50	77	37	35	7	1	23	6	15	21	8
01-02—Colorado	NHL	70	13	35	48	36	8	7	0	19	5	8	13	0
02-03—Colorado	NHL	82	26	41	67	36	34	3	0	7	1	2	3	4
03-04—Colorado	NHL	69	25	54	79	42	30	7	0	8	2	2	4	2
04-05—Lugano	Switzerland	6	3	3	6	4	...	1	0	—	—	—	—	—
NHL Totals (5 years)		379	108	214	322	173	113	29	1	74	16	28	44	16

TAPPER, BRAD — RW — SENATORS

PERSONAL: Born April 28, 1978, in Scarborough, Ont. ... 6-0/190. ... Shoots right.

TRANSACTIONS/CAREER NOTES: Signed as free agent by Atlanta Thrashers (April 11, 2000). ... Traded by Thrashers to Ottawa Senators for C Daniel Corso (January 6, 2004).

		REGULAR SEASON								PLAYOFFS				
Season Team	**League**	**GP**	**G**	**A**	**Pts.**	**PIM**	**+/-**	**PP**	**SH**	**GP**	**G**	**A**	**Pts.**	**PIM**
97-98—Rensselaer Poly. Inst.	ECAC	34	14	11	25	62	...	...	...	—	—	—	—	—
98-99—Rensselaer Poly. Inst.	ECAC	35	20	20	40	60	...	...	...	—	—	—	—	—
99-00—Rensselaer Poly. Inst.	ECAC	37	*31	20	51	81	...	...	...	—	—	—	—	—
00-01—Atlanta	NHL	16	2	3	5	6	1	0	0	—	—	—	—	—
—Orlando	IHL	45	7	9	16	39	...	...	...	2	0	0	0	2
01-02—Atlanta	NHL	20	2	4	6	43	-3	0	0	—	—	—	—	—
—Chicago	AHL	50	14	12	26	62	-7	3	0	19	3	4	7	42
02-03—Atlanta	NHL	35	10	4	14	23	2	1	0	—	—	—	—	—
—Chicago	AHL	28	9	14	23	42	13	5	0	9	1	3	4	10
03-04—Chicago	AHL	20	1	8	9	26	1	1	0	—	—	—	—	—
—Binghamton	AHL	29	9	12	21	26	-1	2	0	—	—	—	—	—
04-05—Nurnberg	Germany	50	26	23	49	101	...	...	...	6	0	2	2	18
NHL Totals (3 years)		71	14	11	25	72	0	1	0					

TARATUKHIN, ANDREI — C — FLAMES

PERSONAL: Born February 22, 1983, in Omsk, U.S.S.R. ... 6-0/198. ... Shoots left. ... Name pronounced tahr-a-TOO-khin.

TRANSACTIONS/CAREER NOTES: Selected by Calgary Flames in second round (second Flames pick, 41st overall) of NHL entry draft (June 23, 2001).

		REGULAR SEASON								PLAYOFFS				
Season Team	**League**	**GP**	**G**	**A**	**Pts.**	**PIM**	**+/-**	**PP**	**SH**	**GP**	**G**	**A**	**Pts.**	**PIM**
01-02—Yaroslavl 2	CIS.2	5	5	2	7	12	...	...	...	—	—	—	—	—
02-03—Avangard Omsk	Russian	21	0	1	1	4	...	...	...	7	1	0	1	18
—Avangard Omsk	Rus. Div.	15	4	13	17	20	...	...	...	—	—	—	—	—
03-04—Avangard Omsk	Russian	8	0	0	0	4	...	...	...	—	—	—	—	—
04-05—Ufa Salavet Yulayev	Russian	54	7	4	11	73	...	...	...	—	—	—	—	—

TARNSTROM, DICK — D — PENGUINS

PERSONAL: Born January 20, 1975, in Sundbyberg, Sweden. ... 6-2/205. ... Shoots left.
TRANSACTIONS/CAREER NOTES: Selected by New York Islanders in 11th round (12th Islanders pick, 272nd overall) of NHL draft (June 29, 1994). ... Injured wrist (March 27, 2002); missed seven games. ... Claimed off waivers by Pittsburgh Penguins (August 6, 2002). ... Fractured foot (November 30, 2002); missed 15 games. ... Strained hamstring (January 7, 2003); missed two games. ... Injured hip (March 20, 2003); missed three games. ... Flu (January 3, 2004); missed one game. ... Flu (January 29, 2004); missed one game.

		REGULAR SEASON								PLAYOFFS				
Season Team	**League**	**GP**	**G**	**A**	**Pts.**	**PIM**	**+/-**	**PP**	**SH**	**GP**	**G**	**A**	**Pts.**	**PIM**
92-93—AIK	Sweden	3	0	0	0	0	...	...	...	—	—	—	—	—
93-94—AIK	Sweden	33	1	4	5	...	...	...	...	—	—	—	—	—
94-95—AIK	Sweden	37	8	4	12	26	...	...	...	—	—	—	—	—
95-96—AIK	Sweden	40	0	5	5	32	...	...	...	—	—	—	—	—
96-97—AIK	Sweden	49	5	3	8	38	...	...	...	7	0	1	1	6
97-98—AIK Solna	Sweden	45	2	12	14	30	...	...	...	—	—	—	—	—
98-99—AIK Solna	Sweden	47	9	14	23	36	...	...	...	—	—	—	—	—
99-00—AIK Solna	Sweden	42	7	15	22	20	...	...	...	—	—	—	—	—
00-01—AIK Solna	Sweden	50	10	18	28	28	...	...	...	5	0	0	0	8
01-02—Bridgeport	AHL	9	0	2	2	2	3	0	0	—	—	—	—	—
—New York Islanders	NHL	62	3	16	19	38	-12	0	0	5	0	0	0	2
02-03—Pittsburgh	NHL	61	7	34	41	50	-11	3	0	—	—	—	—	—
03-04—Pittsburgh	NHL	80	16	36	52	38	-37	12	0	—	—	—	—	—
04-05—Sodertalje	Sweden Dv. 2	50	7	18	25	46	-5	2	0	9	1	0	1	6
NHL Totals (3 years)		203	26	86	112	126	-60	15	0	5	0	0	0	2

TATICEK, PETR — C — PANTHERS

PERSONAL: Born September 22, 1983, in Rakovnik, Czechoslovakia. ... 6-2/188. ... Shoots left. ... Name pronounced TA-tih-chehk.
TRANSACTIONS/CAREER NOTES: Selected by Florida Panthers in first round (second Panthers pick, ninth overall) of NHL entry draft (June 22, 2002).

		REGULAR SEASON								PLAYOFFS				
Season Team	**League**	**GP**	**G**	**A**	**Pts.**	**PIM**	**+/-**	**PP**	**SH**	**GP**	**G**	**A**	**Pts.**	**PIM**
00-01—HC Kladno	Czech Rep.	3	0	0	0	0	...	...	...	—	—	—	—	—
01-02—Sault Ste. Marie	OHL	60	21	42	63	32	...	...	...	6	3	3	6	4
02-03—Sault Ste. Marie	OHL	54	12	45	57	44	...	...	...	4	1	0	1	0
03-04—San Antonio	AHL	63	4	15	19	6	-10	1	0	—	—	—	—	—
04-05—San Antonio	AHL	67	7	15	22	21	-9	0	0	—	—	—	—	—
—Laredo	CHL	4	2	5	7	0	...	...	...	—	—	—	—	—

T

TAYLOR, CHRIS — C — SABRES

PERSONAL: Born March 6, 1972, in Stratford, Ontario. ... 6-2/188. ... Shoots left. ... Brother of Tim Taylor, C, Tampa Bay Lightning.
TRANSACTIONS/CAREER NOTES: Selected by New York Islanders in second round (second Islanders pick, 27th overall) of NHL entry draft (June 16, 1990). ... Signed as free agent by Los Angeles Kings (August 1, 1997). ... Signed as free agent by Boston Bruins (July 22, 1998). ... Signed as free agent by Buffalo Sabres (August 13, 1999).

		REGULAR SEASON								PLAYOFFS				
Season Team	**League**	**GP**	**G**	**A**	**Pts.**	**PIM**	**+/-**	**PP**	**SH**	**GP**	**G**	**A**	**Pts.**	**PIM**
88-89—London	OHL	62	7	16	23	52	...	...	...	15	0	2	2	15
89-90—London	OHL	66	45	60	105	60	...	...	...	6	3	2	5	6
90-91—London	OHL	65	50	78	128	50	...	...	...	7	4	8	12	6
91-92—London	OHL	66	48	74	122	57	...	...	...	10	8	16	24	9
92-93—Roanoke	ECHL	5	2	1	3	0	...	...	...	—	—	—	—	—
—Capital District	AHL	77	19	43	62	32	-15	8	0	4	0	1	1	2
93-94—Raleigh	ECHL	2	0	0	0	0	0	0	0	—	—	—	—	—
—Salt Lake City	IHL	79	21	20	41	38	-28	6	0	—	—	—	—	—
94-95—Denver	IHL	78	38	48	86	47	24	13	2	14	7	6	13	10
—Roanoke	ECHL	1	0	0	0	2	-1	0	0	—	—	—	—	—
—New York Islanders	NHL	10	0	3	3	2	1	0	0	—	—	—	—	—
95-96—Utah	IHL	50	18	23	41	60	...	...	...	22	5	11	16	26
—New York Islanders	NHL	11	0	1	1	2	1	0	0	—	—	—	—	—
96-97—Utah	IHL	71	27	40	67	24	...	...	...	7	1	2	3	0
—New York Islanders	NHL	1	0	0	0	0	0	0	0	—	—	—	—	—
97-98—Utah	IHL	79	28	56	84	66	3	8	4	4	0	2	2	6
98-99—Boston	NHL	37	3	5	8	12	-3	0	1	—	—	—	—	—
—Providence	AHL	21	6	11	17	6	0	5	0	—	—	—	—	—
—Las Vegas	IHL	14	3	12	15	2	0	3	0	—	—	—	—	—
99-00—Rochester	AHL	49	21	28	49	21	...	...	...	—	—	—	—	—
—Buffalo	NHL	11	1	1	2	2	-2	0	0	2	0	0	0	2
00-01—Rochester	AHL	45	20	24	44	25	...	...	...	—	—	—	—	—
—Buffalo	NHL	14	0	2	2	6	1	0	0	—	—	—	—	—
01-02—Rochester	AHL	77	21	45	66	66	-1	7	1	2	0	1	1	0
02-03—Buffalo	NHL	11	1	3	4	2	-1	0	0	—	—	—	—	—
—Rochester	AHL	61	12	55	67	44	-5	5	1	3	3	1	4	2
03-04—Buffalo	NHL	54	6	6	12	22	-2	0	0	—	—	—	—	—
—Rochester	AHL	24	9	19	28	20	-1	4	1	16	5	12	17	0
04-05—Rochester	AHL	79	21	58	79	50	2	10	2	9	1	8	9	4
NHL Totals (8 years)		149	11	21	32	48	-5	0	1	2	0	0	0	2

TAYLOR, TIM — C — LIGHTNING

PERSONAL: Born February 6, 1969, in Stratford, Ont. ... 6-1/190. ... Shoots left. ... Brother of Chris Taylor, C, Buffalo Sabres organization.
TRANSACTIONS/CAREER NOTES: Selected by Washington Capitals in second round (second Capitals pick, 36th overall) of NHL draft (June 11, 1988). ... Traded by Capitals to Vancouver Canucks for C Eric Murano (January 29, 1993). ... Signed as free agent by Detroit Red Wings (July 28, 1993). ... Injured right shoulder (April 5, 1996); missed three games. ... Sprained shoulder (October 15, 1996); missed 16 games. ... Flu (April 9, 1997); missed two games. ... Selected by Boston Bruins from Red Wings in waiver draft (September 28, 1997). ... Injured ribs (March 21, 1998); missed one game. ... Injured hip (March 22, 1998); missed two games. ... Sprained ankle (October 14, 1998); missed 12 games. ... Reinjured ankle (November 13, 1998); missed six games. ... Reinjured ankle (December 10, 1998); missed 14 games. ... Strained groin (April 17, 1999); missed final game of season. ... Signed as free agent by New York Rangers (July 15, 1999). ... Suffered concussion (October 2, 1999); missed two games. ... Injured hand (October 20, 1999); missed one game. ... Injured rib (November 24, 1999); missed one game. ... Flu (February 13, 2000); missed two games. ... Injured shoulder (November 28, 2000); missed one game. ... Tore abdominal muscle (December 31, 2000); missed remainder of season. ... Traded by Rangers to Tampa Bay Lightning for LW Nils Ekman and LW Kyle Freadrich (July 1, 2001). ... Strained groin (January 3, 2002); missed four games. ... Reinjured groin (January 18, 2002); missed four games. ... Reinjured groin (February 4, 2002); missed four games. ... Reinjured groin (March 2, 2002); missed remainder of season.

		REGULAR SEASON								PLAYOFFS				
Season Team	League	GP	G	A	Pts.	PIM	+/-	PP	SH	GP	G	A	Pts.	PIM
86-87—London	OHL	34	7	9	16	11	...	...	...	—	—	—	—	—
87-88—London	OHL	64	46	50	96	66	...	...	...	12	9	9	18	26
88-89—London	OHL	61	34	80	114	93	...	...	...	21	*21	25	*46	58
89-90—Baltimore	AHL	74	22	21	43	63	...	...	...	9	2	2	4	13
90-91—Baltimore	AHL	79	25	42	67	75	...	...	...	5	0	1	1	4
91-92—Baltimore	AHL	65	9	18	27	131	...	...	...	—	—	—	—	—
92-93—Baltimore	AHL	41	15	16	31	49	-7	2	1	—	—	—	—	—
—Hamilton	AHL	36	15	22	37	37	-10	5	1	—	—	—	—	—
93-94—Adirondack	AHL	79	36	*81	117	86	23	13	3	12	2	10	12	12
—Detroit	NHL	1	1	0	1	0	-1	0	0	—	—	—	—	—
94-95—Detroit	NHL	22	0	4	4	16	3	0	0	6	0	1	1	12
95-96—Detroit	NHL	72	11	14	25	39	11	1	1	18	0	4	4	4
96-97—Detroit	NHL	44	3	4	7	52	-6	0	1	2	0	0	0	0
97-98—Boston	NHL	79	20	11	31	57	-16	1	3	6	0	0	0	10
98-99—Boston	NHL	49	4	7	11	55	-10	0	0	12	0	3	3	8
99-00—New York Rangers	NHL	76	9	11	20	72	-4	0	0	—	—	—	—	—
00-01—New York Rangers	NHL	38	2	5	7	16	-6	0	0	—	—	—	—	—
01-02—Tampa Bay	NHL	48	4	4	8	25	-2	0	1	—	—	—	—	—
02-03—Tampa Bay	NHL	82	4	8	12	38	-13	0	0	11	0	1	1	6
03-04—Tampa Bay	NHL	82	7	15	22	25	-5	0	0	23	2	3	5	31
NHL Totals (11 years)		593	65	83	148	395	-49	2	6	78	2	12	14	71

TELLQVIST, MIKAEL — G — MAPLE LEAFS

PERSONAL: Born September 19, 1979, in Sundbyberg, Sweden. ... 5-11/194. ... Name pronounced TEHL-kvihst.
TRANSACTIONS/CAREER NOTES: Selected by Toronto Maple Leafs in third round (third Maple Leafs pick, 70th overall) of NHL entry draft (June 24, 2000).

		REGULAR SEASON									PLAYOFFS							
Season Team	League	GP	Min.	W	L	T	GA	SO	GAA	SV%	GP	Min.	W	L	GA	SO	GAA	SV%
98-99—Djurgarden Stockholm	Sweden	3	124	...	...	...	8	0	3.87	...	4	240	...	...	11	0	2.75	...
99-00—Djurgarden Stockholm	Sweden	30	1909	...	...	...	66	2	2.07	...	13	814	...	...	21	3	1.55	...
00-01—Djurgarden Stockholm	Sweden	43	2622	...	...	...	91	5	*2.08	...	*16	*1006	...	...	*45	1	2.68	...
01-02—St. John's	AHL	28	1521	8	11	6	79	0	3.12	.900	1	14	1	0	0	0	0.00	1.00
02-03—St. John's	AHL	47	2651	17	25	3	148	1	3.35	.910	—	—	—	—	—	—	—	—
—Toronto	NHL	3	86	1	1	0	4	0	2.79	.895	—	—	—	—	—	—	—	—
03-04—Toronto	NHL	11	647	5	3	2	31	0	2.87	.894	—	—	—	—	—	—	—	—
—St. John's	AHL	23	1342	10	11	1	60	1	2.68	.912	—	—	—	—	—	—	—	—
04-05—St. John's	AHL	45	2599	24	16	...	115	0	2.65	.921	5	253	1	4	15	0	3.56	.899
NHL Totals (2 years)		14	733	6	4	2	35	0	2.86	.894								

TETARENKO, JOEY — RW — WILD

PERSONAL: Born March 3, 1978, in Prince Albert, Sask. ... 6-2/210. ... Shoots right.
TRANSACTIONS/CAREER NOTES: Selected by Florida Panthers in fourth round (fourth Panthers pick, 82nd overall) of NHL draft (June 22, 1996). ... Scratched cornea (March 21, 2001); missed one game. ... Dislocated jaw and suffered concussion (October 31, 2001); missed 10 games. ... Tore retina (February 13, 2002); missed one game. ... Injured back (March 20, 2002); missed six games. ... Traded by Panthers to Ottawa Senators for G Simon Lajeunesse (March 4, 2003). ... Signed as free agent by Carolina Hurricanes (July 2, 2003).

		REGULAR SEASON								PLAYOFFS				
Season Team	League	GP	G	A	Pts.	PIM	+/-	PP	SH	GP	G	A	Pts.	PIM
94-95—Portland	WHL	59	0	1	1	134	...	...	...	9	0	0	0	8
95-96—Portland	WHL	71	4	11	15	190	...	...	...	7	0	1	1	17
96-97—Portland	WHL	68	8	18	26	182	30	3	0	2	0	0	0	2
97-98—Portland	WHL	49	2	12	14	148	19	1	0	16	0	2	2	30
98-99—New Haven	AHL	65	4	10	14	154	-2	0	0	—	—	—	—	—
99-00—Louisville	AHL	57	3	11	14	136	...	...	...	4	0	0	0	2
00-01—Florida	NHL	29	3	1	4	44	-1	0	0	—	—	—	—	—
01-02—Florida	NHL	38	1	0	1	123	-5	0	0	—	—	—	—	—
02-03—Florida	NHL	2	0	0	0	4	-1	0	0	—	—	—	—	—
—San Antonio	AHL	50	4	12	16	123	-2	0	0	—	—	—	—	—

Season Team	League	GP	G	A	Pts.	PIM	+/-	PP	SH	PO GP	PO G	PO A	PO Pts.	PO PIM
		REGULAR SEASON								PLAYOFFS				
—Ottawa	NHL	2	0	0	0	5	0	0	0	—	—	—	—	—
—Binghamton	AHL	14	2	2	4	33	0	1	0	14	0	0	0	36
03-04—Lowell	AHL	57	1	6	7	167	-9	0	0	—	—	—	—	—
—Carolina	NHL	2	0	0	0	0	0	0	0	—	—	—	—	—
04-05—Houston	AHL	15	0	1	1	49	1	0	0	0	0	0	0	0
NHL Totals (4 years)		73	4	1	5	176	-7	0	0					

THELEN, A.J. D WILD

PERSONAL: Born March 11, 1986, in Shakopee, Minn. ... 6-3/205. ... Shoots left.
TRANSACTIONS/CAREER NOTES: Selected by Minnesota Wild in 1st round (1st Wild pick, 12th overall) of the entry draft (June 26, 2004).

Season Team	League	GP	G	A	Pts.	PIM	+/-	PP	SH	PO GP	PO G	PO A	PO Pts.	PO PIM
		REGULAR SEASON								PLAYOFFS				
03-04—Michigan State	CCHA	41	11	18	29	50	...	...	...	—	—	—	—	—
04-05—Michigan State	CCHA	33	0	11	11	48	...	...	...	—	—	—	—	—

THEODORE, JOSE G CANADIENS

PERSONAL: Born September 13, 1976, in Laval, Que. ... 5-11/180. ... Catches right. ... Name pronounced JO-zhay THEE-uh-dohr.
TRANSACTIONS/CAREER NOTES: Selected by Montreal Canadiens in 2nd round (2nd Canadiens pick, 44th overall) of entry draft (June 28, 1994). ... Strained groin (March 29, 2000); missed three games. ... Concussion (October 26, 2001); missed four games. ... Injured hip (November 18, 2002); missed two games.

Season Team	League	GP	Min.	W	L	T	GA	SO	GAA	SV%	PO GP	PO Min.	PO W	PO L	PO GA	PO SO	PO GAA	PO SV%
		REGULAR SEASON									PLAYOFFS							
92-93—St. Jean	QMJHL	34	1776	12	16	2	112	0	3.78	...	3	175	0	2	11	0	3.77	...
93-94—St. Jean	QMJHL	57	3225	20	29	6	194	0	3.61	.885	5	296	1	4	18	1	3.65	.910
94-95—Hull	QMJHL	58	3348	32	22	2	193	5	3.46	.890	21	1263	15	6	59	1	2.80	.898
—Fredericton	AHL	...	...	...	...	...	...	...	...	...	1	60	0	1	3	0	3.00	.897
95-96—Hull	QMJHL	48	2803	33	11	2	158	0	3.38	...	5	300	2	3	20	0	4.00	...
—Montreal	NHL	1	9	0	0	0	1	0	6.67	.500	—	—	—	—	—	—	—	—
96-97—Fredericton	AHL	26	1469	12	12	0	87	0	3.55	.898	—	—	—	—	—	—	—	—
—Montreal	NHL	16	821	5	6	2	53	0	3.87	.896	2	168	1	1	7	0	2.50	.935
97-98—Fredericton	AHL	53	3053	20	23	8	145	2	2.85	.918	4	237	1	3	13	0	3.29	.901
—Montreal	NHL	...	...	...	...	...	...	...	...	...	3	120	0	1	1	0	0.50	.971
98-99—Montreal	NHL	18	913	4	12	0	50	1	3.29	.877	—	—	—	—	—	—	—	—
—Fredericton	AHL	27	1609	12	13	2	77	2	2.87	.917	13	694	8	5	35	1	3.03	.926
99-00—Montreal	NHL	30	1655	12	13	2	58	5	2.10	.919	—	—	—	—	—	—	—	—
00-01—Quebec	AHL	3	180	3	0	0	9	0	3.00	.886	—	—	—	—	—	—	—	—
—Montreal	NHL	59	3298	20	29	5	141	2	2.57	.909	—	—	—	—	—	—	—	—
01-02—Montreal	NHL	67	3864	30	24	10	136	7	2.11	*.931	12	686	6	6	35	0	3.06	.915
02-03—Montreal	NHL	57	3419	20	31	6	165	2	2.90	.908	—	—	—	—	—	—	—	—
03-04—Montreal	NHL	67	3961	33	28	5	150	6	2.27	.919	11	678	4	7	27	1	2.39	.919
04-05—Djurgarden Stockholm	Sweden	17	1024	...	...	...	42	0	2.46	.917	12	728	...	...	27	0	2.23	.922
NHL Totals (9 years)		315	17940	124	143	30	754	23	2.52	.914	28	1652	11	15	70	1	2.54	.921

THERIEN, CHRIS D FLYERS

PERSONAL: Born December 14, 1971, in Ottawa. ... 6-5/235. ... Shoots left. ... Name pronounced TAIR-ee-uhn.
TRANSACTIONS/CAREER NOTES: Selected by Philadelphia Flyers in 3ird round (7th Flyers pick, 47th overall) of ntry draft (June 16, 1990). ... Flu (November 3, 1997); missed one game. ... Sprained left knee (April 8, 1998); missed three games. ... Strained shoulder (October 9, 1998); missed first three games of season. ... Bruised left thigh (December 13, 1998); missed three games. ... Injured back (September 14, 2000). ... Injured back (October 17, 2000); missed eight games. ... Concussion (November 15, 2001); missed five games. ... Strained back (November 23, 2002); missed six games. ... Suffered concussion (January 3, 2003); missed four games. ... Strained trunk muscle (February 20, 2003); missed four games. ... Back spasms (December 6, 2003); missed three games. ... Back spasms (December 30, 2003); missed three games. ... Strained left shoulder (March 5, 2004); missed one game. ... Traded by Flyers to Dallas Stars for 8th-round pick in 2004 entry draft and 3rd-round pick in 2005 entry draft (March 8, 2004). ... Signed as a free agent by the Flyers (Aug. 2, 2005).

Season Team	League	GP	G	A	Pts.	PIM	+/-	PP	SH	PO GP	PO G	PO A	PO Pts.	PO PIM
		REGULAR SEASON								PLAYOFFS				
89-90—Northwood School	N.Y. H.S.	31	35	37	72	54	...	...	...	—	—	—	—	—
90-91—Providence College	Hockey East	36	4	18	22	36	...	...	...	—	—	—	—	—
91-92—Providence College	Hockey East	36	16	25	41	38	...	...	...	—	—	—	—	—
92-93—Providence College	Hockey East	33	8	11	19	52	...	...	...	—	—	—	—	—
—Canadian nat'l team	Int'l	8	1	4	5	8	...	...	...	—	—	—	—	—
93-94—Canadian nat'l team	Int'l	59	7	15	22	46	...	...	...	—	—	—	—	—
—Can. Olympic team	Int'l	4	0	0	0	4	1	0	0	—	—	—	—	—
—Hershey	AHL	6	0	0	0	2	-2	0	0	—	—	—	—	—
94-95—Hershey	AHL	34	3	13	16	27	-2	1	0	—	—	—	—	—
—Philadelphia	NHL	48	3	10	13	38	8	1	0	15	0	0	0	10
95-96—Philadelphia	NHL	82	6	17	23	89	16	3	0	12	0	0	0	18
96-97—Philadelphia	NHL	71	2	22	24	64	27	0	0	19	1	6	7	6
97-98—Philadelphia	NHL	78	3	16	19	80	5	1	0	5	0	1	1	4
98-99—Philadelphia	NHL	74	3	15	18	48	16	1	0	6	0	0	0	6
99-00—Philadelphia	NHL	80	4	9	13	66	11	1	0	18	0	1	1	12
00-01—Philadelphia	NHL	73	2	12	14	48	22	1	0	6	1	0	1	8

Season Team	League	GP	G	A	Pts.	PIM	+/-	PP	SH	GP	G	A	Pts.	PIM
		REGULAR SEASON								PLAYOFFS				
01-02—Philadelphia	NHL	77	4	10	14	30	16	0	2	5	0	0	0	2
02-03—Philadelphia	NHL	67	1	6	7	36	10	0	0	13	0	2	2	2
03-04—Philadelphia	AHL	2	0	0	0	0	-1	0	0	—	—	—	—	—
—Philadelphia	NHL	56	1	9	10	50	2	0	0	—	—	—	—	—
—Dallas	NHL	11	0	0	0	2	4	0	0	5	2	0	2	0
NHL Totals (10 years)		717	29	126	155	551	137	8	2	104	4	10	14	68

THIBAULT, JOCELYN G PENGUINS

PERSONAL: Born January 12, 1975, in Montreal. ... 5-11/169. ... Catches left. ... Name pronounced TEE-boh.

TRANSACTIONS/CAREER NOTES: Selected by Quebec Nordiques in 1st round (1st Nordiques pick, 10th overall) of NHL draft (June 26, 1993). ... Sprained shoulder (March 28, 1995); missed 10 games. ... Nordiques franchise moved to Colorado and renamed Avalanche for 1995-96 season (June 21, 1995). ... Traded by Avalanche with LW Martin Rucinsky and RW Andrei Kovalenko to Montreal Canadiens for G Patrick Roy and RW Mike Keane (December 6, 1995). ... Bruised right hand (February 21, 1996); missed two games. ... Fractured finger (October 24, 1996); missed nine games. ... Flu (February 3, 1997); missed two games. ... Bruised collarbone (January 8, 1998); missed one game. ... Traded by Canadiens with D Dave Manson and D Brad Brown to Chicago Blackhawks for G Jeff Hackett, D Eric Weinrich, D Alain Nasreddine and 4th-round pick (D Chris Dyment) in 1999 draft (November 16, 1998). ... Fractured finger (November 27, 1999); missed six games. ... Flu (December 10, 2000); missed one game. ... Suffered concussion (March 23, 2003); missed nine games. ... Injured hip (November 10, 2003) and had surgery (November 16, 2003); missed 60 games. ... Traded by Blackhawks to Pittsburgh Penguins for 6th-round pick in 2006 draft (Aug. 10, 2005).

Season Team	League	GP	Min.	W	L	T	GA	SO	GAA	SV%	GP	Min.	W	L	GA	SO	GAA	SV%
		REGULAR SEASON									PLAYOFFS							
91-92—Trois-Rivieres	QMJHL	30	1497	14	7	1	77	0	3.09	...	3	110	1	1	4	0	2.18	...
92-93—Sherbrooke	QMJHL	56	3190	34	14	5	159	*3	*2.99	*.904	15	883	9	6	57	0	3.87	.862
93-94—Quebec	NHL	29	1504	8	13	3	83	0	3.31	.892	—	—	—	—	—	—	—	—
—Cornwall	AHL	4	240	4	0	0	9	1	2.25	.930	—	—	—	—	—	—	—	—
94-95—Sherbrooke	QMJHL	13	776	6	6	1	38	1	2.94	.903	—	—	—	—	—	—	—	—
—Quebec	NHL	18	898	12	2	2	35	1	2.34	.917	3	148	1	2	8	0	3.24	.895
95-96—Colorado	NHL	10	558	3	4	2	28	0	3.01	.888	—	—	—	—	—	—	—	—
—Montreal	NHL	40	2334	23	13	3	110	3	2.83	.913	6	311	2	4	18	0	3.47	.904
96-97—Montreal	NHL	61	3397	22	24	11	164	1	2.90	.910	3	179	0	3	13	0	4.36	.871
97-98—Montreal	NHL	47	2652	19	15	8	109	2	2.47	.902	2	43	0	0	4	0	5.58	.750
98-99—Montreal	NHL	10	529	3	4	2	23	1	2.61	.908	—	—	—	—	—	—	—	—
—Chicago	NHL	52	3014	21	26	5	136	4	2.71	.905	—	—	—	—	—	—	—	—
99-00—Chicago	NHL	60	3438	25	26	7	158	3	2.76	.906	—	—	—	—	—	—	—	—
00-01—Chicago	NHL	66	3844	27	32	7	180	6	2.81	.895	—	—	—	—	—	—	—	—
01-02—Chicago	NHL	67	3838	33	23	9	159	6	2.49	.902	3	159	1	2	7	0	2.64	.909
02-03—Chicago	NHL	62	3650	26	28	7	144	8	2.37	.915	—	—	—	—	—	—	—	—
03-04—Chicago	NHL	14	821	5	7	2	39	1	2.85	.913	—	—	—	—	—	—	—	—
NHL Totals (11 years)		536	30477	227	217	68	1368	36	2.69	.905	17	840	4	11	50	0	3.57	.891

THOMAS, TIM G BRUINS

PERSONAL: Born April 15, 1974, in Davison, Mich. ... 5-11/181. ... Catches left.

TRANSACTIONS/CAREER NOTES: Selected by Quebec Nordiques in 9th round (11th Nordiques pick, 217th overall) of entry draft (June 29, 1994). ... Nordiques franchise moved to Colorado and renamed Avalanche for 1995-96 season (June 21, 1995). ... Signed as free agent by Edmonton Oilers (June 4, 1998). ... Signed as free agent by Boston Bruins (August 8, 2002).

Season Team	League	GP	Min.	W	L	T	GA	SO	GAA	SV%	GP	Min.	W	L	GA	SO	GAA	SV%
		REGULAR SEASON									PLAYOFFS							
92-93—Lakeland	Tier II	27	1580	...	...	...	87	...	3.30	...	—	—	—	—	—	—	—	—
93-94—Vermont	ECAC	33	1863	15	11	6	95	1	3.06	...	—	—	—	—	—	—	—	—
94-95—Vermont	ECAC	34	2011	18	14	2	90	3	2.69	.914	—	—	—	—	—	—	—	—
95-96—Vermont	ECAC	37	2254	26	7	4	88	3	2.34	...	—	—	—	—	—	—	—	—
96-97—Vermont	ECAC	36	2158	22	11	3	101	2	2.81	.914	—	—	—	—	—	—	—	—
97-98—Birmingham	ECHL	6	360	4	1	1	13	1	2.17	...	—	—	—	—	—	—	—	—
—Houston	IHL	1	60	0	1	0	4	0	4.00	.852	—	—	—	—	—	—	—	—
—HIFK Helsinki	Finland	22	1035	22	4	1	28	2	1.62	...	9	551	9	0	14	3	1.52	...
98-99—Hamilton	AHL	15	837	6	8	0	45	0	3.23	.905	—	—	—	—	—	—	—	—
—HIFK Helsinki	Finland	14	833	8	3	3	31	2	2.23	...	*11	*658	7	4	*25	...	2.28	...
99-00—Detroit	IHL	36	2020	15	21	3	120	1	3.56	...	—	—	—	—	—	—	—	—
00-01—AIK Solna	Sweden	43	2542	...	...	...	105	3	2.48	...	5	299	...	...	20	0	4.01	...
01-02—Karpat Oulu	Finland	32	1937	15	12	5	79	...	2.45	...	3	180	1	2	12	0	4.00	...
02-03—Providence	AHL	35	2048	18	12	5	98	1	2.87	.906	—	—	—	—	—	—	—	—
—Boston	NHL	4	220	3	1	0	11	0	3.00	.907	—	—	—	—	—	—	—	—
03-04—Providence	AHL	43	2549	20	16	6	78	9	1.84	.938	2	84	0	2	10	0	7.14	.474
04-05—Jokerit Helsinki	Finland	54	3267	34	13	7	86	15	1.58	.946	12	721	8	4	22	0	1.83	.938
NHL Totals (1 year)		4	220	3	1	0	11	0	3.00	.907								

THOMPSON, BILLY G SENATORS

PERSONAL: Born September 24, 1982, in Saskatoon, Sask. ... 6-2/180. ... Catches left.

TRANSACTIONS/CAREER NOTES: Selected by Florida Panthers in fifth round (seventh Panthers pick, 136th overall) of NHL entry draft (June 23, 2001). ... Traded by Panthers with C Greg Watson to Ottawa Senators for G Jani Hurme (October 1, 2002).

Season	Team	League	GP	Min.	W	L	T	GA	SO	GAA	SV%	GP	Min.	W	L	GA	SO	GAA	SV%
			REGULAR SEASON									PLAYOFFS							
00-01	—Prince George	WHL	57	3185	24	24	3	178	1	3.35	...	6	324	2	4	22	0	4.07	...
01-02	—Prince George	WHL	42	2375	20	17	2	108	2	2.73	...	7	402	3	4	21	0	3.13	...
02-03	—Binghamton	AHL	1	60	1	0	0	5	0	5.00	.815	—	—	—	—	—	—	—	—
	—Prince George	WHL	50	2776	20	26	0	186	0	4.02	...	—	—	—	—	—	—	—	—
03-04	—Binghamton	AHL	34	1725	13	14	2	83	2	2.89	.897	—	—	—	—	—	—	—	—
04-05	—Binghamton	AHL	34	1868	19	8	...	76	1	2.44	.920	0	0	0	0	0	0	...	...

THOMPSON, ROCKY RW

PERSONAL: Born August 8, 1977, in Calgary. ... 6-2/205. ... Shoots right.

TRANSACTIONS/CAREER NOTES: Selected by Calgary Flames in third round (third Flames pick, 72nd overall) of NHL entry draft (July 8, 1995). ... Injured neck (February 3, 1998); missed two games. ... Suffered concussion (January 16, 1999); missed final 38 games of season. ... Traded by Flames to Florida Panthers for D Filip Kuba (March 16, 2000). ... Injured ankle tendon (September 12, 2001); missed first 27 games of season. ... Signed as free agent by Edmonton Oilers (July 20, 2003). ... Signed as free agent by Edmonton of the AHL (September 29, 2004).

Season	Team	League	GP	G	A	Pts.	PIM	+/-	PP	SH	GP	G	A	Pts.	PIM
			REGULAR SEASON								PLAYOFFS				
93-94	—Medicine Hat	WHL	68	1	4	5	166	...	...	...	3	0	0	0	2
94-95	—Medicine Hat	WHL	63	1	6	7	220	1	0	0	5	0	0	0	17
95-96	—Medicine Hat	WHL	71	9	20	29	260	...	...	...	5	2	3	5	26
	—Saint John	AHL	4	0	0	0	33	...	...	...	—	—	—	—	—
96-97	—Medicine Hat	WHL	47	6	9	15	170	6	1	0	—	—	—	—	—
	—Swift Current	WHL	22	3	5	8	90	13	0	0	10	1	2	3	22
97-98	—Saint John	AHL	51	3	0	3	187	-4	0	0	18	1	1	2	47
	—Calgary	NHL	12	0	0	0	61	0	0	0	—	—	—	—	—
98-99	—Saint John	AHL	27	2	2	4	108	-5	0	0	—	—	—	—	—
	—Calgary	NHL	3	0	0	0	25	0	0	0	—	—	—	—	—
99-00	—Saint John	AHL	53	2	8	10	125	...	...	...	—	—	—	—	—
	—Louisville	AHL	3	0	1	1	54	...	...	...	4	0	0	0	4
00-01	—Louisville	AHL	55	3	5	8	193	...	...	...	—	—	—	—	—
	—Florida	NHL	4	0	0	0	19	0	0	0	—	—	—	—	—
01-02	—Hershey	AHL	42	0	3	3	143	-2	0	0	8	1	0	1	19
	—Florida	NHL	6	0	0	0	12	0	0	0	—	—	—	—	—
02-03	—San Antonio	AHL	79	1	11	12	275	-2	0	0	3	0	0	0	4
03-04	—Toronto	AHL	70	1	8	9	196	-1	0	0	3	1	1	2	0
04-05	—Edmonton	AHL	69	3	3	6	231	-13	0	0	—	—	—	—	—
NHL Totals (4 years)			25	0	0	0	117	0	0	0					

THORNTON, JOE C BRUINS

PERSONAL: Born July 2, 1979, in London, Ontario. ... 6-4/223. ... Shoots left. ... Cousin of Scott Thornton, LW, San Jose Sharks.

TRANSACTIONS/CAREER NOTES: Selected by Boston Bruins in first round (first Bruins pick, first overall) of NHL draft (June 21, 1997). ... Fractured forearm before 1997-98 season; missed first three games. ... Injured ankle (December 13, 1997); missed 10 games. ... Viral infection (March 28, 1998); missed six games. ... Injured chest (April 17, 1999); missed final game of regular season and one playoff game. ... Bruised knee (November 20, 1999); missed one game. ... Charley horse (November 24, 2000); missed six games. ... Suspended two games by NHL for cross-checking incident (December 18, 2000). ... Suspended two games by NHL for cross-checking incident (February 6, 2001). ... Suspended three games by NHL for cross-checking incident (March 1, 2002). ... Injured shoulder (March 7, 2002); missed 13 games. ... Injured elbow (January 7, 2003); missed five games. ... Injured cheekbone (January 19, 2003); missed three games. ... Injured ribs (April 3, 2004); missed final two games of regular season.

STATISTICAL PLATEAUS: Three-goal games: 2000-01 (1), 2001-02 (1). Total: 2.

Season	Team	League	GP	G	A	Pts.	PIM	+/-	PP	SH	GP	G	A	Pts.	PIM
			REGULAR SEASON								PLAYOFFS				
94-95	—St. Thomas	Jr. B	50	40	64	104	53	...	...	...	—	—	—	—	—
95-96	—Sault Ste. Marie	OHL	66	30	46	76	51	...	...	...	4	1	1	2	11
96-97	—Sault Ste. Marie	OHL	59	41	81	122	123	29	11	0	11	11	8	19	24
97-98	—Boston	NHL	55	3	4	7	19	-6	0	0	6	0	0	0	9
98-99	—Boston	NHL	81	16	25	41	69	3	7	0	11	3	6	9	4
99-00	—Boston	NHL	81	23	37	60	82	-5	5	0	—	—	—	—	—
00-01	—Boston	NHL	72	37	34	71	107	-4	19	1	—	—	—	—	—
01-02	—Boston	NHL	66	22	46	68	127	7	6	0	6	2	4	6	10
02-03	—Boston	NHL	77	36	65	101	109	12	12	2	5	1	2	3	4
03-04	—Boston	NHL	77	23	50	73	98	18	4	0	7	0	0	0	14
04-05	—Davos	Switzerland	40	10	44	54	80	...	2	0	14	4	21	25	29
NHL Totals (7 years)			509	160	261	421	611	25	53	3	35	6	12	18	41

THORNTON, SCOTT LW SHARKS

PERSONAL: Born January 9, 1971, in London, Ont. ... 6-3/225. ... Shoots left. ... Cousin of Joe Thornton, C, Boston Bruins.

TRANSACTIONS/CAREER NOTES: Selected by Toronto Maple Leafs in 1st round (1st Maple Leafs pick, 3rd overall) of NHL draft (June 17, 1989). ... Separated shoulder (January 24, 1991); missed eight games. ... Traded by Maple Leafs with LW Vincent Damphousse, D Luke Richardson and G Peter Ing to Edmonton Oilers for G Grant Fuhr, W Glenn Anderson and LW Craig Berube (September 19, 1991). ... Concussion (November 23, 1991); missed one game. ... Sprained ankle (October 6, 1993); missed 13 games. ... Back spasms (November 21, 1993); missed one game. ... Bruised wrist (April 14, 1994); missed one game. ... Cytomegalo virus (January 9, 1996); missed three games. ... Traded by Oilers to Montreal Canadiens for RW Andrei Kovalenko (September 6, 1996). ... Bruised hand (December 28, 1996); missed three games. ... Flu (February 10, 1997); missed one game. ... Arthroscopic knee surgery (March 6, 1997); missed five games. ... Separated shoulder (January 3, 1998); missed two games. ... Injured neck (February 7, 1998); missed one game. ... Fractured rib (March 18, 1998); missed eight games. ... Injured shoulder (April 15, 1998); missed three games. ... Strained abdominal muscle (November 3, 1998) and had surgery; missed 31 games. ... Migraines (February 2, 1999); missed three games. ... Back spasms (April 13, 1999); missed one game. ... Injured tricep (September 20, 1999); missed first two games of 1999-2000 season. ... Reinjured tricep (October 8, 1999); missed three games. ... Strained groin (December 12, 1999); missed one game. ... Traded by Canadiens to Dallas Stars for LW Juha Lind (January 22, 2000). ... Flu (March 8, 2000); missed one game. ... Suspended for three games for high-sticking (March 22, 2000). ... Signed as free agent by San Jose Sharks (July 1, 2000). ... Injured neck (January 4, 2001); missed three games. ... Injured neck (January 30, 2001); missed five games. ... Injured wrist (March 10, 2002); missed one game. ... Injured shoulder (October 10. 2002); missed 14 games. ... Flu (February 17, 2003); missed two games. ... Injured eye (February 24, 2003); missed 21 games. ... Injured groin (November 8, 2003); missed one game.

STATISTICAL PLATEAUS: Three-goal games: 2000-01 (1).

		REGULAR SEASON								PLAYOFFS				
Season Team	**League**	**GP**	**G**	**A**	**Pts.**	**PIM**	**+/-**	**PP**	**SH**	**GP**	**G**	**A**	**Pts.**	**PIM**
86-87—London Diamonds	OPJHL	31	10	7	17	10	...	...	...	—	—	—	—	—
87-88—Belleville	OHL	62	11	19	30	54	...	...	...	6	0	1	1	2
88-89—Belleville	OHL	59	28	34	62	103	...	...	...	5	1	1	2	6
89-90—Belleville	OHL	47	21	28	49	91	...	...	...	11	2	10	12	15
90-91—Belleville	OHL	3	2	1	3	2	...	...	...	6	0	7	7	14
—Newmarket	AHL	5	1	0	1	4	...	...	...	—	—	—	—	—
—Toronto	NHL	33	1	3	4	30	-15	0	0	—	—	—	—	—
91-92—Edmonton	NHL	15	0	1	1	43	-6	0	0	1	0	0	0	0
—Cape Breton	AHL	49	9	14	23	40	...	...	...	5	1	0	1	8
92-93—Cape Breton	AHL	58	23	27	50	102	-17	7	0	16	1	2	3	35
—Edmonton	NHL	9	0	1	1	0	-4	0	0	—	—	—	—	—
93-94—Edmonton	NHL	61	4	7	11	104	-15	0	0	—	—	—	—	—
—Cape Breton	AHL	2	1	1	2	31	-2	1	0	—	—	—	—	—
94-95—Edmonton	NHL	47	10	12	22	89	-4	0	1	—	—	—	—	—
95-96—Edmonton	NHL	77	9	9	18	149	-25	0	2	—	—	—	—	—
96-97—Montreal	NHL	73	10	10	20	128	-19	1	1	5	1	0	1	2
97-98—Montreal	NHL	67	6	9	15	158	0	1	0	9	0	2	2	10
98-99—Montreal	NHL	47	7	4	11	87	-2	1	0	—	—	—	—	—
99-00—Montreal	NHL	35	2	3	5	70	-7	0	0	—	—	—	—	—
—Dallas	NHL	30	6	3	9	38	-5	1	0	23	2	7	9	28
00-01—San Jose	NHL	73	19	17	36	114	4	4	0	6	3	0	3	8
01-02—San Jose	NHL	77	26	16	42	116	11	6	0	12	3	3	6	6
02-03—San Jose	NHL	41	9	12	21	41	-7	4	0	—	—	—	—	—
03-04—San Jose	NHL	80	13	14	27	84	-6	1	0	12	2	2	4	22
04-05—Sodertalje	Sweden	12	2	5	7	10	-7	0	0	10	0	3	3	27
NHL Totals (14 years)		765	122	121	243	1251	-100	19	4	68	11	14	25	76

THORNTON, SHAWN RW

PERSONAL: Born July 23, 1977, in Oshawa, Ont. ... 6-1/209. ... Shoots right.

TRANSACTIONS/CAREER NOTES: Selected by Toronto Maple Leafs in seventh round (sixth Maple Leafs pick, 190th overall) of NHL entry draft (June 21, 1997). ... Traded by Maple Leafs to Chicago Blackhawks for D Marty Wilford (September 30, 2001).

		REGULAR SEASON								PLAYOFFS				
Season Team	**League**	**GP**	**G**	**A**	**Pts.**	**PIM**	**+/-**	**PP**	**SH**	**GP**	**G**	**A**	**Pts.**	**PIM**
95-96—Peterborough	OHL	63	4	10	14	192	...	...	...	24	3	0	3	25
96-97—Peterborough	OHL	61	19	10	29	204	...	...	...	11	2	4	6	20
97-98—St. John's	AHL	59	0	3	3	225	-2	0	0	—	—	—	—	—
98-99—St. John's	AHL	78	8	11	19	354	6	2	0	5	0	0	0	9
99-00—St. John's	AHL	60	4	12	16	316	...	...	...	—	—	—	—	—
00-01—St. John's	AHL	79	5	12	17	320	...	...	...	3	1	2	3	2
01-02—Norfolk	AHL	70	8	14	22	281	-3	0	0	4	0	0	0	4
02-03—Chicago	NHL	13	1	1	2	31	-4	0	0	—	—	—	—	—
—Norfolk	AHL	50	11	2	13	213	-7	4	0	9	0	2	2	28
03-04—Chicago	NHL	8	1	0	1	23	2	0	0	—	—	—	—	—
—Norfolk	AHL	64	6	11	17	259	-7	0	0	8	1	1	2	6
04-05—Norfolk	AHL	71	5	9	14	253	-15	0	1	6	0	0	0	8
NHL Totals (2 years)		21	2	1	3	54	-2	0	0					

TIMANDER, MATTIAS D FLYERS

PERSONAL: Born April 16, 1974, in Solleftea, Sweden. ... 6-3/230. ... Shoots left. ... Name pronounced tih-MAN-duhr.

TRANSACTIONS/CAREER NOTES: Selected by Boston Bruins in seventh round (seventh Bruins pick, 208th overall) of NHL draft (June 21, 1992). ... Injured shoulder (November 26, 1996); missed four games. ... Injured finger (November 17, 1997); missed two games. ... Injured shoulder (March 2, 1999); missed two games. ... Reinjured shoulder (March 13, 1999); missed one game. ... Injured shoulder (November 22, 1999); missed 11 games. ... Selected by Columbus Blue Jackets in expansion draft (June 23, 2000). ... Strained neck (December 16, 2000); missed five games. ... Neck spasms (February 14, 2001); missed one game. ... Bruised hip (November 27, 2001); missed three games. ... Traded by Blue Jackets to New York Islanders for fourth-round pick (D Jekabs Redlihs) in 2002 draft (June 22, 2002). ... Traded by Islanders to Philadelphia Flyers for seventh-round pick in 2004 draft (January 22, 2004).

		REGULAR SEASON								PLAYOFFS				
Season Team	**League**	**GP**	**G**	**A**	**Pts.**	**PIM**	**+/-**	**PP**	**SH**	**GP**	**G**	**A**	**Pts.**	**PIM**
92-93—MoDo Ornskoldsvik	Sweden	1	0	0	0	0	...	...	...	—	—	—	—	—
93-94—MoDo Ornskoldsvik	Sweden	23	2	2	4	6	...	...	...	11	2	0	2	10
94-95—MoDo Ornskoldsvik	Sweden	39	8	9	17	24	...	...	...	—	—	—	—	—
95-96—MoDo Ornskoldsvik	Sweden	37	4	10	14	34	...	...	...	7	1	1	2	8
96-97—Boston	NHL	41	1	8	9	14	-9	0	0	—	—	—	—	—
—Providence	AHL	32	3	11	14	20	6	3	0	10	1	1	2	12
97-98—Boston	NHL	23	1	1	2	6	-9	0	0	—	—	—	—	—

Season Team	League	GP	G	A	Pts.	PIM	+/-	PP	SH	GP	G	A	Pts.	PIM
		REGULAR SEASON								PLAYOFFS				
—Providence	AHL	31	3	7	10	25	-7	3	0	—	—	—	—	—
98-99—Providence	AHL	43	2	22	24	24	6	1	0	—	—	—	—	—
—Boston	NHL	22	0	6	6	10	4	0	0	4	1	1	2	2
99-00—Boston	NHL	60	0	8	8	22	-11	0	0	—	—	—	—	—
—Hershey	AHL	1	0	0	0	2	...	...	...	—	—	—	—	—
00-01—Columbus	NHL	76	2	9	11	24	-8	0	0	—	—	—	—	—
01-02—Columbus	NHL	78	4	7	11	44	-34	1	0	—	—	—	—	—
02-03—New York Islanders	NHL	80	3	13	16	24	-2	0	0	1	0	0	0	0
03-04—Bridgeport	AHL	35	2	6	8	12	6	0	0	—	—	—	—	—
—New York Islanders	NHL	5	1	1	2	2	2	0	0	—	—	—	—	—
—Philadelphia	NHL	34	1	4	5	19	13	0	1	18	2	4	6	6
04-05—MoDo Ornskoldsvik	Sweden	47	3	7	10	60	-13	0	0	6	0	1	1	4
NHL Totals (8 years)		419	13	57	70	165	-54	1	1	23	3	5	8	8

TIMONEN, KIMMO — D — PREDATORS

PERSONAL: Born March 18, 1975, in Kuopio, Finland. ... 5-10/196. ... Shoots left. ... Brother of Jussi Timonen, D, Philadelphia Flyers organization. ... Name pronounced KEE-moh TEE-muh-nehn.

TRANSACTIONS/CAREER NOTES: Selected by Los Angeles Kings in 10th round (11th Kings pick, 250th overall) of NHL draft (June 26, 1993). ... Rights traded by Kings with D Jan Vopat to Nashville Predators for future considerations (June 26, 1998). ... Cut lip (January 26, 1999); missed one game. ... Strained abdominal muscle (December 18, 1999); missed four games. ... Fractured wrist (January 11, 2000); missed 15 games. ... Fractured ankle (March 14, 2000); missed remainder of season. ... Bruised left ankle (November 10, 2002); missed two games. ... Bruised calf (January 6, 2003); missed seven games. ... Bruised foot (January 17, 2004); missed two games. ... Injured knee (January 24, 2004); missed two games.

Season Team	League	GP	G	A	Pts.	PIM	+/-	PP	SH	GP	G	A	Pts.	PIM
		REGULAR SEASON								PLAYOFFS				
91-92—KalPa Kuopio	Finland	5	0	0	0	0	...	...	...	—	—	—	—	—
92-93—KalPa Kuopio	Finland	33	0	2	2	4	...	...	...	—	—	—	—	—
93-94—KalPa Kuopio	Finland	46	6	7	13	55	...	...	...	—	—	—	—	—
94-95—TPS Turku	Finland	45	3	4	7	10	...	...	...	13	0	1	1	6
95-96—TPS Turku	Finland	48	3	21	24	22	...	...	...	9	1	2	3	12
96-97—TPS Turku	Finland	50	10	14	24	18	...	...	...	12	2	7	9	8
97-98—HIFK Helsinki	Finland	45	10	15	25	59	...	...	...	9	3	4	7	8
—Fin. Olympic team	Int'l	6	0	1	1	2	-3	0	0	—	—	—	—	—
98-99—Milwaukee	IHL	29	2	13	15	22	0	0	0	—	—	—	—	—
—Nashville	NHL	50	4	8	12	30	-4	1	0	—	—	—	—	—
99-00—Nashville	NHL	51	8	25	33	26	-5	2	1	—	—	—	—	—
00-01—Nashville	NHL	82	12	13	25	50	-6	6	0	—	—	—	—	—
01-02—Nashville	NHL	82	13	29	42	28	2	9	0	—	—	—	—	—
—Fin. Olympic team	Int'l	4	0	1	1	2	...	...	...	—	—	—	—	—
02-03—Nashville	NHL	72	6	34	40	46	-3	4	0	—	—	—	—	—
03-04—Nashville	NHL	77	12	32	44	52	-7	8	0	6	0	0	0	10
04-05—Lugano	Switzerland	3	0	1	1	0	...	0	0	—	—	—	—	—
—Brynas IF	Sweden	10	5	3	8	8	9	1	0	—	—	—	—	—
—KalPa Kuopio	Finland	12	4	13	17	6	14	...	...	—	—	—	—	—
NHL Totals (6 years)		414	55	141	196	232	-23	30	1	6	0	0	0	10

TJARNQVIST, DANIEL — D — WILD

PERSONAL: Born October 14, 1976, in Umea, Sweden. ... 6-2/200. ... Shoots left. ... Brother of Mathias Tjarnqvist, C, Dallas Stars organization. ... Name pronounced TAHRN-kuh-vihst.

TRANSACTIONS/CAREER NOTES: Selected by Florida Panthers in fourth round (fifth Panthers pick, 88th overall) of NHL draft (July 8, 1995). ... Traded by Panthers with D Gord Murphy, C Herbert Vasiljevs and sixth-round pick (traded to Dallas; Stars selected RW Justin Cox) in 1999 draft to Atlanta Thrashers for G Trevor Kidd (June 25, 1999). ... Had hip pointer (April 2, 2003); missed three games.

Season Team	League	GP	G	A	Pts.	PIM	+/-	PP	SH	GP	G	A	Pts.	PIM
		REGULAR SEASON								PLAYOFFS				
94-95—Rogle Angelholm	Sweden	33	2	4	6	2	...	...	...	—	—	—	—	—
95-96—Rogle Angelholm	Sweden	22	1	7	8	6	...	...	...	—	—	—	—	—
96-97—Jokerit Helsinki	Finland	44	3	8	11	4	...	...	...	9	0	3	3	4
97-98—Djurgarden Stockholm	Sweden	40	5	9	14	12	...	...	...	15	1	1	2	2
98-99—Djurgarden Stockholm	Sweden	40	4	3	7	16	18	...	...	4	0	0	0	2
99-00—Djurgarden Stockholm	Sweden	42	3	16	19	8	...	...	...	5	0	0	0	2
00-01—Djurgarden Stockholm	Sweden	45	9	17	26	26	...	...	...	16	6	5	11	2
01-02—Atlanta	NHL	75	2	16	18	14	-22	1	0	—	—	—	—	—
02-03—Atlanta	NHL	75	3	12	15	26	-20	1	0	—	—	—	—	—
03-04—Atlanta	NHL	68	5	15	20	20	-4	0	2	—	—	—	—	—
04-05—Djurgarden Stockholm	Sweden	49	12	12	24	30	-3	6	1	12	2	5	7	10
NHL Totals (3 years)		218	10	43	53	60	-46	2	2					

TJARNQVIST, MATHIAS — LW — STARS

PERSONAL: Born April 15, 1979, in Umea, Sweden. ... 6-1/183. ... Shoots left. ... Brother of Daniel Tjarnqvist, D, Atlanta Thrashers system.

TRANSACTIONS/CAREER NOTES: Selected by Dallas Stars in third round (third Stars pick, 96th overall) of NHL draft (June 26, 1999). ... Signed as free agent by HV 71of the Swedish league (August 30, 2004).

Season Team	League	REGULAR SEASON GP	G	A	Pts.	PIM	+/-	PP	SH	PLAYOFFS GP	G	A	Pts.	PIM
99-00—Djurgarden Stockholm	Sweden	50	12	12	24	20	...	...	...	13	3	2	5	16
00-01—Djurgarden Stockholm	Sweden	47	11	8	19	53	...	...	...	16	1	2	3	6
01-02—Djurgarden Stockholm	Sweden	6	0	1	1	4	...	...	...	2	0	0	0	2
02-03—Djurgarden Stockholm	Sweden	38	11	13	24	30	...	...	...	9	4	1	5	12
03-04—Dallas	NHL	18	1	1	2	2	-6	0	0	—	—	—	—	—
—Utah	AHL	60	15	13	28	51	-17	6	1	—	—	—	—	—
04-05—HV 71 Jonkoping	Sweden	46	8	9	17	18	-6	4	0	—	—	—	—	—
NHL Totals (1 year)		18	1	1	2	2	-6	0	0					

TKACHUK, KEITH — LW — BLUES

PERSONAL: Born March 28, 1972, in Melrose, Mass. ... 6-2/231. ... Shoots left. ... Cousin of Tom Fitzgerald, RW, Toronto Maple Leafs. ... Name pronounced kuh-CHUHK. ... Nickname: Walt.

TRANSACTIONS/CAREER NOTES: Selected by Winnipeg Jets in first round (first Jets pick, 19th overall) of NHL draft (June 16, 1990). ... Lacerated forearm (November 12, 1993); missed one game. ... Strained groin (October 9, 1995); missed three games. ... Suffered concussion (November 26, 1995); missed one game. ... Suspended two games and fined $1,000 for stick-swinging incident (March 16, 1996). ... Jets franchise moved to Phoenix and renamed Coyotes for 1996-97 season; NHL approved move on January 18, 1996. ... Flu (March 5, 1997); missed one game. ... Injured groin (March 2, 1998); missed two games. ... Fractured rib (March 12, 1998); missed seven games. ... Injured groin (December 14, 1998); missed two games. ... Fractured ribs (December 20, 1998); missed eight games. ... Strained lower back (February 2, 1999); missed two games. ... Injured neck (December 4, 1999); missed three games. ... Back spasms (December 26, 1999); missed four games. ... Sprained ankle (January 31, 2000); missed one game. ... Sprained ankle (February 12, 2000); missed 16 games. ... Suspended two games for high-sticking incident (March 24, 2000). ... Sprained ankle (March 29, 2000); missed final six games of regular season. ... Strained groin (October 12, 2000); missed one game. ... Suffered injury (October 30, 2000); missed one game. ... Suffered concussion (January 26, 2001); missed two games. ... Suffered injury (February 9, 2001); missed one game. ... Traded by Coyotes to St. Louis Blues for C Michal Handzus, RW Ladislav Nagy, C Jeff Taffe and first-round pick (LW Ben Eager) in 2002 draft (March 13, 2001). ... Bruised thigh (February 16, 2002); missed eight games. ... Suspended one game for slashing incident (March 25, 2002). ... Fractured foot (November 2, 2002); missed 11 games. ... Suspended four games for cross-checking incident (February 25, 2003). ... Injured wrist (March 13, 2003); missed nine games. ... Suspended three games for high-sticking incident (November 15, 2003). ... Injured ankle (December 20, 2003); missed three games.

STATISTICAL PLATEAUS: Three-goal games: 1993-94 (1), 1996-97 (1), 1997-98 (3), 1998-99 (1), 2000-01 (1). Total: 7. ... Four-goal games: 1995-96 (1), 1996-97 (1). Total: 2. ... Total hat tricks: 9.

Season Team	League	REGULAR SEASON GP	G	A	Pts.	PIM	+/-	PP	SH	PLAYOFFS GP	G	A	Pts.	PIM
88-89—Malden Catholic H.S.	Mass. H.S.	21	30	16	46	...	...	...	...	—	—	—	—	—
89-90—Malden Catholic H.S.	Mass. H.S.	6	12	14	26	...	...	...	...	—	—	—	—	—
90-91—Boston University	Hockey East	36	17	23	40	70	...	...	...	—	—	—	—	—
91-92—U.S. national team	Int'l	45	10	10	20	141	...	...	...	—	—	—	—	—
—U.S. Olympic team	Int'l	8	1	1	2	12	...	...	...	—	—	—	—	—
—Winnipeg	NHL	17	3	5	8	28	0	2	0	7	3	0	3	30
92-93—Winnipeg	NHL	83	28	23	51	201	-13	12	0	6	4	0	4	14
93-94—Winnipeg	NHL	84	41	40	81	255	-12	22	3	—	—	—	—	—
94-95—Winnipeg	NHL	48	22	29	51	152	-4	7	2	—	—	—	—	—
95-96—Winnipeg	NHL	76	50	48	98	156	11	20	2	6	1	2	3	22
96-97—Phoenix	NHL	81	*52	34	86	228	-1	9	2	7	6	0	6	7
97-98—Phoenix	NHL	69	40	26	66	147	9	11	0	6	3	3	6	10
—U.S. Olympic team	Int'l	4	0	2	2	6	-3	0	0	—	—	—	—	—
98-99—Phoenix	NHL	68	36	32	68	151	22	11	2	7	1	3	4	13
99-00—Phoenix	NHL	50	22	21	43	82	7	5	1	5	1	1	2	4
00-01—Phoenix	NHL	64	29	42	71	108	6	15	0	—	—	—	—	—
—St. Louis	NHL	12	6	2	8	14	-3	2	0	15	2	7	9	20
01-02—St. Louis	NHL	73	38	37	75	117	21	13	0	10	5	5	10	18
—U.S. Olympic team	Int'l	5	2	0	2	2	...	...	...	—	—	—	—	—
02-03—St. Louis	NHL	56	31	24	55	139	1	14	0	7	1	3	4	14
03-04—St. Louis	NHL	75	33	38	71	83	8	18	0	5	0	2	2	10
NHL Totals (13 years)		856	431	401	832	1861	52	161	12	81	27	26	53	162

TOIVONEN, HANNU — G — BRUINS

PERSONAL: Born May 18, 1984, in Kalvola, Finland. ... 6-2/191. ... Catches left. ... Name pronounced HA-noo TOI-voh-nuhn.

TRANSACTIONS/CAREER NOTES: Selected by Boston Bruins in first round (first Bruins pick, 29th overall) of NHL entry draft (June 22, 2002).

Season Team	League	REGULAR SEASON GP	Min.	W	L	T	GA	SO	GAA	SV%	PLAYOFFS GP	Min.	W	L	GA	SO	GAA	SV%
01-02—HPK Hameenlinna	Finland Jr.	31	1877	...	...	...	103	2	3.29	...	—	—	—	—	—	—	—	—
02-03—HPK Hameenlinna	Finland	24	1432	16	2	4	54	2	2.26	...	...	...	1	1	3	1	...	...
03-04—Providence	AHL	36	2163	15	16	4	83	2	2.30	.915	—	—	—	—	—	—	—	—
04-05—Providence	AHL	54	3017	29	18	...	103	7	2.05	.932	17	1037	10	7	42	0	2.43	.923

TOOTOO, JORDIN — RW — PREDATORS

PERSONAL: Born February 2, 1983, in Churchill, Man. ... 5-9/195. ... Shoots right.

TRANSACTIONS/CAREER NOTES: Selected by Nashville Predators in fourth round (sixth Predators pick, 98th overall) of NHL draft (June 23, 2001). ... Flu (February 20, 2004); missed three games.

Season Team	League	REGULAR SEASON GP	G	A	Pts.	PIM	+/-	PP	SH	PLAYOFFS GP	G	A	Pts.	PIM
99-00—Brandon	WHL	45	6	10	16	214	...	...	...	—	—	—	—	—
00-01—Brandon	WHL	60	20	28	48	172	...	...	...	6	2	4	6	18

Season Team	League	REGULAR SEASON GP	G	A	Pts.	PIM	+/-	PP	SH	PLAYOFFS GP	G	A	Pts.	PIM
01-02—Brandon	WHL	64	32	39	71	272	...	...	...	16	4	3	7	*58
02-03—Brandon	WHL	51	35	39	74	216	...	...	...	17	6	3	9	49
03-04—Nashville	NHL	70	4	4	8	137	-6	2	0	5	0	0	0	4
04-05—Milwaukee	AHL	59	10	12	22	266	8	3	0	6	0	0	0	41
NHL Totals (1 year)		70	4	4	8	137	-6	2	0	5	0	0	0	4

TORRES, RAFFI — LW — OILERS

PERSONAL: Born October 8, 1981, in Toronto. ... 6-0/210. ... Shoots left. ... Name pronounced TAN-rehs.

TRANSACTIONS/CAREER NOTES: Selected by New York Islanders in first round (second Islanders pick, fifth overall) of NHL draft (June 24, 2000). ... Traded by Islanders with LW Brad Isbister to Edmonton Oilers for D Janne Niinimaa and second-round pick (C Yevgeny Tanik) in 2003 draft (March 11, 2003). ... Injured ankle (February 16, 2004); missed two games.

Season Team	League	REGULAR SEASON GP	G	A	Pts.	PIM	+/-	PP	SH	PLAYOFFS GP	G	A	Pts.	PIM
97-98—Thornhill	Jr. A	46	17	16	33	90	...	...	...	—	—	—	—	—
98-99—Brampton	OHL	62	35	27	62	32	...	...	...	—	—	—	—	—
99-00—Brampton	OHL	68	43	48	91	40	...	...	...	6	5	2	7	23
00-01—Brampton	OHL	55	33	37	70	76	16	12	5	8	7	4	11	19
01-02—Bridgeport	AHL	59	20	10	30	45	-5	7	0	20	8	9	17	26
—New York Islanders	NHL	14	0	1	1	6	2	0	0	—	—	—	—	—
02-03—New York Islanders	NHL	17	0	5	5	10	0	0	0	—	—	—	—	—
—Bridgeport	AHL	49	17	15	32	54	...	...	...	—	—	—	—	—
—Hamilton	AHL	11	1	7	8	14	...	...	...	23	6	1	7	29
03-04—Edmonton	NHL	80	20	14	34	65	12	5	0	—	—	—	—	—
04-05—Edmonton	AHL	67	21	25	46	165	4	8	0	—	—	—	—	—
NHL Totals (3 years)		111	20	20	40	81	14	5	0					

TOSKALA, VESA — G — SHARKS

PERSONAL: Born May 20, 1977, in Tampere, Finland. ... 5-10/195. ... Catches left. ... Name pronounced TAWS-koh-lah.

TRANSACTIONS/CAREER NOTES: Selected by San Jose Sharks in fourth round (fourth Sharks pick, 90th overall) of NHL draft (July 8, 1995). ... Injured groin (March 13, 2004); missed four games.

Season Team	League	REGULAR SEASON GP	Min.	W	L	T	GA	SO	GAA	SV%	PLAYOFFS GP	Min.	W	L	GA	SO	GAA	SV%
93-94—Ilves Jrs.	Finland	2	...	...	...	...	...	...		...	—	—	—	—	—	—	—	—
94-95—Ilves Jrs.	Finland	17	956	...	...	...	36	...	2.26	...	—	—	—	—	—	—	—	—
95-96—Ilves Tampere	Finland	37	2073	...	...	...	109	1	3.15	...	2	78	...	...	11	0	8.46	...
—Koo Vee	Finland	2	119	...	...	...	5	...	2.52	...	—	—	—	—	—	—	—	—
—Ilves Jrs.	Finland	3	180	...	...	...	3	...	1.00	...	—	—	—	—	—	—	—	—
96-97—Ilves Tampere	Finland	40	2270	22	12	5	108	0	2.85	...	8	479	3	5	29	0	3.63	...
97-98—Ilves Tampere	Finland	48	2555	26	13	3	118	1	2.77	...	9	519	6	3	18	1	2.08	...
98-99—Ilves Tampere	Finland	33	1966	21	12	0	70	5	2.14	...	4	248	1	3	14	...	3.39	...
99-00—Farjestad Karlstad	Sweden	44	2652	...	...	...	118	3	2.67	...	7	439	...	...	19	0	2.60	...
00-01—Kentucky	AHL	44	2466	22	13	5	114	2	2.77	.911	3	197	0	3	8	0	2.44	...
01-02—Cleveland	AHL	*62	*3574	19	*33	7	*178	3	2.99	.904	—	—	—	—	—	—	—	—
—San Jose	NHL	1	10	0	0	0	0	0	0.00	1.00	—	—	—	—	—	—	—	—
02-03—Cleveland	AHL	49	2824	15	30	2	151	1	3.21	.474	—	—	—	—	—	—	—	—
—San Jose	NHL	11	537	4	3	1	21	1	2.35	.927	—	—	—	—	—	—	—	—
03-04—San Jose	NHL	28	1541	12	8	4	53	1	2.06	.930	—	—	—	—	—	—	—	—
04-05—Ilves Tampere	Finland	3	186	0	1	2	8	0	2.58	.930	6	358	3	3	19	0	3.19	.920
NHL Totals (3 years)		40	2088	16	11	5	74	2	2.13	.929								

TRAVERSE, PATRICK — D — STARS

PERSONAL: Born March 14, 1974, in Montreal. ... 6-4/227. ... Shoots left.

TRANSACTIONS/CAREER NOTES: Selected by Ottawa Senators in third round (third Senators pick, 50th overall) of NHL entry draft (June 20, 1992). ... Suffered concussion (January 30, 1999); missed three games. ... Sprained shoulder (February 20, 1999); missed 13 games. ... Bruised right shoulder (February 17, 2000); missed seven games. ... Traded by Senators to Mighty Ducks of Anaheim for D Joel Kwiatkowski (June 12, 2000). ... Traded by Mighty Ducks with LW Andrei Nazarov to Boston Bruins for C Samuel Pahlsson (November 19, 2000). ... Traded by Bruins to Montreal Canadiens for D Eric Weinrich (February 21, 2001). ... Injured neck (April 5, 2001); missed final game of season. ... Sprained knee (November 5, 2001); missed 12 games. ... Suffered concussion (January 10, 2002); missed 12 games. ... Flu (February 27, 2003); missed one game. ... Signed as free agent by Dallas Stars (September 9, 2004). ... Signed as a free agent by Houston of the AHL (September 26, 2004).

Season Team	League	REGULAR SEASON GP	G	A	Pts.	PIM	+/-	PP	SH	PLAYOFFS GP	G	A	Pts.	PIM
91-92—Shawinigan	QMJHL	59	3	11	14	12	...	...	...	10	0	0	0	4
92-93—Shawinigan	QMJHL	53	5	24	29	24	...	...	...	—	—	—	—	—
—New Haven	AHL	2	0	0	0	2	2	0	0	—	—	—	—	—
—St. Jean	QMJHL	15	1	6	7	0	...	...	...	4	0	1	1	2
93-94—Prince Edward	AHL	3	0	1	1	2	-3	0	0	—	—	—	—	—
—St. Jean	QMJHL	66	15	37	52	30	8	3	0	5	0	4	4	4
94-95—Prince Edward	AHL	70	5	13	18	19	-7	1	0	7	0	2	2	0
95-96—Prince Edward	AHL	55	4	21	25	32	...	...	...	5	1	2	3	2
—Ottawa	NHL	5	0	0	0	2	-1	0	0	—	—	—	—	—

T

		REGULAR SEASON								PLAYOFFS				
Season Team	**League**	**GP**	**G**	**A**	**Pts.**	**PIM**	**+/-**	**PP**	**SH**	**GP**	**G**	**A**	**Pts.**	**PIM**
96-97—Worcester	AHL	24	0	4	4	23	-2	0	0	—	—	—	—	—
—Grand Rapids	IHL	10	2	1	3	10	...	...	...	2	0	1	1	2
97-98—Hershey	AHL	71	14	15	29	67	-11	11	0	7	1	3	4	4
98-99—Ottawa	NHL	46	1	9	10	22	12	0	0	—	—	—	—	—
99-00—Ottawa	NHL	66	6	17	23	21	17	1	0	6	0	0	0	2
00-01—Anaheim	NHL	15	1	0	1	6	-6	0	0	—	—	—	—	—
—Boston	NHL	37	2	6	8	14	4	1	0	—	—	—	—	—
—Montreal	NHL	19	2	3	5	10	-8	0	0	—	—	—	—	—
01-02—Montreal	NHL	25	2	3	5	14	-7	2	0	—	—	—	—	—
—Quebec	AHL	4	0	2	2	4	-4	0	0	—	—	—	—	—
02-03—Montreal	NHL	65	0	13	13	24	-9	0	0	—	—	—	—	—
03-04—Hamilton	AHL	80	5	21	26	31	16	2	1	10	1	2	3	0
04-05—Houston	AHL	72	6	9	15	28	0	3	0	5	0	0	0	2
NHL Totals (6 years)		278	14	51	65	113	2	4	0	6	0	0	0	2

TREMBLAY, YANNICK D

PERSONAL: Born November 15, 1975, in Pointe-aux-Trembles, Quebec. ... 6-2/200. ... Shoots right. ... Name pronounced TRAHM-blay.

TRANSACTIONS/CAREER NOTES: Selected by Toronto Maple Leafs in sixth round (fourth Maple Leafs pick, 145th overall) of NHL draft (July 8, 1995). ... Selected by Atlanta Thrashers in expansion draft (June 25, 1999). ... Strained groin (October 23, 1999); missed one game. ... Injured hip (December 8, 1999); missed one game. ... Strained hip flexor (February 7, 2000); missed one game. ... Flu (April 8, 2000); missed two games. ... Flu (December 11, 2000). ... Injured leg (December 19, 2000); missed three games. ... Reinjured leg (December 28, 2000); missed five games. ... Injured shoulder (February 10, 2001); missed remainder of season. ... Dislocated right shoulder (November 4, 2001); missed 10 games. ... Injured groin (March 8, 2002); missed two games. ... Bruised foot (November 16, 2003); missed 13 games. ... Strained hip (January 31, 2004); missed last 29 games of season.

T

		REGULAR SEASON								PLAYOFFS				
Season Team	**League**	**GP**	**G**	**A**	**Pts.**	**PIM**	**+/-**	**PP**	**SH**	**GP**	**G**	**A**	**Pts.**	**PIM**
93-94—St. Thomas Univ.	AUAA	25	2	3	5	10	...	...	...	—	—	—	—	—
94-95—Beauport	QMJHL	70	10	32	42	22	...	...	...	17	6	8	14	6
95-96—Beauport	QMJHL	61	12	33	45	42	...	...	...	20	3	16	19	18
—St. John's	AHL	3	0	1	1	0	...	...	...	—	—	—	—	—
96-97—Sherbrooke	QMJHL	42	21	25	46	212	...	...	...	—	—	—	—	—
—St. John's	AHL	67	7	25	32	34	...	...	...	11	2	9	11	0
—Toronto	NHL	5	0	0	0	0	-4	0	0	—	—	—	—	—
97-98—St. John's	AHL	17	3	6	9	4	-7	2	0	4	0	1	1	5
—Toronto	NHL	38	2	4	6	6	-6	1	0	—	—	—	—	—
98-99—Toronto	NHL	35	2	7	9	16	0	0	0	—	—	—	—	—
99-00—Atlanta	NHL	75	10	21	31	22	-42	4	1	—	—	—	—	—
00-01—Atlanta	NHL	46	4	8	12	30	-6	1	0	—	—	—	—	—
01-02—Atlanta	NHL	66	9	15	24	47	-15	1	0	—	—	—	—	—
02-03—Atlanta	NHL	75	8	22	30	32	-27	5	0	—	—	—	—	—
03-04—Atlanta	NHL	38	2	8	10	13	-13	1	0	—	—	—	—	—
04-05—Mannheim	Germany	14	1	4	5	16	0	0	0	14	2	6	8	6
NHL Totals (8 years)		378	37	85	122	166	-113	13	1					

TREPANIER, PASCAL D/RW

PERSONAL: Born September 4, 1973, in Gaspe, Que. ... 6-0/210. ... Shoots right. ... Name pronounced TREH-puhn-yeh.

TRANSACTIONS/CAREER NOTES: Signed as free agent by Colorado Avalanche (August 30, 1996). ... Selected by Mighty Ducks of Anaheim from Avalanche in waiver draft (October 5, 1998). ... Bruised left leg (March 3, 1999); missed one game. ... Injured in right knee (April 6, 1999) and had surgery; missed remainder of season. ... Suspended five games by NHL for elbowing incident (October 5, 1999). ... Injured head (December 17, 1999); missed six games. ... Bruised left ankle (March 3, 2000); missed nine games. ... Signed as free agent by Nashville Predators (July 16, 2002). ... Traded by Predators to Florida Panthers for G Wade Flaherty (March 9, 2003). ... Signed as free agent by Tampa Bay Lightning (July 23, 2003).

		REGULAR SEASON								PLAYOFFS				
Season Team	**League**	**GP**	**G**	**A**	**Pts.**	**PIM**	**+/-**	**PP**	**SH**	**GP**	**G**	**A**	**Pts.**	**PIM**
90-91—Hull	QMJHL	46	3	3	6	56	...	...	...	4	0	2	2	7
91-92—Trois-Rivieres	QMJHL	53	4	18	22	125	...	...	...	15	3	5	8	21
92-93—Sherbrooke	QMJHL	59	15	33	48	130	...	...	...	15	5	7	12	36
93-94—Sherbrooke	QMJHL	48	16	41	57	67	...	...	...	12	1	8	9	14
94-95—Cornwall	AHL	4	0	0	0	9	...	...	...	—	—	—	—	—
—Dayton	ECHL	36	16	28	44	113	...	...	...	—	—	—	—	—
—Kalamazoo	IHL	14	1	2	3	47	...	...	...	—	—	—	—	—
95-96—Cornwall	AHL	70	13	20	33	142	...	...	...	8	1	2	3	24
96-97—Hershey	AHL	73	14	39	53	151	...	...	...	23	6	13	19	59
97-98—Colorado	NHL	15	0	1	1	18	-2	0	0	—	—	—	—	—
—Hershey	AHL	43	13	18	31	105	3	8	0	7	4	2	6	8
98-99—Anaheim	NHL	45	2	4	6	48	0	0	0	—	—	—	—	—
99-00—Anaheim	NHL	37	0	4	4	54	2	0	0	—	—	—	—	—
00-01—Anaheim	NHL	57	6	4	10	73	-12	3	0	—	—	—	—	—
01-02—Colorado	NHL	74	4	9	13	59	4	2	0	2	0	0	0	0
02-03—Nashville	NHL	1	0	0	0	0	0	0	0	—	—	—	—	—
—Milwaukee	AHL	52	9	15	24	33	0	2	1	—	—	—	—	—
—San Antonio	AHL	12	4	6	10	10	-2	2	0	2	0	0	0	2
03-04—Hershey	AHL	75	11	33	44	53	-31	6	0	—	—	—	—	—
04-05—Nurnberg	Germany	52	15	39	54	66	...	...	...	6	3	1	4	6
NHL Totals (6 years)		229	12	22	34	252	-8	5	0	2	0	0	0	0

TRIPP, JOHN RW

PERSONAL: Born May 4, 1977, in Kingston, Ont. ... 6-3/223. ... Shoots right.
TRANSACTIONS/CAREER NOTES: Selected by Colorado Avalanche in third round (third Avalanche pick, 77th overall) of NHL entry draft (July 8, 1995). ... Returned to draft pool by Avalanche and selected by Calgary Flames in second round (third Flames pick, 42nd overall) of NHL entry draft (June 21, 1997). ... Signed as free agent by New York Rangers (September 3, 2002), ... Signed as free agent by Los Angeles Kings (August 6, 2003). ... Fractured nose (January 20, 2004); missed seven games.

		REGULAR SEASON								PLAYOFFS				
Season Team	**League**	**GP**	**G**	**A**	**Pts.**	**PIM**	**+/-**	**PP**	**SH**	**GP**	**G**	**A**	**Pts.**	**PIM**
93-94—St. Mary's Jr. B	OHA	42	15	29	44	116	...	...	...	—	—	—	—	—
94-95—Oshawa	OHL	58	6	11	17	53	...	2	0	7	0	1	1	4
95-96—Oshawa	OHL	56	13	14	27	95	...	...	...	5	1	1	2	13
96-97—Oshawa	OHL	59	28	20	48	126	30	6	2	18	16	10	26	42
97-98—Roanoke	ECHL	9	0	2	2	22	...	...	...	—	—	—	—	—
—Saint John	AHL	61	1	11	12	66	-4	0	0	2	0	1	1	0
98-99—Saint John	AHL	2	0	0	0	10	0	0	0	—	—	—	—	—
—Johnstown	ECHL	7	2	0	2	12	-1	2	0	—	—	—	—	—
99-00—Johnstown	ECHL	38	13	11	24	64	...	...	...	—	—	—	—	—
—Saint John	AHL	29	8	7	15	38	...	...	...	3	0	0	0	2
00-01—Hershey	AHL	5	0	1	1	0	...	...	...	—	—	—	—	—
—Milwaukee	IHL	6	0	1	1	31	...	...	...	—	—	—	—	—
—Pensacola	ECHL	36	19	14	33	110	...	...	...	—	—	—	—	—
—Houston	IHL	15	0	6	6	14	...	...	...	—	—	—	—	—
01-02—Pensacola	ECHL	49	25	27	52	114	7	10	5	—	—	—	—	—
—Hartford	AHL	23	4	9	13	22	-2	3	0	10	4	2	6	17
02-03—Hartford	AHL	57	29	21	50	68	12	10	0	2	0	0	0	2
—New York Rangers	NHL	9	1	2	3	2	1	0	0	—	—	—	—	—
03-04—Manchester	AHL	24	8	7	15	33	0	4	0	—	—	—	—	—
—Los Angeles	NHL	34	1	5	6	33	-4	0	0	—	—	—	—	—
04-05—Mannheim	Germany	44	9	16	25	136	-10	3	0	14	2	3	5	54
NHL Totals (2 years)		43	2	7	9	35	-3	0	0					

TRNKA, PAVEL D

PERSONAL: Born July 27, 1976, in Plzen, Czechoslovakia. ... 6-2/206. ... Shoots left. ... Name pronounced TRIHN-kuh.
TRANSACTIONS/CAREER NOTES: Selected by Mighty Ducks of Anaheim in 5th round (5th Mighty Ducks pick, 106th overall) of entry draft (1994). ... Concussion (January 12, 1998); missed one game. ... Strained groin (December 8, 1999); missed five games. ... Sprained ankle (March 17, 2000); missed final nine games of season. ... Sprained ankle (October 8, 2000); missed 17 games. ... Strained groin (October 8, 2002); missed 16 games. ... Traded by Mighty Ducks with C Matt Cullen and 4th-round pick (D James Pemberton) in 2003 entry draft to Florida Panthers for D Sandis Ozolinsh and D Lance Ward (January 30, 2003). ... Injured knee (February 22, 2003); missed five games. ... Injured thigh (March 15, 2003); missed one game. ... Injured groin (September 25, 2003); missed two games. ... Injured shoulder (November 18, 2003); missed two games. ... Bruised ribs (December 11, 2003); missed five games. ... Back spasms (March 30, 2004); missed last four games of season.

		REGULAR SEASON								PLAYOFFS				
Season Team	**League**	**GP**	**G**	**A**	**Pts.**	**PIM**	**+/-**	**PP**	**SH**	**GP**	**G**	**A**	**Pts.**	**PIM**
93-94—Skoda Plzen	Czech Rep.	12	0	1	1	...	...	...	...	—	—	—	—	—
94-95—HC Kladno	Czech Rep.	28	0	5	5	...	...	...	...	—	—	—	—	—
—Interconex Plzen	Czech Rep.	6	0	0	0	...	...	...	...	...	...	...	...	...
95-96—Baltimore	AHL	69	2	6	8	44	...	...	...	6	0	0	0	2
96-97—Baltimore	AHL	69	6	14	20	86	5	2	0	3	0	0	0	2
97-98—Cincinnati	AHL	23	3	5	8	28	-2	1	0	—	—	—	—	—
—Anaheim	NHL	48	3	4	7	40	-4	1	0	—	—	—	—	—
98-99—Anaheim	NHL	63	0	4	4	60	-6	0	0	4	0	1	1	2
99-00—Anaheim	NHL	57	2	15	17	34	12	0	0	—	—	—	—	—
00-01—Anaheim	NHL	59	1	7	8	42	-12	0	0	—	—	—	—	—
01-02—Anaheim	NHL	71	2	11	13	66	-5	1	0	—	—	—	—	—
02-03—Anaheim	NHL	24	3	6	9	6	2	1	0	—	—	—	—	—
—Florida	NHL	22	0	3	3	24	-1	0	0	—	—	—	—	—
03-04—Florida	NHL	67	3	13	16	51	2	1	0	—	—	—	—	—
04-05—Plzen	Czech Rep.	47	7	10	17	103	12	...	...	—	—	—	—	—
NHL Totals (7 years)		411	14	63	77	323	-12	4	0	4	0	1	1	2

TSELIOS, NIKOS D

PERSONAL: Born January 20, 1979, in Oak Park, Ill. ... 6-5/210. ... Shoots left. ... Cousin of Chris Chelios, D, Detroit Red Wings. ... Name pronounced NEE-kohz CHEL-yoz.
TRANSACTIONS/CAREER NOTES: Selected by Carolina Hurricanes in first round (first Hurricanes pick, 22nd overall) of NHL entry draft (June 21, 1997). ... Signed as free agent by Phoenix Coyotes (July 21, 2003).

		REGULAR SEASON								PLAYOFFS				
Season Team	**League**	**GP**	**G**	**A**	**Pts.**	**PIM**	**+/-**	**PP**	**SH**	**GP**	**G**	**A**	**Pts.**	**PIM**
95-96—Chicago	MNHL	27	5	8	13	40	...	...	...	—	—	—	—	—
96-97—Belleville	OHL	64	9	37	46	61	...	...	...	—	—	—	—	—
97-98—Belleville	OHL	20	2	10	12	16	...	...	...	—	—	—	—	—
—Plymouth	OHL	41	8	20	28	27	22	...	...	15	1	8	9	27
98-99—Plymouth	OHL	60	21	39	60	60	25	...	...	11	4	10	14	8
99-00—Cincinnati	IHL	80	3	19	22	75	...	...	...	10	0	2	2	4
00-01—Cincinnati	IHL	79	7	18	25	98	...	...	...	5	0	3	3	0
01-02—Lowell	AHL	70	3	16	19	64	13	0	0	—	—	—	—	—

Season Team	League	REGULAR SEASON GP	G	A	Pts.	PIM	+/-	PP	SH	PLAYOFFS GP	G	A	Pts.	PIM
—Carolina	NHL	2	0	0	0	6	-2	0	0	—	—	—	—	—
02-03—Lowell	AHL	61	4	8	12	65	-24	2	0	6	0	0	0	4
—Springfield	AHL	13	0	2	2	12	0	0	0	—	—	—	—	—
03-04—Springfield	AHL	75	5	8	13	105	-16	2	0	—	—	—	—	—
04-05—Springfield	AHL	35	3	6	9	37	-10	0	0	—	—	—	—	—
—Utah	AHL	5	1	1	2	4	-2	1	0	—	—	—	—	—
NHL Totals (1 year)		2	0	0	0	6	-2	0	0					

TUCKER, DARCY RW MAPLE LEAFS

PERSONAL: Born March 15, 1975, in Castor, Alta. ... 5-10/178. ... Shoots left.

TRANSACTIONS/CAREER NOTES: Selected by Montreal Canadiens in sixth round (eighth Canadiens pick, 151st overall) of NHL entry draft (June 26, 1993). ... Bruised knee (December 16, 1996); missed one game. ... Traded by Canadiens with RW Stephane Richer and D David Wilkie to Tampa Bay Lightning for C Patrick Poulin, RW Mick Vukota and D Igor Ulanov (January 15, 1998). ... Suspended two games by NHL for spearing incident (December 28, 1999). ... Traded by Lightning with fourth-round pick (RW Miguel Delisle) in 2000 draft to Toronto Maple Leafs for RW Mike Johnson, D Marek Posmyk and fifth-(RW Pavel Sedov) and sixth-round (D Aaron Gionet) picks in 2000 draft (February 9, 2000). ... Suffered concussion (November 19, 2001); missed three games. ... Suspended five games by NHL for unsportsmanlike conduct (March 5, 2003). ... Suspended five games by NHL for fighting incident (March 6, 2003). ... Injured leg (April 9, 2003); missed one game. ... Injured left eye (January 21, 2004); missed five games. ... Strained abdomen (March 9, 2004); missed remainder of regular season.

Season Team	League	REGULAR SEASON GP	G	A	Pts.	PIM	+/-	PP	SH	PLAYOFFS GP	G	A	Pts.	PIM
91-92—Kamloops	WHL	26	3	10	13	42	...	...	...	9	0	1	1	16
92-93—Kamloops	WHL	67	31	58	89	155	...	...	...	13	7	6	13	34
93-94—Kamloops	WHL	66	52	88	140	143	60	20	2	19	9	*18	*27	43
94-95—Kamloops	WHL	64	64	73	137	94	55	22	3	21	16	15	31	19
95-96—Fredericton	AHL	74	29	64	93	174	...	...	...	7	7	3	10	14
—Montreal	NHL	3	0	0	0	0	-1	0	0	—	—	—	—	—
96-97—Montreal	NHL	73	7	13	20	110	-5	1	0	4	0	0	0	0
97-98—Montreal	NHL	39	1	5	6	57	-6	0	0	—	—	—	—	—
—Tampa Bay	NHL	35	6	8	14	89	-8	1	1	—	—	—	—	—
98-99—Tampa Bay	NHL	82	21	22	43	176	-34	8	2	—	—	—	—	—
99-00—Tampa Bay	NHL	50	14	20	34	108	-15	1	0	—	—	—	—	—
—Toronto	NHL	27	7	10	17	55	3	0	2	12	4	2	6	15
00-01—Toronto	NHL	82	16	21	37	141	6	2	0	11	0	2	2	6
01-02—Toronto	NHL	77	24	35	59	92	24	7	0	17	4	4	8	38
02-03—Toronto	NHL	77	10	26	36	119	-7	4	1	6	0	3	3	6
03-04—Toronto	NHL	64	21	11	32	68	4	8	1	12	2	0	2	14
NHL Totals (9 years)		609	127	171	298	1015	-39	32	7	62	10	11	21	79

TUGNUTT, RON G

PERSONAL: Born October 22, 1967, in Scarborough, Ont. ... 5-11/160. ... Catches left.

TRANSACTIONS/CAREER NOTES: Selected by Quebec Nordiques in fourth round (fourth Nordiques pick, 81st overall) of NHL draft (June 21, 1986). ... Sprained ankle (March 1989). ... Sprained knee (January 13, 1990). ... Injured hamstring (January 29, 1991); missed 11 games. ... Traded by Nordiques with LW Brad Zavisha to Edmonton Oilers for LW Martin Rucinsky (March 10, 1992). ... Selected by Mighty Ducks of Anaheim in NHL expansion draft (June 24, 1993). ... Traded by Mighty Ducks to Montreal Canadiens for C Stephan Lebeau (February 20, 1994). ... Strained knee (January 28, 1995); missed five games. ... Signed as free agent by Washington Capitals (September 20, 1995). ... Signed as free agent by Ottawa Senators (July 17, 1996). ... Strained hip flexor (January 31, 1998); missed two games. ... Injured right knee (March 6, 1999); missed two games. ... Strained left knee before 1999-2000 season; missed two games. ... Reinjured left knee (November 28, 1999); missed three games. ... Flu (January 28, 2000); missed three games. ... Traded by Senators with D Janne Laukkanen to Pittsburgh Penguins for G Tom Barrasso (March 14, 2000). ... Signed as free agent by Columbus Blue Jackets (July 4, 2000). ... Strained hip flexor (December 2, 2000); missed two games. ... Sprained thumb (December 29, 2000); missed five games. ... Traded by Blue Jackets with second-round pick (F Janos Vas) in 2002 draft to Dallas Stars for first-round pick (traded to Buffalo; Sabre selected LW Dan Paille) in 2002 draft (June 18, 2002). ... Injured knee (December 7, 2003); missed four games. ... Injured groin (January 15, 2004); missed 12 games.

Season Team	League	REGULAR SEASON GP	Min.	W	L	T	GA	SO	GAA	SV%	PLAYOFFS GP	Min.	W	L	GA	SO	GAA	SV%
84-85—Peterborough	OHL	18	938	7	4	2	59	0	3.77	...	—	—	—	—	—	—	—	—
85-86—Peterborough	OHL	26	1543	18	7	0	74	1	2.88	...	3	133	2	0	6	0	2.71	...
86-87—Peterborough	OHL	31	1891	21	7	2	88	2	*2.79	...	6	374	3	3	21	1	3.37	...
87-88—Quebec	NHL	6	284	2	3	0	16	0	3.38	.870	—	—	—	—	—	—	—	—
—Fredericton	AHL	34	1962	20	9	4	118	1	3.61	...	4	204	1	2	11	0	3.24	...
88-89—Quebec	NHL	26	1367	10	10	3	82	0	3.60	.892	—	—	—	—	—	—	—	—
—Halifax	AHL	24	1368	14	7	2	79	1	3.46	...	—	—	—	—	—	—	—	—
89-90—Quebec	NHL	35	1978	5	24	3	152	0	4.61	.859	—	—	—	—	—	—	—	—
—Halifax	AHL	6	366	1	5	0	23	0	3.77	...	—	—	—	—	—	—	—	—
90-91—Halifax	AHL	2	100	0	1	0	8	0	4.80	...	—	—	—	—	—	—	—	—
—Quebec	NHL	56	3144	12	29	10	212	0	4.05	8.000	—	—	—	—	—	—	—	—
91-92—Quebec	NHL	30	1583	6	17	3	106	1	4.02	.864	—	—	—	—	—	—	—	—
—Halifax	AHL	8	447	3	3	1	30	0	4.03	...	—	—	—	—	—	—	—	—
—Edmonton	NHL	3	124	1	1	0	10	0	4.84	.863	2	60	0	0	3	0	3.00	.912
92-93—Edmonton	NHL	26	1338	9	12	2	93	0	4.17	.879	—	—	—	—	—	—	—	—
93-94—Anaheim	NHL	28	1520	10	15	1	76	1	3.00	.908	—	—	—	—	—	—	—	—
—Montreal	NHL	8	378	2	3	1	24	0	3.81	.860	1	59	0	1	5	0	5.08	.800
94-95—Montreal	NHL	7	346	1	3	1	18	0	3.12	.895	—	—	—	—	—	—	—	—
95-96—Portland	AHL	58	3067	21	23	6	171	2	3.35	...	13	781	7	6	36	1	2.77	...
96-97—Ottawa	NHL	37	1991	17	15	1	93	3	2.80	.895	7	425	3	4	14	1	1.98	.917

Season Team	League	REGULAR SEASON GP	Min.	W	L	T	GA	SO	GAA	SV%	PLAYOFFS GP	Min.	W	L	GA	SO	GAA	SV%
97-98—Ottawa	NHL	42	2236	15	14	8	84	3	2.25	.905	2	74	0	1	6	0	4.86	.760
98-99—Ottawa	NHL	43	2508	22	10	8	75	3	*1.79	.925	2	118	0	2	6	0	3.05	.854
99-00—Ottawa	NHL	44	2435	18	12	8	103	4	2.54	.899	—	—	—	—	—	—	—	—
—Pittsburgh	NHL	7	374	4	2	0	15	0	2.41	.924	11	746	6	5	22	2	1.77	*.945
00-01—Columbus	NHL	53	3129	22	25	5	127	4	2.44	.917	—	—	—	—	—	—	—	—
01-02—Columbus	NHL	44	2502	12	27	3	119	2	2.85	.900	—	—	—	—	—	—	—	—
02-03—Dallas	NHL	31	1701	15	10	5	70	4	2.47	.896	—	—	—	—	—	—	—	—
03-04—Dallas	NHL	11	548	3	7	0	22	1	2.41	.900	—	—	—	—	—	—	—	—
—Utah	AHL	5	280	1	3	1	14	0	3.00	.881	—	—	—	—	—	—	—	—
NHL Totals (16 years)		537	29486	186	239	62	1497	26	3.05	.895	25	1482	9	13	56	3	2.27	.919

TUKONEN, LAURI — RW — KINGS

PERSONAL: Born September 1, 1986, in Hyvinkaa, Finland. ... 6-2/198. ... Shoots right.
TRANSACTIONS/CAREER NOTES: Selected by Los Angeles Kings in 1st round (1st Kings pick, 11th overall) of entry draft (June 26, 2004).

Season Team	League	REGULAR SEASON GP	G	A	Pts.	PIM	+/-	PP	SH	PLAYOFFS GP	G	A	Pts.	PIM
03-04—Blues Espoo	Finland	35	3	3	6	16	...	...	...	7	0	0	0	0
04-05—Espoo	Finland	43	5	5	10	10	-6	...	...	—	—	—	—	—

TURCO, MARTY — G — STARS

PERSONAL: Born August 13, 1975, in Sault Ste. Marie, Ont. ... 5-11/183. ... Catches left.
TRANSACTIONS/CAREER NOTES: Selected by Dallas Stars in fifth round (fourth Stars pick, 124th overall) of NHL draft (June 29, 1994). ... Suspended one game by NHL for high-sticking (January 21, 2003). ... Sprained ankle (February 11, 2003); missed 18 games. ... Suspended four games by NHL for high-sticking (March 25, 2004).

Season Team	League	REGULAR SEASON GP	Min.	W	L	T	GA	SO	GAA	SV%	PLAYOFFS GP	Min.	W	L	GA	SO	GAA	SV%
93-94—Cambridge Jr. B	OHA	34	1937	...	...	...	114	0	3.53	...	—	—	—	—	—	—	—	—
94-95—Univ. of Michigan	CCHA	37	2064	27	7	1	95	1	2.76	.894	—	—	—	—	—	—	—	—
95-96—Univ. of Michigan	CCHA	42	2334	34	7	1	84	5	2.16	...	—	—	—	—	—	—	—	—
96-97—Univ. of Michigan	CCHA	41	2296	33	4	4	87	4	2.27	.894	—	—	—	—	—	—	—	—
97-98—Univ. of Michigan	CCHA	*45	*2640	*33	10	1	95	3	2.16	...	—	—	—	—	—	—	—	—
98-99—Michigan	IHL	54	3127	24	17	10	136	1	2.61	.920	5	300	2	3	14	0	2.80	.918
99-00—Michigan	IHL	60	3399	28	*27	7	*139	*7	2.45	...	—	—	—	—	—	—	—	—
00-01—Dallas	NHL	26	1266	13	6	1	40	3	*1.90	*.925	—	—	—	—	—	—	—	—
01-02—Dallas	NHL	31	1519	15	6	2	53	2	2.09	.921	—	—	—	—	—	—	—	—
02-03—Dallas	NHL	55	3203	31	10	10	92	7	*1.72	*.932	12	798	6	6	25	0	1.88	.919
03-04—Dallas	NHL	73	4359	37	21	13	144	9	1.98	.913	5	325	1	4	18	0	3.32	.849
04-05—Djurgarden Stockholm	Sweden	6	356	...	...	...	12	1	2.02	.932	—	—	—	—	—	—	—	—
NHL Totals (4 years)		185	10347	96	43	26	329	21	1.91	.922	17	1123	7	10	43	0	2.30	.900

TURGEON, PIERRE — C/LW — AVALANCHE

PERSONAL: Born August 28, 1969, in Rouyn, Que. ... 6-1/200. ... Shoots left. ... Brother of Sylvain Turgeon, LW with four NHL teams (1983-84 through 1994-95). ... Name pronounced TUHR-zhaw.
TRANSACTIONS/CAREER NOTES: Selected by Buffalo Sabres in 1st round (1st Sabres pick, 1rst overall) of entry draft (June 13, 1987). ... Traded by Sabres with RW Benoit Hogue, D Uwe Krupp and C Dave McLlwain to New York Islanders for C Pat LaFontaine, LW Randy Wood, D Randy Hillier and future considerations; Sabres later received 4th-round pick (D Dean Melanson) in 1992 draft to complete deal (October 25, 1991). ... Injured right knee (January 3, 1992); missed three games. ... Separated shoulder (April 28, 1993); missed six playoff games. ... Tendinitis in right wrist (October 5, 1993); missed one game. ... Flu (December 29, 1993); missed one game. ... Fractured cheekbone (January 26, 1994); missed 12 games. ... Traded by Islanders with D Vladimir Malakhov to Montreal Canadiens for LW Kirk Muller, D Mathieu Schneider and C Craig Darby (April 5, 1995). ... Strained shoulder (November 8, 1995); missed two games. ... Bruised thigh (October 24, 1996); missed one game. ... Traded by Canadiens with C Craig Conroy and D Rory Fitzpatrick to St. Louis Blues for LW Shayne Corson, D Murray Baron and 5th-round pick (D Gennady Razin) in 1997 draft (October 29, 1996). ... Fractured right forearm (October 4, 1997); missed 22 games. ... Fractured hand (December 14, 1998); missed 14 games. ... Back spasms (November 20, 1999); missed four games. ... Flu (January 11, 2000); missed one game. ... Injured thumb (January 29, 2000); missed 24 games. ... Suffered concussion (January 11, 2001); missed three games. ... Signed as free agent by Dallas Stars (July 1, 2001). ... Sprained ankle (October 29, 2001); missed 12 games. ... Strained shoulder (March 12, 2002); missed four games. ... Strained hip (February 8, 2003); missed three games. ... Fractured ankle (March 8, 2003); missed 12 games. ... Sprained neck (November 15, 2003); missed three games. ... Injured hip (November 29, 2003); missed two games. ... Flu (December 12, 2003); missed one game. ... Placed on waivers by Stars (July 27, 2005). ... Signed as free agent by Colorado Avalanche (Aug. 3, 2005).
STATISTICAL PLATEAUS: Three-goal games: 1989-90 (1), 1990-91 (1), 1991-92 (2), 1992-93 (4), 1993-94 (2), 1994-95 (1), 1995-96 (1), 1998-99 (1), 1999-00 (1), 2000-01 (1). Total: 15.

Season Team	League	REGULAR SEASON GP	G	A	Pts.	PIM	+/-	PP	SH	PLAYOFFS GP	G	A	Pts.	PIM
85-86—Granby	QMJHL	69	47	67	114	31	...	...	...	—	—	—	—	—
86-87—Granby	QMJHL	58	69	85	154	8	...	...	...	7	9	6	15	15
87-88—Buffalo	NHL	76	14	28	42	34	-8	8	0	6	4	3	7	4
88-89—Buffalo	NHL	80	34	54	88	26	-2	19	0	5	3	5	8	2
89-90—Buffalo	NHL	80	40	66	106	29	10	17	1	6	2	4	6	2
90-91—Buffalo	NHL	78	32	47	79	26	14	13	2	6	3	1	4	6
91-92—Buffalo	NHL	8	2	6	8	4	-1	0	0	—	—	—	—	—
—New York Islanders	NHL	69	38	49	87	16	8	13	0	—	—	—	—	—

T

Season Team	League	GP	G	A	Pts.	PIM	+/-	PP	SH	GP	G	A	Pts.	PIM
		REGULAR SEASON								PLAYOFFS				
92-93—New York Islanders.....	NHL	83	58	74	132	26	-1	24	0	11	6	7	13	0
93-94—New York Islanders.....	NHL	69	38	56	94	18	14	10	4	4	0	1	1	0
94-95—New York Islanders.....	NHL	34	13	14	27	10	-12	3	2	—	—	—	—	—
—Montreal	NHL	15	11	9	20	4	12	2	0	—	—	—	—	—
95-96—Montreal	NHL	80	38	58	96	44	19	17	1	6	2	4	6	2
96-97—Montreal	NHL	9	1	10	11	2	4	0	0	—	—	—	—	—
—St. Louis	NHL	69	25	49	74	12	4	5	0	5	1	1	2	2
97-98—St. Louis	NHL	60	22	46	68	24	13	6	0	10	4	4	8	2
98-99—St. Louis	NHL	67	31	34	65	36	4	10	0	13	4	9	13	6
99-00—St. Louis	NHL	52	26	40	66	8	30	8	0	7	0	7	7	0
00-01—St. Louis	NHL	79	30	52	82	37	14	11	0	15	5	10	15	2
01-02—Dallas..........................	NHL	66	15	32	47	16	-4	7	0	—	—	—	—	—
02-03—Dallas..........................	NHL	65	12	30	42	18	4	3	0	5	0	1	1	0
03-04—Dallas..........................	NHL	76	15	25	40	20	17	6	0	5	1	3	4	2
NHL Totals (17 years)..........		1215	495	779	1274	410	139	182	10	104	35	60	95	30

TVERDOVSKY, OLEG — D — HURRICANES

PERSONAL: Born May 18, 1976, in Donetsk, U.S.S.R. ... 6-1/205. ... Shoots left. ... Name pronounced OH-lehg teh-vuhr-DAHV-skee.
TRANSACTIONS/CAREER NOTES: Selected by Mighty Ducks of Anaheim in 1st round (1st Mighty Ducks pick, 2nd overall) of entry draft (June 28, 1994). ... Pink eye (March 15, 1995); missed two games. ... Traded by Mighty Ducks with C Chad Kilger and 3rd-round pick (D Per-Anton Lundstrom) in 1996 draft to Winnipeg Jets for C Marc Chouinard, RW Teemu Selanne and 4th-round pick (traded to Toronto) in 1996 draft (February 7, 1996). ... Jets franchise moved to Phoenix and renamed Coyotes for 1996-97 season; NHL approved move on January 18, 1996. ... Pulled rib muscle (December 23, 1997); missed one game. ... Traded by Coyotes to Mighty Ducks for C Travis Green and first-round pick (C Scott Kelman) in 1999 draft (June 26, 1999). ... Strained groin (March 24, 2002); missed remainder of season. ... Traded by Mighty Ducks with LW Jeff Friesen and RW Maxim Balmochnykh to New Jersey Devils for RW Petr Sykora, C Igor Pohanka, D Mike Commodore and G J.F. Damphousse (July 7, 2002). ... Bruised back (November 16, 2002); missed one game. ... Flu (December 23, 2002); missed two games. ... Viral illness (January 3, 2003); missed five games. ... Had recurrence of viral illness (January 17, 2003); missed 20 games. ... Signed as free agent by Avangard Omsk of the Russian League (August 29, 2003). ... Signed as free agent by Carolina Hurricanes (Aug. 5, 2005).

T

Season Team	League	GP	G	A	Pts.	PIM	+/-	PP	SH	GP	G	A	Pts.	PIM
		REGULAR SEASON								PLAYOFFS				
92-93—Soviet Wings	CIS	21	0	1	1	6	...	...	...	6	0	0	0	...
93-94—Soviet Wings	CIS	46	4	10	14	22	...	...	...	3	1	0	1	2
94-95—Brandon......................	WHL	7	1	4	5	4	1	0	0	—	—	—	—	—
—Anaheim	NHL	36	3	9	12	14	-6	1	1	—	—	—	—	—
95-96—Anaheim	NHL	51	7	15	22	35	0	2	0	—	—	—	—	—
—Winnipeg	NHL	31	0	8	8	6	-7	0	0	6	0	1	1	0
96-97—Phoenix.......................	NHL	82	10	45	55	30	-5	3	1	7	0	1	1	0
97-98—Hamilton......................	AHL	9	8	6	14	2	12	1	2	—	—	—	—	—
—Phoenix.......................	NHL	46	7	12	19	12	1	4	0	6	0	7	7	0
98-99—Phoenix.......................	NHL	82	7	18	25	32	11	2	0	6	0	2	2	6
99-00—Anaheim	NHL	82	15	36	51	30	5	5	0	—	—	—	—	—
00-01—Anaheim	NHL	82	14	39	53	32	-11	8	0	—	—	—	—	—
01-02—Anaheim	NHL	73	6	26	32	31	0	2	0	—	—	—	—	—
—Russian Oly. team.......	Int'l	6	1	1	2	0	...	...	...	—	—	—	—	—
02-03—New Jersey.................	NHL	50	5	8	13	22	2	2	0	15	0	3	3	0
03-04—Avangard Omsk	Russian	57	16	17	33	58	8	...	...	11	0	2	2	2
04-05—Avangard Omsk	Russian	48	5	15	20	65	8	...	...	11	0	3	3	35
NHL Totals (9 years)...........		615	74	216	290	244	-10	29	2	40	0	14	14	6

TVRDON, ROMAN — C/LW — CAPITALS

PERSONAL: Born January 29, 1981, in Trencin, Czechoslovakia. ... 6-0/200. ... Shoots left. ... Name pronounced tuh-VUHR-duhn.
TRANSACTIONS/CAREER NOTES: Selected by Washington Capitals in fifth round (sixth Capitals pick, 132nd overall) of NHL entry draft (June 26, 1999).

Season Team	League	GP	G	A	Pts.	PIM	+/-	PP	SH	GP	G	A	Pts.	PIM
		REGULAR SEASON								PLAYOFFS				
97-98—Dukla Trencin.............	Slovakia Jrs.	48	4	12	16	...	...	...	...	—	—	—	—	—
98-99—Dukla Trencin.............	Slovakia Jrs.	49	23	23	46	20	...	...	...	6	4	4	8	4
99-00—Spokane......................	WHL	69	26	44	70	40	19	10	0	14	4	7	11	16
00-01—Spokane......................	WHL	62	28	34	62	55	...	...	...	12	5	11	16	0
01-02—Portland......................	AHL	49	5	9	14	22	-5	1	0	—	—	—	—	—
02-03—Portland......................	AHL	35	5	4	9	17	0	1	0	—	—	—	—	—
03-04—Washington	NHL	9	0	1	1	2	-3	0	0	—	—	—	—	—
—Portland......................	AHL	51	2	4	6	20	4	0	0	7	0	0	0	2
NHL Totals (1 year).............		9	0	1	1	2	-3	0	0					

TYUTIN, FEDOR — D — RANGERS

PERSONAL: Born July 19, 1983, in Izhevsk, U.S.S.R. ... 6-2/207. ... Shoots left. ... Name pronounced TOOT-ihn.
TRANSACTIONS/CAREER NOTES: Selected by New York Rangers in second round (second Rangers pick, 40th overall) of NHL draft (June 23, 2001).

Season Team	League	GP	G	A	Pts.	PIM	+/-	PP	SH	GP	G	A	Pts.	PIM
		REGULAR SEASON								PLAYOFFS				
00-01—SKA St. Petersburg.....	Russian	34	2	4	6	20	...	...	...	—	—	—	—	—
01-02—Guelph.........................	OHL	53	19	40	59	54	...	...	...	9	2	8	10	8

Season Team	League	GP	G	A	Pts.	PIM	+/-	PP	SH	GP	G	A	Pts.	PIM
		REGULAR SEASON								PLAYOFFS				
02-03—SKA-2 St. Petersburg .	Rus. Div.	10	1	1	2	16	...	...	...	5	0	0	0	4
—Kazan	Rus. Div.	10	0	0	0	8	...	...	...	—	—	—	—	—
03-04—New York Rangers	NHL	25	2	5	7	14	-4	0	1	—	—	—	—	—
—Hartford	AHL	43	5	9	14	48	7	0	0	16	0	5	5	18
04-05—Hartford	AHL	13	2	1	3	10	0	1	0	—	—	—	—	—
—SKA St. Petersburg	Russian	35	5	3	8	24	-3	...	...	—	—	—	—	—
NHL Totals (1 year)		25	2	5	7	14	-4	0	1					

UCHEVATOV, VICTOR D PANTHERS

PERSONAL: Born February 10, 1983, in Angarsk, U.S.S.R. ... 6-4/205. ... Shoots left. ... Name pronounced oh-shuh-VAH-tahf.
TRANSACTIONS/CAREER NOTES: Selected by New Jersey Devils in second round (fourth Devils pick, 60th overall) of NHL draft (June 23, 2001). ... Traded by Devils with LW Christian Berglund to Florida Panthers for C Viktor Kozlov (March 1, 2004).

Season Team	League	GP	G	A	Pts.	PIM	+/-	PP	SH	GP	G	A	Pts.	PIM
		REGULAR SEASON								PLAYOFFS				
00-01—Yaroslavl 2	CIS.2	28	1	1	2	74	...	...	...	—	—	—	—	—
01-02—Albany	AHL	64	0	2	2	50	-16	0	0	—	—	—	—	—
02-03—Albany	AHL	55	0	2	2	27	-14	0	0	—	—	—	—	—
03-04—Albany	AHL	52	0	3	3	46	-15	0	0	—	—	—	—	—
—San Antonio	AHL	22	3	4	7	6	2	0	0	—	—	—	—	—
04-05—San Antonio	AHL	48	1	1	2	47	-17	0	0	—	—	—	—	—

ULANOV, IGOR D OILERS

PERSONAL: Born October 1, 1969, in Krasnokamsk, U.S.S.R. ... 6-3/215. ... Shoots left. ... Name pronounced EE-gohr yoo-LAH-nahf.
TRANSACTIONS/CAREER NOTES: Selected by Winnipeg Jets in 10th round (8th Jets pick, 203rd overall) of entry draft (June 22, 1991). ... Back spasms (March 7, 1992); missed five games. ... Fractured foot (March 16, 1995); missed 19 games. ... Traded by Jets with C Mike Eagles to Washington Capitals for 3rd-round (traded to Dallas; Stars selected Sergey Gusev) and 5th-round (G Brian Elder) picks in 1995 draft (April 7, 1995). ... Traded by Capitals to Chicago Blackhawks for 3rd-round pick (G Dave Weninger) in 1996 draft (October 17, 1995). ... Traded by Blackhawks with LW Patrick Poulin and 2nd-round pick (D Jeff Paul) in 1996 draft to Tampa Bay Lightning for D Enrico Ciccone (March 20, 1996). ... Injured ribs (October 5, 1996); missed three games. ... Strained groin (February 14, 1997); missed six games. ... Traded by Lightning with C Patrick Poulin and RW Mick Vukota to Montreal Canadiens for RW Stephane Richer, C Darcy Tucker and D David Wilkie (January 15, 1998). ... Torn ligaments in left knee (January 21, 1998); missed remainder of season. ... Fractured left foot (November 3, 1999); missed 13 games. ... Traded by Canadiens with D Alain Nasreddine to Edmonton Oilers for D Christian Laflamme and D Mathieu Descoteaux (March 9, 2000). ... Bruised ankle (November 19, 2000); missed one game. ... Bruised right hand (December 2, 2000); missed two games. ... Suspended two games by NHL for cross-checking incident (December 14, 2000). ... Injured left eye (February 24, 2001); missed three games. ... Reinjured left eye (March 2, 2001); missed six games. ... Signed as free agent by New York Rangers (July 1, 2001). ... Suspended seven games for cross-checking incident (October 12, 2001). ... Traded by Rangers with D Filip Novak, 1st- (traded to Calgary; Flames selected LW Eric Nystrom) and 2nd-round (C/RW Rob Globke) picks in 2002 and 4th-round pick (traded to Atlanta; Thrashers selected RW Guillaume Desbiens) in 2003 draft to Florida Panthers for RW Pavel Bure and 2nd-round pick (C Lee Falardeau) in 2002 draft (March 18, 2002). ... Injured toe (March 5, 2003); missed two games. ... Signed as free agent by Edmonton Oilers (January 5, 2004). ... Injured groin (January 17, 2004); missed one game. ... Signed as free agent by Oilers (Aug. 5, 2005).

Season Team	League	GP	G	A	Pts.	PIM	+/-	PP	SH	GP	G	A	Pts.	PIM
		REGULAR SEASON								PLAYOFFS				
90-91—Khimik	USSR	41	2	2	4	52	...	...	...	—	—	—	—	—
91-92—Khimik	CIS	27	1	4	5	24	...	...	...	—	—	—	—	—
—Winnipeg	NHL	27	2	9	11	67	5	0	0	7	0	0	0	39
—Moncton	AHL	3	0	1	1	16	...	...	...	—	—	—	—	—
92-93—Moncton	AHL	9	1	3	4	26	6	0	0	—	—	—	—	—
—Fort Wayne	IHL	3	0	1	1	29	1	0	0	—	—	—	—	—
—Winnipeg	NHL	56	2	14	16	124	6	0	0	4	0	0	0	4
93-94—Winnipeg	NHL	74	0	17	17	165	-11	0	0	—	—	—	—	—
94-95—Winnipeg	NHL	19	1	3	4	27	-2	0	0	—	—	—	—	—
—Washington	NHL	3	0	1	1	2	3	0	0	2	0	0	0	4
95-96—Indianapolis	IHL	1	0	0	0	0	...	...	...	—	—	—	—	—
—Chicago	NHL	53	1	8	9	92	12	0	0	—	—	—	—	—
—Tampa Bay	NHL	11	2	1	3	24	-1	0	0	5	0	0	0	15
96-97—Tampa Bay	NHL	59	1	7	8	108	2	0	0	—	—	—	—	—
97-98—Tampa Bay	NHL	45	2	7	9	85	-5	1	0	—	—	—	—	—
—Montreal	NHL	4	0	1	1	12	-2	0	0	10	1	4	5	12
98-99—Montreal	NHL	76	3	9	12	109	-3	0	0	—	—	—	—	—
99-00—Montreal	NHL	43	1	5	6	76	-11	0	0	—	—	—	—	—
—Edmonton	NHL	14	0	3	3	10	-3	0	0	5	0	0	0	6
00-01—Edmonton	NHL	67	3	20	23	90	15	1	0	6	0	0	0	4
01-02—New York Rangers	NHL	39	0	6	6	53	-4	0	0	—	—	—	—	—
—Hartford	AHL	6	1	1	2	2	2	0	0	—	—	—	—	—
—Florida	NHL	14	0	4	4	11	-3	0	0	—	—	—	—	—
02-03—San Antonio	AHL	5	1	0	1	4	-2	0	0	—	—	—	—	—
—Florida	NHL	56	1	1	2	39	7	0	0	—	—	—	—	—
03-04—Edmonton	NHL	42	5	13	18	28	19	1	0	—	—	—	—	—
—Toronto	AHL	10	0	5	5	8	4	0	0	—	—	—	—	—
NHL Totals (13 years)		702	24	129	153	1122	24	3	0	39	1	4	5	84

U

ULMER, LAYNE C

PERSONAL: Born September 14, 1980, in North Battleford, Saskatchewan. ... 6-1/201. ... Shoots left.
TRANSACTIONS/CAREER NOTES: Selected by Ottawa Senators in seventh round (eighth Senators pick, 209th overall) of NHL entry draft (June 25, 1999). ... Signed as free agent by New York Rangers (June 13, 2001).

Season Team	League	GP	G	A	Pts.	PIM	+/-	PP	SH	GP	G	A	Pts.	PIM
		REGULAR SEASON								PLAYOFFS				
97-98—Swift Current	WHL	50	8	9	17	23	...	...	...	12	3	1	4	...
98-99—Swift Current	WHL	72	40	35	75	34	...	...	...	6	2	1	3	4
99-00—Swift Current	WHL	71	50	54	104	66	...	...	...	12	12	6	18	16
00-01—Swift Current	WHL	68	*63	56	119	75	...	...	...	19	7	3	10	20
01-02—Charlotte	ECHL	38	18	17	35	12	-1	4	0	5	2	2	4	4
—Hartford	AHL	22	0	5	5	17	1	0	0	—	—	—	—	—
02-03—Hartford	AHL	68	12	20	32	16	15	1	1	2	0	0	0	0
03-04—New York Rangers	NHL	1	0	0	0	0	-1	0	0	—	—	—	—	—
—Hartford	AHL	76	22	16	38	26	14	3	3	7	2	5	7	0
04-05—Hartford	AHL	65	7	30	37	23	16	2	0	6	0	0	0	2
NHL Totals (1 year)		1	0	0	0	0	-1	0	0					

UMBERGER, R.J. C FLYERS

PERSONAL: Born May 3, 1982, in Pittsburgh. ... 6-2/200. ... Shoots left.
TRANSACTIONS/CAREER NOTES: Selected by Vancouver Canucks in first round (first Canucks pick, 16th overall) of NHL draft (June 23, 2001). ... Traded by Canucks with D Martin Grenier to New York Rangers for LW Martin Rucinsky (March 9, 2004). ... Missed 2003-04 season in contract dispute. ... Signed as free agent by Philadelphia Flyers (June 16, 2004).

Season Team	League	GP	G	A	Pts.	PIM	+/-	PP	SH	GP	G	A	Pts.	PIM
		REGULAR SEASON								PLAYOFFS				
99-00—U.S. National	USHL	57	33	35	68	20	...	...	...	—	—	—	—	—
00-01—Ohio State	CCHA	32	14	23	37	18	...	...	...	—	—	—	—	—
01-02—Ohio State	CCHA	37	18	21	39	31	...	...	...	—	—	—	—	—
02-03—Ohio State	CCHA	43	26	27	53	16	...	...	...	—	—	—	—	—
03-04—		Did not play												
04-05—Philadelphia	AHL	80	21	44	65	36	19	2	0	21	3	7	10	12

UNDERHILL, MATT G BLACKHAWKS

PERSONAL: Born September 16, 1979, in Campell River, B.C. ... 6-0/220. ... Catches left.
TRANSACTIONS/CAREER NOTES: Selected by Calgary Flames in sixth round (eighth Flames pick, 170th overall) of NHL entry draft (June 26, 1999). ... Signed as free agent by Chicago Blackhawks (March 4, 2004).

Season Team	League	GP	Min.	W	L	T	GA	SO	GAA	SV%	GP	Min.	W	L	GA	SO	GAA	SV%
		REGULAR SEASON									PLAYOFFS							
98-99—Cornell	ECAC	25	1320	7	11	4	65	1	2.95	.902	—	—	—	—	—	—	—	—
99-00—Cornell	ECAC	17	911	8	7	1	44	1	2.90	...	—	—	—	—	—	—	—	—
00-01—Cornell	ECAC	25	1504	13	8	3	47	1	1.88	...	—	—	—	—	—	—	—	—
01-02—Cornell	ECAC	21	1334	14	6	1	40	3	1.80	...	—	—	—	—	—	—	—	—
02-03—Providence	AHL	7	428	3	3	1	22	0	3.08	.901	—	—	—	—	—	—	—	—
—Pee Dee	ECHL	33	1878	16	13	2	88	0	2.81	...	—	—	—	—	—	—	—	—
03-04—Manchester	AHL	4	185	2	2	0	9	0	2.92	.893	—	—	—	—	—	—	—	—
—Florence	ECHL	29	1686	10	14	1	97	1	3.45	.885	—	—	—	—	—	—	—	—
—Norfolk	AHL	1	19	0	0	0	0	0	0.00	...	—	—	—	—	—	—	—	—
—Chicago	NHL	1	61	0	1	0	4	0	3.93	.879	—	—	—	—	—	—	—	—
04-05—St. John's	AHL	1	38	0	0	...	0	0	0.00	1.00	—	—	—	—	—	—	—	—
—Providence	AHL	5	244	1	2	...	12	1	2.95	.885	—	—	—	—	—	—	—	—
—Alaska	ECHL	3	180	3	0	...	6	0	2.00	.943	3	144	1	1	8	...	3.31	.893
—Mississippi	ECHL	24	1450	13	8	...	64	3	2.65	.923	—	—	—	—	—	—	—	—
NHL Totals (1 year)		1	61	0	1	0	4	0	3.93	.879								

UPSHALL, SCOTTIE RW/LW PREDATORS

PERSONAL: Born October 7, 1983, in Fort McMurray, Alta. ... 6-0/187. ... Shoots left.
TRANSACTIONS/CAREER NOTES: Selected by Nashville Predators in first round (first Predators pick, sixth overall) of NHL entry draft (June 22, 2002). ... Injured knee (December 23, 2003); missed nine games.

Season Team	League	GP	G	A	Pts.	PIM	+/-	PP	SH	GP	G	A	Pts.	PIM
		REGULAR SEASON								PLAYOFFS				
00-01—Kamloops	WHL	70	42	45	87	111	...	...	...	4	0	2	2	10
01-02—Kamloops	WHL	61	32	51	83	139	...	...	...	4	1	2	3	21
02-03—Kamloops	WHL	42	25	31	56	111	...	...	...	6	0	2	2	34
—Milwaukee	AHL	2	1	0	1	2	0	0	0	6	0	0	0	2
—Nashville	NHL	8	1	0	1	0	2	0	0	—	—	—	—	—
03-04—Milwaukee	AHL	31	13	11	24	42	1	3	0	8	3	0	3	4
—Nashville	NHL	7	0	1	1	0	-2	0	0	—	—	—	—	—
04-05—Milwaukee	AHL	62	19	27	46	108	9	8	2	5	2	2	4	8
NHL Totals (2 years)		15	1	1	2	0	0	0	0					

USTRNUL, LIBOR D

PERSONAL: Born February 20, 1982, in Olomouc, Czechoslovakia. ... 6-5/228. ... Shoots left. ... Name pronounced OOS-tuhr-nuhl.
TRANSACTIONS/CAREER NOTES: Selected by Atlanta Thrashers in second round (third Thrashers pick, 42nd overall) of NHL entry draft (June 24, 2000).

U

Season Team	League	GP	G	A	Pts.	PIM	+/-	PP	SH	Playoffs GP	G	A	Pts.	PIM
		REGULAR SEASON								PLAYOFFS				
98-99—Thunder Bay Flyers	USHL	52	2	5	7	65	...	...	...	—	—	—	—	—
99-00—Plymouth	OHL	68	0	15	15	208	...	...	...	23	0	3	3	29
00-01—Plymouth	OHL	35	3	13	16	66	14	1	1	19	1	4	5	19
01-02—Plymouth	OHL	43	1	8	9	84	...	...	...	2	0	0	0	6
—Chicago	AHL	1	0	0	0	0	1	0	0	1	0	0	0	5
02-03—Chicago	AHL	40	1	1	2	94	9	0	0	6	0	0	0	0
04-05—Chicago	AHL	27	0	2	2	35	-2	0	0	—	—	—	—	—
—Gwinnett	ECHL	17	1	5	6	34	9	0	...	2	0	0	0	0

VAANANEN, OSSI — D — AVALANCHE

PERSONAL: Born August 18, 1980, in Vantaa, Finland. ... 6-4/227. ... Shoots left. ... Name pronounced OH-see VAH-nih-nehn.

TRANSACTIONS/CAREER NOTES: Selected by Phoenix Coyotes in 2nd round (2nd Coyotes pick, 43rd overall) of NHL draft (June 27, 1998). ... Bruised shoulder (March 17, 2002); missed six games. ... Bruised foot (October 24, 2002); missed one game. ... Strained right knee (February 1, 2003); missed 14 games. ... Sore neck (December 7, 2003); missed one game. ... Traded by Coyotes with C Chris Gratton and 2nd-round pick in 2005 draft to Colorado Avalanche for D Derek Morris and D Keith Ballard (March 9, 2004).

Season Team	League	GP	G	A	Pts.	PIM	+/-	PP	SH	Playoffs GP	G	A	Pts.	PIM
		REGULAR SEASON								PLAYOFFS				
95-96—Jokerit Helsinki	Finland Jr. B	2	0	0	0	0	...	...	...	—	—	—	—	—
96-97—Jokerit Helsinki	Finland Jr. B	17	1	2	3	43	...	...	...	—	—	—	—	—
97-98—Jokerit Helsinki	Finland Jr.	31	0	6	6	24	...	...	...	—	—	—	—	—
98-99—Jokerit Helsinki	Finland	48	0	1	1	42	...	...	...	3	0	1	1	2
99-00—Jokerit Helsinki	Finland	49	1	6	7	46	...	...	...	11	1	1	2	2
00-01—Phoenix	NHL	81	4	12	16	90	9	0	0	—	—	—	—	—
01-02—Phoenix	NHL	76	2	12	14	74	6	0	1	5	0	0	0	6
—Fin. Olympic team	Int'l	2	0	1	1	0	...	...	...	—	—	—	—	—
02-03—Phoenix	NHL	67	2	7	9	82	1	0	0	—	—	—	—	—
03-04—Phoenix	NHL	67	2	4	6	87	-10	0	0	—	—	—	—	—
—Colorado	NHL	12	0	0	0	2	-4	0	0	11	0	1	1	18
04-05—Jokerit Helsinki	Finland	—	—	—	—	—	—	—	—	12	0	0	0	26
—Jokerit Helsinki	Finland	28	2	2	4	30	6	...	...	—	—	—	—	—
NHL Totals (4 years)		303	10	35	45	335	2	0	1	16	0	1	1	24

VALABIK, BORIS — D — THRASHERS

PERSONAL: Born February 14, 1986, in Nitra, Slovakia. ... 6-7/212. ... Shoots left.

TRANSACTIONS/CAREER NOTES: Selected by Atlanta Thrashers in first round (first Thrashers pick, 10th overall) of NHL entry draft (June 26, 2004).

Season Team	League	GP	G	A	Pts.	PIM	+/-	PP	SH	Playoffs GP	G	A	Pts.	PIM
		REGULAR SEASON								PLAYOFFS				
03-04—Kitchener	OHL	68	3	12	15	278	...	...	...	5	0	0	0	8
04-05—Kitchener	OHL	43	0	4	4	231	0	0	0	15	0	0	0	56

VALICEVIC, ROB — RW — STARS

PERSONAL: Born January 6, 1971, in Detroit. ... 6-2/208. ... Shoots right.

TRANSACTIONS/CAREER NOTES: Selected by New York Islanders in sixth round (sixth Islanders pick, 114th overall) of NHL draft (June 22, 1991). ... Signed as free agent by Nashville Predators (June 8, 1998). ... Suffered concussion (January 31, 2000); missed two games. ... Injured right knee (November 6, 2000); missed three games. ... Knee surgery (November 16, 2000); missed eight games. ... Injured knee (December 4, 2000); missed two games. ... Suffered concussion (March 10, 2001); missed three games. ... Signed as free agent by Los Angeles Kings (August 16, 2001). ... Signed as free agent by Anaheim Mighty Ducks (July 24, 2002). ... Signed as free agent by Dallas Stars (August 28, 2003).

STATISTICAL PLATEAUS: Three-goal games: 1999-00 (1).

Season Team	League	GP	G	A	Pts.	PIM	+/-	PP	SH	Playoffs GP	G	A	Pts.	PIM
		REGULAR SEASON								PLAYOFFS				
90-91—Detroit	USHL	39	31	44	75	54	...	...	...	—	—	—	—	—
91-92—Lake Superior St.	CCHA	32	8	4	12	12	...	...	...	—	—	—	—	—
92-93—Lake Superior St.	CCHA	43	21	20	41	28	...	...	...	—	—	—	—	—
93-94—Lake Superior St.	CCHA	45	18	20	38	46	...	...	...	—	—	—	—	—
94-95—Lake Superior St.	CCHA	37	10	22	32	40	-1	2	1	—	—	—	—	—
95-96—Louisiana	ECHL	60	42	20	62	85	...	...	...	5	2	3	5	8
—Springfield	AHL	2	0	0	0	2	...	...	...	—	—	—	—	—
96-97—Houston	IHL	58	11	12	23	42	...	...	...	12	1	3	4	11
—Louisiana	ECHL	8	7	2	9	21	...	...	...	—	—	—	—	—
97-98—Houston	IHL	72	29	28	57	47	19	8	0	4	2	0	2	2
98-99—Houston	IHL	57	16	33	49	62	18	5	1	19	7	10	17	8
—Nashville	NHL	19	4	2	6	2	4	0	0	—	—	—	—	—
99-00—Nashville	NHL	80	14	11	25	21	-11	2	1	—	—	—	—	—
00-01—Nashville	NHL	60	8	6	14	26	-2	1	0	—	—	—	—	—
01-02—Manchester	AHL	59	11	23	34	25	-2	4	0	5	1	0	1	4
—Los Angeles	NHL	17	1	1	2	8	-4	0	0	—	—	—	—	—
—Cincinnati	AHL	69	17	26	43	38	...	...	...	—	—	—	—	—
02-03—Cincinnati	AHL	69	17	26	43	38	...	...	...	—	—	—	—	—
—Anaheim	NHL	10	1	0	1	2	1	0	0	—	—	—	—	—
03-04—Dallas	NHL	7	0	0	0	2	-1	0	0	—	—	—	—	—
—Utah	AHL	67	11	26	37	44	0	4	2	—	—	—	—	—
04-05—UHL	UHL	78	36	60	96	38	32	10	5	—	—	—	—	—
—TPS Turku	Finland	10	1	1	2	29	2	...	...	—	—	—	—	—
NHL Totals (6 years)		193	28	20	48	61	-13	3	1					

VALIQUETTE, STEPHEN — G — RANGERS

PERSONAL: Born August 20, 1977, in Etobicoke, Ont. ... 6-5/205. ... Catches left. ... Name pronounced val-ih-KEHT.

TRANSACTIONS/CAREER NOTES: Selected by Los Angeles Kings in eighth round (14th Kings pick, 190th overall) of NHL draft (June 22, 1996). ... Signed as free agent by New York Islanders (September 9, 1998). ... Signed as free agent by Edmonton Oilers (July 15, 2003). ... Claimed by Florida Panthers from Oilers in waiver draft (October 3, 2003). ... Claimed by Oilers off waivers from Panthers (October 9, 2003). ... Traded by Oilers with C Dwight Helminen and second-round pick in 2004 draft to New York Rangers for C Petr Nedved and G Jussi Markkanen (March 3, 2004).

		REGULAR SEASON									PLAYOFFS							
Season Team	League	GP	Min.	W	L	T	GA	SO	GAA	SV%	GP	Min.	W	L	GA	SO	GAA	SV%
94-95—Sudbury	OHL	4	138	2	0	0	6	0	2.61	...	—	—	—	—	—	—	—	—
95-96—Sudbury	OHL	39	1887	13	16	2	123	0	3.91	...	—	—	—	—	—	—	—	—
96-97—Sudbury	OHL	61	3311	21	29	7	*232	1	4.20	.904	—	—	—	—	—	—	—	—
97-98—Sudbury	OHL	14	807	5	7	1	50	0	3.72	.904	—	—	—	—	—	—	—	—
—Erie	OHL	28	1525	16	7	3	65	3	2.56	.917	7	467	3	4	15	1	1.93	.941
98-99—Hampton Roads	ECHL	31	1713	18	7	3	84	1	2.94	.916	2	60	0	1	7	0	7.00	.837
—Lowell	AHL	1	59	0	1	0	3	0	3.05	.885	—	—	—	—	—	—	—	—
99-00—Providence	AHL	1	60	1	0	0	3	0	3.00	...	—	—	—	—	—	—	—	—
—Trenton	ECHL	12	692	5	6	1	36	1	3.12	...	—	—	—	—	—	—	—	—
—Lowell	AHL	14	727	8	5	0	36	0	2.97	...	—	—	—	—	—	—	—	—
—New York Islanders	NHL	6	193	2	0	0	6	0	1.87	.949	—	—	—	—	—	—	—	—
00-01—Springfield	AHL	20	1066	7	10	1	54	0	3.04	.907	—	—	—	—	—	—	—	—
01-02—Bridgeport	AHL	20	1070	10	5	1	45	2	2.52	.916	1	18	0	0	1	0	3.33	.800
02-03—Bridgeport	AHL	34	1962	15	14	3	86	2	2.63	.912	4	253	3	1	9	0	2.13	.931
03-04—Edmonton	NHL	1	14	0	0	0	2	0	8.57	.714	—	—	—	—	—	—	—	—
—New York Rangers	NHL	2	120	1	1	0	6	0	3.00	.915	—	—	—	—	—	—	—	—
—Toronto	AHL	35	2064	14	14	5	90	2	2.62	.904	—	—	—	—	—	—	—	—
—Hartford	AHL	7	399	2	4	1	15	1	2.26	.922	1	11	0	0	0	0	0.00	...
04-05—Hartford	AHL	35	1899	19	11	...	56	7	1.77	.935	2	118	1	1	4	0	2.03	.938
NHL Totals (2 years)		9	327	3	1	0	14	0	2.57	.928								

VAN ALLEN, SHAUN — C

PERSONAL: Born August 29, 1967, in Calgary. ... 6-1/207. ... Shoots left.

TRANSACTIONS/CAREER NOTES: Selected by Edmonton Oilers in fifth round (fifth Oilers pick, 105th overall) of NHL entry draft (June 13, 1987). ... Suffered concussion (January 9, 1993); missed 11 games. ... Signed as free agent by Mighty Ducks of Anaheim (July 22, 1993). ... Back spasms (February 7, 1995); missed two games. ... Flu (May 1, 1995); missed one game. ... Dislocated right thumb (November 15, 1995); missed 21 games. ... Back spasms (February 7, 1996); missed four games. ... Traded by Mighty Ducks with D Jason York to Ottawa Senators for C Ted Drury and rights to D Marc Moro (October 1, 1996). ... Back spasms (February 2, 1998); missed one game. ... Strained left knee (December 30, 1999); missed one game. ... Strained muscle in abdomen (January 12, 2000); missed five games. ... Signed as free agent by Dallas Stars (July 12, 2000). ... Back spasms (October 10, 2000); missed five games. ... Injured shoulder (October 28, 2001); missed one game. ... Traded by Stars with RW Donald Audette to Montreal Canadiens for LW Martin Rucinsky and LW Benoit Brunet (November 21, 2001). ... Sprained wrist (November 19, 2001); missed four games. ... Signed as free agent by Senators (July 24, 2002). ... Surgery for kidney stones (March 24, 2003); missed four games. ... Back spasms (February 21, 2004); missed four games.

		REGULAR SEASON								PLAYOFFS				
Season Team	League	GP	G	A	Pts.	PIM	+/-	PP	SH	GP	G	A	Pts.	PIM
84-85—Swift Current	SAJHL	61	12	20	32	136	...	...	...	—	—	—	—	—
85-86—Saskatoon	WHL	55	12	11	23	43	...	...	...	13	4	8	12	28
86-87—Saskatoon	WHL	72	38	59	97	116	...	...	...	11	4	6	10	24
87-88—Nova Scotia	AHL	19	4	10	14	17	...	...	...	4	1	1	2	4
—Milwaukee	IHL	40	14	28	42	34	...	...	...	—	—	—	—	—
88-89—Cape Breton	AHL	76	32	42	74	81	...	...	...	—	—	—	—	—
89-90—Cape Breton	AHL	61	25	44	69	83	...	...	...	4	0	2	2	8
90-91—Edmonton	NHL	2	0	0	0	0	0	0	0	—	—	—	—	—
—Cape Breton	AHL	76	25	75	100	182	...	...	...	4	0	1	1	8
91-92—Cape Breton	AHL	77	29	*84	*113	80	...	...	...	5	3	7	10	14
92-93—Cape Breton	AHL	43	14	62	76	68	12	5	2	15	8	9	17	18
—Edmonton	NHL	21	1	4	5	6	-2	0	0	—	—	—	—	—
93-94—Anaheim	NHL	80	8	25	33	64	0	2	2	—	—	—	—	—
94-95—Anaheim	NHL	45	8	21	29	32	-4	1	1	—	—	—	—	—
95-96—Anaheim	NHL	49	8	17	25	41	13	0	0	—	—	—	—	—
96-97—Ottawa	NHL	80	11	14	25	35	-8	1	1	7	0	1	1	4
97-98—Ottawa	NHL	80	4	15	19	48	4	0	0	11	0	1	1	10
98-99—Ottawa	NHL	79	6	11	17	30	3	0	1	4	0	0	0	0
99-00—Ottawa	NHL	75	9	19	28	37	20	0	2	6	0	1	1	9
00-01—Dallas	NHL	59	7	16	23	16	5	0	2	8	0	2	2	8
01-02—Dallas	NHL	19	2	4	6	6	-5	0	0	—	—	—	—	—
—Montreal	NHL	54	6	9	15	20	5	0	1	7	0	1	1	2
02-03—Ottawa	NHL	78	12	20	32	66	17	2	2	18	1	1	2	12
03-04—Ottawa	NHL	73	2	10	12	80	6	0	1	—	—	—	—	—
NHL Totals (13 years)		794	84	185	269	481	54	6	13	61	1	7	8	45

VAN OENE, DARREN — LW — BRUINS

PERSONAL: Born January 18, 1978, in Edmonton. ... 6-3/207. ... Shoots left. ... Name pronounced van OH-ihn.

TRANSACTIONS/CAREER NOTES: Selected by Buffalo Sabres in second round (third Sabres pick, 33rd overall) of NHL entry draft (June 22, 1996). ... Signed as free agent by Boston Bruins (July 29, 2002).

Season Team	League	GP	G	A	Pts.	PIM	+/-	PP	SH	GP	G	A	Pts.	PIM
		REGULAR SEASON								PLAYOFFS				
94-95—Brandon	WHL	59	5	13	18	108	...	...	...	18	1	1	2	34
95-96—Brandon	WHL	47	10	18	28	126	...	...	...	18	1	6	7	*78
96-97—Brandon	WHL	56	21	27	48	139	27	3	1	6	2	3	5	19
97-98—Brandon	WHL	51	23	24	47	161	26	8	3	17	6	7	13	51
98-99—Rochester	AHL	73	11	20	31	143	...	...	...	12	2	4	6	8
99-00—Rochester	AHL	80	20	18	38	153	...	...	...	21	1	3	4	24
00-01—Rochester	AHL	64	10	12	22	147	...	...	...	4	1	0	1	4
01-02—Rochester	AHL	52	8	6	14	73	-5	2	0	2	0	0	0	4
02-03—Providence	AHL	78	11	17	28	109	1	2	0	4	0	0	0	21
03-04—Providence	AHL	72	9	16	25	111	2	3	1	2	0	0	0	0
04-05—Manchester	AHL	4	0	0	0	10	-1	0	0	—	—	—	—	—
—Elmira	UHL	44	9	15	24	38	...	...	...	—	—	—	—	—
—Providence	AHL	4	0	0	0	7	0	0	0	—	—	—	—	—
—Worcester	AHL	14	0	0	0	6	-7	0	0	—	—	—	—	—

VAN RYN, MIKE — D — PANTHERS

PERSONAL: Born May 14, 1979, in London, Ont. ... 6-1/202. ... Shoots right. ... Name pronounced van RIGHN.

TRANSACTIONS/CAREER NOTES: Selected by New Jersey Devils in first round (first Devils pick, 26th overall) of NHL entry draft (June 27, 1998). ... Signed as free agent by St. Louis Blues (June 30, 2000). ... Traded by Blues to Florida Panthers for RW Valeri Bure and conditional fifth-round pick in 2004 draft (March 11, 2003). ... Suffered concussion (January 23, 2004); missed three games.

Season Team	League	GP	G	A	Pts.	PIM	+/-	PP	SH	GP	G	A	Pts.	PIM
		REGULAR SEASON								PLAYOFFS				
95-96—London Jr. B	OHA	44	9	14	23	24	...	...	...	—	—	—	—	—
96-97—London Jr. B	OHA	46	14	31	45	32	...	...	...	—	—	—	—	—
97-98—Univ. of Michigan	CCHA	25	4	14	18	36	...	...	...	—	—	—	—	—
98-99—Univ. of Michigan	CCHA	37	10	13	23	52	...	...	...	—	—	—	—	—
99-00—Sarnia	OHL	61	6	35	41	34	-2	5	0	7	0	5	5	4
00-01—St. Louis	NHL	1	0	0	0	0	-2	0	0	—	—	—	—	—
—Worcester	AHL	37	3	10	13	12	...	...	...	7	1	1	2	2
01-02—Worcester	AHL	24	2	7	9	17	8	0	0	—	—	—	—	—
—St. Louis	NHL	48	2	8	10	18	10	0	0	9	0	0	0	0
02-03—Worcester	AHL	33	2	8	10	16	-2	2	0	—	—	—	—	—
—St. Louis	NHL	20	0	3	3	8	3	0	0	—	—	—	—	—
—San Antonio	AHL	11	0	3	3	20	2	0	0	3	0	0	0	0
03-04—Florida	NHL	79	13	24	37	52	-16	6	1	—	—	—	—	—
NHL Totals (4 years)		148	15	35	50	78	-5	6	1	9	0	0	0	0

VANDENBUSSCHE, RYAN — RW — PENGUINS

PERSONAL: Born February 28, 1973, in Simcoe, Ont. ... 6-0/205. ... Shoots right. ... Name pronounced VAN-dehn-buhsh.

TRANSACTIONS/CAREER NOTES: Selected by Toronto Maple Leafs in eighth round (173rd overall) of NHL draft (June 20, 1992). ... Signed as free agent by New York Rangers (August 22, 1995). ... Traded by Rangers to Chicago Blackhawks for D Ryan Risidore (March 24, 1998). ... Suspended one game for head-butting incident (March 28, 1999). ... Elbow surgery before 1999-2000 season; missed first six games of season. ... Sore back (December 3, 1999); missed five games. ... Cut left hand (March 3, 2000); missed 10 games. ... Injured wrist (January 5, 2003); missed 14 games. ... Injured wrist (November 29, 2003); missed six games. ... Strained neck (January 29, 2004); missed three games. ... Signed as free agent by Pittsburgh Penguins (July 12, 2004).

Season Team	League	GP	G	A	Pts.	PIM	+/-	PP	SH	GP	G	A	Pts.	PIM
		REGULAR SEASON								PLAYOFFS				
90-91—Cornwall	OHL	49	3	8	11	139	...	...	...	—	—	—	—	—
91-92—Cornwall	OHL	61	13	15	28	232	...	...	...	6	0	2	2	9
92-93—Newmarket	OHL	30	15	12	27	161	...	...	...	—	—	—	—	—
—Guelph	OHL	29	3	14	17	99	...	...	...	5	1	3	4	13
—St. John's	AHL	1	0	0	0	0	...	...	...	—	—	—	—	—
93-94—St. John's	AHL	44	4	10	14	124	...	...	...	—	—	—	—	—
—Springfield	AHL	9	1	2	3	29	...	...	...	5	0	0	0	16
94-95—St. John's	AHL	53	2	13	15	239	...	...	...	—	—	—	—	—
95-96—Binghamton	AHL	68	3	17	20	240	...	...	...	4	0	0	0	9
96-97—Binghamton	AHL	38	8	11	19	133	...	...	...	—	—	—	—	—
—New York Rangers	NHL	11	1	0	1	30	-2	0	0	—	—	—	—	—
97-98—New York Rangers	NHL	16	1	0	1	38	-2	0	0	—	—	—	—	—
—Hartford	AHL	15	2	0	2	45	-2	0	0	—	—	—	—	—
—Chicago	NHL	4	0	1	1	5	0	0	0	—	—	—	—	—
—Indianapolis	IHL	3	1	1	2	4	3	0	0	—	—	—	—	—
98-99—Indianapolis	IHL	34	3	10	13	130	-11	1	0	—	—	—	—	—
—Portland	AHL	37	4	1	5	119	-12	0	0	—	—	—	—	—
—Chicago	NHL	6	0	0	0	17	0	0	0	—	—	—	—	—
99-00—Chicago	NHL	52	0	1	1	143	-3	0	0	—	—	—	—	—
00-01—Chicago	NHL	64	2	5	7	146	-8	0	0	—	—	—	—	—
01-02—Chicago	NHL	50	1	2	3	103	-10	0	0	1	0	0	0	0
02-03—Norfolk	AHL	4	0	1	1	5	1	0	0	—	—	—	—	—
—Chicago	NHL	22	0	0	0	58	0	0	0	—	—	—	—	—
03-04—Chicago	NHL	65	4	1	5	120	-10	2	0	—	—	—	—	—
04-05—Wilkes-Barre/Scranton	AHL	23	4	7	11	67	1	2	0	11	2	2	4	11
NHL Totals (8 years)		290	9	10	19	660	-35	2	0	1	0	0	0	0

VANDERMEER, JIM — D — BLACKHAWKS

PERSONAL: Born February 21, 1980, in Caroline, Alta. ... 6-1/218. ... Shoots left.
TRANSACTIONS/CAREER NOTES: Signed as free agent by Philadelphia Flyers (July 6, 2001). ... Dislocated shoulder (January 20, 2004); missed six games. ... Traded by Flyers with C Colin Fraser and second-round pick in 2004 entry draft (LW Bryan Bickell) to Chicago Blackhawks for C Alexei Zhamnov and fourth-round pick in 2004 entry draft (February 19, 2004).

		REGULAR SEASON								PLAYOFFS				
Season Team	League	GP	G	A	Pts.	PIM	+/-	PP	SH	GP	G	A	Pts.	PIM
97-98—Red Deer	WHL	35	0	3	3	55	...	...	...	2	0	0	0	0
98-99—Red Deer	WHL	70	5	23	28	258	...	...	...	9	0	1	1	24
99-00—Red Deer	WHL	71	8	30	38	221	...	...	...	4	0	1	1	16
00-01—Red Deer	WHL	65	28	37	65	180	...	...	...	22	0	13	13	43
01-02—Philadelphia	AHL	74	1	13	14	88	-8	0	0	5	0	2	2	14
02-03—Philadelphia	AHL	48	4	8	12	122	-9	2	0	—	—	—	—	—
—Philadelphia	NHL	24	2	1	3	27	9	0	0	8	0	1	1	9
03-04—Philadelphia	NHL	23	3	2	5	25	-5	0	0	—	—	—	—	—
—Philadelphia	AHL	26	1	6	7	118	-8	0	0	—	—	—	—	—
—Chicago	NHL	23	2	10	12	58	-6	1	1	—	—	—	—	—
04-05—Norfolk	AHL	52	3	10	13	164	13	2	0	—	—	—	—	—
NHL Totals (2 years)		70	7	13	20	110	-2	1	1	8	0	1	1	9

VANEK, THOMAS — LW — SABRES

PERSONAL: Born January 19, 1984, in Vienna, Austria. ... 6-2/208. ... Shoots right.
TRANSACTIONS/CAREER NOTES: Selected by Buffalo Sabres in first round (first Sabres pick, fifth overall) of NHL entry draft (June 20, 2003).

		REGULAR SEASON								PLAYOFFS				
Season Team	League	GP	G	A	Pts.	PIM	+/-	PP	SH	GP	G	A	Pts.	PIM
02-03—Minnesota	WCHA	45	31	31	62	60	...	...	...	—	—	—	—	—
03-04—Minnesota	WCHA	38	26	25	51	72	...	...	...	—	—	—	—	—
04-05—Rochester	AHL	74	42	26	68	62	-3	25	0	5	2	3	5	10

VARADA, VACLAV — LW/RW — SENATORS

PERSONAL: Born April 26, 1976, in Vsetin, Czechoslovakia. ... 6-0/208. ... Shoots left. ... Name pronounced vuh-RAH-duh.
TRANSACTIONS/CAREER NOTES: Selected by San Jose Sharks in fourth round (fourth Sharks pick, 89th overall) of NHL draft (June 29, 1994). ... Traded by Sharks with LW Martin Spahnel and fourth-round pick (D Mike Martone) in 1996 draft to Buffalo Sabres for D Doug Bodger (November 16, 1995). ... Fractured left hand (February 2, 1997); missed 15 games. ... Sprained ankle (February 9, 1999); missed 10 games. ... Injured ear (January 18, 2000); missed three games. ... Had concussion (February 25, 2001); missed six games. ... Suspended one game for unsportsmanlike conduct (October 27, 2001). ... Suspended three games for high-sticking incident (November 10, 2001). ... Suspended one game for checking from behind (January 20, 2002). ... Sprained right knee (January 7, 2003); missed 17 games. ... Traded by Sabres with fifth-round pick (C Tim Cook) in 2003 draft to Ottawa Senators for C Jakub Klepis (February 25, 2003). ... Sprained knee (March 4, 2003); missed seven games. ... Injured knee (December 13, 2003) and had surgery; missed 52 games.

		REGULAR SEASON								PLAYOFFS				
Season Team	League	GP	G	A	Pts.	PIM	+/-	PP	SH	GP	G	A	Pts.	PIM
92-93—TJ Vitkovice	Czech.	1	0	0	0	...	...	...	...	—	—	—	—	—
93-94—HC Vitkovice	Czech Rep.	24	6	7	13	...	...	...	...	5	1	1	2	...
94-95—Tacoma	WHL	68	50	38	88	108	7	21	4	4	4	3	7	11
—Czech. Jr. nat'l team	Int'l	7	6	4	10	25	...	...	...	—	—	—	—	—
95-96—Kelowna	WHL	59	39	46	85	100	...	...	...	6	3	3	6	16
—Rochester	AHL	5	3	0	3	4	...	...	...	—	—	—	—	—
—Buffalo	NHL	1	0	0	0	0	0	0	0	—	—	—	—	—
—Czech. Jr. nat'l team	Int'l	6	5	1	6	8	...	...	...	—	—	—	—	—
96-97—Rochester	AHL	53	23	25	48	81	8	3	1	10	1	6	7	27
—Buffalo	NHL	5	0	0	0	2	0	0	0	—	—	—	—	—
97-98—Rochester	AHL	45	30	26	56	74	20	14	2	—	—	—	—	—
—Buffalo	NHL	27	5	6	11	15	0	0	0	15	3	4	7	18
98-99—Buffalo	NHL	72	7	24	31	61	11	1	0	21	5	4	9	14
99-00—HC Vitkovice	Czech Rep.	5	2	3	5	12	...	...	...	—	—	—	—	—
—Buffalo	NHL	76	10	27	37	62	12	0	0	5	0	0	0	8
00-01—Buffalo	NHL	75	10	21	31	81	-2	2	0	13	0	4	4	8
01-02—Buffalo	NHL	76	7	16	23	82	-7	1	0	—	—	—	—	—
02-03—Buffalo	NHL	44	7	4	11	23	-2	1	0	—	—	—	—	—
—Ottawa	NHL	11	2	6	8	8	3	1	0	18	2	4	6	18
03-04—Ottawa	NHL	30	5	5	10	26	2	0	0	7	1	1	2	4
04-05—Vitkovice	Czech Rep.	44	8	19	27	83	13	...	...	11	3	3	6	37
NHL Totals (9 years)		417	53	109	162	360	17	6	0	79	11	17	28	70

VARLAMOV, SERGEI — LW/RW — CANUCKS

PERSONAL: Born July 21, 1978, in Kiev, U.S.S.R. ... 5-11/203. ... Shoots left. ... Name pronounced VAHR-luh-mahf.
TRANSACTIONS/CAREER NOTES: Signed as free agent by Calgary Flames (September 18, 1996). ... Traded by Flames with G Fred Brathwaite, C Daniel Tkaczuk, and ninth-round pick (C Grant Jacobsen) in 2001 draft to St. Louis Blues for G Roman Turek and fourth-round pick (LW Egor Shastin) in 2001 draft (June 23, 2001). ... Traded by Blues to Vancouver Canucks for LW Ryan Ready (March 9, 2004).

		REGULAR SEASON								PLAYOFFS				
Season Team	League	GP	G	A	Pts.	PIM	+/-	PP	SH	GP	G	A	Pts.	PIM
95-96—Swift Current	WHL	55	23	21	44	65	...	...	...	—	—	—	—	—
96-97—Swift Current	WHL	72	46	39	85	94	33	13	9	—	—	—	—	—

Season Team	League	GP	G	A	Pts.	PIM	+/-	PP	SH	GP	G	A	Pts.	PIM
		REGULAR SEASON								PLAYOFFS				
—Saint John	AHL	1	0	0	0	2	0	0	0	—	—	—	—	—
97-98—Swift Current	WHL	72	*66	53	*119	132	36	16	8	12	10	5	15	28
—Calgary	NHL	1	0	0	0	0	0	0	0	—	—	—	—	—
—Saint John	AHL	...	...	...	...	...	...	...	...	3	0	0	0	0
98-99—Saint John	AHL	76	24	33	57	66	-8	8	1	7	0	4	4	8
99-00—Saint John	AHL	68	20	21	41	88	...	...	...	3	0	0	0	24
—Calgary	NHL	7	3	0	3	0	0	0	0	—	—	—	—	—
00-01—Saint John	AHL	55	21	30	51	56	...	...	...	19	*15	8	23	10
01-02—St. Louis	NHL	52	5	7	12	26	4	0	0	1	0	0	0	2
—Ukranian Oly. team	Int'l	2	1	0	1	14	...	...	...	—	—	—	—	—
02-03—St. Louis	NHL	3	0	0	0	0	1	0	0	—	—	—	—	—
—Worcester	AHL	72	23	38	61	79	15	10	0	3	2	0	2	0
03-04—Worcester	AHL	43	7	16	23	18	-2	1	0	—	—	—	—	—
—Manitoba	AHL	12	4	2	6	10	-3	0	0	—	—	—	—	—
04-05—Ak Bars Kazan	Russian	2	0	0	0	2	...	...	...	—	—	—	—	—
—Sibir Novosibirsk	Russian	27	2	2	4	55	...	...	...	—	—	—	—	—
NHL Totals (4 years)		63	8	7	15	26	5	0	0	1	0	0	0	2

VASICEK, JOSEF — C/LW — HURRICANES

PERSONAL: Born September 12, 1980, in Havlickuv Brod, Czechoslovakia. ... 6-4/200. ... Shoots left. ... Name pronounced VAHSH-ih-chehk.
TRANSACTIONS/CAREER NOTES: Selected by Carolina Hurricanes in fourth round (fourth Hurricanes pick, 91st overall) of NHL draft (June 27, 1998). ... Injured knee (January 14, 2002); missed four games.
STATISTICAL PLATEAUS: Three-goal games: 2003-04 (1).

Season Team	League	GP	G	A	Pts.	PIM	+/-	PP	SH	GP	G	A	Pts.	PIM
		REGULAR SEASON								PLAYOFFS				
95-96—Havlickuv Brod	Czech. Jrs.	36	25	25	50	...	...	...	...	—	—	—	—	—
96-97—Slavia Praha	Czech. Jrs.	37	20	40	60	...	...	...	...	—	—	—	—	—
97-98—Slavia Praha	Czech. Jrs.	34	13	20	33	...	...	...	...	—	—	—	—	—
98-99—Sault Ste. Marie	OHL	66	21	35	56	30	7	...	...	5	3	0	3	10
99-00—Sault Ste. Marie	OHL	54	26	46	72	49	16	9	1	17	5	15	20	8
00-01—Carolina	NHL	76	8	13	21	53	-8	1	0	6	2	0	2	0
—Cincinnati	IHL	...	...	...	...	...	...	...	...	3	0	0	0	0
01-02—Carolina	NHL	78	14	17	31	53	-7	3	0	23	3	2	5	12
02-03—Carolina	NHL	57	10	10	20	33	-19	4	0	—	—	—	—	—
03-04—Carolina	NHL	82	19	26	45	60	-3	6	0	—	—	—	—	—
04-05—Slavia Praha	Czech Rep.	52	20	23	43	42	13	...	...	7	1	6	7	10
NHL Totals (4 years)		293	51	66	117	199	-37	14	0	29	5	2	7	12

VAUCLAIR, JULIEN — D — SENATORS

PERSONAL: Born October 2, 1979, in Delemont, Switzerland. ... 6-0/200. ... Shoots left. ... Name pronounced voh-CLAIR.
TRANSACTIONS/CAREER NOTES: Selected by Ottawa Senators in third round (fourth Senators pick, 74th overall) of NHL entry draft (June 27, 1998).

Season Team	League	GP	G	A	Pts.	PIM	+/-	PP	SH	GP	G	A	Pts.	PIM
		REGULAR SEASON								PLAYOFFS				
95-96—Ajoie	Switz. Div. 3	20	4	10	14	...	...	...	...	—	—	—	—	—
96-97—Ajoie	Switz. Div. 3	40	0	6	6	24	...	...	...	9	0	2	2	8
97-98—Lugano	Switzerland	36	1	2	3	12	...	...	...	7	0	0	0	25
98-99—Lugano	Switzerland	38	0	3	3	8	...	...	...	—	—	—	—	—
99-00—Lugano	Switzerland	45	3	3	6	16	...	...	...	14	0	0	0	0
00-01—Lugano	Switzerland	42	3	4	7	57	...	...	...	18	0	1	1	4
01-02—Grand Rapids	AHL	71	5	14	19	18	1	2	0	4	0	1	1	4
—Swiss Olympic team	Int'l	4	1	0	1	2	...	...	...	—	—	—	—	—
02-03—Binghamton	AHL	67	6	16	22	30	11	1	1	14	0	1	1	8
03-04—Ottawa	NHL	1	0	0	0	2	1	0	0	—	—	—	—	—
—Binghamton	AHL	78	9	30	39	39	-5	3	0	2	0	0	0	0
04-05—Lugano	Switzerland	42	4	7	11	28	...	0	0	—	—	—	—	—
NHL Totals (1 year)		1	0	0	0	2	1	0	0					

VEILLEUX, STEPHANE — LW/C — WILD

PERSONAL: Born November 16, 1981, in Beauceville, Que. ... 6-1/181. ... Shoots left. ... Name pronounced STEH-fan VAY-oo.
TRANSACTIONS/CAREER NOTES: Selected by Minnesota Wild in third round (fourth Wild pick, 93rd overall) of NHL entry draft (June 23, 2001). ... Signed as free agent by Houston of the AHL (September 25, 2004).

Season Team	League	GP	G	A	Pts.	PIM	+/-	PP	SH	GP	G	A	Pts.	PIM
		REGULAR SEASON								PLAYOFFS				
98-99—Victoriaville	QMJHL	65	6	13	19	35	...	...	...	6	1	3	4	2
99-00—Victoriaville	QMJHL	22	1	4	5	17	...	...	...	—	—	—	—	—
—Val-d'Or	QMJHL	50	14	28	42	100	...	...	...	—	—	—	—	—
00-01—Val-d'Or	QMJHL	68	48	67	115	90	...	...	...	21	15	18	33	42
01-02—Houston	AHL	77	13	22	35	113	5	0	2	14	2	4	6	20
02-03—Minnesota	NHL	38	3	2	5	23	-6	1	0	—	—	—	—	—
—Houston	AHL	29	8	4	12	43	1	2	0	23	7	11	18	12
03-04—Houston	AHL	64	13	25	38	66	-11	3	4	2	1	1	2	2
—Minnesota	NHL	19	2	8	10	20	0	1	1	—	—	—	—	—
04-05—Houston	AHL	59	15	24	39	35	5	7	1	0	0	0	0	0
NHL Totals (2 years)		57	5	10	15	43	-6	2	1					

VERMETTE, ANTOINE — LW/C — SENATORS

PERSONAL: Born July 20, 1982, in St-Agapit, Que. ... 6-0/191. ... Shoots left.

TRANSACTIONS/CAREER NOTES: Selected by Ottawa Senators in second round (third Senators pick, 55th overall) of NHL entry draft (June 24, 2000). ... Separated shoulder (January 9, 2004); missed nine games. ... Injured shoulder (February 3, 2004); missed eight games.

		REGULAR SEASON								PLAYOFFS				
Season Team	League	GP	G	A	Pts.	PIM	+/-	PP	SH	GP	G	A	Pts.	PIM
98-99—Quebec	QMJHL	57	9	17	26	32	...	...	...	13	0	0	0	2
99-00—Victoriaville	QMJHL	71	30	41	71	87	...	...	...	6	0	1	1	6
00-01—Victoriaville	QMJHL	71	57	62	119	102	50	17	3	9	4	6	10	14
01-02—Victoriaville	QMJHL	4	0	2	2	6	...	...	...	22	10	16	26	10
02-03—Binghamton	AHL	80	34	28	62	57	-2	13	3	14	2	9	11	10
03-04—Binghamton	AHL	3	0	0	0	6	-3	0	0	—	—	—	—	—
—Ottawa	NHL	57	7	7	14	16	5	0	1	4	0	1	1	4
04-05—Binghamton	AHL	78	28	45	73	36	20	7	4	6	1	4	5	10
NHL Totals (1 year)		57	7	7	14	16	5	0	1	4	0	1	1	4

VERNARSKY, KRIS — C — BRUINS

PERSONAL: Born April 5, 1982, in Detroit. ... 6-3/201. ... Shoots left.

TRANSACTIONS/CAREER NOTES: Selected by Toronto Maple Leafs in second round (second Maple Leafs pick, 51st overall) of NHL entry draft (June 24, 2000). ... Traded by Maple Leafs to Boston Bruins for D Richard Jackman (May 13, 2002).

		REGULAR SEASON								PLAYOFFS				
Season Team	League	GP	G	A	Pts.	PIM	+/-	PP	SH	GP	G	A	Pts.	PIM
98-99—Plymouth	OHL	45	3	14	17	30	...	...	...	11	0	0	0	2
99-00—Plymouth	OHL	64	16	22	38	63	...	...	...	19	3	6	9	24
00-01—Plymouth	OHL	60	14	21	35	35	10	4	0	19	7	10	17	19
01-02—Plymouth	OHL	59	19	36	55	98	...	...	...	6	1	2	3	15
02-03—Boston	NHL	14	1	0	1	2	-2	0	0	—	—	—	—	—
—Providence	AHL	65	12	15	27	49	-12	2	1	4	0	0	0	20
03-04—Boston	NHL	3	0	0	0	0	-1	0	0	—	—	—	—	—
—Providence	AHL	55	8	9	17	61	-5	3	1	2	0	0	0	4
04-05—Providence	AHL	5	0	1	1	2	-2	0	0	—	—	—	—	—
—Florida	ECHL	53	16	20	36	47	12	2	...	18	2	7	9	33
NHL Totals (2 years)		17	1	0	1	2	-3	0	0					

VEROT, DARCY — C/LW — CAPITALS

PERSONAL: Born July 13, 1976, in Radville, Sask. ... 6-0/202. ... Shoots left.

TRANSACTIONS/CAREER NOTES: Signed as free agent by Pittsburgh Penguins (July 28, 2000). ... Signed as free agent by Calgary Flames (July 9, 2002). ... Signed as free agent by Washington Capitals (September 5, 2003). ... Injured upper body (March 10, 2004); missed four games. ... Suspended three games for elbowing incident (April 1, 2004).

		REGULAR SEASON								PLAYOFFS				
Season Team	League	GP	G	A	Pts.	PIM	+/-	PP	SH	GP	G	A	Pts.	PIM
97-98—Lake Charles	WPHL	68	11	26	37	269	...	...	...	4	0	1	1	25
98-99—Lake Charles	WPHL	68	17	23	40	236	...	...	...	9	2	4	6	53
99-00—Wheeling	ECHL	44	7	12	19	240	...	...	...	—	—	—	—	—
—Wilkes-Barre/Scranton	AHL	23	5	5	10	96	...	...	...	—	—	—	—	—
00-01—Wilkes-Barre/Scranton	AHL	78	10	15	25	347	...	...	...	21	2	3	5	40
01-02—Wilkes-Barre/Scranton	AHL	71	6	10	16	387	-19	0	1	—	—	—	—	—
02-03—Saint John	AHL	73	5	11	16	299	0	2	0	—	—	—	—	—
03-04—Washington	NHL	37	0	2	2	135	-6	0	0	—	—	—	—	—
—Portland	AHL	28	3	5	8	89	-1	1	0	—	—	—	—	—
04-05—Portland	AHL	36	0	1	1	189	-17	0	0	—	—	—	—	—
NHL Totals (1 year)		37	0	2	2	135	-6	0	0					

VIGIER, J.P. — RW — THRASHERS

PERSONAL: Born September 11, 1976, in Notre Dame de Lourdes, Man. ... 6-0/200. ... Shoots right. ... Name pronounced vih-ZHAY.

TRANSACTIONS/CAREER NOTES: Signed as free agent by Atlanta Thrashers (March 24, 2000). ... Injured cheekbone (January 22, 2004); missed three games. ... Injured rib (February 21, 2004); missed seven games. ... Facial cuts (April 3, 2004); missed remainder of regular season. ... Signed as free agent by Chicago of the AHL (September 27, 2004).

		REGULAR SEASON								PLAYOFFS				
Season Team	League	GP	G	A	Pts.	PIM	+/-	PP	SH	GP	G	A	Pts.	PIM
96-97—Northern Michigan	CCHA	36	10	14	24	54	...	...	...	—	—	—	—	—
97-98—Northern Michigan	CCHA	36	12	15	27	60	...	...	...	—	—	—	—	—
98-99—Northern Michigan	CCHA	42	21	18	39	80	...	...	...	—	—	—	—	—
99-00—Northern Michigan	CCHA	39	18	17	35	72	...	...	...	—	—	—	—	—
—Orlando	IHL	1	0	0	0	0	...	...	...	—	—	—	—	—
00-01—Orlando	IHL	78	23	17	40	66	...	...	...	16	6	6	12	14
—Atlanta	NHL	2	0	0	0	0	-2	0	0	—	—	—	—	—
01-02—Chicago	AHL	62	25	16	41	26	4	9	0	21	7	7	14	20
—Atlanta	NHL	15	4	1	5	4	-5	0	0	—	—	—	—	—
02-03—Chicago	AHL	63	29	27	56	54	13	11	2	9	3	1	4	4
—Atlanta	NHL	13	0	0	0	4	-13	0	0	—	—	—	—	—
03-04—Atlanta	NHL	70	10	8	18	22	-18	2	2	—	—	—	—	—
04-05—Chicago	AHL	76	29	41	70	56	26	11	1	18	5	6	11	19
NHL Totals (4 years)		100	14	9	23	30	-38	2	2					

VINCENT, ALEXANDRE — G — CANUCKS

PERSONAL: Born December 11, 1986, in St. Leonard, Que. ... 6-4/195. ... Catches left.

		REGULAR SEASON									PLAYOFFS							
Season Team	League	GP	Min.	W	L	T	GA	SO	GAA	SV%	GP	Min.	W	L	GA	SO	GAA	SV%
03-04—Chicoutimi	QMJHL	...	...	11	11	1	...	...	3.14	.901	—	—	—	—	—	—	—	—
04-05—Chicoutimi	QMJHL	49	2591	24	13	4	130	2	3.01	.904	14	765	7	6	40	1	3.14	.905

VISHNEVSKI, VITALY — D — MIGHTY DUCKS

PERSONAL: Born March 18, 1980, in Kharkov, U.S.S.R. ... 6-2/203. ... Shoots left. ... Name pronounced vihsh-NEHV-skee.

TRANSACTIONS/CAREER NOTES: Selected by Anaheim Mighty Ducks in first round (first Mighty Ducks pick, fifth overall) of NHL draft (June 27, 1998). ... Injured (April 5, 2000); missed final two games of season. ... Strained hip muscle (January 30, 2001); missed three games. ... Strained shoulder (March 16, 2001); missed three games. ... Back spasms (December 23, 2001); missed one game. ... Sprained left wrist (December 26, 2001); missed five games. ... Suspended two games for elbowing incident (March 15, 2002).

		REGULAR SEASON								PLAYOFFS				
Season Team	League	GP	G	A	Pts.	PIM	+/-	PP	SH	GP	G	A	Pts.	PIM
95-96—Torpedo Yaroslavl	CIS Div. II	40	4	4	8	20	...	...	...	—	—	—	—	—
96-97—Torpedo Yaroslavl	Rus. Div.	45	0	2	2	30	...	...	...	—	—	—	—	—
97-98—Torpedo Yaroslavl	Rus. Div.	47	8	9	17	164	...	...	...	—	—	—	—	—
98-99—Torpedo Yaroslavl	Russian	34	3	4	7	38	...	...	...	10	0	0	0	4
99-00—Cincinnati	AHL	35	1	3	4	45	...	...	...	—	—	—	—	—
—Anaheim	NHL	31	1	1	2	26	0	1	0	—	—	—	—	—
00-01—Anaheim	NHL	76	1	10	11	99	-1	0	0	—	—	—	—	—
01-02—Anaheim	NHL	74	0	3	3	60	-10	0	0	—	—	—	—	—
02-03—Anaheim	NHL	80	2	6	8	76	-8	0	1	21	0	1	1	6
03-04—Anaheim	NHL	73	6	10	16	51	0	0	0	—	—	—	—	—
04-05—Khimik Voskresensk	Russian	51	7	17	24	92	-6	...	...	—	—	—	—	—
NHL Totals (5 years)		334	10	30	40	312	-19	1	1	21	0	1	1	6

VISNOVSKY, LUBOMIR — D — KINGS

PERSONAL: Born August 11, 1976, in Topolcany, Czechoslovakia. ... 5-10/188. ... Shoots left. ... Name pronounced LOO-boh-mihr vihsh-NAWV-skee.

TRANSACTIONS/CAREER NOTES: Selected by Los Angeles Kings in fourth round (fourth Kings pick, 118th overall) of NHL draft (June 24, 2000). ... Back spasms (December 3, 2000); missed one game. ... Back spasms (November 19, 2002); missed one game. ... Strained lower back (November 23, 2002); missed nine games. ... Sprained left knee (January 18, 2003); missed 12 games. ... Injured ankle (March 20, 2003); missed one game. ... Had concussion (December 20, 2003); missed six games. ... Injured shoulder (January 31, 2004); missed 17 games.

		REGULAR SEASON								PLAYOFFS				
Season Team	League	GP	G	A	Pts.	PIM	+/-	PP	SH	GP	G	A	Pts.	PIM
94-95—Bratislava	Slovakia	36	11	12	23	10	...	...	...	9	1	3	4	2
95-96—Bratislava	Slovakia	35	8	6	14	22	...	...	...	13	1	5	6	2
96-97—Bratislava	Slovakia	44	11	12	23	...	...	...	...	2	0	1	1	...
97-98—Bratislava	Slovakia	36	7	9	16	16	...	...	...	11	2	4	6	8
98-99—Bratislava	Slovakia	40	9	10	19	31	...	...	...	10	5	5	10	0
99-00—Bratislava	Slovakia	52	21	24	45	38	...	...	...	8	5	3	8	16
00-01—Los Angeles	NHL	81	7	32	39	36	16	3	0	8	0	0	0	0
01-02—Los Angeles	NHL	72	4	17	21	14	-5	1	0	4	0	1	1	0
—Slovakian Oly. team	Int'l	3	1	2	3	0	...	...	...	—	—	—	—	—
02-03—Los Angeles	NHL	57	8	16	24	28	2	1	0	—	—	—	—	—
03-04—Los Angeles	NHL	58	8	21	29	26	8	5	0	—	—	—	—	—
04-05—Bratislava	Slovakia	43	13	24	37	40	12	8	0	14	2	10	12	10
NHL Totals (4 years)		268	27	86	113	104	21	10	0	12	0	1	1	0

VOJTA, JAKUB — D — HURRICANES

PERSONAL: Born February 8, 1987, in Czech Republic. ... 6-0/190. ... Shoots right.

		REGULAR SEASON								PLAYOFFS				
Season Team	League	GP	G	A	Pts.	PIM	+/-	PP	SH	GP	G	A	Pts.	PIM
03-04—Sparta Prague	Czech.	39	3	3	6	22	...	...	...	—	—	—	—	—
04-05—Sparta Prague	Czech Rep.	38	2	7	9	42	...	...	...	—	—	—	—	—

VOKOUN, TOMAS — G — PREDATORS

PERSONAL: Born July 2, 1976, in Karlovy Vary, Czechoslovakia. ... 6-0/195. ... Catches right. ... Name pronounced voh-KOON.

TRANSACTIONS/CAREER NOTES: Selected by Montreal Canadiens in ninth round (11th Canadiens pick, 226th overall) of NHL draft (June 29, 1994). ... Selected by Nashville Predators in expansion draft (June 26, 1998). ... Strained neck (January 19, 1999); missed one game. ... Injured (March 31, 2000); missed final four games of season. ... Bruised foot (October 16, 2000); missed three games. ... Sprained ankle (April 6, 2002); missed remainder of season. ... Flu (January 14, 2003); missed one game. ... Flu (January 8, 2004); missed two games.

		REGULAR SEASON									PLAYOFFS							
Season Team	League	GP	Min.	W	L	T	GA	SO	GAA	SV%	GP	Min.	W	L	GA	SO	GAA	SV%
93-94—Poldi Kladno	Czech Rep.	1	20	...	...	...	2	0	6.00	...	—	—	—	—	—	—	—	—
94-95—Poldi Kladno	Czech Rep.	26	1368	...	...	...	70	...	3.07	...	5	240	...	...	19	...	4.75	...

Season	Team	League	GP	Min.	W	L	T	GA	SO	GAA	SV%	GP	Min.	W	L	GA	SO	GAA	SV%
			REGULAR SEASON									PLAYOFFS							
95-96	—Wheeling	ECHL	35	1911	20	10	2	117	0	3.67	...	7	436	4	3	19	0	2.61	...
	—Fredericton	AHL	...	...	...	...	...	...	...	...	...	1	59	0	1	4	0	4.07	...
96-97	—Fredericton	AHL	47	2645	12	26	7	154	2	3.49	.902	—	—	—	—	—	—	—	—
	—Montreal	NHL	1	20	0	0	0	4	0	12.00	.714	—	—	—	—	—	—	—	—
97-98	—Fredericton	AHL	31	1735	13	13	2	90	0	3.11	.907	—	—	—	—	—	—	—	—
98-99	—Milwaukee	IHL	9	539	3	2	4	22	1	2.45	.920	2	149	0	2	8	0	3.22	.909
	—Nashville	NHL	37	1954	12	18	4	96	1	2.95	.908	—	—	—	—	—	—	—	—
99-00	—Nashville	NHL	33	1879	9	20	1	87	1	2.78	.904	—	—	—	—	—	—	—	—
	—Milwaukee	IHL	7	364	6	2	0	17	0	2.80	...	—	—	—	—	—	—	—	—
00-01	—Nashville	NHL	37	2088	13	17	5	85	2	2.44	.910	—	—	—	—	—	—	—	—
01-02	—Nashville	NHL	29	1471	5	14	4	66	2	2.69	.903	—	—	—	—	—	—	—	—
02-03	—Nashville	NHL	69	3974	25	31	11	146	3	2.20	.918	—	—	—	—	—	—	—	—
03-04	—Nashville	NHL	73	4221	34	29	10	178	3	2.53	.909	6	356	2	4	12	1	2.02	.939
04-05	—HIFK Helsinki	Finland	—	—	—	—	—	—	—	—	—	4	205	0	3	12	0	3.51	.846
	—HC Znojemsti Orli	Czech Rep.	27	1599	10	14	3	69	3	2.59	.927	—	—	—	—	—	—	—	—
NHL Totals (7 years)			279	15607	98	129	35	662	12	2.55	.909	6	356	2	4	12	1	2.02	.939

VOLCHENKOV, ANTON — D — SENATORS

PERSONAL: Born February 25, 1982, in Moscow, U.S.S.R. ... 6-0/237. ... Shoots left.

TRANSACTIONS/CAREER NOTES: Selected by Ottawa Senators in first round (first Senators pick, 21st overall) of NHL draft (June 24, 2000). ... Dental surgery (December 27, 2002); missed one game. ... Injured groin (February 27, 2003); missed four games. ... Injured left shoulder (March 21, 2003); missed seven games. ... Had concussion (October 3, 2003); missed seven games. ... Injured right shoulder (December 9, 2003) and had surgery; missed 52 games.

Season	Team	League	GP	G	A	Pts.	PIM	+/-	PP	SH	GP	G	A	Pts.	PIM
			REGULAR SEASON								PLAYOFFS				
99-00	—CSKA	Rus. Div.	30	2	9	11	36	...	...	...	—	—	—	—	—
00-01	—Krylja Sovetov	Rus. Div.	34	3	4	7	56	...	...	...	—	—	—	—	—
01-02	—Kryla Sov. Moscow	Russian	47	4	16	20	50	...	...	...	3	0	0	0	29
02-03	—Ottawa	NHL	57	3	13	16	40	-4	0	0	17	1	1	2	4
03-04	—Ottawa	NHL	19	1	2	3	8	1	0	0	5	0	0	0	6
04-05	—Binghamton	AHL	69	10	35	45	62	24	3	0	6	0	3	3	0
NHL Totals (2 years)			76	4	15	19	48	-3	0	0	22	1	1	2	10

VOROBIEV, PAVEL — RW — BLACKHAWKS

PERSONAL: Born May 5, 1982, in Karaganda, U.S.S.R. ... 6-3/194. ... Shoots left.

TRANSACTIONS/CAREER NOTES: Selected by Chicago Blackhawks in first round (second Blackhawks pick, 11th overall) of NHL entry draft (June 24, 2000).

Season	Team	League	GP	G	A	Pts.	PIM	+/-	PP	SH	GP	G	A	Pts.	PIM
			REGULAR SEASON								PLAYOFFS				
98-99	—Torpedo Yaroslavl	Rus. Div.	17	0	1	1	0	...	...	...	—	—	—	—	—
99-00	—Torpedo Yaroslavl	Russian	8	2	0	2	4	...	...	...	—	—	—	—	—
	—Torpedo Yaroslavl	Rus. Div.	40	19	15	34	8	...	...	...	—	—	—	—	—
00-01	—Lokomotiv Yaroslavl	Russian	36	8	8	16	28	...	...	...	—	—	—	—	—
01-02	—Lokomotiv Yaroslavl	Russian	9	3	2	5	6	...	...	...	10	4	1	5	8
02-03	—Lokomotiv Yaroslavl	Russian	44	10	18	28	10	...	...	...	7	0	0	0	4
03-04	—Chicago	NHL	18	1	3	4	4	1	1	0	—	—	—	—	—
	—Norfolk	AHL	57	13	16	29	8	4	0	0	4	0	0	0	0
04-05	—Norfolk	AHL	79	19	25	44	48	-1	6	2	6	2	1	3	4
NHL Totals (1 year)			18	1	3	4	4	1	1	0					

VOROS, AARON — C — DEVILS

PERSONAL: Born July 2, 1981, in Vancover. ... 6-3/178. ... Shoots left.

TRANSACTIONS/CAREER NOTES: Selected by New Jersey Devils in eighth round (10th Devils pick, 229th overall) of NHL entry draft (June 24, 2001).

Season	Team	League	GP	G	A	Pts.	PIM	+/-	PP	SH	GP	G	A	Pts.	PIM
			REGULAR SEASON								PLAYOFFS				
00-01	—Victoria	BCJHL	57	34	34	68	196	...	...	...	—	—	—	—	—
01-02	—Alaska-Fairbanks	CCHA	37	18	13	31	101	...	...	...	—	—	—	—	—
02-03	—Alaska-Fairbanks	CCHA	16	2	5	7	42	...	...	...	—	—	—	—	—
03-04	—Alaska-Fairbanks	CCHA	36	16	8	24	132	...	...	...	—	—	—	—	—
	—Albany	AHL	9	2	1	3	14	...	...	...	—	—	—	—	—
04-05	—Albany	AHL	71	11	17	28	220	-11	4	0	—	—	—	—	—

VRBATA, RADIM — RW — HURRICANES

PERSONAL: Born June 13, 1981, in Mlada Boleslav, Czech. ... 6-1/190. ... Shoots right. ... Name pronounced ra-DEEM vuhr-BA-tuh.

TRANSACTIONS/CAREER NOTES: Selected by Colorado Avalanche in eighth round (10th Avalanche pick, 212th overall) of NHL draft (June 26, 1999). ... Injured ribs (December 21, 2001); missed eight games. ... Flu (March 6, 2002); missed one game. ... Injured wrist (March 7, 2003); missed one game. ... Traded by Avalanche to Carolina Hurricanes for LW Bates Battaglia (March 11, 2003). ... Flu (March 4, 2003); missed two games.

STATISTICAL PLATEAUS: Three-goal games: 2001-02 (1), 2003-04 (1). Total: 2.

Season Team	League	REGULAR SEASON								PLAYOFFS				
		GP	G	A	Pts.	PIM	+/-	PP	SH	GP	G	A	Pts.	PIM
98-99—Hull	QMJHL	64	22	38	60	16	...	...	...	23	6	13	19	6
99-00—Hull	QMJHL	58	29	45	74	26	...	...	...	15	3	9	12	8
00-01—Shawinigan	QMJHL	55	56	64	120	67	...	...	...	10	4	7	11	4
—Hershey	AHL	...	...	...	...	...	...	...	...	1	0	1	1	2
01-02—Hershey	AHL	20	8	14	22	8	5	2	0	—	—	—	—	—
—Colorado	NHL	52	18	12	30	14	7	6	0	9	0	0	0	0
02-03—Colorado	NHL	66	11	19	30	16	0	3	0	—	—	—	—	—
—Carolina	NHL	10	5	0	5	2	-7	3	0	—	—	—	—	—
03-04—Carolina	NHL	80	12	13	25	24	-10	4	0	—	—	—	—	—
04-05—Liberec	Czech Rep.	45	18	21	39	91	26	...	...	12	3	2	5	0
—Mlada-Boleslav	Czech. Jrs.	2	0	1	1	6	-2	...	...	—	—	—	—	—
NHL Totals (3 years)		208	46	44	90	56	-10	16	0	9	0	0	0	0

VYBORNY, DAVID — RW — BLUE JACKETS

PERSONAL: Born June 2, 1975, in Jihlava, Czechoslovakia. ... 5-10/189. ... Shoots left. ... Name pronounced vih-BOHR-nee.
TRANSACTIONS/CAREER NOTES: Selected by Edmonton Oilers in second round (third Oilers pick, 33rd overall) of NHL draft (June 26, 1993). ... Signed as free agent by Columbus Blue Jackets (June 7, 2000). ... Strained hip flexor (February 20, 2001); missed one game. ... Strained groin (April 1, 2001); missed two games. ... Strained hip flexor (November 29, 2001); missed one game. ... Sprained knee (January 24, 2002); missed three games.
STATISTICAL PLATEAUS: Three-goal games: 2003-04 (1).

Season Team	League	REGULAR SEASON								PLAYOFFS				
		GP	G	A	Pts.	PIM	+/-	PP	SH	GP	G	A	Pts.	PIM
90-91—Sparta Prague	Czech.	3	0	0	0	0	...	...	...	—	—	—	—	—
91-92—Sparta Prague	Czech.	32	6	9	15	2	...	...	...	—	—	—	—	—
92-93—Sparta Prague	Czech.	52	20	24	44	...	...	...	...	—	—	—	—	—
93-94—Sparta Prague	Czech Rep.	44	15	20	35	...	...	...	...	6	4	7	11	...
94-95—Cape Breton	AHL	76	23	38	61	30	-12	7	0	—	—	—	—	—
95-96—Sparta Praha	Czech Rep.	52	19	36	55	42	...	...	...	—	—	—	—	—
96-97—Sparta Praha	Czech Rep.	47	20	29	49	14	...	...	...	—	—	—	—	—
97-98—MoDo Ornskoldsvik	Sweden	45	16	21	37	34	...	...	...	—	—	—	—	—
98-99—Sparta Praha	Czech Rep.	52	24	46	*70	22	...	...	...	8	1	3	4	...
99-00—Sparta Praha	Czech Rep.	50	25	38	63	30	...	...	...	9	3	8	*11	4
00-01—Columbus	NHL	79	13	19	32	22	-9	5	0	—	—	—	—	—
01-02—Columbus	NHL	75	13	18	31	6	-14	6	0	—	—	—	—	—
02-03—Columbus	NHL	79	20	26	46	16	12	4	1	—	—	—	—	—
03-04—Columbus	NHL	82	22	31	53	40	-26	8	4	—	—	—	—	—
04-05—Sparta Praha	Czech Rep.	51	12	34	46	10	12	...	...	5	2	5	7	4
NHL Totals (4 years)		315	68	94	162	84	-37	23	5					

VYDARENY, RENE — D — CANADIENS

PERSONAL: Born May 6, 1981, in Bratislava, Czechoslovakia. ... 6-1/198. ... Shoots left. ... Name pronounced vih-DAH-reh-nay.
TRANSACTIONS/CAREER NOTES: Selected by Vancouver Canucks in third round (third Canucks pick, 69th overall) of NHL entry draft (June 26, 1999). ... Traded by Canucks to Montreal Canadiens for LW Sylvain Blouin (March 9, 2004).

Season Team	League	REGULAR SEASON								PLAYOFFS				
		GP	G	A	Pts.	PIM	+/-	PP	SH	GP	G	A	Pts.	PIM
97-98—Bratislava	Slov. Jr.	50	5	14	19	74	...	...	...	—	—	—	—	—
98-99—Bratislava	Slov. Jr.	42	4	7	11	65	...	...	...	2	0	0	0	2
99-00—Rimouski	QMJHL	51	7	23	30	41	41	1	1	14	2	2	4	20
00-01—Kansas City	IHL	39	0	1	1	25	...	...	...	—	—	—	—	—
01-02—Manitoba	AHL	61	3	11	14	15	18	0	0	7	0	2	2	4
—Columbia	ECHL	10	2	1	3	9	-4	2	0	—	—	—	—	—
02-03—Manitoba	AHL	71	2	8	10	46	-15	0	0	14	0	2	2	16
03-04—Manitoba	AHL	50	2	10	12	16	-6	0	0	—	—	—	—	—
—Hamilton	AHL	13	0	3	3	2	3	0	0	10	0	1	1	9
04-05—Bratislava	Slovakia	33	0	4	4	22	...	...	...	—	—	—	—	—

WALKER, MATT — D — BLUES

PERSONAL: Born April 7, 1980, in Beaverlodge, Alta. ... 6-3/227. ... Shoots right. ... Nickname: Walks.
TRANSACTIONS/CAREER NOTES: Selected by St. Louis Blues in third round (third Blues pick, 83rd overall) of NHL draft (June 27, 1998). ... Injured groin (September 23, 2003); missed last 51 games of season. ... Signed as free agent by Worcester of the AHL (December 17, 2004).

Season Team	League	REGULAR SEASON								PLAYOFFS				
		GP	G	A	Pts.	PIM	+/-	PP	SH	GP	G	A	Pts.	PIM
97-98—Portland	WHL	64	2	13	15	124	...	...	...	16	0	0	0	21
98-99—Portland	WHL	64	1	10	11	151	-16	0	0	—	—	—	—	—
99-00—Portland	WHL	38	2	7	9	97	...	...	...	—	—	—	—	—
—Kootenay	WHL	69	6	26	32	150	-1	6	0	—	—	—	—	—
00-01—Worcester	AHL	61	4	8	12	131	...	...	...	11	0	0	0	6
—Peoria	ECHL	8	1	0	1	70	...	...	...	—	—	—	—	—
01-02—Worcester	AHL	49	2	11	13	164	5	0	0	3	0	0	0	8
02-03—Worcester	AHL	40	1	8	9	58	15	0	0	—	—	—	—	—
—St. Louis	NHL	16	0	1	1	38	0	0	0	—	—	—	—	—
03-04—St. Louis	NHL	14	0	1	1	25	0	0	0	4	0	0	0	0
—Worcester	AHL	4	0	1	1	7	-2	0	0	—	—	—	—	—
04-05—Worcester	AHL	20	2	4	6	44	1	0	0	—	—	—	—	—
NHL Totals (2 years)		30	0	2	2	63	0	0	0	4	0	0	0	0

WALKER, SCOTT — RW — PREDATORS

PERSONAL: Born July 19, 1973, in Cambridge, Ont. ... 5-10/196. ... Shoots right.

TRANSACTIONS/CAREER NOTES: Selected by Vancouver Canucks in fifth round (fourth Canucks pick, 124th overall) of NHL draft (June 26, 1993). ... Strained abdominal muscle (October 12, 1996); missed eight games. ... Strained groin (December 13, 1996); missed six games. ... Fractured nose (November 16, 1997); missed four games. ... Selected by Nashville Predators in expansion draft (June 26, 1998). ... Separated shoulder (November 19, 1998); missed nine games. ... Ear infection (January 26, 1999); missed two games. ... Suffered concussion (December 6, 1999); missed 10 games. ... Bruised foot (January 21, 2000); missed three games. ... Separated left shoulder (January 19, 2001); missed eight games. ... Suffered concussion (November 13, 2001); missed three games. ... Suffered concussion (December 1, 2001); missed 12 games. ... Suffered post-concussion syndrome (January 10, 2002); missed remainder of season. ... Tore rib cartilage (October 16, 2002); missed 17 games. ... Strained neck (January 4, 2003); missed two games. ... Sprained knee (January 14, 2003); missed three games. ... Injured groin (November 13, 2003); missed six games.

STATISTICAL PLATEAUS: Three-goal games: 2000-01 (1), 2003-04 (1). Total: 2.

		REGULAR SEASON								PLAYOFFS				
Season Team	League	GP	G	A	Pts.	PIM	+/-	PP	SH	GP	G	A	Pts.	PIM
89-90—Kitch.-Cambridge Jr.	OHA	33	7	27	34	91	...	...	...	—	—	—	—	—
90-91—Cambridge Jr. B	OHA	45	10	27	37	241	...	...	...	—	—	—	—	—
91-92—Owen Sound	OHL	53	7	31	38	128	...	...	...	5	0	7	7	8
92-93—Owen Sound	OHL	57	23	68	91	110	...	...	...	8	1	5	6	16
—Canadian nat'l team	Int'l	2	3	0	3	0	...	...	...	—	—	—	—	—
93-94—Hamilton	AHL	77	10	29	39	272	-16	2	0	4	0	1	1	25
94-95—Syracuse	AHL	74	14	38	52	334	6	5	0	—	—	—	—	—
—Vancouver	NHL	11	0	1	1	33	0	0	0	—	—	—	—	—
95-96—Vancouver	NHL	63	4	8	12	137	-7	0	1	—	—	—	—	—
—Syracuse	AHL	15	3	12	15	52	...	...	...	16	9	8	17	39
96-97—Vancouver	NHL	64	3	15	18	132	2	0	0	—	—	—	—	—
97-98—Vancouver	NHL	59	3	10	13	164	-8	0	1	—	—	—	—	—
98-99—Nashville	NHL	71	15	25	40	103	0	0	1	—	—	—	—	—
99-00—Nashville	NHL	69	7	21	28	90	-16	0	1	—	—	—	—	—
00-01—Nashville	NHL	74	25	29	54	66	-2	9	3	—	—	—	—	—
01-02—Nashville	NHL	28	4	5	9	18	-13	1	0	—	—	—	—	—
02-03—Nashville	NHL	60	15	18	33	58	2	7	0	—	—	—	—	—
03-04—Nashville	NHL	75	25	42	67	94	4	9	3	6	0	1	1	6
NHL Totals (10 years)		574	101	174	275	895	-38	26	10	6	0	1	1	6

WALLIN, NICLAS — D — HURRICANES

PERSONAL: Born February 20, 1975, in Boden, Sweden. ... 6-3/220. ... Shoots left. ... Name pronounced VAH-leen.

TRANSACTIONS/CAREER NOTES: Selected by Carolina Hurricanes in 4th round (3rd Hurricanes pick, 97th overall) of entry draft (June 24, 2000). ... Fractured wrist (October 5, 2000); missed six games. ... Strained shoulder (January 29, 2001); missed five games.

		REGULAR SEASON								PLAYOFFS				
Season Team	League	GP	G	A	Pts.	PIM	+/-	PP	SH	GP	G	A	Pts.	PIM
96-97—Brynas Gavle	Sweden	47	1	1	2	16	...	...	...	—	—	—	—	—
97-98—Brynas Gavle	Sweden	44	2	3	5	57	...	...	...	3	0	1	1	4
98-99—Brynas Gavle	Sweden	46	2	4	6	52	...	...	...	14	0	0	0	8
99-00—Brynas Gavle	Sweden	48	7	9	16	73	...	...	...	—	—	—	—	—
00-01—Carolina	NHL	37	2	3	5	21	-11	0	0	3	0	0	0	2
—Cincinnati	IHL	8	1	2	3	4	...	...	...	—	—	—	—	—
01-02—Carolina	NHL	52	1	2	3	36	1	0	0	23	2	1	3	12
02-03—Carolina	NHL	77	2	8	10	71	-19	0	0	—	—	—	—	—
03-04—Carolina	NHL	57	3	7	10	51	-8	0	0	—	—	—	—	—
04-05—Lulea	Sweden	39	6	7	13	89	-15	4	0	3	0	1	1	6
NHL Totals (4 years)		223	8	20	28	179	-37	0	0	26	2	1	3	14

WALLIN, RICKARD — C — WILD

PERSONAL: Born September 9, 1980, in Stockholm, Sweden. ... 6-2/185. ... Shoots left. ... Name pronounced REE-kahrd wah-LEEN.

TRANSACTIONS/CAREER NOTES: Selected by Phoenix Coyotes in sixth round (eighth Coyotes pick, 160th overall) of NHL entry draft (June 27, 1998). ... Traded by Coyotes to Minnesota Wild for C Joe Juneau (June 23, 2000). ... Fractured hand (December 17, 2002); missed 20 games.

		REGULAR SEASON								PLAYOFFS				
Season Team	League	GP	G	A	Pts.	PIM	+/-	PP	SH	GP	G	A	Pts.	PIM
96-97—Vasteras	Sweden Jr.	26	3	3	6	...	...	...	...	—	—	—	—	—
97-98—Farjestad Karlstad	Sweden Jr.	29	20	20	40	32	...	...	...	2	1	1	2	2
98-99—Farjestad Karlstad	Sweden Jr.	5	0	0	0	0	...	...	...	—	—	—	—	—
99-00—Troja-Ljungby	Sweden Dv. 2	46	15	22	37	54	...	...	...	—	—	—	—	—
00-01—Farjestad Karlstad	Sweden	47	9	22	31	24	...	...	...	16	*11	3	14	4
01-02—Farjestad Karlstad	Sweden	50	12	31	43	56	...	...	...	10	4	9	13	8
02-03—Minnesota	NHL	4	1	0	1	0	1	0	0	—	—	—	—	—
—Houston	AHL	52	13	22	35	70	10	4	0	23	4	11	15	22
03-04—Minnesota	NHL	15	5	4	9	14	1	3	0	—	—	—	—	—
—Houston	AHL	47	14	18	32	36	-12	5	1	2	0	0	0	2
04-05—Houston	AHL	79	12	31	43	61	7	4	0	5	1	0	1	29
NHL Totals (2 years)		19	6	4	10	14	2	3	0					

WALSER, DERRICK — D — BLUE JACKETS

PERSONAL: Born May 12, 1978, in New Glasgow, Nova Scotia. ... 5-10/190. ... Shoots left.
TRANSACTIONS/CAREER NOTES: Signed as free agent by Columbus Blue Jackets (September 17, 2001). ... Injured shoulder (November 25, 2003); missed two games.

		REGULAR SEASON								PLAYOFFS				
Season Team	League	GP	G	A	Pts.	PIM	+/-	PP	SH	GP	G	A	Pts.	PIM
95-96—Beauport	QMJHL	69	9	31	40	56	...	...	...	2	2	11	13	16
96-97—Beauport	QMJHL	37	13	25	38	26	...	...	...	—	—	—	—	—
—Rimouski	QMJHL	31	15	30	45	44	...	...	...	4	2	2	4	6
97-98—Rimouski	QMJHL	70	41	69	110	135	...	...	...	18	10	26	36	49
98-99—Johnstown	ECHL	24	8	12	20	29	-9	3	0	—	—	—	—	—
—Saint John	AHL	40	3	7	10	24	-8	1	0	—	—	—	—	—
99-00—Saint John	AHL	14	2	3	5	10	...	...	...	—	—	—	—	—
—Johnstown	ECHL	54	17	26	43	104	...	...	...	7	3	3	6	8
00-01—Saint John	AHL	76	19	36	55	36	...	...	...	19	7	9	16	14
01-02—Syracuse	AHL	73	23	38	61	70	-4	13	0	10	1	5	6	12
—Columbus	NHL	2	1	0	1	0	-2	0	0	—	—	—	—	—
02-03—Syracuse	AHL	28	7	14	21	30	-1	3	1	—	—	—	—	—
—Columbus	NHL	53	4	13	17	34	-9	3	0	—	—	—	—	—
03-04—Columbus	NHL	27	1	8	9	22	-6	1	0	—	—	—	—	—
—Syracuse	AHL	48	10	26	36	82	-10	4	0	3	1	1	2	4
04-05—Eisbaren Berlin	Germany	50	9	14	23	143	...	...	...	12	4	4	8	20
NHL Totals (3 years)		82	6	21	27	56	-17	4	0					

WALZ, WES — C — WILD

PERSONAL: Born May 15, 1970, in Calgary. ... 5-10/180. ... Shoots right.
TRANSACTIONS/CAREER NOTES: Selected by Boston Bruins in third round (third Bruins pick, 57th overall) of NHL draft (June 17, 1989). ... Traded by Bruins with D Garry Galley and a third-round pick (Milos Hoban) in 1993 draft to Philadelphia Flyers for D Gord Murphy, RW Brian Dobbin and third-round pick (LW Sergei Zholtok) in 1992 draft (January 2, 1992). ... Signed as free agent by Calgary Flames (August 31, 1993). ... Strained hip (February 26, 1995); missed one game. ... Signed as free agent by Detroit Red Wings (August 11, 1995). ... Signed as free agent by Minnesota Wild (June 28, 2000). ... Sprained ankle (October 7, 2001); missed eight games. ... Bruised left shoulder (February 25, 2002); missed 10 games. ... Flu (January 4, 2003); missed one game. ... Flu (October 18, 2003); missed two games. ... Separated left shoulder (January 7, 2004); missed 11 games. ... Strained abdomen (February 27, 2004); missed one game. ... Aggravated abdominal strain (March 3, 2004); missed six games.

		REGULAR SEASON								PLAYOFFS				
Season Team	League	GP	G	A	Pts.	PIM	+/-	PP	SH	GP	G	A	Pts.	PIM
87-88—Prince Albert	WHL	1	1	1	2	0	...	...	...	—	—	—	—	—
88-89—Lethbridge	WHL	63	29	75	104	32	...	...	...	8	1	5	6	6
89-90—Boston	NHL	2	1	1	2	0	-1	1	0	—	—	—	—	—
—Lethbridge	WHL	56	54	86	140	69	...	...	...	19	13	*24	37	33
90-91—Maine	AHL	20	8	12	20	19	...	...	...	2	0	0	0	21
—Boston	NHL	56	8	8	16	32	-14	1	0	2	0	0	0	0
91-92—Boston	NHL	15	0	3	3	12	-3	0	0	—	—	—	—	—
—Maine	AHL	21	13	11	24	38	...	...	...	—	—	—	—	—
—Hershey	AHL	41	13	28	41	37	...	...	...	6	1	2	3	0
—Philadelphia	NHL	2	1	0	1	0	1	0	0	—	—	—	—	—
92-93—Hershey	AHL	78	35	45	80	106	-2	5	5	—	—	—	—	—
93-94—Calgary	NHL	53	11	27	38	16	20	1	0	6	3	0	3	2
—Saint John	AHL	15	6	6	12	14	6	2	1	—	—	—	—	—
94-95—Calgary	NHL	39	6	12	18	11	7	4	0	1	0	0	0	0
95-96—Adirondack	AHL	38	20	35	55	58	...	...	...	—	—	—	—	—
—Detroit	NHL	2	0	0	0	0	0	0	0	—	—	—	—	—
96-97—Zug	Switzerland	41	24	22	46	67	...	...	...	—	—	—	—	—
97-98—Zug	Switzerland	38	18	34	52	32	...	...	...	20	16	12	28	18
98-99—Zug	Switzerland	42	22	27	49	75	...	...	...	10	3	9	12	2
99-00—Long Beach	IHL	6	4	3	7	8	...	...	...	—	—	—	—	—
—Lugano	Switzerland	13	7	11	18	14	...	...	...	5	3	4	7	4
00-01—Minnesota	NHL	82	18	12	30	37	-8	0	7	—	—	—	—	—
01-02—Minnesota	NHL	64	10	20	30	43	0	0	2	—	—	—	—	—
02-03—Minnesota	NHL	80	13	19	32	63	11	0	0	18	7	6	13	14
03-04—Minnesota	NHL	57	12	13	25	32	5	0	3	—	—	—	—	—
NHL Totals (10 years)		452	80	115	195	246	18	7	12	27	10	6	16	16

WANVIG, KYLE — RW — WILD

PERSONAL: Born January 29, 1981, in Calgary. ... 6-2/219. ... Shoots right. ... Name pronounced WAHN-vihg.
TRANSACTIONS/CAREER NOTES: Selected by Boston Bruins in third round (third Bruins pick, 89th overall) of NHL entry draft (June 26, 1999). ... Returned to draft pool by Bruins and selected by Minnesota Wild in second round (second Wild pick, 36th overall) of NHL entry draft (June 23, 2001).

		REGULAR SEASON								PLAYOFFS				
Season Team	League	GP	G	A	Pts.	PIM	+/-	PP	SH	GP	G	A	Pts.	PIM
97-98—Edmonton	WHL	62	17	12	29	69	...	...	...	—	—	—	—	—
98-99—Kootenay	WHL	71	12	20	32	119	...	...	...	7	1	3	4	18
99-00—Kootenay	WHL	6	2	2	4	12	...	...	...	—	—	—	—	—
—Red Deer	WHL	58	21	18	39	123	2	5	0	4	1	0	1	4
00-01—Red Deer	WHL	69	55	46	101	202	...	...	...	22	10	12	22	47

Season Team	League	GP	G	A	Pts.	PIM	+/-	PP	SH	GP	G	A	Pts.	PIM
		REGULAR SEASON								PLAYOFFS				
01-02—Houston	AHL	34	6	7	13	43	-7	1	0	9	0	1	1	23
02-03—Minnesota	NHL	7	1	0	1	13	0	0	0	—	—	—	—	—
—Houston	AHL	57	13	16	29	137	...	...	...	21	6	4	10	27
03-04—Houston	AHL	72	25	16	41	147	0	10	0	2	0	1	1	0
—Minnesota	NHL	6	0	1	1	10	-2	0	0	—	—	—	—	—
04-05—Houston	AHL	76	13	17	30	158	-12	7	1	5	1	2	3	8
NHL Totals (2 years)		13	1	1	2	23	-2	0	0					

WARD, AARON D HURRICANES

PERSONAL: Born January 17, 1973, in Windsor, Ont. ... 6-2/225. ... Shoots right.

TRANSACTIONS/CAREER NOTES: Selected by Winnipeg Jets in first round (first Jets pick, fifth overall) of NHL draft (June 22, 1991). ... Traded by Jets with fourth-round pick (D John Jakopin) in 1993 draft and future considerations to Detroit Red Wings for RW Paul Ysebaert (June 11, 1993); Red Wings acquired RW Alan Kerr to complete deal (June 18, 1993). ... Bronchitis (December 22, 1996); missed three games. ... Flu (October 26, 1997); missed two games. ... Bruised knee (November 26, 1997); missed one game. ... Fractured right foot (December 3, 1997); missed 19 games. ... Sprained shoulder (February 7, 1998); missed two games. ... Strained rotator cuff (November 21, 1998); missed two games. ... Injured ribs (October 22, 1999); missed seven games. ... Injured (December 4, 1999); missed four games. ... Injured shoulder (January 22, 2000); missed final 35 games of regular season. ... Flu (January 7, 2001); missed two games. ... Traded by Red Wings to Carolina Hurricanes for second-round pick (C Jiri Hudler) in 2002 draft (July 9, 2001). ... Flu (December 12, 2001); missed one game. ... Injured arm (March 8, 2002); missed one game. ... Injured back (October 29, 2002); missed two games. ... Injured hip (March 15, 2003); missed three games. ... Infection (October 28, 2003); missed seven games. ... Injured upper body (November 26, 2003); missed two games. ... Injured knee (December 9, 2003); missed two games. ... Injured left wrist and had surgery (January 20, 2004); missed 20 games.

Season Team	League	GP	G	A	Pts.	PIM	+/-	PP	SH	GP	G	A	Pts.	PIM
		REGULAR SEASON								PLAYOFFS				
88-89—Nepean	COJHL	56	2	17	19	44	...	...	...	—	—	—	—	—
89-90—Nepean	COJHL	52	6	33	39	85	...	...	...	—	—	—	—	—
90-91—Univ. of Michigan	CCHA	46	8	11	19	126	...	...	...	—	—	—	—	—
91-92—Univ. of Michigan	CCHA	42	7	12	19	64	...	...	...	—	—	—	—	—
92-93—Univ. of Michigan	CCHA	30	5	8	13	73	...	...	...	—	—	—	—	—
—Canadian nat'l team	Int'l	4	0	0	0	8	...	...	...	—	—	—	—	—
93-94—Detroit	NHL	5	1	0	1	4	2	0	0	—	—	—	—	—
—Adirondack	AHL	58	4	12	16	87	31	0	0	9	2	6	8	6
94-95—Adirondack	AHL	76	11	24	35	87	2	2	0	4	0	1	1	0
—Detroit	NHL	1	0	1	1	2	1	0	0	—	—	—	—	—
95-96—Adirondack	AHL	74	5	10	15	133	...	...	...	3	0	0	0	6
96-97—Detroit	NHL	49	2	5	7	52	-9	0	0	19	0	0	0	17
97-98—Detroit	NHL	52	5	5	10	47	-1	0	0	—	—	—	—	—
98-99—Detroit	NHL	60	3	8	11	52	-5	0	0	8	0	1	1	8
99-00—Detroit	NHL	36	1	3	4	24	-4	0	0	3	0	0	0	0
00-01—Detroit	NHL	73	4	5	9	57	-4	0	0	—	—	—	—	—
01-02—Carolina	NHL	79	3	11	14	74	0	0	0	23	1	1	2	22
02-03—Carolina	NHL	77	3	6	9	90	-23	0	0	—	—	—	—	—
03-04—Carolina	NHL	49	3	5	8	37	1	2	0	—	—	—	—	—
04-05—Ingolstadt ERC	Germany	8	0	3	3	16	-5	0	0	11	1	1	2	16
NHL Totals (10 years)		481	25	49	74	439	-42	2	0	53	1	2	3	47

WARD, CAM G HURRICANES

PERSONAL: Born February 29, 1984, in Sherwood Park, Alta. ... 6-0/176. ... Catches left.

TRANSACTIONS/CAREER NOTES: Selected by Carolina Hurricanes in first round (first Hurricanes pick, 25th overall) of NHL entry draft (June 22, 2002).

Season Team	League	GP	Min.	W	L	T	GA	SO	GAA	SV%	GP	Min.	W	L	GA	SO	GAA	SV%
		REGULAR SEASON									PLAYOFFS							
00-01—Red Deer	WHL	1	60	1	0	0	0	1	0.00	...	—	—	—	—	—	—	—	—
01-02—Red Deer	WHL	46	2694	30	11	4	102	1	*2.27	...	*23	*1502	14	*9	*53	2	2.12	...
02-03—Red Deer	WHL	57	3368	40	13	3	118	5	2.10	...	—	—	—	—	—	—	—	—
03-04—Red Deer	WHL	56	3338	31	16	8	114	4	2.05	...	—	—	—	—	—	—	—	—
04-05—Lowell	AHL	50	2828	27	17	...	94	6	1.99	.937	11	663	5	6	28	2	2.53	.918

WARD, JASON RW/C CANADIENS

PERSONAL: Born January 16, 1979, in Chapleau, Ont. ... 6-3/203. ... Shoots right.

TRANSACTIONS/CAREER NOTES: Selected by Montreal Canadiens in 1st round (1st Canadiens pick, 11th overall) of entry draft (June 21, 1997). ... Fractured cheekbone (February 10, 2000); missed seven games. ... Injured knee (January 12, 2001); missed remainder of season. ... Injured elbow (March 27, 2003); missed four games ... Fractured ankle (November 1, 2003); missed 19 games. ... Separated left shoulder (January 24, 2004); missed two games. ... Signed as free agent by New York Rangers (Aug. 4, 2005).

Season Team	League	GP	G	A	Pts.	PIM	+/-	PP	SH	GP	G	A	Pts.	PIM
		REGULAR SEASON								PLAYOFFS				
94-95—Oshawa	Tier II Jr. A	47	30	31	61	75	...	...	...	—	—	—	—	—
95-96—Niagara Falls	OHL	64	15	35	50	139	...	...	...	10	6	4	10	23
96-97—Erie	OHL	58	25	39	64	137	6	4	3	5	1	2	3	2
97-98—Erie	OHL	21	7	9	16	42	...	...	...	—	—	—	—	—
—Windsor	OHL	26	19	27	46	34	...	...	...	—	—	—	—	—
—Fredericton	AHL	7	1	0	1	2	3	0	0	1	0	0	0	2
98-99—Windsor	OHL	12	8	11	19	25	...	...	...	—	—	—	—	—

Season Team	League	GP	G	A	Pts.	PIM	+/-	PP	SH	GP	G	A	Pts.	PIM
		REGULAR SEASON								PLAYOFFS				
—Plymouth	OHL	23	14	13	27	28	...	...	...	11	6	8	14	12
—Fredericton	AHL	...	...	...	...	...	...	...	...	10	4	2	6	22
99-00—Quebec	AHL	40	14	12	26	30	...	...	...	3	2	1	3	4
—Montreal	NHL	32	2	1	3	10	-1	1	0	—	—	—	—	—
00-01—Quebec	AHL	23	7	12	19	69	...	...	...	—	—	—	—	—
—Montreal	NHL	12	0	0	0	12	3	0	0	—	—	—	—	—
01-02—Quebec	AHL	78	24	33	57	128	0	4	1	3	0	0	0	2
02-03—Montreal	NHL	8	3	2	5	0	3	0	0	—	—	—	—	—
—Hamilton	AHL	69	31	41	72	78	20	10	4	23	12	9	21	20
03-04—Montreal	NHL	53	5	7	12	21	3	2	0	5	0	2	2	2
—Hamilton	AHL	2	0	3	3	17	1	0	0	—	—	—	—	—
04-05—Hamilton	AHL	77	20	34	54	66	7	9	1	4	2	1	3	2
NHL Totals (4 years)		105	10	10	20	43	8	3	0	5	0	2	2	2

WARD, LANCE D/LW

PERSONAL: Born June 2, 1978, in Lloydminster, Alberta. ... 6-3/216. ... Shoots left.

TRANSACTIONS/CAREER NOTES: Selected by New Jersey Devils in first round (first Devils pick, 10th overall) of NHL draft (June 22, 1996). ... Returned to draft pool by Devils and selected by Florida Panthers in third round (third Panthers pick, 63rd overall) of NHL entry draft (June 27, 1998). ... Injured back (February 28, 2001); missed 17 games. ... Suffered concussion (March 13, 2002); missed 13 games. ... Suspended one game for unsportsmanlike conduct (October 21, 2002). ... Traded by Panthers with D Sandis Ozolinsh to Mighty Ducks of Anaheim for C Matt Cullen, D Pavel Trnka and fourth-round pick (D James Pemberton) in 2003 (January 30, 2003). ... Injured groin (December 29, 2003); missed one game.

Season Team	League	GP	G	A	Pts.	PIM	+/-	PP	SH	GP	G	A	Pts.	PIM
		REGULAR SEASON								PLAYOFFS				
93-94—Medicine Hat	WHL	68	1	4	5	166	...	...	...	3	0	0	0	2
94-95—Red Deer	WHL	28	0	0	0	57	...	...	...	—	—	—	—	—
95-96—Red Deer	WHL	72	4	13	17	127	...	...	...	10	0	4	4	10
96-97—Red Deer	WHL	70	5	34	39	229	-21	1	0	16	0	3	3	36
97-98—Red Deer	WHL	71	8	25	33	233	-7	4	0	5	0	0	0	16
98-99—Miami	ECHL	6	1	0	1	12	-1	0	0	—	—	—	—	—
—Fort Wayne	IHL	13	0	2	2	28	-4	0	0	—	—	—	—	—
—New Haven	AHL	43	2	5	7	51	-1	0	0	—	—	—	—	—
99-00—Louisville	AHL	80	4	16	20	190	...	...	...	4	0	0	0	6
00-01—Louisville	AHL	35	3	2	5	78	...	...	...	—	—	—	—	—
—Florida	NHL	30	0	2	2	45	-3	0	0	—	—	—	—	—
01-02—Florida	NHL	68	1	4	5	131	-20	0	0	—	—	—	—	—
02-03—Florida	NHL	36	3	1	4	78	-4	0	0	—	—	—	—	—
—Anaheim	NHL	29	0	1	1	43	-2	0	0	—	—	—	—	—
03-04—Anaheim	NHL	46	0	4	4	94	-1	0	0	—	—	—	—	—
—Cincinnati	AHL	5	0	1	1	6	-2	0	0	—	—	—	—	—
NHL Totals (4 years)		209	4	12	16	391	-30	0	0					

WARRENER, RHETT D FLAMES

PERSONAL: Born January 27, 1976, in Shaunavon, Sask. ... 6-2/217. ... Shoots right. ... Name pronounced REHT WAHR-ihn-nuhr.

TRANSACTIONS/CAREER NOTES: Selected by Florida Panthers in second round (second Panthers pick, 27th overall) of NHL draft (June 28, 1994). ... Strained groin (October 20, 1996); missed four games. ... Reinjured groin (November 11, 1996); missed two games. ... Reinjured groin (December 22, 1996); missed 10 games. ... Strained groin (November 2, 1998); missed 12 games. ... Traded by Panthers with fifth-round pick (G Ryan Miller) in 1999 draft to Buffalo Sabres for D Mike Wilson (March 23, 1999). ... Injured shoulder (October 30, 1999); missed two games. ... Strained hip muscle (January 1, 2000); missed four games. ... Injured groin (February 21, 2000); missed eight games. ... Suffered concussion (November 17, 2000); missed five games. ... Injured groin (October 26, 2001); missed 14 games. ... Injured wrist (January 8, 2002); missed one game. ... Suspended two games for receiving third instigator penalty in one season (March 29, 2002). ... Strained abdominal muscle (December 1, 2002); missed three games. ... Injured groin (December 20, 2002); missed nine games. ... Fractured foot (January 10, 2003); missed 10 games. ... Inner-ear imbalance (March 18, 2002); missed one game. ... Traded by Sabres to Calgary Flames with C Steve Reinprecht for C Steve Begin and C/LW Chris Drury (July 2, 2003). ... Injured groin (November 4, 2003); missed two games. ... Injured mouth (January 30, 2004); missed two games.

Season Team	League	GP	G	A	Pts.	PIM	+/-	PP	SH	GP	G	A	Pts.	PIM
		REGULAR SEASON								PLAYOFFS				
91-92—Saskatoon	WHL	2	0	0	0	0	...	...	...	—	—	—	—	—
92-93—Saskatoon	WHL	68	2	17	19	100	...	...	...	9	0	0	0	14
93-94—Saskatoon	WHL	61	7	19	26	131	25	6	0	16	0	5	5	33
94-95—Saskatoon	WHL	66	13	26	39	137	52	4	0	10	0	3	3	6
95-96—Carolina	AHL	9	0	0	0	4	...	...	...	—	—	—	—	—
—Florida	NHL	28	0	3	3	46	4	0	0	21	0	3	3	10
96-97—Florida	NHL	62	4	9	13	88	20	1	0	5	0	0	0	0
97-98—Florida	NHL	79	0	4	4	99	-16	0	0	—	—	—	—	—
98-99—Florida	NHL	48	0	7	7	64	-1	0	0	—	—	—	—	—
—Buffalo	NHL	13	1	0	1	20	3	0	0	20	1	3	4	32
99-00—Buffalo	NHL	61	0	3	3	89	18	0	0	5	0	0	0	2
00-01—Buffalo	NHL	77	3	16	19	78	10	0	0	13	0	2	2	4
01-02—Buffalo	NHL	65	5	5	10	113	15	0	0	—	—	—	—	—
02-03—Buffalo	NHL	50	0	9	9	63	1	0	0	—	—	—	—	—
03-04—Calgary	NHL	77	3	14	17	97	8	0	1	24	0	1	1	6
NHL Totals (9 years)		560	16	70	86	757	62	1	1	88	1	9	10	54

WATSON, GREG — C — SENATORS

PERSONAL: Born March 2, 1983, in Eastend, Sask. ... 6-1/177. ... Shoots left.

TRANSACTIONS/CAREER NOTES: Selected by Florida Panthers in second round (third Panthers pick, 34th overall) of NHL entry draft (June 23, 2001). ... Traded by Panthers with G Billy Thompson to Ottawa Senators for G Jani Hurme (October 1, 2002).

		REGULAR SEASON								PLAYOFFS				
Season Team	**League**	**GP**	**G**	**A**	**Pts.**	**PIM**	**+/-**	**PP**	**SH**	**GP**	**G**	**A**	**Pts.**	**PIM**
98-99—Prince Albert	WHL	2	0	0	0	5	...	...	...	—	—	—	—	—
99-00—Prince Albert	WHL	67	10	5	15	63	...	...	...	6	0	2	2	2
00-01—Prince Albert	WHL	71	22	28	50	72	...	...	...	—	—	—	—	—
01-02—Prince Albert	WHL	51	22	30	52	88	...	...	...	—	—	—	—	—
02-03—Prince Albert	WHL	39	11	15	26	58	...	...	...	—	—	—	—	—
—Brandon	WHL	69	17	29	46	95	...	...	...	17	3	8	11	12
03-04—Binghamton	AHL	69	4	7	11	72	-6	0	0	2	0	0	0	2
04-05—Binghamton	AHL	57	3	4	7	68	1	0	0	1	0	0	0	0

WEAVER, MIKE — D — KINGS

PERSONAL: Born May 2, 1978, in Bramalea, Ont. ... 5-9/185. ... Shoots right.

TRANSACTIONS/CAREER NOTES: Signed as free agent by Atlanta Thrashers (June 15, 2000). ... Signed as free agent by Los Angeles Kings (July 16, 2004).

		REGULAR SEASON								PLAYOFFS				
Season Team	**League**	**GP**	**G**	**A**	**Pts.**	**PIM**	**+/-**	**PP**	**SH**	**GP**	**G**	**A**	**Pts.**	**PIM**
96-97—Michigan State	CCHA	39	0	7	7	46	...	...	...	—	—	—	—	—
97-98—Michigan State	CCHA	44	4	22	26	68	...	...	...	—	—	—	—	—
98-99—Michigan State	CCHA	42	1	6	7	54	...	...	...	—	—	—	—	—
99-00—Michigan State	CCHA	37	0	8	8	34	...	...	...	—	—	—	—	—
00-01—Orlando	IHL	68	0	8	8	34	...	...	...	16	0	2	2	8
01-02—Chicago	AHL	58	2	8	10	67	-9	1	0	25	1	3	4	21
—Atlanta	NHL	16	0	1	1	10	0	0	0	—	—	—	—	—
02-03—Atlanta	NHL	40	0	5	5	20	-5	0	0	—	—	—	—	—
—Chicago	AHL	33	2	2	4	32	2	0	0	9	0	3	3	4
03-04—Atlanta	NHL	1	0	0	0	0	-1	0	0	—	—	—	—	—
—Chicago	AHL	78	3	14	17	89	20	0	0	9	2	2	4	20
04-05—Manchester	AHL	79	1	22	23	61	35	0	0	6	0	1	1	0
NHL Totals (3 years)		57	0	6	6	30	-6	0	0					

WEBB, STEVE — RW

PERSONAL: Born April 30, 1975, in Peterborough, Ont. ... 6-0/218. ... Shoots right.

TRANSACTIONS/CAREER NOTES: Selected by Buffalo Sabres in seventh round (eighth Sabres pick, 176th overall) of NHL draft (June 29, 1994). ... Signed as free agent by New York Islanders (October 14, 1996). ... Injured lower back (October 27, 1999); missed one game. ... Injured back (November 4, 1999); missed four games. ... Flu (April 9, 2000); missed final game of season. ... Strained back (November 7, 2000); missed two games. ... Strained left knee (November 18, 2000); missed 11 games. ... Reinjured knee (December 12, 2000); missed 16 games. ... Reinjured knee (January 21, 2001); missed 22 games. ... Injured hip (October 30, 2001); missed one game. ... Injured hand (January 6, 2002); missed 17 games. ... Suffered concussion (March 27, 2002); missed one game. ... Injured back (October 15, 2002); missed four games. ... Back spasms (December 30, 2002); missed 21 games. ... Signed as free agent by Philadelphia Flyers (October 21, 2003). ... Claimed by Pittsburgh Penguins off waivers from Philadelphia Flyers (October 22, 2003). ... Traded by Penguins to Islanders for D Alain Nasreddine (March 8, 2004).

		REGULAR SEASON								PLAYOFFS				
Season Team	**League**	**GP**	**G**	**A**	**Pts.**	**PIM**	**+/-**	**PP**	**SH**	**GP**	**G**	**A**	**Pts.**	**PIM**
91-92—Peterborough	Jr. B	37	9	9	18	195	...	...	...	—	—	—	—	—
92-93—Windsor	OHL	63	14	25	39	181	...	...	...	—	—	—	—	—
93-94—Windsor	OHL	33	6	15	21	117	...	...	...	—	—	—	—	—
—Peterborough	OHL	2	0	1	1	9	...	...	...	—	—	—	—	—
94-95—Peterborough	OHL	42	8	16	24	109	...	0	...	11	3	3	6	22
95-96—Muskegon	Col.HL	58	18	24	42	263	...	...	...	5	1	2	3	22
—Detroit	IHL	4	0	0	0	24	...	...	...	—	—	—	—	—
96-97—Kentucky	AHL	25	6	6	12	103	5	0	0	2	0	0	0	19
—New York Islanders	NHL	41	1	4	5	144	-10	1	0	—	—	—	—	—
97-98—Kentucky	AHL	37	5	13	18	139	-10	2	0	3	0	1	1	10
—New York Islanders	NHL	20	0	0	0	35	-2	0	0	—	—	—	—	—
98-99—Lowell	AHL	23	2	4	6	80	-9	0	0	—	—	—	—	—
—New York Islanders	NHL	45	0	0	0	32	-10	0	0	—	—	—	—	—
99-00—New York Islanders	NHL	65	1	3	4	103	-4	0	0	—	—	—	—	—
00-01—New York Islanders	NHL	31	0	2	2	35	1	0	0	—	—	—	—	—
01-02—New York Islanders	NHL	60	2	4	6	104	0	0	0	7	0	0	0	12
02-03—New York Islanders	NHL	49	1	0	1	75	-5	0	0	5	0	0	0	10
03-04—Wilkes-Barre/Scranton	AHL	30	4	7	11	48	1	1	0	—	—	—	—	—
—Pittsburgh	NHL	5	0	0	0	2	-3	0	0	—	—	—	—	—
—New York Islanders	NHL	5	0	0	0	2	-1	0	0	2	0	0	0	6
—Bridgeport	AHL	7	1	0	1	29	1	0	0	5	0	0	0	4
NHL Totals (8 years)		321	5	13	18	532	-34	1	0	14	0	0	0	28

WEEKES, KEVIN — G — RANGERS

PERSONAL: Born April 4, 1975, in Toronto. ... 6-0/195. ... Catches left. ... Name pronounced WEEKS.

TRANSACTIONS/CAREER NOTES: Selected by Florida Panthers in second round (second Panthers pick, 41st overall) of NHL draft (June 26, 1993). ... Sprained right knee (March 19, 1998); missed remainder of season. ... Traded by Panthers with D Ed Jovanovski, C Dave Gagner, C

Mike Brown and first-round pick (C Nathan Smith) in 2000 draft to Vancouver Canucks for RW Pavel Bure, D Bret Hedican, D Brad Ference and third-round pick (RW Robert Fried) in 2000 draft (January 17, 1999). ... Injured knee (October 28, 1999); missed three games. ... Traded by Canucks with C Dave Scatchard and RW Bill Muckalt to New York Islanders for G Felix Potvin, second- (traded to New Jersey; Devils selected RW Teemu Laine) and third-round (C Thatcher Bell) picks in 2000 draft (December 19, 1999). ... Sore neck (April 9, 2000); missed final game of season. ... Traded by Islanders with D Kristian Kudroc and second-round pick (traded to Phoenix; Coyotes selected D Matthew Spiller) in 2001 draft to Tampa Bay Lightning for first-(LW Raffi Torres), fourth-(RW/LW Vladimir Gorbunov) and seventh-round (D Ryan Caldwell) picks in 2000 draft (June 24, 2000). ... Injured knee (December 2, 2000); missed three games. ... Strained groin (January 7, 2001); missed three games. ... Strained groin (April 4, 2001); missed final three games of season. ... Traded by Lightning to Carolina Hurricanes for RW Shane Willis and LW Craig Dingman (March 5, 2002). ... Suffered concussion (December 11, 2002); missed eight games. ... Signed as free agent by New York Rangers (August 26, 2004).

		REGULAR SEASON									PLAYOFFS							
Season Team	**League**	**GP**	**Min.**	**W**	**L**	**T**	**GA**	**SO**	**GAA**	**SV%**	**GP**	**Min.**	**W**	**L**	**GA**	**SO**	**GAA**	**SV%**
91-92—Toronto St. Mikes	OJHL	35	1575	...	...	...	68	4	2.59	...	—	—	—	—	—	—	—	—
—St. Michael's	Tier II Jr. A	2	127	...	...	...	11	0	5.20	...	—	—	—	—	—	—	—	—
92-93—Owen Sound	OHL	29	1645	9	12	5	143	0	5.22	...	1	26	0	0	5	0	11.54	...
93-94—Owen Sound	OHL	34	1974	13	19	1	158	0	4.80	.880	—	—	—	—	—	—	—	—
94-95—Ottawa	OHL	41	2266	13	23	4	154	1	4.08	.879	—	—	—	—	—	—	—	—
95-96—Carolina	AHL	60	3403	24	25	8	229	2	4.04	...	—	—	—	—	—	—	—	—
96-97—Carolina	AHL	51	2899	17	28	4	172	1	3.56	.895	—	—	—	—	—	—	—	—
97-98—Fort Wayne	IHL	12	719	9	2	1	34	1	2.84	.918	—	—	—	—	—	—	—	—
—Florida	NHL	11	485	0	5	1	32	0	3.96	.870	—	—	—	—	—	—	—	—
98-99—Detroit	IHL	33	1857	19	5	7	64	*4	*2.07	.919	—	—	—	—	—	—	—	—
—Vancouver	NHL	11	532	0	8	1	34	0	3.83	.868	—	—	—	—	—	—	—	—
99-00—Vancouver	NHL	20	987	6	7	4	47	1	2.86	.898	—	—	—	—	—	—	—	—
—New York Islanders	NHL	36	2026	10	20	4	115	1	3.41	.902	—	—	—	—	—	—	—	—
00-01—Tampa Bay	NHL	61	3378	20	*33	3	177	4	3.14	.898	—	—	—	—	—	—	—	—
01-02—Tampa Bay	NHL	19	830	3	9	0	40	2	2.89	.915	—	—	—	—	—	—	—	—
—Carolina	NHL	2	120	2	0	0	3	0	1.50	.927	8	408	3	2	11	2	1.62	.939
02-03—Carolina	NHL	51	2965	14	24	9	126	5	2.55	.912	—	—	—	—	—	—	—	—
03-04—Carolina	NHL	66	3765	23	30	11	146	6	2.33	.912	—	—	—	—	—	—	—	—
NHL Totals (7 years)		277	15088	78	136	33	720	19	2.86	.904	8	408	3	2	11	2	1.62	.939

WEIGHT, DOUG C BLUES

PERSONAL: Born January 21, 1971, in Warren, Mich. ... 5-11/201. ... Shoots left. ... Name pronounced WAYT.

TRANSACTIONS/CAREER NOTES: Selected by New York Rangers in second round (second Rangers pick, 34th overall) of NHL draft (June 16, 1990). ... Sprained elbow (October 14, 1991); missed three games. ... Damaged ligaments (January 11, 1991). ... Suspended four off-days and fined $500 for cross-checking (November 5, 1992). ... Traded by Rangers to Edmonton Oilers for LW Esa Tikkanen (March 17, 1993). ... Sprained ankle (February 15, 1997); missed one game. ... Injured ankle (February 21, 1997); missed one game. ... Sprained left shoulder (March 15, 1998); missed two games. ... Tore right knee ligament (October 28, 1998); missed 34 games. ... Fractured ribs (December 14, 1999); missed five games. ... Traded by Oilers with LW Michel Riesen to St. Louis Blues for C Marty Reasoner, C Jochen Hecht and D Jan Horacek (July 1, 2001). ... Sprained knee and injured hip (February 28, 2002); missed 20 games. ... Injured ankle (February 5, 2003); missed two games. ... Fractured facial bone (February 11, 2003); missed 10 games. ... Suspended by NHL for four games for high-sticking incident (November 7, 2003). ... Injured groin (November 16, 2003); missed one game. ... Injured groin (December 23, 2003); missed one game.

STATISTICAL PLATEAUS: Three-goal games: 1995-96 (1), 2003-04 (1). Total: 2.

		REGULAR SEASON								PLAYOFFS				
Season Team	**League**	**GP**	**G**	**A**	**Pts.**	**PIM**	**+/-**	**PP**	**SH**	**GP**	**G**	**A**	**Pts.**	**PIM**
88-89—Bloomfield	NAJHL	34	26	53	79	105	...	...	...	—	—	—	—	—
89-90—Lake Superior St.	CCHA	46	21	48	69	44	...	...	...	—	—	—	—	—
90-91—Lake Superior St.	CCHA	42	29	46	75	86	...	...	...	—	—	—	—	—
—New York Rangers	NHL	...	...	...	...	...	...	...	...	1	0	0	0	0
91-92—New York Rangers	NHL	53	8	22	30	23	-3	0	0	7	2	2	4	0
—Binghamton	AHL	9	3	14	17	2	...	...	...	4	1	4	5	6
92-93—New York Rangers	NHL	65	15	25	40	55	4	3	0	—	—	—	—	—
—Edmonton	NHL	13	2	6	8	10	-2	0	0	—	—	—	—	—
93-94—Edmonton	NHL	84	24	50	74	47	-22	4	1	—	—	—	—	—
94-95—Rosenheim	Germany	8	2	3	5	18	...	...	...	—	—	—	—	—
—Edmonton	NHL	48	7	33	40	69	-17	1	0	—	—	—	—	—
95-96—Edmonton	NHL	82	25	79	104	95	-19	9	0	—	—	—	—	—
96-97—Edmonton	NHL	80	21	61	82	80	1	4	0	12	3	8	11	8
97-98—Edmonton	NHL	79	26	44	70	69	1	9	0	12	2	7	9	14
—U.S. Olympic team	Int'l	4	0	2	2	2	-3	0	0	—	—	—	—	—
98-99—Edmonton	NHL	43	6	31	37	12	-8	1	0	4	1	1	2	15
99-00—Edmonton	NHL	77	21	51	72	54	6	3	1	5	3	2	5	4
00-01—Edmonton	NHL	82	25	65	90	91	12	8	0	6	1	5	6	17
01-02—St. Louis	NHL	61	15	34	49	40	20	3	0	10	1	1	2	4
—U.S. Olympic team	Int'l	6	0	3	3	4	...	...	...	—	—	—	—	—
02-03—St. Louis	NHL	70	15	52	67	52	-6	7	0	7	5	8	13	2
03-04—St. Louis	NHL	75	14	51	65	37	-3	6	0	5	2	1	3	6
04-05—Frankfurt	Germany	7	6	9	15	26	8	3	0	11	2	10	12	8
NHL Totals (14 years)		912	224	604	828	734	-36	58	2	69	20	35	55	70

WEINHANDL, MATTIAS RW/LW ISLANDERS

PERSONAL: Born June 1, 1980, in Ljungby, Sweden. ... 6-0/195. ... Shoots right. ... Name pronounced maa-TEE-us WIGHN-hahn-duhl.

TRANSACTIONS/CAREER NOTES: Selected by New York Islanders in third round (fifth Islanders pick, 78th overall) of NHL draft (June 26, 1999). ... Injured shoulder (November 29, 2002); missed eight games. ... Injured ankle (September 10, 2003); missed season's first 12 games.

		REGULAR SEASON								PLAYOFFS				
Season Team	League	GP	G	A	Pts.	PIM	+/-	PP	SH	GP	G	A	Pts.	PIM
97-98—Troja-Ljungby	Sweden Dv. 2	29	4	2	6	10	...	...	...	—	—	—	—	—
98-99—Troja-Ljungby	Sweden Dv. 2	38	20	20	40	30	...	...	...	—	—	—	—	—
99-00—MoDo Ornskoldsvik	Sweden	32	15	9	24	6	...	...	...	13	5	3	8	8
00-01—MoDo Ornskoldsvik	Sweden	48	16	16	32	14	...	...	...	6	1	3	4	6
01-02—MoDo Ornskoldsvik	Sweden	50	18	16	34	10	...	...	...	14	4	*11	*15	4
02-03—Bridgeport	AHL	23	9	12	21	14	2	2	1	—	—	—	—	—
—New York Islanders	NHL	47	6	17	23	10	-2	1	0	—	—	—	—	—
03-04—New York Islanders	NHL	55	8	12	20	26	9	4	0	5	0	0	0	2
—Bridgeport	AHL	10	3	6	9	10	7	0	0	—	—	—	—	—
04-05—MoDo Ornskoldsvik	Sweden	50	26	20	46	18	3	14	0	6	0	0	0	4
NHL Totals (2 years)		102	14	29	43	36	7	5	0	5	0	0	0	2

WEINRICH, ERIC — D — BLUES

PERSONAL: Born December 19, 1966, in Roanoke, Va. ... 6-1/207. ... Shoots left. ... Name pronounced WIGHN-rihch.

TRANSACTIONS/CAREER NOTES: Selected by New Jersey Devils in second round (third Devils pick, 32nd overall) of NHL draft (June 15, 1985). ... Traded by Devils with G Sean Burke to Hartford Whalers for RW Bobby Holik and second-round pick (LW Jay Pandolfo) in 1993 draft (August 28, 1992). ... Suffered concussion (November 25, 1992); missed two games. ... Sprained knee (September 22, 1993); missed five games. ... Injured right knee (October 5, 1993); missed five games. ... Traded with LW Patrick Poulin by Whalers to the Chicago Blackhawks for RW Steve Larmer and D Bryan Marchment (November 2, 1993). ... Fractured jaw (February 24, 1994); missed 17 games. ... Cut eye (November 1, 1995); missed three games. ... Cut thigh (December 31, 1996); missed one game. ... Traded by Blackhawks with G Jeff Hackett, D Alain Nasreddine and fourth-round pick (D Chris Dyment) in 1999 draft to Montreal Canadiens for G Jocelyn Thibault, D Dave Manson and D Brad Brown (November 16, 1998). ... Fractured foot (March 22, 2000); missed five games. ... Traded by Canadiens to Boston Bruins for D Patrick Traverse (February 21, 2001). ... Signed as free agent by Philadelphia Flyers (July 5, 2001). ... Strained left shoulder (October 30, 2001); missed two games, ... Bruised foot (February 4, 2004); missed three games. ... Traded by Flyers to St. Louis Blues for fifth-round pick in 2004 draft (February 9, 2004).

		REGULAR SEASON								PLAYOFFS				
Season Team	League	GP	G	A	Pts.	PIM	+/-	PP	SH	GP	G	A	Pts.	PIM
83-84—North Yarmouth Acad.	Maine H.S.	17	23	33	56	...	...	...	...	—	—	—	—	—
84-85—North Yarmouth Acad.	Maine H.S.	20	6	21	27	...	...	...	...	—	—	—	—	—
85-86—Maine	Hockey East	34	0	15	15	26	...	...	...	—	—	—	—	—
86-87—Maine	Hockey East	41	12	32	44	59	...	...	...	—	—	—	—	—
87-88—Maine	Hockey East	8	4	7	11	22	...	...	...	—	—	—	—	—
—U.S. national team	Int'l	39	3	9	12	24	...	...	...	—	—	—	—	—
—U.S. Olympic team	Int'l	3	0	0	0	24	2	...	...	—	—	—	—	—
88-89—Utica	AHL	80	17	27	44	70	...	...	...	5	0	1	1	8
—New Jersey	NHL	2	0	0	0	0	-1	0	0	—	—	—	—	—
89-90—Utica	AHL	57	12	48	60	38	...	...	...	—	—	—	—	—
—New Jersey	NHL	19	2	7	9	11	1	1	0	6	1	3	4	17
90-91—New Jersey	NHL	76	4	34	38	48	10	1	0	7	1	2	3	6
91-92—New Jersey	NHL	76	7	25	32	55	10	5	0	7	0	2	2	4
92-93—Hartford	NHL	79	7	29	36	76	-11	0	2	—	—	—	—	—
93-94—Hartford	NHL	8	1	1	2	2	-5	1	0	—	—	—	—	—
—Chicago	NHL	54	3	23	26	31	6	1	0	6	0	2	2	6
94-95—Chicago	NHL	48	3	10	13	33	1	1	0	16	1	5	6	4
95-96—Chicago	NHL	77	5	10	15	65	14	0	0	10	1	4	5	10
96-97—Chicago	NHL	81	7	25	32	62	19	1	0	6	0	1	1	4
97-98—Chicago	NHL	82	2	21	23	106	10	0	0	—	—	—	—	—
98-99—Chicago	NHL	14	1	3	4	12	-13	0	0	—	—	—	—	—
—Montreal	NHL	66	6	12	18	77	-12	4	0	—	—	—	—	—
99-00—Montreal	NHL	77	4	25	29	39	4	2	0	—	—	—	—	—
00-01—Montreal	NHL	60	6	19	25	34	-1	2	0	—	—	—	—	—
—Boston	NHL	22	1	5	6	10	-8	1	0	—	—	—	—	—
01-02—Philadelphia	NHL	80	4	20	24	26	27	0	0	5	0	0	0	4
02-03—Philadelphia	NHL	81	2	18	20	40	16	1	1	13	2	3	5	12
03-04—Philadelphia	NHL	54	2	7	9	32	11	1	0	—	—	—	—	—
—St. Louis	NHL	26	2	8	10	14	1	1	0	5	0	1	1	0
04-05—VSV	Austria	10	3	8	11	8	7	1	0	3	0	1	1	6
NHL Totals (16 years)		1082	69	302	371	773	79	23	3	81	6	23	29	67

WEISS, STEPHEN — C — PANTHERS

PERSONAL: Born April 3, 1983, in Toronto. ... 5-11/191. ... Shoots left.

TRANSACTIONS/CAREER NOTES: Selected by Florida Panthers in first round (first Panthers pick, fourth overall) of NHL entry draft (June 23, 2001). ... Fractured toe (February 18, 2003); missed five games. ... Sprained knee (February 1, 2004); missed 16 games. ... Fractured leg (March 29, 2004); missed remained of season.

		REGULAR SEASON								PLAYOFFS				
Season Team	League	GP	G	A	Pts.	PIM	+/-	PP	SH	GP	G	A	Pts.	PIM
99-00—Plymouth	OHL	64	24	42	66	35	...	...	...	23	8	18	26	18
00-01—Plymouth	OHL	62	40	47	87	45	...	...	...	18	7	16	23	10
01-02—Plymouth	OHL	46	25	45	70	69	...	...	...	6	2	7	9	13
—Florida	NHL	7	1	1	2	0	0	1	0	—	—	—	—	—
02-03—Florida	NHL	77	6	15	21	17	-13	0	0	—	—	—	—	—
03-04—Florida	NHL	50	12	17	29	10	-10	3	0	—	—	—	—	—
—San Antonio	AHL	10	6	3	9	14	-1	3	0	—	—	—	—	—
04-05—San Antonio	AHL	62	15	23	38	38	-1	7	0	—	—	—	—	—
—Chicago	AHL	18	7	9	16	12	8	1	0	18	2	7	9	17
NHL Totals (3 years)		134	19	33	52	27	-23	4	0					

WELLWOOD, KYLE — C — MAPLE LEAFS

PERSONAL: Born May 16, 1983, in Windsor, Ont. ... 5-10/180. ... Shoots right.
TRANSACTIONS/CAREER NOTES: Selected by Toronto Maple Leafs in sixth round (sixth Maple Leafs pick, 134th overall) of NHL entry draft (June 23, 2001).

		REGULAR SEASON								PLAYOFFS				
Season Team	League	GP	G	A	Pts.	PIM	+/-	PP	SH	GP	G	A	Pts.	PIM
98-99—Tecumseh	Jr. B	51	22	41	63	12	...	...	...	—	—	—	—	—
99-00—Belleville	OHL	65	14	37	51	14	...	...	...	16	3	7	10	6
00-01—Belleville	OHL	68	35	*83	*118	24	...	...	...	10	3	16	19	4
01-02—Belleville	OHL	28	16	24	40	4	...	...	...	—	—	—	—	—
—Windsor	OHL	26	14	21	35	0	...	...	...	16	12	12	24	0
02-03—Windsor	OHL	57	41	59	100	0	...	...	...	7	5	9	14	0
03-04—Toronto	NHL	1	0	0	0	0	-1	0	0	—	—	—	—	—
—St. John's	AHL	76	20	35	55	6	-14	8	0	—	—	—	—	—
04-05—St. John's	AHL	80	38	49	87	20	11	11	0	5	2	2	4	2
NHL Totals (1 year)		1	0	0	0	0	-1	0	0					

WESLEY, GLEN — D

PERSONAL: Born October 2, 1968, in Red Deer, Alta. ... 6-1/205. ... Shoots left. ... Brother of Blake Wesley, D with four NHL teams (1979-80 through 1985-86).
TRANSACTIONS/CAREER NOTES: Selected by Boston Bruins in first round (first Bruins pick, third overall) of NHL draft (June 13, 1987). ... Sprained left knee (October 1988). ... Fractured foot (November 24, 1992); missed 14 games. ... Injured groin (February 1993); missed one game. ... Injured groin (March 1993); missed three games. ... Injured groin (April 1993); missed two games. ... Injured kidney (March 3, 1994); missed three games. ... Traded by Bruins to Hartford Whalers for first-round picks in 1995 (D Kyle McLaren), 1996 (D Johnathan Aitken) and 1997 (C Sergei Samsonov) drafts (August 26, 1994). ... Bruised shin (November 4, 1995); missed two games. ... Injured groin (December 28, 1995); missed three games. ... Sprained knee (January 6, 1996); missed three games. ... Injured groin (January 17, 1996); missed four games. ... Injured groin (January 25, 1996); missed three games. ... Strained hip flexor (November 4, 1996); missed one game. ... Fractured foot (November 16, 1996); missed 10 games. ... Flu (February 5, 1997); missed one game. ... Whalers franchise moved to North Carolina and renamed Carolina Hurricanes for 1997-98 season; NHL approved move on June 25, 1997. ... Sprained ankle (March 24, 1999); missed eight games. ... Strained groin (November 22, 1999); missed two games. ... Suffered eye injury (February 17, 2000); missed two games. ... Fractured jaw (March 4, 2001); missed 11 games. ... Injured shoulder (April 3, 2002); missed final five games of season. ... Traded by Hurricanes to Toronto Maple Leafs for second-round pick in 2004 draft (March 9, 2003). ... Injured groin (October 11, 2002); missed three games. ... Injured groin (January 25, 2003); missed three games. ... Fractured left ankle (March 25, 2003); missed eight games. ... Signed as free agent by Hurricanes (July 8, 2003). ... Injured shoulder (November 19, 2003); missed seven games.
STATISTICAL PLATEAUS: Three-goal games: 1993-94 (1).

		REGULAR SEASON								PLAYOFFS				
Season Team	League	GP	G	A	Pts.	PIM	+/-	PP	SH	GP	G	A	Pts.	PIM
83-84—Red Deer	AJHL	57	9	20	29	40	...	...	...	—	—	—	—	—
—Portland	WHL	3	1	2	3	0	...	...	...	—	—	—	—	—
84-85—Portland	WHL	67	16	52	68	76	...	...	...	6	1	6	7	8
85-86—Portland	WHL	69	16	75	91	96	...	...	...	15	3	11	14	29
86-87—Portland	WHL	63	16	46	62	72	...	...	...	20	8	18	26	27
87-88—Boston	NHL	79	7	30	37	69	21	1	2	23	6	8	14	22
88-89—Boston	NHL	77	19	35	54	61	23	8	1	10	0	2	2	4
89-90—Boston	NHL	78	9	27	36	48	6	5	0	21	2	6	8	36
90-91—Boston	NHL	80	11	32	43	78	0	5	1	19	2	9	11	19
91-92—Boston	NHL	78	9	37	46	54	-9	4	0	15	2	4	6	16
92-93—Boston	NHL	64	8	25	33	47	-2	4	1	4	0	0	0	0
93-94—Boston	NHL	81	14	44	58	64	1	6	1	13	3	3	6	12
94-95—Hartford	NHL	48	2	14	16	50	-6	1	0	—	—	—	—	—
95-96—Hartford	NHL	68	8	16	24	88	-9	6	0	—	—	—	—	—
96-97—Hartford	NHL	68	6	26	32	40	0	3	1	—	—	—	—	—
97-98—Carolina	NHL	82	6	19	25	36	7	1	0	—	—	—	—	—
98-99—Carolina	NHL	74	7	17	24	44	14	0	0	6	0	0	0	2
99-00—Carolina	NHL	78	7	15	22	38	-4	1	0	—	—	—	—	—
00-01—Carolina	NHL	71	5	16	21	42	-2	3	0	6	0	0	0	0
01-02—Carolina	NHL	77	5	13	18	56	-8	1	0	22	0	2	2	12
02-03—Carolina	NHL	63	1	7	8	40	-5	1	0	—	—	—	—	—
—Toronto	NHL	7	0	3	3	4	3	0	0	5	0	1	1	2
03-04—Carolina	NHL	74	0	6	6	32	18	0	0	—	—	—	—	—
NHL Totals (17 years)		1247	124	382	506	891	48	50	7	144	15	35	50	125

W

WESTCOTT, DUVIE — D — BLUE JACKETS

PERSONAL: Born October 30, 1977, in Winnipeg, Man. ... 5-11/192. ... Shoots right. ... Name pronounced DOO-vee WEHST-kaht.
TRANSACTIONS/CAREER NOTES: Signed as free agent by Columbus Blue Jackets (May 10, 2001). ... Bruised ankle (October 14, 2003); missed eight games. ... Bruised ankle (November 16, 2003); missed 24 games. ... Fractured hand (February 2, 2004); missed 16 games.

		REGULAR SEASON								PLAYOFFS				
Season Team	League	GP	G	A	Pts.	PIM	+/-	PP	SH	GP	G	A	Pts.	PIM
96-97—Winnipeg	MJHL	52	12	47	59	...	...	...	...	—	—	—	—	—
97-98—Alaska-Anchorage	WCHA	25	3	5	8	43	...	...	...	—	—	—	—	—
—Omaha	USHL	12	3	3	6	31	...	...	...	14	0	8	8	84
98-99—St. Cloud State	WCHA	Did not play—transfer student												
99-00—St. Cloud State	WCHA	36	1	18	19	67	...	...	...	—	—	—	—	—
00-01—St. Cloud State	WCHA	38	10	24	34	116	...	...	...	—	—	—	—	—
01-02—Syracuse	AHL	68	4	29	33	99	3	1	1	10	0	1	1	12

		REGULAR SEASON								PLAYOFFS				
Season Team	League	GP	G	A	Pts.	PIM	+/-	PP	SH	GP	G	A	Pts.	PIM
—Columbus	NHL	4	0	0	0	2	-2	0	0	—	—	—	—	—
02-03—Columbus	NHL	39	0	7	7	77	-3	0	0	—	—	—	—	—
—Syracuse	AHL	22	1	10	11	54	...	...	...	—	—	—	—	—
03-04—Columbus	NHL	34	0	7	7	39	-15	0	0	—	—	—	—	—
04-05—JyP Jyvaskyla	Finland	46	11	7	18	106	6	...	...	2	0	2	2	25
NHL Totals (3 years)		77	0	14	14	118	-20	0	0					

WESTRUM, ERIK C COYOTES

PERSONAL: Born July 26, 1979, in Minneapolis, Minn. ... 6-0/204. ... Shoots left.
TRANSACTIONS/CAREER NOTES: Selected by Phoenix Coyotes in seventh round (ninth pick by Coyotes, 187th overall) in 1998 NHL entry draft.

		REGULAR SEASON								PLAYOFFS				
Season Team	League	GP	G	A	Pts.	PIM	+/-	PP	SH	GP	G	A	Pts.	PIM
96-97—Apple Valley	Minn. H.S.	25	23	33	56	...	...	...	...	—	—	—	—	—
97-98—Minnesota	WCHA	39	6	12	18	43	...	...	...	—	—	—	—	—
98-99—Minnesota	WCHA	41	10	26	36	81	...	...	...	—	—	—	—	—
99-00—Minnesota	WCHA	39	27	26	53	99	...	...	...	—	—	—	—	—
00-01—Minnesota	WCHA	42	26	35	61	84	...	...	...	—	—	—	—	—
01-02—Springfield	AHL	73	13	29	42	116	-17	4	1	—	—	—	—	—
02-03 —Springfield	AHL	—	—	—	—	—	—	—	—	6	0	4	4	6
—Springfield	AHL	70	10	22	32	65	2	4	2	—	—	—	—	—
03-04—Phoenix	NHL	15	1	1	2	20	-3	0	0	—	—	—	—	—
—Springfield	AHL	56	14	17	31	81	-1	3	1	—	—	—	—	—
04-05—Utah	AHL	80	18	15	33	117	-16	3	3	—	—	—	—	—
NHL Totals (1 year)		15	1	1	2	20	-3	0	0					

WHEELER, BLAKE RW COYOTES

PERSONAL: Born August 31, 1986, in Robbinsdale, Minn. ... 6-3/185. ... Shoots right.
TRANSACTIONS/CAREER NOTES: Selected by Phoenix Coyotes in first round (first Coyotes pick, fifth overall) of NHL draft (June 26, 2004).

		REGULAR SEASON								PLAYOFFS				
Season Team	League	GP	G	A	Pts.	PIM	+/-	PP	SH	GP	G	A	Pts.	PIM
03-04—Breck	USHS (West)	30	45	55	100	34	...	...	...	—	—	—	—	—
04-05—Green Bay	USHL	58	19	28	47	43	...	...	...	—	—	—	—	—

WHITE, COLIN D DEVILS

PERSONAL: Born December 12, 1977, in New Glasgow, Nova Scotia. ... 6-4/215. ... Shoots left.
TRANSACTIONS/CAREER NOTES: Selected by New Jersey Devils in second round (fifth Devils pick, 49th overall) of NHL draft (June 22, 1996). ... Suffered injury (January 28. 2000); missed two games. ... Stiff neck (March 10, 2000); missed three games. ... Injured neck (December 26, 2001); missed two games. ... Reinjured neck (January 3, 2002); missed two games. ... Strained neck (January 23, 2002); missed two games. ... Injured neck (April 1, 2002); missed one game. ... Sprained knee (February 19, 2003); missed seven games. ... Sore neck (March 28, 2003); missed two games. ... Bruised knee (December 2, 2003); missed four games. ... Stiff neck (March 15, 2004); missed two games.

		REGULAR SEASON								PLAYOFFS				
Season Team	League	GP	G	A	Pts.	PIM	+/-	PP	SH	GP	G	A	Pts.	PIM
94-95—Laval	QMJHL	7	0	1	1	32	...	...	...	—	—	—	—	—
—Hull	QMJHL	5	0	1	1	4	...	...	...	12	0	0	0	23
95-96—Hull	QMJHL	62	2	8	10	303	...	...	...	18	0	4	4	42
96-97—Hull	QMJHL	63	3	12	15	297	...	...	...	14	3	12	15	65
97-98—Albany	AHL	76	3	13	16	235	10	0	0	13	0	0	0	55
98-99—Albany	AHL	77	2	12	14	265	19	0	0	5	0	1	1	8
99-00—Albany	AHL	52	5	21	26	176	...	...	...	—	—	—	—	—
—New Jersey	NHL	21	2	1	3	40	3	0	0	23	1	5	6	18
00-01—New Jersey	NHL	82	1	19	20	155	32	0	0	25	0	3	3	42
01-02—New Jersey	NHL	73	2	3	5	133	6	0	0	6	0	0	0	2
02-03—New Jersey	NHL	72	5	8	13	98	19	0	0	24	0	5	5	29
03-04—New Jersey	NHL	75	2	11	13	96	10	0	0	5	0	0	0	4
NHL Totals (5 years)		323	12	42	54	522	70	0	0	83	1	13	14	95

WHITE, PETER C

PERSONAL: Born March 15, 1969, in Montreal. ... 5-11/201. ... Shoots left.
TRANSACTIONS/CAREER NOTES: Selected by Edmonton Oilers in fifth round (fourth Oilers pick, 92nd overall) of NHL entry draft (June 17, 1989). ... Traded by Oilers with fourth-round pick (RW Jason Sessa) in 1996 draft to Toronto Maple Leafs for LW Kent Manderville (December 4, 1995). ... Signed as free agent by Philadelphia Flyers (July 17, 1996). ... Signed as free agent by Chicago Blackhawks (September 10, 2001). ... Traded by Blackhawks to Flyers for future considerations (March 11, 2003).

		REGULAR SEASON								PLAYOFFS				
Season Team	League	GP	G	A	Pts.	PIM	+/-	PP	SH	GP	G	A	Pts.	PIM
87-88—Pembroke	COJHL	56	90	136	226	32	...	...	...	—	—	—	—	—
88-89—Michigan State	CCHA	46	20	33	53	17	...	...	...	—	—	—	—	—

		REGULAR SEASON								PLAYOFFS				
Season Team	**League**	**GP**	**G**	**A**	**Pts.**	**PIM**	**+/-**	**PP**	**SH**	**GP**	**G**	**A**	**Pts.**	**PIM**
89-90—Michigan State	CCHA	45	22	40	62	6	...	...	...	—	—	—	—	—
90-91—Michigan State	CCHA	37	7	31	38	28	...	...	...	—	—	—	—	—
91-92—Michigan State	CCHA	44	26	51	77	32	...	...	...	—	—	—	—	—
92-93—Cape Breton	AHL	64	12	28	40	10	6	4	1	16	3	3	6	12
93-94—Cape Breton	AHL	45	21	49	70	12	5	7	3	5	2	3	5	2
—Edmonton	NHL	26	3	5	8	2	1	0	0	—	—	—	—	—
94-95—Cape Breton	AHL	65	36	69	*105	30	-5	13	2	—	—	—	—	—
—Edmonton	NHL	9	2	4	6	0	1	2	0	—	—	—	—	—
95-96—Edmonton	NHL	26	5	3	8	0	-14	1	0	—	—	—	—	—
—Toronto	NHL	1	0	0	0	0	0	0	0	—	—	—	—	—
—St. John's	AHL	17	6	7	13	6	...	...	...	—	—	—	—	—
—Atlanta	IHL	36	21	20	41	4	...	...	...	3	0	3	3	2
96-97—Philadelphia	AHL	80	*44	61	*105	28	40	13	1	10	6	8	14	6
97-98—Philadelphia	AHL	80	27	*78	*105	28	18	13	2	20	9	9	18	6
98-99—Philadelphia	AHL	77	31	59	90	20	18	12	4	16	4	13	17	12
—Philadelphia	NHL	3	0	0	0	0	0	0	0	—	—	—	—	—
99-00—Philadelphia	AHL	62	20	41	61	38	...	...	...	—	—	—	—	—
—Philadelphia	NHL	21	1	5	6	6	1	0	0	16	0	2	2	0
00-01—Philadelphia	NHL	77	9	16	25	16	1	1	0	3	0	0	0	0
01-02—Norfolk	AHL	24	4	19	23	18	7	1	1	4	0	1	1	0
—Chicago	NHL	48	3	3	6	10	-8	1	0	—	—	—	—	—
02-03—Philadelphia	AHL	47	17	26	43	16	-4	10	0	—	—	—	—	—
—Chicago	NHL	6	0	1	1	0	0	0	0	—	—	—	—	—
—Norfolk	AHL	31	6	17	23	21	0	5	0	9	2	4	6	5
03-04—Philadelphia	NHL	3	0	0	0	2	-1	0	0	—	—	—	—	—
—Philadelphia	AHL	75	12	48	60	39	20	4	1	12	2	1	3	10
04-05—Philadelphia	AHL	10	2	6	8	6	4	0	0	—	—	—	—	—
—Utah	AHL	70	12	25	37	14	-15	5	0	—	—	—	—	—
NHL Totals (9 years)		220	23	37	60	36	-19	5	0	19	0	2	2	0

WHITE, TODD — C/LW — WILD

PERSONAL: Born May 21, 1975, in Kanata, Ont. ... 5-10/198. ... Shoots left.

TRANSACTIONS/CAREER NOTES: Signed as free agent by Chicago Blackhawks (August 6, 1997). ... Charley horse (October 4, 1997); missed one game. ... Bruised ribs before 1998-99 season; missed first six games of season. ... Traded by Blackhawks to Philadelphia Flyers for future considerations (January 26, 2000). ... Signed as free agent by Ottawa Senators (July 12, 2000). ... Concussion (January 15, 2002); missed one game. ... Injured left hip flexor (March 11, 2003); missed two games. ... Injured shoulder (October 11, 2003); missed one game. ... Reinjured shoulder (October 23, 2003); missed two games. ... Reinjured shoulder (November 7, 2003); missed four games. ... Fractured right foot (February 17, 2004); missed 22 games. ... Traded by Senators to Minnesota Wild for 4th-round pick (C Cody Bass) in entry draft (July 30, 2005).

		REGULAR SEASON								PLAYOFFS				
Season Team	**League**	**GP**	**G**	**A**	**Pts.**	**PIM**	**+/-**	**PP**	**SH**	**GP**	**G**	**A**	**Pts.**	**PIM**
93-94—Clarkson	ECAC	33	10	12	22	28	...	...	...	—	—	—	—	—
94-95—Clarkson	ECAC	34	13	16	29	44	...	...	...	—	—	—	—	—
95-96—Clarkson	ECAC	38	29	43	72	36	...	...	...	—	—	—	—	—
96-97—Clarkson	ECAC	37	38	36	74	22	...	...	...	—	—	—	—	—
97-98—Chicago	NHL	7	1	0	1	2	0	0	0	—	—	—	—	—
—Indianapolis	IHL	65	46	36	82	28	18	21	1	5	2	3	5	4
98-99—Chicago	IHL	25	11	13	24	8	4	2	0	10	1	4	5	8
—Chicago	NHL	35	5	8	13	20	-1	2	0	—	—	—	—	—
99-00—Cleveland	IHL	42	21	30	51	32	...	...	...	—	—	—	—	—
—Chicago	NHL	1	0	0	0	0	0	0	0	—	—	—	—	—
—Philadelphia	AHL	32	19	24	43	12	...	...	...	5	2	1	3	8
—Philadelphia	NHL	3	1	0	1	0	-1	0	0	—	—	—	—	—
00-01—Grand Rapids	IHL	64	22	32	54	20	...	...	...	10	4	4	8	10
—Ottawa	NHL	16	4	1	5	4	5	0	0	2	0	0	0	0
01-02—Ottawa	NHL	81	20	30	50	24	12	4	0	12	2	2	4	6
02-03—Ottawa	NHL	80	25	35	60	28	19	8	1	18	5	1	6	6
03-04—Ottawa	NHL	53	9	20	29	22	12	1	1	7	1	0	1	4
04-05—Sodertalje	Sweden	1	0	1	1	4	-1	0	0	—	—	—	—	—
NHL Totals (7 years)		276	65	94	159	100	46	15	2	39	8	3	11	16

WHITFIELD, TRENT — C — BLUES

PERSONAL: Born June 17, 1977, in Estevan, Sask. ... 5-11/205. ... Shoots left.

TRANSACTIONS/CAREER NOTES: Selected by Boston Bruins in 4th round (5th Bruins pick, 100th overall) of NHL draft (June 22, 1996). ... Signed as free agent by Washington Capitals (September 1, 1998). ... Claimed off waivers by New York Rangers (January 16, 2002). ... Claimed off waivers by Capitals (February 1, 2002). ... Injured chest (March 8, 2004); missed five games. ... Signed as free agent by St. Louis Blues (Aug. 2, 2005).

		REGULAR SEASON								PLAYOFFS				
Season Team	**League**	**GP**	**G**	**A**	**Pts.**	**PIM**	**+/-**	**PP**	**SH**	**GP**	**G**	**A**	**Pts.**	**PIM**
93-94—Spokane	WHL	5	1	1	2	0	...	...	...	—	—	—	—	—
94-95—Spokane	WHL	48	8	17	25	26	-7	2	0	11	7	6	13	5
95-96—Spokane	WHL	72	33	51	84	75	...	...	...	18	8	10	18	10
96-97—Spokane	WHL	58	34	42	76	74	15	12	4	9	5	7	12	10
97-98—Spokane	WHL	65	38	44	82	97	22	11	3	18	9	10	19	15
98-99—Portland	AHL	50	10	8	18	20	-11	1	0	—	—	—	—	—

		REGULAR SEASON								PLAYOFFS				
Season Team	League	GP	G	A	Pts.	PIM	+/-	PP	SH	GP	G	A	Pts.	PIM
—Hampton Roads..........	ECHL	19	13	12	25	12	13	2	1	4	2	0	2	14
99-00—Portland....................	AHL	79	18	35	53	52	...	...	...	3	1	1	2	2
—Washington	NHL	...	...	...	...	...	...	...	...	3	0	0	0	0
00-01—Portland....................	AHL	19	9	11	20	27	...	...	...	—	—	—	—	—
—Washington	NHL	61	2	4	6	35	3	0	0	5	0	0	0	2
01-02—Portland....................	AHL	45	14	20	34	24	-9	8	0	—	—	—	—	—
—New York Rangers......	NHL	1	0	0	0	0	1	0	0	—	—	—	—	—
—Washington	NHL	24	0	1	1	28	-3	0	0	—	—	—	—	—
02-03—Portland....................	AHL	64	27	34	61	42	3	7	5	—	—	—	—	—
—Washington	NHL	14	1	1	2	6	1	0	0	6	0	0	0	10
03-04—Washington	NHL	44	6	5	11	14	-2	0	1	—	—	—	—	—
—Portland....................	AHL	24	8	7	15	22	-5	4	0	—	—	—	—	—
04-05—Portland....................	AHL	67	17	38	55	75	-9	8	2	—	—	—	—	—
NHL Totals (5 years)...........		144	9	11	20	83	0	0	1	14	0	0	0	12

WHITNEY, RAY — LW — HURRICANES

PERSONAL: Born May 8, 1972, in Fort Saskatchewan, Alta. ... 5-10/178. ... Shoots right.

TRANSACTIONS/CAREER NOTES: Selected by San Jose Sharks in 2nd round (2nd Sharks pick, 23rd overall) of NHL draft (June 22, 1991). ... Sprained knee (October 30, 1993); missed 18 games. ... Flu (December 15, 1993); missed one game. ... Injured ankle (February 20, 1995) and suffered eye infection (February 28, 1995); missed seven games. ... Eye infection (March 21, 1995); missed one game. ... Flu (April 9, 1995); missed one game. ... Injured groin (December 15, 1995); missed three games. ... Injured wrist (February 18, 1996); missed 17 games. ... Signed as free agent by Edmonton Oilers (October 1, 1997). ... Claimed off waivers by Florida Panthers (November 6, 1997). ... Strained groin (October 22, 1999); missed one game. ... Injured groin (November 10, 2000). ... Strained back (January 17, 2001); missed six games. ... Strained back (February 9, 2001); missed 28 games, ... Traded by Panthers with future considerations to Columbus Blue Jackets for C Kevyn Adams and 4th-round pick (RW Michael Woodford) in 2001 draft (March 13, 2001). ... Strained chest muscle (October 12, 2001); missed 11 games. ... Flu (December 8, 2001); missed one game. ... Strained lower back (March 25, 2002); missed one game. ... Flu (February 12, 2003); missed one game. ... Signed as free agent by Detroit Red Wings (July 30, 2003). ... Injured groin (November 19, 2003); missed 10 games. ... Injured groin (December 9, 2003); missed five games. ... Placed on waivers by Red Wings (July 25, 2005). ... Signed as free agent by Carolina Hurricanes (Aug. 6, 2005).

STATISTICAL PLATEAUS: Three-goal games: 2002-03 (1).

		REGULAR SEASON								PLAYOFFS				
Season Team	League	GP	G	A	Pts.	PIM	+/-	PP	SH	GP	G	A	Pts.	PIM
88-89—Spokane......................	WHL	71	17	33	50	16	...	...	...	—	—	—	—	—
89-90—Spokane......................	WHL	71	57	56	113	50	...	...	...	6	3	4	7	6
90-91—Spokane......................	WHL	72	67	118	*185	36	...	...	...	15	13	18	*31	12
91-92—San Diego..................	IHL	63	36	54	90	12	...	...	...	4	0	0	0	0
—San Jose....................	NHL	2	0	3	3	0	-1	0	0	—	—	—	—	—
—Koln	Germany	10	3	6	9	4	...	...	...	—	—	—	—	—
92-93—Kansas City................	IHL	46	20	33	53	14	-2	6	1	12	5	7	12	2
—San Jose....................	NHL	26	4	6	10	4	-14	1	0	—	—	—	—	—
93-94—San Jose....................	NHL	61	14	26	40	14	2	1	0	14	0	4	4	8
94-95—San Jose....................	NHL	39	13	12	25	14	-7	4	0	11	4	4	8	2
95-96—San Jose....................	NHL	60	17	24	41	16	-23	4	2	—	—	—	—	—
96-97—Kentucky....................	AHL	9	1	7	8	2	-3	0	0	—	—	—	—	—
—Utah..........................	IHL	43	13	35	48	34	...	...	...	7	3	1	4	6
—San Jose....................	NHL	12	0	2	2	4	-6	0	0	—	—	—	—	—
97-98—Edmonton..................	NHL	9	1	3	4	0	-1	0	0	—	—	—	—	—
—Florida......................	NHL	68	32	29	61	28	10	12	0	—	—	—	—	—
98-99—Florida......................	NHL	81	26	38	64	18	-3	7	0	—	—	—	—	—
99-00—Florida......................	NHL	81	29	42	71	35	16	5	0	4	1	0	1	4
00-01—Florida......................	NHL	43	10	21	31	28	-16	5	0	—	—	—	—	—
—Columbus	NHL	3	0	3	3	2	-1	0	0	—	—	—	—	—
01-02—Columbus	NHL	67	21	40	61	12	-22	6	0	—	—	—	—	—
02-03—Columbus	NHL	81	24	52	76	22	-26	8	2	—	—	—	—	—
03-04—Detroit........................	NHL	67	14	29	43	22	7	3	1	12	1	3	4	4
NHL Totals (13 years)..........		700	205	330	535	219	-85	56	5	41	6	11	17	18

WHITNEY, RYAN — D — PENGUINS

PERSONAL: Born February 19, 1983, in Boston. ... 6-3/202. ... Shoots left.

TRANSACTIONS/CAREER NOTES: Selected by Pittsburgh Penguins in first round (first Penguins pick, fifth overall) of NHL entry draft (June 22, 2002).

		REGULAR SEASON								PLAYOFFS				
Season Team	League	GP	G	A	Pts.	PIM	+/-	PP	SH	GP	G	A	Pts.	PIM
00-01—U.S. National..............	USHL	60	9	31	40	86	...	...	...	—	—	—	—	—
01-02—Boston University.......	Hockey East	31	4	15	19	44	...	...	...	—	—	—	—	—
02-03—Boston University.......	Hockey East	34	3	10	13	48	...	...	...	—	—	—	—	—
03-04—Boston University.......	Hockey East	38	9	16	25	56	...	...	...	—	—	—	—	—
—Wilkes-Barre/Scranton	AHL	...	...	...	...	...	...	...	...	20	1	9	10	0
04-05—Wilkes-Barre/Scranton	AHL	80	6	35	41	101	-12	4	0	11	2	7	9	12

WIDING, DANIEL — RW — PREDATORS

PERSONAL: Born April 13, 1982, in Gavle, Sweden. ... 6-0/185. ... Shoots right.

TRANSACTIONS/CAREER NOTES: Selected by Nashville Predators in 2nd round (2nd Predators pick, 36th overall) of entry draft (June 24, 2000).

Season Team	League	GP	G	A	Pts.	PIM	+/-	PP	SH	GP	G	A	Pts.	PIM
		REGULAR SEASON								PLAYOFFS				
99-00—Leksand	Sweden Jr.	34	15	12	27	65	...	...	...	—	—	—	—	—
—Leksand	Sweden Dv. 2	3	0	0	0	2	...	...	...	—	—	—	—	—
00-01—Leksand	Sweden Dv. 2	40	6	5	11	18	...	...	...	—	—	—	—	—
02-03—Leksand	Sweden Dv. 2	47	2	2	4	8	...	...	...	5	0	0	0	2
03-04—Pelicans-Lahti	Finland	54	6	7	13	62	...	...	...	—	—	—	—	—
04-05—Pelicans-Lahti	Finland	56	13	15	28	74	-24	...	...	—	—	—	—	—

WIEMER, JASON — C/LW — FLAMES

PERSONAL: Born April 14, 1976, in Kimberley, B.C. ... 6-1/225. ... Shoots left. ... Name pronounced WEE-muhr.

TRANSACTIONS/CAREER NOTES: Selected by Tampa Bay Lightning in first round (first Lightning pick, eighth overall) of NHL draft (June 28, 1994). ... Flu (March 2, 1995); missed one game. ... Injured jaw (November 3, 1995); missed one game. ... Injured back (April 12, 1996); missed one game. ... Broke bursa sac in elbow (November 30, 1996); missed 14 games. ... Traded by Lightning to Calgary Flames for RW Sandy McCarthy and third- (LW Brad Richards) and fifth-round (D Curtis Rich) picks in 1998 draft (March 24, 1998). ... Injured hand (March 30, 1999); missed three games. ... Injured knee before start of 1999-2000 season; missed first 10 games of season. ... Reinjured knee (October 28, 1999); missed three games. ... Suffered injury (March 31, 2000); missed final five games of season. ... Suffered concussion (December 31, 2000); missed 17 games. ... Traded by Flames with RW Valeri Bure to Florida Panthers for C Rob Niedermayer and second-round pick (G Andrei Medvedev) in 2001 draft (June 23, 2001). ... Suspended seven games for butt-ending opponent (November 20, 2001). ... Suffered concussion (April 5, 2002); missed remainder of season. ... Traded by Panthers to New York Islanders for D Branislav Mezei (July 3, 2002). ... Bruised ribs (March 13, 2003); missed one game. ... Claimed by Minnesota Wild off waivers from Islanders (November 13, 2003). ... Bruised thigh (December 5, 2003); missed two games. ... Signed as a free agent by Calgary Flames (August 5, 2004).

STATISTICAL PLATEAUS: Three-goal games: 1995-96 (1).

Season Team	League	GP	G	A	Pts.	PIM	+/-	PP	SH	GP	G	A	Pts.	PIM
		REGULAR SEASON								PLAYOFFS				
91-92—Kimberley	RMJHL	45	34	33	67	211	...	...	...	—	—	—	—	—
—Portland	WHL	2	0	1	1	0	...	...	...	—	—	—	—	—
92-93—Portland	WHL	68	18	34	52	159	...	...	...	16	7	3	10	27
93-94—Portland	WHL	72	45	51	96	236	46	17	4	10	4	4	8	32
94-95—Portland	WHL	16	10	14	24	63	-7	6	0	—	—	—	—	—
—Tampa Bay	NHL	36	1	4	5	44	-2	0	0	—	—	—	—	—
95-96—Tampa Bay	NHL	66	9	9	18	81	-9	4	0	6	1	0	1	28
96-97—Tampa Bay	NHL	63	9	5	14	134	-13	2	0	—	—	—	—	—
—Adirondack	AHL	4	1	0	1	7	-2	0	0	—	—	—	—	—
97-98—Tampa Bay	NHL	67	8	9	17	132	-9	2	0	—	—	—	—	—
—Calgary	NHL	12	4	1	5	28	-1	1	0	—	—	—	—	—
98-99—Calgary	NHL	78	8	13	21	177	-12	1	0	—	—	—	—	—
99-00—Calgary	NHL	64	11	11	22	120	-10	2	0	—	—	—	—	—
00-01—Calgary	NHL	65	10	5	15	177	-15	3	0	—	—	—	—	—
01-02—Florida	NHL	70	11	20	31	178	-4	5	1	—	—	—	—	—
02-03—New York Islanders	NHL	81	9	19	28	116	5	0	1	5	0	0	0	23
03-04—New York Islanders	NHL	13	1	3	4	24	-1	0	0	—	—	—	—	—
—Minnesota	NHL	62	7	11	18	106	-6	1	0	—	—	—	—	—
NHL Totals (10 years)		677	88	110	198	1317	-77	21	2	11	1	0	1	51

WILLIAMS, JASON — C/RW — RED WINGS

PERSONAL: Born August 11, 1980, in London, Ont. ... 5-11/185. ... Shoots right.

TRANSACTIONS/CAREER NOTES: Signed as free agent by Detroit Red Wings (September 22, 2000). ... Flu (November 1, 2003); missed one game. ... Injured groin (November 8, 2003); missed two games.

Season Team	League	GP	G	A	Pts.	PIM	+/-	PP	SH	GP	G	A	Pts.	PIM
		REGULAR SEASON								PLAYOFFS				
96-97—Peterborough	OHL	60	4	8	12	8	...	...	...	10	1	0	1	2
97-98—Peterborough	OHL	55	8	27	35	31	...	...	...	4	0	1	1	2
98-99—Peterborough	OHL	68	26	48	74	42	...	...	...	5	1	2	3	2
99-00—Peterborough	OHL	66	36	37	73	64	...	...	...	5	2	1	3	2
00-01—Cincinnati	AHL	76	24	45	69	48	...	...	...	1	0	0	0	2
—Detroit	NHL	5	0	3	3	2	1	0	0	2	0	0	0	0
01-02—Cincinnati	AHL	52	23	27	50	27	-4	6	1	3	0	1	1	6
—Detroit	NHL	25	8	2	10	4	2	4	0	9	0	0	0	2
02-03—Detroit	NHL	16	3	3	6	2	3	1	0	—	—	—	—	—
—Grand Rapids	AHL	45	23	22	45	18	5	9	1	15	1	7	8	16
03-04—Detroit	NHL	49	6	7	13	15	1	0	0	3	0	0	0	2
04-05—Assat Pori	Finland	43	26	17	43	52	-5	...	...	2	1	1	2	4
NHL Totals (4 years)		95	17	15	32	23	7	5	0	14	0	0	0	4

W

WILLIAMS, JUSTIN — RW — HURRICANES

PERSONAL: Born October 4, 1981, in Cobourg, Ont. ... 6-1/190. ... Shoots right.

TRANSACTIONS/CAREER NOTES: Selected by Philadelphia Flyers in first round (first Flyers pick, 28th overall) of NHL draft (June 24, 2000). ... Fractured hand (February 19, 2001); missed 12 games. ... Flu (November 10, 2001); missed one game. ... Strained right shoulder (December 8, 2001); missed two games. ... Sprained knee (September 27, 2002); missed three preseason games. ... Strained left shoulder (November 15, 2002); missed five games. ... Injured knee (January 18, 2003) requiring surgery; missed 36 games. ... Traded by Flyers to Carolina Hurricanes for D Danny Markov (January 20, 2004). ... Fractured left wrist (February 13, 2004); missed three games. ... Signed as free agent by Lulea of the Swedish league (September 21, 2004).

Season Team	League	GP	G	A	Pts.	PIM	+/-	PP	SH	GP	G	A	Pts.	PIM
		REGULAR SEASON								PLAYOFFS				
97-98—Colborne	Jr. C	36	32	35	67	26	...	...	...	—	—	—	—	—
—Cobourg	Tier II Jr. A	17	0	3	3	5	...	...	...	—	—	—	—	—
98-99—Plymouth	OHL	47	4	8	12	28	...	...	...	7	1	2	3	0
99-00—Plymouth	OHL	68	37	46	83	46	...	...	...	23	*14	16	*30	10
00-01—Philadelphia	NHL	63	12	13	25	22	6	0	0	—	—	—	—	—
01-02—Philadelphia	NHL	75	17	23	40	32	11	0	0	5	0	0	0	4
02-03—Philadelphia	NHL	41	8	16	24	22	15	0	0	12	1	5	6	8
03-04—Philadelphia	NHL	47	6	20	26	32	10	3	0	—	—	—	—	—
—Carolina	NHL	32	5	13	18	32	2	1	0	—	—	—	—	—
04-05—Lulea	Sweden	49	14	18	32	61	-5	2	0	4	0	1	1	29
NHL Totals (4 years)		258	48	85	133	140	44	4	0	17	1	5	6	12

WILLIS, SHANE — RW — LIGHTNING

PERSONAL: Born June 13, 1977, in Edmonton. ... 6-1/190. ... Shoots right.

TRANSACTIONS/CAREER NOTES: Selected by Tampa Bay Lightning in third round (third Lightning pick, 56th overall) of NHL draft (July 8, 1995). ... Returned to draft pool by Lightning and selected by Carolina Hurricanes in fourth round (fourth Hurricanes pick, 88th overall) of draft (June 21, 1997). ... Back spasms (December 23, 2000); missed five games. ... Sprained ankle (March 1, 2001); missed four games. ... Injured back (September 26, 2001); missed first three games of season. ... Traded by Hurricanes with LW Craig Dingman to Lightning for G Kevin Weekes (March 5, 2002). ... Signed as free agent by Springfield of the AHL (September 27, 2004).

STATISTICAL PLATEAUS: Three-goal games: 2000-01 (1).

Season Team	League	GP	G	A	Pts.	PIM	+/-	PP	SH	GP	G	A	Pts.	PIM
		REGULAR SEASON								PLAYOFFS				
94-95—Prince Albert	WHL	65	24	19	43	38	14	9	0	13	3	4	7	6
95-96—Prince Albert	WHL	69	41	40	81	47	...	...	...	18	11	10	21	18
96-97—Prince Albert	WHL	41	34	22	56	63	12	14	3	—	—	—	—	—
—Lethbridge	WHL	26	22	17	39	24	17	5	0	19	13	11	24	20
97-98—New Haven	AHL	1	0	1	1	2	-1	0	0	—	—	—	—	—
—Lethbridge	WHL	64	58	54	112	73	25	72	6	4	2	3	5	6
98-99—New Haven	AHL	73	31	50	81	49	-18	9	1	—	—	—	—	—
—Carolina	NHL	7	0	0	0	0	-2	0	0	—	—	—	—	—
99-00—Cincinnati	IHL	80	35	25	60	64	...	...	...	11	5	3	8	8
—Carolina	NHL	2	0	0	0	0	-1	0	0	—	—	—	—	—
00-01—Carolina	NHL	73	20	24	44	45	-6	9	0	2	0	0	0	0
01-02—Carolina	NHL	59	7	10	17	24	-8	2	0	—	—	—	—	—
—Tampa Bay	NHL	21	4	3	7	6	0	0	0	—	—	—	—	—
02-03—Springfield	AHL	56	16	16	32	26	-12	2	0	—	—	—	—	—
03-04—Tampa Bay	NHL	12	0	6	6	2	1	0	0	—	—	—	—	—
—Hershey	AHL	55	27	21	48	71	-3	8	2	—	—	—	—	—
04-05—Springfield	AHL	58	18	16	34	29	-5	3	0	—	—	—	—	—
NHL Totals (5 years)		174	31	43	74	77	-16	11	0	2	0	0	0	0

WILLSIE, BRIAN — RW — CAPITALS

PERSONAL: Born March 16, 1978, in London, Ont. ... 6-1/195. ... Shoots right.

TRANSACTIONS/CAREER NOTES: Selected by Colorado Avalanche in sixth round (seventh Avalanche pick, 146th overall) of NHL draft (June 22, 1996). ... Claimed by Washington Capitals in waiver draft (October 3, 2003). ... Had concussion (December 27, 2003); missed 21 games. ... Signed as free agent by Portland of the AHL (December 15, 2004).

Season Team	League	GP	G	A	Pts.	PIM	+/-	PP	SH	GP	G	A	Pts.	PIM
		REGULAR SEASON								PLAYOFFS				
95-96—Guelph	OHL	65	13	21	34	18	...	...	...	16	4	2	6	6
96-97—Guelph	OHL	64	37	31	68	37	3	10	2	18	15	4	19	10
97-98—Guelph	OHL	57	45	31	76	41	28	...	...	12	9	5	14	18
98-99—Hershey	AHL	72	19	10	29	28	-8	3	1	3	1	0	1	0
99-00—Hershey	AHL	78	20	39	59	44	...	...	...	12	2	6	8	8
—Colorado	NHL	1	0	0	0	0	0	0	0	—	—	—	—	—
00-01—Hershey	AHL	48	18	23	41	20	...	...	...	12	7	2	9	14
01-02—Colorado	NHL	56	7	7	14	14	4	2	0	4	0	1	1	2
02-03—Hershey	AHL	59	29	28	57	49	2	11	4	—	—	—	—	—
—Colorado	NHL	12	0	1	1	15	0	0	0	6	1	0	1	2
03-04—Washington	NHL	49	10	5	15	18	-7	1	1	—	—	—	—	—
04-05—Olimpija	Slovenia	14	7	9	16	38	...	...	...	—	—	—	—	—
—Portland	AHL	53	23	17	40	47	-8	7	0	—	—	—	—	—
NHL Totals (4 years)		118	17	13	30	47	-3	3	1	10	1	1	2	4

WILM, CLARKE — C — MAPLE LEAFS

PERSONAL: Born October 24, 1976, in Central Butte, Sask. ... 6-0/202. ... Shoots left.

TRANSACTIONS/CAREER NOTES: Selected by Calgary Flames in sixth round (fifth Flames pick, 150th overall) of NHL entry draft (July 8, 1995). ... Suffered concussion (November 27, 1998); missed two games. ... Injured eye (January 26, 2002); missed two games. ... Suffered injury (March 9, 2001); missed two games. ... Injured ankle (March 18, 2002); missed remainder of season. ... Signed as free agent by Nashville Predators (July 11, 2002). ... Signed as free agent by Toronto Maple Leafs (October 28, 2003).

Season Team	League	GP	G	A	Pts.	PIM	+/-	PP	SH	GP	G	A	Pts.	PIM
		REGULAR SEASON								PLAYOFFS				
91-92—Saskatoon	WHL	...	...	...	...	...	...	...	...	1	0	0	0	0
92-93—Saskatoon	WHL	69	14	19	33	71	...	...	...	9	4	2	6	13

Season Team	League	GP	G	A	Pts.	PIM	+/-	PP	SH	GP	G	A	Pts.	PIM
		REGULAR SEASON								PLAYOFFS				
93-94—Saskatoon	WHL	70	18	32	50	181	...	...	...	16	0	9	9	19
94-95—Saskatoon	WHL	71	20	39	59	179	30	4	3	10	6	1	7	21
95-96—Saskatoon	WHL	72	49	61	110	83	...	...	...	4	1	1	2	4
96-97—Saint John	AHL	62	9	19	28	107	-4	1	0	5	2	0	2	15
97-98—Saint John	AHL	68	13	26	39	112	7	7	0	21	5	9	14	8
98-99—Calgary	NHL	78	10	8	18	53	11	2	2	—	—	—	—	—
99-00—Calgary	NHL	78	10	12	22	67	-6	1	3	—	—	—	—	—
00-01—Calgary	NHL	81	7	8	15	69	-11	2	0	—	—	—	—	—
01-02—Calgary	NHL	66	4	14	18	61	-1	0	1	—	—	—	—	—
02-03—Nashville	NHL	82	5	11	16	36	-11	0	0	—	—	—	—	—
03-04—Toronto	NHL	10	0	0	0	7	0	0	0	5	0	1	1	2
—St. John's	AHL	47	16	17	33	97	5	3	2	—	—	—	—	—
04-05—St. John's	AHL	69	11	16	27	145	-13	2	0	5	2	2	4	8
NHL Totals (6 years)		395	36	53	89	293	-18	5	6	5	0	1	1	2

WILSON, LANDON — RW

PERSONAL: Born March 13, 1975, in St. Louis. ... 6-3/224. ... Shoots right. ... Son of Rick Wilson, D with three NHL teams (1973-77).

TRANSACTIONS/CAREER NOTES: Selected by Toronto Maple Leafs in first round (second Maple Leafs pick, 19th overall) of NHL draft (June 26, 1993). ... Traded by Maple Leafs with LW Wendel Clark, D Sylvain Lefebvre and first-round pick (D Jeffrey Kealty) in 1994 draft to Quebec Nordiques for C Mats Sundin, D Garth Butcher, LW Todd Warriner and first-round pick (traded to Washington; Capitals selected D Nolan Baumgartner) in 1994 draft (June 28, 1994). ... Nordiques franchise moved to Colorado and renamed Avalanche for 1995-96 season (June 21, 1995). ... Traded by Avalanche with D Anders Myrvold to Boston Bruins for first-round pick (D Robyn Regehr) in 1998 draft (November 22, 1996). ... Sprained shoulder (December 12, 1996); missed 10 games. ... Charley horse (January 7, 1997); missed 12 games. ... Suffered concussion (March 9, 1999); missed two games. ... Strained abdominal muscle (April 15, 1999); missed one game. ... Strained shoulder (April 28, 1999); missed remainder of playoffs. ... Injured shoulder (November 4, 1999); missed seven games. ... Signed as free agent by Phoenix Coyotes (July 7, 2000). ... Back spasms (November 19, 2000); missed one game. ... Strained knee (January 1, 2001); missed six games. ... Strained calf (March 13, 2001); missed five games. ... Sprained ankle (September 5, 2001); missed first 24 games of season. ... Injured eye (December 13, 2002); missed final 51 games of season. ... Injured hip (December 31, 2003); missed 10 games. ... Injured eye (February 11, 2004); missed four games. ... Traded by Coyotes to Pittsburgh Penguins for future considerations (February 22, 2004).

Season Team	League	GP	G	A	Pts.	PIM	+/-	PP	SH	GP	G	A	Pts.	PIM
		REGULAR SEASON								PLAYOFFS				
92-93—Dubuque	USHL	43	29	36	65	284	...	...	...	—	—	—	—	—
93-94—North Dakota	WCHA	35	18	15	33	147	0	5	1	—	—	—	—	—
94-95—North Dakota	WCHA	31	7	16	23	141	...	2	0	—	—	—	—	—
—Cornwall	AHL	8	4	4	8	25	1	1	0	13	3	4	7	68
95-96—Cornwall	AHL	53	21	13	34	154	...	...	...	8	1	3	4	22
—Colorado	NHL	7	1	0	1	6	3	0	0	—	—	—	—	—
96-97—Colorado	NHL	9	1	2	3	23	1	0	0	—	—	—	—	—
—Boston	NHL	40	7	10	17	49	-6	0	0	—	—	—	—	—
—Providence	AHL	2	2	1	3	2	0	1	0	10	3	4	7	16
97-98—Boston	NHL	28	1	5	6	7	3	0	0	1	0	0	0	0
—Providence	AHL	42	18	10	28	146	-14	4	0	—	—	—	—	—
98-99—Providence	AHL	48	31	22	53	89	9	15	0	11	7	1	8	19
—Boston	NHL	22	3	3	6	17	0	0	0	8	1	1	2	8
99-00—Boston	NHL	40	1	3	4	18	-6	0	0	—	—	—	—	—
—Providence	AHL	17	5	5	10	45	...	...	...	9	2	3	5	38
00-01—Phoenix	NHL	70	18	13	31	92	3	2	0	—	—	—	—	—
01-02—Springfield	AHL	2	2	1	3	2	3	0	0	—	—	—	—	—
—Phoenix	NHL	47	7	12	19	46	4	1	0	4	0	0	0	12
02-03—Phoenix	NHL	31	6	8	14	26	1	0	0	—	—	—	—	—
03-04—Phoenix	NHL	35	1	3	4	16	-3	0	0	—	—	—	—	—
—Pittsburgh	NHL	19	5	1	6	31	0	2	0	—	—	—	—	—
04-05—Blues Espoo	Finland	37	8	11	19	80	3	...	...	—	—	—	—	—
NHL Totals (9 years)		348	51	60	111	331	0	5	0	13	1	1	2	20

WILSON, MIKE — D — COYOTES

PERSONAL: Born February 26, 1975, in Brampton, Ont. ... 6-6/229. ... Shoots left.

TRANSACTIONS/CAREER NOTES: Selected by Vancouver Canucks in first round (first Canucks pick, 20th overall) of NHL draft (June 26, 1993). ... Traded by Canucks with RW Michael Peca and first-round pick (D Jay McKee) in 1995 draft to Buffalo Sabres for RW Alexander Mogilny and fifth-round pick (LW Todd Norman) in 1995 draft (July 8, 1995). ... Suffered concussion (January 26, 1996); missed two games. ... Bruised chest (November 13, 1997); missed one game. ... Suffered mild concussion (January 8, 1998); missed two games. ... Missed first 19 games of 1998-99 season in contract dispute. ... Traded by Sabres to Florida Panthers for D Rhett Warrener and fifth-round pick (G Ryan Miller) in 1999 draft (March 23, 1999). ... Suffered concussion (March 31, 1999); missed final nine games of season. ... Injured shoulder (October 22, 2000); missed 61 games. ... Signed as free agent by Pittsburgh Penguins (July 5, 2001). ... Traded by Penguins with RW Alexei Kovalev, LW Dan LaCouture and D Janne Laukkanen to New York Rangers for RW Rico Fata, RW Mikael Samuelsson, D Joel Bouchard, D Richard Lintner and cash (February 10, 2003). ... Signed as free agent by Phoenix Coyotes (September 23, 2003).

Season Team	League	GP	G	A	Pts.	PIM	+/-	PP	SH	GP	G	A	Pts.	PIM
		REGULAR SEASON								PLAYOFFS				
91-92—Georgetown Jr. B	OHA	41	9	13	22	65	...	...	...	—	—	—	—	—
92-93—Sudbury	OHL	53	6	7	13	58	...	...	...	14	1	1	2	21
93-94—Sudbury	OHL	60	4	22	26	62	...	1	0	9	1	3	4	8
94-95—Sudbury	OHL	64	13	34	47	46	...	4	2	18	1	8	9	10
95-96—Rochester	AHL	15	0	5	5	38	...	...	...	—	—	—	—	—
—Buffalo	NHL	58	4	8	12	41	13	1	0	—	—	—	—	—
96-97—Buffalo	NHL	77	2	9	11	51	13	0	0	10	0	1	1	2

Season Team	League	GP	G	A	Pts.	PIM	+/-	PP	SH	GP	G	A	Pts.	PIM
		REGULAR SEASON								PLAYOFFS				
97-98—Buffalo	NHL	66	4	4	8	48	13	0	0	15	0	1	1	13
98-99—Las Vegas	IHL	6	3	1	4	6	-3	2	0	—	—	—	—	—
—Buffalo	NHL	30	1	2	3	47	10	0	0	—	—	—	—	—
—Florida	NHL	4	0	0	0	0	2	0	0	—	—	—	—	—
99-00—Florida	NHL	60	4	16	20	35	10	0	0	4	0	0	0	0
00-01—Florida	NHL	19	0	1	1	25	-7	0	0	—	—	—	—	—
—Louisville	AHL	4	0	2	2	5	...	...	...	—	—	—	—	—
01-02—Pittsburgh	NHL	21	1	1	2	17	-12	0	0	—	—	—	—	—
—Wilkes-Barre/Scranton	AHL	46	3	9	12	59	-3	0	1	—	—	—	—	—
02-03—New York Rangers	NHL	1	0	0	0	0	1	0	0	—	—	—	—	—
—Wilkes-Barre/Scranton	AHL	45	4	5	9	89	-1	2	0	—	—	—	—	—
—Hartford	AHL	5	1	2	3	5	7	0	0	—	—	—	—	—
03-04—Springfield	AHL	45	3	9	12	28	4	1	0	—	—	—	—	—
NHL Totals (8 years)		336	16	41	57	264	43	1	0	29	0	2	2	15

WINCHESTER, BRAD — LW/C — OILERS

PERSONAL: Born March 1, 1981, in Madison, Wis. ... 6-5/208. ... Shoots left.

TRANSACTIONS/CAREER NOTES: Selected by Edmonton Oilers in second round (second Oilers pick, 35th overall) of NHL entry draft (June 24, 2000).

Season Team	League	GP	G	A	Pts.	PIM	+/-	PP	SH	GP	G	A	Pts.	PIM
		REGULAR SEASON								PLAYOFFS				
98-99—U.S. National	USHL	68	21	36	57	...	...	...	...	—	—	—	—	—
99-00—Wisconsin	WCHA	29	8	8	16	48	...	...	...	—	—	—	—	—
00-01—Wisconsin	WCHA	41	7	9	16	71	...	...	...	—	—	—	—	—
01-02—Wisconsin	WCHA	38	14	20	34	38	...	...	...	—	—	—	—	—
02-03—Wisconsin	WCHA	38	10	6	16	58	...	...	...	—	—	—	—	—
03-04—Toronto	AHL	65	13	6	19	85	-10	0	1	3	0	0	0	2
04-05—Edmonton	AHL	76	22	18	40	143	2	10	0	—	—	—	—	—

WISEMAN, CHAD — LW — RANGERS

PERSONAL: Born March 25, 1981, in Burlington, Ont. ... 6-1/201. ... Shoots left.

TRANSACTIONS/CAREER NOTES: Selected by San Jose Sharks in eighth round (eighth Sharks pick, 246th overall) in 2000 NHL draft (June 25, 2000). ... Traded by Sharks to New York Rangers for LW Nils Ekman (August 12, 2003).

Season Team	League	GP	G	A	Pts.	PIM	+/-	PP	SH	GP	G	A	Pts.	PIM
		REGULAR SEASON								PLAYOFFS				
98-99—Mississauga	OHL	64	11	25	36	29	...	...	...	—	—	—	—	—
99-00—Mississauga	OHL	68	23	45	68	53	...	...	...	—	—	—	—	—
00-01—Mississauga	OHL	30	15	29	44	22	...	...	...	—	—	—	—	—
—Plymouth	OHL	32	11	16	27	12	...	...	...	19	12	8	20	22
01-02—Cleveland	AHL	76	21	29	50	61	-21	4	3	—	—	—	—	—
02-03—San Jose	NHL	4	0	0	0	4	-2	0	0	—	—	—	—	—
—Cleveland	AHL	77	17	35	52	44	...	...	...	—	—	—	—	—
03-04—New York Rangers	NHL	4	1	0	1	0	-1	0	0	—	—	—	—	—
—Hartford	AHL	62	25	27	52	45	15	7	4	15	5	6	11	12
04-05—Hartford	AHL	60	17	16	33	74	3	7	1	6	1	1	2	6
NHL Totals (2 years)		8	1	0	1	4	-3	0	0					

WITT, BRENDAN — D

PERSONAL: Born February 20, 1975, in Humboldt, Sask. ... 6-2/231. ... Shoots left.

TRANSACTIONS/CAREER NOTES: Selected by Washington Capitals in first round (first Capitals pick, 11th overall) of NHL draft (June 26, 1993). ... Missed 1994-95 season in contract dispute. ... Fractured wrist (January 28, 1996); missed 34 games. ... Flu (November 15, 1996); missed five games. ... Bruised shoulder (November 27, 1997); missed seven games. ... Flu (January 6, 1998); missed three games. ... Injured wrist (April 6, 1998); missed final six games of regular season and five playoff games. ... Sprained knee (October 18, 1998); missed one game. ... Strained hip flexor (October 28, 1998); missed five games. ... Missed game for personal reasons (January 26, 1999). ... Sprained wrist (February 3, 1999); missed 15 games. ... Sprained knee (October 16, 1999); missed two games. ... Strained back (November 26, 1999); missed one game. ... Strained groin (March 11, 2000); missed one game. ... Injured thigh (March 25, 2000); missed one game. ... Injured left arm (October 17, 2000); missed one game. ... Flu (December 16, 2000); missed three games. ... Separated shoulder (December 29, 2000); missed five games. ... Injured leg (October 10, 2001); missed two games. ... Injured leg (November 6, 2001); missed five games. ... Sprained thumb (January 3, 2002); missed seven games. ... Injured groin (October 26, 2002); missed three games. ... Injured shoulder (November 9, 2002); missed four games. ... Bruised ribs (March 14, 2003); missed two games. ... Aggravated rib injury (March 29, 2003); missed four games. ... Had concussion (October 11, 2003); missed two games. ... Bruised shoulder (December 11, 2003); missed 11 games. ... Injured lower body (March 24, 2004); missed one game.

Season Team	League	GP	G	A	Pts.	PIM	+/-	PP	SH	GP	G	A	Pts.	PIM
		REGULAR SEASON								PLAYOFFS				
90-91—Seattle	WHL	...	...	...	...	...	...	...	...	1	0	0	0	0
91-92—Seattle	WHL	67	3	9	12	212	...	...	...	15	1	1	2	84
92-93—Seattle	WHL	70	2	26	28	239	-14	2	0	5	1	2	3	30
93-94—Seattle	WHL	56	8	31	39	235	18	5	0	9	3	8	11	23
94-95—		Did not play												
95-96—Washington	NHL	48	2	3	5	85	-4	0	0	—	—	—	—	—
96-97—Washington	NHL	44	3	2	5	88	-20	0	0	—	—	—	—	—
—Portland	AHL	30	2	4	6	56	1	0	0	5	1	0	1	30

Season Team	League	GP	G	A	Pts.	PIM	+/-	PP	SH	GP	G	A	Pts.	PIM
		REGULAR SEASON								PLAYOFFS				
97-98—Washington	NHL	64	1	7	8	112	-11	0	0	16	1	0	1	14
98-99—Washington	NHL	54	2	5	7	87	-6	0	0	—	—	—	—	—
99-00—Washington	NHL	77	1	7	8	114	5	0	0	3	0	0	0	0
00-01—Washington	NHL	72	3	3	6	101	2	0	0	6	2	0	2	12
01-02—Washington	NHL	68	3	7	10	78	-1	0	0	—	—	—	—	—
02-03—Washington	NHL	69	2	9	11	106	12	0	0	6	1	0	1	0
03-04—Washington	NHL	72	2	10	12	123	-22	0	0	—	—	—	—	—
04-05—Bracknell	England	3	1	4	5	0	...	...	...	—	—	—	—	—
NHL Totals (9 years)		568	19	53	72	894	-45	0	0	31	4	0	4	26

WOLSKI, WOJTEK — LW — AVALANCHE

PERSONAL: Born February 24, 1986, in Zabrize, Poland. ... 6-3/200. ... Shoots left.
TRANSACTIONS/CAREER NOTES: Selected by Colorado Avalanche in first round (first Avalanche pick, 21st overall) of NHL entry draft (June 26, 2004).

Season Team	League	GP	G	A	Pts.	PIM	+/-	PP	SH	GP	G	A	Pts.	PIM
		REGULAR SEASON								PLAYOFFS				
02-03—Brampton	OHL	64	25	32	57	26	...	...	...	11	5	0	5	6
03-04—Brampton	OHL	66	29	41	70	30	...	...	...	12	5	3	8	8
04-05—Brampton	OHL	67	29	44	73	41	-6	13	2	6	2	5	7	6

WOOLLEY, JASON — D

PERSONAL: Born July 27, 1969, in Toronto. ... 6-0/206. ... Shoots left.
TRANSACTIONS/CAREER NOTES: Selected by Washington Capitals in third round (fourth Capitals pick, 61st overall) of NHL entry draft (June 17, 1989). ... Fractured wrist (October 12, 1992); missed 24 games. ... Tore abdominal muscle (January 2, 1994). ... Signed as free agent by Detroit of the IHL (October 7, 1994). ... Contract sold by Detroit of the IHL to Florida Panthers (February 14, 1995). ... Separated left shoulder (October 15, 1995); missed two games. ... Fractured left thumb (November 18, 1995); missed 13 games. ... Traded by Panthers with C Stu Barnes to Pittsburgh Penguins for C Chris Wells (November 19, 1996). ... Injured groin (November 22, 1996); missed one game. ... Strained groin (February 27, 1997); missed one game. ... Strained groin (March 4, 1997); missed two games. ... Bruised wrist (March 18, 1997); missed two games. ... Traded by Penguins to Buffalo Sabres for fifth-round pick (D Robert Scuderi) in 1998 draft (September 24, 1997). ... Fractured thumb (October 1, 1997); missed nine games. ... Flu (February 15, 1999); missed one game. ... Strained groin (April 14, 1999); missed one game. ... Injured rib (November 12, 1999); missed four games. ... Flu (March 4, 2000); missed two games. ... Injured groin (December 12, 2000); missed four games. ... Injured knee (February 25, 2001); missed two games. ... Flu (November 11, 2001); missed three games. ... Traded by Sabres to Detroit Red Wings for conditional pick in 2003 draft (November 17, 2002). ... Bruised foot (December 28, 2003); missed one game. ... Injured back (February 18, 2004); missed last 21 games of season.

Season Team	League	GP	G	A	Pts.	PIM	+/-	PP	SH	GP	G	A	Pts.	PIM
		REGULAR SEASON								PLAYOFFS				
87-88—St. Michael's Jr. B	ODHA	31	19	37	56	22	...	...	...	—	—	—	—	—
88-89—Michigan State	CCHA	47	12	25	37	26	...	...	...	—	—	—	—	—
89-90—Michigan State	CCHA	45	10	38	48	26	...	...	...	—	—	—	—	—
90-91—Michigan State	CCHA	40	15	44	59	24	...	...	...	—	—	—	—	—
91-92—Canadian nat'l team	Int'l	60	14	30	44	36	...	...	...	—	—	—	—	—
—Can. Olympic team	Int'l	8	0	5	5	4	...	...	...	—	—	—	—	—
—Baltimore	AHL	15	1	10	11	6	...	...	...	—	—	—	—	—
—Washington	NHL	1	0	0	0	0	1	0	0	—	—	—	—	—
92-93—Baltimore	AHL	29	14	27	41	22	4	5	0	1	0	2	2	0
—Washington	NHL	26	0	2	2	10	3	0	0	—	—	—	—	—
93-94—Portland	AHL	41	12	29	41	14	15	5	0	9	2	2	4	4
—Washington	NHL	10	1	2	3	4	2	0	0	4	1	0	1	4
94-95—Detroit	IHL	48	8	28	36	38	7	0	0	—	—	—	—	—
—Florida	NHL	34	4	9	13	18	-1	1	0	—	—	—	—	—
95-96—Florida	NHL	52	6	28	34	32	-9	3	0	13	2	6	8	14
96-97—Florida	NHL	3	0	0	0	2	1	0	0	—	—	—	—	—
—Pittsburgh	NHL	57	6	30	36	28	3	2	0	5	0	3	3	0
97-98—Buffalo	NHL	71	9	26	35	35	8	3	0	15	2	9	11	12
98-99—Buffalo	NHL	80	10	33	43	62	16	4	0	21	4	11	15	10
99-00—Buffalo	NHL	74	8	25	33	52	14	2	0	5	0	2	2	2
00-01—Buffalo	NHL	67	5	18	23	46	0	4	0	8	1	5	6	2
01-02—Buffalo	NHL	59	8	20	28	34	-6	6	0	—	—	—	—	—
02-03—Buffalo	NHL	14	0	3	3	29	-1	0	0	—	—	—	—	—
—Detroit	NHL	62	6	17	23	22	12	1	0	4	1	0	1	0
03-04—Detroit	NHL	55	4	15	19	28	19	0	0	4	0	0	0	0
04-05—UHL	UHL	9	4	2	6	4	2	2	0	—	—	—	—	—
NHL Totals (13 years)		665	67	228	295	402	62	26	0	79	11	36	47	44

WORRELL, PETER — LW

PERSONAL: Born August 18, 1977, in Pierrefonds, Que. ... 6-6/235. ... Shoots left. ... Name pronounced woh-REHL.
TRANSACTIONS/CAREER NOTES: Selected by Florida Panthers in seventh round (seventh Panthers pick, 166th overall) of NHL draft (July 8, 1995). ... Suspended three games and fined $1,000 for elbowing incident (November 18, 1998). ... Sprained knee (September 21, 1999); missed nine games. ... Partially tore anterior collateral ligament in right knee (October 29, 1999); missed 12 games. ... Sprained knee (January 14, 2000); missed six games. ... Suffered head injury (March 19, 2000); missed six games. ... Strained back (March 2, 2001; missed one game. ... Injured shoulder (March 16, 2001); missed final 10 games of the season. ... Strained groin (October 18, 2001); missed one game. ... Injured hand (November 19, 2001); missed one game. ... Injured back (November 29, 2001); missed one game. ... Injured thumb (October 24, 2002); missed three games. ... Injured groin (December 6, 2002); missed two games. ... Suffered concussion (March 1, 2003); missed

W

six games. ... Injured knee (March 15, 2003); missed eight games. ... Traded by Panthers to Colorado Avalanche with 2004 second-round draft pick for LW Eric Messier and C Vaclav Nedorost (July 19, 2003). ... Injured knee (October 9, 2003); missed 27 games. ... Bruised knee (January 27, 2004); missed two games.

		REGULAR SEASON								PLAYOFFS				
Season Team	**League**	**GP**	**G**	**A**	**Pts.**	**PIM**	**+/-**	**PP**	**SH**	**GP**	**G**	**A**	**Pts.**	**PIM**
94-95—Hull	QMJHL	56	1	8	9	243	0	0	0	21	0	1	1	91
95-96—Hull	QMJHL	63	23	36	59	464	...	...	...	18	11	8	19	81
96-97—Hull	QMJHL	62	18	45	63	*495	...	...	...	14	3	13	16	83
97-98—New Haven	AHL	50	15	12	27	309	-3	8	0	1	0	1	1	6
—Florida	NHL	19	0	0	0	153	-4	0	0	—	—	—	—	—
98-99—Florida	NHL	62	4	5	9	258	0	0	0	—	—	—	—	—
—New Haven	AHL	10	3	1	4	65	1	2	0	—	—	—	—	—
99-00—Florida	NHL	48	3	6	9	169	-7	2	0	4	1	0	1	8
00-01—Florida	NHL	71	3	7	10	248	-10	0	0	—	—	—	—	—
01-02—Florida	NHL	79	4	5	9	*354	-15	0	0	—	—	—	—	—
02-03—Florida	NHL	63	2	3	5	193	-14	0	0	—	—	—	—	—
03-04—Colorado	NHL	49	3	1	4	179	2	0	0	—	—	—	—	—
NHL Totals (7 years)		391	19	27	46	1554	-48	2	0	4	1	0	1	8

WOYWITKA, JEFF — D — BLUES

PERSONAL: Born September 1, 1983, in Vermillion, Alta. ... 6-2/197. ... Shoots left.
TRANSACTIONS/CAREER NOTES: Selected by Philadelphia Flyers in first round (first Flyers pick, 27th overall) of NHL entry draft (June 23, 2001). ... Traded by Flyers with 1st-round pick (C Robbie Schremp) in 2004 entry draft and 3rd-round pick in 2005 entry draft to Edmonton Oilers for C Mike Comrie (December 16, 2003). ... Traded by Oilers with D Eric Brewer and D Doug Lynch to St. Louis Blues for D Chris Pronger (Aug. 2, 2005).

		REGULAR SEASON								PLAYOFFS				
Season Team	**League**	**GP**	**G**	**A**	**Pts.**	**PIM**	**+/-**	**PP**	**SH**	**GP**	**G**	**A**	**Pts.**	**PIM**
99-00—Red Deer	WHL	67	4	12	16	40	...	...	...	4	0	3	3	2
00-01—Red Deer	WHL	72	7	28	35	113	...	...	...	22	2	8	10	25
01-02—Red Deer	WHL	72	14	23	37	109	...	...	...	23	2	10	12	22
02-03—Red Deer	WHL	57	16	36	52	65	...	...	...	23	1	9	10	25
03-04—Philadelphia	AHL	29	0	6	6	51	...	...	...	—	—	—	—	—
—Toronto	AHL	53	4	18	22	41	-5	2	0	3	0	0	0	0
04-05—Edmonton	AHL	80	6	20	26	84	-7	1	0	—	—	—	—	—

WRIGHT, TYLER — RW/C — BLUE JACKETS

PERSONAL: Born April 6, 1973, in Kamsack, Sask. ... 6-0/190. ... Shoots right.
TRANSACTIONS/CAREER NOTES: Selected by Edmonton Oilers in first round (first Oilers pick, 12th overall) of NHL draft (June 22, 1991). ... Traded by Oilers to Pittsburgh Penguins for seventh-round pick (RW Brandon LaFrance) in 1996 draft (June 22, 1996). ... Bruised ribs (December 13, 1996); missed one game. ... Back spasms (January 18, 2000); missed two games. ... Strained knee (April 3, 2000); missed two games. ... Selected by Columbus Blue Jackets in NHL expansion draft (June 23, 2000). ... Bruised ribs (December 23, 2000); missed five games. ... Flu (February 21, 2001); missed one game. ... Suffered concussion (November 1, 2001); missed five games. ... Suffered concussion (October 23, 2002); missed one game. ... Fractured hand (November 14, 2002); missed nine games. ... Bruised thigh (March 6, 2003); missed one game. ... Hyperextended elbow (October 14, 2003); missed six games.
STATISTICAL PLATEAUS: Three-goal games: 2000-01 (1), 2002-03 (2). Total: 3.

		REGULAR SEASON								PLAYOFFS				
Season Team	**League**	**GP**	**G**	**A**	**Pts.**	**PIM**	**+/-**	**PP**	**SH**	**GP**	**G**	**A**	**Pts.**	**PIM**
89-90—Swift Current	WHL	67	14	18	32	119	...	...	...	4	0	0	0	12
90-91—Swift Current	WHL	66	41	51	92	157	...	...	...	3	0	0	0	6
91-92—Swift Current	WHL	63	36	46	82	295	...	...	...	8	2	5	7	16
92-93—Swift Current	WHL	37	24	41	65	76	-7	14	2	17	9	17	26	49
—Edmonton	NHL	7	1	1	2	19	-4	0	0	—	—	—	—	—
93-94—Cape Breton	AHL	65	14	27	41	160	-20	2	3	5	2	0	2	11
—Edmonton	NHL	5	0	0	0	4	-3	0	0	—	—	—	—	—
94-95—Cape Breton	AHL	70	16	15	31	184	-16	2	2	—	—	—	—	—
—Edmonton	NHL	6	1	0	1	14	1	0	0	—	—	—	—	—
95-96—Edmonton	NHL	23	1	0	1	33	-7	0	0	—	—	—	—	—
—Cape Breton	AHL	31	6	12	18	158	...	...	...	—	—	—	—	—
96-97—Pittsburgh	NHL	45	2	2	4	70	-7	0	0	—	—	—	—	—
—Cleveland	IHL	10	4	3	7	34	...	...	...	14	4	2	6	44
97-98—Pittsburgh	NHL	82	3	4	7	112	-3	1	0	6	0	1	1	4
98-99—Pittsburgh	NHL	61	0	0	0	90	-2	0	0	13	0	0	0	19
99-00—Wilkes-Barre/Scranton	AHL	25	5	15	20	86	...	...	...	—	—	—	—	—
—Pittsburgh	NHL	50	12	10	22	45	4	0	0	11	3	1	4	17
00-01—Columbus	NHL	76	16	16	32	140	-9	4	1	—	—	—	—	—
01-02—Columbus	NHL	77	13	11	24	100	-40	4	0	—	—	—	—	—
02-03—Columbus	NHL	70	19	11	30	113	-25	3	2	—	—	—	—	—
03-04—Columbus	NHL	68	9	9	18	63	-19	2	0	—	—	—	—	—
04-05—Biel-Bienne	Switz. Div. 2	7	3	4	7	4	...	1	0	12	8	8	16	44
NHL Totals (12 years)		570	77	64	141	803	-114	14	3	30	3	2	5	40

YABLONSKI, JEREMY — RW — PREDATORS

PERSONAL: Born March 21, 1980, in Meadow Lake, Saskatchewan. ... 6-0/232. ... Shoots right.
TRANSACTIONS/CAREER NOTES: Signed as free agent by Worcester of the AHL (July 17, 2003). ... Signed as free agent by St. Louis Blues (December 30, 2003). ... Claimed by Nashville Predators off waivers from Blues (January 30, 2004).

Season Team	League	REGULAR SEASON GP	G	A	Pts.	PIM	+/-	PP	SH	PLAYOFFS GP	G	A	Pts.	PIM
02-03—Peoria	ECHL	24	1	2	3	154	...	...	...	—	—	—	—	—
—Cincinnati	AHL	9	0	0	0	42	...	...	...	—	—	—	—	—
—Worcester	AHL	20	1	0	1	50	...	...	...	1	0	0	0	2
03-04—Worcester	AHL	6	0	0	0	19	-1	0	0	—	—	—	—	—
—Peoria	ECHL	13	0	2	2	62	0	0	0	—	—	—	—	—
—St. Louis	NHL	1	0	0	0	5	-1	0	0	—	—	—	—	—
—Milwaukee	AHL	2	0	0	0	11	0	0	0	—	—	—	—	—
04-05—Milwaukee	AHL	32	3	2	5	116	-2	0	0	—	—	—	—	—
NHL Totals (1 year)		1	0	0	0	5	-1	0	0					

YAKUBOV, MIKHAIL C BLACKHAWKS

PERSONAL: Born February 16, 1982, in Barnaul, U.S.S.R. ... 6-3/202. ... Shoots left. ... Name pronounced YAK-oo-bahf.
TRANSACTIONS/CAREER NOTES: Selected by Chicago Blackhawks in first round (first Blackhawks pick, 10th overall) of NHL entry draft (June 24, 2000).

Season Team	League	REGULAR SEASON GP	G	A	Pts.	PIM	+/-	PP	SH	PLAYOFFS GP	G	A	Pts.	PIM
99-00—Lada Togliatti	Rus. Div.	26	12	19	31	14	...	...	...	—	—	—	—	—
00-01—Lada Togliatti	Russian	25	0	0	0	4	...	...	...	4	0	0	0	0
01-02—Red Deer	WHL	71	32	57	89	54	...	...	...	23	14	9	23	28
02-03—Norfolk	AHL	62	6	5	11	36	-7	3	1	9	0	0	0	8
03-04—Norfolk	AHL	51	9	18	27	22	10	1	0	8	0	3	3	2
—Chicago	NHL	30	1	7	8	8	-12	0	0	—	—	—	—	—
04-05—Norfolk	AHL	59	12	15	27	43	-1	3	0	3	0	0	0	0
NHL Totals (1 year)		30	1	7	8	8	-12	0	0					

YASHIN, ALEXEI C ISLANDERS

PERSONAL: Born November 5, 1973, in Sverdlovsk, U.S.S.R. ... 6-3/220. ... Shoots right. ... Name pronounced uh-LEK-see YA-shihn.
TRANSACTIONS/CAREER NOTES: Selected by Ottawa Senators in first round (first Senators pick, second overall) of NHL draft (June 20, 1992). ... Strep throat (December 4, 1993); missed one game. ... Missed 1999-2000 season in contract dispute. ... Traded by Senators to New York Islanders for RW Bill Muckalt, D Zdeno Chara and first-round pick (C Jason Spezza) in 2001 draft (June 23, 2001). ... Strained groin (April 6, 2002); missed final four games of season. ... Cut right forearm (December 23, 2003); missed 35 games.
STATISTICAL PLATEAUS: Three-goal games: 1993-94 (1), 1994-95 (1), 1995-96 (1), 1997-98 (1), 1998-99 (1), 2000-01 (1), 2001-02 (1). Total: 7. ... Four-goal games: 2002-03 (1). ... Total hat tricks: 8.

Season Team	League	REGULAR SEASON GP	G	A	Pts.	PIM	+/-	PP	SH	PLAYOFFS GP	G	A	Pts.	PIM
90-91—Avtomo. Sverdlovsk	USSR	26	2	1	3	10	...	...	...	—	—	—	—	—
91-92—Dynamo Moscow	CIS	35	7	5	12	19	...	...	...	—	—	—	—	—
92-93—Dynamo Moscow	CIS	27	10	12	22	18	...	...	...	10	7	3	10	18
93-94—Ottawa	NHL	83	30	49	79	22	-49	11	2	—	—	—	—	—
94-95—Las Vegas	IHL	24	15	20	35	32	19	4	0	—	—	—	—	—
—Ottawa	NHL	47	21	23	44	20	-20	11	0	—	—	—	—	—
95-96—Ottawa	NHL	46	15	24	39	28	-15	8	0	—	—	—	—	—
96-97—Ottawa	NHL	82	35	40	75	44	-7	10	0	7	1	5	6	2
97-98—Ottawa	NHL	82	33	39	72	24	6	5	0	11	5	3	8	8
—Russian Oly. team	Int'l	6	3	3	6	0	6	1	0	—	—	—	—	—
98-99—Ottawa	NHL	82	44	50	94	54	16	19	0	4	0	0	0	10
99-00—Ottawa	NHL	Did not play.												
00-01—Ottawa	NHL	82	40	48	88	30	10	13	2	4	0	1	1	0
01-02—New York Islanders	NHL	78	32	43	75	25	-3	15	0	7	3	4	7	2
—Russian Oly. team	Int'l	6	1	1	2	0	...	...	...	—	—	—	—	—
02-03—New York Islanders	NHL	81	26	39	65	32	-12	14	0	5	2	2	4	2
03-04—New York Islanders	NHL	47	15	19	34	10	-1	3	0	5	0	1	1	0
04-05—Lokomotiv Yaroslavl	Russian	10	3	3	6	14	4	...	...	9	3	7	10	10
NHL Totals (11 years)		710	291	374	665	289	-75	109	4	43	11	16	27	24

YEATS, MATT G

PERSONAL: Born April 6, 1979, in Beauport, Que. ... 6-0/180.
TRANSACTIONS/CAREER NOTES: Selected by Los Angeles Kings in ninth round (ninth Kings pick, 248th overall) of NHL entry draft (June 27, 1998). ... Signed as free agent by Washington Capitals (March 19, 2004).

Season Team	League	REGULAR SEASON GP	Min.	W	L	T	GA	SO	GAA	SV%	PLAYOFFS GP	Min.	W	L	GA	SO	GAA	SV%
99-00—Maine	Hockey East	32	1821	20	6	4	79	0	2.60	...	—	—	—	—	—	—	—	—
00-01—Maine	Hockey East	33	1897	18	9	4	76	2	2.40	...	—	—	—	—	—	—	—	—
01-02—Maine	Hockey East	20	1048	6	8	3	54	0	3.09	...	—	—	—	—	—	—	—	—
02-03—Philadelphia	AHL	2	90	1	1	0	4	0	2.67	...	—	—	—	—	—	—	—	—
—Atlantic City	ECHL	48	2811	23	16	8	141	4	3.01	...	8	396	4	0	16	1	2.42	...
03-04—Portland	AHL	7	331	2	1	1	12	1	2.18	.922	—	—	—	—	—	—	—	—
—Washington	NHL	5	258	1	3	0	13	0	3.02	.908	—	—	—	—	—	—	—	—
04-05—Idaho	ECHL	4	246	2	1	...	9	0	2.19	.913	2	66	0	1	3	...	2.72	.864
—Reading	ECHL	13	780	8	2	...	31	1	2.38	.918	—	—	—	—	—	—	—	—
NHL Totals (1 year)		5	258	1	3	0	13	0	3.02	.908								

YELLE, STEPHANE — C — FLAMES

PERSONAL: Born May 9, 1974, in Ottawa. ... 6-1/190. ... Shoots left. ... Name pronounced STEH-fan YEHL.

TRANSACTIONS/CAREER NOTES: Selected by New Jersey Devils in eighth round (ninth Devils pick, 186th overall) of NHL draft (June 20, 1992). ... Traded by Devils with 11th-round pick (D Stephen Low) in 1994 draft to Quebec Nordiques for 11th-round pick (C Mike Hansen) in 1994 draft (June 1, 1994). ... Nordiques franchise moved to Colorado and renamed Avalanche for 1995-96 season (June 21, 1995). ... Pulled groin (February 15, 1996); missed nine games. ... Strained hip flexor (December 14, 1996); missed three games. ... Sprained right wrist (November 28, 1998); missed nine games. ... Sprained knee (May 3, 1999); missed nine playoff games. ... Injured sternum (January 25, 2000); missed two games. ... Strained hip flexor (March 7, 2000); missed one game. ... Injured ankle (October 25, 2000); missed one game. ... Strained groin (November 18, 2000); missed three games. ... Injured back (December 20, 2000); missed three games. ... Herniated disk in back (December 27, 2000); missed 10 games. ... Injured knee (February 17, 2001); missed nine games. ... Sprained knee (March 24, 2001); missed six games. ... Injured ankle (November 16, 2001); missed one game. ... Flu (November 27, 2001); missed one game. ... Bruised foot (December 23, 2001); missed one game. ... Bruised knee (January 3, 2001); missed one game. ... Injured shoulder (March 14, 2002); missed five games. ... Traded by Avalanche with LW Chris Drury to Calgary Flames for D Derek Morris, LW Dean McAmmond and C Jeff Shantz (October 1, 2002). ... Injured head (October 14, 2003); missed one game. ... Injured shoulder (November 15, 2004); missed two games. ... Injured left eye (January 6, 2004); missed three games. ... Sprained right knee (January 16, 2004); missed 18 games.

		REGULAR SEASON								PLAYOFFS				
Season Team	**League**	**GP**	**G**	**A**	**Pts.**	**PIM**	**+/-**	**PP**	**SH**	**GP**	**G**	**A**	**Pts.**	**PIM**
91-92—Oshawa	OHL	55	12	14	26	20	...	...	...	7	2	0	2	1
92-93—Oshawa	OHL	66	24	50	74	20	...	...	...	10	2	4	6	4
93-94—Oshawa	OHL	66	35	69	104	22	...	...	...	5	1	7	8	2
94-95—Cornwall	AHL	40	18	15	33	22	3	11	0	13	7	7	14	8
95-96—Colorado	NHL	71	13	14	27	30	15	0	2	22	1	4	5	8
96-97—Colorado	NHL	79	9	17	26	38	1	0	1	12	1	6	7	2
97-98—Colorado	NHL	81	7	15	22	48	-10	0	1	7	1	0	1	12
98-99—Colorado	NHL	72	8	7	15	40	-8	1	0	10	0	1	1	6
99-00—Colorado	NHL	79	8	14	22	28	9	0	1	17	1	2	3	4
00-01—Colorado	NHL	50	4	10	14	20	-3	0	1	23	1	2	3	8
01-02—Colorado	NHL	73	5	12	17	48	1	0	1	20	0	2	2	14
02-03—Calgary	NHL	82	10	15	25	50	-10	3	0	—	—	—	—	—
03-04—Calgary	NHL	53	4	13	17	24	1	1	0	23	3	3	6	16
NHL Totals (9 years)		640	68	117	185	326	-4	5	7	134	8	20	28	70

YONKMAN, NOLAN — D — CAPITALS

PERSONAL: Born April 1, 1981, in Punnichy, Sask. ... 6-6/236. ... Shoots right.

TRANSACTIONS/CAREER NOTES: Selected by Washington Capitals in second round (fifth Capitals pick, 37th overall) of NHL draft (June 26, 1999).

		REGULAR SEASON								PLAYOFFS				
Season Team	**League**	**GP**	**G**	**A**	**Pts.**	**PIM**	**+/-**	**PP**	**SH**	**GP**	**G**	**A**	**Pts.**	**PIM**
97-98—Kelowna	WHL	65	0	2	2	36	...	...	...	7	0	0	0	2
98-99—Kelowna	WHL	61	1	6	7	129	-33	0	0	6	0	0	0	6
99-00—Kelowna	WHL	71	5	7	12	153	-30	2	0	5	0	0	0	8
00-01—Kelowna	WHL	7	0	1	1	19	...	...	...	—	—	—	—	—
—Brandon	WHL	51	6	10	16	94	...	...	...	6	0	1	1	12
01-02—Portland	AHL	59	4	3	7	116	0	0	0	—	—	—	—	—
—Washington	NHL	11	1	0	1	4	3	0	0	—	—	—	—	—
02-03—Portland	AHL	24	1	4	5	40	4	0	0	3	0	1	1	2
03-04—Portland	AHL	4	0	0	0	11	3	0	0	—	—	—	—	—
—Washington	NHL	1	0	0	0	0	0	0	0	—	—	—	—	—
04-05—Portland	AHL	32	0	3	3	68	-6	0	0	—	—	—	—	—
NHL Totals (2 years)		12	1	0	1	4	3	0	0					

YORK, JASON — D

PERSONAL: Born May 20, 1970, in Nepean, Ont. ... 6-1/208. ... Shoots right.

TRANSACTIONS/CAREER NOTES: Selected by Detroit Red Wings in seventh round (sixth Red Wings pick, 129th overall) of NHL draft (June 16, 1990). ... Traded by Red Wings with C/RW Mike Sillinger to Anaheim Mighty Ducks for LW Stu Grimson, D Mark Ferner and sixth-round pick (LW Magnus Nilsson) in 1996 draft (April 4, 1995). ... Sprained right ankle (December 1, 1995); missed two games. ... Traded by Mighty Ducks with C Shaun Van Allen to Ottawa Senators for C Ted Drury and rights to D Marc Moro (October 1, 1996). ... Strained groin (December 4, 1996); missed six games. ... Had concussion (January 3, 1998); missed four games. ... Injured right eye (April 13, 1998); missed three games. ... Strained shoulder (October 1, 1998); missed first two games of season. ... Strained groin (December 8, 1999); missed three games. ... Strained shoulder (October 27, 2000); missed one game. ... Flu (January 16, 2001); missed one game. ... Fractured leg (February 8, 2001); missed six games. ... Signed as free agent by Mighty Ducks (July 3, 2001). ... Injured right shoulder (January 9, 2002); missed five games. ... Traded by Mighty Ducks to Nashville Predators for future considerations (October 23, 2002). ... Fractured cheekbone (February 25, 2004); missed 13 games.

		REGULAR SEASON								PLAYOFFS				
Season Team	**League**	**GP**	**G**	**A**	**Pts.**	**PIM**	**+/-**	**PP**	**SH**	**GP**	**G**	**A**	**Pts.**	**PIM**
89-90—Windsor	OHL	39	9	30	39	38	...	...	...	—	—	—	—	—
—Kitchener	OHL	25	11	25	36	17	...	...	...	17	3	19	22	10
90-91—Windsor	OHL	66	13	80	93	40	...	...	...	11	3	10	13	12
91-92—Adirondack	AHL	49	4	20	24	32	...	...	...	5	0	1	1	0
92-93—Adirondack	AHL	77	15	40	55	86	29	3	2	11	0	3	3	18
—Detroit	NHL	2	0	0	0	0	0	0	0	—	—	—	—	—
93-94—Adirondack	AHL	74	10	56	66	98	32	2	0	12	3	11	14	22
—Detroit	NHL	7	1	2	3	2	0	0	0	—	—	—	—	—

Y

Season Team	League	REGULAR SEASON								PLAYOFFS				
		GP	G	A	Pts.	PIM	+/-	PP	SH	GP	G	A	Pts.	PIM
94-95—Adirondack	AHL	5	1	3	4	4	0	1	0	—	—	—	—	—
—Detroit	NHL	10	1	2	3	2	0	0	0	—	—	—	—	—
—Anaheim	NHL	15	0	8	8	12	4	0	0	—	—	—	—	—
95-96—Anaheim	NHL	79	3	21	24	88	-7	0	0	—	—	—	—	—
96-97—Ottawa	NHL	75	4	17	21	67	-8	1	0	7	0	0	0	4
97-98—Ottawa	NHL	73	3	13	16	62	8	0	0	7	1	1	2	7
98-99—Ottawa	NHL	79	4	31	35	48	17	2	0	4	1	1	2	4
99-00—Ottawa	NHL	79	8	22	30	60	-3	1	0	6	0	2	2	2
00-01—Ottawa	NHL	74	6	16	22	72	7	3	0	4	0	0	0	4
01-02—Anaheim	NHL	74	5	20	25	60	-11	3	0	—	—	—	—	—
02-03—Cincinnati	AHL	4	3	2	5	8	0	1	0	—	—	—	—	—
—Nashville	NHL	74	4	15	19	52	13	2	0	—	—	—	—	—
03-04—Nashville	NHL	67	2	13	15	64	-4	0	0	6	0	3	3	4
NHL Totals (12 years)		708	41	180	221	589	16	12	0	34	2	7	9	25

YORK, MIKE — C/LW — ISLANDERS

PERSONAL: Born January 3, 1978, in Waterford, Mich. ... 5-10/185. ... Shoots right.
TRANSACTIONS/CAREER NOTES: Selected by New York Rangers in 6th round (7th Rangers pick, 136th overall) of NHL draft (June 21, 1997). ... Bruised ribs (January 22, 2001); missed one game. ... Injured left shoulder (February 9, 2001); missed two games. ... Flu (March 13, 2002); missed one game. ... Traded by Rangers with 4th-round pick (D Ivan Koltsov) in 2002 draft to Edmonton Oilers for D Tom Poti and LW Rem Murray (March 19, 2002). ... Flu (November 15, 2002); missed one game. ... Flu (February 18, 2003); missed one game. ... Fractured wrist (February 25, 2003); missed two games. ... Reinjured wrist (March 6, 2003); missed five games. ... Fractured finger (January 16, 2004); missed 16 games. ... Injured finger (March 10, 2004); missed four games. ... Traded by Oilers with conditional 2006 pick to New York Islanders for Mike Peca (Aug. 3, 2005).

Season Team	League	REGULAR SEASON								PLAYOFFS				
		GP	G	A	Pts.	PIM	+/-	PP	SH	GP	G	A	Pts.	PIM
95-96—Michigan State	CCHA	39	12	27	39	20	...	...	...	—	—	—	—	—
96-97—Michigan State	CCHA	37	18	29	47	42	...	...	...	—	—	—	—	—
97-98—Michigan State	CCHA	40	27	34	61	38	...	...	...	—	—	—	—	—
98-99—Michigan State	CCHA	42	22	32	*54	41	...	...	...	—	—	—	—	—
—Hartford	AHL	3	2	2	4	0	2	1	0	6	3	1	4	0
99-00—New York Rangers	NHL	82	26	24	50	18	-17	8	0	—	—	—	—	—
00-01—New York Rangers	NHL	79	14	17	31	20	1	3	2	—	—	—	—	—
01-02—New York Rangers	NHL	69	18	39	57	16	8	2	0	—	—	—	—	—
—U.S. Olympic team	Int'l	6	0	1	1	0	...	...	...	—	—	—	—	—
—Edmonton	NHL	12	2	2	4	0	-1	1	0	—	—	—	—	—
02-03—Edmonton	NHL	71	22	29	51	10	-8	7	2	6	0	2	2	2
03-04—Edmonton	NHL	61	16	26	42	15	18	1	2	—	—	—	—	—
04-05—Iserlohn	Germany	52	16	46	62	77	-6	9	1	—	—	—	—	—
NHL Totals (5 years)		374	98	137	235	79	1	22	6	6	0	2	2	2

YOUNG, SCOTT — RW

PERSONAL: Born October 1, 1967, in Clinton, Mass. ... 6-1/200. ... Shoots right.
TRANSACTIONS/CAREER NOTES: Selected by Hartford Whalers in first round (first Whalers pick, 11th overall) of NHL draft (June 21, 1986). ... Cut above right eye (October 8, 1988). ... Cut face (February 18, 1990). ... Traded by Whalers to Pittsburgh Penguins for RW Rob Brown (December 21, 1990). ... Traded by Penguins to Quebec Nordiques for D Bryan Fogarty (March 10, 1992). ... Injured rib (February 14, 1993); missed one game. ... Bruised ribs (February 23, 1993); missed one game. ... Sprained right ankle (October 5, 1993); missed eight games. ... Nordiques franchise moved to Colorado and renamed Avalanche for 1995-96 season (June 21, 1995). ... Bruised right shoulder (December 23, 1996); missed five games. ... Traded by Avalanche to Mighty Ducks of Anaheim for third-round pick (traded to Florida) in 1998 draft (September 17, 1997). ... Bruised right foot (November 22, 1997); missed two games. ... Bruised right foot (November 29, 1997); missed five games. ... Eye abrasion (March 9, 1998); missed two games. ... Signed as free agent by St. Louis Blues (July 16, 1998). ... Sore back (February 8, 1999); missed one game. ... Injured back (January 28, 2000); missed three games. ... Separated shoulder (April 5, 2000); missed final two games of regular season. ... Injured shoulder (December 5, 2000); missed one game. ... Back spasms (October 13, 2001); missed four games. ... Injured eye (January 8, 2002); missed 11 games. ... Signed as free agent by Dallas Stars (July 5, 2002). ... Injured hip flexor (March 7, 2003); missed one game. ... Suspended two games for high-sticking incident (March 12, 2003). ... Back spasms (January 19, 2004); missed five games. ... Find $1,000 for high-sticking incident (January 28, 2004). ... Back spasms (February 27, 2004); missed remained of season.
STATISTICAL PLATEAUS: Three-goal games: 1992-93 (1), 1993-94 (1), 1994-95 (1), 1996-97 (1). Total: 4.

Season Team	League	REGULAR SEASON								PLAYOFFS				
		GP	G	A	Pts.	PIM	+/-	PP	SH	GP	G	A	Pts.	PIM
84-85—St. Marks H.S.	Mass. H.S.	23	28	41	69	...	...	...	...	—	—	—	—	—
85-86—Boston University	Hockey East	38	16	13	29	31	...	...	...	—	—	—	—	—
86-87—Boston University	Hockey East	33	15	21	36	24	...	...	...	—	—	—	—	—
87-88—U.S. Olympic team	Int'l	59	13	53	66	...	...	...	...	—	—	—	—	—
—Hartford	NHL	7	0	0	0	2	-6	0	0	4	1	0	1	0
88-89—Hartford	NHL	76	19	40	59	27	-21	6	0	4	2	0	2	4
89-90—Hartford	NHL	80	24	40	64	47	-24	10	2	7	2	0	2	2
90-91—Hartford	NHL	34	6	9	15	8	-9	3	1	—	—	—	—	—
—Pittsburgh	NHL	43	11	16	27	33	3	3	1	17	1	6	7	2
91-92—U.S. national team	Int'l	10	2	4	6	21	...	...	...	—	—	—	—	—
—U.S. Olympic team	Int'l	8	2	1	3	2	...	...	...	—	—	—	—	—
—Bolzano	Italy	18	22	17	39	6	...	...	...	—	—	—	—	—
92-93—Quebec	NHL	82	30	30	60	20	5	9	6	6	4	1	5	0
93-94—Quebec	NHL	76	26	25	51	14	-4	6	1	—	—	—	—	—
94-95—Frankfurt	Germany	1	1	0	1	0	...	...	...	—	—	—	—	—
—Landshut	Germany	4	6	1	7	6	...	...	...	—	—	—	—	—
—Quebec	NHL	48	18	21	39	14	9	3	3	6	3	3	6	2

Season Team	League	GP	G	A	Pts.	PIM	+/-	PP	SH	GP	G	A	Pts.	PIM
		REGULAR SEASON								PLAYOFFS				
95-96—Colorado	NHL	81	21	39	60	50	2	7	0	22	3	12	15	10
96-97—Colorado	NHL	72	18	19	37	14	-5	7	0	17	4	2	6	14
97-98—Anaheim	NHL	73	13	20	33	22	-13	4	2	—	—	—	—	—
98-99—St. Louis	NHL	75	24	28	52	27	8	8	0	13	4	7	11	10
99-00—St. Louis	NHL	75	24	15	39	18	12	6	1	6	6	2	8	8
00-01—St. Louis	NHL	81	40	33	73	30	15	14	3	15	6	7	13	2
01-02—St. Louis	NHL	67	19	22	41	26	11	5	0	10	3	0	3	2
—U.S. Olympic team	Int'l	6	4	0	4	2	...	...	...	—	—	—	—	—
02-03—Dallas	NHL	79	23	19	42	30	24	5	1	10	4	3	7	6
03-04—Dallas	NHL	53	8	8	16	14	-15	2	0	4	1	0	1	2
04-05—Memphis	CHL	3	2	1	3	0	...	...	...	—	—	—	—	—
NHL Totals (16 years)		1102	324	384	708	396	-8	98	21	141	44	43	87	64

YZERMAN, STEVE — C — RED WINGS

PERSONAL: Born May 9, 1965, in Cranbrook, B.C. ... 5-11/185. ... Shoots right. ... Name pronounced IGH-zuhr-muhn.

TRANSACTIONS/CAREER NOTES: Selected by Detroit Red Wings in 1st round (1st Red Wings pick, 4th overall) of NHL draft (June 8, 1983). ... Fractured collarbone (January 31, 1986). ... Injured ligaments of right knee (March 1, 1988) and had surgery. ... Injured right knee in playoff game (April 8, 1991). ... Herniated disc (October 21, 1993); missed 26 games. ... Sprained knee (May 27, 1995); missed three playoff games. ... Flu (March 17, 1996); missed one game. ... Bruised ankle (April 9, 1997); missed one game. ... Sprained knee (January 28, 1998); missed three games. ... Strained groin (April 11, 1998); missed three games. ... Cut forehead and nose and fractured nose (January 21, 1999); missed one game. ... Sprained knee (March 29, 2000); missed final four games of regular season. ... Sprained knee (September 28, 2000); missed first two games of season. ... Knee surgery (October 13, 2000); missed 23 games. ... Bruised ankle (December 26, 2001); missed three games. ... Right knee surgery (January 27, 2002); missed six games. ... Reinjured knee (February 26, 2002); missed 19 games. ... Offseason knee surgery; missed first 66 games of 2002-03 season. ... Injured groin (December 6, 2003); missed six games. ... Eye injury (May 1, 2004); missed remainder of playoffs. ... Signed as free agent by Red Wings (Aug. 2, 2005).

STATISTICAL PLATEAUS: Three-goal games: 1983-84 (1), 1984-85 (1), 1987-88 (2), 1988-89 (2), 1989-90 (2), 1990-91 (3), 1991-92 (3), 1992-93 (3). Total: 17. ... Four-goal games: 1989-90 (1). ... Total hat tricks: 18.

Season Team	League	GP	G	A	Pts.	PIM	+/-	PP	SH	GP	G	A	Pts.	PIM
		REGULAR SEASON								PLAYOFFS				
81-82—Peterborough	OHL	58	21	43	64	65	...	...	...	6	0	1	1	16
82-83—Peterborough	OHL	56	42	49	91	33	...	...	...	4	1	4	5	0
83-84—Detroit	NHL	80	39	48	87	33	-17	13	0	4	3	3	6	0
84-85—Detroit	NHL	80	30	59	89	58	-17	9	0	3	2	1	3	2
85-86—Detroit	NHL	51	14	28	42	16	-24	3	0	—	—	—	—	—
86-87—Detroit	NHL	80	31	59	90	43	-1	9	1	16	5	13	18	8
87-88—Detroit	NHL	64	50	52	102	44	30	10	6	3	1	3	4	6
88-89—Detroit	NHL	80	65	90	155	61	17	17	3	6	5	5	10	2
89-90—Detroit	NHL	79	62	65	127	79	-6	16	7	—	—	—	—	—
90-91—Detroit	NHL	80	51	57	108	34	-2	12	6	7	3	3	6	4
91-92—Detroit	NHL	79	45	58	103	64	26	9	*8	11	3	5	8	12
92-93—Detroit	NHL	84	58	79	137	44	33	13	7	7	4	3	7	4
93-94—Detroit	NHL	58	24	58	82	36	11	7	3	3	1	3	4	0
94-95—Detroit	NHL	47	12	26	38	40	6	4	0	15	4	8	12	0
95-96—Detroit	NHL	80	36	59	95	64	29	16	2	18	8	12	20	4
96-97—Detroit	NHL	81	22	63	85	78	22	8	0	20	7	6	13	4
97-98—Detroit	NHL	75	24	45	69	46	3	6	2	22	6	*18	*24	22
—Can. Olympic team	Int'l	6	1	1	2	10	4	0	0	—	—	—	—	—
98-99—Detroit	NHL	80	29	45	74	42	8	13	2	10	9	4	13	0
99-00—Detroit	NHL	78	35	44	79	34	28	15	2	8	0	4	4	0
00-01—Detroit	NHL	54	18	34	52	18	4	5	0	1	0	0	0	0
01-02—Detroit	NHL	52	13	35	48	18	11	5	1	23	6	17	23	10
—Can. Olympic team	Int'l	6	2	4	6	2	...	...	...	—	—	—	—	—
02-03—Detroit	NHL	16	2	6	8	8	6	1	0	4	0	1	1	2
03-04—Detroit	NHL	75	18	33	51	46	10	7	0	11	3	2	5	0
NHL Totals (21 years)		1453	678	1043	1721	906	177	198	50	192	70	111	181	80

ZAGRAPAN, MAREK — C — SABRES

PERSONAL: Born December 6, 1986, in Presov, Slovakia. ... 6-0/195. ... Shoots left.

TRANSACTIONS/CAREER NOTES: Selected by Buffalo Sabres in 1st round (Sabres 1st pick, 13th overall) of entry draft (July 30, 2005).

Season Team	League	GP	G	A	Pts.	PIM	+/-	PP	SH	GP	G	A	Pts.	PIM
		REGULAR SEASON								PLAYOFFS				
03-04—Zlin	Czech. Jrs.	5	0	0	0	0	...	...	...	—	—	—	—	—
04-05—Chicoutimi	QMJHL	59	32	50	82	50	6	17	0	17	11	6	17	28

ZAJAC, TRAVIS — C — DEVILS

PERSONAL: Born May 13, 1985, in Winnipeg. ... 6-2/205. ... Shoots right.

TRANSACTIONS/CAREER NOTES: Selected by New Jersey Devils in first round (first Devils pick, 20th overall) of NHL draft (June 26, 2004).

Season Team	League	GP	G	A	Pts.	PIM	+/-	PP	SH	GP	G	A	Pts.	PIM
		REGULAR SEASON								PLAYOFFS				
03-04—Salmon Arm	BCHL	59	43	69	112	110	...	...	...	14	10	13	23	10
04-05—Univ. of North Dakota	WCHA	43	17	19	36	16	...	...	...	—	—	—	—	—

ZALESAK, MIROSLAV — RW — CAPITALS

PERSONAL: Born January 2, 1980, in Skalica, Czech. ... 6-0/200. ... Shoots left. ... Name pronounced ZAHL-uh-sak.
TRANSACTIONS/CAREER NOTES: Selected by San Jose Sharks in 4th round (5th Sharks pick, 104th overall) of NHL draft (June 27, 1998). ... Signed as free agent by Washington Capitals (Aug. 8, 2005).

		REGULAR SEASON								PLAYOFFS				
Season Team	League	GP	G	A	Pts.	PIM	+/-	PP	SH	GP	G	A	Pts.	PIM
95-96—HC Nitra	Slovakia Jrs.	49	53	29	82	...	...	...	...	—	—	—	—	—
96-97—HC Nitra	Slovakia Jrs.	58	51	31	82	...	...	...	...	—	—	—	—	—
97-98—HC Nitra	Slovakia Jrs.	23	33	23	56	16	...	...	...	—	—	—	—	—
—Plastika Nitra	Slovakia	30	8	6	14	0	...	...	...	—	—	—	—	—
98-99—Plastika Nitra	Slovakia	15	4	3	7	10	...	...	...	—	—	—	—	—
—Drummondville	QMJHL	45	24	27	51	18	-6	7	0	—	—	—	—	—
99-00—Drummondville	QMJHL	60	50	61	111	40	26	22	0	16	7	11	18	4
00-01—Kentucky	AHL	60	14	11	25	26	...	...	...	3	0	1	1	4
01-02—Cleveland	AHL	74	22	20	42	44	-14	5	1	—	—	—	—	—
02-03—Cleveland	AHL	50	27	22	49	35	-16	11	0	—	—	—	—	—
—San Jose	NHL	10	1	2	3	0	-2	0	0	—	—	—	—	—
03-04—San Jose	NHL	2	0	0	0	0	-1	0	0	—	—	—	—	—
—Cleveland	AHL	72	35	40	75	80	8	13	0	9	1	4	5	14
04-05—Skalica	Slovakia	18	11	14	25	18	11	...	...	—	—	—	—	—
—Chem. Litvinov	Czech Rep.	30	6	6	12	26	-6	...	...	6	1	1	2	0
NHL Totals (2 years)		12	1	2	3	0	-3	0	0					

ZAMUNER, ROB — LW

PERSONAL: Born September 17, 1969, in Oakville, Ont. ... 6-3/200. ... Shoots left. ... Name pronounced ZAM-uh-nuhr.
TRANSACTIONS/CAREER NOTES: Selected by New York Rangers in third round (third Rangers pick, 45th overall) of NHL draft (June 17, 1989). ... Signed as free agent by Tampa Bay Lightning (July 14, 1992). ... Hyperextended elbow (March 19, 1995); missed five games. ... Sprained knee (October 4, 1995); missed 10 games. ... Sore back (April 1, 1998); missed five games. ... Strained groin (October 30, 1998); missed three games. ... Strained groin (November 8, 1998); missed 18 games. ... Strained groin (February 26, 1999); missed three games. ... Traded by Lightning with second-round pick (traded to Philadelphia; traded back to Lightning; traded to Dallas; Stars selected G Tobias Stephan) in 2002 draft to Ottawa Senators for C/LW Andreas Johansson to complete deal that allowed Tampa Bay to sign G.M. Rick Dudley (June 29, 1999). ... Strained groin (October 28, 1999); missed five games. ... Sprained medial collateral ligament in left knee (December 23, 1999); missed 19 games. ... Strained groin (January 25, 2001); missed three games. ... Signed as free agent by Boston Bruins (July 6, 2001). ... Injured shoulder (October 23, 2001); missed 14 games. ... Strained hip flexor (March 1, 2002); missed two games. ... Injured foot (January 10, 2003); missed 22 games. ... Injured groin (March 11, 2003); missed three games. ... Injured hamstring (October 5, 2003); missed 10 games.
STATISTICAL PLATEAUS: Three-goal games: 1997-98 (1).

		REGULAR SEASON								PLAYOFFS				
Season Team	League	GP	G	A	Pts.	PIM	+/-	PP	SH	GP	G	A	Pts.	PIM
86-87—Guelph	OHL	62	6	15	21	8	...	...	...	—	—	—	—	—
87-88—Guelph	OHL	58	20	41	61	18	...	...	...	—	—	—	—	—
88-89—Guelph	OHL	66	46	65	111	38	...	...	...	7	5	5	10	9
89-90—Flint	IHL	77	44	35	79	32	...	...	...	4	1	0	1	6
90-91—Binghamton	AHL	80	25	58	83	50	...	...	...	9	7	6	13	35
91-92—Binghamton	AHL	61	19	53	72	42	...	...	...	11	8	9	17	8
—New York Rangers	NHL	9	1	2	3	2	0	0	0	—	—	—	—	—
92-93—Tampa Bay	NHL	84	15	28	43	74	-25	1	0	—	—	—	—	—
93-94—Tampa Bay	NHL	59	6	6	12	42	-9	0	0	—	—	—	—	—
94-95—Tampa Bay	NHL	43	9	6	15	24	-3	0	3	—	—	—	—	—
95-96—Tampa Bay	NHL	72	15	20	35	62	11	0	3	6	2	3	5	10
96-97—Tampa Bay	NHL	82	17	33	50	56	3	0	4	—	—	—	—	—
97-98—Tampa Bay	NHL	77	14	12	26	41	-31	0	3	—	—	—	—	—
—Can. Olympic team	Int'l	6	1	0	1	8	0	0	0	—	—	—	—	—
98-99—Tampa Bay	NHL	58	8	11	19	24	-15	1	1	—	—	—	—	—
99-00—Ottawa	NHL	57	9	12	21	32	-6	0	1	6	2	0	2	2
00-01—Ottawa	NHL	79	19	18	37	52	7	1	2	4	0	0	0	6
01-02—Boston	NHL	66	12	13	25	24	6	1	2	6	0	2	2	4
02-03—Boston	NHL	55	10	6	16	18	2	3	0	5	0	0	0	4
03-04—Boston	NHL	57	4	5	9	16	3	0	0	7	0	0	0	0
—Providence	AHL	4	0	1	1	2	-2	0	0	—	—	—	—	—
04-05—Basel	Switzerland	40	10	24	34	91	...	5	0	9	7	4	11	20
NHL Totals (13 years)		798	139	172	311	467	-57	7	19	34	4	5	9	26

ZEDNIK, RICHARD — RW/LW — CANADIENS

PERSONAL: Born January 6, 1976, in Bystrica, Czechoslovakia. ... 6-1/196. ... Shoots left. ... Name pronounced ZEHD-nihk.
TRANSACTIONS/CAREER NOTES: Selected by Washington Capitals in 10th round (10th Capitals pick, 249th overall) of NHL draft (June 29, 1994). ... Flu (November 6, 1996); missed two games. ... Flu (December 12, 1997); missed one game. ... Had concussion (March 18, 1998); missed six games. ... Strained abdominal muscle (April 2, 1998); missed final eight games of regular season and four playoff games. ... Bruised shoulder (October 21, 1998); missed 10 games. ... Suspended four games and fined $1,000 by NHL for high-sticking (November 20, 1998). ... Strained groin (December 19, 1998); missed 19 games. ... Had concussion (February 23, 2000); missed 13 games. ... Suspended four games by NHL for cross-checking (October 19, 2000). ... Sprained foot (January 12, 2001); missed two games. ... Traded by Capitals with C Jan Bulis and first-round pick (C Alexander Perezhogin) in 2001 draft to Montreal Canadiens for C Trevor Linden, RW Dainius Zubrus and second-round pick (traded to Tampa Bay; Lightning selected D Andreas Holmqvist) in 2001 draft (March 13, 2001). ... Injured groin (October 14, 2002); missed one game. ... Injured groin (November 15, 2002); missed one game. ... Left team for personal reasons (December 6, 2003); missed one game.
STATISTICAL PLATEAUS: Three-goal games: 2000-01 (1).

Z

Season Team	League	REGULAR SEASON GP	G	A	Pts.	PIM	+/-	PP	SH	PLAYOFFS GP	G	A	Pts.	PIM
93-94—Banska Bystrica	Slovakia	25	3	6	9	...	...	...	...	—	—	—	—	—
94-95—Portland	WHL	65	35	51	86	89	3	15	0	9	5	5	10	20
95-96—Portland	WHL	61	44	37	81	154	...	...	...	7	8	4	12	23
—Portland	AHL	1	1	1	2	0	...	...	...	21	4	5	9	26
—Washington	NHL	1	0	0	0	0	0	0	0	—	—	—	—	—
96-97—Washington	NHL	11	2	1	3	4	-5	1	0	—	—	—	—	—
—Portland	AHL	56	15	20	35	70	5	0	0	5	1	0	1	6
97-98—Washington	NHL	65	17	9	26	28	-2	2	0	17	7	3	10	16
98-99—Washington	NHL	49	9	8	17	50	-6	1	0	—	—	—	—	—
99-00—Washington	NHL	69	19	16	35	54	6	1	0	5	0	0	0	5
00-01—Washington	NHL	62	16	19	35	61	-2	4	0	—	—	—	—	—
—Montreal	NHL	12	3	6	9	10	-2	1	0	—	—	—	—	—
01-02—Montreal	NHL	82	22	22	44	59	-3	4	0	4	4	4	8	6
02-03—Montreal	NHL	80	31	19	50	79	4	9	0	—	—	—	—	—
03-04—Montreal	NHL	81	26	24	50	63	5	7	0	11	3	3	6	2
04-05—Zvolen	Slovakia	37	15	20	35	56	30	...	...	17	9	10	19	12
NHL Totals (9 years)		512	145	124	269	408	-5	30	0	37	14	10	24	29

ZETTERBERG, HENRIK LW/C RED WINGS

PERSONAL: Born October 9, 1980, in Njurunda, Sweden. ... 6-0/190. ... Shoots left.

TRANSACTIONS/CAREER NOTES: Selected by Detroit Red Wings in seventh round (fourth Red Wings pick, 210th overall) of NHL draft (June 27, 1999). ... Injured groin (October 25, 2002); missed three games. ... Fractured leg (November 4, 2003); missed 17 games.

Season Team	League	REGULAR SEASON GP	G	A	Pts.	PIM	+/-	PP	SH	PLAYOFFS GP	G	A	Pts.	PIM
97-98—Timra	Sweden Jr.	18	9	5	14	4	...	...	...	—	—	—	—	—
—Timra	Sweden Dv. 2	16	1	2	3	4	...	...	...	4	0	1	1	0
98-99—Timra	Sweden Dv. 2	37	15	13	28	2	...	...	...	4	2	1	3	2
99-00—Timra	Sweden Dv. 2	11	4	6	10	0	...	...	...	10	10	4	14	4
00-01—Timra	Sweden	47	15	31	46	24	...	...	...	—	—	—	—	—
01-02—Timra	Sweden	48	10	32	42	20	...	...	...	—	—	—	—	—
—Swedish Oly. team	Int'l	4	0	1	1	0	...	...	...	—	—	—	—	—
02-03—Detroit	NHL	79	22	22	44	8	6	5	1	4	1	0	1	0
03-04—Detroit	NHL	61	15	28	43	14	15	7	1	12	2	2	4	4
04-05—Timra	Sweden	50	19	31	50	24	15	5	1	7	6	2	8	2
NHL Totals (2 years)		140	37	50	87	22	21	12	2	16	3	2	5	4

ZHAMNOV, ALEXEI C BRUINS

PERSONAL: Born October 1, 1970, in Moscow, U.S.S.R. ... 6-1/204. ... Shoots left. ... Name pronounced ZHAM-nahf.

TRANSACTIONS/CAREER NOTES: Selected by Winnipeg Jets in 4th round (5th Jets pick, 77th overall) of NHL draft (June 16, 1990). ... Injured hip flexor (November 2, 1992); missed two games. ... Back spasms (January 27, 1993); missed one game. ... Back spasms (February 3, 1993); missed one game. ... Back spasms (February 12, 1993); missed 12 games. ... Bruised leg (October 26, 1993); missed three games. ... Sprained back (December 27, 1993); missed eight games. ... Back spasms (March 19, 1994); missed remainder of season. ... Fractured leg (October 12, 1995); missed eight games. ... Flu (January 5, 1996); missed one game. ... Bruised back (March 7, 1996); missed four games. ... Injured back (March 16, 1996); missed remainder of season. ... Jets franchise moved to Phoenix and renamed Coyotes for 1996-97 season; NHL approved move on January 18, 1996. ... Traded by Coyotes with RW Craig Mills and 1st-round pick (RW Ty Jones) in 1997 draft to Chicago Blackhawks for C Jeremy Roenick (August 16, 1996). ... Fractured toe (November 2, 1997); missed four games. ... Concussion (November 29, 1997); missed one game. ... Concussion (March 3, 1998); missed four games. ... Bruised back (April 4, 1998); missed one game. ... Fractured finger (April 15, 1998); missed two games. ... Bruised ankle (November 10, 1998); missed one game. ... Flu (December 26, 1998); missed one game. ... Injured back (February 6, 1999); missed four games. ... Strained groin (November 7, 1999); missed three games. ... Strained hamstring (January 15, 2000); missed eight games. ... Fractured larynx (January 21, 2001); missed 18 games. ... Hip pointer (March 3, 2002); missed four games. ... Injured hand (January 17, 2003); missed two games. ... Injured hand (March 7, 2003); missed six games ... Back surgery (October 14, 2003); missed 35 games. ... Traded by Blackhawks with 4th-round pick (D Michael R.J. Anderson) in 2004 draft to Philadelphia Flyers for D Jim Vandermeer, C Colin Fraser and 2nd-round pick (LW Bryan Bickell) in 2004 draft (February 19, 2004). ... Signed as free agent by Boston Bruins (Aug. 4, 2005).

STATISTICAL PLATEAUS: Three-goal games: 1993-94 (2), 1994-95 (1), 1995-96 (1), 1996-97 (1). Total: 5. ... Five-goal games: 1994-95 (1). ... Total hat tricks: 6.

Season Team	League	REGULAR SEASON GP	G	A	Pts.	PIM	+/-	PP	SH	PLAYOFFS GP	G	A	Pts.	PIM
88-89—Dynamo Moscow	USSR	4	0	0	0	0	...	...	...	—	—	—	—	—
89-90—Dynamo Moscow	USSR	43	11	6	17	23	...	...	...	—	—	—	—	—
90-91—Dynamo Moscow	USSR	46	16	12	28	24	...	...	...	—	—	—	—	—
91-92—Dynamo Moscow	CIS	39	15	21	36	28	...	...	...	—	—	—	—	—
—Unif. Olympic team	Int'l	8	0	3	3	8	...	...	...	—	—	—	—	—
92-93—Winnipeg	NHL	68	25	47	72	58	7	6	1	6	0	2	2	2
93-94—Winnipeg	NHL	61	26	45	71	62	-20	7	0	—	—	—	—	—
94-95—Winnipeg	NHL	48	30	35	65	20	5	9	0	—	—	—	—	—
95-96—Winnipeg	NHL	58	22	37	59	65	-4	5	0	6	2	1	3	8
96-97—Chicago	NHL	74	20	42	62	56	18	6	1	—	—	—	—	—
97-98—Chicago	NHL	70	21	28	49	61	16	6	2	—	—	—	—	—
—Russian Oly. team	Int'l	6	2	1	3	2	7	1	0	—	—	—	—	—
98-99—Chicago	NHL	76	20	41	61	50	-10	8	1	—	—	—	—	—
99-00—Chicago	NHL	71	23	37	60	61	7	5	0	—	—	—	—	—
00-01—Chicago	NHL	63	13	36	49	40	-12	3	1	—	—	—	—	—
01-02—Chicago	NHL	77	22	45	67	67	8	6	0	5	0	0	0	0
—Russian Oly. team	Int'l	6	1	0	1	4	...	...	...	—	—	—	—	—
02-03—Chicago	NHL	74	15	43	58	70	0	2	3	—	—	—	—	—
03-04—Chicago	NHL	23	6	12	18	14	-8	1	0	—	—	—	—	—
—Philadelphia	NHL	20	5	13	18	14	7	0	0	18	4	10	14	8
04-05—Vityaz Podolsk	Russian	24	5	22	27	20	11	...	...	16	7	7	14	10
NHL Totals (12 years)		783	248	461	709	638	14	64	9	35	6	13	19	18

ZHERDEV, NIKOLAI — RW — BLUE JACKETS

PERSONAL: Born November 5, 1984, in Kiev, U.S.S.R. ... 6-1/186. ... Shoots right. ... Name pronounced ZHAIR-dev.
TRANSACTIONS/CAREER NOTES: Selected by Columbus Blue Jackets in first round (first Blue Jackets pick, fourth overall) in 2003 NHL draft (June 23, 2003). ... Left team for personal reasons (February 25, 2004); missed two games.

		REGULAR SEASON								PLAYOFFS				
Season Team	League	GP	G	A	Pts.	PIM	+/-	PP	SH	GP	G	A	Pts.	PIM
00-01—Elektrostal	Russian Jr.	18	5	8	13	12	...	...	...	—	—	—	—	—
01-02—Elektrostal	Russian Jr.	53	13	15	28	60	...	...	...	—	—	—	—	—
02-03—HC CSKA Moscow	Russian	44	12	12	24	34	...	...	...	—	—	—	—	—
03-04—CSKA Moscow	Russian	20	2	2	4	14	...	...	...	—	—	—	—	—
—Columbus	NHL	57	13	21	34	54	-11	5	0	—	—	—	—	—
04-05—CSKA Moscow	Russian	51	19	21	40	62	17	...	...	—	—	—	—	—
NHL Totals (1 year)		57	13	21	34	54	-11	5	0					

ZHITNIK, ALEXEI — D — ISLANDERS

PERSONAL: Born October 10, 1972, in Kiev, U.S.S.R. ... 5-11/214. ... Shoots left. ... Name pronounced ZHIHT-nihk.
TRANSACTIONS/CAREER NOTES: Selected by Los Angeles Kings in fourth round (third Kings pick, 81st overall) of NHL draft (June 22, 1991). ... Flu (January 12, 1993); missed five games. ... Suspended one game for cross-checking incident (November 30, 1993). ... Traded by Kings with D Charlie Huddy, G Robb Stauber and fifth-round pick (D Marian Menhart) in 1995 draft to Buffalo Sabres for G Grant Fuhr, D Philippe Boucher and D Denis Tsygurov (February 14, 1995). ... Fractured thumb (February 19, 1995); missed three games. ... Reinjured thumb (March 8, 1995); missed one game. ... Ruptured calf muscle (March 19, 1995); missed 11 games. ... Suspended two games and fined $1,000 for high-sticking incident (November 1, 1996). ... Missed first four games of 1997-98 season due to contract dispute. ... Bruised chest (November 29, 1998); missed one game. ... Eye injury (October 17, 1999); missed one game. ... Fractured finger (March 8, 2000); missed six games. ... Suspended one playoff game for high-sticking incident (April 19, 2000). ... Suspended four games for high-sticking incident (October 18, 2000). ... Suspended one game for kneeing incident (November 8, 2002). ... Fractured foot (November 22, 2002); missed 10 games. ... Bruised shoulder (March 10, 2004); missed last 14 games of season. ... Signed as free agent by New York Islanders (Aug, 2, 2005).

		REGULAR SEASON								PLAYOFFS				
Season Team	League	GP	G	A	Pts.	PIM	+/-	PP	SH	GP	G	A	Pts.	PIM
89-90—Sokol Kiev	USSR	31	3	4	7	16	...	...	...	—	—	—	—	—
90-91—Sokol Kiev	USSR	40	1	4	5	46	...	...	...	—	—	—	—	—
91-92—CSKA Moscow	CIS	36	2	7	9	48	...	...	...	—	—	—	—	—
—Unif. Olympic team	Int'l	8	1	0	1	0	...	...	...	—	—	—	—	—
92-93—Los Angeles	NHL	78	12	36	48	80	-3	5	0	24	3	9	12	26
93-94—Los Angeles	NHL	81	12	40	52	101	-11	11	0	—	—	—	—	—
94-95—Los Angeles	NHL	11	2	5	7	27	-3	2	0	—	—	—	—	—
—Buffalo	NHL	21	2	5	7	34	-3	1	0	5	0	1	1	14
95-96—Buffalo	NHL	80	6	30	36	58	-25	5	0	—	—	—	—	—
96-97—Buffalo	NHL	80	7	28	35	95	10	3	1	12	1	0	1	16
97-98—Buffalo	NHL	78	15	30	45	102	19	2	3	15	0	3	3	36
—Russian Oly. team	Int'l	6	0	2	2	2	1	0	0	—	—	—	—	—
98-99—Buffalo	NHL	81	7	26	33	96	-6	3	1	21	4	11	15	*52
99-00—Buffalo	NHL	74	2	11	13	95	-6	1	0	4	0	0	0	8
00-01—Buffalo	NHL	78	8	29	37	75	-3	5	0	13	1	6	7	12
01-02—Buffalo	NHL	82	1	33	34	80	-1	1	0	—	—	—	—	—
02-03—Buffalo	NHL	70	3	18	21	85	-5	0	0	—	—	—	—	—
03-04—Buffalo	NHL	68	4	24	28	102	-13	2	0	—	—	—	—	—
04-05—Ak Bars Kazan	Russian	23	1	8	9	30	9	...	...	4	0	0	0	2
NHL Totals (12 years)		882	81	315	396	1030	-50	41	5	94	9	30	39	164

ZIDLICKY, MAREK — D — PREDATORS

PERSONAL: Born February 3, 1977, in Most, Czechoslovakia. ... 5-11/187. ... Shoots right. ... Name pronounced MAIR-ehk zhihd-LIHTS-kee.
TRANSACTIONS/CAREER NOTES: Selected by New York Rangers in sixth round (sixth Rangers pick, 176th overall) of NHL draft (June 25, 2001). ... Traded by Rangers with LW Rem Murray and D Tomas Kloucek to Nashville Predators for G Mike Dunham (December 12, 2002).

		REGULAR SEASON								PLAYOFFS				
Season Team	League	GP	G	A	Pts.	PIM	+/-	PP	SH	GP	G	A	Pts.	PIM
94-95—HC Kladno	Czech.	30	2	2	4	...	...	...	...	11	1	1	2	...
98-99—HC Kladno	Czech Rep.	50	10	12	22	94	...	...	...	—	—	—	—	—
99-00—HIFK Helsinki	Finland	47	11	10	21	18	...	...	...	9	3	1	4	6
00-01—HIFK Helsinki	Finland	51	12	25	37	146	...	...	...	5	0	1	1	6
01-02—HIFK Helsinki	Finland	56	11	29	40	107	...	...	...	—	—	—	—	—
02-03—HIFK Helsinki	Finland	54	10	37	47	79	...	...	...	4	0	0	0	4
03-04—Nashville	NHL	82	14	39	53	82	-16	9	0	1	0	0	0	0
04-05—HIFK Helsinki	Finland	49	11	20	31	91	2	...	...	5	0	3	3	14
NHL Totals (1 year)		82	14	39	53	82	-16	9	0	1	0	0	0	0

ZIGOMANIS, MIKE — C/RW — HURRICANES

PERSONAL: Born January 17, 1981, in North York, Ont. ... 6-1/200. ... Shoots right. ... Name pronounced zih-goh-MAH-nuhz.
TRANSACTIONS/CAREER NOTES: Selected by Buffalo Sabres in second round (fourth Sabres pick, 64th overall) of NHL draft (June 22, 1999). ... Returned to draft pool by Sabres and selected by Carolina Hurricanes in second round (second Hurricanes pick, 46th overall) of draft (June 23, 2001).

		REGULAR SEASON								PLAYOFFS				
Season Team	League	GP	G	A	Pts.	PIM	+/-	PP	SH	GP	G	A	Pts.	PIM
97-98—Kingston	OHL	62	23	51	74	30	...	...	...	12	1	6	7	2
98-99—Kingston	OHL	67	29	56	85	36	-11	...	...	5	1	7	8	2

		REGULAR SEASON								PLAYOFFS				
Season Team	League	GP	G	A	Pts.	PIM	+/-	PP	SH	GP	G	A	Pts.	PIM
99-00—Kingston	OHL	59	40	54	94	49	21	13	3	5	0	4	4	0
00-01—Kingston	OHL	52	40	37	77	44	21	6	3	—	—	—	—	—
01-02—Lowell	AHL	79	18	30	48	24	-1	4	0	5	1	1	2	2
02-03—Lowell	AHL	38	13	18	31	19	-2	2	0	—	—	—	—	—
—Carolina	NHL	19	2	1	3	0	-4	1	1	—	—	—	—	—
03-04—Carolina	NHL	17	0	3	3	2	-1	0	0	—	—	—	—	—
—Lowell	AHL	61	17	35	52	56	1	5	2	—	—	—	—	—
04-05—Lowell	AHL	76	29	31	60	71	7	7	2	11	4	7	11	8
NHL Totals (2 years)		36	2	4	6	2	-5	1	1					

ZINOVJEV, SERGEI — C — BRUINS

PERSONAL: Born March 4, 1980, in Novokuznetsk, U.S.S.R. ... 5-10/185. ... Shoots left. ... Name pronounced zih-NOH-vee-ehv.
TRANSACTIONS/CAREER NOTES: Selected by Boston Bruins in third round (sixth Bruins pick, 73rd overall) of NHL draft (June 24, 2000). ... Refused assignment to Providence; returned to Russia (December 6, 2003).

		REGULAR SEASON								PLAYOFFS				
Season Team	League	GP	G	A	Pts.	PIM	+/-	PP	SH	GP	G	A	Pts.	PIM
98-99—Magnitogorsk	Russian	31	2	4	6	14	...	...	...	3	0	0	0	0
99-00—Magnitogorsk	Russian	28	0	2	2	16	...	...	...	—	—	—	—	—
00-01—Salavat Yulayev Ufa	Russian	8	4	5	9	6	...	...	...	—	—	—	—	—
—Lokomotiv Yaroslavl	Russian	27	2	10	12	36	...	...	...	—	—	—	—	—
01-02—Spartak Moscow	Russian	51	12	18	30	43	...	...	...	—	—	—	—	—
02-03—Ak Bars Kazan	Russian	47	14	17	31	50	...	...	...	5	1	1	2	6
03-04—Providence	AHL	4	1	2	3	0	3	0	0	—	—	—	—	—
—Boston	NHL	10	0	1	1	2	1	0	0	—	—	—	—	—
—Ak Bars Kazan	Russian	27	5	9	14	73	6	...	...	8	0	1	1	14
04-05—Ak Bars Kazan	Russian	54	17	21	38	82	12	...	...	4	1	0	1	12
NHL Totals (1 year)		10	0	1	1	2	1	0	0					

ZIZKA, TOMAS — D — KINGS

PERSONAL: Born October 10, 1979, in Sternberk, Czechoslovakia. ... 6-1/213. ... Shoots left.
TRANSACTIONS/CAREER NOTES: Selected by Los Angeles Kings in sixth round (sixth Kings pick, 163rd overall) of NHL entry draft (June 27, 1998).

		REGULAR SEASON								PLAYOFFS				
Season Team	League	GP	G	A	Pts.	PIM	+/-	PP	SH	GP	G	A	Pts.	PIM
94-95—ZPS Zlin	Czech. Jrs.	39	1	10	11	...	...	...	...	—	—	—	—	—
95-96—ZPS Zlin	Czech. Jrs.	47	2	8	10	...	...	...	...	—	—	—	—	—
96-97—ZPS Zlin	Czech. Jrs.	14	1	0	1	...	...	...	...	—	—	—	—	—
97-98—ZPS Zlin	Czech Rep.	33	0	3	3	2	...	...	...	—	—	—	—	—
—ZPS Zlin	Czech. Jrs.	11	3	4	7	...	...	...	...	—	—	—	—	—
98-99—ZPS Zlin	Czech Rep.	44	3	7	10	14	...	...	...	11	1	2	3	...
99-00—HC Barum Zlin	Czech Rep.	46	4	6	10	30	...	...	...	4	1	0	1	4
00-01—HC Continental Zlin	Czech Rep.	43	2	11	13	16	...	...	...	6	0	0	0	6
01-02—Manchester	AHL	58	4	17	21	22	4	2	1	4	1	0	1	14
02-03—Los Angeles	NHL	10	0	3	3	4	-4	0	0	—	—	—	—	—
—Manchester	AHL	61	13	30	43	50	15	6	0	3	0	2	2	2
03-04—Manchester	AHL	58	4	24	28	31	2	2	0	5	0	3	3	10
—Los Angeles	NHL	15	2	3	5	12	-4	1	0	—	—	—	—	—
04-05—Spartak Moscow	Russian	23	0	3	3	32	-4	...	...	—	—	—	—	—
—Slavia Praha	Czech Rep.	26	2	4	6	26	1	...	...	2	0	0	0	2
NHL Totals (2 years)		25	2	6	8	16	-8	1	0					

ZUBOV, SERGEI — D — STARS

PERSONAL: Born July 22, 1970, in Moscow, U.S.S.R. ... 6-1/200. ... Shoots right. ... Name pronounced SAIR-gay ZOO-bahf.
TRANSACTIONS/CAREER NOTES: Selected by New York Rangers in fifth round (sixth Rangers pick, 85th overall) of NHL draft (June 16, 1990). ... Suffered concussion (February 26, 1993); missed one game. ... Flu (February 4, 1995); missed one game. ... Wrist surgery (February 27, 1995); missed nine games. ... Traded by Rangers with C Petr Nedved to Pittsburgh Penguins for LW Luc Robitaille and D Ulf Samuelsson (August 31, 1995). ... Fractured finger (October 9, 1995); missed nine games. ... Reinjured finger (November 11, 1995); missed seven games. ... Bruised shoulder (March 31, 1996); missed one game. ... Traded by Penguins to Dallas Stars for D Kevin Hatcher (June 22, 1996). ... Flu (November 20, 1996); missed one game. ... Back spasms (January 24, 1997); missed two games. ... Sprained neck (March 4, 1998); missed nine games. ... Bruised wrist (April 14, 1999); missed one game. ... Sprained knee (March 29, 2000); missed final five games of season. ... Bruised shoulder (January 6, 2001); missed two games. ... Sprained shoulder (December 2, 2001); missed two games. ... Charley horse (March 22, 2004); missed five games.

		REGULAR SEASON								PLAYOFFS				
Season Team	League	GP	G	A	Pts.	PIM	+/-	PP	SH	GP	G	A	Pts.	PIM
88-89—CSKA Moscow	USSR	29	1	4	5	10	...	...	...	—	—	—	—	—
89-90—CSKA Moscow	USSR	48	6	2	8	16	...	...	...	—	—	—	—	—
90-91—CSKA Moscow	USSR	41	6	5	11	12	...	...	...	—	—	—	—	—
91-92—CSKA Moscow	CIS	36	4	7	11	6	...	...	...	—	—	—	—	—
—Unif. Olympic team	Int'l	8	0	1	1	0	...	...	...	—	—	—	—	—
92-93—CSKA Moscow	CIS	1	0	1	1	0	...	...	...	—	—	—	—	—
—Binghamton	AHL	30	7	29	36	14	31	0	1	11	5	5	10	2
—New York Rangers	NHL	49	8	23	31	4	-1	3	0	—	—	—	—	—
93-94—New York Rangers	NHL	78	12	77	89	39	20	9	0	22	5	14	19	0
—Binghamton	AHL	2	1	2	3	0	-2	0	0	—	—	—	—	—

Season Team	League	REGULAR SEASON GP	G	A	Pts.	PIM	+/-	PP	SH	PLAYOFFS GP	G	A	Pts.	PIM
94-95—New York Rangers	NHL	38	10	26	36	18	-2	6	0	10	3	8	11	2
95-96—Pittsburgh	NHL	64	11	55	66	22	28	3	2	18	1	14	15	26
96-97—Dallas	NHL	78	13	30	43	24	19	1	0	7	0	3	3	2
97-98—Dallas	NHL	73	10	47	57	16	16	5	1	17	4	5	9	2
98-99—Dallas	NHL	81	10	41	51	20	9	5	0	23	1	12	13	4
99-00—Dallas	NHL	77	9	33	42	18	-2	3	1	18	2	7	9	6
00-01—Dallas	NHL	79	10	41	51	24	22	6	0	10	1	5	6	4
01-02—Dallas	NHL	80	12	32	44	22	-4	8	0	—	—	—	—	—
02-03—Dallas	NHL	82	11	44	55	26	21	8	0	12	4	10	14	4
03-04—Dallas	NHL	77	7	35	42	20	0	4	1	5	1	1	2	0
NHL Totals (12 years)		856	123	484	607	253	126	61	5	142	22	79	101	50

ZUBRUS, DAINIUS — RW/LW — CAPITALS

PERSONAL: Born June 16, 1978, in Elektrenai, U.S.S.R. ... 6-4/231. ... Shoots left. ... Name pronounced DIGH-nuhz ZOO-bruhz.

TRANSACTIONS/CAREER NOTES: Selected by Philadelphia Flyers in first round (first Flyers pick, 15th overall) of NHL draft (June 22, 1996). ... Bruised right hand (October 8, 1997); missed two games. ... Reinjured right hand (October 15, 1997); missed five games. ... Suspended two games and fined $1,000 in slashing incident (April 2, 1998). ... Strained left hamstring (December 15, 1997); missed one game. ... Traded by Flyers with second-round pick (D Matt Carkner) in 1999 draft to Montreal Canadiens for RW Mark Recchi (March 10, 1999). ... Strained hip flexor (October 20, 1999); missed one game. ... Injured back (October 27, 1999); missed one game. ... Back spasms (January 4, 2000); missed one game. ... Had concussion (February 27, 2000); missed six games. ... Injured rib cage (September 27, 2000); missed first two games of season. ... Had concussion (December 21, 2000); missed 19 games. ... Traded by Canadiens with C Trevor Linden and second-round pick (traded to Tampa Bay; Lightning selected D Andreas Holmqvist) in 2001 draft to Washington Capitals for C Jan Bulis, RW Richard Zednik and first-round pick (C Alexander Perezhogin) in 2001 draft (March 13, 2001). ... Strained groin (December 13, 2001); missed five games. ... Injured foot (January 22, 2002); missed one game. ... Injured right arm (February 26, 2002); missed five games. ... Bruised hand (November 27, 2002); missed 14 games. ... Had concussion (January 17, 2003); missed three games. ... Injured right foot (January 1, 2004); missed 10 games. ... Injured upper body (February 13, 2004); missed two games. ... Injured upper body (February 19, 2004); missed four games. ... Injured chest (March 6, 2004); missed two games. ... Injured chest (March 13, 2004); missed final 11 games of season.

STATISTICAL PLATEAUS: Three-goal games: 2000-01 (1).

Season Team	League	REGULAR SEASON GP	G	A	Pts.	PIM	+/-	PP	SH	PLAYOFFS GP	G	A	Pts.	PIM
95-96—Pembroke	CJHL	28	19	13	32	73	...	...	...	—	—	—	—	—
—Caledon	Jr. A	7	3	7	10	2	...	...	...	17	11	12	23	4
96-97—Philadelphia	NHL	68	8	13	21	22	3	1	0	19	5	4	9	12
97-98—Philadelphia	NHL	69	8	25	33	42	29	1	0	5	0	1	1	2
98-99—Philadelphia	NHL	63	3	5	8	25	-5	0	1	—	—	—	—	—
—Montreal	NHL	17	3	5	8	4	-3	0	0	—	—	—	—	—
99-00—Montreal	NHL	73	14	28	42	54	-1	3	0	—	—	—	—	—
00-01—Montreal	NHL	49	12	12	24	30	-7	3	0	—	—	—	—	—
—Washington	NHL	12	1	1	2	7	-4	1	0	6	0	0	0	2
01-02—Washington	NHL	71	17	26	43	38	5	4	0	—	—	—	—	—
02-03—Washington	NHL	63	13	22	35	43	15	2	0	6	2	2	4	4
03-04—Washington	NHL	54	12	15	27	38	-16	6	1	—	—	—	—	—
04-05—Lada Togliatti	Russian	42	8	11	19	85	9	...	...	10	3	1	4	22
NHL Totals (8 years)		539	91	152	243	303	16	21	2	36	7	7	14	20

ZYUZIN, ANDREI — D — WILD

PERSONAL: Born January 21, 1978, in Ufa, U.S.S.R. ... 6-1/210. ... Shoots left. ... Name pronounced ZYOO-zihn.

TRANSACTIONS/CAREER NOTES: Selected by San Jose Sharks in first round (first Sharks pick, second overall) of NHL draft (June 22, 1996). ... Suspended for remainder of season for leaving team without permission (April 1, 1999) ... Suspended two playoff games for slashing (April 19, 1999). ... Traded by Sharks with D Bill Houlder, LW Shawn Burr and C Steve Guolla to Tampa Bay Lightning for LW Niklas Sundstrom and third-round pick (traded to Chicago; Blackhawks selected LW Igor Radulov) in 2000 draft (August 4, 1999). ... Injured shoulder (October 28, 1999); missed five games. ... Injured shoulder (January 11, 2000); missed remainder of season. ... Had concussion (November 20, 2000); missed five games. ... Had concussion (December 1, 2000); missed five games. ... Injured shoulder (January 30, 2001); missed two games. ... Sprained ankle (March 15, 2001); missed one game. ... Had concussion (March 21, 2001); missed three games. ... Traded by Lightning to New Jersey Devils for D Josef Boumedienne, D Sascha Goc and LW Anton But (November 9, 2001). ... Injured shoulder (December 5, 2001); missed four games. ... Bruised foot (February 27, 2002); missed three games. ... Claimed off waivers by Minnesota Wild (November 3, 2002). ... Flu (December 12, 2002); missed one game. ... Back spasms (October 28, 2003); missed two games. ... Injured ankle (December 18, 2003); missed one game. ... Strained groin (January 16, 2004); missed two games. ... Injured groin (January 21, 2004); missed 10 games.

Season Team	League	REGULAR SEASON GP	G	A	Pts.	PIM	+/-	PP	SH	PLAYOFFS GP	G	A	Pts.	PIM
94-95—Salavat Yulayev Ufa	CIS	30	3	0	3	16	...	...	...	—	—	—	—	—
95-96—Salavat Yulayev Ufa	CIS	41	6	3	9	24	...	...	...	2	0	0	0	4
96-97—Salavet Yulayev Ufa	USSR	32	7	10	17	28	...	...	...	7	1	1	2	4
97-98—San Jose	NHL	56	6	7	13	66	8	2	0	6	1	0	1	14
—Kentucky	AHL	17	4	5	9	28	-2	2	0	—	—	—	—	—
98-99—San Jose	NHL	25	3	1	4	38	5	2	0	—	—	—	—	—
—Kentucky	AHL	23	2	12	14	42	9	1	0	—	—	—	—	—
99-00—Tampa Bay	NHL	34	2	9	11	33	-11	0	0	—	—	—	—	—
00-01—Tampa Bay	NHL	64	4	16	20	76	-8	2	1	—	—	—	—	—
—Detroit	IHL	2	0	1	1	0	...	...	...	—	—	—	—	—
01-02—Tampa Bay	NHL	9	0	2	2	6	-6	0	0	—	—	—	—	—
—New Jersey	NHL	38	1	2	3	25	1	1	0	—	—	—	—	—
—Albany	AHL	3	0	1	1	2	-5	0	0	—	—	—	—	—
02-03—New Jersey	NHL	1	0	1	1	2	-1	0	0	—	—	—	—	—
—Minnesota	NHL	66	4	12	16	34	-7	2	0	18	0	1	1	14
03-04—Minnesota	NHL	65	8	13	21	48	4	4	0	—	—	—	—	—
04-05—Salavat Yulayev Ufa	Russian	14	2	1	3	6	-2	...	...	—	—	—	—	—
—Severstal Cherepovets	Russian	10	2	1	3	8	-2	...	...	—	—	—	—	—
NHL Totals (7 years)		358	28	63	91	328	-15	13	1	24	1	1	2	28

HEAD COACHES

BABCOCK, MIKE — RED WINGS

PERSONAL: Born April 29, 1963, in Manitouwadge, Ont.

HEAD COACHING RECORD

BACKGROUND: Coach, Red Deer (Alta.) College (1988-91). ... Coach, University of Lethbridge, Alta. (1993-94). ... Coach, Spokane of the WHL (1994-95 through 1999-2000). ... Coach, Cincinnati of the AHL (2000-01 through 2001-02). ... Coach, Anaheim Mighty Ducks (May 22, 2002, to June 30, 2005). ... Named coach, Detroit Red Wings (July 15, 2005).

		REGULAR SEASON						PLAYOFFS		
Season Team	League	W	L	T	OL	Pct.	Finish	W	L	Pct.
91-92—Moose Jaw	WHL	33	36	3	...	.479	6th/East Division	0	4	.000
92-93—Moose Jaw	WHL	27	42	3	...	.396	8th/East Division	—	—	—
94-95—Spokane	WHL	32	36	4	...	.472	5th/West Division	3	1	.750
95-96—Spokane	WHL	50	18	4	...	.722	1st/West Division	9	9	.500
96-97—Spokane	WHL	35	33	4	...	.514	3rd/West Division	4	5	.444
97-98—Spokane	WHL	45	23	4	...	.653	2nd/West Division	10	8	.556
98-99—Spokane	WHL	19	44	9	...	.326	7th/West Division	—	—	—
99-00—Spokane	WHL	47	21	4	...	.681	1st/West Division	10	5	.667
00-01—Cincinnati	AHL	41	26	9	4	.569	2nd/Southern Division	1	3	.250
01-02—Cincinnati	AHL	33	33	11	3	.481	3rd/Central Division	1	2	.333
02-03—Anaheim	NHL	40	27	9	6	.543	2nd/Pacific Division	15	6	.714
03-04—Anaheim	NHL	29	35	10	8	.415	4th/Pacific Division	—	—	—
NHL Totals (2 years)		69	62	19	14	.479	**NHL Totals (1 year)**	15	6	.714

NOTES:

91-92—Lost to Prince Albert in East Division preliminary round.
94-95—Lost to Tri-City in West Division quarterfinals.
95-96—Defeated Portland in division quarterfinals; defeated Kamloops in division finals; lost to Brandon in WHL Finals.
96-97—Defeated Kelowna in division quarterfinals; lost to Prince George in division semifinals.
97-98—Defeated Kelowna in division quarterfinals; defeated Prince George in division semifinals; lost to Portland in division finals.
99-00—Defeated Tri-City in division quarterfinals; defeated Prince George in division finals; lost to Kootenay in WHL finals.
00-01—Lost to Norfolk in conference quarterfinals of Calder Cup playoffs.
01-02—Lost to Chicago in qualifying round of Calder Cup playoffs.
02-03—Defeated Detroit in Western Conference quarterfinals; defeated Dallas in Western Conference semifinals; defeated Minnesota in Western Conference finals; lost to New Jersey in Stanley Cup Finals.

CARLYLE, RANDY — MIGHTY DUCKS

PERSONAL: Born April 19, 1956, in Sudbury, Ont. ... 5-10/200. ... Shoots left. ... Played defense.

TRANSACTIONS/CAREER NOTES: Selected by Toronto Maple Leafs from Sudbury Wolves in 2nd round (1st Maple Leafs pick, 30th overall) of entry draft (June 1, 1976). ... Broken ankle; missed parts of 1978-79 season. ... Traded by Maple Leafs with C George Ferguson to Pittsburgh Penguins for D Dave Burrows (June 14, 1978). ... Injured back (October 1982). ... Injured knee (January 1983). ... Injured knee (March 1984). ... Traded by Penguins to Winnipeg Jets for first-round pick in 1984 draft (D Doug Bodger) and player to be named after the 1983-84 season (D Moe Mantha) (March 5, 1984). ... Injured thigh (November 12, 1985); missed eight games. ... Whiplash (November 1986); missed nine games. ... Strained neck muscles (January 18, 1989). ... Bruised left knee (November 5, 1989); missed nine games. ... Missed 10 games due to death of parents (December 1989). ... Torn ligaments in right knee (March 15, 1990). ... Strained groin and bruised thigh (November 11, 1990); missed five games. ... Strained triceps (February 20, 1991); missed seven games. ... Bruised ribs (October 29, 1991); missed three games. ... Strained abdomen (December 14, 1991); missed six games. ... Ankle contusion (January 4, 1992); missed two games. ... Quad strain (October 10, 1992); missed eight games. ... Quad strain (November 2, 1992); missed four games. ... Strained shoulder (December 5, 1992); missed two games. ... Strained groin (December 11, 1992); missed seven games. ... Quad strain (January 8, 1993); missed six games. ... Pulled groin (February 28, 1993); missed three games.

		REGULAR SEASON								PLAYOFFS				
Season Team	League	GP	G	A	Pts.	PIM	+/-	PP	SH	GP	G	A	Pts.	PIM
76-77—Dallas	CHL	26	2	7	9	63	...	...	...	—	—	—	—	—
—Toronto	NHL	45	0	5	5	51	...	...	...	9	0	1	1	20
77-78—Dallas	CHL	21	3	14	17	31	...	...	...	—	—	—	—	—
—Toronto	NHL	49	2	11	13	31	...	...	...	7	0	1	1	8
78-79—Pittsburgh	NHL	70	13	34	47	78	...	...	...	7	0	0	0	12
79-80—Pittsburgh	NHL	67	8	28	36	45	...	...	...	5	1	0	1	4
80-81—Pittsburgh	NHL	76	16	67	83	136	...	...	...	5	4	5	9	9
81-82—Pittsburgh	NHL	73	11	64	75	131	...	...	...	5	1	3	4	16
82-83—Pittsburgh	NHL	61	15	41	56	110	...	...	...	—	—	—	—	—
83-84—Pittsburgh	NHL	50	3	23	26	82	...	...	...	—	—	—	—	—
—Winnipeg	NHL	5	0	3	3	2	...	...	...	3	0	2	2	4
84-85—Winnipeg	NHL	71	13	38	51	98	...	...	...	8	1	5	6	13
85-86—Winnipeg	NHL	68	16	33	49	93	...	...	...	—	—	—	—	—
86-87—Winnipeg	NHL	71	16	26	42	93	...	...	...	10	1	5	6	18
87-88—Winnipeg	NHL	78	15	44	59	210	...	...	...	5	0	2	2	10
88-89—Winnipeg	NHL	78	6	38	44	78	...	...	...	—	—	—	—	—
89-90—Winnipeg	NHL	53	3	15	18	50	8	2	0	—	—	—	—	—
90-91—Winnipeg	NHL	52	9	19	28	44	...	...	...	—	—	—	—	—
91-92—Winnipeg	NHL	66	1	9	10	54	...	...	...	5	1	0	1	6
92-93—Winnipeg	NHL	22	1	1	2	14	-6	0	0	—	—	—	—	—
NHL Totals (17 years)		1055	148	499	647	1400	2	2	0	69	9	24	33	120

HEAD COACHING RECORD

BACKGROUND: Named coach of the Anaheim Mighty Ducks (Aug. 1, 2005).

CRAWFORD, MARC — CANUCKS

PERSONAL: Born February 13, 1961, in Belleville, Ont. ... Shoots left. ... Brother of Bob Crawford, RW with four NHL teams (1979-80 and 1981-87).

TRANSACTIONS/CAREER NOTES: Selected by Vancouver Canucks in fourth round (third Canucks pick, 70th overall) of NHL draft (June 11, 1980). ... Suspended three games for leaving bench to fight (February 3, 1987).

		REGULAR SEASON								PLAYOFFS				
Season Team	**League**	**GP**	**G**	**A**	**Pts.**	**PIM**	**+/-**	**PP**	**SH**	**GP**	**G**	**A**	**Pts.**	**PIM**
81-82—Dallas	CHL	34	13	21	34	71	...	...	...	—	—	—	—	—
—Vancouver	NHL	40	4	8	12	29	0	0	0	14	1	0	1	11
82-83—Vancouver	NHL	41	4	5	9	28	-3	0	0	3	0	1	1	25
—Fredericton	AHL	30	15	9	24	59	...	...	...	9	1	3	4	10
83-84—Vancouver	NHL	19	0	1	1	9	0	0	0	—	—	—	—	—
—Fredericton	AHL	56	9	22	31	96	...	...	...	7	4	2	6	23
84-85—Vancouver	NHL	1	0	0	0	4	-4	0	0	—	—	—	—	—
85-86—Vancouver	NHL	54	11	14	25	92	-7	0	0	3	0	1	1	8
—Fredericton	AHL	26	10	14	24	55	...	...	...	—	—	—	—	—
86-87—Vancouver	NHL	21	0	3	3	67	-8	0	0	—	—	—	—	—
—Fredericton	AHL	25	8	11	19	21	...	...	...	—	—	—	—	—
87-88—Fredericton	AHL	43	5	13	18	90	...	...	...	2	0	0	0	14
88-89—Milwaukee	IHL	53	23	30	53	166	...	...	...	11	2	5	7	26
NHL Totals (6 years)		176	19	31	50	229	-22	0	0	20	1	2	3	44

HEAD COACHING RECORD

BACKGROUND: Player/assistant coach, Fredericton Express of AHL (1987-88). ... Head coach, Quebec Nordiques (1994-95). ... Nordiques franchise moved to Denver for 1995-96 season and renamed Colorado Avalanche. ... Head coach, Colorado Avalanche (1995-1998). ... Hockey analyst, CBC television (1998-January 24, 1999). ... Named coach of Vancouver Canucks (January 24, 1999).

		REGULAR SEASON						PLAYOFFS		
Season Team	**League**	**W**	**L**	**T**	**OL**	**Pct.**	**Finish**	**W**	**L**	**Pct.**
89-90—Cornwall	OHL	24	38	4	...	.394	6th/Leyden Division	2	4	.333
90-91—Cornwall	OHL	23	42	1	...	.356	7th/Leyden Division	—	—	—
91-92—St. John's	AHL	39	29	12	...	.563	2nd/Atlantic Division	11	5	.688
92-93—St. John's	AHL	41	26	13	...	.594	1st/Atlantic Division	4	5	.444
93-94—St. John's	AHL	45	23	12	...	.638	1st/Atlantic Division	6	5	.545
94-95—Quebec	NHL	30	13	5	...	.677	1st/Northeast Division	2	4	.333
95-96—Colorado	NHL	47	25	10	...	.634	1st/Pacific Division	16	6	.727
96-97—Colorado	NHL	49	24	9	...	.652	1st/Pacific Division	10	7	.588
97-98—Colorado	NHL	39	26	17	...	.579	1st/Pacific Division	3	4	.429
98-99—Vancouver	NHL	8	23	6	...	.297	4th/Northwest Division	—	—	—
99-00—Vancouver	NHL	30	29	15	8	.457	3rd/Northwest Division	—	—	—
00-01—Vancouver	NHL	36	28	11	7	.506	3rd/Northwest Division	0	4	.000
01-02—Vancouver	NHL	42	30	7	3	.555	2nd/Northwest Division	2	4	.333
02-03—Vancouver	NHL	45	23	13	1	.628	2nd/Northwest Division	7	7	.500
03-04—Vancouver	NHL	43	24	10	5	.585	1st/Northwest Division	3	4	.429
NHL Totals (10 years)		369	245	103	24	.567	**NHL Totals (8 years)**	43	40	.518

NOTES:

89-90—Lost to Oshawa in Leyden Division quarterfinals.
91-92—Defeated Cape Breton in first round of Calder Cup playoffs; defeated Moncton in second round of Calder Cup playoffs; lost to Adirondack in Calder Cup finals.
92-93—Defeated Moncton in first round of Calder Cup playoffs; lost to Cape Breton in second round of Calder Cup playoffs.
93-94—Defeated Cape Breton in first round of Calder Cup playoffs; lost to Moncton in second round of Calder Cup playoffs.
94-95—Lost to New York Rangers in Eastern Conference quarterfinals.
95-96—Defeated Vancouver in Western Conference quarterfinals; defeated Chicago in Western Conference semifinals; defeated Detroit in Western Conference finals; defeated Florida in Stanley Cup finals.
96-97—Defeated Chicago in Western Conference quarterfinals; defeated Edmonton in conference semifinals; lost to Detroit in conference finals.
97-98—Lost to Edmonton in Western Conference quarterfinals.
98-99—Replaced Mike Keenan as head coach (January 24).
00-01—Lost to Colorado in Western Conference quarterfinals.
01-02—Lost to Detroit in Western Conference quarterfinals.
02-03—Defeated St. Louis in Western Conference quarterfinals; lost to Minnesota in Western Conference semifinals.
03-04—Lost to Calgary in Western Conference quarterfinals.

GALLANT, GERARD — BLUE JACKETS

PERSONAL: Born September 2, 1963, in Summerside, P.E.I. ... 5-10/190. ... Shoots left. ... Played left wing. ... Name pronounced guh-LANT.

TRANSACTIONS/CAREER NOTES: Selected by Detroit Red Wings in sixth round (fourth Red Wings pick, 107th overall) of NHL draft (June 10, 1981). ... Broke jaw (December 11, 1985); missed 25 games. ... Fined $500 for stick-swinging incident (April 8, 1989). ... Suspended five games for slashing (October 7, 1989). ... Suspended three games for hitting linesman (January 13, 1990). ... Suffered sore back (November 1990); missed eight games. ... Back spasms (December 1990); missed 18 games. ... Underwent surgery to remove bone spur in back (March 14, 1991); missed remainder of season. ... Injured hand (February 1992); missed five games. ... Strained back (March 20, 1992); missed five games. ... Injured hip (December 15, 1992); missed three games. ... Flu (January 17, 1993); missed one game. ... Signed as free agent by Tampa Bay Lightning (July 21, 1993). ... Sprained back (November 17, 1993); missed four games. ... Sprained back (April 1, 1994); missed six games.

STATISTICAL PLATEAUS: Three-goal games: 1987-88 (3), 1988-89 (1). Total: 4.

		REGULAR SEASON								PLAYOFFS				
Season Team	**League**	**GP**	**G**	**A**	**Pts.**	**PIM**	**+/-**	**PP**	**SH**	**GP**	**G**	**A**	**Pts.**	**PIM**
83-84—Adirondack	AHL	77	31	33	64	195	...	...	...	7	1	3	4	34
84-85—Adirondack	AHL	46	18	29	47	131	...	...	...	—	—	—	—	—
—Detroit	NHL	32	6	12	18	66	...	...	...	3	0	0	0	11

Season Team	League	REGULAR SEASON GP	G	A	Pts.	PIM	+/-	PP	SH	PLAYOFFS GP	G	A	Pts.	PIM
85-86—Detroit	NHL	52	20	19	39	106	...	...	...	—	—	—	—	—
86-87—Detroit	NHL	80	38	34	72	216	...	...	...	16	8	6	14	43
87-88—Detroit	NHL	73	34	39	73	242	...	...	...	16	6	9	15	55
88-89—Detroit	NHL	76	39	54	93	230	...	...	...	6	1	2	3	40
89-90—Detroit	NHL	69	36	44	80	254	-6	12	3	—	—	—	—	—
90-91—Detroit	NHL	45	10	16	26	111	...	...	...	—	—	—	—	—
91-92—Detroit	NHL	69	14	22	36	187	...	...	...	11	2	2	4	25
92-93—Detroit	NHL	67	10	20	30	188	20	0	0	6	1	2	3	4
93-94—Tampa Bay	NHL	51	4	9	13	74	-6	1	0	—	—	—	—	—
94-95—Atlanta	IHL	16	3	3	6	31	-8	0	0	—	—	—	—	—
—Tampa Bay	NHL	1	0	0	0	0	0	0	0	—	—	—	—	—
95-96—Detroit	IHL	3	2	1	3	6	...	...	...	—	—	—	—	—
NHL Totals (11 years)		615	211	269	480	1674	8	13	3	58	18	21	39	178

HEAD COACHING RECORD

BACKGROUND: Named interim coach of Columbus Blue Jackets (January 1, 2004). ... Named coach of Blue Jackets (June 25, 2004).

Season Team	League	REGULAR SEASON W	L	T	OL	Pct.	Finish	PLAYOFFS W	L	Pct.
03-04—Columbus	NHL	16	24	4	1	.400	4th/Central Division	—	—	—
NHL Totals (1 year)		16	24	4	1	.400				

GRETZKY, WAYNE — COYOTES

PERSONAL: Born January 26, 1961, in Brantford, Ont. ... 6-0/180. ... Shoots left. ... Brother of Brent Gretzky, C with Tampa Bay Lightning (1993-94 and 1994-95). ... Played center.

TRANSACTIONS/CAREER NOTES: Signed as underage junior by Indianapolis Racers to multi-year contract (May 1978). ... Traded by Racers with LW Peter Driscoll and G Ed Mio to Edmonton Oilers for cash and future considerations (November 1978). ... Bruised right shoulder (January 28, 1984). ... Underwent surgery on left ankle to remove benign growth (June 1984). ... Twisted right knee (December 30, 1987). ... Suffered corneal abrasion to left eye (February 19, 1988); missed three games. ... Traded by Oilers with RW//D Marty McSorley and LW//C Mike Krushelnyski to Los Angeles Kings for C Jimmy Carson, LW Martin Gelinas, first-round picks in 1989 (traded to New Jersey), 1991 (LW Martin Rucinsky) and 1993 (D Nick Stajduhar) drafts and cash (August 9, 1988). ... Injured groin (March 17, 1990). ... Strained lower back (March 22, 1990); missed five regular-season games and two playoff games. ... Missed five games due to personal reasons (October 1991). ... Sprained knee (February 25, 1992); missed one game. ... Suffered herniated thoracic disc before 1992-93 season; missed first 39 games of season. ... Sprained left knee (April 9, 1994). ... Traded by Kings to St. Louis Blues for LW Craig Johnson, C Patrice Tardiff, C Roman Vopat, fifth-round pick (D Peter Hogan) in 1996 draft and 1st-round pick (LW Matt Zultek) in 1997 draft (February 27, 1996). ... Bruised lower back (April 4, 1996); missed three games. ... Signed as free agent by New York Rangers (July 21, 1996). ... Suffered from bulging disc in neck (February 22, 1999); missed 12 games. ... Announced retirement to follow 1998-99 season (April 16, 1999).

STATISTICAL PLATEAUS: Three-goal games: 1979-80 (2), 1980-81 (2), 1981-82 (6), 1982-83 (2), 1983-84 (6), 1984-85 (5), 1985-86 (3), 1986-87 (3), 1987-88 (1), 1988-89 (2), 1989-90 (1), 1990-91 (2), 1991-92 (1), 1997-98 (1). Total: 37. ... Four-goal games: 1980-81 (1), 1981-82 (3), 1983-84 (4), 1986-87 (1). Total: 9. ... Five-goal games: 1980-81 (1), 1981-82 (1), 1984-85 (1), 1987-88 (1). Total: 4. ... Total hat tricks: 50.

Season Team	League	REGULAR SEASON GP	G	A	Pts.	PIM	+/-	PP	SH	PLAYOFFS GP	G	A	Pts.	PIM
76-77—Peterborough	OMJHL	3	0	3	3	0	...	...	...	—	—	—	—	—
77-78—Sault Ste. Marie	OMJHL	64	70	112	182	14	...	...	...	13	6	20	26	0
78-79—Indianapolis	WHA	8	3	3	6	0	...	...	...	—	—	—	—	—
—Edmonton	WHA	72	43	61	104	19	...	...	...	13	10	10	*20	2
79-80—Edmonton	NHL	79	51	*86	137	21	15	13	1	3	2	1	3	0
80-81—Edmonton	NHL	80	55	*109	*164	28	41	15	4	9	7	14	21	4
81-82—Edmonton	NHL	80	*92	*120	*212	26	*81	18	6	5	5	7	12	8
82-83—Edmonton	NHL	80	*71	*125	*196	59	60	18	*6	16	12	*26	*38	4
83-84—Edmonton	NHL	74	*87	*118	*205	39	*76	*20	*12	19	13	*22	*35	12
84-85—Edmonton	NHL	80	*73	*135	*208	52	*98	8	*11	18	17	*30	*47	4
85-86—Edmonton	NHL	80	52	*163	*215	46	71	11	3	10	8	11	19	2
86-87—Edmonton	NHL	79	*62	*121	*183	28	*70	13	*7	21	5	*29	*34	6
87-88—Edmonton	NHL	64	40	*109	149	24	39	9	5	19	12	*31	*43	16
88-89—Los Angeles	NHL	78	54	114	168	26	15	11	5	11	5	17	22	0
89-90—Los Angeles	NHL	73	40	*102	*142	42	8	10	4	7	3	7	10	0
90-91—Los Angeles	NHL	78	41	*122	*163	16	30	8	0	12	4	11	15	2
91-92—Los Angeles	NHL	74	31	*90	121	34	-12	12	2	6	2	5	7	2
92-93—Los Angeles	NHL	45	16	49	65	6	6	0	2	24	15	25	*40	4
93-94—Los Angeles	NHL	81	38	*92	*130	20	-25	14	4	—	—	—	—	—
94-95—Los Angeles	NHL	48	11	37	48	6	-20	3	0	—	—	—	—	—
95-96—Los Angeles	NHL	62	15	66	81	32	-7	5	0	—	—	—	—	—
—St. Louis	NHL	18	8	13	21	2	-6	1	1	13	2	14	16	0
96-97—New York Rangers	NHL	82	25	72	97	28	12	6	0	15	10	10	20	2
97-98—New York Rangers	NHL	82	23	67	90	28	-11	6	0	—	—	—	—	—
—Can. Olympic team	Int'l	6	0	4	4	2	3	0	0	—	—	—	—	—
98-99—New York Rangers	NHL	70	9	53	62	14	-23	3	0	—	—	—	—	—
NHL Totals (20 years)		1487	894	1963	2857	577	518	204	73	208	122	260	382	66

HEAD COACHING RECORD

BACKGROUND: Named coach of the Phoenix Coyotes (Aug. 8, 2005).

HANLON, GLEN — CAPITALS

PERSONAL: Born February 20, 1957, in Brandon, Man. ... 6-0/185. ... Shoots right. ... Played goal.

TRANSACTIONS/CAREER NOTES: Selected by Vancouver Canucks from Brandon Wheat Kings in third round (third Canucks pick, 40th overall) of entry draft (June 14, 1977). ... Tore ankle ligaments; missed part of 1977-78 season. ... Injured shoulder; missed part of 1979-80 season. ...

Stretched knee ligaments (October 18, 1980). ... Suffered shoulder separation (March, 1981). ... Traded by Canucks to St. Louis Blues for RW Tony Currie, RW Jim Nill, G Rick Heinz and fourth-round pick (G Shawn Kilroy) in 1982 draft (March 9, 1982). ... Traded by Blues with C Vaclav Nedomansky to New York Rangers for D Andre Dore and future considerations (January 4, 1983). ... Traded by Rangers with third-round picks in 1987 (C Dennis Holland) and 1988 (D Guy Dupuis) drafts and future considerations to Detroit Red Wings for C Kelly Kisio, RW Lane Lambert and D Jim Leavins and fifth-round pick in 1988 draft (July 29, 1986). ... Lacerated finger (October 16, 1987). ... Broke left index finger (January, 1988). ... Injured hip (March, 1989). ... Fractured right hand (January 21, 1991); missed eight games.

HEAD COACHING RECORD

BACKGROUND: Head coach, Portland of the AHL (1999-2000 through 2001-02). ... Named coach of Washington Capitals (December 10, 2003).

		REGULAR SEASON						PLAYOFFS		
Season Team	**League**	**W**	**L**	**T**	**OL**	**Pct.**	**Finish**	**W**	**L**	**Pct.**
99-00—Portland	AHL	46	23	10	1	.638	2nd/Northeast Division	—	—	—
00-01—Portland	AHL	34	40	4	2	.450	5th/Northeast Division	—	—	—
01-02—Portland	AHL	30	31	15	4	.469	4th/Northern Division	—	—	—
03-04—Washington	NHL	15	28	9	2	.361	5th/Southeast Division	—	—	—
NHL Totals (1 year)		15	28	9	2	.361				

NOTES:

99-00—Lost in first round of AHL playoffs.

HARTLEY, BOB — THRASHERS

PERSONAL: Born September 7, 1960, in Hawkesbury, Ont.

HEAD COACHING RECORD

BACKGROUND: Coach, Colorado Avalanche (June 30, 1998 to December 18, 2002). ... Named coach of Atlanta Thrashers (January 14, 2003).

		REGULAR SEASON						PLAYOFFS		
Season Team	**League**	**W**	**L**	**T**	**OL**	**Pct.**	**Finish**	**W**	**L**	**Pct.**
87-88—Hawkesbury	CJHL	9	39	0	...	.188	...	1	4	.200
88-89—Hawkesbury	CJHL	35	20	1	...	.634	...	6	6	.500
89-90—Hawkesbury	CJHL	15	15	1	...	.500	...	12	3	.800
90-91—Hawkesbury	CJHL	42	10	4	...	.786	...	12	0	1.000
91-92—Laval	QMJHL	38	27	5	...	.579	...	4	6	.400
92-93—Laval	QMJHL	43	25	2	...	.629	1st/Robert Le Bel Division	12	1	.923
94-95—Cornwall	AHL	38	33	9	...	.531	2nd/Southern Division	8	6	.571
95-96—Cornwall	AHL	34	39	7	...	.469	4th/Central Division	3	5	.375
96-97—Hershey	AHL	43	22	10	...	.640	2nd/Mid-Atlantic Division	15	8	.652
97-98—Hershey	AHL	36	31	7	...	.534	2nd/Mid-Atlantic Division	3	4	.429
98-99—Colorado	NHL	44	28	10	...	.598	1st/ Northwest Division	11	8	.579
99-00—Colorado	NHL	42	28	11	1	.579	1st/Northwest Division	11	6	.647
00-01—Colorado	NHL	52	16	10	4	.695	1st/Northwest Division	16	7	.696
01-02—Colorado	NHL	45	28	8	1	.598	1st/Northwest Division	11	10	.524
02-03—Atlanta	NHL	19	14	5	1	.551	3rd/Southeast Division	—	—	—
03-04—Atlanta	NHL	33	37	8	4	.451	2nd/Southeast Division	—	—	—
NHL Totals (6 years)		235	151	52	11	.581	**NHL Totals (4 years)**	49	31	.613

NOTES:

92-93—Defeated Verdun in quarterfinals of President Cup playoffs; defeated Drummondville in semifinals of President Cup playoffs; defeated Sherbrooke in finals of President Cup playoffs.

94-95—Defeated Hershey in division semifinals in Calder Cup playoffs; defeated Binghamton in division finals in Calder Cup playoffs; lost to Fredericton in league semifinals in Calder Cup playoffs.

95-96—Defeated Albany in conference quarterfinals in Calder Cup playoffs; lost to Rochester in conference finals in Calder Cup playoffs.

96-97—Defeated Kentucky in conference quarterfinals in Calder Cup playoffs; defeated Phliadelphia in conference semifinals in Calder Cup playoffs; defeated Springfield in conference finals in Calder Cup playoffs; defeated Hamilton in Calder Cup finals.

97-98—Defeated Kentucky in conference quarterfinals in Calder Cup playoffs; lost to Philadelphia in conference semifinals in Calder Cup playoffs.

98-99—Defeated San Jose in Western Conference quarterfinals; defeated Detroit in Western Conference semifinals; lost to Dallas in Western Conference finals.

99-00—Defeated Phoenix in Western Conference quarterfinals; defeated Detroit in Western Conference semifinals; lost to Dallas in Western Conference finals.

00-01—Defeated Vancouver in Western Conference quarterfinals; defeated Los Angeles in Western Conference semifinals; defeated St. Louis in Western Conference finals; defeated New Jersey in Stanley Cup finals.

01-02—Defeated Los Angeles in Western Conference quarterfinals; defeated San Jose in conference semifinals; lost to Detroit in conference finals.

HITCHCOCK, KEN — FLYERS

PERSONAL: Born December 17, 1951, in Edmonton.

HEAD COACHING RECORD

BACKGROUND: Assistant coach, Philadelphia Flyers (1990-93). ... Coach, Dallas Stars (January 8, 1996, through 2001-02). ... Associate coach, Canadian Olympic team (2002). ... Named coach of Flyers (May 14, 2002).

		REGULAR SEASON						PLAYOFFS		
Season Team	**League**	**W**	**L**	**T**	**OL**	**Pct.**	**Finish**	**W**	**L**	**Pct.**
84-85—Kamloops	WHL	52	17	2	...	.746	1st/West Division	10	5	.667
85-86—Kamloops	WHL	49	19	4	...	.708	1st/West Division	14	2	.875
86-87—Kamloops	WHL	55	14	3	...	.785	1st/West Division	8	5	.615
87-88—Kamloops	WHL	45	26	1	...	.632	1st/West Division	12	6	.667
88-89—Kamloops	WHL	34	33	5	...	.507	3rd/West Division	8	8	.500
89-90—Kamloops	WHL	56	16	0	...	.778	1st/West Division	14	3	.824
93-94—Kalamazoo	IHL	48	26	7	...	.636	1st/Atlantic Division	1	4	.200
94-95—Kalamazoo	IHL	43	24	14	...	.617	2nd/Northern Division	10	6	.625

Season Team	League	W	L	T	OL	Pct.	Finish	Playoffs W	Playoffs L	Playoffs Pct.
		REGULAR SEASON						PLAYOFFS		
95-96—Michigan	IHL	19	10	11	...	.613	...	—	—	—
—Dallas	NHL	15	23	5	...	.407	6th/Central Division	—	—	—
96-97—Dallas	NHL	48	26	8	...	.634	1st/Central Division	3	4	.429
97-98—Dallas	NHL	49	22	11	...	.665	1st/Central Division	10	7	.588
98-99—Dallas	NHL	51	19	12	...	.695	1st/Pacific Division	16	7	.696
99-00—Dallas	NHL	43	23	10	6	.585	1st/Pacific Division	14	9	.609
00-01—Dallas	NHL	48	24	8	2	.634	1st/Pacific Division	4	6	.400
01-02—Dallas	NHL	23	17	6	4	.520	...	—	—	—
02-03—Philadelphia	NHL	45	20	13	4	.628	2nd/Atlantic Division	6	7	.462
03-04—Philadelphia	NHL	40	21	15	6	.579	1st/Atlantic Division	11	7	.611
NHL Totals (9 years)		362	195	88	22	.609	**NHL Totals (7 years)**	64	47	.577

NOTES:

84-85—Defeated Portland in West Division semifinals; defeated New Westminster in West Division finals; lost to Prince Albert in WHL finals.
85-86—Defeated Seattle in West Division semifinals; defeated Portland in West Division finals; defeated Medicine Hat in WHL finals.
86-87—Defeated Victoria in West Division semifinals; lost to Portland in West Division finals.
87-88—Defeated New Westminster in West Division semifinals; defeated Spokane in West Division finals; lost to Medicine Hat in WHL finals.
88-89—Defeated Victoria in West Division semifinals; lost to Portland in West Division finals.
89-90—Defeated Spokane in West Division semifinals; defeated Seattle in West Division finals; defeated Lethbridge in WHL finals.
93-94—Lost to Cincinnati in Eastern Conference quarterfinals.
94-95—Defeated Chicago in Eastern Conference quarterfinals; defeated Cincinnati in conference semifinals; lost to Kansas City in conference finals.
95-96—Replaced Bob Gainey as head coach (January 8).
96-97—Lost to Edmonton in Western Conference quarterfinals.
97-98—Defeated San Jose in Western Conference quarterfinals; defeated Edmonton in conference semifinals; lost to Detroit in conference finals.
98-99—Defeated Edmonton in Western Conference quarterfinals; defeated St. Louis in Western Conference semifinals; defeated Colorado in Western Conference finals; defeated Buffalo in Stanley Cup finals.
99-00—Defeated Edmonton in Western Conference quarterfinals; defeated San Jose in Western Conference semifinals; defeated Colorado in Western Conference finals; lost to New Jersey in Stanley Cup finals.
00-01—Defeated Edmonton in Western Conference quarterfinals; lost to St. Louis in Western Conference semifinals.
01-02—Replaced as head coach by Rick Wilson (January 25).
02-03—Defeated Toronto in Eastern Conference quarterfinals; lost to Ottawa in Eastern Conference semifinals.
03-04—Defeated New Jersey in Eastern Conference quarterfinals; defeated Toronto in conference semifinals; lost to Tampa Bay in conference finals.

JULIEN, CLAUDE — CANADIENS

PERSONAL: Born November 11, 1958, in Orleans, Ont. ... 6-0/195. ... Shoots right. ... Played defense.
TRANSACTIONS/CAREER NOTES: Signed as free agent by St. Louis Blues (September 1981). ... Sent with D Gordon Donnelly to Quebec Nordiques as compensation for Blues signing coach Jacques Demers (August 1983). ... Broke nose (February 1, 1986). ... Signed by Fredericton Express after completing a season in Europe (March 1987).

		REGULAR SEASON								PLAYOFFS				
84-85—Fredericton	AHL	77	6	28	34	97	...	...	...	6	2	4	6	13
—Quebec	NHL	1	0	0	0	0	...	...	...	—	—	—	—	—
85-86—Quebec	NHL	13	0	1	1	25	...	...	...	—	—	—	—	—
—Fredericton	AHL	49	3	18	21	74	...	...	...	6	1	4	5	19
NHL Totals (2 years)		14	0	1	1	25	0	0	0					

HEAD COACHING RECORD

BACKGROUND: Named coach of Montreal Canadiens (January 17, 2003).

Season Team	League	W	L	T	OL	Pct.	Finish	Playoffs W	Playoffs L	Playoffs Pct.
		REGULAR SEASON						PLAYOFFS		
96-97—Hull	QMJHL	48	19	3	...	.707	1st/Lebel Conference	—	—	—
97-98—Hull	QMJHL	32	37	1	...	.464	6th/Lebel Conference	—	—	—
98-99—Hull	QMJHL	23	38	9	...	.393	6th/Lebel Conference	—	—	—
99-00—Hull	QMJHL	42	24	6	...	.625	1st/Western Division	—	—	—
00-01—Hamilton	AHL	28	41	6	...	.413	4th/Canadian Division	—	—	—
01-02—Hamilton	AHL	37	30	10	3	.525	2nd/Canadian Division	—	—	—
02-03—Hamilton	AHL	33	6	3	3	.767	...	—	—	—
—Montreal	NHL	12	16	4	4	.389	4th/Northeast Division	—	—	—
03-04—Montreal	NHL	41	30	7	4	.543	4th/Northeast Division	4	7	.364
NHL Totals (2 years)		53	46	11	8	.496	**NHL Totals (1 year)**	4	7	.364

NOTES:

96-97—Won QMJHL championship; won Memorial Cup.
02-03—Replaced Michel Therrien as head coach (January 18).
02-03—Left team to coach Montreal Canadiens.
03-04—Defeated Boston in Eastern Conference quarterfinals; lost to Tampa Bay in Eastern Conference semifinals.

KITCHEN, MIKE — BLUES

PERSONAL: Born February 1, 1956, in Newmarket, Ont. ... Nickname: Kitch.

HEAD COACHING RECORD

BACKGROUND: Assistant coach, AHL Newmarket (1988-89). ... Assistant coach, Toronto Maple Leafs (1989-98). ... Assistant coach, St. Louis Blues (September 1, 1998 through February 24, 2004). ... Named coach of the Blues (February 24, 2004).

Season Team	League	W	L	T	OL	Pct.	Finish	Playoffs W	Playoffs L	Playoffs Pct.
		REGULAR SEASON						PLAYOFFS		
03-04—St. Louis	NHL	10	7	4	0	.571	2nd/Central Division	1	4	.200
NHL Totals (1 year)		10	7	4	0	.571	**NHL Totals (1 year)**	1	4	.200

NOTES:

03-04—Lost to San Jose in Western Conference quarterfinals.

LAVIOLETTE, PETER — HURRICANES

PERSONAL: Born December 7, 1964, in Franklin, Mass. ... 6-2/200. ... Shoots left.

TRANSACTIONS/CAREER NOTES: Signed as free agent by New York Rangers (August 12, 1987). ... Signed as free agent by Boston Bruins (September 8, 1992).

		REGULAR SEASON								PLAYOFFS				
Season Team	League	GP	G	A	Pts.	PIM	+/-	PP	SH	GP	G	A	Pts.	PIM
88-89—Denver	IHL	57	6	19	25	120	...	...	...	3	0	0	0	4
—New York Rangers	NHL	12	0	0	0	6	2	0	0	—	—	—	—	—
NHL Totals (1 year)		12	0	0	0	6	2	0	0					

HEAD COACHING RECORD

BACKGROUND: Coach, ECHL Wheeling (1997-98) ... Named assistant coach of the Boston Bruins, June 30, 2000. ... Coach, AHL Providence (1998-2000); named AHL's most outstanding coach (1999) ... Assistant coach, Boston Bruins (2000-01). ... Coach, New York Islanders (May 23, 2001 to June 3, 2003) ... Named coach of Carolina Hurricanes (December 15, 2003).

		REGULAR SEASON						PLAYOFFS		
Season Team	League	W	L	T	OL	Pct.	Finish	W	L	Pct.
97-98—Wheeling	ECHL	37	24	9	...	.593	2nd/Northeast Division	8	7	.533
98-99—Providence	AHL	56	16	4	...	.763	1st/New England Division	15	4	.789
99-00—Providence	AHL	33	38	6	3	.450	5th/New England Division	10	4	.714
01-02—New York Islanders	NHL	42	28	8	4	.561	2nd/Atlantic Division	3	4	.429
02-03—New York Islanders	NHL	35	34	11	2	.494	3rd/Atlantic Division	1	4	.200
03-04—Carolina	NHL	20	26	6	4	.411	3rd/Southeast Division	—	—	—
NHL Totals (3 years)		97	88	25	10	.498	**NHL Totals (2 years)**	4	8	.333

NOTES:

97-98—Defeated Dayton in preliminary round of playoffs; defeated Toledo in quarterfinals; lost to Hampton Roads in semifinals.

98-99—Defeated Worcester in conference quarterfinals of Calder Cup playoffs; defeated Hartford in conference semifinals of Calder Cup playoffs; defeated Fredericton in conference finals of Calder Cup playoffs; defeated Rochester in Calder Cup finals.

99-00—Defeated Quebec in conference quarterfinals of Calder Cup playoffs; defeated Lowell in conference semifinals of Calder Cup playoffs; lost to Hartford in conference finals of Calder Cup playoffs.

01-02—Lost to Toronto in Eastern Conference quarterfinals.

02-03—Lost to Ottawa in Eastern Conference quarterfinals.

LEMAIRE, JACQUES — WILD

PERSONAL: Born September 7, 1945, in Ville LaSalle, Que. ... Shoots left. ... Uncle of Manny Fernandez, G, Minnesota Wild. ... Name pronounced luh-MAIR.

STATISTICAL PLATEAUS: Three-goal games: 1977-78 (1), 1978-79 (2). Total: 3.

		REGULAR SEASON								PLAYOFFS				
Season Team	League	GP	G	A	Pts.	PIM	+/-	PP	SH	GP	G	A	Pts.	PIM
66-67—Houston	CPHL	69	19	30	49	19	...	...	...	6	0	1	1	0
67-68—Montreal	NHL	69	22	20	42	16	15	3	1	13	7	6	13	6
68-69—Montreal	NHL	75	29	34	63	29	31	5	0	14	4	2	6	6
69-70—Montreal	NHL	69	32	28	60	16	19	13	0	—	—	—	—	—
70-71—Montreal	NHL	78	28	28	56	18	0	6	0	20	9	10	19	17
71-72—Montreal	NHL	77	32	49	81	26	37	8	0	6	2	1	3	2
72-73—Montreal	NHL	77	44	51	95	16	59	9	0	17	7	13	20	2
73-74—Montreal	NHL	66	29	38	67	10	4	10	0	6	0	4	4	2
74-75—Montreal	NHL	80	36	56	92	20	25	12	0	11	5	7	12	4
75-76—Montreal	NHL	61	20	32	52	20	26	6	0	13	3	3	6	2
76-77—Montreal	NHL	75	34	41	75	22	70	5	2	14	7	12	19	6
77-78—Montreal	NHL	75	36	61	97	14	54	6	0	15	6	8	14	10
78-79—Montreal	NHL	50	24	31	55	10	9	6	1	16	11	12	23	6
NHL Totals (12 years)		852	366	469	835	217	349	89	4	145	61	78	139	63

HEAD COACHING RECORD

BACKGROUND: Assistant coach, University of Plattsburgh (1981-82). ... Assistant coach, Montreal Canadiens (October 1982-February 1983). ... Assistant to managing director/director of player personnel, Canadiens (1985-88). ... Assistant to managing director of Verdun, Canadiens organization (1988-89). ... Assistant to managing director, Canadiens (1989-91). ... Assistant to managing director of Fredericton, Canadiens organization (1991-93). ... Served as interim coach of Montreal Canadiens while Jacques Demers was hospitalized with chest pains (March 10 and 11, 1993; team was 1-1 during that time). ... Consultant to general manager, Canadiens (1998-2000). ... Named coach of Minnesota Wild (June 29, 2000).

		REGULAR SEASON						PLAYOFFS		
Season Team	League	W	L	T	OL	Pct.	Finish	W	L	Pct.
82-83—Longueuil	QMJHL	37	29	4	...	.557	3rd/LeBel Division	8	7	.533
83-84—Montreal	NHL	7	10	0	...	.412	4th/Adams Division	9	6	.600
84-85—Montreal	NHL	41	27	12	...	.588	1st/Adams Division	6	6	.500
93-94—New Jersey	NHL	47	25	12	...	.631	2nd/Atlantic Division	11	9	.550
94-95—New Jersey	NHL	22	18	8	...	.542	2nd/Atlantic Division	16	4	.800
95-96—New Jersey	NHL	37	33	12	...	.524	5th/Atlantic Division	—	—	—
96-97—New Jersey	NHL	45	23	14	...	.634	1st/Atlantic Division	5	5	.500
97-98—New Jersey	NHL	48	23	11	...	.652	1st/Atlantic Division	2	4	.333
00-01—Minnesota	NHL	25	39	13	5	.384	5th/Northwest Division	—	—	—
01-02—Minnesota	NHL	26	35	12	9	.390	5th/Northwest Division	—	—	—
02-03—Minnesota	NHL	42	29	10	1	.573	3rd/Northwest Division	8	10	.444
03-04—Minnesota	NHL	30	29	20	3	.488	5th/Northwest Division	—	—	—
NHL Totals (11 years)		370	291	124	18	.538	**NHL Totals (7 years)**	57	44	.564

NOTES:

82-83—Defeated Chicoutimi in President Cup quarterfinals; defeated Laval in President Cup semifinals; lost to Verdun in President Cup finals.
83-84—Defeated Boston in Adams Division semifinals; defeated Quebec in Adams Division finals; lost to New York Islanders in Wales Conference finals.
84-85—Defeated Boston in Adams Division semifinals; lost to Quebec in Adams Division finals.
93-94—Defeated Buffalo in Eastern Conference quarterfinals; defeated Boston in conference semifinals; lost to New York Rangers in conference finals.
94-95—Defeated Boston in Eastern Conference quarterfinals; defeated Pittsburgh in Eastern Conference semifinals; defeated Philadelphia in Eastern Conference finals; defeated Detroit in Stanley Cup finals.
96-97—Defeated Montreal in Eastern Conference quarterfinals; lost to New York Rangers in Eastern Conference semifinals.
97-98—Lost to Ottawa in Eastern Conference quarterfinals.
02-03—Defeated Colorado in Western Conference quarterfinals; defeated Vancouver in conference semifinals; lost to Anaheim in conference finals.

MACTAVISH, CRAIG — OILERS

PERSONAL: Born August 15, 1958, in London, Ont. ... 6-1/195. ... Shoots left.

TRANSACTIONS/CAREER NOTES: Selected by Boston Bruins in ninth round (ninth Bruins pick, 153rd overall) of NHL draft (June 15, 1978). ... Signed as free agent by Edmonton Oilers (February 1, 1985). ... Strained lower back (January 1993); missed one game. ... Suffered concussion (March 10, 1993); missed one game. ... Strained wrist (October 18, 1993); missed one game. ... Reinjured wrist (December 7, 1993); missed one game. ... Suffered whiplash (December 15, 1993); missed four games. ... Bruised foot (December 30, 1993); missed one game. ... Traded by Oilers to New York Rangers for C Todd Marchant (March 21, 1994). ... Signed as free agent by Philadelphia Flyers (July 6, 1994). ... Injured foot (January 24, 1995); missed one game. ... Bruised foot (April 14, 1995); missed two games. ... Underwent knee surgery (September 25, 1995); missed first eight games of season. ... Traded by Flyers to St. Louis Blues for C Dale Hawerchuk (March 15, 1996). ... Announced retirement (April 29, 1997).

STATISTICAL PLATEAUS: Three-goal games: 1985-86 (1), 1990-91 (1). Total: 2.

		REGULAR SEASON								PLAYOFFS				
Season Team	**League**	**GP**	**G**	**A**	**Pts.**	**PIM**	**+/-**	**PP**	**SH**	**GP**	**G**	**A**	**Pts.**	**PIM**
77-78—University of Lowell..	ECAC-II	24	26	19	45	...	...	...	...	—	—	—	—	—
78-79—University of Lowell..	ECAC-II	31	36	52	88	...	...	...	...	—	—	—	—	—
79-80—Binghamton	AHL	34	17	15	32	20	...	...	...	—	—	—	—	—
—Boston	NHL	46	11	17	28	8	...	0	0	10	2	3	5	7
80-81—Boston	NHL	24	3	5	8	13	-1	0	0	—	—	—	—	—
—Springfield	AHL	53	19	24	43	89	...	...	...	7	5	4	9	8
81-82—Erie	AHL	72	23	32	55	37	...	...	...	—	—	—	—	—
—Boston	NHL	2	0	1	1	0	...	...	...	—	—	—	—	—
82-83—Boston	NHL	75	10	20	30	18	15	0	0	17	3	1	4	18
83-84—Boston	NHL	70	20	23	43	35	9	7	0	1	0	0	0	0
84-85—Boston	NHL	Did not play												
85-86—Edmonton	NHL	74	23	24	47	70	17	4	1	10	4	4	8	11
86-87—Edmonton	NHL	79	20	19	39	55	9	1	4	21	1	9	10	16
87-88—Edmonton	NHL	80	15	17	32	47	-3	0	3	19	0	1	1	31
88-89—Edmonton	NHL	80	21	31	52	55	10	2	4	7	0	1	1	8
89-90—Edmonton	NHL	80	21	22	43	89	13	1	6	22	2	6	8	29
90-91—Edmonton	NHL	80	17	15	32	76	-1	2	6	18	3	3	6	20
91-92—Edmonton	NHL	80	12	18	30	98	-1	0	2	16	3	0	3	28
92-93—Edmonton	NHL	82	10	20	30	110	-16	0	3	—	—	—	—	—
93-94—Edmonton	NHL	66	16	10	26	80	-20	0	0	—	—	—	—	—
—New York Rangers	NHL	12	4	2	6	11	6	1	0	23	1	4	5	22
94-95—Philadelphia	NHL	45	3	9	12	23	2	0	0	15	1	4	5	20
95-96—Philadelphia	NHL	55	5	8	13	62	-3	0	0	—	—	—	—	—
—St. Louis	NHL	13	0	1	1	8	-6	0	0	13	0	2	2	6
96-97—St. Louis	NHL	50	2	5	7	33	-12	0	0	1	0	0	0	2
NHL Totals (18 years)		1093	213	267	480	891	18	18	29	193	20	38	58	218

HEAD COACHING RECORD

BACKGROUND: Assistant coach, New York Rangers (1997-98 and 1998-99). ... Assistant coach, Edmonton Oilers (1999-2000). ... Named coach of the Oilers (June 22, 2000).

		REGULAR SEASON						PLAYOFFS		
Season Team	**League**	**W**	**L**	**T**	**OL**	**Pct.**	**Finish**	**W**	**L**	**Pct.**
00-01—Edmonton	NHL	39	28	12	3	.549	2nd/Northwest Division	2	4	.333
01-02—Edmonton	NHL	38	28	12	4	.537	3rd/Northwest Division	—	—	—
02-03—Edmonton	NHL	36	26	11	9	.506	4th/Northwest Division	2	4	.333
03-04—Edmonton	NHL	36	29	12	5	.512	4th/Northwest Division	—	—	—
NHL Totals (4 years)		149	111	47	21	.526	**NHL Totals (2 years)**	4	8	.333

NOTES:

00-01—Lost to Dallas in Western Conference quarterfinals.
02-03—Lost to Dallas in Western Conference quarterfinals.

MARTIN, JACQUES — PANTHERS

PERSONAL: Born October 1, 1952, in Rockland, Ont.

HEAD COACHING RECORD

BACKGROUND: Coach, St. Louis Blues (1986-87 through 1987-88). ... Assistant coach, Chicago Blackhawks (1988-89 through 1989-90). ... Assistant coach, Quebec Nordiques (1990-91 through 1992-93 and 1994-95). ... Assistant coach, Colorado Avalanche (1995 through January 24, 1996). ... Coach, Ottawa Senators (January 24, 1996 through April 22, 2004). ... Associate coach, Canadian Olympic team (2002). ... Named coach of Florida Panthers (May 27, 2004).

Season Team	League	W	L	T	OL	Pct.	Finish	W	L	Pct.
		REGULAR SEASON						PLAYOFFS		
85-86—Guelph	OHL	41	23	2	...	.636	2nd/Emms Division	15	3	.833
86-87—St. Louis	NHL	32	33	15	...	.494	1st/Norris Division	2	4	.333
87-88—St. Louis	NHL	34	38	8	...	.475	2nd/Norris Division	5	5	.500
93-94—Cornwall	AHL	33	36	11	...	.481	T3rd/Southern Division	4	2	.667
95-96—Ottawa	NHL	10	24	4	...	.316	6th/Northeast Division	—	—	—
96-97—Ottawa	NHL	31	36	15	...	.470	T3rd/Northeast Division	3	4	.429
97-98—Ottawa	NHL	34	33	15	...	.506	5th/Northeast Division	5	6	.455
98-99—Ottawa	NHL	44	23	15	...	.628	1st/Northeast Division	0	4	.000
99-00—Ottawa	NHL	41	28	11	2	.567	2nd/Northeast Division	2	4	.333
00-01—Ottawa	NHL	48	21	9	4	.640	1st/Northeast Division	0	4	.000
01-02—Ottawa	NHL	38	26	9	7	.531	3rd/Northwest Division	7	5	.583
02-03—Ottawa	NHL	52	21	8	1	.683	1st/Northeast Division	11	7	.611
03-04—Ottawa	NHL	43	23	10	6	.585	3rd/Northeast Division	3	4	.429
NHL Totals (11 years)		407	306	119	20	.548	**NHL Totals (10 years)**	38	47	.447

NOTES:

85-86—Defeated Sudbury in OHL quarterfinals; defeated Windsor in OHL semifinals; defeated Belleville in J. Ross Robertson Cup finals.
86-87—Lost to Toronto in Norris Division semifinals.
87-88—Defeated Chicago in Norris Division semifinals; lost to Detroit in Norris Division finals.
93-94—Defeated Hamilton in quarterfinals of Calder Cup playoffs; defeated Hershey in division finals of Calder Cup playoffs; lost to Moncton in semifinals of Calder Cup playoffs.
95-96—Replaced Rick Bowness as head coach (January 24).
96-97—Lost to Buffalo in Eastern Conference quarterfinals.
97-98—Defeated New Jersey in Eastern Conference quarterfinals; lost to Washington in Eastern Conference semifinals.
98-99—Lost to Buffalo in Eastern Conference quarterfinals.
99-00—Lost to Toronto in Eastern Conference quarterfinals.
00-01—Lost to Toronto in Eastern Conference quarterfinals.
01-02—Defeated Philadelphia in Eastern Conference quarterfinals; lost to Toronto in Eastern Conference semifinals.
02-03—Defeated New York Islanders in Eastern Conference quarterfinals; defeated Philadelphia in conference semifinals; lost to New Jersey in Eastern Conference finals.
03-04—Lost to Toronto in Eastern Conference quarterfinals.

MURRAY, ANDY — KINGS

PERSONAL: Born March 3, 1951, in Gladstone, Man.

HEAD COACHING RECORD

BACKGROUND: Assistant coach, Brandon University (1973-74). ... Coach, Brandon Travelers of Manitoba Junior A Hockey League (1974-78). ... Coach, Brandon University (1978-81). ... Coach of several of Switzerland Division-A teams (1981-88). ... Assistant coach, Hershey Bears of AHL (1986-87 and 1987-88). ... Assistant coach, Philadelphia Flyers (1988-89 and 1989-90). ... Assistant coach, Minnesota North Stars (1990-92). ... Coach, Lugano of the Swiss League (1991-92). ... Coach, Eisbaren Berlin of German League (1992-93). ... Assistant coach, Winnipeg Jets (1993-95). ... Coach, Canadian national team (1996-98). ... Coach, Shattuck-St. Mary's (Fairbault, Minn.) HS (1998-99). ... General manager, Koln of German League (1998-99). ... Named coach of Los Angeles Kings (June 14, 1999).

Season Team	League	W	L	T	OL	Pct.	Finish	W	L	Pct.
		REGULAR SEASON						PLAYOFFS		
99-00—Los Angeles	NHL	39	27	12	4	.549	2nd/Pacific Division	0	4	.000
00-01—Los Angeles	NHL	38	28	13	3	.543	3rd/Pacific Division	7	6	.538
01-02—Los Angeles	NHL	40	27	11	4	.555	3rd/Pacific Division	3	4	.429
02-03—Los Angeles	NHL	33	37	6	6	.439	3rd/Pacific Division	—	—	—
03-04—Los Angeles	NHL	28	29	16	9	.439	3rd/Pacific Division	—	—	—
NHL Totals (5 years)		178	148	58	26	.505	**NHL Totals (3 years)**	10	14	.417

NOTES:

99-00—Lost to Detroit in Western Conference quarterfinals.
00-01—Defeated Detroit in Western Conference quarterfinals; lost to Colorado in Western Conference semifinals.
01-02—Lost to Colorado in Western Conference quarterfinals.

MURRAY, BRYAN — SENATORS

PERSONAL: Born December 5, 1942, in Shawville, Que. ... Brother of Terry Murray, D with four NHL teams (1972-73 through 1981-82) and head coach of three NHL teams (1989-90 through 1996-97 and 1998-99 through December 10, 2000).

HEAD COACHING RECORD

BACKGROUND: Coach, Washington Capitals, 1981-1990). ... General manager, Detroit Red Wings (1990-94). ... Vice president and general manager, Florida Panthers (1994-95 through December 28, 2000). ... Coach, Anaheim Mighty Ducks (2001-02). ... General manager, Anaheim Mighty Ducks (2002-04). ... Named coach of Ottawa Senators (June 8, 2004).

Season Team	League	W	L	T	OL	Pct.	Finish	W	L	Pct.
		REGULAR SEASON						PLAYOFFS		
78-79—Regina	WHL	18	47	7	...	.299	4th/East Division	—	—	—
79-80—Regina	WHL	47	24	1	...	.660	1st/East Division	14	4	.778
80-81—Hershey	AHL	47	24	9	...	.644	1st/Southern Division	6	4	.600
81-82—Hershey	AHL	6	7	0	...	.462	...	—	—	—
—Washington	NHL	25	28	13	...	.477	5th/Patrick Division	—	—	—
82-83—Washington	NHL	38	25	16	...	.582	3rd/Patrick Division	1	3	.250
83-84—Washington	NHL	48	27	5	...	.631	2nd/Patrick Division	4	4	.500
84-85—Washington	NHL	46	25	9	...	.631	2nd/Patrick Division	2	3	.400
85-86—Washington	NHL	50	23	7	...	.669	2nd/Patrick Division	5	4	.556
86-87—Washington	NHL	38	32	10	...	.538	2nd/Patrick Division	3	4	.429

Season Team	League	W	L	T	OL	Pct.	Finish	W	L	Pct.
		REGULAR SEASON						PLAYOFFS		
87-88—Washington	NHL	38	33	9	...	.531	2nd/Patrick Division	7	7	.500
88-89—Washington	NHL	41	29	10	...	.575	1st/Patrick Division	2	4	.333
89-90—Washington	NHL	18	24	4	...	.435	...	—	—	—
90-91—Detroit	NHL	34	38	8	...	.475	3rd/Norris Division	3	4	.429
91-92—Detroit	NHL	43	25	12	...	.613	1st/Norris Division	4	7	.364
92-93—Detroit	NHL	47	28	9	...	.613	2nd/Norris Division	3	4	.429
97-98—Florida	NHL	17	31	11	...	.381	6th/Atlantic Division	—	—	—
01-02—Anaheim	NHL	29	42	8	3	.402	5th/Pacific Division	—	—	—
NHL Totals (14 years)		512	410	131	3	.547	**NHL Totals (10 years)**	34	44	.436

NOTES:

79-80—Defeated Lethbridge in East Division semifianls; eliminated Brandon in East Division round-robin series; defeated Medicine Hat in East Division finals; defeated Victoria in Monsignor Athol Murray Memorial Trophy finals.
80-81—Defeated New Haven in Calder Cup quarterfinals; lost to Adirondack in Calder Cup semifinals.
82-83—Lost to New York Islanders in Patrick Division semifinals.
83-84—Defeated Philadelphia in Patrick Division semifinals; lost to New York Islanders in Patrick Division finals.
84-85—Lost to New York Islanders in Patrick Division semifinals.
85-86—Defeated New York Islanders in Patrick Division semifinals; lost to to New York Rangers in Patrick Division finals.
86-87—Lost to New York Islanders in Patrick Division semifinals.
87-88—Defeated Philadelphia in Patrick Division semifinals; lost to New Jersey in in Patrick Division finals.
88-89—Lost to Philadelphia in Patrick Division semifinals.
89-90—Replaced as head coach by Terry Murray (January 15).
90-91—Lost to St. Louis in Norris Division semifinals.
91-92—Defeated Minnesota in Norris Division semifinals; lost to Chicago in Norris Division finals.
92-93—Lost to Toronto in Norris Division semifinals.
97-98—Replaced Doug Maclean as head coach on an interim basis (November 24).

OLCZYK, ED — PENGUINS

PERSONAL: Born August 16, 1966, in Chicago. ... 6-1/205. ... Shoots left. ... Played left wing. ... Name pronounced OHL-chehk.

TRANSACTIONS/CAREER NOTES: Selected by Chicago Blackhawks in first round (first Blackhawks pick, third overall) of NHL draft (June 9, 1984). ... Hyperextended knee (September 3, 1984). ... Fractured left foot (December 16, 1984). ... Traded by Blackhawks with LW Al Secord to Toronto Maple Leafs for RW Rick Vaive, LW Steve Thomas and D Bob McGill (September 1987). ... Pinched nerve in left knee (January 3, 1990). ... Traded by Maple Leafs with LW Mark Osborne to Winnipeg Jets for D Dave Ellett and LW Paul Fenton (November 10, 1990). ... Dislocated elbow and sprained ankle (January 8, 1992); missed 15 games. ... Sprained knee (November 24, 1992); missed nine games. ... Traded by Jets to New York Rangers for LW Kris King and RW Tie Domi (December 28, 1992). ... Fractured right thumb (January 31, 1994); missed 24 games. ... Kidney stones (January 24, 1995); missed six games. ... Back spasms (March 3, 1995); missed three games. ... Traded by Rangers to Jets for fifth-round pick (D Alexei Vasiljev) in 1995 draft (April 7, 1995). ... Strained rib cage (October 28, 1995); missed four games. ... Strained back (January 3, 1996); missed four games. ... Sprained knee (March 7, 1996); missed 13 games. ... Signed as free agent by Los Angeles Kings (July 8, 1996). ... Flu (December 12, 1996); missed two games. ... Traded by Kings to Pittsburgh Penguins for RW Glen Murray (March 18, 1997). ... Suffered concussion (October 4, 1997); missed five games. ... Suffered depressed fracture of zygomatic arch in neck (December 1, 1997); missed 18 games. ... Back spasms (March 8, 1998); missed two games. ... Signed as free agent by Chicago Blackhawks (August 26, 1998). ... Suffered sore back before 1999-2000 season; missed first game of season. ... Herniated disc in back (October 16, 1999) and underwent surgery; missed 25 games. ... Bruised ankle (January 15, 2000); missed three games. ... Strained groin (February 20, 2000); missed six games.

STATISTICAL PLATEAUS: Three-goal games: 1988-89 (1), 1989-90 (1), 1992-93 (1), 1995-96 (1), 1996-97 (1). Total: 5.

Season Team	League	GP	G	A	Pts.	PIM	+/-	PP	SH	GP	G	A	Pts.	PIM
		REGULAR SEASON								PLAYOFFS				
83-84—U.S. national team	Int'l	56	19	40	59	36	...	...	...	—	—	—	—	—
—U.S. Olympic team	Int'l	6	2	6	8	0	...	...	...	—	—	—	—	—
84-85—Chicago	NHL	70	20	30	50	67	11	1	1	15	6	5	11	11
85-86—Chicago	NHL	79	29	50	79	47	2	8	1	3	0	0	0	0
86-87—Chicago	NHL	79	16	35	51	119	-4	2	1	4	1	1	2	4
87-88—Toronto	NHL	80	42	33	75	55	-22	14	4	6	5	4	9	2
88-89—Toronto	NHL	80	38	52	90	75	0	11	2	—	—	—	—	—
89-90—Toronto	NHL	79	32	56	88	78	0	6	0	5	1	2	3	14
90-91—Toronto	NHL	18	4	10	14	13	-7	0	0	—	—	—	—	—
—Winnipeg	NHL	61	26	31	57	69	-20	14	0	—	—	—	—	—
91-92—Winnipeg	NHL	64	32	33	65	67	11	12	0	6	2	1	3	4
92-93—Winnipeg	NHL	25	8	12	20	26	-11	2	0	—	—	—	—	—
—New York Rangers	NHL	46	13	16	29	26	9	0	0	—	—	—	—	—
93-94—New York Rangers	NHL	37	3	5	8	28	-1	0	0	1	0	0	0	0
94-95—New York Rangers	NHL	20	2	1	3	4	-2	1	0	—	—	—	—	—
—Winnipeg	NHL	13	2	8	10	8	1	1	0	—	—	—	—	—
95-96—Winnipeg	NHL	51	27	22	49	65	0	16	0	6	1	2	3	6
96-97—Los Angeles	NHL	67	21	23	44	45	-22	5	1	—	—	—	—	—
—Pittsburgh	NHL	12	4	7	11	6	8	0	0	5	1	0	1	12
97-98—Pittsburgh	NHL	56	11	11	22	35	-9	5	1	6	2	0	2	4
98-99—Chicago	NHL	61	10	15	25	29	-3	2	1	—	—	—	—	—
—Chicago	IHL	7	2	2	4	6	-7	0	0	—	—	—	—	—
99-00—Chicago	NHL	33	2	2	4	12	-8	0	0	—	—	—	—	—
NHL Totals (16 years)		1031	342	452	794	874	-67	100	12	57	19	15	34	57

HEAD COACHING RECORD

BACKGROUND: Named coach of Pittsburgh Penguins (June 11, 2003).

Season Team	League	W	L	T	OL	Pct.	Finish	W	L	Pct.
		REGULAR SEASON						PLAYOFFS		
03-04—Pittsburgh	NHL	23	47	8	4	.329	5th/Atlantic Division	—	—	—
NHL Totals (1 year)		23	47	8	4	.329				

QUENNEVILLE, JOEL — AVALANCHE

PERSONAL: Born September 15, 1958, in Windsor, Ont. ... 6-1/200. ... Shoots left. ... Played defense.

TRANSACTIONS/CAREER NOTES: Selected by Toronto Maple Leafs in second round (first Maple Leafs pick, 21st overall) of NHL amateur draft (June 15, 1978). ... Traded by Maple Leafs with RW Lanny McDonald to Colorado Rockies for RW Wilf Paiement and LW Pat Hickey (December 1979). ... Injured ribcage (March 1980). ... Underwent surgery to repair torn ligaments in ring finger of left hand (March 1980). ... Sprained ankle, twisted knee and suffered facial lacerations (January 4, 1982). ... Rockies franchise moved to New Jersey and became the Devils (June 30, 1982). ... Traded by Devils with C Steve Tambellini to Calgary Flames for C Mel Bridgman and D Phil Russell (July 1983). ... Traded by Flames with D Richie Dunn to Hartford Whalers for D Mickey Volcan and third-round pick in 1984 draft (August 1983). ... Fractured right shoulder (December 18, 1986); missed 42 games. ... Separated left shoulder (January 19, 1989); missed nine games. ... Traded by Whalers to Washington Capitals for cash (October 3, 1990). ... Signed as free agent by Maple Leafs (July 30, 1991).

		REGULAR SEASON								PLAYOFFS				
Season Team	League	GP	G	A	Pts.	PIM	+/-	PP	SH	GP	G	A	Pts.	PIM
76-77—Windsor	OMJHL	65	19	59	78	169	...	...	...	9	6	5	11	112
77-78—Windsor	OMJHL	66	27	76	103	114	...	...	...	6	2	3	5	17
78-79—Toronto	NHL	61	2	9	11	60	7	0	0	6	0	1	1	4
—New Brunswick	AHL	16	1	10	11	10	...	...	...	—	—	—	—	—
79-80—Toronto	NHL	32	1	4	5	24	-2	1	0	—	—	—	—	—
—Colorado Rockies	NHL	35	5	7	12	26	-21	1	0	—	—	—	—	—
80-81—Colorado Rockies	NHL	71	10	24	34	86	-24	3	0	—	—	—	—	—
81-82—Colorado Rockies	NHL	64	5	10	15	55	-29	0	0	—	—	—	—	—
82-83—New Jersey	NHL	74	5	12	17	46	-13	0	1	—	—	—	—	—
83-84—Hartford	NHL	80	5	8	13	95	-11	0	2	—	—	—	—	—
84-85—Hartford	NHL	79	6	16	22	96	-15	0	0	—	—	—	—	—
85-86—Hartford	NHL	71	5	20	25	83	20	1	0	10	0	2	2	12
86-87—Hartford	NHL	37	3	7	10	24	8	0	1	6	0	0	0	0
87-88—Hartford	NHL	77	1	8	9	44	-13	0	0	6	0	2	2	2
88-89—Hartford	NHL	69	4	7	11	32	3	0	0	4	0	3	3	4
89-90—Hartford	NHL	44	1	4	5	34	9	0	0	—	—	—	—	—
90-91—Washington	NHL	9	1	0	1	0	-8	0	0	—	—	—	—	—
—Baltimore	AHL	59	6	13	19	58	...	...	...	6	1	1	2	6
91-92—St. John's	AHL	73	7	23	30	58	...	...	...	16	0	1	1	10
NHL Totals (13 years)		803	54	136	190	705	-89	6	4	32	0	8	8	22

HEAD COACHING RECORD

BACKGROUND: Player/coach, St. John's of the AHL (1991-92). ... Assistant coach, St. John's (1992-93). ... Assistant coach, Quebec Nordiques (1994-95). ... Quebec franchise moved in summer 1995 to Denver and renamed Colorado Avalanche. ... Assistant coach, Colorado Avalanche (1995-96 through January 5, 1997). ... Coach, St. Louis Blues (January 7, 1997 through February 24, 2004). ... Named coach of Colorado Avalanche (July 7, 2004).

		REGULAR SEASON						PLAYOFFS		
Season Team	League	W	L	T	OL	Pct.	Finish	W	L	Pct.
93-94—Springfield	AHL	29	38	13	...	.444	4th/Northern Division	2	4	.333
96-97—St. Louis	NHL	18	15	7	...	.538	4th/Central Division	2	4	.333
97-98—St. Louis	NHL	45	29	8	...	.598	3rd/Central Division	6	4	.600
98-99—St. Louis	NHL	37	32	13	...	.530	2nd/Central Division	6	7	.462
99-00—St. Louis	NHL	51	19	11	1	.689	1st/Central Division	3	4	.429
00-01—St. Louis	NHL	43	22	12	5	.598	2nd/Central Division	9	6	.600
01-02—St. Louis	NHL	43	27	8	4	.573	2nd/Central Division	5	5	.500
02-03—St. Louis	NHL	41	24	11	6	.567	2nd/Central Division	3	4	.429
03-04—St. Louis	NHL	29	23	4	2	.534	...	—	—	—
NHL Totals (8 years)		307	191	74	18	.583	**NHL Totals (7 years)**	34	34	.500

NOTES:

93-94—Lost to Adirondack in division semifinals of Calder Cup playoffs.
96-97—Replaced Mike Keenan as coach (January 6); lost to Detroit in Western Conference quarterfinals.
97-98—Defeated Los Angeles in Western Conference quarterfinals; lost to Detroit in Western Conference semifinals.
98-99—Defeated Phoenix in Western Conference quarterfinals; lost to Dallas in Western Conference semifinals.
99-00—Lost to San Jose in Western Conference quarterfinals.
00-01—Defeated San Jose in Western Conference quarterfinals; defeated Dallas in conference semifinals; lost to Colorado in conference finals.
01-02—Defeated Chicago in Western Conference quarterfinals; lost to Detroit in Western Conference semifinals.
02-03—Lost to Vancouver in Western Conference quarterfinals.

QUINN, PAT — MAPLE LEAFS

PERSONAL: Born January 29, 1943, in Hamilton, Ont. ... Shoots left.

TRANSACTIONS/CAREER NOTES: Loaned by Detroit Red Wings to Tulsa Oilers for 1964-65 season. ... Fractured ankle (1965). ... Selected by Montreal Canadiens from Red Wings in intraleague draft (June 1966). ... Sold by Canadiens to St. Louis Blues (June 1967). ... Traded by Blues to Toronto Maple Leafs for rights to LW Dickie Moore (March 1968). ... Selected by Vancouver Canucks in NHL expansion draft (June 1970). ... Selected by Atlanta Flames in NHL expansion draft (June 1972). ... Fractured leg (1976).

		REGULAR SEASON								PLAYOFFS				
Season Team	League	GP	G	A	Pts.	PIM	+/-	PP	SH	GP	G	A	Pts.	PIM
67-68—Tulsa	CPHL	51	3	15	18	178	...	...	...	11	1	4	5	19
68-69—Tulsa	CHL	17	0	6	6	25	...	...	...	—	—	—	—	—
—Toronto	NHL	40	2	7	9	95	10	0	0	4	0	0	0	13
69-70—Tulsa	CHL	2	0	1	1	6	...	...	...	—	—	—	—	—
—Toronto	NHL	59	0	5	5	88	-14	0	0	—	—	—	—	—
70-71—Vancouver	NHL	76	2	11	13	149	2	0	0	—	—	—	—	—
71-72—Vancouver	NHL	57	2	3	5	63	-28	0	0	—	—	—	—	—
72-73—Atlanta	NHL	78	2	18	20	113	2	0	1	—	—	—	—	—

		REGULAR SEASON								PLAYOFFS				
Season Team	League	GP	G	A	Pts.	PIM	+/-	PP	SH	GP	G	A	Pts.	PIM
73-74—Atlanta	NHL	77	5	27	32	94	15	0	0	4	0	0	0	6
74-75—Atlanta	NHL	80	2	19	21	156	12	0	0	—	—	—	—	—
75-76—Atlanta	NHL	80	2	11	13	134	5	0	1	2	0	1	1	2
76-77—Atlanta	NHL	59	1	12	13	58	-7	0	0	1	0	0	0	0
NHL Totals (9 years)		606	18	113	131	950	-3	0	2	11	0	1	1	21

HEAD COACHING RECORD

BACKGROUND: Assistant coach, Philadelphia Flyers (1977-78). ... Coach, Philadelphia Flyers (1978-82). ... Coach, Los Angeles Kings (1984-87). ... Coach, Team Canada (1986). ... President/general manager, Vancouver Canucks (1987-88 through November 4, 1997). ... Coach, Vancouver Canucks (1990-96). ... Assistant general manager, Team Canada (1996 and 1997). ... Head coach, Canadian Olympic team (2002). ... Named coach of Toronto Maple Leafs (June 26, 1998). ... Also general manager (July 14, 1999 to August 29, 2003).

		REGULAR SEASON						PLAYOFFS		
Season Team	League	W	L	T	OL	Pct.	Finish	W	L	Pct.
78-79—Philadelphia	NHL	18	8	4	...	.667	2nd/Patrick Division	3	5	.375
79-80—Philadelphia	NHL	48	12	20	...	.725	1st/Patrick Division	13	6	.684
80-81—Philadelphia	NHL	41	24	15	...	.606	2nd/Patrick Division	6	6	.500
81-82—Philadelphia	NHL	34	29	9	...	.535	3rd/Patrick Division	—	—	—
84-85—Los Angeles	NHL	34	32	14	...	.513	4th/Smythe Division	0	3	.000
85-86—Los Angeles	NHL	23	49	8	...	.338	5th/Smythe Division	—	—	—
86-87—Los Angeles	NHL	18	20	4	...	.476	4th/Smythe Division	—	—	—
90-91—Vancouver	NHL	9	13	4	...	.423	4th/Smythe Division	2	4	.333
91-92—Vancouver	NHL	42	26	12	...	.600	1st/Smythe Division	6	7	.462
92-93—Vancouver	NHL	46	29	9	...	.601	1st/Smythe Division	6	6	.500
93-94—Vancouver	NHL	41	40	3	...	.506	2nd/Pacific Division	15	9	.625
95-96—Vancouver	NHL	3	3	0	...	.500	3rd/Pacific Division	2	4	.333
98-99—Toronto	NHL	45	30	7	...	.591	2nd/Northeast Division	9	8	.529
99-00—Toronto	NHL	45	27	7	3	.591	1st/Northeast Division	6	6	.500
00-01—Toronto	NHL	37	29	11	5	.518	3rd/Northeast Division	7	4	.636
01-02—Toronto	NHL	43	25	10	4	.585	2nd/Northeast Division	10	10	.500
02-03—Toronto	NHL	44	28	7	3	.579	2nd/Northeast Division	3	4	.429
03-04—Toronto	NHL	45	24	10	3	.610	2nd/Northeast Division	6	7	.462
NHL Totals (18 years)		616	448	154	18	.561	**NHL Totals (15 years)**	94	89	.514

NOTES:

78-79—Defeated Vancouver in Stanley Cup preliminary round; lost to New York Rangers in Stanley Cup quarterfinals.
79-80—Defeated Edmonton in Stanley Cup preliminary round; defeated New York Rangers in Stanley Cup quarterfinals; defeated Minnesota in Stanley Cup semifinals; lost to New York Islanders in Stanley Cup finals.
80-81—Defeated Quebec in Stanley Cup preliminary round; lost to Calgary in Stanley Cup quarterfinals.
84-85—Lost to Edmonton in Smythe Division semifinals.
90-91—Replaced Bob McCammon as head coach (January) with club in fifth place; lost to Los Angeles in Smythe Division semifinals.
91-92—Defeated Winnipeg in Smythe Division semifinals; lost to Edmonton in Smythe Division finals.
92-93—Defeated Winnipeg in Smythe Division semifinals; lost to Los Angeles in Smythe Division finals.
93-94—Defeated Calgary in Western Conference quarterfinals; defeated Dallas in Western Conference semifinals; defeated Toronto in Western Conference finals; lost to New York Rangers in Stanley Cup finals.
95-96—Replaced Rick Ley as head coach (March 28) with club in third place; lost to Colorado in Western Conference quarterfinals.
98-99—Defeated Philadelphia in Eastern Conference quarterfinals; defeated Pittsburgh in conference semifinals; lost to Buffalo in conference finals.
99-00—Defeated Ottawa in Eastern Conference quarterfinals; lost to New Jersey in Eastern Conference semifinals.
00-01—Defeated Ottawa in Eastern Conference quarterfinals; lost to New Jersey in Eastern Conference semifinals.
01-02—Defeated New York Islanders in Eastern Conference quarterfinals; defeated Ottawa in conference semifinals; lost to Carolina in conference finals.
02-03—Lost to Philadelphia in Eastern Conference quarterfinal.
03-04—Defeated Ottawa in Eastern Conference quarterfinals; lost to Philadephia in Eastern Conference semifinals.

RENNEY, TOM — RANGERS

PERSONAL: Born March 1, 1955, in Cranbrook, B.C.

HEAD COACHING RECORD

BACKGROUND: Assistant coach, Canadian national team (1992). ... Coach, Canadian national team (1993-94 through 1995-96). ... Coach, Vancouver Canucks (June 1996 through November 1997). ... Coach, Canadian national team (1999-2000). ... Assistant coach, New York Rangers (July 21, 2003 through February 24, 2004). ... Named interim coach, Rangers (February 25, 2004). ... Named coach, Rangers (July 6, 2004).

		REGULAR SEASON						PLAYOFFS		
Season Team	League	W	L	T	OL	Pct.	Finish	W	L	Pct.
90-91—Kamloops	WHL	50	20	2	...	.708	1st/West Division	5	7	.417
91-92—Kamloops	WHL	51	17	4	...	.736	1st/West Division	12	5	.706
96-97—Vancouver	NHL	35	40	7	...	.470	4th/Pacific Division	—	—	—
97-98—Vancouver	NHL	4	13	2	...	.263	...	—	—	—
03-04—New York Rangers	NHL	5	11	0	4	.250	4th/Atlantic Division	—	—	—
NHL Totals (3 years)		44	64	9	4	.401				

NOTES:

90-91—Defeated Tri-City in West Division semifinals; lost to Spokane in West Division Finals.
91-92—Defeated Tacoma in West Division preliminary round; defeated Seattle in West division finals; defeated Saskatoon in WHL finals.
97-98—Replaced as head coach by Mike Keenan (November 13) with club in seventh place.
03-04—Named interim coach, replacing Glen Sather (February 25, 2004).

ROBINSON, LARRY — DEVILS

PERSONAL: Born June 2, 1951, in Winchester, Ont. ... 6-4/225. ... Shoots left. ... Brother of Moe Robinson, D with Canadiens (1979-80).

TRANSACTIONS/CAREER NOTES: Selected by Montreal Canadiens from Kitchener Rangers in 2nd round (4rth Canadiens pick, 20th overall) of amateur draft (June 10, 1971). ... Injured knee; missed part of 1978-79 season. ... Separated right shoulder (March 6, 1980). ... Injured groin (October 1980). ... Separated left shoulder (Nov. 14, 1980). ... Fractured nose (Jan. 8, 1981). ... Injured left shoulder (Oct. 1982). ... Skin infection behind right knee (Oct. 1983). ... Hyperextended left elbow (March 1985). ... Strained ligaments in right ankle (March 9, 1987). ... Fractured right leg (August 1987). ... Sprained right wrist (December 1987). ... Hyperextended knee (May 23, 1989). ... Signed as free agent by Los Angeles Kings (July 26, 1989). ... Suffered food poisoning (March 1990). ... Injured eye (Nov. 26, 1991); missed two games.

STATISTICAL PLATEAUS: Three-goal games: 1985-86 (1).

		REGULAR SEASON								PLAYOFFS				
Season Team	**League**	**GP**	**G**	**A**	**Pts.**	**PIM**	**+/-**	**PP**	**SH**	**GP**	**G**	**A**	**Pts.**	**PIM**
72-73—Nova Scotia	AHL	38	6	33	39	33	...	...	...	—	—	—	—	—
—Montreal	NHL	36	2	4	6	20	3	0	0	11	1	4	5	9
73-74—Montreal	NHL	78	6	20	26	66	32	0	0	6	0	1	1	26
74-75—Montreal	NHL	80	14	47	61	76	61	1	0	11	0	4	4	27
75-76—Montreal	NHL	80	10	30	40	59	50	2	0	13	3	3	6	10
76-77—Montreal	NHL	77	19	66	85	45	*120	3	0	14	2	10	12	12
77-78—Montreal	NHL	80	13	52	65	39	71	3	2	15	4	17	21	6
78-79—Montreal	NHL	67	16	45	61	33	50	4	0	16	6	9	15	8
79-80—Montreal	NHL	72	14	61	75	39	38	6	0	10	0	4	4	2
80-81—Montreal	NHL	65	12	38	50	37	46	7	0	3	0	1	1	2
81-82—Montreal	NHL	71	12	47	59	41	57	5	1	5	0	1	1	8
82-83—Montreal	NHL	71	14	49	63	33	33	6	0	3	0	0	0	2
83-84—Montreal	NHL	74	9	34	43	39	4	4	0	15	0	5	5	22
84-85—Montreal	NHL	76	14	33	47	44	32	6	0	12	3	8	11	8
85-86—Montreal	NHL	78	19	63	82	39	29	10	0	20	0	13	13	22
86-87—Montreal	NHL	70	13	37	50	44	24	6	0	17	3	17	20	6
87-88—Montreal	NHL	53	6	34	40	30	26	2	0	11	1	4	5	4
88-89—Montreal	NHL	74	4	26	30	22	23	0	0	21	2	8	10	12
89-90—Los Angeles	NHL	64	7	32	39	34	7	1	0	10	2	3	5	10
90-91—Los Angeles	NHL	62	1	22	23	16	22	0	0	12	1	4	5	15
91-92—Los Angeles	NHL	56	3	10	13	37	1	0	0	2	0	0	0	0
NHL Totals (20 years)		1384	208	750	958	793	729	66	3	227	28	116	144	211

HEAD COACHING RECORD

BACKGROUND: Assistant coach, New Jersey Devils (1993-94, 1994-95 and 1999-March 23, 2000). ... Named assistant coach of New Jersey Devils, June 30, 1993. ... Named as coach of the New Jersey Devils, July 26, 1995. ... Served as coach of the Los Angeles Kings, 1996-1999. ... Named assistant coach of the New Jersey Devils, May 26, 1999. ... Served as coach of the New Jersey Devils from March 23, 2000, to Jan. 28, 2002. ... Won Stanley Cup, 1999-2000. ... Named assistant coach of the New Jersey Devils, Feb. 25, 2002. ... Named special assignments coach, August 2002. ... Named coach of New Jersey Devils, July 14, 2005.

		REGULAR SEASON						PLAYOFFS		
Season Team	**League**	**W**	**L**	**T**	**OL**	**Pct.**	**Finish**	**W**	**L**	**Pct.**
95-96—Los Angeles	NHL	24	40	18	...	.402	6th/Pacific Division	—	—	—
96-97—Los Angeles	NHL	28	43	11	...	.409	6th/Pacific Division	—	—	—
97-98—Los Angeles	NHL	38	33	11	...	.530	2nd/Pacific Division	0	4	.000
98-99—Los Angeles	NHL	32	45	5	...	.421	5th/Pacific Division	—	—	—
99-00—New Jersey	NHL	4	4	0	0	.500	2nd/Atlantic Division	16	7	.696
00-01—New Jersey	NHL	48	19	12	3	.659	1st/Atlantic Division	15	10	.600
01-02—New Jersey	NHL	51	21	23	7	.613		—	—	—
NHL Totals (7 years)		225	205	80	10	.510	**NHL Totals (3 years)**	31	21	.596

NOTES:

97-98—Lost to St. Louis in Western Conference quarterfinals.

99-00—Replaced Robbie Ftorek as head coach (March 23) with team in first place; defeated Florida in Eastern Conference quarterfinals; defeated Toronto in Eastern Conference semifinals; defeated Philadelphia in Eastern Conference finals; defeated Dallas in Stanl

00-01—Defeated Carolina in Eastern Conference quarterfinals; defeated Toronto in Eastern Conference semifinals; defeated Pittsburgh in Eastern Conference semifinals; lost to Colorado in Stanley Cup finals.

RUFF, LINDY — SABRES

PERSONAL: Born February 17, 1960, in Warburg, Alta. ... 6-2/202. ... Shoots left.

TRANSACTIONS/CAREER NOTES: Selected by Buffalo Sabres in second round (second Sabres pick, 32nd overall) of NHL entry draft (August 9, 1979). ... Fractured ankle (December 1980). ... Fractured hand (March 1983). ... Injured shoulder (January 14, 1984). ... Separated shoulder (October 26, 1984). ... Fractured left clavicle (March 5, 1986). ... Sprained shoulder (November 1988). ... Traded by Sabres to New York Rangers for fifth-round pick (D Richard Smehlik) in 1990 draft (March 7, 1989). ... Fractured rib (January 23, 1990); missed seven games. ... Fractured nose (March 21, 1990). ... Bruised left thigh (April 1990). ... Signed as free agent by Sabres (September 1991).

		REGULAR SEASON								PLAYOFFS				
Season Team	**League**	**GP**	**G**	**A**	**Pts.**	**PIM**	**+/-**	**PP**	**SH**	**GP**	**G**	**A**	**Pts.**	**PIM**
77-78—Lethbridge	WCHL	66	9	24	33	219	...	...	...	8	2	8	10	4
78-79—Lethbridge	WHL	24	9	18	27	108	...	...	...	6	0	1	1	0
79-80—Buffalo	NHL	63	5	14	19	38	-2	1	0	8	1	1	2	19
80-81—Buffalo	NHL	65	8	18	26	121	3	1	0	6	3	1	4	23
81-82—Buffalo	NHL	79	16	32	48	194	1	3	0	4	0	0	0	28
82-83—Buffalo	NHL	60	12	17	29	130	14	2	0	10	4	2	6	47
83-84—Buffalo	NHL	58	14	31	45	101	15	3	0	3	1	0	1	9
84-85—Buffalo	NHL	39	13	11	24	45	-1	2	0	5	2	4	6	15
85-86—Buffalo	NHL	54	20	12	32	158	8	5	1	—	—	—	—	—
86-87—Buffalo	NHL	50	6	14	20	74	-12	0	0	—	—	—	—	—
87-88—Buffalo	NHL	77	2	23	25	179	-9	0	0	6	0	2	2	23
88-89—Buffalo	NHL	63	6	11	17	86	-17	0	0	—	—	—	—	—

Season Team	League	REGULAR SEASON GP	G	A	Pts.	PIM	+/-	PP	SH	PLAYOFFS GP	G	A	Pts.	PIM
—New York Rangers	NHL	13	0	5	5	31	-6	0	0	2	0	0	0	17
89-90—New York Rangers	NHL	56	3	6	9	80	-10	0	0	8	0	3	3	12
90-91—New York Rangers	NHL	14	0	1	1	27	-2	0	0	—	—	—	—	—
91-92—Rochester	AHL	62	10	24	34	110	...	...	...	13	0	4	4	16
92-93—San Diego	IHL	81	10	32	42	100	43	0	1	14	1	6	7	26
NHL Totals (12 years)		691	105	195	300	1264	-18	17	1	52	11	13	24	193

HEAD COACHING RECORD

BACKGROUND: Assistant coach, Florida Panthers (1993-94 through 1996-97). ... Named head coach, Buffalo Sabres (July 21, 1997).

Season Team	League	REGULAR SEASON W	L	T	OL	Pct.	Finish	PLAYOFFS W	L	Pct.
97-98—Buffalo	NHL	36	29	17	...	.543	3rd/Northeast Division	10	5	.667
98-99—Buffalo	NHL	37	28	17	...	.555	3rd/Northeast Division	14	7	.667
99-00—Buffalo	NHL	35	32	11	4	.494	3rd/Northeast Division	1	4	.200
00-01—Buffalo	NHL	46	30	5	1	.591	2nd/Northeast Division	7	6	.538
01-02—Buffalo	NHL	35	35	11	1	.494	5th/Northeast Division	—	—	—
02-03—Buffalo	NHL	27	37	10	8	.390	5th/Northeast Division	—	—	—
03-04—Buffalo	NHL	37	34	7	4	.494	5th/Northeast Division	—	—	—
NHL Totals (7 years)		253	225	78	18	.509	**NHL Totals (4 years)**	32	22	.593

NOTES:

97-98—Defeated Philadelphia in Eastern Conference quarterfinals; defeated Montreal in vonference semifinals; lost to Washington in vonference finals.
98-99—Defeated Ottawa in Eastern Conference quarterfinals; defeated Boston in Eastern Conference semifinals; defeated Toronto in Eastern Conference finals; lost to Dallas in Stanley Cup finals.
99-00—Lost to Philadelphia in Eastern Conference quarterfinals.
00-01—Defeated Philadelphia in Eastern Conference quarterfinals; lost to Pittsburgh in Eastern Conference semifinals.

STIRLING, STEVE — ISLANDERS

PERSONAL: Born November 19, 1949, in Toronto.

TRANSACTIONS/CAREER NOTES: Played for Boston University (1968-71); Boston (AHL), Rochester (AHL), Binghamton (AHL) and in Vienna, Austria (1971-78).

HEAD COACHING RECORD

BACKGROUND: Head coach, Babson College (1978-83 and 1985-93). ... Head coach, Providence College (1983-85). ... Athletic director, Babson College (1986-97). ... Assistant coach, Lowell of the AHL (1998-2001). ... Assistant coach, New York Islanders (2000-01). ... Named coach, New York Islanders (June 3, 2003).

Season Team	League	REGULAR SEASON W	L	T	OL	Pct.	Finish	PLAYOFFS W	L	Pct.
84-85—Providence	ECAC	23	17	...	...	.575	...	—	—	—
01-02—Bridgeport	AHL	43	25	8	4	.588	1st/East Division	12	8	.600
02-03—Bridgeport	AHL	40	26	11	3	.569	2nd/East Division	5	4	.556
03-04—New York Islanders	NHL	38	29	11	4	.530	3rd/Atlantic Division	1	4	.200
NHL Totals (1 year)		38	29	11	4	.530	**NHL Totals (1 year)**	1	4	.200

NOTES:

01-02—Defeated Manitoba in conference quarterfinals; defeated St. John's in conference semifinals; defeated Hamilton in conference finals; lost to Chicago in Calder Cup finals.
02-03—Defeated Manchester in conference quarterfinals; lost to Binghamton in conference semifinals.
03-04—Lost to Tampa Bay in Eastern Conference quarterfinals.

SULLIVAN, MIKE — BRUINS

PERSONAL: Born February 27, 1968, in Marshfield, Mass. ... 6-2/201. ... Shoots left. ... Played center.

TRANSACTIONS/CAREER NOTES: Selected by New York Rangers in fourth round (fourth Rangers pick, 69th overall) of NHL draft (June 13, 1987). ... Traded by Rangers with D Mark Tinordi, D Paul Jerrard, RW Brett Barnett and third-round pick (C Murray Garbutt) in 1989 draft to Minnesota North Stars for LW Igor Liba, C Brian Lawton and rights to LW Eric Bennett (October 11, 1988). ... Signed as free agent by San Jose Sharks (August 9, 1991). ... Sprained left knee (April 6, 1993); missed remainder of season. ... Claimed off waivers by Calgary Flames (January 6, 1994). ... Pulled groin (January 29, 1994); missed 13 games. ... Bruised knee (April 6, 1994); missed one game. ... Bruised left foot (March 17, 1995); missed two games. ... Sprained right ankle (April 13, 1995); missed final eight games of season. ... Concussion (February 15, 1997); missed two games. ... Back spasms (March 16, 1997); missed two games. ... Traded by Flames to Boston Bruins for seventh-round pick (RW Radek Duda) in 1998 draft (June 21, 1997). ... Injured wrist (February 4, 1998); missed two games. ... Selected by Nashville Predators in NHL expansion draft (June 26, 1998). ... Traded by Predators to Phoenix Coyotes for seventh-round pick (G Kyle Kettles) in 1999 draft (June 30, 1998). ... Fractured toe (December 17, 1998); missed three games. ... Fractured rib (January 11, 1999); missed 12 games. ... Separated shoulder (February 26, 1999); missed four games. ... Bruised ankle (January 12, 2000); missed three games. ... Strained muscle in abdomen (November 1, 2000); missed six games. ... Concussion (January 23, 2001); missed three games. ... Strained groin (January 26, 2002); missed eight games. ... Injured ribs (February 26, 2002); missed 12 games.

Season Team	League	REGULAR SEASON GP	G	A	Pts.	PIM	+/-	PP	SH	PLAYOFFS GP	G	A	Pts.	PIM
86-87—Boston University	Hockey East	37	13	18	31	18	...	...	...	—	—	—	—	—
87-88—Boston University	Hockey East	30	18	22	40	30	...	...	...	—	—	—	—	—
88-89—Boston University	Hockey East	36	19	17	36	30	...	...	...	—	—	—	—	—
—Virginia	ECHL	2	0	0	0	0	...	...	...	—	—	—	—	—
89-90—Boston University	Hockey East	38	11	20	31	26	...	...	...	—	—	—	—	—
90-91—San Diego	IHL	74	12	23	35	27	...	...	...	—	—	—	—	—
91-92—Kansas City	IHL	10	2	8	10	8	...	...	...	—	—	—	—	—
—San Jose	NHL	64	8	11	19	15	-18	1	0	—	—	—	—	—

		REGULAR SEASON								PLAYOFFS				
Season Team	League	GP	G	A	Pts.	PIM	+/-	PP	SH	GP	G	A	Pts.	PIM
92-93—San Jose	NHL	81	6	8	14	30	-42	0	2	—	—	—	—	—
93-94—San Jose	NHL	26	2	2	4	4	-3	0	2	—	—	—	—	—
—Kansas City	IHL	6	3	3	6	0	0	2	0	—	—	—	—	—
—Saint John	AHL	5	2	0	2	4	-3	0	0	—	—	—	—	—
—Calgary	NHL	19	2	3	5	6	2	0	0	7	1	1	2	8
94-95—Calgary	NHL	38	4	7	11	14	-2	0	0	7	3	5	8	2
95-96—Calgary	NHL	81	9	12	21	24	-6	0	1	4	0	0	0	0
96-97—Calgary	NHL	67	5	6	11	10	-11	0	3	—	—	—	—	—
—Adirondack	AHL	17	1	3	4	2	...	...	...	—	—	—	—	—
97-98—Boston	NHL	77	5	13	18	34	-1	0	0	6	0	1	1	2
98-99—Phoenix	NHL	63	2	4	6	24	-11	0	1	5	0	0	0	2
99-00—Phoenix	NHL	79	5	10	15	10	-4	0	2	5	0	1	1	0
00-01—Phoenix	NHL	72	5	4	9	16	-6	0	3	—	—	—	—	—
01-02—Phoenix	NHL	42	1	2	3	16	-3	0	0	—	—	—	—	—
NHL Totals (11 years)		709	54	82	136	203	-105	1	14	34	4	8	12	14

HEAD COACHING RECORD

BACKGROUND: Assistant coach, Boston Bruins (March 19, 2003 - April 5, 2003) ... Named coach Boston Bruins (June 23, 2003).

		REGULAR SEASON						PLAYOFFS		
Season Team	League	W	L	T	OL	Pct.	Finish	W	L	Pct.
02-03—Providence	AHL	47	17	9	4	.669	...	—	—	—
03-04—Boston	NHL	41	19	15	7	.591	1st/Northeast Division	3	4	.429
NHL Totals (1 year)		41	19	15	7	.591	**NHL Totals (1 year)**	3	4	.429

NOTES:

03-04—Lost to Montreal in Eastern Conference quarterfinals.

SUTTER, DARRYL — FLAMES

PERSONAL: Born August 19, 1958, in Viking, Alta. ... 5-10. ... Shoots left. ... Brother of Brian Sutter, LW with St. Louis Blues (1976-88) and head coach with Blues (1988-92), Boston Bruins (1992-95) and Calgary Flames (1997-2000); brother of Duane Sutter, RW with New York Islanders (1979-87) and Chicago Blackhawks (1987-90); brother of Rich Sutter, RW, with seven NHL teams (1982-95); brother of Ron Sutter, center, San Jose Sharks; and brother of Brent Sutter, C with Islanders (1980-92) and Blackhawks (1991-98). ... Played left wing.

TRANSACTIONS/CAREER NOTES: Selected by Chicago Blackhawks in 11th round (11th Blackhawks pick, 179th overall) of NHL amateur draft (June 1978). ... Lacerated left elbow, developed infection and underwent surgery (Nov. 27, 1981). ... Fractured nose (Nov. 7, 1982). ... Fractured ribs (Nov. 1983). ... Fracture left cheekbone and injured left eye (Jan. 2, 1984). ... Underwent arthroscopic surgery to right knee (Sept. 1984). ... Bruised ribs (October 1984). ... Fractured left ankle (Dec. 26, 1984). ... Separated right shoulder and underwent surgery (Nov. 13, 1985); missed 30 games. ... Injured knee (February 1987). ... Retired as player to become assistant coach of Blackhawks (June 1987).

		REGULAR SEASON								PLAYOFFS				
Season Team	League	GP	G	A	Pts.	PIM	+/-	PP	SH	GP	G	A	Pts.	PIM
78-79—New Brunswick	AHL	19	7	6	13	6	...	...	...	5	1	2	3	0
—Iwakura	Japan	20	28	13	41	0	...	...	...	—	—	—	—	—
79-80—New Brunswick	AHL	69	35	31	66	69	...	...	...	12	6	6	12	8
—Chicago	NHL	8	2	0	2	2	1	0	0	7	3	1	4	2
80-81—Chicago	NHL	76	40	22	62	86	-1	14	0	3	3	1	4	2
81-82—Chicago	NHL	40	23	12	35	31	0	4	3	3	0	1	1	2
82-83—Chicago	NHL	80	31	30	61	53	18	10	0	13	4	6	10	8
83-84—Chicago	NHL	59	20	20	40	44	-18	8	0	5	1	1	2	0
84-85—Chicago	NHL	49	20	18	38	12	8	2	0	15	12	7	19	12
85-86—Chicago	NHL	50	17	10	27	44	-15	3	0	3	1	2	3	0
86-87—Chicago	NHL	44	8	6	14	16	-3	1	0	2	0	0	0	0
NHL Totals (8 years)		406	161	118	279	288	-10	42	3	51	24	19	43	26

HEAD COACHING RECORD

BACKGROUND: Assistant coach, Chicago Blackhawks (1987-88). ... Associate coach, Blackhawks (1991-92). ... Coach, Blackhawks (1992-93 through 1994-95). ... Special assistant to general manager, Blackhawks (1995-96 and 1996-97). ... Coach, San Jose Sharks (June 9, 1997 to December 2, 2002). ... Named coach of Calgary Flames (December 28, 2002). ... Named general manager of Flames (April 11, 2003). ... Suspended two games for player selection and team conduct (March 21, 2004).

		REGULAR SEASON						PLAYOFFS		
Season Team	League	W	L	T	OL	Pct.	Finish	W	L	Pct.
88-89—Saginaw	IHL	46	26	10	...	.622	2nd/East Division	2	4	.333
89-90—Indianapolis	IHL	53	21	8	...	.695	1st/West Division	12	2	.857
92-93—Chicago	NHL	47	25	12	...	.631	1st/Norris Division	0	4	.000
93-94—Chicago	NHL	39	36	9	...	.518	5th/Central Division	2	4	.333
94-95—Chicago	NHL	24	19	5	...	.552	3rd/Central Division	9	7	.563
97-98—San Jose	NHL	34	38	10	...	.476	4th/Pacific Division	2	4	.333
98-99—San Jose	NHL	31	33	18	...	.488	3rd/Pacific Division	2	4	.333
99-00—San Jose	NHL	35	30	10	7	.488	4th/Pacific Division	5	7	.417
00-01—San Jose	NHL	40	27	12	3	.561	2nd/Pacific Division	2	4	.333
01-02—San Jose	NHL	44	27	8	3	.585	1st/Pacific Division	7	5	.583
02-03—San Jose	NHL	8	12	1	1	.386	...	—	—	—
—Calgary	NHL	19	18	8	1	.500	5th/Northwest Division	—	—	—
03-04—Calgary	NHL	42	30	7	3	.555	3rd/Northwest Division	15	11	.577
NHL Totals (10 years)		363	295	100	18	.532	**NHL Totals (9 years)**	44	50	.468

NOTES:

89-90—Defeated Peoria in quarterfinals of Turner Cup playoffs; defeated Salt Lake City in semifinals; defeated Muskegon in Turner Cup finals.

92-93—Lost to St. Louis in Norris Division semifinals.

93-94—Lost to Toronto in Western Conference quarterfinals.

94-95—Defeated Toronto in Western Conference quarterfinals; defeated Vancouver in conference semifinals; lost to Detroit in conference finals.
97-98—Lost to Dallas in Western Conference quarterfinals.
98-99—Lost to Colorado in Western Conference quarterfinals.
99-00—Defeated St. Louis in Western Conference quarterfinals; lost to Dallas in Western Conference semifinals.
00-01—Lost to St. Louis in Western Conference quarterfinals.
01-02—Defeated Phoenix in Western Conference quarterfinals; lost to Colorado in Western Conference semifinals.
03-04—Defeated Vancouver in Western Conference quarterfinals; defeated Detroit in conference semifinals; defeated San Jose in conference finals; lost to Tampa Bay in Stanley Cup finals.

TIPPETT, DAVE — STARS

PERSONAL: Born August 25, 1961, in Moosomin, Sask. ... 5-10/173. ... Shoots left. ... Played center or left wing.
TRANSACTIONS/CAREER NOTES: Signed as a free agent by Hartford Whalers (February 29, 1984). ... Injured right thumb tendons (Oct. 8, 1989). ... Traded by Whalers to Washington Capitals for 6th-round pick (C Jarret Reid) in 1992 draft (September 30, 1990). ... Separated shoulder (Nov. 28, 1990); missed 11 games. ... Signed as free agent by Pittsburgh Penguins (August 28, 1992). ... Fractured thumb (Nov. 20, 1992); missed six games. ... Signed as free agent by Philadelphia Flyers (Aug. 2, 1993). ... Broken bone in left foot (Nov. 27, 1993); missed eight games.

		REGULAR SEASON								PLAYOFFS				
Season Team	League	GP	G	A	Pts.	PIM	+/-	PP	SH	GP	G	A	Pts.	PIM
81-82—North Dakota	WCHA	43	13	28	41	24	...	...	...	—	—	—	—	—
82-83—North Dakota	WCHA	36	15	31	46	44	...	...	...	—	—	—	—	—
83-84—Can. Olympic team	Int'l	66	14	19	33	24	...	...	...	—	—	—	—	—
—Hartford	NHL	17	4	2	6	2	...	...	...	—	—	—	—	—
84-85—Hartford	NHL	80	7	12	19	12	...	...	...	—	—	—	—	—
85-86—Hartford	NHL	80	14	20	34	18	...	...	...	10	2	2	4	4
86-87—Hartford	NHL	80	9	22	31	42	...	...	...	6	0	2	2	4
87-88—Hartford	NHL	80	16	21	37	32	...	...	...	6	0	0	0	2
88-89—Hartford	NHL	80	17	24	41	45	...	...	...	4	0	1	1	0
89-90—Hartford	NHL	66	8	19	27	32	0	0	1	7	1	3	4	2
90-91—Washington	NHL	61	6	9	15	24	...	...	...	10	2	3	5	8
91-92—Washington	NHL	30	2	10	12	16	...	...	...	7	0	1	1	0
—Canadian nat'l team	Int'l	1	0	0	0	4	...	...	...	—	—	—	—	—
—Can. Olympic team	Int'l	6	1	2	3	10	...	...	...	—	—	—	—	—
92-93—Pittsburgh	NHL	74	6	19	25	56	5	0	1	12	1	4	5	14
93-94—Philadelphia	NHL	73	4	11	15	38	-20	0	2	—	—	—	—	—
94-95—Houston	IHL	75	18	48	66	56	-6	6	0	4	1	2	3	4
NHL Totals (11 years)		721	93	169	262	317	-15	0	4	62	6	16	22	34

HEAD COACHING RECORD

BACKGROUND: Assistant coach, Houston Aeros (1994-95). ... General manager, Aeros (1998-99). ... Assistant coach, Los Angeles Kings (1999-2002). ... Named coach of Dallas Stars (May 16, 2002).

		REGULAR SEASON						PLAYOFFS		
Season Team	League	W	L	T	OL	Pct.	Finish	W	L	Pct.
95-96—Houston	IHL	29	45	8	...	.402	5th/Central Division	—	—	—
96-97—Houston	IHL	44	30	8	...	.585	2nd/Southwest Division	8	5	.615
97-98—Houston	IHL	50	22	10	...	.671	2nd/Southwest Division	1	3	.250
98-99—Houston	IHL	54	15	13	...	.738	1st/Southwest Division	11	8	.579
02-03—Dallas	NHL	46	17	15	4	.652	1st/Pacific Division	6	6	.500
03-04—Dallas	NHL	41	26	13	2	.579	2nd/Pacific Division	1	4	.200
NHL Totals (2 years)		87	43	28	6	.616	**NHL Totals (2 years)**	7	10	.412

NOTES:
96-97—Defeated Las Vegas in conference quarterfinals of Turner Cup playoffs; defeated San Antonio in conference semifinals of Turner Cup playoffs; lost to Long Beach in conference finals of Turner Cup playoffs.
97-98—Lost to Milwaukee in conference quarterfinals of Turner Cup playoffs.
98-99—Defeated Long Beach in conference semifinals of Turner Cup playoffs; defeated Chicago in conference finals; defeated Orlando in Turner Cup finals.
02-03—Defeated Edmonton in Western Conference quarterfinals; lost to Anaheim in Western Conference semifinals.
03-04—Lost to Colorado Avalanche in Western Conference quarterfinals.

TORTORELLA, JOHN — LIGHTNING

PERSONAL: Born June 24, 1958, in Boston.

		REGULAR SEASON								PLAYOFFS				
Season Team	League	GP	G	A	Pts.	PIM	+/-	PP	SH	GP	G	A	Pts.	PIM
79-80—University of Maine	ECAC	31	14	22	36	71	...	...	...	—	—	—	—	—
82-83—Hampton Roads	ACHL	1	1	0	1	2	...	...	...	—	—	—	—	—
—Erie	ACHL	12	2	10	12	4	...	...	...	—	—	—	—	—
83-84—Virginia-Erie	ACHL	64	25	37	62	77	...	...	...	4	1	1	2	18
84-85—Virginia	ACHL	63	33	54	87	66	...	...	...	4	3	4	7	0
85-86—Virginia	ACHL	60	37	59	96	153	...	...	...	5	1	3	4	60

HEAD COACHING RECORD

BACKGROUND: General Manager, Virginia Lancers ACHL (1986-87 and 1987-88). ... Assistant coach, New Haven Nighthawks AHL (1988-89). ... Assistant coach, Buffalo Sabres (1989-90 through 1994-95). ... Assistant coach, Phoenix Coyotes (1997-98 and 1998-99). ... Assistant coach, New York Rangers (1999-March 28, 2000). ... Associate coach, Tampa Bay Lightning (July 7, 2000-January 6, 2001). ... Named coach of Lightning (January 6, 2001).

		REGULAR SEASON						PLAYOFFS		
Season Team	League	W	L	T	OL	Pct.	Finish	W	L	Pct.
86-87—Virginia	ACHL	36	19	3	...	.647	1st overall	8	4	.667
87-88—Virginia	AAHL	37	5	1	...	.872	1st overall	3	5	.375
95-96—Rochester	AHL	37	38	5	...	.494	3rd/Central Division	15	4	.789

Season Team	League	REGULAR SEASON W	L	T	OL	Pct.	Finish	PLAYOFFS W	L	Pct.
96-97—Rochester	AHL	40	30	9	...	.563	1st/Empire State Division	6	4	.600
99-00—New York Rangers	NHL	0	4	0	0	.000	4th/Atlantic Division	—	—	—
00-01—Tampa Bay	NHL	12	27	1	3	.291	5th/Southeast Division	—	—	—
01-02—Tampa Bay	NHL	27	40	11	4	.396	3rd/Southeast Division	—	—	—
02-03—Tampa Bay	NHL	36	25	16	5	.537	1st/Southeast Division	5	6	.455
03-04—Tampa Bay	NHL	46	22	8	6	.610	1st/Southeast Division	16	7	.696
NHL Totals (5 years)		121	118	36	18	.474	**NHL Totals (2 years)**	21	13	.618

NOTES:

86-87—Defeated Carolina in ACHL semifinals; defeated Mohawk Valley in ACHL finals.

87-88—Defeated Johnstown in round-robin series; lost to Carolina in AAHL finals.

95-96—Defeated Adirondack in conference quarterfinals of Calder Cup playoffs; defeated Cornwall in conference semifinals of Calder Cup playoffs; defeated Syracuse in conference finals of Calder Cup playoffs; defeated Portland in Calder Cup finals.

96-97—Defeated Syracuse in conference quarterfinals of Calder Cup playoffs; lost to Albany in conference semifinals of Calder Cup playoffs.

99-00—Replaced John Muckler as head coach on interim basis (March 28).

00-01—Replaced Steve Ludzik as head coach (January 6).

02-03—Defeated Washington in Eastern Conference quarterfinals; lost to New Jersey in Eastern Conference semifinals.

03-04—Defeated New York Islanders in Eastern Conference quarterfinals; defeated Montreal in conference semifinals; defeated Philadelphia in conference finals; defeated Calgary in Stanley Cup finals.

TROTZ, BARRY — PREDATORS

PERSONAL: Born July 15, 1962, in Winnipeg.

HEAD COACHING RECORD

BACKGROUND: Player/assistant coach, University of Manitoba (1983-84). ... Coach/general manager, Dauphin Kings junior team (1984-87). ... Assistant coach, University of Manitoba (1987-88). ... Scout, Washington Capitals (1988-91). ... Assistant coach, Baltimore Skipjacks of the AHL (1991-92). ... Scout, Nashville Predators (1997). ... Named coach of Predators (August 6, 1997).

Season Team	League	REGULAR SEASON W	L	T	OL	Pct.	Finish	PLAYOFFS W	L	Pct.
92-93—Baltimore	AHL	28	40	12	...	.425	4th/Southern Division	3	4	.429
93-94—Portland	AHL	43	27	10	...	.600	2nd/Northern Division	12	5	.706
94-95—Portland	AHL	46	22	12	...	.650	2nd/Northern Division	3	4	.429
95-96—Portland	AHL	32	38	10	...	.463	3rd/Northern Division	14	10	.583
96-97—Portland	AHL	37	26	10	...	.575	3rd/New England Division	2	3	.400
98-99—Nashville	NHL	28	47	7	...	.384	4th/Central Division	—	—	—
99-00—Nashville	NHL	28	40	7	7	.384	4th/Central Division	—	—	—
00-01—Nashville	NHL	34	36	9	3	.470	3rd/Central Division	—	—	—
01-02—Nashville	NHL	28	41	13	0	.421	4th/Central Division	—	—	—
02-03—Nashville	NHL	27	35	13	7	.409	4th/Central Division	—	—	—
03-04—Nashville	NHL	38	29	11	4	.530	3rd/Central Division	2	4	.333
NHL Totals (6 years)		183	228	60	21	.433	**NHL Totals (1 year)**	2	4	.333

NOTES:

92-93—Lost to Binghamton in the first round of Calder Cup playoffs.

93-94—Defeated Albany in Northern Division semifinals; defeated Adirondack in Northern Division finals; defeated Moncton in Calder Cup finals.

94-95—Lost to Providence in Northern Division semifinals.

95-96—Defeated Worcester in Eastern Conference quarterfinals; defeated Springfield in Eastern Conference semifinals; defeated Saint John in Eastern Conference finals; lost to Rochester in Calder Cup finals.

96-97—Lost to Springfield in Southern Conference quarterfinals.

03-04—Lost to Detroit in Western Conference quarterfinals.

WILSON, RON — SHARKS

PERSONAL: Born May 28, 1955, in Windsor, Ont. ... 5-11/175. ... Shoots right. ... Son of Larry Wilson, C with Detroit Red Wings (1949-50, 1951-53) and Chicago Blackhawks (1953-56) and coach with Red Wings (1976-77); and nephew of Johnny Wilson, LW with four NHL teams (1949-62) and coach with four NHL teams and two WHA teams (1969-80). ... Played defense.

TRANSACTIONS/CAREER NOTES: Selected by Toronto Maple Leafs in seventh round (seventh Maple Leafs pick, 132nd overall) in NHL draft (June 3, 1975). ... Loaned by Davos HC to Minnesota North Stars for remainder of NHL season and playoffs (March 1985). ... Loaned by Davos HC to Minnesota North Stars for remainder of NHL season and playoffs (March 1986). ... Traded by Davos HC to Minnesota North Stars for D Craig Levie (May 1986). ... Separated shoulder (March 9, 1987).

Season Team	League	REGULAR SEASON GP	G	A	Pts.	PIM	+/-	PP	SH	PLAYOFFS GP	G	A	Pts.	PIM
73-74—Providence	ECAC	26	16	22	38	...	...	...	...	—	—	—	—	—
74-75—Providence	ECAC	27	26	61	87	12	...	...	...	—	—	—	—	—
—U.S. national team	Int'l	27	5	32	37	42	...	...	...	—	—	—	—	—
75-76—Providence	ECAC	28	19	47	66	44	...	...	...	—	—	—	—	—
76-77—Providence	ECAC	30	17	42	59	62	...	...	...	—	—	—	—	—
—Dallas	CHL	4	1	0	1	2	...	...	...	—	—	—	—	—
77-78—Dallas	CHL	67	31	38	69	18	...	...	...	—	—	—	—	—
—Toronto	NHL	13	2	1	3	0	-5	1	0	—	—	—	—	—
78-79—New Brunswick	AHL	31	11	20	31	13	...	...	...	—	—	—	—	—
—Toronto	NHL	46	5	12	17	4	-10	4	0	3	0	1	1	0
79-80—New Brunswick	AHL	43	20	43	63	10	...	...	...	—	—	—	—	—
—Toronto	NHL	5	0	2	2	0	-2	0	0	3	1	2	3	2
80-81—EHC Kloten	Switzerland	38	22	23	45	...	...	...	...	—	—	—	—	—
81-82—Davos HC	Switzerland	38	24	23	47	...	...	...	...	...	...	...	...	...
82-83—Davos HC	Switzerland	36	32	32	64	...	...	...	...	...	...	...	...	...
83-84—Davos IIC	Switzerland	36	33	39	72	...	...	...	...	...	...	...	...	...
84-85—Davos HC	Switzerland	38	39	62	101	...	...	...	...	...	...	...	...	...
—Minnesota	NHL	13	4	8	12	2	-1	0	0	9	1	6	7	2
85-86—Davos HC	Switzerland	27	28	41	69	...	...	...	...	...	...	...	...	...
—Minnesota	NHL	11	1	3	4	8	-2	1	0	5	2	4	6	4

Season Team	League	GP	G	A	Pts.	PIM	+/-	PP	SH	Playoffs GP	G	A	Pts.	PIM
		REGULAR SEASON								PLAYOFFS				
86-87—Minnesota	NHL	65	12	29	41	36	-9	6	0	—	—	—	—	—
87-88—Minnesota	NHL	24	2	12	14	16	-4	1	0	—	—	—	—	—
NHL Totals (7 years)		177	26	67	93	66	-33	13	0	20	4	13	17	8

HEAD COACHING RECORD

BACKGROUND: Assistant coach, Milwaukee of the IHL (1989-90). ... Served as Milwaukee interim coach while Ron Lapointe underwent cancer treatments (February and March 1990; team went 9-10). ... Assistant coach, Vancouver Canucks (1990-91 through 1992-93). ... Named coach of San Jose Sharks (December 4, 2002).

Season Team	League	W	L	T	OL	Pct.	Finish	Playoffs W	L	Pct.
		REGULAR SEASON						PLAYOFFS		
93-94—Anaheim	NHL	33	46	5	...	.423	4th/Pacific Division	—	—	—
94-95—Anaheim	NHL	16	27	5	...	.385	6th/Pacific Division	—	—	—
95-96—Anaheim	NHL	35	39	8	...	.476	4th/Pacific Division	—	—	—

Season Team	League	W	L	T	OL	Pct.	Finish	Playoffs W	L	Pct.
		REGULAR SEASON						PLAYOFFS		
96-97—Anaheim	NHL	36	33	13	...	.518	2nd/Pacific Division	4	7	.364
97-98—Washington	NHL	40	30	12	...	.561	3rd/Atlantic Division	12	9	.571
98-99—Washington	NHL	31	45	6	...	.415	3rd/Southeast Division	—	—	—
99-00—Washington	NHL	44	24	12	2	.610	1st/Southeast Division	1	4	.200
00-01—Washington	NHL	41	27	10	4	.561	1st/Southeast Division	2	4	.333
01-02—Washington	NHL	36	33	11	2	.506	2nd/Southeast Division	—	—	—
02-03—San Jose	NHL	19	25	7	6	.395	5th/Pacific	—	—	—
03-04—San Jose	NHL	43	21	12	6	.598	1st/Pacific Division	10	7	.588
NHL Totals (11 years)		374	350	101	20	.502	**NHL Totals (5 years)**	29	31	.483

NOTES:

96-97—Defeated Phoenix in Western Conference quarterfinals; lost to Detroit in Western Conference semifinals.
97-98—Defeated Boston in Eastern Conference quarterfinals; defeated Ottawa in Eastern Conference semifinals; defeated Buffalo in Eastern Conference finals; lost to Detroit in Stanley Cup finals.
99-00—Lost to Pittsburgh in Eastern Conference quarterfinals.
00-01—Lost to Pittsburgh in Eastern Conference quarterfinals.
02-03—Replaced Darryl Sutter as head coach (Decemeber 4).
03-04—Defeated St. Louis in Western Conference quarterfinals; defeated Colorado in Western Conference semifinals; lost to Calgary in Western Conference finals.

YAWNEY, TRENT — BLACKHAWKS

PERSONAL: Born September 29, 1965, in Hudson Bay, Sask. ... 6-3/195. ... Shoots left. ... Played defense.

TRANSACTIONS/CAREER NOTES: Selected by Chicago Blackhawks as underage junior in 3rd round (2nd Blackhawks pick, 45th overall) of entry draft (June 9, 1984). ... Bruised left shoulder (March 1989). ... Strained right knee (April 24, 1989). ... Bruised kidney (November 11, 1989). ... Bruised thigh (January 1990). ... Strained knee (October 1990). ... Traded by Blackhawks to Calgary Flames for LW Stephane Matteau (December 16, 1991). ... Fractured right clavicle (September 26, 1992); missed first 20 games of season. ... Tore muscle in shoulder (September 9, 1993); missed 25 games. ... Strained left thumb ligaments (January 28, 1995); missed five games. ... Reinjured left thumb (February 11, 1995); missed two games. ... Strained right thumb ligaments (March 22, 1995); missed one game. ... Suffered from the flu (November 8, 1995); missed two games. ... Lacerated hand (January 5, 1996); missed one game. ... Injured knee (February 3, 1996); missed one game. ... Signed as free agent by St. Louis Blues (July 6, 1996). ... Signed as free agent by Blackhawks (September 25, 1997). ... Sprained thumb (March 14, 1998); missed eight games. ... Fractured arm (Jan. 9, 1999); missed 19 games. ... Retired to become assistant coach with Blackhawks (Feb. 22, 1999).

Season Team	League	GP	G	A	Pts.	PIM	+/-	PP	SH	Playoffs GP	G	A	Pts.	PIM
		REGULAR SEASON								PLAYOFFS				
83-84—Saskatoon	WHL	72	13	46	59	81	...	...	...	—	—	—	—	—
84-85—Saskatoon	WHL	72	16	51	67	158	...	...	...	3	1	6	7	7
85-86—Canadian nat'l team	Int'l	73	6	15	21	60	...	...	...	—	—	—	—	—
86-87—Canadian nat'l team	Int'l	51	4	15	19	37	...	...	...	—	—	—	—	—
87-88—Canadian nat'l team	Int'l	60	4	12	16	81	...	...	...	—	—	—	—	—
—Can. Olympic team	Int'l	8	1	1	2	6	1	...	...	—	—	—	—	—
—Chicago	NHL	15	2	8	10	15	1	2	0	5	0	4	4	8
88-89—Chicago	NHL	69	5	19	24	116	-5	3	1	15	3	6	9	20
89-90—Chicago	NHL	70	5	15	20	82	-6	1	0	20	3	5	8	27
90-91—Chicago	NHL	61	3	13	16	77	6	3	0	1	0	0	0	0
91-92—Indianapolis	IHL	9	2	3	5	12	...	...	...	—	—	—	—	—
—Calgary	NHL	47	4	9	13	45	-5	1	0	—	—	—	—	—
92-93—Calgary	NHL	63	1	16	17	67	9	0	0	6	3	2	5	6
93-94—Calgary	NHL	58	6	15	21	60	21	1	1	7	0	0	0	16
94-95—Calgary	NHL	37	0	2	2	108	-4	0	0	2	0	0	0	2
95-96—Calgary	NHL	69	0	3	3	88	-1	0	0	4	0	0	0	2
96-97—St. Louis	NHL	39	0	2	2	17	2	0	0	—	—	—	—	—
97-98—Chicago	NHL	45	1	0	1	76	-5	0	0	—	—	—	—	—
98-99—Chicago	NHL	20	0	0	0	32	-6	0	0	—	—	—	—	—
NHL Totals (12 years)		593	27	102	129	783	7	11	2	60	9	17	26	81

HEAD COACHING RECORD

BACKGROUND: Named coach of the Chicago Blackhawks (July 7, 2005).

Season Team	League	W	L	T	OL	Pct.	Finish	Playoffs W	L	Pct.
		REGULAR SEASON						PLAYOFFS		
00-01—Norfolk	AHL	36	26	13	5	.531	3rd, Southern Division	4	5	.444
01-02—Norfolk	AHL	38	26	12	4	.550	1st, South Division	1	3	.250
02-03—Norfolk	AHL	37	26	12	5	.538	1st, South Division	5	4	.556
03-04—Norfolk	AHL	35	36	4	5	.463	5th, East Division	4	4	.500
—Norfolk	AHL	43	30	6	1	.575	3rd, East Division	2	4	.333